P9-BHS-937

# *Major British Writers*

WORDSWORTH

COLERIDGE

BYRON

SHELLEY

KEATS

TENNYSON

BROWNING

ARNOLD

SHAW

YEATS

ELIOT

ENLARGED EDITION

# II

HB HARCOURT, BRACE AND COMPANY *New York Burlingame*

[C·1·60]

Library of Congress Catalogue Card Number: 59–6482

COPYRIGHTS AND ACKNOWLEDGMENTS

Selections from Thomas Middleton Raysor's *Coleridge's Shakespearean Criticism* (1930) are used by kind permission of the editor and the Harvard University Press.

"The Love Song of J. Alfred Prufrock," "Sweeney among the Nightingales," "The Waste Land," "The Hollow Men," "Marina," and "Triumphal March," from *Collected Poems*, 1909–1935, by T. S. Eliot, copyright, 1936, by Harcourt, Brace and Company, Inc. "Hamlet" and "The Metaphysical Poets," from *Selected Essays*, 1917–1932, by T. S. Eliot, copyright, 1932, by Harcourt, Brace and Company, Inc. "The Dry Salvages," from *Four Quartets*, copyright, 1943, by T. S. Eliot. Reprinted by permission of Harcourt, Brace and Company, Inc., and Faber and Faber, Ltd.

"The Music of Poetry," by T. S. Eliot, from *Partisan Review*, November–December, 1942. Reprinted by permission of T. S. Eliot, and Faber and Faber, Ltd.

Selections from *The Letters of John Keats* edited by M. Buxton Forman, and used by permission of the publishers, Oxford University Press.

"Man and Superman," copyright, 1903, by George Bernard Shaw. Renewal copyright, 1931, by George Bernard Shaw. Used by permission of the Public Trustee, the Society of Authors, and Dodd, Mead & Company, Inc.

Selections from William Butler Yeats, *Essays*, copyright, 1912 and 1918, by The Macmillan Company, and used with The Macmillan Company's permission.

Selections from *The Autobiography of William Butler Yeats*, copyright 1916 and 1936 by The Macmillan Company and used with The Macmillan Company's permission.

Poems by William Butler Yeats from *Collected Poems*, copyright 1950 by The Macmillan Company and used with The Macmillan Company's permission.

The selections from *The Autobiography of William Butler Yeats*, from *Essays* by William Butler Yeats, and from *Collected Poems* by W. B. Yeats are also reprinted by permission of Mrs. W. B. Yeats, Macmillan & Co., Ltd., and A. P. Watt & Son.

A NOTE ON THE COVER: The coat of arms reproduced on the cover of this book is that of the Worshipful Company of Stationers and Papermakers of London. This ancient City Company was originally a guild of stationers and craftsmen who made and dealt in parchment, paper, quill pens, and materials for binding books. In 1557 (eighty-one years after printing was first introduced into England) the Stationers were granted a charter which gave them the monopoly of the "Art or Mystery of Printing." At the same time they received their coat of arms from the College of Heralds. For many years it was the custom for the titles of books to be printed by members of the Company to be entered in the Stationers' Register, which is thus a record of the first printing of most of the famous works known to students of the literature of the sixteenth and seventeenth centuries.

PRINTED IN THE UNITED STATES OF AMERICA

# CONTENTS

## *WILLIAM WORDSWORTH & SAMUEL TAYLOR COLERIDGE*

*Edited by* GEORGE W. MEYER

## *GEORGE GORDON, LORD BYRON* *Edited by NORTHROP FRYE*

## *PERCY BYSSHE SHELLEY* *Edited by* I. A. RICHARDS



## *JOHN KEATS* *Edited by* WALTER J. BATE

## *ALFRED, LORD TENNYSON* *Edited by DOUGLAS BUSH*



## *ROBERT BROWNING* *Edited by WILLIAM C. DeVANE*

## MATTHEW ARNOLD *Edited by LIONEL TRILLING*

## GEORGE BERNARD SHAW *Edited by REUBEN A. BROWER*



## WILLIAM BUTLER YEATS *Edited by REUBEN A. BROWER*

## T. S. ELIOT *Edited by ELIZABETH DREW*

# PREFACE

Great literature can be studied mainly in two ways. It can be regarded as part of the history and culture of a people; and if so, the student should become acquainted with an extensive collection of many samples and varieties. It can also be regarded as the product of fine minds; and if so, it is better to study the works of great writers with greater intensity.

Either approach has its advantages — and disadvantages. The wide survey gives a nodding acquaintance with many writers and a little of the best of each, but the selections must inevitably be too few and too brief for full understanding of any one author. The study in depth necessitates selection and concentration — certain favorite writers and certain fashionable movements must inevitably be left out. Those who still prefer the study in breadth are well supplied with several good and well-known anthologies, but there is no adequate text for the more intensive study. To supply this need is the aim of *Major British Writers.*

In planning this collection we determined as a first, basic principle that each author should be *fully* represented, preferably by complete works, or, whenever that was physically impossible, by large sections. *Major British Writers* thus offers, within its two volumes, a significant proportion, averaging 75,000 words, of the best writing of twenty-two great authors.

The first — and most difficult — editorial problem in planning these volumes was to select the authors to be represented. Our principle was threefold: the author must be great in himself, representative of his age, and, not least important, significant to the modern reader. In any collection of "major writers," Chaucer, Spenser, Shakespeare, and Milton will first be chosen; but thereafter selection becomes more difficult.

With our principles before us we have chosen Donne to represent the Elizabethan and Jacobean poets because of his great influence on modern poets and critics. Bacon as the father of the modern scientific method and as a master of English prose in his own right was picked as the prose writer of the first half of the seventeenth century rather than Thomas Browne. Dryden, Pope, and Swift represent the "Augustans," though we omitted Addison with regret. Dr. Johnson represents his own inimitable self, but, especially since the discovery of the Boswell Papers, he is inseparable from his biographer, James Boswell. Of the great writers of the early nineteenth century the pre-eminence of Wordsworth, Coleridge, Byron, Shelley, and Keats is hardly disputable. Choice in the Victorian period was far more difficult. While we selected Tennyson, Browning, and Arnold, we realize that some would have substituted for one or another of our preferences Carlyle, Ruskin, Newman, or Mill.

We determined also to include some of the moderns, that is, authors who have been writing during the past half century. Here the choice is embarrassingly difficult. While we doubt whether any reader would reject from the company of the "great moderns" the names of Shaw, Yeats, or Eliot, we realize that every reader would wish to include also at least half a dozen of his own favorites — and thereby have made the second volume of *Major British Writers* impossibly bulky.

The next problem was to plan the editing. We felt that the intensive selections would require equally intensive editing — each writer should be introduced by a full critical essay and should be well annotated. While uniformity was desirable, we regarded the quality of the editing as far more important. We therefore decided to invite a different scholar and critic of well-established reputation to edit each section with the hope that the diversity of gifts of each editor would be fully used. We believe that this hope has been realized and that the critical essays in *Major British Writers* will be recognized as notable contributions to English literary criticism.

Certain general principles were suggested to each editor. Wherever it seemed suitable, they were asked to include in their introductions a biographical sketch of the author, an appreciation of his work as a whole, and a more detailed consideration of some chosen examples of his work. In this way we hoped to meet the differing interests of teachers and students. Further, editors were made aware of what their colleagues were doing, and the selections were correlated. Thus the passages chosen from John Dryden include the remarkable appreciation of Chaucer from the Preface to *Fables, Ancient and Modern* and those from Samuel Johnson include the famous criticism of the "Metaphysical poets" from the *Life of Cowley,* as well as large excerpts from the Preface to Shakespeare and the *Lives of Milton* and *Pope.* Similarly in selecting from the Coleridge lectures on Shakespeare, those on *Hamlet* and *The Tempest* were chosen. The section given to Matthew Arnold includes his essays on Wordsworth and Keats, while Shakespeare and Donne are again illustrated by Mr. Eliot's essays on "*Hamlet*" and "The Metaphysical Poets."

In technical matters it should be noted that while the spelling of Chaucer, Spenser, Byron, Shelley, Keats (in his letters), Tennyson, Shaw, Yeats, and Eliot (the last two in their poetry) has been kept, in general, spelling, use of capitals, punctuation, and other typographical matters conform with modern American usage. In poetry the final *-ed,* when accented, is marked with a diacritical mark and the earlier practice, never consistent, of omitting the silent *e* has been dropped; thus we print *determinèd* and *determined,* and not *determined* and *determin'd.* In the first volume (but not in the second) the sign ° has been used in verse passages to call attention to a word or passage annotated; in prose a superior numeral has been used.

In such a project as this contributors and organizers become acutely aware of each other's personalities. Publisher and General Editor wish to thank the several editors for their patience and forbearance, and for their exceptional, friendly, and ready co-operation at all times.

G. B. H.

*Ann Arbor, Michigan*
*January 10, 1959*

# Major British Writers

GEORGE W. MEYER, *Editor*

# William Wordsworth & Samuel Taylor Coleridge

**WORDSWORTH 1770–1850** **COLERIDGE 1772–1834**

Just south of the Solway Firth and the Scottish border, in the counties of Cumberland and Westmorland, lies the English Lake District, a hilly, glaciated area, some twenty miles across. The District takes its name from the fifteen lakes and innumerable tarns which — along with Scafell, Helvellyn, and Skiddaw, the tallest peaks in England — dominate its landscape. On the northwestern edge of this region of almost incredible natural beauty William Wordsworth was born on April 7, 1770, in the village of Cockermouth, Cumberland. In the heart of these "dear native regions," with which most of his poetry is intimately associated, Wordsworth grew up and lived the greater part of his life.

William was the second in a family of four sons and one daughter born to John and Anne Cookson Wordsworth. The elder Wordsworth was an attorney who served as law agent to Sir James Lowther, later Lord Lonsdale, a tyrannical nobleman known appropriately as "the bad earl." Upon John Wordsworth fell the onerous duty of collecting rents from the Lowther tenants, among whom were acquaintances and neighbors. This circumstance and the fact that the Wordsworths occupied the largest house in town suggest that William and his brothers and sister lived somewhat apart from their Cockermouth contemporaries and were left much to their own resources for society and amusement. From these early years at Cockermouth the poet's habits of solitude, self-dependence, and introspection, as well as his extraordinarily close attachment to his sister Dorothy (born December 25, 1771), probably originate.

We have his own word for it that Wordsworth was a difficult child:

> I was of a stiff, moody, and violent temper; so much so that I remember going once into the attics of my grandfather's house at Penrith, upon some indignity having been put upon me, with an intention of destroying myself with one of the foils which I knew was kept there. I took the foil in hand, but my heart failed. Upon another occasion, while I was at my grandfather's house at Penrith, along with my eldest brother, Richard, we were whipping tops together in the large drawing room, on which the carpet was only laid down upon particular occasions. The walls were hung round with family pictures, and I said to my brother, "Dare you strike your whip through that old lady's petticoat?" He replied, "No, I won't." "Then," said I, "here goes"; and I struck my lash through her hooped petticoat, for which no doubt, though I have forgotten it, I was properly punished.

Wordsworth's childhood comportment filled his mother with mingled hope and despair.

Prior to her death, shortly before his eighth birthday, she confided to a friend that " the only one of her five children about whose future life she was anxious, was William; and he, she said, would be remarkable either for good or for evil." Until several years after his graduation from college this issue remained in doubt.

From 1778 to 1787, when he entered St. John's College, Cambridge, Wordsworth attended Hawkshead Grammar School, an institution founded in 1585 by Edwin Sandys, Archbishop of York. In Wordsworth's day no school in England trained its students better in classics and in mathematics. Here on the shores of Esthwaite Water, hardly two miles from Lake Windermere, Wordsworth shared with his schoolmates the experiences described in the first two books of *The Prelude*. Here he developed the strength and skill that made him the " crack skater on Rydal Lake " and, even at the age of sixty, the equal of the youngest and hardiest mountain climber in the Lake District. Here also his abnormally acute senses awoke to " the mighty world of eye and ear " and began to store away for future imaginative use the materials of his poetry.

The pastoral freedom and excellent training at Hawkshead were not unmixed blessings for Wordsworth. At Cambridge he found himself a year ahead of most of his class and ill-prepared to meet the worldliness and indifference of the college faculty. Left much to his own devices, he indulged a natural adolescent tendency to indolence and, preferring pedestrian tours to study in the vacations, graduated without distinction. When he left Cambridge in January, 1791, he had little to recommend him but scattered translations — one of them obscene — from the poetry of Anacreon, Catullus, and Horace, and a long nostalgic series of octosyllabic couplets called " The Vale of Esthwaite."

For the next few years Wordsworth's behavior exasperated those who thought they knew what was best for him. His father had died in December, 1783, leaving a comfortable estate of £4,700, almost all of which was in the hands of Sir James Lowther, who refused to pay. By a brutal exhibition of feudal power in the English courts, Lowther kept the young Wordsworths from their inheritance until his death in 1802. Meanwhile the Wordsworth children were forced to depend upon guardian relatives, who were not pleased when William failed to equip himself at Cambridge for any profession by which he might earn a living. In his freshman year he had considered becoming a lawyer, but he surrendered this idea when close study provoked headaches and a pain in his side. Later he thought he might emigrate to Barbados with his brother John, a sailor, and then it occurred to him that he might become a general in the army. After his graduation there seemed to Wordsworth and his guardians two possibilities for his future. He wanted to become tutor and companion to some hypothetical rich young man who wished to travel. They wanted him to return to Cambridge for postgraduate work in Oriental languages so that he might become a well-qualified minister in the Anglican Church. The prospect of " vegetating in a paltry curacy " Wordsworth found repulsive, and he persuaded his guardians to finance one more year of freedom from responsibility, this one to be spent in revolutionary France.

Ever since William the Conqueror triumphed at Hastings in 1066 there have been Englishmen who believe that France is the source and center of political and carnal vice. If they had not already shared this belief Wordsworth's guardians must have done so when their nephew returned to England, demonstrating conclusively that he was no longer fitted for the Church. To begin with, Wordsworth had seen enough of the revolution in Paris, Orléans, and Blois to convince him that French republicanism was " nothing out of nature's certain course." Michel Beaupuy, the French captain immortalized in the ninth book of *The Prelude,* had demonstrated to him that the revolutionary cause was the cause of the people, and Wordsworth returned home the champion of radical ideas that were anathema in respectable circles. As if this were not enough, Wordsworth had the effrontery to request still more financial aid so that he might transport to England and marry one Annette Vallon, a French girl several years his senior who had borne him a daughter, Caroline, on December 15, 1792. The guardians refused and, fearing William's influence, denied him permission to see his sister.

In an attempt to raise money Wordsworth published *An Evening Walk* and *Descrip-*

*tive Sketches,* poems which received favorable notice and caught the eye of young Coleridge but did not sell. When in February, 1793, England and France went to war, Wordsworth's sympathies lay with the French, and he faced the future without funds, family, or allegiance to his country. Almost desperate from disappointment and frustration, Wordsworth wrote *A Letter to the Bishop of Llandaff,*[1] which he had the prudence to suppress, and a poem, a watered-down version of which he published in 1842 under the title *Guilt and Sorrow.* Compounded of bitterness towards monarchical society and hopes for the republican future, these two works expressed the extreme radicalism from which Wordsworth, when he had survived the crisis described in the eleventh book of *The Prelude,* wisely retreated.

The rise and decline of Wordsworth's revolutionary ardor between 1793 and 1797 affords a striking parallel to the experience of young radicals in the 1930's and 1940's. Keenly aware of the economic and political injustice suffered by himself and by many of his fellow men, he naïvely assumed that any change must be for the better and grounded his faith in the new world to come on republican principles. He was certain that monarchy was decadent and must die, and for a brief interval he recommended violence to accelerate the destruction of priests and kings. The innate goodness of common humanity, nurtured by modern education, might then be counted upon to produce the millennium. But the course of republican change in France, unlike that in America, produced nothing of the sort. Instead it brought to power Maximilien Robespierre, father of the Terror. After Robespierre fell victim to the guillotine, the revived optimism of Wordsworth and other friends of the revolution turned to despair before the rise of a new dictator-tyrant, Napoleon Bonaparte, who, within a remarkably short time, threatened all of Europe with imperialistic war.

As the political and international horizon darkened, Wordsworth's personal fortunes improved as if by miracle. In 1795 he inherited £900 from a friend[2] and settled with Dorothy[3] at Racedown, Dorsetshire, in a rent-free cottage owned by the Pinney family of Bristol. In September he met the other literary giant of the age, Samuel Taylor Coleridge.

Two years Wordsworth's junior (a fact he later refused to admit) Coleridge, born on October 21, 1772, was the ninth son and the fourteenth child of the Reverend John Coleridge, the absent-minded vicar of Ottery St. Mary, Devonshire. Favored by both parents as the child of their old age, Samuel incurred the resentment of his older brothers, with whom he could not compete physically. For compensation he turned to books (the *Arabian Nights* and other tales of wonder were his favorites) and created a world of imagination in which to live. He liked to read, for example, in the churchyard, where he would converse with gravestones while fancying himself one of the seven champions of Christendom as he struck down weeds with ruthless abandon. When he was eight, after a fight in which (not without provocation) he attempted to stab his brother Frank with a butcher knife, Coleridge ran away from home and slept all night in wet clothes at the edge of the river Otter. When he awoke he could not move his legs. Here began the rheumatic agonies that soon led Coleridge to opium and made his adult life a prolonged disaster.

Within a year of his father's death in 1781, Coleridge became a student at Christ's Hospital, an ancient charity school in London. Here he made a lifelong friend of Charles Lamb and distinguished himself for scholarship. His schoolboy precocity did not, however, stand up well at Jesus College, Cambridge, which he entered in February, 1791, just after Wordsworth's departure from the university. Coleridge began well enough; he wrote his brother George that he was studying mathematics three hours a day and reading and composing Greek verse "like

[1] Richard Watson, the Bishop of Llandaff (Wales), though a native and a resident of the Lake District, had a reputation for political and religious liberalism. When he attacked French republicanism on January 25, 1793, four days after the execution of Louis XVI, Wordsworth was moved to reply.

[2] Raisley Calvert, the brother of a school friend of Wordsworth's, who died of tuberculosis in January, 1795. Wordsworth nursed him in his final illness.

[3] With them was Basil Montagu, the "Edward" of "To My Sister." Basil was the son of a widower friend to whom Wordsworth loaned most of the legacy received from Calvert. The elder Montagu was primarily responsible for the temporary breach between Wordsworth and Coleridge in 1810. Young Basil, who was born in 1793, and who, as Wordsworth put it in 1798, "lies like a little devil," no doubt stimulated Wordsworth's interest in child psychology.

a mad dog." But, alas, many pitfalls — sex, drink, gambling, drugs, and debt, not to mention all-night talk — were available to the undergraduate, then as now, and Coleridge promptly found them all. Owing close to £150, with nothing in his pockets but an Irish lottery ticket, he fled from Cambridge (December, 1793) in a panic of guilt and self-revulsion to enlist in the Fifteenth Light Dragoons under the alias of Silas Tomkyn Comberbacke (S. T. C.). From this preposterous situation (Coleridge could not curry a horse, much less ride one) he was rescued by his brothers who, by judicious application in the right places, secured his discharge on April 7, 1794. The grounds were "insanity."

His debts paid, Coleridge returned to Cambridge within four days, but he was never to graduate. A walking tour in June took him to Oxford where he met Robert Southey, another precocious youth with poetic aspirations. Their common interests in French republicanism and Godwin's *Political Justice* made them fast friends; for most of the next year they considered emigration to America and the establishment of a Utopian community to be called a pantisocracy (for details of this project see the headnote for "To a Young Ass" below). The plan of course failed; meanwhile Coleridge, reacting from unrequited love for one Mary Evans, became engaged to Sara Fricker, a sister of Southey's fiancée. At Southey's insistence, and out of a misguided sense of honor, Coleridge married Sara on October 4, 1795, about a month after his first meeting with William Wordsworth. By June, 1797, Wordsworth and Coleridge had discovered one another's genius, and in July the Wordsworths moved enthusiastically to Alfoxden, a large country house two miles from the Bristol Channel and three miles from Coleridge at Nether Stowey. Here Dorothy began the journals that both poets frequently drew upon for source material, and here began the daily intimacy and collaboration that within fourteen months enabled Wordsworth and Coleridge to produce the revolutionary collection of poems named *Lyrical Ballads*.

After 1798 Wordsworth's life was little more unusual — except for his poetry — than that of the average man working and raising a family in a rural community. In December, 1799, after spending the previous winter in Germany where they had gone with Coleridge, Wordsworth and his sister settled permanently in the vicinity of Grasmere in the Lake District. In 1802, after the Lonsdale debt had been paid — the joint share of William and Dorothy came to £3,825 — Wordsworth married his childhood friend, Mary Hutchinson. Between 1803 and 1810 they had five children, two of whom died in 1812. In 1805 Wordsworth's favorite brother, John, went down with his ship near Weymouth. In 1813, thanks to the new Lord Lonsdale, Wordsworth became Distributor of Stamps for Westmorland, an office that required little work and paid between £400 and £600 a year. Meanwhile, as the numbers and prosperity of the family increased, the Wordsworths made a succession of moves to larger houses — from Dove Cottage to Allan Bank in 1808, to The Rectory in Grasmere in 1811, and finally to Rydal Mount, near Ambleside, in 1813. Here Wordsworth lived until his death on April 23, 1850.

The last decades of Wordsworth's life were years of increasing popularity and triumph. Throughout his great period, 1797–1814, he had withstood the denigrating criticism of conservative reviewers. Steadily, however, he had been creating a new taste and a new audience for poetry, and in the 1820's, aided greatly by Coleridge's praise in his *Biographia Literaria* (1817), Wordsworth came into his own. Edition after edition of his poems was called for, and Wordsworth suddenly found himself the center of a vast tourist traffic — twenty to thirty visitors, among them some of the world's most famous names, would call in a single day — that regarded Rydal as a national park, with Wordsworth the chief attraction. Dr. Thomas Arnold, the headmaster of Rugby, drawn as much by Wordsworth's fame as by the beauty of the region, spent vacations with his family at Fox How on the west bank of the Rothay, less than a mile from Rydal; between his son Matthew and the old poet developed one of the most important literary relationships in the nineteenth century.[1] In 1839 Wordsworth was called to Oxford to receive the degree of Doctor of Civil Law. He was greeted with "thunders of applause, repeated over and over again . . . by undergraduates and Masters of Arts alike." In 1842 he resigned the office of

[1] See p. 582, below.

Stamp Distributor, but was awarded £300 a year on the Civil List. When Robert Southey died in 1843, the young Queen Victoria conferred upon the venerable poet the highest literary honor at her disposal: Wordsworth was appointed poet laureate.

In his later years Wordsworth's poetic powers declined sharply, and he became a political conservative. There is, however, no sound basis for the view that he lost touch with life, became a turncoat reactionary, and could bring himself to speak only disparaging words of younger writers. Shelley and the youthful Browning helped disseminate the idea that Wordsworth sold his political principles for money and the favor of his social superiors. But neither Shelley nor Browning knew Wordsworth, and their opinions are overborne by the testimony of someone who did. The liberal John Stuart Mill, who talked much with Wordsworth as late as 1831, had this to say of his conversation: "He talks on no subject more instructively than on states of society and forms of government. . . . Wordsworth seems always to know the pros and cons of every question; and when you think he strikes the balance wrong it is only because you think he estimates erroneously some matter of fact."

As for the younger writers, Wordsworth, like Dr. Johnson, made some estimates that were foolish but more that stand up well. He disliked Thomas Carlyle, whom he regarded as "sometimes insane" and "a pest to the English tongue."[1] To Wordsworth, Byron also was insane, perverse, and evil, full of power without feeling. Shelley he called the "greatest master of harmonious verse in our modern literature" but "too remote from the humanities," which he tries to "outsoar." Keats was a "youth of promise too great for the sorry company he keeps," and his verse, like that of Tennyson, was jeopardized by "overlusciousness." In 1845 Wordsworth declared Tennyson "decidedly the first of our living poets," and in 1846 — after the publication of "The Lost Leader"[2] — Wordsworth commented as follows upon Elizabeth Barrett's selection of Robert Browning for a husband: "Her choice is a very able man, and I trust that it will be a happy union, not doubting that they will speak more intelligibly to each other than (notwithstanding their abilities) they have yet done to the public."

The later life of Coleridge was less fortunate. After the great year of 1797–98 with the Wordsworths in Somersetshire when he wrote or began his finest poems — the "Ancient Mariner," "Christabel," and "Kubla Khan" — Coleridge's life becomes a tale of sadness almost unrelieved. On a visit to the north of England in 1799 he met and fell in love with Sara Hutchinson, whose sister Wordsworth married three years later. His move with his family in 1800 to Greta Hall, Keswick, within walking distance (for Coleridge) of the Wordsworths, gave no relief. By 1801 Coleridge was a confirmed opium addict; in 1802, in "Dejection: An Ode," he revealed the depths of his domestic misery, the hopelessness of his love for Sara Hutchinson, and the loss of his capacity for sustained creative work, which in his despair he considerably underrated. Having long hoped that a warmer climate might help his rheumatism and impatient to escape from his wife, Coleridge sailed in 1804 for Malta. On his return two years later (his sojourn abroad had not been uneventful; when Coleridge was in Rome, Napoleon ordered his arrest for what he regarded as certain slanders Coleridge had written about him earlier in the *Morning Post*) he was a physical and a mental wreck. Brandy had been added to opium in a vicious circle of hangover and depression, and Coleridge often woke screaming from pain and terror in the night. By 1808 he had begun his brilliant career as a lecturer on Shakespeare; he had also become jealous of Sara Hutchinson's friendship with Wordsworth, and he had separated from Mrs. Coleridge. From 1808 until 1810 he nevertheless lived with the Wordsworths, who had taken Allan Bank, a house large enough to accommodate not only their growing family but also Coleridge and his sons. For nine months of this period Coleridge, with Sara Hutchinson for amanuensis, produced at irregular intervals a periodical called the *Friend*. When Sara, in ill health, left to visit a brother in Wales, publication ceased, and Coleridge had lost over £200.

[1] Carlyle, in turn, did not like Wordsworth, whom he described nevertheless as "a deep, earnest man, who had thought silently and painfully about many things . . . cold, hard, silent, practical . . . a man of immense head and great jaws like a crocodile's, cast in a mold designed for prodigious work."

[2] See headnote to "The Lost Leader," p. 489, below.

In October, 1810, Coleridge, obliged to go to London to find employment, traveled there from Grasmere in the carriage of Basil Montagu, Wordsworth's old friend (see p. 3, n. 3, above), in whose house he planned to live, at least temporarily. Before their departure Wordsworth, fearful of the plan, warned Montagu of what might be expected of Coleridge in a household (Montagu had recently married, for the third time). Coleridge and Montagu soon quarreled in London, and the latter, obviously in a temper ill befitting a lawyer, violated Wordsworth's well-intended confidence and told Coleridge that Wordsworth had called him a "rotten drunkard" and a "nuisance in his family." What was left of Coleridge was of course crushed. A reconciliation of sorts was in time effected, and Coleridge in 1828 toured the Rhineland with Wordsworth and his daughter, but the old love and understanding were forever gone.

Most of the remaining years of his life Coleridge spent in or around London in the households of John Morgan (an old Bristol acquaintance) and Dr. James Gillman of Highgate. These good people helped Coleridge in his not altogether futile struggle with opium, and, when circumstances are considered, Coleridge's performance in these years, especially from 1811 to 1817, seems prodigious. His Shakespeare lectures, 1811–12, were very successful; in 1813 the production at Drury Lane of his play *Remorse* (written in 1797 as *Osorio* and later revised) yielded about £400, more than all of his other literary efforts combined to that date; in 1815 he began collecting his poems (he was never able to finish "Christabel") and writing the preface that grew into the *Biographia Literaria* (1817). His lectures in 1818, again touching upon Shakespeare, represent his last significant venture directly concerned with poetry. In 1825 he published *Aids to Reflection,* an attempt at a Platonic idealization of Trinitarian Christianity, which he regarded as preliminary to a "Magnum Opus" that remained unfinished. Coleridge died on July 25, 1834, and was buried at Highgate, where he had lived since 1816. When Wordsworth in the presence of friends read the letter reporting the death of his old collaborator of the Quantock days, his voice faltered and broke; then Wordsworth declared Coleridge the "most *wonderful* man he had ever known."

## II

Coleridge and Matthew Arnold, the best critics in nineteenth-century England, placed Wordsworth next to Shakespeare and Milton among modern English poets. There were two causes for Wordsworth's greatness: the historical and literary environment into which he was born, and his native genius, the origins and development of which he himself has described in *The Prelude*. The work of no other English writer since Shakespeare better exemplifies Arnold's theory that the creation of the literary masterwork requires a proper conjunction of the man and the moment. Let us consider the appropriateness of the moment and how it assisted Wordsworth and Coleridge to contribute significantly to the development of English poetry.

In the age of Pope, poets dependent upon the patronage of the upper class limited themselves to subjects which would interest their conservative, aristocratic readers. Poet and reader alike, convinced that they enjoyed a civilization and a literature hardly capable of improvement, delighted in the polished reiteration of what they regarded as universal truths. Originality was discouraged, on the theory that if something had not already been said it probably was not worth saying. External nature, the psychology of rustics, children, or the outcasts of society, as well as the private emotions and personal history of the poet himself, were considered to be eccentric, dull, and unrewarding subjects for poetry. The poet might touch upon such matters incidentally, in an effort to illuminate or make momentarily more enjoyable his universal truth, but in so doing he must never become emphatic or betray any enthusiasm for the indecorous subject in its own right. Above all, he must take care to write in a proper form, in the proper measure, and in proper language. The most respectable poetic forms were those tracing their lineage from classical antiquity: the epic, the epistle, the epitaph, the pastoral, the satire. The couplet in iambic pentameter was the preferred measure of expression. And the language was that used by gentle people in polite conversation. Words and phrases vulgarized by everyday use in trade, profession, work on the farm, or even ordinary domestic life, were to be avoided in a poem as in a drawing room. (Dr. Johnson, for example, objected to Shakespeare's use of "knife" and "blanket" in *Macbeth,* I.v.51–55.)

When Wordsworth and Coleridge began to write, there were chinks in the wall of the neoclassical tradition, but the wall had not yet been breached. In poetry James Thomson had achieved fame as an observer of natural appearances; Gray, Goldsmith, and Crabbe had permitted themselves to consider the lot of the poor; the Wartons, Edward Young, Collins, and Cowper had become increasingly emotional and subjective; Chatterton, in writing his medieval poetic forgeries, had used unclassical forms and meters. In prose Jean Jacques Rousseau had published his *Confessions,* and James Boswell, with shocking unrestraint, had told most of what he knew about the life and conversation of Dr. Johnson. Meanwhile, an economic revolution had raised the sentimental and humanitarian middle class to a position of wealth and power. This greatly increased the numbers of the reading public and helped to destroy the power of the aristocracy as arbiters of literary taste. Simultaneously, the forces of republicanism, founded on the idea that all men are essentially virtuous, had triumphed in America, and were ready to erupt across the Channel in monarchical France. All this was the inheritance of Wordsworth and Coleridge, who became the literary embodiment of more than a century of liberating and progressive change.

With a single volume Wordsworth and Coleridge greatly extended the boundaries of poetry. The poems in *Lyrical Ballads* (1798) had little to do with aristocratic men of affairs, except perhaps to warn them that it was sinful to feel contempt for any living thing. This volume of "new" poetry opened with a tale of strange, almost hypnotic, effect told in ballad stanza by an aged sailor who had killed an albatross in southern seas and had suffered compulsive penitential pains ever since. It concluded with a majestic blank-verse meditation in which the speaker, Wordsworth himself, addressing his sister, described a landscape and explained how his memory of the scene had helped him through difficult times and led him to an understanding of his own mind and of its interrelationship with the world of external nature. Between these two poems — Coleridge's "The Rime of the Ancient Mariner" and Wordsworth's "Lines Composed a Few Miles above Tintern Abbey" — came twenty-one other pieces, eighteen of them by Wordsworth. There were poems about abandoned mothers, about convicts rotting in dungeons, about a poor man's instinctive sense of property, and about the victims of war and economic depression. There were poems on disprized love, on a mother's fear for her lost idiot son, on the true nature of the nightingale, and on the psychology of children. And there were poems — the "Ancient Mariner" was one of them — on the sin of pride and the advantages of a life of benevolence, on the limitations of book learning, and on what Wordsworth would later call "Nature's holy plan."

Such subjects were sufficiently unorthodox (some reviewers called them "low," "grotesque," and "childish") to startle many readers from the lethargy into which they had been lulled by the thematic monotony of most eighteenth-century verse. But even more arresting than the matter was the manner of *Lyrical Ballads*. The new subjects demanded a new style, and most of these poems were written in the plain, muscular English that ordinary men use in daily conversation. The studied artificiality of diction that had long been fashionable was rejected. A bird was a bird, not a "feathered chorister," a "wanderer of heaven," a member of the "plumy race," or a "tenant of the sky."[1] What was more, the young poets paid small attention to tradition in rime and meter. In the two-hundred-odd pages of *Lyrical Ballads* there were six poems in blank verse, one in Spenserian stanza, and many examples and adaptations of the ancient ballad stanza resurrected (to the scornful displeasure of Dr. Johnson) by Bishop Percy in his *Reliques of Ancient Poetry* (1765), but there was not a single specimen of the heroic couplet, hitherto the hallmark of major poetry in the eighteenth century.

The range and significance of *Lyrical Ballads* increased with the successive editions of 1800

[1] Had Wordsworth and Coleridge found occasion to refer to what is usually found in any well-stocked barnyard, they would have called it by its given name, "manure," as Whitman soon did in "Song of Myself," even though it cost them the fine humor of Cowper's periphrasis in *The Task:* "The stable yields a stercoraceous heap, / Impregnated with quick-fermenting salts / And potent to resist the freezing blast."

(actually January, 1801) and 1802 (there was a reprinting of this edition in 1805). The 1800 edition, in two volumes, contained many new poems by Wordsworth, among them the "Lucy" poems, the "Matthew" group, and "Michael." In this edition, moreover, Wordsworth expanded the original "Advertisement" into the famous Preface, a document as revolutionary and influential in the history of criticism as *Lyrical Ballads* was in the history of poetry. Written in the summer of 1800 and expanded in 1802, this essay made clear that the poems in *Lyrical Ballads* were not the accidental produce of eccentric poetasters but the thoughtful creations of men learned in poetic theory and willing to defend their practice.

The subjects of these poems, Wordsworth explained, were taken from "humble and rustic life" because there "our elementary feelings coexist in a state of greater simplicity," and there "the passions of men are incorporated with the beautiful and permanent forms of nature." Since a poet, moreover, is a "man speaking to men" — not to the members of one social class, but to all men — the authors thought it proper to present their "incidents and situations from common life" in a "selection of language really used by men" — not rich men living in cities, but humble men living close to nature. Such men "hourly communicate with the best objects from which the best part of language is originally derived"; because they pay little attention to the demands of "social vanity," these men "convey their feelings and notions in simple and unelaborated expressions." [1] Then, as if to underline this deliberate departure from the impersonal and unemotional practice of the eighteenth century, Wordsworth announced that "All good poetry is the spontaneous overflow of powerful feelings."

*Poems in Two Volumes* (1807) revealed even more extensively than *Lyrical Ballads* Wordsworth's imaginative power and his originating and renovating genius in the shorter forms of English poetry. In these volumes were new poems destined to be ranked among the best in the language: "Resolution and Independence," "The Solitary Reaper," "Ode to Duty," the great "Ode" — later subtitled "Intimations of Immortality from Recollections of Early Childhood" — "Elegiac Stanzas," "Character of the Happy Warrior," and the familiar verses on the rainbow, the cuckoo, the daisy, and the daffodils. In addition to these, there were more than fifty sonnets.

Wordsworth's sonnets deserve a special word. In his note to "Nuns Fret Not at Their Convent's Narrow Room," Wordsworth tells us how he began to write sonnets:

> One afternoon in 1801, my sister read to me the sonnets of Milton. I had long been well acquainted with them, but I was particularly struck on that occasion with the dignified simplicity and majestic harmony that runs through most of them — in character so totally different from the Italian, and still more so from Shakespeare's fine sonnets. I took fire . . . and produced three sonnets the same afternoon, the first I ever wrote except an irregular one at school.

Actually, Wordsworth had written several sonnets in his youth, and it was on May 21, 1802, not 1801, that he "took fire" from Dorothy's reading of Milton. Before this flame flickered out, only a few years before his death, Wordsworth wrote more than five hundred and thirty sonnets, most of them very good and many of them among the best ever written. Especially distinguished are those in which he rallied his countrymen against Napoleon and spoke with prophetic indignation against the materialistic dry rot that was sapping England's strength from within. Characteristically, he took liberties with the form and greatly extended its range and variety; he used it to express himself on almost every conceivable subject except romantic love; like Milton, he often rejected the traditional Italianate break in thought at the end of the octave; and he experimented freely with the rhyme scheme of the sestet. In these ways Wordsworth restored to respectability, after a century and a half of almost total neglect, one of the noblest forms of lyrical utterance.

In the spring of 1798 Wordsworth projected a long philosophical poem in three parts, to be entitled *The Recluse.* He then decided that he was not ready for work on so ambitious a project and that he would prepare himself for this

[1] Although Coleridge had regarded the 1800 Preface as "half a child of my own brain," in 1802 he began to differ with some of Wordsworth's ideas, especially his ideas about the language of poetry (see the headnote to *Biographia Literaria* below).

larger task by first writing *The Prelude.* This pseudo-autobiographical poem, which eventually grew to the length of fourteen books, is without precedent in English verse. In form similar to an epic, *The Prelude* traces the development of Wordsworth's imagination from early childhood to 1798. The poem is remarkable for the light it throws on the psychology of the poet and the problems of literary creation, and for its valuable first-hand account of the French Revolution and Wordsworth's reactions to it. Soon after he finished a first draft of *The Prelude* Wordsworth turned to the composition of *The Excursion,* the only part of *The Recluse* that he was to complete.[1] A rambling, discursive poem in nine books, *The Excursion* describes the efforts of a peddler, a poet, and a pastor (all of them thinly disguised portraits of Wordsworth himself) to cure the despondency of the Solitary, a character who, because he has lost wife, children, and faith in the French Revolution, has lost interest in life itself. Totaling together more than seventeen thousand lines of blank verse, *The Prelude* and *The Excursion,* with their many incidents, descriptions, narratives, and reflective passages, represent the most sustained original performance in English poetry since the epics of Milton.

## III

According to Matthew Arnold, "Wordsworth's poetry is great because of the extraordinary power with which Wordsworth feels the joy offered to us in nature, the joy offered to us in the simple primary affections and duties; and because of the extraordinary power with which . . . he shows us this joy, and renders it so as to make us share it." This is sound praise, but when Arnold wrote it he thought chiefly of Wordsworth's shorter poems and neglected the value of Wordsworth's "philosophic" poetry, particularly "Tintern Abbey," *The Prelude,* the "Intimations Ode," and *The Excursion.* In Arnold's opinion, these constituted a large part of the "poetical baggage" of which Wordsworth would have to be relieved if his reputation were to continue to prosper. Ironically, however, these were the poems that Wordsworth valued most, and they are the poems that have attracted most attention from twentieth-century critics, no doubt because they give us a clear and comprehensive expression of what we today so strikingly lack — an organic, unitary vision of man and nature, of the human mind, the earth, and the heavens, all activated by one spirit, all in harmonious relationship and dynamic interaction, inevitably progressing (though not without checks and interruptions) and increasingly characterized by "Beauty, a living presence of the earth."

One of the purposes of Wordsworth's poetry is the purpose of Milton in *Paradise Lost* — to "justify the ways of God to men." Both poets believed that God and his creation constituted a mighty order that, despite the presence of evil and other apparent imperfections, was "in the end / All gratulant, if rightly understood." But the terms in which they expressed their affirmations were as different as the times in which they lived. Milton wrote his great apology in terms of ancient myths and theological arguments that were of great importance in the seventeenth century. Wordsworth, a child of the "enlightened," deistic eighteenth century, turned for his materials not to theology and a superannuated cosmography but to observable nature, particularly the study of the mind of man, which he called "My haunt, and the main region of my song." The world of Milton's epic is a world of miracles and special providences, of divine and angelic intervention in human and natural affairs. The world of Wordsworth's poetry is the modern world, where man exists in and as part of the natural order whose perdurable laws he must discover and adjust to if he is to find happiness in this life.

Wordsworth was convinced that man can find happiness in this life, and he expressed this conviction both in his poetry and in his literary theory. In the Preface to *Lyrical Ballads* he announced that it was the duty of the poet — "who rejoices more than other men in the spirit of life that is in him" — not only to enjoy the air he breathes but also to communicate his special awareness of the joy and dignity of living to his readers. Even when the subjects of poetry are distressing and painful, as they are, for example, in "Michael" and "To Toussaint L'Ouverture"

[1] For a more detailed history of *The Prelude* and for its relationship and that of *The Excursion* to the projected longer poem, see the headnote to *The Prelude* below.

or in *Paradise Lost* and *Samson Agonistes,* the poet must by his art contrive to make the total effect of the individual poem one of pleasure. In "Michael" Wordsworth accomplishes this by emphasizing, not the defection of Luke in the city, but the enduring love and nobility of spirit with which the old shepherd in extreme misfortune "still looked up to sun and cloud, / And listened to the wind." In this way a poem becomes what Wordsworth thought it should be, "an acknowledgment of the beauty of the universe" and an "image of man in nature." By telling of

> Sorrow that is not sorrow, but delight;
> And miserable love, that is not pain
> To hear of, for the glory that redounds
> Therefrom to human kind, and what we are,

such a poem as "Michael" reminds us that the world offers humanity a preponderance of pleasure over pain, and that when associated with stoic dignity even pain can become a source of the deepest joy.

Wordsworth did not easily achieve the cheerful faith on which this view of the world and poetry was based, nor did he easily maintain it when it was achieved. He was not readily persuaded that "God's in his heaven — All's right with the world," or that "Whatever is, is right." Even so, it is reasonable to ask how Wordsworth came to believe that this "unintelligible" world affords us more pleasure than pain and that the ways of God are justifiable to men. Then, once having become convinced, how does any man — even a happy poet — keep his faith in the goodness of the universe when he is everywhere confronted with injustice, tyranny, and war, with the decay of physical and mental powers, with the disappointments and frustrations that accompany the years, with the loss of friends and children, and finally with the certain loss of life itself? Wordsworth faced these questions. They occurred to him as he experienced the two great crises of his imaginative life. The first of these was political in nature; it began in 1793, is reflected in "Tintern Abbey," and provided the climax for *The Prelude*. The second resulted from Wordsworth's disturbing consciousness of mutability and decay. It began in 1798 at Tintern Abbey, provided the impulse for the "Intimations Ode," reached a climax in Wordsworth's personal life in 1805, and yielded one of the main themes of *The Excursion*. Let us see how Wordsworth resolved these troublesome issues in his meditative poetry, especially in "Tintern Abbey" and the "Intimations Ode."

Not until 1797–98 did Wordsworth become thoroughly and thoughtfully convinced that the world and life were good. Because of his unusually happy childhood he had in an unthinking way *felt* this to be true in his earlier years. According to a key passage in *The Prelude* (Book II, lines 231–60), such a sentiment is almost instinctive in all of us; it dates from infancy, when, as babes in arms, we drink in love from our mothers' eyes and in turn bestow a comparable affection on everything we see. In most of us this early love is permanently distorted or destroyed by growing up. In Wordsworth it was obscured, but only temporarily, by the events of 1793. In that year the pleasant order of Wordsworth's youthful imagination fell apart, and he found himself asking: How is it possible to accept life in a world where men and society are unjust?

Wordsworth's first answer, as we have seen, was that acceptance is not possible; the world must be changed. Like the youthful Shelley and the radicals of our own 1930's, Wordsworth wished to destroy the apparent cause of evil, the existing government. But Robespierre and the Terror quickly taught him that violence breeds further violence and settles nothing. Meanwhile, he had been reading Dr. Edward Young's *The Complaint, or Night Thoughts* (1742), David Hartley's *Observations on Man, His Frame, His Duty, and His Expectations* (1749), and William Godwin's *Political Justice* (1793). All these works proclaimed the ability of the human mind to triumph over vicious passions, and two of them asserted that this triumph, with the ultimate promise of a moral and political utopia, was not only possible but inevitable. In the spring of 1794, when he was deep in these books and once more in the Lake District,[1] Wordsworth began to turn again to nature. At this time, more than a year before he met Coleridge and settled at Racedown with

[1] Wordsworth was reunited with his sister at Halifax in the spring of 1794. From there they went to Windy Brow, a farmhouse owned by the Calverts, half a mile from Keswick. Here they were together for a fortnight in April.

Dorothy, he discovered (and recorded in verses that he never published) the value of the

Heart that vibrates evermore, awake
To feeling for all forms that life can take,
That wider still its sympathy extends
And sees not any line where being ends;
Sees sense, through Nature's rudest forms betrayed,
Tremble obscure in fountain, rock, and shade,
And while a secret power those forms endears
Their social accent never vainly hears.

Implicit in these lines is the philosophy of nature Wordsworth expressed in his best poetry, as well as the moral with which Coleridge chose to conclude "The Rime of the Ancient Mariner":

He prayeth best, who loveth best
All things both great and small;
For the dear God who loveth us,
He made and loveth all.

By 1797–98, then, love once again dominated Wordsworth's vision of the world. The feeling heart, sensitive and sympathetic to all nature, was the key to man's happiness, individual and social. Society could be improved and injustice banished not by sudden change in the form of government but by the gradual increase of happiness and virtue in the individuals who made up society. Wordsworth and Coleridge had agreed that their poetry should contribute to the reform of society by educating the reader in the virtues of benevolence and the manifold sources of joy available in nature.

When Wordsworth revisited the Wye, his confidence in the excellence of the world could never again be shaken by the painful awareness of "What man has made of man." He proclaimed this fact in "Tintern Abbey," the first of his great meditative poems. Therein, addressing his sister, he reveals that despite five unusually difficult years, during which he had known times of depression in "lonely rooms, and 'mid the din / Of towns and cities" where the "fretful stir / Unprofitable and the fever of the world" were too much with him — despite such years, his optimistic faith has been firmly re-established. "Therefore," he continues, in the most famous of his affirmatory passages,

am I still
A lover of the meadows and the woods,
And mountains; and of all that we behold
From this green earth; of all the mighty world
Of eye, and ear — both what they half create,
And what perceive; well pleased to recognize
In nature and the language of the sense,
The anchor of my purest thoughts, the nurse,
The guide, the guardian of my heart, and soul
Of all my moral being.

Accordingly, he recommends his view of life to his sister Dorothy and to his readers, assuring them that "Nature never did betray / The heart that loved her," that "'tis her privilege / Through all the years of this our life, to lead / From joy to joy."

This, in very simple summary, is the central statement of the poem. But, skeptics will inquire, is the statement true? Is it possible that the memory and the revisiting of a landscape near Tintern Abbey could assure Wordsworth that life in an unjust and frenzied society is bearable? The answers to these questions are affirmative; they lie in the realm of poetic truth, where what ought to be counts for more than what is. In the poem the introductory description of the landscape is crucial. As Wordsworth sees it, this landscape is no ordinary bit of static rural scenery, but a symbol of the universe itself. It is a perfect organic composition blending apparent opposites into tranquil unity. In the center of the scene Wordsworth discovers unobtrusive evidence of man living in harmony with nature: the cottage grounds and pastoral farms, their orchard plots merging imperceptibly with the undomesticated "groves and copses" which lead to the "houseless woods," whence "wreaths of smoke" ascend "In silence, from among the trees." The scene is peaceful, yet dynamic; serene, though in motion and alive. It is an image of the great world of nature, of which man — even man in cities — is a part. The memory of this image has often filled Wordsworth with the visionary power to "see into the life of things," to look hopefully forward to the time, prophesied by Hartley and Godwin, when all men will participate in the peaceful harmony and joy towards which all nature tends.

Ironically, just as Wordsworth announced his ability to "see into the life of things" and thus answered to his own poetic satisfaction the question of social injustice, a second question, even more difficult, began to disturb him. As he gazed at the landscape, which he had first seen five years before, he made a startling discovery. He saw details that he could recall having seen in 1793, but which he had forgotten during the interval. These were the "gleams of half-extinguished thought," the "many recognitions dim and faint," that brought Wordsworth a moment of "sad perplexity" and caused him to wonder if the memories of this second visit would serve him as had the memories of the first. He was discovering that the memory is ever-changing and imperfect, and that the mind, of which memory is a part, is never from one moment to another the same. This prompted him to compare and contrast in the poem the three stages of his development from childhood to maturity and to notice, perhaps for the first time, that, although he had gained new and greater powers, something which he valued highly had been irretrievably lost. And even though the ability to hear the "still sad music of humanity" and to feel the "sense sublime / Of something far more deeply interfused" were, he was confident, sufficient compensation for the "dizzy raptures" of youthful sensibility, these "aching joys" were unmistakably gone, and Wordsworth now faced the problem of mutability, decay, and death. After 1798, in his deepest meditations Wordsworth struggled with this problem, the second question that anyone who believes that nature leads us on "From joy to joy" must answer or give up his faith: How is it possible to accept life in a world where all men die? The "Intimations Ode" is Wordsworth's answer.

What is important about the "Ode" is not its superficial differences from "Tintern Abbey" but the fact that it is a more mature and complicated meditation on essentially the same subjects. Once again Wordsworth is justifying the ways of God to men and affirming that nature leads us on "From joy to joy," this time at a higher level of experience, with a new and more powerful current of creative energy. "Tintern Abbey" treats of man's position in the order of nature, with nature conceived of as limited in space and time to what mortal man is capable of perceiving. The "Ode" extends this subject and deals not only with the interrelationship of man and nature but also with the relationship of both to what man is capable of intuiting, that is, to God and eternity. In the "Ode," Wordsworth suggests why mortal life, which leads but to the "darkness of the grave," is good, and why the philosophy of nature is not rendered joyless by the fact of universal death.

The "Intimations Ode" is Wordsworth's greatest short poem and one of the most complex utterances in English verse. Here we can only brush the surface of its meaning. In its first four stanzas Wordsworth tells us that, although he is still sensitive to beauty and capable of joy, he can no longer discover anywhere the "celestial" light or glory which as a child he saw everywhere in nature. At the end of stanza 4 he asks: "Where is it now, the glory and the dream?" The next four stanzas attempt to answer the question metaphorically. They suppose that the soul of the child has known a previous existence in Heaven. When the child arrives on earth the celestial radiance trails behind him, glorifying all that he perceives. But the business of the child on this temporal earth is growing up, and, almost imperceptibly as he grows, the celestial light is dimmed by the ordinary light of the natural sun. It is the child's nature to hasten the process of growth. This he does by joyfully mimicking the worldly activities of his elders. The sight of the child thus assisting "custom" to blunt his heavenly potentialities — especially the innocent capacity for joy that is his most priceless heritage — moves Wordsworth to despair in the melancholy closing lines of the eighth stanza. But the poet's recovery is immediate, and sustained to the end. Although the man can no longer see the celestial light, he remembers what he saw and how he felt. These recollections of early childhood he interprets as sufficient evidence for poetic faith in an ideal, immortal world lying behind and above this real one. Meanwhile, as in "Tintern Abbey," for his loss he has had "abundant recompense." The celestial light has been replaced by the light of experience in the "philosophic mind," the "hour / Of splendor in the grass" by the "soothing thoughts that spring / Out of human suffering." As the clouded sun sets at the end of the poet's day, the simplest natural object can provoke thoughts that lead to faith in immortality and are, therefore, "too deep for tears."

Whatever else the "Ode" may affirm, it says, as *The Prelude* says, that the origins of man's joy are fundamental, inevitable, and indestructible. In *The Prelude,* as we have seen, Wordsworth ascribed our love of nature to the love we receive in our mothers' arms. In the "Ode" he tells us metaphorically that our joy in the world comes "from God, who is our home." But this is not its only source. The supernaturalism in the "Ode" has a naturalistic parallel and equivalent in the love the child receives from his parents: in the fourth stanza the "babe leaps up on his mother's arm"; in the seventh the "six-years' darling of a pygmy size" is "Fretted by sallies of his mother's kisses, / With light upon him from his father's eyes"; and in the sixth the poor, tawdry, "homely nurse" of earth with "no unworthy aim" is motivated by "something of a mother's mind." The main point is that joy is born of love, and that it is natural for us to love. As Wordsworth saw it, so marvelously constructed is the human mind, so exquisitely fitted is it to the world in which it lives, that once we experience love nothing can make this earth and this life permanently unattractive. This capacity for joy is the chief characteristic of the human mind, a miraculous compound of celestial and earthly elements. This is what Wordsworth reaffirmed in the ninth stanza of the "Ode," when he acclaimed those

truths that wake,
To perish never;
Which neither listlessness, nor mad endeavor,
Nor man nor boy,
Nor all that is at enmity with joy,
Can utterly abolish or destroy!

Wordsworth does not say, of course, that our joy and faith in life cannot be temporarily disturbed or shaken. He says that it cannot be "utterly" abolished or destroyed. A little less than a year after the completion of the "Ode" there occurred an event that helps to illustrate this point. On the night of February 5, 1805, John Wordsworth went down with his ship, the East Indiaman *Abergavenny,* off the Bill of Portland. A month after receiving word of this catastrophe, Wordsworth wrote to Sir George Beaumont and questioned the ways of God in terms that anticipate Thomas Hardy in his bleakest moments of late nineteenth-century pessimism. The "faith that looks through death" was shaken, and the "philosophic mind" temporarily paralyzed by an intolerable grief. In this time of urgent personal need Wordsworth turned from his new philosophy of immortality based on the psychology of childhood, and sought consolation from the older, more familiar arguments for eternal life contained in the *Night Thoughts* (VII. 205–17) [1] of Dr. Edward Young.

For the time being Wordsworth's happiness was abolished and destroyed. But not "utterly." By May, 1805, in the sober optimism with which he concluded *The Prelude,* Wordsworth had reaffirmed his faith in the indestructibility of joy. Meanwhile, however, he had relearned an old lesson. In "Tintern Abbey" he had spoken of the "still sad music of humanity" and its power to "chasten and subdue." In the intervening years he had not forgotten this power, but he apparently believed that he had paid too little attention to it while he wrote at length in *The Prelude* of the virtually unassailable strength of his imagination rooted deeply in the "spots of time" (XII.208–25). He had perhaps been too well pleased with his own self-sufficiency, and too impatient, too unsympathetic with the plight of those men of stunted imagination who live forever in the "Inanimate cold world" of mechanical custom. The death of his brother reminded Wordsworth of his membership in the fraternity of suffering humanity. This renewed awareness of the brotherhood and of his neglected obligations to his fellow beings he announced in "Elegiac Stanzas, Suggested by a Picture of Peele Castle, in a Storm, Painted by Sir George Beaumont." After confessing, "A deep distress hath humanized my soul," Wordsworth bade solemn farewell to the "heart that lives alone, / Housed in a dream, at distance from the kind!"

It is difficult to think of an English poet, other than Shakespeare, who bore in mind the problems of humanity more consistently than Wordsworth did. Yet in 1805 he clearly felt that he had been living "at distance from the kind." In this sentiment we find the probable explanation for the high value Wordsworth came to place on *The Excursion,* the only one of his major poems not extensively represented in this text. *The Prelude* he regarded as a private work written for himself and for Coleridge, both of them men

[1] In this passage, which Wordsworth transcribed in his letter, Young asserted that a virtuous man must be immortal because it would be wasteful, unjust, and intolerable for him to be otherwise.

of imagination in the highest degree. To us *The Prelude* is infinitely the superior of the two poems. But to Wordsworth it was only the "ante-chapel" to the great cathedral of his verse, the main body of which is represented by *The Excursion*. (See the headnote to *The Prelude*.) The reason is that *The Excursion,* a more explicit, prosaic, and didactic poem, was written in behalf of the average man of little or no imagination. It was designed to ameliorate the condition of those unfortunate men and women whose natural potentialities have been blunted by the world and who lack the inner strength necessary to endure life unassisted.

In *The Excursion* the subject again was "Despondency corrected." The despondency of the Solitary is caused by his inability to answer either of the large questions at issue in Wordsworth's reflective poetry. The three other characters, who know the answers, ply him with a kind of philosophical artificial respiration in eight of the nine books, and it must be admitted that the Solitary is breathing at the end. Meanwhile, the reader has overheard Wordsworth's cogent views on the social, economic, and educational problems which would soon torment those Victorians sufficiently patriotic to care about the "Condition of England." Wordsworth foresaw that in the coming age of industrial materialism fewer and fewer men would grow up in nature and know the opportunities he had enjoyed in his formative years. He knew that the spread of factories, if uncontrolled, would deface and destroy not only England's pleasant landscapes but also England's rugged virtues — "Plain living and high thinking" and "pure religion breathing household laws." To prevent such decadence Wordsworth advocated the strengthening of the church, and, reminding British lawmakers of their responsibility as the center of hope for the world to come, Wordsworth urged them to pass without delay laws governing child labor and establishing compulsory national education.

In *The Excursion* Wordsworth explained again and in great detail why he continued to have faith in the world, and how all men might eventually share in the harmony and joy that are nature's chief characteristics. Wordsworth regarded the poem as the capstone of his great career; Charles Lamb praised it in superlative terms; and Keats declared it one of the three great things of the age. Readers today do not care for it. It belongs to the seventeenth- and eighteenth-century tradition of the long descriptive-didactic poem, a tradition in which the "Romantics" were brought up but which we have long since lost the ability to understand and evaluate. But even if we had not become the victims of such a shift in sensibility we should probably have to agree that, in comparison with most of Wordsworth's earlier work, there is a falling off here. Wordsworth could not write dramatically, and yet that is the way he tried to write in *The Excursion*. For reasons not easy to understand, time and again in this poem he reverted to the manner of the eighteenth-century tradition, which he had done more than anyone else to destroy. The poem contains some of his major banalities — this one, for example, from Book VII: "Rocked by the motion of a trusty ass / Two ruddy children hung." As a result, *The Excursion* is an odd mixture of the sublime and the bathetic, in itself sufficient justification for James Kenneth Stephen's[1] brilliant parodic comment on the unevenness of Wordsworth's performance:

> Two voices are there: one is of the deep;
> It learns the storm cloud's thunderous melody,
> Now roars, now murmurs with the changing sea,
> Now birdlike pipes, now closes soft in sleep;
> And one is of an old half-witted sheep
> Which bleats articulate monotony,
> And indicates that two and one are three,
> That grass is green, lakes damp, and mountains steep:
> And, Wordsworth, both are thine; at certain times,
> Forth from the heart of thy melodious rimes
> The form and pressure of high thoughts will burst;
> At other times — good Lord! I'd rather be
> Quite unacquainted with the ABC
> Than write such hopeless rubbish as thy worst.

But even Wordsworth's "hopeless rubbish" — poems like "The Idiot Boy" or "Goody Blake and Harry Gill" — finds able champions. And in *The Excursion,* as in many of the poems written in his later years (see, for instance, "Extempore Effusion upon the Death of James Hogg"), there are passages like the one which follows from Book IV (ll. 1132–47) that startle

[1] James Kenneth Stephen (1859–92) was a Cambridge wit and football player.

and waylay because they epitomize the multitudinous powers of William Wordsworth at his very best:

I have seen
A curious child, who dwelt upon a tract
Of inland ground, applying to his ear
The convolutions of a smooth-lipped shell;
To which, in silence hushed, his very soul
Listened intensely; and his countenance soon
Brightened with joy; for from within were heard
Murmurings, whereby the monitor expressed
Mysterious union with its native sea.
Even such a shell the universe itself
Is to the ear of Faith; and there are times,
I doubt not, when to you it doth impart
Authentic tidings of invisible things;
Of ebb and flow, and ever-during power;
And central peace, subsisting at the heart
Of endless agitation.

Coleridge's reputation (the better part of it has grown steadily since his death) owes something to his association with the Wordsworths, and more to the irregularity of his personal behavior. With Byron and Shelley, Coleridge set a Romantic example for fantastic eccentricity that was more than emulated later in the century by others — notably Poe in America; Baudelaire, Verlaine, and Rimbaud in France; Wilde and Dowson in England — who helped give poets and poetry a dubious reputation in the first third of the twentieth century. Thanks, however, to the excellence of three poems and to the brilliance of his criticism, in both theory and practice, Coleridge's place high up among the masters of English literature is securely established.

The "Ancient Mariner," "Christabel," and "Kubla Khan" exhibit best the cardinal features of Coleridge's meteoric poetic genius.[1] "Enchantment," "witchery," "magic," and "miraculous" are words frequently and properly used in discussion of these poems because they succeed better than any other works of the period in creating for the reader the pure Romantic sense of wonder, the love of the strange, the remote, and the mysterious. They communicate Coleridge's delight in real and imaginary experience with a naïve freshness and enthusiastic vitality usually found only in the spontaneous verbal responses of children, to whom all things are new. Children lack art and experience; in 1797–98 Coleridge possessed God's plenty of both.

Told in the ancient ballad stanza, ordinarily devoted to tales of heroism or unhappy love, the "Ancient Mariner" seems to be a simple story of minor crime, punishment, repentance, and forgiveness. The speaker, a graybeard bore, buttonholes a youthful wedding guest (he is "next of kin") and causes him to miss the ceremony. The exterior semblance of the poem, like that of Wordsworth's child, belies its true immensity, however, and the mesmeric powers of the mariner's eye hold us for a second reading. As the motto appended to the poem in 1817 suggests, the tale is not of this earth alone: the mariner is the voice of an experience that transcends what man can learn in space and time; his audience represents unsophisticated innocence preoccupied with pleasures of the moment in a universe of whose full dimensions and population he is quite ignorant. The wedding guest is "a sadder and a wiser man" after listening to the mariner's archetypal narrative; he has missed the party, but he has learned vicariously what most men need a lifetime to discover — that life is a voyage of discovery that leads us all, by benevolent necessity, from innocence to sin and the cold isolation of Polar ice, to penitential sacrifice for all humanity, to grace and a return to good standing in the warm society of universal life.

Coleridge, in telling this story, set and maintained a breakneck narrative pace, radically extended the ballad stanza (once to nine lines), and distributed throughout the poem infinite riches of verbal melody, rhythm, and rhyme. Almost as much might be said of "Christabel" and "Kubla Khan," but these remained fragments. In the "Ancient Mariner" alone did Coleridge's "shaping spirit of imagination" work at full stretch. A "cormorant" reader, learned in metaphysics, all poetry, the literature of travel, science, religion, and Gothic romance, Coleridge, when he wrote this poem, unlocked the doors not only of his personal but of the race unconscious, and fused into unity the most disparate elements of his experience in nature and in books. This he did, incidentally, not by argu-

[1] Coleridge's other poems, "Dejection" excepted, are distinctly minor. The "Conversation Poems" (see headnote to "The Eolian Harp") deserve a word, however, for they anticipate the dramatic monologues of Robert Browning, and the introspective colloquial manner of much contemporary poetry.

ment or logical exposition, both of which he thought left too little to the reader's imagination, but by suggestion, evocation, symbol, and association — the favorite methods and devices, since Edgar Allan Poe, of the most influential poets.

Coleridge's poetry nevertheless is limited in bulk and importance when compared with his criticism, which is voluminous and of the highest order of significance. When he began to lecture in 1808, a more than century-old controversy between French and British critics (some English critics took the neoclassic side) over Shakespeare's neglect of the unities of time, place, and action was still unsettled. The French, believing the unities indispensable for verisimilitude, argued that Shakespeare sang as does a bird, because he must; to them he was an untutored butcher-boy, ignorant of taste and art. Reacting against the French insistence upon literal stage delusion, Dr. Johnson went too far in the other direction (see "Preface to Shakespeare," Vol. I, pp. 937–49). Overstressing the rational potential of the audience, he claimed that its members are always aware of the unreality of stage action. Since, therefore, they can assume the truth of Othello's marriage to Desdemona in Venice, they can assume without strain Othello's murder of Desdemona in Cyprus.

Coleridge ended the controversy with his theories of organic unity and dramatic illusion. Observing that the Greeks needed the unities because of the chorus, and that Shakespeare had rejected both unities and chorus, Coleridge refused to accept Greek drama as a criterion for all drama. He saw the unities as artificial restrictions that would, if respected, inhibit modern dramatists and force their material mechanically into predetermined forms. Opposing the neoclassic view he advanced the idea of organic unity — that a play, or any work of art, grows like a tree from the seed which is its origin; it must therefore be judged on its own merits as an individual unit which, ever developing from within, assumes a form and shape innate and proper to it and its species, but peculiarly its own. Well aware of the effectiveness of Shakespeare's plays (even in the garbled versions Garrick prospered with), Coleridge reasoned that a successful dramatist — like a successful poet writing of the supernatural, as Coleridge had done in the "Ancient Mariner" and in "Christabel" — produces in the audience or the reader a "willing suspension of disbelief that constitutes poetic faith." Playwright or poet, in other words, so appeals to and engages the imagination of his audience that the latter voluntarily allows his rational powers to rest in abeyance as he encourages himself temporarily to believe that what he sees and hears or reads is real.

If his theory of dramatic illusion is Coleridge's most important contribution to dramatic criticism, his interpretation of Hamlet's character has been the most influential. Coleridge, like most people, admired Hamlet and found something of himself in him. With typical Romantic interest in the personality of the individual and neglect of the dramatic context in which alone the character exists, Coleridge, the noblest procrastinator of us all, believed that Hamlet failed because he thought too much. Most critics today reject or qualify this view; its tenacity is nowhere better revealed, however, than in the introductory line for Sir Laurence Olivier's movie *Hamlet* (1948): "This is the story of a man who could not make up his mind."

Wordsworth and Coleridge are inseparably linked as poets because of their epoch-making partnership in the composition of *Lyrical Ballads,* to which Coleridge added breadth and brilliance to Wordsworth's depth and solidity. But yet Coleridge's more permanent and pervasive importance is as a critic rather than as a poet. His definition of the imagination (see *Biographia Literaria,* XIII, p. 134, below), his description of the poet (see *ibid.,* XIV, p. 137, below), and his concept of organic as opposed to mechanical unity in works of art — these alone make him one of the greatest of modern literary theorists. When we have also his criticism of Shakespeare, fragmentary but vast and various, no one can question T. S. Eliot's judgment that Coleridge was the greatest of English critics.

## Reading Suggestions

WORDSWORTH:

EDITIONS

Ernest de Selincourt and Helen Darbishire, editors, *The Poetical Works of William Wordsworth,* 5 vols. (1940–49). The definitive variorum edition of the prefaces and of all the poems except *The Prelude.*

Ernest de Selincourt, editor, *The Prelude, or Growth of a Poet's Mind* (1926, 1928, 1932). The great variorum edition of the poem, with the 1805 text (here available for the first time) on the left-hand and the much-revised 1850 text on the right.

BIOGRAPHY AND CRITICISM

Émile Legouis, *The Early Life of William Wordsworth, 1770–1798,* translated by J. W. Matthews (1897). The earliest and still the best commentary based on *The Prelude* as a primary source for Wordsworth's biography. A readable and stimulating book, especially valuable on the French Revolution and on Wordsworth's debt to his eighteenth-century predecessors.

George McLean Harper, *William Wordsworth: His Life, Works, and Influence,* 2 vols. (1916). The only modern attempt to describe the whole of Wordsworth's life, and hence the standard biography. Overemphasizes the contrast between Wordsworth's youthful radicalism and his later conservatism.

Edith Batho, *The Later Wordsworth* (1933). A careful study of Wordsworth's life and thought after 1815. Indispensable as a corrective to the view (out of Shelley, Browning, and others) that the elder Wordsworth was a political and religious apostate and toady whom the younger Wordsworth would have despised.

George Wilbur Meyer, *Wordsworth's Formative Years,* University of Michigan Publications, Language and Literature (1943), Vol. xx. A close study of Wordsworth's development to 1798, based not upon Wordsworth's retrospective and poetically idealized account in *The Prelude,* but upon the letters and poems of the period under discussion.

Samuel Taylor Coleridge, *Biographia Literaria* (1817). Of special value are chaps. 4, 14, and 17–22, which present the great poet-critic's account of the origin of *Lyrical Ballads* and his estimate of Wordsworth's achievements and failures in poetry and literary theory.

Alfred North Whitehead, *Science and the Modern World* (1925), chap. v. One of the greatest modern philosophers discusses Wordsworth's importance in the development of modern thought and shows how his perception of poetic truth transcends the revelations of science.

Oscar James Campbell and Paul Mueschke, "Wordsworth's Aesthetic Development, 1795–1802," *Essays and Studies in English and Comparative Literature,* University of Michigan Publications, Language and Literature (1933), Vol. x.

Oscar James Campbell, "Wordsworth's Conception of the Esthetic Experience," *Wordsworth and Coleridge: Studies in Honor of George McLean Harper,* edited by Earl Leslie Griggs (1939). This study and the one listed immediately above present an invaluable account of the development of Wordsworth's mature aesthetic theory and practice.

Joseph Warren Beach, *The Concept of Nature in Nineteenth-Century English Poetry* (1936). A monumental study in the history of ideas, emphasizing the seventeenth- and eighteenth-century antecedents of Wordsworth's philosophy of nature, and including a valuable note on Wordsworth's reading.

Lionel Trilling, "The Immortality Ode," *The Liberal Imagination* (1950). A successful and stimulating refutation of the widely held notion that the "Intimations Ode" was Wordsworth's conscious farewell to his poetic power.

Helen Darbishire, *The Poet Wordsworth* (1950). A brief but excellent study by the greatest authority on the Wordsworth manuscripts. Especially valuable for students of *The Prelude.*

Frederick A. Pottle, "The Eye and the Object in the Poetry of Wordsworth," *Wordsworth: Centenary Studies Presented at Cornell and Princeton Universities,* edited by Gilbert T. Dunklin (1951). An excellent account of Wordsworth's imagination at work on a poem ("I Wandered Lonely as a Cloud"), and a reconciliation of Wordsworth's seemingly contradictory statements: "Poetry takes its origin from emotion recollected in tranquillity," and "I have at all times endeavored to look steadily at my subject."

## COLERIDGE:

EDITIONS

E. H. Coleridge, editor, *The Complete Poetical Works of S. T. Coleridge,* 2 vols. (1912). The standard edition of the poems and plays.

J. Shawcross, editor, *Biographia Literaria by S. T. Coleridge,* 2 vols. (1907). The standard edition, annotated; introduction perhaps too much concerned with Coleridge's debt to German philosophy.

Thomas Middleton Raysor, editor, *Coleridge's Shakespearean Criticism,* 2 vols. (1930). The definitive edition; a great example of modern editing.

Earl Leslie Griggs, *Collected Letters of Samuel Taylor Coleridge,* 2 vols. (1956). The result of decades of scholarly search, these volumes print the extant letters through December 25, 1806; other volumes forthcoming.

Ernest de Selincourt, "Coleridge's 'Dejection: An Ode,'" *Wordsworthian and Other Studies* (1947). Contains the original draft (April 4, 1802) of the poem.

BIOGRAPHY

E. K. Chambers, *Samuel Taylor Coleridge: A Biographical Study* (1938). An accurate, sensible, and readable chronicle of the significant facts.

Lawrence Hanson, *The Life of S. T. Coleridge: The Early Years* (1938). The fullest account of Coleridge's life to 1800; overestimates his importance to Wordsworth.

CRITICISM

John Livingston Lowes, *The Road to Xanadu* (1927). A classic of source studies; explores Coleridge's omnivorous reading and its links with the "Ancient Mariner" and "Kubla Khan."

D. G. James, *Scepticism and Poetry* (1937). The best discussion of Wordsworth and Coleridge on the imagination.

Donald R. Tuttle, "Christabel Sources in Percy's *Reliques* and the Gothic Romances," *Publications of the Modern Language Association,* LIII (1938), 445–74. An excellent study of Coleridge's poem and its relationship to the eighteenth-century Gothic and ballad traditions.

Arthur H. Nethercot, *The Road to Tryermaine* (1939). Supplements Tuttle and does for "Christabel" what Lowes did for the "Ancient Mariner" and "Kubla Khan."

Robert Penn Warren, editor, *The Rime of the Ancient Mariner* (1946). The critical introduction is the closest, most comprehensive discussion of the poem; the "secondary theme of the imagination" and the idea of the "cursed poet" are, however, very dubious.

Humphry House, *Coleridge* (1953). Delivered as the Clark Lectures (Cambridge University) for 1951–52, this is the best modern discussion of Coleridge's total performance.

Richard Harter Fogle, "Coleridge's Conversation Poems," *Tulane Studies in English,* V (1955). The best discussion of the genre first defined by George McLean Harper in "Coleridge's Conversation Poems," *Spirit of Delight* (1928).

---

# WILLIAM WORDSWORTH

## PREFACE

TO THE SECOND EDITION OF SEVERAL OF THE FOREGOING POEMS, PUBLISHED, WITH AN ADDITIONAL VOLUME, UNDER THE TITLE OF

*Lyrical Ballads*

The first volume of these poems has already been submitted to general perusal. It was published as an experiment, which, I hoped, might be of some use to ascertain how far, by fitting to metrical arrangement a selection of the real language of men in a state of vivid sensation, that sort of pleasure and that quantity of pleasure may be imparted, which a poet may rationally endeavor to impart.

I had formed no very inaccurate estimate of the probable effect of those poems: I flattered myself that they who should be pleased with them would read them with more than common pleasure; and, on the other hand, I was well aware that by those who should dislike them they would be read with more than common dislike. The result has differed from my expectation in this only, that a greater number have been pleased than I ventured to hope I should please.

Several of my friends are anxious for the success of these poems, from a belief that, if the views with which they were composed were indeed realized, a class of poetry would be produced, well adapted to interest mankind permanently, and not unimportant in the quality and in the multiplicty of its moral relations; and on this account they have advised me to prefix a systematic defense of the theory upon which the poems were written. But I was unwilling to undertake the task, knowing that on this occasion the reader would look coldly upon my arguments, since I might be suspected of having been principally influenced by the selfish and foolish hope of *reasoning* him into an approbation of these particular poems; and I was still more unwilling to undertake the task, because adequately to display the opinions, and fully to enforce the arguments, would require a space wholly disproportionate to a preface. For, to treat the subject with the clearness and coherence of which it is susceptible, it would be necessary to give a full account of the present state of the public taste in this country, and to determine how far this taste is healthy or depraved; which, again, could not be determined without pointing out in what manner language and the human mind act and react on each other, and without retracing the revolutions, not of literature alone, but likewise of society itself. I have therefore altogether declined to enter regularly upon this defense; yet I am sensible that there would be something like impropriety in abruptly obtruding upon the public, without a few words of introduction, poems so materially different from those upon which general approbation is at present bestowed.

It is supposed that by the act of writing in verse an author makes a formal engagement that he will gratify certain known habits of association; that he not only thus apprises the reader that certain classes of ideas and expressions will be found in his book, but that others will be carefully excluded. This exponent or symbol held forth by metrical language must in different eras of literature have excited very different expectations: for example, in the age of Catullus, Terence, and Lucretius,[1] and that of Statius or Claudian,[2] and in our own country, in the age of Shakespeare and Beaumont and Fletcher, and that of Donne and Cowley, or Dryden, or Pope. I will not take upon me to determine the exact import of the promise which, by the act of writing in verse, an author in the present day makes to his reader; but it will undoubtedly appear to many persons that I have not fulfilled the terms of an engagement thus voluntarily contracted. They who have been accustomed to the gaudiness and inane phraseology of many modern writers, if they persist in reading this book to its conclusion, will, no doubt, frequently have to struggle with feelings of strangeness and awkwardness; they will look round for poetry, and will be induced to inquire by what species of courtesy these attempts can be permitted to assume that title. I hope, therefore, the reader will not censure me for attempting to state what I have proposed to myself to perform; and also (as far as the limits of a preface will permit) to explain some of the chief reasons which have determined me in the choice of my purpose: that at least he may be spared any unpleasant feeling of disappointment, and that I myself may be protected from one of the most dishonorable accusations which can be brought against an author: namely, that of an indolence which prevents him from endeavoring to ascertain what is his duty, or, when his duty is ascertained, prevents him from performing it.

The principal object, then, proposed in these poems, was to choose incidents and situations from common life, and to relate or describe them throughout, as far as was possible, in a selection of language really used by men, and, at the same time, to throw over them a certain coloring of imagination, whereby ordinary things should be presented to the mind in an unusual aspect; and further, and above all, to make these incidents and situations interesting by tracing in them, truly though not ostentatiously, the primary laws of our nature, chiefly, as far as regards the manner in which we associate ideas in a state of excitement. Humble and rustic life was generally chosen, because in that condition the essential passions of the heart find a better soil in which they can attain their maturity, are less under restraint, and speak a plainer and more emphatic language; because in that condition of life our elementary feelings coexist in a state of greater simplicity, and, consequently, may be more accurately contemplated, and more forcibly communicated; because the manners of rural life germinate from those elementary feelings, and, from the necessary character of rural occupations, are more easily comprehended, and are more durable; and, lastly, because in that condition the passions of men are incorporated with the beautiful and permanent forms of nature. The language, too, of these men has been adopted (purified indeed from what appear to be its real defects, from all lasting and rational causes of dislike or disgust), because such men hourly communicate with the best objects from which the best part of language is originally derived; and because, from their rank in society and the sameness and narrow circle of their intercourse, being less under the influence of social vanity, they convey their feelings and notions in simple and unelaborated expressions. Accordingly, such a language, arising out of repeated experience and regular feelings, is a more permanent, and a far more philosophical language, than that which is frequently substituted for it by poets, who think that they are conferring honor upon themselves and their art in proportion as they separate themselves from the sympathies of men, and indulge in arbitrary and capricious habits of expression, in order to furnish food for fickle tastes and fickle appetites of their own creation.[3]

I cannot, however, be insensible to the present outcry against the triviality and meanness, both of thought and language, which some of my contemporaries have occasionally introduced into their metrical compositions; and I acknowledge that this defect, where it exists, is more dishonorable to the writer's own character than false refinement or arbitrary innovation, though I should contend at the same time that it is far less pernicious in the sum of its consequences. From such verses the poems in these volumes will be found distinguished at least by one mark of difference, that each of them has a worthy *purpose*. Not that I always began to write with a distinct purpose formally conceived, but habits of meditation have, I trust, so prompted

PREFACE TO "LYRICAL BALLADS." **1. Catullus:** a Roman lyric poet (84–54 B.C.) whom Wordsworth imitated in his youth. **Terence:** a Roman comic dramatist (190–159 B.C.). **Lucretius:** the Roman author (96–55 B.C.) of *De Rerum Natura*, a famous philosophical poem. Wordsworth admired these writers for naturalness and purity of style. **2. Statius:** a Roman epic poet (45–96 A.D.), the first book of whose *Thebaid* was translated by Alexander Pope. **Claudian:** a late Roman poet (365–408 A.D.) remarkable for stylistic artificiality.

**3. "It is worth while here to observe that the affecting parts of Chaucer are almost always expressed in language pure and universally intelligible even to this day" [Wordsworth's note].**

and regulated my feelings, that my descriptions of such objects as strongly excite those feelings will be found to carry along with them a *purpose*. If this opinion be erroneous, I can have little right to the name of a poet. For all good poetry is the spontaneous overflow of powerful feelings; and though this be true, poems to which any value can be attached were never produced on any variety of subjects but by a man who, being possessed of more than usual organic sensibility, had also thought long and deeply. For our continued influxes of feeling are modified and directed by our thoughts, which are indeed the representatives of all our past feelings; and as, by contemplating the relation of these general representatives to each other, we discover what is really important to men, so, by the repetition and continuance of this act, our feelings will be connected with important subjects, till at length, if we be originally possessed of much sensibility, such habits of mind will be produced that, by obeying blindly and mechanically the impulses of those habits, we shall describe objects, and utter sentiments, of such a nature, and in such connection with each other, that the understanding of the reader must necessarily be in some degree enlightened, and his affection strengthened and purified.

It has been said that each of these poems has a purpose. Another circumstance must be mentioned which distinguishes these poems from the popular poetry of the day; it is this, that the feeling therein developed gives importance to the action and situation, and not the action and situation to the feeling.

A sense of false modesty shall not prevent me from asserting that the reader's attention is pointed to this mark of distinction, far less for the sake of these particular poems than from the general importance of the subject. The subject is indeed important! For the human mind is capable of being excited without the application of gross and violent stimulants; and he must have a very faint perception of its beauty and dignity who does not know this, and who does not further know that one being is elevated above another in proportion as he possesses this capability. It has therefore appeared to me, that to endeavor to produce or enlarge this capability is one of the best services in which, at any period, a writer can be engaged; but this service, excellent at all times, is especially so at the present day. For a multitude of causes, unknown to former times, are now acting with a combined force to blunt the discriminating powers of the mind and, unfitting it for all voluntary exertion, to reduce it to a state of almost savage torpor. The most effective of these causes are the great national events[4] which are daily taking place, and the increasing accumulation of men in cities, where the uniformity of their occupations produces a craving for extraordinary incident which the rapid communication of intelligence hourly gratifies. To this tendency of life and manners the literature and theatrical exhibitions of the country have conformed themselves. The invaluable works of our elder writers — I had almost said the works of Shakespeare and Milton — are driven into neglect by frantic novels, sickly and stupid German tragedies, and deluges of idle and extravagant stories in verse.[5] When I think upon this degrading thirst after outrageous stimulation, I am almost ashamed to have spoken of the feeble endeavor made in these volumes to counteract it; and, reflecting upon the magnitude of the general evil, I should be oppressed with no dishonorable melancholy, had I not a deep impression of certain inherent and indestructible qualities of the human mind, and likewise of certain powers in the great and permanent objects that act upon it, which are equally inherent and indestructible; and were there not added to this impression a belief that the time is approaching when the evil will be systematically opposed by men of greater powers, and with far more distinguished success.

Having dwelt thus long on the subjects and aim of these poems, I shall request the reader's permission to apprise him of a few circumstances relating to their *style,* in order, among other reasons, that he may not censure me for not having performed what I never attempted. The reader will find that personifications of abstract ideas rarely occur in these volumes, and are utterly rejected as an ordinary device to elevate the style and raise it above prose. My purpose was to imitate, and, as far as is possible, to adopt the very language of men; and assuredly such personifications do not make any natural or regular part of that language. They are, indeed, a figure of speech occasionally prompted by passion, and I have made use of them as such; but have endeavored utterly to reject them as a mechanical device of style, or as a family language which writers in meter seem to lay claim to by prescription. I have wished to keep the reader in the com-

**4. great . . . events:** especially the French Revolution and the Napoleonic Wars. **5. frantic . . . verse:** Wordsworth here deplores the sensational literature popular in the 1790's, particularly the "Gothic" novels of Mrs. Ann Radcliffe and M. G. ("Monk") Lewis, and the translations of German melodramas by August von Kotzebue.

pany of flesh and blood, persuaded that by so doing I shall interest him. Others who pursue a different track will interest him likewise; I do not interfere with their claim, but wish to prefer a claim of my own. There will also be found in these volumes little of what is usually called poetic diction; as much pains has been taken to avoid it as is ordinarily taken to produce it; this has been done for the reason already alleged, to bring my language near to the language of men; and further, because the pleasure which I have proposed to myself to impart is of a kind very different from that which is supposed by many persons to be the proper object of poetry. Without being culpably particular, I do not know how to give my reader a more exact notion of the style in which it was my wish and intention to write, than by informing him that I have at all times endeavored to look steadily at my subject; consequently there is, I hope, in these poems little falsehood of description, and my ideas are expressed in language fitted to their respective importance. Something must have been gained by this practice, as it is friendly to one property of all good poetry, namely, good sense; but it has necessarily cut me off from a large portion of phrases and figures of speech which from father to son have long been regarded as the common inheritance of poets. I have also thought it expedient to restrict myself still further, having abstained from the use of many expressions, in themselves proper and beautiful, but which have been foolishly repeated by bad poets, till such feelings of disgust are connected with them as it is scarcely possible by any art of association to overpower.

If in a poem there should be found a series of lines, or even a single line, in which the language, though naturally arranged and according to the strict laws of meter, does not differ from that of prose, there is a numerous class of critics who, when they stumble upon these prosaisms, as they call them, imagine that they have made a notable discovery, and exult over the poet as over a man ignorant of his own profession. Now these men would establish a canon of criticism which the reader will conclude he must utterly reject, if he wishes to be pleased with these volumes. And it would be a most easy task to prove to him that not only the language of a large portion of every good poem, even of the most elevated character, must necessarily, except with reference to the meter, in no respect differ from that of good prose, but likewise that some of the most interesting parts of the best poems will be found to be strictly the language of prose when prose is well written. The truth of this assertion might be demonstrated by innumerable passages from almost all the poetical writings, even of Milton himself. To illustrate the subject in a general manner, I will here adduce a short composition of Gray,[6] who was at the head of those who, by their reasonings, have attempted to widen the space of separation betwixt prose and metrical composition, and was more than any other man curiously elaborate in the structure of his own poetic diction.

In vain to me the smiling mornings shine,
And reddening Phoebus lifts his golden fire;
The birds in vain their amorous descant join,
Or cheerful fields resume their green attire.
These ears, alas! for other notes repine;
*A different object do these eyes require;*
*My lonely anguish melts no heart but mine;*
*And in my breast the imperfect joys expire;*
Yet morning smiles the busy race to cheer,
And newborn pleasure brings to happier men;
The fields to all their wonted tribute bear;
To warm their little loves the birds complain.
*I fruitless mourn to him that cannot hear,*
*And weep the more because I weep in vain.*

It will easily be perceived that the only part of this sonnet which is of any value is the lines printed in italics; it is equally obvious that, except in the rhyme and in the use of the single word "fruitless" for fruitlessly, which is so far a defect, the language of these lines does in no respect differ from that of prose.

By the foregoing quotation it has been shown that the language of prose may yet be well adapted to poetry; and it was previously asserted that a large portion of the language of every good poem can in no respect differ from that of good prose. We will go further. It may be safely affirmed that there neither is, nor can be, any *essential* difference between the language of prose and metrical composition. We are fond of tracing the resemblance between poetry and painting, and, accordingly, we call them sisters: but where shall we find bonds of connection sufficiently strict to typify the affinity betwixt metrical and prose composition? They both speak by and to the same organs; the bodies in which both of them are clothed may be said to be of the same substance; their affections are kindred,

6. Gray: Thomas Gray (1716–71), English poet and author of "Elegy Written in a Country Churchyard," whose "Sonnet on the Death of Richard West" Wordsworth criticizes immediately below.

and almost identical, not necessarily differing even in degree; poetry[7] sheds no tears "such as angels weep," but natural and human tears; she can boast of no celestial ichor[8] that distinguishes her vital juices from those of prose; the same human blood circulates through the veins of them both.

If it be affirmed that rhyme and metrical arrangement of themselves constitute a distinction which overturns what has just been said on the strict affinity of metrical language with that of prose, and paves the way for other artificial distinctions which the mind voluntarily admits,[9] I answer that the language of such poetry as is here recommended is, as far as is possible, a selection of the language really spoken by men; that this selection, wherever it is made with true taste and feeling, will of itself form a distinction far greater than would at first be imagined, and will entirely separate the composition from the vulgarity and meanness of ordinary life; and, if meter be superadded thereto, I believe that a dissimilitude will be produced altogther sufficient for the gratification of a rational mind. What other distinction would we have? Whence is it to come? And where is it to exist? Not, surely, where the poet speaks through the mouths of his characters; it cannot be necessary here, either for elevation of style, or any of its supposed ornaments; for, if the poet's subject be judiciously chosen, it will naturally, and upon fit occasion, lead him to passions, the language of which, if selected truly and judiciously, must necessarily be dignified and variegated, and alive with metaphors and figures. I forbear to speak of an incongruity which would shock the intelligent reader, should the poet interweave any foreign splendor of his own with that which the passion naturally suggests; it is sufficient to say that such addition is unnecessary. And, surely, it is more probable that those passages, which with propriety abound with metaphors and figures, will have their due effect if, upon other occasions where the passions are of a milder character, the style also be subdued and temperate.

But, as the pleasure which I hope to give by the poems now presented to the reader must depend entirely on just notions upon this subject, and as it is in itself of high importance to our taste and moral feelings, I cannot content myself with these detached remarks. And if, in what I am about to say, it shall appear to some that my labor is unnecessary, and that I am like a man fighting a battle without enemies, such persons may be reminded that, whatever be the language outwardly holden[10] by men, a practical faith in the opinions which I am wishing to establish is almost unknown. If my conclusions are admitted, and carried as far as they must be carried if admitted at all, our judgments concerning the works of the greatest poets, both ancient and modern, will be far different from what they are at present, both when we praise and when we censure, and our moral feelings influencing and influenced by these judgments will, I believe, be corrected and purified.

Taking up the subject, then, upon general grounds, let me ask, what is meant by the word "poet"? What is a poet? To whom does he address himself? And what language is to be expected from him? He is a man speaking to men, a man, it is true, endowed with more lively sensibility, more enthusiasm and tenderness, who has a greater knowledge of human nature, and a more comprehensive soul, than are supposed to be common among mankind; a man pleased with his own passions and volitions, and who rejoices more than other men in the spirit of life that is in him, delighting to contemplate similar volitions and passions as manifested in the goings on of the universe, and habitually impelled to create them where he does not find them. To these qualities he has added a disposition to be affected more than any other men by absent things as if they were present; an ability of conjuring up in himself passions, which are indeed far from being the same as those produced by real events, yet (especially in those parts of the general sympathy which are pleasing and delightful) do more nearly resemble the passions produced by real events than anything which, from the motions of their own minds merely, other men are accustomed to feel in themselves — whence, and from practice, he has acquired a greater readiness and power in expressing what he thinks and feels, and especially those thoughts and feelings which, by his own choice, or from the structure of his

7. "I here use the word 'poetry' (though against my own judgment) as opposed to the word 'prose,' and synonymous with metrical composition. But much confusion has been introduced into criticism by this contradistinction of poetry and prose, instead of the more philosophical one of poetry and matter of fact, or science. The only strict antithesis to prose is meter; nor is this, in truth, a *strict* antithesis, because lines and passages of meter so naturally occur in writing prose that it would be scarcely possible to avoid them, even if it were desirable" [W]. **8. ichor:** a fluid supposed to flow in the veins of celestial creatures. **9.** Here begins the famous description of the poet which Wordsworth added to the Preface in the edition of 1802.

**10. holden:** held.

own mind, arise in him without immediate external excitement.

But whatever portion of this faculty we may suppose even the greatest poet to possess, there cannot be a doubt that the language which it will suggest to him must often, in liveliness and truth, fall short of that which is uttered by men in real life under the actual pressure of those passions, certain shadows of which the poet thus produces, or feels to be produced, in himself.

However exalted a notion we would wish to cherish of the character of a poet, it is obvious that, while he describes and imitates passions, his employment is in some degree mechanical compared with the freedom and power of real and substantial action and suffering. So that it will be the wish of the poet to bring his feelings near to those of the persons whose feelings he describes, nay, for short spaces of time, perhaps, to let himself slip into an entire delusion, and even confound and identify his own feelings with theirs, modifying only the language which is thus suggested to him by a consideration that he describes for a particular purpose, that of giving pleasure. Here, then, he will apply the principle of selection which has been already insisted upon. He will depend upon this for removing what would otherwise be painful or disgusting in the passion; he will feel that there is no necessity to trick out or to elevate nature; and the more industriously he applies this principle the deeper will be his faith that no words which *his* fancy or imagination can suggest will be to be compared with those which are the emanations of reality and truth.

But it may be said by those who do not object to the general spirit of these remarks that, as it is impossible for the poet to produce upon all occasions language as exquisitely fitted for the passion as that which the real passion itself suggests, it is proper that he should consider himself as in the situation of a translator, who does not scruple to substitute excellences of another kind for those which are unattainable by him; and endeavors occasionally to surpass his original, in order to make some amends for the general inferiority to which he feels he must submit. But this would be to encourage idleness and unmanly despair. Further, it is the language of men who speak of what they do not understand; who talk of poetry, as of a matter of amusement and idle pleasure; who will converse with us as gravely about a *taste* for poetry, as they express it, as if it were a thing as indifferent as a taste for rope dancing, or Frontiniac or sherry.[11] Aristotle, I have been told, has said that poetry is the most philosophic of all writing;[12] it is so: its object is truth, not individual and local, but general and operative; not standing upon external testimony, but carried alive into the heart by passion; truth which is its own testimony, which gives competence and confidence to the tribunal to which it appeals, and receives them from the same tribunal. Poetry is the image of man and nature. The obstacles which stand in the way of the fidelity of the biographer and historian, and of their consequent utility, are incalculably greater than those which are to be encountered by the poet who comprehends the dignity of his art. The poet writes under one restriction only, namely, the necessity of giving immediate pleasure to a human being possessed of that information which may be expected from him, not as a lawyer, a physician, a mariner, an astronomer, or a natural philosopher, but as a man. Except this one restriction, there is no object standing between the poet and the image of things; between this, and the biographer and historian, there are a thousand.

Nor let this necessity of producing immediate pleasure be considered as a degradation of the poet's art. It is far otherwise. It is an acknowledgment of the beauty of the universe, an acknowledgment the more sincere because not formal, but indirect; it is a task light and easy to him who looks at the world in the spirit of love; further, it is a homage paid to the native and naked dignity of man, to the grand elementary principle of pleasure, by which he knows, and feels, and lives, and moves. We have no sympathy but what is propagated by pleasure; I would not be misunderstood, but wherever we sympathize with pain, it will be found that the sympathy is produced and carried on by subtle combinations with pleasure. We have no knowledge, that is, no general principles drawn from the contemplation of particular facts, but what has been built up by pleasure, and exists in us by pleasure alone. The man of science, the chemist and mathematician, whatever difficulties and disgusts they may have had to struggle with, know and feel this. However painful may be the objects with which the anatomist's knowledge is connected, he feels that

11. **Frontiniac or sherry:** European wines, the first made in Frontignan, France; the other, originally, near Xeres (Jerez), Spain. 12. **Aristotle . . . writing:** Aristotle (384–322 B.C.) was one of the greatest of Greek philosophers. Wordsworth refers to the *Poetics*, IX.3, in which Aristotle asserts that poetry, because it expresses the universal rather than the particular, is more philosophical than history.

his knowledge is pleasure; and where he has no pleasure he has no knowledge. What then does the poet? He considers man and the objects that surround him as acting and reacting upon each other, so as to produce an infinite complexity of pain and pleasure; he considers man in his own nature and in his ordinary life as contemplating this with a certain quantity of immediate knowledge, with certain convictions, intuitions, and deductions, which from habit acquire the quality of intuitions; he considers him as looking upon this complex scene of ideas and sensations, and finding everywhere objects that immediately excite in him sympathies which, from the necessities of his nature, are accompanied by an overbalance of enjoyment.

To this knowledge which all men carry about with them, and to these sympathies in which, without any other discipline than that of our daily life, we are fitted to take delight, the poet principally directs his attention. He considers man and nature as essentially adapted to each other, and the mind of man as naturally the mirror of the fairest and most interesting properties of nature. And thus the poet, prompted by this feeling of pleasure, which accompanies him through the whole course of his studies, converses with general nature, with affections akin to those which, through labor and length of time, the man of science has raised up in himself, by conversing with those particular parts of nature which are the objects of his studies. The knowledge both of the poet and the man of science is pleasure; but the knowledge of the one cleaves to us as a necessary part of our existence, our natural and unalienable inheritance; the other is a personal and individual acquisition, slow to come to us, and by no habitual and direct sympathy connecting us with our fellow beings. The man of science seeks truth as a remote and unknown benefactor; he cherishes and loves it in his solitude; the poet, singing a song in which all human beings join with him, rejoices in the presence of truth as our visible friend and hourly companion. Poetry is the breath and finer spirit of all knowledge; it is the impassioned expression which is in the countenance of all science. Emphatically may it be said of the poet, as Shakespeare hath said of man, "that he looks before and after." [13] He is the rock of defense for human nature; an upholder and preserver, carrying everywhere with him relationship and love. In spite of difference of soil and climate, of language and manners, of laws and customs; in spite of things silently gone out of mind, and things violently destroyed, the poet binds together by passion and knowledge the vast empire of human society, as it is spread over the whole earth and over all time. The objects of the poet's thoughts are everywhere; though the eyes and senses of man are, it is true, his favorite guides, yet he will follow wheresoever he can find an atmosphere of sensation in which to move his wings. Poetry is the first and last of all knowledge — it is as immortal as the heart of man. If the labors of men of science should ever create any material revolution, direct or indirect, in our condition, and in the impressions which we habitually receive, the poet will sleep then no more than at present; he will be ready to follow the steps of the man of science, not only in those general indirect effects, but he will be at his side, carrying sensation into the midst of the objects of the science itself. The remotest discoveries of the chemist, the botanist, or mineralogist will be as proper objects of the poet's art as any upon which it can be employed, if the time should ever come when these things shall be familiar to us, and the relations under which they are contemplated by the followers of these respective sciences shall be manifestly and palpably material to us as enjoying and suffering beings. If the time should ever come when what is now called science, thus familiarized to men, shall be ready to put on, as it were, a form of flesh and blood, the poet will lend his divine spirit to aid the transfiguration, and will welcome the being thus produced as a dear and genuine inmate of the household of man. It is not, then, to be supposed that anyone who holds that sublime notion of poetry which I have attempted to convey will break in upon the sanctity and truth of his pictures by transitory and accidental ornaments, and endeavor to excite admiration of himself by arts, the necessity of which must manifestly depend upon the assumed meanness of his subject.

What has been thus far said applies to poetry in general, but especially to those parts of compositions where the poet speaks through the mouths of his characters; and upon this point it appears to authorize the conclusion that there are few persons of good sense who would not allow that the dramatic parts of composition are defective in proportion as they deviate from the real language of nature, and are colored by a diction of the poet's own, either peculiar to him as an individual poet or belonging

13. See *Hamlet,* IV.iv.37, in Vol. I.

simply to poets in general; to a body of men who, from the circumstance of their compositions being in meter, it is expected will employ a particular language.

It is not, then, in the dramatic parts of composition that we look for this distinction of language; but still it may be proper and necessary where the poet speaks to us in his own person and character. To this I answer by referring the reader to the description before given of a poet. Among the qualities there enumerated as principally conducing to form a poet, is implied nothing differing in kind from other men, but only in degree. The sum of what was said is, that the poet is chiefly distinguished from other men by a greater promptness to think and feel without immediate external excitement, and a greater power in expressing such thoughts and feelings as are produced in him in that manner. But these passions and thoughts and feelings are the general passions and thoughts and feelings of men. And with what are they connected? Undoubtedly with our moral sentiments and animal sensations, and with the causes which excite these; with the operations of the elements, and the appearances of the visible universe; with storm and sunshine, with the revolutions of the seasons, with cold and heat, with loss of friends and kindred, with injuries and resentments, gratitude and hope, with fear and sorrow. These, and the like, are the sensations and objects which the poet describes, as they are the sensations of other men and the objects which interest them. The poet thinks and feels in the spirit of human passions. How, then, can his language differ in any material degree from that of all other men who feel vividly and see clearly? It might be *proved* that it is impossible. But supposing that this were not the case, the poet might then be allowed to use a peculiar language when expressing his feelings for his own gratification, or that of men like himself. But poets do not write for poets alone, but for men. Unless, therefore, we are advocates for that admiration which subsists upon ignorance, and that pleasure which arises from hearing what we do not understand, the poet must descend from this supposed height; and, in order to excite rational sympathy, he must express himself as other men express themselves. To this it may be added, that while he is only selecting from the real language of men or, which amounts to the same thing, composing accurately in the spirit of such selection, he is treading upon safe ground, and we know what we are to expect from him. Our feelings are the same with respect to meter;[14] for, as it may be proper to remind the reader, the distinction of meter is regular and uniform, and not, like that which is produced by what is usually called "poetic diction," arbitrary, and subject to infinite caprices, upon which no calculation whatever can be made. In the one case, the reader is utterly at the mercy of the poet, respecting what imagery or diction he may choose to connect with the passion; whereas, in the other, the meter obeys certain laws, to which the poet and reader both willingly submit because they are certain, and because no interference is made by them with the passion but such as the concurring testimony of ages has shown to heighten and improve the pleasure which coexists with it.

It will now be proper to answer an obvious question, namely, Why, professing these opinions, have I written in verse? To this, in addition to such answer as is included in what has been already said, I reply, in the first place, because, however I may have restricted myself, there is still left open to me what confessedly constitutes the most valuable object of all writing, whether in prose or verse: the great and universal passions of men, the most general and interesting of their occupations, and the entire world of nature before me — to supply endless combinations of forms and imagery. Now, supposing for a moment that whatever is interesting in these objects may be as vividly described in prose, why should I be condemned for attempting to superadd to such description the charm which, by the consent of all nations, is acknowledged to exist in metrical language? To this, by such as are yet unconvinced, it may be answered that a very small part of the pleasure given by poetry depends upon the meter, and that it is injudicious to write in meter, unless it be accompanied with the other artificial distinctions of style with which meter is usually accompanied, and that, by such deviation, more will be lost from the shock which will thereby be given to the reader's associations than will be counterbalanced by any pleasure which he can derive from the general power of numbers.[15] In answer to those who still contend for the necessity of accompanying meter with certain appropriate colors of style in order to the accomplishment of its appropriate end,

14. Here ends the description of the poet which Wordsworth added to the Preface in the edition of 1802. 15. **from . . . numbers:** from meter and rhyme, as distinct from imagery and metaphor.

and who also, in my opinion, greatly underrate the power of meter in itself, it might, perhaps, as far as relates to these volumes, have been almost sufficient to observe, that poems are extant, written upon more humble subjects, and in a still more naked and simple style, which have continued to give pleasure from generation to generation. Now, if nakedness and simplicity be a defect, the fact here mentioned affords a strong presumption that poems somewhat less naked and simple are capable of affording pleasure at the present day; and, what I wished *chiefly* to attempt, at present, was to justify myself for having written under the impression of this belief.

But various causes might be pointed out why, when the style is manly, and the subject of some importance, words metrically arranged will long continue to impart such a pleasure to mankind as he who proves the extent of that pleasure will be desirous to impart. The end of poetry is to produce excitement in coexistence with an overbalance of pleasure; but, by the supposition, excitement is an unusual and irregular state of the mind; ideas and feelings do not, in that state, succeed each other in accustomed order. If the words, however, by which this excitement is produced be in themselves powerful, or the images and feelings have an undue proportion of pain connected with them, there is some danger that the excitement may be carried beyond its proper bounds. Now the copresence of something regular, something to which the mind has been accustomed in various moods and in a less excited state, cannot but have great efficacy in tempering and restraining the passion by an intertexture of ordinary feeling, and feeling not strictly and necessarily connected with the passion. This is unquestionably true; and hence, though the opinion will at first appear paradoxical, from the tendency of meter to divest language, in a certain degree, of its reality, and thus to throw a sort of half-consciousness of unsubstantial existence over the whole composition, there can be little doubt but that more pathetic situations and sentiments, that is, those which have a greater proportion of pain connected with them, may be endured in metrical composition, especially in rhyme, than in prose. The meter of the old ballads is very artless, yet they contain many passages which would illustrate this opinion; and, I hope, if the following poems be attentively perused, similar instances will be found in them. This opinion may be further illustrated by appealing to the reader's own experience of the reluctance with which he comes to the reperusal of the distressful parts of *Clarissa Harlowe* or *The Gamester;*[16] while Shakespeare's writings, in the most pathetic scenes, never act upon us, as pathetic, beyond the bounds of pleasure — an effect which, in a much greater degree than might at first be imagined, is to be ascribed to small, but continual and regular impulses of pleasurable surprise from the metrical arrangement. On the other hand (what it must be allowed will much more frequently happen), if the poet's words should be incommensurate with the passion, and inadequate to raise the reader to a height of desirable excitement, then (unless the poet's choice of his meter has been grossly injudicious), in the feelings of pleasure which the reader has been accustomed to connect with meter in general, and in the feeling, whether cheerful or melancholy, which he has been accustomed to connect with that particular movement of meter, there will be found something which will greatly contribute to impart passion to the words, and to effect the complex end which the poet proposes to himself.

If I had undertaken a systematic defense of the theory here maintained, it would have been my duty to develop the various causes upon which the pleasure received from metrical language depends. Among the chief of these causes is to be reckoned a principle which must be well known to those who have made any of the arts the object of accurate reflection, namely, the pleasure which the mind derives from the perception of similitude in dissimilitude. This principle is the great spring of the activity of our minds, and their chief feeder. From this principle the direction of the sexual appetite, and all the passions connected with it, take their origin: it is the life of our ordinary conversation; and upon the accuracy with which similitude in dissimilitude, and dissimilitude in similitude, are perceived, depend our taste and our moral feelings. It would not be a useless employment to apply this principle to the consideration of meter, and to show that meter is hence enabled to afford much pleasure, and to point out in what manner that pleasure is produced. But my limits will not permit me to enter upon this subject, and I must content myself with a general summary.

I have said that poetry is the spontaneous overflow of powerful feelings; it takes its origin from

16. *Clarissa Harlowe*- a popular sentimental novel published by Samuel Richardson in 1748. *The Gamester:* a sentimental tragedy (1753) by Edward Moore.

emotion recollected in tranquillity; the emotion is contemplated till, by a species of reaction, the tranquillity gradually disappears, and an emotion, kindred to that which was before the subject of contemplation, is gradually produced, and does itself actually exist in the mind. In this mood successful composition generally begins, and in a mood similar to this it is carried on; but the emotion, of whatever kind, and in whatever degree, from various causes, is qualified by various pleasures, so that in describing any passions whatsoever, which are voluntarily described, the mind will, upon the whole, be in a state of enjoyment. If nature be thus cautious to preserve in a state of enjoyment a being so employed, the poet ought to profit by the lesson held forth to him, and ought especially to take care that, whatever passions he communicates to his reader, those passions, if his reader's mind be sound and vigorous, should always be accompanied with an overbalance of pleasure. Now the music of harmonious metrical language, the sense of difficulty overcome, and the blind association of pleasure which has been previously received from works of rhyme or meter of the same or similar construction, an indistinct perception perpetually renewed of language closely resembling that of real life, and yet, in the circumstance of meter, differing from it so widely — all these imperceptibly make up a complex feeling of delight, which is of the most important use in tempering the painful feeling always found intermingled with powerful descriptions of the deeper passions. This effect is always produced in pathetic and impassioned poetry; while, in lighter compositions, the ease and gracefulness with which the poet manages his numbers are themselves confessedly a principal source of the gratification of the reader. All that it is *necessary* to say, however, upon this subject, may be effected by affirming, what few persons will deny, that of two descriptions, either of passions, manners, or characters, each of them equally well executed, the one in prose and the other in verse, the verse will be read a hundred times where the prose is read once.

Having thus explained a few of my reasons for writing in verse, and why I have chosen subjects from common life, and endeavored to bring my language near to the real language of men, if I have been too minute in pleading my own cause, I have at the same time been treating a subject of general interest; and for this reason a few words shall be added with reference solely to these particular poems, and to some defects which will probably be found in them. I am sensible that my associations must have sometimes been particular instead of general, and that, consequently, giving to things a false importance, I may have sometimes written upon unworthy subjects; but I am less apprehensive on this account, than that my language may frequently have suffered from those arbitrary connections of feelings and ideas with particular words and phrases from which no man can altogether protect himself. Hence I have no doubt that, in some instances, feelings, even of the ludicrous, may be given to my readers by expressions which appeared to me tender and pathetic. Such faulty expressions, were I convinced they were faulty at present, and that they must necessarily continue to be so, I would willingly take all reasonable pains to correct. But it is dangerous to make these alterations on the simple authority of a few individuals, or even of certain classes of men; for where the understanding of an author is not convinced, or his feelings altered, this cannot be done without great injury to himself, for his own feelings are his stay and support; and, if he set them aside in one instance, he may be induced to repeat this act till his mind shall lose all confidence in itself, and become utterly debilitated. To this it may be added, that the critic ought never to forget that he is himself exposed to the same errors as the poet, and, perhaps, in a much greater degree, for there can be no presumption in saying of most readers, that it is not probable they will be so well acquainted with the various stages of meaning through which words have passed, or with the fickleness or stability of the relations of particular ideas to each other; and, above all, since they are so much less interested in the subject, they may decide lightly and carelessly.

Long as the reader has been detained, I hope he will permit me to caution him against a mode of false criticism which has been applied to poetry, in which the language closely resembles that of life and nature. Such verses have been triumphed over in parodies, of which Dr. Johnson's stanza is a fair specimen:

> I put my hat upon my head
> And walked into the Strand,[17]
> And there I met another man
> Whose hat was in his hand.

Immediately under these lines let us place one of the most justly admired stanzas of the "Babes in the Wood":

17. the Strand: a principal business street in London.

These pretty babes with hand in hand
Went wandering up and down;
But never more they saw the man
Approaching from the town.

In both these stanzas the words, and the order of the words, in no respect differ from the most unimpassioned conversation. There are words in both, for example, "the Strand," and "the town," connected with none but the most familiar ideas; yet the one stanza we admit as admirable, and the other as a fair example of the superlatively contemptible. Whence arises this difference? Not from the meter, not from the language, not from the order of the words; but the *matter* expressed in Dr. Johnson's stanza is contemptible. The proper method of treating trivial and simple verses, to which Dr. Johnson's stanza would be a fair parallelism, is not to say, this is a bad kind of poetry, or, this is not poetry; but, this wants sense; it is neither interesting in itself, nor can *lead* to anything interesting; the images neither originate in that sane state of feeling which arises out of thought, nor can excite thought or feeling in the reader. This is the only sensible manner of dealing with such verses. Why trouble yourself about the species till you have previously decided upon the genus? Why take pains to prove that an ape is not a Newton, when it is self-evident that he is not a man?

One request I must make of my reader, which is, that in judging these poems he would decide by his own feelings genuinely, and not by reflection upon what will probably be the judgment of others. How common is it to hear a person say, I myself do not object to this style of composition, or this or that expression, but to such and such classes of people it will appear mean or ludicrous! This mode of criticism, so destructive of all sound unadulterated judgment, is almost universal; let the reader then abide, independently, by his own feelings, and, if he finds himself affected, let him not suffer such conjectures to interfere with his pleasure.

If an author, by any single composition, has impressed us with respect for his talents, it is useful to consider this as affording a presumption that on other occasions where we have been displeased he, nevertheless, may not have written ill or absurdly; and further, to give him so much credit for this one composition as may induce us to review what has displeased us with more care than we should otherwise have bestowed upon it. This is not only an act of justice, but, in our decisions upon poetry especially, may conduce, in a high degree, to the improvement of our own taste, for an *accurate* taste in poetry, and in all the other arts, as Sir Joshua Reynolds has observed, is an *acquired* talent, which can only be produced by thought and a long-continued intercourse with the best models of composition. This is mentioned, not with so ridiculous a purpose as to prevent the most inexperienced reader from judging for himself (I have already said that I wish him to judge for himself), but merely to temper the rashness of decision, and to suggest that, if poetry be a subject on which much time has not been bestowed, the judgment may be erroneous; and that, in many cases, it necessarily will be so.

Nothing would, I know, have so effectually contributed to further the end which I have in view, as to have shown of what kind the pleasure is, and how that pleasure is produced, which is confessedly produced by metrical composition essentially different from that which I have here endeavored to recommend, for the reader will say that he has been pleased by such composition, and what more can be done for him? The power of any art is limited; and he will suspect that, if it be proposed to furnish him with new friends, that can be only upon condition of his abandoning his old friends. Besides, as I have said, the reader is himself conscious of the pleasure which he has received from such composition, composition to which he has peculiarly attached the endearing name of poetry; and all men feel an habitual gratitude, and something of an honorable bigotry, for the objects which have long continued to please them; we not only wish to be pleased, but to be pleased in that particular way in which we have been accustomd to be pleased. There is in these feelings enough to resist a host of arguments; and I should be the less able to combat them successfully, as I am willing to allow that, in order entirely to enjoy the poetry which I am recommending, it would be necessary to give up much of what is ordinarily enjoyed. But would my limits have permitted me to point out how this pleasure is produced, many obstacles might have been removed, and the reader assisted in perceiving that the powers of language are not so limited as he may suppose, and that it is possible for poetry to give other enjoyments, of a purer, more lasting, and more exquisite nature. This part of the subject has not been altogether neglected, but it has not been so much my present aim to prove that the interest excited by some other kinds of poetry is less vivid, and less worthy of the nobler powers of the mind, as to offer reasons for presuming that if my purpose were fulfilled, a species of poetry would be produced which is genuine poetry, in its nature well adapted to interest mankind permanently, and likewise important in the multiplicity and quality of its moral relations.

From what has been said, and from a perusal of the poems, the reader will be able clearly to perceive the object which I had in view; he will determine how far it has been attained, and, what is a much more important question, whether it be worth attaining; and upon the decision of these two questions will rest my claim to the approbation of the public.

*1800*

## LINES

*Left upon a seat in a yew tree which stands near the lake of Esthwaite, on a desolate part of the shore, commanding a beautiful prospect*

" Composed in part at school at Hawkshead. . . . This spot was my favorite walk in the evenings during the latter part of my schooltime. The individual whose habits and character are here given was a gentleman of the neighborhood, a man of talent and learning, who had been educated at one of our universities, and returned to pass his time in seclusion on his own estate. He died a bachelor in middle age " [Wordsworth's note].

Nay, traveler! rest. This lonely yew tree stands
Far from all human dwelling; what if here
No sparkling rivulet spread the verdant herb?
What if the bee love not these barren boughs?
Yet, if the wind breathe soft, the curling waves,
That break against the shore, shall lull thy mind
By one soft impulse saved from vacancy.
Who he was
That piled these stones and with the mossy sod
First covered, and here taught this aged tree
With its dark arms to form a circling bower,
I well remember. He was one who owned
No common soul. In youth by science nursed,
And led by nature into a wild scene
Of lofty hopes, he to the world went forth
A favored being, knowing no desire
Which genius did not hallow; 'gainst the taint
Of dissolute tongues, and jealousy, and hate,
And scorn — against all enemies prepared,
All but neglect. The world, for so it thought,
Owed him no service; wherefore he at once
With indignation turned himself away,
And with the food of pride sustained his soul
In solitude. Stranger! these gloomy boughs
Had charms for him; and here he loved to sit,
His only visitants a straggling sheep,
The stonechat, or the glancing sandpiper;
And on these barren rocks, with fern and heath,
And juniper and thistle, sprinkled o'er,
Fixing his downcast eye, he many an hour
A morbid pleasure nourished, tracing here
An emblem of his own unfruitful life,
And, lifting up his head, he then would gaze
On the more distant scene — how lovely 'tis
Thou seest — and he would gaze till it became
Far lovelier, and his heart could not sustain
The beauty, still more beauteous! Nor, that time,
When Nature had subdued him to herself,
Would he forget those beings to whose minds,
Warm from the labors of benevolence,
The world, and human life, appeared a scene
Of kindred loveliness; then he would sigh,
Inly disturbed, to think that others felt
What he must never feel; and so, lost Man!
On visionary views would fancy feed,
Till his eye streamed with tears. In this deep vale
He died — this seat his only monument.

If thou be one whose heart the holy forms
Of young imagination have kept pure,
Stranger! henceforth be warned; and know that pride,
Howe'er disguised in its own majesty,
Is littleness; that he, who feels contempt
For any living thing, hath faculties
Which he has never used; that thought with him
Is in its infancy. The man whose eye
Is ever on himself doth look on one,
The least of Nature's works, one who might move
The wise man to that scorn which wisdom holds
Unlawful, ever. O be wiser, thou!
Instructed that true knowledge leads to love;
True dignity abides with him alone
Who, in the silent hour of inward thought,
Can still suspect, and still revere himself,
In lowliness of heart.

*1797*

## THE REVERIE OF POOR SUSAN

" This arose out of my observation of the affecting music of these birds hanging in this way in the London streets during the freshness and stillness of the spring morning " [W].

At the corner of Wood Street, when daylight appears,
Hangs a thrush that sings loud, it has sung for three years;

Poor Susan has passed by the spot, and has heard
In the silence of morning the song of the bird.

'Tis a note of enchantment; what ails her? She sees
A mountain ascending, a vision of trees;
Bright volumes of vapor through Lothbury glide,
And a river flows on through the vale of Cheapside.

Green pastures she views in the midst of the dale,
Down which she so often has tripped with her pail;
And a single small cottage, a nest like a dove's,
The one only dwelling on earth that she loves.

She looks, and her heart is in heaven; but they fade,
The mist and the river, the hill and the shade;
The stream will not flow, and the hill will not rise,
And the colors have all passed away from her eyes!

*1797*

# THE RUINED COTTAGE

This is Wordsworth's first sustained narrative in blank verse. Many years later, after he had incorporated the story into *The Excursion* (Book I), Wordsworth recalled that lines 871–916 "were the first written of the whole poem, and were composed at Racedown." This passage, no doubt much expanded, was the first thing read to Samuel Taylor Coleridge when he paid his famous visit to the Wordsworths in June, 1797. But the bulk of the poem dates from the winter of 1797–98, and it was the nearly completed version that Coleridge probably had in mind when he wrote as follows in March, 1798, to Joseph Cottle, who was soon to publish the first edition of *Lyrical Ballads:* "The giant Wordsworth — God love him! When I speak of the terms of admiration due to his intellect, I fear lest these terms should keep out of sight the amiableness of his manners. He has written near twelve hundred lines of blank verse, superior, I hesitate not to aver, to anything in our language which any way resembles it."

Supine the Wanderer lay,
His eyes as if in drowsiness half shut,
The shadows of the breezy elms above
Dappling his face. He had not heard the sound
Of my approaching steps, and in the shade
Unnoticed did I stand some minutes' space.
At length I hailed him, seeing that his hat
Was moist with waterdrops, as if the brim
Had newly scooped a running stream. He rose,
And ere our lively greeting into peace
Had settled, "'Tis," said I, "a burning day;

REVERIE OF POOR SUSAN. **1–8. Wood Street, Lothbury, Cheapside:** places in one of the busiest sections of London.

My lips are parched with thirst, but you, it seems,
Have somewhere found relief." He, at the word,
Pointing towards a sweetbrier, bade me climb
The fence where that aspiring shrub looked out
Upon the public way. It was a plot
Of garden ground run wild, its matted weeds
Marked with the steps of those, whom, as they passed,
The gooseberry trees that shot in long lank slips,
Or currants, hanging from their leafless stems,
In scanty strings, had tempted to o'erleap
The broken wall. I looked around, and there,
Where two tall hedgerows of thick alder boughs
Joined in a cold damp nook, espied a well
Shrouded with willow flowers and plumy fern.
My thirst I slaked, and, from the cheerless spot
Withdrawing, straightway to the shade returned
Where sat the old man on the cottage bench;
And, while, beside him, with uncovered head,
I yet was standing, freely to respire,
And cool my temples in the fanning air,
Thus did he speak. "I see around me here
Things which you cannot see: we die, my friend,
Nor we alone, but that which each man loved
And prized in his peculiar nook of earth
Dies with him, or is changed; and very soon
Even of the good is no memorial left.
— The poets, in their elegies and songs
Lamenting the departed, call the groves,
They call upon the hills and streams, to mourn,
And senseless rocks; nor idly; for they speak,
In these their invocations, with a voice
Obedient to the strong creative power
Of human passion. Sympathies there are
More tranquil, yet perhaps of kindred birth,
That steal upon the meditative mind,
And grow with thought. Beside yon spring I stood,
And eyed its waters till we seemed to feel
One sadness, they and I. For them a bond
Of brotherhood is broken; time has been
When, every day, the touch of human hand
Dislodged the natural sleep that binds them up
In mortal stillness; and they ministered
To human comfort. Stooping down to drink,
Upon the slimy footstone I espied
The useless fragment of a wooden bowl,
Green with the moss of years, and subject only
To the soft handling of the elements:
There let it lie — how foolish are such thoughts!
Forgive them — never — never did my steps
Approach this door but she who dwelt within
A daughter's welcome gave me, and I loved her
As my own child. Oh, sir! the good die first,
And they whose hearts are dry as summer dust
Burn to the socket. Many a passenger
Hath blessed poor Margaret for her gentle looks,
When she upheld the cool refreshment drawn

From that forsaken spring; and no one came
But he was welcome; no one went away
But that it seemed she loved him. She is dead,
The light extinguished of her lonely hut,
The hut itself abandoned to decay,
And she forgotten in the quiet grave.

"I speak," continued he, "of one whose stock
Of virtues bloomed beneath this lonely roof.
She was a woman of a steady mind,
Tender and deep in her excess of love;
Not speaking much, pleased rather with the joy
Of her own thoughts: by some especial care
Her temper had been framed, as if to make
A being, who by adding love to peace
Might live on earth a life of happiness.
Her wedded partner lacked not on his side
The humble worth that satisfied her heart:
Frugal, affectionate, sober, and withal
Keenly industrious. She with pride would tell
That he was often seated at his loom,
In summer, ere the mower was abroad
Among the dewy grass — in early spring,
Ere the last star had vanished. They who passed
At evening, from behind the garden fence
Might hear his busy spade, which he would ply
After his daily work until the light
Had failed, and every leaf and flower were lost
In the dark hedges. So their days were spent
In peace and comfort; and a pretty boy
Was their best hope, next to the God in Heaven.

"Not twenty years ago, but you I think
Can scarcely bear it now in mind, there came
Two blighting seasons, when the fields were left
With half a harvest. It pleased Heaven to add
A worse affliction in the plague of war:
This happy land was stricken to the heart!
A wanderer then among the cottages,
I, with my freight of winter raiment, saw
The hardships of that season: many rich
Sank down, as in a dream, among the poor;
And of the poor did many cease to be,
And their place knew them not. Meanwhile, abridged
Of daily comforts, gladly reconciled
To numerous self-denials, Margaret
Went struggling on through those calamitous years
With cheerful hope, until the second autumn,
When her life's helpmate on a sickbed lay,
Smitten with perilous fever. In disease
He lingered long; and, when his strength returned,
He found the little he had stored, to meet
The hour of accident or crippling age,
Was all consumed. A second infant now
Was added to the troubles of a time
Laden, for them and all of their degree,
With care and sorrow; shoals of artisans
From ill-requited labor turned adrift
Sought daily bread from public charity,
They, and their wives and children — happier far
Could they have lived as do the little birds
That peck along the hedgerows, or the kite
That makes her dwelling on the mountain rocks!

"A sad reverse it was for him who long
Had filled with plenty, and possessed in peace,
This lonely cottage. At the door he stood,
And whistled many a snatch of merry tunes
That had no mirth in them; or with his knife
Carved uncouth figures on the heads of sticks —
Then, not less idly, sought, through every nook
In house or garden, any casual work
Of use or ornament; and with a strange,
Amusing, yet uneasy, novelty,
He mingled, where he might, the various tasks
Of summer, autumn, winter, and of spring.
But this endured not; his good humor soon
Became a weight in which no pleasure was;
And poverty brought on a petted mood
And a sore temper; day by day he drooped,
And he would leave his work — and to the town
Would turn without an errand his slack steps;
Or wander here and there among the fields.
One while he would speak lightly of his babes,
And with a cruel tongue: at other times
He tossed them with a false unnatural joy:
And 'twas a rueful thing to see the looks
Of the poor innocent children. 'Every smile,'
Said Margaret to me, here beneath these trees,
'Made my heart bleed.'"
At this the Wanderer paused;
And, looking up to those enormous elms,
He said, "'Tis now the hour of deepest noon.
At this still season of repose and peace,
This hour when all things which are not at rest
Are cheerful; while this multitude of flies
With tuneful hum is filling all the air;
Why should a tear be on an old man's cheek?
Why should we thus, with an untoward mind,
And in the weakness of humanity,
From natural wisdom turn our hearts away;
To natural comfort shut our eyes and ears;
And, feeding on disquiet, thus disturb
The calm of nature with our restless thoughts?"

He spake with somewhat of a solemn tone,
But, when he ended, there was in his face
Such easy cheerfulness, a look so mild,
That for a little time it stole away
All recollection; and that simple tale
Passed from my mind like a forgotten sound.
A while on trivial things we held discourse,
To me soon tasteless. In my own despite,

I thought of that poor woman as of one
Whom I had known and loved. He had rehearsed
Her homely tale with such familiar power,
With such an active countenance, an eye
So busy, that the things of which he spake
Seemed present; and, attention now relaxed,
A heartfelt chillness crept along my veins;
I rose; and, having left the breezy shade,
Stood drinking comfort from the warmer sun,
That had not cheered me long — ere, looking round
Upon that tranquil ruin, I returned,
And begged of the old man that, for my sake,
He would resume his story.
He replied,
" It were a wantonness, and would demand
Severe reproof, if we were men whose hearts
Could hold vain dalliance with the misery
Even of the dead; contented thence to draw
A momentary pleasure, never marked
By reason, barren of all future good.
But we have known that there is often found
In mournful thoughts, and always might be found,
A power to virtue friendly; were 't not so,
I am a dreamer among men, indeed
An idle dreamer! 'Tis a common tale,
An ordinary sorrow of man's life,
A tale of silent suffering, hardly clothed
In bodily form. But without further bidding
I will proceed.
While thus it fared with them,
To whom this cottage, till those hapless years,
Had been a blessed home, it was my chance
To travel in a country far remote;
And when these lofty elms once more appeared,
What pleasant expectations lured me on
O'er the flat common! With quick step I reached
The threshold, lifted with light hand the latch;
But, when I entered, Margaret looked at me
A little while; then turned her head away
Speechless, and, sitting down upon a chair,
Wept bitterly. I wist not what to do,
Nor how to speak to her. Poor wretch! at last
She rose from off her seat, and then — O sir!
I cannot *tell* how she pronounced my name:
With fervent love, and with a face of grief
Unutterably helpless, and a look
That seemed to cling upon me, she inquired
If I had seen her husband. As she spake
A strange surprise and fear came to my heart,
Nor had I power to answer ere she told
That he had disappeared — not two months gone.
He left his house: two wretched days had passed,
And on the third, as wistfully she raised
Her head from off her pillow, to look forth,
Like one in trouble, for returning light,
Within her chamber casement she espied
A folded paper, lying as if placed
To meet her waking eyes. This tremblingly
She opened — found no writing, but beheld
Pieces of money carefully enclosed,
Silver and gold. 'I shuddered at the sight,'
Said Margaret, 'for I knew it was his hand
That must have placed it there; and ere that day
Was ended, that long anxious day, I learned,
From one who by my husband had been sent
With the sad news, that he had joined a troop
Of soldiers, going to a distant land.
He left me thus — he could not gather heart
To take a farewell of me; for he feared
That I should follow with my babes, and sink
Beneath the misery of that wandering life.'

" This tale did Margaret tell with many tears:
And, when she ended, I had little power
To give her comfort, and was glad to take
Such words of hope from her own mouth as served
To cheer us both. But long we had not talked
Ere we built up a pile of better thoughts,
And with a brighter eye she looked around
As if she had been shedding tears of joy.
We parted. 'Twas the time of early spring;
I left her busy with her garden tools;
And well remember, o'er that fence she looked,
And, while I paced along the footway path,
Called out, and sent a blessing after me,
With tender cheerfulness, and with a voice
That seemed the very sound of happy thoughts.

" I roved o'er many a hill and many a dale,
With my accustomed load; in heat and cold,
Through many a wood and many an open ground,
In sunshine and in shade, in wet and fair,
Drooping or blithe of heart, as might befall;
My best companions now the driving winds,
And now the 'trotting brooks' and whispering
trees,
And now the music of my own sad steps,
With many a short-lived thought that passed be-
tween,
And disappeared.
I journeyed back this way,
When, in the warmth of midsummer, the wheat
Was yellow; and the soft and bladed grass,
Springing afresh, had o'er the hayfield spread
Its tender verdure. At the door arrived,
I found that she was absent. In the shade,
Where now we sit, I waited her return.
Her cottage, then a cheerful object, wore
Its customary look — only, it seemed,
The honeysuckle, crowding round the porch,
Hung down in heavier tufts; and that bright weed,
The yellow stonecrop, suffered to take root
Along the window's edge, profusely grew,
Blinding the lower panes. I turned aside,

And strolled into her garden. It appeared
To lag behind the season, and had lost
Its pride of neatness. Daisy flowers and thrift
Had broken their trim borderlines, and straggled
O'er paths they used to deck: carnations, once
Prized for surpassing beauty, and no less
For the peculiar pains they had required,
Declined their languid heads, wanting support.
The cumbrous bindweed, with its wreaths and bells,
Had twined about her two small rows of peas,
And dragged them to the earth.
                                        Ere this an hour
Was wasted. Back I turned my restless steps;
A stranger passed; and, guessing whom I sought,
He said that she was used to ramble far.
The sun was sinking in the west; and now
I sat with sad impatience. From within
Her solitary infant cried aloud;
Then, like a blast that dies away self-stilled,
The voice was silent. From the bench I rose;
But neither could divert nor soothe my thoughts.
The spot, though fair, was very desolate —
The longer I remained, more desolate;
And, looking round me, now I first observed
The cornerstones, on either side the porch,
With dull red stains discolored, and stuck o'er
With tufts and hairs of wool, as if the sheep,
That fed upon the common, thither came
Familiarly, and found a couching place
Even at her threshold. Deeper shadows fell
From these tall elms; the cottage clock struck eight;
I turned, and saw her distant a few steps.
Her face was pale and thin — her figure, too,
Was changed. As she unlocked the door, she said,
'It grieves me you have waited here so long,
But, in good truth, I've wandered much of late;
And sometimes — to my shame I speak — have need
Of my best prayers to bring me back again.'
While on the board she spread our evening meal,
She told me — interrupting not the work
Which gave employment to her listless hands —
That she had parted with her elder child,
To a kind master on a distant farm
Now happily apprenticed. 'I perceive
You look at me, and you have cause; today
I have been traveling far; and many days
About the fields I wander, knowing this
Only, that what I seek I cannot find;
And so I waste my time: for I am changed;
And to myself,' said she, 'have done much wrong
And to this helpless infant. I have slept
Weeping, and weeping have I waked; my tears
Have flowed as if my body were not such
As others are; and I could never die.
But I am now in mind and in my heart
More easy; and I hope,' said she, 'that God
Will give me patience to endure the things
Which I behold at home.'
                                        It would have grieved
Your very soul to see her. Sir, I feel
The story linger in my heart; I fear
'Tis long and tedious; but my spirit clings
To that poor woman: so familiarly
Do I perceive her manner, and her look,
And presence; and so deeply do I feel
Her goodness, that, not seldom, in my walks
A momentary trance comes over me;
And to myself I seem to muse on one
By sorrow laid asleep; or borne away,
A human being destined to awake
To human life, or something very near
To human life, when he shall come again
For whom she suffered. Yes, it would have grieved
Your very soul to see her; evermore
Her eyelids drooped, her eyes downward were cast;
And, when she at her table gave me food,
She did not look at me. Her voice was low,
Her body was subdued. In every act
Pertaining to her house affairs, appeared
The careless stillness of a thinking mind
Self-occupied; to which all outward things
Are like an idle matter. Still she sighed,
But yet no motion of the breast was seen,
No heaving of the heart. While by the fire
We sat together, sighs came on my ear,
I knew not how, and hardly whence they came.

"Ere my departure, to her care I gave,
For her son's use, some tokens of regard,
Which with a look of welcome she received;
And I exhorted her to place her trust
In God's good love, and seek his help by prayer.
I took my staff, and, when I kissed her babe,
The tears stood in her eyes. I left her then
With the best hope and comfort I could give:
She thanked me for my wish; but for my hope
It seemed she did not thank me.
                                        I returned,
And took my rounds along this road again
When on its sunny bank the primrose flower
Peeped forth, to give an earnest of the spring.
I found her sad and drooping; she had learned
No tidings of her husband; if he lived,
She knew not that he lived; if he were dead,
She knew not he was dead. She seemed the same
In person and appearance; but her house
Bespake a sleepy hand of negligence;
The floor was neither dry nor neat, the hearth
Was comfortless, and her small lot of books,
Which, in the cottage window, heretofore
Had been piled up against the corner panes

In seemly order, now, with straggling leaves
Lay scattered here and there, open or shut,
As they had chanced to fall. Her infant babe
Had from his mother caught the trick of grief,
And sighed among its playthings. I withdrew,
And once again entering the garden saw,
More plainly still, that poverty and grief
Were now come nearer to her: weeds defaced
The hardened soil, and knots of withered grass;
No ridges there appeared of clear back mold,
No winter greenness; of her herbs and flowers,
It seemed the better part was gnawed away
Or trampled into earth; a chain of straw,
Which had been twined about the slender stem
Of a young apple tree, lay at its root;
The bark was nibbled round by truant sheep.
Margaret stood near, her infant in her arms,
And, noting that my eye was on the tree,
She said, 'I fear it will be dead and gone
Ere Robert come again.' When to the house
We had returned together, she inquired
If I had any hope: but for her babe
And for her little orphan boy, she said,
She had no wish to live, that she must die
Of sorrow. Yet I saw the idle loom
Still in its place; his Sunday garments hung
Upon the selfsame nail; his very staff
Stood undisturbed behind the door.
And when,
In bleak December, I retraced this way,
She told me that her little babe was dead,
And she was left alone. She now, released
From her maternal cares, had taken up
The employment common through these wilds, and gained,
By spinning hemp, a pittance for herself;
And for this end had hired a neighbor's boy
To give her needful help. That very time
Most willingly she put her work aside,
And walked with me along the miry road,
Heedless how far; and, in such piteous sort
That any heart had ached to hear her, begged
That, wheresoe'er I went, I still would ask
For him whom she had lost. We parted then—
Our final parting; for from that time forth
Did many seasons pass ere I returned
Into this tract again.
Nine tedious years;
From their first separation, nine long years,
She lingered in unquiet widowhood;
A wife and widow. Needs must it have been
A sore heart-wasting! I have heard, my friend,
That in yon arbor oftentimes she sat
Alone, through half the vacant Sabbath day;
And, if a dog passed by, she still would quit
The shade, and look abroad. On this old bench
For hours she sat; and evermore her eye
Was busy in the distance, shaping things
That made her heart beat quick. You see that path,
Now faint—the grass has crept o'er its gray line;
There, to and fro, she paced through many a day
Of the warm summer, from a belt of hemp
That girt her waist, spinning the long-drawn thread
With backward steps. Yet ever as there passed
A man whose garments showed the soldier's red,
Or crippled mendicant in sailor's garb,
The little child who sat to turn the wheel
Ceased from his task; and she with faltering voice
Made many a fond inquiry; and when they,
Whose presence gave no comfort, were gone by,
Her heart was still more sad. And by yon gate,
That bars the traveler's road, she often stood,
And when a stranger horseman came, the latch
Would lift, and in his face look wistfully;
Most happy, if, from aught discovered there
Of tender feeling, she might dare repeat
The same sad question. Meanwhile her poor hut
Sank to decay; for he was gone, whose hand,
At the first nipping of October frost,
Closed up each chink, and with fresh bands of straw
Checkered the green-grown thatch. And so she lived
Through the long winter, reckless and alone;
Until her house by frost, and thaw, and rain,
Was sapped; and while she slept, the nightly damps
Did chill her breast; and in the stormy day
Her tattered clothes were ruffled by the wind,
Even at the side of her own fire. Yet still
She loved this wretched spot, nor would for worlds
Have parted hence; and still that length of road,
And this rude bench, one torturing hope endeared,
Fast rooted at her heart: and here, my friend,
In sickness she remained; and here she died,
Last human tenant of these ruined walls!"

The old man ceased: he saw that I was moved;
From that low bench, rising instinctively
I turned aside in weakness, nor had power
To thank him for the tale which he had told.
I stood, and leaning o'er the garden wall
Reviewed that woman's sufferings; and it seemed
To comfort me while with a brother's love
I blessed her in the impotence of grief.
Then towards the cottage I returned; and traced
Fondly, though with an interest more mild,
That secret spirit of humanity
Which, 'mid the calm, oblivious tendencies
Of nature, 'mid her plants, and weeds, and flowers,
And silent overgrowings, still survived.

RUINED COTTAGE. **904. checkered . . . thatch: reinforced the roof with fresh straw, giving it a patchwork appearance.**

The old man, noting this, resumed, and said,
"My friend! enough to sorrow you have given,
The purposes of wisdom ask no more:
Nor more would she have craved as due to one
Who, in her worst distress, had ofttimes felt
The unbounded might of prayer; and learned, with soul
Fixed on the cross, that consolation springs,
From sources deeper far than deepest pain,
For the meek sufferer. Why then should we read
The forms of things with an unworthy eye?
She sleeps in the calm earth, and peace is here.
I well remember that those very plumes,
Those weeds, and the high spear grass on that wall,
By mist and silent raindrops silvered o'er,
As once I passed, into my heart conveyed
So still an image of tranquillity,
So calm and still, and looked so beautiful
Amid the uneasy thoughts which filled my mind,
That what we feel of sorrow and despair
From ruin and from change, and all the grief
That passing shows of being leave behind,
Appeared an idle dream, that could maintain,
Nowhere, dominion o'er the enlightened spirit
Whose meditative sympathies repose
Upon the breast of faith. I turned away,
And walked along my road in happiness."

# THE OLD CUMBERLAND BEGGAR

"Observed, and with great benefit to my own heart, when I was a child; written at Racedown and Alfoxden in my twenty-third year. The political economists were about that time beginning their war upon mendicity in all its forms, and by implication, if not directly, on almsgiving also. . . . The class of beggars, to which the old man here described belongs, will probably soon be extinct. It consisted of poor and, mostly, old and infirm persons, who confined themselves to a stated round in their neighborhood, and had certain fixed days on which, at different houses, they regularly received alms, sometimes in money, but mostly in provisions" [W].

I saw an aged beggar in my walk;
And he was seated, by the highway side,
On a low structure of rude masonry
Built at the foot of a huge hill, that they
Who lead their horses down the steep rough road
May thence remount at ease. The aged man
Had placed his staff across the broad smooth stone
That overlays the pile; and, from a bag
All white with flour, the dole of village dames,
He drew his scraps and fragments, one by one;
And scanned them with a fixed and serious look
Of idle computation. In the sun,
Upon the second step of that small pile,
Surrounded by those wild unpeopled hills,
He sat, and ate his food in solitude,
And ever, scattered from his palsied hand,
That, still attempting to prevent the waste,
Was baffled still, the crumbs in little showers
Fell on the ground; and the small mountain birds,
Not venturing yet to peck their destined meal,
Approached within the length of half his staff.

Him from my childhood have I known; and then
He was so old, he seems not older now;
He travels on, a solitary man,
So helpless in appearance, that for him
The sauntering horseman throws not with a slack
And careless hand his alms upon the ground,
But stops, that he may safely lodge the coin
Within the old man's hat; nor quits him so,
But still, when he has given his horse the rein,
Watches the aged beggar with a look
Sidelong, and half-reverted. She who tends
The tollgate, when in summer at her door
She turns her wheel, if on the road she sees
The aged beggar coming, quits her work,
And lifts the latch for him that he may pass.
The postboy, when his rattling wheels o'ertake
The aged beggar in the woody lane,
Shouts to him from behind; and if, thus warned,
The old man does not change his course, the boy
Turns with less noisy wheels to the roadside,
And passes gently by, without a curse
Upon his lips, or anger at his heart.

He travels on, a solitary man;
His age has no companion. On the ground
His eyes are turned, and, as he moves along
*They* move along the ground; and, evermore,
Instead of common and habitual sight
Of fields with rural works, of hill and dale,
And the blue sky, one little span of earth
Is all his prospect. Thus, from day to day,
Bow-bent, his eyes forever on the ground,
He plies his weary journey; seeing still,
And seldom knowing that he sees, some straw,
Some scattered leaf, or marks which, in one track,
The nails of cart or chariot wheel have left
Impressed on the white road — in the same line,
At distance still the same. Poor traveler!
His staff trails with him; scarcely do his feet
Disturb the summer dust; he is so still
In look and motion, that the cottage curs,
Ere he has passed the door, will turn away,
Weary of barking at him. Boys and girls,
The vacant and the busy, maids and youths,

And urchins newly breeched — all pass him by:
Him even the slow-paced wagon leaves behind.

But deem not this man useless. Statesmen! ye
Who are so restless in your wisdom, ye
Who have a broom still ready in your hands
To rid the world of nuisances; ye proud,
Heart-swol'n, while in your pride ye contemplate
Your talents, power, or wisdom, deem him not
A burthen of the earth! 'Tis Nature's law
That none, the meanest of created things,
Or forms created the most vile and brute,
The dullest or most noxious, should exist
Divorced from good — a spirit and pulse of good,
A life and soul, to every mode of being
Inseparably linked. Then be assured
That least of all can aught — that ever owned
The heaven-regarding eye and front sublime
Which man is born to — sink, howe'er depressed,
So low as to be scorned without a sin;
Without offense to God cast out of view;
Like the dry remnant of a garden flower
Whose seeds are shed, or as an implement
Worn out and worthless. While from door to door
This old man creeps, the villagers in him
Behold a record which together binds
Past deeds and offices of charity,
Else unremembered, and so keeps alive
The kindly mood in hearts which lapse of years,
And that half-wisdom half-experience gives,
Make slow to feel, and by sure steps resign
To selfishness and cold oblivious cares.
Among the farms and solitary huts,
Hamlets and thinly scattered villages,
Where'er the aged beggar takes his rounds,
The mild necessity of use compels
To acts of love; and habit does the work
Of reason; yet prepares that afterjoy
Which reason cherishes. And thus the soul,
By that sweet taste of pleasure unpursued,
Doth find herself insensibly disposed
To virtue and true goodness.
Some there are,
By their good works exalted, lofty minds
And meditative, authors of delight
And happiness, which to the end of time
Will live, and spread, and kindle; even such minds
In childhood, from this solitary being,
Or from like wanderer, haply have received
(A thing more precious far than all that books
Or the solicitudes of love can do!)
That first mild touch of sympathy and thought,
In which they found their kindred with a world
Where want and sorrow were. The easy man
Who sits at his own door, and, like the pear
That overhangs his head from the green wall,
Feeds in the sunshine; the robust and young,
The prosperous and unthinking, they who live
Sheltered, and flourish in a little grove
Of their own kindred; all behold in him
A silent monitor, which on their minds
Must needs impress a transitory thought
Of self-congratulation, to the heart
Of each recalling his peculiar boons,
His charters and exemptions; and, perchance,
Though he to no one give the fortitude
And circumspection needful to preserve
His present blessings, and to husband up
The respite of the season, he, at least,
And 'tis no vulgar service, makes them felt.

Yet further. Many, I believe, there are
Who live a life of virtuous decency,
Men who can hear the Decalogue and feel
No self-reproach; who of the moral law
Established in the land where they abide
Are strict observers; and not negligent
In acts of love to those with whom they dwell,
Their kindred, and the children of their blood.
Praise be to such, and to their slumbers peace!
But of the poor man ask, the abject poor;
Go, and demand of him, if there be here
In this cold abstinence from evil deeds,
And these inevitable charities,
Wherewith to satisfy the human soul?
No — man is dear to man; the poorest poor
Long for some moments in a weary life
When they can know and feel that they have been,
Themselves, the fathers and the dealers-out
Of some small blessings; have been kind to such
As needed kindness, for this single cause,
That we have all of us one human heart.
Such pleasure is to one kind being known,
My neighbor, when with punctual care, each week
Duly as Friday comes, though pressed herself
By her own wants, she from her store of meal
Takes one unsparing handful for the scrip
Of this old mendicant, and, from her door
Returning with exhilarated heart,
Sits by her fire, and builds her hope in Heaven.

Then let him pass, a blessing on his head!
And while in that vast solitude to which
The tide of things has borne him, he appears
To breathe and live but for himself alone,
Unblamed, uninjured, let him bear about
The good which the benignant law of Heaven
Has hung around him, and, while life is his,
Still let him prompt the unlettered villagers
To tender offices and pensive thoughts.
Then let him pass, a blessing on his head!
And, long as he can wander, let him breathe

**OLD CUMBERLAND BEGGAR. 158. scrip:** a bag, wallet, or knapsack.

The freshness of the valleys; let his blood
Struggle with frosty air and winter snows;
And let the chartered wind that sweeps the heath
Beat his gray locks against his withered face.
Reverence the hope whose vital anxiousness
Gives the last human interest to his heart.
May never House, misnamed of Industry,
Make him a captive! — for that pent-up din,
Those life-consuming sounds that clog the air,
Be his the natural silence of old age!
Let him be free of mountain solitudes;
And have around him, whether heard or not,
The pleasant melody of woodland birds.
Few are his pleasures; if his eyes have now
Been doomed so long to settle upon earth
That not without some effort they behold
The countenance of the horizontal sun,
Rising or setting, let the light at least
Find a free entrance to their languid orbs.
And let him, *where* and *when* he will, sit down
Beneath the trees, or on a grassy bank
Of highway side, and with the little birds
Share his chance-gathered meal; and, finally,
As in the eye of Nature he has lived,
So in the eye of Nature let him die!

*1797*

## WE ARE SEVEN

— A simple child,
That lightly draws its breath,
And feels its life in every limb,
What should it know of death?

I met a little cottage girl;
She was eight years old, she said;
Her hair was thick with many a curl
That clustered round her head.

She had a rustic, woodland air,
And she was wildly clad;
Her eyes were fair, and very fair;
Her beauty made me glad.

" Sisters and brothers, little maid,
How many may you be? "
" How many? Seven in all," she said,
And wondering looked at me.

" And where are they? I pray you tell."
She answered, " Seven are we;
And two of us at Conway dwell,
And two are gone to sea.

" Two of us in the churchyard lie,
My sister and my brother;
And, in the churchyard cottage, I
Dwell near them with my mother."

" You say that two at Conway dwell,
And two are gone to sea,
Yet ye are seven! I pray you tell,
Sweet maid, how this may be."

Then did the little maid reply,
" Seven boys and girls are we;
Two of us in the churchyard lie,
Beneath the churchyard tree."

" You run about, my little maid,
Your limbs they are alive;
If two are in the churchyard laid,
Then ye are only five."

" Their graves are green, they may be seen,"
The little maid replied,
" Twelve steps or more from my mother's
door,
And they are side by side.

" My stockings there I often knit,
My kerchief there I hem;
And there upon the ground I sit,
And sing a song to them.

" And often after sunset, sir,
When it is light and fair,
I take my little porringer,
And eat my supper there.

" The first that died was sister Jane;
In bed she moaning lay,
Till God released her of her pain;
And then she went away.

" So in the churchyard she was laid;
And, when the grass was dry,
Together round her grave we played,
My brother John and I.

" And when the ground was white with snow,
And I could run and slide,
My brother John was forced to go,
And he lies by her side."

" How many are you, then," said I,
" If they two are in Heaven? "
Quick was the little maid's reply,
" O Master! we are seven."

**179. House . . . Industry:** a poorhouse.

WE ARE SEVEN. **47. porringer:** a deep dish for soup or porridge.

"But they are dead; those two are dead!
Their spirits are in Heaven!"
'Twas throwing words away; for still
The little maid would have her will,
And said, "Nay, we are seven!"

*1798*

## EXPOSTULATION AND REPLY

"This poem is a favorite among the Quakers, as I have learned on many occasions. It was composed in front of the house at Alfoxden, in the spring of 1798" [W].

"Why, William, on that old gray stone,
Thus for the length of half a day,
Why, William, sit you thus alone,
And dream your time away?

"Where are your books? — that light bequeathed
To beings else forlorn and blind!
Up! up! and drink the spirit breathed
From dead men to their kind.

"You look round on your Mother Earth,
As if she for no purpose bore you;
As if you were her first-born birth,
And none had lived before you!"

One morning thus, by Esthwaite Lake,
When life was sweet, I knew not why,
To me my good friend Matthew spake,
And thus I made reply:

"The eye — it cannot choose but see;
We cannot bid the ear be still;
Our bodies feel, where'er they be,
Against or with our will.

"Nor less I deem that there are powers
Which of themselves our minds impress;
That we can feed this mind of ours
In a wise passiveness.

"Think you, 'mid all this mighty sum
Of things forever speaking,
That nothing of itself will come,
But we must still be seeking?

"Then ask not wherefore, here, alone,
Conversing as I may,
I sit upon this old gray stone,
And dream my time away."

*1798*

EXPOSTULATION AND REPLY. **13. Esthwaite Lake:** half a mile from Hawkshead, where Wordsworth went to school. **15. Matthew:** probably William Taylor, headmaster of Hawkshead School (1782–86) and Wordsworth's teacher. He is again referred to in "The Tables Turned," "Matthew," "The Two April Mornings," and "The Fountain," below.

## THE TABLES TURNED

*An Evening Scene on the Same Subject*

Up! up! my friend, and quit your books,
Or surely you'll grow double;
Up! up! my friend, and clear your looks;
Why all this toil and trouble?

The sun, above the mountain's head,
A freshening luster mellow
Through all the long green fields has spread,
His first sweet evening yellow.

Books! 'tis a dull and endless strife;
Come, hear the woodland linnet,
How sweet his music! on my life,
There's more of wisdom in it.

And hark! how blithe the throstle sings!
He, too, is no mean preacher;
Come forth into the light of things,
Let Nature be your teacher.

She has a world of ready wealth,
Our minds and hearts to bless —
Spontaneous wisdom breathed by health,
Truth breathed by cheerfulness.

One impulse from a vernal wood
May teach you more of man,
Of moral evil and of good,
Than all the sages can.

Sweet is the lore which Nature brings;
Our meddling intellect
Misshapes the beauteous forms of things;
We murder to dissect.

Enough of Science and of Art;
Close up those barren leaves;
Come forth, and bring with you a heart
That watches and receives.

*1798*

THE TABLES TURNED. **1. friend:** Matthew. **13. throstle:** the song thrush.

## TO MY SISTER

" Composed in front of Alfoxden House. My little boy-messenger on this occasion was the son of Basil Montagu. The larch mentioned in the first stanza was standing when I revisited the place in May, 1841, more than forty years after " [W].

It is the first mild day of March;
Each minute sweeter than before
The redbreast sings from the tall larch
That stands beside our door.

There is a blessing in the air,
Which seems a sense of joy to yield
To the bare trees, and mountains bare,
And grass in the green field.

My sister! ('tis a wish of mine)
Now that our morning meal is done,
Make haste, your morning task resign;
Come forth and feel the sun.

Edward will come with you; and, pray,
Put on with speed your woodland dress,
And bring no book; for this one day
We'll give to idleness.

No joyless forms shall regulate
Our living calendar;
We from today, my friend, will date
The opening of the year.

Love, now a universal birth,
From heart to heart is stealing,
From earth to man, from man to earth;
It is the hour of feeling.

One moment now may give us more
Than years of toiling reason;
Our minds shall drink at every pore
The spirit of the season.

Some silent laws our hearts will make,
Which they shall long obey:
We for the year to come may take
Our temper from today.

And from the blessed power that rolls
About, below, above,
We'll frame the measure of our souls:
They shall be tuned to love.

Then come, my sister! come, I pray,
With speed put on your woodland dress,
And bring no book; for this one day
We'll give to idleness.

*1798*

TO MY SISTER. **9. sister:** Dorothy Wordsworth. **13. Edward:** young Basil Montagu, who lived with Wordsworth and Dorothy from 1795 to 1798. See Intro., n. 3, p. 3.

## LINES WRITTEN IN EARLY SPRING

" Actually composed while I was sitting by the side of the brook that runs down from the comb in which stands the village of Alford, through the grounds of Alfoxden " [W].

I heard a thousand blended notes,
While in a grove I sat reclined,
In that sweet mood when pleasant thoughts
Bring sad thoughts to the mind.

To her fair works did Nature link
The human soul that through me ran;
And much it grieved my heart to think
What man has made of man.

Through primrose tufts, in that green bower,
The periwinkle trailed its wreaths;
And 'tis my faith that every flower
Enjoys the air it breathes.

The birds around me hopped and played,
Their thoughts I cannot measure;
But the least motion which they made
It seemed a thrill of pleasure.

The budding twigs spread out their fan,
To catch the breezy air;
And I must think, do all I can,
That there was pleasure there.

If this belief from heaven be sent,
If such be Nature's holy plan,
Have I not reason to lament
What man has made of man?

*1798*

LINES WRITTEN IN EARLY SPRING. **10. periwinkle:** a trailing evergreen plant with small blue flowers, usually called myrtle in the United States. **21–22. If this . . . plan:** From 1798 until 1820 these lines read: "If I these thoughts may not prevent, / If such be of my creed the plan."

# LINES

*Composed a few miles above Tintern Abbey, on revisiting the banks of the Wye during a tour. July 13, 1798*

" No poem of mine was composed under circumstances more pleasant for me to remember than this. I began it upon leaving Tintern, after crossing the Wye, and concluded it just as I was entering Bristol in the evening, after a ramble of four or five days, with my sister. Not a line of it was altered, and not any part of it written down till I reached Bristol " [W].

Five years have passed; five summers, with the length
Of five long winters! and again I hear
These waters, rolling from their mountain springs
With a soft inland murmur. Once again
Do I behold these steep and lofty cliffs,
That on a wild secluded scene impress
Thoughts of more deep seclusion; and connect
The landscape with the quiet of the sky.
The day is come when I again repose
Here, under this dark sycamore, and view
These plots of cottage ground, these orchard tufts,
Which at this season, with their unripe fruits,
Are clad in one green hue, and lose themselves
'Mid groves and copses. Once again I see
These hedgerows, hardly hedgerows, little lines
Of sportive wood run wild — these pastoral farms,
Green to the very door; and wreaths of smoke
Sent up, in silence, from among the trees!
With some uncertain notice, as might seem
Of vagrant dwellers in the houseless woods,
Or of some hermit's cave, where by his fire
The hermit sits alone.

These beauteous forms,
Through a long absence, have not been to me
As is a landscape to a blind man's eye;
But oft, in lonely rooms, and 'mid the din
Of towns and cities, I have owed to them
In hours of weariness, sensations sweet,
Felt in the blood, and felt along the heart;
And passing even into my purer mind,
With tranquil restoration; feelings too
Of unremembered pleasure, such, perhaps,
As have no slight or trivial influence
On that best portion of a good man's life,
His little, nameless, unremembered, acts
Of kindness and of love. Nor less, I trust,
To them I may have owed another gift,

TINTERN ABBEY. Tintern Abbey is a picturesque ruin in Monmouthshire. Wordsworth saw it for the first time in the summer of 1793, when he was on his way to visit Robert Jones in Wales.

Of aspect more sublime; that blessed mood,
In which the burthen of the mystery,
In which the heavy and the weary weight
Of all this unintelligible world,
Is lightened: that serene and blessed mood,
In which the affections gently lead us on,
Until, the breath of this corporeal frame
And even the motion of our human blood
Almost suspended, we are laid asleep
In body, and become a living soul,
While with an eye made quiet by the power
Of harmony, and the deep power of joy,
We see into the life of things.

If this
Be but a vain belief, yet, oh! how oft —
In darkness and amid the many shapes
Of joyless daylight; when the fretful stir
Unprofitable, and the fever of the world,
Have hung upon the beatings of my heart —
How oft, in spirit, have I turned to thee,
O sylvan Wye! thou wanderer through the woods,
How often has my spirit turned to thee!

And now, with gleams of half-extinguished thought,
With many recognitions dim and faint,
And somewhat of a sad perplexity,
The picture of the mind revives again:
While here I stand, not only with the sense
Of present pleasure, but with pleasing thoughts
That in this moment there is life and food
For future years. And so I dare to hope,
Though changed, no doubt, from what I was when first
I came among these hills; when like a roe
I bounded o'er the mountains, by the sides
Of the deep rivers, and the lonely streams,
Wherever nature led — more like a man
Flying from something that he dreads, than one
Who sought the thing he loved. For nature then
(The coarser pleasures of my boyish days,
And their glad animal movements all gone by)
To me was all in all. I cannot paint
What then I was. The sounding cataract
Haunted me like a passion; the tall rock,
The mountain, and the deep and gloomy wood,
Their colors and their forms, were then to me
An appetite; a feeling and a love,
That had no need of a remoter charm,
By thought supplied, nor any interest
Unborrowed from the eye. That time is past,
And all its aching joys are now no more,
And all its dizzy raptures. Not for this
Faint I, nor mourn nor murmur; other gifts
Have followed; for such loss, I would believe,

**86. Faint:** lose spirit or courage.

Abundant recompense. For I have learned
To look on nature, not as in the hour
Of thoughtless youth; but hearing oftentimes
The still, sad music of humanity,
Nor harsh nor grating, though of ample power
To chasten and subdue. And I have felt
A presence that disturbs me with the joy
Of elevated thoughts; a sense sublime
Of something far more deeply interfused,
Whose dwelling is the light of setting suns,
And the round ocean and the living air,
And the blue sky, and in the mind of man;
A motion and a spirit, that impels
All thinking things, all objects of all thought,
And rolls through all things. Therefore am I still
A lover of the meadows and the woods,
And mountains; and of all that we behold
From this green earth; of all the mighty world
Of eye, and ear — both what they half-create,
And what perceive; well pleased to recognize
In nature and the language of the sense,
The anchor of my purest thoughts, the nurse,
The guide, the guardian of my heart, and soul
Of all my moral being.
Nor perchance,
If I were not thus taught, should I the more
Suffer my genial spirits to decay;
For thou art with me here upon the banks
Of this fair river, thou my dearest friend,
My dear, dear friend; and in thy voice I catch
The language of my former heart, and read
My former pleasures in the shooting lights
Of thy wild eyes. Oh! yet a little while
May I behold in thee what I was once,
My dear, dear sister! and this prayer I make,
Knowing that Nature never did betray
The heart that loved her; 'tis her privilege,
Through all the years of this our life, to lead
From joy to joy; for she can so inform
The mind that is within us, so impress
With quietness and beauty, and so feed
With lofty thoughts, that neither evil tongues,
Rash judgments, nor the sneers of selfish men,
Nor greetings where no kindness is, nor all
The dreary intercourse of daily life,
Shall e'er prevail against us, or disturb
Our cheerful faith, that all which we behold
Is full of blessings. Therefore let the moon
Shine on thee in thy solitary walk;
And let the misty mountain winds be free
To blow against thee: and, in after years,
When these wild ecstasies shall be matured
Into a sober pleasure; when thy mind
Shall be a mansion for all lovely forms,
Thy memory be as a dwelling place
For all sweet sounds and harmonies; oh! then,
If solitude, or fear, or pain, or grief,
Should be thy portion, with what healing thoughts
Of tender joy wilt thou remember me,
And these my exhortations! Nor, perchance —
If I should be where I no more can hear
Thy voice, nor catch from thy wild eyes these
gleams
Of past existence — wilt thou then forget
That on the banks of this delightful stream
We stood together; and that I, so long
A worshiper of Nature, hither came
Unwearied in that service; rather say
With warmer love — oh! with far deeper zeal
Of holier love. Nor wilt thou then forget,
That after many wanderings, many years
Of absence, these steep woods and lofty cliffs,
And this green pastoral landscape, were to me
More dear, both for themselves and for thy sake!

*1798*

**106 07. both . . . perceive:** "This line has a close resemblance to an admirable line of Young, the exact expression of which I cannot recollect" [W]. The reference is to Edward Young's *The Complaint, or Night Thoughts on Life, Death, and Immortality* (1742–45), VI. 423–25. **113. genial:** cheerful, enlivening. **115. friend:** Dorothy Wordsworth.

# THE PRELUDE

*An Autobiographical Poem*

In March, 1798, Wordsworth determined to write a three-part philosophical poem that would include an account of his own life. He intended to name the poem *The Recluse,* and he expected to finish it within a year and a half. Some time in the spring of 1798 he wrote out or improvised 107 lines of blank verse in which he announced his plans for the long poem in general and for the autobiographical portion in particular.

At Goslar, Germany, in the winter of 1798–99, Wordsworth began the autobiographical part of the long poem, and by the summer of 1799 he had written — except for the introductions — most of what are now Books I and II of *The Prelude.* Then, on October 12, 1799, he announced a change of plan. He had decided to make the account of his life a separate poem which he would address to Samuel Taylor Coleridge. But he added almost nothing to it for four more years.

In the winter of 1803–04, stimulated by increasing

family responsibilities, Coleridge's failing health, and a new and urgent sense of duty (he wrote the "Ode to Duty" at this time), Wordsworth resolved to get on with the autobiography. He wrote down for the first time the 269 lines that introduce *The Prelude,* and by the end of March, 1804, he had completed the first five books. Now he decided to extend the poem to include the history of his development down to 1797–98, the first year of his intimacy with Coleridge. Following this plan, Wordsworth completed the original version of *The Prelude,* substantially as we have it today, in May, 1805.

In 1814 Wordsworth published *The Excursion,* Part II of *The Recluse.* In his 1814 Preface he referred to *The Prelude* as a "preparatory poem" to the larger work. Its relationship to *The Recluse,* he declared, was that of the "ante-chapel . . . to the body of a Gothic church." Unfortunately the main body of the church was left unfinished. Part III and all but Book I of Part I of *The Recluse* ("Home at Grasmere") Wordsworth never wrote. Between 1805 and 1839, however, he repeatedly revised *The Prelude.* Finally, on July 20, 1850, three months after his death, the poem was published. Only then did this, his most famous long poem, receive the title by which we know it. Wordsworth had always referred to it as "the poem to Coleridge" or "the poem on my own earlier life," but Mrs. Wordsworth, with an instinct for brevity in titles which her husband seldom shared, called it simply *The Prelude.* The following selections are from the 1850 text.

## BOOK I

### INTRODUCTION. CHILDHOOD AND SCHOOLTIME

Oh there is blessing in this gentle breeze,
A visitant that while it fans my cheek
Doth seem half-conscious of the joy it brings
From the green fields, and from yon azure sky.
Whate'er its mission, the soft breeze can come
To none more grateful than to me; escaped
From the vast city, where I long had pined
A discontented sojourner, now free,
Free as a bird to settle where I will.
What dwelling shall receive me? in what vale
Shall be my harbor? underneath what grove
Shall I take up my home? and what clear stream
Shall with its murmur lull me into rest?
The earth is all before me. With a heart
Joyous, nor scared at its own liberty,
I look about; and should the chosen guide
Be nothing better than a wandering cloud,
I cannot miss my way. I breathe again!
Trances of thought and mountings of the mind
Come fast upon me; it is shaken off,
That burthen of my own unnatural self,
The heavy weight of many a weary day
Not mine, and such as were not made for me.
Long months of peace (if such bold word accord
With any promises of human life),
Long months of ease and undisturbed delight
Are mine in prospect; whither shall I turn,
By road or pathway, or through trackless field,
Up hill or down, or shall some floating thing
Upon the river point me out my course?

Dear Liberty! Yet what would it avail
But for a gift that consecrates the joy?
For I, methought, while the sweet breath of heaven
Was blowing on my body, felt within
A correspondent breeze, that gently moved
With quickening virtue, but is now become
A tempest, a redundant energy,
Vexing its own creation. Thanks to both,
And their congenial powers, that, while they join
In breaking up a long-continued frost,
Bring with them vernal promises, the hope
Of active days urged on by flying hours—
Days of sweet leisure, taxed with patient thought
Abstruse, nor wanting punctual service high,
Matins and vespers of harmonious verse!

Thus far, O friend! did I, not used to make
A present joy the matter of a song,
Pour forth that day my soul in measured strains
That would not be forgotten, and are here
Recorded; to the open fields I told
A prophecy; poetic numbers came
Spontaneously to clothe in priestly robe
A renovated spirit singled out,
Such hope was mine, for holy services.
My own voice cheered me, and, far more, the mind's
Internal echo of the imperfect sound;
To both I listened, drawing from them both
A cheerful confidence in things to come.

Content and not unwilling now to give
A respite to this passion, I paced on
With brisk and eager steps; and came, at length,
To a green shady place, where down I sat
Beneath a tree, slackening my thoughts by choice
And settling into gentler happiness.
'Twas autumn, and a clear and placid day,
With warmth, as much as needed, from a sun
Two hours declined towards the west; a day
With silver clouds, and sunshine on the grass,
And in the sheltered and the sheltering grove
A perfect stillness. Many were the thoughts
Encouraged and dismissed, till choice was made
Of a known vale, whither my feet should turn,
Nor rest till they had reached the very door
Of the one cottage which methought I saw.

THE PRELUDE. **Book I: 7. city:** London, where Wordsworth lived from January to September, 1795.

**46. friend:** Throughout the poem the friend referred to, unless otherwise noted, is Samuel Taylor Coleridge.

No picture of mere memory ever looked
So fair; and while upon the fancied scene
I gazed with growing love, a higher power
Than Fancy gave assurance of some work
Of glory there forthwith to be begun,
Perhaps too there performed. Thus long I mused,
Nor e'er lost sight of what I mused upon,
Save when, amid the stately grove of oaks,
Now here, now there, an acorn, from its cup
Dislodged, through sere leaves rustled, or at once
To the bare earth dropped with a startling sound.
From that soft couch I rose not, till the sun
Had almost touched the horizon; casting then
A backward glance upon the curling cloud
Of city smoke, by distance ruralized;
Keen as a truant or a fugitive,
But as a pilgrim resolute, I took,
Even with the chance equipment of that hour,
The road that pointed toward the chosen vale.
It was a splendid evening, and my soul
Once more made trial of her strength, nor lacked
Aeolian visitations; but the harp
Was soon defrauded, and the banded host
Of harmony dispersed in straggling sounds,
And lastly utter silence! "Be it so;
Why think of anything but present good?"
So, like a homebound laborer, I pursued
My way beneath the mellowing sun, that shed
Mild influence; nor left in me one wish
Again to bend the Sabbath of that time
To a servile yoke. What need of many words?
A pleasant loitering journey, through three days
Continued, brought me to my hermitage.
I spare to tell of what ensued, the life
In common things — the endless store of things,
Rare, or at least so seeming, every day
Found all about me in one neighborhood —
The self-congratulation, and, from morn
To night, unbroken cheerfulness serene.
But speedily an earnest longing rose
To brace myself to some determined aim,
Reading or thinking; either to lay up
New stores, or rescue from decay the old
By timely interference; and therewith
Came hopes still higher, that with outward life
I might endue some airy fantasies
That had been floating loose about for years,
And to such beings temperately deal forth
The many feelings that oppressed my heart.
That hope hath been discouraged; welcome light
Dawns from the east, but dawns to disappear
And mock me with a sky that ripens not
Into a steady morning; if my mind,
Remembering the bold promise of the past,
Would gladly grapple with some noble theme,
Vain is her wish; where'er she turns she finds
Impediments from day to day renewed.

And now it would content me to yield up
Those lofty hopes awhile, for present gifts
Of humbler industry. But, oh, dear friend!
The poet, gentle creature as he is,
Hath, like the lover, his unruly times;
His fits when he is neither sick nor well,
Though no distress be near him but his own
Unmanageable thoughts; his mind, best pleased
While she as duteous as the mother dove,
Sits brooding, lives not always to that end,
But like the innocent bird, hath goadings on
That drive her as in trouble through the groves;
With me is now such passion, to be blamed
No otherwise than as it lasts too long.

When, as becomes a man who would prepare
For such an arduous work, I through myself
Make rigorous inquisition, the report
Is often cheering; for I neither seem
To lack that first great gift, the vital soul,
Nor general truths, which are themselves a sort
Of elements and agents, underpowers,
Subordinate helpers of the living mind;
Nor am I naked of external things,
Forms, images, nor numerous other aids
Of less regard, though won perhaps with toil
And needful to build up a poet's praise.
Time, place, and manners do I seek, and these
Are found in plenteous store, but nowhere such
As may be singled out with steady choice;
No little band of yet remembered names
Whom I, in perfect confidence, might hope
To summon back from lonesome banishment,
And make them dwellers in the hearts of men
Now living, or to live in future years.
Sometimes the ambitious power of choice, mistaking
Proud spring tide swellings for a regular sea,
Will settle on some British theme, some old
Romantic tale by Milton left unsung;
More often turning to some gentle place
Within the groves of chivalry, I pipe
To shepherd swains, or seated harp in hand,
Amid reposing knights by a riverside
Or fountain, listen to the grave reports
Of dire enchantments faced and overcome
By the strong mind, and tales of warlike feats,
Where spear encountered spear, and sword with sword
Fought, as if conscious of the blazonry
That the shield bore, so glorious was the strife;

**89–93. city . . . vale:** Wordsworth is describing the journey from Bristol, where he first met Coleridge, to Racedown, where he settled with his sister Dorothy in September, 1795. **96. Aeolian visitations:** impulses or thoughts that come and go with the wind, like the sounds made upon an Aeolian harp.

Whence inspiration for a song that winds
Through ever-changing scenes of votive quest
Wrongs to redress, harmonious tribute paid
To patient courage and unblemished truth,
To firm devotion, zeal unquenchable,
And Christian meekness hallowing faithful loves.
Sometimes, more sternly moved, I would relate
How vanquished Mithridates northward passed,
And, hidden in the cloud of years, became
Odin, the father of a race by whom
Perished the Roman Empire; how the friends
And followers of Sertorius, out of Spain
Flying, found shelter in the Fortunate Isles,
And left their usages, their arts and laws,
To disappear by a slow gradual death,
To dwindle and to perish one by one,
Starved in those narrow bounds; but not the soul
Of Liberty, which fifteen hundred years
Survived, and, when the European came
With skill and power that might not be withstood,
Did, like a pestilence, maintain its hold
And wasted down by glorious death that race
Of natural heroes; or I would record
How, in tyrannic times, some high-souled man,
Unnamed among the chronicles of kings,
Suffered in silence for truth's sake; or tell,
How that one Frenchman, through continued force
Of meditation on the inhuman deeds
Of those who conquered first the Indian Isles,
Went single in his ministry across
The ocean; not to comfort the oppressed,
But, like a thirsty wind, to roam about
Withering the oppressor: how Gustavus sought
Help at his need in Dalecarlia's mines:
How Wallace fought for Scotland; left the name
Of Wallace to be found, like a wild flower,
All over his dear country; left the deeds
Of Wallace, like a family of ghosts,
To people the steep rocks and river banks,
Her natural sanctuaries, with a local soul
Of independence and stern liberty.
Sometimes it suits me better to invent
A tale from my own heart, more near akin
To my own passions and habitual thoughts;
Some variegated story, in the main
Lofty, but the unsubstantial structure melts
Before the very sun that brightens it,
Mist into air dissolving! Then a wish,
My last and favorite aspiration, mounts
With yearning toward some philosophic song
Of truth that cherishes our daily life;
With meditations passionate from deep
Recesses in man's heart, immortal verse
Thoughtfully fitted to the Orphean lyre;
But from this awful burthen I full soon
Take refuge and beguile myself with trust
That mellower years will bring a riper mind
And clearer insight. Thus my days are passed
In contradiction; with no skill to part
Vague longing, haply bred by want of power,
From paramount impulse not to be withstood,
A timorous capacity, from prudence,
From circumspection, infinite delay.
Humility and modest awe, themselves
Betray me, serving often for a cloak
To a more subtle selfishness; that now
Locks every function up in blank reserve,
Now dupes me, trusting to an anxious eye
That with intrusive restlessness beats off
Simplicity and self-presented truth.
Ah! better far than this, to stray about
Voluptuously through fields and rural walks,
And ask no record of the hours, resigned
To vacant musing, unreproved neglect
Of all things, and deliberate holiday.
Far better never to have heard the name
Of zeal and just ambition, than to live
Baffled and plagued by a mind that every hour
Turns recreant to her task; takes heart again,
Then feels immediately some hollow thought
Hang like an interdict upon her hopes.
This is my lot; for either still I find
Some imperfection in the chosen theme,
Or see of absolute accomplishment
Much wanting, so much wanting, in myself,
That I recoil and droop, and seek repose
In listlessness from vain perplexity,
Unprofitably traveling toward the grave,
Like a false steward who hath much received
And renders nothing back.
                                        Was it for this
That one, the fairest of all rivers, loved
To blend his murmurs with my nurse's song,
And, from his alder shades and rocky falls,
And from his fords and shallows, sent a voice
That flowed along my dreams? For this, didst thou,

**187–92. Mithridates, Odin, Sertorius, Fortunate Isles:** Mithridates was king of Pontus, a country in northeast Asia Minor. After his defeat by Pompey in 66 B.C., he planned to march around the Black Sea, through what are now the Balkans, and attack Rome from the north. Wordsworth, working imaginatively out of Gibbon's *Decline and Fall of the Roman Empire*, Chapter X, here merges the history of Mithridates with the legend of Odin, a barbarian chieftain who supposedly led his tribe from the shores of Lake Maeotis (now the Sea of Azov) into Sweden, where they developed sufficient strength eventually to defeat the Roman oppressors. Sertorius was a Roman general who, aided by ships and men sent him by Mithridates, opposed the armies of the tyrannical Senatorial party for eight years until his assassination in 72 B.C. Wordsworth supposes that his followers sought refuge in the Fortunate Isles, probably the Canary Islands. **206. Frenchman:** Dominique de Gourges, who went to Florida in 1567 and avenged a massacre of French Protestants by Spaniards. **212–13. Gustavus . . . mines:** Gustavus I (1495–1560), liberator of Sweden from Denmark, evaded capture by disguising himself as a miner in Dalecarlia, a district in west central Sweden. **214. Wallace:** Scottish patriot hero (1272–1305) in the wars against Edward I of England.

O Derwent! winding among grassy holms
Where I was looking on, a babe in arms,
Make ceaseless music that composed my thoughts
To more than infant softness, giving me
Amid the fretful dwellings of mankind
A foretaste, a dim earnest, of the calm
That Nature breathes among the hills and groves.

When he had left the mountains and received
On his smooth breast the shadow of those towers
That yet survive, a shattered monument
Of feudal sway, the bright blue river passed
Along the margin of our terrace walk;
A tempting playmate whom we dearly loved.
Oh, many a time have I, a five-years' child,
In a small millrace severed from his stream,
Made one long bathing of a summer's day;
Basked in the sun, and plunged and basked again
Alternate, all a summer's day, or scoured
The sandy fields, leaping through flowery groves
Of yellow ragwort; or, when rock and hill,
The woods, and distant Skiddaw's lofty height,
Were bronzed with deepest radiance, stood alone
Beneath the sky, as if I had been born
On Indian plains, and from my mother's hut
Had run abroad in wantonness, to sport
A naked savage, in the thundershower.

Fair seedtime had my soul, and I grew up
Fostered alike by beauty and by fear:
Much favored in my birthplace, and no less
In that beloved vale to which erelong
We were transplanted; there were we let loose
For sports of wider range. Ere I had told
Ten birthdays, when among the mountain slopes
Frost, and the breath of frosty wind, had snapped
The last autumnal crocus, 'twas my joy
With store of springes o'er my shoulder hung
To range the open heights where woodcocks run
Along the smooth green turf. Through half the
night,
Scudding away from snare to snare, I plied
That anxious visitation; moon and stars
Were shining o'er my head. I was alone,
And seemed to be a trouble to the peace
That dwelt among them. Sometimes it befell
In these night wanderings, that a strong desire
O'erpowered my better reason, and the bird
Which was the captive of another's toil
Became my prey; and when the deed was done
I heard among the solitary hills
Low breathings coming after me, and sounds
Of undistinguishable motion, steps
Almost as silent as the turf they trod.

Nor less, when spring had warmed the cultured
vale,
Moved we as plunderers where the mother bird
Had in high places built her lodge; though mean
Our object and inglorious, yet the end
Was not ignoble. Oh! when I have hung
Above the raven's nest, by knots of grass
And half-inch fissures in the slippery rock
But ill sustained, and almost (so it seemed)
Suspended by the blast that blew amain,
Shouldering the naked crag, oh, at that time
While on the perilous ridge I hung alone,
With what strange utterance did the loud dry
wind
Blow through my ear! the sky seemed not a sky
Of earth — and with what motion moved the
clouds!

Dust as we are, the immortal spirit grows
Like harmony in music; there is a dark
Inscrutable workmanship that reconciles
Discordant elements, makes them cling together
In one society. How strange, that all
The terrors, pains, and early miseries,
Regrets, vexations, lassitudes interfused
Within my mind, should e'er have borne a part,
And that a needful part, in making up
The calm existence that is mine when I
Am worthy of myself! Praise to the end!
Thanks to the means which Nature deigned to
employ;
Whether her fearless visitings, or those
That came with soft alarm, like hurtless light
Opening the peaceful clouds; or she would use
Severer interventions, ministry
More palpable, as best might suit her aim.

One summer evening (led by her) I found
A little boat tied to a willow tree
Within a rocky cove, its usual home.
Straight I unloosed her chain, and stepping in
Pushed from the shore. It was an act of stealth
And troubled pleasure, nor without the voice
Of mountain echoes did my boat move on;
Leaving behind her still, on either side,
Small circles glittering idly in the moon,
Until they melted all into one track
Of sparkling light. But now, like one who rows,
Proud of his skill, to reach a chosen point
With an unswerving line, I fixed my view
Upon the summit of a craggy ridge,
The horizon's utmost boundary; far above
Was nothing but the stars and the gray sky.

**275. Derwent:** a river that flows through Cockermouth close behind the house in which Wordsworth was born. **283–85. towers . . . sway:** Cockermouth Castle, a medieval ruin, easily seen from the Wordsworth terrace. **295. Skiddaw:** one of the tallest peaks (3054 feet) in the Lake District; about nine miles from Cockermouth. **304. vale:** Esthwaite, where Wordsworth entered school at Hawkshead in 1779. **310. springes:** snares for birds or small animals.

She was an elfin pinnace; lustily
I dipped my oars into the silent lake,
And, as I rose upon the stroke, my boat
Went heaving through the water like a swan;
When, from behind that craggy steep till then
The horizon's bound, a huge peak, black and huge,
As if with voluntary power instinct,
Upreared its head. I struck and struck again,
And growing still in stature the grim shape
Towered up between me and the stars, and still,
For so it seemed, with purpose of its own
And measured motion like a living thing,
Strode after me. With trembling oars I turned,
And through the silent water stole my way
Back to the covert of the willow tree;
There in her mooring place I left my bark,
And through the meadow homeward went, in grave
And serious mood; but after I had seen
That spectacle, for many days, my brain
Worked with a dim and undetermined sense
Of unknown modes of being; o'er my thoughts
There hung a darkness, call it solitude
Or blank desertion. No familiar shapes
Remained, no pleasant images of trees,
Of sea or sky, no colors of green fields;
But huge and mighty forms, that do not live
Like living men, moved slowly through the mind
By day, and were a trouble to my dreams.

Wisdom and Spirit of the universe!
Thou Soul that art the eternity of thought
That givest to forms and images a breath
And everlasting motion, not in vain
By day or starlight thus from my first dawn
Of childhood didst thou intertwine for me
The passions that build up our human soul;
Not with the mean and vulgar works of man,
But with high objects, with enduring things—
With life and nature—purifying thus
The elements of feeling and of thought,
And sanctifying, by such discipline,
Both pain and fear, until we recognize
A grandeur in the beatings of the heart.
Nor was this fellowship vouchsafed to me
With stinted kindness. In November days,
When vapors rolling down the valley made
A lonely scene more lonesome, among woods,
At noon and 'mid the calm of summer nights,
When, by the margin of the trembling lake,
Beneath the gloomy hills homeward I went
In solitude, such intercourse was mine;
Mine was it in the fields both day and night,
And by the waters, all the summer long.

And in the frosty season, when the sun
Was set, and visible for many a mile
The cottage windows blazed through twilight
gloom,
I heeded not their summons; happy time
It was indeed for all of us—for me
It was a time of rapture! Clear and loud
The village clock tolled six—I wheeled about,
Proud and exulting like an untired horse
That cares not for his home. All shod with steel,
We hissed along the polished ice in games
Confederate, imitative of the chase
And woodland pleasures—the resounding horn,
The pack loud chiming, and the hunted hare.
So through the darkness and the cold we flew,
And not a voice was idle; with the din
Smitten, the precipices rang aloud;
The leafless trees and every icy crag
Tinkled like iron; while far distant hills
Into the tumult sent an alien sound
Of melancholy not unnoticed, while the stars
Eastward were sparkling clear, and in the west
The orange sky of evening died away.
Not seldom from the uproar I retired
Into a silent bay, or sportively
Glanced sideway, leaving the tumultuous throng,
To cut across the reflex of a star
That fled, and, flying still before me, gleamed
Upon the glassy plain; and oftentimes,
When we had given our bodies to the wind,
And all the shadowy banks on either side
Came sweeping through the darkness, spinning still
The rapid line of motion, then at once
Have I, reclining back upon my heels,
Stopped short; yet still the solitary cliffs
Wheeled by me—even as if the earth had rolled
With visible motion her diurnal round!
Behind me did they stretch in solemn train,
Feebler and feebler, and I stood and watched
Till all was tranquil as a dreamless sleep.

Ye Presences of Nature in the sky
And on the earth! Ye Visions of the hills!
And Souls of lonely places! can I think
A vulgar hope was yours when ye employed
Such ministry, when ye, through many a year
Haunting me thus among my boyish sports,
On caves and trees, upon the woods and hills,
Impressed, upon all forms, the characters
Of danger or desire; and thus did make
The surface of the universal earth,
With triumph and delight, with hope and fear,
Work like a sea?
Not uselessly employed,
Might I pursue this theme through every change
Of exercise and play, to which the year
Did summon us in his delightful round.

**373. pinnace:** a small boat, usually equipped with a sail. **398–99. forms . . . men:** The punctuation here is debatable; perhaps the only comma should follow l. 398.

We were a noisy crew; the sun in heaven
Beheld not vales more beautiful than ours;
Nor saw a band in happiness and joy
Richer, or worthier of the ground they trod.
I could record with no reluctant voice
The woods of autumn, and their hazel bowers
With milk-white clusters hung; the rod and line,
True symbol of hope's foolishness, whose strong
And unreproved enchantment led us on
By rocks and pools shut out from every star,
All the green summer, to forlorn cascades
Among the windings hid of mountain brooks.
Unfading recollections! at this hour
The heart is almost mine with which I felt,
From some hilltop on sunny afternoons,
The paper kite high among fleecy clouds
Pull at her rein like an impetuous courser;
Or, from the meadows sent on gusty days,
Beheld her breast the wind, then suddenly
Dashed headlong, and rejected by the storm.

Ye lowly cottages wherein we dwelt,
A ministration of your own was yours;
Can I forget you, being as you were
So beautiful among the pleasant fields
In which ye stood? or can I here forget
The plain and seemly countenance with which
Ye dealt out your plain comforts? Yet had ye
Delights and exultations of your own.
Eager and never weary we pursued
Our home amusements by the warm peat fire
At evening, when with pencil, and smooth slate
In square divisions parceled out and all
With crosses and with ciphers scribbled o'er,
We schemed and puzzled, head opposed to head
In strife too humble to be named in verse:
Or round the naked table, snow-white deal,
Cherry or maple, sat in close array,
And to the combat, loo or whist, led on
A thick-ribbed army; not, as in the world,
Neglected and ungratefully thrown by
Even for the very service they had wrought,
But husbanded through many a long campaign.
Uncouth assemblage was it, where no few
Had changed their functions: some, plebeian cards
Which Fate, beyond the promise of their birth,
Had dignified, and called to represent
The persons of departed potentates.
Oh, with what echoes on the board they fell!
Ironic diamonds — clubs, hearts, diamonds, spades,
A congregation piteously akin!
Cheap matter offered they to boyish wit,
Those sooty knaves, precipitated down
With scoffs and taunts, like Vulcan out of heaven:
The paramount ace, a moon in her eclipse,
Queens gleaming through their splendor's last decay,
And monarchs surly at the wrongs sustained
By royal visages. Meanwhile abroad
Incessant rain was falling, or the frost
Raged bitterly, with keen and silent tooth;
And, interrupting oft that eager game,
From under Esthwaite's splitting fields of ice
The pent-up air, struggling to free itself,
Gave out to meadow grounds and hills a loud
Protracted yelling, like the noise of wolves
Howling in troops along the Bothnic main.

Nor, sedulous as I have been to trace
How Nature by extrinsic passion first
Peopled the mind with forms sublime or fair,
And made me love them, may I here omit
How other pleasures have been mine, and joys
Of subtler origin; how I have felt,
Not seldom even in that tempestuous time,
Those hallowed and pure motions of the sense
Which seem, in their simplicity, to own
An intellectual charm; that calm delight
Which, if I err not, surely must belong
To those first-born affinities that fit
Our new existence to existing things,
And, in our dawn of being, constitute
The bond of union between life and joy.

Yes, I remember when the changeful earth,
And twice five summers on my mind had stamped
The faces of the moving year, even then
I held unconscious intercourse with beauty
Old as creation, drinking in a pure
Organic pleasure from the silver wreaths
Of curling mist, or from the level plain
Of waters colored by impending clouds.

The sands of Westmorland, the creeks and bays
Of Cumbria's rocky limits, they can tell
How, when the Sea threw off his evening shade,
And to the shepherd's hut on distant hills
Sent welcome notice of the rising moon,
How I have stood, to fancies such as these
A stranger, linking with the spectacle
No conscious memory of a kindred sight,
And bringing with me no peculiar sense

**499. cottages . . . dwelt:** Hawkshead students lived in the houses of the villagers. For nine years Wordsworth lived in the cottage of Anne Tyson, to whom he refers several times in *The Prelude*. **514. deal:** pine or fir planks usually six feet long and at least seven inches wide. **516–35. combat . . . visages:** an imitation of Pope, *The Rape of the Lock*, III.25–98, pp. 777–78 in Vol. I.

**531. Vulcan . . . heaven:** Vulcan, otherwise known as Hephaestus or Mulciber, was the god of fire and blacksmith of Olympus. He was crippled when Zeus, his father, threw him from Olympus for interfering in a domestic quarrel. See *Paradise Lost*, I.738–46, p. 462 in Vol. I. **543. Bothnic main:** Gulf of Bothnia, between Finland and Sweden. **568. Cumbria:** Cumberland.

Of quietness or peace; yet have I stood,
Even while mine eye hath moved o'er many a league
Of shining water, gathering as it seemed,
Through every hairbreadth in that field of light,
New pleasure like a bee among the flowers.

Thus oft amid those fits of vulgar joy
Which, through all seasons, on a child's pursuits
Are prompt attendants, 'mid that giddy bliss
Which, like a tempest, works along the blood
And is forgotten; even then I felt
Gleams like the flashing of a shield; the earth
And common face of Nature spake to me
Rememberable things; sometimes, 'tis true,
By chance collisions and quaint accidents
(Like those ill-sorted unions, work supposed
Of evil-minded fairies), yet not vain
Nor profitless, if haply they impressed
Collateral objects and appearances,
Albeit lifeless then, and doomed to sleep
Until maturer seasons called them forth
To impregnate and to elevate the mind.
And if the vulgar joy by its own weight
Wearied itself out of the memory,
The scenes which were a witness of that joy
Remained in their substantial lineaments
Depicted on the brain, and to the eye
Were visible, a daily sight; and thus
By the impressive discipline of fear,
By pleasure and repeated happiness,
So frequently repeated, and by force
Of obscure feelings representative
Of things forgotten, these same scenes so bright,
So beautiful, so majestic in themselves,
Though yet the day was distant, did become
Habitually dear, and all their forms
And changeful colors by invisible links
Were fastened to the affections.

I began
My story early — not misled, I trust,
By an infirmity of love for days
Disowned by memory — ere the birth of spring
Planting my snowdrops among winter snows;
Nor will it seem to thee, O friend! so prompt
In sympathy, that I have lengthened out
With fond and feeble tongue a tedious tale.
Meanwhile, my hope has been, that I might fetch
Invigorating thoughts from former years;
Might fix the wavering balance of my mind,
And haply meet reproaches too, whose power
May spur me on, in manhood now mature
To honorable toil. Yet should these hopes
Prove vain, and thus should neither I be taught
To understand myself, nor thou to know
With better knowledge how the heart was framed
Of him thou lovest; need I dread from thee
Harsh judgments, if the song be loath to quit
Those recollected hours that have the charm
Of visionary things, those lovely forms
And sweet sensations that throw back our life,
And almost make remotest infancy
A visible scene, on which the sun is shining?

One end at least hath been attained; my mind
Hath been revived, and if this genial mood
Desert me not, forthwith shall be brought down
Through later years the story of my life.
The road lies plain before me; 'tis a theme
Single and of determined bounds; and hence
I choose it rather at this time, than work
Of ampler or more varied argument,
Where I might be discomfited and lost;
And certain hopes are with me, that to thee
This labor will be welcome, honored friend!

## BOOK II

### SCHOOLTIME (*continued*)

Thus far, O friend! have we, though leaving much
Unvisited, endeavored to retrace
The simple ways in which my childhood walked;
Those chiefly that first led me to the love
Of rivers, woods, and fields. The passion yet
Was in its birth, sustained as might befall
By nourishment that came unsought; for still
From week to week, from month to month, we lived
A round of tumult. Duly were our games
Prolonged in summer till the daylight failed;
No chair remained before the doors; the bench
And threshold steps were empty; fast asleep
The laborer, and the old man who had sat
A later lingerer; yet the revelry
Continued and the loud uproar; at last,
When all the ground was dark, and twinkling stars
Edged the black clouds, home and to bed we went,
Feverish with weary joints and beating minds.
Ah! is there one who ever has been young,
Nor needs a warning voice to tame the pride
Of intellect and virtue's self-esteem?
One is there, though the wisest and the best
Of all mankind, who covets not at times
Union that cannot be; who would not give
If so he might, to duty and to truth
The eagerness of infantine desire?
A tranquilizing spirit presses now
On my corporeal frame, so wide appears
The vacancy between me and those days
Which yet have such self-presence in my mind,
That, musing on them, often do I seem

Two consciousnesses, conscious of myself
And of some other being. A rude mass
Of native rock, left midway in the square
Of our small market village, was the goal
Or center of these sports; and when, returned
After long absence, thither I repaired,
Gone was the old gray stone, and in its place
A smart assembly room usurped the ground
That had been ours. There let the fiddle scream,
And be ye happy! Yet, my friends! I know
That more than one of you will think with me
Of those soft starry nights, and that old dame
From whom the stone was named, who there had sat,
And watched her table with its huckster's wares
Assiduous, through the length of sixty years.

We ran a boisterous course; the year span round
With giddy motion. But the time approached
That brought with it a regular desire
For calmer pleasures, when the winning forms
Of Nature were collaterally attached
To every scheme of holiday delight
And every boyish sport, less grateful else
And languidly pursued.
When summer came,
Our pastime was, on bright half-holidays,
To sweep along the plain of Windermere
With rival oars; and the selected bourn
Was now an island musical with birds
That sang and ceased not; now a sister isle
Beneath the oaks' umbrageous covert, sown
With lilies of the valley like a field;
And now a third small island, where survived
In solitude the ruins of a shrine
Once to Our Lady dedicate, and served
Daily with chanted rites. In such a race
So ended, disappointment could be none,
Uneasiness, or pain, or jealousy;
We rested in the shade, all pleased alike,
Conquered and conqueror. Thus the pride of strength,
And the vainglory of superior skill,
Were tempered; thus was gradually produced
A quiet independence of the heart;
And to my friend who knows me I may add,
Fearless of blame, that hence for future days
Ensued a diffidence and modesty,
And I was taught to feel, perhaps too much,
The self-sufficing power of solitude.

Our daily meals were frugal, Sabine fare!
More than we wished we knew the blessing then
Of vigorous hunger — hence corporeal strength
Unsapped by delicate viands; for, exclude
A little weekly stipend, and we lived
Through three divisions of the quartered year
In penniless poverty. But now to school
From the half-yearly holidays returned,
We came with weightier purses, that sufficed
To furnish treats more costly than the dame
Of the old gray stone, from her scant board, supplied.
Hence rustic dinners on the cool green ground,
Or in the woods, or by a riverside
Or shady fountains, while among the leaves
Soft airs were stirring, and the midday sun
Unfelt shone brightly round us in our joy.
Nor is my aim neglected if I tell
How sometimes, in the length of those half-years,
We from our funds drew largely — proud to curb,
And eager to spur on, the galloping steed;
And with the cautious innkeeper, whose stud
Supplied our want, we haply might employ
Sly subterfuge, if the adventure's bound
Were distant: some famed temple where of yore
The Druids worshiped, or the antique walls
Of that large abbey, where within the Vale
Of Nightshade, to St. Mary's honor built,
Stands yet a moldering pile with fractured arch,
Belfry, and images, and living trees;
A holy scene! Along the smooth green turf
Our horses grazed. To more than inland peace,
Left by the west wind sweeping overhead
From a tumultuous ocean, trees and towers
In that sequestered valley may be seen,
Both silent and both motionless alike;
Such the deep shelter that is there, and such
The safeguard for repose and quietness.

Our steeds remounted and the summons given,
With whip and spur we through the chantry flew
In uncouth race, and left the cross-legged knight,
And the stone abbot, and that single wren
Which one day sang so sweetly in the nave
Of the old church, that — though from recent showers
The earth was comfortless, and, touched by faint
Internal breezes, sobbings of the place
And respirations, from the roofless walls
The shuddering ivy dripped large drops — yet still
So sweetly 'mid the gloom the invisible bird
Sang to herself, that there I could have made
My dwelling place, and lived forever there
To hear such music. Through the walls we flew
And down the valley, and, a circuit made

**Book II: 78. Sabine:** The Sabines were an ancient people, noted for frugality and hardihood, who lived in the Appenine mountains northeast of Rome.

**82. weekly stipend:** between threepence and sixpence (six and twelve cents American money), depending on the age of the boy.
**103. abbey:** Furness Abbey, twenty-one miles from Hawkshead.
**116. chantry:** a chapel attached to the main body of a church, and used for the chanting of masses for the soul of the founder.

In wantonness of heart, through rough and smooth
We scampered homewards. Oh, ye rocks and streams,
And that still spirit shed from evening air!
Even in this joyous time I sometimes felt
Your presence, when with slackened step we breathed
Along the sides of the steep hills, or when
Lighted by gleams of moonlight from the sea
We beat with thundering hoofs the level sand.

Midway on long Winander's eastern shore,
Within the crescent of a pleasant bay,
A tavern stood; no homely featured house,
Primeval like its neighboring cottages,
But 'twas a splendid place, the door beset
With chaises, grooms, and liveries, and within
Decanters, glasses, and the blood-red wine.
In ancient times, or ere the Hall was built
On the large island, had this dwelling been
More worthy of a poet's love, a hut,
Proud of its one bright fire and sycamore shade.
But — though the rhymes were gone that once inscribed
The threshold, and large golden characters,
Spread o'er the spangled signboard, had dislodged
The old Lion and usurped his place, in slight
And mockery of the rustic painter's hand —
Yet, to this hour, the spot to me is dear
With all its foolish pomp. The garden lay
Upon a slope surmounted by a plain
Of a small bowling green; beneath us stood
A grove, with gleams of water through the trees
And over the treetops; nor did we want
Refreshment, strawberries and mellow cream.
There, while through half an afternoon we played
On the smooth platform, whether skill prevailed
Or happy blunder triumphed, bursts of glee
Made all the mountains ring. But, ere nightfall,
When in our pinnace we returned at leisure
Over the shadowy lake, and to the beach
Of some small island streered our course with one,
The minstrel of the troop, and left him there,
And rowed off gently, while he blew his flute
Alone upon the rock — oh, then, the calm
And dead still water lay upon my mind
Even with a weight of pleasure, and the sky,
Never before so beautiful, sank down
Into my heart, and held me like a dream!
Thus were my sympathies enlarged, and thus
Daily the common range of visible things
Grew dear to me; already I began
To love the sun; a boy I loved the sun,
Not as I since have loved him, as a pledge
And surety of our earthly life, a light
Which we behold and feel we are alive;
Nor for his bounty to so many worlds
But for this cause, that I had seen him lay
His beauty on the morning hills, had seen
The western mountain touch his setting orb,
In many a thoughtless hour, when, from excess
Of happiness, my blood appeared to flow
For its own pleasure, and I breathed with joy.
And, from like feelings, humble though intense,
To patriotic and domestic love
Analogous, the moon to me was dear;
For I could dream away my purposes,
Standing to gaze upon her while she hung
Midway between the hills as if she knew
No other region, but belonged to thee,
Yea, appertained by a peculiar right
To thee and thy gray huts, thou one dear vale!

Those incidental charms which first attached
My heart to rural objects, day by day
Grew weaker, and I hasten on to tell
How Nature, intervenient till this time
And secondary, now at length was sought
For her own sake. But who shall parcel out
His intellect by geometric rules,
Split like a province into round and square?
Who knows the individual hour in which
His habits were first sown, even as a seed?
Who that shall point as with a wand and say
" This portion of the river of my mind
Came from yon fountain? " Thou, my friend! art one
More deeply read in thy own thoughts; to thee
Science appears but what in truth she is,
Not as our glory and our absolute boast,
But as a succedaneum, and a prop
To our infirmity. No officious slave
Art thou of that false secondary power
By which we multiply distinctions, then
Deem that our puny boundaries are things
That we perceive, and not that we have made.
To thee, unblinded by these formal arts,
The unity of all hath been revealed,
And thou wilt doubt, with me less aptly skilled
Than many are to range the faculties
In scale and order, class the cabinet
Of their sensations, and in voluble phrase
Run through the history and birth of each
As of a single independent thing.
Hard task, vain hope, to analyze the mind,
If each most obvious and particular thought,
Not in a mystical and idle sense,
But in the words of reason deeply weighed,

**138. Winander:** Windermere, largest of the English lakes.

**214. succedaneum:** a substitute.

Hath no beginning.
Blest the infant babe
(For with my best conjecture I would trace
Our being's earthly progress), blest the babe,
Nursed in his mother's arms, who sinks to sleep
Rocked on his mother's breast; who with his soul
Drinks in the feelings of his mother's eye!
For him, in one dear presence, there exists
A virtue which irradiates and exalts
Objects through widest intercourse of sense;
No outcast he, bewildered and depressed;
Along his infant veins are interfused
The gravitation and the filial bond
Of nature that connect him with the world.
Is there a flower, to which he points with hand
Too weak to gather it, already love
Drawn from love's purest earthly fount for him
Hath beautified that flower; already shades
Of pity cast from inward tenderness
Do fall around him upon aught that bears
Unsightly marks of violence or harm.
Emphatically such a being lives,
Frail creature as he is, helpless as frail,
An inmate of this active universe;
For, feeling has to him imparted power
That through the growing faculties of sense
Doth like an agent of the one great Mind
Create, creator and receiver both,
Working but in alliance with the works
Which it beholds. Such, verily, is the first
Poetic spirit of our human life,
By uniform control of after years,
In most, abated or suppressed; in some,
Through every change of growth and of decay,
Pre-eminent till death.
From early days,
Beginning not long after that first time
In which, a babe, by intercourse of touch
I held mute dialogues with my mother's heart,
I have endeavored to display the means
Whereby this infant sensibility,
Great birthright of our being, was in me
Augmented and sustained. Yet is a path
More difficult before me; and I fear
That in its broken windings we shall need
The chamois' sinews, and the eagle's wing;
For now a trouble came into my mind
From unknown causes. I was left alone
Seeking the visible world, nor knowing why.
The props of my affections were removed,
And yet the building stood, as if sustained
By its own spirit! All that I beheld
Was dear, and hence to finer influxes
The mind lay open to a more exact
And close communion. Many are our joys
In youth, but oh! what happiness to live
When every hour brings palpable access
Of knowledge, when all knowledge is delight,
And sorrow is not there! The seasons came,
And every season wheresoe'er I moved
Unfolded transitory qualities,
Which, but for this most watchful power of love,
Had been neglected; left a register
Of permanent relations, else unknown.
Hence life, and change, and beauty, solitude
More active ever than "best society"—
Society made sweet as solitude
By silent inobtrusive sympathies,
And gentle agitations of the mind
From manifold distinctions, difference
Perceived in things, where, to the unwatchful eye,
No difference is, and hence, from the same source,
Sublimer joy; for I would walk alone,
Under the quiet stars, and at that time
Have felt whate'er there is of power in sound
To breathe an elevated mood, by form
Or image unprofaned; and I would stand,
If the night blackened with a coming storm,
Beneath some rock, listening to notes that are
The ghostly language of the ancient earth,
Or make their dim abode in distant winds.
Thence did I drink the visionary power,
And deem not profitless those fleeting moods
Of shadowy exultation; not for this,
That they are kindred to our purer mind
And intellectual life, but that the soul,
Remembering how she felt, but what she felt
Remembering not, retains an obscure sense
Of possible sublimity, whereto
With growing faculties she doth aspire,
With faculties still growing, feeling still
That whatsoever point they gain, they yet
Have something to pursue.
And not alone,
'Mid gloom and tumult, but no less 'mid fair
And tranquil scenes, that universal power
And fitness in the latent qualities
And essences of things, by which the mind
Is moved with feelings of delight, to me
Came strengthened with a superadded soul,
A virtue not its own. My morning walks
Were early; oft before the hours of school
I traveled round our little lake, five miles
Of pleasant wandering. Happy time! more dear
For this, that one was by my side, a friend,
Then passionately loved; with heart how full
Would he peruse these lines! For many years
Have since flowed in between us, and, our minds
Both silent to each other, at this time
We live as if those hours had never been.
Nor seldom did I lift our cottage latch

**330. hours of school:** Hawkshead work began at six o'clock in summer, seven in winter. **333. friend:** a Hawkshead schoolmate, not S. T. Coleridge.

Far earlier, ere one smoke wreath had risen
From human dwelling, or the vernal thrush
Was audible; and sat among the woods
Alone upon some jutting eminence,
At the first gleam of dawnlight, when the vale,
Yet slumbering, lay in utter solitude.
How shall I seek the origin? where find
Faith in the marvelous things which then I felt?
Oft in these moments such a holy calm
Would overspread my soul, that bodily eyes
Were utterly forgotten, and what I saw
Appeared like something in myself, a dream,
A prospect in the mind.
                                  'Twere long to tell
What spring and autumn, what the winter snows,
And what the summer shade, what day and night,
Evening and morning, sleep and waking, thought
From sources inexhaustible, poured forth
To feed the spirit of religious love
In which I walked with Nature. But let this
Be not forgotten, that I still retained
My first creative sensibility;
That by the regular action of the world
My soul was unsubdued. A plastic power
Abode with me; a forming hand, at times
Rebellious, acting in a devious mood;
A local spirit of his own, at war
With general tendency, but, for the most,
Subservient strictly to external things
With which it communed. An auxiliar light
Came from my mind, which on the setting sun
Bestowed new splendor; the melodious birds,
The fluttering breezes, fountains that run on
Murmuring so sweetly in themselves, obeyed
A like dominion, and the midnight storm
Grew darker in the presence of my eye;
Hence my obeisance, my devotion hence,
And hence my transport.
                                  Nor should this, perchance,
Pass unrecorded, that I still had loved
The exercise and produce of a toil,
Than analytic industry to me
More pleasing, and whose character I deem
Is more poetic as resembling more
Creative agency. The song would speak
Of that interminable building reared
By observation of affinities
In objects where no brotherhood exists
To passive minds. My seventeenth year was come
And, whether from this habit rooted now
So deeply in my mind, or from excess
In the great social principle of life
Coercing all things into sympathy,
To unorganic natures were transferred
My own enjoyments; or the power of truth
Coming in revelation, did converse
With things that really are; I, at this time,
Saw blessings spread around me like a sea.
Thus while the days flew by, and years passed on,
From Nature and her overflowing soul,
I had received so much, that all my thoughts
Were steeped in feeling; I was only then
Contented, when with bliss ineffable
I felt the sentiment of Being spread
O'er all that moves and all that seemeth still;
O'er all that, lost beyond the reach of thought
And human knowledge, to the human eye
Invisible, yet liveth to the heart;
O'er all that leaps and runs, and shouts and sings,
Or beats the gladsome air; o'er all that glides
Beneath the wave, yea, in the wave itself,
And mighty depth of waters. Wonder not
If high the transport, great the joy I felt,
Communing in this sort through earth and Heaven
With every form of creature, as it looked
Towards the Uncreated with a countenance
Of adoration, with an eye of love.
One song they sang, and it was audible,
Most audible, then, when the fleshly ear,
O'ercome by humblest prelude of that strain,
Forgot her functions, and slept undisturbed.

If this be error, and another faith
Find easier access to the pious mind,
Yet were I grossly destitute of all
Those human sentiments that make this earth
So dear, if I should fail with grateful voice
To speak of you, ye mountains, and ye lakes
And sounding cataracts, ye mists and winds
That dwell among the hills where I was born.
If in my youth I have been pure in heart,
If, mingling with the world, I am content
With my own modest pleasures, and have lived
With God and Nature communing, removed
From little enmities and low desires—
The gift is yours; if in these times of fear,
This melancholy waste of hopes o'erthrown,
If, 'mid indifference and apathy,
And wicked exultation when good men
On every side fall off, we know not how,
To selfishness, disguised in gentle names
Of peace and quiet and domestic love
Yet mingled not unwillingly with sneers
On visionary minds; if, in this time
Of dereliction and dismay, I yet
Despair not of our nature, but retain
A more than Roman confidence, a faith
That fails not, in all sorrow my support,
The blessing of my life—the gift is yours,
Ye winds and sounding cataracts! 'tis yours,

**432–51. fear . . . passion:** Wordsworth's expression of continuing faith in the perfectibility of man despite the perversion of the original ideals of the French Revolution and the rise of Napoleon.

Ye mountains! thine, O Nature! Thou hast fed
My lofty speculations; and in thee,
For this uneasy heart of ours, I find
A never-failing principle of joy
And purest passion.
Thou, my friend! wert reared
In the great city, 'mid far other scenes;
But we, by different roads, at length have gained
The selfsame bourn. And for this cause to thee
I speak, unapprehensive of contempt,
The insinuated scoff of coward tongues,
And all that silent language which so oft
In conversation between man and man
Blots from the human countenance all trace
Of beauty and of love. For thou hast sought
The truth in solitude, and, since the days
That gave thee liberty, full long desired,
To serve in Nature's temple, thou hast been
The most assiduous of her ministers;
In many things my brother, chiefly here
In this our deep devotion.
Fare thee well!
Health and the quiet of a healthful mind
Attend thee! seeking oft the haunts of men,
And yet more often living with thyself,
And for thyself, so haply shall thy days
Be many, and a blessing to mankind.

## BOOK III

## RESIDENCE AT CAMBRIDGE

It was a dreary morning when the wheels
Rolled over a wide plain o'erhung with clouds,
And nothing cheered our way till first we saw
The long-roofed chapel of King's College lift
Turrets and pinnacles in answering files,
Extended high above a dusky grove.

Advancing, we espied upon the road
A student clothed in gown and tasseled cap,
Striding along as if o'ertasked by Time,
Or covetous of exercise and air;
He passed — nor was I master of my eyes
Till he was left an arrow's flight behind.
As near and nearer to the spot we drew,
It seemed to suck us in with an eddy's force.
Onward we drove beneath the Castle; caught,
While crossing Magdalene Bridge, a glimpse of
Cam;
And at the *Hoop* alighted, famous inn.

My spirit was up, my thoughts were full of hope;
Some friends I had, acquaintances who there
Seemed friends, poor simple schoolboys, now hung
round
With honor and importance; in a world
Of welcome faces up and down I roved;
Questions, directions, warnings and advice,
Flowed in upon me, from all sides; fresh day
Of pride and pleasure! to myself I seemed
A man of business and expense, and went
From shop to shop about my own affairs,
To tutor or to tailor, as befell,
From street and street with loose and careless mind.

I was the dreamer, they the dream; I roamed
Delighted through the motley spectacle;
Gowns grave, or gaudy, doctors, students, streets,
Courts, cloisters, flocks of churches, gateways, tow-
ers,
Migration strange for a stripling of the hills,
A northern villager.
As if the change
Had waited on some fairy's wand, at once
Behold me rich in moneys, and attired
In splendid garb, with hose of silk, and hair
Powdered like rimy trees, when frost is keen.
My lordly dressing gown, I pass it by,
With other signs of manhood that supplied
The lack of beard. The weeks went roundly on,
With invitations, suppers, wine and fruit,
Smooth housekeeping within, and all without
Liberal, and suiting gentleman's array.

The Evangelist St. John my patron was;
Three Gothic courts are his, and in the first
Was my abiding place, a nook obscure;
Right underneath, the college kitchens made
A humming sound, less tunable than bees,
But hardly less industrious; with shrill notes
Of sharp command and scolding intermixed.
Near me hung Trinity's loquacious clock,
Who never let the quarters, night or day,
Slip by him unproclaimed, and told the hours
Twice over with a male and female voice.
Her pealing organ was my neighbor too;
And from my pillow, looking forth by light
Of moon or favoring stars, I could behold
The antechapel where the statue stood
Of Newton with his prism and silent face,
The marble index of a mind forever
Voyaging through strange seas of thought,
alone.

**452. city:** a reference to Coleridge's early years at Christ's Hospital, a famous and ancient charity school in London, also attended by Charles Lamb and Leigh Hunt. **454. bourn:** destination. **466. Fare . . . well:** probably an echo of Wordsworth's parting from Coleridge after the former's house-hunting expedition into the Lake District in October, 1799. **Book III: 4. chapel:** See the sonnet, "Inside of King's College Chapel, Cambridge," below.

**39. rimy:** covered with rime, a white icy deposit formed from fog or moisture-bearing air. **46. Evangelist St. John:** Wordsworth attended St. John's College, Cambridge University, from 1787 to 1791. **53. Trinity:** another Cambridge college. **62–63. The . . . alone:** the most famous of the later additions to *The Prelude*.

Of college labors, of the lecturer's room
All studded round, as thick as chairs could stand,
With loyal students, faithful to their books,
Half-and-half idlers, hardy recusants,
And honest dunces — of important days,
Examinations, when the man was weighed
As in a balance! of excessive hopes,
Tremblings withal and commendable fears,
Small jealousies, and triumphs good or bad —
Let others that know more speak as they know.
Such glory was but little sought by me,
And little won. Yet from the first crude days
Of settling time in this untried abode,
I was disturbed at times by prudent thoughts,
Wishing to hope without a hope, some fears
About my future worldly maintenance,
And, more than all, a strangeness in the mind,
A feeling that I was not for that hour,
Nor for that place. But wherefore be cast down?
For (not to speak of Reason and her pure
Reflective acts to fix the moral law
Deep in the conscience, nor of Christian Hope,
Bowing her head before her sister Faith
As one far mightier), hither I had come,
Bear witness Truth, endowed with holy powers
And faculties, whether to work or feel.
Oft when the dazzling show no longer new
Had ceased to dazzle, ofttimes did I quit
My comrades, leave the crowd, buildings and groves,
And as I paced alone the level fields
Far from those lovely sights and sounds sublime
With which I had been conversant, the mind
Drooped not; but there into herself returning,
With prompt rebound seemed fresh as heretofore.
At least I more distinctly recognized
Her native instincts; let me dare to speak
A higher language, say that now I felt
What independent solaces were mine,
To mitigate the injurious sway of place
Or circumstance, how far soever changed
In youth, or *to* be changed in after years.
As if awakened, summoned, roused, constrained,
I looked for universal things; perused
The common countenance of earth and sky:
Earth, nowhere unembellished by some trace
Of that first paradise whence man was driven;
And sky, whose beauty and bounty are expressed
By the proud name she bears — the name of heaven.
I called on both to teach me what they might;
Or, turning the mind in upon herself,
Pored, watched, expected, listened, spread my thoughts
And spread them with a wider creeping; felt
Incumbencies more awful, visitings
Of the upholder of the tranquil soul,
That tolerates the indignities of time,
And, from the center of eternity
All finite motions overruling, lives
In glory immutable. But peace! enough
Here to record that I was mounting now
To such community with highest truth.

A track pursuing, not untrod before,
From strict analogies by thought supplied
Or consciousnesses not to be subdued,
To every natural form, rock, fruits, or flower,
Even the loose stones that cover the highway,
I gave a moral life; I saw them feel,
Or linked them to some feeling; the great mass
Lay imbedded in a quickening soul, and all
That I beheld respired with inward meaning.
Add that what'er of terror or of love
Or beauty, Nature's daily face put on
From transitory passion, unto this
I was as sensitive as waters are
To the sky's influence: in a kindred mood
Of passion was obedient as a lute
That waits upon the touches of the wind.
Unknown, unthought of, yet I was most rich —
I had a world about me — 'twas my own;
I made it, for it only lived to me,
And to the God who sees into the heart.
Such sympathies, though rarely, were betrayed
By outward gestures and by visible looks;
Some called it madness — so indeed it was,
If childlike fruitfulness in passing joy,
If steady moods of thoughtfulness matured
To inspiration, sort with such a name;
If prophecy be madness; if things viewed
By poets in old time, and higher up
By the first men, earth's first inhabitants,
May in these tutored days no more be seen
With undisordered sight. But leaving this,
It was no madness, for the bodily eye
Amid my strongest workings evermore
Was searching out the lines of difference
As they lie hid in all external forms,
Near or remote, minute or vast; an eye
Which, from a tree, a stone, a withered leaf,
To the broad ocean and the azure heavens
Spangled with kindred multitudes of stars,
Could find no surface where its power might sleep;
Which spake perpetual logic to my soul,
And by an unrelenting agency
Did bind my feelings even as in a chain.

And here, O friend! have I retraced my life
Up to an eminence, and told a tale
Of matters which not falsely may be called
The glory of my youth. Of genius, power,
Creation and divinity itself
I have been speaking, for my theme has been
What has passed within me. Not of outward things

Done visibly for other minds, words, signs,
Symbols or actions, but of my own heart
Have I been speaking, and my youthful mind.
O heavens! how awful is the might of souls,
And what they do within themselves while yet
The yoke of earth is new to them, the world
Nothing but a wild field where they were sown.
This is, in truth, heroic argument,
This genuine prowess, which I wished to touch
With hand however weak, but in the main
It lies far hidden from the reach of words.
Points have we all of us within our souls
Where all stand single; this I feel, and make
Breathings for incommunicable powers;
But is not each a memory to himself?
And, therefore, now that we must quit this theme,
I am not heartless, for there's not a man
That lives who hath not known his godlike hours,
And feels not what an empire we inherit
As natural beings in the strength of Nature.

No more: for now into a populous plain
We must descend. A traveler I am,
Whose tale is only of himself; even so,
So be it, if the pure of heart be prompt
To follow, and if thou, my honored friend!
Who in these thoughts art ever at my side,
Support, as heretofore, my fainting steps.

It hath been told, that when the first delight
That flashed upon me from this novel show
Had failed, the mind returned into herself;
Yet true it is, that I had made a change
In climate, and my nature's outward coat
Changed also slowly and insensibly.
Full oft the quiet and exalted thoughts
Of loneliness gave way to empty noise
And superficial pastimes; now and then
Forced labor, and more frequently forced hopes;
And, worst of all, a treasonable growth
Of indecisive judgments, that impaired
And shook the mind's simplicity. And yet
This was a gladsome time. Could I behold—
Who, less insensible than sodden clay
In a sea river's bed at ebb of tide,
Could have beheld—with undelighted heart,
So many happy youths, so wide and fair
A congregation in its budding time
Of health, and hope, and beauty, all at once
So many divers samples from the growth
Of life's sweet season—could have seen unmoved
That miscellaneous garland of wild flowers
Decking the matron temples of a place
So famous through the world? To me, at least,
It was a goodly prospect; for, in sooth,
Though I had learned betimes to stand unpropped,
And independent musings pleased me so
That spells seemed on me when I was alone,
Yet could I only cleave to solitude
In lonely places; if a throng was near
That way I leaned by nature; for my heart
Was social, and loved idleness and joy.

Not seeking those who might participate
My deeper pleasures (nay, I had not once,
Though not unused to mutter lonesome songs,
Even with myself divided such delight,
Or looked that way for aught that might be
clothed
In human language), easily I passed
From the remembrances of better things,
And slipped into the ordinary works
Of careless youth, unburthened, unalarmed.
*Caverns* there were within my mind which sun
Could never penetrate, yet did there not
Want store of leafy *arbors* where the light
Might enter in at will. Companionships,
Friendships, acquaintances, were welcome all.
We sauntered, played, or rioted; we talked
Unprofitable talk at morning hours;
Drifted about along the streets and walks,
Read lazily in trivial books, went forth
To gallop through the country in blind zeal
Of senseless horsemanship, or on the breast
Of Cam sailed boisterously, and let the stars
Come forth, perhaps without one quiet thought.

Such was the tenor of the second act
In this new life. Imagination slept,
And yet not utterly. I could not print
Ground where the grass had yielded to the steps
Of generations of illustrious men,
Unmoved. I could not always lightly pass
Through the same gateways, sleep where they had
slept,
Wake where they waked, range that enclosure old,
That garden of great intellects, undisturbed.
Place also by the side of this dark sense
Of nobler feeling, that those spiritual men,
Even the great Newton's own ethereal self,
Seemed humbled in these precincts, thence to be
The more endeared. Their several memories here
(Even like their persons in their portraits clothed
With the accustomed garb of daily life)
Put on a lowly and a touching grace
Of more distinct humanity, that left
All genuine admiration unimpaired.

Beside the pleasant mill of Trompington
I laughed with Chaucer; in the hawthorn shade
Heard him, while birds were warbling, tell his tales
Of amorous passion. And that gentle bard,

**275. mill of Trompington:** three miles from Cambridge; mentioned by Chaucer in the first line of the Reeve's Tale.

Chosen by the Muses for their Page of State—
Sweet Spenser, moving through his clouded heaven
With the moon's beauty and the moon's soft pace,
I called him brother, Englishman, and friend!
Yea, our blind poet, who in his later day,
Stood almost single; uttering odious truth—
Darkness before, and danger's voice behind,
Soul awful—if the earth has ever lodged
An awful soul—I seemed to see him here
Familiarly, and in his scholar's dress
Bounding before me, yet a stripling youth—
A boy, no better, with his rosy cheeks
Angelical, keen eye, courageous look,
And conscious step of purity and pride.
Among the band of my compeers was one
Whom chance had stationed in the very room
Honored by Milton's name. O temperate bard!
Be it confessed that, for the first time, seated
Within thy innocent lodge and oratory,
One of a festive circle, I poured out
Libations, to thy memory drank, till pride
And gratitude grew dizzy in a brain
Never excited by the fumes of wine
Before that hour, or since. Then, forth I ran
From the assembly; through a length of streets,
Ran, ostrich-like, to reach our chapel door
In not a desperate or opprobrious time,
Albeit long after the importunate bell
Had stopped, with wearisome Cassandra voice
No longer haunting the dark winter night.
Call back, O friend! a moment to thy mind,
The place itself and fashion of the rites.
With careless ostentation shouldering up
My surplice, through the inferior throng I clove
Of the plain burghers, who in audience stood
On the last skirts of their permitted ground,
Under the pealing organ. Empty thoughts!
I am ashamed of them; and that great bard,
And thou, O friend! who in thy ample mind
Hast placed me high above my best deserts,
Ye will forgive the weakness of that hour,
In some of its unworthy vanities,
Brother to many more.
In this mixed sort
The months passed on, remissly, not given up
To willful alienation from the right,
Or walks of open scandal, but in vague
And loose indifference, easy likings, aims
Of a low pitch—duty and zeal dismissed,
Yet Nature, or a happy course of things
Not doing in their stead the needful work.
The memory languidly revolved, the heart
Reposed in noontide rest, the inner pulse
Of contemplation almost failed to beat.
Such life might not inaptly be compared
To a floating island, an amphibious spot
Unsound, of spongy texture, yet withal
Not wanting a fair face of water weeds
And pleasant flowers. The thirst of living praise,
Fit reverence for the glorious dead, the sight
Of those long vistas, sacred catacombs,
Where mighty *minds* lie visibly entombed,
Have often stirred the heart of youth, and bred
A fervent love of rigorous discipline.
Alas! such high emotion touched not me.
Look was there none within these walls to shame
My easy spirits, and discountenance
Their light composure, far less to instill
A calm resolve of mind, firmly addressed
To puissant efforts. Nor was this the blame
Of others but my own; I should, in truth,
As far as doth concern my single self,
Misdeem most widely, lodging it elsewhere,
For I, bred up 'mid Nature's luxuries,
Was a spoiled child, and, rambling like the wind,
As I had done in daily intercourse
With those crystalline rivers, solemn heights,
And mountains, ranging like a fowl of the air,
I was ill-tutored for captivity,
To quit my pleasure, and, from month to month,
Take up a station calmly on the perch
Of sedentary peace. Those lovely forms
Had also left less space within my mind,
Which, wrought upon instinctively, had found
A freshness in those objects of her love,
A winning power, beyond all other power.
Not that I slighted books—that were to lack
All sense—but other passions in me ruled,
Passions more fervent, making me less prompt
To indoor study than was wise or well,
Or suited to those years. Yet I, though used
In magisterial liberty to rove,
Culling such flowers of learning as might tempt
A random choice, could shadow forth a place
(If now I yield not to a flattering dream)
Whose studious aspect should have bent me down
To instantaneous service; should at once
Have made me pay to science and to arts
And written lore, acknowledged my liege lord,
A homage frankly offered up, like that
Which I had paid to Nature. Toil and pains
In this recess, by thoughtful fancy built,
Should spread from heart to heart; and stately groves,
Majestic edifices, should not want
A corresponding dignity within.
The congregating temper that pervades
Our unripe years, not wasted, should be taught
To minister to works of high attempt—

**301. Never excited:** a later emendation; in the 1805 version Wordsworth wrote "Never so clouded." **307. Cassandra:** the prophetess daughter of Priam and Hecuba who foretold the doom of Troy but was not believed.

Works which the enthusiast would perform with love.
Youth should be awed, religiously possessed
With a conviction of the power that waits
On knowledge, when sincerely sought and prized
For its own sake, on glory and on praise
If but by labor won, and fit to endure.
The passing day should learn to put aside
Her trappings here, should strip them off abashed
Before antiquity and steadfast truth
And strong book-mindedness; and over all
A healthy sound simplicity should reign,
A seemly plainness, name it what you will,
Republican or pious.
If these thoughts
Are a gratuitous emblazonry
That mocks the recreant age *we* live in, then
Be folly and false-seeming free to affect
Whatever formal gait of discipline
Shall raise them highest in their own esteem —
Let them parade among the schools at will,
But spare the house of God. Was ever known
The witless shepherd who persists to drive
A flock that thirsts not to a pool disliked?
A weight must surely hang on days begun
And ended with such mockery. Be wise,
Ye presidents and deans, and, till the spirit
Of ancient times revive, and youth be trained
At home in pious service, to your bells
Give seasonable rest, for 'tis a sound
Hollow as ever vexed the tranquil air;
And your officious doings bring disgrace
On the plain steeples of our English Church,
Whose worship, 'mid remotest village trees,
Suffers for this. Even Science, too, at hand
In daily sight of this irreverence,
Is smitten thence with an unnatural taint,
Loses her just authority, falls beneath
Collateral suspicion, else unknown.
This truth escaped me not, and I confess,
That having 'mid my native hills given loose
To a schoolboy's vision, I had raised a pile
Upon the basis of the coming time,
That fell in ruins round me. Oh, what joy
To see a sanctuary for our country's youth
Informed with such a spirit as might be
Its own protection; a primeval grove,
Where, though the shades with cheerfulness were filled,
Nor indigent of songs warbled from crowds
In undercoverts, yet the countenance
Of the whole place should bear a stamp of awe;
A habitation sober and demure
For ruminating creatures; a domain
For quiet things to wander in; a haunt
In which the heron should delight to feed
By the shy rivers, and the pelican
Upon the cypress spire in lonely thought
Might sit and sun himself. Alas! Alas!
In vain for such solemnity I looked;
Mine eyes were crossed by butterflies, ears vexed
By chattering popinjays; the inner heart
Seemed trivial, and the impresses without
Of a too gaudy region.
Different sight
Those venerable doctors saw of old,
When all who dwelt within these famous walls
Led in abstemiousness a studious life;
When, in forlorn and naked chambers cooped
And crowded, o'er the ponderous books they hung
Like caterpillars eating out their way
In silence, or with keen devouring noise
Not to be tracked or fathered. Princes then
At matins froze, and couched at curfew time,
Trained up through piety and zeal to prize
Spare diet, patient labor, and plain weeds.
O seat of Arts! renowned throughout the world!
Far different service in those homely days
The Muses' modest nurslings underwent
From their first childhood; in that glorious time
When Learning, like a stranger come from far,
Sounding through Christian lands her trumpet, roused
Peasant and king; when boys and youths, the growth
Of ragged villages and crazy huts,
Forsook their homes, and, errant in the quest
Of patron, famous school or friendly nook,
Where, pensioned, they in shelter might sit down,
From town to town and through wide scattered realms
Journeyed with ponderous folios in their hands;
And often, starting from some covert place,
Saluted the chance comer on the road,
Crying, " An obolus, a penny give
To a poor scholar! " — when illustrious men,
Lovers of truth, by penury constrained,
Bucer, Erasmus, or Melancthon, read
Before the doors or windows of their cells
By moonshine through mere lack of taper light.

But peace to vain regrets! We see but darkly
Even when we look behind us, and best things
Are not so pure by nature that they needs
Must keep to all, as fondly all believe,
Their highest promise. If the mariner,
When at reluctant distance he hath passed
Some tempting island, could but know the ills
That must have fallen upon him had he brought
His bark to land upon the wished-for shore,

**447. venerable doctors:** aged scholars who inhabited Cambridge in its early days. **473. obolus:** an ancient Greek coin worth about a penny and a half in English money. **476. Bucer . . . Melancthon:** distinguished scholars and theologians of the early sixteenth century.

Good cause would oft be his to thank the surf
Whose white belt scared him thence, or wind that blew
Inexorably adverse; for myself
I grieve not; happy is the gownèd youth,
Who only misses what I missed, who falls
No lower than I fell.
I did not love,
Judging not ill perhaps, the timid course
Of our scholastic studies; could have wished
To see the river flow with ampler range
And freer pace; but more, far more, I grieved
To see displayed among an eager few,
Who in the field of contest persevered,
Passions unworthy of youth's generous heart
And mounting spirit, pitiably repaid,
When so disturbed, whatever palms are won.
From these I turned to travel with the shoal
Of more unthinking natures, easy minds
And pillowy; yet not wanting love that makes
The day pass lightly on, when foresight sleeps,
And wisdom and the pledges interchanged
With our own inner being are forgot.

Yet was this deep vacation not given up
To utter waste. Hitherto I had stood
In my own mind remote from social life
(At least from what we commonly so name),
Like a lone shepherd on a promontory,
Who lacking occupation looks far forth
Into the boundless sea, and rather makes
Than finds what he beholds. And sure it is,
That this first transit from the smooth delights
And wild outlandish walks of simple youth
To something that resembles an approach
Towards human business, to a privileged world
Within a world, a midway residence
With all its intervenient imagery,
Did better suit my visionary mind,
Far better, than to have been bolted forth,
Thrust out abruptly into fortune's way
Among the conflicts of substantial life;
By a more just gradation did lead on
To higher things; more naturally matured,
For permanent possession, better fruits,
Whether of truth or virtue, to ensue.
In serious mood, but oftener, I confess,
With playful zest of fancy, did we note
(How could we less?) the manners and the ways
Of those who lived distinguished by the badge
Of good or ill report; or those with whom
By frame of academic discipline
We were perforce connected, men whose sway
And known authority of office served
To set our minds on edge, and did no more.
Nor wanted we rich pastime of this kind,
Found everywhere, but chiefly in the ring
Of the grave elders, men unscoured, grotesque
In character, tricked out like agèd trees
Which through the lapse of their infirmity
Give ready place to any random seed
That chooses to be reared upon their trunks.

Here on my view, confronting vividly
Those shepherd swains whom I had lately left
Appeared a different aspect of old age;
How different! yet both distinctly marked,
Objects embossed to catch the general eye,
Or portraitures for special use designed,
As some might seem, so aptly do they serve
To illustrate Nature's book of rudiments—
That book upheld as with maternal care
When she would enter on her tender scheme
Of teaching comprehension with delight,
And mingling playful with pathetic thoughts.

The surfaces of artificial life
And manners finely wrought, the delicate race
Of colors, lurking, gleaming up and down
Through that state arras woven with silk and gold;
This wily interchange of snaky hues,
Willingly or unwillingly revealed,
I neither knew nor cared for; and as such
Were wanting here, I took what might be found
Of less elaborate fabric. At this day
I smile, in many a mountain solitude
Conjuring up scenes as obsolete in freaks
Of character, in points of wit as broad,
As aught by wooden images performed
For entertainment of the gaping crowd
At wake or fair. And oftentimes do flit
Remembrances before me of old men—
Old humorists, who have been long in their graves,
And having almost in my mind put off
Their human names, have into phantoms passed
Of texture midway between life and books.

I play the loiterer; 'tis enough to note
That here in dwarf proportions were expressed
The limbs of the great world; its eager strifes
Collaterally portrayed, as in mock flight,
A tournament of blows, some hardly dealt
Though short of mortal combat; and whate'er
Might in this pageant be supposed to hit
An artless rustic's notice, this way less,
More that way, was not wasted upon me—
And yet the spectacle may well demand
A more substantial name, no mimic show,
Itself a living part of a live whole,
A creek in the vast sea; for all degrees
And shapes of spurious fame and short-lived praise
Here sat in state, and fed with daily alms
Retainers won away from solid good;

And here was Labor, his own bondslave; Hope,
That never set the pains against the prize;
Idleness halting with his weary clog,
And poor misguided Shame, and witless Fear,
And simple Pleasure foraging for Death;
Honor misplaced, and Dignity astray;
Feuds, factions, flatteries, enmity, and guile,
Murmuring submission, and bald government
(The idol weak as the idolater),
And Decency and Custom starving Truth,
And blind Authority beating with his staff
The child that might have led him; Emptiness
Followed as of good omen, and meek Worth
Left to herself unheard of and unknown.

Of these and other kindred notices
I cannot say what portion is in truth
The naked recollection of that time,
And what may rather have been called to life
By aftermeditation. But delight
That, in an easy temper lulled asleep,
Is still with innocence its own reward,
This was not wanting. Carelessly I roamed
As through a wide museum from whose stores
A casual rarity is singled out
And has its brief perusal, then gives way
To others, all supplanted in their turn;
Till 'mid this crowded neighborhood of things
That are by nature most unneighborly,
The head turns round and cannot right itself;
And though an aching and a barren sense
Of gay confusion still be uppermost,
With few wise longings and but little love,
Yet to the memory something cleaves at last,
Whence profit may be drawn in times to come.

Thus in submissive idleness, my friend!
The laboring time of autumn, winter, spring,
Eight months! rolled pleasingly away; the ninth
Came and returned me to my native hills.

### from BOOK IV
### SUMMER VACATION

Bright was the summer's noon when quickening steps
Followed each other till a dreary moor
Was crossed, a bare ridge clomb, upon whose top
Standing alone, as from a rampart's edge,
I overlooked the bed of Windermere,
Like a vast river, stretching in the sun.
With exultation, at my feet I saw
Lake, islands, promontories, gleaming bays,
A universe of Nature's fairest forms
Proudly revealed with instantaneous burst,
Magnificent, and beautiful, and gay.
I bounded down the hill shouting amain
For the old ferryman; to the shout the rocks
Replied, and when the Charon of the flood
Had stayed his oars, and touched the jutting pier,
I did not step into the well-known boat
Without a cordial greeting. Thence with speed
Up the familiar hill I took my way
Towards that sweet valley where I had been reared;
'Twas but a short hour's walk, ere veering round
I saw the snow-white church upon her hill
Sit like a thronèd lady, sending out
A gracious look all over her domain.
Yon azure smoke betrays the lurking town;
With eager footsteps I advance and reach
The cottage threshold where my journey closed.
Glad welcome had I, with some tears, perhaps,
From my old dame, so kind and motherly,
While she perused me with a parent's pride.
The thoughts of gratitude shall fall like dew
Upon thy grave, good creature! While my heart
Can beat never will I forget thy name.
Heaven's blessing be upon thee where thou liest
After thy innocent and busy stir
In narrow cares, thy little daily growth
Of calm enjoyments, after eighty years,
And more than eighty, of untroubled life;
Childless, yet by the strangers to thy blood
Honored with little less than filial love.
What joy was mine to see thee once again,
Thee and thy dwelling, and a crowd of things
About its narrow precincts all beloved,
And many of them seeming yet my own!
Why should I speak of what a thousand hearts
Have felt, and every man alive can guess?
The rooms, the court, the garden were not left
Long unsaluted, nor the sunny seat
Round the stone table under the dark pine,
Friendly to studious or to festive hours;
Nor that unruly child of mountain birth,
The froward brook, who, soon as he was boxed
Within our garden, found himself at once,
As if by trick insidious and unkind,
Stripped of his voice and left to dimple down
(Without an effort and without a will)
A channel paved by man's officious care.
I looked at him and smiled, and smiled again,
And in the press of twenty thousand thoughts,
"Ha," quoth I, "pretty prisoner, are you there?"
Well might sarcastic Fancy then have whispered,
"An emblem here behold of thy own life;
In its late course of even days with all
Their smooth enthrallment"; but the heart was full,

**Book IV: 3. clomb: climbed.**

**19. valley: Esthwaite. 28. dame: Anne Tyson. 51. froward: unruly, not easily managed.**

Too full for that reproach. My agèd dame
Walked proudly at my side; she guided me,
I willing, nay — nay, wishing to be led.
— The face of every neighbor whom I met
Was like a volume to me; some were hailed
Upon the road, some busy at their work,
Unceremonious greetings interchanged
With half the length of a long field between.
Among my schoolfellows I scattered round
Like recognitions, but with some constraint
Attended, doubtless, with a little pride,
But with more shame, for my habiliments,
The transformation wrought by gay attire.
Not less delighted did I take my place
At our domestic table; and, dear friend!
In this endeavor simply to relate
A poet's history, may I leave untold
The thankfulness with which I laid me down
In my accustomed bed, more welcome now
Perhaps than if it had been more desired
Or been more often thought of with regret?
That lowly bed whence I had heard the wind
Roar, and the rain beat hard; where I so oft
Had lain awake on summer nights to watch
The moon in splendor couched among the leaves
Of a tall ash, that near our cottage stood;
Had watched her with fixed eyes while to and fro
In the dark summit of the waving tree
She rocked with every impulse of the breeze.

Among the favorites whom it pleased me well
To see again, was one by ancient right
Our inmate, a rough terrier of the hills;
By birth and call of nature preordained
To hunt the badger and unearth the fox
Among the impervious crags, but having been
From youth our own adopted, he had passed
Into a gentler service. And when first
The boyish spirit flagged, and day by day
Along my veins I kindled with the stir,
The fermentation, and the vernal heat
Of poesy, affecting private shades
Like a sick lover, then this dog was used
To watch me, an attendant and a friend,
Obsequious to my steps early and late,
Though often of such dilatory walk
Tired, and uneasy at the halts I made.
A hundred times when, roving high and low,
I have been harassed with the toil of verse,
Much pains and little progress, and at once
Some lovely image in the song rose up
Full-formed, like Venus rising from the sea;
Then have I darted forwards to let loose
My hand upon his back with stormy joy,
Caressing him again and yet again.
And when at evening on the public way
I sauntered, like a river murmuring
And talking to itself when all things else
Are still, the creature trotted on before;
Such was his custom; but whene'er he met
A passenger approaching, he would turn
To give me timely notice, and straightway,
Grateful for that admonishment, I hushed
My voice, composed my gait, and, with the air
And mien of one whose thoughts are free, advanced
To give and take a greeting that might save
My name from piteous rumors, such as wait
On men suspected to be crazed in brain.

Those walks well worthy to be prized and loved —
Regretted! — that word, too, was on my tongue,
But they were richly laden with all good,
And cannot be remembered but with thanks
And gratitude, and perfect joy of heart —
Those walks in all their freshness now came back
Like a returning spring. When first I made
Once more the circuit of our little lake,
If ever happiness hath lodged with man,
That day consummate happiness was mine,
Wide-spreading, steady, calm, contemplative.
The sun was set, or setting, when I left
Our cottage door, and evening soon brought on
A sober hour, not winning or serene,
For cold and raw the air was, and untuned;
But as a face we love is sweetest then
When sorrow damps it, or, whatever look
It chance to wear, is sweetest if the heart
Have fullness in herself; even so with me
It fared that evening. Gently did my soul
Put off her veil, and, self-transmuted, stood
Naked, as in the presence of her God.
While on I walked, a comfort seemed to touch
A heart that had not been disconsolate;
Strength came where weakness was not known to be,
At least not felt; and restoration came
Like an intruder knocking at the door
Of unacknowledged weariness. I took
The balance, and with firm hand weighed myself.
Of that external scene which round me lay,
Little, in this abstraction, did I see;
Remembered less; but I had inward hopes
And swellings of the spirit, was rapt and soothed,
Conversed with promises, had glimmering views
How life pervades the undecaying mind;
How the immortal soul with godlike power
Informs, creates, and thaws the deepest sleep
That time can lay upon her; how on earth,
Man, if he do but live within the light
Of high endeavors, daily spreads abroad
His being armed with strength that cannot fail.
Nor was there want of milder thoughts, of love,
Of innocence, and holiday repose;

And more than pastoral quiet, 'mid the stir
Of boldest projects, and a peaceful end
At last, or glorious, by endurance won.
Thus musing, in a wood I sat me down
Alone, continuing there to muse; the slopes
And heights meanwhile were slowly over-spread
With darkness, and before a rippling breeze
The long lake lengthened out its hoary line,
And in the sheltered coppice where I sat,
Around me from among the hazel leaves,
Now here, now there, moved by the straggling wind,
Came ever and anon a breathlike sound,
Quick as the pantings of the faithful dog,
The off and on companion of my walk;
And such, at times, believing them to be,
I turned my head to look if he were there;
Then into solemn thought I passed once more. . . .

Yet in spite
Of pleasure won, and knowledge not withheld,
There was an inner falling off — I loved,
Loved deeply all that had been loved before,
More deeply even than ever; but a swarm
Of heady schemes jostling each other, gauds,
And feast and dance, and public revelry,
And sports and games (too grateful in themselves,
Yet in themselves less grateful, I believe,
Than as they were a badge glossy and fresh
Of manliness and freedom) all conspired
To lure my mind from firm habitual quest
Of feeding pleasures, to depress the zeal
And damp those yearnings which had once been mine —
A wild, unworldly minded youth, given up
To his own eager thoughts. It would demand
Some skill, and longer time than may be spared
To paint these vanities, and how they wrought
In haunts where they, till now, had been unknown.
It seemed the very garments that I wore
Preyed on my strength, and stopped the quiet stream
Of self-forgetfulness.

Yes, that heartless chase
Of trivial pleasures was a poor exchange
For books and nature at that early age.
'Tis true, some casual knowledge might be gained
Of character or life; but at that time,
Of manners put to school I took small note,
And all my deeper passions lay elsewhere.
Far better had it been to exalt the mind
By solitary study, to uphold
Intense desire through meditative peace;
And yet, for chastisement of these regrets,

**281. gauds:** showy ornaments.

The memory of one particular hour
Doth here rise up against me. 'Mid a throng
Of maids and youths, old men, and matrons staid,
A medley of all tempers, I had passed
The night in dancing, gaiety, and mirth,
With din of instruments and shuffling feet,
And glancing forms, and tapers glittering,
And unaimed prattle flying up and down;
Spirits upon the stretch, and here and there
Slight shocks of young love-liking interspersed,
Whose transient pleasure mounted to the head,
And tingled through the veins. Ere we retired,
The cock had crowed, and now the eastern sky
Was kindling, not unseen, from humble copse
And open field, through which the pathway wound,
And homeward led my steps. Magnificent
The morning rose, in memorable pomp,
Glorious as e'er I had beheld — in front,
The sea lay laughing at a distance; near,
The solid mountains shone, bright as the clouds,
Grain-tinctured, drenched in empyrean light;
And in the meadows and the lower grounds
Was all the sweetness of a common dawn —
Dews, vapors, and the melody of birds,
And laborers going forth to till the fields.
Ah! need I say, dear friend! that to the brim
My heart was full; I made no vows, but vows
Were then made for me; bond unknown to me
Was given, that I should be, else sinning greatly,
A dedicated spirit. On I walked
In thankful blessedness, which yet survives. . . .

## BOOK V

## BOOKS

When Contemplation, like the night calm felt
Through earth and sky, spreads widely, and sends deep
Into the soul its tranquilizing power,
Even then I sometimes grieve for thee, O Man,
Earth's paramount creature! not so much for woes
That thou endurest; heavy though that weight be,
Cloudlike it mounts, or touched with light divine
Doth melt away; but for those palms achieved
Through length of time, by patient exercise
Of study and hard thought; there, there, it is
That sadness finds its fuel. Hitherto,
In progress through this verse, my mind hath looked
Upon the speaking face of earth and heaven
As her prime teacher, intercourse with man
Established by the sovereign Intellect,
Who through that bodily image hath diffused,
As might appear to the eye of fleeting time,

**Book V: 17. As . . . time:** In the 1805 version Wordsworth wrote "A soul divine which we participate."

A deathless spirit. Thou also, Man! hast wrought,
For commerce of thy nature with herself,
Things that aspire to unconquerable life;
And yet we feel — we cannot choose but feel —
That they must perish. Tremblings of the heart
It gives, to think that our immortal being
No more shall need such garments; and yet man,
As long as he shall be the child of earth,
Might almost "weep to have" what he may lose,
Nor be himself extinguished, but survive,
Abject, depressed, forlorn, disconsolate.
A thought is with me sometimes, and I say —
Should the whole frame of earth by inward throes
Be wrenched, or fire come down from far to scorch
Her pleasant habitations, and dry up
Old Ocean, in his bed left singed and bare,
Yet would the living Presence still subsist
Victorious, and composure would ensue,
And kindlings like the morning, presage sure
Of day returning and of life revived.
But all the meditations of mankind,
Yea, all the adamantine holds of truth
By reason built, or passion, which itself
Is highest reason in a soul sublime;
The consecrated works of bard and sage,
Sensuous or intellectual, wrought by men,
Twin laborers and heirs of the same hopes;
Where would they be? Oh! why hath not the mind
Some element to stamp her image on
In nature somewhat nearer to her own?
Why, gifted with such powers to send abroad
Her spirit, must it lodge in shrines so frail?

One day, when from my lips a like complaint
Had fallen in presence of a studious friend,
He with a smile made answer, that in truth
'Twas going far to seek disquietude;
But on the front of his reproof confessed
That he himself had oftentimes given way
To kindred hauntings. Whereupon I told,
That once in the stillness of a summer's noon,
While I was seated in a rocky cave
By the seaside, perusing, so it chanced,
The famous history of the errant knight
Recorded by Cervantes, these same thoughts
Beset me, and to height unusual rose,
While listlessly I sat, and, having closed
The book, had turned my eyes toward the wide sea.
On poetry and geometric truth,
And their high privilege of lasting life,
From all internal injury exempt,
I mused; upon these chiefly; and at length,
My senses yielding to the sultry air,
Sleep seized me, and I passed into a dream.
I saw before me stretched a boundless plain
Of sandy wilderness, all black and void,
And as I looked around, distress and fear
Came creeping over me, when at my side,
Close at my side, an uncouth shape appeared
Upon a dromedary, mounted high.
He seemed an Arab of the Bedouin tribes;
A lance he bore, and underneath one arm
A stone, and in the opposite hand a shell
Of a surpassing brightness. At the sight
Much I rejoiced, not doubting but a guide
Was present, one who with unerring skill
Would through the desert lead me; and while yet
I looked and looked, self-questioned what this freight
Which the newcomer carried through the waste
Could mean, the Arab told me that the stone
(To give it in the language of the dream)
Was "Euclid's Elements," and "This," said he,
"Is something of more worth"; and at the word
Stretched forth the shell, so beautiful in shape,
In color so resplendent, with command
That I should hold it to my ear. I did so,
And heard that instant in an unknown tongue,
Which yet I understood, articulate sounds,
A loud prophetic blast of harmony;
An ode, in passion uttered, which foretold
Destruction to the children of the earth
By deluge, now at hand. No sooner ceased
The song, than the Arab with calm look declared
That all would come to pass of which the voice
Had given forewarning, and that he himself
Was going then to bury those two books:
The one that held acquaintance with the stars,
And wedded soul to soul in purest bond
Of reason, undisturbed by space or time;
The other that was a god, yea many gods,
Had voices more than all the winds, with power
To exhilarate the spirit, and to soothe,
Through every clime, the heart of human kind.
While this was uttering, strange as it may seem,
I wondered not, although I plainly saw
The one to be a stone, the other a shell;
Nor doubted once but that they both were books,
Having a perfect faith in all that passed.
Far stronger, now, grew the desire I felt
To cleave unto this man; but when I prayed
To share his enterprise, he hurried on
Reckless of me; I followed, not unseen,
For oftentimes he cast a backward look,
Grasping his twofold treasure. Lance in rest,
He rode, I keeping pace with him; and now
He, to my fancy, had become the knight
Whose tale Cervantes tells; yet not the knight,
But was an Arab of the desert too;
Of these was neither, and was both at once.

**26. "weep to have"**: quoted from Shakespeare, Sonnet LXIV, l. 14. **60. errant knight**: Don Quixote.

His countenance, meanwhile, grew more disturbed;
And, looking backwards when he looked, mine eyes
Saw, over half the wilderness diffused,
A bed of glittering light; I asked the cause.
"It is," said he, "the waters of the deep
Gathering upon us"; quickening then the pace
Of the unwieldy creature he bestrode,
He left me; I called after him aloud;
He heeded not; but, with his twofold charge
Still in his grasp, before me, full in view,
Went hurrying o'er the illimitable waste,
With the fleet waters of a drowning world
In chase of him; whereat I waked in terror,
And saw the sea before me, and the book,
In which I had been reading, at my side.

Full often, taking from the world of sleep
This Arab phantom, which I thus beheld,
This semi-Quixote, I to him have given
A substance, fancied him a living man,
A gentle dweller in the desert, crazed
By love and feeling, and internal thought
Protracted among endless solitudes;
Have shaped him wandering upon this quest!
Nor have I pitied him; but rather felt
Reverence was due to a being thus employed;
And thought that, in the blind and awful lair
Of such a madness, reason did lie couched.
Enow there are on earth to take in charge
Their wives, their children, and their virgin loves,
Or whatsoever else the heart holds dear;
Enow to stir for these; yea, will I say,
Contemplating in soberness the approach
Of an event so dire, by signs in earth
Or heaven made manifest, that I could share
That maniac's fond anxiety, and go
Upon like errand. Oftentimes at least
Me hath such strong entrancement overcome,
When I have held a volume in my hand,
Poor earthly casket of immortal verse,
Shakespeare, or Milton, laborers divine!

Great and benign, indeed, must be the power
Of living nature, which could thus so long
Detain me from the best of other guides
And dearest helpers, left unthanked, unpraised.
Even in the time of lisping infancy,
And later down, in prattling childhood even,
While I was traveling back among those days,
How could I ever play an ingrate's part?
Once more should I have made those bowers resound,
By intermingling strains of thankfulness
With their own thoughtless melodies; at least
It might have well beseemed me to repeat
Some simply fashioned tale, to tell again,
In slender accents of sweet verse, some tale
That did bewitch me then, and soothes me now.
O friend! O poet! brother of my soul,
Think not that I could pass along untouched
By these remembrances. Yet wherefore speak?
Why call upon a few weak words to say
What is already written in the hearts
Of all that breathe? — what in the path of all
Drops daily from the tongue of every child,
Wherever man is found? The trickling tear
Upon the cheek of listening Infancy
Proclaims it, and the insuperable look
That drinks as if it never could be full.

That portion of my story I shall leave
There registered; whatever else of power
Of pleasure sown, or fostered thus, may be
Peculiar to myself, let that remain
Where still it works, though hidden from all search
Among the depths of time. Yet is it just
That here, in memory of all books which lay
Their sure foundations in the heart of man,
Whether by native prose, or numerous verse,
That in the name of all inspirèd souls —
From Homer the great thunderer, from the voice
That roars along the bed of Jewish song,
And that more varied and elaborate,
Those trumpet tones of harmony that shake
Our shores in England — from those loftiest notes
Down to the low and wrenlike warblings, made
For cottagers and spinners at the wheel,
And sunburnt travelers resting their tired limbs,
Stretched under wayside hedgerows, ballad tunes,
Food for the hungry ears of little ones,
And of old men who have survived their joys —
'Tis just that in behalf of these, the works,
And of the men that framed them, whether known
Or sleeping nameless in their scattered graves,
That I should here assert their rights, attest
Their honors, and should, once for all, pronounce
Their benediction; speak of them as powers
Forever to be hallowed; only less,
For what we are and what we may become,
Than Nature's self, which is the breath of God,
Or his pure Word by miracle revealed.

Rarely and with reluctance would I stoop
To transitory themes; yet I rejoice,
And, by these thoughts admonished, will pour out
Thanks with uplifted heart, that I was reared
Safe from an evil which these days have laid
Upon the children of the land, a pest
That might have dried me up, body and soul.
This verse is dedicate to Nature's self,
And things that teach as Nature teaches, then,
Oh! where had been the man, the poet where,

168. best . . . guides: the authors of books.

Where had we been, we two, beloved friend!
If in the season of unperilous choice,
In lieu of wandering, as we did, through vales
Rich with indigenous produce, open ground
Of Fancy, happy pastures ranged at will,
We had been followed, hourly watched, and noosed,
Each in his several melancholy walk
Stringed like a poor man's heifer at its feed,
Led through the lanes in forlorn servitude;
Or rather like a stallèd ox debarred
From touch of growing grass, that may not taste
A flower till it have yielded up its sweets
A prelibation to the mower's scythe.
  Behold the parent hen amid her brood,
Though fledged and feathered, and well pleased to part
And straggle from her presence, still a brood,
And she herself from the maternal bond
Still undischarged; yet doth she little more
Than move with them in tenderness and love,
A center to the circle which they make;
And now and then, alike from need of theirs
And call of her own natural appetites,
She scratches, ransacks up the earth for food,
Which they partake at pleasure. Early died
My honored mother, she who was the heart
And hinge of all our learnings and our loves;
She left us destitute, and, as we might,
Trooping together. Little suits it me
To break upon the sabbath of her rest
With any thought that looks at others' blame;
Nor would I praise her but in perfect love.
Hence am I checked, but let me boldly say,
In gratitude, and for the sake of truth,
Unheard by her, that she, not falsely taught,
Fetching her goodness rather from times past,
Than shaping novelties for times to come,
Had no presumption, no such jealousy,
Nor did by habit of her thoughts mistrust
Our nature, but had virtual faith that He
Who fills the mother's breast with innocent milk,
Doth also for our nobler part provide,
Under His great correction and control,
As innocent instincts, and as innocent food;
Or draws, for minds that are left free to trust
In the simplicities of opening life,
Sweet honey out of spurned or dreaded weeds.
This was her creed, and therefore she was pure
From anxious fear of error or mishap,
And evil, overweeningly so called;
Was not puffed up by false unnatural hopes,
Nor selfish with unnecessary cares,
Nor with impatience from the season asked
More than its timely produce; rather loved
The hours for what they are, than from regard
Glanced on their promises in restless pride.
Such was she — not from faculties more strong
Than others have, but from the times, perhaps,
And spot in which she lived, and through a grace
Of modest meekness, simple-mindedness,
A heart that found benignity and hope,
Being itself benign.
                    My drift I fear
Is scarcely obvious; but, that common sense
May try this modern system by its fruits,
Leave let me take to place before her sight
A specimen portrayed with faithful hand.
Full early trained to worship seemliness,
This model of a child is never known
To mix in quarrels; that were far beneath
Its dignity; with gifts he bubbles o'er
As generous as a fountain; selfishness
May not come near him, nor the little throng
Of flitting pleasures tempt him from his path;
The wandering beggars propagate his name,
Dumb creatures find him tender as a nun,
And natural or supernatural fear,
Unless it leap upon him in a dream,
Touches him not. To enhance the wonder, see
How arch his notices, how nice his sense
Of the ridiculous; not blind is he
To the broad follies of the licensed world,
Yet innocent himself withal, though shrewd,
And can read lectures upon innocence;
A miracle of scientific lore,
Ships he can guide across the pathless sea,
And tell you all their cunning; he can read
The inside of the earth, and spell the stars;
He knows the policies of foreign lands;
Can string you names of districts, cities, towns,
The whole world over, tight as beads of dew
Upon a gossamer thread; he sifts, he weighs;
All things are put to question; he must live
Knowing that he grows wiser every day
Or else not live at all, and seeing too
Each little drop of wisdom as it falls
Into the dimpling cistern of his heart;
For this unnatural growth the trainer blame,
Pity the tree. Poor human vanity,
Wert thou extinguished, little would be left
Which he could truly love; but how escape?
For, ever as a thought of purer birth
Rises to lead him toward a better clime,
Some intermeddler still is on the watch
To drive him back, and pound him, like a stray,
Within the pinfold of his own conceit.
Meanwhile old grandame Earth is grieved to find
The playthings, which her love designed for him,
Unthought of: in their woodland beds the flowers
Weep, and the riversides are all forlorn.
Oh! give us once again the wishing cap

245. **prelibation:** a previous or preliminary tasting.

Of Fortunatus, and the invisible coat
Of Jack the Giant Killer, Robin Hood,
And Sabra in the forest with St. George!
The child, whose love is here, at least, doth reap
One precious gain, that he forgets himself.

These mighty workmen of our later age,
Who, with a broad highway, have overbridged
The froward chaos of futurity,
Tamed to their bidding; they who have the skill
To manage books, and things, and make them act
On infant minds as surely as the sun
Deals with a flower; the keepers of our time,
The guides and wardens of our faculties,
Sages who in their prescience would control
All accidents, and to the very road
Which they have fashioned would confine us down,
Like engines; when will their presumption learn,
That in the unreasoning progress of the world
A wiser spirit is at work for us,
A better eye than theirs, most prodigal
Of blessings, and most studious of our good,
Even in what seem our most unfruitful hours?

There was a boy; ye knew him well, ye cliffs
And islands of Winander! many a time
At evening, when the earliest stars began
To move along the edges of the hills,
Rising or setting, would he stand alone
Beneath the trees or by the glimmering lake,
And there, with fingers interwoven, both hands
Pressed closely palm to palm, and to his mouth
Uplifted, he, as through an instrument,
Blew mimic hootings to the silent owls,
That they might answer him; and they would shout
Across the watery vale, and shout again,
Responsive to his call, with quivering peals,
And long halloos and screams, and echoes loud,
Redoubled and redoubled, concourse wild
Of jocund din; and, when a lengthened pause
Of silence came and baffled his best skill,
Then sometimes, in that silence while he hung
Listening, a gentle shock of mild surprise
Has carried far into his heart the voice
Of mountain torrents; or the visible scene
Would enter unawares into his mind,
With all its solemn imagery, its rocks,
Its woods, and that uncertain heaven, received
Into the bosom of the steady lake.

This boy was taken from his mates, and died
In childhood, ere he was full twelve years old.
Fair is the spot, most beautiful the vale
Where he was born; the grassy churchyard hangs
Upon a slope above the village school,
And through that churchyard when my way has led
On summer evenings, I believe that there
A long half hour together I have stood
Mute, looking at the grave in which he lies!
Even now appears before the mind's clear eye
That selfsame village church; I see her sit
(The thronèd lady whom erewhile we hailed)
On her green hill, forgetful of this boy
Who slumbers at her feet — forgetful, too,
Of all her silent neighborhood of graves,
And listening only to the gladsome sounds
That, from the rural school ascending, play
Beneath her and about her. May she long
Behold a race of young ones like to those
With whom I herded! — (easily, indeed,
We might have fed upon a fatter soil
Of arts and letters — but be that forgiven) —
A race of real children; not too wise,
Too learned, or too good; but wanton, fresh,
And bandied up and down by love and hate;
Not unresentful where self-justified;
Fierce, moody, patient, venturous, modest, shy;
Mad at their sports like withered leaves in winds;
Though doing wrong and suffering, and full oft
Bending beneath our life's mysterious weight
Of pain, and doubt, and fear, yet yielding not
In happiness to the happiest upon earth.
Simplicity in habit, truth in speech,
Be these the daily strengtheners of their minds;
May books aand Nature be their early joy!
And knowledge, rightly honored with that name —
Knowledge not purchased by the loss of power!

Well do I call to mind the very week
When I was first intrusted to the care
Of that sweet valley; when its paths, its shores,
And brooks were like a dream of novelty
To my half-infant thoughts; that very week,
While I was roving up and down alone,
Seeking I knew not what, I chanced to cross
One of those open fields, which, shaped like ears,
Make green peninsulas on Esthwaite's lake:
Twilight was coming on, yet through the gloom
Appeared distinctly on the opposite shore
A heap of garments, as if left by one
Who might have there been bathing. Long I watched,

**342. Fortunatus:** a character in German folk story whose purse would always supply him with ten pieces of gold, and whose cap would magically transport him anywhere he wished. **344. Sabra:** an Egyptian princess in Richard Johnson's romance, *The Seven Champions of Christendom* (*c.* 1597). She married St. George of England after he rescued her from a dragon. **364–97. There . . . lies!:** written in Germany, 1798, and first published as an independent poem in *Lyrical Ballads,* 1800. In the earliest extant version of the passage Wordsworth mentioned Esthwaite and used the first instead of the third person.

But no one owned them; meanwhile the calm lake
Grew dark with all the shadows on its breast,
And, now and then, a fish upleaping snapped
The breathless stillness. The succeeding day,
Those unclaimed garments telling a plain tale
Drew to the spot an anxious crowd; some looked
In passive expectation from the shore,
While from a boat others hung o'er the deep,
Sounding with grappling irons and long poles.
At last, the dead man, 'mid that beauteous scene
Of trees and hills and water, bolt upright
Rose, with his ghastly face, a specter shape
Of terror; yet no soul-debasing fear,
Young as I was, a child not nine years old,
Possessed me, for my inner eye had seen
Such sights before, among the shining streams
Of faëry land, the forest of romance.
Their spirit hallowed the sad spectacle
With decoration of ideal grace;
A dignity, a smoothness, like the works
Of Grecian art, and purest poesy.

A precious treasure had I long possessed,
A little yellow, canvas-covered book,
A slender abstract of the Arabian tales;
And, from companions in a new abode,
When first I learned that this dear prize of mine
Was but a block hewn from a mighty quarry—
That there were four large volumes, laden all
With kindred matter, 'twas to me, in truth,
A promise scarcely earthly. Instantly,
With one not richer than myself, I made
A covenant that each should lay aside
The moneys he possessed, and hoard up more
Till our joint savings had amassed enough
To make this book our own. Through several months,
In spite of all temptation, we preserved
Religiously that vow; but firmness failed,
Nor were we ever masters of our wish.

And when thereafter to my father's house
The holidays returned me, there to find
That golden store of books which I had left,
What joy was mine! How often in the course
Of those glad respites, though a soft west wind
Ruffled the waters to the angler's wish,
For a whole day together, have I lain
Down by thy side, O Derwent! murmuring stream,
On the hot stones, and in the glaring sun,
And there have read, devouring as I read,
Defrauding the day's glory, desperate!
Till with a sudden bound of smart reproach,
Such as an idler deals with in his shame,
I to the sport betook myself again.

A gracious spirit o'er this earth presides,
And o'er the heart of man; invisibly
It comes, to works of unreproved delight,
And tendency benign, directing those
Who care not, know not, think not, what they do.
The tales that charm away the wakeful night
In Araby; romances; legends penned
For solace by dim light of monkish lamps;
Fictions, for ladies of their love, devised
By youthful squires; adventures endless, spun
By the dismantled warrior in old age,
Out of the bowels of those very schemes
In which his youth did first extravagate;
These spread like day, and something in the shape
Of these will live till man shall be no more.
Dumb yearnings, hidden appetites, are ours,
And *they must* have their food. Our childhood sits,
Our simple childhood, sits upon a throne
That hath more power than all the elements.
I guess not what this tells of being past,
Nor what it augurs of the life to come;
But so it is; and, in that dubious hour—
That twilight—when we first begin to see
This dawning earth, to recognize, expect,
And, in the long probation that ensues,
The time of trial, ere we learn to live
In reconcilement with our stinted powers;
To endure this state of meager vassalage,
Unwilling to forgo, confess, submit,
Uneasy and unsettled, yokefellows
To custom, mettlesome, and not yet tamed
And humbled down—oh! then we feel, we feel,
We know where we have friends. Ye dreamers, then,
Forgers of daring tales! we bless you then,
Impostors, drivelers, dotards, as the ape
Philosophy will call you; *then* we feel
With what, and how great might ye are in league,
Who make our wish our power, our thought a deed,
An empire, a possession—ye whom time
And seasons serve; all faculties; to whom
Earth crouches, the elements are potter's clay,
Space like a heaven filled up with northern lights,
Here, nowhere, there, and everywhere at once.

Relinquishing this lofty eminence
For ground, though humbler, not the less a tract
Of the same isthmus, which our spirits cross
In progress from their native continent
To earth and human life, the song might dwell
On that delightful time of growing youth,
When craving for the marvelous gives way
To strengthening love for things that we have seen;
When sober truth and steady sympathies,
Offered to notice by less daring pens,
Take firmer hold of us, and words themselves

Move us with conscious pleasure.
I am sad
At thought of rapture now forever flown;
Almost to tears I sometimes could be sad
To think of, to read over, many a page,
Poems withal of name, which at that time
Did never fail to entrance me, and are now
Dead in my eyes, dead as a theater
Fresh emptied of spectators. Twice five years
Or less I might have seen, when first my mind
With conscious pleasure opened to the charm
Of words in tuneful order, found them sweet
For their own *sakes*, a passion, and a power;
And phrases pleased me chosen for delight,
For pomp, or love. Oft, in the public roads
Yet unfrequented, while the morning light
Was yellowing the hilltops, I went abroad
With a dear friend, and for the better part
Of two delightful hours we strolled along
By the still borders of the misty lake,
Repeating favorite verses with one voice,
Or conning more, as happy as the birds
That round us chanted. Well might we be glad.
Lifted above the ground by airy fancies,
More bright than madness or the dreams of wine;
And, though full oft the objects of our love
Were false, and in their splendor overwrought,
Yet was there surely then no vulgar power
Working within us — nothing less, in truth,
Than that most noble attribute of man,
Though yet untutored and inordinate,
That wish for something loftier, more adorned,
Than is the common aspect, daily garb,
Of human life. What wonder, then, if sounds
Of exultation echoed through the groves!
For, images, and sentiments, and words,
And everything encountered or pursued
In that delicious world of poesy,
Kept holiday, a never-ending show,
With music, incense, festival, and flowers!

Here must we pause; this only let me add,
From heart experience, and in humblest sense
Of modesty, that he, who in his youth
A daily wanderer among woods and fields
With living Nature hath been intimate,
Not only in that raw unpracticed time
Is stirred to esctasy, as others are,
By glittering verse; but further, doth receive,
In measure only dealt out to himself,
Knowledge and increase of enduring joy
From the great Nature that exists in works
Of mighty poets. Visionary power
Attends the motions of the viewless winds,
Embodied in the mystery of words;
There, darkness makes abode, and all the host
Of shadowy things work endless changes — there,
As in a mansion like their proper home,
Even forms and substances are circumfused
By that transparent veil with light divine,
And, through the turnings intricate of verse,
Present themselves as objects recognized,
In flashes, and with glory not their own.

**552–53. Twice . . . less:** probably inaccurate; Wordsworth first wrote "Thirteen years / Or haply less." **561. friend:** a schoolmate, not S. T. Coleridge.

## from BOOK VI

## CAMBRIDGE AND THE ALPS

When the third summer freed us from restraint,
A youthful friend, he too a mountaineer,
Not slow to share my wishes, took his staff,
And sallying forth, we journeyed side by side,
Bound to the distant Alps. A hardy slight,
Did this unprecedented course imply,
Of college studies and their set rewards;
Nor had, in truth, the scheme been formed by me
Without uneasy forethought of the pain,
The censures, and ill-omening, of those
To whom my worldly interests were dear.
But Nature then was sovereign in my mind,
And mighty forms, seizing a youthful fancy,
Had given a charter to irregular hopes.
In any age of uneventful calm
Among the nations, surely would my heart
Have been possessed by similar desire;
But Europe at that time was thrilled with joy,
France standing on the top of golden hours,
And human nature seeming born again.

Lightly equipped, and but a few brief looks
Cast on the white cliffs of our native shore
From the receding vessel's deck, we chanced
To land at Calais on the very eve
Of that great federal day; and there we saw,
In a mean city, and among a few,
How bright a face is worn when joy of one
Is joy for tens of millions. Southward thence
We held our way, direct through hamlets, towns,
Gaudy with relics of that festival,
Flowers left to wither on triumphal arcs,
And window garlands. On the public roads,
And, once, three days successively, through paths
By which our toilsome journey was abridged,
Among sequestered villages we walked
And found benevolence and blessedness

**Book VI: 322. third summer:** 1790. **323. youthful friend:** Robert Jones (see "Tintern Abbey" note, above), a college friend to whom Wordsworth dedicated *Descriptive Sketches* (1793), his first account in verse of his tour of the Alps. **345–46. eve . . . day:** the night before July 14, 1790, the first anniversary of the fall of the Bastille.

Spread like a fragrance everywhere, when spring
Hath left no corner of the land untouched;
Where elms for many and many a league in files
With their thin umbrage, on the stately roads
Of that great kingdom, rustled o'er our heads,
Forever near us as we paced along:
How sweet at such a time, with such delight
On every side, in prime of youthful strength,
To feed a poet's tender melancholy
And fond conceit of sadness, with the sound
Of undulations varying as might please
The wind that swayed them; once, and more than once,
Unhoused beneath the evening star we saw
Dances of liberty, and, in late hours
Of darkness, dances in the open air
Deftly prolonged, though gray-haired lookers-on
Might waste their breath in chiding.
Under hills—
The vine-clad hills and slopes of Burgundy,
Upon the bosom of the gentle Saône
We glided forward with the flowing stream.
Swift Rhone! thou wert the *wings* on which we cut
A winding passage with majestic ease
Between thy lofty rocks. Enchanting show
Those woods and farms and orchards did present,
And single cottages and lurking towns,
Reach after reach, succession without end
Of deep and stately vales! A lonely pair
Of strangers, till day closed, we sailed along
Clustered together with a merry crowd
Of those emancipated, a blithe host
Of travelers, chiefly delegates, returning
From the great spousals newly solemnized
At their chief city, in the sight of Heaven.
Like bees they swarmed, gaudy and gay as bees;
Some vapored in the unruliness of joy,
And with their swords flourished as if to fight
The saucy air. In this proud company
We landed—took with them our evening meal,
Guests welcome almost as the angels were
To Abraham of old. The supper done,
With flowing cups elate and happy thoughts
We rose at signal given, and formed a ring
And, hand in hand, danced round and round the board;
All hearts were open, every tongue was loud
With amity and glee; we bore a name
Honored in France, the name of Englishmen,
And hospitably did they give us hail,
As their forerunners in a glorious course;
And round and round the board we danced again.
With these blithe friends our voyage we renewed
At early dawn. . . .

When from the Valais we had turned, and clomb
Along the Simplon's steep and rugged road,
Following a band of muleteers, we reached
A halting place, where all together took
Their noontide meal. Hastily rose our guide,
Leaving us at the board; awhile we lingered,
Then paced the beaten downward way that led
Right to a rough stream's edge, and there broke off;
The only track now visible was one
That from the torrent's further brink held forth
Conspicuous invitation to ascend
A lofty mountain. After brief delay
Crossing the unbridged stream, that road we took,
And clomb with eagerness, till anxious fears
Intruded, for we failed to overtake
Our comrades gone before. By fortunate chance,
While every moment added doubt to doubt,
A peasant met us, from whose mouth we learned
That to the spot which had perplexed us first
We must descend, and there should find the road,
Which in the stony channel of the stream
Lay a few steps, and then along its banks;
And, that our future course, all plain to sight,
Was downwards, with the current of that stream.
Loath to believe what we so grieved to hear,
For still we had hopes that pointed to the clouds,
We questioned him again, and yet again;
But every word that from the peasant's lips
Came in reply, translated by our feelings,
Ended in this—*that we had crossed the Alps.*

Imagination—here the power so called
Through sad incompetence of human speech,
That awful power rose from the mind's abyss
Like an unfathered vapor that enwraps,
At once, some lonely traveler. I was lost;
Halted without an effort to break through;
But to my conscious soul I now can say—
"I recognize thy glory": in such strength
Of usurpation, when the light of sense
Goes out, but with a flash that has revealed
The invisible world, doth greatness make abode,
There harbors; whether we be young or old,
Our destiny, our being's heart and home,
Is with infinitude, and only there;
With hope it is, hope that can never die,
Effort, and expectation, and desire,
And something evermore about to be.
Under such banners militant, the soul
Seeks for no trophies, struggles for no spoils
That may attest her prowess, blest in thoughts
That are their own perfection and reward,
Strong in herself and in beatitude
That hides her, like the mighty flood of Nile

**361. umbrage:** foliage. **389–90. spousals . . . city:** the national Festival of Confederation, held in Paris on Bastille Day, 1790, at which Louis XVI swore an oath of allegiance to the new constitution. **392. vapored:** behaved in a swaggering manner. **396–97. Guests . . . old:** See Gen. 18 and 22.

Poured from his fount of Abyssinian clouds
To fertilize the whole Egyptian plain.

The melancholy slackening that ensued
Upon those tidings by the peasant given
Was soon dislodged. Downwards we hurried fast,
And, with the half-shaped road which we had
missed,
Entered a narrow chasm. The brook and road
Were fellow travelers in this gloomy strait,
And with them did we journey several hours
At a slow pace. The immeasurable height
Of woods decaying, never to be decayed,
The stationary blasts of waterfalls,
And in the narrow rent at every turn
Winds thwarting winds, bewildered and forlorn,
The torrents shooting from the clear blue sky,
The rocks that muttered close upon our ears,
Black drizzling crags that spake by the wayside
As if a voice were in them, the sick sight
And giddy prospect of the raving stream,
The unfettered clouds and region of the heavens,
Tumult and peace, the darkness and the light—
Were all like workings of one mind, the features
Of the same face, blossoms upon one tree;
Characters of the great Apocalypse,
The types and symbols of Eternity,
Of first, and last, and midst, and without end. . . .

## from BOOK VII

## RESIDENCE IN LONDON

Rise up, thou monstrous anthill on the plain
Of a too busy world! Before me flow,
Thou endless stream of men and moving things!
Thy everyday appearance, as it strikes—
With wonder heightened, or sublimed by awe—
On strangers, of all ages; the quick dance
Of colors, lights, and forms; the deafening din;
The comers and the goers face to face,
Face after face; the string of dazzling wares,
Shop after shop, with symbols, blazoned names,
And all the tradesman's honors overhead:
Here, fronts of houses, like a title page,
With letters huge inscribed from top to toe,
Stationed above the door, like guardian saints;
There, allegoric shapes, female or male,
Or physiognomies of real men,
Land warriors, kings, or admirals of the sea,
Boyle, Shakespeare, Newton, or the attractive head
Of some quack doctor, famous in his day. . . .

As the black storm upon the mountaintop
Sets off the sunbeam in the valley, so
That huge fermenting mass of humankind
Serves as a solemn background, or relief,
To single forms and objects, whence they draw,
For feeling and contemplative regard,
More than inherent liveliness and power.
How oft, amid those overflowing streets,
Have I gone forward with the crowd, and said
Unto myself, "The face of everyone
That passes by me is a mystery!"
Thus have I looked, nor ceased to look, oppressed
By thoughts of what and whither, when and how,
Until the shapes before my eyes became
A second-sight procession, such as glides
Over still mountains, or appears in dreams;
And once, far-traveled in such mood, beyond
The reach of common indication, lost
Amid the moving pageant, I was smitten
Abruptly, with the view (a sight not rare)
Of a blind beggar, who, with upright face,
Stood, propped against a wall, upon his chest
Wearing a written paper, to explain
His story, whence he came, and who he was.
Caught by the spectacle my mind turned round
As with the might of waters; and apt type
This label seemed of the utmost we can know,
Both of ourselves and of the universe;
And, on the shape of that unmoving man,
His steadfast face and sightless eyes, I gazed,
As if admonished from another world. . . .

From these sights
Take one—that ancient festival, the Fair,
Holden where martyrs suffered in past time,
And named of St. Bartholomew; there, see
A work completed to our hands, that lays,
If any spectacle on earth can do,
The whole creative powers of man asleep!
For once, the Muse's help will we implore,
And she shall lodge us, wafted on her wings,
Above the press and danger of the crowd,
Upon some showman's platform. What a shock
For eyes and ears! what anarchy and din,
Barbarian and infernal—a phantasma,
Monstrous in color, motion, shape, sight, sound!
Below, the open space, through every nook
Of the wide area, twinkles, is alive
With heads; the midway region, and above,
Is thronged with staring pictures and huge
scrolls,
Dumb proclamations of the prodigies;

**638. Apocalypse:** the Revelation of St. John the Divine, the highly symbolic last book in the New Testament. **Book VII: 166. Boyle:** Robert Boyle (1627–91), British natural philosopher and chemist, formulator of the law which states that, the temperature remaining constant, the volume of a confined gas decreases in proportion to the pressure exerted upon it.

**676–78. Fair . . . St. Bartholomew:** The Fair, for hundreds of years a popular exhibition, was last held in 1855; it began on St. Bartholomew's Day (August 24) in Smithfield, where Protestants were executed in the reign of Queen Mary (1553–58). **687. phantasma:** a fantastic creation of the imagination.

With chattering monkeys dangling from their poles,
And children whirling in their roundabouts;
With those that stretch the neck and strain the eyes,
And crack the voice in rivalship, the crowd
Inviting; with buffoons against buffoons
Grimacing, writhing, screaming — him who grinds
The hurdy-gurdy, at the fiddle weaves,
Rattles the salt box, thumps the kettledrum,
And him who at the trumpet puffs his cheeks,
The silver-collared Negro with his timbrel,
Equestrians, tumblers, women, girls, and boys,
Blue-breeched, pink-vested, with high-towering plumes.
All movables of wonder, from all parts,
Are here — Albinos, painted Indians, Dwarfs,
The Horse of knowledge, and the learned Pig,
The Stone Eater, the man that swallows fire,
Giants, Ventriloquists, the Invisible Girl,
The Bust that speaks and moves its goggling eyes,
The Waxwork, Clockwork, all the marvelous craft
Of modern Merlins, Wild Beasts, Puppet Shows,
All out-o'-the-way, farfetched, perverted things,
All freaks of nature, all Promethean thoughts
Of man, his dullness, madness, and their feats
All jumbled up together, to compose
A Parliament of Monsters. Tents and booths
Meanwhile, as if the whole were one vast mill,
Are vomiting, receiving on all sides,
Men, women, three-years' children, babes in arms.

Oh, blank confusion! true epitome
Of what the mighty city is herself,
To thousands upon thousands of her sons,
Living amid the same perpetual whirl
Of trivial objects, melted and reduced
To one identity, by differences
That have no law, no meaning, and no end —
Oppression, under which even highest minds
Must labor, whence the strongest are not free.
But though the picture weary out the eye,
By nature an unmanageable sight,
It is not wholly so to him who looks
In steadiness, who hath among least things
An undersense of greatest; sees the parts
As parts, but with a feeling of the whole.
This, of all acquisitions first, awaits
On sundry and most widely different modes
Of education, nor with least delight
On that through which I passed. Attention springs,
And comprehensiveness and memory flow,
From early converse with the works of God
Among all regions; chiefly where appear
Most obviously simplicity and power.
Think, how the everlasting streams and woods,
Stretched and still stretching far and wide, exalt
The roving Indian: on his desert sands,
What grandeur not unfelt, what pregnant show
Of beauty, meets the sunburnt Arab's eye:
And, as the sea propels, from zone to zone,
Its currents; magnifies its shoals of life
Beyond all compass; spreads, and sends aloft
Armies of clouds — even so, its powers and aspects
Shape for mankind, by principles as fixed,
The views and aspirations of the soul
To majesty. Like virtue have the forms
Perennial of the ancient hills; nor less
The changeful language of their countenances
Quickens the slumbering mind, and aids the thoughts,
However multitudinous, to move
With order and relation. . . .

**695. roundabouts:** merry-go-rounds. **713. Merlins:** Merlin was the magician famous in Arthurian romance. **715. Promethean:** a loose reference to Prometheus, a foresighted Titan who fashioned men out of clay, taught them various arts, and stole fire from Olympus. Here Wordsworth seems to mean "daringly creative, fantastically original."

## from BOOK VIII

### RETROSPECT — LOVE OF NATURE LEADING TO LOVE OF MAN

What sounds are those, Helvellyn, that are heard
Up to thy summit, through the depth of air
Ascending, as if distance had the power
To make the sounds more audible? What crowd
Covers, or sprinkles o'er, yon village green?
Crowd seems it, solitary hill! to thee,
Though but a little family of men,
Shepherds and tillers of the ground — betimes
Assembled with their children and their wives,
And here and there a stranger interspersed.
They hold a rustic fair — a festival,
Such as, on this side now, and now on that,
Repeated through his tributary vales,
Helvellyn, in the silence of his rest,
Sees annually, if clouds towards either ocean
Blown from their favorite resting place, or mists
Dissolved, have left him an unshrouded head.
Delightful day it is for all who dwell
In this secluded glen, and eagerly
They give it welcome. Long ere heat of noon,
From byre or field the kine were brought; the sheep
Are penned in cotes; the chaffering is begun.
The heifer lows, uneasy at the voice
Of a new master; bleat the flocks aloud.

**Book VIII: 21. byre:** a cow barn.

Booths are there none; a stall or two is here;
A lame man or a blind, the one to beg,
The other to make music; hither, too,
From far, with basket, slung upon her arm,
Of hawker's wares — books, pictures, combs, and
  pins —
Some agèd woman finds her way again,
Year after year, a punctual visitant!
There also stands a speechmaker by rote,
Pulling the strings of his boxed raree show;
And in the lapse of many years may come
Prouder intinerant, mountebank, or he
Whose wonders in a covered wain lie hid.
But one there is, the loveliest of them all,
Some sweet lass of the valley, looking out
For gains, and who that sees her would not buy?
Fruits of her father's orchard are her wares,
And with the ruddy produce she walks round
Among the crowd, half-pleased with, half-ashamed
Of, her new office, blushing restlessly.
The children now are rich, for the old today
Are generous as the young; and, if content
With looking on, some ancient wedded pair
Sit in the shade together; while they gaze,
"A cheerful smile unbends the wrinkled brow,
The days departed start again to life,
And all the scenes of childhood reappear,
Faint, but more tranquil, like the changing sun
To him who slept at noon and wakes at eve."
Thus gaiety and cheerfulness prevail,
Spreading from young to old, from old to young,
And no one seems to want his share. Immense
Is the recess, the circumambient world
Magnificent, by which they are embraced;
They move about upon the soft green turf;
How little they, they and their doings, seem,
And all that they can further or obstruct!
Through utter weakness pitiably dear,
As tender infants are, and yet how great!
For all things serve them: them the morning
  light
Loves, as it glistens on the silent rocks;
And them the silent rocks, which now from high
Look down upon them; the reposing clouds;
The wild brooks prattling from invisible haunts;
And old Helvellyn, conscious of the stir
Which animates this day their calm abode. . . .

For me, when my affections first were led
From kindred, friends, and playmates, to partake
Love for the human creature's absolute self,
That noticeable kindliness of heart
Sprang out of fountains, there abounding most,
Where sovereign Nature dictated the tasks
And occupations which her beauty adorned,
And shepherds were the men that pleased me
  first. . . .

Smooth life had flock and shepherd in old time,
Long springs and tepid winters, on the banks
Of delicate Galesus; and no less
Those scattered along Adria's myrtle shores;
Smooth life had herdsman, and his snow-white
  herd
To triumphs and to sacrificial rites
Devoted, on the inviolable stream
Of rich Clitumnus; and the goatherd lived
As calmly, underneath the pleasant brows
Of cool Lucretilis, where the pipe was heard
Of Pan, invisible god, thrilling the rocks
With tutelary music, from all harm
The fold protecting. I myself, mature
In manhood then, have seen a pastoral tract
Like one of these, where Fancy might run wild,
Though under skies less generous, less serene;
There, for her own delight had Nature framed
A pleasure ground, diffused a fair expanse
Of level pasture, islanded with groves
And banked with woody risings; but the plain
Endless, here opening widely out, and there
Shut up in lesser lakes or beds of lawn
And intricate recesses, creek or bay
Sheltered within a shelter, where at large
The shepherd strays, a rolling hut his home.
Thither he comes with springtime, there abides
All summer, and at sunrise ye may hear
His flageolet to liquid notes of love
Attuned, or sprightly fife resounding far.
Nook is there none, nor tract of that vast space
Where passage opens, but the same shall have
In turn its visitant, telling there his hours
In unlaborious pleasure, with no task
More toilsome than to carve a beechen bowl
For spring or fountain, which the traveler finds,
When through the region he pursues at will
His devious course. A glimpse of such sweet life
I saw when, from the melancholy walls
Of Goslar, once imperial, I renewed
My daily walk along that wide champaign,
That, reaching to her gates, spreads east and west,
And northwards, from beneath the mountainous
  verge
Of the Hercynian forest. Yet, hail to you
Moors, mountains, headlands, and ye hollow vales,
Ye long deep channels for the Atlantic's voice,
Powers of my native region! Ye that seize

**33. raree show**: a peep show. **36. wain**: a wagon.

**175–82. Galesus . . . Lucretilis**: The proper names in this passage refer to Italian pastoral centers of classical antiquity celebrated in the poetry of Virgil and Horace. **200. flageolet**: a small flute. **211. Goslar . . . imperial**: the German town, formerly the seat of German emperors, where Wordsworth and his sister spent the winter of 1798–99. **215. Hercynian forest**: ancient name for the region in southeastern Germany now known as the Harz.

The heart with firmer grasp! Your snows and streams
Ungovernable, and your terrifying winds,
That howl so dismally for him who treads
Companionless your awful solitudes!
There, 'tis the shepherd's task the winter long
To wait upon the storms; of their approach
Sagacious, into sheltering coves he drives
His flock, and thither from the homestead bears
A toilsome burden up the craggy ways,
And deals it out, their regular nourishment
Strewn on the frozen snow. And when the spring
Looks out, and all the pastures dance with lambs,
And when the flock, with warmer weather, climbs
Higher and higher, him his office leads
To watch their goings, whatsoever track
The wanderers choose. For this he quits his home
At dayspring, and no sooner doth the sun
Begin to strike him with a firelike heat,
Than he lies down upon some shining rock,
And breakfasts with his dog. When they have stolen,
As is their wont, a pittance from strict time,
For rest not needed or exchange of love,
Then from his couch he starts; and now his feet
Crush out a livelier fragrance from the flowers
Of lowly thyme, by Nature's skill enwrought
In the wild turf; the lingering dews of morn
Smoke round him, as from hill to hill he hies,
His staff protending like a hunter's spear,
Or by its aid leaping from crag to crag,
And o'er the brawling beds of unbridged streams.
Philosophy, methinks, at Fancy's call,
Might deign to follow him through what he does
Or sees in his day's march; himself he feels,
In those vast regions where his service lies,
A freeman, wedded to his life of hope
And hazard, and hard labor interchanged
With that majestic indolence so dear
To native man. A rambling schoolboy, thus,
I felt his presence in his own domain,
As of a lord and master, or a power,
Or genius, under Nature, under God,
Presiding; and severest solitude
Had more commanding looks when he was there.
When up the lonely brooks on rainy days
Angling I went, or trod the trackless hills
By mists bewildered, suddenly mine eyes
Have glanced upon him distant a few steps,
In size a giant, stalking through thick fog,
His sheep like Greenland bears; or, as he stepped
Beyond the boundary line of some hill shadow,
His form hath flashed upon me, glorified
By the deep radiance of the setting sun;
Or him have I descried in distant sky,
A solitary object and sublime,
Above all height! like an aerial cross
Stationed alone upon a spiry rock
Of the Chartreuse, for worship. Thus was man
Ennobled outwardly before my sight,
And thus my heart was early introduced
To an unconscious love and reverence
Of human nature; hence the human form
To me became an index of delight,
Of grace and honor, power and worthiness.
Meanwhile this creature — spiritual almost
As those of books, but more exalted far;
Far more of an imaginative form
Than the gay Corin of the groves, who lives
For his own fancies, or to dance by the hour,
In coronal, with Phyllis in the midst —
Was, for the purposes of kind, a man
With the most common; husband, father; learned,
Could teach, admonish; suffered with the rest
From vice and folly, wretchedness and fear;
Of this I little saw, cared less for it,
But something must have felt.
                                        Call ye these appearances —
Which I beheld of shepherds in my youth,
This sanctity of Nature given to man —
A shadow, a delusion, ye who pore
On the dead letter, miss the spirit of things;
Whose truth is not a motion or a shape
Instinct with vital functions, but a block
Or waxen image which yourselves have made,
And ye adore! But blessèd be the God
Of Nature and of Man that this was so;
That men before my inexperienced eyes
Did first present themselves thus purified,
Removed, and to a distance that was fit;
And so we all of us in some degree
Are led to knowledge, wheresoever led,
And howsoever; were it otherwise,
And we found evil fast as we find good
In our first years, or think that it is found,
How could the innocent heart bear up and live!
But doubly fortunate my lot; not here
Alone, that something of a better life
Perhaps was round me than it is the privilege
Of most to move in, but that first I looked
At Man through objects that were great or fair;
First communed with him by their help. And thus
Was founded a sure safeguard and defense
Against the weight of meanness, selfish cares,
Coarse manners, vulgar passions, that beat in
On all sides from the ordinary world
In which we traffic. . . .

**246. protending:** extending.

**275. Chartreuse:** a Carthusian monastery in the French Alps near Grenoble. See Arnold's "Stanzas from the Grande Chartreuse," pp. 612–15, below. **285–87. Corin . . . Phyllis:** common names of stock characters in pastoral literature. See, for example, Milton's "L'Allegro," ll. 83 and 86, p. 418 in Vol. I.

### from BOOK IX
### RESIDENCE IN FRANCE

France lured me forth, the realm that I had crossed
So lately, journeying toward the snow-clad Alps.
But now, relinquishing the scrip and staff,
And all enjoyment which the summer sun
Sheds round the steps of those who meet the day
With motion constant as his own, I went
Prepared to sojourn in a pleasant town,
Washed by the current of the stately Loire.

Through Paris lay my readiest course, and there
Sojourning a few days, I visited
In haste, each spot of old or recent fame,
The latter chiefly; from the field of Mars
Down to the suburbs of St. Antony,
And from Mont Martre southward to the dome
Of Geneviève. In both her clamorous halls,
The National Synod and the Jacobins,
I saw the revolutionary power
Toss like a ship at anchor, rocked by storms;
The arcades I traversed, in the palace huge
Of Orléans; coasted round and round the line
Of tavern, brothel, gaming house, and shop,
Great rendezvous of worst and best, the walk
Of all who had a purpose, or had not;
I stared and listened, with a stranger's ears,
To hawkers and haranguers, hubbub wild!
And hissing factionists with ardent eyes,
In knots, or pairs, or single. Not a look
Hope takes, or Doubt or Fear is forced to wear,
But seemed there present; and I scanned them all,
Watched every gesture uncontrollable,
Of anger, and vexation, and despite,
All side by side, and struggling face to face,
With gaicty and dissolute idleness. . . .

A band of military officers,
Then stationed in the city, were the chief
Of my associates; some of these wore swords
That had been seasoned in the wars, and all
Were men wellborn, the chivalry of France.
In age and temper differing, they had yet
One spirit ruling in each heart; alike
(Save only one, hereafter to be named)
Were bent upon undoing what was done;
This was their best and only hope; therewith
No fear had they of bad becoming worse,
For worst to them was come; nor would have stirred,
Or deemed it worth a moment's thought to stir,
In anything, save only as the act
Looked thitherward. . . .

Among that band of officers was one,
Already hinted at, of other mold—
A patriot, thence rejected by the rest,
And with an oriental loathing spurned,
As of a different caste. A meeker man
Than this lived never, nor a more benign,
Meek though enthusiastic. Injuries
Made *him* more gracious, and his nature then
Did breathe its sweetness out most sensibly,
As aromatic flowers on Alpine turf,
When foot hath crushed them. He through the events
Of that great change wandered in perfect faith,
As through a book, an old romance, or tale
Of fairy, or some dream of actions wrought
Behind the summer clouds. By birth he ranked
With the most noble, but unto the poor
Among mankind he was in service bound,
As by some tie invisible, oaths professed
To a religious order. Man he loved
As man; and, to the mean and the obscure,
And all the homely in their homely works,
Transferred a courtesy which had no air
Of condescension; but did rather seem
A passion and a gallantry, like that
Which he, a soldier, in his idler day
Had paid to woman; somewhat vain he was,
Or seemed so, yet it was not vanity,
But fondness, and a kind of radiant joy
Diffused around him, while he was intent
On works of love or freedom, or revolved
Complacently the progress of a cause,
Whereof he was a part; yet this was meek
And placid, and took nothing from the man
That was delightful. Oft in solitude
With him did I discourse about the end
Of civil government, and its wisest forms;
Of ancient loyalty, and chartered rights,
Custom and habit, novelty and change;
Of self-respect, and virtue in the few
For patrimonial honor set apart,

**Book IX: 36. scrip:** bag, wallet, or knapsack. **40–41. town . . . Loire:** Actually Wordsworth sojourned in two towns situated on the Loire, Orléans and Blois. **45. field of Mars:** the Champ de Mars, in the western part of Paris, where Louis XVI took the oath of allegiance in 1790. **46. suburbs of St. Antony:** the Faubourg St. Antoine in the eastern part of the city, famous as the home of revolutionary workers. **47. Mont Martre:** a hilly section in the northern part of Paris. **47–48. dome of Geneviève:** the Pantheon, burial place of Voltaire and Rousseau, in the southern part of Paris. **49. National Synod:** the National Assembly, the newly formed French legislative body which met in the Riding Hall on the Rue de Rivoli. **Jacobins:** a famous club of revolutionists, so called after the convent (originally named after St. Jacques) in which they held their meetings. **52–53. arcades . . . Orléans:** the arcades in the courtyard of the Palais Royal, a Parisian shopping center.

**288. one:** Michel Beaupuy (1755–96), whose conversation seems to have wakened Wordsworth's political and social consciousness. The memory of Beaupuy helped to inspire the "Character of the Happy Warrior," below. **289. Already . . . at:** See *Prelude*, IX.132, above.

And ignorance in the laboring multitude.
For he, to all intolerance indisposed,
Balanced these contemplations in his mind;
And I, who at that time was scarcely dipped
Into the turmoil, bore a sounder judgment
Than later days allowed; carried about me,
With less alloy to its integrity,
The experience of past ages, as, through help
Of books and common life, it makes sure way
To youthful minds, by objects over near
Not pressed upon, nor dazzled or misled
By struggling with the crowd for present ends. . . .

Yet not the less,
Hatred of absolute rule, where will of one
Is law for all, and of that barren pride
In them who, by immunities unjust,
Between the sovereign and the people stand,
His helper and not theirs, laid stronger hold
Daily upon me, mixed with pity too
And love; for where hope is, there love will be
For the abject multitude. And when we chanced
One day to meet a hunger-bitten girl,
Who crept along fitting her languid gait
Unto a heifer's motion, by a cord
Tied to her arm, and picking thus from the lane
Its sustenance, while the girl with pallid hands
Was busy knitting in a heartless mood
Of solitude, and at the sight my friend
In agitation said, "'Tis against *that*
That we are fighting," I with him believed
That a benignant spirit was abroad
Which might not be withstood, that poverty
Abject as this would in a little time
Be found no more, that we should see the earth
Unthwarted in her wish to recompense
The meek, the lowly, patient child of toil,
All institutes forever blotted out
That legalized exclusion, empty pomp
Abolished, sensual state and cruel power
Whether by edict of the one or few;
And finally, as sum and crown of all,
Should see the people having a strong hand
In framing their own laws; whence better days
To all mankind. . . .

## from BOOK X

## RESIDENCE IN FRANCE (*continued*)

In this frame of mind,
Dragged by a chain of harsh necessity,
So seemed it — now I thankfully acknowledge,
Forced by the gracious providence of Heaven —
To England I returned, else (though assured
That I both was and must be of small weight,
No better than a landsman on the deck
Of a ship struggling with a hideous storm)
Doubtless, I should have then made common cause
With some who perished; haply perished too,
A poor mistaken and bewildered offering —
Should to the breast of Nature have gone back,
With all my resolutions, all my hopes,
A poet only to myself, to men
Useless, and even, beloved friend! a soul
To thee unknown! . . .

What, then, were my emotions, when in arms
Britain put forth her freeborn strength in league,
Oh, pity and shame! with those confederate powers!
Not in my single self alone I found,
But in the minds of all ingenuous youth,
Change and subversion from that hour. No shock
Given to my moral nature had I known
Down to that very moment; neither lapse
Nor turn of sentiment that might be named
A revolution, save at this one time;
All else was progress on the selfsame path
On which, with a diversity of pace,
I had been traveling; this a stride at once
Into another region. As a light
And pliant harebell, swinging in the breeze
On some gray rock — its birthplace — so had I
Wantoned, fast-rooted on the ancient tower
Of my beloved country, wishing not
A happier fortune than to wither there;
Now was I from that pleasant station torn
And tossed about in whirlwind. I rejoiced,
Yea, afterwards — truth most painful to record! —
Exulted, in the triumph of my soul,
When Englishmen by thousands were o'erthrown,
Left without glory on the field, or driven,
Brave hearts! to shameful flight. It was a grief —
Grief call it not, 'twas anything but that —
A conflict of sensations without name,
Of which *he* only, who may love the sight
Of a village steeple, as I do, can judge,
When, in the congregation bending all
To their great Father, prayers were offered up,
Or praises for our country's victories;
And, 'mid the simple worshipers, perchance
I only, like an uninvited guest
Whom no one owned, sat silent, shall I add,
Fed on the day of vengeance yet to come. . . .

**Book X: 222–25. Dragged . . . returned:** Lack of money forced Wordsworth to return to England late in December, 1792.

**263–65. What . . . powers!:** On February 1, 1793, France declared war on England and Holland. England retaliated on February 11 and, along with Holland, Austria, Prussia, Spain, and Sardinia, became a member of the First Coalition. **286–88. Englishmen . . . flight:** At the battle of Hondschoote (September 6, 1793) the French defeated the English under the Duke of York and forced them to retreat.

Most melancholy at that time, O friend!
Were my day thoughts — my nights were miserable;
Through months, through years, long after the last beat
Of those atrocities, the hour of sleep
To me came rarely charged with natural gifts,
Such ghastly visions had I of despair
And tyranny, and implements of death;
And innocent victims sinking under fear,
And momentary hope, and worn-out prayer,
Each in his separate cell, or penned in crowds
For sacrifice, and struggling with forced mirth
And levity in dungeons, where the dust
Was laid with tears. Then suddenly the scene
Changed, and the unbroken dream entangled me
In long orations, which I strove to plead
Before unjust tribunals — with a voice
Laboring, a brain confounded, and a sense,
Deathlike, of treacherous desertion, felt
In the last place of refuge — my own soul. . . .

## from BOOK XI

## FRANCE (*concluded*)

O pleasant exercise of hope and joy!
For mighty were the auxiliars which then stood
Upon our side, us who were strong in love!
Bliss was it in that dawn to be alive,
But to be young was very heaven! O times,
In which the meager, stale, forbidding ways
Of custom, law, and statute, took at once
The attraction of a country in romance!
When Reason seemed the most to assert her rights,
When most intent on making of herself
A prime enchantress — to assist the work,
Which then was going forward in her name!
Not favored spots alone, but the whole earth,
The beauty wore of promise — that which sets
(As at some moments might not be unfelt
Among the bowers of paradise itself)
The budding rose above the rose full-blown.
What temper at the prospect did not wake
To happiness unthought of? The inert
Were roused, and lively natures rapt away!
They who had fed their childhood upon dreams,
The playfellows of fancy, who had made
All powers of swiftness, subtlety, and strength
Their ministers, who in lordly wise had stirred
Among the grandest objects of the sense,
And dealt with whatsoever they found there
As if they had within some lurking right
To wield it; they, too, who of gentle mood
Had watched all gentle motions, and to these
Had fitted their own thoughts, schemers more mild,
And in the region of their peaceful selves —
Now was it that *both* found, the meek and lofty
Did both find, helpers to their hearts' desire,
And stuff at hand, plastic as they could wish,
Were called upon to exercise their skill,
Not in Utopia — subterranean fields —
Or some secreted island, Heaven knows where!
But in the very world, which is the world
Of all of us — the place where, in the end,
We find our happiness, or not at all! . . .

But now, become oppressors in their turn,
Frenchmen had changed a war of self-defense
For one of conquest, losing sight of all
Which they had struggled for; up mounted now,
Openly in the eye of earth and heaven,
The scale of liberty. I read her doom.
With anger vexed, with disappointment sore,
But not dismayed, nor taking to the shame
Of a false prophet. While resentment rose,
Striving to hide, what nought could heal, the wounds
Of mortified presumption, I adhered
More firmly to old tenets, and, to prove
Their temper, strained them more; and thus, in heat
Of contest, did opinions every day
Grow into consequence, till round my mind
They clung, as if they were its life, nay more,
The very being of the immortal soul. . . .

So I fared,
Dragging all precepts, judgments, maxims, creeds,
Like culprits to the bar; calling the mind,
Suspiciously, to establish in plain day
Her titles and her honors; now believing,
Now disbelieving; endlessly perplexed
With impulse, motive, right and wrong, the ground
Of obligation, what the rule and whence
The sanction; till, demanding formal *proof,*
And seeking it in everything, I lost
All feeling of conviction, and, in fine,
Sick, wearied out with contrarieties,
Yielded up moral questions in despair. . . .

Then it was —
Thanks to the bounteous Giver of all good! —
That the belovèd sister in whose sight
Those days were passed, now speaking in a voice
Of sudden admonition — like a brook
That did but *cross* a lonely road, and now
Is seen, heard, felt, and caught at every turn,

**Book XI: 105–44. O . . . all!:** These lines were first published as an independent poem in Coleridge's periodical *The Friend,* for October 26, 1809.

**335. sister:** Dorothy Wordsworth, who joined her brother for several weeks in the spring of 1794 at Windy Brow, half a mile from Keswick, and lived with him permanently after the settlement at Racedown in September, 1795.

Companion never lost through many a league —
Maintained for me a saving intercourse
With my true self; for, though bedimmed and changed
Much, as it seemed, I was no further changed
Than as a clouded, not a waning moon;
She whispered still that brightness would return;
She, in the midst of all, preserved me still
A poet, made me seek beneath that name,
And that alone, my office upon earth;
And, lastly, as hereafter will be shown,
If willing audience fail not, Nature's self,
By all varieties of human love
Assisted, led me back through opening day
To those sweet counsels between head and heart
Whence grew that genuine knowledge, fraught with peace,
Which, through the later sinkings of this cause,
Hath still upheld me, and upholds me now. . . .

## from BOOK XII

## IMAGINATION AND TASTE, HOW IMPAIRED AND RESTORED

There are in our existence spots of time,
That with distinct pre-eminence retain
A renovating virtue, whence — depressed
By false opinion and contentious thought,
Or aught of heavier or more deadly weight,
In trivial occupations, and the round
Of ordinary intercourse — our minds
Are nourished and invisibly repaired;
A virtue, by which pleasure is enhanced,
That penetrates, enables us to mount,
When high, more high, and lifts us up when fallen.
This efficacious spirit chiefly lurks
Among those passages of life that give
Profoundest knowledge to what point, and how,
The mind is lord and master — outward sense
The obedient servant of her will. Such moments
Are scattered everywhere, taking their date
From our first childhood. I remember well,
That once, while yet my inexperienced hand
Could scarcely hold a bridle, with proud hopes
I mounted, and we journeyed towards the hills;
An ancient servant of my father's house
Was with me, my encourager and guide;
We had not traveled long, ere some mischance
Disjoined me from my comrade; and, through fear
Dismounting, down the rough and stony moor
I led my horse, and, stumbling on, at length
Came to a bottom, where in former times
A murderer had been hung in iron chains.
The gibbet mast had moldered down, the bones
And iron case were gone; but on the turf,
Hard by, soon after that fell deed was wrought,
Some unknown hand had carved the murderer's name.
The monumental letters were inscribed
In times long past; but still, from year to year
By superstition of the neighborhood,
The grass is cleared away, and to this hour
The characters are fresh and visible;
A casual glance had shown them, and I fled,
Faltering and faint, and ignorant of the road;
Then, reascending the bare common, saw
A naked pool that lay beneath the hills,
The beacon on the summit, and, more near,
A girl, who bore a pitcher on her head,
And seemed with difficult steps to force her way
Against the blowing wind. It was, in truth,
An ordinary sight; but I should need
Colors and words that are unknown to man,
To paint the visionary dreariness
Which, while I looked all round for my lost guide,
Invested moorland waste and naked pool,
The beacon crowning the lone eminence,
The female and her garments vexed and tossed
By the strong wind. When, in the blessèd hours
Of early love, the loved one at my side,
I roamed, in daily presence of this scene,
Upon the naked pool and dreary crags,
And on the melancholy beacon, fell
A spirit of pleasure and youth's golden gleam;
And think ye not with radiance more sublime
For these remembrances, and for the power
They had left behind? So feeling comes in aid
Of feeling, and diversity of strength
Attends us, if but once we have been strong.
Oh! mystery of man, from what a depth
Proceed thy honors. I am lost, but see
In simple childhood something of the base
On which thy greatness stands; but this I feel,
That from thyself it comes, that thou must give,
Else never canst receive. The days gone by
Return upon me almost from the dawn
Of life: the hiding places of man's power
Open; I would approach them, but they close.
I see by glimpses now; when age comes on,
May scarcely see at all; and I would give,
While yet we may, as far as words can give,
Substance and life to what I feel, enshrining,
Such is my hope, the spirit of the past
For future restoration. Yet another
Of these memorials:
One Christmastime,
On the glad eve of its dear holidays,
Feverish, and tired, and restless, I went forth

**Book XII: 281–82. I . . . all:** sometimes interpreted erroneously as reflecting Wordsworth's acknowledgment of declining poetic power. The context makes it clear that Wordsworth refers to the difficulty in middle age of remembering the experiences of early childhood.

Into the fields, impatient for the sight
Of those led palfreys that should bear us home,
My brothers and myself. There rose a crag,
That, from the meeting point of two highways
Ascending, overlooked them both, far stretched;
Thither, uncertain on which road to fix
My expectation, thither I repaired,
Scoutlike, and gained the summit; 'twas a day
Tempestuous, dark and wild, and on the grass
I sat half-sheltered by a naked wall;
Upon my right hand couched a single sheep,
Upon my left a blasted hawthorn stood;
With those companions at my side, I watched,
Straining my eyes intensely, as the mist
Gave intermitting prospect of the copse
And plain beneath. Ere we to school returned—
That dreary time—ere we had been ten days
Sojourners in my father's house, he died;
And I and my two brothers, orphans then,
Followed his body to the grave. The event,
With all the sorrow that it brought, appeared
A chastisement; and when I called to mind
That day so lately past, when from the crag
I looked in such anxiety of hope;
With trite reflections of morality,
Yet in the deepest passion, I bowed low
To God, who thus corrected my desires;
And, afterwards, the wind and sleety rain,
And all the business of the elements,
The single sheep, and the one blasted tree,
And the bleak music from that old stone wall,
The noise of wood and water, and the mist
That on the line of each of those two roads
Advanced in such indisputable shapes;
All these were kindred spectacles and sounds
To which I oft repaired, and thence would drink,
As at a fountain; and on winter nights,
Down to this very time, when storm and rain
Beat on my roof, or, haply, at noonday,
While in a grove I walk, whose lofty trees,
Laden with summer's thickest foliage, rock
In a strong wind, some working of the spirit,
Some inward agitations thence are brought,
Whate'er their office, whether to beguile
Thoughts overbusy in the course they took,
Or animate an hour of vacant ease.

from BOOK XIII

## IMAGINATION AND TASTE, HOW IMPAIRED AND RESTORED (*concluded*)

From Nature doth emotion come, and moods
Of calmness equally are Nature's gift;
This is her glory; these two attributes
Are sister horns that constitute her strength.
Hence Genius, born to thrive by interchange
Of peace and excitation, finds in her
His best and purest friend; from her receives
That energy by which he seeks the truth,
From her that happy stillness of the mind
Which fits him to receive it when unsought.

Such benefit the humblest intellects
Partake of, each in their degree; 'tis mine
To speak, what I myself have known and felt;
Smooth task! for words find easy way, inspired
By gratitude, and confidence in truth.
Long time in search of knowledge did I range
The field of human life, in heart and mind
Benighted; but, the dawn beginning now
To reappear, 'twas proved that not in vain
I had been taught to reverence a power
That is the visible quality and shape
And image of right reason; that matures
Her processes by steadfast laws; gives birth
To no impatient or fallacious hopes,
No heat of passion or excessive zeal,
No vain conceits; provokes to no quick turns
Of self-applauding intellect; but trains
To meekness, and exalts by humble faith;
Holds up before the mind intoxicate
With present objects, and the busy dance
Of things that pass away, a temperate show
Of objects that endure; and by this course
Disposes her, when overfondly set
On throwing off incumbrances, to seek
In man, and in the frame of social life,
Whate'er there is desirable and good
Of kindred permanence, unchanged in form
And function, or, through strict vicissitude
Of life and death, revolving. Above all
Were re-established now those watchful thoughts
Which, seeing little worthy or sublime
In what the historian's pen so much delights
To blazon—power and energy detached
From moral purpose—early tutored me
To look with feelings of fraternal love
Upon the unassuming things that hold
A silent station in this beauteous world. . . .

Here, calling up to mind what then I saw,
A youthful traveler, and see daily now
In the familiar circuit of my home,
Here might I pause, and bend in reverence
To Nature, and the power of human minds,
To men as they are men within themselves.
How oft high service is performed within,
When all the external man is rude in show,
Not like a temple rich with pomp and gold,
But a mere mountain chapel, that protects
Its simple worshipers from sun and shower.

**307. died:** Wordsworth's father died on December 30, 1783.

Of these, said I, shall be my song; of these,
If future years mature me for the task,
Will I record the praises, making verse
Deal boldly with substantial things; in truth
And sanctity of passion, speak of these,
That justice may be done, obeisance paid
Where it is due; thus haply shall I teach,
Inspire; through unadulterated ears
Pour rapture, tenderness, and hope, my theme
No other than the very heart of man,
As found among the best of those who live —
Not unexalted by religious faith,
Nor uninformed by books, good books, though few —
In Nature's presence; thence may I select
Sorrow, that is not sorrow, but delight;
And miserable love, that is not pain
To hear of, for the glory that redounds
Therefrom to human kind, and what we are. . . .

## from BOOK XIV
## CONCLUSION

It was a close, warm, breezeless summer night,
Wan, dull, and glaring, with a dripping fog
Low-hung and thick that covered all the sky;
But, undiscouraged, we began to climb
The mountainside. The mist soon girt us round,
And, after ordinary travelers' talk
With our conductor, pensively we sank
Each into commerce with his private thoughts;
Thus did we breast the ascent, and by myself
Was nothing either seen or heard that checked
Those musings or diverted, save that once
The shepherd's lurcher, who, among the crags,
Had to his joy unearthed a hedgehog, teased
His coiled-up prey with barkings turbulent.
This small adventure, for even such it seemed
In that wild place and at the dead of night,
Being over and forgotten, on we wound
In silence as before. With forehead bent
Earthward, as if in opposition set
Against an enemy, I panted up
With eager pace, and no less eager thoughts.
Thus might we wear a midnight hour away,
Ascending at loose distance each from each,
And I, as chanced, the foremost of the band;
When at my feet the ground appeared to brighten,
And with a step or two seemed brighter still;
Nor was time given to ask or learn the cause,
For instantly a light upon the turf
Fell like a flash, and lo! as I looked up
The moon hung naked in a firmament
Of azure without cloud, and at my feet
Rested a silent sea of hoary mist.
A hundred hills their dusky backs upheaved
All over this still ocean; and beyond,
Far, far beyond, the solid vapors stretched,
In headlands, tongues, and promontory shapes,
Into the main Atlantic, that appeared
To dwindle, and give up his majesty,
Usurped upon far as the sight could reach.
Not so the ethereal vault; encroachment none
Was there, nor loss; only the inferior stars
Had disappeared, or shed a fainter light
In the clear presence of the full-orbed moon,
Who, from her sovereign elevation, gazed
Upon the billowy ocean, as it lay
All meek and silent, save that through a rift —
Not distant from the shore whereon we stood,
A fixed, abysmal, gloomy, breathing place —
Mounted the roar of waters, torrents, streams
Innumerable, roaring with one voice!
Heard over earth and sea, and, in that hour,
For so it seemed, felt by the starry heavens.

When into air had partially dissolved
That vision, given to spirits of the night
And three chance human wanderers, in calm thought
Reflected, it appeared to me the type
Of a majestic intellect, its acts
And its possessions, what it has and craves,
What in itself it is, and would become.
There I beheld the emblem of a mind
That feeds upon infinity, that broods
Over the dark abyss, intent to hear
Its voices issuing forth to silent light
In one continuous stream; a mind sustained
By recognitions of transcendent power,
In sense conducting to ideal form,
In soul of more than mortal privilege.
One function, above all, of such a mind
Had Nature shadowed there, by putting forth,
'Mid circumstances awful and sublime,
That mutual domination which she loves
To exert upon the face of outward things,
So molded, joined, abstracted, so endowed
With interchangeable supremacy,
That men, least sensitive, see, hear, perceive,
And cannot choose but feel. The power, which all
Acknowledge when thus moved, which Nature thus
To bodily sense exhibits, is the express
Resemblance of that glorious faculty
That higher minds bear with them as their own.
This is the very spirit in which they deal
With the whole compass of the universe:

**Book XIV: 11–15. summer . . . mountainside: In 1791 or 1793 Wordsworth and his friend Jones climbed Mt. Snowdon (3560 feet), the tallest peak in England and Wales. 22. lurcher: a mongrel hunting dog.**

They from their native selves can send abroad
Kindred mutations; for themselves create
A like existence; and, whene'er it dawns
Created for them, catch it, or are caught
By its inevitable mastery,
Like angels stopped upon the wing by sound
Of harmony from Heaven's remotest spheres.
Them the enduring and the transient both
Serve to exalt; they build up greatest things
From least suggestions; ever on the watch,
Willing to work and to be wrought upon,
They need not extraordinary calls
To rouse them; in a world of life they live,
By sensible impressions not enthralled,
But by their quickening impulse made more
 prompt
To hold fit converse with the spiritual world,
And with the generations of mankind
Spread over time, past, present, and to come,
Age after age, till time shall be no more.
Such minds are truly from the Deity,
For they are powers; and hence the highest bliss
That flesh can know is theirs — the consciousness
Of whom they are, habitually infused
Through every image and through every thought,
And all affections by communion raised
From earth to heaven, from human to divine;
Hence endless occupation for the soul,
Whether discursive or intuitive;
Hence cheerfulness for acts of daily life,
Emotions which best foresight need not fear,
Most worthy then of trust when most intense.
Hence, amid ills that vex and wrongs that crush
Our hearts — if here the words of Holy Writ
May with fit reverence be applied — that peace
Which passeth understanding, that repose
In moral judgments which from this pure source
Must come, or will by man be sought in vain. . . .

This spiritual love acts not nor can exist
Without Imagination, which, in truth,
Is but another name for absolute power
And clearest insight, amplitude of mind,
And Reason in her most exalted mood.
This faculty hath been the feeding source
Of our long labor: we have traced the stream
From the blind cavern whence is faintly heard
Its natal murmur; followed it to light
And open day; accompanied its course
Among the ways of Nature, for a time
Lost sight of it bewildered and engulfed;
Then given it greeting as it rose once more
In strength, reflecting from its placid breast
The works of man and face of human life;
And lastly, from its progress have we drawn
Faith in life endless, the sustaining thought
Of human Being, Eternity, and God. . . .

Whether to me shall be allotted life,
And, with life, power to accomplish aught of
 worth,
That will be deemed no insufficient plea
For having given the story of myself,
Is all uncertain; but, beloved friend!
When, looking back, thou seest, in clearer view
Than any liveliest sight of yesterday,
That summer, under whose indulgent skies,
Upon smooth Quantock's airy ridge we roved
Unchecked, or loitered 'mid her sylvan combs,
Thou in bewitching words, with happy heart,
Didst chant the vision of that Ancient Man,
The bright-eyed Mariner, and rueful woes
Didst utter of the Lady Christabel;
And I, associate with such labor, steeped
In soft forgetfulness the livelong hours,
Murmuring of him who, joyous hap, was found,
After the perils of his moonlight ride,
Near the loud waterfall; or her who sat
In misery near the miserable Thorn —
When thou dost to that summer turn thy thoughts,
And hast before thee all which then we were,
To thee, in memory of that happiness,
It will be known, by thee at least, my friend!
Felt, that the history of a poet's mind
Is labor not unworthy of regard;
To thee the work shall justify itself. . . .

Oh! yet a few short years of useful life,
And all will be complete, thy race be run,
Thy monument of glory will be raised;
Then, though (too weak to tread the ways of truth)
This age fall back to old idolatry,
Though men returned to servitude as fast
As the tide ebbs, to ignominy and shame,
By nations, sink together, we shall still
Find solace — knowing what we have learned to
 know,
Rich in true happiness if allowed to be
Faithful alike in forwarding a day
Of firmer trust, joint laborers in the work
(Should Providence such grace to us vouchsafe)
Of their deliverance, surely yet to come.
Prophets of Nature, we to them will speak
A lasting inspiration, sanctified
By reason, blessed by faith; what we have loved,
Others will love, and we will teach them how;
Instruct them how the mind of man becomes

**395–407. That . . . Thorn:** Wordsworth refers to the summer of 1797, when he and Dorothy, living at Alfoxden in Somersetshire, began their intimate association with Coleridge. Walking together almost daily on the Quantock Hills, Wordsworth and Coleridge in this year began to write many of the poems published in *Lyrical Ballads*, 1798. Here Wordsworth mentions specifically Coleridge's "The Rime of the Ancient Mariner" and "Christabel" (rejected for *Lyrical Ballads*, but published independently in 1816), and his own poems, "The Idiot Boy" and "The Thorn."
**397. combs:** narrow valleys.

A thousand times more beautiful than the earth
On which he dwells, above this frame of things
(Which, 'mid all revolution in the hopes
And fears of men, doth still remain unchanged)
In beauty exalted, as it is itself
Of quality and fabric more divine.

## LUCY GRAY

### *or, Solitude*

The following five poems, together with "I Traveled among Unknown Men," are known as the "Lucy" poems. Except for "I Traveled among Unknown Men," written in 1801, Wordsworth wrote these poems in Germany in the winter of 1798–99. The name Lucy appears in four of them, and all six resemble one another in sentiment and tone. The Lucy Gray who disappears from the bridge in the snowstorm, however, is obviously unrelated to the girls referred to in the other poems. We have no evidence that Wordsworth ever knew anyone named Lucy. Consequently there has been much speculation about Lucy's identity, just as there has been much speculation about Matthew Arnold's Marguerite. Was Lucy a real person? Was she Dorothy Wordsworth, or was she imaginary?

Probably we shall never know. Wordsworth first used the name in an unpublished fragment he wrote in the summer of 1798. Therein he seems to have been addressing his sister Dorothy. But Dorothy Wordsworth lived until 1855, and in all but one of the "Lucy" poems Lucy is dead. Perhaps Coleridge was close to the truth in April, 1799, when he wrote Thomas Poole: "Some months ago Wordsworth transmitted to me a most sublime epitaph ["A Slumber Did My Spirit Seal"]. Whether it had any reality I cannot say. Most probably, in some gloomier moment he had fancied the moment in which his sister might die."

Oft I had heard of Lucy Gray;
And, when I crossed the wild,
I chanced to see at break of day
The solitary child.

No mate, no comrade Lucy knew;
She dwelt on a wide moor,
— The sweetest thing that ever grew
Beside a human door!

You yet may spy the fawn at play,
The hare upon the green;
But the sweet face of Lucy Gray
Will nevermore be seen.

"Tonight will be a stormy night —
You to the town must go;
And take a lantern, child, to light
Your mother through the snow."

"That, Father! will I gladly do;
'Tis scarcely afternoon —
The minster clock has just struck two,
And yonder is the moon!"

At this the father raised his hook,
And snapped a fagot band;
He plied his work, and Lucy took
The lantern in her hand.

Not blither is the mountain roe;
With many a wanton stroke
Her feet disperse the powdery snow,
That rises up like smoke.

The storm came on before its time;
She wandered up and down;
And many a hill did Lucy climb,
But never reached the town.

The wretched parents all that night
Went shouting far and wide;
But there was neither sound nor sight
To serve them for a guide.

At daybreak on a hill they stood
That overlooked the moor;
And thence they saw the bridge of wood,
A furlong from their door.

They wept — and, turning homeward, cried,
"In Heaven we all shall meet";
When in the snow the mother spied
The print of Lucy's feet.

Then downwards from the steep hill's edge
They tracked the footmarks small;
And through the broken hawthorn hedge,
And by the long stone wall;

And then an open field they crossed;
The marks were still the same;
They tracked them on, nor ever lost;
And to the bridge they came.

They followed from the snowy bank
Those footmarks, one by one,
Into the middle of the plank;
And further there were none!

Yet some maintain that to this day
She is a living child;
That you may see sweet Lucy Gray
Upon the lonesome wild.

LUCY GRAY. **19. minster clock:** church clock. **22. snapped . . . band:** broke the cord around a bundle of small branches to be used as fuel. **40. furlong:** an eighth of a mile.

O'er rough and smooth she trips along,
And never looks behind;
And sings a solitary song
That whistles in the wind.

*1799*

## STRANGE FITS OF PASSION HAVE I KNOWN

Strange fits of passion have I known,
And I will dare to tell,
But in the lover's ear alone,
What once to me befell.

When she I loved looked every day
Fresh as a rose in June,
I to her cottage bent my way,
Beneath an evening moon.

Upon the moon I fixed my eye,
All over the wide lea;
With quickening pace my horse drew nigh
Those paths so dear to me.

And now we reached the orchard plot;
And, as we climbed the hill,
The sinking moon to Lucy's cot
Came near, and nearer still.

In one of those sweet dreams I slept,
Kind Nature's gentlest boon!
And all the while my eyes I kept
On the descending moon.

My horse moved on; hoof after hoof
He raised, and never stopped;
When down behind the cottage roof,
At once, the bright moon dropped.

What fond and wayward thoughts will slide
Into a lover's head!
"O mercy!" to myself I cried,
"If Lucy should be dead!"

*1799*

## SHE DWELT AMONG THE UNTRODDEN WAYS

She dwelt among the untrodden ways
Beside the springs of Dove,
A maid whom there were none to praise
And very few to love;

A violet by a mossy stone
Half-hidden from the eye!
Fair as a star, when only one
Is shining in the sky.

She lived unknown, and few could know
When Lucy ceased to be;
But she is in her grave, and, oh,
The difference to me!

*1799*

SHE DWELT AMONG UNTRODDEN WAYS. **2. Dove**: a small stream in central England, which takes its rise on the border of the counties of Stafford and Derby.

## THREE YEARS SHE GREW IN SUN AND SHOWER

Three years she grew in sun and shower,
Then Nature said, "A lovelier flower
On earth was never sown;
This child I to myself will take;
She shall be mine, and I will make
A lady of my own.

"Myself will to my darling be
Both law and impulse; and with me
The girl, in rock and plain,
In earth and heaven, in glade and bower,
Shall feel an overseeing power
To kindle or restrain.

"She shall be sportive as the fawn
That wild with glee across the lawn,
Or up the mountain springs;
And hers shall be the breathing balm,
And hers the silence and the calm
Of mute insensate things.

"The floating clouds their state shall lend
To her; for her the willow bend;
Nor shall she fail to see
Even in the motions of the storm
Grace that shall mold the maiden's form
By silent sympathy.

"The stars of midnight shall be dear
To her; and she shall lean her ear
In many a secret place
Where rivulets dance their wayward round,
And beauty born of murmuring sound
Shall pass into her face.

"And vital feelings of delight
Shall rear her form to stately height,
Her virgin bosom swell;
Such thoughts to Lucy I will give

While she and I together live
Here in this happy dell."

Thus Nature spake — the work was done —
How soon my Lucy's race was run!
She died, and left to me
This heath, this calm, and quiet scene;
The memory of what has been,
And nevermore will be.

*1799*

## A SLUMBER DID MY SPIRIT SEAL

A slumber did my spirit seal;
I had no human fears;
She seemed a thing that could not feel
The touch of earthly years.

No motion has she now, no force;
She neither hears nor sees;
Rolled round in earth's diurnal course,
With rocks, and stones, and trees.

*1799*

## A POET'S EPITAPH

Art thou a statist in the van
Of public conflicts trained and bred?
First learn to love one living man;
*Then* may'st thou think upon the dead.

A lawyer art thou? — draw not nigh!
Go, carry to some fitter place
The keenness of that practiced eye,
The hardness of that sallow face.

Art thou a man of purple cheer?
A rosy man, right plump to see?
Approach; yet, doctor, not too near,
This grave no cushion is for thee.

Or art thou one of gallant pride,
A soldier and no man of chaff?
Welcome! — but lay thy sword aside,
And lean upon a peasant's staff.

Physician art thou? one, all eyes,
Philosopher! a fingering slave,
One that would peep and botanize
Upon his mother's grave?

Wrapped closely in thy sensual fleece,
O turn aside, and take, I pray,
That he below may rest in peace,
Thy ever-dwindling soul, away!

A moralist perchance appears;
Led, Heaven knowns how! to this poor sod;
And he has neither eyes nor ears;
Himself his world, and his own god;

One to whose smooth-rubbed soul can cling
Nor form, nor feeling, great or small;
A reasoning, self-sufficing thing,
An intellectual all-in-all!

Shut close the door; press down the latch;
Sleep in thy intellectual crust;
Nor lose ten tickings of thy watch
Near this unprofitable dust.

But who is he, with modest looks,
And clad in homely russet brown?
He murmurs near the running brooks
A music sweeter than their own.

He is retired as noontide dew,
Or fountain in a noonday grove;
And you must love him, ere to you
He will seem worthy of your love.

The outward shows of sky and earth,
Of hill and valley, he has viewed;
And impulses of deeper birth
Have come to him in solitude.

In common things that round us lie
Some random truths he can impart —
The harvest of a quiet eye
That broods and sleeps on his own heart.

But he is weak; both man and boy,
Hath been an idler in the land;
Contented if he might enjoy
The things which others understand.

— Come hither in thy hour of strength;
Come, weak as is a breaking wave!
Here stretch thy body at full length;
Or build thy house upon this grave.

*1799*

## MATTHEW

" In the School of —— is a tablet, on which are inscribed, in gilt letters, the names of the several persons who have been schoolmasters there since the foundation of the school, with the time at which they entered upon

**A SLUMBER. 7. diurnal:** daily. **A POET'S EPITAPH. 1. statist:** Until 1837 this word was "statesman." **11–12. doctor . . . cushion:** a doctor of divinity, accustomed to kneel on a cushion when at prayer. **14. no . . . chaff:** one who speaks or tolerates no foolishness.

and quitted their office. Opposite to one of those names the author wrote the following lines.

Such a tablet as is here spoken of continued to be preserved in Hawkshead School, though the inscriptions were not brought down to our time. This and other poems connected with Matthew would not gain by a literal detail of facts. Like the Wanderer in *The Excursion,* this schoolmaster was made up of several both of his class and men of other occupations. I do not ask pardon for what there is of untruth in such verses, considered strictly as matters of fact. It is enough if, being true and consistent in spirit, they move and teach in a manner not unworthy of a poet's calling" [W].

See also "Expostulation and Reply," l. 15n.

If Nature, for a favorite child,
In thee hath tempered so her clay,
That every hour thy heart runs wild,
Yet never once doth go astray,

Read o'er these lines; and then review
This tablet, that thus humbly rears
In such diversity of hue
Its history of two hundred years.

When through this little wreck of fame,
Cipher and syllable! thine eye
Has traveled down to Matthew's name,
Pause with no common sympathy.

And, if a sleeping tear should wake,
Then be it neither checked nor stayed;
For Matthew a request I make
Which for himself he had not made.

Poor Matthew, all his frolics o'er,
Is silent as a standing pool;
Far from the chimney's merry roar,
And murmur of the village school.

The sighs which Matthew heaved were sighs
Of one tired out with fun and madness;
The tears which came to Matthew's eyes
Were tears of light, the dew of gladness.

Yet, sometimes, when the secret cup
Of still and serious thought went round,
It seemed as if he drank it up—
He felt with spirit so profound.

Thou soul of God's best earthly mold!
Thou happy soul! and can it be
That these two words of glittering gold
Are all that must remain of thee?

*1799*

## THE TWO APRIL MORNINGS

We walked along, while bright and red
Uprose the morning sun;
And Matthew stopped, he looked, and said,
"The will of God be done!"

A village schoolmaster was he,
With hair of glittering gray;
As blithe a man as you could see
On a spring holiday.

And on that morning, through the grass,
And by the steaming rills,
We traveled merrily, to pass
A day among the hills.

"Our work," said I, "was well begun,
Then, from thy breast what thought,
Beneath so beautiful a sun,
So sad a sigh has brought?"

A second time did Matthew stop;
And fixing still his eye
Upon the eastern mountaintop,
To me he made reply:

"Yon cloud with that long purple cleft
Brings fresh into my mind
A day like this which I have left
Full thirty years behind.

"And just above yon slope of corn
Such colors, and no other,
Were in the sky, that April morn,
Of this the very brother.

"With rod and line I sued the sport
Which that sweet season gave,
And, to the churchyard come, stopped short
Beside my daughter's grave.

"Nine summers had she scarcely seen,
The pride of all the vale;
And then she sang;—she would have been
A very nightingale.

"Six feet in earth my Emma lay;
And yet I loved her more,
For so it seemed, than till that day
I e'er had loved before.

"And, turning from her grave, I met,
Beside the churchyard yew,

TWO APRIL MORNINGS. 29. sued: pursued.

A blooming girl, whose hair was wet
With points of morning dew.

" A basket on her head she bare;
Her brow was smooth and white;
To see a child so very fair,
It was a pure delight!

" No fountain from its rocky cave
E'er tripped with foot so free;
She seemed as happy as a wave
That dances on the sea.

" There came from me a sigh of pain
Which I could ill confine;
I looked at her, and looked again,
And did not wish her mine! "

Matthew is in his grave, yet now,
Methinks, I see him stand,
As at that moment, with a bough
Of wilding in his hand.

*1799*

## THE FOUNTAIN

### *A Conversation*

We talked with open heart, and tongue
Affectionate and true,
A pair of friends, though I was young,
And Matthew seventy-two.

We lay beneath a spreading oak,
Beside a mossy seat;
And from the turf a fountain broke,
And gurgled at our feet.

" Now, Matthew! " said I, " let us match
This water's pleasant tune
With some old Border song, or catch
That suits a summer's noon;

" Or of the church clock and the chimes
Sing here beneath the shade,
That half-mad thing of witty rhymes
Which you last April made! "

In silence Matthew lay, and eyed
The spring beneath the tree;
And thus the dear old man replied,
The gray-haired man of glee:

" No check, no stay, this streamlet fears;
How merrily it goes!
'Twill murmur on a thousand years,
And flow as now it flows.

" And here, on this delightful day,
I cannot choose but think
How oft, a vigorous man, I lay
Beside this fountain's brink.

" My eyes are dim with childish tears,
My heart is idly stirred,
For the same sound is in my ears
Which in those days I heard.

" Thus fares it still in our decay;
And yet the wiser mind
Mourns less for what age takes away
Than what it leaves behind.

" The blackbird amid leafy trees,
The lark above the hill,
Let loose their carols when they please,
Are quiet when they will.

" With Nature never do *they* wage
A foolish strife; they see
A happy youth, and their old age
Is beautiful and free;

" But we are pressed by heavy laws;
And often, glad no more,
We wear a face of joy, because
We have been glad of yore.

" If there be one who need bemoan
His kindred laid in earth,
The household hearts that were his own,
It is the man of mirth.

" My days, my friend, are almost gone,
My life has been approved,
And many love me; but by none
Am I enough beloved."

" Now both himself and me he wrongs,
The man who thus complains;
I live and sing my idle songs
Upon these happy plains;

" And, Matthew, for thy children dead
I'll be a son to thee! "
At this he grasped my hand, and said,
" Alas! that cannot be."

We rose up from the fountainside;
And down the smooth descent
Of the green sheep track did we glide;
And through the wood we went;

**60. wilding:** any wild plant; here, probably an apple. **THE FOUNTAIN. 11. catch:** a musical round of humorous effect.

And, ere we came to Leonard's rock,
He sang those witty rhymes
About the crazy old church clock,
And the bewildered chimes.

*1799*

## ELLEN IRWIN

### *or, The Braes of Kirtle*

Fair Ellen Irwin, when she sate
Upon the braes of Kirtle,
Was lovely as a Grecian maid
Adorned with wreaths of myrtle;
Young Adam Bruce beside her lay,
And there did they beguile the day
With love and gentle speeches,
Beneath the budding beeches.

From many knights and many squires
The Bruce had been selected;
And Gordon, fairest of them all,
By Ellen was rejected.
Sad tidings to that noble youth!
For it may be proclaimed with truth,
If Bruce hath loved sincerely,
That Gordon loves as dearly.

But what are Gordon's form and face,
His shattered hopes and crosses,
To them, 'mid Kirtle's pleasant braes,
Reclined on flowers and mosses?
Alas that ever he was born!
The Gordon, couched behind a thorn,
Sees them and their caressing;
Beholds them blest and blessing.

Proud Gordon, maddened by the thoughts
That through his brain are traveling,
Rushed forth, and at the heart of Bruce
He launched a deadly javelin!
Fair Ellen saw it as it came,
And, starting up to meet the same,
Did with her body cover
The youth, her chosen lover.

And, falling into Bruce's arms,
Thus died the beauteous Ellen,
Thus, from the heart of her true love,
The mortal spear repelling.
And Bruce, as soon as he had slain
The Gordon, sailed away to Spain;
And fought with rage incessant
Against the Moorish crescent.

But many days, and many months,
And many years ensuing,
This wretched knight did vainly seek
The death that he was wooing.
So, coming his last help to crave,
Heartbroken, upon Ellen's grave
His body he extended,
And there his sorrow ended.

Now ye, who willingly have heard
The tale I have been telling,
May in Kirkconnel churchyard view
The grave of lovely Ellen:
By Ellen's side the Bruce is laid;
And, for the stone upon his head,
May no rude hand deface it,
And its forlorn *Hic jacet!*

*1800*

## MICHAEL

### *A Pastoral Poem*

"Written at Town End, Grasmere. . . . The sheep-fold, on which so much of the poem turns, remains, or rather the ruins of it. The character and circumstances of Luke were taken from a family to whom had belonged, many years before, the house we lived in at Town End, along with some fields and woodlands on the eastern shore of Grasmere. The name of the Evening Star was not in fact given to this house, but to another on the same side of the valley, more to the north" [W].

If from the public way you turn your steps
Up the tumultuous brook of Greenhead Ghyll,
You will suppose that with an upright path
Your feet must struggle; in such bold ascent
The pastoral mountains front you, face to face.
But, courage! for around the boisterous brook
The mountains have all opened out themselves,
And made a hidden valley of their own.
No habitation can be seen; but they
Who journey thither find themselves alone
With a few sheep, with rocks and stones, and kites
That overhead are sailing in the sky.
It is in truth an utter solitude;
Nor should I have made mention of this dell
But for one object which you might pass by,
Might see and notice not. Beside the brook
Appears a straggling heap of unhewn stones!
And to that simple object appertains
A story — unenriched with strange events,
Yet not unfit, I deem, for the fireside,
Or for the summer shade. It was the first
Of those domestic tales that spake to me

MICHAEL. 2. **Greenhead Ghyll**: a steep and narrow valley less than a mile from Dove Cottage.

Of shepherds, dwellers in the valleys, men
Whom I already loved; not verily
For their own sakes, but for the fields and hills
Where was their occupation and abode.
And hence this tale, while I was yet a boy
Careless of books, yet having felt the power
Of Nature, by the gentle agency
Of natural objects, led me on to feel
For passions that were not my own, and think
(At random and imperfectly indeed)
On man, the heart of man, and human life.
Therefore, although it be a history
Homely and rude, I will relate the same
For the delight of a few natural hearts;
And, with yet fonder feeling, for the sake
Of youthful poets, who among these hills
Will be my second self when I am gone.

Upon the forest side in Grasmere Vale
There dwelt a shepherd, Michael was his name;
An old man, stout of heart, and strong of limb.
His bodily frame had been from youth to age
Of an unusual strength; his mind was keen,
Intense, and frugal, apt for all affairs,
And in his shepherd's calling he was prompt
And watchful more than ordinary men.
Hence had he learned the meaning of all winds,
Of blasts of every tone; and, oftentimes,
When others heeded not, he heard the south
Make subterraneous music, like the noise
Of bagpipers on distant Highland hills.
The shepherd, at such warning, of his flock
Bethought him, and he to himself would say,
"The winds are now devising work for me!"
And, truly, at all times, the storm, that drives
The traveler to a shelter, summoned him
Up to the mountains; he had been alone
Amid the heart of many thousand mists,
That came to him, and left him, on the heights.
So lived he till his eightieth year was past.
And grossly that man errs, who should suppose
That the green valleys, and the streams and rocks,
Were things indifferent to the shepherd's thoughts.
Fields, where with cheerful spirits he had breathed
The common air; hills, which with vigorous step
He had so often climbed; which had impressed
So many incidents upon his mind
Of hardship, skill or courage, joy or fear;
Which, like a book, preserved the memory
Of the dumb animals, whom he had saved,
Had fed or sheltered, linking to such acts
The certainty of honorable gain;
Those fields, those hills—what could they less? had laid
Strong hold on his affections, were to him
A pleasurable feeling of blind love,
The pleasure which there is in life itself.

His days had not been passed in singleness.
His helpmate was a comely matron, old—
Though younger than himself full twenty years.
She was a woman of a stirring life,
Whose heart was in her house; two wheels she had
Of antique form: this large, for spinning wool;
That small, for flax; and if one wheel had rest
It was because the other was at work.
The pair had but one inmate in their house,
An only child, who had been born to them
When Michael, telling o'er his years, began
To deem that he was old—in shepherd's phrase,
With one foot in the grave. This only son,
With two brave sheep dogs tried in many a storm,
The one of an inestimable worth,
Made all their household. I may truly say,
That they were as a proverb in the vale
For endless industry. When day was gone,
And from their occupations out of doors
The son and father were come home, even then,
Their labor did not cease; unless when all
Turned to the cleanly supper board, and there,
Each with a mess of pottage and skimmed milk,
Sat round the basket piled with oaten cakes,
And their plain homemade cheese. Yet when the meal
Was ended, Luke (for so the son was named)
And his old father both betook themselves
To such convenient work as might employ
Their hands by the fireside; perhaps to card
Wool for the housewife's spindle, or repair
Some injury done to sickle, flail, or scythe,
Or other implement of house or field.

Down from the ceiling, by the chimney's edge,
That in our ancient uncouth country style
With huge and black projection overbrowed
Large space beneath, as duly as the light
Of day grew dim the housewife hung a lamp;
An aged utensil, which had performed
Service beyond all others of its kind.
Early at evening did it burn—and late,
Surviving comrade of uncounted hours,
Which, going by from year to year, had found,
And left, the couple neither gay perhaps
Nor cheerful, yet with objects and with hopes,
Living a life of eager industry.
And now, when Luke had reached his eighteenth year,
There by the light of this old lamp they sat,
Father and son, while far into the night
The housewife plied her own peculiar work,
Making the cottage through the silent hours
Murmur as with the sound of summer flies.
This light was famous in its neighborhood,
And was a public symbol of the life
That thrifty pair had lived. For, as it chanced,

Their cottage on a plot of rising ground
Stood single, with large prospect, north and south,
High into Easedale, up to Dunmail Raise,
And westward to the village near the lake;
And from this constant light, so regular
And so far seen, the house itself, by all
Who dwelt within the limits of the vale,
Both old and young, was named the Evening Star.

Thus living on through such a length of years,
The shepherd, if he loved himself, must needs
Have loved his helpmate; but to Michael's heart
This son of his old age was yet more dear —
Less from instinctive tenderness, the same
Fond spirit that blindly works in the blood of all —
Than that a child, more than all other gifts
That earth can offer to declining man,
Brings hope with it, and forward-looking thoughts,
And stirrings of inquietude, when they
By tendency of nature needs must fail.
Exceeding was the love he bare to him,
His heart and his heart's joy! For oftentimes
Old Michael, while he was a babe in arms,
Had done him female service, not alone
For pastime and delight, as is the use
Of fathers, but with patient mind enforced
To acts of tenderness; and he had rocked
His cradle, as with a woman's gentle hand.

And, in a later time, ere yet the boy
Had put on boy's attire, did Michael love,
Albeit of a stern unbending mind,
To have the young one in his sight, when he
Wrought in the field, or on his shepherd's stool
Sat with a fettered sheep before him stretched
Under the large old oak, that near his door
Stood single, and, from matchless depth of shade,
Chosen for the shearer's covert from the sun,
Thence in our rustic dialect was called
The Clipping Tree, a name which yet it bears.
There, while they two were sitting in the shade,
With others round them, earnest all and blithe,
Would Michael exercise his heart with looks
Of fond correction and reproof bestowed
Upon the child, if he disturbed the sheep
By catching at their legs, or with his shouts
Scared them, while they lay still beneath the shears.

And when by Heaven's good grace the boy grew up
A healthy lad, and carried in his cheek
Two steady roses that were five years old;
Then Michael from a winter coppice cut
With his own hand a sapling, which he hooped
With iron, making it throughout in all
Due requisites a perfect shepherd's staff,
And gave it to the boy; wherewith equipped
He as a watchman oftentimes was placed
At gate or gap, to stem or turn the flock;
And, to his office prematurely called,
There stood the urchin, as you will divine,
Something between a hindrance and a help;
And for this cause not always, I believe,
Receiving from his father hire of praise;
Though nought was left undone which staff, or voice,
Or looks, or threatening gestures, could perform.

But soon as Luke, full ten years old, could stand
Against the mountain blasts; and to the heights,
Not fearing toil, nor length of weary ways,
He with his father daily went, and they
Were as companions, why should I relate
That objects which the shepherd loved before
Were dearer now? that from the boy there came
Feelings and emanations — things which were
Light to the sun and music to the wind;
And that the old man's heart seemed born again?

Thus in his father's sight the boy grew up:
And now, when he had reached his eighteenth year,
He was his comfort and his daily hope.

While in this sort the simple household lived
From day to day, to Michael's ear there came
Distressful tidings. Long before the time
Of which I speak, the shepherd had been bound
In surety for his brother's son, a man
Of an industrious life, and ample means;
But unforeseen misfortunes suddenly
Had pressed upon him; and old Michael now
Was summoned to discharge the forfeiture,
A grievous penalty, but little less
Than half his substance. This unlooked-for claim,
At the first hearing, for a moment took
More hope out of his life than he supposed
That any old man ever could have lost.
As soon as he had armed himself with strength
To look his trouble in the face, it seemed
The shepherd's sole resource to sell at once
A portion of his patrimonial fields.
Such was his first resolve; he thought again,
And his heart failed him. "Isabel," said he,
Two evenings after he had heard the news,
"I have been toiling more than seventy years,
And in the open sunshine of God's love
Have we all lived; yet if these fields of ours
Should pass into a stranger's hand, I think
That I could not lie quiet in my grave.

**134. Easedale:** a hilly region northwest of Grasmere. **Dunmail Raise:** a pass in the mountains about three miles north of Grasmere on the road to Keswick.

Our lot is a hard lot; the sun himself
Has scarcely been more diligent than I;
And I have lived to be a fool at last
To my own family. An evil man
That was, and made an evil choice, if he
Were false to us; and if he were not false,
There are ten thousand to whom loss like this
Had been no sorrow. I forgive him — but
'Twere better to be dumb than to talk thus.

"When I began, my purpose was to speak
Of remedies and of a cheerful hope.
Our Luke shall leave us, Isabel; the land
Shall not go from us, and it shall be free;
He shall possess it, free as is the wind
That passes over it. We have, thou know'st,
Another kinsman — he will be our friend
In this distress. He is a prosperous man,
Thriving in trade — and Luke to him shall go,
And with his kinsman's help and his own thrift
He quickly will repair this loss, and then
He may return to us. If here he stay,
What can be done? Where everyone is poor,
What can be gained?"
At this the old man paused,
And Isabel sat silent, for her mind
Was busy, looking back into past times.
There's Richard Bateman, thought she to herself,
He was a parish boy — at the church door
They made a gathering for him, shillings, pence,
And halfpennies, wherewith the neighbors bought
A basket, which they filled with pedlar's wares;
And, with this basket on his arm, the lad
Went up to London, found a master there,
Who, out of many, chose the trusty boy
To go and overlook his merchandise
Beyond the seas; where he grew wondrous rich,
And left estates and moneys to the poor.
And, at his birthplace, built a chapel, floored
With marble which he sent from foreign lands.
These thoughts, and many others of like sort,
Passed quickly through the mind of Isabel,
And her face brightened. The old man was glad,
And thus resumed: "Well, Isabel! this scheme
These two days, has been meat and drink to me.
Far more than we have lost is left us yet.
We have enough — I wish indeed that I
Were younger — but this hope is a good hope.
Make ready Luke's best garments, of the best
Buy for him more, and let us send him forth
Tomorrow, or the next day, or tonight;
If he *could* go, the boy should go tonight."

Here Michael ceased, and to the fields went forth
With a light heart. The housewife for five days
Was restless morn and night, and all day long
Wrought on with her best fingers to prepare
Things needful for the journey of her son.
But Isabel was glad when Sunday came
To stop her in her work; for, when she lay
By Michael's side, she through the last two nights
Heard him, how he was troubled in his sleep;
And when they rose at morning she could see
That all his hopes were gone. That day at noon
She said to Luke, while they two by themselves
Were sitting at the door, "Thou must not go;
We have no other child but thee to lose —
None to remember — do not go away,
For if thou leave thy father he will die."
The youth made answer with a jocund voice;
And Isabel, when she had told her fears,
Recovered heart. That evening her best fare
Did she bring forth, and all together sat
Like happy people round a Christmas fire.
With daylight Isabel resumed her work;
And all the ensuing week the house appeared
As cheerful as a grove in spring; at length
The expected letter from their kinsman came,
With kind assurances that he would do
His utmost for the welfare of the boy;
To which, requests were added, that forthwith
He might be sent to him. Ten times or more
The letter was read over; Isabel
Went forth to show it to the neighbors round;
Nor was there at that time on English land
A prouder heart than Luke's. When Isabel
Had to her house returned, the old man said,
"He shall depart tomorrow." To this word
The housewife answered, talking much of things
Which, if at such short notice he should go,
Would surely be forgotten. But at length
She gave consent, and Michael was at ease.

Near the tumultuous brook of Greenhead Ghyll,
In that deep valley, Michael had designed
To build a sheepfold; and, before he heard
The tidings of his melancholy loss,
For this same purpose he had gathered up
A heap of stones, which by the streamlet's edge
Lay thrown together, ready for the work.
With Luke that evening thitherward he walked;
And soon as they had reached the place he stopped,
And thus the old man spake to him: "My son,

**258–70. Bateman . . . lands:** "The story alluded to here is well known in the country. The chapel is called Ings Chapel and is on the road from Kendal to Ambleside" [W]. Robert Bateman, a merchant of Leghorn and a native of Ings (about ten miles southeast of Grasmere), ordered the chapel rebuilt in 1743.

**324–28. sheepfold . . . work:** "It may be proper to inform some readers that a sheepfold in these mountains is an unroofed building of stone walls, with different divisions. It is generally placed by the side of a brook, for the convenience of washing the sheep; but it is also useful as a shelter for them, and as a place to drive them into, to enable the shepherds conveniently to single out one or more for any particular purpose" [W].

Tomorrow thou wilt leave me; with full heart
I look upon thee, for thou art the same
That wert a promise to me ere thy birth,
And all thy life hast been my daily joy.
I will relate to thee some little part
Of our two histories; 'twill do thee good
When thou art from me, even if I should touch
On things thou canst not know of. After thou
First cam'st into the world — as oft befalls
To newborn infants — thou didst sleep away
Two days, and blessings from thy father's tongue
Then fell upon thee. Day by day passed on,
And still I loved thee with increasing love.
Never to living ear came sweeter sounds
Than when I heard thee by our own fireside
First uttering, without words, a natural tune;
While thou, a feeding babe, didst in thy joy
Sing at thy mother's breast. Month followed month,
And in the open fields my life was passed
And on the mountains; else I think that thou
Hadst been brought up upon thy father's knees.
But we were playmates, Luke; among these hills,
As well thou knowest, in us the old and young
Have played together, nor with me didst thou
Lack any pleasure which a boy can know."
Luke had a manly heart; but at these words
He sobbed aloud. The old man grasped his hand,
And said, "Nay, do not take it so — I see
That these are things of which I need not speak.
Even to the utmost I have been to thee
A kind and a good father, and herein
I but repay a gift which I myself
Received at others' hands; for, though now old
Beyond the common life of man, I still
Remember them who loved me in my youth.
Both of them sleep together; here they lived,
As all their forefathers had done; and when
At length their time was come, they were not loath
To give their bodies to the family mold.
I wished that thou shouldst live the life they lived;
But, 'tis a long time to look back, my son,
And see so little gain from threescore years.
These fields were burthened when they came to me;
Till I was forty years of age, not more
Than half of my inheritance was mine.
I toiled and toiled; God blessed me in my work,
And till these three weeks past the land was free.
It looks as if it never could endure
Another master. Heaven forgive me, Luke,
If I judge ill for thee, but it seems good
That thou shouldst go."
At this the old man paused;
Then, pointing to the stones near which they stood,
Thus, after a short silence, he resumed:
"This was a work for us, and now, my son,
It is a work for me. But, lay one stone —
Here, lay it for me, Luke, with thine own hands.
Nay, boy, be of good hope — we both may live
To see a better day. At eighty-four
I still am strong and hale; do thou thy part;
I will do mine. I will begin again
With many tasks that were resigned to thee:
Up to the heights, and in among the storms,
Will I without thee go again, and do
All works which I was wont to do alone,
Before I knew thy face. Heaven bless thee, boy!
Thy heart these two weeks has been beating fast
With many hopes; it should be so — yes — yes —
I knew that thou couldst never have a wish
To leave me, Luke; thou hast been bound to me
Only by links of love; when thou art gone,
What will be left to us! But I forget
My purposes. Lay now the cornerstone,
As I requested; and hereafter, Luke,
When thou art gone away, should evil men
Be thy companions, think of me, my son,
And of this moment; hither turn thy thoughts,
And God will strengthen thee; amid all fear
And all temptation, Luke, I pray that thou
Mayst bear in mind the life thy fathers lived,
Who, being innocent, did for that cause
Bestir them in good deeds. Now, fare thee well —
When thou return'st, thou in this place wilt see
A work which is not here: a covenant
'Twill be between us; but, whatever fate
Befall thee, I shall love thee to the last,
And bear thy memory with me to the grave."

The shepherd ended here; and Luke stooped down,
And, as his father had requested, laid
The first stone of the sheepfold. At the sight
The old man's grief broke from him; to his heart
He pressed his son, he kissed him and wept;
And to the house together they returned.
Hushed was that house in peace, or seeming peace,
Ere the night fell; with morrow's dawn the boy
Began his journey, and when he had reached
The public way, he put on a bold face;
And all the neighbors, as he passed their doors,
Came forth with wishes and with farewell prayers,
That followed him till he was out of sight.

A good report did from their kinsman come,
Of Luke and his well doing; and the boy
Wrote loving letters, full of wondrous news,
Which, as the housewife phrased it, were throughout
"The prettiest letters that were ever seen."
Both parents read them with rejoicing hearts.
So, many months passed on; and once again
The shepherd went about his daily work
With confident and cheerful thoughts; and now
Sometimes when he could find a leisure hour

He to that valley took his way, and there
Wrought at the sheepfold. Meantime Luke began
To slacken in his duty; and, at length,
He in the dissolute city gave himself
To evil courses; ignominy and shame
Fell on him, so that he was driven at last
To seek a hiding place beyond the seas.

There is a comfort in the strength of love;
'Twill make a thing endurable, which else
Would overset the brain, or break the heart;
I have conversed with more than one who well
Remember the old man, and what he was
Years after he had heard this heavy news.
His bodily frame had been from youth to age
Of an unusual strength. Among the rocks
He went, and still looked up to sun and cloud,
And listened to the wind; and, as before,
Performed all kinds of labor for his sheep,
And for the land, his small inheritance.
And to that hollow dell from time to time
Did he repair, to build the fold of which
His flock had need. 'Tis not forgotten yet
The pity which was then in every heart
For the old man — and 'tis believed by all
That many and many a day he thither went,
And never lifted up a single stone.

There, by the sheepfold, sometimes was he seen
Sitting alone, or with his faithful dog,
Then old, beside him, lying at his feet.
The length of full seven years, from time to time,
He at the building of this sheepfold wrought,
And left the work unfinished when he died.
Three years, or little more, did Isabel
Survive her husband; at her death the estate
Was sold, and went into a stranger's hand.
The cottage which was named the Evening Star
Is gone — the plowshare has been through the ground
On which it stood; great changes have been wrought
In all the neighborhood; yet the oak is left
That grew beside their door; and the remains
Of the unfinished sheepfold may be seen
Beside the boisterous brook of Greenhead Ghyll.

*1800*

## I TRAVELED AMONG UNKNOWN MEN

" Written in Germany " [W].

I traveled among unknown men,
In lands beyond the sea;
Nor, England! did I know till then
What love I bore to thee.

'Tis past, that melancholy dream!
Nor will I quit thy shore
A second time; for still I seem
To love thee more and more.

Among thy mountains did I feel
The joy of my desire;
And she I cherished turned her wheel
Beside an English fire.

Thy mornings showed, thy nights concealed
The bowers where Lucy played;
And thine too is the last green field
That Lucy's eyes surveyed.

*1801*

## TO THE CUCKOO

O blithe newcomer! I have heard,
I hear thee and rejoice.
O cuckoo! shall I call thee bird,
Or but a wandering voice?

While I am lying on the grass
Thy twofold shout I hear,
From hill to hill it seems to pass,
At once far off, and near.

Though babbling only to the vale,
Of sunshine and of flowers,
Thou bringest unto me a tale
Of visionary hours.

Thrice welcome, darling of the spring!
Even yet thou art to me
No bird, but an invisible thing,
A voice, a mystery;

The same whom in my schoolboy days
I listened to; that cry
Which made me look a thousand ways
In bush, and tree, and sky.

To seek thee did I often rove
Through woods and on the green;
And thou wert still a hope, a love;
Still longed for, never seen.

And I can listen to thee yet;
Can lie upon the plain
And listen, till I do beget
That golden time again.

**TO THE CUCKOO. In England the note of the first cuckoo, usually heard on St. George's Day (April 23), is regularly reported to the London *Times* as a sign that spring has come again.**

O blessed bird! the earth we pace
Again appears to be
An unsubstantial, faery place,
That is fit home for thee!

*1802*

## MY HEART LEAPS UP WHEN I BEHOLD

My heart leaps up when I behold
A rainbow in the sky;
So was it when my life began;
So is it now I am a man;
So be it when I shall grow old,
Or let me die!
The child is father of the man;
And I could wish my days to be
Bound each to each by natural piety.

*1802*

## RESOLUTION AND INDEPENDENCE

"Written at Town End, Grasmere. This old man I met a few hundred yards from my cottage; and the account of him is taken from his own mouth. I was in the state of feeling described in the beginning of the poem, while crossing over Barton Fell from Mr. Clarkson's, at the foot of Ullswater, towards Askham. The image of the hare I then observed on the ridge of the Fell" [W].

1

There was a roaring in the wind all night;
The rain came heavily and fell in floods;
But now the sun is rising calm and bright;
The birds are singing in the distant woods;
Over his own sweet voice the stock dove broods;
The jay makes answer as the magpie chatters;
And all the air is filled with pleasant noise of waters.

2

All things that love the sun are out of doors;
The sky rejoices in the morning's birth;
The grass is bright with raindrops; on the moors
The hare is running races in her mirth;
And with her feet she from the plashy earth
Raises a mist, that, glittering in the sun,
Runs with her all the way, wherever she doth run.

3

I was a traveler then upon the moor,
I saw the hare that raced about with joy;
I heard the woods and distant waters roar,
Or heard them not, as happy as a boy;
The pleasant season did my heart employ;
My old remembrances went from me wholly;
And all the ways of men, so vain and melancholy.

4

But, as it sometimes chanceth, from the might
Of joy in minds that can no further go,
As high as we have mounted in delight
In our dejection do we sink as low;
To me that morning did it happen so;
And fears and fancies thick upon me came;
Dim sadness — and blind thoughts, I knew not, nor could name.

5

I heard the skylark warbling in the sky,
And I bethought me of the playful hare:
Even such a happy child of earth am I;
Even as these blissful creatures do I fare;
Far from the world I walk, and from all care;
But there may come another day to me —
Solitude, pain of heart, distress, and poverty.

6

My whole life I have lived in pleasant thought,
As if life's business were a summer mood;
As if all needful things would come unsought
To genial faith, still rich in genial good;
But how can he expect that others should
Build for him, sow for him, and at his call
Love him, who for himself will take no heed at all?

7

I thought of Chatterton, the marvelous boy,
The sleepless soul that perished in his pride;
Of him who walked in glory and in joy
Following his plow, along the mountainside:
By our own spirits are we deified;
We poets in our youth begin in gladness,
But thereof come in the end despondency and madness.

8

Now, whether it were by peculiar grace,
A leading from above, a something given,
Yet it befell, that, in this lonely place,
When I with these untoward thoughts had striven,
Beside a pool bare to the eye of Heaven
I saw a man before me unawares:
The oldest man he seemed that ever wore gray hairs.

**RESOLUTION AND INDEPENDENCE. 43. Chatterton:** Thomas Chatterton (1752–70), a promising poet from Bristol who committed suicide at the age of seventeen by taking arsenic. **45. him:** Robert Burns (1759–96).

9

As a huge stone is sometimes seen to lie
Couched on the bald top of an eminence;
Wonder to all who do the same espy,
By what means it could thither come, and whence;
So that it seems a thing endued with sense;
Like a sea beast crawled forth, that on a shelf
Of rock or sand reposeth, there to sun itself;

10

Such seemed this man, not all alive nor dead,
Nor all asleep — in his extreme old age;
His body was bent double, feet and head
Coming together in life's pilgrimage;
As if some dire constraint of pain, or rage
Of sickness felt by him in times long past,
A more than human weight upon his frame had
 cast.

11

Himself he propped, limbs, body, and pale face,
Upon a long gray staff of shaven wood;
And, still as I drew near with gentle pace,
Upon the margin of that moorish flood
Motionless as a cloud the old man stood,
That heareth not the loud winds when they call
And moveth all together, if it move at all.

12

At length, himself unsettling, he the pond
Stirred with his staff, and fixedly did look
Upon the muddy water, which he conned,
As if he had been reading in a book;
And now a stranger's privilege I took,
And, drawing to his side, to him did say,
"This morning gives us promise of a glorious
 day."

13

A gentle answer did the old man make,
In courteous speech which forth he slowly drew;
And him with further words I thus bespake,
"What occupation do you there pursue?
This is a lonesome place for one like you."
Ere he replied, a flash of mild surprise
Broke from the sable orbs of his yet vivid eyes,

**57–77. As . . . all:** "In these images, the conferring, the abstracting, and the modifying powers of the Imagination, immediately and mediately acting, are all brought into conjunction. The stone is endowed with something of the power of life to approximate it to the sea beast; and the sea beast stripped of some of its vital qualities to assimilate it to the stone; which intermediate image is thus treated for the purpose of bringing the original image, that of the stone, to a nearer resemblance to the figure and condition of the aged man, who is divested of so much of the indications of life and motion as to bring him to the point where the two objects unite and coalesce in just such comparison. After what has been said, the image of the cloud need not be commented upon" [W., Preface to the Edition of 1815].

14

His words came feebly, from a feeble chest,
But each in solemn order followed each,
With something of a lofty utterance dressed —
Choice word and measured phrase, above the reach
Of ordinary men; a stately speech;
Such as grave livers do in Scotland use,
Religious men, who give to God and man their
 dues.

15

He told, that to these waters he had come
To gather leeches, being old and poor —
Employment hazardous and wearisome!
And he had many hardships to endure:
From pond to pond he roamed, from moor to
 moor;
Housing, with God's good help, by choice or
 chance,
And in this way he gained an honest maintenance.

16

The old man still stood talking by my side;
But now his voice to me was like a stream
Scarce heard; nor word from word could I divide;
And the whole body of the man did seem
Like one whom I had met with in a dream;
Or like a man from some far region sent,
To give me human strength, by apt admonishment.

17

My former thoughts returned: the fear that kills;
And hope that is unwilling to be fed;
Cold, pain, and labor, and all fleshly ills;
And mighty poets in their misery dead.
Perplexed, and longing to be comforted,
My question eagerly did I renew,
"How is it that you live, and what is it you do?"

18

He with a smile did then his words repeat;
And said, that, gathering leeches, far and wide
He traveled, stirring thus above his feet
The waters of the pools where they abide.
"Once I could meet with them on every side,
But they have dwindled long by slow decay;
Yet still I persevere, and find them where I may."

19

While he was talking thus, the lonely place,
The old man's shape, and speech — all troubled
 me;
In my mind's eye I seemed to see him pace
About the weary moors continually,

**100. leeches:** aquatic, bloodsucking worms formerly much used for medical purposes.

Wandering about alone and silently.
While I these thoughts within myself pursued,
He, having made a pause, the same discourse re-
newed.

20

And soon with this he other matter blended,
Cheerfully uttered, with demeanor kind,
But stately in the main; and when he ended,
I could have laughed myself to scorn to find
In that decrepit man so firm a mind.
"God," said I, "be my help and stay secure;
I'll think of the leech gatherer on the lonely
moor!"

*1802*

## TO H. C.

*Six Years Old*

O thou! whose fancies from afar are brought;
Who of thy words dost make a mock apparel,
And fittest to unutterable thought
The breezelike motion and the self-born carol;
Thou faery voyager! that dost float
In such clear water, that thy boat
May rather seem
To brood on air than on an earthly stream;
Suspended in a stream as clear as sky,
Where earth and heaven do make one imagery;
O blessed vision! happy child!
Thou art so exquisitely wild,
I think of thee with many fears
For what may be thy lot in future years.
I thought of times when Pain might be thy guest,
Lord of thy house and hospitality;
And Grief, uneasy lover! never rest
But when she sat within the touch of thee.
O too industrious folly!
O vain and causeless melancholy!
Nature will either end thee quite,
Or, lengthening out thy season of delight,
Preserve for thee, by individual right,
A young lamb's heart among the full-grown flocks.
What hast thou to do with sorrow,
Or the injuries of tomorrow?
Thou art a dewdrop, which the morn brings forth,
Ill fitted to sustain unkindly shocks,
Or to be trailed along the soiling earth;
A gem that glitters while it lives,
And no forewarning gives;
But, at the touch of wrong, without a strife
Slips in a moment out of life.

*1802*

**139. stay:** support. TO H. C. **H.C.:** Hartley Coleridge, born September 19, 1796.

## I GRIEVED FOR BUONAPARTÉ

I grieved for Buonaparté, with a vain
And an unthinking grief! The tenderest mood
Of that man's mind—what can it be? what food
Fed his first hopes? what knowledge could *he*
gain?
'Tis not in battles that from youth we train
The governor who must be wise and good,
And temper with the sternness of the brain
Thoughts motherly, and meek as womanhood.
Wisdom doth live with children round her knees;
Books, leisure, perfect freedom, and the talk
Man holds with weekday man in the hourly walk
Of the mind's business: these are the degrees
By which true sway doth mount; this is the stalk
True power doth grow on; and her rights are these.

*1802*

## COMPOSED UPON WESTMINSTER BRIDGE

"Written on the roof of a coach, on my way to France" [W].

Earth has not anything to show more fair;
Dull would he be of soul who could pass by
A sight so touching in its majesty:
This city now doth, like a garment, wear
The beauty of the morning; silent, bare,
Ships, towers, domes, theaters, and temples lie
Open unto the fields, and to the sky;
All bright and glittering in the smokeless air.
Never did sun more beautifully steep
In his first splendor, valley, rock, or hill;
Ne'er saw I, never felt, a calm so deep!
The river glideth at his own sweet will;
Dear God! the very houses seem asleep;
And all that mighty heart is lying still!

*1802*

## ON THE EXTINCTION OF THE VENETIAN REPUBLIC

Once did she hold the gorgeous east in fee;
And was the safeguard of the west; the worth
Of Venice did not fall below her birth,
Venice, the eldest child of Liberty.

THE VENETIAN REPUBLIC. **1–2. Once . . . west:** During the Middle Ages and the early Renaissance Venice was the leading commercial and naval power in the Mediterranean. **4. Venice . . . Liberty:** Along with England and Switzerland, Venice symbolized for Wordsworth the incessant struggle of liberty against tyrannical power.

She was a maiden city, bright and free;
No guile seduced, no force could violate;
And, when she took unto herself a mate,
She must espouse the everlasting sea.
And what if she had seen those glories fade,
Those titles vanish, and that strength decay;
Yet shall some tribute of regret be paid
When her long life hath reached its final day:
Men are we, and must grieve when even the shade
Of that which once was great, is passed away.

*1802*

## COMPOSED BY THE SEASIDE, NEAR CALAIS, AUGUST, 1802

Fair star of evening, splendor of the west,
Star of my country!—on the horizon's brink
Thou hangest, stooping, as might seem, to sink
On England's bosom; yet well pleased to rest,
Meanwhile, and be to her a glorious crest
Conspicuous to the nations. Thou, I think,
Shouldst be my country's emblem; and shouldst wink,
Bright star! with laughter on her banners, dressed
In thy fresh beauty. There! that dusky spot
Beneath thee, that is England; there she lies.
Blessings be on you both! one hope, one lot,
One life, one glory!—I, with many a fear
For my dear country, many heartfelt sighs,
Among men who do not love her, linger here.

*1802*

## TO TOUSSAINT L'OUVERTURE

Toussaint, the most unhappy man of men!
Whether the whistling rustic tend his plow
Within thy hearing, or thy head be now
Pillowed in some deep dungeon's earless den—
O miserable chieftain! where and when
Wilt thou find patience? Yet die not; do thou
Wear rather in thy bonds a cheerful brow;
Though fallen thyself, never to rise again,
Live, and take comfort. Thou hast left behind
Powers that will work for thee: air, earth, and skies;
There's not a breathing of the common wind
That will forget thee; thou hast great allies;
Thy friends are exultations, agonies,
And love, and man's unconquerable mind.

*1802*

**8. She . . . sea:** In 1000 the Venetians defeated the Dalmatians in a naval battle. Thereafter each year on Ascension Day (the fortieth day after Easter) a ring was cast into the sea to signify the wedding of the Doge to the Adriatic, of which he was unmistakably master. See also Browning's "A Toccata of Galuppi's, ll. 5–6, p. 500, below. **11–14. Yet . . . away:** After a long and gradual decline in power Venice in 1797 fell to Napoleon, who divided her territory between France and Austria. TO TOUSSAINT L'OUVERTURE. **1. Toussaint:** a Negro revolutionist (b. 1743) who declared the independence of Haiti from Napoleon and France in 1801. Defeated by the French, Toussaint was thrown into prison at Fort de Joux, near Besançon, France, where he died on April 27, 1803, soon after Wordsworth wrote this sonnet.

## IT IS A BEAUTEOUS EVENING, CALM AND FREE

"This was composed on the beach near Calais, in the autumn of 1802" [W].

It is a beauteous evening, calm and free;
The holy time is quiet as a nun
Breathless with adoration; the broad sun
Is sinking down in its tranquillity;
The gentleness of heaven broods o'er the sea.
Listen! the mighty Being is awake,
And doth with his eternal motion make
A sound like thunder—everlastingly.
Dear child! dear girl! that walkest with me here,
If thou appear untouched by solemn thought,
Thy nature is not therefore less divine;
Thou liest in Abraham's bosom all the year;
And worship'st at the temple's inner shrine,
God being with thee when we know it not.

*1802*

## NEAR DOVER, SEPTEMBER, 1802

Inland, within a hollow vale, I stood,
And saw, while sea was calm and air was clear,
The coast of France—the coast of France how near!
Drawn almost into frightful neighborhood.
I shrunk; for verily the barrier flood
Was like a lake, or river bright and fair,
A span of waters; yet what power is there!
What mightiness for evil and for good!
Even so doth God protect us if we be
Virtuous and wise. Winds blow, and waters roll,
Strength to the brave, and power, and deity;
Yet in themselves are nothing! One decree
Spake laws to *them,* and said that by the soul
Only, the nations shall be great and free.

*1802*

IT IS A BEAUTEOUS EVENING. **9. Dear . . . girl!:** Caroline Wordsworth, born December, 1792, the natural daughter of Wordsworth and Annette Vallon. **12. Abraham's bosom:** the name given by some theologians to a place nearer Heaven than earth where the departed souls of the blessed prepare for their final ascent to God (see Luke 16:19–31).

## IN LONDON, SEPTEMBER, 1802

"This was written immediately after my return from France to London, when I could not but be struck, as here described, with the vanity and parade of our own country, especially in great towns and cities, as contrasted with the quiet and, I may say, the desolation, that the Revolution had produced in France. This must be borne in mind, or else the reader may think that in this and the succeeding sonnets I have exaggerated the mischief engendered and fostered among us by undisturbed wealth. It would not be easy to conceive with what a depth of feeling I entered into the struggle carried on by the Spaniards for their deliverance from the usurped power of the French. Many times have I gone from Allan Bank in Grasmere Vale, where we were then residing, to the top of the Raise Gap, as it is called, so late as two o'clock in the morning, to meet the carrier bringing the newspaper from Keswick" [W].

O friend! I know not which way I must look
For comfort, being, as I am, oppressed,
To think that now our life is only dressed
For show; mean handiwork of craftsman, cook,
Or groom! We must run glittering like a brook
In the open sunshine, or we are unblessed;
The wealthiest man among us is the best;
No grandeur now in Nature or in book
Delights us. Rapine, avarice, expense,
This is idolatry, and these we adore;
Plain living and high thinking are no more;
The homely beauty of the good old cause
Is gone; our peace, our fearful innocence,
And pure religion breathing household laws.

*1802*

## LONDON, 1802

Milton! thou shouldst be living at this hour;
England hath need of thee; she is a fen
Of stagnant waters: altar, sword, and pen,
Fireside, the heroic wealth of hall and bower,
Have forfeited their ancient English dower
Of inward happiness. We are selfish men;
Oh! raise us up, return to us again;
And give us manners, virtue, freedom, power.
Thy soul was like a star, and dwelt apart;
Thou hadst a voice whose sound was like the sea;
Pure as the naked heavens, majestic, free, 11
So didst thou travel on life's common way,
In cheerful godliness; and yet thy heart
The lowliest duties on herself did lay.

*1802*

## GREAT MEN HAVE BEEN AMONG US

Great men have been among us; hands that penned
And tongues that uttered wisdom — better none:
The later Sidney, Marvell, Harrington,
Young Vane, and others who called Milton friend.
These moralists could act and comprehend;
They knew how genuine glory was put on,
Taught us how rightfully a nation shone
In splendor; what strength was, that would not bend
But in magnanimous meekness. France, 'tis strange,
Hath brought forth no such souls as we had then.
Perpetual emptiness! unceasing change! 11
No single volume paramount, no code,
No master spirit, no determined road;
But equally a want of books and men!

*1802*

## IT IS NOT TO BE THOUGHT OF

It is not to be thought of that the flood
Of British freedom, which, to the open sea
Of the world's praise, from dark antiquity
Hath flowed, "with pomp of waters, unwithstood,"
Roused though it be full often to a mood
Which spurns the check of salutary bands,
That this most famous stream in bogs and sands
Should perish, and to evil and to good
Be lost forever. In our halls is hung
Armory of the invincible knights of old;
We must be free or die, who speak the tongue
That Shakespeare spake, the faith and morals hold
Which Milton held. In everything we are sprung
Of earth's first blood, have titles manifold.

*1802*

## ENGLAND! THE TIME IS COME WHEN THOU SHOULDST WEAN

England! the time is come when thou shouldst wean
Thy heart from its emasculating food;
The truth should now be better understood;
Old things have been unsettled; we have seen

GREAT MEN AMONG US. **3–4. Sidney . . . Vane:** seventeenth-century English political heroes (Marvell was also a poet) who helped establish the Puritan Commonwealth and championed the republican principles which Wordsworth endorsed more than a century later. IT IS NOT TO BE THOUGHT OF. **4. "with . . . unwithstood":** quoted from *Civil Wars*, I.7, by Samuel Daniel (1562–1619), an Elizabethan poet and historian whom Wordsworth admired.

Fair seedtime, better harvest might have been
But for thy trespasses; and, at this day,
If for Greece, Egypt, India, Africa,
Aught good were destined, thou wouldst step between.
England! all nations in this charge agree;
But worse, more ignorant in love and hate,
Far — far more abject, is thine enemy;
Therefore the wise pray for thee, though the freight
Of thy offenses be a heavy weight;
Oh grief that earth's best hopes rest all with thee!

*1803*

## SHE WAS A PHANTOM OF DELIGHT

She was a phantom of delight
When first she gleamed upon my sight,
A lovely apparition, sent
To be a moment's ornament;
Her eyes as stars of twilight fair;
Like twilight's, too, her dusky hair;
But all things else about her drawn
From Maytime and the cheerful dawn;
A dancing shape, an image gay,
To haunt, to startle, and waylay.

I saw her upon nearer view,
A spirit, yet a woman too!
Her household motions light and free,
And steps of virgin liberty;
A countenance in which did meet
Sweet records, promises as sweet;
A creature not too bright or good
For human nature's daily food;
For transient sorrows, simple wiles,
Praise, blame, love, kisses, tears, and smiles.

And now I see with eye serene
The very pulse of the machine;
A being breathing thoughtful breath,
A traveler between life and death;
The reason firm, the temperate will,
Endurance, foresight, strength, and skill;
A perfect woman, nobly planned,
To warn, to comfort, and command;
And yet a spirit still, and bright
With something of angelic light.

*1804*

## I WANDERED LONELY AS A CLOUD

I wandered lonely as a cloud
That floats on high o'er vales and hills,
When all at once I saw a crowd,
A host, of golden daffodils,
Beside the lake, beneath the trees,
Fluttering and dancing in the breeze.

Continuous as the stars that shine
And twinkle on the milky way,
They stretched in never-ending line
Along the margin of a bay;
Ten thousand saw I at a glance,
Tossing their heads in sprightly dance.

The waves beside them danced, but they
Outdid the sparkling waves in glee;
A poet could not but be gay,
In such a jocund company;
I gazed — and gazed — but little thought
What wealth the show to me had brought:

For oft, when on my couch I lie
In vacant or in pensive mood,
They flash upon that inward eye
Which is the bliss of solitude;
And then my heart with pleasure fills,
And dances with the daffodils.

*1804*

## THE SOLITARY REAPER

Behold her, single in the field,
Yon solitary Highland lass!
Reaping and singing by herself;
Stop here, or gently pass!
Alone she cuts and binds the grain,

SHE WAS A PHANTOM OF DELIGHT. Wordsworth acknowledged that he wrote this poem about his wife, Mary Hutchinson Wordsworth.

I WANDERED LONELY. This poem was based on a personal experience first described by Dorothy Wordsworth in her *Journal* for April 15, 1802: "The wind seized our breath. The lake was rough. There was a boat by itself floating in the middle of the bay below Water Millock. We rested again in the Water Millock Lane. The hawthorns are black and green, the birches here and there greenish, but there is yet more of purple to be seen on the twigs. We got over into a field to avoid some cows — people working. A few primroses by the roadside — woodsorrel flower, the anemone, scentless violets, strawberries, and that starry, yellow flower which Mrs. C. calls pile wort. When we were in the woods beyond Gowbarrow Park we saw a few daffodils close to the waterside. We fancied that the lake had floated the seeds ashore, and that the little colony had so sprung up. But as we went along there were more and yet more; and at last, under the boughs of the trees, we saw that there was a long belt of them along the shore, about the breadth of a country turnpike road. I never saw daffodils so beautiful. They grew among the mossy stones about and about them; some rested their heads upon these stones as on a pillow for weariness; and the rest tossed and reeled and danced, and seemed as if they verily laughed with the wind, that blew upon them over the lake, they looked so gay, ever glancing, ever changing. This wind blew directly over the lake to them. There was here and there a little knot, and a few stragglers a few yards higher up; but they were so few as not to disturb the simplicity, unity, and life of that one busy highway. We rested again and again. The bays were stormy, and we heard the waves at different distances, and in the middle of the water. Rain came on — we were wet when we reached Luff's. . . ."

And sings a melancholy strain;
O listen! for the vale profound
Is overflowing with the sound.

No nightingale did ever chant
More welcome notes to weary bands
Of travelers in some shady haunt,
Among Arabian sands;
A voice so thrilling ne'er was heard
In springtime from the cuckoo bird,
Breaking the silence of the seas
Among the farthest Hebrides.

Will no one tell me what she sings? —
Perhaps the plaintive numbers flow
For old, unhappy, far-off things,
And battles long ago;
Or is it some more humble lay,
Familiar matter of today?
Some natural sorrow, loss, or pain,
That has been, and may be again?

Whate'er the theme, the maiden sang
As if her song could have no ending;
I saw her singing at her work,
And o'er the sickle bending;
I listened, motionless and still;
And, as I mounted up the hill
The music in my heart I bore,
Long after it was heard no more.

*1805*

## ODE TO DUTY

"This ode is on the model of Gray's 'Ode to Adversity,' which is copied from Horace's 'Ode to Fortune.' Many and many a time have I been twitted by my wife and sister for having forgotten this dedication of myself to the stern lawgiver. Transgressor indeed I have been, from hour to hour, from day to day: I would fain hope, however, not more flagrantly or in a worse way than most of my tuneful brethren. But these last words are in a wrong strain. We should be rigorous to ourselves and forbearing, if not indulgent, to others, and, if we make comparisons at all, it ought to be with those who have morally excelled us" [W].

---

*Jam non consilio bonus, sed more eò perductus, ut non tantum rectè facere possim, sed nisi rectè facere non possim.*

ODE TO DUTY. *Jam . . . possim:* This motto ("Guided not so much by counsel or design as by habit or custom, I am not only capable of doing good but incapable of doing evil") Wordsworth took from Seneca's *Moral Epistles*, CXX.x, and used for the first time in the edition of 1837.

Stern Daughter of the Voice of God!
O Duty! if that name thou love
Who art a light to guide, a rod
To check the erring, and reprove;
Thou, who art victory and law
When empty terrors overawe;
From vain temptations dost set free;
And calm'st the weary strife of frail humanity!

There are who ask not if thine eye
Be on them; who, in love and truth,
Where no misgiving is, rely
Upon the genial sense of youth;
Glad hearts! without reproach or blot
Who do thy work, and know it not;
Oh! if through confidence misplaced
They fail, thy saving arms, dread Power! around
them cast.

Serene will be our days and bright,
And happy will our nature be,
When love is an unerring light,
And joy its own security.
And they a blissful course may hold
Even now, who, not unwisely bold,
Live in the spirit of this creed;
Yet seek thy firm support, according to their need.

I, loving freedom, and untried,
No sport of every random gust,
Yet being to myself a guide,
Too blindly have reposed my trust;
And oft, when in my heart was heard
Thy timely mandate, I deferred
The task, in smoother walks to stray;
But thee I now would serve more strictly, if I may.

Through no disturbance of my soul,
Or strong compunction in me wrought,
I supplicate for thy control;
But in the quietness of thought:
Me this unchartered freedom tires;
I feel the weight of chance desires;
My hopes no more must change their name,
I long for a repose that ever is the same.

Stern Lawgiver! yet thou dost wear
The Godhead's most benignant grace;
Nor know we anything so fair
As is the smile upon thy face;
Flowers laugh before thee on their beds,
And fragrance in thy footing treads;
Thou dost preserve the stars from wrong;
And the most ancient heavens, through Thee, are
fresh and strong.

12. **genial:** cheerful, enlivening.

To humbler functions, awful Power!
I call thee; I myself commend
Unto thy guidance from this hour;
Oh, let my weakness have an end!
Give unto me, made lowly wise,
The spirit of self-sacrifice;
The confidence of reason give;
And in the light of truth thy bondman let me live!

*1804*

# ODE

## *Intimations of Immortality from Recollections of Early Childhood*

"This was composed during my residence at Town End, Grasmere. Two years at least passed between the writing of the four first stanzas and the remaining part. To the attentive and competent reader the whole sufficiently explains itself, but there may be no harm in adverting here to particular feelings or *experiences* of my own mind on which the structure of the poem partly rests. Nothing was more difficult for me in childhood than to admit the notion of death as a state applicable to my own being. I have said elsewhere

A simple child,
That lightly draws its breath,
And feels its life in every limb,
What should it know of death?

But it was not so much from feelings of animal vivacity that *my* difficulty came as from a sense of the indomitableness of the spirit within me. I used to brood over the stories of Enoch and Elijah, and almost to persuade myself that, whatever might become of others, I should be translated, in something of the same way, to Heaven. With a feeling congenial to this, I was often unable to think of external things as having external existence, and I communed with all that I saw as something not apart from, but inherent in, my own immaterial nature. Many times while going to school have I grasped at a wall or tree to recall myself from this abyss of idealism to the reality. At that time I was afraid of such processes. In later periods of life I have deplored, as we have all reason to do, a subjugation of an opposite character, and have rejoiced over the remembrances, as is expressed in the lines:

Obstinate questionings
Of sense and outward things,
Fallings from us, vanishings. . . .

To that dreamlike vividness and splendor which invest objects of sight in childhood, everyone, I believe, if he would look back, could bear testimony, and I need not dwell upon it here, but having in the poem regarded it as presumptive evidence of a prior state of existence, I think it right to protest against a conclusion, which has given pain to some good and pious persons, that I meant to inculcate such a belief. It is far too shadowy a notion to be recommended to faith, as more than an element in our instincts of immortality. But let us bear in mind that, though the idea is not advanced in revelation, there is nothing there to contradict it, and the fall of man presents an analogy in its favor. Accordingly, a pre-existent state has entered into the popular creeds of many nations, and, among all persons acquainted with classic literature, is known as an ingredient in Platonic philosophy. Archimedes said that he could move the world if he had a point whereon to rest his machine. Who has not felt the same aspirations as regards the world of his own mind? Having to wield some of its elements when I was impelled to write this poem on the "Immortality of the Soul," I took hold of the notion of pre-existence as having sufficient foundation in humanity for authorizing me to make for my purpose the best use of it I could as a poet" [W].

---

The child is father of the man;
And I could wish my days to be
Bound each to each by natural piety.

1

There was a time when meadow, grove, and
stream,
The earth, and every common sight,
To me did seem
Appareled in celestial light,
The glory and the freshness of a dream.
It is not now as it hath been of yore;
Turn wheresoe'er I may,
By night or day,
The things which I have seen I now can see no
more.

2

The rainbow comes and goes,
And lovely is the rose,
The moon doth with delight
Look round her when the heavens are bare;
Waters on a starry night
Are beautiful and fair;
The sunshine is a glorious birth;
But yet I know, where'er I go,
That there hath passed away a glory from the earth.

3

Now, while the birds thus sing a joyous song,
And while the young lambs bound
As to the tabor's sound,
To me alone there came a thought of grief,
A timely utterance gave that thought relief,
And I again am strong;
The cataracts blow their trumpets from the steep;
No more shall grief of mine the season wrong;
I hear the echoes through the mountains throng,
The winds come to me from the fields of sleep,
And all the earth is gay;
Land and sea
Give themselves up to jollity,

And with the heart of May
Doth every beast keep holiday;
Thou child of joy,
Shout round me, let me hear thy shouts, thou happy
Shepherd boy!

4

Ye blessed creatures, I have heard the call
Ye to each other make; I see
The heavens laugh with you in your jubilee;
My heart is at your festival,
My head hath its coronal,
The fullness of your bliss, I feel — I feel it all.
Oh evil day! if I were sullen
While Earth herself is adorning,
This sweet May morning,
And the children are culling
On every side,
In a thousand valleys far and wide,
Fresh flowers; while the sun shines warm,
And the babe leaps up on his mother's arm:
I hear, I hear, with joy I hear!
— But there's a tree, of many, one,
A single field which I have looked upon,
Both of them speak of something that is gone;
The pansy at my feet
Doth the same tale repeat:
Whither is fled the visionary gleam?
Where is it now, the glory and the dream?

5

Our birth is but a sleep and a forgetting;
The soul that rises with us, our life's star,
Hath had elsewhere its setting,
And cometh from afar;
Not in entire forgetfulness,
And not in utter nakedness,
But trailing clouds of glory do we come
From God, who is our home;
Heaven lies about us in our infancy!
Shades of the prison house begin to close
Upon the growing boy,
But he beholds the light, and whence it flows,
He sees it in his joy;
The youth, who daily farther from the east
Must travel, still is Nature's priest,
And by the vision splendid
Is on his way attended;
At length the man perceives it die away,
And fade into the light of common day.

6

Earth fills her lap with pleasures of her own;
Yearnings she hath in her own natural kind,
And, even with something of a mother's mind,
And no unworthy aim,
The homely nurse doth all she can
To make her foster child, her inmate man,
Forget the glories he hath known,
And that imperial palace whence he came.

7

Behold the child among his newborn blisses,
A six-years' darling of a pygmy size!
See, where 'mid work of his own hand he lies,
Fretted by sallies of his mother's kisses,
With light upon him from his father's eyes!
See, at his feet, some little plan or chart,
Some fragment from his dream of human life,
Shaped by himself with newly learnèd art;
A wedding or a festival,
A mourning or a funeral;
And this hath now his heart,
And unto this he frames his song;
Then will he fit his tongue
To dialogues of business, love, or strife;
But it will not be long
Ere this be thrown aside,
And with new joy and pride
The little actor cons another part,
Filling from time to time his "humorous stage"
With all the persons, down to palsied age,
That life brings with her in her equipage;
As if his whole vocation
Were endless imitation.

8

Thou, whose exterior semblance doth belie
Thy soul's immensity;
Thou best philosopher, who yet dost keep
Thy heritage, thou eye among the blind,
That, deaf and silent, read'st the eternal deep,
Haunted forever by the eternal mind —
Mighty prophet! Seer blest!
On whom those truths do rest,
Which we are toiling all our lives to find,
In darkness lost, the darkness of the grave;
Thou, over whom thy immortality
Broods like the day, a master o'er a slave,
A presence which is not to be put by;
Thou little child, yet glorious in the might
Of heaven-born freedom on thy being's height,
Why with such earnest pains dost thou provoke
The years to bring the inevitable yoke,
Thus blindly with thy blessedness at strife?

INTIMATIONS OF IMMORTALITY. **104. "humorous stage"**: quoted from the dedicatory sonnet to Samuel Daniel's *Musophilus* (1599). **121–22. presence . . . might**: In the first published version of the poem these lines read: "To whom the grave / Is but a lonely bed without the sense or sight / Of day or the warm light, / A place of thought where we in waiting lie." The idea of lying awake in the grave, which Wordsworth thus expressed, proved "frightful" to Coleridge, and Wordsworth deleted these lines after 1815.

Full soon thy soul shall have her earthly freight,
And custom lie upon thee with a weight,
Heavy as frost, and deep almost as life!

9

O joy! that in our embers
Is something that doth live,
That nature yet remembers
What was so fugitive!
The thought of our past years in me doth breed
Perpetual benediction: not indeed
For that which is most worthy to be blessed;
Delight and liberty, the simple creed
Of childhood, whether busy or at rest,
With new-fledged hope still fluttering in his breast:
Not for these I raise
The song of thanks and praise;
But for those obstinate questionings
Of sense and outward things,
Fallings from us, vanishings;
Blank misgivings of a creature
Moving about in worlds not realized,
High instincts before which our mortal nature
Did tremble like a guilty thing surprised;
But for those first affections,
Those shadowy recollections,
Which, be they what they may,
Are yet the fountain light of all our day,
Are yet a master light of all our seeing;
Uphold us, cherish, and have power to make
Our noisy years seem moments in the being
Of the eternal silence; truths that wake,
To perish never;
Which neither listlessness, nor mad endeavor,
Nor man nor boy,
Nor all that is at enmity with joy,
Can utterly abolish or destroy!
Hence in a season of calm weather
Though inland far we be,
Our souls have sight of that immortal sea
Which brought us hither,
Can in a moment travel thither,
And see the children sport upon the shore,
And hear the mighty waters rolling evermore.

10

Then sing, ye birds, sing, sing a joyous song!
And let the young lambs bound
As to the tabor's sound!
We in thought will join your throng,
Ye that pipe and ye that play,
Ye that through your hearts today
Feel the gladness of the May!
What though the radiance which was once so bright
Be now forever taken from my sight,
Though nothing can bring back the hour
Of splendor in the grass, of glory in the flower;
We will grieve not, rather find
Strength in what remains behind;
In the primal sympathy
Which having been must ever be;
In the soothing thoughts that spring
Out of human suffering;
In the faith that looks through death,
In years that bring the philosophic mind.

11

And O, ye fountains, meadows, hills, and groves,
Forebode not any severing of our loves!
Yet in my heart of hearts I feel your might;
I only have relinquished one delight
To live beneath your more habitual sway.
I love the brooks which down their channels fret,
Even more than when I tripped lightly as they;
The innocent brightness of a newborn day
Is lovely yet;
The clouds that gather round the setting sun
Do take a sober coloring from an eye
That hath kept watch o'er man's mortality;
Another race hath been, and other palms are won.
Thanks to the human heart by which we live,
Thanks to its tenderness, its joys, and fears;
To me the meanest flower that blows can give
Thoughts that do often lie too deep for tears.

*1802–04*

## "WITH HOW SAD STEPS, O MOON, THOU CLIMB'ST THE SKY"

"With how sad steps, O Moon, thou climb'st the sky,
How silently, and with how wan a face!"
Where art thou? Thou so often seen on high
Running among the clouds a wood nymph's race!
Unhappy nuns, whose common breath's a sigh
Which they would stifle, move at such a pace!
The northern wind, to call thee to the chase,
Must blow tonight his bugle horn. Had I
The power of Merlin, goddess! this should be:
And all the stars, fast as the clouds were riven,
Should sally forth, to keep thee company,
Hurrying and sparkling through the clear blue heaven.
But, Cynthia! should to thee the palm be given,
Queen both for beauty and for majesty.

*1804*

**148. tremble . . . surprised**: an echo of Shakespeare's *Hamlet*, I.i.148–49, p. 240 in Vol. I.

WITH HOW SAD STEPS. **1–2**: These lines Wordsworth took from Sir Philip Sidney's *Astrophel and Stella*, Sonnet XXI. **9. Merlin**: magician famous in Arthurian romance. **13. Cynthia**: Artemis, or Diana, goddess of the moon.

## NUNS FRET NOT AT THEIR CONVENT'S NARROW ROOM

Nuns fret not at their convent's narrow room;
And hermits are contented with their cells;
And students with their pensive citadels;
Maids at the wheel, the weaver at his loom,
Sit blithe and happy; bees that soar for bloom,
High as the highest peak of Furness Fells,
Will murmur by the hour in foxglove bells.
In truth, the prison, into which we doom
Ourselves, no prison is; and hence for me,
In sundry moods, 'twas pastime to be bound
Within the sonnet's scanty plot of ground;
Pleased if some souls (for such there needs must be)
Who have felt the weight of too much liberty,
Should find brief solace there, as I have found.

*1804*

## THE WORLD IS TOO MUCH WITH US; LATE AND SOON

The world is too much with us; late and soon,
Getting and spending, we lay waste our powers;
Little we see in Nature that is ours;
We have given our hearts away, a sordid boon!
The sea that bares her bosom to the moon,
The winds that will be howling at all hours,
And are upgathered now like sleeping flowers;
For this, for everything, we are out of tune;
It moves us not. Great God! I'd rather be
A pagan suckled in a creed outworn,
So might I, standing on this pleasant lea,
Have glimpses that would make me less forlorn;
Have sight of Proteus rising from the sea;
Or hear old Triton blow his wreathèd horn.

*1804*

## WHERE LIES THE LAND TO WHICH YON SHIP MUST GO?

Where lies the land to which yon ship must go?
Fresh as a lark mounting at break of day,
Festively she puts forth in trim array;
Is she for tropic suns, or polar snow?
What boots the inquiry? Neither friend nor foe
She cares for; let her travel where she may,
She finds familiar names, a beaten way
Ever before her, and a wind to blow.
Yet still I ask, what haven is her mark?
And, almost as it was when ships were rare,
(From time to time, like pilgrims, here and there
Crossing the waters) doubt, and something dark,
Of the old sea some reverential fear,
Is with me at thy farewell, joyous bark!

*1804*

## WITH SHIPS THE SEA WAS SPRINKLED FAR AND NIGH

With ships the sea was sprinkled far and nigh,
Like stars in heaven, and joyously it showed;
Some lying fast at anchor in the road,
Some veering up and down, one knew not why.
A goodly vessel did I then espy
Come like a giant from a haven broad;
And lustily along the bay she strode,
Her tackling rich, and of apparel high.
This ship was nought to me, nor I to her,
Yet I pursued her with a lover's look;
This ship to all the rest did I prefer;
When will she turn, and whither? She will brook
No tarrying; where she comes the winds must stir;
On went she, and due north her journey took.

*1804*

## TO SLEEP

A flock of sheep that leisurely pass by,
One after one; the sound of rain, and bees
Murmuring; the fall of rivers, winds, and seas,
Smooth fields, white sheets of water, and pure sky;
I have thought of all by turns, and yet do lie
Sleepless! and soon the small birds' melodies
Must hear, first uttered from my orchard trees;
And the first cuckoo's melancholy cry.
Even thus last night, and two nights more, I lay,
And could not win thee, Sleep! by any stealth:
So do not let me wear tonight away;
Without thee what is all the morning's wealth?
Come, blessed barrier between day and day,
Dear mother of fresh thoughts and joyous health!

*1804*

## ELEGIAC STANZAS

*Suggested by a Picture of Peele Castle, in a Storm, Painted by Sir George Beaumont*

I was thy neighbor once, thou rugged pile!
Four summer weeks I dwelt in sight of thee;

NUNS FRET NOT. **6. Furness Fells:** hills west of Lake Windermere. The tallest peak is the Old Man of Coniston, 2633 feet high.
THE WORLD IS TOO MUCH WITH US. **13–14. Proteus . . . Triton:** sons of Poseidon, or Neptune, god of the sea. Proteus tended his father's herd of seals, and could change shape at will. Triton was the herald of the seas, and used a conch shell for a trumpet.

I saw thee every day; and all the while
Thy form was sleeping on a glassy sea.

So pure the sky, so quiet was the air!
So like, so very like, was day to day!
Whene'er I looked, thy image still was there;
It trembled, but it never passed away.

How perfect was the calm! it seemed no sleep;
No mood, which season takes away, or brings:
I could have fancied that the mighty deep
Was even the gentlest of all gentle things.

Ah! then, if mine had been the painter's hand,
To express what then I saw; and add the gleam,
The light that never was, on sea or land,
The consecration, and the poet's dream;

I would have planted thee, thou hoary pile
Amid a world how different from this!
Beside a sea that could not cease to smile;
On tranquil land, beneath a sky of bliss.

Thou shouldst have seemed a treasure house divine
Of peaceful years, a chronicle of heaven;
Of all the sunbeams that did ever shine
The very sweetest had to thee been given.

A picture had it been of lasting ease,
Elysian quiet, without toil or strife;
No motion but the moving tide, a breeze,
Or merely silent Nature's breathing life.

Such, in the fond illusion of my heart,
Such picture would I at that time have made,
And seen the soul of truth in every part,
A steadfast peace that might not be betrayed.

So once it would have been — 'tis so no more;
I have submitted to a new control;
A power is gone, which nothing can restore;
A deep distress hath humanized my soul.

Not for a moment could I now behold
A smiling sea, and be what I have been;
The feeling of my loss will ne'er be old;
This, which I know, I speak with mind serene.

Then, Beaumont, friend! who would have been the friend,
If he had lived, of him whom I deplore,
This work of thine I blame not, but commend;
This sea in anger, and that dismal shore.

O 'tis a passionate work! — yet wise and well,
Well chosen is the spirit that is here;
That hulk which labors in the deadly swell,
This rueful sky, this pageantry of fear!

And this huge castle, standing here sublime,
I love to see the look with which it braves,
Cased in the unfeeling armor of old time,
The lightning, the fierce wind, and trampling waves.

Farewell, farewell, the heart that lives alone,
Housed in a dream, at distance from the kind!
Such happiness, wherever it be known,
Is to be pitied; for 'tis surely blind.

But welcome fortitude, and patient cheer,
And frequent sights of what is to be borne!
Such sights, or worse, as are before me here.
Not without hope we suffer and we mourn.

*1805*

# CHARACTER OF THE HAPPY WARRIOR

Who is the happy warrior? Who is he
That every man in arms should wish to be?
It is the generous spirit, who, when brought
Among the tasks of real life, hath wrought
Upon the plan that pleased his boyish thought;
Whose high endeavors are an inward light
That makes the path before him always bright;
Who, with a natural instinct to discern
What knowledge can perform, is diligent to learn;
Abides by this resolve, and stops not there,
But makes his moral being his prime care;
Who, doomed to go in company with Pain,
And Fear, and Bloodshed, miserable train!
Turns his necessity to glorious gain;
In face of these doth exercise a power
Which is our human nature's highest dower;
Controls them and subdues, transmutes, bereaves
Of their bad influence, and their good receives;
By objects, which might force the soul to abate
Her feeling, rendered more compassionate;
Is placable — because occasions rise
So often that demand such sacrifice;
More skillful in self-knowledge, even more pure,
As tempted more; more able to endure,
As more exposed to suffering and distress;

ELEGIAC STANZAS. **1–3. I . . . day:** In 1794 Wordsworth spent four weeks with his cousin, Mrs. Barker, at Rampside in Lancashire. Peele Castle stands on a promontory near Rampside. **36. deep . . . soul:** a reference to the drowning of John Wordsworth, February 5, 1805. **41. Beaumont:** Sir George Beaumont (1753–1827), a landscape painter, patron of the arts, and the intimate friend of Wordsworth. Beaumont was largely responsible for the founding of the National Gallery.

**54. kind:** humanity, humankind.

Thence, also, more alive to tenderness.
'Tis he whose law is reason; who depends
Upon that law as on the best of friends;
Whence, in a state where men are tempted still
To evil for a guard against worse ill,
And what in quality or act is best
Doth seldom on a right foundation rest,
He labors good on good to fix, and owes
To virtue every triumph that he knows;
Who, if he rise to station of command,
Rises by open means; and there will stand
On honorable terms, or else retire,
And in himself possess his own desire;
Who comprehends his trust, and to the same
Keeps faithful with a singleness of aim;
And therefore does not stoop, nor lie in wait
For wealth, or honors, or for worldly state;
Whom they must follow; on whose head must fall,
Like showers of manna, if they come at all;
Whose powers shed round him in the common strife,
Or mild concerns of ordinary life,
A constant influence, a peculiar grace;
But who, if he be called upon to face
Some awful moment to which Heaven has joined
Great issues, good or bad for humankind,
Is happy as a lover; and attired
With sudden brightness, like a man inspired;
And, through the heat of conflict, keeps the law
In calmness made, and sees what he foresaw;
Or if an unexpected call succeed,
Come when it will, is equal to the need;
He who, though thus endued as with a sense
And faculty for storm and turbulence,
Is yet a soul whose master bias leans
To homefelt pleasures and to gentle scenes;
Sweet images! which, wheresoe'er he be,
Are at his heart; and such fidelity
It is his darling passion to approve;
More brave for this, that he hath much to love:
'Tis, finally, the man, who, lifted high,
Conspicuous object in a nation's eye,
Or left unthought-of in obscurity—
Who, with a toward or untoward lot,
Prosperous or adverse, to his wish or not—
Plays, in the many games of life, that one
Where what he most doth value must be won;
Whom neither shape of danger can dismay,
Nor thought of tender happiness betray;
Who, not content that former worth stand fast,
Looks forward, persevering to the last,
From well to better, daily self-surpassed;
Who, whether praise of him must walk the earth
Forever, and to noble deeds give birth,
Or he must fall, to sleep without his fame,
And leave a dead unprofitable name—
Finds comfort in himself and in his cause;
And, while the mortal mist is gathering, draws
His breath in confidence of Heaven's applause:
This is the happy warrior; this is he
That every man in arms should wish to be.

*1806*

## THOUGHT OF A BRITON ON THE SUBJUGATION OF SWITZERLAND

Two voices are there; one is of the sea,
One of the mountains; each a mighty voice;
In both from age to age thou didst rejoice;
They were thy chosen music, Liberty!
There came a tyrant, and with holy glee
Thou fought'st against him, but hast vainly striven;
Thou from thy Alpine holds at length art driven,
Where not a torrent murmurs heard by thee.
Of one deep bliss thine ear hath been bereft:
Then cleave, O cleave to that which still is left;
For, high-souled maid, what sorrow would it be
That mountain floods should thunder as before,
And ocean bellow from his rocky shore,
And neither awful voice be heard by thee!

*1806*

## LINES

"Composed at Grasmere, during a walk one evening, after a stormy day, the author having just read in a newspaper that the dissolution of Mr. Fox was hourly expected" [W].

Loud is the vale! the voice is up
With which she speaks when storms are gone,
A mighty unison of streams!
Of all her voices, one!

Loud is the vale—this inland depth
In peace is roaring like the sea;
Yon star upon the mountaintop
Is listening quietly.

Sad was I, even to pain depressed,
Importunate and heavy load!
The Comforter hath found me here,
Upon this lonely road;

THOUGHT OF A BRITON. 1. Two voices: England and Switzerland. 5. tyrant: Napoleon, who invaded Switzerland in 1797 and completed her subjugation in 1802–03, while threatening England with invasion. LINES. Mr. Fox: Charles James Fox (b. 1749), William Pitt's successor as Minister of Foreign Affairs, died September 13, 1806. Once known as the "idol of the people," Fox had opposed British policy in the American and French revolutionary wars and had worked for the abolition of the slave trade, which was finally declared illegal in March, 1807.

And many thousands now are sad —
Wait the fulfillment of their fear;
For he must die who is their stay,
Their glory disappear.

A power is passing from the earth
To breathless Nature's dark abyss;
But when the great and good depart
What is it more than this —

That man, who is from God sent forth,
Doth yet again to God return?
Such ebb and flow must ever be,
Then wherefore should we mourn?

*1806*

# LAODAMÍA

" Written at Rydal Mount. The incident of the trees growing and withering put the subject into my thoughts, and I wrote with the hope of giving it a loftier tone than, so far as I know, has been given to it by any of the ancients who have treated of it. It cost me more trouble than almost anything of equal length I have ever written " [W].

" With sacrifice before the rising morn
Vows have I made by fruitless hope inspired;
And from the infernal gods, 'mid shades forlorn
Of night, my slaughtered lord have I required:
Celestial pity I again implore;
Restore him to my sight — great Jove, restore! "

So speaking, and by fervent love endowed
With faith, the suppliant heavenward lifts her hands;
While, like the sun emerging from a cloud,
Her countenance brightens — and her eye expands;
Her bosom heaves and spreads, her stature grows;
And she expects the issue in repose.

O terror! what hath she perceived? — O joy!
What doth she look on? — whom doth she behold?
Her hero slain upon the beach of Troy?
His vital presence? his corporeal mold?
It is — if sense deceive her not — 'tis he!
And a god leads him, wingèd Mercury!

Mild Hermes spake — and touched her with his wand
That calms all fear: " Such grace hath crowned thy prayer,
Laodamía! that at Jove's command
Thy husband walks the paths of upper air;
He comes to tarry with thee three hours' space;
Accept the gift, behold him face to face! "

Forth sprang the impassioned queen her lord to clasp;
Again that consummation she essayed;
But unsubstantial form eludes her grasp
As often as that eager grasp was made.
The phantom parts — but parts to reunite,
And reassume his place before her sight.

" Protesiláus, lo! thy guide is gone!
Confirm, I pray, the vision with thy voice;
This is our palace — yonder is thy throne;
Speak, and the floor thou tread'st on will rejoice.
Not to appall me have the gods bestowed
This precious boon, and blessed a sad abode."

" Great Jove, Laodamía! doth not leave
His gifts imperfect; specter though I be,
I am not sent to scare thee or deceive;
But in reward of thy fidelity.
And something also did my worth obtain;
For fearless virtue bringeth boundless gain.

" Thou knowest, the Delphic oracle foretold
That the first Greek who touched the Trojan strand
Should die; but me the threat could not withhold;
A generous cause a victim did demand;
And forth I leapt upon the sandy plain;
A self-devoted chief — by Hector slain."

" Supreme of heroes — bravest, noblest, best!
Thy matchless courage I bewail no more,
Which then, when tens of thousands were depressed
By doubt, propelled thee to the fatal shore;
Thou found'st — and I forgive thee — here thou art —
A nobler counselor than my poor heart.

" But thou, though capable of sternest deed,
Wert kind as resolute, and good as brave;
And he, whose power restores thee, hath decreed
Thou should'st elude the malice of the grave;
Redundant are thy locks, thy lips as fair
As when their breath enriched Thessalian air.

" No specter greets me — no vain shadow this;
Come, blooming hero, place thee by my side!
Give, on this well-known couch, one nuptial kiss
To me, this day, a second time thy bride! "
Jove frowned in heaven: the conscious Parcae threw
Upon those roseate lips a Stygian hue.

LAODAMÍA. **15. hero . . . Troy:** Protesilaus, the husband of Laodamía, was the first Greek ashore and the first to be killed in the Trojan war. **19. Hermes:** Mercury, messenger of the gods.

**65. Parcae:** the Fates, controllers of human destiny. **66. Stygian:** dark and gloomy, characteristic of the river Styx and the lower world.

"This visage tells thee that my doom is past:
Nor should the change be mourned, even if the joys
Of sense were able to return as fast
And surely as they vanish. Earth destroys
Those raptures duly — Erebus disdains;
Calm pleasures there abide — majestic pains.

"Be taught, O faithful consort, to control
Rebellious passion, for the Gods approve
The depth, and not the tumult, of the soul;
A fervent, not ungovernable, love.
Thy transports moderate; and meekly mourn
When I depart, for brief is my sojourn —"

"Ah, wherefore? — Did not Hercules by force
Wrest from the guardian monster of the tomb
Alcestis, a reanimated corse,
Given back to dwell on earth in vernal bloom?
Medea's spells dispersed the weight of years,
And Aeson stood a youth 'mid youthful peers.

"The gods to us are merciful — and they
Yet further may relent; for mightier far
Than strength of nerve and sinew, or the sway
Of magic potent over sun and star,
Is love, though oft to agony distressed,
And though his favorite seat be feeble woman's
breast.

"But if thou goest, I follow —" "Peace!" he
said —
She looked upon him and was calmed and cheered;
The ghastly color from his lips had fled;
In his deportment, shape, and mien, appeared
Elysian beauty, melancholy grace,
Brought from a pensive though a happy place.

He spake of love, such love as spirits feel
In worlds whose course is equable and pure;
No fears to beat away — no strife to heal —
The past unsighed for, and the future sure;
Spake of heroic arts in graver mood
Revived, with finer harmony pursued;

Of all that is most beauteous — imaged there
In happier beauty; more pellucid streams,
An ampler ether, a diviner air,
And fields invested with purpureal gleams;
Climes which the sun, who sheds the brightest day
Earth knows, is all unworthy to survey.

**79–81. Hercules . . . Alcestis:** Alcestis, a patient Griselda of ancient mythology, died so that her husband, Admetus, might live. Hercules, to repay Admetus for his hospitality, defeated Death in a wrestling match, and Alcestis was restored to life. See Milton's Sonnet XXIII, p. 453 in Vol. I. **83–84. Medea's . . . youth:** By means of a magical transfusion, Medea, the sorceress wife of Jason, restored Aeson, her aged father-in-law, to youthfulness.

Yet there the soul shall enter which hath earned
That privilege by virtue. "Ill," said he,
"The end of man's existence I discerned,
Who from ignoble games and revelry
Could draw, when we had parted, vain delight,
While tears were thy best pastime, day and night;

"And while my youthful peers before my eyes
(Each hero following his peculiar bent)
Prepared themselves for glorious enterprise
By martial sports — or, seated in the tent,
Chieftains and kings in council were detained;
What time the fleet at Aulis lay enchained.

"The wished-for wind was given — I then revolved
The oracle, upon the silent sea;
And, if no worthier led the way, resolved
That, of a thousand vessels, mine should be
The foremost prow in pressing to the strand,
Mine the first blood that tinged the Trojan sand.

"Yet bitter, oftimes bitter, was the pang
When of thy loss I thought, beloved wife!
On thee too fondly did my memory hang,
And on the joys we shared in mortal life,
The paths which we had trod — these fountains,
flowers,
My new-planned cities, and unfinished towers.

"But should suspense permit the foe to cry,
'Behold they tremble! — haughty their array,
Yet of their number no one dares to die?'
In soul I swept the indignity away;
Old frailties then recurred, but lofty thought,
In act embodied, my deliverance wrought.

"And thou, though strong in love, art all too weak
In reason, in self-government too slow;
I counsel thee by fortitude to seek
Our blest reunion in the shades below.
The invisible world with thee hath sympathized;
Be thy affections raised and solemnized.

"Learn, by a mortal yearning, to ascend —
Seeking a higher object. Love was given,
Encouraged, sanctioned, chiefly for that end;
For this the passion to excess was driven —
That self might be annulled; her bondage prove
The fetters of a dream, opposed to love."

Aloud she shrieked! for Hermes reappears!
Round the dear shade she would have clung — 'tis
vain:
The hours are past — too brief had they been years;

**120. Aulis:** a port in Boeotia where the Greek fleet was delayed until — to appease the wrath of Artemis, whose stag he had killed — Agamemnon offered to sacrifice his daughter Iphigeuia.

And him no mortal effort can detain:
Swift, toward the realms that know not earthly day,
He through the portal takes his silent way,
And on the palace floor a lifeless corse she lay.

Thus, all in vain exhorted and reproved,
She perished; and, as for a willful crime,
By the just gods whom no weak pity moved,
Was doomed to wear out her appointed time,
Apart from happy ghosts, that gather flowers
Of blissful quiet 'mid unfading bowers.

Yet tears to human suffering are due;
And mortal hopes defeated and o'erthrown
Are mourned by man, and not by man alone,
As fondly he believes. Upon the side
Of Hellespont (such faith was entertained)
A knot of spiry trees for ages grew
From out the tomb of him for whom she died;
And ever, when such stature they had gained
That Ilium's walls were subject to their view,
The trees' tall summits withered at the sight;
A constant interchange of growth and blight!

*1814*

## WEAK IS THE WILL OF MAN, HIS JUDGMENT BLIND

"Weak is the will of man, his judgment blind;
Remembrance persecutes, and hope betrays;
Heavy is woe; and joy, for humankind,
A mournful thing, so transient is the blaze!"
Thus might *he* paint our lot of mortal days
Who wants the glorious faculty assigned
To elevate the more-than-reasoning mind,
And color life's dark cloud with orient rays.
Imagination is that sacred power,
Imagination lofty and refined;
'Tis hers to pluck the amaranthine flower
Of faith, and round the sufferer's temples bind
Wreaths that endure affliction's heaviest shower,
And do not shrink from sorrow's keenest wind.

*1815*

**158–63. Thus . . . bowers:** This passage troubled Wordsworth, and he changed it many times. Originally he wrote:

Ah, judge her gently who so deeply loved!
Her, who, in reason's spite, yet without crime,
Was in a trance of passion thus removed;
Delivered from the galling yoke of time
And these frail elements — to gather flowers
Of blissful quiet 'mid unfailing bowers.

**WEAK IS THE WILL OF MAN. 11. amaranthine:** everlasting.

## COMPOSED UPON AN EVENING OF EXTRAORDINARY SPLENDOR AND BEAUTY

1

Had this effulgence disappeared
With flying haste, I might have sent,
Among the speechless clouds, a look
Of blank astonishment;
But 'tis endued with power to stay,
And sanctify one closing day,
That frail mortality may see —
What is? — ah no, but what *can* be!
Time was when field and watery cove
With modulated echoes rang,
While choirs of fervent angels sang
Their vespers in the grove;
Or, crowning, starlike, each some sovereign height,
Warbled, for heaven above and earth below,
Strains suitable to both. Such holy rite,
Methinks, if audibly repeated now
From hill or valley, could not move
Sublimer transport, purer love,
Than doth this silent spectacle — the gleam —
The shadow — and the peace supreme!

2

No sound is uttered, but a deep
And solemn harmony pervades
The hollow vale from steep to steep,
And penetrates the glades.
Far-distant images draw nigh,
Called forth by wondrous potency
Of beamy radiance, that imbues,
Whate'er it strikes, with gemlike hues!
In vision exquisitely clear,
Herds range along the mountainside;
And glistening antlers are descried;
And gilded flocks appear.
Thine is the tranquil hour, purpureal eve!
But long as godlike wish, or hope divine,
Informs my spirit, ne'er can I believe
That this magnificence is wholly thine!
From worlds not quickened by the sun
A portion of the gift is won;
An intermingling of Heaven's pomp is spread
On ground which British shepherds tread!

3

And, if there be whom broken ties
Afflict, or injuries assail,
Yon hazy ridges to their eyes
Present a glorious scale,
Climbing suffused with sunny air,
To stop — no record hath told where!

And tempting fancy to ascend,
And with immortal spirits blend!
Wings at my shoulders seem to play;
But, rooted here, I stand and gaze
On those bright steps that heavenward raise
Their practicable way.
Come forth, ye drooping old men, look abroad,
And see to what fair countries ye are bound!
And if some traveler, weary of his road,
Hath slept since noontide on the grassy ground,
Ye genii! to his covert speed;
And wake him with such gentle heed
As may attune his soul to meet the dower
Bestowed on this transcendent hour!

4

Such hues from their celestial urn
Were wont to stream before mine eye,
Where'er it wandered in the morn
Of blissful infancy.
This glimpse of glory, why renewed?
Nay, rather speak with gratitude;
For, if a vestige of those gleams
Survived, 'twas only in my dreams.
Dread Power! whom peace and calmness serve
No less than Nature's threatening voice,
If aught unworthy be my choice,
From thee if I would swerve;
Oh, let thy grace remind me of the light
Full early lost, and fruitlessly deplored;
Which, at this moment, on my waking sight
Appears to shine, by miracle restored;
My soul, though yet confined to earth,
Rejoices in a second birth!
— 'Tis past, the visionary splendor fades;
And night approaches with her shades.

*1817*

## AFTERTHOUGHT

I thought of thee, my partner and my guide,
As being passed away. — Vain sympathies!
For, backward, Duddon, as I cast my eyes,
I see what was, and is, and will abide;
Still glides the stream, and shall forever glide;
The form remains, the function never dies;
While we, the brave, the mighty, and the wise,
We men, who in our morn of youth defied
The elements, must vanish — be it so!
Enough, if something from our hands have power
To live, and act, and serve the future hour;
And if, as toward the silent tomb we go,
Through love, through hope, and faith's transcendent dower,
We feel that we are greater than we know.

*1820*

## INSIDE OF KING'S COLLEGE CHAPEL, CAMBRIDGE

Tax not the royal saint with vain expense,
With ill-matched aims the architect who planned —
Albeit laboring for a scanty band
Of white-robed scholars only — this immense
And glorious work of fine intelligence!
Give all thou canst; high Heaven rejects the lore
Of nicely calculated less or more;
So deemed the man who fashioned for the sense
These lofty pillars, spread that branching roof
Self-poised, and scooped into ten thousand cells,
Where light and shade repose, where music dwells
Lingering — and wandering on as loath to die;
Like thoughts whose very sweetness yieldeth proof
That they were born for immortality.

*1820*

## MUTABILITY

From low to high doth dissolution climb,
And sink from high to low, along a scale
Of awful notes, whose concord shall not fail;
A musical but melancholy chime,
Which they can hear who meddle not with crime,
Nor avarice, nor overanxious care.
Truth fails not; but her outward forms that bear
The longest date do melt like frosty rime,
That in the morning whitened hill and plain
And is no more; drop like the tower sublime
Of yesterday, which royally did wear
His crown of weeds, but could not even sustain
Some casual shout that broke the silent air,
Or the unimaginable touch of time.

*1821*

AFTERTHOUGHT. This is the thirty-fourth and concluding sonnet of the sequence entitled *The River Duddon*. **1. partner . . . guide:** the river Duddon, whose course, emblematic of the life of man, Wordsworth had followed from its source in the clouds and mountains to its termination in the sea. **3. Duddon:** The river, in northwest England, takes its rise in Wrynose Pass — about five miles west of Grasmere — where the counties of Westmorland, Cumberland, and Lancashire come together. **7. we . . . wise:** an adaptation of Moschus's *Lament for Bion*, part of which Wordsworth had translated at Cambridge. **14. We . . . know:** an echo of Milton's *Paradise Lost*, VIII.282. KING'S COLLEGE CHAPEL. **1. royal . . . expense:** Henry VI (1421–71), a devout but impractical monarch, founded King's College in 1441 and laid the first stone of its chapel in 1446. Although the college boasted but few scholars, Henry's chapel was colossal (289 feet long, 40 feet wide, and 80 feet high), one of the most superb and lavish examples of late Gothic architecture of the ornate perpendicular variety. MUTABILITY. This is the thirty-fourth sonnet in the third part of the sequence entitled *Ecclesiastical Sonnets*.

## SCORN NOT THE SONNET

Scorn not the sonnet; critic, you have frowned,
Mindless of its just honors; with this key
Shakespeare unlocked his heart; the melody
Of this small lute gave ease to Petrarch's wound;
A thousand times this pipe did Tasso sound;
With it Camoëns soothed an exile's grief;
The sonnet glittered a gay myrtle leaf
Amid the cypress with which Dante crowned
His visionary brow: a glowworm lamp,
It cheered mild Spenser, called from faeryland
To struggle through dark ways; and, when a damp
Fell round the path of Milton, in his hand
The thing became a trumpet; whence he blew
Soul-animating strains—alas, too few!

*1827*

## WHY ART THOU SILENT!

Why art thou silent! Is thy love a plant
Of such weak fiber that the treacherous air
Of absence withers what was once so fair?
Is there no debt to pay, no boon to grant?
Yet have my thoughts for thee been vigilant—
Bound to thy service with unceasing care,
The mind's least generous wish a mendicant
For nought but what thy happiness could spare.
Speak—though this soft warm heart, once free to hold
A thousand tender pleasures, thine and mine,
Be left more desolate, more dreary cold
Than a forsaken bird's nest filled with snow
'Mid its own bush of leafless eglantine—
Speak, that my torturing doubts their end may know!

*1830*

## THE TROSSACHS

There's not a nook within this solemn pass,
But were an apt confessional for one
Taught by his summer spent, his autumn gone,
That life is but a tale of morning grass
Withered at eve. From scenes of art which chase
That thought away, turn, and with watchful eyes
Feed it 'mid Nature's old felicities,
Rocks, rivers, and smooth lakes more clear than glass,
Untouched, unbreathed upon. Thrice happy quest,
If from a golden perch of aspen spray
(October's workmanship to rival May)
The pensive warbler of the ruddy breast
That moral sweeten by a heaven-taught lay,
Lulling the year, with all its cares, to rest!

*1831*

## EXTEMPORE EFFUSION UPON THE DEATH OF JAMES HOGG

When first, descending from the moorlands,
I saw the stream of Yarrow glide
Along a bare and open valley,
The Ettrick Shepherd was my guide.

When last along its banks I wandered,
Through groves that had begun to shed
Their golden leaves upon the pathways,
My steps the Border Minstrel led.

The mighty minstrel breathes no longer;
'Mid moldering ruins low he lies;
And death upon the braes of Yarrow
Has closed the shepherd poet's eyes;

Nor has the rolling year twice measured,
From sign to sign, its steadfast course,
Since every mortal power of Coleridge
Was frozen at its marvelous source;

The rapt one, of the godlike forehead,
The heaven-eyed creature sleeps in earth:
And Lamb, the frolic and the gentle,
Has vanished from his lonely hearth.

Like clouds that rake the mountain summits,
Or waves that own no curbing hand,
How fast has brother followed brother
From sunshine to the sunless land!

Yet I, whose lids from infant slumber
Were earlier raised, remain to hear
A timid voice, that asks in whispers,
"Who next will drop and disappear?"

SCORN NOT THE SONNET. **2–3. with . . . heart:** See Browning's reply to this idea in "House," ll. 38–40, p. 575, below. **4. Petrarch's wound:** Wordsworth refers to the sonnets written by the Italian poet (1304–74) to Laura after her death. **5. Tasso:** Italian poet (1544–95), author of *Jerusalem Delivered*. **6. Camoëns . . . grief:** Portuguese epic and lyric poet (1524–80) who, in exile at Goa, wrote laments for the death of Donna Caterina. **7–9. myrtle . . . brow:** Dante Alighiere (1265–1321), greatest of Italian poets and author of the *Divine Comedy*, loved Beatrice, who died in 1290 at the age of twenty-four. To her he addressed sonnets of love, symbolized by the myrtle, and of mourning, symbolized by the cypress. THE TROSSACHS. This sonnet is named after a valley in central Scotland which Wordsworth, with his sister Dorothy and Coleridge, saw for the first time in 1803.

EXTEMPORE EFFUSION. **2. Yarrow:** a river in southeastern Scotland. **4. Ettrick Shepherd:** James Hogg, a Scottish poet, who died November 21, 1835. **8. Border Minstrel:** Sir Walter Scott, who died September 21, 1832. **13–18. Nor . . . earth:** Coleridge died July 25, 1834. **19. Lamb:** Charles Lamb, the essayist, died December 27, 1834.

Our haughty life is crowned with darkness,
Like London with its own black wreath,
On which with thee, O Crabbe! forth looking,
I gazed from Hampstead's breezy heath.

As if but yesterday departed,
Thou too art gone before; but why,
O'er ripe fruit, seasonably gathered,
Should frail survivors heave a sigh?

Mourn rather for that holy spirit,
Sweet as the spring, as ocean deep;
For her who, ere her summer faded,
Has sunk into a breathless sleep.

No more of old romantic sorrows,
For slaughtered youth or lovelorn maid!
With sharper grief is Yarrow smitten,
And Ettrick mourns with her their poet dead.

*1835*

**31. Crabbe:** George Crabbe, an English poet, died February 3, 1832. **32. Hampstead's . . . heath:** now a borough in northwest London.

**37–40. holy . . . sleep:** Felicia Hemans, British poetess, who died in her forty-second year (May 16, 1835); author of "Casabianca" ("The boy stood on the burning deck") and "The Landing of the Pilgrim Fathers in New England."

---

# SAMUEL TAYLOR COLERIDGE

## TO A YOUNG ASS

### ITS MOTHER BEING TETHERED NEAR IT

This poem exhibits some of the pre-Romantic characteristics of Coleridge's early poetry: absurd sentimentalism, the factitious personification of abstract ideas (against which Wordsworth was to inveigh in the Preface to *Lyrical Ballads*), and a naïve social and political philosophy. Confident of the ultimate triumph of French republican principles, but impatient of delays in England, Coleridge and Southey proposed to emigrate to America with ten other young men (each was to take a wife) and establish a "pantisocracy" (equal government for all) on the banks of the Susquehanna in Pennsylvania. They were attracted by the euphony of the river's name, by reports that the great scientist and liberal, Joseph Priestley, resided there, and by the assurances of an inspired real estate agent that a few hours' work a day would suffice to support the community, leaving its members ample time for philosophical discussion and for the generation of an unspoiled progeny that might be educated in a Rousseauistic state of nature. Little came of the project except a few bad poems and Coleridge's unfortunate marriage to Sara Fricker, to whose sister Southey had for some time been engaged.

Poor little foal of an oppressèd race!
I love the languid patience of thy face:
And oft with gentle hand I give thee bread,
And clap thy ragged coat, and pat thy head.
But what thy dulled spirits hath dismayed,
That never thou dost sport along the glade?
And (most unlike the nature of things young)
That earthward still thy moveless head is hung?
Do thy prophetic fears anticipate,
Meek Child of Misery! thy future fate?
The starving meal, and all the thousand aches
"Which patient Merit of the Unworthy takes"?
Or is thy sad heart thrilled with filial pain
To see thy wretched mother's shortened chain?
And truly, very piteous is *her* lot—
Chained to a log within a narrow spot,
Where the close-eaten grass is scarcely seen,
While sweet around her waves the tempting green!

Poor Ass! thy master should have learnt to show
Pity—best taught by fellowship of Woe!
For much I fear me that *He* lives like thee,
Half famished in a land of Luxury!
How *askingly* its footsteps hither bend!
It seems to say, "And have I then *one* friend?"
Innocent foal! thou poor despised forlorn!
I hail thee *Brother*—spite of the fool's scorn!
And fain would take thee with me, in the Dell
Of Peace and mild Equality to dwell,
Where Toil shall call the charmer Health his bride,
And Laughter tickle Plenty's ribless side!
How thou wouldst toss thy heels in gamesome play,
And frisk about, as lamb or kitten gay!
Yea! and more musically sweet to me
Thy dissonant harsh bray of joy would be,
Than warbled melodies that soothe to rest
The aching of pale Fashion's vacant breast!

*1794*

TO A YOUNG ASS. **12. "Which . . . takes":** from *Hamlet*, III.i.74. See Vol. I, p. 259. **27–28. Dell . . . Equality:** the pantisocratic community (see headnote).

## THE EOLIAN HARP[1]

### COMPOSED AT CLEVEDON, SOMERSETSHIRE[2]

This is the first and, in Coleridge's opinion, the best of his "Conversation Poems" (other examples of the type included in this selection are "This Lime Tree Bower My Prison" and "Frost at Midnight"). Invariably written in blank verse, these poems begin with the speaker, always Coleridge (he may or may not have an audience), in a mood of "wise passiveness": his mind is relaxed, almost quiescent, but his senses are exquisitely awake to the objects at hand, indoors or out. Gradually the involuntary activity of the senses rouses the mind from lethargy; an idea or emotion, usually the product of association and memory, comes into focus, and the poem gains in intensity and mounts to a crisis. Then in gentle decrescendo poem and speaker come full circle as they return to the random peacefulness of the beginning. Meanwhile, however, something of value has been added, and the reader turns from the poem a wiser, if not a sadder, man.

My pensive Sara! thy soft cheek reclined
Thus on mine arm, most soothing sweet it is
To sit beside our cot, our cot o'ergrown
With white-flowered jasmin, and the broad-leaved myrtle,
(Meet emblems they of Innocence and Love!)
And watch the clouds, that late were rich with light,
Slow saddening round, and mark the star of eve
Serenely brilliant (such should Wisdom be)
Shine opposite! How exquisite the scents
Snatched from yon beanfield! and the world *so* hushed!
The stilly murmur of the distant sea
Tells us of silence.
And that simplest lute,
Placed lengthways in the clasping casement, hark!
How by the desultory breeze caressed,
Like some coy maid half yielding to her lover,
It pours such sweet upbraiding, as must needs
Tempt to repeat the wrong! And now, its strings
Boldlier swept, the long sequacious notes
Over delicious surges sink and rise,
Such a soft floating witchery of sound
As twilight elfins make, when they at eve
Voyage on gentle gales from fairyland,
Where melodies round honey-dropping flowers,
Footless and wild, like birds of paradise,
Nor pause, nor perch, hovering on untamed wing!
O! the one life within us and abroad,
Which meets all motion and becomes its soul,
A light in sound, a sound-like power in light,
Rhythm in all thought, and joyance every where—
Methinks, it should have been impossible
Not to love all things in a world so filled;
Where the breeze warbles, and the mute still air
Is Music slumbering on her instrument.

And thus, my love! as on the midway slope
Of yonder hill I stretch my limbs at noon,
Whilst through my half-closed eyelids I behold
The sunbeams dance, like diamonds, on the main,
And tranquil muse upon tranquility;
Full many a thought uncalled and undetained,
And many idle flitting fantasies,
Traverse my indolent and passive brain,
As wild and various as the random gales
That swell and flutter on this subject lute!
And what if all of animated nature
Be but organic harps diversely framed,
That tremble into thought, as o'er them sweeps
Plastic and vast, one intellectual breeze,
At once the soul of each, and God of all?
But thy more serious eye a mild reproof
Darts, O beloved woman! nor such thoughts
Dim and unhallowed dost thou not reject,
And biddest me walk humbly with my God.
Meek daughter in the family of Christ!
Well hast thou said and holily dispraised
These shapings of the unregenerate mind;
Bubbles that glitter as they rise and break
On vain philosophy's aye-babbling spring.
For never guiltless may I speak of him,
The Incomprehensible! save when with awe
I praise him, and with faith that inly *feels;*
Who with his saving mercies healed me,
A sinful and most miserable man,
Wildered and dark, and gave me to possess
Peace, and this cot, and thee, heart-honored maid!

*1795*

**THE EOLIAN HARP.** **1. Eolian Harp:** Named after Eolus, god of the winds, the harp was box-shaped with strings stretched across its open ends; a movement of air would cause the strings to vibrate and produce crude music. The Eolian harp became for the Romantics a symbol for the creative process. **2. Clevedon, Somersetshire:** a village on the Bristol Channel where Coleridge spent his honeymoon in 1795; also the place where Tennyson's friend, Arthur Henry Hallam, was buried on January 3, 1834 (see *In Memoriam,* XVIII–XIX, p. 412, below). **1. Sara:** Sara Fricker, Coleridge's wife. **3. cot:** cottage. **12. lute:** Eolian harp. **18. sequacious:** successive. **24. birds of paradise:** fabulous birds; lacking feet, they live on the wing and feed on air. **26–33. O! . . . instrument:** These lines first appeared in the 1817 edition.

## THIS LIME TREE BOWER MY PRISON

### ADDRESSED TO CHARLES LAMB, OF THE INDIA HOUSE, LONDON

In the June of 1797 some long-expected friends[1] paid a visit to the author's cottage; and on the morning of their arrival, he met with an accident,[2] which disabled him from walking during the whole time of their stay.

**THIS LIME TREE BOWER MY PRISON.** **1. friends:** William and Dorothy Wordsworth, and Charles Lamb. **2. accident:** His wife, Sara, "emptied a skillet

One evening, when they had left him for a few hours, he composed the following lines in the garden-bower [STC].

Well, they are gone, and here must I remain,
This lime tree bower my prison! I have lost
Beauties and feelings, such as would have been
Most sweet to my remembrance even when age
Had dimmed mine eyes to blindness! They, meanwhile,
Friends, whom I never more may meet again,
On springy heath, along the hilltop edge,
Wander in gladness, and wind down, perchance,
To that still roaring dell of which I told;
The roaring dell, o'erwooded, narrow, deep,
And only speckled by the midday sun;
Where its slim trunk the ash from rock to rock
Flings arching like a bridge; — that branchless ash,
Unsunned and damp, whose few poor yellow leaves
Ne'er tremble in the gale, yet tremble still,
Fanned by the waterfall! and there my friends
Behold the dark green file of long lank weeds,
That all at once (a most fantastic sight!)
Still nod and drip beneath the dripping edge
Of the blue clay stone.

Now my friends emerge
Beneath the wide wide heaven — and view again
The many-steepled tract magnificent
Of hilly fields and meadows, and the sea,
With some fair bark, perhaps, whose sails light up
The slip of smooth clear blue betwixt two isles
Of purple shadow! Yes! they wander on
In gladness all; but thou, methinks, most glad,
My gentle-hearted Charles! for thou hast pined
And hungered after nature, many a year,
In the great city pent, winning thy way
With sad yet patient soul, through evil and pain
And strange calamity! Ah! slowly sink
Behind the western ridge, thou glorious sun!
Shine in the slant beams of the sinking orb,
Ye purple heath flowers! richlier burn, ye clouds!
Live in the yellow light, ye distant groves!
And kindle, thou blue ocean! So my friend
Struck with deep joy may stand, as I have stood,
Silent with swimming sense; yea, gazing round
On the wide landscape, gaze till all doth seem
Less gross than bodily; and of such hues
As veil the Almighty Spirit, when yet he makes
Spirits perceive his presence.

A delight
Comes sudden on my heart, and I am glad
As I myself were there! Nor in this bower,
This little lime tree bower, have I not marked
Much that has soothed me. Pale beneath the blaze
Hung the transparent foliage; and I watched
Some broad and sunny leaf, and loved to see
The shadow of the leaf and stem above
Dappling its sunshine! And that walnut tree
Was richly tinged, and a deep radiance lay
Full on the ancient ivy which usurps
Those fronting elms, and now, with blackest mass
Makes their dark branches gleam a lighter hue
Through the late twilight: and though now the bat
Wheels silent by, and not a swallow twitters,
Yet still the solitary humblebee
Sings in the bean flower! Henceforth I shall know
That nature ne'er deserts the wise and pure;
No plot so narrow, be but nature there,
No waste so vacant, but may well employ
Each faculty of sense, and keep the heart
Awake to love and beauty! and sometimes
'Tis well to be bereft of promised good,
That we may lift the soul, and contemplate
With lively joy the joys we cannot share.
My gentle-hearted Charles! when the last rook
Beat its straight path along the dusky air
Homewards, I blest it! deeming its black wing
(Now a dim speck, now vanishing in light)
Had crossed the mighty orb's dilated glory,
While thou stood'st gazing; or, when all was still,
Flew creeking o'er thy head, and had a charm
For thee, my gentle-hearted Charles, to whom
No sound is dissonant which tells of life.

1797

of boiling milk" on Coleridge's foot. **28. gentle-hearted Charles:** This epithet displeased Lamb who replied, "For God's sake, don't make me ridiculous any more by terming me gentle-hearted in print. . . ." **33. strange calamity:** the insanity of Lamb's sister Mary, who had killed their mother in 1796.

# THE RIME OF THE ANCIENT MARINER

### IN SEVEN PARTS

Originally Coleridge and Wordsworth intended to write this poem in collaboration. Wordsworth's manner proved unsuited for the purpose, however, and after contributing half a dozen lines (particularly ll. 13–16 and 226–27) and suggesting the shooting of the albatross and the "reanimation of the dead bodies to work the ship," Wordsworth withdrew, and Coleridge proceeded alone. The details of the origin of the poem are contained in the opening paragraphs of Chapter XIV of Coleridge's *Biographia Literaria* (pp. 134–35, below), and in the Fenwick note (1843) to Wordsworth's "We Are Seven."

The effectiveness of the first (1798) version of the poem was reduced by Coleridge's overenthusiasm for archaic words and spellings, many of which he removed in subsequent editions. The Latin motto below was added in 1817, as was the marginal gloss, although the latter may have been written much earlier.

---

Facile credo, plures esse Naturas invisibiles quam visibiles in rerum universitate. Sed horum omnium familiam quis nobis enarrabit? et gradus et cognationes et discrimina et singulorum munera? Quid agunt? quae loca habitant? Harum rerum notitiam semper ambivit ingenium humanum, nunquam attigit. Juvat, interea, non diffiteor, quandoque in animo, tanquam in tabulà, majoris et melioris mundi imaginem contemplari: ne mens assuefacta hodiernae vitae minutiis se contrahat nimis, et tota subsidat in pusillas cogitationes. Sed veritati interea invigilandum est, modusque servandus, ut certa ab incertis, diem a nocte, distinguamus.[1]

[Thomas Burnet,[2] *Archaeologiae Philosophicae* (1692), p. 68]

## ARGUMENT

*How a Ship having passed the Line was driven by storms to the cold Country towards the South Pole; and how from thence she made her course to the tropical Latitude of the Great Pacific Ocean; and of the strange things that befell; and in what manner the Ancient Mariner came back to his own Country.*

## PART I

An ancient Mariner meeteth three Gallants bidden to a wedding-feast, and detaineth one.

It is an ancient Mariner,
And he stoppeth one of three.
"By thy long gray beard and glittering eye,
Now wherefore stopp'st thou me?

The Bridegroom's doors are opened wide,
And I am next of kin;
The guests are met, the feast is set:
May'st hear the merry din."

He holds him with his skinny hand,
"There was a ship," quoth he.
"Hold off! unhand me, graybeard loon!"
Eftsoons his hand dropt he.

The Wedding Guest is spellbound by the eye of the old seafaring man, and constrained to hear his tale.

He holds him with his glittering eye—
The Wedding Guest stood still,
And listens like a three years' child:
The Mariner hath his will.

The Wedding Guest sat on a stone:
He cannot choose but hear;
And thus spake on that ancient man,
The bright-eyed Mariner.

"The ship was cheered, the harbor cleared,
Merrily did we drop
Below the kirk, below the hill,
Below the lighthouse top.

The Mariner tells how the ship sailed southward with a good wind and fair weather, till it reached the line.

The Sun came up upon the left,
Out of the sea came he!
And he shone bright, and on the right
Went down into the sea.

Higher and higher every day,
Till over the mast at noon—"
The Wedding Guest here beat his breast,
For he heard the loud bassoon.

The Wedding Guest heareth the bridal music; but the Mariner continueth his tale.

The bride hath paced into the hall,
Red as a rose is she;
Nodding their heads before her goes
The merry minstrelsy.

The Wedding Guest he beat his breast,
Yet he cannot choose but hear;
And thus spake on that ancient man,
The bright-eyed Mariner.

The ship driven by a storm toward the south pole.

"And now the STORM-BLAST came, and he
Was tyrannous and strong:
He struck with his o'ertaking wings,
And chased us south along.

With sloping masts and dipping prow,
As who pursued with yell and blow
Still treads the shadow of his foe,
And forward bends his head,
The ship drove fast, loud roared the blast,
And southward aye we fled.

And now there came both mist and snow,
And it grew wondrous cold:

THE RIME OF THE ANCIENT MARINER. **1. Facile . . . distinguamus:** "I find it easy to believe that there are more invisible than visible things in the universe. But who shall describe for us the families of all of them, their rank and relationships, the distinguishing features and singularities of each. What do they do? What places inhabit? The human mind has always circled about but never attained knowledge of these things. I do not doubt, however, that it is sometimes good to contemplate in the mind, as in a picture, the image of a greater and better world; otherwise the mind, accustomed to the minutiae of daily life, may contract too much and sink altogether to trivial thoughts. Meanwhile, however, we must be vigilant for truth and keep proportion, so that we may distinguish certainty from uncertainty, day from night." **2. Thomas Burnet:** Anglican divine (1635?–1715); a favorite author of Coleridge and Wordsworth (see p. 137, n. 12, below). **12. Eftsoons:** at once.

**13–16.** Wordsworth wrote this stanza. **23. kirk:** church **36. minstrelsy:** musicians.

And ice, mast-high, came floating by,
As green as emerald.

*The land of ice, and of fearful sounds where no living thing was to be seen.*

And through the drifts the snowy clifts
Did send a dismal sheen:
Nor shapes of men nor beasts we ken—
The ice was all between.

The ice was here, the ice was there,
The ice was all around:
It cracked and growled, and roared and howled,
Like noises in a swound!

*Till a great seabird, called the Albatross, came through the snow-fog, and was received with great joy and hospitality.*

At length did cross an Albatross,
Thorough the fog it came;
As if it had been a Christian soul,
We hailed it in God's name.

It ate the food it ne'er had eat,
And round and round it flew.
The ice did split with a thunder-fit;
The helmsman steered us through!

*And lo! the Albatross proveth a bird of good omen, and followeth the ship as it returned northward through fog and floating ice.*

And a good south wind sprung up behind;
The Albatross did follow,
And every day, for food or play,
Came to the mariners' hollo!

In mist or cloud, on mast or shroud,
It perched for vespers nine;
Whiles all the night, through fog-smoke white,
Glimmered the white Moon shine."

"God save thee, ancient Mariner!
From the fiends, that plague thee thus!—

*The ancient Mariner inhospitably killeth the pious bird of good omen.*

Why look'st thou so?"—With my crossbow
I shot the ALBATROSS.

PART II

The Sun now rose upon the right:
Out of the sea came he,
Still hid in mist, and on the left
Went down into the sea.

And the good south wind still blew behind,
But no sweet bird did follow,
Nor any day for food or play
Came to the mariners' hollo!

*His shipmates cry out against the ancient Mariner, for killing the bird of good luck.*

And I had done a hellish thing,
And it would work 'em woe:
For all averred, I had killed the bird
That made the breeze to blow.
Ah wretch! said they, the bird to slay,
That made the breeze to blow!

*But when the fog cleared off, they justify the same, and thus make themselves accomplices in the crime.*

Nor dim nor red, like God's own head,
The glorious Sun uprist:
Then all averred, I had killed the bird
That brought the fog and mist.
'Twas right, said they, such birds to slay,
That bring the fog and mist.

*The fair breeze continues; the ship enters the Pacific Ocean, and sails northward, even till it reaches the Line.*

The fair breeze blew, the white foam flew,
The furrow followed free;
We were the first that ever burst
Into that silent sea.

*The ship hath been suddenly becalmed.*

Down dropt the breeze, the sails dropt down,
'Twas sad as sad could be;
And we did speak only to break
The silence of the sea!

All in a hot and copper sky,
The bloody Sun, at noon,
Right up above the mast did stand,
No bigger than the Moon.

Day after day, day after day,
We stuck, nor breath nor motion;
As idle as a painted ship
Upon a painted ocean.

*And the Albatross begins to be avenged.*

Water, water, everywhere,
And all the boards did shrink;
Water, water, everywhere,
Nor any drop to drink.

The very deep did rot: O Christ!
That ever this should be!
Yea, slimy things did crawl with legs
Upon the slimy sea.

*A Spirit had followed them; one of the invisible inhabitants of*

About, about, in reel and rout
The death-fires danced at night;
The water, like a witch's oils,
Burnt green, and blue and white.

**55. clifts:** cliffs. **62. swound:** swoon. **64. Thorough:** through. **75. shroud:** rope or line. **76. vespers:** evening religious services. **83. The . . . right:** The ship, having rounded the Horn, is now he ding no-th into the Pacific.

**128. death-fires:** St. Elmo's fire, phosphorescent lights on a ship's rigging, believed by sailors to be prophetic of disaster.

**this planet, neither departed souls nor angels; concerning whom the learned Jew, Josephus, and the Platonic Constantinopolitan, Michael Psellus, may be consulted. They are very numerous, and there is no climate or element without one or more.**

And some in dreams assurèd were
Of the Spirit that plagued us so;
Nine fathom deep he had followed us
From the land of mist and snow.

And every tongue, through utter drought,
Was withered at the root;
We could not speak, no more than if
We had been choked with soot.

**The shipmates, in their sore distress, would fain throw the whole guilt on the ancient Mariner: in sign whereof they hang the dead sea bird round his neck.**

Ah! wel-a-day! what evil looks
Had I from old and young!
Instead of the cross, the Albatross
About my neck was hung.

## Part III

There passed a weary time. Each throat
Was parched, and glazed each eye.
A weary time! a weary time!
How glazed each weary eye,

**The ancient Mariner beholdeth a sign in the element afar off.**

When looking westward, I beheld
A something in the sky.

At first it semed a little speck,
And then it seemed a mist;
It moved and moved, and took at last
A certain shape, I wist.

A speck, a mist, a shape, I wist!
And still it neared and neared:
As if it dodged a water sprite,
It plunged and tacked and veered.

**At its nearer approach, it seemeth him to be a ship; and at a dear ransom he freeth his speech from the bonds of thirst.**

With throats unslaked, with black lips baked,
We could nor laugh nor wail;
Through utter drought all dumb we stood!
I bit my arm, I sucked the blood,
And cried, A sail! a sail!

With throats unslaked, with black lips baked,
Agape they heard me call:
Gramercy! they for joy did grin,

**A flash of joy;**

And all at once their breath drew in,
As they were drinking all.

**And horror follows. For can it be a ship that comes onward without wind or tide?**

See! see! (I cried) she tacks no more!
Hither to work us weal;
Without a breeze, without a tide,
She steadies with upright keel!

The western wave was all aflame.
The day was well nigh done!
Almost upon the western wave
Rested the broad bright Sun;
When that strange shape drove suddenly
Betwixt us and the Sun.

**It seemeth him but the skeleton of a ship. And its ribs are seen as bars on the face of the setting Sun.**

And straight the Sun was flecked with bars,
(Heaven's Mother send us grace!)
As if through a dungeon grate he peered
With broad and burning face.

Alas! (thought I, and my heart beat loud)
How fast she nears and nears!
Are those *her* sails that glance in the Sun,
Like restless gossameres?

**The Specter-Woman and her Death-mate, and no other on board the skeleton ship.**

Are those *her* ribs through which the Sun
Did peer, as through a grate?
And is that Woman all her crew?
Is that a Death? and are there two?
Is Death that woman's mate?

**Like vessel, like crew!**

*Her* lips were red, *her* looks were free,
Her locks were yellow as gold:
Her skin was as white as leprosy,
The Nightmare Life-in-Death was she,
Who thicks man's blood with cold.

**Death and Life-in-Death have diced for the ship's crew, and she (the latter) winneth the ancient Mariner.**

The naked hulk alongside came,
And the twain were casting dice;
"The game is done! I've won! I've won!"
Quoth she, and whistles thrice.

**No twilight within the courts of the Sun.**

The Sun's rim dips; the stars rush out:
At one stride comes the dark;
With far-heard whisper, o'er the sea,
Off shot the specter bark.

**At the rising of the Moon,**

We listened and looked sideways up!
Fear at my heart, as at a cup,
My lifeblood seemed to sip!
The stars were dim, and thick the night,
The steersman's face by his lamp gleamed white;

**152. wist:** knew. **164. Gramercy:** great thanks. **168. weal:** good.

**184. gossameres:** cobwebs floating in the air.

From the sails the dew did drip—
Till clomb above the eastern bar
The hornèd Moon, with one bright
star
Within the nether tip.

One after another,

One after one, by the star-dogged Moon,
Too quick for groan or sigh,
Each turned his face with a ghastly
pang,
And cursed me with his eye.

His shipmates drop down dead.

Four times fifty living men,
(And I heard nor sigh nor groan)
With heavy thump, a lifeless lump,
They dropped down one by one.

But Life-in-Death begins her work on the ancient Mariner.

The souls did from their bodies fly—
They fled to bliss or woe!
And every soul, it passed me by,
Like the whizz of my crossbow!

## Part IV

The Wedding Guest feareth that a Spirit is talking to him;

"I fear thee, ancient Mariner!
I fear thy skinny hand!
And thou art long, and lank, and
brown,
As is the ribbed sea-sand.

I fear thee and thy glittering eye,
And thy skinny hand, so brown."—

But the ancient Mariner assureth him of his bodily life, and proceedeth to relate his horrible penance.

Fear not, fear not, thou Wedding
Guest!
This body dropt not down.

Alone, alone, all, all alone,
Alone on a wide wide sea!
And never a saint took pity on
My soul in agony.

He despiseth the creatures of the calm,

The many men, so beautiful!
And they all dead did lie:
And a thousand thousand slimy things
Lived on; and so did I.

And envieth that *they* should live, and so many lie dead.

I looked upon the rotting sea,
And drew my eyes away;
I looked upon the rotting deck,
And there the dead men lay.

I looked to heaven, and tried to pray;
But or ever a prayer had gusht,
A wicked whisper came, and made
My heart as dry as dust.

I closed my lids, and kept them close,
And the balls like pulses beat;
For the sky and the sea, and the sea
and the sky
Lay like a load on my weary eye,
And the dead were at my feet.

But the curse liveth for him in the eye of the dead men.

The cold sweat melted from their limbs,
Nor rot nor reek did they:
The look with which they looked on
me
Had never passed away.

An orphan's curse would drag to hell
A spirit from on high;
But oh! more horrible than that
Is the curse in a dead man's eye!
Seven days, seven nights, I saw that
curse,
And yet I could not die.

In his loneliness and fixedness he yearneth towards the journeying Moon, and the stars that still sojourn, yet still move onward; and everywhere the blue sky belongs to them, and is their appointed rest, and their native country and their own natural homes, which they enter unannounced, as lords that are certainly expected and yet there is a silent joy at their arrival.

The moving Moon went up the sky,
And nowhere did abide:
Softly she was going up,
And a star or two beside—

Her beams bemocked the sultry main,
Like April hoarfrost spread;
But where the ship's huge shadow
lay,
The charmèd water burnt alway
A still and awful red.

By the light of the Moon he beholdeth God's creatures of the great calm.

Beyond the shadow of the ship,
I watched the water snakes:
They moved in tracks of shining white,
And when they reared, the elfish light
Fell off in hoary flakes.

Within the shadow of the ship
I watched their rich attire:
Blue, glossy green, and velvet black,
They coiled and swam; and every track
Was a flash of golden fire.

Their beauty and their happiness.

O happy living things! no tongue
Their beauty might declare:

He blesseth them in his heart.

A spring of love gushed from my heart,
And I blessed them unaware:
Sure my kind saint took pity on me,
And I blessed them unaware.

The spell begins to break.

The selfsame moment I could pray;
And from my neck so free
The Albatross fell off, and sank
Like lead into the sea.

209. clomb: climbed. 226–27. Wordsworth wrote these lines

## Part V

Oh sleep! it is a gentle thing,
Beloved from pole to pole!
To Mary Queen the praise be given!
She sent the gentle sleep from Heaven,
That slid into my soul.

By grace of the holy Mother, the ancient Mariner is refreshed with rain.

The silly buckets on the deck,
That had so long remained,
I dreamt that they were filled with dew;
And when I awoke, it rained.

My lips were wet, my throat was cold,
My garments all were dank;
Sure I had drunken in my dreams,
And still my body drank.

I moved, and could not feel my limbs:
I was so light — almost
I thought that I had died in sleep,
And was a blessèd ghost.

He heareth sounds and seeth strange sights and commotions in the sky and the element.

And soon I heard a roaring wind:
It did not come anear;
But with its sound it shook the sails,
That were so thin and sere.

The upper air burst into life!
And a hundred fireflags sheen,
To and fro they were hurried about!
And to and fro, and in and out,
The wan stars danced between.

And the coming wind did roar more loud,
And the sails did sigh like sedge;
And the rain poured down from one black cloud;
The Moon was at its edge.

The thick black cloud was cleft, and still
The Moon was at its side:
Like waters shot from some high crag,
The lightning fell with never a jag,
A river steep and wide.

The bodies of the ship's crew are inspired and the ship moves on;

The loud wind never reached the ship,
Yet now the ship moved on!
Beneath the lightning and the Moon
The dead men gave a groan.

They groaned, they stirred, they all uprose,
Nor spake, nor moved their eyes;
It had been strange, even in a dream,
To have seen those dead men rise.

The helmsman steered, the ship moved on;
Yet never a breeze upblew;
The mariners all 'gan work the ropes,
Where they were wont to do;
They raised their limbs like lifeless tools —
We were a ghastly crew.

The body of my brother's son
Stood by me, knee to knee:
The body and I pulled at one rope,
But he said nought to me.

But not by the souls of the men, nor by demons of earth or middle air, but by a blessed troop of angelic spirits, sent down by the invocation of the guardian saint.

"I fear thee, ancient Mariner!"
Be calm, thou Wedding Guest!
'Twas not those souls that fled in pain,
Which to their corses came again,
But a troop of spirits blest:

For when it dawned — they dropped their arms,
And clustered round the mast;
Sweet sounds rose slowly through their mouths,
And from their bodies passed.

Around, around, flew each sweet sound,
Then darted to the Sun;
Slowly the sounds came back again,
Now mixed, now one by one.

Sometimes a-dropping from the sky
I heard the skylark sing;
Sometimes all little birds that are,
How they seemed to fill the sea and air
With their sweet jargoning!

And now 'twas like all instruments,
Now like a lonely flute;
And now it is an angel's song,
That makes the heavens be mute.

It ceased; yet still the sails made on
A pleasant noise till noon,
A noise like of a hidden brook
In the leafy month of June,

**297. silly:** because empty and useless. **313–17. The . . . between:** Aurora Australis or Southern Lights. **319. sedge:** marsh grass.

**348. corses:** corpses. **362. jargoning:** singing.

That to the sleeping woods all night
Singeth a quiet tune.

Till noon we quietly sailed on,
Yet never a breeze did breathe:
Slowly and smoothly went the ship,
Moved onward from beneath.

The lonesome Spirit from the South Pole carries on the ship as far as the Line, in obedience to the angelic troop, but still requireth vengeance.

Under the keel nine fathom deep,
From the land of mist and snow,
The spirit slid; and it was he
That made the ship to go.
The sails at noon left off their tune,
And the ship stood still also.

The Sun, right up above the mast,
Had fixed her to the ocean:
But in a minute she 'gan stir,
With a short uneasy motion —
Backwards and forwards half her length
With a short uneasy motion.

Then like a pawing horse let go,
She made a sudden bound:
It flung the blood into my head,
And I fell down in a swound.

The Polar Spirit's fellow-demons, the invisible inhabitants of the element, take part in his wrong; and two of them relate, one to the other, that penance long and heavy for the ancient Mariner hath been accorded to the Polar Spirit, who returneth southward.

How long in that same fit I lay,
I have not to declare;
But ere my living life returned,
I heard and in my soul discerned
Two voices in the air.

"Is it he?" quoth one, "Is this the
man?
By him who died on cross,
With his cruel bow he laid full low
The harmless Albatross.

The spirit who bideth by himself
In the land of mist and snow,
He loved the bird that loved the man
Who shot him with his bow."

The other was a softer voice,
As soft as honeydew:
Quoth he, "The man hath penance
done,
And penance more will do."

## Part VI

FIRST VOICE

"But tell me, tell me! speak again,
Thy soft response renewing —
What makes that ship drive on so fast?
What is the ocean doing?"

SECOND VOICE

"Still as a slave before his lord,
The ocean hath no blast;
His great bright eye most silently
Up to the Moon is cast —

If he may know which way to go;
For she guides him smooth or grim.
See, brother, see! how graciously
She looketh down on him."

FIRST VOICE

The Mariner hath been cast into a trance; for the angelic power causeth the vessel to drive northward faster than human life could endure.

"But why drives on that ship so fast,
Without or wave or wind?"

SECOND VOICE

"The air is cut away before,
And closes from behind.

Fly, brother, fly! more high, more high!
Or we shall be belated:
For slow and slow that ship will go,
When the Mariner's trance is abated."

The supernatural motion is retarded; the Mariner awakes, and his penance begins anew.

I woke, and we were sailing on
As in a gentle weather:
'Twas night, calm night, the moon was
high;
The dead men stood together.

All stood together on the deck,
For a charnel-dungeon fitter:
All fixed on me their stony eyes,
That in the Moon did glitter.

The pang, the curse, with which they
died,
Had never passed away:
I could not draw my eyes from theirs,
Nor turn them up to pray.

The curse is finally expiated.

And now this spell was snapt: once
more
I viewed the ocean green,
And looked far forth, yet little saw
Of what had else been seen —

Like one, that on a lonesome road
Doth walk in fear and dread,
And having once turned round walks
on,

394. I . . . declare: I cannot say.

435. charnel-dungeon: an underground prison, its occupants

And turns no more his head;
Because he knows, a frightful fiend
Doth close behind him tread.

But soon there breathed a wind on me,
Nor sound nor motion made:
Its path was not upon the sea,
In ripple or in shade.

It raised my hair, it fanned my cheek
Like a meadow-gale of spring—
It mingled strangely with my fears,
Yet it felt like a welcoming.

Swiftly, swiftly flew the ship,
Yet she sailed softly too:
Sweetly, sweetly blew the breeze—
On me alone it blew.

*And the ancient Mariner beholdeth his native country.*

Oh! dream of joy! is this indeed
The lighthouse top I see?
Is this the hill? is this the kirk?
Is this mine own countree?

We drifted o'er the harbor-bar,
And I with sobs did pray—
O let me be awake, my God!
Or let me sleep alway.

The harbor-bay was clear as glass,
So smoothly it was strewn!
And on the bay the moonlight lay,
And the shadow of the Moon.

The rock shone bright, the kirk no less,
That stands above the rock:
The moonlight steeped in silentness
The steady weathercock.

And the bay was white with silent light,
Till rising from the same,
Full many shapes, that shadows were,
In crimson colors came.

*The angelic spirits leave the dead bodies,*

A little distance from the prow
Those crimson shadows were:
I turned my eyes upon the deck—
Oh, Christ! what saw I there!

*And appear in their own forms of light.*

Each corse lay flat, lifeless and flat,
And, by the holy rood!
A man all light, a seraph man,
On every corse there stood.

This seraph band, each waved his hand:
It was a heavenly sight!
They stood as signals to the land,
Each one a lovely light;

This seraph band, each waved his hand,
No voice did they impart—
No voice; but oh! the silence sank
Like music on my heart.

But soon I heard the dash of oars,
I heard the Pilot's cheer;
My head was turned perforce away
And I saw a boat appear.

The Pilot and the Pilot's boy,
I heard them coming fast:
Dear Lord in Heaven! it was a joy
The dead men could not blast.

I saw a third—I heard his voice:
It is the Hermit good!
He singeth loud his godly hymns
That he makes in the wood.
He'll shrieve my soul, he'll wash away
The Albatross's blood.

## PART VII

*The Hermit of the Wood,*

This Hermit good lives in that wood
Which slopes down to the sea.
How loudly his sweet voice he rears!
He loves to talk with mariners
That come from a far countree.

He kneels at morn, and noon, and eve—
He hath a cushion plump:
It is the moss that wholly hides
The rotted old oak stump.

The skiff boat neared: I heard them talk,
"Why, this is strange, I trow!
Where are those lights so many and fair,
That signal made but now?"

*Approacheth the ship with wonder.*

"Strange, by my faith!" the Hermit said—
"And they answered not our cheer!
The planks looked warped! and see those sails,
How thin they are and sere!

abandoned to death and decay. **489. rood:** cross. **490. seraph:** luminiferous angel, higher in rank than a cherub.

**512. shrieve:** shrive, listen to penitential confession.

I never saw aught like to them,
Unless perchance it were

Brown skeletons of leaves that lag
My forest-brook along;
When the ivy tod is heavy with snow,
And the owlet whoops to the wolf below,
That eats the she-wolf's young."

"Dear Lord! it hath a fiendish look—
(The Pilot made reply)
I am afeared"—"Push on, push on!"
Said the Hermit cheerily.

The boat came closer to the ship,
But I nor spake nor stirred;
The boat came close beneath the ship,
And straight a sound was heard.

*The ship suddenly sinketh.*

Under the water it rumbled on,
Still louder and more dread:
It reached the ship, it split the bay;
The ship went down like lead.

*The ancient Mariner is saved in the Pilot's boat.*

Stunned by that loud and dreadful sound,
Which sky and ocean smote,
Like one that hath been seven days drowned
My body lay afloat;
But swift as dreams, myself I found
Within the Pilot's boat.

Upon the whirl, where sank the ship,
The boat spun round and round;
And all was still, save that the hill
Was telling of the sound.

I moved my lips—the Pilot shrieked
And fell down in a fit;
The holy Hermit raised his eyes,
And prayed where he did sit.

I took the oars: the Pilot's boy,
Who now doth crazy go,
Laughed loud and long, and all the while
His eyes went to and fro.
"Ha! ha!" quoth he, "full plain I see,
The Devil knows how to row."

And now, all in my own countree,
I stood on the firm land!

535. tod: bush.

The Hermit stepped forth from the boat,
And scarcely he could stand.

*The ancient Mariner earnestly entreateth the Hermit to shrieve him; and the penance of life falls on him.*

"O shrieve me, shrieve me, holy man!"
The Hermit crossed his brow.
"Say quick," quoth he, "I bid thee say—
What manner of man art thou?"

Forthwith this frame of mine was wrenched
With a woful agony,
Which forced me to begin my tale;
And then it left me free.

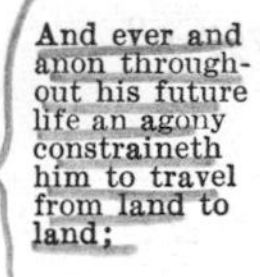

*And ever and anon throughout his future life an agony constraineth him to travel from land to land;*

Since then, at an uncertain hour,
That agony returns:
And till my ghastly tale is told,
This heart within me burns.

I pass, like night, from land to land;
I have strange power of speech;
That moment that his face I see,
I know the man that must hear me:
To him my tale I teach.

What loud uproar bursts from that door!
The wedding guests are there:
But in the garden-bower the bride
And bridemaids singing are:
And hark the little vesper bell,
Which biddeth me to prayer!

O Wedding Guest! this soul hath been
Alone on a wide wide sea:
So lonely 'twas, that God himself
Scarce seemèd there to be.

O sweeter than the marriage feast,
'Tis sweeter far to me,
To walk together to the kirk
With a goodly company!—

To walk together to the kirk,
And all together pray,
While each to his great Father bends,
Old men, and babes, and loving friends
And youths and maidens gay!

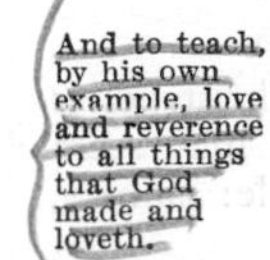

*And to teach, by his own example, love and reverence to all things that God made and loveth.*

Farewell, farewell! but this I tell
To thee, thou Wedding Guest!
He prayeth well, who loveth well
Both man and bird and beast.

575. crossed: made the sign of the cross.

He prayeth best, who loveth best
All things both great and small;
For the dear God who loveth us,
He made and loveth all.

The Mariner, whose eye is bright,
Whose beard with age is hoar,
Is gone: and now the Wedding Guest
Turned from the bridegroom's door.

He went like one that hath been
stunned,
And is of sense forlorn:
A sadder and a wiser man,
He rose the morrow morn.

*1797–98*

# CHRISTABEL

## PREFACE

The first part of the following poem was written in the year 1797 at Stowey, in the county of Somerset. The second part, after my return from Germany, in the year 1800, at Keswick, Cumberland. It is probable that if the poem had been finished at either of the former periods, or if even the first and second part had been published in the year 1800, the impression of its originality would have been much greater than I dare at present expect. But for this I have only my own indolence to blame. The dates are mentioned for the exclusive purpose of precluding charges of plagiarism or servile imitation from myself. For there is amongst us a set of critics who seem to hold that every possible thought and image is traditional; who have no notion that there are such things as fountains in the world, small as well as great; and who would therefore charitably derive every rill they behold flowing from a perforation made in some other man's tank. I am confident, however, that as far as the present poem is concerned, the celebrated poets[1] whose writings I might be suspected of having imitated, either in particular passages, or in the tone and the spirit of the whole, would be among the first to vindicate me from the charge, and who, on any striking coincidence, would permit me to address them in this doggerel version of two monkish Latin hexameters.

'Tis mine and it is likewise yours;
But an if this will not do;
Let it be mine, good friend! for I
Am the poorer of the two.

I have only to add that the meter of Christabel is not, properly speaking, irregular, though it may seem so from its being founded on a new principle: namely, that of counting in each line the accents, not the syllables. Though the latter may vary from seven to twelve, yet in each line the accents will be found to be only four. Nevertheless, this occasional variation in number of syllables is not introduced wantonly, or for the mere ends of convenience, but in correspondence with some transition in the nature of the imagery or passion [STC].

### Part I

'Tis the middle of night by the castle clock,
And the owls have awakened the crowing cock;
Tu—whit!—— Tu—whoo!
And hark, again! the crowing cock,
How drowsily it crew.

Sir Leoline, the Baron rich,
Hath a toothless mastiff bitch;
From her kennel beneath the rock
She maketh answer to the clock,
Four for the quarters, and twelve for the hour;
Ever and aye, by shine and shower,
Sixteen short howls, not over loud;
Some say, she sees my lady's shroud.

Is the night chilly and dark?
The night is chilly, but not dark.
The thin gray cloud is spread on high,
It covers but not hides the sky.
The moon is behind, and at the full;
And yet she looks both small and dull.
The night is chill, the cloud is gray:
'Tis a month before the month of May,
And the spring comes slowly up this way.

The lovely lady, Christabel,
Whom her father loves so well,
What makes her in the wood so late,
A furlong from the castle gate?
She had dreams all yesternight
Of her own betrothèd knight;
And she in the midnight wood will pray
For the weal of her lover that's far away.

She stole along, she nothing spoke,
The sighs she heaved were soft and low,
And naught was green upon the oak
But moss and rarest mistletoe:
She kneels beneath the huge oak tree,
And in silence prayeth she.

The lady sprang up suddenly,
The lovely lady, Christabel!
It moaned as near, as near can be,
But what it is she cannot tell.—
On the other side it seems to be,
Of the huge, broad-breasted, old oak tree.

**623. forlorn:** deprived. CHRISTABEL. **1. poets:** Scott and Byron.

The night is chill; the forest bare;
Is it the wind that moaneth bleak?
There is not wind enough in the air
To move away the ringlet curl
From the lovely lady's cheek —
There is not wind enough to twirl
The one red leaf, the last of its clan,
That dances as often as dance it can,
Hanging so light, and hanging so high,
On the topmost twig that looks up at the sky.

Hush, beating heart of Christabel!
Jesu, Maria, shield her well!
She folded her arms beneath her cloak,
And stole to the other side of the oak.
What sees she there?

There she sees a damsel bright,
Drest in a silken robe of white,
That shadowy in the moonlight shone:
The neck that made that white robe wan,
Her stately neck, and arms were bare;
Her blue-veined feet unsandeled were,
And wildly glittered here and there
The gems entangled in her hair.

I guess, 'twas frightful there to see
A lady so richly clad as she —
Beautiful exceedingly!

Mary mother, save me now!
(Said Christabel,) And who art thou?

The lady strange made answer meet,
And her voice was faint and sweet: —
Have pity on my sore distress,
I scarce can speak for weariness:
Stretch forth thy hand, and have no fear!
Said Christabel, How camest thou here?
And the lady, whose voice was faint and sweet,
Did thus pursue her answer meet: —

My sire is of a noble line,
And my name is Geraldine:
Five warriors seized me yestermorn,
Me, even me, a maid forlorn:
They choked my cries with force and fright,
And tied me on a palfrey white.
The palfrey was as fleet as wind,
And they rode furiously behind.
They spurred amain, their steeds were white:
And once we crossed the shade of night.
As sure as Heaven shall rescue me,
I have no thought what men they be;
Nor do I know how long it is

87. amain: at full speed.

(For I have lain entranced I wis)
Since one, the tallest of the five,
Took me from the palfrey's back,
A weary woman, scarce alive.
Some muttered words his comrades spoke:
He placed me underneath this oak;
He swore they would return with haste;
Whither they went I cannot tell —
I thought I heard, some minutes past,
Sounds as of a castle bell.
Stretch forth thy hand (thus ended she),
And help a wretched maid to flee.

Then Christabel stretched forth her hand,
And comforted fair Geraldine:
O well, bright dame! may you command
The service of Sir Leoline;
And gladly our stout chivalry
Will he send forth and friends withal
To guide and guard you safe and free
Home to your noble father's hall.

She rose: and forth with steps they passed
That strove to be, and were not, fast.
Her gracious stars the lady blest,
And thus spake on sweet Christabel:
All our household are at rest,
The hall as silent as the cell;
Sir Leoline is weak in health,
And may not well awakened be,
But we will move as if in stealth,
And I beseech your courtesy,
This night, to share your couch with me.

They crossed the moat, and Christabel
Took the key that fitted well;
A little door she opened straight,
All in the middle of the gate;
The gate that was ironed within and without,
Where an army in battle array had marched out.
The lady sank, belike through pain,
And Christabel with might and main
Lifted her up, a weary weight,
Over the threshold of the gate:
Then the lady rose again,
And moved, as she were not in pain.

So free from danger, free from fear,
They crossed the court: right glad they were.
And Christabel devoutly cried
To the lady by her side,
Praise we the Virgin all divine
Who hath rescued thee from thy distress!

Alas, alas! said Geraldine,
I cannot speak for weariness.

So free from danger, free from fear,
They crossed the court: right glad they were.

Outside her kennel, the mastiff old
Lay fast asleep, in moonshine cold.
The mastiff old did not awake,
Yet she an angry moan did make!
And what can ail the mastiff bitch?
Never till now she uttered yell
Beneath the eye of Christabel.
Perhaps it is the owlet's scritch:
For what can ail the mastiff bitch?

They passed the hall, that echoes still,
Pass as lightly as you will!
The brands were flat, the brands were dying,
Amid their own white ashes lying;
But when the lady passed, there came
A tongue of light, a fit of flame;
And Christabel saw the lady's eye,
And nothing else saw she thereby,
Save the boss of the shield of Sir Leoline tall,
Which hung in a murky old niche in the wall.
O softly tread, said Christabel,
My father seldom sleepeth well.

Sweet Christabel her feet doth bare,
And jealous of the listening air
They steal their way from stair to stair,
Now in glimmer, and now in gloom,
And now they pass the Baron's room,
As still as death, with stifled breath!
And now have reached her chamber door;
And now doth Geraldine press down
The rushes of the chamber floor.

The moon shines dim in the open air,
And not a moonbeam enters here.
But they without its light can see
The chamber carved so curiously,
Carved with figures strange and sweet,
All made out of the carver's brain,
For a lady's chamber meet:
The lamp with twofold silver chain
Is fastened to an angel's feet.

The silver lamp burns dead and dim;
But Christabel the lamp will trim.
She trimmed the lamp, and made it bright,
And left it swinging to and fro,
While Geraldine, in wretched plight,
Sank down upon the floor below.

O weary lady, Geraldine,
I pray you, drink this cordial wine!
It is a wine of virtuous powers;
My mother made it of wild flowers.

And will your mother pity me,
Who am a maiden most forlorn?
Christabel answered—Woe is me!
She died the hour that I was born.
I have heard the gray-haired friar tell
How on her deathbed she did say,
That she should hear the castle bell
Strike twelve upon my wedding day.
O mother dear! that thou wert here!
I would, said Geraldine, she were!

But soon with altered voice, said she—
"Off, wandering mother! Peak and pine!
I have power to bid thee flee."
Alas! what ails poor Geraldine?
Why stares she with unsettled eye?
Can she the bodiless dead espy?
And why with hollow voice cries she,
"Off, woman, off! this hour is mine—
Though thou her guardian spirit be,
Off, woman, off! 'tis given to me."

Then Christabel knelt by the lady's side,
And raised to heaven her eyes so blue—
Alas! said she, this ghastly ride—
Dear lady! it hath wildered you!
The lady wiped her moist cold brow,
And faintly said, " 'Tis over now!"

Again the wild-flower wine she drank:
Her fair large eyes 'gan glitter bright,
And from the floor whereon she sank,
The lofty lady stood upright:
She was most beautiful to see,
Like a lady of a far countree.

And thus the lofty lady spake—
"All they who live in the upper sky,
Do love you, holy Christabel!
And you love them, and for their sake
And for the good which me befell,
Even I in my degree will try,
Fair maiden, to requite you well.
But now unrobe yourself; for I
Must pray, ere yet in bed I lie."

Quoth Christabel, So let it be!
And as the lady bade, did she.
Her gentle limbs did she undress,
And lay down in her loveliness.

**152. scritch:** screech.

**205. Peak:** grow thin.

But through her brain of weal and woe
So many thoughts moved to and fro,
That vain it were her lids to close;
So halfway from the bed she rose,
And on her elbow did recline
To look at the lady Geraldine.

Beneath the lamp the lady bowed,
And slowly rolled her eyes around;
Then drawing in her breath aloud,
Like one that shuddered, she unbound
The cincture from beneath her breast:
Her silken robe, and inner vest,
Dropt to her feet, and full in view,
Behold! her bosom and half her side——
A sight to dream of, not to tell!
O shield her! shield sweet Christabel!

Yet Geraldine nor speaks nor stirs;
Ah! what a stricken look was hers!
Deep from within she seems halfway
To lift some weight with sick assay,
And eyes the maid and seeks delay;
Then suddenly, as one defied,
Collects herself in scorn and pride,
And lay down by the Maiden's side!—
And in her arms the maid she took,
        Ah wel-a-day!
And with low voice and doleful look
These words did say:
"In the touch of this bosom there worketh a spell,
Which is lord of thy utterance, Christabel!
Thou knowest tonight, and wilt know tomorrow,
This mark of my shame, this seal of my sorrow;
    But vainly thou warrest,
        For this is alone in
    Thy power to declare,
        That in the dim forest
    Thou heard'st a low moaning,
And found'st a bright lady, surpassingly fair;
And didst bring her home with thee in love and in charity,
To shield her and shelter her from the damp air."

### The Conclusion to Part I

It was a lovely sight to see
The lady Christabel, when she
Was praying at the old oak tree.
    Amid the jaggèd shadows
    Of mossy leafless boughs,
    Kneeling in the moonlight,
    To make her gentle vows;
Her slender palms together prest,
Heaving sometimes on her breast;
Her face resigned to bliss or bale—
Her face, oh call it fair not pale,
And both blue eyes more bright than clear,
Each about to have a tear.

With open eyes (ah woe is me!)
Asleep, and dreaming fearfully,
Fearfully dreaming, yet, I wis,
Dreaming that alone, which is—
O sorrow and shame! Can this be she,
The lady, who knelt at the old oak tree?
And lo! the worker of these harms,
That holds the maiden in her arms,
Seems to slumber still and mild,
As a mother with her child.

A star hath set, a star hath risen,
O Geraldine! since arms of thine
Have been the lovely lady's prison.
O Geraldine! one hour was thine—
Thou'st had thy will! By tairn and rill,
The night birds all that hour were still.
But now they are jubilant anew,
From cliff and tower, tu—whoo! tu—whoo!
Tu—whoo! tu—whoo! from wood and fell!

And see! the lady Christabel
Gathers herself from out her trance;
Her limbs relax, her countenance
Grows sad and soft; the smooth thin lids
Close o'er her eyes; and tears she sheds—
Large tears that leave the lashes bright!
And oft the while she seems to smile
As infants at a sudden light!

Yea, she doth smile, and she doth weep,
Like a youthful hermitess,
Beauteous in a wilderness,
Who, praying always, prays in sleep.
And, if she move unquietly,
Perchance, 'tis but the blood so free
Comes back and tingles in her feet.
No doubt, she hath a vision sweet.
What if her guardian spirit 'twere,
What if she knew her mother near?
But this she knows, in joys and woes,
That saints will aid if men will call:
For the blue sky bends over all!

### Part II

Each matin bell, the Baron saith,
Knells us back to a world of death.

**256–61.** These lines were added in 1828.

**306. tairn:** small mountain lake. **310. fell:** mountain.

These words Sir Leoline first said,
When he rose and found his lady dead:
These words Sir Leoline will say
Many a morn to his dying day!

And hence the custom and law began
That still at dawn the sacristan,
Who duly pulls the heavy bell,
Five and forty beads must tell
Between each stroke — a warning knell,
Which not a soul can choose but hear
From Bratha Head to Wyndermere.

Saith Bracy the bard, So let it knell!
And let the drowsy sacristan
Still count as slowly as he can!
There is no lack of such, I ween,
As well fill up the space between.
In Langdale Pike and Witch's Lair,
And Dungeon Ghyll so foully rent,
With ropes of rock and bells of air
Three sinful sextons' ghosts are pent,
Who all give back, one after t'other,
The death-note to their living brother;
And oft too, by the knell offended,
Just as their one! two! three! is ended,
The devil mocks the doleful tale
With a merry peal from Borodale.

The air is still! through mist and cloud
That merry peal comes ringing loud;
And Geraldine shakes off her dread,
And rises lightly from the bed;
Puts on her silken vestments white,
And tricks her hair in lovely plight,
And nothing doubting of her spell
Awakens the lady Christabel.
"Sleep you, sweet lady Christabel?
I trust that you have rested well."

And Christabel awoke and spied
The same who lay down by her side —
O rather say, the same whom she
Raised up beneath the old oak tree!
Nay, fairer yet! and yet more fair!
For she belike hath drunken deep
Of all the blessedness of sleep!
And while she spake, her looks, her air
Such gentle thankfulness declare,
That (so it seemed) her girded vests
Grew tight beneath her heaving breasts.

"Sure I have sinned!" said Christabel,
"Now heaven be praised if all be well!"
And in low faltering tones, yet sweet,
Did she the lofty lady greet
With such perplexity of mind
As dreams too lively leave behind.

So quickly she rose, and quickly arrayed
Her maiden limbs, and having prayed
That He, who on the cross did groan,
Might wash away her sins unknown,
She forthwith led fair Geraldine
To meet her sire, Sir Leoline.

The lovely maid and the lady tall
Are pacing both into the hall,
And pacing on through page and groom,
Enter the Baron's presence room.

The Baron rose, and while he prest
His gentle daughter to his breast,
With cheerful wonder in his eyes
The lady Geraldine espies,
And gave such welcome to the same,
As might beseem so bright a dame!

But when he heard the lady's tale,
And when she told her father's name,
Why waxed Sir Leoline so pale,
Murmuring o'er the name again,
Lord Roland de Vaux of Tryermaine?

Alas! they had been friends in youth;
But whispering tongues can poison truth;
And constancy lives in realms above;
And life is thorny; and youth is vain;
And to be wroth with one we love
Doth work like madness in the brain.
And thus it chanced, as I divine,
With Roland and Sir Leoline.
Each spake words of high disdain
And insult to his heart's best brother:
They parted — ne'er to meet again!
But never either found another
To free the hollow heart from paining —
They stood aloof, the scars remaining,
Like cliffs which had been rent asunder;
A dreary sea now flows between; —
But neither heat, nor frost, nor thunder,
Shall wholly do away, I ween,
The marks of that which once hath been.

Sir Leoline, a moment's space,
Stood gazing on the damsel's face:

**339. sacristan:** sexton. **341. beads:** prayers. **344–59. Bratha . . . Borodale:** The places named in this passage are in the Lake District. **350. Pike:** peak. **351. Ghyll:** valley. **365. plight:** plait, or condition.

**408–26. Alas! . . . been:** These lines appear to have been in-

And the youthful Lord of Tryermaine
Came back upon his heart again.

O then the Baron forgot his age,
His noble heart swelled high with rage;
He swore by the wounds in Jesu's side
He would proclaim it far and wide,
With trump and solemn heraldry,
That they, who thus had wronged the dame,
Were base as spotted infamy!
" And if they dare deny the same,
My herald shall appoint a week,
And let the recreant traitors seek
My tourney court — that there and then
I may dislodge their reptile souls
From the bodies and forms of men!"
He spake: his eye in lightning rolls!
For the lady was ruthlessly seized; and he kenned
In the beautiful lady the child of his friend!

And now the tears were on his face,
And fondly in his arms he took
Fair Geraldine, who met the embrace,
Prolonging it with joyous look.
Which when she viewed, a vision fell
Upon the soul of Christabel,
The vision of fear, the touch and pain!
She shrunk and shuddered, and saw again —
(Ah, woe is me! Was it for thee,
Thou gentle maid! such sights to see?)

Again she saw that bosom old,
Again she felt that bosom cold,
And drew in her breath with a hissing sound:
Whereat the Knight turned wildly round,
And nothing saw, but his own sweet maid
With eyes upraised, as one that prayed.

The touch, the sight, had passed away,
And in its stead that vision blest,
Which comforted her after rest
While in the lady's arms she lay,
Had put a rapture in her breast,
And on her lips and o'er her eyes
Spread smiles like light!
With new surprise,
" What ails then my belovèd child? "
The Baron said — His daughter mild
Made answer, " All will yet be well! "
I ween, she had no power to tell
Aught else: so mighty was the spell.

Yet he, who saw this Geraldine,
Had deemed her sure a thing divine:
Such sorrow with such grace she blended,
As if she feared she had offended
Sweet Christabel, that gentle maid!
And with such lowly tones she prayed
She might be sent without delay
Home to her father's mansion.
"Nay!
Nay, by my soul!" said Leoline.
" Ho! Bracy the bard, the charge be thine!
Go thou, with music sweet and loud,
And take two steeds with trappings proud,
And take the youth whom thou lov'st best
To bear thy harp, and learn thy song,
And clothe you both in solemn vest,
And over the mountains haste along,
Lest wandering folk, that are abroad,
Detain you on the valley road.

" And when he has crossed the Irthing flood,
My merry bard! he hastes, he hastes
Up Knorren Moor, through Halegarth Wood,
And reaches soon that castle good
Which stands and threatens Scotland's wastes.

" Bard Bracy! bard Bracy! your horses are fleet,
Ye must ride up the hall, your music so sweet,
More loud than your horses' echoing feet!
And loud and loud to Lord Roland call,
Thy daughter is safe in Langdale hall!
Thy beautiful daughter is safe and free —
Sir Leoline greets thee thus through me!
He bids thee come without delay
With all thy numerous array
And take thy lovely daughter home:
And he will meet thee on the way
With all his numerous array
White with their panting palfreys' foam:
And, by mine honor! I will say,
That I repent me of the day
When I spake words of fierce disdain
To Roland de Vaux of Tryermaine! —
— For since that evil hour hath flown,
Many a summer's sun hath shone;
Yet ne'er found I a friend again
Like Roland de Vaux of Tryermaine.

The lady fell, and clasped his knees,
Her face upraised, her eyes o'erflowing;
And Bracy replied, with faltering voice,
His gracious Hail on all bestowing! —
" Thy words, thou sire of Christabel,
Are sweeter than my harp can tell;
Yet might I gain a boon of thee,
This day my journey should not be,
So strange a dream hath come to me,
That I had vowed with music loud

spired by Coleridge's temporary estrangement from Robert Southey.

To clear yon wood from thing unblest,
Warned by a vision in my rest!
For in my sleep I saw that dove,
That gentle bird, whom thou dost love,
And call'st by thy own daughter's name —
Sir Leoline! I saw the same
Fluttering, and uttering fearful moan,
Among the green herbs in the forest alone.
Which when I saw and when I heard,
I wondered what might ail the bird;
For nothing near it could I see,
Save the grass and green herbs underneath the old tree.

"And in my dream methought I went
To search out what might there be found;
And what the sweet bird's trouble meant,
That thus lay fluttering on the ground.
I went and peered, and could descry
No cause for her distressful cry;
But yet for her dear lady's sake
I stooped, methought, the dove to take,
When lo! I saw a bright green snake
Coiled around its wings and neck.
Green as the herbs on which it couched,
Close by the dove's its head it crouched;
And with the dove it heaves and stirs,
Swelling its neck as she swelled hers!
I woke; it was the midnight hour,
The clock was echoing in the tower;
But though my slumber was gone by,
This dream it would not pass away —
It seems to live upon my eye!
And thence I vowed this selfsame day
With music strong and saintly song
To wander through the forest bare,
Lest aught unholy loiter there."

Thus Bracy said: the Baron, the while,
Half listening heard him with a smile;
Then turned to Lady Geraldine,
His eyes made up of wonder and love;
And said in courtly accents fine,
"Sweet maid, Lord Roland's beauteous dove,
With arms more strong than harp or song,
Thy sire and I will crush the snake!"
He kissed her forehead as he spake,
And Geraldine in maiden wise
Casting down her large bright eyes,
With blushing cheek and courtesy fine
She turned her from Sir Leoline;
Softly gathering up her train,
That o'er her right arm fell again;
And folded her arms across her chest,
And couched her head upon her breast,
And looked askance at Christabel —
Jesu, Maria, shield her well!

A snake's small eye blinks dull and shy;
And the lady's eyes they shrunk in her head,
Each shrunk up to a serpent's eye,
And with somewhat of malice, and more of dread,
At Christabel she looked askance! —
One moment — and the sight was fled!
But Christabel in dizzy trance
Stumbling on the unsteady ground
Shuddered aloud, with a hissing sound;
And Geraldine again turned round,
And like a thing that sought relief,
Full of wonder and full of grief,
She rolled her large bright eyes divine
Wildly on Sir Leoline.

The maid, alas! her thoughts are gone,
She nothing sees — no sight but one!
The maid, devoid of guile and sin,
I know not how, in fearful wise,
So deeply had she drunken in
That look, those shrunken serpent eyes,
That all her features were resigned
To this sole image in her mind;
And passively did imitate
That look of dull and treacherous hate!
And thus she stood, in dizzy trance,
Still picturing that look askance
With forced unconscious sympathy
Full before her father's view ——
As far as such a look could be
In eyes so innocent and blue!

And when the trance was o'er, the maid
Paused awhile, and inly prayed:
Then falling at the Baron's feet,
"By my mother's soul do I entreat
That thou this woman send away!"
She said: and more she could not say:
For what she knew she could not tell,
O'ermastered by the mighty spell.

Why is thy cheek so wan and wild,
Sir Leoline? Thy only child
Lies at thy feet, thy joy, thy pride,
So fair, so innocent, so mild;
The same, for whom thy lady died!
O by the pangs of her dear mother
Think thou no evil of thy child!
For her, and thee, and for no other,
She prayed the moment ere she died:
Prayed that the babe for whom she died,
Might prove her dear lord's joy and pride!
That prayer her deadly pangs beguiled,
Sir Leoline!
And wouldst thou wrong thy only child,
Her child and thine?

Within the Baron's heart and brain
If thoughts, like these, had any share,
They only swelled his rage and pain,
And did but work confusion there.
His heart was cleft with pain and rage,
His cheeks they quivered, his eyes were wild,
Dishonored thus in his old age;
Dishonored by his only child,
And all his hospitality
To the wronged daughter of his friend
By more than woman's jealousy
Brought thus to a disgraceful end —
He rolled his eye with stern regard
Upon the gentle minstrel bard,
And said in tones abrupt, austere —
"Why, Bracy! dost thou loiter here?
I bade thee hence!" The bard obeyed;
And turning from his own sweet maid,
The agèd knight, Sir Leoline,
Led forth the lady Geraldine!

THE CONCLUSION TO PART II

A little child, a limber elf,
Singing, dancing to itself,
A fairy thing with red round cheeks,
That always finds, and never seeks,
Makes such a vision to the sight
As fills a father's eyes with light;
And pleasures flow in so thick and fast
Upon his heart, that he at last
Must needs express his love's excess
With words of unmeant bitterness.
Perhaps 'tis pretty to force together
Thoughts so all unlike each other;
To mutter and mock a broken charm,
To dally with wrong that does no harm.
Perhaps 'tis tender too and pretty
At each wild word to feel within
A sweet recoil of love and pity.
And what, if in a world of sin
(O sorrow and shame should this be true!)
Such giddiness of heart and brain
Comes seldom save from rage and pain,
So talks as it's most used to do.

*1797?–1801*

## FROST AT MIDNIGHT

The frost performs its secret ministry,
Unhelped by any wind. The owlet's cry
Came loud — and hark, again! loud as before.
The inmates of my cottage, all at rest,
Have left me to that solitude, which suits
Abstruser musings: save that at my side
My cradled infant slumbers peacefully.
'Tis calm indeed! so calm, that it disturbs
And vexes meditation with its strange
And extreme silentness. Sea, hill, and wood,
This populous village! Sea, and hill, and wood,
With all the numberless goings-on of life,
Inaudible as dreams! the thin blue flame
Lies on my low-burnt fire, and quivers not;
Only that film, which fluttered on the grate,
Still flutters there, the sole unquiet thing.
Methinks, its motion in this hush of nature
Gives it dim sympathies with me who live,
Making it a companionable form,
Whose puny flaps and freaks the idling spirit
By its own moods interprets, everywhere
Echo or mirror seeking of itself,
And makes a toy of thought.

But O! how oft,
How oft, at school, with most believing mind,
Presageful, have I gazed upon the bars,
To watch that fluttering *stranger!* and as oft
With unclosed lids, already had I dreamt
Of my sweet birthplace, and the old church tower,
Whose bells, the poor man's only music, rang
From morn to evening, all the hot fair-day,
So sweetly, that they stirred and haunted me
With a wild pleasure, falling on mine ear
Most like articulate sounds of things to come!
So gazed I, till the soothing things, I dreamt,
Lulled me to sleep, and sleep prolonged my dreams!
And so I brooded all the following morn,
Awed by the stern preceptor's face, mine eye
Fixed with mock study on my swimming book:
Save if the door half opened, and I snatched
A hasty glance, and still my heart leaped up,
For still I hoped to see the *stranger's* face,
Townsman, or aunt, or sister more beloved,
My playmate when we both were clothed alike!

Dear babe, that sleepest cradled by my side,
Whose gentle breathings, heard in this deep calm,
Fill up the interspersèd vacancies
And momentary pauses of the thought!
My babe so beautiful! it thrills my heart
With tender gladness, thus to look at thee,
And think that thou shalt learn far other lore,
And in far other scenes! For I was reared

FROST AT MIDNIGHT. **7. infant**: Hartley Coleridge. **15. film**: "In all parts of the kingdom these films are called *strangers* and supposed to portend the arrival of some absent friend" [C]. **24. school**: Christ's Hospital, London. **37. stern preceptor**: Boyer, master of Christ's Hospital; he once knocked Coleridge down and flogged him for saying that because he was an infidel he wished to become a cobbler instead of a clergyman. **43. playmate**: his sister Ann. **51–53. For . . . stars**: Compare these lines with *The Prelude,* VIII.433–34 ("I did not pine like one in cities bred,/As was thy melancholy lot, dear friend").

In the great city, pent 'mid cloisters dim,
And saw nought lovely but the sky and stars.
But *thou*, my babe! shalt wander like a breeze
By lakes and sandy shores, beneath the crags
Of ancient mountain, and beneath the clouds,
Which image in their bulk both lakes and shores
And mountain crags: so shalt thou see and hear
The lovely shapes and sounds intelligible
Of that eternal language, which thy God
Utters, who from eternity doth teach
Himself in all, and all things in himself.
Great universal Teacher! he shall mold
Thy spirit, and by giving make it ask.

Therefore all seasons shall be sweet to thee,
Whether the summer clothe the general earth
With greenness, or the redbreast sit and sing
Betwixt the tufts of snow on the bare branch
Of mossy apple tree, while the nigh thatch
Smokes in the sun-thaw; whether the eave drops
fall
Heard only in the trances of the blast,
Or if the secret ministry of frost
Shall hang them up in silent icicles,
Quietly shining to the quiet moon.

*1798*

## FRANCE: AN ODE

I

Ye Clouds! that far above me float and pause,
Whose pathless march no mortal may control!
Ye Ocean Waves! that, wheresoe'er ye roll,
Yield homage only to eternal laws!
Ye Woods! that listen to the night birds sing-
ing,
Midway the smooth and perilous slope reclined,
Save when your own imperious branches swing-
ing,
Have made a solemn music of the wind!
Where, like a man beloved of God,
Through glooms, which never woodman trod,
How oft, pursuing fancies holy,
My moonlight way o'er flowering weeds I wound,
Inspired, beyond the guess of folly,
By each rude shape and wild unconquerable sound!
O ye loud Waves! and O ye Forests high!
And O ye Clouds that far above me soared!
Thou rising Sun! thou blue rejoicing Sky!
Yea, every thing that is and will be free!
Bear witness for me, wheresoe'er ye be,
With what deep worship I have still adored
The spirit of divinest Liberty.

II

When France in wrath her giant limbs upreared,
And with that oath, which smote air, earth, and
sea,
Stamped her strong foot and said she would be
free,
Bear witness for me, how I hoped and feared!
With what a joy my lofty gratulation
Unawed I sang, amid a slavish band:
And when to whelm the disenchanted nation,
Like fiends embattled by a wizard's wand,
The monarchs marched in evil day,
And Britain joined the dire array;
Though dear her shores and circling ocean,
Though many friendships, many youthful loves
Had swoln the patriot emotion
And flung a magic light o'er all her hills and
groves;
Yet still my voice, unaltered, sang defeat
To all that braved the tyrant-quelling lance,
And shame too long delayed and vain retreat!
For ne'er, O Liberty! with partial aim
I dimmed thy light or damped thy holy flame;
But blessed the paeans of delivered France,
And hung my head and wept at Britain's name.

III

"And what," I said, "though Blasphemy's loud
scream
With that sweet music of deliverance strove!
Though all the fierce and drunken passions
wove
A dance more wild than e'er was maniac's dream!
Ye storms, that round the dawning East as-
sembled,
The Sun was rising, though ye hid his light!"
And when, to soothe my soul, that hoped and
trembled,
The dissonance ceased, and all seemed calm and
bright;
When France her front deep scarred and gory
Concealed with clustering wreaths of glory;
When, insupportably advancing,
Her arm made mockery of the warrior's ramp;
While timid looks of fury glancing,
Domestic treason, crushed beneath her fatal
stamp,
Writhed like a wounded dragon in his gore;
Then I reproached my fears that would not flee;
"And soon," I said, "shall Wisdom teach her lore

FRANCE: AN ODE. **31. dire array:** Prussia and Austria went to war against France in 1792; England and Holland joined the alliance in 1793. **43. Blasphemy's . . . scream:** In November, 1793, a woman, euphemistically referred to as an actress, was enthroned at the high altar in Notre Dame and worshiped as the Goddess of Reason. **48. Sun:** of liberty. **54. warrior's ramp:** truculent posture or attitude.

In the low huts of them that toil and groan!
And, conquering by her happiness alone,
Shall France compel the nations to be free,
Till Love and Joy look round, and call the earth their own."

IV

Forgive me, Freedom! O forgive those dreams!
I hear thy voice, I hear thy loud lament,
From bleak Helvetia's icy caverns sent—
I hear thy groans upon her bloodstained streams!
Heroes, that for your peaceful country perished,
And ye that, fleeing, spot your mountain snows
With bleeding wounds; forgive me, that I cherished
One thought that ever blessed your cruel foes!
To scatter rage, and traitorous guilt,
Where Peace her jealous home had built;
A patriot race to disinherit
Of all that made their stormy wilds so dear;
And with inexpiable spirit
To taint the bloodless freedom of the mountaineer—
O France, that mockest Heaven, adulterous, blind,
And patriot only in pernicious toils!
Are these thy boasts, champion of human kind?
To mix with kings in the low lust of sway,
Yell in the hunt, and share the murderous prey;
To insult the shrine of Liberty with spoils
From freemen torn; to tempt and to betray?

V

The Sensual and the Dark rebel in vain,
Slaves by their own compulsion! In mad game
They burst their manacles and wear the name
Of Freedom, graven on a heavier chain!
O Liberty! with profitless endeavor
Have I pursued thee, many a weary hour;
But thou nor swell'st the victor's strain, nor ever
Didst breathe thy soul in forms of human power.
Alike from all, howe'er they praise thee,
(Nor prayer, nor boastful name delays thee)
Alike from Priestcraft's harpy minions,
And factious Blasphemy's obscener slaves,
Thou speedest on thy subtle pinions,
The guide of homeless winds, and playmate of the waves!
And there I felt thee!—on that sea cliff's verge,
Whose pines, scarce traveled by the breeze above,
Had made one murmur with the distant surge!
Yes, while I stood and gazed, my temples bare,
And shot my being through earth, sea, and air,
Possessing all things with intensest love,
O Liberty! my spirit felt thee there.

*1798*

**66. Helvetia**: Switzerland.

# KUBLA KHAN

### OR, A VISION IN A DREAM. A FRAGMENT.

The following fragment is here published at the request of a poet of great and deserved celebrity,[1] and, as far as the author's own opinions are concerned, rather as a psychological curiosity than on the ground of any supposed *poetic* merits.

In the summer of the year 1797, the author, then in ill health, had retired to a lonely farmhouse between Porlock and Linton, on the Exmoor confines of Somerset and Devonshire. In consequence of a slight indisposition, an anodyne had been prescribed, from the effects of which he fell asleep in his chair at the moment that he was reading the following sentence, or words of the same substance, in "Purchas's Pilgrimage": "Here the Khan Kubla commanded a palace to be built, and a stately garden thereunto. And thus ten miles of fertile ground were inclosed with a wall." The author continued for about three hours in a profound sleep, at least of the external senses, during which time he has the most vivid confidence, that he could not have composed less than from two to three hundred lines; if that indeed can be called composition in which all the images rose up before him as *things,* with a parallel production of the correspondent expressions, without any sensation or consciousness of effort. On awaking he appeared to himself to have a distinct recollection of the whole, and taking his pen, ink, and paper, instantly and eagerly wrote down the lines that are here preserved. At this moment he was unfortunately called out by a person on business from Porlock and detained by him above an hour, and on his return to his room, found, to his no small surprise and mortification, that though he still retained some vague and dim recollection of the general purport of the vision, yet, with the exception of some eight or ten scattered lines and images, all the rest had passed away like the images on the surface of a stream into which a stone has been cast, but, alas! without the after restoration of the latter!

Then all the charm
Is broken—all that phantom world so fair
Vanishes, and a thousand circlets spread,
And each misshape[s] the other. Stay awhile,
Poor youth! who scarcely dar'st lift up thine eyes—
The stream will soon renew its smoothness, soon
The visions will return! And lo, he stays,
And soon the fragments dim of lovely forms
Come trembling back, unite, and now once more
The pool becomes a mirror.

["The Picture, or the Lover's Resolution," ll. 91–100]

Yet from the still surviving recollections in his mind, the author has frequently purposed to finish for himself what had been originally, as it were, given to him. Σαμερον αδιον ασω:[2] but the tomorrow is yet to come [STC].

KUBLA KHAN. **1. celebrity**: Byron. **2.** "I will sing you a sweeter song tomorrow" (Theocritus, *Idylls,* I.145).

In Xanadu did Kubla Khan
A stately pleasure dome decree:
Where Alph, the sacred river, ran
Through caverns measureless to man
  Down to a sunless sea.
So twice five miles of fertile ground
With walls and towers were girdled round:
And there were gardens bright with sinuous rills,
Where blossomed many an incense-bearing tree;
And here were forests ancient as the hills,
Enfolding sunny spots of greenery.
But oh! that deep romantic chasm which slanted
Down the green hill athwart a cedarn cover!
A savage place! as holy and enchanted
As e'er beneath a waning moon was haunted
By woman wailing for her demon lover!
And from this chasm, with ceaseless turmoil seething,
As if this earth in fast thick pants were breathing,
A mighty fountain momently was forced:
Amid whose swift half-intermitted burst
Huge fragments vaulted like rebounding hail,
Or chaffy grain beneath the thresher's flail:
And 'mid these dancing rocks at once and ever
It flung up momently the sacred river.
Five miles meandering with a mazy motion
Through wood and dale the sacred river ran,
Then reached the caverns measureless to man,
And sank in tumult to a lifeless ocean:
And 'mid this tumult Kubla heard from far
Ancestral voices prophesying war!
  The shadow of the dome of pleasure
  Floated midway on the waves;
  Where was heard the mingled measure
  From the fountain and the caves.
It was a miracle of rare device,
A sunny pleasure dome with caves of ice!

  A damsel with a dulcimer
  In a vision once I saw:
  It was an Abyssinian maid,
  And on her dulcimer she played,
  Singing of Mount Abora.
  Could I revive within me
  Her symphony and song,
  To such a deep delight 'twould win me,
That with music loud and long,
I would build that dome in air,
That sunny dome! those caves of ice!
And all who heard should see them there,
And all should cry, Beware! Beware!
His flashing eyes, his floating hair!
Weave a circle round him thrice,
And close your eyes with holy dread,
For he on honeydew hath fed,
And drunk the milk of Paradise.

*1797?–1800*

**1. Xanadu . . . Khan:** Xanadu, named variously Xamdu, Xaindu, and Xandu by Samuel Purchas, was probably situated near what is now Peiping; it was the seat of Kublai Khan (1216–94), grandson of Genghis Khan and founder of the Mongol dynasty in China.

# DEJECTION: AN ODE

WRITTEN APRIL 4, 1802

Coleridge wrote the first draft of this poem after hearing Dorothy Wordsworth read from her brother's most recently composed poems, "The Rainbow" and the opening stanzas of the "Intimations Ode" among them. Originally "Dejection" was a verse letter to Sara Hutchinson that ran to 338 lines in which Coleridge expatiated on his domestic misery and its sad contrast with Wordsworth's happiness. During the summer Coleridge worked at the poem, reduced it to its present length and changed the name "Sara" first to "William" (Wordsworth), then to "Edmund," and finally to "Lady." When it first appeared, in the *Morning Post* of October 4, 1802 — Wordsworth's wedding day — "Dejection," the poem in which Coleridge announced the loss of his "shaping spirit of imagination," turned out paradoxically to be one of the best poems his imagination had ever shaped.

Late, late yestreen I saw the new moon,
With the old moon in her arms;
And I fear, I fear, my master dear!
We shall have a deadly storm.
  ["Ballad of Sir Patrick Spence"]

I

Well! If the bard was weather-wise, who made
  The grand old ballad of Sir Patrick Spence,
  This night, so tranquil now, will not go hence
Unroused by winds, that ply a busier trade
Than those which mold yon cloud in lazy flakes,
Or the dull sobbing draft, that moans and rakes
Upon the strings of this Eolian lute,
    Which better far were mute.
  For lo! the new moon winter-bright!
  And overspread with phantom light,
  (With swimming phantom light o'erspread
  But rimmed and circled by a silver thread)
I see the old moon in her lap, foretelling
  The coming on of rain and squally blast.
And oh! that even now the gust were swelling,
  And the slant night shower driving loud and fast!
Those sounds which oft have raised me, whilst they awed,
  And sent my soul abroad,

**51. Weave . . . thrice:** to exorcise or forestall any evil spirit which might possess him. DEJECTION: AN ODE. **7. Eolian lute:** See "The Eolian Harp," p. 110, n. 1, above.

Might now perhaps their wonted impulse give,
Might startle this dull pain, and make it move and live!

II

A grief without a pang, void, dark, and drear,
A stifled, drowsy, unimpassioned grief,
Which finds no natural outlet, no relief,
In word, or sigh, or tear—
O Lady! in this wan and heartless mood,
To other thoughts by yonder throstle wooed,
All this long eve, so balmy and serene,
Have I been gazing on the western sky,
And its peculiar tint of yellow green:
And still I gaze—and with how blank an eye!
And those thin clouds above, in flakes and bars,
That give away their motion to the stars;
Those stars, that glide behind them or between,
Now sparkling, now bedimmed, but always seen:
Yon crescent moon, as fixed as if it grew
In its own cloudless, starless lake of blue;
I see them all so excellently fair,
I see, not feel, how beautiful they are!

III

My genial spirits fail;
And what can these avail
To lift the smothering weight from off my breast?
It were a vain endeavor,
Though I should gaze forever
On that green light that lingers in the west:
I may not hope from outward forms to win
The passion and the life, whose fountains are within.

IV

O Lady! we receive but what we give,
And in our life alone does Nature live:
Ours is her wedding garment, ours her shroud!
And would we aught behold, of higher worth,
Than that inanimate cold world allowed
To the poor loveless ever-anxious crowd,
Ah! from the soul itself must issue forth
A light, a glory, a fair luminous cloud
Enveloping the earth—
And from the soul itself must there be sent
A sweet and potent voice, of its own birth,
Of all sweet sounds the life and element!

V

O pure of heart! thou need'st not ask of me
What this strong music in the soul may be!
What, and wherein it doth exist,
This light, this glory, this fair luminous mist,
This beautiful and beauty-making power.
Joy, virtuous Lady! joy that ne'er was given,
Save to the pure, and in their purest hour,
Life, and life's effluence, cloud at once and shower,
Joy, Lady! is the spirit and the power,
Which wedding Nature to us gives in dower
A new earth and new heaven,
Undreamt of by the sensual and the proud—
Joy is the sweet voice, joy the luminous cloud—
We in ourselves rejoice!
And thence flows all that charms or ear or sight,
All melodies the echoes of that voice,
All colors a suffusion from that light.

VI

There was a time when, though my path was rough,
This joy within me dallied with distress,
And all misfortunes were but as the stuff
Whence fancy made me dreams of happiness:
For hope grew round me, like the twining vine,
And fruits, and foliage, not my own, seemed mine.
But now afflictions bow me down to earth:
Nor care I that they rob me of my mirth;
But oh! each visitation
Suspends what nature gave me at my birth,
My shaping spirit of imagination.
For not to think of what I needs must feel,
But to be still and patient, all I can;
And haply by abstruse research to steal
From my own nature all the natural man—
This was my sole resource, my only plan:
Till that which suits a part infects the whole,
And now is almost grown the habit of my soul.

VII

Hence, viper thoughts, that coil around my mind,
Reality's dark dream!
I turn from you, and listen to the wind,
Which long has raved unnoticed. What a scream
Of agony by torture lengthened out
That lute sent forth! Thou wind, that rav'st without,
Bare crag, or mountain tairn, or blasted tree,
Or pine grove whither woodman never clomb,
Or lonely house, long held the witches' home,
Methinks were fitter instruments for thee,
Mad lutanist! who in this month of showers,
Of dark-brown gardens, and of peeping flowers,
Mak'st devils' yule, with worse than wintry song,
The blossoms, buds, and timorous leaves among.
Thou actor, perfect in all tragic sounds!
Thou mighty poet, e'en to frenzy bold!
What tell'st thou now about?
'Tis of the rushing of an host in rout,

**19. wonted:** usual. **25. Lady:** Sara Hutchinson (see headnote).

**100. tairn:** small mountain lake. **104. Mad lutan st:** the wind. **106. yule:** Christmas.

With groans, of trampled men, with smarting wounds —
At once they groan with pain, and shudder with the cold!
But hush! there is a pause of deepest silence!
And all that noise, as of a rushing crowd,
With groans, and tremulous shudderings — all is over —
It tells another tale, with sounds less deep and loud!
A tale of less affright,
And tempered with delight,
As Otway's self had framed the tender lay, —
'Tis of a little child
Upon a lonesome wild,
Not far from home, but she hath lost her way:
And now moans low in bitter grief and fear,
And now screams loud, and hopes to make her mother hear.

VIII

'Tis midnight, but small thoughts have I of sleep:
Full seldom may my friend such vigils keep!
Visit her, gentle sleep! with wings of healing,
And may this storm be but a mountain birth,
May all the stars hang bright above her dwelling,
Silent as though they watched the sleeping earth!
With light heart may she rise,
Gay fancy, cheerful eyes,
Joy lift her spirit, joy attune her voice;
To her may all things live, from pole to pole,
Their life the eddying of her living soul!
O simple spirit, guided from above,
Dear Lady! friend devoutest of my choice,
Thus mayest thou ever, evermore rejoice.

*1802*

## TO WILLIAM WORDSWORTH

COMPOSED ON THE NIGHT AFTER HIS RECITATION OF A POEM [1] ON THE GROWTH OF AN INDIVIDUAL MIND

Friend of the wise! and teacher of the good!
Into my heart have I received that lay
More than historic, that prophetic lay
Wherein (high theme by thee first sung aright)
Of the foundations and the building up
Of a human spirit thou hast dared to tell
What may be told, to the understanding mind
Revealable; and what within the mind
By vital breathings secret as the soul
Of vernal growth, oft quickens in the heart
Thoughts all too deep for words! —

Theme hard as high!
Of smiles spontaneous, and mysterious fears
(The first-born they of reason and twin birth),
Of tides obedient to external force,
And currents self-determined, as might seem,
Or by some inner power; of moments awful,
Now in thy inner life, and now abroad,
When power streamed from thee, and thy soul received
The light reflected as a light bestowed —
Of fancies fair, and milder hours of youth,
Hyblean murmurs of poetic thought
Industrious in its joy, in vales and glens
Native or outland, lakes and famous hills!
Or on the lonely highroad, when the stars
Were rising; or by secret mountain streams,
The guides and the companions of thy way!

Of more than fancy, of the social sense
Distending wide, and man beloved as man,
Where France in all her towns lay vibrating
Like some becalmèd bark beneath the burst
Of heaven's immediate thunder, when no cloud
Is visible, or shadow on the main.
For thou wert there, thine own brows garlanded,
Amid the tremor of a realm aglow,
Amid a mighty nation jubilant,
When from the general heart of human kind
Hope sprang forth like a full-born deity!
— Of that dear hope afflicted and struck down,
So summoned homeward, thenceforth calm and sure
From the dread watch tower of man's absolute self,
With light unwaning on her eyes, to look
Far on — herself a glory to behold,
The angel of the vision! Then (last strain)
Of duty, chosen laws controlling choice,
Action and joy! — An Orphic song indeed,
A song divine of high and passionate thoughts
To their own music chanted!

O great bard!
Ere yet that last strain dying awed the air,
With steadfast eye I viewed thee in the choir

**120. Otway:** Thomas Otway (1652–85), English tragic dramatist, noted for pathos. Originally the "tender lay" was "William's"; the "little child" (l. 121) is clearly Lucy Gray. TO WILLIAM WORDSWORTH. **1. Night . . . Poem:** On the night of January 7, 1807, Wordsworth finished reading (it had taken almost two weeks) *The Prelude* (pp. 41–80, above) to Coleridge. Previously Coleridge had seen only the first five books of the poem. **2. lay:** *The Prelude.* **11. Thoughts . . . words:** an echo of the last line of Wordsworth's "Intimations Ode" ("Thoughts that do often lie too deep for tears," p. 100, above). **21. Hyblean:** Hybla was an ancient Sicilian town famous for honey. **45. Orphic song:** a reference to *The Prelude,* I.233, p. 44, above (see also Matthew Arnold, "Memorial Verses," 34–39, p. 603, below).

Of ever-enduring men. The truly great
Have all one age, and from one visible space
Shed influence! They, both in power and act,
Are permanent, and time is not with them,
Save as it worketh for them, they in it.
Nor less a sacred roll, than those of old,
And to be placed, as they, with gradual fame
Among the archives of mankind, thy work
Makes audible a linkèd lay of truth,
Of truth profound a sweet continuous lay,
Not learnt, but native, her own natural notes!
Ah! as I listened with a heart forlorn,
The pulses of my being beat anew:
And even as life returns upon the drowned,
Life's joy rekindling roused a throng of pains—
Keen pangs of love, awakening as a babe
Turbulent, with an outcry in the heart;
And fears self-willed, that shunned the eye of hope;
And hope that scarce would know itself from fear;
Sense of past youth, and manhood come in vain,
And genius given, and knowledge won in vain;
And all which I had culled in wood-walks wild,
And all which patient toil had reared, and all,
Commune with thee had opened out—but flowers
Strewed on my corse, and borne upon my bier
In the same coffin, for the selfsame grave!

That way no more! and ill beseems it me,
Who came a welcomer in herald's guise,
Singing of glory, and futurity,
To wander back on such unhealthful road,
Plucking the poisons of self-harm! And ill
Such intertwine beseems triumphal wreaths
Strewed before thy advancing!

Nor do thou,
Sage bard! impair the memory of that hour
Of thy communion with my nobler mind
By pity or grief, already felt too long!
Nor let my words import more blame than needs.
The tumult rose and ceased: for peace is nigh
Where wisdom's voice has found a listening heart.
Amid the howl of more than wintry storms,
The halcyon hears the voice of vernal hours
Already on the wing.

Eve following eve,
Dear tranquil time, when the sweet sense of home
Is sweetest! moments for their own sake hailed
And more desired, more precious, for thy song,
In silence listening, like a devout child,
My soul lay passive, by thy various strain
Driven as in surges now beneath the stars,
With momentary stars of my own birth,
Fair constellated foam, still darting off
Into the darkness; now a tranquil sea,
Outspread and bright, yet swelling to the moon.

And when—O friend! my comforter and guide!
Strong in thyself, and powerful to give strength!—
Thy long sustainèd song finally closed,
And thy deep voice had ceased—yet thou thyself
Wert still before my eyes, and round us both
That happy vision of belovèd faces—
Scarce conscious, and yet conscious of its close
I sat, my being blended in one thought
(Thought was it? or aspiration? or resolve?)
Absorbed, yet hanging still upon the sound—
And when I rose, I found myself in prayer.

*1807*

83–84. **that . . . mind:** the healthy years of 1797–98 when Wordsworth and Coleridge wrote *Lyrical Ballads* (see *The Prelude*, XIV.388–414, p. 79, above).

## WORK WITHOUT HOPE

LINES COMPOSED 21ST FEBRUARY 1825

All nature seems at work. Slugs leave their lair—
The bees are stirring—birds are on the wing—
And Winter slumbering in the open air,
Wears on his smiling face a dream of Spring!
And I the while, the sole unbusy thing,
Nor honey make, nor pair, nor build, nor sing.

Yet well I ken the banks where amaranths blow,
Have traced the fount whence streams of nectar flow.
Bloom, O ye amaranths! bloom for whom ye may,
For me ye bloom not! Glide, rich streams, away!
With lips unbrightened, wreathless brow, I stroll:
And would you learn the spells that drowse my soul?
Work without Hope draws nectar in a sieve,
And Hope without an object cannot live.

*1825*

WORK WITHOUT HOPE. 1. **Slugs:** snail-like creatures, slow and slothful.

## from
# BIOGRAPHIA LITERARIA

The *Biographia Literaria* found its origin in the summer of 1802 when Coleridge, having read Wordsworth's additions to the Preface to *Lyrical Ballads* (third edition; see pp. 18–29, above), announced in letters to friends his disagreement with some of Wordsworth's theories and his intention to discuss these differences in a "disquisition on the nature and essence of poetry."

Characteristically Coleridge did nothing but talk about this project for the next thirteen years. Then, stimulated by Wordsworth's publication in March, 1815, of his collected poems, with a new preface and supplementary essay, Coleridge determined to collect his poems and write a preface of his own. This grew until, two years later and after incredible difficulties with his printers, Coleridge produced his *Biographia Literaria,* in two volumes.

The title is a misnomer. Occasional autobiographical details serve primarily to introduce and enliven discussions of Coleridge's views on philosophy, psychology, poetry, and contemporary book reviewers. In the first volume Coleridge undertook to demonstrate that the imagination and the fancy differed in kind, and not, as Wordsworth had argued in 1815, merely in degree. But, after twelve chapters of labored preliminary exposition Coleridge wrote himself a letter, which he attributed to a friend, and, arguing that it would be unintelligible to the unprepared public mind, advised himself not to print the great "Chapter on the Imagination." The only part of this "Chapter" which he had in fact written was the brief and cryptic "conclusion" which appears below from Chapter XIII.

In the second volume Coleridge, working closely with the poetry of Shakespeare and Wordsworth, exhibits brilliantly the "symptoms" of poetic and imaginative power. Along the way, in chapters too lengthy for publication here, Coleridge defends the general purpose and direction of Wordsworth's theory and practice while expressing his dissent from the notion that the best language for poetry may be found among rustics, and from the argument that the language of poetry does not differ essentially from that of prose.

## from CHAPTER XIII

The imagination, then, I consider either as primary, or secondary. The primary imagination I hold to be the living power and prime agent of all human perception, and as a repetition in the finite mind of the eternal act of creation in the infinite I AM. The secondary imagination I consider as an echo of the former, coexisting with the conscious will, yet still as identical with the primary in the *kind* of its agency, and differing only in *degree* and in the *mode* of its operation. It dissolves, diffuses, dissipates, in order to recreate; or where this process is rendered impossible, yet still at all events it struggles to idealize and to unify. It is essentially *vital,* even as all objects (*as* objects) are essentially fixed and dead.

Fancy, on the contrary, has no other counters to play with, but fixities and definites. The fancy is indeed no other than a mode of memory emancipated from the order of time and space; while it is blended with, and modified by that empirical phenomenon of the will, which we express by the word *choice.* But equally with the ordinary memory the fancy must receive all its materials ready made from the law of association.

## CHAPTER XIV

*Occasion of the Lyrical Ballads, and the objects originally proposed — Preface to the second edition — The ensuing controversy, its causes and acrimony — Philosophic definitions of a poem and poetry with scholia.*

During the first year [1] that Mr. Wordsworth and I were neighbors, our conversations turned frequently on the two cardinal points of poetry, the power of exciting the sympathy of the reader by a faithful adherence to the truth of nature, and the power of giving the interest of novelty by the modifying colors of imagination. The sudden charm, which accidents of light and shade, which moonlight or sunset diffused over a known and familiar landscape, appeared to represent the practicability of combining both. These are the poetry of nature. The thought suggested itself (to which of us I do not recollect) that a series of poems might be composed of two sorts. In the one, the incidents and agents were to be, in part at least, supernatural; and the excellence aimed at was to consist in the interesting of the affections by the dramatic truth of such emotions as would naturally accompany such situations, supposing them real. And real in *this* sense they have been to every human being who, from whatever source of delusion, has at any time believed himself under supernatural agency. For the second class, subjects were to be chosen from ordinary life; the characters and incidents were to be such as will be found in every village and its vicinity where there is a meditative and feeling mind to seek after them or to notice them when they present themselves.

In this idea originated the plan of the *Lyrical Ballads* [2]; in which it was agreed that my endeavors should be directed to persons and characters supernatural, or at least romantic; yet so as to transfer from our inward nature a human interest and a semblance of truth sufficient to procure for these

BIOGRAPHIA LITERARIA. **1. first year:** 1797, at Alfoxden and Nether Stowey. **2.** ***Lyrical Ballads:*** the first edition, 1798.

shadows of imagination that willing suspension of disbelief for the moment which constitutes poetic faith. Mr. Wordsworth, on the other hand, was to propose to himself as his object to give the charm of novelty to things of every day, and to excite a feeling analogous to the supernatural, by awakening the mind's attention from the lethargy of custom and directing it to the loveliness and the wonders of the world before us; an inexhaustible treasure, but for which, in consequence of the film of familiarity and selfish solicitude we have eyes, yet see not, ears that hear not, and hearts that neither feel nor understand.[3]

With this view I wrote "The Ancient Mariner," and was preparing among other poems, "The Dark Ladie," and the "Christabel," in which I should have more nearly realized my ideal than I had done in my first attempt. But Mr. Wordsworth's industry had proved so much more successful, and the number of his poems so much greater, that my compositions, instead of forming a balance, appeared rather an interpolation of heterogeneous matter. Mr. Wordsworth added two or three poems written in his own character, in the impassioned, lofty, and sustained diction, which is characteristic of his genius. In this form the *Lyrical Ballads*[4] were published; and were presented by him as an *experiment,* whether subjects, which from their nature rejected the usual ornaments and extracolloquial style of poems in general, might not be so managed in the language of ordinary life as to produce the pleasurable interest which it is the peculiar business of poetry to impart. To the second edition he added a preface of considerable length in which, notwithstanding some passages of apparently a contrary import, he was understood to contend for the extension of this style to poetry of all kinds, and to reject as vicious and indefensible all phrases and forms of style that were not included in what he (unfortunately, I think, adopting an equivocal expression) called the language of *real* life. From this preface, prefixed to poems in which it was impossible to deny the presence of original genius, however mistaken its direction might be deemed, arose the whole long-continued controversy.[5] For from the conjunction of perceived power with supposed heresy I explain the inveteracy and in some instances, I grieve to say, the acrimonious passions, with which the controversy has been conducted by the assailants.

Had Mr. Wordsworth's poems been the silly, the childish things, which they were for a long time described as being; had they been really distinguished from the compositions of other poets merely by meanness of language and inanity of thought; had they indeed contained nothing more than what is found in the parodies and pretended imitations of them; they must have sunk at once, a dead weight, into the slough of oblivion, and have dragged the preface along with them. But year after year increased the number of Mr. Wordsworth's admirers. They were found, too, not in the lower classes of the reading public, but chiefly among young men of strong sensibility and meditative minds; and their admiration (inflamed perhaps in some degree by opposition) was distinguished by its intensity, I might almost say, by its *religious* fervor. These facts, and the intellectual energy of the author, which was more or less consciously felt, where it was outwardly and even boisterously denied, meeting with sentiments of aversion to his opinions and of alarm at their consequences, produced an eddy of criticism which would of itself have borne up the poems by the violence, with which it whirled them round and round. With many parts of this preface, in the sense attributed to them, and which the words undoubtedly seem to authorize, I never concurred; but on the contrary objected to them as erroneous in principle, and as contradictory (in appearance at least) both to other parts of the same preface, and to the author's own practice in the greater number of the poems themselves. Mr. Wordsworth in his recent collection has, I find, degraded this prefatory disquisition to the end of his second volume, to be read or not at the reader's choice. But he has not, as far as I can discover, announced any change in his poetic creed. At all events, considering it as the source of a controversy, in which I have been honored more than I deserve by the frequent conjunction of my name with his, I think it expedient to declare once for all in what points I coincide with his opinions and in what points I altogether differ. But in order to render myself intelligible I must previously, in as few words as possible, explain my ideas, first, of a poem; and secondly, of poetry itself, in *kind,* and in *essence.*

**3. eyes . . . understand:** see Isa. 6:9–10. **4. *Lyrical Ballads:*** the second edition, 1800 (actually publication was in January, 1801). **5. long-continued controversy:** over Wordsworth's poetic theory and practice.

The office of philosophical *disquisition* consists in just *distinction;* while it is the privilege of the philosopher to preserve himself constantly aware, that distinction is not division. In order to obtain adequate notions of any truth, we must intellectually separate its distinguishable parts; and this is the technical *process* of philosophy. But having so done, we must then restore them in our conceptions to the unity, in which they actually coexist; and this is the *result* of philosophy. A poem contains the same elements as a prose composition; the difference therefore must consist in a different combination of them, in consequence of a different object being proposed. According to the difference of the object will be the difference of the combination. It is possible, that the object may be merely to facilitate the recollection of any given facts or observations by artificial arrangement; and the composition will be a poem merely because it is distinguished from prose by meter or by rhyme, or by both conjointly. In this, the lowest sense, a man might attribute the name of a poem to the well-known enumeration of the days in the several months;

Thirty days hath September,
April, June, and November, &c.

and others of the same class and purpose. And as a particular pleasure is found in anticipating the recurrence of sounds and quantities, all compositions that have this charm superadded, whatever be their contents, *may* be entitled poems.

So much for the superficial *form*. A difference of object and contents supplies an additional ground of distinction. The immediate purpose may be the communication of truths; either of truth absolute and demonstrable, as in works of science; or of facts experienced and recorded, as in history. Pleasure, and that of the highest and most permanent kind, may *result* from the *attainment* of the end; but it is not itself the immediate end. In other works the communication of pleasure may be the immediate purpose; and though truth, either moral or intellectual, ought to be the *ultimate* end, yet this will distinguish the character of the author, not the class to which the work belongs. Blest indeed is that state of society in which the immediate purpose would be baffled by the perversion of the proper ultimate end; in which no charm of diction or imagery could exempt the Bathyllus even of an Anacreon,[6] or the Alexis of Virgil,[7] from disgust and aversion!

But the communication of pleasure may be the immediate object of a work not metrically composed; and that object may have been in a high degree attained, as in novels and romances. Would then the mere superaddition of meter, with or without rhyme, entitle *these* to the name of poems? The answer is, that nothing can permanently please which does not contain in itself the reason why it is so, and not otherwise. If meter be superadded, all other parts must be made consonant with it. They must be such as to justify the perpetual and distinct attention to each part which an exact correspondent recurrence of accent and sound are calculated to excite. The final definition then, so deduced, may be thus worded. A poem is that species of composition which is opposed to works of science by proposing for its *immediate* object pleasure, not truth; and from all other species (having *this* object in common with it) it is discriminated by proposing to itself such delight from the *whole,* as is compatible with a distinct gratification from each component *part.*

Controversy is not seldom excited in consequence of the disputants attaching each a different meaning to the same word; and in few instances has this been more striking than in disputes concerning the present subject. If a man chooses to call every composition a poem which is rhyme, or measure, or both, I must leave his opinion uncontroverted. The distinction is at least competent to characterize the writer's intention. If it were subjoined that the whole is likewise entertaining or affecting as a tale, or as a series of interesting reflections, I of course admit this as another fit ingredient of a poem, and an additional merit. But if the definition sought for be that of a *legitimate* poem, I answer it must be one the parts of which mutually support and explain each other; all in their proportion harmonizing with and supporting the purpose and known influences of metrical arrangement. The philosophic critics of all ages coincide with the ultimate judgment of all countries in equally denying the praises of a just poem, on the one hand, to a series of striking lines or distichs,[8] each of which,

**6. Bathyllus . . . Anacreon:** Bathyllus was a beautiful boy celebrated in the odes of Anacreon, a Greek lyric poet (*ca.* 560–475 B.C.). **7. Alexis . . . Virgil:** Alexis was a male slave loved by the shepherd Corydon (Virgil, *Eclogues*, II); Virgil (70–19 B.C.) was the author of the *Aeneid* and the most famous Roman poet. **8. distichs:** pairs of lines, not necessarily couplets.

absorbing the whole attention of the reader to itself, disjoins it from its context, and makes it a separate whole, instead of a harmonizing part; and on the other hand, to an unsustained composition from which the reader collects rapidly the general result, unattracted by the component parts. The reader should be carried forward, not merely or chiefly by the mechanical impulse of curiosity, or by a restless desire to arrive at the final solution; but by the pleasurable activity of mind excited by the attractions of the journey itself. Like the motion of a serpent, which the Egyptians made the emblem of intellectual power; or like the path of sound through the air; at every step he pauses and half recedes, and from the retrogressive movement collects the force which again carries him onward. "Praecipitandus est *liber* spiritus,"[9] says Petronius Arbiter[10] most happily. The epithet, *liber,* here balances the preceding verb; and it is not easy to conceive more meaning condensed in fewer words.

But if this should be admitted as a satisfactory character of a poem, we have still to seek for a definition of poetry. The writings of Plato, and Bishop Taylor,[11] and the *Theoria Sacra*[12] of Burnet, furnish undeniable proofs that poetry of the highest kind may exist without meter, and even without the contradistinguishing objects of a poem. The first chapter of Isaiah (indeed a very large portion of the whole book) is poetry in the most emphatic sense; yet it would be not less irrational than strange to assert, that pleasure, and not truth, was the immediate object of the prophet. In short, whatever *specific* import we attach to the word, poetry, there will be found involved in it, as a necessary consequence, that a poem of any length neither can be, or ought to be, all poetry. Yet if a harmonious whole is to be produced, the remaining parts must be preserved *in keeping* with the poetry; and this can be no otherwise effected than by such a studied selection and artificial arrangement as will partake of *one,* though not a *peculiar* property of poetry. And this again can be no other than the property of exciting a more continuous and equal attention than the language of prose aims at, whether colloquial or written.

My own conclusions on the nature of poetry, in the strictest use of the word, have been in part anticipated in the preceding disquisition on the fancy and imagination. What is poetry? is so nearly the same question with, what is a poet? that the answer to the one is involved in the solution of the other. For it is a distinction resulting from the poetic genius itself, which sustains and modifies the images, thoughts, and emotions of the poet's own mind.

The poet, described in *ideal* perfection, brings the whole soul of man into activity, with the subordination of its faculties to each other, according to their relative worth and dignity. He diffuses a tone and spirit of unity that blends, and (as it were) *fuses,* each into each, by that synthetic and magical power to which we have exclusively appropriated the name of imagination. This power, first put in action by the will and understanding, and retained under their irremissive, though gentle and unnoticed, control (*laxis effertur habenis*[13]) reveals itself in the balance or reconciliation of opposite or discordant qualities: of sameness with difference; of the general with the concrete; the idea with the image; the individual with the representative; the sense of novelty and freshness with old and familiar objects; a more than usual state of emotion with more than usual order; judgment ever awake and steady self-possession with enthusiasm and feeling profound or vehement; and while it blends and harmonizes the natural and the artificial, still subordinates art to nature; the manner to the matter; and our admiration of the poet to our sympathy with the poetry. "Doubtless," as Sir John Davies[14] observes of the soul (and his words may with slight alteration be applied, and even more appropriately, to the poetic imagination)

Doubtless this could not be, but that she turns
  Bodies to spirit by sublimation strange,
As fire converts to fire the things it burns,
  As we our food into our nature change.

From their gross matter she abstracts their forms,
  And draws a kind of quintessence from things;
Which to her proper nature she transforms,
  To bear them light on her celestial wings.

Thus does she, when from individual states
  She doth abstract the universal kinds;

9. **"Praecipitandus . . . spiritus"**: "The free spirit is hurried onwards" (*Satyricon,* 118). 10. **Petronius Arbiter**: Roman satirist (?–65 A.D.) and director of amusement at the court of Nero. 11. **Bishop Taylor**: Jeremy Taylor (1613–67), an English divine whose sermons Coleridge much admired. 12. ***Theoria Sacra:*** *Telluris Theoria Sacra* (*The Sacred Theory of the Earth*), 1681–89, by Thomas Burnet, from whom Coleridge took the Latin motto for the "Ancient Mariner" (see p. 112, n. 1, above). Coleridge once contemplated rendering the *Sacred Theory* into English blank verse.

13. ***laxis . . . habenis:*** driven along with loose reins. 14. **Sir John Davies**: a minor English poet (1569–1626).

Which then re-clothed in divers names and fates
Steal access through our senses to our minds.

Finally, good sense is the body of poetic genius, fancy its drapery, motion its life, and imagination the soul that is everywhere and in each; and forms all into one graceful and intelligent whole.

## CHAPTER XV

*The specific symptoms of poetic power elucidated in a critical analysis of Shakespeare's* Venus and Adonis, *and* Lucrece.[15]

In the application of these principles to purposes of practical criticism as employed in the appraisal of works more or less imperfect, I have endeavored to discover what the qualities in a poem are, which may be deemed promises and specific symptoms of poetic power as distinguished from general talent determined to poetic composition by accidental motives, by an act of the will, rather than by the inspiration of a genial and productive nature. In this investigation I could not, I thought, do better than keep before me the earliest work of the greatest genius that perhaps human nature has yet produced, our myriad-minded Shakespeare. I mean the *Venus and Adonis,* and the *Lucrece;* works which give at once strong promises of the strength, and yet obvious proofs of the immaturity of his genius. From these I abstracted the following marks, as characteristics of original poetic genius in general.

1. In the *Venus and Adonis,* the first and most obvious excellence is the perfect sweetness of the versification; its adaptation to the subject; and the power displayed in varying the march of the words without passing into a loftier and more majestic rhythm than was demanded by the thoughts, or permitted by the propriety of preserving a sense of melody predominant. The delight in richness and sweetness of sound, even to a faulty excess, if it be evidently original and not the result of an easily imitable mechanism, I regard as a highly favorable promise in the compositions of a young man. "The man that hath not music in his soul"[16] can indeed never be a genuine poet. Imagery (even taken from nature, much more when transplanted from books, as travels, voyages, and works of natural history); affecting incidents; just thoughts; interesting personal or domestic feelings; and with these the art of their combination or intertexture in the form of a poem; may all by incessant effort be acquired as a trade, by a man of talents and much reading, who, as I once before observed, has mistaken an intense desire of poetic reputation for a natural poetic genius; the love of the arbitrary end for a possession of the peculiar means. But the sense of musical delight, with the power of producing it, is a gift of imagination; and this together with the power of reducing multitude into unity of effect, and modifying a series of thoughts by some one predominant thought or feeling, may be cultivated and improved but can never be learned. It is in these that "poeta nascitur non fit."[17]

2. A second promise of genius is the choice of subjects very remote from the private interests and circumstances of the writer himself. At least I have found, that where the subject is taken immediately from the author's personal sensations and experiences, the excellence of a particular poem is but an equivocal mark, and often a fallacious pledge, of genuine poetic power. We may perhaps remember the tale of the statuary, who had acquired considerable reputation for the legs of his goddesses, though the rest of the statue accorded but indifferently with ideal beauty; till his wife, elated by her husband's praises, modestly acknowledged that she herself had been his constant model. In the *Venus and Adonis* this proof of poetic power exists even to excess. It is throughout as if a superior spirit more intuitive, more intimately conscious even than the characters themselves, not only of every outward look and act, but of the flux and reflux of the mind in all its subtlest thoughts and feelings, were placing the whole before our view; himself meanwhile unparticipating in the passions and actuated only by that pleasurable excitement, which had resulted from the energetic fervor of his own spirit in so vividly exhibiting what it had so accurately and profoundly contemplated. I think I should have conjectured from these poems that even then the great instinct which impelled the poet to the drama was secretly working in him, prompting him by a series and never broken chain of imagery, always vivid and, because unbroken, often minute; by the highest effort of the picturesque in words

15. *Venus . . . Lucrece* [*The Rape of*]: narrative poems by Shakespeare, published respectively in 1593 and 1594. 16. "The . . . soul": misquoted from Shakespeare's *The Merchant of Venice,* V.i.83.

17. "poeta . . . fit": "The poet is born, not made."

of which words are capable, higher perhaps than was ever realized by any other poet, even Dante not excepted; to provide a substitute for that visual language, that constant intervention and running comment by tone, look and gesture, which in his dramatic works he was entitled to expect from the players. His Venus and Adonis seem at once the characters themselves and the whole representation of those characters by the most consummate actors. You seem to be told nothing, but to see and hear everything. Hence it is that from the perpetual activity of attention required on the part of the reader; from the rapid flow, the quick change, and the playful nature of the thoughts and images; and above all from the alienation, and, if I may hazard such an expression, the utter *aloofness* of the poet's own feelings from those of which he is at once the painter and the analyst; that though the very subject cannot but detract from the pleasure of a delicate mind, yet never was poem less dangerous on a moral account. Instead of doing as Ariosto,[18] and as, still more offensively, Wieland[19] has done, instead of degrading and deforming passion into appetite, the trials of love into the struggles of concupiscence; Shakespeare has here represented the animal impulse itself, so as to preclude all sympathy with it, by dissipating the reader's notice among the thousand outward images, and now beautiful, now fanciful circumstances, which form its dresses and its scenery; or by diverting our attention from the main subject by those frequent witty or profound reflections which the poet's ever-active mind has deduced from, or connected with, the imagery and the incidents. The reader is forced into too much action to sympathize with the merely passive of our nature. As little can a mind thus roused and awakened be brooded on by mean and indistinct emotion as the low, lazy mist can creep upon the surface of a lake while a strong gale is driving it onward in waves and billows.

3. It has been before observed that images, however beautiful, though faithfully copied from nature, and as accurately represented in words, do not of themselves characterize the poet. They become proofs of original genius only as far as they are modified by a predominant passion; or by associated thoughts or images awakened by that passion; or when they have the effect of reducing multitude to unity, or succession to an instant; or lastly, when a human and intellectual life is transferred to them from the poet's own spirit

Which shoots its being through earth, sea, and air.[20]

In the two following lines, for instance, there is nothing objectionable, nothing which would preclude them from forming, in their proper place, part of a descriptive poem:

Behold yon row of pines, that shorn and bowed
Bend from the sea-blast, seen at twilight eve.

But with a small alteration of rhythm the same words would be equally in their place in a book of topography or in a descriptive tour. The same image will rise into semblance of poetry if thus conveyed:

Yon row of bleak and visionary pines,
By twilight glimpse discerned, mark! how they flee
From the fierce sea-blast, all their tresses wild
Streaming before them.

I have given this as an illustration, by no means as an instance, of that particular excellence which I had in view, and in which Shakespeare even in his earliest, as in his latest, works surpasses all other poets. It is by this, that he still gives a dignity and a passion to the objects which he presents. Unaided by any previous excitement, they burst upon us at once in life and in power.

Full many a glorious morning have I seen
*Flatter* the mountain tops with sovereign eye.
[Shakespeare, Sonnet 33]

Not mine own fears, nor the prophetic soul
Of the wide world dreaming on things to come,

. . . . . .

The mortal moon hath her eclipse endured,
And the sad augurs mock their own presage;
Incertainties now crown themselves assured,
And peace proclaims olives of endless age.
Now with the drops of this most balmy time
My love looks fresh, and death to me subscribes!
Since spite of him, I'll live in this poor rhyme,
While he insults o'er dull and speechless tribes.
And thou in this shalt find thy monument,
When tyrants' crests, and tombs of brass are spent.
[Sonnet 107]

As of higher worth, so doubtless still more characteristic of poetic genius does the imagery become, when it molds and colors itself to the circumstances, passion, or character, present and foremost in the mind. For unrivaled instances of this excellence

**18. Ariosto**: Lodovico Ariosto, an Italian poet (1474–1533).
**19. Wieland**: Christoph Martin Wieland, a German author (1733–1813).

**20. Which . . . air**: altered from Coleridge's "France: An Ode," 103. See p. 129, above.

the reader's own memory will refer him to the *Lear, Othello,* in short to which not of the "great, ever living, dead man's" dramatic works? "Inopem me copia fecit." [21] How true it is to nature, he has himself finely expressed in the instance of love in Sonnet 98.

From you have I been absent in the spring,
When proud pied April drest in all its trim
Hath put a spirit of youth in every thing,
That heavy Saturn laughed and leaped with him.
Yet nor the lays of birds, nor the sweet smell
Of different flowers in odor and in hue,
Could make me any summer's story tell,
Or from their proud lap pluck them, where they grew:
Nor did I wonder at the lilies white,
Nor praise the deep vermilion in the rose;
They were, tho' sweet, but figures of delight,
Drawn after you, you pattern of all those.
Yet seemed it winter still, and, you away,
*As with your shadow I with these did play!*

Scarcely less sure, or if a less valuable, not less indispensable mark

Γονίμου μὲν ποιητοῦ ——
—— ὅστις ῥῆμα γενναῖον λάκοι,[22]

will the imagery supply, when, with more than the power of the painter, the poet gives us the liveliest image of succession with the feeling of simultaneousness!

With this, he breaketh from the sweet embrace
Of those fair arms, that held him to her heart,
And homeward through the dark lawns runs apace:
*Look! how a bright star shooteth from the sky,*
*So glides he in the night from Venus' eye.*[23]

4. The last character I shall mention, which would prove indeed but little, except as taken conjointly with the former; yet without which the former could scarce exist in a high degree, and (even if this were possible) would give promises only of transitory flashes and a meteoric power; is depth, and energy of thought. No man was ever yet a great poet without being at the same time a profound philosopher. For poetry is the blossom and the fragrancy of all human knowledge, human thoughts, human passions, emotions, language. In Shakespeare's poems the creative power and the intellectual energy wrestle as in a war embrace. Each in its excess of strength seems to threaten the extinction of the other. At length in the drama they were reconciled, and fought each with its shield before the breast of the other. Or like two rapid streams that, at their first meeting within narrow and rocky banks, mutually strive to repel each other and intermix reluctantly and in tumult; but soon finding a wider channel and more yielding shores blend, and dilate, and flow on in one current and with one voice. The *Venus and Adonis* did not perhaps allow the display of the deeper passions. But the story of Lucretia seems to favor and even demand their intensest workings. And yet we find in Shakespeare's management of the tale neither pathos, nor any other dramatic quality. There is the same minute and faithful imagery as in the former poem, in the same vivid colors, inspirited by the same impetuous vigor of thought, and diverging and contracting with the same activity of the assimilative and of the modifying faculties; and with a yet larger display, a yet wider range of knowledge and reflection; and lastly, with the same perfect dominion, often domination, over the whole world of language. What then shall we say? even this; that Shakespeare, no mere child of nature; no automaton of genius; no passive vehicle of inspiration possessed by the spirit, not possessing it; first studied patiently, meditated deeply, understood minutely, till knowledge, become habitual and intuitive, wedded itself to his habitual feelings, and at length gave birth to that stupendous power by which he stands alone, with no equal or second in his own class; to that power which seated him on one of the two glory-smitten summits of the poetic mountain, with Milton as his compeer, not rival. While the former darts himself forth and passes into all the forms of human character and passion, the one Proteus [24] of the fire and the flood; the other attracts all forms and things to himself, into the unity of his own ideal. All things and modes of action shape themselves anew in the being of Milton; while Shakespeare becomes all things, yet for ever remaining himself. O what great men hast thou not produced, England! my country! truly indeed —

Must *we* be free or die, who speak the tongue
Which Shakespeare spake; the faith and morals hold
Which Milton held. In everything we are sprung
Of earth's first blood, have titles manifold!
[Wordsworth [25]]

**21. "Inopem . . . fecit"**: "Abundance has made me poor." **22.** "There's not one poet among them/Fit to risk a valiant phrase" (Aristophanes [448?–380? B.C.], *Frogs*, 96–97). **23. With . . . eye**: misquoted from *Venus and Adonis*, 811–15.

**24. Proteus**: a son of Poseidon, or Neptune, god of the sea. Proteus tended his father's herd of seals, and could change shape at will. **25. Wordsworth**: misquoted from his sonnet, "It Is Not to Be Thought Of." See p. 95, above.

# SHAKESPEAREAN CRITICISM

Coleridge published no book under this title. On no other subject, however, did he talk and write so much or so well. When he died in 1834 he left behind in notes and marginalia tens of thousands of words devoted to England's greatest writer and his works. Jotted down in the course of Coleridge's lecture commitments from 1808 to 1818, these fragments were first collected and given a semblance of coherence by H. N. Coleridge, the poet's nephew, in *Literary Remains* (1836–39). In 1930 Professor Thomas Middleton Raysor, working from the manuscripts, and from shorthand reports of the lectures not available to H. N. Coleridge, produced an expertly edited, definitive text from which the selections below are reprinted by permission of the Harvard University Press.

## from HAMLET

. . . We will now pass to *Hamlet,* in order to obviate some of the general prejudices against the author, in reference to the character of the hero. Much has been objected to which ought to have been praised, and many beauties of the highest kind have been neglected because they are somewhat hidden.

The first question we should ask ourselves is — What did Shakespeare mean when he drew the character of Hamlet? He never wrote anything without design, and what was his design when he sat down to produce this tragedy? My belief is that he always regarded his story, before he began to write, much in the same light as a painter regards his canvas, before he begins to paint — as a mere vehicle for his thoughts — as the ground upon which he was to work. What then was the point to which Shakespeare directed himself in Hamlet? He intended to portray a person in whose view the external world and all its incidents and objects were comparatively dim and of no interest in themselves, and which began to interest only when they were reflected in the mirror of his mind. Hamlet beheld external things in the same way that a man of vivid imagination, who shuts his eyes, sees what has previously made an impression on his organs.

The poet places him in the most stimulating circumstances that a human being can be placed in. He is the heir apparent of a throne; his father dies suspiciously; his mother excludes her son from his throne by marrying his uncle. This is not enough; but the Ghost of the murdered father is introduced to assure the son that he was put to death by his own brother. What is the effect upon the son? — instant action and pursuit of revenge? No: endless reasoning and hesitating — constant urging and solicitation of the mind to act, and as constant an escape from action; ceaseless reproaches of himself for sloth and negligence, while the whole energy of his resolution evaporates in these reproaches. This, too, not from cowardice, for he is drawn as one of the bravest of his time — not from want of forethought or slowness of apprehension, for he sees through the very souls of all who surround him, but merely from that aversion to action which prevails among such as have a world in themselves.

How admirable, too, is the judgment of the poet! Hamlet's own disordered fancy has not conjured up the spirit of his father; it has been seen by others: he is prepared by them to witness its reappearance, and when he does see it, Hamlet is not brought forward as having long brooded on the subject. The moment before the Ghost enters Hamlet speaks of other matters: he mentions the coldness of the night and observes that he has not heard the clock strike, adding, in reference to the custom of drinking, that it is

> More honored in the breach than the observance.
> [I.iv.16]

Owing to the tranquil state of his mind, he indulges in some moral reflections. Afterwards, the Ghost suddenly enters.

> HOR. Look, my lord, it comes.
> HAM. Angels and ministers of grace defend us!
> [I.iv.38–39]

The same thing occurs in *Macbeth:* in the dagger-scene,[1] the moment before the hero sees it, he has his mind applied to some indifferent matters; "Go, tell thy mistress," &c. Thus in both cases the preternatural appearance has all the effect of abruptness, and the reader is totally divested of the notion that the figure is a vision of a highly wrought imagination.

Here Shakespeare adapts himself so admirably to the situation — in other words, so puts himself into it — that, though poetry, his language is the very language of nature. No terms associated with such feelings can occur to us so proper as those which he has employed, especially on the highest, the most august, and the most awful subjects that can interest a human being in this sentient world. That this is

SHAKESPEAREAN CRITICISM: 1. dagger-scene: II.i.

no mere fancy I can undertake to establish from hundreds, I might say thousands, of passages. No character he has drawn in the whole list of his plays could so well and fitly express himself as in the language Shakespeare has put into his mouth.

There is no indecision about Hamlet as far as his own sense of duty is concerned; he knows well what he ought to do, and over and over again he makes up his mind to do it. The moment the players, and the two spies set upon him, have withdrawn, of whom he takes leave with a line so expressive of his contempt,

> Aye, so, God be wi' ye! — Now I am alone,
> [II.ii.575]

he breaks out into a delirium of rage against himself for neglecting to perform the solemn duty he had undertaken, and contrasts the factitious and artificial display of feeling by the player with his own apparent indifference;

> What's Hecuba to him or he to Hecuba,
> That he should weep for her?
> [II.ii.585–6]

Yet the player did weep for her, and was in an agony of grief at her sufferings, while Hamlet is unable to rouse himself to action in order that he may perform the command of his father, who had come from the grave to incite him to revenge: —

> This is most brave,
> That I, the son of a dear father murdered,
> Prompted to my revenge by Heaven and Hell,
> Must, like a whore, unpack my heart with words,
> And fall a-cursing like a very drab,
> A scullion.
> [II.ii.611–16]

It is the same feeling, the same conviction of what is his duty, that makes Hamlet exclaim in a subsequent part of the tragedy:

> How all occasions do inform against me
> And spur my dull revenge! What is a man
> If his chief good and market of his time
> Be but to sleep and feed? A beast, no more.
> . . . I do not know
> Why yet I live to say "this thing's to do,"
> Sith I have cause, and will, and strength, and means
> To do't.
> [IV.iv.32–35, 43–46]

Yet with all this strong conviction of duty, and with all this resolution arising out of strong conviction, nothing is done. This admirable and consistent character, deeply acquainted with his own feelings, painting them with such wonderful power and accuracy, and firmly persuaded that a moment ought not to be lost in executing the solemn charge committed to him, still yields to the same retiring from reality which is the result of having, what we express by the terms, a world within himself.

Such a mind as Hamlet's is near akin to madness. Dryden has somewhere said,

> Great wit to madness nearly is allied,[2]

and he was right; for he means by "wit" that greatness of genius, which led Hamlet to a perfect knowledge of his own character, which, with all strength of motive, was so weak as to be unable to carry into act his own most obvious duty.

With all this he has a sense of imperfectness which becomes apparent when he is moralizing on the skull in the churchyard. Something is wanting to his completeness — something is deficient which remains to be supplied, and he is therefore described as attached to Ophelia. His madness is assumed, when he finds that witnesses have been placed behind the arras to listen to what passes, and when the heroine has been thrown in his way as a decoy.

Another objection has been taken by Dr. Johnson, and Shakespeare has been taxed very severely. I refer to the scene where Hamlet enters and finds his uncle praying, and refuses to take his life, excepting when he is in the height of his iniquity. To assail him at such a moment of confession and repentance, Hamlet declares,

> Oh, this is hire and salary, not revenge.
> [III.iii.79]

He therefore forbears and postpones his uncle's death until he can catch him in some act

> That has no relish of salvation in't.
> [III.iii.92]

This conduct, and this sentiment, Dr. Johnson has pronounced to be so atrocious and horrible as to be unfit to be put into the mouth of a human being. The fact, however, is that Dr. Johnson did not understand the character of Hamlet and censured accordingly: the determination to allow the guilty King to escape at such a moment is only part of the indecision and irresoluteness of the hero. Hamlet seizes hold of a pretext for not acting, when he might have acted so instantly and effectually: therefore, he again defers the revenge he was

2. **Great . . . allied**: misquoted from *Absalom and Achitophel*, 163. See Vol. I, p. 576.

bound to seek and declares his determination to accomplish it at some time,

> When he is drunk asleep, or in his rage,
> Or in the incestuous pleasure of his bed.
> [III.iii.89–90]

This, allow me to impress upon you most emphatically, was merely the excuse Hamlet made to himself for not taking advantage of this particular and favorable moment for doing justice upon his guilty uncle at the urgent instance of the spirit of his father.

Dr. Johnson farther states that in the voyage to England Shakespeare merely follows the novel as he found it, as if the poet had no other reason for adhering to his original; but Shakespeare never followed a novel because he found such and such an incident in it, but because he saw that the story, as he read it, contributed to enforce or to explain some great truth inherent in human nature. He never could lack invention to alter or improve a popular narrative; but he did not wantonly vary from it when he knew that, as it was related, it would so well apply to his own great purpose. He saw at once how consistent it was with the character of Hamlet that, after still resolving, and still deferring, still determining to execute, and still postponing execution, he should finally, in the infirmity of his disposition, give himself up to his destiny and hopelessly place himself in the power and at the mercy of his enemies.

Even after the scene with Osric,[3] we see Hamlet still indulging in reflection, and hardly thinking of the task he has just undertaken: he is all dispatch and resolution as far as words and present intentions are concerned, but all hesitation and irresolution when called upon to carry his words and intentions into effect; so that, resolving to do everything, he does nothing. He is full of purpose but void of that quality of mind which accomplishes purpose.

Anything finer than this conception and working out of a great character is merely impossible. Shakespeare wished to impress upon us the truth that action is the chief end of existence — that no faculties of intellect, however brilliant, can be considered valuable, or indeed otherwise than as misfortunes, if they withdraw us from or render us repugnant to action, and lead us to think and think of doing until the time has elapsed when we can do anything effectually. In enforcing this moral truth, Shakespeare has shown the fulness and force of his powers: all that is amiable and excellent in nature is combined in Hamlet, with the exception of one quality. He is a man living in meditation, called upon to act by every motive human and divine, but the great object of his life is defeated by continually resolving to do, yet doing nothing but resolve.

## THE TEMPEST

Once more, tho' in a somewhat different and, I would fain believe, in a more instructive form, I have undertaken the task of criticizing the works of that great dramatist whose own name has become their best and most expressive epithet. The task will be genial in proportion as the criticism is reverential. Assuredly the Englishman who without reverence, who without a proud and affectionate reverence, can utter the name of Shakespeare, stands disqualified for the office. He wants one at least of the very senses the language of which he is to employ, and will discourse at best [but as a blind man], while the whole harmonious creation of light and shade with all its subtle interchange of deepening and dissolving colors rises in silence to the silent fiat of the uprising Apollo. However inferior in ability to some who have followed me, I am proud that I was the first in time who publicly demonstrated to the full extent of the position that the supposed irregularity and extravagances of Shakespeare were the mere dreams of a pedantry that arraigned the eagle because it had not the dimensions of the swan. In all the successive courses delivered by me since my first attempt at the Royal Institution,[4] it has been and it still remains my object to prove that in all points from the most important to the most minute, the judgment of Shakespeare is commensurate with his genius — nay, that his genius reveals itself in his judgment as in its most exalted form. And the more gladly do I recur to the subject from the clear conviction that to judge aright, and with the distinct consciousness of the grounds of our judgment, concerning the works of Shakespeare, implies the power and the means of judging rightly of all other works, those of abstract science alone excepted.

3. **scene with Osric:** V.ii.80–190.

4. **Royal Institution:** founded in 1799 to promote scientific and literary research.

We commence with *The Tempest* as a specimen of the romantic drama. But whatever play of Shakespeare's we had selected there is one preliminary point to be first settled, as the indispensable condition not only of just and genial criticism, but of all consistency in our opinions. This point is contained in the words *probable, natural.* We are all in the habit of praising Shakespeare or of hearing him extolled for his fidelity to nature. Now what are we to understand by these words in their application to the drama? Assuredly not the ordinary meaning of them. Farquhar,[5] the most ably, and if we except a few sentences in one of Dryden's prefaces [6] (written for a particular purpose and in contradiction to the opinions elsewhere supported by him) first exposed the ludicrous absurdities involved in the supposition, and demolished as with the single sweep of a careless hand the whole edifice of French criticism respecting the so-called unities of time and place. But a moment's reflection suffices to make every man conscious of what every man must have before felt, that the drama is an *imitation* of reality, not a *copy* — and that imitation is contradistinguished from copy by this: that a certain quantum of difference is essential to the former, and an indispensable condition and cause of the pleasure we derive from it; while in a copy it is a defect, contravening its name and purpose. If illustration were needed, it should be sufficient to ask why we prefer a fruit view of Van Huysum's [7] to a marble peach on a mantelpiece, or why we prefer an historical picture of West to Mrs. Salmon's [8] wax-figure gallery. Not only that we ought, but that we actually do, all of us, judge of the drama under this impression, we need no other proof than the impassive slumber of our sense of probability when we hear an actor announce himself as a Greek, Roman, Venetian, or Persian in good mother English. And how little our great dramatist feared awakening in it we have a lively instance in proof in Portia's answer to Nerissa's question, "What say you then to Falconbridge, the young baron of England?" — to which she replies, "You know I say nothing to him; for he understands not me, nor I him. He hath neither Latin, French, nor Italian, and you will come into the court and swear that I have a poor pennyworth in the English." [9]

Still, however, there is a sort of improbability with which we are shocked in dramatic representation no less than in the narrative of real life. Consequently, there must be rules respecting it; and as rules are nothing but means to an end previously ascertained (the inattention to which simple truth has been the occasion of all the pedantry of the French school), we must first ascertain what the immediate end or object of the drama is. Here I find two extremes in critical decision: the French, which evidently presupposes that a perfect delusion is to be aimed at — an opinion which now needs no fresh confutation; [10] the opposite, supported by Dr. Johnson,[11] supposes the auditors throughout as in the full and positive reflective knowledge of the contrary. In evincing the impossibility of delusion, he makes no sufficient allowance for an intermediate state, which we distinguish by the term *illusion.*

In what this consists I cannot better explain than by referring you to the highest degree of it; namely, dreaming. It is laxly said that during sleep we take our dreams for realities, but this is irreconcilable with the nature of sleep, which consists in the suspension of the voluntary and, therefore, of the comparative power. The fact is that we pass no judgment either way: we simply do not judge them to be unreal, in consequence of which the images act on our minds, as far as they act at all, by their own force as images. Our state while we are dreaming differs from that in which we are in the perusal of a deeply interesting novel in the degree rather than in the kind, and from three causes: First, from the exclusion of all outward impressions on our senses the images in sleep become proportionally more vivid than they can be when the organs of sense are in their active state. Secondly, in sleep the sensations, and with these the emotions and passions which they counterfeit, are the causes of our dream images, while in our waking hours our emotions are the effects of the images presented to us. (Apparitions [are] *so detectable.*) Lastly, in sleep we pass at once by a sudden collapse into this suspension of will and the comparative power: whereas in an interesting play, read or represented, we are

5. **Farquhar:** George Farquhar, an Irish comic dramatist (1678–1707). Coleridge here refers to his *A Discourse upon Comedy.*
6. **Dryden's prefaces:** see particularly his *Essay of Dramatic Poesy*, Vol. I, pp. 540 ff.
7. **Van Huysum:** Jan van Huysum, a Dutch still-life painter (1682–1749) noted for fullness and precision of detail.
8. **Mrs. Salmon:** early nineteenth-century rival of Mme. Tussaud.
9. **"What . . . English":** *Merchant of Venice*, I.ii.71–77.
10. **no . . . confutation:** See Dryden's *Essay of Dramatic Poesy*, Vol. I, pp. 536–65.
11. **Dr. Johnson:** See his "Preface to Shakespeare," Vol. I, pp. 940–42, 944–45.

brought up to this point, as far as it is requisite or desirable, gradually, by the art of the poet and the actors, and with the consent and positive aidance of our own will. We *choose* to be deceived. The rule, therefore, may be easily inferred. Whatever tends to prevent the mind from placing it[self] or from being gradually placed in this state in which the images have a negative reality must be a defect, and consequently anything that must force itself on the auditors' mind as improbable, not because it *is* improbable (for that the whole play is foreknown to be) but because it cannot but *appear* as such.

But this again depends on the degree of excitement in which the mind is supposed to be. Many things would be intolerable in the first scene of a play that would not at all interrupt our enjoyment in the height of the interest. The narrow cockpit may hold

> The vasty fields of France, or we may cram
> Within its wooden O the very casques
> That did affright the air at Agincourt.
> [*Henry V,* Prologue, 12–14]

And again, on the other hand, many obvious improbabilities will be endured as belonging to the groundwork of the story rather than to the drama, in the first scenes, which would disturb or disentrance us from all illusion in the acme of our excitement, as, for instance, Lear's division of his realm and banishment of Cordelia.[12] But besides this dramatic probability, all the other excellencies of the drama, as unity of interest, with distinctness and subordination of the characters, appropriateness of style, nay, and the charm of language and sentiment for their own sakes, yet still as far as they tend to increase the inward excitement, are all means to this chief end, that of producing and supporting this willing illusion.

I have but one point more to add — namely, that tho' the excellencies above mentioned are means to this end, they do not therefore cease to be themselves *ends,* and as such carry their own justification with them as long as they do not contravene or interrupt the illusion. It is not even always or of necessity an objection to them that they prevent it from rising to as great a height as it might otherwise have attained; it is enough if they are compatible with as high a degree as is requisite. If the panorama had been invented in the time of Leo X,[13] Raphael [14] would still have smiled at the regret that the broom-twigs, etc., at the back of his grand pictures were not as probable trees as those in the panorama. Let me venture to affirm that certain obvious, if not palpable, improbabilities may be hazarded in order to keep down a scene, [to keep it] merely instrumental and to preserve it in its due proportion of interest. I now quit this subject for the time with less regret, because in my next lecture I shall have occasion to take it up again, in application to Shakespeare's historical dramas.

*The Tempest,* I repeat, has been selected as a specimen of the romantic drama; *i.e.,* of a drama, the interests of which are independent of all historical facts and associations, and arise from their fitness to that faculty of our nature, the imagination I mean, which owes no allegiance to time and place — a species of drama, therefore, in which errors in chronology and geography, no mortal sins in any species, are venial, or count for nothing.

---

Exquisite judgment — first the noise and confusion — then the silence of a deserted island — and Prospero and Miranda. I have often thought of Shakespeare as the mighty wizard himself introducing as the first and fairest [?] pledge of his so potent art, the female character in all its charms, as if conscious that he first had represented womanhood as a dramatist.

---

It addresses itself entirely to the imaginative faculty; and although the illusion may be assisted by the effect on the senses of the complicated scenery and decorations of modern times, yet this sort of assistance is dangerous. For the principal and only genuine excitement ought to come from within — from the moved and sympathetic imagination; whereas, where so much is addressed to the mere external senses of seeing and hearing, the spiritual vision is apt to languish, and the attraction from without will withdraw the mind from the proper and only legitimate interest which is intended to spring from within.

The romance opens with a busy scene admirably appropriate to the kind of drama, and giving, as it were, the keynote to the whole harmony. It pre-

12. **Lear's . . . Cordelia:** I.i.

13. **Leo X:** a Pope (1513–21), patron of Raphael. 14. **Raphael:** Raphael Sanzio (1483–1520), one of the greatest of Italian Renaissance painters.

pares and initiates the excitement required for the entire piece, and yet does not demand anything from the spectators which their previous habits had not fitted them to understand. It is the bustle of a tempest from which the real horrors are abstracted; — therefore it is poetical, though not in strictness natural — (the distinction to which I have so often alluded) — and is purposely restrained from concentering the interest on itself, but used merely as an induction or tuning for what is to follow.

In the second scene Prospero's speeches, till the entrance of Ariel, contain the finest example I remember of retrospective narration for the purpose of exciting immediate interest and putting the audience in possession of all the information necessary for the understanding of the plot. Observe, too, the perfect probability of the moment chosen by Prospero (the very Shakespeare himself, as it were, of the tempest) to open out the truth to his daughter, his own romantic bearing, and how completely anything that might have been disagreeable to us in the magician, is reconciled and shaded in the humanity and natural feelings of the father. In the very first speech of Miranda the simplicity and tenderness of her character are at once laid open — it would have been lost in direct contact with the agitation of the first scene. The opinion once prevailed, but, happily, is now abandoned, that Fletcher alone wrote for women; the truth is, that with very few, and those partial, exceptions, the female characters in the plays of Beaumont and Fletcher[15] are, when of the light kind, not decent; when heroic, complete viragos. But in Shakespeare all the elements of womanhood are holy, and there is the sweet, yet dignified feeling of all that *continuates* society, as sense of ancestry and of sex, with a purity unassailable by sophistry because it rests not in the analytic processes, but in that sane equipoise of the faculties, during which the feelings are representative of all past experience, — not of the individual only, but of all those by whom she has been educated, and their predecessors even up to the first mother that lived. Shakespeare saw that the want of prominence, which Pope notices for sarcasm, was the blessèd beauty of the woman's character, and knew that it arose not from any deficiency, but from the more exquisite harmony of all the parts of the moral being constituting one living total of head and heart. He has drawn it, indeed, in all its distinctive energies of faith, patience, constancy, fortitude — shown in all of them as following the heart, which gives its results by a nice tact and happy intuition, without the intervention of the discursive faculty — sees all things in and by the light of the affections, and errs, if it ever err, in the exaggerations of love alone. In all the Shakespearean women there is essentially the same foundation and principle; the distinct individuality and variety are merely the result of the modification of circumstances, whether in Miranda the maiden, in Imogen the wife, or in Katharine the queen.

But to return. The appearance and characters of the super or ultranatural servants are finely contrasted. Ariel has in everything the airy tint which gives the name; and it is worthy of remark that Miranda is never directly brought into comparison with Ariel, lest the natural and human of the one and the supernatural of the other should tend to neutralize each other; Caliban, on the other hand, is all earth, all condensed and gross in feelings and images; he has the dawnings of understanding without reason or the moral sense, and in him, as in some brute animals, this advance to the intellectual faculties, without the moral sense, is marked by the appearance of vice. For it is in the primacy of the moral being only that man is truly human; in his intellectual powers he is certainly approached by the brutes, and, man's whole system duly considered, those powers cannot be considered other than means to an end, that is, to morality.

In this scene, as it proceeds, is displayed the impression made by Ferdinand and Miranda on each other; it is love at first sight; —

at the first sight
They have changed eyes: —
[I.ii.440–01]

and it appears to me that in all cases of real love it is at one moment that it takes place. That moment may have been prepared by previous esteem, admiration, or even affection; yet love seems to require a momentary act of volition by which a tacit bond of devotion is imposed, a bond not to be thereafter broken without violating what should be sacred in our nature. How finely is the true Shakespearean scene contrasted with Dryden's vulgar alteration of it, in which a mere ludicrous psychological experiment, as it were, is tried — displaying nothing but indelicacy without passion. Prospero's interruption of the courtship has often seemed to

**15. Beaumont and Fletcher**: Francis Beaumont (1584–1616) and John Fletcher (1579–1625), a famous team of Jacobean playwrights.

me to have no sufficient motive; still his alleged reason —

lest too light winning
Make the prize light —
[II.ii.451–52]

is enough for the ethereal connections of the romantic imagination, although it would not be so for the historical. The whole courting scene, indeed, in the beginning of the third act, between the lovers is a masterpiece; and the first dawn of disobedience in the mind of Miranda to the command of her father is very finely drawn, so as to seem the working of the Scriptural command, *Thou shalt leave father and mother,* &c. O! with what exquisite purity this scene is conceived and executed! Shakespeare may sometimes be gross, but I boldly say that he is always moral and modest. Alas! in this our day decency of manners is preserved at the expense of morality of heart, and delicacies for vice are allowed, whilst grossness against it is hypocritically, or at least morbidly, condemned.

In this play are admirably sketched the vices generally accompanying a low degree of civilization; and in the first scene of the second act Shakespeare has, as in many other places, shown the tendency in bad men to indulge in scorn and contemptuous expressions as a mode of getting rid of their own uneasy feelings of inferiority to the good, and also, by making the good ridiculous, of rendering the transition of others to wickedness easy. Shakespeare never puts habitual scorn into the mouths of other than bad men, as here in the instances of Antonio and Sebastian. The scene of the intended assassination of Alonzo and Gonzalo is an exact counterpart of the scene between Macbeth and his lady, only pitched in a lower key throughout, as designed to be frustrated and concealed, and exhibiting the same profound management in the manner of familiarizing a mind, not immediately recipient, to the suggestion of guilt by associating the proposed crime with something ludicrous or out of place — something not habitually matter of reverence. By this kind of sophistry the imagination and fancy are first bribed to contemtemplate the suggested act, and at length to become acquainted with it. Observe how the effect of this scene is heightened by contrast with another counterpart of it in low life — that between the conspirators Stephano, Caliban, and Trinculo in the second scene of the third act, in which there are the same essential characteristics.

In this play and in this scene of it are also shown the springs of the vulgar in politics, of that kind of politics which is inwoven with human nature. In his treatment of this subject, wherever it occurs, Shakespeare is quite peculiar. In other writers we find the particular opinions of the individual; in Massinger [16] it is rank republicanism; in Beaumont and Fletcher even *jure divino* [17] principles are carried to excess; but Shakespeare never promulgates any party tenets. He is always the philosopher and the moralist, but at the same time with a profound veneration for all the established institutions of society, and for those classes which form the permanent elements of the state — especially never introducing a professional character, as such, otherwise than as respectable. If he must have any name, he should be styled a philosophical aristocrat, delighting in those hereditary institutions which have a tendency to bind one age to another, and in that distinction of ranks, of which, although few may be in possession, all enjoy the advantages. Hence, again, you will observe the good nature with which he seems always to make sport with the passions and follies of a mob, as with an irrational animal. He is never angry with it, but hugely content with holding up its absurdities to its face; and sometimes you may trace a tone of almost affectionate superiority, something like that in which a father speaks of the rogueries of a child. See the good-humored way in which he describes Stephano passing from the most licentious freedom to absolute despotism over Trinculo and Caliban. The truth is, Shakespeare's characters are all *genera* [18] intensely individualized, the results of meditation of which observation supplied the drapery and the colors necessary to combine them with each other. He had virtually surveyed all the great component powers and impulses of human nature, had seen that their different combinations and subordinations were in fact the individualizers of men, and showed how their harmony was produced by reciprocal disproportions of excess or deficiency. The language in which these truths are expressed was not drawn from any set fashion, but from the profoundest depths of his moral being, and is therefore for all ages.

16. **Massinger**: Philip Massinger, an English dramatist (1583–1640). 17. ***jure divino:*** divine right or justice. 18. ***genera:*** species.

**NORTHROP FRYE, *Editor***

# George Gordon, Lord Byron

**1788–1824**

It is hardly possible to discuss Byron's poetry without telling the story of his life in some detail. His father was Captain Jack Byron, a nephew of the fifth Baron Byron, and a psychopathic spendthrift and sponger on women who had run through the fortunes of two heiresses. The first, a marchioness, he had acquired by divorce from her husband, and by her he had a daughter, Augusta Byron, later Augusta Leigh, the poet's half-sister. The second was a Scotswoman, Catherine Gordon of Gight, an explosive, unbalanced, ill-educated but affectionate woman whose only child was the poet. Byron was born in London on January 22, 1788, in great poverty and distress as his mother was returning from France to Scotland to get some relief from her rapacious spouse. He was handicapped at birth with a lameness that embittered his life (what was wrong, and which leg was affected, are still uncertain points), and he also had some glandular imbalance that forced him to a starvation diet in order to avoid grotesque corpulence. The mother brought up her boy in Aberdeen, where his religious training was naturally Presbyterian, giving many a later critic a somewhat dubious cliché about the "persisting Calvinism" in Byron's mind. When Byron was three his father died; when he was six his cousin, the heir to the Byron title, was killed, and when he was ten his great-uncle, who held the title, died and the poet became the sixth Lord Byron. The fact that Byron made so professional a job of being a lord is perhaps the result of his entering on that state when he was old enough to notice the difference his title made in the attitude that society took toward him.

He was then educated at Harrow and at Trinity College, Cambridge. The most important of the friendships he formed there was with John Cam Hobhouse, in later life Lord Broughton, who founded a "Whig Club" at Cambridge, and whose influence had much to do with Byron's left-of-center political views. Byron's chief athletic interests were swimming and pistol-shooting, the latter a useful accomplishment in the days when gentlemen were expected to fight the odd duel, and he got around a regulation against keeping a dog at Cambridge by keeping a bear instead. What with his extravagance, his lack of discipline, and the liberties he took with his rank, he was anything but a model student. He announced more than once that he wished he had gone to Oxford instead, and the Cambridge authorities must often have wished so too. However, he acquired the usual gentleman's classical education, and while still an undergraduate he produced a slim volume of melodious if not very arresting lyrics. This volume was, after some vicissitudes, published in 1807 under the title given it by the publisher, *Hours of Idleness. Hours of Idleness* got roughly handled in the *Edinburgh Review,* and the result was Byron's first major satire, *English Bards and Scotch Reviewers* (1809). Although the motivation for this poem was revenge on the Edinburgh reviewer, Byron took the opportunity to satirize most of his poetic contemporaries, including Scott, Southey, Wordsworth and Coleridge.

Meanwhile Byron had been planning a variant

of the "Grand Tour" that it was fashionable for young well-to-do Englishmen to take. Instead of the usual journey to France and Italy, he decided to go first to Portugal and Spain, bypass Italy by way of Malta, and then travel in what were at that time Turkish dominions: Greece, Asia Minor, and the practically unknown Albania. He set out with Hobhouse on July 2, 1809, on the "Lisbon Packet." The Peninsular War was in progress, but life was made easy for people in Byron's social position, and one would never dream from his letters that this was the time and place of Goya's *Disasters of War*. The travelers passed through Malta, where a Mrs. Spencer Smith became the "Florence" of some of Byron's love poems, and on to Albania. Byron and his party were hospitably received by a local ruler, Ali Pasha, who found Byron as attractive as most people did, besides having political reasons for welcoming English visitors. Once, on suspicion that was no more than gossip, he had had fifteen women kidnapped and flung into the sea. Another woman narrowly escaped the same fate on a charge of infidelity: this incident was used by Byron as the basis for his tale *The Giaour,* and rumor maintained that Byron himself had been her lover. Next came Greece and Asia Minor, where Byron duplicated Leander's famous swim across the Hellespont, pondered over the sites of Marathon and Troy, and deplored the activities of Lord Elgin, who was engaged in hacking off the sculptures now called the Elgin Marbles from the ruined Parthenon and transporting them to England. Byron's satire on Lord Elgin's enterprise, "The Curse of Minerva" (i.e., Athene, the patron of Athens), was not published until 1815. Meanwhile he had begun to write a poem about his travels, *Childe Harold,* the first two cantos of the poem we now have.

On his return to England in July, 1811, he went back to Newstead, the estate of the Byrons, where he had established himself before he left, a rambling "Gothic" mansion he was later forced to sell. His mother died suddenly soon after his arrival, and the deaths of three close friends occurred about the same time. The relations between Byron and his mother had always been tense, especially after she had begun to see some of his father's extravagance reappearing in him, but they were fond enough of each other when they were not living together. Byron now entered upon a phenomenally successful literary and social career. *Childe Harold,* as he said, made him famous overnight, and it was followed by a series of Oriental tales, *The Giaour, The Bride of Abydos, The Corsair,* and *Lara,* which appeared in 1813 and 1814. He wrote with great speed, completing the thousand-odd lines of *The Bride of Abydos* in four days, and he seldom revised. "I am like the tyger," he said: "If I miss my first Spring, I go growling back to my Jungle. There is no second. I can't correct; I can't, and I won't."

When Byron said in *Beppo:*

> I've half a mind to tumble down to prose,
> But verse is more in fashion — so here goes.

the last statement, incredible as it may seem now, was true when he wrote. Nobody would turn to poetry for stories nowadays, but in Byron's day there was a popular demand for verse tales that Byron did not create, though he did much to expand it. The melancholy misanthropy, so full of romantic *frisson,* the pirates and the harems, the exotic Orientalism, the easy and pleasant versification, swept London as they were later to sweep the Continent. As a celebrity Byron could hold his own even in the most absorbing period of the Napoleonic War. *The Corsair* sold 10,000 copies on the day of its publication by John Murray, and ran through seven editions in a month. Byron probably made more money from his poetry than any other English poet, though being a lord who derived his income from rents, he often gave his royalties away to friends. The first money he accepted on his own account was £700 for the copyright of *Lara.*

Apart from literature Byron had many other activities, both serious and scandalous. Before he had left England he had taken the seat in the House of Lords that his title gave him, and he now became active in Whig circles. His first speech was made in defence of the "framebreakers," or workers who had destroyed some textile machines through fear of unemployment. He also supported a number of other liberal causes, including the relief of Catholics in Ireland. When Napoleon was banished to Elba, Byron wrote an ode on him in which he contrasted him unfavorably with Washington as a fighter for liberty. (There is an impressive musical setting of this ode, for orchestra and *Sprechgesang* solo, by Arnold Schönberg.) But his hatred of the reactionary English government, especially Lord Castlereagh, was strong enough to give him a considerable admiration for Napoleon, even to the point of regretting the outcome of Waterloo: he had hoped, he said, to see Castlereagh's head on a pole. In fact his attitude to Napoleon always retained a good deal of self-identification.

Meanwhile Byron was carrying on some highly publicized affairs with several women of fashion. Lady Caroline Lamb, always something of an emotional exhibitionist, kept London, which on Byron's social level was still a small town, buzzing with gossip over her pursuit of Byron, her visits to him disguised, her tantrums, and her public scenes. Lady Oxford, whose children, in an erudite contemporary joke, were known as the Harleian Miscellany, was another mistress of his, and there were briefer encounters with others. Despite his crowded schedule, Byron began seriously to consider marriage, making a trusted confidante of Lady Melbourne, Caroline Lamb's mother-in-law, to whom he wrote many frank and unaffected letters. Given Byron's temperament, he could only marry some kind of *femme fatale;* and the only really fatal type of woman for him would be an earnest, humorless, rather inhibited female who would represent everything that was insular and respectable in English society. His choice fell on Annabella Milbanke, heiress to a title in her own right and niece of Lady Melbourne, and who otherwise reminds one a little of Mary Bennett in *Pride and Prejudice*. She was highly intelligent and had many interests, including mathematics (Byron called her the "Princess of Parallelograms," as in those days any woman with such an interest could expect to be teased about it), but her mind ran to rather vague maxims of general conduct, and to an interest in the moral reformation of other people which boded ill for marriage to an unreformed poet with an unusually concrete view of life.

The marriage lasted a year (January, 1815, to January, 1816) and then fell apart. A separation (they were never divorced) was agreed upon, and Lady Byron obtained custody of their daughter, Augusta Ada. Byron appears to have gone somewhat berserk in his matrimonial bonds, and his wife's doubts about his sanity were probably genuine. The situation was aggravated by financial difficulties and by the fact that gossip had begun to whisper about Byron and his half-sister Augusta. That there were sexual relations between them seems obvious enough, though the matter is hotly disputed, and the relevant documents have been carefully removed from the prying eyes of scholars. The combination of this exceptionally delicious scandal with the matrimonial one, along with his expression of some perverse pro-French political views, made things unpleasant for Byron, and although social disapproval was perhaps not as intense as he pretended or thought, he felt forced to leave England once more. He set out for the Continent on April 25, 1816, never to return to England.

He made his way to Geneva, where he met, by prearrangement, Shelley and his wife Mary Godwin, along with her stepsister, Claire (or Jane) Clairmont. The last named had visited Byron before his departure from England and had thrown herself, as biographers say, at his head, the result of this accurate if morally unguided missile being a daughter, Allegra, whom Byron eventually placed in an Italian convent to be brought up as a Roman Catholic, and who died there at the age of eight. The association with Shelley, one of Byron's few intellectual friends, is marked in the new poetry that Byron now began writing—the third canto of *Childe Harold; Manfred;* the two remarkable poems "Darkness" and "The Dream"; and the most poignant of his tales, "The Prisoner of Chillon." Shelley's reaction to Byron may be found in his poem "Julian and Maddalo," but for all the skepticism he ascribes to Byron, he was unable to convince him that Christianity was less reasonable than his own brand of Platonism.

In the fall of 1817 Byron went over the Alps and settled in Venice. His "Ode to Venice," *Beppo,* the opening of the fourth canto of *Childe Harold,* and two of his dramas, *Marino Faliero* and *The Two Foscari*, are some of the evidence for the fascination that this dreamlike World's Fair of a city had for him. At Venice he plunged into an extraordinary sexual debauch, but he also wrote some of his best poetry, including the fourth canto of *Childe Harold* and the beginning of his greatest work, *Don Juan*. In the spring of 1819 he met Teresa Guiccioli, the wife of an elderly Count, who was both attractive enough to hold Byron and astute enough to keep other women away from him. Byron moved into the Guiccioli household in Ravenna, and settled down with Teresa into what by Byronic standards was practically an old-fashioned marriage. Ravenna saw the composition of *Sardanapalus* and *Cain,* as well as *The Vision of Judgment,* but his poetic energies were increasingly absorbed by *Don Juan*.

At that time the two great centers of classical civilization, Greece and Italy, were under foreign occupation: Greece was a Turkish dependency, and most of northern Italy was controlled by Austria. Byron and Shelley were passionate supporters of the efforts of Italian and Greek nationalists to get free of their foreign yokes. Teresa's family, the Gambas, were also Italian nationalists in sympathy, and hence were, as was Byron, closely watched and reported on by the Austrian police. The Gambas were forced to move from Ravenna to Pisa, and Byron followed them. At Pisa Byron rejoined the Shelleys, and here Shelley, on July 8, 1822, was drowned at sea and cremated on the shore. The cremation was carried out by Byron and their friend Edward Trelawny, an extraordinarily circumstantial liar who had reconstructed his past life along the general lines of a Byronic hero. Meanwhile Byron had broken with his publisher John Murray, and had formed an alliance through Shelley with Leigh Hunt, whom he brought to Pisa. The plan was to found a literary and left-wing political magazine, and this magazine, called *The Liberal,* printed a good deal of Byron's poetry, including *The Vision of Judgment,* in its four numbers. Hunt, however, was somewhat irresponsible (he is the original of Harold Skimpole in Dickens' *Bleak House*), and his absurd and even more Dickensian wife and their demonic children helped to keep relations strained.

Eventually the Gamba-Byron menage was forced to move on to Genoa, where Byron wrote some unimportant poems and finished what we have of *Don Juan* — sixteen cantos and a fragment of a seventeenth. Meanwhile a group of revolutionaries in Greece had been planning an insurrection against the Turkish authority, and knowing of Byron's sympathy with their cause, they offered him membership in their Committee. Byron had been meditating the possibility of going to Greece for some time, and on July 23, 1823, he left in the company of Trelawny and Pietro Gamba, Teresa's brother. He established connection at Missolonghi on January 5, 1824, with Prince Alexander Mavrocordato, the leader of the Western Greek revolutionaries, and put his money and his very real qualities of leadership at the service of the Greek cause. His health, which had been precarious for some time, broke down in a series of fevers, and he died at Missolonghi on April 19, 1824, three months after he had passed the thirty-sixth birthday which his valedictory poem records.

## II

The main appeal of Byron's poetry is in the fact that it is Byron's. To read Byron's poetry is to hear all about Byron's marital difficulties, flirtations, love for Augusta, friendships, travels, and political and social views. And Byron is a consistently interesting person to hear about, this being why Byron, even at his worst of self-pity and egotism and blither and doggerel, is still so incredibly readable. He proves what many critics declare to be impossible, that a poem can make its primary impact as a historical and biographical document. The critical problem involved here is crucial to our understanding of not only Byron but literature as a whole. Even when Byron's poetry is not objectively very good, it is still important, because it is Byron's. But who was Byron to be so important? certainly not an exceptionally good or wise man. Byron is, strictly, neither a great poet nor a great man who wrote poetry, but something in between: a tremendous cultural force that was life and literature at once. How he came to be this is what we must try to explain as we review the four chief genres of his work: the lyrics, the tales (including *Childe Harold*), the dramas, and the later satires.

Byron's lyrical poetry affords a good exercise in critical catholicity, because it contains nothing that "modern" critics look for: no texture, no ambiguities, no intellectualized ironies, no intensity, no vividness of phrasing, the words and images being vague to the point of abstraction.

The poetry seems to be a plain man's poetry, making poetic emotion out of the worn and blunted words of ordinary speech. Yet it is not written by a plain man: it is written, as Arnold said, with the careless ease of a man of quality, and its most striking and obvious feature is its gentlemanly amateurism. It is, to be sure, in an amateur tradition, being a romantic, subjective, personal development of the kind of Courtly Love poetry that was written by Tudor and Cavalier noblemen in earlier ages. Byron's frequent statements in prefaces that this would be his last work to trouble the public with, his offhand deprecating comments on his work, his refusal to revise, all give a studious impression of a writer who can take poetry or leave it alone. Byron held the view that lyrical poetry was an expression of passion, and that passion was essentially fitful, and he distrusted professional poets, who pretended to be able to summon passion at will and sustain it indefinitely. Poe was later to hold much the same view of poetry, but more consistently, for he drew the inference that a continuous long poem was impossible, whereas *Childe Harold* has the stretches of perfunctory, even slapdash writing that one would expect with such a theory.

In Byron's later lyrics, especially the *Hebrew Melodies* of 1815, where he was able to add some of his Oriental technicolor to the Old Testament, more positive qualities emerge, particularly in the rhythm. "The Destruction of Sennacherib" is a good reciter's piece (though not without its difficulties, as Tom Sawyer discovered), and anticipates some of the later experiments in verbal jazz by Poe and Swinburne. Some of the best of his poems bear the title "Stanzas for Music," and they have the flat conventional diction appropriate to poems that depend partly on another art for their sound:

One shade the more, one ray the less,
  Had half impaired the nameless grace
Which waves in every raven tress,
  Or softly lightens o'er her face;
Where thoughts serenely sweet express
  How pure, how dear their dwelling-place.

(If the reader would like a clue to the caressing rhythm of this stanza, he should read the iambic meters so as to give the stresses twice the length of the unstressed syllables. Then the lines will fall into four bars of three-four time, beginning on the third beat, and the rhythm of a nineteenth-century waltz will emerge.) We notice that while Byron's amateur predecessors wrote in a convention and Byron from personal experience, Byron was equally conventional, because his personal experience conformed to a literary pattern. Byron's life imitated literature: this is where his unique combination of the poetic and the personal begins.

Byron was naturally an extroverted person, fond of company, of travel, of exploring new scenes, making new friends, falling in love with new women. Like Keats, in a much more direct way, he wanted a life of sensations rather than of thoughts. As he said: "I can not repent me (I try very often) so much of any thing I have done, as of anything I have left undone. Alas! I have been but idle, and have the prospect of an early decay, without having seized every available instant of our pleasurable years." In the records of his journeys in his letters and Hobhouse's diaries, it is the more introverted Hobhouse who dwells on the dirt and the fleas, and it is Hobhouse too who does the serious studying and takes an interest in archaeology. It is Byron who swims across the Hellespont, learns the songs of Albanian mountaineers, makes friends with a Moslem vizier, amuses himself with the boys in a monastery school, flirts with Greek girls, and picks up a smattering of Armenian. He was continually speculating about unknown sensations, such as how it would feel to have committed a murder, and he had the nervous dread of growing older that goes with the fear of slowing down in the rhythm of experience. His writing depends heavily on experience; he seldom describes any country that he has not seen, and for all his solitary role he shows, especially in *Don Juan,* a novelist's sense of established society.

It was an essential part of his strongly extroverted and empirical bent that he should not be a systematic thinker, nor much interested in people who were. He used his intelligence to make common-sense judgements on specific situations, and found himself unable to believe anything that he did not find confirmed in his own experience. In his numerous amours, for example, the absence of any sense of sin was as unanswerable a fact of his experience as the presence of it would have been to St. Augustine. He thought of sexual love as a product of reflex and mechanical habit, not of inner emotional drives. When he said: "I do not believe in the existence of what is called love," we are probably to take him quite literally. Nevertheless, his extroversion made him easily confused by efforts at self-analysis, and he flew into rages when he was accused of any lack of feeling. One reason why his marriage demoralized him so was that it forced such efforts on him.

Now if we look into Byron's tales and *Childe Harold* we usually find as the central character an inscrutable figure with hollow cheeks and blazing eyes, wrapped in a cloud of gloom, full of mysterious and undefined remorse, an outcast from society, a wanderer of the race of Cain. At times he suggests something demonic rather than human, a Miltonic Satan or fallen angel. He may be a sinister brigand like the Corsair, or an aloof and icily polite aristocrat like the Lucifer of *The Vision of Judgment,* but he is always haughty and somber of demeanor; his glance is difficult to meet; he will not brook questioning, though he himself questions all established social standards, and he is associated with lonely and colorful predatory animals, as ordinary society is with gregarious ones like sheep and domestic fowl. "The lion is alone, and so am I," says Manfred. The name of the Corsair is "linked with one virtue, and a thousand crimes": the virtue is manifested when he refuses, as a prisoner, to assassinate his captor to escape being impaled. Fortunately his mistress Gulnare was less scrupulous. As for Lara, who is the Corsair returned from exile to his estates:

> He stood a stranger in this breathing world,
> An erring spirit from another hurled.

This type of character is now known as the "Byronic hero," and wherever he has appeared since in literature there has been the influence, direct or indirect, of Byron. And if we ask how a witty, sociable, extroverted poet came to create such a character, we can see that it must have arisen as what psychologists call a projection of his inner self, that inner self that was so mysterious and inscrutable even to its owner.

It happened that this type of character had already been popularized in the "Gothic" thrillers or "horrid stories" of Mrs. Radcliffe, M. G. Lewis (a friend of Byron's, known as "Monk" Lewis from his violent and sadistic tale *The Monk*), John Moore, whose *Zeluco,* a much more serious work, Byron greatly admired, and lesser writers. The period of their greatest popularity was the last decade of the eighteenth century, but they survived through Byron's lifetime. Jane Austen's *Northanger Abbey* was written as a parody of them in 1798, but it still had a point when it was published in 1818. These thrillers were intended for an English Protestant middle-class reading public: consequently their horrid surroundings were normally Continental, Catholic and upper class, though Oriental settings also had a vogue. Into such settings stalked a character type, sometimes a villain, sometimes presented in a more sympathetic, or more-sinned-against-than-sinning, role, but in either case misanthropic, misunderstood, and solitary, with strong diabolical overtones. The devil is a powerfully erotic figure, his horns and hoofs descending from the ancient satyrs, and the various forms of sadism and masochism glanced at in these thrillers helped to make them extremely popular, not least with the female part of the reading public.

Childe Harold and the other lowering heroes of Byron's tales not only popularized a conventional type of hero, but popularized Byron himself in that role. For Byron was a dark and melancholy-looking lord with a reputation for wickedness and free thought; he seemed to prefer the Continent to England, and took a detached view of middle-class and even Christian morality. He owned a gloomy Gothic castle and spent evenings with revelers in it; he was pale and thin with his ferocious dieting; he even had a lame foot. No wonder he said that strangers whom he met at dinner "looked as if his Satanic Majesty had been among them." The prince of darkness is a gentleman, and so was Byron. Again, when a "nameless vice" was introduced into a Gothic thriller, as part of the villain's or hero's background, it generally turned out, when named, to be incest. This theme recurs all through Romantic literature, being almost obsessive in Shelley as well as Byron, and here again a literary convention turns up in Byron's life. Even a smaller detail, like the disguising of the ex-Corsair's mistress in *Lara* as the page-boy Kaled, recurs in Byron's liaison with Caroline Lamb, who looked well in a page's costume.

Byron did not find the Byronic hero as enthralling as his public did, and he made several efforts to detach his own character from Childe Harold and his other heroes, with limited success. He says of Childe Harold that he wanted to make him an objective study of gloomy misanthropy, hence he deliberately cut humor out of the poem in order to preserve a unity of tone. But Byron's most distinctive talents did not have full scope in this part of his work. Most of the Gothic thriller writers were simple-minded popular novelists, but the same convention had also been practised on a much higher level of literary intelligence. Apart from Goethe's early *Sorrows of Werther,* an extraordinarily popular tale of a solemn suicide, Addison in *The Vision of Mirza* and Johnson in *Rasselas* had used the Oriental tale for serious literary purposes. Also, Horace Walpole in *The Castle of Otranto* (1764) and William Beckford in *Vathek* (1786) had written respectively a Gothic and an Oriental romance in which melodrama and fantasy were shot through with flickering lights of irony. They were addressed to a reading public capable, to use modern phraseology, of taking their corn with a pinch of salt. It was this higher level of sophistication that Byron naturally wanted to reach, and he was oppressed by the humorless solemnity of his own creations. His sardonic and ribald wit, his sense of the concrete, his almost infallible feeling for the common-sense perspective on every situation, crackles all through his letters and journals, even through his footnotes. But it seems to be locked out of his serious poetry, and only in the very last canto of *Don Juan* did he succeed in uniting fantasy and humor.

Byron's tales are, on the whole, well-told and well-shaped stories. Perhaps he learned something from his own ridicule of Southey, who was also a popular writer of verse tales, sometimes of mammoth proportions. In any case he is well able to exploit the capacity of verse for dramatizing one or two central situations, leaving all the cumbersome apparatus of plot to be ignored or taken for granted. But he seemed unable to bring his various projections of his inner ghost to life: his heroes, like the characters of a detective story, are thin, bloodless, abstract, and popular. Nor could he seem to vary the tone, from romance to irony, from fantasy to humor, as Beckford does in *Vathek*. Byron was strongly attracted by Beckford, and is thinking of him at the very opening of *Childe Harold,* as Beckford had lived for two years in Portugal. When Byron writes:

> Deep in yon cave Honorius long did dwell,
> In hope to merit Heaven by making earth a Hell.

he obviously has in mind the demure remark in the opening of *Vathek:* "He did not think . . . that it was necessary to make a hell of this world to enjoy paradise in the next." But though Byron is the wittiest of writers, the Byronic hero cannot manage much more than a gloomy smile. Here, for instance, is Childe Harold on the "Lisbon Packet":

> The sails were filled, and fair the light winds
> blew,
> As glad to waft him from his native home . . .
> And then, it may be, of his wish to roam
> Repented he, but in his bosom slept
> The silent thought, nor from his lips did come
> One word of wail, whilst others sate and wept,
> And to the reckless gales unmanly moaning kept.

and here is Byron himself in the same situation:

> Hobhouse muttering fearful curses,
> As the hatchway down he rolls,
> Now his breakfast, now his verses,
> Vomits forth — and damns our souls . . .
> "Zounds! my liver's coming up:
> I shall not survive the racket
> Of this brutal Lisbon Packet."

The same inability to combine seriousness and humor is also to be found in the plays, where one would expect more variety of tone. The central character is usually the Byronic hero again, and again he seems to cast a spell over the whole action. Byron recognized this deficiency in his dramas, and to say that his plays were not intended for the stage would be an understatement. Byron had a positive phobia of stage production, and once tried to get an injunction issued to prevent a performance of *Marino Faliero*. "I never risk *rivalry* in anything," he wrote to Lady Melbourne, and being directly dependent on the applause or booing of a crowd (modern theaters give us no notion of what either form of demonstration was like in Byron's day) was something he could not face, even in absence. Besides, he had no professional sense, and nothing of the capacity to write for an occasion that the practising dramatist needs. Hence, with the exception of *Werner,* a lively and well-written melodrama based on a plot by somebody else, Byron's plays are so strictly closet dramas that they differ little in structure from the tales.

The establishing of the Byronic hero was a major feat of characterization, but Byron had little power of characterization apart from this figure. Like many brilliant talkers, he had not much ear for the rhythms and nuances of other people's speech. Here again we find a close affinity between Byron's personality and the conventions of his art. For instance, in his life Byron seemed to have curiously little sense of women as human beings. Except for Lady Melbourne, he addressed himself to the female in them, took a hearty-male view of their intellectual interests, and concentrated on the ritual of love-making with the devotion of what an earlier age would have called a clerk of Venus. This impersonal and ritualistic approach to women is reflected in his tales and plays, where again it fits the conventions of Byronic romance. It is difficult for a heroine of strong character to make much headway against a gloomy misanthropic hero, and Byron's heroines, like the heroines of Gothic romance in general, are insipid prodigies of neurotic devotion.

But if Byron's plays are not practicable stage plays, they are remarkable works. *Manfred,* based on what Byron had heard about Goethe's *Faust,* depicts the Byronic hero as a student of magic whose knowledge has carried him beyond the limits of human society and given him superhuman powers, but who is still held to human desire by his love for his sister (apparently) Astarte. At the moment of his death the demons he has controlled, with a sense of what is customary in stories about magicians, come to demand his soul, but Manfred, in a crisp incisive speech which retains its power to surprise through any number of rereadings, announces that he has made no bargain with them, that whatever he has done, they can go to hell, and he will not go with them. The key to this final scene is the presence of the Abbot. Manfred and the Abbot differ on all points of theory, but the Abbot is no coward and Manfred is no villain: they face the crisis together, linked in a common bond of humanity which enables Manfred to die and to triumph at the same time.

Two of Byron's plays, *Cain* and *Heaven and Earth,* are described by Byron as "mysteries," by which he meant Biblical plays like those of the Middle Ages. Wherever we turn in Byron's poetry, we meet the figure of Cain, the first man who never knew Paradise, and whose sexual love was necessarily incestuous. In Byron's "mystery" Cain is Adam's eldest son and heir, but what he really inherits is the memory of a greater dispossession. "Dost thou not live?" asks Adam helplessly. "Must I not die?" retorts Cain. Adam cannot comprehend the mentality of one who has been born with the consciousness of death. But Lucifer can, for he too has been disinherited. He comes to Cain and gives him what he gave Adam: fruit of the tree of knowledge, of a kind that Raphael, in the eighth book of *Paradise Lost,* warned Adam against: a knowledge of other worlds and other beings, a realization that the fortunes of humanity are of less account in the scheme of things than he had assumed. From such knowledge develops the resentment that leads to the murder of Abel and to Cain's exile. And just as Milton tries to show us that we in Adam's place would have committed Adam's sin, so Byron makes us feel that we all have something of Cain in us: everybody has killed something that he wishes he had kept alive, and the fullest of lives is wrapped around the taint of an inner death. As the princess says in *The Castle of Otranto:* "This can be no evil spirit: it is undoubtedly one of the family."

The other "mystery," *Heaven and Earth,* deals with the theme of the love of angels for human women recorded in some mysterious verses of Genesis, and ends with the coming of Noah's flood. Angels who fall through sexual love are obvious enough subjects for Byron, but *Heaven and Earth* lacks the clear dramatic outline of *Cain.* All Byron's plays are tragedies, and as Byron moved further away from the easy sentiment of his earlier tales he moved toward intellectual paradox rather than tragedy. It is particularly in the final scenes that we observe Byron becoming too self-conscious for the full emotional resonance of tragedy. In *Sardanapalus,* for example, we see the downfall of a king who pursued pleasure because he was too intelligent to want to keep his people plunged into warfare. His intelligence is identified by his people with weakness, and his pursuit of pleasure is inseparably attached to selfishness. What we are left with, despite his final death on a funeral pyre, is less tragedy than an irony of a kind that is very close to satire. Byron's creative powers were clearly running in the direction of satire, and it was to satire that he turned in his last and greatest period.

In *English Bards and Scotch Reviewers* Byron spoke of Wordsworth as "that mild apostate from poetic rule." This poem is early, but Byron never altered his opinion of the Lake Poets as debasers of the currency of English poetry. His own poetic idol was Pope, whom he called "the moral poet of all civilization," and he thought of himself as continuing Pope's standards of clarity, craftsmanship and contact with real life against the introverted metaphysical mumblings of Coleridge and Wordsworth. Byron's early models were standard, even old-fashioned, later eighteenth-century models. *English Bards* is in the idiom of eighteenth-century satire, less of Pope than of Pope's successors, Churchill, Wolcot, and Gifford, and the first part of *Childe Harold,* with its pointless Spenserian stanza and its semi-facetious antique diction — fortunately soon dropped by Byron — is also an eighteenth-century stock pattern. Byron was friendly with Shelley, but owes little to him technically, and in his letters he expressed a vociferous dislike for the poetry of Keats (considerably toned down in the eleventh canto of *Don Juan*). His literary friends, Sheridan, Rogers, Gifford, were of the older generation, and even Tom Moore, his biographer and by far his closest friend among his poetic contemporaries, preserved, like so many Irish writers, something of the eighteenth-century manner.

It was also an eighteenth-century model that gave him the lead for the phase of poetry that began with *Beppo* in September, 1817, and exploited the possibilities of the eight-line (*ottava rima*) stanza used there and in *Don Juan* and *The Vision of Judgment.* Byron seems to have derived this stanza from a heroi-comical poem, "Whistlecraft," by John Hookham Frere, whom Byron had met in Spain, and which in its turn had owed something to the Italian romantic epics of the early Renaissance. Byron went on to study the Italian poems, and translated the first canto of one of the best of them, Pulci's tale of a good-natured giant, *Morgante Maggiore.* But there was one feature in Frere that he could not have found in the Italians, and that was the burlesque rhyme. In Italian the double rhyme is normal, but it is a peculiarity of English that even double rhymes have to be used with great caution in serious poetry, and that all obtrusive or ingenious rhymes belong to comic verse. This is a major principle of the wit of *Hudibras* before Byron's time, as of W. S. Gilbert and Ogden Nash since, and without it the wit of *Don Juan* is hardly conceivable:

> But — Oh! ye lords of ladies intellectual,
> Inform us truly, have they not hen-pecked you all?

Armed with this new technique, Byron was ready to tackle a narrative satire, and in narrative satire he found not only a means of exploiting all his best qualities, but of turning his very faults as a poet into virtues. He could digress to his heart's content, for digression is part of the fun in satire — one thinks of *Tristram Shandy* and the "Digression in Praise of Digressions" in *A Tale of a Tub.* He could write doggerel, but doggerel in satire is a sign of wit rather than incompetence. He could be serious if he liked, for sudden changes of mood belong to the form, and he could swing back to burlesque again as soon as he was bored with seriousness, or thought the reader might be. It is particularly the final couplet that he uses to undercut his own romantic Byronism, as in the description of Daniel Boone in Canto VIII:

> Crime came not near him — she is not the child
> Of solitude; Health shrank not from him — for
> Her home is in the rarely trodden wild,
> Where if men seek her not, and death be more
> Their choice than life, forgive them, as beguiled
> By habit to what their own hearts abhor —
> In cities caged. The present case in point I
> Cite is, that Boon lived hunting up to ninety.

In the new flush of discovery, Byron wrote exultantly to his friend Douglas Kinnaird: "[*Don Juan*] is the sublime of *that there* sort of writing — it may be bawdy, but is it not good English? It may be profligate but is it not *life,* is it not *the thing?* Could any man have written it who has not lived in the world?" But even Byron was soon made aware that he was not at popular as he had been. The women who loved *The Corsair* hated *Don Juan,* for the reason that Byron gives with his usual conciseness on such subjects: "the wish of all women to exalt the *sentiment* of the passions, and to keep up the illusion which is their empire." Teresa, as soon as she understood anything of the poem, boycotted it, and forced Byron to promise not to go on with it, a promise he was able to evade only with great difficulty. His friend Harriet Wilson, significantly enough a courtesan who lived partly by blackmail, wrote him: "Dear *Adorable* Lord Byron, *don't* make a mere *coarse* old libertine of yourself."

Don Juan is traditionally the incautious amorist, the counterpart in love to Faust in knowledge, whose pursuit of women is so ruthless that he is eventually damned, as in the last scene of Mozart's opera *Don Giovanni.* Consequently he is a logical choice as a mask for Byron, but he is a mask that reveals the whole Byronic personality, instead of concealing the essence of it as Childe Harold does. The extroversion of Byron's temperament has full scope in *Don Juan*. There is hardly any characterization in the poem: even Don Juan never emerges clearly as a character. We see only what happens to him, and the other characters, even Haidée, float past as phantasmagoria of romance and adventure. What one misses in the poem is the sense of engagement or participation. Everything happens to Don Juan, but he is never an active agent, and seems to take no responsibility for his life. He drifts from one thing to the next, appears to find one kind of experience as good as another, makes no judgements and no commitments. As a result the gloom and misanthropy, the secret past sins, the gnawing remorse of the earlier heroes is finally identified as a shoddier but more terrifying evil—boredom, the sense of the inner emptiness of life that is one of Byron's most powerfully compelling moods, and has haunted literature ever since, from the *ennui* of Baudelaire to the *Angst* and *nausée* of our own day.

The episodes of the poem are all stock Byronic scenes: Spain, the pirates of the Levant, the odalisques of Turkish harems, battlefields, and finally English high society. But there is as little plot as characterization: the poem exists for the sake of its author's comment. As Byron says:

This narrative is not meant for narration,
But a mere airy and fantastic basis,
To build up common things with common places.

Its wit is constantly if not continuously brilliant, and Byron's contempt of cant and prudery, his very real hatred of cruelty, his detached view of all social icons, whether conservative or popular, are well worth having. Not many poets give us as much common sense as Byron does. On the other hand the opposition to the poem made him increasingly self-conscious as he went on, and his technique of calculated bathos and his deliberate refusal to "grow metaphysical"—that is, pursue any idea beyond the stage of initial reaction—keep the poem too resolutely on one level. The larger imaginative vistas that we are promised ("a panoramic view of hell's in training") do not materialize, and by the end of the sixteenth canto we have a sense of a rich but not inexhaustible vein rapidly thinning out. As *Don Juan* is not Don Juan's poem but Byron's poem, it could hardly have been ended, but only abandoned or cut short by its author's death. The Mozartian ending of the story Byron had already handled, in his own way, in *Manfred.*

*The Vision of Judgment* is Byron's most original poem, and therefore his most conventional one; it is his wittiest poem, and therefore his most serious one. Southey, Byron's favorite target among the Lake poets, had become poet laureate, and his political views, like those of Coleridge and Wordsworth, had shifted from an early liberalism to a remarkably complacent Toryism. On the death of George III in 1820 he was ill-advised enough to compose, in his laureate capacity, a "Vision of Judgment" describing the apotheosis and entry into heaven of the stammering, stupid, obstinate, and finally lunatic and blind monarch whose sixty-year reign had lost America, alienated Ireland, plunged the country into the longest and bloodiest war in its history, and ended in a desolate scene of domestic misery and repression. George III was not personally responsible for all the evils of his reign, but in those days royalty was not the projection of middle-class virtue that it is now, and was consequently less popular and more open to attack. The apotheosis of a dead monarch, as a literary form, is of classical origin, and so is its parody, Byron's poem being in the tradition of Seneca's brilliant mockery of the entry into heaven of the Emperor Claudius.

Byron's religious views were certainly unusual in his day, but if we had to express them in a formula, it would be something like this: the best that we can imagine man doing is where our conception of God ought to start. Religions that foment cruelty and induce smugness, or ascribe cruelty and smugness to God, are superstitions. In *Heaven and Earth,* for example, the offstage deity who decrees the deluge at the end is clearly the moral inferior of every human creature he drowns. In *The Vision of Judgment* the sycophantic Southey is contrasted with John Wilkes, who fought King George hard all his life, but who, when encouraged to go on persecuting him after death, merely says:

> I don't like ripping up old stories, since
> His conduct was but natural in a prince.

This is a decent human attitude, consequently it must be the least we can expect from heaven, and so the poet takes leave of the poor old king "practising the hundredth Psalm."

### III

Byron has probably had more influence outside England than any other English poet except Shakespeare. In English literature, though he is always classified with the Romantic poets, he is Romantic only because the Byronic hero is a Romantic figure: as we have seen, he has little technically in common with other English Romantics. But on the Continent Byron has been the arch-romantic of modern literature, and European nineteenth-century culture is as unthinkable without Byron as its history would be without Napoleon. From the painting of Delacroix to the music of Berlioz, from the poetry of Pushkin to the philosophy of Nietzsche, the spell of Byron is everywhere. Modern fiction would be miserably impoverished without the Byronic hero: Balzac, Stendhal, Dostoevsky, have all used him in crucial roles. In the more advanced political atmosphere of England, Byron was only a Whig intellectual, whereas in Greece and Italy he was a revolutionary fighter for freedom, a poetic Mazzini or Bolivar, though, like them, not a class leveler. As he said:

> I wish men to be free
> As much from mobs as kings — from you as me.

Among English readers the reputation of the Romantic and sentimental Byron has not kept pace with his reputation as a satirist, but it would be wrong to accept the assertion, so often made today, that Byron is of little importance apart from his satires and letters. An immense amount of imitation and use of Byron, conscious or unconscious, direct or indirect, has taken place in English literature, too, and nearly all of it is of the Romantic Byron. Melville (whose Ishmael is in the line of Cain), Conrad, Hemingway, A. E. Housman, Thomas Wolfe, D. H. Lawrence, W. H. Auden — these writers have little in common except that they all Byronize.

The most important reason for Byron's great influence is that he was a portent of a new kind of sensibility. For many centuries poets had assumed a hierarchy of nature with a moral principle built into it. For Dante, for Shakespeare, for Milton, there was a top level of divine providence; a level of distinctively human nature which included education, reason and law; a level of physical nature, which was morally neutral and which man could not, like the animals, adjust to; and a bottom level of sin and corruption. This hierarchy corresponded to the teachings of religion and science alike. But from Rousseau's time on a profound change in the cultural framework of the arts takes place. Man is now thought of as a product of the energy of physical nature, and as this nature is subhuman in morality and intelligence and capacity for pleasure, the origin of art is morally ambivalent, and may even be demonic. The Byronic hero, for whom, as for Manfred, pride, lack of sympathy with humanity and a destructive influence even in love are inseparable from genius, dramatizes this new conception of art and life alike more vividly than anything else in the culture of the time. Hence it is no exaggeration to say that Byron released a mainspring of creative energy in modern culture.

Byron's immediate influence in his own country, on the other hand, though certainly very great, was qualified in many ways, by queasiness about his morality, by a refusal to separate him from his posing heroes, by a feeling that he lacked the sterner virtues and wrote with too much pleasure and too few pains. The first canto of *Don Juan* centers on the nervous prudery of Donna Inez, who is, not surprisingly, modeled on Byron's wife. But Donna Inez was Britannia as well. The sands of the Regency aristocracy were running out, the tide of middle-class morality had already set in, and the age that we think of as Victorian, with its circulating libraries, its custom of reading aloud to large family circles, and its tendency not to be amused, at any rate by anything approaching the ribald, was on the way. As Byron admitted ruefully of the opening cantos:

> . . . the publisher declares, in sooth,
> Through needles' eyes it easier for the camel is
> To pass, than those two cantos into families.

A more important barrier was raised by the lack of any sense of moral involvement in *Don Juan,* already mentioned. With the British Empire developing, and a greater number of poets and intellectuals issuing stentorian calls to duty, such detachment seemed inadequate, except for the fact that Byron himself took matters out of Don Juan's hands and died for a cause in Greece. In *Sartor Resartus* Carlyle summed up the later view of Byron as a poet who had gone through a gloomy stage of denial and defiance, an " Everlasting No," had then moved into a " Centre of Indifference," but had never gone on to the final " Everlasting Yea." For this final stage, Carlyle recommended: " Close thy Byron; open thy Goethe."

However, Carlyle himself hardly succeeded in closing his Byron, as when he went on to work out his conception of the Great Man what he actually produced was a vulgarization of the Byronic hero. The author of *The Corsair* would have raised a quizzical eyebrow at Carlyle's hero journeying forward " escorted by the Terrors and the Splendours, the Archdemons and Archangels." This tendency to underestimate Byron without surpassing him has recurred more than once. Bernard Shaw, in the preface to his Don Juan play, *Man and Superman,* dismissed Byron's Don Juan as a mere " libertine vagabond." Yet Byron had certainly anticipated Shaw's central idea, that woman takes the lead in sexual relations and that Don Juan is consequently as much a victim as a pursuer. No, Byron will not stay closed. It is a better idea to open Goethe, and when we do we find a more liberal view of Byron. Goethe in fact was fascinated by Byron, who dedicated *Sardanapalus* to him, and he referred to him in the second part of *Faust* as Euphorion, a kind of Eros-figure whose passion for liberty, if self-destructive, is also an acceptance of life simply because it is there, and has nothing of the compulsion to justify existence that is often close to a distrust of its worth.

We have not yet shaken off our nineteenth-century inhibitions about Byron. A frequent twentieth-century jargon term for him is " immature," which endorses the Carlyle view that Byron is a poet to be outgrown. One thinks of Yeats's penetrating remark that we are never satisfied with the maturity of those whom we have admired in boyhood. Even those who have not admired Byron in boyhood have gone through a good deal of Byronism at that stage. There is certainly something youthful about the Byronic hero, and for some reason we feel more defensive about youth than about childhood, and more shamefaced about liking a poet who has captured a youthful imagination. If we replace " youthful " with the loaded term " adolescent " we can see how deeply ingrained this feeling is.

Among intellectuals the Southey type, who makes a few liberal gestures in youth to quiet his conscience and then plunges into a rapturous authoritarianism for the rest of his life, is much more common than the Byron type, who continues to be baffled by unanswered questions and simple anomalies, to make irresponsible jokes, to set his face against society, to respect the authority of his own mood — in short, to retain the rebellious or irreverent qualities of youth. Perhaps it is as dangerous to eliminate the adolescent in us as it is to eliminate the child. In any case the kind of poetic experience that Byronism represents should be obtained young, and in Byron. It may later be absorbed into more complex experiences, but to miss or renounce it is to impoverish whatever else we may attain.

### *Reading Suggestions*

The poems of Byron were edited in seven volumes by Ernest Hartley Coleridge, and the letters and journals in six volumes by Rowland E. Prothero, later Lord

Ernle, in 1898–1904. This edition may be supplemented by *Lord Byron's Correspondence,* 2 Vols., ed. John Murray (1922); *Byron: A Self-Portrait,* 2 Vols., ed. Peter Quennell (1950); *Ravenna Journal,* ed. Lord Ernle (1928); Marchesa Iris Origo, *Byron: The Last Attachment* (letters to Teresa Guiccioli, 1949); *His Very Self and Voice* (collected conversations), ed. Ernest J. Lovell, Jr. (1954).

Most scholarship on Byron has been biographical rather than critical. The fullest and most up-to-date biography is Leslie A. Marchand, *Byron: A Biography,* 3 Vols. (1957). Despite its length and the exhaustiveness of its scholarship, it is also extremely readable. It is recommended in preference to the older general biographies, though André Maurois, *Byron* (tr. Hamish Miles, 1930), and Charles Du Bos, *Byron and the Need of Fatality* (tr. Ethel Colburn Mayne, 1932), with its strongly psychological approach, may be mentioned. Studies of parts of Byron's career include: W. W. Pratt, *Byron at Southwell* (1948); William A. Borst, *Lord Byron's First Pilgrimage* (1948); Peter Quennell, *Byron: The Years of Fame* (1934) and *Byron in Italy* (1941); C. L. Cline, *Byron, Shelley and Their Pisan Circle* (1952): Harold Nicolson, *Byron: The Last Journey: 1823–1824* (1924; new ed. 1948). See also E. R. P. Vincent, *Byron, Hobhouse and Foscolo* (1949) and E. M. Butler, *Byron and Goethe* (1956).

For general criticism, often with a strongly biographical slant, see especially William J. Calvert, *Byron: Romantic Paradox* (1935); G. Wilson Knight, *The Burning Oracle* (1939) and *Lord Byron: Christian Virtues* (1952); E. J. Lovell, *Byron: The Record of a Quest* (1949). For the background of the Byronic hero see Mario Praz, *The Romantic Agony* (1933). On *Don Juan* see P. G. Trueblood, *The Flowering of Byron's Genius: Studies in Don Juan* (1945), and E. F. Boyd, *Byron's Don Juan: A Critical Study* (1945).

---

## WRITTEN AFTER SWIMMING FROM SESTOS TO ABYDOS

The story of Leander, the youth of Abydos who swam nightly across the Hellespont to Hero, priestess of Aphrodite at Sestos, and was drowned one stormy night, causing Hero's suicide, was the theme of an Alexandrian poem ascribed to the legendary pre-Homeric poet Musaeus. This poem in its turn was the basis of Christopher Marlowe's unfinished *Hero and Leander* (1598). Byron accomplished the swim (in the opposite direction) in an hour and ten minutes on May 3, 1810, and wrote this poem on May 9. His note reads in part: "On the 3rd of May, 1810 . . . Lieutenant Ekenhead . . . and the writer of these rhymes, swam from the European shore to the Asiatic. . . . The whole distance . . . was . . . upwards of four English miles, though the actual breadth is barely one. The rapidity of the current is such that no boat can row directly across. . . . The water was extremely cold, from the melting of the mountain snows. . . . The only thing that surprised me was that, as doubts had been entertained of the truth of Leander's story, no traveller had ever endeavoured to ascertain its practicability." In a letter to Henry Drury, Byron remarks: " . . . the immediate distance is not above a mile but the current renders it hazardous, so much so, that I doubt whether Leander's conjugal powers must not have been exhausted in his passage to Paradise." Byron also made his Don Juan a good swimmer:

> He could, perhaps, have passed the Hellespont,
> As once (a feat on which ourselves we prided)
> Leander, Mr. Ekenhead, and I did.
>
> [*Don Juan,* II.105]

I

If, in the month of dark December,
  Leander, who was nightly wont
(What maid will not the tale remember?)
  To cross thy stream, broad Hellespont!

II

If, when the wintry tempest roared,
  He sped to Hero, nothing loth,
And thus of old thy current poured,
  Fair Venus! how I pity both!

III

For *me,* degenerate modern wretch,
  Though in the genial month of May
My dripping limbs I faintly stretch,
  And think I've done a feat to-day.

IV

But since he crossed the rapid tide,
  According to the doubtful story,
To woo, — and — Lord knows what beside,
  And swam for Love, as I for Glory;

V

'Twere hard to say who fared the best:
  Sad mortals! thus the Gods still plague you!
He lost his labour, I my jest:
  For he was drowned, and I've the ague.

## MAID OF ATHENS, ERE WE PART

Ζωή μου, σᾶς ἀγαπῶ.[1]

The Maid of Athens was a twelve-year-old girl named Theresa Macri, the youngest of three daughters

MAID OF ATHENS. 1. *Zoe mou sas agapo.*

of the widow of the English vice-consul, in whose house Byron stayed in Athens. That she had some claim to the title of maid seems clear from a later letter in which Byron speaks of bargaining with her mother, who at first "was mad enough to imagine I was going to marry the girl," and then, failing marriage, held out for 30,000 piastres. Theresa eventually married a Mr. Black, and died in the odor of Byronism. Byron's note on the refrain reads: "Romaic expression of tenderness: If I translate it, I shall affront the gentlemen, as it may seem that I supposed they could not; and if I do not, I may affront the ladies. For fear of any misconstruction on the part of the latter, I shall do so, begging pardon of the learned. It means, 'My life, I love you!' which sounds very prettily in all languages, and is as much in fashion in Greece at this day as, Juvenal tells us, the two first words were amongst the Roman ladies, whose erotic expressions were all Hellenised." The poem is dated Athens, 1810.

I

Maid of Athens, ere we part,
Give, oh give me back my heart!
Or, since that has left my breast,
Keep it now, and take the rest!
Hear my vow before I go,
Ζωή μου, σᾶς ἀγαπῶ.

II

By those tresses unconfined,
Wooed by each Aegean wind;
By those lids whose jetty fringe
Kiss thy soft cheeks' blooming tinge;
By those wild eyes like the roe,
Ζωή μου, σᾶς ἀγαπῶ.

III

By that lip I long to taste;
By that zone-encircled waist;
By all the token-flowers that tell
What words can never speak so well;
By Love's alternate joy and woe,
Ζωή μου, σᾶς ἀγαπῶ.

IV

Maid of Athens! I am gone:
Think of me, sweet! when alone.
Though I fly to Istambol,
Athens holds my heart and soul:
Can I cease to love thee? No!
Ζωή μου, σᾶς ἀγαπῶ.

## REMEMBER THEE! REMEMBER THEE!

Written in a fit of ill temper as a rejoinder to Lady Caroline Lamb, who, calling one morning and finding the poet out, wrote "Remember me!" in a copy of *Vathek* lying on his table.

I

Remember thee! remember thee!
Till Lethe quench Life's burning stream
Remorse and Shame shall cling to thee,
And haunt thee like a feverish dream!

II

Remember thee! Aye, doubt it not.
Thy husband too shall think of thee:
By neither shalt thou be forgot,
Thou *false* to him, thou *fiend* to me!

## SHE WALKS IN BEAUTY

This and the following poem appeared in a volume called *Hebrew Melodies*, published in 1815 with the following advertisement: "The subsequent poems were written at the request of my friend, the Hon. Douglas Kinnaird, for a Selection of Hebrew Melodies, and have been published, with the music, arranged by Mr. Braham and Mr. Nathan." The poems are based on Biblical themes, and "She Walks in Beauty" has no place in the volume except that it was written about the same time. The inspiration is said to have been a beautiful woman, Lady Wilmot Horton, whom Byron had seen at a ball dressed in mourning with spangles on her dress. The poem is dated June 12, 1814.

I

She walks in Beauty, like the night
Of cloudless climes and starry skies;
And all that's best of dark and bright
Meet in her aspect and her eyes:
Thus mellowed to that tender light
Which Heaven to gaudy day denies.

II

One shade the more, one ray the less,
Had half impaired the nameless grace
Which waves in every raven tress,
Or softly lightens o'er her face;
Where thoughts serenely sweet express,
How pure, how dear their dwelling-place.

III

And on that cheek, and o'er that brow,
So soft, so calm, yet eloquent,
The smiles that win, the tints that glow,
But tell of days in goodness spent,
A mind at peace with all below,
A heart whose love is innocent!

## THE DESTRUCTION OF SENNACHERIB

This poem, one of the *Hebrew Melodies*, is dated Seaham, February 17, 1815. For the story told in the poem see II Kings 19.

I

The Assyrian came down like the wolf on the fold,
And his cohorts were gleaming in purple and gold;
And the sheen of their spears was like stars on the sea,
When the blue wave rolls nightly on deep Galilee.

II

Like the leaves of the forest when Summer is green,
That host with their banners at sunset were seen:
Like the leaves of the forest when Autumn hath blown,
That host on the morrow lay withered and strown.

III

For the angel of Death spread his wings on the blast,
And breathed in the face of the foe as he passed;
And the eyes of the sleepers waxed deadly and chill,
And their hearts but once heaved — and for ever grew still!

IV

And there lay the steed with his nostril all wide,
But through it there rolled not the breath of his pride;
And the foam of his gasping lay white on the turf,
And cold as the spray of the rock-beating surf.

V

And there lay the rider distorted and pale,
With the dew on his brow, and the rust on his mail:
And the tents were all silent — the banners alone —
The lances unlifted — the trumpet unblown.

VI

And the widows of Ashur are loud in their wail,
And the idols are broke in the temple of Baal;
And the might of the Gentile, unsmote by the sword,
Hath melted like snow in the glance of the Lord!

## STANZAS FOR MUSIC

Published in 1816, and usually ascribed to March 28 of that year, but the date and occasion are unknown.

I

There be none of Beauty's daughters
With a magic like thee;
And like music on the waters
Is thy sweet voice to me:
When, as if its sound were causing
The charméd Ocean's pausing,
The waves lie still and gleaming,
And the lulled winds seem dreaming:

II

And the Midnight Moon is weaving
Her bright chain o'er the deep;
Whose breast is gently heaving,
As an infant's asleep:
So the spirit bows before thee,
To listen and adore thee;
With a full but soft emotion,
Like the swell of Summer's ocean.

## SONNET ON CHILLON

This sonnet forms a prelude to Byron's tale *The Prisoner of Chillon*, pp. 174–78, below, which commemorates the political and religious martyrdom of François Bonivard, a sixteenth-century Genevese imprisoned for seven years by the Duke of Savoy. Byron and Shelley visited the Castle of Chillon, on Lake Geneva, on June 26, 1816; Byron's poem was written soon after, and the sonnet, which stresses the political rather than the religious aspect of persecution, was appended later.

Eternal Spirit of the chainless Mind!
Brightest in dungeons, Liberty! thou art,
For there thy habitation is the heart —
The heart which love of thee alone can bind;
And when thy sons to fetters are consigned —
To fetters, and the damp vault's dayless gloom,
Their country conquers with their martyrdom,
And Freedom's fame finds wings on every wind.
Chillon! thy prison is a holy place,
And thy sad floor an altar — for 'twas trod,
Until his very steps have left a trace
Worn, as if thy cold pavement were a sod,
By Bonnivard! — May none those marks efface!
For they appeal from tyranny to God.

## DARKNESS

Written at Diodati, Switzerland, in July, 1816, during the sojourn with the Shelleys on Lake Geneva. The somberness of the poem reflects the interest of the

THE DESTRUCTION OF SENNACHERIB. 21. Ashur: Assyria.

group in reading and writing ghost stories, an interest of which the most remarkable result was Mary Shelley's *Frankenstein.*

I had a dream, which was not all a dream.
The bright sun was extinguished, and the stars
Did wander darkling in the eternal space,
Rayless, and pathless, and the icy Earth
Swung blind and blackening in the moonless air;
Morn came and went — and came, and brought no day,
And men forgot their passions in the dread
Of this their desolation; and all hearts
Were chilled into a selfish prayer for light:
And they did live by watchfires — and the thrones,
The palaces of crownèd kings — the huts,
The habitations of all things which dwell,
Were burnt for beacons; cities were consumed,
And men were gathered round their blazing homes
To look once more into each other's face;
Happy were those who dwelt within the eye
Of the volcanoes, and their mountain-torch:
A fearful hope was all the World contained;
Forests were set on fire — but hour by hour
They fell and faded — and the crackling trunks
Extinguished with a crash — and all was black.
The brows of men by the despairing light
Wore an unearthly aspect, as by fits
The flashes fell upon them; some lay down
And hid their eyes and wept; and some did rest
Their chins upon their clenchèd hands, and smiled;
And others hurried to and fro, and fed
Their funeral piles with fuel, and looked up
With mad disquietude on the dull sky,
The pall of a past World; and then again
With curses cast them down upon the dust,
And gnashed their teeth and howled: the wild birds shrieked,
And, terrified, did flutter on the ground
And flap their useless wings; the wildest brutes
Came tame and tremulous; and vipers crawled
And twined themselves among the multitude,
Hissing, but stingless — they were slain for food:
And War, which for a moment was no more,
Did glut himself again: — a meal was bought
With blood, and each sate sullenly apart
Gorging himself in gloom: no Love was left;
All earth was but one thought — and that was Death,
Immediate and inglorious; and the pang
Of famine fed upon all entrails — men
Died, and their bones were tombless as their flesh;
The meagre by the meagre were devoured,
Even dogs assailed their masters, all save one,
And he was faithful to a corse, and kept
The birds and beasts and famished men at bay,
Till hunger clung them, or the dropping dead
Lured their lank jaws; himself sought out no food,
But with a piteous and perpetual moan,
And a quick desolate cry, licking the hand
Which answered not with a caress — he died.
The crowd was famished by degrees; but two
Of an enormous city did survive,
And they were enemies: they met beside
The dying embers of an altar-place
Where had been heaped a mass of holy things
For an unholy usage; they raked up,
And shivering scraped with their cold skeleton hands
The feeble ashes, and their feeble breath
Blew for a little life, and made a flame
Which was a mockery; then they lifted up
Their eyes as it grew lighter, and beheld
Each other's aspects — saw, and shrieked, and died —
Even of their mutual hideousness they died,
Unknowing who he was upon whose brow
Famine had written Fiend. The World was void,
The populous and the powerful was a lump,
Seasonless, herbless, treeless, manless, lifeless —
A lump of death — a chaos of hard clay.
The rivers, lakes, and ocean all stood still,
And nothing stirred within their silent depths;
Ships sailorless lay rotting on the sea,
And their masts fell down piecemeal: as they dropped
They slept on the abyss without a surge —
The waves were dead; the tides were in their grave,
The Moon, their mistress, had expired before;
The winds were withered in the stagnant air,
And the clouds perished; Darkness had no need
Of aid from them — She was the Universe.

## SO WE'LL GO NO MORE A-ROVING

In a letter to Thomas Moore dated Venice, February 28, 1817, Byron says: "The Carnival — that is, the latter part of it, and sitting up late o' nights, had knocked me up a little. . . . The mumming closed with a masked ball . . . where I went . . . and, though I did not dissipate much upon the whole, yet I find 'the sword wearing out the scabbard,' though I have but just turned the corner of twenty-nine." The poem below follows.

I

So we'll go no more a-roving
  So late into the night,
Though the heart be still as loving,
  And the moon be still as bright.

II

For the sword outwears its sheath,
  And the soul wears out the breast,

And the heart must pause to breathe,
  And Love itself have rest.

III

Though the night was made for loving,
  And the day returns too soon,
Yet we'll go no more a-roving
  By the light of the moon.

## SONNET TO THE PRINCE REGENT

ON THE REPEAL OF
LORD EDWARD FITZGERALD'S FORFEITURE

Dated Bologna, August 12, 1819, and also known as "Sonnet to George the Fourth," which the Prince Regent became the next year. Lord Edward Fitzgerald was involved in the Irish uprising of 1798, was shot when captured and died from the wound. A bill of attainder was passed against him which was repealed in 1819. Byron's interest in him was probably due to Thomas Moore, who later wrote a life of Fitzgerald.

To be the father of the fatherless,
  To stretch the hand from the throne's height, and raise
*His* offspring, who expired in other days
To make thy sire's sway by a kingdom less,—
*This* is to be a monarch, and repress
  Envy into unutterable praise.
  Dismiss thy guard, and trust thee to such traits,
For who would lift a hand, except to bless?
  Were it not easy, sir, and is't not sweet
  To make thyself beloved? and to be
Omnipotent by mercy's means? for thus
  Thy sovereignty would grow but more complete:
A despot thou, and yet thy people free,
  And by the heart, not hand, enslaving us.

## ON MY THIRTY-THIRD BIRTHDAY

Byron's thirty-third birthday was on January 22, 1821. On January 21 he wrote in his diary: "To-morrow is my birthday—that is to say, at twelve o' the clock, midnight, *i.e.,* in twelve minutes, I shall have completed thirty and three years of age!—and I go to my bed with a heaviness of heart at having lived so long, and to so little purpose. . . . I don't regret them [the years] so much for what I have done, as for what I *might* have done." The quatrain below follows.

Through Life's dull road, so dim and dirty,
  I have dragged to three-and-thirty.
  What have these years left to me?
Nothing—except thirty-three.

## ON THIS DAY I COMPLETE MY THIRTY-SIXTH YEAR

Written at Missolonghi, Greece, on January 22, 1824, and published in the *Morning Chronicle* on October 29, after the poet's death. Pietro Gamba tells how Byron came out of his bedroom and said to his friends: "You were complaining that I never write any poetry now:—this is my birthday, and I have just finished something, which, I think, is better than what I usually write." It is not quite his last poem, but is still essentially his farewell to the world.

I

'Tis time this heart should be unmoved,
  Since others it hath ceased to move:
Yet, though I cannot be beloved,
  Still let me love!

II

My days are in the yellow leaf;
  The flowers and fruits of Love are gone;
The worm, the canker, and the grief
  Are mine alone!

III

The fire that on my bosom preys
  Is lone as some Volcanic isle;
No torch is kindled at its blaze—
  A funeral pile.

IV

The hope, the fear, the zealous care,
  The exalted portion of the pain
And power of love, I cannot share,
  But wear the chain.

V

But 'tis not *thus*—and 'tis not *here*—
  Such thoughts should shake my soul, nor *now*
Where Glory decks the hero's bier,
  Or binds his brow.

VI

The Sword, the Banner, and the Field,
  Glory and Greece, around me see!
The Spartan, borne upon his shield,
  Was not more free.

VII

Awake! (not Greece—she *is* awake!)
  Awake, my spirit! Think through *whom*
Thy life-blood tracks its parent lake,
  And then strike home!

VIII

Tread those reviving passions down,
 Unworthy manhood! — unto thee
Indifferent should the smile or frown
 Of Beauty be.

IX

If thou regret'st thy youth, *why live?*
 The land of honourable death
Is here: — up to the Field, and give
 Away thy breath!

X

Seek out — less often sought than found —
 A soldier's grave, for thee the best;
Then look around, and choose thy ground,
 And take thy Rest.

# CHILDE HAROLD'S PILGRIMAGE

*A Romaunt*

Hobhouse records in his diary under October 31, 1809, that Byron had begun a new poem in Spenserian stanzas. This was at Janina in Epirus: the second canto was finished at Smyrna on March 28, 1810. After various changes the two cantos were published in 1812, after Byron's return to England, and instantly made him famous, the poem running through four editions between March and September. Byron's preface reads in part: "The following poem was written, for the most part, amidst the scenes which it attempts to describe. . . . The scenes attempted to be sketched are in Spain, Portugal, Epirus, Acarnania, and Greece. There, for the present, the poem stops: its reception will determine whether the author may venture to conduct his readers to the capital of the East. . . . A fictitious character is introduced for the sake of giving some connection to the piece. . . . It has been suggested to me by friends . . . that in this fictitious character, Childe[1] Harold, I may incur the suspicion of having intended some real personage: this I beg leave, once for all, to disclaim. . . ."

The hint that Byron intended to continue the poem was not picked up until after the collapse of his marriage and his second journey abroad. The third canto was written in Switzerland in May and June of 1816. It depicts Byron's journey from the Low Countries (the field of Waterloo) down the Rhine to Lake Leman and the Rhone, and contains appropriate reflections, mainly on the careers of Napoleon and Rousseau, and many personal comments on his wife, his daughter, and his own situation. The third canto was published in November of 1816.

The fourth canto was written, in its original form, in July, 1817, but considerably expanded before publication in the following April. Its scene is entirely Italian, beginning in Venice and passing through Ferrara and Florence to Rome, and it is accompanied by extensive historical notes, mainly by Hobhouse. In an epistolary dedication to Hobhouse, Byron speaks of the poem as "the longest, the most thoughtful and comprehensive of my compositions," and states that he had finally given up the effort to separate his own character from Childe Harold's, as a separation that no one paid any attention to anyway.

From Canto I we give some of the opening stanzas and the first lyric; also the lyric "To Inez," which is inserted between stanzas 84 and 85. This poem replaced the much more cheerful ballad, "The Girl of Cadiz," as more suitable to Harold's melancholy temperament. From the third canto are included the opening and some of the closing stanzas on Byron's daughter, and the famous Waterloo and Napoleon passages. From the fourth canto we give the "Bridge of Sighs" opening and the intensely personal conclusion.

CHILDE HAROLD'S PILGRIMAGE. 1. Childe: "It is almost superfluous to mention that the appellation 'Childe' . . . is used as more consonant with the old structure of versification which I have adopted" [from Byron's preface].

## from CANTO I

1

Oh, thou! in Hellas deemed of heavenly birth,
Muse! formed or fabled at the Minstrel's will!
Since shamed full oft by later lyres on earth,
Mine dares not call thee from thy sacred Hill:
Yet there I've wandered by thy vaunted rill;
Yes! sighed o'er Delphi's long deserted shrine,
Where, save that feeble fountain, all is still;
Nor mote my shell awake the weary Nine
To grace so plain a tale — this lowly lay of mine.

2

Whilome in Albion's isle there dwelt a youth,
Who ne in Virtue's ways did take delight;
But spent his days in riot most uncouth,
And vexed with mirth the drowsy ear of Night.
Ah me! in sooth he was a shameless wight,

Canto I: 6. Delphi's . . . shrine: "The little village of Castri stands partly on the site of Delphi. Along the path of the mountain, from Chrysso, are the remains of sepulchres hewn in and from the rock:—'One,' said the guide, 'of a king who broke his neck hunting.' His majesty had certainly chosen the fittest spot for such an achievement. A little above Castri is a cave, supposed the Pythian, of immense depth; the upper part of it is paved, and now a cowhouse" [part of Byron's note]. 8. mote: might. 10. Whilome: once upon a time.

Sore given to revel, and ungodly glee;
Few earthly things found favour in his sight
Save concubines and carnal companie,
And flaunting wassailers of high and low degree.

3

Childe Harold was he hight: — but whence his name
And lineage long, it suits me not to say;
Suffice it, that perchance they were of fame,
And had been glorious in another day:
But one sad losel soils a name for ay,
However mighty in the olden time;
Nor all that heralds rake from coffined clay,
Nor florid prose, nor honied lies of rhyme,
Can blazon evil deeds, or consecrate a crime.

4

Childe Harold basked him in the Noontide sun,
Disporting there like any other fly;
Nor deemed before his little day was done
One blast might chill him into misery.
But long ere scarce a third of his passed by,
Worse than Adversity the Childe befell;
He felt the fulness of Satiety:
Then loathed he in his native land to dwell,
Which seemed to him more lone than Eremite's sad cell.

5

For he through Sin's long labyrinth had run,
Nor made atonement when he did amiss,
Had sighed to many though he loved but one,
And that loved one, alas! could ne'er be his.
Ah, happy she! to 'scape from him whose kiss
Had been pollution unto aught so chaste;
Who soon had left her charms for vulgar bliss,
And spoiled her goodly lands to gild his waste,
Nor calm domestic peace had ever deigned to taste. . . .

9

And none did love him! — though to hall and bower
He gathered revellers from far and near,
He knew them flatterers of the festal hour,
The heartless Parasites of present cheer.
Yea! none did love him — not his lemans dear —
But pomp and power alone are Woman's care,
And where these are light Eros finds a feere;
Maidens, like moths, are ever caught by glare,
And Mammon wins his way where Seraphs might despair.

**18. flaunting wassailers:** shameless drunkards. **23. losel:** scoundrel. **36. Eremite's:** hermit's. **50. lemans:** mistresses. **52. feere:** companion.

10

Childe Harold had a mother — not forgot,
Though parting from that mother he did shun:
A sister whom he loved, but saw her not
Before his weary pilgrimage begun:
If friends he had, he bade adieu to none.
Yet deem not thence his breast a breast of steel:
Ye, who have known what 'tis to dote upon
A few dear objects, will in sadness feel
Such partings break the heart they fondly hope to heal.

11

His house, his home, his heritage, his lands,
The laughing dames in whom he did delight,
Whose large blue eyes, fair locks, and snowy hands,
Might shake the Saintship of an Anchorite,
And long had fed his youthful appetite;
His goblets brimmed with every costly wine,
And all that mote to luxury invite,
Without a sigh he left, to cross the brine,
And traverse Paynim shores, and pass Earth's central line.

12

The sails were filled, and fair the light winds blew,
As glad to waft him from his native home;
And fast the white rocks faded from his view,
And soon were lost in circumambient foam:
And then, it may be, of his wish to roam
Repented he, but in his bosom slept
The silent thought, nor from his lips did come
One word of wail, whilst others sate and wept,
And to the reckless gales unmanly moaning kept.

13

But when the Sun was sinking in the sea
He seized his harp, which he at times could string,
And strike, albeit with untaught melody,
When deemed he no strange ear was listening:
And now his fingers o'er it he did fling,
And tuned his farewell in the dim twilight;
While flew the vessel on her snowy wing,
And fleeting shores receded from his sight,
Thus to the elements he poured his last " Good Night."

## CHILDE HAROLD'S GOOD NIGHT

1

" Adieu, adieu! my native shore
Fades o'er the waters blue;

**72. Paynim:** pagan (or Mohammedan). **Childe Harold's Good Night:** In his preface Byron remarks that this poem was suggested

The night-winds sigh, the breakers roar,
And shrieks the wild sea-mew.
Yon Sun that sets upon the sea
We follow in his flight;
Farewell awhile to him and thee,
My native Land — Good Night!

2

" A few short hours and He will rise
To give the Morrow birth;
And I shall hail the main and skies,
But not my mother Earth.
Deserted is my own good Hall,
Its hearth is desolate;
Wild weeds are gathering on the wall;
My Dog howls at the gate.

3

" Come hither, hither, my little page!
Why dost thou weep and wail?
Or dost thou dread the billows' rage,
Or tremble at the gale?
But dash the tear-drop from thine eye;
Our ship is swift and strong:
Our fleetest falcon scarce can fly
More merrily along."

4

" Let winds be shrill, let waves roll high,
I fear not wave nor wind:
Yet marvel not, Sir Childe, that I
Am sorrowful in mind;
For I have from my father gone,
A mother whom I love,
And have no friends, save these alone,
But thee — and One above.

5

" My father blessed me fervently,
Yet did not much complain;
But sorely will my mother sigh
Till I come back again."—
" Enough, enough, my little lad!
Such tears become thine eye;
If I thy guileless bosom had,
Mine own would not be dry.

6

" Come hither, hither, my staunch yeoman,
Why dost thou look so pale?
Or dost thou dread a French foeman?
Or shiver at the gale? "—
" Deem'st thou I tremble for my life?
Sir Childe, I'm not so weak;
But thinking on an absent wife
Will blanch a faithful cheek.

7

" My spouse and boys dwell near thy hall,
Along the bordering Lake,
And when they on their father call,
What answer shall she make?"—
" Enough, enough, my yeoman good,
Thy grief let none gainsay;
But I, who am of lighter mood,
Will laugh to flee away.

8

" For who would trust the seeming sighs
Of wife or paramour?
Fresh feeres will dry the bright blue eyes
We late saw streaming o'er.
For pleasures past I do not grieve,
Nor perils gathering near;
My greatest grief is that I leave
No thing that claims a tear.

9

" And now I'm in the world alone,
Upon the wide, wide sea:
But why should I for others groan,
When none will sigh for me?
Perchance my Dog will whine in vain,
Till fed by stranger hands;
But long ere I come back again,
He'd tear me where he stands.

10

" With thee, my bark, I'll swiftly go
Athwart the foaming brine;
Nor care what land thou bear'st me to,
So not again to mine.
Welcome, welcome, ye dark-blue waves!
And when you fail my sight,
Welcome, ye deserts, and ye caves!
My native Land — Good Night! "

## TO INEZ

1

Nay, smile not at my sullen brow;
Alas! I cannot smile again:
Yet Heaven avert that ever thou
Shouldst weep, and haply weep in vain.

2

And dost thou ask what secret woe
I bear, corroding Joy and Youth?

by "Lord Maxwell's Good Night," in the *Border Minstrelsy*, edited by Sir Walter Scott.

And wilt thou vainly seek to know
  A pang, ev'n thou must fail to soothe?

3

It is not love, it is not hate,
  Nor low Ambition's honours lost,
That bids me loathe my present state,
  And fly from all I prized the most:

4

It is that weariness which springs
  From all I meet, or hear, or see:
To me no pleasure Beauty brings;
  Thine eyes have scarce a charm for me.

5

It is that settled, ceaseless gloom
  The fabled Hebrew Wanderer bore;
That will not look beyond the tomb,
  But cannot hope for rest before.

6

What Exile from himself can flee?
  To zones though more and more remote,
Still, still pursues, where'er I be,
  The blight of Life — the Demon Thought.

7

Yet others rapt in pleasure seem,
  And taste of all that I forsake;
Oh! may they still of transport dream,
  And ne'er — at least like me — awake!

8

Through many a clime 'tis mine to go,
  With many a retrospection curst;
And all my solace is to know,
  Whate'er betides, I've known the worst.

9

What is that worst? Nay do not ask —
  In pity from the search forbear:
Smile on — nor venture to unmask
  Man's heart, and view the Hell that's there.

### from CANTO III

1

Is thy face like thy mother's, my fair child!
Ada! sole daughter of my house and heart?
When last I saw thy young blue eyes they
  smiled,

To Inez: 18. fabled Hebrew Wanderer: the Wandering Jew.

And then we parted, — not as now we part,
But with a hope. —
                Awaking with a start,
The waters heave around me; and on high
The winds lift up their voices: I depart,
Whither I know not; but the hour's gone by,
When Albion's lessening shores could grieve or
  glad mine eye.

2

Once more upon the waters! yet once more!
And the waves bound beneath me as a steed
That knows his rider. Welcome to their roar!
Swift be their guidance, wheresoe'er it lead!
Though the strained mast should quiver as a reed,
And the rent canvass fluttering strew the gale,
Still must I on; for I am as a weed,
Flung from the rock, on Ocean's foam, to sail
Where'er the surge may sweep, the tempest's breath
  prevail.

3

In my youth's summer I did sing of One,
The wandering outlaw of his own dark mind;
Again I seize the theme, then but begun,
And bear it with me, as the rushing wind
Bears the cloud onwards: in that Tale I find
The furrows of long thought, and dried-up tears,
Which, ebbing, leave a sterile track behind,
O'er which all heavily the journeying years
Plod the last sands of life, — where not a flower
  appears.

4

Since my young days of passion — joy or pain —
Perchance my heart and harp have lost a string —
And both may jar: it may be that in vain
I would essay, as I have sung, to sing:
Yet, though a dreary strain, to this I cling;
So that it wean me from the weary dream
Of selfish grief or gladness — so it fling
Forgetfulness around me — it shall seem
To me, though to none else, a not ungrateful theme.

5

He, who grown agéd in this world of woe,
In deeds, not years, piercing the depths of life,
So that no wonder waits him — nor below
Can Love or Sorrow, Fame, Ambition, Strife,
Cut to his heart again with the keen knife
Of silent, sharp endurance — he can tell
Why Thought seeks refuge in lone caves, yet
  rife
With airy images, and shapes which dwell
Still unimpaired, though old, in the Soul's haunted
  cell.

6

'Tis to create, and in creating live
A being more intense, that we endow
With form our fancy, gaining as we give
The life we image, even as I do now—
What am I? Nothing: but not so art thou,
Soul of my thought! with whom I traverse earth,
Invisible but gazing, as I glow
Mixed with thy spirit, blended with thy birth,
And feeling still with thee in my crushed feelings' dearth.

7

Yet must I think less wildly: — I *have* thought
Too long and darkly, till my brain became,
In its own eddy boiling and o'erwrought,
A whirling gulf of phantasy and flame:
And thus, untaught in youth my heart to tame,
My springs of life were poisoned. 'Tis too late!
Yet am I changed; though still enough the same
In strength to bear what Time can not abate,
And feed on bitter fruits without accusing Fate.

8

Something too much of this: — but now 'tis past,
And the spell closes with its silent seal:
Long absent HAROLD re-appears at last —
He of the breast which fain no more would feel,
Wrung with the wounds which kill not, but ne'er heal;
Yet Time, who changes all, had altered him
In soul and aspect as in age: years steal
Fire from the mind as vigour from the limb;
And Life's enchanted cup but sparkles near the brim.

21

There was a sound of revelry by night,
And Belgium's Capital had gathered then
Her Beauty and her Chivalry — and bright
The lamps shone o'er fair women and brave men;
A thousand hearts beat happily; and when
Music arose with its voluptuous swell,
Soft eyes looked love to eyes which spake again,
And all went merry as a marriage bell;
But hush! hark! a deep sound strikes like a rising knell!

22

Did ye not hear it? — No — 'twas but the Wind,
Or the car rattling o'er the stony street;
On with the dance! let joy be unconfined;
No sleep till morn, when Youth and Pleasure meet
To chase the glowing Hours with flying feet —
But hark! — that heavy sound breaks in once more,
As if the clouds its echo would repeat;
And nearer — clearer — deadlier than before!
Arm! Arm! it is — it is — the cannon's opening roar!

23

Within a windowed niche of that high hall
Sate Brunswick's fated Chieftain; he did hear
That sound the first amidst the festival,
And caught its tone with Death's prophetic ear;
And when they smiled because he deemed it near,
His heart more truly knew that peal too well
Which stretched his father on a bloody bier,
And roused the vengeance blood alone could quell;
He rushed into the field, and, foremost fighting, fell.

24

Ah! then and there was hurrying to and fro —
And gathering tears, and tremblings of distress,
And cheeks all pale, which but an hour ago
Blushed at the praise of their own loveliness —
And there were sudden partings, such as press
The life from out young hearts, and choking sighs
Which ne'er might be repeated; who could guess
If ever more should meet those mutual eyes,
Since upon night so sweet such awful morn could rise!

25

And there was mounting in hot haste — the steed,
The mustering squadron, and the clattering car,
Went pouring forward with impetuous speed,
And swiftly forming in the ranks of war —
And the deep thunder peal on peal afar;
And near, the beat of the alarming drum
Roused up the soldier ere the Morning Star;
While thronged the citizens with terror dumb,
Or whispering, with white lips — "The foe! They come! they come!"

26

And wild and high the "Cameron's Gathering" rose!
The war-note of Lochiel, which Albyn's hills
Have heard, and heard, too, have her Saxon foes: —
How in the noon of night that pibroch thrills,
Savage and shrill! But with the breath which fills

**Canto III: 80. And . . . bell:** "On the night previous to the action, it is said that a ball was given at Brussels" [B].

**92. Brunswick's . . . Chieftain:** The Duke of Brunswick, nephew of George III, was killed at the battle of Quatre Bras, two days before Waterloo. **118. Cameron's Gathering:** the clan song of the Camerons. **119. Lochiel:** the title of the chief of the clan Cameron. **Albyn's:** Albyn is the Gaelic name for Scotland.

Their mountain pipe, so fill the mountaineers
With the fierce native daring which instils
The stirring memory of a thousand years,
And Evan's — Donald's — fame rings in each clansman's ears! . .

36

There sunk the greatest, nor the worst of men,
Whose Spirit, antithetically mixed,
One moment of the mightiest, and again
On little objects with like firmness fixed;
Extreme in all things! hadst thou been betwixt,
Thy throne had still been thine, or never been;
For Daring made thy rise as fall: thou seek'st
Even now to re-assume the imperial mien,
And shake again the world, the Thunderer of the scene!

37

Conqueror and Captive of the Earth art thou!
She trembles at thee still, and thy wild name
Was ne'er more bruited in men's minds than now
That thou art nothing, save the jest of Fame,
Who wooed thee once, thy Vassal, and became
The flatterer of thy fierceness — till thou wert
A God unto thyself; nor less the same
To the astounded kingdoms all inert,
Who deemed thee for a time whate'er thou didst assert.

38

Oh, more or less than man — in high or low —
Battling with nations, flying from the field;
Now making monarchs' necks thy footstool, now
More than thy meanest soldier taught to yield;
An Empire thou couldst crush, command, rebuild,
But govern not thy pettiest passion, nor,
However deeply in men's spirits skilled,
Look through thine own, nor curb the lust of War,
Nor learn that tempted Fate will leave the loftiest Star.

39

Yet well thy soul hath brooked the turning tide
With that untaught innate philosophy,
Which, be it Wisdom, Coldness, or deep Pride,
Is gall and wormwood to an enemy.
When the whole host of hatred stood hard by,
To watch and mock thee shrinking, thou hast smiled
With a sedate and all-enduring eye; —
When Fortune fled her spoiled and favourite child,
He stood unbowed beneath the ills upon him piled.

40

Sager than in thy fortunes; for in them
Ambition steeled thee on too far to show
That just habitual scorn, which could contemn
Men and their thoughts; 'twas wise to feel, not so
To wear it ever on thy lip and brow,
And spurn the instruments thou wert to use
Till they were turned unto thine overthrow:
'Tis but a worthless world to win or lose;
So hath it proved to thee, and all such lot who choose.

41

If, like a tower upon a headlong rock,
Thou hadst been made to stand or fall alone,
Such scorn of man had helped to brave the shock;
But men's thoughts were the steps which paved thy throne,
*Their* admiration thy best weapon shone;
The part of Philip's son was thine — not then
(Unless aside thy Purple had been thrown)
Like stern Diogenes to mock at men:
For sceptred Cynics Earth were far too wide a den.

42

But Quiet to quick bosoms is a Hell,
And *there* hath been thy bane; there is a fire
And motion of the Soul which will not dwell
In its own narrow being, but aspire
Beyond the fitting medium of desire;
And, but once kindled, quenchless evermore,
Preys upon high adventure, nor can tire
Of aught but rest; a fever at the core,
Fatal to him who bears, to all who ever bore.

93

I have not loved the World, nor the World me;
I have not flattered its rank breath, nor bowed
To its idolatries a patient knee,
Nor coined my cheek to smiles, — nor cried aloud
In worship of an echo: in the crowd
They could not deem me one of such — I stood
Among them, but not of them — in a shroud

**126. Evan's—Donald's:** "Sir Evan Cameron, and his descendant Donald, the 'gentle Lochiel' of the 'forty-five'" [B]. Sir Evan fought for James II; Donald for the Young Pretender in the 1745 rebellion.

**177. Philip's son:** Alexander the Great. **180. sceptred Cynics:** "The great error of Napoleon, 'if we have writ our annals true,' was a continued obtrusion on mankind of his want of all community of feeling for or with them; perhaps more offensive to human vanity than the active cruelty of more trembling and suspicious tyranny. Such were his speeches to public assemblies as well as individuals; and the single expression which he is said to have used on returning to Paris after the Russian winter had destroyed his army, rubbing his hands over a fire, 'This is pleasanter than Moscow,' would probably alienate more favour from his cause than the destruction and reverses which led to the remark" [B].

Of thoughts which were not their thoughts, and still could,
Had I not filed my mind, which thus itself subdued.

94

I have not loved the World, nor the World me,—
But let us part fair foes; I do believe,
Though I have found them not, that there may be
Words which are things,—Hopes which will not deceive,
And Virtues which are merciful, nor weave
Snares for the failing: I would also deem
O'er others' griefs that some sincerely grieve—
That two, or one, are almost what they seem,—
That Goodness is no name—and Happiness no dream.

95

My daughter! with thy name this song begun!
My daughter! with thy name thus much shall end!—
I see thee not—I hear thee not—but none
Can be so wrapt in thee; Thou art the Friend
To whom the shadows of far years extend:
Albeit my brow thou never should'st behold,
My voice shall with thy future visions blend,
And reach into thy heart,—when mine is cold,—
A token and a tone, even from thy father's mould.

## from CANTO IV

1

I stood in Venice, on the "Bridge of Sighs";
A Palace and a prison on each hand:
I saw from out the wave her structures rise
As from the stroke of the Enchanter's wand:
A thousand Years their cloudy wings expand
Around me, and a dying Glory smiles
O'er the far times, when many a subject land
Looked to the wingéd Lion's marble piles,
Where Venice sate in state, throned on her hundred isles!

2

She looks a sea Cybele, fresh from Ocean,
Rising with her tiara of proud towers
At airy distance, with majestic motion,
A Ruler of the waters and their powers:
And such she was;—her daughters had their dowers
From spoils of nations, and the exhaustless East
Poured in her lap all gems in sparkling showers:
In purple was she robed, and of her feast
Monarchs partook, and deemed their dignity increased.

3

In Venice Tasso's echoes are no more,
And silent rows the songless Gondolier;
Her palaces are crumbling to the shore,
And Music meets not always now the ear:
Those days are gone—but Beauty still is here.
States fall—Arts fade—but Nature doth not die,
Nor yet forget how Venice once was dear,
The pleasant place of all festivity,
The Revel of the earth—the Masque of Italy!

95

I speak not of men's creeds—they rest between
Man and his maker—but of things allowed,
Averred, and known, and daily, hourly seen—
The yoke that is upon us doubly bowed,
And the intent of Tyranny avowed,
The edict of Earth's rulers, who are grown
The apes of him who humbled once the proud,
And shook them from their slumbers on the throne;
Too glorious, were this all his mighty arm had done.

96

Can tyrants but by tyrants conquered be,
And Freedom find no Champion and no Child,
Such as Columbia saw arise when she
Sprung forth a Pallas, armed and undefiled?
Or must such minds be nourished in the wild,
Deep in the unpruned forest, 'midst the roar
Of cataracts, where nursing Nature smiled
On infant Washington? Has Earth no more
Such seeds within her breast, or Europe no such shore?

97

But France got drunk with blood to vomit crime;
And fatal have her Saturnalia been
To Freedom's cause, in every age and clime;
Because the deadly days which we have seen,
And vile Ambition, that built up between
Man and his hopes an adamantine wall,

**198. filed:** Byron refers to *Macbeth*, III.i.65. **Canto IV: 2. Palace . . . prison:** The Bridge of Sighs connects the Doge's Palace with the San Marco prison. **8. Lion's:** The lion is the emblem of St. Mark, patron saint of Venice. **10. Cybele:** "Sabellicus, describing the appearance of Venice, has made use of the above image, which would not be poetical were it not true" [B]. Sabellicus was a fifteenth-century historian of Venice. Cybele, the mother of the gods in some Roman cults, was often represented as crowned with a tower.

**19. Tasso's echoes:** There used to be a custom of gondoliers' reciting stanzas of Tasso's sixteenth-century poem, *Gerusalemme Liberata* (*Jerusalem Delivered*) which had practically disappeared in Byron's day. **40. Sprung . . . Pallas:** Pallas Athene was fabled to have sprung full-grown from the forehead of Zeus.

And the base pageant last upon the scene,
Are grown the pretext for the eternal thrall
Which nips Life's tree, and dooms man's worst—
his second fall

98

Yet, Freedom! yet thy banner, torn but flying,
Streams like the thunder-storm *against* the wind!
Thy trumpet voice, though broken now and dying,
The loudest still the Tempest leaves behind;
Thy tree hath lost its blossoms, and the rind,
Chopped by the axe, looks rough and little worth,
But the sap lasts,—and still the seed we find
Sown deep, even in the bosom of the North;
So shall a better spring less bitter fruit bring forth.

133

It is not that I may not have incurred,
For my ancestral faults or mine, the wound
I bleed withal; and, had it been conferred
With a just weapon, it had flowed unbound;
But now my blood shall not sink in the ground—
To thee I do devote it—*Thou* shalt take
The vengeance, which shall yet be sought and
found—
Which if *I* have not taken for the sake—
But let that pass—I sleep—but Thou shalt yet
awake.

134

And if my voice break forth, 'tis not that now
I shrink from what is suffered: let him speak
Who hath beheld decline, upon my brow,
Or seen my mind's convulsion leave it weak;
But in this page a record will I seek.
Not in the air shall these my words disperse,
Though I be ashes; a far hour shall wreak
The deep prophetic fulness of this verse,
And pile on human heads the mountain of my
curse!

135

That curse shall be Forgiveness.—Have I not—
Hear me, my mother Earth! behold it, Heaven!—
Have I not had to wrestle with my lot?
Have I not suffered things to be forgiven?
Have I not had my brain seared, my heart riven,
Hopes sapped, name blighted, Life's life lied away?
And only not to desperation driven,
Because not altogether of such clay
As rots into the souls of those whom I survey.

136

From mighty wrongs to petty perfidy
Have I not seen what human things could do?
From the loud roar of foaming calumny
To the small whisper of the as paltry few—
And subtler venom of the reptile crew,
The Janus glance of whose significant eye,
Learning to lie with silence, would *seem* true—
And without utterance, save the shrug or sigh,
Deal round to happy fools its speechless obloquy.

137

But I have lived, and have not lived in vain:
My mind may lose its force, my blood its fire,
And my frame perish even in conquering pain;
But there is that within me which shall tire
Torture and Time, and breathe when I expire;
Something unearthly, which they deem not of,
Like the remembered tone of a mute lyre,
Shall on their softened spirits sink, and move
In hearts all rocky now the late remorse of Love.

177

Oh! that the Desert were my dwelling-place,
With one fair Spirit for my minister,
That I might all forget the human race,
And, hating no one, love but only her!
Ye elements!—in whose ennobling stir
I feel myself exalted—Can ye not
Accord me such a Being? Do I err
In deeming such inhabit many a spot?
Though with them to converse can rarely be our
lot.

178

There is a pleasure in the pathless woods,
There is a rapture on the lonely shore,
There is society, where none intrudes,
By the deep Sea, and Music in its roar:
I love not Man the less, but Nature more,
From these our interviews, in which I steal
From all I may be, or have been before,
To mingle with the Universe, and feel
What I can ne'er express—yet can not all conceal.

179

Roll on, thou deep and dark blue Ocean—roll!
Ten thousand fleets sweep over thee in vain;
Man marks the earth with ruin—his control
Stops with the shore;—upon the watery plain
The wrecks are all thy deed, nor doth remain
A shadow of man's ravage, save his own,
When, for a moment, like a drop of rain,
He sinks into thy depths with bubbling groan—
Without a grave—unknelled, uncoffined, and un-
known.

**96. Janus glance: Janus, the god of doorways who gave his name to January, was represented as double-faced.**

184

And I have loved thee, Ocean! and my joy
Of youthful sports was on thy breast to be
Borne, like thy bubbles, onward: from a boy
I wantoned with thy breakers — they to me
Were a delight; and if the freshening sea
Made them a terror — 'twas a pleasing fear,
For I was as it were a Child of thee,
And trusted to thy billows far and near,
And laid my hand upon thy mane — as I do here.

185

My task is done — my song hath ceased — my theme
Has died into an echo; it is fit
The spell should break of this protracted dream.
The torch shall be extinguished which hath lit
My midnight lamp — and what is writ, is writ, —
Would it were worthier! but I am not now
That which I have been — and my visions flit
Less palpably before me — and the glow
Which in my Spirit dwelt is fluttering, faint, and low.

186

Farewell! a word that must be, and hath been —
A sound which makes us linger; — yet — farewell!
Ye! who have traced the Pilgrim to the scene
Which is his last — if in your memories dwell
A thought which once was his — if on ye swell
A single recollection — not in vain
He wore his sandal-shoon, and scallop-shell;
Farewell! with *him* alone may rest the pain,
If such there were — with *you*, the Moral of his Strain.

# THE PRISONER OF CHILLON

See the headnote to the "Sonnet on Chillon," p. 163. Byron gave this tale the subtitle of "A Fable," to indicate that it was not intended as a historically accurate account of Bonivard's imprisonment, but as a protest against man's inhumanity to man. "When this poem was composed," says Byron, "I was not sufficiently aware of the history of Bonnivard, or I should have endeavoured to dignify the subject by an attempt to celebrate his courage and his virtues." He then proceeds to give a long extract from (without naming it) the *Histoire Littéraire de Genève,* by Jean Sénebier, 1786. The chief literary sources for Byron are Rousseau's romance *La Nouvelle Héloïse* and the account of the imprisonment of Ugolino at the end of Dante's *Inferno.*

*The Prisoner of Chillon* was probably written in July, 1816, and was published in December of the same year.

I

My hair is grey, but not with years,
Nor grew it white
In a single night,
As men's have grown from sudden fears:
My limbs are bowed, though not with toil,
But rusted with a vile repose,
For they have been a dungeon's spoil,
And mine has been the fate of those
To whom the goodly earth and air
Are banned, and barred — forbidden fare;
But this was for my father's faith
I suffered chains and courted death;
That father perished at the stake
For tenets he would not forsake;
And for the same his lineal race
In darkness found a dwelling place;
We were seven — who now are one,
Six in youth, and one in age,
Finished as they had begun,
Proud of Persecution's rage;
One in fire, and two in field,
Their belief with blood have sealed,
Dying as their father died,
For the God their foes denied; —
Three were in a dungeon cast,
Of whom this wreck is left the last.

II

There are seven pillars of Gothic mould,
In Chillon's dungeons deep and old,
There are seven columns, massy and grey,
Dim with a dull imprisoned ray,
A sunbeam which hath lost its way,
And through the crevice and the cleft
Of the thick wall is fallen and left;
Creeping o'er the floor so damp,
Like a marsh's meteor lamp:
And in each pillar there is a ring,
And in each ring there is a chain;
That iron is a cankering thing,
For in these limbs its teeth remain,
With marks that will not wear away,
Till I have done with this new day,
Which now is painful to these eyes,
Which have not seen the sun so rise
For years — I cannot count them o'er,
I lost their long and heavy score

THE PRISONER OF CHILLON. **3. single night:** "Ludovico Sforza, and others.—The same is asserted of Marie Antoinette's, the wife of Louis the Sixteenth, though not in quite so short a period. Grief is said to have the same effect: to such, and not to fear, this change in *hers* was to be attributed" [B]. Ludovico Sforza (1451–1508), named "The Moor," was Duke of Milan and patron of Leonardo da Vinci. Driven from his dukedom by the French and reinstated by the Swiss, he was finally betrayed by the Swiss and died in a French dungeon.

When my last brother dropped and died,
And I lay living by his side.

III

They chained us each to a column stone,
And we were three — yet, each alone;
We could not move a single pace,
We could not see each other's face,
But with that pale and livid light
That made us strangers in our sight:
And thus together — yet apart,
Fettered in hand, but joined in heart,
'Twas still some solace in the dearth
Of the pure elements of earth,
To hearken to each other's speech,
And each turn comforter to each
With some new hope, or legend old,
Or song heroically bold;
But even these at length grew cold.
Our voices took a dreary tone,
An echo of the dungeon stone,
A grating sound, not full and free,
As they of yore were wont to be:
It might be fancy — but to me
They never sounded like our own.

IV

I was the eldest of the three,
And to uphold and cheer the rest
I ought to do — and did my best —
And each did well in his degree.
The youngest, whom my father loved,
Because our mother's brow was given
To him, with eyes as blue as heaven —
For him my soul was sorely moved:
And truly might it be distressed
To see such bird in such a nest;
For he was beautiful as day —
(When day was beautiful to me
As to young eagles, being free) —
A polar day, which will not see
A sunset till its summer's gone,
Its sleepless summer of long light,
The snow-clad offspring of the sun:
And thus he was as pure and bright,
And in his natural spirit gay,
With tears for naught but others' ills,
And then they flowed like mountain rills,
Unless he could assuage the woe
Which he abhorred to view below.

V

The other was as pure of mind,
But formed to combat with his kind;
Strong in his frame, and of a mood
Which 'gainst the world in war had stood.
And perished in the foremost rank
With joy: — but not in chains to pine:
His spirit withered with their clank,
I saw it silently decline —
And so perchance in sooth did mine:
But yet I forced it on to cheer
Those relics of a home so dear.
He was a hunter of the hills,
Had followed there the deer and wolf
To him this dungeon was a gulf,
And fettered feet the worse of ills.

VI

Lake Leman lies by Chillon's walls:
A thousand feet in depth below
Its massy waters meet and flow;
Thus much the fathom-line was sent
From Chillon's snow-white battlement,
Which round about the wave inthralls:
A double dungeon wall and wave
Have made — and like a living grave.
Below the surface of the lake
The dark vault lies wherein we lay:
We heard it ripple night and day;
Sounding o'er our heads it knocked;
And I have felt the winter's spray
Wash through the bars when winds were high
And wanton in the happy sky;
And then the very rock hath rocked,
And I have felt it shake, unshocked,
Because I could have smiled to see
The death that would have set me free.

VII

I said my nearer brother pined,
I said his mighty heart declined,
He loathed and put away his food;
It was not that 'twas coarse and rude,
For we were used to hunter's fare,
And for the like had little care:
The milk drawn from the mountain goat
Was changed for water from the moat,

55. **joined in heart**: the early editions read "pined in heart."

111. **snow-white battlement**: "The Chateau de Chillon is situated between Clarens and Villeneuve, which last is at one extremity of the Lake of Geneva. . . . Near it, on a hill behind, is a torrent: below it, washing its walls, the lake has been fathomed to the depth of 800 feet French measure: within it are a range of dungeons, in which the early reformers, and subsequently prisoners of state, were confined. . . . In the cells are seven pillars, or, rather, eight, one being half merged in the wall; in some of these are rings for the fetters and the fettered: in the pavement the steps of Bonnivard have left their traces . . ." [B]. 115. **Below the surface**: This detail is derived from Rousseau's *La Nouvelle Héloïse*, and is not true of the room in which the historical Bonivard was confined.

Our bread was such as captives' tears
Have moistened many a thousand years,
Since man first pent his fellow men
Like brutes within an iron den;
But what were these to us or him?
These wasted not his heart or limb;
My brother's soul was of that mould
Which in a palace had grown cold,
Had his free breathing been denied
The range of the steep mountain's side;
But why delay the truth? — he died.
I saw, and could not hold his head,
Nor reach his dying hand — nor dead, —
Though hard I strove, but strove in vain,
To rend and gnash my bonds in twain.
He died — and they unlocked his chain,
And scooped for him a shallow grave
Even from the cold earth of our cave.
I begged them, as a boon, to lay
His corse in dust whereon the day
Might shine — it was a foolish thought,
But then within my brain it wrought,
That even in death his freeborn breast
In such a dungeon could not rest.
I might have spared my idle prayer —
They coldly laughed — and laid him there:
The flat and turfless earth above
The being we so much did love;
His empty chain above it leant,
Such Murder's fitting monument!

VIII

But he, the favourite and the flower,
Most cherished since his natal hour,
His mother's image in fair face,
The infant love of all his race,
His martyred father's dearest thought,
My latest care, for whom I sought
To hoard my life, that his might be
Less wretched now, and one day free;
He, too, who yet had held untired
A spirit natural or inspired —
He, too, was struck, and day by day
Was withered on the stalk away.
Oh, God! it is a fearful thing
To see the human soul take wing
In any shape, in any mood:
I've seen it rushing forth in blood,
I've seen it on the breaking ocean
Strive with a swoln convulsive motion,
I've seen the sick and ghastly bed
Of Sin delirious with its dread:
But these were horrors — this was woe
Unmixed with such — but sure and slow:
He faded, and so calm and meek,
So softly worn, so sweetly weak,
So tearless, yet so tender — kind,
And grieved for those he left behind;
With all the while a cheek whose bloom
Was as a mockery of the tomb,
Whose tints as gently sunk away
As a departing rainbow's ray;
An eye of most transparent light,
That almost made the dungeon bright;
And not a word of murmur — not
A groan o'er his untimely lot, —
A little talk of better days,
A little hope my own to raise,
For I was sunk in silence — lost
In this last loss, of all the most;
And then the sighs he would suppress
Of fainting Nature's feebleness,
More slowly drawn, grew less and less:
I listened, but I could not hear;
I called, for I was wild with fear;
I knew 'twas hopeless, but my dread
Would not be thus admonishèd;
I called, and thought I heard a sound —
I burst my chain with one strong bound,
And rushed to him: — I found him not,
*I* only stirred in this black spot,
*I* only lived, *I* only drew
The accursèd breath of dungeon-dew;
The last, the sole, the dearest link
Between me and the eternal brink,
Which bound me to my failing race,
Was broken in this fatal place.
One on the earth, and one beneath —
My brothers — both had ceased to breathe!
I took that hand which lay so still,
Alas! my own was full as chill;
I had not strength to stir, or strive,
But felt that I was still alive —
A frantic feeling, when we know
That what we love shall ne'er be so.
I know not why
I could not die,
I had no earthly hope — but faith,
And that forbade a selfish death.

IX

What next befell me then and there
I know not well — I never knew —
First came the loss of light, and air,
And then of darkness too:
I had no thought, no feeling — none —
Among the stones I stood a stone,
And was, scarce conscious what I wist,
As shrubless crags within the mist;
For all was blank, and bleak, and grey;

It was not night — it was not day;
It was not even the dungeon-light,
So hateful to my heavy sight,
But vacancy absorbing space,
And fixedness — without a place;
There were no stars — no earth — no time —
No check — no change — no good — no crime —
But silence, and a stirless breath
Which neither was of life nor death;
A sea of stagnant idleness,
Blind, boundless, mute, and motionless!

X

A light broke in upon my brain, —
It was thc carol of a bird;
It ceased, and then it came again,
The sweetest song ear ever heard,
And mind was thankful till my eyes
Ran over with the glad surprise,
And they that moment could not see
I was the mate of misery;
But then by dull degrees came back
My senses to their wonted track;
I saw the dungeon walls and floor
Close slowly round me as before,
I saw the glimmer of the sun
Creeping as it before had done,
But through the crevice where it came
That bird was perched, as fond and tame,
And tamer than upon the tree;
A lovely bird, with azure wings,
And song that said a thousand things,
And seemed to say them all for me!
I never saw its like before,
I ne'er shall see its likeness more:
It seemed like me to want a mate,
But was not half so desolate,
And it was come to love me when
None lived to love me so again,
And cheering from my dungeon's brink,
Had brought me back to feel and think.
I know not if it late were free,
Or broke its cage to perch on mine,
But knowing well captivity,
Sweet bird! I could not wish for thine!
Or if it were, in wingèd guise,
A visitant from Paradise;
For — Heaven forgive that thought! the while
Which made me both to weep and smile —
I sometimes deemed that it might be
My brother's soul come down to me;
But then at last away it flew,
And then 'twas mortal well I knew,
For he would never thus have flown —
And left me twice so doubly lone, —
Lone — as the corse within its shroud,
Lone — as a solitary cloud,
A single cloud on a sunny day,
While all the rest of heaven is clear,
A frown upon the atmosphere,
That hath no business to appear
When skies are blue, and earth is gay.

XI

A kind of change came in my fate,
My keepers grew compassionate;
I know not what had made them so,
They were inured to sights of woe,
But so it was: — my broken chain
With links unfastened did remain,
And it was liberty to stride
Along my cell from side to side,
And up and down, and then athwart,
And tread it over every part;
And round the pillars one by one,
Returning where my walk begun,
Avoiding only, as I trod,
My brothers' graves without a sod;
For if I thought with heedless tread
My step profaned their lowly bed,
My breath came gaspingly and thick,
And my crushed heart felt blind and sick.

XII

I made a footing in the wall,
It was not therefrom to escape,
For I had buried one and all,
Who loved me in a human shape;
And the whole earth would henceforth be
A wider prison unto me:
No child — no sire — no kin had I,
No partner in my misery;
I thought of this, and I was glad,
For thought of them had made me mad;
But I was curious to ascend
To my barred windows, and to bend
Once more, upon the mountains high,
The quiet of a loving eye.

XIII

I saw them — and they were the same,
They were not changed like me in frame;
I saw their thousand years of snow
On high — their wide long lake below,
And the blue Rhone in fullest flow;
I heard the torrents leap and gush
O'er channelled rock and broken bush;
I saw the white-walled distant town,

339. **distant town**: Villeneuve; see note to l. 111.

And whiter sails go skimming down;
And then there was a little isle,
Which in my very face did smile,
  The only one in view;
A small green isle, it seemed no more,
Scarce broader than my dungeon floor,
But in it there were three tall trees,
And o'er it blew the mountain breeze,
And by it there were waters flowing,
And on it there were young flowers growing,
  Of gentle breath and hue.
The fish swam by the castle wall,
And they seemed joyous each and all;
The eagle rode the rising blast,
Methought he never flew so fast
As then to me he seemed to fly;
And then new tears came in my eye,
And I felt troubled — and would fain
I had not left my recent chain;
And when I did descend again,
The darkness of my dim abode
Fell on me as a heavy load;
It was as is a new-dug grave,
Closing o'er one we sought to save, —
And yet my glance, too much opprest,
Had almost need of such a rest.

XIV

It might be months, or years, or days —
  I kept no count, I took no note —
I had no hope my eyes to raise,
  And clear them of their dreary mote;
At last men came to set me free;
  I asked not why, and recked not where;
It was at length the same to me,
Fettered or fetterless to be,
  I learned to love despair.
And thus when they appeared at last,
And all my bonds aside were cast,
These heavy walls to me had grown
A hermitage — and all my own!
And half I felt as they were come
To tear me from a second home:
With spiders I had friendship made,
And watched them in their sullen trade,
Had seen the mice by moonlight play,
And why should I feel less than they?
We were all inmates of one place,
And I, the monarch of each race,
Had power to kill — yet, strange to tell!
In quiet we had learned to dwell;
My very chains and I grew friends,
So much a long communion tends
To make us what we are; — even I
Regained my freedom with a sigh.

**341. little isle:** "Between the entrances of the Rhone and Villeneuve, not far from Chillon, is a very small island. . . . It contains a few trees (I think not above three), and from its singleness and diminutive size has a peculiar effect upon the view" [B]. The island is called the Île de Peilx.

# MANFRED

### A DRAMATIC POEM

The first two acts of *Manfred* were written in the autumn of 1816, under the inspiration of Alpine scenery. Byron said: "It was the *Staubach,* and the *Jungfrau,* and something else . . . that made me write *Manfred.*" Biographers usually identify the "something else" with his love for Augusta. The name Manfred comes (probably) from Horace Walpole's *Castle of Otranto* (1764), and the opening scene is heavily dependent on Goethe's *Faust,* parts of which had been translated to him (Byron did not read German) by "Monk" Lewis. Byron admitted that "The first Scene and that of Faustus are very similar," but later became impatient with the parallels pointed out with not only Goethe's *Faust* but Christopher Marlowe's *Faustus.* "The devil may take both Faustuses, German and English," said Byron: "I have taken neither." Nietzsche maintained that *Manfred* was a better work of art than *Faust.*

The "Incantation" of the opening scene, lines 192–261, was written and published in an earlier volume of Byron's: possibly it referred originally to Lady Byron. Byron's note to it in the earlier volume reads: "The following Poem was a Chorus in an unfinished Witch Drama, which was begun some years ago." What he meant by "some years ago," no one knows. The third act of *Manfred* was written later at Venice, during the Carnival of 1817, but revised and rewritten before publication on June 16 of that year. John Murray paid Byron three hundred guineas for the whole drama, which he knew would not sell as well as the tales.

In the original version of the third act the Abbot had little of the dignity he was eventually given, and was treated more like a buffoon. Manfred is a typical Byronic hero, but the incest theme and the superhuman qualities assigned to him made the public identification of Byron with his heroes unusually embarrassing. Hence, although it is perhaps Byron's greatest serious work, he always spoke of it slightingly as "of a very wild, metaphysical, and inexplicable kind."

# Manfred

## DRAMATIS PERSONAE

MANFRED
CHAMOIS HUNTER
ABBOT OF ST. MAURICE
MANUEL
HERMAN

WITCH OF THE ALPS
ARIMANES
NEMESIS
THE DESTINIES
SPIRITS, ETC.

*The Scene of the Drama is amongst the Higher Alps — partly in the Castle of Manfred, and partly in the Mountains.*

---

## Act I

### SCENE I. MANFRED *alone. — Scene, a Gothic Gallery. — Time, Midnight.*

MANFRED. The lamp must be replenished, but even then
It will not burn so long as I must watch:
My slumbers — if I slumber — are not sleep,
But a continuance of enduring thought,
Which then I can resist not: in my heart
There is a vigil, and these eyes but close
To look within; and yet I live, and bear
The aspect and the form of breathing men.
But Grief should be the Instructor of the wise;
Sorrow is Knowledge: they who know the most
Must mourn the deepest o'er the fatal truth —
The Tree of Knowledge is not that of Life.
Philosophy and Science, and the springs
Of Wonder, and the wisdom of the World,
I have essayed, and in my mind there is
A power to make these subject to itself —
But they avail not: I have done men good,
And I have met with good even among men —
But this availed not: I have had my foes,
And none have baffled, many fallen before me —
But this availed not: — Good — or evil — life —
Powers, passions — all I see in other beings,
Have been to me as rain unto the sands,
Since that all-nameless hour. I have no dread,
And feel the curse to have no natural fear,
Nor fluttering throb that beats with hopes or wishes,
Or lurking love of something on the earth.
Now to my task. —
Mysterious Agency!
Ye Spirits of the unbounded Universe!
Whom I have sought in darkness and in light —
Ye, who do compass earth about, and dwell
In subtler essence — ye, to whom the tops
Of mountains inaccessible are haunts,
And Earth's and Ocean's caves familiar things —
I call upon ye by the written charm
Which gives me power upon you — Rise! Appear!
[*A pause*]
They come not yet. — Now by the voice of him
Who is the first among you — by this sign,
Which makes you tremble — by the claims of him
Who is undying, — Rise! Appear! —— Appear!
[*A pause*]
If it be so. — Spirits of Earth and Air,
Ye shall not so elude me! By a power,
Deeper than all yet urged, a tyrant-spell,
Which had its birthplace in a star condemned,
The burning wreck of a demolished world,
A wandering hell in the eternal Space;
By the strong curse which is upon my Soul,
The thought which is within me and around me,
I do compel ye to my will. — Appear!
[*A star is seen at the darker end of the gallery; it is stationary; and a voice is heard singing.*]

FIRST SPIRIT.
Mortal! to thy bidding bowed,
From my mansion in the cloud,
Which the breath of Twilight builds,
And the Summer's sunset gilds
With the azure and vermilion,
Which is mixed for my pavilion;
Though thy quest may be forbidden,
On a star-beam I have ridden,
To thine adjuration bowed:
Mortal — be thy wish avowed!

*Voice of the* SECOND SPIRIT.
Mont Blanc is the Monarch of mountains;
They crowned him long ago
On a throne of rocks, in a robe of clouds,
With a Diadem of snow.
Around his waist are forests braced,
The Avalanche in his hand;

MANFRED. Act I, Sc. i: 12. not . . . Life: See Gen. 3:22. Byron's Cain asks Adam why he failed to eat of the Tree of Life.

But ere it fall, that thundering ball
Must pause for my command.
The Glacier's cold and restless mass
Moves onward day by day;
But I am he who bids it pass,
Or with its ice delay.
I am the Spirit of the place,
Could make the mountain bow
And quiver to his caverned base —
And what with me would'st *Thou?*

*Voice of the* THIRD SPIRIT.
In the blue depth of the waters,
Where the wave hath no strife,
Where the Wind is a stranger,
And the Sea-snake hath life,
Where the Mermaid is decking
Her green hair with shells,
Like the storm on the surface
Came the sound of thy spells;
O'er my calm Hall of Coral
The deep Echo rolled —
To the Spirit of Ocean
Thy wishes unfold!

FOURTH SPIRIT.
Where the slumbering Earthquake
Lies pillowed on fire,
And the lakes of bitumen
Rose boilingly higher;
Where the roots of the Andes
Strike deep in the earth,
As their summits to heaven
Shoot soaringly forth;
I have quitted my birthplace,
Thy bidding to bide —
Thy spell hath subdued me,
Thy will be my guide!

FIFTH SPIRIT.
I am the rider of the wind,
The stirrer of the storm;
The hurricane I left behind
Is yet with lightning warm;
To speed to thee, o'er shore and sea
I swept upon the blast:
The fleet I met sailed well — and yet
'Twill sink ere night be past.

SIXTH SPIRIT.
My dwelling is the shadow of the Night,
Why doth thy magic torture me with light?

SEVENTH SPIRIT.
The Star which rules thy destiny
Was ruled, ere earth began, by me:
It was a World as fresh and fair
As e'er revolved round Sun in air;
Its course was free and regular,
Space bosomed not a lovelier star.
The Hour arrived — and it became
A wandering mass of shapeless flame,
A pathless Comet, and a curse,
The menace of the Universe;
Still rolling on with innate force,
Without a sphere, without a course,
A bright deformity on high,
The monster of the upper sky!
And Thou! beneath its influence born —
Thou worm! whom I obey and scorn —
Forced by a Power (which is not thine,
And lent thee but to make thee mine)
For this brief moment to descend,
Where these weak Spirits round thee bend
And parley with a thing like thee —
What would'st thou, Child of Clay! with me?

*The* SEVEN SPIRITS. Earth — ocean — air — night
— mountains — winds — thy Star,
Are at thy beck and bidding, Child of Clay!
Before thee at thy quest their Spirits are —
What would'st thou with us, Son of mortals —
say?

MANFRED. Forgetfulness —

FIRST SPIRIT. Of what — of whom
— and why?

MANFRED. Of that which is within me; read it
there —
Ye know it — and I cannot utter it.

FIRST SPIRIT. We can but give thee that which we
possess:
Ask of us subjects, sovereignty, the power
O'er earth — the whole, or portion — or a sign
Which shall control the elements, whereof
We are the dominators, — each and all,
These shall be thine.

MANFRED. Oblivion — self-oblivion!
Can ye not wring from out the hidden realms
Ye offer so profusely — what I ask?

FIRST SPIRIT. It is not in our essence, in our skill;
But — thou may'st die.

MANFRED. Will Death bestow it on
me?

FIRST SPIRIT. We are immortal, and do not forget;
We are eternal; and to us the past
Is, as the future, present. Art thou answered?

MANFRED. Ye mock me — but the Power which
brought ye here
Hath made you mine. Slaves, scoff not at my will!
The Mind — the Spirit — the Promethean spark,
The lightning of my being, is as bright,
Pervading, and far darting as your own,
And shall not yield to yours, though cooped in clay!
Answer, or I will teach you what I am.

FIRST SPIRIT. We answer — as we answered; our
reply
Is even in thine own words.

MANFRED. Why say ye so?

FIRST SPIRIT. If, as thou say'st, thine essence be as ours,
We have replied in telling thee, the thing
Mortals call death hath nought to do with us.

MANFRED. I then have called ye from your realms in vain;
Ye cannot, or ye will not, aid me.

FIRST SPIRIT. Say—
What we possess we offer; it is thine:
Bethink ere thou dismiss us;—ask again;
Kingdom, and sway, and strength, and length of days—

MANFRED. Accursèd! what have I to do with days?
They are too long already.—Hence—begone!

FIRST SPIRIT. Yet pause: being here, our will would do thee service;
Bethink thee, is there then no other gift
Which we can make not worthless in thine eyes?

MANFRED. No, none: yet stay—one moment, ere we part,
I would behold ye face to face. I hear
Your voices, sweet and melancholy sounds,
As Music on the waters; and I see
The steady aspect of a clear large Star—
But nothing more. Approach me as ye are,
Or one—or all—in your accustomed forms.

FIRST SPIRIT. We have no forms, beyond the elements
Of which we are the mind and principle:
But choose a form—in that we will appear.

MANFRED. I have no choice; there is no form on earth
Hideous or beautiful to me. Let him,
Who is most powerful of ye, take such aspect
As unto him may seem most fitting—Come!

SEVENTH SPIRIT [*appearing in the shape of a beautiful female figure*]. Behold!

MANFRED. Oh God! if it be thus, and *thou*
Art not a madness and a mockery,
I yet might be most happy. I will clasp thee,
And we again will be—— [*The figure vanishes.*]
My heart is crushed!

[MANFRED *falls senseless. A voice is heard in the Incantation which follows.*]

VOICE.

When the Moon is on the wave,
  And the glow-worm in the grass,
And the meteor on the grave,
  And the wisp on the morass;
When the falling stars are shooting,
And the answered owls are hooting,
And the silent leaves are still
In the shadow of the hill,
Shall my soul be upon thine,
With a power and with a sign.

Though thy slumber may be deep,
Yet thy Spirit shall not sleep;
There are shades which will not vanish,
There are thoughts thou canst not banish;
By a Power to thee unknown,
Thou canst never be alone;
Thou art wrapt as with a shroud,
Thou art gathered in a cloud;
And for ever shalt thou dwell
In the spirit of this spell.

Though thou seest me not pass by,
Thou shalt feel me with thine eye
As a thing that, though unseen,
Must be near thee, and hath been;
And when in that secret dread
Thou hast turned around thy head,
Thou shalt marvel I am not
As thy shadow on the spot,
And the power which thou dost feel
Shall be what thou must conceal.

And a magic voice and verse
Hath baptized thee with a curse;
And a Spirit of the air
Hath begirt thee with a snare;
In the wind there is a voice
Shall forbid thee to rejoice;
And to thee shall Night deny
All the quiet of her sky;
And the day shall have a sun,
Which shall make thee wish it done.

From thy false tears I did distil
An essence which hath strength to kill;
From thy own heart I then did wring
The black blood in its blackest spring;
From thy own smile I snatched the snake,
For there it coiled as in a brake;
From thy own lip I drew the charm
Which gave all these their chiefest harm;
In proving every poison known,
I found the strongest was thine own.

By the cold breast and serpent smile,
By thy unfathomed gulfs of guile,
By that most seeming virtuous eye,
By thy shut soul's hypocrisy;
By the perfection of thine art
Which passed for human thine own heart:
By thy delight in others' pain,
And by thy brotherhood of Cain,
I call upon thee! and compel
Thyself to be thy proper Hell!

And on thy head I pour the vial
Which doth devote thee to this trial;
Nor to slumber, nor to die,

Shall be in thy destiny;
Though thy death shall still seem near
To thy wish, but as a fear;
Lo! the spell now works around thee,
And the clankless chain hath bound thee;
O'er thy heart and brain together
Hath the word been passed — now wither!

## SCENE II. *The Mountain of the Jungfrau. — Time, Morning. —* MANFRED *alone upon the cliffs.*

MANFRED. The spirits I have raised abandon me,
The spells which I have studied baffle me,
The remedy I recked of tortured me:
I lean no more on superhuman aid;
It hath no power upon the past, and for
The future, till the past be gulfed in darkness,
It is not of my search. — My Mother Earth!
And thou fresh-breaking Day, and you, ye Mountains,
Why are ye beautiful? I cannot love ye.
And thou, the bright Eye of the Universe,
That openest over all, and unto all
Art a delight — thou shin'st not on my heart.
And you ye crags, upon whose extreme edge
I stand, and on the torrent's brink beneath
Behold the tall pines dwindled as to shrubs
In dizziness of distance; when a leap,
A stir, a motion, even a breath, would bring
My breast upon its rocky bosom's bed
To rest for ever — wherefore do I pause?
I feel the impulse — yet I do not plunge;
I see the peril — yet do not recede;
And my brain reels — and yet my foot is firm:
There is a power upon me which withholds,
And makes it my fatality to live, —
If it be life to wear within myself
This barrenness of Spirit, and to be
My own Soul's sepulchre, for I have ceased
To justify my deeds unto myself —
The last infirmity of evil. Aye,
Thou winged and cloud-cleaving minister,
[*An Eagle passes.*]
Whose happy flight is highest into heaven,
Well may'st thou swoop so near me — I should be
The prey, and gorge thine eaglets; thou art gone
Where the eye cannot follow thee; but thine
Yet pierces downward, onward, or above,
With a pervading vision. — Beautiful!
How beautiful is all this visible world!
How glorious in its action and itself!
But we, who name ourselves its sovereigns, we,
Half dust, half deity, alike unfit
To sink or soar, with our mixed essence make
A conflict of its elements, and breathe
The breath of degradation and of pride,
Contending with low wants and lofty will,
Till our Mortality predominates,
And men are — what they name not to themselves,
And trust not to each other. Hark! the note,
[*The Shepherd's pipe in the distance is heard.*]
The natural music of the mountain reed —
For here the patriarchal days are not
A pastoral fable — pipes in the liberal air,
Mixed with the sweet bells of the sauntering herd;
My soul would drink those echoes. Oh, that I were
The viewless spirit of a lovely sound,
A living voice, a breathing harmony
A bodiless enjoyment — born and dying
With the blest tone which made me!
[*Enter from below a* CHAMOIS HUNTER.]

CHAMOIS HUNTER. Even so
This way the Chamois leapt: her nimble feet
Have baffled me; my gains to-day will scarce
Repay my break-neck travail. — What is here?
Who seems not of my trade, and yet hath reached
A height which none even of our mountaineers,
Save our best hunters, may attain: his garb
Is goodly, his mien manly, and his air
Proud as a free-born peasant's, at this distance:
I will approach him nearer.

MANFRED [*not perceiving the other*]. To be thus —
Grey-haired with anguish, like these blasted pines,
Wrecks of a single winter, barkless, branchless,
A blighted trunk upon a cursèd root,
Which but supplies a feeling to Decay —
And to be thus, eternally but thus,
Having been otherwise! Now furrowed o'er
With wrinkles, ploughed by moments, not by years
And hours, all tortured into ages — hours
Which I outlive! — Ye toppling crags of ice!
Ye Avalanches, whom a breath draws down
In mountainous o'erwhelming, come and crush me!
I hear ye momently above, beneath,
Crash with a frequent conflict; but ye pass,
And only fall on things that still would live;
On the young flourishing forest, or the hut
And hamlet of the harmless villager.

CHAMOIS HUNTER. The mists begin to rise from up the valley;
I'll warn him to descend, or he may chance
To lose at once his way and life together.

MANFRED. The mists boil up around the glaciers; clouds
Rise curling fast beneath me, white and sulphury,
Like foam from the roused ocean of deep Hell,
Whose every wave breaks on a living shore,
Heaped with the damned like pebbles. — I am giddy.

CHAMOIS HUNTER. I must approach him cautiously; if near,
A sudden step will startle him, and he
Seems tottering already.
MANFRED. Mountains have fallen,
Leaving a gap in the clouds, and with the shock
Rocking their Alpine brethren; filling up
The ripe green valleys with Destruction's splinters;
Damming the rivers with a sudden dash,
Which crushed the waters into mist, and made
Their fountains find another channel — thus,
Thus, in its old age, did Mount Rosenberg —
Why stood I not beneath it?
CHAMOIS HUNTER. Friend! have a care,
Your next step may be fatal! — for the love
Of Him who made you, stand not on that brink!
MANFRED [*not hearing him*]. Such would have been for me a fitting tomb;
My bones had then been quiet in their depth;
They had not then been strewn upon the rocks
For the wind's pastime — as thus — thus they shall be —
In this one plunge. — Farewell, ye opening Heavens!
Look not upon me thus reproachfully —
You were not meant for me — Earth! take these atoms!

[*As* MANFRED *is in act to spring from the cliff, the* CHAMOIS HUNTER *seizes and retains him with a sudden grasp.*]

CHAMOIS HUNTER. Hold, madman! — though aweary of thy life,
Stain not our pure vales with thy guilty blood:
Away with me — I will not quit my hold.
MANFRED. I am most sick at heart — nay, grasp me not —
I am all feebleness — the mountains whirl,
Spinning around me —— I grow blind —— What art thou?
CHAMOIS HUNTER. I'll answer that anon. — Away with me ——
The clouds grow thicker —— there — now lean on me —
Place your foot here — here, take this staff, and cling
A moment to that shrub — now give me your hand,
And hold fast my girdle — softly — well —
The Chalet will be gained within an hour:
Come on, we'll quickly find a surer footing,
And something like a pathway, which the torrent
Hath washed since winter. — Come, 'tis bravely done —
You should have been a hunter. — Follow me.

[*As they descend the rocks with difficulty, the scene closes.*]

**Sc. ii: 99. Mount Rosenberg:** A landslide down the slope of the Rossberg destroyed four villages 1806.

# Act II

## SCENE I. *A Cottage among the Bernese Alps.* — MANFRED *and the* CHAMOIS HUNTER.

CHAMOIS HUNTER. No — no — yet pause — thou must not yet go forth:
Thy mind and body are alike unfit
To trust each other, for some hours, at least;
When thou art better, I will be thy guide —
But whither?
MANFRED. It imports not: I do know
My route full well, and need no further guidance.
CHAMOIS HUNTER. Thy garb and gait bespeak thee of high lineage —
One of the many chiefs, whose castled crags
Look o'er the lower valleys — which of these
May call thee lord? I only know their portals;
My way of life leads me but rarely down
To bask by the huge hearths of those old halls,
Carousing with the vassals; but the paths,
Which step from out our mountains to their doors,
I know from childhood — which of these is thine?
MANFRED. No matter.
CHAMOIS HUNTER. Well, Sir, pardon me the question,
And be of better cheer. Come, taste my wine;
'Tis of an ancient vintage; many a day
'T has thawed my veins among our glaciers, now
Let it do thus for thine — Come, pledge me fairly!
MANFRED. Away, away! there's blood upon the brim!
Will it then never — never sink in the earth?
CHAMOIS HUNTER. What dost thou mean? thy senses wander from thee.
MANFRED. I say 'tis blood — my blood! the pure warm stream
Which ran in the veins of my fathers, and in ours
When we were in our youth, and had one heart,
And loved each other as we should not love,
And this was shed: but still it rises up,
Colouring the clouds, that shut me out from Heaven,
Where thou art not — and I shall never be.
CHAMOIS HUNTER. Man of strange words, and some half-maddening sin,
Which makes thee people vacancy, whate'er
Thy dread and sufferance be, there's comfort yet —
The aid of holy men, and heavenly patience ——

MANFRED. Patience — and patience! Hence — that word was made
For brutes of burthen, not for birds of prey!
Preach it to mortals of a dust like thine, —
I am not of thine order.
CHAMOIS HUNTER. Thanks to Heaven!
I would not be of thine for the free fame
Of William Tell; but whatsoe'er thine ill,
It must be borne, and these wild starts are useless.
MANFRED. Do I not bear it? — Look on me — I live.
CHAMOIS HUNTER. This is convulsion, and no healthful life.
MANFRED. I tell thee, man! I have lived many years,
Many long years, but they are nothing now
To those which I must number: ages — ages —
Space and eternity — and consciousness,
With the fierce thirst of death — and still unslaked!
CHAMOIS HUNTER. Why, on thy brow the seal of middle age
Hath scarce been set; I am thine elder far.
MANFRED. Think'st thou existence doth depend on time?
It doth; but actions are our epochs: mine
Have made my days and nights imperishable,
Endless, and all alike, as sands on the shore,
Innumerable atoms; and one desert,
Barren and cold, on which the wild waves break,
But nothing rests, save carcasses and wrecks,
Rocks, and the salt-surf weeds of bitterness.
CHAMOIS HUNTER. Alas! he's mad — but yet I must not leave him.
MANFRED. I would I were — for then the things I see
Would be but a distempered dream.
CHAMOIS HUNTER. What is it
That thou dost see, or think thou look'st upon?
MANFRED. Myself, and thee — a peasant of the Alps —
Thy humble virtues, hospitable home,
And spirit patient, pious, proud, and free;
Thy self-respect grafted on innocent thoughts;
Thy days of health, and nights of sleep: thy toils,
By danger dignified, yet guiltless; hopes
Of cheerful old age and a quiet grave,
With cross and garland over its green turf,
And thy grandchildren's love for epitaph!
This do I see — and then I look within —
It matters not — my Soul was scorched already!
CHAMOIS HUNTER. And would'st thou then exchange thy lot for mine?
MANFRED. No, friend! I would not wrong thee, nor exchange
My lot with living being: I can bear —
However wretchedly, 'tis still to bear —
In life what others could not brook to dream,
But perish in their slumber.
CHAMOIS HUNTER. And with this —
This cautious feeling for another's pain,
Canst thou be black with evil? — say not so.
Can one of gentle thoughts have wreaked revenge
Upon his enemies?
MANFRED. Oh! no, no, no!
My injuries came down on those who loved me —
On those whom I best loved: I never quelled
An enemy, save in my just defence —
But my embrace was fatal.
CHAMOIS HUNTER. Heaven give thee rest!
And Penitence restore thee to thyself;
My prayers shall be for thee.
MANFRED. I need them not,
But can endure thy pity. I depart —
'Tis time — farewell! — Here's gold, and thanks for thee —
No words — it is thy due. — Follow me not —
I know my path — the mountain peril's past:
And once again I charge thee, follow not!
[*Exit* MANFRED.]

## SCENE II. *A lower Valley in the Alps. — A Cataract.*

[*Enter* MANFRED.]

MANFRED. It is not noon — the Sunbow's rays still arch
The torrent with the many hues of heaven,
And roll the sheeted silver's waving column
O'er the crag's headlong perpendicular,
And fling its line of foaming light along,
And to and fro, like the pale courser's tail,
The Giant steed, to be bestrode by Death,
As told in the Apocalypse. No eyes
But mine now drink this sight of loveliness;
I should be sole in this sweet solitude,
And with the Spirit of the place divide
The homage of these waters. — I will call her.
[MANFRED *takes some of the water into the palm of his hand and flings it into the air, muttering the adjuration. After a pause, the* WITCH OF THE ALPS *rises beneath the arch of the sunbow of the torrent.*]
Beautiful Spirit! with thy hair of light,
And dazzling eyes of glory, in whose form
The charms of Earth's least mortal daughters grow
To an unearthly stature, in an essence
Of purer elements; while the hues of youth, —
Carnationed like a sleeping Infant's cheek,

**Act II, Sc. ii: 8. Apocalypse:** See Rev. 6:8. Byron in his journal compares a mountain torrent to the tail of a white horse "such as it might be conceived would be that of the 'pale horse' on which Death is mounted in the Apocalypse."

Rocked by the beating of her mother's heart,
Or the rose tints, which Summer's twilight leaves
Upon the lofty Glacier's virgin snow,
The blush of earth embracing with her Heaven, —
Tinge thy celestial aspect, and make tame
The beauties of the Sunbow which bends o'er thee.
Beautiful Spirit! in thy calm clear brow,
Wherein is glassed serenity of Soul,
Which of itself shows immortality,
I read that thou wilt pardon to a Son
Of Earth, whom the abstruser powers permit
At times to commune with them — if that he
Avail him of his spells — to call thee thus,
And gaze on thee a moment.

WITCH. Son of Earth!
I know thee, and the Powers which give thee power!
I know thee for a man of many thoughts,
And deeds of good and ill, extreme in both,
Fatal and fated in thy sufferings.
I have expected this — what would'st thou with me?

MANFRED. To look upon thy beauty — nothing further.
The face of the earth hath maddened me, and I
Take refuge in her mysteries, and pierce
To the abodes of those who govern her —
But they can nothing aid me. I have sought
From them what they could not bestow, and now
I search no further.

WITCH. What could be the quest
Which is not in the power of the most powerful,
The rulers of the invisible?

MANFRED. A boon; —
But why should I repeat it? 'twere in vain.

WITCH. I know not that; let thy lips utter it.

MANFRED. Well, though it torture me, 'tis but the same;
My pang shall find a voice. From my youth upwards
My Spirit walked not with the souls of men,
Nor looked upon the earth with human eyes;
The thirst of their ambition was not mine,
The aim of their existence was not mine;
My joys — my griefs — my passions — and my powers,
Made me a stranger; though I wore the form,
I had no sympathy with breathing flesh,
Nor midst the Creatures of Clay that girded me
Was there but One who — but of her anon.
I said with men, and with the thoughts of men,
I held but slight communion; but instead,
My joy was in the wilderness, — to breathe
The difficult air of the iced mountain's top,
Where the birds dare not build — nor insect's wing
Flit o'er the herbless granite; or to plunge
Into the torrent, and to roll along
On the swift whirl of the new-breaking wave
Of river-stream, or ocean, in their flow.
In these my early strength exulted; or
To follow through the night the moving moon,
The stars and their development; or catch
The dazzling lightnings till my eyes grew dim;
Or to look, list'ning, on the scattered leaves,
While Autumn winds were at their evening song.
These were my pastimes, and to be alone;
For if the beings, of whom I was one, —
Hating to be so, — crossed me in my path,
I felt myself degraded back to them,
And all was clay again. And then I dived,
In my lone wanderings, to the caves of Death,
Searching its cause in its effect; and drew
From withered bones, and skulls, and heaped up dust,
Conclusions most forbidden. Then I passed
The nights of years in sciences untaught,
Save in the old-time; and with time and toil,
And terrible ordeal, and such penance
As in itself hath power upon the air,
And spirits that do compass air and earth,
Space, and the peopled Infinite, I made
Mine eyes familiar with Eternity,
Such as, before me, did the Magi, and
He who from out their fountain-dwellings raised
Eros and Anteros, at Gadara,
As I do thee; — and with my knowledge grew
The thirst of knowledge, and the power and joy
Of this most bright intelligence, until ——

WITCH. Proceed.

MANFRED. Oh! I but thus prolonged my words,
Boasting these idle attributes, because
As I approach the core of my heart's grief —
But — to my task. I have not named to thee
Father or mother, mistress, friend, or being,
With whom I wore the chain of human ties;
If I had such, they seemed not such to me —
Yet there was One ——

WITCH. Spare not thyself — proceed.

MANFRED. She was like me in lineaments — her eyes —
Her hair — her features — all, to the very tone
Even of her voice, they said were like to mine;
But softened all, and tempered into beauty:
She had the same lone thoughts and wanderings,
The quest of hidden knowledge, and a mind
To comprehend the Universe: nor these

92. **He**: the Neoplatonic philosopher Iamblichus is said to have summoned Eros (Cupid, or the god of love) and his brother Anteros (the avenger of rejected love) from two fountains which supplied water to the hot baths at Gadara, in Syria.

Alone, but with them gentler powers than mine,
Pity, and smiles, and tears — which I had not;
And tenderness — but that I had for her;
Humility — and that I never had.
Her faults were mine — her virtues were her
own —
I loved her, and destroyed her!

WITCH. With thy hand?

MANFRED. Not with my hand, but heart, which
broke her heart;
It gazed on mine, and withered. I have shed
Blood, but not hers — and yet her blood was shed;
I saw — and could not stanch it.

WITCH. And for this —
A being of the race thou dost despise —
The order, which thine own would rise above,
Mingling with us and ours, — thou dost forgo
The gifts of our great knowledge, and shrink'st
back
To recreant mortality — Away!

MANFRED. Daughter of Air! I tell thee, since that
hour —
But words are breath — look on me in my sleep,
Or watch my watchings — Come and sit by me!
My solitude is solitude no more,
But peopled with the Furies; — I have gnashed
My teeth in darkness till returning morn,
Then cursed myself till sunset; — I have prayed
For madness as a blessing — 'tis denied me.
I have affronted Death — but in the war
Of elements the waters shrunk from me,
And fatal things passed harmless; the cold hand
Of an all-pitiless Demon held me back,
Back by a single hair, which would not break
In Fantasy, Imagination, all
The affluence of my soul — which one day was
A Croesus in creation — I plunged deep,
But, like an ebbing wave, it dashed me back
Into the gulf of my unfathomed thought.
I plunged amidst Mankind — Forgetfulness
I sought in all, save where 'tis to be found —
And that I have to learn — my Sciences,
My long pursued and superhuman art,
Is mortal here: I dwell in my despair —
And live — and live for ever.

WITCH. It may be
That I can aid thee.

MANFRED. To do this thy power
Must wake the dead, or lay me low with them.
Do so — in any shape — in any hour —
With any torture — so it be the last.

WITCH. That is not in my province; but if thou
Wilt swear obedience to my will, and do
My bidding, it may help thee to thy wishes.

MANFRED. I will not swear — Obey! and whom?
the Spirits
Whose presence I command, and be the slave
Of those who served me — Never!

WITCH. Is this all?
Hast thou no gentler answer? — Yet bethink thee,
And pause ere thou rejectest.

MANFRED. I have said it.

WITCH. Enough! I may retire then — say!

MANFRED. Retire!

[*The* WITCH *disappears.*]

MANFRED (*alone*). We are the fools of Time and
Terror: Days
Steal on us, and steal from us; yet we live,
Loathing our life, and dreading still to die.
In all the days of this detested yoke —
This vital weight upon the struggling heart,
Which sinks with sorrow, or beats quick with pain,
Or joy that ends in agony or faintness —
In all the days of past and future — for
In life there is no present — we can number
How few — how less than few — wherein the soul
Forbears to pant for death, and yet draws back
As from a stream in winter, though the chill
Be but a moment's. I have one resource
Still in my science — I can call the dead,
And ask them what it is we dread to be:
The sternest answer can but be the Grave,
And that is nothing: if they answer not —
The buried Prophet answered to the Hag
Of Endor; and the Spartan Monarch drew
From the Byzantine maid's unsleeping spirit
An answer and his destiny — he slew
That which he loved, unknowing what he slew,
And died unpardoned — though he called in aid
The Phyxian Jove, and in Phigalia roused
The Arcadian Evocators to compel
The indignant shadow to depose her wrath,
Or fix her term of vengeance — she replied
In words of dubious import, but fulfilled.
If I had never lived, that which I love
Had still been living; had I never loved
That which I love would still be beautiful,
Happy and giving happiness. What is she?
What is she now? — a sufferer for my sins —
A thing I dare not think upon — or nothing.
Within few hours I shall not call in vain —
Yet in this hour I dread the thing I dare:
Until this hour I never shrunk to gaze
On spirit, good or evil — now I tremble,
And feel a strange cold thaw upon my heart.

182. **Endor**: See I Sam. 28. **Spartan Monarch**: according to Plutarch in his life of Cimon, Pausanias, King of Sparta, stabbed by misadventure a maiden named Cleonice when he was in Byzantium. Her ghost haunted him, and when he asked her forgiveness she merely foretold his death. Another Pausanias, the author of the *Description of Greece*, adds the details about his consulting the oracle of Phyxian Jove and the necromancers of Phigalia in Arcadia.

But I can act even what I most abhor,
And champion human fears. — The night approaches. [*Exit.*]

SCENE III. *The summit of the Jungfrau Mountain.*

[*Enter* FIRST DESTINY.]

FIRST DESTINY. The Moon is rising broad, and round, and bright;
And here on snows, where never human foot
Of common mortal trod, we nightly tread,
And leave no traces: o'er the savage sea,
The glassy ocean of the mountain ice,
We skim its rugged breakers, which put on
The aspect of a tumbling tempest's foam
Frozen in a moment — a dead Whirlpool's image:
And this most steep fantastic pinnacle,
The fretwork of some earthquake — where the clouds
Pause to repose themselves in passing by —
Is sacred to our revels, or our vigils;
Here do I wait my sisters, on our way
To the Hall of Arimanes — for to-night
Is our great festival — 'tis strange they come not.

FIRST VOICE [*without, singing*].
The Captive Usurper,
Hurled down from the throne,
Lay buried in torpor,
Forgotten and lone;
I broke through his slumbers,
I shivered his chain,
I leagued him with numbers —
He's Tyrant again!
With the blood of a million he'll answer my care,
With a Nation's destruction — his flight and despair!

SECOND VOICE [*without*]. The Ship sailed on, the Ship sailed fast,
But I left not a sail, and I left not a mask;
There is not a plank of the hull or the deck,
And there is not a wretch to lament o'er his wreck;
Save one, whom I held, as he swam, by the hair,
And he was a subject well worthy my care;
A traitor on land, and a pirate at sea —
But I saved him to wreak further havoc for me!

FIRST DESTINY [*answering*].
The City lies sleeping;
The morn, to deplore it,
May dawn on it weeping:
Sullenly, slowly,
The black plague flew o'er it —
Thousands lie lowly;
Tens of thousands shall perish;
The living shall fly from
The sick they should cherish;
But nothing can vanquish
The touch that they die from.
Sorrow and anguish,
And evil and dread,
Envelop a nation;
The blest are the dead,
Who see not the sight
Of their own desolation;
This work of a night —
This wreck of a realm — this deed of my doing —
For ages I've done, and shall still be renewing!

[*Enter the* SECOND *and* THIRD DESTINIES.]

DESTINIES.
Our hands contain the hearts of men,
Our footsteps are their graves;
We only give to take again
The Spirits of our slaves!

FIRST DESTINY. Welcome! — Where's Nemesis?
SECOND DESTINY. At some great work;
But what I know not, for my hands were full.
THIRD DESTINY. Behold she cometh.

[*Enter* NEMESIS.]

FIRST DESTINY. Say, where hast thou been?
My Sisters and thyself are slow to-night.
NEMESIS. I was detained repairing shattered thrones —
Marrying fools, restoring dynasties —
Avenging men upon their enemies,
And making them repent their own revenge;
Goading the wise to madness; from the dull
Shaping out oracles to rule the world
Afresh — for they were waxing out of date,
And mortals dared to ponder for themselves,
To weigh kings in the balance — and to speak
Of Freedom, the forbidden fruit. — Away!
We have outstayed the hour — mount we our clouds! [*Exeunt.*]

SCENE IV. *The Hall of Arimanes. — Arimanes on his Throne, a Globe of Fire, surrounded by the Spirits.*

*Hymn of the* SPIRITS.
Hail to our Master! — Prince of Earth and Air!
Who walks the clouds and waters — in his hand
The sceptre of the Elements, which tear
Themselves to chaos at his high command!
He breatheth — and a tempest shakes the sea;
He speaketh — and the clouds reply in thunder;
He gazeth — from his glance the sunbeams flee;

**Sc. iii: 16. Captive Usurper**: Napoleon, whom Byron sometimes expected to return from St. Helena as he had done from Elba.

**62. shattered thrones**: referring to the period of reaction which followed Napoleon's downfall at Waterloo.

He moveth — Earthquakes rend the world asunder.
Beneath his footsteps the Volcanoes rise;
His shadow is the Pestilence: his path
The comets herald through the crackling skies;
And Planets turn to ashes at his wrath.
To him War offers daily sacrifice;
To him Death pays his tribute; Life is his,
With all its Infinite of agonies —
And his the Spirit of whatever is!

[*Enter the* DESTINIES *and* NEMESIS.]

FIRST DESTINY. Glory to Arimanes! on the earth
His power increaseth — both my sisters did
His bidding, nor did I neglect my duty!

SECOND DESTINY. Glory to Arimanes! we who bow
The necks of men, bow down before his throne!

THIRD DESTINY. Glory to Arimanes! we await His nod!

NEMESIS. Sovereign of Sovereigns! we are thine,
And all that liveth, more or less, is ours,
And most things wholly so; still to increase
Our power, increasing thine, demands our care,
And we are vigilant. Thy late commands
Have been fulfilled to the utmost.

[*Enter* MANFRED.]

A SPIRIT. What is here?
A mortal! — Thou most rash and fatal wretch,
Bow down and worship!

SECOND SPIRIT. I do know the man —
A Magian of great power, and fearful skill!

THIRD SPIRIT. Bow down and worship, slave! — What, know'st thou not
Thine and our Sovereign? — Tremble, and obey!

ALL THE SPIRITS. Prostrate thyself, and thy condemnèd clay,
Child of the Earth! or dread the worst.

MANFRED. I know it;
And yet ye see I kneel not.

FOURTH SPIRIT. 'Twill be taught thee.

MANFRED. 'Tis taught already; — many a night on the earth,
On the bare ground, have I bowed down my face,
And strewed my head with ashes; I have known
The fulness of humiliation — for
I sunk before my vain despair, and knelt
To my own desolation.

FIFTH SPIRIT. Dost thou dare
Refuse to Arimanes on his throne
What the whole earth accords, beholding not
The terror of his Glory? — Crouch! I say.

MANFRED. Bid *him* bow down to that which is above him,
The overruling Infinite — the Maker
Who made him not for worship — let him kneel,
And we will kneel together.

ALL THE SPIRITS. Crush the worm!
Tear him in pieces! —

FIRST DESTINY. Hence! Avaunt! — he's mine.
Prince of the Powers invisible! This man
Is of no common order, as his port
And presence here denote: his sufferings
Have been of an immortal nature — like
Our own; his knowledge, and his powers and will,
As far as is compatible with clay,
Which clogs the ethereal essence, have been such
As clay hath seldom borne; his aspirations
Have been beyond the dwellers of the earth,
And they have only taught him what we know —
That knowledge is not happiness, and science
But an exchange of ignorance for that
Which is another kind of ignorance.
This is not all — the passions, attributes
Of Earth and Heaven, from which no power nor being,
Nor breath from the worm upwards is exempt,
Have pierced his heart; and in their consequence
Made him a thing — which — I who pity not,
Yet pardon those who pity. He is mine —
And thine it may be; be it so, or not —
No other Spirit in this region hath
A soul like his — or power upon his soul.

NEMESIS. What doth he here then?

FIRST DESTINY. Let *him* answer that.

MANFRED. Ye know what I have known; and without power
I could not be amongst ye: but there are
Powers deeper still beyond — I come in quest
Of such, to answer unto what I seek.

NEMESIS. What would'st thou?

MANFRED. *Thou* canst not reply to me.
Call up the dead — my question is for them.

NEMESIS. Great Arimanes, doth thy will avouch
The wishes of this mortal?

ARIMANES. Yea.

NEMESIS. Whom wouldst thou
Uncharnel?

MANFRED. One without a tomb — call up Astarte.

NEMESIS.

Shadow! or Spirit!
Whatever thou art,
Which still doth inherit
The whole or a part
Of the form of thy birth,
Of the mould of thy clay,
Which returned to the earth,
Re-appear to the day!
Bear what thou borest,
The heart and the form,
And the aspect thou worest
Redeem from the worm.
Appear! — Appear! — Appear!
Who sent thee there requires thee here!

[*The* PHANTOM OF ASTARTE *rises and stands in the midst.*]

MANFRED. Can this be death? there's bloom upon her cheek;
But now I see it is no living hue,
But a strange hectic — like the unnatural red
Which Autumn plants upon the perished leaf,
It is the same! Oh, God! that I should dread
To look upon the same — Astarte! — No,
I cannot speak to her — but bid her speak —
Forgive me or condemn me.

NEMESIS.
By the Power which hath broken
The grave which enthralled thee,
Speak to him who hath spoken,
Or those who have called thee!

MANFRED. She is silent,
And in that silence I am more than answered.

NEMESIS. My power extends no further. Prince of Air!
It rests with thee alone — command her voice.

ARIMANES. Spirit — obey this sceptre!

NEMESIS. Silent still!
She is not of our order, but belongs
To the other powers. Mortal! thy quest is vain,
And we are baffled also.

MANFRED. Hear me, hear me —
Astarte! my belovèd! speak to me:
I have so much endured — so much endure —
Look on me! the grave hath not changed thee more
Than I am changed for Thee. Thou lovedst me
Too much, as I loved thee: we were not made
To torture thus each other —though it were
The deadliest sin to love as we have loved.
Say that thou loath'st me not — that I do bear
This punishment for both — that thou wilt be
One of the blessèd — and that I shall die;
For hitherto all hateful things conspire
To bind me in existence — in a life
Which makes me shrink from Immortality —
A future like the past. I cannot rest.
I know not what I ask, nor what I seek:
I feel but what thou art, and what I am;
And I would hear yet once before I perish
The voice which was my music — speak to me!
For I have called on thee in the still night,
Startled the slumbering birds from the hushed boughs,
And woke the mountain wolves, and made the caves
Acquainted with thy vainly echoed name,
Which answered me — many things answered me —
Spirits and men — but thou wert silent all.
Yet speak to me! I have outwatched the stars,
And gazed o'er heaven in vain in search of thee.
Speak to me! I have wandered o'er the earth,
And never found thy likeness — Speak to me!
Look on the fiends around — they feel for me:
I fear them not, and feel for thee alone.
Speak to me! though it be in wrath; — but say —
I reck not what — but let me hear thee once —
This once — once more!

PHANTOM OF ASTARTE. Manfred!

MANFRED. Say on, say on —
I live but in the sound — it is thy voice!

PHANTOM. Manfred! to-morrow ends thine earthly ills.
Farewell!

MANFRED. Yet one word more — am I forgiven?

PHANTOM. Farewell!

MANFRED. Say, shall we meet again?

PHANTOM. Farewell!

MANFRED. One word for mercy! Say thou lovest me.

PHANTOM. Manfred!

[*The Spirit of* ASTARTE *disappears.*]

NEMESIS. She's gone, and will not be recalled:
Her words will be fulfilled. Return to the earth.

A SPIRIT. He is convulsed — This is to be a mortal,
And seek the things beyond mortality.

ANOTHER SPIRIT. Yet, see, he mastereth himself, and makes
His torture tributary to his will.
Had he been one of us, he would have made
An awful Spirit.

NEMESIS. Hast thou further question
Of our great sovereign, or his worshippers?

MANFRED. None.

NEMESIS. Then, for a time, farewell.

MANFRED. We meet then! Where? On the earth? —
Even as thou wilt: and for the grace accorded
I now depart a debtor. Fare ye well!

[*Exit* MANFRED.]

[*Scene closes.*]

# Act III

## SCENE I. *A Hall in the Castle of Manfred.* — MANFRED *and* HERMAN.

MANFRED. What is the hour?

HERMAN. It wants but one till sunset,
And promises a lovely twilight.

MANFRED. Say,
Are all things so disposed of in the tower
As I directed?

HERMAN. All, my Lord, are ready:

Here is the key and casket.
MANFRED. It is well:
Thou mayst retire. [*Exit* HERMAN.]
MANFRED (*alone*). There is a calm upon me —
Inexplicable stillness! which till now
Did not belong to what I knew of life.
If that I did not know Philosophy
To be of all our vanities the motliest,
The merest word that ever fooled the ear
From out the schoolman's jargon, I should deem
The golden secret, the sought "Kalon," found,
And seated in my soul. It will not last,
But it is well to have known it, though but once:
It hath enlarged my thoughts with a new sense,
And I within my tablets would note down
That there is such a feeling. Who is there?
[*Re-enter* HERMAN.]
HERMAN. My Lord, the Abbot of St. Maurice craves
To greet your presence.
[*Enter the* ABBOT OF ST. MAURICE.]
ABBOT. Peace be with Count Manfred!
MANFRED. Thanks, holy father! welcome to these walls;
Thy presence honours them, and blesseth those
Who dwell within them.
ABBOT. Would it were so, Count! —
But I would fain confer with thee alone.
MANFRED. Herman, retire. — What would my reverend guest?
ABBOT. Thus, without prelude: — Age and zeal — my office —
And good intent must plead my privilege;
Our near, though not acquainted neighbourhood,
May also be my herald. Rumours strange,
And of unholy nature, are abroad,
And busy with thy name — a noble name
For centuries: may he who bears it now
Transmit it unimpaired!
MANFRED. Proceed, — I listen.
ABBOT. 'Tis said thou holdest converse with the things
Which are forbidden to the search of man;
That with the dwellers of the dark abodes,
The many evil and unheavenly spirits
Which walk the valley of the Shade of Death,
Thou communest. I know that with mankind,
Thy fellows in creation, thou dost rarely
Exchange thy thoughts, and that thy solitude
Is as an Anchorite's — were it but holy.
MANFRED. And what are they who do avouch these things?

**Act III, Sc. i: 13. "Kalon"**: in Greek philosophy, the good which is also the beautiful; the supreme good. **19. St. Maurice**: There is an Abbey of St. Maurice in a town of the same name in the Rhone valley.

ABBOT. My pious brethren — the scared peasantry —
Even thy own vassals — who do look on thee
With most unquiet eyes. Thy life's in peril!
MANFRED. Take it.
ABBOT. I come to save, and not destroy:
I would not pry into thy secret soul;
But if these things be sooth, there still is time
For penitence and pity: reconcile thee
With the true church, and through the church to Heaven.
MANFRED. I hear thee. This is my reply — whate'er
I may have been, or am, doth rest between
Heaven and myself — I shall not choose a mortal
To be my mediator — Have I sinned
Against your ordinances? prove and punish!
ABBOT. My son! I did not speak of punishment,
But penitence and pardon; — with thyself
The choice of such remains — and for the last,
Our institutions and our strong belief
Have given me power to smooth the path from sin
To higher hope and better thoughts; the first
I leave to Heaven, — "Vengeance is mine alone!"
So saith the Lord, and with all humbleness
His servant echoes back the awful word.
MANFRED. Old man! there is no power in holy men,
Nor charm in prayer, nor purifying form
Of penitence, nor outward look, nor fast,
Nor agony — nor, greater than all these,
The innate tortures of that deep Despair,
Which is Remorse without the fear of Hell,
But all in all sufficient to itself
Would make a hell of Heaven — can exorcise
From out the unbounded spirit the quick sense
Of its own sins — wrongs — sufferance — and revenge
Upon itself; there is no future pang
Can deal that justice on the self-condemned
He deals on his own soul.
ABBOT. All this is well;
For this will pass away, and be succeeded
By an auspicious hope, which shall look up
With calm assurance to that blessed place,
Which all who seek may win, whatever be
Their earthly errors, so they be atoned:
And the commencement of atonement is
The sense of its necessity. Say on —
And all our church can teach thee shall be taught;
And all we can absolve thee shall be pardoned.
MANFRED. When Rome's sixth Emperor was near his last,
The victim of a self-inflicted wound,

**88. sixth Emperor**: This story is actually told of Nero, the fifth emperor.

To shun the torments of a public death
From senates once his slaves, a certain soldier,
With show of loyal pity, would have stanched
The gushing throat with his officious robe;
The dying Roman thrust him back, and said —
Some empire still in his expiring glance —
" It is too late — is this fidelity? "

ABBOT. And what of this?

MANFRED. I answer with the Roman —
" It is too late! "

ABBOT. It never can be so,
To reconcile thyself with thy own soul,
And thy own soul with Heaven. Hast thou no hope?
'Tis strange — even those who do despair above,
Yet shape themselves some fantasy on earth,
To which frail twig they cling, like drowning men.

MANFRED. Aye — father! I have had those early visions,
And noble aspirations in my youth,
To make my own the mind of other men,
The enlightener of nations; and to rise
I knew not whither — it might be to fall;
But fall, even as the mountain-cataract,
Which having leapt from its more dazzling height,
Even in the foaming strength of its abyss,
(Which casts up misty columns that become
Clouds raining from the re-ascended skies,)
Lies low but mighty still. — But this is past,
My thoughts mistook themselves.

ABBOT. And wherefore so?

MANFRED. I could not tame my nature down; for he
Must serve who fain would sway; and soothe, and sue,
And watch all time, and pry into all place,
And be a living Lie, who would become
A mighty thing amongst the mean — and such
The mass are; I disdained to mingle with
A herd, though to be leader — and of wolves.
The lion is alone, and so am I.

ABBOT. And why not live and act with other men?

MANFRED. Because my nature was averse from life;
And yet not cruel; for I would not make,
But find a desolation. Like the Wind,
The red-hot breath of the most lone Simoom,
Which dwells but in the desert, and sweeps o'er
The barren sands which bear no shrubs to blast,
And revels o'er their wild and arid waves,
And seeketh not, so that it is not sought,
But being met is deadly, — such hath been
The course of my existence; but there came
Things in my path which are no more.

ABBOT. Alas!
I 'gin to fear that thou art past all aid
From me and from my calling; yet so young,
I still would —

MANFRED. Look on me! there is an order
Of mortals on the earth, who do become
Old in their youth, and die ere middle age,
Without the violence of warlike death;
Some perishing of pleasure — some of study —
Some worn with toil, some of mere weariness, —
Some of disease — and some insanity —
And some of withered, or of broken hearts;
For this last is a malady which slays
More than are numbered in the lists of Fate,
Taking all shapes, and bearing many names.
Look upon me! for even of all these things
Have I partaken; and of all these things
One were enough; then wonder not that I
Am what I am, but that I ever was,
Or having been, that I am still on earth.

ABBOT. Yet, hear me still —

MANFRED. Old man! I do respect
Thine order, and revere thine years; I deem
Thy purpose pious, but it is in vain:
Think me not churlish; I would spare thyself,
Far more than me, in shunning at this time
All further colloquy — and so — farewell.

[*Exit* MANFRED.]

ABBOT. This should have been a noble creature: he
Hath all the energy which would have made
A goodly frame of glorious elements,
Had they been wisely mingled; as it is,
It is an awful chaos — Light and Darkness —
And mind and dust — and passions and pure thoughts
Mixed, and contending without end or order, —
All dormant or destructive. He will perish —
And yet he must not — I will try once more,
For such are worth redemption; and my duty
Is to dare all things for a righteous end.
I'll follow him — but cautiously, though surely.

[*Exit* ABBOT.]

## SCENE II. *Another Chamber.* —

MANFRED *and* HERMAN.

HERMAN. My lord, you bade me wait on you at sunset:
He sinks behind the mountain.

MANFRED. Doth he so?
I will look on him.

[MANFRED *advances to the Window of the Hall.*]

Glorious Orb! the idol
Of early nature, and the vigorous race
Of undiseased mankind, the giant sons

**Sc. ii : 5. giant sons :** See Gen. 6:1–4. This passage is the source of Byron's "mystery" play, *Heaven and Earth.*

Of the embrace of Angels, with a sex
More beautiful than they, which did draw down
The erring Spirits who can ne'er return.—
Most glorious Orb! that wert a worship, ere
The mystery of thy making was revealed!
Thou earliest minister of the Almighty,
Which gladdened, on their mountain tops, the hearts
Of the Chaldean shepherds, till they poured
Themselves in orisons! Thou material God!
And representative of the Unknown—
Who chose thee for his shadow! Thou chief Star!
Centre of many stars! which mak'st our earth
Endurable, and temperest the hues
And hearts of all who walk within thy rays!
Sire of the seasons! Monarch of the climes,
And those who dwell in them! for near or far,
Our inborn spirits have a tint of thee
Even as our outward aspects;—thou dost rise,
And shine, and set in glory. Fare thee well!
I ne'er shall see thee more. As my first glance
Of love and wonder was for thee, then take
My latest look: thou wilt not beam on one
To whom the gifts of life and warmth have been
Of a more fatal nature. He is gone—
I follow. [*Exit* MANFRED.]

SCENE III. *The Mountains—The Castle of Manfred at some distance—A Terrace before a Tower.—Time, Twilight.*—HERMAN, MANUEL, *and other dependants of* MANFRED.

HERMAN. 'Tis strange enough! night after night, for years,
He hath pursued long vigils in this tower,
Without a witness. I have been within it,—
So have we all been oft-times; but from it,
Or its contents, it were impossible
To draw conclusions absolute, of aught
His studies tend to. To be sure, there is
One chamber where none enter: I would give
The fee of what I have to come these three years,
To pore upon its mysteries.
MANUEL. 'Twere dangerous;
Content thyself with what thou know'st already.
HERMAN. Ah! Manuel! thou art elderly and wise,
And couldst say much; thou hast dwelt within the castle—
How many years is't?
MANUEL. Ere Count Manfred's birth,
I served his father, whom he nought resembles.
HERMAN. There be more sons in like predicament!
But wherein do they differ?
MANUEL. I speak not
Of features or of form, but mind and habits;
Count Sigismund was proud, but gay and free,—
A warrior and a reveller; he dwell not
With books and solitude, nor made the night
A gloomy vigil, but a festal time,
Merrier than day; he did not walk the rocks
And forests like a wolf, nor turn aside
From men and their delights.
HERMAN. Beshrew the hour,
But those were jocund times! I would that such
Would visit the old walls again; they look
As if they had forgotten them.
MANUEL. These walls
Must change their chieftain first. Oh! I have seen
Some strange things in them, Herman.
HERMAN. Come, be friendly;
Relate me some to while away our watch:
I've heard thee darkly speak of an event
Which happened hereabouts, by this same tower.
MANUEL. That was a night indeed! I do remember
'Twas twilight, as it may be now, and such
Another evening:—yon red cloud, which rests
On Eigher's pinnacle, so rested then,—
So like that it might be the same; the wind
Was faint and gusty, and the mountain snows
Began to glitter with the climbing moon;
Count Manfred was, as now, within his tower,—
How occupied, we knew not, but with him
The sole companion of his wanderings
And watchings—her, whom of all earthly things
That lived, the only thing he seemed to love,—
As he, indeed, by blood was bound to do,
The Lady Astarte, his—
Hush! who comes here?
[*Enter the* ABBOT.]
ABBOT. Where is your master?
HERMAN. Yonder in the tower.
ABBOT. I must speak with him.
MANUEL. 'Tis impossible;
He is most private, and must not be thus
Intruded on.
ABBOT. Upon myself I take
The forfeit of my fault, if fault there be—
But I must see him.
HERMAN. Thou hast seen him once
This eve already.
ABBOT. Herman! I command thee,
Knock, and apprize the Count of my approach.
HERMAN. We dare not.
ABBOT. Then it seems I must be herald
Of my own purpose.

**Sc. iii: 37. Eigher's pinnacle:** Mount Eiger is east of the Jungfrau.

MANUEL. Reverend father, stop—
I pray you pause.
ABBOT. Why so?
MANUEL. But step this way,
And I will tell you further. [*Exeunt.*]

### SCENE IV. *Interior of the Tower.—* MANFRED *alone.*

MANFRED. The stars are forth, the moon above the tops
Of the snow-shining mountains.—Beautiful!
I linger yet with Nature, for the Night
Hath been to me a more familiar face
Than that of man; and in her starry shade
Of dim and solitary loveliness,
I learned the language of another world.
I do remember me, that in my youth,
When I was wandering,—upon such a night
I stood within the Coliseum's wall,
'Midst the chief relics of almighty Rome;
The trees which grew along the broken arches
Waved dark in the blue midnight, and the stars
Shone through the rents of ruin; from afar
The watch-dog bayed beyond the Tiber; and
More near from out the Caesar's palace came
The owl's long cry, and, interruptedly,
Of distant sentinels the fitful song
Begun and died upon the gentle wind.
Some cypresses beyond the time-worn breach
Appeared to skirt the horizon, yet they stood
Within a bowshot. Where the Caesars dwelt,
And dwell the tuneless birds of night, amidst
A grove which springs through levelled battlements,
And twines its roots with the imperial hearths,
Ivy usurps the laurel's place of growth;—
But the gladiators' bloody Circus stands,
A noble wreck in ruinous perfection,
While Caesar's chambers, and the Augustan halls,
Grovel on earth in indistinct decay.—
And thou didst shine, thou rolling Moon, upon
All this, and cast a wide and tender light,
Which softened down the hoar austerity
Of rugged desolation, and filled up,
As 'twere anew, the gaps of centuries;
Leaving that beautiful which still was so,
And making that which was not—till the place
Became religion, and the heart ran o'er
With silent worship of the Great of old,—
The dead, but sceptred, Sovereigns, who still rule
Our spirits from their urns.
'Twas such a night!
'Tis strange that I recall it at this time;
But I have found our thoughts take wildest flight
Even at the moment when they should array
Themselves in pensive order.
[*Enter the* ABBOT.]
ABBOT. My good Lord!
I crave a second grace for this approach;
But yet let not my humble zeal offend
By its abruptness—all it hath of ill
Recoils on me; its good in the effect
May light upon your head—could I say *heart*—
Could I touch *that,* with words or prayers, I should
Recall a noble spirit which hath wandered,
But is not yet all lost.
MANFRED. Thou know'st me not;
My days are numbered, and my deeds recorded:
Retire, or 'twill be dangerous—Away!
ABBOT. Thou dost not mean to menace me?
MANFRED. Not I!
I simply tell thee peril is at hand,
And would preserve thee.
ABBOT. What dost thou mean?
MANFRED. Look there!
What dost thou see?
ABBOT. Nothing.
MANFRED. Look there, I say,
And steadfastly;—now tell me what thou see'st?
ABBOT. That which should shake me,—but I fear it not:
I see a dusk and awful figure rise,
Like an infernal god, from out the earth;
His face wrapt in a mantle, and his form
Robed as with angry clouds: he stands between
Thyself and me—but I do fear him not.
MANFRED. Thou hast no cause—he shall not harm thee—but
His sight may shock thine old limbs into palsy.
I say to thee—Retire!
ABBOT. And I reply—
Never—till I have battled with this fiend:—
What doth he here?
MANFRED. Why—aye—what doth he here?
I did not send for him,—he is unbidden.
ABBOT. Alas! lost Mortal! what with guests like these
Hast thou to do? I tremble for thy sake:
Why doth he gaze on thee, and thou on him?
Ah! he unveils his aspect: on his brow
The thunder-scars are graven; from his eye
Glares forth the immortality of Hell—
Avaunt!—
MANFRED. Pronounce—what is thy mission?
SPIRIT. Come!
ABBOT. What art thou, unknown being? answer!—speak!
SPIRIT. The genius of this mortal.—Come! 'tis time.
MANFRED. I am prepared for all things, but deny

The Power which summons me. Who sent thee here?
SPIRIT. Thou'lt know anon — Come! come!
MANFRED. I have commanded
Things of an essence greater far than thine,
And striven with thy masters. Get thee hence!
SPIRIT. Mortal! thine hour is come — Away! I say.
MANFRED. I knew, and know my hour is come, but not
To render up my soul to such as thee:
Away! I'll die as I have lived — alone.
SPIRIT. Then I must summon up my brethren. — Rise!

[*Other* SPIRITS *rise up.*]

ABBOT. Avaunt! ye evil ones! — Avaunt! I say, —
Ye have no power where Piety hath power,
And I do charge ye in the name —
SPIRIT. Old man!
We know ourselves, our mission and thine order;
Waste not thy holy words on idle uses —
It were in vain: this man is forfeited.
Once more — I summon him — Away! Away!
MANFRED. I do defy ye, — though I feel my soul
Is ebbing from me, yet I do defy ye;
Nor will I hence, while I have earthly breath
To breathe my scorn upon ye — earthly strength
To wrestle, though with spirits; what ye take
Shall be ta'en limb by limb.
SPIRIT. Reluctant mortal!
Is this the Magian who would so pervade
The world invisible, and make himself
Almost our equal? Can it be that thou
Art thus in love with life? the very life
Which made thee wretched?
MANFRED. Thou false fiend, thou liest!
My life is in its last hour, — *that* I know,
Nor would redeem a moment of that hour;
I do not combat against Death, but thee
And thy surrounding angels; my past power
Was purchased by no compact with thy crew,
But by superior science — penance, daring,
And length of watching, strength of mind, and skill
In knowledge of our Fathers — when the earth
Saw men and spirits walking side by side,
And gave ye no supremacy: I stand
Upon my strength — I do defy — deny —
Spurn back, and scorn ye! —
SPIRIT. But thy many crimes
Have made thee ——
MANFRED. What are they to such as thee?
Must crimes be punished but by other crimes,
And greater criminals? — Back to thy hell!
Thou hast no power upon me, *that* I feel;
Thou never shalt possess me, *that* I know:
What I have done is done; I bear within
A torture which could nothing gain from thine:
The Mind which is immortal makes itself
Requital for its good or evil thoughts, —
Is its own origin of ill and end —
And its own place and time: its innate sense,
When stripped of this mortality, derives
No colour from the fleeting things without,
But is absorbed in sufferance or in joy,
Born from the knowledge of its own desert.
*Thou* didst not tempt me, and thou couldst not tempt me;
I have not been thy dupe, nor am thy prey —
But was my own destroyer, and will be
My own hereafter. — Back, ye baffled fiends!
The hand of Death is on me — but not yours!

[*The Demons disappear.*]

ABBOT. Alas! how pale thou art — thy lips are white —
And thy breast heaves — and in thy gasping throat
The accents rattle: Give thy prayers to Heaven —
Pray — albeit but in thought, — but die not thus.
MANFRED. 'Tis over — my dull eyes can fix thee not;
But all things swim around me, and the earth
Heaves as it were beneath me. Fare thee well —
Give me thy hand.
ABBOT. Cold — cold — even to the heart —
But yet one prayer — Alas! how fares it with thee?
MANFRED. Old man! 'tis not so difficult to die.

[MANFRED *expires.*]

ABBOT. He's gone — his soul hath ta'en its earthless flight;
Whither? I dread to think — but he is gone.

# THE VISION OF JUDGMENT

*The Vision of Judgment* was written in Ravenna in the fall of 1821; Robert Southey's poem with the same title had been published in the spring of the same year. Byron's poem was refused by two publishers, Murray and Longman, and it finally appeared in the first issue of *The Liberal* in October, 1822, under the pseudonym "Quevedo Redivivus," i.e., Quevedo reborn, Quevedo (1580–1645) being a Spanish satirist who in 1635 published a number of "Visions," one called "A Vision in Jest to the Empire of Death." Three days after Byron's burial, John Hunt, Leigh Hunt's brother, as publisher of *The Liberal,* was prosecuted and fined £100 for publishing a poem "calculated to destroy the comfort and happiness of his present Majesty," i.e., George IV.

The immediate occasion for Byron's poem was not so much Southey's poem as his preface, which spoke of poets who produced "monstrous combinations of horrors and mockery, lewdness and impiety," referred to a "Satanic school" of poetry, and prophesied for Byron, without naming him directly, a bad time on his deathbed. Byron replied briefly in a note added to his play *The Two Foscari,* and Southey replied more personally in a letter to a periodical called the *Courier,* in which he called Byron, among many other things, a public pander. Of his epithet "Satanic school," he said: "I have sent a stone from my sling which has smitten their Goliath in the forehead. I have fastened his name upon the gibbet for reproach and ignominy as long as it shall endure." Southey then added, with the fatal arrogance of a doomed tragic hero: "When he attacks me again let it be in rhyme."

Byron's poem bears the subtitle "Suggested by the Composition So Entitled by the Author of 'Wat Tyler.'" Southey's *Wat Tyler* was an early poem on the leader of the fourteenth-century Peasants' Revolt, and it showed some liberal sympathies. The unauthorized publication of this poem in 1817 had been a source of acute embarrassment to Southey, and is the basis for Byron's attacks on him as an apostate and renegade. Byron's preface (not included in the original *Liberal* publication) reads in part: "If Mr. Southey had not rushed in where he had no business, and where he never was before, and never will be again, the following poem would not have been written. It is not impossible that it may be as good as his own, seeing that it cannot, by any species of stupidity, natural or acquired, be *worse*. The gross flattery, the dull impudence, the renegado intolerance, and impious cant, of the poem by the author of 'Wat Tyler,' are something so stupendous as to form the sublime of himself. . . . In this preface it has pleased the magnanimous Laureate to draw the picture of a supposed 'Satanic School,' the which he doth recommend to the notice of the legislature; thereby adding to his other laurels the ambition of those of an informer. . . . The way in which that poor insane creature, the Laureate, deals about his judgments in the next world, is like his own judgment in this. If it were not completely ludicrous, it would be something worse. . . ."

Southey's *Vision of Judgment* is written, like Longfellow's *Evangeline,* in dactylic hexameters (see lines 719–21 below), and Byron, however prejudiced, is not wholly wrong in ridiculing it as broken-winded in rhythm. Byron's poem is among other things a close and deadly parody of Southey's. Southey also introduces Wilkes and Junius as witnesses against King George's entry into heaven, though in his poem they are unable to say anything, and one of the King's "absolvers," as they are called, George Washington, has clearly contributed to Byron's portrait of Lucifer:

Thoughtful awhile he gazed; severe, but serene, was his aspect;
Calm, but stern; like one whom no compassion could weaken,
Neither could doubt deter, nor violent impulses alter;
Lord of his own resolves,—of his own heart absolute master.
Awful Spirit; his place was with ancient sages and heroes;
Fabius, Aristides, and Solon, and Epaminondas.

I

Saint Peter sat by the celestial gate:
  His keys were rusty, and the lock was dull,
So little trouble had been given of late;
  Not that the place by any means was full,
But since the Gallic era "eighty-eight"
  The Devils had ta'en a longer, stronger pull,
And "a pull altogether," as they say
At sea—which drew most souls another way.

II

The Angels all were singing out of tune,
  And hoarse with having little else to do,
Excepting to wind up the sun and moon,
  Or curb a runaway young star or two,
Or wild colt of a comet, which too soon
  Broke out of bounds o'er the ethereal blue,
Splitting some planet with its playful tail,
As boats are sometimes by a wanton whale.

III

The Guardian Seraphs had retired on high,
  Finding their charges past all care below;
Terrestrial business filled nought in the sky
  Save the Recording Angel's black bureau;
Who found, indeed, the facts to multiply
  With such rapidity of vice and woe,
That he had stripped off both his wings in quills,
And yet was in arrear of human ills.

IV

His business so augmented of late years,
  That he was forced, against his will, no doubt,

THE VISION OF JUDGMENT. 5. **"eighty-eight"**: taken as the opening year of the French Revolution, more usually dated from the fall of the Bastille on July 14, 1789.

(Just like those cherubs, earthly ministers,)
For some resource to turn himself about,
And claim the help of his celestial peers,
To aid him ere he should be quite worn out
By the increased demand for his remarks:
Six Angels and twelve Saints were named his clerks.

V

This was a handsome board — at least for Heaven;
And yet they had even then enough to do,
So many Conquerors' cars were daily driven,
So many kingdoms fitted up anew;
Each day, too, slew its thousands six or seven,
Till at the crowning carnage, Waterloo,
They threw their pens down in divine disgust —
The page was so besmeared with blood and dust.

VI

This by the way; 'tis not mine to record
What Angels shrink from: even the very Devil
On this occasion his own work abhorred,
So surfeited with the infernal revel:
Though he himself had sharpened every sword,
It almost quenched his innate thirst of evil.
(Here Satan's sole good work deserves insertion —
'Tis, that he has both Generals in reversion.)

VII

Let's skip a few short years of hollow peace,
Which peopled earth no better, Hell as wont,
And Heaven none — they form the tyrant's lease,
With nothing but new names subscribed upon't;
'Twill one day finish: meantime they increase,
"With seven heads and ten horns," and all in front,
Like Saint John's foretold beast; but ours are born
Less formidable in the head than horn.

VIII

In the first year of Freedom's second dawn
Died George the Third; although no tyrant, one
Who shielded tyrants, till each sense withdrawn
Left him nor mental nor external sun:
A better farmer ne'er brushed dew from lawn,
A worse king never left a realm undone!
He died — but left his subjects still behind,
One half as mad — and t'other no less blind.

IX

He died! his death made no great stir on earth:
His burial made some pomp; there was profusion
Of velvet — gilding — brass — and no great dearth
Of aught but tears — save those shed by collusion:
For these things may be bought at their true worth;
Of elegy there was the due infusion —
Bought also; and the torches, cloaks and banners,
Heralds, and relics of old Gothic manners,

X

Formed a sepulchral melodrame. Of all
The fools who flocked to swell or see the show,
Who cared about the corpse? The funeral
Made the attraction, and the black the woe.
There throbbed not there a thought which pierced the pall;
And when the gorgeous coffin was laid low.
It seemed the mockery of hell to fold
The rottenness of eighty years in gold.

XI

So mix his body with the dust! It might
Return to what it *must* far sooner, were
The natural compound left alone to fight
Its way back into earth, and fire, and air;
But the unnatural balsams merely blight
What Nature made him at his birth, as bare
As the mere million's base unmummied clay —
Yet all his spices but prolong decay.

XII

He's dead — and upper earth with him has done;
He's buried; save the undertaker's bill,
Or lapidary scrawl, the world is gone
For him, unless he left a German will:
But where's the proctor who will ask his son?
In whom his qualities are reigning still,
Except that household virtue, most uncommon,
Of constancy to a bad, ugly woman.

XIII

"God save the king!" It is a large economy
In God to save the like; but if he will
Be saving, all the better; for not one am I
Of those who think damnation better still:
I hardly know too if not quite alone am I
In this small hope of bettering future ill
By circumscribing, with some slight restriction,
The eternity of Hell's hot jurisdiction.

XIV

I know this is unpopular; I know
'Tis blasphemous; I know one may be damned

**48. reversion:** i.e., both Napoleon and Wellington belong to him. **55. foretold beast:** See Rev. 13:1. **57. freedom's . . . dawn:** the year 1820 was a year of great political unrest in southern Europe, including the beginning of the Greek revolt against Turkey.

**91. lapidary scrawl:** inscription on a tombstone. **93. proctor:** an official of the court of probate; there was a rumor that George IV had stolen his father's will, referred to also in *Don Juan*, Canto XI, st. 78. Or the reference may be to a similar rumor about George III's having stolen George II's will in 1760.

For hoping no one else may e'er be so;
I know my catechism; I know we're crammed
With the best doctrines till we quite o'erflow;
I know that all save England's Church have shammed,
And that the other twice two hundred churches
And synagogues have made a *damned* bad purchase.

XV

God help us all! God help me too! I am,
God knows, as helpless as the Devil can wish,
And not a whit more difficult to damn,
Than is to bring to land a late-hooked fish,
Or to the butcher to purvey the lamb;
Not that I'm fit for such a noble dish,
As one day will be that immortal fry
Of almost every body born to die.

XVI

Saint Peter sat by the celestial gate,
And nodded o'er his keys: when, lo! there came
A wondrous noise he had not heard of late —
A rushing sound of wind, and stream, and flame;
In short, a roar of things extremely great,
Which would have made aught save a Saint exclaim;
But he, with first a start and then a wink,
Said, "There's another star gone out, I think!"

XVII

But ere he could return to his repose,
A Cherub flapped his right wing o'er his eyes —
At which Saint Peter yawned, and rubbed his nose:
"Saint porter," said the angel, "prithee rise!"
Waving a goodly wing, which glowed, as glows
An earthly peacock's tail, with heavenly dyes:
To which the saint replied, "Well, what's the matter?
Is Lucifer come back with all this clatter?"

XVIII

"No," quoth the Cherub: "George the Third is dead."
"And who *is* George the Third?" replied the apostle:
"*What George? What Third?*" "The King of England," said
The angel. "Well! he won't find kings to jostle
Him on his way; but does he wear his head?
Because the last we saw here had a tustle,
And ne'er would have got into Heaven's good graces,
Had he not flung his head in all our faces.

XIX

"He was — if I remember — King of France;
That head of his, which could not keep a crown
On earth, yet ventured in my face to advance
A claim to those of martyrs — like my own:
If I had had my sword, as I had once
When I cut ears off, I had cut him down;
But having but my *keys,* and not my brand,
I only knocked his head from out his hand.

XX

"And then he set up such a headless howl,
That all the Saints came out and took him in;
And there he sits by Saint Paul, cheek by jowl;
That fellow Paul — the parvenù! The skin
Of Saint Bartholomew, which makes his cowl
In heaven, and upon earth redeemed his sin,
So as to make a martyr, never sped
Better than did this weak and wooden head.

XXI

"But had it come up here upon its shoulders,
There would have been a different tale to tell:
The fellow-feeling in the Saint's beholders
Seems to have acted on them like a spell;
And so this very foolish head Heaven solders
Back on its trunk: it may be very well,
And seems the custom here to overthrow
Whatever has been wisely done below."

XXII

The Angel answered, "Peter! do not pout:
The King who comes has head and all entire,
And never knew much what it was about —
He did as doth the puppet — by its wire,
And will be judged like all the rest, no doubt:
My business and your own is not to inquire
Into such matters, but to mind our cue —
Which is to act as we are bid to do."

XXIII

While thus they spake, the angelic caravan,
Arriving like a rush of mighty wind,
Cleaving the fields of space, as doth the swan
Some silver stream (say Ganges, Nile, or Inde,
Or Thames, or Tweed), and midst them an old man
With an old soul, and both extremely blind,
Halted before the gate, and, in his shroud,
Seated their fellow-traveller on a cloud.

**142. last . . . here:** Louis XVI of France, beheaded in 1793.

**150. cut . . . off:** See John 18:10. **156. parvenù:** Byron pretends that Peter still resents the authority of Paul, as a more recent convert in the Christian Church. **157. Bartholomew:** who according to legend was flayed alive in his martyrdom.

XXIV

But bringing up the rear of this bright host
A Spirit of a different aspect waved
His wings, like thunder-clouds above some coast
Whose barren beach with frequent wrecks is paved;
His brow was like the deep when tempest-tossed;
Fierce and unfathomable thoughts engraved
Eternal wrath on his immortal face,
And *where* he gazed a gloom pervaded space.

XXV

As he drew near, he gazed upon the gate
Ne'er to be entered more by him or Sin,
With such a glance of supernatural hate,
As made Saint Peter wish himself within;
He pottered with his keys at a great rate,
And sweated through his Apostolic skin:
Of course his perspiration was but ichor,
Or some such other spiritual liquor.

XXVI

The very Cherubs huddled all together,
Like birds when soars the falcon; and they felt
A tingling to the tip of every feather,
And formed a circle like Orion's belt
Around their poor old charge; who scarce knew whither
His guards had led him, though they gently dealt
With Royal Manes (for by many stories,
And true, we learn the Angels all are Tories).

XXVII

As things were in this posture, the gate flew
Asunder, and the flashing of its hinges
Flung over space an universal hue
Of many-coloured flame, until its tinges
Reached even our speck of earth, and made a new
Aurora borealis spread its fringes
O'er the North Pole; the same seen, when ice-bound,
By Captain Parry's crew, in "Melville's Sound."

XXVIII

And from the gate thrown open issued beaming
A beautiful and mighty Thing of Light,
Radiant with glory, like a banner streaming
Victorious from some world-o'erthrowing fight:
My poor comparisons must needs be teeming
With earthly likenesses, for here the night
Of clay obscures our best conceptions, saving
Johanna Southcote, or Bob Southey raving.

XXIX

'Twas the Archangel Michael: all men know
The make of Angels and Archangels, since
There's scarce a scribbler has not one to show,
From the fiends' leader to the Angels' Prince.
There also are some altar-pieces, though
I really can't say that they much evince
One's inner notions of immortal spirits;
But let the connoisseurs explain *their* merits.

XXX

Michael flew forth in glory and in good;
A goodly work of him from whom all Glory
And Good arise; the portal past — he stood;
Before him the young Cherubs and Saints hoary —
(I say *young,* begging to be understood
By looks, not years; and should be very sorry
To state, they were not older than St. Peter,
But merely that they seemed a little sweeter).

XXXI

The Cherubs and the Saints bowed down before
That arch-angelic Hierarch, the first
Of Essences angelical who wore
The aspect of a god; but this ne'er nursed
Pride in his heavenly bosom, in whose core
No thought, save for his Maker's service, durst
Intrude — however glorified and high,
He knew him but the Viceroy of the sky.

XXXII

He and the sombre, silent Spirit met —
They knew each other both for good and ill;
Such was their power, that neither could forget
His former friend and future foe; but still
There was a high, immortal, proud regret
In either's eye, as if 'twere less their will
Than destiny to make the eternal years
Their date of war, and their "Champ Clos" the spheres.

XXXIII

But here they were in neutral space: we know
From Job, that Satan hath the power to pay
A heavenly visit thrice a-year or so;
And that the "Sons of God," like those of clay,
Must keep him company; and he might show

**207. Manes:** spirits. **216. Parry's crew:** Captain Edward Parry had attempted to discover a Northwest Passage in 1819–20 and had written an account of the voyage, from which Byron quotes in a note at this point. **224. Johanna Southcote:** leader of a fanatical millennial sect who announced in 1814, at the age of sixty-four, that she was virginally pregnant with a new Messiah, whom she called "Shiloh." Her influence waned when her pregnancy turned out to be dropsy, of which she died; see *DJ*, l. 236, p. 233, below. **256. "Champ Clos":** enclosed field of a tournament. **258. Job:** See Job 1, 2.

From the same book, in how polite a way
The dialogue is held between the Powers
Of Good and Evil — but 'twould take up hours.

XXXIV

And this is not a theologic tract,
To prove with Hebrew and with Arabic,
If Job be allegory or a fact,
But a true narrative; and thus I pick
From out the whole but such and such an act
As sets aside the slightest thought of trick.
'Tis every tittle true, beyond suspicion,
And accurate as any other vision.

XXXV

The spirits were in neutral space, before
The gate of Heaven; like eastern thresholds is
The place where Death's grand cause is argued o'er
And souls despatched to that world or to this;
And therefore Michael and the other wore
A civil aspect: though they did not kiss,
Yet still between his Darkness and his Brightness
There passed a mutual glance of great politeness.

XXXVI

The Archangel bowed, not like a modern beau,
But with a graceful oriental bend,
Pressing one radiant arm just where below
The heart in good men is supposed to tend;
He turned as to an equal, not too low,
But kindly; Satan met his ancient friend
With more hauteur, as might an old Castilian
Poor Noble meet a mushroom rich civilian.

XXXVII

He merely bent his diabolic brow
An instant; and then raising it, he stood
In act to assert his right or wrong, and show
Cause why King George by no means could or should
Make out a case to be exempt from woe
Eternal, more than other kings, endued
With better sense and hearts, whom History mentions,
Who long have "paved Hell with their good intentions."

XXXVIII

Michael began: "What wouldst thou with this man,
Now dead, and brought before the Lord? What ill
Hath he wrought since his mortal race began,
That thou canst claim him? Speak! and do thy will,
If it be just: if in this earthly span
He hath been greatly failing to fulfil
His duties as a king and mortal, say,
And he is thine; if not — let him have way."

XXXIX

"Michael!" replied the Prince of Air, "even here
Before the gate of Him thou servest, must
I claim my subject: and will make appear
That as he was my worshipper in dust,
So shall he be in spirit, although dear
To thee and thine, because nor wine nor lust
Were of his weaknesses; yet on the throne
He reigned o'er millions to serve me alone.

XL

"Look to *our* earth, or rather *mine;* it was,
*Once, more* thy master's: but I triumph not
In this poor planet's conquest; nor, alas!
Need he thou servest envy me my lot:
With all the myriads of bright worlds which pass
In worship round him, he may have forgot
Yon weak creation of such paltry things:
I think few worth damnation save their kings,

XLI

"And these but as a kind of quit-rent, to
Assert my right as Lord: and even had
I such an inclination, 'twere (as you
Well know) superfluous; they are grown so bad,
That Hell has nothing better left to do
Than leave them to themselves: so much more mad
And evil by their own internal curse,
Heaven cannot make them better, nor I worse.

XLII

"Look to the earth, I said, and say again:
When this old, blind, mad, helpless, weak, poor worm
Began in youth's first bloom and flush to reign,
The world and he both wore a different form,
And much of earth and all the watery plain
Of Ocean called him king: through many a storm
His isles had floated on the abyss of Time;
For the rough virtues chose them for their clime.

XLIII

"He came to his sceptre young; he leaves it old:
Look to the state in which he found his realm,
And left it; and his annals too behold,
How to a minion first he gave the helm;

**305. Prince of Air**: Cf. Eph. 2:2. **330. poor worm**: With the epithets given George III here cf. Shelley, "England in 1819."

How grew upon his heart a thirst for gold,
  The beggar's vice, which can but overwhelm
The meanest hearts; and for the rest, but glance
Thine eye along America and France.

XLIV

" 'Tis true, he was a tool from first to last
  (I have the workmen safe); but as a tool
So let him be consumed. From out the past
  Of ages, since mankind have known the rule
Of monarchs — from the bloody rolls amassed
  Of Sin and Slaughter — from the Caesars' school,
Take the worst pupil; and produce a reign
More drenched with gore, more cumbered with the slain.

XLV

" He ever warred with freedom and the free:
  Nations as men, home subjects, foreign foes,
So that they uttered the word 'Liberty!'
  Found George the Third their first opponent. Whose
History was ever stained as his will be
  With national and individual woes?
I grant his household abstinence; I grant
His neutral virtues, which most monarchs want;

XLVI

" I know he was a constant consort; own
  He was a decent sire, and middling lord.
All this is much, and most upon a throne;
  As temperance, if at Apicius' board,
Is more than at an anchorite's supper shown.
  I grant him all the kindest can accord;
And this was well for him, but not for those
Millions who found him what Oppression chose.

XLVII

" The New World shook him off; the Old yet groans
  Beneath what he and his prepared, if not
Completed: he leaves heirs on many thrones
  To all his vices, without what begot
Compassion for him — his tame virtues; drones
  Who sleep, or despots who have now forgot
A lesson which shall be retaught them, wake
Upon the thrones of earth; but let them quake!

XLVIII

" Five millions of the primitive, who hold
  The faith which makes ye great on earth, implored
A *part* of that vast *all* they held of old, —
  Freedom to worship — not alone your Lord,
Michael, but you, and you, Saint Peter! Cold
  Must be your souls, if you have not abhorred
The foe to Catholic participation
In all the license of a Christian nation.

XLIX

" True! he allowed them to pray God; but as
  A consequence of prayer, refused the law
Which would have placed them upon the same base
  With those who did not hold the Saints in awe."
But here Saint Peter started from his place
  And cried, " You may the prisoner withdraw:
Ere Heaven shall ope her portals to this Guelph,
While I am guard, may I be damned myself!

L

" Sooner will I with Cerberus exchange
  My office (and *his* is no sinecure)
Than see this royal Bedlam-bigot range
  The azure fields of Heaven, of that be sure!"
" Saint!" replied Satan, " you do well to avenge
  The wrongs he made your satellites endure;
And if to this exchange you should be given,
I'll try to coax *our* Cerberus up to Heaven!"

LI

Here Michael interposed: " Good Saint! and Devil!
  Pray, not so fast; you both outrun discretion.
Saint Peter! you were wont to be more civil:
  Satan! excuse this warmth of his expression,
And condescension to the vulgar's level:
  Even Saints sometimes forget themselves in session.
Have you got more to say?" — " No." — " If you please,
I'll trouble you to call your witnesses."

LII

Then Satan turned and waved his swarthy hand,
  Which stirred with its electric qualities
Clouds farther off than we can understand,
  Although we find him sometimes in our skies;
Infernal thunder shook both sea and land
  In all the planets — and Hell's batteries
Let off the artillery, which Milton mentions
As one of Satan's most sublime inventions.

**364. Apicius' board:** Apicius was a gourmet of the time of Tiberius, who hanged himself when he found he had spent a large part of his fortune on his luxuries. **377. five millions:** the Roman Catholics in Ireland, whose cause Byron had supported in the House of Lords. **391. Guelph:** the family name of the House of Hanover, to which George III belonged; also the name of the party which in the Middle Ages supported the temporal supremacy of the Pope—the exact opposite of what George III stood for. **393. Cerberus:** the three-headed dog who guarded the gate of hell. **415. Milton:** See *Paradise Lost,* VI.484 ff.

LIII

This was a signal unto such damned souls
  As have the privilege of their damnation
Extended far beyond the mere controls
  Of worlds past, present, or to come; no station
Is theirs particularly in the rolls
  Of Hell assigned; but where their inclination
Or business carries them in search of game,
They may range freely — being damned the same.

LIV

They are proud of this — as very well they may,
  It being a sort of knighthood, or gilt key
Stuck in their loins; or like to an " entré "
  Up the back stairs, or such free-masonry.
I borrow my comparisons from clay,
  Being clay myself. Let not those spirits be
Offended with such base low likenesses;
We know their posts are nobler far than these.

LV

When the great signal ran from Heaven to Hell —
  About ten million times the distance reckoned
From our sun to its earth, as we can tell
  How much time it takes up, even to a second,
For every ray that travels to dispel
  The fogs of London, through which, dimly beaconed,
The weathercocks are gilt some thrice a year,
If that the *summer* is not too severe:

LVI

I say that I can tell — 'twas half a minute;
  I know the solar beams take up more time
Ere, packed up for their journey, they begin it;
  But then their Telegraph is less sublime,
And if they ran a race, they would not win it
  'Gainst Satan's couriers bound for their own clime.
The sun takes up some years for every ray
To reach its goal — the Devil not half a day.

LVII

Upon the verge of space, about the size
  Of half-a-crown, a little speck appeared
(I've seen a something like it in the skies
  In the Aegean, ere a squall); it neared,
And, growing bigger, took another guise;
  Like an aërial ship it tacked, and steered,
Or *was* steered (I am doubtful of the grammar
Of the last phrase, which makes the stanza stammer;

LVIII

But take your choice): and then it grew a cloud;
  And so it was — a cloud of witnesses.
But such a cloud! No land ere saw a crowd
  Of locusts numerous as the heavens saw these;
They shadowed with their myriads Space; their loud
  And varied cries were like those of wild geese,
(If nations may be likened to a goose),
And realised the phrase of " Hell broke loose."

LIX

Here crashed a sturdy oath of stout John Bull,
  Who damned away his eyes as heretofore:
There Paddy brogued " By Jasus! " — " What's your wull? "
  The temperate Scot exclaimed: the French ghost swore
In certain terms I shan't translate in full,
  As the first coachman will; and 'midst the war,
The voice of Jonathan was heard to express,
" *Our* President is going to war, I guess."

LX

Besides there were the Spaniard, Dutch, and Dane;
  In short, an universal shoal of shades
From Otaheite's isle to Salisbury Plain,
  Of all climes and professions, years and trades,
Ready to swear against the good king's reign,
  Bitter as clubs in cards are against spades:
All summoned by this grand " subpoena," to
Try if kings mayn't be damned like me or you.

LXI

When Michael saw this host, he first grew pale,
  As Angels can; next, like Italian twilight,
He turned all colours — as a peacock's tail,
  Or sunset streaming through a Gothic skylight
In some old abbey, or a trout not stale,
  Or distant lightning on the horizon *by* night,
Or a fresh rainbow, or a grand review
Of thirty regiments in red, green, and blue.

LXII

Then he addressed himself to Satan: " Why —
  My good old friend, for such I deem you, though
Our different parties make us fight so shy,
  I ne'er mistake you for a *personal* foe;
Our difference is *political*, and I
  Trust that, whatever may occur below,

**426. gilt key:** a gold key hanging below the edge of a coat is the insignia of a lord chamberlain.

**458. cloud of witnesses:** the phrase is Biblical; see Heb. 12:1. **464. Hell . . . loose:** See *Paradise Lost,* IV.918. **475. Otaheite's isle:** an island in the South Seas, prominent during the "noble savage" craze of the late eighteenth century.

You know my great respect for you: and this
Makes me regret whate'er you do amiss —

LXIII

" Why, my dear Lucifer, would you abuse
  My call for witnesses? I did not mean
That you should half of Earth and Hell produce;
  'Tis even superfluous, since two honest, clean,
True testimonies are enough: we lose
  Our Time, nay, our Eternity, between
The accusation and defence: if we
Hear both, 'twill stretch our immortality."

LXIV

Satan replied, " To me the matter is
  Indifferent, in a personal point of view:
I can have fifty better souls than this
  With far less trouble than we have gone through
Already; and I merely argued his
  Late Majesty of Britain's case with you
Upon a point of form: you may dispose
Of him; I've kings enough below, God knows! "

LXV

Thus spoke the Demon (late called " multi-faced "
  By multo-scribbling Southey). " Then we'll call
One or two persons of the myriads placed
  Around our congress, and dispense with all
The rest," quoth Michael: " Who may be so graced
  As to speak first? there's choice enough — who shall
It be? " Then Satan answered, " There are many;
But you may choose Jack Wilkes as well as any."

LXVI

A merry, cock-eyed, curious-looking Sprite
  Upon the instant started from the throng,
Dressed in a fashion now forgotten quite;
  For all the fashions of the flesh stick long
By people in the next world; where unite
  All the costumes since Adam's, right or wrong,
From Eve's fig-leaf down to the petticoat,
Almost as scanty, of days less remote.

LXVII

The Spirit looked around upon the crowds
  Assembled, and exclaimed, " My friends of all
The spheres, we shall catch cold amongst these clouds;

**520. Wilkes**: John Wilkes (1727–97), a sharp critic of George III and his ministers, elected MP three times for Middlesex, his election being arbitrarily annulled each time, but who finally entered Parliament without opposition in 1774 (hence l. 557). His victory ensured the right of free elections, but his interest in pornography and his membership in the notorious "Hellfire Club" helped to make him a symbol of the depravity of opponents of Toryism.

  So let's to business: why this general call?
If those are freeholders I see in shrouds,
  And 'tis for an election that they bawl,
Behold a candidate with unturned coat!
Saint Peter, may I count upon your vote? "

LXVIII

" Sir," replied Michael, " you mistake; these things
  Are of a former life, and what we do
Above is more august; to judge of kings
  Is the tribunal met: so now you know."
" Then I presume those gentlemen with wings,"
  Said Wilkes, " are Cherubs; and that soul below
Looks much like George the Third, but to my mind
A good deal older — bless me! is he blind? "

LXIX

" He is what you behold him, and his doom
  Depends upon his deeds," the Angel said;
" If you have aught to arraign in him, the tomb
  Gives license to the humblest beggar's head
To lift itself against the loftiest." — " Some,"
  Said Wilkes, " don't wait to see them laid in lead,
For such a liberty — and I, for one,
Have told them what I thought beneath the sun."

LXX

" *Above* the sun repeat, then, what thou hast
  To urge against him," said the Archangel. " Why,"
Replied the Spirit, " since old scores are past,
  Must I turn evidence? In faith, not I.
Besides, I beat him hollow at the last,
  With all his Lords and Commons: in the sky
I don't like ripping up old stories, since
His conduct was but natural in a prince.

LXXI

" Foolish, no doubt, and wicked, to oppress
  A poor unlucky devil without a shilling;
But then I blame the man himself much less
  Than Bute and Grafton, and shall be unwilling
To see him punished here for their excess,
  Since they were both damned long ago, and still in
Their place below: for me, I have forgiven,
And vote his *habeas corpus* into Heaven."

LXXII

" Wilkes," said the Devil, " I understand all this;
  You turned to half a courtier ere you died,
And seem to think it would not be amiss
  To grow a whole one on the other side
Of Charon's ferry; you forget that *his*

**564. Bute and Grafton**: early ministers of George III.

Reign is concluded; whatsoe'er betide,
He won't be sovereign more: you've lost your labour,
For at the best he will but be your neighbour.

LXXIII

"However, I knew what to think of it,
When I beheld you in your jesting way,
Flitting and whispering round about the spit
Where Belial, upon duty for the day,
With Fox's lard was basting William Pitt,
His pupil; I knew what to think, I say:
That fellow even in Hell breeds farther ills;
I'll have him *gagged* — 'twas one of his own Bills.

LXXIV

"Call Junius!" From the crowd a shadow stalked,
And at the name there was a general squeeze,
So that the very ghosts no longer walked
In comfort, at their own aërial ease,
But were all rammed, and jammed (but to be balked,
As we shall see), and jostled hands and knees,
Like wind compressed and pent within a bladder,
Or like a human colic, which is sadder.

LXXV

The shadow came — a tall, thin, grey-haired figure,
That looked as it had been a shade on earth;
Quick in its motions, with an air of vigour,
But nought to mark its breeding or its birth;
Now it waxed little, then again grew bigger,
With now an air of gloom, or savage mirth;
But as you gazed upon its features, they
Changed every instant — to *what,* none could say.

LXXVI

The more intently the ghosts gazed, the less
Could they distinguish whose the features were;
The Devil himself seemed puzzled even to guess;
They varied like a dream — now here, now there;
And several people swore from out the press,
They knew him perfectly; and one could swear
He was his father; upon which another
Was sure he was his mother's cousin's brother:

LXXVII

Another, that he was a duke, or knight,
An orator, a lawyer, or a priest,
A nabob, a man-midwife; but the wight
Mysterious changed his countenance at least
As oft as they their minds: though in full sight
He stood, the puzzle only was increased;
The man was a phantasmagoria in
Himself — he was so volatile and thin.

LXXVIII

The moment that you had pronounced him *one,*
Presto! his face changed, and he was another;
And when that change was hardly well put on,
It varied, till I don't think his own mother
(If that he had a mother) would her son
Have known, he shifted so from one to t'other;
Till guessing from a pleasure grew a task,
At this epistolary "Iron Mask."

LXXIX

For sometimes he like Cerberus would seem —
"Three gentlemen at once" (as sagely says
Good Mrs. Malaprop); then you might deem
That he was not even *one;* now many rays
Were flashing round him; and now a thick steam
Hid him from sight — like fogs on London days:
Now Burke, now Tooke, he grew to people's fancies,
And certes often like Sir Philip Francis.

LXXX

I've an hypothesis — 'tis quite my own;
I never let it out till now, for fear
Of doing people harm about the throne,
And injuring some minister or peer,
On whom the stigma might perhaps be blown;
It is — my gentle public, lend thine ear!
'Tis, that what Junius we are wont to call,
Was *really* — *truly* — nobody at all.

LXXXI

I don't see wherefore letters should not be
Written without hands, since we daily view
Them written without heads; and books, we see,
Are filled as well without the latter too:
And really till we fix on somebody
For certain sure to claim them as his due,
Their author, like the Niger's mouth, will bother
The world to say if *there* be mouth or author.

**581. Fox's . . . Pitt:** Charles James Fox and William Pitt are both treated by Byron as renegade Whigs. Pitt, while Prime Minister, passed in 1795 a bill restricting freedom of speech and the press, known as the "gagging bill" (l. 584). Fox's corpulence suggests the word "lard." **585. Junius:** the pseudonym of an unknown author of a series of letters vigorously attacking George III and his ministers, which appeared in the *Public Advertiser* from 1769 to 1771. The authorship is still uncertain, but is often assigned to Sir Philip Francis (l. 632).

**624. Iron Mask:** The "Man in the Iron Mask" was a prisoner confined in the Bastille in the reign of Louis XIV; his identity has never been fully established. **627. Mrs. Malaprop:** The character in Sheridan's *School for Scandal* who has given the word "malapropism" to the language. **647. Niger's mouth:** referring to recent explorations in what is now Nigeria by Mungo Park.

LXXXII

"And who and what art thou?" the Archangel said.
"For *that* you may consult my title-page,"
Replied this mighty shadow of a shade:
"If I have kept my secret half an age,
I scarce shall tell it now." — "Canst thou upbraid,"
Continued Michael, "George Rex, or allege
Aught further?" Junius answered, "You had better
First ask him for *his* answer to my letter:

LXXXIII

"My charges upon record will outlast
The brass of both his epitaph and tomb."
"Repent'st thou not," said Michael, "of some past
Exaggeration? something which may doom
Thyself if false, as him if true? Thou wast
Too bitter — is it not so? — in thy gloom
Of passion?" — "Passion!" cried the phantom dim,
"I loved my country, and I hated him.

LXXXIV

"What I have written, I have written: let
The rest be on his head or mine!" So spoke
Old "*Nominis Umbra*"; and while speaking yet,
Away he melted in celestial smoke.
Then Satan said to Michael, "Don't forget
To call George Washington, and John Horne Tooke,
And Franklin;" — but at this time there was heard
A cry for room, though not a phantom stirred.

LXXXV

At length with jostling, elbowing, and the aid
Of Cherubim appointed to that post,
The devil Asmodeus to the circle made
His way, and looked as if his journey cost
Some trouble. When his burden down he laid,
"What's this?" cried Michael; "why, 'tis not a ghost?"
"I know it," quoth the Incubus; "but he
Shall be one, if you leave the affair to me.

LXXXVI

"Confound the renegado! I have sprained
My left wing, he's so heavy; one would think
Some of his works about his neck were chained.
But to the point; while hovering o'er the brink
Of Skiddaw (where as usual it still rained),
I saw a taper, far below me, wink,
And stooping, caught this fellow at a libel —
No less on History — than the Holy Bible.

LXXXVII

"The former is the Devil's scripture, and
The latter yours, good Michael: so the affair
Belongs to all of us, you understand.
I snatched him up just as you see him there,
And brought him off for sentence out of hand:
I've scarcely been ten minutes in the air —
At least a quarter it can hardly be:
I dare say that his wife is still at tea."

LXXXVIII

Here Satan said, "I know this man of old,
And have expected him for some time here;
A sillier fellow you will scarce behold,
Or more conceited in his petty sphere:
But surely it was not worth while to fold
Such trash below your wing, Asmodeus dear:
We had the poor wretch safe (without being bored
With carriage) coming of his own accord.

LXXXIX

"But since he's here, let's see what he has done."
"Done!" cried Asmodeus, "he anticipates
The very business you are now upon,
And scribbles as if head clerk to the Fates.
Who knows to what his ribaldry may run,
When such an ass as this, like Balaam's, prates?
"Let's hear," quoth Michael, "what he has to say:
You know we're bound to that in every way."

XC

Now the Bard, glad to get an audience, which
By no means often was his case below,
Began to cough, and hawk, and hem, and pitch
His voice into that awful note of woe
To all unhappy hearers within reach
Of poets when the tide of rhyme's in flow;
But stuck fast with his first hexameter,
Not one of all whose gouty feet would stir.

XCI

But ere the spavined dactyls could be spurred
Into recitative, in great dismay
Both Cherubim and Seraphim were heard
To murmur loudly through their long array;
And Michael rose ere he could get a word
Of all his foundered verses under way,

667. **"*Nominis Umbra*"**: "shadow of a name," part of the motto of Junius. 670. **Tooke**: a supporter of Wilkes, fined and imprisoned for sedition, and once tried, though acquitted, for high treason. He was also a student of Gothic and Anglo-Saxon. 675. **Asmodeus**: a devil mentioned in the Book of Tobit (see the Apocrypha) and in Le Sage's *Diable Boiteux* (1707).

685. **Skiddaw**: a mountain in the Lake Country, near where Southey lived. 710. **Balaam's**: See Num. 22:28.

And cried, "For God's sake stop, my friend! 'twere best —
*'Non Di, non homines'* — you know the rest."

XCII

A general bustle spread throughout the throng,
Which seemed to hold all verse in detestation;
The Angels had of course enough of song
When upon service; and the generation
Of ghosts had heard too much in life, not long
Before, to profit by a new occasion:
The Monarch, mute till then, exclaimed, "What! what!
*Pye* come again? No more — no more of that!"

XCIII

The tumult grew; an universal cough
Convulsed the skies, as during a debate,
When Castlereagh has been up long enough
(Before he was first minister of state,
I mean — the *slaves hear now*); some cried "Off, off!"
As at a farce; till, grown quite desperate,
The Bard Saint Peter prayed to interpose
(Himself an author) only for his prose.

XCIV

The varlet was not an ill-favoured knave;
A good deal like a vulture in the face,
With a hook nose and a hawk's eye, which gave
A smart and sharper-looking sort of grace
To his whole aspect, which, though rather grave,
Was by no means so ugly as his case;
But that, indeed, was hopeless as can be,
Quite a poetic felony *"de se."*

XCV

Then Michael blew his trump, and stilled the noise
With one still greater, as is yet the mode
On earth besides; except some grumbling voice,
Which now and then will make a slight inroad
Upon decorous silence, few will twice
Lift up their lungs when fairly overcrowed
And now the Bard could plead his own bad cause,
With all the attitudes of self-applause.

XCVI

He said — (I only give the heads) — he said,
He meant no harm in scribbling; 'twas his way
Upon all topics; 'twas, besides, his bread,
Of which he buttered both sides; 'twould delay
Too long the assembly (he was pleased to dread),
And take up rather more time than a day,
To name his works — he would but cite a few —
"Wat Tyler" — "Rhymes on Blenheim" — "Waterloo."

XCVII

He had written praises of a Regicide;
He had written praises of all kings whatever;
He had written for republics far and wide,
And then against them bitterer than ever;
For pantisocracy he once had cried
Aloud, a scheme less moral than 'twas clever;
Then grew a hearty anti-jacobin —
Had turned his coat — and would have turned his skin.

XCVIII

He had sung against all battles, and again
In their high praise and glory; he had called
Reviewing "the ungentle craft," and then
Became as base a critic as e'er crawled —
Fed, paid, and pampered by the very men
By whom his muse and morals had been mauled:
He had written much blank verse, and blanker prose,
And more of both than any body knows.

XCIX

He had written Wesley's life: — here turning round
To Satan, "Sir, I'm ready to write yours,
In two octavo volumes, nicely bound,
With notes and preface, all that most allures
The pious purchaser; and there's no ground
For fear, for I can choose my own reviewers:
So let me have the proper documents,
That I may add you to my other saints."

C

Satan bowed, and was silent. "Well, if you,
With amiable modesty, decline

**728. *'Non . . . homines'*:** part of a quotation from Horace's *Ars Poetica*, which states that "neither gods nor men" can endure a mediocre poet. **736. *Pye:*** James Pye (1745–1813), known as "Poetical Pye," was Southey's predecessor in the Laureateship, and one of the worst poets to hold even that office. Byron imitates George III's famous stammer. **745. not . . . knave:** a letter of Byron's to Thomas Moore, written in 1813, calls Southey "the best-looking bard I have seen for some time. To have that poet's head and shoulders, I would almost have written his Sapphics." **752. felony *"de se"*:** suicide.

**768. Blenheim:** Southey's "Battle of Blenheim" (1798) is one of his best-known poems; *The Poet's Pilgrimage to Waterloo* (1816), in two parts and eight long sections, is not so well known. **769. Regicide:** Henry Marten, one of the judges at Charles I's trial in 1649, imprisoned from the Restoration in 1660 till his death in 1680 in Chepstow Castle. An early poem of Southey's on his imprisonment was not included in Southey's collected works. **773. pantisocracy:** Southey's early plan with Coleridge to found an ideal community on the banks of the Susquehanna; see p. 109, above. **779. "ungentle craft":** in his life of the poet Kirke White (1808).

My offer, what says Michael? There are few
  Whose memoirs could be rendered more divine.
Mine is a pen of all work; not so new
  As it was once, but I would make you shine
Like your own trumpet. By the way, my own
Has more of brass in it, and is as well blown.

CI

" But talking about trumpets, here's my 'Vision' !
  Now you shall judge, all people — yes — you shall
Judge with my judgment! and by my decision
  Be guided who shall enter heaven or fall.
I settle all these things by intuition,
  Times present, past, to come — Heaven — Hell — and all,
Like King Alfonso. When I thus see double,
I save the Deity some worlds of trouble."

CII

He ceased, and drew forth an MS.; and no
  Persuasion on the part of Devils, Saints,
Or Angels, now could stop the torrent; so
  He read the first three lines of the contents;
But at the fourth, the whole spiritual show
  Had vanished, with variety of scents,
Ambrosial and sulphureous, as they sprang,
Like lightning, off from his " melodious twang."

CIII

Those grand heroics acted as a spell;
  The Angels stopped their ears and plied their pinions;
The Devils ran howling, deafened, down to Hell;
  The ghosts fled, gibbering, for their own dominions —
(For 'tis not yet decided where they dwell,
  And I leave every man to his opinions);
Michael took refuge in his trump — but, lo!
His teeth were set on edge, he could not blow!

CIV

Saint Peter, who has hitherto been known
  For an impetuous saint, upraised his keys,
And at the fifth line knocked the poet down;
  Who fell like Phaeton, but more at ease,
Into his lake, for there he did not drown;
  A different web being by the Destinies
Woven for the Laureate's final wreath, whene'er
Reform shall happen either here or there.

CV

He first sank to the bottom — like his works,
  But soon rose to the surface — like himself;
For all corrupted things are buoyed like corks,
  By their own rottenness, light as an elf,
Or wisp that flits o'er a morass: he lurks,
  It may be, still, like dull books on a shelf,
In his own den, to scrawl some " Life " or " Vision,"
As Welborn says — " the Devil turned precisian."

CVI

As for the rest, to come to the conclusion
  Of this true dream, the telescope is gone
Which kept my optics free from all delusion,
  And showed me what I in my turn have shown;
All I saw farther, in the last confusion,
  Was, that King George slipped into Heaven for one;
And when the tumult dwindled to a calm,
I left him practising the hundredth psalm.

**807. King Alfonso**: "Alfonso, speaking of the Ptolomean system, said that 'had he been consulted at the creation of the world, he would have spared the Maker some absurdities' " [B]. The reference is to Alphonso X (1252–81), King of Castile; the story is probably misunderstood. **816. "melodious twang"**: "See Aubrey's account of the apparition which disappeared 'with a curious perfume, and a *most melodious twang*' " [B]. The story is in Aubrey's *Miscellanies upon Various Subjects* (1696); Byron got it from Scott's *Antiquary*, ch. ix.

**828. Phaeton**: the son of Apollo who failed to drive his father's chariot of the sun across the sky. **835. corrupted things**: "A drowned body lies at the bottom till rotten; it then floats, as most people know" [B]. **840. precisian**: Puritan. The reference is to Massinger's play *A New Way to Pay Old Debts* (1633), of which Welborn is the hero.

# DON JUAN

The first hint that Byron was working on *Don Juan* is in a letter to John Murray, dated July 10, 1818, where he says that he has begun a "ludicrous" story in the style of *Beppo*. With his usual amazing facility he completed the first canto in September, accompanying it with a mock dedication to Southey, which contains one of his most violent assaults on that poet, along with some equally bitter reflections on "the intellectual eunuch Castlereagh." The professed reason for the attack on Southey was the malicious gossip that had been allegedly spread by Southey about the Shelley-Byron menage in Switzerland, or, as Byron said in a letter to Hobhouse, "On his return from Switzerland, two years ago, [Southey] said that Shelley and I 'had formed a League of Incest, and practised our precepts.'" The second canto was finished in January, 1819.

It is difficult for us to understand today how passionately sincere Byron's best friends, Kinnaird, Hobhouse, and John Murray, were in believing that *Don Juan* was a disgrace to Byron's reputation. They could not understand Byron's assertion that "it is the most moral of poems," nor the seriousness of his fight to maintain its integrity. "You shan't make *Canticles* of My Cantos," said Byron in response to pleas to bowdlerize the poem, and again: "You have so many '*divine*' poems, is it nothing to have written a *Human* one?" Eventually Murray, with great hesitation, published the first two cantos on July 15, 1819—anonymously, with only the printer's name on the title-page, and with the Southey "dedication" withdrawn.

Byron was chagrined by the unfavorable reaction, but went on with the poem, saying to Murray that "the outcry has not frightened but it has *hurt* me." Murray had paid Byron fifteen hundred guineas for the first two cantos (along with the "Ode on Venice"), and twenty-five hundred for the next three along with three of Byron's plays. But his disapproval of the poem was so marked that Byron eventually gave the sixth, seventh and eighth cantos to John Hunt, Leigh Hunt's brother, which were published with a separate prose preface. Before the middle of 1823 he had finished sixteen cantos, and took the first fourteen stanzas of a seventeenth to Greece with him, hoping to be able to continue it there. But nothing was added to the poem in Greece, and the final fragment, left among his private papers, was not published until 1903.

After Don Juan's misadventure in the first canto, he was sent abroad, but his vessel was shipwrecked and the survivors suffered great hardships, only partly alleviated by eating first Juan's spaniel and then his tutor. Juan himself however refused to "dine with them on his pastor and his master." Juan was then cast up on a Greek island and tenderly nursed by Haidée, the lovely daughter of a Greek pirate named Lambro, described as "the mildest mannered man/ That ever scuttled ship or cut a throat." The latter returned unexpectedly, kidnapped Juan and sold him as a slave in Constantinople, while Haidée went mad with grief and died. Juan then became a slave in the harem of his mistress, a sultana who had fallen in love with him. After several adventures he escaped to the Russian army, then at war with Turkey, attracted favorable attention by his valor, and was sent to the court of Catherine II at St. Petersburg. The Empress then sent him on a diplomatic mission to England, and England is the scene of the poem from the tenth canto to the end. Byron says in the first canto that he plans a regular mock epic in the conventional epic number of twelve cantos, the last to be a satiric vision of "hell," which, as Byron explains elsewhere, could also be a symbol of marriage. This scheme soon broke down: Byron promised first fifty, then, in the poem itself, a hundred cantos. But, aside from a hint that he intended to make Don Juan become a Methodist for a while, we have little indication of how the poem was to proceed.

In such an embarrassment of riches it is hard to make anything but an arbitrary choice. The first canto, a superb piece of leisurely storytelling, is here given complete, along with the end of the third, with its famous lyric, its equally famous ridicule of the Lake poets, and the sudden changes of mood that are so characteristic of the poem.

## CANTO I

1

I want a hero: an uncommon want,
  When every year and month sends forth a new
    one,
Till, after cloying the gazettes with cant,
  The age discovers he is not the true one:
Of such as these I should not care to vaunt,
  I'll therefore take our ancient friend Don Juan—
We all have seen him, in the pantomime,
Sent to the devil somewhat ere his time.

2

Vernon, the butcher Cumberland, Wolfe, Hawke,
  Prince Ferdinand, Granby, Burgoyne, Keppel,
    Howe,
Evil and good, have had their tithe of talk,
  And filled their sign-posts then, like Wellesley
    now;
Each in their turn like Banquo's monarchs stalk,
  Followers of fame, "nine farrow" of that sow:

DON JUAN. **Canto I: 7. pantomime:** The story of Don Juan had been popular in English pantomime for over a century. **9–10. Vernon . . . Howe:** British eighteenth-century army commanders. The Duke of Cumberland (1721–65) was called "Butcher" because of his brutality to the defeated Jacobites after the rebellion of 1745. **12. Wellesley:** the Duke of Wellington. **14. "nine farrow":** See *Macbeth,* IV.i.65.

France, too, had Buonaparté and Dumourier
Recorded in the Moniteur and Courier.

3

Barnave, Brissot, Condorcet, Mirabeau,
  Pétion, Clootz, Danton, Marat, La Fayette,
Were French, and famous people, as we know
  And there were others, scarce forgotten yet,
Joubert, Hoche, Marceau, Lannes, Desaix, Moreau,
  With many of the military set,
Exceedingly remarkable at times,
But not at all adapted to my rhymes.

4

Nelson was once Britannia's god of war,
  And still should be so, but the tide is turned;
There's no more to be said of Trafalgar,
  'Tis with our hero quietly inurned;
Because the army's grown more popular,
  At which the naval people are concerned,
Besides, the prince is all for the land-service,
Forgetting Duncan, Nelson, Howe, and Jervis.

5

Brave men were living before Agamemnon
  And since, exceeding valorous and sage,
A good deal like him too, though quite the same
    none;
  But then they shone not on the poet's page,
And so have been forgotten: — I condemn none,
  But can't find any in the present age
Fit for my poem (that is, for my new one);
So, as I said, I'll take my friend Don Juan.

6

Most epic poets plunge "in medias res"
  (Horace makes this the heroic turnpike road),
And then your hero tells, whene'er you please,
  What went before — by way of episode,
While seated after dinner at his ease,
  Beside his mistress in some soft abode,
Palace, or garden, paradise, or cavern,
Which serves the happy couple for a tavern.

7

That is the usual method, but not mine —
  My way is to begin with the beginning;
The regularity of my design
  Forbids all wandering as the worst of sinning,
And therefore I shall open with a line
  (Although it cost me half an hour in spinning)
Narrating somewhat of Don Juan's father,
And also of his mother, if you'd rather.

8

In Seville was he born, a pleasant city,
  Famous for oranges and women — he
Who has not seen it will be much to pity,
  So says the proverb — and I quite agree;
Of all the Spanish towns is none more pretty,
  Cadiz, perhaps — but that you soon may see: —
Don Juan's parents lived beside the river,
A noble stream, and called the Guadalquivir.

9

His father's name was Jóse — *Don,* of course,
  A true Hidalgo, free from every strain
Of Moor or Hebrew blood, he traced his source
  Through the most Gothic gentlemen of Spain;
A better cavalier ne'er mounted horse,
  Or, being mounted, e'er got down again,
Than Jóse, who begot our hero, who
Begot — but that's to come —— Well, to renew:

10

His mother was a learned lady, famed
  For every branch of every science known —
In every Christian language ever named,
  With virtues equalled by her wit alone:
She made the cleverest people quite ashamed,
  And even the good with inward envy groan,
Finding themselves so very much exceeded
In their own way by all the things that she did.

11

Her memory was a mine: she knew by heart
  All Calderon and greater part of Lopé,
So that if any actor missed his part
  She could have served him for the prompter's
    copy;
For her Feinagle's were an useless art,
  And he himself obliged to shut up shop — he
Could never make a memory so fine as
That which adorned the brain of Donna Inez.

12

Her favourite science was the mathematical,
  Her noblest virtue was her magnanimity;
Her wit (she sometimes tried at wit) was Attic all,
  Her serious sayings darkened to sublimity;

**15. Dumourier:** or Dumouriez, a revolutionary turned royalist who lived on a pension in England. **17–20. Barnave . . . Moreau:** French Napoleonic and Revolutionary military leaders. **32. Duncan . . . Jervis:** British naval commanders. The Prince Regent's boasts about his military capacities were a common joke. He was never in any battle. **41. "in . . . res":** "in the midst of things." The practice of Homer and Virgil of beginning their epics at a well-advanced point in the action was noted in Horace's *Ars Poetica.*

**82. Calderon . . . Lopé:** Calderon de la Barca (1600–81) and Lope de Vega (1562–1635) are the greatest dramatists of Spanish literature. **85. Feinagle's:** Professor Gregor von Feinagle, who had invented a mnemonic system, had lectured in London in 1811.

In short, in all things she was fairly what I call
  A prodigy — her morning dress was dimity,
Her evening silk, or, in the summer, muslin,
And other stuffs, with which I won't stay puzzling.

13

She knew the Latin — that is, " the Lord's prayer,"
  And Greek — the alphabet — I'm nearly sure;
She read some French romances here and there,
  Although her mode of speaking was not pure;
For native Spanish she had no great care,
  At least her conversation was obscure;
Her thoughts were theorems, her words a problem,
As if she deemed that mystery would ennoble 'em.

14

She liked the English and the Hebrew tongue,
  And said there was analogy between 'em;
She proved it somehow out of sacred song,
  But I must leave the proofs to those who've seen 'em,
But this I heard her say, and can't be wrong,
  And all may think which way their judgments lean 'em,
" 'Tis strange — the Hebrew noun which means ' I am,'
The English always use to govern d—n."

15

Some women use their tongues — she *looked* a lecture,
  Each eye a sermon, and her brow a homily,
An all-in-all sufficient self-director,
  Like the lamented late Sir Samuel Romilly,
The Law's expounder, and the State's corrector,
  Whose suicide was almost an anomaly —
One sad example more, that " All is vanity," —
(The jury brought their verdict in " Insanity.")

16

In short, she was a walking calculation,
  Miss Edgeworth's novels stepping from their covers,
Or Mrs. Trimmer's books on education,
  Or " Coelebs' Wife " set out in quest of lovers,
Morality's grim personification,
  In which not Envy's self a flaw discovers;
To others' share let " female errors fall,"
For she had not even one — the worst of all.

17

Oh! she was perfect past all parallel —
  Of any modern female saint's comparison;
So far above the cunning powers of hell,
  Her guardian angel had given up his garrison;
Even her minutest motions went as well
  As those of the best time-piece made by Harrison:
In virtues nothing earthly could surpass her,
Save thine " incomparable oil," Macassar!

18

Perfect she was, but as perfection is
  Insipid in this naughty world of ours,
Where our first parents never learned to kiss
  Till they were exiled from their earlier bowers,
Where all was peace, and innocence, and bliss
  (I wonder how they got through the twelve hours),
Don José, like a lineal son of Eve,
Went plucking various fruit without her leave.

19

He was a mortal of the careless kind,
  With no great love for learning, or the learn'd,
Who chose to go where'er he had a mind,
  And never dreamed his lady was concerned;
The world, as usual, wickedly inclined
  To see a kingdom or a house o'erturned,
Whispered he had a mistress, some said *two,*
But for domestic quarrels *one* will do.

20

Now Donna Inez had, with all her merit,
  A great opinion of her own good qualities;
Neglect, indeed, requires a saint to bear it,
  And such, indeed, she was in her moralities;
But then she had a devil of a spirit,
  And sometimes mixed up fancies with realities,
And let few opportunities escape
Of getting her liege lord into a scrape.

21

This was an easy matter with a man
  Oft in the wrong, and never on his guard;
And even the wisest, do the best they can,
  Have moments, hours, and days, so unprepared,
That you might " brain them with their lady's fan ";

111. **'I am':** i.e., God; see Exod. 3:14. 116. **Romilly:** Sir Samuel Romilly was Lady Byron's legal adviser, and Byron called him one of the "assassins" of his character. He committed suicide in 1818, a few days after his wife's death. This suicide is the subject of a savage letter from Byron to his wife, dated November 18, 1818. 122–24. **Miss . . . lovers:** Maria Edgeworth (1767–1849), Sarah Trimmer (1741–1810), and Hannah More (1745–1833) were all purveyors of improving fiction for adolescent females. The last named was the author of *Coelebs in Search of a Wife* (1809).

134. **Harrison:** John "Longitude" Harrison was a famous watchmaker, and the inventor of watch compensation. 136. **Macassar:** Macassar oil was used in hair dressing; its lethal effect on velvet-covered furniture was the reason for the "antimacassar" protective covering. 165. **"brain . . . fan":** See *I Henry IV*, II.iii.25.

And sometimes ladies hit exceeding hard,
And fans turn into falchions in fair hands,
And why and wherefore no one understands.

22

'Tis pity learned virgins ever wed
With persons of no sort of education,
Or gentlemen, who, though well born and bred,
Grow tired of scientific conversation;
I don't choose to say much upon this head,
I'm a plain man, and in a single station,
But — Oh! ye lords of ladies intellectual,
Inform us truly, have they not hen-pecked you all?

23

Don Jóse and his lady quarrelled — *why,*
Not any of the many could divine,
Though several thousand people chose to try,
'Twas surely no concern of theirs nor mine;
I loathe that low vice — curiosity;
But if there's anything in which I shine,
'Tis in arranging all my friends' affairs,
Not having, of my own, domestic cares.

24

And so I interfered, and with the best
Intentions, but their treatment was not kind;
I think the foolish people were possessed,
For neither of them could I ever find,
Although their porter afterwards confessed —
But that's no matter, and the worst's behind,
For little Juan o'er me threw, down stairs,
A pail of housemaid's water unawares.

25

A little curly-headed, good-for-nothing,
And mischief-making monkey from his birth;
His parents ne'er agreed except in doting
Upon the most inquiet imp on earth;
Instead of quarrelling, had they been but both in
Their senses, they'd have sent young master forth
To school, or had him soundly whipped at home,
To teach him manners for the time to come.

26

Don Jóse and the Donna Inez led
For some time an unhappy sort of life,
Wishing each other, not divorced, but dead;
They lived respectably as man and wife,
Their conduct was exceedingly well-bred,
And gave no outward signs of inward strife,
Until at length the smothered fire broke out,
And put the business past all kind of doubt.

27

For Inez called some druggists and physicians,
And tried to prove her loving lord was *mad,*
But as he had some lucid intermissions,
She next decided he was only *bad;*
Yet when they asked her for her depositions,
No sort of explanation could be had,
Save that her duty both to man and God
Required this conduct — which seemed very odd.

28

She kept a journal, where his faults were noted,
And opened certain trunks of books and letters,
All which might, if occasion served, be quoted;
And then she had all Seville for abettors,
Besides her good old grandmother (who doted);
The hearers of her case became repeaters,
Then advocates, inquisitors, and judges,
Some for amusement, others for old grudges.

29

And then this best and meekest woman bore
With such serenity her husband's woes,
Just as the Spartan ladies did of yore,
Who saw their spouses killed, and nobly chose
Never to say a word about them more —
Calmly she heard each calumny that rose,
And saw *his* agonies with such sublimity,
That all the world exclaimed, "What magnanimity!"

30

No doubt this patience, when the world is damning us,
Is philosophic in our former friends;
'Tis also pleasant to be deemed magnanimous,
The more so in obtaining our own ends;
And what the lawyers call a *"malus animus"*
Conduct like this by no means comprehends:
Revenge in person's certainly no virtue,
But then 'tis not *my* fault, if *others* hurt you.

31

And if our quarrels should rip up old stories,
And help them with a lie or two additional,
*I'm* not to blame, as you well know — no more is
Any one else — they were become traditional;
Besides, their resurrection aids our glories
By contrast, which is what we just were wishing all:
And science profits by this resurrection —
Dead scandals form good subjects for dissection.

237. **"*malus animus*"**: malice aforethought.

32

Their friends had tried at reconciliation,
  Then their relations, who made matters worse,
('Twere hard to tell upon a like occasion
  To whom it may be best to have recourse —
I can't say much for friend or yet relation):
  The lawyers did their utmost for divorce,
But scarce a fee was paid on either side
Before, unluckily, Don Jóse died.

33

He died; and most unluckily, because,
  According to all hints I could collect
From counsel learned in those kinds of laws
  (Although their talk's obscure and circumspect),
His death contrived to spoil a charming cause;
  A thousand pities also with respect
To public feeling, which on this occasion
Was manifested in a great sensation.

34

But ah! he died; and buried with him lay
  The public feeling and the lawyer's fees:
His house was sold, his servants sent away,
  A Jew took one of his two mistresses,
A priest the other — at least so they say:
  I asked the doctors after his disease —
He died of the slow fever called the tertian,
And left his widow to her own aversion.

35

Yet Jóse was an honourable man,
  That I must say, who knew him very well;
Therefore his frailties I'll no further scan,
  Indeed there were not many more to tell:
And if his passion now and then outran
  Discretion, and were not so peaceable
As Numa's (who was also named Pompilius),
He had been ill brought up, and was born bilious.

36

Whate'er might be his worthlessness or worth,
  Poor fellow! he had many things to wound
    him,
Let's own — since it can do no good on earth —
  It was a trying moment that which found him
Standing alone beside his desolate hearth,
  Where all his household gods lay shivered round
    him:
No choice was left his feelings or his pride,
Save death or Doctors' Commons — so he died.

**279. Numa's:** Numa Pompilius, the second king of Rome, had a long and peaceful reign as the result of taking the advice of the nymph Egeria, who loved him. **288. Doctors' Commons:** i.e., the divorce courts.

37

Dying intestate, Juan was sole heir
  To a chancery suit, and messuages and lands,
Which, with a long minority and care,
  Promised to turn out well in proper hands:
Inez became sole guardian, which was fair,
  And answered but to nature's just demands;
An only son left with an only mother
Is brought up much more wisely than another.

38

Sagest of women, even of widows, she
  Resolved that Juan should be quite a paragon,
And worthy of the noblest pedigree:
  (His sire was of Castile, his dam from Aragon).
Then for accomplishments of chivalry,
  In case our lord the king should go to war again,
He learned the arts of riding, fencing, gunnery,
And how to scale a fortress — or a nunnery.

39

But that which Donna Inez most desired,
  And saw into herself each day before all
The learned tutors whom for him she hired,
  Was, that his breeding should be strictly moral:
Much into all his studies she inquired,
  And so they were submitted first to her, all,
Arts, sciences, no branch was made a mystery
To Juan's eyes, excepting natural history.

40

The languages, especially the dead,
  The sciences, and most of all the abstruse,
The arts, at least all such as could be said
  To be the most remote from common use,
In all these he was much and deeply read:
  But not a page of anything that's loose,
Or hints continuation of the species,
Was ever suffered, lest he should grow vicious.

41

His classic studies made a little puzzle,
  Because of filthy loves of gods and goddesses,
Who in the earlier ages raised a bustle,
  But never put on pantaloons or bodices;
His reverend tutors had at times a tussle,
  And for their Aeneids, Iliads, and Odysseys,
Were forced to make an odd sort of apology,
But Donna Inez dreaded the Mythology.

42

Ovid's a rake, as half his verses show him,
  Anacreon's morals are a still worse sample,

**290. messuages:** dwelling houses along with their outbuildings and lands. **329–36. Ovid's . . . Corydon:** the obscenity of

Catullus scarcely has a decent poem,
  I don't think Sappho's Ode a good example,
Although Longinus tells us there is no hymn
  Where the sublime soars forth on wings more ample;
But Virgil's songs are pure, except that horrid one
Beginning with "Formosum Pastor Corydon."

43

Lucretius' irreligion is too strong
  For early stomachs, to prove wholesome food;
I can't help thinking Juvenal was wrong,
  Although no doubt his real intent was good,
For speaking out so plainly in his song,
  So much indeed as to be downright rude;
And then what proper person can be partial
To all those nauseous epigrams of Martial?

44

Juan was taught from out the best edition,
  Expurgated by learned men, who place,
Judiciously, from out the schoolboy's vision,
  The grosser parts; but, fearful to deface
Too much their modest bard by this omission,
  And pitying sore his mutilated case,
They only add them all in an appendix,
Which saves, in fact, the trouble of an index;

45

For there we have them all "at one fell swoop,"
  Instead of being scattered through the pages;
They stand forth marshalled in a handsome troop,
  To meet the ingenuous youth of future ages,
Till some less rigid editor shall stoop
  To call them back into their separate cages,
Instead of standing staring all together,
Like garden gods — and not so decent either.

46

The Missal too (it was the family Missal)
  Was ornamented in a sort of way
Which ancient mass-books often are, and this all
  Kinds of grotesques illumined; and how they,
Who saw those figures on the margin kiss all,
  Could turn their optics to the text and pray,
Is more than I know — But Don Juan's mother
Kept this herself, and gave her son another.

47

Sermons he read, and lectures he endured,
  And homilies and lives of all the saints;
To Jerome and to Chrysostom inured,
  He did not take such studies for restraints;
But how faith is acquired, and then insured,
  So well not one of the aforesaid paints
As Saint Augustine in his fine Confessions,
Which make the reader envy his transgressions.

48

This, too, was a sealed book to little Juan —
  I can't but say that his mamma was right,
If such an education was the true one.
  She scarcely trusted him from out her sight;
Her maids were old, and if she took a new one,
  You might be sure she was a perfect fright,
She did this during even her husband's life —
I recommend as much to every wife.

49

Young Juan waxed in godliness and grace;
  At six a charming child, and at eleven
With all the promise of as fine a face
  As e'er to man's maturer growth was given.
He studied steadily and grew apace,
  And seemed, at least, in the right road to heaven,
For half his days were passed at church, the other
Between his tutors, confessor, and mother.

50

At six, I said, he was a charming child,
  At twelve he was a fine, but quiet boy;
Although in infancy a little wild,
  They tamed him down amongst them: to destroy
His natural spirit not in vain they toiled,
  At least it seemed so; and his mother's joy
Was to declare how sage, and still, and steady,
Her young philosopher was grown already.

51

I had my doubts, perhaps, I have them still,
  But what I say is neither here nor there:
I knew his father well, and have some skill
  In character — but it would not be fair
From sire to son to augur good or ill:
  He and his wife were an ill sorted pair —
But scandal's my aversion — I protest
Against all evil speaking, even in jest.

Ovid's *Ars Amatoria* was the excuse given by Augustus for banishing him; Anacreon celebrated drunkenness; Sappho's home in Lesbos has given the word "Lesbian" to the language, though her "Ode" was highly praised in Longinus' *On the Sublime*, sec. 10; Virgil's second *Eclogue* is an expression of homosexual love.
**351. appendix:** "Fact! There is, or was, such an edition, with all the obnoxious epigrams of Martial placed by themselves at the end" [B].

**375. Confessions:** "See his *Confessions*, I.ix. By the representation which Saint Augustine gives of himself in his youth, it is easy to see that he was what we should call a rake. He avoided the school as the plague; he loved nothing but gaming and public shows; he robbed his father of everything he could find; he invented a thousand lies to escape the rod, which they were obliged to make use of to punish his irregularities" [B].

52

For my part I say nothing — nothing — but
  *This* I will say — my reasons are my own —
That if I had an only son to put
  To school (as God be praised that I have none),
'Tis not with Donna Inez I would shut
  Him up to learn his catechism alone,
No — no — I'd send him out betimes to college,
For there it was I picked up my own knowl-
    edge.

53

For there one learns — 'tis not for me to boast,
  Though I acquired — but I pass over *that,*
As well as all the Greek I since have lost:
  I say that there's the place — but "*Verbum
    sat,*"
I think I picked up too, as well as most,
  Knowledge of matters — but no matter *what* —
I never married — but, I think, I know
That sons should not be educated so.

54

Young Juan now was sixteen years of age,
  Tall, handsome, slender, but well knit: he seemed
Active, though not so sprightly, as a page;
  And everybody but his mother deemed
Him almost man; but she flew in a rage
  And bit her lips (for else she might have
    screamed)
If any said so, for to be precocious
Was in her eyes a thing the most atrocious.

55

Amongst her numerous acquaintances, all
  Selected for discretion and devotion,
There was the Donna Julia, whom to call
  Pretty were but to give a feeble notion
Of many charms in her as natural
  As sweetness to the flower, or salt to ocean,
Her zone to Venus, or his bow to Cupid,
(But this last simile is trite and stupid).

56

The darkness of her Oriental eye
  Accorded with her Moorish origin;
(Her blood was not all Spanish, by the by;
  In Spain, you know, this is a sort of sin).
When proud Granada fell, and, forced to fly,
  Boabdil wept, of Donna Julia's kin
Some went to Africa, some stayed in Spain,
Her great great grandmamma chose to remain.

57

She married (I forget the pedigree)
  With an Hidalgo, who transmitted down
His blood less noble than such blood should be;
  At such alliances his sires would frown,
In that point so precise in each degree
  That they bred *in and in,* as might be shown,
Marrying their cousins — nay, their aunts, and
    nieces,
Which always spoils the breed, if it increases.

58

This heathenish cross restored the breed again,
  Ruined its blood, but much improved its flesh;
For from a root the ugliest in old Spain
  Sprung up a branch as beautiful as fresh;
The sons no more were short, the daughters plain:
  But there's a rumour which I fain would hush,
'Tis said that Donna Julia's grandmamma
Produced her Don more heirs at love than law.

59

However this might be, the race went on
  Improving still through every generation,
Until it centered in an only son,
  Who left an only daughter: my narration
May have suggested that this single one
  Could be but Julia (whom on this occasion
I shall have much to speak about), and she
Was married, charming, chaste, and twenty-three.

60

Her eye (I'm very fond of handsome eyes)
  Was large and dark, suppressing half its fire
Until she spoke, then through its soft disguise
  Flashed an expression more of pride than ire,
And love than either; and there would arise
  A something in them which was not desire,
But would have been, perhaps, but for the soul
Which struggled through and chastened down the
    whole.

61

Her glossy hair was clustered o'er a brow
  Bright with intelligence, and fair, and smooth;
Her eyebrow's shape was like the aërial bow,
  Her cheek all purple, with the beam of youth,
Mounting, at times, to a transparent glow,
  As if her veins ran lightning; she, in sooth,
Possessed an air and grace by no means common:
Her stature tall — I hate a dumpy woman.

62

Wedded she was some years, and to a man
  Of fifty, and such husbands are in plenty;

420. "*Verbum sat*": "A word [to the wise] is enough." 446. **Boabdil**: the last Moorish King of Granada, in Southern Spain, finally conquered by King Ferdinand in 1492.

And yet, I think, instead of such a ONE
 'Twere better to have TWO of five-and-twenty,
Especially in countries near the sun:
 And now I think on't, "mi vien in mente,"
Ladies even of the most uneasy virtue
Prefer a spouse whose age is short of thirty.

63

'Tis a sad thing, I cannot choose but say,
 And all the fault of that indecent sun,
Who cannot leave alone our helpless clay,
 But will keep baking, broiling, burning on,
That howsoever people fast and pray,
 The flesh is frail, and so the soul undone:
What men call gallantry, and gods adultery,
Is much more common where the climate's sultry.

64

Happy the nations of the moral North!
 Where all is virtue, and the winter season
Sends sin, without a rag on, shivering forth
 ('Twas snow that brought St. Anthony to reason);
Where juries cast up what a wife is worth,
 By laying whate'er sum, in mulct, they please on
The lover, who must pay a handsome price,
Because it is a marketable vice.

65

Alfonso was the name of Julia's lord,
 A man well looking for his years, and who
Was neither much beloved nor yet abhorred:
 They lived together as most people do,
Suffering each other's foibles by accord,
 And not exactly either *one* or *two;*
Yet he was jealous, though he did not show it,
For jealousy dislikes the world to know it.

66

Julia was — yet I never could see why —
 With Donna Inez quite a favourite friend;
Between their tastes there was small sympathy,
 For not a line had Julia ever penned:
Some people whisper (but, no doubt, they lie,
 For malice still imputes some private end)
That Inez had, ere Don Alfonso's marriage,
Forgot with him her very prudent carriage;

67

And that still keeping up the old connexion,
 Which time had lately rendered much more chaste,
She took his lady also in affection,
 And certainly this course was much the best:
She flattered Julia with her sage protection,
 And complimented Don Alfonso's taste;
And if she could not (who can?) silence scandal,
At least she left it a more slender handle.

68

I can't tell whether Julia saw the affair
 With other people's eyes, or if her own
Discoveries made, but none could be aware
 Of this, at least no symptom e'er was shown;
Perhaps she did not know, or did not care,
 Indifferent from the first, or callous grown:
I'm really puzzled what to think or say,
She kept her counsel in so close a way.

69

Juan she saw, and, as a pretty child,
 Caressed him often — such a thing might be
Quite innocently done, and harmless styled,
 When she had twenty years, and thirteen he;
But I am not so sure I should have smiled
 When he was sixteen, Julia twenty-three;
These few short years make wondrous alterations,
Particularly amongst sun-burnt nations.

70

Whate'er the cause might be, they had become
 Changed; for the dame grew distant, the youth shy,
Their looks cast down, their greetings almost dumb,
 And much embarrassment in either eye;
There surely will be little doubt with some
 That Donna Julia knew the reason why,
But as for Juan, he had no more notion
Than he who never saw the sea of ocean.

71

Yet Julia's very coldness still was kind,
 And tremulously gentle her small hand
Withdrew itself from his, but left behind
 A little pressure, thrilling, and so bland
And slight, so very slight, that to the mind
 'Twas but a doubt; but ne'er magician's wand
Wrought change with all Armida's fairy art
Like what this light touch left on Juan's heart.

72

And if she met him, though she smiled no more,
 She looked a sadness sweeter than her smile,

**494. "mi . . . mente"**: "It comes into my mind." **508. snow**: "For the particulars of St. Anthony's recipe for hot blood in cold weather, see Mr. Alban Butler's *Lives of the Saints*" [B].

**567. Armida's**: the enchantress in Tasso's *Jerusalem Delivered.*

As if her heart had deeper thoughts in store
  She must not own, but cherished more the while
For that compression in its burning core;
  Even innocence itself has many a wile,
And will not dare to trust itself with truth,
And love is taught hypocrisy from youth.

73

But passion most dissembles, yet betrays
  Even by its darkness; as the blackest sky
Foretells the heaviest tempest, it displays
  Its workings through the vainly guarded eye,
And in whatever aspect it arrays
  Itself, 'tis still the same hypocrisy:
Coldness or anger, even disdain or hate,
Are masks it often wears, and still too late.

74

Then there were sighs, the deeper for suppression,
  And stolen glances, sweeter for the theft,
And burning blushes, though for no transgression,
  Tremblings when met, and restlessness when
    left;
All these are little preludes to possession,
  Of which young passion cannot be bereft,
And merely tend to show how greatly love is
Embarrassed at first starting with a novice.

75

Poor Julia's heart was in an awkward state;
  She felt it going, and resolved to make
The noblest efforts for herself and mate,
  For honour's, pride's, religion's, virtue's sake,
Her resolutions were most truly great,
  And almost might have made a Tarquin quake:
She prayed the Virgin Mary for her grace,
As being the best judge of a lady's case.

76

She vowed she never would see Juan more,
  And next day paid a visit to his mother
And looked extremely at the opening door,
  Which, by the Virgin's grace, let in another;
Grateful she was, and yet a little sore —
  Again it opens, it can be no other,
'Tis surely Juan now — No! I'm afraid
That night the Virgin was no further prayed.

77

She now determined that a virtuous woman
  Should rather face and overcome temptation,
That flight was base and dastardly, and no man
  Should ever give her heart the least sensation;
That is to say, a thought beyond the common
  Preference, that we must feel upon occasion,
For people who are pleasanter than others,
But then they only seem so many brothers.

78

And even if by chance — and who can tell?
  The devil's so very sly — she should discover
That all within was not so very well,
  And, if still free, that such or such a lover
Might please perhaps, a virtuous wife can quell
  Such thoughts, and be the better when they're
    over;
And if the man should ask, 'tis but denial:
I recommend young ladies to make trial.

79

And then there are such things as love divine,
  Bright and immaculate, unmixed and pure,
Such as the angels think so very fine,
  And matrons, who would be no less secure,
Platonic, perfect, " just such love as mine: "
  Thus Julia said — and thought so, to be sure;
And so I'd have her think, were I the man
On whom her reveries celestial ran.

80

Such love is innocent, and may exist
  Between young persons without any danger:
A hand may first, and then a lip be kist;
  For my part, to such doings I'm a stranger,
But *hear* these freedoms form the utmost list
  Of all o'er which such love may be a ranger:
If people go beyond, 'tis quite a crime,
But not my fault — I tell them all in time.

81

Love, then, but love within its proper limits
  Was Julia's innocent determination
In young Don Juan's favour, and to him its
  Exertion might be useful on occasion;
And, lighted at too pure a shrine to dim its
  Ethereal lustre, with what sweet persuasion
He might be taught, by love and her together —
I really don't know what, nor Julia either.

82

Fraught with this fine intention, and well fenced
  In mail of proof — her purity of soul,
She, for the future of her strength convinced,
  And that her honour was a rock, or mole,
Exceedingly sagely from that hour dispensed
  With any kind of troublesome control;
But whether Julia to the task was equal
Is that which must be mentioned in the sequel.

598. **Tarquin**: Tarquinius Superbus, the last king of Rome, was expelled after his son Sextus made the famous assault on Lucretia celebrated in Shakespeare's *Rape of Lucrece*.

83

Her plan she deemed both innocent and feasible,
And, surely, with a stripling of sixteen
Not scandal's fangs could fix on much that's seizable,
Or if they did so, satisfied to mean
Nothing but what was good, her breast was peaceable:
A quiet conscience makes one so serene!
Christians have burnt each other, quite persuaded
That all the Apostles would have done as they did.

84

And if in the mean time her husband died,
But Heaven forbid that such a thought should cross
Her brain, though in a dream! (and then she sighed)
Never could she survive that common loss;
But just suppose that moment should betide,
I only say suppose it—*inter nos*.
(This should be *entre nous,* for Julia thought
In French, but then the rhyme would go for nought.)

85

I only say, suppose this supposition:
Juan being then grown up to man's estate
Would fully suit a widow of condition,
Even seven years hence it would not be too late;
And in the interim (to pursue this vision)
The mischief, after all, could not be great,
For he would learn the rudiments of love,
I mean the seraph way of those above.

86

So much for Julia. Now we'll turn to Juan.
Poor little fellow! he had no idea
Of his own case, and never hit the true one;
In feelings quick as Ovid's Miss Medea,
He puzzled over what he found a new one,
But not as yet imagined it could be a
Thing quite in course, and not at all alarming,
Which, with a little patience, might grow charming.

87

Silent and pensive, idle, restless, slow,
His home deserted for the lonely wood,
Tormented with a wound he could not know,
His, like all deep grief, plunged in solitude:
I'm fond myself of solitude or so,
But then, I beg it may be understood,
By solitude I mean a Sultan's, not
A hermit's, with a haram for a grot.

88

"Oh Love! in such a wilderness as this,
Where transport and security entwine,
Here is the empire of thy perfect bliss,
And here thou art a god indeed divine."
The bard I quote from does not sing amiss,
With the exception of the second line,
For that same twining "transport and security"
Are twisted to a phrase of some obscurity.

89

The poet meant, no doubt, and thus appeals
To the good sense and senses of mankind,
The very thing which everybody feels,
As all have found on trial, or may find,
That no one likes to be disturbed at meals
Or love.—I won't say more about "entwined"
Or "transport," as we knew all that before,
But beg "Security" will bolt the door.

90

Young Juan wandered by the glassy brooks,
Thinking unutterable things; he threw
Himself at length within the leafy nooks
Where the wild branch of the cork forest grew;
There poets find materials for their books,
And every now and then we read them through,
So that their plan and prosody are eligible,
Unless, like Wordsworth, they prove unintelligible.

91

He, Juan (and not Wordsworth), so pursued
His self-communion with his own high soul,
Until his mighty heart, in its great mood,
Had mitigated part, though not the whole
Of its disease; he did the best he could
With things not very subject to control,
And turned, without perceiving his condition,
Like Coleridge, into a metaphysician.

92

He thought about himself, and the whole earth,
Of man the wonderful, and of the stars,
And how the deuce they ever could have birth;
And then he thought of earthquakes, and of wars,
How many miles the moon might have in girth,
Of air-balloons, and of the many bars
To perfect knowledge of the boundless skies;—
And then he thought of Donna Julia's eyes.

**684. Ovid's . . . Medea:** Byron refers to Ovid's *Ars Amatoria,* II

**697. "Oh . . . divine":** "Campbell's *Gertrude of Wyoming*—(I think)—the opening of Canto Second—but quote from memory"

93

In thoughts like these true wisdom may discern
  Longings sublime, and aspirations high,
Which some are born with, but the most part learn
  To plague themselves withal, they know not why:
'Twas strange that one so young should thus concern
  His brain about the action of the sky;
If *you* think 'twas philosophy that this did,
I can't help thinking puberty assisted.

94

He pored upon the leaves, and on the flowers,
  And heard a voice in all the winds; and then
He thought of wood-nymphs and immortal bowers,
  And how the goddesses came down to men:
He missed the pathway, he forgot the hours,
  And when he looked upon his watch again,
He found how much old Time had been a winner—
He also found that he had lost his dinner.

95

Sometimes he turned to gaze upon his book,
  Boscan, or Garcilasso;—by the wind
Even as the page is rustled while we look,
  So by the poesy of his own mind
Over the mystic leaf his soul was shook,
  As if 'twere one whereon magicians bind
Their spells, and give them to the passing gale
According to some good old woman's tale.

96

Thus would he while his lonely hours away
  Dissatisfied, nor knowing what he wanted;
Nor glowing reverie, nor poet's lay,
  Could yield his spirit that for which it panted,
A bosom whereon he his head might lay,
  And hear the heart beat with the love it granted,
With —— several other things, which I forget,
Or which, at least, I need not mention yet.

97

Those lonely walks, and lengthening reveries,
  Could not escape the gentle Julia's eyes;
She saw that Juan was not at his ease;
  But that which chiefly may, and must surprise,
Is, that the Donna Inez did not tease
  Her only son with question or surmise;
Whether it was she did not see, or would not,
Or, like all very clever people, could not.

98

This may seem strange, but yet 'tis very common;
  For instance—gentlemen, whose ladies take
Leave to o'erstep the written rights of woman,
  And break the —— Which commandment is't they break?
(I have forgot the number, and think no man
  Should rashly quote, for fear of a mistake.)
I say, when these same gentlemen are jealous,
They make some blunder, which their ladies tell us.

99

A real husband always is suspicious,
  But still no less suspects in the wrong place,
Jealous of some one who had no such wishes,
  Or pandering blindly to his own disgrace,
By harbouring some dear friend extremely vicious;
  The last indeed's infallibly the case:
And when the spouse and friend are gone off wholly,
He wonders at their vice, and not his folly.

100

Thus parents also are at times short-sighted;
  Though watchful as the lynx, they ne'er discover,
The while the wicked world beholds delighted,
  Young Hopeful's mistress, or Miss Fanny's lover,
Till some confounded escapade has blighted
  The plan of twenty years, and all is over;
And then the mother cries, the father swears,
And wonders why the devil he got heirs.

101

But Inez was so anxious, and so clear
  Of sight, that I must think, on this occasion,
She had some other motive much more near
  For leaving Juan to this new temptation,
But what that motive was, I shan't say here;
  Perhaps to finish Juan's education,
Perhaps to open Don Alfonso's eyes,
In case he thought his wife too great a prize.

102

It was upon a day, a summer's day;—
  Summer's indeed a very dangerous season,
And so is spring about the end of May;
  The sun, no doubt, is the prevailing reason;
But whatsoe'er the cause is, one may say,
  And stand convicted of more truth than treason,
That there are months which nature grows more merry in,—
March has its hares, and May must have its heroine.

[B]. The passage occurs at the opening of the third part of Campbell's poem. **754. Boscan, or Garcilasso**: Juan Boscan and Garcilaso de la Vega were Spanish poets of the early sixteenth century.

103

'Twas on a summer's day — the sixth of June: —
I like to be particular in dates,
Not only of the age, and year, but moon;
They are a sort of post-house, where the Fates
Change horses, making history change its tune,
Then spur away o'er empires and o'er states,
Leaving at last not much besides chronology,
Excepting the post-obits of theology.

104

'Twas on the sixth of June, about the hour
Of half-past six — perhaps still nearer seven —
When Julia sate within as pretty a bower
As e'er held houri in that heathenish heaven
Described by Mahomet, and Anacreon Moore,
To whom the lyre and laurels have been given,
With all the trophies of triumphant song —
He won them well, and may he wear them long!

105

She sate, but not alone; I know not well
How this same interview had taken place,
And even if I knew, I should not tell —
People should hold their tongues in any case;
No matter how or why the thing befell,
But there were she and Juan, face to face —
When two such faces are so, 'twould be wise,
But very difficult, to shut their eyes.

106

How beautiful she looked! her conscious heart
Glowed in her cheek, and yet she felt no wrong,
Oh Love! how perfect is thy mystic art,
Strengthening the weak, and trampling on the strong!
How self-deceitful is the sagest part
Of mortals whom thy lure hath led along! —
The precipice she stood on was immense,
So was her creed in her own innocence.

107

She thought of her own strength, and Juan's youth,
And of the folly of all prudish fears,
Victorious virtue, and domestic truth,
And then of Don Alfonso's fifty years:
I wish these last had not occurred, in sooth,
Because that number rarely much endears,
And through all climes, the snowy and the sunny,
Sounds ill in love, whate'er it may in money.

108

When people say, "I've told you *fifty* times,"
They mean to scold, and very often do;
When poets say, "I've written *fifty* rhymes,"
They make you dread that they'll recite them too;
In gangs of *fifty,* thieves commit their crimes;
At *fifty* love for love is rare, 'tis true,
But then, no doubt, it equally as true is,
A good deal may be bought for *fifty* Louis.

109

Julia had honour, virtue, truth, and love
For Don Alfonso; and she inly swore,
By all the vows below to powers above,
She never would disgrace the ring she wore,
Nor leave a wish which wisdom might reprove;
And while she pondered this, besides much more,
One hand on Juan's carelessly was thrown,
Quite by mistake — she thought it was her own;

110

Unconsciously she leaned upon the other,
Which played within the tangles of her hair;
And to contend with thoughts she could not smother
She seemed, by the distraction of her air.
'Twas surely very wrong in Juan's mother
To leave together this imprudent pair,
She who for many years had watched her son so —
I'm very certain *mine* would not have done so.

111

The hand which still held Juan's, by degrees
Gently, but palpably confirmed its grasp,
As if it said, "Detain me, if you please;"
Yet there's no doubt she only meant to clasp
His fingers with a pure Platonic squeeze;
She would have shrunk as from a toad, or asp,
Had she imagined such a thing could rouse
A feeling dangerous to a prudent spouse.

112

I cannot know what Juan thought of this,
But what he did, is much what you would do;
His young lip thanked it with a grateful kiss,
And then, abashed at its own joy, withdrew
In deep despair, lest he had done amiss, —
Love is so very timid when 'tis new:
She blushed, and frowned not, but she strove to speak,
And held her tongue, her voice was grown so weak.

113

The sun set, and up rose the yellow moon:
The devil's in the moon for mischief; they
Who called her CHASTE, methinks, began too soon

**829. Anacreon Moore:** Byron's friend the poet Thomas Moore is called Anacreon because he translated the odes of that Greek lyrical poet in his youth.

Their nomenclature; there is not a day,
The longest, not the twenty-first of June,
Sees half the business in a wicked way,
On which three single hours of moonshine smile—
And then she looks so modest all the while.

114

There is a dangerous silence in that hour,
A stillness, which leaves room for the full soul
To open all itself, without the power
Of calling wholly back its self-control;
The silver light which, hallowing tree and tower,
Sheds beauty and deep softness o'er the whole,
Breathes also to the heart, and o'er it throws
A loving languor, which is not repose.

115

And Julia sate with Juan, half embraced
And half retiring from the glowing arm,
Which trembled like the bosom where 'twas placed;
Yet still she must have thought there was no harm,
Or else 'twere easy to withdraw her waist;
But then the situation had its charm,
And then —— God knows what next—I can't go on;
I'm almost sorry that I e'er begun.

116

Oh Plato! Plato! you have paved the way,
With your confounded fantasies, to more
Immoral conduct by the fancied sway
Your system feigns o'er the controlless core
Of human hearts, than all the long array
Of poets and romancers:—You're a bore,
A charlatan, a coxcomb—and have been,
At best, no better than a go-between.

117

And Julia's voice was lost, except in sighs,
Until too late for useful conversation;
The tears were gushing from her gentle eyes,
I wish, indeed, they had not had occasion;
But who, alas! can love, and then be wise?
Not that remorse did not oppose temptation;
A little still she strove, and much repented,
And whispering "I will ne'er consent"—consented.

118

'Tis said that Xerxes offered a reward
To those who could invent him a new pleasure;
Methinks the requisition's rather hard,
And must have cost his majesty a treasure:
For my part, I'm a moderate-minded bard,
Fond of a little love (which I call leisure);
I care not for new pleasures, as the old
Are quite enough for me, so they but hold.

119

Oh Pleasure! you're indeed a pleasant thing,
Although one must be damned for you, no doubt:
I make a resolution every spring
Of reformation, ere the year run out,
But somehow, this my vestal vow takes wing,
Yet still, I trust, it may be kept throughout:
I'm very sorry, very much ashamed,
And mean, next winter, to be quite reclaimed.

120

Here my chaste Muse a liberty must take—
Start not! still chaster reader—she'll be nice hence-
Forward, and there is no great cause to quake;
This liberty is a poetic licence,
Which some irregularity may make
In the design, and as I have a high sense
Of Aristotle and the Rules, 'tis fit
To beg his pardon when I err a bit.

121

This licence is to hope the reader will
Suppose from June the sixth (the fatal day
Without whose epoch my poetic skill
For want of facts would all be thrown away),
But keeping Julia and Don Juan still
In sight, that several months have passed; we'll say
'Twas in November, but I'm not so sure
About the day—the era's more obscure.

122

We'll talk of that anon.—'Tis sweet to hear
At midnight on the blue and moonlit deep
The song and oar of Adria's gondolier,
By distance mellowed, o'er the waters sweep;
'Tis sweet to see the evening star appear;
'Tis sweet to listen as the night-winds creep
From leaf to leaf; 'tis sweet to view on high
The rainbow, based on ocean, span the sky.

123

'Tis sweet to hear the watch-dog's honest bark
Bay deep-mouthed welcome as we draw near home;
'Tis sweet to know there is an eye will mark

**937. Xerxes**: the King of Persia who invaded Greece and was defeated in the naval battle of Salamis. He is also the Ahasuerus of the Biblical Book of Esther.

Our coming, and look brighter when we come;
'Tis sweet to be awakened by the lark,
Or lulled by falling waters; sweet the hum
Of bees, the voice of girls, the song of birds,
The lisp of children, and their earliest words.

124

Sweet is the vintage when the showering grapes
In Bacchanal profusion reel to earth,
Purple and gushing; sweet are our escapes
From civic revelry to rural mirth;
Sweet to the miser are his glittering heaps,
Sweet to the father is his first-born's birth,
Sweet is revenge — especially to women,
Pillage to soldiers, prize-money to seamen.

125

Sweet is a legacy, and passing sweet
The unexpected death of some old lady
Or gentleman of seventy years complete,
Who've made "us youth" wait too — too long already
For an estate, or cash, or country seat,
Still breaking, but with stamina so steady
That all the Israelites are fit to mob its
Next owner for their double-damned post-obits.

126

'Tis sweet to win, no matter how, one's laurels,
By blood or ink; 'tis sweet to put an end
To strife; 'tis sometimes sweet to have our quarrels,
Particularly with a tiresome friend:
Sweet is old wine in bottles, ale in barrels;
Dear is the helpless creature we defend
Against the world; and dear the schoolboy spot
We ne'er forget, though there we are forgot.

127

But sweeter still than this, than these, than all,
Is first and passionate love — it stands alone,
Like Adam's recollection of his fall;
The tree of knowledge has been plucked — all's known —
And life yields nothing further to recall
Worthy of this ambrosial sin, so shown,
No doubt in fable, as the unforgiven
Fire which Prometheus filched for us from heaven.

128

Man's a strange animal, and makes strange use
Of his own nature, and the various arts,
And likes particularly to produce
Some new experiment to show his parts;
This is the age of oddities let loose,
Where different talents find their different marts;
You'd best begin with truth, and when you've lost your
Labour, there's a sure market for imposture.

129

What opposite discoveries we have seen!
(Signs of true genius, and of empty pockets.)
One makes new noses, one a guillotine,
One breaks your bones, one sets them in their sockets;
But vaccination certainly has been
A kind of antithesis to Congreve's rockets,
With which the Doctor paid off an old pox,
By borrowing a new one from an ox.

130

Bread has been made (indifferent) from potatoes;
And galvanism has set some corpses grinning,
But has not answered like the apparatus
Of the Humane Society's beginning,
By which men are unsuffocated gratis:
What wondrous new machines have late been spinning!
I said the small pox has gone out of late;
Perhaps it may be followed by the great.

131

'Tis said the great came from America;
Perhaps it may set out on its return, —
The population there so spreads, they say
'Tis grown high time to thin it in its turn,
With war, or plague, or famine, any way,
So that civilisation they may learn;
And which in ravage the more loathsome evil is —
Their real lues, or our pseudo-syphilis?

132

This is the patent age of new inventions
For killing bodies, and for saving souls,
All propagated with the best intentions;
Sir Humphrey Davy's lantern, by which coals
Are safely mined for in the mode he mentions,
Tombuctoo travels, voyages to the Poles,
Are ways to benefit mankind, as true,
Perhaps, as shooting them at Waterloo.

**1000. post-obits:** loans to an heir falling due at the death of the person whose property he inherits.

**1030. rockets:** a new kind of artillery shell invented by Sir William Congreve and used during the Napoleonic wars. **1031. Doctor:** i.e., Edward Jenner, the discoverer of vaccination. **1034. galvanism:** experiments on dead bodies with electricity were made by Galvani's nephew in 1803. **1040. great:** The "great pox," as distinct from smallpox, was syphilis, or "lues" (l. 1048), said to have entered Europe for the first time after the discovery of America. **1052. lantern:** Sir Humphrey Davy invented the safety lamp for miners in 1815. **1054. travels,**

133

Man's phenomenon, one knows not what,
And wonderful beyond all wondrous measure;
'Tis pity, though, in this sublime world, that
Pleasure's a sin, and sometimes sin's a pleasure;
Few mortals know what end they would be at,
But whether glory, power, or love, or treasure,
The path is through perplexing ways, and when
The goal is gained, we die, you know — and then ——

134

What then? — I do not know, no more do you ——
And so good night. — Return we to our story:
'Twas in November, when fine days are few,
And the far mountains wax a little hoary,
And clap a white cape on their mantles blue;
And the sea dashes round the promontory,
And the loud breaker boils against the rock,
And sober suns must set at five o'clock.

135

'Twas, as the watchmen say, a cloudy night;
No moon, no stars, the wind was low or loud
By gusts, and many a sparkling hearth was bright
With the piled wood, round which the family crowd;
There's something cheerful in that sort of light,
Even as a summer sky's without a cloud:
I'm fond of fire, and crickets, and all that,
A lobster salad, and champagne, and chat.

136

'Twas midnight — Donna Julia was in bed,
Sleeping, most probably — when at her door
Arose a clatter might awake the dead,
If they had never been awoke before,
And that they have been so we all have read,
And are to be so, at the least, once more; —
The door was fastened, but with voice and fist
First knocks were heard, then " Madam — Madam — hist!

137

" For God's sake, Madam — Madam — here's my master,
With more than half the city at his back —
Was ever heard of such a curst disaster!
'Tis not my fault — I kept good watch — Alack!
Do pray undo the bolt a little faster —
They're on the stair just now, and in a crack
Will all be here; perhaps he yet may fly —
Surely the window's not so *very* high! "

138

By this time Don Alfonso was arrived,
With torches, friends, and servants in great number;
The major part of them had long been wived,
And therefore paused not to disturb the slumber
Of any wicked woman, who contrived
By stealth her husband's temples to encumber:
Examples of this kind are so contagious,
Were *one* not punished, *all* would be outrageous.

139

I can't tell how, or why, or what suspicion
Could enter into Don Alfonso's head;
But for a cavalier of his condition
It surely was exceedingly ill-bred,
Without a word of previous admonition,
To hold a levée round his lady's bed,
And summon lackeys, armed with fire and sword,
To prove himself the thing he most abhorred.

140

Poor Donna Julia! starting as from sleep
(Mind — that I do not say — she had not slept),
Began at once to scream, and yawn, and weep;
Her maid, Antonia, who was an adept,
Contrived to fling the bed-clothes in a heap,
As if she had just now from out them crept;
I can't tell why she should take all this trouble
To prove her mistress had been sleeping double.

141

But Julia mistress, and Antonia maid,
Appeared like two poor harmless women, who
Of goblins, but still more of men afraid,
Had thought one man might be deterred by two,
And therefore side by side were gently laid,
Until the hours of absence should run through,
And truant husband should return, and say,
" My dear, I was the first who came away."

142

Now Julia found at length a voice, and cried,
" In heaven's name, Don Alfonso, what d'ye mean?
Has madness seized you? would that I had died
Ere such a monster's victim I had been!
What may this midnight violence betide,
A sudden fit of drunkenness or spleen?
Dare you suspect me, whom the thought would kill?
Search, then, the room! " — Alfonso said, " I will."

**voyages**: Byron refers to recent books of travels in Morocco and the Arctic Ocean.

143

*He* searched, *they* searched, and rummaged every-
where,
Closet and clothes-press, chest and window-
seat,
And found much linen, lace, and several pair
Of stockings, slippers, brushes, combs, com-
plete,
With other articles of ladies fair,
To keep them beautiful, or leave them neat:
Arras they pricked and curtains with their swords,
And wounded several shutters, and some boards.

144

Under the bed they searched, and there they
found —
No matter what — it was not that they sought;
They opened the windows, gazing if the ground
Had signs of footmarks, but the earth said
naught;
And then they stared each other's faces round:
'Tis odd, not one of all these seekers thought,
And seems to me almost a sort of blunder,
Of looking *in* the bed as well as under.

145

During this inquisition Julia's tongue
Was not asleep — "Yes, search and search," she
cried,
"Insult on insult heap, and wrong on wrong!
It was for this that I became a bride!
For this in silence I have suffered long
A husband like Alfonso at my side;
But now I'll bear no more, nor here remain,
If there be law or lawyers in all Spain.

146

"Yes, Don Alfonso! husband now no more,
If ever you indeed deserved the name,
Is't worthy of your years? — you have three-score —
Fifty, or sixty, it is all the same —
Is't wise or fitting, causeless to explore
For facts against a virtuous woman's fame?
Ungrateful, perjured, barbarous Don Alfonso,
How dare you think your lady would go on so?

147

"Is it for this I have disdained to hold
The common privileges of my sex?
That I have chosen a confessor so old
And deaf, that any other it would vex,
And never once he has had cause to scold,
But found my very innocence perplex
So much, he always doubted I was married —
How sorry you will be when I've miscarried!

148

"Was it for this that no Cortejo e'er
I yet have chosen from out the youth of Seville?
Is it for this I scarce went anywhere,
Except to bull-fights, mass, play, rout, and revel?
Is it for this, whate'er my suitors were,
I favoured none — nay, was almost uncivil?
Is it for this that General Count O'Reilly,
Who took Algiers, declares I used him vilely?

149

"Did not the Italian Musico Cazzani
Sing at my heart six months at least in vain?
Did not his countryman, Count Corniani,
Call me the only virtuous wife in Spain?
Were there not also Russians, English, many?
The Count Strongstroganoff I put in pain,
And Lord Mount Coffeehouse, the Irish peer,
Who killed himself for love (with wine) last year.

150

"Have I not had two bishops at my feet?
The Duke of Ichar, and Don Fernan Nunez?
And is it thus a faithful wife you treat?
I wonder in what quarter now the moon is:
I praise your vast forbearance not to beat
Me also, since the time so opportune is —
Oh, valiant man! with sword drawn and cocked
trigger,
Now, tell me, don't you cut a pretty figure?

151

"Was it for this you took your sudden journey,
Under pretence of business indispensable,
With that sublime of rascals your attorney,
Whom I see standing there, and looking sensible
Of having played the fool? though both I spurn,
he
Deserves the worst, his conduct's less defensible,
Because, no doubt, 'twas for his dirty fee,
And not from any love to you nor me.

152

"If he comes here to take a deposition,
By all means let the gentleman proceed;
You've made the apartment in a fit condition: —
There's pen and ink for you, sir, when you
need —
Let everything be noted with precision,

**1177. Cortejo**: "The Spanish 'Cortejo' is much the same as the Italian 'Cavalier Servente'" [B]. Both terms refer to the acknowledged lover of a married woman. **1184. took Algiers**: "Donna Julia here made a mistake. Count O'Reilly did not take Algiers—but Algiers very nearly took him; he and his army and fleet retreated with great loss, and not much credit, from before that city, in the year 1775" [B].

I would not you for nothing should be feed —
But as my maid's undrest, pray turn your spies out."
"Oh!" sobbed Antonia, "I could tear their eyes out."

153

"There is the closet, there the toilet, there
The antechamber — search them under, over;
There is the sofa, there the great arm-chair,
The chimney — which would really hold a lover.
I wish to sleep, and beg you will take care
And make no further noise, till you discover
The secret cavern of this lurking treasure —
And when 'tis found, let me, too, have that pleasure.

154

"And now, Hidalgo! now that you have thrown
Doubt upon me, confusion over all,
Pray have the courtesy to make it known
*Who* is the man you search for? how d'ye call
Him? what's his lineage? let him but be shown —
I hope he's young and handsome — is he tall?
Tell me — and be assured, that since you stain
Mine honour thus; it shall not be in vain.

155

"At least, perhaps, he has not sixty years,
At that age he would be too old for slaughter,
Or for so young a husband's jealous fears —
(Antonia! let me have a glass of water.)
I am ashamed of having shed these tears,
They are unworthy of my father's daughter;
My mother dreamed not in my natal hour,
That I should fall into a monster's power.

156

"Perhaps 'tis of Antonia you are jealous,
You saw that she was sleeping by my side,
When you broke in upon us with your fellows;
Look where you please — we've nothing, sir, to hide;
Only another time, I trust, you'll tell us,
Or for the sake of decency abide
A moment at the door, that we may be
Drest to receive so much good company.

157

"And now, sir, I have done, and say no more;
The little I have said may serve to show
The guileless heart in silence may grieve o'er
The wrongs to whose exposure it is slow: —
I leave you to your conscience as before,
'Twill one day ask you, *why* you used me so?
God grant you feel not then the bitterest grief!
Antonia! where's my pocket-handkerchief?"

158

She ceased, and turned upon her pillow; pale
She lay, her dark eyes flashing through their tears,
Like skies that rain and lighten; as a veil,
Waved and o'ershading her wan cheek, appears
Her streaming hair; the black curls strive, but fail,
To hide the glossy shoulder, which uprears
Its snow through all; — her soft lips lie apart,
And louder than her breathing beats her heart.

159

The Senhor Don Alfonso stood confused;
Antonia bustled round the ransacked room,
And, turning up her nose, with looks abused
Her master, and his myrmidons, of whom
Not one, except the attorney, was amused;
He, like Achates, faithful to the tomb,
So there were quarrels, cared not for the cause,
Knowing they must be settled by the laws.

160

With prying snub-nose, all small eyes, he stood.
Following Antonia's motions here and there,
With much suspicion in his attitude;
For reputations he had little care;
So that a suit or action were made good,
Small pity had he for the young and fair,
And ne'er believed in negatives, till these
Were proved by competent false witnesses.

161

But Don Alfonso stood with downcast looks,
And, truth to say, he made a foolish figure;
When, after searching in five hundred nooks,
And treating a young wife with so much rigour,
He gained no point, except some self-rebukes,
Added to those his lady with such vigour
Had poured upon him for the last half-hour,
Quick, thick, and heavy — as a thunder-shower.

162

At first he tried to hammer an excuse,
To which the sole reply was tears and sobs,
And indications of hysterics, whose
Prologue is always certain throes, and throbs,
Gasps, and whatever else the owners choose:
Alfonso saw his wife, and thought of Job's;
He saw too, in perspective, her relations,
And then he tried to muster all his patience.

**1270. Achates:** the companion of Aeneas, whose fidelity has become proverbial.

163

He stood in act to speak, or rather stammer,
  But sage Antonia cut him short before
The anvil of his speech received the hammer,
  With "Pray, sir, leave the room, and say no more,
Or madam dies." — Alfonso mutter'd, "D—n her."
  But nothing else, the time of words was o'er;
He cast a rueful look or two, and did,
He knew not wherefore, that which he was bid.

164

With him retired his "*posse comitatus,*"
  The attorney last, who lingered near the door
Reluctantly, still tarrying there as late as
  Antonia let him — not a little sore
At this most strange and unexplained "*hiatus*"
  In Don Alfonso's facts, which just now wore
An awkward look; as he revolved the case,
The door was fastened in his legal face.

165

No sooner was it bolted, than — O shame!
  Oh sin! Oh sorrow! and Oh womankind!
How can you do such things and keep your fame,
  Unless this world, and t'other too, be blind?
Nothing so dear as an unfilched good name!
  But to proceed — for there is more behind:
With much heartfelt reluctance be it said,
Young Juan slipped, half-smothered, from the bed.

166

He had been hid — I don't pretend to say
  How, nor can I indeed describe the where —
Young, slender, and packed easily, he lay,
  No doubt, in little compass, round or square;
But pity him I neither must nor may
  His suffocation by that pretty pair;
'Twere better, sure, to die so, than be shut
With maudlin Clarence in his Malmsey butt.

167

And, secondly, I pity not, because
  He had no business to commit a sin,
Forbid by heavenly, fined by human laws,
  At least 'twas rather early to begin;
But at sixteen the conscience rarely gnaws
  So much as when we call our old debts in
At sixty years, and draw the accompts of evil,
And find a deuced balance with the devil.

168

Of his position I can give no notion;
  'Tis written in the Hebrew Chronicle,
How the physicians, leaving pill and potion,
  Prescribed, by way of blister, a young belle,
When old King David's blood grew dull in motion,
  And that the medicine answered very well;
Perhaps 'twas in a different way applied,
For David lived, but Juan nearly died.

169

What's to be done? Alfonso will be back
  The moment he has sent his fools away.
Antonia's skill was put upon the rack,
  But no device could be brought into play —
And how to parry the renewed attack?
  Besides, it wanted but few hours of day:
Antonia puzzled; Julia did not speak,
But pressed her bloodless lip to Juan's cheek.

170

He turned his lip to hers, and with his hand
  Called back the tangles of her wandering hair;
Even then their love they could not all command,
  And half forgot their danger and despair:
Antonia's patience now was at a stand —
  "Come, come, 'tis no time now for fooling there,"
She whispered, in great wrath — "I must deposit
This pretty gentleman within the closet:

171

"Pray, keep your nonsense for some luckier night —
  *Who* can have put my master in this mood?
What will become on't — I'm in such a fright,
  The devil's in the urchin, and no good —
Is this a time for giggling? this a plight?
  Why, don't you know that it may end in blood?
You'll lose your life, and I shall lose my place,
My mistress all, for the half-girlish face.

172

"Had it but been for a stout cavalier
  Of twenty-five or thirty — (come, make haste)
But for a child, what piece of work is here!
  I really, madam, wonder at your taste —
(Come, sir, get in) — my master must be near:
  There, for the present, at the least, he's fast,
And if we can but till the morning keep
Our counsel — Juan, mind, you must not sleep."

173

Now, Don Alfonso entering, but alone,
  Closed the oration of the trusty maid:

**1305. "*posse comitatus*"**: the full form of the modern word "posse." **1328. With . . . butt**: referring to the legend that the Duke of Clarence, brother of Edward IV and Richard III, was drowned in a butt of his favorite wine; see Shakespeare's *Richard III*, I.iv.

**1338. Hebrew Chronicle**: See I Kings 1.

She loitered, and he told her to be gone,
An order somewhat sullenly obeyed;
However, present remedy was none,
And no great good seemed answered if she staid;
Regarding both with slow and sidelong view,
She snuffed the candle, curtsied, and withdrew.

174

Alfonso paused a minute — then begun
Some strange excuses for his late proceeding;
He would not justify what he had done,
To say the best, it was extreme ill-breeding;
But there were ample reasons for it, none
Of which he specified in this his pleading:
His speech was a fine sample, on the whole,
Of rhetoric, which the learned call "*rigmarole.*"

175

Julia said nought; though all the while there rose
A ready answer, which at once enables
A matron, who her husband's foible knows,
By a few timely words to turn the tables,
Which, if it does not silence, still must pose, —
Even if it should comprise a pack of fables;
'Tis to retort with firmness, and when he
Suspects with *one,* do you reproach with *three.*

176

Julia, in fact, had tolerable grounds, —
Alfonso's loves with Inez were well known;
But whether 'twas that one's own guilt confounds —
But that can't be, as has been often shown,
A lady with apologies abounds; —
It might be that her silence sprang alone
From delicacy to Don Juan's ear,
To whom she knew his mother's fame was dear.

177

There might be one more motive, which makes two,
Alfonso ne'er to Juan had alluded, —
Mentioned his jealousy, but never who
Had been the happy lover, he concluded,
Concealed amongst his premises; 'tis true,
His mind the more o'er this its mystery brooded
To speak of Inez now were, one may say,
Like throwing Juan in Alfonso's way.

178

A hint, in tender cases, is enough;
Silence is best: besides there is a *tact* —
(That modern phrase appears to me sad stuff,
But it will serve to keep my verse compact) —
Which keeps, when pushed by questions rather rough,
A lady always distant from the fact:
The charming creatures lie with such a grace,
There's nothing so becoming to the face.

179

They blush, and we believe them, at least I
Have always done so; 'tis of no great use,
In any case, attempting a reply,
For then their eloquence grows quite profuse;
And when at length they're out of breath, they sigh,
And cast their languid eyes down, and let loose
A tear or two, and then we make it up;
And then — and then — and then — sit down and sup.

180

Alfonso closed his speech, and begged her pardon,
Which Julia half withheld, and then half granted,
And laid conditions, he thought very hard, on,
Denying several little things he wanted:
He stood like Adam lingering near his garden,
With useless penitence perplexed and haunted,
Beseeching she no further would refuse,
When, lo! he stumbled o'er a pair of shoes.

181

A pair of shoes! — what then? not much, if they
Are such as fit with ladies' feet, but these
(No one can tell how much I grieve to say)
Were masculine; to see them, and to seize,
Was but a moment's act. — Ah! well-a-day!
My teeth begin to chatter, my veins freeze —
Alfonso first examined well their fashion,
And then flew out into another passion.

182

He left the room for his relinquished sword,
And Julia instant to the closet flew.
" Fly, Juan, fly! for heaven's sake — not a word —
The door is open — you may yet slip through
The passage you so often have explored —
Here is the garden-key — Fly — fly — Adieu!
Haste — haste! I hear Alfonso's hurrying feet —
Day has not broke — there's no one in the street."

183

None can say that this was not good advice,
The only mischief was, it came too late;
Of all experience 'tis the usual price,
A sort of income-tax laid on by fate:
Juan had reached the room-door in a trice,
And might have done so by the garden-gate,
But met Alfonso in his dressing-gown,
Who threatened death — so Juan knocked him down.

184

Dire was the scuffle, and out went the light;
  Antonia cried out "Rape!" and Julia "Fire!"
But not a servant stirred to aid the fight.
  Alfonso, pommelled to his heart's desire,
Swore lustily he'd be revenged this night;
  And Juan, too, blasphemed an octave higher;
His blood was up; though young, he was a Tartar,
And not at all disposed to prove a martyr.

185

Alfonso's sword had dropped ere he could draw it,
  And they continued battling hand to hand,
For Juan very luckily ne'er saw it;
  His temper not being under great command,
If at that moment he had chanced to claw it,
  Alfonso's days had not been in the land
Much longer.—Think of husbands', lovers' lives!
And how ye may be doubly widows—wives!

186

Alfonso grappled to detain the foe,
  And Juan throttled him to get away,
And blood ('twas from the nose) began to flow;
  At last, as they more faintly wrestling lay,
Juan contrived to give an awkward blow,
  And then his only garment quite gave way;
He fled, like Joseph, leaving it; but there,
I doubt, all likeness ends between the pair.

187

Lights came at length, and men, and maids, who found
  An awkward spectacle their eyes before;
Antonia in hysterics, Julia swooned,
  Alfonso leaning, breathless, by the door;
Some half-torn drapery scattered on the ground,
  Some blood, and several footsteps, but no more:
Juan the gate gained, turned the key about,
And liking not the inside, locked the out.

188

Here ends this canto.—Need I sing, or say,
  How Juan, naked, favoured by the night,
Who favours what she should not, found his way,
  And reached his home in an unseemly plight?
The pleasant scandal which arose next day,
  The nine days' wonder which was brought to light,
And how Alfonso sued for a divorce,
Were in the English newspapers, of course.

189

If you would like to see the whole proceedings,
  The depositions and the cause at full,
The names of all the witnesses, the pleadings
  Of counsel to nonsuit, or to annul,
There's more than one edition, and the readings
  Are various, but they none of them are dull;
The best is that in short-hand ta'en by Gurney,
Who to Madrid on purpose made a journey.

190

But Donna Inez, to divert the train
  Of one of the most circulating scandals
That had for centuries been known in Spain,
  At least since the retirement of the Vandals,
First vowed (and never had she vowed in vain)
  To Virgin Mary several pounds of candles;
And then, by the advice of some old ladies,
She sent her son to be shipped off from Cadiz.

191

She had resolved that he should travel through
  All European climes, by land or sea,
To mend his former morals, and get new,
  Especially in France and Italy
(At least this is the thing most people do).
  Julia was sent into a convent: she
Grieved, but, perhaps, her feelings may be better
Shown in the following copy of her Letter:—

192

"They tell me 'tis decided you depart:
  'Tis wise—'tis well, but not the less a pain;
I have no further claim on your young heart,
  Mine is the victim, and would be again:
To love too much has been the only art
  I used;—I write in haste, and if a stain
Be on this sheet, 'tis not what it appears;
My eyeballs burn and throb, but have no tears.

193

"I loved, I love you, for this love have lost
  State, station, heaven, mankind's, my own esteem,
And yet cannot regret what it hath cost,
  So dear is still the memory of that dream;
Yet, if I name my guilt, 'tis not to boast,
  None can deem harshlier of me than I deem:
I trace this scrawl because I cannot rest—
I've nothing to reproach or to request.

194

"Man's love is of man's life a thing apart,
  'Tis woman's whole existence; man may range

**1488. all . . . ends:** Joseph's resistance to the blandishments of Potiphar's wife has made his name proverbial for chastity, as in Fielding's *Joseph Andrews;* see Gen. 39.

**1511. Gurney:** William B. Gurney was a famous shorthand writer and court reporter. **1516. Vandals:** The Vandals invaded Spain

The court, camp, church, the vessel, and the mart;
  Sword, gown, gain, glory, offer in exchange
Pride, fame, ambition, to fill up his heart,
  And few there are whom these cannot estrange;
Men have all these resources, we but one,
To love again, and be again undone.

195

"You will proceed in pleasure, and in pride,
  Beloved and loving many; all is o'er
For me on earth, except some years to hide
  My shame and sorrow deep in my heart's core:
These I could bear, but cannot cast aside
  The passion which still rages as before,—
And so farewell—forgive me, love me—No,
That word is idle now—but let it go.

196

"My breast has been all weakness, is so yet;
  But still I think I can collect my mind;
My blood still rushes where my spirit's set,
  As roll the waves before the settled wind;
My heart is feminine, nor can forget—
  To all, except one image, madly blind;
So shakes the needle, and so stands the pole,
As vibrates my fond heart to my fixed soul.

197

"I have no more to say, but linger still,
  And dare not set my seal upon this sheet,
And yet I may as well the task fulfil,
  My misery can scarce be more complete:
I had not lived till now, could sorrow kill;
  Death shuns the wretch who fain the blow would meet,
And I must even survive this last adieu,
And bear with life to love and pray for you!"

198

This note was written upon gilt-edged paper
  With a neat little crow-quill, slight and new;
Her small white hand could hardly reach the taper,
  It trembled as magnetic needles do,
And yet she did not let one tear escape her;
  The seal a sun-flower; "*Elle vous suit partout,*"
The motto, cut upon a white cornelian;
The wax was superfine, its hue vermilion.

199

This was Don Juan's earliest scrape; but whether
  I shall proceed with his adventures is
Dependent on the public altogether;
  We'll see, however, what they say to this,
Their favour in an author's cap's a feather,
  And no great mischief's done by their caprice;
And if their approbation we experience,
Perhaps they'll have some more about a year hence.

200

My poem's epic, and is meant to be
  Divided in twelve books; each book containing,
With love, and war, a heavy gale at sea,
  A list of ships, and captains, and kings reigning,
New characters; the episodes are three:
  A panoramic view of hell's in training,
After the style of Virgil and of Homer,
So that my name of Epic's no misnomer.

201

All these things will be specified in time,
  With strict regard to Aristotle's rules,
The *Vade Mecum* of the true sublime,
  Which makes so many poets, and some fools:
Prose poets like blank-verse, I'm fond of rhyme,
  Good workmen never quarrel with their tools;
I've got new mythological machinery,
And very handsome supernatural scenery.

202

There's only one slight difference between
  Me and my epic brethren gone before,
And here the advantage is my own, I ween
  (Not that I have not several merits more,
But this will more peculiarly be seen);
  They so embellish, that 'tis quite a bore
Their labyrinth of fables to thread through,
Whereas this story's actually true.

203

If any person doubt it, I appeal
  To history, tradition, and to facts,
To newspapers, whose truth all know and feel,
  To plays in five, and operas in three acts;
All these confirm my statement a good deal,
  But that which more completely faith exacts
Is, that myself, and several now in Seville,
*Saw* Juan's last elopement with the devil.

204

If ever I should condescend to prose,
  I'll write poetical commandments, which
Shall supersede beyond all doubt all those

in the fifth century and gave their name to Andalusia. Their thoroughness in violating the women in the cities they sacked is described by Gibbon, Byron's authority on late Roman history. 1582. *"Elle . . . partout"*: "She follows you everywhere," an allusion to the sunflower's keeping its face towards the sun. 1603. *Vade Mecum:* handbook. "Aristotle's rules" were generally supposed to be rules for observing the unities of time, place, and action, none of which Byron observes.

That went before; in these I shall enrich
My text with many things that no one knows,
And carry precept to the highest pitch:
I'll call the work "Longinus o'er a Bottle,
Or, Every Poet his *own* Aristotle."

205

Thou shalt believe in Milton, Dryden, Pope;
Thou shalt not set up Wordsworth, Coleridge, Southey;
Because the first is crazed beyond all hope,
The second drunk, the third so quaint and mouthy:
With Crabbe it may be difficult to cope,
And Campbell's Hippocrene is somewhat drouthy:
Thou shalt not steal from Samuel Rogers, nor
Commit — flirtation with the muse of Moore.

206

Thou shalt not covet Mr. Sotheby's Muse,
His Pegasus, nor anything that's his;
Thou shalt not bear false witness like "the Blues" —
(There's one, at least, is very fond of this);
Thou shalt not write, in short, but what I choose:
This is true criticism, and you may kiss —
Exactly as you please, or not, — the rod;
But if you don't, I'll lay it on, by G—d!

207

If any person should presume to assert
This story is not moral, first, I pray,
That they will not cry out before they're hurt,
Then that they'll read it o'er again, and say
(But, doubtless, nobody will be so pert),
That this is not a moral tale, though gay;
Beside, in Canto Twelfth, I mean to show
The very place where wicked people go.

208

If, after all, there should be some so blind
To their own good this warning to despise,

**1631. "Longinus . . . Aristotle"**: Longinus' *On the Sublime* and Aristotle's *Poetics* were the two Classical authorities on literary criticism. **1637–40. Crabbe . . . Rogers**: George Crabbe (1754–1832), author of *The Village*, Thomas Campbell (1777–1844), author of *The Pleasures of Hope* and *Gertrude of Wyoming* (quoted in st. 88, above), and Samuel Rogers (1763–1855), author of *The Pleasures of Memory*, were minor poets of the Romantic period. Rogers was a friend of Byron's, hence the difference of tone in the allusion. For "Hippocrene" see Keats, "Ode to a Nightingale," st. 2, p. 343, below. **1641. Sotheby**: William Sotheby (1757–1833), best known as the translator of Homer and Virgil, had a substantial private income and was often a patron of other poets, hence the allusion in l. 1642. **1643. "the Blues"**: i.e., bluestockings, or pedantic women. The allusion in the next line is to Lady Byron.

Let by some tortuosity of mind,
Not to believe my verse and their own eyes,
And cry that they "the moral cannot find,"
I tell him, if a clergyman, he lies;
Should captains the remark, or critics, make,
They also lie too — under a mistake.

209

The public approbation I expect,
And beg they'll take my word about the moral,
Which I with their amusement will connect
(So children cutting teeth receive a coral);
Meantime they'll doubtless please to recollect
My epical pretensions to the laurel:
For fear some prudish readers should grow skittish,
I've bribed my grandmother's review — the British.

210

I sent it in a letter to the Editor,
Who thanked me duly by return of post —
I'm for a handsome article his creditor;
Yet, if my gentle Muse he please to roast,
And break a promise after having made it her,
Denying the receipt of what it cost,
And smear his page with gall instead of honey,
All I can say is — that he had the money.

211

I think that with this holy new alliance
I may ensure the public, and defy
All other magazines of art or science,
Daily, or monthly or three monthly; I
Have not essayed to multiply their clients,
Because they tell me 'twere in vain to try,
And that the Edinburgh Review and Quarterly
Treat a dissenting author very martyrly.

212

"*Non ego hoc ferrem calida juventâ*
*Consule Planco*," Horace said, and so
Say I; by which quotation there is meant a
Hint that some six or seven good years ago
(Long ere I dreamt of dating from the Brenta)
I was most ready to return a blow,
And would not brook at all this sort of thing
In my hot youth — when George the Third was King.

213

But now at thirty years my hair is grey —
(I wonder what it will be like at forty?
I thought of a peruke the other day — )

**1689. "*Non . . . Planco*"**: "I should not have borne this in the heat of my youth when Plancus was consul" (Horace, *Odes*, III.xiv). **1693. Brenta**: a river near Venice. The line means "before I went abroad for the last time."

My heart is not much greener; and, in short, I
Have squandered my whole summer while 'twas May,
And feel no more the spirit to retort; I
Have spent my life, both interest and principal,
And deem not, what I deemed, my soul invincible.

214

No more — no more — Oh! never more on me
The freshness of the heart can fall like dew,
Which out of all the lovely things we see
Extracts emotions beautiful and new;
Hived in our bosoms like the bag o' the bee.
Think'st thou the honey with those objects grew?
Alas! 'twas not in them, but in thy power
To double even the sweetness of a flower.

215

No more — no more — Oh! never more, my heart,
Canst thou be my sole world, my universe!
Once all in all, but now a thing apart,
Thou canst not be my blessing or my curse:
The illusion's gone for ever, and thou art
Insensible, I trust, but none the worse,
And in thy stead I've got a deal of judgment,
Though heaven knows how it ever found a lodgment.

216

My days of love are over; me no more
The charms of maid, wife, and still less of widow,
Can make the fool of which they made before, —
In short, I must not lead the life I did do;
The credulous hope of mutual minds is o'er,
The copious use of claret is forbid too,
So for a good old-gentlemanly vice,
I think I must take up with avarice.

217

Ambition was my idol, which was broken
Before the shrines of Sorrow, and of Pleasure;
And the two last have left me many a token
O'er which reflection may be made at leisure;
Now, like Friar Bacon's brazen head, I've spoken,
"Time is, Time was, Time's past:" — a chymic treasure
Is glittering youth, which I have spent betimes —
My heart in passion, and my head on rhymes.

218

What is the end of fame? 'tis but to fill
A certain portion of uncertain paper:
Some liken it to climbing up a hill,
Whose summit, like all hills, is lost in vapour;
For this men write, speak, preach, and heroes kill,
And bards burn what they call their "midnight taper,"
To have, when the original is dust,
A name, a wretched picture, and worst bust.

219

What are the hopes of man? Old Egypt's King
Cheops erected the first pyramid
And largest, thinking it was just the thing
To keep his memory whole, and mummy hid:
But somebody or other rummaging,
Burglariously broke his coffin's lid.
Let not a monument give you or me hopes,
Since not a pinch of dust remains of Cheops.

220

But I, being fond of true philosophy,
Say very often to myself, "Alas!
All things that have been born were born to die,
And flesh (which Death mows down to hay) is grass;
You've passed your youth not so unpleasantly.
And if you had it o'er again — 'twould pass —
So thank your stars that matters are no worse,
And read your Bible, sir, and mind your purse."

221

But for the present, gentle reader! and
Still gentler purchaser! the bard — that's I —
Must, with permission, shake you by the hand,
And so your humble servant, and good-bye!
We meet again, if we should understand
Each other; and if not, I shall not try
Your patience further than by this short sample —
'Twere well if others followed my example.

222

"Go, little book, from this my solitude!
I cast thee on the waters — go thy ways!
And if, as I believe, thy vein be good,
The world will find thee after many days."
When Southey's read, and Wordsworth understood,
I can't help putting in my claim to praise —
The four first rhymes are Southey's, every line:
For God's sake, reader! take them not for mine!

## from CANTO III

78

And now they were diverted by their suite,
Dwarfs, dancing-girls, black eunuchs, and a poet,
Which made their new establishment complete;

**1733. Friar Bacon's:** The story of the legendary speaking brazen head made by the medieval philosopher Roger Bacon is told in Robert Greene's play, *Friar Bacon and Friar Bungay* (1594).

**1775. Southey's:** The lines are from the last stanza of Southey's "Epilogue to the Lay of the Laureate."

The last was of great fame, and liked to show it;
His verses rarely wanted their due feet—
And for this theme—he seldom sung below it,
He being paid to satirise or flatter,
As the psalm says, "inditing a good matter."

79

He praised the present, and abused the past,
Reversing the good custom of old days,
An Eastern anti-jacobin at last
He turned, preferring pudding to *no* praise—
For some few years his lot had been o'ercast
By his seeming independent in his lays,
But now he sung the Sultan and the Pacha
With truth like Southey, and with verse like Crashaw.

80

He was a man who had seen many changes,
And always changed as true as any needle;
His polar star being one which rather ranges,
And not the fixed—he knew the way to wheedle:
So vile he 'scaped the doom which oft avenges;
And being fluent (save indeed when feed ill),
He lied with such a fervour of intention—
There was no doubt he earned his laureate pension.

81

But he had genius,—when a turncoat has it,
The "Vates irritabilis" takes care
That without notice few full moons shall pass it;
Even good men like to make the public stare:—
But to my subject—let me see—what was it?—
Oh!—the third canto—and the pretty pair—
Their loves, and feasts, and house, and dress, and mode
Of living in their insular abode.

82

Their poet, a sad trimmer, but no less
In company a very pleasant fellow,
Had been the favourite of full many a mess
Of men, and made them speeches when half mellow;
And though his meaning they could rarely guess,
Yet still they deigned to hiccup or to bellow
The glorious meed of popular applause,
Of which the first ne'er knows the second cause.

83

But now being lifted into high society,
And having picked up several odds and ends
Of free thoughts in his travels, for variety,
He deemed, being in a lone isle, among friends,
That without any danger of a riot, he
Might for long lying make himself amends;
And singing as he sung in his warm youth,
Agree to a short armistice with truth.

84

He had travelled 'mongst the Arabs, Turks, and Franks,
And he knew the self-loves of the different nations;
And having lived with people of all ranks,
Had something ready upon most occasions—
Which got him a few presents and some thanks.
He varied with some skill his adulations;
To "do at Rome as Romans do," a piece
Of conduct was which he observed in Greece.

85

Thus, usually, when he was asked to sing,
He gave the different nations something national;
'Twas all the same of him—"God save the king,"
Or "*ça ira*," according to the fashion all:
His muse made increment of anything,
From the high lyric down to the low rational:
If Pindar sang horse-races, what should hinder
Himself from being as pliable as Pindar?

86

In France, for instance, he would write a chanson;
In England a six canto quarto tale;
In Spain he'd make a ballad or romance on
The last war—much the same in Portugal;
In Germany, the Pegasus he'd prance on
Would be old Goethe's—(see what says De Staël);
In Italy he'd ape the "Trecentisti";
In Greece, he'd sing some sort of hymn like this t'ye:

i

The isles of Greece, the isles of Greece!
Where burning Sappho loved and sung,
Where grew the arts of war and peace,
Where Delos rose, and Phoebus sprung!
Eternal summer gilds them yet,
But all, except their sun, is set.

ii

The Scian and the Teian muse,
The hero's harp, the lover's lute,

**Canto III: 8. psalm:** Ps. 45:1. **16. Crashaw:** Richard Crashaw (1613–50), poet and Roman Catholic convert, whose "metaphysical" style of writing was out of fashion in Byron's day. **26. "Vates irritabilis":** the irritable poet; see Coleridge, *Biographia Literaria*, II. **33. trimmer:** time-serving compromiser.

**60. "ça ira":** a French Revolutionary song. **70. De Staël:** Madame de Staël, whom Byron had met in England, said in her book *De L'Allemagne* (1810) that Goethe represented the entire literature of Germany. **71. "Trecentisti":** Italian poets of the fourteenth century: Dante, Petrarch, Boccaccio. **76. Delos:** the island in the Cyclades said to have been originally a floating island, and the place where Phoebus Apollo and his sister Artemis

Have found the fame your shores refuse:
 Their place of birth alone is mute
To sounds which echo further west
Than your sires' "Islands of the Blest."

iii

The mountains look on Marathon —
 And Marathon looks on the sea;
And musing there an hour alone,
 I dreamed that Greece might still be free;
For standing on the Persians' grave,
I could not deem myself a slave.

iv

A king sate on the rocky brow
 Which looks o'er sea-born Salamis;
And ships, by thousands, lay below,
 And men in nations; — all were his!
He counted them at break of day —
And when the sun set where were they?

v

And where are they? and where art thou,
 My country? On thy voiceless shore
The heroic lay is tuneless now —
 The heroic bosom beats no more!
And must thy lyre, so long divine,
Degenerate into hands like mine?

vi

'Tis something, in the dearth of fame,
 Though linked among a fettered race,
To feel at least a patriot's shame,
 Even as I sing, suffuse my face;
For what is left the poet here?
For Greeks a blush — for Greece a tear.

vii

Must *we* but weep o'er days more blest?
 Must *we* but blush? — Our fathers bled.
Earth! render back from out thy breast
 A remnant of our Spartan dead!
Of the three hundred grant but three,
To make a new Thermopylae!

viii

What, silent still? and silent all?
 Ah! no; — the voices of the dead
Sound like a distant torrent's fall,
 And answer, "Let one living head,
But one arise, — we come, we come!"
'Tis but the living who are dumb.

ix

In vain — in vain: strike other chords;
 Fill high the cup with Samian wine!
Leave battles to the Turkish hordes,
 And shed the blood of Scio's vine!
Hark! rising to the ignoble call —
How answers each bold Bacchanal!

x

You have the Pyrrhic dance as yet;
 Where is the Pyrrhic phalanx gone?
Of two such lessons, why forget
 The nobler and the manlier one?
You have the letters Cadmus gave —
Think ye he meant them for a slave?

xi

Fill high the bowl with Samian wine!
 We will not think of themes like these!
It made Anacreon's song divine:
 He served — but served Polycrates —
A tyrant; but our masters then
Were still, at least, our countrymen.

xii

The tyrant of the Chersonese
 Was freedom's best and bravest friend;
*That* tyrant was Miltiades!
 Oh! that the present hour would lend
Another despot of the kind!
Such chains as his were sure to bind.

xiii

Fill high the bowl with Samian wine!
 On Suli's rock, and Parga's shore,
Exists the remnant of a line
 Such as the Doric mothers bore;
And there, perhaps, some seed is sown,
The Heracleidan blood might own.

xiv

Trust not for freedom to the Franks
 They have a king who buys and sells;
In native swords, and native ranks,
 The only hope of courage dwells:
But Turkish force, and Latin fraud,
Would break your shield, however broad.

were born. **79. Scian . . . Teian:** Scio and Teos were traditionally the birthplaces of Homer and Anacreon, respectively. **84. "Islands . . . Blest":** "The *nesoi makaron* of the Greek poets were supposed to have been the Cape de Verd islands or the Canaries" [B]. **91. king:** Xerxes. See the note on Canto I, I, 937. He watched the battle of Salamis from a nearby mountain.

**127. Pyrrhic:** Pyrrhus, king of Epirus in the third century B.C. and winner of a "Pyrrhic victory" (i.e., one in which the victor's losses are great enough to amount to a defeat) over the Romans, fought with the Macedonian phalanx and is said to have invented a war dance. **136. Polycrates:** a tyrant of Samos in the sixth century B.C.; Anacreon was one of his court poets. **139. Chersonese:** a peninsula in Thrace, the modern Gallipoli. Miltiades, its ruler in the fifth century B.C., was the leader of the Greeks at Marathon. **146. Suli's . . . Parga's:** towns in Albania. **148. Doric:** The Dorian invasion of Greece after the Trojan War was called the "Return of the Heracleidae," because the Dorians claimed descent from Hercules. **151. Franks:** Western Europeans.

xv

Fill high the bowl with Samian wine!
  Our virgins dance beneath the shade—
I see their glorious black eyes shine;
  But gazing on each glowing maid,
My own the burning tear-drop loves,
To think such breasts must suckle slaves.

xvi

Place me on Sunium's marbled steep,
  Where nothing, save the waves and I,
May hear our mutual murmurs sweep;
  There, swan-like, let me sing and die:
A land of slaves shall ne'er be mine—
Dash down yon cup of Samian wine!

87

Thus sung, or would, or could, or should have sung,
  The modern Greek, in tolerable verse;
If not like Orpheus quite, when Greece was young,
  Yet in these times he might have done much worse:
His strain displayed some feeling—right or wrong;
  And feeling, in a poet, is the source
Of others' feeling; but they are such liars,
And take all colours—like the hands of dyers.

88

But words are things, and a small drop of ink,
  Falling like dew, upon a thought, produces
That which makes thousands, perhaps millions, think;
  'Tis strange, the shortest letter which man uses
Instead of speech, may form a lasting link
  Of ages; to what straits old Time reduces
Frail man, when paper—even a rag like this,
Survives himself, his tomb, and all that's his!

89

And when his bones are dust, his grave a blank,
  His station, generation, even his nation,
Become a thing, or nothing, save to rank
  In chronological commemoration,
Some dull MS. oblivion long has sank,
  Or graven stone found in a barrack's station
In digging the foundation of a closet,
May turn his name up, as a rare deposit.

90

And glory long has made the sages smile;
  'Tis something, nothing, words, illusion, wind—
Depending more upon the historian's style
  Than on the name a person leaves behind:
Troy owes to Homer what whist owes to Hoyle:
  The present century was growing blind
To the great Marlborough's skill in giving knocks,
Until his late Life by Archdeacon Coxe.

91

Milton's the prince of poets—so we say;
  A little heavy, but no less divine:
An independent being in his day—
  Learn'd, pious, temperate in love and wine;
But his life falling into Johnson's way,
  We're told this great high priest of all the Nine
Was whipt at college—a harsh sire—odd spouse,
For the first Mrs. Milton left his house.

92

All these are, *certes,* entertaining facts,
  Like Shakespeare's stealing deer, Lord Bacon's bribes;
Like Titus' youth, and Caesar's earliest acts;
  Like Burns (whom Doctor Currie well describes);
Like Cromwell's pranks;—but although truth exacts
  These amiable descriptions from the scribes,
As most essential to their hero's story,
They do not much contribute to his glory.

93

All are not moralists, like Southey, when
  He prated to the world of "Pantisocrasy;"
Or Wordsworth unexcised, unhired, who then
  Seasoned his pedlar poems with democracy;
Or Coleridge, long before his flighty pen
  Let to the Morning Post its aristocracy;
When he and Southey, following the same path,
Espoused two partners (milliners of Bath).

94

Such names at present cut a convict figure,
  The very Botany Bay in moral geography;

**163. Sunium's:** the promontory at the southeastern tip of Attica.

**200. late Life:** *Memoirs of John, Duke of Marlborough,* by William Coxe, Archdeacon of Wilts, appeared in 1818–19. **206. Nine:** i.e., the nine Muses. **208. For . . . house:** "See Johnson's Life of Milton" [B], for which see Vol. I, pp. 951–61. **210–13. Like . . . pranks:** For the Shakespeare legend see any annotated edition of the opening scene of *The Merry Wives of Windsor;* Bacon was convicted by Parliament of taking bribes as Chancellor; Titus practised forgery in his youth; Caesar betrayed and crucified some pirates after making friends with them; the dissipation of Burns is described (and much exaggerated) in James Currie's life, published in 1800; Cromwell is said to have robbed orchards in his youth. **217–24. All . . . Bath:** for "Pantisocracy" see headnote to "To a Young Ass," p. 109, above; Wordsworth was appointed Distributor of Stamps in Westmoreland, a position in the excise, in 1813; the central figures of Wordsworth's *Peter Bell* and *The Excursion* are pedlars, hence "pedlar poems"; Coleridge began writing for the *Morning Post* in 1800 after giving up his earlier radical views; Southey and Coleridge married sisters, Edith and Sara Fricker, who were not milliners and came not from Bath but from Bristol. **226. Botany Bay:** penal settlement in Australia.

Their loyal treason, renegado rigour,
  Are good manure for their more bare biography,
Wordsworth's last quarto, by the way, is bigger
  Than any since the birthday of typography;
A drowsy frowzy poem, called the "Excursion,"
Writ in a manner which is my aversion.

95

He there builds up a formidable dyke
  Between his own and others' intellect:
But Wordsworth's poem, and his followers, like
  Joanna Southcote's Shiloh, and her sect,
Are things which in this century don't strike
  The public mind,—so few are the elect;
And the new births of both their stale virginities
Have proved but dropsies, taken for divinities.

96

But let me to my story: I must own,
  If I have any fault, it is digression,
Leaving my people to proceed alone,
  While I soliloquize beyond expression:
But these are my addresses from the throne,
  Which put off business to the ensuing session:
Forgetting each omission is a loss to
The world, not quite so great as Ariosto.

97

I know that what our neighbours call *"longueurs,"*
  (We've not so good a *word,* but have the *thing,*
In that complete perfection which insures
  An epic from Bob Southey every Spring—)
Form not the true temptation which allures
  The reader; but 'twould not be hard to bring
Some fine examples of the *epopée,*
To prove its grand ingredient is *ennui.*

98

We learn from Horace, "Homer sometimes sleeps;"
  We feel without him, Wordsworth sometimes wakes,—
To show with what complacency he creeps,
  With his dear *"Waggoners,"* around his lakes.
He wishes for "a boat" to sail the deeps—
  Of ocean?—No, of air; and then he makes
Another outcry for "a little boat,"
And drivels seas to set it well afloat.

99

If he must fain sweep o'er the ethereal plain,
  And Pegasus runs restive in his "Waggon,"
Could he not beg the loan of Charles's Wain?
  Or pray Medea for a single dragon?
Or if, too classic for his vulgar brain,
  He feared his neck to venture such a nag on,
And he must needs mount nearer to the moon,
Could not the blockhead ask for a balloon?

100

"Pedlars," and "Boats," and "Waggons!" Oh! ye shades
  Of Pope and Dryden, are we come to this?
That trash of such sort not alone evades
  Contempt, but from the bathos' vast abyss
Floats scumlike uppermost, and these Jack Cades
  Of sense and song above your graves may hiss—
The "little boatman" and his "Peter Bell"
Can sneer at him who drew "Achitophel"!

101

T'our tale.—The feast was over, the slaves gone,
  The dwarfs and dancing girls had all retired;
The Arab lore and poet's song were done,
  And every sound of revelry expired;
The lady and her lover, left alone,
  The rosy flood of twilight's sky admired;—
Ave Maria! o'er the earth and sea,
That heavenliest hour of Heaven is worthiest thee!

102

Ave Maria! blessed be the hour!
  The time, the clime, the spot, where I so oft
Have felt that moment in its fullest power
  Sink o'er the earth so beautiful and soft,
While swung the deep bell in the distant tower
  Or the faint dying day-hymn stole aloft,
And not a breath crept through the rosy air,
And yet the forest leaves seemed stirred with prayer.

103

Ave Maria! 'tis the hour of prayer!
  Ave Maria! 'tis the hour of love!

**231. "Excursion":** Wordsworth's *The Excursion,* in nine books, was published in 1814. **236. Joanna . . . Shiloh:** See *The Vision of Judgment,* l. 224 and note, p. 198, above. **248. Ariosto:** the Italian poet (1474–1533) whose romantic epic, *Orlando Furioso,* is one of Byron's models. **257. Horace:** in the *Ars Poetica,* l. 359. **260. "*Waggoners*":** Wordsworth's *The Waggoner,* to which this refers, was published in 1819, just after *Peter Bell.* The first stanza of *Peter Bell* reads:

> There's something in a flying horse,
> There's something in a huge balloon;
> But through the clouds I'll never float
> Until I have a little Boat,
> Shaped like a crescent-moon.

**267. Charles's Wain:** the constellation usually called the Big Dipper. "Wain" means waggon. **277. Jack Cades:** Jack Cade was the leader of a rebellion against King Henry VI in 1450. See Shakespeare's *II Henry VI.* **280. "Achitophel":** The author of the satire *Absalom and Achitophel* (Vol. I, pp. 574–84) was John Dryden, of whom Wordsworth had remarked in one of his critical essays: "The verses of Dryden, once so highly celebrated, are forgotten" [quoted by Byron in a note]. **287. Ave Maria!:** Hail, Mary; an invocation used in the vesper prayer, hence symbolic of the close of the day.

Ave Maria! may our spirits dare
  Look up to thine and to thy Son's above!
Ave Maria! oh that face so fair!
  Those downcast eyes beneath the Almighty dove —
What though 'tis but a pictured image strike,
That painting is no idol, — 'tis too like.

104

Some kinder casuits are pleased to say,
  In nameless print — that I have no devotion;
But set those persons down with me to pray,
  And you shall see who has the properest notion
Of getting into heaven the shortest way;
  My altars are the mountains and the ocean,
Earth, air, stars, — all that springs from the great Whole,
Who hath produced, and will receive the soul.

105

Sweet hour of twilight! — in the solitude
  Of the pine forest, and the silent shore
Which bounds Ravenna's immemorial wood,
  Rooted where once the Adrian wave flowed o'er,
To where the last Caesarean fortress stood,
  Evergreen forest — which Boccacio's lore
And Dryden's lay made haunted ground to me,
How have I loved the twilight hour and thee!

106

The shrill cicalas, people of the pine,
  Making their summer lives one ceaseless song,
Were the sole echoes, save my steed's and mine,
  And vesper bell's that rose the boughs along;
The spectre huntsman of Onesti's line,
  His hell-dogs, and their chase, and the fair throng
Which learned from this example not to fly
From a true lover, — shadowed my mind's eye.

107

Oh, Hesperus! thou bringest all good things —
  Home to the weary, to the hungry cheer,
To the young bird the parent's brooding wings,
  The welcome stall to the o'erlaboured steer;
Whate'er of peace about our hearthstone clings,
  Whate'er our household gods protect of dear,
Are gathered round us by thy look of rest;
Thou bring'st the child, too, to the mother's breast.

108

Soft hour! which wakes the wish and melts the heart
  Of those who sail the seas, on the first day
When they from their sweet friends are torn apart;
  Or fills with love the pilgrim on his way
As the far bell of vesper makes him start,
  Seeming to weep the dying day's decay;
Is this a fancy which our reason scorns?
Ah! surely nothing dies but something mourns!

109

When Nero perished by the justest doom
  Which ever the destroyer yet destroyed,
Amidst the road of liberated Rome,
  Of nations freed, and the world overjoyed,
Some hands unseen strewed flowers upon his tomb:
  Perhaps the weakness of a heart not void
Of feeling for some kindness done, when power
Had left the wretch an uncorrupted hour.

110

But I'm digressing; what on earth has Nero,
  Or any such like sovereign buffoons,
To do with the transactions of my hero,
  More than such madmen's fellow man — the moon's?
Sure my invention must be down at zero,
  And I grown one of many "wooden spoons"
Of verse (the name with which we Cantabs please
To dub the last of honours in degrees).

111

I feel this tediousness will never do —
  'Tis being *too* epic, and I must cut down
(In copying) this long canto into two;
  They'll never find it out, unless I own
The fact, excepting some experienced few;
  And then as an improvement 'twill be shown:
I'll prove that such the opinion of the critic is
From Aristotle *passim*. — See Ποιητικῆς.

**315. wood:** Ravenna, where Byron lived in 1820–21, was originally a port on the Adriatic, and is now five miles inland, separated from the sea by a pine forest. **317. fortress:** The old fortified port of Augustus was demolished and turned into a grove in the sixth century A.D. **318. Boccacio's lore:** one of the tales in Boccaccio's *Decameron* was retold in Dryden's poem *Theodore and Honoria*. The "Theodore" of Dryden is the "Onesti" (l. 325) of Boccaccio. Byron's purpose in referring to Dryden's poem is to show that there is more genuine feeling for nature in Dryden than in Wordsworth. **329. Hesperus:** the evening star. Byron is paraphrasing a fragment of Sappho.

**359. Cantabs:** graduates of Cambridge. **368. Aristotle:** Aristotle remarks in ch. xxiv of the *Ars Poetica* that in epic "the beginning and the end must be capable of being brought within a single view" [Butcher trans.].

**I. A. RICHARDS, *Editor***

# *Percy Bysshe Shelley*

**1792–1822**

"I am one whom men love not," Shelley wrote one day in a dejected mood. It was not true of his personal life, for he was exceptionally beloved by all his friends. But there was no public for his poetry; the critics derided it and the law condemned it. Almost to the present day he has suffered from popular misconceptions that have made him out either a softie or a villain. A weak, girlish portrait painted by a woman who knew it was a failure; the label "ineffectual angel" clamped on by a Victorian critic who had not studied his subject; a story-biography by a twentieth century Frenchman done for entertainment — these form one side of the picture. On the reverse we have the atheistic author of blasphemous poems, the immoral seducer of schoolgirls who drove his wife to suicide, practiced free love and preached subversive doctrines.

The two incompatible pictures are the extreme travesties of a central unity, since "a passion for reforming the world" was combined in Shelley with grace and tenderness beyond all common measure. A truer description of him was given by a fellow poet, Walter Savage Landor, who regretted that through ignorant prejudice he had never visited Shelley when both were living in Italy. He had come to appreciate how much he had missed:

> Innocent and careless as a boy, he possessed all the delicate feelings of a gentleman, all the discrimination of a scholar, and united, in just degree, the ardour of the poet with the patience and forbearance of the philosopher. His generosity and charity went far beyond those of any man (I believe) at present in existence.[1]

This was the mature Shelley of his final phase. Though he did not live to be thirty, so much intense experience and so much thought were crowded into his short life that in five years he developed more than other men in fifty, and remarked once that if he should die tomorrow he had yet lived to be older than his father. By more ordinary reckoning the baronet, Sir Timothy, was to survive his unruly son by twenty-two years — his peaceful existence disturbed by eddies and reactions. Behind him stretched a dignified line of Sussex aristocrats traceable back to the fifteenth century; but although the poet's grandfather, Sir Bysshe Shelley, was a man of enterprise, oddity and humor, convention had settled solidly on Timothy, who slid smoothly through Oxford and the Grand Tour of Europe, besides winning a seat in Parliament through the safe assets of family connections and party influence. When his wife Elizabeth — a correct and cold-hearted lady — gave birth to their first son on August 4, 1792, this hard-headed country squire no doubt expected Percy Bysshe to follow in his tracks. And reasonably enough. As Santayana observes: "Few revolutionists would be such if they were heirs to a baronetcy." The boy was to be educated first at Syon House Academy, a respectable private school at Brentford, then at Eton and at Oxford, as befitted the son of a country squire.

[1] *Imaginary Conversations,* Vol. III, 1828.

Shelley, however, while learning Latin from the age of six and enjoying rural pranks on his father's estate, an only son surrounded by adoring sisters, found his own type and degree of education. Looking back on his boyhood — in "Hymn to Intellectual Beauty," V — he recalled how the fashionable Gothic tales of ghosts and haunted ruins (read in the school library) enthralled him until, puzzling deeply on the mystery of man's life and love and hatred, he awoke suddenly to a realizing sense of the Beauty there addressed. To that light, which "gives grace and truth to life's unquiet dream," he vowed to dedicate his own powers. And again, in dedicating *The Revolt of Islam* to Mary Shelley:

I will be wise,
And just, and free, and mild, if in me lies
Such power, for I grow weary to behold
The selfish and the strong still tyrannise
Without reproach or check.

Great commitments, not only recorded but, to a degree seldom equaled, kept.

Already, then, Shelley had burst through the bounds of personal pleasures and comforts to fight all tyranny and slavery, whether practiced on nations or on individuals, and to attempt to lead men, so far as a single mind could do it, to a life of freedom, love, and apprehension of the beautiful. Poem after poem of his maturer years expresses the same striving. To name a few, it is the motivating power in *The Revolt of Islam,* the "Ode to Liberty," and *Hellas;* it is savage and denunciatory in "The Mask of Anarchy" and "Lines Written During the Castlereagh Administration"; it is transcendental in the great verse drama *Prometheus Unbound.* He was impatient of conventionalized creeds and cramping laws. Development, with Shelley, lay not in altering his basic ideas but in maturing the comprehension and expression of them through study and understanding, and in learning by hard experience that practical efforts were often a waste owing to lack of co-operation. In a community alien to his ideals his only hope of raising a firm edifice was to build it in words and images. These came, almost too readily, at his call.

Not surprisingly, at Eton the young Shelley looked on some of its customs as forms of tyranny. He had something better to do; his expanding mind had taken a decided turn to the scientific, and while he studied the "general principles of electricity" his experiments were so practical as to look like practical jokes. His interest in astronomy was to serve him well as a poet; many of his apparently airy fantasies, when examined closely, show an unusually clear grasp of the solar system and the stellar universe. At the same time, besides going ahead with Greek and Latin, he was scribbling a Gothic romance, *Zastrozzi,* replete with the horrors of its kind.

These activities, scientific, classical, and literary, were pursued with ever-growing zeal when at Michaelmas, 1810, Shelley went up to University College, Oxford. He had the luck of the wealthy in that Sir Timothy, thinking no harm could come of it, asked a friendly firm of printers to indulge his son's literary freaks. But Messrs. Slatter & Munday shook their heads over the bold opinions in a novel called *Leonora,* written jointly by Shelley and another odd fish of his year. Thomas Jefferson Hogg shared his friend's passion for the Greek philosophers and his hatred of the orthodox, though he was far from sharing Shelley's sensitivity. He claimed, too, a hand in Shelley's notorious pamphlet on *The Necessity of Atheism,* copies of which were burning in the booksellers' back kitchen twenty minutes after their first appearance in the shop. Shelley and Hogg exasperated the Master and Fellows by their pride and obstinacy when called up to be questioned. After only two terms at Oxford they were "publicly expelled from the College for contumacy in refusing to answer certain questions put to them."

The months that followed give us Shelley's least attractive period. His career was broken, his aim uncertain, his friend was a coarsening influence, and his inspired revolt was growing harsh and petulant. To banish uncertainty he tried hyperbole, and determined in this mood to enact the knight-errant by "rescuing" his sisters' discontented school-friend, Harriet Westbrook. They hurried to Edinburgh and were married in a fashion, despite Shelley's principles — as a conscientious revolutionary of the period he regarded the marriage bond as a degrading concession to false social conventions. For a while they moved about restlessly — as all moved who lived with Shelley — from town to town. Harriet welcomed her "tyrant" sister Eliza; Hogg tried to seduce the bride in Shelley's absence. All this was disillusioning to the idealist; but his enthusiasm mounted in politics and he set out for Dublin, armed with an "Address to the Irish People," pleading for charity to their ill-used Catholics. To this day the "Address" makes lively reading; the adventure ended in a resolve to labor for "an effect which will take place ages after I have mouldered in the dust." At the same time he was pressing acquaintanceship on the aging William Godwin, author of *Political Justice,* whose radical ideas matched and influenced his own. Shelley had still to find his feet.

Yet he had been working on a long, philosophical, allegorical poem with the misleading title of *Queen Mab.* Highly and variously derivative, yet charged with the images and ideas of future work, this premature concoction—or news of it, since it was printed privately—got around, and branded the author at the very start of his mission. "There is no God!" he had written, and in his formidably learned notes used rational arguments to prove his case. What he upheld was the bleak doctrine of "Necessity," by which he meant, at this date, that a chain of undisplaceable causes and effects composed the universe. He was soon to progress to a conviction of man's own power over good and evil, but the symbolism of the later poems shrouded his meaning. The four monosyllables "There is no God" were thought to explain themselves.[1] From now onward he was handicapped with the social world which had, as ever, a keener ear for scandal than for poetry; so that when, in the following spring, the news went round that Shelley had left his wife and eloped with Godwin's daughter Mary his reputation as villain and blasphemer was complete.

His own friends—Hogg; Leigh Hunt, the encourager of all young poets; Thomas Love Peacock, the classical scholar and satiric novelist—knew that Shelley was in a turmoil of conflicting loyalties and indecisions. His poetry reflects it: in May of 1814 he was writing to Harriet,

> Thy look of love has power to calm
> The stormiest passion of my soul;

in the following month he was addressing Mary,

> We are not happy, sweet! our state
> Is strange and full of doubt and fear.

He has been laughed at by the worldly-wise for inviting the abandoned Harriet to Switzerland where he had fled with his new love. Yet in a truly Shelleyan community such a solution might have worked. Already they had with them Mary's step-sister Claire Clairmont, from whom there was to be almost no escape until Shelley's death. She was a thorn too in Mary's side. These two women, for all their love of Shelley, did not inhabit his ideal world. He came to know that, but tried for the most part to forget it. Shelley abhorred the limitation and exclusiveness of marriage; his Platonic search for Intellectual Beauty had its counterpart in human love. To worship of the beautiful there should be no boundaries; and in Shelley himself it was not only possible but natural to love many women, each for her own distinctiveness. This interdependence of idea and action make it difficult to consider his writings apart from some attention to the outward pattern of his life.

Idealism and chivalry came up against spates of practical perplexities. Shelley wrote on, harried by financial troubles, by the predicament of Harriet and their children, by the pettifogging attacks of Mary's philosopher-father whose behavior was so much meaner than his principles. It was an escape, in 1816, to visit Lake Geneva, meet the self-exiled Byron and indulge his passion for boating with his fellow poet. There was already a curious indifference about Shelley's hold on physical life. His desire for freedom had begun to include freedom from the body, which seemed to hamper and imprison his mental powers. When a tempest blew up on the lake one day, Byron and the boatmen sprang to the alert while Shelley sat motionless, declaring he was content to go to the bottom. Contemplating the high serenity of Mont Blanc he speculated:

> Has some unknown omnipotence unfurled
> The veil of life and death?
>
> [53–54]

and he was later to describe life as a "dome of many-coloured glass" that *stained* the white radiance of eternity until death should shatter it.

[1] This despite Shelley's note: "This negation must be understood solely to affect a creative Deity. The hypothesis of a pervading Spirit co-eternal with the universe remains unshaken."

From such happy companionship and transcendent musing Shelley was to return that autumn to the shock of Harriet's apparent suicide, and to the stunning legal decision by Lord Chancellor Eldon to deprive so unprincipled a rebel of the care of their children. It was a first-fruit of *Queen Mab,* and could only fan the poet's revolt against tyrannical law.

I curse thee by a parent's outraged love,
By hopes long cherished and too lately lost,
By gentle feelings thou couldst never prove,
By griefs which thy stern nature never crossed,
["To the Lord Chancellor, V]

he wrote in the flood of his bitterness. But defeat and negation were not natural to Shelley without their converse of rebirth and hope. The following summer, on the Thames at Marlow, he wrote his twelve-canto poem *Laon and Cythna* which was again a plea for liberty and justice even in the face of the French Revolution's galling aftermath. To his timid publisher the poem looked both blasphemous and immoral, and Shelley was constrained to tone it down. It then appeared—and, like most of his publications, remained unsold—as *The Revolt of Islam.* It was his last big-scale work before he left with Mary, their two children (both destined to die shortly) and the inevitable Claire, for Italy.

Again they led a roving, restless, traveling existence. Shelley was frequently unwell, and while his intellect and creative mind raced forward, his body lagged, encumbering him so that he deplored the "heavy weight of hours" that chained and bowed a tameless spirit. Incessantly reading and thinking, broadening his intellect, he had now come to a maturity of imaginative power that was matched by an astonishing ability to manage human beings. He kept peace between Mary and Claire Clairmont, eased the strains of Claire and Byron over their joint offspring, by his salutary company rescued Byron from a condition bordering on degeneracy. He even fell in cheerfully with milord's inverted living habits; "I don't suppose this will kill me in a week or a fortnight," he commented in a letter to Peacock, "but I shall not try it longer."

A group known usually as the Pisan Circle revolved around Shelley in those years. Conspicuous among them was the adventurous Cornish seafarer E. J. Trelawny—a man with a glib tongue and a hearty egotism, except where Shelley was concerned. Thomas Medwin, a clever unscrupulous cousin from Sussex, hovered about the two poets seeking journalistic gossip. His best service was to introduce Edward and Jane Williams who fell most happily into the picture, the one as enthusiastic over yachts as Shelley, and more competent, the other a fair if not profound young lady who possessed, what all the circle lacked, the gift of tranquilizing. Contrary to popular ideas, Shelley's was still the practical mind of the community. He might be heard of sitting in the ruined Baths of Caracalla to compose *Prometheus Unbound,* but he was also house-hunting for himself and Byron, ordering books and medicines from England, stretching inadequate finances, replying sternly to Godwin's insatiable demands for money—while in consideration for Mary he continued to send him sums beyond his means.

This was the prose of his Italian years. The poetry does not seem to have suffered from it. Shelley never expected his *Prometheus Unbound* to sell, but asked his publisher to "pet him and feed him with fine ink and good paper" believing it "the most perfect of my productions." He felt he had truly expressed, though not for popular understanding, the conviction that still moved him. Man was to overthrow evil and secure his liberation when he could not only "defy Power which seems omnipotent" but also "forgive wrongs darker than death or night," motivated by love even for his enemies. (The atheist was by this time close to Christianity, though he balked at the label on account of the dead matter it covered.)

As his major poetic and philosophic utterance, he could afford to see *Prometheus* miss the common market. But *The Cenci,* a stage play in the Elizabethan manner built on a true Roman story, was a bid for immediate fame. He hoped to see it staged at Covent Garden with his favourite actress as the heroine. However, the managers shuddered at the theme of incest. It was Shelley's usual luck. Even a humorous political jest could not get by: *Swellfoot the Tyrant* gaily satirized George IV's indictment of Queen Caroline. Authority threatened prosecution, and the whole edition had to be suppressed.

The guardians of public morals would have

been equally outraged by *Epipsychidion* in 1821, could they have pierced the obscurities in both poem and title. They would have found Shelley's most emphatic rejection of the narrowing principle of monogamy. No less than in *Prometheus,* he was urging the power and infinitude of love. That he was enchanted, on the personal side, by another imprisoned maiden, is less than half the story. While Emilia Viviani, the Italian girl in a convent, moved him to his utterance, he knew, or came to realize, her inadequacy as a symbol of that "light, and love, and immortality" beyond the mutations of human lives. The same spirit of Intellectual Beauty — "the Vision I had sought through grief and shame" — now penetrated him with its intensity. But Emily — though he exalted her as the shadow or incarnation of that love and truth — could never be "one with nature"; she was mortal and mutable like the rest of them. To Claire Clairmont he wrote critically, "Her moral nature is fine — but not above circumstances."

After that impassioned, frustrated urge for coalescence Shelley found a way to separate his worship of immortal beauty from his pleasure in the company of women. When Keats died in February, 1821, Shelley, knowing little of him personally, was the freer to generalize elegiacally on the untimely passing of a poetic soul. In *Adonais* mourning changed into triumph as he pictured the freed spirit flowing back to be "a portion of the Eternal, which must glow through time and change." Without fear of disillusion he could rejoice in the poet's merging into universal light and beauty and pervading love.

There was a freshening and partial relaxation of Shelley's own spirits in the spring of 1822. Captain Roberts was building a boat for him and Williams, and in expectation of the "perfect plaything for the summer" they looked for houses on the seacoast east of La Spezia, and found one only, "a white house with arches" that would take both families. Shelley delighted in the sweet serenity of Jane Williams, without feeling constrained to tear his soul apart. There is no more than a whisper of regret and loneliness in the gracious, dancing lines he addressed to her — "The Invitation," "The Recollection," "With a Guitar," and "In the Bay of Lerici." He was almost happy, though never at peace: a peace he valued more than life. Mortality sat ever more lightly on him. Should they not overturn the boat, he proposed to the unwilling Jane, and explore the unknown together? What life truly was, and for what, he was perhaps on the way to determining, by his own beliefs and standards, in the long poem, *The Triumph of Life,* that he was writing, mostly on the water. Trelawny records that Shelley, reflecting on "the System of the Universe," remarked to him, "I have no fears and some hopes. In our present gross material state our faculties are clouded — when Death removes our clay coverings the mystery will be solved."

A more practical project was afoot. Leigh Hunt, with wife and family, was on his way to Italy to launch a new periodical — the *Liberal* — with the editorial help of Shelley and Byron. Shelley sailed eagerly to Leghorn with Williams in the "perfect plaything" and spent a lively week with Hunt. When they set out on July 8 to return to Lerici a storm blew up and the schooner vanished. After days of fruitless search the remains of both were washed ashore near Viareggio. In Shelley's pocket was a copy of Keats' *Lamia* volume which seemed to have been hastily stuffed there. Trelawny, in whom was a touch of the dramatic, made a ceremony out of the quarantine law's requirement and, in the presence of Hunt and Byron, burned the bodies to ashes. *The Triumph of Life* remained an unfinished poem.

## II

Poetry is made of words and images. The most striking surface character of Shelley's poetic style is the return again and again of a limited number of words and images: *cave (cavern), dew, chariot, cloud, mist, flower, tower, stream, wilderness, veil, tyrant, throne . . . ; azure, aerial, daedal, bright, aetherial, sweet, weak . . . ;* "the desire of the moth for the star" (in many variants), "fountain-lighted caves" (*Prometheus Unbound,* II.i.184), the "enchanted boat" (*PU,* II.v.72), "Elysian garden islets" (*PU,* II.v.91), "watery paths that wind between Wildernesses" (*PU,* II.v.106), "crystàlline streams" (*"Ode to the West Wind"*) which equally are "the clear hyaline" (*PU,* II.v.21) from which Asia "Daughter of Ocean" (who is also "Life of Life," too beautiful to be seen, and "Shadow of beauty unbeheld") has arisen — such words and such images, recurring sometimes with and sometimes without variation of phrasing, comprise a considerable proportion of Shelley's work.

They have often been pointed to by unsympathetic readers as showing that the poet was too easily satisfied, facile rather than critical with his inspiration. The extraordinary difference between his use of any one of these words, or images, on the great occasions and his other uses of it has not enough been remarked. Very often, it is true, Shelley does seem to be using the first thing which comes to mind, as a sufficient notation with which to catch and pin down part at least of what is being offered him, his sight focused rather upon what is about to be borne down upon the rapid stream of an all but overwhelming inspiration. "When my brain gets heated with thought it soon boils and throws off images and words faster than I can skim them off" (Shelley to Trelawny; see Neville Rogers, *Shelley at Work,* pp. 3–4).

In such moments of ebullition a poet may well try to serve the general good of the whole composition rather than sacrifice the remainder by attempting to give adequate treatment to each detail as it comes. Be it granted, however, that Shelley did have favorite words and figures which, under stress, he would often use as though they had an indwelling magic of their own apart from context. The effect then is that of a carpet or curtain into which all sorts of symbols may be inwoven, but as figures not to be especially remarked. It may have been this which led Keats to offer his famous advice: "You might curb your magnanimity and be more of an artist, and 'load every rift' of your subject with ore" (see p. 367, below). But "curb your magnanimity" also suggests Keats' uneasiness with and suspicion of the fine gentleman in Shelley. If Keats was echoing Spenser, and if Shelley, as a specialist in caves, noted the echo, he may well have burst out with his celebrated "fiendish laugh" — for Spenser's "rifts" belong to the description of the Cave of Mammon. (See *Faerie Queene,* II.vii.28, 5, Vol. I, p. 130.)

Nothing of this casualness, which makes Shelley seem to the end to write sometimes so badly, should dull us to what in the great original passages these same words and images can achieve. There, in the supporting contexts, interacting with one another in ways for which a Shelley today would find comparisons in nuclear physics, they have powers of which it is hard to speak moderately. In Shelleyan terms these symbolic passages can release us into susceptibility to nothing less than Intellectual Beauty, and to discover more about *that* is, of course, why reasonable people read Shelley. He himself best describes what his poetry at its highest attains:

> The mind, arising bright
> From the embrace of beauty (whence the forms
> Of which these are the phantoms) casts on them
> The gathered rays which are reality.
> [*PU,* III.iii.50–53]

"These," you will find, are "the echoes of the human world": love, pity, music . . . "all that tempers or improves man's life" — in brief, our deepest concern — and

> The progeny immortal
> Of Painting, Sculpture, and rapt Poesy,
> And arts, though unimagined, yet to be,
> [54–56]

are the "them" on which the mind, refreshed by beauty, casts these gathered rays. Anything becomes unreal as it is disconnected from what is relevant to it; it becomes real as it is brought into its due connections with what can illuminate it. Poetry (along with the other arts, and we may wonder if the cinema, for example, is among the arts "yet to be") is for Shelley a means, as he describes it in *A Defence of Poetry,* of defeating

> the curse which binds us to be subjected to the accident of surrounding impressions. And whether it spreads its own figured curtain, or withdraws life's dark veil from before the scene of things, it equally creates for us a being within our being. It makes us the inhabitants of a world to which the familiar world is a chaos. It reproduces the common universe of which we are portions and percipients, and it purges from our inward sight the film of familiarity which obscured from us the wonder of our being. It compels us to feel that which we perceive, and to imagine that which we know.

The parenthesis " (whence the forms of which these are the phantoms) " points us to Shelley's Platonism. Platonism in general is easy enough to sum up in a formula: the belief in a world of Forms or Ideas — an *idea* being, as the dictionary has it, "a supposed eternally existing pattern or archetype of any class of things, of which the individual things in that class are imperfect copies, and from which they derive their existence." It is another undertaking to enter, as Shelley did, into imaginative realization of what this doctrine has to offer. In its historic roots it was two things. Logically, it was a theory of Sameness: how can there be any stability or constancy in anything, in our own selves, for example? Many things are white, say (or beautiful), at many different times and in many different places. But how? Plato suggested that it is Whiteness (or Beauty) — a being not in time or space — which makes them white (or beautiful).[1] Though A. N. Whitehead truly said that the history of Western philosophy consists largely of footnotes to footnotes . . . to this theory, none of it all does more to explain how Sameness is possible. The other root is less intellectual; it is an offered hope of immortality. The soul may even be among the Forms. For Plato there is something more, even beyond the world of Forms; there is the Idea of the Good, from which the Forms receive their Being — as beautiful things in their turn receive their beauty from Beauty. In this passage Shelley has shifted terms up the scale, to call the Idea of the Good *beauty,* whence the *forms* arise, from which the *phantoms* in turn derive.

Once alerted to it, any reader of Shelley will find himself noting echoes and reflections of this Platonism everywhere. Innumerable readers in fact have learned Platonism from Shelley without knowing it by that name. Thus, as even Asia (even for Prometheus) is "Shadow of beauty unbeheld," so too, all that we can see, hear, touch, etc., is only shadow, phantom, reflection, echo, image, dream; the real things — represented by such shadows . . . on the "figured curtain" or by "life's dark veil" — are other. Shelley, while sure of this, maintains a speculative openmindedness matching that of Socrates as to how the world of shadows, phantoms, reflections, echoes, images, dreams stands to "the common universe of which we are portions and percipients." Neither he nor Socrates pretends to know; both, none the less, are sure that man's chief concern, his "virtue and power," his *arete,* is to pursue such knowledge, far off though it may be.

Shelley tried many paths in this pursuit. One of them is represented by "the gathered rays which are reality." Can we, perhaps, by being more inclusive, by seeing things at once from more angles and in more universal perspective, manage to reach Reality through appearances? "All things exist as they are perceived; at least in relation to the percipient" (*A Defence of Poetry*). Shelley held to this as firmly and as far as any reasonable man can; his "at least" shows his reservations. It is deeply true, as anyone who has ever observed a lover will recognize, that "The Eye altering alters All," as Blake put it. Can the Eye be so altered that it is enabled to perceive not the shadow merely but the Reality which casts it? That might be said to be the aim and end of Poetry for Shelley, but he would permit (or even require) us to qualify it, I think. What the Eye sees depends on what is looking through it. Here is a sentence from Shelley's *Essay on Christianity:* "Our most imperial and stupendous qualities — those on which the majesty and the power of humanity is erected — are, relatively to the inferior portion of its mechanism, active and imperial; but they are *the passive slaves* of some higher and more omnipotent Power." Strong language. Shelley is speaking from the depths of his experience of inspiration. Maybe, when the Eye does perceive Reality, something other than "our most imperial and stupendous qualities" does the beholding? But "Poetry," the *Defence* maintains, "expresses those arrangements of language . . . which are created by that imperial faculty, whose throne is curtained within the invisible nature of man."

Another path is represented by: "withdraws life's dark veil from before the scene of things." Shelley seems to have taken increasingly to heart the Earth's utterance in *Prometheus Unbound* (III.iii.113–14):

> Death is the veil which those who live call life:
> They sleep, and it is lifted.

This is an echo of a passage in Plato's *Gorgias* (492e): "For I should not be surprised, if Euripides were right when he says:

> But who knows if to live is to be dead
> And to be dead to live."

[1] *Phaedo,* 100d. For an expansion of this summary, see I. A. Richards, *How to Read a Page,* pp. 148 and Index.

But such an origin would give it by no means less authority to Shelley. On this image of the veil it is perhaps helpful to recall a remark which F. H. Bradley, author of *Appearance and Reality,* quotes from Hegel: "There is nothing behind the curtain other than that which is before it."

On these matters — central to a poetry such as Shelley's which would initiate a revelation — that central mystery of *Prometheus Unbound,* Demogorgon, should probably have the last word:

DEMOGORGON. If the abysm
Could vomit forth its secrets. . . . But a voice
Is wanting, the deep truth is imageless.
[II.iv.114–16]

III

"I have re-read," wrote W. B. Yeats in 1900, "*Prometheus Unbound,* which I had hoped my fellow students would have studied as a sacred book, and it seems to me to have an even more certain place than I had thought, among the sacred books of the world." There have been many to whom it is natural to read Shelley at his best in this way, and as many to whom such respect seems outrageous. That is what sacred books are like.

As with other sacred books, *Prometheus Unbound* requires to be read and reread until separate lines and phrases come to reflect light and heat one upon another, and images that at first may seem meaningless, or mere decoration, or mechanical re-use of stock material . . . begin to swing together like some incalculable cyclotron. "There is little enjoyment to be derived from his works," wrote F. S. Ellis, compiler of the *Shelley Lexicon,* "by those who read as they run; but they afford an ever-increasing and permanent treasure of delight to those who will be at the pains to study them." To use Shelley's own language, "transforming enlargements of the imagination" are offered: see *A Defence of Poetry* for explanations of this phrase. It may be added that such "enlargement" means not only increased power but a widened and heightened range of operations.

An attempt to summarize[1] the plot-structure of *Prometheus Unbound* shows that it hardly has one. Shelley knew better than to give his Mystery much overt action. The drama is in the moral transformations which his superhuman figures reflect and enact. Within sixty lines it is clear that Prometheus is deeply changed through his long ordeal: "aught evil wish Is dead within" (70). To measure this change he wishes to hear again the Curse he originally flung at his oppressor. But, though all remember, none who heard will repeat it; the dangers from Jupiter's vengeance are too evident. In the end the Phantasm of Jupiter himself gives the fierce and prophetic words utterance. Jupiter's response is immediate. More hideous Furies are directed to inflict new pangs. The last of these Furies, who speaks heartbroken philosophy, vanishes (634) at Prometheus' pitying reply. Jupiter has lost and his hour of doom is on its way. But so immense a change entails a time lag. In Act II, Asia and Panthea visit Demogorgon (see below) and Asia's question — "When shall the destined hour arrive? (II.iv.129) — is answered by action. Demogorgon ascends and (III.i) overthrows Jupiter. In the remaining scenes of Act III the transformation of the world is described. Act IV (added later) displays and celebrates the Renovation further and ends with a reminder from Demogorgon of how it has been achieved. In all this a central challenge to speculation is Demogorgon.

Not much that matters can be learned from inquiry into the possible sources, for Shelley, of this enigmatic Being — *Paradise Lost,* II.959–67; *Faerie Queene,* I.i.37, and IV.ii.47; Boccaccio, *De Genealogia Deorum,* and behind him cloudy references. Shelley may have known all or most of this, but very likely it was Peacock's note[2] to his poem *Rhododaphne* which led Shelley to choose this majestic and horrific name for what is essentially a creation of his own. Let us see just what the play offers us as rays which may be gathered into Demogorgon's reality.

[1] A useful detailed account will be found in Hughes, pp. 184–89.

[2] "The dreaded name of Demogorgon" is familiar to every reader, in Milton's enumeration of the Powers of chaos. Mythological writers in general afford but little information concerning this terrible Divinity. . . . He was the Genius of the Earth, and the Sovereign Power of the Terrestrial Daemons. He dwelt originally with Eternity and Chaos, till, becoming weary of inaction, he organized the chaotic elements, and surrounded the earth with the heavens. In addition to Pan and the Fates, his children were Uranus, Titaea, Pytho, Eris, and Erebus. This awful Power was so sacred among the Arcadians, that it was held impious to pronounce his name. (Note to VI.149.)

To begin with the first mention (II.ii.43) it is " By Demogorgon's mighty law " that certain echoes, " music tongued," draw

> All spirits on that secret way;
> As inland boats are driven to Ocean.
>
> [45–46]

It is not merely " that lovely twain," Asia and Panthea, who are so drawn (as at the end of II.i) but " All spirits." And " that secret way " is to be compared with nothing less than the courses of rivers, and yet none the less it is " secret." Then follows an account of inspiration as it appears to the inspired and to the observer. The inspired (and we may learn from *A Defence of Poetry* that legislation, for example, along with " all that tempers or improves man's life " is a product of poetic inspiration)

> Believe their own swift wings and feet
> The sweet desires within obey
>
> [55–56]

but it is not so. The observers, " those who saw," give an account which carries suggestions of the " oracular vapour " used in Apollo's Temple at Delphi, suggestions taken further in the next scene and elaborated in III.iii.124–30. The observers

> Say from the breathing earth behind
> There streams a plume-uplifting wind
> Which drives them on their path.
>
> [52–54]

It is " the breathing earth " (compare *Kubla Khan,* " As if this earth in fast thick pants were breathing," p. 130, above) which bestows this impulsion. The phrase " plume-uplifting " has baffled some readers, but whoever has watched a breeze ruffling up, say, a pigeon's plumage will not be at a loss. This fidelity of description is here combined with the boldest use of that Platonic watchword, " wings of the spirit ":

> More than any other bodily thing the wing partakes of the divine. But this is beauty, wisdom, goodness and all such qualities. It is by these that the wings of the soul are nourished and grow.
>
> [*Phaedrus,* 246e]

(Shelley was studying the *Phaedrus* between writing Act I and Acts II and III.)

Such traditional images are not exactly, themselves, " shapes which haunt thought's *wildernesses"*; they are rather viewpoints on Plato's great highway of the spirit. But this does not in the least diminish Shelley's achievement in that from such traditional material " create he can " what seem by now, evidently enough, " nurslings of immortality."

These " enchanted eddies " of echoes (it is always proper, with an echo, to wonder what it is an echo of; and possibly it may be relevant to recall Coleridge's line in " Dejection," " Their life the eddying of thy living soul ") become a " storm of sound . . . / Sucked up and hurrying," whose " gathering billows " in the end bear all spirits to " the fatal mountain " — the mountain where Jove's fate lingers, awaiting its hour. At the opening of the next scene Panthea and Asia are on this fatal mountain: " A Pinnacle of Rock among mountains." They recognize and comment on the place. It is the realm of Demogorgon. That " plume-uplifting wind " is described by Panthea as

> the oracular vapour . . .
> Which lonely men drink wandering in their youth,
> And call truth, virtue, love, genius, or joy
>
> [II.iii.4–6]

— different names here for what in the *Defence* is to be defined as poetry (as to " joy," see Coleridge's account of it in " Dejection "). Here it becomes, somewhat surprisingly, in the next line:

> That maddening wine of life, whose dregs they drain
> To deep intoxication.
>
> [7–8]

Both " maddening " and " dregs " invite more reflection than they may receive. " Maddening " carries many echoes — from Plato's discussions, in *Phaedrus, Ion, Apology,* and elsewhere, to Shakespeare's " The lunatic, the lover and the poet " or Yeats' choice of Crazy Jane (or Cracked Mary) as a mouthpiece. To connect inspiration with madness is traditional. But " dregs " — what are we to make of that? Poetry of this order does not hobble its words. Is there a measure of protest in Panthea's mode of reference to " the lees and settlings " of " truth, virtue, love, genius, or joy "? Compare the last stanza of *Hellas.* But equally here as with all exalted themes,

> of such truths
> Each to itself must be the oracle.
> [II.iv.122–23]

However we incline, we have to weigh " dregs " together with another violent word which is coming. What these " lonely men . . . wandering in their youth " have to declare (or sing) is " *contagion* to the world," and will be shunned by it as the plague — the world (in this sense) being composed of the priests and slaves of Jupiter, extremely averse to becoming " pestilence stricken multitudes." It is worth noting that these men are " lonely " and " wandering " because they are seeking " that secret way " whose names now seem to be " truth, virtue, love, genius, or joy "; a way " unknown to the poor, loveless, ever-anxious crowd " of Jove's adherents; and, note further, though all this is " By Demogorgon's mighty law," this " maddening wine of life " is the Earth's who has here provided, in this Pinnacle of Rock, as Asia observes, " Fit throne for such a Power! "

No one who reads much in Shelley can fail to notice how favorite a word " throne " is with him in his prose as in his verse. He uses it 146 times; Shakespeare, who might be supposed to have had more occasion, only 75 times: a proof of how radical was Shelley's concern with questions of government and control — in the state and in the individual. Demogorgon, indeed, is the unknown quantity in Shelley's Theory of Government or Power, a symbol for a speculative possibility that must, to many, seem overdaring. Thus Ralph Cudworth, the Cambridge Platonist, in his *The Intellectual History of the Universe* (1658), declares: " There is another Wild and Extravagant Conceit which some of the Pagans had, who, though they verbally acknowledged a Deity, yet supposed a certain Fate superior to it, and not only to all their other Petty Gods, but also to *Jupiter* himself." This, he considers, is " an odd kind of Intimation, that, however the name of God be used in compliance with Vulgar Speech and Opinion, yet indeed it signifies nothing but material necessity " (I.i.3). Cudworth, for all his Platonism, would evidently have been of Jupiter's party rather than Demogorgon's.

" Necessity," indeed, has been the label under which Demogorgon has chiefly been discussed. It is a less informative label than it may seem: even Milton's fiends in Hell got nothing more than pastime from investigating it:

> Fixed fate, free will, foreknowledge absolute,
> And found no end, in wandering mazes lost.
> [*Paradise Lost,* II.560–61 (See Vol. I, p. 469)]

Demogorgon himself speaks later on as though he would agree with Milton on this; and when Jupiter demands his name replies " Eternity " — not " Necessity." He adds, it is true, " Demand no direr name; " — the name, perhaps, that in Peacock's note the Arcadians held it impious to pronounce: not " Demogorgon," for Jupiter has used that twice, but the real name of the new incarnation.

The consultation or spell scene (II.iv) has received almost as many interpretations as there have been authorities, and this is no place in which to add another. I would only remark that its great theme — the Ultimate Authority, Principle of Principles — is not one upon which it seems proper to be vocally positive. Negatively, I doubt whether Asia is here receiving any course preparing her for her union with Prometheus as much as I doubt whether Demogorgon's Cave has anything to do with Plato's.[1] I do not see that she needs one; there is Panthea's last speech in Act I to consider: the aether of Asia's transforming presence has long been mingled with that of Prometheus.

At first the sisters see a " veiled form " upon the " ebon throne." When the veil falls it is as though a false hypothesis has been discarded and now it is a " mighty darkness " that the sisters see; the falling of the veil has increased the mystery. Those " rays of gloom " are not illumination but its inverse. The more Asia questions this source the less she learns. A moment comes when under Asia's pressure, Demogorgon's response grows suddenly violent:

> ASIA. Who is the master of the slave?
> DEMOGORGON. If the abysm
> Could vomit forth its secrets. . . .
> [114–15]

It is as though Demogorgon were here using great self-control; almost as though any question or utterance on such themes were a sort of vomiting. There are things which can be thought and perhaps known but not said. As the Tao Tê Ching, LVI, has it:

[1] See Neville Rogers, *Shelley at Work,* p. 156.

He who speaks does not know;
He who knows does not speak.

or, as Ludwig Wittgenstein put it:

Whereof one cannot speak, thereof one must be silent.[1]

Asia's insistence — which is the spell that brings forth the event — does, however, wring a denial and a declaration from Demogorgon. The denial is as to the utility here of talk about Fate or Necessity:

For what would it avail . . .
What to bid speak
Fate, Time, Occasion, Chance and Change?
[117–19]

They will have nothing to say upon this — which is beyond their realm, vast though that be. The declaration is:

To these
All things are subject but eternal Love.
[119–20]

Asia's feminine style of agreement with this leads to her last demand and the arrival of the destiny.

Those who think Shelley lacking in humor or in dramatic invention may consider what is happening in Heaven through these very minutes during which Asia is releasing the Doom. Jupiter, who is far indeed from being only a symbol, is luxuriating in a superlative vaunt. He has everything, he fancies, to exult in: the congregated powers of heaven have at last really an occasion for indulgence, via nectar, in "the soul of joy."

Rejoice! henceforth I am omnipotent.
[III.i.3]

That irrepressible nuisance, the soul of man, is to meet its match at last, for Jove and Thetis have begotten a strange wonder, Demogorgon:

The dreadful might of ever-living limbs
[22]

now to clothe

that awful spirit unbeheld
[23]

will soon deal with the human being's "unextinguishable fire," "and trample out the spark."

[1] The closing sentence of *Tractatus Logico-Philosophicus.*

Turning to Thetis, whom he hails in the very images used by Panthea and the Voice in the Air (which may be the voice of Prometheus, or the "familiar voice" of love — see II.v.41) he produces, ventriloquizing for her, a superb burlesque parody:

all my being

(she is supposed to cry)

Like him whom the Numidian seps did thaw
Into a dew with poison, is dissolved.
[39–41]

No nastier reptile[2] ever than this seps (sepsis, septic) is on record; and it is on this that Jove's inspiration swoops as "the thunder of the fiery wheels" is heard "griding the winds." And he lives his part, if any character did, until his most involuntary exit. The skill with which the possibility of any pity — except from Prometheus — is avoided is remarkable.

After this cosmic convulsion, so briefly executed, a pause is necessary. Shelley fills it with the most delicious passage in the drama. Apollo, who has been "held in heaven by wonder" (II.v.11) adds his eye-witness report and Asia's father, Jupiter's brother, Ocean, breathes his satisfaction. The close of this scene is poetry at its highest, a poetry of inexhaustible simplicity:

[*A sound of waves is heard.*]
OCEAN. It is the unpastured sea hungering for calm.
Peace, monster; I come now. Farewell.
APOLLO. Farewell.

## IV

The action of *Prometheus Unbound* has an elemental simplicity. The crisis comes as early as I.53 with the words "I pity thee"; the rest is outcome and description. After Jupiter's fall there remains only the spelling out of what has happened. One of the marvels of the play is the continued invention with which this is kept, on the whole, from flagging. This is the more astonishing because what might well have seemed

[2] See Lucan, *Pharsalia,* IX.763–88. A count of Shelley's uses of serpents shows the following proportion: as sympathetic 14; as odious 63. See "Reptile Lore in Shelley," Lloyd N. Jeffrey, *Keats-Shelley Journal,* VII.29. Yet Brailsford can write: "The snake is everywhere in his poems the incarnation of good."

at the start a disabling weakness of the design is so deftly handled. So long as Prometheus and the Oceanides remain symbols of "exultations, agonies, and love, and man's unconquerable mind," all is well. But as soon as Prometheus starts to describe how they will contrive henceforward to kill time Shelley recognizes the danger. He reveals it in the phrase: "our unexhausted spirits" (III.iii.36). In fact, Prometheus and the sisters are near dwindling into nothing more than the poet's own ideal household.

The little company, however, are only by intermittent analogy human. They have, when prosperous, the inherent insipidity of immortals, and the more human their behavior the greater the danger. It is a proof of Shelley's tact that he makes them fade out almost as soon as they cease to be interesting. The moment of risk is in III.iii.26–36. Prometheus has just described the cave which is to be their "simple dwelling." No doubt it is more than it appears: a sanctum of the poetic consciousness where

> a fountain
> Leaps in the midst with an awakening sound.
> [13–14]

There they "will sit and talk." But the terrible words "ourselves unchanged" are uttered and the ennui of perfection hangs over them. What rescues them (40–63) is the arts. But in their concern with how, through the arts,

> . . . veil by veil, evil and error fall
> [62]

they have really become human again. We see why to Blake "Eternity is in love with the productions of time" is one of the "Proverbs of Hell."

Act IV of *Prometheus Unbound* is hard to speak of worthily. Edmund Blunden, however, can do so. After noting how it opens like a hunting horn, he says:

> It must have been Shelley's opinion as he reconsidered the work that [the end of Act III] inclined too much towards a speech at a reformist's meeting to end such a lyric drama. The reformed world was certainly outlined there with a decisive mind: not with the extremist impossibility which is imputed to Shelley. . . . Feeling that the victory of Prometheus should not be concluded in that way, as if he had been writing a political poem and nothing more, Shelley presently caught the music which inspired the appropriate ending. It must be jubilant, aerial, adventurous — and the fourth act appears to have been his equivalent of a ballet, springing from all he had enjoyed of spectacle, dance and music.
> [*Shelley,* p. 220]

The new action, so far as there is one, is supplied by the courtship between Moon and Earth. The Spirit of the Earth has taken a hint offered by Asia (III.iv.86–90) who seems there to have been more than ordinarily prescient. Of this transcendent colloquy Blunden remarks:

> It is the utmost assertion in all his writings of his creed of love, one and the same whether felt by man and woman or by whatever is, and while we hear with wonder the voices of his "lamps of heaven," and confess that they are the imaginary voices of nature, we know that human wooing has never been more beautifully remembered.
> [p. 222]

## V

Of the characters in *Prometheus Unbound* the stature of the Earth seems to have been the least recognized. She is Prometheus' mother, is conversant with the language of the dead, can command "the shadows of all forms that think and live," is, Asia surmises, herself

> The shadow of some spirit lovelier still
> Though evil stain its work.
> [II.iii.13]

She, moreover, as we have seen, is the source of inspiration, "from the breathing earth . . . steams the plume-uplifting wind." To Earth the most authoritative words on life and death are given and it is she who — immediately before her rejuvenation as the Spirit of the Earth (the spirit lovelier still?) — appoints to Prometheus and his company "the destined cave." She, if anyone, knows why that cave must be

> Beside the windless and crystàlline pool,
> Where ever lies, on unerasing waves,
> The image of a temple.
> [III.iii.159]

*Crystàlline* — the word, so accented, occurs at several places in which Shelley seems not so much to be speaking as being spoken through. Some meaning not yet fully present to him seems to be shaping the passage and we may have to look to lines he is going to write a year or two years later to feel it if not see. One of the most familiar of these passages is in the third stanza of "Ode to the West Wind":

Thou who didst waken from his summer dreams
The blue Mediterranean, where he lay,
Lulled by the coil of his crystàlline streams . . .

To not a few readers this third stanza has seemed, I believe, an odd interlude in the ode — not in any very living relation to the rest. Why should the Mediterranean need awakening? What are these summer dreams? What are this coil and these streams? And in the next tercet what is the force of the insistent "in sleep"? Why "towers"? And why are they "quivering within the wave's intenser day"? And how is that wave "intenser"?

References to other places in Shelley where these words, phrases and images play more openly significant parts in his over-all poetic outlook will, I believe, at least give this third stanza a clearer relevance in the ode as a whole. I do not pretend that these bits and pieces which I am about to lay out can speak in any mode but that of a somewhat occult poetry, but reasons may perhaps appear why this should be so.

To take the last questions first, reflections, along with echoes and images, had a very complex interest for Shelley. In the "Ode to Liberty," written some six months later, we have

Within the surface of Time's fleeting river
  Its wrinkled image lies, as then it lay,
Immovably unquiet, and for ever
  It trembles, but it cannot pass away!
[VI]

And these lines he uses merely descriptively elsewhere. A hint for them came to him from a depiction of Peele Castle by Wordsworth (pp. 101–02, above), but Shelley made it Time's river and turned a visual observation into a meditation on memory and on the Permanence which triumphs endlessly *within* the universal flux: "Immovably unquiet." He is being philosophical here without ceasing to be intently concerned with minutiae of appearance: witness "wrinkled." Shelley's curiosity about what is manifest goes along with his concern with representation itself. How does anything stand for something else? Here is a note written perhaps a year later than the "Ode to Liberty":

Why is the reflection in that canal far more beautiful than the objects it reflects? The colours more vivid yet blended with more harmony; the openings from within into the soft and tender colours of the distant wood and the intersection of the mountain lines surpass and misrepresent truth.
[Bod. MS. 1821. See Rogers, *Shelley at Work*, p. 149*n*.]

This (which might have been in a Coleridge notebook) is not only an observation beside which anyone could place supporting examples, and a clearly formulated question for aesthetics; it is a posing of the problem of the image. That recollections can glow as the recollected scenes and incidents never glowed themselves is a commonplace of sentiment. But poetry (as we have seen above) "equally creates for us a being within our being" free "from the curse which binds us to be subjected to the accident of surrounding impressions" (a piece, we may think, of Jupiter's tyranny). And the greatest and most permanent representations of "Man, oh, not men," of "Man . . . / Whose nature is its own divine control," of that whose "words waken Oblivion," lie likewise "Within the surface of Time's fleeting river . . . / Immovably unquiet."

In this instance — and here is the connection with "the blue Mediterranean" and "his summer dreams" — the "wrinkled image" which "lies, as then it lay," is Athens; and to learn what the Mediterranean "saw in sleep" "where he lay" we will do well to consider how Athens is presented in stanzas IV and V of the "Ode to Liberty." While reading them through let us keep the "Ode to the West Wind" in mind, too, especially stanza II and the second half of III.

The danger here is to press too much; to try to find "a chain of linkèd thought" where, at most, highly indefinite connections are alone to be suspected. Has "far below / The sea-blooms and the oozy woods which wear / The sapless foliage of the ocean" anything to do with "unfolded flowers beneath the sea"? Perhaps they should be "enfolded" flowers, since they are being compared with "art's deathless dreams" while these "Lay veiled in many a vein of Parian stone" — sculptures still in the unopened quarry. They are also being compared with "the man's thought dark in the infant's brain" and with

" aught that is which wraps what is to be." We may look back to the place given to " Art's deathless dreams " in *Prometheus Unbound* (III.iii.50–62). There, " the progeny immortal / Of Painting, Sculpture and rapt Poesy, / And arts, though unimagined, yet to be " are " The wandering voices and the shadows . . . / Of all that man becomes." With " all that man becomes " (in its double sense: *should be* as well as *will be*) we are near enough to Athens as it is described in the *Defence* and not far from the " new birth " prayed for in " Ode to the West Wind."

In " Ode to Liberty " Athens is first described as a cloud city. Then as " paved " (one of Shelley's prime words; could the proverb: " The road to Hell is paved with good intentions " have had anything to do with such special favor?) by the ocean-floors. Then " The evening sky pavilions it." If Athens rather than this cloud city were being described we might expect " morning sky," not " evening "; but evening is the time for " cloud-capped palaces." It is " black Vesper's pageants " we are being treated to here. These " purple crags and silver towers / Of battlemented cloud " take on the semblance of a temple next. Perhaps the temple which stands

> Beside the windless and crystàlline pool
> Where ever lies, on unerasing waves,

its image. " Its portals are inhabited / By thunder-zonèd winds." So stand the Guardians of the Gates to keep in order the profane who would approach. Each head, like " the head of some fierce Maenad " is " within its cloudy wings with sun-fire garlanded." It is as though something of the mood in which " the locks of the approaching storm " had been described were active — " A divine work! "

Suddenly " Athens, diviner yet," shoulders aside the cloudy construction, and we take a long step towards the elucidation of *crystàlline streams* which we are pursuing. Athens is " on the will / Of man, as on a mount of diamond, set." Put that beside " the ocean-floors / Pave it " and add this from *Hellas* (1821):

> But Greece and her foundations are
> Built below the tide of war
> Based on the crystàlline sea
> Of thought and its eternity.

" Diamond " and " crystàlline " are variants of one image. Both are so transparent as to be invisible except through refraction and reflection and are emblems of endurance and impenetrability. And they have important association with Power — not only with " that imperial faculty whose throne is curtained within the invisible nature of man," to quote the *Defence* once more; but with Power in Shakespeare and in the Bible:

> Man, proud man,
> Dressed in a little brief authority,
> Most ignorant of what he's most assured,
> His glassy essence . . .
> [*Measure for Measure,* II.ii.117–20]

" And before the throne there was a sea of glass like unto crystal " (Rev. 4:6). As to connections with " old palaces and towers," compare *PU,* IV:99–104. Palaces, towers, crowns, and thrones are alternates in such a context as this.[1] Whatever else stanza III of " Ode to the West Wind " may be also about, it seems hardly rash to suggest that this sleeping Mediterranean's " summer dreams " were of the ultimate control of power and its source in the " crystàlline sea / Of thought and its eternity."

But there are still " coil " and " streams " to be touched on. Experiments in inviting free comment on

> Lulled by the coil of his crystàlline streams

show that to a majority of should-be well-qualified readers, " coil " will be taken as " noise, confused sound of plashing and so on " of " streams " taken as rivers, torrents, falling into the Mediterranean (Arethusa-wise) from its mountainous shores. But a further reading takes " streams " as " currents " — as in " the Gulf Stream," or in Swinburne's line on the birth of Venus-Asia: " and bluer, the sea-blue stream of the bays." If so, " coil " takes on reverberation, a " consentaneity " — to use a word that Shelley liked — with " The snake-line Doom coiled underneath his throne " (*PU,* II.iii.97), if not with " The serpent that would clasp her with his length " (IV.567). How far any reader will find it well to follow this path, of that again

> Each to itself must be the oracle,
> [II.iv.123]

[1] Cf. " Athwart the glowing steps and the crystàlline throne . . . ," *Revolt of Islam,* I.630, from a passage which strangely prefigures and illuminates much in *Prometheus Unbound.*

an oracle, however, which has submitted itself to as much of Shelley and of his peers as possible: "The jury which sits in judgment upon a poet, belonging as he does to all time, must be composed of his peers: it must be impannelled by Time from the selectest of the wise of many generations" (*Defence,* p. 308, below).

Here a standard is set up which might well make us all cautious and modest in our opinions. But opinion about Shelley's poetry has often, alas, been neither. From Arnold on to very recent pundits have come pronouncements more than fulfilling Shelley's most sardonic expectations as to judgments on "this jingling food for the hunger of oblivion" (Letter to Peacock, January 11, 1822). It has been the recipient of condescension from Authorities suffering under the disability of somehow supposing themselves superior to the poet and feeling sure that when they could not comprehend him the fault could only be his. Coleridge in the opening of Chapter XII of *Biographia Literaria* declares himself to have been greatly benefited by the following resolve: "Until you understand a writer's ignorance, presume yourself ignorant of his understanding"—this "in the perusal of philosophic works." At his best Shelley's poetry is philosophical—as in the passages I have commented on. His incidental, personal, and autobiographical poems, though they have had great popular appeal, do not seem to me of the same order. I have accordingly not discussed them; my comments would not help.

The philosophic and prophetic character of his most exalted work makes it difficult: difficult sometimes to conceive the aim, difficult in any case to use the means with which he reaches toward that. And there is this additional difficulty. Shelley's *world* of thought has to an extreme degree the nature of a poem. The most certain things in it have the status of words in a poem, whose main virtue is that they represent and can convey something else, something quite different from any word—a meaning, or rather, an unending series or hierarchy of meanings, intricate and irregular. This is not to say that Shelley lived in a world of words; no man was more concerned with actuals throughout, or more live-hearted and immediate with people and with scenes; but it is the case that these actuals—living men and women, political situations, ideas . . . —were to him, incessantly, as to few others, *symbols* or, in a strict sense, *images.* This visible, audible, tangible . . . world —the world we can have our opinions of—is an image of the eternal. This, as F. M. Cornford remarks (*Plato's Cosmology,* p. 28) is "the cardinal doctrine of Platonism." Shelley is one of those who have been possessed by this doctrine. His "Hymn to Intellectual Beauty" gives a true account.

Accordingly, in his politics and his personal relations as in his poetry, he was concerned with people, things, and events as conveying, representing, symbolizing something forever beyond themselves and yet their essence. And what they might represent would often in turn represent, and so on and on. In his last and most elaborate use of the fountain-lighted cavern image (*The Triumph of Life,* 308–65)

the bright omnipresence
Of morning through the orient cavern flowed,
And the sun's image radiantly intense

Burned on the waters of the well that glowed
Like gold, and threaded all the forest's maze
With winding paths of emerald fire; there stood

Amid the sun, as he amid the blaze
Of his own glory, on the vibrating
Floor of the fountain, paved with flashing rays,

A Shape all light.

This is both a dazzlingly exact depiction of what the eye could see by gazing into such reflections *and* a symbolic presentation of the awakening mind with every other word overcharged. For example, "winding paths." Cf. note to *PU,* I.742, p. 267, below.

This Shape, which is to undergo disguising transformations even in what is left of this unfinished poem, stood enclosed within "the bright omnipresence," within "the sun's image" and within the "flashing rays" of the reflection "in the waters" as "he [the sun] amid the blaze / Of his own glory." Is not this in analogy with the way in which a word, however illuminating, seems to enclose a meaning, and that again a further interpretation: or with the fashion in which a poem or work of art creates "a being within our being," "a world within a world"? That Shelley, in writing so, is aware of and deliberately using such parallels may be what he means in the Preface to *Prometheus Unbound* by "The imagery which I have employed will be found, in many instances, to have been drawn from the operations of the human mind"; a singularity he is willing to have imputed to his study of the Greek poets.

It may be hoped that these characteristics of Shelley's poetry will come to be more widely recognized. Meanwhile, the fact that a critic, however eminent, does not understand something, if a point at all, is a point against the critic, not against the poet. As with his peers, when we judge Shelley, it is not Shelley who is judged.

## *Reading Suggestions*

EDITIONS

Thomas Hutchinson, *The Poems of Percy Bysshe Shelley* (1904).

A. M. D. Hughes, *Prometheus Unbound, etc., 1820* (2nd edition, 1957). Shelley's poetry is full of echoes and of conscious parallels, and the conduct of these was the occasion for deeply ingenious design. References and elucidations for much of this will be found in this critical edition.

H. F. B. Brett-Smith, *Peacock's Four Ages of Poetry, Shelley's Defence of Poetry, Browning's Essay on Shelley* (1929). A model of judicious editing.

BIOGRAPHY

Edmund Blunden, *Shelley: A Life Story* (1946). A balanced account with vivid illustrative detail from a poet and Shelleyan steeped in the period.

Newman, I. White, *Shelley,* 2 Vols. (1940). The most recent full-scale biography.

CRITICISM AND COMMENT

Stephen Spender, *Shelley,* Supplement to British Book News No. 29 (1952). A compact discussion of the life and work, with select bibliography, by a modern poet whose autobiography "World Within World" takes its title from Shelley.

W. B. Yeats, "The Philosophy of Shelley's Poetry," *Ideas of Good and Evil* (1900; reprinted in *Essays,* 1924). "I only made my pleasure in him contented pleasure by massing in my imagination his recurring images of towers and rivers and caves with fountains in them and that one star of his, till his world had grown solid underfoot and consistent enough for the soul's habitation."

George Santayana, "Shelley, or the Poetic Value of Revolutionary Principles," *Winds of Doctrine* (1913). "An angel cannot be ineffectual if the standard of efficiency is moral."

C. H. Baker, *Shelley's Major Poetry: The Fabric of a Vision* (1948). A careful and detailed study.

H. N. Brailsford, *Shelley, Godwin, and Their Circle,* Home University Library (1913). Exaggerates the influence of Godwin and is inaccurate, but presents background.

Olwen Ward Campbell, *Shelley and the Unromantics* (1924). Vigorous, informative, and enthusiastic.

Neville Rogers, *Shelley at Work* (1956). Based on the study of Shelley's Notebooks with many illuminating quotations from them. The interpretations offered, however, seem at times in need of defense.

Sylva Norman, *Flight of the Skylark* (1954). A rewarding account of opinion on Shelley from his day to ours.

---

# STANZAS—APRIL, 1814

Composed at Bracknell where Shelley had been the guest of Mrs. de Boinville and her daughter, Cornelia Turner. The poem may be read as an imaginary construction or as a record of experience.

Away! the moor is dark beneath the moon,
  Rapid clouds have drank the last pale beam of even:
Away! the gathering winds will call the darkness soon,
  And profoundest midnight shroud the serene lights of heaven.

Pause not! the time is past! Every voice cries, Away!
  Tempt not with one last tear thy friend's ungentle mood:
Thy lover's eye, so glazed and cold, dares not entreat thy stay:
  Duty and dereliction guide thee back to solitude.

Away, away! to thy sad and silent home;
  Pour bitter tears on its desolated hearth;
Watch the dim shades as like ghosts they go and come,
  And complicate strange webs of melancholy mirth.

The leaves of wasted autumn woods shall float around thine head:
  The blooms of dewy spring shall gleam beneath thy feet:
But thy soul or this world must fade in the frost that binds the dead,
  Ere midnight's frown and morning's smile, ere thou and peace may meet.

The cloud shadows of midnight possess their own repose,
  For the weary winds are silent, or the moon is in the deep:

Some respite to its turbulence unresting ocean knows;
Whatever moves, or toils, or grieves, hath its appointed sleep.

Thou in the grave shalt rest — yet till the phantoms flee
Which that house and heath and garden made dear to thee erewhile,
Thy remembrance, and repentance, and deep musings are not free
From the music of two voices and the light of one sweet smile.

*1814*

## HYMN TO INTELLECTUAL BEAUTY

Planned on the voyage (June, 1816) with Byron round Lake Geneva; written soon after.

I

The awful shadow of some unseen Power
Floats though unseen among us, — visiting
This various world with as inconstant wing
As summer winds that creep from flower to flower, —
Like moonbeams that behind some piny mountain shower,
It visits with inconstant glance
Each human heart and countenance;
Like hues and harmonies of evening, —
Like clouds in starlight widely spread, —
Like memory of music fled, —
Like aught that for its grace may be
Dear, and yet dearer for its mystery.

II

Spirit of Beauty, that dost consecrate
With thine own hues all thou dost shine upon
Of human thought or form, — where art thou gone?
Why dost thou pass away and leave our state,
This dim vast vale of tears, vacant and desolate?
Ask why the sunlight not for ever
Weaves rainbows o'er yon mountain-river,
Why aught should fail and fade that once is shown,
Why fear and dream and death and birth
Cast on the daylight of this earth
Such gloom, — why man has such a scope
For love and hate, despondency and hope?

III

No voice from some sublimer world hath ever
To sage or poet these responses given —
Therefore the names of Demon, Ghost, and Heaven,
Remain the records of their vain endeavour,
Frail spells — whose uttered charm might not avail to sever,
From all we hear and all we see,
Doubt, chance, and mutability.
Thy light alone — like mist o'er mountains driven,
Or music by the night-wind sent
Through strings of some still instrument,
Or moonlight on a midnight stream,
Gives grace and truth to life's unquiet dream.

IV

Love, Hope, and Self-esteem, like clouds depart
And come, for some uncertain moments lent.
Man were immortal, and omnipotent,
Didst thou, unknown and awful as thou art,
Keep with thy glorious train firm state within his heart.
Thou messenger of sympathies,
That wax and wane in lovers' eyes —
Thou — that to human thought art nourishment,
Like darkness to a dying flame!
Depart not as thy shadow came,
Depart not — lest the grave should be,
Like life and fear, a dark reality.

V

While yet a boy I sought for ghosts, and sped
Through many a listening chamber, cave and ruin,
And starlight wood, with fearful steps pursuing
Hopes of high talk with the departed dead.
I called on poisonous names with which our youth is fed;
I was not heard — I saw them not —
When musing deeply on the lot
Of life, at that sweet time when winds are wooing
All vital things that wake to bring
News of birds and blossoming, —
Sudden, thy shadow fell on me;
I shrieked, and clasped my hands in ecstasy!

VI

I vowed that I would dedicate my powers
To thee and thine — have I not kept the vow?
With beating heart and streaming eyes, even now
I call the phantoms of a thousand hours
Each from his voiceless grave: they have in visioned bowers
Of studious zeal or love's delight
Outwatched with me the envious night —
They know that never joy illumed my brow

Unlinked with hope that thou wouldst free
This world from its dark slavery,
That thou — O awful LOVELINESS,
Wouldst give whate'er these words cannot express.

VII

The day becomes more solemn and serene
When moon is past — there is a harmony
In autumn, and a lustre in its sky,
Which through the summer is not heard or seen,
As if it could not be, as if it had not been!
Thus let thy power, which like the truth
Of nature on my passive youth
Descended, to my onward life supply
Its calm — to one who worships thee,
And every form containing thee,
Whom, SPIRIT fair, thy spells did bind
To fear himself, and love all human kind.

*1816*

## MONT BLANC

"... composed under the immediate impression of the deep and powerful feelings excited by the objects which it attempts to describe; and, as an undisciplined overflowing of the soul, the piece rests its claim to approbation on an attempt to imitate the untamable wildness and inaccessible solemnity from which those feelings sprang" [Shelley's note].

However much an "undisciplined overflowing" Shelley may later have thought it, this poem has seemed to many to be an inexhaustible presentation of his philosophic position.

I

The everlasting universe of things
Flows through the mind, and rolls its rapid waves,
Now dark — now glittering — now reflecting gloom —
Now lending splendour, where from secret springs
The source of human thought its tribute brings
Of waters, — with a sound but half its own,
Such as a feeble brook will oft assume
In the wild woods, among the mountains lone,
Where waterfalls around it leap for ever,
Where woods and winds contend, and a vast river
Over its rocks ceaselessly bursts and raves.

II

Thus thou, Ravine of Arve — dark, deep Ravine —
Thou many-coloured, many voicèd vale,
Over whose pines, and crags, and caverns sail
Fast cloud-shadows and sunbeams: awful scene,
Where Power in likeness of the Arve comes down
From the ice-gulfs that gird his secret throne,
Bursting through these dark mountains like the flame
Of lightning through the tempest; — thou dost lie,
Thy giant brood of pines around thee clinging,
Children of elder time, in whose devotion
The chainless winds still come and ever came
To drink their odours, and their mighty swinging
To hear — an old and solemn harmony;
Thine earthly rainbows stretched across the sweep
Of the aethereal waterfall, whose veil
Robes some unsculptured image; the strange sleep
Which when the voices of the desert fail
Wraps all in its own deep eternity; —
Thy caverns echoing to the Arve's commotion,
A loud, lone sound no other sound can tame;
Thou art pervaded with that ceaseless motion,
Thou art the path of that unresting sound —
Dizzy Ravine! and when I gaze on thee
I seem as in a trance sublime and strange
To muse on my own separate fantasy,
My own, my human mind, which passively
Now renders and receives fast influencings,
Holding an unremitting interchange
With the clear universe of things around;
One legion of wild thoughts, whose wandering wings
Now float above thy darkness, and now rest
Where that or thou art no unbidden guest,
In the still cave of the witch Poesy,
Seeking among the shadows that pass by
Ghosts of all things that are, some shade of thee,
Some phantom, some faint image; till the breast
From which they fled recalls them, thou art there!

III

Some say that gleams of a remoter world
Visit the soul in sleep, — that death is slumber,
And that its shapes the busy thoughts outnumber
Of those who wake and live. — I look on high;
Has some unknown omnipotence unfurled
The veil of life and death? or do I lie
In dream, and does the mightier world of sleep
Spread far around and inaccessibly
Its circles? For the very spirit fails,

MONT BLANC. **12. Ravine:** "Our route still lay through the valley, or rather, as it had become, the vast ravine, which is at once the couch and the creation of the terrible Arve," Shelley to Peacock, July 22, 1816. **35–36. I . . . fantasy:** Cf. Preface to *Prometheus Unbound*, p. 256, "The imagery which I have employed will be found, in many instances, to have been drawn from the operations of the human mind, or from those external actions by which they are expressed." **37. My . . . mind:** as opposed to some universal Mind. **41–42. One . . . darkness:** Cf. "Lines Written among the Euganean Hills" (two years later), 70–75, "I stood listening to the paean/With which the legioned rooks did hail/The sun's uprise majestical;/Gathering round with wings all hoar,/Through the dewy mist they soar/Like gray shades . . ." **46. of thee:** of the ravine, but also of the poet's mind.

Driven like a homeless cloud from steep to steep
That vanishes among the viewless gales!
Far, far above, piercing the infinite sky,
Mont Blanc appears, — still, snowy, and serene —
Its subject mountains their unearthly forms
Pile around it, ice and rock; broad vales between
Of frozen floods, unfathomable deeps,
Blue as the overhanging heaven, that spread
And wind among the accumulated steeps;
A desert peopled by the storms alone,
Save when the eagle brings some hunter's bone,
And the wolf tracks her there — how hideously
Its shapes are heaped around! rude, bare, and high,
Ghastly, and scarred, and riven. — Is this the scene
Where the old Earthquake-daemon taught her
young
Ruin? Were these their toys? or did a sea
Of fire envelop once this silent snow?
None can reply — all seems eternal now.
The wilderness has a mysterious tongue
Which teaches awful doubt, or faith so mild,
So solemn, so serene, that man may be,
But for such faith, with nature reconciled;
Thou hast a voice, great Mountain, to repeal
Large codes of fraud and woe; not understood
By all, but which the wise, and great, and good
Interpret, or make felt, or deeply feel.

IV

The fields, the lakes, the forests, and the streams,
Ocean, and all the living things that dwell
Within the daedal earth; lightning, and rain,
Earthquake, and fiery flood, and hurricane,
The torpor of the year when feeble dreams
Visit the hidden buds, or dreamless sleep
Holds every future leaf and flower; — the bound
With which from that detested trance they leap;
The works and ways of man, their death and birth,
And that of him and all that his may be;
All things that move and breathe with toil and
sound
Are born and die; revolve, subside, and swell.
Power dwells apart in its tranquillity,
Remote, serene, and inaccessible:
And *this,* the naked countenance of earth,
On which I gaze, even these primaeval mountains
Teach the adverting mind. The glaciers creep

**62. subject mountains:** "Pinnacles of snow, intolerably bright, part of the chain connected with Mont Blanc, shone through the clouds at intervals on high. I never knew—I never imagined—what mountains were before. The immensity of these aerial summits excited, when they suddenly burst upon the sight, a sentiment of ecstatic wonder, not unallied to madness," Shelley to Peacock, July 22, 1816. **77. awful doubt:** doubt that fills the mind with awe. **79. But . . . faith:** through such faith apart from all else. **86. daedal:** rich, variegated, as though the work of Daedalus who built the Cretan Labyrinth. **96. dwells apart:** as does Mont Blanc.

Like snakes that watch their prey, from their far
fountains,
Slow rolling on; there, many a precipice,
Frost and the Sun in scorn of mortal power
Have piled: dome, pyramid, and pinnacle,
A city of death, distinct with many a tower
And wall impregnable of beaming ice.
Yet not a city, but a flood of ruin
Is there, that from the boundaries of the sky
Rolls its perpetual stream; vast pines are strewing
Its destined path, or in the mangled soil
Branchless and shattered stand; the rocks, drawn
down
From yon remotest waste, have overthrown
The limits of the dead and living world,
Never to be reclaimed. The dwelling-place
Of insects, beasts, and birds, becomes its spoil;
Their food and their retreat for ever gone,
So much of life and joy is lost. The race
Of man flies far in dread; his work and dwelling
Vanish, like smoke before the tempest's stream,
And their place is not known. Below, vast caves
Shine in the rushing torrents' restless gleam,
Which from those secret chasms in tumult welling
Meet in the vale, and one majestic River,
The breath and blood of distant lands, for ever
Rolls its loud waters to the ocean-waves,
Breathes its swift vapours to the circling air.

V

Mont Blanc yet gleams on high: — the power is
there,
The still and solemn power of many sights,
And many sounds, and much of life and death.
In the calm darkness of the moonless nights,
In the lone glare of day, the snows descend
Upon that Mountain; none beholds them there,
Nor when the flakes burn in the sinking sun,
Or the star-beams dart through them: — Winds
contend
Silently there, and heap the snow with breath
Rapid and strong, but silently! Its home
The voiceless lightning in these solitudes
Keeps innocently, and like vapour broods
Over the snow. The secret Strength of things
Which governs thought, and to the infinite dome
Of Heaven is as a law, inhabits thee!
And what were thou, and earth, and stars, and sea,

**105. many a tower:** the *séracs* of the glacier. **109–14. vast . . . reclaimed:** Shelley is describing an advancing glacier; for many decades glaciers everywhere have been retreating. **122. in . . . welling:** Cf. "Kubla Khan," "sank in tumult to a lifeless ocean." **123. one . . . River:** The Arve joins the Rhone at Geneva. **142–44: And . . . vacancy?** Cf. Wordsworth, "Intimations Ode," IX, ". . . have power to make/Our noisy years seem moments in the being/Of the eternal silence,"

If to the human mind's imaginings
Silence and solitude were vacancy?

*1816*

## OZYMANDIAS

I met a traveller from an antique land
Who said: Two vast and trunkless legs of stone
Stand in the desert . . . Near them, on the sand,
Half sunk, a shattered visage lies, whose frown,
And wrinkled lip, and sneer of cold command,
Tell that its sculptor well those passions read
Which yet survive, stamped on these lifeless things,
The hand that mocked them, and the heart that fed:
And on the pedestal these words appear:
'My name is Ozymandias, king of kings:
Look on my works, ye Mighty, and despair!'
Nothing beside remains. Round the decay
Of that colossal wreck, boundless and bare
The lone and level sands stretch far away.

*1817*

## ODE TO THE WEST WIND

"This poem was conceived and chiefly written in a wood that skirts the Arno, near Florence, and on a day when that tempestuous wind, whose temperature is at once mild and animating, was collecting the vapours which pour down the autumnal rains. They began, as I foresaw, at sunset with a violent tempest of hail and rain, attended by that magnificent thunder and lightning peculiar to the Cisalpine regions.

"The phenomenon alluded to at the conclusion of the third stanza is well known to naturalists. The vegetation at the bottom of the sea, of rivers, and of lakes, sympathizes with that of the land in the change of seasons, and is consequently influenced by the winds which announce it" [S].

In stanza III Shelley recalls an excursion made in a small boat on December 8, 1818, to the Bay of Baiae, at the northwestern end of the Bay of Naples, sheltered by the promontory of Posilipo. To Peacock (December 22) he described how they observed at Baiae "the ruins of its antique grandeur standing like rocks in the transparent sea under our boat." Passing through the cavern of the Cumaean Sibyl, they "came to a calm and lovely basin of water, surrounded by dark woody hills, and profoundly solitary. Some vast ruins of the Temple of Pluto stand on a lawny hill one side of it, and are reflected in its windless mirror."

The Being to whom this prayer is addressed is at once the West Wind and that Power the Wind symbolizes. How this may be conceived must extend an inexhaustible invitation to speculation: Expiration, the necessary prelude to Inspiration; the cyclic return of the Destruction required for Preservation; the death which is the condition for "a new birth"—in a thought, a feeling, a culture; in a day, a year, an epoch; in a cell, in an individual, in a society, in the Universe. The poem is speaking of and for the poet, but also of and for that which speaks through him. And his words (as with a Hosea or an Isaiah) are an "incantation" or spell or ritual bringing about that which they utter.

"Self-surrender, through which everything is lost, and renewed, and identified with that power (the wind), is here the essential moment expressed. We begin to be aware that the 'Wind' is spirit itself, or a medium to its expression . . . Shelley explicitly calls the West Wind 'spirit,' or 'Wild Spirit,' which is 'moving everywhere.' But this does not, or might not, mean very much; and 'spirit' and 'wind' are terms which possess an old common history. What matters is that the actual and yet self-transcending cause of life is real, and known, in the image of the West Wind" (Leone Vivante, *English Poetry,* pp. 165–67).

"The stanzaic form is a highly original invention consisting of fourteen lines (three tercets and a couplet) wrought out of the preliminary terza rima so that while each moves along with the whole, each, in itself, has the strength and compactness of a sonnet" (Neville Rogers, *Shelley at Work,* p. 226). These five stanzas are as intricately organized: in sense, image, emotion, concept—passing from the woods to the atmosphere to the seas, and then collecting what the comparisons with "a dead leaf," "a swift cloud," "a wave" can say of spiritual stress into a prayer that such submission may become complete Possession (see *A Defence of Poetry,* p. 305).

I

O wild West Wind, thou breath of Autumn's being,
Thou, from whose unseen presence the leaves dead
Are driven, like ghosts from an enchanter fleeing,

Yellow, and black, and pale, and hectic red,
Pestilence-stricken multitudes: O thou,
Who chariotest to their dark wintry bed

The wingèd seeds, where they lie cold and low,
Each like a corpse within its grave, until
Thine azure sister of the Spring shall blow

Her clarion o'er the dreaming earth, and fill
(Driving sweet buds like flocks to feed in air)
With living hues and odours plain and hill:

and Plotinus, *Enneads*, "On Beauty," I.vi.7, "Each in the solitude of himself shall behold that solitary-dwelling Existence, the Apart, the Unmingled, the Pure. . . ." OZYMANDIAS. **6–8. those . . . fed**: The pride and cruelty depicted in the sculpture outlive the artist and his subject. **mocked**: both imitated and derided.

Wild Spirit, which art moving everywhere;
Destroyer and preserver; hear, oh, hear!

II

Thou on whose stream, mid the steep sky's commotion,
Loose clouds like earth's decaying leaves are shed,
Shook from the tangled boughs of Heaven and Ocean,

Angels of rain and lightning: there are spread
On the blue surface of thine aëry surge,
Like the bright hair uplifted from the head

Of some fierce Maenad, even from the dim verge
Of the horizon to the zenith's height,
The locks of the approaching storm. Thou dirge

Of the dying year, to which this closing night
Will be the dome of a vast sepulchre,
Vaulted with all thy congregated might

Of vapours, from whose solid atmosphere
Black rain, and fire, and hair will burst: oh, hear!

III

Thou who didst waken from his summer dreams
The blue Mediterranean, where he lay,
Lulled by the coil of his crystàlline streams,

Beside a pumice isle in Baiae's bay,
And saw in sleep old palaces and towers
Quivering within the wave's intenser day,

All overgrown with azure moss and flowers
So sweet, the sense faints picturing them! Thou
For whose path the Atlantic's level powers

Cleave themselves into chasms, while far below
The sea-blooms and the oozy woods which wear
The sapless foliage of the ocean, know

Thy voice, and suddenly grow gray with fear,
And tremble and despoil themselves: oh, hear!

IV

If I were a dead leaf thou mightest bear;
If I were a swift cloud to fly with thee;
A wave to pant beneath thy power, and share

The impulse of thy strength, only less free
Than thou, O uncontrollable! If even
I were as in my boyhood, and could be

The comrade of thy wanderings over Heaven,
As then, when to outstrip thy skiey speed
Scarce seemed a vision; I would ne'er have striven

As thus with thee in prayer in my sore need.
Oh, lift me as a wave, a leaf, a cloud!
I fall upon the thorns of life! I bleed!

A heavy weight of hours has chained and bowed
One too like thee: tameless, and swift, and proud.

V

Make me thy lyre, even as the forest is:
What if my leaves are falling like its own!
The tumult of thy mighty harmonies

Will take from both a deep, autumnal tone,
Sweet though in sadness. Be thou, Spirit fierce,
My spirit! Be thou me, impetuous one!

Drive my dead thoughts over the universe
Like withered leaves to quicken a new birth!
And, by the incantation of this verse,

Scatter, as from an unextinguished hearth
Ashes and sparks, my words among mankind!
Be through my lips to unawakened earth

The trumpet of a prophecy! O, Wind,
If Winter comes, can Spring be far behind?

*1819*

ODE TO THE WEST WIND. **14. Destroyer and preserver:** Apollo was destroyer and healer, and, among the gods of India, Siva and Vishnu. **17. tangled boughs:** waterspouts; waves swept up into the sky by whirlwinds. **20–23:** Hughes quotes from Shelley's *Critical Notices* of some Maenad figures on the pedestal of the Minerva in the Florence Gallery, "The tremendous spirit of superstition seems to have caught them in its whirlwinds and to bear them over the earth as the rapid volutions of a tempest have the ever-changing trunk of a waterspout, or as the torrent of a mountain river whirls the autumnal leaves resistlessly along in its full eddies. The hair, loose and flowing, seems caught in the tempest of their own tumultuous motion." The Maenads were devoted women who danced and sang in honor of Dionysus. **31–34. Lulled . . . day:** See Intro., p. 247, above. **35. azure moss:** Shelley to Peacock, December 22, 1818, "The sea was so translucent that you could see the caverns clothed with glaucous sea-moss and the leaves and branches of those delicate weeds that pave the bottom of the water." **47. O uncontrollable:** Cf. John 3:7–8, "Marvel not that I said unto thee, Ye must be born again. The wind bloweth where it listeth, and thou hearest the sound thereof, but canst not tell whence it cometh, and wither it goeth: so is every one that is born of the Spirit." **57. thy lyre:** "We live and move and think; but we are not the creators of our own origin and existence. We are not the arbiters of every motion of our own complicated nature; we are not the masters of our own imaginations and moods of mental being. There is a Power by which we are surrounded, like the atmosphere in which some motionless lyre is suspended, which visits with its breath our silent chords at will," Shelley, *Essay on Christianity*. See also *A Defence of Poetry*, p. 305, Paragraph 2, below. **67. Ashes and sparks:** Cf. "It is brought to birth in the soul on a sudden, as light that is kindled by a leaping spark, and thereafter it nourishes itself," Plato, *Epistles*, VII.341d. **68. unawakened:** Cf. 29.

# PROMETHEUS UNBOUND

### A LYRICAL DRAMA IN FOUR ACTS

### SHELLEY'S PREFACE

The Greek tragic writers, in selecting as their subject any portion of their national history or mythology, employed in their treatment of it a certain arbitrary discretion. They by no means conceived themselves bound to adhere to the common interpretation or to imitate in story as in title their rivals and predecessors. Such a system would have amounted to a resignation of those claims to preference over their competitors which incited the composition. The Agamemnonian story was exhibited on the Athenian theatre with as many variations as dramas.

I have presumed to employ a similar licence. The *Prometheus Unbound* of Aeschylus supposed the reconciliation of Jupiter with his victim as the price of the disclosure of the danger threatened to his empire by the consummation of his marriage with Thetis. Thetis, according to this view of the subject, was given in marriage to Peleus, and Prometheus, by the permission of Jupiter, delivered from his captivity by Hercules. Had I framed my story on this model, I should have done no more than have attempted to restore the lost drama of Aeschylus; an ambition which, if my preference to this mode of treating the subject had incited me to cherish, the recollection of the high comparison such an attempt would challenge might well abate. But, in truth, I was averse from a catastrophe so feeble as that of reconciling the Champion with the Oppressor of mankind. The moral interest of the fable, which is so powerfully sustained by the sufferings and endurance of Prometheus, would be annihilated if we could conceive of him as unsaying his high language and quailing before his successful and perfidious adversary. The only imaginary being resembling in any degree Prometheus, is Satan; and Prometheus is, in my judgement, a more poetical character than Satan, because, in addition to courage, and majesty, and firm and patient opposition to omnipotent force, he is susceptible of being described as exempt from the taints of ambition, envy, revenge, and a desire for personal aggrandisement, which, in the Hero of *Paradise Lost,* interfere with the interest. The character of Satan engenders in the mind a pernicious casuistry which leads us to weigh his faults with his wrongs, and to excuse the former because the latter exceed all measure. In the minds of those who consider that magnificent fiction with a religious feeling it engenders something worse. But Prometheus is, as it were, the type of the highest perfection of moral and intellectual nature, impelled by the purest and the truest motives to the best and noblest ends.

This Poem was chiefly written upon the mountainous ruins of the Baths of Caracalla, among the flowery glades, and thickets of odoriferous blossoming trees, which are extended in ever winding labyrinths upon its immense platforms and dizzy arches suspended in the air. The bright blue sky of Rome, and the effect of the vigorous awakening spring in that divinest climate, and the new life with which it drenches the spirits even to intoxication, were the inspiration of this drama.

The imagery which I have employed will be found, in many instances, to have been drawn from the operations of the human mind, or from those external actions by which they are expressed. This is unusual in modern poetry, although Dante and Shakespeare are full of instances of the same kind: Dante indeed more than any other poet, and with greater success. But the Greek poets, as writers to whom no resource of awakening the sympathy of their contemporaries was unknown, were in the habitual use of this power; and it is the study of their works (since a higher merit would probably be denied me) to which I am willing that my readers should impute this singularity.

One word is due in candour to the degree in which the study of contemporary writings may have tinged my composition, for such has been a topic of censure with regard to poems far more popular, and indeed more deservedly popular, than mine. It is impossible that any one who inhabits the same age with such writers as those who stand in the foremost ranks of our own, can conscientiously assure himself that his language and tone of thought may not have been modified by the study of the productions of those extraordinary intellects. It is true, that, not the spirit of their genius, but the forms in which it has manifested itself, are due less to the peculiarities of their own minds than to the peculiarity of the moral and intellectual condition of the minds among which they have been produced. Thus a number of writers possess the form, whilst they want the spirit of those whom, it is alleged, they imitate; because the former is the endowment of the age in which they live, and the latter must be the uncommunicated lightning of their own mind.

The peculiar style of intense and comprehensive imagery which distinguishes the modern literature of England, has not been, as a general power, the product of the imitation of any particular writer. The mass of capabilities remains at every period materially the same; the circumstances which awaken it to action perpetually change. If England were divided into forty republics, each equal in population and extent to Athens, there is no reason to suppose but that, under institutions not more perfect than those of Athens, each would produce philosophers and poets equal to those who (if we except Shakespeare) have never been surpassed. We owe the great writers of the golden age of our literature to that fervid awakening of the public mind which shook to dust the oldest and most oppressive form of the Christian religion.[1] We owe

PROMETHEUS UNBOUND. 1. **Christian religion:** that is, pre-Reformation Roman Catholicism.

Milton to the progress and development of the same spirit: the sacred Milton was, let it ever be remembered, a republican, and a bold inquirer into morals and religion. The great writers of our own age are, we have reason to suppose, the companions and forerunners of some unimagined change in our social condition or the opinions which cement it. The cloud of mind is discharging its collected lightning, and the equilibrium between institutions and opinions is now restoring, or is about to be restored.

As to imitation, poetry is a mimetic art. It creates, but it creates by combination and representation. Poetical abstractions are beautiful and new, not because the portions of which they are composed had no previous existence in the mind of man or in nature, but because the whole produced by their combination has some intelligible and beautiful analogy with those sources of emotion and thought, and with the contemporary condition of them: one great poet is a masterpiece of nature which another not only ought to study but must study. He might as wisely and as easily determine that his mind should no longer be the mirror of all that is lovely in the visible universe, as exclude from his contemplation the beautiful which exists in the writings of a great contemporary. The pretence of doing it would be a presumption in any but the greatest; the effect, even in him, would be strained, unnatural, and ineffectual. A poet is the combined product of such internal powers as modify the nature of others; and of such external influences as excite and sustain these powers; he is not one, but both. Every man's mind is, in this respect, modified by all the objects of nature and art; by every word and every suggestion which he ever admitted to act upon his consciousness; it is the mirror upon which all forms are reflected, and in which they compose one form. Poets, not otherwise than philosophers, painters, sculptors, and musicians, are, in one sense, the creators, and, in another, the creations, of their age. From this subjection the loftiest do not escape. There is a similarity between Homer and Hesiod, between Aeschylus and Euripides, between Virgil and Horace, between Dante and Petrarch, between Shakespeare and Fletcher, between Dryden and Pope; each has a generic resemblance under which their specific distinctions are arranged. If this similarity be the result of imitation, I am willing to confess that I have imitated.

Let this opportunity be conceded to me of acknowledging that I have, what a Scotch philosopher characteristically terms, 'a passion for reforming the world:' what passion incited him to write and publish his book, he omits to explain. For my part I had rather be damned with Plato and Lord Bacon, than go to Heaven with Paley and Malthus.[2] But it is a mistake to suppose that I dedicate my poetical compositions solely to the direct enforcement of reform, or that I consider them in any degree as containing a reasoned system on the theory of human life. Didactic poetry is my abhorrence; nothing can be equally well expressed in prose that is not tedious and supererogatory in verse. My purpose has hitherto been simply to familiarise the highly refined imagination of the more select classes of poetical readers with beautiful idealisms of moral excellence; aware that until the mind can love, and admire, and trust, and hope, and endure, reasoned principles of moral conduct are seeds cast upon the highway of life which the unconscious passenger tramples into dust, although they would bear the harvest of his happiness. Should I live to accomplish what I purpose, that is, produce a systematical history of what appear to me to be the genuine elements of human society, let not the advocates of injustice and superstition flatter themselves that I should take Aeschylus rather than Plato as my model.

The having spoken of myself with unaffected freedom will need little apology with the candid; and let the uncandid consider that they injure me less than their own hearts and minds by misrepresentation. Whatever talents a person may possess to amuse and instruct others, be they ever so inconsiderable, he is yet bound to exert them: if his attempt be ineffectual, let the punishment of an unaccomplished purpose have been sufficient; let none trouble themselves to heap the dust of oblivion upon his efforts; the pile they raise will betray his grave which might otherwise have been unknown.

2. **I . . . Malthus:** In the *Essay on Christianity* Shelley wrote: "Every human mind has what Lord Bacon calls its 'idola specus,' peculiar images which reside in the inner cave of thought." Some of these are images of man's future. See *PU* I.659–63. William Paley, English divine and philosopher (1743–1805), in his *Natural Theology* (1802) gave "Evidences of the Existence and Attributes of the Deity from the Appearances of Nature." Robert Malthus, English economist (1766–1834), was the author of *An Essay on the Principle of Population As It Affects the Future Improvement of Society.* In this he combatted Godwin's and all idealist theories of man's perfectibility, arguing that population tends to outgrow its means of subsistence. Thus Paley and Malthus brought forward ethical and pseudoscientific arguments in support of the *status quo.*

# Prometheus Unbound

## DRAMATIS PERSONAE

PROMETHEUS
DEMOGORGON
JUPITER
THE EARTH
OCEAN

APOLLO
MERCURY
ASIA }
PANTHEA } *Oceanides.*
IONE }

HERCULES
THE PHANTASM OF JUPITER
THE SPIRIT OF THE EARTH
THE SPIRIT OF THE MOON
SPIRITS OF THE HOURS
SPIRITS, ECHOES, FAUNS, FURIES

---

# Act I

SCENE. — *A Ravine of Icy Rocks in the Indian Caucasus.* PROMETHEUS *is discovered bound to the Precipice.* PANTHEA *and* IONE *are seated at his feet. Time, night. During the Scene, morning slowly breaks.*

PROMETHEUS. Monarch of Gods and Daemons, and all Spirits
But One, who throng those bright and rolling worlds
Which Thou and I alone of living things
Behold with sleepless eyes! regard this Earth
Made multitudinous with thy slaves, whom thou
Requitest for knee-worship, prayer, and praise,
And toil, and hecatombs of broken hearts,
With fear and self-contempt and barren hope.
Whilst me, who am thy foe, eyeless in hate,
Hast thou made reign and triumph, to thy scorn,
O'er mine own misery and thy vain revenge.
Three thousand years of sleep-unsheltered hours,
And moments aye divided by keen pangs
Till they seemed years, torture and solitude,
Scorn and despair, — these are mine empire: —
More glorious far than that which thou surveyest
From thine unenvied throne, O Mighty God!
Almighty, had I deigned to share the shame
Of thine ill tyranny, and hung not here
Nailed to this wall of eagle-baffling mountain,
Black, wintry, dead, unmeasured; without herb,
Insect, or beast, or shape or sound of life.
Ah me! alas, pain, pain ever, for ever!

No change, no pause, no hope! Yet I endure.
I ask the Earth, have not the mountains felt?
I ask yon Heaven, the all-beholding Sun,
Has it not seen? The Sea, in storm or calm,
Heaven's ever-changing Shadow, spread below,
Have its deaf waves not heard my agony?
Ah me! alas, pain, pain ever, for ever!
The crawling glaciers pierce me with the spears
Of their moon-freezing crystals, the bright chains
Eat with their burning cold into my bones.
Heaven's winged hound, polluting from thy lips
His beak in poison not his own, tears up
My heart; and shapeless sights come wandering by,
The ghastly people of the realm of dream,
Mocking me: and the Earthquake-fiends are charged
To wrench the rivets from my quivering wounds
When the rocks split and close again behind:
While from their loud abysses howling throng
The genii of the storm, urging the rage
Of whirlwind, and afflict me with keen hail.
And yet to me welcome is day and night,
Whether one breaks the hoar frost of the morn,
Or starry, dim, and slow, the other climbs
The leaden-coloured east; for then they lead
The wingless, crawling hours, one among whom
— As some dark Priest hales the reluctant victim
Shall drag thee, cruel King, to kiss the blood
From these pale feet, which then might trample thee
If they disdained not such a prostrate slave.
Disdain! Ah no! I pity thee. What ruin
Will hunt thee undefended through wide Heaven!

**Act I. 1–2. Monarch . . . One**: Jupiter rules tyrannically over all spirits but Prometheus, the mind of man, who has defied and cursed him. **8. barren**: without fruit. **9. eyeless in hate**: Jupiter is blinded by hate. **10. to . . . scorn**: Jupiter scorns such a triumph and thereby is made a scorn himself. **18. Almighty**: If Prometheus had yielded, Jupiter's power would have been limitless.

**24. no hope**: Cf. 808, "Most vain all hope but love," and 701, 706. **28. Heaven's . . . Shadow**: Cf. "Mont Blanc," p. 252, above, 15, 37–42. The Sea is often an image for the multitudes of mankind. **29. deaf**: even such uncaring ones. See *Triumph of Life*, 477, "For deaf as is a sea, which wrath makes hoary . . .". **32. moon-freezing**: cold as if on the moon? **34–35: wingèd . . . own**: the vulture, kissed by Jupiter as reward on his return. The phrase "heaven's winged hound" is from Aeschylus, *Prometheus Bound*, 1021–22. **53–57. I . . . more**: the redeeming spring and release of the play.

How will thy soul, cloven to its depth with terror,
Gape like a hell within! I speak in grief,
Not exultation, for I hate no more,
As then ere misery made me wise. The curse
Once breathed on thee I would recall. Ye Mountains,
Whose many-voicèd Echoes, through the mist
Of cataracts, flung the thunder of that spell!
Ye icy Springs, stagnant with wrinkling frost,
Which vibrated to hear me, and then crept
Shuddering through India! Thou serenest Air,
Through which the Sun walks burning without beams!
And ye swift Whirlwinds, who on poisèd wings
Hung mute and moveless o'er yon hushed abyss,
As thunder, louder than your own, made rock
The orbèd world! If then my words had power,
Though I am changed so that aught evil wish
Is dead within; although no memory be
Of what is hate, let them not lose it now!
What was that curse? for ye all heard me speak.

FIRST VOICE [*from the Mountains*].

Thrice three hundred thousand years
O'er the Earthquake's couch we stood:
Oft, as men convulsed with fears,
We trembled in our multitude.

SECOND VOICE [*from the Springs*].

Thunderbolts had parched our water,
We had been stained with bitter blood,
And had run mute, 'mid shrieks of slaughter,
Thro' a city and a solitude.

THIRD VOICE [*from the Air*].

I had clothed, since Earth uprose,
Its wastes in colours not their own,
And oft had my serene repose
Been cloven by many a rending groan.

FOURTH VOICE [*from the Whirlwinds*].

We had soared beneath these mountains
Unresting ages; nor had thunder,
Nor yon volcano's flaming fountains,
Nor any power above or under
Ever made us mute with wonder.

FIRST VOICE

But never bowed our snowy crest
As at the voice of thine unrest.

**65. burning . . . beams**: "Beyond the atmosphere the sun would appear a rayless orb of fire in the midst of a black concave," Shelley's first note to *Queen Mab*. But see also *Paradise Lost* I.594–96 (Vol. I, p. 461). **69–72. If . . . now**: Though he no longer knows what hate is, let his former words have a power, though a changed power.



SECOND VOICE

Never such a sound before
To the Indian waves we bore.
A pilot asleep on the howling sea
Leaped up from the deck in agony,
And heard, and cried, 'Ah, woe is me!'
And died as mad as the wild waves be.

THIRD VOICE

By such dread words from Earth to Heaven
My still realm was never riven:
When its wound was closed, there stood
Darkness o'er the day like blood.

FOURTH VOICE

And we shrank back: for dreams of ruin
To frozen caves our flight pursuing
Made us keep silence — thus — and thus —
Though silence is as hell to us.

THE EARTH. The tongueless Caverns of the craggy hills
Cried, 'Misery!' then; the hollow Heaven replied,
'Misery!' And the Ocean's purple waves,
Climbing the land, howled to the lashing winds,
And the pale nations heard it, 'Misery!'

PROMETHEUS. I heard a sound of voices: not the voice
Which I gave forth. Mother, thy sons and thou
Scorn him, without whose all-enduring will
Beneath the fierce omnipotence of Jove,
Both they and thou had vanished, like thin mist
Unrolled on the morning wind. Know ye not me,
The Titan? He who made his agony
The barrier to your else all-conquering foe?
Oh, rock-embosomed lawns, and snow-fed streams,
Now seen athwart frore vapours, deep below,
Through whose o'ershadowing woods I wandered once
With Asia, drinking life from her loved eyes;
Why scorns the spirit which informs ye, now
To commune with me? me alone, who checked,
As one who checks a fiend-drawn charioteer,
The falsehood and the force of him who reigns
Supreme, and with the groans of pining slaves

**102. Darkness . . . day**: Matt. 27:45, "Now from the sixth hour there was darkness over all the land unto the ninth hour"; 51, ". . . and the earth did quake; and the rocks were rent." **114–16. without . . . vanished**: Only Prometheus had kept Jove from destroying them. **118. The Titan**: Strictly speaking, Prometheus is not a Titan; but the name is also given to divine and semidivine beings descended from Titans. **121. frore**: frosty. **123. Asia**: "Asia, one of the Oceanides, is the wife of Prometheus—she was, according to other mythological interpretations, the same as Venus and Nature. When the benefactor of mankind is liberated, Nature resumes the beauty of her prime, and is united to her husband, the emblem of the human race, in perfect and happy union," Mrs. Shelley's note. See III.iii,iv.

Fills your dim glens and liquid wildernesses:
Why answer ye not, still? Brethren!
THE EARTH. They dare not.
PROMETHEUS. Who dares? for I would hear that curse again.
Ha, what an awful whisper rises up!
'Tis scarce like sound: it tingles through the frame
As lightning tingles, hovering ere it strike.
Speak, Spirit! from thine inorganic voice
I only know that thou art moving near
And love. How cursed I him?
THE EARTH. How canst thou hear
Who knowest not the language of the dead?
PROMETHEUS. Thou art a living spirit; speak as they.
THE EARTH. I dare not speak like life, lest Heaven's fell King
Should hear, and link me to some wheel of pain
More torturing than the one whereon I roll.
Subtle thou art and good, and though the Gods
Hear not this voice, yet thou art more than God,
Being wise and kind: earnestly hearken now.
PROMETHEUS. Obscurely through my brain, like shadows dim,
Sweep awful thoughts, rapid and thick. I feel
Faint, like one mingled in entwining love;
Yet 'tis not pleasure.
THE EARTH. No, thou canst not hear:
Thou art immortal, and this tongue is known
Only to those who die.
PROMETHEUS. And what art thou,
O, melancholy Voice?
THE EARTH. I am the Earth,
Thy mother; she within whose stony veins,
To the last fibre of the loftiest tree
Whose thin leaves trembled in the frozen air,
Joy ran, as blood within a living frame,
When thou didst from her bosom, like a cloud
Of glory, arise, a spirit of keen joy!
And at thy voice her pining sons uplifted
Their prostrate brows from the polluting dust,
And our almighty Tyrant with fierce dread
Grew pale, until his thunder chained thee here.
Then, see those million worlds which burn and roll
Around us: their inhabitants beheld
My spherèd light wane in wide Heaven; the sea
Was lifted by strange tempest, and new fire
From earthquake-rifted mountains of bright snow
Shook its portentous hair beneath Heaven's frown;
Lightning and Inundation vexed the plains;
Blue thistles bloomed in cities; foodless toads
Within voluptuous chambers panting crawled:
When Plague had fallen on man, and beast, and worm,
And Famine; and black blight on herb and tree;
And in the corn, and vines, and meadow-grass,
Teemed ineradicable poisonous weeds
Draining their growth, for my wan breast was dry
With grief; and the thin air, my breath was stained
With the contagion of a mother's hate
Breathed on her child's destroyer; ay, I heard
Thy curse, the which, if thou rememberest not,
Yet my innumerable seas and streams,
Mountains, and caves, and winds, and yon wide air,
And the inarticulate people of the dead,
Preserve, a treasured spell. We meditate
In secret joy and hope those dreadful words,
But dare not speak them.
PROMETHEUS. Venerable mother!
All else who live and suffer take from thee
Some comfort; flowers, and fruits, and happy sounds,
And love, though fleeting; these may not be mine.
But mine own words, I pray, deny me not.
THE EARTH. They shall be told. Ere Babylon was dust,
The Magus Zoroaster, my dead child,
Met his own image walking in the garden.
That apparition, sole of men, he saw.
For know there are two worlds of life and death:
One that which thou beholdest; but the other
Is underneath the grave, where do inhabit
The shadows of all forms that think and live
Till death unite them and they part no more;
Dreams and the light imaginings of men,
And all that faith creates or love desires,
Terrible, strange, sublime and beauteous shapes.
There thou art, and dost hang, a writhing shade,
'Mid whirlwind-peopled mountains; all the gods
Are there, and all the powers of nameless worlds,
Vast, sceptred phantoms; heroes, men, and beasts;
And Demogorgon, a tremendous gloom;
And he, the supreme Tyrant, on his throne
Of burning gold. Son, one of these shall utter
The curse which all remember. Call at will
Thine own ghost, or the ghost of Jupiter,
Hades or Typhon, or what mightier Gods

**129. liquid wildernesses:** the seas. Cf. III.ii.29–31. **135. inorganic:** the parts not making sense with one another. **138. language . . . dead:** There are three languages in this passage: of the dead, of living mortals, and of immortals. Cf. III.iii.111. **151. And . . . thou?:** mortal? immortal?—or, possibly, who is speaking now? **153. stony veins:** The Earth and all upon her were cold as stone before Prometheus came. Cf. III.iii.85–90.

**191. Ere . . . dust:** before the 6th century B.C. **192. Zoroaster:** Zarathustra, the founder of the occult Magian religion. Morally dualistic and puritanical, mystically ecstatic, the Zoroastrians believed in the eternal war of good and evil "powers." Shelley perhaps had this story from Peacock. **197. underneath the grave:** In *Odyssey*, XI.601–14, Heracles is represented as being a phantom in Hades *and* at the banquet among the immortal gods. **199. unite them:** the shadows with the forms. The passage seems to promise death even to immortals. **207. Demogorgon:** see Intro., p. 244, above. **209. burning gold:** Cf. 291. **212. Hades or Typhon:** Pluto, god of the underworld;

From all-prolific Evil, since thy ruin
Have sprung, and trampled on my prostrate sons.
Ask, and they must reply: so the revenge
Of the Supreme may sweep through vacant shades,
As rainy wind through the abandoned gate
Of a fallen palace.
  PROMETHEUS. Mother, let not aught
Of that which may be evil, pass again
My lips, or those of aught resembling me.
Phantasm of Jupiter, arise, appear!

IONE.

My wings are folded o'er mine ears:
  My wings are crossèd o'er mine eyes:
Yet through their silver shade appears,
  And through their lulling plumes arise,
A Shape, a throng of sounds;
  May it be no ill to thee
O thou of many wounds!
Near whom, for our sweet sister's sake,
Ever thus we watch and wake.

PANTHEA.

The sound is of whirlwind underground,
  Earthquake, and fire, and mountains cloven;
The shape is awful like the sound,
  Clothed in dark purple, star-inwoven.
A sceptre of pale gold
  To stay steps proud, o'er the slow cloud
His veinèd hand doth hold.
Cruel he looks, but calm and strong,
Like one who does, not suffers wrong.

  PHANTASM OF JUPITER. Why have the secret powers of this strange world
Driven me, a frail and empty phantom, hither
On direst storms? What unaccustomed sounds
Are hovering on my lips, unlike the voice
With which our pallid race hold ghastly talk
In darkness? And, proud sufferer, who art thou?
  PROMETHEUS. Tremendous Image, as thou art must be
He whom thou shadowest forth. I am his foe,
The Titan. Speak the words which I would hear,
Although no thought inform thine empty voice.
  THE EARTH. Listen! And though your echoes must be mute,
Gray mountains, and old woods, and haunted springs,
Prophetic caves, and isle-surrounding streams,
Rejoice to hear what yet ye cannot speak.
  PHANTASM. A spirit seizes me and speaks within:
It tears me as fire tears a thunder-cloud.
  PANTHEA. See, how he lifts his mighty looks, the Heaven
Darkens above.
  IONE. He speaks! O shelter me!
  PROMETHEUS. I see the curse on gestures proud and cold,
And looks of firm defiance, and calm hate,
And such despair as mocks itself with smiles,
Written as on a scroll: yet speak: Oh, speak!

PHANTASM.

Fiend, I defy thee! with a calm, fixed mind,
  All that thou canst inflict I bid thee do;
Foul Tyrant both of Gods and Human-kind,
  One only being shalt thou not subdue.
Rain then thy plagues upon me here,
Ghastly disease, and frenzying fear;
And let alternate frost and fire
Eat into me, and be thine ire
Lightning, and cutting hail, and legioned forms
Of furies, driving by upon the wounding storms.

Ay, do thy worst. Thou art omnipotent. 272
  O'er all things but thyself I gave thee power,
And my own will. Be thy swift mischiefs sent
  To blast mankind, from yon ethereal tower.
Let thy malignant spirit move
In darkness over those I love:
On me and mine I imprecate
The utmost torture of thy hate;
And thus devote to sleepless agony,
This undeclining head while thou must reign on high.

But thou, who art the God and Lord: O, thou,
  Who fillest with thy soul this world of woe,
To whom all things of Earth and Heaven do bow
  In fear and worship: all-prevailing foe!
I curse thee! let a sufferer's curse
Clasp thee, his torturer, like remorse;
Till thin Infinity shall be
A robe of envenomed agony;
And thine Omnipotence a crown of pain,
To cling like burning gold round thy dissolving brain.

Heap on thy soul, by virtue of this Curse,
  Ill deeds, then be thou damned, beholding good;

Typhon, a hundred-headed monster, son of Earth; the embodiment of volcanoes and earthquakes, and of storms accompanying volcanic disturbances. **236. stay:** support. **252. Prophetic caves:** Cf. 658–63. **254. A spirit:** the curse.

**258. gestures:** The Phantasm resembles Prometheus as he spoke the curse. **273. I . . . power:** Cf. II.iv.43–46. **283. Who fillest:** The source of evil is the soul of "Heaven's fell king."

Both infinite as is the universe,
And thou, and thy self-torturing solitude.
An awful image of calm power
Though now thou sittest, let the hour
Come, when thou must appear to be
That which thou art internally;
And after many a false and fruitless crime
Scorn track thy lagging fall through boundless space and time.

PROMETHEUS. Were these my words, O Parent?
THE EARTH. They were thine.
PROMETHEUS. It doth repent me: words are quick and vain;
Grief for awhile is blind, and so was mine.
I wish no living thing to suffer pain.

THE EARTH.

Misery, Oh misery to me,
That Jove at length should vanquish thee.
Wail, howl aloud, Land and Sea,
The Earth's rent heart shall answer ye.
Howl, Spirits of the living and the dead,
Your refuge, your defence lies fallen and vanquishèd.

FIRST ECHO.

Lies fallen and vanquishèd!

SECOND ECHO.

Fallen and vanquishèd!

IONE.

Fear not: 'tis but some passing spasm,
The Titan is unvanquished still.
But see, where through the azure chasm
Of yon forked and snowy hill
Trampling the slant winds on high
With golden-sandalled feet, that glow
Under plumes of purple dye,
Like rose-ensanguined ivory,
A Shape comes now,
Stretching on high from his right hand
A serpent-cinctured wand.

PANTHEA. 'Tis Jove's world-wandering herald, Mercury.

IONE.

And who are those with hydra tresses
And iron wings that climb the wind,
Whom the frowning God represses
Like vapours steaming up behind,
Clanging loud, an endless crowd —

PANTHEA.

These are Jove's tempest-walking hounds,
Whom he gluts with groans and blood,
When charioted on sulphurous cloud
He bursts Heaven's bounds.

IONE.

Are they now led, from the thin dead
On new pangs to be fed?

PANTHEA.

The Titan looks as ever, firm, not proud.

FIRST FURY. Ha! I scent life!
SECOND FURY. Let me but look into his eyes!
THIRD FURY. The hope of torturing him smells like a heap
Of corpses, to a death-bird after battle.
FIRST FURY. Darest thou delay, O Herald! take cheer, Hounds
Of Hell: what if the Son of Maia soon
Should make us food and sport — who can please long
The Omnipotent?
MERCURY. Back to your towers of iron,
And gnash, beside the streams of fire, and wail
Your foodless teeth. Geryon, arise! and Gorgon,
Chimaera, and thou Sphinx, subtlest of fiends
Who ministered to Thebes Heaven's poisoned wine,
Unnatural love, and more unnatural hate:
These shall perform your task.
FIRST FURY. Oh, mercy! mercy!
We die with our desire: drive us not back!
MERCURY. Crouch then in silence.
Awful Sufferer!
To thee unwilling, most unwillingly
I come, by the great Father's will driven down,
To execute a doom of new revenge.
Alas! I pity thee, and hate myself

**294. Both**: ill deeds and good. **301. lagging**: long-delayed, always falling behind in time. **324. serpent-cinctured wand**: the caduceus of Hermes (Mercury), which signified both health and cunning. It was his official token of authority when he guided souls to the other world. **326. hydra**: snakelike, from Hydra, a snake-headed monster. **331–32. These . . . blood**: Cf. *Paradise Lost*, X.616, "See with what heat these dogs of Hell advance/To waste and havoc yonder World." **342. Son of Maia**: Mercury. Shelley translated the Homeric *Hymn to Mercury*, where the winged messenger's life and character are described. **345–47. gnash . . . teeth**: Gnash your teeth and bewail that they are not to be fed. **Geryon**: a three-bodied giant killed by Hercules. **Chimaera**: a fire-breathing monster. **Sphinx**: a she-monster who murdered all Thebans unable to guess her riddle. For solving it, Oedipus was given the kingdom and Iocasta—his mother—as wife. **349. Unnatural**: Here the word applies both to Oedipus' marriage with his mother and to the conflict between his sons.

That I can do no more: aye from thy sight
Returning, for a season, Heaven seems Hell,
So thy worn form pursues me night and day,
Smiling reproach. Wise art thou, firm and good,
But vainly wouldst stand forth alone in strife
Against the Omnipotent; as yon clear lamps
That measure and divide the weary years
From which there is no refuge, long have taught
And long must teach. Even now thy Torturer arms
With the strange might of unimagined pains
The powers who scheme slow agonies in Hell,
And my commission is to lead them here,
Or what more subtle, foul, or savage fiends
People the abyss, and leave them to their task.
Be it not so! there is a secret known
To thee, and to none else of living things,
Which may transfer the sceptre of wide Heaven,
The fear of which perplexes the Supreme:
Clothe it in words, and bid it clasp his throne
In intercession; bend thy soul in prayer,
And like a suppliant in some gorgeous fane,
Let the will kneel within thy haughty heart:
For benefits and meek submission tame
The fiercest and the mightiest.

PROMETHEUS. Evil minds
Change good to their own nature. I gave all
He has; and in return he chains me here
Years, ages, night and day: whether the Sun
Split my parched skin, or in the moony night
The crystal-wingèd snow cling round my hair:
Whilst my belovèd race is trampled down
By his thought-executing ministers.
Such is the tyrant's recompense: 'tis just:
He who is evil can receive no good;
And for a world bestowed, or a friend lost,
He can feel hate, fear, shame; not gratitude:
He but requites me for his own misdeed.
Kindness to such is keen reproach, which breaks
With bitter stings the light sleep of Revenge.
Submission, thou dost know I cannot try:
For what submission but that fatal word,
The death-seal of mankind's captivity,
Like the Sicilian's hair-suspended sword,
Which trembles o'er his crown, would he accept,
Or could I yield? Which yet I will not yield.
Let others flatter Crime, where it sits throned
In brief Omnipotence: secure are they:
For Justice, when triumphant, will weep down
Pity, not punishment, on her own wrongs,
Too much avenged by those who err. I wait,
Enduring thus, the retributive hour
Which since we spake is even nearer now.
But hark, the hell-hounds clamour: fear delay:
Behold! Heaven lowers under thy Father's frown.

MERCURY. Oh, that we might be spared: I to inflict
And thou to suffer! Once more answer me:
Thou knowest not the period of Jove's power?

PROMETHEUS. I know but this, that it must come.

MERCURY. Alas!
Thou canst not count thy years to come of pain?

PROMETHEUS. They last while Jove must reign: nor more, nor less
Do I desire or fear.

MERCURY. Yet pause, and plunge
Into Eternity, where recorded time,
Even all that we imagine, age on age,
Seems but a point, and the reluctant mind
Flags wearily in its unending flight,
Till it sink, dizzy, blind, lost, shelterless;
Perchance it has not numbered the slow years
Which thou must spend in torture, unreprieved?

PROMETHEUS. Perchance no thought can count them, yet they pass.

MERCURY. If thou might'st dwell among the Gods the while
Lapped in voluptuous joy?

PROMETHEUS. I would not quit
This bleak ravine, these unrepentant pains.

MERCURY. Alas! I wonder at, yet pity thee.

PROMETHEUS. Pity the self-despising slaves of Heaven,
Not me, within whose mind sits peace serene,
As light in the sun, throned: how vain is talk!
Call up the fiends.

IONE. O, sister, look! White fire
Has cloven to the roots yon huge snow-loaded cedar;
How fearfully God's thunder howls behind!

MERCURY. I must obey his words and thine: alas!
Most heavily remorse hangs at my heart!

PANTHEA. See where the child of Heaven, with wingèd feet,
Runs down the slanted sunlight of the dawn.

IONE. Dear sister, close thy plumes over thine eyes
Lest thou behold and die: they come: they come
Blackening the birth of day with countless wings,
And hollow underneath, like death.

FIRST FURY. Prometheus!

SECOND FURY. Immortal Titan!

THIRD FURY. Champion of Heaven's slaves!

375. **it**: the secret. 381–82. **I . . . has**: Cf. 273–74, and II.iv.43–44. 387. **thought-executing ministers**: carrying out Jove's thoughts. Cf. *King Lear*, III.ii.4, "You sulph'rous and thought-executing fires." 390. **friend**: Prometheus had been Jove's friend. 396. **that . . . word**: the secret. 398. **Like . . . sword**: Damocles, having extolled the felicity of his king, Dionysius of Sicily, for his wealth and power, was placed at a banquet under a naked sword suspended by a single horse-hair, to teach him what a tyrant's happiness is.

405. **avenged**: As virtue is its own reward, vice is its own punishment. 409. **lowers**: frowns, threatens. 412. **period**: end point; also, duration. 436–37. **child**: Mercury, whose departure marks the coming of day. Cf. *Paradise Lost*, IV.555–56 (Vol. I, p. 481).

PROMETHEUS. He whom some dreadful voice invokes is here,
Prometheus, the chained Titan. Horrible forms,
What and who are ye? Never yet there came
Phantasms so foul through monster-teeming Hell
From the all-miscreative brain of Jove;
Whilst I behold such execrable shapes,
Methinks I grow like what I contemplate,
And laugh and stare in loathsome sympathy.

FIRST FURY. We are the ministers of pain, and fear,
And disappointment, and mistrust, and hate,
And clinging crime; and as lean dogs pursue
Through wood and lake some struck and sobbing fawn,
We track all things that weep, and bleed, and live,
When the great King betrays them to our will.

PROMETHEUS. Oh! many fearful natures in one name,
I know ye; and these lakes and echoes know
The darkness and the clangour of your wings.
But why more hideous than your loathèd selves
Gather ye up in legions from the deep?

SECOND FURY. We knew not that: Sisters, rejoice, rejoice!

PROMETHEUS. Can aught exult in its deformity?

SECOND FURY. The beauty of delight makes lovers glad,
Gazing on one another: so are we.
As from the rose which the pale priestess kneels
To gather for her festal crown of flowers
The aëreal crimson falls, flushing her cheek,
So from our victim's destined agony
The shade which is our form invests us round,
Else we are shapeless as our mother Night.

PROMETHEUS. I laugh your power, and his who sent you here,
To lowest scorn. Pour forth the cup of pain.

FIRST FURY. Thou thinkest we will rend thee bone from bone,
And nerve from nerve, working like fire within?

PROMETHEUS. Pain is my element, as hate is thine;
Ye rend me now: I care not.

SECOND FURY. Dost imagine
We will but laugh into thy lidless eyes?

PROMETHEUS. I weigh not what ye do, but what ye suffer,
Being evil. Cruel was the power which called
You, or aught else so wretched, into light.

THIRD FURY. Thou think'st we will live through thee, one by one,
Like animal life, and though we can obscure not
The soul which burns within, that we will dwell
Beside it, like a vain loud multitude
Vexing the self-content of wisest men:
That we will be dread thought beneath thy brain,
And foul desire round thine astonished heart,
And blood within thy labyrinthine veins
Crawling like agony?

PROMETHEUS. Why, ye are thus now;
Yet am I king over myself, and rule
The torturing and conflicting throngs within,
As Jove rules you when Hell grows mutinous.

CHORUS OF FURIES.

From the ends of the earth, from the ends of the earth,
Where the night has its grave and the morning its birth,
Come, come, come!
Oh, ye who shake hills with the scream of your mirth,
When cities sink howling in ruin; and ye
Who with wingless footsteps trample the sea,
And close upon Shipwreck and Famine's track,
Sit chattering with joy on the foodless wreck;
Come, come, come!
Leave the bed, low, cold, and red,
Strewed beneath a nation dead;
Leave the hatred, as in ashes
Fire is left for future burning:
It will burst in bloodier flashes
When ye stir it, soon returning:
Leave the self-contempt implanted
In young spirits, sense-enchanted,
Misery's yet unkindled fuel:
Leave Hell's secrets half unchanted
To the maniac dreamer; cruel
More than ye can be with hate
Is he with fear.
Come, come, come!
We are steaming up from Hell's wide gate
And we burthen the blast of the atmosphere,
But vainly we toil till ye come here.

IONE. Sister, I hear the thunder of new wings.

PANTHEA. These solid mountains quiver with the sound
Even as the tremulous air: their shadows make
The space within my plumes more black than night.

FIRST FURY.

Your call was as a wingèd car
Driven on whirlwinds fast and far;
It rapt us from red gulfs of war.

**458. one name:** Furies. **461–62. But . . . deep?:** Why are they worse than ever known before? **479. lidless:** eyes unable to close their lids to shut out this.

**527. rapt:** snatched away bodily, or carried away in spirit, from earth, consciousness, or occupation.

SECOND FURY.

From wide cities, famine-wasted;

THIRD FURY.

Groans half heard, and blood untasted;

FOURTH FURY.

Kingly conclaves stern and cold,
Where blood with gold is bought and sold;

FIFTH FURY.

From the furnace, white and hot,
In which —

A FURY.

Speak not: whisper not:
I know all that ye would tell,
But to speak might break the spell
Which must bend the Invincible,
The stern of thought;
He yet defies the deepest power of Hell.

A FURY.

Tear the veil!

ANOTHER FURY.

It is torn.

CHORUS.

The pale stars of the morn
Shine on a misery, dire to be borne.
Dost thou faint, mighty Titan? We laugh thee to scorn.
Dost thou boast the clear knowledge thou waken'dst for man?
Then was kindled within him a thirst which outran
Those perishing waters; a thirst of fierce fever,
Hope, love, doubt, desire, which consume him for ever.
One came forth of gentle worth
Smiling on the sanguine earth;
His words outlived him, like swift poison
Withering up truth, peace, and pity.
Look! where round the wide horizon
Many a million-peopled city
Vomits smoke in the bright air.
Hark that outcry of despair!
'Tis his mild and gentle ghost
Wailing for the faith he kindled:
Look again, the flames almost
To a glow-worm's lamp have dwindled:
The survivors round the embers
Gather in dread.
Joy, joy, joy!
Past ages crowd on thee, but each one remembers,
And the future is dark, and the present is spread
Like a pillow of thorns for thy slumberless head.

SEMICHORUS I.

Drops of bloody agony flow
From his white and quivering brow.
Grant a little respite now:
See a disenchanted nation
Springs like day from desolation;
To Truth its state is dedicate,
And Freedom leads it forth, her mate;
A legioned band of linkèd brothers
Whom Love calls children —

SEMICHORUS II.

'Tis another's:
See how kindred murder kin:
'Tis the vintage-time for death and sin:
Blood, like new wine, bubbles within:
Till Despair smothers
The struggling world, which slaves and tyrants win.

[*All the* FURIES *vanish, except one.*]

IONE. Hark, sister! what a low yet dreadful groan
Quite unsuppressed is tearing up the heart
Of the good Titan, as storms tear the deep,
And beasts hear the sea moan in inland caves.
Darest thou observe how the fiends torture him?

PANTHEA. Alas! I looked forth twice, but will no more.

IONE. What didst thou see?

PANTHEA. A woful sight: a youth
With patient looks nailed to a crucifix.

IONE. What next?

PANTHEA. The heaven around, the earth below
Was peopled with thick shapes of human death,
All horrible, and wrought by human hands,
And some appeared the work of human hearts,
For men were slowly killed by frowns and smiles:
And other sights too foul to speak and live
Were wandering by. Let us not tempt worse fear
By looking forth: those groans are grief enough.

FURY. Behold an emblem: those who do endure

**540. dire . . . borne**: an echo of much English used in translation of Greek tragedy. **544. perishing**: "clear knowledge" which can be said ironically to be forever dying? **546. One**: Jesus of Nazareth. In the subsequent passage instances of evil coming from good intentions and beginnings are cited: through the growth of Christianity, 546–66, 586–631; and through the French Revolution, 567–77, 648–54. **547. sanguine**: hopeful, *and* bloodstained.

**567. disenchanted nation**: France. **584. youth**: Jesus.

Deep wrongs for man, and scorn, and chains, but heap
Thousandfold torment on themselves and him.

PROMETHEUS. Remit the anguish of that lighted stare;
Close those wan lips; let that thorn-wounded brow
Stream not with blood; it mingles with thy tears!
Fix, fix those tortured orbs in peace and death,
So thy sick throes shake not that crucifix,
So those pale fingers play not with thy gore.
O, horrible! Thy name I will not speak,
It hath become a curse. I see, I see
The wise, the mild, the lofty, and the just,
Whom thy slaves hate for being like to thee,
Some hunted by foul lies from their heart's home,
An early-chosen, late-lamented home;
As hooded ounces cling to the driven hind;
Some linked to corpses in unwholesome cells:
Some — Hear I not the multitude laugh loud? —
Impaled in lingering fire: and mighty realms
Float by my feet, like sea-uprooted isles,
Whose sons are kneaded down in common blood
By the red light of their own burning homes.

FURY. Blood thou canst see, and fire; and canst hear groans;
Worse things, unheard, unseen, remain behind.

PROMETHEUS. Worse?

FURY. In each human heart terror survives
The ravin it has gorged: the loftiest fear
All that they would disdain to think were true:
Hypocrisy and custom make their minds
The fanes of many a worship, now outworn.
They dare not devise good for man's estate,
And yet they know not that they do not dare.
The good want power, but to weep barren tears.
The powerful goodness want: worse need for them.
The wise want love; and those who love want wisdom;
And all best things are thus confused to ill.
Many are strong and rich, and would be just,
But live among their suffering fellow-men
As if none felt: they know not what they do.

PROMETHEUS. Thy words are like a cloud of wingèd snakes;
And yet I pity those they torture not.

FURY. Thou pitiest them? I speak no more!
[*Vanishes.*]

PROMETHEUS. Ah woe!
Ah woe! Alas! pain, pain ever, for ever!
I close my tearless eyes, but see more clear
Thy works within my woe-illumèd mind,
Thou subtle tyrant! Peace is in the grave.
The grave hides all things beautiful and good:
I am a God and cannot find it there,
Nor would I seek it: for, though dread revenge,
This is defeat, fierce king, not victory.
The sights with which thou torturest gird my soul
With new endurance, till the hour arrives
When they shall be no types of things which are.

PANTHEA. Alas! what sawest thou more?

PROMETHEUS. There are two woes:
To speak, and to behold; thou spare me one.
Names are there, Nature's sacred watchwords, they
Were borne aloft in bright emblazonry;
The nations thronged around, and cried aloud,
As with one voice, Truth, liberty, and love!
Suddenly fierce confusion fell from heaven
Among them: there was strife, deceit, and fear:
Tyrants rushed in, and did divide the spoil.
This was the shadow of the truth I saw.

THE EARTH. I felt thy torture, son; with such mixed joy
As pain and virtue give. To cheer thy state
I bid ascend those subtle and fair spirits,
Whose homes are the dim caves of human thought,
And who inhabit, as birds wing the wind,
Its world-surrounding aether: they behold
Beyond that twilight realm, as in a glass,
The future: may they speak comfort to thee!

PANTHEA. Look, sister, where a troop of spirits gather,
Like flocks of clouds in spring's delightful weather,
Thronging in the blue air!

IONE. And see! more come,
Like fountain-vapours when the winds are dumb,
That climb up the ravine in scattered lines.
And, hark! is it the music of the pines?
Is it the lake? Is it the waterfall?

PANTHEA. 'Tis something sadder, sweeter far than all.

CHORUS OF SPIRITS.

From unremembered ages we
Gentle guides and guardians be
Of heaven-oppressed mortality;
And we breathe, and sicken not,
The atmosphere of human thought:
Be it dim, and dank, and gray,
Like a storm-extinguished day,

**597. lighted stare:** Jesus' gaze, penetrating to the meaning of his torment. **609. hooded ounces:** leopards used in hunting, hooded as a means of control, suggesting the blindness of the "foul lies." **619. The . . . gorged:** the prey it has devoured. **625. want:** lack. **627.** Cf. Lucifer's speech in Byron's *Cain*, I, "Choose betwixt love and knowledge—since there is/No other choice." **631. they . . . not:** See Luke 23:34.

**643. gird:** armor. **659. Whose homes:** Cf. 675–76. **661. aether:** "Light consists either of vibrations propagated through a subtle medium (the aether), or of numerous minute particles . . . ," Shelley's first note to *Queen Mab*.

Travelled o'er by dying gleams;
Be it bright as all between
Cloudless skies and windless streams,
Silent, liquid, and serene;
As the birds within the wind,
As the fish within the wave,
As the thoughts of man's own mind
Float through all above the grave;
We make there our liquid lair,
Voyaging cloudlike and unpent
Through the boundless element:
Thence we bear the prophecy
Which begins and ends in thee!

IONE. More yet come, one by one: the air around them
Looks radiant as the air around a star.

FIRST SPIRIT.

On a battle-trumpet's blast
I fled hither, fast, fast, fast,
'Mid the darkness upward cast.
From the dust of creeds outworn,
From the tyrant's banner torn,
Gathering 'round me, onward borne,
There was mingled many a cry —
Freedom! Hope! Death! Victory!
Till they faded through the sky;
And one sound, above, around,
One sound beneath, around, above,
Was moving; 'twas the soul of Love;
'Twas the hope, the prophecy,
Which begins and ends in thee.

SECOND SPIRIT.

A rainbow's arch stood on the sea,
Which rocked beneath, immovably;
And the triumphant storm did flee,
Like a conqueror, swift and proud,
Between, with many a captive cloud,
A shapeless, dark and rapid crowd,
Each by lightning riven in half:
I heard the thunder hoarsely laugh:
Mighty fleets were strewn like chaff
And spread beneath a hell of death
O'er the white waters. I alit
On a great ship lightning-split,
And speeded hither on the sigh
Of one who gave an enemy
His plank, then plunged aside to die.

**685–86. As . . . grave:** one of Shelley's characteristic spiraling, self-encompassing comparisons; these spirits voyage through the atmosphere of human thought as thoughts float through all who live. Cf. IV.81–82. **688. unpent:** unrestricted. **694 ff.:** The four spirits celebrate the victory of Love in different situations: heroic war, self-sacrifice, wise decision, creative imagining. **707. in thee:** in Prometheus.

THIRD SPIRIT.

I sate beside a sage's bed,
And the lamp was burning red
Near the book where he had fed,
When a Dream with plumes of flame.
To his pillow hovering came,
And I knew it was the same
Which had kindled long ago
Pity, eloquence, and woe;
And the world awhile below
Wore the shade, its lustre made.
It has borne me here as fleet
As Desire's lightning feet:
I must ride it back ere morrow,
Or the sage will wake in sorrow.

FOURTH SPIRIT.

On a poet's lips I slept
Dreaming like a love-adept
In the sound his breathing kept;
Nor seeks nor finds he mortal blisses,
But feeds on the aëreal kisses
Of shapes that haunt thought's wildernesses.
He will watch from dawn to gloom
The lake-reflected sun illume
The yellow bees in the ivy-bloom,
Nor heed nor see, what things they be;
But from these create he can
Forms more real than living man,
Nurslings of immortality!
One of these awakened me,
And I sped to succour thee.

IONE.

Behold'st thou not two shapes from the east and west
Come, as two doves to one belovèd nest,
Twin nurslings of the all-sustaining air
On swift still wings glide down the atmosphere?
And, hark! their sweet, sad voices! 'tis despair
Mingled with love and then dissolved in sound.

**724. red:** fuel almost exhausted. **732. shade:** The world's illumination is as shadow to reality. **742. thought's wildernesses:** the not yet explored. "In the Greek Shakespeare, Sophocles, we find this image, 'Coming to many ways in the wanderings of careful thought'—a line of almost unfathomable depth of poetry; yet how simple are the images in which it is arrayed! . . . What a picture does this line suggest of the mind as a wilderness of intricate paths wide as the universe, which is here made its symbol; a world within a world which he who seeks some knowledge with respect to what he ought to do searches throughout . . . ," Shelley's notebook. See Neville Rogers, *Shelley at Work*, p. 15. **744. lake-reflected sun:** Cf. *Epipsychidion*, 88–90, "The sun-beams of those wells which ever leap/Under the lightnings of the soul—too deep/For the brief fathom-line of thought or sense."

PANTHEA. Canst thou speak, sister? all my words
are drowned.

IONE. Their beauty gives me voice. See how they
float
On their sustaining wings of skiey grain,
Orange and azure deepening into gold:
Their soft smiles light the air like a star's fire.

CHORUS OF SPIRITS.

Hast thou beheld the form of Love?

FIFTH SPIRIT.

As over wide dominions
I sped, like some swift cloud that wings the wide
air's wildernesses,
That planet-crested shape swept by on lightning-
braided pinions,
Scattering the liquid joy of life from his am-
brosial tresses:
His footsteps paved the world with light; but as I
passed 'twas fading,
And hollow Ruin yawned behind: great sages
bound in madness,
And headless patriots, and pale youths who perished,
unupbraiding,
Gleamed in the night. I wandered o'er, till thou,
O King of sadness,
Turned by thy smile the worst I saw to recollected
gladness.

SIXTH SPIRIT.

Ah, sister! Desolation is a delicate thing:
It walks not on the earth, it floats not on the air,
But treads with lulling footstep, and fans with silent
wing
The tender hopes which in their hearts the best
and gentlest bear;
Who, soothed to false repose by the fanning plumes
above
And the music-stirring motion of its soft and busy
feet,
Dream visions of aëreal joy, and call the monster,
Love,
And wake, and find the shadow Pain, as he
whom now we greet.

CHORUS.

Though Ruin now Love's shadow be,
Following him, destroyingly,
On Death's white and wingèd steed,
Which the fleetest cannot flee,
Trampling down both flower and weed,
Man and beast, and foul and fair,
Like a tempest through the air;
Thou shalt quell this horseman grim,
Woundless though in heart or limb.

PROMETHEUS. Spirits! how know ye this shall be?

CHORUS.

In the atmosphere we breathe,
As buds grow red when the snow-storms flee,
From Spring gathering up beneath,
Whose mild winds shake the elder brake,
And the wandering herdsmen know
That the white-thorn soon will blow:
Wisdom, Justice, Love, and Peace,
When they struggle to increase,
Are to us as soft winds be
To shepherd boys, the prophecy
Which begins and ends in thee.

IONE. Where are the Spirits fled?

PANTHEA Only a sense
Remains of them, like the omnipotence
Of music, when the inspired voice and lute
Languish, ere yet the responses are mute,
Which through the deep and labyrinthine soul,
Like echoes through long caverns, wind and roll.

PROMETHEUS. How fair these airborn shapes! and
yet I feel
Most vain all hope but love; and thou art far,
Asia! who, when my being overflowed,
Wert like a golden chalice to bright wine
Which else had sunk into the thirsty dust.
All things are still: alas! how heavily
This quiet morning weighs upon my heart;
Though I should dream I could even sleep with
grief
If slumber were denied not. I would fain
Be what it is my destiny to be,
The saviour and the strength of suffering man,
Or sink into the original gulf of things:
There is no agony, and no solace left;
Earth can console, Heaven can torment no more.

PANTHEA. Hast thou forgotten one who watches
thee
The cold dark night, and never sleeps but when
The shadow of thy spirit falls on her?

**760. On . . . grain:** In *Paradise Lost,* V.284–85, the Seraph's wings shadowed his feet "from either heel with feathered mail,/ Sky-tinctured grain . . ." **772 ff. Desolation . . . :** "For Homer says that the Goddess Calamity is delicate, and that her feet are tender. 'Her feet are soft', he says, 'for she treads not upon the ground but makes her path upon the heads of men,'" Shelley's translation of *Symposium,* 195d. **778. the monster:** the false joy. **779. he:** Prometheus, who likewise misjudged?

**782. Death's . . . steed:** Rev. 6:8, ". . . and behold a pale horse; and his name that sat on him was Death, and Hell followed with him . . ." **788. Woundless though:** After the victory thou shalt be woundless. **818. original gulf:** primordial Chaos. **820. Earth . . . more:** Neither can Earth console nor Heaven torment now. **823. The . . . her:** Cf. 732; II.i.31; III.iii.7.

PROMETHEUS. I said all hope was vain but love: thou lovest.
PANTHEA. Deeply in truth; but the eastern star looks white,
And Asia waits in that far Indian vale,
The scene of her sad exile; rugged once
And desolate and frozen, like this ravine;
But now invested with fair flowers and herbs,
And haunted by sweet airs and sounds, which flow
Among the woods and waters, from the aether
Of her transforming presence, which would fade
If it were mingled not with thine. Farewell!

[*End of the First Act*]

# Act II

SCENE I. — *Morning. A lovely Vale in the Indian Caucasus.* ASIA *alone.*

ASIA. From all the blasts of heaven thou hast descended:
Yes, like a spirit, like a thought, which makes
Unwonted tears throng to the horny eyes,
And beatings haunt the desolated heart,
Which should have learnt repose: thou hast descended
Cradled in tempests; thou dost wake, O Spring!
O child of many winds! As suddenly
Thou comest as the memory of a dream,
Which now is sad because it hath been sweet;
Like genius, or like joy which riseth up
As from the earth, clothing with golden clouds
The desert of our life.
This is the season, this the day, the hour;
At sunrise thou shouldst come, sweet sister mine,
Too long desired, too long delaying, come!
How like death-worms the wingless moments crawl!
The point of one white star is quivering still
Deep in the orange light of widening morn
Beyond the purple mountains: through a chasm
Of wind-divided mist the darker lake
Reflects it: now it wanes: it gleams again
As the waves fade, and as the burning threads
Of woven cloud unravel in pale air:
'Tis lost! and through yon peaks of cloud-like snow
The roseate sunlight quivers: hear I not
The Aeolian music of her sea-green plumes
Winnowing the crimson dawn?
[PANTHEA *enters.*]
I feel, I see
Those eyes which burn through smiles that fade in tears,
Like stars half quenched in mists of silver dew.
Belovèd and most beautiful, who wearest
The shadow of that soul by which I live,
How late thou art! the spherèd sun had climbed
The sea; my heart was sick with hope, before
The printless air felt thy belated plumes.
PANTHEA. Pardon, great Sister! but my wings were faint
With the delight of a remembered dream,
As are the noontide plumes of summer winds
Satiate with sweet flowers. I was wont to sleep
Peacefully, and awake refreshed and calm
Before the sacred Titan's fall, and thy
Unhappy love, had made, through use and pity,
Both love and woe familiar to my heart
As they had grown to thine: erewhile I slept
Under the glaucous caverns of old Ocean
Within dim bowers of green and purple moss,
Our young Ione's soft and milky arms
Locked then, as now, behind my dark, moist hair,
While my shut eyes and cheeks were pressed within
The folded depth of her life-breathing bosom:
But not as now, since I am made the wind
Which fails beneath the music that I bear
Of thy most wordless converse; since dissolved
Into the sense with which love talks, my rest
Was troubled and yet sweet; my waking hours
Too full of care and pain.
ASIA. Lift up thine eyes,
And let me read thy dream.
PANTHEA. As I have said
With our sea-sister at his feet I slept.
The mountain mists, condensing at our voice
Under the moon, had spread their snowy flakes,
From the keen ice shielding our linkèd sleep.
Then two dreams came. One, I remember not.
But in the other his pale wound-worn limbs
Fell from Prometheus, and the azure night
Grew radiant with the glory of that form
Which lives unchanged within, and his voice fell
Like music which makes giddy the dim brain,
Faint with intoxication of keen joy:
'Sister of her whose footsteps pave the world
With loveliness — more fair than aught but her,

**831. aether:** here, a life-giving atmosphere. **832–33:** Cf. "Love's Philosophy" (1819), "Nothing in the world is single;/All things by a law divine/In one spirit meet and mingle . . ."
**Act II, Sc. i. 1. thou:** Spring. See I.829–34; Preface, paragraphs 3 and 4. **3. horny:** dry, calloused, insensitive. **17. white:** See I.825. **26. Aeolian music:** made by the winds sweeping through the harp of Aeolus, god of the winds.

**27. Winnowing . . . dawn:** See *Paradise Lost,* V.268–70; the winged Raphael, descending, "then with quick fan/Winnows the buxom air." **31. that soul:** Prometheus. **34. printless:** used as if the air were a ground to be walked on, or solid enough to feel the imprint of a wing. **37–38. As . . . flowers:** Cf. "To a Skylark," 55. **43. erewhile:** formerly. **44. glaucous:** dull grayish green or blue. **58. voice:** command. **61. two . . . One:** See 132.

Whose shadow thou art — lift thine eyes on me.'
I lifted them: the overpowering light
Of that immortal shape was shadowed o'er
By love; which, from his soft and flowing limbs,
And passion-parted lips, and keen, faint eyes,
Steamed forth like vaporous fire; an atmosphere
Which wrapped me in its all-dissolving power,
As the warm aether of the morning sun
Wraps ere it drinks some cloud of wandering dew.
I saw not, heard not, moved not, only felt
His presence flow and mingle through my blood
Till it became his life, and his grew mine,
And I was thus absorbed, until it passed,
And like the vapours when the sun sinks down,
Gathering again in drops upon the pines,
And tremulous as they, in the deep night
My being was condensed; and as the rays
Of thought were slowly gathered, I could hear
His voice, whose accents lingered ere they died
Like footsteps of weak melody: thy name
Among the many sounds alone I heard
Of what might be articulate; though still
I listened through the night when sound was none.
Ione wakened then, and said to me:
'Canst thou divine what troubles me to-night?
I always knew what I desired before,
Nor ever found delight to wish in vain.
But now I cannot tell thee what I seek;
I know not; something sweet, since it is sweet
Even to desire; it is thy sport, false sister;
Thou hast discovered some enchantment old,
Whose spells have stolen my spirit as I slept
And mingled it with thine: for when just now
We kissed, I felt within thy parted lips
The sweet air that sustained me, and the warmth
Of the life-blood, for loss of which I faint,
Quivered between our intertwining arms.'
I answered not, for the Eastern star grew pale,
But fled to thee.

ASIA. Thou speakest, but thy words
Are as the air: I feel them not: Oh, lift
Thine eyes, that I may read his written soul!

PANTHEA. I lift them though they droop beneath the load
Of that they would express: what canst thou see
But thine own fairest shadow imaged there?

ASIA. Thine eyes are like the deep, blue, boundless heaven
Contracted to two circles underneath
Their long, fine lashes; dark, far, measureless,
Orb within orb, and line through line inwoven.

PANTHEA. Why lookest thou as if a spirit passed?

ASIA. There is a change: beyond their inmost depth
I see a shade, a shape: 'tis He, arrayed
In the soft light of his own smiles, which spread
Like radiance from the cloud-surrounded moon.
Prometheus, it is thine! depart not yet!
Say not those smiles that we shall meet again
Within that bright pavilion which their beams
Shall build o'er the waste world? The dream is told.
What shape is that between us? Its rude hair
Roughens the wind that lifts it, its regard
Is wild and quick, yet 'tis a thing of air,
For through its gray robe gleams the golden dew
Whose stars the noon has quenched not.

DREAM. Follow! Follow!

PANTHEA. It is mine other dream.

ASIA. It disappears.

PANTHEA. It passes now into my mind. Methought
As we sate here, the flower-infolding buds
Burst on yon lightning-blasted almond-tree,
When swift from the white Scythian wilderness
A wind swept forth wrinkling the Earth with frost:
I looked, and all the blossoms were blown down;
But on each leaf was stamped, as the blue bells
Of Hyacinth tell Apollo's written grief,
O, FOLLOW, FOLLOW!

ASIA. As you speak, your words
Fill, pause by pause, my own forgotten sleep
With shapes. Methought among these lawns together
We wandered, underneath the young gray dawn,
And multitudes of dense white fleecy clouds
Were wandering in thick flocks along the mountains
Shepherded by the slow, unwilling wind;
And the white dew on the new-bladed grass,
Just piercing the dark earth, hung silently;
And there was more which I remember not:
But on the shadows of the morning clouds,
Athwart the purple mountain slope, was written
FOLLOW, O, FOLLOW! as they vanished by;
And on each herb, from which Heaven's dew had fallen,
The like was stamped, as with a withering fire;
A wind arose among the pines; it shook
The clinging music from their boughs, and then
Low, sweet, faint sounds, like the farewell of ghosts,
Were heard: O, FOLLOW, FOLLOW, FOLLOW ME!
And then I said: 'Panthea, look on me.'
But in the depth of those beloved eyes
Still I saw, FOLLOW, FOLLOW!

ECHO. Follow, follow!

PANTHEA. The crags, this clear spring morning, mock our voices

**81–82. it**: the ecstasy. Cf. Donne, Vol. I, p. 372, and Shakespeare, "The Phoenix and the Turtle." **86. the rays**: Cf. III.iii.53.

**136. Scythian**: of an unbounded country stretching beyond the Black Sea, far into India. **140. Hyacinth**: When inadvertently Apollo killed Hyacinthus, whom he loved, the youth was turned into a flower on whose leaves might be seen the Greek word expressing anguish, *AI*.

As they were spirit-tongued.
ASIA. It is some being
Around the crags. What fine clear sounds! O, list!

ECHOES [*unseen*].

Echoes we: listen!
We cannot stay:
As dew-stars glisten
Then fade away—
Child of Ocean!

ASIA. Hark! Spirits speak. The liquid responses
Of their aëreal tongues yet sound.
PANTHEA. I hear.

ECHOES.

O, follow, follow,
As our voice recedeth
Through the caverns hollow,
Where the forest spreadeth;
[*More distant*]
O, follow, follow!
Through the caverns hollow,
As the song floats thou pursue,
Where the wild bee never flew,
Through the noontide darkness deep,
By the odour-breathing sleep
Of faint night flowers, and the waves
At the fountain-lighted caves,
While our music, wild and sweet,
Mocks thy gently falling feet,
Child of Ocean!

ASIA. Shall we pursue the sound? It grows more faint
And distant.
PANTHEA. List! the strain floats nearer now.

ECHOES.

In the world unknown
Sleeps a voice unspoken;
By thy step alone
Can its rest be broken;
Child of Ocean!

ASIA. How the notes sink upon the ebbing wind!

ECHOES.

O, follow, follow!
Through the caverns hollow,
As the song floats thou pursue,
By the woodland noontide dew;
By the forest, lakes, and fountains,
Through the many-folded mountains;
To the rents, and gulfs, and chasms,
Where the Earth reposed from spasms,
On the day when He and thou
Parted, to commingle now;
Child of Ocean!

ASIA. Come, sweet Panthea, link thy hand in mine,
And follow, ere the voices fade away.

SCENE II.—*A Forest, intermingled with Rocks and Caverns.* ASIA *and* PANTHEA *pass into it. Two young Fauns are sitting on a Rock listening.*

SEMICHORUS I. OF SPIRITS.

The path through which that lovely twain
Have passed, by cedar, pine, and yew,
And each dark tree that ever grew,
Is curtained out from Heaven's wide blue;
Nor sun, nor moon, nor wind, nor rain,
Can pierce its interwoven bowers,
Nor aught, save where some cloud of dew,
Drifted along the earth-creeping breeze,
Between the trunks of the hoar trees,
Hangs each a pearl in the pale flowers
Of the green laurel, blown anew;
And bends, and then fades silently,
One frail and fair anemone:
Or when some star of many a one
That climbs and wanders through steep night,
Has found the cleft through which alone
Beams fall from high those depths upon
Ere it is borne away, away,
By the swift Heavens that cannot stay,
It scatters drops of golden light,
Like lines of rain that ne'er unite:
And the gloom divine is all around,
And underneath is the mossy ground.

SEMICHORUS II.

There the voluptuous nightingales,
Are awake through all the broad noonday.
When one with bliss or sadness fails,
And through the windless ivy-boughs,
Sick with sweet love, droops dying away
On its mate's music-panting bosom;
Another from the swinging blossom,
Watching to catch the languid close
Of the last strain, then lifts on high
The wings of the weak melody,

184. fountain-lighted: Cf. II.iii.26.

Sc. ii. 10. Hangs . . . flowers: Cf. *A Midsummer Night's Dream*, II.i.15, "And hang a pearl in every cowslip's ear."

'Till some new strain of feeling bear
The song, and all the woods are mute;
When there is heard through the dim air
The rush of wings, and rising there
Like many a lake-surrounded flute,
Sounds overflow the listener's brain
So sweet, that joy is almost pain.

SEMICHORUS I.

There those enchanted eddies play
Of echoes, music-tongued, which draw,
By Demogorgon's mighty law,
With melting rapture, or sweet awe,
All spirits on that secret way;
As inland boats are driven to Ocean
Down streams made strong with mountain-thaw:
And first there comes a gentle sound
To those in talk or slumber bound,
And wakes the destined soft emotion,—
Attracts, impels them; those who saw
Say from the breathing earth behind
There steams a plume-uplifting wind
Which drives them on their path, while they
Believe their own swift wings and feet
The sweet desires within obey:
And so they float upon their way,
Until, still sweet, but loud and strong,
The storm of sound is driven along,
Sucked up and hurrying: as they fleet
Behind, its gathering billows meet
And to the fatal mountain bear
Like clouds amid the yielding air.

FIRST FAUN. Canst thou imagine where those spirits live
Which make such delicate music in the woods?
We haunt within the least frequented caves
And closest coverts, and we know these wilds,
Yet never meet them, though we hear them oft:
Where may they hide themselves?
SECOND FAUN. 'Tis hard to tell:
I have heard those more skilled in spirits say,
The bubbles, which the enchantment of the sun
Sucks from the pale faint water-flowers that pave
The oozy bottom of clear lakes and pools,
Are the pavilions where such dwell and float
Under the green and golden atmosphere
Which noontide kindles through the woven leaves;
And when these burst, and the thin fiery air,
The which they breathed within those lucent domes,
Ascends to flow like meteors through the night,
They ride on them, and rein their headlong speed,
And bow their burning crests, and glide in fire
Under the waters of the earth again.
FIRST FAUN. If such live thus, have others other lives,
Under pink blossoms or within the bells
Of meadow flowers, or folded violets deep,
Or on their dying odours, when they die,
Or in the sunlight of the spherèd dew?
SECOND FAUN. Ay, many more which we may well divine.
But, should we stay to speak, noontide would come,
And thwart Silenus find his goats undrawn,
And grudge to sing those wise and lovely songs
Of Fate, and Chance, and God, and Chaos old,
And Love, and the chained Titan's woful doom,
And how he shall be loosed, and make the earth
One brotherhood: delightful strains which cheer
Our solitary twilights, and which charm
To silence the unenvying nightingales.

## SCENE III.—*A Pinnacle of Rock among Mountains.* ASIA *and* PANTHEA.

PANTHEA. Hither the sound has borne us—to the realm
Of Demogorgon, and the mighty portal,
Like a volcano's meteor-breathing chasm,
Whence the oracular vapour is hurled up
Which lonely men drink wandering in their youth,
And call truth, virtue, love, genius, or joy,
That maddening wine of life, whose dregs they drain
To deep intoxication; and uplift,
Like Maenads who cry loud, Evoe! Evoe!
The voice which is contagion to the world.
ASIA. Fit throne for such a Power! Magnificent!
How glorious art thou, Earth! And if thou be
The shadow of some spirit lovelier still,
Though evil stain its work, and it should be
Like its creation, weak yet beautiful,
I could fall down and worship that and thee.
Even now my heart adoreth: Wonderful!
Look, sister, ere the vapour dim thy brain:

**38. Like . . . flute:** Like reeds in a lake. Or the sweetness of a flute's sound borne across a lake. **43. Demogorgon's . . . law:** See Intro., p. 243. **46–47. As . . . mountain-thaw:** This uses what is perhaps Shelley's supreme symbol. Cf. Asia's song ending II. **51. those . . . saw:** seers who understood that Demogorgon's law moves men by necessity, yet allows them the sense of their own free will. **62. fatal mountain:** the mountain toward which Panthea and Asia are moving, where they arrive at the opening of the next scene.

**90. And . . . undrawn:** See Virgil, *Eclogue*, VI. Two shepherds bind the drunken Silenus in a cave, and force him to sing. Silenus, a wood god, had the power of prophecy; he was chief of the Satyrs, and the teacher of Dionysus. Plato likened Socrates to him, in the *Symposium*. **thwart:** stubborn, contradictious. **undrawn:** not milked.

**Sc. iii: 3. chasm:** Cf. III.iii.125–28. **9. Maenads:** See note to "Ode to the West Wind," p. 255, l. 23, above. **Evoe:** the cry the Maenads shouted to their god. **10. contagion:** destroying what "the world" most cares for.

Beneath is a wide plain of billowy mist,
As a lake, paving in the morning sky,
With azure waves which burst in silver light,
Some Indian vale. Behold it, rolling on
Under the curdling winds, and islanding
The peak whereon we stand, midway, around,
Encinctured by the dark and blooming forests,
Dim twilight-lawns, and stream-illumèd caves,
And wind-enchanted shapes of wandering mist;
And far on high the keen sky-cleaving mountains
From icy spires of sun-like radiance fling
The dawn, as lifted Ocean's dazzling spray,
From some Atlantic islet scattered up,
Spangles the wind with lamp-like water-drops.
The vale is girdled with their walls, a howl
Of cataracts from their thaw-cloven ravines,
Satiates the listening wind, continuous, vast,
Awful as silence. Hark! the rushing snow!
The sun-awakened avalanche! whose mass,
Thrice sifted by the storm, had gathered there
Flake after flake, in heaven-defying minds
As thought by thought is piled, till some great truth
Is loosened, and the nations echo round,
Shaken to their roots, as do the mountains now.

PANTHEA. Look how the gusty sea of mist is breaking
In crimson foam, even at our feet! it rises
As Ocean at the enchantment of the moon
Round foodless men wrecked on some oozy isle.

ASIA. The fragments of the cloud are scattered up;
The wind that lifts them disentwines my hair;
Its billows now sweep o'er mine eyes; my brain
Grows dizzy; see'st thou shapes within the mist?

PANTHEA. A countenance with beckoning smiles: there burns
An azure fire within its golden locks!
Another and another: hark! they speak!

SONG OF SPIRITS.

To the deep, to the deep,
Down, down!
Through the shade of sleep,
Through the cloudy strife
Of Death and of Life;
Through the veil and the bar
Of things which seem and are
Even to the steps of the remotest throne,
Down, down!

While the sound whirls around,
Down, down!
As the fawn draws the hound,
As the lightning the vapour,
As a weak moth the taper;
Death, despair; love, sorrow;
Time both; to-day, to-morrow;
As steel obeys the spirit of the stone,
Down, down!

Through the gray, void abysm,
Down, down!
Where the air is no prism,
And the moon and stars are not,
And the cavern-crags wear not
The radiance of Heaven,
Nor the gloom to Earth given,
Where there is One pervading, One alone,
Down, down!

In the depth of the deep,
Down, down!
Like veiled lightning asleep,
Like the spark nursed in embers,
The last look Love remembers,
Like a diamond, which shines
On the dark wealth of mines,
A spell is treasured but for thee alone.
Down, down!

We have bound thee, we guide thee;
Down, down!
With the bright form beside thee;
Resist not the weakness,
Such strength is in meekness
That the Eternal, the Immortal,
Must unloose through life's portal
The snake-like Doom coiled underneath his throne
By that alone.

SCENE IV. — *The Cave of* DEMOGORGON. ASIA *and* PANTHEA.

PANTHEA. What veilèd form sits on that ebon throne?

ASIA. The veil has fallen.

**66–69. As . . . to-morrow:** Vapor, taper, despair, and sorrow attract lightning, the moth, death, and love; Time draws both love and sorrow; today is pursued by tomorrow. **74. Where . . . prism:** where space is totally empty, and according to the Newtonian theory of light, does not transmit the light rays. **86. Like a diamond:** Cf. Milton, *Comus*, 732–36, ". . . and the unsought diamonds/Would so emblaze the forehead of the deep,/And so bestud with stars, that they below/Would grow inured to light, and come at last/To gaze upon the sun with shameless brows." **88. thee:** Asia, who is accompanied by "the bright form" of Panthea. **93–94. Resist . . . meekness:** Shelley has a peculiar feeling for the word "weak." Cf. II.i.89; II.iii.15. **97. coiled underneath:** Between his returns in the unending cycle, Vishnu sleeps on the coils of the serpent.

**Sc. iv. 2. fallen:** The falling of the veil leaves this Spirit as inapprehensible as before.

PANTHEA. I see a mighty darkness
Filling the seat of power, and rays of gloom
Dart round, as light from the meridian sun.
— Ungazed upon and shapeless; neither limb,
Nor form, nor outline; yet we feel it is
A living Spirit.

DEMOGORGON. Ask what thou wouldst know.

ASIA. What canst thou tell?

DEMOGORGON. All things thou dar'st demand.

ASIA. Who made the living world?

DEMOGORGON. God.

ASIA. Who made all
That it contains? thought, passion, reason, will,
Imagination?

DEMOGORGON. God: Almighty God.

ASIA. Who made that sense which, when the winds of Spring
In rarest visitation, or the voice
Of one belovèd heard in youth alone,
Fills the faint eyes with falling tears which dim
The radiant looks of unbewailing flowers,
And leaves this peopled earth a solitude
When it returns no more?

DEMOGORGON. Merciful God.

ASIA. And who made terror, madness, crime, remorse,
Which from the links of the great chain of things,
To every thought within the mind of man
Sway and drag heavily, and each one reels
Under the load towards the pit of death;
Abandoned hope, and love that turns to hate;
And self-contempt, bitterer to drink than blood;
Pain, whose unheeded and familiar speech
Is howling, and keen shrieks, day after day;
And Hell, or the sharp fear of Hell?

DEMOGORGON. He reigns.

ASIA. Utter his name: a world pining in pain
Asks but his name: curses shall drag him down.

DEMOGORGON. He reigns.

ASIA. I feel, I know it: who?

DEMOGORGON. He reigns.

ASIA. Who reigns? There was the Heaven and Earth at first,
And Light and Love; then Saturn, from whose throne
Time fell, an envious shadow: such the state
Of the earth's primal spirits beneath his sway,
As the calm joy of flowers and living leaves
Before the wind or sun has withered them
And semivital worms; but he refused
The birthright of their being, knowledge, power,
The skill which wields the elements, the thought
Which pierces this dim universe like light,
Self-empire, and the majesty of love;
For thirst of which they fainted. Then Prometheus
Gave wisdom, which is strength, to Jupiter,
And with this law alone, 'Let man be free,'
Clothed him with the dominion of wide Heaven.
To know nor faith, nor love, nor law; to be
Omnipotent but friendless is to reign;
And Jove now reigned; for on the race of man
First famine, and then toil, and then disease,
Strife, wounds, and ghastly death unseen before,
Fell; and the unseasonable seasons drove
With alternating shafts of frost and fire,
Their shelterless, pale tribes to mountain caves:
And in their desert hearts fierce wants he sent,
And mad disquietudes, and shadows idle
Of unreal good, which levied mutual war,
So ruining the lair wherein they raged.
Prometheus saw, and waked the legioned hopes
Which sleep within folded Elysian flowers,
Nepenthe, Moly, Amaranth, fadeless blooms,
That they might hide with thin and rainbow wings
The shape of Death; and Love he sent to bind
The disunited tendrils of that vine
Which bears the wine of life, the human heart;
And he tamed fire which, like some beast of prey,
Most terrible, but lovely, played beneath
The frown of man; and tortured to his will
Iron and gold, the slaves and signs of power,
And gems and poisons, and all subtlest forms
Hidden beneath the mountains and the waves.
He gave man speech, and speech created thought,
Which is the measure of the universe;
And Science struck the thrones of earth and heaven,
Which shook, but fell not; and the harmonious mind
Poured itself forth in all-prophetic song;
And music lifted up the listening spirit
Until it walked, exempt from mortal care.
Godlike, o'er the clear billows of sweet sound;

**8. dar'st demand:** "We are on that verge where words abandon us, and what wonder if we grow dizzy to look down the dark abyss of how little we know," Shelley's essay, *On Life*. **16. unbewailing:** having a surety we do not have. **24–28. Abandoned . . . Hell:** Who made all these? **30. curses . . . down:** Asia (not Prometheus) is speaking. Cf. I.303–05. **31. who?:** Asia is fulfilling the promise of the Echoes of II.i.190.

**47–48. To . . . reign:** Cf. Lord Acton, "Power corrupts; absolute power corrupts absolutely," and Shelley, *Queen Mab*, III.176–77, "Power like a desolating pestilence/Pollutes whate'er it touches." **59–70. Prometheus . . . poisons:** "The alleviations of his state Prometheus gave to man," 98–99, were not all good for him. **Nepenthe:** See Spenser, *Faerie Queene*, IV.iii.43, "Nepenthe is a drinck of sovrayne grace,/Devized by the gods for to asswage/Harts grief, and bitter gall away to chace . . .", and Milton, *Comus*, 675–77, "Not that Nepenthes which the wife of Thone/In Egypt gave to Jove-born Helena/Is of such power to stir up joy as this. . . ." See also "Triumph of Life," 358–59, "In her right hand she bore a crystal glass,/Mantling with bright Nepenthe." **Moly:** See *Comus*, 635–36, "And yet more med'cinal is it than that moly/That Hermes once to wise Ulysses gave." **Amaranth:** See *Paradise Lost*, III.353–55, "Immortal amarant, a flower which once/In Paradise, fast by the Tree of Life,/Began to bloom." **tortured:** twisted, bent, misused.

And human hands first mimicked and then
mocked,
With moulded limbs more lovely than its own,
The human form, till marble grew divine;
And mothers, gazing, drank the love men see
Reflected in their race, behold, and perish.
He told the hidden power of herbs and springs,
And Disease drank and slept. Death grew like sleep.
He taught the implicated orbits woven
Of the wide-wandering stars; and how the sun
Changes his lair, and by what secret spell
The pale moon is transformed, when her broad eye
Gazes not on the interlunar sea:
He taught to rule, as life directs the limbs,
The tempest-wingèd chariots of the Ocean,
And the Celt knew the Indian. Cities then
Were built, and through their snow-like columns
flowed
The warm winds, and the azure aether shone,
And the blue sea and shadowy hills were seen.
Such, the alleviations of his state,
Prometheus gave to man, for which he hangs
Withering in destined pain: but who rains down
Evil, the immedicable plague, which, while
Man looks on his creation like a God
And sees that it is glorious, drives him on,
The wreck of his own will, the scorn of earth,
The outcast, the abandoned, the alone?
Not Jove: while yet his frown shook Heaven, ay,
when
His adversary from adamantine chains
Cursed him, he trembled like a slave. Declare
Who is his master? Is he too a slave?

DEMOGORGON. All spirits are enslaved which serve
things evil:
Thou knowest if Jupiter be such or no.

ASIA. Whom calledst thou God?

DEMOGORGON. I spoke but as ye speak,
For Jove is the supreme of living things.

ASIA. Who is the master of the slave?

DEMOGORGON. If the abysm
Could vomit forth its secrets. . . . But a voice
Is wanting, the deep truth is imageless;
For what would it avail to bid thee gaze
On the revolving world? What to bid speak
Fate, Time, Occasion, Chance, and Change? To
these
All things are subject but eternal Love.

ASIA. So much I asked before, and my heart gave
The response thou hast given; and of such truths
Each to itself must be the oracle.
One more demand; and do thou answer me
As mine own soul would answer, did it know
That which I ask. Prometheus shall arise
Henceforth the sun of this rejoicing world:
When shall the destined hour arrive?

DEMOGORGON. Behold!

ASIA. The rocks are cloven, and through the pur-
ple night
I see cars drawn by rainbow-wingèd steeds
Which trample the dim winds: in each there stands
A wild-eyed charioteer urging their flight.
Some look behind, as fiends pursued them there,
And yet I see no shapes but the keen stars:
Others, with burning eyes, lean forth, and drink
With eager lips the wind of their own speed,
As if the thing they loved fled on before,
And now, even now, they clasped it. Their bright
locks
Stream like a comet's flashing hair: they all
Sweep onward.

DEMOGORGON. These are the immortal Hours,
Of whom thou didst demand. One waits for thee.

ASIA. A spirit with a dreadful countenance
Checks its dark chariot by the craggy gulf.
Unlike thy brethren, ghastly charioteer,
Who art thou? Whither wouldst thou bear me?
Speak!

SPIRIT. I am the shadow of a destiny
More dread than is my aspect: ere yon planet
Has set, the darkness which ascends with me
Shall wrap in lasting night heaven's kingless throne.

ASIA. What meanest thou?

PANTHEA. That terrible shadow floats
Up from its throne, as may the lurid smoke
Of earthquake-ruined cities o'er the sea.
Lo! it ascends the car; the coursers fly
Terrified: watch its path among the stars
Blackening the night!

ASIA. Thus I am answered: strange!

PANTHEA. See, near the verge, another chariot
stays;

**80. mimicked . . . mocked:** See *Ozymandias*, "the hand that mocked them." The sculptor improves on the human form by the loveliness of his enduring creations. **82–84. marble . . . perish:** Mothers-to-be were to look at statues in order to have beautiful offspring; men beholding such beauty die of love. **88. wide-wandering stars:** planets. **90–91. The . . . sea:** Between lunations, the bright face of the moon does not shine down upon the sea. Cf. *A Defence of Poetry*, p. 314, below, "it arrests the vanishing apparitions which haunt the interlunations of life." And see Milton, *Samson Agonistes*, 87–89 (Vol. I, p. 505). **92–94. He . . . Indian:** Prometheus taught man how to navigate sailing ships; the Briton could cross the sea and reach India. **101. immedicable:** incurable. **103. drives . . . on:** For Asia evil may have a function? Shelley had written much earlier of "the woe-fertilized world" (Rogers, 29). **104–05. The . . . earth:** Cf. Pope, *Essay on Man*, 18, "The glory, jest, and riddle of the world" (Vol. I, p. 793).

**117–120. For . . . Love:** Asia is answered; eternal Love alone is beyond mutability. See *Triumph of Life*, 475–76, "the wondrous story/How all things are transfigured except Love." **128. Behold!:** Demogorgon's answer is not in speech. Asia does not realize what is happening. Cf. 155. **148. the darkness:** Demogorgon, "that terrible shadow," 150, who is himself, it may be, the shadow of another.

An ivory shell inlaid with crimson fire,
Which comes and goes within its sculptured rim
Of delicate strange tracery; the young spirit
That guides it has the dove-like eyes of hope;
How its soft smiles attract the soul! as light
Lures wingèd insects through the lampless air.

SPIRIT.

My coursers are fed with the lightning,
They drink of the whirlwind's stream,
And when the red morning is bright'ning
They bathe in the fresh sunbeam;
They have strength for their swiftness I deem,
Then ascend with me, daughter of Ocean.

I desire: and their speed makes night kindle;
I fear: they outstrip the Typhoon;
Ere the cloud piled on Atlas can dwindle
We encircle the earth and the moon:
We shall rest from long labours at noon:
Then ascend with me, daughter of Ocean.

SCENE V. — *The Car pauses within a Cloud on the top of a snowy Mountain.* ASIA, PANTHEA, *and the* SPIRIT OF THE HOUR.

SPIRIT.

On the brink of the night and the morning
My coursers are wont to respire;
But the Earth has just whispered a warning
That their flight must be swifter than fire:
They shall drink the hot speed of desire!

ASIA. Thou breathest on their nostrils, but my breath
Would give them swifter speed.

SPIRIT. Alas! it could not.

PANTHEA. Oh Spirit! pause, and tell whence is the light
Which fills this cloud? the sun is yet unrisen.

SPIRIT. The sun will rise not until noon. Apollo
Is held in heaven by wonder; and the light
Which fills this vapour, as the aëreal hue
Of fountain-gazing roses fills the water,
Flows from thy mighty sister.

PANTHEA. Yes, I feel —

ASIA. What is it with thee, sister? Thou art pale.

PANTHEA. How thou art changed! I dare not look on thee;
I feel but see thee not. I scarce endure
The radiance of thy beauty. Some good change
Is working in the elements, which suffer
Thy presence thus unveiled. The Nereids tell
That on the day when the clear hyaline
Was cloven at thine uprise, and thou didst stand
Within a veinèd shell, which floated on
Over the calm floor of the crystal sea,
Among the Aegean isles, and by the shores
Which bear thy name; love, like the atmosphere
Of the sun's fire filling the living world,
Burst from thee, and illumined earth and heaven
And the deep ocean and the sunless caves
And all that dwells within them; till grief cast
Eclipse upon the soul from which it came:
Such art thou now; nor is it I alone,
Thy sister, thy companion, thine own chosen one,
But the whole world which seeks thy sympathy.
Hearest thou not sounds i' the air which speak the love
Of all articulate beings? Feelest thou not
The inanimate winds enamoured of thee? List!
[*Music.*]

ASIA. Thy words are sweeter than aught else but his
Whose echoes they are: yet all love is sweet,
Given or returned. Common as light is love,
And its familiar voice wearies not ever.
Like the wide heaven, the all-sustaining air,
It makes the reptile equal to the God:
They who inspire it most are fortunate,
As I am now; but those who feel it most
Are happier still, after long sufferings,
As I shall soon become.

PANTHEA. List! Spirits speak.

VOICE IN THE AIR [*singing*].

Life of Life! thy lips enkindle
With their love the breath between them;
And thy smiles before they dwindle
Make the cold air fire; then screen them
In those looks, where whoso gazes
Faints, entangled in their mazes.

Child of Light! thy limbs are burning
Through the vest which seems to hide them;
As the radiant lines of morning

**162. lampless:** "the desire of the moth for the star." A strange image for the smiles of hope. This, and the song which follows, may be thought to lapse from the height of the rest of this scene. But the song establishes this as the dawn hour.
**Sc. v. 10–14. The . . . sister:** See Milton, "On the Morning of Christ's Nativity," 7, 79–84 (Vol. I, p. 415).

**17. but . . . not:** Cf. 64–65. **20–28. The . . . thee:** See "Ode to the West Wind," 31. Asia now appears as the spirit of Love, or Intellectual Beauty, and is therefore identified with Aphrodite (Venus), who was said to be born of the sea foam. The Nereids, daughters of the Ocean king, tell of her rising from the sea, standing on a shell. This seems to be a description of Botticelli's picture "The Birth of Venus" in the Uffizi Gallery, Florence. Shelley, who took a keen interest in Italian paintings, was in Florence during the fall of 1819. **hyaline:** transparent, glassy, crystalline. **44–47. They . . . become:** a study of the depth meanings of *fortunate* and *happy*.

Through the clouds ere they divide them;
And this atmosphere divinest
Shrouds thee wheresoe'er thou shinest.

Fair are others; none beholds thee,
But thy voice sounds low and tender
Like the fairest, for it folds thee
From the sight, that liquid splendour,
And all feel, yet see thee never,
As I feel now, lost for ever!

Lamp of Earth! where'er thou movest
Its dim shapes are clad with brightness,
And the souls of whom thou lovest
Walk upon the winds with lightness,
Till they fail, as I am failing,
Dizzy, lost, yet unbewailing!

ASIA.

My soul is an enchanted boat,
Which, like a sleeping swan, doth float
Upon the silver waves of thy sweet singing;
And thine doth like an angel sit
Beside a helm conducting it,
Whilst all the winds with melody are ringing.
It seems to float ever, for ever,
Upon that many-winding river,
Between mountains, woods, abysses,
A paradise of wildernesses!
Till, like one in slumber bound,
Borne to the ocean, I float down, around,
Into a sea profound, of ever-spreading sound:

Meanwhile thy spirit lifts its pinions
In music's most serene dominions;
Catching the winds that fan that happy heaven.
And we sail on, away, afar,
Without a course, without a star,
But, by the instinct of sweet music driven;
Till through Elysian garden islets
By thee, most beautiful of pilots,
Where never mortal pinnace glided,
The boat of my desire is guided:
Realms where the air we breathe is love,
Which in the winds and on the waves doth move,
Harmonizing this earth with what we feel above.

We have passed Age's icy caves,
And Manhood's dark and tossing waves,
And Youth's smooth ocean, smiling to betray:
Beyond the glassy gulfs we flee
Of shadow-peopled Infancy,
Through Death and Birth, to a diviner day;
A paradise of vaulted bowers,
Lit by downward-gazing flowers,
And watery paths that wind between
Wildernesses calm and green,
Peopled by shapes too bright to see,
And rest, having beheld; somewhat like thee;
Which walk upon the sea, and chant melodiously!

[*End of the Second Act*]

# Act III

SCENE I.—*Heaven.* JUPITER *on his Throne;* THETIS *and the other Deities assembled.*

JUPITER. Ye congregated powers of heaven, who share
The glory and the strength of him ye serve,
Rejoice! henceforth I am omnipotent.
All else had been subdued to me; alone
The soul of man, like unextinguished fire,
Yet burns towards heaven with fierce reproach, and doubt,
And lamentation, and reluctant prayer,
Hurling up insurrection, which might make
Our antique empire insecure, though built
On eldest faith, and hell's coeval, fear;
And though my curses through the pendulous air,
Like snow on herbless peaks, fall flake by flake,
And cling to it; though under my wrath's night
It climbs the crags of life, step after step,
Which wound it, as ice wounds unsandalled feet,
It yet remains supreme o'er misery,
Aspiring, unrepressed, yet soon to fall:
Even now have I begotten a strange wonder,
That fatal child, the terror of the earth,
Who waits but till the destined hour arrive,
Bearing from Demogorgon's vacant throne
The dreadful might of ever-living limbs
Which clothed that awful spirit unbeheld,

**64–65. feel**: a more inclusive mode of knowing. **lost**: a reversal of the ordinary sense; Cf. Matt. 16:25, "whosoever will lose his life for my sake shall find it." **71. unbewailing**: Cf. II.iv.16. **81. wildernesses**: the unexplored. Cf. I.742. **98–103**: By this music Time is reversed. **We**: Asia, "shadow of beauty unbeheld," is here speaking for regenerated Man. **caves**: places of thought. **smooth ocean**: Cf. Gray, "The Bard," "Youth on the prow and Pleasure at the helm." **glassy gulfs**: invisible intervals. **shadow-peopled**: Cf. Wordsworth, "Heaven lies about us in our infancy" (p. 99, above). **109. And . . . beheld**: Cf. Milton, "On Time," "Then long Eternity shall greet our bliss/With an individual kiss,/And joy shall overtake us as a flood . . . Attired with stars we shall for ever sit/Triumphing over Death, and Chance, and thee, O Time." **110. sea**: Cf. 74.

**Act III, Sc. i. 8. Hurling up insurrection**: Cf. *Paradise Lost*, I.669, "Hurling defiance toward the vault of Heaven" (Vol. I, p. 462). **11. pendulous air**: See *King Lear*, III.iv.66, "Now all the plagues that in the pendulous air . . ." **20–24. Who . . . spark**: His and Thetis' "fatal child . . . mightier than either" is to be the incarnation of Demogorgon.

To redescend, and trample out the spark.
Pour forth heaven's wine, Idaean Ganymede,
And let it fill the Daedal cups like fire,
And from the flower-inwoven soil divine
Ye all-triumphant harmonies arise,
As dew from earth under the twilight stars:
Drink! be the nectar circling through your veins
The soul of joy, ye ever-living Gods,
Till exultation burst in one wide voice
Like music from Elysian winds.
And thou
Ascend beside me, veilèd in the light
Of the desire which makes thee one with me,
Thetis, bright image of eternity!
When thou didst cry, 'Insufferable might!
God! Spare me! I sustain not the quick flames,
The penetrating presence; all my being,
Like him whom the Numidian seps did thaw
Into a dew with poison, is dissolved,
Sinking through its foundations:' even then
Two mighty spirits, mingling, made a third
Mightier than either, which, unbodied now,
Between us floats, felt, although unbeheld,
Waiting the incarnation, which ascends,
(Hear ye the thunder of the fiery wheels
Griding the winds?) from Demogorgon's throne.
Victory! victory! Feel'st thou not, O world,
The earthquake of his chariot thundering up
Olympus?

[*The Car of the* HOUR *arrives.* DEMOGORGON *descends, and moves towards the Throne of* JUPITER.]

Awful shape, what art thou? Speak!

DEMOGORGON. Eternity. Demand no direr name.
Descend, and follow me down the abyss.
I am thy child, as thou wert Saturn's child;
Mightier than thee: and we must dwell together
Henceforth in darkness. Lift thy lightnings not.
The tyranny of heaven none may retain,
Or reassume, or hold, succeeding thee:
Yet if thou wilt, as 'tis the destiny
Of trodden worms to writhe till they are dead,
Put forth thy might.

JUPITER. Detested prodigy!
Even thus beneath the deep Titanian prisons
I trample thee! thou lingerest?
Mercy! mercy!
No pity, no release, no respite! Oh,
That thou wouldst make mine enemy my judge,
Even where he hangs, seared by my long revenge,
On Caucasus! he would not doom me thus.
Gentle, and just, and dreadless, is he not
The monarch of the world? What then art thou?
No refuge! no appeal!
Sink with me then,
We two will sink on the wide waves of ruin,
Even as a vulture and a snake outspent
Drop, twisted in inextricable fight,
Into a shoreless sea. Let hell unlock
Its mounded oceans of tempestuous fire,
And whelm on them into the bottomless void
This desolated world, and thee, and me,
The conqueror and the conquered, and the wreck
Of that for which they combated.
Ai! Ai!
The elements obey me not. I sink
Dizzily down, ever, for ever, down.
And, like a cloud, mine enemy above
Darkens my fall with victory! Ai, Ai!

SCENE II.—*The Mouth of a great River in the Island Atlantis.* OCEAN *is discovered reclining near the Shore;* APOLLO *stands beside him.*

OCEAN. He fell, thou sayest, beneath his conqueror's frown?

APOLLO. Ay, when the strife was ended which made dim
The orb I rule, and shook the solid stars,
The terrors of his eye illumined heaven
With sanguine light, through the thick ragged skirts
Of the victorious darkness, as he fell:
Like the last glare of day's red agony,
Which, from a rent among the fiery clouds,
Burns far along the tempest-wrinkled deep.

OCEAN. He sunk to the abyss? To the dark void?

APOLLO. An eagle so caught in some bursting cloud
On Caucasus, his thunder-baffled wings
Entangled in the whirlwind, and his eyes
Which gazed on the undazzling sun, now blinded
By the white lightning, while the ponderous hail
Beats on his struggling form, which sinks at length

**26. Daedal**: skillful, inventive, variegated. In the manner of Daedalus, the Greek artificer. A word favored by Shelley; see "Ode to Liberty," "Hymn of Pan," "Mont Blanc," 86. **27. flower-inwoven**: Cf. Milton, "On the Morning of Christ's Nativity," 20, 187–88 (Vol. I, pp. 414, 416). **40. seps**: a skink or serpent lizard, from Greek *sepo*—rot; referring to the effect of its bite. Hence *sepsis:* putrefaction. Shelley is concerned with every mode of radical transformation, in this instance one suitably atrocious. **45. felt . . . unbeheld**: In his infatuate ignorance Jupiter uses the very distinction being used (in II.v.17) at this moment. This feeling can be as deceitful as other modes of knowledge. **48. Griding**: cutting through with a strident or grating sound; see *Paradise Lost*, VI.329–30, "The griding sword with discontinuous wound/Passed through him." And *Faerie Queene*, II.viii.36, "That through his thigh the mortall steele did gryde." **52. Eternity**: Cf. 36, "no direr name." See Intro., p. 244, above.

**72–74. Even . . . sea**: an ancient image used repeatedly by Shelley for an eternal opposition.

Prone, and the aëreal ice clings over it.

OCEAN. Henceforth the fields of heaven-reflecting sea
Which are my realm, will heave, unstained with blood,
Beneath the uplifting winds, like plains of corn
Swayed by the summer air; my streams will flow
Round many-peopled continents, and round
Fortunate isles; and from their glassy thrones
Blue Proteus and his humid nymphs shall mark
The shadow of fair ships, as mortals see
The floating bark of the light-laden moon
With that white star, its sightless pilot's crest,
Borne down the rapid sunset's ebbing sea;
Tracking their path no more by blood and groans,
And desolation, and the mingled voice
Of slavery and command; but by the light
Of wave-reflected flowers, and floating odours,
And music soft, and mild, free, gentle voices,
And sweetest music, such as spirits love.

APOLLO. And I shall gaze not on the deeds which make
My mind obscure with sorrow, as eclipse
Darkens the sphere I guide; but list, I hear
The small, clear, silver lute of the young Spirit
That sits i' the morning star.

OCEAN. Thou must away;
Thy steeds will pause at even, till when farewell:
The loud deep calls me home even now to feed it
With azure calm out of the emerald urns
Which stand for ever full beside my throne.
Behold the Nereids under the green sea,
Their wavering limbs borne on the wind-like stream,
Their white arms lifted o'er their streaming hair
With garlands pied and starry sea-flower crowns,
Hastening to grace their mighty sister's joy.
[*A sound of waves is heard.*]
It is the unpastured sea hungering for calm.
Peace, monster; I come now. Farewell.

APOLLO. Farewell.

SCENE III.—*Caucasus,* PROMETHEUS, HERCULES, IONE, *the* EARTH, SPIRITS, ASIA, *and* PANTHEA, *borne in the Car with the* SPIRIT OF THE HOUR. HERCULES *unbinds* PROMETHEUS, *who descends.*

HERCULES. Most glorious among Spirits, thus doth strength

**Sc. ii. 27. sightless:** invisible. **pilot:** The evening star seems to guide the moon to the horizon. **49. Burns . . . deep:** This line perhaps takes some of its surpassing poetry from its place in the action of the play, but goes far beyond explanation.

To wisdom, courage, and long-suffering love,
And thee, who art the form they animate,
Minister like a slave.

PROMETHEUS. Thy gentle words
Are sweeter even than freedom long desired
And long delayed.
Asia, thou light of life,
Shadow of beauty unbeheld: and ye,
Fair sister nymphs, who made long years of pain
Sweet to remember, through your love and care:
Henceforth we will not part. There is a cave,
All overgrown with trailing odorous plants,
Which curtain out the day with leaves and flowers,
And paved with veinèd emerald, and a fountain
Leaps in the midst with an awakening sound.
From its curved roof the mountain's frozen tears
Like snow, or silver, or long diamond spires,
Hang downward, raining forth a doubtful light:
And there is heard the ever-moving air,
Whispering without from tree to tree, and birds,
And bees; and all around are mossy seats,
And the rough walls are clothed with long soft grass;
A simple dwelling, which shall be our own;
Where we will sit and talk of time and change,
As the world ebbs and flows, ourselves unchanged.
What can hide man from mutability?
And if ye sigh, then I will smile; and thou,
Ione, shalt chant fragments of sea-music,
Until I weep, when ye shall smile away
The tears she brought, which yet were sweet to shed.
We will entangle buds and flowers and beams
Which twinkle on the fountain's brim, and make
Strange combinations out of common things,
Like human babes in their brief innocence;
And we will search, with looks and words of love,
For hidden thoughts, each lovelier than the last,
Our unexhausted spirits; and like lutes
Touched by the skill of the enamoured wind,
Weave harmonies divine, yet ever new,
From difference sweet where discord cannot be;
And hither come, sped on the charmèd winds,
Which meet from all the points of heaven, as bees
From every flower aëreal Enna feeds,
At their known island-homes in Himera,
The echoes of the human world, which tell
Of the low voice of love, almost unheard,
And dove-eyed pity's murmured pain, and music,
Itself the echo of the heart, and all
That tempers or improves man's life, now free;

**Sc. iii. 24. ebbs and flows:** Cf. *King Lear,* V.iii.17–19, "And we'll wear out,/In a walled prison, packs and sects of great ones/That ebb and flow by the moon." **42–43:** Enna is a plain and Himera a river in Sicily. **47. echo:** Cf. *Twelfth Night,* II.iv. 21–22, "It gives a very echo to the seat/Where Love is throned."

And lovely apparitions,— dim at first,
Then radiant, as the mind, arising bright
From the embrace of beauty (whence the forms
Of which these are the phantoms) casts on them
The gathered rays which are reality—
Shall visit us, the progeny immortal
Of Painting, Sculpture, and rapt Poesy,
And arts, though unimagined, yet to be.
The wandering voices and the shadows these
Of all that man becomes, the mediators
Of that best worship, love, by him and us
Given and returned; swift shapes and sounds, which grow
More fair and soft as man grows wise and kind,
And, veil by veil, evil and error fall:
Such virtue has the cave and place around.

[*Turning to the* SPIRIT OF THE HOUR]

For thee, fair Spirit, one toil remains. Ione,
Give her that curvèd shell, which Proteus old
Made Asia's nuptial boon, breathing within it
A voice to be accomplished, and which thou
Didst hide in grass under the hollow rock.

IONE. Thou most desired Hour, more loved and lovely
Than all thy sisters, this is the mystic shell;
See the pale azure fading into silver
Lining it with a soft yet glowing light:
Looks it not like lulled music sleeping there?

SPIRIT. It seems in truth the fairest shell of Ocean:
Its sound must be at once both sweet and strange.

PROMETHEUS. Go, borne over the cities of mankind
On whirlwind-footed coursers: once again
Outspeed the sun around the orbèd world;
And as thy chariot cleaves the kindling air,
Thou breathe into the many-folded shell,
Loosening its mighty music; it shall be
As thunder mingled with clear echoes: then
Return; and thou shalt dwell beside our cave.
And thou, O, Mother Earth!—

THE EARTH. I hear, I feel;
Thy lips are on me, and their touch runs down
Even to the adamantine central gloom
Along these marble nerves; 'tis life, 'tis joy,
And through my withered, old, and icy frame
The warmth of an immortal youth shoots down
Circling. Henceforth the many children fair
Folded in my sustaining arms; all plants,
And creeping forms, and insects rainbow-winged,
And birds, and beasts, and fish, and human shapes,
Which drew disease and pain from my wan bosom,
Draining the poison of despair, shall take
And interchange sweet nutriment; to me
Shall they become like sister-antelopes
By one fair dam, snow-white and swift as wind,
Nursed among lilies near a brimming stream.
The dew-mists of my sunless sleep shall float
Under the stars like balm: night-folded flowers
Shall suck unwithering hues in their repose:
And men and beasts in happy dreams shall gather
Strength for the coming day, and all its joy:
And death shall be the last embrace of her
Who takes the life she gave, even as a mother
Folding her child, says, 'Leave me not again.'

ASIA. Oh, mother! wherefore speak the name of death?
Cease they to love, and move, and breathe, and speak,
Who die?

THE EARTH. It would avail not to reply:
Thou art immortal, and this tongue is known
But to the uncommunicating dead.
Death is the veil which those who live call life:
They sleep, and it is lifted: and meanwhile
In mild variety the seasons mild
With rainbow-skirted showers, and odorous winds,
And long blue meteors cleansing the dull night,
And the life-kindling shafts of the keen sun's
All-piercing bow, and the dew-mingled rain
Of the calm moonbeams, a soft influence mild,
Shall clothe the forests and the fields, ay, even
The crag-built deserts of the barren deep,
With ever-living leaves, and fruits, and flowers.
And thou! There is a cavern where my spirit
Was panted forth in anguish whilst thy pain
Made my heart mad, and those who did inhale it
Became mad too, and built a temple there,
And spoke, and were oracular, and lured
The erring nations round to mutual war,
And faithless faith, such as Jove kept with thee;
Which breath now rises, as amongst tall weeds
A violet's exhalation, and it fills
With a serener light and crimson air
Intense, yet soft, the rocks and woods around;
It feeds the quick growth of the serpent vine,
And the dark linkèd ivy tangling wild,
And budding, blown, or odour-faded blooms
Which star the winds with points of coloured light,
As they rain through them, and bright golden globes
Of fruit, suspended in their own green heaven,
And through their veinèd leaves and amber stems
The flowers whose purple and translucid bowls
Stand ever mantling with aëreal dew,
The drink of spirits: and it circles round,
Like the soft waving wings of noonday dreams,
Inspiring calm and happy thoughts, like mine,

**50. as**: in the measure that. So too in 61. **58. becomes**: in both senses—that which is fitting to man and that to which he will change.

**113–14. Death . . . lifted**: See Intro., p. 241, above.

Now thou art thus restored. This cave is thine.
Arise! Appear!
[*A* SPIRIT *rises in the likeness of a winged child.*]
This is my torch-bearer;
Who let his lamp out in old time with gazing
On eyes from which he kindled it anew
With love, which is as fire, sweet daughter mine,
For such is that within thine own. Run, wayward,
And guide this company beyond the peak
Of Bacchic Nysa, Maenad-haunted mountain,
And beyond Indus and its tribute rivers,
Trampling the torrent streams and glassy lakes
With feet unwet, unwearied, undelaying,
And up the green ravine, across the vale,
Beside the windless and crystàlline pool,
Where ever lies, on unerasing waves,
The image of a temple, built above,
Distinct with column, arch, and architrave,
And palm-like capital, and over-wrought,
And populous with most living imagery,
Praxitelean shapes, whose marble smiles
Fill the hushed air with everlasting love.
It is deserted now, but once it bore
Thy name, Prometheus; there the emulous youths
Bore to thy honour through the divine gloom
The lamp which was thine emblem; even as those
Who bear the untransmitted torch of hope
Into the grave, across the night of life,
As thou hast borne it most triumphantly
To this far goal of Time. Depart, farewell.
Beside that temple is the destined cave.

SCENE IV. — *A Forest. In the Background a Cave.* PROMETHEUS, ASIA, PANTHEA, IONE, *and the* SPIRIT OF THE EARTH.

IONE. Sister, it is not earthly: how it glides
Under the leaves! how on its head there burns
A light, like a green star, whose emerald beams
Are twined with its fair hair! how, as it moves,
The splendour drops in flakes upon the grass!
Knowest thou it?
PANTHEA. It is the delicate spirit
That guides the earth through heaven. From afar
The populous constellations call that light
The loveliest of the planets; and sometimes
It floats along the spray of the salt sea,
Or makes its chariot of a foggy cloud,
Or walks through fields or cities while men sleep,
Or o'er the mountain tops, or down the rivers,
Or through the green waste wilderness, as now,
Wondering at all it sees. Before Jove reigned
It loved our sister Asia, and it came
Each leisure hour to drink the liquid light
Out of her eyes, for which it said it thirsted
As one bit by a dipsas, and with her
It made its childish confidence, and told her
All it had known or seen, for it saw much,
Yet idly reasoned what it saw; and called her —
For whence it sprung it knew not, nor do I —
Mother, dear mother.
THE SPIRIT OF THE EARTH [*running to* ASIA].
Mother, dearest mother;
May I then talk with thee as I was wont?
May I then hide my eyes in thy soft arms,
After thy looks have made them tired of joy?
May I then play beside thee the long noons,
When work is none in the bright silent air?
ASIA. I love thee, gentlest being, and henceforth
Can cherish thee unenvied: speak, I pray:
Thy simple talk once solaced, now delights.
SPIRIT OF THE EARTH. Mother, I am grown wiser, though a child
Cannot be wise like thee, within this day;
And happier too; happier and wiser both.
Thou knowest that toads, and snakes, and loathly worms,
And venomous and malicious beasts, and boughs
That bore ill berries in the woods, were ever
An hindrance to my walks o'er the green world:
And that, among the haunts of humankind,
Hard-featured men, or with proud, angry looks,
Or cold, staid gait, or false and hollow smiles,
Or the dull sneer of self-loved ignorance,
Or other such foul masks, with which ill thoughts
Hide that fair being whom we spirits call man;
And women too, ugliest of all things evil
(Though fair, even in a world where thou art fair,
When good and kind, free and sincere like thee),
When false or frowning, made me sick at heart
To pass them, though they slept, and I unseen,
Well, my path lately lay through a great city
Into the woody hills surrounding it:
A sentinel was sleeping at the gate:
When there was heard a sound, so loud, it shook
The towers amid the moonlight, yet more sweet
Than any voice but thine, sweetest of all;
A long, long sound, as it would never end:
And all the inhabitants leaped suddenly
Out of their rest, and gathered in the streets,
Looking in wonder up to Heaven, while yet
The music pealed along. I hid myself
Within a fountain in the public square,

**150. kindled it:** Cf. III.iv.116–19. **154. Nysa:** the mountain on which Dionysus was nursed by nymphs. **158. across the vale:** Many Indian readers of Shelley are convinced that this is the vale of Kashmir and the "destined cave" the cavern of Amarnath, sacred to Siva. **171. untransmitted:** This hope no one can receive from another. **172. night of life:** Cf. III.iii.113–14.

**Sc. iv. 19. dipsas:** a serpent whose bite caused intense thirst.

Where I lay like the reflex of the moon
Seen in a wave under green leaves; and soon
Those ugly human shapes and visages
Of which I spoke as having wrought me pain,
Passed floating through the air, and fading still
Into the winds that scattered them; and those
From whom they passed seemed mild and lovely forms
After some foul disguise had fallen, and all
Were somewhat changed, and after brief surprise
And greetings of delighted wonder, all
Went to their sleep again: and when the dawn
Came, wouldst thou think that toads, and snakes, and efts,
Could e'er be beautiful? yet so they were,
And that with little change of shape or hue:
All things had put their evil nature off:
I cannot tell my joy, when o'er a lake
Upon a drooping bough with nightshade twined,
I saw two azure halcyons clinging downward
And thinning one bright bunch of amber berries,
With quick long beaks, and in the deep there lay
Those lovely forms imaged as in a sky;
So, with my thoughts full of these happy changes,
We meet again, the happiest change of all.

ASIA. And never will we part, till thy chaste sister
Who guides the frozen and inconstant moon
Will look on thy more warm and equal light
Till her heart thaw like flakes of April snow
And love thee.

SPIRIT OF THE EARTH. What; as Asia loves Prometheus?

ASIA. Peace, wanton, thou art yet not old enough.
Think ye by gazing on each other's eyes
To multiply your lovely selves, and fill
With spherèd fires the interlunar air?

SPIRIT OF THE EARTH. Nay, mother, while my sister trims her lamp
'Tis hard I should go darkling.

ASIA. Listen; look!

[*The* SPIRIT OF THE HOUR *enters.*]

PROMETHEUS. We feel what thou hast heard and seen: yet speak.

SPIRIT OF THE HOUR. Soon as the sound had ceased whose thunder filled
The abysses of the sky and the wide earth,
There was a change: the impalpable thin air
And the all-circling sunlight were transformed,
As if the sense of love dissolved in them
Had folded itself round the spherèd world.
My vision then grew clear, and I could see
Into the mysteries of the universe:
Dizzy as with delight I floated down,
Winnowing the lightsome air with languid plumes,
My coursers sought their birthplace in the sun,
Where they henceforth will live exempt from toil,
Pasturing flowers of vegetable fire;
And where my moonlike car will stand within
A temple, gazed upon by Phidian forms
Of thee, and Asia, and the Earth, and me,
And you fair nymphs looking the love we feel,—
In memory of the tidings it has borne,—
Beneath a dome fretted with graven flowers,
Poised on twelve columns of resplendent stone,
And open to the bright and liquid sky.
Yoked to it by an amphisbaenic snake
The likeness of those wingèd steeds will mock
The flight from which they find repose. Alas,
Whither has wandered now my partial tongue
When all remains untold which ye would hear?
As I have said, I floated to the earth:
It was, as it is still, the pain of bliss
To move, to breathe, to be; I wandering went
Among the haunts and dwellings of mankind,
And first was disappointed not to see
Such mighty change as I had felt within
Expressed in outward things; but soon I looked,
And behold, thrones were kingless, and men walked
One with the other even as spirits do,
None fawned, none trampled; hate, disdain, or fear,
Self-love or self-contempt, on human brows
No more inscribed, as o'er the gate of hell,
'All hope abandon ye who enter here;'
None frowned, none trembled, none with eager fear
Gazed on another's eye of cold command,
Until the subject of a tyrant's will
Became, worse fate, the abject of his own,
Which spurred him, like an outspent horse, to death.
None wrought his lips in truth-entangling lines
Which smiled the lie his tongue disdained to speak;
None, with firm sneer, trod out in his own heart
The sparks of love and hope till there remained
Those bitter ashes, a soul self-consumed,
And the wretch crept a vampire among men,
Infecting all with his own hideous ill;
None talked that common, false, cold, hollow talk
Which makes the heart deny the *yes* it breathes,
Yet question that unmeant hypocrisy
With such a self-mistrust as has no name.

**80–81. halcyons . . . berries:** Kingfishers feed on the fruit of the deadly nightshade which has ceased to be poisonous. **94. interlunar air:** Cf. II.iv.91.

**110. vegetable fire:** Cf. *Paradise Lost*, IV.218–20 (Vol. I, pp. 477–78). **112. Phidian forms:** figures wrought by the Greek sculptor Phidias. **119. amphisbaenic snake:** a fabulous serpent with a head at each end, able to move both ways. **136.** See Dante, *Inferno*, III.9. **140. abject:** a person of the meanest condition, a menial. Cf. I.450–51. **150. the *yes* . . . breathes:** Cf. Blake, "If the Sun and Moon should doubt,/They'd immediately go out."

And women, too, frank, beautiful, and kind
As the free heaven which rains fresh light and dew
On the wide earth, past; gentle radiant forms,
From custom's evil taint exempt and pure;
Speaking the wisdom once they could not think,
Looking emotions once they feared to feel,
And changed to all which once they dared not be,
Yet being now, made earth like heaven; nor pride,
Nor jealousy, nor envy, nor ill shame,
The bitterest of those drops of treasured gall,
Spoilt the sweet taste of the nepenthe, love.

Thrones, altars, judgement-seats, and prisons; wherein,
And beside which, by wretched men were borne
Sceptres, tiaras, swords, and chains, and tomes
Of reasoned wrong, glozed on by ignorance,
Were like those monstrous and barbaric shapes,
The ghost of a no-more-remembered fame,
Which, from their unworn obelisks, look forth
In triumph o'er the palaces and tombs
Of those who were their conquerors: mouldering round,
These imaged to the pride of kings and priests
A dark yet mighty faith, a power as wide
As is the world it wasted, and are now
But an astonishment; even so the tools
And emblems of its last captivity,
Amid the dwellings of the peopled earth,
Stand, not o'erthrown, but unregarded now.
And those foul shapes, abhorred by god and man, —
Which, under many a name and many a form
Strange, savage, ghastly, dark and execrable,
Were Jupiter, the tyrant of the world;
And which the nations, panic-stricken, served
With blood, and hearts broken by long hope, and love
Dragged to his altars soiled and garlandless,
And slain amid men's unreclaiming tears,
Flattering the thing they feared, which fear was hate, —
Frown, mouldering fast, o'er their abandoned shrines:
The painted veil, by those who were, called life,
Which mimicked, as with colours idly spread,
All men believed or hoped, is torn aside;
The loathsome mask has fallen, the man remains
Sceptreless, free, uncircumscribed, but man
Equal, unclassed, tribeless, and nationless,
Exempt from awe, worship, degree, the king
Over himself; just, gentle, wise: but man
Passionless? —— no, yet free from guilt or pain,

167. **glozed**: commented, also fawned. 168–76: Cf. "Ozymandias," p. 254, above. 180–88. **foul . . . hate**: e.g., Moloch and other deities placated by human sacrifice. 190: Cf. III.iii.113; and "Sonnet," "Lift not the painted veil . . ."



Which were, for his will made or suffered them,
Nor yet exempt, though ruling them like slaves,
From chance, and death, and mutability,
The clogs of that which else might oversoar
The loftiest star of unascended heaven,
Pinnacled dim in the intense inane.

[*End of the Third Act*]

# Act IV

SCENE. — *A Part of the Forest near the Cave of* PROMETHEUS. PANTHEA *and* IONE *are sleeping: they awaken gradually during the first Song.*

VOICE OF UNSEEN SPIRITS.

The pale stars are gone!
For the sun, their swift shepherd,
To their folds them compelling,
In the depths of the dawn,
Hastes, in meteor-eclipsing array, and they flee
Beyond his blue dwelling,
As fawns flee the leopard.
But where are ye?

[*A Train of dark Forms and Shadows passes by confusedly, singing.*]

Here, oh, here:
We bear the bier
Of the Father of many a cancelled year.
Spectres we
Of the dead Hours be,
We bear Time to his tomb in eternity.

Strew, oh, strew
Hair, not yew!
Wet the dusty pall with tears, not dew!
Be the faded flowers
Of Death's bare bowers
Spread on the corpse of the King of Hours!

Haste, oh, haste!
As shades are chased,
Trembling, by day, from heaven's blue waste.
We melt away,
Like dissolving spray,
From the children of a diviner day,
With the lullaby
Of winds that die
On the bosom of their own harmony!

IONE.

What dark forms were they?

PANTHEA.

The past Hours weak and gray,
With the spoil which their toil
Raked together
From the conquest but One could foil.

IONE.

Have they passed?

PANTHEA.

They have passed;
They outspeeded the blast,
While 'tis said, they are fled:

IONE.

Whither, oh, whither?

PANTHEA.

To the dark, to the past, to the dead.

VOICE OF UNSEEN SPIRITS.

Bright clouds float in heaven,
Dew-stars gleam on earth,
Waves assemble on ocean,
They are gathered and driven
By the storm of delight, by the panic of glee!
They shake with emotion,
They dance in their mirth.
But where are ye?

The pine boughs are singing
Old songs with new gladness,
The billows and fountains
Fresh music are flinging,
Like the notes of a spirit from land and from sea;
The storms mock the mountains
With the thunder of gladness.
But where are ye?

IONE. What charioteers are these?
PANTHEA. Where are their chariots?

SEMICHORUS OF HOURS.

The voice of the Spirits of Air and of Earth
Have drawn back the figured curtain of sleep
Which covered our being and darkened our birth
In the deep.

A VOICE.

In the deep?

SEMICHORUS II.

Oh, below the deep.

SEMICHORUS I.

An hundred ages we had been kept
Cradled in visions of hate and care,
And each one who waked as his brother slept,
Found the truth—

SEMICHORUS II.

Worse than his visions were!

SEMICHORUS I.

We have heard the lute of Hope in sleep;
We have known the voice of Love in dreams;
We have felt the wand of Power, and leap—

SEMICHORUS II.

As the billows leap in the morning beams!

CHORUS.

Weave the dance on the floor of the breeze,
Pierce with song heaven's silent light,
Enchant the day that too swiftly flees,
To check its flight ere the cave of Night.

Once the hungry Hours were hounds
Which chased the day like a bleeding deer,
And it limped and stumbled with many wounds
Through the nightly dells of the desert year.

But now, oh weave the mystic measure
Of music, and dance, and shapes of light,
Let the Hours, and the spirits of might and pleasure,
Like the clouds and sunbeams, unite.

A VOICE.

Unite!

PANTHEA. See, where the Spirits of the human mind
Wrapped in sweet sounds, as in bright veils, approach.

CHORUS OF SPIRITS.

We join the throng
Of the dance and the song,
By the whirlwind of gladness borne along;
As the flying-fish leap
From the Indian deep,
And mix with the sea-birds, half asleep.

CHORUS OF HOURS.

Whence come ye, so wild and so fleet,
For sandals of lightning are on your feet,
And your wings are soft and swift as thought,
And your eyes are as love which is veilèd not?

CHORUS OF SPIRITS.

We come from the mind
Of human kind
Which was late so dusk, and obscene, and blind,
Now 'tis an ocean
Of clear emotion,
A heaven of serene and mighty motion.

From that deep abyss
Of wonder and bliss,
Whose caverns are crystal palaces;
From those skiey towers
Where Thought's crowned powers
Sit watching your dance, ye happy Hours!

From the dim recesses
Of woven caresses,
Where lovers catch ye by your loose tresses
From the azure isles,
Where sweet Wisdom smiles,
Delaying your ships with her siren wiles.

From the temples high
Of Man's ear and eye,
Roofed over Sculpture and Poesy;
From the murmurings
Of the unsealed springs
Where Science bedews her Daedal wings.

Years after years,
Through blood, and tears,
And a thick hell of hatreds, and hopes, and fears;
We waded and flew,
And the islets were few
Where the bud-blighted flowers of happiness grew.

Our feet now, every palm,
Are sandalled with calm,
And the dew of our wings is a rain of balm;
And, beyond our eyes,
The human love lies
Which makes all it gazes on Paradise.

CHORUS OF SPIRITS AND HOURS.

Then weave the web of the mystic measure;
From the depths of the sky and the ends of the earth,
Come, swift Spirits of might and of pleasure,
Fill the dance and the music of mirth,
As the waves of a thousand streams rush by
To an ocean of splendour and harmony!

CHORUS OF SPIRITS.

Our spoil is won,
Our task is done,
We are free to dive, or soar, or run;
Beyond and around,
Or within the bound
Which clips the world with darkness round.

We'll pass the eyes
Of the starry skies
Into the hoar deep to colonize:
Death, Chaos, and Night,
From the sound of our flight,
Shall flee, like mist from a tempest's might

And Earth, air, and Light,
And the Spirit of Might,
Which drives round the stars in their fiery flight;
And Love, Thought, and Breath,
The powers that quell Death,
Wherever we soar shall assemble beneath.

And our singing shall build
In the void's loose field
A world for the Spirit of Wisdom to wield;
We will take our plan
From the new world of man,
And our work shall be called the Promethean.

CHORUS OF HOURS.

Break the dance, and scatter the song;
Let some depart, and some remain.

SEMICHORUS I.

We, beyond heaven, are driven along:

SEMICHORUS II.

Us the enchantments of earth retain:

SEMICHORUS I.

Ceaseless, and rapid, and fierce, and free,
With the Spirits which build a new earth and sea,
And a heaven where yet heaven could never be.

SEMICHORUS II.

Solemn, and slow, and serene, and bright,
Leading the Day and outspeeding the Night,
With the powers of a world of perfect light.

SEMICHORUS I.

We whirl, singing loud, round the gathering sphere,
Till the trees, and the beasts, and the clouds appear
From its chaos made calm by love, not fear.

**Act IV. 96–103. ocean . . . powers:** Cf. "Ode to the West Wind," III.

**141–43: We'll . . . colonize:** a prophecy of space travel—"mur-

SEMICHORUS II.

We encircle the ocean and mountains of earth,
And the happy forms of its death and birth
Change to the music of our sweet mirth.

CHORUS OF HOURS AND SPIRITS.

Break the dance, and scatter the song,
  Let some depart, and some remain,
Wherever we fly we lead along
In leashes, like starbeams, soft yet strong,
  The clouds that are heavy with love's sweet rain.

PANTHEA. Ha! they are gone!
IONE. Yet feel you no delight
From the past sweetness?
PANTHEA. As the bare green hill
When some soft cloud vanishes into rain,
Laughs with a thousand drops of sunny water
To the unpavilioned sky!
IONE. Even whilst we speak
New notes arise. What is that awful sound?
PANTHEA. 'Tis the deep music of the rolling world
Kindling within the strings of the waved air
Aeolian modulations.
IONE. Listen too,
How every pause is filled with under-notes,
Clear, silver, icy, keen, awakening tones,
Which pierce the sense, and live within the soul,
As the sharp stars pierce winter's crystal air
And gaze upon themselves within the sea.
PANTHEA. But see where through two openings in the forest
Which hanging branches overcanopy,
And where two runnels of a rivulet,
Between the close moss violet-inwoven,
Have made their path of melody, like sisters
Who part with sighs that they may meet in smiles,
Turning their dear disunion to an isle
Of lovely grief, a wood of sweet sad thoughts;
Two visions of strange radiance float upon
The ocean-like enchantment of strong sound,
Which flows intenser, keener, deeper yet
Under the ground and through the windless air.
IONE. I see a chariot like that thinnest boat,
In which the Mother of the Months is borne
By ebbing light into her western cave,
When she upsprings from interlunar dreams;
O'er which is curved an orblike canopy
Of gentle darkness, and the hills and woods,
Distinctly seen through that dusk aery veil,
Regard like shapes in an enchanter's glass;
Its wheels are solid clouds, azure and gold,
Such as the genii of the thunderstorm
Pile on the floor of the illumined sea
When the sun rushes under it; they roll
And move and grow as with an inward wind;
Within it sits a wingèd infant, white
Its countenance, like the whiteness of bright snow,
Its plumes are as feathers of sunny frost,
Its limbs gleam white, through the wind-flowing folds
Of its white robe, woof of ethereal pearl.
Its hair is white, the brightness of white light
Scattered in strings; yet its two eyes are heavens
Of liquid darkness, which the Deity
Within seems pouring, as a storm is poured
From jaggèd clouds, out of their arrowy lashes,
Tempering the cold and radiant air around,
With fire that is not brightness; in its hand
It sways a quivering moonbeam, from whose point
A guiding power directs the chariot's prow
Over its wheelèd clouds, which as they roll
Over the grass, and flowers, and waves, wake sounds,
Sweet as a singing rain of silver dew.
PANTHEA. And from the other opening in the wood
Rushes, with loud and whirlwind harmony,
A sphere, which is as many thousand spheres,
Solid as crystal, yet through all its mass
Flow, as through empty space, music and light:
Ten thousand orbs involving and involved,
Purple and azure, white, and green, and golden,
Sphere within sphere; and every space between
Peopled with unimaginable shapes,
Such as ghosts dream dwell in the lampless deep,
Yet each inter-transpicuous, and they whirl
Over each other with a thousand motions,
Upon a thousand sightless axles spinning,
And with the force of self-destroying swiftness,
Intensely, slowly, solemnly roll on,
Kindling with mingled sounds, and many tones,
Intelligible words and music wild.
With mighty whirl the multitudinous orb
Grinds the bright brook into an azure mist
Of elemental subtlety, like light;
And the wild odour of the forest flowers,
The music of the living grass and air,
The emerald light of leaf-entangled beams
Round its intense yet self-conflicting speed,

murings/Of the unsealed springs/Where Science bedews her Daedal wings," 114–16. **184. unpavilioned:** no longer roofed over. **185. awful:** full of awe. **190–93. awakening . . . sea:** Ione's description shadows forth the poet's aim—to bring powers within the soul to gaze upon themselves. Cf. Coleridge, *Biographia Literaria*, XII, "The postulate of philosophy . . . the heaven-descended KNOW THYSELF." **200. dear disunion:** parallel to the past disunion of Moon and Earth. **207. Mother . . . Months:** the moon. **209. When . . . dreams:** Cf. II.iv.90–91. **210. orblike canopy:** Cf. Coleridge, "Dejection: An Ode," 13, p. 130, above, "the old Moon in her lap." **213. Regard like:** I see as. **214. wheels:** Cf. Ezek. 10. **238. many thousand:** the Earth's inconceivable complexity. **249. self-destroying:** stability as the outcome of innumerable interdependent activities.

Seem kneaded into one aëreal mass
Which drowns the sense. Within the orb itself,
Pillowed upon its alabaster arms,
Like to a child o'erwearied with sweet toil,
On its own folded wings, and wavy hair,
The Spirit of the Earth is laid asleep,
And you can see its little lips are moving,
Amid the changing light of their own smiles,
Like one who talks of what he loves in dream.

IONE. 'Tis only mocking the orb's harmony.

PANTHEA. And from a star upon its forehead, shoot,
Like swords of azure fire, or golden spears
With tyrant-quelling myrtle overtwined,
Embleming heaven and earth united now,
Vast beams like spokes of some invisible wheel
Which whirl as the orb whirls, swifter than thought,
Filling the abyss with sun-like lightenings,
And perpendicular now, and now transverse,
Pierce the dark soil, and as they pierce and pass,
Make bare the secrets of the earth's deep heart;
Infinite mines of adamant and gold,
Valueless stones, and unimagined gems,
And caverns on crystalline columns poised
With vegetable silver overspread;
Wells of unfathomed fire, and water springs
Whence the great sea, even as a child is fed,
Whose vapours clothe earth's monarch mountain-tops
With kingly, ermine snow. The beams flash on
And make appear the melancholy ruins
Of cancelled cycles; anchors, beaks of ships;
Planks turned to marble; quivers, helms, and spears,
And gorgon-headed targes, and the wheels
Of scythèd chariots, and the emblazonry
Of trophies, standards, and armorial beasts,
Round which death laughed, sepulchred emblems
Of dead destruction, ruin within ruin!
The wrecks beside of many a city vast,
Whose population which the earth grew over
Was mortal, but not human; see, they lie,
Their monstrous works, and uncouth skeletons,
Their statues, homes and fanes; prodigious shapes
Huddled in gray annihilation, split,
Jammed in the hard, black deep; and over these,
The anatomies of unknown wingèd things,
And fishes which were isles of living scale,
And serpents, bony chains, twisted around
The iron crags, or within heaps of dust
To which the tortuous strength of their last pangs
Had crushed the iron crags; and over these
The jaggèd alligator, and the might
Of earth-convulsing behemoth, which once
Were monarch beasts, and on the slimy shores,
And weed-overgrown continents of earth,
Increased and multiplied like summer worms
On an abandoned corpse, till the blue globe
Wrapped deluge round it like a cloak, and they
Yelled, gasped, and were abolished; or some God
Whose throne was in a comet, passed, and cried,
'Be not!' And like my words they were no more.

THE EARTH.

The joy, the triumph, the delight, the madness!
The boundless, overflowing, bursting gladness,
The vaporous exultation not to be confined!
Ha! ha! the animation of delight
Which wraps me, like an atmosphere of light,
And bears me as a cloud is borne by its own wind.

THE MOON.

Brother mine, calm wanderer,
Happy globe of land and air,
Some Spirit is darted like a beam from thee,
Which penetrates my frozen frame,
And passes with the warmth of flame,
With love, and odour, and deep melody
Through me, through me!

THE EARTH.

Ha! ha! the caverns of my hollow mountains,
My cloven fire-crags, sound-exulting fountains
Laugh with a vast and inextinguishable laughter.
The oceans, and the deserts, and the abysses,
And the deep air's unmeasured wildernesses,
Answer from all their clouds and billows, echoing after.

They cry aloud as I do. Sceptred curse,
Who all our green and azure universe
Threatenedst to muffle round with black destruction, sending
A solid cloud to rain hot thunderstones,
And splinter and kneed down my children's bones,
All I bring forth, to one void mass battering and blending,—

Until each crag-like tower, and storied column,
Palace, and obelisk, and temple solemn,
My imperial mountains crowned with cloud, and snow, and fire;
My sea-like forests, every blade and blossom
Which finds a grave or cradle in my bosom,

**272. tyrant-quelling myrtle:** Cf. Milton, "Lycidas," 2 (Vol. I, p. 421). **283. vegetable silver:** See III.iv.110, and note. **291. targes:** shields with petrifying faces on them. **292. scythèd chariots:** The ancient Britons used chariots having wheels mounted with sharp, sickle-shaped blades.

**310. behemoth:** See Job 40:15–24. **325. wanderer:** The planets (from Greek *planetes*—wanderer) change their places relative to the fixed stars. **338. Sceptred curse:** Jupiter.

Were stamped by thy strong hate into a lifeless
mire:

How art thou sunk, withdrawn, covered, drunk
up
By thirsty nothing, as the brackish cup
Drained by a desert-troop, a little drop for all;
And from beneath, around, within, above,
Filling thy void annihilation, love
Burst in like light on caves cloven by the thunder-
ball.

THE MOON.

The snow upon my lifeless mountains
Is loosened into living fountains,
My solid oceans flow, and sing, and shine:
A spirit from my heart bursts forth,
It clothes with unexpected birth
My cold bare bosom: Oh! it must be thine
On mine, on mine!

Gazing on thee I feel, I know
Green stalks burst forth, and bright flowers
grow,
And living shapes upon my bosom move:
Music is in the sea and air,
Wingèd clouds soar here and there,
Dark with the rain new buds are dreaming of:
'Tis love, all love!

THE EARTH.

It interpenetrates my granite mass,
Through tangled roots and trodden clay doth pass
Into the utmost leaves and delicatest flowers;
Upon the winds, among the clouds 'tis spread,
It wakes a life in the forgotten dead,
They breathe a spirit up from their obscurest
bowers.

And like a storm bursting its cloudy prison
With thunder, and with whirlwind, has arisen
Out of the lampless caves of unimagined being:
With earthquake shock and swiftness making
shiver
Thought's stagnant chaos, unremoved for ever,
Till hate, and fear, and pain, light-vanquished
shadows, fleeing,

Leave Man, who was a many-sided mirror,
Which could distort to many a shape of error,
This true fair world of things, a sea reflecting love;
Which over all his kind, as the sun's heaven
Gliding o'er ocean, smooth, serene, and even,
Darting from starry depths radiance and life, doth
move:

Leave Man, even as a leprous child is left,
Who follows a sick beast to some warm cleft
Of rocks, through which the might of healing
springs is poured;
Then when it wanders home with rosy smile,
Unconscious, and its mother fears awhile
It is a spirit, then, weeps on her child restored.

Man, oh, not men! a chain of linkèd thought,
Of love and might to be divided not,
Compelling the elements with adamantine stress;
As the sun rules, even with a tyrant's gaze,
The unquiet republic of the maze
Of planets, struggling fierce towards heaven's free
wilderness.

Man, one harmonious soul of many a soul,
Whose nature is its own divine control,
Where all things flow to all, as rivers to the sea;
Familiar acts are beautiful through love;
Labour, and pain, and grief, in life's green grove
Sport like tame beasts, none knew how gentle they
could be!

His will, with all mean passions, bad delights,
And selfish cares, its trembling satellites,
A spirit ill to guide, but mighty to obey,
Is as a tempest-wingèd ship, whose helm
Love rules, through waves which dare not over-
whelm,
Forcing life's wildest shores to own its sovereign
sway.

All things confess his strength. Through the cold
mass
Of marble and of colour his dreams pass;
Bright threads whence mothers weave the robes
their children wear;
Language is a perpetual Orphic song,
Which rules with Daedal harmony a throng
Of thoughts and forms, which else senseless and
shapeless were.

The lightning is his slave; heaven's utmost deep
Gives up her stars, and like a flock of sheep
They pass before his eye, are numbered, and roll on!
The tempest is his steed, he strides the air;
And the abyss shouts from her depth laid bare,
Heaven, hast thou secrets? Man unveils me; I have
none.

THE MOON.

The shadow of white death has passed
From my path in heaven at last,

**380. unremoved for ever:** never to be moved until hate, fear, and pain permit Man to be healed, as in 390. Cf. 404–05. **415. Orphic:** As Orpheus with his music made trees and rocks follow him, so Language gives life, motion, and order. **421. strides**

A clinging shroud of solid frost and sleep;
And through my newly-woven bowers,
Wander happy paramours,
Less mighty, but as mild as those who keep
Thy vales more deep.

THE EARTH.

As the dissolving warmth of dawn may fold
A half unfrozen dew-globe, green, and gold,
And crystalline, till it becomes a wingèd mist,
And wanders up the vault of the blue day,
Outlives the noon, and on the sun's last ray
Hangs o'er the sea, a fleece of fire and amethyst.

THE MOON.

Thou art folded, thou art lying
In the light which is undying
Of thine own joy, and heaven's smile divine;
All suns and constellations shower
On thee a light, a life, a power
Which doth array thy sphere; thou pourest thine
On mine, on mine!

THE EARTH.

I spin beneath my pyramid of night,
Which points into the heavens dreaming delight,
Murmuring victorious joy in my enchanted sleep;
As a youth lulled in love-dreams faintly sighing,
Under the shadow of his beauty lying,
Which round his rest a watch of light and warmth doth keep.

THE MOON.

As in the soft and sweet eclipse,
When soul meets soul on lovers' lips,
High hearts are calm, and brightest eyes are dull;
So when thy shadow falls on me,
Then am I mute and still, by thee
Covered; of thy love, Orb most beautiful,
Full, oh, too full!

Thou art speeding round the sun
Brightest world of many a one;
Green and azure sphere which shinest
With a light which is divinest
Among all the lamps of Heaven
To whom life and light is given;
I, thy crystal paramour
Borne beside thee by a power
Like the polar Paradise,
Magnet-like of lovers' eyes;
I, a most enamoured maiden
Whose weak brain is overladen
With the pleasure of her love,
Maniac-like around thee move
Gazing, an insatiate bride,
On thy form from every side
Like a Maenad, round the cup
Which Agave lifted up
In the weird Cadmaean forest.
Brother, wheresoe'er thou soarest
I must hurry, whirl and follow
Through the heavens wide and hollow,
Sheltered by the warm embrace
Of thy soul from hungry space,
Drinking from thy sense and sight
Beauty, majesty, and might,
As a lover or a chameleon
Grows like what it looks upon,
As a violet's gentle eye
Gazes on the azure sky
Until its hue grows like what it beholds,
As a gray and watery mist
Glows like solid amethyst
Athwart the western mountain it enfolds,
When the sunset sleeps
Upon its snow—

THE EARTH.

And the weak day weeps
That it should be so.
Oh, gentle Moon, the voice of thy delight
Falls on me like thy clear and tender light
Soothing the seaman, borne the summer night,
Through isles for ever calm;
Oh, gentle Moon, thy crystal accents pierce
The caverns of my pride's deep universe,
Charming the tiger joy, whose tramplings fierce
Made wounds which need thy balm.

PANTHEA. I rise as from a bath of sparkling water,
A bath of azure light, among dark rocks,
Out of the stream of sound.
IONE. Ah me! sweet sister,
The stream of sound has ebbed away from us,
And you pretend to rise out of its wave,
Because your words fall like the clear, soft dew
Shaken from a bathing wood-nymph's limbs and hair.
PANTHEA. Peace! peace! A mighty Power, which is as darkness,
Is rising out of Earth, and from the sky
Is showered like night, and from within the air
Bursts, like eclipse which had been gathered up
Into the pores of sunlight: the bright visions,

**the air:** May the poet's other prophecies come true as fully. **444. pyramid of night:** Cf. A. E. Housman, *Last Poems*, XXXVI, "[Earth's] towering foolscap of eternal shade." **465. polar Paradise:** The moon keeps her face forever turned to the earth.

**474. Agave:** daughter of Cadmus, king of Thebes. In a frenzy, she tore her son Pentheus to pieces for trying to prohibit the women's Dionysiac festivals. **493–94. weeps . . . so:** that it is at an end. The dewfall.

Wherein the singing spirits rode and shone,
Gleam like pale meteors through a watery night.

IONE. There is a sense of words upon mine ear.

PANTHEA. An universal sound like words: Oh, list!

DEMOGORGON.

Thou, Earth, calm empire of a happy soul,
Sphere of divinest shapes and harmonies,
Beautiful orb! gathering as thou dost roll
The love which paves thy path along the skies:

THE EARTH.

I hear: I am as a drop of dew that dies.

DEMOGORGON.

Thou, Moon, which gazest on the nightly Earth
With wonder, as it gazes upon thee;
Whilst each to men, and beasts, and the swift birth
Of birds, is beauty, love, calm, harmony:

THE MOON.

I hear: I am a leaf shaken by thee!

DEMOGORGON.

Ye Kings of suns and stars, Daemons and Gods,
Aetherial Dominations, who possess
Elysian, windless, fortunate abodes
Beyond Heaven's constellated wilderness:

A VOICE FROM ABOVE.

Our great Republic hears, we are blest, and bless.

DEMOGORGON.

Ye happy Dead, whom beams of brightest verse
Are clouds to hide, not colours to portray,
Whether your nature is that universe
Which once ye saw and suffered —

A VOICE FROM BENEATH.

Or as they
Whom we have left, we change and pass away.

DEMOGORGON.

Ye elemental Genii, who have homes
From man's high mind even to the central stone
Of sullen lead; from heaven's star-fretted domes
To the dull weed some sea-worm battens on:

A CONFUSED VOICE.

We hear: thy words waken Oblivion.

DEMOGORGON.

Spirits, whose homes are flesh: ye beasts and birds,
Ye worms, and fish; ye living leaves and buds;
Lightning and wind; and ye untameable herds,
Meteors and mists, which throng air's solitudes: —

A VOICE.

Thy voice to us is wind among still woods.

DEMOGORGON.

Man, who wert once a despot and a slave;
A dupe and a deceiver; a decay;
A traveller from the cradle to the grave
Through the dim night of this immortal day:

ALL.

Speak: thy strong words may never pass away.

DEMOGORGON.

This is the day, which down the void abysm
At the Earth-born's spell yawns for Heaven's despotism,
And Conquest is dragged captive through the deep:
Love, from its awful throne of patient power
In the wise heart, from the last giddy hour
Of dread endurance, from the slippery, steep,
And narrow verge of crag-like agony, springs
And folds over the world its healing wings.

Gentleness, Virtue, Wisdom, and Endurance,
These are the seals of that most firm assurance
Which bars the pit over Destruction's strength;
And if, with infirm hand, Eternity,
Mother of many acts and hours, should free
The serpent that would clasp her with his length;
These are the spells by which to reassume
An empire o'er the disentangled doom.

To suffer woes which Hope thinks infinite;
To forgive wrongs darker than death or night;
To defy Power, which seems omnipotent;
To love, and bear; to hope till Hope creates
From its own wreck the thing it contemplates;
Neither to change, nor falter, nor repent;
This, like thy glory, Titan, is to be
Good, great and joyous, beautiful and free;
This is alone Life, Joy, Empire, and Victory.

*1818–19*

**523. dew dies**: so universal is the sound. Cf. 518, 431–36; and the last line of Edwin Arnold's "The Light of Asia," "The Dew-drop slips into the shining Sea." **530. Aetherial Dominations**: Cf. *Paradise Lost*, V.601, "Thrones, Dominations, Princedoms, Virtues, Powers . . ." (Vol. I, p. 485). **555. Earth-born's spell**: Prometheus' spell. Cf. 568. **560. crag-like agony**: The image takes us back to the opening scene. **567. The . . . length**: Cf. II.iii.97. **569. disentangled**: The disentangling is

## THE CLOUD

I bring fresh showers for the thirsting flowers,
From the seas and the streams;
I bear light shade for the leaves when laid
In their noonday dreams.
From my wings are shaken the dews that waken
The sweet buds every one,
When rocked to rest on their mother's breast,
As she dances about the sun.
I wield the flail of the lashing hail,
And whiten the green plains under,
And then again I dissolve it in rain,
And laugh as I pass in thunder.

I sift the snow on the mountains below,
And their great pines groan aghast;
And all the night 'tis my pillow white,
While I sleep in the arms of the blast.
Sublime on the towers of my skiey bowers,
Lightning my pilot sits;
In a cavern under is fettered the thunder,
It struggles and howls at fits;
Over earth and ocean, with gentle motion,
This pilot is guiding me,
Lured by the love of the genii that move
In the depths of the purple sea;
Over the rills, and the crags, and the hills,
Over the lakes and the plains,
Wherever he dream, under mountain or stream,
The Spirit he loves remains;
And I all the while bask in Heaven's blue smile,
Whilst he is dissolving in rains.

The sanguine Sunrise, with his meteor eyes,
And his burning plumes outspread,
Leaps on the back of my sailing rack,
When the morning star shines dead;
As on the jag of a mountain crag,
Which an earthquake rocks and swings,
An eagle alit one moment may sit
In the light of its golden wings.
And when Sunset may breathe, from the lit sea beneath,
Its ardours of rest and of love,
And the crimson pall of eve may fall
From the depth of Heaven above,
With wings folded I rest, on mine aëry nest,
As still as a brooding dove.

That orbèd maiden with white fire laden,
Whom mortals call the Moon,
Glides glimmering o'er my fleece-like floor,
By the midnight breezes strewn;
And wherever the beat of her unseen feet,
Which only the angels hear,
May have broken the woof of my tent's thin roof,
The stars peep behind her and peer;
And I laugh to see them whirl and flee,
Like a swarm of golden bees,
When I widen the rent in my wind-built tent,
Till the calm rivers, lakes, and seas,
Like strips of the sky fallen through me on high,
Are each paved with the moon and these.

I bind the Sun's throne with a burning zone,
And the Moon's with a girdle of pearl;
The volcanoes are dim, and the stars reel and swim,
When the whirlwinds my banner unfurl.
From cape to cape, with a bridge-like shape,
Over a torrent sea,
Sunbeam-proof, I hang like a roof,—
The mountains its columns be.
The triumphal arch through which I march
With hurricane, fire, and snow,
When the Powers of the air are chained to my chair,
Is the million-coloured bow;
The sphere-fire above its soft colours wove,
While the moist Earth was laughing below.

I am the daughter of Earth and Water,
And the nursling of the Sky;
I pass through the pores of the ocean and shores;
I change, but I cannot die.
For after the rain when with never a stain
The pavilion of Heaven is bare,
And the winds and sunbeams with their convex gleams
Build up the blue dome of air,
I silently laugh at my own cenotaph,
And out of the caverns of rain,
Like a child from the womb, like a ghost from the tomb,
I arise and unbuild it again.

*1820*

## TO A SKYLARK

Hail to thee, blithe Spirit!
Bird thou never wert,
That from Heaven, or near it,
Pourest thy full heart
In profuse strains of unpremeditated art.

a prerequisite for regaining control. THE CLOUD. **20. at fits:** intermittently? **23–30. Lured . . . rains:** speculative electrical theory.

**47. floor:** as seen from above. **51. roof:** as seen from below. TO A SKYLARK. **2. Bird . . . wert:** The blithe Spirit here addressed is even more the joy than the bird it animates. **3. or near it:** Cf. Browning, 98, p. 511, below, "what's a heaven for?"

Higher still and higher
From the earth thou springest
Like a cloud of fire;
The blue deep thou wingest,
And singing still dost soar, and soaring ever singest.

In the golden lightning
Of the sunken sun,
O'er which clouds are bright'ning,
Thou dost float and run;
Like an unbodied joy whose race is just begun.

The pale purple even
Melts around thy flight;
Like a star of Heaven,
In the broad daylight
Thou art unseen, but yet I hear thy shrill delight,

Keen as are the arrows
Of that silver sphere,
Whose intense lamp narrows
In the white dawn clear
Until we hardly see — we feel that it is there.

All the earth and air
With thy voice is loud,
As, when night is bare,
From one lonely cloud
The moon rains out her beams, and Heaven is overflowed.

What thou art we know not;
What is most like thee?
From rainbow clouds there flow not
Drops so bright to see
As from thy presence showers a rain of melody.

Like a Poet hidden
In the light of thought,
Singing hymns unbidden,
Till the world is wrought
To sympathy with hopes and fears it heeded not:

Like a high-born maiden
In a palace-tower,
Soothing her love-laden
Soul in secret hour
With music sweet as love, which overflows her bower:

Like a glow-worm golden
In a dell of dew,
Scattering unbeholden
Its aëreal hue
Among the flowers and grass, which screen it from the view!

Like a rose embowered
In its own green leaves,
By warm winds deflowered,
Till the scent it gives
Makes faint with too much sweet those heavy-wingèd thieves:

Sound of vernal showers
On the twinkling grass,
Rain-awakened flowers,
All that ever was
Joyous, and clear, and fresh, thy music doth surpass:

Teach us, Sprite or Bird,
What sweet thoughts are thine:
I have never heard
Praise of love or wine
That panted forth a flood of rapture so divine.

Chorus Hymeneal,
Or triumphal chant,
Matched with thine would be all
But an empty vaunt,
A thing wherein we feel there is some hidden want.

What objects are the fountains
Of thy happy strain?
What fields, or waves, or mountains?
What shapes of sky or plain?
What love of thine own kind? what ignorance of pain?

With thy clear keen joyance
Languor cannot be:
Shadow of annoyance
Never came near thee:
Thou lovest — but ne'er knew love's sad satiety.

Waking or asleep,
Thou of death must deem
Things more true and deep
Than we mortals dream,
Or how could thy notes flow in such a crystal stream?

We look before and after,
And pine for what is not:

**15. unbodied:** a joy escaped from the body. **22. that . . . sphere:** the Morning Star, Phosphor, Lucifer, Light bringer. **25. feel:** Cf. *PU*, II.v.17. **36. hidden:** a description of Shelley's poetry at its highest.

**53. deflowered:** a metaphorical word here used literally. **66. Hymeneal:** celebrating a marriage. **81. Waking or asleep:** Cf. *PU*, III.iii.113–14.

Our sincerest laughter
With some pain is fraught;
Our sweetest songs are those that tell of saddest thought.

Yet if we could scorn
Hate, and pride, and fear;
If we were things born
Not to shed a tear,
I know not how thy joy we ever should come near.

Better than all measures
Of delightful sound,
Better than all treasures
That in books are found,
Thy skill to poet were, thou scorner of the ground!

Teach me half the gladness
That thy brain must know,
Such harmonious madness
From my lips would flow
The world should listen then — as I am listening now.

*1820*

## ODE TO LIBERTY

Yet, Freedom, yet, thy banner, torn but flying,
Streams like a thunder-storm against the wind.
[Byron, *Childe Harold,* IV.98]

Unlike the "Ode to the West Wind," this Ode is in the English "Pindaric" manner, and is correspondingly more elaborate in rhetoric, heavier in rhythm, slower in pace. It draws not only on the political situation of its time, a period of popular uprisings in Spain, Italy and Greece, but more deeply on its finest English precedent, Milton's *Areopagitica,* to which it refers obliquely in line 75, as its "latest oracle." Even after the Reformation, Shelley saw orthodox Christianity as an oppression, effecting tyranny by superstition. This attitude prevails from his earliest writings, despite his "exceeding faith in the spirit of Christianity" (Leigh Hunt). Shelley's notion of political liberty needs always to be considered as an aspect of "intellectual beauty." Thus, the two might be interchangeable in the following canceled passage of the "Ode to Liberty":

Within a cavern of man's trackless spirit
Is throned an Image, so intensely fair
That the adventurous thoughts that wander near it
Worship, and as they kneel, tremble and wear
The splendour of its presence, and the light
Penetrates their dreamlike frame
Till they become charged with the strength of flame.

I

A glorious people vibrated again
The lightning of the nations: Liberty
From heart to heart, from tower to tower, o'er Spain,
Scattering contagious fire into the sky,
Gleamed. My soul spurned the chains of its dismay,
And in the rapid plumes of song
Clothed itself, sublime and strong,
(As a young eagle soars the morning clouds among,)
Hovering in verse o'er its accustomed prey;
Till from its station in the Heaven of fame
The Spirit's whirlwind rapt it, and the ray
Of the remotest sphere of living flame
Which paves the void was from behind it flung,
As foam from a ship's swiftness, when there came
A voice out of the deep: I will record the same.

II

The Sun and the serenest Moon sprang forth:
The burning stars of the abyss were hurled
Into the depths of Heaven. The daedal earth,
That island in the ocean of the world,
Hung in its cloud of all-sustaining air:
But this divinest universe
Was yet a chaos and a curse,
For thou wert not: but, power from worst producing worse,
The spirit of the beasts was kindled there,
And of the birds, and of the watery forms,
And there was war among them, and despair
Within them, raging without truce or terms:
The bosom of their violated nurse
Groaned, for beasts warred on beasts, and worms on worms,
And men on men; each heart was as a hell of storms.

III

Man, the imperial shape, then multiplied
His generations under the pavilion
Of the Sun's throne: palace and pyramid,
Temple and prison, to many a swarming million
Were, as to mountain-wolves their raggèd caves.
This human living multitude
Was savage, cunning, blind, and rude,
For thou wert not; but o'er the populous solitude,
Like one fierce cloud over a waste of waves,
Hung Tyranny; beneath, sate deified
The sister-pest, congregator of slaves;
Into the shadow of her pinions wide

ODE TO LIBERTY. **16 ff.:** The voice is speaking. **23. thou:** Liberty. **28. violated nurse:** the Earth. **33–45. palace . . . side:** The masters of "palace and pyramid, temple and

Anarchs and priests, who feed on gold and blood
  Till with the stain their inmost souls are dyed,
  Drove the astonished herds of men from every side.

IV

The nodding promontories, and blue isles,
  And cloud-like mountains, and dividuous waves
Of Greece, basked glorious in the open smiles
  Of favouring Heaven: from their enchanted caves
Prophetic echoes flung dim melody.
    On the unapprehensive wild
    The vine, the corn, the olive mild,
Grew savage yet, to human use unreconciled;
  And, like unfolded flowers beneath the sea,
    Like the man's thought dark in the infant's brain,
  Like aught that is which wraps what is to be,
    Art's deathless dreams lay veiled by many a vein
Of Parian stone; and, yet a speechless child,
  Verse murmured, and Philosophy did strain
  Her lidless eyes for thee; when o'er the Aegean main

V

Athens arose: a city such as vision
  Builds from the purple crags and silver towers
Of battlemented cloud, as in derision
  Of kingliest masonry: the ocean-floors
Pave it; the evening sky pavilions it;
    Its portals are inhabited
    By thunder-zonèd winds, each head
Within its cloudy wings with sun-fire garlanded,—
  A divine work! Athens, diviner yet,
    Gleamed with its crest of columns, on the will
  Of man, as on a mount of diamond, set;
    For thou wert, and thine all-creative skill
Peopled, with forms that mock the eternal dead
  In marble immortality, that hill
  Which was thine earliest throne and latest oracle.

VI

Within the surface of Time's fleeting river
  Its wrinkled image lies, as then it lay
Immovably unquiet, and for ever
  It trembles, but it cannot pass away!
The voices of thy bards and sages thunder
    With an earth-awakening blast
    Through the caverns of the past:
(Religion veils her eyes; Oppression shrinks aghast:)
  A wingèd sound of joy, and love, and wonder,
    Which soars where Expectation never flew,
  Rending the veil of space and time asunder!
    One ocean feeds the clouds, and streams, and dew;
One Sun illumines Heaven; one Spirit vast
  With life and love makes chaos ever new,
  As Athens doth the world with thy delight renew.

. . . . . . .

The voice then relates the vicissitudes of Liberty in Rome, in the dark ages, in Alfred's England, in Italy, in Luther's Germany and Milton's England, in the French Revolution, in Greece and Spain and Germany again . . . and concludes:

. . . . . . .

XVIII

Come thou, but lead out of the inmost cave
  Of man's deep spirit, as the morning-star
Beckons the Sun from the Eoan wave,
  Wisdom. I hear the pennons of her car
Self-moving, like cloud charioted by flame;
    Comes she not, and come ye not,
    Rulers of eternal thought,
To judge, with solemn truth, life's ill-apportioned lot?
  Blind Love, and equal Justice, and the Fame
    Of what has been, the Hope of what will be?
  O Liberty! if such could be thy name
    Wert thou disjoined from these, or they from thee:
If thine or theirs were treasures to be bought
  By blood or tears, have not the wise and free
  Wept tears, and blood like tears?—The solemn harmony

prison" were as wolves to the "astonished herds of men." **populous solitude**: the lonely crowd. **sister-pest**: organized religion; cf. 83. **Anarchs**: Tyranny knows no rule and therefore is anarchy. **46. nodding**: their motion as watched from a small sailing boat. **47. dividuous**: separating. Cf. *Iliad*, XIV, "Too many things lie between: shadowy mountains and sounding seas." **51. unapprehensive**: unaware and unfearing. **54. unfolded**: perhaps a misprint for "enfolded"—not yet unfolded: cf. 56, "wraps what is to be." **58. Parian stone**: marble from Paros. **60. lidless**: Philosophy can close its eyes to nothing. **63. in derision**: making the triumphs of royal builders seem petty. **65. pavilions**: roofs. **66–68. portals . . . garlanded**: within its gates stand, as guardians, thunderbolt belted winds, their heads lit "like the bright hair uplifted from the head of some fierce Maenad" (see Intro., p. 248). **69. A . . . yet**: This visionary city is less divine than Athens. **70. crest of columns**: the Acropolis. **70–71. on . . . set**: Cf. *Hellas*, 696–99, "But Greece and her foundations are/Built below the tide of war,/Based on the crystalline sea/Of thought and its eternity." **73. mock . . . dead**: imitate those who, though they are dead, are eternal. **74–75. hill . . . oracle**: the Areopagus from which Milton named his *Areopagitica* (Vol. I, p. 428). **86. Rending the veil**: as Plato shows what is beyond the illusive flux. **89. makes . . . new**: Cf. "Destroyer and preserver", "Ode to the West Wind," 14, p. 255. **256. thou**: Liberty. **258. Eoan wave**: eastern, from Eos, the dawn. **262. Rulers . . . thought**: Love, Justice, Fame, Hope. **266. if . . . name**: Liberty, Love, Justice, must be inseparable.

XIX

Paused, and the Spirit of that mighty singing
To its abyss was suddenly withdrawn;
Then, as a wild swan, when sublimely winging
Its path athwart the thunder-smoke of dawn,
Sinks headlong through the aëreal golden light
On the heavy-sounding plain,
When the bolt has pierced its brain;
As summer clouds dissolve, unburthened of their rain;
As a far taper fades with fading night,
As a brief insect dies with dying day, —
My song, its pinions disarrayed of might,
Drooped; o'er it closed the echoes far away
Of the great voice which did its flight sustain,
As waves which lately paved his watery way
Hiss round a drowner's head in their tempestuous play.

*1820*

## ARETHUSA

In 1820 Mary Shelley, whose novel *Frankenstein* had been published anonymously in 1818, wrote two short mythological verse dramas, *Proserpine* and *Midas*. Shelley contributed lyrics that far outshine their setting. "Arethusa" was written for *Proserpine,* and the "Hymn of Apollo" and "Hymn of Pan" for *Midas*. In all three Shelley transcends the classical myth, turning it to his own imaginative conception.

I

Arethusa arose
From her couch of snows
In the Acroceraunian mountains, —
From cloud and from crag,
With many a jag,
Shepherding her bright fountains.
She leapt down the rocks,
With her rainbow locks
Streaming among the streams; —
Her steps paved with green
The downward ravine
Which slopes to the western gleams;
And gliding and springing
She went, ever singing,
In murmurs as soft as sleep;
The Earth seemed to love her,
And Heaven smiled above her,
As she lingered towards the deep.

II

Then Alpheus bold,
On his glacier cold,
With his trident the mountains strook;
And opened a chasm
In the rocks — with the spasm
All Erymanthus shook.
And the black south wind
It unsealed behind
The urns of the silent snow,
And earthquake and thunder
Did rend in sunder
The bars of the springs below.
And the beard and the hair
Of the River-god were
Seen through the torrent's sweep,
As he followed the light
Of the fleet nymph's flight
To the brink of the Dorian deep.

III

'Oh, save me! Oh, guide me!
And bid the deep hide me,
For he grasps me now by the hair!'
The loud Ocean heard,
To its blue depth stirred,
And divided at her prayer;
And under the water
The Earth's white daughter
Fled like a sunny beam;
Behind her descended
Her billows, unblended
With the brackish Dorian stream: —
Like a gloomy stain
On the emerald main
Alpheus rushed behind, —
As an eagle pursuing
A dove to its ruin,
Down the streams of the cloudy wind.

IV

Under the bowers
Where the Ocean Powers
Sit on their pearlèd thrones;
Through the coral woods
Of the weltering floods,

**273–82. Then . . . away:** What the lines describe happens in them till the last three take up again. ARETHUSA. **3. Acroceraunian:** literally, thunder-smitten; the name of a storm-enclouded mountain range in Albania.

**19. Alpheus:** Here depicted as the frozen god of the glacier, also the god of a river in the Peloponnesus. He fell in love with the water-nymph Arethusa, and pursued her downstream, and across the Mediterranean to the Sicilian island of Ortygia, where, to escape him, yet remain always in his reach, she was metamorphosed into a fountain. See Ovid, *Metamorphoses*. **24. Erymanthus:** Arcadia, where lived the Erymanthian boar, which Hercules killed to fulfill one of his twelve labors.

Over heaps of unvalued stones;
  Through the dim beams
  Which amid the streams
Weave a network of coloured light;
  And under the caves,
  Where the shadowy waves
Are as green as the forest's night:—
  Outspeeding the shark,
  And the sword-fish dark,
Under the Ocean's foam,
  And up through the rifts
  Of the mountain clifts
They passed to their Dorian home.

V

  And now from their fountains
  In Enna's mountains,
Down one vale where the morning basks,
  Like friends once parted
  Grown single-hearted,
They ply their watery tasks.
  At sunrise they leap
  From their cradles steep
In the cave of the shelving hill;
  At noontide they flow
  Through the woods below
And the meadows of asphodel;
  And at night they sleep
  In the rocking deep
Beneath the Ortygian shore;—
  Like spirits that lie
  In the azure sky
When they love but live no more.

*1820*

## HYMN OF APOLLO

Pan has challenged Apollo
  Saying his Syrinx can give sweeter notes
  Than the stringèd instrument Apollo boasts.

Old Tmolus, God of the bare hill on which the contest takes place, judges in Apollo's favour. Syrinx, pursued by Pan, was transformed into the reed of which Pan-pipes are made.

I

The sleepless Hours who watch me as I lie,
  Curtained with star-inwoven tapestries
From the broad moonlight of the sky,
  Fanning the busy dreams from my dim eyes,—
Waken me when their Mother, the gray Dawn,
Tells them that dreams and that the moon is gone.

**72. They**: Alpheus and Arethusa. **74. Enna**: a plain in Sicily within sight of Mt. Etna.

II

Then I arise, and climbing Heaven's blue dome,
  I walk over the mountains and the waves,
Leaving my robe upon the ocean foam;
  My footsteps pave the clouds with fire; the caves
Are filled with my bright presence, and the air
Leaves the green Earth to my embraces bare.

III

The sunbeams are my shafts, with which I kill
  Deceit, that loves the night and fears the day;
All men who do or even imagine ill
  Fly me, and from the glory of my ray
Good minds and open actions take new might,
Until diminished by the reign of Night.

IV

I feed the clouds, the rainbows and the flowers
  With their aethereal colours; the moon's globe
And the pure stars in their eternal bowers
  Are cinctured with my power as with a robe;
Whatever lamps on Earth or Heaven may shine
Are portions of one power, which is mine.

V

I stand at noon upon the peak of Heaven,
  Then with unwilling steps I wander down
Into the clouds of the Atlantic even;
  For grief that I depart they weep and frown:
What look is more delightful than the smile
With which I soothe them from the western isle?

VI

I am the eye with which the Universe
  Beholds itself and knows itself divine;
All harmony of instrument or verse,
  All prophecy, all medicine is mine,
All light of art or nature;—to my song
Victory and praise in its own right belong.

*1820*

## HYMN OF PAN

I

  From the forests and highlands
    We come, we come;
  From the river-girt islands,
    Where loud waves are dumb
      Listening to my sweet pipings.
  The wind in the reeds and the rushes,
    The bees on the bells of thyme,
  The birds on the myrtle bushes,
    The cicale above in the lime,

And the lizards below in the grass,
Were as silent as ever old Tmolus was,
Listening to my sweet pipings.

II

Liquid Peneus was flowing,
And all dark Tempe lay
In Pelion's shadow, outgrowing
The light of the dying day,
Speeded by my sweet pipings.
The Sileni, and Sylvans, and Fauns,
And the Nymphs of the woods and the waves,
To the edge of the moist river-lawns,
And the brink of the dewy caves,
And all that did then attend and follow,
Were silent with love, as you now, Apollo,
With envy of my sweet pipings.

III

I sang of the dancing stars,
I sang of the daedal Earth,
And of Heaven — and the giant wars,
And Love, and Death, and Birth, —
And then I changed my pipings, —
Singing how down the vale of Maenalus
I pursued a maiden and clasped a reed.
Gods and men, we are all deluded thus!
It breaks in our bosom and then we bleed:
All wept, as I think both ye now would,
If envy or age had not frozen your blood,
At the sorrow of my sweet pipings.

*1820*

## TO THE MOON

I

Art thou pale for weariness
Of climbing heaven and gazing on the earth,
Wandering companionless
Among the stars that have a different birth, —
And ever changing, like a joyless eye
That finds no object worth its constancy?

*1820*

## from EPIPSYCHIDION

VERSES ADDRESSED TO THE NOBLE AND UNFORTUNATE LADY, EMILIA V——,

NOW IMPRISONED IN THE CONVENT OF ——

In his Preface Shelley attributes the poem to a fictitious author recently dead and is at some pains to increase its enigmatic character: "The present Poem, like the *Vita Nuova* of Dante, is sufficiently intelligible to a certain class of readers without a matter-of-fact history of the circumstances; and to a certain other class it must ever remain incomprehensible, from a defect of a common organ of perception for the ideas of which it treats." Eloquent, impassioned, ecstatic, there is an air of improvization about much of it, and the stress of an awareness of a need for defence. A summary would have little significance. As Stephen Spender observes, it "contains his philosophy of love expressed in words which have profoundly influenced many people in their lives." The same words, especially the third paragraph of this selection, have also moved eminent critics to stern disapproval. Compare, however, C. S. Lewis' remarks on Prince Arthur's search for Gloriana (Vol. I, p. 103, col. 1). Shelley's own comment of the following year is: "The error consists in seeking in a mortal image the likeness of what is perhaps eternal" (Letter to Gisborne, June 18, 1822).

It may be added that to take in this compact poetry we have to read far more slowly and reflectively than usual; whereas the movement of the verses frequently invites us to read faster. To use words Shelley uses of Plato, we have here "the rare union of close and subtle logic with the Pythian enthusiasm of poetry, melted by the splendour and harmony of his periods into one irresistible stream of musical impressions, which hurry the persuasions onward, as in a breathless career."

See where she stands! a mortal shape indued
With love and life and light and deity,
And motion which may change but cannot die;
An image of some bright Eternity;
A shadow of some golden dream; a Splendour
Leaving the third sphere pilotless; a tender
Reflection of the eternal Moon of Love
Under whose motions life's dull billows move;
A Metaphor of Spring and Youth and Morning;
A Vision like incarnate April, warning, 121
With smiles and tears, Frost the Anatomy
Into his summer grave.

Ah, woe is me!
What have I dared? where am I lifted? how
Shall I descend, and perish not? I know
That Love makes all things equal: I have heard
By mine own heart this joyous truth averred:
The spirit of the worm beneath the sod
In love and worship, blends itself with God.

Spouse! Sister! Angel! Pilot of the Fate
Whose course has been so starless! O too late
Belovèd! O too soon adored, by me!
For in the fields of Immortality
My spirit should at first have worshipped thine,
A divine presence in a place divine;
Or should have moved beside it on this earth,

EPIPSYCHIDION. 134. at first: before birth.

A shadow of that substance, from its birth;
But not as now: — I love thee; yes, I feel
That on the fountain of my heart a seal
Is set, to keep its waters pure and bright
For thee, since in those *tears* thou hast delight.
We — are we not formed, as notes of music are,
For one another, though dissimilar;
Such difference without discord, as can make
Those sweetest sounds, in which all spirits shake
As trembling leaves in a continuous air?

Thy wisdom speaks in me, and bids me dare
Beacon the rocks on which high hearts are wrecked.
I never was attached to that great sect,
Whose doctrine is, that each one should select
Out of the crowd a mistress or a friend,
And all the rest, though fair and wise, commend
To cold oblivion, though it is in the code
Of modern morals, and the beaten road
Which those poor slaves with weary footsteps tread,
Who travel to their home among the dead
By the broad highway of the world, and so
With one chained friend, perhaps a jealous foe,
The dreariest and the longest journey go.

True Love in this differs from gold and clay,
That to divide is not to take away.
Love is like understanding, that grows bright,
Gazing on many truths; 'tis like thy light,
Imagination! which from earth and sky,
And from the depths of human fantasy,
As from a thousand prisms and mirrors, fills
The Universe with glorious beams, and kills
Error, the worm, with many a sun-like arrow
Of its reverberated lightning. Narrow
The heart that loves, the brain that contemplates,
The life that wears, the spirit that creates
One object, and one form, and builds thereby
A sepulchre for its eternity.

Mind from its object differs most in this:
Evil from good; misery from happiness;
The baser from the nobler; the impure
And frail, from what is clear and must endure.
If you divide suffering and dross, you may
Diminish till it is consumed away;
If you divide pleasure and love and thought,
Each part exceeds the whole; and we know not
How much, while any yet remains unshared,
Of pleasure may be gained, of sorrow spared:
This truth is that deep well, whence sages draw
The unenvied light of hope; the eternal law
By which those live, to whom this world of life
Is as a garden ravaged, and whose strife
Tills for the promise of a later birth
The wilderness of this Elysian earth.

There was a Being whom my spirit oft
Met on its visioned wanderings, far aloft,
In the clear golden prime of my youth's dawn,
Upon the fairy isles of sunny lawn,
Amid the enchanted mountains, and the caves
Of divine sleep, and on the air-like waves
Of wonder-level dream, whose tremulous floor
Paved her light steps; — on an imagined shore,
Under the gray beak of some promontory
She met me, robed in such exceeding glory,
That I beheld her not. In solitudes
Her voice came to me through the whispering woods,
And from the fountains, and the odours deep
Of flowers, which, like lips murmuring in their sleep
Of the sweet kisses which had lulled them there,
Breathed but of *her* to the enamoured air;
And from the breezes whether low or loud,
And from the rain of every passing cloud,
And from the singing of the summer-birds,
And from all sounds, all silence. In the words
Of antique verse and high romance, — in form
Sound, colour — in whatever checks that Storm
Which with the shattered present chokes the past;
And in that best philosophy, whose taste
Makes this cold common hell, our life, a doom
As glorious as a fiery martyrdom;
Her Spirit was the harmony of truth. —

Then, from the caverns of my dreamy youth
I sprang, as one sandalled with plumes of fire,
And towards the lodestar of my one desire,
I flitted, like a dizzy moth, whose flight
Is as a dead leaf's in the owlet light,
When it would seek in Hesper's setting sphere
A radiant death, a fiery sepulchre,
As if it were a lamp of earthly flame. —
But She, whom prayers or tears then could not tame,
Passed, like a God throned on a wingèd planet,
Whose burning plumes to tenfold swiftness fan it,
Into the dreary cone of our life's shade;
And as a man with mighty loss dismayed,
I would have followed, though the grave between
Yawned like a gulf whose spectres are unseen:

137. **A . . . substance**: a derivative of that beauty which she represents. 148. **Beacon**: set up warning lights on. 159. **longest journey**: E. M. Forster so entitled his first (and still his favorite) novel. 164–69. **Imagination . . . lightning**: gathering the "rays which are reality"?

189. **Elysian**: which might and should be like the Elysian fields. 191. **visioned wanderings**: imagined, and attended by, and in pursuit of, visions. 200. **beheld . . . not**: Cf. Panthea to Asia, *PU*, III.v.17. 222. **Hesper**: the evening star. 228. **Into . . . shade**: Cf. 215.

When a voice said: — 'O thou of hearts the weakest,
The phantom is beside thee whom thou seekest.'
Then I — 'Where?' — the world's echo answered 'where?'
And in that silence, and in my despair,
I questioned every tongueless wind that flew
Over my tower of mourning, if it knew
Whither 'twas fled, this soul out of my soul . . .

*1821*

# EPIGRAMS

## TO STELLA

FROM THE GREEK OF PLATO

Thou wert the morning star among the living,
Ere thy fair light had fled; —
Now, having died, thou art as Hesperus, giving
New splendour to the dead.

*1821?*

## CIRCUMSTANCE

FROM THE GREEK

A man who was about to hang himself,
Finding a purse, then threw away his rope;
The owner, coming to reclaim his pelf,
The halter found, and used it. So is Hope
Changed for Despair — one laid upon the shelf,
We take the other. Under Heaven's high cope
Fortune is God — all you endure and do
Depends on circumstance as much as you.

*1821?*

# from ADONAIS[1]

AN ELEGY ON THE DEATH OF JOHN KEATS, AUTHOR OF ENDYMION, HYPERION, ETC.

John Keats died in Rome on February 23, 1821. Shelley's Elegy was written four months later and printed at Pisa in July under the author's name and supervision, part of the edition being sent to his London publishers. Its first English imprint was at Cambridge in 1829, by the efforts of Shelley's young admirers, among them Hallam, on whose death Tennyson was to write *In Memoriam*. The poet speaks of "Adonais" in his letters as a "highly wrought piece of art," a character blindly neglected by its first English reviewers, who did not, for example, see its parentage with Milton's "Lycidas." Whereas Johnson had at least recognized, and *then* criticized Milton's conventional devices, the early critics of "Adonais" seem to have been unaware of the tradition in which the poet wrote. See Vol. I, pp. 952–53. Shelley had translated fragments of the two classic Greek elegies of Bion and Moschus, from which the modern elegiac tradition stemmed.

I

I weep for Adonais — he is dead!
O, weep for Adonais! though our tears
Thaw not the frost which binds so dear a head!
And thou, sad Hour, selected from all years
To mourn our loss, rouse thy obscure compeers,
And teach them thine own sorrow, say: 'With me
Died Adonais; till the Future dares
Forget the Past, his fate and fame shall be
An echo and a light unto eternity!'

II

Where wert thou, mighty Mother, when he lay,
When thy Son lay, pierced by the shaft which flies
In darkness? where was lorn Urania
When Adonais died? With veilèd eyes,
'Mid listening Echoes, in her Paradise
She sate, while one, with soft enamoured breath,
Rekindled all the fading melodies,
With which, like flowers that mock the corse beneath,
He had adorned and hid the coming bulk of Death.

III

Oh, weep for Adonais — he is dead!
Wake, melancholy Mother, wake and weep!
Yet wherefore? Quench within their burning bed
Thy fiery tears, and let thy loud heart keep
Like his, a mute and uncomplaining sleep;
For he is gone, where all things wise and fair
Descend; — oh, dream not that the amorous Deep
Will yet restore him to the vital air;
Death feeds on his mute voice, and laughs at our despair.

**233. The phantom**: the ideal Being or any of its living representatives—which? **238. this . . . soul**: "Epipsychidion" can mean "the soul within the soul." ADONAIS. **1.** The adonai was a festival celebrating the death and resurrection of Adonis.

**12. Urania**: the Muse of astronomy, also Aphrodite as goddess of the Heavens. Cf. XLVI.

. . . . . . .

In stanzas IV–XXXVIII other poets, dead or still toiling, are recalled. The youngest and loveliest of them will wake no more; his creative dreams and desires, personified as spirits, are seen mourning him. But while, after winter's passing, nature is everywhere renewed in spring, Urania challenges Death and laments her lifeless son again. She is joined by the mountain shepherds, who stand for Byron, Moore and Shelley himself — "a pardlike Spirit, beautiful and swift." These deplore the poisoning of Adonais by a detractor's infamous words. Yet his pure spirit, now beyond venom's reach, flows back to its origin, a portion of the Eternal, beyond time and change.

. . . . . . .

XXXIX

Peace, peace! he is not dead, he doth not sleep —
He hath awakened from the dream of life —
'Tis we, who lost in stormy visions, keep
With phantoms an unprofitable strife,
And in mad trance, strike with our spirit's knife
Invulnerable nothings. — *We* decay
Like corpses in a charnel; fear and grief
Convulse us and consume us day by day,
And cold hopes swarm like worms within our living clay.

XL

He has outsoared the shadow of our night;
Envy and calumny and hate and pain,
And that unrest which men miscall delight,
Can touch him not and torture not again;
From the contagion of the world's slow stain
He is secure, and now can never mourn
A heart grown cold, a head grown gray in vain;
Nor, when the spirit's self has ceased to burn,
With sparkless ashes load an unlamented urn.

XLI

He lives, he wakes — 'tis Death is dead, not he;
Mourn not for Adonais. — Thou young Dawn,
Turn all thy dew to splendour, for from thee
The spirit thou lamentest is not gone;
Ye caverns and ye forests, cease to moan!
Cease, ye faint flowers and fountains, and thou Air,
Which like a mourning veil thy scarf hadst thrown
O'er the abandoned Earth, now leave it bare
Even to the joyous stars which smile on its despair!

XLII

He is made one with Nature: there is heard
His voice in all her music, from the moan
Of thunder, to the song of night's sweet bird;
He is a presence to be felt and known
In darkness and in light, from herb and stone,
Spreading itself where'er that Power may move
Which has withdrawn his being to its own;
Which wields the world with never-wearied love,
Sustains it from beneath, and kindles it above.

XLIII

He is a portion of the loveliness
Which once he made more lovely: he doth bear
His part, while the one Spirit's plastic stress
Sweeps through the dull dense world, compelling there,
All new successions to the forms they wear;
Torturing th' unwilling dross that checks its flight
To its own likeness, as each mass may bear;
And bursting in its beauty and its might
From trees and beasts and men into the Heaven's light.

XLIV

The splendours of the firmament of time
May be eclipsed, but are extinguished not;
Like stars to their appointed height they climb,
And death is a low mist which cannot blot
The brightness it may veil. When lofty thought
Lifts a young heart above its mortal lair,
And love and life contend in it, for what
Shall be its earthly doom, the dead live there
And move like winds of light on dark and stormy air.

XLV

The inheritors of unfulfilled renown
Rose from their thrones, built beyond mortal thought,
Far in the Unapparent. Chatterton
Rose pale, — his solemn agony had not
Yet faded from him; Sidney, as he fought
And as he fell and as he lived and loved
Sublimely mild, a Spirit without spot,
Arose; and Lucan, by his death approved:
Oblivion as they rose shrank like a thing reproved.

XLVI

And many more, whose names on Earth are dark,
But whose transmitted effluence cannot die
So long as fire outlives the parent spark,

**361. 'tis . . . dead:** Cf. Donne's sonnet "Death be not proud" (Vol. I, p. 386). **385. as . . . bear:** as much as every material allows. **399. Chatterton:** English poet (1752–70) who died by his own hand at the age of seventeen. **404. Lucan:** Latin poet, author of *Pharsalia*, who took part in a plot against Nero and killed himself when this was discovered.

Rose, robed in dazzling immortality.
'Thou art become as one of us,' they cry,
'It was for thee yon kingless sphere has long
Swung blind in unascended majesty,
Silent alone amid an Heaven of Song.
Assume thy wingèd throne, thou Vesper of our throng!'

XLVII

Who mourns for Adonais? Oh, come forth,
Fond wretch! and know thyself and him aright.
Clasp with thy panting soul the pendulous Earth;
As from a centre, dart thy spirit's light
Beyond all worlds, until its spacious might
Satiate the void circumference: then shrink
Even to a point within our day and night;
And keep thy heart light lest it make thee sink
When hope has kindled hope, and lured thee to the brink.

XLVIII

Or go to Rome, which is the sepulchre,
Oh, not of him, but of our joy: 'tis nought
That ages, empires, and religions there
Lie buried in the ravage they have wrought;
For such as he can lend, — they borrow not
Glory from those who made the world their prey;
And he is gathered to the kings of thought
Who waged contention with their time's decay,
And of the past are all that cannot pass away.

XLIX

Go thou to Rome, — at once the Paradise,
The grave, the city, and the wilderness;
And where its wrecks like shattered mountains rise,
And flowering weeds, and fragrant copses dress
The bones of Desolation's nakedness
Pass, till the spirit of the spot shall lead
Thy footsteps to a slope of green access
Where, like an infant's smile, over the dead
A light of laughing flowers along the grass is spread;

L

And gray walls moulder round, on which dull Time
Feeds, like slow fire upon a hoary brand;
And one keen pyramid with wedge sublime,
Pavilioning the dust of him who planned
This refuge for his memory, doth stand
Like flame transformed to marble; and beneath,
A field is spread, on which a newer band
Have pitched in Heaven's smile their camp of death,
Welcoming him we lose with scarce extinguished breath.

LI

Here pause: these graves are all too young as yet
To have outgrown the sorrow which consigned
Its charge to each; and if the seal is set,
Here, on one fountain of a mourning mind,
Break it not thou! too surely shalt thou find
Thine own well full, if thou returnest home,
Of tears and gall. From the world's bitter wind
Seek shelter in the shadow of the tomb.
What Adonais is, why fear we to become?

LII

The One remains, the many change and pass;
Heaven's light forever shines, Earth's shadows fly;
Life, like a dome of many-coloured glass,
Stains the white radiance of Eternity,
Until Death tramples it to fragments. — Die,
If thou wouldst be with that which thou dost seek!
Follow where all is fled! — Rome's azure sky,
Flowers, ruins, statues, music, words, are weak
The glory they transfuse with fitting truth to speak.

LIII

Why linger, why turn back, why shrink, my Heart?
Thy hopes are gone before: from all things here
They have departed; thou shouldst now depart!
A light is passed from the revolving year,
And man, and woman; and what still is dear
Attracts to crush, repels to make thee wither.
The soft sky smiles, — the low wind whispers near:
'Tis Adonais calls! oh, hásten thither,
No more let Life divide what Death can join together.

LIV

That Light whose smile kindles the Universe,
That Beauty in which all things work and move,
That Benediction which the eclipsing Curse
Of birth can quench not, that sustaining Love
Which through the web of being blindly wove
By man and beast and earth and air and sea,
Burns bright or dim, as each are mirrors of
The fire for which all thirst; now beams on me,
Consuming the last clouds of cold mortality.

**417. pendulous**: hanging or floating. Cf. "The pendulous round Earth," *Paradise Lost*, IV.1000. **424. Rome**: Keats was buried in the Old Protestant Cemetery in Rome.

**448. a newer band**: Shelley s three-year-old son, William, was also

LV

The breath whose might I have invoked in song
Descends on me; my spirit's bark is driven,
Far from the shore, far from the trembling throng
Whose sails were never to the tempest given;
The massy earth and spherèd skies are riven!
I am borne darkly, fearfully, afar;
Whilst, burning through the inmost veil of Heaven,
The soul of Adonais, like a star,
Beacons from the abode where the Eternal are.

*1821*

## LINES: "WHEN THE LAMP IS SHATTERED"

I

When the lamp is shattered
The light in the dust lies dead —
When the cloud is scattered
The rainbow's glory is shed.
When the lute is broken,
Sweet tones are remembered not;
When the lips have spoken,
Loved accents are soon forgot.

II

As music and splendour
Survive not the lamp and the lute,
The heart's echoes render
No song when the spirit is mute: —
No song but sad dirges,
Like the wind through a ruined cell,
Or the mournful surges
That ring the dead seaman's knell.

III

When hearts have once mingled
Love first leaves the well-built nest;
The weak one is singled
To endure what it once possessed.
O Love! who bewailest
The frailty of all things here,
Why choose you the frailest
For your cradle, your home, and your bier?

IV

Its passions will rock thee
As the storms rock the ravens on high;
Bright reason will mock thee,
Like the sun from a wintry sky.
From thy nest every rafter
Will rot, and thine eagle home
Leave thee naked to laughter,
When leaves fall and cold winds come.

*1822*

## TO JANE: THE INVITATION

Best and brightest, come away!
Fairer far than this fair Day,
Which, like thee to those in sorrow,
Comes to bid a sweet good-morrow
To the rough Year just awake
In its cradle on the brake.
The brightest hour of unborn Spring,
Through the winter wandering,
Found, it seems, the halcyon Morn
To hoar February born.
Bending from Heaven, in azure mirth,
It kissed the forehead of the Earth,
And smiled upon the silent sea,
And bade the frozen streams be free,
And waked to music all their fountains,
And breathed upon the frozen mountains,
And like a prophetess of May
Strewed flowers upon the barren way,
Making the wintry world appear
Like one on whom thou smilest, dear.
Away, away, from men and towns,
To the wild wood and the downs —
To the silent wilderness
Where the soul need not repress
Its music lest it should not find
An echo in another's mind,
While the touch of Nature's art
Harmonizes heart to heart.
I leave this notice on my door
For each accustomed visitor: —
'I am gone into the fields
To take what this sweet hour yields; —
Reflection, you may come to-morrow,
Sit by the fireside with Sorrow. —
You with the unpaid bill, Despair, —
You, tiresome verse-reciter, Care, —
I will pay you in the grave, —
Death will listen to your stave.
Expectation too, be off!
To-day is for itself enough;
Hope, in pity mock not Woe
With smiles, nor follow where I go;
Long having lived on thy sweet food,
At length I find one moment's good

buried there. **495. Beacons**: lights the way; beckons.

After long pain — with all your love,
This you never told me of.'

Radiant Sister of the Day,
Awake! arise! and come away!
To the wild woods and the plains,
And the pools where winter rains
Image all their roof of leaves,
Where the pine its garland weaves
Of sapless green and ivy dun
Round stems that never kiss the sun;
Where the lawns and pastures be,
And the sandhills of the sea; —
Where the melting hoar-frost wets
The daisy-star that never sets,
And wind-flowers, and violets,
Which yet join not scent to hue,
Crown the pale year weak and new;
When the night is left behind
In the deep east, dun and blind,
And the blue noon is over us,
And the multitudinous
Billows murmur at our feet,
Where the earth and ocean meet,
And all things seem only one
In the universal sun.

*1822*

## TO JANE: THE RECOLLECTION

I

Now the last day of many days,
 All beautiful and bright as thou,
 The loveliest and the last, is dead,
Rise, Memory, and write its praise!
 Up, — to thy wonted work! come, trace
 The epitaph of glory fled, —
For now the Earth has changed its face,
 A frown is on the Heaven's brow.

II

We wandered to the Pine Forest
 That skirts the Ocean's foam,
The lightest wind was in its nest,
 The tempest in its home.
The whispering waves were half asleep,
 The clouds were gone to play,
And on the bosom of the deep
 The smile of Heaven lay;
It seemed as if the hour were one
 Sent from beyond the skies,
Which scattered from above the sun
 A light of Paradise.

III

We paused amid the pines that stood
 The giants of the waste,
Tortured by storms to shapes as rude
 As serpents interlaced,
And soothed by every azure breath,
 That under Heaven is blown,
To harmonies and hues beneath,
 As tender as its own;
Now all the tree-tops lay asleep,
 Like green waves on the sea,
As still as in the silent deep
 The ocean woods may be.

IV

How calm it was! — the silence there
 By such a chain was bound
That even the busy woodpecker
 Made stiller by her sound
The inviolable quietness;
 The breath of peace we drew
With its soft motion made not less
 The calm that round us grew.
There seemed from the remotest seat
 Of the white mountain waste,
To the soft flower beneath our feet,
 A magic circle traced, —
A spirit interfused around,
 A thrilling, silent life, —
To momentary peace it bound
 Our mortal nature's strife;
And still I felt the center of
 The magic circle there
Was one fair form that filled with love
 The lifeless atmosphere.

V

We paused beside the pools that lie
 Under the forest bough, —
Each seemed as 'twere a little sky
 Gulfed in a world below;
A firmament of purple light
 Which in the dark earth lay,
More boundless than the depth of night,
 And purer than the day —
In which the lovely forests grew,
 As in the upper air,
More perfect both in shape and hue
 Than any spreading there.
There lay the glade and neighbouring lawn,
 And through the dark green wood
The white sun twinkling like the dawn
 Out of a speckled cloud.
Sweet views which in our world above
 Can never well be seen,
Were imaged by the water's love

Of that fair forest green.
And all was interfused beneath
With an Elysian glow,
An atmosphere without a breath,
A softer day below.
Like one beloved the scene had lent
To the dark water's breast,
Its every leaf and lineament
With more than truth expressed;
Until an envious wind crept by,
Like an unwelcome thought,
Which from the mind's too faithful eye
Blots one dear image out.
Though thou art ever fair and kind,
The forests ever green,
Less oft is peace in Shelley's mind,
Than calm in waters, seen.

*1822*

# A DEFENCE OF POETRY

"The profoundest essay on the foundation of poetry in English" (W. B. Yeats): Shelley's *Defence* has been all this to many poets and students of poetry. We may well wonder, therefore, how a critic as learned as René Wellek can write, after quoting its final sentence: "It must be obvious today that this kind of defence of poetry defeats its own purpose." (*A History of Modern Criticism,* Vol. II, p. 125.) In part the mistake is as to this purpose and as to what Shelley is writing about. Many things can be named "poetry" — from a mass of reading matter upon which courses are given and examinations held, up to the creative, imaginative activities themselves. Shelley is writing about these last and what he has to say is again and again literally exact, as in that final sentence. If we understand his words aright, poets *are* "the unacknowledged legislators of the world." To affirm such things nobly enough protects and restores the connections of imagination with the reading matter, connections forever in danger from academic silt. It is these creative activities — not the printed pages nor the biographer's subjects — which are these "unacknowledged legislators." C. H. Baker has well pointed out how much the *Defence* and Shelley's highest poetry illumine one another. It is itself at many points "high poetry," not to be hastily assessed. "All high poetry is infinite; it is as the first acorn, which contained all oaks potentially."

Another part of the mistake is in accepting a passing fashion in criticism as a secured result ("must be obvious today"). The *Defence* has helped and will continue to help creative minds "to serve the power which is seated on the throne of their own soul" — that soul "Whose nature is its own divine control" (*PU,* IV.401). Its prime theme is a perennial concern, though its historical illustrations may in places seem, to some professorial eyes, uninformed.

Shelley's immediate purpose was to answer, philosophically, *The Four Ages of Poetry,* a diverting attack on poetic endeavor as an anachronism, written by his friend Peacock, whose portrait-caricature of Shelley as Scythrop in *Nightmare Abbey* had so delighted the poet. The attack aroused in him, he writes to Peacock, "the greatest possible desire to break a lance with you, within the lists of a magazine, in honour of my mistress *Urania,*" though he dubs himself "the knight of the shield of shadow and the lance of gossamere." As first written, it contained many references and allusions to *The Four Ages* and to Peacock. These were cut out before publication, but echoes of Peacock's phrasing as well as of Plato's *Ion* and *Symposium* and of Sidney's *Apologie* are frequent. A few sentences from *The Four Ages* will show why it stirred Shelley so deeply: "While the historian and the philosopher are advancing in, and accelerating, the progress of knowledge, the poet is wallowing in the rubbish of departed ignorance, and raking up the ashes of dead savages to find gewgaws and rattles for the grown babies of the age. . . . A poet in our times is a semi-barbarian in a civilized community. . . . In whatever degree poetry is cultivated, it must necessarily be to the neglect of some branch of useful study: and it is a lamentable spectacle to see minds capable of better things, running to seed in the specious indolence of these empty aimless mockeries of intellectual exertion." It was to counter his friend's chuckling onslaught that Shelley wrote the *Defence.*

## PART I

According to one mode of regarding those two classes of mental action, which are called reason and imagination, the former may be considered as mind contemplating the relations borne by one thought to another, however produced; and the latter, as mind acting upon those thoughts so as to colour them with its own light, and composing from them, as from elements, other thoughts, each containing within itself the principle of its own integrity.[1] The one [2] is the τὸ ποιεῖν, or the principle of synthesis, and has for its object those forms which are common to universal nature and existence itself; the other is the τὸ λογίζειν, or principle of analysis, and its action regards the relations of things, simply as relations; considering thoughts, not in their integral unity, but as the algebraical representations which conduct to certain general

A DEFENCE OF POETRY. **1. each . . . integrity**: Cf. "Nothing can permanently please which does not contain in itself the reason why it is so, and not otherwise." Coleridge, *Biographia Literaria,* XIV, p. 136, above. **2. one**: imagination. Cf. Sidney, "The Greeks called him a Poet, which name hath, as the most excellent, gone through other Languages. It commeth of this word *Poiein,* which is to make: wherein, I know not whether by lucke or wisedome, wee Englishmen have mette with the Greekes in calling him a maker."

results. Reason is the enumeration of quantities already known; imagination is the perception of the value of those quantities, both separately and as a whole. Reason respects the differences, and imagination the similitudes of things. Reason is to the imagination as the instrument to the agent, as the body to the spirit, as the shadow to the substance.

Poetry, in a general sense, may be defined to be 'the expression of the imagination': and poetry is connate with the origin of man. Man is an instrument over which a series of external and internal impressions are driven, like the alternations of an ever-changing wind over an Aeolian lyre, which move it by their motion to ever-changing melody. But there is a principle within the human being, and perhaps within all sentient beings, which acts otherwise than in the lyre, and produces not melody alone, but harmony, by an internal adjustment of the sounds or motions thus excited to the impressions which excite them. It is as if the lyre could accommodate its chords to the motions of that which strikes them, in a determined proportion of sound; even as the musician can accommodate his voice to the sound of the lyre. A child at play by itself will express its delight by its voice and motions; and every inflexion of tone and every gesture will bear exact relation to a corresponding antitype in the pleasurable impressions which awakened it; it will be the reflected image of that impression; and as the lyre trembles and sounds after the wind has died away, so the child seeks, by prolonging in its voice and motions the duration of the effect, to prolong also a consciousness of the cause. In relation to the objects which delight a child, these expressions are, what poetry is to higher objects. The savage (for the savage is to ages what the child is to years) expresses the emotions produced in him by surrounding objects in a similar manner; and language and gesture, together with plastic or pictorial imitation, become the image of the combined effect of those objects, and of his apprehension of them. Man in society, with all his passions and his pleasures, next becomes the object of the passions and pleasures of man; an additional class of emotions produces an augmented treasure of expressions; and language, gesture, and the imitative arts, become at once the representation and the medium, the pencil and the picture, the chisel and the statue, the chord and the harmony. The social sympathies, or those laws from which, as from its elements, society results, begin to develop themselves from the moment that two human beings coexist; the future is contained within the present, as the plant within the seed; and equality, diversity, unity, contrast, mutual dependence, become the principles alone capable of affording the motives according to which the will of a social being is determined to action, inasmuch as he is social; and constitute pleasure in sensation, virtue in sentiment, beauty in art, truth in reasoning, and love in the intercourse of kind. Hence men, even in the infancy of society, observe a certain order in their words and actions, distinct from that of the objects and the impressions represented by them, all expression being subject to the laws of that from which it proceeds. But let us dismiss those more general considerations which might involve an inquiry into the principles of society itself, and restrict our view to the manner in which the imagination is expressed upon its forms.

In the youth of the world, men dance and sing and imitate natural objects, observing in these actions, as in all others, a certain rhythm or order. And, although all men observe a similar, they observe not the same order, in the motions of the dance, in the melody of the song, in the combinations of language, in the series of their imitations of natural objects. For there is a certain order or rhythm belonging to each of these classes of mimetic representation, from which the hearer and the spectator receive an intenser and purer pleasure than from any other: the sense of an approximation to this order has been called taste by modern writers. Every man in the infancy of art observes an order which approximates more or less closely to that from which this highest delight results: but the diversity is not sufficiently marked, as that its gradations should be sensible, except in those instances where the predominance of this faculty of approximation to the beautiful (for so we may be permitted to name the relation between this highest pleasure and its cause) is very great. Those in whom it exists in excess are poets, in the most universal sense of the word; and the pleasure resulting from the manner in which they express the influence of society or nature upon their own minds, communicates itself to others, and gathers a sort of reduplication from that community. Their language is vitally metaphorical; that is, it marks the before unapprehended relations of things and perpetuates their apprehension, until the words which represent them become, through time, signs for portions or classes of thoughts[3] instead of pictures of integral thoughts; and then if no new poets should arise to create afresh the associations which have been thus disorganized, language will be dead to all the nobler purposes of human intercourse. These similitudes or relations are finely said by Lord Bacon to be 'the same footsteps of nature impressed upon the various subjects of the world';[4] and he considers the faculty which perceives them as the storehouse of axioms common to all knowledge. In the infancy of society every author is necessarily a poet, because language itself is poetry; and to be a poet is to apprehend the true and the beautiful, in a word, the good which exists in the relation, subsisting, first between existence and perception, and secondly between perception and expression. Every original language near to its source is in itself the chaos of a cyclic poem: the copiousness of lexicography and the distinctions of grammar are the works of a later age, and are merely the catalogue and the form of the creations of poetry.

But poets, or those who imagine and express this indestructible order, are not only the authors of language and of music, of the dance, and architecture, and statuary, and painting; they are the institutors of laws, and the founders of civil society, and the inventors of the arts of life, and the teachers, who draw into a certain propinquity with the beautiful and the true, that partial apprehension of the agencies of the invisible world which is called religion.[5] Hence all original religions are allegorical, or susceptible of allegory, and, like Janus,[6] have a double face of false and true. Poets, according to the circumstances of the age and nation in which they appeared, were called, in the earlier epochs of the world, legislators, or prophets: a poet essentially comprises and unites both these characters. For he not only beholds intensely the present as it is, and discovers those laws according to which present things ought to be ordered, but he beholds the future in the present, and his thoughts are the germs of the flower and the fruit of latest time. Not that I assert poets to be prophets in the gross sense of the word, or that they can foretell the form as surely as they foreknow the spirit of events: such is the pretence of superstition, which would make poetry an attribute of prophecy, rather than prophecy an attribute of poetry. A poet participates in the eternal, the infinite, and the one; as far as relates to his conceptions, time and place and number are not. The grammatical forms which express the moods of time, and the difference of persons, and the distinction of place, are convertible with respect to the highest poetry without injuring it as poetry; and the choruses of Aeschylus, and the book of *Job,* and Dante's *Paradise,* would afford, more than any other writings, examples of this fact, if the limits of this essay did not forbid citation. The creations of sculpture, painting, and music, are illustrations still more decisive.

Language, colour, form, and religious and civil habits of action, are all the instruments and materials of poetry; they may be called poetry by that figure of speech which considers the effect as a synonym of the cause.[7] But poetry in a more restricted sense expresses those arrangements of language, and especially metrical language, which are created by that imperial faculty, whose throne is curtained within the invisible nature of man. And this springs from the nature itself of language, which is a more direct representation of the actions and passions of our internal being, and is susceptible of more various and delicate combinations, than colour, form, or motion, and is more plastic and obedient to the control of that faculty of which it is the creation. For language is arbitrarily produced by the imagination, and has relation to thoughts alone; but all other materials, instruments, and conditions of art, have relations among each other, which limit and interpose between conception and expression. The former is as a mirror which reflects, the latter as a cloud which enfeebles, the light of which both are mediums of communication. Hence the fame of sculptors, painters, and musicians, although the intrinsic powers of the great masters of these arts may yield in no degree to that of those who have employed language as the hieroglyphic of their thoughts, has never equalled that of poets in the restricted sense of the term; as two performers of equal skill will produce unequal effects from a guitar and a harp. The fame of legislators and founders of religions, so long as their institutions last, alone seems to exceed that of poets in the restricted sense; but it can scarcely be

3. **thoughts:** concepts merely, abstract notions. 4. **'the . . . world':** *De Augment. Scient.,* i., lib. iii [Shelley's note]. 5. **But . . . religion:** all this by virtue of the definition following "and to be a poet" in the preceding paragraph. Shelley is here following Plato, "The exercise of every inventive art is poetry, and all such artists poets" *Symposium,* Shelley's translation. 6. **Janus:** a Roman god represented as looking before and behind.

7. **effect . . . cause:** being, by Shelley's definition, produced by poets.

a question, whether, if we deduct the celebrity which their flattery of the gross opinions of the vulgar usually conciliates, together with [8] that which belonged to them in their higher character of poets, any excess will remain.

We have thus circumscribed the word poetry within the limits of that art which is the most familiar and the most perfect expression of the faculty itself. It is necessary, however, to make the circle still narrower, and to determine the distinction between measured and unmeasured language; for the popular division into prose and verse is inadmissible in accurate philosophy.

Sounds as well as thoughts have relation both between each other and towards that which they represent, and a perception of the order of those relations has always been found connected with a perception of the order of the relations of thoughts. Hence the language of poets has ever affected a certain uniform and harmonious recurrence of sound, without which it were not poetry, and which is scarcely less indispensable to the communication of its influence, than the words themselves, without reference to that peculiar order. Hence the vanity of translation; it were as wise to cast a violet into a crucible that you might discover the formal principle of its colour and odour, as seek to transfuse from one language into another the creations of a poet. The plant must spring again from its seed, or it will bear no flower — and this is the burthen of the curse of Babel.

An observation of the regular mode of the recurrence of harmony in the language of poetical minds, together with its relation to music, produced metre, or a certain system of traditional forms of harmony and language. Yet it is by no means essential that a poet should accommodate his language to this traditional form, so that the harmony, which is its spirit, be observed. The practice is indeed convenient and popular, and to be preferred, especially in such composition as includes much action: but every great poet must inevitably innovate upon the example of his predecessors in the exact structure of his peculiar versification. The distinction between poets and prose writers is a vulgar error. The distinction between philosophers and poets has been anticipated. Plato was essentially a poet — the truth and splendour of his imagery, and the melody of his language, are the most intense that it is possible to conceive. He rejected the measure of the epic, dramatic, and lyrical forms, because he sought to kindle a harmony in thoughts divested of shape and action, and he forbore to invent any regular plan of rhythm which would include, under determinate forms, the varied pauses of his style. Cicero sought to imitate the cadence of his periods, but with little success. Lord Bacon was a poet.[9] His language has a sweet and majestic rhythm, which satisfies the sense, no less than the almost superhuman wisdom of his philosophy satisfies the intellect; it is a strain which distends, and then bursts the circumference of the reader's mind, and pours itself forth together with it into the universal element with which it has perpetual sympathy. All the authors of revolutions in opinion are not only necessarily poets as they are inventors, nor even as their words unveil the permanent analogy of things by images which participate in the life of truth; but as their periods are harmonious and rhythmical, and contain in themselves the elements of verse; being the echo of the eternal music. Nor are those supreme poets, who have employed traditional forms of rhythm on account of the form and action of their subjects, less capable of perceiving and teaching the truth of things, than those who have omitted that form. Shakespeare, Dante, and Milton (to confine ourselves to modern writers) are philosophers of the very loftiest power.

A poem is the very image of life expressed in its eternal truth. There is this difference between a story and a poem, that a story is a catalogue of detached facts, which have no other connexion than time, place, circumstance, cause and effect; the other is the creation of actions according to the unchangeable forms of human nature, as existing in the mind of the Creator, which is itself the image of all other minds. The one is partial, and applies only to a definite period of time, and a certain combination of events which can never again recur; the other is universal, and contains within itself the germ of a relation to whatever motives or actions have place in the possible varieties of human nature. Time, which destroys the beauty and the use of the story of particular facts, stripped of the poetry which should invest them, augments that of poetry, and for ever develops new and wonderful applications

8. **together with:** Shelley's point would have been clearer if he had written "from."

9. **Lord . . . poet:** See the *Filum Labyrinthi*, and the *Essay on Death* particularly [S]. It may be added that it was Bacon who called epitomies the moths of history, in *The Advancement of Learning*, II.ii.5.

of the eternal truth which it contains. Hence epitomes have been called the moths of just history; they eat out the poetry of it. A story of particular facts is as a mirror which obscures and distorts that which should be beautiful: poetry is a mirror which makes beautiful that which is distorted.

The parts of a composition may be poetical, without the composition as a whole being a poem. A single sentence may be considered as a whole, though it may be found in the midst of a series of unassimilated portions: a single word even may be a spark of inextinguishable thought. And thus all the great historians, Herodotus, Plutarch, Livy, were poets; and although the plan of these writers, especially that of Livy, restrained them from developing this faculty in its highest degree, they made copious and ample amends for their subjection, by filling all the interstices of their subjects with living images.

Having determined what is poetry, and who are poets, let us proceed to estimate its effects upon society.

Poetry is ever accompanied with pleasure: all spirits on which it falls open themselves to receive the wisdom which is mingled with its delight. In the infancy of the world, neither poets themselves nor their auditors are fully aware of the excellence of poetry: for it acts in a divine and unapprehended manner, beyond and above consciousness; and it is reserved for future generations to contemplate and measure the mighty cause and effect in all the strength and splendour of their union. Even in modern times, no living poet ever arrived at the fullness of his fame; the jury which sits in judgement upon a poet, belonging as he does to all time, must be composed of his peers: it must be impanelled by Time from the selectest of the wise of many generations. A poet is a nightingale, who sits in darkness and sings to cheer its own solitude with sweet sounds; his auditors are as men entranced by the melody of an unseen musician, who feel that they are moved and softened, yet know not whence or why. The poems of Homer and his contemporaries were the delight of infant Greece; they were the elements of that social system which is the column upon which all succeeding civilization has reposed. Homer embodied the ideal perfection of his age in human character; nor can we doubt that those who read his verses were awakened to an ambition of becoming like to Achilles, Hector, and Ulysses: the truth and beauty of friendship, patriotism, and persevering devotion to an object, were unveiled to the depths in these immortal creations: the sentiments of the auditors must have been refined and enlarged by a sympathy with such great and lovely impersonations, until from admiring they imitated, and from imitation they identified themselves with the objects of their admiration. Nor let it be objected, that these characters are remote from moral perfection, and that they can by no means be considered as edifying patterns for general imitation. Every epoch, under names more or less specious, has deified its peculiar errors; Revenge is the naked idol of the worship of a semibarbarous age; and Self-deceit is the veiled image of unknown evil, before which luxury and satiety lie prostrate. But a poet considers the vices of his contemporaries as a temporary dress in which his creations must be arrayed, and which cover without concealing the eternal proportions of their beauty. An epic or dramatic personage is understood to wear them around his soul, as he may the ancient armour or the modern uniform around his body; whilst it is easy to conceive a dress more graceful than either. The beauty of the internal nature cannot be so far concealed by its accidental vesture, but that the spirit of its form shall communicate itself to the very disguise, and indicate the shape it hides from the manner in which it is worn. A majestic form and graceful motions will express themselves through the most barbarous and tasteless costume. Few poets of the highest class have chosen to exhibit the beauty of their conceptions in its naked truth and splendour; and it is doubtful whether the alloy of costume, habit, &c., be not necessary to temper this planetary music for mortal ears.

The whole objection, however, of the immorality of poetry rests upon a misconception of the manner in which poetry acts to produce the moral improvement of man. Ethical science arranges the elements which poetry has created, and propounds schemes and proposes examples of civil and domestic life: nor is it for want of admirable doctrines that men hate, and despise, and censure, and deceive, and subjugate one another. But poetry acts in another and diviner manner. It awakens and enlarges the mind itself by rendering it the receptacle of a thousand unapprehended combinations of thought. Poetry lifts the veil from the hidden beauty of the world, and makes familiar objects be as if they were not familiar; it reproduces all that it represents, and the impersonations clothed in its Elysian light stand thenceforward in the minds of those who have once contemplated them as memorials of that gentle and exalted content[10] which extends itself over all thoughts and actions with which it coexists. The great secret of morals is love; or a going out of our own nature, and an identification of ourselves with the beautiful which exists in thought, action, or person, not our own. A man, to be greatly good, must imagine intensely and comprehensively; he must put himself in the place of another and of many others; the pains and pleasures of his species must become his own. The great instrument of moral good is the imagination; and poetry administers to the effect by acting upon the cause. Poetry enlarges the circumference of the imagination by replenishing it with thoughts of ever new delight, which have the power of attracting and assimilating to their own nature all other thoughts, and which form new intervals and interstices whose void for ever craves fresh food. Poetry strengthens the faculty which is the organ of the moral nature of man, in the same manner as exercise strengthens a limb. A poet therefore would do ill to embody his own conceptions of right and wrong, which are usually those of his place and time, in his poetical creations, which participate in neither. By this assumption of the inferior office of interpreting the effect, in which perhaps after all he might acquit himself but imperfectly, he would resign a glory in a participation in the cause. There was little danger that Homer, or any of the eternal poets, should have so far misunderstood themselves as to have abdicated this throne of their widest dominion. Those in whom the poetical faculty, though great, is less intense, as Euripides, Lucan, Tasso, Spenser, have frequently affected a moral aim, and the effect of their poetry is diminished in exact proportion to the degree in which they compel us to advert to this purpose.

Homer and the cyclic[11] poets were followed at a certain interval by the dramatic and lyrical poets of Athens, who flourished contemporaneously with all that is most perfect in the kindred expressions of the poetical faculty; architecture, painting, music, the dance, sculpture, philosophy, and, we may add, the forms of civil life. For although the scheme of Athenian society was deformed by many imperfections[12] which the poetry existing in chivalry and Christianity has erased from the habits and institutions of modern Europe; yet never at any other period has so much energy, beauty, and virtue, been developed; never was blind strength and stubborn form so disciplined and rendered subject to the will of man, or that will less repugnant to the dictates of the beautiful and the true, as during the century which preceded the death of Socrates. Of no other epoch in the history of our species have we records and fragments stamped so visibly with the image of the divinity in man. But it is poetry alone, in form, in action, or in language, which has rendered this epoch memorable above all others, and the storehouse of examples to everlasting time. For written poetry existed at that epoch simultaneously with the other arts, and it is an idle inquiry to demand which gave and which received the light, which all, as from a common focus, have scattered over the darkest periods of succeeding time. We know no more of cause and effect than a constant conjunction of events: poetry is ever found to coexist with whatever other arts contribute to the happiness and perfection of man. I appeal to what has already been established to distinguish between the cause and the effect.

It was at the period here adverted to, that the drama had its birth; and however a succeeding writer may have equalled or surpassed those few great specimens of the Athenian drama which have been preserved to us, it is indisputable that the art itself never was understood or practised according to the true philosophy of it, as at Athens. For the Athenians employed language, action, music, painting, the dance, and religious institutions, to produce a common effect in the representation of the highest idealisms of passion and of power; each division in the art was made perfect in its kind by artists of the most consummate skill, and was disciplined into a beautiful proportion and unity one towards the other. On the modern stage a few only of the elements capable of expressing the image of the poet's conception are employed at once. We have tragedy without music and dancing; and music and dancing without the highest impersonations of which they are the fit accompaniment, and both without religion and solemnity. Religious institution has indeed been usually banished from the stage. Our system of divesting the actor's face of a

10. **content**: fulfillment. 11. **Cyclic poets**: poets of the cycle or body of epic poetry of which the *Iliad* and *Odyssey* alone survive.

12. **imperfections**: notably, as Shelley elsewhere insists, slavery and the inferior status of women.

mask, on which the many expressions appropriated to his dramatic character might be moulded into one permanent and unchanging expression, is favourable only to a partial and inharmonious effect; it is fit for nothing but a monologue, where all the attention may be directed to some great master of ideal mimicry. The modern practice of blending comedy with tragedy, though liable to great abuse in point of practice, is undoubtedly an extension of the dramatic circle; but the comedy should be as in *King Lear,* universal, ideal, and sublime. It is perhaps the intervention of this principle which determines the balance in favour of *King Lear* against the *Oedipus Tyrannus* or the *Agamemnon,* or, if you will, the trilogies with which they are connected; unless the intense power of the choral poetry, especially that of the latter, should be considered as restoring the equilibrium. *King Lear,* if it can sustain this comparison, may be judged to be the most perfect specimen of the dramatic art existing in the world; in spite of the narrow conditions to which the poet was subjected by the ignorance of the philosophy of the drama which has prevailed in modern Europe. Calderon,[13] in his religious *Autos,* has attempted to fulfil some of the high conditions of dramatic representation neglected by Shakespeare; such as the establishing a relation between the drama and religion, and the accommodating them to music and dancing; but he omits the observation of conditions still more important, and more is lost than gained by the substitution of the rigidly-defined and ever-repeated idealisms of a distorted superstition for the living impersonations of the truth of human passion.

But I digress. — The connexion of scenic exhibitions with the improvement or corruption of the manners of men, has been universally recognized: in other words, the presence or absence of poetry in its most perfect and universal form, has been found to be connected with good and evil in conduct or habit. The corruption which has been imputed to the drama as an effect, begins, when the poetry employed in its constitution ends: I appeal to the history of manners whether the periods of the growth of the one and the decline of the other have not corresponded with an exactness equal to any example of moral cause and effect.

The drama at Athens, or wheresoever else it may have approached to its perfection, ever co-existed with the moral and intellectual greatness of the age. The tragedies of the Athenian poets are as mirrors in which the spectator beholds himself, under a thin disguise of circumstance, stript of all but that ideal perfection and energy which every one feels to be the internal type of all that he loves, admires, and would become. The imagination is enlarged by a sympathy with pains and passions so mighty, that they distend in their conception the capacity of that by which they are conceived; the good affections are strengthened by pity, indignation, terror, and sorrow; and an exalted calm is prolonged from the satiety of this high exercise of them into the tumult of familiar life:[14] even crime is disarmed of half its horror and all its contagion by being represented as the fatal consequence of the unfathomable agencies of nature; error is thus divested of its wilfulness; men can no longer cherish it as the creation of their choice. In a drama of the highest order there is little food for censure or hatred; it teaches rather self-knowledge and self-respect. Neither the eye nor the mind can see itself, unless reflected upon that which it resembles. The drama, so long as it continues to express poetry, is as a prismatic and many-sided mirror, which collects the brightest rays[15] of human nature and divides and reproduces them from the simplicity of these elementary forms, and touches them with majesty and beauty, and multiplies all that it reflects, and endows it with the power of propagating its like wherever it may fall.

But in periods of the decay of social life, the drama sympathizes with that decay. Tragedy becomes a cold imitation of the form of the great masterpieces of antiquity, divested of all harmonious accompaniment of the kindred arts; and often the very form misunderstood, or a weak attempt to teach certain doctrines, which the writer considers as moral truths; and which are usually no more than specious flatteries of some gross vice or weakness, with which the author, in common with his auditors, is infected. Hence what has been called the classical and domestic drama. Addison's *Cato* is a specimen of the one; and would it were not

13. **Calderon**: Pedro Calderón de la Barca (1600–1681), Spanish poet and dramatist. The *Autos sacramentales* are allegorical plays, of which he is the master. Shelley translated scenes from his drama, *El Magico Prodigioso.*

14. **The imagination . . . life**: Shelley's comment on Aristotle's doctrine of the catharsis of tragedy: "effecting, through pity and terror, the purgation of such passions," *Poetics*, 6. Cf. the last line of Milton's *Samson Agonistes:* "And calm of mind, all passion spent" (Vol. I, p. 522). 15. **as . . . rays**: Cf. *PU*, III.iii.53; and Intro., p. 240, above.

superfluous to cite examples of the other! To such purposes poetry cannot be made subservient. Poetry is a sword of lightning, ever unsheathed, which consumes the scabbard that would contain it. And thus we observe that all dramatic writings of this nature are unimaginative in a singular degree; they affect sentiment and passion, which, divested of imagination, are other names for caprice and appetite. The period in our own history of the grossest degradation of the drama is the reign of Charles II, when all forms in which poetry had been accustomed to be expressed became hymns to the triumph of kingly power over liberty and virtue. Milton stood alone illuminating an age unworthy of him. At such periods the calculating principle pervades all the forms of dramatic exhibition, and poetry ceases to be expressed upon them. Comedy loses its ideal universality: wit succeeds to humour; we laugh from self-complacency and triumph, instead of pleasure; malignity, sarcasm, and contempt, succeed to sympathetic merriment; we hardly laugh, but we smile. Obscenity, which is ever blasphemy against the divine beauty in life, becomes, from the very veil which it assumes, more active if less disgusting: it is a monster for which the corruption of society for ever brings forth new food, which it devours in secret.

The drama being that form under which a greater number of modes of expression of poetry are susceptible of being combined than any other, the connexion of poetry and social good is more observable in the drama than in whatever other form. And it is indisputable that the highest perfection of human society has ever corresponded with the highest dramatic excellence; and that the corruption or the extinction of the drama in a nation where it has once flourished, is a mark of a corruption of manners, and an extinction of the energies which sustain the soul of social life. But, as Machiavelli says of political institutions, that life may be preserved and renewed, if men should arise capable of bringing back the drama to its principles. And this is true with respect to poetry in its most extended sense: all language, institution and form, require not only to be produced but to be sustained: the office and character of a poet participates in the divine nature as regards providence, no less than as regards creation.

. . . . . . . . .

About seven pages of a historical sketch are here omitted as of less permanent interest.

. . . . . . . .

Dante and Milton were both deeply penetrated with the ancient religion of the civilised world; and its spirit exists in their poetry probably in the same proportion as its forms survived in the unreformed worship of modern Europe. The one preceded and the other followed the Reformation at almost equal intervals. Dante was the first religious reformer, and Luther surpassed him rather in the rudeness and acrimony, than in the boldness of his censures of papal usurpation. Dante was the first awakener of entranced Europe; he created a language, in itself music and persuasion, out of a chaos of inharmonious barbarisms. He was the congregator of those great spirits who presided over the resurrection of learning; the Lucifer of that starry flock which in the thirteenth century shone forth from republican Italy, as from a heaven, into the darkness of the benighted world. His very words are instinct with spirit; each is as a spark, a burning atom of inextinguishable thought; and many yet lie covered in the ashes of their birth, and pregnant with the lightning which has yet found no conductor. All high poetry is infinite; it is as the first acorn, which contained all oaks potentially. Veil after veil may be undrawn, and the inmost naked beauty of the meaning never exposed. A great poem is a fountain for ever overflowing with the waters of wisdom and delight; and after one person and one age has exhausted all its divine effluence which their peculiar relations enable them to share, another and yet another succeeds, and new relations are ever developed, the source of an unforeseen and an unconceived delight.

The age immediately succeeding to that of Dante, Petrarch, and Boccaccio, was characterised by a revival of painting, sculpture, and architecture. Chaucer caught the sacred inspiration, and the superstructure of English literature is based upon the materials of Italian invention.

But let us not be betrayed from a defence into a critical history of poetry and its influence on society. Be it enough to have pointed out the effects of poets, in the large and true sense of the word, upon their own and all succeeding times.

But poets have been challenged to resign the civic crown to reasoners and mechanists, on another plea. It is admitted that the exercise of the imagination is most delightful, but it is alleged that that of reason is more useful. Let us examine as the grounds of this distinction, what is here meant by utility.

Pleasure or good, in a general sense, is that which the consciousness of a sensitive and intelligent being seeks, and in which, when found, it acquiesces. There are two kinds of pleasure, one durable, universal and permanent; the other transitory and particular. Utility may either express the means of producing the former or the latter. In the former sense, whatever strengthens and purifies the affections, enlarges the imagination, and adds spirit to sense, is useful. But a narrower meaning may be assigned to the word utility, confining it to express that which banishes the importunity of the wants of our animal nature, the surrounding men with security of life, the dispersing the grosser delusions of superstition, and the conciliating such a degree of mutual forbearance among men as may consist with the motives of personal advantage.

Undoubtedly the promoters of utility, in this limited sense, have their appointed office in society. They follow the footsteps of poets, and copy the sketches of their creations into the book of common life. They make space, and give time. Their exertions are of the highest value, so long as they confine their administration of the concerns of the inferior powers of our nature within the limits due to the superior ones. But whilst the sceptic destroys gross superstitions, let him spare to deface, as some of the French writers have defaced, the eternal truths charactered upon the imaginations of men. Whilst the mechanist abridges, and the political economist combines labour, let them beware that their speculations, for want of correspondence with those first principles which belong to the imagination, do not tend, as they have in modern England, to exasperate at once the extremes of luxury and want. They have exemplified the saying, 'To him that hath, more shall be given; and from him that hath not, the little that he hath shall be taken away.'[16] The rich have become richer, and the poor have become poorer; and the vessel of the state is driven between the Scylla and Charybdis of anarchy and despotism. Such are the effects which must ever flow from an unmitigated exercise of the calculating faculty.

It is difficult to define pleasure in its highest sense; the definition involving a number of apparent paradoxes. For, from an inexplicable defect of harmony in the constitution of human nature, the pain of the inferior is frequently connected with the pleasures of the superior portions of our being. Sorrow, terror, anguish, despair itself, are often the chosen expressions of an approximation to the highest good. Our sympathy in tragic fiction depends on this principle; tragedy delights by affording a shadow of the pleasure which exists in pain. This is the source also of the melancholy which is inseparable from the sweetest melody. The pleasure that is in sorrow is sweeter than the pleasure of pleasure itself. And hence the saying, 'It is better to go to the house of mourning, than to the house of mirth.'[17] Not that this highest species of pleasure is necessarily linked with pain. The delight of love and friendship, the ecstasy of the admiration of nature, the joy of the perception and still more of the creation of poetry, is often wholly unalloyed.

The production and assurance of pleasure in this highest sense is true utility. Those who produce and preserve this pleasure are poets or poetical philosophers.

The exertions of Locke, Hume, Gibbon, Voltaire, Rousseau,[18] and their disciples, in favour of oppressed and deluded humanity, are entitled to the gratitude of mankind. Yet it is easy to calculate the degree of moral and intellectual improvement which the world would have exhibited, had they never lived. A little more nonsense would have been talked for a century or two; and perhaps a few more men, women, and children, burnt as heretics. We might not at this moment have been congratulating each other on the abolition of the Inquisition in Spain. But it exceeds all imagination to conceive what would have been the moral condition of the world if neither Dante, Petrarch, Boccaccio, Chaucer, Shakespeare, Calderon, Lord Bacon, nor Milton, had ever existed; if Raphael and Michael Angelo had never been born; if the Hebrew poetry had never been translated; if a revival of the study of Greek literature had never taken place; if no monuments of ancient sculpture had been handed down to us; and if the poetry of the religion of the ancient world had been extinguished together with its belief. The human mind could never, except by the intervention of these excitements, have been awakened to the invention of the grosser sciences, and that application of analytical reasoning to the aberrations of society, which it is now attempted to exalt over the direct

16. **'To . . . away'**: See Mark 4:25.

17. **'It . . . mirth'**: See Eccles. 7:2.

18. **Rousseau**: Although Rousseau has been thus classed, he was essentially a poet. The others, even Voltaire, were mere reasoners [S].

expression of the inventive and creative faculty itself.

We have more moral, political and historical wisdom, than we know how to reduce into practice; we have more scientific and economical knowledge than can be accommodated to the just distribution of the produce which it multiplies. The poetry in these systems of thought, is concealed by the accumulation of facts and calculating processes. There is no want of knowledge respecting what is wisest and best in morals, government, and political economy, or at least, what is wiser and better than what men now practise and endure. But we let '*I dare not* wait upon *I would,* like the poor cat in the adage.'[19] We want the creative faculty to imagine that which we know; we want the generous impulse to act that which we imagine; we want the poetry of life: our calculations have outrun conception; we have eaten more than we can digest. The cultivation of those sciences which have enlarged the limits of the empire of man over the external world, has, for want of the poetical faculty, proportionally circumscribed those of the internal world; and man, having enslaved the elements, remains himself a slave. To what but a cultivation of the mechanical arts in a degree disproportioned to the presence of the creative faculty, which is the basis of all knowledge, is to be attributed the abuse of all invention for abridging and combining labour, to the exasperation of the inequality of mankind? From what other cause has it arisen that the discoveries which should have lightened, have added a weight to the curse imposed on Adam? Poetry, and the principle of Self, of which money is the visible incarnation, are the God and Mammon of the world.

The functions of the poetical faculty are two-fold; by one it creates new materials of knowledge and power and pleasure; by the other it engenders in the mind a desire to reproduce and arrange them according to a certain rhythm and order which may be called the beautiful and the good. The cultivation of poetry is never more to be desired than at periods when, from an excess of the selfish and calculating principle, the accumulation of the materials of external life exceed the quantity of the power of assimilating them to the internal laws of human nature. The body has then become too unwieldy for that which animates it.

Poetry is indeed something divine. It is at once the centre and circumference of knowledge; it is that which comprehends all science, and that to which all science must be referred. It is at the same time the root and blossom of all other systems of thought; it is that from which all spring, and that which adorns all; and that which, if blighted, denies the fruit and the seed, and withholds from the barren world the nourishment and the succession of the scions of the tree of life. It is the perfect and consummate surface and bloom of all things; it is as the odour and the colour of the rose to the texture of the elements which compose it, as the form and splendour of unfaded beauty to the secrets of anatomy and corruption. What were virtue, love, patriotism, friendship — what were the scenery of this beautiful universe which we inhabit; what were our consolations on this side of the grave — and what were our aspirations beyond it, if poetry did not ascend to bring light and fire from those eternal regions where the owl-winged faculty of calculation dare not ever soar? Poetry is not like reasoning, a power to be exerted according to the determination of the will. A man cannot say, 'I will compose poetry.' The greatest poet even cannot say it; for the mind in creation is as a fading coal, which some invisible influence, like an inconstant wind, awakens to transitory brightness; this power arises from within, like the colour of a flower which fades and changes as it is developed, and the conscious portions of our natures are unprophetic either of its approach or its departure. Could this influence be durable in its original purity and force, it is impossible to predict the greatness of the results; but when composition begins, inspiration is already on the decline, and the most glorious poetry that has ever been communicated to the world is probably a feeble shadow of the original conceptions of the poet. I appeal to the greatest poets of the present day, whether it is not an error to assert that the finest passages of poetry are produced by labour and study. The toil and the delay recommended by critics, can be justly interpreted to mean no more than a careful observation of the inspired moments, and an artificial connexion of the spaces between their suggestions by the intertexture of conventional expressions; a necessity only imposed by the limitedness of the poetical faculty itself; for Milton conceived the *Paradise Lost* as a whole before he executed it in portions. We have his own authority also for the muse having 'dictated' to him the 'unpremeditated song.'[20] And

19. **'I . . . adage':** *Macbeth,* I.vii.44.

20. **unpremeditated song:** *Paradise Lost,* IX.21–24.

let this be an answer to those who would allege the fifty-six various readings of the first line of the *Orlando Furioso.* Compositions so produced are to poetry what mosaic is to painting. This instinct and intuition of the poetical faculty is still more observable in the plastic and pictorial arts; a great statue or picture grows under the power of the artist as a child in the mother's womb; and the very mind which directs the hands in formation is incapable of accounting to itself for the origin, the gradations, or the media of the process.

Poetry is the record of the best and happiest moments of the happiest and best minds. We are aware of evanescent visitations of thought and feeling sometimes associated with place or person, sometimes regarding our own mind alone, and always arising unforeseen and departing unbidden, but elevating and delightful beyond all expression: so that even in the desire and regret they leave, there cannot but be pleasure, participating as it does in the nature of its object. It is as it were the interpenetration of a diviner nature [21] through our own; but its footsteps are like those of a wind over the sea, which the coming calm erases, and whose traces remain only, as on the wrinkled sand which paves it. These and corresponding conditions of being are experienced principally by those of the most delicate sensibility and the most enlarged imagination; and the state of mind produced by them is at war with every base desire. The enthusiasm of virtue, love, patriotism, and friendship, is essentially linked with such emotions; and whilst they last, self appears as what it is, an atom to a universe. Poets are not only subject to these experiences as spirits of the most refined organization, but they can colour all that they combine with the evanescent hues of this ethereal world; a word, a trait in the representation of a scene or a passion, will touch the enchanted chord, and reanimate, in those who have ever experienced these emotions, the sleeping, the cold, the buried image of the past. Poetry thus makes immortal all that is best and most beautiful in the world; it arrests the vanishing apparitions which haunt the interlunations of life, and veiling them, or in language or in form, sends them forth among mankind, bearing sweet news of kindred joy to those with whom their sisters abide—abide, because there is no portal of expression from the caverns of the spirit which they inhabit into the universe of things. Poetry redeems from decay the visitations of the divinity in man.

Poetry turns all things to loveliness; it exalts the beauty of that which is most beautiful, and it adds beauty to that which is most deformed; it marries exultation and horror, grief and pleasure, eternity and change; it subdues to union under its light yoke, all irreconcilable things. It transmutes all that it touches, and every form moving within the radiance of its presence is changed by wondrous sympathy to an incarnation of the spirit which it breathes: its secret alchemy turns to potable gold the poisonous waters which flow from death through life; it strips the veil of familiarity from the world, and lays bare the naked and sleeping beauty, which is the spirit of its forms.

All things exist as they are perceived; at least in relation to the percipient. "The mind is its own place, and of itself can make a heaven of hell, a hell of heaven.' [22] But poetry defeats the curse which binds us to be subjected to the accident of surrounding impressions. And whether it spreads its own figured curtain, or withdraws life's dark veil from before the scene of things, it equally creates for us a being within our being. It makes us the inhabitants of a world to which the familiar world is a chaos. It reproduces the common universe of which we are portions and percipients, and it purges from our inward sight the film of familiarity [23] which obscures from us the wonder of our being. It compels us to feel that which we perceive, and to imagine that which we know. It creates anew the universe, after it has been annihilated in our minds by the recurrence of impressions blunted by reiteration. It justifies the bold and true words of Tasso: *Non merita nome di creatore, se non Iddio ed il Poeta.*[24]

A poet, as he is the author to others of the highest wisdom, pleasure, virtue and glory, so he ought personally to be the happiest, the best, the wisest, and the most illustrious of men. As to his glory, let time be challenged to declare whether the fame of any other institutor of human life be comparable

**21. diviner nature:** Cf. "A Poet is indeed a thing etherially light, winged, and sacred; nor can he compose any thing worth calling poetry until he becomes inspired, and, as it were, mad, or whilst any reason remains in him," Plato, *Ion,* Shelley's translation. **22. 'The . . . heaven':** See *Paradise Lost,* I.254. **23. film of familiarity:** Cf. "by awakening the mind's attention from the lethargy of custom and directing it to the loveliness and the wonders of the world before us; an inexhaustible treasure, but for which, in consequence of the film of familiarity and selfish solicitude we have eyes, yet see not, ears that hear not, and hearts that neither feel nor understand" (Coleridge, *Biographia Literaria,* XIV, p. 135, above). **24. *Non . . . Poeta:*** No one de-to that of a poet. That he is the wisest, the happiest, and the best, inasmuch as he is a poet, is equally incontrovertible: the greatest poets have been men of the most spotless virtue, of the most consummate prudence, and, if we would look into the interior of their lives, the most fortunate of men: and the exceptions, as they regard those who possessed the poetic faculty in a high yet inferior degree, will be found on consideration to confine rather than destroy the rule. Let us for a moment stoop to the arbitration of popular breath, and usurping and uniting in our own persons the incompatible characters of accuser, witness, judge, and executioner, let us decide without trial, testimony, or form, that certain motives of those who are 'there sitting where we dare not soar',[25] are reprehensible. Let us assume that Homer was a drunkard, that Virgil was a flatterer, that Horace was a coward, that Tasso was a madman, that Lord Bacon was a peculator, that Raphael was a libertine, that Spenser was a poet laureate. It is inconsistent with this division of our subject to cite living poets, but posterity has done ample justice to the great names now referred to. Their errors have been weighed and found to have been dust in the balance; if their sins 'were as scarlet, they are now white as snow': [26] they have been washed in the blood of the mediator and redeemer, Time. Observe in what a ludicrous chaos the imputations of real or fictitious crime have been confused in the contemporary calumnies against poetry and poets; consider how little is, as it appears — or appears, as it is; look to your own motives, and judge not, lest ye be judged.

Poetry, as has been said, differs in this respect from logic, that it is not subject to the control of the active powers of the mind, and that its birth and recurrence have no necessary connexion with the consciousness or will. It is presumptuous to determine that these are the necessary conditions of all mental causation, when mental effects are experienced unsusceptible of being referred to them. The frequent recurrence of the poetical power, it is obvious to suppose, may produce in the mind a habit of order and harmony correlative with its own nature and with its effects upon other minds. But in the intervals of inspiration, and they may be frequent without being durable, a poet becomes a man, and is abandoned to the sudden reflux of the influences under which others habitually live. But as he is more delicately organized than other men, and sensible to pain and pleasure, both his own and that of others, in a degree unknown to them, he will avoid the one and pursue the other with an ardour proportioned to this difference. And he renders himself obnoxious to calumny, when he neglects to observe the circumstances under which these objects of universal pursuit and flight have disguised themselves in one another's garments.

But there is nothing necessarily evil in this error, and thus cruelty, envy, revenge, avarice, and the passions purely evil, have never formed any portion of the popular imputations on the lives of poets.

I have thought it most favourable to the cause of truth to set down these remarks according to the order in which they were suggested to my mind, by a consideration of the subject itself, instead of observing the formality of a polemical reply; but if the view which they contain be just, they will be found to involve a refutation of the arguers against poetry, so far at least as regards the first division of the subject. I can readily conjecture what should have moved the gall of some learned and intelligent writers who quarrel with certain versifiers; I confess myself, like them, unwilling to be stunned by the Theseids [27] of the hoarse Codri [28] of the day. Bavius and Maevius [29] undoubtedly are, as they ever were, insufferable persons. But it belongs to a philosophical critic to distinguish rather than confound.

The first part of these remarks has related to poetry in its elements and principles; and it has been shown, as well as the narrow limits assigned them would permit, that what is called poetry, in a restricted sense, has a common source with all other forms of order and of beauty, according to which the materials of human life are susceptible of being arranged, and which is poetry in a universal sense.

The second part will have for its object an application of these principles to the present state of the cultivation of poetry, and a defence of the attempt to idealize the modern forms of manners and opinions, and compel them into a subordination to the imaginative and creative faculty. For the literature of England, an energetic development of which has ever preceded or accompanied a great

serves the name of creator except God and the Poet. **25. there . . . soar:** See *Paradise Lost*, IV.829. **26. were . . . snow:** Isa. 1:18. **27. Theseids:** inferior epics. **28. Codri:** Codrus was satirized by Juvenal. **29. Bavius and Maevius:** poetasters satirized by Virgil.

and free development of the national will, has arisen as it were from a new birth. In spite of the low-thoughted envy which would undervalue contemporary merit, our own will be a memorable age in intellectual achievements, and we live among such philosophers and poets as surpass beyond comparison any who have appeared since the last national struggle for civil and religious liberty. The most unfailing herald, companion, and follower of the awakening of a great people to work a beneficial change in opinion or institution, is poetry. At such periods there is an accumulation of the power of communicating and receiving intense and impassioned conceptions respecting man and nature. The persons in whom this power resides may often, as far as regards many portions of their nature, have little apparent correspondence with that spirit of good of which they are the ministers. But even whilst they deny and abjure, they are yet compelled to serve, the power which is seated on the throne of their own soul. It is impossible to read the compositions of the most celebrated writers of the present day without being startled with the electric life which burns within their words. They measure the circumference and sound the depths of human nature with a comprehensive and all-penetrating spirit, and they are themselves perhaps the most sincerely astonished at its manifestations; for it is less their spirit than the spirit of the age. Poets are the hierophants of an unapprehended inspiration; the mirrors of the gigantic shadows which futurity casts upon the present; the words which express what they understand not; the trumpets which sing to battle, and feel not what they inspire; the influence which is moved not, but moves. Poets are the unacknowledged legislators of the world.

*1821*

WALTER J. BATE, *Editor*

# John Keats

1795–1821

More than any other great poet, not only in English but in European literature, Keats is distinguished by his unusual promise. He is the classic example of the gifted poet who died young. Before his death at the age of twenty-five, he succeeded in writing verse that, in latent imaginative power and in mastery of phrase, ranks among the highest achievements in English poetry. Yet it is plain that his ability had only started to unfold. Far from being a mere youthful prodigy, he hardly began to write poetry until he was eighteen years old, and little of what he wrote before the age of twenty-two was of high value. In every way, his talent was clearly the sort that grows and improves with time and experience. Moreover, he possessed unusual sincerity and honesty. Such qualities are not only admirable in themselves; they also encourage an eager and open readiness of mind, a constant desire to improve. They prevent a poet from settling, with self-satisfaction or defensive pride, into one specialized manner. Keats's development after the age of twenty-two took massive and sure strides every few months. It is characteristic that, at the close of his brief career, we find him preparing virtually to discard the kinds of poetry with which he had been experimenting in favor of one that was very different and more demanding than any attained during the nineteenth century. Few English poets, therefore, have appealed to a greater variety of readers than Keats. For, besides the attraction of the high quality of the poetry he did write, there is a perennial fascination in speculating about the direction his talent would ultimately have taken. Finally, his rapid development provides us with a rare opportunity to discover what qualities and influences most stimulate and direct poetic genius.

## LIFE OF KEATS

Keats was born in London at the end of October, 1795. The trials, anxieties, and loneliness of his brief life make a moving story. But his ability to prevent them from embittering and thwarting his character is even more moving to contemplate. When Keats was only eight years of age, his father, who kept a livery stable, was killed by a fall from a horse. Before he was fifteen his mother died of tuberculosis, leaving Keats the eldest of four orphans. By the time he was trying seriously to write poetry, his brother George left England and emigrated to America; and the same year (1818) his brother Tom died of tuberculosis, foreshadowing Keats's own death from tuberculosis three years later. Alone, bewildered, financially pressed, rendered still more anxious by an intense but unsatisfactory love affair, and with his poetry relatively unappreciated, he continued to hold before himself the ideals of sincerity, open-mindedness, and generosity. As a result, his outlook — as much as that of any other poet since Shakespeare — is characterized by a cheerful humor, an enthusiastic gusto, and an extraordinarily sympathetic and tolerant understanding of other people.

After the death of his parents, Keats, his two younger brothers, and a still younger sister were left in the hands of his maternal grandmother. Doubting her ability to look after them adequately, the grandmother, who was to die herself in another four years, appointed two businessmen as guardians to the four orphans, and placed in trust a substantial sum of money which, if Keats had received his share, would have freed him from want and possibly have lengthened his life. But the money had become tied up through unforeseen complications; there was a lawsuit that was to last almost twenty years; and the guardians proved to have been poorly selected. Keats, meanwhile, was attending a small school at Enfield, where he had become a close friend of Charles Cowden Clarke, the son of the headmaster. Clarke, eight years older, was struck by Keats's "high-mindedness, his utter unconsciousness of a mean motive, his placability, his generosity." Clarke, more than anyone else, awakened Keats's interest in literature. The two enthusiastically read and studied poetry together. When Keats came to Spenser's *Faerie Queene,* he went through it, said Clarke, "as a young horse would through a spring meadow—ramping." The magic of Spenser's phrasing opened a new door to him, and Keats responded with an excited imagination. In reading one line of *The Faerie Queene,* for example, he hoisted himself up, according to Clarke, "and looked burly and dominant, as he said, 'What an image that is—*sea-shouldering whales!*'" But the young Keats was to have less opportunity than he hoped for reading and helpful guidance. A year after his mother's death, his narrow and opinionated guardian, Richard Abbey, who felt that schooling beyond the elementary stage had little practical use, withdrew him from Enfield, and had him apprenticed to an apothecary-surgeon at Edmonton. Keats still made efforts, however, to walk over to the school at Enfield in order to visit Clarke and borrow books.

After four years of his apprenticeship (1811–15), Keats entered Guy's and St. Thomas's hospitals, London, as a medical student, remained there for almost a year, and received a certificate allowing him to practice. Keats, who was now twenty-one, had meanwhile tried to write some poetry; and the ambition to become a poet was taking a strong hold on his imagination. He hoped to become acquainted with some of the literary figures of the day, although he had no idea where to turn or how to discriminate among them. He read some of the poorer poets who were fashionable at the time, as well as some of the better ones. But at the back of his mind there was still a vivid sense of the great poets of England's past, especially Shakespeare; and it is these models rather than his contemporaries that were ultimately to nourish and develop his latent genius. Shortly before the close of his term of study at Guy's and St. Thomas's hospitals, Keats had met Leigh Hunt, well-known as a London literary figure, liberal in politics, a copious writer in both verse and prose, and editor of a magazine called the *Examiner.* Keats, who was attracted by Hunt's amiability and political liberalism, frequently visited him and his family at Hampstead, just outside London, and through Hunt met various men of literary interests, such as Charles Lamb, and Benjamin Robert Haydon, the painter. Touched by this attention, Keats wrote sonnets to Hunt and Haydon expressing his enthusiasm. Early in 1817 his first volume of *Poems* was published. It was Haydon who took Keats to see the Elgin marbles, a remarkable collection of sculpture and fragments, chiefly from the Parthenon at Athens. The sight of the collection increased Keats's interest in Greek art, and was to leave its effect on the calm and sculptural imagery of his later poetry, especially the great "Ode on a Grecian Urn."

In the spring of 1817, Keats went to the Isle of Wight and began his long poem *Endymion,* which he finished the following autumn. Both the small volume that preceded it and *Endymion* received little more than unfavorable notice. Political sentiment, at this time, frequently biased literary criticism; and, since Keats, when he was noticed at all, was regarded as a disciple of the radical Hunt, the unfavorable reviews in the Tory magazines were sharpened even further by political animosity. *Blackwood's* published a series of articles on "The Cockney School of Poetry," one of which (August, 1818) contained a heavy-handed attack on Keats, and sarcastically advised him to return to the apothecary business. The following month, the *Quarterly* ridiculed *Endymion.* The attacks were sufficiently venomous to encourage the rise of the sentimental legend, spread by Byron and Shelley, that Keats's early death was hastened by the hostile reception of his poems. But, however sensitive Keats was to the hostility of the reviews, he took it with manly courage. In fact, he was already becoming a severe and discriminating critic of his own work. During the previous winter (1817–18) he had been trying to write a more compact poetry, and to some extent had succeeded in *Isabella* (written early in 1818) and in shorter poems. Also, he had become interested in the theater, and had written for the *Champion* magazine on Edmund Kean, the Shakespearean actor. This sharpened his growing interest in the drama. The year 1818 also marks a sudden enlarging and maturing of his conception of the function of poetry — a conception in which poetry is of value only to the degree that it rises above the poet's own personality and is able to render the concrete world with objective truth and sympathetic warmth. Measured by this high standard, *Endymion,* he now realized, was "mawkish," and his mind, in writing it, had been "like a pack of scattered cards."

In the summer of 1818, Keats went on a walking tour through northern England, Scotland, and Ireland with his friend Charles Brown. A severe sore throat, the first sign of his fatal illness, forced him to conclude the trip early. Meanwhile, his brother George had already left for America. His other brother, Tom, was now gravely ill; and Keats nursed him until his death in December. Also, Keats had now met Fanny Brawne, the young daughter of a widow living at Hampstead. This moving, pathetic love affair, greatly intensified by his loneliness, seemed to bring Keats little except further anxiety and, after his illness became pronounced, an almost wild despair. His financial difficulties were growing. Yet, from the autumn of 1818 through the summer of the next year, Keats composed his greatest poetry: *Hyperion, The Eve of St. Agnes,* then the great odes, and, finally, during the summer of 1819, *Lamia* and a thorough revision of *Hyperion.* After the fall of 1819, Keats was able to do little except revise some of the poems that were to be published in his third and last volume (1820). He was soon suffering continual hemorrhages in the lungs, and, being assured by his physician that another English winter would kill him, he borrowed money and sailed in September, 1820, for Italy in the care of his friend, Joseph Severn. More even than the prolonged physical pain, the sense that everything in his life was now lost at last made him feel, he said, as though he had "coals of fire in my breast. It surprises me that the human heart is capable of containing and bearing so much misery." He died in Rome on February 23, 1821.

## GENERAL CHARACTER OF KEATS'S POETRY

When we think of Keats's poetry, certain qualities at once stand out that distinguish it from the work of other poets. To begin with, his poetry is unusually concrete. The images and allusions are not abstract, as they often are in the verse of some of his contemporaries. For example, Shelley and even Wordsworth often *describe* an object, enumerating or suggesting its characteristics, whereas Keats actually *presents* the object. Thus Wordsworth begins one of his sonnets:

> It is a beauteous evening, calm and free;
> The holy time is quiet as a nun
> Breathless with adoration; . . .

The evening is described successively as "beauteous," "calm," "free," and "quiet" — words which state the effect of the evening on the poet. The evening in Keats's "Ode to a Nightingale" is not "described." Specific, concrete objects are presented as they appear in the growing dark; and the general character of the evening and its effect on the poet are inferred from these by the reader:

> I cannot see what flowers are at my feet,
> Nor what soft incense hangs upon the boughs,
> But, in embalmèd darkness, guess each sweet
> Wherewith the seasonable month endows
> The grass, the thicket, and the fruit-tree wild; . . .

Because of this strong and confident sense of concrete objects, Keats's poetry is sensuous. The reader's own senses are stimulated as if the object were physically present. Keats speaks, in the "Ode on Melancholy," of "the wealth of *globèd* peonies"; and one can virtually feel their roundness. Again, there is a vigorous, almost sculpturesque sense of outline and spatial depth about the great figures in *Hyperion,* as when Hyperion at night arose, "and on the stars / Lifted his *curvèd lids,* and kept them wide," or in Thea kneeling before the "frozen" despairing figure of Saturn:

One moon, with alteration slow, had shed
Her silver seasons four upon the night,
And still these two were postured motionless,
*Like natural sculpture in cathedral cavern;* . . .

The physical firmness of Keats's imagery has intensity as well as depth and dimension. Thus he writes of the bitter Titan, Hyperion (Book I, ll. 186–89),

when he would *taste the spicy wreaths*
Of incense, breathed aloft from sacred hills,
Instead of *sweets, his ample palate took*
*Savor of poisonous brass and metal sick:* . . .

The last example is typical in another way. For more than any other English poet, with the possible exception of Shakespeare, Keats exploits the physically direct senses of taste and touch in his imagery, as when the two interplay in the last stanza of the " Ode on Melancholy ":

and *aching* Pleasure nigh,
Turning to Poison *while the bee-mouth sips* . . .
Though seen of none save him whose *strenuous tongue*
Can *burst* Joy's grape *against his palate fine;*
His soul shall *taste* the sadness of her might, . . .

Keats's alert and immediate sensuousness is also made active and complete by his ability to focus more than one kind of sense impression into a single image. This would partly include the use of " synaesthesia," that is, the use of one sense impression to interpret or suggest another. Examples would be Keats's phrases, " the *touch* of *scent,*" " *fragrant* and enwreathèd *light,*" " embalmèd darkness," or " But here there is no *light,* / Save what from heaven is *with the breezes blown.*" Keats's brilliant use of synaesthetic imagery was to leave a pronounced effect on English and American poetry from the beginning of the Victorian era to the present day. But more uniquely characteristic of Keats is the use of one sense impression not to *replace* but to *supplement* others, and thus secure a richer, more massive completeness. In such instances, an appeal to several senses becomes actively unified into a single perception, sometimes through a direct listing, as " hushed, cool-rooted flowers, fragrant-eyed," but more often through indirect suggestion, as in the " draught of vintage," in the " Ode to a Nightingale," which is described as *" Tasting of . . . sunburnt* mirth "; or as when the senses of sight, touch, and odor are brought to bear in " fragrance soft and coolness to the eye," or " the small warm rain / Melts out the frozen incense from all flowers."

In addition to its firm, physical sensuousness, Keats's poetry, like that of Shakespeare, has a sympathetic depth, a penetrating and clairvoyant " in-feeling " that captures the inner vital character of the object. In *The Eve of St. Agnes,* for example, Madeline, retiring for the night, " unclasps her *warmèd* jewels." And the stained-glass casement is so suffused by the actively flowing moonlight that the multitude of soft colors interplay like " the tiger-moth's *deep-damasked* wings "; while in the midst is " a shielded scutcheon *blushed* with blood of queens and kings." Often, when joined with Keats's strong sense for tactile imagery, this sympathetic in-feeling can arouse a direct, organically felt participation: in *Endymion,* there are the active and nervous minnows " staying their wavy bodies 'gainst the stream "; in *The Eve of St. Agnes,* " The hare *limped trembling* through the frozen grass "; and, in the " Ode to a Nightingale," the sense of muscular pressure is felt in the description of the bird singing of summer " in *full-throated* ease." So, in his reading, Keats responded immediately to Spenser's *" sea-shouldering* whales " or to Shakespeare's description, in *Venus and Adonis,* of the delicate withdrawal of a snail: " He has left nothing," exclaimed Keats, " to say about nothing or anything: for look at snails . . ."; and he quotes

As the snail, whose *tender horns being hit,*
*Shrinks back* into its shelly cave *with pain*
And there all *smothered up* in shade doth sit, . . .

If a sparrow, he wrote in another letter, " comes before my window I take part in its existence and pick about the gravel."

We may describe the principal characteristic of Keats's poetry, therefore, as a firm and tenacious grasp of external objects — an ability to absorb himself in them to such a degree, and to render them with such completeness and such sympathetic insight, that the mind of the poet does not (as in so much other romantic poetry) stand as a veil between the reader and the object. Instead, the identity of the poet becomes transparent, the object itself emerging untrammeled and in its total individuality.

This characteristic of Keats exemplifies his

own ideal of the poet as a chameleon who is himself "the most unpoetical of any thing in existence; because he has no identity — he is continually informing — and filling some other body." Keats was gradually coming to understand the nature and value of this sympathetic openness of the imagination, and wrote illuminating comments on it. This theoretical understanding greatly encouraged and guided his own instinctive potentiality to fulfill it. With most of the literary acquaintances he met through Leigh Hunt, the high-minded young Keats had had less in common than his generosity led him to assume. Meanwhile, however, he had been reading one of the greatest of English critics and journalists, William Hazlitt (1778–1830), and had come to admire him from a distance. This energetic, penetrating journalist, who saw so clearly the weaknesses of much of the literature of his own day, had evolved a conception of poetry which assumed that greatness of any sort — in art, in morality, in every act of life — consisted in the ability to lose oneself in something bigger. Shakespeare, above all, stood out for Hazlitt as the great example of a mind that could enter into the life and character that was outside him, instead of merely projecting his own *ego*. What appealed most to Keats in Hazlitt was his emphasis on sincerity, and with it a conception of poetry that lifted it beyond mere cleverness and fashion and viewed it as a vital form of awareness and understanding. Already, at twenty-two, he had felt disconcerted to find that so many literary men seemed less eagerly interested in the concrete reality without, and in attaining a large and vivid poetic sense of its meaning, than in asserting their own sense of importance, and in saying "things which make one *start,* without making one *feel.*" After attending a party in which they talked mainly of "fashionables," and, in everything they said and did, showed a self-conscious "mannerism," it struck him "what quality went to form a man of achievement, especially in Literature, and which Shakespeare possessed so enormously — I mean *Negative Capability*" (December 21, 1817); the capacity to shed one's egoistic sense of one's own identity through a vital and sincere interest in other things. He was learning, as Goethe said at a much more advanced age, that "a subjective nature has soon talked out his little internal material, and is at last ruined by mannerism," whereas the poet whose mind becomes a window to reality "is inexhaustible, and can be always new." This concept of the function of the poet was henceforth to affect Keats's life and thought in the most valuable way. It is this salutary and fruitful ideal, more than any other, that underlay and guided his sudden, remarkable development, and that offers the surest sign of his future growth.

## KEATS'S POETIC DEVELOPMENT

The development of Keats's poetry is a progressive and rapid maturing of precisely the qualities we have been emphasizing: an increasing development in the range and importance of the objects in which he became absorbed; a constantly more objective and penetrating sympathetic insight; and a greater richness and more concentrated strength in the expression of it.

In Keats's early verse, written before he was twenty-three (1818), we may already sense his eager impulse to commit himself to his subject, and virtually lose himself in it. To be sure, this headlong impulsiveness was unselective and immature. When his enthusiasm for poetry was first aroused, it was natural that he should be most attracted by images and themes that had little to do with actual life, and by the sentimental expression of the most obvious emotions. It is also natural that so young a poet, when he begins to write verse, should follow fashionable conventions; for his first hope is to be accepted by writers currently successful and in the public eye. To remember this will help to explain such early poems as the stereotyped "Imitation of Spenser" and the sentimental, plaintive sonnet, "To Byron." And when, at the age of twenty-one, he met Leigh Hunt — the first writer with any literary pretensions he was to encounter — and when Hunt went out of his way to show interest, it was also inevitable that the young medical student at Guy's Hospital should be eager to follow in the footsteps of his mentor. Now Hunt was conducting a side skirmish in the romantic revolt from conventional eighteenth-century poetry — a revolt against what Hunt felt was a prosaic concern with the everyday world, and a lack of direct human feeling. This attitude toward poetry appealed to both the rebellious instincts and the open sentiment of the young Keats; and his early sonnets and his longer poems up through *Endymion* show the direct influence of Hunt. But Hunt was not a desirable model. His verse lacked spine, and tended toward a coquettish looseness, partly because he was too eager to make it as unlike the neoclassic poetry of the preceding century as possible. For example, he had disliked the strict form of the couplet as it was used by Dryden and Pope. He therefore tried to break the closed unity of the couplet, run the second line of it on to the next couplet, and, by greatly varying the pause or *caesura,* give his lines a sort of falling rhythm. He also cultivated a deliberately casual and conversational manner which often resulted in slackness, while at the same time he used a soft, languishing poetic diction. In all these respects, Keats followed Hunt. The couplet is almost completely broken. There is an embarrassing use of such coy, conversational expressions as "giggle" or "turn, damsels! *hist!* one word I have to say." Moreover, his verse, up through *Endymion,* is often soft, gushing, and verbose. It is studded with such mannerisms as the use of adverbs made from participles — "lingeringly," "cooingly," "dreamingly." Even worse are such affected expressions as "*so* elegantly" and "*so* invitingly." Abstract nouns like "smotherings," "pleasurings," "flutterings," "embracements," and "languishment," and adjectives like "pillowy," also furnish some of the stock props of Keats's early verse. Joined with the influence of Hunt was that of Elizabethan and seventeenth-century poets, particularly Spenser. However, their work attracted him mainly because of their treatment of mythology and enchantment and because it provided an extensive storehouse of images and unusual words.

As far as his early verse is concerned, therefore, Keats's instinctive impulse toward self-absorption in the object is associated with having the "soul," as he said, "lost in pleasant smotherings." It shows itself, that is, in a luxurious abandoning of himself to the conventionally "poetic" imagery and themes that he found ready at hand in the poetry of Hunt and of the writers Hunt held up as a model. But within a year after he had met Hunt, Keats's energetic enthusiasm was becoming more informed and discriminating. "I shall have," he said of *Endymion,* "the Reputation of Hunt's elevé. His corrections and amputations will by the knowing ones be traced in the Poem." Although he had grown "tired" of the "slipshod" *Endymion,* he completed it simply because the sheer need to "make 4000 Lines . . . and fill them with Poetry" would be a challenging "trial of invention." It thus served, he thought, as a kind of "go-cart" in learning to write poetry. But immediately after finishing *Endymion,* he made a deliberate effort to rid his poetry of its lax exuberance and "Cockney" mannerisms. In his poem *Isabella* (written early in 1818), he tried to tell a story in a briefer, more vivid and dramatic style, though he felt that it too was "weak-sided," sentimental, with too much "inexperience of life." He was more successful with his shorter poems. He continued to write sonnets. But the form he now chose was the Shakespearean rhyme scheme (*abab cdcd efef gg*) instead of the Petrarchan pattern (*abba abba,* with varying sestets) that he had earlier followed Hunt in using. Meanwhile Keats was rereading, with a new and enlarged insight, the work of Shakespeare and Milton.

The influence of Shakespeare, though ultimately greater than that of Milton, was more indirect and subterraneous: it was to color first Keats's *thinking* about poetry rather than his actual verse. When Keats was forced by ill health to cut short his walking tour in the summer of 1818, he returned to Hampstead intent on writing a poem of epic proportions, *Hyperion,* which was to be treated "in a more naked and Grecian Manner" than *Endymion;* and his imagination was now dominated by the greatest of English epics, Milton's *Paradise Lost. Hyperion* abounds with some of the more obvious Miltonic mannerisms. The adjective, for example, is often used in place of an adverb ("through all his bulk an agony / Crept *gradual*"). There are also the "Miltonic inversions" that Keats later decided were "unEnglish," such as putting the noun before the adjective ("palace bright," "hieroglyphics old"), or the verb before the subject ("Pale wox I"). In versification, also, Keats closely followed Milton's blank verse. But the influence of Milton far transcends the mere copying of stylistic devices, and pervades the entire conception of the poem.

The reading of Kant, said Coleridge, took hold of him "as with a giant's hand." The experience of studying Milton was similar in its effect on Keats. The powerful influence of Milton at once lifted him above the petty literary interests, the stereotyped and routine opinions, of the fashionable literary society of the time. In doing so, it bestowed on him a new freedom. The experience illustrates the premise of ancient classical thought that the imaginative imitation of great models, far from stifling genius, is able to free and sustain it — to free it, above all, from whatever fashionable customs and stock responses happen to prevail in our environment. But so valuable a result from imitation necessitates not only greatness in the model but also a potential greatness in the imitator. Milton has influenced many writers, often in the most trivial and unessential ways. But no student so gifted as Keats ever sat at his feet. The imposing fragment of *Hyperion,* which Keats wrote when he was only twenty-three, is, as one critic has said, only a magnificent façade. After one passes through the façade, there is nothing else. But the unfinished *Hyperion* is still the most truly Miltonic of all poems after *Paradise Lost.* One result of the new independence Keats acquired from Milton was to feel that the Miltonic style, whatever its greatness, was too unique and individual a manner to be closely followed by other writers. Indeed, the greatest tribute to the educative effect of Milton on Keats is that, after the few months devoted to writing *Hyperion,* he was sufficiently able to walk on his own feet to turn to very different kinds of poetry with an imaginative strength and technical virtuosity far beyond that of his earlier verse.

Most of *Hyperion* was written during the anxious and lonely autumn and winter of 1818 when Keats's brother Tom died. It was then shelved, partly because the story was proving too slender as a basis, and partly because Keats was eager to apply himself to other kinds of verse. *The Eve of St. Agnes,* written early in 1819, marks a temporary return to openly romantic narrative. But the richly sumptuous phrasing and the grave music of the Spenserian stanzas of this poem show an enormous advance over *Endymion* and *Isabella* in imaginative resourcefulness and technical sureness. Despite the comparative sentimentality of its story, therefore, *The Eve of St. Agnes* remains the most successful of the many English romantic poems that take the Middle Ages as their setting. Meanwhile, Keats was continuing to write sonnets in the Shakespearean pattern. But he was looking for a lyrical form that would permit a more leisurely and weighted expression. In the spring of 1819, he abandoned the sonnet. He believed that the three couplets in the first eight lines of the Petrarchan form (*a bb aa bb a*) gave a " pouncing " effect; the rhymes seemed to leap out obtrusively at the reader. In the Shakespearean form, the continual alternate rhyming of the quatrains (*abab,* etc.) was languid and monotonous; while its concluding couplet, with which even Shakespeare had trouble, tended to turn into a mere tag. He therefore combined some of the features of both forms into what was to serve as the basic stanza of the great odes he wrote in May, 1819. With some variations, this ten-line stanza consisted largely of one alternate-rhyming quatrain from the Shakespearean form (*abab*) together with one of the common sestets of the Petrarchan (*cde cde*). Both the continual alternate rhyming and the " pouncing " couplets were thus avoided.

In the poetry of the ten months from August, 1818, through the following May — from *Hyperion* through *The Eve of St. Agnes* to the great odes — certain common tendencies prevail, despite Keats's constant experimentation. These are discussed above in the separate section devoted to the general character of Keats's poetry. The development from the awkward sonnet " To Byron " of four years earlier (" thou thy griefs dost dress / With a bright halo, shining beamily ") to the remarkable achievement of this ten months offers the most encouraging example in literary history to the beginning poet. But during the spring of 1819, shortly before the writing of the odes, Keats was far from satisfied with what he had attained. Indeed, there is every indication that he was about to enter on the second great transition in his career. Questionings that had long since risen in his mind about the function of poetry now became more firmly crystallized. Until this time, more often than not, reality, for Keats, was to be found in the concrete, material world of sense experience. The individual object, simply by *being,* by asserting its individual character and " identity," possesses an " instinctive " grace: its fulfilling of its particular nature (its " truth ") is — when vitally felt and understood — what we mean by " beauty." The object of poetry is to capture and express this elusive and fluid character, caught as it shines forth in momentary fulfillment, whether it be the " alertness " of a stoat or a field mouse " peeping out of the withered grass," or, on a more complex level, the interplay in a drama of human motivations and passions. The poet, he had written the previous year, " lives in gusto, be it foul or fair. . . . What shocks the virtuous philosopher, delights the chameleon poet." But Keats now feels that, if poetry is devoted solely to the relish and expression of the concrete object, apart from general values, then poetry " is not so fine a thing as philosophy — For the same reason that an eagle is not so fine a thing as a truth." The fullest possible knowledge of the " dark side of things " is as necessary as the " taste for the bright one." Whatever science and philosophy disclose must in some way be faced by the poet; and if this knowledge cuts through the poetry of romance and sheer delight, then such a poetry is inadequate. The argument is not advanced that such feelings were entirely new to Keats at this time but simply that they had now become dominant. " I hope," he wrote at the beginning of the summer of 1819, " I am a little more of a philosopher than I was, consequently less of a versifying pet-lamb." Not " fresh feathers and wings " are what he now wishes but " patient sublunary legs."

The two long poems that he wrote during this final summer, though they point to no definite direction, at least mirror his feeling of what, at all costs, he does *not* want to be — the " dreaming " and escapist poet. In the allegorical *Lamia,* the romantic and relatively mindless Lycius becomes entranced with a beautiful serpent that has assumed a woman's shape. At the time of the wedding, his old tutor, the philosopher Apollonius, sees through Lamia's guise, and the shock kills Lycius. In style, the poem represents a departure, almost a break from Keats's previous verse. He uses the epigrammatic heroic couplet of Dryden and Pope. The imagery is at times brilliantly colored, but it deliberately lacks the richness and sympathetic depth that had increasingly characterized Keats's style. His revision of *Hyperion,* also written during the summer and early autumn of 1819, is mellower in style. It suggests that Keats was developing a staid and quiet, but latently powerful, blank verse without the Miltonic idiom of the earlier version. The theme of the revised *Hyperion,* however, is far from mellow or calm. It is a vigorous and troubled insistence that " the poet and the dreamer are distinct," in fact, " sheer opposite, antipodes." Moreover, it is applied directly to Keats himself, with a strong, implicit condemnation of his earlier poetry. Only in the last of Keats's great poems, the ode " To Autumn," written in September, 1819, is there a momentary return to the intense but restrained richness of the verse written before *Lamia;* and the result is paradoxically the most flawlessly serene of all the great lyrics in English. Beginning as a direct address to autumn, the poem in the second stanza envisages autumn first as the benign lord of an estate, sitting " amid thy store," and then as the various hands on the estate reclining on a " half-reaped furrow," carrying grain, or watching the cider press. In the final stanza, autumn is no longer pictured as acting: it is occupied in *being,* as a general and pervading spirit. The music of autumn — the mourning, funereal choir of the small gnats, the bleating of the " full-grown lambs," the chorus of hedge crickets and birds — signifies both the death and the serene culminating fulfillment of the year.

Though there is every indication that a second major change was about to take place in Keats's approach to poetry — a transition quite as significant as that from his early verse to the great Miltonic fragment of *Hyperion* and the odes of May, 1819 — it is doubtful whether his Shakespearean relish for concrete life would have altered. It is more likely that it would have been supplemented and deepened by his belief that poetry must justify itself on broader grounds than he had previously assumed. Had this been the case, it is not improbable that he might even have fulfilled his " greatest ambition when I do feel ambitious " — to try within another six years or so to write " a few fine plays," and perhaps eventually accomplish " a revolution in modern dramatic writing." But after the final spurt of effort during the summer of 1819, Keats was able to write very little. From now until his death, there remain only the poignant letters to continue suggesting that his poetic gift was the greatest England has witnessed during the past two centuries and a half.

## Reading Suggestions

EDITIONS

C. D. Thorpe, editor, *Complete Poems and Selected Letters* (1935). The best selection of Keats's work for the general student.

M. B. Forman, editor, *Letters of John Keats* (1931 and later revised editions).

H. W. Garrod, editor, *The Poetical Works of John Keats* (1939). The standard text of Keats's verse.

BIOGRAPHY

Sir Sidney Colvin, *John Keats* (1917). One of the two standard biographies.

Amy Lowell, *John Keats,* 2 vols. (1925). Compared with that of Colvin, the Lowell biography lacks proportion and inclines to ramble, but it is both more enthusiastic and more detailed.

Hyder E. Rollins, editor, *The Keats Circle,* 2 vols. (1948). Contains valuable supplementary material relating to Keats's life, letters, and friends.

STYLE

M. R. Ridley, *Keats's Craftsmanship* (1933). An illuminating study of Keats's manuscript revisions.

W. J. Bate, *The Stylistic Development of Keats* (1945). Primarily concerned with versification and diction.

R. H. Fogle, *The Imagery of Keats and Shelley* (1949).

OTHER COMMENTARY

J. Middleton Murry, *Keats and Shakespeare* (1926). A provocative study of some aspects of Keats's thought, and its similarity to that of Shakespeare.

C. D. Thorpe, *The Mind of John Keats* (1926). Perhaps the best general consideration of Keats's ideals and the character of his mind.

W. J. Bate, *Negative Capability* (1939). Concerned with Keats's conception of the poetic imagination.

---

## IMITATION OF SPENSER

The first of Keats's extant poems, this was written in 1812 or 1813, when he was seventeen or eighteen. The tone and style follow the eighteenth-century imitators of Spenser rather than Spenser himself.

Now Morning from her orient chamber came,
And her first footsteps touched a verdant hill;
Crowning its lawny crest with amber flame,
Silv'ring the untainted gushes of its rill;
Which, pure from mossy beds, did down distill,
And after parting beds of simple flowers,
By many streams a little lake did fill,
Which round its marge reflected woven bowers,
And, in its middle space, a sky that never lowers.

There the king-fisher saw his plumage bright
Vying with fish of brilliant dye below;
Whose silkèn fins, and golden scales' light
Cast upward, through the waves, a ruby glow:
There saw the swan his neck of archèd snow,
And oared himself along with majesty;
Sparkled his jetty eyes; his feet did show
Beneath the waves like Afric's ebony,
And on his back a fay reclined voluptuously.

Ah! could I tell the wonders of an isle
That in that fairest lake had placèd been,
I could e'en Dido of her grief beguile;
Or rob from aged Lear his bitter teen:
For sure so fair a place was never seen,
Of all that ever charmed romantic eye:
It seemed an emerald in the silver sheen
Of the bright waters; or as when on high,
Through clouds of fleecy white, laughs the cœrulean sky.

And all around it dipped luxuriously
Slopings of verdure through the glossy tide,
Which, as it were in gentle amity,
Rippled delighted up the flowery side;
As if to glean the ruddy tears, it tried,
Which fell profusely from the rose-tree stem!
Haply it was the workings of its pride,
In strife to throw upon the shore a gem
Outvying all the buds in Flora's diadem.

IMITATION OF SPENSER. **21. Dido:** Queen of Carthage, loved and then abandoned by Aeneas. **22. teen:** grief.

## TO BYRON

Written in December, 1814, this sonnet is included in order to give one brief example of Keats's early verse at its lowest point. Conventional both in its sentimental plaintiveness and in its stock diction ("plaintive lute," "dying swan," and "pleasing woe"), it also illustrates the mannered laxity Keats caught from Leigh Hunt (for example, the adverb "beamily," l. 8). The sonnet, written when Keats was nineteen, is a clear indication of how far he was from being merely "precocious."

Byron! how sweetly sad thy melody!
Attuning still the soul to tenderness,
As if soft Pity, with unusual stress,
Had touched her plaintive lute, and thou, being by,
Hadst caught the tones, nor suffered them to die.
O'ershadowing sorrow doth not make thee less
Delightful: thou thy griefs dost dress
With a bright halo, shining beamily,
As when a cloud the golden moon doth veil,
Its sides are tinged with a resplendent glow,
Through the dark robe oft amber rays prevail,

And like fair veins in sable marble flow;
Still warble, dying swan! still tell the tale,
The enchanting tale, the tale of pleasing woe.

## TO ONE WHO HAS BEEN LONG

To one who has been long in city pent,
'Tis very sweet to look into the fair
And open face of heaven — to breathe a prayer
Full in the smile of the blue firmament.
Who is more happy, when, with heart's content,
Fatigued he sinks into some pleasant lair
Of wavy grass, and reads a debonair
And gentle tale of love and languishment?
Returning home at evening, with an ear
Catching the notes of Philomel — an eye
Watching the sailing cloudlet's bright career,
He mourns that day so soon has glided by:
E'en like the passage of an angel's tear
That falls through the clear ether silently.

*June, 1816*

## ON FIRST LOOKING INTO CHAPMAN'S HOMER

This, the first of Keats's great sonnets, was composed (October, 1816) after his friend, Charles Cowden Clarke, introduced him to Homer in the translation of the Elizabethan poet, George Chapman.

Much have I traveled in the realms of gold,
And many goodly states and kingdoms seen;
Round many western islands have I been
Which bards in fealty to Apollo hold.
Oft of one wide expanse had I been told
That deep-browed Homer ruled as his demesne;
Yet did I never breathe its pure serene
Till I heard Chapman speak out loud and bold:
Then felt I like some watcher of the skies
When a new planet swims into his ken;
Or like stout Cortez when with eagle eyes
He stared at the Pacific — and all his men
Looked at each other with a wild surmise —
Silent, upon a peak in Darien.

## KEEN, FITFUL GUSTS

Keen, fitful gusts are whisp'ring here and there
Among the bushes half leafless, and dry;
The stars look very cold about the sky,
And I have many miles on foot to fare.
Yet feel I little of the cool bleak air,
Or of the dead leaves rustling drearily,
Or of those silver lamps that burn on high,
Or of the distance from home's pleasant lair:
For I am brimful of the friendliness
That in a little cottage I have found;
Of fair-haired Milton's eloquent distress,
And all his love for gentle Lycid drowned;
Of lovely Laura in her light green dress,
And faithful Petrarch gloriously crowned.

*Autumn, 1816*

## TO HAYDON

Great spirits now on earth are sojourning;
He of the cloud, the cataract, the lake,
Who on Helvellyn's summit, wide awake,
Catches his freshness from Archangel's wing:
He of the rose, the violet, the spring,
The social smile, the chain for Freedom's sake:
And lo! — whose stedfastness would never take
A meaner sound than Raphael's whispering.
And other spirits there are standing apart
Upon the forehead of the age to come;
These, these will give the world another heart,
And other pulses. Hear ye not the hum
Of mighty workings? ——
Listen awhile ye nations, and be dumb.

*November, 1816*

## ON THE GRASSHOPPER AND CRICKET

The poetry of earth is never dead:
When all the birds are faint with the hot sun,
And hide in cooling trees, a voice will run
From hedge to hedge about the new-mown mead;
That is the Grasshopper's — he takes the lead
In summer luxury — he has never done
With his delights; for when tired out with fun
He rests at ease beneath some pleasant weed.
The poetry of earth is ceasing never:
On a lone winter evening, when the frost
Has wrought a silence, from the stove there shrills
The Cricket's song, in warmth increasing ever,

TO ONE WHO HAS BEEN LONG. **10. Philomel:** nightingale. See Arnold, "Philomela," below. CHAPMAN'S HOMER. **6. demesne:** realm. **11. Cortez:** mistaken for Balboa.

KEEN, FITFUL GUSTS. **11. Milton's . . . distress:** his elegy, "Lycidas," p. 421 in Vol. I. **13. Laura:** the woman to whom Petrarch's sonnets were addressed. TO HAYDON. **2. He . . . cloud:** Wordsworth. **3. Helvellyn:** a mountain in the Lake District in northern England. **5. He . . . rose:** Leigh Hunt. **7. And lo:** Haydon himself. See Intro., p. 318. Of the "great spirits," only Wordsworth somewhat survived Keats's increasing taste and knowledge.

And seems to one in drowsiness half lost,
  The Grasshopper's among some grassy hills.

*December, 1816*

## ON SEEING THE ELGIN MARBLES FOR THE FIRST TIME

My spirit is too weak; mortality
  Weighs heavily on me like unwilling sleep,
  And each imagined pinnacle and steep
Of godlike hardship tells me I must die
Like a sick eagle looking at the sky.
  Yet 'tis a gentle luxury to weep,
  That I have not the cloudy winds to keep
Fresh for the opening of the morning's eye.
Such dim-conceivèd glories of the brain
  Bring round the heart an indescribable feud;
So do these wonders a most dizzy pain,
  That mingles Grecian grandeur with the rude
Wasting of old Time — with a billowy main,
  A sun, a shadow of a magnitude.

*March, 1817*

## ON THE SEA

It keeps eternal whisperings around
  Desolate shores, and with its mighty swell
  Gluts twice ten thousand Caverns, till the spell
Of Hecate leaves them their old shadowy sound.
Often 'tis in such gentle temper found,
  That scarcely will the very smallest shell
  Be moved for days from where it sometime fell,
When last the winds of Heaven were unbound.
Oh ye! who have your eye-balls vexed and tired,
  Feast them upon the wideness of the Sea;
    Oh ye! whose ears are dinned with uproar rude,
  Or fed too much with cloying melody —
    Sit ye near some old Cavern's mouth, and brood
Until ye start, as if the sea-nymphs quired!

*April, 1818*

# ENDYMION

Begun in April, 1817, and finished the following November, *Endymion* was Keats's first attempt to write a long poem. He threw himself into the work with an enthusiasm that later turned into a dogged determination to complete the poem as an exercise and "test of Invention." The story is an allegory, with Endymion representing the human imagination — especially the imagination of the poet — in quest of ideal beauty. For a poet as young as Keats, the Preface is a remarkable example of clear and objective self-criticism.

ON THE SEA. 4. **Hecate:** Greek goddess, associated with the moon, the underworld, and with magic and witchcraft. 11. **whose ears:** The sonnet is enclosed in a letter (April 17, 1817) in which Keats describes the scene, and adds that "the passage in Lear — 'Do you not hear the sea?' — has haunted me intensely." See *King Lear*, IV.vi.4.

---

### PREFACE

Knowing within myself the manner in which this Poem has been produced, it is not without a feeling of regret that I make it public.

What manner I mean, will be quite clear to the reader, who must soon perceive great inexperience, immaturity, and every error denoting a feverish attempt, rather than a deed accomplished. The two first books, and indeed the two last, I feel sensible are not of such completion as to warrant their passing the press; nor should they if I thought a year's castigation would do them any good; — it will not: the foundations are too sandy. It is just that this youngster should die away: a sad thought for me, if I had not some hope that while it is dwindling I may be plotting, and fitting myself for verses fit to live.

This may be speaking too presumptuously, and may deserve a punishment: but no feeling man will be forward to inflict it: he will leave me alone, with the conviction that there is not a fiercer hell than the failure in a great object. This is not written with the least atom of purpose to forestall criticisms of course, but from the desire I have to conciliate men who are competent to look, and who do look with a zealous eye, to the honor of English literature.

The imagination of a boy is healthy, and the mature imagination of a man is healthy; but there is a space of life between, in which the soul is in a ferment, the character undecided, the way of life uncertain, the ambition thick-sighted: thence proceeds mawkishness, and all the thousand bitters which those men I speak of must necessarily taste in going over the following pages.

I hope I have not in too late a day touched the beautiful mythology of Greece, and dulled its brightness: for I wish to try once more, before I bid it farewell.

### from BOOK I

A thing of beauty is a joy forever:
Its loveliness increases; it will never
Pass into nothingness; but still will keep
A bower quiet for us, and a sleep
Full of sweet dreams, and health, and quiet breathing.
Therefore, on every morrow, are we wreathing
A flowery band to bind us to the earth,
Spite of despondence, of the inhuman dearth
Of noble natures, of the gloomy days,
Of all the unhealthy and o'er-darkened ways
Made for our searching: yes, in spite of all,
Some shape of beauty moves away the pall

From our dark spirits. Such the sun, the moon,
Trees old, and young, sprouting a shady boon
For simple sheep; and such are daffodils
With the green world they live in; and clear rills
That for themselves a cooling covert make
'Gainst the hot season; the mid-forest brake,
Rich with a sprinkling of fair musk-rose blooms:
And such too is the grandeur of the dooms
We have imagined for the mighty dead;
All lovely tales that we have heard or read:
An endless fountain of immortal drink,
Pouring unto us from the heaven's brink.

Nor do we merely feel these essences
For one short hour; no, even as the trees
That whisper round a temple become soon
Dear as the temple's self, so does the moon,
The passion poesy, glories infinite,
Haunt us till they become a cheering light
Unto our souls, and bound to us so fast,
That, whether there be shine, or gloom o'ercast,
They always must be with us, or we die.

Therefore, 'tis with full happiness that I
Will trace the story of Endymion.
The very music of the name has gone
Into my being, and each pleasant scene
Is growing fresh before me as the green
Of our own vallies: so I will begin
Now while I cannot hear the city's din;
Now while the early budders are just new,
And run in mazes of the youngest hue
About old forests; while the willow trails
Its delicate amber; and the dairy pails
Bring home increase of milk. And, as the year
Grows lush in juicy stalks, I'll smoothly steer
My little boat, for many quiet hours,
With streams that deepen freshly into bowers.
Many and many a verse I hope to write,
Before the daisies, vermeil rimmed and white,
Hide in deep herbage; and ere yet the bees
Hum about globes of clover and sweet peas,
I must be near the middle of my story.
O may no wintry season, bare and hoary,
See it half finished: but let Autumn bold,
With universal tinge of sober gold,
Be all about me when I make an end.
And now at once, adventuresome, I send
My herald thought into a wilderness:
There let its trumpet blow, and quickly dress
My uncertain path with green, that I may speed
Easily onward, thorough flowers and weed.

Upon the sides of Latmos was outspread
A mighty forest; for the moist earth fed
So plenteously all weed-hidden roots
Into o'er-hanging boughs, and precious fruits.
And it had gloomy shades, sequestered deep,
When no man went; and if from shepherd's keep
A lamb strayed far a-down those inmost glens,
Never again saw he the happy pens
Whither his brethren, bleating with content,
Over the hills at every nightfall went.
Among the shepherds, 'twas believèd ever,
That not one fleecy lamb which thus did sever
From the white flock, but passed unworried
By angry wolf, or pard with prying head,
Until it came to some unfooted plains
Where fed the herds of Pan: ay great his gains
Who thus one lamb did lose. Paths there were many,
Winding through palmy fern, and rushes fenny,
And ivy banks; all leading pleasantly
To a wide lawn, whence one could only see
Stems thronging all around between the swell
Of turf and slanting branches: who could tell
The freshness of the space of heaven above,
Edged round with dark tree tops? through which a dove
Would often beat its wings, and often too
A little cloud would move across the blue.

Full in the middle of this pleasantness
There stood a marble altar, with a tress
Of flowers budded newly; and the dew
Had taken fairy phantasies to strew
Daisies upon the sacred sward last eve,
And so the dawnèd light in pomp receive.
For 'twas the morn: Apollo's upward fire
Made every eastern cloud a silvery pyre
Of brightness so unsullied, that therein
A melancholy spirit well might win
Oblivion, and melt out his essence fine
Into the winds: rain-scented eglantine
Gave temperate sweets to that well-wooing sun;
The lark was lost in him; cold springs had run
To warm their chilliest bubbles in the grass;
Man's voice was on the mountains; and the mass
Of nature's lives and wonders pulsed tenfold,
To feel this sun-rise and its glories old.

Now while the silent workings of the dawn
Were busiest, into that self-same lawn
All suddenly, with joyful cries, there sped
A troop of little children garlanded;
Who gathering round the altar, seemed to pry
Earnestly round as wishing to espy
Some folk of holiday: nor had they waited
For many moments, ere their ears were sated
With a faint breath of music, which ev'n then
Filled out its voice, and died away again.
Within a little space again it gave

ENDYMION. **Book I: 18. brake:** thicket of shrubs. **63. Latmos:** Mount Latmus, in Caria, Asia Minor.

Its airy swellings, with a gentle wave,
To light-hung leaves, in smoothest echoes breaking
Through copse-clad vallies, — ere their death, o'ertaking
The surgy murmurs of the lonely sea.

And now, as deep into the wood as we
Might mark a lynx's eye, there glimmered light
Fair faces and a rush of garments white,
Plainer and plainer showing, till at last
Into the widest alley they all passed,
Making directly for the woodland altar.
O kindly muse! let not my weak tongue falter
In telling of this goodly company,
Of their old piety, and of their glee:
But let a portion of ethereal dew
Fall on my head, and presently unmew
My soul; that I may dare, in wayfaring,
To stammer where old Chaucer used to sing.

Leading the way, young damsels danced along,
Bearing the burden of a shepherd song;
Each having a white wicker over brimmed
With April's tender younglings: next, well trimmed,
A crowd of shepherds with as sunburnt looks
As may be read of in Arcadian books;
Such as sat listening round Apollo's pipe,
When the great deity, for earth too ripe,
Let his divinity o'erflowing die
In music, through the vales of Thessaly:
Some idly trailed their sheep-hooks on the ground,
And some kept up a shrilly mellow sound
With ebon-tippèd flutes: close after these,
Now coming from beneath the forest trees,
A venerable priest full soberly,
Begirt with minist'ring looks: always his eye
Stedfast upon the matted turf he kept,
And after him his sacred vestments swept.
From his right hand there swung a vase, milk-white,
Of mingled wine, out-sparkling generous light;
And in his left he held a basket full
Of all sweet herbs that searching eye could cull:
Wild thyme, and valley-lillies whiter still
Than Leda's love, and cresses from the rill.
His aged head, crowned with beechen wreath,
Seemed like a poll of ivy in the teeth
Of winter hoar. Then came another crowd
Of shepherds, lifting in due time aloud
Their share of the ditty. After them appeared,
Up-followed by a multitude that reared
Their voices to the clouds, a fair wrought car,
Easily rolling so as scarce to mar
The freedom of three steeds of dapple brown:
Who stood therein did seem of great renown
Among the throng. His youth was fully blown,
Showing like Ganymede to manhood grown;
And, for those simple times, his garments were
A chieftain king's: beneath his breast, half bare,
Was hung a silver bugle, and between
His nervy knees there lay a boar-spear keen.
A smile was on his countenance; he seemed,
To common lookers on, like one who dreamed
Of idleness in groves Elysian:
But there were some who feelingly could scan
A lurking trouble in his nether lip,
And see that oftentimes the reins would slip
Through his forgotten hands: then would they sigh,
And think of yellow leaves, of owlets' cry,
Of logs piled solemnly. — Ah, well-a-day,
Why should our young Endymion pine away!

Soon the assembly, in a circle ranged,
Stood silent round the shrine: each look was changed
To sudden veneration: women meek
Beckoned their sons to silence; while each cheek
Of virgin bloom paled gently for slight fear.
Endymion too, without a forest peer,
Stood, wan, and pale, and with an awèd face,
Among his brothers of the mountain chase.
In midst of all, the venerable priest
Eyed them with joy from greatest to the least,
And, after lifting up his aged hands,
Thus spake he: "Men of Latmos! shepherd bands!
Whose care it is to guard a thousand flocks:
Whether descended from beneath the rocks
That overtop your mountains; whether come
From vallies where the pipe is never dumb;
Or from your swelling downs, where sweet air stirs
Blue hare-bells lightly, and where prickly furze
Buds lavish gold; or ye, whose precious charge
Nibble their fill at ocean's very marge,
Whose mellow reeds are touched with sounds forlorn
By the dim echoes of old Triton's horn:
Mothers and wives! who day by day prepare
The scrip, with needments, for the mountain air;
And all ye gentle girls who foster up
Udderless lambs, and in a little cup
Will put choice honey for a favored youth:
Yea, everyone attend! for in good truth
Our vows are wanting to our great god Pan.
Are not our lowing heifers sleeker than
Night-swollen mushrooms? Are not our wide plains
Speckled with countless fleeces? Have not rains
Greened over April's lap? No howling sad
Sickens our fearful ewes; and we have had

**140. Arcadian:** See "Ode on a Grecian Urn," l. 7n., below. **144. Thessaly:** a pastoral district of Greece. **158. Leda:** Zeus, in the shape of a swan, seduced her, and she gave birth to Helen. See Yeats's "Leda and the Swan," p. 798.

**170. Ganymede:** the cupbearer to the Greek gods.

Great bounty from Endymion our lord.
The earth is glad: the merry lark has poured
His early song against yon breezy sky,
That spreads so clear o'er our solemnity."

Thus ending, on the shrine he heaped a spire
Of teeming sweets, enkindling sacred fire;
Anon he stained the thick and spongy sod
With wine, in honor of the shepherd-god.
Now while the earth was drinking it, and while
Bay leaves were crackling in the fragrant pile,
And gummy frankincense was sparkling bright
'Neath smothering parsley, and a hazy light
Spread greyly eastward, thus a chorus sang:

"O thou, whose mighty palace roof doth hang
From jagged trunks, and overshadoweth
Eternal whispers, glooms, the birth, life, death
Of unseen flowers in heavy peacefulness;
Who lov'st to see the hamadryads dress
Their ruffled locks where meeting hazels darken;
And through whole solemn hours dost sit, and hearken
The dreary melody of bedded reeds —
In desolate places, where dank moisture breeds
The pipy hemlock to strange overgrowth;
Bethinking thee, how melancholy loth
Thou wast to lose fair Syrinx — do thou now,
By thy love's milky brow!
By all the trembling mazes that she ran,
Hear us, great Pan!

"O thou, for whose soul-soothing quiet, turtles
Passion their voices cooingly 'mong myrtles,
What time thou wanderest at eventide
Through sunny meadows, that outskirt the side
Of thine enmossèd realms: O thou, to whom
Broad leavèd fig trees even now foredoom
Their ripened fruitage; yellow girted bees
Their golden honeycombs; our village leas
Their fairest blossomed beans and poppied corn;
The chuckling linnet its five young unborn,
To sing for thee; low creeping strawberries
Their summer coolness; pent up butterflies
Their freckled wings; yea, the fresh budding year
All its completions — be quickly near,
By every wind that nods the mountain pine,
O forester divine!

"Thou, to whom every faun and satyr flies
For willing service; whether to surprise
The squatted hare while in half sleeping fit;
Or upward ragged precipices flit
To save poor lambkins from the eagle's maw;
Or by mysterious enticement draw
Bewildered shepherds to their path again;
Or to tread breathless round the frothy main,
And gather up all fancifullest shells
For thee to tumble into Naiads' cells,
And, being hidden, laugh at their out-peeping;
Or to delight thee with fantastic leaping,
The while they pelt each other on the crown
With silvery oak apples, and fir cones brown —
By all the echoes that about thee ring,
Hear us, O satyr king!

"O Hearkener to the loud clapping shears
While ever and anon to his shorn peers
A ram goes bleating: Winder of the horn,
When snouted wild-boars routing tender corn
Anger our huntsmen: Breather round our farms,
To keep off mildews, and all weather harms:
Strange ministrant of undescribèd sounds,
That come a-swooning over hollow grounds,
And wither drearily on barren moors:
Dread opener of the mysterious doors
Leading to universal knowledge — see,
Great son of Dryope,
The many that are come to pay their vows
With leaves about their brows!

"Be still the unimaginable lodge
For solitary thinkings; such as dodge
Conception to the very bourn of heaven,
Then leave the naked brain: be still the leaven,
That spreading in this dull and clodded earth
Gives it a touch ethereal — a new birth:
Be still a symbol of immensity;
A firmament reflected in a sea;
An element filling the space between;
An unknown — but no more: we humbly screen
With uplift hands our foreheads, lowly bending,
And giving out a shout most heaven rending,
Conjure thee to receive our humble Paean,
Upon thy Mount Lycean!"

**243. Syrinx:** a nymph pursued by Pan; her fellow nymphs rescued her by turning her into a thicket of reeds. **247. turtles:** turtle-doves. **255. poppied corn:** fields of corn sprinkled with poppies.

**272. Naiads:** water nymphs. **290. Dryope:** daughter of King Dryops; not actually Pan's mother, but probably associated with him since she was a playmate of the wood nymphs. **295. bourn:** See below, "To Autumn," l. 30 n. **305. Paean:** choral ode or song of joy. **306. Lycean:** having to do with Apollo.

## ON SITTING DOWN TO READ *KING LEAR* ONCE AGAIN

This and the sonnet "To Spenser," below, illustrate Keats's divided attitude at this time toward two kinds of poetry which he increasingly felt were impossible to reconcile. Compare his contrast of the "noble poet of romance" with the "miserable and mighty poet of the human Heart" in the letter of June 9, 1819, below.

O golden-tongued Romance with serene lute!
  Fair plumèd Syren! Queen of far away!
  Leave melodizing on this wintry day,
Shut up thine olden pages, and be mute:
Adieu! for once again the fierce dispute,
  Betwixt damnation and impassioned clay
  Must I burn through; once more humbly assay
The bitter-sweet of this Shakespearean fruit.
Chief Poet! and ye clouds of Albion,
  Begetters of our deep eternal theme,
When through the old oak forest I am gone,
  Let me not wander in a barren dream,
But when I am consumèd in the fire,
Give me new Phoenix wings to fly at my desire.

*January, 1818*

## WHEN I HAVE FEARS

This is Keats's first and probably most effective sonnet in the Shakespearean form.

When I have fears that I may cease to be
  Before my pen has gleaned my teeming brain,
Before high-pilèd books, in charact'ry,
  Hold like rich garners the full-ripened grain;
When I behold, upon the night's starred face,
  Huge cloudy symbols of a high romance,
And think that I may never live to trace
  Their shadows, with the magic hand of chance;
And when I feel, fair creature of an hour,
  That I shall never look upon thee more,
Never have relish in the faery power
  Of unreflecting love! — then on the shore
Of the wide world I stand alone, and think
Till Love and Fame to nothingness do sink.

*January, 1818*

## TO SPENSER

Spenser! a jealous honorer of thine,
  A forester deep in thy midmost trees,
Did, last eve, ask my promise to refine
  Some English, that might strive thine ear to
    please.
But, Elfin Poet! 'tis impossible
  For our inhabitant of wintry earth
To rise, like Phoebus, with a golden quell,
  Fire-winged and make a morning in his mirth.
It is impossible to 'scape from toil
  O' the sudden, and receive thy spiriting:
The flower must drink the nature of the soil
  Before it can put forth its blossoming:
Be with me in the summer days, and I
Will for thine honor and his pleasure try.

*February, 1818*

## WHAT THE THRUSH SAID

LINES FROM A LETTER
TO JOHN HAMILTON REYNOLDS

This experimental sonnet has no rhymes, but attains its lyrical music through vowel assonance and through an effective use of balance (ll. 9–12).

O thou whose face hath felt the Winter's wind,
  Whose eye has seen the snow-clouds hung in
    mist,
  And the black elm tops 'mong the freezing stars,
  To thee the spring will be a harvest-time.
O thou whose only book has been the light
  Of supreme darkness, which thou feddest on
  Night after night, when Phoebus was away!
  To thee the Spring shall be a triple morn.
O fret not after knowledge — I have none,
  And yet my song comes native with the warmth.
O fret not after knowledge — I have none,
  And yet the Evening listens. He who saddens
At thought of idleness cannot be idle,
And he's awake who thinks himself asleep.

*February, 1818*

## TO HOMER

Standing aloof in giant ignorance,
  Of thee I hear and of the Cyclades,
As one who sits ashore and longs perchance
  To visit dolphin-coral in deep seas.
So thou wast blind! — but then the veil was rent;
  For Jove uncurtained Heaven to let thee live,
And Neptune made for thee a spumy tent,
  And Pan made sing for thee his forest-hive;
Aye, on the shores of darkness there is light,
  And precipices show untrodden green;
There is a budding morrow in midnight, —
  There is a triple sight in blindness keen;
Such seeing hadst thou, as it once befell
To Dian, Queen of Earth, and Heaven, and Hell.

*Spring, 1818*

"KING LEAR." **14. Phoenix:** in Egyptian mythology, a bird able to rise in youthful vigor from its own ashes after being burned. WHEN I HAVE FEARS. **3. charact'ry:** expressing character by signs and symbols. TO SPENSER. **2. forester:** probably Leigh Hunt. **7. quell:** quill.

TO HOMER. **2. Cyclades:** Greek isles in the Aegean Sea. **14. Dian:** In later classical mythology, Diana was viewed as a goddess with three forms — Selene in the sky, Artemis on earth, and Hecate in the lower world.

## FRAGMENT OF AN ODE TO MAIA

Written on May Day, 1818, this fragment anticipates the restraint and richness of phrase of the great odes written in May of the following year.

Mother of Hermes! and still youthful Maia!
May I sing to thee
As thou wast hymnèd on the shores of Baiae?
Or may I woo thee
In earlier Sicilian? or thy smiles
Seek as they once were sought, in Grecian isles,
By bards who died content on pleasant sward,
Leaving great verse unto a little clan?
O, give me their old vigor, and unheard
Save of the quiet primrose, and the span
Of heaven and few ears,
Rounded by thee, my song should die away
Content as theirs,
Rich in the simple worship of a day.

## WHERE'S THE POET?

Where's the Poet? show him! show him,
Muses nine! that I may know him.
'Tis the man who with a man
Is an equal, be he King,
Or poorest of the beggar-clan,
Or any other wondrous thing
A man may be 'twixt ape and Plato;
'Tis the man who with a bird,
Wren or Eagle, finds his way to
All its instincts; he hath heard
The Lion's roaring, and can tell
What his horny throat expresseth,
And to him the Tiger's yell
Comes articulate and presseth
On his ear like mother-tongue.

*1818*

# from HYPERION

Keats began *Hyperion* in September, 1818. Within three or four months, he had probably completed the two and a half books of the poem as it now stands, though it was not definitely abandoned till the following April, just before Keats turned to the writing of the great odes. As originally planned, *Hyperion* was to be of truly epic cast. It was based on the classical myth of the creation of the world, and the rise of the Olympic hierarchy of gods. After the Chaos that existed at the beginning came the age of the Titans, who were the offspring of Uranus (the Sky) and Gaea (the Earth). Among the Titans were Saturn and the god of the sun, Hyperion. The Titans in turn were overthrown by Zeus and the new hierarchy of gods. At the beginning of the poem, all the Titans except Hyperion have been deposed. The story was then to relate the defeat of Hyperion by Apollo, the rise of the new order fulfilling "the eternal law / That first in beauty should be first in might." Keats wished to treat this theme, as he said, "in a more naked and Grecian manner" than *Endymion*. The unexpected grandeur of the style certainly represents a marked departure from Keats's earlier verse, and easily distinguishes *Hyperion* as the most successful of all the many imitations of Milton. Moreover, in power of image and diction, in surety of phrasing, this remarkable fragment stands out, in its own right, as one of the great examples of English blank verse.

### BOOK I

Deep in the shady sadness of a vale
Far sunken from the healthy breath of morn,
Far from the fiery noon, and eve's one star,
Sat grey-haired Saturn, quiet as a stone,
Still as the silence round about his lair;
Forest on forest hung about his head
Like cloud on cloud. No stir of air was there,
Not so much life as on a summer's day
Robs not one light seed from the feathered grass,
But where the dead leaf fell, there did it rest.
A stream went voiceless by, still deadened more
By reason of his fallen divinity
Spreading a shade: the Naiad 'mid her reeds
Pressed her cold finger closer to her lips.

Along the margin-sand large foot-marks went,
No further than to where his feet had strayed,
And slept there since. Upon the sodden ground
His old right hand lay nerveless, listless, dead,
Unsceptered; and his realmless eyes were closed;
While his bowed head seemed list'ning to the Earth,
His ancient mother, for some comfort yet.

It seemed no force could wake him from his place;
But there came one, who with a kindred hand
Touched his wide shoulders, after bending low
With reverence, though to one who knew it not.
She was a Goddess of the infant world;

ODE TO MAIA. **1. Hermes:** See "Lamia," l. 7n., below. **Maia:** one of the seven daughters (the Pleiades) of Atlas. **3. Baiae:** a village and general district west of Naples, Italy. WHERE'S THE POET? **9–10: Wren . . . instincts:** "if a sparrow comes before my window I take part in its existence and pick about the gravel" (letter to Bailey, Nov. 22, 1817, below). Compare the poem as a whole with the discussion of the poet's character in letter to Woodhouse, Oct. 27, 1818, below.

HYPERION. **Book I: 23. came one:** Thea, Hyperion's sister and wife.

By her in stature the tall Amazon
Had stood a pigmy's height: she would have ta'en
Achilles by the hair and bent his neck;
Or with a finger stayed Ixion's wheel.
Her face was large as that of Memphian sphinx,
Pedestaled haply in a palace court,
When sages looked to Egypt for their lore.
But oh! how unlike marble was that face:
How beautiful, if sorrow had not made
Sorrow more beautiful than Beauty's self.
There was a listening fear in her regard,
As if calamity had but begun;
As if the vanward clouds of evil days
Had spent their malice, and the sullen rear
Was with its storèd thunder laboring up.
One hand she pressed upon that aching spot
Where beats the human heart, as if just there,
Though an immortal, she felt cruel pain:
The other upon Saturn's bended neck
She laid, and to the level of his ear
Leaning with parted lips, some words she spake
In solemn tenor and deep organ tone:
Some mourning words, which in our feeble tongue
Would come in these like accents; O how frail
To that large utterance of the early Gods!
"Saturn, look up! — though wherefore, poor old King?
I have no comfort for thee, no not one:
I cannot say, 'O wherefore sleepest thou?'
For heaven is parted from thee, and the earth
Knows thee not, thus afflicted, for a God;
And ocean too, with all its solemn noise,
Has from thy scepter passed; and all the air
Is emptied of thine hoary majesty.
Thy thunder, conscious of the new command,
Rumbles reluctant o'er our fallen house;
And thy sharp lightning in unpracticed hands
Scorches and burns our once serene domain.
O aching time! O moments big as years!
All as ye pass swell out the monstrous truth,
And press it so upon our weary griefs
That unbelief has not a space to breathe.
Saturn, sleep on: — O thoughtless, why did I
Thus violate thy slumbrous solitude?
Why should I ope thy melancholy eyes?
Saturn, sleep on! while at thy feet I weep."

As when, upon a trancèd summer night,
Those green-robed senators of mighty woods,
Tall oaks, branch-charmèd by the earnest stars,
Dream, and so dream all night without a stir,
Save from one gradual solitary gust
Which comes upon the silence, and dies off,
As if the ebbing air had but one wave;
So came these words and went; the while in tears
She touched her fair large forehead to the ground,
Just where her falling hair might be outspread 81
A soft and silken mat for Saturn's feet.
One moon, with alteration slow, had shed
Her silver seasons four upon the night,
And still these two were postured motionless,
Like natural sculpture in cathedral cavern;
The frozen God still couchant on the earth,
And the sad Goddess weeping at his feet:
Until at length old Saturn lifted up
His faded eyes, and saw his kingdom gone,
And all the gloom and sorrow of the place,
And that fair kneeling Goddess; and then spake,
As with a palsied tongue, and while his beard
Shook horrid with such aspen-malady:
"O tender spouse of gold Hyperion,
Thea, I feel thee ere I see thy face;
Look up, and let me see our doom in it;
Look up, and tell me if this feeble shape
Is Saturn's; tell me, if thou hear'st the voice
Of Saturn; tell me, if this wrinkling brow,
Naked and bare of its great diadem,
Peers like the front of Saturn. Who had power
To make me desolate? whence came the strength?
How was it nurtured to such bursting forth,
While Fate seemed strangled in my nervous grasp?
But it is so; and I am smothered up,
And buried from all godlike exercise
Of influence benign on planets pale,
Of admonitions to the winds and seas,
Of peaceful sway above man's harvesting,
And all those acts which Deity supreme
Doth ease its heart of love in. — I am gone
Away from my own bosom: I have left
My strong identity, my real self,
Somewhere between the throne, and where I sit
Here on this spot of earth. Search, Thea, search!
Open thine eyes eterne, and sphere them round
Upon all space: space starred, and lorn of light;
Space regioned with life-air; and barren void;
Spaces of fire, and all the yawn of hell. —
Search, Thea, search! and tell me, if thou seest
A certain shape or shadow, making way
With wings or chariot fierce to repossess
A heaven he lost erewhile: it must — it must
Be of ripe progress — Saturn must be King.
Yes, there must be a golden victory;
There must be Gods thrown down, and trumpets blown
Of triumph calm, and hymns of festival
Upon the gold clouds metropolitan,
Voices of soft proclaim, and silver stir
Of strings in hollow shells: and there shall
Beautiful things made new, for the surprise

**27. Amazon:** nation of female warriors; hence, a tall masculine woman. **30. Ixion:** For aspiring to love the goddess Hera Ixion was condemned to be bound to a continually revolving wheel. **31. Memphian:** Memphis, Egypt; Keats is probably thinking of an account he read of the colossal statue of Memnon.

Of the sky-children; I will give command:
Thea! Thea! Thea! where is Saturn?"

This passion lifted him upon his feet,
And made his hands to struggle in the air,
His Druid locks to shake and ooze with sweat,
His eyes to fever out, his voice to cease.
He stood, and heard not Thea's sobbing deep;
A little time, and then again he snatched
Utterance thus. — "But cannot I create?
Cannot I form? Cannot I fashion forth
Another world, another universe,
To overbear and crumble this to naught?
Where is another chaos? Where?" — That word
Found way unto Olympus, and made quake
The rebel three. — Thea was startled up,
And in her bearing was a sort of hope,
As thus she quick-voiced spake, yet full of awe.

"This cheers our fallen house: come to our friends,
O Saturn! come away, and give them heart;
I know the covert, for thence came I hither."
Thus brief; then with beseeching eyes she went
With backward footing through the shade a space:
He followed, and she turned to lead the way
Through aged boughs, that yielded like the mist
Which eagles cleave upmounting from their nest.

Meanwhile in other realms big tears were shed,
More sorrow like to this, and such like woe,
Too huge for mortal tongue or pen of scribe:
The Titans fierce, self-hid, or prison-bound,
Groaned for the old allegiance once more,
And listened in sharp pain for Saturn's voice.
But one of the whole mammoth-brood still kept
His sov'reignty, and rule, and majesty; —
Blazing Hyperion on his orbèd fire
Still sat, still snuffed the incense, teeming up
From man to the sun's God; yet unsecure:
For as among us mortals omens drear
Fright and perplex, so also shuddered he —
Not at dog's howl, or gloom-bird's hated screech,
Or the familiar visiting of one
Upon the first toll of his passing-bell,
Or prophesyings of the midnight lamp;
But horrors, portioned to a giant nerve,
Oft made Hyperion ache. His palace bright
Bastioned with pyramids of glowing gold,
And touched with shade of bronzèd obelisks,
Glared a blood-red through all its thousand courts,
Arches, and domes, and fiery galleries;
And all its curtains of Aurorian clouds
Flushed angerly: while sometimes eagle's wings,
Unseen before by Gods or wondering men,
Darkened the place; and neighing steeds were heard,
Not heard before by Gods or wondering men.
Also, when he would taste the spicy wreaths
Of incense, breathed aloft from sacred hills,
Instead of sweets, his ample palate took
Savor of poisonous brass and metal sick:
And so, when harbored in the sleepy west,
After the full completion of fair day —
For rest divine upon exalted couch
And slumber in the arms of melody,
He paced away the pleasant hours of ease
With stride colossal, on from hall to hall;
While far within each aisle and deep recess,
His wingèd minions in close clusters stood,
Amazed and full of fear; like anxious men
Who on wide plains gather in panting troops,
When earthquakes jar their battlements and towers.
Even now, while Saturn, roused from icy trance,
Went step for step with Thea through the woods,
Hyperion, leaving twilight in the rear,
Came slope upon the threshold of the west;
Then, as was wont, his palace-door flew ope
In smoothest silence, save what solemn tubes,
Blown by the serious Zephyrs, gave of sweet
And wandering sounds, slow-breathèd melodies;
And like a rose in vermeil tint and shape,
In fragrance soft, and coolness to the eye,
That inlet to severe magnificence
Stood full blown, for the God to enter in.

He entered, but he entered full of wrath;
His flaming robes streamed out beyond his heels,
And gave a roar, as if of earthly fire,
That scared away the meek ethereal Hours
And made their dove-wings tremble. On he flared,
From stately nave to nave, from vault to vault,
Through bowers of fragrant and enwreathèd light,
And diamond-pavèd lustrous long arcades,
Until he reached the great main cupola;
There standing fierce beneath, he stamped his foot,
And from the basements deep to the high towers
Jarred his own golden region; and before
The quavering thunder thereupon had ceased,
His voice leapt out, despite of godlike curb,
To this result: "O dreams of day and night!
O monstrous forms! O effigies of pain!
O specters busy in a cold, cold gloom!
O lank-eared Phantoms of black-weeded pools!
Why do I know ye? why have I seen ye? why
Is my eternal essence thus distraught
To see and to behold these horrors new?
Saturn is fallen, am I too to fall?
Am I to leave this haven of my rest,

**Aurorian:** from Aurora, Roman goddess of dawn.

207. **Zephyrs:** light breezes from the west.

This cradle of my glory, this soft clime,
This calm luxuriance of blissful light,
These crystalline pavilions, and pure fanes,
Of all my lucent empire? It is left
Deserted, void, nor any haunt of mine.
The blaze, the splendor, and the symmetry,
I cannot see — but darkness, death and darkness.
Even here, into my center of repose,
The shady visions come to domineer,
Insult, and blind, and stifle up my pomp. —
Fall! — No, by Tellus and her briny robes!
Over the fiery frontier of my realms
I will advance a terrible right arm
Shall scare that infant thunderer, rebel Jove,
And bid old Saturn take his throne again." —
He spake, and ceased, the while a heavier threat
Held struggle with his throat but came not forth;
For as in theaters of crowded men
Hubbub increases more they call out "Hush!"
So at Hyperion's words the Phantoms pale
Bestirred themselves, thrice horrible and cold;
And from the mirrored level where he stood
A mist arose, as from a scummy marsh.
At this, through all his bulk an agony
Crept gradual, from the feet unto the crown,
Like a lithe serpent vast and muscular
Making slow way, with head and neck convulsed
From over-strainèd might. Released, he fled
To the eastern gates, and full six dewy hours
Before the dawn in season due should blush,
He breathed fierce breath against the sleepy
portals,
Cleared them of heavy vapors, burst them wide
Suddenly on the ocean's chilly streams.
The planet orb of fire, whereon he rode
Each day from east to west the heavens through,
Spun round in sable curtaining of clouds;
Not therefore veilèd quite, blindfold, and hid,
But ever and anon the glancing spheres,
Circles, and arcs, and broad-belting colure,
Glowed through, and wrought upon the muffling
dark
Sweet-shapèd lightnings from the nadir deep
Up to the zenith — hieroglyphics old
Which sages and keen-eyed astrologers
Then living on the earth, with laboring thought
Won from the gaze of many centuries:
Now lost, save what we find on remnants huge
Of stone, or marble swart; their import gone,
Their wisdom long since fled. — Two wings this
orb
Possessed for glory, two fair argent wings,
Ever exalted at the God's approach:

**246. Tellus:** goddess of the earth, especially cultivated ground. **274. colure:** one of the circles of the celestial sphere intersecting at the poles. **276. nadir:** the point, in the celestial sphere, directly beneath the spot where one is standing; hence, the opposite of zenith. **284. argent:** silver.

And now, from forth the gloom their plumes immense
Rose, one by one, till all outspreaded were;
While still the dazzling globe maintained eclipse,
Awaiting for Hyperion's command.
Fain would he have commanded, fain took throne
And bid the day begin, if but for change.
He might not: — No, though a primeval God:
The sacred seasons might not be disturbed.
Therefore the operations of the dawn
Stayed in their birth, even as here 'tis told.
Those silver wings expanded sisterly,
Eager to sail their orb; the porches wide
Opened upon the dusk demesnes of night;
And the bright Titan, phrenzied with new woes,
Unused to bend, by hard compulsion bent
His spirit to the sorrow of the time;
And all along a dismal rack of clouds,
Upon the boundaries of day and night,
He stretched himself in grief and radiance faint.
There as he lay, the Heaven with its stars
Looked down on him with pity, and the voice
Of Coelus, from the universal space,
Thus whispered low and solemn in his ear:
"O brightest of my children dear, earth-born
And sky-engendered, Son of Mysteries
All unrevealèd even to the powers
Which met at thy creating; at whose joys
And palpitations sweet, and pleasures soft,
I, Coelus, wonder, how they came and whence;
And at the fruits thereof what shapes they be,
Distinct, and visible; symbols divine,
Manifestations of that beauteous life
Diffused unseen throughout eternal space:
Of these new-formed art thou, oh brightest child!
Of these, thy brethren and the Goddesses!
There is sad feud among ye, and rebellion
Of son against his sire. I saw him fall,
I saw my first-born tumbled from his throne!
To me his arms were spread, to me his voice
Found way from forth the thunders round his
head!
Pale wox I, and in vapors hid my face.
Art thou, too, near such doom? vague fear there is:
For I have seen my sons most unlike Gods.
Divine ye were created, and divine
In sad demeanor, solemn, undisturbed,
Unruffled, like high Gods, ye lived and ruled:
Now I behold in you fear, hope, and wrath;
Actions of rage and passion; even as
I see them, on the mortal world beneath,
In men who die. — This is the grief, O Son!
Sad sign of ruin, sudden dismay, and fall!
Yet do thou strive; as thou art capable,
As thou canst move about, an evident God;

**307. Coelus:** Uranus (the sky).

And canst oppose to each malignant hour
Ethereal presence: — I am but a voice;
My life is but the life of winds and tides,
No more than winds and tides can I avail: —
But thou canst. — Be thou therefore in the van
Of circumstance; yea, seize the arrow's barb
Before the tense string murmur. — To the earth!
For there thou wilt find Saturn, and his woes.
Meantime I will keep watch on thy bright sun,
And of thy seasons be a careful nurse." —
Ere half this region-whisper had come down,
Hyperion arose, and on the stars
Lifted his curvèd lids, and kept them wide
Until it ceased; and still he kept them wide:
And still they were the same bright, patient stars.
Then with a slow incline of his broad breast,
Like to a diver in the pearly seas,
Forward he stooped over the airy shore,
And plunged all noiseless into the deep night.

# THE EVE OF ST. AGNES

Begun late in January, 1819, the first draft was completed a month later, though Keats continued making substantial changes in the wording. For the story, he drew on various sources, especially the episode of Biancofiore and Florio in Boccaccio's *Il Filocolo*. According to legend, maidens who performed the proper ceremony might be able on the Eve (January 21) of St. Agnes, the patron saint of virgins, to dream of the man they were destined to marry.

1

St. Agnes' Eve — Ah, bitter chill it was!
The owl, for all his feathers, was a-cold;
The hare limped trembling through the frozen grass,
And silent was the flock in woolly fold:
Numb were the Beadsman's fingers, while he told
His rosary, and while his frosted breath,
Like pious incense from a censer old,
Seemed taking flight for heaven, without a death,
Past the sweet Virgin's picture, while his prayer he saith.

2

His prayer he saith, this patient, holy man;
Then takes his lamp, and riseth from his knees,
And back returneth, meager, barefoot, wan,
Along the chapel aisle by slow degrees:
The sculptured dead, on each side, seem to freeze,
Emprisoned in black, purgatorial rails:
Knights, ladies, praying in dumb orat'ries,
He passeth by; and his weak spirit fails
To think how they may ache in icy hoods and mails.

3

Northward he turneth through a little door,
And scarce three steps, ere Music's golden tongue
Flattered to tears this aged man and poor;
But no — already had his deathbell rung:
The joys of all his life were said and sung:
His was harsh penance on St. Agnes' Eve:
Another way he went, and soon among
Rough ashes sat he for his soul's reprieve,
And all night kept awake, for sinner's sake to grieve.

4

That ancient Beadsman heard the prelude soft;
And so it chanced, for many a door was wide,
From hurry to and fro. Soon, up aloft,
The silver, snarling trumpets 'gan to chide:
The level chambers, ready with their pride,
Were glowing to receive a thousand guests:
The carvèd angels, ever eager-eyed,
Stared, where upon their heads the cornice rests,
With hair blown back, and wings put cross-wise on their breasts.

5

At length burst in the argent revelry,
With plume, tiara, and all rich array,
Numerous as shadows haunting fairily
The brain, new stuffed, in youth, with triumphs gay
Of old romance. These let us wish away,
And turn, sole-thoughted, to one Lady there,
Whose heart had brooded, all that wintry day,
On love, and winged St. Agnes' saintly care,
As she had heard old dames full many times declare.

6

They told her how, upon St. Agnes' Eve,
Young virgins might have visions of delight,
And soft adorings from their loves receive
Upon the honeyed middle of the night,
If ceremonies due they did aright;
As, supperless to bed they must retire,
And couch supine their beauties, lily white;
Nor look behind, nor sideways, but require
Of Heaven with upward eyes for all that they desire.

EVE OF ST. AGNES. **5. Beadsman:** one pensioned to pray for a benefactor.

**16. orat'ries:** small chapels for private devotion. **37. argent revelry:** revelers clad in silver.

**7**

Full of this whim was thoughtful Madeline:
The music, yearning like a god in pain,
She scarcely heard: her maiden eyes divine,
Fixed on the floor, saw many a sweeping train
Pass by — she heeded not at all: in vain
Came many a tiptoe, amorous cavalier,
And back retired; not cooled by high disdain,
But she saw not: her heart was otherwhere:
She sighed for Agnes' dreams, the sweetest of the
year.

8

She danced along with vague, regardless eyes,
Anxious her lips, her breathing quick and short:
The hallowed hour was near at hand: she sighs
Amid the timbrels, and the thronged resort
Of whispers in anger, or in sport;
'Mid looks of love, defiance, hate, and scorn,
Hoodwinkled with faery fancy; all amort,
Save to St. Agnes and her lambs unshorn,
And all the bliss to be before to-morrow morn.

9

So, purposing each moment to retire,
She lingered still. Meantime, across the moors,
Had come young Porphyro, with heart on fire
For Madeline. Beside the portal doors,
Buttressed from moonlight, stands he, and im-
plores
All saints to give him sight of Madeline,
But for one moment in the tedious hours,
That he might gaze and worship all unseen;
Perchance speak, kneel, touch, kiss — in sooth such
things have been.

10

He ventures in: let no buzzed whisper tell:
All eyes be muffled, or a hundred swords
Will storm his heart, Love's fev'rous citadel:
For him, those chambers held barbarian hordes,
Hyena foemen, and hot-blooded lords,
Whose very dogs would execrations howl
Against his lineage; not one breast affords
Him any mercy, in that mansion foul,
Save one old beldame, weak in body and in
soul.

11

Ah, happy chance! the aged creature came,
Shuffling along with ivory-headed wand,
To where he stood, hid from the torch's flame,
Behind a broad hall-pillar, far beyond
The sound of merriment and chorus bland:
He startled her; but soon she knew his face,
And grasped his fingers in her palsied hand,
Saying, "Mercy, Porphyro! hie thee from this
place;
They are all here to-night, the whole blood-thirsty
race!

12

"Get hence! get hence! there's dwarfish Hilde-
brand;
He had a fever late, and in the fit
He cursèd thee and thine, both house and land:
Then there's that old Lord Maurice, not a whit
More tame for his gray hairs — Alas me! flit!
Flit like a ghost away." — "Ah, Gossip dear,
We're safe enough; here in this arm-chair sit,
And tell me how" — "Good Saints; not here,
not here;
Follow me, child, or else these stones will be thy
bier."

13

He followed through a lowly archèd way,
Brushing the cobwebs with his lofty plume,
And as she muttered "Well-a — well-a-day!"
He found him in a little moonlight room,
Pale, latticed, chill, and silent as a tomb.
"Now tell me where is Madeline," said he,
"O tell me, Angela, by the holy loom
Which none but secret sisterhood may see,
When they St. Agnes' wool are weaving
piously."

14

"St. Agnes! Ah! it is St. Agnes' Eve —
Yet men will murder upon holy days:
Thou must hold water in a witch's sieve,
And be liege-lord of all the Elves and Fays,
To venture so: it fills me with amaze
To see thee, Porphyro! — St. Agnes' Eve!
God's help! my lady fair the conjuror plays
This very night: good angels her deceive!
But let me laugh awhile, I've mickle time to
grieve."

15

Feebly she laugheth in the languid moon,
While Porphyro upon her face doth look,
Like puzzled urchin on an aged crone
Who keepeth closed a wondrous riddle-book,
As spectacled she sits in chimney nook.
But soon his eyes grew brilliant, when she told
His lady's purpose; and he scarce could brook

**70. amort:** dead. **71. St. Agnes . . . unshorn:** On St. Agnes' Day, when lambs were brought as an offering to the altar, the wool was given to the nuns to be spun and woven (ll. 115–17). **86. Hyena:** hyena-like. **90. beldame:** old woman.

**120. witch's sieve:** sieve made by witchcraft to hold water. **121. Fays:** fairies. **124. conjuror:** magician; that is, by performing certain rites, Madeline hopes to conjure up a true vision.

Tears, at the thought of those enchantments cold,
And Madeline asleep in lap of legends old.

16

Sudden a thought came like a full-blown rose,
Flushing his brow, and in his painèd heart
Made purple riot: then doth he propose
A stratagem, that makes the beldame start:
"A cruel man and impious thou art:
Sweet lady, let her pray, and sleep, and dream
Alone with her good angels, far apart
From wicked men like thee. Go, go! — I deem
Thou canst not surely be the same that thou didst seem."

17

"I will not harm her, by all saints I swear,"
Quoth Porphyro: "O may I ne'er find grace
When my weak voice shall whisper its last prayer,
If one of her soft ringlets I displace,
Or look with ruffian passion in her face:
Good Angela, believe me by these tears;
Or I will, even in a moment's space,
Awake, with horrid shout, my foemen's ears,
And beard them, though they be more fanged than wolves and bears."

18

"Ah! why wilt thou affright a feeble soul?
A poor, weak, palsy-stricken, churchyard thing,
Whose passing-bell may ere the midnight toll;
Whose prayers for thee, each morn and evening,
Were never missed." — Thus plaining, doth she bring
A gentler speech from burning Porphyro;
So woeful, and of such deep sorrowing,
That Angela gives promise she will do
Whatever he shall wish, betide her weal or woe.

19

Which was, to lead him, in close secrecy,
Even to Madeline's chamber, and there hide
Him in a closet, of such privacy
That he might see her beauty unespied,
And win perhaps that night a peerless bride,
While legioned faeries paced the coverlet,
And pale enchantment held her sleepy-eyed.
Never on such a night have lovers met,
Since Merlin paid his Demon all the monstrous debt.

20

"It shall be as thou wishest," said the Dame:
"All cates and dainties shall be storèd there
Quickly on this feast-night: by the tambour frame
Her own lute thou wilt see: no time to spare,
For I am slow and feeble, and scarce dare
On such a catering trust my dizzy head.
Wait here, my child, with patience; kneel in prayer
The while: Ah! thou must needs the lady wed,
Or may I never leave my grave among the dead."

21

So saying, she hobbled off with busy fear.
The lover's endless minutes slowly passed:
The dame returned, and whispered in his ear
To follow her; with aged eyes aghast
From fright of dim espial. Safe at last,
Through many a dusky gallery, they gain
The maiden's chamber, silken, hushed, and chaste;
Where Porphyro took covert, pleased amain.
His poor guide hurried back with agues in her brain.

22

Her falt'ring hand upon the balustrade,
Old Angela was feeling for the stair,
When Madeline, St. Agnes' charmèd maid,
Rose, like a missioned spirit, unaware:
With silver taper's light, and pious care,
She turned, and down the aged gossip led
To a safe level matting. Now prepare,
Young Porphyro, for gazing on that bed;
She comes, she comes again, like ring-dove frayed and fled.

23

Out went the taper as she hurried in;
Its little smoke, in pallid moonshine, died:
She closed the door, she panted, all akin
To spirits of the air, and visions wide:
No uttered syllable, or, woe betide!
But to her heart, her heart was voluble,
Paining with eloquence her balmy side;
As though a tongueless nightingale should swell
Her throat in vain, and die, heart-stifled, in her dell.

24

A casement high and triple-arched there was,
All garlanded with carven imag'ries
Of fruits, and flowers, and bunches of knot-grass,
And diamonded with panes of quaint device,
Innumerable of stains and splendid dyes,
As are the tiger-moth's deep-damasked wings;
And in the midst, 'mong thousand heraldries,
And twilight saints, and dim emblazonings,
A shielded scutcheon blushed with blood of queens and kings.

**156. passing-bell:** bell that announces death. **171. Merlin . . . debt:** the magician Merlin, who owed his life to a devil, and paid for it by committing evil deeds. **173. cates:** choice food. **174. tambour frame:** drum-shaped embroidery frame. **198. frayed:** frightened.

25

Full on this casement shone the wintry moon,
And threw warm gules on Madeline's fair breast,
As down she knelt for heaven's grace and boon;
Rose-bloom fell on her hands, together pressed,
And on her silver cross soft amethyst,
And on her hair a glory, like a saint:
She seemed a splendid angel, newly dressed,
Save wings, for heaven: — Porphyro grew faint:
She knelt, so pure a thing, so free from mortal taint.

26

Anon his heart revives: her vespers done,
Of all its wreathèd pearls her hair she frees;
Unclasps her warmèd jewels one by one;
Loosens her fragrant bodice; by degrees
Her rich attire creeps rustling to her knees:
Half-hidden, like a mermaid in sea-weed,
Pensive awhile she dreams awake, and sees,
In fancy, fair St. Agnes in her bed,
But dares not look behind, or all the charm is fled.

27

Soon, trembling in her soft and chilly nest,
In sort of wakeful swoon, perplexed she lay,
Until the poppied warmth of sleep oppressed
Her soothèd limbs, and soul fatigued away;
Flown, like a thought, until the morrow-day;
Blissfully havened both from joy and pain;
Clasped like a missal where swart Paynims pray;
Blinded alike from sunshine and from rain,
As though a rose should shut, and be a bud again.

28

Stol'n to this paradise, and so entranced,
Porphyro gazed upon her empty dress,
And listened to her breathing, if it chanced
To wake into a slumberous tenderness;
Which when he heard, that minute did he bless,
And breathed himself: then from the closet crept,
Noiseless as fear in a wide wilderness,
And over the hushed carpet, silent, stepped,
And 'tween the curtains peeped, where, lo! — how fast she slept.

29

Then by the bed-side, where the faded moon
Made a dim, silver twilight, soft he set
A table, and, half anguished, threw thereon
A cloth of woven crimson, gold, and jet: —
O for some drowsy Morphean amulet!
The boisterous, midnight, festive clarion,
The kettle-drum, and far-heard clarinet,
Affray his ears, though but in dying tone: —
The hall door shuts again, and all the noise is gone.

30

And still she slept an azure-lidded sleep,
In blanchèd linen, smooth, and lavendered,
While he from forth the closet brought a heap
Of candied apple, quince, and plum, and gourd;
With jellies soother than the creamy curd,
And lucent syrops, tinct with cinnamon;
Manna and dates, in argosy transferred
From Fez; and spicèd dainties, every one,
From silken Samarkand to cedared Lebanon.

31

These delicates he heaped with glowing hand
On golden dishes and in baskets bright
Of wreathèd silver: sumptuous they stand
In the retired quiet of the night,
Filling the chilly room with perfume light. —
"And now, my love, my seraph fair, awake!
Thou art my heaven, and I thine eremite:
Open thine eyes, for meek St. Agnes' sake,
Or I shall drowse beside thee, so my soul doth ache."

32

Thus whispering, his warm, unnervèd arm
Sank in her pillow. Shaded was her dream
By the dusk curtains: — 'twas a midnight charm
Impossible to melt as icèd stream:
The lustrous salvers in the moonlight gleam;
Broad golden fringe upon the carpet lies:
It seemed he never, never could redeem
From such a stedfast spell his lady's eyes;
So mused awhile, entoiled in woofèd phantasies.

33

Awakening up, he took her hollow lute —
Tumultuous — and, in chords that tenderest be,
He played an ancient ditty, long since mute,
In Provence called, "La belle dame sans mercy":
Close to her ear touching the melody; —
Wherewith disturbed, she uttered a soft moan:
He ceased — she panted quick — and suddenly
Her blue affrayèd eyes wide open shone:
Upon his knees he sank, pale as smooth-sculptured stone.

34

Her eyes were open, but she still beheld,
Now wide awake, the vision of her sleep:
There was a painful change, that nigh expelled
The blisses of her dream so pure and deep
At which fair Madeline began to weep,
And moan forth witless words with many a sigh;

**218. gules:** the color red as used in heraldry; Keats is probably thinking of its original meaning (a fur necklace dyed red). **241. Clasped . . . pray:** clasped shut, as a prayer book (missal) would be in a country of dark pagans (Paynims). **257. Morpheus:** god of sleep.

**277. eremite:** hermit. **292. Provence:** district in southern France noted for its troubadours. **"La . . . mercy":** "the fair lady without mercy".

While still her gaze on Porphyro would keep;
Who knelt, with joinèd hands and piteous eye,
Fearing to move or speak, she looked so dreamingly.

35

"Ah, Porphyro!" said she, "but even now
Thy voice was at sweet tremble in mine ear,
Made tuneable with every sweetest vow;
And those sad eyes were spiritual and clear:
How changed thou art! how pallid, chill, and drear!
Give me that voice again, my Porphyro,
Those looks immortal, those complainings dear!
Oh leave me not in this eternal woe,
For if thou diest, my Love, I know not where to go."

36

Beyond a mortal man impassioned far
At these voluptuous accents, he arose,
Ethereal, flushed, and like a throbbing star
Seen mid the sapphire heaven's deep repose;
Into her dream he melted, as the rose
Blended its odor with the violet —
Solution sweet: meantime the frost-wind blows
Like Love's alarum pattering the sharp sleet
Against the window-panes; St. Agnes' moon hath set.

37

'Tis dark: quick pattereth the flaw-blown sleet:
"This is no dream, my bride, my Madeline!"
'Tis dark: the icèd gusts still rave and beat:
"No dream, alas! alas! and woe is mine!
Porphyro will leave me here to fade and pine. —
Cruel! what traitor could thee hither bring?
I curse not, for my heart is lost in thine,
Though thou forsakest a deceivèd thing; —
A dove forlorn and lost with sick unprunèd wing."

38

"My Madeline! sweet dreamer! lovely bride!
Say, may I be for aye thy vassal blest?
Thy beauty's shield, heart-shaped and vermeil dyed?
Ah, silver shrine, here will I take my rest
After so many hours of toil and quest,
A famished pilgrim — saved by miracle.
Though I have found, I will not rob thy nest
Saving of thy sweet self; if thou think'st well
To trust, fair Madeline, to no rude infidel.

39

"Hark! 'tis an elfin-storm from faery land,
Of haggard seeming, but a boon indeed:
Arise — arise! the morning is at hand; —
The bloated wassailers will never heed: —
Let us away, my love, with happy speed;
There are no ears to hear, or eyes to see —
Drowned all in Rhenish and the sleepy mead:
Awake! arise! my love, and fearless be,
For o'er the southern moors I have a home for thee."

40

She hurried at his words, beset with fears,
For there were sleeping dragons all around,
At glaring watch, perhaps, with ready spears —
Down the wide stairs a darkling way they found. —
In all the house was heard no human sound.
A chain-drooped lamp was flickering by each door;
The arras, rich with horseman, hawk, and hound,
Fluttered in the besieging wind's uproar;
And the long carpets rose along the gusty floor.

41

They glide, like phantoms, into the wide hall;
Like phantoms, to the iron porch, they glide;
Where lay the Porter, in uneasy sprawl,
With a huge empty flagon by his side:
The wakeful bloodhound rose, and shook his hide,
But his sagacious eye an inmate owns:
By one, and one, the bolts full easy slide: —
The chains lie silent on the footworn stones; —
The key turns, and the door upon its hinges groans.

42

And they are gone: aye, ages long ago
These lovers fled away into the storm.
That night the Baron dreamt of many a woe,
And all his warrior-guests, with shade and form
Of witch, and demon, and large coffin-worm,
Were long be-nightmared. Angela the old
Died palsy-twitched, with meager face deform;
The Beadsman, after thousands aves told,
For aye unsought-for slept among his ashes cold.

**325. flaw-blown:** A flaw is a short, gusty storm. **336. vermeil:** vermilion.

**349. Rhenish:** wine from the Rhine district. **358. arras:** tapestry.

## WHY DID I LAUGH?

Why did I laugh to-night? No voice will tell:
No God, no Demon of severe response,
Deigns to reply from Heaven or from Hell.
Then to my human heart I turn at once.
Heart! Thou and I are here sad and alone;
Say, wherefore did I laugh? O mortal pain!
O Darkness! Darkness! ever must I moan,

To question Heaven and Hell and Heart in vain.
Why did I laugh? I know this Being's lease,
My fancy to its utmost blisses spreads;
Yet would I on this very midnight cease,
And the world's gaudy ensigns see in shreds;
Verse, Fame, and Beauty are intense indeed,
But Death intenser — Death is Life's high meed.

*March, 1819*

## BRIGHT STAR

Bright star, would I were stedfast as thou art —
Not in lone splendor hung aloft the night
And watching, with eternal lids apart,
Like nature's patient, sleepless Eremite,
The moving waters at their priestlike task
Of pure ablution round earth's human shores,
Or gazing on the new soft fallen mask
Of snow upon the mountains and the moors —
No — yet still stedfast, still unchangeable,
Pillowed upon my fair love's ripening breast,
To feel forever its soft fall and swell,
Awake forever in a sweet unrest,
Still, still to hear her tender-taken breath,
And so live ever — or else swoon to death.

*April, 1819*

## ON A DREAM

After reading the episode of Paolo and Francesca in Dante, Keats had a dream "of being in that region of Hell. . . . I floated about the whirling atmosphere as it is described with a beautiful figure to whose lips mine were joined, as it seemed for an age. . . . I tried a Sonnet upon it" (journal letter to George and Georgiana Keats, Feb. 14–May 3, 1819).

As Hermes once took to his feathers light,
When lullèd Argus, baffled, swooned and slept,
So on a Delphic reed, my idle spright
So played, so charmed, so conquered, so bereft
The dragon-world of all its hundred eyes;
And seeing it asleep, so fled away,
Not to pure Ida with its snow-cold skies,
Nor unto Tempe where Jove grieved a day;
But to that second circle of sad Hell,
Where 'mid the gust, the whirlwind, and the flaw
Of rain and hail-stones, lovers need not tell
Their sorrows — pale were the sweet lips I saw,
Pale were the lips I kissed, and fair the form
I floated with, about that melancholy storm.

*April, 1819*

WHY DID I LAUGH? **11. Yet . . . cease:** Compare the line in the "Ode to a Nightingale" (l. 56), written a month later: "To cease upon the midnight with no pain." The state of feeling that the entire ode elaborates is close to that of this sonnet. BRIGHT STAR. **4. Eremite:** hermit. ON A DREAM. **2. Argus:** in Greek mythology, a monster with a hundred eyes. **3. Delphic:** like that of Apollo. **reed:** reed pipe. **7. Ida:** ancient name for the highest mountain of Crete. **8. Tempe:** valley in Thessaly, Greece.

## LA BELLE DAME SANS MERCI

Keats took the title, "The Fair Lady Without Pity," from a medieval French poem by Alain Chartier, the translation of which was mistakenly assumed in Keats's time to have been made by Chaucer.

O what can ail thee, Knight at arms,
Alone and palely loitering?
The sedge has withered from the Lake
And no birds sing!

O what can ail thee, Knight at arms,
So haggard, and so woebegone?
The Squirrel's granary is full
And the harvest's done.

I see a lily on thy brow
With anguish moist and fever dew,
And on thy cheeks a fading rose
Fast withereth too.

"I met a Lady in the Meads,
Full beautiful, a faery's child
Her hair was long, her foot was light,
And her eyes were wild.

"I made a Garland for her head,
And bracelets too, and fragrant Zone
She looked at me as she did love
And made sweet moan.

"I set her on my pacing steed
And nothing else saw all day long
For sidelong would she bend and sing
A faery's song.

"She found me roots of relish sweet
And honey wild and manna dew
And sure in language strange she said
I love thee true.

"She took me to her elfin grot
And there she wept and sighed full sore,
And there I shut her wild wild eyes
With kisses four.

"And there she lullèd me asleep
And there I dreamed, Ah woe betide!

The latest dream I ever dreamt
  On the cold hill side.

"I saw pale Kings, and Princes too
  Pale warriors, death pale were they all;
They cried, La belle dame sans merci
  Thee hath in thrall.

"I saw their starved lips in the gloam
  With horrid warning gapèd wide,
And I awoke, and found me here
  On the cold hill's side.

"And this is why I sojourn here
  Alone and palely loitering;
Though the sedge is withered from the Lake
  And no birds sing."

*April, 1819*

## TO SLEEP

O soft embalmer of the still midnight,
  Shutting, with careful fingers and benign,
Our gloom-pleased eyes, embowered from the light,
  Enshaded in forgetfulness divine;
O soothest Sleep! if so it please thee, close
  In midst of this thine hymn, my willing eyes,
Or wait the Amen, ere thy poppy throws
  Around my bed its lulling charities;
Then save me, or the passèd day will shine
Upon my pillow, breeding many woes;
  Save me from curious conscience, that still hoards
Its strength for darkness, burrowing like a mole;
  Turn the key deftly in the oilèd wards,
And seal the hushèd casket of my soul.

*April, 1819*

## ON THE SONNET

This sonnet and the "Ode to Psyche" mark Keats's abandonment of the sonnet as a lyrical form in favor of the ode. "I have been endeavoring," he wrote before copying out the sonnet in a letter, "to discover a better Sonnet Stanza than we have. The legitimate [Petrarchan form] does not suit the language over-well from the pouncing rhymes — the other appears too elegiac — and the couplet at the end of it has seldom a pleasing effect — I do not pretend to have succeeded" (May 3, 1819).

If by dull rhymes our English must be chained,
  And, like Andromeda, the Sonnet sweet
Fettered, in spite of painèd loveliness;
Let us find out, if we must be constrained,
  Sandals more interwoven and complete
To fit the naked foot of poesy;
Let us inspect the lyre, and weigh the stress
Of every chord, and see what may be gained
  By ear industrious, and attention meet;
Misers of sound and syllable, no less
Than Midas of his coinage, let us be
  Jealous of dead leaves in the bay-wreath crown;
So, if we may not let the Muse be free,
  She will be bound with garlands of her own.

*April, 1819*

ON THE SONNET. **2. Andromeda:** She was chained to a cliff, left to be devoured by a monster, and rescued by Perseus.

**11. Midas:** a king of Phrygia, whose prayer that everything he touched might turn to gold was granted by Dionysus; Midas found the results disastrous when he touched food.

## ODE TO PSYCHE

The "Ode to Psyche" is the first of the great odes that were written from the latter part of April through May, 1819, and it is thus Keats's first attempt to construct a new lyrical form that would lack the features he disliked in both the Petrarchan and Shakespearean sonnets (see "On the Sonnet," above). In the same letter as that in which he mentions his attempt to find a better sonnet form, he states, before copying out the "Ode to Psyche": "The following poem . . . is the first and the only one with which I have taken even moderate pains. I have for the most part dash'd off my lines in a hurry. This I have done leisurely — I think it reads the more richly for it. . . ." In classical mythology, Psyche (the Greek word for "soul") was a princess loved by Cupid, son of Venus. After difficulties with Venus, she was united with Cupid and given immortality.

O Goddess! hear these tuneless numbers, wrung
  By sweet enforcement and remembrance dear,
And pardon that thy secrets should be sung
  Even into thine own soft-conchèd ear:
Surely I dreamt today, or did I see
  The wingèd Psyche with awakened eyes?
I wandered in a forest thoughtlessly,
  And, on the sudden, fainting with surprise,
Saw two fair creatures, couchèd side by side
  In deepest grass, beneath the whisp'ring roof
  Of leaves and trembled blossoms, where there ran
    A brooklet, scarce espied:
'Mid hushed, cool-rooted flowers, fragrant-eyed,
  Blue, silver-white, and budded Tyrian,
They lay calm-breathing on the bedded grass;
  Their arms embracèd, and their pinions too;
  Their lips touched not, but had not bade adieu,

ODE TO PSYCHE. **4. conched:** formed like a shell. **14. Tyrian:** "Tyrian purple," a dye used by the Greeks and Romans and made from shellfish.

As if disjoinèd by soft-handed slumber,
And ready still past kisses to outnumber
At tender eye-dawn of aurorean love:
The wingèd boy I knew;
But who wast thou, O happy, happy dove?
His Psyche true!

O latest born and loveliest vision far
Of all Olympus' faded hierarchy!
Fairer than Phoebe's sapphire-regioned star,
Or Vesper, amorous glow-worm of the sky;
Fairer than these, though temple thou hast none,
Nor altar heaped with flowers;
Nor virgin-choir to make delicious moan
Upon the midnight hours;
No voice, no lute, no pipe, no incense sweet
From chain-swung censer teeming;
No shrine, no grove, no oracle, no heat
Of pale-mouthed prophet dreaming!

O brightest! though too late for antique vows,
Too, too late for the fond believing lyre,
When holy were the haunted forest boughs,
Holy the air, the water, and the fire;
Yet even in these days so far retired
From happy pieties, thy lucent fans,
Fluttering among the faint Olympians,
I see, and sing, by my own eyes inspired.
So let me be thy choir, and make a moan
Upon the midnight hours;
Thy voice, thy lute, thy pipe, thy incense sweet
From swingèd censer teeming;
Thy shrine, thy grove, thy oracle, thy heat
Of pale-mouthed prophet dreaming.

Yes, I will be thy priest, and build a fane
In some untrodden region of my mind,
Where branchèd thoughts, new grown with pleasant pain,
Instead of pines shall murmur in the wind:
Far, far around shall those dark-clustered trees
Fledge the wild-ridgèd mountains steep by steep;
And there by zephyrs, streams, and birds, and bees,
The moss-lain Dryads shall be lulled to sleep;
And in the midst of this wide quietness
A rosy sanctuary will I dress
With the wreathed trellis of a working brain,
With buds, and bells, and stars without a name,
With all the gardener Fancy e'er could feign,
Who breeding flowers, will never breed the same:

**20. aurorean:** dawning (from Aurora, the Roman goddess of the dawn). **24. latest born:** See l. 36n., below. **25. Olympus' . . . hierarchy:** the hierarchy or collective group of classical deities. **26. Phoebe's . . . star:** the moon, of which Diana (or Phoebe) was the goddess. **36. too late:** regarded as a goddess too late (in Roman times) to have been officially worshiped in Greece. **41. fans:** wings.

And there shall be for thee all soft delight
That shadowy thought can win,
A bright torch, and a casement ope at night,
To let the warm Love in!

## ODE TO A NIGHTINGALE

Composed in early May, 1819, this was probably the first of Keats's great odes to be written in the set ten-line stanza form that would combine, as he thought, the virtues of both the Petrarchan and Shakespearean sonnets.

1

My heart aches, and a drowsy numbness pains
My sense, as though of hemlock I had drunk,
Or emptied some dull opiate to the drains
One minute past, and Lethe-wards had sunk:
'Tis not through envy of thy happy lot,
But being too happy in thine happiness —
That thou, light-wingèd Dryad of the trees,
In some melodious plot
Of beechen green, and shadows numberless,
Singest of summer in full-throated ease.

2

O, for a draught of vintage! that hath been
Cooled a long age in the deep-delvèd earth,
Tasting of Flora and the country green,
Dance, and Provençal song, and sunburnt mirth!
O for a beaker full of the warm South,
Full of the true, the blushful Hippocrene,
With beaded bubbles winking at the brim,
And purple-stainèd mouth;
That I might drink, and leave the world unseen,
And with thee fade away into the forest dim:

3

Fade far away, dissolve, and quite forget
What thou among the leaves hast never known,
The weariness, the fever, and the fret
Here, where men sit and hear each other groan;
Where palsy shakes a few, sad, last gray hairs,
Where youth grows pale, and specter-thin, and dies;

**66. casement ope:** The image of open windows fascinated Keats. Compare the "magic casements" in "Ode to a Nightingale" (l. 69), or the mention of a "Window opening on Winandermere" in a letter to his brother (Oct. 14–31, 1818). ODE TO A NIGHTINGALE. **4. Lethe:** the river in Hades, whose waters brought forgetfulness. **7. Dryad:** tree nymph. **13. Flora:** goddess of flowers. **14. Provençal:** See *Eve of St. Agnes*, l. 292n., above. **16. Hippocrene:** a fountain, on Mt. Helicon, the waters of which would inspire the poet who drank from it. **26. youth . . . dies:** probably an allusion to Keats's brother, Tom, who had died the preceding winter.

Where but to think is to be full of sorrow
 And leaden-eyed despairs,
Where Beauty cannot keep her lustrous eyes,
 Or new Love pine at them beyond to-morrow.

4

Away! away! for I will fly to thee,
 Not charioted by Bacchus and his pards,
But on the viewless wings of Poesy,
 Though the dull brain perplexes and retards:
Already with thee! tender is the night,
 And haply the Queen-Moon is on her throne,
  Clustered around by all her starry Fays;
   But here there is no light,
 Save what from heaven is with the breezes blown
  Through verdurous glooms and winding mossy ways.

5

I cannot see what flowers are at my feet,
 Nor what soft incense hangs upon the boughs,
But, in embalmèd darkness, guess each sweet
 Wherewith the seasonable month endows
The grass, the thicket, and the fruit-tree wild;
 White hawthorn, and the pastoral eglantine;
  Fast fading violets covered up in leaves;
   And mid-May's eldest child,
 The coming musk-rose, full of dewy wine,
  The murmurous haunt of flies on summer eves.

6

Darkling I listen; and, for many a time
 I have been half in love with easeful Death,
Called him soft names in many a musèd rhyme,
 To take into the air my quiet breath;
Now more than ever seems it rich to die,
 To cease upon the midnight with no pain,
  While thou art pouring forth thy soul abroad
   In such an ecstasy!
 Still wouldst thou sing, and I have ears in vain —
  To thy high requiem become a sod.

**32–33. Not . . . Poesy:** not rescued from the ugliness of life by Bacchus, the god of wine (whose chariot was often pictured as being drawn by leopards), but by the poetic imagination. **37. Fays:** fairies. **44–50. seasonable . . . fading violets . . . musk-rose . . . wine . . . summer eves:** The cluster of images here (as of others throughout the ode) appears nostalgically in Keats's letters of the spring of 1819, before the writing of the ode, and offers a vivid example of the use of its materials by the poetic imagination. For example, in a letter to his sister (April 17), he speaks of securing some "seasonable" plants for her at a nursery, and mentions desiring "claret-*wine cool* out of a cellar a mile *deep*," and a "strawberry bed to say your prayers to *Flora* in." In a letter to his brother (Feb. 14–May 3), he mentions drinking claret, "cool and *feverless*," on "summer evenings," and concludes his letter, on May 3, by adding that "the *violets* are not withered before the peeping of the first *rose*." **51. Darkling:** in the dark.

7

Thou wast not born for death, immortal Bird!
 No hungry generations tread thee down;
The voice I hear this passing night was heard
 In ancient days by emperor and clown:
Perhaps the self-same song that found a path
 Through the sad heart of Ruth, when, sick for home,
  She stood in tears amid the alien corn;
   The same that oft-times hath
 Charmed magic casements, opening on the foam
  Of perilous seas, in faery lands forlorn.

8

Forlorn! the very word is like a bell
 To toll me back from thee to my sole self!
Adieu! the fancy cannot cheat so well
 As she is famed to do, deceiving elf.
Adieu! adieu! thy plaintive anthem fades
 Past the near meadows, over the still stream,
  Up the hill-side; and now 'tis buried deep
   In the next valley-glades:
 Was it a vision, or a waking dream?
  Fled is that music: — Do I wake or sleep?

## ODE ON MELANCHOLY

The theme of the interconnection of melancholy and joy is similar to that previously touched on in the sonnet, "Why Did I Laugh?" and in the "Ode to a Nightingale" (ll. 1–6).

I

No, no, go not to Lethe, neither twist
 Wolf's-bane, tight-rooted, for its poisonous wine;
Nor suffer thy pale forehead to be kissed
 By nightshade, ruby grape of Proserpine;
Make not your rosary of yew-berries,
 Nor let the beetle, nor the death-moth be

**66–67. Through . . . corn:** See the book of Ruth 2. **70. forlorn:** now passed and lost. ODE ON MELANCHOLY: A first stanza, later canceled, reads:

Though you should build a bark of dead men's bones,
 And rear a phantom gibbet for a mast,
Stitch creeds together for a sail, with groans
 To fill it out, blood-stainèd and aghast;
Although your rudder be a dragon's tail
 Long severed, yet still hard with agony,
  Your cordage large uprootings from the skull
Of bald Medusa, certes you would fail
 To find the Melancholy — whether she
  Dreameth in any isle of Lethe dull.

**1. Lethe:** See "Ode to a Nightingale," l. 4n. **2. Wolf's-bane:** aconite, a yellow-flowered plant the roots of which contain poison. **4. Proserpine:** bride of Pluto, ruler of the underworld. See *Fall of Hyperion*, ll. 37–38, below. **6–7. death-moth . . . Psyche:**

Your mournful Psyche, nor the downy owl
A partner in your sorrow's mysteries;
For shade to shade will come too drowsily,
And drown the wakeful anguish of the soul.

2

But when the melancholy fit shall fall
Sudden from heaven like a weeping cloud,
That fosters the droop-headed flowers all,
And hides the green hill in an April shroud;
Then glut thy sorrow on a morning rose,
Or on the rainbow of the salt sand-wave,
Or on the wealth of globèd peonies;
Or if thy mistress some rich anger shows,
Emprison her soft hand, and let her rave,
And feed deep, deep upon her peerless eyes.

3

She dwells with Beauty — Beauty that must die;
And Joy, whose hand is ever at his lips
Bidding adieu; and aching Pleasure nigh,
Turning to Poison while the bee-mouth sips:
Aye, in the very temple of Delight
Veiled Melancholy has her sovran shrine,
Though seen of none save him whose strenuous tongue
Can burst Joy's grape against his palate fine;
His soul shall taste the sadness of her might,
And be among her cloudy trophies hung.

*May, 1819*

Psyche (the "soul") was symbolized by a butterfly. Hence, "Do not take the death-moth instead of the butterfly as the symbol of your soul." **9–10. For . . . soul:** For the shades, or ghosts, of melancholy and death will steal on you gradually; and in that growing numbness you will lose the keen edge of perception with which the full meaning of melancholy, as it is inextricably bound up with joy, can be sensed and known. **21. She:** Melancholy, not the "mistress." **24. Turning to Poison:** Two months before the ode, Keats had written to his brother George (March 19): "While we are laughing, the seed of some trouble is put into the wide arable land of events — While we are laughing, it sprouts, it grows, and suddenly bears a *poison* fruit which we must pluck."

## ODE ON A GRECIAN URN

The theme and much of the imagery of this ode were suggested by the sight of the Elgin marbles and the Grecian urns in the British Museum. The last two lines of the poem are probably the most widely known lines of Keats. If they have also proved the most puzzling, it is probably because the statement "that is all / Ye know on earth, and all ye need to know" is usually regarded as Keats's own observation on the maxim, "Beauty is truth, truth beauty." Construed in this way, the last two lines seem merely a bald assertion rather than a convincing conclusion organically following from the body of the poem. In his interpretation of the ode (*The Finer Tone* [1953], pp. 58–62), Earl Wasserman persuasively argues that the statement "that is all / Ye know on earth . . ." applies, not merely to the maxim, "Beauty is truth," but also to the previous three lines (ll. 46–48). In other words, in a world of change and decay, all we can know is that the sort of insight the urn embodies is able to remain "a friend to man," reminding him that, at one level at least, "Beauty is truth." It can continue, as Mr. Wasserman says, to hold out to man "the promise that somewhere . . . songs are forever new, love is forever young, . . . beauty is truth. . . . The knowledge that in art this insight is forever available is the height of earthly wisdom; and it is all man needs to know, for it endows his earthly existence with a purpose and a meaning."

1

Thou still unravished bride of quietness,
Thou foster-child of silence and slow time,
Sylvan historian, who canst thus express
A flowery tale more sweetly than our rhyme:
What leaf-fringed legend haunts about thy shape
Of deities or mortals, or of both,
In Tempe or the dales of Arcady?
What men or gods are these? What maidens loth?
What mad pursuit? What struggle to escape?
What pipes and timbrels? What wild ecstasy?

2

Heard melodies are sweet, but those unheard
Are sweeter; therefore, ye soft pipes, play on;
Not to the sensual ear, but, more endeared,
Pipe to the spirit ditties of no tone:
Fair youth, beneath the trees, thou canst not leave
Thy song, nor ever can those trees be bare;
Bold Lover, never, never canst thou kiss,
Though winning near the goal — yet, do not grieve;
She cannot fade, though thou hast not thy bliss,
Forever wilt thou love, and she be fair!

3

Ah, happy, happy boughs! that cannot shed
Your leaves, nor ever bid the Spring adieu;
And, happy melodist, unwearied,
Forever piping songs forever new;
More happy love! more happy, happy love!
Forever warm and still to be enjoyed,
Forever panting, and forever young;
All breathing human passion far above,
That leaves a heart high-sorrowful and cloyed,
A burning forehead, and a parching tongue.

ODE ON A GRECIAN URN. **3. Sylvan:** woodlike or rustic. **7. Tempe:** See the sonnet, "On a Dream," above, l. 8. **Arcady:** a hilly district, in southern Greece, noted as a center of pastoral life. **13. sensual ear:** sensuous ear — the physical sense of hearing. **15–18. Fair . . . goal:** Compare the passage from Keats's letter cited in the headnote to "On a Dream," above.

4

Who are these coming to the sacrifice?
  To what green altar, O mysterious priest,
Lead'st thou that heifer lowing at the skies,
  And all her silken flanks with garlands dressed?
What little town by river or sea shore,
  Or mountain-built with peaceful citadel,
    Is emptied of this folk, this pious morn?
And, little town, thy streets forevermore
  Will silent be; and not a soul to tell
    Why thou art desolate, can e'er return.

5

O Attic shape! Fair attitude! with brede
  Of marble men and maidens overwrought,
With forest branches and the trodden weed;
  Thou, silent form, dost tease us out of thought
As doth eternity: Cold Pastoral!
  When old age shall this generation waste,
    Thou shalt remain, in midst of other woe
  Than ours, a friend to man, to whom thou say'st,
"Beauty is truth, truth beauty,"—that is all
    Ye know on earth, and all ye need to know.

*May, 1819*

# LAMIA

*Lamia* was composed during July and August, 1819. The allegory of the poem—for it is obviously allegorical—is based on a story Keats found in Robert Burton's *Anatomy of Melancholy* (1621): "Philostratus, in his fourth book *De Vita Apollonii,* hath a memorable instance . . . of one Menippus Lycius, a young man twenty-five years of age, that going betwixt Cenchreas and Corinth, met such a phantasm in the habit of a fair gentlewoman, which, taking him by the hand, carried him home to her house, in the suburbs of Corinth . . . The young man, a philosopher, otherwise staid and discreet, able to moderate his passions, though not this of love, tarried with her a while to his great content, and at last married her, to whose wedding, amongst other guests, came Apollonius; who . . . found her out to be a serpent, a lamia; and that all her furniture was, like Tantalus' gold, . . . no substance but mere illusions. When she saw herself descried, she wept, and desired Apollonius to be silent, but he would not be moved, and thereupon she, plate, house, and all that was in it, vanished in an instant. . . ."

The poem is variously interpreted. The most probable explanation is that Lamia is the phantasm she is said to be; that Lycius—if he is indeed the "poet"—is not the highest type of one; and that the philosopher, Apollonius, though uncongenial, is at least partly right. In this case, two interpretations seem more satisfactory than others: (1) The poem is an attack on the "dreaming poet," later castigated in the *Fall of Hyperion:* he is deluded by a phantasm, and cannot survive the shock of seeing through the delusion; or (2), more probable, Lamia (representing the unreal poetry of dreams) and Apollonius (cold, analytic philosophy) are both inadequate, both injurious to poetry; and what is wanted is a larger, more vital grasp of reality than can be had through either. The form and style mark a break with Keats's preceding poetry. (See Introduction, p. 324.)

## PART I

Upon a time, before the faery broods
Drove Nymph and Satyr from the prosperous
    woods,
Before King Oberon's bright diadem,
Scepter, and mantle, clasped with dewy gem,
Frightened away the Dryads and the Fauns
From rushes green, and brakes, and cowslipped
    lawns,
The ever-smitten Hermes empty left
His golden throne, bent warm on amorous theft:
From high Olympus had he stolen light,
On this side of Jove's clouds, to escape the sight
Of his great summoner, and made retreat
Into a forest on the shores of Crete.
For somewhere in that sacred island dwelt
A nymph, to whom all hoofèd Satyrs knelt;
At whose white feet the languid Tritons poured
Pearls, while on land they withered and adored.
Fast by the springs where she to bathe was wont,
And in those meads where sometimes she might
    haunt,
Were strewn rich gifts, unknown to any Muse,
Though Fancy's casket were unlocked to choose.
Ah, what a world of love was at her feet!
So Hermes thought, and a celestial heat
Burnt from his wingèd heels to either ear,
That from a whiteness, as the lily clear,
Blushed into roses 'mid his golden hair,
Fallen in jealous curls about his shoulders bare.
From vale to vale, from wood to wood, he flew,
Breathing upon the flowers his passion new,
And wound with many a river to its head,
To find where this sweet nymph prepared her se-
    cret bed:
In vain; the sweet nymph might nowhere be
    found,
And so he rested, on the lonely ground,
Pensive, and full of painful jealousies
Of the Wood-Gods, and even the very trees.
There as he stood, he heard a mournful voice,

**41. Attic:** of Attica (Athens). **brede:** design. **45. Cold Pastoral:** pastoral scene, coolly aloof from human bustle, and rendered fixed and immortal on the face of the urn. **46–50. When . . . know:** See headnote above.

LAMIA. **Part I: 3. Oberon:** in medieval folklore, king of the fairies. **7. ever-smitten Hermes:** The winged messenger of the gods was unusually prone to fall in love.

Such as once heard, in gentle heart, destroys
All pain but pity: thus the lone voice spake:
" When from this wreathèd tomb shall I awake!
When move in a sweet body fit for life,
And love, and pleasure, and the ruddy strife
Of hearts and lips! Ah, miserable me!"
The God, dove-footed, glided silently
Round bush and tree, soft-brushing, in his speed,
The taller grasses and full-flowering weed,
Until he found a palpitating snake,
Bright, and cirque-couchant in a dusky brake.

She was a gordian shape of dazzling hue,
Vermilion-spotted, golden, green, and blue;
Striped like a zebra, freckled like a pard,
Eyed like a peacock, and all crimson barred;
And full of silver moons, that, as she breathed,
Dissolved or brighter shone, or interwreathed
Their lusters with the gloomier tapestries —
So rainbow-sided, touched with miseries,
She seemed, at once, some penanced lady elf,
Some demon's mistress, or the demon's self.
Upon her crest she wore a wannish fire
Sprinkled with stars, like Ariadne's tiar:
Her head was serpent, but ah, bitter-sweet!
She had a woman's mouth with all its pearls complete:
And for her eyes: what could such eyes do there
But weep, and weep, that they were born so fair?
As Proserpine still weeps for her Sicilian air.
Her throat was serpent, but the words she spake
Came, as through bubbling honey, for Love's sake,
And thus; while Hermes on his pinions lay,
Like a stooped falcon ere he takes his prey.

" Fair Hermes, crowned with feathers, fluttering light,
I had a splendid dream of thee last night:
I saw thee sitting, on a throne of gold,
Among the Gods, upon Olympus old,
The only sad one; for thou didst not hear
The soft, lute-fingered Muses chaunting clear,
Nor even Apollo when he sang alone,
Deaf to his throbbing throat's long, long melodious moan.
I dreamt I saw thee, robed in purple flakes,
Break amorous through the clouds, as morning breaks,
And, swiftly as a bright Phoebean dart,
Strike for the Cretan isle; and here thou art!
Too gentle Hermes, hast thou found the maid?"
Whereat the star of Lethe not delayed
His rosy eloquence, and thus inquired:
" Thou smooth-lipped serpent, surely high inspired!
Thou beauteous wreath, with melancholy eyes,
Possess whatever bliss thou canst devise,
Telling me only where my nymph is fled —
Where she doth breathe!" " Bright planet, thou hast said,"
Returned the snake, " but seal with oaths, fair God!"
" I swear," said Hermes, " by my serpent rod,
And by thine eyes, and by thy starry crown!"
Light flew his earnest words, among the blossoms blown.
Then thus again the brilliance feminine:
" Too frail of heart! for this lost nymph of thine,
Free as the air, invisibly, she strays
About these thornless wilds; her pleasant days
She tastes unseen; unseen her nimble feet
Leave traces in the grass and flowers sweet;
From weary tendrils, and bowed branches green,
She plucks the fruit unseen, she bathes unseen:
And by my power is her beauty veiled
To keep it unaffronted, unassailed
By the love-glances of unlovely eyes,
Of Satyrs, Fauns, and bleared Silenus' sighs.
Pale grew her immortality, for woe
Of all these lovers, and she grievèd so
I took compassion on her, bade her steep
Her hair in weïrd syrops, that would keep
Her loveliness invisible, yet free
To wander as she loves, in liberty.
Thou shalt behold her, Hermes, thou alone,
If thou wilt, as thou swearest, grant my boon!"
Then, once again, the charmèd God began
An oath, and through the serpent's ears it ran
Warm, tremulous, devout, psalterian.
Ravished, she lifted her Circean head,
Blushed a live damask, and swift-lisping said,
" I was a woman, let me have once more
A woman's shape, and charming as before.
I love a youth of Corinth — O the bliss!
Give me my woman's form, and place me where he is.
Stoop, Hermes, let me breathe upon thy brow,
And thou shalt see thy sweet nymph even now."
The God on half-shut feathers sank serene,
She breathed upon his eyes, and swift was seen
Of both the guarded nymph near-smiling on the green.
It was no dream; or say a dream it was,

**46. cirque-couchant:** crouched or coiled in the form of a circle. **47. gordian:** intricate (from Gordius, who tied the famous knot). **58. Ariadne's tiar:** the crown of Ariadne, lover of Theseus and daughter of King Minos of Crete, who became a constellation after her death. **63. Proserpine:** daughter of Ceres, carried off to Hades by Pluto, but allowed to return once a year. See *Fall of Hyperion*, I. 37–38, below. **78. Phoebean dart:** dart of Apollo, god of the sun.

**81. star of Lethe:** Hermes, one of whose duties was to guide the souls of the dead to Hades, in the midst of which flowed the river of forgetfulness, Lethe. **103. Silenus:** a woodland god, tutor and companion of Bacchus; usually portrayed as a drunken old man with a flat nose and pointed ears; also applied as a term to a group of woodland gods, half man and half goat. **114. psalterian:** from psaltery, a stringed instrument like a zither. **115. Circean:** like Circe, the enchantress.

Real are the dreams of Gods, and smoothly pass
Their pleasures in a long immortal dream.
One warm, flushed moment, hovering, it might
seem
Dashed by the wood-nymph's beauty, so he burned;
Then, lighting on the printless verdure, turned
To the swooned serpent, and with languid arm,
Delicate, put to proof the lithe Caducean charm.
So done, upon the nymph his eyes he bent
Full of adoring tears and blandishment,
And towards her stepped: she, like a moon in wane,
Faded before him, cowered, nor could restrain
Her fearful sobs, self-folding like a flower
That faints into itself at evening hour:
But the God fostering her chillèd hand,
She felt the warmth, her eyelids opened bland,
And, like new flowers at morning song of bees,
Bloomed, and gave up her honey to the lees.
Into the green-recessèd woods they flew;
Nor grew they pale, as mortal lovers do.

Left to herself, the serpent now began
To change; her elfin blood in madness ran,
Her mouth foamed, and the grass, therewith be-
sprent,
Withered at dew so sweet and virulent;
Her eyes in torture fixed, and anguish drear,
Hot, glazed, and wide, with lid-lashes all sear,
Flashed phosphor and sharp sparks, without one
cooling tear.
The colors all inflamed throughout her train,
She writhed about, convulsed with scarlet pain:
A deep volcanian yellow took the place
Of all her milder-moonèd body's grace;
And, as the lava ravishes the mead,
Spoilt all her silver mail, and golden brede;
Made gloom of all her frecklings, streaks and bars,
Eclipsed her crescents, and licked up her stars:
So that, in moments few, she was undressed
Of all her sapphires, greens, and amethyst,
And rubious-argent: of all these bereft,
Nothing but pain and ugliness were left.
Still shone her crown; that vanished, also she
Melted and disappeared as suddenly;
And in the air, her new voice luting soft,
Cried, "Lycius! gentle Lycius!" — Borne aloft
With the bright mists about the mountains hoar
These words dissolved: Crete's forests heard no
more.

Whither fled Lamia, now a lady bright,
A full-born beauty new and exquisite?
She fled into that valley they pass o'er
Who go to Corinth from Cenchreas' shore;
And rested at the foot of those wild hills,
The rugged founts of the Peraean rills,
And of that other ridge whose barren back
Stretches, with all its mist and cloudy rack,
South-westward to Cleone. There she stood
About a young bird's flutter from a wood,
Fair, on a sloping green of mossy tread,
By a clear pool, wherein she passioned
To see herself escaped from so sore ills,
While her robes flaunted with the daffodils.

Ah, happy Lycius! — for she was a maid
More beautiful than ever twisted braid,
Or sighed, or blushed, or on spring-flowered lea
Spread a green kirtle to the minstrelsy:
A virgin purest lipped, yet in the lore
Of love deep learnèd to the red heart's core:
Not one hour old, yet of sciential brain
To unperplex bliss from its neighbor pain;
Define their pettish limits, and estrange
Their points of contact, and swift counterchange;
Intrigue with the specious chaos, and dispart
Its most ambiguous atoms with sure art;
As though in Cupid's college she had spent
Sweet days a lovely graduate, still unshent,
And kept his rosy terms in idle languishment.

Why this fair creature chose so faerily
By the wayside to linger, we shall see;
But first 'tis fit to tell how she could muse
And dream, when in the serpent prison-house,
Of all she list, strange or magnificent:
How, ever, where she willed, her spirit went;
Whether to faint Elysium, or where
Down through tress-lifting waves the Nereids fair
Wind into Thetis' bower by many a pearly stair;
Or where God Bacchus drains his cups divine,
Stretched out, at ease, beneath a glutinous pine;
Or where in Pluto's gardens palatine
Mulciber's columns gleam in far piazzian line.
And sometimes into cities she would send
Her dream, with feast and rioting to blend;
And once, while among mortals dreaming thus,
She saw the young Corinthian Lycius
Charioting foremost in the envious race,

**133. Caducean:** The Caduceus was the name of Hermes' magic wand. **158. brede:** embroidery. **174. Cenchreas:** ancient city in Asia Minor. **192. unperplex . . . pain:** Cf. "Ode on Melancholy," ll. 23–30. **198. unshent:** innocent. **199. terms:** college terms. **203. serpent prison-house:** Keats had been struck by the sympathetic identification in Milton's description of Satan entering the serpent, and had written in the margin of his copy of *Paradise Lost*, IX. 179–91: "Satan having enter'd the Serpent, and inform'd his brutal sense — might seem sufficient — but Milton goes on *'but his sleep disturbed not.'* Whose spirit does not ache at the smothering and confinement — the unwilling stillness — the *'waiting close'*? Whose head is not dizzy at the possible speculations of Satan in the serpent prison? No passage of poetry can ever give a greater pain of suffocation." **207. Nereids:** sea nymphs, formed like mermaids, who attended Poseidon (or Neptune), god of the sea. Thetis, mother of Achilles, was one of them. **212. Mulciber:** Vulcan, god of fire and metalworking,

Like a young Jove with calm uneager face,
And fell into a swooning love of him.
Now on the moth-time of that evening dim
He would return that way, as well she knew,
To Corinth from the shore; for freshly blew
The eastern soft wind, and his galley now
Grated the quaystones with her brazen prow
In port Cenchreas, from Egina isle
Fresh anchored; whither he had been awhile
To sacrifice to Jove, whose temple there
Waits with high marble doors for blood and incense rare.
Jove heard his vows, and bettered his desire;
For by some freakful chance he made retire
From his companions, and set forth to walk,
Perhaps grown wearied of their Corinth talk:
Over the solitary hills he fared,
Thoughtless at first, but ere eve's star appeared
His phantasy was lost, where reason fades,
In the calmed twilight of Platonic shades.
Lamia beheld him coming, near, more near —
Close to her passing, in indifference drear,
His silent sandals swept the mossy green;
So neighbored to him, and yet so unseen
She stood: he passed, shut up in mysteries,
His mind wrapped like his mantle, while her eyes
Followed his steps, and her neck regal white
Turned — syllabling thus, "Ah, Lycius bright,
And will you leave me on the hills alone?
Lycius, look back! and be some pity shown."
He did; not with cold wonder fearingly,
But Orpheus-like at an Eurydice;
For so delicious were the words she sung,
It seemed he had loved them a whole summer long:
And soon his eyes had drunk her beauty up,
Leaving no drop in the bewildering cup,
And still the cup was full — while he, afraid
Lest she should vanish ere his lip had paid
Due adoration, thus began to adore;
Her soft look growing coy, she saw his chain so sure:
"Leave thee alone! Look back! Ah, Goddess, see
Whether my eyes can ever turn from thee!
For pity do not this sad heart belie —
Even as thou vanishest so shall I die.
Stay! though a Naiad of the rivers, stay!
To thy far wishes will thy streams obey:
Stay! though the greenest woods be thy domain,
Alone they can drink up the morning rain:
Through a descended Pleiad, will not one
Of thine harmonious sisters keep in tune
Thy spheres, and as thy silver proxy shine?
So sweetly to these ravished ears of mine
Came thy sweet greeting, that if thou shouldst fade
Thy memory will waste me to a shade: —
For pity do not melt!" — "If I should stay,"
Said Lamia, "here, upon this floor of clay,
And pain my steps upon these flowers too rough,
What canst thou say or do of charm enough
To dull the nice remembrance of my home?
Thou canst not ask me with thee here to roam
Over these hills and vales, where no joy is —
Empty of immortality and bliss!
Thou art a scholar, Lycius, and must know
That finer spirits cannot breathe below
In human climes, and live: Alas! poor youth,
What taste of purer air hast thou to soothe
My essence? What serener palaces,
Where I may all my many senses please,
And by mysterious sleights a hundred thirsts appease?
It cannot be — Adieu!" So said, she rose
Tiptoe with white arms spread. He, sick to lose
The amorous promise of her lone complain,
Swooned, murmuring of love, and pale with pain.
The cruel lady, without any show
Of sorrow for her tender favorite's woe,
But rather, if her eyes could brighter be,
With brighter eyes and slow amenity,
Put her new lips to his, and gave afresh
The life she had so tangled in her mesh:
And as he from one trance was wakening
Into another, she began to sing,
Happy in beauty, life, and love, and everything,
A song of love, too sweet for earthly lyres,
While, like held breath, the stars drew in their panting fires.
And then she whispered in such trembling tone,
As those who, safe together met alone
For the first time through many anguished days,
Use other speech than looks; bidding him raise
His drooping head, and clear his soul of doubt,
For that she was a woman, and without
Any more subtle fluid in her veins
Than throbbing blood, and that the self-same pains
Inhabited her frail-strung heart as his.
And next she wondered how his eyes could miss
Her face so long in Corinth, where, she said,
She dwelt but half retired, and there had led
Days happy as the gold coin could invent
Without the aid of love; yet in content
Till she saw him, as once she passed him by,
Where 'gainst a column he leant thoughtfully
At Venus' temple porch, 'mid baskets heaped
Of amorous herbs and flowers, newly reaped
Late on that eve, as 'twas the night before
The Adonian feast; whereof she saw no more,
But wept alone those days, for why should she adore?

**248. Orpheus:** allowed by Pluto to bring his wife, Eurydice, back to earth from Hades provided he did not look at her; he could not resist doing so, and therefore lost her. **265. Pleiad:** one of the seven daughters of Atlas who were later changed into a group of stars. Cf. "Ode to Maia," above.

**320. Adonian:** feast of Adonis, loved by Venus.

Lycius from death awoke into amaze,
To see her still, and singing so sweet lays;
Then from amaze into delight he fell
To hear her whisper woman's lore so well;
And every word she spake enticed him on
To unperplexed delight and pleasure known.
Let the mad poets say whate'er they please
Of the sweets of Faeries, Peris, Goddesses,
There is not such a treat among them all,
Haunters of caverns, lake, and waterfall,
As a real woman, lineal indeed
From Pyrrha's pebbles or old Adam's seed.
Thus gentle Lamia judged, and judged aright,
That Lycius could not love in half a fright,
So threw the goddess off, and won his heart
More pleasantly by playing woman's part,
With no more awe than what her beauty gave,
That, while it smote, still guaranteed to save.
Lycius to all made eloquent reply,
Marrying to every word a twinborn sigh;
And last, pointing to Corinth, asked her sweet,
If 'twas too far that night for her soft feet.
The way was short, for Lamia's eagerness
Made, by a spell, the triple league decrease
To a few paces; not at all surmised
By blinded Lycius, so in her comprized.
They passed the city gates, he knew not how,
So noiseless, and he never thought to know.

As men talk in a dream, so Corinth all,
Throughout her palaces imperial,
And all her populous streets and temples lewd,
Muttered, like tempest in the distance brewed,
To the wide-spreaded night above her towers.
Men, women, rich and poor, in the cool hours,
Shuffled their sandals o'er the pavement white,
Companioned or alone; while many a light
Flared, here and there, from wealthy festivals,
And threw their moving shadows on the walls,
Or found them clustered in the corniced shade
Of some arched temple door, or dusky colonnade.

Muffling his face, of greeting friends in fear,
Her fingers he pressed hard, as one came near
With curled grey beard, sharp eyes, and smooth bald crown,
Slow-stepped, and robed in philosophic gown:
Lycius shrank closer, as they met and passed,
Into his mantle, adding wings to haste,
While hurried Lamia trembled: "Ah," said he,
"Why do you shudder, love, so ruefully?
Why does your tender palm dissolve in dew?"
"I'm wearied," said fair Lamia: "tell me who
Is that old man? I cannot bring to mind
His features: — Lycius! wherefore did you blind
Yourself from his quick eyes?" Lycius replied,
"'Tis Apollonius sage, my trusty guide
And good instructor; but tonight he seems
The ghost of folly haunting my sweet dreams."

While yet he spake they had arrived before
A pillared porch, with lofty portal door,
Where hung a silver lamp, whose phosphor glow
Reflected in the slabbèd steps below,
Mild as a star in water; for so new,
And so unsullied was the marble hue,
So through the crystal polish, liquid fine,
Ran the dark veins, that none but feet divine
Could e'er have touched there. Sounds Aeolian
Breathed from the hinges, as the ample span
Of the wide doors disclosed a place unknown
Some time to any, but those two alone,
And a few Persian mutes, who that same year
Were seen about the markets: none knew where
They could inhabit; the most curious
Were foiled, who watched to trace them to their house:
And but the flittered-wingèd verse must tell,
For truth's sake, what woe afterwards befell,
'Twould humor many a heart to leave them thus,
Shut from the busy world of more incredulous.

## PART II

Love in a hut, with water and a crust,
Is — Love, forgive us! — cinders, ashes, dust;
Love in a palace is perhaps at last
More grievous torment than a hermit's fast: —
That is a doubtful tale from faery land,
Hard for the non-elect to understand.
Had Lycius lived to hand his story down,
He might have given the moral a fresh frown,
Or clenched it quite: but too short was their bliss
To breed distrust and hate, that make the soft voice hiss.
Beside, there, nightly, with terrific glare,
Love, jealous grown of so complete a pair,
Hovered and buzzed his wings, with fearful roar,
Above the lintel of their chamber door,
And down the passage cast a glow upon the floor.

For all this came a ruin: side by side
They were enthronèd, in the eventide,
Upon a couch, near to a curtaining
Whose airy texture, from a golden string,
Floated into the room, and let appear
Unveiled the summer heaven, blue and clear,

**329. Peris:** winged creatures in Persian mythology, who were descended from the rebel angels. **333. Pyrrha's pebbles:** After the flood, in classical mythology, Pyrrha and her husband repeopled the earth by strewing pebbles that became men. **352. temples lewd:** temples of Venus, frequently the scene of sexual rites.

**386. Aeolian:** like an Aeolian harp (named for Aeolus, god of winds), which is played when passing currents of air touch it.

Betwixt two marble shafts: — there they reposed,
Where use had made it sweet, with eyelids closed,
Saving a tithe which love still open kept,
That they might see each other while they almost slept;
When from the slope side of a suburb hill,
Deafening the swallow's twitter, came a thrill
Of trumpets — Lycius started — the sounds fled,
But left a thought, a buzzing in his head.
For the first time, since first he harbored in
That purple-linèd palace of sweet sin,
His spirit passed beyond its golden bourn
Into the noisy world almost forsworn.
The lady, ever watchful, penetrant,
Saw this with pain, so arguing a want
Of something more, more than her empery
Of joys; and she began to moan and sigh
Because he mused beyond her, knowing well
That but a moment's thought is passion's passing bell.
"Why do you sigh, fair creature?" whispered he:
"Why do you think?" returned she tenderly:
"You have deserted me; — where am I now?
Not in your heart while care weighs on your brow:
No, no, you have dismissed me; and I go
From your breast houseless: aye, it must be so."
He answered, bending to her open eyes,
Where he was mirrored small in paradise,
"My silver planet, both of eve and morn!
Why will you plead yourself so sad forlorn,
While I am striving how to fill my heart
With deeper crimson, and a double smart?
How to entangle, trammel up and snare
Your soul in mine, and labyrinth you there
Like the hid scent in an unbudded rose?
Aye, a sweet kiss — you see your mighty woes.
My thoughts! shall I unveil them? Listen then!
What mortal hath a prize, that other men
May be confounded and abashed withal,
But lets it sometimes pace abroad majestical,
And triumph, as in thee I should rejoice
Amid the hoarse alarm of Corinth's voice.
Let my foes choke, and my friends shout afar,
While through the throngèd streets your bridal car
Wheels round its dazzling spokes." — The lady's cheek
Trembled; she nothing said, but, pale and meek,
Arose and knelt before him, wept a rain
Of sorrows at his words; at last with pain
Beseeching him, the while his hand she wrung,
To change his purpose. He thereat was stung,
Perverse, with stronger fancy to reclaim
Her wild and timid nature to his aim:
Besides, for all his love, in self despite,
Against his better self, he took delight
Luxurious in her sorrows, soft and new.
His passion, cruel grown, took on a hue
Fierce and sanguineous as 'twas possible
In one whose brow had no dark veins to swell.
Fine was the mitigated fury, like
Apollo's presence when in act to strike
The serpent — Ha, the serpent! certes, she
Was none. She burnt, she loved the tyranny,
And, all subdued, consented to the hour
When to the bridal he should lead his paramour.
Whispering in midnight silence, said the youth,
"Sure some sweet name thou hast, though, by my truth,
I have not asked it, ever thinking thee
Not mortal, but of heavenly progeny,
As still I do. Hast any mortal name,
Fit appellation for this dazzling frame?
Or friends or kinsfolk on the citied earth,
To share our marriage feast and nuptial mirth?"
"I have no friends," said Lamia, "no, not one;
My presence in wide Corinth hardly known:
My parents' bones are in their dusty urns
Sepulchered, where no kindled incense burns,
Seeing all their luckless race are dead, save me,
And I neglect the holy rite for thee.
Even as you list invite your many guests;
But if, as now it seems, your vision rests
With any pleasure on me, do not bid
Old Apollonius — from him keep me hid."
Lycius, perplexed at words so blind and blank,
Made close inquiry; from whose touch she shrank,
Feigning a sleep; and he to the dull shade
Of deep sleep in a moment was betrayed.

It was the custom then to bring away
The bride from home at blushing shut of day,
Veiled, in a chariot, heralded along
By strewn flowers, torches, and a marriage song,
With other pageants: but this fair unknown
Had not a friend. So being left alone,
(Lycius was gone to summon all his kin)
And knowing surely she could never win
His foolish heart from its mad pompousness,
She set herself, high-thoughted, how to dress
The misery in fit magnificence.
She did so, but 'tis doubtful how and whence
Came, and who were her subtle servitors.
About the halls, and to and from the doors,
There was a noise of wings, till in short space
The glowing banquet-room shone with wide-archèd grace.
A haunting music, sole perhaps and lone
Supportress of the faery-roof, made moan
Throughout, as fearful the whole charm might fade.
Fresh carvèd cedar, mimicking a glade
Of palm and plantain, met from either side,

Part II: 36. empery: empire. 48. My . . . planet: Lycius thinks of her again as a Pleiad. See above, I.265n.

High in the midst, in honor of the bride:
Two palms and then two plantains, and so on,
From either side their stems branched one to one
All down the aislèd place; and beneath all
There ran a stream of lamps straight on from wall
to wall.
So canopied, lay an untasted feast
Teeming with odors. Lamia, regal dressed,
Silently paced about, and as she went,
In pale contented sort of discontent,
Missioned her viewless servants to enrich
The fretted splendor of each nook and niche.
Between the tree-stems, marbled plain at first,
Came jasper pannels; then, anon, there burst
Forth creeping imagery of slighter trees,
And with the larger wove in small intricacies.
Approving all, she faded at self-will,
And shut the chamber up, close, hushed and still,
Complete and ready for the revels rude,
When dreadful guests would come to spoil her soli-
tude.

The day appeared, and all the gossip rout.
O senseless Lycius! Madman! wherefore flout
The silent-blessing fate, warm cloistered hours,
And show to common eyes these secret bowers?
The herd approached; each guest, with busy brain,
Arriving at the portal, gazed amain,
And entered marveling: for they knew the street,
Remembered it from childhood all complete
Without a gap, yet ne'er before had seen
That royal porch, that high-built fair demesne;
So in they hurried all, mazed, curious and keen:
Save one, who looked thereon with eye severe,
And with calm-planted steps walked in austere;
'Twas Apollonius: something too he laughed,
As though some knotty problem, that had daft
His patient thought, had now begun to thaw,
And solve and melt: — 'twas just as he foresaw.

He met within the murmurous vestibule
His young disciple. " 'Tis no common rule,
Lycius," said he, " for uninvited guest
To force himself upon you, and infest
With an unbidden presence the bright throng
Of younger friends; yet must I do this wrong,
And you forgive me." Lycius blushed, and led
The old man through the inner doors broad-spread;
With reconciling words and courteous mien
Turning into sweet milk the sophist's spleen.

Of wealthy luster was the banquet-room,
Filled with pervading brilliance and perfume:
Before each lucid pannel fuming stood
A censer fed with myrrh and spicèd wood,
Each by a sacred tripod held aloft,

**160. daft:** bewildered, made giddy.

Whose slender feet wide-swerved upon the soft
Wool-woofèd carpets: fifty wreaths of smoke
From fifty censers their light voyage took
To the high roof, still mimicked as they rose
Along the mirrored walls by twin-clouds odorous.
Twelve spherèd tables, by silk seats insphered,
High as the level of a man's breast reared
On libbard's paws, upheld the heavy gold
Of cups and goblets, and the store thrice told
Of Ceres' horn, and, in huge vessels, wine
Come from the gloomy tun with merry shine.
Thus loaded with a feast the tables stood,
Each shrining in the midst the image of a God.

When in an antechamber every guest
Had felt the cold full sponge to pleasure pressed,
By minist'ring slaves, upon his hands and feet,
And fragrant oils with ceremony meet
Poured on his hair, they all moved to the feast
In white robes, and themselves in order placed
Around the silken couches, wondering
Whence all this mighty cost and blaze of wealth
could spring.

Soft went the music the soft air along,
While fluent Greek, a voweled undersong,
Kept up among the guests, discoursing low
At first, for scarcely was the wine at flow;
But when the happy vintage touched their brains,
Louder they talk, and louder come the strains
Of powerful instruments: — the gorgeous dyes,
The space, the splendor of the draperies,
The roof of awful richness, nectarous cheer,
Beautiful slaves, and Lamia's self, appear,
Now, when the wine has done its rosy deed,
And every soul from human trammels freed,
No more so strange; for merry wine, sweet wine,
Will make Elysian shades not too fair, too divine.
Soon was God Bacchus at meridian height;
Flushed were their cheeks, and bright eyes double
bright:
Garlands of every green, and every scent
From vales deflowered, or forest-trees branch-rent,
In baskets of bright osiered gold were brought
High as the handles heaped, to suit the thought
Of every guest; that each, as he did please,
Might fancy-fit his brows, silk-pillowed at his ease.

What wreath for Lamia? What for Lycius?
What for the sage, old Apollonius?
Upon her aching forehead be there hung
The leaves of willow and of adder's tongue;
And for the youth, quick, let us strip for him
The thyrsus, that his watching eyes may swim

**185. libbard:** leopard. **187. Ceres' horn:** Ceres, goddess of growth and vegetation; her horn signified abundance (*Fall of Hyperion*, I. 35–36). **226. thyrsus:** the staff of Bacchus, the sight of which could intoxicate.

Into forgetfulness; and, for the sage,
Let spear-grass and the spiteful thistle wage
War on his temples. Do not all charms fly
At the mere touch of cold philosophy?
There was an awful rainbow once in heaven:
We know her woof, her texture; she is given
In the dull catalogue of common things.
Philosophy will clip an Angel's wings,
Conquer all mysteries by rule and line,
Empty the haunted air, and gnomèd mine—
Unweave a rainbow, as it erewhile made
The tender-personed Lamia melt into a shade.

By her glad Lycius sitting, in chief place,
Scarce saw in all the room another face,
Till, checking his love trance, a cup he took
Full brimmed, and opposite sent forth a look
'Cross the broad table, to beseech a glance
From his old teacher's wrinkled countenance,
And pledge him. The bald-head philosopher
Had fixed his eye, without a twinkle or stir
Full on the alarmèd beauty of the bride,
Brow-beating her fair form, and troubling her sweet pride.
Lycius then pressed her hand, with devout touch,
As pale it lay upon the rosy couch:
'Twas icy, and the cold ran through his veins;
Then sudden it grew hot, and all the pains
Of an unnatural heat shot to his heart.
"Lamia, what means this? Wherefore dost thou start?
Know'st thou that man?" Poor Lamia answered not.
He gazed into her eyes, and not a jot
Owned they the lovelorn piteous appeal:
More, more he gazed: his human senses reel:
Some hungry spell that loveliness absorbs;
There was no recognition in those orbs.
"Lamia!" he cried—and no soft-toned reply.
The many heard, and the loud revelry
Grew hush; the stately music no more breathes;
The myrtle sickened in a thousand wreaths.
By faint degrees, voice, lute, and pleasure ceased;
A deadly silence step by step increased,
Until it seemed a horrid presence there,
And not a man but felt the terror in his hair.
"Lamia!" he shrieked; and nothing but the shriek
With its sad echo did the silence break.
"Begone, foul dream!" he cried, gazing again
In the bride's face, where now no azure vein
Wandered on fair-spaced temples; no soft bloom
Misted the cheek; no passion to illume
The deep-recessèd vision:—all was blight;
Lamia, no longer fair, there sat a deadly white.
"Shut, shut those juggling eyes, thou ruthless man!
Turn them aside, wretch! or the righteous ban
Of all the Gods, whose dreadful images
Here represent their shadowy presences,
May pierce them on the sudden with the thorn
Of painful blindness; leaving thee forlorn,
In trembling dotage to the feeblest fright
Of conscience, for their long offended might,
For all thine impious proud-heart sophistries,
Unlawful magic, and enticing lies.
Corinthians! look upon that grey-beard wretch!
Mark how, possessed, his lashless eyelids stretch
Around his demon eyes! Corinthians, see!
My sweet bride withers at their potency."
"Fool!" said the sophist, in an under-tone
Gruff with contempt; which a death-nighing moan
From Lycius answered, as heart-struck and lost,
He sank supine beside the aching ghost.
"Fool! Fool!" repeated he, while his eyes still
Relented not, nor moved; "from every ill
Of life have I preserved thee to this day,
And shall I see thee made a serpent's prey?"
Then Lamia breathed death breath; the sophist's eye,
Like a sharp spear, went through her utterly,
Keen, cruel, perceant, stinging: she, as well
As her weak hand could any meaning tell
Motioned him to be silent; vainly so,
He looked and looked again a level—No!
"A serpent!" echoed he; no sooner said,
Than with a frightful scream she vanished:
And Lycius' arms were empty of delight,
As were his limbs of life, from that same night.
On the high couch he lay!—his friends came round—
Supported him—no pulse, or breath they found.
And, in its marriage robe, the heavy body wound.

**229–33. all things:** The passage has occasionally been taken too literally as an indication of Keats's opposition to science and philosophy. It has also been associated with the story that, at a party, Keats and Charles Lamb condemned Newton for destroying "the beauty of the rainbow by reducing it to the prismatic colors." Keats and possibly Lamb were half joking, however. The passage, moreover, cannot be considered apart from Keats's general emphasis at this time on the importance of philosophy. **231. awful:** awe-inspiring.

# THE FALL OF HYPERION

*A Dream*

Keats's revision of *Hyperion* was begun in August, 1819, while he was still at work on *Lamia*. He probably discontinued it by the end of September. The revision, especially the first canto, is a quite different poem from the former *Hyperion*. Much of the Miltonic style of the first version has evaporated; the blank verse of the revision is quieter, more relaxed, mellow, and idiomatic. What remains of the original story seems to have been destined for another purpose, though the revision, like the original, is incomplete. The new first canto carries further the condemnation of the "dreaming" poet already implied in *Lamia.*

### from CANTO I

Fanatics have their dreams, wherewith they weave
A paradise for a sect; the savage, too,
From forth the loftiest fashion of his sleep
Guesses at Heaven; pity these have not
Traced upon vellum or wild Indian leaf
The shadows of melodious utterance.
But bare of laurel they live, dream, and die;
For Poesy alone can tell her dreams —
With the fine spell of words alone can save
Imagination from the sable chain
And dumb enchantment — Who alive can say,
"Thou art no Poet — may'st not tell thy dreams"?
Since every man whose soul is not a clod
Hath visions, and would speak, if he had loved,
And been well nurtured in his mother tongue.
Whether the dream now purposed to rehearse
Be poet's or fanatic's will be known
When this warm scribe, my hand, is in the grave.

Methought I stood where trees of every clime,
Palm, myrtle, oak, and sycamore, and beech,
With plantane, and spice-blossoms, made a screen;
In neighborhood of fountains by the noise
Soft-showering in mine ears and by the touch
Of scent, not far from roses. Turning round
I saw an arbor with a drooping roof
Of trellis vines, and bells, and larger blooms,
Like floral censers, swinging light in air;
Before its wreathèd doorway, on a mound
Of moss, was spread a feast of summer fruits,
Which, nearer seen, seemed refuse of a meal
By angel tasted or our Mother Eve;
For empty shells were scattered on the grass,
And grape-stalks but half bare, and remnants more,
Sweet-smelling, whose pure kinds I could not know.
Still was more plenty than the fabled horn
Thrice emptied could pour forth, at banqueting
For Proserpine returned to her own fields,
Where the white heifers low. And appetite,
More yearning than on earth I ever felt,
Growing within, I ate deliciously;
And, after not long, thirsted; for thereby
Stood a cool vessel of transparent juice,
Sipped by the wandered bee, the which I took,
And, pledging all the mortals of the world,
And all the dead whose names are in our lips,
Drank. That full draught is parent of my theme.
No Asian poppy nor elixir fine
Of the soon-fading, jealous Caliphat,
No poison gendered in close monkish cell,
To thin the scarlet conclave of old men,
Could so have rapt unwilling life away.
Among the fragrant husks and berries crushed
Upon the grass, I struggled hard against
The domineering potion, but in vain.
The cloudy swoon came on, and down I sunk,
Like a Silenus on an antique vase.
How long I slumbered 'tis a chance to guess.
When sense of life returned, I started up
As if with wings, but the fair trees were gone,
The mossy mound and arbor were no more:
I looked around upon the carvèd sides
Of an old sanctuary with roof august,
Builded so high, it seemed that filmèd clouds
Might spread beneath, as o'er the stars of heaven.
So old the place was, I remembered none
The like upon the earth: what I had seen
Of grey cathedrals, buttressed walls, rent towers,
The superannuations of sunk realms,
Or Nature's rocks toiled hard in waves and winds,
Seemed but the faulture of decrepit things
To that eternal domèd monument.
Upon the marble at my feet there lay
Store of strange vessels, and large draperies,
Which needs had been of dyed asbestos wove,
Or in that place the moth could not corrupt,
So white the linen, so, in some, distinct
Ran imageries from a somber loom.
All in a mingled heap confused there lay
Robes, golden tongs, censer and chafing-dish,
Girdles, and chains, and holy jewelries.

Turning from these with awe, once more I raised
My eyes to fathom the space every way;
The embossèd roof, the silent massy range
Of columns north and south, ending in mist
Of nothing; then to eastward, where black gates
Were shut against the sunrise evermore.
Then to the west I looked, and saw far off
An image, huge of feature as a cloud,
At level of whose feet an altar slept,
To be approached on either side by steps
And marble balustrade, and patient travail
To count with toil the innumerable degrees.
Towards the altar sober-paced I went,
Repressing haste, as too unholy there;
And, coming nearer, saw beside the shrine
One minist'ring; and there arose a flame.
When in mid-May the sickening east-wind
Shifts sudden to the south, the small warm rain

**FALL OF HYPERION. Canto I: 37. Proserpine:** See *Lamia* I. 63n., above.

**48. soon-fading . . . Caliphat:** The implication is that the caliphs (descendants or successors of Mohammed — the title was often assumed by the Turkish sultans) so frequently murdered each other or were murdered by others that their reigns were short. **50. scarlet . . . men:** secret meeting of cardinals. **56. Silenus:** See *Lamia*, I. 103n., above.

Melts out the frozen incense from all flowers,
And fills the air with so much pleasant health
That even the dying man forgets his shroud; —
Even so that lofty sacrificial fire,
Sending forth Maian incense, spread around
Forgetfulness of everything but bliss,
And clouded all the altar with soft smoke;
From whose white fragrant curtains thus I heard
Language pronounced: " If thou canst not ascend
These steps, die on that marble where thou art.
Thy flesh, near cousin to the common dust,
Will parch for lack of nutriment — thy bones
Will wither in few years, and vanish so
That not the quickest eye could find a grain
Of what thou now art on that pavement cold.
The sands of thy short life are spent this hour,
And no hand in the universe can turn
Thy hourglass, if these gummèd leaves be burnt
Ere thou canst mount up these immortal steps."
I heard, I looked: two senses both at once,
So fine, so subtle, felt the tyranny
Of that fierce threat and the hard task proposed.
Prodigious seemed the toil; the leaves were yet
Burning, — when suddenly a palsied chill
Struck from the pavèd level up my limbs,
And was ascending quick to put cold grasp
Upon those streams that pulse beside the throat!
I shrieked, and the sharp anguish of my shriek
Stung my own ears — I strove hard to escape
The numbness, strove to gain the lowest step.
Slow, heavy, deadly was my pace: the cold
Grew stifling, suffocating, at the heart;
And when I clasped my hands I felt them not.
One minute before death, my icèd foot touched
The lowest stair; and, as it touched, life seemed
To pour in at the toes: I mounted up,
As once fair angels on a ladder flew
From the green turf to heaven. " Holy Power,"
Cried I, approaching near the hornèd shrine,
" What am I that should be so saved from death?
What am I that another death come not
To choke my utterance, sacrilegious, here? "
Then said the veilèd Shadow: " Thou hast felt
What 'tis to die and live again before
Thy fated hour; that thou hadst power to do so
Is thy own safety; thou hast dated on
Thy doom." " High Prophetess," said I, " purge off,
Benign, if so it please thee, my mind's film."
" None can usurp this height," returned that shade,
" But those to whom the miseries of the world
Are misery, and will not let them rest.
All else who find a haven in the world,
Where they may thoughtless sleep away their days,
If by a chance into this fane they come,
Rot on the pavement where thou rotted'st half."
" Are there not thousands in the world," said I,
Encouraged by the sooth voice of the shade,
" Who love their fellows even to the death;
Who feel the giant agony of the world;
And more, like slaves to poor humanity,
Labor for mortal good? I sure should see
Other men here, but I am here alone."
" Those whom thou spakest of are no visionaries,"
Rejoined that voice — " they are no dreamers weak;
They seek no wonder but the human face,
No music but a happy-noted voice —
They come not here, they have no thought to come —
And thou art here, for thou art less than they.
What benefit canst thou do, or all thy tribe,
To the great world? Thou art a dreaming thing,
A fever of thyself — think of the earth;
What bliss, even in hope, is there for thee?
What haven? every creature hath its home;
Every sole man hath days of joy and pain,
Whether his labors be sublime or low —
The pain alone, the joy alone, distinct:
Only the dreamer venoms all his days,
Bearing more woe than all his sins deserve.
Therefore, that happiness be somewhat shared,
Such things as thou art are admitted oft
Into like gardens thou didst pass erewhile,
And suffered in these temples: for that cause
Thou standest safe beneath this statue's knees."
" That I am favored for unworthiness,
By such propitious parley medicined
In sickness not ignoble, I rejoice,
Aye, and could weep for love of such award."
So answered I, continuing, " If it please,
Majestic Shadow, tell me: sure not all
Those melodies sung into the world's ear
Are useless: sure a poet is a sage;
A humanist, physician to all men.
That I am none I feel, as vultures feel
They are no birds when eagles are abroad.
What am I then: thou spakest of my tribe:
What tribe? " The tall shade veiled in drooping white
Then spake, so much more earnest, that the breath
Moved the thin linen folds that drooping hung
About a golden censer, from the hand
Pendent — " Art thou not of the dreamer tribe?
The poet and the dreamer are distinct,
Diverse, sheer opposite, antipodes.
The one pours out a balm upon the world,
The other vexes it." Then shouted I
Spite of myself, and with a Pythia's spleen,
" Apollo! faded! O far-flown Apollo!

**103. Maian:** See "Ode to Maia," above. **147. None . . . usurp:** See Keats's letter to his brother, Feb. 14–May 3, 1819, below.

**203. Pythia:** priestess of the oracle at Delphi.

Where is thy misty pestilence to creep
Into the dwellings, through the door crannies
Of all mock lyrists, large self-worshipers
And careless Hectorers in proud bad verse?
Though I breathe death with them it will be life
To see them sprawl before me into graves.
Majestic Shadow, tell me where I am,
Whose altar this, for whom this incense curls;
What image this whose face I cannot see
For the broad marble knees; and who thou art,
Of accent feminine so courteous?"

Then the tall shade, in drooping linens veiled,
Spake out, so much more earnest, that her breath
Stirred the thin folds of gauze that drooping hung
About a golden censer, from her hand
Pendent; and by her voice I knew she shed
Long-treasured tears. "This temple, sad and lone,
Is all spared from the thunder of a war
Foughten long since by giant Hierarchy
Against rebellion: this old Image here,
Whose carvèd features wrinkled as he fell,
Is Saturn's; I, Moneta, left supreme,
Sole priestess of his desolation." —
I had no words to answer, for my tongue,
Useless, could find about its roofèd home
No syllable of a fit majesty
To make rejoinder to Moneta's mourn:
There was a silence, while the altar's blaze
Was fainting for sweet food. I looked thereon,
And on the pavèd floor, where nigh were piled
Faggots of cinnamon, and many heaps
Of other crispèd spicewood: then again
I looked upon the altar, and its horns
Whitened with ashes, and its lang'rous flame,
And then upon the offerings again;
And so by turns — till sad Moneta cried:
"The sacrifice is done, but not the less
Will I be kind to thee for thy good will.
My power, which to me is still a curse,
Shall be to thee a wonder; for the scenes
Still swooning vivid through my globèd brain,
With an electral changing misery,
Thou shalt with these dull mortal eyes behold
Free from all pain, if wonder pain thee not."
As near as an immortal's spherèd words
Could to a mother's soften, were these last:
And yet I had a terror of her robes,
And chiefly of the veils, that from her brow
Hung pale, and curtained her in mysteries,
That made my heart too small to hold its blood.
This saw that Goddess, and with sacred hand
Parted the veils. Then saw I a wan face,
Not pined by human sorrows, but bright-blanched
By an immortal sickness which kills not;
It works a constant change, which happy death
Can put no end to; deathwards progressing
To no death was that visage; it had passed
The lily and the snow; and beyond these
I must not think now, though I saw that face.
But for her eyes I should have fled away.
They held me back with a benignant light,
Soft mitigated by divinest lids
Half closed, and visionless entire they seemed
Of all external things — they saw me not,
But, in blank splendor, beamed like the mild
moon,
Who comforts those she sees not, who knows not
What eyes are upward cast. As I had found
A grain of gold upon a mountain's side,
And, twinged with avarice, strained out my eyes
To search its sullen entrails rich with ore,
So, at the view of sad Moneta's brow,
I ached to see what things the hollow brain
Behind enwombèd: what high tragedy
In the dark secret Chambers of her skull
Was acting, that could give so dread a stress
To her cold lips, and fill with such a light
Her planetary eyes, and touch her voice
With such a sorrow. . . .

**208. Hectorers:** bullying, browbeating writers; possibly an allusion to Byron. **246. electral:** vital, vivid.

## THIS LIVING HAND

Probably written in 1819, these lines are commonly supposed to have been addressed to Fanny Brawne.

This living hand, now warm and capable
Of earnest grasping, would, if it were cold
And in the icy silence of the tomb,
So haunt thy days and chill thy dreaming nights
That thou wouldst wish thine own heart dry of
blood
So in my veins red life might stream again,
And thou be conscience-calmed — see here it is —
I hold it towards you.

## TO AUTUMN

Written September 19, 1819. Three days later, Keats wrote to his friend, J. H. Reynolds, from Winchester, "How beautiful the season is now. How fine the air. . . . I never liked stubble-fields so much as now — Aye better than the chilly green of the spring. Somehow a stubble-field looks warm — in the same way that some pictures look warm. This struck me so much in my Sunday's walk that I composed upon it." For general discussion of the ode, see the Introduction, p. 324.

I

Season of mists and mellow fruitfulness,
  Close bosom-friend of the maturing sun;

Conspiring with him how to load and bless
With fruit the vines that round the thatch-eaves run;
To bend with apples the mossed cottage-trees,
And fill all fruit with ripeness to the core;
To swell the gourd, and plump the hazel shells
With a sweet kernel; to set budding more,
And still more, later flowers for the bees,
Until they think warm days will never cease,
For Summer has o'er-brimmed their clammy cells.

2

Who hath not seen thee oft amid thy store?
Sometimes whoever seeks abroad may find
Thee sitting careless on a granary floor,
Thy hair soft-lifted by the winnowing wind;
Or on a half-reaped furrow sound asleep,
Drowsed with the fume of poppies, while thy hook
Spares the next swath and all its twinèd flowers:
And sometimes like a gleaner thou dost keep
Steady thy laden head across a brook;
Or by a cyder-press, with patient look,
Thou watchest the last oozings hours by hours.

3

Where are the songs of Spring? Ay, where are they?
Think not of them, thou hast thy music too,—
While barrèd clouds bloom the soft-dying day,
And touch the stubble-plains with rosy hue;
Then in a wailful choir the small gnats mourn
Among the river sallows, borne aloft
Or sinking as the light wind lives or dies;
And full-grown lambs loud bleat from hilly bourn;
Hedge-crickets sing; and now with treble soft
The red-breast whistles from a garden-croft; 32
And gathering swallows twitter in the skies.

TO AUTUMN. **28. sallows:** willows. **30. bourn:** region. **32. croft:** a small, enclosed field

# LETTERS

The letters of Keats are among the most appealing in English literature. They touch upon both ideas and ordinary daily experiences with insight, gusto, warmth, and humor. Particularly valuable for interpreting what was best in Keats, and sensing the direction in which his unique promise lay, are his searching remarks on poetry and the poetic character. Among them, as T. S. Eliot has said, there is hardly one statement that "will not be found to be true; and what is more, true for greater and more mature poetry than anything that Keats ever wrote."

The text of the letters is basically that of M. B. Forman (Oxford, 1931, and later revised editions). Capitalization has in general been changed to conform more closely with modern usage, but the original spelling and punctuation have been retained.

## I. To JOHN HAMILTON REYNOLDS [1]

*Saturday 22 Nov. 1817*

Saturday

My Dear Reynolds,

There are two things which tease me here—one of them Crips,[2] and the other that I cannot go with Tom into Devonshire—however I hope to do my duty to myself in a week or so; and then I'll try what I can do for my neighbour—now is not this virtuous? on returning to town—I'll damn all idleness—indeed, in superabundance of employment, I must not be content to run here and there on little two-penny errands—but turn rake-hell, i e go a masking [3] or Bailey will think me just as great a promise keeper as *he* thinks you—for myself I do not,—and do not remember above one complaint against you for matter o' that—Bailey writes so abominable a hand, to give his letter a fair reading requires a little time: so I had not seen, when I saw you last, his invitation to Oxford at Christmas—I'll go with you. You know how poorly Rice was—I do not think it was all corporeal—bodily pain was not used to keep him silent. I'll tell you what; he was hurt at what your sisters said about his joking with your mother, he was, soothly to sain—It will all blow over. God knows, my dear Reynolds, I should not talk any sorrow to you—you must have enough vexations—so I won't any more—If I ever start a rueful subject in a letter to you—blow me! Why don't you—Now I was agoing to ask a very silly question neither you nor any body else could answer, under a folio, or at least a pamphlet—you shall judge—Why don't you, as I do, look unconcerned at what may be called more particularly Heart-vexations? They never surprize me—lord! a man should have the fine point of his soul taken off to become fit for this world—I like this place very much. There is hill & dale and a little river—I

LETTERS. **1.** Reynolds, a young clerk, slightly older than Keats, had been writing poetry for some years. Keats met him through Leigh Hunt. **2. Crips:** Charles Cripps; see n. 17, below. **3. go a masking:** wear a mask, as rakes of the time often did when they roamed the town at night.

went up Box hill this evening after the moon—you a' seen the moon—came down—and wrote some lines. Whenever I am separated from you, and not engaged in a continued poem—every letter shall bring you a lyric—but I am too anxious for you to enjoy the whole, to send you a particle. One of the three books I have with me is Shakespear's Poems: I neer found so many beauties in the Sonnets—they seem to be full of fine things said unintentionally—in the intensity of working out conceits. Is this to be borne? Hark ye!

When lofty trees I see barren of leaves
  Which erst from heat did canopy the herd,
And Summer's green all girded up in sheaves,
  Borne on the bier with white and bristly beard.[4]

He has left nothing to say about nothing or anything: for look at snails, you know what he says about snails, you know where he talks about "cockled snails"[5]—well, in one of these sonnets, he says—the chap slips into—no! I lie! this is in the Venus and Adonis: the simile brought it to my mind.

Audi—As the snail, whose tender horns being hit,
  Shrinks back into his shelly cave with pain
And there all smothered up in shade doth sit,
  Long after fearing to put forth again:
So at his bloody view her eyes are fled,
Into the deep dark cabins of her head.[6]

He overwhelms a genuine lover of Poesy with all manner of abuse, talking about—

"a poet's rage
And stretchèd metre of an antique song."[7]

Which by the by will be a capital motto for my Poem,[8] won't it?—He speaks too of "Time's antique pen"—and "April's first born flowers"—and "deaths eternal cold".—By the Whim King! I'll give you a stanza, because it is not material in connection and when I wrote it I wanted you to—give your vote, pro or con.—

Crystalline Brother of the belt of Heaven,
Aquarius! to whom King Jove hath given
Two liquid pulse-streams! 'stead of feathered
  wings—
Two fan-like fountains—thine illuminings
For Dian play:
Dissolve the frozen purity of air;
Let thy white shoulders silvery and bare,
Show cold through watery pinions: make more
  bright
The Star-Queen's Crescent on her marriage night:
Haste Haste away!—[9]

Now I hope I shall not fall off in the winding up, as the woman said to the ———[10]—I mean up and down. I see there is an advertizement in the Chronicle to poets—he is so overloaded with poems on the late Princess.[11]—I suppose you do not lack—send me a few—lend me thy hand to laugh a little—send me a little pullet sperm, a few finch eggs[12]—and remember me to each of our card playing club—When you die you will all be turned into dice, and be put in pawn with the Devil—for cards they crumple up[13] like any king—I mean John in the stage play what pertains Prince Arthur.

I rest
Your affectionate friend
John Keats

Give my love to both houses[14]—hinc atque illinc.[15]

## II. To BENJAMIN BAILEY[16]

*Saturday 22 Nov. 1817*

My dear Bailey,

I will get over the first part of this (*un*said)[17] letter as soon as possible for it relates to the affair of poor Crips—To a man of your nature such a letter as Haydon's must have been extremely cutting—What occasions the greater part of the world's quarrels? simply this, two minds meet and do not understand each other time enough to prevent any shock or surprise at the conduct of either

4. *Sonnets*, XII. 5. *Love's Labor's Lost*, IV.iii.338. 6. Lines 1033–38. 7. This and the following three quotations are from the *Sonnets*, XVII, XIX, XXI, XIII. 8. **Poem:** *Endymion*, the title page of which bore this quotation.

9. *Endymion*, IV. 581–90. 10. Word illegible. 11. **the . . . Princess:** Princess Charlotte, only daughter of the Prince Regent (later George IV) had just died. As in the eighteenth century, deaths in the royal family were mourned publicly in mediocre verse. 12. The preceding three phrases are from Shakespeare's *I Henry IV*, II.iv.2; *Merry Wives of Windsor*, III.v.32; and *Troilus and Cressida*, V.i.41. The letters of Keats abound with Shakespearean allusions of this sort. 13. **crumple up:** *King John*, V.vii.31. 14. **to . . . houses:** *Romeo and Juliet*, III.i.94, 111. 15. **hinc . . . illinc:** hence and thence. 16. Bailey was an undergraduate at Oxford, preparing to enter the Church, when Keats first met him. Keats wrote Book III of *Endymion* while visiting him at Oxford. 17. ***unsaid*:** Keats is playing on the legal phrase "said letter"; the "said letter" would be Haydon's to Bailey, the "unsaid" Keats's. Benjamin Robert Haydon (1786–1846), the historical painter, had for a year been friendly with Keats. See "To Haydon," l. 7n., above. The background of the present incident is not clear. Cripps, a young artist, had attracted Haydon's attention. Haydon implied he would help to train Cripps, and then demanded an apprentice fee which Keats tried to raise.

party—As soon as I had known Haydon three days I had got enough of his character not to have been surprised at such a letter as he has hurt you with. Nor when I knew it was it a principle with me to drop his acquaintance although with you it would have been an imperious feeling. I wish you knew all that I think about Genius and the Heart—and yet I think you are thoroughly acquainted with my innermost breast in that respect, or you could not have known me even thus long and still hold me worthy to be your dear friend. In passing however I must say of one thing that has pressed upon me lately and encreased my humility and capability of submission and that is this truth—Men of Genius are great as certain ethereal chemicals operating on the mass of neutral intellect—but they have not any individuality, any determined character—I would call the top and head of those who have a proper self Men of Power—

But I am running my head into a subject which I am certain I could not do justice to under five years study and 3 vols octavo—and moreover long to be talking about the Imagination—so my dear Bailey do not think of this unpleasant affair if possible—do not—I defy any harm to come of it—I defy. I'll shall write to Crips this week and request him to tell me all his goings on from time to time by letter wherever I may be—it will all go on well so don't because you have suddenly discover'd a coldness in Haydon suffer yourself to be teased. Do not my dear fellow. O I wish I was as certain of the end of all your troubles as that of your momentary start about the authenticity of the Imagination. I am certain of nothing but of the holiness of the Heart's affections and the truth of Imagination—What the Imagination seizes as Beauty must be Truth—whether it existed before or not—for I have the same idea of all our passions as of love they are all in their sublime, creative of essential Beauty. In a word, you may know my favorite speculation by my first book and the little song I sent in my last—which is a representation from the fancy of the probable mode of operating in these matters. The Imagination may be compared to Adam's dream[18]—he awoke and found it truth. I am the more zealous in this affair, because I have never yet been able to perceive how any thing can be known for truth by consequitive reasoning[19]—and yet it must be. Can it be that even the greatest philosopher ever arrived at his goal without putting aside numerous objections. However it may be, O for a life of sensations rather than of thoughts! It is "a Vision in the form of Youth" a shadow of reality to come—and this consideration has further convinced me for it has come as auxiliary to another favorite speculation of mine, that we shall enjoy ourselves here after by having what we called happiness on earth repeated in a finer tone and so repeated. And yet such a fate can only befall those who delight in sensation rather than hunger as you do after Truth. Adam's dream will do here and seems to be a conviction that Imagination and its empyreal reflection is the same as human life and its spiritual repetition. But as I was saying—the simple imaginative mind may have its rewards in the repetition of its own silent working coming continually on the spirit with a fine suddenness—to compare great things with small—have you never by being surprised with an old melody—in a delicious place—by a delicious voice, felt over again your very speculations and surmises at the time it first operated on your soul—do you not remember forming to yourself the singer's face more beautiful than it was possible and yet with the elevation of the moment you did not think so—even then you were mounted on the wings of Imagination so high—that the prototype must be here after—that delicious face you will see. What a time! I am continually running away from the subject—sure this cannot be exactly the case with a complex mind—one that is imaginative and at the same time careful of its fruits—who would exist partly on sensation partly on thought—to whom it is necessary that years should bring the philosophic mind[20]—such an one I consider your's and therefore it is necessary to your eternal happiness that you not only drink this old wine of Heaven, which I shall call the redigestion of our most ethereal musings on earth; but also increase in knowledge and know all things. I am glad to hear you are in a fair way for Easter—you will soon get through your unpleasant reading and then!—but the world is full of troubles and I have not much reason to think myself pesterd with many—I think Jane or Marianne has a better opinion of me than I deserve—for really and truly I do not think my brothers illness connected with mine—you know more of the real cause than they do nor have I any chance of being rack'd as

**18. Adam's dream:** *Paradise Lost,* VIII. 460–90. **19. consequitive reasoning:** abstract analysis, and consecutive, step-by-step logic.

**20. years . . . mind:** Keats is echoing Wordsworth, "Intimations of Immortality," l. 187, above.

you have been — You perhaps at one time thought there was such a thing as worldly happiness to be arrived at, at certain periods of time marked out — you have of necessity from your disposition been thus led away — I scarcely remember counting upon my happiness — I look not for it if it be not in the present hour — nothing startles me beyond the moment. The setting sun will always set me to rights — or if a sparrow come before my window I take part in its existince and pick about the gravel. The first thing that strikes me on hearing a misfortune having befalled another is this. "Well it cannot be helped — he will have the pleasure of trying the resources of his spirit" — and I beg now my dear Bailey that hereafter should you observe any thing cold in me not to put it to the account of heartlessness but abstraction — for I assure you I sometimes feel not the influence of a passion or affection during a whole week — and so long this sometimes continues I begin to suspect myself and the genuineness of my feelings at other times — thinking them a few barren tragedy-tears — My brother Tom is much improved — he is going to Devonshire — whither I shall follow him — at present I am just arrived at Dorking to change the scene — change the air and give me a spur to wind up my Poem, of which there are wanting 500 lines. I should have been here a day sooner but the Reynoldses persuaded me to stop in town to meet your friend Christie. There were Rice and Martin — we talked about ghosts. I will have some talk with Taylor and let you know — when please God I come down at Christmas. I will find that Examiner if possible. My best regards to Gleig. My brothers to you and M[rs] Bentley's

Your affectionate friend
John Keats —

## III. To GEORGE and THOMAS KEATS

*Sunday 21 Dec. 1817*

Hampstead Sunday

My dear Brothers,

I must crave your pardon for not having written ere this. . . .[21] I saw Kean [22] return to the public in 'Richard III.', and finely he did it, and, at the request of Reynolds, I went to criticize his Luke in Riches. The critique is in to-day's 'Champion', which I send you, with the Examiner, in which you will find very proper lamentation on the obsoletion of Christmas gambols and pastimes: [23] but it was mixed up with so much egotism of that drivelling nature that pleasure is entirely lost. Hone, the publisher's trial, you must find very amusing; and, as Englishmen, very encouraging — his *Not Guilty* is a thing, which not to have been, would have dulled still more Liberty's emblazoning — Lord Ellenborough has been paid in his own coin — Wooler and Hone [24] have done us an essential service — I have had two very pleasant evenings with Dilke,[25] yesterday and to-day, and am at this moment just come from him, and feel in the humour to go on with this, began in the morning, and from which he came to fetch me. I spent Friday evening with Wells,[26] and went next morning to see Death on the Pale Horse.[27] It is a wonderful picture, when West's age is considered; But there is nothing to be intense upon; no women one feels mad to kiss, no face swelling into reality — The excellence of every art is its intensity, capable of making all disagreeables evaporate, from their being in close relationship with Beauty and Truth.[28] Examine 'King Lear,' and you will find this exemplified throughout; but in this picture we have unpleasantness without any momentous depth of speculation excited, in which to bury its repulsiveness — The picture is larger than 'Christ rejected.'

I dined with Haydon the Sunday after you left, and had a very pleasant day, I dined too (for I have been out too much lately) with Horace Smith, and met his two brothers, with Hill and Kingston, and one Du Bois.[29] They only served to convince me, how superior humour is to wit in respect to enjoyment — These men say things which make one start, without making one feel; they are all alike;

**21.** A passage was here omitted in the only copy of the letter that has survived. **22. Kean:** Edmund Kean (1787–1833), the noted tragic actor. Keats's review of his performance appeared in the *Champion,* Dec. 21, 1817.

**23. lamentation . . . pastimes:** The reference is to an essay of Leigh Hunt on this subject in the *Examiner*, Dec. 21 and 28, 1817. **24. Wooler . . . Hone:** publishers. William Hone had been tried for libel. **25. Dilke:** Charles Dilke (1789–1864), later known as an editor and scholar. **26. Wells:** Charles Wells (1800–79), author of *Stories after Nature.* **27. Death . . . Horse:** Benjamin West (1738–1820). His "Christ Rejected," referred to later in the paragraph, was criticized in the same terms by Hazlitt, whose critical opinions Keats closely followed. **28. The . . . Truth:** If the imaginative grasp of an object is sufficiently intense, it takes so strong a hold of the mind that whatever qualities are irrelevant to its central character (the "disagreeables") evaporate. Its truth (or character) then "swells into reality" for us so vividly that the dynamic awareness of it is also "beautiful." In other words, reality taking form and meaning is "beauty" if it is vitally enough known and felt. Cf. "Ode on a Grecian Urn," ll. 49–50, above. **29. Smith . . . Du Bois:** writers who contributed to magazines of the time.

their manners are alike; they all know fashionables; they have a mannerism in their very eating and drinking, in their mere handling a decanter — They talked of Kean and his low company — Would I were with that company instead of yours, said I to myself! I know such like acquaintance will never do for me, and yet I am going to Reynolds on Wednesday. Brown and Dilke walked with me and back from the Christmas pantomime. I had not a dispute but a disquisition, with Dilke on various subjects; several things dove-tailed in my mind, and at once it struck me what quality went to form a Man of Achievement, especially in Literature, and which Shakespeare possessed so enormously — I mean *Negative Capability,*[30] that is, when a man is capable of being in uncertainties, mysteries, doubts, without any irritable reaching after fact and reason — Coleridge, for instance, would let go by a fine isolated verisimilitude caught from the penetralium of mystery, from being incapable of remaining content with half-knowledge. This pursued through volumes would perhaps take us no further than this, that with a great poet the sense of Beauty overcomes every other consideration, or rather obliterates all consideration.

Shelley's poem [31] is out, and there are words about its being objected to as much as "Queen Mab" was. Poor Shelley, I think he has his quota of good qualities, in sooth la!! Write soon to your most sincere friend and affectionate brother

John.

**30.** We may interpret these difficult remarks, from here to the end of the paragraph, as follows: Our life is filled with change, uncertainties, mysteries; no one complete system of rigid categories will explain it fully. We can grasp and understand the elusive flux of life only by being imaginatively open-minded, sympathetic, receptive — by extending every possible feeler that we may have potentially in us. But we can achieve this active awareness only by ***negating*** our own ***egos.*** We must not only rise above our own vanity and prejudices, but resist the temptation to make up our minds on everything, and to have always ready a neat answer. If we discard a momentary insight, for example, because we cannot fit it into a static category or systematic framework, we are selfishly asserting our own "identity." A great poet is less concerned with himself, and has his eyes on what is without. With him "the sense of Beauty" — the capacity to relish concrete reality in its full, if elusive, meaning — "overcomes every other consideration." In fact, it goes beyond and "obliterates" the act of "consideration" — of deliberating, analyzing, and piecing together experience in a logical structure. For related remarks, see the letter to Woodhouse, Oct. 27, 1818, below. **31. Shelley's poem:** "Laon and Cythna."

## IV. *From* To JOHN HAMILTON REYNOLDS

*Tuesday 3 Feb. 1818*

It may be said that we ought to read our contemporaries — that Wordsworth &c. should have their due from us. But, for the sake of a few fine imaginative or domestic passages, are we to be bullied into a certain philosophy engendered in the whims of an egotist — Every man has his speculations, but every man does not brood and peacock over them till he makes a false coinage and deceives himself.[32] Many a man can travel to the very bourne of Heaven, and yet want confidence to put down his half-seeing. Sancho will invent a journey heavenward as well as any body. We hate poetry that has a palpable design upon us — and if we do not agree, seems to put its hand in its breeches pocket. Poetry should be great and unobtrusive, a thing which enters into one's soul, and does not startle it or amaze it with itself, but with its subject. — How beautiful are the retired flowers! how would they lose their beauty were they to throng into the highway crying out, "admire me I am a violet! — dote upon me I am a primrose!" Modern poets differ from the Elizabethans in this. Each of the moderns like an Elector of Hanover governs his petty state, and knows how many straws are swept daily from the causeways in all his dominions and has a continual itching that all the housewives should have their coppers well scoured: the antients were emperors of vast provinces, they had only heard of the remote ones and scarcely cared to visit them. — I will cut all this — I will have no more of Wordsworth or Hunt in particular — Why should we be of the tribe of Manasseh, when we can wander with Esau? why should we kick against the pricks, when we can walk on roses? Why should we be owls, when we can be eagles? Why be teased with "nice eyed wagtails",[33] when we have in sight "the Cherub Contemplation"? [34] — Why with Wordsworth's "Matthew with a bough of wilding in his hand" [35] when we can have Jacques "under an oak &c."? [36] — The secret of the bough of wilding will run through your head faster than I can write it — Old Matthew spoke to him some years ago on some

**32.** Keats, in his contrast of Wordsworth with the Elizabethans, is following Hazlitt, for whom much of the poetry of the Romantic movement, especially that of Wordsworth, was subjective self-expression. **33.** Leigh Hunt, *The Nymphs,* II.170. **34.** Milton, "Il Penseroso," l. 54 in Vol. I. **35.** "The Two April Mornings," ll. 59–60, above. **36.** *As You Like It,* II.i.31.

nothing, and because he happens in an evening walk to imagine the figure of the old man — he must stamp it down in black and white, and it is henceforth sacred — I don't mean to deny Wordsworth's grandeur and Hunt's merit, but I mean to say we need not be teazed with grandeur and merit when we can have them uncontaminated and unobtrusive. Let us have the old poets, and Robin Hood. Your letter and its sonnets gave me more pleasure than will the 4th Book of Childe Harold [37] and the whole of anybody's life and opinions. In return for your dish of filberts, I have gathered a few catkins,[38] I hope they'll look pretty.

## V. To JOHN TAYLOR [39]

*Friday 27 Feb. 1818*

Hampstead 27 Feby ——

My dear Taylor,

Your alteration strikes me as being a great improvement — the page looks much better. And now I will attend to the punctuations you speak of — the comma should be at *soberly,* and in the other passage the comma should follow *quiet.* I am extremely indebted to you for this attention and also for your after admonitions — It is a sorry thing for me that any one should have to overcome prejudices in reading my verses — that affects me more than any hypercriticism on any particular passage. In *Endymion* I have most likely but moved into the go-cart from the leading strings. In poetry I have a few axioms and you will see how far I am from their centre. 1st. I think poetry should surprise by a fine excess and not by singularity — it should strike the reader as a wording of his own highest thoughts, and appear almost a remembrance —2nd. Its touches of Beauty should never be half way thereby making the reader breathless instead of content: the rise, the progress, the setting of imagery should like the sun come natural too him — shine over him and set soberly although in magnificence leaving him in the luxury of twilight — but it is easier to think what poetry should be than to write it — and this leads me on to another axiom. That if poetry comes not as naturally as the leaves to a tree it had better not come at all. However it may be with me I cannot help looking into new countries with 'O for a Muse of fire to ascend!' [40] If Endymion serves me as a pioneer perhaps I ought to be content. I have great reason to be content, for thank God I can read and perhaps understand Shakspeare to his depths, and I have I am sure many friends, who, if I fail, will attribute any change in my life and temper to humbleness rather than to pride — to a cowering under the wings of great poets rather than to a bitterness that I am not appreciated. I am anxious to get *Endymion* printed that I may forget it and proceed. I have coppied the 3rd Book and have begun the 4th. On running my eye over the proofs — I saw one mistake I will notice it presently and also any others if there be any. There should be no comma in "the raft branch down sweeping from a tall ash top". I have besides made one or two alterations and also altered the 13 line page 32 to make sense of it as you will see. I will take care the printer shall not trip up my heels. There should be no dash after Dryope in this line "Dryope's lone lulling of her Child." Remember me to Percy Street.

Your sincere and obligd friend

John Keats —

P.S. You shall have a short *Preface* in good time —

## VI. *From* To JOHN HAMILTON REYNOLDS

*Sunday 3 May 1818*

. . . I will return to Wordsworth — whether or no he has an extended vision or a circumscribed grandeur — whether he is an eagle in his nest, or on the wing — And to be more explicit and to show you how tall I stand by the giant, I will put down a simile of human life as far as I now perceive it; that is, to the point to which I say we both have arrived at — Well — I compare human life to a large mansion of many apartments, two of which I can only describe, the doors of the rest being as yet shut upon me. The first we step into we call the infant or thoughtless chamber, in which we remain as long as we do not think — We remain there a long while, and notwithstanding the doors of the second chamber remain wide open, showing a bright appearance, we care not to hasten to it; but are at length imperceptibly impelled by the awakening of this thinking principle within us — we no sooner get into the second chamber, which I shall

37. Byron's *Childe Harold*, which was to be published on April 28.
38. **filberts . . . catkins:** Filberts are hazelnuts. catkins their blossom.
39. **Taylor:** of the firm of Taylor and Hessey, publishers of Keats's *Endymion*.

40. Prologue to Shakespeare's *Henry V*.

call the chamber of maiden-thought, than we become intoxicated with the light and the atmosphere, we see nothing but pleasant wonders, and think of delaying there for ever in delight: However among the effects this breathing is father of is that tremendous one of sharpening one's vision into the heart and nature of man — of convincing one's nerves that the world is full of misery and heartbreak, pain, sickness and oppression — whereby this chamber of maiden thought becomes gradually darken'd and at the same time on all sides of it many doors are set open — but all dark — all leading to dark passages — We see not the ballance of good and devil. We are in a mist. *We* are now in that state — We feel the "burden of the mystery", To this point was Wordsworth come, as far as I can conceive when he wrote 'Tintern Abbey' and it seems to me that his Genius is explorative of those dark passages. Now if we live, and go on thinking, we too shall explore them — he is a Genius and superior to us, in so far as he can, more than we, make discoveries, and shed a light in them — Here I must think Wordsworth is deeper than Milton — though I think it has depended more upon the general and gregarious advance of intellect, than individual greatness of mind — From the Paradise Lost and the other works of Milton, I hope it is not too presuming, even between ourselves to say, that his philosophy, human and divine, may be tolerably understood by one not much advanced in years, In his time Englishmen were just emancipated from a great superstition — and men had got hold of certain points and resting places in reasoning which were too newly born to be doubted, and too much opposed by the mass of Europe not to be thought etherial and authentically divine — who could gainsay his ideas on virtue, vice, and chastity in Comus, just at the time of the dismissal of cod-pieces and a hundred other disgraces? who would not rest satisfied with his hintings at good and evil in the Paradise Lost, when just free from the inquisition and burning in Smithfield? The Reformation produced such immediate and great benefits, that Protestantism was considered under the immediate eye of Heaven, and its own remaining dogmas and superstitions, then, as it were, regenerated, constituted those resting places and seeming sure points of reasoning — from that I have mentioned, Milton, whatever he may have thought in the sequel, appears to have been content with these by his writings — He did not think into the human heart, as Wordsworth has done — Yet Milton as a philosopher, had sure as great powers as Wordsworth — What is then to be inferr'd? O many things — It proves there is really a grand march of intellect —, It proves that a mighty providence subdues the mightiest minds to the service of the time being, whether it be in human knowledge or religion — I have often pitied a tutor who has to hear "Nom: Musa"[41] — so often dinn'd into his ears — I hope you may not have the same pain in this scribbling — I may have read these things before, but I never had even a thus dim perception of them; and moreover I like to say my lesson to one who will endure my tediousness for my own sake — After all there is certainly something real in the world — Moore's present to Hazlitt[42] is real — I like that Moore, and am glad I saw him at the theatre just before I left town. Tom has spit a leetle blood this afternoon, and that is rather a damper — but I know — the truth is there is something real in the world. Your third chamber of life shall be a lucky and a gentle one — stored with the wine of love — and the bread of friendship. When you see George if he should not have received a letter from me tell him he will find one at home most likely — tell Bailey I hope soon to see him — Remember me to all. The leaves have been out here, for mony a day — I have written to George for the first stanzas of my Isabel[43] — I shall have them soon and will copy the whole out for you.

Your affectionate friend
John Keats.

## VII. To RICHARD WOODHOUSE[44]

*Tuesday 27 Oct. 1818*

My dear Woodhouse,

Your letter gave me a great satisfaction; more on account of its friendliness, than any relish of that matter in it which is accounted so acceptable in the "genus irritabile". The best answer I can give you is in a clerk-like manner to make some observations on two principle points, which seem to point like indices into the midst of the whole pro and con, about genius, and views and atchievements

41. **"Nom: Musa"**: the first lesson in Latin grammar: "Nominative: Musa," etc. 42. Probably a copy of one of Thomas Moore's books. 43. **Isabel**: Keats's poem, *Isabella*. 44. Woodhouse, a few years older than Keats, was a young lawyer with an intelligent approach to literature. He collected valuable information about Keats and his work, and perhaps understood the character of his mind better than any of Keats's other friends.

and ambition and cœtera. 1st. As to the poetical character itself (I mean that sort of which, if I am any thing, I am a member; that sort distinguished from the Wordsworthian or egotistical sublime; which is a thing per se and stands alone) it is not itself — it has no self — it is every thing and nothing — It has no character — it enjoys light and shade; it lives in gusto, be it foul or fair, high or low, rich or poor, mean or elevated — It has as much delight in conceiving an Iago as an Imogen. What shocks the virtuous philosopher, delights the camelion poet.[45] It does no harm from its relish of the dark side of things any more than from its taste for the bright one; because they both end in speculation. A poet is the most unpoetical of any thing in existence; because he has no identity — he is continually in for[46] — and filling some other body — The sun, the moon, the sea and men and women who are creatures of impulse are poetical and have about them an unchangeable attribute — the poet has none; no identity — he is certainly the most unpoetical of all God's creatures. If then he has no self, and if I am a poet, where is the wonder that I should say I would write no more? Might I not at that very instant have been cogitating on the characters of Saturn and Ops? It is a wretched thing to confess; but is a very fact that not one word I ever utter can be taken for granted as an opinion growing out of my identical nature — how can it, when I have no nature? When I am in a room with people if I ever am free from speculating on creations of my own brain, then not myself goes home to myself: but the identity of every one in the room begins to press upon me that I am in a very little time annihilated — not only among men; it would be the same in a nursery of children: I know not whether I make myself wholly understood: I hope enough so to let you see that no dependence is to be placed on what I said that day.

In the second place I will speak of my views, and of the life I purpose to myself. I am ambitious of doing the world some good: if I should be spared that may be the work of maturer years — in the interval I will assay to reach to as high a summit in poetry as the nerve bestowed upon me will suffer. The faint conceptions I have of poems to come brings the blood frequently into my forehead. All I hope is that I may not lose all interest in human affairs — that the solitary indifference I feel for applause even from the finest spirits, will not blunt any acuteness of vision I may have. I do not think it will — I feel assured I should write from the mere yearning and fondness I have for the beautiful even if my night's labours should be burnt every morning, and no eye ever shine upon them. But even now I am perhaps not speaking from myself: but from some character in whose soul I now live. I am sure however that this next sentence is from myself. I feel your anxiety, good opinion and friendliness in the highest degree, and am

Your's most sincerely
John Keats

**45. camelion poet:** See Intro., p. 324. **46. in for:** probably "informing."

## VIII. *From* To GEORGE and GEORGIANA KEATS

*Sunday 14 Feb.–Monday 3 May 1819*

. . . Very few have been influenced by a pure desire of the benefit of others — in the greater part of the benefactors to humanity some meretricious motive has sullied their greatness — some melodramatic scenery has fascinated them — From the manner in which I feel Haslam's misfortune I perceive how far I am from any humble standard of disinterestedness[47] — Yet this feeling ought to be carried to its highest pitch as there is no fear of its ever injuring society — which it would do I fear pushed to an extremity — For in wild nature the hawk would loose his breakfast of robins and the robin his of worms — the lion must starve as well as the swallow. The greater part of men make their way with the same instinctiveness, the same unwandering eye from their purposes, the same animal eagerness as the hawk. The hawk wants a mate, so does the man — look at them both they set about it and procure one in the same manner. They want both a nest and they both set about one in the same manner — they get their food in the same manner — The noble animal man for his amusement smokes his pipe — the hawk balances about the clouds — that is the only difference of their leisures. This it is that makes the amusement of life — to a speculative Mind. I go among the fields and catch a glimpse of a stoat or a fieldmouse peeping out of the withered grass — the creature hath a purpose and its eyes are bright with it. I go amongst the buildings of a city and I see a man

**47. disinterestedness:** freedom from all selfish motives. Keats is referring to the approaching death of the father of his close friend, William Haslam, a young businessman.

hurrying along — to what? the creature has a purpose and his eyes are bright with it. But then, as Wordsworth says, "we have all one human heart"[48] — there is an ellectric fire in human nature tending to purify — so that among these human creatures there is continually some birth of new heroism. The pity is that we must wonder at it: as we should at finding a pearl in rubbish. I have no doubt that thousands of people never heard of have had hearts completely disinterested: I can remember but two — Socrates and Jesus — their histories evince it. What I heard a little time ago, Taylor observe with respect to Socrates may be said of Jesus — That he was so great a man that though he transmitted no writing of his own to posterity, we have his Mind and his sayings and his greatness handed to us by others. It is to be lamented that the history of the latter was written and revised by men interested in the pious frauds of religion. Yet through all this I see his splendour. Even here[49] though I myself am pursueing the same instinctive course as the veriest human animal you can think of — I am however young writing at random — straining at particles of light in the midst of a great darkness — without knowing the bearing of any one assertion of any one opinion. Yet may I not in this be free from sin? May there not be superior beings amused with any graceful, though instinctive attitude my mind may fall into, as I am entertained with the alertness of a stoat or the anxiety of a deer? Though a quarrel in the streets is a thing to be hated, the energies displayed in it are fine; the commonest man shows a grace in his quarrel — By a superior being our reasonings may take the same tone — though erroneous they may be fine — This is the very thing in which consists poetry; and if so it is not so fine a thing as philosophy — For the same reason that an eagle is not so fine a thing as a truth — Give me this credit — Do you not think I strive — to know myself? Give me this credit — and you will not think that on my own account I repeat Milton's lines

"How charming is divine Philosophy  
Not harsh and crabbed as dull fools suppose  
But musical as is Apollo's lute" —[50] . . .

Call the world if you please "The vale of Soul-making." Then you will find out the use of the world (I am speaking now in the highest terms for human nature admitting it to be immortal which I will here take for granted for the purpose of showing a thought which has struck me concerning it) I say *'Soul making'* Soul as distinguished from an Intelligence — There may be intelligences or sparks of the divinity in millions — but they are not Souls till they acquire identities, till each one is personally itself.[51] Intelligences are atoms of perception — they know and they see and they are pure, in short they are God — How then are Souls to be made? How then are these sparks which are God to have identity given them — so as ever to possess a bliss peculiar to each one's individual existence? How, but by the medium of a world like this? This point I sincerely wish to consider because I think it a grander system of salvation than the chrystiain religion — or rather it is a system of spirit-creation — This is effected by three grand materials acting the one upon the other for a series of years. These three materials are the *Intelligence* — the *human Heart* (as distinguished from Intelligence or Mind) and the *world* or *elemental space* suited for the proper action of *Mind and Heart* on each other for the purpose of forming the *Soul* or *Intelligence destined to possess the sense of identity.* I can scarcely express what I but dimly perceive — and yet I think I perceive it — that you may judge the more clearly I will put it in the most homely form possible — I will call the *world* a school instituted for the purpose of teaching little children to read — I will call the *human Heart* the *horn book* used in that school — and I will call the *child able to read, the Soul* made from that *school* and its *hornbook.* Do you not see how necessary a world of pains and troubles is to school an Intelligence and make it a Soul? A place where the Heart must feel and suffer in a thousand diverse ways! Not merely is the Heart a hornbook, It is the Minds Bible, it is the Minds experience, it is

48. "The Old Cumberland Beggar," l. 153, above. 49. This and the following two sentences may be paraphrased thus: I myself am far from being completely "disinterested" — that is, completely free from all selfish motivations. In fact, like all human animals, I am pursuing my own instinctive course of action. (Also, I am young, groping without much light as yet; and I still do not know very well what would be the full, logical result of attitudes I instinctively adopt.) Yet is this to be greatly condemned? This following of one's instinctive course, this assertion of "self-identity," is not complete "selfishness" so much as it is the instinctive activity of the animal world, innocent and to be expected. It is not, to be sure, the highest development of what human nature can and should be. As Keats's later remarks about the "vale of Soul-making" suggest, the developing of human character comes about by gradual concrete experience. From this experience, provided one is endowed with intelligence and sensitivity, wisdom (or philosophy) emerges, man's heart is deepened, and his nature is increasingly "fortified" and perfected into a "soul."

50. *Comus*, ll. 476–78. 51. See n. 49, above.

the teat from which the Mind or Intelligence sucks its identity. . . . If what I have said should not be plain enough, as I fear it may not be, I will put you in the place where I began in this series of thoughts — I mean, I began by seeing how man was formed by circumstances — and what are circumstances? — but touchstones of his Heart — ? and what are touchstones? but proovings of his Heart? and what are proovings of his Heart but fortifiers or alterers of his nature? and what is his altered nature but his Soul? — and what was his Soul before it came into the world and had these provings and alterations and perfectionings? — An Intelligence — without identity — and how is this identity to be made? Through the medium of the Heart? And how is the Heart to become this medium but in a world of circumstances?

## IX. To MISS JEFFREY [52]

*Wednesday 9 June 1819*

Wentworth Place

My Dear young Lady,

I am exceedingly obliged by your two letters — Why I did not answer your first immediately was that I have had a little aversion to the south of Devon from the continual remembrance of my brother Tom. On that account I do not return to my old lodgings in Hampstead though the people of the house have become friends of mine — This however I could think nothing of, it can do no more than keep one's thoughts employed for a day or two. I like your description of Bradley [53] very much and I dare say shall be there in the course of the summer; it would be immediately but that a friend with ill health and to whom I am greatly attached call'd on me yesterday and proposed my spending a month with him at the back of the Isle of Wight. This is just the thing at present — the morrow will take care of itself — I do not like the name of Bishop's Teigntown — I hope the road from Teignmouth to Bradley does not lie that way — Your advice about the Indiaman is a very wise advice, because it justs suits me, though you are a little in the wrong concerning its destroying the energies of mind: [54] on the contrary it would be the finest thing in the world to strengthen them — To be thrown among people who care not for you, with whom you have no sympathies forces the mind upon its own resources, and leaves it free to make its speculations of the differences of human character and to class them with the calmness of a botanist. An Indiaman is a little world. One of the great reasons that the English have produced the finest writers in the world is, that the English world has ill-treated them during their lives and foster'd them after their deaths. They have in general been trampled aside into the bye paths of life and seen the festerings of society. They have not been treated like the Raphaels of Italy. And where is the Englishman and poet who has given a magnificent entertainment at the christening of one of his hero's horses as Boyardo [55] did? He had a castle in the Appenine. He was a noble poet of romance; not a miserable and mighty poet of the human Heart. The middle age of Shakespeare was all clouded over; his days were not more happy than Hamlet's who is perhaps more like Shakspeare himself in his common every day life than any other of his characters — Ben Johnson was a common Soldier and in the Low Countries, in the face of two armies, fought a single combat with a French trooper and slew him — For all this I will not go on board an Indiaman, nor for example's sake run my head into dark alleys: I dare say my discipline is to come, and plenty of it too. I have been very idle lately, very averse to writing; both from the overpowering idea of our dead poets and from abatement of my love of fame. I hope I am a little more of a philosopher than I was, consequently a little less of a versifying pet-lamb.[56] I have put no more in print or you should have had it. You will judge of my 1819 temper when I tell you that the thing I have most enjoyed this year has been writing an ode to Indolence. Why did you not make your long-haired sister put her great brown hard fist to paper and cross your letter? Tell her when you write again that I expect chequer-work — My friend M^r^ Brown is sitting opposite me employed in writing a life of *David*. He reads me passages as he writes them stuffing my infidel mouth as though I were a young rook — Infidel rooks do not provender with Elisha's ravens.[57] If he goes on as he has begun your new

**52. Miss Jeffrey:** A member of a family friendly to Keats, at Teignmouth, Devon. It is uncertain to which of the daughters of the family the letter is addressed. **53. Bradley:** in South Devon. **54. Your . . . mind:** Keats had been speculating about the advisability of becoming a surgeon on an East India trade ship. In an earlier letter to Miss Jeffrey, he had mentioned this as a possibility.

**55. Boyardo:** Matteo Maria Boiardo (1434–94), an Italian poet who wrote chivalric romances based on the legends of Arthur and Charlemagne. **56.** Cf. the letter to George and Georgiana Keats (Feb. 14–May 3, 1819), above, n. 49, and the discussion in the headnote to *Lamia*. **57. Elisha's ravens:** Elijah, not Elisha, was fed by the ravens (I Kings 17:6).

church had better not proceed, for parsons will be superseeded — and of course the clerks must follow. Give my love to your mother with the assurance that I can never forget her anxiety for my brother Tom. Believe also that I shall ever remember our leave-taking with *you*.

Ever sincerely yours
John Keats.

## X. To BENJAMIN BAILEY

*Saturday 14 Aug. 1819*

We removed to Winchester for the convenience of a library and find it an exceeding pleasant town, enriched with a beautiful cathedrall and surrounded by a fresh-looking country. We are in tolerably good and cheap lodgings. Within these two months I have written 1500 lines, most of which besides many more of prior composition you will probably see by next winter. I have written two tales, one from Boccaccio call'd the Pot of Basil; and another call'd St. Agnes' Eve on a popular superstition; and a third call'd Lamia — half finished — I have also been writing parts of my Hyperion and completed 4 acts of a tragedy.[58] It was the opinion of most of my friends that I should never be able to write a scene. I will endeavour to wipe away the prejudice — I sincerely hope you will be pleased when my labours since we last saw each other shall reach you. One of my ambitions is to make as great a revolution in modern dramatic writing as Kean has done in acting — another to upset the drawling of the blue stocking literary world — if in the course of a few years I do these two things I ought to die content — and my friends should drink a dozen of claret on my tomb — I am convinced more and more every day that (excepting the human friend philosopher) [59] a fine writer is the most genuine being in the world. Shakspeare and the Paradise Lost every day become greater wonders to me. I look upon fine phrases like a lover. I was glad to see, by a passage in one of Brown's letters some time ago from the north that you were in such good spirits. Since that you have been married and in congratulating you I wish you every continuance of them. Present my respects to Mrs Bailey. This sounds oddly to me, and I dare say I do it awkwardly enough: but I suppose by this time it is nothing new to you — Brown's remembrances to you — As far as I know we shall remain at Winchester for a goodish while —

Ever your sincere friend
John Keats.

58. **tragedy:** *Otho the Great,* which was written rapidly, amid much distraction, and gives little indication of Keats's potential dramatic ability. 59. **excepting . . . philosopher:** This exception should be kept in mind in reading ***Lamia*** and the *Fall of Hyperion.*

## XI. To PERCY BYSSHE SHELLEY

*Wednesday 16 Aug. 1820*

Hampstead August 16th

My dear Shelley,

I am very much gratified that you, in a foreign country, and with a mind almost overoccupied, should write to me in the strain of the letter beside me. If I do not take advantage of your invitation it will be prevented by a circumstance I have very much at heart to prophesy. There is no doubt that an English winter would put an end to me, and do so in a lingering hateful manner, therefore I must either voyage or journey to Italy as a soldier marches up to a battery. My nerves at present are the worst part of me, yet they feel soothed when I think that come what extreme may, I shall not be destined to remain in one spot long enough to take a hatred of any four particular bedposts. I am glad you take any pleasure in my poor poem; — which I would willingly take the trouble to unwrite, if possible, did I care so much as I have done about reputation. I received a copy of the Cenci, as from yourself from Hunt. There is only one part of it I am judge of; the poetry, and dramatic effect, which by many spirits now a days is considered the mammon. A modern work it is said must have a purpose, which may be the God — *an artist* must serve Mammon — he must have "self concentration" selfishness perhaps. You I am sure will forgive me for sincerely remarking that you might curb your magnanimity and be more of an artist, and "load every rift" of your subject with ore.[60] The thought of such discipline must fall like cold chains upon you, who perhaps never sat with your wings furl'd for six months together. And is not this extraordinary talk for the writer of Endymion! whose mind was like a pack of scattered cards — I am pick'd up and sorted to a pip. My Imagination is a monastry and I am its monk — you must explain my metaprs to yourself. I am in expectation of Pro-

60. Cf. Spenser, *Faerie Queene*, II.vii.28, p. 130, in Vol. I.

metheus [61] every day. Could I have my own wish for its interest effected you would have it still in manuscript — or be but now putting an end to the second act. I remember you advising me not to publish my first-blights, on Hampstead heath — I am returning advice upon your hands. Most of the poems in the volume [62] I send you have been written above two years, and would never have been publish'd but from a hope of gain; so you see I am inclined enough to take your advice now. I must express once more my deep sense of your kindness, adding my sincere thanks and respects for M[rs] Shelley. In the hope of soon seeing you I remain

most sincerely yours,

John Keats —

## XII. To CHARLES BROWN

*Thursday 30 Nov. 1820*

Rome, 30 November 1820.

My dear Brown,

'Tis the most difficult thing in the world to me to write a letter. My stomach continues so bad, that I feel it worse on opening any book, — yet I am much better than I was in quarantine. Then I am afraid to encounter the pro-ing and con-ing of anything interesting to me in England. I have an habitual feeling of my real life having passed, and that I am leading a posthumous existence. God knows how it would have been — but it appears to me — however, I will not speak of that subject. I must have been at Bedhampton nearly at the time you were writing to me from Chichester — how unfortunate — and to pass on the river too! There was my star predominant! I cannot answer anything in your letter, which followed me from Naples to Rome, because I am afraid to look it over again. I am so weak (in mind) that I cannot bear the sight of any handwriting of a friend I love so much as I do you. Yet I ride the little horse, and, at my worst, even in quarantine, summoned up more puns, in a sort of desperation, in one week than in any year of my life. There is one thought enough to kill me; I have been well, healthy, alert, &c., walking with her,[63] and now — the knowledge of contrast, feeling for light and shade, all that information (primitive sense) necessary for a poem, are great enemies to the recovery of the stomach. There, you rogue, I put you to the torture; but you must bring your philosophy to bear, as I do mine, really, or how should I be able to live? Dr. Clark is very attentive to me; he says, there is very little the matter with my lungs, but my stomach, he says, is very bad. I am well disappointed in hearing good news from George, for it runs in my head we shall all die young. I have not written to Reynolds yet, which he must think very neglectful; being anxious to send him a good account of my health, I have delayed it from week to week. If I recover, I will do all in my power to correct the mistakes made during sickness; and if I should not, all my faults will be forgiven. Severn [64] is very well, though he leads so dull a life with me. Remember me to all friends, and tell Haslam [65] I should not have left London without taking leave of him, but from being so low in body and mind. Write to George as soon as you receive this, and tell him how I am, as far as you can guess; and also a note to my sister — who walks about my imagination like a ghost — she is so like Tom. I can scarcely bid you good-bye, even in a letter. I always made an awkward bow.

God bless you!

John Keats.

61. **Prometheus:** Shelley's verse drama, *Prometheus Unbound* (1820). 62. **volume:** Keats's new volume, which contained *Lamia, Isabella, Eve of St. Agnes, Hyperion,* and the odes.

63. **her:** Fanny Brawne. 64. **Severn:** Joseph Severn, a young painter who befriended Keats and nursed him in his last illness. 65. See n. 47, above.

**DOUGLAS BUSH,** ***Editor***

# Alfred, Lord Tennyson

1809–1892

Tennyson was born at Somersby in Lincolnshire on August 6, 1809, the birth year of Gladstone and Darwin and Lincoln and Poe; he was the third of eleven children, seven sons and four daughters. Like other lively and cultivated families of the pre-electronic era, and isolated as they were in the rectory of a rural parish, the young Tennysons made their own good times. Indoors there were the books of their father's library, from Shakespeare to Buffon, and writing, carving, clay-modeling, and such games as are mentioned in *In Memoriam,* LXXVIII; outdoors there were the Lincolnshire wolds and the life of birds and animals and, not far away, the North Sea. Mrs. Tennyson, evidently a robust mother, was a woman of simple piety; she lived to welcome the early *Idylls.* One moist and sulphurous element in the family was a Calvinistic aunt who could weep for hours in contemplation of the goodness of a God who had elected her while damning most of her friends, and who could impale the small boy with "Alfred, Alfred, when I look at you, I think of the words of Holy Scripture — 'Depart from me, ye cursed, into everlasting fire.'"

The father, Rev. George Clayton Tennyson, was a sterner and more complex personality than his wife, and his moods determined the barometric pressures of the household. The elder son of a rich man, he had the normal expectations of inheritance; but he was displaced in favor of the younger son and forced into the church. Though he had no vocation, he was a zealous clergyman and was well liked in his parish; his brilliant talk was enjoyed in higher circles. In his normal role as father he was also zealous. He himself educated his sons at home in Latin and Greek (Alfred had had only four or five years of formal schooling), and he encouraged the verse-writing of the three older boys, Frederick, Alfred, and Charles. On the other hand, Dr. Tennyson had his full share of the "black blood" of the Tennysons and brooded on his father's injustice and his own fate — while the favored younger brother enjoyed wealth and worldly prominence (later, like the "new-made lord" of *Maud,* he built himself a "gewgaw castle"). Dr. Tennyson's despondency drove him increasingly to alcoholic consolation and then to spells of insane violence. This story, which may well have contributed to "Locksley Hall" and *Maud,* was barely touched in the official *Memoir* of the poet (1897) and was first told fully in the biography (1949) by the poet's grandson, Sir Charles Tennyson. One can readily imagine how, for a sensitive young boy, even the happy periods of home life would be darkened by such an atmosphere, and why, when his father was in one of his spells, he more than once went out in the night and threw himself on a grave in the churchyard, praying for his own death.

*Poems by Two Brothers* was published by a provincial printer in the spring of 1827. In October Alfred and Charles went up to Trinity College, Cambridge, where Frederick already was. Tennyson, who had hardly been away from home before, did not much like the flat fen country or crowded communal life or the predominantly mathematical studies, which could be enjoyed by "None but dry-headed, calculating, angular little gentlemen." In October, 1828, Arthur Hallam became a fellow student and in the course of the year the famous friendship began. Hallam, a year and a half Tennyson's junior, was the son of Henry Hallam, the historian, and had the literary and social sophistication of Eton and London along with his own quick intelligence and charm; Tennyson's mind and frame were noble, his dress and manner rustic. Both were elected to a society of undergraduate intellectuals commonly known as the "Apostles," a group that included a number of young men destined for eminence. They were seriously concerned with religion, philosophy, and science, with social and political problems, and with literature; they were in advance of conventional opinion in admiring Wordsworth, Coleridge, Shelley, and Keats. Tennyson, who shrank from giving papers, occupied a sort of honorary niche on the strength of his poems. In June, 1829, his poem "Timbuctoo" won the university medal. In 1830 his first independent volume, *Poems, Chiefly Lyrical,* was published. In the summer of this year Tennyson and Hallam manifested their liberal sentiments by going to Spain with money from English sympathizers for Spanish rebels; the scenery of the Pyrenees left its impress on some of Tennyson's poems.

Early in 1831 Tennyson was called home from Cambridge by the illness of his father, who died in March, and he did not return to the university. Inheriting chiefly responsibilities, he lived with his mother and the family at Somersby. In July, 1832, he and Hallam made a tour on the Rhine. Another collection, *Poems,* dated 1833, appeared at the end of 1832 (it is cited under either date). This volume, which contained the first versions of a number of Tennyson's best-known early poems, had in the main a fair press; the notorious exception was a brutal article in the all-powerful *Quarterly Review* by John Wilson Croker, who hoped to do for the new poet what he had done for Keats. Tennyson, who was always morbidly sensitive to criticism, and who at this time, we may remember, was only twenty-three, was "almost crushed," though Croker's savagery had the effect of provoking some defenses, including one — two years later — from John Stuart Mill. Tennyson published no more books until 1842; he spent this "ten years' silence" in revising poems of 1832 and writing new ones. But hostile criticism — and harassing family problems — were not the only reasons for silence; there was also what may be called the one shattering event of his life, the sudden death of Arthur Hallam, at the age of twenty-two (September 15, 1833). During the next seventeen years Tennyson was sporadically composing the lyrics that became *In Memoriam.*

In 1837 the family moved from the familiar associations of Somersby to High Beech, Epping Forest, near London (an uprooting recorded in *In Memoriam,* c–cv), where they lived until 1840; other migrations cannot be chronicled here. Rural life was now varied by more frequent visits to London, where Tennyson became acquainted with Carlyle, Thackeray, Dickens, and many other writers. He kept up friendship with such old "Apostles" as James Spedding, and especially with another Cambridge friend, Edward FitzGerald, the future translator of the *Rubáiyát.* In 1837–38 Tennyson had become engaged to Emily Sellwood, but his lack of both money and religious orthodoxy led to her father's breaking off the relation in 1840; these obstacles were not overcome until 1850.

Tennyson was, in face and figure, perhaps the most impressively bardlike of all English poets, tall, handsome, dark, a sort of gypsy Apollo. Sydney Dobell, the "Spasmodic" poet, when asked to describe him, said that, if he were pointed out to you as the man who had written the *Iliad,* you would answer "I can well believe it." For a more specific picture one may quote the much-quoted letter from Carlyle to Emerson (1844):

> Alfred is one of the few British or Foreign Figures (a not increasing number I think!) who are and remain beautiful to me; — a true human soul, or some authentic approximation thereto, to whom your own soul can say, Brother! — However, I doubt he will not come; he often skips me, in these brief visits to Town; skips everybody indeed; being a man solitary and sad, as certain men are, dwelling in an element of gloom, — carrying a bit of Chaos about him, in short, which he is manufacturing into Cosmos! . . . He had his breeding at Cambridge, as if for the Law or Church; being master of a small annuity on his Father's decease, he preferred clubbing with his Mother and some Sisters, to live unpromoted and write Poems. In

this way he lives still, now here, now there; the family always within reach of London, never in it; he himself making rare and brief visits, lodging in some old comrade's rooms. I think he must be under forty, not much under it. One of the finest-looking men in the world. A great shock of rough dusty-dark hair; bright-laughing hazel eyes; massive aquiline face, most massive yet most delicate; of sallow-brown complexion, almost Indian-looking; clothes cynically loose, free-and-easy; — smokes infinite tobacco. His voice is musical metallic, — fit for loud laughter and piercing wail, and all that may lie between; speech and speculation free and plenteous: I do not meet, in these late decades, such company over a pipe! — We shall see what he will grow to.

As man and as poet, Tennyson embodied at least the normal quota of apparent contradictions. We may think of the tenderly devoted son who reminded his teary mother of her handkerchief with a "Dam your eyes, mother, dam your eyes!" of the shy and slovenly young man from the country still present in the poet and prophet who received universal homage; of the friend of dukes and royalty who measured the airs of county families in the light of the starry spheres; of the mystic who clung to "the Reality of the Unseen" and the native of Lincolnshire who relished anecdotes of earthy reality; of the man whose "most passionate desire" was "to have a clearer and fuller vision of God" and whose notion of the height of luxury (Aldworth had some plumbing) was "to sit in a hot bath and read about little birds"; who knew the depths of melancholy and cherished the "glorious power" of humor in the greatest writers; who wrote (and was praised for) sentimental verses that embarrass us and who read aloud his poem on the pathological St. Simeon Stylites with gusts of laughter — but we need not pile up antitheses, however wholesome they were. And Tennyson's conversational phrases were not always in the exalted vein. He observed that the bland portrait of an elderly politician was "rather like a retired panther," and pronounced a source-hunting scholar "a louse upon the locks of literature"; thinking of nature's blind profusion and overpopulation, he shuddered at "the torrent of babies"; and one cannot forget his picture of the common English conception of God "as of an immeasurable clergyman."

The two volumes of collected poems, old and new, of 1842 established Tennyson, among the more literary, as the chief active poet of the time. But Tennyson and the family were having financial trouble that came to a head in 1843; he had invested their meager resources in a wood-carving enterprise that failed (a good deal was recovered in 1845 on the death of the manufacturer, whose life had been insured by the poet's brother-in-law, Edmund Lushington). One concrete and welcome proof of Tennyson's poetical standing was a pension of £200, secured by the efforts of Henry Hallam, Gladstone, Carlyle, and Richard Monckton Milnes (the last an old "Apostle," now an M.P. and noted host); the Prime Minister, Sir Robert Peel, gave in when Milnes persuaded him to read "Ulysses."

*The Princess* (1847) sold better than any previous book, but it disappointed Carlyle and FitzGerald and a number of critics; for most modern readers only the songs survive. In 1850 came *In Memoriam*, Tennyson's greatest work and probably the central poetic document of the Victorian age. The same year brought his long-delayed marriage to Emily Sellwood and his appointment as Poet Laureate in succession to Wordsworth. In 1853 the married pair settled at Farringford on the Isle of Wight, which remained their home for the rest of Tennyson's life; he was able, in 1868, to build a house, named Aldworth, in Sussex, which in the summer became a refuge from the tourists who swarmed over the Isle of Wight. *Maud* (1855) evoked, in the unhappy time of the Crimean War, a good deal of hostility. So too, among leading writers and other critical minds, did *Idylls of the King*, which were published from 1859 onward, but these poems greatly extended Tennyson's popular following in both England and America — and had some critical esteem as well. There is no need to chronicle the later years of multiplying books, editions, friends, and visitors, of growing prosperity and fame. In 1883 Gladstone persuaded the poet to accept a peerage, which provoked some unpleasant squibs in the press. Like Dickens and like no other English writer, Tennyson lived the last third of his life as a national or international institution — and the theatrical novelist enjoyed the Hollywood glare more than the poet. Tennyson died on October 6, 1892, at the age of eighty-three.

The outward culmination of his immense success was his funeral; never had an English writer been borne to Westminster Abbey with such pomp and circumstance.

This biographical sketch has dwelt very disproportionately on Tennyson's earlier years of comparative loneliness, unhappiness, poverty, and modest critical repute (and some harsh abuse), the years in which he grew up and wrote many of his best and best-known poems, including *In Memoriam.* It has often been said that, because of moralistic critics, Mrs. Tennyson, and an equally conventional and worshipful public, a bold and original poet was eventually tamed into a purveyor of edifying lollipops. To pass by the supposed causes, one must dispute the supposed fact. In the first place, Tennyson could hardly escape altogether the taste that largely prevailed among both writers and readers when he was first publishing, and, like Dickens and many lesser authors, the early Tennyson had in him, along with much else, a streak of popular sentimentalism that yielded "O Darling Room," "Lady Clara Vere de Vere," "The May Queen," and "The Lord of Burleigh"; it was natural enough that, without any external influence, these should lead on to "Enoch Arden," the weaker *Idylls,* and other more or less regrettable things. Likewise, an early sonnet on Buonaparte as a madman who thought to quell English hearts of oak led on to some too simply patriotic and martial verses by the Laureate, though even these few pieces cannot be dismissed with a blanket condemnation; the "Ode on the Death of the Duke of Wellington" contained noble poetry as well as editorial eulogy, "The Charge of the Light Brigade" was effective journalism, and the vigorous "ballad of the fleet," "The Revenge," reproduced, quite properly, the Elizabethan man of action's feelings about Spain. (We might remember, too, Tennyson's opinion of the English as "the most beastly self-satisfied nation in the world.") Most great authors, from Shakespeare down, have been betrayed by their own tincture of popular taste into some bad writing; if Tennyson, coming at a notoriously bad time, suffered in the usual way, he also did a great deal to raise the level of poetry and taste. And, in the second place, if like other men he grew more conservative with age, he could still write many great and original poems, such as the two "Northern Farmers," "Lucretius," "The Holy Grail," "The Last Tournament," "The Ancient Sage," and "Demeter and Persephone," not to mention the plays.

Any writer who achieves an enormous reputation in his own lifetime is assured of a reaction, for both legitimate and illegitimate reasons; recent cases, on a smaller scale than Tennyson's, are Shaw and Mr. Eliot. Younger writers must escape from a dominant mode, which may have been carried as far as it can go, and find new ways of expressing the ideas and feelings of their generations. During the Victorian age, in addition to the older Browning and Arnold, various groups and individuals, of whom some owed much to Tennyson and none could be untouched by his influence, naturally struck out on different lines — the "Spasmodics," the Pre-Raphaelites, Swinburne, Hardy, Meredith, Hopkins, and others. Then, as we have observed, reaction did not wait for Tennyson's death; throughout his career both the young innovator and the elderly popular oracle received a good deal of severe criticism as well as praise. And part of his popular fame was based on the appeal of his inferior or positively bad work, or on an uncritical clutching at his "message" of faith and hope. Finally, for late Victorian rebels and moderns reacting in the normal way against their predecessors, Tennyson was the most conspicuous scapegoat for all the supposedly Victorian shams and sins. It is now clear, if it was not long ago, that much of the general reaction against "Victorianism" was not only uninformed and uncritical but hypocritical, since we have, often in inverted or disguised forms, our full share of smugness, sentimentality, and the other "Victorian" vices.

At any rate the first crude reaction against Tennyson and his age has long spent itself, and both can now be seen in a clearer perspective. Tennyson is naturally prominent in such recent general reassessments as Jerome H. Buckley's *The Victorian Temper* (1951) and Walter E. Houghton's *The Victorian Frame of Mind, 1830–1870* (1957). The claims upon us of any bygone writer are of two kinds, and Tennyson's are strong in both ways. First, he is of prime historical importance as the most fully representative mirror and interpreter of his great age, an age of bewildering progress and bewildering anxiety. (The offbeat Browning was much less so, as his long-delayed arrival indicates; and Arnold, whose relatively small body of poetry has worn signally well, was representative in a far more limited degree.) Secondly, when Tennyson's mediocre and bad writing has been stripped away, he still has, to quote Eliot, three qualities rarely found together except in the greatest poets: abundance, variety, and complete competence. We may survey Tennyson's long career and large output and try to illustrate these general criteria; and, though material, ideas, and attitudes cannot be separated from technique, a short sketch seems to require such a separation (and once in a while we may glance outside our restricted table of contents).

One astonishing item among Tennyson's abundant juvenilia is *The Devil and the Lady,* a play he wrote at fourteen and revised somewhat in the next year or two. This pseudo-Elizabethan frolic already shows its author's scientific and metaphysical concern: picturing the earth as a " petty clod " amid " suns and spheres and stars and belts and systems," he goes on to pose questions of Berkeleyan idealism. In the same period — in 1824 — on " a day when the whole world seemed to be darkened " for him — the boy went out and carved on a stone " Byron is dead "; Byron was the one great romantic poet who, in the first third of the century, made an impact that reached even the Somersby parsonage. Tennyson's share in *Poems by Two Brothers* (1827) was mostly thin, tinkling imitations of the lyrics of Byron and Moore; he had written far better things, but these were excluded from the book as unsuited to popular taste. Though academic prize poems are seldom memorable, " Timbuctoo " (1829), a revised version of a youthful piece, must be noticed because it marks the appearance of a question Tennyson was to handle variously in later poems, a question already current in the prose of Hazlitt, Peacock, and Macaulay — that is, the effects of advancing civilization upon poetry. In " Timbuctoo " the poet, on a mountain above the strait of Gibraltar (the ancient Pillars of Hercules), is told by the Spirit of Fable that her fair city of myth and imagination and idealism will, under the pressure of science and technology, decay into " Low-built, mud-wall'd, barbarian settlements."

*Poems, Chiefly Lyrical* (1830) contained, along with the merely or mainly melodious, some poems that were to hold a place in the select canon of posterity. " Mariana " was Tennyson's first elaborate expression of the deeply felt theme of loneliness, his first elaborate interweaving of scene and mood. " The Poet " was a confident proclamation of the high prophetic power the romantic poets had claimed. " The Poet's Mind " asserted another tenet of the romantic creed and was a link between " Timbuctoo " and " The Hesperides "; it warned cold, skeptical reason away from the holy ground of imagination. And we must note the first disclosure of a central and enduring problem, the undermining of traditional religious faith, in the poem that bore the self-mocking title " Supposed Confessions of a Second-Rate Sensitive Mind Not in Unity with Itself "; the piece ended with a despairing cry significantly close to the refrain of " Mariana." " The Kraken " perhaps had no successors except that massive miniature of naked energy, " The Eagle."

This volume received a quite favorable welcome from a number of reviewers, including Leigh Hunt. The *Westminster Review* trusted that the young author would live up to the noble creed of " The Poet," and we might have expected a similar exhortation from Arthur Hallam in his review; but Hallam named the purely pictorial " Recollections of the Arabian Nights " as perhaps the best poem in the book. Setting the poetry of sensation (Shelley, Keats) above the poetry of reflection (Wordsworth), Hallam found Tennyson a highly original poet of sensation, distinguished by controlled luxuriance of imagination, the power of embodying himself in ideal characters or moods, the vivid, picturesque delineation of objects and the fusing of these in a medium of strong emotion (such a fusion, we may note, was a romantic inheritance that Tennyson developed to the full), the variety of his lyrical measures, and his elevated habits of thought. Despite this last quality, which was to become a main text in the critical response to Tennyson, Hallam's emphasis was on the creation of beauty, art for art's sake; a little later, apparently, the two friends were at one in the conviction that they must not " lose hold of the Real in seeking the Ideal " — a phrase that might serve as a summary of Keats's

*Endymion.* In general, the reception of the volume of 1830, and also of that of 1832, seemed to promise Tennyson a fairly rapid rise to eminence as the lineal successor of Keats; but we have observed the effect upon him of Croker's onslaught and of Hallam's death.

In the *Poems* of 1832 the Tennyson we know began to take shape clearly, even though we read the more famous pieces — "The Lady of Shalott," "Œnone," "The Palace of Art," and "The Lotos-Eaters" — in the much-revised versions that appeared in 1842. In these four poems, and in "The Hesperides," Tennyson was dealing with a problem that was evidently personal, a problem that had preoccupied Keats from "Sleep and Poetry" to *The Fall of Hyperion:* the artist's choice — which of course depends on his gifts as well as his will — between contemplative detachment from life and the acceptance of social and ethical responsibility, whether in action or in "public" poetry. (Modern words, in the continuing debate, are "involvement," "engagement," "commitment.") The young Tennyson, in spite of "The Poet" and the perhaps ambivalent "Palace of Art," seems to have been temperamentally inclined toward aesthetic detachment; but his revision, for 1842, of some poems of 1832 suggests a shift in the other direction. Along with critics' complaints, a partial change of heart may explain the unaccountable failure to reprint the unique and magical "Hesperides." In the original conclusion of "The Lady of Shalott" an unexpected jab at "The well-fed wits at Camelot" seems to set the secluded and now dead "artist" above and against an insensitive bourgeois world; the ending of 1842 invites the verdict, however sympathetic, that detachment from reality is fatal. Much more obvious evidence of Tennyson's getting into the stream of the contemporary and actual is the many new poems of 1842, poems written at various times in the preceding decade, such as "You Ask Me, Why," "Love Thou Thy Land," "Locksley Hall," and — by implication — "Morte d'Arthur," along with a number of tales and vignettes of English life which have a rather tepid attraction for modern readers. One must mention three poems that unhappily could not be included in these selections, the grimly bizarre "St. Simeon Stylites," the macabre ballad of "The Vision of Sin," and "The Two Voices." In this last, written after Hallam's death, the poet's faith in life and God struggles against the temptation of suicide upheld by nihilistic skepticism. These two voices of resolution and despair might be said to speak in the two great monologues, "Ulysses" and "Tithonus." Apropos of Tennyson's series of mythological poems, and the age's increasing demand that poetry should draw its material from modern life, a word may be added. Carlyle, though he was deeply stirred by "Ulysses," was apparently complaining of Tennyson's remote and antique themes when he described him as "sitting on a dung-heap among innumerable dead dogs." But all of Tennyson's fine mythological poems (except the last and weakest, "The Death of Œnone") were more or less intensely personal and modern in inspiration — and usually much better than his modern treatments of parallel themes. Much later, when he resolved to write "Demeter and Persephone," Tennyson indicated what had always been his way of approach: "when I write an antique like this I must put it into a frame — something modern about it. It is no use giving a mere *réchauffé* of old legends" *(Memoir,* II, 364). In this Tennyson was following the example of Keats and Shelley, who had revived classical myth as a vehicle for both private and public themes.

Modern scientific skepticism, even if it came partly from the "lying lips" of Sorrow, was a main source of tension and despair in *In Memoriam,* which was largely composed in the decade 1833–43. The sudden shock of Hallam's death brought together and greatly deepened all Tennyson's questionings of earlier years — in somewhat the same way as the death of a virtuous and promising young man had forced Milton to a questioning of God's providence and justice. But for Tennyson, two centuries later, the religious problem was immensely complicated by science and the general growth of rationalism. From boyhood to old age he kept in touch with science, especially astronomy, more closely perhaps than any other poet of the century, partly because of scientific curiosity but mainly because of the impact of scientific discovery and thought upon man's religious sense of his own being, of his place in nature, and his belief in survival after death. Even if law was the foundation, and the fetish, of nineteenth-century science — as it was, for instance, in that very successful work of popularizing, *Vestiges of the Natural History of Creation* (1844), by Robert Chambers — there was cold comfort in cosmic and biological law that was utterly indifferent to man. Sir Charles Lyell's *Principles of Geology* (1830–33), which Tennyson read in 1837 if not earlier, stressed the immense tract of time required for natural processes, such as erosion, to work immense changes in land and sea, processes that went on in entire disregard of sentient life; both individuals and species appeared and disappeared, leaving only fossil records. Though *In Memoriam* was often acclaimed as a "reconciliation" of science and faith, modern readers may be more conscious of the poet's stark despair in "the night of fear," in the face of a blind, mechanical, meaningless universe in which man seems an insignificant and perhaps ephemeral accident. If we have grown used to living with such specters (or have been diverted by more immediate specters of universal destruction), they are still there; and no one has put the great questions more powerfully than Tennyson put them in sections LV–LVI.

Some modern writers and readers cling tenaciously to despair and look down their noses at anything that savors of affirmation. Tennyson, like most other Victorian writers, sought for something positive. His efforts toward affirmation in *In Memoriam* are of two kinds, and, for us, they are likely to seem of quite unequal validity. One was his "lesser faith" or hope in the general progress, the upward movement, of the race. Such a faith or hope had been current or intermittent for ages, and in the nineteenth century it had gained momentum and concreteness through the evolutionary doctrines of Lamarck and others and through the scientific and technological discoveries that were working radical changes in modes of life and thought. Tennyson's hope of progress, of the emergence of a higher type of man (exemplified by Hallam), could in expression be tinged with scientific language but was much more ethical than scientific — and was attended, or attenuated, by an increasingly dark view of his own age. Since many people vaguely associate *In Memoriam* with monkey business, we may remember that Tennyson was not concerned with Lamarckian or Darwinian mutation of species; the leading English scientists before 1850 — or before (and often after) 1859 — upheld the successive creation of distinct species, along with the general concept of unity and analogy in the biological world.

Tennyson's central affirmation, which worked its way out of despair, was subjective, intuitive faith in love as the supreme experience and reality of life, a reality that implied a God of love and individual immortality. He had profound reverence for Christ but was not apparently an orthodox Christian. "There's a Something that watches over us; and our individuality endures," he said once; "that's my faith, and that's all my faith." Holding with passionate intensity to these minimal beliefs, Tennyson, without attempting to deny the grim facts of nature and history, took his stand on ground above both skeptical science and the traditional "argument from design" of rational religion. His answer, "I have felt" (*In Memoriam,* CXXIV), has been condemned by some readers in both skeptical and religious camps — though the former seldom quarrel with the equally intuitive negations of other writers, and the latter might find it difficult to prove the objectivity of their own faith. Tennyson had always had a mystical strain in him. The boy who, by repeating his own name, could have a disembodied, trancelike experience of partaking of pure and boundless being (*Memoir,* I, 320) grew into the man who wrote section XCV of *In Memoriam* and the last words of Arthur in "The Holy Grail." Like some mystical minds of other ages, he had a strong conviction of the nothingness of flesh and the eternal reality of spirit (*Memoir,* II, 90). Tennyson's idea, expressed in *In Memoriam* and elsewhere, of successive existences after death may have come from non-Christian religions.

According to the author (*Memoir,* I, 404) the central idea of *Maud* (1855) was "the holy power of Love," and according to James Russell Lowell this work was "the antiphonal voice to 'In Memoriam.'" But modern readers, while recognizing extraordinary technical resourcefulness and power of a kind, would put *Maud* far below its predecessor. Lyrical and authentic ecstasies of love there are, though it is youthful romantic love; and the antiheroic hero, however justified his railing at society, may suggest "the angry young men" who of late years have been making such a tiresome noise in English fiction and drama. The hero's salvation (of which something is said in the headnote to the poem) can be defended as dramatically sound, but it may be thought less impressive than the overthrow and death of King Arthur. *Idylls of the King* (1859 ff.), which grew slowly in Tennyson's mind and became the fulfillment of a major ambition, were sniffed or snorted at in their own time by Carlyle, Browning, Swinburne, Meredith, Hopkins, and others, and they have been largely dismissed and ignored in ours; but, if some *Idylls* are weak and satiny romance or parable, some are powerful and moving pictures of an ideal society in decay, the waste land of a civilization without conscience and without love. These, rather than *Maud,* are the antiphonal voice to *In Memoriam;* the ape and the tiger have not died but triumphed, and the one far-off divine event can now be hardly even imagined. Though Tennyson had never had anything like Milton's early militant faith in a great reformation here and now, in his later years he may be said to have had some affinity with the disillusioned Milton who in *Paradise Lost* saw the great reformation only as the new heaven and new earth beyond the day of judgment. Tennyson's faith in progress — in the sense of regeneration, not of multiplying gadgets — had always been fixed on a dim and distant future (the far-off world, he said, often seemed nearer than the present) and was less of a belief than a hope and a dream. The conclusion of "Tiresias" (1885), the testament of "an old man in a dry month," celebrates heroic greatness — in Pindaric images — as it lives in the world of the dead:

But for me,
I would that I were gather'd to my rest,
And mingled with the famous kings of old,
On whom about their ocean-islets flash
The faces of the Gods — the wise man's word,
Here trampled by the populace underfoot,
There crown'd with worship — and these eyes will find
The men I knew, and watch the chariot whirl
About the goal again, and hunters race
The shadowy lion, and the warrior-kings,
In height and prowess more than human, strive
Again for glory, while the golden lyre
Is ever sounding in heroic ears
Heroic hymns, and every way the vales
Wind, clouded with the grateful incense-fume
Of those who mix all odor to the Gods
On one far height in one far-shining fire.

No doubt one may, if one likes, call this an escapist vision.

Our rapid glance at some of Tennyson's major works, themes, and attitudes is also a partial reminder of the bulk and variety of his output, and variety as well as bulk would be much extended if we had space for many other good poems, long and short. Nor should we forget the plays written from 1875 onward, *Queen Mary, Becket, The Foresters,* and several others; all but one were produced, most of them with more or less success. If Tennyson had not done so, we would never have expected that he could write for the stage; he received cordial congratulations from Browning, who, in spite of his finely dramatic and colloquial monologues, had, many years earlier, failed lamentably in the theater.

To look over even a small selection from Tennyson is to be reminded also of the wide variety of style and tone that goes along with a wide variety of theme. Such major poets of our time as Yeats and Mr. Eliot and Mr. Frost — not to mention the host of good smaller poets — have a relatively limited range; we hear somewhat varied intonations of one always recognizable voice. But Tennyson is a ventriloquist, or a troupe of ventriloquists; to put the matter in another way, his poems are diverse objects made, as it were, by a whole corps of different craftsmen. We may think of the gulf between "The Hesperides" and the two "Northern Farmers," between "The Lady of Shalott" and "Ulysses," between "Tears, Idle Tears" and "Lucretius," between "Tithonus" and *Maud,* between *In Memoriam* and "The Holy Grail" — but there is no need of repeating a table of contents. In his art as well as in his thought and feeling Tennyson was inevitably the heir of the romantic poets, and criticism soon aligned him with Keats, but he was almost from the start an original master himself. Our space forbids any broad account of his varied qualities and we might concentrate chiefly on one, the studied refinement of phrase and rhythm which, in countless modulations, runs through much of his work.

Tennyson's poetic powers were no less precocious than long-lived; he was writing from the age of five up to eighty-three. We have already noticed, in the play he wrote at fourteen, the presence of astronomy and metaphysics, and here we may observe in the same play the minutely accurate, carefully composed scene-painting that bears the Tennysonian hallmark:

> Each hoar wave
> With crispèd undulation arching rose,
> Thence falling in white ridge with sinuous slope
> Dash'd headlong to the shore and spread along
> The sands its tender fringe of creamy spray.

And one must quote another phrase, not as characteristic Tennyson, but as something that might have been written yesterday, about a reed bed that may wave

> Its trembling shadows to the ambiguity
> Of moonlight.[1]

The virtues of sensibility and expression that Hallam praised in the volume of 1830, virtues more generally conspicuous in the volume of 1832, had their obverse side. The poet was very young — at the end of his life he said that he had been nearer thirty than twenty before he was anything of an artist; the substance of some early poems was thin or worse, luxuriance of imagination could be overluxuriant and descriptive details under uncertain control, and there were some stylistic mannerisms such as an excess of compound words. Although there was no excuse for Croker's violence, and not much for his blindness and deafness, he and some other critics in their flailing about hit on real as well as superficial faults. Tennyson, while suffering from reviewers as well as from his grief for Hallam, was attaining poetic maturity. In the process of selecting and rejecting early poems for the next edition, and of revising a number of those retained, he was wise enough to heed critical strictures and wise enough also to rely on his own increasingly disciplined taste. The story of early criticism and the poet's reactions, 1827–51, is expertly told in Edgar F. Shannon's *Tennyson and the Reviewers* (1952); a discerning complementary study is Joyce Green's "Tennyson's Development during the 'Ten Years' Silence' (1832–1842)," *Publications of the Modern Language Association,* LXVI (1951). Tennyson's rapid growth in power and depth as well as artistry is sufficiently illustrated by some of the new poems of 1842 that had been written in 1833, such as "St. Simeon Stylites" and "Ulysses," and "Morte d'Arthur," written in 1833–35.

What early unfavorable criticism called affectation was in Tennyson's mature work subdued, deepened, and enriched into the refinement and elaboration that came to be regarded as the dominant quality of his style. This view may be said to have become canonical with Walter Bagehot's critique of 1864, "Wordsworth, Tennyson, and Browning; or, Pure, Ornate, and Grotesque in English Poetry." But Tennysonian refinement was in the main a potent virtue and only on occasion a vice — and sometimes, most obviously in the "Northern Farmers" — it was far away. Of course if a reader can be imagined as coming to Tennyson from modern poetry, which does not carve "jewels five-words long" (the phrase is Tennyson's) and which has so largely cultivated the colloquial and casual in language and rhythm, nearly all of Tennyson may appear studiously composed and hence artificial; but such an impression would by no means constitute a valid condemnation. For one thing, modern colloquialism is quite as consciously artificial as any more formal style; like "natural acting" on the stage, it only gives the illusion of naturalness. For another, Tennyson was in accord with the immemorial tradition of European poetry which prescribed that the poet should wear his singing robes, not an open shirt and slacks. Everything depends upon what the theme and attitude require; and, since the house of poetry has many mansions, we could ill afford to lose the one dedicated to golden splendor — one to which Yeats and Eliot also have the key. At his frequent best, Tennyson's inlaid, beautifully contrived texture is akin to Virgil's; it has long been a commonplace that he is the most Virgilian of English poets. One half-humorous and inadequate reminder of what he learned from the classics is his saying that he knew the quantity of every English word except "scissors."

We might look at some examples and first

[1] *The Devil and the Lady,* ed. Sir Charles Tennyson (1930), pp. 62, 6, and quoted by Sir Charles' kind permission.

at some bad ones — which are not very numerous. Over-refinement may become inflation. Criticism has made sufficiently merry with King Arthur's mustache, "the knightly growth that fringed his lips." At the beginning and end of *In Memoriam,* Holy Communion and wedding champagne are described in much the same kind of overwrought periphrasis:

> Or where the kneeling hamlet drains
> The chalice of the grapes of God.

> My drooping memory will not shun
> The foaming grape of eastern France.

Another kind of overrefinement (likewise uncommon) is the excessive and obvious use of devices for creating an effect, as in the harsh epithets, verbs, and consonants piled up in lines 237–41 of "Morte d'Arthur." The opposite effect of softness overreaches itself in the same kind of elementary onomatopoeia in two lines from a song in *The Princess* which used to be more admired than they are now:

> The moan of doves in immemorial elms,
> And murmuring of innumerable bees.

Many similar but somewhat less obviously calculated effects may be debatable matters of individual taste. Probably most readers would approve of the slow succession of long vowels, followed by the choppy sound of waves, in these lines from "Ulysses":

> The long day wanes; the slow moon climbs; the deep
> Moans round with many voices.

The stanzaic pictures in "The Palace of Art" are among Tennyson's most conscious contrivances, and these are sometimes debatable in another way as well. On the one hand, the note of artifice and excess may be justified by the theme of aesthetic surfeit; or, on the other, is the poet's instinctive relish undercutting his nominal "moral"? The soft, languorous beauty of the Lotos-eaters' Choric Song is manifestly required by the escapist theme. Two lines from "Morte d'Arthur" — on which Tennyson, reading aloud to FitzGerald, commented in his innocent way, "Not bad that, Fitz, is it?" — carry, in their highly wrought phrasing, an appropriate suggestion of a remote, mysterious artifact:

> Nine years she wrought it, sitting in the deeps
> Upon the hidden bases of the hills.

(One wonders if the time taken by the Lady of the Lake was linked in Tennyson's mind with the nine years that, according to Horace, the true artist should keep his work by him.) He liked, too, the sound of

> only the rounded moon
> Thro' the tall oriel on the rolling sea

("The Holy Grail," 827–28); here the chosen adjectives, one for each noun, make a visual pattern of contrasted geometrical planes and again, in their very artifice, create a sense of mystery. Thus we are led almost imperceptibly from Tennyson's few excesses into one mode of his finest writing. Even such flaws as those noticed in *In Memoriam* are a sort of oblique reminder of the prevailing "metaphysical" density — and occasional difficulty — of that poem.

The poems on mythological themes, though they differ a good deal among themselves in manner as in mood, are almost all among Tennyson's great and original achievements. The irregular rhythms and pure incantation of "The Hesperides" he never repeated; all the others, from "Œnone" onward, are in blank verse. Tennyson liked to quote the conclusion of "Tiresias," which was given above, as a diploma specimen of his blank verse, but that, grand as it is, does not perhaps surpass many other parts of these poems and the whole of "Tithonus." In such dramatic monologues the movement is slow and reflective, more akin to that of Keats's *Hyperion* than to the onward rush and intricate paragraphs of Milton; the unit, as in Keats, is in the main the heavily weighted single line, for example, in the opening of "Tithonus." That same passage may serve to illustrate Tennyson's kind of contrived simplicity: "Man comes and tills the field and lies beneath" is not like Wordsworth's "And never lifted up a single stone," yet Tennyson's simplicity is biblical. So, too, on a lower level, in "Œnone,"

> With narrow moonlit slips of silver cloud,
> Between the loud stream and the trembling stars,

or, in "The Lotos-Eaters,"

> They sat them down upon the yellow sand,
> Between the sun and moon upon the shore,

we have largely the simple words and simple order of prose, but decidedly not the character and tone of prose. Yet Tennyson's phrasing, for its purposes, has its own absolute rightness; and hundreds of examples would support the same conclusion. In *Idylls of the King* Tennyson, like any poet embarked on a long work, was bound to adopt a more or less stylized manner, and it seems to be agreed that the semi-archaic style he created was not an ideal success. Whereas the style of the classical poems, however refined or exalted, comes to us as the poet's own voice, in the *Idylls* the voice has come through Malory, and we may have the feeling we get in reading the Homeric translations of Andrew Lang and his collaborators. To say that is not to unsay remarks already made about the total impact of some of the *Idylls.*

Great as Tennyson is in many modes, by instinct and endowment he is perhaps most of all a lyric poet, a poet of personal emotion. Many of his lyrics, both individual pieces and parts of larger works, could not be included here, but those we have — separate poems, a few of the songs from *The Princess,* about half of *In Memoriam,* the lyrics in *Maud* — are more than enough to place Tennyson easily first among the lyrists of the century. Within the lyrical range his fecundity, versatility, and felicity are astonishing. One of his deepest wells of inspiration — and not lyrical inspiration only — is what he called " the passion of the past," the indefinable regret and yearning (which in him had been especially strong in youth) for things in life that seem to have passed away for ever. Of this rich, somber, more or less universal feeling the most perfect expression is " Tears, Idle Tears," Tennyson's masterpiece among the lyrics outside *In Memoriam* and, one might add, the most Virgilian of his lyrics. In *In Memoriam* the passion of the past naturally becomes remembrance of communion with Hallam, and ranges from the time when

all the lavish hills would hum
The murmur of a happy Pan

to the picture of the dark house in London where

ghastly thro' the drizzling rain
On the bald street breaks the blank day.

This last poem (section VII) has naturally attracted Mr. Eliot's notice; the final line is at once a piece of modernity and, in its alliteration, monosyllables, and broken rhythm, a Tennysonian contrivance — completely and powerfully effective.

*In Memoriam* enshrines many themes and moods, and Tennyson's instinct served him well when it led him into " Short swallow-flights of song " rather than into a long philosophical poem. Some lyrics, naturally, are weak, and some have incidental flaws, but in the work as a whole the stylization of language and rhythm is marvellously right (one uses the adverb partly because the poems were written over so long a time). Even the best lyrics do not yield their full strength if read in isolation; each gains from its full context. And as the grave quatrains proceed in their undulating ebb and flow, variety is achieved within a general uniformity of style and movement that has a high ritualistic value. The intimately personal is raised to the universal and timeless. Since Tennyson had always been given to rendering states of mind through description of nature, we might note a few examples. In section XI, each of the five stanzas begins with " Calm," yet apparent rhetorical artifice becomes a kind of sublimation; the effect is of a man who can retain self-control only and barely by a ceremonial ordering of landscape and emotion. A later and happier mood, the sense of rebirth, is rendered through scene-painting in the single magnificent sentence that constitutes section LXXXVI. In section XCV, which many critics regard as the poetic pinnacle of *In Memoriam,* the mystical experience rises out of a homely everyday scene and then subsides into it again, though now objects are not just their familiar selves but have taken on a symbolic life. A doctrinaire modernist might conceivably ask, " Why the ' white kine ' instead of ' white cows '? " The not very difficult answer would cover many similar questions.

These sketchy remarks on some elements in Tennyson's thinking, feeling, and artistry do not go very far, and they pass by many important things, but perhaps they go far enough to suggest the nature of his many strong claims upon us. If I, a Victorian by birth, may testify from my own experience in a course on several Victorian poets, it is always inspiriting to find that many intelligent young students, who had acquired the condescending or hostile view of Tennyson, change their minds when they really read him. They discover that he is an interpreter not only of his own great and troubled age but in some respects of ours, and that he is, simply, one of the enduring poets who give enduring and very individual stimulus and satisfaction, that his artifice partakes of "the artifice of eternity."

### *Reading Suggestions*

Annotated editions are: *Works,* ed. Hallam, Lord Tennyson, 9 vols. (1907–08); the same, 1 vol. (1913); *Poetic and Dramatic Works,* ed. W. J. Rolfe (1898); *Early Poems,* ed. J. C. Collins (1900); *Selections,* ed. W. C. and M. P. DeVane (1940); *Representative Poems,* ed. S. C. Chew (1941); *Poems,* ed. J. H. Buckley (1958); and selections (with bibliographies) in various college anthologies of Victorian poetry.

For biography the indispensable books are *Alfred Lord Tennyson: A Memoir,* by Hallam, Lord Tennyson, 2 vols. (1897) — cited here as *Memoir* — and Sir Charles Tennyson's *Alfred Tennyson* (1949).

Criticism down to recent years is listed in the *Cambridge Bibliography of English Literature,* ed. F. W. Bateson (1941), III, 255–58, and in the *Supplement,* ed. George Watson (1957), pp. 584–86.

Some recent studies of the age and of Tennyson — by Jerome H. Buckley, Walter E. Houghton, Edgar F. Shannon, and Joyce Green — are mentioned in the Introduction; and some more special criticism is cited in the headnotes to *In Memoriam* and "The Holy Grail."

The great mass of Victorian criticism may be represented by Walter Bagehot's essay of 1864 (cited in the Introduction), reprinted in his *Literary Studies,* and Richard H. Hutton, *Literary Essays* (1888).

Some modern books and essays are:

Paull F. Baum, *Tennyson Sixty Years After* (1948). A full, expert, and not oversympathetic reassessment.

Joseph Warren Beach, *The Concept of Nature in Nineteenth Century English Poetry* (1936), chap. xv. On Tennyson's place in scientific and religious thought.

Douglas Bush, *Mythology and the Romantic Tradition in English Poetry* (1937), chap. vi.

Arthur J. Carr, "Tennyson as a Modern Poet." *University of Toronto Quarterly,* XIX (1949–50), 361–82. The theme of loss and frustration and other anticipations of modernity.

T. S. Eliot, "In Memoriam." *Essays Ancient and Modern* (1936). Of special interest as an appreciation by a major modern poet.

Oliver Elton, *A Survey of English Literature 1780–1880,* 4 vols. (1920), vol. IV, chap. xiii. A compendious estimate by a scholar-critic of Victorian vintage.

E. D. H. Johnson, *The Alien Vision of Victorian Poetry: Sources of the Poetic Imagination in Tennyson, Browning, and Arnold* (1952). A study, in partial opposition to the usual picture, of Tennyson's interior, imaginative nonconformity.

Georg Roppen, *Evolution and Poetic Belief* (1956), chap. ii, "Alfred Tennyson."

Basil Willey, "Tennyson." *More Nineteenth Century Studies* (1956). Chiefly on religion and science.

---

## THE KRAKEN

Published in 1830. A massive, "primitive" fusion of a sea monster of Scandinavian folklore with apocalyptic imagery concerning the fiery end of the world: "And I stood upon the sand of the sea, and saw a beast rise up out of the sea" (Rev. 13:1).

Below the thunders of the upper deep,
Far, far beneath in the abysmal sea,
His ancient, dreamless, uninvaded sleep
The Kraken sleepeth: faintest sunlights flee
About his shadowy sides; above him swell
Huge sponges of millennial growth and height;
And far away into the sickly light,
From many a wondrous grot and secret cell
Unnumber'd and enormous polypi
Winnow with giant arms the slumbering green.
There hath he lain for ages, and will lie
Battening upon huge sea-worms in his sleep,
Until the latter fire shall heat the deep;
Then once by man and angels to be seen,
In roaring he shall rise and on the surface die.

*1830* [1]

## MARIANA

"Mariana in the moated grange."
*Measure for Measure*

This poem of 1830, Tennyson's first notable treatment of isolation and the "death-wish," is more characteristic in its rendering of mood through scenic details, skillfully grouped, than in its blending of everyday realism with romantic and ominous mystery. There seems to be little Shakespearian suggestion beyond the name and echoes of the epigraph, adapted from *Measure for Measure,* III.i.277: "There at the moated grange resides this dejected Mariana."

1. Dates at the end of poems indicate publication (left) and composition (right).

With blackest moss the flower-plots
  Were thickly crusted, one and all;
The rusted nails fell from the knots
  That held the pear to the gable-wall.
The broken sheds look'd sad and strange:
  Unlifted was the clinking latch;
  Weeded and worn the ancient thatch
Upon the lonely moated grange.
    She only said, "My life is dreary,
      He cometh not," she said;
    She said, "I am aweary, aweary,
      I would that I were dead!"

Her tears fell with the dews at even;
  Her tears fell ere the dews were dried;
She could not look on the sweet heaven,
  Either at morn or eventide.
After the flitting of the bats,
  When thickest dark did trance the sky,
  She drew her casement-curtain by,
And glanced athwart the glooming flats.
    She only said, "The night is dreary,
      He cometh not," she said;
    She said, "I am aweary, aweary,
      I would that I were dead!"

Upon the middle of the night,
  Waking she heard the night-fowl crow;
The cock sung out an hour ere light;
  From the dark fen the oxen's low
Came to her; without hope of change,
  In sleep she seem'd to walk forlorn,
  Till cold winds woke the gray-eyed morn
About the lonely moated grange.
    She only said, "The day is dreary,
      He cometh not," she said;
    She said, "I am aweary, aweary,
      I would that I were dead!"

About a stone-cast from the wall
  A sluice with blacken'd waters slept,
And o'er it many, round and small,
  The cluster'd marish-mosses crept.
Hard by a poplar shook alway,
  All silver-green with gnarlèd bark:
  For leagues no other tree did mark
The level waste, the rounding gray.
    She only said, "My life is dreary,
      He cometh not," she said;
    She said, "I am aweary, aweary,
      I would that I were dead!"

And ever when the moon was low,
  And the shrill winds were up and away,
In the white curtain, to and fro,
  She saw the gusty shadow sway.
But when the moon was very low,
  And wild winds bound within their cell,
  The shadow of the poplar fell
Upon her bed, across her brow.
    She only said, "The night is dreary,
      He cometh not," she said;
    She said, "I am aweary, aweary,
      I would that I were dead!"

All day within the dreamy house,
  The doors upon their hinges creak'd;
The blue fly sung in the pane; the mouse
  Behind the moldering wainscot shriek'd,
Or from the crevice peer'd about.
  Old faces glimmer'd thro' the doors,
  Old footsteps trod the upper floors,
Old voices called her from without.
    She only said, "My life is dreary,
      He cometh not," she said;
    She said, "I am aweary, aweary,
      I would that I were dead!"

The sparrow's chirrup on the roof,
  The slow clock ticking, and the sound
Which to the wooing wind aloof
  The poplar made, did all confound
Her sense; but most she loathed the hour
  When the thick-moted sunbeam lay
  Athwart the chambers, and the day
Was sloping toward his western bower.
    Then, said she, "I am very dreary,
      He will not come," she said;
    She wept, "I am aweary, aweary,
      Oh God, that I were dead!"

*1830*

MARIANA. 18. **trance**: entrance, put under a spell.

## THE POET

This openly didactic and confident proclamation of the poet's social responsibility and power (1830) is not in line with other early poems in which Tennyson reveals more sympathy with contemplative detachment. It may reflect the influence of the Cambridge "Apostles" (see the Introduction). Such messianic assurance may be called Shelleyan (though Shelley's *Defence of Poetry* was not published until 1840), and Tennyson's imagery is somewhat in the vein of Shelley's poetry.

The poet in a golden clime was born,
    With golden stars above;
Dower'd with the hate of hate, the scorn of scorn,
    The love of love.

THE POET. 3–4. Tennyson at first meant love for love, etc.; later he preferred the idea of the quintessence of love, etc.

He saw thro' life and death, thro' good and ill,
He saw thro' his own soul.
The marvel of the everlasting will,
An open scroll,

Before him lay; with echoing feet he threaded
The secretest walks of fame:
The viewless arrows of his thoughts were headed
And wing'd with flame,

Like Indian reeds blown from his silver tongue,
And of so fierce a flight,
From Calpè unto Caucasus they sung,
Filling with light

And vagrant melodies the winds which bore
Them earthward till they lit;
Then, like the arrow-seeds of the field flower,
The fruitful wit

Cleaving, took root, and springing forth anew
Where'er they fell, behold,
Like to the mother plant in semblance, grew
A flower all gold,

And bravely furnish'd all abroad to fling
The wingèd shafts of truth,
To throng with stately blooms the breathing spring
Of Hope and Youth.

So many minds did gird their orbs with beams,
Tho' one did fling the fire;
Heaven flow'd upon the soul in many dreams
Of high desire.

Thus truth was multiplied on truth, the world
Like one great garden show'd,
And thro' the wreaths of floating dark upcurl'd,
Rare sunrise flow'd.

And Freedom rear'd in that august sunrise
Her beautiful bold brow,
When rites and forms before his burning eyes
Melted like snow.

There was no blood upon her maiden robes
Sunn'd by those orient skies;
But round about the circles of the globes
Of her keen eyes

And in her raiment's hem was traced in flame
Wisdom, a name to shake
All evil dreams of power — a sacred name.
And when she spake,

Her words did gather thunder as they ran,
And as the lightning to the thunder
Which follows it, riving the spirit of man,
Making earth wonder,

So was their meaning to her words. No sword
Of wrath her right arm whirl'd,
But one poor poet's scroll, and with *his* word
She shook the world.

*1830*

11. **viewless**: invisible. 13. **blown**: from a blowpipe. 15. **Calpè**: Gibraltar (the ancient limit of the western world). **Caucasus**: the mountains between the Black and the Caspian Seas. 19. **field flower**: dandelion.

## THE HESPERIDES

"Hesperus and his daughters three
That sing about the golden tree."
*Comus*

"The Hesperides" (1832), Tennyson's first elaborate treatment of myth, is much less familiar than it should be, since he never reprinted it (and came to regret not having done so). It is the most purely magical, and most elusive, poem he ever wrote. The difficulty, of a kind common in modern poetry but rare in Tennyson's age, is that there is next to nothing in the way of "prose statement," that the theme is developed wholly in images. Other early writings (Act I, Scene iii, of the youthful play, *The Devil and the Lady;* "Timbuctoo"; "The Poet's Mind"; "The Lady of Shalott") suggest that "The Hesperides" celebrates the value of myth and the precious seclusion of the artistic imagination in the face of the encroachments of scientific progress and the world of action. G. R. Stange has a study of the poem in *Publications of the Modern Language Association,* LXVII (1952).

The Hesperides were the nymphs who, with the aid of a dragon, guarded the golden apples that had been given to Hera when she wedded Zeus. They were placed, in different versions of the myth, on an Atlantic island or near Mount Atlas in northwest Africa; Tennyson's use of Hanno implies that he has the African scene in mind. Heracles, coming from the east, carried off the apples, but they were eventually restored. Tennyson might have seen the curious book by Edward Davies, *Celtic Researches* (1804), which says (p. 193): "Hercules had the task of procuring three yellow apples, from the garden of the Hesperides. These apples were metaphorical, and pointed at science, discipline, or mystery."

The North wind fall'n, in the new-starrèd night
Zidonian Hanno, voyaging beyond

THE HESPERIDES. **Epigraph.** Milton, *Comus,* 981–82. 2. Hanno, a Carthaginian navigator (Carthage was founded by Phoenicians from Sidon and Tyre), wrote an account of his

The hoary promontory of Soloë
Past Thymiaterion, in calmèd bays,
Between the southern and the western Horn,
Heard neither warbling of the nightingale,
Nor melody o' the Libyan lotus flute
Blown seaward from the shore; but from a slope
That ran bloom-bright into the Atlantic blue,
Beneath a highland leaning down a weight
Of cliffs, and zoned below with cedar shade,
Came voices, like the voices in a dream,
Continuous, till he reached the outer sea.

SONG

I

The golden apple, the golden apple, the hallowed
fruit,
Guard it well, guard it warily,
Singing airily,
Standing about the charmèd root.
Round about all is mute,
As the snow-field on the mountain-peaks,
As the sand-field at the mountain-foot.
Crocodiles in briny creeks
Sleep and stir not: all is mute.
If ye sing not, if ye make false measure,
We shall lose eternal pleasure,
Worth eternal want of rest.
Laugh not loudly: watch the treasure
Of the wisdom of the west.
In a corner wisdom whispers. Five and three
(Let it not be preached abroad) make an awful
mystery.
For the blossom unto threefold music bloweth;
Evermore it is born anew;
And the sap to threefold music floweth,
From the root
Drawn in the dark,
Up to the fruit,
Creeping under the fragrant bark,
Liquid gold, honeysweet, thro' and thro'.
Keen-eyed Sisters, singing airily,
Looking warily
Every way,
Guard the apple night and day,
Lest one from the East come and take it away.

II

Father Hesper, Father Hesper, watch, watch, ever
and aye,
Looking under silver hair with a silver eye.
Father, twinkle not thy steadfast sight;
Kingdoms lapse, and climates change, and races
die;
Honor comes with mystery;
Hoarded wisdom brings delight.
Number, tell them over and number
How many the mystic fruit-tree holds,
Lest the red-combed dragon slumber
Rolled together in purple folds.
Look to him, father, lest he wink, and the golden
apple be stol'n away,
For his ancient heart is drunk with overwatchings
night and day,
Round about the hallowed fruit-tree curled —
Sing away, sing aloud evermore in the wind, with-
out stop,
Lest his scalèd eyelid drop,
For he is older than the world.
If he waken, we waken,
Rapidly leveling eager eyes.
If he sleep, we sleep,
Dropping the eyelid over the eyes.
If the golden apple be taken,
The world will be overwise.
Five links, a golden chain, are we,
Hesper, the dragon, and sisters three,
Bound about the golden tree.

III

Father Hesper, Father Hesper, watch, watch, night
and day,
Lest the old wound of the world be healèd,
The glory unsealèd,
The golden apple stol'n away,
And the ancient secret revealèd.
Look from west to east along:
Father, old Himala weakens, Caucasus is bold and
strong.
Wandering waters unto wandering waters call;
Let them clash together, foam and fall.
Out of watchings, out of wiles,
Comes the bliss of secret smiles.
All things are not told to all.
Half-round the mantling night is drawn,
Purple-fringèd with even and dawn.
Hesper hateth Phosphor, evening hateth morn.

IV

Every flower and every fruit the redolent breath
Of this warm sea-wind ripeneth,

voyage (*c.* 490 B.C.) along the northwest coast of Africa. Tennyson presumably used *The Voyage of Hanno*, tr. T. Falconer (1797); Falconer has, with much else, remarks on the island of the Hesperides. **3. Soloë**: "Soloeis, a promontory of Libya" (Falconer, p. 7); modern Cape Cantin in Morocco. **4. Thymiaterion**: the name in Falconer's Greek text (Thymiaterium in his translation); modern Mehedia. **5. southern . . . Horn**: so named in Falconer, pp. 11, 13; modern Sherbro Sound and Bissagos Bay. **21. Crocodiles**: "another river . . . full of crocodiles and river horses" (Falconer, pp. 9–11).

**74. Himala**: the Himalayan mountains of India. **Caucasus**: See the note on "The Poet," 15. **82. Hesper**: the evening star.

Arching the billow in his sleep;
But the land-wind wandereth,
Broken by the highland-steep,
Two streams upon the violet deep;
For the western sun and the western star,
And the low west-wind, breathing afar,
The end of day and beginning of night
Make the apple holy and bright;
Holy and bright, round and full, bright and blest,
Mellowed in a land of rest;
Watch it warily day and night;
All good things are in the west.
Till mid noon the cool east light
Is shut out by the round of the tall hillbrow;
But when the full-faced sunset yellowly
Stays on the flowering arch of the bough,
The luscious fruitage clustereth mellowly,
Golden-kerneled, golden-cored,
Sunset-ripened above on the tree.
The world is wasted with fire and sword,
But the apple of gold hangs over the sea.
Five links, a golden chain, are we,
Hesper, the dragon, and sisters three,
Daughters three,
Bound about
All round about
The gnarlèd bole of the charmèd tree.
The golden apple, the golden apple, the hallowed
 fruit,
Guard it well, guard it warily,
Watch it warily,
Singing airily,
Standing about the charmèd root.

*1832*

Phosphor: the morning star. 109. "Bound" in 1832 edition; "Round" in *Memoir,* I, 64, and *Works,* ed. Hallam, Lord Tennyson.

# THE LADY OF SHALOTT

Published in 1832; much revised, 1842. Tennyson's "plot" is quite different, except in its denouement, from Malory's story of the maid of Astolat (*Morte d'Arthur,* XVIII.ix–xx), which he followed in his later Idyll, "Lancelot and Elaine." Editors cite a brief Italian tale (in *The Italian Novelists,* tr. Thomas Roscoe [1825], I, 45–46), which Tennyson may have read, but this is only a condensed equivalent of Malory's chaps. xix–xx and tells how "the lady of Scalot," dying for love of Lancelot, was by her own wish floated down to Camelot and how she was received there. The lyrical tale, at once crisp and incantatory, clearly has allegorical overtones. Tennyson's summary — "The new-born love for something, for some one in the wide world from which she has been so long secluded, takes her out of the region of shadows into that of realities" (*Memoir,* I, 117) — would be somewhat altered in focus by modern critics, who would link this poem with his other early treatments of personal or artistic isolation. Here the shock of reality is fatal to the secluded artist.

PART I

On either side the river lie
Long fields of barley and of rye,
That clothe the wold and meet the sky;
And thro' the field the road runs by
  To many-tower'd Camelot;
And up and down the people go,
Gazing where the lilies blow
Round an island there below,
  The island of Shalott.

Willows whiten, aspens quiver,
Little breezes dusk and shiver
Thro' the wave that runs for ever
By the island in the river
  Flowing down to Camelot.
Four gray walls, and four gray towers,
Overlook a space of flowers,
And the silent isle imbowers
  The Lady of Shalott.

By the margin, willow-veil'd,
Slide the heavy barges trail'd
By slow horses; and unhail'd
The shallop flitteth silken-sail'd
  Skimming down to Camelot:
But who hath seen her wave her hand?
Or at the casement seen her stand?
Or is she known in all the land,
  The Lady of Shalott?

Only reapers, reaping early
In among the bearded barley,
Hear a song that echoes cheerly
From the river winding clearly,
  Down to tower'd Camelot;
And by the moon the reaper weary,
Piling sheaves in uplands airy,
Listening, whispers "'Tis the fairy
  Lady of Shalott."

PART II

There she weaves by night and day
A magic web with colors gay.
She has heard a whisper say,
A curse is on her if she stay

THE LADY OF SHALOTT. **5. Camelot:** King Arthur's capital; symbolically, the outer world in general. **7. blow:** blossom.

To look down to Camelot.
She knows not what the curse may be,
And so she weaveth steadily,
And little other care hath she,
The Lady of Shalott.

And moving thro' a mirror clear
That hangs before her all the year,
Shadows of the world appear.
There she sees the highway near
Winding down to Camelot;
There the river eddy whirls,
And there the surly village-churls,
And the red cloaks of market girls,
Pass onward from Shalott.

Sometimes a troop of damsels glad,
An abbot on an ambling pad,
Sometimes a curly shepherd-lad,
Or long-hair'd page in crimson clad,
Goes by to tower'd Camelot;
And sometimes thro' the mirror blue
The knights come riding two and two:
She hath no loyal knight and true,
The Lady of Shalott.

But in her web she still delights
To weave the mirror's magic sights,
For often thro' the silent nights
A funeral, with plumes and lights
And music, went to Camelot;
Or when the moon was overhead,
Came two young lovers lately wed:
"I am half sick of shadows," said
The Lady of Shalott.

PART III

A bow-shot from her bower-eaves,
He rode between the barley-sheaves,
The sun came dazzling thro' the leaves,
And flamed upon the brazen greaves
Of bold Sir Lancelot.
A red-cross knight for ever kneel'd
To a lady in his shield,
That sparkled on the yellow field,
Beside remote Shalott.

The gemmy bridle glitter'd free,
Like to some branch of stars we see
Hung in the golden Galaxy.
The bridle bells rang merrily
As he rode down to Camelot;
And from his blazon'd baldric slung
A mighty silver bugle hung,
And as he rode his armor rung,
Beside remote Shalott.

All in the blue unclouded weather
Thick-jewel'd shone the saddle-leather,
The helmet and the helmet-feather
Burn'd like one burning flame together,
As he rode down to Camelot;
As often thro' the purple night,
Below the starry clusters bright,
Some bearded meteor, trailing light,
Moves over still Shalott.

His broad clear brow in sunlight glow'd;
On burnish'd hooves his war-horse trode;
From underneath his helmet flow'd
His coal-black curls as on he rode,
As he rode down to Camelot.
From the bank and from the river
He flash'd into the crystal mirror,
"Tirra lirra," by the river
Sang Sir Lancelot.

She left the web, she left the loom,
She made three paces thro' the room,
She saw the water-lily bloom,
She saw the helmet and the plume,
She look'd down to Camelot.
Out flew the web and floated wide;
The mirror crack'd from side to side;
"The curse is come upon me," cried
The Lady of Shalott.

PART IV

In the stormy east-wind straining,
The pale yellow woods were waning,
The broad stream in his banks complaining,
Heavily the low sky raining
Over tower'd Camelot;
Down she came and found a boat
Beneath a willow left afloat,
And round about the prow she wrote
*The Lady of Shalott.*

And down the river's dim expanse
Like some bold seër in a trance,
Seeing all his own mischance —
With a glassy countenance
Did she look to Camelot.
And at the closing of the day
She loosed the chain, and down she lay,
The broad stream bore her far away,
The Lady of Shalott.

Lying, robed in snowy white
That loosely flew to left and right —

56. **pad**: road horse.

The leaves upon her falling light—
Thro' the noises of the night
She floated down to Camelot;
And as the boat-head wound along
The willowy hills and fields among,
They heard her singing her last song,
The Lady of Shalott.

Heard a carol, mournful, holy,
Chanted loudly, chanted lowly,
Till her blood was frozen slowly,
And her eyes were darken'd wholly,
Turn'd to tower'd Camelot.
For ere she reach'd upon the tide
The first house by the water-side,
Singing in her song she died,
The Lady of Shalott.

Under tower and balcony,
By garden-wall and gallery,
A gleaming shape she floated by,
Dead-pale between the houses high,
Silent into Camelot.
Out upon the wharfs they came,
Knight and burgher, lord and dame,
And round the prow they read her name,
*The Lady of Shalott.*

Who is this? and what is here?
And in the lighted palace near
Died the sound of royal cheer;
And they cross'd themselves for fear,
All the knights at Camelot:
But Lancelot mused a little space;
He said, "She has a lovely face;
God in his mercy lend her grace,
The Lady of Shalott."

*1832, 1842*

## ŒNONE

First published in 1832; much revised, 1842. The poem was begun in Spain, in the valley of Cauteretz, in 1830, and the scenery is more Spanish than Trojan. "Œnone" is an epyllion in the manner of Theocritus, a miniature epic or mythic tale closely interwoven with the natural setting; and the refrain is Theocritean. The main sources were presumably the epistles of Paris to Helen and of the deserted Œnone to Paris in Ovid's *Heroides.* The poem is related on one side to Tennyson's early and personal concern with loneliness and the desire for death—Œnone is a mythological Mariana. But in the central episode, the judgment of Paris, the poet shapes Pallas' traditional offer in terms of his own excellent political and social creed, and the poem can hardly sustain the sermon imposed upon it; nor do we feel any ethical impact from Paris' choice of beauty over wisdom (cf. "The Palace of Art"). But the clear-cut scene-painting is in Tennyson's best vein; and the last paragraph, perhaps because of Virgilian and Aeschylean inspiration, rises above Theocritus to the epic or tragic level.

There lies a vale in Ida, lovelier
Than all the valleys of Ionian hills.
The swimming vapor slopes athwart the glen,
Puts forth an arm, and creeps from pine to pine,
And loiters, slowly drawn. On either hand
The lawns and meadow-ledges midway down
Hang rich in flowers, and far below them roars
The long brook falling thro' the clov'n ravine
In cataract after cataract to the sea.
Behind the valley topmost Gargarus
Stands up and takes the morning; but in front
The gorges, opening wide apart, reveal
Troas and Ilion's column'd citadel,
The crown of Troas.
Hither came at noon
Mournful Œnone, wandering forlorn
Of Paris, once her playmate on the hills.
Her cheek had lost the rose, and round her neck
Floated her hair or seem'd to float in rest.
She, leaning on a fragment twined with vine,
Sang to the stillness, till the mountain-shade
Sloped downward to her seat from the upper cliff.

"O mother Ida, many-fountain'd Ida,
Dear mother Ida, harken ere I die.
For now the noonday quiet holds the hill;
The grasshopper is silent in the grass;
The lizard, with his shadow on the stone,
Rests like a shadow, and the winds are dead.
The purple flower droops, the golden bee
Is lily-cradled; I alone awake.
My eyes are full of tears, my heart of love,
My heart is breaking, and my eyes are dim,
And I am all aweary of my life.

"O mother Ida, many-fountain'd Ida,
Dear mother Ida, harken ere I die.
Hear me, O earth, hear me, O hills, O caves
That house the cold crown'd snake! O mountain
brooks,
I am the daughter of a River-God,
Hear me, for I will speak, and build up all
My sorrow with my song, as yonder walls
Rose slowly to a music slowly breathed,

ŒNONE. **1. Ida**: a mountain range near Troy, in Ionia (northern Asia Minor); the epithet is Homeric. **10. Gargarus**: the highest peak of Ida. **13. Troas**: the city of Troy (Ilion) and the region around it. **39–40.** The walls of Troy were said to have been built by Apollo's music.

A cloud that gather'd shape; for it may be
That, while I speak of it, a little while
My heart may wander from its deeper woe.

"O mother Ida, many-fountain'd Ida,
Dear mother Ida, harken ere I die.
I waited underneath the dawning hills;
Aloft the mountain lawn was dewy-dark,
And dewy-dark aloft the mountain pine.
Beautiful Paris, evil-hearted Paris,
Leading a jet-black goat white-horn'd, white-hooved,
Came up from reedy Simois all alone.

"O mother Ida, harken ere I die.
Far-off the torrent call'd me from the cleft;
Far up the solitary morning smote
The streaks of virgin snow. With down-dropt eyes
I sat alone; white-breasted like a star
Fronting the dawn he moved; a leopard skin
Droop'd from his shoulder, but his sunny hair
Cluster'd about his temples like a God's;
And his cheek brighten'd as the foam-bow brightens
When the wind blows the foam, and all my heart
Went forth to embrace him coming ere he came.

"Dear mother Ida, harken ere I die.
He smiled, and opening out his milk-white palm
Disclosed a fruit of pure Hesperian gold,
That smelt ambrosially, and while I look'd
And listen'd, the full-flowing river of speech
Came down upon my heart:
"'My own Œnone,
Beautiful-brow'd Œnone, my own soul,
Behold this fruit, whose gleaming rind ingrav'n
"For the most fair," would seem to award it thine,
As lovelier than whatever Oread haunt
The knolls of Ida, loveliest in all grace
Of movement, and the charm of married brows.'

"Dear mother Ida, harken ere I die.
He prest the blossom of his lips to mine,
And added, 'This was cast upon the board,
When all the full-faced presence of the Gods
Ranged in the halls of Peleus; whereupon
Rose feud, with question unto whom 't were due;
But light-foot Iris brought it yester-eve,
Delivering, that to me, by common voice
Elected umpire, Herè comes to-day,
Pallas and Aphrodite, claiming each

**51. Simois:** a river. **60. foam-bow:** rainbow. **65. Hesperian gold:** See the headnote to "The Hesperides." **74. married brows:** meeting eyebrows, an ancient mark of beauty. **79.** The marriage of Peleus and Thetis (parents of Achilles) was attended by the gods. **83. Herè:** wife of Zeus and queen of the gods (Juno). **84. Pallas:** Athene, goddess of wisdom and war (Minerva).

This meed of fairest. Thou, within the cave
Behind yon whispering tuft of oldest pine,
Mayst well behold them unbeheld, unheard
Hear all, and see thy Paris judge of Gods.'

"Dear mother Ida, harken ere I die.
It was the deep midnoon; one silvery cloud
Had lost his way between the piny sides
Of this long glen. Then to the bower they came,
Naked they came to that smooth-swarded bower,
And at their feet the crocus brake like fire,
Violet, amaracus, and asphodel,
Lotos and lilies; and a wind arose,
And overhead the wandering ivy and vine,
This way and that, in many a wild festoon
Ran riot, garlanding the gnarlèd boughs
With bunch and berry and flower thro' and thro'.

"O mother Ida, harken ere I die.
On the tree-tops a crested peacock lit,
And o'er him flow'd a golden cloud, and lean'd
Upon him, slowly dropping fragrant dew.
Then first I heard the voice of her to whom
Coming thro' heaven, like a light that grows
Larger and clearer, with one mind the Gods
Rise up for reverence. She to Paris made
Proffer of royal power, ample rule
Unquestion'd, overflowing revenue
Wherewith to embellish state, 'from many a vale
And river-sunder'd champaign clothed with corn,
Or labor'd mine undrainable of ore.
Honor,' she said, 'and homage, tax and toll,
From many an inland town and haven large,
Mast-throng'd beneath her shadowing citadel
In glassy bays among her tallest towers.'

"O mother Ida, harken ere I die.
Still she spake on and still she spake of power,
'Which in all action is the end of all;
Power fitted to the season; wisdom-bred
And throned of wisdom — from all neighbor crowns
Alliance and allegiance, till thy hand
Fail from the scepter-staff. Such boon from me,
From me, heaven's queen, Paris, to thee king-born,
A shepherd all thy life but yet king-born,
Should come most welcome, seeing men, in power
Only, are likest Gods, who have attain'd
Rest in a happy place and quiet seats
Above the thunder, with undying bliss
In knowledge of their own supremacy.'

**95. amaracus:** marjoram. **102. peacock:** the bird of Herè. **111–17.** Evidently imitated from, and more studiously "composed" than, Milton's *Paradise Regained,* III.254–62. **112. corn:** grain.

"Dear mother Ida, harken ere I die.
She ceased, and Paris held the costly fruit
Out at arm's-length, so much the thought of power
Flatter'd his spirit; but Pallas where she stood
Somewhat apart, her clear and barèd limbs
O'erthwarted with the brazen-headed spear
Upon her pearly shoulder leaning cold,
The while, above, her full and earnest eye
Over her snow-cold breast and angry cheek
Kept watch, waiting decision, made reply:

"'Self-reverence, self-knowledge, self-control,
These three alone lead life to sovereign power.
Yet not for power (power of herself
Would come uncall'd for) but to live by law,
Acting the law we live by without fear;
And, because right is right, to follow right
Were wisdom in the scorn of consequence.'

"Dear mother Ida, harken ere I die.
Again she said: 'I woo thee not with gifts.
Sequel of guerdon could not alter me
To fairer. Judge thou me by what I am,
So shalt thou find me fairest.
Yet, indeed,
If gazing on divinity disrobed
Thy mortal eyes are frail to judge of fair,
Unbias'd by self-profit, O, rest thee sure
That I shall love thee well and cleave to thee,
So that my vigor, wedded to thy blood,
Shall strike within thy pulses, like a God's,
To push thee forward thro' a life of shocks,
Dangers, and deeds, until endurance grow
Sinew'd with action, and the full-grown will,
Circled thro' all experiences, pure law,
Commeasure perfect freedom.'
"Here she ceas'd,
And Paris ponder'd, and I cried, 'O Paris,
Give it to Pallas!' but he heard me not,
Or hearing would not hear me, woe is me!

"O mother Ida, many-fountain'd Ida,
Dear mother Ida, harken ere I die.
Idalian Aphrodite beautiful,
Fresh as the foam, new-bathed in Paphian wells,
With rosy slender fingers backward drew
From her warm brows and bosom her deep hair
Ambrosial, golden round her lucid throat
And shoulder; from the violets her light foot
Shone rosy-white, and o'er her rounded form
Between the shadows of the vine-bunches
Floated the glowing sunlights, as she moved.

"Dear mother Ida, harken ere I die.
She with a subtle smile in her mild eyes,
The herald of her triumph, drawing nigh
Half-whisper'd in his ear, 'I promise thee
The fairest and most loving wife in Greece.'
She spoke and laugh'd; I shut my sight for fear;
But when I look'd, Paris had raised his arm,
And I beheld great Herè's angry eyes,
As she withdrew into the golden cloud,
And I was left alone within the bower;
And from that time to this I am alone,
And I shall be alone until I die.

"Yet, mother Ida, harken ere I die.
Fairest — why fairest wife? am I not fair?
My love hath told me so a thousand times.
Methinks I must be fair, for yesterday,
When I past by, a wild and wanton pard,
Eyed like the evening star, with playful tail
Crouch'd fawning in the weed. Most loving is she?
Ah me, my mountain shepherd, that my arms
Were wound about thee, and my hot lips prest
Close, close to thine in that quick-falling dew
Of fruitful kisses, thick as autumn rains
Flash in the pools of whirling Simois!

"O mother, hear me yet before I die.
They came, they cut away my tallest pines,
My tall dark pines, that plumed the craggy ledge
High over the blue gorge, and all between
The snowy peak and snow-white cataract
Foster'd the callow eaglet — from beneath
Whose thick mysterious boughs in the dark morn
The panther's roar came muffled, while I sat
Low in the valley. Never, never more
Shall lone Œnone see the morning mist
Sweep thro' them; never see them overlaid
With narrow moonlit slips of silver cloud,
Between the loud stream and the trembling stars.

"O mother, hear me yet before I die.
I wish that somewhere in the ruin'd folds,
Among the fragments tumbled from the glens,
Or the dry thickets, I could meet with her
The Abominable, that uninvited came
Into the fair Peleïan banquet-hall,
And cast the golden fruit upon the board,
And bred this change; that I might speak my mind,
And tell her to her face how much I hate
Her presence, hated both of Gods and men.

**151. Sequel of guerdon:** Paris' judgment in her favor, following upon a gift offered to him, would not make her fairer than she is. **161–64.** Cf. "You Ask Me, Why" and "Love Thou Thy Land." **170. Idalian:** from Idalium in Cyprus, the island near which Aphrodite rose from the sea. **171. Paphian:** Paphos, in Cyprus, was a center of the worship of Aphrodite.

**195. pard:** leopard. **204.** The pines were used for ships to take Paris to Greece in quest of Helen, wife of King Menelaus, promised Paris by Aphrodite. **220. The Abominable:** Eris, goddess of discord.

"O mother, hear me yet before I die.
Hath he not sworn his love a thousand times,
In this green valley, under this green hill,
Even on this hand, and sitting on this stone?
Seal'd it with kisses? water'd it with tears?
O happy tears, and how unlike to these!
O happy heaven, how canst thou see my face?
O happy earth, how canst thou bear my weight?
O death, death, death, thou ever-floating cloud,
There are enough unhappy on this earth,
Pass by the happy souls, that love to live;
I pray thee, pass before my light of life,
And shadow all my soul, that I may die.
Thou weighest heavy on the heart within,
Weigh heavy on my eyelids; let me die.

"O mother, hear me yet before I die.
I will not die alone, for fiery thoughts
Do shape themselves within me, more and more,
Whereof I catch the issue, as I hear
Dead sounds at night come from the inmost hills,
Like footsteps upon wool. I dimly see
My far-off doubtful purpose, as a mother
Conjectures of the features of her child
Ere it is born. Her child!—a shudder comes
Across me: never child be born of me,
Unblest, to vex me with his father's eyes!

"O mother, hear me yet before I die.
Hear me, O earth. I will not die alone,
Lest their shrill happy laughter come to me
Walking the cold and starless road of death
Uncomforted, leaving my ancient love
With the Greek woman. I will rise and go
Down into Troy, and ere the stars come forth
Talk with the wild Cassandra, for she says
A fire dances before her, and a sound
Rings ever in her ears of armèd men.
What this may be I know not, but I know
That, wheresoe'er I am by night and day,
All earth and air seem only burning fire."

*1832, 1842*

# THE PALACE OF ART

Published in 1832; much revised, 1842. This parable is Tennyson's most open treatment of the problem that runs through so many of his earlier poems, the conflicting claims of aesthetic detachment and social or ethical responsibility. Another title for this piece might be the cliché of a later age, "The Ivory Tower." The *Memoir* (I, 118) records the saying of a Cambridge friend, R. C. Trench: "Tennyson, we cannot live in art." Critics have suggested that the poet took hints from such diverse sources as Eccles. 2 and Shelley's *Queen Mab,* II.55–66. The poet undoubtedly felt a real conflict, though it is a question here if it comes through to us; the victory seems to be won in advance. Or perhaps it is won, subconsciously, by the instincts that get such full expression in the body of the poem; lines 237–44, however, anticipate "the romantic agony" of later aestheticism.

**246–47. I . . . purpose:** Œnone later refused to heal the wounded Paris and, having let him die, killed herself (see Tennyson's "The Death of Œnone"). **253–56.** An inspired echo of Dido's dream, *Aeneid,* IV.466–68. **257. Greek woman:** Helen. **259–61. Cassandra . . . men:** a prophetess, daughter of King Priam and sister of Paris; cf. Aeschylus, *Agamemnon,* 1256.

TO ——
WITH THE FOLLOWING POEM

I send you here a sort of allegory—
For you will understand it—of a soul,
A sinful soul possess'd of many gifts,
A spacious garden full of flowering weeds,
A glorious devil, large in heart and brain,
That did love beauty only—beauty seen
In all varieties of mold and mind—
And knowledge for its beauty; or if good,
Good only for its beauty, seeing not
That Beauty, Good, and Knowledge are three sisters
That dote upon each other, friends to man,
Living together under the same roof,
And never can be sunder'd without tears.
And he that shuts Love out, in turn shall be
Shut out from Love, and on her threshold lie
Howling in outer darkness. Not for this
Was common clay ta'en from the common earth
Molded by God, and temper'd with the tears
Of angels to the perfect shape of man.

THE PALACE OF ART

I built my soul a lordly pleasure-house,
Wherein at ease for aye to dwell.
I said, "O Soul, make merry and carouse,
Dear soul, for all is well."

A huge crag-platform, smooth as burnish'd brass,
I chose. The rangèd ramparts bright
From level meadow-bases of deep grass
Suddenly scaled the light.

Thereon I built it firm. Of ledge or shelf
The rock rose clear, or winding stair.
My soul would live alone unto herself
In her high palace there.

THE PALACE OF ART. **3–4.** Cf. Luke 12:19.

And "While the world runs round and round," I said,
"Reign thou apart, a quiet king,
Still as, while Saturn whirls, his steadfast shade
Sleeps on his luminous ring."

To which my soul made answer readily:
"Trust me, in bliss I shall abide
In this great mansion, that is built for me,
So royal-rich and wide."

. . . . . . . .

Four courts I made, East, West and South and North,
In each a squarèd lawn, wherefrom
The golden gorge of dragons spouted forth
A flood of fountain-foam.

And round the cool green courts there ran a row
Of cloisters, branch'd like mighty woods,
Echoing all night to that sonorous flow
Of spouted fountain-floods;

And round the roofs a gilded gallery
That lent broad verge to distant lands,
Far as the wild swan wings, to where the sky
Dipt down to sea and sands.

From those four jets four currents in one swell
Across the mountain stream'd below
In misty folds, that floating as they fell
Lit up a torrent-bow.

And high on every peak a statue seem'd
To hang on tiptoe, tossing up
A cloud of incense of all odor steam'd
From out a golden cup.

So that she thought, "And who shall gaze upon
My palace with unblinded eyes,
While this great bow will waver in the sun,
And that sweet incense rise?"

For that sweet incense rose and never fail'd,
And, while day sank or mounted higher,
The light aerial gallery, golden-rail'd,
Burnt like a fringe of fire.

Likewise the deep-set windows, stain'd and traced,
Would seem slow-flaming crimson fires
From shadow'd grots of arches interlaced,
And tipt with frost-like spires.

. . . . . . . .

15–16. As the planet Saturn revolves, its shadow, thrown upon the bright ring around it, seems to be motionless.

Full of long-sounding corridors it was,
That over-vaulted grateful gloom,
Thro' which the livelong day my soul did pass,
Well-pleased, from room to room.

Full of great rooms and small the palace stood,
All various, each a perfect whole
From living Nature, fit for every mood
And change of my still soul.

For some were hung with arras green and blue,
Showing a gaudy summer-morn,
Where with puff'd cheek the belted hunter blew
His wreathèd bugle-horn.

One seem'd all dark and red — a tract of sand,
And some one pacing there alone,
Who paced for ever in a glimmering land,
Lit with a low large moon.

One show'd an iron coast and angry waves.
You seem'd to hear them climb and fall
And roar rock-thwarted under bellowing caves,
Beneath the windy wall.

And one, a full-fed river winding slow
By herds upon an endless plain,
The ragged rims of thunder brooding low,
With shadow-streaks of rain.

And one, the reapers at their sultry toil.
In front they bound the sheaves. Behind
Were realms of upland, prodigal in oil,
And hoary to the wind.

And one a foreground black with stones and slags;
Beyond, a line of heights; and higher
All barr'd with long white cloud the scornful crags;
And highest, snow and fire.

And one, an English home — gray twilight pour'd
On dewy pastures, dewy trees,
Softer than sleep — all things in order stored,
A haunt of ancient Peace.

Nor these alone, but every landscape fair,
As fit for every mood of mind,
Or gay, or grave, or sweet, or stern, was there,
Not less than truth design'd.

. . . . .

Or the maid-mother by a crucifix,
In tracts of pasture sunny-warm,
Beneath branch-work of costly sardonyx
Sat smiling, babe in arm.

54. grateful: pleasing. 64. wreathèd: coiled.

Or in a clear-wall'd city on the sea,
  Near gilded organ-pipes, her hair
Wound with white roses, slept Saint Cecily;
  An angel look'd at her.

Or thronging all one porch of Paradise
  A group of Houris bow'd to see
The dying Islamite, with hands and eyes
  That said, We wait for thee.

Or mythic Uther's deeply-wounded son
  In some fair space of sloping greens
Lay, dozing in the vale of Avalon,
  And watch'd by weeping queens.

Or hollowing one hand against his ear,
  To list a foot-fall, ere he saw
The wood-nymph, stay'd the Ausonian king to hear
  Of wisdom and of law.

Or over hills with peaky tops engrail'd,
  And many a tract of palm and rice,
The throne of Indian Cama slowly sail'd
  A summer fann'd with spice.

Or sweet Europa's mantle blew unclasp'd,
  From off her shoulder backward borne;
From one hand droop'd a crocus; one hand grasp'd
  The mild bull's golden horn.

Or else flush'd Ganymede, his rosy thigh
  Half-buried in the eagle's down,
Sole as a flying star shot thro' the sky
  Above the pillar'd town.

Nor these alone; but every legend fair
  Which the supreme Caucasian mind
Carved out of Nature for itself was there,
  Not less than life, design'd.

. . . . . . .

Then in the towers I placed great bells that swung,
  Moved of themselves, with silver sound;
And with choice paintings of wise men I hung
  The royal dais round.

For there was Milton like a seraph strong,
  Beside him Shakespeare bland and mild;
And there the world-worn Dante grasp'd his song,
  And somewhat grimly smiled.

And there the Ionian father of the rest;
  A million wrinkles carved his skin;
A hundred winters snow'd upon his breast,
  From cheek and throat and chin.

Above, the fair hall-ceiling stately-set
  Many an arch high up did lift,
And angels rising and descending met
  With interchange of gift.

Below was all mosaic choicely plann'd
  With cycles of the human tale
Of this wide world, the times of every land
  So wrought, they will not fail.

The people here, a beast of burden slow,
  Toil'd onward, prick'd with goads and stings;
Here play'd, a tiger, rolling to and fro
  The heads and crowns of kings;

Here rose, an athlete, strong to break or bind
  All force in bonds that might endure,
And here once more like some sick man declined,
  And trusted any cure.

But over these she trod; and those great bells
  Began to chime. She took her throne;
She sat betwixt the shining oriels,
  To sing her songs alone.

And thro' the topmost oriels' colored flame
  Two godlike faces gazed below;
Plato the wise, and large-brow'd Verulam,
  The first of those who know.

And all those names that in their motion were
  Full-welling fountain-heads of change,
Betwixt the slender shafts were blazon'd fair
  In diverse raiment strange;

Thro' which the lights, rose, amber, emerald, blue,
  Flush'd in her temples and her eyes,
And from her lips, as morn from Memnon, drew
  Rivers of melodies.

No nightingale delighteth to prolong
  Her low preamble all alone,
More than my soul to hear her echo'd song
  Throb thro' the ribbèd stone;

99. St. Cecilia, the patron saint of music, was in legend the inventor of the organ. **105–09.** Uther was Arthur's father. See "Morte d'Arthur." **107. Avalon:** the island paradise of Celtic legend. **111. Ausonian king:** Numa, a legendary king of Rome, who received counsel from the nymph Egeria. Ausonia is a name for Italy (as in Virgil). **113. engrail'd:** indented. **115. Cama:** the Hindu god of love. **126. Caucasian:** of the white race.

**137. Ionian father:** Homer, born in Asia Minor. **148. fail:** fade. **153. athlete:** democracy. **155–56.** Anarchy. **163. Verulam:** Francis Bacon, created Baron Verulam. **164.** Cf. Dante, *Inferno*, IV.131 (of Aristotle). **171–72.** An Egyptian statue, supposedly of Memnon (an Ethiopian prince who fought at Troy), was said to emit sounds when touched by the sun's rays.

Singing and murmuring in her feastful mirth,
  Joying to feel herself alive,
Lord over Nature, lord of the visible earth,
    Lord of the senses five;

Communing with herself: "All these are mine,
  And let the world have peace or wars,
'Tis one to me." She — when young night divine
    Crown'd dying day with stars,

Making sweet close of his delicious toils —
  Lit light in wreaths and anadems,
And pure quintessences of precious oils
    In hollow'd moons of gems,

To mimic heaven; and clapt her hands and cried,
  "I marvel if my still delight
In this great house so royal-rich and wide
    Be flatter'd to the height.

"O all things fair to sate my various eyes!
  O shapes and hues that please me well!
O silent faces of the Great and Wise,
    My Gods, with whom I dwell!

"O Godlike isolation which art mine,
  I can but count thee perfect gain,
What time I watch the darkening droves of swine
    That range on yonder plain.

"In filthy sloughs they roll a prurient skin,
  They graze and wallow, breed and sleep;
And oft some brainless devil enters in,
    And drives them to the deep."

Then of the moral instinct would she prate
  And of the rising from the dead,
As hers by right of full-accomplish'd Fate;
    And at the last she said:

"I take possession of man's mind and deed.
  I care not what the sects may brawl.
I sit as God holding no form of creed,
    But contemplating all."

. . . . . . . .

Full oft the riddle of the painful earth
  Flash'd thro' her as she sat alone,
Yet not the less held she her solemn mirth,
    And intellectual throne.

And so she throve and prosper'd; so three years
  She prosper'd; on the fourth she fell,
Like Herod, when the shout was in his ears,
    Struck thro' with pangs of hell.

Lest she should fail and perish utterly,
  God, before whom ever lie bare
The abysmal deeps of personality,
    Plagued her with sore despair.

When she would think, where'er she turn'd her sight
  The airy hand confusion wrought,
Wrote, "Mene, mene," and divided quite
    The kingdom of her thought.

Deep dread and loathing of her solitude
  Fell on her, from which mood was born
Scorn of herself; again, from out that mood
    Laughter at her self-scorn.

"What! is not this my place of strength," she said,
  "My spacious mansion built for me,
Whereof the strong foundation-stones were laid
    Since my first memory?"

But in dark corners of her palace stood
  Uncertain shapes; and unawares
On white-eyed phantasms weeping tears of blood,
    And horrible nightmares,

And hollow shades enclosing hearts of flame,
  And, with dim fretted foreheads all,
On corpses three-months-old at noon she came,
    That stood against the wall.

A spot of dull stagnation, without light
  Or power of movement, seem'd my soul,
Mid onward-sloping motions infinite
    Making for one sure goal;

A still salt pool, lock'd in with bars of sand,
  Left on the shore, that hears all night
The plunging seas draw backward from the land
    Their moon-led waters white;

A star that with the choral starry dance
  Join'd not, but stood, and standing saw
The hollow orb of moving Circumstance
    Roll'd round by one fix'd law.

Back on herself her serpent pride had curl'd.
  "No voice," she shriek'd in that lone hall,
"No voice breaks thro' the stillness of this world;
    One deep, deep silence all!"

**188.** Gems hollowed out in moonlike shapes, to serve as lamps. **203–04.** See Matt. 8:32, Luke 8:33.

**219–20.** See Acts 12:21–23. **227.** See Dan. 5:25. **242. fretted**: worm-eaten. **247–48.** World progress—in which "my soul" could not participate. **255. Circumstance**: the celestial order, the heavens.

She, moldering with the dull earth's moldering sod,
Inwrapt tenfold in slothful shame,
Lay there exilèd from eternal God,
Lost to her place and name;

And death and life she hated equally,
And nothing saw, for her despair,
But dreadful time, dreadful eternity,
No comfort anywhere;

Remaining utterly confused with fears,
And ever worse with growing time,
And ever unrelieved by dismal tears,
And all alone in crime.

Shut up as in a crumbling tomb, girt round
With blackness as a solid wall,
Far off she seem'd to hear the dully sound
Of human footsteps fall:

As in strange lands a traveler walking slow,
In doubt and great perplexity,
A little before moonrise hears the low
Moan of an unknown sea;

And knows not if it be thunder, or a sound
Of rocks thrown down, or one deep cry
Of great wild beasts; then thinketh, "I have found
A new land, but I die."

She howl'd aloud, "I am on fire within.
There comes no murmur of reply.
What is it that will take away my sin,
And save me lest I die?"

So when four years were wholly finishèd,
She threw her royal robes away.
"Make me a cottage in the vale," she said,
"Where I may mourn and pray.

"Yet pull not down my palace towers, that are
So lightly, beautifully built;
Perchance I may return with others there
When I have purged my guilt."

*1832, 1842*

# THE LOTOS-EATERS

Published in 1832; much revised, 1842. The prelude of five Spenserian stanzas embodies recollections of Spanish scenes from the visit of 1830 (cf. "Œnone"). Tennyson adapts the Homeric episode (*Odyssey*, IX.82 ff.) to his recurrent theme of these years: man's, or the artist's, acceptance or evasion of social responsibility. He also transforms the epic material and manner into his own most luxuriant lyrical vein. Escapist languor is rendered with a verbal and rhythmical felicity that is both exquisite and enervated—and the mood is not condemned, unless by general implication or comparison with other poems, such as "Ulysses." In the Choric Song alternate stanzas are given to pleasurable apathy and the pains of action at sea or at home, and, to some degree, images are correspondingly given a downward or upward movement.

"Courage!" he said, and pointed toward the land,
"This mounting wave will roll us shoreward soon."
In the afternoon they came unto a land
In which it seemèd always afternoon.
All around the coast the languid air did swoon,
Breathing like one that hath a weary dream.
Full-faced above the valley stood the moon;
And, like a downward smoke, the slender stream
Along the cliff to fall and pause and fall did seem.

A land of streams! some, like a downward smoke,
Slow-dropping veils of thinnest lawn, did go;
And some thro' wavering lights and shadows broke,
Rolling a slumbrous sheet of foam below.
They saw the gleaming river seaward flow
From the inner land; far off, three mountain-tops,
Three silent pinnacles of aged snow,
Stood sunset-flush'd; and, dew'd with showery drops,
Up-clomb the shadowy pine above the woven copse.

The charmèd sunset linger'd low adown
In the red West; thro' mountain clefts the dale
Was seen far inland, and the yellow down
Border'd with palm, and many a winding vale
And meadow, set with slender galingale;
A land where all things always seem'd the same!
And round about the keel with faces pale,
Dark faces pale against that rosy flame,
The mild-eyed melancholy Lotos-eaters came.

Branches they bore of that enchanted stem,
Laden with flower and fruit, whereof they gave
To each, but whoso did receive of them
And taste, to him the gushing of the wave
Far far away did seem to mourn and rave
On alien shores; and if his fellow spake,
His voice was thin, as voices from the grave;
And deep-asleep he seem'd, yet all awake,
And music in his ears his beating heart did make.

They sat them down upon the yellow sand,
Between the sun and moon upon the shore;

**275. dully**: dull.

THE LOTOS-EATERS. **1. he**: Odysseus.

And sweet it was to dream of Fatherland,
Of child, and wife, and slave; but evermore
Most weary seem'd the sea, weary the oar,
Weary the wandering fields of barren foam.
Then some one said, "We will return no more;"
And all at once they sang, "Our island home
Is far beyond the wave; we will no longer roam."

CHORIC SONG

I

There is sweet music here that softer falls
Than petals from blown roses on the grass,
Or night-dews on still waters between walls
Of shadowy granite, in a gleaming pass;
Music that gentlier on the spirit lies,
Than tired eyelids upon tired eyes;
Music that brings sweet sleep down from the bliss-
ful skies.
Here are cool mosses deep,
And thro' the moss the ivies creep,
And in the stream the long-leaved flowers weep,
And from the craggy ledge the poppy hangs in
sleep.

II

Why are we weigh'd upon with heaviness,
And utterly consumed with sharp distress,
While all things else have rest from weariness?
All things have rest: why should we toil alone,
We only toil, who are the first of things,
And make perpetual moan,
Still from one sorrow to another thrown;
Nor ever fold our wings,
And cease from wanderings,
Nor steep our brows in slumber's holy balm;
Nor harken what the inner spirit sings,
"There is no joy but calm!" —
Why should we only toil, the roof and crown of
things?

III

Lo! in the middle of the wood,
The folded leaf is woo'd from out the bud
With winds upon the branch, and there
Grows green and broad, and takes no care,
Sun-steep'd at noon, and in the moon
Nightly dew-fed; and turning yellow
Falls, and floats adown the air.
Lo! sweeten'd with the summer light,
The full-juiced apple, waxing over-mellow,
Drops in a silent autumn night.
All its allotted length of days
The flower ripens in its place,
Ripens and fades, and falls, and hath no toil,
Fast rooted in the fruitful soil.

IV

Hateful is the dark-blue sky,
Vaulted o'er the dark-blue sea.
Death is the end of life; ah, why
Should life all labor be?
Let us alone. Time driveth onward fast,
And in a little while our lips are dumb.
Let us alone. What is it that will last?
All things are taken from us, and become
Portions and parcels of the dreadful past.
Let us alone. What pleasure can we have
To war with evil? Is there any peace
In ever climbing up the climbing wave?
All things have rest, and ripen toward the grave
In silence — ripen, fall, and cease:
Give us long rest or death, dark death, or dreamful
ease.

V

How sweet it were, hearing the downward stream,
With half-shut eyes ever to seem
Falling asleep in a half-dream!
To dream and dream, like yonder amber light,
Which will not leave the myrrh-bush on the height;
To hear each other's whisper'd speech;
Eating the Lotos day by day,
To watch the crisping ripples on the beach,
And tender curving lines of creamy spray;
To lend our hearts and spirits wholly
To the influence of mild-minded melancholy;
To muse and brood and live again in memory,
With those old faces of our infancy
Heap'd over with a mound of grass,
Two handfuls of white dust, shut in an urn of
brass!

VI

Dear is the memory of our wedded lives,
And dear the last embraces of our wives
And their warm tears; but all hath suffer'd change;
For surely now our household hearths are cold,
Our sons inherit us, our looks are strange,
And we should come like ghosts to trouble joy.
Or else the island princes over-bold
Have eat our substance, and the minstrel sings
Before them of the ten years' war in Troy,
And our great deeds, as half-forgotten things.

**44. island home:** Ithaca, west of Greece. **Choric Song. 2. blown:** past maturity.

**61. crisping:** curling. **69–87.** Stanza VI was added in 1842. Though it is relatively Homeric in substance, line 79 seems to glance at social and political unrest in England. **76. eat:** the past participle, in English usage; pronounced "et."

Is there confusion in the little isle?
Let what is broken so remain.
The Gods are hard to reconcile;
'Tis hard to settle order once again.
There *is* confusion worse than death,
Trouble on trouble, pain on pain,
Long labor unto aged breath,
Sore tasks to hearts worn out by many wars
And eyes grown dim with gazing on the pilot-stars.

VII

But, propt on beds of amaranth and moly,
How sweet — while warm airs lull us. blowing lowly —
With half-dropt eyelid still,
Beneath a heaven dark and holy,
To watch the long bright river drawing slowly
His waters from the purple hill —
To hear the dewy echoes calling
From cave to cave thro' the thick-twinèd vine —
To watch the emerald-color'd water falling
Thro' many a woven acanthus-wreath divine!
Only to hear and see the far-off sparkling brine,
Only to hear were sweet, stretch'd out beneath the pine.

VIII

The Lotos blooms below the barren peak,
The Lotos blows by every winding creek;
All day the wind breathes low with mellower tone;
Thro' every hollow cave and alley lone
Round and round the spicy downs the yellow Lotos-dust is blown.
We have had enough of action, and of motion we,
Roll'd to starboard, roll'd to larboard, when the surge was seething free,
Where the wallowing monster spouted his foam-fountains in the sea.
Let us swear an oath, and keep it with an equal mind,
In the hollow Lotos-land to live and lie reclined
On the hills like Gods together, careless of mankind.
For they lie beside their nectar, and the bolts are hurl'd
Far below them in the valleys, and the clouds are lightly curl'd
Round their golden houses, girdled with the gleaming world;
Where they smile in secret, looking over wasted lands,
Blight and famine, plague and earthquake, roaring deeps and fiery sands,
Clanging fights, and flaming towns, and sinking ships, and praying hands.
But they smile, they find a music centered in a doleful song
Steaming up, a lamentation and an ancient tale of wrong,
Like a tale of little meaning tho' the words are strong;
Chanted from an ill-used race of men that cleave the soil,
Sow the seed, and reap the harvest with enduring toil,
Storing yearly little dues of wheat, and wine and oil;
Till they perish and they suffer — some, 'tis whisper'd — down in hell
Suffer endless anguish, others in Elysian valleys dwell,
Resting weary limbs at last on beds of asphodel.
Surely, surely, slumber is more sweet than toil, the shore
Than labor in the deep mid-ocean, wind and wave and oar;
O, rest ye, brother mariners, we will not wander more.

*1832, 1842*

## ULYSSES

Written in October, 1833; published in 1842. Tennyson's first dramatic monologue on a classical theme is characteristic in its use of a universally familiar mythic figure and of an antique frame for modern and personal feelings, and in its elevated style. The Homeric Odysseus' motive (though he did sojourn with Circe and Calypso) was to get home to Ithaca and stay there. But the *Odyssey* itself (XI.100–37) foretold death at sea, a hint somewhat developed in later writings, and in Dante (*Inferno,* XXVI.90 ff.) he makes a fatal voyage into the unknown west in search of knowledge. While for Dante Ulysses is a type of pride (and deceitful counsel), for Tennyson, stricken by the death of Hallam (of which he received word on October 1, 1833), he represents the courageous facing of life — though resolution and fortitude are touched with weariness and despair. The poet's own comment, apropos of *In Memoriam,* was: "There is more about myself in 'Ulysses,' which was written under the sense of loss and all that had gone by, but that still life must be fought out to the end. It was more written with the

**88. amaranth**: a supposedly unfading flower. **moly**: the magical herb that protected Odysseus from Circe's spells, though here only a Homeric plant. **105–28.** Completely altered from the original and inferior ending—though the new ending, with its access of energy, is perhaps less in harmony with the tone of the whole. **107. monster**: whale. **110 ff.** The picture of the indifferent gods is developed from the Epicurean Lucretius (*De Rerum Natura,* II.646 ff., V.83 ff., VI.58 ff.). **111. bolts**: thunderbolts.

**124.** Elysium was the Greek paradise for heroes. **125. asphodel**: daffodils (in the Homeric Elysium).

feeling of his loss upon me than many poems in 'In Memoriam.'" (*Nineteenth Century,* XXXIII, 1893, p. 182; cf. *Memoir,* I, 196.) The poem is placed in its long tradition in W. B. Stanford's *The Ulysses Theme* (1954), pp. 202–04.

It little profits that an idle king,
By this still hearth, among these barren crags,
Match'd with an aged wife, I mete and dole
Unequal laws unto a savage race,
That hoard, and sleep, and feed, and know not me.
I cannot rest from travel; I will drink
Life to the lees. All times I have enjoy'd
Greatly, have suffer'd greatly, both with those
That loved me, and alone; on shore, and when
Thro' scudding drifts the rainy Hyades
Vext the dim sea. I am become a name;
For always roaming with a hungry heart
Much have I seen and known, — cities of men
And manners, climates, councils, governments,
Myself not least, but honor'd of them all, —
And drunk delight of battle with my peers,
Far on the ringing plains of windy Troy.
I am a part of all that I have met;
Yet all experience is an arch wherethro'
Gleams that untravel'd world whose margin fades
For ever and for ever when I move. 21
How dull it is to pause, to make an end,
To rust unburnish'd, not to shine in use!
As tho' to breathe were life! Life piled on life
Were all too little, and of one to me
Little remains; but every hour is saved
From that eternal silence, something more,
A bringer of new things; and vile it were
For some three suns to store and hoard myself,
And this gray spirit yearning in desire
To follow knowledge like a sinking star,
Beyond the utmost bound of human thought.
  This is my son, mine own Telemachus,
To whom I leave the scepter and the isle, —
Well-loved of me, discerning to fulfil
This labor, by slow prudence to make mild
A rugged people, and thro' soft degrees
Subdue them to the useful and the good.
Most blameless is he, centered in the sphere
Of common duties, decent not to fail
In offices of tenderness, and pay
Meet adoration to my household gods,
When I am gone. He works his work, I mine.
  There lies the port; the vessel puffs her sail;
There gloom the dark, broad seas. My mariners,
Souls that have toil'd, and wrought, and thought with me, —
That ever with a frolic welcome took
The thunder and the sunshine, and opposed
Free hearts, free foreheads, — you and I are old;
Old age hath yet his honor and his toil.
Death closes all; but something ere the end,
Some work of noble note, may yet be done,
Not unbecoming men that strove with Gods.
The lights begin to twinkle from the rocks;
The long day wanes; the slow moon climbs; the deep
Moans round with many voices. Come, my friends,
'Tis not too late to seek a newer world.
Push off, and sitting well in order smite
The sounding furrows; for my purpose holds
To sail beyond the sunset, and the baths
Of all the western stars, until I die.
It may be that the gulfs will wash us down;
It may be we shall touch the Happy Isles,
And see the great Achilles, whom we knew.
Tho' much is taken, much abides; and tho'
We are not now that strength which in old days
Moved earth and heaven, that which we are, we are, —
One equal temper of heroic hearts,
Made weak by time and fate, but strong in will
To strive, to seek, to find, and not to yield.

*1842* *1833*

ULYSSES. **5.** Cf. *Hamlet,* IV.iv.35. **23.** Cf. *Hamlet,* IV.iv.39. **34–43.** In view of Tennyson's early and prolonged concern over contemplative detachment versus social responsibility, the latter might seem to be fulfilled by Telemachus, but in this poem the issue is rather between giving up and going on. **45 ff.** In Homer, Odysseus had lost all his comrades by the time he reached Ithaca; in Dante, he sails westward from Circe's island, so that they are still with him. Tennyson obviously needs to have them. **54–55.** Homeric voyages commonly begin in the evening; here the accent is on the evening of life. **63. Happy Isles:** Elysium. **64. Achilles:** Arthur Hallam?

## TITHONUS

The mortal Tithonus loved Eos, the goddess of dawn, who obtained for him from Zeus the gift of immortality but neglected to ask for eternal youth, so that he withered away into a repulsive subhuman creature ("Homeric Hymn to Aphrodite"). The theme of isolation and of death as an escape from the burden of living, which had haunted Tennyson from boyhood onward (cf. "Mariana," "Œnone"), is here greatly deepened by the loss of Hallam. This monologue is at the opposite pole from "Ulysses" (though even there the thought of death is not unwelcome), and is of perhaps still finer texture; and, not unnaturally, it has a more mythic quality. "Tithonus" was written apparently in 1833–34, revised in 1859, and published in 1860 (*Memoir,* I, 459; II, 9); the first version was printed and compared with the final one by M. J. Donahue, *Publications of the Modern Language Association,* LXIV (1949), 400 ff.

The woods decay, the woods decay and fall,
The vapors weep their burthen to the ground,
Man comes and tills the field and lies beneath,
And after many a summer dies the swan.
Me only cruel immortality
Consumes; I wither slowly in thine arms,
Here at the quiet limit of the world,
A white-hair'd shadow roaming like a dream
The ever-silent spaces of the East,
Far-folded mists, and gleaming halls of morn.
  Alas! for this gray shadow, once a man —
So glorious in his beauty and thy choice,
Who madest him thy chosen, that he seem'd
To his great heart none other than a God!
I ask'd thee, "Give me immortality."
Then didst thou grant mine asking with a smile,
Like wealthy men who care not how they give.
But thy strong Hours indignant work'd their wills,
And beat me down and marr'd and wasted me,
And tho' they could not end me, left me maim'd
To dwell in presence of immortal youth,
Immortal age beside immortal youth,
And all I was in ashes. Can thy love,
Thy beauty, make amends, tho' even now,
Close over us, the silver star, thy guide,
Shines in those tremulous eyes that fill with tears
To hear me? Let me go; take back thy gift.
Why should a man desire in any way
To vary from the kindly race of men,
Or pass beyond the goal of ordinance
Where all should pause, as is most meet for all?
  A soft air fans the cloud apart; there comes
A glimpse of that dark world where I was born.
Once more the old mysterious glimmer steals
From thy pure brows, and from thy shoulders pure,
And bosom beating with a heart renew'd.
Thy cheek begins to redden thro' the gloom,
Thy sweet eyes brighten slowly close to mine,
Ere yet they blind the stars, and the wild team
Which love thee, yearning for thy yoke, arise,
And shake the darkness from their loosen'd manes,
And beat the twilight into flakes of fire.
  Lo! ever thus thou growest beautiful
In silence, then before thine answer given
Departest, and thy tears are on my cheek.
  Why wilt thou ever scare me with thy tears,
And make me tremble lest a saying learnt,
In days far-off, on that dark earth, be true?
"The Gods themselves cannot recall their gifts."
  Ay me! ay me! with what another heart
In days far-off, and with what other eyes
I used to watch — if I be he that watch'd —
The lucid outline forming round thee; saw
The dim curls kindle into sunny rings;
Changed with thy mystic change, and felt my blood
Glow with the glow that slowly crimson'd all
Thy presence and thy portals, while I lay,
Mouth, forehead, eyelids, growing dewy-warm
With kisses balmier than half-opening buds
Of April, and could hear the lips that kiss'd
Whispering I knew not what of wild and sweet,
Like that strange song I heard Apollo sing,
While Ilion like a mist rose into towers.
  Yet hold me not for ever in thine East;
How can my nature longer mix with thine?
Coldly thy rosy shadows bathe me, cold
Are all thy lights, and cold my wrinkled feet
Upon thy glimmering thresholds, when the steam
Floats up from those dim fields about the homes
Of happy men that have the power to die,
And grassy barrows of the happier dead.
Release me, and restore me to the ground.
Thou seest all things, thou wilt see my grave;
Thou wilt renew thy beauty morn by morn,
I earth in earth forget these empty courts,
And thee returning on thy silver wheels.

*1860* *1833–34, 1859*

TITHONUS. **6. thine arms:** the arms of Eos. **25. silver star:** Venus, the morning star. **29. kindly:** following the course of their nature.

62–63. The walls of Troy were said to have been built by Apollo's music.

## BREAK, BREAK, BREAK

This lyric was composed, Tennyson said, in a Lincolnshire lane at five in the morning between blossoming hedges (probably in the spring of 1834). His lifelong "passion of the past" (cf. "Tears, Idle Tears") is here channeled into grief for Hallam's death — grief to which nature and man, pursuing their normal course, are indifferent. The meter is predominantly anapaestic.

Break, break, break,
  On thy cold gray stones, O Sea!
And I would that my tongue could utter
  The thoughts that arise in me.

O, well for the fisherman's boy,
  That he shouts with his sister at play!
O, well for the sailor lad,
  That he sings in his boat on the bay!

And the stately ships go on
  To their haven under the hill;
But O for the touch of a vanish'd hand,
  And the sound of a voice that is still!

Break, break, break,
 At the foot of thy crags, O Sea!
But the tender grace of a day that is dead
 Will never come back to me.

*1842* *1834?*

## YOU ASK ME, WHY

This and the following poem (both written in 1833–34) express, in more or less gnomic fashion, Tennyson's political attitude in the disturbed period of the first Reform Act (1832); his liberal conservatism is in the tradition of Burke. The two pieces are in the stanza, though not the style, of *In Memoriam*.

You ask me, why, tho' ill at ease,
 Within this region I subsist,
 Whose spirits falter in the mist,
And languish for the purple seas.

It is the land that freemen till,
 That sober-suited Freedom chose,
 The land, where girt with friends or foes
A man may speak the thing he will;

A land of settled government,
 A land of just and old renown,
 Where Freedom slowly broadens down
From precedent to precedent;

Where faction seldom gathers head,
 But, by degrees to fullness wrought,
 The strength of some diffusive thought
Hath time and space to work and spread.

Should banded unions persecute
 Opinion, and induce a time
 When single thought is civil crime,
And individual freedom mute,

Tho' power should make from land to land
 The name of Britain trebly great—
 Tho' every channel of the State
Should fill and choke with golden sand—

Yet waft me from the harbor-mouth,
 Wild wind! I seek a warmer sky,
 And I will see before I die
The palms and temples of the South.

*1842* *1833–34*

YOU ASK ME, WHY. 1–4 (and 25–28). Cf. "Locksley Hall," 153–72. 15–16. Cf. "The Poet."

## LOVE THOU THY LAND

Love thou thy land, with love far-brought
 From out the storied past, and used
 Within the present, but transfused
Thro' future time by power of thought;

True love turn'd round on fixèd poles,
 Love, that endures not sordid ends,
 For English natures, freemen, friends,
Thy brothers and immortal souls.

But pamper not a hasty time,
 Nor feed with crude imaginings
 The herd, wild hearts and feeble wings
That every sophister can lime.

Deliver not the tasks of might
 To weakness, neither hide the ray
 From those, not blind, who wait for day,
Tho' sitting girt with doubtful light.

Make knowledge circle with the winds;
 But let her herald, Reverence, fly
 Before her to whatever sky
Bear seed of men and growth of minds.

Watch what main-currents draw the years;
 Cut Prejudice against the grain.
 But gentle words are always gain;
Regard the weakness of thy peers.

Nor toil for title, place, or touch
 Of pension, neither count on praise—
 It grows to guerdon after-days.
Nor deal in watch-words overmuch;

Not clinging to some ancient saw,
 Not master'd by some modern term,
 Not swift nor slow to change, but firm;
And in its season bring the law,

That from Discussion's lip may fall
 With Life, that, working strongly, binds—
 Set in all lights by many minds,
To close the interests of all.

For Nature also, cold and warm,
 And moist and dry, devising long,
 Thro' many agents making strong,
Matures the individual form.

LOVE THOU THY LAND. 12. lime: catch (as birds used to be caught with a sticky substance). 17–18. Cf. "Locksley Hall," 141; *In Memoriam*, Prologue, 25–26. 37–40. cold . . . dry: the traditional four elements.

Meet is it changes should control
  Our being, lest we rust in ease.
  We all are changed by still degrees,
All but the basis of the soul.

So let the change which comes be free
  To ingroove itself with that which flies,
  And work, a joint of state, that plies
Its office, moved with sympathy.

A saying hard to shape in act;
  For all the past of Time reveals
  A bridal dawn of thunder-peals,
Wherever Thought hath wedded Fact.

Even now we hear with inward strife
  A motion toiling in the gloom —
  The Spirit of the years to come
Yearning to mix himself with Life.

A slow-develop'd strength awaits
  Completion in a painful school;
  Phantoms of other forms of rule,
New Majesties of mighty States —

The warders of the growing hour,
  But vague in vapor, hard to mark;
  And round them sea and air are dark
With great contrivances of Power.

Of many changes, aptly join'd,
  Is bodied forth the second whole.
  Regard gradation, lest the soul
Of Discord race the rising wind;

A wind to puff your idol-fires,
  And heap their ashes on the head;
  To shame the boast so often made,
That we are wiser than our sires.

O, yet, if Nature's evil star
  Drive men in manhood, as in youth,
  To follow flying steps of Truth
Across the brazen bridge of war —

If New and Old, disastrous feud,
  Must ever shock, like armèd foes,
  And this be true, till Time shall close,
That Principles are rain'd in blood;

Not yet the wise of heart would cease
  To hold his hope thro' shame and guilt,
  But with his hand against the hilt,
Would pace the troubled land, like Peace;

68. rising wind: of revolution.

Not less, tho' dogs of Faction bay,
  Would serve his kind in deed and word,
  Certain, if knowledge bring the sword,
That knowledge takes the sword away —

Would love the gleams of good that broke
  From either side, nor veil his eyes;
  And if some dreadful need should rise
Would strike, and firmly, and one stroke.

To-morrow yet would reap to-day,
  As we bear blossom of the dead;
  Earn well the thrifty months, nor wed
Raw Haste, half-sister to Delay.

*1842* *1833–34*

## MORTE D'ARTHUR

This poem was written by 1835 (the Prologue and Epilogue were apparently added several years later) and published in 1842. The *Memoir,* I, 109, 129 records the significant facts that Tennyson was working on it at least as early as November, 1833, and that the first draft was written in a manuscript book between sections XXX and XXXI of *In Memoriam* — which, along with internal elements, suggest the association between King Arthur and Arthur Hallam. Tennyson already had in mind something of the symbolism developed — and altered — later in *Idylls of the King* (see the headnote to "The Holy Grail"), and touches of that symbolism enrich the atmosphere of this early piece. The poem, based on Sir Thomas Malory's *Morte d'Arthur,* XXI.iv–vi, is not merely the story of a good king defeated and fatally wounded in a battle with his wicked and rebellious nephew Modred; Arthur is the dedicated servant of God and man, the ideal not only of the soul or conscience but of selfless, beneficent action. And, though the Round Table is now broken up and its chief dies in failure, his life and reign receive mystical sanction; and in his last speech (291–315) he can himself accept the historical process as God's way of working. With some additions, this poem was later made the last of the *Idylls* as "The Passing of Arthur."

### THE EPIC

At Francis Allen's on the Christmas-eve, —
The game of forfeits done — the girls all kiss'd
Beneath the sacred bush and past away —
The parson Holmes, the poet Everard Hall,
The host, and I sat round the wassail-bowl,
Then half-way ebb'd; and there we held a talk,
How all the old honor had from Christmas gone,
Or gone or dwindled down to some odd games
In some odd nooks like this; till I, tired out
With cutting eights that day upon the pond,

Where, three times slipping from the outer edge,
I bump'd the ice into three several stars,
Fell in a doze; and half-awake I heard
The parson taking wide and wider sweeps,
Now harping on the church-commissioners,
Now hawking at geology and schism;
Until I woke, and found him settled down
Upon the general decay of faith
Right thro' the world: "at home was little left,
And none abroad; there was no anchor, none,
To hold by." Francis, laughing, clapt his hand
On Everard's shoulder, with "I hold by him."
"And I," quoth Everard, "by the wassail-bowl."
"Why yes," I said, "we knew your gift that way
At college; but another which you had —
I mean of verse (for so we held it then),
What came of that?" "You know," said Frank, "he burnt
His epic, his King Arthur, some twelve books" —
And then to me demanding why: "O, sir,
He thought that nothing new was said, or else
Something so said 'twas nothing — that a truth
Looks freshest in the fashion of the day;
God knows; he has a mint of reasons; ask.
It pleased *me* well enough." "Nay, nay," said Hall,
"Why take the style of those heroic times?
For nature brings not back the mastodon,
Nor we those times; and why should any man
Remodel models? these twelve books of mine
Were faint Homeric echoes, nothing-worth,
Mere chaff and draff, much better burnt." "But I,"
Said Francis, "pick'd the eleventh from this hearth,
And have it; keep a thing, its use will come.
I hoard it as a sugar-plum for Holmes."
He laugh'd, and I, tho' sleepy, like a horse
That hears the corn-bin open, prick'd my ears;
For I remember'd Everard's college fame
When we were Freshmen. Then at my request
He brought it; and the poet, little urged,
But with some prelude of disparagement,
Read, mouthing out his hollow oes and aes,
Deep-chested music, and to this result.

## MORTE D'ARTHUR

So all day long the noise of battle roll'd
Among the mountains by the winter sea,
Until King Arthur's table, man by man,
Had fallen in Lyonnesse about their lord,
King Arthur; then, because his wound was deep,
The bold Sir Bedivere uplifted him,
Sir Bedivere, the last of all his knights,
And bore him to a chapel nigh the field,
A broken chancel with a broken cross,
That stood on a dark strait of barren land.
On one side lay the ocean, and on one
Lay a great water, and the moon was full.
Then spake King Arthur to Sir Bedivere:
"The sequel of to-day unsolders all
The goodliest fellowship of famous knights
Whereof this world holds record. Such a sleep
They sleep — the men I loved. I think that we
Shall never more, at any future time,
Delight our souls with talk of knightly deeds,
Walking about the gardens and the halls
Of Camelot, as in the days that were.
I perish by this people which I made, —
Tho' Merlin sware that I should come again
To rule once more — but let what will be be,
I am so deeply smitten thro' the helm
That without help I cannot last till morn.
Thou therefore take my brand Excalibur,
Which was my pride; for thou rememberest how
In those old days, one summer noon, an arm
Rose up from out the bosom of the lake,
Clothed in white samite, mystic, wonderful,
Holding the sword — and how I row'd across
And took it, and have worn it, like a king;
And, wheresoever I am sung or told
In aftertime, this also shall be known.
But now delay not; take Excalibur,
And fling him far into the middle mere;
Watch what thou seest, and lightly bring me word."
To him replied the bold Sir Bedivere:
"It is not meet, Sir King, to leave thee thus,
Aidless, alone, and smitten thro' the helm.
A little thing may harm a wounded man.
Yet I thy hest will all perform at full,
Watch what I see, and lightly bring thee word."
So saying, from the ruin'd shrine he stept
And in the moon athwart the place of tombs,
Where lay the mighty bones of ancient men,
Old knights, and over them the sea-wind sang
Shrill, chill, with flakes of foam. He, stepping down
By zigzag paths and juts of pointed rock,
Came on the shining levels of the lake.
There drew he forth the brand Excalibur,
And o'er him, drawing it, the winter moon,
Brightening the skirts of a long cloud, ran forth
And sparkled keen with frost against the hilt;
For all the haft twinkled with diamond sparks,
Myriads of topaz-lights, and jacinth work
Of subtlest jewelry. He gazed so long

MORTE D'ARTHUR. **15. church-commissioners:** a body set up in 1835–36 to administer the Church of England's revenues. **16. geology:** as affecting traditional views of Genesis, the creation and age of the world, etc. **45. corn-bin:** grain-bin. **55. Lyonnesse:** a mythical part of England, beyond Cornwall, that figures in the Arthurian stories.

**72. Camelot:** Arthur's capital. **74. Merlin:** the magician of the Arthurian romances. **78. Excalibur:** Arthur's sword, given him by the Lady of the Lake; a symbol of his Christ-like activities. **82. samite:** silken fabric. **88. middle mere:** middle of the lake.

That both his eyes were dazzled, as he stood,
This way and that dividing the swift mind,
In act to throw; but at the last it seem'd
Better to leave Excalibur conceal'd
There in the many-knotted water-flags,
That whistled stiff and dry about the marge.
So strode he back slow to the wounded king.
Then spake King Arthur to Sir Bedivere:
"Hast thou perform'd my mission which I gave?
What is it thou hast seen, or what hast heard?"
And answer made the bold Sir Bedivere:
"I heard the ripple washing in the reeds,
And the wild water lapping on the crag."
To whom replied King Arthur, faint and pale:
"Thou hast betray'd thy nature and thy name,
Not rendering true answer, as beseem'd
Thy fealty, nor like a noble knight;
For surer sign had follow'd, either hand,
Or voice, or else a motion of the mere.
This is a shameful thing for men to lie.
Yet now, I charge thee, quickly go again
As thou art lief and dear, and do the thing
I bade thee, watch, and lightly bring me word."
Then went Sir Bedivere the second time
Across the ridge, and paced beside the mere,
Counting the dewy pebbles, fix'd in thought;
But when he saw the wonder of the hilt,
How curiously and strangely chased, he smote
His palms together, and he cried aloud:
"And if indeed I cast the brand away,
Surely a precious thing, one worthy note,
Should thus be lost forever from the earth,
Which might have pleased the eyes of many men.
What good should follow this, if this were done?
What harm, undone? deep harm to disobey,
Seeing obedience is the bond of rule.
Were it well to obey then, if a king demand
An act unprofitable, against himself?
The king is sick, and knows not what he does.
What record, or what relic of my lord
Should be to aftertime, but empty breath
And rumors of a doubt? but were this kept,
Stored in some treasure-house of mighty kings,
Some one might show it at a joust of arms,
Saying, 'King Arthur's sword, Excalibur,
Wrought by the lonely maiden of the lake;
Nine years she wrought it, sitting in the deeps
Upon the hidden bases of the hills.'
So might some old man speak in the aftertime
To all the people, winning reverence;
But now much honor and much fame were lost."
So spake he, clouded with his own conceit,
And hid Excalibur the second time,
And so strode back slow to the wounded king.

**137. curiously:** elaborately. **161. conceit:** idea, along with the feeling of superior wisdom.

Then spoke King Arthur, breathing heavily:
"What is it thou hast seen, or what hast heard?"
And answer made the bold Sir Bedivere:
"I heard the water lapping on the crag,
And the long ripple washing in the reeds."
To whom replied King Arthur, much in wrath:
"Ah, miserable and unkind, untrue,
Unknightly, traitor-hearted! Woe is me!
Authority forgets a dying king,
Laid widow'd of the power in his eye
That bow'd the will. I see thee what thou art,
For thou, the latest-left of all my knights,
In whom should meet the offices of all,
Thou wouldst betray me for the precious hilt;
Either from lust of gold, or like a girl
Valuing the giddy pleasure of the eyes.
Yet, for a man may fail in duty twice,
And the third time may prosper, get thee hence;
But, if thou spare to fling Excalibur,
I will arise and slay thee with my hands."
Then quickly rose Sir Bedivere, and ran,
And, leaping down the ridges lightly, plunged
Among the bulrush-beds, and clutch'd the sword,
And strongly wheel'd and threw it. The great brand
Made lightnings in the splendor of the moon,
And flashing round and round, and whirl'd in an arch,
Shot like a streamer of the northern morn,
Seen where the moving isles of winter shock
By night, with noises of the northern sea.
So flash'd and fell the brand Excalibur;
But ere he dipt the surface, rose an arm
Cloth'd in white samite, mystic, wonderful,
And caught him by the hilt, and brandish'd him
Three times, and drew him under in the mere.
And lightly went the other to the king.
Then spoke King Arthur, drawing thicker breath:
"Now see I by thine eyes that this is done.
Speak out; what is it thou hast heard, or seen?"
And answer made the bold Sir Bedivere:
"Sir King, I closed mine eyelids, lest the gems
Should blind my purpose, for I never saw,
Nor shall see, here or elsewhere, till I die,
Not tho' I live three lives of mortal men,
So great a miracle as yonder hilt.
Then with both hands I flung him, wheeling him;
But when I look'd again, behold an arm,
Clothed in white samite, mystic, wonderful,
That caught him by the hilt, and brandish'd him
Three times, and drew him under in the mere."
And answer made King Arthur, breathing hard:
"My end draws nigh; 'tis time that I were gone.
Make broad thy shoulders to receive my weight,
And bear me to the margin; yet I fear
My wound hath taken cold, and I shall die."

**190–92.** The northern lights. **191. isles of winter:** icebergs.

So saying, from the pavement he half rose,
Slowly, with pain, reclining on his arm,
And looking wistfully with wide blue eyes
As in a picture. Him Sir Bedivere
Remorsefully regarded thro' his tears,
And would have spoken, but he found not words,
Then took with care, and kneeling on one knee,
O'er both his shoulders drew the languid hands,
And rising bore him thro' the place of tombs.
But, as he walk'd, King Arthur panted hard,
Like one that feels a nightmare on his bed
When all the house is mute. So sigh'd the king,
Muttering and murmuring at his ear, "Quick, quick!
I fear it is too late, and I shall die."
But the other swiftly strode from ridge to ridge,
Clothed with his breath, and looking, as he walk'd,
Larger than human on the frozen hills.
He heard the deep behind him, and a cry
Before. His own thought drove him like a goad.
Dry clash'd his harness in the icy caves
And barren chasms, and all to left and right
The bare black cliff clang'd round him, as he based
His feet on juts of slippery crag that rang
Sharp-smitten with the dint of armèd heels—
And on a sudden, lo! the level lake,
And the long glories of the winter moon.
Then saw they how there hove a dusky barge,
Dark as a funeral scarf from stem to stern,
Beneath them; and descending they were ware
That all the decks were dense with stately forms
Black-stoled, black-hooded, like a dream—by these
Three queens with crowns of gold—and from them rose
A cry that shiver'd to the tingling stars,
And, as it were one voice, an agony
Of lamentation, like a wind that shrills
All night in a waste land, where no one comes,
Or hath come, since the making of the world.
Then murmur'd Arthur, "Place me in the barge,"
And to the barge they came. There those three queens
Put forth their hands, and took the king, and wept.
But she that rose the tallest of them all
And fairest laid his head upon her lap,
And loosed the shatter'd casque, and chafed his hands,
And call'd him by his name, complaining loud,
And dropping bitter tears against his brow
Striped with dark blood; for all his face was white
And colorless, and like the wither'd moon
Smote by the fresh beam of the springing east;
And all his greaves and cuisses dash'd with drops
Of onset; and the light and lustrous curls—
That made his forehead like a rising sun
High from the dais-throne—were parch'd with dust;
Or, clotted into points and hanging loose,
Mix'd with the knightly growth that fringed his lips.
So like a shatter'd column lay the king;
Not like that Arthur who, with lance in rest,
From spur to plume a star of tournament,
Shot thro' the lists at Camelot, and charged
Before the eyes of ladies and of kings.
Then loudly cried the bold Sir Bedivere:
"Ah! my Lord Arthur, whither shall I go?
Where shall I hide my forehead and my eyes?
For now I see the true old times are dead,
When every morning brought a noble chance,
And every chance brought out a noble knight.
Such times have been not since the light that led
The holy Elders with the gift of myrrh.
But now the whole ROUND TABLE is dissolved
Which was an image of the mighty world;
And I, the last, go forth companionless,
And the days darken round me, and the years,
Among new men, strange faces, other minds."
And slowly answer'd Arthur from the barge:
"The old order changeth, yielding place to new,
And God fulfils himself in many ways,
Lest one good custom should corrupt the world.
Comfort thyself: what comfort is in me?
I have lived my life, and that which I have done
May He within himself make pure! but thou,
If thou shouldst never see my face again,
Pray for my soul. More things are wrought by prayer
Than this world dreams of. Wherefore, let thy voice
Rise like a fountain for me night and day.
For what are men better than sheep or goats
That nourish a blind life within the brain,
If, knowing God, they lift not hands of prayer
Both for themselves and those who call them friend?
For so the whole round earth is every way
Bound by gold chains about the feet of God.
But now farewell. I am going a long way
With these thou seest—if indeed I go—
For all my mind is clouded with a doubt—

**249. Three queens:** In Malory (XXI.vi) these are Morgan le Fay, the queen of Northgalis, and the queen of the Waste Lands. Tennyson, when asked if they represented Faith, Hope, and Charity, would not accept this one meaning only.

**266–67. drops of onset:** blood of battle. **281. chance:** adventure, enterprise. **283–84.** The Wise Men who followed the star to Bethlehem (Matt. 2:7–12). **285. Round Table:** the band of Arthur's knights, dedicated to the righting of wrongs; they sat at a round table which obviated questions of precedence. For Tennyson's later conception, perhaps present here, see the headnote to "The Holy Grail." **293. custom:** chivalry. **305–06.** This image goes back through centuries of symbolic interpretation to the *Iliad*, VIII.18–22. Arthur's speech is entirely Tennyson's invention.

To the island-valley of Avilion;
Where falls not hail, or rain, or any snow,
Nor ever wind blows loudly, but it lies
Deep-meadow'd, happy, fair with orchard lawns
And bowery hollows crown'd with summer sea,
Where I will heal me of my grievous wound."
  So said he, and the barge with oar and sail
Moved from the brink, like some full-breasted swan
That, fluting a wild carol ere her death,
Ruffles her pure cold plume, and takes the flood
With swarthy webs. Long stood Sir Bedivere
Revolving many memories, till the hull
Look'd one black dot against the verge of dawn,
And on the mere the wailing died away.

  Here ended Hall, and our last light, that long
Had wink'd and threaten'd darkness, flared and fell;
At which the parson, sent to sleep with sound,
And waked with silence, grunted "Good!" but we
Sat rapt: it was the tone with which he read—
Perhaps some modern touches here and there
Redeem'd it from the charge of nothingness—
Or else we loved the man, and prized his work;
I know not; but we sitting, as I said,
The cock crew loud, as at that time of year
The lusty bird takes every hour for dawn.
Then Francis, muttering, like a man ill-used,
"There now—that's nothing!" drew a little back,
And drove his heel into the smolder'd log,
That sent a blast of sparkles up the flue.
And so to bed, where yet in sleep I seem'd
To sail with Arthur under looming shores,
Point after point; till on to dawn, when dreams
Begin to feel the truth and stir of day,
To me, methought, who waited with a crowd,
There came a bark that, blowing forward, bore
King Arthur, like a modern gentleman
Of stateliest port; and all the people cried,
"Arthur is come again: he cannot die."
Then those that stood upon the hills behind
Repeated—"Come again, and thrice as fair;"
And, further inland, voices echoed—"Come
With all good things, and war shall be no more."
At this a hundred bells began to peal,
That with the sound I woke, and heard indeed
The clear church-bells ring in the Christmas morn.

*1842* *1833–35*

**310. Avilion:** Avalon, the paradise of Celtic legend. **333–34.** Cf. *Hamlet,* I.i.157–60. **347.** According to medieval legend, Arthur was to return and resume his rule (cf. 74–75).

# LOCKSLEY HALL

Published in 1842. Writing to G. M. Hopkins in 1879, R. W. Dixon described "Locksley Hall" as an "ungentlemanly row," but such a representative of an earlier generation as Charles Kingsley said in 1850 that this poem had "most influence on the minds of the young men of our day"—an influence akin to that of the social verse of the 1930's, though doubtless more in accord with public opinion and faith in progress. Tennyson said that, while he was indebted to some Arabian poems translated by Sir William Jones, the narrative situation was imaginary (*Memoir,* I, 195); the attack on Mammonism may in part reflect the feud in the Tennyson family (see the Introduction). Some of the attitudes expressed are Tennyson's, though he is not to be identified with the speaker. It is odd that a poet who normally has the most sensitive metrical tact should have put a reflective monologue into galloping trochaics because English people liked that meter (*Memoir,* l.c.); at any rate the lines were highly quotable.

Comrades, leave me here a little, while as yet 'tis early morn;
Leave me here, and when you want me, sound upon the bugle-horn.

'Tis the place, and all around it, as of old, the curlews call,
Dreary gleams about the moorland flying over Locksley Hall;

Locksley Hall, that in the distance overlooks the sandy tracts,
And the hollow ocean-ridges roaring into cataracts.

Many a night from yonder ivied casement, ere I went to rest,
Did I look on great Orion sloping slowly to the west.

Many a night I saw the Pleiads, rising thro' the mellow shade,
Glitter like a swarm of fireflies tangled in a silver braid.

Here about the beach I wander'd, nourishing a youth sublime
With the fairy tales of science, and the long result of time;

When the centuries behind me like a fruitful land reposed;
When I clung to all the present for the promise that it closed;

LOCKSLEY HALL. **4. gleams:** of light. **14. closed:** enclosed.

When I dipt into the future far as human eye could see,
Saw the vision of the world and all the wonder that would be. —

In the spring a fuller crimson comes upon the robin's breast;
In the spring the wanton lapwing gets himself another crest;

In the spring a livelier iris changes on the burnish'd dove;
In the spring a young man's fancy lightly turns to thoughts of love.

Then her cheek was pale and thinner than should be for one so young,
And her eyes on all my motions with a mute observance hung.

And I said, "My cousin Amy, speak, and speak the truth to me,
Trust me, cousin, all the current of my being sets to thee."

On her pallid cheek and forehead came a color and a light,
As I have seen the rosy red flushing in the northern night.

And she turn'd — her bosom shaken with a sudden storm of sighs —
All the spirit deeply dawning in the dark of hazel eyes —

Saying, "I have hid my feelings, fearing they should do me wrong;"
Saying, "Dost thou love me, cousin?" weeping, "I have loved thee long."

Love took up the glass of Time, and turn'd it in his glowing hands;
Every moment, lightly shaken, ran itself in golden sands.

Love took up the harp of Life, and smote on all the chords with might;
Smote the chord of Self, that, trembling, past in music out of sight.

Many a morning on the moorland did we hear the copses ring,
And her whisper throng'd my pulses with the fullness of the spring.

Many an evening by the waters did we watch the stately ships,
And our spirits rush'd together at the touching of the lips.

O my cousin, shallow-hearted! O my Amy, mine no more!
O the dreary, dreary moorland! O the barren, barren shore!

Falser than all fancy fathoms, falser than all songs have sung,
Puppet to a father's threat, and servile to a shrewish tongue!

Is it well to wish thee happy? — having known me — to decline
On a range of lower feelings and a narrower heart than mine!

Yet it shall be; thou shalt lower to his level day by day,
What is fine within thee growing coarse to sympathize with clay.

As the husband is, the wife is; thou art mated with a clown,
And the grossness of his nature will have weight to drag thee down.

He will hold thee, when his passion shall have spent its novel force,
Something better than his dog, a little dearer than his horse.

What is this? his eyes are heavy; think not they are glazed with wine.
Go to him, it is thy duty; kiss him, take his hand in thine.

It may be my lord is weary, that his brain is overwrought;
Soothe him with thy finer fancies, touch him with thy lighter thought.

He will answer to the purpose, easy things to understand —
Better thou wert dead before me, tho' I slew thee with my hand!

Better thou and I were lying, hidden from the heart's disgrace,
Roll'd in one another's arms, and silent in a last embrace.

Cursèd be the social wants that sin against the strength of youth!

**17.** The English robin is a little garden bird with a vivid scarlet breast.

Cursèd be the social lies that warp us from the living truth!
Cursèd be the sickly forms that err from honest Nature's rule!
Cursèd be the gold that gilds the straiten'd forehead of the fool!

Well — 'tis well that I should bluster! — Hadst thou less unworthy proved —
Would to God — for I had loved thee more than ever wife was loved.

Am I mad, that I should cherish that which bears but bitter fruit?
I will pluck it from my bosom, tho' my heart be at the root.

Never, tho' my mortal summers to such length of years should come
As the many-winter'd crow that leads the clanging rookery home.

Where is comfort? in division of the records of the mind?
Can I part her from herself, and love her, as I knew her, kind?

I remember one that perish'd; sweetly did she speak and move;
Such a one do I remember, whom to look at was to love.

Can I think of her as dead, and love her for the love she bore?
No — she never loved me truly; love is love for evermore.

Comfort? comfort scorn'd of devils! this is truth the poet sings,
That a sorrow's crown of sorrow is remembering happier things.

Drug thy memories, lest thou learn it, lest thy heart be put to proof,
In the dead unhappy night, and when the rain is on the roof.

Like a dog, he hunts in dreams, and thou art staring at the wall,
Where the dying night-lamp flickers, and the shadows rise and fall.

Then a hand shall pass before thee, pointing to his drunken sleep,
To thy widow'd marriage-pillows, to the tears that thou wilt weep.

Thou shalt hear the "Never, never," whisper'd by the phantom years,
And a song from out the distance in the ringing of thine ears;

And an eye shall vex thee, looking ancient kindness on thy pain.
Turn thee, turn thee on thy pillow; get thee to thy rest again.

Nay, but Nature brings thee solace; for a tender voice will cry.
'Tis a purer life than thine, a lip to drain thy trouble dry.

Baby lips will laugh me down; my latest rival brings thee rest.
Baby fingers, waxen touches, press me from the mother's breast.

O, the child too clothes the father with a dearness not his due.
Half is thine and half is his; it will be worthy of the two.

O, I see thee old and formal, fitted to thy petty part,
With a little hoard of maxims preaching down a daughter's heart.

"They were dangerous guides the feelings — she herself was not exempt —
Truly, she herself had suffer'd" — Perish in thy self-contempt!

Overlive it — lower yet — be happy! wherefore should I care?
I myself must mix with action, lest I wither by despair.

What is that which I should turn to, lighting upon days like these?
Every door is barr'd with gold, and opens but to golden keys.

Every gate is throng'd with suitors, all the markets overflow.
I have but an angry fancy; what is that which I should do?

I had been content to perish, falling on the foeman's ground,
When the ranks are roll'd in vapor, and the winds are laid with sound.

75. poet: Dante (*Inferno*, V.121–23).

But the jingling of the guinea helps the hurt that Honor feels,
And the nations do but murmur, snarling at each other's heels.

Can I but relive in sadness? I will turn that earlier page.
Hide me from my deep emotion, O thou wondrous Mother-Age!

Make me feel the wild pulsation that I felt before the strife,
When I heard my days before me, and the tumult of my life;

Yearning for the large excitement that the coming years would yield,
Eager-hearted as a boy when first he leaves his father's field,

And at night along the dusky highway near and nearer drawn,
Sees in heaven the light of London flaring like a dreary dawn;

And his spirit leaps within him to be gone before him then,
Underneath the light he looks at, in among the throngs of men;

Men, my brothers, men the workers, ever reaping something new;
That which they have done but earnest of the things that they shall do.

For I dipt into the future, far as human eye could see,
Saw the Vision of the world, and all the wonder that would be;

Saw the heavens fill with commerce, argosies of magic sails,
Pilots of the purple twilight, dropping down with costly bales;

Heard the heavens fill with shouting, and there rain'd a ghastly dew
From the nations' airy navies grappling in the central blue;

Far along the world-wide whisper of the south-wind rushing warm,
With the standards of the peoples plunging thro' the thunderstorm;

Till the war-drum throbb'd no longer, and the battle-flags were furl'd
In the Parliament of man, the Federation of the world.

There the common sense of most shall hold a fretful realm in awe,
And the kindly earth shall slumber, lapt in universal law.

So I triumph'd ere my passion sweeping thro' me left me dry,
Left me with the palsied heart, and left me with the jaundiced eye;

Eye, to which all order festers, all things here are out of joint.
Science moves, but slowly, slowly, creeping on from point to point;

Slowly comes a hungry people, as a lion, creeping nigher,
Glares at one that nods and winks behind a slowly-dying fire.

Yet I doubt not thro' the ages one increasing purpose runs,
And the thoughts of men are widen'd with the process of the suns.

What is that to him that reaps not harvest of his youthful joys,
Tho' the deep heart of existence beat for ever like a boy's?

Knowledge comes, but wisdom lingers, and I linger on the shore,
And the individual withers, and the world is more and more.

Knowledge comes, but wisdom lingers, and he bears a laden breast,
Full of sad experience, moving toward the stillness of his rest.

Hark, my merry comrades call me, sounding on the bugle-horn,
They to whom my foolish passion were a target for their scorn.

Shall it not be scorn to me to harp on such a molder'd string?
I am shamed thro' all my nature to have loved so slight a thing.

**121–25.** These lines probably reflect contemporary interest in balloons, though they are, for us, grimly prophetic.

**135–36.** One English manifestation of political and social unrest was the Chartist movement, which reached its peak in 1842.

Weakness to be wroth with weakness! woman's pleasure, woman's pain—
Nature made them blinder motions bounded in a shallower brain.

Woman is the lesser man, and all thy passions, match'd with mine,
Are as moonlight unto sunlight, and as water unto wine—

Here at least, where nature sickens, nothing. Ah, for some retreat
Deep in yonder shining Orient, where my life began to beat,

Where in wild Mahratta-battle fell my father evil-starr'd;—
I was left a trampled orphan, and a selfish uncle's ward.

Or to burst all links of habit—there to wander far away,
On from island unto island at the gateways of the day.

Larger constellations burning, mellow moons and happy skies,
Breadths of tropic shade and palms in cluster, knots of Paradise.

Never comes the trader, never floats an European flag,
Slides the bird o'er lustrous woodland, swings the trailer from the crag;

Droops the heavy-blossom'd bower, hangs the heavy-fruited tree—
Summer isles of Eden lying in dark-purple spheres of sea.

There methinks would be enjoyment more than in this march of mind,
In the steamship, in the railway, in the thoughts that shake mankind.

There the passions cramp'd no longer shall have scope and breathing space;
I will take some savage woman, she shall rear my dusky race.

Iron-jointed, supple-sinew'd, they shall dive, and they shall run,
Catch the wild goat by the hair, and hurl their lances in the sun;

Whistle back the parrot's call, and leap the rainbows of the brooks,
Not with blinded eyesight poring over miserable books—

Fool, again the dream, the fancy! but I *know* my words are wild,
But I count the gray barbarian lower than the Christian child.

I, to herd with narrow foreheads, vacant of our glorious gains,
Like a beast with lower pleasures, like a beast with lower pains!

Mated with a squalid savage—what to me were sun or clime?
I the heir of all the ages, in the foremost files of time—

I that rather held it better men should perish one by one,
Than that earth should stand at gaze like Joshua's moon in Ajalon!

Not in vain the distance beacons. Forward, forward let us range,
Let the great world spin for ever down the ringing grooves of change.

Thro' the shadow of the globe we sweep into the younger day;
Better fifty years of Europe than a cycle of Cathay.

Mother-Age,—for mine I knew not,—help me as when life begun;
Rift the hills, and roll the waters, flash the lightnings, weigh the sun.

O, I see the crescent promise of my spirit hath not set.
Ancient founts of inspiration well thro' all my fancy yet.

Howsoever these things be, a long farewell to Locksley Hall!
Now for me the woods may wither, now for me the roof-tree fall.

Comes a vapor from the margin, blackening over heath and holt,

**155.** The Mahrattas were a people of India who gave trouble to their British rulers. **162. trailer:** vine.

**180.** See Josh. 10:12. **182.** When in 1830 Tennyson made his first journey by train, he thought—in nocturnal darkness—that the wheels ran in grooves (*Memoir*, I, 195). **184. Cathay:** an old name for China, here as a land of immemorial stagnation. **187. crescent:** growing. **190. for me:** so far as I am concerned.

Cramming all the blast before it, in its breast a thunderbolt.

Let it fall on Locksley Hall, with rain or hail, or fire or snow;
For the mighty wind arises, roaring seaward, and I go.

*1842* *1835–42*

# SONGS from *THE PRINCESS*

*The Princess,* published in 1847 — the year of *Jane Eyre* — was a serio-comic-romantic poem on the education and emancipation of women. The stern intellectual, Princess Ida, founds a college of like-minded young women from which men are excluded, but she eventually succumbs to love. While parts of the narrative have their interest, as a whole it cannot be said to make strong claims upon the modern reader. But some of the eleven interspersed lyrics, which reflect phases of the story, are among Tennyson's finest. "Sweet and Low" and "The Splendor Falls" (the latter inspired by a boatman's echoing bugle on the lakes of Killarney) were added in 1850. The richest of the group in depth and verbal and rhythmical felicity is "Tears, Idle Tears" — which is also that rare thing, a blank-verse lyric. It expresses "the yearning that young people occasionally experience for that which seems to have passed away from them for ever" (*Memoir,* II, 73); and Tennyson's own profound "passion of the past" carries his Virgilian "sadness at the doubtful doom of human kind." He composed the poem in "the yellowing autumn-tide at Tintern Abbey, full for me of its bygone memories" (*Memoir,* I, 253) — memories of Wordsworth's poem (which, like his own, rendered the sense of "the abiding in the transient") and of Hallam, whose burial place was not far away (cf. *In Memoriam,* XIX).

## SWEET AND LOW

Sweet and low, sweet and low,
  Wind of the western sea,
Low, low, breathe and blow,
  Wind of the western sea!
Over the rolling waters go,
Come from the dying moon, and blow,
  Blow him again to me;
While my little one, while my pretty one, sleeps.

Sleep and rest, sleep and rest,
  Father will come to thee soon;
Rest, rest, on mother's breast,
  Father will come to thee soon;
Father will come to his babe in the nest,
Silver sails all out of the west
  Under the silver moon;
Sleep, my little one, sleep, my pretty one, sleep.

*1850*

## THE SPLENDOR FALLS

The splendor falls on castle walls
  And snowy summits old in story;
The long light shakes across the lakes,
  And the wild cataract leaps in glory.
Blow, bugle, blow, set the wild echoes flying,
Blow, bugle; answer, echoes, dying, dying, dying.

O, hark, O, hear! how thin and clear,
  And thinner, clearer, farther going!
O, sweet and far from cliff and scar
  The horns of Elfland faintly blowing!
Blow, let us hear the purple glens replying,
Blow, bugle; answer, echoes, dying, dying, dying.

O love, they die in yon rich sky,
  They faint on hill or field or river;
Our echoes roll from soul to soul,
  And grow for ever and for ever.
Blow, bugle, blow, set the wild echoes flying,
And answer, echoes, answer, dying, dying, dying.

*1850*

## TEARS, IDLE TEARS

  Tears, idle tears, I know not what they mean,
Tears from the depth of some divine despair
Rise in the heart, and gather to the eyes,
In looking on the happy autumn-fields,
And thinking of the days that are no more.

  Fresh as the first beam glittering on a sail,
That brings our friends up from the underworld,
Sad as the last which reddens over one
That sinks with all we love below the verge;
So sad, so fresh, the days that are no more.

  Ah, sad and strange as in dark summer dawns
The earliest pipe of half-awaken'd birds
To dying ears, when unto dying eyes
The casement slowly grows a glimmering square;
So sad, so strange, the days that are no more.

  Dear as remember'd kisses after death,
And sweet as those by hopeless fancy feign'd
On lips that are for others; deep as love,

Deep as first love, and wild with all regret;
O Death in Life, the days that are no more!

*1847*

## NOW SLEEPS THE CRIMSON PETAL

Now sleeps the crimson petal, now the white;
Nor waves the cypress in the palace walk;
Nor winks the gold fin in the porphyry font.
The fire-fly wakens; waken thou with me.

Now droops the milk-white peacock like a ghost,
And like a ghost she glimmers on to me.

Now lies the Earth all Danaë to the stars,
And all thy heart lies open unto me.

Now slides the silent meteor on, and leaves
A shining furrow, as thy thoughts in me.

Now folds the lily all her sweetness up,
And slips into the bosom of the lake.
So fold thyself, my dearest, thou, and slip
Into my bosom and be lost in me.

*1847*

## THE EAGLE

FRAGMENT

He clasps the crag with crooked hands;
Close to the sun in lonely lands,
Ring'd with the azure world, he stands.

The wrinkled sea beneath him crawls;
He watches from his mountain walls,
And like a thunderbolt he falls.

*1851*

# IN MEMORIAM A.H.H.

OBIIT MDCCCXXXIII

Something has been said of Arthur Hallam at several points in the Introduction. His friendship with Tennyson and his visits at Somersby led to his becoming engaged to Tennyson's sister Emily. After taking his degree in 1832, Hallam commenced the study of law in London. While traveling with his father he died in Vienna of apoplexy on September 15, 1833, at the age of twenty-two. His writings in verse and prose, which have been edited by T. H. Vail Motter (1943), are of some interest; his review of Tennyson's volume of 1830 was noticed in the Introduction. Hallam's "Theodicæa Novissima," an essay read to the "Apostles" in 1831, was an attempt to grapple with the problem of evil, to find a valid religious and philosophical faith (cf. *In Memoriam,* XCVI); one phrase in it, "God's election, with whom alone rest the abysmal secrets of personality" (Motter, pp. 210–11), was echoed in "The Palace of Art," lines 221–23. Some of Hallam's distinguished contemporaries at Cambridge thought him the most brilliant of their set. Although their estimate may have been heightened by his early death, he clearly possessed a very quick, keen intellect, a breadth of literary and philosophical knowledge, fine integrity, and a charming blend of seriousness and gaiety. Still clearer is the depth of love and admiration he inspired in Tennyson. His death brought together and greatly intensified all the feelings that had long troubled the poet — loneliness and self-distrust, questionings about life and God and immortality, about the destiny of the individual and society in a world increasingly given over by scientific skepticism to blind and ruthless Nature.

Immediately after Hallam's death Tennyson began to seek relief in lyric utterance; the collection of lyrics, growing through seventeen years, was published in 1850. Written thus over a long period, and not for some time conceived of as a publishable whole, the poems have, in T. S. Eliot's phrase, "only the unity and continuity of a diary." (Although, as Mr. Eliot also says, "It is a diary of which we have to read every word," in an anthology lack of space admits of no appeal.) The long process of time naturally affected both Tennyson's private grief and the religious and philosophic questions it involved. Eleanor B. Mattes (*In Memoriam: The Way of a Soul* [1951]) has tried, so far as evidence and inference allow, to trace the currents of his feeling and thought, the impact of various books and ideas, and the dates of individual poems. The arrangement of poems does not, except in some small sequences, follow the order of composition, and has only the appearance of a chronological pattern. Four large divisions are established by the Christmastide sections (XXVIII, LXXVIII, CIV), which make the imagined time of the poem seem to be less than three years. In the standard general study, *A Commentary on Tennyson's In Memoriam* (3rd ed., 1910), A. C. Bradley sets up these divisions and their main themes in the following way (to give only a skeleton and leave out subdivisions):

*Part I.* I–XXVII: Absorption in grief.

*Part II.* XXVIII–LXXVII: Preoccupation with the question of individual survival after death and related problems.

*Part III.* LXXVIII–CIII: Section LXXVIII may be said to inaugurate the upward, affirmative movement of faith and hope. The question of immortality recedes, though sections XC–XCV deal with possible communion between the living and the dead.

*Part IV.* CIV–CXXXI: A forward-looking conclusion based on the assurance of love as the soul of the world and of the dead man as the type of a nobler race to come.

Tennyson thought that he had invented the stanza (which he used in the previously published "You Ask

Me, Why" and "Love Thou Thy Land"), but critics have pointed out examples in Sir Philip Sidney, Ben Jonson, and Lord Herbert.

Strong Son of God, immortal Love,
  Whom we, that have not seen thy face,
  By faith, and faith alone, embrace,
Believing where we cannot prove;

Thine are these orbs of light and shade;
  Thou madest Life in man and brute;
  Thou madest Death; and lo, thy foot
Is on the skull which thou hast made.

Thou wilt not leave us in the dust:
  Thou madest man, he knows not why,
  He thinks he was not made to die;
And thou hast made him: thou art just.

Thou seemest human and divine,
  The highest, holiest manhood, thou.
  Our wills are ours, we know not how;
Our wills are ours, to make them thine.

Our little systems have their day;
  They have their day and cease to be;
  They are but broken lights of thee,
And thou, O Lord, art more than they.

We have but faith: we cannot know,
  For knowledge is of things we see;
  And yet we trust it comes from thee,
A beam in darkness: let it grow.

Let knowledge grow from more to more,
  But more of reverence in us dwell;
  That mind and soul, according well,
May make one music as before,

But vaster. We are fools and slight;
  We mock thee when we do not fear:
  But help thy foolish ones to bear;
Help thy vain worlds to bear thy light.

Forgive what seem'd my sin in me,
  What seem'd my worth since I began;
  For merit lives from man to man,
And not from man, O Lord, to thee.

Forgive my grief for one removed,
  Thy creature, whom I found so fair.
  I trust he lives in thee, and there
I find him worthier to be loved.

Forgive these wild and wandering cries,
  Confusions of a wasted youth;
  Forgive them where they fail in truth,
And in thy wisdom make me wise.

*1849*

I

I held it truth, with him who sings
  To one clear harp in divers tones,
  That men may rise on stepping-stones
Of their dead selves to higher things.

But who shall so forecast the years
  And find in loss a gain to match?
  Or reach a hand thro' time to catch
The far-off interest of tears?

Let Love clasp Grief lest both be drown'd,
  Let darkness keep her raven gloss.
  Ah, sweeter to be drunk with loss,
To dance with Death, to beat the ground,

Than that the victor Hours should scorn
  The long result of love, and boast,
  "Behold the man that loved and lost,
But all he was is overworn."

II

Old yew, which graspest at the stones
  That name the underlying dead,
  Thy fibers net the dreamless head,
Thy roots are wrapt about the bones.

The seasons bring the flower again,
  And bring the firstling to the flock;
  And in the dusk of thee the clock
Beats out the little lives of men.

O, not for thee the glow, the bloom,
  Who changest not in any gale,
  Nor branding summer suns avail
To touch thy thousand years of gloom;

And gazing on thee, sullen tree,
  Sick for thy stubborn hardihood,

IN MEMORIAM. **Prologue.** This section, written shortly before publication, should perhaps be read last—and even then appears as a more positively Christian affirmation than the work as a whole seems to warrant. **1. immortal Love:** Cf. I John 4,5; and George Herbert, "Immortal Love, author of this great frame . . . on that dust which thou has made." **5. orbs . . . shades:** the sun, the earth, and the planets, and the cycle of light and darkness—and life and death. **17. systems:** of belief and thought. **19. broken:** refracted. **28. as before:** as in the age of secure faith.

**42. wasted:** desolated. **I.1. him:** Goethe. **8. interest:** a commercial metaphor (cf. "loss" and "gain," 6). **II.1–4.** Cf. Job 8:17. **7. clock:** on the church tower. **14. for:** with desire for.

I seem to fail from out my blood
And grow incorporate into thee.

III

O Sorrow, cruel fellowship,
O Priestess in the vaults of Death,
O sweet and bitter in a breath,
What whispers from thy lying lip?

"The stars," she whispers, "blindly run;
A web is woven across the sky;
From out waste places comes a cry,
And murmurs from the dying sun;

"And all the phantom, Nature, stands—
With all the music in her tone,
A hollow echo of my own,—
A hollow form with empty hands."

And shall I take a thing so blind,
Embrace her as my natural good;
Or crush her, like a vice of blood,
Upon the threshold of the mind?

V

I sometimes hold it half a sin
To put in words the grief I feel;
For words, like Nature, half reveal
And half conceal the Soul within.

But, for the unquiet heart and brain,
A use in measured language lies;
The sad mechanic exercise,
Like dull narcotics, numbing pain.

In words, like weeds, I'll wrap me o'er,
Like coarsest clothes against the cold;
But that large grief which these enfold
Is given in outline and no more.

VII

Dark house, by which once more I stand
Here in the long unlovely street,
Doors, where my heart was used to beat
So quickly, waiting for a hand,

A hand that can be clasp'd no more—
Behold me, for I cannot sleep,
And like a guilty thing I creep
At earliest morning to the door.

He is not here; but far away
The noise of life begins again,
And ghastly thro' the drizzling rain
On the bald street breaks the blank day.

X

I hear the noise about thy keel;
I hear the bell struck in the night;
I see the cabin-window bright;
I see the sailor at the wheel.

Thou bring'st the sailor to his wife,
And travel'd men from foreign lands;
And letters unto trembling hands;
And, thy dark freight, a vanish'd life.

So bring him; we have idle dreams;
This look of quiet flatters thus
Our home-bred fancies. O, to us,
The fools of habit, sweeter seems

To rest beneath the clover sod,
That takes the sunshine and the rains,
Or where the kneeling hamlet drains
The chalice of the grapes of God;

Than if with thee the roaring wells
Should gulf him fathom-deep in brine,
And hands so often clasp'd in mine,
Should toss with tangle and with shells.

XI

Calm is the morn without a sound,
Calm as to suit a calmer grief,
And only thro' the faded leaf
The chestnut pattering to the ground;

Calm and deep peace on this high wold,
And on these dews that drench the furze,
And all the silvery gossamers
That twinkle into green and gold;

Calm and still light on yon great plain
That sweeps with all its autumn bowers,
And crowded farms and lessening towers,
To mingle with the bounding main;

Calm and deep peace in this wide air,
These leaves that redden to the fall,
And in my heart, if calm at all,
If any calm, a calm despair;

**III.** The first statement of one major theme: the mechanistic view of a dying universe denies a providential order and leaves man an insignificant atom. The idea is made the deceptive utterance of Sorrow, but her voice is the poet's. **V.9. weeds:** clothes. **VII.1–2.** The Hallam house in Wimpole Street, London.

**X.1–8.** The ship bringing Hallam's body to England. **13–16.** An over-refined image of alternative places of burial—the churchyard or the chancel where villagers kneel for Holy Communion. **20. tangle:** seaweed. **XI.7. gossamers:** cobwebs. **12. bounding:** bordering, limiting.

Calm on the seas, and silver sleep,
  And waves that sway themselves in rest,
  And dead calm in that noble breast
Which heaves but with the heaving deep.

XV

To-night the winds begin to rise
  And roar from yonder dropping day;
  The last red leaf is whirl'd away,
The rooks are blown about the skies;

The forest crack'd, the waters curl'd,
  The cattle huddled on the lea;
  And wildly dash'd on tower and tree
The sunbeam strikes along the world:

And but for fancies, which aver
  That all thy motions gently pass
  Athwart a plane of molten glass,
I scarce could brook the strain and stir

That makes the barren branches loud;
  And but for fear it is not so,
  The wild unrest that lives in woe
Would dote and pore on yonder cloud

That rises upward always higher,
  And onward drags a laboring breast,
  And topples round the dreary west,
A looming bastion fringed with fire.

XVI

What words are these have fall'n from me?
  Can calm despair and wild unrest
  Be tenants of a single breast,
Or Sorrow such a changeling be?

Or doth she only seem to take
  The touch of change in calm or storm,
  But knows no more of transient form
In her deep self, than some dead lake

That holds the shadow of a lark
  Hung in the shadow of a heaven?
  Or has the shock, so harshly given,
Confused me like the unhappy bark

That strikes by night a craggy shelf,
  And staggers blindly ere she sink?
  And stunn'd me from my power to think
And all my knowledge of myself;

And made me that delirious man
  Whose fancy fuses old and new,
  And flashes into false and true,
And mingles all without a plan?

XVIII

'T is well; 't is something; we may stand
  Where he in English earth is laid,
  And from his ashes may be made
The violet of his native land.

'T is little; but it looks in truth
  As if the quiet bones were blest
  Among familiar names to rest
And in the places of his youth.

Come then, pure hands, and bear the head
  That sleeps or wears the mask of sleep,
  And come, whatever loves to weep,
And hear the ritual of the dead.

Ah yet, even yet, if this might be,
  I, falling on his faithful heart,
  Would breathing thro' his lips impart
The life that almost dies in me;

That dies not, but endures with pain,
  And slowly forms the firmer mind,
  Treasuring the look it cannot find,
The words that are not heard again.

XIX

The Danube to the Severn gave
  The darken'd heart that beat no more;
  They laid him by the pleasant shore,
And in the hearing of the wave.

There twice a day the Severn fills;
  The salt sea-water passes by,
  And hushes half the babbling Wye,
And makes a silence in the hills.

The Wye is hush'd nor moved along,
  And hush'd my deepest grief of all,
  When fill'd with tears that cannot fall,
I brim with sorrow drowning song.

The tide flows down, the wave again
  Is vocal in its wooded walls;
  My deeper anguish also falls,
And I can speak a little then.

**XV.2. dropping day**: the west. **10. thy**: the ship's (cf. X.1–8). **11. plane . . . glass**: a calm sea (cf. Job 37:18, Rev. 15:2). **XVI.2. calm . . . unrest**: Cf. XI and XV.

**XVIII.2.** Hallam was actually buried in Clevedon Church, not in the churchyard. **XIX.** Written at Tintern Abbey on the Wye (see the note on "Tears, Idle Tears"). **1. Danube . . . Severn.** Hallam died in Vienna; Clevedon overlooks the Severn river where it flows into the Bristol Channel. The tidal ebb and flow of the Severn and its tributary, the Wye, are applied to the poet's utterance and silence.

XXI

I sing to him that rests below,
  And, since the grasses round me wave,
  I take the grasses of the grave,
And make them pipes whereon to blow.

The traveler hears me now and then,
  And sometimes harshly will he speak:
  "This fellow would make weakness weak,
And melt the waxen hearts of men."

Another answers: "Let him be,
  He loves to make parade of pain,
  That with his piping he may gain
The praise that comes to constancy."

A third is wroth: "Is this an hour
  For private sorrow's barren song,
  When more and more the people throng
The chairs and thrones of civil power?

"A time to sicken and to swoon,
  When Science reaches forth her arms
  To feel from world to world, and charms
Her secret from the latest moon?"

Behold, ye speak an idle thing;
  Ye never knew the sacred dust.
  I do but sing because I must,
And pipe but as the linnets sing;

And one is glad; her note is gay,
  For now her little ones have ranged;
  And one is sad; her note is changed,
Because her brood is stolen away.

XXII

The path by which we twain did go,
  Which led by tracts that pleased us well,
  Thro' four sweet years arose and fell,
From flower to flower, from snow to snow;

And we with singing cheer'd the way,
  And, crown'd with all the season lent,
  From April on to April went,
And glad at heart from May to May.

But where the path we walk'd began
  To slant the fifth autumnal slope,
  As we descended following Hope,
There sat the Shadow fear'd of man;

Who broke our fair companionship,
  And spread his mantle dark and cold,
  And wrapt thee formless in the fold,
And dull'd the murmur on thy lip,

And bore thee where I could not see
  Nor follow, tho' I walk in haste,
  And think that somewhere in the waste
The Shadow sits and waits for me.

XXIII

Now, sometimes in my sorrow shut,
  Or breaking into song by fits,
  Alone, alone, to where he sits,
The Shadow cloak'd from head to foot,

Who keeps the keys of all the creeds,
  I wander, often falling lame,
  And looking back to whence I came,
Or on to where the pathway leads;

And crying, How changed from where it ran
  Thro' lands where not a leaf was dumb,
  But all the lavish hills would hum
The murmur of a happy Pan;

When each by turns was guide to each,
  And Fancy light from Fancy caught,
  And Thought leapt out to wed with Thought
Ere Thought could wed itself with Speech;

And all we met was fair and good,
  And all was good that Time could bring,
  And all the secret of the Spring
Moved in the chambers of the blood;

And many an old philosophy
  On Argive heights divinely sang,
  And round us all the thicket rang
To many a flute of Arcady.

XXIV

And was the day of my delight
  As pure and perfect as I say?
  The very source and fount of day
Is dash'd with wandering isles of night.

If all was good and fair we met,
  This earth had been the Paradise

**XXI.** Tennyson's old theme—here in new circumstances—of private versus public poetry. **4.** The musical pipes of the pastoral poet. **15–16.** Cf. "The Palace of Art," 149 ff., "Locksley Hall," 135–36. **20. moon:** the planet Neptune and its moon, discovered in 1846. **XXII.** Sections XXII–XXV contrast the past and the present. **3. four . . . years:** 1829–32. **10.** September, 1833.

**12. Shadow:** Death. **XXIII.22. Argive:** Greek. **24. Arcady:** Arcadia, a region of Greece, has been in literary tradition an ideal pastoral world. **XXIV.3–4.** Even the sun has spots.

It never look'd to human eyes
Since our first sun arose and set.

And is it that the haze of grief
Makes former gladness loom so great?
The lowness of the present state,
That sets the past in this relief?

Or that the past will always win
A glory from its being far,
And orb into the perfect star
We saw not when we moved therein?

XXV

I know that this was Life,—the track
Whereon with equal feet we fared;
And then, as now, the day prepared
The daily burden for the back.

But this it was that made me move
As light as carrier-birds in air;
I loved the weight I had to bear,
Because it needed help of Love;

Nor could I weary, heart or limb,
When mighty Love would cleave in twain
The lading of a single pain,
And part it, giving half to him.

XXVI

Still onward winds the dreary way;
I with it, for I long to prove
No lapse of moons can canker Love,
Whatever fickle tongues may say.

And if that eye which watches guilt
And goodness, and hath power to see
Within the green the molder'd tree,
And towers fall'n as soon as built—

O, if indeed that eye foresee
Or see—in Him is no before—
In more of life true life no more
And Love the indifference to be,

Then might I find, ere yet the morn
Breaks hither over Indian seas,
That Shadow waiting with the keys,
To shroud me from my proper scorn.

XXVII

I envy not in any moods
The captive void of noble rage,
The linnet born within the cage,
That never knew the summer woods;

I envy not the beast that takes
His license in the field of time,
Unfetter'd by the sense of crime,
To whom a conscience never wakes;

Nor, what may count itself as blest,
The heart that never plighted troth
But stagnates in the weeds of sloth;
Nor any want-begotten rest.

I hold it true, whate'er befall;
I feel it, when I sorrow most;
'Tis better to have loved and lost
Than never to have loved at all.

XXVIII

The time draws near the birth of Christ.
The moon is hid, the night is still;
The Christmas bells from hill to hill
Answer each other in the mist.

Four voices of four hamlets round,
From far and near, on mead and moor,
Swell out and fail, as if a door
Were shut between me and the sound;

Each voice four changes on the wind,
That now dilate, and now decrease,
Peace and goodwill, goodwill and peace,
Peace and goodwill, to all mankind.

This year I slept and woke with pain,
I almost wish'd no more to wake,
And that my hold on life would break
Before I heard those bells again;

But they my troubled spirit rule,
For they controll'd me when a boy;
They bring me sorrow touch'd with joy,
The merry, merry bells of Yule.

XXX

With trembling fingers did we weave
The holly round the Christmas hearth;
A rainy cloud possess'd the earth,
And sadly fell our Christmas-eve.

**15.** As the earth, viewed from outer space, would seem a perfect disk. **XXV.11. lading:** burden. **XXVI.12.** Love turning with time into indifference. **15. Shadow:** See XXII.12, 20, XXIII.4. **16. my . . . scorn:** scorn of myself.

**XXVII.6. field of time:** earthly life. **12. want-begotten:** the result of a deficiency. **XXVIII.** The first Christmas (at Somersby) since Hallam's death. In XXVIII–LXXVII the predominant theme is the continuance of life and love after death. **5–12.** The phrases imitate the sound of the bells. **9. changes:** tunes. **13. This year:** 1833.

At our old pastimes in the hall
We gambol'd, making vain pretense
Of gladness, with an awful sense
Of one mute Shadow watching all.

We paused: the winds were in the beech;
We heard them sweep the winter land;
And in a circle hand-in-hand
Sat silent, looking each at each.

Then echo-like our voices rang;
We sung, tho' every eye was dim,
A merry song we sang with him
Last year; impetuously we sang.

We ceased; a gentler feeling crept
Upon us: surely rest is meet.
"They rest," we said, "their sleep is sweet,"
And silence follow'd, and we wept.

Our voices took a higher range;
Once more we sang: "They do not die
Nor lose their mortal sympathy,
Nor change to us, altho' they change;

"Rapt from the fickle and the frail
With gather'd power, yet the same,
Pierces the keen seraphic flame
From orb to orb, from veil to veil."

Rise, happy morn, rise, holy morn,
Draw forth the cheerful day from night:
O Father, touch the east, and light
The light that shone when Hope was born.

XXXIV

My own dim life should teach me this,
That life shall live for evermore,
Else earth is darkness at the core,
And dust and ashes all that is;

This round of green, this orb of flame,
Fantastic beauty; such as lurks
In some wild poet, when he works
Without a conscience or an aim.

What then were God to such as I?
'T were hardly worth my while to choose
Of things all mortal, or to use
A little patience ere I die;

'T were best at once to sink to peace,
Like birds the charming serpent draws,
To drop head-foremost in the jaws
Of vacant darkness and to cease.

XXXV

Yet if some voice that man could trust
Should murmur from the narrow house,
"The cheeks drop in, the body bows;
Man dies, nor is there hope in dust;"

Might I not say? "Yet even here,
But for one hour, O Love, I strive
To keep so sweet a thing alive."
But I should turn mine ears and hear

The moanings of the homeless sea,
The sound of streams that swift or slow
Draw down Æonian hills, and sow
The dust of continents to be;

And Love would answer with a sigh,
"The sound of that forgetful shore
Will change my sweetness more and more,
Half-dead to know that I shall die."

O me, what profits it to put
An idle case? If Death were seen
At first as Death, Love had not been,
Or been in narrowest working shut,

Mere fellowship of sluggish moods,
Or in his coarsest Satyr-shape
Had bruised the herb and crush'd the grape,
And bask'd and batten'd in the woods.

XXXVI

Tho' truths in manhood darkly join,
Deep-seated in our mystic frame,
We yield all blessing to the name
Of Him that made them current coin;

For Wisdom dealt with mortal powers,
Where truth in closest words shall fail,
When truth embodied in a tale
Shall enter in at lowly doors.

**XXX.8. Shadow:** here, not Death, but the spirit of Hallam. **22 ff.** The first appearance of the theme of immortality. **25–28.** The soul, freed from the temporal, goes through life after life. **27. flame:** the subject of "Pierces." **32. Hope:** Christ, as the agent of human immortality. **XXXIV.** Consciousness alone, without revelation, should compel belief in immortality, since without it the world and life would be meaningless. **5.** Earth and sun.

**XXXV.2. narrow house:** the grave. **11. Æonian:** lasting for aeons. Sir Charles Lyell's *Principles of Geology* (1830–33), which Tennyson read in 1837, emphasized the changes in the earth's surface caused by erosion and silt. **14. forgetful shore:** the mythological Lethe, river of oblivion; here, death as the end of consciousness. **18–19.** If man recognized death as extinction, love would not exist, or would be reduced to animal moods. Richard Ellmann describes Yeats's parallel argument in words that would fit Tennyson (*The Identity of Yeats*, 1954, p. 40). **XXXVI.1–2.** Though human consciousness in itself obscurely arrives at truths (here, immortality). **5. dealt with:** adapted itself to. **6.** Where formal philosophy fails.

And so the Word had breath, and wrought
  With human hands the creed of creeds
  In loveliness of perfect deeds,
More strong than all poetic thought;

Which he may read that binds the sheaf,
  Or builds the house, or digs the grave,
  And those wild eyes that watch the wave
In roarings round the coral reef.

XXXIX

Old warder of these buried bones,
  And answering now my random stroke
  With fruitful cloud and living smoke,
Dark yew, that graspest at the stones

And dippest toward the dreamless head,
  To thee too comes the golden hour
  When flower is feeling after flower;
But Sorrow, — fixt upon the dead,

And darkening the dark graves of men, —
  What whisper'd from her lying lips?
  Thy gloom is kindled at the tips,
And passes into gloom again.

XLI

Thy spirit ere our fatal loss
  Did ever rise from high to higher,
  As mounts the heavenward altar-fire,
As flies the lighter thro' the gross.

But thou art turn'd to something strange,
  And I have lost the links that bound
  Thy changes; here upon the ground,
No more partaker of thy change.

Deep folly! yet that this could be —
  That I could wing my will with might
  To leap the grades of life and light,
And flash at once, my friend, to thee!

For tho' my nature rarely yields
  To that vague fear implied in death,
  Nor shudders at the gulfs beneath,
The howlings from forgotten fields;

Yet oft when sundown skirts the moor
  An inner trouble I behold,
  A spectral doubt which makes me cold,
That I shall be thy mate no more,

Tho' following with an upward mind
  The wonders that have come to thee,
  Thro' all the secular to-be,
But evermore a life behind.

XLIII

If Sleep and Death be truly one,
  And every spirit's folded bloom
  Thro' all its intervital gloom
In some long trance should slumber on;

Unconscious of the sliding hour,
  Bare of the body, might it last,
  And silent traces of the past
Be all the color of the flower:

So then were nothing lost to man;
  So that still garden of the souls
  In many a figured leaf enrolls
The total world since life began;

And love will last as pure and whole
  As when he loved me here in Time,
  And at the spiritual prime
Rewaken with the dawning soul.

XLIV

How fares it with the happy dead?
  For here the man is more and more;
  But he forgets the days before
God shut the doorways of his head.

The days have vanish'd, tone and tint,
  And yet perhaps the hoarding sense
  Gives out at times — he knows not whence —
A little flash, a mystic hint;

And in the long harmonious years —
  If Death so taste Lethean springs —
  May some dim touch of earthly things
Surprise thee ranging with thy peers.

If such a dreamy touch should fall,
  O, turn thee round, resolve the doubt;

**9. the Word.** Tennyson (*Memoir*, I, 312) cited John 1, for "the Revelation of the Eternal Thought of the Universe." **10. creed of creeds**: the life of Christ. **XXXIX.** This section, written in 1868, glances back at II and III. **3. cloud . . . smoke**: pollen. **11. tips**: flowers. **XLI.9. Deep folly**: what is to be said in 10–12. **16. forgotten**: by God (cf. Dante's *Inferno*).

**23. secular**: age-long. **XLIII.** The image of a flower is carried throughout. **3. intervital**: between earthly life and the next life. **10. garden**: the unconscious state described in 1–8. **12. total world**: all experience. **15. spiritual prime**: dawn of another life. **XLIV.** This section rejects the idea, raised in XLIII, of a sleep between death and the next life. **2.** On earth man's consciousness stores up increasing experience. **3–4.** Man forgets early infancy, before the skull hardened. **5–8.** The dead may dimly recall life on earth as a person may at times have a strange sense of recollection from earliest infancy.

My guardian angel will speak out
In that high place, and tell thee all.

XLV

The baby new to earth and sky,
  What time his tender palm is prest
  Against the circle of the breast,
Has never thought that "this is I";

But as he grows he gathers much,
  And learns the use of "I" and "me,"
  And finds "I am not what I see,
And other than the things I touch."

So rounds he to a separate mind
  From whence clear memory may begin,
  As thro' the frame that binds him in
His isolation grows defined.

This use may lie in blood and breath,
  Which else were fruitless of their due,
  Had man to learn himself anew
Beyond the second birth of death.

XLVI

We ranging down this lower track,
  The path we came by, thorn and flower,
  Is shadow'd by the growing hour,
Lest life should fail in looking back.

So be it: there no shade can last
  In that deep dawn behind the tomb,
  But clear from marge to marge shall bloom
The eternal landscape of the past;

A lifelong tract of time reveal'd,
  The fruitful hours of still increase;
  Days order'd in a wealthy peace,
And those five years its richest field.

O Love, thy province were not large,
  A bounded field, nor stretching far;
  Look also, Love, a brooding star,
A rosy warmth from marge to marge.

XLVII

That each, who seems a separate whole,
  Should move his rounds, and fusing all
  The skirts of self again, should fall
Remerging in the general Soul,

Is faith as vague as all unsweet.
  Eternal form shall still divide
  The eternal soul from all beside;
And I shall know him when we meet;

And we shall sit at endless feast,
  Enjoying each the other's good.
  What vaster dream can hit the mood
Of Love on earth? He seeks at least

Upon the last and sharpest height,
  Before the spirits fade away,
  Some landing-place, to clasp and say,
"Farewell! We lose ourselves in light."

XLVIII

If these brief lays, of Sorrow born,
  Were taken to be such as closed
  Grave doubts and answers here proposed,
Then these were such as men might scorn.

Her care is not to part and prove;
  She takes, when harsher moods remit,
  What slender shade of doubt may flit,
And makes it vassal unto love;

And hence, indeed, she sports with words,
  But better serves a wholesome law,
  And holds it sin and shame to draw
The deepest measure from the chords;

Nor dare she trust a larger lay,
  But rather loosens from the lip
  Short swallow-flights of song, that dip
Their wings in tears, and skim away.

L

Be near me when my light is low,
  When the blood creeps, and the nerves prick
  And tingle; and the heart is sick,
And all the wheels of being slow.

Be near me when the sensuous frame
  Is rack'd with pangs that conquer trust;
  And Time, a maniac scattering dust,
And Life, a Fury slinging flame.

Be near me when my faith is dry,
  And men the flies of latter spring,

**XLV.** The birth of consciousness in the growing infant. The development of personal identity may be the purpose of earthly life. **XLVI.1. lower track**: earthly life. **2–3.** Memory of the past is obscured as life proceeds. **5. there**: in the next life. **12. five years**: of friendship. **13–14.** Love on earth. **15–16.** Love enlarged in heaven. **XLVII.** The poet rules out the idea, recurrent in religious thought, that the individual soul does not survive but is merged in the world-soul—though this is apparently admitted in 14–16 as an ultimate stage. **13.** In the last of many existences (*Memoir*, I, 319). **XLVIII.5. Her**: Sorrow's. **part**: sort out. **L.8.** The Furies carried torches.

That lay their eggs, and sting and sing
And weave their petty cells and die.

Be near me when I fade away,
To point the term of human strife,
And on the low dark verge of life
The twilight of eternal day.

LIV

O, yet we trust that somehow good
Will be the final goal of ill,
To pangs of nature, sins of will,
Defects of doubt, and taints of blood;

That nothing walks with aimless feet;
That not one life shall be destroy'd,
Or cast as rubbish to the void,
When God hath made the pile complete;

That not a worm is cloven in vain;
That not a moth with vain desire
Is shrivel'd in a fruitless fire,
Or but subserves another's gain.

Behold, we know not anything;
I can but trust that good shall fall
At last — far off — at last, to all,
And every winter change to spring.

So runs my dream; but what am I?
An infant crying in the night;
An infant crying for the light,
And with no language but a cry.

LV

The wish, that of the living whole
No life may fail beyond the grave,
Derives it not from what we have
The likest God within the soul?

Are God and Nature then at strife,
That Nature lends such evil dreams?
So careful of the type she seems,
So careless of the single life,

That I, considering everywhere
Her secret meaning in her deeds,
And finding that of fifty seeds
She often brings but one to bear,

I falter where I firmly trod,
And falling with my weight of cares
Upon the great world's altar-stairs
That slope thro' darkness up to God,

I stretch lame hands of faith, and grope,
And gather dust and chaff, and call
To what I feel is Lord of all,
And faintly trust the larger hope.

LVI

"So careful of the type?" but no.
From scarpèd cliff and quarried stone
She cries, "A thousand types are gone;
I care for nothing, all shall go.

"Thou makest thine appeal to me:
I bring to life, I bring to death;
The spirit does but mean the breath:
I know no more." And he, shall he,

Man, her last work, who seem'd so fair,
Such splendid purpose in his eyes,
Who roll'd the psalm to wintry skies,
Who built him fanes of fruitless prayer,

Who trusted God was love indeed
And love Creation's final law —
Tho' Nature, red in tooth and claw
With ravine, shriek'd against his creed —

Who loved, who suffer'd countless ills,
Who battled for the True, the Just,
Be blown about the desert dust,
Or seal'd within the iron hills?

No more? A monster then, a dream,
A discord. Dragons of the prime,
That tare each other in their slime,
Were mellow music match'd with him.

O life as futile, then, as frail!
O for thy voice to soothe and bless!
What hope of answer, or redress?
Behind the veil, behind the veil.

LVII

Peace; come away: the song of woe
Is after all an earthly song.

**14. term:** limit. **LV.7–8.** Nature's concern for the species and indifference to the individual was current, e.g., from Buffon to Robert Chambers' *Vestiges* (1844); but see the note on LVI. **11–12.** The example is like one in Bishop Butler's *Analogy of Religion*, 1736 (Everyman ed., p. 80).

**20. larger hope:** "that the whole human race would through, perhaps, ages of suffering, be at length purified and saved" (*Memoir*, I, 321–22). **LVI.** Lyell (see the note on XXXV.11) presented full evidence for the extinction of species as well as individuals. **2. scarpèd:** shorn away. **3. She:** Nature. **15.** This, the most famous phrase in *In Memoriam*, crystallizes the idea of the ruthless struggle for survival that had been present in men's minds since antiquity. Cf. Erasmus Darwin (grandfather of Charles): "And one great Slaughter-house the warring world." **20.** Like other fossils. **26. thy:** Hallam's. **28. veil:** of death (see Eleanor B. Mattes, pp. 62–63).

Peace; come away: we do him wrong
To sing so wildly: let us go.

Come; let us go: your cheeks are pale;
But half my life I leave behind.
Methinks my friend is richly shrined;
But I shall pass, my work will fail.

Yet in these ears, till hearing dies,
One set slow bell will seem to toll
The passing of the sweetest soul
That ever look'd with human eyes.

I hear it now, and o'er and o'er,
Eternal greetings to the dead;
And "Ave, Ave, Ave," said,
"Adieu, adieu," for evermore.

LXX

I cannot see the features right,
When on the gloom I strive to paint
The face I know; the hues are faint
And mix with hollow masks of night;

Cloud-towers by ghostly masons wrought,
A gulf that ever shuts and gapes,
A hand that points, and pallèd shapes
In shadowy thoroughfares of thought;

And crowds that stream from yawning doors,
And shoals of pucker'd faces drive;
Dark bulks that tumble half alive,
And lazy lengths on boundless shores;

Till all at once beyond the will
I hear a wizard music roll,
And thro' a lattice on the soul
Looks thy fair face and makes it still.

LXXVIII

Again at Christmas did we weave
The holly round the Christmas hearth;
The silent snow possess'd the earth,
And calmly fell our Christmas-eve.

The yule-clog sparkled keen with frost,
No wing of wind the region swept,
But over all things brooding slept
The quiet sense of something lost.

As in the winters left behind,
Again our ancient games had place,
The mimic picture's breathing grace,
And dance and song and hoodman-blind.

Who show'd a token of distress?
No single tear, no mark of pain —
O sorrow, then can sorrow wane?
O grief, can grief be changed to less?

O last regret, regret can die!
No — mixt with all this mystic frame,
Her deep relations are the same,
But with long use her tears are dry.

LXXXII

I wage not any feud with Death
For changes wrought on form and face;
No lower life that earth's embrace
May breed with him can fright my faith.

Eternal process moving on,
From state to state the spirit walks;
And these are but the shatter'd stalks,
Or ruin'd chrysalis of one.

Nor blame I Death, because he bare
The use of virtue out of earth;
I know transplanted human worth
Will bloom to profit, otherwhere.

For this alone on Death I wreak
The wrath that garners in my heart:
He put our lives so far apart
We cannot hear each other speak.

LXXXVI

Sweet after showers, ambrosial air,
That rollest from the gorgeous gloom
Of evening over brake and bloom
And meadow, slowly breathing bare

The round of space, and rapt below
Thro' all the dewy-tassel'd wood,
And shadowing down the hornèd flood
In ripples, fan my brows and blow

The fever from my cheek, and sigh
The full new life that feeds thy breath
Throughout my frame, till Doubt and Death,
Ill brethren, let the fancy fly

**LVII.15. Ave:** hail. Cf. "Frater Ave atque Vale." **LXX.7. pallèd:** wrapped in palls. **13–16.** As sleep comes on, he sees the face he could not picture when awake. **LXXVIII.** The second Christmas (1834) inaugurates a more acceptant and cheerful mood than the first (XXX) had allowed. **5. clog** (a dialect word): log. **11. mimic picture's:** tableau's. **12. hoodman-blind:** blindman's buff. **LXXXII.6.** Cf. XXX.27–28 and XLVII.13. **7. these:** See 2–3. **9. bare:** bore away. **LXXXVI.** The poet's sense of peace and rebirth, rendered in one exquisitely modulated sentence. **4–5.** Clearing the sky of clouds. **7. hornèd:** winding.

From belt to belt of crimson seas
 On leagues of odor streaming far,
 To where in yonder orient star
A hundred spirits whisper "Peace."

LXXXVII

I past beside the reverend walls
 In which of old I wore the gown;
 I roved at random thro' the town,
And saw the tumult of the halls;

And heard once more in college fanes
 The storm their high-built organs make,
 And thunder-music, rolling, shake
The prophet blazon'd on the panes;

And caught once more the distant shout,
 The measured pulse of racing oars
 Among the willows; paced the shores
And many a bridge, and all about

The same gray flats again, and felt
 The same, but not the same; and last
 Up that long walk of limes I past
To see the rooms in which he dwelt.

Another name was on the door.
 I linger'd; all within was noise
 Of songs, and clapping hands, and boys
That crash'd the glass and beat the floor;

Where once we held debate, a band
 Of youthful friends, on mind and art,
 And labor, and the changing mart,
And all the framework of the land;

When one would aim an arrow fair,
 But send it slackly from the string;
 And one would pierce an outer ring,
And one an inner, here and there;

And last the master-bowman, he,
 Would cleave the mark. A willing ear
 We lent him. Who but hung to hear
The rapt oration flowing free

From point to point, with power and grace
 And music in the bounds of law,
 To those conclusions when we saw
The God within him light his face,

And seem to lift the form, and glow
 In azure orbits heavenly-wise;
 And over those ethereal eyes
The bar of Michael Angelo?

LXXXIX

Witch-elms that counterchange the floor
 Of this flat lawn with dusk and bright;
 And thou, with all thy breadth and height
Of foliage, towering sycamore;

How often, hither wandering down,
 My Arthur found your shadows fair,
 And shook to all the liberal air
The dust and din and steam of town!

He brought an eye for all he saw;
 He mixt in all our simple sports;
 They pleased him, fresh from brawling courts
And dusty purlieus of the law.

O joy to him in this retreat,
 Inmantled in ambrosial dark,
 To drink the cooler air, and mark
The landscape winking thro' the heat!

O sound to rout the brood of cares,
 The sweep of scythe in morning dew,
 The gust that round the garden flew,
And tumbled half the mellowing pears!

O bliss, when all in circle drawn
 About him, heart and ear were fed
 To hear him, as he lay and read
The Tuscan poets on the lawn!

Or in the all-golden afternoon
 A guest, or happy sister, sung,
 Or here she brought the harp and flung
A ballad to the brightening moon.

Nor less it pleased in livelier moods,
 Beyond the bounding hill to stray,
 And break the livelong summer day
With banquet in the distant woods;

Whereat we glanced from theme to theme,
 Discuss'd the books to love or hate,
 Or touch'd the changes of the state,
Or threaded some Socratic dream;

But if I praised the busy town,
 He loved to rail against it still,
 For "ground in yonder social mill
We rub each other's angles down,

**13. crimson:** in successive sunsets. **LXXXVII.** A visit to Cambridge. **21. band:** the "Apostles." **29. he:** Hallam. **40.** A ridge over the eyes, once remarked upon by Hallam himself (*Memoir*, I, 38). **LXXXIX.** Hallam's visits at Somersby. **1. counterchange:** checker. **7. liberal:** open, spacious. **24. Tuscan poets:** Dante *et al.* **30. bounding:** limiting.

" And merge," he said, " in form and gloss
The picturesque of man and man."
We talk'd: the stream beneath us ran,
The wine-flask lying couch'd in moss,

Or cool'd within the glooming wave;
And last, returning from afar,
Before the crimson-circled star
Had fall'n into her father's grave,

And brushing ankle-deep in flowers,
We heard behind the woodbine veil
The milk that bubbled in the pail,
And buzzings of the honeyed hours.

XCV

By night we linger'd on the lawn,
For underfoot the herb was dry;
And genial warmth; and o'er the sky
The silvery haze of summer drawn;

And calm that let the tapers burn
Unwavering: not a cricket chirr'd;
The brook alone far-off was heard,
And on the board the fluttering urn.

And bats went round in fragrant skies,
And wheel'd or lit the filmy shapes
That haunt the dusk, with ermine capes
And woolly breasts and beaded eyes;

While now we sang old songs that peal'd
From knoll to knoll, where, couch'd at ease,
The white kine glimmer'd, and the trees
Laid their dark arms about the field.

But when those others, one by one,
Withdrew themselves from me and night,
And in the house light after light
Went out, and I was all alone,

A hunger seized my heart; I read
Of that glad year which once had been,
In those fall'n leaves which kept their green,
The noble letters of the dead.

And strangely on the silence broke
The silent-speaking words, and strange
Was love's dumb cry defying change
To test his worth; and strangely spoke

The faith, the vigor, bold to dwell
On doubts that drive the coward back,
And keen thro' wordy snares to track
Suggestion to her inmost cell.

So word by word, and line by line,
The dead man touch'd me from the past,
And all at once it seem'd at last
The living soul was flash'd on mine,

And mine in this was wound, and whirl'd
About empyreal heights of thought,
And came on that which is, and caught
The deep pulsations of the world,

Æonian music measuring out
The steps of Time — the shocks of Chance —
The blows of Death. At length my trance
Was cancel'd, stricken thro' with doubt.

Vague words! but ah, how hard to frame
In matter-molded forms of speech,
Or even for intellect to reach
Thro' memory that which I became;

Till now the doubtful dusk reveal'd
The knolls once more where, couch'd at ease,
The white kine glimmer'd, and the trees
Laid their dark arms about the field;

And suck'd from out the distant gloom
A breeze began to tremble o'er
The large leaves of the sycamore,
And fluctuate all the still perfume,

And gathering freshlier overhead
Rock'd the full-foliaged elms, and swung
The heavy-folded rose, and flung
The lilies to and fro, and said,

" The dawn, the dawn," and died away;
And East and West, without a breath,
Mixt their dim lights, like life and death,
To broaden into boundless day.

XCVI

You say, but with no touch of scorn,
Sweet-hearted, you, whose light-blue eyes

**47–48.** Before the evening star (Venus) is lost in the setting sun. According to the nebular hypothesis, the planets originated from the sun. **XCV.** This account of the poet's trance-like apprehension of the dead Hallam's presence, and of the divine order of the world, is commonly regarded as one of his supreme achievements. **1. lawn:** at Somersby. **8. urn:** the boiling tea urn. **10. shapes:** moths. **22. year:** for the whole period of friendship that seemed so short.

**36. living soul:** the Deity, maybe (said Tennyson), as including the lesser soul of Hallam. The original reading was "His living soul," i.e., Hallam's. **41. Æonian:** comprehending ages. **XCVI. 1. You:** any simple-minded woman.

Are tender over drowning flies,
You tell me, doubt is Devil-born.

I know not: one indeed I knew
  In many a subtle question versed,
  Who touch'd a jarring lyre at first,
But ever strove to make it true;

Perplext in faith, but pure in deeds,
  At last he beat his music out.
  There lives more faith in honest doubt,
Believe me, than in half the creeds.

He fought his doubts and gather'd strength,
  He would not make his judgment blind,
  He faced the specters of the mind
And laid them; thus he came at length

To find a stronger faith his own,
  And Power was with him in the night,
  Which makes the darkness and the light,
And dwells not in the light alone,

But in the darkness and the cloud,
  As over Sinaï's peaks of old,
  While Israel made their gods of gold,
Altho' the trumpet blew so loud.

CIV

The time draws near the birth of Christ;
  The moon is hid, the night is still;
  A single church below the hill
Is pealing, folded in the mist.

A single peal of bells below,
  That wakens at this hour of rest
  A single murmur in the breast,
That these are not the bells I know.

Like strangers' voices here they sound,
  In lands where not a memory strays,
  Nor landmark breathes of other days,
But all is new unhallow'd ground.

CV

To-night ungather'd let us leave
  This laurel, let this holly stand:
  We live within the stranger's land,
And strangely falls our Christmas-eve.

Our father's dust is left alone
  And silent under other snows:
  There in due time the woodbine blows,
The violet comes, but we are gone.

No more shall wayward grief abuse
  The genial hour with mask and mime;
  For change of place, like growth of time,
Has broke the bond of dying use.

Let cares that petty shadows cast,
  By which our lives are chiefly proved,
  A little spare the night I loved,
And hold it solemn to the past.

But let no footstep beat the floor,
  Nor bowl of wassail mantle warm;
  For who would keep an ancient form
Thro' which the spirit breathes no more?

Be neither song, nor game, nor feast;
  Nor harp be touch'd, nor flute be blown;
  No dance, no motion, save alone
What lightens in the lucid East

Of rising worlds by yonder wood.
  Long sleeps the summer in the seed;
  Run out your measured arcs, and lead
The closing cycle rich in good.

CVI

Ring out, wild bells, to the wild sky,
  The flying cloud, the frosty light:
  The year is dying in the night;
Ring out, wild bells, and let him die.

Ring out the old, ring in the new,
  Ring, happy bells, across the snow:
  The year is going, let him go;
Ring out the false, ring in the true.

Ring out the grief that saps the mind,
  For those that here we see no more;
  Ring out the feud of rich and poor,
Ring in redress to all mankind.

Ring out a slowly dying cause,
  And ancient forms of party strife;
  Ring in the nobler modes of life,
With sweeter manners, purer laws.

Ring out the want, the care, the sin,
  The faithless coldness of the times;
  Ring out, ring out my mournful rhymes,
But ring the fuller minstrel in.

**5. One**: Hallam. **21–22.** In Exod. 19 God appeared to Moses in a cloud. **23.** See Exod. 32. **24.** See Exod. 19:19. **CIV–CV.** The third Christmas of the poem, actually 1837, at the Tennysons' new home at High Beech, Epping Forest, north of London. **CV.5.** The poet's father was buried at Somersby in 1831.

**7. blows**: blossoms. **14. proved**: tested. **18. mantle**: froth. **25. worlds**: stars. **CVI.** New Year's Eve.

Ring out false pride in place and blood,
The civic slander and the spite;
Ring in the love of truth and right,
Ring in the common love of good.

Ring out old shapes of foul disease;
Ring out the narrowing lust of gold;
Ring out the thousand wars of old,
Ring in the thousand years of peace.

Ring in the valiant man and free,
The larger heart, the kindlier hand;
Ring out the darkness of the land,
Ring in the Christ that is to be.

CXIV

Who loves not Knowledge? Who shall rail
Against her beauty? May she mix
With men and prosper! Who shall fix
Her pillars? Let her work prevail.

But on her forehead sits a fire;
She sets her forward countenance
And leaps into the future chance,
Submitting all things to desire.

Half-grown as yet, a child, and vain—
She cannot fight the fear of death.
What is she, cut from love and faith,
But some wild Pallas from the brain

Of demons? fiery-hot to burst
All barriers in her onward race
For power. Let her know her place;
She is the second, not the first.

A higher hand must make her mild,
If all be not in vain, and guide
Her footsteps, moving side by side
With Wisdom, like the younger child;

For she is earthly of the mind,
But Wisdom heavenly of the soul.
O friend, who camest to thy goal
So early, leaving me behind,

I would the great world grew like thee,
Who grewest not alone in power
And knowledge, but by year and hour
In reverence and in charity.

**28.** See Rev. 20. **32.** The true spirit of Christlike goodness and love, free from bigotry and controversy (*Memoir*, I, 325–26). **CXIV.3–4. Who . . . pillars?** See Prov. 9:1, Job 38. **12.** Pallas Athene, goddess of wisdom, sprang full-armed from the brain of Zeus.

CXV

Now fades the last long streak of snow,
Now burgeons every maze of quick
About the flowering squares, and thick
By ashen roots the violets blow.

Now rings the woodland loud and long,
The distance takes a lovelier hue,
And drown'd in yonder living blue
The lark becomes a sightless song.

Now dance the lights on lawn and lea,
The flocks are whiter down the vale,
And milkier every milky sail
On winding stream or distant sea;

Where now the seamew pipes, or dives
In yonder greening gleam, and fly
The happy birds, that change their sky
To build and brood, that live their lives

From land to land; and in my breast
Spring wakens too, and my regret
Becomes an April violet,
And buds and blossoms like the rest.

CXVIII

Contemplate all this work of Time,
The giant laboring in his youth;
Nor dream of human love and truth,
As dying Nature's earth and lime;

But trust that those we call the dead
Are breathers of an ampler day
For ever nobler ends. They say,
The solid earth whereon we tread

In tracts of fluent heat began,
And grew to seeming-random forms,
The seeming prey of cyclic storms,
Till at the last arose the man;

Who throve and branch'd from clime to clime,
The herald of a higher race,
And of himself in higher place,
If so he type this work of time

**CXV.2. maze of quick:** hawthorn hedges. **3. squares:** fields. **4. blow:** blossom. **8. sightless:** invisible. **14. gleam:** the sea. **CXVIII.** The analogy between cosmic and human evolution, between material and spiritual process. **1. Contemplate:** accented on the second syllable. **4. Nature:** here the flesh-and-bone body of man. **7–9.** The nebular hypothesis concerning the origin of the solar system. **11.** Apparently a reference to Cuvier's theory of cataclysmic change. **12–14.** The general advance of man (not Darwinian mutation of species). **14. higher race:** humanity of a higher type (cf. Epilogue 137–39). **15. higher place:** life after death. **16. type:** parallel, emulate.

Within himself, from more to more;
  Or, crown'd with attributes of woe
  Like glories, move his course, and show
That life is not as idle ore,

But iron dug from central gloom,
  And heated hot with burning fears,
  And dipt in baths of hissing tears,
And batter'd with the shocks of doom

To shape and use. Arise and fly
  The reeling Faun, the sensual feast;
  Move upward, working out the beast,
And let the ape and tiger die.

CXIX

Doors, where my heart was used to beat
  So quickly, not as one that weeps
  I come once more; the city sleeps;
I smell the meadow in the street;

I hear a chirp of birds; I see
  Betwixt the black fronts long-withdrawn
  A light-blue lane of early dawn,
And think of early days and thee,

And bless thee, for thy lips are bland,
  And bright the friendship of thine eye;
  And in my thoughts with scarce a sigh
I take the pressure of thine hand.

CXX

I trust I have not wasted breath:
  I think we are not wholly brain,
  Magnetic mockeries; not in vain,
Like Paul with beasts, I fought with Death;

Not only cunning casts in clay:
  Let Science prove we are, and then
  What matters Science unto men,
At least to me? I would not stay.

Let him, the wiser man who springs
  Hereafter, up from childhood shape
  His action like the greater ape,
But I was *born* to other things.

CXXI

Sad Hesper o'er the buried sun
  And ready, thou, to die with him,
  Thou watchest all things ever dim
And dimmer, and a glory done.

The team is loosen'd from the wain,
  The boat is drawn upon the shore;
  Thou listenest to the closing door,
And life is darken'd in the brain.

Bright Phosphor, fresher for the night,
  By thee the world's great work is heard
  Beginning, and the wakeful bird;
Behind thee comes the greater light.

The market boat is on the stream,
  And voices hail it from the brink;
  Thou hear'st the village hammer clink,
And see'st the moving of the team.

Sweet Hesper-Phosphor, double name
  For what is one, the first, the last,
  Thou, like my present and my past,
Thy place is changed; thou art the same.

CXXII

O, wast thou with me, dearest, then,
  While I rose up against my doom,
  And yearn'd to burst the folded gloom,
To bare the eternal heavens again,

To feel once more, in placid awe,
  The strong imagination roll
  A sphere of stars about my soul,
In all her motion one with law?

If thou wert with me, and the grave
  Divide us not, be with me now,
  And enter in at breast and brow,
Till all my blood, a fuller wave,

Be quicken'd with a livelier breath,
  And like an inconsiderate boy,
  As in the former flash of joy,
I slip the thoughts of life and death;

And all the breeze of Fancy blows,
  And every dewdrop paints a bow,
  The wizard lightnings deeply glow,
And every thought breaks out a rose.

CXXIII

There rolls the deep where grew the tree.
  O earth, what changes hast thou seen!

**CXIX.** Cf. VII. **CXX.3. Magnetic mockeries:** electric machines. **4.** See I Cor. 15:32. **9. wiser man:** an ironical reference to the scientist who insists on man's merely animal nature and inheritance. **CXXI.1. Hesper:** the evening star (symbol of the past). **9. Phosphor:** the morning star (the present). **CXXII.1. then:** such moments as those described in LXXXVI and XCV. **2. doom:** grief for Hallam. **16. slip:** escape. **18. bow:** rainbow. **CXXIII.** See the note on XXXV.11.

There where the long street roars hath been
The stillness of the central sea.

The hills are shadows, and they flow
  From form to form, and nothing stands;
  They melt like mist, the solid lands,
Like clouds they shape themselves and go.

But in my spirit will I dwell,
  And dream my dream, and hold it true;
  For tho' my lips may breathe adieu,
I cannot think the thing farewell.

CXXIV

That which we dare invoke to bless;
  Our dearest faith; our ghastliest doubt;
  He, They, One, All; within, without;
The Power in darkness whom we guess,—

I found Him not in world or sun,
  Or eagle's wing, or insect's eye,
  Nor thro' the questions men may try,
The petty cobwebs we have spun.

If e'er when faith had fallen asleep,
  I heard a voice, "believe no more,"
  And heard an ever-breaking shore
That tumbled in the Godless deep,

A warmth within the breast would melt
  The freezing reason's colder part,
  And like a man in wrath the heart
Stood up and answer'd, "I have felt."

No, like a child in doubt and fear:
  But that blind clamor made me wise;
  Then was I as a child that cries,
But, crying, knows his father near;

And what I am beheld again
  What is, and no man understands;
  And out of darkness came the hands
That reach thro' nature, molding men.

CXXV

Whatever I have said or sung,
  Some bitter notes my harp would give,
  Yea, tho' there often seem'd to live
A contradiction on the tongue,

Yet Hope had never lost her youth,
  She did but look through dimmer eyes;
  Or Love but play'd with gracious lies,
Because he felt so fix'd in truth;

And if the song were full of care,
  He breathed the spirit of the song;
  And if the words were sweet and strong
He set his royal signet there;

Abiding with me till I sail
  To seek thee on the mystic deeps,
  And this electric force, that keeps
A thousand pulses dancing, fail.

CXXVI

Love is and was my lord and king,
  And in his presence I attend
  To hear the tidings of my friend,
Which every hour his couriers bring.

Love is and was my king and lord,
  And will be, tho' as yet I keep
  Within his court on earth, and sleep
Encompass'd by his faithful guard,

And hear at times a sentinel
  Who moves about from place to place,
  And whispers to the worlds of space,
In the deep night, that all is well.

CXXVII

And all is well, tho' faith and form
  Be sunder'd in the night of fear;
  Well roars the storm to those that hear
A deeper voice across the storm,

Proclaiming social truth shall spread,
  And justice, even tho' thrice again
  The red fool-fury of the Seine
Should pile her barricades with dead.

But ill for him that wears a crown,
  And him, the lazar, in his rags!
  They tremble, the sustaining crags;
The spires of ice are toppled down,

And molten up, and roar in flood;
  The fortress crashes from on high,

**9–12.** Man is not part of the temporal flux. **CXXIV.** A major assertion of the poet's intuitive faith. **1–4.** The God present in all faith and doubt and fear, however dimly or variously conceived. **5–6.** A rejection of the traditional "argument from design," the rational proof of God's existence derived from the order of nature. **14.** The cold rationalism that sees the world and man as a meaningless flux. **18. blind clamor**: of 10–12. **22. What is**: spiritual reality. **23–24.** Faith built on the inner consciousness can now partly admit what was rejected in 5–6 as inadequate, that God can work through nature.

**CXXVII.1–4.** All is well, not in the sense that life is smooth, but that love is the supreme power, as in CXXVI; "faith and form" seems to mean faith and its varying forms, and also enduring reality and social change. **7–8.** Apparently the French revolution of July, 1830.

The brute earth lightens to the sky,
And the great Æon sinks in blood,

And compass'd by the fires of hell;
While thou, dear spirit, happy star,
O'erlook'st the tumult from afar,
And smilest, knowing all is well.

CXXVIII

The love that rose on stronger wings,
Unpalsied when he met with Death,
Is comrade of the lesser faith
That sees the course of human things.

No doubt vast eddies in the flood
Of onward time shall yet be made,
And thronèd races may degrade;
Yet, O ye mysteries of good,

Wild Hours that fly with Hope and Fear,
If all your office had to do
With old results that look like new—
If this were all your mission here,

To draw, to sheathe a useless sword,
To fool the crowd with glorious lies,
To cleave a creed in sects and cries,
To change the bearing of a word,

To shift an arbitrary power,
To cramp the student at his desk,
To make old bareness picturesque
And tuft with grass a feudal tower,

Why, then my scorn might well descend
On you and yours. I see in part
That all, as in some piece of art,
Is toil coöperant to an end.

CXXIX

Dear friend, far off, my lost desire,
So far, so near in woe and weal,
O loved the most, when most I feel
There is a lower and a higher;

Known and unknown, human, divine;
Sweet human hand and lips and eye;
Dear heavenly friend that canst not die,
Mine, mine, for ever, ever mine;

Strange friend, past, present, and to be;
Loved deeplier, darklier understood;

Behold, I dream a dream of good,
And mingle all the world with thee.

CXXX

Thy voice is on the rolling air;
I hear thee where the waters run;
Thou standest in the rising sun,
And in the setting thou art fair.

What art thou then? I cannot guess;
But tho' I seem in star and flower
To feel thee some diffusive power,
I do not therefore love thee less.

My love involves the love before;
My love is vaster passion now;
Tho' mix'd with God and Nature thou,
I seem to love thee more and more.

Far off thou art, but ever nigh;
I have thee still, and I rejoice;
I prosper, circled with thy voice;
I shall not lose thee tho' I die.

CXXXI

O living will that shalt endure
When all that seems shall suffer shock,
Rise in the spiritual rock,
Flow thro' our deeds and make them pure,

That we may lift from out of dust
A voice as unto him that hears,
A cry above the conquer'd years
To one that with us works, and trust,

With faith that comes of self-control,
The truths that never can be proved
Until we close with all we loved,
And all we flow from, soul in soul.

---

O true and tried, so well and long,
Demand not thou a marriage lay;
In that it is thy marriage day
Is music more than any song.

Nor have I felt so much of bliss
Since first he told me that he loved

**16. Æon**: the modern age. **CXXVIII.3. lesser faith**: in social progress. **7. degrade**: degenerate. **22–24. I . . . end**: Cf. LIV. **CXXIX–CXXX.** The poet can feel Hallam in all the goodness and beauty of the world.

**CXXXI. 1. living will**: man's free will. **2. seems**: merely seems. **3. rock**: Christ (I Cor. 10:4). **7. conquer'd years**: the situation of I.13 is reversed. **Epilogue.** A celebration of the marriage of the poet's sister Cecilia and Edmund Lushington, October 10, 1842. Tennyson spoke of *In Memoriam* as a sort of *Divine Comedy*, beginning with death and ending with marriage and the promise of a new life (*Memoir*, I, 304; Bradley, pp. 237–38). **6. he**: Hallam.

A daughter of our house, nor proved
Since that dark day a day like this;

Tho' I since then have number'd o'er
 Some thrice three years; they went and came,
 Remade the blood and changed the frame,
And yet is love not less, but more;

No longer caring to embalm
 In dying songs a dead regret,
 But like a statue solid-set,
And molded in colossal calm.

Regret is dead, but love is more
 Than in the summers that are flown,
 For I myself with these have grown
To something greater than before;

Which makes appear the songs I made
 As echoes out of weaker times,
 As half but idle brawling rhymes,
The sport of random sun and shade.

But where is she, the bridal flower,
 That must be made a wife ere noon?
 She enters, glowing like the moon
Of Eden on its bridal bower.

On me she bends her blissful eyes
 And then on thee; they meet thy look
 And brighten like the star that shook
Betwixt the palms of Paradise.

O, when her life was yet in bud,
 He too foretold the perfect rose.
 For thee she grew, for thee she grows
For ever, and as fair as good.

And thou art worthy, full of power;
 As gentle; liberal-minded, great,
 Consistent; wearing all that weight
Of learning lightly like a flower.

But now set out: the noon is near,
 And I must give away the bride;
 She fears not, or with thee beside
And me behind her, will not fear.

For I that danced her on my knee,
 That watch'd her on her nurse's arm,
 That shielded all her life from harm,
At last must part with her to thee;

Now waiting to be made a wife,
 Her feet, my darling, on the dead;
 Their pensive tablets round her head,
And the most living words of life

Breathed in her ear. The ring is on,
 The "Wilt thou?" answer'd, and again
 The "Wilt thou?" ask'd, till out of twain
Her sweet "I will" has made you one.

Now sign your names, which shall be read,
 Mute symbols of a joyful morn,
 By village eyes as yet unborn.
The names are sign'd, and overhead

Begins the clash and clang that tells
 The joy to every wandering breeze;
 The blind wall rocks, and on the trees
The dead leaf trembles to the bells.

O happy hour, and happier hours
 Await them. Many a merry face
 Salutes them—maidens of the place,
That pelt us in the porch with flowers.

O happy hour, behold the bride
 With him to whom her hand I gave.
 They leave the porch, they pass the grave
That has to-day its sunny side.

To-day the grave is bright for me,
 For them the light of life increased,
 Who stay to share the morning feast,
Who rest to-night beside the sea.

Let all my genial spirits advance
 To meet and greet a whiter sun;
 My drooping memory will not shun
The foaming grape of eastern France.

It circles round, and fancy plays,
 And hearts are warm'd and faces bloom,
 As drinking health to bride and groom
We wish them store of happy days.

Nor count me all to blame if I
 Conjecture of a stiller guest,
 Perchance, perchance, among the rest,
And, tho' in silence, wishing joy.

But they must go, the time draws on,
 And those white-favor'd horses wait;
 They rise, but linger; it is late;
Farewell, we kiss, and they are gone.

**7. daughter:** Emily Tennyson. **8. dark day:** of Hallam's death. **30. thee:** Lushington. **31–32.** The stars shook when Zeus nodded approval of the marriage of Peleus and Thetis (Catullus, LXIV.204–06). **34. He:** Hallam. **39–40.** Lushington was professor of Greek at Glasgow University.

**50. on the dead:** on the tombs under the church floor. **51. tablets:** on the walls. **80.** Champagne. **86. guest:** Hallam.

A shade falls on us like the dark
  From little cloudlets on the grass,
  But sweeps away as out we pass
To range the woods, to roam the park,

Discussing how their courtship grew,
  And talk of others that are wed,
  And how she look'd, and what he said,
And back we come at fall of dew.

Again the feast, the speech, the glee,
  The shade of passing thought, the wealth
  Of words and wit, the double health,
The crowning cup, the three-times-three,

And last the dance; — till I retire.
  Dumb is that tower which spake so loud,
  And high in heaven the streaming cloud,
And on the downs a rising fire:

And rise, O moon, from yonder down,
  Till over down and over dale
  All night the shining vapor sail
And pass the silent-lighted town,

The white-faced halls, the glancing rills,
  And catch at every mountain head,
  And o'er the friths that branch and spread
Their sleeping silver thro' the hills;

And touch with shade the bridal doors,
  With tender gloom the roof, the wall;
  And breaking let the splendor fall
To spangle all the happy shores

By which they rest, and ocean sounds,
  And, star and system rolling past,
  A soul shall draw from out the vast
And strike his being into bounds,

And, moved thro' life of lower phase,
  Result in man, be born and think,
  And act and love, a closer link
Betwixt us and the crowning race

Of those that, eye to eye, shall look
  On knowledge; under whose command
  Is Earth and Earth's, and in their hand
Is Nature like an open book;

No longer half-akin to brute,
  For all we thought and loved and did,
  And hoped, and suffer'd, is but seed
Of what in them is flower and fruit;

Whereof the man that with me trod
  This planet was a noble type
  Appearing ere the times were ripe,
That friend of mine who lives in God,

That God, which ever lives and loves,
  One God, one law, one element,
  And one far-off divine event,
To which the whole creation moves.

*1850* *1833–50*

**125.** According to a current biological theory, the stages of life in the embryo paralleled the lower forms of animal life. **128–39.** See the note on CXVIII.12–14.

**143–44.** See the note on LV.20.

# MAUD

### *A Monodrama*

*Maud* (1855) grew out of or around the lyric "O that 'twere possible," which was printed as an individual poem in 1837 and later, in much altered form, became section iv of Part II; the first draft of the lyric was written apparently in the autumn of 1833, after Hallam's death, and expressed the longing for reunion that animates parts of *In Memoriam. Maud* as a whole was written in 1854–55; some additions were made in 1856. The story may suggest Victorian melodramas, but it doubtless — like the situation in "Locksley Hall" — had a partial origin in the feud within the Tennyson clan which was referred to in the Introduction. Lonely and half-hysterical at the outset, the antiheroic hero assails the corruptions of business, the class barriers built on money, and so on. He has fallen below Maud's level because his father had been ruined by her father, his supposed friend. Though he wins her love, in spite of her hostile brother and the aristocratic suitor the brother favors, his happiness, his sense of a life reborn, is quickly blighted; the brother provokes a duel in which he is killed, Maud dies of the shock, and the hero, when he emerges from a period of madness, escapes from himself and his hollow world by going to war. The ending was condemned as jingoistic by a number of contemporary readers, who were living in the shadow of the Crimean War, but it may be thought dramatically consistent with the personality and experience of the hero; one of the "lost generation," he has, like some of Hemingway's heroes, alternated between violence and apathy, between self-centered complaint and selfless devotion, and he can now welcome the chance to enlist in a cause beyond himself.

Tennyson was very fond of *Maud,* his "little *Hamlet,*" and regularly read it to visitors. The work is a tour de force, in that "different phases of passion in one person take the place of different characters" (*Memoir,* I, 396). Such different phases of passion and the high-pitched tone of the poem suggest that Tennyson breathed some of the same air as the "Spasmodic" school of minor poets, who made some stir in the early 1850's. His technical virtuosity is amply apparent. And there are threads of symbolism, such as that of lilies and roses (the red color extends to blood and cannon fire). To some readers the poem as a whole may seem a mixture of the sour and the sentimental; but Tennyson's lyrical — and satirical — powers achieve some notable things, and, in a poet and a man who seems to have known little of romantic passion, "the new strong wine of love" inspires ecstasies that are surely not mere froth.

## *Part I*

### i

1

I hate the dreadful hollow behind the little wood;
Its lips in the field above are dabbled with blood-red heath,
The red-ribb'd ledges drip with a silent horror of blood,
And Echo there, whatever is ask'd her, answers "Death."

2

For there in the ghastly pit long since a body was found,
His who had given me life — O father! O God! was it well? —
Mangled, and flatten'd, and crush'd, and dinted into the ground;
There yet lies the rock that fell with him when he fell.

3

Did he fling himself down? who knows? for a vast speculation had fail'd,
And ever he mutter'd and madden'd, and ever wann'd with despair,
And out he walk'd when the wind like a broken worldling wail'd,
And the flying gold of the ruin'd woodlands drove thro' the air.

4

I remember the time, for the roots of my hair were stirr'd
By a shuffled step, by a dead weight trail'd, by a whisper'd fright,
And my pulses closed their gates with a shock on my heart as I heard
The shrill-edged shriek of a mother divide the shuddering night.

5

Villainy somewhere! whose? One says, we are villains all.
Not he; his honest fame should at least by me be maintained;
But that old man, now lord of the broad estate and the Hall,
Dropt off gorged from a scheme that had left us flaccid and drain'd.

6

Why do they prate of the blessings of peace? we have made them a curse,
Pickpockets, each hand lusting for all that is not its own;
And lust of gain, in the spirit of Cain, is it better or worse
Than the heart of the citizen hissing in war on his own hearthstone?

7

But these are the days of advance, the works of the men of mind,
When who but a fool would have faith in a tradesman's ware or his word?
Is it peace or war? Civil war, as I think, and that of a kind
The viler, as underhand, not openly bearing the sword.

8

Sooner or later I too may passively take the print
Of the golden age — why not? I have neither hope nor trust;
May make my heart as a millstone, set my face as a flint,
Cheat and be cheated, and die — who knows? we are ashes and dust.

9

Peace sitting under her olive, and slurring the days gone by,
When the poor are hovel'd and hustled together, each sex, like swine,
When only the ledger lives, and when only not all men lie;
Peace in her vineyard — yes! — but a company forges the wine.

10

And the vitriol madness flushes up in the ruffian's head,
Till the filthy by-lane rings to the yell of the trampled wife,

MAUD. **I.36. forges: adulterates.**

And chalk and alum and plaster are sold to the poor for bread,
And the spirit of murder works in the very means of life,

11

And Sleep must lie down arm'd, for the villainous center-bits
Grind on the wakeful ear in the hush of the moonless nights,
While another is cheating the sick of a few last gasps, as he sits
To pestle a poison'd poison behind his crimson lights.

12

When a Mammonite mother kills her babe for a burial fee,
And Timour-Mammon grins on a pile of children's bones,
Is it peace or war? better, war! loud war by land and by sea,
War with a thousand battles, and shaking a hundred thrones!

13

For I trust if an enemy's fleet came yonder round by the hill,
And the rushing battle-bolt sang from the three-decker out of the foam,
That the smooth-faced, snub-nosed rogue would leap from his counter and till,
And strike, if he could, were it but with his cheating yardwand, home.—

14

What! am I raging alone as my father raged in his mood?
Must *I* too creep to the hollow and dash myself down and die
Rather than hold by the law that I made, nevermore to brood
On a horror of shatter'd limbs and a wretched swindler's lie?

15

Would there be sorrow for *me?* there was *love* in the passionate shriek,
Love for the silent thing that had made false haste to the grave—
Wrapt in a cloak, as I saw him, and thought he would rise and speak
And rave at the lie and the liar, ah God, as he used to rave.

16

I am sick of the Hall and the hill, I am sick of the moor and the main.
Why should I stay? can a sweeter chance ever come to me here?
O, having the nerves of motion as well as the nerves of pain,
Were it not wise if I fled from the place and the pit and the fear?

17

Workmen up at the Hall!—they are coming back from abroad;
The dark old place will be gilt by the touch of a millionaire.
I have heard, I know not whence, of the singular beauty of Maud;
I play'd with the girl when a child; she promised then to be fair.

18

Maud, with her venturous climbings and tumbles and childish escapes,
Maud, the delight of the village, the ringing joy of the Hall,
Maud, with her sweet purse-mouth when my father dangled the grapes,
Maud, the beloved of my mother, the moon-faced darling of all,—

19

What is she now? My dreams are bad. She may bring me a curse.
No, there is fatter game on the moor; she will let me alone.
Thanks; for the fiend best knows whether woman or man be the worse.
I will bury myself in myself, and the Devil may pipe to his own.

ii

Long have I sigh'd for a calm; God grant I may find it at last!
It will never be broken by Maud; she has neither savor nor salt.
But a cold and clear-cut face, as I found when her carriage past,
Perfectly beautiful; let it be granted her; where is the fault?
All that I saw—for her eyes were downcast, not to be seen—

**41. center-bits**: burglar's drills. **43. another**: a pharmacist. **45. Mammonite**: devotee of Mammon, money. **46. Timour**: Tamerlane (Marlowe's Tamburlaine), an example of ruthless conquest and slaughter, in his modern commercial form, exploiting children in factories and mines. **58. made . . . grave**: committed suicide.

Faultily faultless, icily regular, splendidly null,
Dead perfection, no more; nothing more, if it had not been
For a chance of travel, a paleness, an hour's defect of the rose,
Or an underlip, you may call it a little too ripe, too full,
Or the least little delicate aquiline curve in a sensitive nose,
From which I escaped heart-free, with the least little touch of spleen.

iii

Cold and clear-cut face, why come you so cruelly meek,
Breaking a slumber in which all spleenful folly was drown'd?
Pale with the golden beam of an eyelash dead on the cheek,
Passionless, pale, cold face, star-sweet on a gloom profound;
Womanlike, taking revenge too deep for a transient wrong
Done but in thought to your beauty, and ever as pale as before
Growing and fading and growing upon me without a sound,
Luminous, gemlike, ghostlike, deathlike, half the night long
Growing and fading and growing, till I could bear it no more,
But arose, and all by myself in my own dark garden ground,
Listening now to the tide in its broad-flung ship-wrecking roar,
Now to the scream of a madden'd beach dragg'd down by the wave,
Walk'd in a wintry wind by a ghastly glimmer, and found
The shining daffodil dead, and Orion low in his grave.

iv

I

A million emeralds break from the ruby-budded lime
In the little grove where I sit — ah, wherefore cannot I be
Like things of the season gay, like the bountiful season bland,
When the far-off sail is blown by the breeze of a softer clime,
Half-lost in the liquid azure bloom of a crescent of sea,
The silent sapphire-spangled marriage ring of the land?

2

Below me, there, is the village, and looks how quiet and small!
And yet bubbles o'er like a city, with gossip, scandal, and spite;
And Jack on his ale-house bench has as many lies as a Czar;
And here on the landward side, by a red rock, glimmers the Hall;
And up in the high Hall-garden I see her pass like a light;
But sorrow seize me if ever that light be my leading star!

3

When have I bow'd to her father, the wrinkled head of the race?
I met her to-day with her brother, but not to her brother I bow'd;
I bow'd to his lady-sister as she rode by on the moor,
But the fire of a foolish pride flash'd over her beautiful face.
O child, you wrong your beauty, believe it, in being so proud;
Your father has wealth well-gotten, and I am nameless and poor.

4

I keep but a man and a maid, ever ready to slander and steal;
I know it, and smile a hard-set smile, like a stoic, or like
A wiser epicurean, and let the world have its way.
For nature is one with rapine, a harm no preacher can heal;
The Mayfly is torn by the swallow, the sparrow spear'd by the shrike,
And the whole little wood where I sit is a world of plunder and prey.

5

We are puppets, Man in his pride, and Beauty fair in her flower;
Do we move ourselves, or are moved by an unseen hand at a game
That pushes us off from the board, and others ever succeed?
Ah yet, we cannot be kind to each other here for an hour;
We whisper, and hint, and chuckle, and grin at a brother's shame;

101. The lowness of Orion marks the approach of spring.

110. The first explicit reference to the Crimean War of 1854–55.

However we brave it out, we men are a little breed.

6

A monstrous eft was of old the lord and master of earth,
For him did his high sun flame, and his river billowing ran,
And he felt himself in his force to be Nature's crowning race.
As nine months go to the shaping an infant ripe for his birth,
So many a million of ages have gone to the making of man:
He now is first, but is he the last? is he not too base?

7

The man of science himself is fonder of glory, and vain,
An eye well-practised in nature, a spirit bounded and poor;
The passionate heart of the poet is whirl'd into folly and vice.
I would not marvel at either, but keep a temperate brain;
For not to desire or admire, if a man could learn it, were more
Than to walk all day like the sultan of old in a garden of spice.

8

For the drift of the Maker is dark, an Isis hid by the veil.
Who knows the ways of the world, how God will bring them about?
Our planet is one, the suns are many, the world is wide.
Shall I weep if a Poland fall? shall I shriek if a Hungary fail?
Or an infant civilization be ruled with rod or with knout?
*I* have not made the world, and He that made it will guide.

9

Be mine a philosopher's life in the quiet woodland ways,
Where if I cannot be gay let a passionless peace be my lot,
Far-off from the clamor of liars belied in the hubbub of lies;
From the long-neck'd geese of the world that are ever hissing dispraise
Because their natures are little, and, whether he heed it or not,
Where each man walks with his head in a cloud of poisonous flies.

10

And most of all would I flee from the cruel madness of love,
The honey of poison-flowers and all the measureless ill.
Ah, Maud, you milk-white fawn, you are all unmeet for a wife.
Your mother is mute in her grave as her image in marble above;
Your father is ever in London, you wander about at your will;
You have but fed on the roses and lain in the lilies of life.

V

1

A voice by the cedar tree
In the meadow under the Hall!
She is singing an air that is known to me,
A passionate ballad gallant and gay,
A martial song like a trumpet's call!
Singing alone in the morning of life,
In the happy morning of life and of May,
Singing of men that in battle array,
Ready in heart and ready in hand,
March with banner and bugle and fife
To the death, for their native land.

2

Maud with her exquisite face,
And wild voice pealing up to the sunny sky,
And feet like sunny gems on an English green,
Maud in the light of her youth and her grace,
Singing of Death, and of Honor that cannot die,
Till I well could weep for a time so sordid and mean,
And myself so languid and base.

3

Silence, beautiful voice!
Be still, for you only trouble the mind
With a joy in which I cannot rejoice,
A glory I shall not find.
Still! I will hear you no more,
For your sweetness hardly leaves me a choice
But to move to the meadow and fall before

**132. eft**: one of "the great old lizards of geology" (Tennyson). **135–36.** See the note on *In Memoriam*, Epilogue, 125. **142. admire**: wonder (Horace, *Epistles*, I.vi.1).

Her feet on the meadow grass, and adore,
Not her, who is neither courtly nor kind,
Not her, not her, but a voice.

vi

1

Morning arises stormy and pale,
No sun, but a wannish glare
In fold upon fold of hueless cloud;
And the budded peaks of the wood are bow'd,
Caught, and cuff'd by the gale:
I had fancied it would be fair.

2

Whom but Maud should I meet
Last night, when the sunset burn'd
On the blossom'd gable-ends
At the head of the village street,
Whom but Maud should I meet?
And she touch'd my hand with a smile so sweet,
She made me divine amends
For a courtesy not return'd.

3

And thus a delicate spark
Of glowing and growing light
Thro' the livelong hours of the dark
Kept itself warm in the heart of my dreams,
Ready to burst in a color'd flame;
Till at last, when the morning came
In a cloud, it faded, and seems
But an ashen-gray delight.

4

What if with her sunny hair,
And smile as sunny as cold,
She meant to weave me a snare
Of some coquettish deceit,
Cleopatra-like as of old
To entangle me when we met,
To have her lion roll in a silken net
And fawn at a victor's feet.

5

Ah, what shall I be at fifty
Should Nature keep me alive,
If I find the world so bitter
When I am but twenty-five?
Yet, if she were not a cheat,
If Maud were all that she seem'd,
And her smile were all that I dream'd,
Then the world were not so bitter
But a smile could make it sweet.

6

What if, tho' her eye seem'd full
Of a kind intent to me,
What if that dandy-despot, he,
That jewel'd mass of millinery,
That oil'd and curl'd Assyrian bull
Smelling of musk and of insolence,
Her brother, from whom I keep aloof,
Who wants the finer politic sense
To mask, tho' but in his own behoof,
With a glassy smile his brutal scorn—
What if he had told her yestermorn
How prettily for his own sweet sake
A face of tenderness might be feign'd,
And a moist mirage in desert eyes,
That so, when the rotten hustings shake
In another month to his brazen lies,
A wretched vote may be gain'd?

7

For a raven ever croaks, at my side,
Keep watch and ward, keep watch and ward,
Or thou wilt prove their tool.
Yea, too, myself from myself I guard,
For often a man's own angry pride
Is cap and bells for a fool.

8

Perhaps the smile and tender tone
Came out of her pitying womanhood,
For am I not, am I not, here alone
So many a summer since she died,
My mother, who was so gentle and good?
Living alone in an empty house,
Here half-hid in the gleaming wood,
Where I hear the dead at midday moan,
And the shrieking rush of the wainscot mouse,
And my own sad name in corners cried,
When the shiver of dancing leaves is thrown
About its echoing chambers wide,
Till a morbid hate and horror have grown
Of a world in which I have hardly mixt,
And a morbid eating lichen fixt
On a heart half-turn'd to stone.

9

O heart of stone, are you flesh, and caught
By that you swore to withstand?
For what was it else within me wrought
But, I fear, the new strong wine of love,
That made my tongue so stammer and trip
When I saw the treasured splendor, her hand,

**203. courtesy**: bow (cf. I.114–19).

233. With hair curled like that of sculptured Assyrian bulls.

**251. cap and bells**: insignia of a medieval court fool.

Come sliding out of her sacred glove,
And the sunlight broke from her lip?

10

I have play'd with her when a child;
She remembers it now we meet.
Ah, well, well, well, I *may* be beguiled
By some coquettish deceit.
Yet, if she were not a cheat,
If Maud were all that she seem'd,
And her smile had all that I dream'd,
Then the world were not so bitter
But a smile could make it sweet.

vii

1

Did I hear it half in a doze
Long since, I know not where?
Did I dream it an hour ago,
When asleep in this arm-chair?

2

Men were drinking together,
Drinking and talking of me:
"Well, if it prove a girl, the boy
Will have plenty; so let it be."

3

Is it an echo of something
Read with a boy's delight,
Viziers nodding together
In some Arabian night?

4

Strange, that I hear two men,
Somewhere, talking of me:
"Well, if it prove a girl, my boy
Will have plenty; so let it be."

viii

She came to the village church,
And sat by a pillar alone;
An angel watching an urn
Wept over her, carved in stone;
And once, but once, she lifted her eyes,
And suddenly, sweetly, strangely blush'd
To find they were met by my own;
And suddenly, sweetly, my heart beat stronger
And thicker, until I heard no longer
The snowy-banded, dilettante,
Delicate-handed priest intone;
And thought, is it pride? and mused and sigh'd,
"No surely, now it cannot be pride."

ix

I was walking a mile,
More than a mile from the shore,
The sun look'd out with a smile
Betwixt the cloud and the moor;
And riding at set of day
Over the dark moor land,
Rapidly riding far away,
She waved to me with her hand.
There were two at her side,
Something flash'd in the sun,
Down by the hill I saw them ride,
In a moment they were gone;
Like a sudden spark
Struck vainly in the night,
Then returns the dark
With no more hope of light.

x

1

Sick, am I sick of a jealous dread?
Was not one of the two at her side
This new-made lord, whose splendor plucks
The slavish hat from the villager's head?
Whose old grandfather has lately died,
Gone to a blacker pit, for whom
Grimy nakedness dragging his trucks
And laying his trams in a poison'd gloom
Wrought, till he crept from a gutted mine
Master of half a servile shire,
And left his coal all turn'd into gold
To a grandson, first of his noble line,
Rich in the grace all women desire,
Strong in the power that all men adore,
And simper and set their voices lower,
And soften as if to a girl, and hold
Awe-stricken breaths at a work divine,
Seeing his gewgaw castle shine,
New as his title, built last year,
There amid perky larches and pine,
And over the sullen-purple moor—
Look at it—pricking a cockney ear.

2

What, has he found my jewel out?
For one of the two that rode at her side
Bound for the Hall, I am sure was he;
Bound for the Hall, and I think for a bride.
Blithe would her brother's acceptance be.
Maud could be gracious too, no doubt,
To a lord, a captain, a padded shape,
A bought commission, a waxen face,

**289–300.** The two fathers, long ago, planning marriage for their children; cf. I.720–26. **310. snowy-banded:** wearing the clerical white neckband, or stock, with two pendent strips.

A rabbit mouth that is ever agape—
Bought? what is it he cannot buy?
And therefore splenetic, personal, base,
A wounded thing with a rancorous cry,
At war with myself and a wretched race,
Sick, sick to the heart of life, am I.

3

Last week came one to the county town,
To preach our poor little army down,
And play the game of the despot kings,
Tho' the state has done it and thrice as well.
This broad-brimm'd hawker of holy things,
Whose ear is cramm'd with his cotton, and rings
Even in dreams to the chink of his pence,
This huckster put down war! can he tell
Whether war be a cause or a consequence?
Put down the passions that make earth hell!
Down with ambition, avarice, pride,
Jealousy, down! cut off from the mind
The bitter springs of anger and fear!
Down too, down at your own fireside,
With the evil tongue and the evil ear,
For each is at war with mankind!

4

I wish I could hear again
The chivalrous battle-song
That she warbled alone in her joy!
I might persuade myself then
She would not do herself this great wrong,
To take a wanton dissolute boy
For a man and leader of men.

5

Ah God, for a man with heart, head, hand,
Like some of the simple great ones gone
For ever and ever by,
One still strong man in a blatant land,
Whatever they call him—what care I?—
Aristocrat, democrat, autocrat—one
Who can rule and dare not lie!

6

And ah for a man to arise in me,
That the man I am may cease to be!

xi

1

O, let the solid ground
Not fail beneath my feet
Before my life has found
What some have found so sweet!
Then let come what come may,
What matter if I go mad,
I shall have had my day.

2

Let the sweet heavens endure,
Not close and darken above me
Before I am quite sure
That there is one to love me!
Then let come what come may
To a life that has been so sad,
I shall have had my day.

xii

1

Birds in the high Hall-garden
When twilight was falling,
Maud, Maud, Maud, Maud,
They were crying and calling.

2

Where was Maud? in our wood;
And I—who else?—was with her,
Gathering woodland lilies,
Myriads blow together.

3

Birds in our wood sang
Ringing thro' the valleys,
Maud is here, here, here
In among the lilies.

4

I kiss'd her slender hand,
She took the kiss sedately;
Maud is not seventeen,
But she is tall and stately.

5

I to cry out on pride
Who have won her favor!
O, Maud were sure of heaven
If lowliness could save her!

6

I know the way she went
Home with her maiden posy,
For her feet have touch'd the meadows
And left the daisies rosy.

370–73. The allusion to a Quaker pacifist and manufacturer was thought to be to John Bright, who opposed the Crimean War, but Tennyson said he did not know that Bright was a Quaker and that he had no individual in mind.

414. The repeated name is like the rook's caw. **419. blow:** blossom. 420–24. These birds, unlike those of 412–15, are on the lovers' side (*Memoir*, I, 379, 403). 435. The daisies' heads were tilted and showed their rosy underpetals.

7

Birds in the high Hall-garden
  Were crying and calling to her,
Where is Maud, Maud, Maud?
  One is come to woo her.

8

Look, a horse at the door,
  And little King Charley snarling!
Go back, my lord, across the moor,
  You are not her darling.

xiii

1

Scorn'd, to be scorn'd by one that I scorn,
Is that a matter to make me fret?
That a calamity hard to be borne?
Well, he may live to hate me yet.
Fool that I am to be vext with his pride!
I past him, I was crossing his lands;
He stood on the path a little aside;
His face, as I grant, in spite of spite,
Has a broad-blown comeliness, red and white,
And six feet two, as I think, he stands;
But his essences turn'd the live air sick,
And barbarous opulence jewel-thick
Sunn'd itself on his breast and his hands.

2

Who shall call me ungentle, unfair?
I long'd so heartily then and there
To give him the grasp of fellowship;
But while I past he was humming an air,
Stopt, and then with a riding-whip
Leisurely tapping a glossy boot,
And curving a contumelious lip,
Gorgonized me from head to foot
With a stony British stare.

3

Why sits he here in his father's chair?
That old man never comes to his place;
Shall I believe him ashamed to be seen?
For only once, in the village street,
Last year, I caught a glimpse of his face,
A gray old wolf and a lean.
Scarcely, now, would I call him a cheat;
For then, perhaps, as a child of deceit,
She might by a true descent be untrue;
And Maud is as true as Maud is sweet,
Tho' I fancy her sweetness only due
To the sweeter blood by the other side;
Her mother has been a thing complete,
However she came to be so allied.
And fair without, faithful within,
Maud to him is nothing akin.
Some peculiar mystic grace
Made her only the child of her mother,
And heap'd the whole inherited sin
On that huge scapegoat of the race,
All, all upon the brother.

4

Peace, angry spirit, and let him be!
Has not his sister smiled on me?

xiv

1

Maud has a garden of roses
And lilies fair on a lawn;
There she walks in her state
And tends upon bed and bower,
And thither I climb'd at dawn
And stood by her garden-gate.
A lion ramps at the top,
He is claspt by a passion-flower.

2

Maud's own little oak-room—
Which Maud, like a precious stone
Set in the heart of the carven gloom,
Lights with herself, when alone
She sits by her music and books
And her brother lingers late
With a roystering company—looks
Upon Maud's own garden-gate;
And I thought as I stood, if a hand, as white
As ocean-foam in the moon, were laid
On the hasp of the window, and my Delight
Had a sudden desire, like a glorious ghost, to glide,
Like a beam of the seventh heaven, down to my side,
There were but a step to be made.

3

The fancy flatter'd my mind,
And again seem'd overbold;
Now I thought that she cared for me,
Now I thought she was kind
Only because she was cold.

4

I heard no sound where I stood
But the rivulet on from the lawn
Running down to my own dark wood,
Or the voice of the long sea-wave as it swell'd
Now and then in the dim-gray dawn;

**441.** The King Charles is a small, silky breed of spaniel **464.** The Gorgon Medusa's head turned beholders to stone.

But I look'd, and round, all round the house I
  beheld
The death-white curtain drawn,
Felt a horror over me creep,
Prickle my skin and catch my breath,
Knew that the death-white curtain meant but sleep,
Yet I shudder'd and thought like a fool of the
  sleep of death.

xv

So dark a mind within me dwells,
  And I make myself such evil cheer,
That if *I* be dear to some one else,
  Then some one else may have much to fear;
But if *I* be dear to some one else,
  Then I should be to myself more dear.
Shall I not take care of all that I think,
Yea, even of wretched meat and drink,
If I be dear,
If I be dear to some one else?

xvi

1

This lump of earth has left his estate
The lighter by the loss of his weight;
And so that he find what he went to seek,
And fulsome pleasure clog him, and drown
His heart in the gross mud-honey of town,
He may stay for a year who has gone for a week.
But this is the day when I must speak,
And I see my Oread coming down,
O, this is the day!
O beautiful creature, what am I
That I dare to look her way?
Think I may hold dominion sweet,
Lord of the pulse that is lord of her breast,
And dream of her beauty with tender dread,
From the delicate Arab arch of her feet
To the grace that, bright and light as the crest
Of a peacock, sits on her shining head,
And she knows it not — O, if she knew it,
To know her beauty might half undo it!
I know it the one bright thing to save
My yet young life in the wilds of Time,
Perhaps from madness, perhaps from crime,
Perhaps from a selfish grave.

2

What, if she be fasten'd to this fool lord,
Dare I bid her abide by her word?
Should I love her so well if she
Had given her word to a thing so low?
Shall I love her as well if she
Can break her word were it even for me?
I trust that it is not so.

3

Catch not my breath, O clamorous heart,
Let not my tongue be a thrall to my eye,
For I must tell her before we part,
I must tell her, or die.

xvii

Go not, happy day,
  From the shining fields,
Go not, happy day,
  Till the maiden yields.
Rosy is the West,
  Rosy is the South,
Roses are her cheeks,
  And a rose her mouth.
When the happy Yes
  Falters from her lips,
Pass and blush the news
  Over glowing ships;
Over blowing seas,
  Over seas at rest,
Pass the happy news,
  Blush it thro' the West;
Till the red man dance
  By his red cedar-tree,
And the red man's babe
  Leap, beyond the sea.
Blush from West to East,
  Blush from East to West,
Till the West is East,
  Blush it thro' the West.
Rosy is the West,
  Rosy is the South,
Roses are her cheeks,
  And a rose her mouth.

xviii

1

I have led her home, my love, my only friend.
There is none like her, none.
And never yet so warmly ran my blood
And sweetly, on and on,
Calming itself to the long-wish'd-for end,
Full to the banks, close on the promised good.

2

None like her, none.
Just now the dry-tongued laurels' pattering talk
Seem'd her light foot along the garden walk,
And shook my heart to think she comes once more.
But even then I heard her close the door;
The gates of heaven are closed, and she is gone.

**529–31. some one else:** Maud. **551. Arab arch:** high instep.

3

There is none like her, none,
Nor will be when our summers have deceased.
O, art thou sighing for Lebanon
In the long breeze that streams to thy delicious East,
Sighing for Lebanon,
Dark cedar, tho' thy limbs have here increased,
Upon a pastoral slope as fair,
And looking to the South and fed
With honey'd rain and delicate air,
And haunted by the starry head
Of her whose gentle will has changed my fate,
And made my life a perfumed altar-flame;
And over whom thy darkness must have spread
With such delight as theirs of old, thy great
Forefathers of the thornless garden, there
Shadowing the snow-limb'd Eve from whom she
came?

4

Here will I lie, while these long branches sway,
And you fair stars that crown a happy day
Go in and out as if at merry play,
Who am no more so all forlorn
As when it seem'd far better to be born
To labor and the mattock-harden'd hand
Than nursed at ease and brought to understand
A sad astrology, the boundless plan
That makes you tyrants in your iron skies,
Innumerable, pitiless, passionless eyes,
Cold fires, yet with power to burn and brand
His nothingness into man.

5

But now shine on, and what care I,
Who in this stormy gulf have found a pearl
The countercharm of space and hollow sky,
And do accept my madness, and would die
To save from some slight shame one simple girl? —

6

Would die, for sullen-seeming Death may give
More life to Love than is or ever was
In our low world, where yet 'tis sweet to live.
Let no one ask me how it came to pass;
It seems that I am happy, that to me
A livelier emerald twinkles in the grass,
A purer sapphire melts into the sea.

7

Not die, but live a life of truest breath,
And teach true life to fight with mortal wrongs.
O, why should Love, like men in drinking-songs,
Spice his fair banquet with the dust of death?
Make answer, Maud my bliss,
Maud made my Maud by that long loving kiss,
Life of my life, wilt thou not answer this?
"The dusky strand of Death inwoven here
With dear Love's tie, makes Love himself more
dear."

8

Is that enchanted moan only the swell
Of the long waves that roll in yonder bay?
And hark the clock within, the silver knell
Of twelve sweet hours that past in bridal white,
And died to live, long as my pulses play;
But now by this my love has closed her sight
And given false death her hand, and stolen away
To dreamful wastes where footless fancies dwell
Among the fragments of the golden day.
May nothing there her maiden grace affright!
Dear heart, I feel with thee the drowsy spell.
My bride to be, my evermore delight,
My own heart's heart, my ownest own, farewell;
It is but for a little space I go.
And ye meanwhile far over moor and fell
Beat to the noiseless music of the night!
Has our whole earth gone nearer to the glow
Of your soft splendors that you look so bright?
*I* have climb'd nearer out of lonely hell.
Beat, happy stars, timing with things below,
Beat with my heart more blest than heart can tell,
Blest, but for some dark undercurrent woe
That seems to draw — but it shall not be so;
Let all be well, be well.

xix

1

Her brother is coming back to-night,
Breaking up my dream of delight.

2

My dream? do I dream of bliss?
I have walk'd awake with Truth.
O, when did a morning shine
So rich in atonement as this
For my dark-dawning youth,
Darken'd watching a mother decline
And that dead man at her heart and mine;
For who was left to watch her but I?
Yet so did I let my freshness die.

3

I trust that I did not talk
To gentle Maud in our walk —
For often in lonely wanderings

**613–16.** Cf. the cedars of Lebanon, Song of Sol. 5:15, etc.

**666.** false death: sleep.

I have cursed him even to lifeless things—
But I trust that I did not talk,
Not touch on her father's sin.
I am sure I did but speak
Of my mother's faded cheek
When it slowly grew so thin
That I felt she was slowly dying
Vext with lawyers and harass'd with debt;
For how often I caught her with eyes all wet,
Shaking her head at her son and sighing
A world of trouble within!

4

And Maud too, Maud was moved
To speak of the mother she loved
As one scarce less forlorn,
Dying abroad and it seems apart
From him who had ceased to share her heart,
And ever mourning over the feud,
The household Fury sprinkled with blood
By which our houses are torn.
How strange was what she said,
When only Maud and the brother
Hung over her dying bed—
That Maud's dark father and mine
Had bound us one to the other,
Betrothed us over their wine,
On the day when Maud was born;
Seal'd her mine from her first sweet breath!
Mine, mine by a right, from birth till death!
Mine, mine—our fathers have sworn!

5

But the true blood spilt had in it a heat
To dissolve the precious seal on a bond,
That, if left uncancel'd, had been so sweet;
And none of us thought of a something beyond,
A desire that awoke in the heart of the child,
As it were a duty done to the tomb,
To be friends for her sake, to be reconciled;
And I was cursing them and my doom,
And letting a dangerous thought run wild
While often abroad in the fragrant gloom
Of foreign churches—I see her there,
Bright English lily, breathing a prayer
To be friends, to be reconciled!

6

But then what a flint is he!
Abroad, at Florence, at Rome,
I find whenever she touch'd on me
This brother had laugh'd her down,
And at last, when each came home,
He had darken'd into a frown,
Chid her, and forbid her to speak
To me, her friend of the years before;
And this was what had redden'd her cheek
When I bow'd to her on the moor.

7

Yet Maud, altho' not blind
To the faults of his heart and mind,
I see she cannot but love him,
And says he is rough but kind,
And wishes me to approve him,
And tells me, when she lay
Sick once, with a fear of worse,
That he left his wine and horses and play,
Sat with her, read to her, night and day,
And tended her like a nurse.

8

Kind? but the death-bed desire
Spurn'd by this heir of the liar—
Rough but kind? yet I know
He has plotted against me in this,
That he plots against me still.
Kind to Maud? that were not amiss.
Well, rough but kind; why, let it be so,
For shall not Maud have her will?

9

For, Maud, so tender and true,
As long as my life endures
I feel I shall owe you a debt
That I never can hope to pay;
And if ever I should forget
That I owe this debt to you
And for your sweet sake to yours,
O, then, what then shall I say?—
If ever I *should* forget,
May God make me more wretched
Than ever I have been yet!

10

So now I have sworn to bury
All this dead body of hate,
I feel so free and so clear
By the loss of that dead weight,
That I should grow light-headed, I fear,
Fantastically merry,
But that her brother comes, like a blight
On my fresh hope, to the Hall to-night.

XX

1

Strange, that I felt so gay,
Strange, that *I* tried to-day
To beguile her melancholy;

720–26. Cf. I.289–300.

The Sultan, as we name him —
She did not wish to blame him —
But he vext her and perplext her
With his worldly talk and folly.
Was it gentle to reprove her
For stealing out of view
From a little lazy lover
Who but claims her as his due?
Or for chilling his caresses
By the coldness of her manners,
Nay, the plainness of her dresses?
Now I know her but in two,
Nor can pronounce upon it
If one should ask me whether
The habit, hat, and feather,
Or the frock and gipsy bonnet
Be the neater and completer;
For nothing can be sweeter
Than maiden Maud in either.

2

But to-morrow, if we live,
Our ponderous squire will give
A grand political dinner
To half the squirelings near;
And Maud will wear her jewels,
And the bird of prey will hover,
And the titmouse hope to win her
With his chirrup at her ear.

3

A grand political dinner
To the men of many acres,
A gathering of the Tory,
A dinner and then a dance
For the maids and marriage-makers,
And every eye but mine will glance
At Maud in all her glory.

4

For I am not invited,
But, with the Sultan's pardon,
I am all as well delighted,
For I know her own rose-garden,
And mean to linger in it
Till the dancing will be over;
And then, O, then, come out to me
For a minute, but for a minute,
Come out to your own true lover,
That your true lover may see
Your glory also, and render
All homage to his own darling,
Queen Maud in all her splendor.

**790. Sultan**: Maud's brother. **796. lover**: the "new-made lord" of I.332 ff.

xxi

Rivulet crossing my ground,
And bringing me down from the Hall
This garden-rose that I found,
Forgetful of Maud and me,
And lost in trouble and moving round
Here at the head of a tinkling fall,
And trying to pass to the sea;
O rivulet, born at the Hall,
My Maud has sent it by thee —
If I read her sweet will right —
On a blushing mission to me,
Saying in odor and color, "Ah, be
Among the roses to-night."

xxii

1

Come into the garden, Maud,
  For the black bat, night, has flown,
Come into the garden, Maud,
  I am here at the gate alone;
And the woodbine spices are wafted abroad,
  And the musk of the rose is blown.

2

For a breeze of morning moves,
  And the planet of Love is on high,
Beginning to faint in the light that she loves
  On a bed of daffodil sky,
To faint in the light of the sun she loves,
  To faint in his light, and to die.

3

All night have the roses heard
  The flute, violin, bassoon;
All night has the casement jessamine stirr'd
  To the dancers dancing in tune;
Till a silence fell with the waking bird,
  And a hush with the setting moon.

4

I said to the lily, "There is but one,
  With whom she has heart to be gay.
When will the dancers leave her alone?
  She is weary of dance and play."
Now half to the setting moon are gone,
  And half to the rising day;
Low on the sand and loud on the stone
  The last wheel echoes away.

5

I said to the rose, "The brief night goes
  In babble and revel and wine.

**857. planet of Love**: Venus.

O young lord-lover, what sighs are those,
For one that will never be thine?
But mine, but mine," so I sware to the rose,
"For ever and ever, mine."

6

And the soul of the rose went into my blood,
As the music clash'd in the hall;
And long by the garden lake I stood,
For I heard your rivulet fall
From the lake to the meadow and on to the wood,
Our wood, that is dearer than all;

7

From the meadow your walks have left so sweet
That whenever a March-wind sighs
He sets the jewel-print of your feet
In violets blue as your eyes,
To the woody hollows in which we meet
And the valleys of Paradise.

8

The slender acacia would not shake
One long milk-bloom on the tree;
The white lake-blossom fell into the lake
As the pimpernel dozed on the lea;
But the rose was awake all night for your sake,
Knowing your promise to me;
The lilies and roses were all awake,
They sigh'd for the dawn and thee.

9

Queen rose of the rosebud garden of girls,
Come hither, the dances are done,
In gloss of satin and glimmer of pearls,
Queen lily and rose in one;
Shine out, little head, sunning over with curls,
To the flowers, and be their sun.

10

There has fallen a splendid tear
From the passion-flower at the gate.
She is coming, my dove, my dear;
She is coming, my life, my fate.
The red rose cries, "She is near, she is near;"
And the white rose weeps, "She is late;"
The larkspur listens, "I hear, I hear;"
And the lily whispers, "I wait."

11

She is coming, my own, my sweet;
Were it ever so airy a tread,
My heart would hear her and beat,
Were it earth in an earthy bed;
My dust would hear her and beat,
Had I lain for a century dead,
Would start and tremble under her feet,
And blossom in purple and red.

## *Part II*

### i

1

"The fault was mine, the fault was mine"—
Why am I sitting here so stunn'd and still,
Plucking the harmless wild-flower on the hill?—
It is this guilty hand!—
And there rises ever a passionate cry
From underneath in the darkening land—
What is it, that has been done?
O dawn of Eden bright over earth and sky,
The fires of hell brake out of thy rising sun,
The fires of hell and of hate;
For she, sweet soul, had hardly spoken a word,
When her brother ran in his rage to the gate,
He came with the babe-faced lord,
Heap'd on her terms of disgrace;
And while she wept, and I strove to be cool,
He fiercely gave me the lie,
Till I with as fierce an anger spoke,
And he struck me, madman, over the face,
Struck me before the languid fool,
Who was gaping and grinning by;
Struck for himself an evil stroke,
Wrought for his house an irredeemable woe.
For front to front in an hour we stood,
And a million horrible bellowing echoes broke
From the red-ribb'd hollow behind the wood,
And thunder'd up into heaven the Christless code
That must have life for a blow.
Ever and ever afresh they seem'd to grow.
Was it he lay there with a fading eye?
"The fault was mine," he whisper'd, "fly!"
Then glided out of the joyous wood
The ghastly Wraith of one that I know,
And there rang on a sudden a passionate cry,
A cry for a brother's blood;
It will ring in my heart and my ears, till I die, till I die.

2

Is it gone? my pulses beat—
What was it? a lying trick of the brain?
Yet I thought I saw her stand,
A shadow there at my feet,
High over the shadowy land.
It is gone; and the heavens fall in a gentle rain,
When they should burst and drown with deluging storms
The feeble vassals of wine and anger and lust,

II.31–35. A vision of Maud.

The little hearts that know not how to forgive.
Arise, my God, and strike, for we hold Thee just,
Strike dead the whole weak race of venomous worms,
That sting each other here in the dust;
We are not worthy to live.

ii

1

See what a lovely shell,
Small and pure as a pearl,
Lying close to my foot,
Frail, but a work divine,
Made so fairily well
With delicate spire and whorl,
How exquisitely minute,
A miracle of design!

2

What is it? a learned man
Could give it a clumsy name.
Let him name it who can,
The beauty would be the same.

3

The tiny cell is forlorn,
Void of the little living will
That made it stir on the shore.
Did he stand at the diamond door
Of his house in a rainbow frill?
Did he push, when he was uncurl'd,
A golden foot or a fairy horn
Thro' his dim water-world?

4

Slight, to be crush'd with a tap
Of my finger-nail on the sand,
Small, but a work divine,
Frail, but of force to withstand,
Year upon year, the shock
Of cataract seas that snap
The three-decker's oaken spine
Athwart the ledges of rock,
Here on the Breton strand!

5

Breton, not Briton; here
Like a shipwreck'd man on a coast
Of ancient fable and fear —
Plagued with a flitting to and fro,
A disease, a hard mechanic ghost
That never came from on high
Nor ever arose from below,
But only moves with the moving eye,
Flying along the land and the main —
Why should it look like Maud?
Am I to be overawed
By what I cannot but know
Is a juggle born of the brain?

6

Back from the Breton coast,
Sick of a nameless fear,
Back to the dark sea-line
Looking, thinking of all I have lost;
An old song vexes my ear,
But that of Lamech is mine.

7

For years, a measureless ill,
For years, for ever, to part —
But she, she would love me still;
And as long, O God, as she
Have a grain of love for me,
So long, no doubt, no doubt,
Shall I nurse in my dark heart,
However weary, a spark of will
Not to be trampled out.

8

Strange, that the mind, when fraught
With a passion so intense
One would think that it well
Might drown all life in the eye, —
That it should, by being so overwrought,
Suddenly strike on a sharper sense
For a shell, or a flower, little things
Which else would have been past by!
And now I remember, I,
When he lay dying there,
I noticed one of his many rings —
For he had many, poor worm — and thought,
It is his mother's hair.

9

Who knows if he be dead?
Whether I need have fled?
Am I guilty of blood?
However this may be,
Comfort her, comfort her, all things good,
While I am over the sea!
Let me and my passionate love go by,
But speak to her all things holy and high,
Whatever happen to me!

**49 ff.** The shell, surviving storms, perhaps symbolizes the hero's "first and highest nature preserved amid the storms of passion" (*Memoir*, I, 404). **77. Breton strand:** Brittany, in France, whither the hero has fled after the duel.

**96. Lamech:** See Gen. 4:23.

Me and my harmful love go by;
But come to her waking, find her asleep,
Powers of the height, Powers of the deep,
And comfort her tho' I die!

iii

Courage, poor heart of stone!
I will not ask thee why
Thou canst not understand
That thou art left for ever alone;
Courage, poor stupid heart of stone!—
Or if I ask thee why,
Care not thou to reply:
She is but dead, and the time is at hand
When thou shalt more than die.

iv

1

O that 'twere possible
After long grief and pain
To find the arms of my true love
Round me once again!

2

When I was wont to meet her
In the silent woody places
By the home that gave me birth,
We stood tranced in long embraces
Mixt with kisses sweeter, sweeter
Than anything on earth.

3

A shadow flits before me,
Not thou, but like to thee.
Ah, Christ, that it were possible
For one short hour to see
The souls we loved, that they might tell us
What and where they be!

4

It leads me forth at evening,
It lightly winds and steals
In a cold white robe before me,
When all my spirit reels
At the shouts, the leagues of lights,
And the roaring of the wheels.

5

Half the night I waste in sighs,
Half in dreams I sorrow after
The delight of early skies;
In a wakeful doze I sorrow
For the hand, the lips, the eyes,
For the meeting of the morrow,
The delight of happy laughter,
The delight of low replies.

6

'T is a morning pure and sweet,
And a dewy splendor falls
On the little flower that clings
To the turrets and the walls;
'T is a morning pure and sweet,
And the light and shadow fleet.
She is walking in the meadow,
And the woodland echo rings;
In a moment we shall meet.
She is singing in the meadow,
And the rivulet at her feet
Ripples on in light and shadow
To the ballad that she sings.

7

Do I hear her sing as of old,
My bird with the shining head,
My own dove with the tender eye?
But there rings on a sudden a passionate cry,
There is some one dying or dead,
And a sullen thunder is roll'd;
For a tumult shakes the city,
And I wake, my dream is fled.
In the shuddering dawn, behold,
Without knowledge, without pity,
By the curtains of my bed
That abiding phantom cold!

8

Get thee hence, nor come again,
Mix not memory with doubt,
Pass, thou deathlike type of pain,
Pass and cease to move about!
'T is the blot upon the brain
That *will* show itself without.

9

Then I rise, the eave-drops fall,
And the yellow vapors choke
The great city sounding wide;
The day comes, a dull red ball
Wrapt in drifts of lurid smoke
On the misty river-tide.

10

Thro' the hubbub of the market
I steal, a wasted frame;
It crosses here, it crosses there,
Thro' all that crowd confused and loud,
The shadow still the same;

141–238. The germ of *Maud*. See the headnote.

And on my heavy eyelids
My anguish hangs like shame.

11

Alas for her that met me,
That heard me softly call,
Came glimmering thro' the laurels
At the quiet evenfall,
In the garden by the turrets
Of the old manorial hall!

12

Would the happy spirit descend
From the realms of light and song,
In the chamber or the street,
As she looks among the blest,
Should I fear to greet my friend
Or to say "Forgive the wrong,"
Or to ask her, "Take me, sweet,
To the regions of thy rest"?

13

But the broad light glares and beats,
And the shadow flits and fleets
And will not let me be;
And I loathe the squares and streets,
And the faces that one meets,
Hearts with no love for me.
Always I long to creep
Into some still cavern deep,
There to weep, and weep, and weep
My whole soul out to thee.

V

1

Dead, long dead,
Long dead!
And my heart is a handful of dust,
And the wheels go over my head,
And my bones are shaken with pain,
For into a shallow grave they are thrust,
Only a yard beneath the street,
And the hoofs of the horses beat, beat,
The hoofs of the horses beat,
Beat into my scalp and my brain,
With never an end to the stream of passing feet,
Driving, hurrying, marrying, burying,
Clamor and rumble, and ringing and clatter;
And here beneath it is all as bad,
For I thought the dead had peace, but it is not so.
To have no peace in the grave, is that not sad?
But up and down and to and fro,
Ever about me the dead men go;
And then to hear a dead man chatter
Is enough to drive one mad.

2

Wretchedest age, since Time began,
They cannot even bury a man;
And tho' we paid our tithes in the days that are gone,
Not a bell was rung, not a prayer was read.
It is that which makes us loud in the world of the dead;
There is none that does his work, not one.
A touch of their office might have sufficed,
But the churchmen fain would kill their church,
As the churches have kill'd their Christ.

3

See, there is one of us sobbing,
No limit to his distress;
And another, a lord of all things, praying
To his own great self, as I guess;
And another, a statesman there, betraying
His party-secret, fool, to the press;
And yonder a vile physician, blabbing
The case of his patient — all for what?
To tickle the maggot born in an empty head,
And wheedle a world that loves him not,
For it is but a world of the dead.

4

Nothing but idiot gabble!
For the prophecy given of old
And then not understood,
Has come to pass as foretold;
Not let any man think for the public good,
But babble, merely for babble.
For I never whisper'd a private affair
Within the hearing of cat or mouse,
No, not to myself in the closet alone,
But I heard it shouted at once from the top of the house;
Everything came to be known.
Who told *him* we were there?

5

Not that gray old wolf, for he came not back
From the wilderness, full of wolves, where he used to lie;
He has gather'd the bones for his o'ergrown whelp to crack —
Crack them now for yourself, and howl, and die.

**239 ff.** The hero goes through a period of insanity.

**259 ff.** Imagining that he is dead, he feels the restlessness that, according to superstition, was felt by those buried without due rites. **280. prophecy:** See Luke 12:2–3. **290. him:** Maud's brother. **291. wolf:** Maud's father (cf. I.471).

6

Prophet, curse me the blabbing lip,
And curse me the British vermin, the rat;
I know not whether he came in the Hanover ship,
But I know that he lies and listens mute
In an ancient mansion's crannies and holes.
Arsenic, arsenic, sure, would do it,
Except that now we poison our babes, poor souls!
It is all used up for that.

7

Tell him now: she is standing here at my head;
Not beautiful now, not even kind;
He may take her now; for she never speaks her
mind,
But is ever the one thing silent here.
She is not *of* us, as I divine;
She comes from another stiller world of the dead,
Stiller, not fairer than mine.

8

But I know where a garden grows,
Fairer than aught in the world beside,
All made up of the lily and rose
That blow by night, when the season is good,
To the sound of dancing music and flutes:
It is only flowers, they had no fruits,
And I almost fear they are not roses, but blood;
For the keeper was one, so full of pride,
He linkt a dead man there to a spectral bride;
For he, if he had not been a Sultan of brutes,
Would he have that hole in his side?

9

But what will the old man say?
He laid a cruel snare in a pit
To catch a friend of mine one stormy day;
Yet now I could even weep to think of it;
For what will the old man say
When he comes to the second corpse in the pit?

10

Friend, to be struck by the public foe,
Then to strike him and lay him low,
That were a public merit, far,
Whatever the Quaker holds, from sin;
But the red life spilt for a private blow —
I swear to you, lawful and lawless war
Are scarcely even akin.

11

O me, why have they not buried me deep enough?
Is it kind to have made me a grave so rough,
Me, that was never a quiet sleeper?
Maybe still I am but half-dead;
Then I cannot be wholly dumb.
I will cry to the steps above my head
And somebody, surely, some kind heart will come
To bury me, bury me
Deeper, ever so little deeper.

297. The Norwegian rat appeared in England in the early eighteenth century; the phrase "Hanover rat" was applied by adherents of the Stuarts to followers of the early Hanoverian kings of England, who came to the throne in the person of George I, in 1714. **317. keeper**: Maud's brother. **318. dead man**: the hero. **319. Sultan**: Cf. I.790. **321. old man**: Maud's father. **323. friend of mine**: the hero's father (see I.5 ff.). **326. second corpse**: Maud's brother (the first was the hero's father). **330. Quaker**: as opposed to fighting (cf. I.370).

## *Part III*

1

My life has crept so long on a broken wing
Thro' cells of madness, haunts of horror and fear,
That I come to be grateful at last for a little thing.
My mood is changed, for it fell at a time of year
When the face of night is fair on the dewy downs,
And the shining daffodil dies, and the Charioteer
And starry Gemini hang like glorious crowns
Over Orion's grave low down in the west,
That like a silent lightning under the stars
She seem'd to divide in a dream from a band of the
blest,
And spoke of a hope for the world in the coming
wars —
"And in that hope, dear soul, let trouble have rest,
Knowing I tarry for thee," and pointed to Mars
As he glow'd like a ruddy shield on the Lion's
breast.

2

And it was but a dream, yet it yielded a dear de-
light
To have look'd, tho' but in a dream, upon eyes so
fair,
That had been in a weary world my one thing
bright;
And it was but a dream, yet it lighten'd my despair
When I thought that a war would arise in defense
of the right,
That an iron tyranny now should bend or cease,
The glory of manhood stand on his ancient height,
Nor Britain's one sole God be the millionaire.
No more shall commerce be all in all, and Peace
Pipe on her pastoral hillock a languid note,
And watch her harvest ripen, her herd increase,

III.6. **Charioteer**: the constellation Auriga. **7. Gemini**: the twin stars Castor and Pollux. **10. She**: Maud. **13–14.** The planet Mars and the constellation of the Lion (suggesting war and the symbolic British lion). **20. tyranny**: of the Czar.

Nor the cannon-bullet rust on a slothful shore,
And the cobweb woven across the cannon's throat
Shall shake its threaded tears in the wind no more.

3

And as months ran on and rumor of battle grew,
"It is time, it is time, O passionate heart," said I,—
For I cleaved to a cause that I felt to be pure and true,—
"It is time, O passionate heart and morbid eye,
That old hysterical mock-disease should die."
And I stood on a giant deck and mixt my breath
With a loyal people shouting a battle-cry,
Till I saw the dreary phantom arise and fly
Far into the North, and battle, and seas of death.

4

Let it go or stay, so I wake to the higher aims
Of a land that has lost for a little her lust of gold,
And love of a peace that was full of wrongs and shames,
Horrible, hateful, monstrous, not to be told;
And hail once more to the banner of battle unroll'd!
Tho' many a light shall darken, and many shall weep
For those that are crush'd in the clash of jarring claims,
Yet God's just wrath shall be wreak'd on a giant liar,
And many a darkness into the light shall leap,
And shine in the sudden making of splendid names,
And noble thought be freer under the sun,
And the heart of a people beat with one desire;
For the peace, that I deem'd no peace, is over and done,
And now by the side of the Black and the Baltic deep,
And deathful-grinning mouths of the fortress, flames
The blood-red blossom of war with a heart of fire.

5

Let it flame or fade, and the war roll down like a wind,
We have proved we have hearts in a cause, we are noble still,
And myself have awaked, as it seems, to the better mind.
It is better to fight for the good than to rail at the ill;
I have felt with my native land, I am one with my kind,
I embrace the purpose of God, and the doom assign'd.

*1855, 1856*

36. **phantom**: Editors suggest the phantom of Maud (cf. II.iv), but would it be called "dreary"? It seems rather the "old hysterical mock-disease" of 33, just above. 45. **giant liar**: the Czar (cf. I.110). 51. The Crimean peninsula is in the Black Sea.

# IN THE VALLEY OF CAUTERETZ

Written in the Pyrenees in 1861; published in 1864. Tennyson is recalling the visit made to Spain with Hallam in 1830 — actually thirty-one years earlier.

All along the valley, stream that flashest white,
Deepening thy voice with the deepening of the night,
All along the valley, where thy waters flow,
I walk'd with one I loved two and thirty years ago.
All along the valley, while I walk'd to-day,
The two and thirty years were a mist that rolls away;
For all along the valley, down thy rocky bed,
Thy living voice to me was as the voice of the dead,
And all along the valley, by rock and cave and tree,
The voice of the dead was a living voice to me.

*1864* *1861*

# NORTHERN FARMER

## OLD STYLE

In this poem and the companion poem following, published in 1864 and 1869 respectively, there is much social history as well as humor and flavor. The new kind of farmer — who speaks less dialectal English than the old one — is self-seeking in his mercenary independence, in contrast with his predecessor, who had pride in his work and was loyal to the land and its owner. Each poem grew out of a saying Tennyson had heard: the germ of the first is lines 45 and 47, that of the second is lines 1–2 (*Memoir*, II, 9).

I

Wheer 'asta beän saw long and meä liggin' 'ere aloän?
Noorse? thourt nowt o' a noorse; whoy, Doctor's abeän an' agoän;
Says that I moänt 'a naw moor aäle, but I beänt a fool;
Git ma my aäle, fur I beänt a-gawin' to breäk my rule.

NORTHERN FARMER (OLD STYLE). 1. **'asta beän**: hast thou been. **saw**: so. **liggin'**: lying. 2. **noorse**: nurse. **nowt**: nought 3. **moänt 'a**: may not have. 4. **ma**: me.

II

Doctors, they knaws nowt, fur a says what 's naw-ways true;
Naw soort o' koind o' use to saäy the things that a do.
I've 'ed my point o' aäle ivry noight sin' I beän 'ere.
An' I've 'ed my quart ivry market-noight for foorty year.

III

Parson's a beän loikewoise, an' a sittin' 'ere o' my bed.
"The Amoighty's a taäkin o' you to 'issén, my friend," a said,
An' a towd ma my sins, an's toithe were due, an' I gied it in hond;
I done moy duty boy 'um, as I 'a done boy the lond.

IV

Larn'd a ma' beä. I reckons I 'annot sa mooch to larn.
But a cast oop, thot a did, 'bout Bessy Marris's barne.
Thaw a knaws I hallus voäted wi' Squoire an' choorch an' staäte,
An' i' the woost o' toimes I wur niver agin the raäte.

V

An' I hallus coom'd to 's choorch afoor moy Sally wur deäd,
An' 'eärd 'um a bummin' awaäy loike a buzzard-clock ower my 'eäd,
An' I niver knaw'd whot a meän'd but I thowt a 'ad summut to saäy,
An' I thowt a said whot a owt to 'a said, an I coom'd awaäy.

VI

Bessy Marris's barne! tha knaws she laäid it to meä.
Mowt a beän, mayhap, for she wur a bad un, sheä.
'Siver, I kep 'um, I kep 'um, my lass, tha mun understond;
I done moy duty boy 'um, as I 'a done boy the lond.

**5. a**: he. **7. point**: pint. **10. you**: *ou* as in *hour*. **'issén**: himself. **11. towd**: told. **toithe**: tithe. **12. boy**: by. **13. Larn'd a ma' beä**: learned he may be. **14. a cast oop**: he brought up against me. **barne**: bairn. **15. Thaw**: though. **hallus**: always. **16. raäte**: poor-tax. **18. buzzard-clock**: cockchafer. **19. summut**: somewhat. **20. owt**: ought. **22. Mowt a beän**: might have been. **23. 'Siver**: howsoever. **mun**: must.

VII

But Parson a cooms an' a goäs, an 'a says it eäsy an' freeä:
"The Amoighty 's a taäkin o' you to 'issén, my friend," says 'eä.
I weänt saäy men be loiars, thaw summun said it in 'aäste;
But 'e reäds woon sarmin a weeäk, an' I 'a stubb'd Thurnaby waäste.

VIII

D' ya moind the waäste, my lass? naw, naw, tha was not born then;
Theer wur a boggle in it, I often 'eärd 'um mysen;
Moäst loike a butter-bump, fur I 'eärd 'um about an' about,
But I stubb'd 'um oop wi' the lot, an' raäved an' rembled 'um out.

IX

Keäper's it wur; fo' they fun 'um theer a-laäid of 'is faäce
Down i' the woild 'enemies afoor I coom'd to the plaäce.
Noäks or Thimbleby — toäner 'ed shot 'um as deäd as a naäil.
Noäks wur 'ang'd for it oop at 'soize — but git ma my aäle.

X

Dubbut looök at the waäste; theer warn't not feeäd for a cow;
Nowt at all but bracken an' fuzz, an' looök at it now —
Warn't worth nowt a haäcre, an' now theer 's lots o' feeäd,
Fourscoor yows upon it, an' some on it down i' seeäd.

XI

Nobbut a bit on it 's left, an' I meän'd to 'a stubb'd it at fall,
Done it ta-year I meän'd, an' runn'd plow thruff it an' all,
If Godamoighty an' Parson 'ud nobbut let ma aloän, —

**27. summun**: someone (Ps. 116:11). **28. wonn sarmin**: one sermon. **stubb'd**: cleared. **29. moind**: mind, remember. **30. boggle**: bogy, ghost. **31. butter-bump**: bittern. **32. raäved an' rembled**: tore up and threw away. **33. Keäper's**: the gamekeeper's. **fun**: found. **34. 'enemies**: anemones. **35. toäner**: one or other. **36. 'soize**: assizes. **37. Dobbut**: do but. **feeäd**: feed. **38. fuzz**: furze. **40. fourscoor**: *ou* as in *hour*. **yows**: ewes. **seeäd**: clover. **41. Nobbut**: nought but. **42. ta-year**: this year. **thruff**: through. **43. 'ud nobbut**: would only.

Meä, wi' haäte hoonderd haäcre o' Squoire's, an' lond o' my oän.

XII

Do Godamoighty knaw what a's doing a-taäkin' o' meä?
I beänt wonn as saws 'ere a beän an' yonder a peä;
An' Squoire 'ull be sa mad an' all — a' dear, a' dear!
And I 'a managed for Squoire coom Michaelmas thutty year.

XIII

A mowt 'a taäen owd Joänes, as 'ant not a 'aäpoth o' sense,
Or a mowt 'a taäen young Robins — a niver mended a fence;
But Godamoighty a moost taäke meä an' taäke ma now,
Wi' aäf the cows to cauve an' Thurnaby hoälms to plow!

XIV

Looök 'ow quoloty smoiles when they seeäs ma a passin' boy,
Says to thessén, naw doubt, "What a man a beä sewer-loy!"
Fur they knaws what I beän to Squoire sin' fust a coom'd to the 'All;
I done moy duty by Squoire an' I done moy duty boy hall.

XV

Squoire 's i' Lunnon, an' summun I reckons 'ull 'a to wroite,
For whoä 's to howd the lond ater meä thot muddles ma quoit;
Sartin-sewer I beä thot a weänt niver give it to Joänes,
Naw, nor a moänt to Robins — a niver rembles the stoäns.

XVI

But summun 'ull come ater meä mayhap wi' 'is kittle o' steäm
Huzzin' an' maäzin' the blessed feälds wi' the divil's oän teäm.

Sin' I mun doy I mun doy, thaw loife they says is sweet,
But sin' I mun doy I mun doy, for I couldn abeär to see it.

XVII

What atta stannin' theer fur, an' doesn bring ma the aäle?
Doctor 's a 'toättler, lass, an a 's hallus i' the owd taäle;
I weänt breäk rules fur Doctor, a knaws naw moor nor a floy;
Git ma my aäle, I tell tha, an' if I mun doy I mun doy.

*1864*

## NORTHERN FARMER

### NEW STYLE

I

Dosn't thou 'ear my 'erse's legs, as they canters awaäy?
Proputty, proputty, proputty — that's what I 'ears 'em saäy.
Proputty, proputty, proputty — Sam, thou 's an ass for thy paains;
Theer's moor sense i' one o' 'is legs, nor in all thy braaïns.

II

Woä — theer 's a craw to pluck wi' tha, Sam: yon's Parson's 'ouse —
Dosn't thou knaw that a man mun be eäther a man or a mouse?
Time to think on it then; for thou 'll be twenty to weeäk.
Proputty, proputty — woä then, woä — let ma 'ear mysén speäk.

III

Me an' thy muther, Sammy, 'as beän a-talkin' o' thee;
Thou 's beän talkin' to muther, an' she beän a-tellin' it me.
Thou 'll not marry for munny — thou 's sweet upo' Parson's lass —
Noä — thou 'll marry for luvv — an' we boäth on us thinks tha an ass.

**46. wonn as saws**: one that sows. **49. owd**: old. **'ant**: has not. **'aäpoth**: halfpenny-worth. **52. aäf**: half. **cauve**: calve. **hoälms**: holms, low land by a stream. **53. quoloty**: quality, the gentry. **54. thessén**: themselves. **sewer-loy**: surely. **55. sin fust**: since first. **58. howd**: hold. **ater**: after. **thot**: that. **quoit**: quite. **59. Sartin-sewer**: certain sure. **a weänt niver**: he won't ever. **60. moänt**: must not. **rembles**: removes. **61. kittle o' steäm**: steam thresher. **62. Huzzin' an' maäzin'**: worrying and confusing.

**63. doy**: die. **65. atta**: art thou. **66. 'toättler**: teetotaler. **taäle**: tale. **67. floy**: fly. NORTHERN FARMER (NEW STYLE) **1. 'erse's**: horse's. **2. Proputty**: property. **5. craw**: crow **7. to weeäk**: this week. **8. mysén**: myself.

IV

Seeä'd her to-daäy goä by — Saäint's-daäy — they was ringing the bells.
She 's a beauty, thou thinks — an' soä is scoors o' gells,
Them as 'as munny an' all — wot 's a beauty? — the flower as blaws.
But proputty, proputty sticks, an' proputty, proputty graws.

V

Do'ant be stunt; taäke time. I knaws what maäkes tha sa mad.
Warn't I craäzed fur the lasses mysén when I wur a lad?
But I knaw'd a Quaäker feller as often 'as towd ma this:
"Doänt thou marry for munny, but goä wheer munny is!"

VI

An' I went wheer munny war; an' thy muther coom to 'and,
Wi' lots o' munny laaïd by, an' a nicetish bit o' land.
Maäybe she warn't a beauty — I niver giv it a thowt —
But warn't she as good to cuddle an' kiss as a lass as 'ant nowt?

VII

Parson's lass 'ant nowt, an' she weant 'a nowt when 'e 's deäd,
Mun be a guvness, lad, or summut, and addle her breäd.
Why? fur 'e 's nobbut a curate, an' weänt niver get hissén clear,
An' 'e maäde the bed as 'e ligs on afoor 'e coom'd to the shere.

VIII

An' thin 'e coom'd to the parish wi' lots o' Varsity debt,
Stook to his taaïl they did, an' 'e 'ant got shut on 'em yet.
An' 'e ligs on 'is back i' the grip, wi' noän to lend 'im a shuvv,
Woorse nor a far-welter'd yowe; fur, Sammy, 'e married fur luvv.

IX

Luvv? what's luvv? thou can luvv thy lass an' 'er munny too,
Maäkin' 'em goä togither, as they've good right to do.
Couldn I luvv thy muther by cause o' 'er munny laaïd by?
Naäy — fur I luvv'd 'er a vast sight moor fur it; reäson why.

X

Ay, an' thy muther says thou wants to marry the lass,
Cooms of a gentleman burn; an' we boäth on us thinks tha an ass.
Woä then, proputty, wiltha? — an ass as near as mays nowt —
Woä then, wiltha? dangtha! — the bees is as fell as owt.

XI

Breäk me a bit o' the esh for his 'eäd, lad, out o' the fence!
Gentleman burn! what 's gentleman burn? is it shillins an' pence?
Proputty, proputty's ivrything 'ere, an', Sammy, I'm blest
If it isn't the saäme oop yonder, fur them as 'as it's the best.

XII

Tis 'n them as 'as munny as breäks into 'ouses an' steäls,
Them as 'as coäts to their backs an' taäkes their regular meäls.
Noä, but it 's them as niver knaws wheer a meäl's to be 'ad.
Taäke my word for it, Sammy, the poor in a loomp is bad.

XIII

Them or thir feythers, tha sees, mun 'a beän a laäzy lot,
Fur work mun 'a gone to the gittin' whiniver munny was got.
Feyther 'ad ammost nowt; leästways 'is munny was 'id.
But 'e tued an' moil'd issén deäd, an' 'e died a good un, 'e did.

**14. scoors o' gells:** scores of girls. **17. stunt:** stubborn. **19. towd:** told. **24. 'ant nowt:** has nothing. **25. weänt 'a:** will not have. **26. addle:** earn. **27. nobbut:** nothing but. **clear:** of debt. **28. ligs:** lies. **shere:** shire. **30. shut on:** clear of. **31. grip:** ditch. **shuvv:** shove. **32. far-welter'd yowe:** ewe lying helpless on her back.

**38. burn:** born. **39. wiltha:** wilt thou. **mays nowt:** makes no difference. **40. bees . . . owt:** flies are as fierce as anything. **41. esh:** ash. **49. mun 'a beän:** must have been. **51. ammost:** almost. **52. tued an' moil'd:** toiled and drudged.

XIV

Looök thou theer wheer Wrigglesby beck cooms out by the 'ill!
Feyther run oop to the farm, an' I runs oop to the mill;
An' I 'll run oop to the brig, an' that thou 'll live to see;
And if thou marries a good un I 'll leäve the land to thee.

XV

Thim 's my noätions, Sammy, wheerby I meäns to stick;
But if thou marries a bad un, I 'll leäve the land to Dick.—
Coom oop, proputty, proputty—that 's what I 'ears 'im saäy—
Proputty, proputty, proputty—canter an' canter awaäy.

*1869*

53. **beck**: brook. 54. **Feyther . . . oop**: father's land ran up. 55. **brig**: bridge.

# LUCRETIUS

In his long poem *De Rerum Natura* (*On the Nature of Things*), Lucretius (?94–?55 B.C.) expounded the philosophy of Epicurus with a messianic fire of his own; his great aim was to free mankind from religious superstition and the fear of death. According to a tradition preserved by St. Jerome, Lucretius was driven mad by a love-potion, in lucid intervals wrote his unfinished poem, and committed suicide. Whether or not there is any truth in the tradition, the use of it for this poem and the rendering of the speaker's efforts to maintain his reason against the sensual potency of the drug, along with the background of the night of storm—all this has a result that is, for Tennyson, relatively "Spasmodic" or Browningesque. And into his violent picture of a noble Roman mind breaking with the Roman republic the poet contrives, with inspired skill, to weave many echoes of *De Rerum Natura,* from the concourse of atoms to the twitching foot of the dreaming dog. Apart from, or along with, the intrinsic power of the monologue, Tennyson apparently suggests, though without any overt hint, the fatal inadequacy of a materialistic philosophy. "Lucretius" was written in 1865 and published in 1868.

Lucilia, wedded to Lucretius, found
Her master cold; for when the morning flush
Of passion and the first embrace had died
Between them, tho' he loved her none the less,
Yet often when the woman heard his foot
Return from pacings in the field, and ran
To greet him with a kiss, the master took
Small notice, or austerely, for—his mind
Half buried in some weightier argument,
Or fancy-borne perhaps upon the rise
And long roll of the hexameter—he past
To turn and ponder those three hundred scrolls
Left by the Teacher, whom he held divine.
She brook'd it not, but wrathful, petulant,
Dreaming some rival, sought and found a witch
Who brew'd the philter which had power, they said,
To lead an errant passion home again.
And this, at times, she mingled with his drink,
And this destroy'd him; for the wicked broth
Confused the chemic labor of the blood,
And tickling the brute brain within the man's
Made havoc among those tender cells, and check'd
His power to shape. He loathed himself, and once
After a tempest woke upon a morn
That mock'd him with returning calm, and cried:

"Storm in the night! for thrice I heard the rain
Rushing; and once the flash of a thunderbolt—
Methought I never saw so fierce a fork—
Struck out the streaming mountain-side, and show'd
A riotous confluence of watercourses
Blanching and billowing in a hollow of it,
Where all but yester-eve was dusty-dry.

"Storm, and what dreams, ye holy Gods, what dreams!
For thrice I waken'd after dreams. Perchance
We do but recollect the dreams that come
Just ere the waking. Terrible: for it seem'd
A void was made in Nature; all her bonds
Crack'd; and I saw the flaring atom-streams
And torrents of her myriad universe,
Ruining along the illimitable inane,
Fly on to clash together again, and make
Another and another frame of things
For ever. That was mine, my dream, I knew it—
Of and belonging to me, as the dog
With inward yelp and restless forefoot plies
His function of the woodland; but the next!
I thought that all the blood by Sylla shed
Came driving rainlike down again on earth,
And where it dash'd the reddening meadow, sprang
No dragon warriors from Cadmean teeth,
For these I thought my dream would show to me,
But girls, Hetairai, curious in their art,
Hired animalisms, vile as those that made
The mulberry-faced Dictator's orgies worse
Than aught they fable of the quiet Gods.

LUCRETIUS. 13. **the Teacher**: Epicurus. 47 (and 54): the military dictator Sulla. 50. The warriors who, in the Greek myth, sprang from the dragon's teeth Cadmus sowed in the ground.

And hands they mixt, and yell'd and round me drove
In narrowing circles till I yell'd again
Half-suffocated, and sprang up, and saw—
Was it the first beam of my latest day?

"Then, then, from utter gloom stood out the breasts,
The breasts of Helen, and hoveringly a sword
Now over and now under, now direct,
Pointed itself to pierce, but sank down shamed
At all that beauty; and as I stared, a fire,
The fire that left a roofless Ilion,
Shot out of them, and scorch'd me that I woke.

"Is this thy vengeance, holy Venus, thine,
Because I would not one of thine own doves,
Not even a rose, were offer'd to thee? thine,
Forgetful how my rich prœmion makes
Thy glory fly along the Italian field,
In lays that will outlast thy deity?

"Deity? nay, thy worshipers. My tongue
Trips, or I speak profanely. Which of these
Angers thee most, or angers thee at all?
Not if thou be'st of those who, far aloof
From envy, hate and pity, and spite and scorn,
Live the great life which all our greatest fain
Would follow, centered in eternal calm.

"Nay, if thou canst, O Goddess, like ourselves
Touch, and be touch'd, then would I cry to thee
To kiss thy Mavors, roll thy tender arms
Round him, and keep him from the lust of blood
That makes a steaming slaughter-house of Rome.

"Ay, but I meant not thee; I meant not her
Whom all the pines of Ida shook to see
Slide from that quiet heaven of hers, and tempt
The Trojan, while his neatherds were abroad;
Nor her that o'er her wounded hunter wept
Her deity false in human-amorous tears;
Nor whom her beardless apple-arbiter
Decided fairest. Rather, O ye Gods,
Poet-like, as the great Sicilian called
Calliope to grace his golden verse—
Ay, and this Kypris also—did I take
That popular name of thine to shadow forth
The all generating powers and genial heat
Of Nature, when she strikes thro' the thick blood
Of cattle, and light is large, and lambs are glad
Nosing the mother's udder, and the bird
Makes his heart voice amid the blaze of flowers;
Which things appear the work of mighty Gods.

"The Gods! and if I go *my* work is left
Unfinish'd—*if* I go. The Gods, who haunt
The lucid interspace of world and world,
Where never creeps a cloud, or moves a wind,
Nor ever falls the least white star of snow,
Nor ever lowest roll of thunder moans,
Nor sound of human sorrow mounts to mar
Their sacred everlasting calm! and such,
Not all so fine, nor so divine a calm,
Not such, nor all unlike it, man may gain
Letting his own life go. The Gods, the Gods!
If all be atoms, how then should the Gods
Being atomic not be dissoluble,
Not follow the great law? My master held
That Gods there are, for all men so believe.
I prest my footsteps into his, and meant
Surely to lead my Memmius in a train
Of flowery clauses onward to the proof
That Gods there are, and deathless. Meant? I meant?
I have forgotten what I meant; my mind
Stumbles, and all my faculties are lamed.

"Look where another of our Gods, the Sun,
Apollo, Delius, or of older use
All-seeing Hyperion—what you will—
Has mounted yonder; since he never sware,
Except his wrath were wreak'd on wretched man,
That he would only shine among the dead
Hereafter—tales! for never yet on earth
Could dead flesh creep, or bits of roasting ox
Moan round the spit—nor knows he what he sees;
King of the East altho' he seem, and girt
With song and flame and fragrance, slowly lifts
His golden feet on those empurpled stairs
That climb into the windy halls of heaven.
And here he glances on an eye new-born,
And gets for greeting but a wail of pain;
And here he stays upon a freezing orb
That fain would gaze upon him to the last;
And here upon a yellow eyelid fallen
And closed by those who mourn a friend in vain,
Not thankful that his troubles are no more.

61. Helen of Troy (for this incident, see Euripides, *Andromache,* 628–31). **70. prœmion:** In the introductory part of his poem Lucretius celebrated Venus, not as the goddess of popular religion, but as the generative power in nature (see below, 85–102). **82. Mavors:** Mars. **88. Trojan:** Anchises, the mortal father, by Venus, of Aeneas ("Homeric Hymn to Aphrodite"). **89. hunter:** Adonis. **91. apple-arbiter:** Paris (see "Œnone"). **93. Sicilian:** the philosopher-poet Empedocles. **94. Calliope:** the Muse of epic poetry. **95. Kypris:** Cypris, an epithet for Venus, who rose from the sea near Cyprus.

**97. genial:** fruitful. **116. my master:** Epicurus. **119. Memmius:** the Roman to whom Lucretius dedicated his poem. **125. Delius:** an epithet for Apollo, who was born on the island of Delos. **126. Hyperion:** the sun god, before Apollo; the name is accented correctly, as here, on the *i.*

And me, altho' his fire is on my face
Blinding, he sees not, nor at all can tell
Whether I mean this day to end myself,
Or lend an ear to Plato where he says,
That men like soldiers may not quit the post
Allotted by the Gods. But he that holds
The Gods are careless, wherefore need he care
Greatly for them, nor rather plunge at once,
Being troubled, wholly out of sight, and sink
Past earthquake — ay, and gout and stone, that break
Body toward death, and palsy, death-in-life,
And wretched age — and worst disease of all,
These prodigies of myriad nakednesses,
And twisted shapes of lust, unspeakable,
Abominable, strangers at my hearth
Not welcome, harpies miring every dish,
The phantom husks of something foully done,
And fleeting thro' the boundless universe,
And blasting the long quiet of my breast
With animal heat and dire insanity?

"How should the mind, except it loved them, clasp
These idols to herself? or do they fly
Now thinner, and now thicker, like the flakes
In a fall of snow, and so press in, perforce
Of multitude, as crowds that in an hour
Of civic tumult jam the doors, and bear
The keepers down, and throng, their rags and they
The basest, far into that council-hall
Where sit the best and stateliest of the land?

"Can I not fling this horror off me again,
Seeing with how great ease Nature can smile,
Balmier and nobler from her bath of storm,
At random ravage? and how easily
The mountain there has cast his cloudy slough,
Now towering o'er him in serenest air,
A mountain o'er a mountain, — ay, and within
All hollow as the hopes and fears of men?

"But who was he that in the garden snared
Picus and Faunus, rustic Gods? a tale
To laugh at — more to laugh at in myself —
For look! what is it? there? yon arbutus
Totters; a noiseless riot underneath
Strikes through the wood, sets all the tops quivering —
The mountain quickens into Nymph and Faun;
And here an Oread — how the sun delights
To glance and shift about her slippery sides,
And rosy knees and supple roundedness,
And budded bosom-peaks — who this way runs
Before the rest! — A satyr, a satyr, see,
Follows; but him I proved impossible;
Twy-natured is no nature. Yet he draws
Nearer and nearer, and I scan him now
Beastlier than any phantom of his kind
That ever butted his rough brother-brute
For lust or lusty blood or provender.
I hate, abhor, spit, sicken at him; and she
Loathes him as well; such a precipitate heel,
Fledged as it were with Mercury's ankle-wing,
Whirls her to me — but will she fling herself
Shameless upon me? Catch her, goat-foot! nay,
Hide, hide them, million-myrtled wilderness,
And cavern-shadowing laurels, hide! do I wish —
What? — that the bush were leafless? or to whelm
All of them in one massacre? O ye Gods,
I know you careless, yet, behold, to you
From childly wont and ancient use I call —
I thought I lived securely as yourselves —
No lewdness, narrowing envy, monkey-spite,
No madness of ambition, avarice, none;
No larger feast than under plane or pine
With neighbors laid along the grass, to take
Only such cups as left us friendly-warm,
Affirming each his own philosophy —
Nothing to mar the sober majesties
Of settled, sweet, Epicurean life.
But now it seems some unseen monster lays
His vast and filthy hands upon my will,
Wrenching it backward into his, and spoils
My bliss in being; and it was not great,
For save when shutting reasons up in rhythm,
Or Heliconian honey in living words,
To make a truth less harsh, I often grew
Tired of so much within our little life,
Or of so little in our little life —
Poor little life that toddles half an hour
Crown'd with a flower or two, and there an end —
And since the nobler pleasure seems to fade,
Why should I, beastlike as I find myself,
Not manlike end myself? — our privilege —
What beast has heart to do it? And what man,
What Roman would be dragg'd in triumph thus?
Not I; not he, who bears one name with her
Whose death-blow struck the dateless doom of kings,
When, brooking not the Tarquin in her veins,
She made her blood in sight of Collatine
And all his peers, flushing the guiltless air,

147. See Plato, *Phaedo*, 62. 159. **harpies**: the birds which befouled the food of King Phineus (*Aeneid*, III.212 ff.). 165. **idols**: images. 181. **he**: Numa, the legendary king of Rome (the story alluded to is in Ovid, *Fasti*, III.291 ff.).

194. **Twy-natured**: of double nature, part man, part goat. 235. **her**: Lucretia, raped by Sextus, son of the Roman King Tarquin, told her story to her husband Collatine and her uncle, and then stabbed herself; in Roman legend, this led to the expulsion of the Tarquins and the founding of the republic.

Spout from the maiden fountain in her heart.
And from it sprang the Commonwealth, which breaks
As I am breaking now!

"And therefore now
Let her, that is the womb and tomb of all,
Great Nature, take, and forcing far apart
Those blind beginnings that have made me man,
Dash them anew together at her will
Thro' all her cycles — into man once more,
Or beast or bird or fish, or opulent flower.
But till this cosmic order everywhere
Shatter'd into one earthquake in one day
Cracks all to pieces, — and that hour perhaps
Is not so far when momentary man
Shall seem no more a something to himself,
But he, his hopes and hates, his homes and fanes,
And even his bones long laid within the grave,
The very sides of the grave itself shall pass,
Vanishing, atom and void, atom and void,
Into the unseen for ever, — till that hour,
My golden work in which I told a truth
That stays the rolling Ixionian wheel,
And numbs the Fury's ringlet-snake, and plucks
The mortal soul from out immortal hell,
Shall stand. Ay, surely; then it fails at last
And perishes as I must; for O Thou,
Passionless bride, divine Tranquillity,
Yearn'd after by the wisest of the wise,
Who fail to find thee, being as thou art
Without one pleasure and without one pain,
Howbeit I know thou surely must be mine
Or soon or late, yet out of season, thus
I woo thee roughly, for thou carest not
How roughly men may woo thee so they win —
Thus — thus — the soul flies out and dies in the air."

With that he drove the knife into his side.
She heard him raging, heard him fall, ran in,
Beat breast, tore hair, cried out upon herself
As having fail'd in duty to him, shriek'd
That she but meant to win him back, fell on him,
Clasp'd, kiss'd him, wail'd. He answer'd, "Care not thou!
Thy duty? What is duty? Fare thee well!"

*1868* *1865*

**245. blind beginnings:** atoms. **257. atom and void:** in Epicurean physics, the constituents of the universe. **260.** Ixion, having offered violence to Hera, wife of Zeus, was bound to a turning wheel in Hades. **261.** The Furies, avengers of crime, had snakes in their hair.

# from IDYLLS OF THE KING

## THE HOLY GRAIL

Tennyson's interest in Arthurian legend began with his youthful reading of Malory, and bore such early fruit as "The Lady of Shalott" and "Morte d'Arthur." It was not until the 1850's that plans for a large connected series gradually took shape. Four of the *Idylls of the King* were published in 1859, four more (of which two were "The Holy Grail" and "The Passing of Arthur," the latter somewhat expanded from the early "Morte d'Arthur") in 1869; the cycle of twelve *Idylls* was not completed until 1885. If allegory is defined as a story with a continuous double meaning, the term is less descriptive of Tennyson's method than symbolism; and his general and sometimes modified conceptions — of Arthur as the soul (in action), his queen Guinevere as sense, the knights of the Round Table as human passions and capacities, and Camelot as the growth of beliefs and institutions, the spiritual development of man — he would not allow to be tied down to too definite interpretation. The *Idylls* differ a good deal in symbolic content. "The Holy Grail" (which was written rapidly in September, 1868) is perhaps the most substantial and original and — along with "The Last Tournament" — the most impressive to a modern reader. Tennyson used material from Malory, Books XI–XVIII, but quite altered its spirit. Whereas in medieval lore the Grail — a dish or cup used by Christ at the Last Supper — was a supreme object of religious devotion, Tennyson makes the quest of it, for most of the knights, a mistaken and neurotic quest for certitude or mere excitement, an escape from the real righteousness and performance of duty exemplified by Arthur. Here and in "The Last Tournament" the corruption that began with the adulterous love of Guinevere and Lancelot has largely undermined Arthur's ideals and work. The two *Idylls* are a sort of Victorian *Waste Land,* a picture of a society in feverish decay. In addition to such books as M. W. MacCallum, *Tennyson's Idylls and Arthurian Story from the XVIth Century* (1894) and M. J. C. Reid, *The Arthurian Legend: Comparison of Treatment in Modern and Mediaeval Literature* (1939), a valuable short study is that of F. E. L. Priestley, *University of Toronto Quarterly,* XIX (1949).

From noiseful arms, and acts of prowess done
In tournament or tilt, Sir Percivale,
Whom Arthur and his knighthood call'd the Pure,
Had past into the silent life of prayer,
Praise, fast, and alms; and leaving for the cowl
The helmet in an abbey far away
From Camelot, there, and not long after, died.

And one, a fellow-monk among the rest,
Ambrosius, loved him much beyond the rest,

THE HOLY GRAIL. **1. noiseful:** famous.

And honor'd him, and wrought into his heart
A way by love that waken'd love within,
To answer that which came; and as they sat
Beneath a world-old yew-tree, darkening half
The cloisters, on a gustful April morn
That puff'd the swaying branches into smoke
Above them, ere the summer when he died,
The monk Ambrosius question'd Percivale:

"O brother, I have seen this yew-tree smoke,
Spring after spring, for half a hundred years;
For never have I known the world without,
Nor ever stray'd beyond the pale. But thee,
When first thou camest — such a courtesy
Spake thro' the limbs and in the voice — I knew
For one of those who eat in Arthur's hall;
For good ye are and bad, and like to coins,
Some true, some light, but every one of you
Stamp'd with the image of the King; and now
Tell me, what drove thee from the Table Round,
My brother? was it earthly passion crost?"

"Nay," said the knight; "for no such passion mine.
But the sweet vision of the Holy Grail
Drove me from all vainglories, rivalries,
And earthly heats that spring and sparkle out
Among us in the jousts, while women watch
Who wins, who falls, and waste the spiritual strength
Within us, better offer'd up to heaven."

To whom the monk: "The Holy Grail! — I trust
We are green in Heaven's eyes; but here too much
We molder — as to things without I mean —
Yet one of your own knights, a guest of ours,
Told us of this in our refectory,
But spake with such a sadness and so low
We heard not half of what he said. What is it?
The phantom of a cup that comes and goes?"

"Nay, monk! what phantom?" answer'd Percivale.
"The cup, the cup itself, from which our Lord
Drank at the last sad supper with his own.
This, from the blessed land of Aromat —
After the day of darkness, when the dead
Went wandering o'er Moriah — the good saint
Arimathæan Joseph, journeying brought
To Glastonbury, where the winter thorn
Blossoms at Christmas, mindful of our Lord.
And there awhile it bode; and if a man
Could touch or see it, he was heal'd at once,
By faith, of all his ills. But then the times
Grew to such evil that the holy cup
Was caught away to heaven, and disappear'd."

To whom the monk: "From our old books I know
That Joseph came of old to Glastonbury,
And there the heathen Prince, Arviragus,
Gave him an isle of marsh whereon to build;
And there he built with wattles from the marsh
A little lonely church in days of yore,
For so they say, these books of ours, but seem
Mute of this miracle, far as I have read.
But who first saw the holy thing to-day?"

"A woman," answer'd Percivale, "a nun,
And one no further off in blood from me
Than sister; and if ever holy maid
With knees of adoration wore the stone,
A holy maid; tho' never maiden glow'd,
But that was in her earlier maidenhood,
With such a fervent flame of human love,
Which, being rudely blunted, glanced and shot
Only to holy things; to prayer and praise
She gave herself, to fast and alms. And yet,
Nun as she was, the scandal of the Court,
Sin against Arthur and the Table Round,
And the strange sound of an adulterous race,
Across the iron grating of her cell
Beat, and she pray'd and fasted all the more.

"And he to whom she told her sins, or what
Her all but utter whiteness held for sin,
A man wellnigh a hundred winters old,
Spake often with her of the Holy Grail,
A legend handed down thro' five or six,
And each of these a hundred winters old,
From our Lord's time. And when King Arthur made
His Table Round, and all men's hearts became
Clean for a season, surely he had thought
That now the Holy Grail would come again;
But sin broke out. Ah, Christ, that it would come,
And heal the world of all their wickedness!
'O Father!' ask'd the maiden, 'might it come
To me by prayer and fasting?' 'Nay,' said he,
'I know not, for thy heart is pure as snow.'
And so she pray'd and fasted, till the sun

**15. smoke**: give out a cloud of pollen when shaken by the wind. **21. pale**: boundary. **48. Aromat**: Arimathea. **49. of darkness**: of Christ's crucifixion. **50. Moriah**: a hill at Jerusalem, the site of Solomon's temple (see Matt. 27:52–53). **51. Joseph** of Arimathea, who is named in the gospels as having taken Christ's body for burial. **52.** In medieval legend Joseph carried the Grail, the cup used at the Last Supper which later received Christ's blood, to England and founded the abbey of Glastonbury. The thorn tree there that bloomed at Christmas was said to have sprung from his staff. **61. Arviragus**: a legendary king of Britain.

Shone, and the wind blew, thro' her, and I thought
She might have risen and floated when I saw her.

"For on a day she sent to speak with me.
And when she came to speak, behold her eyes
Beyond my knowing of them, beautiful,
Beyond all knowing of them, wonderful,
Beautiful in the light of holiness!
And 'O my brother Percivale,' she said,
'Sweet brother, I have seen the Holy Grail;
For, waked at dead of night, I heard a sound
As of a silver horn from o'er the hills
Blown, and I thought, "It is not Arthur's use
To hunt by moonlight." And the slender sound
As from a distance beyond distance grew
Coming upon me — O never harp nor horn,
Nor aught we blow with breath, or touch with hand,
Was like that music as it came; and then
Stream'd thro' my cell a cold and silver beam,
And down the long beam stole the Holy Grail,
Rose-red with beatings in it, as if alive,
Till all the white walls of my cell were dyed
With rosy colors leaping on the wall;
And then the music faded, and the Grail
Past, and the beam decay'd, and from the walls
The rosy quiverings died into the night.
So now the Holy Thing is here again
Among us, brother, fast thou too and pray,
And tell thy brother knights to fast and pray,
That so perchance the vision may be seen
By thee and those, and all the world be heal'd.'

"Then leaving the pale nun, I spake of this
To all men; and myself fasted and pray'd
Always, and many among us many a week
Fasted and pray'd even to the uttermost,
Expectant of the wonder that would be.

"And one there was among us, ever moved
Among us in white armor, Galahad.
'God make thee good as thou art beautiful!'
Said Arthur, when he dubb'd him knight, and none
In so young youth was ever made a knight
Till Galahad; and this Galahad, when he heard
My sister's vision, fill'd me with amaze;
His eyes became so like her own, they seem'd
Hers, and himself her brother more than I.

"Sister or brother none had he; but some
Call'd him a son of Lancelot, and some said
Begotten by enchantment — chatterers they,
Like birds of passage piping up and down,
That gape for flies — we know not whence they come;
For when was Lancelot wanderingly lewd?

**118. beatings:** pulsations.

"But she, the wan sweet maiden, shore away
Clean from her forehead all that wealth of hair
Which made a silken mat-work for her feet;
And out of this she plaited broad and long
A strong sword-belt, and wove with silver thread
And crimson in the belt a strange device,
A crimson grail within a silver beam;
And saw the bright boy-knight, and bound it on him,
Saying: 'My knight, my love, my knight of heaven,
O thou, my love, whose love is one with mine,
I, maiden, round thee, maiden, bind my belt.
Go forth, for thou shalt see what I have seen,
And break thro' all, till one will crown thee king
Far in the spiritual city;' and as she spake
She sent the deathless passion in her eyes
Thro' him, and made him hers, and laid her mind
On him, and he believed in her belief.

"Then came a year of miracle. O brother,
In our great hall there stood a vacant chair,
Fashion'd by Merlin ere he past away,
And carven with strange figures; and in and out
The figures, like a serpent, ran a scroll
Of letters in a tongue no man could read.
And Merlin call'd it 'the Siege Perilous,'
Perilous for good and ill; 'for there,' he said,
'No man could sit but he should lose himself.'
And once by misadvertence Merlin sat
In his own chair, and so was lost; but he,
Galahad, when he heard of Merlin's doom,
Cried, 'If I lose myself, I save myself!'

"Then on a summer night it came to pass,
While the great banquet lay along the hall,
That Galahad would sit down in Merlin's chair.

"And all at once, as there we sat, we heard
A cracking and a riving of the roofs,
And rending, and a blast, and overhead
Thunder, and in the thunder was a cry.
And in the blast there smote along the hall
A beam of light seven times more clear than day;
And down the long beam stole the Holy Grail
All over cover'd with a luminous cloud,
And none might see who bare it, and it past.
But every knight beheld his fellow's face
As in a glory, and all the knights arose,
And staring each at other like dumb men
Stood, till I found a voice and sware a vow.

**162. spiritual city:** heaven, the new Jerusalem (Rev. 21:2). **168. Merlin:** the magician of the Arthurian tales. **172. Siege Perilous:** the perilous seat, here "the spiritual imagination." 178. See Matt. 10:39.

"I sware a vow before them all, that I,
Because I had not seen the Grail, would ride
A twelvemonth and a day in quest of it,
Until I found and saw it, as the nun
My sister saw it; and Galahad sware the vow,
And good Sir Bors, our Lancelot's cousin, sware,
And Lancelot sware, and many among the knights,
And Gawain sware, and louder than the rest."

Then spake the monk Ambrosius, asking him,
"What said the King? Did Arthur take the vow?"

"Nay, for my lord," said Percivale, "the King,
Was not in hall; for early that same day,
Scaped thro' a cavern from a bandit hold,
An outraged maiden sprang into the hall
Crying on help; for all her shining hair
Was smear'd with earth, and either milky arm
Red-rent with hooks of bramble, and all she wore
Torn as a sail that leaves the rope is torn
In tempest. So the King arose and went
To smoke the scandalous hive of those wild bees
That made such honey in his realm. Howbeit
Some little of this marvel he too saw,
Returning o'er the plain that then began
To darken under Camelot; whence the King
Look'd up, calling aloud, 'Lo, there! the roofs
Of our great hall are roll'd in thunder-smoke!
Pray heaven, they be not smitten by the bolt!'
For dear to Arthur was that hall of ours,
As having there so oft with all his knights
Feasted, and as the stateliest under heaven.

"O brother, had you known our mighty hall,
Which Merlin built for Arthur long ago!
For all the sacred mount of Camelot,
And all the dim rich city, roof by roof,
Tower after tower, spire beyond spire,
By grove, and garden-lawn, and rushing brook,
Climbs to the mighty hall that Merlin built.
And four great zones of sculpture, set betwixt
With many a mystic symbol, gird the hall;
And in the lowest beasts are slaying men,
And in the second men are slaying beasts,
And on the third are warriors, perfect men,
And on the fourth are men with growing wings,
And over all one statue in the mold
Of Arthur, made by Merlin, with a crown,
And peak'd wings pointed to the Northern Star.
And eastward fronts the statue, and the crown
And both the wings are made of gold, and flame
At sunrise till the people in far fields,
Wasted so often by the heathen hordes,
Behold it, crying, 'We have still a king.'

"And, brother, had you known our hall within,
Broader and higher than any in all the lands!
Where twelve great windows blazon Arthur's wars,
And all the light that falls upon the board
Streams thro' the twelve great battles of our King.
Nay, one there is, and at the eastern end,
Wealthy with wandering lines of mount and mere,
Where Arthur finds the brand Excalibur.
And also one to the west, and counter to it,
And blank; and who shall blazon it? when and how? —
O, there, perchance, when all our wars are done,
The brand Excalibur will be cast away!

"So to this hall full quickly rode the King,
In horror lest the work by Merlin wrought,
Dreamlike, should on the sudden vanish, wrapt
In unremorseful folds of rolling fire.
And in he rode, and up I glanced, and saw
The golden dragon sparkling over all;
And many of those who burnt the hold, their arms
Hack'd, and their foreheads grimed with smoke and sear'd,
Follow'd, and in among bright faces, ours,
Full of the vision, prest; and then the King
Spake to me, being nearest, 'Percivale,' —
Because the hall was all in tumult — some
Vowing, and some protesting, — 'what is this?'

"O brother, when I told him what had chanced,
My sister's vision and the rest, his face
Darken'd, as I have seen it more than once,
When some brave deed seem'd to be done in vain,
Darken; and 'Woe is me, my knights,' he cried,
'Had I been here, ye had not sworn the vow.'
Bold was mine answer, 'Had thyself been here,
My King, thou wouldst have sworn.' 'Yea, yea,' said he,
'Art thou so bold and hast not seen the Grail?'

"'Nay, lord, I heard the sound, I saw the light,
But since I did not see the holy thing,
I sware a vow to follow it till I saw.'

"Then when he ask'd us, knight by knight, if any
Had seen it, all their answers were as one:
'Nay, lord, and therefore have we sworn our vows.'

"'Lo, now,' said Arthur, 'have ye seen a cloud?
What go ye into the wilderness to see?'

**232 ff.** The course of human development; cf. *In Memoriam*, CXVIII. **240.** Northern Star: a symbol of fixity and fidelity. **241. eastward**: toward the home of Christianity.

**253. Excalibur**: See "Morte d'Arthur," above. **263. dragon**: a British emblem. **287.** See Matt. 11:7.

"Then Galahad on the sudden, and in a voice
Shrilling along the hall to Arthur, call'd,
'But I, Sir Arthur, saw the Holy Grail,
I saw the Holy Grail and heard a cry—
"O Galahad, and O Galahad, follow me!"'

"'Ah, Galahad, Galahad,' said the King, 'for such
As thou art is the vision, not for these.
Thy holy nun and thou have seen a sign—
Holier is none, my Percivale, than she—
A sign to maim this Order which I made.
But ye that follow but the leader's bell,'—
Brother, the King was hard upon his knights,—
'Taliessin is our fullest throat of song,
And one hath sung and all the dumb will sing.
Lancelot is Lancelot, and hath overborne
Five knights at once, and every younger knight,
Unproven, holds himself as Lancelot,
Till overborne by one, he learns—and ye,
What are ye? Galahads?—no, nor Percivales'—
For thus it pleased the King to range me close
After Sir Galahad;—'nay,' said he, 'but men
With strength and will to right the wrong'd, of power
To lay the sudden heads of violence flat,
Knights that in twelve great battles splash'd and dyed
The strong White Horse in his own heathen blood—
But one hath seen, and all the blind will see.
Go, since your vows are sacred, being made.
Yet—for ye know the cries of all my realm
Pass thro' this hall—how often, O my knights,
Your places being vacant at my side,
This chance of noble deeds will come and go
Unchallenged, while ye follow wandering fires
Lost in the quagmire! Many of you, yea most,
Return no more. Ye think I show myself
Too dark a prophet. Come now, let us meet
The morrow morn once more in one full field
Of gracious pastime, that once more the King,
Before ye leave him for this quest, may count
The yet-unbroken strength of all his knights,
Rejoicing in that Order which he made.'

"So when the sun broke next from underground,
All the great Table of our Arthur closed
And clash'd in such a tourney and so full,
So many lances broken—never yet
Had Camelot seen the like since Arthur came;
And I myself and Galahad, for a strength
Was in us from the vision, overthrew
So many knights that all the people cried,

298. Sheep following the bellwether. **300. Taliessin:** a Welsh bard of the sixth century. **312. White Horse:** a Saxon emblem.

And almost burst the barriers in their heat,
Shouting, 'Sir Galahad and Sir Percivale!'

"But when the next day brake from underground—
O brother, had you known our Camelot,
Built by old kings, age after age, so old
The King himself had fears that it would fall,
So strange, and rich, and dim; for where the roofs
Totter'd toward each other in the sky,
Met foreheads all along the street of those
Who watch'd us pass; and lower, and where the long
Rich galleries, lady-laden, weigh'd the necks
Of dragons clinging to the crazy walls,
Thicker than drops from thunder, showers of flowers
Fell as we past; and men and boys astride
On wyvern, lion, dragon, griffin, swan,
At all the corners, named us each by name,
Calling 'God speed!' but in the ways below
The knights and ladies wept, and rich and poor
Wept, and the King himself could hardly speak
For grief, and all in middle street the Queen,
Who rode by Lancelot, wail'd and shriek'd aloud,
'This madness has come on us for our sins.'
So to the Gate of the Three Queens we came,
Where Arthur's wars are render'd mystically,
And thence departed every one his way.

"And I was lifted up in heart, and thought
Of all my late-shown prowess in the lists,
How my strong lance had beaten down the knights,
So many and famous names; and never yet
Had heaven appear'd so blue, nor earth so green,
For all my blood danced in me, and I knew
That I should light upon the Holy Grail.

"Thereafter, the dark warning of our King,
That most of us would follow wandering fires,
Came like a driving gloom across my mind.
Then every evil word I had spoken once,
And every evil thought I had thought of old,
And every evil deed I ever did,
Awoke and cried, 'This quest is not for thee.'
And lifting up mine eyes, I found myself
Alone, and in a land of sand and thorns,
And I was thirsty even unto death;
And I, too, cried, 'This quest is not for thee.'

"And on I rode, and when I thought my thirst
Would slay me, saw deep lawns, and then a brook,

350. Heraldic emblems. **358. Three Queens:** See the note on "Morte d'Arthur," 249. **379 ff.** Percivale won no content from gratification of sense (379–90), love of wife and family (391–400), wealth (401–20), or glory (421–39).

With one sharp rapid, where the crisping white
Play'd ever back upon the sloping wave
And took both ear and eye; and o'er the brook
Were apple-trees, and apples by the brook
Fallen, and on the lawns. 'I will rest here,'
I said, 'I am not worthy of the quest;'
But even while I drank the brook, and ate
The goodly apples, all these things at once
Fell into dust, and I was left alone
And thirsting in a land of sand and thorns.

"And then behold a woman at a door
Spinning; and fair the house whereby she sat,
And kind the woman's eyes and innocent,
And all her bearing gracious; and she rose
Opening her arms to meet me, as who should say,
'Rest here;' but when I touch'd her, lo! she, too,
Fell into dust and nothing, and the house
Became no better than a broken shed,
And in it a dead babe; and also this
Fell into dust, and I was left alone.

"And on I rode, and greater was my thirst.
Then flash'd a yellow gleam across the world,
And where it smote the plowshare in the field
The plowman left his plowing and fell down
Before it; where it glitter'd on her pail
The milkmaid left her milking and fell down
Before it, and I knew not why, but thought
'The sun is rising,' tho' the sun had risen.
Then was I ware of one that on me moved
In golden armor with a crown of gold
About a casque all jewels, and his horse
In golden armor jeweled everywhere;
And on the splendor came, flashing me blind,
And seem'd to me the lord of all the world,
Being so huge. But when I thought he meant
To crush me, moving on me, lo! he, too,
Open'd his arms to embrace me as he came,
And up I went and touch'd him, and he, too,
Fell into dust, and I was left alone
And wearying in a land of sand and thorns.

"And I rode on and found a mighty hill,
And on the top a city wall'd; the spires
Prick'd with incredible pinnacles into heaven.
And by the gateway stirr'd a crowd; and these
Cried to me climbing, 'Welcome, Percivale!
Thou mightiest and thou purest among men!'
And glad was I and clomb, but found at top
No man, nor any voice. And thence I past
Far thro' a ruinous city, and I saw
That man had once dwelt there; but there I found
Only one man of an exceeding age.
'Where is that goodly company,' said I,
'That so cried out upon me?' and he had
Scarce any voice to answer, and yet gasp'd,
'Whence and what art thou?' and even as he spoke
Fell into dust and disappear'd, and I
Was left alone once more and cried in grief,
'Lo, if I find the Holy Grail itself
And touch it, it will crumble into dust!'

"And thence I dropt into a lowly vale,
Low as the hill was high, and where the vale
Was lowest found a chapel, and thereby
A holy hermit in a hermitage,
To whom I told my phantoms, and he said:

"'O son, thou hast not true humility,
The highest virtue, mother of them all;
For when the Lord of all things made Himself
Naked of glory for His mortal change,
"Take thou my robe," she said, "for all is thine,"
And all her form shone forth with sudden light
So that the angels were amazed, and she
Follow'd Him down, and like a flying star
Led on the gray-hair'd wisdom of the east.
But her thou hast not known; for what is this
Thou thoughtest of thy prowess and thy sins?
Thou hast not lost thyself to save thyself
As Galahad.' When the hermit made an end,
In silver armor suddenly Galahad shone
Before us, and against the chapel door
Laid lance and enter'd, and we knelt in prayer.
And there the hermit slaked my burning thirst,
And at the sacring of the mass I saw
The holy elements alone; but he,
'Saw ye no more? I, Galahad, saw the Grail,
The Holy Grail, descend upon the shrine.
I saw the fiery face as of a child
That smote itself into the bread and went;
And hither am I come; and never yet
Hath what thy sister taught me first to see,
This holy thing, fail'd from my side, nor come
Cover'd, but moving with me night and day,
Fainter by day, but always in the night
Blood-red, and sliding down the blacken'd marsh
Blood-red, and on the naked mountain top
Blood-red, and in the sleeping mere below
Blood-red. And in the strength of this I rode,
Shattering all evil customs everywhere,
And past thro' Pagan realms, and made them mine,
And clash'd with Pagan hordes, and bore them down,
And broke thro' all, and in the strength of this
Come victor. But my time is hard at hand,
And hence I go, and one will crown me king
Far in the spiritual city; and come thou, too,
For thou shalt see the vision when I go.'

**449. she:** humility. **453.** The three Wise Men (Matt. 2).
**462. sacring:** consecration of bread and wine.

"While thus he spake, his eye, dwelling on mine,
Drew me, with power upon me, till I grew
One with him, to believe as he believed.
Then, when the day began to wane, we went.

"There rose a hill that none but man could climb,
Scarr'd with a hundred wintry watercourses —
Storm at the top, and when we gain'd it, storm
Round us and death; for every moment glanced
His silver arms and gloom'd, so quick and thick
The lightnings here and there to left and right
Struck, till the dry old trunks about us, dead,
Yea, rotten with a hundred years of death,
Sprang into fire. And at the base we found
On either hand, as far as eye could see,
A great black swamp and of an evil smell,
Part black, part whiten'd with the bones of men,
Not to be crost, save that some ancient king
Had built a way, where, link'd with many a bridge,
A thousand piers ran into the great Sea.
And Galahad fled along them bridge by bridge,
And every bridge as quickly as he crost
Sprang into fire and vanish'd, tho' I yearn'd
To follow; and thrice above him all the heavens
Open'd and blazed with thunder such as seem'd
Shoutings of all the sons of God. And first
At once I saw him far on the great Sea,
In silver-shining armor starry-clear;
And o'er his head the Holy Vessel hung
Clothed in white samite or a luminous cloud.
And with exceeding swiftness ran the boat,
If boat it were — I saw not whence it came.
And when the heavens open'd and blazed again
Roaring, I saw him like a silver star —
And had he set the sail, or had the boat
Become a living creature clad with wings?
And o'er his head the Holy Vessel hung
Redder than any rose, a joy to me,
For now I knew the veil had been withdrawn.
Then in a moment when they blazed again
Opening, I saw the least of little stars
Down on the waste, and straight beyond the star
I saw the spiritual city and all her spires
And gateways in a glory like one pearl —
No larger, tho' the goal of all the saints —
Strike from the sea; and from the star there shot
A rose-red sparkle to the city, and there
Dwelt, and I knew it was the Holy Grail,
Which never eyes on earth again shall see.
Then fell the floods of heaven drowning the deep.
And how my feet recrost the deathful ridge
No memory in me lives; but that I touch'd
The chapel-doors at dawn I know, and thence
Taking my war-horse from the holy man,
Glad that no phantom vext me more, return'd
To whence I came, the gate of Arthur's wars."

"O brother," ask'd Ambrosius, — "for in sooth
These ancient books — and they would win thee — teem,
Only I find not there this Holy Grail,
With miracles and marvels like to these,
Not all unlike; which oftentime I read,
Who read but on my breviary with ease,
Till my head swims, and then go forth and pass
Down to the little thorpe that lies so close,
And almost plaster'd like a martin's nest
To these old walls — and mingle with our folk;
And knowing every honest face of theirs
As well as ever shepherd knew his sheep,
And every homely secret in their hearts,
Delight myself with gossip and old wives,
And ills and aches, and teethings, lyings-in,
And mirthful sayings, children of the place,
That have no meaning half a league away;
Or lulling random squabbles when they rise,
Chafferings and chatterings at the market-cross,
Rejoice, small man, in this small world of mine,
Yea, even in their hens and in their eggs —
O brother, saving this Sir Galahad,
Came ye on none but phantoms in your quest,
No man, no woman?"

Then Sir Percivale:
"All men, to one so bound by such a vow,
And women were as phantoms. O, my brother,
Why wilt thou shame me to confess to thee
How far I falter'd from my quest and vow?
For after I had lain so many nights,
A bed-mate of the snail and eft and snake,
In grass and burdock, I was changed to wan
And meager, and the vision had not come;
And then I chanced upon a goodly town
With one great dwelling in the middle of it.
Thither I made, and there was I disarm'd
By maidens each as fair as any flower;
But when they led me into hall, behold,
The princess of that castle was the one,
Brother, and that one only, who had ever
Made my heart leap; for when I moved of old
A slender page about her father's hall,
And she a slender maiden, all my heart
Went after her with longing, yet we twain
Had never kiss'd a kiss or vow'd a vow.
And now I came upon her once again,
And one had wedded her, and he was dead,
And all his land and wealth and state were hers.
And while I tarried, every day she set
A banquet richer than the day before
By me, for all her longing and her will

509. Cf. Job 38:7. 513. samite: silken fabric. 526–27. Cf. Rev. 21: 2, 10, 21. 539. Cf. 358–59.

Was toward me as of old; till one fair morn,
I walking to and fro beside a stream
That flash'd across her orchard underneath
Her castle-walls, she stole upon my walk,
And calling me the greatest of all knights,
Embraced me, and so kiss'd me the first time,
And gave herself and all her wealth to me.
Then I remember'd Arthur's warning word,
That most of us would follow wandering fires,
And the quest faded in my heart. Anon,
The heads of all her people drew to me,
With supplication both of knees and tongue:
'We have heard of thee; thou art our greatest knight,
Our Lady says it, and we well believe.
Wed thou our Lady, and rule over us,
And thou shalt be as Arthur in our land.'
O me, my brother! but one night my vow
Burnt me within, so that I rose and fled,
But wail'd and wept, and hated mine own self,
And even the holy quest, and all but her;
Then after I was join'd with Galahad
Cared not for her nor anything upon earth."

Then said the monk: "Poor men, when yule is cold,
Must be content to sit by little fires.
And this am I, so that ye care for me
Ever so little; yea, and blest be heaven
That brought thee here to this poor house of ours
Where all the brethren are so hard, to warm
My cold heart with a friend; but O the pity
To find thine own first love once more — to hold,
Hold her a wealthy bride within thine arms,
Or all but hold, and then — cast her aside,
Foregoing all her sweetness, like a weed!
For we that want the warmth of double life,
We that are plagued with dreams of something sweet
Beyond all sweetness in a life so rich, —
Ah, blessed Lord, I speak too earthly-wise,
Seeing I never stray'd beyond the cell,
But live like an old badger in his earth,
With earth about him everywhere, despite
All fast and penance. Saw ye none beside,
None of your knights?"

"Yea, so," said Percivale:
"One night my pathway swerving east, I saw
The pelican on the casque of our Sir Bors
All in the middle of the rising moon,
And toward him spurr'd, and hail'd him, and he me,
And each made joy of either. Then he ask'd:
'Where is he? hast thou seen him — Lancelot? — Once,'
Said good Sir Bors, 'he dash'd across me — mad,
And maddening what he rode; and when I cried,
"Ridest thou then so hotly on a quest
So holy?" Lancelot shouted, "Stay me not!
I have been the sluggard, and I ride apace,
For now there is a lion in the way!"
So vanish'd.'

"Then Sir Bors had ridden on
Softly, and sorrowing for our Lancelot,
Because his former madness, once the talk
And scandal of our table, had return'd;
For Lancelot's kith and kin so worship him
That ill to him is ill to them, to Bors
Beyond the rest. He well had been content
Not to have seen, so Lancelot might have seen,
The Holy Cup of healing; and, indeed,
Being so clouded with his grief and love,
Small heart was his after the holy quest.
If God would send the vision, well; if not,
The quest and he were in the hands of Heaven.

"And then, with small adventure met, Sir Bors
Rode to the lonest tract of all the realm,
And found a people there among their crags,
Our race and blood, a remnant that were left
Paynim amid their circles, and the stones
They pitch up straight to heaven; and their wise men
Were strong in that old magic which can trace
The wandering of the stars, and scoff'd at him
And this high quest as at a simple thing,
Told him he follow'd — almost Arthur's words —
A mocking fire: 'what other fire than he
Whereby the blood beats, and the blossom blows,
And the sea rolls, and all the world is warm'd?'
And when his answer chafed them, the rough crowd,
Hearing he had a difference with their priests,
Seized him, and bound and plunged him into a cell
Of great piled stones; and lying bounden there
In darkness thro' innumerable hours
He heard the hollow-ringing heavens sweep
Over him till by miracle — what else? —
Heavy as it was, a great stone slipt and fell,
Such as no wind could move; and thro' the gap
Glimmer'd the streaming scud. Then came a night
Still as the day was loud, and thro' the gap
The seven clear stars of Arthur's Table Round —
For, brother, so one night, because they roll

**612. yule**: the big fires of Christmas. Cf. *In Memoriam*, LXXVIII. 5.

**642–43.** See Prov. 22:13, 26:13. **646–47.** In Malory (XI.vii–x) Lancelot's madness was brought on by Guinevere's anger over his relations with King Pelles' daughter. **659 ff.** A people of Druidic religion. **661. circles**: like Stonehenge. **667. he**: the sun. **668. blows**: blooms. **679. scud**: cloud.

Thro' such a round in heaven, we named the stars,
Rejoicing in ourselves and in our King —
And these, like bright eyes of familiar friends,
In on him shone: 'And then to me, to me,'
Said good Sir Bors, 'beyond all hopes of mine,
Who scarce had pray'd or ask'd it for myself —
Across the seven clear stars — O grace to me! —
In color like the fingers of a hand
Before a burning taper, the sweet Grail
Glided and past, and close upon it peal'd
A sharp quick thunder.' Afterwards, a maid,
Who kept our holy faith among her kin
In secret, entering, loosed and let him go."

To whom the monk: "And I remember now
That pelican on the casque. Sir Bors it was
Who spake so low and sadly at our board,
And mighty reverent at our grace was he;
A square-set man and honest, and his eyes,
An outdoor sign of all the warmth within,
Smiled with his lips — a smile beneath a cloud,
But heaven had meant it for a sunny one.
Ay, ay, Sir Bors, who else? But when ye reach'd
The city, found ye all your knights return'd,
Or was there sooth in Arthur's prophecy,
Tell me, and what said each, and what the King?"

Then answer'd Percivale: "And that can I,
Brother, and truly; since the living words
Of so great men as Lancelot and our King
Pass not from door to door and out again,
But sit within the house. O, when we reach'd
The city, our horses stumbling as they trode
On heaps of ruin, hornless unicorns,
Crack'd basilisks, and splinter'd cockatrices,
And shatter'd talbots, which had left the stones
Raw that they fell from, brought us to the hall.

"And there sat Arthur on the dais throne,
And those that had gone out upon the quest,
Wasted and worn, and but a tithe of them,
And those that had not, stood before the King,
Who, when he saw me, rose and bade me hail,
Saying: 'A welfare in thine eyes reproves
Our fear of some disastrous chance for thee
On hill or plain, at sea or flooding ford.
So fierce a gale made havoc here of late
Among the strange devices of our kings,
Yea, shook this newer, stronger hall of ours,
And from the statue Merlin molded for us
Half-wrench'd a golden wing; but now — the quest,
This vision — hast thou seen the Holy Cup
That Joseph brought of old to Glastonbury?'

"So when I told him all thyself hast heard,
Ambrosius, and my fresh but fixt resolve
To pass away into the quiet life,
He answer'd not, but, sharply turning, ask'd
Of Gawain, 'Gawain, was this quest for thee?'

"'Nay, lord,' said Gawain, 'not for such as I.
Therefore I communed with a saintly man,
Who made me sure the quest was not for me;
For I was much a-wearied of the quest,
But found a silk pavilion in a field,
And merry maidens in it; and then this gale
Tore my pavilion from the tenting-pin,
And blew my merry maidens all about
With all discomfort; yea, and but for this,
My twelvemonth and a day were pleasant to me.'

"He ceased; and Arthur turn'd to whom at first
He saw not, for Sir Bors, on entering, push'd
Athwart the throng to Lancelot, caught his hand,
Held it, and there, half-hidden by him, stood,
Until the King espied him, saying to him,
'Hail, Bors! if ever loyal man and true
Could see it, thou hast seen the Grail;' and Bors,
'Ask me not, for I may not speak of it;
I saw it;' and the tears were in his eyes.

"Then there remain'd but Lancelot, for the rest
Spake but of sundry perils in the storm.
Perhaps, like him of Cana in Holy Writ,
Our Arthur kept his best until the last;
'Thou, too, my Lancelot,' ask'd the King, 'my friend,
Our mightiest, hath this quest avail'd for thee?'

"'Our mightiest!' answer'd Lancelot, with a groan;
'O King!' — and when he paused methought I spied
A dying fire of madness in his eyes —
'O King, my friend, if friend of thine I be,
Happier are those that welter in their sin,
Swine in the mud, that cannot see for slime,
Slime of the ditch; but in me lived a sin
So strange, of such a kind, that all of pure,
Noble, and knightly in me twined and clung
Round that one sin, until the wholesome flower
And poisonous grew together, each as each,
Not to be pluck'd asunder; and when thy knights
Sware, I sware with them only in the hope
That could I touch or see the Holy Grail
They might be pluck'd asunder. Then I spake
To one most holy saint, who wept and said

681. The constellation of the Great Bear, revolving around the North Star. 714–16. Carvings of fabulous animals torn from buildings by the wind and not restored. 716. talbots: dogs.

759. See John 2:2–11. 769. sin: his adulterous love for Guinevere.

That, save they could be pluck'd asunder, all
My quest were but in vain; to whom I vow'd
That I would work according as he will'd.
And forth I went, and while I yearn'd and strove
To tear the twain asunder in my heart,
My madness came upon me as of old,
And whipt me into waste fields far away.
There was I beaten down by little men,
Mean knights, to whom the moving of my sword
And shadow of my spear had been enow
To scare them from me once; and then I came
All in my folly to the naked shore,
Wide flats, where nothing but coarse grasses grew;
But such a blast, my King, began to blow,
So loud a blast along the shore and sea,
Ye could not hear the waters for the blast,
Tho' heapt in mounds and ridges all the sea
Drove like a cataract, and all the sand
Swept like a river, and the clouded heavens
Were shaken with the motion and the sound.
And blackening in the sea-foam sway'd a boat,
Half-swallow'd in it, anchor'd with a chain;
And in my madness to myself I said,
"I will embark and I will lose myself,
And in the great sea wash away my sin."
I burst the chain, I sprang into the boat.
Seven days I drove along the dreary deep,
And with me drove the moon and all the stars;
And the wind fell, and on the seventh night
I heard the shingle grinding in the surge,
And felt the boat shock earth, and looking up,
Behold, the enchanted towers of Carbonek,
A castle like a rock upon a rock,
With chasm-like portals open to the sea,
And steps that met the breaker! There was none
Stood near it but a lion on each side
That kept the entry, and the moon was full.
Then from the boat I leapt, and up the stairs,
There drew my sword. With sudden-flaring manes
Those two great beasts rose upright like a man,
Each gript a shoulder, and I stood between,
And, when I would have smitten them, heard a
 voice,
"Doubt not, go forward; if thou doubt, the beasts
Will tear thee piecemeal." Then with violence
The sword was dash'd from out my hand, and fell.
And up into the sounding hall I past;
But nothing in the sounding hall I saw,
No bench nor table, painting on the wall
Or shield of knight, only the rounded moon
Thro' the tall oriel on the rolling sea.
But always in the quiet house I heard,
Clear as a lark, high o'er me as a lark,
A sweet voice singing in the topmost tower
To the eastward. Up I climb'd a thousand steps
With pain; as in a dream I seem'd to climb
For ever; at the last I reach'd a door,
A light was in the crannies, and I heard,
"Glory and joy and honor to our Lord
And to the Holy Vessel of the Grail!"
Then in my madness I essay'd the door;
It gave, and thro' a stormy glare, a heat
As from a seven-times-heated furnace, I,
Blasted and burnt, and blinded as I was,
With such a fierceness that I swoon'd away —
O, yet methought I saw the Holy Grail,
All pall'd in crimson samite, and around
Great angels, awful shapes, and wings and eyes!
And but for all my madness and my sin,
And then my swooning, I had sworn I saw
That which I saw; but what I saw was veil'd
And cover'd, and this quest was not for me.'

"So speaking, and here ceasing, Lancelot left
The hall long silent, till Sir Gawain — nay,
Brother, I need not tell thee foolish words, —
A reckless and irreverent knight was he,
Now bolden'd by the silence of his King, —
Well, I will tell thee: 'O King, my liege,' he said,
'Hath Gawain fail'd in any quest of thine?
When have I stinted stroke in foughten field?
But as for thine, my good friend Percivale,
Thy holy nun and thou have driven men mad,
Yea, made our mightiest madder than our least.
But by mine eyes and by mine ears I swear,
I will be deafer than the blue-eyed cat,
And thrice as blind as any noonday owl,
To holy virgins in their ecstasies,
Henceforward.'

"'Deafer,' said the blameless King,
'Gawain, and blinder unto holy things,
Hope not to make thyself by idle vows,
Being too blind to have desire to see.
But if indeed there came a sign from heaven,
Blessed are Bors, Lancelot, and Percivale,
For these have seen according to their sight.
For every fiery prophet in old times,
And all the sacred madness of the bard,
When God made music thro' them, could but speak
His music by the framework and the chord;
And as ye saw it ye have spoken truth.

"'Nay — but thou errest, Lancelot; never yet
Could all of true and noble in knight and man
Twine round one sin, whatever it might be,
With such a closeness but apart there grew,
Save that he were the swine thou spakest of,

**810. Carbonek**: the castle in which the Grail was said to be kept.

**862.** The deafness of the white, blue-eyed cat is an unexpected item from Darwin's *Origin of Species*, ch. 1.

Some root of knighthood and pure nobleness;
Whereto see thou, that it may bear its flower.

"'And spake I not too truly, O my knights?
Was I too dark a prophet when I said
To those who went upon the Holy Quest,
That most of them would follow wandering fires,
Lost in the quagmire? — lost to me and gone,
And left me gazing at a barren board,
And a lean Order — scarce return'd a tithe —
And out of those to whom the vision came
My greatest hardly will believe he saw.
Another hath beheld it afar off,
And, leaving human wrongs to right themselves,
Cares but to pass into the silent life.
And one hath had the vision face to face,
And now his chair desires him here in vain,
However they may crown him otherwhere.

"'And some among you held that if the King
Had seen the sight he would have sworn the vow.
Not easily, seeing that the King must guard
That which he rules, and is but as the hind
To whom a space of land is given to plow,
Who may not wander from the allotted field
Before his work be done, but, being done,
Let visions of the night or of the day
Come as they will; and many a time they come,
Until this earth he walks on seems not earth,
This light that strikes his eyeball is not light,
This air that smites his forehead is not air
But vision — yea, his very hand and foot —
In moments when he feels he cannot die,
And knows himself no vision to himself,
Nor the high God a vision, nor that One
Who rose again. Ye have seen what ye have seen.'

"So spake the King; I knew not all he meant."

*1869*

## "FRATER AVE ATQUE VALE"

During an Italian tour in 1880 Tennyson lingered on Sirmione, a peninsula in the Lago di Garda where Catullus (?84–?54 B.C.) had a cherished retreat. Tennyson had a special regard for the Roman lyrist, and here he recalls, in a melodious pattern of *o*'s and *a*'s, both a scene of happy associations and Catullus' lament for his dead brother. Tennyson himself had lately lost his favorite brother, Charles.

Row us out from Desenzano, to your Sirmione row!
So they row'd, and there we landed — "O venusta Sirmio!"
There to me thro' all the groves of olive in the summer glow,
There beneath the Roman ruin where the purple flowers grow,
Came that "Ave atque Vale" of the Poet's hopeless woe,
Tenderest of Roman poets nineteen hundred years ago,
"Frater Ave atque Vale" — as we wander'd to and fro
Gazing at the Lydian laughter of the Garda Lake below
Sweet Catullus's all-but-island, olive-silvery Sirmio!

*1883* *1880*

## TO VIRGIL

WRITTEN AT THE REQUEST OF THE MANTUANS FOR THE NINETEENTH CENTENARY OF VIRGIL'S DEATH

Virgil was born near Mantua in 70 B.C. and died in 19 B.C. Mantua celebrated the nineteenth centenary of his death in 1881; Tennyson's poem was published in 1882. This tribute from the most Virgilian of English poets includes phrases that would fit much of his own work. The rolling trochaic lines suggest something of the sound of the Virgilian hexameter.

I

Roman Virgil, thou that singest Ilion's lofty temples robed in fire,
Ilion falling, Rome arising, wars, and filial faith, and Dido's pyre;

II

Landscape-lover, lord of language more than he that sang the "Works and Days,"

892. **he**: Lancelot. 893. **Another**: Percivale. 896. **one**: Galahad. 899–915. Tennyson said that in "The Holy Grail" he expressed his "strong feeling as to the Reality of the Unseen" (*Memoir*, II, 90). Arthur's last speech was "intended to be the summing up of all in the highest note by the highest of human men"; and the lines "In moments . . . nor the high God a vision" (912–14) "are the (spiritually) central lines of the Idylls." "The general English view of God," he added, "is as of an immeasurable clergyman; and some mistake the devil for God." 916. Percivale, the ascetic who withdrew from life, could not understand Arthur's ideal, at once active and mystical.

"FRATER AVE ATQUE VALE." 1. **Desenzano**: a town on Lake Garda near Sirmione. 2. **O venusta [lovely] Sirmio**: from Catullus, XXXI.12. 4. **Roman ruin**: traditionally said to be the remains of Catullus' villa. 5. **Ave atque Vale**: hail and farewell (Catullus, CI.10). The Roman poet's woe was hopeless because he could not look forward to reunion in an afterlife (*Memoir*, II, 239). 8. **Lydian laughter**: from Catullus, XXXI.13. The ancient Etruscans of this region were said to be descended from the Lydians of Asia Minor. 9. **all-but-island**: peninsula (Catullus, XXXI.1). TO VIRGIL. 1–2. **singest**: in the *Aeneid*. 2. **Ilion**: Troy. 3. **he**: the Greek poet Hesiod.

All the chosen coin of fancy flashing out from many
a golden phrase;

III

Thou that singest wheat and woodland, tilth and
vineyard, hive and horse and herd;
All the charm of all the Muses often flowering in a
lonely word;

IV

Poet of the happy Tityrus piping underneath his
beechen bowers;
Poet of the poet-satyr whom the laughing shepherd
bound with flowers;

V

Chanter of the Pollio, glorying in the blissful years
again to be,
Summers of the snakeless meadow, unlaborious
earth and oarless sea;

VI

Thou that seest Universal Nature moved by Universal Mind;
Thou majestic in thy sadness at the doubtful doom
of human kind;

VII

Light among the vanish'd ages; star that gildest
yet this phantom shore;
Golden branch amid the shadows, kings and realms
that pass to rise no more;

VIII

Now thy Forum roars no longer, fallen every purple
Caesar's dome —
Tho' thine ocean-roll of rhythm sound for ever of
Imperial Rome —

IX

Now the Rome of slaves hath perish'd, and the
Rome of freemen holds her place,
I, from out the Northern Island sunder'd once from
all the human race,

X

I salute thee, Mantovano, I that loved thee since
my day began,
Wielder of the stateliest measure ever molded by
the lips of man.

*1882*

5. Virgil's four *Georgics*. 7. *Eclogue* I. 8. *Eclogue* VI. 9–10. The fourth or "Messianic" *Eclogue*, celebrating a new golden age of peace, in which Virgil addresses his patron, the consul Asinius Pollio. 11–12. The *Aeneid*, especially VI. 14. Virgil shines out of the past like the golden bough that Aeneas carried into the underworld (*Aeneid*, VI.208 ff.). 17. With the liberation and unification of Italy in 1870, Rome was freed from foreign and papal control. 18. An echo of *Eclogue* I.66.

# DEMETER AND PERSEPHONE

(IN ENNA)

This poem, the last of Tennyson's dramatic monologues based on classical myth, was written in May, 1887, and published in 1889; it is an astonishing production for a poet in his seventy-eighth year. Moreover, though his initial or ostensible theme, suggested by his son Hallam, was "Motherhood" (*Memoir,* II, 364) — which might sound ominous — his treatment is more "mythic" and "primitive" than most of the earlier poems had been. Tennyson has not, to be sure, abandoned his old and fruitful habit of reinterpretation, and the conclusion presents, in mythological terms, his hope of progress, the "one far-off divine event, To which the whole creation moves." Yet the speech of Demeter (Ceres) to her daughter Persephone (Proserpine), now wife of the king of the underworld, while it ends on the note of spring and rebirth and love, creates a dominant effect of vague foreboding, of the mysterious terrors that envelop life, of the menace of sterility and death. As befits a poem concerned with the visit to earth of the queen of Hades, much use is made of images of light and darkness. Tennyson's main source was apparently the "Homeric Hymn to Demeter," which tells of the mother's long and agonized search for her daughter after Pluto had carried her off. There are studies of the poem by G. R. Stange, *ELH, A Journal of English Literary History,* XXI (1954), and C. Dahl, *Victorian Studies,* I (1958).

Faint as a climate-changing bird that flies
All night across the darkness, and at dawn
Falls on the threshold of her native land,
And can no more, thou camest, O my child,
Led upward by the God of ghosts and dreams,
Who laid thee at Eleusis, dazed and dumb
With passing thro' at once from state to state,
Until I brought thee hither, that the day,
When here thy hands let fall the gather'd flower,
Might break thro' clouded memories once again
On thy lost self. A sudden nightingale
Saw thee, and flash'd into a frolic of song
And welcome; and a gleam as of the moon,
When first she peers along the tremulous deep,
Fled wavering o'er thy face, and chased away

19. **Mantovano:** Mantuan. DEMETER AND PERSEPHONE. 5. **God . . . dreams:** Hermes (Mercury), who conducted the dead to Hades. 6. **Eleusis:** a town in Attica which had a great temple to Demeter and was the seat of the Eleusinian mysteries. 9. Persephone, gathering flowers in the Sicilian vale of Enna, let them fall when she was seized by Pluto.

That shadow of a likeness to the king
Of shadows, thy dark mate. Persephone!
Queen of the dead no more — my child! Thine eyes
Again were human-godlike, and the Sun
Burst from a swimming fleece of winter gray,
And robed thee in his day from head to feet —
"Mother!" and I was folded in thine arms.

Child, those imperial, disimpassion'd eyes
Awed even me at first, thy mother — eyes
That oft had seen the serpent-wanded power
Draw downward into Hades with his drift
Of flickering specters, lighted from below
By the red race of fiery Phlegethon;
But when before have Gods or men beheld
The Life that had descended re-arise,
And lighted from above him by the Sun?
So mighty was the mother's childless cry,
A cry that rang thro' Hades, Earth, and Heaven!

So in this pleasant vale we stand again,
The field of Enna, now once more ablaze
With flowers that brighten as thy footstep falls,
All flowers — but for one black blur of earth
Left by that closing chasm, thro' which the car
Of dark Aïdoneus rising rapt thee hence.
And here, my child, tho' folded in thine arms,
I feel the deathless heart of motherhood
Within me shudder, lest the naked glebe
Should yawn once more into the gulf, and thence
The shrilly whinnyings of the team of Hell,
Ascending, pierce the glad and songful air,
And all at once their arch'd necks, midnight-maned,
Jet upward thro' the midday blossom. No!
For, see, thy foot has touch'd it; all the space
Of blank earth-baldness clothes itself afresh,
And breaks into the crocus-purple hour
That saw thee vanish.

Child, when thou wert gone,
I envied human wives, and nested birds,
Yea, the cubb'd lioness; went in search of thee
Thro' many a palace, many a cot, and gave
Thy breast to ailing infants in the night,
And set the mother waking in amaze
To find her sick one whole; and forth again
Among the wail of midnight winds, and cried,
"Where is my loved one? Wherefore do ye wail?"
And out from all the night an answer shrill'd,
"We know not, and we know not why we wail."
I climb'd on all the cliffs of all the seas,
And ask'd the waves that moan about the world,
"Where? do ye make your moaning for my child?"
And round from all the world the voices came,
"We know not, and we know not why we moan."
"Where?" and I stared from every eagle-peak,
I thridded the black heart of all the woods,
I peer'd thro' tomb and cave, and in the storms
Of autumn swept across the city, and heard
The murmur of their temples chanting me,
Me, me, the desolate Mother! "Where?" — and turn'd,
And fled by many a waste, forlorn of man,
And grieved for man thro' all my grief for thee, —
The jungle rooted in his shatter'd hearth,
The serpent coil'd about his broken shaft,
The scorpion crawling over naked skulls; —
I saw the tiger in the ruin'd fane
Spring from his fallen God, but trace of thee
I saw not; and far on, and, following out
A league of labyrinthine darkness, came
On three gray heads beneath a gleaming rift.
"Where?" and I heard one voice from all the three,
"We know not, for we spin the lives of men,
And not of Gods, and know not why we spin!
There is a Fate beyond us." Nothing knew.

Last as the likeness of a dying man,
Without his knowledge, from him flits to warn
A far-off friendship that he comes no more,
So he, the God of dreams, who heard my cry,
Drew from thyself the likeness of thyself
Without thy knowledge, and thy shadow past
Before me, crying, "The Bright one in the highest
Is brother of the Dark one in the lowest,
And Bright and Dark have sworn that I, the child
Of thee, the great Earth-Mother, thee, the Power
That lifts her buried life from gloom to bloom,
Should be for ever and for evermore
The Bride of Darkness."

So the Shadow wail'd.
Then I, Earth-Goddess, cursed the Gods of Heaven.
I would not mingle with their feasts; to me
Their nectar smack'd of hemlock on the lips,
Their rich ambrosia tasted aconite.
The man, that only lives and loves an hour,
Seem'd nobler than their hard Eternities.
My quick tears kill'd the flower, my ravings hush'd
The bird, and lost in utter grief I fail'd
To send my life thro' olive-yard and vine
And golden-grain, my gift to helpless man.
Rain-rotten died the wheat, the barley-spears

**25. serpent-wanded power:** Hermes. **28. Phlegethon:** the river of fire in Hades. **39. Aïdoneus:** Pluto, who drove his chariot up through the earth to carry off Persephone. **55. Thy breast:** Demeter's breast, which had nurs ed Persephone in her infancy.

**68. thridded:** threaded. **82. three . . . heads:** the Fates. **87–89.** The idea may come from Lucretius, *De Rerum Natura,* IV.34–37, 760–61. **93. Bright one:** Zeus. **94. Dark one:** Pluto.

Were hollow-husk'd, the leaf fell, and the Sun,
Pale at my grief, drew down before his time
Sickening, and Ætna kept her winter snow.

Then He, the brother of this Darkness, He
Who still is highest, glancing from his height
On earth a fruitless fallow, when he miss'd
The wonted steam of sacrifice, the praise
And prayer of men, decreed that thou shouldst dwell
For nine white moons of each whole year with me,
Three dark ones in the shadow with thy King.

Once more the reaper in the gleam of dawn
Will see me by the landmark far away,
Blessing his field, or seated in the dusk
Of even, by the lonely threshing-floor,
Rejoicing in the harvest and the grange.

Yet I, Earth-Goddess, am but ill-content
With them who still are highest. Those gray heads,
What meant they by their "Fate beyond the Fates"
But younger kindlier Gods to bear us down,
As we bore down the Gods before us? Gods,
To quench, not hurl the thunderbolt, to stay,
Not spread the plague, the famine; Gods indeed,
To send the noon into the night and break
The sunless halls of Hades into Heaven?
Till thy dark lord accept and love the Sun,
And all the Shadow die into the Light,
When thou shalt dwell the whole bright year with me,
And souls of men, who grew beyond their race,
And made themselves as Gods against the fear
Of Death and Hell; and thou that hast from men,
As Queen of Death, that worship which is Fear,
Henceforth, as having risen from out the dead,
Shalt ever send thy life along with mine
From buried grain thro' springing blade, and bless
Their garner'd autumn also, reap with me,
Earth-Mother, in the harvest hymns of Earth
The worship which is Love, and see no more
The Stone, the Wheel, the dimly-glimmering lawns
Of that Elysium, all the hateful fires
Of torment, and the shadowy warrior glide
Along the silent field of Asphodel.

*1889* *1887*

## CROSSING THE BAR

The poem was written and published in 1889, in Tennyson's eighty-first year; he said that it came to him in a moment. A few days before his death he expressed the wish that it should be printed at the end of all editions of his poems (*Memoir*, II, 366–67). However one regards the poem, which has been both admired and detested, it may be thought that Tennyson faces death with a dignity and a sense of mystery that are somewhat lacking in Browning's equally characteristic "Prospice" and "Epilogue."

Sunset and evening star,
And one clear call for me!
And may there be no moaning of the bar,
When I put out to sea,

But such a tide as moving seems asleep,
Too full for sound and foam,
When that which drew from out the boundless deep
Turns again home.

Twilight and evening bell,
And after that the dark!
And may there be no sadness of farewell,
When I embark;

For tho' from out our bourne of Time and Place
The flood may bear me far,
I hope to see my Pilot face to face
When I have crost the bar.

*1889* *1889*

**114. He:** Zeus. **129–30.** Cf. Aeschylus, *Prometheus Bound*, 907 ff.; Keats, *Hyperion*, II.188 ff. **148.** Traditional punishments in Hades: the stone forever rolled by Sisyphus, the wheel of Ixion (for Ixion, see the note on "Lucretius," 260). **150–51.** Cf. the ghost of Achilles, *Odyssey*, XI.538–39, and the note on "The Lotos-Eaters," 125. CROSSING THE BAR. **7–8. that:** the soul (cf. *In Memoriam*, Epilogue, 123–24). **15.** It has been objected that a pilot would be seen while navigating, and would be dropped when the ship left harbor. Tennyson's image is governed by the idea of the Pilot as "That Divine and Unseen Who is always guiding us" (*Memoir*, II, 367).

**WILLIAM C. DeVANE, *Editor***

# Robert Browning

**1812–1889**

The mental picture that most of us have of famous men in history is a static rather than a developing one. The usual image of Robert Browning in the popular mind is an apt illustration of this generality. The poet is most often remembered as he was at the height of his fame during the last two decades of his life, that is, from 1868 to 1889. This is to see him as a robust, hearty, elderly man, a great diner-out and visitor in fashionable homes, a constant attender at concerts and art exhibitions, honored by both of the great English universities, and also beloved and cared for by wealthy ladies, British as well as American. He was immensely successful, it seemed, in his public and his private life. Societies of earnest people, led by the London Browning Society, had sprung up in England and America to study the writings of the sage and prophet of the age. An observer watching him move at his ease in London's high society might have remembered the words that Ben Jonson had written about Francis Bacon: "His fate was spun out of the finest and the softest wool." So busy was he, and so much a man of the social world, that the legend rose, abetted by his friend Henry James the American novelist, that the familiar man people saw was not the author of the rich body of poetry which everyone knew, but that Browning kept a "ghost" to write his verse.

Of course, there was nothing to the legend. Nor was this the Browning who had struggled hard, and for years desperately, from the beginning of his literary career in 1833 almost until he published *The Ring and the Book* in 1868–69, to make his voice as a poet heard by a deaf world. The British public had grossly and undeservedly neglected him in his best days as a poet, and now honored and rewarded him, perhaps extravagantly. With his keen sense of irony, the words of his fellow poet, Matthew Arnold, in a poem that was probably written as an answer to his own "Rabbi Ben Ezra," must have come home to him. In "Growing Old" Arnold remarks how bitter it is "To hear the world applaud the hollow ghost / Which blamed the living man." But few people who saw the stocky, bearded, brisk, and cheerful Browning of the 70's and 80's thought of him as "ghostly" in any sense. He was all too palpably there in the flesh. Henry James thought of him as an "accomplished, saturated, sane, sound man of the London world."

Under the impact of the Industrial Revolution and the growth of empire, the London of the late nineteenth century was a very different place from what it was in Browning's youth. The suburb, Camberwell, where the poet was born on May 7, 1812, was across the Thames and south of the city. It is now a mass of brick buildings, alleys, and noisy streets. But when Browning was a boy, it was a green and pleasant place, and he remembered it all his life with nostalgia.

The Browning family was in modest circumstances. The poet's father, Robert Browning, Sr., was a clerk in the Bank of England on a small salary. In his youth he had been sent out to the family plantation in the West Indies, but when he revolted from the slavery and cruelty there and returned to England, his father, the first

Robert Browning about whom we know much, found him a minor place in the Bank, which he held until his retirement in 1852. The poet's father was an amiable, mild, self-effacing person, more of a scholar than a man of business. In his youth he had hoped to be an artist, and all his life he drew sketches and illustrations to amuse his children and friends. His chief delight was in collecting odd and rare books, and much of his salary must have gone into that pleasure. In his library of 6000 volumes, made up of Greek, Latin, and recondite English books, the poet got most of his education.

Browning's mother, Sarah Anna Wiedemann, was of German and Scotch descent, and of a rigid and somewhat unimaginative mind and temperament. It was she who controlled the destinies of the family and made all decisions. Apart from her family her interest in life was almost wholly religious. She was an ardent member of the Congregational chapel, and in time brought all her family to worship there. Beyond that we know little of her, except that she had some gift in music, spent a good deal of time in her rose garden, and that her son and her daughter, Sarianna, who much resembled her, were passionately devoted to her all their lives. Her character and temperament influenced the poet far more than her husband's did.

Here, then, in Camberwell and later at New Cross, further to the southeast from London, young Browning was reared. He was a precocious schoolboy, and was often unruly and impatient. It is recorded that at his mother's chapel the preacher, George Clayton, publicly reproved "for restlessness and inattention Master Robert Browning." He rebelled from school, as he was later to rebel from London University, and was mainly taught by his father and a series of tutors and masters in Greek, Latin, French, music, and Italian. The odd learning for which he became famous was chiefly acquired at home by omnivorous reading. For his pleasure, he roamed the fields and woods nearby, rode horseback in the country lanes, or walked to the Dulwich Gallery to see its notable pictures. He grew up to be a passionate, brilliant, undisciplined boy with an inordinate estimate of his own powers, which were yet very great.

Such was the environment of this richly endowed young man. As he grew older his problem was how to break out of the physical and intellectual suburb into the great world of London, how to employ his extraordinary powers to become a significant and recognized person, how to escape from the constricting — and to him almost suffocating — ideas of the middle-class chapel-going and business world in which he found himself. His home was an oasis in a desert of materialism and smug provincialism. Early Victorian middle-class society had two main preoccupations — the daily task of making a living in an aggressive and expanding city, and the illiberal and narrow piety of the Dissenting chapel on Sunday. Very few of the young men of Camberwell and New Cross had the advantages of the great public schools like Arnold's Rugby, and even fewer went on to Oxford and Cambridge. For the most part, they were excluded by their poverty and by their limited abilities and imaginations from ever attaining a fuller and freer life. But for a young man of Browning's ambition, power, and taste, escape to the larger world was as necessary as breathing. For three-quarters of his life he struggled in various ways to establish himself among his peers in this larger world — like his own *dramatis persona* Paracelsus he aspired and was defeated, aspired again and was baffled, and aspired again to achieve success at last.

One of the victories of Browning's adolescence was his triumph in persuading his family that he should become a poet. The Brownings' financial resources were limited, and the reasonable expectancy was that their son at manhood would enter some trade or profession by which he could support himself. Instead, until his marriage at 33, his family supported him, and in addition paid for the publication of most of his poetry, which brought practically no financial return. He had to borrow money for his wedding journey to Italy, and then for many years he and his wife were mainly dependent upon her income. The world has reason to be grateful to him for this conduct, which at the time must have seemed extraordinarily selfish and stubborn.

When Browning was fourteen years old the first great avenue of escape into the intellectual world seemed to open before him. This was his discovery of Shelley, a poet little appreciated in 1826. From that poet's *Miscellaneous Poems* Browning went on to devour all of Shelley's works he could come by, including *Queen Mab,* and a new world was revealed to him. He became a disciple, and like his master a vegetarian in diet, an extreme liberal in politics, and an atheist in religion. For the better part of six years he preached Shelley, grinning with devilish delight when he upset the orthodox faith of a young lady of his affections or discomfited his friends. The young lady, Sarah Flower, soon recovered her faith sufficiently to write the famous hymn, "Nearer My God to Thee."

But there were strong and subtle forces working against Browning's rebellion. Of the pain that the wildness of the young man's opinions, especially his atheism, brought to his matter-of-fact and pious mother we have no record. But it must have been great. It is clear that Browning's intense affection for her gradually won him back from his atheism, and in his first poem *Pauline,* published in 1833, the young poet professes to believe in "God and truth" rather than Shelley. He disavows Shelley's doctrine as he was late in life to disavow Shelley himself. Mrs. Browning had won, not by the employment of reason, but by the tender ties of love, and her son's intellectual independence in religious inquiry was permanently impaired. He never managed to free himself entirely from the narrow and emotional bases of his mother's religion.

As he grew older, other avenues of possible escape opened before him. The chief one was literary. Shelley's religious opinions were repudiated, but his poetry and poetic method were still compelling. From 1833, when *Pauline* was published, until 1840, when *Sordello* appeared, Browning tried strenuously to make his voice heard in the literary world of London through the long "confessional" poem, recounting his deepest aspirations and defeats in the intensely personal manner of Shelley. But *Pauline* sold no copies and was hardly noticed by the reviewers, and survived only to shame its author. *Paracelsus* (1835) enjoyed a brief success and took Browning for a little while into the company of the great artistic and literary world of London. The society into which Browning came was brilliant: it included Macready, the greatest tragic actor of the day; John Forster, the influential literary critic; Wordsworth, who was in a few years to become poet laureate; and Maclise, the painter and friend of Dickens. At a dinner in 1836 Wordsworth himself proposed a toast to Browning and welcomed him to the company of the poets of England. But the colossal failure of *Sordello,* upon which he had spent seven years of hard labor, was a serious blow to Browning's reputation in literary London, and one from which he recovered only slowly.

In the meanwhile he made a different attempt in drama for the stage, and this lasted from 1837, when *Strafford* was produced, until his marriage in 1846. Upon this effort Browning broke his heart and his head, but his peculiar analytical talents were not suited to the acting stage, and none of his eight plays achieved success upon the boards. The plays are often full of magnificent poetry and superb analysis of character and motive, but are frequently lacking in external action and are recondite to the point of obscurity. In his attempts to become an accepted playwright Browning quarreled with Macready the tragedian and Forster the critic, and once again was baffled.

Though admired by a few and defended by his friends, such as Alfred Dommett and Joseph Arnould (who like the poet were not typical of their environment and were later in life to become important colonial administrators), Browning was at thirty-two a social figure in a limited circle, and a poet read by a small intellectual coterie. He was hardly prepared for the change in his way of life that was soon to come to him. In 1844 he went off to Italy to refresh his jaded spirit. Upon his return to England toward the end of the year, he found waiting for him two volumes of poems by Elizabeth Barrett. These poems, mainly lays, ballads, and romances, had been widely praised and had won for Miss Barrett the position of being, after Tennyson and Wordsworth, the foremost poet of the age. Browning read the poems with a rising excitement, and on January 10, 1845, wrote the lady: "I love your poems, dear Miss Barrett, and I love you too." But it was not until May of that year that Browning was permitted to call. He found Miss Barrett in her invalid's darkened room, a frail, small lady chained by weakness to her couch, her dark, heavy hair framing her sensitive and intelligent face. She saw few people beyond her family and wrote her poetry from her reading and her vivid imagination. She was then thirty-eight years old and had been an invalid for ten years. The passionate and jealous love which her father had for her was an even greater chain than her illness. The visits of Browning, or indeed of any man, were not welcomed by Mr. Barrett, and Browning had to come when Mr. Barrett was not at home. On Browning's side it was a case of love at first sight, or even before he had seen Miss Barrett. He proposed marriage after his first visit to her. Of course it was impossible, but his visits became more frequent, letters flew between them, and before a year was out an understanding had been reached. Miss Barrett began secretly to write her famous sonnet sequence, *Sonnets from the Portuguese*. Her health improved almost miraculously. Her father, perhaps sensing that he was losing control over his daughter's affections and actions, became more tyrannous than ever. And thus it came about that in September, 1846, Browning and Miss Barrett were married secretly and a week later fled to Italy.

The Browning who entered Miss Barrett's room in 1845 was assuredly not the confident, aggressive character we see in the modern play, *The Barretts of Wimpole Street*. Rather, while hopeful still that one day his genius would be recognized, he was humbled by his failure to obtain readers, and needed to have his confidence in himself restored by the admiration of a successful poet. In this, Miss Barrett succeeded and continued to succeed for a while after they were married and lived in Italy. But in those happy years of marriage it was Mrs. Browning that the visitors from America and England came to see. She was the poet and Browning only the husband — a man of talent, to be sure, extremely well informed about many things, a good man of business and entertaining company, a man one might rely upon. He could be seen in the streets of Florence with an old dog at his heels, poking into art shops or merely watching the bustling life of the city.

In 1850 Browning's long poem, "Christmas Eve and Easter Day," sold only 200 copies. This was disheartening, but after two years he resolved to try his fortune again. In the 40's a few of his shorter poems, such as "The Bishop Orders His Tomb" and "My Last Duchess," had been well received; Walter Savage Landor, the revered veteran among the poets, had praised him; and he now resolved to try to make his voice heard with two volumes of short poems, dramatic monologues, and lyrics, dealing in part with art and music. The result is the two volumes of *Men and Women* (1855), one of the great achievements of English literature. But his great hopes were soon dashed when the reviewers found the poems obscure; John Ruskin, who by his great books on painting, architecture, and literature had become the arbiter of taste, disapproved; and the public refused to buy and read them. It was a wounded and resentful Browning who turned back from London to life in Italy. There he resumed his place, overshadowed by his wife and allowed by that passionate and strong-minded lady to have little voice in the bringing up of their child. He was, rather, the stable element in the household, tempering as best he could the ardently held ideas of his wife upon public and private affairs. The Brownings were now financially in good condition through the immense sales of Mrs. Browning's *Aurora Leigh* (1856) and the beneficence of John Kenyon, a relative of Mrs. Browning's and a patron of poetry, who left them £11,000.

In 1861 Mrs. Browning died, and the grief-stricken husband and his thirteen-year-old son returned to London to make their home. There was much to be done. For the first time Browning had to assume in a real sense the role of parent and to make decisions. A home had to be established. An authoritative final edition of his wife's poetry had to be prepared. And yet, even in these dark hours of loneliness and grief, his own fortunes began to take a better turn. A selection of his poems prepared by friends enjoyed a considerable success in 1863, and his volume of new poems, *Dramatis Personae* (1864) achieved a second edition. News also came from America of the increasing popularity of his works. Greatly heartened, he resolved to produce a monumental work which would establish him once and forever among the great poets of England.

In 1864 he was fifty-two years old, and he had finally made an impression upon the public mind, mainly by his amazing short poems, lyrics, and dramatic monologues. But he wished to be remembered by an altogether greater achievement. He now aspired to write a poem of epic length in which he would employ all his peculiar techniques and talents — his mastery of the dramatic monologue in blank verse, his forte in reinterpreting fact, his defense of innocent and misunderstood virtue, his analysis of motive and character, the mobility and variety of his expression. Above all he wished to give the public his reading of life in all its variety and scope. His great work was, after four years of constant labor, *The Ring and the Book,* a poem upon an obscure Roman murder case of the seventeenth century in twelve dramatic monologues, amounting to more than 21,000 lines. It was published in four volumes in 1868–69.

The effect upon the reading public was impressive. Browning's reputation had been growing quietly at the universities among the younger men, and now his poem was called "the greatest spiritual treasure since Shakespeare," and he was accepted almost everywhere as the peer of the laureate, Alfred Tennyson. Henceforth he was established by his contemporaries among the great poets of English literature, even though many readers objected to the nature of his subject, the inordinate length of the poem, and the poet's mannerisms. It was a somewhat superficial view of his reading of life that made an appeal to his fellow Victorians; it has remained for our own day to discover the full subtlety and depth of Browning's art.

In the two decades of life that remained to him he wrote an immense amount that added little to his fame, and his poetry grew more craggy and wayward as he allowed himself to indulge more and more in his peculiarities of style and subject. In his pride of accomplishment he bore prosperity less well than he had adversity. But the goal of a lifetime had been achieved; however imperfectly he was understood, the public was listening to his voice. And he had good reason to feel, in spite of life's ironies and disappointments — such as the failure of his son to achieve anything worthy of note — that for the valiant and enduring man old age was "the last of life, for which the first was made."

## II

It has been said that in literature as in life sympathy often skips a generation. A reaction is especially likely to follow when a group of strong authors has captured the minds and imaginations of its generation almost completely. This was the case with the great figures of Victorian literature. During the first four decades of the twentieth century the critics, led by T. S. Eliot, were scornful of the Victorian poets, but now there are clear evidences of a reviving interest in them and a willingness once again to rank the greatest of them with their peers of older times in the main tradition of English literature. Browning has weathered the reaction, and now may be spoken of in the same breath with Chaucer, Spenser, Shakespeare, Donne, Milton, Dryden, Wordsworth, and Keats.

There had been, however, no very violent reaction on the part of the Victorian poets from their Romantic predecessors. There was, indeed, change, but also continuity. Tennyson carried on in the manner of Keats, and Arnold championed and followed Wordsworth. Browning, as we have seen, modeled his first long poems upon the practice of Shelley, and his plays, written early in his career, owe a great debt to the Shakespeare of the Romantic poets and critics, the Shakespeare of Coleridge, Lamb, Hazlitt, De Quincey, and Byron. This was the Shakespeare of the study rather than the writer of successful plays for the stage, the infallible Shakespeare whose management of the psychology of character and dramatic action was to be explained rather than questioned, the Shakespeare of the lofty and resounding blank verse.

Browning, like most great poets who deal with character and important moral issues, matured slowly, and the models provided for him by Shelley and Shakespeare were not the right ones for him. He had to work his way through the long, personal "confessional" poem of the Romantic tradition in *Pauline, Paracelsus,* and *Sordello* in order to find out what he could and could not do. From the process he learned a great deal about psychology, and he learned to watch and analyze his emotions and thoughts as they rose to the surface of his consciousness. In his career as a playwright also, he learned what he could not do, namely, endow and project a character in action on the stage with life and expression independent of its author. He was too much an analyst of motive to be a great playwright, but from his struggle to become one he learned such things as form, situation, order, and control. In the long partly autobiographical poems, and even more in the plays, there is a great deal of psychological action in the minds of the speakers, but Browning was not able to translate the feelings and thoughts of his characters into the external action and language required for success on the stage and for complete comprehension by readers. He made considerable progress in the swift dramatic episodes of *Pippa Passes* (1841). But only gradually did he find the right ground for himself, the soliloquy of a character (not himself) who, usually in a moment of crisis, speaks out his deepest thoughts and feelings, and is generally not conscious of how profoundly he is disclosing his true nature. This is, of course, the dramatic monologue.

In many aspects of poetry Browning was an innovator, but never more happily than in his development of the dramatic monologue. He can hardly be called the inventor of this form. Chaucer had used it, and so had Shakespeare in the monologues of *Hamlet*. And so had Tennyson, among Browning's contemporaries. But it was Browning who developed the dramatic monologue so completely, so subtly, and so penetratingly that he gave it new life and dimensions. It is most fitting that the form should be attached to his name. In it he has given English literature such great and memorable figures as the Duke in "My Last Duchess," the Bishop who orders his tomb, Lippi and Andrea, Pompilia, Caponsacchi, Guido, and the Pope, to name only a few from a great host. The dramatic monologue became a habit of Browning's thinking, and his natural mode of expression was at last to break the clear white light of his thought and feeling into its prismatic hues through the medium of a borrowed ego.

The dramatic monologue is at its best when the poet employs all its elements: a speaker; his audience; interplay between them; dramatic occasion and present action; and, above all, revelation of character.

It must not be imagined that Browning arrived at perfection in the form at once and easily, or having reached that perfection was always able to sustain it. Many rival interests make claims against the pure delineation of personality which is the ideal of the monologue. For example, in "Porphyria's Lover" Browning is too much interested in the strange event, and the rhymed verse is not the best vehicle; in "My Last Duchess," which is nearly perfect, the character of the Duke looks like an afterthought, as if Browning's interest began with the plight of the young duchess, and the verse, though muted, is still rhymed. Even in "The Bishop Orders His Tomb," where blank verse is at last arrived at as the right verse form, the poet may be suspected of being more concerned with illustrating the corruption of Renaissance clergy than he is with the Bishop himself. The danger of caricature is not escaped in the speaker of the "Soliloquy of the Spanish Cloister" and in the Italian Person of Quality in "Up at the Villa." There is frequently, also, the intrusion of doctrine or purpose — Browning's doctrine — into the utterances of his characters, and one may cite in this regard David in "Saul," Cleon, Fra Lippo Lippi, Caponsacchi, and the Pope. Browning's personality even in his full maturity is sometimes stronger than his art, and he is unable often to achieve that complete subjugation of his own person and opinions which so distinguishes Shakespeare. These are impurities in the substance and form of the poems. Perhaps "Andrea del Sarto" is as near perfection in the dramatic monologue as Browning ever attained, and the primary reason for this perfection may be that Andrea's nature was as unlike Browning's as it could be. A similar claim may be made for several monologues in which Browning's villains speak — such as Guido in *The Ring and the Book*. When all is said, Browning is one of the great creators of character and types in our literature, and he has stamped the dramatic monologue as peculiarly his own. His method of subtle analysis, penetrating even to the secret recesses of the heart, has had a palpable and lasting effect upon later English and American literature.

Closely connected with this achievement was another. Because he was the close observer and the conscientious recorder of life, Browning achieved an objectivity in his treatment of men and women which had not been characteristic of the Romantic poets, or of English poetry since the eighteenth century. The exception to this generalization was the Byron of "Beppo" and *Don Juan,* and it was this aspect of Byron that Browning particularly liked. The predilection toward objectivity led Browning to be realistic in his description of life, in the characters he created, and in the language he employed —

a language that sometimes shocked his fellow Victorians into thinking him vulgar. He dealt daringly with subjects that offended the proprieties of his time, and also with socially unapproved characters. He reintroduced new, racy, common words into the prevailing bardic utterances of the age of Tennyson. He put into verse such things as corsetstrings and bottles of ether and aching corns. It was sarcastically remarked that his finest lines were those from "Up at a Villa":

*Bang-whang-whang* goes the drum, *tootle-te-tootle* the fife;
No keeping one's haunches still; it's the greatest pleasure in life.

An eminently characteristic phrase occurs in "Bishop Blougram's Apology": "don't jog the ice."

The pure and simple language of everyday life which Wordsworth had advocated in his Preface to the *Lyrical Ballads* (see above in this volume) and had sometimes employed was hardly what Wordsworth thought it was. Coleridge observed that Wordsworth had purified that language even when it was most simple, and Wordsworth himself found it inadequate to express the ideas of "Tintern Abbey" and the "Ode on the Intimations of Immortality." Tennyson, following Wordsworth at a distance, had a natural richness and deliberateness in his use of language that led him inevitably to the grand style, and by the time he was deeply engaged upon his *Idylls of the King,* dealing with lofty subjects and noble personages, the formal, dignified language of the bard was fastened upon him and upon nineteenth-century poetry. Far from being vulgar, Browning's habit of familiar language is the very breath of life to modern verse, and Browning deserves the title of liberator from the crushing formality that had been fastened upon poetry.

His immense gusto for life and his determination to find out the deepest motives that moved men led him to pay close attention to the criminal and sensational event, and ultimately to base his masterpiece upon a sordid murder story. In the process of allowing each character to justify himself he created such a gallery of rogues as had not been seen in English literature since the days of the first Elizabeth — notable among them being the Duke of "My Last Duchess," the Bishop who orders his tomb, Sludge, Blougram, Guido Franceschini, Napoleon III, and the elderly man of *The Inn Album.* His practice, here too, broadened the range of modern poetry, and placed him in the line of Chaucer, Shakespeare, and the great novelists, such as Fielding and Dickens.

Using the same penetrating powers, but as if in contrast, Browning devoted a very large proportion of his poetry to the subject of love between men and women. Indeed, not since John Donne, a poet almost idolized by Browning, had the whole anatomy of love been so scrutinized. Donne taught Browning many things — the use of strong vivid language, the value of beginning a poem abruptly to arouse the reader's interest, and the delight in surprise and paradox. But chiefly, perhaps, Donne delighted Browning by his candid and fearless treatment of passion between men and women.

Browning's lovers are a varied lot: there is the lover of Porphyria with his mad logic; the insanely jealous woman of "The Laboratory"; the triumphantly successful and chivalric Count Gismond; and the dying but happy lover of "Confessions," who remembers

How sad and bad and mad it was —
But then, how it was sweet!

There are numbers of rejected lovers who behave with incredible nobility. Examples may be seen in "The Last Ride Together" and "Serenade at the Villa." There are lovers who let the good minute pass without acting upon it, such as the man and woman of "Youth and Art" and "The Statue and the Bust"; and there are others, like the speakers in "Cristina" and "Evelyn Hope," who, having failed in their present lives, expect to catch up with their loves in some epoch of their future lives.

Perhaps more interesting than these unsuccessful lovers are the subtle relationships between men and women in love. The situations here are often imagined as between husband and wife, and some of them are personal to Browning and Mrs. Browning rather than objective and "dramatic." The form of these poems also is more often lyrical than dramatic. Such is the record of the perfect fusion of souls in "By the Fireside":

A moment after, and hands unseen
  Were hanging the night around us fast;
But we knew that a bar was broken between
  Life and life: we were mixed at last
In spite of the mortal screen.

But these moments are rare, and are recorded only when John Donne writes "The Ecstasy" or Browning this poem or "One Word More." There is a fainter recollection of a similar experience when he looks back in memory at the end of his life to "What came once when a woman leant / To feel for my brow where her kiss might fall."

More often by far the fusion of souls is not accomplished, as in "Two in the Campagna"; the good minute goes, and we are left with

Infinite passion, and the pain
Of finite hearts that yearn.

These are but two aspects of Browning's treatment of the nature of love; elsewhere we find love eager and strenuous or satiated and dull, illicit or saintly, reminiscent and tender, rueful at lost opportunity, or triumphant over the ruins of time as it is in the small masterpiece, "Love Among the Ruins." But everywhere it is a matter of grave moment and is seriously dealt with. It is not too much to say that his hopes for mankind were staked on the gospel of love between men and women.

In the twentieth century Browning has been praised most for his development of the dramatic monologue, his analysis of the passion of love, and for his refreshing diction. He has suffered most criticism where he attempted to erect a formal system of thought. In their troubled age the Victorians were hot for certainties in religious and philosophical matters and made their great poets assume the mantles of seers and sages. It was not enough to create beauty or depict men and women or illuminate the subtle complexities of secular life. The poet, if he aspired to be a nation's heritage, had to be the wise leader of the people, bearing a message from Heaven. Both Tennyson and Browning were coerced by the climate of their times into offering answers to ultimate questions — the nature of God, the purpose of the universe and man's destiny in it, good and evil. The answers to these questions had to be given to a society which was shaken by momentous changes — the Industrial Revolution, the crumbling of the literal interpretation of the Scriptures under the impact of the Higher Criticism,[1] the advances in the sciences of astronomy and geology, and biological evolution. Both Tennyson and Browning gave answers that seemed satisfactory to many people in the Victorian period, but the solutions of these eternal problems made by one age seldom satisfy a later time.

This is especially true in Browning's case because he was not a philosopher and had little faith in man's intellect. After his brief youthful rebellion from his mother's religious beliefs when he was under the influence of Shelley, he fell back upon a profoundly felt intuition that love, divine and human, is the motive force of the world. The central fact of history, he felt, was that God so loved mankind that He sent his Son in the flesh to demonstrate that love. This theme is nobly treated in such poems as "Saul," "Cleon," and the Pope's soliloquy in *The Ring and the Book*. His faith, in this respect, was the orthodox Christian one, and can hardly be attacked. But upon it Browning erected a metaphysical system that argued that God's intelligence and strength were evident in the physical world around us. This superstructure to his central faith, and his further "proofs" of immortality were much more vulnerable to the attack of reason. As the years advanced Browning spent great resourcefulness and ingenuity in defending, with less and less success, the intellectualized system he had constructed, and he finally had to retreat into a nescience that almost admitted defeat and intellectual despair. He was at his best in his thought and melody when he forgot his formal message to his age and wrote meditatively of his deeper intuitions, as in "Abt Vogler," where he falls back upon the timeless idealism of man:

On the earth the broken arcs; in the heaven
  a perfect round.

Darwin's conception of evolution came too late in Browning's life for him to grasp it. He

[1] The Higher Criticism was a movement which started in Germany among scholars of the Bible and swept into England toward the middle of the century. It challenged at many points the idea that the Bible was a literal transcription of the word of God, and tended to reduce the Old Testament merely to a literary document of the ancient Hebrews. It also challenged the authenticity of parts of the New Testament. George Eliot's translation of Strauss's *Leben Jesu* in 1846 introduced the movement to the public.

thought he was "Darwinized," and was accustomed as proof to point to his "Caliban" and to passages in "Paracelsus" that he had written twenty-five years before *The Origin of Species* appeared in 1859. His conception of evolution was not, however, a scientific one, and he was adamant against any theory of the process of life which would exclude belief in a cause exterior to matter and acting upon it. Browning's conception was rather an extension of the older doctrines of progress and perfectibility which he had learned in his youth from Shelley. The decay of the doctrine of inevitable progress and the continuous advance of scientific knowledge have dated Browning's noble but patchwork philosophy. Later generations have found his position untenable.

In the area of history, also, Browning can hardly be reckoned a scholar. With all his immense and irregular learning, such as his knowledge of the Renaissance as we see it in "The Bishop Orders His Tomb," he had never endured the discipline of collecting and sifting evidence with an open mind, prepared to follow truth and reason wherever they led. Instead, he approached his material with strong prejudgments, and his native creative imagination habitually wrenched the facts to suit his predilections. He surely did himself wrong in his insistence that his great poem, *The Ring and the Book,* was an accurate, but artistic, transcription of what he found in his source, *The Old Yellow Book.* He read his source eight times and culled details from it most extensively, but it is clear from the poem itself that his moral judgments were made on the first day he possessed the volume. Whatever the facts were in the sordid story of the old Roman murder case, Pompilia was to represent wronged and outraged virtue in captivity to evil, and Caponsacchi to be St. George, the rescuer. The habit of prejudgment in Browning can be illustrated many times, and the only point of concern is that he represented himself as an historian, which he was not, and did not give himself credit for the imaginative, intuitive poet he was. Great poetry may be truer than history.

Perhaps one of Browning's greatest assets as a poet is his cheerful and tonic view of life. His was not the hard-won and determined cheerfulness of Wordsworth, but rather the intuitive expression of a healthy, active, and courageous man. It is sometimes too strenuous and aggressive for a generation less certain of its part and of its future. We "greet the unseen with a cheer" far less heartily than he. But we can still appreciate and profit from the belief in the worth of action and endurance in "How They Brought the Good News," and the courage of "Childe Roland." These and other poems like them in Browning's works have supported many men in the hour of need.

Another aspect of the poet's cheerfulness was his strong faith that "if virtue feeble were, Heaven itself would stoop to her," to use the words of another idealist. Early in his career Browning placed before him on his desk a picture of Caravaggio's "Andromeda," "the perfect picture" as he called it, showing Andromeda being rescued from the sea beast by Perseus, and it became the lifelong symbol of his faith. He was sure that in the nick of time "Some god would come in thunder from the stars" to rescue the imperiled maiden. The legend of Andromeda and its Christian cognate, the legend of St. George, appears in one form or another thirty times in *The Ring and the Book,* and how each speaker deals with the legend is a touchstone of his character. This chivalric idea not only informed a great many of Browning's poems, such as "Count Gismond," "The Glove," "The Flight of the Duchess," and "Pompilia," but it directed his life as well, as we may see in his elopement and marriage.

When Browning was at the peak of his powers, he elaborated twice in notable poems his conception of the function of art. Succinctly stated, the function of the artist was to interpret this earthly show of men and women under the eye of God, and with reference always to God. His conception was essentially moral and religious, and his religious feeling penetrates all his dramatic and lyrical poems. The creation of men and women was God's province; the poet's task was one of observation, interpretation, imitation in his faint degree, and then communication, both to God and man.

In 1851 Browning had been rereading Shelley and Shakespeare for the purpose of writing an introductory essay to a volume of Shelley's letters. The letters proved to be spurious, and the volume was withdrawn, but Shelley's notion that poets were "the unacknowledged legislators of mankind" combined with a sentence from *King Lear,* "We'll take upon 's the mystery of things / As if we were God's spies," to conjure up in Browning's mind an image of a poet. The result was the compact and sharply drawn monologue, "How It Strikes a Contemporary." The speaker, or "contemporary," is a sprucely dressed young man in the streets of Valladolid, and what "strikes" him is the figure of a poet (a good deal like Browning) who goes about observing everything, but never speaking, and who becomes the legend of the town. The heart of the matter is caught in these lines, spoken by the young man:

We merely kept a governor for form,
While this man walked about and took account
Of all thought, said and acted, then went
home,
And wrote it fully to our Lord the King
Who has an itch to know things, he knows why,
And reads them in his bedroom of a night.

A more explicit statement of the function of the artist appears in "Fra Lippo Lippi," one of Browning's most successful dramatic monologues. Lippi, it will be remembered, with his irrepressible gaiety and his incorruptible innocence, has just escaped from the house of his patron because it is carnival time and he has not been able to resist the excitement of the streets. As the monologue begins he has been captured by the constables as a lawbreaker. Sitting upon the curb at the corner, he pours out the story of his life and his conception of his function as an artist. The world to him is no abstraction but the contemporary things and people he sees all about him. He has thrown over the traditional formalized art of the Church and instinctively reproduces as faithfully as he can the people and scenes around him. In so doing he teaches men to see, and he returns thanks and praise to God for the privilege of living.

However, you're my man, you've seen the world
— The beauty and the wonder and the power,
The shapes of things, their colors, lights and shades,
Changes, surprises — and God made it all!
— For what? Do you feel thankful, aye or no,
For this fair town's face, yonder river's line,
The mountain round it and the sky above,
Much more the figures of man, woman, child,
These are the frame to? What's it all about?
To be passed over, despised? or dwelt upon,
Wondered at? oh, this last of course! — you say.
But why not do as well as say — paint these
Just as they are, careless what comes of it?
God's works — paint any one, and count it
crime
To let a truth slip. Don't object, "His works
Are here already; nature is complete:
Suppose you reproduce her — (which you can't)
There's no advantage! you must beat her, then."
For, don't you mark? we're made so that we
love
First when we see them painted, things we have
passed
Perhaps a hundred times nor cared to see;
And so they are better, painted — better to us,
Which is the same thing. Art was given for
that;
God uses us to help each other so,
Lending our minds out. Have you noticed, now,
Your cullion's hanging face? A bit of chalk,
And trust me but you should, though! How much
more,
If I drew higher things with the same truth!
That were to take the Prior's pulpit-place,
Interpret God to all of you! Oh, oh,
It makes me mad to see what men shall do
And we in our graves! This world's no blot
for us,
Nor blank; it means intensely, and means good:
To find its meaning is my meat and drink.

Like Lippi, Browning has broken away from the formal and traditional ideas of the art of his time and prefers to depict the contemporary life around him in all its familiar realism. The artist cannot reproduce the scene he sees in all its beauty and completeness, but it is his peculiar gift to call our attention to things we have missed, to interpret them for us, and thus to communicate God's purpose and benevolence to us. Like Lippi, again, Browning thought of himself as a pioneer in art, and foresaw a time when the artist would be free of restricting conventions. The artist's responsibility is primarily to God, and only secondarily to his fellow men and society.

These are some of the major strands in the warp and woof of Browning's poetry. He wrote with great insight upon timeless themes — life and duty, the personalities of men and women and their dilemmas and solutions. He appreciated and honored bold and noble character and action. He dealt in an intensely original manner with all kinds of human relationships, and endowed us with a poetry of great richness and variety. He left us a great store of delight, and taught us to see many familiar things that we had failed to notice. At his best, Browning deserved the generous praise which (putting Shakespeare out of the question) Landor accorded him in 1846:

> Since Chaucer was alive and hale
> No man has walked along our road with step
> So active, so inquiring eye, and tongue
> So varied in discourse.

## III

It is becoming increasingly apparent to the critics of our own century that Browning was a far more skillful and conscious artist in poetry than his own age was inclined to think him. He was laughing at his critics when he made one of his characters say of a versifier:

> That bard's a Browning, he neglects the form
> But, ah, the sense, ye gods, the weighty sense!

It will be useful, therefore, to point out a few of Browning's special peculiarities in imagery, patterns of thought, meter, diction, and grammar — matters that come under the general heading of style.

The images which Browning uses in his poetry are innumerable and varied, but we may single out a few that come most frequently to him and are most characteristic. The symbol which he uses from the beginning of his career to the end for his central faith and hope is the Andromeda–St. George legend and has already been commented upon. It only needs to be added that the conception involved in the legend so penetrates Browning's thought and feeling that it appears a hundred times in his poetry. The figure that is central to Browning's love poetry, the mortal screen that the lovers are always striving to break through, has also been mentioned above, and needs no fuller illustration. But there are certain other characteristic images always at hand. Whenever Mrs. Browning appears in his verse the figure is likely to be of the heavens — a star in "My Star," or more usually the moon with its "Silent silver lights and darks undreamed of." Browning is also fond of contrasting light and dark, or heaven and hell, or heaven and the dim twilight of our earth, and these shades are used to apply to persons as well as situations, as we may see in the Pope's monologue in *The Ring and the Book*. A favorite figure, akin to the spectrum of light to dark, expresses the Platonic notion of the imperfection of earth and the perfection of heaven in terms of the arc of the rainbow, broken and incomplete here, but perfect there.

Whenever Browning is writing heroic poetry, dramatic or personal, he is apt to imagine the act of heroism as a journey taken over rough land and with many difficulties, usually by a single and lonely person. There is generally, also, the atmosphere of a military exploit. In his carefree younger days the journey is a stirring gallop from Ghent to Aix with companions, at least at the beginning. In "The Lost Leader" the march is made by a company of faithful men. Childe Roland must endure alone the quest through the terrible country and the more terrifying psychological hazards until he comes to the dark tower and the tragic triumph that awaits him there. In "Prospice" the poet himself takes the imaginary journey up the steep pass of death, like his "peers / The heroes of old." In the Epilogue to his last volume of poems, *Asolando,* he looks back on his life and thinks of himself as one who "marched breast forward." As a small matter of interest it may be noted that the name "Roland," the epic warrior of Charlemagne's army, has heroic connotations for Browning. This characteristic figure well expresses the poet's energetic spirit of faith and courage.

When we turn to Browning's meters we find that the prevailing impulse in him is to be free, to be natural and expressive, to be inventive in meeting the necessities of the moment. He found that the dramatic monologue fares best in blank verse, but there is no uniform pattern to his blank verse. It adapts itself to the speaker; it is broken and sometimes properly incoherent in the mouth of the dying Bishop of St. Praxed's; it is joyous and conversational in "Fra Lippo Lippi"; intensely colorful in "How It Strikes a Contemporary"; stately and reasoned in "Cleon"; sober and nerveless in "Andrea del Sarto"; simple and innocent in "Pompilia"; fierce and biting in "Guido"; and grave and deliberate in "The Pope." The great characteristics of Browning's blank verse are its variety and its resilience.

In his lyric measures Browning is equally inventive, and seems to fling down his verse as the opportunity occurs, often with what looks like amazingly good luck. He can flow softly and smoothly when he pleases, as he does in "In a Gondola" or in the running long lines of "A Toccata of Galuppi's," or in the alternating long and short lines of "Love among the Ruins,"

> Where the quiet-colored end of evening smiles
> Miles and miles. . . .

Or he can manage well the undulating harmonies of the long lines of "Saul" or the speculative melody of "Abt Vogler," as the improviser meditates over his music:

> But here is the finger of God, a flash of the will that can,
> Existent behind all laws, that made them and, lo, they are!
> And I know not if, save in this, such gift be allowed to man,
> That out of three sounds he frame, not a fourth sound, but a star.

But softness and sweetness are not usually Browning's aims. He likes on occasion to employ short abrupt measures, often scornful and informal, as in "Youth and Art":

> Each life unfulfilled, you see;
> It hangs still, patchy and scrappy:
> We have not sighed deep, laughed free,
> Starved, feasted, despaired — been happy.

Sometimes the short line is used for point and command:

> Look not thou down but up!
> To uses of a cup, . . .

Frequently, Browning's love of the grotesque invades his language and meter. This is to be seen in the playful tumbling lines of "The Pied Piper," with its haphazard rhymes, and also in "A Grammarian's Funeral," where the grotesque is used in the service of greatness, as the disciples of the scholar, defiant of the world's estimate of the man and fond of their master, climb up the mountain to the sepulcher.

> Let us begin and carry up this corpse,
> Singing together.
> Leave we the common crofts, the vulgar thorpes
> Each in its tether
> Sleeping safe on the bosom of the plain,
> Cared-for till cock-crow:
> Look out if yonder be not day again
> Rimming the rock-row!

Such comment by no means exhausts the endless variety of Browning's measures, but it is only necessary to add that in meter, as in most other things, he breaks away from all tradition, and is entirely original. He is especially fond of a five-line stanza, rhyming *ababa,* but that too undergoes many variations.

In creating his vast and varied body of poetry, Browning gradually hammered out a personal idiom. By nature strong-headed and intensely individualistic, he allowed himself considerable license with the language. His English was never that of the great public schools or the universities, and to his early contemporaries it appeared altogether eccentric. Frequently his mental force outranged his artistic powers, and he was obscure in his moral and emotional appeal because he could not manage his language. His problem, therefore, was to find a means of communication through poetry and still retain his individuality. Though he courted his oddities and was sometimes deliberately unusual, yet his primary aim was to achieve a natural broken speech. Browning was strong, but the English language was stronger. He was forced to compromise, and the compromise is an idiom that can be recognized instantly as Browning's. He writes characteristically a stiff and elliptical language, more expressive than beautiful. He is often colloquial, but equally often richly allusive from his recondite learning. He retains many learned and Latinate words, but moves toward the native English monosyllable which often makes his verse creak and grind with its knots of consonants:

> Irks care the crop-full bird? Frets doubt the maw-crammed beast?

Often these discords are useful to his purpose. They show life and impulse and individuality, a congested expression struggling to break through. He may justly be called a "great though irregular master of English."

Browning's grammar, too, is his own, free and somewhat hit or miss. His sentences are frequently interrupted by a long parenthesis, but with patience the grammar will usually come right in the end. He is often fettered by rhyme, but keeps plunging forward. His most characteristic mark of punctuation is the impatient dash. He omits articles and relative pronouns. He likes to heap alliteration on his verse, as when Lippi describes himself as he appears in his own painting:

Mazed, motionless, and moon-struck — . . .

One of his more superficial, but amusing, habits is to cut off the final consonants of prepositions and articles, as his parodist, Calverly, and others have noticed,

I love to dock the smaller parts o' speech,
As we curtail the already curtailed cur.

And this gives a staccato effect, one of speed.

All these eccentricities no doubt delayed his acceptance by the English public. But they do not ultimately obscure his strong imaginative and emotional appeal. He did not concede too much to his readers in subject or in manner. In his verse we find preserved his temperament with all its oddity and originality, its splendor and its color, and his passionate belief in the value of the individual. He was something new among the poets. "I like Browning," said Lockhart, Sir Walter Scott's son-in-law. "He's not the least like one of your damned literary men."

The order followed in this selection from Browning's poems is chronological. The poems are grouped under the volume headings in which they first appeared, that is, *Dramatic Lyrics, Dramatic Romances, Men and Women,* and so forth. Within each volume the order is Browning's as the poems were first published in book form. The exception to this is "Porphyria's Lover," which is put first because it was written and printed several years before the other *Dramatic Lyrics* included here.

## Reading Suggestions

EDITION

Augustine Birrell, editor, *The Complete Poetical Works of Robert Browning, New Edition with Additional Poems First Published in 1914* (1915). This edition has an excellent text, and it is the most nearly complete of all the editions of Browning's works.

BIOGRAPHY

W. H. Griffin and H. C. Minchin, *The Life of Robert Browning* (1910) (2nd edition, revised, 1938). The standard life of the poet. Reliable and informative.

Mrs. Betty Miller, *Robert Browning, A Portrait* (1952). A lively and challenging volume, with a good deal of new information, which attempts to apply twentieth-century psychology to the interpretation of Browning's character.

LETTERS

*The Letters of Robert Browning and Elizabeth Barrett Browning,* 2 vols. (1899). The famous love letters — sometimes hard to follow because of their elliptical expression, but rewarding.

Sir F. G. Kenyon, editor, *Robert Browning and Alfred Domett* (1910). These letters record the friendship of Browning and Domett between 1840 and 1846. They shed much light on the young poet.

Thurman L. Hood, editor, *Letters of Robert Browning, Collected by Thomas J. Wise* (1933). A large collection of letters from the poet's whole career, well edited and useful.

Edward C. McAleer, editor, *Dearest Isa, Robert Browning's Letters to Isabella Blagden* (1951). Well edited and interesting letters covering the years from 1861 to 1872. A good record of Browning's activities and opinions after Mrs. Browning's death.

CRITICISM

A. K. Cook, *A Commentary upon Browning's The Ring and the Book* (1920). Indispensable for the study of the whole poem.

F. G. R. Duckworth, *Browning, Background and Conflict* (1931). Excellent chapters upon Browning's methods of thinking and writing poetry.

W. L. Phelps, *Robert Browning, How to Know Him* (1931). Witty, chatty, and often wise interpretation.

W. C. DeVane, *A Browning Handbook* (1935). A useful and authoritative account of the genesis, source, and history of each poem.

W. O. Raymond, *The Infinite Moment and Other Essays in Robert Browning* (1950). A collection of penetrating and informative essays upon the poet's ideas, moods, and practices, by a lifelong student of Browning. Very helpful.

Besides these volumes there are many separate essays upon Browning of particular interest. Among them are the following:

W. Bagehot, "Wordsworth, Tennyson and Browning," in *Literary Studies* (1895).

O. Elton, "The Brownings," in the *Survey of English Literature, 1830–1880,* vol. ii (1949).

H. J. C. Grierson, "Tennyson, Browning and Some Others," in *Lyrical Poetry of the Nineteenth Century* (1929).

B. Groom, "On the Diction of Tennyson, Browning, and Arnold," Society for Pure English, Tract 53 (1939).

E. D. H. Johnson, "Browning," in *The Alien Vision of Victorian Poetry* (1952).

G. Santayana, "The Poetry of Barbarism," in *Interpretations of Poetry and Religion* (1900).

Dixon Scott, "The Homeliness of Robert Browning," in *Men of Letters* (1923).

# from DRAMATIC LYRICS, 1842

## PORPHYRIA'S LOVER

This poem was first printed as "Porphyria" in *The Monthly Repository* for January, 1836. In *Dramatic Lyrics* it was linked with a poem called "Johannes Agricola" under the title "Madhouse Cells." It was probably written in St. Petersburg, Russia, in March or April, 1834.

The rain set early in tonight,
  The sullen wind was soon awake,
It tore the elm tops down for spite,
  And did its worst to vex the lake;
I listened with heart fit to break.
When glided in Porphyria; straight
  She shut the cold out and the storm,
And kneeled and made the cheerless grate
  Blaze up, and all the cottage warm;
Which done, she rose, and from her form
Withdrew the dripping cloak and shawl,
  And laid her soiled gloves by, untied
Her hat and let the damp hair fall,
  And, last, she sat down by my side
And called me. When no voice replied,
She put my arm about her waist,
  And made her smooth white shoulder bare
And all her yellow hair displaced,
  And, stooping, made my cheek lie there,
And spread, o'er all, her yellow hair,
Murmuring how she loved me — she
  Too weak, for all her heart's endeavor,
To set its struggling passion free
  From pride, and vainer ties dissever,
And give herself to me forever.
But passion sometimes would prevail,
  Nor could tonight's gay feast restrain
A sudden thought of one so pale
  For love of her, and all in vain:
So, she was come through wind and rain.
Be sure I looked up at her eyes
  Happy and proud; at last I knew
Porphyria worshiped me; surprise
  Made my heart swell, and still it grew
While I debated what to do.
That moment she was mine, mine, fair,
  Perfectly pure and good; I found
A thing to do, and all her hair
  In one long yellow string I wound
Three times her little throat around,
And strangled her. No pain felt she;
  I am quite sure she felt no pain.
As a shut bud that holds a bee,
  I warily oped her lids; again
Laughed the blue eyes without a stain.
And I untightened next the tress
  About her neck; her cheek once more
Blushed bright beneath my burning kiss:
  I propped her head up as before,
Only, this time my shoulder bore
Her head, which droops upon it still;
  The smiling rosy little head,
So glad it has its utmost will,
  That all it scorned at once is fled,
And I, its love, am gained instead!
Porphyria's love: she guessed not how
  Her darling one wish would be heard.
And thus we sit together now,
  And all night long we have not stirred,
And yet God has not said a word!

## MY LAST DUCHESS

*Ferrara*

When this poem was first published in *Dramatic Lyrics,* it was paired with "Count Gismond" under the title "Italy and France." It received its present title in the collected edition of 1849. A product of the poet's interest in Italian life and art, "My Last Duchess" is an early example of Browning's study of the Italian Renaissance, and also a milestone in his development of the dramatic monologue. It is probable that Browning had Alfonso II (1533–98), fifth Duke of Ferrara, as his model for the portrait of the duke of the poem.

That's my last Duchess painted on the wall,
Looking as if she were alive. I call
That piece a wonder, now; Frà Pandolf's hands
Worked busily a day, and there she stands.
Will 't please you sit and look at her? I said
"Frà Pandolf" by design, for never read
Strangers like you that pictured countenance,
The depth and passion of its earnest glance,
But to myself they turned (since none puts by
The curtain I have drawn for you, but I)
And seemed as they would ask me, if they durst,
How such a glance came there; so, not the first
Are you to turn and ask thus. Sir, 'twas not
Her husband's presence only, called that spot
Of joy into the Duchess' cheek; perhaps
Frà Pandolf chanced to say, "Her mantle laps
Over my lady's wrist too much," or, "Paint
Must never hope to reproduce the faint
Half-flush that dies along her throat." Such stuff
Was courtesy, she thought, and cause enough
For calling up that spot of joy. She had
A heart — how shall I say? — too soon made glad,
Too easily impressed; she liked whate'er
She looked on, and her looks went everywhere.
Sir, 'twas all one! My favor at her breast,

MY LAST DUCHESS. **3. Fra Pandolf:** an imaginary artist who was a friar. **13. Sir:** the ambassador of Ferdinand II, Duke of Tyrol, with his capital at Innsbruck, with whom the Duke is negotiating for another wife. This lady was Barbara, Ferdinand's sister.

The dropping of the daylight in the west,
The bough of cherries some officious fool
Broke in the orchard for her, the white mule
She rode with round the terrace — all and each
Would draw from her alike the approving speech,
Or blush, at least. She thanked men — good! but thanked
Somehow — I know not how — as if she ranked
My gift of a nine-hundred-years-old name
With anybody's gift. Who'd stoop to blame
This sort of trifling? Even had you skill
In speech — (which I have not) — to make your will
Quite clear to such an one, and say, "Just this
Or that in you disgusts me; here you miss,
Or there exceed the mark" — and if she let
Herself be lessoned so, nor plainly set
Her wits to yours, forsooth, and made excuse,
— E'en then would be some stooping; and I choose
Never to stoop. Oh, sir, she smiled, no doubt,
Whene'er I passed her; but who passed without
Much the same smile? This grew; I gave commands;
Then all smiles stopped together. There she stands
As if alive. Will 't please you rise? We'll meet
The company below, then. I repeat,
The Count your master's known munificence
Is ample warrant that no just pretense
Of mine for dowry will be disallowed;
Though his fair daughter's self, as I avowed
At starting, is my object. Nay, we'll go
Together down, sir. Notice Neptune, though,
Taming a sea horse, thought a rarity,
Which Claus of Innsbruck cast in bronze for me!

## COUNT GISMOND

*Aix in Provence*

See the headnote on "My Last Duchess," above. "Count Gismond" is in the medieval chivalric tradition and thus illustrates a strong trait in Browning's character. The scene is laid in Provence in southeastern France, the home of troubadour romance. The speaker is the heroine of the story, now Gismond's wife.

Christ God who savest man, save most
  Of men Count Gismond who saved me!
Count Gauthier, when he chose his post,
  Chose time and place and company
To suit it; when he struck at length
My honor, 'twas with all his strength.

And doubtlessly ere he could draw
  All points to one, he must have schemed!
That miserable morning saw
  Few half so happy as I seemed,
While being dressed in queen's array
To give our tourney prize away.

I thought they loved me, did me grace
  To please themselves; 'twas all their deed;
God makes, or fair or foul, our face;
  If showing mine so caused to bleed
My cousins' hearts, they should have dropped
A word, and straight the play had stopped.

They, too, so beauteous! Each a queen
  By virtue of her brow and breast;
Not needing to be crowned, I mean,
  As I do. E'en when I was dressed,
Had either of them spoke, instead
Of glancing sideways with still head!

But no: they let me laugh, and sing
  My birthday song quite through, adjust
The last rose in my garland, fling
  A last look on the mirror, trust
My arms to each an arm of theirs,
And so descend the castle stairs —

And come out on the morning-troop
  Of merry friends who kissed my cheek,
And called me queen, and made me stoop
  Under the canopy — (a streak
That pierced it, of the outside sun,
Powdered with gold its gloom's soft dun) —

And they could let me take my state
  And foolish throne amid applause
Of all come there to celebrate
  My queen's-day — Oh, I think the cause
Of much was, they forgot no crowd
Makes up for parents in their shroud!

Howe'er that be, all eyes were bent
  Upon me, when my cousins cast
Theirs down; 'twas time I should present
  The victor's crown, but . . . there, 'twill last
No long time . . . the old mist again
Blinds me as then it did. How vain!

See! Gismond's at the gate, in talk
  With his two boys: I can proceed.
Well, at that moment, who should stalk
  Forth boldly — to my face, indeed —

45–46. **I . . . together:** Alfonso II had three wives, the first of whom was Lucrezia, daughter of Cosimo de' Medici, Duke of Florence. She was married at 14, and died at 17 — it was rumored of poison. When Browning was asked the meaning of these lines he said that "the commands were that she should be put to death, . . . or he might have had her shut up in a convent." **56. Claus:** an imaginary artist.

COUNT GISMOND. **13. they:** the speaker's cousins.

But Gauthier, and he thundered, "Stay!"
And all stayed. "Bring no crowns, I say!

"Bring torches! Wind the penance sheet
  About her! Let her shun the chaste,
Or lay herself before their feet!
  Shall she whose body I embraced
A night long, queen it in the day?
For honor's sake no crowns, I say!"

I? What I answered? As I live,
  I never fancied such a thing
As answer possible to give.
  What says the body when they spring
Some monstrous torture engine's whole
Strength on it? No more says the soul.

Till out strode Gismond; then I knew
  That I was saved. I never met
His face before, but, at first view,
  I felt quite sure that God had set
Himself to Satan; who would spend
A minute's mistrust on the end?

He strode to Gauthier, in his throat
  Gave him the lie, then struck his mouth
With one backhanded blow that wrote
  In blood men's verdict there. North, south,
East, west, I looked. The lie was dead,
And damned, and truth stood up instead.

This glads me most, that I enjoyed
  The heart of the joy, with my content
In watching Gismond unalloyed
  By any doubt of the event;
God took that on him — I was bid
Watch Gismond for my part: I did.

Did I not watch him while he let
  His armorer just brace his greaves,
Rivet his hauberk, on the fret
  The while! His foot . . . my memory leaves
No least stamp out, nor how anon
He pulled his ringing gauntlets on.

And e'en before the trumpet's sound
  Was finished, prone lay the false knight,
Prone as his lie, upon the ground;
  Gismond flew at him, used no sleight
O' the sword, but open-breasted drove,
Cleaving till out the truth he clove.

Which done, he dragged him to my feet
  And said, "Here die, but end thy breath
In full confession, lest thou fleet
  From my first, to God's second death!
Say, hast thou lied?" And, "I have lied
To God and her," he said, and died.

Then Gismond, kneeling to me, asked
  — What safe my heart holds, though no word
Could I repeat now, if I tasked
  My powers forever, to a third
Dear even as you are. Pass the rest
Until I sank upon his breast.

Over my head his arm he flung
  Against the world; and scarce I felt
His sword (that dripped by me and swung)
  A little shifted in its belt;
For he began to say the while
How south our home lay many a mile.

So 'mid the shouting multitude
  We two walked forth to nevermore
Return. My cousins have pursued
  Their life, untroubled as before
I vexed them. Gauthier's dwelling place
God lighten! May his soul find grace!

Our elder boy has got the clear
  Great brow; though when his brother's black
Full eye shows scorn, it . . . Gismond here?
  And have you brought my tercel back?
I just was telling Adela
How many birds it struck since May.

83. **God**: The story is founded upon the medieval idea that "God will have a stroke in every battle." 86. **greaves**: armor for the shins. 87. **hauberk**: coat of mail.

124. **tercel**: male falcon.

## INCIDENT OF THE FRENCH CAMP

This poem was probably written in December, 1841, when a second funeral of Napoleon was held in Paris. It is founded on oral legend. On April 23, 1809, Napoleon's army captured Ratisbon (Regensburg) from the Austrians. The city was stormed by Marshal Lannes (1769–1809), Duc de Montebello, who led the attackers in person. Lannes was fatally wounded a month later at the battle of Aspern.

You know, we French stormed Ratisbon:
  A mile or so away,
On a little mound, Napoleon
  Stood on our storming day;
With neck outthrust, you fancy how,
  Legs wide, arms locked behind,
As if to balance the prone brow
  Oppressive with its mind.

Just as perhaps he mused, "My plans
  That soar, to earth may fall,

Let once my army-leader Lannes
  Waver at yonder wall" —
Out 'twixt the battery smokes there flew
  A rider, bound on bound
Full-galloping; nor bridle drew
  Until he reached the mound.

Then off there flung in smiling joy,
  And held himself erect
By just his horse's mane, a boy;
  You hardly could suspect —
(So tight he kept his lips compressed,
  Scarce any blood came through)
You looked twice ere you saw his breast
  Was all but shot in two.

"Well," cried he, "Emperor, by God's grace
  We've got you Ratisbon!
The Marshal's in the market place,
  And you'll be there anon
To see your flag-bird flap his vans
  Where I, to heart's desire,
Perched him!" The chief's eye flashed; his plans
  Soared up again like fire.

The chief's eye flashed; but presently
  Softened itself, as sheathes
A film the mother-eagle's eye
  When her bruised eaglet breathes;
"You're wounded!" "Nay," the soldier's pride
  Touched to the quick, he said:
"I'm killed, Sire!" And his chief beside,
  Smiling the boy fell dead.

## SOLILOQUY OF THE SPANISH CLOISTER

When this poem was published in 1842, it was linked with "Incident of the French Camp." It illustrates Browning's early attempts to depict national characteristics. He had never been to Spain but had seen monasteries on his travels in Italy in 1838.

Gr-r-r — there go, my heart's abhorrence!
  Water your damned flowerpots, do!
If hate killed men, Brother Lawrence,
  God's blood, would not mine kill you!
What? your myrtle bush wants trimming?
  Oh, that rose has prior claims —
Needs its leaden vase filled brimming?
  Hell dry you up with its flames!

INCIDENT OF THE FRENCH CAMP. **29. flag-bird:** Napoleon's emblem, the imperial eagle.

At the meal we sit together:
  *Salve tibi!* I must hear
Wise talk of the kind of weather,
  Sort of season, time of year:
*Not a plenteous cork crop; scarcely*
  *Dare we hope oak galls, I doubt;*
*What's the Latin name for "parsley"?*
  What's the Greek name for "swine's snout"?

Whew! We'll have our platter burnished,
  Laid with care on our own shelf!
With a fire-new spoon we're furnished,
  And a goblet for ourself,
Rinsed like something sacrificial
  Ere 'tis fit to touch our chaps —
Marked with L for our initial!
  (He-he! There his lily snaps!)

*Saint,* forsooth! While brown Dolores
  Squats outside the Convent bank
With Sanchicha, telling stories,
  Steeping tresses in the tank,
Blue-black, lustrous, thick like horsehairs
  — Can't I see his dead eye glow,
Bright as 'twere a Barbary corsair's?
  (That is, if he'd let it show!)

When he finishes refection,
  Knife and fork he never lays
Crosswise, to my recollection,
  As do I, in Jesu's praise.
I the Trinity illustrate,
  Drinking watered orange pulp—
In three sips the Arian frustrate;
  While he drains his at one gulp.

Oh, those melons! If he's able
  We're to have a feast! so nice!
One goes to the Abbot's table,
  All of us get each a slice.
How go on your flowers? None double?
  Not one fruit-sort can you spy?
Strange! — And I, too, at such trouble
  Keep them close-nipped on the sly!

There's a great text in Galatians,
  Once you trip on it, entails
Twenty-nine distinct damnations,
  One sure, if another fails;

SOLILOQUY OF SPANISH CLOISTER. **10.** ***Salve tibi!:*** "Hail to you." **31. Barbary corsair:** Pirates infested the northwestern coast of Africa early in the nineteenth century. **39. Arian:** Arius, a heretic of the fourth century, denied the equality of Christ with God the Father and attacked the doctrine of the Trinity. **49. text in Galatians:** In Gal. 2 and 3 there are many texts difficult to interpret. The speaker in this stanza hopes to trap Lawrence in a heresy just as the good brother is dying, and thus damn his soul. (See Gal. 3:21.) In the next stanza the speaker hopes to trap Lawrence in a moral sin.

If I trip him just a-dying,
  Sure of heaven as sure can be,
Spin him round and send him flying
  Off to hell, a Manichee?

Or, my scrofulous French novel
  On gray paper with blunt type!
Simply glance at it, you grovel
  Hand and foot in Belial's gripe;
If I double down its pages
  At the woeful sixteenth print,
When he gathers his greengages,
  Ope a sieve and slip in 't?

Or, there's Satan! — one might venture
  Pledge one's soul to him, yet leave
Such a flaw in the indenture
  As he'd miss till, past retrieve,
Blasted lay that rose acacia
  We're so proud of! *Hy, Zy, Hine . . .*
'St, there's Vespers! *Plena gratia,*
  *Ave, Virgo!* Gr-r-r — you swine!

## CRISTINA

In fancy a lover addresses Cristina, Queen of Spain under Ferdinand VII, and Queen Regent from 1833 to 1840. She was forced to abdicate in 1840 when it was discovered that she had secretly married an officer in the Army. The scandal of her abdication was probably the occasion of the poem. Cristina had a great reputation as a coquette and a lover of pleasure.

"Cristina" has usually been taken to illustrate Browning's interest in the "doctrine of elective affinity," a notion promulgated by Goethe in 1809 in his novel, *Wahlverwandschaften* (*Elective Affinities*). The term is taken from chemistry and implies that, as in physical substances, so in human beings there is a natural force which draws together certain persons of opposite sexes, instantaneously and almost irresistibly, no matter what their different stations, circumstances, and ages. It has been suggested, however, that Browning means to depict the speaker as a rationalizing egoist who is arguing with a skeptical friend.

She should never have looked at me
  If she meant I should not love her!
There are plenty . . . men, you call such,
  I suppose . . . she may discover
All her soul to, if she pleases,
  And yet leave much as she found them;
But I'm not so, and she knew it
  When she fixed me, glancing round them.

What? To fix me thus meant nothing?
  But I can't tell (there's my weakness)
What her look said! — no vile cant, sure,
  About "need to strew the bleakness
Of some lone shore with its pearl seed
  That the sea feels" — no "strange yearning
That such souls have, most to lavish
  Where there's chance of least returning."

Oh, we're sunk enough here, God knows!
  But not quite so sunk that moments,
Sure though seldom, are denied us,
  When the spirit's true endowments
Stand out plainly from its false ones,
  And apprise it if pursuing
Or the right way or the wrong way,
  To its triumph or undoing.

There are flashes struck from midnights,
  There are fire flames noondays kindle,
Whereby piled-up honors perish,
  Whereby swollen ambitions dwindle,
While just this or that poor impulse,
  Which for once had play unstifled,
Seems the sole work of a lifetime,
  That away the rest have trifled.

Doubt you if, in some such moment,
  As she fixed me, she felt clearly,
Ages past the soul existed,
  Here an age 'tis resting merely,
And hence fleets again for ages,
  While the true end, sole and single,
It stops here for is, this love-way,
  With some other soul to mingle?

Else it loses what it lived for,
  And eternally must lose it;
Better ends may be in prospect,
  Deeper blisses (if you choose it),
But this life's end and this love-bliss
  Have been lost here. Doubt you whether
This she felt as, looking at me,
  Mine and her souls rushed together?

Oh, observe! Of course, next moment,
  The world's honors, in derision,
Trampled out the light forever.
  Never fear but there's provision

**56. Manichee:** a follower of the Manichean heresy, which interprets the world as the region of eternal struggle between good and evil, neither of which is strong enough to defeat the other. This neutrality showed a lack of Christian faith in an all-powerful and benevolent God. **60. Belial:** the Devil. **62. woeful:** "awful" in the colloquial sense. **70. *Hy, Zy, Hine:*** often assumed to represent the sound of the vesper bells, but it may be the first words of a spell to conjure up the Devil. **71–72. *Plena . . . Virgo!:*** "Hail, Virgin, full of grace!"; the beginning of one of the prayers often used at the vespers service.

CRISTINA. **12–16. About . . . returning:** The speaker is sure that Cristina's glance was not a condescending pity for him because of his lower station in life. In the figure Browning uses here, the speaker is the "lone shore" and Cristina's favor is the "pearl seed."

Of the devil's to quench knowledge
  Lest we walk the earth in rapture!
— Making those who catch God's secret
  Just so much more prize their capture!

Such am I: the secret's mine now!
  She has lost me, I have gained her;
Her soul's mine; and thus, grown perfect,
  I shall pass my life's remainder.
Life will just hold out the proving
  Both our powers, alone and blended;
And then, come the next life quickly!
  This world's use will have been ended.

## THE PIED PIPER OF HAMELIN

### *A Child's Story*

WRITTEN FOR, AND INSCRIBED TO, W. M. THE YOUNGER

This poem was written in May, 1842, for Willie Macready, son of the tragedian, who was ill and wished something to illustrate. When the printers reported in October that more copy was needed to make up the pamphlet of *Dramatic Lyrics,* the poet sent "The Pied Piper." It has become one of the most widely known of all Browning's poems. The legend from which it was made was well known in the Browning family. The poet's father also wrote a rhymed version at about the same time.

1

  Hamelin town's in Brunswick,
By famous Hanover city;
  The river Weser, deep and wide,
  Washes its wall on the southern side;
  A pleasanter spot you never spied;
But, when begins my ditty,
  Almost five hundred years ago,
  To see the townsfolk suffer so
    From vermin, was a pity.

2

  Rats!
They fought the dogs and killed the cats,
  And bit the babies in the cradles,
And ate the cheeses out of the vats,
  And licked the soup from the cooks' own ladles,
Split open the kegs of salted sprats,
Made nests inside men's Sunday hats,
And even spoiled the women's chats
  By drowning their speaking
  With shrieking and squeaking
In fifty different sharps and flats.

3

At last the people in a body
  To the Town Hall came flocking:
"'Tis clear," cried they, "our Mayor's a noddy;
  And as for our Corporation — shocking
To think we buy gowns lined with ermine
For dolts that can't or won't determine
What's best to rid us of our vermin!
You hope, because you're old and obese,
To find in the furry civic robe ease?
Rouse up, sirs! Give your brains a racking
To find the remedy we're lacking,
Or, sure as fate, we'll send you packing!"
At this the Mayor and Corporation
Quaked with a mighty consternation.

4

An hour they sat in council;
  At length the Mayor broke silence:
"For a guilder I'd my ermine gown sell,
  I wish I were a mile hence!
It's easy to bid one rack one's brain —
I'm sure my poor head aches again,
I've scratched it so, and all in vain.
Oh for a trap, a trap, a trap!"
Just as he said this, what should hap
At the chamber door but a gentle tap?
"Bless us," cried the Mayor, "what's that?
(With the Corporation as he sat,
Looking little though wondrous fat;
Nor brighter was his eye, nor moister
Than a too-long-opened oyster,
Save when at noon his paunch grew mutinous
For a plate of turtle green and glutinous)
"Only a scraping of shoes on the mat?
Anything like the sound of a rat
Makes my heart go pit-a-pat!"

5

"Come in!" — the Mayor cried, looking bigger;
And in did come the strangest figure!
His queer long coat from heel to head
Was half of yellow and half of red,
And he himself was tall and thin,
With sharp blue eyes, each like a pin,
And light loose hair, yet swarthy skin,
No tuft on cheek nor beard on chin,
But lips where smiles went out and in;
There was no guessing his kith and kin;
And nobody could enough admire
The tall man and his quaint attire.
Quoth one: "It's as my great-grandsire,
Starting up at the Trump of Doom's tone,
Had walked this way from his painted tombstone!"

6

He advanced to the council table:
And, "Please your honors," said he, "I'm able,
By means of a secret charm, to draw

THE PIED PIPER. 65. admire: wonder at.

All creatures living beneath the sun,
That creep or swim or fly or run,
After me so as you never saw!
And I chiefly use my charm
On creatures that do people harm,
The mole and toad and newt and viper;
And people call me the Pied Piper."
(And here they noticed round his neck
A scarf of red and yellow stripe,
To match with his coat of the selfsame check;
And at the scarf's end hung a pipe;
And his fingers, they noticed, were ever straying
As if impatient to be playing
Upon this pipe, as low it dangled
Over his vesture so oldfangled.)
"Yet," said he, "poor piper as I am,
In Tartary I freed the Cham,
Last June, from his huge swarms of gnats;
I eased in Asia the Nizam
Of a monstrous brood of vampire bats;
And as for what your brain bewilders,
If I can rid your town of rats
Will you give me a thousand guilders?"
"One? fifty thousand!" — was the exclamation
Of the astonished Mayor and Corporation.

7

Into the street the Piper stepped,
  Smiling first a little smile,
As if he knew what magic slept
  In his quiet pipe the while;
Then, like a musical adept,
To blow the pipe his lips he wrinkled,
And green and blue his sharp eyes twinkled,
Like a candle flame where salt is sprinkled;
And ere three shrill notes the pipe uttered,
You heard as if an army muttered;
And the muttering grew to a grumbling;
And the grumbling grew to a mighty rumbling;
And out of the houses the rats came tumbling.
Great rats, small rats, lean rats, brawny rats,
Brown rats, black rats, gray rats, tawny rats,
Grave old plodders, gay young friskers,
  Fathers, mothers, uncles, cousins,
Cocking tails and pricking whiskers,
  Families by tens and dozens,
Brothers, sisters, husbands, wives —
Followed the Piper for their lives.
From street to street he piped advancing,
And step for step they followed dancing,
Until they came to the river Weser,
Wherein all plunged and perished!
— Save one who, stout as Julius Caesar,
Swam across and lived to carry
(As he, the manuscript he cherished)
To Rat-land home his commentary:
Which was, "At the first shrill notes of the
  pipe,
I heard a sound as of scraping tripe,
And putting apples, wondrous ripe,
Into a cider press's gripe;
And a moving away of pickle-tub boards,
And a leaving ajar of conserve cupboards,
And a drawing the corks of train-oil flasks,
And a breaking the hoops of butter casks;
And it seemed as if a voice
(Sweeter far than by harp or by psaltery
Is breathed) called out, 'Oh rats, rejoice!
The world is grown to one vast drysaltery!
So munch on, crunch on, take your nuncheon,
Breakfast, supper, dinner, luncheon!'
And just as a bulky sugar puncheon,
All ready staved, like a great sun shone
Glorious scarce an inch before me,
Just as methought it said, 'Come, bore me!'
— I found thee Weser rolling o'er me."

8

You should have heard the Hamelin people
Ringing the bells till they rocked the steeple.
"Go," cried the Mayor, "and get long poles,
Poke out the nests and block up the holes!
Consult with carpenters and builders,
And leave in our town not even a trace
Of the rats!" — when suddenly, up the face
Of the Piper perked in the market place,
With a, "First, if you please, my thousand
  guilders!"

9

A thousand guilders! The Mayor looked blue;
So did the Corporation too.
For council dinners made rare havoc
With Claret, Moselle, Vin-de-Grave, Hock;
And half the money would replenish
Their cellar's biggest butt with Rhenish.
To pay this sum to a wandering fellow
With a gypsy coat of red and yellow!
"Beside," quoth the Mayor with a knowing
  wink,
"Our business was done at the river's brink;
We saw with our eyes the vermin sink,
And what's dead can't come to life, I think.
So, friend, we're not the folks to shrink
From the duty of giving you something for
  drink,

**89. Tartary . . . Cham:** The Cham was the ruler of the Tartar empire in central Asia. **91. Nizam:** the ruler of Hyderabad, a state in India. **123. Caesar:** At the siege of Alexandria in 48 B.C., Caesar, when his ship was captured, swam to safety carrying the manuscript of his *Commentaries on the Gallic Wars* in his hand. **133. train-oil flasks:** flasks of whale oil. **138. drysaltery:** a store dealing in dried and salted meats. **139. nuncheon:** light luncheon. **141. sugar puncheon:** a cask containing sugar.

And a matter of money to put in your poke;
But as for the guilders, what we spoke
Of them, as you very well know, was in joke.
Beside, our losses have made us thrifty.
A thousand guilders! Come, take fifty!"

10

The Piper's face fell, and he cried,
"No trifling! I can't wait, beside!
I've promised to visit by dinner time
Bagdat, and accept the prime
Of the Head Cook's pottage, all he's rich in,
For having left, in the Caliph's kitchen,
Of a nest of scorpions no surivivor;
With him I proved no bargain-driver,
With you, don't think I'll bate a stiver!
And folks who put me in a passion
May find me pipe after another fashion."

11

"How?" cried the Mayor, "d'ye think I brook
Being worse treated than a Cook?
Insulted by a lazy ribald
With idle pipe and vesture piebald?
You threaten us, fellow? Do your worst,
Blow your pipe there till you burst!"

12

Once more he stepped into the street,
  And to his lips again
Laid his long pipe of smooth straight cane;
  And ere he blew three notes (such sweet
Soft notes as yet musician's cunning
  Never gave the enraptured air)
There was a rustling that seemed like a bustling
Of merry crowds justling at pitching and hustling;
Small feet were pattering, wooden shoes clattering,
Little hands clapping and little tongues chattering
And, like fowls in a farmyard when barley is scattering,
Out came the children running.
All the little boys and girls,
With rosy cheeks and flaxen curls,
And sparkling eyes and teeth like pearls,
Tripping and skipping, ran merrily after
The wonderful music with shouting and laughter.

13

The Mayor was dumb, and the Council stood
As if they were changed into blocks of wood,
Unable to move a step, or cry
To the children merrily skipping by
—Could only follow with the eye
That joyous crowd at the piper's back.

**182. stiver:** a Dutch coin worth about two cents.

But how the Mayor was on the rack,
And the wretched Council's bosoms beat,
As the Piper turned from the High Street
To where the Weser rolled its waters
Right in the way of their sons and daughters!
However, he turned from south to west,
And to Koppelberg Hill his steps addressed,
And after him the children pressed;
Great was the joy in every breast.
"He never can cross that mighty top!
He's forced to let the piping drop,
And we shall see our children stop!"
When, lo, as they reached the mountainside,
A wondrous portal opened wide,
As if a cavern was suddenly hollowed;
And the Piper advanced and the children followed,
And when all were in to the very last,
The door in the mountainside shut fast.
Did I say, all? No! One was lame,
And could not dance the whole of the way;
And in after years, if you would blame
His sadness, he was used to say—
"It's dull in our town since my playmates left!
I can't forget that I'm bereft
Of all the pleasant sights they see,
Which the Piper also promised me.
For he led us, he said, to a joyous land,
Joining the town and just at hand,
Where waters gushed and fruit trees grew
And flowers put forth a fairer hue,
And everything was strange and new;
The sparrows were brighter than peacocks here,
And their dogs outran our fallow deer,
And honeybees had lost their stings,
And horses were born with eagles' wings;
And just as I became assured
My lame foot would be speedily cured,
The music stopped and I stood still,
And found myself outside the hill,
Left alone against my will,
To go now limping as before,
And never hear of that country more!"

14

Alas, alas for Hamelin!
  There came into many a burgher's pate
  A text which says that heaven's gate
  Opes to the rich at as easy rate
As the needle's eye takes a camel in!
The Mayor sent east, west, north, and south,
To offer the Piper, by word of mouth,
  Wherever it was men's lot to find him,

**258. a text:** Matt. 19:24.

Silver and gold to his heart's content,
If he'd only return the way he went,
  And bring the children behind him.
But when they saw 'twas a lost endeavor,
And Piper and dancers were gone forever,
They made a decree that lawyers never
  Should think their records dated duly
If, after the day of the month and year,
These words did not as well appear,
" And so long after what happened here
  On the Twenty-second of July,
Thirteen hundred and seventy-six ";
And the better in memory to fix
The place of the children's last retreat,
They called it, the Pied Pipers Street —
Where anyone playing on pipe or tabor
Was sure for the future to lose his labor.
Nor suffered they hostelry or tavern
  To shock with mirth a street so solemn;
But opposite the place of the cavern
  They wrote the story on a column.
And on the great church window painted
The same, to make the world acquainted
How their children were stolen away,
And there it stands to this very day.
And I must not omit to say
That in Transylvania there's a tribe
Of alien people who ascribe
The outlandish ways and dress
On which their neighbors lay such stress,
To their fathers and mothers having risen
Out of some subterraneous prison
Into which they were trepanned
Long time ago in a mighty band
Out of Hamelin town in Brunswick land,
But how or why, they don't understand.

15

So, Willy, let me and you be wipers
Of scores out with all men — especially pipers!
And, whether they pipe us free fróm rats or fróm mice,
If we've promised them aught, let us keep our promise!

**288. this . . . day:** The date used by Browning is that given by the legend in Verstegen's *Restitution of Decayed Intelligence in Antiquities* (1605), but he may have seen the column and window as he passed through Hamelin on his journey to Russia in 1834. **290. Transylvania:** now in northwestern Rumania. The legend of the children may have risen to explain the presence of Saxon people in that part of Europe. It may owe something to the Children's Crusade of 1212.

# from DRAMATIC ROMANCES, 1845

## HOW THEY BROUGHT THE GOOD NEWS FROM GHENT TO AIX

[*16—*]

" How They Brought the Good News " was written on the flyleaf of Bartoli's *Simboli* while Browning's ship was off the north coast of Africa in August, 1844. The *Simboli* was a collection of moral essays and legends of saints, which Browning's tutor in Italian had edited as a model of good Italian style. It is possible that Bartoli's legends spurred Browning to imagine a secular story more to his own taste. The poem records no historical incident but catches the spirit of the wars in Flanders in the seventeenth century. Browning had twice passed through Flanders, but his memory of places and distances was inaccurate, and he made the rider travel 120 miles in one night. Aix-la-Chapelle in West Prussia is about one hundred miles from Ghent in Belgium. Looz and Tongres are about twenty miles out of the direct route from Ghent to Aix.

I sprang to the stirrup, and Joris, and he;
I galloped, Dirck galloped, we galloped all three;
" Good speed! " cried the watch, as the gatebolts undrew;
" Speed! " echoed the wall to us galloping through;
Behind shut the postern, the lights sank to rest,
And into the midnight we galloped abreast.

Not a word to each other; we kept the great pace
Neck by neck, stride by stride, never changing our place;
I turned in my saddle and made its girths tight,
Then shortened each stirrup, and set the pique right,
Rebuckled the cheek strap, chained slacker the bit,
Nor galloped less steadily Roland a whit.

'Twas moonset at starting; but while we drew near
Lokeren, the cocks crew and twilight dawned clear;
At Boom, a great yellow star came out to see;
At Düffeld, 'twas morning as plain as could be;
And from Mecheln church steeple we heard the half-chime,
So, Joris broke silence with, " Yet there is time! "

At Aershot, up leaped of a sudden the sun,
And against him the cattle stood black every one,
To stare through the mist at us galloping past
And I saw my stout galloper Roland at last,

HOW THEY BROUGHT THE GOOD NEWS. **5. postern:** a back or side gate. **10. pique:** possibly the spur; from the French verb *piquer*.

With resolute shoulders, each butting away
The haze, as some bluff river headland its spray:

And his low head and crest, just one sharp ear bent back
For my voice, and the other pricked out on his track;
And one eye's black intelligence — ever that glance
O'er its white edge at me, his own master, askance!
And the thick heavy spume flakes which aye and anon
His fierce lips shook upwards in galloping on.

By Hasselt, Dirck groaned; and cried Joris, "Stay spur!
Your Roos galloped bravely, the fault's not in her,
We'll remember at Aix" — for one heard the quick wheeze
Of her chest, saw the stretched neck and staggering knees,
And sunk tail, and horrible heave of the flank,
As down on her haunches she shuddered and sank.

So, we were left galloping, Joris and I,
Past Looz and past Tongres, no cloud in the sky;
The broad sun above laughed a pitiless laugh,
'Neath our feet broke the brittle bright stubble like chaff;
Till over by Dalhem a dome-spire sprang white,
And "Gallop," gasped Joris, "for Aix is in sight!"

"How they'll greet us!" — and all in a moment his roan
Rolled neck and croup over, lay dead as a stone;
And there was my Roland to bear the whole weight
Of the news which alone could save Aix from her fate,
With his nostrils like pits full of blood to the brim,
And with circles of red for his eye sockets' rim.

Then I cast loose my buffcoat, each holster let fall,
Shook off both my jack boots, let go belt and all,
Stood up in the stirrup, leaned, patted his ear,
Called my Roland his pet name, my horse without peer;
Clapped my hands, laughed and sang, any noise, bad or good,
Till at length into Aix Roland galloped and stood.

And all I remember is — friends flocking round
As I sat with his head 'twixt my knees on the ground;
And no voice but was praising this Roland of mine,
As I poured down his throat our last measure of wine,
Which (the burgesses voted by common consent)
Was no more than his due who brought good news from Ghent.

# THE LOST LEADER

Browning admitted that "The Lost Leader" was a "fancy portrait" of William Wordsworth, whose acceptance of a Civil List pension of £300 on October 15, 1842, and the laureateship on April 4, 1843, seemed like apostasy to the young poet devoted to the liberalism of Shelley, Byron, Hazlitt, and Leigh Hunt. The poem seems to have been written just before October 22, 1845, when Miss Barrett first saw it. In his later years Browning qualified his charges against Wordsworth but never entirely abandoned them.

Just for a handful of silver he left us,
  Just for a riband to stick in his coat —
Found the one gift of which fortune bereft us,
  Lost all the others she lets us devote;
They, with the gold to give, doled him out silver,
  So much was theirs who so little allowed;
How all our copper had gone for his service!
  Rags — were they purple, his heart had been proud!
We that had loved him so, followed him, honored him,
  Lived in his mild and magnificent eye,
Learned his great language, caught his clear accents,
  Made him our pattern to live and to die!
Shakespeare was of us, Milton was for us,
  Burns, Shelley were with us — they watch from their graves!
He alone breaks from the van and the freemen,
  — He alone sinks to the rear and the slaves!

We shall march prospering — not through his presence;
  Songs may inspirit us — not from his lyre;
Deeds will be done — while he boasts his quiescence,
  Still bidding crouch whom the rest bade aspire;
Blot out his name, then, record one lost soul more,
  One task more declined, one more footpath untrod,
One more devils' triumph and sorrow for angels,
  One wrong more to man, one more insult to God!
Life's night begins; let him never come back to us!
  There would be doubt, hesitation, and pain,
Forced praise on our part — the glimmer of twilight,
  Never glad confident morning again!
Best fight on well, for we taught him — strike gallantly,
  Menace our heart ere we master his own;
Then let him receive the new knowledge and wait us,
  Pardoned in heaven, the first by the throne!

THE LOST LEADER. 1. **handful of silver**: the pension referred to in the headnote. 2. **riband**: the laureateship.

## HOME-THOUGHTS, FROM ABROAD

This poem was probably written in England in the early spring of 1845, after Browning's return from Italy. Compare "De Gustibus," below.

Oh, to be in England
Now that April's there,
And whoever wakes in England
Sees, some morning, unaware,
That the lowest boughs and the brushwood sheaf
Round the elm-tree bole are in tiny leaf,
While the chaffinch sings on the orchard bough
In England — now!

And after April, when May follows,
And the whitethroat builds, and all the swallows!
Hark, where my blossomed pear tree in the hedge
Leans to the field and scatters on the clover
Blossoms and dewdrops — at the bent spray's edge —
That's the wise thrush; he sings each song twice over,
Lest you should think he never could recapture
The first fine careless rapture!
And though the fields look rough with hoary dew,
All will be gay when noontide wakes anew
The buttercups, the little children's dower
— Far brighter than this gaudy melon flower!

## HOME-THOUGHTS, FROM THE SEA

The tradition that "Home-Thoughts, from the Sea" was written on Browning's first voyage to Italy in 1838 seems untenable. It is more likely that it was written in August, 1844, when Browning's ship, bound for Italy, lay off Cape St. Vincent, the southwestern point of Portugal. Here, on February 14, 1797, Nelson received the surrender of the Spanish fleet.

Nobly, nobly Cape St. Vincent to the northwest died away;
Sunset ran, one glorious blood-red, reeking into Cadiz Bay;
Bluish 'mid the burning water, full in face Trafalgar lay;
In the dimmest northeast distance dawned Gibraltar grand and gray;
"Here and here did England help me; how can I help England?" — say,
Whoso turns as I, this evening, turn to God to praise and pray,
While Jove's planet rises yonder, silent over Africa.

HOME-THOUGHTS, FROM THE SEA. **3. Trafalgar:** a cape east of Cadiz Bay. Here on Oct. 21, 1805, Nelson defeated the French and Spanish fleets and was himself fatally wounded. **7. Jove's planet:** Jupiter, the evening star.

## THE BISHOP ORDERS HIS TOMB AT ST. PRAXED'S CHURCH

*Rome, 15—*

Under the title, "The Tomb at St. Praxed's," this poem was first published in *Hood's Magazine* for March, 1845. It was probably conceived in October, 1844, in Rome, when Browning visited the ornately decorated Church of S. Prassede, so-called for the virgin daughter of Pudens, a Roman senator of the second century. It may have been written in England early in 1845.

Although the particular tomb, the bishop, and Gandolf are all imaginary, the substance of the poem was provided by Browning's wide knowledge of Renaissance history, both secular and religious. Ruskin said admiringly of it: "I know of no other piece of modern English, prose or poetry, in which there is so much told, as in these lines, of the Renaissance spirit — its worldliness, inconsistency, pride, hypocrisy, ignorance of itself, love of art, of luxury, and of good Latin. . . ." In her letter of November 15, 1845, Miss Barrett reserved first place for it among the *Dramatic Romances.* The poem shows Browning's early mastery of the dramatic monologue as a type of poetry he was to make peculiarly his own.

Vanity, saith the preacher, vanity!
Draw round my bed; is Anselm keeping back?
Nephews — sons mine . . . ah, God, I know not! Well —
She, men would have to be your mother once,
Old Gandolf envied me, so fair she was!
What's done is done, and she is dead beside,
Dead long ago, and I am Bishop since,
And as she died so must we die ourselves,
And thence ye may perceive the world's a dream.
Life, how and what is it? As here I lie
In this state chamber, dying by degrees,
Hours and long hours in the dead night, I ask,
"Do I live, am I dead?" Peace, peace seems all.
St. Praxed's ever was the church for peace;
And so, about this tomb of mine. I fought
With tooth and nail to save my niche, ye know —
Old Gandolf cozened me, despite my care;
Shrewd was that snatch from out the corner south
He graced his carrion with, God curse the same!
Yet still my niche is not so cramped but thence
One sees the pulpit o' the epistle side,
And somewhat of the choir, those silent seats,
And up into the aery dome where live
The angels, and a sunbeam's sure to lurk;
And I shall fill my slab of basalt there,

THE BISHOP ORDERS HIS TOMB. **1.** The bishop is thinking of the passage in Eccles. 1:2: "Vanity of vanities, saith the Preacher, vanity of vanities; all is vanity." **3. Nephews:** as he has called his sons for the sake of propriety. **17. cozened:** cheated. **21. epistle side:** The epistle side is the right as one faces the altar.

And 'neath my tabernacle take my rest,
With those nine columns round me, two and
two,
The odd one at my feet where Anselm stands:
Peach-blossom marble all, the rare, the ripe
As fresh-poured red wine of a mighty pulse.
— Old Gandolf with his paltry onion stone,
Put me where I may look at him! True peach,
Rosy and flawless; how I earned the prize!
Draw close; that conflagration of my church
— What then? So much was saved if aught were
missed!
My sons, ye would not be my death? Go dig
The white-grape vineyard where the oil press stood,
Drop water gently till the surface sink,
And if ye find . . . Ah, God, I know not, I! . . .
Bedded in store of rotten fig leaves soft,
And corded up in a tight olive-frail,
Some lump, ah, God, of *lapis lazuli*,
Big as a Jew's head cut off at the nape,
Blue as a vein o'er the Madonna's breast . . .
Sons, all have I bequeathed you, villas, all,
That brave Frascati villa with its bath,
So, let the blue lump poise between my knees,
Like God the Father's globe on both his hands
Ye worship in the Jesu Church so gay,
For Gandolf shall not choose but see and burst!
Swift as a weaver's shuttle fleet our years;
Man goeth to the grave, and where is he?
Did I say basalt for my slab, sons? Black—
'Twas ever antique-black I meant! How else
Shall ye contrast my frieze to come beneath?
The bas-relief in bronze ye promised me,
Those Pans and Nymphs ye wot of, and perchance
Some tripod, thyrsus, with a vase or so,
The Saviour at his sermon on the mount,
St. Praxed in a glory, and one Pan
Ready to twitch the Nymph's last garment off,
And Moses with the tables . . . but I know
Ye mark me not! What do they whisper thee,
Child of my bowels, Anselm? Ah, ye hope
To revel down my villas while I gasp
Bricked o'er with beggar's moldy travertine
Which Gandolf from his tomb top chuckles at!
Nay, boys, ye love me — all of jasper, then!
'Tis jasper ye stand pledged to, lest I grieve
My bath must needs be left behind, alas!
One block, pure green as a pistachio nut,
There's plenty jasper somewhere in the world —
And have I not St. Praxed's ear to pray
Horses for ye, and brown Greek manuscripts,
And mistresses with great smooth marbly limbs?
— That's if ye carve my epitaph aright,
Choice Latin, picked phrase, Tully's every word,
No gaudy ware like Gandolf's second line —
Tully, my masters? Ulpian serves his need!
And then how I shall lie through centuries,
And hear the blessed mutter of the mass,
And see God made and eaten all day long,
And feel the steady candle flame, and taste
Good strong thick stupefying incense smoke!
For as I lie here, hours of the dead night,
Dying in state and by such slow degrees,
I fold my arms as if they clasped a crook,
And stretch my feet forth straight as stone can
point,
And let the bedclothes, for a mortcloth, drop
Into great laps and folds of sculptor's work:
And as yon tapers dwindle, and strange thoughts
Grow, with a certain humming in my ears,
About the life before I lived this life,
And this life too, popes, cardinals, and priests,
St. Praxed at his sermon on the mount,
Your tall pale mother with her talking eyes,
And new-found agate urns as fresh as day,
And marble's language, Latin pure, discreet,
— Aha, ELUCESCEBAT quoth our friend?
No Tully, said I, Ulpian at the best!
Evil and brief hath been my pilgrimage.
All *lapis*, all, sons! Else I give the Pope
My villas! Will ye ever eat my heart?
Ever your eyes were as a lizard's quick,
They glitter like your mother's for my soul,
Or ye would heighten my impoverished frieze,
Piece out its starved design, and fill my vase
With grapes, and add a visor and a term,
And to the tripod ye would tie a lynx
That in his struggle throws the thyrsus down,
To comfort me on my entablature
Whereon I am to lie till I must ask
"Do I live, am I dead?" There, leave me, there!
For ye have stabbed me with ingratitude

**26. tabernacle:** canopy. **30. pulse:** strength. **31. onion stone:** a cheap marble that peels in layers, green and yellow. **41. olive-frail:** basket for olives. **42. *lapis lazuli*:** a semiprecious blue stone. **46. Frascati:** a wealthy suburb southeast of Rome. **49. Jesu Church:** Il Jesu, the Jesuit church in Rome. **51. Swift . . . years:** Job 7:6: "My days are swifter than a weaver's shuttle, and are spent without hope." **58. tripod, thyrsus:** The tripod was the three-legged stool connected with the Delphic oracle; the thyrsus was a staff used by the followers of Bacchus. Observe the pagan nature of the bishop's ornaments. **60. St. Praxed:** See headnote. **62. Moses . . . tables:** Moses brought the tablets down from Mount Sinai with the Ten Commandments written upon them. See Exod. 24. **66. travertine:** a form of limestone commonly used in building.

**74. brown . . . manuscripts:** Because of their hunger for learning, Renaissance society greatly prized Greek manuscripts. **77. Tully:** Marcus Tullius Cicero, whose style was classic. **79. Ulpian:** Domitius Ulpianus (170–228), whose style was ornate and regarded as degenerate. **82. God . . . eaten:** In the Mass the priest is believed to convert the bread into the body of Christ which is eaten by the communicants. **87. crook:** a crozier, a symbol of episcopal rank. **89. mortcloth:** funeral pall. **99.** ELUCESCEBAT: "he was famous." Cicero would have written *elucebat*. **108. visor:** mask. **term:** a bust on a pedestal.

To death — ye wish it — God, ye wish it! Stone —
Gritstone, a-crumble! Clammy squares which sweat
As if the corpse they keep were oozing through —
And no more *lapis* to delight the world!
Well, go! I bless ye. Fewer tapers there,
But in a row; and, going, turn your backs
— Aye, like departing altar ministrants,
And leave me in my church, the church for peace,
That I may watch at leisure if he leers —
Old Gandolf — at me, from his onion stone,
As still he envied me, so fair she was!

## MEETING AT NIGHT

In 1845 this poem and the poem which follows appeared under the title "Night and Morning." They assumed their present titles in 1849. They were called "new poems" by Miss Barrett when she first saw them in October, 1845, and it is likely that they had only recently been written. The landscapes suggest Italy. Browning declared that both poems were written from the point of view of the man.

The gray sea and the long black land;
And the yellow half-moon large and low;
And the startled little waves that leap
In fiery ringlets from their sleep,
As I gain the cove with pushing prow,
And quench its speed i' the slushy sand.

Then a mile of warm sea-scented beach;
Three fields to cross till a farm appears;
A tap at the pane, the quick sharp scratch
And blue spurt of a lighted match,
And a voice less loud, through its joys and fears,
Than the two hearts beating each to each!

## PARTING AT MORNING

See the headnote for "Meeting at Night," above. According to Browning, this second poem "is *his* confession of how fleeting is the belief (implied in the first part) that such raptures are self-sufficient and enduring — as for the time they appear."

Round the cape of a sudden came the sea,
And the sun looked over the mountain's rim;
And straight was a path of gold for him,
And the need of a world of men for me.

PARTING AT MORNING. 3. him: the sun.



# from MEN AND WOMEN, 1855

## LOVE AMONG THE RUINS

"Love among the Ruins" was written on January 1, 1852, in Paris. It reflects the immense rise of interest in these years in archaeological exploration in Europe and the Near East; the ancient city as Browning describes it resembles Herodotus' description of Babylon, but owes some details to the Apocalypse of St. John, and perhaps to I Chronicles 18 and 21. The city, however, seems to be a composite containing elements from the descriptions of Tarquinia, Nineveh, Thebes, and others as well. The modern scene may owe something to the Italian Campagna, or to pictures of it.

Where the quiet-colored end of evening smiles
Miles and miles
On the solitary pastures where our sheep
Half-asleep
Tinkle homeward through the twilight, stray or stop
As they crop —
Was the site once of a city great and gay,
(So they say)
Of our country's very capital, its prince
Ages since
Held his court in, gathered councils, wielding far
Peace or war.

Now — the country does not even boast a tree,
As you see,
To distinguish slopes of verdure, certain rills
From the hills
Intersect and give a name to (else they run
Into one),
Where the domed and daring palace shot its spires
Up like fires
O'er the hundred-gated circuit of a wall
Bounding all,
Made of marble, men might march on nor be pressed,
Twelve abreast.

And such plenty and perfection, see, of grass
Never was!
Such a carpet as, this summer time, o'erspreads
And embeds
Every vestige of the city, guessed alone,
Stock or stone —
Where a multitude of men breathed joy and woe
Long ago;
Lust of glory pricked their hearts up, dread of shame
Struck them tame;
And that glory and that shame alike, the gold
Bought and sold.

Now — the single little turret that remains
  On the plains,
By the caper overrooted, by the gourd
  Overscored,
While the patching houseleek's head of blossom winks
  Through the chinks —
Marks the basement whence a tower in ancient time
  Sprang sublime,
And a burning ring, all round, the chariots traced
  As they raced,
And the monarch and his minions and his dames
  Viewed the games.

And I know, while thus the quiet-colored eve
  Smiles to leave
To their folding, all our many-tinkling fleece
  In such peace,
And the slopes and rills in undistinguished gray
  Melt away —
That a girl with eager eyes and yellow hair
  Waits me there
In the turret whence the charioteers caught soul
  For the goal,
When the king looked, where she looks now, breathless, dumb
  Till I come.

But he looked upon the city, every side,
  Far and wide,
All the mountains topped with temples, all the glades'
  Colonnades,
All the causeys, bridges, aqueducts — and then,
  All the men!
When I do come, she will speak not, she will stand,
  Either hand
On my shoulder, give her eyes the first embrace
  Of my face,
Ere we rush, ere we extinguish sight and speech
  Each on each.

In one year they sent a million fighters forth
  South and north,
And they built their gods a brazen pillar high
  As the sky,
Yet reserved a thousand chariots in full force —
  Gold, of course.
Oh, heart! oh, blood that freezes, blood that burns!
  Earth's returns
For whole centuries of folly, noise, and sin!
  Shut them in,
With their triumphs and their glories and the rest!
  Love is best.

LOVE AMONG THE RUINS. **39. caper**: a low, brambly bush. **41. houseleek**: a small, spreading plant. **47. minions**: favorites, lesser persons. **65. causeys**: causeways, or raised roads over low ground or swamps.

# EVELYN HOPE

From its interest in the idea of successive reincarnations one is inclined to link this poem with "Cristina," and to assume that it was written early, possibly in 1846. The idea of successive lives is implicit in the whole poem, and the elderly lover is confident, as we see in lines 29–32, that in some future life he and Evelyn Hope will be lovers. The poem is not autobiographical.

Beautiful Evelyn Hope is dead!
  Sit and watch by her side an hour.
That is her book shelf, this her bed;
  She plucked that piece of geranium flower,
Beginning to die too, in the glass;
  Little has yet been changed, I think:
The shutters are shut, no light may pass
  Save two long rays through the hinge's chink.

Sixteen years old when she died!
  Perhaps she had scarcely heard my name;
It was not her time to love; beside,
  Her life had many a hope and aim,
Duties enough and little cares,
  And now was quiet, now astir,
Till God's hand beckoned unawares —
  And the sweet white brow is all of her.

Is it too late then, Evelyn Hope?
  What, your soul was pure and true,
The good stars met in your horoscope,
  Made you of spirit, fire, and dew —
And, just because I was thrice as old
  And our paths in the world diverged so wide,
Each was nought to each, must I be told?
  We were fellow mortals, naught beside?

No, indeed! for God above
  Is great to grant, as mighty to make,
And creates the love to reward the love:
  I claim you still, for my own love's sake!
Delayed it may be for more lives yet,
  Through worlds I shall traverse, not a few;
Much is to learn, much to forget
  Ere the time be come for taking you.

But the time will come — at last it will,
  When, Evelyn Hope, what meant (I shall say)
In the lower earth, in the years long still,
  That body and soul so pure and gay?
Why your hair was amber, I shall divine,
  And your mouth of your own geranium's red —
And what you would do with me, in fine,
  In the new life come in the old one's stead.

I have lived (I shall say) so much since then,
  Given up myself so many times,

Gained me the gains of various men,
  Ransacked the ages, spoiled the climes;
Yet one thing, one, in my soul's full scope,
  Either I missed or itself missed me:
And I want and find you, Evelyn Hope!
  What is the issue? let us see!

I loved you, Evelyn, all the while!
  My heart seemed full as it could hold;
There was place and to spare for the frank young smile,
  And the red young mouth, and the hair's young gold.
So, hush — I will give you this leaf to keep:
  See, I shut it inside the sweet cold hand!
There, that is our secret: go to sleep!
  You will wake, and remember, and understand.

## UP AT A VILLA — DOWN IN THE CITY

### *As Distinguished by an Italian Person of Quality*

"Up at a Villa" was possibly written in September, 1850, when the Brownings occupied a villa on the hills near Siena, or in the summer of 1853 at Bagni di Lucca where conditions were similar to those in Siena. It illustrates Browning's acute and humorous observation of Italian life.

Had I but plenty of money, money enough and to spare,
The house for me, no doubt, were a house in the city square;
Ah, such a life, such a life, as one leads at the window there!

Something to see, by Bacchus, something to hear, at least!
There, the whole day long, one's life is a perfect feast;
While up at a villa one lives, I maintain it, no more than a beast.

Well now, look at our villa! stuck like the horn of a bull
Just on a mountain edge as bare as the creature's skull,
Save a mere shag of a bush with hardly a leaf to pull!
— I scratch my own, sometimes, to see if the hair's turned wool.

But the city, oh, the city — the square with the houses! Why?
They are stone-faced, white as a curd, there's something to take the eye!
Houses in four straight lines, not a single front awry;
You watch who crosses and gossips, who saunters, who hurries by;
Green blinds, as a matter of course, to draw when the sun gets high;
And the shops with fanciful signs which are painted properly.

What of a villa? Though winter be over in March by rights,
'Tis May perhaps ere the snow shall have withered well off the heights;
You've the brown plowed land before, where the oxen steam and wheeze,
And the hills oversmoked behind by the faint gray olive trees.

Is it better in May, I ask you? You've summer all at once;
In a day he leaps complete with a few strong April suns.
'Mid the sharp short emerald wheat, scarce risen three fingers well,
The wild tulip, at end of its tube, blows out its great red bell
Like a thin clear bubble of blood, for the children to pick and sell.

Is it ever hot in the square? There's a fountain to spout and splash!
In the shade it sings and springs; in the shine such foam-bows flash
On the horses with curling fish tails, that prance and paddle and pash
Round the lady atop in her conch — fifty gazers do not abash,
Though all that she wears is some weeds round her waist in a sort of sash.

All the year long at the villa, nothing to see though you linger,
Except yon cypress that points like death's lean lifted forefinger.
Some think fireflies pretty, when they mix i' the corn and mingle,
Or thrid the stinking hemp till the stalks of it seem a-tingle.
Late August or early September, the stunning cicala is shrill,
And the bees keep their tiresome whine round the resinous firs on the hill.
Enough of the seasons — I spare you the months of the fever and chill.

UP AT A VILLA. 4. by Bacchus: a mild Italian oath.

29. conch: shell. 34. thrid: thread, fly through.

Ere you open your eyes in the city, the blessed church bells begin;
No sooner the bells leave off than the diligence rattles in;
You get the pick of the news, and it costs you never a pin.
By and by there's the traveling doctor gives pills, lets blood, draws teeth;
Or the Pulcinello trumpet breaks up the market beneath.
At the post office such a scene-picture — the new play, piping hot!
And a notice how, only this morning, three liberal thieves were shot.
Above it, behold the Archbishop's most fatherly of rebukes,
And beneath, with his crown and his lion, some little new law of the Duke's!
Or a sonnet with flowery marge, to the Reverend Don So-and-so,
Who is Dante, Boccaccio, Petrarca, St. Jerome, and Cicero,
"And moreover" (the sonnet goes rhyming) "the skirts of St. Paul has reached,
Having preached us those six Lent lectures more unctuous than ever he preached."
Noon strikes — here sweeps the procession! Our Lady borne smiling and smart
With a pink gauze gown all spangles, and seven swords stuck in her heart!
*Bang-whang-whang* goes the drum, *tootle-te-tootle* the fife;
No keeping one's haunches still; it's the greatest pleasure in life.

But bless you, it's dear — it's dear! fowls, wine, at double the rate.
They have clapped a new tax upon salt, and what oil pays passing the gate
It's a horror to think of. And so, the villa for me, not the city!
Beggars can scarcely be choosers; but still — ah, the pity, the pity!
Look, two and two go the priests, then the monks with cowls and sandals,
And the penitents dressed in white shirts, a-holding the yellow candles;
One, he carries a flag up straight, and another a cross with handles,
And the Duke's guard brings up the rear, for the better prevention of scandals.
*Bang-whang-whang* goes the drum, *tootle-te-tootle* the fife.
Oh, a day in the city square, there is no such pleasure in life!

**39. diligence:** coach. **42. Pulcinello trumpet:** the trumpet, used by strolling players, to announce the arrival of Pulcinello, the buffoon of the puppet show. **43. scene-picture:** picture advertising the coming play. **44. liberal thieves:** men of the revolutionary party against Austria (which then controlled Italy), who practiced thievery on the side. **47. sonnet:** First written in Italy, the sonnet was used for all occasions, especially, as here, to compliment prominent persons. **51. Our Lady:** the Virgin, here Our Lady of Sorrows. The seven swords represent her seven sorrows: (1) the prophecy that a sword should pierce her soul because of her Son; (2) her suffering in the flight into Egypt; (3) her grief when her Son was lost in Jerusalem before he was found in the Temple; (4) her pain when she saw Jesus bearing the cross; (5) her suffering when she saw the agony of Christ; (6) her pain when the side of her Son was pierced; and (7) her grief at the burial of Christ. **56. tax . . . salt:** Salt was a favorite commodity for taxation in Italy and other nations. All country produce was subject to tax as it entered the city.

## FRA LIPPO LIPPI

Early in 1853 Browning was "writing — a first step towards popularity for me — lyrics with more music and painting than before, so as to get people to hear and see. . . ." "Fra Lippo Lippi" was one of these. In Florence and elsewhere, Browning saw many of Lippi's pictures, especially "The Coronation of the Virgin," which is described at the end of the poem. In the story of the poem he mainly follows the colorful account of Lippi's life in Vasari's *Delle Vite Pittori* (1550), now available in English as *The Lives of the Painters,* although for some details he used Baldinucci's *Account of the Artists,* published in Italian at Florence in 1767–74. Baldinucci emphasized more strongly than Vasari the idea that Lippi was one of the first painters to break with the stiff formal tradition of ecclesiastical painting, to become a naturalistic and realistic artist, and to introduce contemporary scenes and figures into his work. In Lippi's view of the nature and function of art Browning saw a parallel to his own conception of the nature and function of poetry in the nineteenth century in England, and he thought of himself as a pioneer among his fellow poets as Lippi was among the painters of his day. Also, like Lippi, Browning's temperament was cheerful and energetic, and the sympathy with which he wrote this dramatic monologue accounts for much of its success. Many of the opinions expressed in the poem are more Browning's than Lippi's.

This poem illustrates well Browning's difference from other Victorian poets. When in 1855 he was called upon to read one of his new poems before Tennyson and D. G. Rossetti, he selected "Fra Lippo Lippi." He could not have chosen a poem of his which by its opinions on the nature of art, as well as by its conversational blank verse and its colloquial language, would challenge more effectively the formality and remoteness from reality of the poetry of that time. Just as pointedly "Fra Lippo Lippi" runs counter to the pronouncement of Matthew Arnold in his famous Preface to his *Poems* of 1853. Arnold had contended against the "false contemporary view" that poets must write upon "matters of present import," and said, "A great human action of a thousand years ago is more interesting

. . . than a smaller human action of today, even though upon the representation of this last the most consummate skill may have been expended, and though it has the advantage of appealing by its modern language, familiar manners, and contemporary allusions, to all our transient feelings and interests. . . ." (See Arnold's Preface and the Introduction to Arnold, below.) Though Browning frequently used subjects from the past, especially the Renaissance, he usually gave such subjects a relevance to nineteenth-century England and contemporary problems, and, as here, he employed distinctly modern, colloquial language and familiar manners. In his later poetry he more and more dealt directly and frankly with the contemporary scene.

Vasari's account of Lippi records that he was born in 1412. At two years of age he became an orphan and fell into the care of his father's sister, Mona Lapaccia. When he was eight years old he was entered in the Carmine monastery at Florence. There he filled his schoolbooks with drawings, mainly caricatures. He took holy orders, but soon left the monastery to follow the career of a painter. He won the patronage of Cosimo de' Medici, and on one occasion, when Cosimo had him locked in the Medici Palace in order to force him to finish a picture, he escaped by tying his bedclothes together and letting himself down into the street. It is at this point that Browning's poem begins. Lippi was a gay and cheerful person. After the time which Browning represents in the poem, Lippi fell in love with a nun and abducted her, and later had this relationship recognized by the Church. He died in 1469.

I am poor brother Lippo, by your leave!
You need not clap your torches to my face.
Zooks, what's to blame? you think you see a monk!
What, 'tis past midnight, and you go the rounds,
And here you catch me at an alley's end
Where sportive ladies leave their doors ajar?
The Carmine's my cloister; hunt it up,
Do — harry out, if you must show your zeal,
Whatever rat, there, haps on his wrong hole,
And nip each softling of a wee white mouse,
*Weke, weke,* that's crept to keep him company!
Aha, you know your betters! Then, you'll take
Your hand away that's fiddling on my throat,
And please to know me likewise. Who am I?
Why, one, sir, who is lodging with a friend
Three streets off — he's a certain . . . how d' ye call?
Master — a . . . Cosimo of the Medici,
I' the house that caps the corner. Boh! you were best!
Remember and tell me, the day you're hanged,
How you affected such a gullet's gripe!
But you, sir, it concerns you that your knaves
Pick up a manner nor discredit you;
Zooks, are we pilchards, that they sweep the streets
And count fair prize what comes into their net?
He's Judas to a tittle, that man is!
Just such a face! Why, sir, you make amends.
Lord, I'm not angry! Bid your hangdogs go
Drink out this quarter-florin to the health
Of the munificent House that harbors me
(And many more beside, lads! more beside!)
And all's come square again. I'd like his face —
His, elbowing on his comrade in the door
With the pike and lantern — for the slave that holds
John Baptist's head a-dangle by the hair
With one hand ("Look you, now," as who should say)
And his weapon in the other, yet unwiped!
It's not your chance to have a bit of chalk,
A wood coal or the like? or you should see!
Yes, I'm the painter, since you style me so.
What, brother Lippo's doings, up and down,
You know them and they take you? like enough!
I saw the proper twinkle in your eye —
'Tell you, I liked your looks at very first.
Let's sit and set things straight now, hip to haunch.
Here's spring come, and the nights one makes up bands
To roam the town and sing out carnival,
And I've been three weeks shut within my mew,
A-painting for the great man, saints and saints
And saints again. I could not paint all night —
Ouf! I leaned out of window for fresh air.
There came a hurry of feet and little feet,
A sweep of lute strings, laughs, and whifts of song —
*Flower o' the broom,*
*Take away love, and our earth is a tomb!*
*Flower o' the quince,*
*I let Lisa go, and what good in life since?*
*Flower o' the thyme* — and so on. Round they went.
Scarce had they turned the corner when a titter
Like the skipping of rabbits by moonlight — three slim shapes,
And a face that looked up . . . zooks, sir, flesh and blood,
That's all I'm made of! Into shreds it went,
Curtain and counterpane and coverlet,
All the bed furniture — a dozen knots,
There was a ladder! Down I let myself,

FRA LIPPO LIPPI. **3. Zooks:** a mild oath. **17–18. Cosimo . . . best!:** Statesman, banker, and patron of the arts, Cosimo (1389–1464) was head of the Medici family at the time. Lippi roguishly delays the shock to the guards of the name of his great patron.

They remove their hands from his throat. **21. sir:** officer of the guard. **23. pilchards:** a small, common Mediterranean fish. **28. quarter-florin:** a small coin of Florence. **34. John Baptist:** a favorite subject of Lippi's. **38. wood coal:** charcoal. **41. they . . . you:** engage your interest. **53. *Flower . . . broom:*** The flower songs interspersed in the narrative are called ***stornelli*** by the Italians. They are usually three lines each.

Hands and feet, scrambling somehow, and so dropped,
And after them. I came up with the fun
Hard by St. Laurence, hail fellow, well met—
*Flower o' the rose,*
*If I've been merry, what matter who knows?*
And so as I was stealing back again
To get to bed and have a bit of sleep
Ere I rise up tomorrow and go work
On Jerome knocking at his poor old breast
With his great round stone to subdue the flesh,
You snap me of the sudden. Ah, I see!
Though your eye twinkles still, you shake your head—
Mine's shaved—a monk, you say—the sting's in that!
If Master Cosimo announced himself,
Mum's the word naturally; but a monk!
Come, what am I a beast for? tell us, now!
I was a baby when my mother died
And father died and left me in the street.
I starved there, God knows how, a year or two
On fig skins, melon parings, rinds and shucks,
Refuse and rubbish. One fine frosty day,
My stomach being empty as your hat,
The wind doubled me up and down I went.
Old Aunt Lapaccia trussed me with one hand,
(Its fellow was a stinger as I knew)
And so along the wall, over the bridge,
By the straight cut to the convent. Six words there,
While I stood munching my first bread that month:
"So, boy, you're minded," quoth the good fat father,
Wiping his own mouth, 'twas refection time—
"To quit this very miserable world?
Will you renounce" . . . "the mouthful of bread?" thought I;
By no means! Brief, they made a monk of me;
I did renounce the world, its pride and greed,
Palace, farm, villa, shop, and banking house,
Trash, such as these poor devils of Medici
Have given their hearts to—all at eight years old.
Well, sir, I found in time, you may be sure,
'Twas not for nothing—the good bellyful,
The warm serge and the rope that goes all round,
And day-long blessèd idleness beside!
"Let's see what the urchin's fit for"—that came next.
Not overmuch their way, I must confess.
Such a to-do! They tried me with their books;
Lord, they'd have taught me Latin in pure waste!
*Flower o' the clove,*
*All the Latin I construe is "amo," I love!*
But, mind you, when a boy starves in the streets
Eight years together, as my fortune was,
Watching folk's faces to know who will fling
The bit of half-stripped grape bunch he desires,
And who will curse or kick him for his pains—
Which gentleman processional and fine,
Holding a candle to the Sacrament,
Will wink and let him lift a plate and catch
The droppings of the wax to sell again,
Or holla for the Eight and have him whipped—
How say I?—nay, which dog bites, which lets drop
His bone from the heap of offal in the street—
Why, soul and sense of him grow sharp alike,
He learns the look of things, and none the less
For admonition from the hunger pinch.
I had a store of such remarks, be sure,
Which, after I found leisure, turned to use.
I drew men's faces on my copy books,
Scrawled them within the antiphonary's marge,
Joined legs and arms to the long music notes,
Found eyes and nose and chin for A's and B's,
And made a string of pictures of the world
Betwixt the ins and outs of verb and noun,
On the wall, the bench, the door. The monks looked black.
"Nay," quoth the Prior, "turn him out, d' ye say?
In no wise. Lose a crow and catch a lark.
What if at last we get our man of parts,
We Carmelites, like those Camaldolese
And Preaching Friars, to do our church up fine
And put the front on it that ought to be!"
And hereupon he bade me daub away.
Thank you! my head being crammed, the walls a blank,
Never was such prompt disemburdening.
First, every sort of monk, the black and white,
I drew them, fat and lean; then, folk at church,
From good old gossips waiting to confess
Their cribs of barrel droppings, candle ends—
To the breathless fellow at the altar foot,
Fresh from his murder, safe and sitting there
With the little children round him in a row
Of admiration, half for his beard and half
For that white anger of his victim's son
Shaking a fist at him with one fierce arm,
Signing himself with the other because of Christ
(Whose sad face on the cross sees only this
After the passion of a thousand years)
Till some poor girl, her apron o'er her head,
(Which the intense eyes looked through) came at eve
On tiptoe, said a word, dropped in a loaf,
Her pair of earrings and a bunch of flowers
(The brute took growling), prayed, and so was gone.

**67. St. Laurence:** the Church of San Lorenzo. **73. Jerome:** Lippi painted a picture of St. Jerome (340–420) for Cosimo. **81–135:** See headnote, above.

**121. the Eight:** the magistrates of Florence. **130. antiphonary:** the book of responses sung by the choirboys. **139. Camaldolese:** a religious order with a monastery in Florence. **140. Preaching Friars:** the Dominicans, another order. **148. cribs:** small thefts.

I painted all, then cried, "'Tis ask and have;
Choose, for more's ready!" — laid the ladder flat,
And showed my covered bit of cloister wall.
The monks closed in a circle and praised loud
Till checked, taught what to see and not to see,
Being simple bodies — "That's the very man!
Look at the boy who stoops to pat the dog!
That woman's like the Prior's niece who comes
To care about his asthma; it's the life!"
But there my triumph's straw fire flared and funked;
Their betters took their turn to see and say;
The Prior and the learned pulled a face
And stopped all that in no time. "How? what's here?
Quite from the mark of painting, bless us all!
Faces, arms, legs, and bodies like the true
As much as pea and pea! it's devil's game!
Your business is not to catch men with show,
With homage to the perishable clay,
But lift them over it, ignore it all,
Make them forget there's such a thing as flesh.
Your business is to paint the souls of men —
Man's soul, and it's a fire, smoke . . . no, it's not . . .
Its vapor done up like a newborn babe —
(In that shape when you die it leaves your mouth)
It's . . . well, what matters talking, it's the soul!
Gives us no more of body than shows soul!
Here's Giotto, with his Saint a-praising God,
That sets us praising — why not stop with him?
Why put all thoughts of praise out of our head
With wonder at lines, colors, and what not?
Paint the soul, never mind the legs and arms!
Rub all out, try at it a second time.
Oh, that white smallish female with the breasts,
She's just my niece . . . Herodias, I would say —
Who went and danced and got men's heads cut off!
Have it all out!" Now, is this sense, I ask?
A fine way to paint soul, by painting body
So ill, the eye can't stop there, must go further
And can't fare worse! Thus, yellow does for white
When what you put for yellow's simply black,
And any sort of meaning looks intense
When all beside itself means and looks naught.
Why can't a painter lift each foot in turn,
Left foot and right foot, go a double step,
Make his flesh liker and his soul more like,
Both in their order? Take the prettiest face,
The Prior's niece . . . patron saint — is it so pretty
You can't discover if it means hope, fear,
Sorrow or joy? won't beauty go with these?
Suppose I've made her eyes all right and blue,
Can't I take breath and try to add life's flash,
And then add soul and heighten them threefold?
Or say there's beauty with no soul at all —
(I never saw it — put the case the same — )
If you get simple beauty and naught else,
You get about the best thing God invents:
That's somewhat; and you'll find the soul you have missed,
Within yourself, when you return him thanks.
"Rub all out!" Well, well, there's my life, in short,
And so the thing has gone on ever since.
I'm grown a man no doubt, I've broken bounds;
You should not take a fellow eight years old
And make him swear to never kiss the girls.
I'm my own master, paint now as I please —
Having a friend, you see, in the Corner-house!
Lord, it's fast holding by the rings in front —
Those great rings serve more purposes than just
To plant a flag in, or tie up a horse!
And yet the old schooling sticks, the old grave eyes
Are peeping o'er my shoulder as I work,
The heads shake still — "It's art's decline, my son!
You're not of the true painters, great and old;
Brother Angelico's the man, you'll find;
Brother Lorenzo stands his single peer;
Fag on at flesh, you'll never make the third!"
*Flower o' the pine,*
*You keep your mistr . . . manners, and I'll stick to mine!*
I'm not the third, then; bless us, they must know!
Don't you think they're the likeliest to know,
They with their Latin? So, I swallow my rage,
Clench my teeth, suck my lips in tight, and paint
To please them — sometimes do and sometimes don't;
For, doing most, there's pretty sure to come
A turn, some warm eve finds me at my saints —
A laugh, a cry, the business of the world —
(*Flower o' the peach,*
*Death for us all, and his own life for each!*)
And my whole soul revolves, the cup runs over,
The world and life's too big to pass for a dream,
And I do these wild things in sheer despite,
And play the fooleries you catch me at,
In pure rage! The old mill horse, out at grass
After hard years, throws up his stiff heels so,

**172. funked:** turned to smoke. **189. Giotto:** Giotto di Bondone (1276–1337), the most famous of early Italian painters, also a sculptor and architect of renown. Browning is here describing the monastic tradition in painting against which Lippi revolts. **196. Herodias:** the wife of Philip, Herod's brother, and the mother of Salome. When John the Baptist objected to Herod's marrying his brother's wife, Herodias plotted the revenge which led to John's decapitation.

**227. Corner-house:** the palace in which Cosimo de' Medici lived, now known as the Palazzo Riccardi, at the corner of Via Cavour and Via Gori. **235–36. Angelico, Lorenzo:** Fra Angelico, Giovanni da Fiesole (1387–1455), and Lorenzo Monaco (*c.* 1370–*c.* 1425) are cited as representatives of the traditional school of religious painters against which Lippi sets himself. Angelico is said to have knelt while painting; Lorenzo, the Monk, was of the Camaldolese order. Lippi hardly does justice to Angelico here

Although the miller does not preach to him
The only good of grass is to make chaff.
What would men have? Do they like grass or no—
May they or mayn't they? all I want's the thing
Settled forever one way. As it is,
You tell too many lies and hurt yourself;
You don't like what you only like too much,
You do like what, if given you at your word,
You find abundantly detestable.
For me, I think I speak as I was taught;
I always see the garden and God there
A-making man's wife; and, my lesson learned,
The value and significance of flesh,
I can't unlearn ten minutes afterwards.

You understand me; I'm a beast, I know.
But see, now—why, I see as certainly
As that the morning star's about to shine,
What will hap some day. We've a youngster here
Comes to our convent, studies what I do,
Slouches and stares and lets no atom drop.
His name is Guidi—he'll not mind the monks—
They call him Hulking Tom, he lets them talk—
He picks my practice up—he'll paint apace,
I hope so—though I never live so long,
I know what's sure to follow. You be judge!
You speak no Latin more than I, belike;
However, you're my man, you've seen the world
—The beauty and the wonder and the power,
The shapes of things, their colors, lights and shades,
Changes, surprises—and God made it all!
—For what? Do you feel thankful, aye or no,
For this fair town's face, yonder river's line,
The mountain round it and the sky above,
Much more the figures of man, woman, child,
These are the frame to? What's it all about?
To be passed over, despised? or dwelt upon,
Wondered at? oh, this last of course!—you say.
But why not do as well as say—paint these
Just as they are, careless what comes of it?
God's works—paint any one, and count it crime
To let a truth slip. Don't object, "His works
Are here already; nature is complete:
Suppose you reproduce her—(which you can't)
There's no advantage! you must beat her, then."
For, don't you mark? we're made so that we love
First when we see them painted, things we have passed
Perhaps a hundred times nor cared to see;
And so they are better, painted—better to us,
Which is the same thing. Art was given for that;
God uses us to help each other so,
Lending our minds out. Have you noticed, now,
Your cullion's hanging face? A bit of chalk,
And trust me but you should, though! How much more,
If I drew higher things with the same truth!
That were to take the Prior's pulpit-place,
Interpret God to all of you! Oh, oh,
It makes me mad to see what men shall do
And we in our graves! This world's no blot for us,
Nor blank; it means intensely, and means good:
To find its meaning is my meat and drink.
"Aye, but you don't so instigate to prayer!"
Strikes in the Prior; "when your meaning's plain
It does not say to folk—remember matins,
Or, mind you fast next Friday!" Why, for this
What need of art at all? A skull and bones,
Two bits of stick nailed crosswise, or, what's best,
A bell to chime the hour with, does as well.
I painted a St. Laurence six months since
At Prato, splashed the fresco in fine style;
"How looks my painting, now the scaffold's down?"
I ask a brother. "Hugely," he returns—
"Already not one phiz of your three slaves
Who turn the Deacon off his toasted side,
But's scratched and prodded to our heart's content,
The pious people have so eased their own
With coming to say prayers there in a rage;
We get on fast to see the bricks beneath.
Expect another job this time next year,
For pity and religion grow i' the crowd—
Your painting serves its purpose!" Hang the fools!

—That is—you'll not mistake an idle word
Spoke in a huff by a poor monk, God wot,
Tasting the air this spicy night which turns
The unaccustomed head like Chianti wine!
Oh, the Church knows! don't misreport me, now
It's natural a poor monk out of bounds
Should have his apt word to excuse himself;
And hearken how I plot to make amends.
I have bethought me: I shall paint a piece
. . . There's for you! Give me six months, then go, see
Something in Sant' Ambrogio's! Bless the nuns!
They want a cast o' my office. I shall paint
God in the midst, Madonna and her babe,
Ringed by a bowery, flowery angel brood,

**273–77. youngster . . . Tom:** Tomaso Guidi or Masaccio (1401–28). The best opinion now is that Masaccio who painted the famous Branacci frescoes was not Lippi's pupil, but possibly his master. Like Lippi he was a realist.

**307. cullion:** low fellow. **323. St. Laurence:** This saint was martyred in 258 by being roasted on a gridiron. **324. Prato:** a town near Florence in whose church is some of Lippi's work. **327. phiz:** face. **339. Chianti wine:** a famous wine from a region south of Florence. **344–77.** The picture which Lippi here plans to paint at St. Ambrose's Convent, so named for an early Father of the Church, is "The Coronation of the Virgin." It is now in the Accademia delle Velle Arti in Florence, where Browning saw it. The identification of the figure near the words in the lower right-hand corner of the picture *"Iste perfecit opus"* ("This man made the work") as Lippi has been seriously challenged. **347. cast . . . office:** a painting by me.

Lilies and vestments and white faces, sweet
As puff on puff of grated orris root
When ladies crowd to church at midsummer.
And then i' the front, of course a saint or two —
St. John, because he saves the Florentines,
St. Ambrose, who puts down in black and white
The convent's friends and gives them a long day,
And Job, I must have him there past mistake,
The man of Uz (and Us without the z,
Painters who need his patience). Well, all these
Secured at their devotion, up shall come
Out of a corner when you least expect,
As one by a dark stair into a great light,
Music and talking, who but Lippo! I! —
Mazed, motionless, and moonstruck — I'm the man!
Back I shrink — what is this I see and hear?
I, caught up with my monk's things by mistake,
My old serge gown and rope that goes all round,
I, in this presence, this pure company!
Where's a hole, where's a corner for escape?
Then steps a sweet angelic slip of a thing
Forward, puts out a soft palm — " Not so fast! "
— Addresses the celestial presence, " nay —
He made you and devised you, after all,
Though he's none of you! Could St. John there draw —
His camel hair make up a painting brush?
We come to brother Lippo for all that,
*Iste perfecit opus!* " So, all smile —
I shuffle sideways with my blushing face
Under the cover of a hundred wings
Thrown like a spread of kirtles when you're gay
And play hot cockles, all the doors being shut,
Till, wholly unexpected, in there pops
The hothead husband! Thus I scuttle off
To some safe bench behind, not letting go
The palm of her, the little lily thing
That spoke the good word for me in the nick,
Like the Prior's niece . . . St. Lucy, I would say.
And so all's saved for me, and for the church
A pretty picture gained. Go, six months hence!
Your hand, sir, and good-by; no lights, no lights!
The street's hushed, and I know my own way back,
Don't fear me! There's the gray beginning. Zooks!

## A TOCCATA OF GALUPPI'S

This poem may have been written as early as 1847, but more probably is one of the " lyrics with more music and painting" in them which Browning referred to in the letter of February 24, 1853, quoted from above. (See the headnote to " Fra Lippo Lippi.")

Baldassaro Galuppi (1706–85) made his great fame in Venice as a composer of light operas, church music, and sonatas. Browning, who was a skillful pianist, encountered Galuppi's music in quantity in Italy. The contrast in the poem is between the intellectual music of Galuppi's toccata (a touchpiece illustrating technique) and the pleasure-seeking lovers of the decadent city, between thought and flesh, immortality and mortality. The speaker in the poem is an Englishman, interested in mathematics and science and troubled by the cold brilliance of Galuppi's music. Venice was to his unsophisticated mind the symbol of romance — gaiety, youth, and love. Instead of these things he finds Galuppi satirizing them in his music. Compare the use of music here with that in " Abt Vogler," below.

Oh, Galuppi, Baldassare, this is very sad to find!
I can hardly misconceive you; it would prove me deaf and blind;
But although I take your meaning, 'tis with such a heavy mind!

Here you come with your old music, and here's all the good it brings.
What, they lived once thus at Venice where the merchants were the kings,
Where St. Mark's is, where the Doges used to wed the sea with rings?

Aye, because the sea's the street there; and 'tis arched by . . . what you call
. . . Shylock's bridge with houses on it, where they kept the carnival.
I was never out of England — it's as if I saw it all.

Did young people take their pleasure when the sea was warm in May?
Balls and masks begun at midnight, burning ever to mid-day,
When they made up fresh adventures for the morrow, do you say?

Was a lady such a lady, cheeks so round and lips so red —
On her neck the small face buoyant, like a bell-flower on its bed,
O'er the breast's superb abundance where a man might base his head?

Well, and it was graceful of them — they'd break talk off and afford
— She, to bite her mask's black velvet — he, to finger on his sword,

**351. orris root**: fragrant iris root, used as perfume. **354. St. John**: the patron saint of Florence. **375. camel hair**: "And John was clothed with camel's hair" (Mark 1:6). **380. kirtles**: gowns. **381. hot cockles**: a form of blindman's buff; here, not so innocent as usual.

A TOCCATA OF GALUPPI'S. **6. St. . . . rings**: St. Mark's is the great cathedral of Venice. The Doge was the chief magistrate of the city. For several centuries, beginning with the year 1000, the Doge annually performed the ceremony of wedding the Adriatic to Venice by throwing a ring into the sea, as wife to husband. **8. Shylock's bridge**: the Rialto over the Grand Canal. See Shakespeare's *Merchant of Venice*. **9. England**: The speaker is an imaginary person. Browning had been in Venice several times.

While you sat and played toccatas, stately at the clavichord?

What? Those lesser thirds so plaintive, sixths diminished, sigh on sigh,
Told them something? Those suspensions, those solutions — " Must we die? "
Those commiserating sevenths — " Life might last! we can but try! "

" Were you happy? " — " Yes." — " And are you still as happy? " — " Yes. And you? "
— " Then, more kisses! " — " Did *I* stop them, when a million seemed so few? "
Hark, the dominant's persistence till it must be answered to!

So, an octave struck the answer. Oh, they praised you, I dare say!
" Brave Galuppi! that was music! good alike at grave and gay!
I can always leave off talking when I hear a master play! "

Then they left you for their pleasure; till in due time, one by one,
Some with lives that came to nothing, some with deeds as well undone,
Death stepped tacitly and took them where they never see the sun.

But when I sit down to reason, think to take my stand nor swerve,
While I triumph o'er a secret wrung from nature's close reserve,
In you come with your cold music till I creep through every nerve.

Yes, you, like a ghostly cricket, creaking where a house was burned:
" Dust and ashes, dead and done with, Venice spent what Venice earned.
The soul, doubtless, is immortal — where a soul can be discerned.

" Yours, for instance: you know physics, something of geology,
Mathematics are your pastime; souls shall rise in their degree;
Butterflies may dread extinction — you'll not die, it cannot be!

" As for Venice and her people, merely born to bloom and drop,
Here on earth they bore their fruitage, mirth and folly were the crop;
What of soul was left, I wonder, when the kissing had to stop?

" Dust and ashes! " So you creak it, and I want the heart to scold.
Dear dead women, with such hair, too — what's become of all the gold
Used to hang and brush their bosoms? I feel chilly and grown old.

**18. clavichord:** an ancestor of the modern piano. **19–25.** The emotional significance of these technical terms is given in the phrases attached to each. The effect upon the hearer is to induce a melancholy fatalism, touched with transient hope. Suspensions cause a moving dissonance which craves to be resolved; the seventh commiserates because it sees hope for unity, and urges towards the octaves. The "dominant" implies the masculine, the imperial theme, and traditionally requires a return to the tonic, to the octave, what Milton calls "the perfect diapason." **26. grave . . . gay:** See the headnote above. **32. nature's . . . reserve:** That the speaker has scientific interests is implied in ll. 37–38, where Galuppi seems to be answering his English critic. **35–43.** The passage in quotation marks records the effect of the music upon the speaker. Though expressed ironically, Galuppi's meaning is that the scientist will die just as surely as the gay Venetians.

## BY THE FIRESIDE

In essence " By the Fireside " is autobiographical, but not literally so. The meeting of souls described in the poem actually occurred, but in Wimpole Street, London, in 1845. In September, 1853, the Brownings made an expedition to the ruined chapel beside the mountain path to Prato Fiorito, the probable scene of the poem, and the verses were written soon afterward at Bagni di Lucca or in Florence by their fireside in November. The poem is notable for its portrait of Mrs. Browning (Leonor) and for its illustration of a favorite doctrine of Browning's that the fate of men and women is usually decided in a moment of decision to which all past life leads. Contrast " Two in the Campagna," below, and compare Shakespeare's " The Phoenix and the Turtle " and Donne's " The Ecstasy " (p. 372 in Vol. I). See the Introduction, pp. 473–74.

How well I know what I mean to do
  When the long dark autumn evenings come;
And where, my soul, is thy pleasant hue?
  With the music of all thy voices, dumb
In life's November too!

I shall be found by the fire, suppose,
  O'er a great wise book as beseemeth age,
While the shutters flap as the cross-wind blows,
  And I turn the page, and I turn the page,
Not verse now, only prose!

Till the young ones whisper, finger on lip,
  " There he is at it, deep in Greek;
Now then, or never, out we slip

To cut from the hazels by the creek
A mainmast for our ship!"

I shall be at it indeed, my friends!
Greek puts already on either side
Such a branch-work forth as soon extends
To a vista opening far and wide,
And I pass out where it ends.

The outside frame, like your hazel trees —
But the inside archway widens fast,
And a rarer sort succeeds to these,
And we slope to Italy at last
And youth, by green degrees.

I follow wherever I am led,
Knowing so well the leader's hand;
Oh woman-country, wooed not wed,
Loved all the more by earth's male-lands,
Laid to their hearts instead!

Look at the ruined chapel again
Halfway up in the Alpine gorge!
Is that a tower, I point you plain,
Or is it a mill, or an iron forge
Breaks solitude in vain?

A turn, and we stand in the heart of things;
The woods are round us, heaped and dim;
From slab to slab how it slips and springs,
The thread of water single and slim,
Through the ravage some torrent brings!

Does it feed the little lake below?
That speck of white just on its marge
Is Pella; see, in the evening glow,
How sharp the silver spearheads charge
When Alp meets heaven in snow!

On our other side is the straight-up rock;
And a path is kept 'twixt the gorge and it
By boulder stones where lichens mock
The marks on a moth, and small ferns fit
Their teeth to the polished block.

Oh the sense of the yellow mountain flowers,
And thorny balls, each three in one,
The chestnuts throw on our path in showers!
For the drop of the woodland fruit's begun,
These early November hours,

That crimson the creeper's leaf across
Like a splash of blood, intense, abrupt,
O'er a shield else gold from rim to boss,
And lay it for show on the fairy-cupped
Elf-needled mat of moss,

By the rose-flesh mushrooms, undivulged
Last evening — nay, in today's first dew
Yon sudden coral nipple bulged,
Where a freaked fawn-colored flaky crew
Of toadstools peep indulged.

And yonder, at foot of the fronting ridge
That takes the turn to a range beyond,
Is the chapel reached by the one-arched bridge
Where the water is stopped in a stagnant pond
Danced over by the midge.

The chapel and bridge are of stone alike,
Blackish gray and mostly wet;
Cut hemp stalks steep in the narrow dike.
See here again, how the lichens fret
And the roots of the ivy strike!

Poor little place, where its one priest comes
On a festa-day, if he comes at all,
To the dozen folk from their scattered homes,
Gathered within that precinct small
By the dozen ways one roams —

To drop from the charcoal-burners' huts,
Or climb from the hemp-dressers' low shed,
Leave the grange where the woodman stores his nuts,
Or the wattled cote where the fowlers spread
Their gear on the rock's bare juts.

It has some pretension too, this front,
With its bit of fresco half-moon-wise
Set over the porch, Art's early wont.
'Tis John in the Desert, I surmise,
But has borne the weather's brunt —

Not from the fault of the builder, though,
For a penthouse properly projects
Where three carved beams make a certain show,
Dating — good thought of our architect's —
'Five, six, nine, he lets you know.

And all day long a bird sings there,
And a stray sheep drinks at the pond at times;
The place is silent and aware;
It has had its scenes, its joys and crimes,
But that is its own affair.

**BY THE FIRESIDE. 24–25.** These lines serve as a transition from the interior scene described above to the mountain scene which follows. **43. Pella:** This Italian town is considerably farther north than Prato Fiorito, and has led some commentators to think the scene an imaginary one.

**83. grange:** granary. **84. wattled cote:** a thatched shelter, made of stakes interwoven with twigs or strips of wood. **89. John . . . Desert:** St. John the Evangelist, who died in the desert. See Browning's poem, "A Death in the Desert."

My perfect wife, my Leonor,
  Oh heart, my own, oh eyes, mine too,
Whom else could I dare look backward for,
  With whom beside should I dare pursue
The path gray heads abhor?

For it leads to a crag's sheer edge with them;
  Youth, flowery all the way, there stops —
Not they; age threatens and they contemn,
  Till they reach the gulf wherein youth drops,
One inch from life's safe hem!

With me, youth led . . . I will speak now,
  No longer watch you as you sit
Reading by firelight, that great brow
  And the spirit-small hand propping it,
Mutely, my heart knows how —

When, if I think but deep enough,
  You are wont to answer, prompt as rhyme;
And you, too, find without rebuff
  Response your soul seeks many a time
Piercing its fine flesh-stuff.

My own, confirm me! If I tread
  This path back, is it not in pride
To think how little I dreamed it led
  To an age so blest that, by its side,
Youth seems the waste instead?

My own, see where the years conduct!
  At first, 'twas something our two souls
Should mix as mists do; each is sucked
  In each now; on, the new stream rolls,
Whatever rocks obstruct.

Think, when our one soul understands
  The great Word which makes all things new,
When earth breaks up and heaven expands,
  How will the change strike me and you
In the house not made with hands?

Oh, I must feel your brain prompt mine,
  Your heart anticipate my heart,
You must be just before, in fine,
  See and make me see, for your part,
New depths of the divine!

But who could have expected this
  When we two drew together first
Just for the obvious human bliss,
  To satisfy life's daily thirst
With a thing men seldom miss?

Come back with me to the first of all,
  Let us lean and love it over again,
Let us now forget and now recall,
  Break the rosary in a pearly rain
And gather what we let fall!

What did I say? — that a small bird sings
  All day long, save when a brown pair
Of hawks from the wood float with wide wings
  Strained to a bell; 'gainst noonday glare
You count the streaks and rings.

But at afternoon or almost eve
  'Tis better; then the silence grows
To that degree, you half believe
  It must get rid of what it knows,
Its bosom does so heave.

Hither we walked then, side by side,
  Arm in arm and cheek to cheek,
And still I questioned or replied,
  While my heart, convulsed to really speak
Lay choking in its pride.

Silent the crumbling bridge we cross,
  And pity and praise the chapel sweet,
And care about the fresco's loss,
  And wish for our souls a like retreat,
And wonder at the moss.

Stoop and kneel on the settle under,
  Look through the window's grated square:
Nothing to see! For fear of plunder,
  The cross is down and the altar bare,
As if thieves don't fear thunder.

We stoop and look in through the grate,
  See the little porch and rustic door,
Read duly the dead builder's date;
  Then cross the bridge that we crossed before,
Take the path again — but wait!

Oh moment, one and infinite!
  The water slips o'er stock and stone;
The west is tender, hardly bright;
  How gray at once is the evening grown —
One star its chrysolite!

We two stood there with never a third,
  But each by each, as each knew well;
The sights we saw and the sounds we heard,
  The lights and the shades made up a spell
Till the trouble grew and stirred.

**101. Leonor:** a name for Mrs. Browning, adapted from Beethoven's opera, *Fidelio*, where Leonore is the devoted wife. **132. The . . . Word:** Rev. 21:1–7, "Behold, I make all things new."

**171. settle:** seat or ledge. **185. chrysolite:** an olive-green stone, used as a gem.

Oh, the little more, and how much it is!
  And the little less, and what worlds away!
How a sound shall quicken content to bliss,
  Or a breath suspend the blood's best play,
And life be a proof of this!

Had she willed it, still had stood the screen
  So slight, so sure, 'twixt my love and her;
I could fix her face with a guard between,
  And find her soul as when friends confer,
Friends — lovers that might have been.

For my heart had a touch of the woodland-time,
  Wanting to sleep now over its best.
Shake the whole tree in the summer-prime,
  But bring to the last leaf no such test!
"Hold the last fast!" runs the rhyme.

For a chance to make your little much,
  To gain a lover and lose a friend,
Venture the tree and a myriad such,
  When nothing you mar but the year can mend;
But a last leaf — fear to touch!

Yet should it unfasten itself and fall
  Eddying down till it find your face
At some slight wind — best chance of all!
  Be your heart henceforth its dwelling place
You trembled to forestall!

Worth how well, those dark gray eyes,
  That hair so dark and dear, how worth
That a man should strive and agonize,
  And taste a veriest hell on earth
For the hope of such a prize!

You might have turned and tried a man,
  Set him a space to weary and wear,
And prove which suited more your plan,
  His best of hope or his worst despair,
Yet end as he began.

But you spared me this, like the heart you are,
  And filled my empty heart at a word.
If two lives join, there is oft a scar,
  They are one and one, with a shadowy third;
One near one is too far.

A moment after, and hands unseen
  Were hanging the night around us fast;
But we knew that a bar was broken between
  Life and life: we were mixed at last
In spite of the mortal screen.

The forests had done it; there they stood;
  We caught for a moment the powers at play;
They had mingled us so, for once and good,
  Their work was done — we might go or stay,
They relapsed to their ancient mood.

How the world is made for each of us!
  How all we perceive and know in it
Tends to some moment's product thus,
  When a soul declares itself — to wit,
By its fruit, the thing it does!

Be hate that fruit or love that fruit,
  It forwards the general deed of man,
And each of the Many helps to recruit
  The life of the race by a general plan;
Each living his own, to boot.

I am named and known by that moment's feat;
  There took my station and degree;
So grew my own small life complete,
  As nature obtained her best of me —
One born to love you, sweet!

And to watch you sink by the fireside now
  Back again, as you mutely sit
Musing by firelight, that great brow
  And the spirit-small hand propping it,
Yonder, my heart knows how!

So, earth has gained by one man the more,
  And the gain of earth must be heaven's gain too;
And the whole is well worth thinking o'er
  When autumn comes: which I mean to do
One day, as I said before.

## MY STAR

"My Star" is traditionally interpreted as referring to Mrs. Browning. The imagery fits that interpretation, though later the poet more often used the moon to symbolize his wife. When Browning made a selection from his poems in 1872 he chose this one to be first in the volume.

All that I know
  Of a certain star
Is, it can throw
  (Like the angled spar)
Now a dart of red,
  Now a dart of blue;
Till my friends have said
  They would fain see, too,
My star that dartles the red and the blue!
Then it stops like a bird; like a flower, hangs furled;

MY STAR. **4. angled spar:** the Iceland spar, or prism, which breaks light into its component colors.

They must solace themselves with the Saturn
above it.
What matter to me if their star is a world?
Mine has opened its soul to me; therefore
I love it.

## CHILDE ROLAND TO THE DARK TOWER CAME

(See Edgar's song in *Lear.*)

"Childe Roland to the Dark Tower Came" was written, Browning tells us, on January 2, 1852, when he had resolved to write a poem each day. On January 1 he wrote "Women and Roses," the record of a vivid dream; on January 3 he wrote "Love among the Ruins," containing much reminiscence.

In forcing himself to write, Browning drew upon dream, nightmare, and reminiscence. His sources for "Childe Roland" went much deeper into his subconscious than is indicated by his reference to Edgar's line in *King Lear* (III.iv.187), his favorite play, which he had recently been reading. He realized later that a tower he had seen in the Carrara Mountains, a painting he had seen in Paris, and the figure of a horse in a tapestry in his drawing room in Florence had entered into his conception. Even more fundamentally, fairy tales vaguely remembered and a favorite book he had almost memorized in his youth, Gerard de Lairesse's *The Art of Painting in All Its Branches* (1778), supplied most of the details for his fantasy, especially Lairesse's chapter "Of Things Deformed and Broken, Falsely Called Painter-Like."

When he was asked late in life if he agreed with an allegorical interpretation of the poem, Browning said, "Oh, no, not at all. Understand I don't repudiate it, either. I only mean I was conscious of no allegorical intention in writing it." When a friend asked the poet if the meaning of the poem could be expressed in the phrase, "He that endureth to the end shall be saved," he replied, "Yes, just about that." Browning, writing in a dream, had employed one of the most characteristic patterns of his poetry. In "Childe Roland" a journey is imagined, a march with military overtones is made, as it is in "The Lost Leader," "How They Brought the Good News," "Prospice," the Epilogue to *Asolando,* and many other poems by Browning. The goal is not so important as the manner in which the journey is accomplished. In "Childe Roland," as in "How They Brought the Good News," we do not know the outcome, but how Roland endures the physical and psychological terrors which assail him on his quest tells us the quality of his character. Compare T. S. Eliot's *Waste Land,* pp. 830–38, below. A "childe" was a young esquire, a candidate for knighthood.

My first thought was, he lied in every word,
  That hoary cripple, with malicious eye
  Askance to watch the working of his lie
On mine, and mouth scarce able to afford
Suppression of the glee, that pursed and scored
  Its edge, at one more victim gained thereby.

What else should he be set for, with his staff?
  What, save to waylay with his lies, ensnare
  All travelers who might find him posted there,
And ask the road? I guessed what skull-like laugh
Would break, what crutch 'gin write my epitaph
  For pastime in the dusty thoroughfare,

If at his counsel I should turn aside
  Into that ominous tract which, all agree,
  Hides the Dark Tower. Yet acquiescingly
I did turn as he pointed; neither pride
Nor hope rekindling at the end descried,
  So much as gladness that some end might be.

For, what with my whole world-wide wandering,
  What with my search drawn out through years, my hope
  Dwindled into a ghost not fit to cope
With that obstreperous joy success would bring—
I hardly tried now to rebuke the spring
  My heart made, finding failure in its scope.

As when a sick man very near to death
  Seems dead indeed, and feels begin and end
  The tears, and takes the farewell of each friend,
And hears one bid the other go, draw breath
Freelier outside ("since all is o'er," he saith,
  "And the blow fallen no grieving can amend"),

While some discuss if near the other graves
  Be room enough for this, and when a day
  Suits best for carrying the corpse away,
With care about the banners, scarves, and staves:
And still the man hears all, and only craves
  He may not shame such tender love and stay.

Thus, I had so long suffered in this quest,
  Heard failure prophesied so oft, been writ
  So many times among "The Band"—to wit,
The knights who to the Dark Tower's search addressed
Their steps—that just to fail as they, seemed best,
  And all the doubt was now—should I be fit?

So, quiet as despair, I turned from him,
  That hateful cripple, out of his highway
  Into the path he pointed. All the day
Had been a dreary one at best, and dim
Was settling to its close, yet shot one grim
  Red leer to see the plain catch its estray.

11. **Saturn:** the planet.

CHILDE ROLAND. 48. **estray:** the victim who has strayed.

For mark! no sooner was I fairly found
Pledged to the plain, after a pace or two,
Than, pausing to throw backward a last view
O'er the safe road, 'twas gone; gray plain all round;
Nothing but plain to the horizon's bound.
I might go on; naught else remained to do.

So, on I went. I think I never saw
Such starved ignoble nature; nothing throve;
For flowers — as well expect a cedar grove!
But cockle, spurge, according to their law
Might propagate their kind, with none to awe,
You'd think; a burr had been a treasure trove.

No! penury, inertness, and grimace,
In some strange sort, were the land's portion. "See
Or shut your eyes," said Nature peevishly,
"It nothing skills; I cannot help my case;
'Tis the Last Judgment's fire must cure this place,
Calcine its clods and set my prisoners free."

If there pushed any ragged thistle stalk
Above its mates, the head was chopped; the bents
Were jealous else. What made those holes and rents
In the dock's harsh swarth leaves, bruised as to balk
All hope of greenness? 'tis a brute must walk
Pashing their life out, with a brute's intents.

As for the grass, it grew as scant as hair
In leprosy; thin dry blades pricked the mud
Which underneath looked kneaded up with blood.
One stiff blind horse, his every bone a-stare,
Stood stupefied, however he came there;
Thrust out past service from the devil's stud!

Alive? he might be dead for aught I know,
With that red gaunt and colloped neck a-strain,
And shut eyes underneath the rusty mane;
Seldom went such grotesqueness with such woe;
I never saw a brute I hated so;
He must be wicked to deserve such pain.

I shut my eyes and turned them on my heart.
As a man calls for wine before he fights,
I asked one draught of earlier, happier sights,
Ere fitly I could hope to play my part.
Think first, fight afterwards — the soldier's art;
One taste of the old time sets all to rights.

Not it! I fancied Cuthbert's reddening face
Beneath its garniture of curly gold,
Dear fellow, till I almost felt him fold
An arm in mine to fix me to the place,
That way he used. Alas, one night's disgrace!
Out went my heart's new fire and left it cold.

Giles then, the soul of honor — there he stands
Frank as ten years ago when knighted first.
What honest man should dare (he said) he durst.
Good — but the scene shifts — faugh! what hangman hands
Pin to his breast a parchment? His own bands
Read it. Poor traitor, spit upon and cursed!

Better this present than a past like that;
Back therefore to my darkening path again!
No sound, no sight as far as eye could strain.
Will the night send a howlet or a bat?
I asked: when something on the dismal flat
Came to arrest my thoughts and change their train.

A sudden little river crossed my path
As unexpected as a serpent comes.
No sluggish tide congenial to the glooms;
This, as it frothed by, might have been a bath
For the fiend's glowing hoof — to see the wrath
Of its black eddy bespate with flakes and spumes.

So petty yet so spiteful! All along,
Low scrubby alders kneeled down over it;
Drenched willows flung them headlong in a fit
Of mute despair, a suicidal throng;
The river which had done them all the wrong,
Whate'er that was, rolled by, deterred no whit.

Which, while I forded — good saints, how I feared
To set my foot upon a dead man's cheek,
Each step, or feel the spear I thrust to seek
For hollows, tangled in his hair or beard!
— It may have been a water rat I speared,
But, ugh! it sounded like a baby's shriek.

Glad was I when I reached the other bank.
Now for a better country. Vain presage!
Who were the strugglers, what war did they wage,
Whose savage trample thus could pad the dank
Soil to a plash? Toads in a poisoned tank,
Or wild cats in a red-hot iron cage —

**66. Calcine:** to turn to powder by means of heat. **68. bents:** coarse grasses. **80. colloped:** ridged.

**94. fix . . . place:** strengthen my resolve. **106. howlet:** owl. **114. bespate:** spattered.

The fight must so have seemed in that fell cirque.
What penned them there, with all the plain to choose?
No footprint leading to that horrid mews,
None out of it. Mad brewage set to work
Their brains, no doubt, like galley slaves the Turk
Pits for his pastime, Christians against Jews.

And more than that — a furlong on — why, there!
What bad use was that engine for, that wheel,
Or brake, not wheel — that harrow fit to reel
Men's bodies out like silk? with all the air
Of Tophet's tool, on earth left unaware,
Or brought to sharpen its rusty teeth of steel.

Then came a bit of stubbed ground, once a wood,
Next a marsh, it would seem, and now mere earth
Desperate and done with; (so a fool finds mirth,
Makes a thing and then mars it, till his mood
Changes and off he goes!) within a rood —
Bog, clay, and rubble, sand and stark black dearth.

Now blotches rankling, colored gay and grim,
Now patches where some leanness of the soil's
Broke into moss or substances like boils;
Then came some palsied oak, a cleft in him
Like a distorted mouth that splits its rim
Gaping at death, and dies while it recoils.

And just as far as ever from the end!
Naught in the distance but the evening, naught
To point my footstep further! At the thought,
A great black bird, Apollyon's bosom friend,
Sailed past, nor beat his wide wing dragon-penned
That brushed my cap — perchance the guide I sought.

For, looking up, aware I somehow grew,
'Spite of the dusk, the plain had given place
All round to mountains — with such name to grace
Mere ugly heights and heaps now stolen in view.
How thus they had surprised me — solve it, you!
How to get from them was no clearer case.

Yet half I seemed to recognize some trick
Of mischief happened to me, God knows when —
In a bad dream perhaps. Here ended, then,
Progress this way. When, in the very nick
Of giving up, one time more, came a click
As when a trap shuts — you're inside the den!

Burningly it came on me all at once,
This was the place! those two hills on the right,
Crouched like two bulls locked horn in horn in fight;
While to the left, a tall scalped mountain . . . Dunce,
Dotard, a-dozing at the very nonce,
After a life spent training for the sight!

What in the midst lay but the Tower itself?
The round squat turret, blind as the fool's heart,
Built of brown stone, without a counterpart
In the whole world. The tempest's mocking elf
Points to the shipman thus the unseen shelf
He strikes on, only when the timbers start.

Not see? because of night perhaps? — why, day
Came back again for that! before it left,
The dying sunset kindled through a cleft;
The hills, like giants at a hunting, lay,
Chin upon hand, to see the game at bay —
"Now stab and end the creature — to the heft!"

Not hear? when noise was everywhere! it tolled
Increasing like a bell. Names in my ears
Of all the lost adventurers my peers —
How such a one was strong, and such was bold,
And such was fortunate, yet each of old
Lost, lost! one moment knelled the woe of years.

There they stood, ranged along the hillsides, met
To view the last of me, a living frame
For one more picture! in a sheet of flame
I saw them and I knew them all. And yet
Dauntless the slug-horn to my lips I set,
And blew. *"Childe Roland to the Dark Tower came."*

**133. cirque:** circular arena. **141. brake:** a machine for separating fiber, such as flax or hemp. **143. Tophet:** Hell. **149. rood:** a rod, about $5^1/_2$ yards. **154. palsied:** paralyzed, here struck by lightning. **160. Apollyon:** another name for the Devil. **161. dragon-penned:** with pinions like a dragon.

**178. scalped:** bare at the peak. **179. nonce:** moment. **189. cleft:** an opening in the hills. **203. slug-horn:** trumpet. Actually there is no such horn. Browning borrowed the word from Chatterton, who misunderstood the word "slogan."

## RESPECTABILITY

This poem was probably written in February, 1852, when François Guizot (1787–1874), the statesman and historian, delivered the *discours de reception* to Charles Montalembert (1810–70) upon the latter's election to the Académie Française, a branch of the Institut de France. Convention compelled Guizot to receive Montalembert, though there was enmity between the two men. It has been suggested that Browning had in mind as his unconventional lovers George Sand, the novelist and radical, and Jules Sandeau, with whom she lived after leaving her husband. The scene is Paris.

Dear, had the world in its caprice
 Deigned to proclaim, "I know you both,
 Have recognized your plighted troth,
Am sponsor for you; live in peace!" —
How many precious months and years
 Of youth had passed, that speed so fast,
 Before we found it out at last,
The world, and what it fears!

How much of priceless life were spent
 With men that every virtue decks,
 And women models of their sex,
Society's true ornament —
Ere we dared wander, nights like this,
 Through wind and rain, and watch the Seine,
 And feel the Boulevard break again
To warmth and light and bliss!

I know! the world proscribes not love;
 Allows my finger to caress
 Your lips' contour and downiness,
Provided it supply a glove.
The world's good word! — the Institute!
 Guizot receives Montalembert!
 Eh? Down the court three lampions flare;
Put forward your best foot!

## HOW IT STRIKES A CONTEMPORARY

This poem may have been written in Paris early in 1852. In considering the nature and function of poetry, Browning had been reading Shelley and Shakespeare as contrasting kinds of poets, subjective and dramatic. (See the Introduction, pp. 475–76.) Browning's own view was expressed in his "Introductory Essay" to *Letters of Percy Bysshe Shelley* as follows: "The whole poet's function [is that] of beholding with an understanding keenness the universe, nature, and man, in their actual state of perfection in imperfection. . . ." "Fra Lippo Lippi" expresses essentially the same conception of the nature and function of painting. Browning was never in Valladolid, a town in north central Spain, and the details of the poem are imaginary. For Browning's admiration of Shelley see "Memorabilia," below.

I only knew one poet in my life;
And this, or something like it, was his way.
 You saw go up and down Valladolid,
A man of mark, to know next time you saw.
His very serviceable suit of black
Was courtly once and conscientious still,
And many might have worn it, though none did;
The cloak, that somewhat shone and showed the threads,
Had purpose, and the ruff, significance.
He walked and tapped the pavement with his cane,
Scenting the world, looking it full in face,
An old dog, bald and blindish, at his heels.
They turned up, now, the alley by the church,
That leads nowhither; now, they breathed themselves
On the main promenade just at the wrong time;
You'd come upon his scrutinizing hat,
Making a peaked shade blacker than itself
Against the single window spared some house
Intact yet with its moldered Moorish work —
Or else surprise the ferrel of his stick
Trying the mortar's temper 'tween the chinks
Of some new shop a-building, French and fine.
He stood and watched the cobbler at his trade,
The man who slices lemons into drink,
The coffee roaster's brazier, and the boys
That volunteer to help him turn its winch.
He glanced o'er books on stalls with half an eye,
And flyleaf ballads on the vendor's string,
And broad-edge bold-print posters by the wall.
He took such cognizance of men and things,
If any beat a horse, you felt he saw;
If any cursed a woman, he took note;
Yet stared at nobody — you stared at him,
And found, less to your pleasure than surprise,
He seemed to know you and expect as much.
So, next time that a neighbor's tongue was loosed,
It marked the shameful and notorious fact,
We had among us, not so much a spy,
As a recording chief inquisitor,
The town's true master if the town but knew!
We merely kept a governor for form,
While this man walked about and took account
Of all thought, said, and acted, then went home,
And wrote it fully to our Lord the King
Who has an itch to know things, he knows why,
And reads them in his bedroom of a night.
Oh, you might smile! there wanted not a touch,
A tang of . . . well, it was not wholly ease
As back into your mind the man's look came.
Stricken in years a little — such a brow
His eyes had to live under! — clear as flint
On either side the formidable nose

RESPECTABILITY. **23. lampions:** lamps. As they come to the lighted court of the Institute, the woman remarks ironically that they must appear at their best.

HOW IT STRIKES A CONTEMPORARY. **19. Moorish work:** a survival of the time when the Moors were masters of Spain. **20. ferrel:** the metal point. **28. flyleaf ballads:** broadsides, ballads printed on single sheets of paper. **44. our . . . King:** The king symbolizes God. In the first edition all the pronouns referring to him were capitalized.

Curved, cut, and colored like an eagle's claw.
Had he to do with A's surprising fate?
When altogether old B disappeared
And young C got his mistress — was't our friend,
His letter to the King, that did it all?
What paid the bloodless man for so much pains?
Our Lord the King has favorites manifold,
And shifts his ministry some once a month;
Our city gets new governors at whiles —
But never word or sign, that I could hear,
Notified to this man about the streets
The King's approval of those letters conned
The last thing duly at the dead of night.
Did the man love his office? Frowned our Lord,
Exhorting when none heard — "Beseech me not!
Too far above my people — beneath me!
I set the watch — how should the people know?
Forget them, keep me all the more in mind!"
Was some such understanding 'twixt the two?

I found no truth in one report at least —
That if you tracked him to his home, down lanes
Beyond the Jewry, and as clean to pace,
You found he ate his supper in a room
Blazing with lights, four Titians on the wall,
And twenty naked girls to change his plate!
Poor man, he lived another kind of life
In that new stuccoed third house by the bridge,
Fresh-painted, rather smart than otherwise!
The whole street might o'erlook him as he sat,
Leg crossing leg, one foot on the dog's back,
Playing a decent cribbage with his maid
(Jacynth, you're sure her name was) o'er the cheese
And fruit, three red halves of starved winter pears,
Or treat of radishes in April. Nine,
Ten, struck the church clock, straight to bed went
he.

My father, like the man of sense he was,
Would point him out to me a dozen times;
"'St — 'St," he'd whisper, "the Corregidor!"
I had been used to think that personage
Was one with lacquered breeches, lustrous belt,
And feathers like a forest in his hat,
Who blew a trumpet and proclaimed the news,
Announced the bullfights, gave each church its turn,
And memorized the miracle in vogue!
He had a great observance from us boys;
We were in error; that was not the man.

I'd like now, yet had haply been afraid,
To have just looked, when this man came to die,
And seen who lined the clean gay garret sides 101
And stood about the neat low truckle-bed,
With the heavenly manner of relieving guard.
Here had been, mark, the general-in-chief,
Through a whole campaign of the world's life and
death,
Doing the King's work all the dim day long,
In his old coat and up to knees in mud,
Smoked like a herring, dining on a crust —
And, now the day was won, relieved at once!
No further show or need for that old coat,
You are sure, for one thing! Bless us, all the
while
How sprucely we are dressed out, you and I!
A second, and the angels alter that.
Well, I could never write a verse — could you?
Let's to the Prado and make the most of time.

74. **the Jewry**: the ghetto. 76. **Titians**: paintings by the great Italian, Titian (1477–1575). 90. **the Corregidor**: the chief magistrate.

111–12. **Bless . . . I!**: This passage is an aside. 115. **Prado**: the promenade where fashion and gaiety congregate.

## MEMORABILIA

"Memorabilia" is a monument to Browning's early adoration of Shelley, and is possibly a product of his labors for the "Introductory Essay" that he wrote in the fall of 1851 to accompany a collection of Shelley letters which later proved to be spurious. According to a friend, W. G. Kingsland, Browning was in the shop of a London bookseller when a stranger entered and began a conversation with the bookseller about Shelley, remarking that he had seen and spoken to Shelley. The stranger turned and broke into a laugh when he saw Browning "staring at him with a blanched face." Browning added to Kingsland, "I still remember vividly how strangely the presence of a man who had seen and spoken with Shelley affected me." The title signifies "things worth remembering." See the headnote to "How It Strikes a Contemporary," above, and the Introduction, p. 476.

Ah, did you once see Shelley plain,
  And did he stop and speak to you,
And did you speak to him again?
  How strange it seems and new!

But you were living before that,
  And also you are living after;
And the memory I started at —
  My starting moves your laughter!

I crossed a moor, with a name of its own
  And a certain use in the world no doubt,
Yet a handsbreadth of it shines alone
  'Mid the blank miles round about;

For there I picked up on the heather,
  And there I put inside my breast
A molted feather, an eagle feather!
  Well, I forget the rest.

## ANDREA DEL SARTO

*Called " The Faultless Painter "*

In the fall of 1852, or early in 1853, John Kenyon, the benefactor of the Brownings, requested the poet to get for him a photograph of a picture in the Pitti Palace in Florence which purported to be portraits by the painter Andrea del Sarto of himself and his wife, Lucrezia. When he could not obtain a photograph, Browning wrote the poem and sent it to Kenyon instead.

For the facts of Andrea's career, as well as for the interpretation of the painter's character, Browning relied upon Vasari's *Lives of the Painters* and most likely went to the first edition of Vasari's work where Lucrezia's character is depicted in darker colors than it is in later editions. Vasari was Andrea's pupil, and his account was made from firsthand observation and knowledge.

Andrea was the son of a Florentine tailor and from this fact got the name " del Sarto." He was born in 1486. Early in his career he won great fame as a painter with faultless technique, " Il Pittore senzi Errori." In 1513, he married Lucrezia, who served as a model for many of his pictures, notably for his famous *Madonna del Sacco*. His infatuation with Lucrezia was most unfortunate for his career. At the invitation of Francis I, King of France, Andrea went to the French court in 1518 and there did some of his best work. According to Vasari, he was lured back to Florence by Lucrezia and persuaded to spend money which King Francis had given him to buy pictures for the French court upon a house for himself and his wife. Andrea died of the plague on January 22, 1531, deserted in his last illness by his wife and his servants.

As well as supplying the facts of Andrea's life, Vasari also provided Browning with most of the moral and artistic judgments made in the poem. Vasari calls Andrea timid and uxorious and emphasizes the painter's lack of spirit in spite of his great skill. He recounts with scorn Andrea's infatuation with Lucrezia and his abandonment of his own parents in order to support her relatives. Vasari records also what Michelangelo is reported to have said to Raphael about Andrea: " There is a little man in Florence, who if he were employed upon such great works as have been given to you, would make you sweat." And there is throughout Vasari's account, as in Browning's poem, a running comparison of Andrea with the greater artists of the time, Leonardo, Michelangelo, and Raphael.

Scholars of the twentieth century are inclined to be kinder to Andrea's character and art than Vasari and Browning were. The painter's great skill has been highly praised, and historians now cast doubt upon the story that Andrea misappropriated King Francis's money. As a minor matter, but one of interest, the portrait of Andrea and his wife of which Kenyon wished to have a photograph and upon which Browning wrote his poem is now not thought to be authentic, at least not in the form in which it appears in the Pitti Palace. It seems to be two portraits joined together. The poem is generally regarded as one of Browning's finest dramatic monologues.

But do not let us quarrel any more,
No, my Lucrezia; bear with me for once;
Sit down and all shall happen as you wish.
You turn your face, but does it bring your heart?
I'll work then for your friend's friend, never fear,
Treat his own subject after his own way,
Fix his own time, accept too his own price,
And shut the money into this small hand
When next it takes mine. Will it? tenderly?
Oh, I'll content him — but tomorrow, Love!
I often am much wearier than you think,
This evening more than usual, and it seems
As if — forgive now — should you let me sit
Here by the window with your hand in mine
And look a half-hour forth on Fiesole,
Both of one mind, as married people use,
Quietly, quietly the evening through,
I might get up tomorrow to my work
Cheerful and fresh as ever. Let us try.
Tomorrow, how you shall be glad for this!
Your soft hand is a woman of itself,
And mine the man's bared breast she curls inside.
Don't count the time lost, neither; you must serve
For each of the five pictures we require;
It saves a model. So! keep looking so —
My serpentining beauty, rounds on rounds!
— How could you ever prick those perfect ears,
Even to put the pearl there! oh, so sweet —
My face, my moon, my everybody's moon,
Which everybody looks on and calls his,
And, I suppose, is looked on by in turn,
While she looks — on one's; very dear, no less.
You smile? why, there's my picture ready made,
There's what we painters call our harmony!
A common grayness silvers everything —
All in a twilight, you and I alike
— You, at the point of your first pride in me
(That's gone you know) — but I, at every point;
My youth, my hope, my art, being all toned down
To yonder sober pleasant Fiesole.
There's the bell clicking from the chapel top;
That length of convent wall across the way
Holds the trees safer, huddled more inside;
The last monk leaves the garden; days decrease,
And autumn grows, autumn in everything.
Eh? the whole seems to fall into a shape
As if I saw alike my work and self
And all that I was born to be and do,
A twilight piece. Love, we are in God's hand.
How strange now looks the life he makes us lead;
So free we seem, so fettered fast we are!
I feel he laid the fetter; let it lie!

ANDREA DEL SARTO. **5. friend's friend:** Lucrezia's "friend" is the "Cousin" mentioned later in the poem. Who *his* friend is we do not know. **15. Fiesole:** a suburb on the hills east of Florence. **24. five pictures:** probably those to be painted for the "friend's friend." **26. rounds on rounds:** The reference is possibly to her hair.

This chamber for example — turn your head —
All that's behind us! You don't understand
Nor care to understand about my art,
But you can hear at least when people speak;
And that cartoon, the second from the door
— It is the thing, Love! so such thing should
be —
Behold Madonna! — I am bold to say.
I can do with my pencil what I know,
What I see, what at bottom of my heart
I wish for, if I ever wish so deep —
Do easily, too — when I say, perfectly,
I do not boast, perhaps; yourself are judge,
Who listened to the Legate's talk last week,
And just as much they used to say in France.
At any rate 'tis easy, all of it!
No sketches first, no studies, that's long past;
I do what many dream of all their lives
— Dream? strive to do, and agonize to do,
And fail in doing. I could count twenty such
On twice your fingers, and not leave this town,
Who strive — you don't know how the others strive
To paint a little thing like that you smeared
Carelessly passing with your robes afloat —
Yet do much less, so much less, Someone says,
(I know his name, no matter) — so much less!
Well, less is more, Lucrezia; I am judged.
There burns a truer light of God in them,
In their vexed beating stuffed and stopped-up brain,
Heart, or whate'er else, than goes on to prompt
This low-pulsed forthright craftsman's hand of
mine.
Their works drop groundward, but themselves, I
know,
Reach many a time a heaven that's shut to me,
Enter and take their place there sure enough,
Though they come back and cannot tell the world.
My works are nearer heaven, but I sit here.
The sudden blood of these men! at a word —
Praise them, it boils, or blame them, it boils too.
I, painting from myself and to myself,
Know what I do, am unmoved by men's blame
Or their praise either. Somebody remarks
Morello's outline there is wrongly traced,
His hue mistaken; what of that? or else,
Rightly traced and well ordered; what of that?
Speak as they please, what does the mountain
care?
Ah, but a man's reach should exceed his grasp,
Or what's a heaven for? All is silver-gray
Placid and perfect with my art: the worse!
I know both what I want and what might gain,
And yet how profitless to know, to sigh
"Had I been two, another and myself,
Our head would have o'erlooked the world!" No
doubt.
Yonder's a work now, of that famous youth
The Urbinate who died five years ago.
('Tis copied, George Vasari sent it me.)
Well, I can fancy how he did it all,
Pouring his soul, with kings and popes to see,
Reaching, that heaven might so replenish him,
Above and through his art — for it gives way;
That arm is wrongly put — and there again —
A fault to pardon in the drawing's lines,
Its body, so to speak; its soul is right,
He means right — that, a child may understand.
Still, what an arm! and I could alter it:
But all the play, the insight, and the stretch —
Out of me, out of me! And wherefore out?
Had you enjoined them on me, given me soul,
We might have risen to Rafael, I and you!
Nay, Love, you did give all I asked, I think —
More than I merit, yes, by many times.
But had you — oh, with the same perfect brow,
And perfect eyes, and more than perfect mouth,
And the low voice my soul hears, as a bird
The fowler's pipe, and follows to the snare —
Had you, with these the same, but brought a
mind!
Some women do so. Had the mouth there urged,
"God and the glory! never care for gain.
The present by the future, what is that?
Live for fame, side by side with Agnolo!
Rafael is waiting; up to God, all three!"
I might have done it for you. So it seems;
Perhaps not. All is as God overrules.
Beside, incentives come from the soul's self;
The rest avail not. Why do I need you?
What wife had Rafael, or has Agnolo?
In this world, who can do a thing, will not;
And who would do it, cannot, I perceive;
Yet the will's somewhat — somewhat, too, the
power —
And thus we half-men struggle. At the end,
God, I conclude, compensates, punishes.
'Tis safer for me, if the award be strict,
That I am something underrated here,
Poor this long while, despised, to speak the truth.
I dared not, do you know, leave home all day,
For fear of chancing on the Paris lords.
The best is when they pass and look aside;
But they speak sometimes; I must bear it all.
Well may they speak! That Francis, that first time,
And that long festal year at Fontainebleau!
I surely then could sometimes leave the ground,
Put on the glory, Rafael's daily wear,
In that humane great monarch's golden look —

**57. cartoon:** a preliminary drawing. **65. Legate:** envoy of the Pope. **76. Someone:** Michelangelo; see l. 199. **93. Morello:** a mountain north of Florence.

**105. The Urbinate:** Raphael, born at Urbino. **130. Agnolo:** Michelangelo Buonarotti (1475–1564), a universal genius. **146. Paris lords:** See headnote.

One finger in his beard or twisted curl
Over his mouth's good mark that made the smile,
One arm about my shoulder, round my neck,
The jingle of his gold chain in my ear,
I painting proudly with his breath on me,
All his court round him, seeing with his eyes,
Such frank French eyes, and such a fire of souls
Profuse, my hand kept plying by those hearts —
And, best of all, this, this, this face beyond,
This in the background, waiting on my work,
To crown the issue with a last reward!
A good time, was it not, my kingly days?
And had you not grown restless . . . but I know —
'Tis done and past; 'twas right, my instinct said;
Too live the life grew, golden and not gray,
And I'm the weak-eyed bat no sun should tempt
Out of the grange whose four walls make his world.
How could it end in any other way?
You called me, and I came home to your heart.
The triumph was — to reach and stay there; since
I reached it ere the triumph, what is lost?
Let my hands frame your face in your hair's gold
You beautiful Lucrezia that are mine!
"Rafael did this, Andrea painted that;
The Roman's is the better when you pray,
But still the other's Virgin was his wife" —
Men will excuse me. I am glad to judge
Both pictures in your presence; clearer grows
My better fortune, I resolve to think.
For, do you know, Lucrezia, as God lives,
Said one day Agnolo, his very self,
To Rafael . . . I have known it all these years . . .
(When the young man was flaming out his thoughts
Upon a palace wall for Rome to see,
Too lifted up in heart because of it),
"Friend, there's a certain sorry little scrub
Goes up and down our Florence, none cares how,
Who, were he set to plan and execute
As you are, pricked on by your popes and kings,
Would bring the sweat into that brow of yours!"
To Rafael's! — And indeed the arm is wrong.
I hardly dare . . . yet, only you to see,
Give the chalk here — quick, thus the line should go!
Aye, but the soul! he's Rafael! rub it out!
Still, all I care for, if he spoke the truth
(What he? why, who but Michel Agnolo?
Do you forget already words like those?)
If really there was such a chance, so lost —
Is, whether you're — not grateful — but more pleased.
Well, let me think so. And you smile indeed!
This hour has been an hour! Another smile?
If you would sit thus by me every night
I should work better, do you comprehend?
I mean that I should earn more, give you more.
See, it is settled dusk now; there's a star;
Morello's gone, the watch lights show the wall,
The cue-owls speak the name we call them by.
Come from the window, love — come in, at last,
Inside the melancholy little house
We built to be so gay with. God is just.
King Francis may forgive me; oft at nights
When I look up from painting, eyes tired out,
The walls become illumined, brick from brick
Distinct, instead of mortar, fierce bright gold,
That gold of his I did cement them with!
Let us but love each other. Must you go?
That Cousin here again? he waits outside?
Must see you — you, and not with me? Those loans?
More gaming debts to pay? you smiled for that?
Well, let smiles buy me! have you more to spend?
While hand and eye and something of a heart
Are left me, work's my ware, and what's it worth?
I'll pay my fancy. Only let me sit
The gray remainder of the evening out,
Idle, you call it, and muse perfectly
How I could paint, were I but back in France,
One picture, just one more — the Virgin's face,
Not yours this time! I want you at my side
To hear them — that is, Michel Agnolo —
Judge all I do and tell you of its worth.
Will you? Tomorrow, satisfy your friend.
I take the subjects for his corridor,
Finish the portrait out of hand — there, there,
And throw him in another thing or two
If he demurs; the whole should prove enough
To pay for this same Cousin's freak. Beside,
What's better and what's all I care about,
Get you the thirteen scudi for the ruff!
Love, does that please you? Ah, but what does he,
The Cousin! what does he to please you more?

I am grown peaceful as old age tonight.
I regret little, I would change still less.
Since there my past life lies, why alter it?
The very wrong to Francis! — it is true
I took his coin, was tempted and complied,
And built this house and sinned, and all is said.
My father and my mother died of want.
Well, had I riches of my own? you see
How one gets rich! Let each one bear his lot.
They were born poor, lived poor, and poor they died;

**155. mouth's . . . mark:** the line of the lips through the beard and moustache. **178. The Roman:** Raphael. **184–93. Said . . . yours:** See Michelangelo's words in headnote. It is doubtful if these words were addressed to Raphael. **186–87. When . . . see:** possibly a reference to Raphael's painting of the rooms in the Vatican when Julius II was pope.

**210. cue-owls:** little owls, so named from the sound they make. **220. Cousin:** Lucrezia's lover, as Andrea well knows. **241. scudi:** A scudo was worth about a dollar. **250. father:** Vasari charged that Andrea neglected his parents.

And I have labored somewhat in my time
And not been paid profusely. Some good son
Paint my two hundred pictures — let him try!
No doubt, there's something strikes a balance. Yes,
You loved me quite enough, it seems tonight.
This must suffice me here. What would one have?
In heaven, perhaps, new chances, one more
    chance —
Four great walls in the New Jerusalem,
Meted on each side by the angel's reed,
For Leonard, Rafael, Agnolo, and me
To cover — the three first without a wife,
While I have mine! So — still they overcome
Because there's still Lucrezia — as I choose.

Again the Cousin's whistle! Go, my Love.

261. **New Jerusalem:** See Rev. 21:10–21. 262. **Meted:** measured. **reed:** measuring rod. 263. **Leonard:** Leonardo da Vinci (1452–1519), great in all arts, but especially in painting.

## SAUL

The first nine sections of "Saul" were published as a fragment in the *Dramatic Romances* in 1845 at Miss Barrett's insistence; in 1855 ten new sections were added, with a few changes to accommodate the new matter. The first part of "Saul" was conceived in January, 1845, when Browning read Christopher Smart's great "Song to David." In his foreword to his "Ode to Musick on Saint Cecelia's Day" Smart said: "It would not be right to conclude without taking notice of a fine subject for an Ode on S. Cecelia's Day, . . . that is David's playing to King Saul when he was troubled with the evil spirit. He," continued Smart speaking of himself, "was much pleased with the hint [of the subject] at first, but at length was deterred from improving it by the greatness of the subject, and he thinks not without reason. The chusing [sic] of too high subjects has been the ruin of many a tolerable Genius." Browning's Biblical source is, of course, I Samuel 16:4–23. The first nine sections of "Saul" are written in the manner of Smart's poetry, as we shall see below.

In 1845, Browning was unable to bring the poem to a conclusion which satisfied him. In "Christmas Eve and Easter Day" (1850) he succeeded, with Mrs. Browning's help, in clarifying his religious ideas, and in 1852–53 he completed "Saul." The last ten sections of the poem are on a different philosophical and religious plane from the first nine. Sir Thomas Wyatt's *Seven Penitential Psalms,* a copy of which was in the Brownings' library in Florence, seems to have provided the framework for Browning's poem.

The poem progresses in the following manner: Christopher Smart, under whose spirit the first nine sections of the poem were written, devoted his whole genius to recording the good things of the earth in his poetry for the purpose of praising God. Browning adopts this manner and makes David praise the good things of the earth as arguments why King Saul should wish to live. David sings (sections 5 and 6) of the innocent happiness of nature, of the joys and comforts of the community of men and their ceremonies (7 and 9), and of the pride of the warrior all "brought to blaze on the head of one creature — King Saul!" At this point David has restored life to Saul. The medical aspect of the cure is complete.

But this is insufficient to move Saul to a zest for life. In the next nine sections Browning develops the theology which informs many of his poems, such as "Cleon," "Karshish," and "The Pope" in *The Ring and the Book,* to name only a few. David agrees with Saul (13) that the King is right in rejecting the mere comforts of earth as a reason for living. Even earthly fame (13 and 15) is not enough. Man needs a larger hope. God's power is evident in the universe and so is his wisdom (17). What is needed is overwhelming evidence of God's love for man. David, inspired suddenly to see that his own love for Saul is a microscopic representation of God's love for man, rises to prophetic vision at this point (18) and foretells the coming of Christ, sent to earth to assure us of God's love for man, and the immortality which is a consequence of that love. The end of the eighteenth section parallels the end of the ninth; the nineteenth section records the dazed ecstasy of David as he stumbles away from the healed king. The poem begins as David, keeping his flock in the fields again the next day, recollects his encounter with Saul.

1

Said Abner, "At last thou art come! Ere I tell, ere
    thou speak,
Kiss my cheek, wish me well!" Then I wished it,
    and did kiss his cheek.
And he: "Since the King, O my friend, for thy
    countenance sent,
Neither drunken nor eaten have we; nor until from
    his tent
Thou return with the joyful assurance the King
    liveth yet,
Shall our lip with the honey be bright, with the
    water be wet.
For out of the black mid-tent's silence, a space of
    three days,
Not a sound hath escaped to thy servants, of prayer
    nor of praise,
To betoken that Saul and the Spirit have ended
    their strife,
And that, faint in his triumph, the monarch sinks
    back upon life.

2

"Yet now my heart leaps, O beloved! God's child
    with his dew
On thy gracious gold hair, and those lilies still living and blue
Just broken to twine round thy harpstrings, as if no
    wild heat
Were now raging to torture the desert!"

SAUL. 1. **Abner:** Saul's uncle and general of his army. 3. **the King:** Saul.

3

Then I, as was meet,
Knelt down to the God of my fathers, and rose on my feet,
And ran o'er the sand burnt to powder. The tent was unlooped;
I pulled up the spear that obstructed, and under I stooped;
Hands and knees on the slippery grass patch, all withered and gone,
That extends to the second enclosure, I groped my way on
Till I felt where the foldskirts fly open. Then once more I prayed,
And opened the foldskirts and entered, and was not afraid
But spoke, "Here is David, thy servant!" And no voice replied.
At the first I saw nought but the blackness; but soon I descried
A something more black than the blackness—the vast, the upright
Main prop which sustains the pavilion; and slow into sight
Grew a figure against it, gigantic and blackest of all.
Then a sunbeam, that burst through the tent roof, showed Saul.

4

He stood as erect as that tent prop, both arms stretched out wide
On the great cross-support in the center, that goes to each side;
He relaxed not a muscle, but hung there as, caught in his pangs
And waiting his change, the king-serpent all heavily hangs,
Far away from his kind, in the pine, till deliverance come
With the springtime—so agonized Saul, drear and stark, blind and dumb.

5

Then I tuned my harp—took off the lilies we twine round its chords
Lest they snap 'neath the stress of the noontide—those sunbeams like swords!
And I first played the tune all our sheep know, as, one after one,
So docile they come to the pen door till folding be done.
They are white and untorn by the bushes, for lo, they have fed
Where the long grasses stifle the water within the stream's bed;
And now one after one seeks its lodging, as star follows star
Into eve and the blue far above us—so blue and so far!

6

—Then the tune for which quails on the cornland will each leave his mate
To fly after the player; then, what makes the crickets elate
Till for boldness they fight one another; and then, what has weight
To set the quick jerboa a-musing outside his sand house—
There are none such as he for a wonder, half-bird and half-mouse!
God made all the creatures and gave them our love and our fear,
To give sign, we and they are his children, one family here.

7

Then I played the help-tune of our reapers, their wine song, when hand
Grasps at hand, eye lights eye in good friendship, and great hearts expand
And grow one in the sense of this world's life.—And then, the last song
When the dead man is praised on his journey—"Bear, bear him along,
With his few faults shut up like dead flowerets! Are balm seeds not here
To console us? The land has none left such as he on the bier.
Oh, would we might keep thee, my brother!"—And then, the glad chaunt
Of the marriage—first go the young maidens; next, she whom we vaunt
As the beauty, the pride of our dwelling. And then, the great march
Wherein man runs to man to assist him and buttress an arch
Nought can break; who shall harm them, our friends? Then, the chorus intoned
As the Levites go up to the altar in glory enthroned.
But I stopped here; for here in the darkness Saul groaned.

8

And I paused, held my breath in such silence, and listened apart;

**31. the king-serpent:** perhaps the boa-constrictor, awaiting the change of his skin in the spring.

**45. jerboa:** the leaping hare of the rodent family. It is called "half-bird" in the next line because of its speed and height in leaping. **57. the . . . march:** of the battle. **60. Levites:** priests, the sons of Levi.

And the tent shook, for mighty Saul shuddered; and sparkles 'gan dart
From the jewels that woke in his turban, at once with a start,
All its lordly male-sapphires, and rubies courageous at heart.
So the head; but the body still moved not, still hung there erect.
And I bent once again to my playing, pursued it unchecked,
As I sang:

9

"Oh, our manhood's prime vigor! No spirit feels waste,
Not a muscle is stopped in its playing nor sinew unbraced.
Oh, the wild joys of living! the leaping from rock up to rock,
The strong rending of boughs from the fir tree, the cool silver shock
Of the plunge in a pool's living water, the hunt of the bear,
And the sultriness showing the lion is couched in his lair.
And the meal, the rich dates yellowed over with gold dust divine,
And the locust flesh steeped in the pitcher, the full draught of wine,
And the sleep in the dried river channel where bulrushes tell
That the water was wont to go warbling so softly and well.
How good is man's life, the mere living! how fit to employ
All the heart and the soul and the senses forever in joy!
Hast thou loved the white locks of thy father, whose sword thou didst guard
When he trusted thee forth with the armies, for glorious reward?
Didst thou see the thin hands of thy mother held up as men sung
The low song of the nearly departed, and hear her faint tongue
Joining in while it could to the witness, 'Let one more attest,
I have lived, seen God's hand through a lifetime, and all was for best'?
Then they sung through their tears in strong triumph, not much, but the rest.
And thy brothers, the help and the contest, the working whence grew
Such result as, from seething grape bundles, the spirit strained true;
And the friends of thy boyhood — that boyhood of wonder and hope,
Present promise and wealth of the future beyond the eye's scope —
Till lo, thou art grown to a monarch; a people is thine;
And all gifts, which the world offers singly, on one head combine!
On one head, all the beauty and strength, love and rage (like the throe
That, a-work in the rock, helps its labor and lets the gold go)
High ambition and deeds which surpass it, fame crowning them — all
Brought to blaze on the head of one creature — King Saul!"

10

And lo, with that leap of my spirit — heart, hand, harp, and voice,
Each lifting Saul's name out of sorrow, each bidding rejoice
Saul's fame in the light it was made for — as when, dare I say,
The Lord's army, in rapture of service, strains through its array,
And upsoareth the cherubim chariot — "Saul!" cried I, and stopped,
And waited the thing that should follow. Then Saul, who hung propped
By the tent's cross-support in the center, was struck by his name.
Have ye seen when spring's arrowy summons goes right to the aim,
And some mountain, the last to withstand her, that held (he alone,
While the vale laughed in freedom and flowers) on a broad bust of stone
A year's snow bound about for a breastplate — leaves grasp of the sheet?
Fold on fold all at once it crowds thunderously down to his feet,
And there fronts you, stark, black, but alive yet, your mountain of old,
With his rents, the successive bequeathings of ages untold —
Yea, each harm got in fighting your battles, each furrow and scar
Of his head thrust 'twixt you and the tempest — all hail, there they are!
— Now again to be softened with verdure, again hold the nest
Of the dove, tempt the goat and its young to the green on his crest
For their food in the ardors of summer. One long shudder thrilled

**65. male-sapphires:** brilliant blue gems, sometimes called starstones.

**96. King Saul:** Cf. l. 312.

All the tent till the very air tingled, then sank and was stilled
At the King's self left standing before me, released and aware.
What was gone, what remained? All to traverse 'twixt hope and despair,
Death was past, life not come; so he waited. Awhile his right hand
Held the brow, helped the eyes left too vacant forthwith to remand
To their place what new objects should enter: 'twas Saul as before.
I looked up and dared gaze at those eyes, nor was hurt any more
Than by slow pallid sunsets in autumn, ye watch from the shore,
At their sad level gaze o'er the ocean — a sun's slow decline
Over hills which, resolved in stern silence, o'erlap and entwine
Base with base to knit strength more intensely; so, arm folded arm
O'er the chest whose slow hearings subsided.

11

What spell or what charm
(For awhile there was trouble within me) what next should I urge
To sustain him where song had restored him? — Song filled to the verge
His cup with the wine of this life, pressing all that it yields
Of mere fruitage, the strength and the beauty; beyond, on what fields,
Glean a vintage more potent and perfect to brighten the eye
And bring blood to the lip, and commend them the cup they put by?
He saith, "It is good"; still he drinks not; he lets me praise life,
Gives assent, yet would die for his own part.

12

Then fancies grew rife
Which had come long ago on the pasture, when round me the sheep
Fed in silence — above, the one eagle wheeled slow as in sleep;
And I lay in my hollow and mused on the world that might lie
'Neath his ken, though I saw but the strip 'twixt the hill and the sky;
And I laughed — "Since my days are ordained to be passed with my flocks,
Let me people at least, with my fancies, the plains and the rocks,
Dream the life I am never to mix with, and image the show
Of mankind as they live in those fashions I hardly shall know!
Schemes of life, its best rules and right uses, the courage that gains,
And the prudence that keeps what men strive for." And now these old trains
Of vague thought came again; I grew surer; so, once more the string
Of my harp made response to my spirit, as thus —

13

"Yea, my King,"
I began — "thou dost well in rejecting mere comforts that spring
From the mere mortal life held in common by man and by brute;
In our flesh grows the branch of this life, in our soul it bears fruit.
Thou hast marked the slow rise of the tree — how its stem trembled first
Till it passed the kid's lip, the stag's antler; then safely outburst
The fan-branches all round; and thou mindest when these too, in turn,
Broke a-bloom and the palm tree seemed perfect; yet more was to learn,
E'en the good that comes in with the palm fruit. Our dates shall we slight,
When their juice brings a cure for all sorrow? or care for the plight
Of the palm's self whose slow growth produced them? Not so! stem and branch
Shall decay, nor be known in their place, while the palm wine shall stanch
Every wound of man's spirit in winter. I pour thee such wine.
Leave the flesh to the fate it was fit for! the spirit be thine!
By the spirit, when age shall o'ercome thee, thou still shalt enjoy
More indeed, than at first when inconscious, the life of a boy.
Crush that life, and behold its wine running! Each deed thou hast done
Dies, revives, goes to work in the world; until e'en as the sun
Looking down on the earth, though clouds spoil him, though tempests efface,
Can find nothing his own deed produced not, must everywhere trace
The results of his past summer-prime — so, each ray of thy will,

**162. inconscious: not conscious.**

Every flash of thy passion and prowess, long over, shall thrill
Thy whole people, the countless, with ardor, till they too give forth
A like cheer to their sons, who in turn, fill the south and the north
With the radiance thy deed was the germ of. Carouse in the past!
But the license of age has its limit; thou diest at last:
As the lion when age dims his eyeball, the rose at her height,
So with man — so his power and his beauty forever take flight.
No! Again a long draught of my soul-wine! Look forth o'er the years!
Thou hast done now with eyes for the actual; begin with the seer's!
Is Saul dead? In the depth of the vale make his tomb — bid arise
A gray mountain of marble heaped four-square, till, built to the skies,
Let it mark where the great First King slumbers: whose frame would ye know?
Up above see the rock's naked face, where the record shall go
In great characters cut by the scribe — Such was Saul, so he did;
With the sages directing the work, by the populace chid —
For not half, they'll affirm, is comprised there! Which fault to amend,
In the grove with his kind grows the cedar, whereon they shall spend
(See, in tablets 'tis level before them) their praise, and record
With the gold of the graver, Saul's story — the statesman's great word
Side by side with the poet's sweet comment. The river's a-wave
With smooth paper-reeds grazing each other when prophet winds rave:
So the pen gives unborn generations their due and their part
In thy being! Then, first of the mighty, thank God that thou art!"

14

And behold while I sang . . . but O Thou who didst grant me that day,
And before it not seldom hast granted thy help to essay,
Carry on and complete an adventure — my shield and my sword
In that act where my soul was thy servant, thy word was my word —
Still be with me, who then at the summit of human endeavor
And scaling the highest, man's thought could, gazed hopeless as ever
On the new stretch of heaven above me — till, mighty to save,
Just one lift of thy hand cleared that distance — God's throne from man's grave!
Let me tell out my tale to its ending — my voice to my heart
Which can scarce dare believe in what marvels last night I took part,
As this morning I gather the fragments, alone with my sheep,
And still fear lest the terrible glory evanish like sleep!
For I wake in the gray dewy covert, while Hebron upheaves
The dawn struggling with night on his shoulder, and Kidron retrieves
Slow the damage of yesterday's sunshine.

15

I say then — my song
While I sang thus, assuring the monarch, and ever more strong
Made a proffer of good to console him — he slowly resumed
His old motions and habitudes kingly. The right hand replumed
His black locks to their wonted composure, adjusted the swathes
Of his turban, and see — the huge sweat that his countenance bathes,
He wipes off with the robe; and he girds now his loins as of yore,
And feels slow for the armlets of price, with the clasp set before.
He is Saul, ye remember in glory — ere error had bent
The broad brow from the daily communion; and still, though much spent
Be the life and the bearing that front you, the same, God did choose,
To receive what a man may waste, desecrate, never quite lose.

175. **soul-wine:** insight into spiritual truth. 176. **actual:** that which exists to the senses. 188. **paper-reeds:** reeds from which papyrus was made.

203. **Hebron:** a mountain in Judea with the ancient city of Hebron upon it. 204. **Kidron:** a small stream near Jerusalem. 213. **error:** Saul had disobeyed God's command to exterminate all the Amalekites, and kept their king, Agag, and the best of their livestock. His disobedience caused God to decide that he should not remain king. See I Sam. 15. 216. **what . . . lose:** namely, his humanity, his likeness to God in spirit and mind.

So sank he along by the tent prop till, stayed by the pile
Of his armor and war cloak and garments, he leaned there awhile,
And sat out my singing — one arm round the tent prop, to raise
His bent head, and the other hung slack — till I touched on the praise
I foresaw from all men in all time, to the man patient there;
And thus ended, the harp falling forward. Then first I was 'ware
That he sat, as I say, with my head just above his vast knees
Which were thrust out on each side around me, like oak roots which please
To encircle a lamb when it slumbers. I looked up to know
If the best I could do had brought solace; he spoke not, but slow
Lifted up the hand slack at his side, till he laid it with care
Soft and grave, but in mild settled will, on my brow; through my hair
The large fingers were pushed, and he bent back my head, with kind power —
All my face back, intent to peruse it, as men do a flower.
Thus held he me there with his great eyes that scrutinized mine —
And oh, all my heart how it loved him! but where was the sign?
I yearned — "Could I help thee, my father, inventing a bliss,
I would add, to that life of the past, both the future and this;
I would give thee new life altogether, as good, ages hence,
As this moment — had love but the warrant, love's heart to dispense!"

16

Then the truth came upon me. No harp more — no song more! outbroke —

17

"I have gone the whole round of creation; I saw and I spoke;
I, a work of God's hand for that purpose, received in my brain
And pronounced on the rest of his handwork — returned him again
His creation's approval or censure; I spoke as I saw:
I report, as a man may of God's work — all's love, yet all's law.
Now I lay down the judgeship he lent me. Each faculty tasked
To perceive him, has gained an abyss, where a dewdrop was asked.
Have I knowledge? confounded it shrivels at Wisdom laid bare.
Have I forethought? how purblind, how blank, to the Infinite Care!
Do I task any faculty highest, to image success?
I but open my eyes — and perfection, no more and no less,
In the kind I imagined, full-fronts me, and God is seen God
In the star, in the stone, in the flesh, in the soul and the clod.
And thus looking within and around me, I ever renew
(With that stoop of the soul which in bending upraises it too)
The submission of man's nothing-perfect to God's all-complete,
As by each new obeisance in spirit, I climb to his feet.
Yet with all this abounding experience, this deity known,
I shall dare to discover some province, some gift of my own.
There's a faculty pleasant to exercise, hard to hoodwink,
I am fain to keep still in abeyance (I laugh as I think)
Lest, insisting to claim and parade in it, wot ye, I worst
E'en the Giver in one gift. Behold, I could love if I durst!
But I sink the pretension as fearing a man may o'ertake
God's own speed in the one way of love; I abstain for love's sake.
— What, my soul? see thus far and no farther? when doors great and small,
Nine and ninety flew ope at our touch, should the hundredth appall?
In the least things have faith, yet distrust in the greatest of all?
Do I find love so full in my nature, God's ultimate gift,
That I doubt his own love can compete with it? Here, the parts shift?
Here, the creature surpass the Creator — the end, what Began?
Would I fain in my impotent yearning do all for this man,
And dare doubt he alone shall not help him, who yet alone can?
Would it ever have entered my mind, the bare will, much less power,

To bestow on this Saul what I sang of, the marvellous dower
Of the life he was gifted and filled with? to make such a soul,
Such a body, and then such an earth for insphering the whole?
And doth it not enter my mind (as my warm tears attest)
These good things being given, to go on, and give one more, the best?
Aye, to save and redeem and restore him, maintain at the height
This perfection — succeed with life's dayspring, death's minute of night?
Interpose at the difficult minute, snatch Saul the mistake,
Saul the failure, the ruin he seems now — and bid him awake
From the dream, the probation, the prelude, to find himself set
Clear and safe in new light and new life — a new harmony yet
To be run, and continued, and ended — who knows? — or endure!
The man taught enough by life's dream, of the rest to make sure;
By the pain throb, triumphantly winning intensified bliss,
And the next world's reward and repose, by the struggles in this.

18

"I believe it! 'Tis thou, God, that givest, 'tis I who receive;
In the first is the last, in thy will is my power to believe.
All's one gift; thou canst grant it moreover, as prompt to my prayer
As I breathe out this breath, as I open these arms to the air.
From thy will stream the worlds, life and nature, thy dread Sabaoth;
*I* will? — the mere atoms despise me! Why am I not loath
To look that, even that in the face too? Why is it I dare
Think but lightly of such impuissance? What stops my despair?
This — 'tis not what man Does which exalts him, but what man Would do!
See the King — I would help him but cannot, the wishes fall through.
Could I wrestle to raise him from sorrow, grow poor to enrich,

**291. Sabaoth:** hosts or armies, here expressing God's omnipotence.

To fill up his life, starve my own out, I would — knowing which,
I know that my service is perfect. Oh, speak through me now!
Would I suffer for him that I love? So wouldst thou — so wilt thou!
So shall crown thee the topmost, ineffablest, uttermost crown —
And thy Love fill infinitude wholly, nor leave up nor down
One spot for the creature to stand in! It is by no breath,
Turn of eye, wave of hand, that salvation joins issue with death!
As thy Love is discovered almighty, almighty be proved
Thy power, that exists with and for it, of being Beloved!
He who did most, shall bear most; the strongest shall stand the most weak.
'Tis the weakness in strength, that I cry for! my flesh, that I seek
In the Godhead! I seek and I find it. O Saul, it shall be
A Face like my face that receives thee; a Man like to me,
Thou shalt love and be loved by, forever; a Hand like this hand
Shall throw open the gates of new life to thee! See the Christ stand!"

19

I know not too well how I found my way home in the night.
There were witnesses, cohorts about me, to left and to right,
Angels, powers, the unuttered, unseen, the alive, the aware;
I repressed, I got through them as hardly, as strugglingly there,
As a runner beset by the populace famished for news —
Life or death. The whole earth was awakened, hell loosed with her crews;
And the stars of night beat with emotion, and tingled and shot
Out in fire the strong pain of pent knowledge; but I fainted not,
For the Hand still impelled me at once and supported, suppressed
All the tumult, and quenched it with quiet, and holy behest,
Till the rapture was shut in itself, and the earth sank to rest.
Anon at the dawn, all that trouble had withered from earth —

**322. behest:** command.

Not so much, but I saw it die out in the day's tender birth;
In the gathered intensity brought to the gray of the hills;
In the shuddering forests' held breath; in the sudden wind-thrills;
In the startled wild beasts that bore off, each with eye sidling still
Though averted with wonder and dread; in the birds stiff and chill
That rose heavily, as I approached them, made stupid with awe;
E'en the serpent that slid away silent — he felt the new law.
The same stared in the white humid faces upturned by the flowers;
The same worked in the heart of the cedar and moved the vine bowers;
And the little brooks witnessing murmured, persistent and low,
With their obstinate, all but hushed voices — " E'en so, it is so! "

## DE GUSTIBUS —

Browning possibly wrote this poem at Bagni di Lucca in 1849 when he was feeling a nostalgia for England. The second part of the poem presents a scene in southern Italy. Years later Browning wrote to a friend, "Tell me all the news about Rome and Naples. I am always thereabout in spirit." The title is a reference to the Latin proverb, *De gustibus non est disputandum,* "There is no arguing about tastes." In Browning's regrouping of his poems in 1863 this poem stood just before "Home-Thoughts from Abroad" and "Home-Thoughts from the Sea."

Your ghost will walk, you lover of trees,
(If our loves remain)
In an English lane,
By a cornfield-side a-flutter with poppies.
Hark, those two in the hazel coppice —
A boy and a girl, if the good fates please,
Making love, say —
The happier they!
Draw yourself up from the light of the moon,
And let them pass, as they will too soon,
With the beanflowers' boon,
And the blackbird's tune,
And May, and June!

What I love best in all the world
Is a castle, precipice-encurled,
In a gash of the wind-grieved Apennine.
Or look for me, old fellow of mine
(If I get my head from out the mouth
O' the grave, and loose my spirit's bands,
And come again to the land of lands) —
In a seaside house to the farther south,
Where the baked cicala dies of drouth,
And one sharp tree — 'tis a cypress — stands
By the many hundred years red-rusted,
Rough iron-spiked, ripe fruit-o'ercrusted,
My sentinel to guard the sands
To the water's edge. For, what expands
Before the house, but the great opaque
Blue breadth of sea without a break?
While, in the house, forever crumbles
Some fragment of the frescoed walls,
From blisters where a scorpion sprawls.
A girl barefooted brings, and tumbles
Down on the pavement, green-flesh melons,
And says there's news today — the king
Was shot at, touched in the liver-wing,
Goes with his Bourbon arm in a sling
— She hopes they have not caught the felons.
Italy, my Italy!
Queen Mary's saying serves for me —
(When fortune's malice
Lost her, Calais)
Open my heart and you will see
Graved inside of it, " Italy."
Such lovers old are I and she;
So it always was, so shall ever be!

## CLEON

After clarifying his religious beliefs in "Christmas Eve and Easter Day" (1850) and "Saul," Browning, it is clear from several poems written about this time, became interested in speculating upon how Christianity with its immense new hope struck the near contemporaries of its beginning. In the imaginary figure of Cleon, who is supposed to be speaking about 50 A.D., Browning gives us a Greek poet, artist, musician, and philosopher. He is a figure of the Greek decadence, and though he has not the genius of the great Greeks in any single art, he is nevertheless a complete epitome of Greek culture, and argues from this fact that he represents a natural progress. He also possesses a Greek arrogance that impels him to question whether any good can come from a region outside Greece. It is probable that Matthew Arnold's "Empedocles on Etna" (1852)

331. **new law:** the conception, fundamental to all Browning's religious thinking, that God is infinite in love, as proved by the incarnation of Christ; that his love is equal to his power on the one hand and his intelligence on the other.

DE GUSTIBUS —. 35. **the king:** Ferdinand II, a Bourbon, Tyrant of the Two Sicilies. He acquired the name, "King Bomba," a term of scorn conferred upon him in 1849, when with the help of the Austrians he crushed an uprising in his kingdom and bombarded his chief cities. 36. **liver-wing:** right arm. 40–42. **Queen . . . Calais:** Calais was lost to the English in 1558, when Mary Tudor was on the throne. In her grief at the loss she said that at her death "Calais" would be found written on her heart.

suggested the subject to Browning. In the character of Empedocles Arnold had presented a figure of the Greek decadence, a philosopher in the condition of despair to which, Browning believed, Greek paganism in its hopelessness would lead a profound mind. Empedocles plunges into the crater. Cleon is a comparable figure. The irony of the poem is that, as gifted as he is, he is blinded by his arrogance from seeing that Christianity, here at his hand, offers everything that he yearns for and everything that his reason tells him would perfect God's plan for the world. The quotation which heads the poem is taken from Acts 17:28 and is a part of the address of St. Paul to the Greeks from the Areopagus in Athens. "Cleon" was probably written in 1854.

---

"As certain also of your own poets have said"—

Cleon the poet (from the sprinkled isles,
Lily on lily, that o'erlace the sea,
And laugh their pride when the light wave lisps,
"Greece")—
To Protus in his Tyranny: much health!

They give thy letter to me, even now;
I read and seem as if I heard thee speak.
The master of thy galley still unlades
Gift after gift; they block my court at last
And pile themselves along its portico
Royal with sunset, like a thought of thee;
And one white she-slave from the group dispersed
Of black and white slaves (like the checkerwork
Pavement, at once my nation's work and gift,
Now covered with this settle-down of doves),
One lyric woman, in her crocus vest
Woven of sea-wools, with her two white hands
Commends to me the strainer and the cup
Thy lip hath bettered ere it blesses mine.

Well-counseled, king in thy munificence!
For so shall men remark, in such an act
Of love for him whose song gives life its joy,
Thy recognition of the use of life;
Nor call thy spirit barely adequate
To help on life in straight ways, broad enough
For vulgar souls, by ruling and the rest.
Thou, in the daily building of thy tower—
Whether in fierce and sudden spasms of toil,
Or through dim lulls of unapparent growth,
Or when the general work 'mid good acclaim
Climbed with the eye to cheer the architect—
Didst ne'er engage in work for mere work's sake—
Hadst ever in thy heart the luring hope
Of some eventual rest atop of it,
Whence, all the tumult of the building hushed,
Thou first of men mightst look out to the east;
The vulgar saw thy tower, thou sawest the sun.
For this, I promise on thy festival
To pour libation, looking o'er the sea,
Making this slave narrate thy fortunes, speak
Thy great words, and describe thy royal face—
Wishing thee wholly where Zeus lives the most,
Within the eventual element of calm.

Thy letter's first requirement meets me here.
It is as thou hast heard: in one short life
I, Cleon, have effected all those things
Thou wonderingly dost enumerate.
That epos on thy hundred plates of gold
Is mine—and also mine the little chant,
So sure to rise from every fishing bark
When, lights at prow, the seamen haul their net.
The image of the sun god on the phare,
Men turn from the sun's self to see, is mine;
The Poecile, o'erstoried its whole length,
As thou didst hear, with painting, is mine too.
I know the true proportions of a man
And woman also, not observed before;
And I have written three books on the soul,
Proving absurd all written hitherto,
And putting us to ignorance again.
For music—why, I have combined the moods,
Inventing one. In brief, all arts are mine;
Thus much the people know and recognize,
Throughout our seventeen islands. Marvel not.
We of these latter days, with greater mind
Than our forerunners, since more composite,
Look not so great, beside their simple way,
To a judge who only sees one way at once,
One mind-point and no other at a time—
Compares the small part of a man of us
With some whole man of the heroic age,
Great in his way—not ours, nor meant for ours.
And ours is greater, had we skill to know;
For, what we call this life of men on earth,
This sequence of the soul's achievements here
Being, as I find much reason to conceive,
Intended to be viewed eventually
As a great whole, not analyzed to parts,
But each part having reference to all—
How shall a certain part, pronounced complete,
Endure effacement by another part?
Was the thing done?—then, what's to do again?
See, in the checkered pavement opposite,
Suppose the artist made a perfect rhomb,

CLEON. 1. **sprinkled isles:** the Sporades, east of the Greek mainland. 4. **Tyranny:** used in its Greek sense; a tyrant was a ruler having absolute power. No implication of oppression is intended. 16. **sea-wools:** fibers of sea plants.

47. **epos:** epic poem. 51. **sun . . . phare:** the statue of Apollo on the lighthouse. 53. **Poecile:** the portico at Athens, covered with paintings. 60. **moods:** The moods or modes in Greek music were the equivalent of the scales in our music.

And next a lozenge, then a trapezoid —
He did not overlay them, superimpose
The new upon the old and blot it out,
But laid them on a level in his work,
Making at last a picture; there it lies.
So, first the perfect separate forms were made,
The portions of mankind; and after, so,
Occurred the combination of the same.
For where had been a progress, otherwise?
Mankind, made up of all the single men —
In such a synthesis the labor ends.
Now mark me! those divine men of old time
Have reached, thou sayest well, each at one point
The outside verge that rounds our faculty;
And where they reached, who can do more than reach?
It takes but little water just to touch
At some one point the inside of a sphere,
And, as we turn the sphere, touch all the rest
In due succession; but the finer air
Which not so palpably nor obviously,
Though no less universally, can touch
The whole circumference of that emptied sphere
Fills it more fully than the water did;
Holds thrice the weight of water in itself
Resolved into a subtler element.
And yet the vulgar call the sphere first full
Up to the visible height — and after, void;
Not knowing air's more hidden properties.
And thus our soul, misknown, cries out to Zeus
To vindicate his purpose in our life;
Why stay we on the earth unless to grow?
Long since, I imaged, wrote the fiction out,
That he or other god descended here
And, once for all, showed simultaneously
What, in its nature, never can be shown,
Piecemeal or in succession — showed, I say,
The worth both absolute and relative
Of all his children from the birth of time,
His instruments for all appointed work.
I now go on to image — might we hear
The judgment which should give the due to each,
Show where the labor lay and where the ease,
And prove Zeus' self, the latent everywhere!
This is a dream — but no dream, let us hope,
That years and days, the summers and the springs,
Follow each other with unwaning powers.
The grapes which dye thy wine are richer far,
Through culture, than the wild wealth of the rock;
The suave plum than the savage-tasted drupe;
The pastured honeybee drops choicer sweet;
The flowers turn double, and the leaves turn flowers;
That young and tender crescent moon, thy slave,
Sleeping above her robe as buoyed by clouds,
Refines upon the women of my youth.
What, and the soul alone deteriorates?
I have not chanted verse like Homer, no —
Nor swept string like Terpander, no — nor carved
And painted men like Phidias and his friend;
I am not great as they are, point by point.
But I have entered into sympathy
With these four, running these into one soul,
Who, separate, ignored each other's art.
Say, is it nothing that I know them all?
The wild flower was the larger; I have dashed
Rose-blood upon its petals, pricked its cup's
Honey with wine, and driven its seed to fruit,
And show a better flower if not so large;
I stand myself. Refer this to the gods
Whose gift alone it is! which, shall I dare
(All pride apart) upon the absurd pretext
That such a gift by chance lay in my hand,
Discourse of lightly or depreciate?
It might have fallen to another's hand; what then?
I pass too surely; let at least truth stay!

And next, of what thou followest on to ask.
This being with me as I declare, O king,
My works, in all these varicolored kinds,
So done by me, accepted so by men —
Thou askest, if (my soul thus in men's hearts)
I must not be accounted to attain
The very crown and proper end of life?
Inquiring thence how, now life closeth up,
I face death with success in my right hand:
Whether I fear death less than dost thyself
The fortunate of men? "For" (writest thou)
"Thou leavest much behind, while I leave nought.
Thy life stays in the poems men shall sing,
The pictures men shall study; while my life,
Complete and whole now in its power and joy,
Dies altogether with my brain and arm,
Is lost indeed; since, what survives myself?
The brazen statue to o'erlook my grave,
Set on the promontory which I named.
And that — some supple courtier of my heir
Shall use its robed and sceptered arm, perhaps,
To fix the rope to, which best drags it down.
I go then; triumph thou, who dost not go!"

Nay, thou art worthy of hearing my whole mind.
Is this apparent, when thou turn'st to muse

**97. outside . . . faculty:** the apex of human ability. **126. latent everywhere:** Cleon is moving in his speculations toward the Christian and pantheistic positions which Browning developed often in his later poetry. **132. drupe:** any fruit in which the pulp encloses a stone, or seed; here a plum.

**140. Terpander:** a musician of the seventh century B.C., the founder of Greek classical music. **141. Phidias:** Greek sculptor of the fifth century B.C., who helped to decorate the Parthenon. His friend was Pericles (490?–429 B.C.), the ruler who gave his name to the great Athenian age.

Upon the scheme of earth and man in chief,
That admiration grows as knowledge grows?
That imperfection means perfection hid,
Reserved in part, to grace the aftertime?
If, in the morning of philosophy,
Ere aught had been recorded, nay perceived,
Thou, with the light now in thee, couldst have looked
On all earth's tenantry, from worm to bird,
Ere man, her last, appeared upon the stage —
Thou wouldst have seen them perfect, and deduced
The perfectness of others yet unseen.
Conceding which — had Zeus then questioned thee,
"Shall I go on a step, improve on this,
Do more for visible creatures than is done?"
Thou wouldst have answered, "Aye, by making each
Grow conscious in himself — by that alone.
All's perfect else; the shell sucks fast the rock,
The fish strikes through the sea, the snake both swims
And slides, forth range the beasts, the birds take flight,
Till life's mechanics can no further go —
And all this joy in natural life is put
Like fire from off thy finger into each,
So exquisitely perfect is the same.
But 'tis pure fire, and they mere matter are;
It has them, not they it; and so I choose
For man, thy last premeditated work
(If I might add a glory to the scheme)
That a third thing should stand apart from both,
A quality arise within his soul,
Which, intro-active, made to supervise
And feel the force it has, may view itself,
And so be happy." Man might live at first
The animal life; but is there nothing more?
In due time, let him critically learn
How he lives; and, the more he gets to know
Of his own life's adaptabilities,
The more joy-giving will his life become.
Thus man, who hath this quality, is best.

But thou, king, hadst more reasonably said:
"Let progress end at once — man make no step
Beyond the natural man, the better beast,
Using his senses, not the sense of sense."
In man there's failure, only since he left
The lower and inconscious forms of life.
We called it an advance, the rendering plain
Man's spirit might grow conscious of man's life,
And, by new lore so added to the old,
Take each step higher over the brute's head.
This grew the only life, the pleasure house,
Watchtower and treasure fortress of the soul,
Which whole surrounding flats of natural life
Seemed only fit to yield subsistence to;
A tower that crowns a country. But alas,
The soul now climbs it just to perish there!
For thence we have discovered ('tis no dream —
We know this, which we had not else perceived)
That there's a world of capability
For joy, spread round about us, meant for us,
Inviting us; and still the soul craves all,
And still the flesh replies, "Take no jot more
Than ere thou comb'st the tower to look abroad!
Nay, so much less as that fatigue has brought
Deduction to it." We struggle, fain to enlarge
Our bounded physical recipiency,
Increase our power, supply fresh oil to life,
Repair the waste of age and sickness; no,
It skills not! life's inadequate to joy,
As the soul sees joy, tempting life to take.
They praise a fountain in my garden here
Wherein a naiad sends the water-bow
Thin from her tube; she smiles to see it rise.
What if I told her, it is just a thread
From that great river which the hills shut up,
And mock her with my leave to take the same?
The artificer has given her one small tube
Past power to widen or exchange — what boots
To know she might spout oceans if she could?
She cannot lift beyond her first thin thread;
And so a man can use but a man's joy
While he sees God's. Is it for Zeus to boast,
"See, man, how happy I live, and despair —
That I may be still happier — for thy use!"
If this were so, we could not thank our lord,
As hearts beat on to doing; 'tis not so —
Malice it is not. Is it carelessness?
Still, no. If care — where is the sign? I ask,
And get no answer, and agree in sum,
O king, with thy profound discouragement,
Who seest the wider but to sigh the more.
Most progress is most failure; thou sayest well.

The last point now: thou dost except a case —
Holding joy not impossible to one
With artist gifts — to such a man as I
Who leave behind me living works indeed;
For, such a poem, such a painting lives.
What? dost thou verily trip upon a word,
Confound the accurate view of what joy is
(Caught somewhat clearer by my eyes than thine)
With feeling joy? confound the knowing how
And showing how to live (my faculty)
With actually living? — Otherwise
Where is the artist's vantage o'er the king?
Because in my great epos I display
How divers men young, strong, fair, wise, can act —
Is this as though I acted? if I paint,
Carve the young Phoebus, am I therefore young?
Methinks I'm older that I bowed myself

The many years of pain that taught me art!
Indeed, to know is something, and to prove
How all this beauty might be enjoyed, is more;
But, knowing nought, to enjoy is something too.
Yon rower, with the molded muscles there,
Lowering the sail, is nearer it than I.
I can write love odes; thy fair slave's an ode.
I get to sing of love, when grown too gray
For being beloved; she turns to that young man,
The muscles all a-ripple on his back.
I know the joy of kingship; well, thou art king!

"But," sayest thou (and I marvel, I repeat,
To find thee trip on such a mere word) "what
Thou writest, paintest, stays; that does not die;
Sappho survives, because we sing her songs,
And Aeschylus, because we read his plays!"
Why, if they live still, let them come and take
Thy slave in my despite, drink from thy cup,
Speak in my place. Thou diest while I survive?
Say rather that my fate is deadlier still,
In this, that every day my sense of joy
Grows more acute, my soul (intensified
By power and insight) more enlarged, more keen;
While every day my hairs fall more and more,
My hand shakes, and the heavy years increase —
The horror quickening still from year to year,
The consummation coming past escape,
When I shall know most, and yet least enjoy —
When all my works wherein I prove my worth,
Being present still to mock me in men's mouths,
Alive still, in the praise of such as thou,
I, I the feeling, thinking, acting man,
The man who loved his life so overmuch,
Sleep in my urn. It is so horrible,
I dare at times imagine to my need
Some future state revealed to us by Zeus,
Unlimited in capability
For joy, as this is in desire for joy
— To seek which, the joy-hunger forces us:
That, stung by straitness of our life, made strait
On purpose to make prized the life at large —
Freed by the throbbing impulse we call death,
We burst there as the worm into the fly,
Who, while a worm still, wants his wings. But no!
Zeus has not yet revealed it; and alas,
He must have done so, were it possible!

Live long and happy, and in that thought die:
Glad for what was! Farewell. And for the rest,
I cannot tell thy messenger aright
Where to deliver what he bears of thine
To one called Paulus; we have heard his fame

**304. Sappho:** the great lyric poetess of Lesbos, born about 500 B.C. **305. Aeschylus:** the earliest (525–456 B.C.) of the great writers of tragedy. **340. Paulus:** St. Paul of Tarsus, "the apostle to the Gentiles." Paul began his "European mission" about the year 50 A.D. and soon afterwards was in Athens.

Indeed, if Christus be not one with him —
I know not, nor am troubled much to know.
Thou canst not think a mere barbarian Jew,
As Paulus proves to be, one circumcised,
Hath access to a secret shut from us?
Thou wrongest our philosophy, O king,
In stooping to inquire of such an one,
As if his answer could impose at all!
He writeth, doth he? well, and he may write.
Oh, the Jew findeth scholars! certain slaves
Who touched on this same isle, preached him and Christ;
And (as I gathered from a bystander)
Their doctrine could be held by no sane man.

## TWO IN THE CAMPAGNA

This poem was the product of explorations by the Brownings in May, 1854, of the great open plain called the Campagna which surrounds Rome. The Campagna, with the ruins of the tombs of ancient Romans everywhere upon it, is appropriately known as "Rome's ghost." The poem records a mood between lovers. Contrast it with "By the Fireside" and compare it with Matthew Arnold's poem, "Isolation: To Marguerite, No. 5."

I wonder do you feel today
  As I have felt since, hand in hand,
We sat down on the grass, to stray
  In spirit better through the land,
This morn of Rome and May?

For me, I touched a thought, I know,
  Has tantalized me many times,
(Like turns of thread the spiders throw
  Mocking across our path) for rhymes
To catch at and let go.

Help me to hold it! First it left
  The yellowing fennel, run to seed
There, branching from the brickwork's cleft,
  Some old tomb's ruin; yonder weed
Took up the floating weft,

Where one small orange cup amassed
  Five beetles — blind and green they grope
Among the honey-meal; and last,
  Everywhere on the grassy slope
I traced it. Hold it fast!

The champaign with its endless fleece
  Of feathery grasses everywhere!
Silence and passion, joy and peace,
  An everlasting wash of air —
Rome's ghost since her decease.

Such life here, through such lengths of hours,
  Such miracles performed in play,
Such primal naked forms of flowers,
  Such letting nature have her way
While heaven looks from its towers!

How say you? Let us, O my dove,
  Let us be unashamed of soul,
As earth lies bare to heaven above!
  How is it under our control
To love or not to love?

I would that you were all to me,
  You that are just so much, no more.
Nor yours nor mine, nor slave nor free!
  Where does the fault lie? What the core
O' the wound, since wound must be?

I would I could adopt your will,
  See with your eyes, and set my heart
Beating by yours, and drink my fill
  At your soul's springs — your part my part
In life, for good and ill.

No. I yearn upward, touch you close,
  Then stand away. I kiss your cheek,
Catch your soul's warmth, — I pluck the rose
  And love it more than tongue can speak —
Then the good minute goes.

Already how am I so far
  Out of that minute? Must I go
Still like the thistle ball, no bar,
  Onward, whenever light winds blow,
Fixed by no friendly star?

Just when I seemed about to learn!
  Where is the thread now? Off again!
The old trick! Only I discern —
  Infinite passion, and the pain
Of finite hearts that yearn.

## A GRAMMARIAN'S FUNERAL

*Shortly after the Revival of Learning in Europe*

It is Browning's purpose in "A Grammarian's Funeral" to catch the thirst for knowledge of the scholars of the early Renaissance. The Grammarian illustrates the "philosophy of the imperfect," a favorite idea of the nineteenth century that it is better to aim high and fail than to succeed in a low aim. Compare "Andrea del Sarto," lines 77–98, above, and "Rabbi Ben Ezra," lines 25–42, below. The meter is adapted to the motion and voices of the disciples of the Grammarian as they carry his body to the mountaintop at daybreak. The poem was probably written in Florence in the summer of 1854.

Let us begin and carry up this corpse,
  Singing together.
Leave we the common crofts, the vulgar thorpes
  Each in its tether
Sleeping safe on the bosom of the plain,
  Cared-for till cock-crow:
Look out if yonder be not day again
  Rimming the rock-row!
That's the appropriate country; there, man's
    thought,
  Rarer, intenser,
Self-gathered for an outbreak, as it ought,
  Chafes in the censer.
Leave we the unlettered plain its herd and crop;
  Seek we sepulture
On a tall mountain, citied to the top,
  Crowded with culture!
All the peaks soar, but one the rest excels;
  Clouds overcome it;
No! yonder sparkle is the citadel's
  Circling its summit.
Thither our path lies; wind we up the heights;
  Wait ye the warning?
Our low life was the level's and the night's;
  He's for the morning.
Step to a tune, square chests, erect each head,
  'Ware the beholders!
This is our master, famous, calm, and dead,
  Borne on our shoulders.

Sleep, crop and herd! sleep, darkling thorpe and
    croft,
  Safe from the weather!
He, whom we convoy to his grave aloft,
  Singing together,
He was a man born with thy face and throat,
  Lyric Apollo!
Long he lived nameless; how should spring take
    note
  Winter would follow?
Till lo, the little touch, and youth was gone!
  Cramped and diminished,
Moaned he, "New measures, other feet anon!
  My dance is finished"?
No, that's the world's way: (keep the mountain-
    side,
  Make for the city!)
He knew the signal, and stepped on with pride
  Over men's pity;
Left play for work, and grappled with the world
  Bent on escaping;
"What's in the scroll," quoth he, "thou keepest
    furled?

A GRAMMARIAN'S FUNERAL. **3. crofts:** enclosed fields. **thorpes:** villages. **26. 'Ware:** be aware of. **34. Lyric Apollo:** The sun god was renowned for his beauty and his music. **47. scroll:** The Grammarian wished to get the authority of the manuscript. He is the kind of fundamental scholar who made the later Renaissance possible in Europe.

Show me their shaping,
Theirs who most studied man, the bard and sage —
Give!" — So, he gowned him,
Straight got by heart that book to its last page;
Learnèd, we found him.
Yea, but we found him bald too, eyes like lead,
Accents uncertain;
"Time to taste life," another would have said,
"Up with the curtain!"
This man said rather, "Actual life comes next?
Patience a moment!
Grant I have mastered learning's crabbed text,
Still there's the comment.
Let me know all! Prate not of most or least,
Painful or easy!
Even to the crumbs I'd fain eat up the feast,
Aye, nor feel queasy."
Oh, such a life as he resolved to live,
When he had learned it,
When he had gathered all books had to give!
Sooner, he spurned it.
Image the whole, then execute the parts —
Fancy the fabric
Quite, ere you build, ere steel strike fire from quartz,
Ere mortar dab brick!

(Here's the town gate reached; there's the market place
Gaping before us.)
Yea, this in him was the peculiar grace
(Hearten our chorus!)
That before living he'd learn how to live —
No end to learning;
Earn the means first — God surely will contrive
Use for our earning.
Others mistrust and say, "But time escapes;
Live now or never!"
He said, "What's time? Leave Now for dogs and apes!
Man has Forever."
Back to his book then; deeper drooped his head;
*Calculus* racked him;
Leaden before, his eyes grew dross of lead;
*Tussis* attacked him.
"Now, master, take a little rest!" — not he!
(Caution redoubled,
Step two abreast, the way winds narrowly!)
Not a whit troubled,
Back to his studies, fresher than at first,
Fierce as a dragon
He (soul-hydroptic with a sacred thirst)
Sucked at the flagon.
Oh, if we draw a circle premature,
Heedless of far gain,
Greedy for quick returns of profit, sure
Bad is our bargain!
Was it not great? did not he throw on God,
(He loves the burthen)
God's task to make the heavenly period
Perfect the earthen?
Did not he magnify the mind, show clear
Just what it all meant?
He would not discount life, as fools do here,
Paid by installment.
He ventured neck or nothing — heaven's success
Found, or earth's failure;
"Wilt thou trust death or not?" He answered, "Yes!
Hence with life's pale lure!"
That low man seeks a little thing to do,
Sees it and does it;
This high man, with a great thing to pursue,
Dies ere he knows it.
That low man goes on adding one to one,
His hundred's soon hit;
This high man, aiming at a million,
Misses an unit.
That, has the world here — should he need the next,
Let the world mind him!
This, throws himself on God, and unperplexed
Seeking shall find him.
So, with the throttling hands of death at strife,
Ground he at grammar;
Still, through the rattle, parts of speech were rife;
While he could stammer
He settled *Hoti's* business — let it be! —
Properly based *Oun* —
Gave us the doctrine of the enclitic *De*,
Dead from the waist down.
Well, here's the platform, here's the proper place:
Hail to your purlieus,
All ye highfliers of the feathered race,
Swallows and curlews!
Here's the top-peak; the multitude below
Live, for they can, there;
This man decided not to Live but Know —
Bury this man there?
Here — here's his place, where meteors shoot, clouds form,
Lightnings are loosened,

**50. gowned:** became a scholar; i.e., put on the gown. **86. *Calculus:*** a disease called the stone, as a stone in the bladder. **88. *Tussis:*** a bronchial cough. **95. soul-hydroptic:** thirsty of soul.

**103. period:** a span of time with beginning and end. **120. unit:** one part of many parts. **127. rattle:** the death rattle in his throat. **129–131. *Hoti . . . Oun. . . De:*** These are Greek particles meaning respectively "that," "therefore," and "towards." In the "enclitic *De*" the *De* would be so unemphatic as to be pronounced as a part of the preceding word. In their efforts to reach perfection in their knowledge such matters were of great concern to linguistic scholars.

Stars come and go! Let joy break with the storm,
  Peace let the dew send!
Lofty designs must close in like effects;
  Loftily lying,
Leave him — still loftier than the world suspects,
  Living and dying.

## from DRAMATIS PERSONAE, 1864

### ABT VOGLER

*After He Has Been Extemporizing upon the Musical Instrument of His Invention*

"Abt Vogler" was probably written in London soon after Mrs. Browning's death in 1861. Browning sought consolation in music, and the career of Abbé Georg Vogler (1749–1814) fitted the poet's need for a subject, for Vogler was at once a devout person and a notable extemporizer upon the organ. The musical instrument upon which he extemporized was a small portable organ of about 900 pipes, called an "orchestrion." Browning knew Vogler's system well, because John Relfe, Browning's music teacher and Musician in Ordinary to the king, had been a pupil of Vogler's at the same time as Weber and Meyerbeer. What we know of Vogler does not allow us to think him capable of the speculation which we find in the poem. He was inventive rather than meditative or profound. "Abt Vogler" should be compared to Browning's other poems on music. The thought of the poem is Browning's and may be called Christian-Platonic; that is, its idea that all things on earth are but faint and imperfect copies of perfect prototypes in Heaven is derived from Plato, and this notion is combined with the Christian conception that our lives on earth are merely periods of trial and struggle toward the perfection we shall find only in Heaven. This poem is near the peak of Browning's metaphysical verse.

Would that the structure brave, the manifold music I build,
  Bidding my organ obey, calling its keys to their work,
Claiming each slave of the sound, at a touch, as when Solomon willed
  Armies of angels that soar, legions of demons that lurk,
Man, brute, reptile, fly — alien of end and of aim,
  Adverse, each from the other heaven-high, hell-deep removed —
Should rush into sight at once as he named the ineffable Name,
  And pile him a palace straight, to pleasure the princess he loved!

Would it might tarry like his, the beautiful building of mine,
  This which my keys in a crowd pressed and importuned to raise!
Ah, one and all, how they helped, would dispart now and now combine,
  Zealous to hasten the work, heighten their master his praise!
And one would bury his brow with a blind plunge down to hell,
  Burrow awhile and build, broad on the roots of things,
Then up again swim into sight, having based me my palace well,
  Founded it, fearless of flame, flat on the nether springs.

And another would mount and march, like the excellent minion he was,
  Aye, another and yet another, one crowd but with many a crest,
Raising my rampired walls of gold as transparent as glass,
  Eager to do and die, yield each his place to the rest;
For higher still and higher (as a runner tips with fire,
  When a great illumination surprises a festal night —
Outlined round and round Rome's dome from space to spire)
  Up, the pinnacled glory reached, and the pride of my soul was in sight.

In sight? Not half! for it seemed, it was certain, to match man's birth,
  Nature in turn conceived, obeying an impulse as I;
And the emulous heaven yearned down, made effort to reach the earth,
  As the earth had done her best, in my passion, to scale the sky;
Novel splendors burst forth, grew familiar and dwelt with mine,
  Not a point nor peak but found and fixed its wandering star;
Meteor-moons, balls of blaze; and they did not pale nor pine,
  For earth had attained to heaven, there was no more near nor far.

ABT VOGLER. **3. Solomon:** Talmudic legend says that Solomon possessed a seal with the "ineffable Name" of God upon it, and by this seal he had power over supernatural beings. He spent thirteen years in building his palace.

**17. minion:** servant. **21–23. For . . . spire:** The structure of Vogler's music rises in his imagination like the fire which ascends by streamers to illuminate the dome of St. Peter's to the cross on the top. Browning had witnessed such an event at Easter time in 1854 when he was in Rome.

Nay more; for there wanted not who walked in the glare and glow,
Presences plain in the place; or, fresh from the Protoplast,
Furnished for ages to come, when a kindlier wind should blow,
Lured now to begin and live, in a house to their liking at last;
Or else the wonderful Dead who have passed through the body and gone,
But were back once more to breathe in an old world worth their new;
What never had been, was now; what was, as it shall be anon;
And what is — shall I say, matched both? for I was made perfect too.

All through my keys that gave their sounds to a wish of my soul,
All through my soul that praised as its wish flowed visibly forth,
All through music and me! For think, had I painted the whole,
Why, there it had stood, to see, nor the process so wonder-worth;
Had I written the same, made verse — still, effect proceeds from cause,
Ye know why the forms are fair, ye hear how the tale is told;
It is all triumphant art, but art in obedience to laws,
Painter and poet are proud in the artist-list enrolled —

But here is the finger of God, a flash of the will that can,
Existent behind all laws, that made them and, lo, they are!
And I know not if, save in this, such gift be allowed to man,
That out of three sounds he frame, not a fourth sound, but a star.
Consider it well: each tone of our scale in itself is nought;
It is everywhere in the world — loud, soft, and all is said;
Give it to me to use! I mix it with two in my thought;
And there! Ye have heard and seen: consider and bow the head!

Well, it is gone at last, the palace of music I reared;
Gone! and the good tears start, the praises that come too slow;
For one is assured at first, one scarce can say that he feared,
That he even gave it a thought, the gone thing was to go.
Never to be again! But many more of the kind
As good, nay, better perchance; is this your comfort to me?
To me, who must be saved because I cling with my mind
To the same, same self, same love, same God; aye, what was, shall be.

Therefore to whom turn I but to thee, the ineffable Name?
Builder and maker, thou, of houses not made with hands!
What, have fear of change from thee who art ever the same?
Doubt that thy power can fill the heart that thy power expands?
There shall never be one lost good! What was, shall live as before;
The evil is null, is nought, is silence implying sound;
What was good shall be good, with, for evil, so much good more;
On the earth the broken arcs; in the heaven a perfect round.

All we have willed or hoped or dreamed of good shall exist;
Not its semblance, but itself; no beauty, nor good, nor power
Whose voice has gone forth, but each survives for the melodist
When eternity affirms the conception of an hour.
The high that proved too high, the heroic for earth too hard,
The passion that left the ground to lose itself in the sky,
Are music sent up to God by the lover and the bard;
Enough that he heard it once; we shall hear it by and by.

And what is our failure here but a triumph's evidence
For the fullness of the days? Have we withered or agonized?
Why else was the pause prolonged but that singing might issue thence?
Why rushed the discords in, but that harmony should be prized?
Sorrow is hard to bear, and doubt is slow to clear,
Each sufferer says his say, his scheme of the weal and woe;

**34. Protoplast:** freshly created from the elemental stuff of life. **43. had I painted:** Here Browning deals with a favorite idea: a comparison of the effects of the various arts. Music is usually judged the most affecting by Browning, but also the most transient in its effects.

**66. houses . . . hands:** See II Cor. 5:1.

But God has a few of us whom he whispers in the ear;
The rest may reason and welcome: 'tis we musicians know.

Well, it is earth with me; silence resumes her reign;
I will be patient and proud, and soberly acquiesce.
Give me the keys. I feel for the common chord again,
Sliding by semitones till I sink to the minor — yes,
And I blunt it into a ninth, and I stand on alien ground,
Surveying awhile the heights I rolled from into the deep;
Which, hark, I have dared and done, for my resting place is found,
The C Major of this life; so, now I will try to sleep.

## RABBI BEN EZRA

"Rabbi Ben Ezra" was possibly written in 1862. Browning had known the work of Abraham Ibn Ezra since 1854 and probably was familiar with the Jewish philosopher's *Commentary on Isaiah.* The figure which dominates the poem occurs in Isaiah 64:8: "But now, O Lord, thou art our father; we are clay, and thou our potter; and we all are the work of thy hand." The image of the potter had been used extensively by Edward Fitzgerald in his *Rubáiyát of Omar Khayyám* (1859), and that poem possibly was the spark that set Browning off. Browning's poem may itself be answered by Matthew Arnold's "Growing Old" (1867).

Abraham Ibn Ezra (1092?–1167) was a Spanish rabbi who in his middle years was driven by persecution from Spain into a life of travel and scholarship. He was a theologian, a philosopher, a linguist, and a scientist. A strong believer in immortality, he found the second half of his life much more productive and satisfactory in every way than the first. The ideas in the poem are Browning's, though in accord with what we know of the rabbi's temperament.

Grow old along with me!
The best is yet to be,
The last of life, for which the first was made;
Our times are in His hand
Who saith, "A whole I planned,
Youth shows but half; trust God; see all, nor be afraid!"

Not that, amassing flowers,
Youth sighed, "Which rose make ours,
Which lily leave and then as best recall?"
Not that, admiring stars,
It yearned, "Nor Jove, nor Mars;
Mine be some figured flame which blends, transcends them all!"

Not for such hopes and fears
Annulling youth's brief years,
Do I remonstrate: folly wide the mark!
Rather I prize the doubt
Low kinds exist without,
Finished and finite clods, untroubled by a spark.

Poor vaunt of life indeed,
Were man but formed to feed
On joy, to solely seek and find and feast;
Such feasting ended, then
As sure an end to men;
Irks care the crop-full bird? Frets doubt the maw-crammed beast?

Rejoice we are allied
To That which doth provide
And not partake, effect and not receive!
A spark disturbs our clod;
Nearer we hold of God
Who gives, than of his tribes that take, I must believe.

Then, welcome each rebuff
That turns earth's smoothness rough,
Each sting that bids nor sit nor stand but go!
Be our joys three-parts pain!
Strive, and hold cheap the strain;
Learn, nor account the pang; dare, never grudge the throe!

For thence — a paradox
Which comforts while it mocks —
Shall life succeed in that it seems to fail;
What I aspired to be,
And was not, comforts me;
A brute I might have been, but would not sink i' the scale.

What is he but a brute
Whose flesh has soul to suit,
Whose spirit works lest arms and legs want play?
To man, propose this test —
Thy body at its best,
How far can that project thy soul on its lone way?

Yet gifts should prove their use;
I own the Past profuse

**91. common chord:** the fundamental tone, a major or minor third, and a perfect fifth. The C Major is the natural scale, without sharps or flats, and is thus symbolic of the common level of ordinary life.

RABBI BEN EZRA. **12. figured:** imagined.

Of power each side, perfection every turn:
Eyes, ears took in their dole,
Brain treasured up the whole;
Should not the heart beat once, " How good to live and learn "?

Not once beat, " Praise be thine!
I see the whole design,
I, who saw power, see now Love perfect too;
Perfect I call Thy plan;
Thanks that I was a man!
Maker, remake, complete — I trust what Thou shalt do! "

For pleasant is this flesh;
Our soul, in its rose-mesh
Pulled ever to the earth, still yearns for rest;
Would we some prize might hold
To match those manifold
Possessions of the brute — gain most, as we did best!

Let us not always say,
" Spite of this flesh today
I strove, made head, gained ground upon the whole! "
As the bird wings and sings,
Let us cry, " All good things
Are ours, nor soul helps flesh more, now, than flesh helps soul! "

Therefore I summon age
To grant youth's heritage,
Life's struggle having so far reached its term;
Thence shall I pass, approved
A man, for aye removed
From the developed brute; a God though in the germ.

And I shall thereupon
Take rest, ere I be gone
Once more on my adventure brave and new;
Fearless and unperplexed,
When I wage battle next,
What weapons to select, what armor to indue.

Youth ended, I shall try
My gain or loss thereby;
Leave the fire ashes, what survives is gold;
And I shall weigh the same,
Give life its praise or blame;
Young, all lay in dispute; I shall know, being old.

For note, when evening shuts,
A certain moment cuts
The deed off, calls the glory from the gray;
A whisper from the west
Shoots — " Add this to the rest,
Take it and try its worth; here dies another day."

So, still within this life,
Though lifted o'er its strife,
Let me discern, compare, pronounce at last,
" This rage was right i' the main,
That acquiescence vain;
The Future I may face now I have proved the Past."

For more is not reserved
To man, with soul just nerved
To act tomorrow what he learns today;
Here, work enough to watch
The Master work, and catch
Hints of the proper craft, tricks of the tool's true play.

As it was better, youth
Should strive, through acts uncouth,
Toward making, than repose on aught found made;
So, better, age, exempt
From strife, should know, than tempt
Further. Thou waitedst age: wait death nor be afraid!

Enough now, if the Right
And Good and Infinite
Be named here, as thou callest thy hand thine own,
With knowledge absolute,
Subject to no dispute
From fools that crowded youth, nor let thee feel alone.

Be there, for once and all,
Severed great minds from small,
Announced to each his station in the Past!
Was I, the world arraigned,
Where they, my soul disdained,
Right? Let age speak the truth and give us peace at last!

Now, who shall arbitrate?
Ten men love what I hate,
Shun what I follow, slight what I receive;
Ten, who in ears and eyes
Match me; we all surmise,
They this thing, and I that; whom shall my soul believe?

56–57. **I . . . too:** God's power is equaled by his love. Compare "Cleon," "Karshish," "Saul" and "The Pope." 74. **youth's heritage:** what youth should give us, a strong physical being, to be linked with the thoughtfulness of age. 75. **term:** limit. 81. **adventure:** life beyond the grave. 84. **indue:** to put on.

102. **proved:** tried and judged. 110. **uncouth:** awkward and unsure. 113. **tempt:** experiment or attempt.

Not on the vulgar mass
Called "work" must sentence pass,
Things done, that took the eye and had the price;
O'er which, from level stand,
The low world laid its hand,
Found straightway to its mind, could value in a trice;

But all the world's coarse thumb
And finger failed to plumb,
So passed in making up the main account;
All instincts immature,
All purposes unsure,
That weighed not as his work, yet swelled the man's amount;

Thoughts hardly to be packed
Into a narrow act,
Fancies that broke through language and escaped;
All I could never be,
All, men ignored in me,
This, I was worth to God, whose wheel the pitcher shaped.

Ay, note that Potter's wheel,
That metaphor! and feel
Why time spins fast, why passive lies our clay —
Thou, to whom fools propound,
When the wine makes its round,
"Since life fleets, all is change; the Past gone, seize today!"

Fool! All that is, at all,
Lasts ever, past recall;
Earth changes, but thy soul and God stand sure;
What entered into thee,
*That* was, is, and shall be;
Time's wheel runs back or stops: Potter and clay endure.

He fixed thee 'mid this dance
Of plastic circumstance,
This Present, thou, forsooth, would fain arrest;
Machinery just meant
To give thy soul its bent,
Try thee, and turn thee forth, sufficiently impressed.

What though the earlier grooves,
Which ran the laughing loves
Around thy base, no longer pause and press?
What though, about thy rim,
Skull-things in order grim
Grow out, in graver mood, obey the sterner stress?

Look not thou down but up!
To uses of a cup,
The festal board, lamp's flash, and trumpet's peal,
The new wine's foaming flow,
The Master's lips aglow!
Thou, heaven's consummate cup, what need'st thou with earth's wheel?

But I need, now as then,
Thee, God, who moldest men;
And since, not even while the whirl was worst,
Did I — to the wheel of life
With shapes and colors rife,
Bound dizzily — mistake my end, to slake thy thirst;

So, take and use thy work;
Amend what flaws may lurk,
What strain o' the stuff, what warpings past the aim!
My times be in thy hand!
Perfect the cup as planned!
Let age approve of youth, and death complete the same!

**141. passed:** neglected. **154–56. fools . . . today:** possibly addressed to the hedonistic philosophy *carpe diem* of Fitzgerald's *Rubáiyát*, sts. 82–90. **164. plastic:** molding, forming.

## CONFESSIONS

This poem was probably written in Italy in 1859. It was part of Browning's purpose to pluck romance from familiar realism.

What is he buzzing in my ears?
"Now that I come to die,
Do I view the world as a vale of tears?"
Ah, reverend sir, not I!

What I viewed there once, what I view again
Where the physic bottles stand
On the table's edge — is a suburb lane,
With a wall to my bedside hand.

That lane sloped, much as the bottles do,
From a house you could descry
O'er the garden wall; is the curtain blue
Or green to a healthy eye?

To mine, it serves for the old June weather
Blue above lane and wall;
And that farthest bottle labeled "Ether"
Is the house o'ertopping all.

At a terrace, somewhere near the stopper,
There watched for me, one June,
A girl; I know, sir, it's improper,
My poor mind's out of tune.

Only, there was a way . . . you crept
  Close by the side, to dodge
Eyes in the house, two eyes except;
  They styled their house "The Lodge."

What right had a lounger up their lane?
  But, by creeping very close,
With the good wall's help — their eyes might strain
  And stretch themselves to Oes,

Yet never catch her and me together,
  As she left the attic, there,
By the rim of the bottle labeled "Ether,"
  And stole from stair to stair,

And stood by the rose-wreathed gate. Alas,
  We loved, sir — used to meet;
How sad and bad and mad it was —
  But then, how it was sweet!

## MAY AND DEATH

First published in a literary annual, *The Keepsake,* for 1857, this poem was revised when it was republished in 1864. It commemorates James (called Charles in the poem) Silverthorne, Browning's cousin and companion of his youth, who died in May, 1852. The "wood" referred to in the poem is the Dulwich Wood, and the plant of line 13 is the "spotted persicaria." Because its leaves are spotted with purple, the legend is that it grew beneath the Cross, and received its color from the blood of Christ.

I wish that when you died last May,
  Charles, there had died along with you
Three parts of spring's delightful things;
  Aye, and, for me, the fourth part too.

A foolish thought, and worse, perhaps!
  There must be many a pair of friends
Who, arm in arm, deserve the warm
  Moon-births and the long evening-ends.

So, for their sake, be May still May!
  Let their new time, as mine of old,
Do all it did for me; I bid
  Sweet sights and sounds throng manifold.

Only, one little sight, one plant,
  Woods have in May, that starts up green
Save a sole streak which, so to speak,
  Is spring's blood, spilt its leaves between —

That, they might spare; a certain wood
  Might miss the plant; their loss were small;
But I — whene'er the leaf grows there,
  Its drop comes from my heart, that's all.

## PROSPICE

This poem first appeared in the *Atlantic Monthly* for June, 1864. It was probably written soon after the death of Mrs. Browning on June 29, 1861. After his wife's death Browning wrote in her testament the words that Dante had written concerning Beatrice (*Convito,* II.9): "Thus I believe, thus I affirm, thus I am certain it is, that from this life I shall pass to another, there, where that lady lives of whom my soul was enamoured." As an expression of courage, compare "Prospice" with Tennyson's "Ulysses." The title means "look forward."

Fear death? — to feel the fog in my throat,
  The mist in my face,
When the snows begin, and the blasts denote
  I am nearing the place,
The power of the night, the press of the storm,
  The post of the foe;
Where he stands, the Arch-Fear in a visible form,
  Yet the strong man must go;
For the journey is done and the summit attained,
  And the barriers fall,
Though a battle's to fight ere the guerdon be gained,
  The reward of it all.
I was ever a fighter, so — one fight more,
  The best and the last!
I would hate that death bandaged my eyes, and forbore,
  And bade me creep past.
No! let me taste the whole of it, fare like my peers
  The heroes of old,
Bear the brunt, in a minute pay glad life's arrears
  Of pain, darkness, and cold.
For sudden the worst turns the best to the brave,
  The black minute's at end,
And the elements' rage, the fiend-voices that rave,
  Shall dwindle, shall blend,
Shall change, shall become first a peace out of pain,
  Then a light, then thy breast,
O thou soul of my soul! I shall clasp thee again,
  And with God be the rest!

## YOUTH AND ART

This poem was probably written early in 1861. The setting is the artistic group in Rome; the speaker and the sculptor she addresses are imaginary English persons. The style of the poem is designed to express the

CONFESSIONS. 28. **Oes:** that is, their eyes would be stretched wide open, each like the letter O, in their efforts to see.

embittered ruefulness of the speaker at having lost the opportunity afforded by love.

It once might have been, once only:
  We lodged in a street together,
You, a sparrow on the housetop lonely,
  I, a lone she-bird of his feather.

Your trade was with sticks and clay,
  You thumbed, thrust, patted and polished,
Then laughed, "They will see some day
  Smith made, and Gibson demolished."

My business was song, song, song;
  I chirped, cheeped, trilled, and twittered,
"Kate Brown's on the boards ere long,
  And Grisi's existence embittered!"

I earned no more by a warble
  Than you by a sketch in plaster;
You wanted a piece of marble,
  I needed a music master.

We studied hard in our styles,
  Chipped each at a crust like Hindoos,
For air, looked out on the tiles,
  For fun, watched each other's windows.

You lounged, like a boy of the south,
  Cap and blouse — nay, a bit of beard, too;
Or you got it, rubbing your mouth
  With fingers the clay adhered to.

And I — soon managed to find
  Weak points in the flower-fence facing,
Was forced to put up a blind
  And be safe in my corset lacing.

No harm! It was not my fault
  If you never turned your eye's tail up,
As I shook upon E *in alt*,
  Or ran the chromatic scale up:

For spring bade the sparrows pair,
  And the boys and girls gave guesses,
And stalls in our street looked rare
  With bulrush and watercresses.

Why did not you pinch a flower
  In a pellet of clay and fling it?
Why did not I put a power
  Of thanks in a look, or sing it?

I did look, sharp as a lynx
  (And yet the memory rankles),
When models arrived, some minx
  Tripped upstairs, she and her ankles.

But I think I gave you as good!
  "That foreign fellow — who can know
How she pays, in a playful mood,
  For his tuning her that piano?"

Could you say so, and never say,
  "Suppose we join hands and fortunes,
And I fetch her from over the way,
  Her, piano, and long tunes and short tunes"?

No, no; you would not be rash,
  Nor I rasher and something over;
You've to settle yet Gibson's hash,
  And Grisi yet lives in clover.

But you meet the Prince at the Board,
  I'm queen myself at *bals-paré,*
I've married a rich old lord,
  And you're dubbed knight and an R. A.

Each life unfulfilled, you see;
  It hangs still, patchy and scrappy:
We have not sighed deep, laughed free,
  Starved, feasted, despaired — been happy.

And nobody calls you a dunce,
  And people suppose me clever;
This could but have happened once,
  And we missed it, lost it forever.

YOUTH AND ART. **8. Gibson:** John Gibson (1790–1866), regarded as the foremost English sculptor of his day. He was a friend of Browning's. **12. Grisi:** Giulia Grisi (1811–69), the great Italian operatic soprano. **31. E *in alt:*** high E.

**57. Prince:** Albert, the Prince Consort, who was interested in the Royal Academy of Art. He died in 1861. **58. *bals-paré:*** fancy-dress balls. **60. R.A.:** member of the British Royal Academy of Arts.

## from THE RING AND THE BOOK

*The Ring and the Book,* a poem of more than 21,000 lines in twelve books, was published in four parts, two in 1868 and two in 1869. Browning had spent four years writing the poem. His main source was a volume of documents in Latin and Italian, mainly printed but part in manuscript, relating to the trial of Guido Franceschini for the murder of his wife Francesca (whom Browning calls Pompilia) in Rome in 1698. This collection had been made by a Florentine lawyer at the time of the trial. Browning found it on a bookstall in Florence in 1860. In 1908 an American professor, C. W. Hodell, published the collection in facsimile with a translation under the title, *The Old Yellow Book,* a name for it which he had borrowed from Browning. The translation is also available in Everyman's Library.

The story of the poem is as follows: Count Guido Franceschini, an impoverished and middle-aged nobleman of Arezzo, in 1693 married Francesca Pompilia, the supposed daughter of Pietro and Violante Comparini, middle-class citizens of Rome. The Comparini moved to Arezzo with Pompilia after the marriage, and friction soon developed. Each side had deceived the other concerning its wealth. The Comparini returned to Rome and brought suit for the return of Pompilia's dowry, alleging that she was not their daughter, but the child of a prostitute. Guido treated Pompilia with great cruelty and, according to her account, fostered an intrigue between her and a priest of Arezzo, Guiseppe Caponsacchi. About to become a mother, Pompilia in 1697 fled from Arezzo toward Rome accompanied by Caponsacchi. They were overtaken by Guido at Castelnuovo, a town in the Papal State, and were arrested on the charge of adultery. The Papal court condemned Caponsacchi to three years banishment to Civita Vecchia for seduction and adultery and detained Pompilia in a nunnery until her case could be examined further. She was soon released under bond to the Comparini and bore her child at their house in Rome.

Two weeks after the birth of the child, Guido and four hired accomplices entered the house, killed the Comparini, and wounded Pompilia so that she died four days later. Guido and his associates were arrested almost at once and were brought to trial. The murders were admitted, but Guido's lawyers argued that his crimes were justified by his wife's flight and adultery and the Comparini's complicity. The court sentenced Guido to beheading and his accomplices to hanging. Guido, who had been in minor clerical orders, appealed to the Pope, but the Pope refused to set aside the sentence of the court, and Guido was executed.

The poem is developed by Browning in a series of dramatic monologues. The first book introduces the case with Browning himself as the speaker explaining his purpose and method; the second, third, and fourth books give opinions on the case as it was seen outside by representatives of three groups of Roman society. The fifth book consists of Guido's plea imagined as given before the judges a few days after the murder; the sixth book is imagined as spoken by Caponsacchi to the judges while Pompilia is still alive; the seventh is spoken by Pompilia on her deathbed. The next three books are devoted to the law: the eighth and ninth are speeches by the opposing lawyers, Archangelis and Bottinius, and the tenth is the review of the case and the decision by the Pope. The eleventh book is Guido's defiant statement as he awaits execution, and the twelfth is Browning's conclusion.

The title of the poem is developed in a figure which the poet stresses early and late. The "ring" refers to to a ring of Etruscan manufacture which was once Mrs. Browning's and which Browning kept always with him after her death. The "book" is the crude mass of facts about the case in the collection of documents. An Etruscan jeweler had explained to Browning how the ring was made: in order to work the gold an alloy was added, but when the final form of the ring was attained, an acid made the alloy fly off in fume and left the ring pure gold. Thus, the poet's imagination worked as an alloy with the crude facts of the "book," and at the end of the process the poet's imagination went off in fume and left the pure substance and form in the poem. This was Browning's figure and it provided his title, but happily Browning's personality did not disappear from the poem. His analogy was imperfect, or, at least, not clearly expressed.

*The Ring and the Book* is certainly one of the most original, as it is one of the greatest, of long English poems. Thomas Carlyle in congratulating Browning on his "wonderful poem" added characteristically that it is "all made out of an Old Bayley story that might have been told in ten lines and only wants forgetting." It is true that Browning has glorified by his imagination a sordid and all too commonplace murder story. He has transformed his characters from what they appear to be in his source: Caponsacchi is changed from a light, adventurous, carefree young man into a chivalric St. George with many of the qualities of Browning himself; Pompilia, from an ignorant and flirtatious young wife in trouble into the very symbol of virtuous motherhood, Mrs. Browning herself; Guido is changed from a poor-spirited and degenerate hanger-on of the Church into a villain of terrifying intelligence, worthy to be compared with Iago. Browning seems to have been unaware of the elevation which he had introduced into the vulgar story, and insisted that he found it all in his source.

In architectonics Browning's art is consummate. Through the first four books we gradually become steeped in the facts of the case; in the fifth, Guido's plea, full of artifice and subterfuge, is so plausible that a person reading no further might be convinced that he was justified in his outrageous acts. With rising tension we hear Caponsacchi's anguished statement in the sixth book. The first apex of the poem is reached in Pompilia's pitiful deposition from her deathbed. Having reached that first peak, Browning deliberately courts the anticlimax of the lawyers' speeches in the eighth and ninth books as he makes an expansive buffoon of Archangelis and a solemn ass of Bottinius. From this low ground he rises swiftly and steeply to the lofty utterance of the Pope in Book X, a second great height. In the eleventh book we are given the frightening revelation of Guido's true nature as he bares his hate and scorn until his courage collapses as the executioners approach. In the twelfth book we are brought down to earth again, the C major of this life. The design is as daring as it is successful.

## POMPILIA

Browning believed that the Francesca he found in the documents of *The Old Yellow Book* was the same as the Pompilia of his poem. He wrote, "I assure you I found her in the book just as she speaks and acts in my poem." Critics, however, differ sharply with the poet and think his interpretation of the character is strongly colored by his love of Mrs. Browning, who had died in 1861, his pride in having freed her from the tyranny of her father, and his chivalric nature. To a considerable extent he identified Caponsacchi's part in the story with his own elopement with his wife. In the poem Pompilia speaks from her deathbed. The reader should observe the gradual and skillful revelation of Pompilia's character as the poem progresses from the account of her childhood to her full maturity.

I am just seventeen years and five months old,
And, if I lived one day more, three full weeks;
'Tis writ so in the church's register,
Lorenzo in Lucina, all my names
At length, so many names for one poor child
— Francesca Camilla Vittoria Angela
Pompilia Comparini — laughable!
Also 'tis writ that I was married there
Four years ago; and they will add, I hope,
When they insert my death, a word or two —
Omitting all about the mode of death —
This, in its place, this which one cares to know,
That I had been a mother of a son
Exactly two weeks. It will be through grace
O' the Curate, not through any claim I have;
Because the boy was born at, so baptized
Close to, the Villa, in the proper church:
A pretty church, I say no word against,
Yet stranger-like — while this Lorenzo seems
My own particular place, I always say.
I used to wonder, when I stood scarce high
As the bed here, what the marble lion meant,
With half his body rushing from the wall,
Eating the figure of a prostrate man —
(To the right, it is, of entry by the door) —
An ominous sign to one baptized like me,
Married, and to be buried there, I hope.
And they should add, to have my life complete,
He is a boy and Gaetan by name —
Gaetano, for a reason — if the friar
Don Celestine will ask this grace for me
Of Curate Ottoboni; he it was
Baptized me; he remembers my whole life
As I do his gray hair.

All these few things
I know are true — will you remember them?
Because time flies. The surgeon cared for me,
To count my wounds — twenty-two dagger
wounds,
Five deadly, but I do not suffer much —
Or too much pain — and am to die tonight.
Oh, how good God is that my babe was born,
— Better than born, baptized and hid away
Before this happened, safe from being hurt!
That had been sin God could not well forgive:
He was too young to smile and save himself.
When they took, two days after he was born,
My babe away from me to be baptized
And hidden awhile, for fear his foe should find —
The country woman, used to nursing babes,
Said, "Why take on so? where is the great loss?
These next three weeks he will but sleep and feed,
Only begin to smile at the month's end;
He would not know you, if you kept him here,
Sooner than that; so, spend three merry weeks
Snug in the Villa, getting strong and stout,
And then I bring him back to be your own,
And both of you may steal to — we know where!"
The month — there wants of it two weeks this day!
Still, I half fancied when I heard the knock
At the Villa in the dusk, it might prove she —
Come to say, "Since he smiles before the time,
Why should I cheat you out of one good hour?
Back I have brought him; speak to him and
judge!"
Now I shall never see him; what is worse,
When he grows up and gets to be my age,
He will seem hardly more than a great boy;
And if he asks, "What was my mother like?"
People may answer, "Like girls of seventeen" —
And how can he but think of this and that,
Lucias, Marias, Sofias, who titter or blush
When he regards them as such boys may do?
Therefore I wish someone will please to say
I looked already old though I was young;
Do I not . . . say, if you are by to speak . . .
Look nearer twenty? No more like, at least,
Girls who look arch or redden when boys laugh,
Than the poor Virgin that I used to know
At our street corner in a lonely niche —
The babe, that sat upon her knees, broke off —
Thin white glazed clay, you pitied her the more;
She, not the gay ones, always got my rose.

How happy those are who know how to write!
Such could write what their son should read in time,
Had they a whole day to live out like me.
Also my name is not a common name,
"Pompilia," and may help to keep apart
A little the thing I am from what girls are.
But then how far away, how hard to find
Will anything about me have become,
Even if the boy bethink himself and ask!
No father that ever knew at all,
Nor ever had — no, never had, I say!

**POMPILIA. 4. Lorenzo in Lucina:** the Roman church where Pompilia was baptized and later married. **6. Francesca:** She is known by this name in the documents. **17. the Villa:** the home of the Comparini in the suburbs. **30. Gaetano:** See ll. 100–06. The saint was canonized in 1671. **30–31. friar . . . Celestine:** Celestino Angelo of St. Anna, who attended Pompilia upon her deathbed and attested his admiration for her character and his conviction of her innocence. Since he was her confessor, he was bound to take that position.

**41.** The child was born on Dec. 18, 1697; Guido's assault upon Pompilia and the Comparini took place on Jan. 2; Pompilia died on Jan. 6. **81.** Critical opinion now believes she could both write and read.

That is the truth — nor any mother left,
Out of the little two weeks that she lived,
Fit for such memory as might assist;
As good too as no family, no name,
Not even poor old Pietro's name, nor hers,
Poor kind unwise Violante, since it seems
They must not be my parents any more.
That is why something put it in my head
To call the boy " Gaetano " — no old name
For sorrow's sake; I looked up to the sky
And took a new saint to begin anew.
One who has only been made saint — how long?
Twenty-five years; so, carefuller, perhaps,
To guard a namesake than those old saints grow,
Tired out by this time — see my own five saints!

On second thoughts, I hope he will regard
The history of me as what someone dreamed,
And get to disbelieve it at the last,
Since to myself it dwindles fast to that,
Sheer dreaming and impossibility —
Just in four days too! All the seventeen years,
Not once did a suspicion visit me
How very different a lot is mine
From any other woman's in the world.
The reason must be, 'twas by step and step
It got to grow so terrible and strange.
These strange woes stole on tiptoe, as it were,
Into my neighborhood and privacy,
Sat down where I sat, laid them where I lay;
And I was found familiarized with fear,
When friends broke in, held up a torch and cried,
" Why, you Pompilia in the cavern thus,
How comes that arm of yours about a wolf?
And the soft length — lies in and out your feet
And laps you round the knee — a snake it is! "
And so on.

Well, and they are right enough,
By the torch they hold up now: for first, observe,
I never had a father — no, nor yet
A mother; my own boy can say at least,
" I had a mother whom I kept two weeks! "
Not I, who little used to doubt . . . *I* doubt
Good Pietro, kind Violante, gave me birth?
They loved me always as I love my babe
( — Nearly so, that is — quite so could not be — )
Did for me all I meant to do for him,
Till one surprising day, three years ago,
They both declared, at Rome, before some judge
In some court where the people flocked to hear,
That really I had never been their child,
Was a mere castaway, the careless crime
Of an unknown man, the crime and care too much
Of a woman known too well — little to these,
Therefore, of whom I was the flesh and blood;
What then to Pietro and Violante, both
No more my relatives than you or you?
Nothing to them! You know what they declared.

So with my husband — just such a surprise,
Such a mistake, in that relationship!
Everyone says that husbands love their wives,
Guard them and guide them, give them happiness;
'Tis duty, law, pleasure, religion; well,
You see how much of this comes true in mine!
People indeed would fain have somehow proved
He was no husband, but he did not hear,
Or would not wait, and so has killed us all.
Then there is . . . only let me name one more!
There is the friend — men will not ask about,
But tell untruths of, and give nicknames to,
And think my lover, most surprise of all!
Do only hear, it is the priest they mean,
Guiseppe Caponsacchi: a priest — love,
And love me! Well, yet people think he did.
I am married, he has taken priestly vows,
They know that, and yet go on, say, the same,
" Yes, how he loves you! " " That was love " — they say,
When anything is answered that they ask;
Or else " No wonder you love him " — they say.
Then they shake heads, pity much, scarcely blame —
As if we neither of us lacked excuse,
And anyhow are punished to the full,
And downright love atones for everything!
Nay, I heard read out in the public court
Before the judge, in presence of my friends,
Letters 'twas said the priest had sent to me,
And other letters sent him by myself,
We being lovers!

Listen what this is like!
When I was a mere child, my mother . . . that's
Violante, you must let me call her so,
Nor waste time, trying to unlearn the word, . . .
She brought a neighbor's child of my own age
To play with me of rainy afternoons,
And, since there hung a tapestry on the wall,

138. The Comparini, in 1694, disclosed that Pompilia was not their daughter in order to escape paying the dowry to which they had agreed. They resented the treatment which they had received from Guido. Recently discovered documents show that Pompilia was the daughter of a poor but legitimate widow.

**148. my husband:** Pompilia was married to Guido in 1693 at the age of 13. **175. Letters:** Browning follows Pompilia and Caponsacchi in insisting that these were forgeries. Modern critics believe them genuine. **183. tapestry:** The tapestry in which Tisbe and Pompilia see their own likenesses are two different subjects: Tisbe is likened to Diana, goddess of hunting, and Pompilia to Daphne, a beautiful nymph who changed herself into a laurel tree to escape capture by Apollo. The significance of the legend's being allotted to Pompilia lies in her purity and her captivity.

We two agreed to find each other out
Among the figures. "Tisbe, that is you,
With half-moon on your hair knot, spear in hand,
Flying, but no wings, only the great scarf
Blown to a bluish rainbow at your back;
Call off your hound and leave the stag alone!"
"— And there are you, Pompilia, such green leaves
Flourishing out of your five finger ends,
And all the rest of you so brown and rough;
Why is it you are turned a sort of tree?"
You know the figures never were ourselves
Though we nicknamed them so. Thus, all my life —
As well what was, as what, like this, was not —
Looks old, fantastic and impossible:
I touch a fairy thing that fades and fades.
— Even to my babe! I thought, when he was born,
Something began for once that would not end,
Nor change into a laugh at me, but stay
Forevermore, eternally quite mine.
Well, so he is — but yet they bore him off,
The third day, lest my husband should lay traps
And catch him, and by means of him catch me.
Since they have saved him so, it was well done;
Yet thence comes such confusion of what was
With what will be — that late seems long ago,
And, what years should bring round, already come,
Till even he withdraws into a dream
As the rest do; I fancy him grown great,
Strong, stern, a tall young man who tutors me,
Frowns with the others, "Poor imprudent child!
Why did you venture out of the safe street?
Why go so far from help to that lone house?
Why open at the whisper and the knock?"

Six days ago when it was New Year's Day,
We bent above the fire and talked of him,
What he should do when he was grown and great.
Violante, Pietro, each had given the arm
I leant on, to walk by, from couch to chair
And fireside — laughed, as I lay safe at last,
"Pompilia's march from bed to board is made,
Pompilia back again and with a babe,
Shall one day lend his arm and help her walk!"
Then we all wished each other more New Years.
Pietro began to scheme — "Our cause is gained;
The law is stronger than a wicked man:
Let him henceforth go his way, leave us ours!
We will avoid the city, tempt no more
The greedy ones by feasting and parade —
Live at the other villa, we know where,
Still farther off, and we can watch the babe
Grow fast in the good air; and wood is cheap
And wine sincere outside the city gate.
I still have two or three old friends will grope
Their way along the mere half-mile of road,
With staff and lantern on a moonless night
When one needs talk; they'll find me, never fear,
And I'll find them a flask of the old sort yet!"
Violante said, "You chatter like a crow;
Pompilia tires o' the tattle, and shall to bed;
Do not too much the first day — somewhat more
Tomorrow, and, the next, begin the cape
And hood and coat! I have spun wool enough."
Oh, what a happy friendly eve was that!

And, next day, about noon, out Pietro went —
He was so happy and would talk so much,
Until Violante pushed and laughed him forth
Sight-seeing in the cold — "So much to see
I' the churches! Swathe your throat three times!" she cried,
"And, above all, beware the slippery ways,
And bring us all the news by suppertime!"
He came back late, laid by cloak, staff, and hat,
Powdered so thick with snow it made us laugh,
Rolled a great log upon the ash o' the hearth,
And bade Violante treat us to a flask,
Because he had obeyed her faithfully,
Gone sight-see through the seven, and found no church
To his mind like San Giovanni — "There's the fold,
And all the sheep together, big as cats!
And such a shepherd, half the size of life,
Starts up and hears the angel" — when, at the door,
A tap: we started up: you know the rest.

Pietro at least had done no harm, I know;
Nor even Violante, so much harm as makes
Such revenge lawful. Certainly she erred —
Did wrong, how shall I dare say otherwise? —
In telling that first falsehood, buying me
From my poor faulty mother at a price,
To pass off upon Pietro as his child.
If one should take my babe, give him a name,
Say he was not Gaetano and my own,
But that some other woman made his mouth
And hands and feet — how very false were that!
No good could come of that; and all harm did.
Yet if a stranger were to represent,
"Needs must you either give your babe to me
And let me call him mine forevermore,
Or let your husband get him" — ah, my God,
That were a trial I refuse to face!

**227. Our cause:** probably the suit brought by the Comparini to recover Pompilia's dowry. **232. other villa:** The Comparini owned two houses. They lived in the Strada Paolina in a house with shops attached.

**260. San Giovanni:** the church of St. John Lateran, one of the most splendid in Rome. **269–71.** The motive in Violante's action in passing off Pompilia as her own child was to obtain an inheritance which would not come to the Comparini if they were childless.

Well, just so here; it proved wrong but seemed right
To poor Violante — for there lay, she said,
My poor real dying mother in her rags,
Who put me from her with the life and all,
Poverty, pain, shame, and disease at once,
To die the easier by what price I fetched —
Also (I hope) because I should be spared
Sorrow and sin — why may not that have helped?
My father — he was no one, anyone —
The worse, the likelier — call him — he who came,
Was wicked for his pleasure, went his way,
And left no trace to track by; there remained
Nothing but me, the unnecessary life,
To catch up or let fall — and yet a thing
She could make happy, be made happy with,
This poor Violante — who would frown thereat?

Well, God, you see! God plants us where we grow.
It is not that, because a bud is born
At a wild brier's end, full i' the wild beast's way,
We ought to pluck and put it out of reach
On the oak-tree top — say, "There the bud belongs!"
She thought, moreover, real lies were lies told
For harm's sake; whereas this had good at heart,
Good for my mother, good for me, and good
For Pietro who was meant to love a babe,
And needed one to make his life of use,
Receive his house and land when he should die.
Wrong, wrong, and always wrong! how plainly wrong!
For see, this fault kept pricking, as faults do,
All the same at her heart; this falsehood hatched,
She could not let it go nor keep it fast.
She told me so — the first time I was found
Locked in her arms once more after the pain,
When the nuns let me leave them and go home,
And both of us cried all the cares away —
This it was set her on to make amends,
This brought about the marriage — simply this!
Do let me speak for her you blame so much!
When Paul, my husband's brother, found me out,
Heard there was wealth for who should marry me,
So, came and made a speech to ask my hand
For Guido — she, instead of piercing straight
Through the pretense to the ignoble truth,
Fancied she saw God's very finger point,
Designate just the time for planting me
(The wild-brier slip she plucked to love and wear)
In soil where I could strike real root, and grow,
And get to be the thing I called myself;
For, wife and husband are one flesh, God says,
And I, whose parents seemed such and were none,
Should in a husband have a husband now,
Find nothing, this time, but was what it seemed,
— All truth and no confusion any more.
I know she meant all good to me, all pain
To herself — since how could it be aught but pain
To give me up, so, from her very breast,
The wilding flower-tree branch that, all those years,
She had got used to feel for and find fixed?
She meant well; has it been so ill i' the main?
That is but fair to ask; one cannot judge
Of what has been the ill or well of life,
The day that one is dying — sorrows change
Into not altogether sorrow-like;
I do see strangeness but scarce misery,
Now it is over, and no danger more.
My child is safe; there seems not so much pain.
It comes, most like, that I am just absolved,
Purged of the past, the foul in me, washed fair —
One cannot both have and not have, you know —
Being right now, I am happy and color things.
Yes, everybody that leaves life sees all
Softened and bettered; so with other sights:
To me at least was never evening yet
But seemed far beautifuller than its day,
For past is past.

There was a fancy came,
When somewhere, in the journey with my friend,
We stepped into a hovel to get food;
And there began a yelp here, a bark there —
Misunderstanding creatures that were wroth
And vexed themselves and us till we retired.
The hovel is life; no matter what dogs bit
Or cat scratched in the hovel I break from,
All outside is lone field, moon, and such peace —
Flowing in, filling up as with a sea
Whereon comes Someone, walks fast on the white,
Jesus Christ's self, Don Celestine declares,
To meet me and calm all things back again.

Beside, up to my marriage, thirteen years
Were, each day, happy as the day was long;
This may have made the change too terrible.
I know that when Violante told me first
The cavalier — she meant to bring next morn,
Whom I must also let take, kiss my hand —
Would be at San Lorenzo the same eve
And marry me — which over, we should go
Home both of us without him as before,
And, till she bade speak, I must hold my tongue,
Such being the correct way with girl brides,
From whom one word would make a father blush —
I know, I say, that when she told me this
— Well, I no more saw sense in what she said

**320. Paul:** Father Paolo Franceschini was the oldest of the family. He held the important position of secretary to the Order of St. John of Malta.

**357. my friend:** Caponsacchi.

Than a lamb does in people clipping wool;
Only lay down and let myself be clipped.
And when next day the cavalier who came —
(Tisbe had told me that the slim young man
With wings at head, and wings at feet, and sword
Threatening a monster, in our tapestry,
Would eat a girl else — was a cavalier) —
When he proved Guido Franceschini — old
And nothing like so tall as I myself,
Hook-nosed and yellow in a bush of beard,
Much like a thing I saw on a boy's wrist,
He called an owl and used for catching birds —
And when he took my hand and made a smile —
Why, the uncomfortableness of it all
Seemed hardly more important in the case
Than — when one gives you, say, a coin to spend —
Its newness or its oldness; if the piece
Weigh properly and buy you what you wish,
No matter whether you get grime or glare!
Men take the coin, return you grapes and figs.
Here, marriage was the coin, a dirty piece
Would purchase me the praise of those I loved;
About what else should I concern myself?

So, hardly knowing what a husband meant,
I supposed this or any man would serve,
No whit the worse for being so uncouth;
For I was ill once and a doctor came
With a great ugly hat, no plume thereto,
Black jerkin and black buckles and black sword,
And white sharp beard over the ruff in front,
And oh, so lean, so sour-faced and austere! —
Who felt my pulse, made me put out my tongue,
Then oped a phial, dripped a drop or two
Of a black bitter something — I was cured!
What mattered the fierce beard or the grim face?
It was the physic beautified the man,
Master Malpichi — never met his match
In Rome, they said — so ugly all the same!

However, I was hurried through a storm,
Next dark eve of December's deadest day —
How it rained! — through our street and the Lion's Mouth
And the bit of Corso — cloaked round, covered close,
I was like something strange or contraband —
Into blank San Lorenzo, up the aisle,
My mother keeping hold of me so tight,
I fancied we were come to see a corpse
Before the altar which she pulled me toward.
There we found waiting an unpleasant priest
Who proved the brother, not our parish friend,
But one with mischief-making mouth and eye,
Paul, whom I know since to my cost. And then
I heard the heavy church door lock out help
Behind us; for the customary warmth,
Two tapers shivered on the altar. "Quick —
Lose no time!" cried the priest. And straightway down
From . . . what's behind the altar where he hid —
Hawk nose and yellowness and bush and all,
Stepped Guido, caught my hand, and there was I
O' the chancel, and the priest had opened book,
Read here and there, made me say that and this,
And after, told me I was now a wife,
Honored indeed, since Christ thus weds the Church,
And therefore turned he water into wine,
To show I should obey my spouse like Christ.
Then the two slipped aside and talked apart,
And I, silent and scared, got down again
And joined my mother, who was weeping now.
Nobody seemed to mind us any more,
And both of us on tiptoe found our way
To the door which was unlocked by this, and wide.
When we were in the street, the rain had stopped,
All things looked better. At our own house door,
Violante whispered, "No one syllable
To Pietro! Girl brides never breathe a word!"
"— Well treated to a wetting, draggletails!"
Laughed Pietro as he opened — "Very near
You made me brave the gutter's roaring sea
To carry off from roost old dove and young,
Trussed up in church, the cote, by me, the kite!
What do these priests mean, praying folk to death
On stormy afternoons, with Christmas close
To wash our sins off nor require the rain?"
Violante gave my hand a timely squeeze,
Madonna saved me from immodest speech,
I kissed him and was quiet, being a bride.

When I saw nothing more, the next three weeks,
Of Guido — "Nor the Church sees Christ" thought I;
"Nothing is changed however, wine is wine
And water only water in our house.
Nor did I see that ugly doctor since
That cure of the illness; just as I was cured,
I am married — neither scarecrow will return."

Three weeks, I chuckled — "How would Giulia stare,
And Tecla smile and Tisbe laugh outright,
Were it not impudent for brides to talk!" —
Until one morning, as I sat and sang
At the broidery frame alone i' the chamber — loud
Voices, two, three together, sobbings too,
And my name, "Guido," "Paolo," flung like stones
From each to the other! In I ran to see.

386. **young man:** Perseus, who rescued Andromeda from the dragon. 419. **Malpichi:** Malpighi, a papal physician who died in 1694. 423. **Lion's Mouth:** Via della Bocca di Leone, the Street of the Lion's Mouth. 424. **Corso:** one of the main avenues of the city.

There stood the very Guido and the priest
With sly face — formal but nowise afraid —
While Pietro seemed all red and angry, scarce
Able to stutter out his wrath in words;
And this it was that made my mother sob,
As he reproached her — " You have murdered us,
Me and yourself and this our child beside! "
Then Guido interposed, " Murdered or not,
Be it enough your child is now my wife!
I claim and come to take her." Paul put in,
" Consider — kinsman, dare I term you so? —
What is the good of your sagacity
Except to counsel in a strait like this?
I guarantee the parties man and wife
Whether you like or loathe it, bless or ban.
May spilt milk be put back within the bowl —
The done thing, undone? You, it is, we look
For counsel to, you fitliest will advise!
Since milk, though spilt and spoilt, does marble good,
Better we down on knees and scrub the floor,
Than sigh, ' the waste would make a syllabub! '
Help us so turn disaster to account,
So predispose the groom, he needs shall grace
The bride with favor from the very first,
Not begin marriage an embittered man! "
He smiled — the game so wholly in his hands!
While fast and faster sobbed Violante — " Aye,
All of us murdered, past averting now!
O my sin, O my secret! " and such like.

Then I began to half surmise the truth;
Something had happened, low, mean, underhand,
False, and my mother was to blame, and I
To pity, whom all spoke of, none addressed;
I was the chattel that had caused a crime.
I stood mute — those who tangled must untie
The embroilment. Pietro cried, " Withdraw, my child!
She is not helpful to the sacrifice
At this stage — do you want the victim by
While you discuss the value of her blood?
For her sake, I consent to hear you talk;
Go, child, and pray God help the innocent! "

I did go and was praying God, when came
Violante, with eyes swollen and red enough,
But movement on her mouth for make-believe
Matters were somehow getting right again.
She bade me sit down by her side and hear.
" You are too young and cannot understand,
Nor did your father understand at first.
I wished to benefit all three of us,
And when he failed to take my meaning — why,
I tried to have my way at unaware —
Obtained him the advantage he refused.
As if I put before him wholesome food
Instead of broken victual — he finds change
I' the viands, never cares to reason why,
But falls to blaming me, would fling the plate
From window, scandalize the neighborhood,
Even while he smacks his lips — men's way, my child!
But either you have prayed him unperverse
Or I have talked him back into his wits;
And Paolo was a help in time of need —
Guido, not much — my child, the way of men!
A priest is more a woman than a man,
And Paul did wonders to persuade. In short,
Yes, he was wrong, your father sees and says;
My scheme was worth attempting, and bears fruit,
Gives you a husband and a noble name,
A palace and no end of pleasant things.
What do you care about a handsome youth?
They are so volatile, and tease their wives!
This is the kind of man to keep the house.
We lose no daughter — gain a son, that's all:
For 'tis arranged we never separate,
Nor miss, in our gray time of life, the tints
Of you that color eve to match with morn.
In good or ill, we share and share alike,
And cast our lots into a common lap,
And all three die together as we lived!
Only, at Arezzo — that's a Tuscan town,
Not so large as this noisy Rome, no doubt,
But older far and finer much, say folk —
In a great palace where you will be queen,
Know the Archbishop and the Governor,
And we see homage done you ere we die.
Therefore, be good and pardon! " — " Pardon what?
You know things, I am very ignorant:
All is right if you only will not cry! "

And so an end! Because a blank begins
From when, at the word, she kissed me hard and hot,
And took me back to where my father leaned
Opposite Guido — who stood eying him,
As eyes the butcher the cast panting ox
That feels his fate is come, nor struggles more —
While Paul looked archly on, pricked brow at whiles
With the pen point as to punish triumph there —
And said, " Count Guido, take your lawful wife
Until death part you! "

All since is one blank,
Over and ended; a terrific dream.
It is the good of dreams — so soon they go!
Wake in a horror of heartbeats, you may —

**511.** Violante is thinking of her deception in passing off Pompilia as her child and also of having agreed to Pompilia's marriage without Pietro's knowledge. Her guilt was well established in the historical source.

Cry, "The dread thing will never from my
thoughts!"
Still, a few daylight doses of plain life,
Cockcrow and sparrow-chirp, or bleat and bell
Of goats that trot by, tinkling, to be milked;
And when you rub your eyes awake and wide,
Where is the harm o' the horror? Gone! So here.
I know I wake — but from what? Blank, I say!
This is the note of evil; for good lasts.
Even when Don Celestine bade, "Search and find!
For your soul's sake, remember what is past,
The better to forgive it" — all in vain!
What was fast getting indistinct before,
Vanished outright. By special grace perhaps,
Between that first calm and this last, four years
Vanish — one quarter of my life, you know.
I am held up, amid the nothingness,
By one or two truths only — thence I hang,
And there I live — the rest is death or dream,
All but those points of my support. I think
Of what I saw at Rome once in the Square
O' the Spaniards, opposite the Spanish House;
There was a foreigner had trained a goat,
A shuddering white woman of a beast,
To climb up, stand straight on a pile of sticks
Put close, which gave the creature room enough;
When she was settled there, he, one by one,
Took away all the sticks, left just the four
Whereon the little hoofs did really rest,
There she kept firm, all underneath was air.
So, what I hold by, are my prayer to God,
My hope, that came in answer to the prayer,
Some hand would interpose and save me — hand
Which proved to be my friend's hand, and — blest
bliss —
That fancy which began so faint at first,
That thrill of dawn's suffusion through my dark,
Which I perceive was promise of my child,
The light his unborn face sent long before —
God's way of breaking the good news to flesh.
That is all left now of those four bad years.
Don Celestine urged, "But remember more!
Other men's faults may help me find your own.
I need the cruelty exposed, explained,
Or how can I advise you to forgive?"
He thought I could not properly forgive
Unless I ceased forgetting — which is true;
For, bringing back reluctantly to mind
My husband's treatment of me — by a light
That's later than my lifetime, I review
And comprehend much and imagine more,
And have but little to forgive at last.
For now — be fair and say — is it not true
He was ill-used and cheated of his hope
To get enriched by marriage? Marriage gave
Me and no money, broke the compact so;
He had a right to ask me on those terms,
As Pietro and Violante to declare
They would not give me; so the bargain stood;
They broke it, and he felt himself aggrieved,
Became unkind with me to punish them.
They said 'twas he began deception first,
Nor, in one point whereto he pledged himself,
Kept promise; what of that, suppose it were?
Echoes die off, scarcely reverberate
Forever — why should ill keep echoing ill,
And never let our ears have done with noise?
Then my poor parents took the violent way
To thwart him — he must needs retaliate — wrong,
Wrong, and all wrong — better say, all blind!
As I myself was, that is sure, who else
Had understood the mystery; for his wife
Was bound in some sort to help somehow there.
It seems as if I might have interposed,
Blunted the edge of their resentment so,
Since he vexed me because they first vexed him;
"I will entreat them to desist, submit,
Give him the money and be poor in peace —
Certainly not go tell the world; perhaps
He will grow quiet with his gains."
Yes, say
Something to this effect and you do well!
But then you have to see first: I was blind.
That is the fruit of all such wormy ways,
The indirect, the unapproved of God:
You cannot find their author's end and aim,
Not even to substitute your good for bad,
Your straight for the irregular; you stand
Stupefied, profitless, as cow or sheep
That miss a man's mind; anger him just twice
By trial at repairing the first fault.
Thus, when he blamed me, "You are a coquette,
A lure-owl posturing to attract birds,
You look love-lures at theater and church,
In walk, at window!" — that, I knew, was false;
But why he charged me falsely, whither sought
To drive me by such charge — how could I know?
So, unaware, I only made things worse.
I tried to soothe him by abjuring walk,
Window, church, theater, for good and all,
As if he had been in earnest; that, you know,
Was nothing like the object of his charge.
Yes, when I got my maid to supplicate
The priest, whose name she read when she would
read
Those feigned false letters I was forced to hear
Though I could read no word of — he should cease
Writing — nay, if he minded prayer of mine,

602–03. **Square . . . Spaniards:** the Piazza di Spagna, a square in Rome frequented by foreigners. It takes its name from the palace of the Spanish ambassador.

663. **wormy:** crooked and ignoble. 685. Pompilia contended that she could not read or write. See l. 81n.

Cease from so much as even pass the street
Whereon our house looked — in my ignorance
I was just thwarting Guido's true intent,
Which was, to bring about a wicked change
Of sport to earnest, tempt a thoughtless man
To write indeed, and pass the house, and more,
Till both of us were taken in a crime.
He ought not to have wished me thus act lies,
Simulate folly, but — wrong or right, the wish —
I failed to apprehend its drift. How plain
It follows — if I fell into such fault,
He also may have overreached the mark,
Made mistake, by perversity of brain,
I' the whole sad strange plot, the grotesque intrigue
To make me and my friend unself ourselves,
Be other man and woman than we were!
Think it out, you who have the time! for me —
I cannot say less; more I will not say.
Leave it to God to cover and undo!
Only, my dullness should not prove too much!
— Not prove that in a certain other point
Wherein my husband blamed me — and you blame,
If I interpret smiles and shakes of head —
I was dull, too. Oh, if I dared but speak!
Must I speak? I am blamed that I forwent
A way to make my husband's favor come.
That is true; I was firm, withstood, refused . . .
— Women as you are, how can I find the words?

I felt there was just one thing Guido claimed
I had no right to give nor he to take,
We being in estrangement, soul from soul;
Till, when I sought help, the Archbishop smiled,
Inquiring into privacies of life
— Said I was blamable — (he stands for God)
Nowise entitled to exemption there.
Then I obeyed — as surely had obeyed
Were the injunction, " Since your husband bids,
Swallow the burning coal he proffers you! "
But I did wrong, and he gave wrong advice
Though he were thrice Archbishop — that, I know! —
Now I have got to die and see things clear.
Remember I was barely twelve years old —
A child at marriage; I was let alone
For weeks, I told you, lived my child-life still
Even at Arezzo, when I woke and found
First . . . but I need not think of that again —
Over and ended! Try and take the sense
Of what I signify, if it must be so.
After the first, my husband, for hate's sake,
Said one eve, when the simpler cruelty
Seemed somewhat dull at edge and fit to bear,
" We have been man and wife six months almost;
How long is this your comedy to last?
Go this night to my chamber, not your own! "
At which word, I did rush — most true the charge —
And gain the Archbishop's house — he stands for God —
And fall upon my knees and clasp his feet,
Praying him hinder what my estranged soul
Refused to bear, though patient of the rest;
" Place me within a convent," I implored —
" Let me henceforward lead the virgin life
You praise in her you bid me imitate! "
What did he answer? " Folly of ignorance!
Know, daughter, circumstances make or mar
Virginity — 'tis virtue or 'tis vice.
That which was glory in the Mother of God
Had been, for instance, damnable in Eve
Created to be mother of mankind.
Had Eve, in answer to her Maker's speech
' Be fruitful, multiply, replenish earth ' —
Pouted ' But I choose rather to remain
Single ' — why, she had spared herself forthwith
Further probation by the apple and snake,
Been pushed straight out of Paradise! For see —
If motherhood be qualified impure,
I catch you making God command Eve sin!
— A blasphemy so like these Molinists',
I must suspect you dip into their books."
Then he pursued, " 'Twas in your covenant! "

No! There my husband never used deceit.
He never did by speech nor act imply
" Because of our souls' yearning that we meet
And mix in soul through flesh, which yours and mine
Wear and impress, and make their visible selves
— All which means, for the love of you and me,
Let us become one flesh, being one soul! "
He only stipulated for the wealth;
Honest so far. But when he spoke as plain —
Dreadfully honest also — " Since our souls
Stand each from each, a whole world's width between,
Give me the fleshly vesture I can reach
And rend and leave just fit for hell to burn! " —
Why, in God's name, for Guido's soul's own sake
Imperiled by polluting mine — I say,
I did resist; would I had overcome!

My heart died out at the Archbishop's smile
— It seemed so stale and worn a way o' the world,
As though 'twere nature frowning — " Here is spring,

**728. twelve:** really thirteen.

**763. Molinists:** followers of Molinos, a Spanish priest. His heresies were condemned in 1687. He recanted, but died in prison in 1696, two years before Pompilia is supposed to be speaking.
**765. covenant:** the marriage ceremony.

The sun shines as he shone at Adam's fall,
The earth requires that warmth reach everywhere;
What, must your patch of snow be saved forsooth
Because you rather fancy snow than flowers?"
Something in this style he began with me.
Last he said, savagely for a good man,
"This explains why you call your husband harsh,
Harsh to you, harsh to whom you love. God's Bread!
The poor Count has to manage a mere child
Whose parents leave untaught the simplest things
Their duty was and privilege to teach —
Goodwives' instruction, gossips' lore; they laugh
And leave the Count the task — or leave it me!"
Then I resolved to tell a frightful thing.
"I am not ignorant — know what I say,
Declaring this is sought for hate, not love.
Sir, you may hear things like almighty God.
I tell you that my housemate, yes — the priest
My husband's brother, Canon Girolamo —
Has taught me what depraved and misnamed love
Means, and what outward signs denote the sin,
For he solicits me and says he loves,
The idle young priest with nought else to do.
My husband sees this, knows this, and lets be.
Is it your counsel I bear this beside?"
"— More scandal, and against a priest this time!
What, 'tis the Canon now?" — less snappishly —
"Rise up, my child, for such a child you are,
The rod were too advanced a punishment!
Let's try the honeyed cake. A parable!
'Without a parable spake he not to them.'
There was a ripe round long black toothsome fruit,
Even a flower-fig, the prime boast of May;
And, to the tree, said . . . either the spirit o' the fig,
Or, if we bring in men, the gardener,
Archbishop of the orchard — had I time
To try o' the two which fits in best; indeed
It might be the Creator's self, but then
The tree should bear an apple, I suppose —
Well, anyhow, one with authority said,
'Ripe fig, burst skin, regale the fig-pecker —
The bird whereof thou art a perquisite!'
'Nay,' with a flounce, replied the restive fig,
'I much prefer to keep my pulp myself:
He may go breakfastless and dinnerless,
Supperless of one crimson seed, for me!'
So, back she flopped into her bunch of leaves.
He flew off, left her — did the natural lord —
And lo, three hundred thousand bees and wasps
Found her out, feasted on her to the shuck;
Such gain the fig's that gave its bird no bite!
The moral — fools elude their proper lot,
Tempt other fools, get ruined all alike.

**792. God's Bread!**: an oath referring to the Lord's Supper. See "The Bishop Orders His Tomb," l. 82n.

Therefore go home, embrace your husband quick!
Which if his Canon brother chance to see,
He will the sooner back to book again."

So, home I did go; so, the worst befell;
So, I had proof the Archbishop was just man,
And hardly that, and certainly no more.
For, miserable consequence to me,
My husband's hatred waxed nor waned at all,
His brother's boldness grew effrontery soon,
And my last stay and comfort in myself
Was forced from me; henceforth I looked to God
Only, nor cared my desecrated soul
Should have fair walls, gay windows for the world.
God's glimmer, that came through the ruin-top,
Was witness why all lights were quenched inside;
Henceforth I asked God counsel, not mankind.

So, when I made the effort, freed myself,
They said — "No care to save appearance here!
How cynic — when, how wanton, were enough!"
— Adding, it all came of my mother's life —
My own real mother, whom I never knew,
Who did wrong (if she needs must have done wrong)
Through being all her life, not my four years,
At mercy of the hateful; every beast
O' the field was wont to break that fountain fence,
Trample the silver into mud so murk
Heaven could not find itself reflected there.
Now they cry, "Out on her, who, plashy pool,
Bequeathed turbidity and bitterness
To the daughter stream where Guido dipped and drank!"

Well, since she had to bear this brand — let me!
The rather do I understand her now —
From my experience of what hate calls love —
Much love might be in what their love called hate.
If she sold . . . what they call, sold . . . me, her child —
I shall believe she hoped in her poor heart
That I at least might try be good and pure,
Begin to live untempted, not go doomed
And done with ere once found in fault, as she.
Oh and, my mother, it all came to this?
Why should I trust those that speak ill of you,
When I mistrust who speaks even well of them?
Why, since all bound to do me good, did harm,
May not you, seeming as you harmed me most,
Have meant to do most good — and feed your child
From bramble-bush, whom not one orchard tree
But drew bough back from, nor let one fruit fall?
This it was for you sacrificed your babe?

**879. them**: the Comparini.

Gained just this, giving your heart's hope away
As I might give mine, loving it as you,
If . . . but that never could be asked of me!

There, enough! I have my support again,
Again the knowledge that my babe was, is,
Will be mine only. Him, by death, I give
Outright to God, without a further care —
But not to any parent in the world —
So to be safe; why is it we repine?
What guardianship were safer could we choose?
All human plans and projects come to nought:
My life, and what I know of other lives,
Prove that: no plan nor project! God shall care!

And now you are not tired? How patient then
All of you — oh yes, patient this long while
Listening, and understanding, I am sure!
Four days ago, when I was sound and well
And like to live, no one would understand.
People were kind, but smiled, "And what of him,
Your friend, whose tonsure the rich dark brown hides?
There, there! — your lover, do we dream he was?
A priest, too — never were such naughtiness!
Still, he thinks many a long think, never fear,
After the shy pale lady — lay so light
For a moment in his arms, the lucky one!"
And so on; wherefore should I blame you much?
So we are made, such difference in minds,
Such difference too in eyes that see the minds!
That man, you misinterpert and misprize —
The glory of his nature, I had thought,
Shot itself out in white light, blazed the truth
Through every atom of his act with me;
Yet where I point you, through the crystal shrine,
Purity in quintessence, one dewdrop,
You all descry a spider in the midst.
One says, "The head of it is plain to see,"
And one, "They are the feet by which I judge,"
All say, "Those films were spun by nothing else."

Then, I must lay my babe away with God,
Nor think of him again for gratitude.
Yes, my last breath shall wholly spend itself
In one attempt more to disperse the stain,
The mist from other breath fond mouths have made,
About a lustrous and pellucid soul;
So that, when I am gone but sorrow stays,
And people need assurance in their doubt
If God yet have a servant, man a friend,
The weak a saviour, and the vile a foe —
Let him be present, by the name invoked,
Giuseppe-Maria Caponsacchi!

There,
Strength comes already with the utterance!
I will remember once more for his sake
The sorrow; for he lives and is belied.
Could he be here, how he would speak for me!

I had been miserable three drear years
In that dread palace and lay passive now,
When I first learned there could be such a man.
Thus it fell: I was at a public play,
In the last days of Carnival last March,
Brought there I knew not why, but now know well.
My husband put me where I sat, in front;
Then crouched down, breathed cold through me from behind,
Stationed i' the shadow — none in front could see —
I, it was, faced the stranger throng beneath,
The crowd with upturned faces, eyes one stare,
Voices one buzz. I looked but to the stage,
Whereon two lovers sang and interchanged
"True life is only love, love only bliss;
I love thee — thee I love!" then they embraced.
I looked thence to the ceiling and the walls —
Over the crowd, those voices and those eyes —
My thoughts went through the roof and out, to Rome
On wings of music, waft of measured words —
Set me down there, a happy child again,
Sure that tomorrow would be festa day,
Hearing my parents praise past festas more,
And seeing they were old if I was young,
Yet wondering why they still would end discourse
With, "We must soon go, you abide your time,
And — might we haply see the proper friend
Throw his arm over you and make you safe!"

Sudden I saw him; into my lap there fell
A foolish twist of comfits, broke my dream
And brought me from the air and laid me low,
As ruined as the soaring bee that's reached
(So Pietro told me at the Villa once)
By the dust-handful. There the comfits lay;
I looked to see who flung them, and I faced
This Caponsacchi, looking up in turn.
Ere I could reason out why, I felt sure,
Whoever flung them, his was not the hand —
Up rose the round face and good-natured grin
Of one who, in effect, had played the prank,
From covert close beside the earnest face —
Fat waggish Conti, friend of all the world.
He was my husband's cousin, privileged
To throw the thing; the other, silent, grave,
Solemn almost, saw me, as I saw him.

There is a psalm Don Celestine recites,
"Had I a dove's wings, how I fain would flee!"

944. **Carnival**: the gay season just before Lent. 960. **festa day**: feast day. 980. **Conti**: He was the brother of Guido's sister's husband.

The psalm runs not, "I hope, I pray for wings," —
Not "If wings fall from heaven, I fix them fast," —
Simply "How good it were to fly and rest,
Have hope now, and one day expect content!
How well to do what I shall never do!"
So I said, "Had there been a man like that,
To lift me with his strength out of all strife
Into the calm, how I could fly and rest!
I have a keeper in the garden here
Whose sole employment is to strike me low
If ever I, for solace, seek the sun.
Life means with me successful feigning death,
Lying stonelike, eluding notice so,
Forgoing here the turf and there the sky.
Suppose that man had been instead of this!"

Presently Conti laughed into my ear,
— Had tripped up to the raised place where I sat —
"Cousin, I flung them brutishly and hard!
Because you must be hurt, to look austere
As Caponsacchi yonder, my tall friend
A-gazing now. Ah, Guido, you so close?
Keep on your knees, do! Beg her to forgive!
My cornet battered like a cannonball.
Good-by, I'm gone!" — nor waited the reply.

That night at supper, out my husband broke,
"Why was that throwing, that buffoonery?
Do you think I am your dupe? What man would dare
Throw comfits in a stranger lady's lap?
'Twas knowledge of you bred such insolence
In Caponsacchi; he dared shoot the bolt,
Using that Conti for his stalking-horse.
How could you see him this once and no more,
When he is always haunting hereabout
At the street corner or the palace side,
Publishing my shame and your impudence?
You are a wanton — I a dupe, you think?
O Christ, what hinders that I kill her quick?"
Whereat he drew his sword and feigned a thrust.

All this, now — being not so strange to me,
Used to such misconception day by day
And broken-in to bear — I bore, this time.
More quietly than woman should perhaps;
Repeated the mere truth and held my tongue.

Then he said, "Since you play the ignorant,
I shall instruct you. This amour — commenced
Or finished or midway in act, all's one —
'Tis the town talk; so my revenge shall be.
Does he presume because he is a priest?
I warn him that the sword I wear shall pink
His lily-scented cassock through and through,
Next time I catch him underneath your eaves!"
But he had threatened with the sword so oft
And, after all, not kept his promise. All
I said was, "Let God save the innocent!
Moreover, death is far from a bad fate.
I shall go pray for you and me, not him;
And then I look to sleep, come death or, worse,
Life." So, I slept.

There may have elapsed a week,
When Margherita — called my waiting maid,
Whom it is said my husband found too fair —
Who stood and heard the charge and the reply,
Who never once would let the matter rest
From that night forward, but rang changes still
On this the thrust and that the shame, and how
Good cause for jealousy cures jealous fools,
And what a paragon was this same priest
She talked about until I stopped my ears —
She said, "A week is gone; you comb your hair,
Then go mope in a corner, cheek on palm,
Till night comes round again — so, waste a week
As if your husband menaced you in sport.
Have not I some acquaintance with his tricks?
Oh, no, he did not stab the servingman
Who made and sang the rhymes about me once!
For why? They sent him to the wars next day.
Nor poisoned he the foreigner, my friend,
Who wagered on the whiteness of my breast —
The swarth skins of our city in dispute;
For, though he paid me proper compliment,
The Count well knew he was besotted with
Somebody else, a skin as black as ink
(As all the town knew save my foreigner) —
He found and wedded presently — 'Why need
Better revenge?' — the Count asked. But what's here?
A priest that does not fight, and cannot wed,
Yet must be dealt with! If the Count took fire
For the poor pastime of a minute — me —
What were the conflagration for yourself,
Countess and lady-wife and all the rest?
The priest will perish; you will grieve too late;
So shall the city-ladies' handsomest,
Frankest, and liberalest gentleman
Die for you, to appease a scurvy dog
Hanging's too good for. Is there no escape?
Were it not simple Christian charity
To warn the priest be on his guard — save him
Assured death, save yourself from causing it?
I meet him in the street. Give me a glove,
A ring to show for token! Mum's the word!"
I answered, "If you were, as styled, my maid,
I would command you; as you are, you say,
My husband's intimate — assist his wife
Who can do nothing but entreat 'Be still!'
Even if you speak truth and a crime is planned,

1008. cornet: a conical twist of paper.

Leave help to God as I am forced to do!
There is no other help, or we should craze,
Seeing such evil with no human cure.
Reflect that God, who makes the storm desist,
Can make an angry violent heart subside.
Why should we venture teach him governance?
Never address me on this subject more!"

Next night she said, "But I went, all the same
— Ay, saw your Caponsacchi in his house,
And come back stuffed with news I must outpour.
I told him, 'Sir, my mistress is a stone;
Why should you harm her for no good you get?
For you do harm her — prowl about our place
With the Count never distant half the street,
Lurking at every corner, would you look!
'Tis certain she has witched you with a spell.
Are there not other beauties at your beck?
We all know, Donna This and Monna That
Die for a glance of yours, yet here you gaze!
Go make them grateful, leave the stone its cold!'
And he — oh, he turned first white and then red,
And then — 'To her behest I bow myself,
Whom I love with my body and my soul:
Only a word i' the bowing! See, I write
One little word, no harm to see or hear!
Then, fear no further!' This is what he wrote.
I know you cannot read — therefore, let me!
*'My idol!'"* . . .

But I took it from her hand
And tore it into shreds. "Why join the rest
Who harm me? Have I ever done you wrong?
People have told me 'tis you wrong myself;
Let it suffice I either feel no wrong
Or else forgive it — yet you turn my foe!
The others hunt me and you throw a noose!"

She muttered, "Have your willful way!" I slept.

Whereupon . . . no, I leave my husband out!
It is not to do him more hurt, I speak.
Let it suffice, when misery was most,
One day, I swooned and got a respite so.
She stooped as I was slowly coming to,
This Margherita, ever on my trace,
And whispered — "Caponsacchi!"

If I drowned,
But woke afloat i' the wave with upturned eyes,
And found their first sight was a star! I turned —
For the first time, I let her have her will,
Heard passively, "The imposthume at such head,
One touch, one lancet puncture would relieve —
And still no glance the good physician's way
Who rids you of the torment in a trice!
Still he writes letters you refuse to hear.
He may prevent your husband, kill himself,
So desperate and all fordone is he!
Just hear the pretty verse he made today!
A sonnet from Mirtillo. *'Peerless fair. . . .'*
All poetry is difficult to read
— The sense of it is, anyhow, he seeks
Leave to contrive you an escape from hell,
And for that purpose asks an interview.
I can write, I can grant it in your name,
Or, what is better, lead you to his house.
Your husband dashes you against the stones;
This man would place each fragment in a shrine;
You hate him, love your husband!"

I returned,
"It is not true I love my husband — no,
Nor hate this man. I listen while you speak
— Assured that what you say is false, the same;
Much as when once, to me a little child,
A rough gaunt man in rags, with eyes on fire,
A crowd of boys and idlers at his heels,
Rushed as I crossed the Square, and held my head
In his two hands, 'Here's she will let me speak!
You little girl, whose eyes do good to mine,
I am the Pope, am Sextus, now the Sixth;
And that Twelfth Innocent, proclaimed today,
Is Lucifer disguised in human flesh!
The angels, met in conclave, crowned me!' — thus
He gibbered and I listened; but I knew
All was delusion, ere folk interposed,
'Unfasten him, the maniac!' Thus I know
All your report of Caponsacchi false,
Folly or dreaming; I have seen so much
By that adventure at the spectacle,
The face I fronted that one first, last time;
He would belie it by such words and thoughts.
Therefore while you profess to show him me,
I ever see his own face. Get you gone!"

"— That will I, nor once open mouth again —
No, by St. Joseph and the Holy Ghost!
On your head be the damage, so adieu!"

And so more days, more deeds I must forget,
Till . . . what a strange thing now is to declare!
Since I say anything, say all if true!
And how my life seems lengthened as to serve!
It may be idle or inopportune,
But, true? — why, what was all I said but truth,
Even when I found that such as are untrue
Could only take the truth in through a lie?

**1135. imposthume:** abscess.

**1143. Mirtillo:** a traditional name of a lover in pastoral poetry, used in the original letters. **1162. Sextus:** The speaker here is mad. No pope has chosen this title. The last Pope Sixtus was the fifth of that name.

Now — I am speaking truth to the Truth's self:
God will lend credit to my words this time.

It had got half through April. I arose
One vivid daybreak — who had gone to bed
In the old way my wont those last three years,
Careless until, the cup drained, I should die.
The last sound in my ear, the overnight,
Had been a something let drop on the sly
In prattle by Margherita, "Soon enough
Gaieties end, now Easter's past: a week,
And the Archbishop gets him back to Rome, —
Everyone leaves the town for Rome, this spring —
Even Caponsacchi, out of heart and hope,
Resigns himself and follows with the flock."
I heard this drop and drop like rain outside
Fast-falling through the darkness while she spoke;
So had I heard with like indifference,
"And Michael's pair of wings will arrive first
At Rome, to introduce the company,
And bear him from our picture where he fights
Satan — expect to have that dragon loose
And never a defender!" — my sole thought
Being still, as night came, "Done, another day!
How good to sleep and so get nearer death!" —
When, what, first thing at daybreak, pierced the sleep
With a summons to me? Up I sprang alive,
Light in me, light without me, everywhere
Change! A broad yellow sunbeam was let fall
From heaven to earth — a sudden drawbridge lay,
Along which marched a myriad merry motes,
Mocking the flies that crossed them and recrossed
In rival dance, companions newborn too.
On the house eaves, a dripping shag of weed
Shook diamonds on each dull gray lattice square,
As first one, then another bird leapt by,
And light was off, and lo was back again,
Always with one voice — where are two such joys? —
The blessed building sparrow! I stepped forth,
Stood on the terrace — o'er the roofs, such sky!
My heart sang, "I too am to go away,
I too have something I must care about,
Carry away with me to Rome, to Rome!
The bird brings hither sticks and hairs and wool,
And nowhere else i' the world; what fly breaks rank,
Falls out of the procession that befits,
From window here to window there, with all
The world to choose — so well he knows his course?
I have my purpose and my motive, too,
My march to Rome, like any bird or fly!
Had I been dead! How right to be alive!
Last night I almost prayed for leave to die,
Wished Guido all his pleasure with the sword
Or the poison — poison, sword, was but a trick,
Harmless, may God forgive him the poor jest!
My life is charmed, will last till I reach Rome!
Yesterday, but for the sin — ah, nameless be
The deed I could have dared against myself!
Now — see if I will touch an unripe fruit,
And risk the health I want to have and use!
Not to live, now, would be the wickedness —
For life means to make haste and go to Rome
And leave Arezzo, leave all woes at once!"

Now, understand here, by no means mistake!
Long ago had I tried to leave that house
When it seemed such procedure would stop sin;
And still failed more the more I tried — at first
The Archbishop, as I told you — next, our lord
The Governor — indeed I found my way,
I went to the great palace where he rules,
Though I knew well 'twas he who — when I gave
A jewel or two, themselves had given me,
Back to my parents — since they wanted bread,
They who had never let me want a nosegay — he
Spoke of the jail for felons, if they kept
What was first theirs, then mine, so doubly theirs,
Though all the while my husband's most of all!
I knew well who had spoke the word wrought this;
Yet, being in extremity, I fled
To the Governor, as I say — scarce opened lip
When — the cold cruel snicker close behind —
Guido was on my trace, already there,
Exchanging nod and wink for shrug and smile,
And I — pushed back to him and, for my pains,
Paid with . . . but why remember what is past?
I sought out a poor friar the people call
The Roman, and confessed my sin which came
Of their sin — that fact could not be repressed —
The frightfulness of my despair in God;
And feeling, through the grate, his horror shake.
Implored him, "Write for me who cannot write
Apprise my parents, make them rescue me!
You bid me be courageous and trust God;
Do you in turn dare somewhat, trust and write,
'Dear friends, who used to be my parents once,
And now declare you have no part in me,
This is some riddle I want wit to solve,
Since you must love me with no difference.
Even suppose you altered — there's your hate,
To ask for; hate of you two dearest ones
I shall find liker love than love found here,
If husbands love their wives. Take me away
And hate me as you do the gnats and fleas,
Even the scorpions! How I shall rejoice!'

**1254. the Governor:** Marzi-Medici, governor of Arezzo. **1256–57. gave . . . two:** Guido's charge that Pompilia improperly restored such things to the Comparini was believed by the governor. **1272. The Roman:** Pompilia appealed to a fellow townsman, an Augustinian priest, to help her to communicate with the Comparini.

Write that and save me!" And he promised—wrote
Or did not write; things never changed at all;
He was not like the Augustinian here!
Last, in a desperation I appealed
To friends, whoever wished me better days,
To Guillichini, that's of kin—"What, I—
Travel to Rome with you? A flying gout
Bids me deny my heart and mind my leg!"
Then I tried Conti, used to brave—laugh back
The louring thunder when his cousin scowled
At me protected by his presence: "You—
Who well know what you cannot save me from—
Carry me off! What frightens you, a priest?"
He shook his head, looked grave—"Above my strength!
Guido has claws that scratch, shows feline teeth;
A formidabler foe than I dare fret;
Give me a dog to deal with, twice the size!
Of course I am a priest and canon too,
But . . . by the bye . . . though both, not quite so bold
As he, my fellow-canon, brother priest,
The personage in such ill odor here
Because of the reports—pure birth o' the brain!
Our Caponsacchi, he's your true St. George
To slay the monster, set the Princess free,
And have the whole High Altar to himself;
I always think so when I see that piece
I' the Pieve, that's his church and mine, you know,
Though you drop eyes at mention of his name!"

That name had got to take a half-grotesque
Half-ominous, wholly enigmatic sense,
Like any byword, broken bit of song
Born with a meaning, changed by mouth and mouth
That mix it in a sneer or smile, as chance
Bids, till it now means nought but ugliness
And perhaps shame.

—All this intends to say,
That, overnight, the notion of escape
Had seemed distemper, dreaming; and the name—
Not the man, but the name of him, thus made
Into a mockery and disgrace—why, she
Who uttered it persistently, had laughed,
"I name his name, and there you start and wince
As criminal from the red tongs' touch!"—yet now,
Now, as I stood letting morn bathe me bright,
Choosing which butterfly should bear my news—
The white, the brown one, or that tinier blue,—
The Margherita, I detested so,
In she came—"The fine day, the good springtime!
What, up and out at window? That is best.
No thought of Caponsacchi?—who stood there
All night on one leg, like the sentry crane,
Under the pelting of your waterspout—
Looked last look at your lattice ere he leave
Our city, bury his dead hope at Rome.
Aye, go to looking glass and make you fine,
While he may die ere touch one least loose hair
You drag at with the comb in such a rage!"

I turned—"Tell Caponsacchi he may come!"
"Tell him to come? Ah, but, for charity,
A truce to fooling! Come? What—come this eve?
Peter and Paul! But I see through the trick!
Yes, come, and take a flowerpot on his head,
Flung from your terrace! No joke, sincere truth?"

How plainly I perceived hell flash and fade
O' the face of her—the doubt that first paled joy,
Then, final reassurance I indeed
Was caught now, never to be free again!
What did I care?—who felt myself of force
To play with silk, and spurn the horsehair springe.

"But—do you know that I have bade him come,
And in your own name? I presumed so much,
Knowing the thing you needed in your heart.
But somehow—what had I to show in proof?
He would not come; half-promised, that was all,
And wrote the letters you refused to read.
What is the message that shall move him now?"

"After the Ave Maria, at first dark,
I will be standing on the terrace, say!"

"I would I had a good long lock of hair
Should prove I was not lying! Never mind!"

Off she went—"May he not refuse, that's all—
Fearing a trick!"

I answered, "He will come."
And, all day, I sent prayer like incense up
To God the strong, God the beneficent,
God ever mindful in all strife and strait,
Who, for our own good, makes the need extreme,
Till at the last he puts forth might and saves.
An old rhyme came into my head and rang
Of how a virgin, for the faith of God,
Hid herself, from the paynims that pursued,

**1295. Guillichini:** In spite of Guillichini's refusal to accompany Pompilia to Rome, Guido proceeded against him in court, and he was sentenced to the galleys. **1312. St. George:** Compare the tapestry described in ll. 386 ff. **1315–16. that . . . Pieve:** Vasari's statue of St. George. The church was the one in which Caponsacchi and Conti were canons.

**1375. old rhyme:** The miracles which follow seem to be such legends as occur in quantity in Bartoli's *Simboli*, a book Browning read for its Italian style. See headnote to "How They Brought the Good News," above.

In a cave's heart; until a thunderstone,
Wrapped in a flame, revealed the couch and prey:
And they laughed — " Thanks to lightning, ours at last! "
And she cried, " Wrath of God, assert his love!
Servant of God, thou fire, befriend his child! "
And lo, the fire she grasped at, fixed its flash,
Lay in her hand a calm cold dreadful sword
She brandished till pursuers strewed the ground,
So did the souls within them die away,
As o'er the prostrate bodies, sworded, safe,
She walked forth to the solitudes and Christ:
So should I grasp the lightning and be saved!

And still, as the day wore, the trouble grew
Whereby I guessed there would be born a star,
Until at an intense throe of the dusk,
I started up, was pushed, I dare to say,
Out on the terrace, leaned and looked at last
Where the deliverer waited me: the same
Silent and solemn face, I first descried
At the spectacle, confronted mine once more.

So was that minute twice vouchsafed me, so
The manhood, wasted then, was still at watch
To save me yet a second time; no change
Here, though all else changed in the changing world!

I spoke on the instant, as my duty bade,
In some such sense as this, whatever the phrase:

" Friend, foolish words were borne from you to me;
Your soul behind them is the pure strong wind,
Not dust and feathers which its breath may bear;
These to the witless seem the wind itself,
Since proving thus the first of it they feel.
If by mischance you blew offense my way,
The straws are dropped, the wind desists no whit,
And how such strays were caught up in the street
And took a motion from you, why inquire?
I speak to the strong soul, no weak disguise.
If it be truth — why should I doubt it truth? —
You serve God specially, as priests are bound,
And care about me, stranger as I am,
So far as wish my good, that — miracle
I take to imitate he wills you serve
By saving me — what else can he direct?
Here is the service. Since a long while now,
I am in course of being put to death;
While death concerned nothing but me, I bowed
The head and bade, in heart, my husband strike.
Now I imperil something more, it seems,
Something that's trulier me than this myself,
Something I trust in God and you to save.
You go to Rome, they tell me; take me there,
Put me back with my people! "

He replied —
The first word I heard ever from his lips,
All himself in it — an eternity
Of speech, to match the immeasurable depth
O' the soul that then broke silence — " I am yours."

So did the star rise, soon to lead my step,
Lead on, nor pause before it should stand still
Above the House o' the Babe — my babe to be,
That knew me first and thus made me know him,
That had his right of life and claim on mine,
And would not let me die till he was born,
But pricked me at the heart to save us both,
Saying, " Have you the will? Leave God the way! "
And the way was Caponsacchi — " mine," thank God!
He was mine, he is mine, he will be mine.

No pause i' the leading and the light! I know.
Next night there was a cloud came, and not he,
But I prayed through the darkness till it broke
And let him shine. The second night, he came.

" The plan is rash; the project desperate;
In such a flight needs must I risk your life,
Give food for falsehood, folly or mistake,
Ground for your husband's rancor and revenge " —
So he began again, with the same face.
I felt that, the same loyalty — one star
Turning now red that was so white before —
One service apprehended newly: just
A word of mine and there the white was back!

" No, friend, for you will take me! 'Tis yourself
Risk all, not I — who let you, for I trust
In the compensating great God: enough!
I know you; when is it that you will come? "

" Tomorrow at the day's dawn." Then I heard
What I should do: how to prepare for flight
And where to fly.

That night my husband bade
" — You, whom I loathe, beware you break my sleep
This whole night! Couch beside me like the corpse
I would you were! " The rest you know, I think —
How I found Caponsacchi and escaped.

And this man, men call sinner? Jesus Christ!
Of whom men said, with mouths Thyself mad'st once,

**1436. House . . . Babe:** in Bethlehem

" He hath a devil " — say he was Thy saint,
My Caponsacchi! Shield and show — unshroud
In Thine own time the glory of the soul
If aught obscure — if inkspot, from vile pens
Scribbling a charge against him (I was glad
Then, for the first time, that I could not write)
Flirted his way, have flecked the blaze!

For me,
'Tis otherwise; let men take, sift my thoughts
— Thoughts I throw like the flax for sun to bleach!
I did pray, do pray, in the prayer shall die,
" Oh, to have Caponsacchi for my guide! "
Ever the face upturned to mine, the hand
Holding my hand across the world — a sense
That reads, as only such can read, the mark
God sets on woman, signifying so
She should — shall peradventure — be divine;
Yet 'ware, the while, how weakness mars the print
And makes confusion, leaves the thing men see
— Not this man sees — who from his soul, rewrites
The obliterated charter — love and strength
Mending what's marred. " So kneels a votarist,
Weeds some poor waste traditionary plot
Where shrine once was, where temple yet may be,
Purging the place but worshiping the while,
By faith and not by sight, sight clearest so —
Such way the saints work," — says Don Celestine.
But I, not privileged to see a saint
Of old when such walked earth with crown and
palm,
If I call " saint " what saints call something else —
The saints must bear with me, impute the fault
To a soul i' the bud, so starved by ignorance,
Stinted of warmth, it will not blow this year
Nor recognize the orb which spring flowers know.
But if meanwhile some insect with a heart
Worth floods of lazy music, spendthrift joy —
Some firefly renounced spring for my dwarfed cup,
Crept close to me, brought luster for the dark,
Comfort against the cold — what though excess
Of comfort should miscall the creature — sun?
What did the sun to hinder while harsh hands
Petal by petal, crude and colorless,
Tore me? This one heart gave me all the spring!

Is all told? There's the journey; and where's time
To tell you how that heart burst out in shine?
Yet certain points do press on me too hard.
Each place must have a name, though I forget;
How strange it was — there where the plain begins
And the small river mitigates its flow —
When eve was fading fast, and my soul sank,
And he divined what surge of bitterness,
In overtaking me, would float me back
Whence I was carried by the striding day —
So — "This gray place was famous once," said
he —
And he began that legend of the place
As if in answer to the unspoken fear,
And told me all about a brave man dead,
Which lifted me and let my soul go on!
How did he know too — at that town's approach
By the rock-side — that in coming near the signs
Of life, the house roofs and the church and tower,
I saw the old boundary and wall o' the world
Rise plain as ever round me, hard and cold,
As if the broken circlet joined again,
Tightened itself about me with no break —
As if the town would turn Arezzo's self —
The husband there — the friends my enemies,
All ranged against me, not an avenue
To try, but would be blocked and drive me back
On him — this other . . . oh, the heart in that!
Did not he find, bring, put into my arms
A newborn babe? — and I saw faces beam
Of the young mother proud to teach me joy,
And gossips round expecting my surprise
At the sudden hole through earth that lets in
heaven.
I could believe himself by his strong will
Had woven around me what I thought the world
We went along in, every circumstance,
Towns, flowers and faces, all things helped so well!
For, through the journey, was it natural
Such comfort should arise from first to last?
As I look back, all is one milky way;
Still bettered more, the more remembered, so
Do new stars bud while I but search for old,
And fill all gaps i' the glory, and grow him —
Him I now see make the shine everywhere.
Even at the last when the bewildered flesh,
The cloud of weariness about my soul
Clogging too heavily, sucked down all sense —
Still its last voice was, " He will watch and care;
Let the strength go, I am content; he stays! "
I doubt not he did stay and care for all —
From that sick minute when the head swam round,
And the eyes looked their last and died on him,
As in his arms he caught me, and, you say,
Carried me in, that tragical red eve,
And laid me where I next returned to life
In the other red of morning, two red plates
That crushed together, crushed the time between,
And are since then a solid fire to me —
When in, my dreadful husband and the world
Broke — and I saw him, master, by hell's right,
And saw my angel helplessly held back
By guards that helped the malice — the lamb prone,

**1470. "He . . . devil"**: see Matt. 9:34. This charge was made by the Pharisees when Jesus cast out devils. **1490. votarist:** devotee. **1501. blow:** bloom. **1512.** Pompilia is confused in her account of the journey from Arezzo to Castelnuovo. The way was about Perugia, Assisi, and Foligno to Castelnuovo.

The serpent towering and triumphant — then
Came all the strength back in a sudden swell,
I did for once see right, do right, give tongue
The adequate protest; for a worm must turn
If it would have its wrong observed by God.
I did spring up, attempt to thrust aside
That ice block 'twixt the sun and me, lay low
The neutralizer of all good and truth.
If I sinned so — never obey voice more
O' the Just and Terrible, who bids us — "Bear!"
Not — "Stand by, bear to see my angels bear!"
I am clear it was on impulse to serve God
Not save myself — no — nor my child unborn!
Had I else waited patiently till now? —
Who saw my old kind parents, silly-sooth
And too much trustful, for their worst of faults,
Cheated, browbeaten, stripped, and starved, cast out
Into the kennel; I remonstrated,
Then sank to silence, for — their woes at end,
Themselves gone — only I was left to plague.
If only I was threatened and belied,
What matter? I could bear it and did bear;
It was a comfort, still one lot for all;
They were not persecuted for my sake
And I, estranged, the single happy one.
But when at last, all by myself I stood
Obeying the clear voice which bade me rise,
Not for my own sake but my babe unborn,
And take the angel's hand was sent to help —
And found the old adversary athwart the path —
Not my hand simply struck from the angel's, but
The very angel's self made foul i' the face
By the fiend who struck there — that I would not bear,
That only I resisted! So, my first
And last resistance was invincible.
Prayers move God; threats, and nothing else, move men!
I must have prayed a man as he were God
When I implored the Governor to right
My parents' wrongs; the answer was a smile.
The Archbishop — did I clasp his feet enough,
Hide my face hotly on them, while I told
More than I dared make my own mother know?
The profit was — compassion and a jest.
This time, the foolish prayers were done with, right
Used might, and solemnized the sport at once.
All was against the combat; vantage, mine?
The runaway avowed, the accomplice-wife,
In company with the plan-contriving priest?
Yet, shame thus rank and patent, I struck, bare,
At foe from head to foot in magic mail,
And off it withered, cobweb armory
Against the lightning! 'Twas truth singed the lies
And saved me, not the vain sword nor weak speech!

You see, I will not have the service fail!
I say, the angel saved me; I am safe!
Others may want and wish, I wish nor want
One point o' the circle plainer, where I stand
Traced round about with white to front the world.
What of the calumny I came across,
What o' the way to end? — the end crowns all.
The judges judged aright i' the main, gave me
The uttermost of my heart's desire, a truce
From torture and Arezzo, balm for hurt,
With the quiet nuns — God recompense the good!
Who said and sang away the ugly past.
And, when my final fortune was revealed,
What safety, while, amid my parents' arms,
My babe was given me! Yes, he saved my babe;
It would not have peeped forth, the birdlike thing,
Through that Arezzo noise and trouble; back
Had it returned nor ever let me see!
But the sweet peace cured all, and let me live
And give my bird the life among the leaves
God meant him! Weeks and months of quietude,
I could lie in such peace and learn so much —
Begin the task, I see how needful now,
Of understanding somewhat of my past —
Know life a little, I should leave so soon.
Therefore, because this man restored my soul,
All has been right; I have gained my gain, enjoyed
As well as suffered — nay, got foretaste too
Of better life beginning where this ends —
All through the breathing-while allowed me thus,
Which let good premonitions reach my soul
Unthwarted, and benignant influence flow
And interpenetrate and change my heart,
Uncrossed by what was wicked — nay, unkind.
For, as the weakness of my time drew nigh,
Nobody did me one disservice more,
Spoke coldly or looked strangely, broke the love
I lay in the arms of, till my boy was born,
Born all in love, with nought to spoil the bliss
A whole long fortnight; in a life like mine
A fortnight filled with bliss is long and much.
All women are not mothers of a boy,
Though they live twice the length of my whole life,
And, as they fancy, happily all the same.
There I lay, then, all my great fortnight long,
As if it would continue, broaden out
Happily more and more, and lead to heaven;
Christmas before me — was not that a chance?
I never realized God's birth before —
How he grew likest God in being born.
This time I felt like Mary, had my babe
Lying a little on my breast like hers.

1633. The judgment of the court in Pompilia's case had not been final. She was put in the charge of the Roman nuns while further inquiries were made, and then transferred to the Comparini when the birth of her child was imminent.

So all went on till, just four days ago —
The night and the tap.

Oh, it shall be success
To the whole of our poor family! My friends
. . . Nay, father and mother — give me back my word!
They have been rudely stripped of life, disgraced
Like children who must needs go clothed too fine,
Carry the garb of Carnival in Lent.
If they too much affected frippery,
They have been punished and submit themselves,
Say no word; all is over, they see God
Who will not be extreme to mark their fault
Or he had granted respite; they are safe.

For that most woeful man my husband once,
Who, needing respite, still draws vital breath,
I — pardon him? So far as lies in me,
I give him for his good the life he takes,
Praying the world will therefore acquiesce.
Let him make God amends — none, none to me,
Who thank him rather that, whereas strange fate
Mockingly styled him husband and me wife,
Himself this way at least pronounced divorce,
Blotted the marriage bond; this blood of mine
Flies forth exultingly at any door,
Washes the parchment white, and thanks the blow.
We shall not meet in this world nor the next,
But where will God be absent? In his face
Is light, but in his shadow healing too;
Let Guido touch the shadow and be healed!
And as my presence was importunate —
My earthly good, temptation and a snare —
Nothing about me but drew somehow down
His hate upon me — somewhat so excused
Therefore, since hate was thus the truth of him —
May my evanishment forevermore
Help further to relieve the heart that cast
Such object of its natural loathing forth!
So he was made; he nowise made himself;
I could not love him, but his mother did.
His soul has never lain beside my soul;
But for the unresisting body — thanks!
He burned that garment spotted by the flesh.
Whatever he touched is rightly ruined; plague
It caught, and disinfection it had craved
Still but for Guido; I am saved through him
So as by fire; to him — thanks and farewell!

Even for my babe, my boy, there's safety thence —
From the sudden death of me, I mean; we poor
Weak souls, how we endeavor to be strong!
I was already using up my life —
This portion, now, should do him such a good,
This other go to keep off such an ill!
The great life; see, a breath and it is gone!
So is detached, so left all by itself
The little life, the fact which means so much.
Shall not God stoop the kindlier to his work,
His marvel of creation, foot would crush,
Now that the hand he trusted to receive
And hold it, lets the treasure fall perforce?
The better; he shall have in orphanage
His own way all the clearlier; if my babe
Outlived the hour — and he has lived two weeks —
It is through God who knows I am not by.
Who is it makes the soft gold hair turn black,
And sets the tongue, might lie so long at rest,
Trying to talk? Let us leave God alone!
Why should I doubt he will explain in time
What I feel now, but fail to find the words?
My babe nor was, nor is, nor yet shall be
Count Guido Franceschini's child at all —
Only his mother's, born of love, not hate!
So shall I have my rights in aftertime.
It seems absurd, impossible today;
So seems so much else, not explained but known!

Ah! Friends, I thank and bless you every one!
No more now; I withdraw from earth and man
To my own soul, compose myself for God.

Well, and there is more! Yes, my end of breath
Shall bear away my soul in being true!
He is still here, not outside with the world,
Here, here, I have him in his rightful place!
'Tis now, when I am most upon the move,
I feel for what I verily find — again
The face, again the eyes, again, through all,
The heart and its immeasurable love
Of my one friend, my only, all my own,
Who put his breast between the spears and me.
Ever with Caponsacchi! Otherwise
Here alone would be failure, loss to me —
How much more loss to him, with life debarred
From giving life, love locked from love's display,
The daystar stopped its task that makes night morn!
O lover of my life, O soldier-saint,
No work begun shall ever pause for death!
Love will be helpful to me more and more
I' the coming course, the new path I must tread —
My weak hand in thy strong hand, strong for that!
Tell him that if I seem without him now,
That's the world's insight! Oh, he understands!
He is at Civita — do I once doubt
The world again is holding us apart?
He had been here, displayed in my behalf
The broad brow that reverberates the truth,

1776. Civita: Civita Vecchia, a coastal city north of Rome to which Caponsacchi was banished for three years.

And flashed the word God gave him, back to man!
I know where the free soul is flown! My fate
Will have been hard for even him to bear;
Let it confirm him in the trust of God,
Showing how holily he dared the deed!
And, for the rest — say, from the deed, no touch
Of harm came, but all good, all happiness,
Not one faint fleck of failure! Why explain?
What I see, oh, he sees and how much more!
Tell him — I know not wherefore the true word
Should fade and fall unuttered at the last —
It was the name of him I sprang to meet
When came the knock, the summons and the end.
"My great heart, my strong hand are back again!"
I would have sprung to these, beckoning across
Murder and hell gigantic and distinct
O' the threshold, posted to exclude me heaven;
He is ordained to call and I to come!
Do not the dead wear flowers when dressed for God?
Say — I am all in flowers from head to foot!
Say — not one flower of all he said and did,
Might seem to flit unnoticed, fade unknown,
But dropped a seed, has grown a balsam tree
Whereof the blossoming perfumes the place
At this supreme of moments! He is a priest;
He cannot marry, therefore, which is right;
I think he would not marry if he could.
Marriage on earth seems such a counterfeit,
Mere imitation of the inimitable;
In heaven we have the real and true and sure.
'Tis there they neither marry nor are given
In marriage but are as the angels; right,
Oh, how right that is, how like Jesus Christ
To say that! Marriage-making for the earth,
With gold so much — birth, power, repute so much,
Or beauty, youth so much, in lack of these!
Be as the angels rather, who, apart,
Know themselves into one, are found at length
Married, but marry never, no, nor give
In marriage; they are man and wife at once
When the true time is; here we have to wait
Not so long neither! Could we by a wish
Have what we will and get the future now,
Would we wish aught done undone in the past?
So, let him wait God's instant men call years;
Meantime hold hard by truth and his great soul,
Do out the duty! Through such souls alone
God stooping shows sufficient of his light
For us i' the dark to rise by. And I rise.

**1825–28. Through . . . by:** For this estimate of Pompilia's true character Browning relied heavily upon the eloquent and admiring deposition of Father Celestine, who was with her at the end. The account is highly colored, however, by Browning's recollection of Mrs. Browning.

## THE POPE

Antonio Pignatelli was elevated to the papacy in 1691 and assumed the title of Innocent XII. He occupied the throne until his death in 1700. Before his elevation he had served as papal legate in foreign countries and had been Archbishop of Naples. Browning's delineation of his personality is quite faithful. The Pope cared only, according to a contemporary, for "God, the poor, and the reform of abuses." He abolished the sale of appointments, was readily accessible to the poor, and devoted himself without regard for his health to his duties. As faithful as Browning is to the character of Innocent XII, however, the thoughts which the poet puts in the Pope's mouth are altogether ideas of a nineteenth-century English Protestant, that is, of Browning himself. This may be seen at its most flagrant in the theology which the Pope speaks and in the magnificent appeal of Euripides, a favorite of Browning's.

The Pope hardly appears in Browning's source. There we have only the entry: "Judging it expedient not to postpone the execution of the sentence already determined His Holiness thought well, by a special decree under his signature, to deny all clerical privilege [to Guido]. . . . Last evening at two hours of the night [about 8 P.M.] my Lord signed the death-warrant, disallowing the clericate."

Like to Ahasuerus, that shrewd prince,
I will begin as is, these seven years now,
My daily wont — and read a history
(Written by one whose deft right hand was dust
To the last digit, ages ere my birth)
Of all my predecessors, Popes of Rome;
For though mine ancient early dropped the pen,
Yet others picked it up and wrote it dry,
Since of the making books there is no end.
And so I have the Papacy complete
From Peter first to Alexander last;
Can question each and take instruction so.
Have I to dare! — I ask, how dared this Pope?
To suffer? Such an one, how suffered he?
Being about to judge, as now, I seek
How judged once, well or ill, some other Pope;
Study some signal judgment that subsists
To blaze on, or else blot, the page which seals
The sum up of what gain or loss to God
Came of his one more Vicar in the world.
So, do I find example, rule of life;
So, square and set in order the next page,
Shall be stretched smooth o'er my own funeral cyst.

THE POPE. **1. Ahasuerus:** See Esther 1:1. Ahasuerus reigned "from India even unto Ethiopia." When he was unable to sleep he had chronicles read to him. **2.** Innocent XII had been pope for seven years. **7. mine ancient:** We are not told the name of the historian the Pope consulted upon this occasion. The swift succession of popes between 867 and 1073 illustrates the degradation of the papacy in these years by imperialistic factions. To Innocent XII the chronicle means that the claim of infallibility is dubious, at best. **11.** St. Peter was the first pope; Alexander VIII immediately preceded Innocent XII. **23. funeral cyst:** coffin.

Eight hundred years exact before the year
I was made Pope, men made Formosus Pope,
Say Sigebert and other chroniclers.
Ere I confirm or quash the trial here
Of Guido Franceschini and his friends,
Read — How there was a ghastly trial once
Of a dead man by a live man, and both Popes:
Thus — in the antique penman's very phrase:

" Then Stephen, Pope and seventh of the name,
Cried out, in synod as he sat in state,
While choler quivered on his brow and beard,
' Come into court, Formosus, thou lost wretch,
That claimedst to be late Pope as even I! '

" And at the word, the great door of the church
Flew wide, and in they brought Formosus' self,
The body of him, dead, even as embalmed
And buried duly in the Vatican
Eight months before, exhumed thus for the nonce.
They set it, that dead body of a Pope,
Clothed in pontific vesture now again,
Upright on Peter's chair as if alive.

" And Stephen, springing up, cried furiously,
' Bishop of Porto, wherefore didst presume
To leave that see and take this Roman see,
Exchange the lesser for the greater see,
— A thing against the canons of the Church? '

" Then one (a Deacon who, observing forms,
Was placed by Stephen to repel the charge,
Be advocate and mouthpiece of the corpse)
Spoke as he dared, set stammeringly forth
With white lips and dry tongue — as but a youth,
For frightful was the corpse face to behold —
How nowise lacked there precedent for this.

" But when, for his last precedent of all,
Emboldened by the Spirit, out he blurts,
' And, Holy Father, didst not thou thyself
Vacate the lesser for the greater see,
Half a year since change Arago for Rome? '
' — Ye have the sin's defense now, synod mine! '
Shrieks Stephen in a beastly froth of rage;
' Judge now betwixt him dead and me alive!
Hath he intruded, or do I pretend?
Judge, judge! ' — breaks wavelike one whole foam of wrath.

" Whereupon they, being friends and followers,
Said, ' Aye, thou art Christ's Vicar, and not he!
Away with what is frightful to behold!
This act was uncanonic and a fault.'

" Then, swallowed up in rage, Stephen exclaimed,
' So, guilty! So, remains I punish guilt!
He is unpoped, and all he did I damn;
The Bishop, that ordained him, I degrade;
Depose to laics those he raised to priests;
What they have wrought is mischief nor shall stand,
It is confusion, let it vex no more!
Since I revoke, annul, and abrogate
All his decrees in all kinds: they are void!
In token whereof and warning to the world,
Strip me yon miscreant of those robes usurped,
And clothe him with vile serge befitting such!
Then hale the carrion to the market place;
Let the town hangman chop from his right hand
Those same three fingers which he blessed withal;
Next cut the head off, once was crowned forsooth;
And last go fling them, fingers, head and trunk,
To Tiber that my Christian fish may sup! '
— Either because of ΙΧΘΥΣ which means Fish
And very aptly symbolizes Christ,
Or else because the Pope is Fisherman,
And seals with Fisher's signet.

" Anyway,
So said, so done: himself, to see it done,
Followed the corpse they trailed from street to street
Till into Tiber wave they threw the thing.
The people, crowded on the banks to see,
Were loud or mute, wept or laughed, cursed or jeered,
According as the deed addressed their sense;
A scandal verily; and out spake a Jew,
' Wot ye your Christ had vexed our Herod thus? '

" Now when, Formosus being dead a year,
His judge Pope Stephen tasted death in turn,
Made captive by the mob and strangled straight,
Romanus, his successor for a month,
Did make protest Formosus was with God,
Holy, just, true in thought and word and deed.
Next Theodore, who reigned but twenty days,
Therein convoked a synod, whose decree
Did reinstate, repope the late unpoped,
And do away with Stephen as accursed.
So that when presently certain fisherfolk
(As if the queasy river could not hold
Its swallowed Jonas, but discharged the meal)
Produced the timely product of their nets,

**25. Formosus:** pope from 891 to 896. He had been bishop of Porto (see ll. 46–48).

**89. ΙΧΘΥΣ:** These Greek letters, which spell the word for "fish," are also the initial letters of the five Greek words for Jesus, Christ, God's, son, saviour. Therefore the symbol of a fish was much used in early Christian times to signify the presence of Christians. **91. Fisherman:** Peter was a fisherman whom Christ said he would convert into a fisher of men. **104. Romanus:** In his short tenure of the Holy See he strove to undo all that Stephen had done. **107. Theodore:** Theodore II attempted to restore the conditions existing before Stephen.

The mutilated man, Formosus — saved
From putrefaction by the embalmer's spice,
Or, as some said, by santity of flesh —
'Why, lay the body again,' bade Theodore,
'Among his predecessors, in the church
And burial place of Peter!' which was done.
'And,' addeth Luitprand, 'many of repute,
Pious and still alive, avouch to me
That, as they bore the body up the aisle,
The saints in imaged row bowed each his head
For welcome to a brother saint come back.'
As for Romanus and this Theodore,
These two Popes, through the brief reign granted each,
Could but initiate what John came to close
And give the final stamp to: he it was,
Ninth of the name (I follow the best guides)
Who — in full synod at Ravenna held
With Bishops seventy-four, and present too
Eude King of France with his Archbishopry —
Did condemn Stephen, anathematize
The disinterment, and make all blots blank.
'For,' argueth here Auxilius in a place
*De Ordinationibus,* 'precedents
Had been, no lack, before Formosus long,
Of Bishops so transferred from see to see —
Marinus, for example': read the tract.

"But, after John, came Sergius, reaffirmed
The right of Stephen, cursed Formosus, nay
Cast out, some say, his corpse a second time,
And here — because the matter went to ground,
Fretted by new griefs, other cares of the age —
Here is the last pronouncing of the Church,
Her sentence that subsists unto this day.
Yet constantly opinion hath prevailed
I' the Church, Formosus was a holy man."

Which of the judgments was infallible?
Which of my predecessors spoke for God?
And what availed Formosus that this cursed,
That blessed, and then this other cursed again?
"Fear ye not those whose power can kill the body
And not the soul," saith Christ, "but rather those
Can cast both soul and body into hell!"

**121. Luitprand:** a papal historian. **128. John:** Having a somewhat longer reign than his immediate predecessors, John IX (898–900) called a synod at Ravenna, which condemned Stephen in full judicial form. **133. Eude:** king of France from 888 to 898. **136. Auxilius:** a French theologian who wrote on the subject of Stephen's decision. **141. Sergius:** According to Platina, papal historian, Sergius III abolished all that Formosus had done, had his body again taken out of the grave, beheaded it, and had it thrown into the Tiber. Some fishermen found it and brought it to St. Peter's church. While the funeral rites were being performed, the images of the saints in the church bowed in veneration. Browning uses this legend in ll. 121 ff.

John judged thus in eight hundred ninety eight,
Exact eight hundred years ago today
When, sitting in his stead, Vicegerent here,
I must give judgment on my own behoof.
So worked the predecessor; now, my turn!

In God's name! Once more on this earth of God's,
While twilight lasts and time wherein to work,
I take his staff with my uncertain hand,
And stay my six and fourscore years, my due
Labor and sorrow, on his judgment seat,
And forthwith think, speak, act, in place of him —
The Pope for Christ. Once more appeal is made
From man's assize to mine; I sit and see
Another poor weak trembling human wretch
Pushed by his fellows, who pretend the right,
Up to the gulf which, where I gaze, begins
From this world to the next — gives way and way,
Just on the edge over the awful dark;
With nothing to arrest him but my feet.
He catches at me with convulsive face,
Cries, "Leave to live the natural minute more!"
While hollowly the avengers echo, "Leave?
None! So has he exceeded man's due share
In man's fit license, wrung by Adam's fall,
To sin and yet not surely die — that we,
All of us sinful, all with need of grace,
All chary of our life — the minute more
Or minute less of grace which saves a soul —
Bound to make common cause with who craves time
— We yet protest against the exorbitance
Of sin in this one sinner, and demand
That his poor sole remaining piece of time
Be plucked from out his clutch: put him to death!
Punish him now! As for the weal or woe
Hereafter, God grant mercy! Man be just.
Nor let the felon boast he went scot free!"
And I am bound, the solitary judge,
To weigh the worth, decide upon the plea,
And either hold a hand out, or withdraw
A foot and let the wretch drift to the fall.
Aye, and while thus I dally, dare perchance
Put fancies for a comfort 'twixt this calm
And yonder passion that I have to bear —
As if reprieve were possible for both
Prisoner and Pope — how easy were reprieve!
A touch o' the handbell here, a hasty word
To those who wait, and wonder they wait long,
I' the passage there, and I should gain the life! —
Yea, though I flatter me with fancy thus,
I know it is but Nature's craven trick.

**168. Once . . . made:** Because he was in a minor sense a member of the clergy, Guido claimed the right to have his cause referred to an ecclesiastical tribunal. **203. wonder . . . long:** They wait long because of the rank of the accused and his connection with the papal court.

The case is over, judgment at an end,
And all things done now and irrevocable:
A mere dead man is Franceschini here,
Even as Formosus centuries ago.
I have worn through this somber wintry day,
With winter in my soul beyond the world's,
Over these dismalest of documents
Which drew night down on me ere eve befell —
Pleadings and counterpleadings, figure of fact
Beside fact's self, these summaries, to wit —
How certain three were slain by certain five;
I read here why it was, and how it went,
And how the chief o' the five preferred excuse,
And how law rather chose defense should lie —
What argument he urged by wary word
When free to play off wile, start subterfuge,
And what the unguarded groan told, torture's feat
When law grew brutal, outbroke, overbore
And glutted hunger on the truth, at last —
No matter for the flesh and blood between.
All's a clear rede and no more riddle now.
Truth, nowhere, lies yet everywhere in these —
Not absolutely in a portion, yet
Evolvable from the whole; evolved at last
Painfully, held tenaciously by me.
Therefore there is not any doubt to clear
When I shall write the brief word presently
And chink the handbell, which I pause to do.
Irresolute? Not I, more than the mound
With the pine trees on it yonder! Some surmise,
Perchance, that since man's wit is fallible,
Mine may fail here? Suppose it so — what then?
Say — Guido, I count guilty, there's no babe
So guiltless, for I misconceive the man!
What's in the chance should move me from my mind?
If, as I walk in a rough countryside,
Peasants of mine cry, "Thou art he can help,
Lord of the land and counted wise to boot:
Look at our brother, strangling in his foam,
He fell so where we find him — prove thy worth!"
I may presume, pronounce, "A frenzy fit,
A falling sickness or a fever stroke!
Breathe a vein, copiously let blood at once!"
So perishes the patient, and anon
I hear my peasants — "All was error, lore!
Our story, thy prescription; for there crawled
In due time from our hapless brother's breast
The serpent which had stung him; bleeding slew
Whom a prompt cordial had restored to health."
What other should I say than, "God so willed;
Mankind is ignorant, a man am I;
Call ignorance my sorrow, not my sin!"
So and not otherwise, in aftertime,
If some acuter wit, fresh probing, sound
This multifarious mass of words and deeds
Deeper, and reach through guilt to innocence,
I shall face Guido's ghost nor blench a jot.
"God who set me to judge thee, meted out
So much of judging faculty, no more;
Ask him if I was slack in use thereof!"
I hold a heavier fault imputable
Inasmuch as I changed a chaplain once,
For no cause — no, if I must bare my heart —
Save that he snuffled somewhat saying mass.
For I am 'ware it is the seed of act,
God holds appraising in his hollow palm,
Not act grown great thence on the world below,
Leafage and branchage, vulgar eyes admire.
Therefore I stand on my integrity,
Nor fear at all; and if I hesitate,
It is because I need to breathe awhile,
Rest, as the human right allows, review
Intent the little seeds of act, my tree —
The thought, which, clothed in deed, I give the world
At chink of bell and push of arrased door.

O pale departure, dim disgrace of day!
Winter's in wane, his vengeful worst art thou,
To dash the boldness of advancing March!
Thy chill persistent rain has purged our streets
Of gossipry; pert tongue and idle ear
By this, consort 'neath archway, portico.
But wheresoe'er Rome gathers in the gray,
Two names now snap and flash from mouth to mouth —
(Sparks, flint, and steel strike) — Guido and the Pope.
By this same hour tomorrow eve — aha,
How do they call him? — the sagacious Swede
Who finds by figures how the chances prove,
Why one comes rather than another thing,
As, say, such dots turn up by throw of dice,
Or, if we dip in Virgil here and there
And prick for such a verse, when such shall point.
Take this Swede, tell him, hiding name and rank,
Two men are in our city this dull eve;
One doomed to death — but hundreds in such plight
Slip aside, clean escape by leave of law
Which leans to mercy in this latter time;
Moreover in the plenitude of life
Is he, with strength of limb and brain adroit,
Presumably of service here; beside,

**211. wintry day:** February 21. **217. certain five:** Guido and his four accomplices. **220.** That is, what line of defense Guido's lawyers thought it best to take. **227. rede:** design.

**292. sagacious Swede:** The identity of this wise student of the laws of probability has remained one of the most tantalizing mysteries of Browning scholarship. **296–97.** The reference is to an old practice called *sortes Virgilianae* (Virgilian lots), by which one opened a copy of Virgil at random and placed a tip of the finger on a line without looking. The line gave guidance to the person performing the act.

The man is noble, backed by nobler friends;
Nay, they so wish him well, the city's self
Makes common cause with who — house magistrate,
Patron of hearth and home, domestic lord —
But ruled his own, let aliens cavil. Die?
He'll bribe a jailer or break prison first!
Nay, a sedition may be helpful, give
Hint to the mob to batter wall, burn gate,
And bid the favorite malefactor march.
Calculate now these chances of escape!
"It is not probable, but well may be."
Again, there is another man, weighed now
By twice eight years beyond the seven-times-ten,
Appointed overweight to break our branch.
And this man's loaded branch lifts, more than snow,
All the world's cark and care, though a bird's nest
Were a superfluous burden; notably
Hath he been pressed, as if his age were youth,
From today's dawn till now that day departs,
Trying one question with true sweat of soul,
"Shall the said doomed man fitlier die or live?"
When a straw swallowed in his posset, stool
Stumbled on where his path lies, any puff
That's incident to such a smoking flax,
Hurries the natural end and quenches him!
Now calculate, thou sage, the chances here,
Say, which shall die the sooner, this or that?
"That, possibly, this in all likelihood."
I thought so; yet thou tripp'st, my foreign friend!
No, it will be quite otherwise — today
Is Guido's last; my term is yet to run.

But say the Swede were right, and I forthwith
Acknowledge a prompt summons and lie dead;
Why, then I stand already in God's face
And hear, "Since by its fruit a tree is judged,
Show me thy fruit, the latest act of thine!
For in the last is summed the first and all —
What thy life last put heart and soul into,
There shall I taste thy product." I must plead
This condemnation of a man today.

Not so! Expect nor question nor reply
At what we figure as God's judgment bar!
None of this vile way by the barren words
Which, more than any deed, characterize
Man as made subject to a curse; no speech —
That still bursts o'er some lie which lurks inside,
As the split skin across the coppery snake,
And most denotes man! since, in all beside,
In hate or lust or guile or unbelief,
Out of some core of truth the excrescence comes,
And, in the last resort, the man may urge
"So was I made, a weak thing that gave way
To truth, to impulse only strong since true,
And hated, lusted, used guile, forwent faith."
But when man walks the garden of this world
For his own solace, and, unchecked by law,
Speaks or keeps silence as himself sees fit,
Without the least incumbency to lie
— Why, can he tell you what a rose is like,
Or how the birds fly, and not slip to false
Though truth serve better? Man must tell his mate
Of you, me and himself, knowing he lies,
Knowing his fellow knows the same — will think
"He lies, it is the method of a man!"
And yet will speak for answer, "It is truth,"
To him who shall rejoin, "Again a lie!"
Therefore these filthy rags of speech, this coil
Of statement, comment, query, and response,
Tatters all too contaminate for use,
Have no renewing; He the Truth is, too,
The Word. We men, in our degree, may know
There, simply, instantaneously, as here
After long time and amid many lies,
Whatever we dare think we know indeed
— That I am I, as He is He — what else?
But be man's method for man's life at least!
Wherefore, Antonio Pignatelli, thou
My ancient self, who wast no Pope so long
But studiedst God and man, the many years
I' the school, i' the cloister, in the diocese
Domestic, legate rule in foreign lands —
Thou other force in those old busy days
Than this gray ultimate decrepitude —
Yet sensible of fires that more and more
Visit a soul, in passage to the sky,
Left nakeder than when flesh-robe was new —
Thou, not Pope but the mere old man o' the world,
Supposed inquisitive and dispassionate,
Wilt thou, the one whose speech I somewhat trust,
Question the after-me, this self now Pope,
Hear his procedure, criticize his work?
Wise in its generation is the world.

This is why Guido is found reprobate.
I see him furnished forth for his career,
On starting for the life chance in our world,
With nearly all we count sufficient help:
Body and mind in balance, a sound frame,
A solid intellect; the wit to seek,
Wisdom to choose, and courage wherewithal
To deal in whatsoever circumstance
Should minister to man, make life succeed.
Oh, and much drawback! what were earth without?
Is this our ultimate stage, or starting place
To try man's foot, if it will creep or climb,
'Mid obstacles in seeming, points that prove

**327. posset:** a drink in which milk is mingled with wine or ale. **346–97.** Here the Pope (and Browning) recognizes the impossibility of getting the full and perfect truth into or out of human words, but since language is all we have, he must act upon it as best he can.

**375. He:** Christ. **385–86. diocese . . . rule:** a bishopric at home in Italy, and a nunciature abroad.

Advantage for who vaults from low to high
And makes the stumbling block a steppingstone?
So, Guido, born with appetite, lacks food;
Is poor, who yet could deftly play off wealth;
Straitened, whose limbs are restless till at large.
He, as he eyes each outlet of the cirque
And narrow penfold for probation, pines
After the good things just outside its grate,
With less monition, fainter conscience twitch,
Rarer instinctive qualm at the first feel
Of greed unseemly, prompting grasp undue,
Than nature furnishes her main mankind —
Making it harder to do wrong than right
The first time, careful lest the common ear
Break measure, miss the outstep of life's march.
Wherein I see a trial fair and fit
For one else too unfairly fenced about,
Set above sin, beyond his fellows here;
Guarded from the archtempter all must fight,
By a great birth, traditionary name,
Diligent culture, choice companionship,
Above all, conversancy with the faith
Which puts forth for its base of doctrine just,
"Man is born nowise to content himself,
But please God." He accepted such a rule,
Recognized man's obedience; and the Church,
Which simply is such rule's embodiment,
He clave to, he held on by — nay, indeed,
Near pushed inside of, deep as layman durst,
Professed so much of priesthood as might sue
For priest's exemption where the layman sinned —
Go this arm frocked which, bare, the law would bruise,
Hence, at this moment, what's his last resource,
His extreme stay and utmost stretch of hope
But that — convicted of such crime as law
Wipes not away save with a worldling's blood —
Guido, the three-parts consecrate, may 'scape?
Nay, the portentous brothers of the man
Are veritably priests, protected each
May do his murder in the Church's pale,
Abate Paul, Canon Girolamo!
This is the man proves irreligiousest
Of all mankind, religion's parasite!
This may forsooth plead dinned ear, jaded sense,
The vice o' the watcher who bides near the bell,
Sleeps sound because the clock is vigilant,
And cares not whether it be shade or shine,
Doling out day and night to all men else!
Why was the choice o' the man to niche himself
Perversely 'neath the tower where Time's own tongue
Thus undertakes to sermonize the world?
Why, but because the solemn is safe too,
The belfry proves a fortress of a sort,
Has other uses than to teach the hour;
Turns sunscreen, paravent, and ombrifuge
To whoso seeks a shelter in its pale
— Aye, and attractive to unwary folk
Who gaze at storied portal, statued spire,
And go home with full head but empty purse,
Nor dare suspect the sacristan the thief!
Shall Judas — hard upon the donor's heel,
To filch the fragments of the basket — plead
He was too near the preacher's mouth, nor sat
Attent with fifties in a company?
No — closer to promulgated decree,
Clearer the censure of default. Proceed!

I find him bound, then, to begin life well;
Fortified by propitious circumstance,
Great birth, good breeding, with the Church for guide,
How lives he? Cased thus in a coat of proof,
Mailed like a man-at-arms, though all the while
A puny starveling — does the breast pant big,
The limb swell to the limit, emptiness
Strive to become solidity indeed?
Rather, he shrinks up like the ambiguous fish,
Detaches flesh from shell and outside show,
And steals by moonlight (I have seen the thing)
In and out, now to prey and now to skulk.
Armor he boasts when a wave breaks on beach,
Or bird stoops for the prize; with peril nigh —
The man of rank, the much-befriended man,
The man almost affiliate to the Church,
Such is to deal with, let the world beware!
Does the world recognize, pass prudently?
Do tides abate and seafowl hunt i' the deep?
Already is the slug from out its mew,
Ignobly faring with all loose and free,
Sand fly and slush-worm at their garbage feast,
A naked blotch no better than they all;
Guido has dropped nobility, slipped the Church,
Plays trickster if not cutpurse, body and soul
Prostrate among the filthy feeders — faugh!
And when Law takes him by surprise at last,
Catches the foul thing on its carrion prey,
Behold, he points to shell left high and dry,
Pleads, "But the case out yonder is myself!"
Nay, it is thou, Law prongs amid thy peers,
Congenial vermin; that was none of thee,
Thine outside — give it to the soldier crab!

For I find this black mark impinge the man,
That he believes in just the vile of life.
Low instinct, base pretension, are these truth?

**416. cirque:** arena. **441. priest's exemption:** clerical privilege; the right of one connected with the clergy to appeal to the religious rather than secular courts for judgment.

**465. paravent:** screen. **ombrifuge:** shade or shelter. **474. attent . . . fifties:** See Mark 6:39–40. When Jesus fed the five thousand, he caused them to sit in groups of fifty and one hundred. **509. soldier crab:** a crab which occupies the shells of others.

Then, that aforesaid armor, probity,
He figures in, is falsehood scale on scale;
Honor and faith — a lie and a disguise,
Probably for all livers in this world,
Certainly for himself! All say good words
To who will hear, all do thereby bad deeds
To who must undergo; so thrive mankind!
See this habitual creed exemplified
Most in the last deliberate act; as last,
So, very sum and substance of the soul
Of him that planned and leaves one perfect piece,
The sin brought under jurisdiction now,
Even the marriage of the man; this act
I sever from his life as sample, show
For Guido's self, intend to test him by,
As, from a cup filled fairly at the fount,
By the components we decide enough
Or to let flow as late, or stanch the source.

He purposes this marriage, I remark,
On no one motive that should prompt thereto —
Farthest, by consequence, from ends alleged
Appropriate to the action; so they were;
The best, he knew and feigned, the worst he took.
Not one permissible impulse moves the man,
From the mere liking of the eye and ear,
To the true longing of the heart that loves,
No trace of these; but all to instigate,
Is what sinks man past level of the brute,
Whose appetite if brutish is a truth.
All is the lust for money: to get gold —
Why, lie, rob, if it must be, murder! Make
Body and soul wring gold out, lured within
The clutch of hate by love, the trap's pretense!
What good else get from bodies and from souls?
This got, there were some life to lead thereby
— What, where or how, appreciate those who tell
How the toad lives: it lives — enough for me!
To get this good — but with a groan or so,
Then, silence of the victims — were the feat.
He foresaw, made a picture in his mind —
Of father and mother stunned and echoless
To the blow, as they lie staring at fate's jaws
Their folly danced into, till the woe fell;
Edged in a month by strenuous cruelty
From even the poor nook whence they watched the wolf
Feast on their heart, the lamblike child his prey;
Plundered to the last remnant of their wealth,
(What daily pittance pleased the plunderer dole)
Hunted forth to go hide head, starve, and die,
And leave the pale awe-stricken wife, past hope
Of help i' the world now, mute and motionless,
His slave, his chattel, to first use, then destroy.
All this, he bent mind how to bring about,
Put plain in act and life, as painted plain,
So have success, reach crown of earthly good,
In this particular enterprise of man,
By marriage — undertaken in God's face
With all these lies so opposite God's truth,
For end so other than man's end.

Thus schemes
Guido, and thus would carry out his scheme;
But when an obstacle first blocks the path,
When he finds none may boast monopoly
Of lies and trick i' the tricking lying world —
That sorry timid natures, even this sort
O' the Comparini, want nor trick nor lie
Proper to the kind — that as the gorcrow treats
The bramble finch, so treats the finch the moth,
And the great Guido is minutely matched
By this same couple — whether true or false
The revelation of Pompilia's birth,
Which in a moment brings his scheme to nought —
Then, he is piqued, advances yet a stage,
Leaves the low region to the finch and fly,
Soars to the zenith whence the fiercer fowl
May dare the inimitable swoop. I see.
He draws now on the curious crime, the fine
Felicity and flower of wickedness;
Determines, by the utmost exercise
Of violence, made safe and sure by craft.
To satiate malice, pluck one last archpang
From the parents, else would triumph out of reach,
By punishing their child, within reach yet,
Who, by thought, word, or deed, could nowise wrong
I' the matter that now moves him. So plans he,
Always subordinating (note the point!)
Revenge, the manlier sin, to interest
The meaner — would pluck pang forth, but unclench
No gripe in the act, let fall no moneypiece.
Hence a plan for so plaguing, body and soul,
His wife, so putting, day by day, hour by hour,
The untried torture to the untouched place,
As must precipitate an end foreseen,
Goad her into some plain revolt, most like
Plunge upon patent suicidal shame,
Death to herself, damnation by rebound
To those whose hearts he, holding hers, holds still:
Such plan as, in its bad completeness, shall
Ruin the three together and alike,
Yet leave himself in luck and liberty,
No claim renounced, no right a forfeiture,
His person unendangered, his good fame
Without a flaw, his pristine worth intact —
While they, with all their claims and rights that cling,
Shall forthwith crumble off him every side,
Scorched into dust, a plaything for the winds.

578. gorcrow: carrion crow.

As when, in our Campagna, there is fired
The nestlike work that overruns a hut;
And, as the thatch burns here, there, everywhere,
Even to the ivy and wild vine, that bound
And blessed the home where men were happy once,
There rises gradual, black amid the blaze,
Some grim and unscathed nucleus of the nest—
Some old malicious tower, some obscene tomb
They thought a temple in their ignorance,
And clung about and thought to lean upon—
There laughs it o'er their ravage—where are they?
So did his cruelty burn life about,
And lay the ruin bare in dreadfulness,
Try the persistency of torment so
Upon the wife, that, at extremity,
Some crisis brought about by fire and flame,
The patient frenzy-stung must needs break loose,
Fly anyhow, find refuge anywhere,
Even in the arms of who should front her first,
No monster but a man—while Nature shrieked,
"Or thus escape, or die!" The spasm arrived,
Not the escape by way of sin—O God,
Who shall pluck sheep thou holdest, from thy
    hand?
Therefore she lay resigned to die—so far
The simple cruelty was foiled. Why then,
Craft to the rescue, let craft supplement
Cruelty and show hell a masterpiece!
Hence this consummate lie, this love intrigue,
Unmanly simulation of a sin,
With place and time and circumstance to suit—
These letters false beyond all forgery—
Not just handwriting and mere authorship,
But false to body and soul they figure forth—
As though the man had cut out shape and shape
From fancies of that other Aretine,
To paste below—incorporate the filth
With cherub faces on a missal page!

Whereby the man so far attains his end
That strange temptation is permitted—see?
Pompilia, wife, and Caponsacchi, priest,
Are brought together as nor priest nor wife
Should stand, and there is passion in the place,
Power in the air for evil as for good,
Promptings from heaven and hell, as if the stars
Fought in their courses for a fate to be.
Thus stand the wife and priest, a spectacle,
I doubt not, to unseen assemblage there.
No lamp will mark that window for a shrine,
No tablet signalize the terrace, teach
New generations which succeed the old,
The pavement of the street is holy ground:
No bard describe in verse how Christ prevailed
And Satan fell like lightning! Why repine?
What does the world, told truth, but lie the
    more?

A second time the plot is foiled; nor, now,
By corresponding sin for countercheck,
No wile and trick that baffle trick and wile—
The play o' the parents! Here the blot is blanched
By God's gift of a purity of soul
That will not take pollution, ermine-like
Armed from dishonor by its own soft snow.
Such was this gift of God who showed for once
How he would have the world go white; it seems
As a new attribute were born of each
Champion of truth, the priest and wife I praise—
As a new safeguard sprang up in defense
Of their new noble nature; so a thorn
Comes to the aid of and completes the rose—
Courage to wit, no woman's gift nor priest's,
I' the crisis; might leaps vindicating right.
See how the strong aggressor, bad and bold,
With every vantage, preconcerts surprise,
Leaps of a sudden at his victim's throat
In a byway—how fares he when face to face
With Caponsacchi? Who fights, who fears now?
There quails Count Guido, armed to the chattering
    teeth,
Cowers at the steadfast eye and quiet word
O' the Canon of the Pieve! There skulks crime
Behind law called in to back cowardice!
While out of the poor trampled worm the wife
Springs up a serpent!

                    But anon of these!
Him I judge now—of him proceed to note,
Failing the first, a second chance befriends
Guido, gives pause ere punishment arrive.
The law he called, comes, hears, adjudicates,
Nor does amiss i' the main—secludes the wife
From the husband, respites the oppressed one,
    grants
Probation to the oppressor, could he know
The mercy of a minute's fiery purge!
The furnace coals alike of public scorn,
Private remorse, heaped glowing on his head,
What if—the force and guile, the ore's alloy,
Eliminate, his baser soul refined—
The lost be saved even yet, so as by fire?
Let him, rebuked, go softly all his days
And, when no graver musings claim their due,
Meditate on a man's immense mistake

**652. Aretine:** an inhabitant of Arezzo. Here Browning refers to Pietro Aretino, a notorious Renaissance literary figure, who blackmailed kings by his sonnets. **662. for . . . be:** The ancient belief was that the stars determined human destinies. Here Browning adds the notion of the stars in conflict to determine a particular human issue.

**695. the Pieve:** the church in Arezzo of which Caponsacchi was a canon. **697–98.** Pompilia brandished a sword when Guido caught up with her and Caponsacchi at the inn in Castelnuovo. Compare Pompilia's account at ll. 1619 ff. of her monologue.

Who, fashioned to use feet and walk, deigns crawl —
Takes the unmanly means — aye, though to ends
Man scarce should make for, would but reach through wrong —
May sin, but nowise needs shame manhood so,
Since fowlers hawk, shoot, nay, and snare the game,
And yet eschew vile practice, nor find sport
In torchlight treachery or the luring owl.

But how hunts Guido? Why, the fraudful trap —
Late spurned to ruin by the indignant feet
Of fellows in the chase who loved fair play —
Here he picks up its fragments to the least,
Lades him and hies to the old lurking place
Where haply he may patch again, refit
The mischief, file its blunted teeth anew,
Make sure, next time, first snap shall break the bone.
Craft, greed, and violence complot revenge:
Craft, for its quota, schemes to bring about
And seize occasion and be safe withal;
Greed craves its act may work both far and near,
Crush the tree, branch and trunk and root beside,
Whichever twig or leaf arrests a streak
Of possible sunshine else would coin itself,
And drop down one more gold piece in the path;
Violence stipulates, " Advantage proved,
And safety sure, be pain the overplus!
Murder with jagged knife! Cut but tear too!
Foiled oft, starved long, glut malice for amends! "
And what, craft's scheme? scheme sorrowful and strange
As though the elements, whom mercy checked,
Had mustered hate for one eruption more,
One final deluge to surprise the Ark
Cradled and sleeping on its mountaintop:
Their outbreak-signal — what but the dove's coo,
Back with the olive in her bill for news
Sorrow was over? 'Tis an infant's birth,
Guido's first-born, his son and heir, that gives
The occasion; other men cut free their souls
From care in such a case, fly up in thanks
To God, reach, recognize his love for once;
Guido cries, " Soul, at last the mire is thine!
Lie there in likeness of a moneybag,
My babe's birth so pins down past moving now,
That I dare cut adrift the lives I late
Scrupled to touch lest thou escape with them!
These parents and their child my wife — touch one,
Lose all! Their rights determined on a head
I could but hate, not harm, since from each hair
Dangled a hope for me; now — chance and change!
No right was in their child but passes plain
To that child's child and through such child to me.
I am a father now — come what come will,
I represent my child; he comes between —
Cuts sudden off the sunshine of this life
From those three; why, the gold is in his curls!
Not with old Pietro's, Violante's head,
Not his gray horror, her more hideous black —
Go these, devoted to the knife! "

'Tis done:
Wherefore should mind misgive, heart hesitate?
He calls to counsel, fashions certain four
Colorless natures counted clean till now
— Rustic simplicity, uncorrupted youth,
Ignorant virtue! Here's the gold o' the prime
When Saturn ruled, shall shock our leaden day —
The clown abash the courtier! Mark it, bards!
The courtier tries his hand on clownship here,
Speaks a word, names a crime, appoints a price —
Just breathes on what, suffused with all himself,
Is red-hot henceforth past distinction now
I' the common glow of hell. And thus they break
And blaze on us at Rome. Christ's birthnight eve!
Oh, angels that sang erst, " On the earth, peace!
To man, good will! " — such peace finds earth today!
After the seventeen hundred years, so man
Wills good to man, so Guido makes complete
His murder! what is it I said? — cuts loose
Three lives that hitherto he suffered cling,
Simply because each served to nail secure,
By a corner of the moneybag, his soul —
Therefore, lives sacred till the babe's first breath
O'erweights them in the balance — off they fly!

So is the murder managed, sin conceived
To the full; and why not crowned with triumph too?
Why must the sin, conceived thus, bring forth death?
I note how, within hairsbreath of escape,
Impunity and the thing supposed success,
Guido is found when the check comes, the change,
The monitory touch o' the tether — felt
By few, not marked by many, named by none
At the moment, only recognized aright
I' the fullness of the days, for God's, lest sin
Exceed the service, leap the line; such check —
A secret which this life finds hard to keep,
And, often guessed, is never quite revealed —
Needs must trip Guido on a stumbling block
Too vulgar, too absurdly plain i' the path!

745–49. See Gen. 8. The dove on its second flight from Noah's Ark brought back an olive branch.

777. **When . . . ruled:** According to Greek mythology, Saturn ruled in a golden age before Zeus brought law and order into the world. The Pope is satirizing the glorification of rural simplicity and the notion of natural virtue in men.

Study this single oversight of care,
This hebetude that marred sagacity,
Forgetfulness of all the man best knew—
How any stranger having need to fly,
Needs but to ask and have the means of flight.
Why, the first urchin tells you, to leave Rome,
Get horses, you must show the warrant, just
The banal scrap, clerk's scribble, a fair word buys,
Or foul one, if a ducat sweeten word—
And straight authority will back demand,
Give you the pick o' the posthouse!—how should he,
Then, resident at Rome for thirty years,
Guido, instruct a stranger! And himself
Forgets just this poor paper scrap, wherewith
Armed, every door he knocks at opens wide
To save him; horsed and manned, with such advance
O' the hunt behind, why, 'twere the easy task
Of hours told on the fingers of one hand,
To reach the Tuscan frontier, laugh at home,
Lighthearted with his fellows of the place—
Prepared by that strange shameful judgment, that
Satire upon a sentence just pronounced
By the Rota and confirmed by the Grand Duke—
Ready in a circle to receive their peer,
Appreciate his good story how, when Rome,
The Pope-King, and the populace of priests
Made common cause with their confederate
The other priestling who seduced his wife,
He, all unaided, wiped out the affront
With decent bloodshed and could face his friends,
Frolic it in the world's eye. Aye, such tale
Missed such applause, and by such oversight!
So, tired and footsore, those blood-flustered five
Went reeling on the road through dark and cold,
The few permissible miles, to sink at length,
Wallow and sleep in the first wayside straw,
As the other herd quenched, i' the wash o' the wave
—Each swine, the devil inside him; so slept they,
And so were caught and caged—all through one trip,
One touch of fool in Guido the astute!
He curses the omission, I surmise,
More than the murder. Why, thou fool and blind,
It is the mercy stroke that stops thy fate,
Hamstrings and holds thee to thy hurt—but how?
On the edge o' the precipice! One minute more,
Thou hadst gone farther and fared worse, my son,
Fathoms down on the flint and fire beneath!
Thy comrades each and all were of one mind,
Thy murder done, to straightway murder thee
In turn, because of promised pay withheld.
So, to the last, greed found itself at odds
With craft in thee, and, proving conqueror,
Had sent thee, the same night that crowned thy hope,
Thither where, this same day, I see thee not,
Nor, through God's mercy, need, tomorrow, see.
Such I find Guido, midmost blotch of black
Discernible in this group of clustered crimes
Huddling together in the cave they call
Their palace, outraged day thus penetrates.
Around him ranged, now close and now remote,
Prominent or obscure to meet the needs
O' the mage and master, I detect each shape
Subsidiary i' the scene nor loathed the less,
All alike colored, all descried akin
By one and the same pitchy furnace stirred
At the center; see, they lick the master's hand—
This fox-faced horrible priest, this brother brute
The Abate—why, mere wolfishness looks well,
Guido stands honest in the red o' the flame,
Beside this yellow that would pass for white,
Twice Guido, all craft but no violence,
This copier of the mien and gait and garb
Of Peter and Paul, that he may go disguised,
Rob halt and lame, sick folk i' the temple porch!
Armed with religion, fortified by law,
A man of peace, who trims the midnight lamp
And turns the classic page—and all for craft,
All to work harm with, yet incur no scratch!
While Guido brings the struggle to a close,
Paul steps back the due distance, clear o' the trap
He builds and baits. Guido I catch and judge;
Paul is past reach in this world and my time;
That is a case reserved. Pass to the next,
The boy of the brood, the young Girolamo,
Priest, Canon, and what more? nor wolf nor fox,
But hybrid, neither craft nor violence
Wholly; part violence, part craft; such cross
Tempts speculation—will both blend one day,
And prove hell's better product? Or subside
And let the simple quality emerge,
Go on with Satan's service the old way?
Meanwhile, what promise—what performance too!
For there's a new distinctive touch, I see,
Lust—lacking in the two—hell's own blue tint
That gives a character and marks the man
More than a match for yellow and red. Once more,
A case reserved; why should I doubt? Then comes
The gaunt gray nightmare in the furthest smoke,
The hag that gave these three abortions birth,

811. **hebetude**: stupidity. 816. **warrant**: a pass to leave or enter the city gates. 820. **pick . . . posthouse**: the best horses for traveling. 828. **Tuscan frontier**: Arezzo was under the grand duke of Tuscany. 832. **Rota**: the supreme court.

877. **Abate**: Guido's brother, Paul, an abbot in the Church. 891. Paolo Franceschini left Rome in 1697 before the murder. He lost his position when his part in the marriage was discovered. 903–05. Girolamo Franceschini had also fled. According to Pompilia, he had made improper advances to her.

Unmotherly mother and unwomanly
Woman, that near turns motherhood to shame,
Womanliness to loathing; no one word,
No gesture to curb cruelty a whit
More than the she-pard thwarts her playsome whelps
Trying their milkteeth on the soft o' the throat
O' the first fawn, flung, with those beseeching eyes,
Flat in the covert! How should she but couch,
Lick the dry lips, unsheathe the blunted claw,
Catch 'twixt her placid eyewinks at what chance
Old bloody half-forgotten dream may flit,
Born when herself was novice to the taste,
The while she lets youth take its pleasure. Last,
These God-abandoned wretched lumps of life,
These four companions — countryfolk this time,
Not tainted by the unwholesome civic breath,
Much less the curse o' the court! Mere striplings too,
Fit to do human nature justice still!
Surely when impudence in Guido's shape
Shall propose crime and proffer money's worth
To these stout tall rough bright-eyed black-haired boys,
The blood shall bound in answer to each cheek
Before the indignant outcry break from lip!
Are these i' the mood to murder, hardly loosed
From healthy autumn finish of plowed glebe,
Grapes in the barrel, work at happy end,
And winter near with rest and Christmas play?
How greet they Guido with his final task —
(As if he but proposed, "One vineyard more
To dig, ere frost come, then relax indeed!")
"Anywhere, anyhow, and anywhy,
Murder me some three people, old and young,
Ye never hear the names of — and be paid
So much!" And the whole four accede at once.
Demur? Do cattle bidden march or halt?
Is it some lingering habit, old fond faith
I' the lord o' the land, instructs them — birthright badge
Of feudal tenure claims its slaves again?
Not so at all, thou noble human heart!
All is done purely for the pay — which, earned,
And not forthcoming at the instant, makes
Religion heresy, and the lord o' the land
Fit subject for a murder in his turn.
The patron with cut throat and rifled purse,
Deposited i' the roadside ditch, his due,
Nought hinders each good fellow trudging home,
The heavier by a piece or two in poke,
And so with new zest to the common life,
Mattock and spade, plowtail and wagon shaft,
Till some such other piece of luck betide,
Who knows? Since this is a mere start in life,
And none of them exceeds the twentieth year.
Nay, more i' the background yet? Unnoticed forms
Claim to be classed, subordinately vile?
Complacent lookers-on that laugh — perchance
Shake head as their friend's horseplay grows too rough
With the mere child he manages amiss —
But would not interfere and make bad worse
For twice the fractious tears and prayers; thou know'st
Civility better, Marzi-Medici,
Governor for thy kinsman the Grand Duke!
Fit representative of law, man's lamp
I' the magistrate's grasp full flare, no rushlight end
Sputtering 'twixt thumb and finger of the priest!
Whose answer to the couple's cry for help
Is a threat — whose remedy of Pompilia's wrong,
A shrug o' the shoulder, and facetious word
Or wink, traditional with Tuscan wits,
To Guido in the doorway. Laud to law!
The wife is pushed back to the husband, he
Who knows how these home squabblings persecute
People who have the public good to mind,
And work best with a silence in the court!

Ah, but I save my word at least for thee,
Archbishop, who art under, i' the Church,
As I am under God — thou, chosen by both
To do the shepherd's office, feed the sheep —
How of this lamb that panted at thy foot
While the wolf pressed on her within crook's reach?
Wast thou the hireling that did turn and flee?
With thee at least anon the little word!

Such denizens o' the cave now cluster round
And heat the furnace sevenfold; time indeed
A bolt from heaven should cleave roof and clear place,
Transfix and show the world, suspiring flame,
The main offender, scar and brand the rest
Hurrying, each miscreant to his hole; then flood
And purify the scene with outside day —
Which yet, in the absolutest drench of dark,
Ne'er wants a witness, some stray beauty-beam
To the despair of hell.

First of the first,
Such I pronounce Pompilia, then as now
Perfect in whiteness; stoop thou down, my child,
Give one good moment to the poor old Pope
Heartsick at having all his world to blame —
Let me look at thee in the flesh as erst,

**955. poke:** pocket.

**969.** No evidence of the kinship has come to light. **983. Archbishop:** really the Bishop of Arezzo. **987. crook:** crozier. The word is used in a double sense — the shepherd's staff, and the bishop's, he being also a shepherd.

Let me enjoy the old clean linen garb,
Not the new splendid vesture! Armed and crowned,
Would Michael, yonder, be, nor crowned nor armed,
The less pre-eminent angel? Everywhere
I see in the world the intellect of man,
That sword, the energy his subtle spear,
The knowledge which defends him like a shield —
Everywhere; but they make not up, I think,
The marvel of a soul like thine, earth's flower
She holds up to the softened gaze of God!
It was not given Pompilia to know much,
Speak much, to write a book, to move mankind,
Be memorized by who records my time.
Yet if in purity and patience, if
In faith held fast despite the plucking fiend,
Safe like the signet stone with the new name
That saints are known by — if in right returned
For wrong, most pardon for worst injury,
If there be any virtue, any praise —
Then will this woman-child have proved — who knows? —
Just the one prize vouchsafed unworthy me,
Seven years a gardener of the untoward ground
I till — this earth, my sweat and blood manure
All the long day that barrenly grows dusk;
At least one blossom makes me proud at eve
Born 'mid the briers of my enclosure! Still
(Oh, here as elsewhere, nothingness of man!)
Those be the plants, imbedded yonder south
To mellow in the morning, those made fat
By the master's eye, that yield such timid leaf,
Uncertain bud, as product of his pains!
While — see how this mere chance-sown, cleft-nursed seed,
That sprang up by the wayside 'neath the foot
Of the enemy, this breaks all into blaze,
Spreads itself, one wide glory of desire
To incorporate the whole great sun it loves
From the inch height whence it looks and longs!
My flower,
My rose, I gather for the breast of God;
This I praise most in thee, where all I praise,
That having been obedient to the end
According to the light allotted, law
Prescribed thy life, still tried, still standing test —
Dutiful to the foolish parents first,
Submissive next to the bad husband — nay,
Tolerant of those meaner miserable
That did his hests, eked out the dole of pain —
Thou, patient thus, couldst rise from law to law,
The old to the new, promoted at one cry
O' the trump of God to the new service, not
To longer bear, but henceforth fight, be found
Sublime in new impatience with the foe!
Endure man and obey God; plant firm foot
On neck of man, tread man into the hell
Meet for him, and obey God all the more!
Oh, child that didst despise thy life so much
When it seemed only thine to keep or lose,
How the fine ear felt fall the first low word
"Value life, and preserve life for My sake!"
Thou didst . . . how shall I say? . . . receive so long
The standing ordinance of God on earth,
What wonder if the novel claim had clashed
With old requirement, seemed to supersede
Too much the customary law? But, brave,
Thou at first prompting of what I call God,
And fools call Nature, didst hear, comprehend,
Accept the obligation laid on thee,
Mother-elect, to save the unborn child,
As brute and bird do, reptile and the fly,
Aye, and, I nothing doubt, even tree, shrub, plant,
And flower o' the field, all in a common pact
To worthily defend the trust of trusts,
Life from the Ever-Living — didst resist —
Anticipate the office that is mine —
And with his own sword stay the upraised arm,
The endeavor of the wicked, and defend
Him who — again in my default — was there
For visible providence; one less true than thou
To touch, i' the past, less practiced in the right,
Approved less far in all docility
To all instruction — how had such an one
Made scruple, "Is this motion a decree?"
It was authentic to the experienced ear
O' the good and faithful servant. Go past me
And get thy praise — and be not far to seek
Presently when I follow if I may!

And surely not so very much apart
Need I place thee, my warrior-priest — in whom
What if I gain the other rose, the gold,
We grave to imitate God's miracle,
Greet monarchs with, good rose in its degree?
Irregular noble scapegrace — son the same!
Faulty — and peradventure ours the fault
Who still misteach, mislead, throw hook and line,
Thinking to land leviathan forsooth,
Tame the scaled neck, play with him as a bird,
And bind him for our maidens! Better bear
The King of Pride go wantoning awhile,
Unplagued by cord in nose and thorn in jaw,
Through deep to deep, followed by all that shine,
Churning the blackness hoary; He who made

**1006. splendid vesture:** what she shall wear in Heaven. **1017. memorized:** recorded to remind posterity. **1020. signet . . . name:** See Rev. 7:2–4.

**1060. only thine:** up to the time when she realized that she was pregnant. **1080. Him:** Caponsacchi. **1092. other rose:** The Pope blesses a golden rose on the fourth Sunday in Lent and sends it to some distinguished person or group. **1096. ours . . . fault:** that is, the Church's fault. **1098. leviathan:** the great whale of Job 41.

The comely terror, He shall make the sword
To match that piece of netherstone his heart,
Aye, nor miss praise thereby; who else shut fire
I' the stone, to leap from mouth at sword's first stroke,
In lamps of love and faith, the chivalry
That dares the right and disregards alike
The yea and nay o' the world? Self-sacrifice —
What if an idol took it? Ask the Church
Why she was wont to turn each Venus here —
Poor Rome perversely lingered round, despite
Instruction, for the sake of purblind love —
Into Madonna's shape, and waste no whit
Of aught so rare on earth as gratitude!
All this sweet savor was not ours but thine,
Nard of the rock, a natural wealth we name
Incense, and treasure up as food for saints,
When flung to us — whose function was to give
Not find the costly perfume. Do I smile?
Nay, Caponsacchi, much I find amiss,
Blameworthy, punishable in this freak
Of thine, this youth prolonged, though age was ripe,
This masquerade in sober day, with change
Of motley too — now hypocrite's disguise,
Now fool's costume; which lie was least like truth,
Which the ungainlier, more discordant garb,
With that symmetric soul inside my son,
The churchman's or the worldling's — let him judge,
Our adversary who enjoys the task!
I rather chronicle the healthy rage —
When the first moan broke from the martyr maid
At that uncaging of the beasts — made bare
My athlete on the instant, gave such good
Great undisguised leap over post and pale
Right into the midcirque, free fighting place.
There may have been rash stripping — every rag
Went to the winds — infringement manifold
Of laws prescribed pudicity, I fear,
In this impulsive and prompt self-display!
Ever such tax comes of the foolish youth;
Men mulct the wiser manhood, and suspect
No veritable star swims out of cloud.
Bear thou such imputation, undergo
The penalty I nowise dare relax —
Conventional chastisement and rebuke.
But for the outcome, the brave starry birth
Conciliating earth with all that cloud,
Thank heaven as I do! Aye, such championship
Of God at first blush, such prompt cheery thud
Of glove on ground that answers ringingly
The challenge of the false knight — watch we long,
And wait we vainly for its gallant like
From those appointed to the service, sworn
His bodyguard with pay and privilege —
White-cinct, because in white walks sanctity,
Red-socked, how else proclaim fine scorn of flesh,
Unchariness of blood when blood faith begs!
Where are the men-at-arms with cross on coat?
Aloof, bewraying their attire, whilst thou
In mask and motley, pledged to dance, not fight,
Sprang'st forth the hero! In thought, word, and deed,
How throughout all thy warfare thou wast pure,
I find it easy to believe; and if
At any fateful moment of the strange
Adventure, the strong passion of that strait,
Fear and surprise, may have revealed too much —
As when a thundrous midnight, with black air
That burns, raindrops that blister, breaks a spell,
Draws out the excessive virtue of some sheathed
Shut unsuspected flower that hoards and hides
Immensity of sweetness — so, perchance,
Might the surprise and fear release too much
The perfect beauty of the body and soul
Thou savedst in thy passion for God's sake,
He who is Pity. Was the trial sore?
Temptation sharp? Thank God a second time!
Why comes temptation but for man to meet
And master and make crouch beneath his foot,
And so be pedestaled in triumph? Pray,
"Lead us into no such temptations, Lord!"
Yea, but, O Thou whose servants are the bold,
Lead such temptations by the head and hair,
Reluctant dragons, up to who dares fight,
That so he may do battle and have praise!
Do I not see the praise? — that while thy mates
Bound to deserve i' the matter, prove at need
Unprofitable through the very pains
We gave to train them well and start them fair —
Are found too stiff, with standing ranked and ranged,
For onset in good earnest, too obtuse
Of ear, through iteration of command,
For catching quick the sense of the real cry —
Thou, whose sword hand was used to strike the lute,
Whose sentry station graced some wanton's gate,
Thou didst push forward and show mettle, shame
The laggards, and retrieve the day. Well done!
Be glad thou hast let light into the world,

**1112–22:** Here the Pope, in thinking of Caponsacchi's sacrifice for Pompilia, sees the error of the priest in giving his love to a human being instead of giving it directly to God, just as the half-pagan Romans worshiped Venus and only indirectly the Madonna. But he honors self-sacrifice in Caponsacchi, though its aim be mistaken. **1119. nard:** spikenard, a fragrant ointment. **1132. Our adversary:** the Devil. **1134–35. When . . . beasts:** Browning's figure is drawn from the legends of Christian martyrs forced to fight wild animals in the early days at Rome.

**1156–60. those . . . begs:** Those appointed to defend the right are, of course, the clergy. The red stockings of the cardinals are explained whimsically as showing a scorn of flesh. **1163. mask . . . motley:** Caponsacchi was expected by the Bishop to take part in dances and masked balls.

Through that irregular breach o' the boundary — see
The same upon thy path and march assured,
Learning anew the use of soldiership,
Self-abnegation, freedom from all fear,
Loyalty to the life's end! Ruminate,
Deserve the initiatory spasm — once more
Work, be unhappy but bear life, my son!

And troop you, somewhere 'twixt the best and worst,
Where crowd the indifferent product, all too poor
Makeshift, starved samples of humanity!
Father and mother, huddle there and hide!
A gracious eye may find you! Foul and fair,
Sadly mixed natures; self-indulgent — yet
Self-sacrificing too; how the love soars,
How the craft, avarice, vanity, and spite
Sink again! So they keep the middle course,
Slide into silly crime at unaware,
Slip back upon the stupid virtue, stay
Nowhere enough for being classed, I hope
And fear. Accept the swift and rueful death,
Taught, somewhat sternlier than is wont, what waits
The ambiguous creature — how the one black tuft
Steadies the aim of the arrow just as well
As the wide faultless white on the bird's breast!
Nay, you were punished in the very part
That looked most pure of speck, 'twas honest love
Betrayed you — did love seem most worthy pains,
Challenge such purging, since ordained survive
When all the rest of you was done with? Go!
Never again elude the choice of tints!
White shall not neutralize the black, nor good
Compensate bad in man, absolve him so,
Life's business being just the terrible choice.

So do I see, pronounce on all and some
Grouped for my judgment now — profess no doubt
While I pronounce; dark, difficult enough
The human sphere, yet eyes grow sharp by use,
I find the truth, dispart the shine from shade,
As a mere man may, with no special touch
O' the lynx-gift in each ordinary orb;
Nay, if the popular notion class me right,
One of well-nigh decayed intelligence —
What of that? Through hard labor and good will,
And habitude that gives a blind man sight
At the practiced finger ends of him, I do
Discern, and dare decree in consequence,
Whatever prove the peril of mistake.
Whence, then, this quite new quick cold thrill — cloudlike,
This keen dread creeping from a quarter scarce
Suspected in the skies I nightly scan?
What slacks the tense nerve, saps the wound-up spring
Of the act that should and shall be, sends the mount
And mass o' the whole man's strength — conglobed so late —
Shudderingly into dust, a moment's work?
While I stand firm, go fearless, in this world,
For this life recognize and arbitrate,
Touch and let stay, or else remove a thing,
Judge, "This is right, this object out of place,"
Candle in hand that helps me and to spare —
What if a voice deride me, "Perk and pry!
Brighten each nook with thine intelligence!
Play the good householder, ply man and maid
With tasks prolonged into the midnight, test
Their work and nowise stint of the due wage
Each worthy worker; but with gyves and whip
Pay thou misprision of a single point
Plain to thy happy self who lift'st the light,
Lament'st the darkling — bold to all beneath!
What if thyself adventure, now the place
Is purged so well? Leave pavement and mount roof,
Look round thee for the light of the upper sky,
The fire which lit thy fire which finds default
In Guido Franceschini to his cost!
What if, above in the domain of light,
Thou miss the accustomed signs, remark eclipse?
Shalt thou still gaze on ground nor lift a lid —
Steady in thy superb prerogative,
Thy inch of inkling — nor once face the doubt
I' the sphere above thee, darkness to be felt?"

Yet my poor spark had for its source, the sun;
Thither I sent the great looks which compel
Light from its fount; all that I do and am
Comes from the truth, or seen or else surmised,
Remembered or divined, as mere man may;
I know just so, nor otherwise. As I know,
I speak — what should I know, then, and how speak
Were there a wild mistake of eye or brain
As to recorded governance above?
If my own breath, only, blew coal alight
I styled celestial and the morning star?
I, who in this world act resolvedly,
Dispose of men, their bodies and their souls,
As they acknowledge or gainsay the light
I show them — shall I too lack courage? — leave
I, too, the post of me, like those I blame?
Refuse, with kindred inconsistency,
To grapple danger whereby souls grow strong?
I am near the end, but still not at the end;
All to the very end is trial in life;

**1238. dispart:** separate. **1240. lynx-gift:** gift of lynx-like (that is, sharp) eyes. **orb:** eye.

**1266. misprision:** mistake.

At this stage is the trial of my soul
Danger to face, or danger to refuse?
Shall I dare try the doubt now, or not dare?

O Thou — as represented here to me
In such conception as my soul allows —
Under Thy measureless, my atom width! —
Man's mind, what is it but a convex glass
Wherein are gathered all the scattered points
Picked out of the immensity of sky,
To reunite there, be our heaven for earth,
Our known unknown, our God revealed to man?
Existent somewhere, somehow, as a whole;
Here, as a whole proportioned to our sense —
There (which is nowhere, speech must babble thus!)
In the absolute immensity, the whole
Appreciable solely by Thyself —
Here, by the little mind of man, reduced
To littleness that suits his faculty,
In the degree appreciable too;
Between Thee and ourselves — nay even, again,
Below us, to the extreme of the minute,
Appreciable by how many and what diverse
Modes of the life Thou madest be! (why live
Except for love — how love unless they know?)
Each of them, only filling to the edge,
Insect or angel, his just length and breadth,
Due facet of reflection — full, no less,
Angel or insect, as Thou framedst things.
I it is who have been appointed here
To represent Thee, in my turn, on earth,
Just as, if new philosophy know aught,
This one earth, out of all the multitude
Of peopled worlds, as stars are now supposed —
Was chosen, and no sun-star of the swarm,
For stage and scene of Thy transcendent act
Beside which even the creation fades
Into a puny exercise of power.
Choice of the world, choice of the thing I am,
Both emanate alike from Thy dread play
Of operation outside this our sphere
Where things are classed and counted small or great —
Incomprehensibly the choice is Thine!
I therefore bow my head and take Thy place.
There is, beside the works, a tale of Thee
In the world's mouth, which I find credible;
I love it with my heart; unsatisfied,
I try it with my reason, nor discept
From any point I probe and pronounce sound.
Mind is not matter nor from matter, but
Above — leave matter then, proceed with mind!
Man's be the mind recognized at the height —
Leave the inferior minds and look at man!
Is he the strong, intelligent, and good
Up to his own conceivable height? Nowise.
Enough o' the low — soar the conceivable height,
Find cause to match the effect in evidence,
The work i' the world, not man's but God's; leave man!
Conjecture of the worker by the work:
Is there strength there? — enough; intelligence?
Ample; but goodness in a like degree?
Not to the human eye in the present state,
An isoscele deficient in the base.
What lacks, then, of perfection fit for God
But just the instance which this tale supplies
Of love without a limit? So is strength,
So is intelligence; let love be so,
Unlimited in its self-sacrifice,
Then is the tale true and God shows complete.
Beyond the tale, I reach into the dark,
Feel what I cannot see, and still faith stands;
I can believe this dread machinery
Of sin and sorrow, would confound me else,
Devised — all pain, at most expenditure
Of pain by Who devised pain — to evolve,
By new machinery in counterpart,
The moral qualities of man — how else? —
To make him love in turn and be beloved,
Creative and self-sacrificing too,
And thus eventually Godlike (aye,
"I have said ye are Gods" — shall it be said for nought?)
Enable man to wring, from out all pain,
All pleasure for a common heritage
To all eternity; this may be surmised,
The other is revealed — whether a fact,
Absolute, abstract, independent truth,
Historic, not reduced to suit man's mind —
Or only truth reverberate, changed, made pass
A spectrum into mind, the narrow eye —
The same and not the same, else unconceived —
Though quite conceivable to the next grade
Above it in intelligence — as truth
Easy to man were blindness to the beast
By parity of procedure — the same truth
In a new form, but changed in either case;
What matter so intelligence be filled?
To a child, the sea is angry, for it roars:
Frost bites, else why the toothlike fret on face?
Man makes acoustics deal with the sea's wrath,
Explains the choppy cheek by chymic law —

**1303 ff.** These religious and philosophical ideas are Browning's, and could hardly be held by a pope, and especially by one of the seventeenth century. **1330. new philosophy:** new science. The science of physics was called natural philosophy well into the nineteenth century. **1334. Thy . . . act:** To Browning the most important event of history was that Christ, God's Son, took on human form and life. It proved God's love for man. See Intro., p. 474, and headnote to "Saul," above. **1346. discept:** reject.

**1361. isoscele:** an isosceles triangle, one with equal sides. The three sides in Browning's thinking are Power, Intelligence, and Love, as attributes of the Deity. **1398. choppy:** chapped.

To man and child remains the same effect
On drum of ear and root of nose, change cause
Never so thoroughly; so my heart be struck,
What care I — by God's gloved hand or the bare?
Nor do I much perplex me with aught hard,
Dubious in the transmitting of the tale —
No, nor with certain riddles set to solve.
This life is training and a passage; pass —
Still, we march over some flat obstacle
We made give way before us; solid truth
In front of it, what motion for the world?
The moral sense grows but by exercise.
'Tis even as man grew probatively
Initiated in Godship, set to make
A fairer moral world than this he finds,
Guess now what shall be known hereafter. Deal
Thus with the present problem: as we see,
A faultless creature is destroyed, and sin
Has had its way i' the world where God should rule.
Aye, but for this irrelevant circumstance
Of inquisition after blood, we see
Pompilia lost and Guido saved; how long?
For his whole life; how much is that whole life?
We are not babes, but know the minute's worth,
And feel that life is large and the world small,
So, wait till life have passed from out the world.
Neither does this astonish at the end,
That whereas I can so receive and trust,
Other men made with hearts and souls the same,
Reject and disbelieve — subordinate
The future to the present — sin, nor fear.
This I refer still to the foremost fact,
Life is probation and the earth no goal
But starting point of man; compel him strive,
Which means, in man, as good as reach the goal —
Why institute that race, his life, at all?
But this does overwhelm me with surprise,
Touch me to terror — not that faith, the pearl,
Should be let lie by fishers wanting food —
Nor, seen and handled by a certain few
Critical and contemptuous, straight consigned
To shore and shingle for the pebble it proves —
But that, when haply found and known and named
By the residue made rich forevermore,
These — that these favored ones, should in a trice
Turn, and with double zest go dredge for whelks,
Mudworms that make the savory soup! Enough
O' the disbelievers, see the faithful few!
How do the Christians here deport them, keep
Their robes of white unspotted by the world?
What is this Aretine Archbishop, this
Man under me as I am under God,
This champion of the faith, I armed and decked,
Pushed forward, put upon a pinnacle,
To show the enemy his victor — see!
What's the best fighting when the couple close?
Pompilia cries, " Protect me from the wolf! "
He — " No, thy Guido is rough, heady, strong,
Dangerous to disquiet; let him bide!
He needs some bone to mumble, help amuse
The darkness of his den with; so, the fawn
Which limps up bleeding to my foot and lies
— Come to me, daughter! — thus I throw him back! "
Have we misjudged here, overarmed our knight,
Given gold and silk where plain hard steel serves best,
Enfeebled whom we sought to fortify,
Made an archbishop and undone a saint?
Well, then, descend these heights, this pride of life,
Sit in the ashes with a barefoot monk
Who long ago stamped out the worldly sparks,
By fasting, watching, stone cell, and wire scourge
— No such indulgence as unknits the strength —
These breed the tight nerve and tough cuticle,
And the world's praise or blame runs rillet-wise
Off the broad back and brawny breast, we know!
He meets the first cold sprinkle of the world,
And shudders to the marrow. " Save this child?
Oh, my superiors, oh, the Archbishop's self!
Who was it dared lay hand upon the ark
His betters saw fall nor put finger forth?
Great ones could help yet help not; why should small?
I break my promise; let her break her heart! "
These are the Christians not the worldlings, not
The skeptics, who thus battle for the faith!
If foolish virgins disobey and sleep,
What wonder? But, this time, the wise that watch
Sell lamps and buy lutes, exchange oil for wine,
The mystic Spouse betrays the Bridegroom here.
To our last resource, then! Since all flesh is weak,
Bind weakness together, we get strength;
The individual weighed, found wanting, try
Some institution, honest artifice
Whereby the units grow compact and firm!
Each props the other, and so stand is made
By our embodied cowards that grow brave.
The Monastery called of Convertites,
Meant to help women because these helped Christ —

**1472. rillet-wise:** like a very small stream. **1480.** The Comparini received no message. See "Pompilia," ll. 1271 ff. The Pope is not surprised to find that the worldlings have not helped Pompilia, but the Bishop of Arezzo might have been expected to do better. But he had been spoiled by the Church. The friar, however, into whose mouth the lines here (1475–80) are put as a justification of his failure to help, was not spoiled by soft treatment. It is no surprise if the foolish virgins sleep (see Matt. 25), but it is shocking that the wise virgins — that is, people and orders connected with the Church — should be moved by motives of gain to themselves. **1494. Convertites:** This community had been founded to assist immoral women, and had the legal right to claim the property of such women if they died in Rome.

A thing existent only while it acts,
Does as designed, else a nonentity —
For what is an idea unrealized? —
Pompilia is consigned to these for help.
They do help; they are prompt to testify
To her pure life and saintly dying days.
She dies, and lo, who seemed so poor, proves rich!
What does the body that lives through helpfulness
To women for Christ's sake? The kiss turns bite,
The dove's note changes to the crow's cry: judge!
" Seeing that this our Convent claims of right
What goods belong to those we succor, be
The same proved women of dishonest life —
And seeing that this trial made appear
Pompilia was in such predicament —
The Convent hereupon pretends to said
Succession of Pompilia, issues writ,
And takes possession by the Fisc's advice."
Such is their attestation to the cause
Of Christ, who had one saint at least, they hoped;
But, is a title deed to filch, a corpse
To slander, and an infant heir to cheat?
Christ must give up his gains then! They unsay
All the fine speeches — who was saint is whore.
Why, scripture yields no parallel for this!
The soldiers only threw dice for Christ's coat;
We want another legend of the Twelve
Disputing if it was Christ's coat at all,
Claiming as prize the woof of price — for why?
The Master was a thief, purloined the same,
Or paid for it out of the common bag!
Can it be this is end and outcome, all
I take with me to show as stewardship's fruit,
The best yield of the latest time, this year
The seventeen-hundredth since God died for man?
Is such effect proportionate to cause?
And still the terror keeps on the increase
When I perceive . . . how can I blink the fact?
That the fault, the obduracy to good,
Lies not with the impracticable stuff
Whence man is made, his very nature's fault,
As if it were of ice the moon may gild
Not melt, or stone 'twas meant the sun should warm
Not make bear flowers — nor ice nor stone to blame;
But it can melt, that ice, can bloom, that stone,
Impassible to rule of day and night!
This terrifies me, thus compelled perceive,
Whatever love and faith we looked should spring
At advent of the authoritative star,
Which yet lie sluggish, curdled at the source —
These have leaped forth profusely in old time,
These still respond with promptitude today,
At challenge of — what unacknowledged powers
O' the air, what uncommissioned meteors warmth
By law, and light by rule should supersede?
For see this priest, this Caponsacchi, stung
At the first summons — " Help for honor's sake,
Play the man, pity the oppressed! " — no pause,
How does he lay about him in the midst,
Strike any foe, right wrong at any risk,
All blindness, bravery, and obedience! — blind?
Aye, as a man would be inside the sun,
Delirious with the plenitude of light
Should interfuse him to the finger ends —
Let him rush straight, and how shall he go wrong?
Where are the Christians in their panoply?
The loins we girt about with truth, the breasts
Righteousness plated round, the shield of faith,
The helmet of salvation, and that sword
O' the Spirit, even the word of God — where these?
Slunk into corners! Oh, I hear at once
Hubbub of protestation! " What, we monks,
We friars, of such an order, such a rule,
Have not we fought, bled, left our martyr mark
At every point along the boundary line
'Twixt true and false, religion and the world,
Where this or the other dogma of our Church
Called for defense? " And I, despite myself,
How can I but speak loud what truth speaks low,
" Or better than the best, or nothing serves!
What boots deed, I can cap and cover straight
With such another doughtiness to match,
Done at an instinct of the natural man? "
Immolate body, sacrifice soul too —
Do not these publicans the same? Outstrip!
Or else stop race you boast runs neck and neck,
You with the wings, they with the feet — for shame!
Oh, I remark your diligence and zeal!
Five years long, now, rounds faith into my ears,
" Help thou, or Christendom is done to death! "
Five years since, in the Province of To-kien,
Which is in China as some people know,
Maigrot, my Vicar Apostolic there,
Having a great qualm, issues a decree.
Alack, the converts use as God's name, not
*Tien-chu* but plain *Tien* or else mere *Shang-ti*,

1499. Pompilia had not been in the charge of the Convertites, but rather in that of the nuns of the convent of Scalette. **1513. the Fisc**: Bottinius. Book IX records the argument of Bottinius, the representative of the treasury and the reverend apostolic chamber. **1522. legend . . . Twelve**: the twelve apostles. Of course, there is no such legend. **1542–50. This . . . supersede**: There was a great deal of love and faith at the beginning when the Church needed them, that is, at the "advent of the authoritative star." Now, however, love and faith no longer respond to the Church's warmth and light, but rather to the instinct of the natural man, that is, the "uncommissioned meteors." Caponsacchi has responded to these instincts: honor, pity, manliness. **1561 ff.** See Eph. 6:13–17. **1586. Tokien**: Fukien. **1588. Maigrot**: vicar apostolic in China. In 1693 he condemned the Jesuit position, which would allow Chinese modifications of Christian truth.

As Jesuits please to fancy politic,
While, say Dominicans, it calls down fire —
For *Tien* means heaven, and *Shang-ti* supreme
prince,
While *Tien-chu* means the lord of heaven; all cry,
"There is no business urgent for dispatch
As that thou send a legate, specially
Cardinal Tournon, straight to Pekin, there
To settle and compose the difference!"
So have I seen a potentate all fume
For some infringement of his realm's just right,
Some menace to a mud-built straw-thatched farm
O' the frontier; while inside the mainland lie,
Quite undisputed-for in solitude,
Whole cities plague may waste or famine sap;
What if the sun crumble, the sands encroach,
While he looks on sublimely at his ease?
How does their ruin touch the empire's bound?

And is this little all that was to be?
Where is the gloriously decisive change,
Metamorphosis the immeasurable
Of human clay to divine gold, we looked
Should, in some poor sort, justify its price?
Had an adept of the mere Rosy Cross
Spent his life to consummate the Great Work,
Would not we start to see the stuff it touched
Yield not a grain more than the vulgar got
By the old smelting process years ago?
If this were sad to see in just the sage
Who should profess so much, perform no more,
What is it when suspected in that Power
Who undertook to make and made the world,
Devised and did effect man, body and soul,
Ordained salvation for them both, and yet . . .
Well, is the thing we see, salvation?
I
Put no such dreadful question to myself,
Within whose circle of experience burns
The central truth, Power, Wisdom, Goodness —
God;
I must outlive a thing ere know it dead;
When I outlive the faith there is a sun,
When I lie, ashes to the very soul —
Someone, not I, must wail above the heap,
"He died in dark whence never morn arose."
While I see day succeed the deepest night —
How can I speak but as I know? — my speech
Must be, throughout the darkness, "It will end;
The light that did burn, will burn!" Clouds ob-
scure —
But for which obscuration all were bright?
Too hastily concluded! Sun-suffused,
A cloud may soothe the eye made blind by blaze —
Better the very clarity of heaven;
The soft streaks are the beautiful and dear.
What but the weakness in a faith supplies
The incentive to humanity, no strength
Absolute, irresistible, comports?
How can man love but what he yearns to help?
And that which men think weakness within
strength,
But angels know for strength and stronger yet —
What were it else but the first things made new,
But repetition of the miracle,
The divine instance of self-sacrifice
That never ends and aye begins for man?
So, never I miss footing in the maze,
No — I have light nor fear the dark at all.

But are mankind not real, who pace outside
My petty circle, world that's measured me?
And when they stumble even as I stand,
Have I a right to stop ear when they cry,
As they were phantoms who took clouds for crags,
Tripped and fell, where man's march might safely
move?
Beside, the cry is other than a ghost's,
When out of the old time there pleads some bard,
Philosopher, or both, and — whispers not,
But words it boldly. "The inward work and worth
Of any mind, what other mind may judge
Save God who only knows the thing he made,
The veritable service he exacts?
It is the outward product men appraise.
Behold, an engine hoists a tower aloft:
'I looked that it should move the mountain too!'
Or else, 'Had just a turret toppled down,
Success enough!' — may say the Machinist
Who knows what less or more result might be;
But we, who see that done we cannot do,
'A feat beyond man's force,' we men must say.
Regard me and that shake I gave the world!
I was born, not so long before Christ's birth
As Christ's birth haply did precede thy day —
But many a watch before the star of dawn;
Therefore I lived — it is thy creed affirms,
Pope Innocent, who art to answer me! —
Under conditions, nowise to escape,
Whereby salvation was impossible.
Each impulse to achieve the good and fair,

**1598. Tournon:** made a cardinal in 1707. He was legate to India, but was later sent to China. **1614. Rosy Cross:** a Rosicrucian. This group claimed to have discovered the secret of changing baser metals into gold. **1615. Great Work:** the act of transmutation. **1625 ff.** As he sees how far the performance of the clergy falls short of the ideal of Christian principles, the Pope is shaken, almost to the point of asking if the Christian doctrine is salvation, after all. But he refuses to put such a "dreadful question" to himself, and confirms his faith in the power, wisdom, and goodness of God. We have not seen the end, and it is too hasty to conclude that what we see at the moment is the ultimate truth. His faith gives him light in the dark. **1633. "He . . . arose":** See Matt. 27:45. There was darkness over all the land for three hours as Jesus died on the cross.

**1664 ff.** Euripides, Browning's favorite Greek dramatist, is imagined as speaking here.

Each aspiration to the pure and true,
Being without a warrant or an aim,
Was just as sterile a felicity
As if the insect, born to spend his life
Soaring his circles, stopped them to describe
(Painfully motionless in the mid-air)
Some word of weighty counsel for man's sake,
Some 'Know thyself' or 'Take the golden mean!'
— Forwent his happy dance and the glad ray,
Died half an hour the sooner and was dust.
I, born to perish like the brutes, or worse,
Why not live brutishly, obey brutes' law?
But I, of body as of soul complete,
A gymnast at the games, philosopher
I' the schools, who painted, and made music — all
Glories that met upon the tragic stage
When the Third Poet's tread surprised the Two —
Whose lot fell in a land where life was great
And sense went free and beauty lay profuse,
I, untouched by one adverse circumstance,
Adopted virtue as my rule of life,
Waived all reward, loved but for loving's sake,
And, what my heart taught me, I taught the world,
And have been teaching now two thousand years.
Witness my work — plays that should please, forsooth!
'They might please, they may displease, they shall teach,
For truth's sake,' so I said, and did, and do.
Five hundred years ere Paul spoke, Felix heard —
How much of temperance and righteousness,
Judgment to come, did I find reason for,
Corroborate with my strong style that spared
No sin, nor swerved the more from branding brow
Because the sinner was called Zeus and God?
How nearly did I guess at that Paul knew?
How closely come, in what I represent
As duty, to his doctrine yet a blank?
And as that limner not untruly limns
Who draws an object round or square, which square
Or round seems to the unassisted eye,
Though Galileo's tube display the same
Oval or oblong — so, who controverts
I rendered rightly what proves wrongly wrought
Beside Paul's picture? Mine was true for me.
I saw that there are, first and above all,
The hidden forces, blind necessities,
Named Nature, but the thing's self unconceived;
Then follow — how dependent upon these,
We know not, how imposed above ourselves,
We well know — what I name the gods, a power
Various or one; for great and strong and good
Is there, and little, weak, and bad there too,
Wisdom and folly; say, these make no God —
What is it else that rules outside man's self?
A fact then — always, to the naked eye —
And so, the one revealment possible
Of what were unimagined else by man.
Therefore, what gods do, man may criticize,
Applaud, condemn — how should he fear the truth? —
But likewise have in awe because of power,
Venerate for the main munificence,
And give the doubtful deed its due excuse
From the acknowledged creature of a day
To the Eternal and Divine. Thus, bold
Yet self-mistrusting, should man bear himself,
Most assured on what now concerns him most —
The law of his own life, the path he prints —
Which law is virtue and not vice, I say —
And least inquisitive where search least skills,
I' the nature we best give the clouds to keep.
What could I paint beyond a scheme like this
Out of the fragmentary truths where light
Lay fitful in a tenebrific time?
You have the sunrise now, joins truth to truth,
Shoots life and substance into death and void;
Themselves compose the whole we made before;
The forces and necessity grow God —
The beings so contrarious that seemed gods,
Prove just his operation manifold
And multiform, translated, as must be,
Into intelligible shape so far
As suits our sense and sets us free to feel.
What if I let a child think, childhood-long,
That lightning, I would have him spare his eye,
Is a real arrow shot at naked orb?
The man knows more, but shuts his lids the same;
Lightning's cause comprehends nor man nor child.
Why then, my scheme, your better knowledge broke,
Presently readjusts itself, the small
Proportioned largelier, parts and whole named new;
So much, no more two thousand years have done!
Pope, dost thou dare pretend to punish me,
For not descrying sunshine at midnight,
Me who crept all fours, found my way so far —
While thou rewardest teachers of the truth,
Who miss the plain way in the blaze of noon —
Though just a word from that strong style of mine,
Grasped honestly in hand as guiding-staff,
Had pricked them a sure path across the bog,
That mire of cowardice and slush of lies
Wherein I find them wallow in wide day!"

**1701. the Two:** Aeschylus and Sophocles. **1712. Paul . . . heard:** See Acts 24. Felix was the governor in Jerusalem. **1716–17.** Euripides, a rebel in doctrine as well as in dramatic techniques, was critical of the Greek legends of the gods. **1721–25.** Euripides is made to assert here that he had the gist of St. Paul's doctrine, though not in the precise form. A celestial body which appears square to the naked eye is proved to be round when seen better through Galileo's telescope, but it is a star just the same. The figure is not especially happy.

How should I answer this Euripides?
Paul — 'tis a legend — answered Seneca,
But that was in the dayspring; noon is now,
We have got too familiar with the light.
Shall I wish back once more that thrill of dawn?
When the whole truth-touched man burned up, one fire?
— Assured the trial, fiery, fierce, but fleet,
Would, from his little heap of ashes, lend
Wings to that conflagration of the world
Which Christ awaits ere he makes all things new:
So should the frail become the perfect, rapt
From glory of pain to glory of joy; and so,
Even in the end — the act renouncing earth,
Lands, houses, husbands, wives, and children here —
Begin that other act which finds all, lost,
Regained, in this time even, a hundredfold,
And, in the next time, feels the finite love
Blent and embalmed with the eternal life.
So does the sun ghastily seem to sink
In those north parts, lean all but out of life,
Desist a dread mere breathing-stop, then slow
Reassert day, begin the endless rise.
Was this too easy for our afterstage?
Was such a lighting up of faith, in life,
Only allowed initiate, set man's step
In the true way by help of the great glow?
A way wherein it is ordained he walk,
Bearing to see the light from heaven still more
And more encroached on by the light of earth,
Tentatives earth puts forth to rival heaven,
Earthly incitements that mankind serve God
For man's sole sake, not God's and therefore man's.
Till at last, who distinguishes the sun
From a mere Druid fire on a far mount?
More praise to him who with his subtle prism
Shall decompose both beams and name the true
In such sense, who is last proves first indeed;
For how could saints and martyrs fail see truth
Streak the night's blackness? Who is faithful now,
Who untwists heaven's white from the yellow flare
O' the world's gross torch, without night's foil that helped
Produce the Christian act so possible
When in the way stood Nero's cross and stake —
So hard now when the world smiles, "Right and wise!
Faith points the politic, the thrifty way,
Will make who plods it in the end returns
Beyond mere fool's sport and improvidence.
We fools dance through the cornfield of this life,
Pluck ears to left and right and swallow raw
— Nay, tread, at pleasure, a sheaf underfoot,
To get the better at some poppy flower —
Well aware we shall have so much less wheat
In the eventual harvest; you meantime
Waste not a spike — the richlier will you reap!
What then? There will be always garnered meal
Sufficient for our comfortable loaf,
While you enjoy the undiminished sack!"
Is it not this ignoble confidence,
Cowardly hardihood, that dulls and damps,
Makes the old heroism impossible?

Unless . . . what whispers me of times to come?
What if it be the mission of that age
My death will usher into life, to shake
This torpor of assurance from our creed,
Reintroduce the doubt discarded, bring
That formidable danger back, we drove
Long ago to the distance and the dark?
No wild beast now prowls round the infant camp;
We have built wall and sleep in city safe;
But if some earthquake try the towers that laugh,
To think they once saw lions rule outside,
And man stand out again, pale, resolute,
Prepared to die — which means, alive at last?
As we broke up that old faith of the world,
Have we, next age, to break up this the new —
Faith, in the thing, grown faith in the report —
Whence need to bravely disbelieve report
Through increased faith i' the thing reports belie?
Must we deny — do they, these Molinists,
At peril of their body and their soul —
Recognized truths, obedient to some truth
Unrecognized yet, but perceptible? —
Correct the portrait by the living face,
Man's God, by God's God in the mind of man?
Then, for the few that rise to the new height,
The many that must sink to the old depth,
The multitude found fall away! A few,
E'en ere new law speak clear, may keep the old,
Preserve the Christian level, call good good
And evil evil (even though razed and blank
The old titles) helped by custom, habitude,
And all else they mistake for finer sense
O' the fact that reason warrants — as before.
They hope perhaps, fear not impossibly,
At least some one Pompilia left the world
Will say, "I know the right place by foot's feel,
I took it and tread firm there; wherefore change?"
But what a multitude will surely fall
Quite through the crumbling truth, late subjacent,
Sink to the next discoverable base,
Rest upon human nature, settle there
On what is firm, the lust and pride of life!
A mass of men, whose very souls even now
Seem to need re-creating — so they slink
Wormlike into the mud, light now lays bare —
Whose future we dispose of with shut eyes
And whisper — "They are grafted, barren twigs,

**1786.** Legend had it that Paul corresponded with Seneca, the Roman philosopher. **1827. Nero's cross:** for crucifixion.

**1863.** See "Pompilia," l. 763n.

Into the living stock of Christ; may bear
One day, till when they lie deathlike, not dead" —
Those who with all the aid of Christ succumb,
How, without Christ, shall they, unaided, sink?
Whither but to this gulf before my eyes?
Do not we end, the century and I?
The impatient antimasque treads close on kibe
O' the very masque's self it will mock — on me,
Last lingering personage, the impatient mime
Pushes already — will I block the way?
Will my slow trail of garments ne'er leave space
For pantaloon, sock, plume, and castanet?
Here comes the first experimentalist
In the new order of things — he plays a priest;
Does he take inspiration from the Church,
Directly make her rule his law of life?
Not he: his own mere impulse guides the man —
Happily sometimes, since ourselves allow
He has danced, in gaiety of heart, i' the main
The right step through the maze we bade him foot.
But if his heart had prompted him break loose
And mar the measure? Why, we must submit,
And thank the chance that brought him safe so far.
Will he repeat the prodigy? Perhaps.
Can he teach others how to quit themselves,
Show why this step was right while that were wrong?
How should he? " Ask your hearts as I asked mine,
And get discreetly through the morrice too;
If your hearts misdirect you — quit the stage,
And make amends — be there amends to make! "
Such is, for the Augustin that was once,
This Canon Caponsacchi we see now.
" But my heart answers to another tune,"
Puts in the Abate, second in the suite;
" I have my taste too, and tread no such step!
You choose the glorious life, and may, for me!
I like the lowest of life's appetites —
So you judge — but the very truth of joy
To my own apprehension which decides.
Call me knave and you get yourself called fool!
I live for greed, ambition, lust, revenge;
Attain these ends by force, guile; hypocrite,
Today perchance tomorrow recognized
The rational man, the type of common sense."
There's Loyola adapted to our time!
Under such guidance Guido plays his part,
He also influencing in the due turn
These last clods where I track intelligence
By any glimmer, these four at his beck
Ready to murder any, and, at their own,
As ready to murder him — such make the world!

**1898. antimasque:** a comic or burlesque interlude between the acts of a masque. **kibe:** heel. **1904. experimentalist:** Caponsacchi. **1919. morrice:** an intricate dance. **1936. Loyola:** St. Ignatius of Loyola (1491–1556), who founded the Society of Jesus, known as the Jesuits.

And, first effect of the new cause of things,
There they lie also duly — the old pair
Of the weak head and not so wicked heart,
With the one Christian mother, wife, and girl,
— Which three gifts seem to make an angel up —
The world's first foot o' the dance is on their heads!
Still, I stand here, not off the stage though close
On the exit; and my last act, as my first,
I owe the scene, and Him who armed me thus
With Paul's sword as with Peter's key. I smite
With my whole strength once more, ere end my part,
Ending, so far as man may, this offense.
And when I raise my arm, who plucks my sleeve?
Who stops me in the righteous function — foe
Or friend? Oh, still as ever, friends are they
Who, in the interest of outraged truth
Deprecate such rough handling of a lie!
The facts being proved and incontestable,
What is the last word I must listen to?
Perchance — " Spare yet a term this barren stock,
We pray thee dig about and dung and dress
Till he repent and bring forth fruit even yet! "
Perchance — " So poor and swift a punishment
Shall throw him out of life with all that sin;
Let mercy rather pile up pain on pain
Till the flesh expiate what the soul pays else! "
Nowise! Remonstrants on each side commence
Instructing, there's a new tribunal now
Higher than God's — the educated man's!
Nice sense of honor in the human breast
Supersedes here the old coarse oracle —
Confirming nonetheless a point or so
Wherein blind predecessors worked aright
By rule of thumb, as when Christ said — when, where?
Enough, I find it pleaded in a place —
" All other wrongs done, patiently I take:
But touch my honor and the case is changed!
I feel the due resentment — *nemini*
*Honorem trado* is my quick retort."
Right of Him, just as if pronounced today!
Still, should the old authority be mute
Or doubtful, or in speaking clash with new,
The younger takes permission to decide.
At last we have the instinct of the world
Ruling its household without tutelage;
And while the two laws, human and divine,
Have busied finger with this tangled case,
In pushes the brisk junior, cuts the knot,
Pronounces for acquittal. How it trips
Silverly o'er the tongue! " Remit the death!
Forgive . . . well, in the old way, if thou please,
Decency and the relics of routine
Respected — let the Count go free as air!

**1980–81.** ***nemini . . . trado:*** "I give my glory into no man's keeping" (see Isa. 42:9).

Since he may plead a priest's immunity —
The minor orders help enough for that,
With Farinacci's license — who decides
That the mere implication of such man,
So privileged, in any cause, before
Whatever Court except the Spiritual,
Straight quashes law procedure — quash it, then!
Remains a pretty loophole of escape
Moreover, that, beside the patent fact
O' the law's allowance, there's involved the weal
O' the Popedom: a son's privilege at stake,
Thou wilt pretend the Church's interest,
Ignore all finer reasons to forgive!
But herein lies the crowning cogency —
(Let thy friends teach thee while thou tellest beads)
That in this case the spirit of culture speaks,
Civilization is imperative.
To her shall we remand all delicate points
Henceforth, nor take irregular advice
O' the sly, as heretofore; she used to hint
Remonstrances, when law was out of sorts
Because a saucy tongue was put to rest,
An eye that roved was cured of arrogance;
But why be forced to mumble under breath
What soon shall be acknowledged as plain fact,
Outspoken, say, in thy successor's time?
Methinks we see the golden age return!
Civilization and the Emperor
Succeed to Christianity and Pope.
One Emperor then, as one Pope now; meanwhile,
Anticipate a little! We tell thee 'Take
Guido's life, sapped society shall crash,
Whereof the main prop was, is, and shall be
— Supremacy of husband over wife!'
Does the man rule i' the house, and may his mate
Because of any plea dispute the same?
Oh, pleas of all sorts shall abound, be sure,
One but allowed validity — for, harsh
And savage, for, inept and silly-sooth,
For, this and that, will the ingenious sex
Demonstrate the best master e'er graced slave;
And there's but one short way to end the coil —
Acknowledge right and reason steadily
I' the man and master; then the wife submits
To plain truth broadly stated. Does the time
Advise we shift — a pillar? nay, a stake
Out of its place i' the social tenement?
One touch may send a shudder through the heap
And bring it toppling on our children's heads!
Moreover, if ours breed a qualm in thee,
Give thine own better feeling play for once!
Thou, whose own life winks o'er the socket edge,
Wouldst thou it went out in such ugly snuff
As dooming sons dead, e'en though justice prompt?

**1998. Farinacci:** procurator-general to Pope Paul V, and an authority on canon law.

Why, on a certain feast, Barabbas' self
Was set free, not to cloud the general cheer:
Neither shalt thou pollute thy Sabbath close!
Mercy is safe and graceful. How one hears
The howl begin, scarce the three little taps
O' the silver mallet silent on thy brow —
'His last act was to sacrifice a Count
And thereby screen a scandal of the Church!
Guido condemned, the Canon justified
Of course — delinquents of his cloth go free!'
And so the Luthers chuckle, Calvins scowl,
So thy hand helps Molinos to the chair
Whence he may hold forth till doomsday on just
These *petit-maître* priestlings — in the choir,
*Sanctus et Benedictus,* with a brush
Of soft guitar strings that obey the thumb,
Touched by the bedside, for accompaniment!
Does this give umbrage to a husband? Death
To the fool, and to the priest impunity!
But no impunity to any friend
So simply overloyal as these four
Who made religion of their patron's cause,
Believed in him and did his bidding straight,
Asked not one question but laid down the lives
This Pope took — all four lives together make
Just his own length of days — so, dead they lie,
As these were times when loyalty's a drug,
And zeal in a subordinate too cheap
And common to be saved when we spend life!
Come, 'tis too much good breath we waste in words:
The pardon, Holy Father! Spare grimace,
Shrugs, and reluctance! Are not we the world,
Art not thou Priam? let soft culture plead
Hecuba-like, *'non tali'* (Virgil serves)
*'Auxilio,'* and the rest! Enough, it works!
The Pope relaxes, and the Prince is loath,
The father's bowels yearn, the man's will bends,
Reply is apt. Our tears on tremble, hearts
Big with a benediction, wait the word
Shall circulate through the city in a trice,
Set every window flaring, give each man
O' the mob his torch to wave for gratitude.
Pronounce then, for our breath and patience fail!"

I will, Sirs; but a voice other than yours
Quickens my spirit. *"Quis pro Domino?*
Who is upon the Lord's side?" asked the Count.
I, who write —

**2050. Barabbas:** See Matt. 27:17. Pilate offered to free either Jesus or Barabbas. **2054. three . . . taps:** When a pope dies the camerlingo cardinal is supposed to tap on his forehead thrice with a silver mallet. **2063.** ***petit-maître*** **priestlings:** small-minded, worldly priests. **2064.** ***Sanctus et Benedictus:*** "holy and blessed." **2082. Priam:** the aged king of Troy. **2083. Hecuba:** Priam's wife. **2083–84. "*non . . . Auxilio*":** "not with such aid" (see *Aeneid,* II.521).

"On receipt of this command,
Acquaint Count Guido and his fellows four
They die tomorrow; could it be tonight,
The better, but the work to do, takes time.
Set with all diligence a scaffold up,
Not in the customary place, by Bridge
St. Angelo, where die the common sort;
But since the man is noble, and his peers
By predilection haunt the People's Square,
There let him be beheaded in the midst,
And his companions hanged on either side;
So shall the quality see, fear, and learn.
All which work takes time: till tomorrow,
then,
Let there be prayer incessant for the five!"

For the main criminal I have no hope
Except in such a suddenness of fate.
I stood at Naples once, a night so dark
I could have scarce conjectured there was earth
Anywhere, sky or sea or world at all:
But the night's black was burst through by a
blaze —
Thunder struck blow on blow, earth groaned and
bore,
Through her whole length of mountain visible;
There lay the city thick and plain with spires,
And, like a ghost disshrouded, white the sea.
So may the truth be flashed out by one blow,
And Guido see, one instant, and be saved.
Else I avert my face, nor follow him
Into that sad obscure sequestered state
Where God unmakes but to remake the soul
He else made first in vain; which must not be
Enough, for I may die this very night:
And how should I dare die, this man let live?

Carry this forthwith to the Governor!

# from PACCHIAROTTO, 1876

## HOUSE

This poem was written on February 1, 1874. Superficially Browning is answering Wordsworth's statement in "Scorn Not the Sonnet" (p. 108, above) that Shakespeare unlocked his heart in his sonnets. More profoundly Browning is defending the dramatic method of poetry as opposed to personal utterance and at the same time reminding the reader, once again, of the dramatic quality of his own poetry — that his poems are the "utterances of so many imaginary characters — not mine." The occasion which may have caused Browning to write "House" was the publication in 1870 of D. G. Rossetti's sonnet sequence on married love, *The House of Life.*

Shall I sonnet-sing you about myself?
Do I live in a house you would like to see?
Is it scant of gear, has it store of pelf?
"Unlock my heart with a sonnet-key?"

Invite the world, as my betters have done?
"Take notice: this building remains on view,
Its suites of reception every one,
Its private apartment and bedroom too;

"For a ticket, apply to the Publisher."
No; thanking the public, I must decline.
A peep through my window, if folk prefer;
But, please you, no foot over threshold of
mine!

I have mixed with a crowd and heard free talk
In a foreign land where an earthquake chanced
And a house stood gaping, nought to balk
Man's eye wherever he gazed or glanced.

The whole of the frontage shaven sheer,
The inside gaped, exposed to day,
Right and wrong and common and queer,
Bare, as the palm of your hand, it lay.

The owner? Oh, he had been crushed, no doubt!
"Odd tables and chairs for a man of wealth!
What a parcel of musty old books about!
He smoked — no wonder he lost his health!

"I doubt if he bathed before he dressed.
A brasier? — the pagan, he burned perfumes!
You see it is proved, what the neighbors guessed;
His wife and himself had separate rooms."

Friends, the good man of the house at least
Kept house to himself till an earthquake
came;
'Tis the fall of its frontage permits you feast
On the inside arrangement you praise or blame.

Outside should suffice for evidence;
And whoso desires to penetrate
Deeper, must dive by the spirit-sense —
No optics like yours, at any rate!

"Hoity-toity! A street to explore,
Your house the exception! '*With this same key*
*Shakespeare unlocked his heart,* once more!"
Did Shakespeare? If so, the less Shakespeare he!

**2104. People's Square:** the Piazza del Popolo, one of Rome's great squares.

# from DRAMATIC IDYLS

## (Second Series), 1880

### EPILOGUE

The first ten lines of this untitled poem served as an epilogue to the Second Series of *Dramatic Idyls* in 1880 and were probably written earlier the same year. The second part, "Thus I wrote in London," was written in the album of Miss Edith Longfellow, daughter of the American poet, in Venice, October 14, 1880. Browning was chagrined when Miss Longfellow published these lines in the *Century Magazine* in 1882, and he never included them in his collected works. His preference in 1880 for the poet who was "a nation's heritage" instead of for the poet as singer is significant. Compare "How It Strikes a Contemporary," above.

"Touch him ne'er so lightly, into song he broke;
Soil so quick-receptive — not one feather-seed,
Not one flower-dust fell but straight its fall awoke
Vitalizing virtue; song would song succeed
Sudden as spontaneous — prove a poet-soul!"
Indeed?
Rock's the song-soil rather, surface hard and bare;
Sun and dew their mildness, storm and frost their
rage
Vainly both expend — few flowers awaken there;
Quiet in its cleft broods — what the after-age
Knows and names a pine, a nation's heritage.

---

Thus I wrote in London, musing on my betters,
Poets dead and gone; and lo, the critics cried,
"Out on such a boast!" as if I dreamed that fetters
Binding Dante bind up — me! as if true pride
Were not also humble!
So I smiled and sighed
As I oped your book in Venice this bright morning,
Sweet new friend of mine! and felt the clay or sand,
Whatsoe'er my soil be, break — for praise or scorning —
Out in grateful fancies — weeds; but weeds expand
Almost into flowers, held by such a kindly hand.

# from JOCOSERIA, 1883

### WANTING IS — WHAT?

This lyric served as prologue to the volume called *Jocoseria* in 1883.

Wanting is — what?
Summer redundant,
Blueness abundant,
— Where is the blot?
Beamy the world, yet a blank all the same,
— Framework which waits for a picture to
frame:
What of the leafage, what of the flower?
Roses embowering with nought they embower!
Come then, complete incompletion,
O comer,
Pant through the blueness, perfect the
summer!
Breathe but one breath
Rose-beauty above,
And all that was death
Grows life, grows love,
Grows love!

### NEVER THE TIME AND THE PLACE

Probably written in May, 1882, this lyric refers with longing to the memory of Elizabeth Barrett Browning. The "enemy" seems to be time or change, which threatens memories and shakes faith. Only love can overcome this enemy.

Never the time and the place
And the loved one all together!
This path — how soft to pace!
This May — what magic weather!
Where is the loved one's face?
In a dream that loved one's face meets
mine,
But the house is narrow, the place is
bleak
Where, outside, rain and wind combine
With a furtive ear, if I strive to speak,
With a hostile eye at my flushing cheek,
With a malice that marks each word, each
sign!
O enemy sly and serpentine,
Uncoil thee from the waking man!
Do I hold the Past
Thus firm and fast
Yet doubt if the Future hold I can?
This path so soft to pace shall lead
Through the magic of May to herself
indeed!
Or narrow if needs the house must be,
Outside are the storms and strangers;
we —
Oh, close, safe, warm sleep I and she,
— I and she!

# from ASOLANDO, 1889

## DUBIETY

This poem was written in Asolo, Italy, in the autumn of 1889. In reverie, the poet recalls something that once happened to him. The memory is of his wife.

I will be happy if but for once;
  Only help me, autumn weather,
Me and my cares to screen, ensconce
  In luxury's sofa-lap of leather!

Sleep? Nay, comfort — with just a cloud
  Suffusing day too clear and bright;
Eve's essence, the single drop allowed
  To sully, like milk, noon's water-white.

Let gauziness shade, not shroud — adjust,
  Dim and not deaden — somehow sheathe
Aught sharp in the rough world's busy thrust,
  If it reach me through dreaming's vapor wreath.

Be life so, all things ever the same!
  For, what has disarmed the world? Outside,
Quiet and peace; inside, nor blame
  Nor want, nor wish whate'er betide.

What is it like that has happened before?
  A dream? No dream, more real by much.
A vision? But fanciful days of yore
  Brought many; mere musing seems not such.

Perhaps but a memory, after all!
  —Of what came once when a woman leant
To feel for my brow where her kiss might fall.
  Truth ever, truth only the excellent!

## EPILOGUE

This poem concluded the *Asolando* volume. It bears the marks of being a final utterance and was probably written in the autumn of 1889. It has become famous as an expression of Browning's spirit and usually concludes all editions of his poetry. Compare it with "Prospice," above.

At the midnight in the silence of the sleep-time,
  When you set your fancies free,
Will they pass to where — by death, fools think, imprisoned —
Low he lies who once so loved you, whom you loved so,
      — Pity me?

Oh, to love so, be so loved, yet so mistaken!
  What had I on earth to do
With the slothful, with the mawkish, the unmanly?
Like the aimless, helpless, hopeless, did I drivel
      — Being — who?

One who never turned his back but marched breast forward,
  Never doubted clouds would break,
Never dreamed, though right were worsted, wrong would triumph,
Held we fall to rise, are baffled to fight better,
      Sleep to wake.

No, at noonday in the bustle of man's work-time
  Greet the unseen with a cheer!
Bid him forward, breast and back as either should be,
"Strive and thrive!" cry, "Speed — fight on, fare ever
      There as here!"

**LIONEL TRILLING, *Editor***

# *Matthew Arnold*

**1822–1888**

If it were possible for Matthew Arnold to know of the existence of this book, he would approve of it and take pleasure in it. In his lifetime he was much concerned with the purpose to which the book addresses itself — with, that is, the continuing of the literary tradition from one generation to the next, with the choosing of the best authors and works of the past. But Arnold, I think, would be surprised to learn that he had been included among the small company of authors whose work is represented in this volume. Not that he was a man given to excessive modesty and self-depreciation. He loved the considerable measure of fame that came to him in his lifetime. He took pleasure in the influence over people's minds that he knew he had gained. But his strong sense of fact and his passionate desire to make accurate judgments would lead him to observe that he was here in the company of genius and that he himself, whatever high virtues might be ascribed to him, was not a genius. In this observation he might very possibly be correct. Matthew Arnold has been the object of attention, admiration, and affection, yet with but two exceptions that I know of, no one has spoken of him as a genius. The exceptions, to be sure, are notable. The great Benjamin Jowett, the famous translator of Plato, spoke of Arnold as a man of genius in order to say that he was "the most sensible man of genius I have ever known." And no less a poet than Gerard Manley Hopkins said that, although he disagreed with Arnold in essential ways, he nevertheless thought him a "rare genius." These remarks are pleasant to read, yet I confess to being somewhat surprised whenever I read them.

Arnold did not, we must observe, give to genius the unqualified admiration which it receives from most people. He was even a little suspicious of it. He thought that the definitive element of genius was *energy* — and he thought that energy needed to be modified by other qualities before it deserved our full admiration. In social and political life he was concerned with the question of how energy could be organized and made to serve the right ends; and in the intellectual life he was no less concerned with the right disposition of energy, with the ordering and distribution and continuation of creative power. And yet, for all his reservations about it, Arnold loved energy almost above any other human trait; he loved genius, and it pained him to realize that he was not of the company to whom the word is commonly, or without qualification, applied. At a certain point in his career as a poet he consciously surrendered the poetic hopes of his young manhood. The business of life so occupied him and so fatigued him that it was no longer possible for him to write poetry. The writing of poetry, he said, "demands not merely an effort and a labor, but an actual tearing of oneself to pieces, which one does not readily consent to . . . unless one can devote one's whole life to poetry," and this entire devotion was not possible for him.

If, then, we consider Arnold only as a poet, it is not hard to understand the surprise I impute to him at his being included here among the pre-eminent geniuses of English literature. His total production in poetry was relatively small, and only a very few items of it may be judged perfect or of the very highest quality. And then, if we look at the work which occupied him when poetry was no longer of the first importance to him, we see that it is not of the kind that usually entitles a man to a place among the greatest spirits of his country's literature. Not that we do not habitually treat literary criticism with great respect, but we do not often consider it to be the kind of literature that is of the very first importance; as compared with the literature of imagination, the literature of judgment is quite properly thought to be secondary. Then too it must be said that as a critic Arnold could often be wrong. Nothing is more common as a strategic opening for a contemporary essay in literary criticism than to quote some judgment of Arnold's and to show how mistaken it was.

And yet — and this is one of the curious facts of English literature — Arnold holds a great and permanent place in our minds. The relatively small and often imperfect body of Arnold's poetry has a reality for us and a power over us which seem quite out of proportion to its poetic quality as we usually judge poetic quality. The merest novice in the criticism of poetry can point out where Arnold goes wrong. Everyone can quote, "Who prop, thou ask'st, in these bad days, my mind?" in order to demonstrate that it is a virtually unsayable line; yet everyone knows the line and, in some way, loves it. The fact is that Arnold's poetic lapses seem not to matter. Tennyson, in almost everything that makes a poet, was far more happily endowed than Arnold, and of recent years we have learned to know how great a poet Tennyson at his best really is. And yet Arnold interests us more than Tennyson; indeed, it is probably true that of all the poets of the later nineteenth century, it is Arnold to whom we listen most attentively. We listen to him as if he were a friend speaking to us, which is to say that, although we are aware of his faults and weaknesses, we are essentially indifferent to them. And if to make us listen in this way is not one of the things we think poetry properly should do, then perhaps we must examine afresh our notions of the task of poetry.

And when we consider Arnold as a critic, no matter how often we note his errors of opinion, we cannot avoid coming to the judgment that Arnold was one of the greatest critics in English literature, or, indeed, in the literature of the world. It is never really of consequence how wrong a critic is on one point or another, or even on many points. What is of consequence is that he should, by what he says about a work of literature, induce us to look at it with a renovated curiosity, and that he should lead us to judge it not merely by the highest literary standards but also by our own sense of life. To do this, a critic must take large chances. He must unsettle old established notions and propose new ones, and this is never without its risk. We can go so far as to say that a critic who is essentially right may be most interesting and most powerful and most useful when he is wrong, that his mistakes may sometimes be the most vital part of him, for they represent his passion and commitment.

Arnold's peculiar greatness as a critic lies in his having made so many and such large issues in literature. Nothing can be easier than to quarrel with his guiding principle, that "literature is the criticism of life," especially if what he meant by the phrase is not truly understood. Yet the phrase has established itself in our minds, and it has become the principle of criticism — and, indeed, of literature itself — in the modern world. For English-speaking people, Arnold is the father of criticism. Coleridge is in some respects a greater critical mind than Arnold — he is no doubt larger, more subtle, more complex and systematic. But Coleridge, great as he is, never has had the effect upon criticism that Arnold has had.

If we look for the clue to Arnold's greatness, both as poet and as critic, we find it, I think, in his particular relation to the historical period in which he lived. Perhaps more than any other Englishman of his time, Arnold submitted himself to the stresses of his age, experiencing its pains and its contradictions in a personal way. G. K. Chesterton, who by temperament and belief, could not be wholly sympathetic to Arnold, says of him that of all the Victorians he was the one who naturally *knew*. And if one were to say what it was that Arnold knew, it might well be this: that he, better than anyone else of his time, knew the relation of the part to the whole, of the individual to his class, of the class to the national society, of the national society to the society of nations. And overarching this knowledge was a brooding wonder about the relation of all men to the universe. It is this knowledge and this wonder, implicit in all that he wrote, that make his criticism and his poetry so full of meaning for us today.

## II

Matthew Arnold was born in 1822, on the twenty-fourth of December. He was the son of a remarkable father. Thomas Arnold was at this time a young clergyman of the Church of England, who, in the little village of Laleham on the upper Thames, made a modest livelihood by taking young gentlemen into his home and preparing them for the universities. He was not long to remain thus obscure. In 1827, at the age of thirty-two, he was elected headmaster of Rugby School, an ancient but much deteriorated foundation. The story of Thomas Arnold's reform of Rugby, of his raising it from the shabby slackness in which he found it to the position of one of the most famous and influential of schools, has become one of the legends of Victorian England, and even today people who do not know another name in the long history of scholastic education know the name of Dr. Arnold.

It was, however, not only his striking success as a schoolmaster that made Dr. Arnold one of the most notable figures of early Victorian England. He was an historian of considerable eminence, although not actually of great originality, and he was a leader in the religious controversies of the time, controversies which are likely to seem the more important to us today because they involved great political issues. As one of the moving spirits of the so-called Broad Church movement in the Church of England, it was Thomas Arnold's aim to make the Established Church more nearly a national church than in fact it was. He wanted to so liberalize the Church and its doctrines and organizations that the many sects of Protestant dissenters which, since the seventeenth century, had detached themselves from the Establishment, would find it possible to return to the fold and help toward the formation of a coherent body of Protestant Christianity. He believed too that it was the clear duty of the Church to take upon itself the responsibility for the physical, intellectual, and social well-being of its communicants. Far more than most men of his time and class, he understood the meaning of the great social changes that were taking place in England, most especially of the development of the great new class of industrial workers whom the Church was not reaching and who were indeed, as Arnold was aware, growing hostile to the Church.

As we consider the later intellectual development of Matthew Arnold, we cannot help perceiving the many respects in which his ideas are similar to those of his father. Yet we are no less aware that the principle of his early life was to be as different from his father as possible. Dr. Arnold was known for his enormous seriousness, his intense moral conviction, and his strong, simple will. Matthew, even as a boy, and all through his youth and young manhood, saw to it that he was known for his airy elegance, his vivacity, and his irony; and something of these qualities stayed with him all through his life. He was remarkably handsome as a boy and as a young man, and he cultivated his appearance with an ostentatious though humorous vanity which, in a family and social group that valued seriousness and gravity, was thought of as very odd.

He seems to have derived something of his manner from his mother. Mrs. Arnold, the daughter of a well-known clerical family of Cornwall, was certainly anything but a frivolous woman, and yet we know that she quite shocked Charlotte Brontë by her lighthearted social manner. Miss Brontë's visit was paid to Mrs. Arnold after the famous Doctor's death. Matthew was present during the call, and Miss Brontë was troubled by the tone both of the mother and the son, which was marked, she said, by a lack of genuineness and sympathy. Of Mrs. Arnold she said that it was hard to believe that she could have been a proper wife for Dr. Arnold. Of Matthew she observed that, although he was "striking and prepossessing in appearance," yet his manner "displeases from his seeming foppery." But even this stern judge found herself, before the visit was out, charmed by both the mother and the son, and she was able to say of Matthew that she perceived a "real modesty beneath the assumed conceit."

It was an accurate judgment, and, apparently, it was not very difficult to make — the young Matthew Arnold was the recipient of much warm affection from his friends, even when they were most annoyed with him for his airs. Yet they worried about his superciliousness, his affectations, his extravagant waistcoats, and his hair allowed to grow long in the French fashion. Arnold was young in a day when the most elaborate dandyism of dress and deportment was still possible, and he took a pretty full advantage of its license.

There is, I believe, no record of what William Wordsworth made of this. In 1833, Thomas Arnold had built a summer and holiday home at Westmorland in the Lake Country and thus became a neighbor and eventually a close friend of Wordsworth. The poet grew fond of Matthew, who had early shown a literary bent, and followed his young friend's career with affectionate interest. If, with Charles Lamb, we speculate on persons one would wish to have seen, we could do no better for our amusement than to ask for the sight of the craggy old Wordsworth in conversation with Matthew Arnold either as a supercilious boy or as a dandified young man. Yet, strikingly different as their temperaments were, the influence of the old man on the young was very great. The meaning which Arnold was to give to the word "nature" in his poetry was to be very different from that which Wordsworth gave, but at least one of its several senses is Wordsworth's own — that which relates to the strong response, both aesthetic and moral, to unspoiled country, to field and stream, to mountain and firmament. Arnold lived part of his boyhood where Wordsworth had lived his. He skated on the same lakes and climbed the same mountains. The effect of this experience on him was certainly not so intense as it had been on Wordsworth, but it was decisive in Arnold's life.

At Rugby, young Matthew's friends were the boys upon whom his father was having the greatest influence — an influence which was to continue all through their lives. Among these was Thomas Hughes, later to be known as a leader of the Christian Socialist movement and chiefly remembered as the author of *Tom Brown's Schooldays,* the book which has done most to establish the legend of the great Doctor, and which even now can best suggest the effect which he had upon his pupils. Another was Arthur Penrhyn Stanley, Thomas Arnold's biographer, a historian of considerable eminence and eventually Dean of Westminister Abbey. It was, however, with Arthur Hugh Clough that Matthew was most intimate. Clough[1] was a brilliant boy of extreme moral earnestness, all that Dr. Arnold might have wished a Rugby boy to be. Perhaps because he was an orphan and was therefore impelled to make Dr. Arnold and the school stand in the place of the parents he had lost, he committed himself to the Doctor's view of things in a way that was surely excessive. He planned a career in the university, and there is every reason to suppose that this should have been in most respects suitable to his temperament; but during his incumbency of a fellowship at Oriel College, he began to experience religious doubts, which, when he was unable to resolve them, led him to resign his fellowship, for he believed that he could not in good conscience make the formal subscription to the doctrines of the Church of England which was at that time required of fellows. He had great difficulty in establishing himself in secular life. His moral sensitivity went with an extreme indecisiveness and with bouts of melancholy depression which kept him from exercising his considerable, if limited, abilities as a poet and critic. He was appointed head of University Hall at the University of London, but the post did not suit him, nor did he discharge his duties well. A year in America, where he lived under the friendly eye of Emerson, did nothing to advance his fortunes, but after his return to England he received a post as examiner in the Education Office. He died in 1861 at the age of forty-two, and he is commemorated in all his sad frustration by one of Arnold's most successful poems, "Thyrsis," which stands with Milton's "Lycidas" and Shelley's "Adonais," although below them, as one of the three most famous elegies in English poetry.

The temperament of Clough and its relation to the moral influence of Dr. Arnold suggest an explanation of Matthew Arnold's manner as he developed and exercised it during his years at Oxford. The letters that passed between Arnold and Clough — Clough's have been lost but Arnold's were fortunately preserved — during the first years after college indicate very clearly that Arnold was in profound opposition to the earnestness and the moral intensity of his school

[1] His name is pronounced to rhyme with *rough.*

and college friends. For Arnold wanted to be a poet, and he had come to believe, nor can we doubt that he was right, that poetry could never be written out of the solemn wish to write poetry, that it could not be written out of the conscience or out of intellectual preoccupation. Arnold never does say, of course, that poetry is written out of an indifference to serious matters and to ideas, or that poetry is written out of a commitment to fancy waistcoats and hair worn in the French fashion; but Clough must have understood him to be saying something very much like this, for Arnold does indeed say that poetry is primarily a matter of surfaces rather than of depths, of style rather than of matter, that a poem is great when it is a thing perceived, not an organization of ideas understood. Arnold is putting forward a view of poetry which has been summed up in our time by Archibald MacLeish's famous statement, "A poem should not mean, / But be." And he is quite open in saying to Clough that he had intentionally isolated himself from his friends, even, for a time, from Clough himself, because their intense moralism, their piety, their intellectuality and self-scrutiny were hostile to the condition of mind in which poetry could be written. What seemed to Arnold at this time to make the writing of poetry possible was gaiety, and openness to experience, and the cultivation of the ego in fantasy and dream.

And so his friends were right when they felt that he kept them at a distance and refused to be serious with them. We cannot, of course, suppose that his affectations and frivolities were wholly and merely programmatic. When he told the passengers of a coach that his traveling companion, his friend Walrond, was a poor insane gentleman and that he was the madman's keeper, he was simply giving vent to high spirits. Yet we cannot help feeling that the whole course of his life during the Oxford time and shortly after — the practical jokes and the affectations, the French novels and the heterodox philosophers that he read, and the ribaldry of his letters — had in it an element of consciousness, a desire not to succumb to literalness, or to solemnity, or to the piousness of English life.

It was at this time that Arnold conceived his intense admiration for two French women, one the great actress Rachel, possibly the greatest actress the world has known, the other the French novelist George Sand. In one of his late essays Arnold tells us that he once followed Rachel to Paris after her London season. And in another essay he recalls his visit to George Sand, who, when he had plucked up his courage to write to her, asking if he might call, responded most kindly; she received him at her country home, among a party of friends which included Chopin, her lover at the time. The two women tell us much about the aspirations of Arnold's youthful mind. Rachel, especially as she performed Racine, stood for style — style so perfect that her most intense passions, and she was the most passionate of players, could not shatter its perfection. And George Sand stood for freedom and sentiment. Both, we may suppose Arnold to have thought, were incomprehensible to the serious, good young men of Rugby and Oxford. To Arnold they were the image of artistic salvation.

In the Oxford days, Clough, with his extravagant love of rectitude, fussed over his unreliable friend like a mother hen who has hatched a pheasant. "Matt is full of Parisianism," he wrote in a letter. "Theaters in general, and Rachel in special: he enters the room with a chanson of Béranger's on his lips — for the sake of French words almost conscious of tune: his carriage shows him in fancy parading the Rue de Rivoli; and his hair is guiltless of English scissors: he breakfasts at 12, and never dines in Hall, and in the week or 8 days rather (for 2 Sundays must be included) he has been in chapel *once*." As the time for Arnold's last examinations approached, the good Clough was determined that his friend should justify the expectations that were had of him and take his degree with first-class honors. Following the Oxford custom, they went on a reading party with a group of friends, and Clough fatigued himself by his efforts to pace Arnold in the work of each day. But to no avail, and Clough must report in a letter that "M. Arnold has gone fishing when he should properly be working." When the examination results were posted, Arnold was found to have taken his degree with only second-class honors, which in the Rugby circle was considered a sad defeat.

There is no record of Arnold's spirits having been lowered by the event. He was provided with a post as classical undermaster at Rugby, at which he spent a year. His father had died in

1842, and Arnold did not hold the new headmaster in great esteem. His letters to Clough are irreverent and raffish, and he was still given to hoaxes. But at the end of the year he was elected to a fellowship at Oriel College, which, in the eyes of his friends, wiped out the Balliol defeat. He held the fellowship for a year, and then, having been appointed secretary to Lord Lansdowne, a political peer of liberal opinions, he settled in London, where his reputation as a handsome and dandified young man was reinforced.

But this reputation underwent a considerable modification when, in 1849, Arnold published his first volume of verse, *The Strayed Reveler and Other Poems*. The book, like Arnold's next volume of verse, *Empedocles on Etna and Other Poems,* published in 1852, was signed only with the initial A, but it was pretty much an open secret that the author was the son of Dr. Arnold. Among some who had known the Doctor it was a cause of surprise that any son of his should be able to write poetry at all. And many who knew the son were astonished that so dandified a young man should have written poetry that was so serious and sad.

On the whole, the critical reception of the two volumes was not good. Where Arnold's early verses made an appeal at all, it was to " intellectuals " and to " advanced " readers, those who had a special ability to respond to what was new and good in poetry. More conventional readers spoke of the verse as being difficult, even incomprehensible, and they commented adversely on the unorthodox religious attitudes, and also on the pervasive tone of personal melancholy, which seemed so at odds with what any healthy-minded Englishman ought to feel about the state of the world and the possibility of progress. The year of Arnold's *Empedocles* volume, 1852, was the year of the height of the Great Exhibition, which marked England's sense of past achievement and her expectation of greater material good to come.

The personal melancholy of Arnold's early verse is sometimes, although not always, expressed in connection with an incident of disappointed love. As with Wordsworth's Lucy, we have no real knowledge of the Marguerite of Arnold's poems beyond what the poems themselves give us, nor can we be sure that she had an actual existence. Arnold himself disclosed but very little of his private life, and even forbade that any biography of him ever be written. His family concurred in his wish, and presumably made sure that it be carried out by destroying letters which might have given us knowledge of the actuality of the affair, and denied that it had any actuality at all, insisting that Marguerite was a fictitious person. This is possible, although the tone of the poems in which she is spoken of makes against it, suggesting a real rather than an imagined suffering, and there is at least one passage in one of the letters to Clough which substantiates the supposition that the love affair was actual. If there was indeed a Marguerite, we may conclude from the poems that Arnold met her in Switzerland, that she was French, that the reason for the unhappiness was in part caused by the poet's notion of her national temperament; for, much as Arnold admired French culture and felt the deep need of it for himself, he seems to have had a conventional Englishman's notion of French women, and he ascribes to Marguerite, delightful as she is, a lightness and lack of seriousness and depth of feeling, and a lack of propriety, even of chastity, which make it impossible for them to continue as lovers. The separation and its heartache became for Arnold the symbol of human separateness in the modern world, which is one of the dominant themes of his verse.

In 1851 Arnold married Frances Lucy Wightman, the daughter of an eminent judge, and he had to confront the necessity of finding an income sufficient to support domestic life. He had not been trained for any profession, and he could not hope to live by his pen. Lord Lansdowne was able to secure for him a post in the Education Department as an inspector of schools. No work could have been less suited to a poet. It involved constant traveling under most uncomfortable conditions, the grind of petty detail in stuffy schoolrooms, long evenings spent reading examination papers in depressing hotel rooms after solitary dinners. The fastidious Arnold had become the most dutiful of men; he discharged his responsibilities with consummate earnestness and skill. He soon won the confidence of his superiors and, as he rose in the service, the affection of his subordinates. With time, the sphere of his duties widened; he was given assignments to survey the schools of France, Germany, and Switzerland. His interest in the work grew, for he involved its problems with his general view of the social life of England, and his influence on the developing system of free schools in the nation was considerable. Yet the work made it impossible for him to go on with the writing of poetry, except infrequently, and it is indeed to be wondered at that his prose writings are so extensive as in fact they are.

In 1857 Arnold was elected to the professorship of poetry at Oxford, a post of considerable distinction which he held for two terms of five years each. It had always been the custom for the professor to lecture in Latin. At his request Arnold was granted permission to speak in English. His inaugural lecture was called " On the Modern Element in Literature," and the title is suggestive of the nature of Arnold's work in criticism. Many of Arnold's first essays in criticism were delivered as lectures to Oxford audiences before they were published, and this in part accounts for the tone of the prose, which, having something of the formality that befits public discourse, is at the same time intimate and easy.

From the first, Arnold's reputation as a poet established itself, despite the hostile reception of his early volumes, despite his small subsequent production. His reputation as a critic was no less steady and rather more rapid in its growth. In his middle and later years he moved by natural stages from the discussion of literature to what was always implicit in his literary criticism, the discussion of politics and of religion. *Culture and Anarchy,* the first chapter of which was the last of his Oxford lectures, is one of the central works of the nineteenth century, and, if his writings on religion are now less well remembered, they were of the first importance in their time.

From the end of youth on, Arnold's life was a quiet one, and both happy and sad. His happiness came from the domestic affections, as indeed came the sadness, for he endured the death of three of his sons; in the face of his terrible grief he maintained the fortitude of the Stoics whom he so much admired. It is a charming and touching paradox of his nature that, although he kept most in mind the books and ideas that enforce upon us the tragic seriousness of life and the high necessity of dutifulness and fortitude, he nevertheless not only loved gaiety but believed that it was the sign of the health of individuals and societies.

By 1883 Arnold's fame was as great in America as in England, possibly greater. Upon the invitation of an American lecture agency, Arnold undertook to make a lecture tour of America. The auguries were good, for the American interest in Arnold was by no means confined to a small group of intellectuals but extended to people of all ranks of society. At the beginning of the tour there were some difficulties, for Arnold's manner of lecturing was not what Americans were accustomed to, and he could not be heard in Carnegie Hall. Then the lecture on Emerson, one of the three he had prepared, gave offense to some by denying final greatness to Emerson. And Arnold's English manners and sometimes his personal manner seemed to antagonize some people. Arnold was thought of as the " prophet of culture," and it was perhaps natural that Americans, uneasy about their own condition of culture, should be antagonistic to Arnold almost in the degree that they were interested in what he would say on the subject. Nevertheless, the trip was a success, and Arnold, who all his intellectual life had been uneasy about American social and political manifestations, acquired an affection for this country and a considerable admiration for its manner of life. He made a second visit in 1886; one of his daughters had married an American, and he came to see his new grandchild. In that same year he retired from his school post. He had had signs of the heart disease which had taken off his father at a much younger age, but he nevertheless lived very actively. In 1888, on the fourteenth of April he went to Liverpool to meet his daughter and granddaughter on a visit from America, and in his eagerness to see them he leaped over a fence and fell dead.

## III

Arnold's poetry in its most characteristic mood is elegiac — it mourns a loss, celebrates the lost thing, and tries to come to terms with the deprivation. What is the thing that is grieved for? The contemporary reader of English literature need not be long over this question. He will quite easily see that Arnold's loss is much the same as that which is at the center of the thought and feeling of such modern writers as T. S. Eliot, D. H. Lawrence, and W. B. Yeats. It is the loss of a certain culture — that is to say, of a certain body of assumptions, a certain way of looking at the world and of responding to it, a certain quality of temperament which seems no longer available.

For Arnold, as for so many intellectuals of his time, the essential element of this sense of loss was the diminution of the intensity of religious faith. Arnold's age was not an irreligious age — indeed, a case might be made out for its having been one of the notable epochs of religious intensity. And Arnold himself was by no means a man without religious faith. But we may say of the religion of Arnold's day that it was of a kind that did not suffuse the consciousness of men of intellect. It was not an element of their imaginations, although it might be an element of their morality or of their disciplined thought. The poets, of course, were, of all men, the most likely to be aware of this change in the constitution of the imagination or, as they were more likely to say, in the object of their imaginations. The world, they felt, did not have the look and feel that it had once had to earlier poets. Something had gone out of the universe, some element of wonder, of mystery, of life itself. Schiller mourned the passing of the Greek gods, the pagan spirits and genii of places, but he had in mind the attrition of Christian belief by the scientific world view which made it easier to think of the world as a mechanism than as an organic, animated entity. Keats spoke of philosophy — science — conquering "all mysteries by rule and line" and emptying "the haunted air." John Dewey, writing of Arnold, thus describes Arnold's sense of the world: "No longer, he seems to say, may man believe in his oneness with the dear nature about him: the sense of a common purpose outworking in both has fled. Nature, in ceasing to be divine, has ceased to be human." Again and again in the early verse Arnold expresses the shock and pain of perceiving that the laws of nature are not the laws of man, that, as he says, "Nature and man can never be fast friends."

One of the traditional ways of understanding the Romantic movement is as an effort to compensate for the loss of religion by creating a vision of the universe which, even though it might not have the awful sanctions of orthodox Christianity, would still allow men to be in a vivid relation to a sentient world. Blake undertook to people the universe with newly conceived spirits. Coleridge tells how he and Wordsworth divided between them the empire of poetic subjects, Wordsworth to treat commonplace objects in a supernatural light, Coleridge to deal with supernatural objects as matters of common experience. Shelley, who was hostile to established religion, was yet at pains to evolve from ancient sources a complex pantheism, a view of the material universe in which spirit should have a dominant part. Arnold is in the line and under the influence of these Romantic poets, as, indeed, are Eliot, Lawrence, and Yeats. All seek to reanimate a world from which the animating imagination of religion had withdrawn.

But the efforts of the Romantic poets, although certainly related to religion, were not in themselves essentially religious. Rather, they were directed to assuring, to validating, man's power to *feel*. The fear of the loss of the power to feel — this is one of the great themes of the literature of the last century and a half. For Arnold, as for the more recent writers I have mentioned, the instinctual life is depressed and attenuated by the pre-eminence of rationality. As early as in the letters to Clough, Arnold expressed his apprehension of the dominance of intellect in the life of contemporary man, of its desiccating effect. His youthful extravagances, as I have tried to suggest, were a way of protecting himself from this drying up of the springs of the emotions and the imagination. Again and again he recurs to the passing of the freshness of youth, either in death, as with the young god Balder, or in old age and in the withering and hardening of the spirit.

Dear saints, it is not sorrow, as I hear,
Not suffering, that shuts up eye and ear
To all which has delighted them before,
And lets us be what we were once no more.
No: we may suffer deeply, yet retain
Power to be moved and soothed, for all our pain,
By what of old pleased us, and will again.
No: 'tis the gradual furnace of the world,
In whose hot air our spirits are upcurled
Until they crumble, or else grow like steel —
Which kills in us the bloom, the youth, the spring —
Which leaves the fierce necessity to feel,
But takes away the power — . . .

Almost inevitably the power to feel finds its focus in the sexual passions, and the checking or diminution or warping of sexuality is likely to serve in literature as the most dramatic instance of the effect of modern civilization upon the instinctual life of man. Of the preoccupation with sexuality as the summary of the instinctual life, D. H. Lawrence will probably come to mind as the most striking example. But Eliot, in his most famous poem, *The Waste Land,* makes use of the symbol of sexual impotence to represent the deprived condition of modern culture, and for Yeats the sexual power is the index of force and grace of life. And Arnold, although to be sure he is more reticent than these writers, represents modern man as being deprived of his sexual freedom and energy; this, in the face of all his efforts to rationalize and moralize it, is the real theme of all his love poems.

One of Arnold's most successful poems, "The Scholar Gypsy," is a peculiarly interesting example of the conjunction which the poet makes between the power to feel and the kind of belief which the individual is permitted by his culture to hold. The poem is based on an Oxford legend of the seventeenth century, which Arnold found in Joseph Glanvill's *Vanity of Dogmatizing* (1661), of a gifted scholar who, because of poverty, left his college to join the gypsies. He became a master of their esoteric lore, and Arnold imagines him thus to have gained the gifts of immortality and perpetual youth. As Glanvill tells the story, the scholar, in a chance meeting with three friends of his college days, "told them that the people he went with were not such impostors as they were taken for, but that they had a traditional kind of learning among them, and could do wonders by the power of imagination, their fancy binding that of others. . . ." We are immediately put in mind of Lawrence's interest in the ancient "dark" peoples — Etruscans, Aztecs, and the gypsies themselves — to whom Lawrence turns for ancient wisdom and continuing organic power. Yeats too involves himself in occult, esoteric knowledges, and Eliot finds power in ritual, magic, and myth, and in ancient Indian thought.

For Arnold, the dominance of the rational intellect, the loss of the old intuitive knowledge, is the sign of the aging and decay not merely of the individual but of the whole culture. Fancying that he has caught a glimpse of the scholar wandering still through the woods around nineteenth-century Oxford, he cries out to him in warning:

But fly our paths, our feverish contact fly!
For strong the infection of our mental strife,
Which, though it gives no bliss, yet spoils for rest;
And we should win thee from thy own fair life,
Like us distracted, and like us unblessed.
Soon, soon thy cheer would die,
Thy hopes grow timorous, and unfixed thy powers,
And thy clear aims be cross and shifting made;
And then thy glad perennial youth would fade,
Fade, and grow old at last, and die like ours.

That the legend upon which he bases his poem has its source in the seventeenth century is of great importance to Arnold, and he writes with the strong nostalgic sense of the youthfulness of that former time, of the "days when wits were fresh and clear, / And life ran gaily as the sparkling Thames." In similar fashion — perhaps even with a reminiscence of "The Scholar Gypsy" — Eliot in *The Waste Land* gives us a picture of the Thames in Elizabethan days, contrasting it with the soiled, sad river of our own day. The awareness, or imagination, of the lost virtue of a richer, freer life in the past, and not necessarily in the far-distant past of a far-off land, is an element also of the thought of Yeats and Lawrence. Yeats looks back to the Anglo-Irish culture of eighteenth-century Dublin as a golden age, and Lawrence, among the many other times and cultures to which he turns, includes the England of Jane Austen. In *Women in Love,* Birkin and Ursula have found in the market an old chair of birchwood, simple and beautiful, and Birkin (who "is" Lawrence) speaks of it in this way:

"So beautiful, so pure!" Birkin said. "It almost breaks my heart. . . . My beloved country — it had something to express even when it made that chair."

"And hasn't it now?" asked Ursula. She was always angry when he took this tone.

"No, it hasn't. When I see that clear, beautiful chair, and I think of England, even Jane Austen's England — it had living thoughts to unfold even then, and pure happiness in unfolding them. And now, we can only fish among the rubbish heaps for the remnants of their old expression. There is no production in us now, only sordid and foul mechanicalness."

Lawrence's word "mechanicalness" leads us to another cause of Arnold's sense of loss. The "mechanicalness" of the universe as conceived of by science seemed to be reflected in the mechanicalness of social life itself. In this feeling, actual mechanical contrivances played a large part. The Industrial Revolution, which had been brought about by — or which itself had brought about — the increased invention of machinery, is no doubt all too frequently invoked as being responsible for all the emotional troubles that have occurred since its inception. Yet the image of the factory, the emblem of the machine, were always present in the minds of the men of the nineteenth century as, indeed, they are in the minds of the men of the twentieth. And for all the sentimentality that is likely to inhere in the harsh words we use about the factory and the machine, we are right to have them so centrally in our thought. It is indisputable that they made a substantive difference in the relation between men and their work, and a difference no less great in the relation of men to their fellows. What Lawrence meant when he had his hero admire the handmade chair was what Lawrence had learned from the teachers and "prophets" of the nineteenth century, especially from Ruskin, the idea of the moral relation between men and their work, between men and the things they make with their own hands and minds.

Possibly of even wider significance is the effect which the Industrial Revolution had upon the large aspects of social life. Industrialism brought the great city as we nowadays know it, the overgrown, sordid, sprawling city, of men living together in hitherto unknown numbers. The smaller units of social life — the estate, the farm, the town, the small compact city of earlier times — ceased to be typical of England. The old forms of social organization, more or less intimate, were lost, and the emotions which tied men to particular localities and to the people in them seemed less and less relevant to the modern situation. And those who had something to gain from the new system felt free to say that the only bond between man and man was the "cash nexus," the wages paid when work was done, and that what they called the "iron law of wages" was not to be tampered with. The mechanistic conception of the universe was made to serve as the model for the conception of the economic and social life of man, and to certain theorists of the manufacturing class, any interference with the "laws" of economics, any attempt to be one's brother's keeper, was a step toward anarchy and ruin.

In the light of this ever-accelerating revision of the old social arrangements we can understand the repeated note of loneliness in Arnold's poetry. He speaks of men as being "in the sea of life enisled" — they are, in the literal sense of the word, isolated, sundered from each other by the "unplumbed, salt, estranging sea" of modern society. The incident of the affair with Marguerite, whether it was actual or only a poetic fantasy, serves as the occasion for hopelessness over the possibility of two souls truly and fully meeting.

I have referred to the influence of Wordsworth on Arnold's life and thought, and it is not surprising that Nature should have served Arnold as the principle which stood in opposition to all that was inorganic and "mechanical" in the life of his time. He never doubted the beneficent power of Nature in the simplest and most limited meaning of the word — in the sense, that is, of Wordsworth's "mighty world of ear and eye," the world of growing things. Nature as an aesthetic experience genuinely served him as an anodyne or even as a healing agent. The English countryside in its charm, which Arnold was inclined to see as already archaic, soothed and calmed him, no doubt in part because it spoke of a vanished time and way of life. The Alps in their majesty seemed always to him a "refuge." The procession of the stars was his symbol of law and duty. He had a passion for the clear water of flowing streams, which figures again and again in his verse, often as the contrast to the "heat" and "fever" of modern life.

It was inevitable that he should be led further in his dealings with Nature, that he should try to advance to the full Wordsworthian response to Nature as, if not actually divine, having something of the quality of divinity, as being the source of human values. Yet we cannot help feeling that this effort is rather more wistful than decisive. The image of Nature such as Spinoza gives it to us in his *Ethics* — a work which Arnold read with great attention in his college days — the image of Nature which must rationally be seen as indifferent to man and operating by laws not analogous to the laws of humanity, was too deeply ingrained in Arnold's thought to permit him to accept without reservation the Wordsworthian view.

I have spoken of Arnold's poetry as being, in

its characteristic mood, elegiac. Its most successful moments are those of melancholy and nostalgia, even of despair. Yet it is of the essence of elegy that it should pass beyond the expression of grief and move toward reconciliation. Certainly it was Arnold's conscious intention that his poetry should do this. If Arnold perceived a kind of sickness in the life of his time, he was not perversely and sentimentally attracted to it. He has no wish to be passive to the ideas that depress him. In one of his letters he says that what the men of his day want "is something to *animate* and ennoble them — not to add zest to their melancholy or grace to their dreams." His feeling is for energy and health, and his poems, as much as they dwell upon the reasons for despair, seek to find countervailing reasons for hope. And if they do not find what they seek, we may still say of them that they served to realize and discharge the negative emotions and made possible the affirmative qualities which become manifest in Arnold's prose.

It is significant that Arnold's first important writing in prose is his Preface to his *Poems* of 1853, a critical essay in which he explains why he is omitting one of the most important and extensive of his poems from this new collection of his work. The poem in question is "Empedocles on Etna," and Arnold tells us that he has excluded it because he could not approve of its psychological and moral effect upon the reader. He quotes with approval Schiller's dictum, "All Art is dedicated to Joy," and goes on to say that "Empedocles on Etna" cannot give joy, not because it is sad, but because it represents a situation in which "a continuous state of mental distress is prolonged, unrelieved by incident, hope, or resistance; in which there is everything to be endured, nothing to be done."

The sentence implies Arnold's whole position as a critic of literature. Arnold is concerned not merely with the nature and quality of the work under consideration but also with the effect of the work upon the reader and, eventually, upon the polity. In this concern Arnold is equally in the tradition of Plato and Aristotle, who, although their theories of poetry are radically opposed, yet agreed that a prime consideration of criticism must be the effect of the work upon the emotional and the moral *health* of the individual and the State. In his inaugural lecture as professor of poetry at Oxford, "On the Modern Element in Literature," Arnold continues and develops his preoccupation with the effect of literature. To be called great, he says, a work of literature must be both *adequate* and *fortifying*. The quality of "adequacy" refers to the intellectual completeness and cogency of a work; the "fortifying" quality refers to its power of giving the reader the energy and courage to confront a difficult world. In his lectures *On Translating Homer* he makes his well-known summary of the essential qualities of Homer, saying that these are rapidity of movement, plainness and directness of diction and syntax, plainness of thought, and nobility. And this characterization of Homer, which would seem to have only the poet in mind, actually implies the qualities that Arnold hoped to establish in the English culture of his time. His exposition of the "grand style" in art has in view the virtues of a grand style in life: Homer serves as the criterion of a middle class which Arnold characterized as being "drugged with business," small in its aims, petty in its view of the world. Many readers of Arnold's great and famous essay "On the Function of Criticism at the Present Time" have wondered whether Arnold means literary criticism at all, for so many of his examples are drawn from the actualities of social and political life rather than from literature.

Arnold saw it as a characteristic of the modern world that it was moved by ideas to an extent that had never before been known, and he conceived it to be the function of criticism to subject all ideas to examination and refinement and to make available the best ideas of past and present. Criticism, he said, is "a disinterested endeavor to learn and propagate the best that is known and thought in the world." Arnold's theory of criticism grows naturally into his more elaborate theory of "culture." What Arnold means by culture is most fully suggested by the word with which he links it in one of his best-known works, *Culture and Anarchy:* culture is that totality of the imaginative reason which must be applied to our social and political life if anarchy is not to prevail. What led him to imagine the possibility of anarchy was the unenlightened dominance of the middle classes in English life, their inability to deal in an imaginative and reasonable way with the rising power of an industrial proletariat, their lack of the generosity of mind which might lead them to conceive of the nation as an entity not to be judged by the criteria of their narrow class interest.

The power of the imaginative reason, the immediate necessity of bringing the imaginative reason to bear upon the conduct of practical life — this is what Arnold tried to make the people of England understand. It was to this end that in *Culture and Anarchy* he expounded the opposing ways of thought that he called "Hebraism" and "Hellenism," Hebraism being the way of the conscience and of religion, Hellenism being the way of intelligence and culture. Arnold is entirely sincere in saying that these two ways of dealing with the world are of equal value, but that at certain historical moments one is more appropriate than the other, more relevant to the given situation, more practical, and that at the moment at which he is writing what England needs is a great access of Hellenism, for of Hebraism it has a sufficiency and more than that. Arnold has in mind the sincere but narrow religion of the puritan middle classes of England which has the effect of preventing the free play of mind. The practical point that Arnold wishes to enforce is the desirability of establishing in England a strong State; against such an idea the middle classes have traditionally maintained the most intense opposition, and not without reason, for in their rise to power they had had to overcome the often indefensible restrictions put upon their liberty of conscience and action by the agencies of the State as it had been constituted since Tudor times. But the occasion for the middle-class fear of the State, Arnold argued, has long ago disappeared; the middle classes are no longer in danger of being oppressed, as once they were, by a State which represents the aristocracy. What culture suggests as necessary is a State which, while representing all the classes — the newly enfranchised working class as well as the middle class and the aristocracy — shall be superior to all classes by being the representation of what Arnold calls "the best self" of each, and which will thus serve as the principle of authority and the agency of organization for the whole nation. Some readers have been inclined to criticize Arnold's theory of the State as being too idealistic for practice, yet the fact is that, taking into account all the hostilities of actual politics, all the acrimonies of class opposition, the nature of the English State became substantially what Arnold hoped it would be, and England, at a time of crisis, has achieved a greater degree of national unity than might ever have been supposed possible from an inspection of its class structure.

Arnold's opposing Hellenism to Hebraism, culture to religion, made him seem in the eyes of many an avowed enemy of religion, perhaps the more effective because he was so gentle and good-natured a foe. The judgment was not accurate. To certain forms of religion Arnold was indeed hostile, yet it is clear that his very conception of culture itself had in it a strong infusion of religious assumption. Culture, he said, has for its prime function the task of making "reason and the will of God prevail," and the phrase, "the will of God," was not for Arnold a mere manner of speaking. He meant it sincerely, even though he did not mean it as the average religious Englishman of his time meant it. For all his quarrels with religion, Arnold loved religion, even those aspects of it to which he could not give his assent. So much so, indeed, that for some ten years after *Culture and Anarchy,* Arnold devoted himself to the attempt to make religion real and acceptable at a time when, as he believed, it was in danger of being despised and dismissed by many. He undertook to purge religion of all the elements that might confuse or repel the modern mind. What his method was may almost be inferred in its entirety from the title of his book about the Bible, *Literature and Dogma*. The Bible, Arnold said, is not to be understood as dogma or the source of dogma — not to be understood, that is, as making statements of a scientific or quasi-scientific or metaphysical kind. Rather, it is to be understood as literature, as the greatest poetry on the greatest of subjects, which is man's effort to live the good life and to be in a right relation to God. Whatever in the Bible seems to controvert reason or science is to be understood by the aid of our historical imagination, as having been uttered by men who were inevitably conditioned by their time and place, as we are by ours, who used the scientific or philosophic concepts that were available to them, and the forms of language that were theirs. Concepts change and forms of language change, but what does not ever change, Arnold insisted, is the essential nature of the moral life and its central importance. The truth of the Bible is for him a moral truth, and its utterance is, if properly understood, an inspired utterance. The unchanging truth of the Bible is a simple truth — that righteousness makes for life. In the light of its simplicity Arnold defines religion as being in its essence "morality touched with emotion," and he defines God "as the power not ourselves that makes for righteousness." Whatever in religion seems to the modern mind extraneous to this moral essence is to be sympathetically comprehended as the result of the effort, sometimes excessive or misguided, to make morality real and present and moving to mankind — to touch it, that is, with a sufficiently powerful emotion.

In its day Arnold's religious writing won a very considerable acceptance from people who, doubting one or another aspect of religion, were nevertheless reluctant to abandon their faith, who felt that life without some sense of connection with the Divine would be lacking in meaning, grace, and fullness. People of full religious commitment, however, have never been able to grant that Arnold's religious writings have very much to do with religion as they know and experience it. Arnold undertook to relieve religion of its intellectual difficulties, and it may indeed be true, as many feel, that the intellectual difficulties are of the very essence of religion. Yet Arnold's religious writings do still speak to men who, unable to accept dogma and orthodoxy, are yet impelled to connect their moral commitment and their passion for human good and their vision of human fate with something beyond the merely temporal and the wholly conditioned. It is the fashion nowadays to represent Arnold's work on religion as naïve, yet it is worth remarking that when in our day a man so little susceptible to the accusation of naïveté as André Gide speculates upon the large ultimate questions, doing so in a culture pre-eminent for its religious and philosophical sophistication, his conclusions of faith are like no one's so much as Matthew Arnold's.

With his religious writings the pattern of Arnold's intellectual life was complete. He had moved from poetry to literary criticism, thence to politics, thence to religion; each stage of his activity grows with a charming logicality out of the one before, and perhaps as much as anything else that accounts for his continuing interest for us, it is this unity of his life in its diverse activities. Arnold's last decade of work — and he worked, and at his best, up to the very end — is chiefly given to literary criticism. In these last great essays — which include "The Study of Poetry," "Literature and Science," and the essays on the Romantic poets — Arnold is more than ever committed to the idea of the importance of literature in the modern world, of the imaginative reason as a practical power in the social and political life of man. With one or another point of literary doctrine we now inevitably disagree — we do not think it obvious that Wordsworth is only interesting in his shorter poems, and we regard with astonishment Arnold's judgment of Keats's letters as vulgar. Yet quarrel with these essays as we may — and should — we can never ignore them, for we know that they still express, as once they helped to form, the best of our modern feeling about literature.

The dates of the composition of Arnold's poems cannot be established with any satisfactory degree of accuracy. The dates in brackets at the end of each poem indicate the year in which the poem was first published.

### Reading Suggestions

EDITIONS

C. B. Tinker and H. F. Lowry, *The Poetical Works of Matthew Arnold* (1950). The standard edition of Arnold's complete poetical works.

BIOGRAPHY

Arnold forbade that any biography of him be written, and none has been written. For the main facts of Arnold's life, consult the works of Louis Bonnerot and Lionel Trilling listed under *criticism.*

LETTERS AND NOTEBOOKS

G. W. E. Russell, editor, *Letters of Matthew Arnold, 1848–1888,* 2 vols. (1895). Howard Foster Lowry, editor, *The Letters of Matthew Arnold to Arthur Hugh Clough* (1932). The letters to Clough, fully and admirably annotated, make the best possible introduction to Arnold as a personality.

Howard Foster Lowry, Karl Young, and Waldo Hilary Dunn, *The Notebooks of Matthew Arnold* (1952). Arnold's notes of his reading in six languages from 1852 until his death.

COMMENTARY

Chauncey Brewster Tinker and Howard Lowry, *The Poetry of Matthew Arnold: A Commentary* (1940). A useful handbook to Arnold's verse.

CRITICISM

R. H. Hutton, "The Two Great Oxford Thinkers, Cardinal Newman and Matthew Arnold," in *Essays on Some of the Modern Guides of English Thought on Matters of Faith* (1887); and "The Poetry of Matthew Arnold," in *Essays in Literary Criticism* (1888). Essays by an intelligent and too-little-known contemporary who respected Arnold but differed from him.

John Dewey, "Arnold and Browning," in vol. i of *Characters and Events* (1929).

H. W. Garrod, *Poetry and the Criticism of Life* (1931). An excellent discussion of some of Arnold's critical principles by one of his successors in the chair of poetry at Oxford.

T. S. Eliot, "Arnold and Pater," in *Selected Essays* (1932); and "Matthew Arnold," in *The Use of Poetry and the Use of Criticism* (1932). Two essays by the poet and critic whose criticism holds the place in our literary life that Arnold's held in his time.

F. R. Leavis, "Arnold as Critic," in the English critical review, *Scrutiny* (December, 1938). The essay is reprinted in *The Importance of Scrutiny,* edited by Eric Bentley (1948). A very useful essay by the well-known English critic.

Lionel Trilling, *Matthew Arnold* (1939). An account by the present editor of the development and background of Arnold's thought.

Louis Bonnerot, *Matthew Arnold, Essai de Biographie Psychologique* (1947). A sympathetic account, by an eminent French scholar, of Arnold's emotional and intellectual life.

# THE STRAYED REVELER

"The Strayed Reveler," the quasi-dramatic poem from which Arnold's first volume took its title, is unlike any other of his poems in its imagistic clarity and vivaciousness. Its verse form — unrhymed lines that are cadenced rather than metrical — is daring and singularly successful. Arnold was to use the form, in one or another variation, in other poems, but perhaps it shows to best advantage here. The theme of the poem is that of the initiation of a young man into the life of poetry. Much of its point and charm derive from Arnold's divergence from the characterization of Circe as given in *The Odyssey*. Homer represents her as a beautiful sorceress; when Ulysses, returning from the Trojan war, visited her island, his companions rushed headlong into the voluptuousness which marked her way of life and were changed by her potions into swine. Ulysses, protected from her charms by the magic herb called moly which had been given to him by Mercury, forced her at the point of his sword to restore his men to human form, and then spent a year of luxury and sensuality with her, forgetful of his home and glory. But Arnold gives us a Circe who is a goddess rather than a sorceress and who, although not without her sensual charm, has no interest in turning men into swine. She is, rather, tender and solicitous of the youthful shepherd poet, and her wine brings him the great poetic visions he desires.

*The Portico of Circe's Palace. Evening*

A YOUTH. CIRCE

THE YOUTH

Faster, faster,
O Circe, Goddess,
Let the wild, thronging train,
The bright procession
Of eddying forms,
Sweep through my soul!
Thou standest, smiling
Down on me! thy right arm,
Leaned up against the column there,
Props thy soft cheek;
Thy left holds, hanging loosely,
The deep cup, ivy-cinctured,
I held but now.

Is it, then, evening
So soon? I see, the night dews,
Clustered in thick beads, dim
The agate brooch stones
On thy white shoulder;
The cool night wind, too,
Blows through the portico,
Stirs thy hair, Goddess,
Waves thy white robe!

CIRCE

Whence art thou, sleeper?

THE YOUTH

When the white dawn first
Through the rough fir planks
Of my hut, by the chestnuts,
Up at the valley head,
Came breaking, Goddess!
I sprang up, I threw round me
My dappled fawn skin;
Passing out, from the wet turf,
Where they lay, by the hut door,
I snatched up my vine crown, my fir staff,
All drenched in dew —
Came swift down to join
The rout early gathered
In the town, round the temple,
Iacchus' white fane
On yonder hill.

STRAYED REVELER. **38. Iacchus:** another name for Bacchus, or Dionysus, often used to suggest the god in his more spiritual aspect.

Quick I passed, following
The woodcutters' cart track
Down the dark valley; — I saw
On my left, through the beeches,
Thy palace, Goddess,
Smokeless, empty!
Trembling, I entered; beheld
The court all silent,
The lions sleeping,
On the altar this bowl.
I drank, Goddess!
And sank down here, sleeping,
On the steps of thy portico.

CIRCE

Foolish boy! Why tremblest thou?
Thou lovest it, then, my wine?
Wouldst more of it? See, how glows,
Through the delicate, flushed marble,
The red, creaming liquor,
Strown with dark seeds!
Drink, then! I chide thee not,
Deny thee not my bowl.
Come, stretch forth thy hand, then — so!
Drink — drink again!

THE YOUTH

Thanks, gracious one!
Ah, the sweet fumes again!
More soft, ah me,
More subtle-winding
Than Pan's flute music!
Faint — faint! Ah me,
Again the sweet sleep!

CIRCE

Hist! Thou — within there!
Come forth, Ulysses!
Art tired with hunting?
While we range the woodland,
See what the day brings.

ULYSSES

Ever new magic!
Hast thou then lured hither,
Wonderful Goddess, by thy art,
The young, languid-eyed Ampelus,
Iacchus' darling —
Or some youth beloved of Pan,
Of Pan and the Nymphs?
That he sits, bending downward
His white, delicate neck
To the ivy-wreathed marge
Of thy cup; the bright, glancing vine leaves
That crown his hair,
Falling forward, mingling
With the dark ivy plants —
His fawn skin, half untied,
Smeared with red wine stains? Who is he,
That he sits, overweighed
By fumes of wine and sleep,
So late, in thy portico?
What youth, Goddess — what guest
Of Gods or mortals?

CIRCE

Hist! he wakes
I lured him not hither, Ulysses.
Nay, ask him!

THE YOUTH

Who speaks? Ah, who comes forth
To thy side, Goddess, from within?
How shall I name him?
This spare, dark-featured,
Quick-eyed stranger?
Ah, and I see too
His sailor's bonnet,
His short coat, travel-tarnished,
With one arm bare! —
Art thou not he, whom fame
This long time rumors
The favored guest of Circe, brought by the waves?
Art thou he, stranger?
The wise Ulysses,
Laertes' son?

ULYSSES

I am Ulysses.
And thou, too, sleeper?
Thy voice is sweet.
It may be thou hast followed
Through the islands some divine bard,
By age taught many things,
Age and the Muses;
And heard him delighting
The chiefs and people
In the banquet, and learned his songs,
Of Gods and heroes,
Of war and arts,
And peopled cities,
Inland, or built
By the gray sea. — If so, then hail!
I honor and welcome thee.

THE YOUTH

The Gods are happy.
They turn on all sides
Their shining eyes,
And see below them
The earth and men.

**78. Ampelus:** a boy, son of a satyr and a nymph, who was a favorite of Bacchus. After his death he became a constellation.

They see Tiresias
Sitting, staff in hand,
On the warm, grassy
Asopus bank,
His robe drawn over
His old, sightless head,
Revolving inly
The doom of Thebes.

They see the centaurs
In the upper glens
Of Pelion, in the streams,
Where red-berried ashes fringe
The clear brown shallow pools,
With streaming flanks, and heads
Reared proudly, snuffing
The mountain wind.

They see the Indian
Drifting, knife in hand,
His frail boat moored to
A floating isle thick-matted
With large-leaved, low-creeping melon plants,
And the dark cucumber.
He reaps, and stows them,
Drifting — drifting — round him,
Round his green harvest plot,
Flow the cool lake waves,
The mountains ring them.

They see the Scythian
On the wide steppe, unharnessing
His wheeled house at noon.
He tethers his beast down, and makes his meal —
Mares' milk, and bread
Baked on the embers; — all around
The boundless, waving grass plains stretch, thick-starred
With saffron and the yellow hollyhock
And flag-leaved iris flowers.
Sitting in his cart
He makes his meal; before him, for long miles,
Alive with bright green lizards,
And the springing bustard fowl,
The track, a straight black line,
Furrows the rich soil; here and there
Clusters of lonely mounds
Topped with rough-hewn,
Gray, rain-bleared statues, overpeer
The sunny waste.

They see the ferry
On the broad, clay-laden
Lone Chorasmian stream; — thereon,
With snort and strain,
Two horses, strongly swimming, tow
The ferryboat, with woven ropes
To either bow
Firm harnessed by the mane; a chief,
With shout and shaken spear,
Stands at the prow, and guides them; but astern
The cowering merchants, in long robes,
Sit pale beside their wealth
Of silk bales and balsam drops,
Of gold and ivory,
Of turquoise-earth and amethyst,
Jasper and chalcedony,
And milk-barred onyx stones.
The loaded boat swings groaning
In the yellow eddies;
The Gods behold them.
They see the heroes
Sitting in the dark ship
On the foamless, long-heaving
Violet sea,
At sunset nearing
The Happy Islands.

These things, Ulysses,
The wise bards also
Behold and sing.
But oh, what labor!
O prince, what pain!

They too can see
Tiresias; — but the Gods,
Who give them vision,
Added this law:
That they should bear too
His groping blindness,
His dark foreboding,
His scorned white hairs;
Bear Hera's anger
Through a life lengthened
To seven ages.

**135. Tiresias:** a celebrated prophet of Thebes who lived to an extraordinary age. He figures in Sophocles' *Oedipus the King* and in T. S. Eliot's *Waste Land*. See p. 831, below. **138. Asopus:** a river in Boeotia, Teresias' country. **142. Thebes:** principal city of Boeotia, the scene of *Oedipus the King* and other tragedies dealing with the fate of Oedipus' family. **145. Pelion:** a mountain in Thessaly on which the centaurs lived. **162. Scythian:** Scythia was the general name of the ancients for the northern part of Europe and Asia, much of it uninhabited, most of it unknown to the Greeks.

**183. Chorasmian stream:** the river Oxus, because it flows through the country anciently known as Chorasmia. See, below, the conclusion of Arnold's *Sohrab and Rustum*. **206. Happy Islands:** It was here that the heroes lived after death. **220. Hera's anger:** Hera, or Juno, punished Tiresias by blindness because he decided an argument in favor of Zeus, or Jupiter, rather than herself. The matter at issue was whether men or women derived the greater pleasure from sexuality, and the question was put to Tiresias because, according to the legend, he had been for a time transformed into a woman. It was his opinion that women's pleasure was ten times greater than that of men. To compensate him for the loss of his eyesight, Jupiter bestowed on him the gift of prophecy.

They see the centaurs
On Pelion; — then they feel,
They too, the maddening wine
Swell their large veins to bursting; in wild pain
They feel the biting spears
Of the grim Lapithae, and Theseus, drive,
Drive crashing through their bones; they feel
High on a jutting rock in the red stream
Alcmena's dreadful son
Ply his bow; — such a price
The Gods exact for song:
To become what we sing.

They see the Indian
On his mountain lake; but squalls
Make their skiff reel, and worms
In the unkind spring have gnawn
Their melon harvest to the heart. — They see
The Scythian; but long frosts
Parch them in wintertime on the bare steppe,
Till they too fade like grass; they crawl
Like shadows forth in spring.

They see the merchants
On the Oxus stream; — but care
Must visit first them too, and make them pale.
Whether, through whirling sand,
A cloud of desert robber-horse have burst
Upon their caravan; or greedy kings,
In the walled cities the way passes through,
Crushed them with tolls; or fever airs,
On some great river's marge,
Mown them down, far from home.

They see the heroes
Near harbor; — but they share
Their lives, and former violent toil in Thebes,
Seven-gated Thebes, or Troy;
Or where the echoing oars
Of Argo first
Startled the unknown sea.

The old Silenus
Came, lolling in the sunshine,
From the dewy forest coverts,
This way, at noon.
Sitting by me, while his Fauns
Down at the waterside
Sprinkled and smoothed
His drooping garland,
He told me these things.

But I, Ulysses,
Sitting on the warm steps,
Looking over the valley,
All day long, have seen,
Without pain, without labor,
Sometimes a wild-haired Maenad —
Sometimes a Faun with torches —
And sometimes, for a moment,
Passing through the dark stems
Flowing-robed, the beloved,
The desired, the divine,
Beloved Iacchus.

Ah, cool night wind, tremulous stars!
Ah, glimmering water,
Fitful earth murmur,
Dreaming woods!
Ah, golden-haired, strangely smiling Goddess,
And thou, proved, much enduring,
Wave-tossed wanderer!
Who can stand still?
Ye fade, ye swim, ye waver before me —
The cup again!

Faster, faster,
O Circe, Goddess,
Let the wild, thronging train,
The bright procession
Of eddying forms,
Sweep through my soul!
[*1849*]

## TO A FRIEND

Who prop, thou ask'st, in these bad days, my mind? —
He much, the old man, who, clearest-souled of men,
Saw the Wide Prospect, and the Asian Fen,
And Tmolus hill, and Smyrna bay, though blind.

**228. Lapithae:** the Lapiths were a people in Thessaly who invited the centaurs to the marriage of one of their number. One of the centaurs got drunk at the party and made rough advances to the bride. This resulted in a battle which was frequently described in ancient poetry and represented in art. The Lapiths were said to have invented bits and bridles for horses. **Theseus:** the famous king of Athens who was the hero of many Greek stories. He was present at the battle between the Lapiths and the centaurs, aiding the Lapiths, whose guest he was, for the bridegroom was Parithous, his close friend and his companion in many adventures. **231. Alcmena's . . . son:** Hercules, who also fought the centaurs. **259. Argo:** the name of the ship of the adventuring Argonauts who, under the command of Jason, sailed to capture the Golden Fleece. **261. Silenus:** a faun or satyr, the nurse, teacher, and constant companion of Bacchus. He is represented as a fat, jolly, old man riding on an ass.

**275. Maenad:** a priestess of Bacchus. The name derives from the Greek word meaning "to be furious" and suggests the behavior of the women who celebrated the Bacchic rites. TO A FRIEND. The friend is probably Arthur Hugh Clough. **1–4. Who . . . blind:** The blind old man of the first quatrain is Homer. **3. Wide . . . Fen:** Arnold explained the line in this note: "The name Europe (Εὐρώπη, *the wide prospect*) probably describes the appearance of the European coast to the Greeks on the coast of Asia Minor opposite. The name Asia, again, comes, it has been thought, from the muddy fens of the rivers of Asia Minor, such as the Cayster or Maeander, which struck the imagination of the Greeks living near them." **4. Tmolus . . . Smyrna:** Tmolus, a mountain range in Asia Minor near Smyrna, one of the seven cities which claimed the honor of being Homer's birthplace.

Much he, whose friendship I not long since won,
That halting slave, who in Nicopolis
Taught Arrian, when Vespasian's brutal son
Cleared Rome of what most shamed him. But be
his

My special thanks, whose even-balanced soul,
From first youth tested up to extreme old age,
Business could not make dull, nor passion wild;

Who saw life steadily, and saw it whole;
The mellow glory of the Attic stage,
Singer of sweet Colonus, and its child.
[*1849*]

## SHAKESPEARE

Others abide our question. Thou art free.
We ask and ask — Thou smilest and art still,
Out-topping knowledge. For the loftiest hill,
Who to the stars uncrowns his majesty,

Planting his steadfast footsteps in the sea,
Making the heaven of heavens his dwelling place,
Spares but the cloudy border of his base
To the foiled searching of mortality;

And thou, who didst the stars and sunbeams know,
Self-schooled, self-scanned, self-honored, self-secure,
Didst tread on earth unguessed at. — Better so!

All pains the immortal spirit must endure,
All weakness which impairs, all griefs which bow,
Find their sole speech in that victorious brow.
[*1849*]

## WRITTEN IN BUTLER'S SERMONS

Affections, instincts, principles, and powers,
Impulse and reason, freedom and control —
So men, unraveling God's harmonious whole,
Rend in a thousand shreds this life of ours.

Vain labor! Deep and broad, where none may see,
Spring the foundations of that shadowy throne
Where man's one nature, queenlike, sits alone,
Centered in a majestic unity;

And rays her powers, like sister islands seen
Linking their coral arms under the sea,
Or clustered peaks with plunging gulfs between

Spanned by aërial arches all of gold,
Whereo'er the chariot wheels of life are rolled
In cloudy circles to eternity.
[*1849*]

## IN HARMONY WITH NATURE

*To a Preacher*

"In harmony with Nature?" Restless fool,
Who with such heat dost preach what were to
thee,
When true, the last impossibility —
To be like Nature strong, like Nature cool!

Know, man hath all which Nature hath, but more,
And in that *more* lie all his hopes of good.
Nature is cruel, man is sick of blood;
Nature is stubborn, man would fain adore;

Nature is fickle, man hath need of rest;
Nature forgives no debt, and fears no grave;
Man would be mild, and with safe conscience
blessed.

Man must begin, know this, where Nature ends;
Nature and man can never be fast friends.
Fool, if thou canst not pass her, rest her slave!
[*1849*]

## TO A REPUBLICAN FRIEND, 1848

God knows it, I am with you. If to prize
Those virtues, prized and practiced by too
few,
But prized, but loved, but eminent in you,
Man's fundamental life; if to despise

The barren optimistic sophistries
Of comfortable moles, whom what they do

**6. halting slave:** Epictetus, the Greek Stoic philosopher, who was lame, was a liberated slave who taught philosophy at Rome. **6–8. Nicopolis . . . him:** Nicopolis was the city to which Epictetus went when the Emperor Domitian, son of the Emperor Vespasian, issued an edict banishing all philosophers from Rome. Arrian was his pupil who summarized and preserved the teachings of his master. **8–14. But . . . child:** It is for Sophocles that Arnold reserves his special thanks. Colonus, a suburb of Athens, was the birthplace of Sophocles and the scene of Sophocles' last play, *Oedipus at Colonus,* written when he was nearly ninety, in which the town is the object of beautiful praise. **BUTLER'S SERMONS.** Joseph Butler (1692–1752), a bishop of the Church of England, was perhaps the most famous and influential of English theologians of the eighteenth century. He is best known for his *Analogy of Religion, Natural and Revealed, to the Constitution and Course of Nature,* but his *Sermons* were also highly prized. Butler was required reading for undergraduates at Oxford in Arnold's day. As the poem implies, he is an exponent of the "faculty psychology" of the eighteenth century, which taught that the mind is composed of certain powers, such as will and reason, each of which has a particular discrete function in mental activity. **REPUBLICAN FRIEND.** Arthur Hugh Clough, who witnessed the 1848 Revolution in Paris and was generally in sympathy with it.

Teaches the limit of the just and true
(And for such doing they require not eyes);

If sadness at the long heart-wasting show
Wherein earth's great ones are disquieted;
If thoughts, not idle, while before me flow

The armies of the homeless and unfed —
If these are yours, if this is what you are,
Then am I yours, and what you feel, I share.

[*1849*]

## TO A REPUBLICAN FRIEND, 1848, CONTINUED

Yet, when I muse on what life is, I seem
Rather to patience prompted, than that proud
Prospect of hope which France proclaims so loud —
France, famed in all great arts, in none supreme;

Seeing this vale, this earth, whereon we dream,
Is on all sides o'ershadowed by the high
Uno'erleaped Mountains of Necessity,
Sparing us narrower margin than we deem.

Nor will that day dawn at a human nod,
When, bursting through the network superposed
By selfish occupation — plot and plan,

Lust, avarice, envy — liberated man,
All difference with his fellow mortal closed,
Shall be left standing face to face with God.

[*1849*]

## RELIGIOUS ISOLATION

*To the Same Friend*

Children (as such forgive them) have I known,
Ever in their own eager pastime bent
To make the incurious bystander, intent
On his own swarming thoughts, an interest own —

Too fearful or too fond to play alone.
Do thou, whom light in thine own inmost soul
(Not less thy boast) illuminates, control
Wishes unworthy of a man full-grown.

What though the holy secret, which molds thee,
Mold not the solid earth? though never winds
Have whispered it to the complaining sea,

Nature's great law, and law of all men's minds? —
To its own impulse every creature stirs;
Live by thy light, and earth will live by hers!

[*1849*]

## THE FORSAKEN MERMAN

Although Arnold usually indicates the sources of the stories and legends that he uses, he tells us nothing of how he derived the subject of "The Forsaken Merman." The story is of Danish origin and is told in a Danish ballad, "The Deceived Merman." Arnold may have become acquainted with it through the reference which Hans Christian Andersen makes to it in his autobiography, of which an English translation appeared in 1847. George Borrow had translated the ballad in his *Romantic Ballads Translated from the Danish,* published in 1826, and the year before he had given a prose version of it in a magazine review of a book of Danish folk tales. The story is an inversion of the more familiar Undine legend, in which a girl, a lovely habitant of the waters, lives for a time with the people of earth, and it is one of many stories — Keats's "La Belle Dame sans Merci" is another — which tell of the unhappiness which results from the meeting of the creatures of diverse elements.

From the first, "The Forsaken Merman" was one of the most popular of Arnold's poems. Although it intrudes no meaning beyond the pathos of the given situation, it can scarcely be read without reference to Arnold's reiterated melancholy over the desolation of modern man, and of course it is not without significance that the suffering speaker in the poem should be a king of the sea, of what Arnold called the "estranging sea," which was so often for him the symbol of loneliness.

Come, dear children, let us away;
Down and away below!
Now my brothers call from the bay,
Now the great winds shoreward blow,
Now the salt tides seaward flow;
Now the wild white horses play,
Champ and chafe and toss in the spray.
Children dear, let us away!
This way, this way!

Call her once before you go —
Call once yet!
In a voice that she will know:
"Margaret! Margaret!"
Children's voices should be dear
(Call once more) to a mother's ear;
Children's voices, wild with pain —
Surely she will come again!
Call her once and come away;
This way, this way!
"Mother dear, we cannot stay!
The wild white horses foam and fret."
Margaret! Margaret!

Come, dear children, come away down;
Call no more!
One last look at the white-walled town,

And the little gray church on the windy shore,
Then come down!
She will not come though you call all day;
Come away, come away!

Children dear, was it yesterday
We heard the sweet bells over the bay?
In the caverns where we lay,
Through the surf and through the swell,
The far-off sound of a silver bell?
Sand-strewn caverns, cool and deep,
Where the winds are all asleep;
Where the spent lights quiver and gleam,
Where the salt weed sways in the stream,
Where the sea beasts, raged all round,
Feed in the ooze of their pasture ground;
Where the sea snakes coil and twine,
Dry their mail and bask in the brine;
Where great whales come sailing by,
Sail and sail, with unshut eye,
Round the world for ever and aye?
When did music come this way?
Children dear, was it yesterday?

Children dear, was it yesterday
(Call yet once) that she went away?
Once she sate with you and me,
On a red gold throne in the heart of the sea,
And the youngest sate on her knee.
She combed its bright hair, and she tended it well,
When down swung the sound of a far-off bell.
She sighed, she looked up through the clear green sea;
She said: "I must go, for my kinsfolk pray
In the little gray church on the shore today.
'Twill be Easter time in the world—ah me!
And I lose my poor soul, Merman! here with thee."
I said: "Go up, dear heart, through the waves;
Say thy prayer, and come back to the kind sea caves!"
She smiled, she went up through the surf in the bay.
Children dear, was it yesterday?

Children dear, were we long alone?
"The sea grows stormy, the little ones moan.
Long prayers," I said, "in the world they say;
Come!" I said; and we rose through the surf in the bay.
We went up the beach, by the sandy down
Where the sea stocks bloom, to the white-walled town;
Through the narrow paved streets, where all was still,
To the little gray church on the windy hill.
From the church came a murmur of folk at their prayers,
But we stood without in the cold blowing airs.
We climbed on the graves, on the stones worn with rains,
And we gazed up the aisle through the small leaded panes.
She sate by the pillar; we saw her clear:
"Margaret, hist! come quick, we are here!
Dear heart," I said, "we are long alone;
The sea grows stormy, the little ones moan."
But, ah, she gave me never a look,
For her eyes were sealed to the holy book!
Loud prays the priest; shut stands the door.
Come away, children, call no more!
Come away, come down, call no more!

Down, down, down!
Down to the depths of the sea!
She sits at her wheel in the humming town,
Singing most joyfully.
Hark, what she sings: "O joy, O joy,
For the humming street, and the child with its toy!
For the priest, and the bell, and the holy well,
For the wheel where I spun,
And the blessed light of the sun!"
And so she sings her fill,
Singing most joyfully,
Till the shuttle falls from her hand,
And the whizzing wheel stands still.
She steals to the window, and looks at the sand,
And over the sand at the sea;
And her eyes are set in a stare;
And anon there breaks a sigh,
And anon there drops a tear,
From a sorrow-clouded eye,
And a heart sorrow-laden,
A long, long sigh,
For the cold strange eyes of a little Mermaiden,
And the gleam of her golden hair.

Come away, away, children!
Come children, come down!
The hoarse wind blows coldly;
Lights shine in the town.
She will start from her slumber
When gusts shake the door;
She will hear the winds howling,
Will hear the waves roar.
We shall see, while above us
The waves roar and whirl,
A ceiling of amber,
A pavement of pearl.
Singing: "Here came a mortal,
But faithless was she!
And alone dwell forever
The kings of the sea."

But, children, at midnight,
When soft the winds blow,
When clear falls the moonlight,
When spring tides are low;
When sweet airs come seaward
From heaths starred with broom,
And high rocks throw mildly
On the blanched sands a gloom;
Up the still, glistening beaches,
Up the creeks we will hie,
Over banks of bright seaweed
The ebb tide leaves dry.
We will gaze, from the sand hills,
At the white, sleeping town;
At the church on the hillside —
And then come back down.
Singing: "There dwells a loved one,
But cruel is she!
She left lonely forever
The kings of the sea."
[*1849*]

## URANIA

I too have suffered; yet I know
She is not cold, though she seems so.
She is not cold, she is not light;
But our ignoble souls lack might.

She smiles and smiles, and will not sigh,
While we for hopeless passion die;
Yet she could love, those eyes declare,
Were but men nobler than they are.

Eagerly once her gracious ken
Was turned upon the sons of men;
But light the serious visage grew —
She looked, and smiled, and saw them through.

Our petty souls, our strutting wits,
Our labored, puny passion fits —
Ah, may she scorn them still, till we
Scorn them as bitterly as she!

Yet show her once, ye heavenly Powers,
One of some worthier race than ours!
One for whose sake she once might prove
How deeply she who scorns can love.

His eyes be like the starry lights —
His voice like sounds of summer nights —
In all his lovely mien let pierce
The magic of the universe!

And she to him will reach her hand,
And gazing in his eyes will stand,
And know her friend, and weep for glee,
And cry: *Long, long I've looked for thee.*

Then will she weep; with smiles, till then,
Coldly she mocks the sons of men.
Till then, her lovely eyes maintain
Their pure, unwavering, deep disdain.
[*1852*]

URANIA. The Muse of astronomy and the heavenly forces — her name means "the Heavenly One."

## EUPHROSYNE

I must not say that thou wast true,
Yet let me say that thou wast fair;
And they, that lovely face who view,
Why should they ask if truth be there?

Truth — what is truth? Two bleeding hearts,
Wounded by men, by fortune tried,
Outwearied with their lonely parts,
Vow to beat henceforth side by side.

The world to them was stern and drear
Their lot was but to weep and moan.
Ah, let them keep their faith sincere,
For neither could subsist alone!

But souls whom some benignant breath
Hath charmed at birth from gloom and care,
These ask no love, these plight no faith,
For they are happy as they are.

The world to them may homage make,
And garlands for their forehead weave;
And what the world can give, they take —
But they bring more than they receive.

They shine upon the world! Their ears
To one demand alone are coy;
They will not give us love and tears,
They bring us light and warmth and joy.

It was not love which heaved thy breast,
Fair child! — it was the bliss within.
Adieu! and say that one, at least,
Was just to what he did not win.
[*1852*]

EUPHROSYNE. In Greek mythology, one of the three Graces Her name means "mirth."

## MEETING

Again I see my bliss at hand,
The town, the lake are here;

My Marguerite smiles upon the strand,
Unaltered with the year.

I know that graceful figure fair,
That cheek of languid hue;
I know that soft, enkerchiefed hair,
And those sweet eyes of blue.

Again I spring to make my choice;
Again in tones of ire
I hear a God's tremendous voice:
" Be counseled, and retire."

Ye guiding Powers who join and part,
What would ye have with me?
Ah, warn some more ambitious heart,
And let the peaceful be!

[*1852*]

## A FAREWELL

My horse's feet beside the lake,
Where sweet the unbroken moonbeams lay,
Sent echoes through the night to wake
Each glistening strand, each heath-fringed bay.

The poplar avenue was passed,
And the roofed bridge that spans the stream;
Up the steep street I hurried fast,
Led by thy taper's starlike beam.

I came! I saw thee rise! — the blood
Poured flushing to thy languid cheek.
Locked in each other's arms we stood,
In tears, with hearts too full to speak.

Days flew; — ah, soon I could discern
A trouble in thine altered air!
Thy hand lay languidly in mine,
Thy cheek was grave, thy speech grew rare.

I blame thee not! — this heart, I know,
To be long loved was never framed;
For something in its depths doth glow
Too strange, too restless, too untamed.

And women — things that live and move
Mined by the fever of the soul —
They seek to find in those they love
Stern strength, and promise of control.

They ask not kindness, gentle ways —
These they themselves have tried and known;
They ask a soul which never sways
With the blind gusts that shake their own.

I too have felt the load I bore
In a too strong emotion's sway;
I too have wished, no woman more,
This starting, feverish heart away.

I too have longed for trenchant force,
And will like a dividing spear;
Have praised the keen, unscrupulous course,
Which knows no doubt, which feels no fear.

But in the world I learnt, what there
Thou too wilt surely one day prove,
That will, that energy, though rare,
Are yet far, far less rare than love.

Go, then! — till time and fate impress
This truth on thee, be mine no more!
They will! — for thou, I feel, not less
Than I, wast destined to this lore.

We school our manners, act our parts —
But He, who sees us through and through,
Knows that the bent of both our hearts
Was to be gentle, tranquil, true.

And though we wear out life, alas!
Distracted as a homeless wind,
In beating where we must not pass,
In seeking what we shall not find;

We shall one day gain, life past,
Clear prospect o'er our being's whole;
Shall see ourselves, and learn at last
Our true affinities of soul.

We shall not then deny a course
To every thought the mass ignore;
We shall not then call hardness force,
Nor lightness wisdom any more.

Then in the eternal Father's smile,
Our soothed, encouraged souls will dare
To seem as free from pride and guile,
As good, as generous, as they are.

Then we shall know our friends! — though much
Will have been lost — the help in strife,
The thousand sweet, still joys of such
As hand in hand face earthly life —

Though these be lost, there will be yet
A sympathy august and pure;
Ennobled by a vast regret,
And by contrition sealed thrice sure.

And we, whose ways were unlike here,
May then more neighboring courses ply;
May to each other be brought near,
And greet across infinity.

How sweet, unreached by earthly jars,
My sister! to maintain with thee
The hush among the shining stars,
The calm upon the moonlit sea!

How sweet to feel, on the boon air,
All our unquiet pulses cease!
To feel that nothing can impair
The gentleness, the thirst for peace —

The gentleness too rudely hurled
On this wild earth of hate and fear;
The thirst for peace a raving world
Would never let us satiate here.

[*1852*]

## ISOLATION

*To Marguerite*

We were apart; yet, day by day,
I bade my heart more constant be.
I bade it keep the world away,
And grow a home for only thee;
Nor feared but thy love likewise grew,
Like mine, each day, more tried, more true.

The fault was grave! I might have known,
What far too soon, alas! I learned —
The heart can bind itself alone,
And faith may oft be unreturned.
Self-swayed our feelings ebb and swell —
Thou lov'st no more; — Farewell! Farewell!

Farewell! — and thou, thou lonely heart,
Which never yet without remorse
Even for a moment didst depart
From thy remote and spherèd course
To haunt the place where passions reign —
Back to thy solitude again!

Back! with the conscious thrill of shame
Which Luna felt, that summer night,
Flash through her pure immortal frame,
When she forsook the starry height
To hang over Endymion's sleep
Upon the pine-grown Latmian steep.

Yet she, chaste queen, had never proved
How vain a thing is mortal love,
Wandering in Heaven, far removed.
But thou has long had place to prove
This truth — to prove, and make thine own:
"Thou hast been, shalt be, art, alone."

Or, if not quite alone, yet they
Which touch thee are unmating things —
Ocean and clouds and night and day;
Lorn autumns and triumphant springs;
And life, and others' joy and pain,
And love, if love, of happier men.

Of happier men — for they, at least,
Have *dreamed* two human hearts might blend
In one, and were through faith released
From isolation without end
Prolonged; nor knew, although not less
Alone than thou, their loneliness.

[*1857*]

ISOLATION. **23. Endymion:** The Greek legend tells of this beautiful youth loved by the moon goddess (Luna or Diana or Artemis) on Mount Latmos. The incident is a favorite theme of English poets, among them Keats, of whose long poem *Endymion* an extract is given in this volume.

## TO MARGUERITE — CONTINUED

Yes! in the sea of life enisled,
With echoing straits between us thrown,
Dotting the shoreless watery wild,
We mortal millions live *alone*.
The islands feel the enclasping flow,
And then their endless bounds they know.

But when the moon their hollows lights,
And they are swept by balms of spring,
And in their glens, on starry nights,
The nightingales divinely sing;
And lovely notes, from shore to shore,
Across the sounds and channels pour —

Oh! then a longing like despair
Is to their farthest caverns sent;
For surely once, they feel, we were
Parts of a single continent!
Now round us spreads the watery plain —
Oh might our marges meet again!

Who ordered, that their longing's fire
Should be, as soon as kindled, cooled?
Who renders vain their deep desire? —
A God, a God their severance ruled!
And bade betwixt their shores to be
The unplumbed, salt, estranging sea.

[*1852*]

## ABSENCE

In this fair stranger's eyes of gray
Thine eyes, my love! I see.

I shiver; for the passing day
Had borne me far from thee.

This is the curse of life! that not
A nobler, calmer train
Of wiser thoughts and feelings blot
Our passions from our brain;

But each day brings its petty dust
Our soon-choked souls to fill,
And we forget because we must
And not because we will.

I struggle towards the light; and ye,
Once-longed-for storms of love!
If with the light ye cannot be,
I bear that ye remove.

I struggle towards the light—but oh,
While yet the night is chill,
Upon time's barren, stormy flow,
Stay with me, Marguerite, still!

[*1852*]

## LONGING

Come to me in my dreams, and then
By day I shall be well again!
For then the night will more than pay
The hopeless longing of the day.

Come, as thou cam'st a thousand times,
A messenger from radiant climes,
And smile on thy new world, and be
As kind to others as to me!

Or, as thou never cam'st in sooth,
Come now, and let me dream in truth;
And part my hair, and kiss my brow,
And say: *My love! why sufferest thou?*

Come to me in my dreams, and then
By day I shall be well again!
For then the night will more than pay
The hopeless longing of the day.

[*1852*]

## DESTINY

Why each is striving, from of old,
To love more deeply than he can?
Still would be true, yet still grows cold?
—Ask of the Powers that sport with man!

They yoked in him, for endless strife,
A heart of ice, a soul of fire;
And hurled him on the Field of Life,
An aimless unallayed Desire.

[*1852*]

## HUMAN LIFE

What mortal, when he saw,
Life's voyage done, his heavenly Friend,
Could ever yet dare tell him fearlessly:
"I have kept uninfringed my nature's law;
The inly written chart thou gavest me,
To guide me, I have steered by to the end"?

Ah! let us make no claim,
On life's incognizable sea,
To too exact a steering of our way;
Let us not fret and fear to miss our aim,
If some fair coast have lured us to make stay,
Or some friend hailed us to keep company.

Ay! we would each fain drive
At random, and not steer by rule.
Weakness! and worse, weakness bestowed in vain!
Winds from our side the unsuiting consort rive,
We rush by coasts where we had lief remain;
Man cannot, though he would, live chance's fool.

No! as the foaming swath
Of torn-up water, on the main,
Falls heavily away with long-drawn roar
On either side the black deep-furrowed path
Cut by an onward-laboring vessel's prore,
And never touches the ship side again;

Even so we leave behind,
As, chartered by some unknown Powers,
We stem across the sea of life by night,
The joys which were not for our use designed;
The friends to whom we had no natural right,
The homes that were not destined to be ours.

[*1852*]

## SELF-DECEPTION

Say, what blinds us, that we claim the glory
Of possessing powers not our share?
—Since man woke on earth, he knows his story,
But, before we woke on earth, we were.

Long, long since, undowered yet, our spirit
Roamed, ere birth, the treasuries of God;
Saw the gifts, the powers it might inherit,
Asked an outfit for its earthly road.

HUMAN LIFE. 23. prore: prow.

Then, as now, this tremulous, eager being
Strained and longed and grasped each gift it saw;
Then, as now, a Power beyond our seeing
Staved us back, and gave our choice the law.

Ah, whose hand that day through Heaven guided
Man's new spirit, since it was not we?
Ah, who swayed our choice, and who decided
What our gifts, and what our wants should be?

For, alas! he left us each retaining
Shreds of gifts which he refused in full.
Still these waste us with their hopeless straining,
Still the attempt to use them proves them null.

And on earth we wander, groping, reeling;
Powers stir in us, stir and disappear.
Ah! and he, who placed our master feeling,
Failed to place that master feeling clear.

We but dream we have our wished-for powers,
Ends we seek we never shall attain.
Ah! *some* power exists there, which is ours?
*Some* end is there, we indeed may gain?

[*1852*]

## YOUTH AND CALM

'Tis death! and peace, indeed, is here,
And ease from shame, and rest from fear.
There's nothing can dismarble now
The smoothness of that limpid brow.
But is a calm like this, in truth,
The crowning end of life and youth,
And when this boon rewards the dead,
Are all debts paid, has all been said?
And is the heart of youth so light,
Its step so firm, its eye so bright,
Because on its hot brow there blows
A wind of promise and repose
From the far grave, to which it goes;
Because it hath the hope to come,
One day, to harbor in the tomb?
Ah no, the bliss youth dreams is one
For daylight, for the cheerful sun,
For feeling nerves and living breath —
Youth dreams a bliss on this side death.
It dreams a rest, if not more deep,
More grateful than this marble sleep;
It hears a voice within it tell:
*Calm's not life's crown, though calm is well.*
'Tis all perhaps which man acquires,
But 'tis not what our youth desires.

[*1852*]

## MEMORIAL VERSES

*April, 1850*

Goethe in Weimar sleeps, and Greece,
Long since, saw Byron's struggle cease.
But one such death remained to come;
The last poetic voice is dumb —
We stand today by Wordsworth's tomb.

When Byron's eyes were shut in death,
We bowed our head and held our breath.
He taught us little; but our soul
Had *felt* him like the thunder's roll.
With shivering heart the strife we saw
Of passion with eternal law;
And yet with reverential awe
We watched the fount of fiery life
Which served for that Titanic strife.

When Goethe's death was told, we said:
Sunk, then, is Europe's sagest head.
Physician of the iron age,
Goethe has done his pilgrimage.
He took the suffering human race,
He read each wound, each weakness clear;
And struck his finger on the place,
And said: *Thou ailest here, and here!*
He looked on Europe's dying hour
Of fitful dream and feverish power;
His eye plunged down the weltering strife,
The turmoil of expiring life —
He said: *The end is everywhere,*
*Art still has truth, take refuge there!*
And he was happy, if to know
Causes of things, and far below
His feet to see the lurid flow
Of terror, and insane distress,
And headlong fate, be happiness.

And Wordsworth! — Ah, pale ghosts, rejoice!
For never has such soothing voice
Been to your shadowy world conveyed,
Since erst, at morn, some wandering shade
Heard the clear song of Orpheus come
Through Hades, and the mournful gloom.

MEMORIAL VERSES. **April, 1850:** Wordsworth died at Rydal Mount on April 23, 1850, at the age of eighty. Goethe had died in 1832, Byron in 1824. Goethe had always been an object of Arnold's admiration. Byron, however, fluctuated in Arnold's esteem. After the usual boyish submission to Byron's influence, Arnold came to dislike him. But his mind changed again, and in this poem, as in the poem "Courage," which follows, we have the evidence of his deep commitment to Byron, which finds final expression in his essay on the poet prefixed to a selection of his work and included in *Essays in Criticism: Second Series.* **34–39. Ah . . . gloom:** Arnold refers to the journey to Hades made by Orpheus to regain his dead wife Eurydice. He won his way through the perils of the underworld by the quieting powers

Wordsworth has gone from us — and ye,
Ah, may ye feel his voice as we!
He too upon a wintry clime
Had fallen — on this iron time
Of doubts, disputes, distractions, fears.
He found us when the age had bound
Our souls in its benumbing round;
He spoke, and loosed our heart in tears.
He laid us as we lay at birth
On the cool flowery lap of earth,
Smiles broke from us and we had ease;
The hills were round us, and the breeze
Went o'er the sunlit fields again;
Our foreheads felt the wind and rain.
Our youth returned; for there was shed
On spirits that had long been dead,
Spirits dried up and closely furled,
The freshness of the early world.

Ah! since dark days still bring to light
Man's prudence and man's fiery might,
Time may restore us in his course
Goethe's sage mind and Byron's force;
But where will Europe's latter hour
Again find Wordsworth's healing power?
Others will teach us how to dare,
And against fear our breast to steel;
Others will strengthen us to bear —
But who, ah! who, will make us feel?
The cloud of mortal destiny,
Others will front it fearlessly —
But who, like him, will put it by?

Keep fresh the grass upon his grave
O Rotha, with thy living wave!
Sing him thy best! for few or none
Hears thy voice right, now he is gone.

[*1850*]

## COURAGE

True, we must tame our rebel will:
True, we must bow to Nature's law:
Must bear in silence many an ill;
Must learn to wait, renounce, withdraw.

Yet now, when boldest wills give place,
When Fate and Circumstance are strong,
And in their rush the human race
Are swept, like huddling sheep, along;

Those sterner spirits let me prize,
Who, though the tendence of the whole
They less than us might recognize,
Kept, more than us, their strength of soul.

Yes, be the second Cato praised!
Not that he took the course to die —
But that, when 'gainst himself he raised
His arm, he raised it dauntlessly.

And, Byron! let us dare admire,
If not thy fierce and turbid song,
Yet that, in anguish, doubt, desire,
Thy fiery courage still was strong.

The sun that on thy tossing pain
Did with such cold derision shine,
He crushed thee not with his disdain —
He had his glow, and thou hadst thine.

Our bane, disguise it as we may,
Is weakness, is a faltering course.
Oh that past times could give our day,
Joined to its clearness, of their force!

[*1852*]

## SELF-DEPENDENCE

Weary of myself, and sick of asking
What I am, and what I ought to be,
At this vessel's prow I stand, which bears me
Forwards, forwards, o'er the starlit sea.

And a look of passionate desire
O'er the sea and to the stars I send:
" Ye who from my childhood up have calmed me,
Calm me, ah, compose me to the end!

" Ah, once more," I cried, " ye stars, ye waters,
On my heart your mighty charm renew;
Still, still let me, as I gaze upon you,
Feel my soul becoming vast like you! "

From the intense, clear, star-sown vault of heaven,
Over the lit sea's unquiet way,
In the rustling night air came the answer:
" Wouldst thou *be* as these are? *Live* as they.

" Unaffrighted by the silence round them,
Undistracted by the sights they see,
These demand not that the things without them
Yield them love, amusement, sympathy.

" And with joy the stars perform their shining,
And the sea its long moon-silvered roll;
For self-poised they live, nor pine with noting
All the fever of some differing soul.

of his harping and singing. **72. Rotha:** the river that flows near the churchyard at Grasmere, where Wordsworth is buried.

COURAGE. **13. Cato:** "The second Cato" is Marcus Porius Cato (95 B.C.–46 B.C.), a Roman patriot and Stoic philosopher, great-grandson of Cato the Censor. He sided with Pompey against Caesar in the civil war which broke out in 49 B.C. He committed suicide upon hearing that Caesar had won the battle of Thapsus.

"Bounded by themselves, and unregardful
In what state God's other works may be,
In their own tasks all their powers pouring,
These attain the mighty life you see."

O air-born voice! long since, severely clear,
A cry like thine in mine own heart I hear:
"Resolve to be thyself; and know that he,
Who finds himself, loses his misery!"

[*1852*]

## A SUMMER NIGHT

In the deserted, moon-blanched street,
How lonely rings the echo of my feet!
Those windows, which I gaze at, frown,
Silent and white, unopening down,
Repellent as the world — but see,
A break between the housetops shows
The moon! and, lost behind her, fading dim
Into the dewy dark obscurity
Down at the far horizon's rim,
Doth a whole tract of heaven disclose!

And to my mind the thought
Is on a sudden brought
Of a past night, and a far different scene.
Headlands stood out into the moonlit deep
As clearly as at noon;
The spring tide's brimming flow
Heaved dazzlingly between;
Houses, with long white sweep,
Girdled the glistening bay;
Behind, through the soft air,
The blue haze-cradled mountains spread away,
That night was far more fair —
But the same restless pacings to and fro,
And the same vainly throbbing heart was there,
And the same bright, calm moon.
And the calm moonlight seems to say:
*Hast thou then still the old unquiet breast,*
*Which neither deadens into rest,*
*Nor ever feels the fiery glow*
*That whirls the spirit from itself away,*
*But fluctuates to and fro,*
*Never by passion quite possessed*
*And never quite benumbed by the world's sway?* —
And I, I know not if to pray
Still to be what I am, or yield and be
Like all the other men I see.

For most men in a brazen prison live,
Where, in the sun's hot eye,
With heads bent o'er their toil, they languidly
Their lives to some unmeaning taskwork give,
Dreaming of nought beyond their prison wall.
And as, year after year,
Fresh products of their barren labor fall
From their tired hands, and rest
Never yet comes more near,
Gloom settles slowly down over their breast;
And while they try to stem
The waves of mournful thought by which they are pressed,
Death in their prison reaches them,
Unfreed, having seen nothing, still unblessed.

And the rest, a few,
Escape their prison and depart
On the wide ocean of life anew.
There the freed prisoner, where'er his heart
Listeth, will sail;
Nor doth he know how there prevail,
Despotic on that sea,
Trade winds which cross it from eternity.
Awhile he holds some false way, undebarred
By thwarting signs, and braves
The freshening wind and blackening waves.
And then the tempest strikes him; and between
The lightning bursts is seen
Only a driving wreck,
And the pale master on his spar-strewn deck
With anguished face and flying hair
Grasping the rudder hard,
Still bent to make some port he knows not where,
Still standing for some false, impossible shore.
And sterner comes the roar
Of sea and wind, and through the deepening gloom
Fainter and fainter wreck and helmsman loom,
And he too disappears, and comes no more.

Is there no life, but these alone?
Madman or slave, must man be one?

Plainness and clearness without shadow of stain!
Clearness divine!
Ye heavens, whose pure dark regions have no sign
Of languor, though so calm, and, though so great,
Are yet untroubled and unpassionate;
Who, though so noble, share in the world's toil,
And, though so tasked, keep free from dust and soil!
I will not say that your mild deeps retain
A tinge, it may be, of their silent pain
Who have longed deeply once, and longed in vain —
But I will rather say that you remain
A world above man's head, to let him see
How boundless might his soul's horizons be,
How vast, yet of what clear transparency!
How it were good to abide there, and breathe free;
How fair a lot to fill
Is left to each man still!

[*1852*]

## THE BURIED LIFE

Light flows our war of mocking words, and yet,
Behold, with tears mine eyes are wet!
I feel a nameless sadness o'er me roll.
Yes, yes, we know that we can jest,
We know, we know that we can smile!
But there's a something in this breast,
To which thy light words bring no rest,
And thy gay smiles no anodyne.
Give me thy hand, and hush awhile,
And turn those limpid eyes on mine,
And let me read there, love! thy inmost soul.

Alas! is even love too weak
To unlock the heart, and let it speak?
Are even lovers powerless to reveal
To one another what indeed they feel?
I knew the mass of men concealed
Their thoughts, for fear that if revealed
They would by other men be met
With blank indifference, or with blame reproved;
I knew they lived and moved
Tricked in disguises, alien to the rest
Of men, and alien to themselves—and yet
The same heart beats in every human breast!

But we, my love!—doth a like spell benumb
Our hearts, our voices?—must we too be dumb?

Ah! well for us, if even we,
Even for a moment, can get free
Our heart, and have our lips unchained;
For that which seals them hath been deep-ordained!

Fate, which foresaw
How frivolous a baby man would be—
By what distractions he would be possessed,
How he would pour himself in every strife,
And well-nigh change his own identity—
That it might keep from his capricious play
His genuine self, and force him to obey
Even in his own despite his being's law,
Bade through the deep recesses of our breast
The unregarded river of our life
Pursue with indiscernible flow its way;
And that we should not see
The buried stream, and seem to be
Eddying at large in blind uncertainty,
Though driving on with it eternally.

But often, in the world's most crowded streets,
But often, in the din of strife,
There rises an unspeakable desire
After the knowledge of our buried life;
A thirst to spend our fire and restless force
In tracking out our true, original course;
A longing to inquire
Into the mystery of this heart which beats
So wild, so deep in us—to know
Whence our lives come and where they go.
And many a man in his own breast then delves,
But deep enough, alas! none ever mines.
And we have been on many thousand lines,
And we have shown, on each, spirit and power;
But hardly have we, for one little hour,
Been on our own line, have we been ourselves—
Hardly had skill to utter one of all
The nameless feelings that course through our breast,
But they course on forever unexpressed.
And long we try in vain to speak and act
Our hidden self, and what we say and do
Is eloquent, is well—but 'tis not true!
And then we will no more be racked
With inward striving, and demand
Of all the thousand nothings of the hour
Their stupefying power;
Ah yes, and they benumb us at our call!
Yet still, from time to time, vague and forlorn,
From the soul's subterranean depth upborne
As from an infinitely distant land,
Come airs, and floating echoes, and convey
A melancholy into all our day.

Only—but this is rare—
When a beloved hand is laid in ours,
When, jaded with the rush and glare
Of the interminable hours,
Our eyes can in another's eyes read clear,
When our world-deafened ear
Is by the tones of a loved voice caressed—
A bolt is shot back somewhere in our breast,
And a lost pulse of feeling stirs again.
The eye sinks inward, and the heart lies plain,
And what we mean, we say, and what we would, we know.
A man becomes aware of his life's flow,
And hears its winding murmur; and he sees
The meadows where it glides, the sun, the breeze.

And there arrives a lull in the hot race
Wherein he doth forever chase
That flying and elusive shadow, rest.
An air of coolness plays upon his face,
An an unwonted calm pervades his breast.
And then he thinks he knows
The hills where his life rose,
And the sea where it goes.

[*1852*]

## LINES

*Written in Kensington Gardens*

In this lone, open glade I lie,
Screened by deep boughs on either hand;
And at its end, to stay the eye,
Those black-crowned, red-boled pine trees stand!

Birds here make song, each bird has his,
Across the girdling city's hum.
How green under the boughs it is!
How thick the tremulous sheep cries come!

Sometimes a child will cross the glade
To take his nurse his broken toy;
Sometimes a thrush flit overhead
Deep in her unknown day's employ.

Here at my feet what wonders pass,
What endless, active life is here!
What blowing daisies, fragrant grass!
An air-stirred forest, fresh and clear.

Scarce fresher is the mountain sod
Where the tired angler lies, stretched out,
And, eased of basket and of rod,
Counts his day's spoil, the spotted trout.

In the huge world, which roars hard by,
Be others happy if they can!
But in my helpless cradle I
Was breathed on by the rural Pan.

I, on men's impious uproar hurled,
Think often, as I hear them rave,
That peace has left the upper world
And now keeps only in the grave.

Yet here is peace forever new!
When I who watch them am away,
Still all things in this glade go through
The changes of their quiet day.

Then to their happy rest they pass!
The flowers upclose, the birds are fed,
The night comes down upon the grass,
The child sleeps warmly in his bed.

Calm soul of all things! make it mine
To feel, amid the city's jar,
That there abides a peace of thine,
Man did not make, and cannot mar.

The will to neither strive nor cry,
The power to feel with others give!
Calm, calm me more! nor let me die
Before I have begun to live.

[*1852*]

KENSINGTON GARDENS. A London park.

## from SOHRAB AND RUSTUM

*Sohrab and Rustum* first appeared in the 1853 edition of Arnold's *Poems.* In its entirety the poem is 892 lines long. It is made memorable by its conclusion, which is given here.

Rustum is the great epic hero of Persia; Sohrab is Rustum's son by a Tartar princess whom he had loved in his youth. Sohrab's mother has told her son who his father is, and the young hero — for Sohrab early became famous for his prowess — is eager to find and claim a father so glorious. But Rustum does not know that he has a son because Sohrab's mother, fearful lest her child be taken away from her to be trained for war, had sent word to Rustum that their child was a girl. Sohrab takes military service with the Tartars. When the Persian and the Tartar forces meet, a single combat is arranged between the champions of each army. Rustum represents the Persians, Sohrab the Tartars. Rustum hides his identity from his opponent, but Sohrab, when they confront each other, suspects that he is face to face with the great Rustum at last. As for Rustum, he is drawn to the youth and tries to prevail upon him to withdraw from the fight. Sohrab, of course, will not do so. They fight, and Rustum is hard pressed as never before; indeed, Sohrab has the advantage over his father until his sword breaks. Then Rustum cries aloud his own name as a battle cry, and Sohrab, astonished, lowers his shield, and Rustum's spear strikes his exposed side. As Sohrab lies at the point of death, he threatens the victor with the revenge that his father, the great Rustum, will take upon him. Rustum admits his identity but says that he never had a son. Sohrab shows the family insignia pricked on his shoulder, which, for Rustum, is proof not to be denied, and he is overcome by grief for the son who is lost as soon as found.

Then, at the point of death, Sohrab replied:
"A life of blood indeed, thou dreadful man!
But thou shalt yet have peace; only not now,
Not yet! but thou shalt have it on that day,
When thou shalt sail in a high-masted ship,
Thou and the other peers of Kai Khosroo,
Returning home over the salt blue sea,
From laying thy dear master in his grave."
And Rustum gazed in Sohrab's face, and said:
"Soon be that day, my son, and deep that sea!
Till then, if fate so wills, let me endure."
He spoke; and Sohrab smiled on him, and took

SOHRAB AND RUSTUM. **6. Kai Khosroo:** the king of the Persians, perhaps the great Cyrus. **7–8. Returning . . . grave:** It is not precisely clear to what event Sohrab refers; presumably he is prophesying a death journey of the great king, Kai Khosroo, Rustum to be of the party of warriors who accompany their master.

The spear, and drew it from his side, and eased
His wound's imperious anguish; but the blood
Came welling from the open gash, and life
Flowed with the stream — all down his cold white side
The crimson torrent ran, dim now and soiled,
Like the soiled tissue of white violets
Left, freshly gathered, on their native bank,
By children whom their nurses call with haste
Indoors from the sun's eye; his head drooped low,
His limbs grew slack; motionless, white, he lay —
White, with eyes closed; only when heavy gasps,
Deep heavy gasps quivering through all his frame,
Convulsed him back to life, he opened them,
And fixed them feebly on his father's face;
Till now all strength was ebbed, and from his limbs
Unwillingly the spirit fled away,
Regretting the warm mansion which it left,
And youth, and bloom, and this delightful world.
  So, on the bloody sand, Sohrab lay dead;
And the great Rustum drew his horseman's cloak
Down o'er his face, and sate by his dead son.
As those black granite pillars, once high-reared
By Jemshid in Persepolis, to bear
His house, now 'mid their broken flights of steps
Lie prone, enormous, down the mountainside —
So in the sand lay Rustum by his son.
  And night came down over the solemn waste,
And the two gazing hosts, and that sole pair,
And darkened all; and a cold fog, with night,
Crept from the Oxus. Soon a hum arose,
As of a great assembly loosed, and fires
Began to twinkle through the fog; for now
Both armies moved to camp, and took their meal;
The Persians took it on the open sands
Southward, the Tartars by the river marge;
And Rustum and his son were left alone.
  But the majestic river floated on,
Out of the mist and hum of that low land,
Into the frosty starlight, and there moved,
Rejoicing, through the hushed Chorasmian waste,
Under the solitary moon — he flowed
Right for the polar star, past Orgunjè,
Brimming, and bright, and large; then sands begin
To hem his watery march, and dam his streams,
And split his currents; that for many a league
The shorn and parceled Oxus strains along
Through beds of sand and matted rushy isles —
Oxus, forgetting the bright speed he had
In his high mountain cradle in Pamere,
A foiled circuitous wanderer — till at last
The longed-for dash of waves is heard, and wide
His luminous home of waters opens, bright
And tranquil, from whose floor the new-bathed stars
Emerge, and shine upon the Aral Sea.

**35. Jemshid:** a legendary Persian king. **Persepolis:** the ancient capital of Persia. **42. Oxus:** a river in western Asia. **52. Chorasmian waste:** the desert of Chorasmia. **54. Orgunjè:** a small town on the Oxus. **61. Pamere:** now Pamirs, a mountain system and high tableland in Tadzhik, in central Asia, now one of the republics of the U. S. S. R. The native name for the range means "roof of the world."

## PHILOMELA

Hark! ah, the nightingale —
The tawny-throated!
Hark, from that moonlit cedar what a burst!
What triumph! hark! — what pain!

O wanderer from a Grecian shore,
Still, after many years, in distant lands,
Still nourishing in thy bewildered brain
That wild, unquenched, deep-sunken, old-world pain —
Say, will it never heal?
And can this fragrant lawn
With its cool trees, and night,
And the sweet, tranquil Thames,
And moonshine, and the dew,
To thy racked heart and brain
Afford no balm?

Dost thou tonight behold,
Here, through the moonlight on this English grass,
The unfriendly palace in the Thracian wild?
Dost thou again peruse
With hot cheeks and seared eyes
The too-clear web, and thy dumb sister's shame?

**66. Aral Sea:** sometimes called Aral Lake; an inland sea in central Asia, somewhat larger than our Lake Huron. PHILOMELA. A poetic name for the nightingale, sometimes in the form "philomel." There are various versions of the story of how the girl Philomela was changed into the bird, all of them in essential agreement, although they contradict each other in details. As Arnold uses it, the tale is as follows: Philomela and Procne were the daughters of a king of Athens. Procne was married to Tereus, King of Thrace. Falling in love with Philomela, Tereus cut out Procne's tongue and hid her away, telling Philomela that her sister was dead. He then married Philomela. But Procne wove a tapestry ("the too-clear web" of l. 21) in which she portrayed what had been done to her, and had it conveyed to her sister. Philomela released Procne, and the two sisters now avenged themselves on Tereus: they killed the little son of Procne and Tereus, Itylus by name, and cooked him in a stew which they served to his father. They revealed what they had done when Tereus had eaten of the dish, producing the head of Itylus by way of proof. Arnold does not refer to this incident, but he probably felt that it would come to the minds of many of his readers when he spoke (l. 26) of "love and hate." Philomela and Procne fled from Tereus, and, just as he was about to catch them to slay them, Philomela was changed by the gods into a nightingale, Procne into a swallow. (It was sometimes said that Tereus became a hoopoe and Itylus a pheasant.) In some versions Tereus ravishes Philomela and cuts out *her* tongue; it is she whom he conceals; and it is she who sends the web to Procne. It would seem that Arnold had this version also in mind; we can feel that the beautiful song of the nightingale is a "triumph" (l. 4) over dumbness; and the "shame" attributed (l. 21) to Procne might better apply to the ravished Philomela.

Dost thou once more assay
Thy flight, and feel come over thee,
Poor fugitive, the feathery change
Once more, and once more seem to make resound
With love and hate, triumph and agony,
Lone Daulis, and the high Cephissian vale?
Listen, Eugenia —
How thick the bursts come crowding through the leaves!
Again — thou hearest?
Eternal passion!
Eternal pain!

[*1853*]

## REQUIESCAT

Strew on her roses, roses,
And never a spray of yew!
In quiet she reposes;
Ah, would that I did too!

Her mirth the world required;
She bathed it in smiles of glee.
But her heart was tired, tired,
And now they let her be.

Her life was turning, turning,
In mazes of heat and sound.
But for peace her soul was yearning,
And now peace laps her round.

Her cabined, ample spirit,
It fluttered and failed for breath.
Tonight it doth inherit
The vasty hall of death.

[*1853*]

## THE SCHOLAR GYPSY

In explanation of the legend upon which he based this poem, Arnold quoted the following passage from Joseph Glanvill's *Vanity of Dogmatizing* (1661):

"There was very lately a lad in the University of Oxford, who was by his poverty forced to leave his studies there; and at last to join himself to a company of vagabond gypsies. Among these extravagant people, by the insinuating subtlety of his carriage, he quickly got so much of their love and esteem as that they discovered to him their mystery. After he had been a pretty while exercised in the trade, there chanced to ride by a couple of scholars, who had formerly been of his acquaintance. They quickly spied out their old friend among the gypsies; and he gave them an account of the necessity which drove him to that kind of life, and told them that the people he went with were not such impostors as they were taken for, but that they had a traditional kind of learning among them, and could do wonders by the power of imagination, their fancy binding that of others: that himself had learned much of their art, and when he had compassed the whole secret, he intended, he said, to leave their company, and give the world an account of what he had learned."

See the discussion of this poem in the Introduction, p. 587.

Go, for they call you, shepherd, from the hill;
Go, shepherd, and untie the wattled cotes!
No longer leave thy wistful flock unfed,
Nor let thy bawling fellows rack their throats,
Nor the cropped herbage shoot another head.
But when the fields are still,
And the tired men and dogs all gone to rest,
And only the white sheep are sometimes seen
Cross and recross the strips of moon-blanched green,
Come, shepherd, and again begin the quest!

Here, where the reaper was at work of late —
In this high field's dark corner, where he leaves
His coat, his basket, and his earthen cruse,
And in the sun all morning binds the sheaves,
Then here, at noon, comes back his stores to use —
Here will I sit and wait,
While to my ear from uplands far away
The bleating of the folded flocks is borne,
With distant cries of reapers in the corn —
All the live murmur of a summer's day.

Screened is this nook o'er the high, half-reaped field,
And here till sundown, shepherd! will I be.
Through the thick corn the scarlet poppies peep,
And round green roots and yellowing stalks I see
Pale pink convolvulus in tendrils creep;
And air-swept lindens yield
Their scent, and rustle down their perfumed showers
Of bloom on the bent grass where I am laid,
And bower me from the August sun with shade;
And the eye travels down to Oxford's towers.

27. **Daulis:** a city in Phocis. It was here that Philomela and Procne took their revenge on Tereus and here that they became birds. **Cephissian vale:** The Cephissus was a river that took its rise in Phocis. 28. **Eugenia:** an imaginary person whom the poet represents as being by his side and whom he addresses directly. The presence of this nineteenth-century English girl has the effect of making the barbaric passions of the ancient myth seem very far off — yet very real. REQUIESCAT. "May she rest."

SCHOLAR GYPSY. 19. **corn:** In England the word means wheat, not our Indian corn.

And near me on the grass lies Glanvill's book —
Come, let me read the oft-read tale again!
The story of the Oxford scholar poor,
Of pregnant parts and quick inventive brain,
Who, tired of knocking at preferment's door,
One summer morn forsook
His friends, and went to learn the gypsy lore,
And roamed the world with that wild brother-hood,
And came, as most men deemed, to little good,
But came to Oxford and his friends no more.

But once, years after, in the country lanes,
Two scholars, whom at college erst he knew,
Met him, and of his way of life inquired;
Whereat he answered, that the gypsy crew,
His mates, had arts to rule as they desired
The workings of men's brains,
And they can bind them to what thoughts they will.
"And I," he said, "the secret of their art,
When fully learned, will to the world impart;
But it needs heaven-sent moments for this skill."

This said, he left them, and returned no more. —
But rumors hung about the countryside,
That the lost Scholar long was seen to stray,
Seen by rare glimpses, pensive and tongue-tied,
In hat of antique shape, and cloak of gray,
The same the gypsies wore.
Shepherds had met him on the Hurst in spring;
At some lone alehouse in the Berkshire moors,
On the warm ingle bench, the smock-frocked boors
Had found him seated at their entering,

But, 'mid their drink and clatter, he would fly.
And I myself seem half to know thy looks,
And put the shepherds, wanderer! on thy trace;
And boys who in lone wheatfields scare the rooks
I ask if thou hast passed their quiet place;
Or in my boat I lie
Moored to the cool bank in the summer heats,
'Mid wide grass meadows which the sunshine fills,
And watch the warm, green-muffled Cumner hills,
And wonder if thou haunt'st their shy retreats.

For most, I know, thou lov'st retired ground!
Thee at the ferry Oxford riders blithe,
Returning home on summer nights, have met
Crossing the stripling Thames at Bab-lock-hithe,
Trailing in the cool stream thy fingers wet,
As the punt's rope chops round;
And leaning backward in a pensive dream,
And fostering in thy lap a heap of flowers
Plucked in shy fields and distant Wychwood bowers,
And thine eyes resting on the moonlit stream.

And then they land, and thou art seen no more! —
Maidens, who from the distant hamlets come
To dance around the Fyfield elm in May,
Oft through the darkening fields have seen thee roam,
Or cross a stile into the public way.
Oft thou hast given them store
Of flowers — the frail-leafed, white anemone,
Dark bluebells drenched with dews of summer eves,
And purple orchises with spotted leaves —
But none hath words she can report of thee.

And, above Godstow Bridge, when haytime's here
In June, and many a scythe in sunshine flames,
Men who through those wide fields of breezy grass
Where black-winged swallows haunt the glitter-ing Thames,
To bathe in the abandoned lasher pass,
Have often passed thee near
Sitting upon the river bank o'ergrown;
Marked thine outlandish garb, thy figure spare,
Thy dark vague eyes, and soft abstracted air —
But, when they came from bathing, thou wast gone!

At some lone homestead in the Cumner hills,
Where at her open door the housewife darns,
Thou hast been seen, or hanging on a gate
To watch the threshers in the mossy barns.
Children, who early range these slopes and late
For cresses from the rills,
Have known thee eying, all an April day,
The springing pastures and the feeding kine;
And marked thee, when the stars come out and shine,
Through the long dewy grass move slow away.

In autumn, on the skirts of Bagley Wood —
Where most the gypsies by the turf-edged way
Pitch their smoked tents, and every bush you see

**57. Hurst:** Cumner Hurst is a hill near Oxford, one of the Cumner hills referred to in l. 69. **58. Berkshire:** the county adjacent to Oxfordshire. **74. Bab-lock-hithe:** a ferry about two miles west of the village of Cumner.

**79. Wychwood bowers:** Wychwood Forest is some twelve miles to the northwest of Oxford. **83. Fyfield elm:** Fyfield is a village about seven miles southwest of Oxford, not far from which was a great elm. **91. Godstow Bridge:** across the Thames about two miles above Oxford. **95. lasher:** a pool below a dam. **111. Bagley Wood:** some three miles below Oxford, on the far side of the Thames.

With scarlet patches tagged and shreds of gray,
Above the forest ground called Thessaly —
The blackbird, picking food,
Sees thee, nor stops his meal, nor fears at all;
So often has he known thee past him stray,
Rapt, twirling in thy hand a withered spray,
And waiting for the spark from heaven to fall.

And once, in winter, on the causeway chill
Where home through flooded fields foot travelers go,
Have I not passed thee on the wooden bridge,
Wrapped in thy cloak and battling with the snow,
Thy face toward Hinksey and its wintry ridge?
And thou hast climbed the hill,
And gained the white brow of the Cumner range;
Turned once to watch, while thick the snowflakes fall,
The line of festal light in Christ Church hall —
Then sought thy straw in some sequestered grange.

But what — I dream! Two hundred years are flown
Since first thy story ran through Oxford halls,
And the grave Glanvill did the tale inscribe
That thou wert wandered from the studious walls
To learn strange arts, and join a gypsy tribe;
And thou from earth art gone
Long since, and in some quiet churchyard laid —
Some country nook, where o'er thy unknown grave
Tall grasses and white flowering nettles wave,
Under a dark, red-fruited yew tree's shade.

— No, no, thou hast not felt the lapse of hours!
For what wears out the life of mortal men?
'Tis that from change to change their being rolls;
'Tis that repeated shocks, again, again,
Exhaust the energy of strongest souls
And numb the elastic powers.
Till having used our nerves with bliss and teen,
And tired upon a thousand schemes our wit,
To the just-pausing Genius we remit
Our worn-out life, and are — what we have been.

Thou hast not lived, why should'st thou perish, so?
Thou hadst *one* aim, *one* business, *one* desire;
Else wert thou long since numbered with the dead!
Else hadst thou spent, like other men, thy fire!
The generations of thy peers are fled,
And we ourselves shall go;
But thou possessest an immortal lot,
And we imagine thee exempt from age
And living as thou liv'st on Glanvill's page,
Because thou hadst — what we, alas! have not.

For early didst thou leave the world, with powers
Fresh, undiverted to the world without,
Firm to their mark, not spent on other things;
Free from the sick fatigue, the languid doubt,
Which much to have tried, in much been baffled, brings.
O life unlike to ours!
Who fluctuate idly without term or scope,
Of whom each strives, nor knows for what he strives,
And each half lives a hundred different lives;
Who wait like thee, but not, like thee, in hope.

Thou waitest for the spark from heaven! and we,
Light half-believers of our casual creeds,
Who never deeply felt, nor clearly willed,
Whose insight never has borne fruit in deeds,
Whose vague resolves never have been fulfilled;
For whom each year we see
Breeds new beginnings, disappointments new;
Who hesitate and falter life away,
And lose tomorrow the ground won today —
Ah! do not we, wanderer! await it too?

Yes, we await it! — but it still delays,
And then we suffer! and amongst us one,
Who most has suffered, takes dejectedly
His seat upon the intellectual throne;
And all his store of sad experience he
Lays bare of wretched days;
Tells us his misery's birth and growth and signs,
And how the dying spark of hope was fed,
And how the breast was soothed, and how the head,
And all his hourly varied anodynes.

This for our wisest! and we others pine,
And wish the long unhappy dream would end,
And waive all claim to bliss, and try to bear;
With close-lipped patience for our only friend,
Sad patience, too near neighbor to despair —
But none has hope like thine!
Thou through the fields and through the woods dost stray,

**115. Thessaly:** the name given by Oxford students to a piece of land between Bagley Wood and the river. Thessaly was a region of ancient Greece; among other legendary reasons, it is noted because Mount Olympus, the home of the gods, was situated there. **125. Hinksey:** There are two Hinkseys, North and South. They lie between Oxford and Cumner. **129. Christ Church hall:** the dining hall of Christ Church College can be seen from the Cumner hills.

**182–90. one . . . anodynes:** Although there has been some question of who it is that Arnold refers to in this passage, it is virtually certain that he means Goethe.

Roaming the countryside, a truant boy,
Nursing thy project in unclouded joy,
And every doubt long blown by time away.

O born in days when wits were fresh and clear,
And life ran gaily as the sparkling Thames;
Before this strange disease of modern life,
With its sick hurry, its divided aims,
Its heads o'ertaxed, its palsied hearts, was rife —
Fly hence, our contact fear!
Still fly, plunge deeper in the bowering wood!
Averse, as Dido did with gesture stern
From her false friend's approach in Hades turn,
Wave us away, and keep thy solitude!

Still nursing the unconquerable hope,
Still clutching the inviolable shade,
With a free, onward impulse brushing through,
By night, the silvered branches of the glade —
Far on the forest skirts, where none pursue,
On some mild pastoral slope
Emerge, and resting on the moonlit pales
Freshen thy flowers as in former years
With dew, or listen with enchanted ears,
From the dark dingles, to the nightingales!

But fly our paths, our feverish contact fly!
For strong the infection of our mental strife,
Which, though it gives no bliss, yet spoils for rest;
And we should win thee from thy own fair life,
Like us distracted, and like us unblessed.
Soon, soon thy cheer would die,
Thy hopes grow timorous, and unfixed thy powers,
And thy clear aims be cross and shifting made;
And then thy glad perennial youth would fade,
Fade, and grow old at last, and die like ours.

Then fly our greetings, fly our speech and smiles!
As some grave Tyrian trader, from the sea,
Descried at sunrise an emerging prow
Lifting the cool-haired creepers stealthily,
The fringes of a southward-facing brow
Among the Aegean isles;
And saw the merry Grecian coaster come,
Freighted with amber grapes, and Chian wine,
Green, bursting figs, and tunnies steeped in brine —
And knew the intruders on his ancient home,

The young lighthearted masters of the waves —
And snatched his rudder, and shook out more sail;
And day and night held on indignantly
O'er the blue Midland waters with the gale,
Betwixt the Syrtes and soft Sicily,
To where the Atlantic raves
Outside the western straits; and unbent sails
There, where down cloudy cliffs, through sheets of foam,
Shy traffickers, the dark Iberians come;
And on the beach undid his corded bales.

[*1853*]

**208–09. Dido . . . turn:** Dido was the queen of Carthage who loved the Trojan hero, Aeneas. When, at the behest of the gods, he deserted her to follow his fate and found Rome, she committed suicide in her despair. In a famous passage of the *Aeneid*, Aeneas descends into Hades and, meeting Dido, tenderly addresses her, but she turns from him in horror. **232. Tyrian:** Tyre was one of the two cities of the Phoenicians, who were the great navigators and traders of the ancient world.

# STANZAS FROM THE GRANDE CHARTREUSE

Through Alpine meadows soft-suffused
With rain, where thick the crocus blows,
Past the dark forges long disused,
The mule track from St. Laurent goes.
The bridge is crossed, and slow we ride,
Through forest, up the mountainside.

The autumnal evening darkens round,
The wind is up, and drives the rain;
While, hark! far down, with strangled sound
Doth the Dead Guier's stream complain,
Where that wet smoke, among the woods,
Over his boiling caldron broods.

Swift rush the spectral vapors white
Past limestone scars with ragged pines,
Showing — then blotting from our sight! —
Halt — through the cloud drift something shines!
High in the valley, wet and drear,
The huts of Courrerie appear.

**244. Midland waters:** "Midland" translates literally the word Mediterranean. **245. the Syrtes:** the ancient Greek name for two large sand banks on the coast of Africa. They were considered very dangerous to navigation because their position shifted; sometimes they were under high water, sometimes under low water. **249. Iberians:** the ancient name for the people of the Spanish peninsula. THE GRANDE CHARTREUSE. A *chartreuse* is a monastery of the very austere monastic order of Carthusians, founded by St. Bruno in 1086 in the French Alpine town of Chartreuse, near Grenoble. The word Carthusian derives from the name of the town. The English word for a *chartreuse*, arrived at by "folk etymology," is charterhouse. The original and chief home of the order came to be called La Grande Chartreuse. **4. St. Laurent:** a village some five miles from the monastery. **10. Dead . . . stream:** The river Guiers, which flows into the Rhone, divides into two streams, *Guiers vif* and *Guiers mort*, Live Guiers and Dead Guiers. Arnold spells the name without the final *s*. **18. Courrerie:** a mountain village near the monastery.

*Strike leftward!* cries our guide; and higher
Mounts up the stony forest way.
At last the encircling trees retire;
Look! through the showery twilight gray
What pointed roofs are these advance? —
A palace of the Kings of France?

Approach, for what we seek is here!
Alight, and sparely sup, and wait
For rest in this outbuilding near;
Then cross the sward and reach that gate.
Knock; pass the wicket! Thou art come
To the Carthusians' world-famed home.

The silent courts, where night and day
Into their stone-carved basins cold
The splashing icy fountains play —
The humid corridors behold!
Where, ghostlike in the deepening night,
Cowled forms brush by in gleaming white.

The chapel, where no organ's peal
Invests the stern and naked prayer —
With penitential cries they kneel
And wrestle; rising then, with bare
And white uplifted faces stand,
Passing the Host from hand to hand;

Each takes, and then his visage wan
Is buried in his cowl once more.
The cells! — the suffering Son of Man
Upon the wall — the knee-worn floor —
And where they sleep, that wooden bed,
Which shall their coffin be, when dead!

The library, where tract and tome
Not to feed priestly pride are there,
To hymn the conquering march of Rome,
Nor yet to amuse, as ours are!
They paint of souls the inner strife,
Their drops of blood, their death in life.

The garden, overgrown — yet mild,
See, fragrant herbs are flowering there!
Strong children of the Alpine wild
Whose culture is the brethren's care;
Of human tasks their only one,
And cheerful works beneath the sun.

Those halls, too, destined to contain
Each its own pilgrim host of old,
From England, Germany, or Spain —
All are before me! I behold
The House, the Brotherhood austere!
— And what am I, that I am here?

**56. fragrant herbs:** From these herbs the monks make the pleasant cordial called *chartreuse.*

For rigorous teachers seized my youth,
And purged its faith, and trimmed its fire,
Showed me the high, white star of Truth,
There bade me gaze, and there aspire.
Even now their whispers pierce the gloom:
*What dost thou in this living tomb?*

Forgive me, masters of the mind!
At whose behest I long ago
So much unlearned, so much resigned —
I come not here to be your foe!
I seek these anchorites, not in ruth,
To curse and to deny your truth;

Not as their friend, or child, I speak!
But as, on some far northern strand,
Thinking of his own gods, a Greek
In pity and mournful awe might stand
Before some fallen runic stone —
For both were faiths, and both are gone.

Wandering between two worlds, one dead,
The other powerless to be born,
With nowhere yet to rest my head,
Like these, on earth I wait forlorn.
Their faith, my tears, the world deride —
I come to shed them at their side.

Oh, hide me in your gloom profound,
Ye solemn seats of holy pain!
Take me, cowled forms, and fence me round,
Till I possess my soul again;
Till free my thoughts before me roll,
Not chafed by hourly false control!

For the world cries your faith is now
But a dead time's exploded dream;
My melancholy, sciolists say,
Is a passed mode, an outworn theme —
As if the world had ever had
A faith, or sciolists been sad!

Ah, if it *be* passed, take away,
At least, the restlessness, the pain;
Be man henceforth no more a prey
To these outdated stings again!
The nobleness of grief is gone —
Ah, leave us not the fret alone!

But — if you cannot give us ease —
Last of the race of them who grieve
Here leave us to die out with these
Last of the people who believe!
Silent, while years engrave the brow;
Silent — the best are silent now.

Achilles ponders in his tent,
The kings of modern thought are dumb;
Silent they are, though not content,
And wait to see the future come.
They have the grief men had of yore,
But they contend and cry no more.

Our fathers watered with their tears
This sea of time whereon we sail,
Their voices were in all men's ears
Who passed within their puissant hail.
Still the same ocean round us raves,
But we stand mute, and watch the waves.

For what availed it, all the noise
And outcry of the former men? —
Say, have their sons achieved more joys,
Say, is life lighter now than then?
The sufferers died, they left their pain —
The pangs which tortured them remain.

What helps it now, that Byron bore,
With haughty scorn which mocked the smart,
Through Europe to the Aetolian shore
The pageant of his bleeding heart?
That thousands counted every groan,
And Europe made his woe her own?

What boots it, Shelley! that the breeze
Carried thy lovely wail away,
Musical through Italian trees
Which fringe thy soft blue Spezian bay?
Inheritors of thy distress
Have restless hearts one throb the less?

Or are we easier, to have read,
O Obermann! the sad, stern page,
Which tells us how thou hidd'st thy head
From the fierce tempest of thine age
In the lone brakes of Fontainebleau,
Or chalets near the Alpine snow?

Ye slumber in your silent grave! —
The world, which for an idle day
Grace to your mood of sadness gave,
Long since hath flung her weeds away.
The eternal trifler breaks your spell;
But we — we learned your lore too well!

Years hence, perhaps, may dawn an age,
More fortunate, alas! than we,
Which without hardness will be sage,
And gay without frivolity.
Sons of the world, oh, speed those years;
But, while we wait, allow our tears!

Allow them! We admire with awe
The exulting thunder of your race;
You give the universe your law,
You triumph over time and space!
Your pride of life, your tireless powers,
We laud them, but they are not ours.

We are like children reared in shade
Beneath some old-world abbey wall,
Forgotten in a forest glade,
And secret from the eyes of all.
Deep, deep the greenwood round them waves,
Their abbey, and its close of graves!

But, where the road runs near the stream,
Oft through the trees they catch a glance
Of passing troops in the sun's beam —
Pennon, and plume, and flashing lance!
Forth to the world those soldiers fare,
To life, to cities, and to war!

And through the wood, another way,
Faint bugle notes from far are borne,
Where hunters gather, staghounds bay,
Round some fair forest lodge at morn.
Gay dames are there, in sylvan green;
Laughter and cries — those notes between!

The banners flashing through the trees
Make their blood dance and chain their eyes;
That bugle music on the breeze
Arrests them with a charmed surprise.
Banner by turns and bugle woo:
*Ye shy recluses, follow too!*

O children, what do ye reply? —
"Action and pleasure, will ye roam
Through these secluded dells to cry
And call us? — but too late ye come!
Too late for us your call ye blow,
Whose bent was taken long ago.

"Long since we pace this shadowed nave;
We watch those yellow tapers shine,
Emblems of hope over the grave,
In the high altar's depth divine;

**115. Achilles . . . tent:** At the siege of Troy, Achilles, the greatest warrior of the Greeks, sulked in his tent, refusing to take part in the fighting because he had been unjustly treated by Agamemnon. **135. Aetolian shore:** Missolonghi, where Byron met his death aiding the cause of Greek national independence, is on the shores of Aetolia, a region in western Greece. **142. Spezian bay:** Shelley was drowned in the Gulf of Spezia. **146. Obermann:** the suppositious writer of the letters from Switzerland which make up the volume *Obermann* by Étienne Pivert de Senancour (1770–1846). Arnold had great affection for this book; it expressed almost unrelieved despair over the spiritual bereavements of modern man. **149. Fontainebleau:** a town near Paris, famous as the site of a palace which used to be the residence of the kings of France. But Arnold, referring to the "lone brakes" or thickets, had in mind the nearby picturesque forest rather than the town itself.

The organ carries to our ear
Its accents of another sphere.

" Fenced early in this cloistral round
Of reverie, of shade, of prayer,
How should we grow in other ground?
How can we flower in foreign air?
— Pass, banners, pass, and bugles, cease;
And leave our desert to its peace!"
[*1855*]

# THYRSIS

*A Monody, to Commemorate the Author's Friend, Arthur Hugh Clough, who Died at Florence, 1861*

" Thyrsis," Arnold's elegy for his friend, Arthur Hugh Clough, is the masterpiece of his later poetic production. It is a poem which is the more moving if we perceive it to be the lament not only for a vanished friend but also for a vanished friendship. There can be no doubt that the connection between Arnold and Clough (see the Introduction, p. 582) had attenuated since their youthful days together. The passing years do not usually allow school and college friendships to endure in their early force, and in the case of Arnold and Clough it seems clear that the friends were aware of their growing incompatibility. Arnold's letters to Clough in the years just after Oxford, and what we can deduce of Clough's letters to which Arnold was replying, indicate that their judgment of the things that were most important to each was becoming more and more divergent. In any such lessening of friendship it is never possible to say that one party or another is at fault. Clough was increasingly difficult; he was depressed, often sunk in the deepest neurotic melancholy, and Arnold, who knew what possibilities of depression and melancholy he had within himself and who was determined to fight them, seems to have withdrawn from the intimacy. Also, Clough may well have been alienated by Arnold's determination to deal with life in as positive a way as he could and not to be withdrawn from living by the doubts and fears which were the stuff of Clough's existence.

The friendship never actually came to an end. The two men were bound not only by the memory of the affection of the past but also by a present warmth of good will. Each was an important figure in the life of the other, even if they no longer confided in each other. As Clough approached middle life, his spirits revived considerably. His post in the Education Office made possible his long-postponed marriage, and he seemed in a fair way to contentment and even happiness. But he gave alarming signs of physical illness, and, in 1861, on a visit to Italy in search of health, he died in Florence, at the age of forty-two.

" Thyrsis" appeared in 1866 in *Macmillan's Magazine*. Arnold, just after the news of the death, had spoken movingly of Clough in one of his lectures " On Translating Homer," but there was some speculation on why he had found it necessary to wait so long to speak in verse of his dead friend, to which the only answer can be that this much passage of time was needed. There was also some comment on the emphasis which Arnold seemed to put on Clough's extreme sensitivity, even weakness. But these objections are virtually of the nature of gossip; they have no merit in themselves, and they did not keep the poem from establishing itself with the two great examples of the pastoral elegy in English, Milton's " Lycidas" and Shelley's " Adonais."

In a note to the poem, Arnold said that " Thyrsis" makes reference throughout to " The Scholar Gypsy." And indeed the later poem may be said to be based on the earlier and to be continuous with it. Its verse form is the same, its tone is the same. Its setting, the Oxford country, is the same; Oxford was, of course, inevitable for a poem by Arnold about Clough, as being the scene in which the early friendship had flourished; it was, indeed, inevitable for any poem about Clough, as being the scene of Clough's early promise and glory. Almost all the paraphernalia of " The Scholar Gypsy," including the Fyfield elm, is brought into use. " The Scholar Gypsy" was in itself an elegy — for Arnold's youth and for a vanished England. Now, in " Thyrsis," Arnold laments the time of the earlier poem, written some thirteen years earlier, with a sadness twice compounded.

One of the charms of " The Scholar Gypsy" is the vista of time that it gives us. Set in the present of its date of publication, it goes back to the poet's youth, thence to the seventeenth century with the legend of the Oxford Gypsy; and then, when we have gone as far into the past as we think we can go, it carries us beyond, to the world of the ancient Aegean. The same device of unfolding time is used in " Thyrsis": it starts in the immediate present, goes back to the time of the writing of " The Scholar Gypsy," thence back to the seventeenth century with its evocation of the Gypsy, and its furthest reach is the half-real, half-imagined world of the Greek pastoral poets of the third century B.C. The name Thyrsis is one of the traditional names of the shepherds who, according to the convention of the pastoral, lived their lives in an entire devotion to poetry and friendship; a common theme of the tradition was the lament of one shepherd-poet for a friend who has died. Again we have been carried beyond the fever and the fret of the modern world to the imagination of a fresh, young, sunlit age.

How changed is here each spot man makes or fills!
  In the two Hinkseys nothing keeps the same;
    The village street its haunted mansion lacks,
  And from the sign is gone Sibylla's name,
    And from the roofs the twisted chimney stacks —
      Are ye too changed, ye hills?
  See, 'tis no foot of unfamiliar men

**THYRSIS. 2. two Hinkseys:** See "The Scholar Gypsy," l. 125n. **4. Sibylla's name:** There had been a public house at South Hinksey kept by a woman named Sibylla Kerr.

Tonight from Oxford up your pathway strays!
Here came I often, often, in old days —
Thyrsis and I; we still had Thyrsis then.

Runs it not here, the track by Childsworth Farm,
Past the high wood, to where the elm tree crowns
The hill behind whose ridge the sunset flames?
The signal elm, that looks on Ilsley Downs,
The Vale, the three lone weirs, the youthful Thames? —
This winter eve is warm,
Humid the air! leafless, yet soft as spring,
The tender purple spray on copse and briers!
And that sweet city with her dreaming spires,
She needs not June for beauty's heightening,

Lovely all times she lies, lovely tonight! —
Only, methinks, some loss of habit's power
Befalls me wandering through this upland dim.
Once passed I blindfold here, at any hour;
Now seldom come I, since I came with him.
That single elm tree bright
Against the west — I miss it! is it gone?
We prized it dearly; while it stood, we said,
Our friend, the Gypsy Scholar, was not dead;
While the tree lived, he in these fields lived on.

Too rare, too rare, grow now my visits here,
But once I knew each field, each flower, each stick;
And with the countryfolk acquaintance made
By barn in threshing time, by new-built rick.
Here, too, our shepherd pipes we first assayed.
Ah me! this many a year
My pipe is lost, my shepherd's holiday!
Needs must I lose them, needs with heavy heart
Into the world and wave of men depart;
But Thyrsis of his own will went away.

It irked him to be here, he could not rest.
He loved each simple joy the country yields,
He loved his mates; but yet he could not keep,
For that a shadow lowered on the fields,
Here with the shepherds and the silly sheep.
Some life of men unblessed
He knew, which made him droop, and filled his head.
He went; his piping took a troubled sound
Of storms that rage outside our happy ground;
He could not wait their passing, he is dead.

So, some tempestuous morn in early June,
When the year's primal burst of bloom is o'er,
Before the roses and the longest day —
When garden walks and all the grassy floor
With blossoms red and white of fallen May
And chestnut flowers are strewn —
So have I heard the cuckoo's parting cry,
From the wet field, through the vexed garden trees,
Come with the volleying rain and tossing breeze:
*The bloom is gone, and with the bloom go I!*

Too quick despairer, wherefore wilt thou go?
Soon will the high Midsummer pomps come on,
Soon will the musk carnations break and swell,
Soon shall we have gold-dusted snapdragon,
Sweet William with his homely cottage smell,
And stocks in fragrant blow;
Roses that down the alleys shine afar,
And open, jasmine-muffled lattices,
And groups under the dreaming garden trees,
And the full moon, and the white evening star.

He harkens not! light comer, he is flown!
What matters it? next year he will return,
And we shall have him in the sweet spring days,
With whitening hedges, and uncrumpling fern,
And bluebells trembling by the forest ways,
And scent of hay new mown.
But Thyrsis never more we swains shall see;
See him come back, and cut a smoother reed,
And blow a strain the world at last shall heed —
For Time, not Corydon, hath conquered thee!

Alack, for Corydon no rival now! —
But when Sicilian shepherds lost a mate,
Some good survivor with his flute would go,
Piping a ditty sad for Bion's fate;
And cross the unpermitted ferry's flow,
And relax Pluto's brow,

**11. Childsworth Farm:** about three miles from Oxford. **26. single . . . bright:** Attempts have been made to identify this tree, but it doesn't much matter what tree it was. Compare its use in the poem with that of the "Tree, of many, one" and the "single field which I have looked upon" in st. iv of Wordsworth's "Ode: Intimations of Immortality," above. **40. of . . . away:** Thyrsis' going away, of his own will, does not, despite the last phrase of l. 50, refer to Clough's death but rather to his having resigned his fellowship at Oriel College and left Oxford because of his religious opinions.

**80. Corydon:** like Thyrsis, a traditional name for a shepherd in pastoral poetry, here used by Arnold to refer to himself. The rivalry mentioned in l. 81 refers to the friendly contests in song which were part of the pastoral tradition. Clough wrote poetry which is by no means without its interest. **82. Sicilian shepherds:** The tradition of pastoral poetry took its rise in Sicily. **84. Bion:** an actual poet, one of the founders of the pastoral convention. Arnold refers to the poem of Bion's friend Moschus, "Lament for Bion." It should perhaps be said that, when Arnold speaks of these poets as "shepherds," he is assimilating them to the fanciful subjects of their poetry — they were very elegant poets and had no more to do with sheep than Milton had, or Arnold and Clough!

And make leap up with joy the beauteous head
Of Proserpine, among whose crownèd hair
Are flowers first opened on Sicilian air,
And flute his friends, like Orpheus, from the dead.

O easy access to the hearer's grace
When Dorian shepherds sang to Proserpine!
For she herself had trod Sicilian fields,
She knew the Dorian water's gush divine,
She knew each lily white which Enna yields,
Each rose with blushing face;
She loved the Dorian pipe, the Dorian strain.
But ah, of our poor Thames she never heard!
Her foot the Cumner cowslips never stirred;
And we should tease her with our plaint in vain!

Well! wind-dispersed and vain the words will be,
Yet, Thyrsis, let me give my grief its hour
In the old haunt, and find our tree-topped hill!
Who, if not I, for questing here hath power?
I know the wood which hides the daffodil,
I know the Fyfield tree,
I know what white, what purple fritillaries
The grassy harvest of the river fields,
Above by Ensham, down by Sandford, yields,
And what sedged brooks are Thames's tributaries;

I know these slopes; who knows them if not I? —
But many a dingle on the loved hillside,
With thorns once studded, old, white-blossomed trees,
Where thick the cowslips grew, and far descried
High towered the spikes of purple orchises,
Hath since our day put by
The coronals of that forgotten time;
Down each green bank hath gone the plowboy's team,
And only in the hidden brookside gleam
Primroses, orphans of the flowery prime.

Where is the girl, who by the boatman's door,
Above the locks, above the boating throng,
Unmoored our skiff when through the Wytham flats,
Red loosestrife and blond meadowsweet among
And darting swallows and light water gnats,
We tracked the shy Thames shore?
Where are the mowers, who, as the tiny swell
Of our boat passing heaved the river grass,
Stood with suspended scythe to see us pass? —
They all are gone, and thou art gone as well!

Yes, thou art gone! and round me too the night
In ever-nearing circle weaves her shade.
I see her veil draw soft across the day,
I feel her slowly chilling breath invade
The cheek grown thin, the brown hair sprent with gray;
I feel her finger light
Laid pausefully upon life's headlong train; —
The foot less prompt to meet the morning dew,
The heart less bounding at emotion new,
And hope, once crushed, less quick to spring again.

And long the way appears, which seemed so short
To the less practiced eye of sanguine youth;
And high the mountaintops, in cloudy air,
The mountaintops where is the throne of Truth,
Tops in life's morning sun so bright and bare!
Unbreachable the fort
Of the long-battered world uplifts its wall;
And strange and vain the earthly turmoil grows,
And near and real the charm of thy repose,
And night as welcome as a friend would fall.

But hush! the upland hath a sudden loss
Of quiet! — Look, adown the dusk hillside,
A troop of Oxford hunters going home,
As in old days, jovial and talking, ride!
From hunting with the Berkshire hounds they come.
Quick! let me fly, and cross
Into yon farther field! — 'Tis done; and see,
Backed by the sunset, which doth glorify
The orange and pale violet evening sky,
Bare on its lonely ridge, the Tree! the Tree!

I take the omen! Eve lets down her veil,
The white fog creeps from bush to bush about,
The west unflushes, the high stars grow bright,
And in the scattered farms the lights come out.
I cannot reach the signal tree tonight,
Yet, happy omen, hail!
Hear it from thy broad lucent Arno vale
(For there thine earth-forgetting eyelids keep
The morningless and unawakening sleep
Under the flowery oleanders pale),

Hear it, O Thyrsis, still our tree is there! —
Ah, vain! These English fields, this upland dim,

**90. Orpheus:** His power of song was so great that he was able to penetrate to Hades, though alive, and win permission to lead his wife Eurydice back to the upper world. **92. Dorian:** Sicilian. **95. Enna:** the Sicilian town from which Proserpine was carried off by Pluto. **106. Fyfield tree:** See "The Scholar Gipsy," l. 83n. **107. fritillaries:** a name both for a spotted flower of the lily family and for butterflies with spotted wings. Arnold means the flower. **109. Ensham . . . Sandford:** villages near Oxford. **123. Wytham flats:** the low land between Oxford and the village of Wytham.

**167. Arno vale:** Clough died in Italy and was buried in Florence near the river Arno.

These brambles pale with mist engarlanded,
That lone sky-pointing tree are not for him;
To a boon southern country he is fled,
And now in happier air,
Wandering with the great Mother's train divine
(And purer or more subtle soul than thee,
I trow, the mighty Mother doth not see)
Within a folding of the Apennine,

Thou hearest the immortal chants of old!—
Putting his sickle to the perilous grain
In the hot cornfield of the Phrygian king,
For thee the Lityerses song again
Young Daphnis with his silver voice doth sing;
Sings his Sicilian fold,
His sheep, his hapless love, his blinded eyes—
And how a call celestial round him rang,
And heavenward from the fountain brink he sprang,
And all the marvel of the golden skies.

There thou art gone, and me thou leavest here
Sole in these fields! yet will I not despair.
Despair I will not, while I yet descry
'Neath the mild canopy of English air
That lonely tree against the western sky.
Still, still these slopes, 'tis clear,
Our Gypsy Scholar haunts, outliving thee!
Fields where soft sheep from cages pull the hay,
Woods with anemones in flower till May,
Know him a wanderer still; then why not me?

A fugitive and gracious light he seeks,
Shy to illumine; and I seek it too.
This does not come with houses or with gold,
With place, with honor, and a flattering crew;
'Tis not in the world's market bought and sold—
But the smooth-slipping weeks
Drop by, and leave its seeker still untired;
Out of the heed of mortals he is gone,
He wends unfollowed, he must house alone;
Yet on he fares, by his own heart inspired.

**183–85. Phrygian . . . sing:** "Daphnis, the ideal Sicilian shepherd of Greek pastoral poetry, was said to have followed into Phrygia his mistress Piplea, who had been carried off by robbers, and to have found her in the power of the king of Phrygia, Lityerses. Lityerses used to make strangers try a contest with him in reaping corn, and to put them to death if he overcame them. Hercules arrived in time to save Daphnis, took upon himself the reaping contest with Lityerses, overcame him, and slew him. The Lityerses song connected with this tradition was, like the Linus song, one of the early plaintive strains of Greek popular poetry, and used to be sung by corn reapers. Other traditions represented Daphnis as beloved by a nymph who exacted from him an oath to love no one else. He fell in love with a princess, and was struck blind by the jealous nymph. Mercury, who was his father, raised him to heaven, and made a fountain spring up in the place from which he ascended. At this fountain the Sicilians offered yearly sacrifices" [Arnold's note].

Thou too, O Thyrsis, on like quest wast bound;
Thou wanderedst with me for a little hour!
Men gave thee nothing; but this happy quest,
If men esteemed thee feeble, gave thee power,
If men procured thee trouble, gave thee rest.
And this rude Cumner ground,
Its fir-topped Hurst, its farms, its quiet fields,
Here cam'st thou in thy jocund youthful time,
Here was thine height of strength, thy golden prime!
And still the haunt beloved a virtue yields.

What though the music of thy rustic flute
Kept not for long its happy, country tone;
Lost it too soon, and learned a stormy note
Of men contention-tossed, of men who groan,
Which tasked thy pipe too sore, and tired thy throat—
It failed, and thou wast mute!
Yet hadst thou always visions of our light,
And long with men of care thou couldst not stay,
And soon thy foot resumed its wandering way,
Left human haunt, and on alone till night.

Too rare, too rare, grow now my visits here!
'Mid city noise, not, as with thee of yore,
Thyrsis! in reach of sheepbells is my home.
—Then through the great town's harsh, heart-wearying roar,
Let in thy voice a whisper often come,
To chase fatigue and fear:
*Why faintest thou? I wandered till I died.*
*Roam on! The light we sought is shining still.*
*Dost thou ask proof? Our tree yet crowns the hill,*
*Our Scholar travels yet the loved hillside.*
[*1866*]

## PERSISTENCY OF POETRY

Though the Muse be gone away,
Though she move not earth today,
Souls, erewhile who caught her word,
Ah! still harp on what they heard.
[*1867*]

## DOVER BEACH

The sea is calm tonight.
The tide is full, the moon lies fair
Upon the straits;—on the French coast the light
Gleams and is gone; the cliffs of England stand,

**216–17. Cumner . . . Hurst:** See "The Scholar Gypsy," l. 57n.

Glimmering and vast, out in the tranquil bay.
Come to the window, sweet is the night air!

Only, from the long line of spray
Where the sea meets the moon-blanched land,
Listen! you hear the grating roar
Of pebbles which the waves draw back, and
fling,
At their return, up the high strand,
Begin, and cease, and then again begin,
With tremulous cadence slow, and bring
The eternal note of sadness in.

Sophocles long ago
Heard it on the Aegean, and it brought
Into his mind the turbid ebb and flow
Of human misery; we
Find also in the sound a thought,
Hearing it by this distant northern sea.

The Sea of Faith
Was once, too, at the full, and round earth's
shore
Lay like the folds of a bright girdle furled.
But now I only hear
Its melancholy, long, withdrawing roar,
Retreating, to the breath
Of the night wind, down the vast edges drear
And naked shingles of the world.

Ah, love, let us be true
To one another! for the world, which seems
To lie before us like a land of dreams,
So various, so beautiful, so new,
Hath really neither joy, nor love, nor light,
Nor certitude, nor peace, nor help for pain;
And we are here as on a darkling plain
Swept with confused alarms of struggle and
flight,
Where ignorant armies clash by night.

[*1867*]

## FRAGMENT OF CHORUS OF A "DEJANEIRA"

O frivolous mind of man,
Light ignorance, and hurrying, unsure thoughts!
Though man bewails you not,
How *I* bewail you!

Little in your prosperity
Do you seek counsel of the Gods.
Proud, ignorant, self-adored, you live alone.
In profound silence stern,
Among their savage gorges and cold springs,
Unvisited remain
The great oracular shrines.

Thither in your adversity
Do you betake yourselves for light,
But strangely misinterpret all you hear.
For you will not put on
New hearts with the inquirer's holy robe,
And purged, considerate minds.

And him on whom, at the end
Of toil and dolor untold,
The Gods have said that repose
At last shall descend undisturbed—
Him you expect to behold
In an easy old age, in a happy home;
No end but this you praise.

But him, on whom, in the prime
Of life, with vigor undimmed,
With unspent mind, and a soul
Unworn, undebased, undecayed,
Mournfully grating, the gates
Of the city of death have forever closed—
*Him,* I count *him,* well starred.

[*1867*]

DOVER BEACH. 28. shingles: (usually in the singular) the large coarse gravel of a beach. "DEJANEIRA." Dejaneira was the wife of Hercules. She unwittingly caused her husband's death by sending him a tunic which she believed had the magic power of making him love her once more but which was actually poisoned. The incident is the subject of Sophocles' tragedy *Trachinae* and of Euripides' *Hercules*.

## EARLY DEATH AND FAME

For him who must see many years,
I praise the life which slips away
Out of the light and mutely; which avoids
Fame, and her less fair followers, envy, strife,
Stupid detraction, jealousy, cabal,
Insincere praises; which descends
The quiet mossy track to age.

But, when immature death
Beckons too early the guest
From the half-tried banquet of life,
Young, in the bloom of his days;
Leaves no leisure to press,
Slow and surely, the sweets
Of a tranquil life in the shade—

Fuller for him be the hours!
Give him emotion, though pain!
Let him live, let him feel: *I have lived.*
Heap up his moments with life!
Triple his pulses with fame!

[*1867*]

## GROWING OLD

What is it to grow old?
Is it to lose the glory of the form,
The luster of the eye?
Is it for beauty to forgo her wreath?
— Yes, but not this alone.

Is it to feel our strength —
Not our bloom only, but our strength — decay?
Is it to feel each limb
Grow stiffer, every function less exact,
Each nerve more loosely strung?

Yes, this, and more; but not
Ah, 'tis not what in youth we dreamed 'twould be!
'Tis not to have our life
Mellowed and softened as with sunset glow,
A golden day's decline.

'Tis not to see the world
As from a height, with rapt prophetic eyes,
And heart profoundly stirred;
And weep, and feel the fullness of the past,
The years that are no more.

It is to spend long days
And not once feel that we were ever young;
It is to add, immured
In the hot prison of the present, month
To month with weary pain.

It is to suffer this,
And feel but half, and feebly, what we feel.
Deep in our hidden heart
Festers the dull remembrance of a change,
But no emotion — none.

It is — last stage of all —
When we are frozen up within, and quite
The phantom of ourselves,
To hear the world applaud the hollow ghost
Which blamed the living man.
[*1867*]

## THE PROGRESS OF POESY

*A Variation*

Youth rambles on life's arid mount,
And strikes the rock, and finds the vein,
And brings the water from the fount,
The fount which shall not flow again.

PROGRESS OF POESY. Arnold probably implies that his poem is a variation on Thomas Gray's Pindaric ode, "The Progress of Poesy."

The man mature with labor chops
For the bright stream a channel grand,
And sees not that the sacred drops
Ran off and vanished out of hand.

And then the old man totters nigh,
And feebly rakes among the stones.
The mount is mute, the channel dry;
And down he lays his weary bones.
[*1867*]

## THE LAST WORD

Creep into thy narrow bed,
Creep, and let no more be said!
Vain thy onset! all stands fast.
Thou thyself must break at last.

Let the long contention cease!
Geese are swans, and swans are geese.
Let them have it how they will!
Thou art tired; best be still.

They out-talked thee, hissed thee, tore thee?
Better men fared thus before thee;
Fired their ringing shot and passed,
Hotly charged — and sank at last.

Charge once more, then, and be dumb!
Let the victors, when they come,
When the forts of folly fall,
Find thy body by the wall!
[*1867*]

# RUGBY CHAPEL

Dr. Thomas Arnold, Matthew Arnold's father, was buried in the chapel of the school of which he had been headmaster. For an account of Thomas Arnold's place in the life of Victorian England see the Introduction to these selections, p. 581. It will be apparent from this moving tribute that Matthew Arnold in middle age had long left behind him his youthful resistance to his father's stern commitment to duty.

*November, 1857*

Coldly, sadly descends
The autumn evening. The field
Strewn with its dank yellow drifts
Of withered leaves, and the elms,
Fade into dimness apace,
Silent; — hardly a shout
From a few boys late at their play!
The lights come out in the street,
In the schoolroom windows; — but cold,

Solemn, unlighted, austere,
Through the gathering darkness, arise
The chapel walls, in whose bound
Thou, my father! art laid.

There thou dost lie, in the gloom
Of the autumn evening. But ah!
That word, *gloom,* to my mind
Brings thee back, in the light
Of thy radiant vigor, again;
In the gloom of November we passed

Days not dark at thy side;
Seasons impaired not the ray
Of thy buoyant cheerfulness clear.
Such thou wast! and I stand
In the autumn evening, and think
Of bygone autumns with thee.

Fifteen years have gone round
Since thou arosest to tread,
In the summer morning, the road
Of death, at a call unforeseen,
Sudden. For fifteen years,
We who till then in thy shade
Rested as under the boughs
Of a mighty oak, have endured
Sunshine and rain as we might,
Bare, unshaded, alone,
Lacking the shelter of thee.

O strong soul, by what shore
Tarriest thou now? For that force,
Surely, has not been left vain!
Somewhere, surely, afar,
In the sounding laborhouse vast
Of being, is practiced that strength,
Zealous, beneficent, firm!

Yes, in some far-shining sphere,
Conscious or not of the past,
Still thou performest the word
Of the Spirit in whom thou dost live—
Prompt, unwearied, as here!
Still thou upraisest with zeal
The humble good from the ground,
Sternly repressest the bad!
Still, like a trumpet, dost rouse
Those who with half-open eyes
Tread the borderland dim
'Twixt vice and virtue; revivest,
Succourest!—this was thy work,
This was thy life upon earth.

What is the course of the life
Of mortal men on the earth?—
Most men eddy about
Here and there—eat and drink,
Chatter and love and hate,
Gather and squander, are raised
Aloft, are hurled in the dust,
Striving blindly, achieving
Nothing; and then they die—
Perish—and no one asks
Who or what they have been,
More than he asks what waves,
In the moonlit solitudes mild
Of the midmost ocean, have swelled,
Foamed for a moment, and gone.

And there are some, whom a thirst
Ardent, unquenchable, fires,
Not with the crowd to be spent,
Not without aim to go round
In an eddy of purposeless dust,
Effort unmeaning and vain.
Ah yes! some of us strive
Not without action to die
Fruitless, but something to snatch
From dull oblivion, nor all
Glut the devouring grave!
We, we have chosen our path—
Path to a clear-purposed goal,
Path of advance!—but it leads
A long, steep journey, through sunk
Gorges, o'er mountains in snow.
Cheerful, with friends, we set forth—
Then, on the height, comes the storm.
Thunder crashes from rock
To rock, the cataracts reply,
Lightnings dazzle our eyes.
Roaring torrents have breached
The track, the stream bed descends
In the place where the wayfarer once
Planted his footsteps—the spray
Boils o'er its borders! aloft
The unseen snow beds dislodge
Their hanging ruin; alas,
Havoc is made in our train!
Friends, who set forth at our side,
Falter, are lost in the storm.
We, we only are left!
With frowning foreheads, with lips
Sternly compressed, we strain on,
On—and at nightfall at last
Come to the end of our way,
To the lonely inn 'mid the rocks;
Where the gaunt and taciturn host
Stands on the threshold, the wind
Shaking his thin white hairs—
Holds his lantern to scan
Our storm-beat figures, and asks:
Whom in our party we bring?
Whom we have left in the snow?

Sadly we answer: We bring
Only ourselves! we lost
Sight of the rest in the storm.
Hardly ourselves we fought through,
Stripped, without friends, as we are.
Friends, companions, and train,
The avalanche swept from our side.
But thou would'st not *alone*
Be saved, my father! *alone*
Conquer and come to thy goal,
Leaving the rest in the wild.
We were weary, and we
Fearful, and we in our march
Fain to drop down and to die.
Still thou turnedst, and still
Beckonedst the trembler, and still
Gavest the weary thy hand.

If, in the paths of the world,
Stones might have wounded thy feet,
Toil or dejection have tried
Thy spirit, of that we saw
Nothing — to us thou wast still
Cheerful, and helpful, and firm!
Therefore to thee it was given
Many to save with thyself;
And, at the end of thy day,
O faithful shepherd! to come,
Bringing thy sheep in thy hand.

And through thee I believe
In the noble and great who are gone;
Pure souls honored and blessed
By former ages, who else —
Such, so soulless, so poor,
Is the race of men whom I see —
Seemed but a dream of the heart,
Seemed but a cry of desire.
Yes! I believe that there lived
Others like thee in the past,
Not like the men of the crowd
Who all round me today
Bluster or cringe, and make life
Hideous, and arid, and vile;
But souls tempered with fire,
Fervent, heroic, and good,
Helpers and friends of mankind.

Servants of God! — or sons
Shall I not call you? because
Not as servants ye knew
Your Father's innermost mind,
His, who unwillingly sees
One of his little ones lost —
Yours is the praise, if mankind
Hath not as yet in its march
Fainted, and fallen, and died!

See! In the rocks of the world
Marches the host of mankind,
A feeble, wavering line.
Where are they tending? — A God
Marshaled them, gave them their goal.
Ah, but the way is so long!
Years they have been in the wild!
Sore thirst plagues them, the rocks,
Rising all round, overawe;
Factions divide them, their host
Threatens to break, to dissolve.
— Ah, keep, keep them combined!
Else, of the myriads who fill
That army, not one shall arrive;
Sole they shall stray; in the rocks
Stagger forever in vain,
Die one by one in the waste.

Then, in such hour of need
Of your fainting, dispirited race,
Ye, like angels, appear,
Radiant with ardor divine!
Beacons of hope, ye appear!
Languor is not in your heart,
Weakness is not in your word,
Weariness not on your brow.
Ye alight in our van! at your voice,
Panic, despair, flee away.
Ye move through the ranks, recall
The stragglers, refresh the outworn,
Praise, reinspire the brave!
Order, courage, return.
Eyes rekindling, and prayers,
Follow your steps as ye go.
Ye fill up the gaps in our files,
Strengthen the wavering line,
Stablish, continue our march,
On, to the bound of the waste,
On, to the City of God.

[*1867*]

# PREFACE TO *POEMS*, EDITION OF 1853

The Introduction to Arnold (p. 589) gives the circumstance under which the Preface, the first of Arnold's critical essays, was written. In 1867 Arnold restored "Empedocles on Etna" to the canon of his work with this note: "I cannot deny myself the pleasure of saying that I reprint (I cannot say *republish*, for it was withdrawn from circulation before fifty copies were sold) this poem at the request of a man of genius, whom it had the honor and the good fortune to interest — Mr. Robert Browning."

In two small volumes of Poems, published anonymously, one in 1849, the other in 1852,[1] many of the Poems which compose the present volume have already appeared. The rest are now published for the first time.

I have, in the present collection, omitted the Poem from which the volume published in 1852 took its title. I have done so, not because the subject of it was a Sicilian Greek born between two and three thousand years ago, although many persons would think this a sufficient reason. Neither have I done so because I had, in my own opinion, failed in the delineation which I intended to effect. I intended to delineate the feelings of one of the last of the Greek religious philosophers, one of the family of Orpheus and Musaeus,[2] having survived his fellows, living on into a time when the habits of Greek thought and feeling had begun fast to change, character to dwindle, the influence of the Sophists to prevail. Into the feelings of a man so situated there entered much that we are accustomed to consider as exclusively modern; how much, the fragments of Empedocles himself which remain to us are sufficient at least to indicate. What those who are familiar only with the great monuments of early Greek genius suppose to be its exclusive characteristics, have disappeared; the calm, the cheerfulness, the disinterested objectivity have disappeared; the dialogue of the mind with itself has commenced; modern problems have presented themselves; we hear already the doubts, we witness the discouragement, of Hamlet and of Faust.

The representation of such a man's feelings must be interesting, if consistently drawn. We all naturally take pleasure, says Aristotle, in any imitation or representation whatever: this is the basis of our love of Poetry; and we take pleasure in them, he adds, because all knowledge is naturally agreeable to us; not to the philosopher only, but to mankind at large. Every representation therefore which is consistently drawn may be supposed to be interesting, inasmuch as it gratifies this natural interest in knowledge of all kinds. What is *not* interesting, is that which does not add to our knowledge of any kind; that which is vaguely conceived and loosely drawn; a representation which is general, indeterminate, and faint, instead of being particular, precise, and firm.

Any accurate representation may therefore be expected to be interesting; but, if the representation be a poetical one, more than this is demanded. It is demanded, not only that it shall interest, but also that it shall inspirit and rejoice the reader: that it shall convey a charm, and infuse delight. For the Muses, as Hesiod[3] says, were born that they might be "a forgetfulness of evils, and a truce from cares," and it is not enough that the Poet should add to the knowledge of men; it is required of him also that he should add to their happiness. "All Art," says Schiller, "is dedicated to Joy, and there is no higher and no more serious problem, than how to make men happy. The right Art is that alone, which creates the highest enjoyment."

A poetical work, therefore, is not yet justified when it has been shown to be an accurate, and therefore interesting, representation; it has to be shown also that it is a representation from which men can derive enjoyment. In presence of the most tragic circumstances, represented in a work of Art, the feeling of enjoyment, as is well known, may still subsist; the representation of the most utter calamity, of the liveliest anguish, is not sufficient to destroy it; the more tragic the situation, the deeper becomes the enjoyment; and the situation is more tragic in proportion as it becomes more terrible.

What then are the situations, from the representation of which, though accurate, no poetical enjoyment can be derived? They are those in which the suffering finds no vent in action; in which a continuous state of mental distress is prolonged, unrelieved by incident, hope, or resistance; in which there is everything to be endured, nothing to be done. In such situations there is inevitably something morbid, in the description of them something monotonous. When they occur in actual life, they are painful, not tragic; the representation of them in poetry is painful also.

To this class of situations, poetically faulty as it appears to me, that of Empedocles, as I have endeavored to represent him, belongs; and I have therefore excluded the Poem from the present collection.

And why, it may be asked, have I entered into this explanation respecting a matter so unimportant as the admission or exclusion of the Poem in question? I have done so, because I was anxious to

PREFACE TO POEMS. 1. **one . . . 1852:** The volume published in 1849 was *The Strayed Reveler, and Other Poems;* the volume of 1852 was *Empedocles on Etna, and Other Poems.* 2. **Orpheus . . . Musaeus:** Orpheus was the son of Apollo; Musaeus was the son of Orpheus. Both were famous for their power of song. Arnold wishes to imply that Empedocles' philosophy was more intuitive, more poetic, and less rationalistic than that of his successors.

3. **Hesiod:** an early Greek poet, probably of the eighth century B.C.

avow that the sole reason for its exclusion was that which has been stated above; and that it has not been excluded in deference to the opinion which many critics of the present day appear to entertain against subjects chosen from distant times and countries, against the choice, in short, of any subjects but modern ones.

"The Poet," it is said,[4] and by an intelligent critic, "the Poet who would really fix the public attention must leave the exhausted past, and draw his subjects from matters of present import, and *therefore* both of interest and novelty."

Now this view I believe to be completely false. It is worth examining, inasmuch as it is a fair sample of a class of critical dicta everywhere current at the present day, having a philosophical form and air, but no real basis in fact; and which are calculated to vitiate the judgment of readers of poetry, while they exert, so far as they are adopted, a misleading influence on the practice of those who write it.

What are the eternal objects of Poetry, among all nations and at all times? They are actions, human actions, possessing an inherent interest in themselves, and which are to be communicated in an interesting manner by the art of the Poet. Vainly will the latter imagine that he has everything in his own power; that he can make an intrinsically inferior action equally delightful with a more excellent one by his treatment of it; he may indeed compel us to admire his skill, but his work will possess, within itself, an incurable defect.

The Poet, then, has in the first place to select an excellent action; and what actions are the most excellent? Those, certainly, which most powerfully appeal to the great primary human affections: to those elementary feelings which subsist permanently in the race, and which are independent of time. These feelings are permanent and the same; that which interests them is permanent and the same also. The modernness or antiquity of an action, therefore, has nothing to do with its fitness for poetical representation; this depends upon its inherent qualities. To the elementary part of our nature, to our passions, that which is great and passionate is eternally interesting; and interesting solely in proportion to its greatness and to its passion. A great human action of a thousand years ago is more interesting to it than a smaller human action of today, even though upon the representation of this last the most consummate skill may have been expended, and though it has the advantage of appealing by its modern language, familiar manners, and contemporary allusions, to all our transient feelings and interests. These, however, have no right to demand of a poetical work that it shall satisfy them; their claims are to be directed elsewhere. Poetical works belong to the domain of our permanent passions: let them interest these, and the voice of all subordinate claims upon them is at once silenced.

Achilles, Prometheus, Clytemnestra, Dido[5]—what modern poem presents personages as interesting, even to us moderns, as these personages of an "exhausted past"? We have the domestic epic dealing with the details of modern life which pass daily under our eyes; we have poems representing modern personages in contact with the problems of modern life, moral, intellectual, and social; these works have been produced by poets the most distinguished of their nation and time; yet I fearlessly assert that *Hermann and Dorothea, Childe Harold, Jocelyn, The Excursion,*[6] leave the reader cold in comparison with the effect produced upon him by the latter books of the *Iliad,* by the *Oresteia*[7] or by the episode of Dido. And why is this? Simply because in the three latter cases the action is greater, the personage nobler, the situations more intense; and this is the true basis of the interest in a poetical work, and this alone.

It may be urged, however, that past actions may be interesting in themselves, but that they are not to be adopted by the modern Poet, because it is impossible for him to have them clearly present to his own mind, and he cannot therefore feel them deeply, nor represent them forcibly. But this is not necessarily the case. The externals of a past action, indeed, he cannot know with the precision of a contemporary; but his business is with its essentials. The outward man of Oedipus or of Macbeth, the houses in which they lived, the ceremonies of their courts, he cannot accurately figure to himself; but neither do they essentially concern him. His business is with their inward man; with their feelings and behavior in certain tragic situations, which en-

4. "In the *Spectator* of April 2, 1853. The words quoted were not used with reference to poems of mine"[A].

5. **Achilles . . . Dido:** Achilles is the hero of Homer's *Iliad;* Prometheus is the hero of Aeschylus' tragedy, *Prometheus Bound;* Clytemnestra is the wife and murderer of Agamemnon in Aeschylus' tragedy, *Agamemnon;* Dido is the queen of Carthage in Virgil's *Aeneid* who kills herself when Aeneas, whom she loves, leaves her to found the city of Rome. 6. ***Hermann and Dorothea . . . The Excursion:*** long narrative poems by, respectively, Goethe, Byron, Lamartine, Wordsworth. 7. ***Oresteia:*** See note 8, below.

gage their passions as men; these have in them nothing local and casual; they are as accessible to the modern Poet as to a contemporary.

The date of an action, then, signifies nothing; the action itself, its selection and construction, this is what is all-important. This the Greeks understood far more clearly than we do. The radical difference between their poetical theory and ours consists, as it appears to me, in this: that, with them, the poetical character of the action in itself, and the conduct of it, was the first consideration; with us, attention is fixed mainly on the value of the separate thoughts and images which occur in the treatment of an action. They regarded the whole; we regard the parts. With them, the action predominated over the expression of it; with us, the expression predominates over the action. Not that they failed in expression, or were inattentive to it; on the contrary, they are the highest models of expression, the unapproached masters of the *grand style,* but their expression is so excellent because it is so admirably kept in its right degree of prominence; because it is so simple and so well subordinated; because it draws its force directly from the pregnancy of the matter which it conveys. For what reason was the Greek tragic poet confined to so limited a range of subjects? Because there are so few actions which unite in themselves, in the highest degree, the conditions of excellence; and it was not thought that on any but an excellent subject could an excellent Poem be constructed. A few actions, therefore, eminently adapted for tragedy, maintained almost exclusive possesssion of the Greek tragic stage; their significance appeared inexhaustible; they were as permanent problems, perpetually offered to the genius of every fresh poet. This too is the reason of what appears to us moderns a certain baldness of expression in Greek tragedy; of the triviality with which we often reproach the remarks of the chorus, where it takes part in the dialogue: that the action itself, the situation of Orestes, or Merope, or Alcmaeon,[8] was to stand the central point of interest, unforgotten, absorbing, principal; that no accessories were for a moment to distract the spectator's attention from this; that the tone of the parts was to be perpetually kept down, in order not to impair the grandiose effect of the whole. The terrible old mythic story on which the drama was founded stood, before he entered the theater, traced in its bare outlines upon the spectator's mind; it stood in his memory, as a group of statuary, faintly seen, at the end of a long and dark vista; then came the Poet, embodying outlines, developing situations, not a word wasted, not a sentiment capriciously thrown in: stroke upon stroke, the drama proceeded; the light deepened upon the group; more and more it revealed itself to the riveted gaze of the spectator, until at last, when the final words were spoken, it stood before him in broad sunlight, a model of immortal beauty.

This was what a Greek critic demanded; this was what a Greek poet endeavored to effect. It signified nothing to what time an action belonged; we do not find that the *Persae* occupied a particularly high rank among the dramas of Aeschylus, because it represented a matter of contemporary interest:[9] this was not what a cultivated Athenian required; he required that the permanent elements of his nature should be moved; and dramas of which the action, though taken from a long-distant mythic time, yet was calculated to accomplish this in a higher degree than that of the *Persae,* stood higher in his estimation accordingly. The Greeks felt, no doubt, with their exquisite sagacity of taste, that an action of present times was too near them, too much mixed up with what was accidental and passing, to form a sufficiently grand, detached, and self-subsistent object for a tragic poem: such objects belonged to the domain of the comic poet, and of the lighter kinds of poetry. For the more serious kinds, for *pragmatic* poetry, to use an excellent expression of Polybius,[10] they were more difficult and severe in the range of subjects which they permitted. Their theory and practice alike, the admirable treatise of Aristotle, and the unrivaled works of their poets, exclaim with a thousand tongues — "All depends upon the subject; choose a fitting action, penetrate yourself with the feeling of its situations; this done, everything else will follow."

But for all kinds of poetry alike there was one point on which they were rigidly exacting: the

**8. Orestes . . . Alcmaeon:** Orestes, the son of Agamemnon and Clytemnestra, kills his mother and her lover to avenge the death of his father; he is the hero of plays by Aeschylus, Sophocles, and Euripides. Merope was a Greek queen whose husband and two children were murdered by Polyphontes; the murders were avenged by her third son, Aepytus. Aristotle, for reasons that are hard to understand, speaks of the subject as one of the "most tragic" a dramatist could use — perhaps because of its most famous scene in which Merope, not knowing the identity of Aepytus, is on the point of murdering her own son as he sleeps. Euripides wrote a drama on the subject, and so did Voltaire and others, including Arnold himself. Alcmaeon killed his mother to avenge his father; he is the subject of tragedies now lost.

**9. matter . . . interest:** *Persae — The Persians* — was produced in 472 B.C. It dealt with the defeat of the Persians by the Greeks in 480 B.C. **10. Polybius:** a Greek historian who lived 205?–125? B.C.

adaptability of the subject to the kind of poetry selected, and the careful construction of the poem.

How different a way of thinking from this is ours! We can hardly at the present day understand what Menander [11] meant, when he told a man who inquired as to the progress of his comedy that he had finished it, not having yet written a single line, because he had constructed the action of it in his mind. A modern critic would have assured him that the merit of his piece depended on the brilliant things which arose under his pen as he went along. We have poems which seem to exist merely for the sake of single lines and passages, not for the sake of producing any total impression. We have critics who seem to direct their attention merely to detached expressions, to the language about the action, not to the action itself. I verily think that the majority of them do not in their hearts believe that there is such a thing as a total impression to be derived from a poem at all, or to be demanded from a poet; they think the term a commonplace of metaphysical criticism. They will permit the Poet to select any action he pleases, and to suffer that action to go as it will, provided he gratifies them with occasional bursts of fine writing, and with a shower of isolated thoughts and images. That is, they permit him to leave their poetical sense ungratified, provided that he gratifies their rhetorical sense and their curiosity. Of his neglecting to gratify these, there is little danger; he needs rather to be warned against the danger of attempting to gratify these alone; he needs rather to be perpetually reminded to prefer his action to everything else; so to treat this, as to permit its inherent excellences to develop themselves, without interruption from the intrusion of his personal peculiarities: most fortunate, when he most entirely succeeds in effacing himself, and in enabling a noble action to subsist as it did in nature.

But the modern critic not only permits a false practice; he absolutely prescribes false aims. "A true allegory of the state of one's own mind in a representative history," the Poet is told, "is perhaps the highest thing that one can attempt in the way of poetry." And accordingly he attempts it. An allegory of the state of one's own mind, the highest problem of an art which imitates actions! No, assuredly it is not, it never can be so; no great poetical work has ever been produced with such an aim. *Faust* itself, in which something of the kind is attempted, wonderful passages as it contains, and in spite of the unsurpassed beauty of the scenes which relate to Margaret, *Faust* itself, judged as a whole, and judged strictly as a poetical work, is defective; its illustrious author, the greatest poet of modern times, the greatest critic of all times, would have been the first to acknowledge it; he only defended his work, indeed, by asserting it to be "something incommensurable."

The confusion of the present times is great, the multitude of voices counseling different things bewildering, the number of existing works capable of attracting a young writer's attention and of becoming his models, immense; what he wants is a hand to guide him through the confusion, a voice to prescribe to him the aim which he should keep in view, and to explain to him that the value of the literary works which offer themselves to his attention is relative to their power of helping him forward on his road towards this aim. Such a guide the English writer at the present day will nowhere find. Failing this, all that can be looked for, all indeed that can be desired, is that his attention should be fixed on excellent models; that he may reproduce, at any rate, something of their excellence, by penetrating himself with their works and by catching their spirit, if he cannot be taught to produce what is excellent independently.

Foremost among these models for the English writer stands Shakespeare: a name the greatest perhaps of all poetical names; a name never to be mentioned without reverence. I will venture, however, to express a doubt, whether the influence of his works, excellent and fruitful for the readers of poetry, for the great majority, has been of unmixed advantage to the writers of it. Shakespeare indeed chose excellent subjects; the world could afford no better than Macbeth, or Romeo and Juliet, or Othello; he had no theory respecting the necessity of choosing subjects of present import, or the paramount interest attaching to allegories of the state of one's own mind; like all great poets, he knew well what constituted a poetical action; like them, wherever he found such an action, he took it; like them, too, he found his best in past times. But to these general characteristics of all great poets he added a special one of his own; a gift, namely, of happy, abundant, and ingenious expression, eminent and unrivaled: so eminent as irresistibly to strike the attention first in him, and even to throw into comparative shade his other excellences as a poet. Here

11. **Menander**: a Greek dramatist (343?–291? B.C.), the author of many comedies considered by the ancients to be of the highest excellence, most of which have been lost.

has been the mischief. These other excellences were his fundamental excellences *as a poet;* what distinguishes the artist from the mere amateur, says Goethe, is *Architectonicè* in the highest sense; that power of execution, which creates, forms, and constitutes; not the profoundness of single thoughts, not the richness of imagery, not the abundance of illustration. But these attractive accessories of a poetical work being more easily seized than the spirit of the whole, and these accessories being possessed by Shakespeare in an unequaled degree, a young writer having recourse to Shakespeare as his model runs great risk of being vanquished and absorbed by them, and, in consequence, of reproducing, according to the measure of his power, these, and these alone. Of this preponderating quality of Shakespeare's genius, accordingly, almost the whole of modern English poetry has, it appears to me, felt the influence. To the exclusive attention on the part of his imitators to this it is in a great degree owing, that of the majority of modern poetical works the details alone are valuable, the composition worthless. In reading them one is perpetually reminded of that terrible sentence on a modern French poet—*il dit tout ce qu'il veut, mais malheureusement il n'a rien à dire.*[12]

Let me give an instance of what I mean. I will take it from the works of the very chief among those who seem to have been formed in the school of Shakespeare: of one whose exquisite genius and pathetic death render him forever interesting. I will take the poem of "Isabella, or the Pot of Basil," by Keats. I choose this rather than the *Endymion,* because the latter work (which a modern critic has classed with *The Faerie Queene!*), although undoubtedly there blows through it the breath of genius, is yet as a whole so utterly incoherent, as not strictly to merit the name of a poem at all. The poem of "Isabella," then, is a perfect treasure house of graceful and felicitous words and images; almost in every stanza there occurs one of those vivid and picturesque turns of expression, by which the object is made to flash upon the eye of the mind, and which thrill the reader with a sudden delight. This one short poem contains, perhaps, a greater number of happy single expressions which one could quote than all the extant tragedies of Sophocles. But the action, the story? The action in itself is an excellent one; but so feebly is it conceived by the Poet, so loosely constructed, that the effect produced by it, in and for itself, is absolutely null. Let the reader, after he has finished the poem of Keats, turn to the same story in the *Decameron;*[13] he will then feel how pregnant and interesting the same action has become in the hands of a great artist, who above all things delineates his object, who subordinates expression to that which it is designed to express.

I have said that the imitators of Shakespeare, fixing their attention on his wonderful gift of expression, have directed their imitation to this, neglecting his other excellences. These excellences, the fundamental excellences of poetical art, Shakespeare no doubt possessed them—possessed many of them in a splendid degree, but it may perhaps be doubted whether even he himself did not sometimes give scope to his faculty of expression to the prejudice of a higher poetical duty. For we must never forget that Shakespeare is the great poet he is from his skill in discerning and firmly conceiving an excellent action, from his power of intensely feeling a situation, of intimately associating himself with a character; not from his gift of expression, which rather even leads him astray, degenerating sometimes into a fondness for curiosity of expression, into an irritability of fancy, which seems to make it impossible for him to say a thing plainly, even when the press of the action demands the very directest language, or its level character the very simplest. Mr. Hallam,[14] than whom it is impossible to find a saner and more judicious critic, has had the courage (for at the present day it needs courage) to remark, how extremely and faultily difficult Shakespeare's language often is. It is so: you may find main scenes in some of his greatest tragedies, *King Lear* for instance, where the language is so artificial, so curiously tortured, and so difficult, that every speech has to be read two or three times before its meaning can be comprehended. This overcuriousness of expression is indeed but the excessive employment of a wonderful gift—of the power of saying a thing in a happier way than any other man; nevertheless, it is carried so far that one understands what M. Guizot[15] meant, when he said that Shakespeare appears in his language to have tried all styles except that of simplicity. He has not the severe and scrupulous self-restraint of the ancients, partly no doubt because he had a far

12. *il . . . dire:* "he says all that he wants to say, but unhappily he has nothing to say."

13. turn . . . *Decameron:* the fifth story of the fourth day in Boccaccio's famous collection of stories. 14. Mr. Hallam: Henry Hallam (1777–1859) the historian, father of Arthur Hallam, who was Tennyson's friend celebrated in *In Memoriam.* 15. Guizot: François Pierre Guillaume Guizot (1787–1874), French historian, statesman, premier of France (1840–48).

less cultivated and exacting audience; he has indeed a far wider range than they had, a far richer fertility of thought; in this respect he rises above them; in his strong conception of his subject, in the genuine way in which he is penetrated with it, he resembles them, and is unlike the moderns; but in the accurate limitation of it, the conscientious rejection of superfluities, the simple and rigorous development of it from the first line of his work to the last, he falls below them, and comes nearer to the moderns. In his chief works, besides what he has of his own, he has the elementary soundness of the ancients; he has their important action and their large and broad manner, but he has not their purity of method. He is therefore a less safe model, for what he has of his own is personal, and inseparable from his own rich nature; it may be imitated and exaggerated; it cannot be learned or applied as an art; he is above all suggestive; more valuable, therefore, to young writers as men than as artists. But clearness of arrangement, rigor of development, simplicity of style — these may to a certain extent be learned: and these may, I am convinced, be learned best from the ancients, who although infinitely less suggestive than Shakespeare, are thus, to the artist, more instructive.

What, then, it will be asked, are the ancients to be our sole models? the ancients with their comparatively narrow range of experience, and their widely different circumstances? Not, certainly, that which is narrow in the ancients, nor that in which we can no longer sympathize. An action like the action of the *Antigone* of Sophocles, which turns upon the conflict between the heroine's duty to her brother's corpse and that to the laws of her country, is no longer one in which it is possible that we should feel a deep interest. I am speaking too, it will be remembered, not of the best sources of intellectual stimulus for the general reader, but of the best models of instruction for the individual writer. This last may certainly learn of the ancients, better than anywhere else, three things which it is vitally important for him to know: the all-importance of the choice of a subject; the necessity of accurate construction; and the subordinate character of expression. He will learn from them how unspeakably superior is the effect of the one moral impression left by a great action treated as a whole, to the effect produced by the most striking single thought or by the happiest image. As he penetrates into the spirit of the great classical works, as he becomes gradually aware of their intense significance, their noble simplicity, and their calm pathos, he will be convinced that it is this effect, unity and profoundness of moral impression, at which the ancient Poets aimed; that it is this which constitutes the grandeur of their works, and which makes them immortal. He will desire to direct his own efforts towards producing the same effect. Above all, he will deliver himself from the jargon of modern criticism, and escape the danger of producing poetical works conceived in the spirit of the passing time, and which partake of its transitoriness.

The present age makes great claims upon us: we owe it service; it will not be satisfied without our admiration. I know not how it is, but their commerce with the ancients appears to me to produce, in those who constantly practice it, a steady and composing effect upon their judgment, not of literary works only, but of men and events in general. They are like persons who have had a very weighty and impressive experience: they are more truly than others under the empire of facts, and more independent of the language current among those with whom they live. They wish neither to applaud nor to revile their age: they wish to know what it is, what it can give them, and whether this is what they want. What they want, they know very well; they want to educe and cultivate what is best and noblest in themselves: they know, too, that this is no easy task —χαλεπὸν, as Pittacus said, χαλεπὸν ἐσθλὸν ἔμμεναι[16] — and they ask themselves sincerely whether their age and its literature can assist them in the attempt. If they are endeavoring to practice any art, they remember the plain and simple proceedings of the old artists, who attained their grand results by penetrating themselves with some noble and significant action, not by inflating themselves with a belief in the pre-eminent importance and greatness of their own times. They do not talk of their mission, nor of interpreting their age, nor of the coming Poet; all this, they know, is the mere delirium of vanity; their business is not to praise their age, but to afford to the men who live in it the highest pleasure which they are capable of feeling. If asked to afford this by means of subjects drawn from the age itself, they ask what special fitness the present age has for supplying them; they are told that it is an era of progress, an age commissioned to carry out the

16. χαλεπὸυ . . . ἔμμεναι: "it is hard to be excellent." Pittacus (c. 652–570 B.C.), became king of Mitylene. He was celebrated for his virtue and wisdom, was numbered among the Seven Wise Men of Greece, and his sayings were inscribed on the walls of Apollo's temple at Delphi.

great ideas of industrial development and social amelioration. They reply that with all this they can do nothing; that the elements they need for the exercise of their art are great actions, calculated powerfully and delightfully to affect what is permanent in the human soul; that so far as the present age can supply such actions, they will gladly make use of them; but that an age wanting in moral grandeur can with difficulty supply such, and an age of spiritual discomfort with difficulty be powerfully and delightfully affected by them.

A host of voices will indignantly rejoin that the present age is inferior to the past neither in moral grandeur nor in spiritual health. He who possesses the discipline I speak of will content himself with remembering the judgments passed upon the present age, in this respect, by the two men, the one of strongest head, the other of widest culture, whom it has produced; by Goethe and by Niebuhr.[17] It will be sufficient for him that he knows the opinions held by these two great men respecting the present age and its literature; and that he feels assured in his own mind that their aims and demands upon life were such as he would wish, at any rate, his own to be; and their judgment as to what is impeding and disabling such as he may safely follow. He will not, however, maintain a hostile attitude towards the false pretensions of his age; he will content himself with not being overwhelmed by them. He will esteem himself fortunate if he can succeed in banishing from his mind all feelings of contradiction, and irritation, and impatience, in order to delight himself with the contemplation of some noble action of a heroic time, and to enable others, through his representation of it, to delight in it also.

I am far indeed from making any claim, for myself, that I possess this discipline; or for the following Poems, that they breathe its spirit. But I say, that in the sincere endeavor to learn and practice, amid the bewildering confusion of our times, what is sound and true in poetical art, I seemed to myself to find the only sure guidance, the only solid footing, among the ancients. They, at any rate, knew what they wanted in Art, and we do not. It is this uncertainty which is disheartening, and not hostile criticism. How often have I felt this when reading words of disparagement or of cavil: that it is the uncertainty as to what is really to be aimed at which makes our difficulty, not the dissatisfaction of the critic, who himself suffers from the same uncertainty. *Non me tua fervida terrent Dicta: Dii me terrent, et Jupiter hostis.*[18]

Two kinds of *dilettanti,* says Goethe, there are in poetry: he who neglects the indispensable mechanical part, and thinks he has done enough if he shows spirituality and feeling; and he who seeks to arrive at poetry merely by mechanism, in which he can acquire an artisan's readiness, and is without soul and matter. And he adds, that the first does most harm to Art, and the last to himself. If we must be *dilettanti:* if it is impossible for us, under the circumstances amidst which we live, to think clearly, to feel nobly, and to delineate firmly; if we cannot attain to the mastery of the great artists — let us, at least, have so much respect for our Art as to prefer it to ourselves; let us not bewilder our successors; let us transmit to them the practice of Poetry, with its boundaries and wholesome regulative laws, under which excellent works may again, perhaps, at some future time, be produced, not yet fallen into oblivion through our neglect, not yet condemned and canceled by the influence of their eternal enemy, Caprice.

## ADVERTISEMENT TO THE SECOND EDITION OF *POEMS*

I have allowed the Preface to the former edition of these Poems to stand almost without change, because I still believe it to be, in the main, true. I must not, however, be supposed insensible to the force of much that has been alleged against portions of it, or unaware that it contains many things incompletely stated, many things which need limitation. It leaves, too, untouched the question, how far, and in what manner, the opinions there expressed respecting the choice of subjects apply to lyric poetry, that region of the poetical field which is chiefly cultivated at present. But neither have I time now to supply these deficiencies, nor is this the proper place for attempting it; on one or two points alone I wish to offer, in the briefest possible way, some explanation.

An objection has been ably urged to the classing together, as subjects equally belonging to a past time, Oedipus and Macbeth. And it is no doubt true that to Shakespeare, standing on the verge of the Middle Ages, the epoch of Macbeth was more

17. Niebuhr: Barthold Georg Niebuhr (1776–1831), a German statesman, famous as one of the most influential historians of his time.

18. *Non . . . hostis:* "Your fierce words do not frighten me: The Gods frighten me and the idea of having Jupiter as my enemy" (Virgil, *Aeneid,* XII.894–95).

familiar than that of Oedipus. But I was speaking of actions as they presented themselves to us moderns; and it will hardly be said that the European mind, since Voltaire, has much more affinity with the times of Macbeth than with those of Oedipus. As moderns, it seems to me, we have no longer any direct affinity with the circumstances and feelings of either; as individuals, we are attracted towards this or that personage, we have a capacity for imagining him, irrespective of his times, solely according to a law of personal sympathy; and those subjects for which we feel this personal attraction most strongly, we may hope to treat successfully. Alcestis or Joan of Arc, Charlemagne or Agamemnon — one of these is not really nearer to us now than another; each can be made present only by an act of poetic imagination, but this man's imagination has an affinity for one of them, and that man's for another.

It has been said that I wish to limit the Poet in his choice of subjects to the period of Greek and Roman antiquity, but it is not so; I only counsel him to choose for his subjects great actions, without regarding to what time they belong. Nor do I deny that the poetic faculty can and does manifest itself in treating the most trifling action, the most hopeless subject. But it is a pity that power should be wasted, and that the Poet should be compelled to impart interest and force to his subject, instead of receiving them from it, and thereby doubling his impressiveness. There is, it has been excellently said, an immortal strength in the stories of great actions; the most gifted poet, then, may well be glad to supplement with it that mortal weakness, which, in presence of the vast spectacle of life and the world, he must forever feel to be his individual portion.

Again, with respect to the study of the classical writers of antiquity: it has been said that we should emulate rather than imitate them. I make no objection; all I say is, let us study them. They can help to cure us of what is, it seems to me, the great vice of our intellect, manifesting itself in our incredible vagaries in literature, in art, in religion, in morals; namely, that it is *fantastic,* and wants *sanity*. Sanity — that is the great virtue of the ancient literature; the want of that is the great defect of the modern, in spite of all its variety and power. It is impossible to read carefully the great ancients, without losing something of our caprice and eccentricity; and to emulate them we must at least read them.

[*1855*]

# THE FUNCTION OF CRITICISM AT THE PRESENT TIME

If one were required to name the one piece of Arnold's prose that is likely to speak most directly to readers of today, it would almost inevitably be the great essay, "The Function of Criticism at the Present Time." The first essay in Arnold's *Essays in Criticism* (1865), it is the classic statement in English of the role of intelligence in the modern world, of an intelligence truly objective and disinterested.

The word "disinterested" as Arnold uses it needs explanation, else the whole point of the essay is in danger of being lost. It is a misfortune of the English language in modern times that the word "disinterested" is commonly confused with the word "uninterested." The modern lexicographers who work on the principle that whatever is the usage of people is acceptable are beginning to accept the confusion, and perhaps they are very wise in their principle, but in this instance the usage of people — or at least of some people — has deprived us of our only word for a very important virtue. Up until recently the meanings of the two words were kept distinct, and it was a mark of ignorance to confuse them. "Disinterested" meant that one had nothing to gain from the matter at hand, that one was objective in one's judgment, that one had no selfish motive but was impartial and unbiased. "Uninterested" meant that one was bored by the matter at hand, that it did not engage one's attention. The distinction is still in force among almost all careful writers and speakers; they blame, say, a labor arbitrator who is *uninterested* in the case he is hearing, but they praise him for being *disinterested* in the way he decides it.

Many objections have been made to a proposition which, in some remarks of mine on translating Homer,[1] I ventured to put forth: a proposition about criticism, and its importance at the present day. I said: "Of the literature of France and Germany, as of the intellect of Europe in general, the main effort, for now many years, has been a critical effort; the endeavor, in all branches of knowledge, theology, philosophy, history, art, science, to see the object as in itself it really is." I added that, owing to the operation in English literature of certain causes, "almost the last thing for which one would come to English literature is just that very thing which now Europe most desires — criticism"; and that the power and value of English literature was thereby impaired. More than one rejoinder declared that the importance I here assigned to criticism was excessive, and asserted the inherent superiority of the creative effort of the human spirit over its critical effort. And the other day, having been led by a

FUNCTION OF CRITICISM. **1. on . . . Homer: the last paragraph of Lecture II, from *On Translating Homer* (1861).**

Mr. Shairp's excellent notice of Wordsworth [2] to turn again to his biography, I found, in the words of this great man, whom I, for one, must always listen to with the profoundest respect, a sentence passed on the critic's business, which seems to justify every possible disparagement of it. Wordsworth says in one of his letters:

The writers in these publications [the Reviews], while they prosecute their inglorious employment, cannot be supposed to be in a state of mind very favorable for being affected by the finer influences of a thing so pure as genuine poetry.

And a trustworthy reporter of his conversation quotes a more elaborate judgment to the same effect:

Wordsworth holds the critical power very low, infinitely lower than the inventive; and he said today that if the quantity of time consumed in writing critiques on the works of others were given to original composition, of whatever kind it might be, it would be much better employed; it would make a man find out sooner his own level, and it would do infinitely less mischief. A false or malicious criticism may do much injury to the minds of others; a stupid invention, either in prose or verse, is quite harmless.

It is almost too much to expect of poor human nature, that a man capable of producing some effect in one line of literature, should, for the greater good of society, voluntarily doom himself to impotence and obscurity in another. Still less is this to be expected from men addicted to the composition of the "false or malicious criticism" of which Wordsworth speaks. However, everybody would admit that a false or malicious criticism had better never have been written. Everybody, too, would be willing to admit, as a general proposition, that the critical faculty is lower than the inventive. But is it true that criticism is really, in itself, a baneful and injurious employment; is it true that all time given to writing critiques on the works of others would be much better employed if it were given to original composition, of whatever kind this may be? Is it true that Johnson had better have gone on producing more *Irenes* instead of writing his *Lives of the Poets;* [3] is it certain that Wordsworth himself was better employed in making his *Ecclesiastical Sonnets* than when he made his celebrated Preface [4] so full of criticism, and criticism of the works of others? Wordsworth was himself a great critic, and it is to be sincerely regretted that he has not left us more criticism; Goethe was one of the greatest of critics, and we may sincerely congratulate ourselves that he has left us so much criticism. Without wasting time over the exaggeration which Wordsworth's judgment on criticism clearly contains, or over an attempt to trace the causes — not difficult, I think, to be traced — which may have led Wordsworth to this exaggeration, a critic may with advantage seize an occasion for trying his own conscience, and for asking himself of what real service, at any given moment, the practice of criticism either is or may be made to his own mind and spirit, and to the minds and spirits of others.

The critical power is of lower rank than the creative. True; but in assenting to this proposition, one or two things are to be kept in mind. It is undeniable that the exercise of a creative power, that a free creative activity, is the highest function of man; it is proved to be so by man's finding in it his true happiness. But it is undeniable, also, that men may have the sense of exercising this free creative activity in other ways than in producing great works of literature or art; if it were not so, all but a very few men would be shut out from the true happiness of all men. They may have it in well-doing, they may have it in learning, they may have it even in criticizing. This is one thing to be kept in mind. Another is, that the exercise of the creative power in the production of great works of literature or art, however high this exercise of it may rank, is not at all epochs and under all conditions possible; and that therefore labor may be vainly spent in attempting it, which might with more fruit be used in preparing for it, in rendering it possible. This creative power works with elements, with materials; what if it has not those materials, those elements, ready for its use? In that case it must surely wait till they are ready. Now, in literature — I will limit myself to literature, for it is about literature that the question arises — the elements with which the creative power works are ideas; the best ideas on every matter which litera-

2. "I cannot help thinking that a practice, common in England during the last century, and still followed in France, of printing a notice of this kind — a notice by a competent critic — to serve as an introduction to an eminent author's works, might be revived among us with advantage. To introduce all succeeding editions of Wordsworth, Mr. Shairp's notice might, it seems to me, excellently serve; it is written from the point of view of an admirer, nay, of a disciple, and that is right; but then the disciple must be also, as in this case he is, a critic, a man of letters, not, as too often happens, some relation or friend with no qualification for his task except affection for his author" [A].

3. See selections from Johnson's *Lives*, in Vol. I. 4. See Wordsworth's Preface to *Lyrical Ballads*, above.

ture touches, current at the time. At any rate we may lay it down as certain that in modern literature no manifestation of the creative power not working with these can be very important or fruitful. And I say *current* at the time, not merely accessible at the time; for creative literary genius does not principally show itself in discovering new ideas; that is rather the business of the philosopher. The grand work of literary genius is a work of synthesis and exposition, not of analysis and discovery; its gift lies in the faculty of being happily inspired by a certain intellectual and spiritual atmosphere, by a certain order of ideas, when it finds itself in them; of dealing divinely with these ideas, presenting them in the most effective and attractive combinations — making beautiful works with them, in short. But it must have the atmosphere, it must find itself amidst the order of ideas, in order to work freely; and these it is not so easy to command. This is why great creative epochs in literature are so rare, this is why there is so much that is unsatisfactory in the productions of many men of real genius; because, for the creation of a masterwork of literature two powers must concur, the power of the man and the power of the moment, and the man is not enough without the moment; the creative power has, for its happy exercise, appointed elements, and those elements are not in its own control.

Nay, they are more within the control of the critical power. It is the business of the critical power, as I said in the words already quoted, " in all branches of knowledge, theology, philosophy, history, art, science, to see the object as in itself it really is." Thus it tends, at last, to make an intellectual situation of which the creative power can profitably avail itself. It tends to establish an order of ideas, if not absolutely true, yet true by comparison with that which it displaces; to make the best ideas prevail. Presently these new ideas reach society; the touch of truth is the touch of life, and there is a stir and growth everywhere; out of this stir and growth, the creative epochs of literature.

Or, to narrow our range, and quit these considerations of the general march of genius and of society — considerations which are apt to become too abstract and impalpable — everyone can see that a poet, for instance, ought to know life and the world before dealing with them in poetry; and life and the world being in modern times very complex things, the creation of a modern poet, to be worth much, implies a great critical effort behind it; else it must be a comparatively poor, barren, and short-lived affair. This is why Byron's poetry had so little endurance in it, and Goethe's so much; both Byron and Goethe had a great productive power, but Goethe's was nourished by a great critical effort providing the true materials for it, and Byron's was not; Goethe knew life and the world, the poet's necessary subjects, much more comprehensively and thoroughly than Byron. He knew a great deal more of them, and he knew them much more as they really are.

It has long seemed to me that the burst of creative activity in our literature, through the first quarter of this century, had about it in fact something premature; and that from this cause its productions are doomed, most of them, in spite of the sanguine hopes which accompanied and do still accompany them, to prove hardly more lasting than the productions of far less splendid epochs. And this prematureness comes from its having proceeded without having its proper data, without sufficient materials to work with. In other words, the English poetry of the first quarter of this century, with plenty of energy, plenty of creative force, did not know enough. This makes Byron so empty of matter, Shelley so incoherent, Wordsworth even, profound as he is, yet so wanting in completeness and variety. Wordsworth cared little for books, and disparaged Goethe. I admire Wordsworth, as he is, so much that I cannot wish him different; and it is vain, no doubt, to imagine such a man different from what he is, to suppose that he *could* have been different. But surely the one thing wanting to make Wordsworth an even greater poet than he is — his thought richer, and his influence of wider application — was that he should have read more books, among them, no doubt, those of that Goethe whom he disparaged without reading him.

But to speak of books and reading may easily lead to a misunderstanding here. It was not really books and reading that lacked to our poetry at this epoch: Shelley had plenty of reading, Coleridge had immense reading. Pindar and Sophocles — as we all say so glibly, and often with so little discernment of the real import of what we are saying — had not many books; Shakespeare was no deep reader. True; but in the Greece of Pindar and Sophocles, in the England of Shakespeare, the poet lived in a current of ideas in the highest degree animating and nourishing to the creative power; society was, in the fullest measure, permeated by fresh thought, intelligent and alive. And this state of things is the true basis for the creative power's exercise, in this it finds its data, its materials, truly ready for its hand; all the books and reading in the world are only valuable as they are helps to this. Even when this does not actually exist, books and reading may enable a man to construct a kind of semblance of it in his own mind, a world of knowledge and intelligence in which he may live and work. This is by no means an equivalent to the artist for the nationally diffused life and thought of the epochs of Sophocles or Shakespeare; but, besides that it may be a means of preparation for such epochs, it does really constitute, if many share in it, a quickening and sustaining atmosphere of great value. Such an atmosphere the many-sided learning and the long and widely combined critical effort of Germany formed for Goethe, when he lived and worked. There was no national glow of life and thought there as in the Athens of Pericles or the England of Elizabeth. That was the poet's weakness. But there was a sort of equivalent for it in the complete culture and unfettered thinking of a large body of Germans. That was his strength. In the England of the first quarter of this century there was neither a national glow of life and thought, such as we had in the age of Elizabeth, nor yet a culture and a force of learning and criticism such as were to be found in Germany. Therefore the creative power of poetry wanted, for success in the highest sense, materials and a basis; a thorough interpretation of the world was necessarily denied to it.

At first sight it seems strange that out of the immense stir of the French Revolution and its age should not have come a crop of works of genius equal to that which came out of the stir of the great productive time of Greece, or out of that of the Renaissance, with its powerful episode, the Reformation. But the truth is that the stir of the French Revolution took a character which essentially distinguished it from such movements as these. These were, in the main, disinterestedly intellectual and spiritual movements, movements in which the human spirit looked for its satisfaction in itself and in the increased play of its own activity. The French Revolution took a political, practical character. The movement which went on in France under the old *régime,* from 1700 to 1789, was far more really akin than that of the Revolution itself to the movement of the Renaissance; the France of Voltaire and Rousseau told far more powerfully upon the mind of Europe than the France of the Revolution. Goethe reproached this last expressly with having "thrown quiet culture back." Nay, and the true key to how much in our Byron, even in our Wordsworth, is this! — that they had their source in a great movement of feeling, not in a great movement of mind. The French Revolution, however — that object of so much blind love and so much blind hatred — found undoubtedly its motive power in the intelligence of men, and not in their practical sense; this is what distinguishes it from the English Revolution of Charles I's time. This is what makes it a more spiritual event than our Revolution, an event of much more powerful and world-wide interest, though practically less successful; it appeals to an order of ideas which are universal, certain, permanent. 1789 asked of a thing, "Is it rational?" 1642 asked of a thing, "Is it legal?" or, when it went furthest, "Is it according to conscience?" This is the English fashion, a fashion to be treated, within its own sphere, with the highest respect; for its success, within its own sphere, has been prodigious. But what is law in one place is not law in another; what is law here today is not law even here tomorrow; and as for conscience, what is binding on one man's conscience is not binding on another's. The old woman who threw her stool at the head of the surpliced minister in St. Giles's Church at Edinburgh[5] obeyed an impulse to which millions of the human race may be permitted to remain strangers. But the prescriptions of reason are absolute, unchanging, of universal validity; *to count by tens is the easiest way of counting* — that is a proposition of which everyone, from here to the antipodes, feels the force; at least I should say so if we did not live in a country where it is not impossible that any morning we may find a letter in the *Times* declaring that a decimal coinage is an absurdity. That a whole nation should have been penetrated with an enthusiasm for pure reason, and with an ardent zeal for making its prescriptions triumph, is a very remarkable thing, when we consider how little of mind, or anything so worthy and quickening as mind, comes into the motives which alone, in general, impel great masses of men. In spite of the extravagant direction given to this enthusiasm, in spite of the crimes and follies in which it lost itself, the French Revolution derives from the force, truth, and universality of the ideas which it took for its law, and from the passion with which it could inspire a multitude for these ideas, a

5. **The . . . Edinburgh:** Charles I prescribed a new church service for Scotland, and the violent protest against it is said to have been started by an old woman, Janet Geddes, in the manner Arnold refers to.

unique and still living power; it is — it will probably long remain — the greatest, the most animating event in history. And as no sincere passion for the things of the mind, even though it turn out in many respects an unfortunate passion, is ever quite thrown away and quite barren of good, France has reaped from hers one fruit — the natural and legitimate fruit though not precisely the grand fruit she expected: she is the country in Europe where *the people* is most alive.

But the mania for giving an immediate political and practical application to all these fine ideas of the reason was fatal. Here an Englishman is in his element: on this theme we can all go on for hours. And all we are in the habit of saying on it has undoubtedly a great deal of truth. Ideas cannot be too much prized in and for themselves, cannot be too much lived with; but to transport them abruptly into the world of politics and practice, violently to revolutionize this world to their bidding — that is quite another thing. There is the world of ideas and there is the world of practice; the French are often for suppressing the one and the English the other; but neither is to be suppressed. A member of the House of Commons said to me the other day: "That a thing is an anomaly, I consider to be no objection to it whatever." I venture to think he was wrong; that a thing is an anomaly *is* an objection to it, but absolutely and in the sphere of ideas: it is not necessarily, under such and such circumstances, or at such and such a moment, an objection to it in the sphere of politics and practice. Joubert [6] has said beautifully: *"C'est la force et le droit qui règlent toutes choses dans le monde; la force en attendant le droit."* (Force and right are the governors of this world; force till right is ready.) *Force till right is ready;* and till right is ready, force, the existing order of things, is justified, is the legitimate ruler. But right is something moral, and implies inward recognition, free assent of the will; we are not ready for right — *right,* so far as we are concerned, *is not ready* — until we have attained this sense of seeing it and willing it. The way in which for us it may change and transform force, the existing order of things, and become, in its turn, the legitimate ruler of the world, should depend on the way in which, when our time comes, we see it and will it. Therefore for other people enamored of their own newly discerned right, to attempt to impose it upon us as ours, and violently to substitute their right for our force, is an act of tyranny, and to be resisted. It sets at nought the second great half of our maxim, *force till right is ready.* This was the grand error of the French Revolution; and its movement of ideas, by quitting the intellectual sphere and rushing furiously into the political sphere, ran, indeed, a prodigious and memorable course, but produced no such intellectual fruit as the movement of ideas of the Renaissance, and created, in opposition to itself, what I may call an *epoch of concentration.* The great force of that epoch of concentration was England; and the great voice of that epoch of concentration was Burke. It is the fashion to treat Burke's writings on the French Revolution as superannuated and conquered by the event, as the eloquent but unphilosophical tirades of bigotry and prejudice. I will not deny that they are often disfigured by the violence and passion of the moment, and that in some directions Burke's view was bounded, and his observation therefore at fault. But on the whole, and for those who can make the needful corrections, what distinguishes these writings is their profound, permanent, fruitful, philosophical truth. They contain the true philosophy of an epoch of concentration, dissipate the heavy atmosphere which its own nature is apt to engender round it, and make its resistance rational instead of mechanical.

But Burke is so great because, almost alone in England, he brings thought to bear upon politics, he saturates politics with thought. It is his accident that his ideas were at the service of an epoch of concentration, not of an epoch of expansion; it is his characteristic that he so lived by ideas, and had such a source of them welling up within him, that he could float even an epoch of concentration and English Tory politics with them. It does not hurt him that Dr. Price and the Liberals [7] were enraged with him; it does not even hurt him that George III and the Tories were enchanted with him. His greatness is that he lived in a world which neither English Liberalism nor English Toryism is apt to enter — the world of ideas, not the world of catchwords and party habits. So far is it from being really true of him that he "to party gave up what

**6. Joubert:** Joseph Joubert (1754–1824), French moralist, writer of essays and *pensées.* Arnold held him in high esteem and devoted one of the essays of *Essays in Criticism* to him.

**7. Dr. Price . . . Liberals:** Dr. Richard Price (1723–91) was a nonconformist minister and a writer on political and moral subjects one of whose speeches in support of the French Revolution was extensively criticized and satirized by Burke in *Reflections on the French Revolution.* In the first years of the Revolution, until the Reign of Terror, many Englishmen of liberal sentiment regarded the events in France with warm sympathy and hope.

was meant for mankind,"[8] that at the very end of his fierce struggle with the French Revolution, after all his invectives against its false pretensions, hollowness, and madness, with his sincere convictions of its mischievousness, he can close a memorandum on the best means of combating it, some of the last pages he ever wrote — the *Thoughts on French Affairs,* in December, 1791 — with these striking words:

> The evil is stated, in my opinion, as it exists. The remedy must be where power, wisdom, and information, I hope, are more united with good intentions than they can be with me. I have done with this subject, I believe, forever. It has given me many anxious moments for the last two years. *If a great change is to be made in human affairs, the minds of men will be fitted to it; the general opinions and feelings will draw that way. Every fear, every hope will forward it; and then they who persist in opposing this mighty current in human affairs, will appear rather to resist the decrees of Providence itself, than the mere designs of men. They will not be resolute and firm, but perverse and obstinate.*

That return of Burke upon himself has always seemed to me one of the finest things in English literature, or indeed in any literature. That is what I call living by ideas: when one side of a question has long had your earnest support, when all your feelings are engaged, when you hear all round you no language but one, when your party talks this language like a steam engine and can imagine no other — still to be able to think, still to be irresistibly carried, if so it be, by the current of thought to the opposite side of the question, and, like Balaam, to be unable to speak anything *but what the Lord has put in your mouth.* I know nothing more striking, and I must add that I know nothing more un-English.

For the Englishman in general is like my friend the member of Parliament, and believes, point-blank, that for a thing to be an anomaly is absolutely no objection to it whatever. He is like the Lord Auckland of Burke's day, who, in a memorandum on the French Revolution, talks of certain "miscreants, assuming the name of philosophers, who have presumed themselves capable of establishing a new system of society." The Englishman has been called a political animal, and he values what is political and practical so much that ideas easily become objects of dislike in his eyes, and thinkers, "miscreants," because ideas and thinkers have rashly meddled with politics and practice. This would be all very well if the dislike and neglect confined themselves to ideas transported out of their own sphere, and meddling rashly with practice; but they are inevitably extended to ideas as such, and to the whole life of intelligence; practice is everything, a free play of the mind is nothing. The notion of the free play of the mind upon all subjects being a pleasure in itself, being an object of desire, being an essential provider of elements without which a nation's spirit, whatever compensations it may have for them, must, in the long run, die of inanition, hardly enters into an Englishman's thoughts. It is noticeable that the word "curiosity," which in other languages is used in a good sense, to mean, as a high and fine quality of man's nature, just this disinterested love of a free play of the mind on all subjects, for its own sake — it is noticeable, I say, that this word has in our language no sense of the kind, no sense but a rather bad and disparaging one. But criticism, real criticism, is essentially the exercise of this very quality. It obeys an instinct prompting it to try to know the best that is known and thought in the world, irrespectively of practice, politics, and everything of the kind; and to value knowledge and thought as they approach this best, without the intrusion of any other considerations whatever. This is an instinct for which there is, I think, little original sympathy in the practical English nature, and what there was of it has undergone a long benumbing period of blight and suppression in the epoch of concentration which followed the French Revolution.

But epochs of concentration cannot well endure forever; epochs of expansion, in the due course of things, follow them. Such an epoch of expansion seems to be opening in this country. In the first place all danger of a hostile forcible pressure of foreign ideas upon our practice has long disappeared; like the traveler in the fable, therefore, we begin to wear our cloak a little more loosely. Then, with a long peace, the ideas of Europe steal gradually and amicably in, and mingle, though in infinitesimally small quantities at a time, with our own notions. Then, too, in spite of all that is said about the absorbing and brutalizing influence of our passionate material progress, it seems to me indisputable that this progress is likely, though not certain, to lead in the end to an apparition of intellectual life; and that man, after he has made

8. "to . . . mankind": Oliver Goldsmith's humorous "epitaph" on Burke in his poem, "Retaliation."

himself perfectly comfortable and has now to determine what to do with himself next, may begin to remember that he has a mind, and that the mind may be made the source of great pleasure. I grant it is mainly the privilege of faith, at present, to discern this end to our railways, our business, and our fortune-making; but we shall see if, here as elsewhere, faith is not in the end the true prophet. Our ease, our traveling, and our unbounded liberty to hold just as hard and securely as we please to the practice to which our notions have given birth, all tend to beget an inclination to deal a little more freely with these notions themselves, to canvass them a little, to penetrate a little into their real nature. Flutterings of curiosity, in the foreign sense of the word, appear amongst us, and it is in these that criticism must look to find its account. Criticism first; a time of true creative activity, perhaps — which, as I have said, must inevitably be preceded amongst us by a time of criticism — hereafter, when criticism has done its work.

It is of the last importance that English criticism should clearly discern what rule for its course, in order to avail itself of the field now opening to it, and to produce fruit for the future, it ought to take. The rule may be summed up in one word — *disinterestedness*. And how is criticism to show disinterestedness? By keeping aloof from what is called "the practical view of things"; by resolutely following the law of its own nature, which is to be a free play of the mind on all subjects which it touches. By steadily refusing to lend itself to any of those ulterior, political, practical considerations about ideas, which plenty of people will be sure to attach to them, which perhaps ought often to be attached to them, which in this country at any rate are certain to be attached to them quite sufficiently. but which criticism has really nothing to do with. Its business is, as I have said, simply to know the best that is known and thought in the world, and by in its turn making this known, to create a current of true and fresh ideas. Its business is to do this with inflexible honesty, with due ability; but its business is to do no more, and to leave alone all questions of practical consequences and applications, questions which will never fail to have due prominence given to them. Else criticism, besides being really false to its own nature, merely continues in the old rut which it has hitherto followed in this country, and will certainly miss the chance now given to it. For what is at present the bane of criticism in this country? It is that practical considerations cling to it and stifle it. It subserves interests not its own. Our organs of criticism are organs of men and parties having practical ends to serve, and with them those practical ends are the first thing and the play of mind the second; so much play of mind as is compatible with the prosecution of those practical ends is all that is wanted. An organ like the *Revue des Deux Mondes,*[9] having for its main function to understand and utter the best that is known and thought in the world, existing, it may be said, as just an organ for a free play of the mind, we have not. But we have the *Edinburgh Review,* existing as an organ of the old Whigs, and for as much play of mind as may suit its being that; we have the *Quarterly Review,* existing as an organ of the Tories, and for as much play of mind as may suit its being that; we have the *British Quarterly Review,* existing as an organ of the political Dissenters, and for as much play of mind as may suit its being that; we have the *Times,* existing as an organ of the common, satisfied, well-to-do Englishman, and for as much play of mind as may suit its being that. And so on through all the various fractions, political and religious, of our society; every fraction has, as such, its organ of criticism, but the notion of combining all fractions in the common pleasure of a free disinterested play of mind meets with no favor. Directly this play of mind wants to have more scope, and to forget the pressure of practical considerations a little, it is checked, it is made to feel the chain. We saw this the other day in the extinction, so much to be regretted, of the *Home and Foreign Review*. Perhaps in no organ of criticism in this country was there so much knowledge, so much play of mind; but these could not save it. The *Dublin Review* subordinates play of mind to the practical business of English and Irish Catholicism, and lives. It must needs be that men should act in sects and parties, that each of these sects and parties should have its organ, and should make this organ subserve the interests of its action; but it would be well, too, that there should be a criticism, not the minister of these interests, not their enemy, but absolutely and entirely independent of them. No other criticism will ever attain any real authority or make any real way towards its end — the creating a current of true and fresh ideas.

9. ***Revue . . . Mondes:*** perhaps the most impressive of French periodicals in the nineteenth century. Founded in 1829, the *Revue* published the work of almost all the great writers of France. Arnold regarded it as representative of the high quality of French culture, the kind of enterprise that the English could not even conceive the value of.

It is because criticism has so little kept in the pure intellectual sphere, has so little detached itself from practice, has been so directly polemical and controversial, that it has so ill accomplished, in this country, its best spiritual work, which is to keep man from a self-satisfaction which is retarding and vulgarizing, to lead him towards perfection, by making his mind dwell upon what is excellent in itself, and the absolute beauty and fitness of things. A polemical practical criticism makes men blind even to the ideal imperfection of their practice, makes them willingly assert its ideal perfection, in order the better to secure it against attack; and clearly this is narrowing and baneful for them. If they were reassured on the practical side, speculative considerations of ideal perfection they might be brought to entertain, and their spiritual horizon would thus gradually widen. Sir Charles Adderley [10] says to the Warwickshire farmers:

> Talk of the improvement of breed! Why, the race we ourselves represent, the men and women, the old Anglo-Saxon race, are the best breed in the whole world. . . . The absence of a too enervating climate, too unclouded skies, and a too luxurious nature, has produced so vigorous a race of people, and has rendered us so superior to all the world.

Mr. Roebuck [11] says to the Sheffield cutlers:

> I look around me and ask what is the state of England? Is not property safe? Is not every man able to say what he likes? Can you not walk from one end of England to the other in perfect security? I ask you whether, the world over or in past history, there is anything like it? Nothing. I pray that our unrivaled happiness may last.

Now obviously there is a peril for poor human nature in words and thoughts of such exuberant self-satisfaction, until we find ourselves safe in the streets of the Celestial City.

*Das wenige verschwindet leicht dem Blicke*
*Der vorwärts sieht, wie viel noch übrig bleibt*—

says Goethe; "the little that is done seems nothing when we look forward and see how much we have yet to do." Clearly this is a better line of reflection for weak humanity, so long as it remains on this earthly field of labor and trial.

But neither Sir Charles Adderley nor Mr. Roebuck is by nature inaccessible to considerations of this sort. They only lose sight of them owing to the controversial life we all lead, and the practical form which all speculation takes with us. They have in view opponents whose aim is not ideal, but practical; and in their zeal to uphold their own practice against these innovators, they go so far as even to attribute to this practice an ideal perfection. Somebody has been wanting to introduce a six-pound franchise, or to abolish church rates, or to collect agricultural statistics by force, or to diminish local self-government. How natural, in reply to such proposals, very likely improper or ill-timed, to go a little beyond the mark and to say stoutly, "Such a race of people as we stand, so superior to all the world! The old Anglo-Saxon race, the best breed in the whole world! I pray that our unrivaled happiness may last! I ask you whether, the world over or in past history, there is anything like it?" And so long as criticism answers this dithyramb by insisting that the old Anglo-Saxon race would be still more superior to all others if it had no church rates, or that our unrivaled happiness would last yet longer with a six-pound franchise, so long will the strain, "The best breed in the whole world!" swell louder and louder, everything ideal and refining will be lost out of sight, and both the assailed and their critics will remain in a sphere, to say the truth, perfectly unvital, a sphere in which spiritual progression is impossible. But let criticism leave church rates and the franchise alone, and in the most candid spirit, without a single lurking thought of practical innovation, confront with our dithyramb this paragraph on which I stumbled in a newspaper immediately after reading Mr. Roebuck:

> A shocking child murder has just been committed at Nottingham. A girl named Wragg left the workhouse there on Saturday morning with her young illegitimate child. The child was soon afterwards found dead on Mapperly Hills, having been strangled. Wragg is in custody.

Nothing but that; but, in juxtaposition with the absolute eulogies of Sir Charles Adderley and Mr. Roebuck, how eloquent, how suggestive are those few lines! "Our old Anglo-Saxon breed, the best in the whole world!"—how much that is harsh and ill-favored there is in this best! *Wragg!* If we are to talk of ideal perfection, of "the best in the whole world," has anyone reflected what a touch of grossness in our race, what an original shortcoming in the more delicate spiritual perceptions, is shown by the natural growth amongst us of such hideous names—Higginbottom, Stiggins, Bugg! In Ionia

10. **Adderley:** Sir Charles Bowyer Adderley, later first Baron Norton (1814–1905), was a wealthy landowner and a Conservative politician. 11. **Roebuck:** John Arthur Roebuck (1801–79) was well known as a radical and reformer. He was a member of parliament for Sheffield.

and Attica they were luckier in this respect than "the best race in the world"; by the Ilissus there was no Wragg, poor thing! And "our unrivaled happiness"— what an element of grimness, bareness, and hideousness mixes with it and blurs it; the workhouse, the dismal Mapperly Hills — how dismal those who have seen them will remember — the gloom, the smoke, the cold, the strangled illegitimate child! "I ask you whether, the world over or in past history, there is anything like it?" Perhaps not, one is inclined to answer; but at any rate, in that case, the world is very much to be pitied. And the final touch — short, bleak, and inhuman: *Wragg is in custody.* The sex lost in the confusion of our unrivaled happiness; or (shall I say?) the superfluous Christian name lopped off by the straightforward vigor of our old Anglo-Saxon breed! There is profit for the spirit in such contrasts as this; criticism serves the cause of perfection by establishing them. By eluding sterile conflict, by refusing to remain in the sphere where alone narrow and relative conceptions have any worth and validity, criticism may diminish its momentary importance, but only in this way has it a chance of gaining admittance for those wider and more perfect conceptions to which all its duty is really owed. Mr. Roebuck will have a poor opinion of an adversary who replies to his defiant songs of triumph only by murmuring under his breath, *Wragg is in custody;* but in no other way will these songs of triumph be induced gradually to moderate themselves, to get rid of what in them is excessive and offensive, and to fall into a softer and truer key.

It will be said that it is a very subtle and indirect action which I am thus prescribing for criticism, and that, by embracing in this manner the Indian virtue of detachment and abandoning the sphere of practical life, it condemns itself to a slow and obscure work. Slow and obscure it may be, but it is the only proper work of criticism. The mass of mankind will never have any ardent zeal for seeing things as they are; very inadequate ideas will always satisfy them. On these inadequate ideas reposes, and must repose, the general practice of the world. That is as much as saying that whoever sets himself to see things as they are will find himself one of a very small circle, but it is only by this small circle resolutely doing its own work that adequate ideas will ever get current at all. The rush and roar of practical life will always have a dizzying and attracting effect upon the most collected spectator, and tend to draw him into its vortex; most of all will this be the case where that life is so powerful as it is in England. But it is only by remaining collected, and refusing to lend himself to the point of view of the practical man, that the critic can do the practical man any service; and it is only by the greatest sincerity in pursuing his own course, and by at last convincing even the practical man of his sincerity, that he can escape misunderstandings which perpetually threaten him.

For the practical man is not apt for fine distinctions, and yet in these distinctions truth and the highest culture greatly find their account. But it is not easy to lead a practical man — unless you reassure him as to your practical intentions, you have no chance of leading him, — to see that a thing which he has always been used to look at from one side only, which he greatly values, and which, looked at from that side, quite deserves, perhaps, all the prizing and admiring which he bestows upon it, — that this thing, looked at from another side, may appear much less beneficent and beautiful, and yet retain all its claims to our practical allegiance. Where shall we find language innocent enough, how shall we make the spotless purity of our intentions evident enough, to enable us to say to the political Englishman that the British Constitution itself, which, seen from the practical side, looks such a magnificent organ of progress and virtue, seen from the speculative side — with its compromises, its love of facts, its horror of theory, its studied avoidance of clear thoughts — that, seen from this side, our august Constitution sometimes looks — forgive me, shade of Lord Somers![12] — a colossal machine for the manufacture of Philistines?[13] How is Cobbett[14] to say this and not be misunderstood, blackened as he is with the smoke of a lifelong conflict in the field of political practice? how is Mr. Carlyle to say it and not be misunderstood, after his furious raid into this field with his *Latter-Day Pamphlets?* how is Mr. Ruskin, after his pugnacious political economy? I say, the critic must keep out of the region of immediate

**12. Somers:** John Somers, Baron Somers (1657–1716) was famous as a lawyer and a defender of the English Constitution. His name is associated with the drafting of the Bill of Rights after the abdication of James II. **13. Philistines:** the name Arnold liked to use for members of the middle class who lacked culture or despised it and who were chiefly interested in material and practical pursuits. In the Bible the Philistines are the enemies of the children of Israel, "the chosen people." The word, through Arnold's agency, is now established in the language in the sense in which he uses it. **14. Cobbett:** William Cobbett (1762–1835), a well-known reformer and democrat, notable for the violence of his eloquence.

practice in the political, social, humanitarian sphere if he wants to make a beginning for that more free speculative treatment of things, which may perhaps one day make its benefits felt even in this sphere, but in a natural and thence irresistible manner.

Do what he will, however, the critic will still remain exposed to frequent misunderstandings, and nowhere so much as in this country. For here people are particularly indisposed even to comprehend that without this free disinterested treatment of things, truth and the highest culture are out of the question. So immersed are they in practical life, so accustomed to take all their notions from this life and its processes, that they are apt to think that truth and culture themselves can be reached by the processes of this life, and that it is an impertinent singularity to think of reaching them in any other. "We are all *terrae filii,*"[15] cries their eloquent advocate; "all Philistines together. Away with the notion of proceeding by any other course than the course dear to the Philistines; let us have a social movement, let us organize and combine a party to pursue truth and new thought, let us call it *the liberal party,* and let us all stick to each other, and back each other up. Let us have no nonsense about independent criticism, and intellectual delicacy, and the few and the many. Don't let us trouble ourselves about foreign thought; we shall invent the whole thing for ourselves as we go along. If one of us speaks well, applaud him; if one of us speaks ill, applaud him too; we are all in the same movement, we are all liberals, we are all in pursuit of truth." In this way the pursuit of truth becomes really a social, practical pleasurable affair, almost requiring a chairman, a secretary, and advertisements; with the excitement of an occasional scandal, with a little resistance to give the happy sense of difficulty overcome; but, in general, plenty of bustle and very little thought. To act is so easy, as Goethe says; to think is so hard! It is true that the critic has many temptations to go with the stream, to make one of the party movement, one of these *terrae filii;* it seems ungracious to refuse to be a *terrae filius* when so many excellent people are; but the critic's duty is to refuse, or, if resistance is vain, at least to cry with Obermann: *Périssons en résistant.*[16]

15. *terrae filii:* sons of the earth. 16. **Obermann . . . résistant:** Obermann is the suppositious writer of the philosophical letters from Switzerland which make up the volume *Obermann* by Étienne Pivert de Senancour (1770–1846). See "The Grande Chartreuse," l. 146n, above. The French phrase means "Let us die resisting."

How serious a matter it is to try and resist, I had ample opportunity of experiencing when I ventured some time ago to criticize the celebrated first volume of Bishop Colenso.[17] The echoes of the storm which was then raised I still, from time to time, hear grumbling round me. That storm arose out of a misunderstanding almost inevitable. It is a result of no little culture to attain to a clear perception that science and religion are two wholly different things. The multitude will forever confuse them; but happily that is of no great real importance, for while the multitude imagines itself to live by its false science, it does really live by its true religion. Dr. Colenso, however, in his first volume did all he could to strengthen the confusion, and to make it dangerous. He did this with the best intentions, I freely admit, and with the most candid ignorance that this was the natural effect of what he was doing; but, says Joubert, "Ignorance, which in matters of morals extenuates the crime, is itself, in intellectual matters, a crime of the first order." I criticized Bishop Colenso's speculative confusion. Immediately there was a cry raised: "What is this? here is a liberal attacking a liberal. Do not you belong to the movement? are you not a friend of truth? Is not Bishop Colenso in pursuit of truth? then speak with proper respect of his book. Dr. Stanley is another friend of truth, and you speak with proper respect of his book; why make these invidious differences? both books are excellent, ad-

17. **first . . . Colenso:** "So sincere is my dislike to all personal attack and controversy, that I abstain from reprinting, at this distance of time from the occasion which called them forth, the essays in which I criticized Dr. Colenso's book; I feel bound, however, after all that has passed, to make here a final declaration of my sincere impenitence for having published them. Nay, I cannot forbear repeating yet once more, for his benefit and that of his readers, this sentence from my original remarks upon him: *There is truth of science and truth of religion; truth of science does not become truth of religion till it is made religious.* And I will add: Let us have all the science there is from the men of science; from the men of religion let us have religion" [A]. In 1862 John William Colenso (1814–83), Bishop of Natal in Africa, published the first volume of *The Pentateuch and Book of Joshua Critically Examined* in which he undertook to demonstrate that the Bible could not be accepted as literal fact. Arnold attacked the book in an essay, "The Bishop and the Philosopher," published in *Macmillan's Magazine,* January, 1863. Arnold, who had no objection to Colenso's general conclusion, thought that his method of demonstration was silly and trivial and far below that of the great Biblical scholars of the Continent, who, indeed, had nothing but contempt for Colenso's work. The book, Arnold said, could not tell educated people anything they did not know, and it could only confuse the uneducated classes. For an understanding of what Arnold is saying about his position in regard to Colenso, it will be helpful to have in mind that Colenso was tried for heresy and that the case was the occasion for very intense partisan feeling. Arnold had no sympathy for the prosecutors of Colenso, but he would not allow partisan considerations to lead him to say that Colenso's book was a good book, or anything but a foolish book.

mirable, liberal; Bishop Colenso's perhaps the most so, because it is the boldest, and will have the best practical consequences for the liberal cause. Do you want to encourage to the attack of a brother liberal his, and your, and our implacable enemies, the *Church and State Review* or the *Record*—the High Church rhinoceros and the Evangelical hyena? Be silent, therefore; or rather speak, speak as loud as ever you can! and go into ecstasies over the eighty and odd pigeons." [18]

But criticism cannot follow this coarse and indiscriminate method. It is unfortunately possible for a man in pursuit of truth to write a book which reposes upon a false conception. Even the practical consequences of a book are to genuine criticism no recommendation of it, if the book is, in the highest sense, blundering. I see that a lady who herself, too, is in pursuit of truth, and who writes with great ability, but a little too much, perhaps, under the influence of the practical spirit of the English liberal movement, classes Bishop Colenso's book and M. Renan's [19] together, in her survey of the religious state of Europe, as facts of the same order, works, both of them, of "great importance"; "great ability, power, and skill"; Bishop Colenso's, perhaps, the most powerful; at least, Miss Cobbe [20] gives special expression to her gratitude that to Bishop Colenso "has been given the strength to grasp, and the courage to teach, truths of such deep import." In the same way, more than one popular writer has compared him to Luther. Now it is just this kind of false estimate which the critical spirit is, it seems to me, bound to resist. It is really the strongest possible proof of the low ebb at which, in England, the critical spirit is, that while the critical hit in the religious literature of Germany is Dr. Strauss's book,[21] in that of France M. Renan's book, the book of Bishop Colenso is the critical hit in the religious literature of England. Bishop Colenso's book reposes on a total misconception of the essential elements of the religious problem, as that problem is now presented for solution. To criticism, therefore, which seeks to have the best that is known and thought on this problem, it is, however well meant, of no importance whatever. M. Renan's book attempts a new synthesis of the elements furnished to us by the Four Gospels. It attempts, in my opinion, a synthesis, perhaps premature, perhaps impossible, certainly not successful. Up to the present time, at any rate, we must acquiesce in Fleury's sentence on such recastings of the Gospel story: *Quiconque s'imagine la pouvoir mieux écrire, ne l'entend pas*.[22] M. Renan had himself passed by anticipation a like sentence on his own work, when he said: "If a new presentation of the character of Jesus were offered to me, I would not have it; its very clearness would be, in my opinion, the best proof of its insufficiency." His friends may with perfect justice rejoin that at the sight of the Holy Land, and of the actual scene of the Gospel story, all the current of M. Renan's thoughts may have naturally changed, and a new casting of that story irresistibly suggested itself to him; and that this is just a case for applying Cicero's maxim: Change of mind is not inconsistency—*nemo doctus unquam mutationem consilii inconstantiam dixit esse*.[23] Nevertheless, for criticism, M. Renan's first thought must still be the truer one, as long as his new casting so fails more fully to commend itself, more fully (to use Coleridge's happy phrase about the Bible) to *find* us. Still M. Renan's attempt is, for criticism, of the most real interest and importance, since, with all its difficulty, a fresh synthesis of the New Testament data—not a making war on them, in Voltaire's fashion, not a leaving them out of mind, in the world's fashion, but the putting a new construction upon them, the taking them from under the old, traditional, conventional point of view and placing them under a new one—is the very essence of the religious problem, as now presented; and only by efforts in this direction can it receive a solution.

Again, in the same spirit in which she judges Bishop Colenso, Miss Cobbe, like so many earnest liberals of our practical race, both here and in America, herself sets vigorously about a positive reconstruction of religion, about making a religion of the future out of hand, or at least setting about making it. We must not rest, she and they are always thinking and saying, in negative criticism, we

18. **eighty . . . pigeons:** a reference to a passage in "The Bishop and the Philosopher" in which Arnold, by way of demonstrating how trivial is Colenso's arithmetical method of dealing with Biblical statements, cites satirically his analysis of a prescription in Leviticus requiring three priests to eat 264 pigeons. 19. **Renan:** Ernest Renan (1823–92), the French Oriental scholar and student of religion, had published in 1863 his famous *Life of Jesus*, the first volume of his extensive *History of the Origins of Christianity*. 20. **Miss Cobbe:** Frances Power Cobbe (1822–1904), a writer on religious and moral subjects. 21. **Dr. . . . book:** David Friedrich Strauss (1808–74), the German theologian and scholar, had published his *Life of Jesus* in 1835. It appeared in English translation—by George Eliot—in 1846 and had considerable fame. In 1864 it was published in a cheap popular edition.

22. ***Quiconque . . . pas:*** "Whoever thinks he can write it better does not understand it." 23. ***nemo . . . esse:*** "no learned man ever said that to change one's mind is to be inconsistent."

must be creative and constructive; hence we have such works as her recent *Religious Duty,* and works still more considerable, perhaps, by others, which will be in everyone's mind. These works often have much ability; they often spring out of sincere convictions, and a sincere wish to do good; and they sometimes, perhaps, do good. Their fault is (if I may be permitted to say so) one which they have in common with the British College of Health,[24] in the New Road. Everyone knows the British College of Health; it is that building with the lion and the statue of the Goddess Hygeia before it; at least I am sure about the lion, though I am not absolutely certain about the Goddess Hygeia. This building does credit, perhaps, to the resources of Dr. Morison and his disciples; but it falls a good deal short of one's idea of what a British College of Health ought to be. In England, where we hate public interference and love individual enterprise, we have a whole crop of places like the British College of Heath — the grand name without the grand thing. Unluckily, creditable to individual enterprise as they are, they tend to impair our taste by making us forget what more grandiose, noble, or beautiful character properly belongs to a public institution. The same may be said of the religions of the future of Miss Cobbe and others. Creditable, like the British College of Health, to the resources of their authors, they yet tend to make us forget what more grandiose, noble, or beautiful character properly belongs to religious constructions. The historic religions, with all their faults, have had this; it certainly belongs to the religious sentiment, when it truly flowers, to have this; and we impoverish our spirit if we allow a religion of the future without it. What then is the duty of criticism here? To take the practical point of view, to applaud the liberal movement and all its works — its New Road religions of the future into the bargain — for their general utility's sake? By no means; but to be perpetually dissatisfied with these works, while they perpetually fall short of a high and perfect ideal.

For criticism, these are elementary laws; but they never can be popular, and in this country they have been very little followed, and one meets with immense obstacles in following them. That is a reason for asserting them again and again. Criticism must maintain its independence of the practical spirit and its aims. Even with well-meant efforts of the practical spirit it must express dissatisfaction, if in the sphere of the ideal they seem impoverishing and limiting. It must not hurry on to the goal because of its practical importance. It must be patient, and know how to wait; and flexible, and know how to attach itself to things and how to withdraw from them. It must be apt to study and praise elements that for the fullness of spiritual perfection are wanted, even though they belong to a power which in the practical sphere may be maleficent. It must be apt to discern the spiritual shortcomings or illusions of powers that in the practical sphere may be beneficent. And this without any notion of favoring or injuring, in the practical sphere, one power or the other; without any notion of playing off, in this sphere, one power against the other. When one looks, for instance, at the English Divorce Court — an institution which perhaps has its practical conveniences, but which in the ideal sphere is so hideous; an institution which neither makes divorce impossible nor makes it decent, which allows a man to get rid of his wife, or a wife of her husband, but makes them drag one another first, for the public edification, through a mire of unutterable infamy — when one looks at this charming institution, I say, with its crowded trials, its newspaper reports, and its money compensations, this institution in which the gross unregenerate British Philistine has indeed stamped an image of himself — one may be permitted to find the marriage theory of Catholicism refreshing and elevating. Or when Protestantism, in virtue of its supposed rational and intellectual origin, gives the law to criticism too magisterially, criticism may and must remind it that its pretensions, in this respect, are illusive and do it harm; that the Reformation was a moral rather than an intellectual event; that Luther's theory of grace no more exactly reflects the mind of the spirit than Bossuet's philosophy of history[25] reflects it; and that there is no more antecedent probability of the Bishop of Durham's stock of ideas being agreeable to perfect reason than of Pope Pius IX's. But criticism will not on that account forget the achievements of Protestantism in the practical and moral sphere; nor that, even in the intellectual sphere, Protestantism, though in a blind and stumbling manner, carried forward the Renaissance, while Catholicism threw itself violently across its path.

**24. British . . . Health:** The British College of Health was not British and not a college but merely the grandiosely named place of business of the enterprising James Morison, who sold "Morison's Pills," extensively advertised as the cure for almost all ailments.

**25. Bossuet's . . . history:** Jacques Bénigne Bossuet (1627–1704) a French bishop, noted for his eloquence, held the belief that all of history demonstrated that God had ordered events for the good of Christianity.

I lately heard a man of thought and energy contrasting the want of ardor and movement which he now found amongst young men in this country with what he remembered in his own youth, twenty years ago. "What reformers we were then!" he exclaimed. "What a zeal we had! how we canvassed every institution in Church and State, and were prepared to remodel them all on first principles!" He was inclined to regret, as a spiritual flagging, the lull which he saw. I am disposed rather to regard it as a pause in which the turn to a new mode of spiritual progress is being accomplished. Everything was long seen, by the young and ardent amongst us, in inseparable connection with politics and practical life. We have pretty well exhausted the benefits of seeing things in this connection, we have got all that can be got by so seeing them. Let us try a more disinterested mode of seeing them; let us betake ourselves more to the serener life of the mind and spirit. This life, too, may have its excesses and dangers; but they are not for us at present. Let us think of quietly enlarging our stock of true and fresh ideas, and not, as soon as we get an idea or half an idea, be running out with it into the street, and trying to make it rule there. Our ideas will, in the end, shape the world all the better for maturing a little. Perhaps in fifty years' time it will in the English House of Commons be an objection to an institution that it is an anomaly, and my friend the member of Parliament will shudder in his grave. But let us in the meanwhile rather endeavor that in twenty years' time it may, in English literature, be an objection to a proposition that it is absurd. That will be a change so vast, that the imagination almost fails to grasp it. *Ab integro saeclorum nascitur ordo.*[26]

If I have insisted so much on the course which criticism must take where politics and religion are concerned, it is because, where these burning matters are in question, it is most likely to go astray. I have wished, above all, to insist on the attitude which criticism should adopt towards things in general; on its right tone and temper of mind. But then comes another question as to the subject matter which literary criticisms should most seek. Here, in general, its course is determined for it by the idea which is the law of its being: the idea of a disinterested endeavor to learn and propagate the best that is known and thought in the world, and thus to establish a current of fresh and true ideas. By the very nature of things, as England is not all the world, much of the best that is known and thought in the world cannot be of English growth, must be foreign; by the nature of things, again, it is just this that we are least likely to know, while English thought is streaming in upon us from all sides, and takes excellent care that we shall not be ignorant of its existence. The English critic of literature, therefore, must dwell much on foreign thought, and with particular heed on any part of it, which, while significant and fruitful in itself, is for any reason specially likely to escape him. Again, judging is often spoken of as the critic's one business, and so in some sense it is; but the judgment which almost insensibly forms itself in a fair and clear mind, along with fresh knowledge, is the valuable one; and thus knowledge, and ever fresh knowledge, must be the critic's great concern for himself. And it is by communicating fresh knowledge, and letting his own judgment pass along with it — but insensibly, and in the second place, not the first, as a sort of companion and clue, not as an abstract lawgiver — that the critic will generally do most good to his readers. Sometimes, no doubt, for the sake of establishing an author's place in literature, and his relation to a central standard (and if this is not done, how are we to get at our *best in the world?*) criticism may have to deal with a subject matter so familiar that fresh knowledge is out of the question, and then it must be all judgment; an enunciation and detailed application of principles. Here the great safeguard is never to let oneself become abstract, always to retain an intimate and lively consciousness of the truth of what one is saying, and, the moment this fails us, to be sure that something is wrong. Still under all circumstances, this mere judgment and application of principles is, in itself, not the most satisfactory work to the critic; like mathematics, it is tautological, and cannot well give us, like fresh learning, the sense of creative activity.

But stop, someone will say; all this talk is of no practical use to us whatever; this criticism of yours is not what we have in our minds when we speak of criticism; when we speak of critics and criticism, we mean critics and criticism of the current English literature of the day; when you offer to tell criticism its function, it is to this criticism that we expect you to address yourself. I am sorry for it, for I am afraid I must disappoint these expectations. I am bound by my own definition of criticism: *a disin-*

26. ***Ab . . . ordo:*** "The order of the ages begins anew." The phrase is quoted from the famous fourth *Eclogue* of Virgil (l. 5), which speaks of the Golden Age to come and which has often been read as prophesying the birth of Christ.

*terested endeavor to learn and propagate the best that is known and thought in the world.* How much of current English literature comes into this "best that is known and thought in the world"? Not very much, I fear; certainly less, at this moment, than of the current literature of France or Germany. Well, then, am I to alter my definition of criticism, in order to meet the requirements of a number of practicing English critics, who, after all, are free in their choice of a business? That would be making criticism lend itself just to one of those alien practical considerations which, I have said, are so fatal to it. One may say, indeed, to those who have to deal with the mass — so much better disregarded — of current English literature, that they may at all events endeavor, in dealing with this, to try it, so far as they can, by the standard of the best that is known and thought in the world; one may say, that to get anywhere near this standard, every critic should try and possess one great literature, at least, besides his own; and the more unlike his own, the better. But, after all, the criticism I am really concerned with — the criticism which alone can much help us for the future, the criticism which, throughout Europe, is at the present day meant, when so much stress is laid on the importance of criticism and the critical spirit — is a criticism which regards Europe as being, for intellectual and spiritual purposes, one great confederation, bound to a joint action and working to a common result, and whose members have, for their proper outfit, a knowledge of Greek, Roman, and Eastern antiquity, and of one another. Special, local, and temporary advantages being put out of account, that modern nation will in the intellectual and spiritual sphere make most progress, which most thoroughly carries out this program. And what is that but saying that we too, all of us, as individuals, the more thoroughly we carry it out, shall make the more progress?

There is so much inviting us! — what are we to take? what will nourish us in growth towards perfection? That is the question which, with the immense field of life and of literature lying before him, the critic has to answer; for himself first, and afterwards for others. In this idea of the critic's business the essays brought together in the following pages have had their origin; in this idea, widely different as are their subjects, they have, perhaps, their unity.

I conclude with what I said at the beginning: to have the sense of creative activity is the great happiness and the great proof of being alive, and it is not denied to criticism to have it; but then criticism must be sincere, simple, flexible, ardent, ever widening its knowledge. Then it may have, in no contemptible measure, a joyful sense of creative activity; a sense which a man of insight and conscience will prefer to what he might derive from a poor, starved, fragmentary, inadequate creation. And at some epochs no other creation is possible.

Still, in full measure, the sense of creative activity belongs only to genuine creation; in literature we must never forget that. But what true man of letters ever can forget it? It is no such common matter for a gifted nature to come into possession of a current of true and living ideas, and to produce amidst the inspiration of them, that we are likely to underrate it. The epochs of Aeschylus and Shakespeare make us feel their pre-eminence. In an epoch like those is, no doubt, the true life of literature; there is the promised land, towards which criticism can only beckon. That promised land it will not be ours to enter, and we shall die in the wilderness: but to have desired to enter it, to have saluted it from afar, is already, perhaps, the best distinction among contemporaries; it will certainly be the best title to esteem with posterity.

# LITERATURE AND SCIENCE

"Literature and Science" was one of the three lectures which Arnold prepared for his American tour of 1883, the two others being "Emerson" and "Numbers." It is perhaps the classic statement of the claims which literature makes to have a pre eminent place in education, even in an "age of science."

Practical people talk with a smile of Plato and of his absolute ideas;[1] and it is impossible to deny that Plato's ideas do often seem unpractical and impracticable, and especially when one views them in connection with the life of a great workaday world like the United States. The necessary staple of the life of such a world Plato regards with disdain; handicraft and trade and the working professions he regards with disdain; but what becomes of the life of an industrial modern community if you take

LITERATURE AND SCIENCE. 1. **Plato . . . ideas:** Plato expounded the doctrine that there existed, beyond human knowledge, the perfect ideas or archetypes of all things, of which the existent things that we perceive are but imperfect "copies." It was in this way that Plato set forth his theory of knowledge, that is, of the relation of what we know to ultimate reality.

handicraft and trade and the working professions out of it? The base mechanic arts and handicrafts, says Plato, bring about a natural weakness in the principle of excellence in a man, so that he cannot govern the ignoble growths in him, but nurses them, and cannot understand fostering any other. Those who exercise such arts and trades, as they have their bodies, he says, marred by their vulgar businesses, so they have their souls, too, bowed and broken by them. And if one of these uncomely people has a mind to seek self-culture and philosophy, Plato compares him to a bald little tinker, who has scraped together money, and has got his release from service, and has had a bath, and bought a new coat, and is rigged out like a bridegroom about to marry the daughter of his master who has fallen into poor and helpless estate.

Nor do the working professions fare any better than trade at the hands of Plato. He draws for us an inimitable picture of the working lawyer, and of his life of bondage; he shows how this bondage from his youth up has stunted and warped him, and made him small and crooked of soul, encompassing him with difficulties which he is not man enough to rely on justice and truth as means to encounter, but has recourse, for help out of them, to falsehood and wrong. And so, says Plato, this poor creature is bent and broken, and grows up from boy to man without a particle of soundness in him, although exceedingly smart and clever in his own esteem.

One cannot refuse to admire the artist who draws these pictures. But we say to ourselves that his ideas show the influence of a primitive and obsolete order of things, when the warrior caste and the priestly caste were alone in honor, and the humble work of the world was done by slaves. We have now changed all that; the modern majesty [2] consists in work, as Emerson declares; and in work, we may add, principally of such plain and dusty kind as the work of cultivators of the ground, handicraftsmen, men of trade and business, men of the working professions. Above all is this true in a great industrious community such as that of the United States.

Now education, many people go on to say, is still mainly governed by the ideas of men like Plato, who lived when the warrior caste and the priestly or philosophical class were alone in honor, and the really useful part of the community were slaves. It is an education fitted for persons of leisure in such a community. This education passed from Greece and Rome to the feudal communities of Europe, where also the warrior caste and the priestly caste were alone held in honor, and where the really useful and working part of the community, though not nominally slaves as in the pagan world, were practically not much better off than slaves, and not more seriously regarded. And how absurd it is, people end by saying, to inflict this education upon an industrious modern community, where very few indeed are persons of leisure, and the mass to be considered has not leisure, but is bound, for its own great good, and for the great good of the world at large, to plain labor and to industrial pursuits, and the education in question tends necessarily to make men dissatisfied with these pursuits and unfitted for them!

That is what is said. So far I must defend Plato, as to plead that his view of education and studies is in the general, as it seems to me, sound enough, and fitted for all sorts and conditions of men, whatever their pursuits may be. "An intelligent man," says Plato, "will prize those studies which result in his soul getting soberness, righteousness, and wisdom, and will less value the others." I cannot consider *that* a bad description of the aim of education, and of the motives which should govern us in the choice of studies, whether we are preparing ourselves for a hereditary seat in the English House of Lords or for the pork trade in Chicago.

Still I admit that Plato's world was not ours, that his scorn of trade and handicraft is fantastic, that he had no conception of a great industrial community such as that of the United States, and that such a community must and will shape its education to suit its own needs. If the usual education handed down to it from the past does not suit it, it will certainly before long drop this and try another. The usual education in the past has been mainly literary. The question is whether the studies which were long supposed to be the best for all of us are practically the best now; whether others are not better. The tyranny of the past, many think, weighs on us injuriously in the predominance given to letters in education. The question is raised whether, to meet the needs of our modern life, the predominance ought not now to pass from letters to science; and naturally the question is nowhere raised with more energy than here in the United

2. **majesty:** All editions of Arnold read "the modern majority." But this is clearly an error; what Emerson wrote (in his essay, "Literary Ethics") was: "Feudalism and Orientalism had long enough thought it majestic to do nothing; the modern majesty consists in work." The error was noted and corrected by C. F. Harrold and W. D. Templeman in their ***English Prose of the Victorian Era.***

States. The design of abasing what is called "mere literary instruction and education," and of exalting what is called "sound, extensive, and practical scientific knowledge," is, in this intensely modern world of the United States, even more perhaps than in Europe, a very popular design, and makes great and rapid progress.

I am going to ask whether the present movement for ousting letters from their old predominance in education, and for transferring the predominance in education to the natural sciences, whether this brisk and flourishing movement ought to prevail, and whether it is likely that in the end it really will prevail. An objection may be raised which I will anticipate. My own studies have been almost wholly in letters, and my visits to the field of the natural sciences have been very slight and inadequate, although those sciences have always strongly moved my curiosity. A man of letters, it will perhaps be said, is not competent to discuss the comparative merits of letters and natural sciences as means of education. To this objection I reply, first of all, that his incompetence, if he attempts the discussion but is really incompetent for it, will be abundantly visible; nobody will be taken in; he will have plenty of sharp observers and critics to save mankind from that danger. But the line I am going to follow is, as you will soon discover, so extremely simple, that perhaps it may be followed without failure even by one who for a more ambitious line of discussion would be quite incompetent.

Some of you may possibly remember a phrase of mine which has been the object of a good deal of comment; an observation to the effect that in our culture, the aim being *to know ourselves and the world,* we have, as the means to this end, *to know the best which has been thought and said in the world.*[3] A man of science, who is also an excellent writer and the very prince of debaters, Professor Huxley,[4] in a discourse at the opening of Sir Josiah Mason's college at Birmingham, laying hold of this phrase, expanded it by quoting some more words of mine, which are these: "The civilized world is to be regarded as now being, for intellectual and spiritual purposes, one great confederation, bound to a joint action and working to a common result; and whose members have for their proper outfit a knowledge of Greek, Roman, and Eastern antiquity, and of one another. Special local and temporary advantages being put out of account, that modern nation will in the intellectual and spiritual sphere make most progress, which most thoroughly carries out this program."

Now on my phrase, thus enlarged, Professor Huxley remarks that when I speak of the above-mentioned knowledge as enabling us to know ourselves and the world, I assert *literature* to contain the materials which suffice for thus making us know ourselves and the world. But it is not by any means clear, says he, that after having learned all which ancient and modern literatures have to tell us, we have laid a sufficiently broad and deep foundation for that criticism of life, that knowledge of ourselves and the world, which constitutes culture. On the contrary, Professor Huxley declares that he finds himself "wholly unable to admit that either nations or individuals will really advance, if their outfit draws nothing from the stores of physical science. An army without weapons of precision, and with no particular base of operations, might more hopefully enter upon a campaign on the Rhine, than a man, devoid of a knowledge of what physical science has done in the last century, upon a criticism of life."

This shows how needful it is for those who are to discuss any matter together, to have a common understanding as to the sense of the terms they employ — how needful, and how difficult. What Professor Huxley says implies just the reproach which is so often brought against the study of belles-lettres, as they are called: that the study is an elegant one, but slight and ineffectual; a smattering of Greek and Latin and other ornamental things, of little use for anyone whose object is to get at truth, and to be a practical man. So, too, M. Renan[5] talks of the "superficial humanism" of a school course which treats us as if we were all going to be poets, writers, preachers, orators, and he opposes this humanism to positive science, or the critical search after truth. And there is always a tendency in those who are remonstrating against the predominance of letters in education, to understand by letters belles-lettres, and by belles-lettres a superficial humanism, the opposite of science or true knowledge.

But when we talk of knowing Greek and Roman antiquity, for instance, which is the knowledge people have called the humanities, I for my part mean a knowledge which is something more than a su-

3. *know . . . world*: See "The Function of Criticism at the Present Time," above. 4. **Huxley**: Thomas Henry Huxley (1825–95), the famous scientist and exponent of the Darwinian theory of evolution.

5. Ernest Renan (1823–92), the French Orientalist and student of religions.

perficial humanism, mainly decorative. "I call all teaching *scientific,*" says Wolf,[6] the critic of Homer, "which is systematically laid out and followed up to its original sources. For example: a knowledge of classical antiquity is scientific when the remains of classical antiquity are correctly studied in the original languages." There can be no doubt that Wolf is perfectly right; that all learning is scientific which is systematically laid out and followed up to its original sources, and that a genuine humanism is scientific.

When I speak of knowing Greek and Roman antiquity, therefore, as a help to knowing ourselves and the world, I mean more than a knowledge of so much vocabulary, so much grammar, so many portions of authors in the Greek and Latin languages. I mean knowing the Greeks and Romans, and their life and genius, and what they were and did in the world; what we get from them, and what is its value. That, at least, is the ideal; and when we talk of endeavoring to know Greek and Roman antiquity, as a help to knowing ourselves and the world, we mean endeavoring so to know them as to satisfy this ideal, however much we may still fall short of it.

The same also as to knowing our own and other modern nations, with the like aim of getting to understand ourselves and the world. To know the best that has been thought and said by the modern nations, is to know, says Professor Huxley, "only what modern *literatures* have to tell us; it is the criticism of life contained in modern literature." And yet "the distinctive character of our times," he urges, "lies in the vast and constantly increasing part which is played by natural knowledge." And how, therefore, can a man, devoid of knowledge of what physical science has done in the last century, enter hopefully upon a criticism of modern life?

Let us, I say, be agreed about the meaning of the terms we are using. I talk of knowing the best which has been thought and uttered in the world; Professor Huxley says this means knowing *literature*. Literature is a large word; it may mean everything written with letters or printed in a book. Euclid's *Elements* and Newton's *Principia* are thus literature. All knowledge that reaches us through books is literature. But by literature Professor Huxley means belles-lettres. He means to make me say, that knowing the best which has been thought and said by the modern nations is knowing their belles-lettres and no more. And this is no sufficient equipment, he argues, for a criticism of modern life. But as I do not mean, by knowing ancient Rome, knowing merely more or less of Latin belles-lettres, and taking no account of Rome's military, and political, and legal, and administrative work in the world; and as, by knowing ancient Greece, I understand knowing her as the giver of Greek art, and the guide to a free and right use of reason and to scientific method, and the founder of our mathematics and physics and astronomy and biology — I understand knowing her as all this, and not merely knowing certain Greek poems, and histories, and treatises, and speeches — so as to the knowledge of modern nations also. By knowing modern nations, I mean not merely knowing their belles-lettres, but knowing also what has been done by such men as Copernicus, Galileo, Newton, Darwin. "Our ancestors learned," says Professor Huxley, "that the earth is the center of the visible universe, and that man is the cynosure of things terrestrial; and more especially was it inculcated that the course of nature had no fixed order, but that it could be, and constantly was, altered." But for us now, continues Professor Huxley, "the notions of the beginning and the end of the world entertained by our forefathers are no longer credible. It is very certain that the earth is not the chief body in the material universe, and that the world is not subordinated to man's use. It is even more certain that nature is the expression of a definite order, with which nothing interferes." "And yet," he cries, "the purely classical education advocated by the representatives of the humanists in our day gives no inkling of all this!"

In due place and time I will just touch upon that vexed question of classical education, but at present the question is as to what is meant by knowing the best which modern nations have thought and said. It is not knowing their belles-lettres merely which is meant. To know Italian belles-lettres is not to know Italy, and to know English belles-lettres is not to know England. Into knowing Italy and England there comes a great deal more, Galileo and Newton amongst it. The reproach of being a superficial humanism, a tincture of belles-lettres, may attach rightly enough to some other disciplines; but to the particular discipline recommended when I proposed knowing the best that has been thought and said in the world, it does not apply. In that best I certainly include what in modern times has

6. **Wolf**: Friedrich August Wolf (1759–1824).

been thought and said by the great observers and knowers of nature.

There is, therefore, really no question between Professor Huxley and me as to whether knowing the great results of the modern scientific study of nature is not required as a part of our culture, as well as knowing the products of literature and art. But to follow the processes by which those results are reached, ought, say the friends of physical science, to be made the staple of education for the bulk of mankind. And here there does arise a question between those whom Professor Huxley calls with playful sarcasm "the Levites of culture," and those whom the poor humanist is sometimes apt to regard as its Nebuchadnezzars.[7]

The great results of the scientific investigation of nature we are agreed upon knowing, but how much of our study are we bound to give to the processes by which those results are reached? The results have their visible bearing on human life. But all the processes, too, all the items of fact, by which those results are reached and established, are interesting. All knowledge is interesting to a wise man, and the knowledge of nature is interesting to all men. It is very interesting to know, that, from the albuminous white of the egg, the chick in the egg gets the materials for its flesh, bones, blood, and feathers; while, from the fatty yolk of the egg, it gets the heat and energy which enable it at length to break its shell and begin the world. It is less interesting, perhaps, but still it is interesting, to know that when a taper burns, the wax is converted into carbonic acid and water. Moreover, it is quite true that the habit of dealing with facts, which is given by the study of nature, is, as the friends of physical science praise it for being, an excellent discipline. The appeal, in the study of nature, is constantly to observation and experiment; not only is it said that the thing is so, but we can be made to see that it is so. Not only does a man tell us that when a taper burns the wax is converted into carbonic acid and water, as a man may tell us, if he likes, that Charon is punting his ferryboat on the river Styx, or that Victor Hugo is a sublime poet, or Mr. Gladstone the most admirable of statesmen; but we are made to see that the conversion into carbonic acid and water does actually happen. This reality of natural knowledge it is, which makes the friends of physical science contrast it, as a knowledge of things, with the humanist's knowledge, which is, say they, a knowledge of words. And hence Professor Huxley is moved to lay it down that, "for the purpose of attaining real culture, an exclusively scientific education is at least as effectual as an exclusively literary education." And a certain president of the Section for Mechanical Science in the British Association is, in Scripture phrase, "very bold," and declares that if a man, in his mental training, "has substituted literature and history for natural science, he has chosen the less useful alternative." But whether we go these lengths or not, we must all admit that in natural science the habit gained of dealing with facts is a most valuable discipline, and that everyone should have some experience of it.

More than this, however, is demanded by the reformers. It is proposed to make the training in natural science the main part of education, for the great majority of mankind at any rate. And here, I confess, I part company with the friends of physical science, with whom up to this point I have been agreeing. In differing from them, however, I wish to proceed with the utmost caution and diffidence. The smallness of my own acquaintance with the disciplines of natural science is ever before my mind, and I am fearful of doing these disciplines an injustice. The ability and pugnacity of the partisans of natural science makes them formidable persons to contradict. The tone of tentative inquiry, which befits a being of dim faculties and bounded knowledge, is the tone I would wish to take and not to depart from. At present it seems to me, that those who are for giving to natural knowledge, as they call it, the chief place in the education of the majority of mankind, leave one important thing out of their account: the constitution of human nature. But I put this forward on the strength of some facts not at all recondite, very far from it; facts capable of being stated in the simplest possible fashion, and to which, if I so state them, the man of science will, I am sure, be willing to allow their due weight.

Deny the facts altogether, I think, he hardly can. He can hardly deny, that when we set ourselves to enumerate the powers which go to the building up of human life, and say that they are the power of conduct, the power of intellect and knowledge, the power of beauty, and the power of social life and manners — he can hardly deny that this scheme,

7. **Levites . . . Nebuchadnezzars:** The Levites were the Jewish tribe assigned the task of assisting the high priest in ceremonial matters and of doing the physical work of the Temple. Nebuchadnezzar was the Babylonian king who captured Jerusalem and destroyed the temple. Huxley is saying that those who favor a classical education are merely ritualistic; Arnold is saying that those who attack classical education may be thought of as destroying the "Temple" of education.

though drawn in rough and plain lines enough, and not pretending to scientific exactness, does yet give a fairly true representation of the matter. Human nature is built up by these powers; we have the need for them all. When we have rightly met and adjusted the claims of them all, we shall then be in a fair way for getting soberness and righteousness, with wisdom. This is evident enough, and the friends of physical science would admit it.

But perhaps they may not have sufficiently observed another thing, namely, that the several powers just mentioned are not isolated, but there is, in the generality of mankind, a perpetual tendency to relate them one to another in divers ways. With one such way of relating them I am particularly concerned now. Following our instinct for intellect and knowledge, we acquire pieces of knowledge; and presently, in the generality of men, there arises the desire to relate these pieces of knowledge to our sense for conduct, to our sense for beauty — and there is weariness and dissatisfaction it the desire is balked. Now in this desire lies, I think, the strength of that hold which letters have upon us.

All knowledge is, as I said just now, interesting; and even items of knowledge which from the nature of the case cannot well be related, but must stand isolated in our thoughts, have their interest. Even lists of exceptions have their interest. If we are studying Greek accents, it is interesting to know that *pais* and *pas,* and some other monosyllables of the same form of declension, do not take the circumflex upon the last syllable of the genitive plural, but vary, in this respect, from the common rule. If we are studying physiology, it is interesting to know that the pulmonary artery carries dark blood and the pulmonary vein carries bright blood, departing in this respect from the common rule for the division of labor between the veins and the arteries. But everyone knows how we seek naturally to combine the pieces of our knowledge together, to bring them under general rules, to relate them to principles; and how unsatisfactory and tiresome it would be to go on forever learning lists of exceptions, or accumulating items of fact which must stand isolated.

Well, that same need of relating our knowledge, which operates here within the sphere of our knowledge itself, we shall find operating, also, outside that sphere. We experience, as we go on learning and knowing — the vast majority of us experience — the need of relating what we have learned and known to the sense which we have in us for conduct, to the sense which we have in us for beauty.

A certain Greek prophetess of Mantinea in Arcadia, Diotima by name, once explained to the philosopher Socrates that love, and impulse, and bent of all kinds, is, in fact, nothing else but the desire in men that good should forever be present to them.[8] This desire for good, Diotima assured Socrates, is our fundamental desire, of which fundamental desire every impulse in us is only some one particular form. And therefore this fundamental desire it is, I suppose — this desire in men that good should be forever present to them — which acts in us when we feel the impulse for relating our knowledge to our sense for conduct and to our sense for beauty. At any rate, with men in general the instinct exists. Such is human nature. And the instinct, it will be admitted, is innocent, and human nature is preserved by our following the lead of its innocent instincts. Therefore, in seeking to gratify this instinct in question, we are following the instinct of self-preservation in humanity.

But, no doubt, some kinds of knowledge cannot be made to directly serve the instinct in question, cannot be directly related to the sense for beauty, to the sense for conduct. These are instrument knowledges; they lead on to other knowledges, which can. A man who passes his life in instrument knowledges is a specialist. They may be invaluable as instruments to something beyond, for those who have the gift thus to employ them; and they may be disciplines in themselves wherein it is useful for everyone to have some schooling. But it is inconceivable that the generality of men should pass all their mental life with Greek accents or with formal logic. My friend Professor Sylvester, who is one of the first mathematicians in the world, holds transcendental doctrines as to the virtue of mathematics, but those doctrines are not for common men. In the very Senate House and heart of our English Cambridge I once ventured, though not without an apology for my profaneness, to hazard the opinion that for the majority of mankind a little of mathematics, even, goes a long way.[9] Of course this is quite consistent with their being of immense importance as an instrument to something else, but it is the few who have the aptitude for thus using them, not the bulk of mankind.

The natural sciences do not, however, stand on the same footing with these instrument knowledges. Experience shows us that the generality of men will find more interest in learning that, when a taper

**8. Diotima . . . them:** In Plato's *Symposium* Socrates gives this account of Diotima and her doctrine. **9. Cambridge . . . way:** The point of this remark is that Cambridge University always put great emphasis upon mathematics, far more than Oxford.

burns, the wax is converted into carbonic acid and water, or in learning the explanation of the phenomenon of dew, or in learning how the circulation of the blood is carried on, than they find in learning that the genitive plural of *pais* and *pas* does not take the circumflex on the termination. And one piece of natural knowledge is added to another, and others are added to that, and at last we come to propositions so interesting as Mr. Darwin's famous proposition that "our ancestor was a hairy quadruped furnished with a tail and pointed ears, probably arboreal in his habits." Or we come to propositions of such reach and magnitude as those which Professor Huxley delivers, when he says that the notions of our forefathers about the beginning and the end of the world were all wrong, and that nature is the expression of a definite order with which nothing interferes.

Interesting, indeed, these results of science are, important they are, and we should all of us be acquainted with them. But what I now wish you to mark is, that we are still, when they are propounded to us and we receive them, we are still in the sphere of intellect and knowledge. And for the generality of men there will be found, I say, to arise, when they have duly taken in the proposition that their ancestor was "a hairy quadruped furnished with a tail and pointed ears, probably arboreal in his habits," there will be found to arise an invincible desire to relate this proposition to the sense in us for conduct, and to the sense in us for beauty. But this the men of science will not do for us, and will hardly even profess to do. They will give us other pieces of knowledge, other facts, about other animals and their ancestors, or about plants, or about stones, or about stars; and they may finally bring us to those great "general conceptions of the universe, which are forced upon us all," says Professor Huxley, "by the progress of physical science." But still it will be *knowledge* only which they give us; knowledge not put for us into relation with our sense for conduct, our sense for beauty, and touched with emotion by being so put; not thus put for us, and therefore, to the majority of mankind, after a certain while, unsatisfying, wearying.

Not to the born naturalist, I admit. But what do we mean by a born naturalist? We mean a man in whom the zeal for observing nature is so uncommonly strong and eminent, that it marks him off from the bulk of mankind. Such a man will pass his life happily in collecting natural knowledge and reasoning upon it, and will ask for nothing, or hardly anything, more. I have heard it said that the sagacious and admirable naturalist whom we lost not very long ago, Mr. Darwin, once owned to a friend that for his part he did not experience the necessity for two things which most men find so necessary to them — religion and poetry; science and the domestic affections, he thought, were enough. To a born naturalist, I can well understand that this should seem so. So absorbing is his occupation with nature, so strong his love for his occupation, that he goes on acquiring natural knowledge and reasoning upon it, and has little time or inclination for thinking about getting it related to the desire in man for conduct, the desire in man for beauty. He relates it to them for himself as he goes along, so far as he feels the need; and he draws from the domestic affections all the additional solace necessary. But then Darwins are extremely rare. Another great and admirable master of natural knowledge, Faraday, was a Sandemanian.[10] That is to say, he related his knowledge to his instinct for conduct and to his instinct for beauty, by the aid of that respectable Scottish sectary, Robert Sandeman. And so strong, in general, is the demand of religion and poetry to have their share in a man, to associate themselves with his knowing, and to relieve and rejoice it, that, probably, for one man amongst us with the disposition to do as Darwin did in this respect, there are at least fifty with the disposition to do as Faraday.

Education lays hold upon us, in fact, by satisfying this demand. Professor Huxley holds up to scorn medieval education, with its neglect of the knowledge of nature, its poverty even of literary studies, its formal logic devoted to "showing how and why that which the Church said was true must be true." But the great medieval universities were not brought into being, we may be sure, by the zeal for giving a jejune and contemptible education. Kings have been their nursing fathers, and queens have been their nursing mothers, but not for this. The medieval universities came into being because the supposed knowledge, delivered by Scripture and the Church, so deeply engaged men's hearts, by so simply, easily, and powerfully relating itself to their desire for conduct, their desire for beauty. All other knowledge was dominated by this supposed knowledge and was subordinated to it, because of the surpassing strength of the hold which it gained upon the affections of men, by

10. **Faraday . . . Sandemanian:** Michael Faraday (1791–1867) was a great chemist and physicist. The Sandemanians were a Protestant sect, followers of Robert Sandeman (1718–1871).

allying itself profoundly with their sense for conduct, their sense for beauty.

But now, says Professor Huxley, conceptions of the universe fatal to the notions held by our forefathers have been forced upon us by physical science. Grant to him that they are thus fatal, that the new conceptions must and will soon become current everywhere, and that everyone will finally perceive them to be fatal to the beliefs of our forefathers. The need of humane letters, as they are truly called, because they serve the paramount desire in men that good should be forever present to them — the need of humane letters, to establish a relation between the new conceptions, and our instinct for beauty, our instinct for conduct, is only the more visible. The Middle Age could do without humane letters, as it could do without the study of nature, because its supposed knowledge was made to engage its emotions so powerfully. Grant that the supposed knowledge disappears, its power of being made to engage the emotions will of course disappear along with it — but the emotions themselves, and their claim to be engaged and satisfied, will remain. Now if we find by experience that humane letters have an undeniable power of engaging the emotions, the importance of humane letters in a man's training becomes not less, but greater, in proportion to the success of modern science in extirpating what it calls "medieval thinking."

Have humane letters, then, have poetry and eloquence, the power here attributed to them of engaging the emotions, and do they exercise it? And if they have it and exercise it, *how* do they exercise it, so as to exert an influence upon man's sense for conduct, his sense for beauty? Finally, even if they both can and do exert an influence upon the senses in question, how are they to relate to them the results — the modern results — of natural science? All these questions may be asked. First, have poetry and eloquence the power of calling out the emotions? The appeal is to experience. Experience shows that for the vast majority of men, for mankind in general, they have the power. Next, do they exercise it? They do. But then, *how* do they exercise it so as to affect man's sense for conduct, his sense for beauty? And this is perhaps a case for applying the Preacher's words: "Though a man labor to seek it out, yet he shall not find it; yea, farther, though a wise man think to know it, yet shall he not be able to find it." [11] Why should it be one thing, in its effect upon the emotions, to say, "Patience is a virtue," and quite another thing, in its effect upon the emotions, to say with Homer,

*τλητὸν γὰρ Μοῖραι θυμὸν θέσαν ἀνθρώποισιν* [12]—

"for an enduring heart have the destinies appointed to the children of men"? Why should it be one thing, in its effect upon the emotions, to say with the philosopher Spinoza, *Felicitas in eo consistit quod homo suum esse conservare potest* — "Man's happiness consists in his being able to preserve his own essence," and quite another thing, in its effect upon the emotions, to say with the Gospel, "What is a man advantaged, if he gain the whole world, and lose himself, forfeit himself?" How does this difference of effect arise? I cannot tell, and I am not much concerned to know; the important thing is that it does arise, and that we can profit by it. But how, finally, are poetry and eloquence to exercise the power of relating the modern results of natural science to man's instinct for conduct, his instinct for beauty? And here again I answer that I do not know *how* they will exercise it, but that they can and will exercise it I am sure. I do not mean that modern philosophical poets and modern philosophical moralists are to come and relate for us, in express terms, the results of modern scientific research to our instinct for conduct, our instinct for beauty. But I mean that we shall find, as a matter of experience, if we know the best that has been thought and uttered in the world, we shall find that the art and poetry and eloquence of men who lived, perhaps, long ago, who had the most limited natural knowledge, who had the most erroneous conceptions about many important matters, we shall find that this art, and poetry, and eloquence, have in fact not only the power of refreshing and delighting us, they have also the power — such is the strength and worth, in essentials, of their authors' criticism of life — they have a fortifying, and elevating, and quickening, and suggestive power, capable of wonderfully helping us to relate the results of modern science to our need for conduct, our need for beauty. Homer's conceptions of the physical universe were, I imagine, grotesque; but really, under the shock of hearing from modern science that "the world is not subordinated to man's use, and that man is not the cynosure of things terrestrial," I could, for my own part, desire no better comfort than Homer's line which I quoted just now,

11. "Though . . . it": Eccles. 8:17 [A].

12. *Iliad*, XXIV.49 [A].

τλητὸν γὰρ Μοῖραι θυμὸν θέσαν ἀνθρώποισιν—
"for an enduring heart have the destinies appointed to the children of men"!

And the more that men's minds are cleared, the more that the results of science are frankly accepted, the more that poetry and eloquence come to be received and studied as what in truth they really are — the criticism of life by gifted men, alive and active with extraordinary power at an unusual number of points — so much the more will the value of humane letters, and of art also, which is an utterance having a like kind of power with theirs, be felt and acknowledged, and their place in education be secured.

Let us therefore, all of us, avoid indeed as much as possible any invidious comparison between the merits of humane letters, as means of education, and the merits of the natural sciences. But when some president of a Section for Mechanical Science insists on making the comparison, and tells us that "he who in his training has substituted literature and history for natural science has chosen the less useful alternative," let us make answer to him that the student of humane letters only, will, at least, know also the great general conceptions brought in by modern physical science; for science, as Professor Huxley says, forces them upon us all. But the student of the natural sciences only, will, by our very hypothesis, know nothing of humane letters, not to mention that in setting himself to be perpetually accumulating natural knowledge, he sets himself to do what only specialists have in general the gift for doing genially.[13] And so he will probably be unsatisfied, or at any rate incomplete, and even more incomplete than the student of humane letters only.

I once mentioned in a school report, how a young man in one of our English training colleges having to paraphrase the passage in *Macbeth* beginning,

Canst thou not minister to a mind diseased? [14]

turned this line into, "Can you not wait upon the lunatic?" And I remarked what a curious state of things it would be, if every pupil of our national schools knew, let us say, that the moon is two thousand one hundred and sixty miles in diameter, and thought at the same time that a good paraphrase for

Canst thou not minister to a mind diseased?

was, "Can you not wait upon the lunatic?" If one is driven to choose, I think I would rather have a young person ignorant about the moon's diameter, but aware that "Can you not wait upon the lunatic?" is bad, than a young person whose education had been such as to manage things the other way.

Or to go higher than the pupils of our national schools. I have in my mind's eye a member of our British parliament who comes to travel here in America, who afterwards relates his travels, and who shows a really masterly knowledge of the geology of this great country and of its mining capabilities, but who ends by gravely suggesting that the United States should borrow a prince from our royal family, and should make him their king, and should create a House of Lords of great landed proprietors after the pattern of ours; and then America, he thinks, would have her future happily and perfectly secured. Surely, in this case, the president of the Section for Mechanical Science would himself hardly say that our member of Parliament, by concentrating himself upon geology and mineralogy, and so on, and not attending to literature and history, had "chosen the more useful alternative."

If then there is to be separation and option between humane letters on the one hand, and the natural sciences on the other, the great majority of mankind, all who have not exceptional and overpowering aptitudes for the study of nature, would do well, I cannot but think, to choose to be educated in humane letters rather than in the natural sciences. Letters will call out their being at more points, will make them live more.

I said that before I ended I would just touch on the question of classical education, and I will keep my word. Even if literature is to retain a large place in our education, yet Latin and Greek, say the friends of progress, will certainly have to go. Greek is the grand offender in the eyes of these gentlemen. The attackers of the established course of study think that against Greek, at any rate, they have irresistible arguments. Literature may perhaps be needed in education, they say, but why on earth should it be Greek literature? Why not French or German? Nay, "has not an Englishman models in his own literature of every kind of excellence?" [15] As before, it is not on any weak pleadings of my own that I rely for convincing the gainsayers; it is on the constitution of human nature itself, and on

13. **genially**: Arnold is using the word in its meaning of "good for life and growth." 14. *Macbeth*, V.iii.40.

15. **"has . . . excellence"**: Arnold is quoting from Huxley's address.

the instinct of self-preservation in humanity. The instinct for beauty is set in human nature, as surely as the instinct for knowledge is set there, or the instinct for conduct. If the instinct for beauty is served by Greek literature and art as it is served by no other literature and art, we may trust to the instinct of self-preservation in humanity for keeping Greek as part of our culture. We may trust to it for even making the study of Greek more prevalent than it is now. Greek will come, I hope, some day to be studied more rationally than at present, but it will be increasingly studied as men increasingly feel the need in them for beauty, and how powerfully Greek art and Greek literature can serve this need. Women will again study Greek, as Lady Jane Grey [16] did; I believe that in that chain of forts, with which the fair host of the Amazons are now engirdling our English universities,[17] I find that here in America, in colleges like Smith College in Massachusetts, and Vassar College in the state of New York, and in the happy families of the mixed universities out West, they are studying it already.

*Defuit una mihi symmetria prisca* — "The antique symmetry was the one thing wanting to me," said Leonardo da Vinci, and he was an Italian. I will not presume to speak for the Americans, but I am sure that, in the Englishman, the want of this admirable symmetry of the Greeks is a thousand times more great and crying than in any Italian. The results of the want show themselves most glaringly, perhaps, in our architecture, but they show themselves, also, in all our art. *Fit details strictly combined, in view of a large general result nobly conceived;* that is just the beautiful *symmetria prisca* of the Greeks, and it is just where we English fail, where all our art fails. Striking ideas we have, and well-executed details we have; but that high symmetry which, with satisfying and delightful effect, combines them, we seldom or never have. The glorious beauty of the Acropolis at Athens did not come from single fine things stuck about on that hill, a statue here, a gateway there; no, it arose from all things being perfectly combined for a supreme total effect. What must not an Englishman feel about our deficiencies in this respect, as the sense for beauty, whereof this symmetry is an essential element, awakens and strengthens within him! what will not one day be his respect and desire for Greece and its *symmetria prisca,* when the scales drop from his eyes as he walks the London streets, and he sees such a lesson in meanness as the Strand, for instance, in its true deformity! But here we are coming to our friend Mr. Ruskin's province, and I will not intrude upon it, for he is its very sufficient guardian.

And so we at last find, it seems, we find flowing in favor of the humanities the natural and necessary stream of things, which seemed against them when we started. The "hairy quadruped furnished with a tail and pointed ears, probably arboreal in his habits," this good fellow carried hidden in his nature, apparently, something destined to develop into a necessity for humane letters. Nay, more; we seem finally to be even led to the further conclusion that our hairy ancestor carried in his nature, also, a necessity for Greek.

And therefore, to say the truth, I cannot really think that humane letters are in much actual danger of being thrust out from their leading place in education, in spite of the array of authorities against them at this moment. So long as human nature is what it is, their attractions will remain irresistible. As with Greek, so with letters generally: they will some day come, we may hope, to be studied more rationally, but they will not lose their place. What will happen will rather be that there will be crowded into education other matters besides, far too many; there will be, perhaps, a period of unsettlement and confusion and false tendency; but letters will not in the end lose their leading place. If they lose it for a time, they will get it back again. We shall be brought back to them by our wants and aspirations. And a poor humanist may possess his soul in patience, neither strive nor cry, admit the energy and brilliancy of the partisans of physical science, and their present favor with the public, to be far greater than his own, and still have a happy faith that the nature of things works silently on behalf of the studies which he loves, and that, while we shall all have to acquaint ourselves with the great results reached by modern science, and to give ourselves as much training in its disciplines as we can conveniently carry, yet the majority of men will always require humane letters; and so much the more, as they have the more and the greater results of science to relate to the need in man for conduct, and to the need in him for beauty.

**16. Grey:** Lady Jane Grey (1537–54), the daughter of the Duke of Suffolk, was noted for her abilities as a Greek scholar. As a result of the intrigues of Dudley, Duke of Northumberland, the dying Edward VI designated her his successor to the throne. But the scheme failed, and both Northumberland and Lady Jane Grey were executed. **17.** Arnold's rather arch irony takes note of the fact that women's colleges at Oxford and Cambridge were at first regarded with suspicion and even hostility.

# THE STUDY OF POETRY

It is possible to say of "The Study of Poetry" that no single piece of literary criticism of the Victorian age had so wide an influence in England and America. It controlled the educated taste in poetry until the critical ascendancy of T. S. Eliot and the powerful critical movement that arose with him and the early writings of I. A. Richards. The degree of one's acceptance of Arnold's judgments as expressed in the essay depends largely on how far one goes in agreeing with his conception of "seriousness." Nowadays we are likely to feel that seriousness takes more forms than Arnold was inclined to admit, much of our taste having been formed by critics who have insisted upon the seriousness as well as upon the charms of the wit and paradox of the so-called Metaphysical poets. We have learned, too, to respond more freely to those very "prosaic" qualities, in Dryden and Pope, or in other and different poets, that Arnold deprecated. But it would be a rash critic and an insensitive reader who, even while perceiving the limits of Arnold's canons, would not admit their cogency and power.

---

"The future of poetry is immense, because in poetry, where it is worthy of its high destinies, our race, as time goes on, will find an ever surer and surer stay. There is not a creed which is not shaken, not an accredited dogma which is not shown to be questionable, not a received tradition which does not threaten to dissolve. Our religion has materialized itself in the fact, in the supposed fact; it has attached its emotion to the fact, and now the fact is failing it. But for poetry the idea is everything; the rest is a world of illusion, of divine illusion. Poetry attaches its emotion to the idea; the idea *is* the fact. The strongest part of our religion today is its unconscious poetry."

Let me be permitted to quote these words of my own,[1] as uttering the thought which should, in my opinion, go with us and govern us in all our study of poetry. In the present work [2] it is the course of one great contributory stream to the world river of poetry that we are invited to follow. We are here invited to trace the stream of English poetry. But whether we set ourselves, as here, to follow only one of the several streams that make the mighty river of poetry, or whether we seek to know them all, our governing thought should be the same. We should conceive of poetry worthily, and more highly than it has been the custom to conceive of it. We should conceive of it as capable of higher uses, and called to higher destinies, than those which in general men have assigned to it hitherto. More and more mankind will discover that we have to turn to poetry to interpret life for us, to console us, to sustain us. Without poetry, our science will appear incomplete; and most of what now passes with us for religion and philosophy will be replaced by poetry. Science, I say, will appear incomplete without it. For finely and truly does Wordsworth call poetry "the impassioned expression which is in the countenance of all science"; and what is a countenance without its expression? Again, Wordsworth finely and truly calls poetry "the breath and finer spirit of all knowledge": our religion, parading evidences such as those on which the popular mind relies now; our philosophy, pluming itself on its reasonings about causation and finite and infinite being; what are they but the shadows and dreams and false shows of knowledge? The day will come when we shall wonder at ourselves for having trusted to them, for having taken them seriously; and the more we perceive their hollowness, the more we shall prize "the breath and finer spirit of knowledge" offered to us by poetry.

But if we conceive thus highly of the destinies of poetry, we must also set our standard for poetry high, since poetry, to be capable of fulfilling such high destinies, must be poetry of a high order of excellence. We must accustom ourselves to a high standard and to a strict judgment. Sainte-Beuve [3] relates that Napoleon one day said, when somebody was spoken of in his presence as a charlatan: "Charlatan as much as you please, but where is there *not* charlatanism?" — "Yes," answers Sainte-Beuve, "in politics, in the art of governing mankind, that is perhaps true. But in the order of thought, in art, the glory, the eternal honor is that charlatanism shall find no entrance; herein lies the inviolableness of that noble portion of man's being." It is admirably said, and let us hold fast to it. In poetry, which is thought and art in one, it is the glory, the eternal honor, that charlatanism shall find no entrance; that this noble sphere be kept inviolate and inviolable. Charlatanism is for confusing or obliterating the distinctions between excellent and inferior, sound and unsound or only

STUDY OF POETRY. **1. Let . . . own:** The paragraph is quoted, in slightly condensed form, from the introduction which Arnold wrote to a volume called *The Hundred Greatest Men* (1879). **2. present work:** The essay first appeared in 1880 as the general introduction to *The English Poets*, a comprehensive anthology in several volumes edited by T. H. Ward.

**3. Sainte-Beuve:** Charles Augustin Sainte-Beuve (1804–69), the most famous of modern French critics, was much admired by Arnold. The two men were acquainted with each other.

half-sound, true and untrue or only half-true. It is charlatanism, conscious or unconscious, whenever we confuse or obliterate these. And in poetry, more than anywhere else, it is unpermissible to confuse or obliterate them. For in poetry the distinction between excellent and inferior, sound and unsound or only half-sound, true and untrue or only half-true, is of paramount importance. It is of paramount importance because of the high destinies of poetry. In poetry, as a criticism of life under the conditions fixed for such a criticism by the laws of poetic truth and poetic beauty, the spirit of our race will find, we have said, as time goes on and as other helps fail, its consolation and stay. But the consolation and stay will be of power in proportion to the power of the criticism of life. And the criticism of life will be of power in proportion as the poetry conveying it is excellent rather than inferior, sound rather than unsound or half-sound, true rather than untrue or half-true.

The best poetry is what we want; the best poetry will be found to have a power of forming, sustaining, and delighting us, as nothing else can. A clearer, deeper sense of the best in poetry, and of the strength and joy to be drawn from it, is the most precious benefit which we can gather from a poetical collection such as the present. And yet in the very nature and conduct of such a collection there is inevitably something which tends to obscure in us the consciousness of what our benefit should be, and to distract us from the pursuit of it. We should therefore steadily set it before our minds at the outset, and should compel ourselves to revert constantly to the thought of it as we proceed.

Yes; constantly in reading poetry, a sense for the best, the really excellent, and of the strength and joy to be drawn from it, should be present in our minds and should govern our estimate of what we read. But this real estimate, the only true one, is liable to be superseded, if we are not watchful, by two other kinds of estimate, the historic estimate and the personal estimate, both of which are fallacious. A poet or a poem may count to us historically, they may count to us on grounds personal to ourselves, and they may count to us really. They may count to us historically. The course of development of a nation's language, thought, and poetry, is profoundly interesting; and by regarding a poet's work as a stage in this course of development we may easily bring ourselves to make it of more importance as poetry than in itself it really is; we may come to use a language of quite exaggerated praise in criticizing it, in short, to overrate it. So arises in our poetic judgments the fallacy caused by the estimate which we may call historic. Then, again, a poet or a poem may count to us on grounds personal to ourselves. Our personal affinities, likings, and circumstances have great power to sway our estimate of this or that poet's work, and to make us attach more importance to it as poetry than in itself it really possesses, because to us it is, or has been, of high importance. Here also we overrate the object of our interest, and apply to it a language of praise which is quite exaggerated. And thus we get the source of a second fallacy in our poetic judgments — the fallacy caused by an estimate which we may call personal.

Both fallacies are natural. It is evident how naturally the study of the history and development of a poetry may incline a man to pause over reputations and works once conspicuous but now obscure, and to quarrel with a careless public for skipping, in obedience to mere tradition and habit, from one famous name or work in its national poetry to another, ignorant of what it misses, and of the reason for keeping what it keeps, and of the whole process of growth in its poetry. The French have become diligent students of their own early poetry, which they long neglected; the study makes many of them dissatisfied with their so-called classical poetry, the court tragedy of the seventeenth century, a poetry which Pellisson [4] long ago reproached with its want of the true poetic stamp, with its *politesse stérile et rampante,*[5] but which nevertheless has reigned in France as absolutely as if it had been the perfection of classical poetry indeed. The dissatisfaction is natural; yet a lively and accomplished critic, M. Charles d'Héricault, the editor of Clément Marot,[6] goes too far when he says that "the cloud of glory playing round a classic is a mist as dangerous to the future of a literature as it is intolerable for the purposes of history." "It hinders," he goes on, "it hinders us from seeing more than one single point, the culminating and exceptional point; the summary, fictitious and arbitrary, of a thought and of a work. It substitutes a halo for a physiognomy, it puts a statue where there was once a man, and, hiding from us all trace of the labor, the attempts,

**4. Pellisson:** Paul Pellisson (1624–93), a French critic. **5. *politesse . . . rampante:*** "desiccated and servile propriety." (The French word *rampant* has virtually the opposite sense from the English word.) **6. d'Héricault . . . Marot:** D'Héricault, a French critic and journalist, brought out his edition of Marot's poems between 1868 and 1872. Clément Marot (1496–1544) was court poet to Francis I.

the weaknesses, the failures, it claims not study but veneration; it does not show us how the thing is done; it imposes upon us a model. Above all, for the historian this creation of classic personages is inadmissible, for it withdraws the poet from his time, from his proper life, it breaks historical relationships, it blinds criticism by conventional admiration, and renders the investigation of literary origins unacceptable. It gives us a human personage no longer, but a god seated immovable amidst his perfect work, like Jupiter on Olympus; and hardly will it be possible for the young student, to whom such work is exhibited at such a distance from him, to believe that it did not issue ready-made from that divine head."

All this is brilliantly and tellingly said, but we must plead for a distinction. Everything depends on the reality of a poet's classic character. If he is a dubious classic, let us sift him; if he is a false classic, let us explode him. But if he is a real classic, if his work belongs to the class of the very best (for this is the true and right meaning of the word "classic," "classical"), then the great thing for us is to feel and enjoy his work as deeply as ever we can, and to appreciate the wide difference between it and all work which has not the same high character. This is what is salutary, this is what is formative; this is the great benefit to be got from the study of poetry. Everything which interferes with it, which hinders it, is injurious. True, we must read our classic with open eyes, and not with eyes blinded with superstition; we must perceive when his work comes short, when it drops out of the class of the very best, and we must rate it, in such cases, at its proper value. But the use of this negative criticism is not in itself, it is entirely in its enabling us to have a clearer sense and a deeper enjoyment of what is truly excellent. To trace the labor, the attempts, the weaknesses, the failures of a genuine classic, to acquaint oneself with his time and his life and his historical relationships, is mere literary dilettantism unless it has that clear sense and deeper enjoyment for its end. It may be said that the more we know about a classic, the better we shall enjoy him; and, if we lived as long as Methuselah and had all of us heads of perfect clearness and wills of perfect steadfastness, this might be true in fact as it is plausible in theory. But the case here is much the same as the case with the Greek and Latin studies of our schoolboys. The elaborate philological groundwork which we require them to lay is in theory an admirable preparation for appreciating the Greek and Latin authors worthily. The more thoroughly we lay the groundwork, the better we shall be able, it may be said, to enjoy the authors. True, if time were not so short, and schoolboys' wits not so soon tired and their power of attention exhausted; only, as it is, the elaborate philological preparation goes on, but the authors are little known and less enjoyed. So with the investigator of "historic origins" in poetry. He ought to enjoy the true classic all the better for his investigations; he often is distracted from the enjoyment of the best, and with the less good he overbusies himself, and is prone to overrate it in proportion to the trouble which it has cost him.

The idea of tracing historic origins and historical relationships cannot be absent from a compilation like the present. And naturally the poets to be exhibited in it will be assigned to those persons for exhibition who are known to prize them highly, rather than to those who have no special inclination towards them. Moreover, the very occupation with an author, and the business of exhibiting him, disposes us to affirm and amplify his importance. In the present work, therefore, we are sure of frequent temptation to adopt the historic estimate, or the personal estimate, and to forget the real estimate; which latter, nevertheless, we must employ if we are to make poetry yield us its full benefit. So high is that benefit, the benefit of clearly feeling and of deeply enjoying the really excellent, the truly classic in poetry, that we do well, I say, to set it fixedly before our minds as our object in studying poets and poetry, and to make the desire of attaining it the one principle to which, as the *Imitation*[7] says, whatever we may read or come to know, we always return. *Cum multa legeris et cognoveris, ad unum semper oportet redire principium.*

This historic estimate is likely in especial to affect our judgment and our language when we are dealing with ancient poets; the personal estimate when we are dealing with poets our contemporaries, or at any rate modern. The exaggerations due to the historic estimate are not in themselves, perhaps, of very much gravity. Their report hardly enters the general ear; probably they do not always impose even on the literary men who adopt them. But they lead to a dangerous abuse of language. So we hear Caedmon, amongst our own poets, compared to Milton. I have already noticed the en-

7. *Imitation: The Imitation of Christ*, a famous devotional work usually said to have been written by Thomas à Kempis (1380–1471), a German monk.

thusiasm of one accomplished French critic for "historic origins." Another eminent French critic, M. Vitet, comments upon that famous document of the early poetry of his nation, the *Chanson de Roland*. It is indeed a most interesting document. The *joculator* or *jongleur* Taillefer, who was with William the Conqueror's army at Hastings, marched before the Norman troops, so said the tradition, singing "of Charlemagne and of Roland and of Oliver, and of the vassals who died at Roncevaux"; and it is suggested that in the *Chanson de Roland* by one Turoldus or Théroulde, a poem preserved in a manuscript of the twelfth century in the Bodleian Library at Oxford, we have certainly the matter, perhaps even some of the words, of the chant which Taillefer sang. The poem has vigor and freshness; it is not without pathos. But M. Vitet is not satisfied with seeing in it a document of some poetic value, and of very high historic and linguistic value; he sees in it a grand and beautiful work, a monument of epic genius. In its general design he finds the grandiose conception, in its details he finds the constant union of simplicity with greatness, which are the marks, he truly says, of the genuine epic, and distinguish it from the artificial epic of literary ages. One thinks of Homer; this is the sort of praise which is given to Homer, and justly given. Higher praise there cannot well be, and it is the praise due to epic poetry of the highest order only, and to no other. Let us try, then, the *Chanson de Roland* at its best. Roland, mortally wounded, lays himself down under a pine tree, with his face turned towards Spain and the enemy —

> *De plusurs choses à remembrer li prist,*
> *De tantes tres cume li bers cunquist,*
> *De dulce France, des humes de sun lign,*
> *De Charlemagne sun seignor ki l'nurrit.*[8]

That is primitive work, I repeat, with an undeniable poetic quality of its own. It deserves such praise, and such praise is sufficient for it. But now turn to Homer —

> Ὣς φάτο· τοὺς δ ἤδη κατέχεν φυσίζοος αἶα
> ἐν Λακεδαίμονι αὖθι, φίλῃ ἐν πατρίδι γαίῃ.[9]

We are here in another world, another order of poetry altogether; here is rightly due such supreme praise as that which M. Vitet gives to the *Chanson de Roland*. If our words are to have any meaning, if our judgments are to have any solidity, we must not heap that supreme praise upon poetry of an order immeasurably inferior.

Indeed there can be no more useful help for discovering what poetry belongs to the class of the truly excellent, and can therefore do us most good, than to have always in one's mind lines and expressions of the great masters, and to apply them as a touchstone to other poetry. Of course we are not to require this other poetry to resemble them; it may be very dissimilar. But if we have any tact we shall find them, when we have lodged them well in our minds, an infallible touchstone for detecting the presence or absence of high poetic quality, and also the degree of this quality, in all other poetry which we may place beside them. Short passages, even single lines, will serve our turn quite sufficiently. Take the two lines which I have just quoted from Homer, the poet's comment on Helen's mention of her brothers; — or take his

> Ἆ δειλώ, τί σφῶϊ δόμεν Πηλῆϊ ἄνακτι
> θνητῷ; ὑμεῖς δ' ἐστὸν ἀγήρω τ' ἀθανάτω τε.
> ἦ ἵνα δυστήνοισι μετ' ἀνδράσιν ἄλγἐ ἔχητον;[10]

the address of Zeus to the horses of Peleus; — or take finally his

> Καὶ σέ, γέρον, τὸ πρὶν μὲν ἀκούομεν ὄλβιον εἶναι·[11]

the words of Achilles to Priam, a suppliant before him. Take that incomparable line and a half of Dante, Ugolino's tremendous words —

> *Io no piangeva; sì dentro impietrai.*
> *Piangevan elli . . .*[12]

take the lovely words of Beatrice to Virgil —

> *Io son fatta da Dio, sua mercè, tale,*
> *Che la vostra miseria non mi tange,*
> *Nè fiamma d'esto incendio non m'assale . . .*[13]

take the simple, but perfect, single line —

> *In la sua volontade è nostra pace. . . .*[14]

8. "'Then began he to call many things to remembrance, all the lands which his valor conquered, and pleasant France, and the men of his lineage, and Charlemagne his liege lord who nourished him.' (*Chanson de Roland*, III.939–42)" [A]. 9. "'So said she; they long since in Earth's soft arms were reposing, there in their own dear land, their fatherland, Lacedaemon.' (*Iliad*, III.243–44) (translated by Dr. Hawtrey)" [A].

10. "'Ah, unhappy pair, why gave we you to King Peleus, to a mortal? but ye are without old age, and immortal. Was it that with men born to misery ye might have sorrow?' (*Iliad*, X.vii. 443–45)" [A]. 11. "Nay, and thou too, old man, in former days, wast, as we hear, happy" [A]. 12. "'I wailed not, so of stone I grew within; they wailed.' (*Inferno*, XXXIII.49–50)" [A]. 13. "'Of such sort hath God, thanked be his mercy, made me, that your misery toucheth me not, neither doth the flame of this fire strike me.' (*Inferno*, II.91–93)" [A]. 14. "'In his will is our peace.' (*Paradiso*, III.85)" [A].

Take of Shakespeare a line or two of Henry IV's expostulation with sleep —

> Wilt thou upon the high and giddy mast
> Seal up the ship-boy's eyes, and rock his brains
> In cradle of the rude imperious surge . . .[15]

and take, as well, Hamlet's dying request to Horatio —

> If thou didst ever hold me in thy heart,
> Absent thee from felicity awhile,
> And in this harsh world draw thy breath in pain
> To tell my story. . . .[16]

Take of Milton that Miltonic passage —

> Darken'd so, yet shone
> Above them all the archangel; but his face
> Deep scars of thunder had intrench'd, and care
> Sat on his faded cheek, . . .[17]

add two such lines as —

> And courage never to submit or yield
> And what is else not to be overcome . . .[18]

and finish with the exquisite close to the loss of Proserpine, the loss

> . . . which cost Ceres all that pain
> To seek her through the world.[19]

These few lines, if we have tact and can use them, are enough even of themselves to keep clear and sound our judgments about poetry, to save us from fallacious estimates of it, to conduct us to a real estimate.

The specimens I have quoted differ widely from one another, but they have in common this: the possession of the very highest poetical quality. If we are thoroughly penetrated by their power, we shall find that we have acquired a sense enabling us, whatever poetry may be laid before us, to feel the degree in which a high poetical quality is present or wanting there. Critics give themselves great labor to draw out what in the abstract constitutes the characters of a high quality of poetry. It is much better simply to have recourse to concrete examples, to take specimens of poetry of the high, the very highest quality, and to say: The characters of a high quality of poetry are what is expressed *there.* They are far better recognized by being felt in the verse of the master, than by being perused in the prose of the critic. Nevertheless if we are urgently pressed to give some critical account of them, we may safely, perhaps, venture on laying down, not indeed how and why the characters arise, but where and in what they arise. They are in the matter and substance of the poetry, and they are in its manner and style. Both of these, the substance and matter on the one hand, the style and manner on the other, have a mark, an accent, of high beauty, worth, and power. But if we are asked to define this mark and accent in the abstract, our answer must be: No, for we should thereby be darkening the question, not clearing it. The mark and accent are as given by the substance and matter of that poetry, by the style and manner of that poetry, and of all other poetry which is akin to it in quality.

Only one thing we may add as to the substance and matter of poetry, guiding ourselves by Aristotle's profound observation that the superiority of poetry over history consists in its possessing a higher truth and a higher seriousness (φιλοσοφώτερον καὶ σπουδαιότερον). Let us add, therefore, to what we have said, this: that the substance and matter of the best poetry acquire their special character from possessing, in an eminent degree, truth and seriousness. We may add yet further, what is in itself evident, that to the style and manner of the best poetry their special character, their accent, is given by their diction, and, even yet more, by their movement. And though we distinguish between the two characters, the two accents, of superiority, yet they are nevertheless vitally connected one with the other. The superior character of truth and seriousness, in the matter and substance of the best poetry, is inseparable from the superiority of diction and movement marking its style and manner. The two superiorities are closely related, and are in steadfast proportion one to the other. So far as high poetic truth and seriousness are wanting to a poet's matter and substance, so far also, we may be sure, will a high poetic stamp of diction and movement be wanting to his style and manner. In proportion as this high stamp of diction and movement, again, is absent from a poet's style and manner, we shall find, also, that high poetic truth and seriousness are absent from his substance and matter.

So stated, these are but dry generalities; their whole force lies in their application. And I could wish every student of poetry to make the application of them for himself. Made by himself, the application would impress itself upon his mind far

15. *II Henry IV,* III.i.18–20. 16. *Hamlet,* V.ii.357–60. 17. *Paradise Lost,* I.599–602. 18. *Paradise Lost,* I.108–09. 19. *Paradise Lost,* IV.271–72. See Vol. I for quotations from *Hamlet* and *Paradise Lost.*

more deeply than made by me. Neither will my limits allow me to make any full application of the generalities above propounded; but in the hope of bringing out, at any rate, some significance in them, and of establishing an important principle more firmly by their means, I will, in the space which remains to me, follow rapidly from the commencement the course of our English poetry with them in my view.

Once more I return to the early poetry of France, with which our own poetry, in its origins, is indissolubly connected. In the twelfth and thirteenth centuries, that seedtime of all modern language and literature, the poetry of France had a clear predominance in Europe. Of the two divisions of that poetry, its productions in the *langue d'oïl*[20] and its productions in the *langue d'oc*,[21] the poetry of the *langue d'oc,* of southern France, of the troubadours, is of importance because of its effect on Italian literature — the first literature of modern Europe to strike the true and grand note, and to bring forth, as in Dante and Petrarch it brought forth, classics. But the predominance of French poetry in Europe, during the twelfth and thirteenth centuries, is due to its poetry of the *langue d'oïl,* the poetry of northern France and of the tongue which is now the French language. In the twelfth century the bloom of this romance poetry was earlier and stronger in England, at the court of our Anglo-Norman kings, than in France itself. But it was a bloom of French poetry; and as our native poetry formed itself, it formed itself out of this. The romance poems which took possession of the heart and imagination of Europe in the twelfth and thirteenth centuries are French; "they are," as Southey justly says, "the pride of French literature, nor have we anything which can be placed in competition with them." Themes were supplied from all quarters; but the romance setting which was common to them all, and which gained the ear of Europe, was French. This constituted for the French poetry, literature, and language, at the height of the Middle Age, an unchallenged predominance. The Italian Brunetto Latini, the master of Dante, wrote his *Treasure* in French because, he says, "*la parleure en est plus délitable et plus commune à toutes gens.*"[22] In the same century, the thirteenth, the French romance writer, Christian of Troyes, formulates the claims, in chivalry and letters, of France, his native country, as follows:

*Or vous ert par ce livre apris,*
*Que Gresse ot de chevalerie*
*Le premier los et de clergie;*
*Puis vint chevalerie à Rome,*
*Et de la clergie la some,*
*Qui ore est en France venue.*
*Diex doinst qu'ele i soit retenue,*
*Et que li lius li abelisse*
*Tant que de France n'isse*
*L'onor qui s'i est arestée!*

[Now by this book you will learn that first Greece had the renown for chivalry and letters; then chivalry and the primacy in letters passed to Rome, and now it is come to France. God grant it may be kept there; and that the place may please it so well, that the honor which has come to make stay in France may never depart thence!][23]

Yet it is now all gone, this French romance poetry, of which the weight of substance and the power of style are not unfairly represented by this extract from Christian of Troyes. Only by means of the historic estimate can we persuade ourselves now to think that any of it is of poetical importance.

But in the fourteenth century there comes an Englishman nourished on this poetry, taught his trade by this poetry, getting words, rhyme, meter from this poetry; for even of that stanza which the Italians used, and which Chaucer derived immediately from the Italians, the basis and suggestion was probably given in France. Chaucer (I have already named him) fascinated his contemporaries, but so too did Christian of Troyes and Wolfram of Eschenbach.[24] Chaucer's power of fascination, however, is enduring; his poetical importance does not need the assistance of the historic estimate; it is real. He is a genuine source of joy and strength, which is flowing still for us and will flow always. He will be read, as time goes on, far more generally than he is read now. His language is a cause of difficulty for us; but so also, and I think in quite as great a degree, is the language of Burns. In Chaucer's case, as in that of Burns, it is a difficulty to be unhesitatingly accepted and overcome.

If we ask ourselves wherein consists the immense

**20.** *langue d'oïl:* a group of French dialects spoken in most of central and northern France in the Middle Ages, so called from the characteristic use of *oïl* (*oui*) for *yes*. It is from these dialects that modern French is derived. **21.** *langue d'oc:* a group of French dialects spoken in southern France in the Middle Ages, so called from the characteristic use of *oc* for *yes*. These dialects survive in the Provençal language.

**22.** "*la . . . gens*": "the speech is pleasanter and more common to all peoples." Latini's work is called *Livres dou Trésor*. **23.** *Or . . .* thence: *Cligès*, ll. 30–39. **24.** Wolfram von Eschenbach (*c.* 1165–*c.* 1220), a German poet, known chiefly for his *Parsifal*, a long Arthurian poem.

superiority of Chaucer's poetry over the romance poetry — why it is that in passing from this to Chaucer we suddenly feel ourselves to be in another world, we shall find that his superiority is both in the substance of his poetry and in the style of his poetry. His superiority in substance is given by his large, free, simple, clear yet kindly view of human life — so unlike the total want, in the romance poets, of all intelligent command of it. Chaucer has not their helplessness; he has gained the power to survey the world from a central, a truly human point of view. We have only to call to mind the Prologue to *The Canterbury Tales*.[25] The right comment upon it is Dryden's: "It is sufficient to say, according to the proverb, that *here is God's plenty*." And again: "He is a perpetual fountain of good sense."[26] It is by a large, free, sound representation of things, that poetry, this high criticism of life, has truth of substance; and Chaucer's poetry has truth of substance.

Of his style and manner, if we think first of the romance poetry and then of Chaucer's divine liquidness of diction, his divine fluidity of movement, it is difficult to speak temperately. They are irresistible, and justify all the rapture with which his successors speak of his "gold dewdrops of speech."[27] Johnson misses the point entirely when he finds fault with Dryden for ascribing to Chaucer the first refinement of our numbers, and says that Gower also can show smooth numbers and easy rhymes. The refinement of our numbers means something far more than this. A nation may have versifiers with smooth numbers and easy rhymes, and yet may have no real poetry at all. Chaucer is the father of our splendid English poetry; he is our "well of English undefiled,"[28] because by the lovely charm of his diction, the lovely charm of his movement, he makes an epoch and founds a tradition. In Spenser, Shakespeare, Milton, Keats, we can follow the tradition of that liquid diction, the fluid movement, of Chaucer; at one time it is his liquid diction of which in these poets we feel the virtue, and at another time it is his fluid movement. And the virtue is irresistible.

Bounded as is my space, I must yet find room for an example of Chaucer's virtue, as I have given examples to show the virtue of the great classics. I feel disposed to say that a single line is enough to show the charm of Chaucer's verse; that merely one line like this —

O martyr souded[29] in virginitee!

has a virtue of manner and movement such as we shall not find in all the verse of romance poetry — but this is saying nothing. The virtue is such as we shall not find, perhaps, in all English poetry, outside the poets whom I have named as the special inheritors of Chaucer's tradition. A single line, however, is too little if we have not the strain of Chaucer's verse well in our memory; let us take a stanza. It is from the Prioress's Tale,[30] the story of the Christian child murdered in a Jewry —

My throte is cut unto my nekke-bone  
Saidè this child, and as by way of kinde  
I should have deyd, yea, longè time agone;  
But Jesu Christ, as ye in bookès finde,  
Will that his glory last and be in minde,  
And for the worship of his mother dere  
Yet may I sing *O Alma* loud and clere.

Wordsworth has modernized this Tale, and to feel how delicate and evanescent is the charm of verse, we have only to read Wordsworth's first three lines of this stanza after Chaucer's —

My throat is cut unto the bone, I trow,  
Said this young child, and by the law of kind  
I should have died, yea, many hours ago.

The charm is departed. It is often said that the power of liquidness and fluidity in Chaucer's verse was dependent upon a free, a licentious dealing with language, such as is now impossible; upon a liberty, such as Burns too enjoyed, of making words like "neck," "bird," into a dissyllable by adding to them, and words like "cause," "rhyme," into a dissyllable by sounding the *e* mute. It is true that Chaucer's fluidity is conjoined with this liberty, and is admirably served by it; but we ought not to say that it was dependent upon it. It was dependent upon his talent. Other poets with a like liberty do not attain to the fluidity of Chaucer; Burns himself does not attain to it. Poets, again, who have a talent akin to Chaucer's, such as Shakespeare or Keats, have known how to attain to his fluidity without the like liberty.

And yet Chaucer is not one of the great classics. His poetry transcends and effaces, easily and with-

25. See pp. 13-24 of Vol. I. 26. The quotations are from the Preface to Dryden's *Fables*. 27. "gold . . . speech" : This was said in praise of Chaucer by John Lydgate (1370–1451?) in his poem, "The Life of Our Lady." 28. "well . . . undefiled": said of Chaucer by Spenser; see *Faerie Queene*, IV.ii.32.

29. "The French *soudé*: soldered, fixed fast" [A]. Arnold misquotes the line (The Prioress's Tale, l. 127); Chaucer wrote "souded to," not "souded in." 30. See pp. 33–35 in Vol. I.

out effort, all the romance poetry of Catholic Christendom; it transcends and effaces all the English poetry contemporary with it, it transcends and effaces all the English poetry subsequent to it down to the age of Elizabeth. Of such avail is poetic truth of substance, in its natural and necessary union with poetic truth of style. And yet, I say, Chaucer is not one of the great classics. He has not their accent. What is wanting to him is suggested by the mere mention of the name of the first great classic of Christendom, the immortal poet who died eighty years before Chaucer — Dante. The accent of such verse as

*In la sua volontade è nostra pace . . .*

is altogether beyond Chaucer's reach; we praise him, but we feel that this accent is out of the question for him. It may be said that it was necessarily out of the reach of any poet in the England of that stage of growth. Possibly; but we are to adopt a real, not a historic, estimate of poetry. However we may account for its absence, something is wanting, then, to the poetry of Chaucer, which poetry must have before it can be placed in the glorious class of the best. And there is no doubt what that something is. It is the σπουδαιότης, the high and excellent seriousness, which Aristotle assigns as one of the grand virtues of poetry. The substance of Chaucer's poetry, his view of things and his criticism of life, has largeness, freedom, shrewdness, benignity; but it has not this high seriousness. Homer's criticism of life has it, Dante's has it, Shakespeare's has it. It is this chiefly which gives to our spirits what they can rest upon; and with the increasing demands of our modern ages upon poetry, this virtue of giving us what we can rest upon will be more and more highly esteemed. A voice from the slums of Paris, fifty or sixty years after Chaucer, the voice of poor Villon out of his life of riot and crime, has at its happy moments (as, for instance, in the last stanza of "La Belle Heaulmière" [31]) more of this important poetic virtue of seriousness than all the productions of Chaucer. But its apparition in Villon, and in men like Villon, is fitful; the greatness of the great poets, the power of their criticism of life, is that their virtue is sustained.

To our praise, therefore, of Chaucer as a poet there must be this limitation: he lacks the high seriousness of the great classics, and therewith an important part of their virtue. Still, the main fact for us to bear in mind about Chaucer is his sterling value according to that real estimate which we firmly adopt for all poets. He has poetic truth of substance, though he has not high poetic seriousness, and corresponding to his truth of substance he has an exquisite virtue of style and manner. With him is born our real poetry.

For my present purpose I need not dwell on our Elizabethan poetry, or on the continuation and close of this poetry in Milton. We all of us profess to be agreed in the estimate of this poetry; we all of us recognize it as great poetry, our greatest, and Shakespeare and Milton as our poetical classics. The real estimate, here, has universal currency. With the next age of our poetry divergency and difficulty begin. An historic estimate of that poetry has established itself; and the question is, whether it will be found to coincide with the real estimate.

The age of Dryden, together with our whole eighteenth century which followed it, sincerely believed itself to have produced poetical classics of its own, and even to have made advance, in poetry, beyond all its predecessors. Dryden regards as not seriously disputable the opinion "that the sweetness of English verse was never understood or practiced by our fathers." Cowley could see nothing at all in Chaucer's poetry. Dryden heartily admired it, and, as we have seen, praised its matter admirably; but of its exquisite manner and movement all he can find to say is that "there is the rude sweetness of a Scotch tune in it, which is natural and pleasing, though not perfect." Addison, wishing to praise Chaucer's numbers, compares them with Dryden's own. And all through the eighteenth century, and down even into our own times, the stereotyped phrase of approbation for good verse found in our early poetry has been, that it even approached the verse of Dryden, Addison, Pope, and Johnson.

Are Dryden and Pope poetical classics? Is the historic estimate, which represents them as such,

31. "The name *Heaulmière* is said to be derived from a headdress (helm) worn as a mark by courtesans. In Villon's ballad, a poor old creature of this class laments her days of youth and beauty. The last stanza of the ballad runs thus:

*Ainsi le bon temps regretons*
*Entre nous, pauvres vieilles sottes,*
*Assisses bas, à croppetons,*
*Tout en ung tas comme pellotes;*
*A petit feu de chenevottes*
*Tost allumées, tost estainctes.*
*Et jadis fusmes si mignottes!*
*Ainsi en prend à maintz et maintes.*

'Thus amongst ourselves we regret the good time, poor silly old things, low-seated on our heels, all in a heap like so many balls; by a little fire of hemp stalks, soon lighted, soon spent. And once we were such darlings! So fares it with many and many a one'" [A].

and which has been so long established that it cannot easily give way, the real estimate? Wordsworth and Coleridge, as is well known, denied it; but the authority of Wordsworth and Coleridge does not weigh much with the young generation, and there are many signs to show that the eighteenth century and its judgments are coming into favor again. Are the favorite poets of the eighteenth century classics?

It is impossible within my present limits to discuss the question fully. And what man of letters would not shrink from seeming to dispose dictatorially of the claims of two men who are, at any rate, such masters in letters as Dryden and Pope; two men of such admirable talent, both of them, and one of them, Dryden, a man, on all sides, of such energetic and genial power? And yet, if we are to gain the full benefit from poetry, we must have the real estimate of it. I cast about for some mode of arriving, in the present case, at such an estimate without offense. And perhaps the best way is to begin, as it is easy to begin, with cordial praise.

When we find Chapman, the Elizabethan translator of Homer, expressing himself in his preface thus: "Though truth in her very nakedness sits in so deep a pit, that from Gades to Aurora and Ganges few eyes can sound her, I hope yet those few here will so discover and confirm that, the date being out of her darkness in this morning of our poet, he shall now gird his temples with the sun," we pronounce that such a prose is intolerable. When we find Milton writing: "And long it was not after, when I was confirmed in this opinion, that he, who would not be frustrate of his hope to write well hereafter in laudable things, ought himself to be a true poem,"[32] we pronounce that such a prose has its own grandeur, but that it is obsolete and inconvenient. But when we find Dryden telling us: "What Virgil wrote in the vigor of his age, in plenty and at ease, I have undertaken to translate in my declining years; struggling with wants, oppressed with sickness, curbed in my genius, liable to be misconstrued in all I write"[33] — then we exclaim that here at last we have the true English prose, a prose such as we would all gladly use if we only knew how. Yet Dryden was Milton's contemporary.

But after the Restoration the time had come when our nation felt the imperious need of a fit prose. So, too, the time had likewise come when our nation felt the imperious need of freeing itself from the absorbing preoccupation which religion in the Puritan age had exercised. It was impossible that this freedom should be brought about without some negative excess, without some neglect and impairment of the religious life of the soul; and the spiritual history of the eighteenth century shows us that the freedom was not achieved without them. Still, the freedom was achieved; the preoccupation, an undoubtedly baneful and retarding one if it had continued, was got rid of. And as with religion amongst us at that period, so it was also with letters. A fit prose was a necessity; but it was impossible that a fit prose should establish itself amongst us without some touch of frost to the imaginative life of the soul. The needful qualities for a fit prose are regularity, uniformity, precision, balance. The men of letters, whose destiny it may be to bring their nation to the attainment of a fit prose, must of necessity, whether they work in prose or in verse, give a predominating, an almost exclusive attention to the qualities of regularity, uniformity, precision, balance. But an almost exclusive attention to these qualities involves some repression and silencing of poetry.

We are to regard Dryden as the puissant and glorious founder, Pope as the splendid high priest, of our age of prose and reason, of our excellent and indispensable eighteenth century. For the purposes of their mission and destiny their poetry, like their prose, is admirable. Do you ask me whether Dryden's verse, take it almost where you will, is not good?

> A milk-white Hind, immortal and unchanged,
> Fed on the lawns and in the forest ranged.[34]

I answer: Admirable for the purposes of the inaugurator of an age of prose and reason. Do you ask me whether Pope's verse, take it almost where you will, is not good?

> To Hounslow Heath I point, and Banstead Down;
> Thence comes your mutton, and these chicks my own.[35]

I answer: Admirable for the purposes of the high priest of an age of prose and reason. But do you ask me whether such verse proceeds from men with an adequate poetic criticism of life, from men whose criticism of life has a high seriousness, or even, without that high seriousness, has poetic largeness, freedom, insight, benignity? Do you ask me whether the application of ideas to life in

32. "And . . . poem": See *An Apology for Smectymnuus*, p. 427 in Vol. I. 33. "What . . . write": Dryden's Postscript to the Reader in his translation of Virgil.

34. *The Hind and the Panther*, I.1–2. 35. *Imitations of Horace*, Sat. II.ii.143–44.

the verse of these men, often a powerful application, no doubt, is a powerful *poetic* application? Do you ask me whether the poetry of these men has either the matter or the inseparable manner of such an adequate poetic criticism; whether it has the accent of

Absent thee from felicity awhile,

or of

And what is else not to be overcome . . .

or of

O martyr souded in virginitee!

I answer: It has not and cannot have them; it is the poetry of the builders of an age of prose and reason. Though they may write in verse, though they may in a certain sense be masters of the art of versification, Dryden and Pope are not classics of our poetry, they are classics of our prose.

Gray is our poetical classic of that literature and age; the position of Gray is singular, and demands a word of notice here. He has not the volume or the power of poets who, coming in times more favorable, have attained to an independent criticism of life. But he lived with the great poets, he lived, above all, with the Greeks, through perpetually studying and enjoying them; and he caught their poetic point of view for regarding life, caught their poetic manner. The point of view and the manner are not self-sprung in him; he caught them of others; and he had not the free and abundant use of them. But whereas Addison and Pope never had the use of them, Gray had the use of them at times. He is the scantiest and frailest of classics in our poetry, but he is a classic.

And now, after Gray, we are met, as we draw towards the end of the eighteenth century, we are met by the great name of Burns. We enter now on times where the personal estimate of poets begins to be rife, and where the real estimate of them is not reached without difficulty. But in spite of the disturbing pressures of personal partiality, of national partiality, let us try to reach a real estimate of the poetry of Burns.

By his English poetry Burns in general belongs to the eighteenth century, and has little importance for us.

Mark ruffian Violence, distain'd with crimes,
Rousing elate in these degenerate times;
View unsuspecting Innocence a prey,
As guileful Fraud points out the erring way;
While subtle Litigation's pliant tongue
The life-blood equal sucks of Right and Wrong! [36]

Evidently this is not the real Burns, or his name and fame would have disappeared long ago. Nor is Clarinda's love poet, Sylvander,[37] the real Burns either. But he tells us himself: "These English songs gravel me to death. I have not the command of the language that I have of my native tongue. In fact, I think that my ideas are more barren in English than in Scotch. I have been at 'Duncan Gray' to dress it in English, but all I can do is desperately stupid." We English turn naturally, in Burns, to the poems in our own language, because we can read them easily; but in those poems we have not the real Burns.

The real Burns is of course in his Scotch poems. Let us boldly say that of much of this poetry, a poetry dealing perpetually with Scotch drink, Scotch religion, and Scotch manners, a Scotchman's estimate is apt to be personal. A Scotchman is used to this world of Scotch drink, Scotch religion, and Scotch manners; he has a tenderness for it; he meets its poet halfway. In this tender mood he reads pieces like the "Holy Fair" or "Halloween." But this world of Scotch drink, Scotch religion, and Scotch manners is against a poet, not for him, when it is not a partial countryman who reads him; for in itself it is not a beautiful world, and no one can deny that it is of advantage to a poet to deal with a beautiful world. Burns's world of Scotch drink, Scotch religion, and Scotch manners, is often a harsh, a sordid, a repulsive world; even the world of his "Cotter's Saturday Night" is not a beautiful world. No doubt a poet's criticism of life may have such truth and power that it triumphs over its world and delights us. Burns may triumph over his world, often he does triumph over his world, but let us observe how and where. Burns is the first case we have had where the bias of the personal estimate tends to mislead; let us look at him closely; he can bear it.

Many of his admirers will tell us that we have Burns, convivial, genuine, delightful, here—

Leeze me on drink! it gies us mair
Than either school or college;
It kindles wit, it waukens lair,
It pangs us fou o' knowledge.

36. "On the Death of Lord President Dundas." 37. **Clarinda . . . Sylvander**: Burns, engaged in an elaborate correspondence with a Mrs. Maclehose, calling himself Sylvander and the lady Clarinda. The names are derived from the tradition of eighteenth-century pastoral, which is highly artificial.

Be 't whisky gill or penny wheep
  Or ony stronger potion,
It never fails, on drinking deep,
  To kittle up our notion
    By night or day.[38]

There is a great deal of that sort of thing in Burns, and it is unsatisfactory, not because it is bacchanalian poetry, but because it has not that accent of sincerity which bacchanalian poetry, to do it justice, very often has. There is something in it of bravado, something which makes us feel that we have not the man speaking to us with his real voice; something, therefore, poetically unsound.

With still more confidence will his admirers tell us that we have the genuine Burns, the great poet, when his strain asserts the independence, equality, dignity, of men, as in the famous song "For A' That and A' That" —

A prince can mak' a belted knight,
  A marquis, duke, and a' that;
But an honest man's aboon his might,
  Guid faith he mauna fa' that!
    For a' that, and a' that,
      Their dignities, and a' that,
    The pith o' sense, and pride o' worth,
      Are higher rank than a' that.

Here they find his grand, genuine touches; and still more, when this puissant genius, who so often set morality at defiance, falls moralizing —

The sacred lowe o' weel-placed love
  Luxuriantly indulge it;
But never tempt th' illicit rove,
  Tho' naething should divulge it.
I waive the quantum o' the sin,
  The hazard o' concealing,
But och! it hardens a' within,
  And petrifies the feeling.[39]

Or in a higher strain —

Who made the heart, 'tis He alone
  Decidedly can try us;
He knows each chord, its various tone;
  Each spring, its various bias.
Then at the balance let's be mute,
  We never can adjust it;
What's *done* we partly may compute,
  But know not what's resisted.[40]

Or in a better strain yet, a strain, his admirers will say, unsurpassable —

To make a happy fire-side clime
  To weans and wife,
That's the true pathos and sublime
  Of human life.[41]

There is a criticism of life for you, the admirers of Burns will say to us; there is the application of ideas to life! There is, undoubtedly. The doctrine of the last-quoted lines coincides almost exactly with what was the aim and end, Xenophon tells us, of all the teaching of Socrates. And the application is a powerful one, made by a man of vigorous understanding, and (need I say?) a master of language.

But for supreme poetical success more is required than the powerful application of ideas to life; it must be an application under the conditions fixed by the laws of poetic truth and poetic beauty. Those laws fix as an essential condition, in the poet's treatment of such matters as are here in question, high seriousness — the high seriousness which comes from absolute sincerity. The accent of high seriousness, born of absolute sincerity, is what gives to such verse as

*In la sua volontade è nostra pace . . .*

to such criticism of life as Dante's, its power. Is this accent felt in the passages which I have been quoting from Burns? Surely not; surely, if our sense is quick, we must perceive that we have not in those passages a voice from the very inmost soul of the genuine Burns; he is not speaking to us from these depths, he is more or less preaching. And the compensation for admiring such passages less, from missing the perfect poetic accent in them, will be that we shall admire more the poetry where that accent is found.

No; Burns, like Chaucer, comes short of the high seriousness of the great classics, and the virtue of matter and manner which goes with that high seriousness is wanting to his work. At moments he touches it in a profound and passionate melancholy, as in those four immortal lines taken by Byron as a motto for *The Bride of Abydos,* but which have in them a depth of poetic quality such as resides in no verse of Byron's own —

Had we never loved sae kindly,
Had we never loved sae blindly,
Never met, or never parted,
We had nee'r been broken-hearted.

But a whole poem of that quality Burns cannot make; the rest, in the "Farewell to Nancy," is verbiage.

We arrive best at the real estimate of Burns, I think, by conceiving his work as having truth of matter and truth of manner, but not the accent or

38. "The Holy Fair," ll. 163–71. 39. "Epistle to a Young Friend." 40. "Address to the Unco Guid."

41. "Epistle to Dr. Blacklock."

the poetic virtue of the highest masters. His genuine criticism of life, when the sheer poet in him speaks, is ironic; it is not —

Thou Power Supreme, whose mighty scheme
These woes of mine fulfil,
Here firm I rest, they must be best
Because they are Thy will! [42]

It is far rather: "Whistle owre the lave o't!" [43] Yet we may say of him as of Chaucer, that of life and the world, as they come before him, his view is large, free, shrewd, benignant — truly poetic, therefore; and his manner of rendering what he sees is to match. But we must note, at the same time, his great difference from Chaucer. The freedom of Chaucer is heightened, in Burns, by a fiery, reckless energy; the benignity of Chaucer deepens, in Burns, into an overwhelming sense of the pathos of things — of the pathos of human nature, the pathos, also, of nonhuman nature. Instead of the fluidity of Chaucer's manner, the manner of Burns has spring, bounding swiftness. Burns is by far the greater force, though he has perhaps less charm. The world of Chaucer is fairer, richer, more significant than that of Burns; but when the largeness and freedom of Burns get full sweep, as in "Tam o' Shanter," or still more in that puissant and splendid production, "The Jolly Beggars," his world may be what it will, his poetic genius triumphs over it. In the world of "The Jolly Beggars" there is more than hideousness and squalor, there is bestiality; yet the piece is a superb poetic success. It has a breadth, truth, and power which make the famous scene in Auerbach's cellar, of Goethe's *Faust,*[44] seem artificial and tame beside it, and which are only matched by Shakespeare and Aristophanes.

Here, where his largeness and freedom serve him so admirably, and also in those poems and songs where to shrewdness he adds infinite archness and wit, and to benignity infinite pathos, where his manner is flawless, and a perfect poetic whole is the result — in things like the address to the mouse whose home he had ruined, in things like "Duncan Gray," "Tam Glen," "Whistle and I'll Come to You, My Lad," "Auld Lang Syne" (this list might be made much longer) — here we have the genuine Burns, of whom the real estimate must be high indeed. Not a classic, nor with the excellent σπουδαιότης of the great classics, nor with a verse rising to a criticism of life and a virtue like theirs; but a poet with thorough truth of substance and an answering truth of style, giving us a poetry sound to the core. We all of us have a leaning towards the pathetic, and may be inclined perhaps to prize Burns most for his touches of piercing, sometimes almost intolerable, pathos; for verse like —

We twa hae paidl't i' the burn
From mornin' sun till dine;
But seas between us braid hae roar'd
Sin auld lang syne . . .[45]

where he is as lovely as he is sound. But perhaps it is by the perfection of soundness of his lighter and archer masterpieces that he is poetically most wholesome for us. For the votary misled by a personal estimate of Shelley — as so many of us have been, are, and will be — of that beautiful spirit building his many-colored haze of words and images

Pinnacled dim in the intense inane — [46]

no contact can be wholesomer than the contact with Burns at his archest and soundest. Side by side with the

On the brink of the night and the morning
My coursers are wont to respire,
But the Earth has just whispered a warning
That their flight must be swifter than fire . . .[47]

of *Prometheus Unbound,* how salutary, how very salutary, to place this from "Tam Glen" —

My minnie does constantly deave me
And bids me beware o' young men;
They flatter, she says, to deceive me;
But wha can think sae o' Tam Glen?

But we enter on burning ground as we approach the poetry of times so near to us — poetry like that of Byron, Shelley, and Wordsworth — of which the estimates are so often not only personal, but personal with passion. For my purpose, it is enough to have taken the single case of Burns, the first poet we come to of whose work the estimate formed is evidently apt to be personal, and to have suggested how we may proceed, using the poetry of the great classics as a sort of touchstone, to correct this estimate, as we had previously corrected by the same means the historic estimate where we met with it. A collection like the present, with its succession of celebrated names and celebrated poems, offers a good opportunity to us for resolutely endeavoring

42. "Winter: A Dirge." 43. **"Whistle . . . o't"**: "Whistle over the rest of it." The line is the title and the refrain of one of Burns's poems. 44. The first of Faust's experiences with Mephistopheles takes place in Auerbach's wine cellar with a group of drinking, brawling students.

45. "Auld Lang Syne," ll. 17–20. 46. Shelley's *Prometheus Unbound*, III.iv.204, above. 47. *PU*, II.v.1–4, above.

to make our estimates of poetry real. I have sought to point out a method which will help us in making them so, and to exhibit it in use so far as to put anyone who likes in a way of applying it for himself.

At any rate the end to which the method and the estimate are designed to lead, and from leading to which, if they do lead to it, they get their whole value — the benefit of being able clearly to feel and deeply to enjoy the best, the truly classic, in poetry — is an end, let me say it once more at parting, of supreme importance. We are often told that an era is opening in which we are to see multitudes of a common sort of readers, and masses of a common sort of literature; that such readers do not want and could not relish anything better than such literature, and that to provide it is becoming a vast and profitable industry. Even if good literature entirely lost currency with the world, it would still be abundantly worth while to continue to enjoy it by oneself. But it never will lose currency with the world, in spite of momentary appearances; it never will lose supremacy. Currency and supremacy are insured to it, not indeed by the world's delicate and conscious choice, but by something far deeper — by the instinct of self-preservation in humanity.

## WORDSWORTH

Arnold's essay on Wordsworth first appeared as the Preface to *The Poems of Wordsworth,* a selection from the large body of Wordsworth's work which Arnold published in 1879. The choice was made with impeccable taste according to the principles which Arnold sets forth in the essay, and the book, coming when it did, served to rehabilitate Wordsworth for many readers who had turned away from him. Nowadays, we are inclined to question Arnold's depreciation of Wordsworth's longer poems and of his pretensions to systematic thought. Granting that Wordsworth's highest art appears in his shorter poems, we yet feel that *The Prelude* is a great and interesting poem and that the systematic elements of Wordsworth's thought are interesting in themselves and of high importance for the full understanding of all his poetry. Yet Wordsworth as Arnold saw him is Wordsworth as he should be seen by everyone who is making a first acquaintance with him.

I remember hearing Lord Macaulay say, after Wordsworth's death, when subscriptions were being collected to found a memorial of him, that ten years earlier more money could have been raised in Cambridge alone, to do honor to Wordsworth, than was now raised all through the country. Lord Macaulay had, as we know, his own heightened and telling way of putting things, and we must always make allowance for it. But probably it is true that Wordsworth has never, either before or since, been so accepted and popular, so established in possession of the minds of all who profess to care for poetry, as he was between the years 1830 and 1840, and at Cambridge. From the very first, no doubt, he had his believers and witnesses. But I have myself heard him declare that, for he knew not how many years, his poetry had never brought him in enough to buy his shoestrings. The poetry-reading public was very slow to recognize him, and was very easily drawn away from him. Scott effaced him with this public, Byron effaced him.

The death of Byron seemed, however, to make an opening for Wordsworth. Scott, who had for some time ceased to produce poetry himself, and stood before the public as a great novelist — Scott, too genuine himself not to feel the profound genuineness of Wordsworth, and with an instinctive recognition of his firm hold on nature and of his local truth, always admired him sincerely, and praised him generously. The influence of Coleridge upon young men of ability was then powerful, and was still gathering strength; this influence told entirely in favor of Wordsworth's poetry. Cambridge was a place where Coleridge's influence had great action, and where Wordsworth's poetry, therefore, flourished especially. But even amongst the general public its sale grew large, the eminence of its author was widely recognized, and Rydal Mount became an object of pilgrimage. I remember Wordsworth relating how one of the pilgrims, a clergyman, asked him if he had ever written anything besides the *Guide to the Lakes*. Yes, he answered modestly, he had written verses. Not every pilgrim was a reader, but the vogue was established, and the stream of pilgrims came.

Mr. Tennyson's decisive appearance dates from 1842. One cannot say that he effaced Wordsworth as Scott and Byron had effaced him. The poetry of Wordsworth had been so long before the public, the suffrage of good judges was so steady and so strong in its favor, that by 1842 the verdict of posterity, one may almost say, had been already pronounced, and Wordsworth's English fame was secure. But the vogue, the ear and applause of the great body of poetry readers, never quite thoroughly perhaps his, he gradually lost more and more, and Mr. Tennyson gained them. Mr. Tennyson drew to himself, and away from Wordsworth, the poetry-reading public, and the new generations.

Even in 1850, when Wordsworth died, this diminution of popularity was visible, and occasioned the remark of Lord Macaulay which I quoted at starting.

The diminution has continued. The influence of Coleridge has waned, and Wordsworth's poetry can no longer draw succor from this ally. The poetry has not, however, wanted eulogists, and it may be said to have brought its eulogists luck, for almost everyone who has praised Wordsworth's poetry has praised it well. But the public has remained cold or, at least, undetermined. Even the abundance of Mr. Palgrave's fine and skillfully chosen specimens of Wordsworth, in the *Golden Treasury,* surprised many readers, and gave offense to not a few. To tenth-rate critics and compilers, for whom any violent shock to the public taste would be a temerity not to be risked, it is still quite permissible to speak of Wordsworth's poetry, not only with ignorance, but with impertinence. On the Continent he is almost unknown.

I cannot think, then, that Wordsworth has, up to this time, at all obtained his deserts. "Glory," said M. Renan [1] the other day, "glory after all is the thing which has the best chance of not being altogether vanity." Wordsworth was a homely man, and himself would certainly never have thought of talking of glory as that which, after all, has the best chance of not being altogether vanity. Yet we may well allow that few things are less vain than *real* glory. Let us conceive of the whole group of civilized nations as being, for intellectual and spiritual purposes, one great confederation, bound to a joint action and working towards a common result; a confederation whose members have a due knowledge both of the past, out of which they all proceed, and of one another. This was the ideal of Goethe, and it is an ideal which will impose itself upon the thoughts of our modern societies more and more. Then to be recognized by the verdict of such a confederation as a master, or even as a seriously and eminently worthy workman, in one's own line of intellectual or spiritual activity, is indeed glory, a glory which it would be difficult to rate too highly. For what could be more beneficent, more salutary? The world is forwarded by having its attention fixed on the best things; and here is a tribunal, free from all suspicion of national and provincial partiality, putting a stamp on the best things, and recommending them for general honor and acceptance. A nation, again, is furthered by recognition of its real gifts and successes; it is encouraged to develop them further. And here is an honest verdict, telling us which of our supposed successes are really, in the judgment of the great impartial world, and not in our own private judgment only, successes, and which are not.

It is so easy to feel pride and satisfaction in one's own things, so hard to make sure that one is right in feeling it! We have a great empire. But so had Nebuchadnezzar. We extol the "unrivaled happiness" of our national civilization. But then comes a candid friend, and remarks that our upper class is materialized, our middle class vulgarized, and our lower class brutalized.[2] We are proud of our painting, our music. But we find that in the judgment of other people our painting is questionable, and our music nonexistent. We are proud of our men of science. And here it turns out that the world is with us; we find that in the judgment of other people, too, Newton among the dead, and Mr. Darwin among the living, hold as high a place as they hold in our national opinion.

Finally, we are proud of our poets and poetry. Now poetry is nothing less than the most perfect speech of man, that in which he comes nearest to being able to utter the truth. It is no small thing, therefore, to succeed eminently in poetry. And so much is required for duly estimating success here, that about poetry it is perhaps hardest to arrive at a sure general verdict, and takes longest. Meanwhile, our own conviction of the superiority of our national poets is not decisive, is almost certain to be mingled, as we see constantly in English eulogy of Shakespeare, with much of provincial infatuation. And we know what was the opinion current amongst our neighbors the French — people of taste, acuteness, and quick literary tact — not a hundred years ago, about our great poets. The old *Biographie Universelle* notices the pretension of the English to a place for their poets among the chief poets of the world, and says that this is a pretension which to no one but an Englishman can ever seem admissible. And the scornful, disparaging things said by foreigners about Shakespeare and Milton, and about our national overestimate of them, have been often quoted, and will be in everyone's remembrance.

WORDSWORTH. 1. **Renan:** Ernest Renan (1823–92), the French Orientalist and student of religion. The sentence occurs in the address he made on the occasion of being received into the French Academy in 1879.

2. **But . . . brutalized:** The "candid friend" is Arnold himself; his characterization of the three English social classes appeared in his essay, "Equality."

A great change has taken place, and Shakespeare is now generally recognized, even in France, as one of the greatest of poets. Yes, some anti-Gallican cynic will say, the French rank him with Corneille and with Victor Hugo! But let me have the pleasure of quoting a sentence about Shakespeare, which I met with by accident not long ago in the *Correspondant,* a French review which not a dozen English people, I suppose, look at. The writer is praising Shakespeare's prose. With Shakespeare, he says, "prose comes in whenever the subject being more familiar, is unsuited to the majestic English iambic." And he goes on: "Shakespeare is the king of poetic rhythm and style, as well as the king of the realm of thought; along with his dazzling prose, Shakespeare has succeeded in giving us the most varied, the most harmonious verse which has ever sounded upon the human ear since the verse of the Greeks." M. Henry Cochin, the writer of this sentence, deserves our gratitude for it; it would not be easy to praise Shakespeare, in a single sentence, more justly. And when a foreigner and a Frenchman writes thus of Shakespeare, and when Goethe says of Milton, in whom there was so much to repel Goethe rather than to attract him, that "nothing has been ever done so entirely in the sense of the Greeks as *Samson Agonistes,*" and that "Milton is in very truth a poet whom we must treat with all reverence," then we understand what constitutes a European recognition of poets and poetry as contradistinguished from a merely national recognition, and that in favor both of Milton and of Shakespeare the judgment of the high court of appeal has finally gone.

I come back to M. Renan's praise of glory, from which I started. Yes, real glory is a most serious thing, glory authenticated by the Amphictyonic Court[3] of final appeal, definitive glory. And even for poets and poetry, long and difficult as may be the process of arriving at the right award, the right award comes at last, the definitive glory rests where it is deserved. Every establishment of such a real glory is good and wholesome for mankind at large, good and wholesome for the nation which produced the poet crowned with it. To the poet himself it can seldom do harm; for he, poor man, is in his grave, probably, long before his glory crowns him.

Wordsworth has been in his grave for some thirty years, and certainly his lovers and admirers cannot flatter themselves that this great and steady light of glory as yet shines over him. He is not fully recognized at home; he is not recognized at all abroad. Yet I firmly believe that the poetical performance of Wordsworth is, after that of Shakespeare and Milton, of which all the world now recognizes the worth, undoubtedly the most considerable in our language from the Elizabethan age to the present time. Chaucer is anterior; and on other grounds, too, he cannot well be brought into the comparison. But taking the roll of our chief poetical names, besides Shakespeare and Milton, from the age of Elizabeth downwards, and going through it — Spenser, Dryden, Pope, Gray, Goldsmith, Cowper, Burns, Coleridge, Scott, Campbell, Moore, Byron, Shelley, Keats (I mention those only who are dead) — I think it certain that Wordsworth's name deserves to stand, and will finally stand, above them all. Several of the poets named have gifts and excellences which Wordsworth has not. But taking the performance of each as a whole, I say that Wordsworth seems to me to have left a body of poetical work superior in power, in interest, in the qualities which give enduring freshness, to that which any one of the others has left.

But this is not enough to say. I think it certain, further, that if we take the chief poetical names of the Continent since the death of Molière, and, omitting Goethe, confront the remaining names with that of Wordsworth, the result is the same. Let us take Klopstock, Lessing, Schiller, Uhland, Rückert, and Heine for Germany; Filicaia, Alfieri, Manzoni, and Leopardi for Italy; Racine, Boileau, Voltaire, André Chenier, Béranger, Lamartine, Musset, M. Victor Hugo (he has been so long celebrated that although he still lives I may be permitted to name him) for France. Several of these, again, have evidently gifts and excellences to which Wordsworth can make no pretension. But in real poetical achievement it seems to me indubitable that to Wordsworth, here again, belongs the palm. It seems to me that Wordsworth has left behind him a body of poetical work which wears, and will wear, better on the whole than the performance of any one of these personages, so far more brilliant and celebrated, most of them, than the homely poet of Rydal. Wordsworth's performance in poetry is on the whole, in power, in interest, in the qualities which give enduring freshness, superior to theirs.

This is a high claim to make for Wordsworth. But if it is a just claim, if Wordsworth's place among the poets who have appeared in the last

3. **Amphictyonic Court:** a confederation of ancient Greek states organized to maintain and protect a particular temple or shrine.

two or three centuries is after Shakespeare, Molière, Milton, Goethe, indeed, but before all the rest, then in time Wordsworth will have his due. We shall recognize him in his place, as we recognize Shakespeare and Milton; and not only we ourselves shall recognize him, but he will be recognized by Europe also. Meanwhile, those who recognize him already may do well, perhaps, to ask themselves whether there are not in the case of Wordsworth certain special obstacles which hinder or delay his due recognition by others, and whether these obstacles are not in some measure removable.

*The Excursion* and *The Prelude,* his poems of greatest bulk, are by no means Wordsworth's best work. His best work is in his shorter pieces, and many indeed are there of these which are of first-rate excellence. But in his seven volumes the pieces of high merit are mingled with a mass of pieces very inferior to them, so inferior to them that it seems wonderful how the same poet should have produced both. Shakespeare frequently has lines and passages in a strain quite false, and which are entirely unworthy of him. But one can imagine his smiling if one could meet him in the Elysian fields and tell him so; smiling and replying that he knew it perfectly well himself, and what did it matter? But with Wordsworth the case is different. Work altogether inferior, work quite uninspired, flat and dull, is produced by him with evident unconsciousness of its defects, and he presents it to us with the same faith and seriousness as his best work. Now a drama or an epic fill the mind, and one does not look beyond them; but in a collection of short pieces the impression made by one piece requires to be continued and sustained by the piece following. In reading Wordsworth the impression made by one of his fine pieces is too often dulled and spoiled by a very inferior piece coming after it.

Wordsworth composed verses during a space of some sixty years; and it is no exaggeration to say that within one single decade of those years, between 1798 and 1808, almost all his really first-rate work was produced. A mass of inferior work remains, work done before and after this golden prime, imbedding the first-rate work and clogging it, obstructing our approach to it, chilling, not unfrequently, the high-wrought mood with which we leave it. To be recognized far and wide as a great poet, to be possible and receivable as a classic, Wordsworth needs to be relieved of a great deal of the poetical baggage which now encumbers him. To administer this relief is indispensable, unless he is to continue to be a poet for the few only — a poet valued far below his real worth by the world.

There is another thing. Wordsworth classified his poems not according to any commonly received plan of arrangement, but according to a scheme of mental physiology. He has poems of the fancy, poems of the imagination, poems of sentiment and reflection, and so on. His categories are ingenious but farfetched, and the result of his employment of them is unsatisfactory. Poems are separated one from another which possess a kinship of subject or of treatment far more vital and deep than the supposed unity of mental origin, which was Wordsworth's reason for joining them with others.

The tact of the Greeks in matters of this kind was infallible. We may rely upon it that we shall not improve upon the classification adopted by the Greeks for kinds of poetry; that their categories of epic, dramatic, lyric, and so forth, have a natural propriety, and should be adhered to. It may sometimes seem doubtful to which of two categories a poem belongs; whether this or that poem is to be called, for instance, narrative or lyric, lyric or elegiac. But there is to be found in every good poem a strain, a predominant note, which determines the poem as belonging to one of these kinds rather than the other; and here is the best proof of the value of the classification, and of the advantage of adhering to it. Wordsworth's poems will never produce their due effect until they are freed from their present artificial arrangement, and grouped more naturally.

Disengaged from the quantity of inferior work which now obscures them, the best poems of Wordsworth, I hear many people say, would indeed stand out in great beauty, but they would prove to be very few in number, scarcely more than half a dozen. I maintain, on the other hand, that what strikes me with admiration, what establishes in my opinion Wordsworth's superiority, is the great and ample body of powerful work which remains to him, even after all his inferior work has been cleared away. He gives us so much to rest upon, so much which communicates his spirit and engages ours!

This is of very great importance. If it were a comparison of single pieces, or of three or four pieces, by each poet, I do not say that Wordsworth would stand decisively above Gray, or Burns, or Coleridge, or Keats, or Manzoni, or Heine. It is in his ampler body of powerful work that I find his superiority. His good work itself, his work which counts, is not all of it, of course, of equal value. Some kinds of poetry are in themselves lower kinds than others. The ballad kind is a lower kind; the didactic kind, still more, is a lower kind. Poetry of this latter sort counts, too, sometimes, by its biographical interest partly, not by its poetical interest pure and simple; but then this can only be when the poet producing it has the power and importance of Wordsworth, a power and importance which he assuredly did not establish by such didactic poetry alone. Altogether, it is, I say, by the great body of powerful and significant work which remains to him, after every reduction and deduction has been made, that Wordsworth's superiority is proved.

To exhibit this body of Wordsworth's best work, to clear away obstructions from around it, and to let it speak for itself, is what every lover of Wordsworth should desire. Until this has been done, Wordsworth, whom we, to whom he is dear, all of us know and feel to be so great a poet, has not had a fair chance before the world. When once it has been done, he will make his way best, not by our advocacy of him, but by his own worth and power. We may safely leave him to make his way thus, we who believe that a superior worth and power in poetry finds in mankind a sense responsive to it and disposed at last to recognize it. Yet at the outset, before he has been duly known and recognized, we may do Wordsworth a service, perhaps, by indicating in what his superior power and worth will be found to consist, and in what it will not.

Long ago, in speaking of Homer, I said that the noble and profound application of ideas to life is the most essential part of poetic greatness. I said that a great poet receives his distinctive character of superiority from his application, under the conditions immutably fixed by the laws of poetic beauty and poetic truth, from his application, I say, to his subject, whatever it may be, of the ideas

> On man, on nature, and on human life,[4]

which he has acquired for himself. The line quoted is Wordsworth's own, and his superiority arises from his powerful use, in his best pieces, his powerful application to his subject, of ideas "on man, on nature, and on human life."

Voltaire, with his signal acuteness, most truly remarked that "no nation has treated in poetry moral ideas with more energy and depth than the English nation." And he adds: "There, it seems to me, is the great merit of the English poets." Voltaire does not mean, by "treating in poetry moral ideas," the composing moral and didactic poems; — that brings us but a very little way in poetry. He means just the same thing as was meant when I spoke above "of the noble and profound application of ideas to life"; and he means the application of these ideas under the conditions fixed for us by the laws of poetic beauty and poetic truth. If it is said that to call these ideas *moral* ideas is to introduce a strong and injurious limitation, I answer that it is to do nothing of the kind, because moral ideas are really so main a part of human life. The question, *how to live,* is itself a moral idea; and it is the question which most interests every man, and with which, in some way or other, he is perpetually occupied. A large sense is of course to be given to the term *moral.* Whatever bears upon the question, "how to live," comes under it.

> Nor love thy life, nor hate; but, what thou liv'st,
> Live well; how long or short, permit to Heaven.[5]

In those fine lines Milton utters, as everyone at once perceives, a moral idea. Yes, but so too, when Keats consoles the forward-bending lover on the Grecian urn, the lover arrested and presented in immortal relief by the sculptor's hand before he can kiss, with the line,

> Forever wilt thou love, and she be fair![6]

he utters a moral idea. When Shakespeare says, that

> We are such stuff
> As dreams are made of, and our little life
> Is rounded with a sleep,[7]

he utters a moral idea.

Voltaire was right in thinking that the energetic and profound treatment of moral ideas, in this large sense, is what distinguishes the English poetry. He sincerely meant praise, not dispraise or hint of limitation; and they err who suppose that poetic limitation is a necessary consequence of the fact, the fact being granted as Voltaire states it. If what distinguishes the greatest poets is their powerful and profound application of ideas to life, which surely no good critic will deny, then to prefix to the term "ideas" here the term "moral" makes hardly any difference, because human life itself is in so preponderating a degree moral.

4. Wordsworth, *The Recluse,* l. 754.

5. *Paradise Lost,* XI.553–54. 6. "Ode on a Grecian Urn," l. 20. See above. 7. *The Tempest,* IV.i.156–58. Arnold misquotes — Shakespeare wrote "made on," not "made of." See p. 310 in Vol. I.

It is important, therefore, to hold fast to this: that poetry is at bottom a criticism of life; that the greatness of a poet lies in his powerful and beautiful application of ideas to life — to the question: How to live. Morals are often treated in a narrow and false fashion; they are bound up with systems of thought and belief which have had their day; they are fallen into the hands of pedants and professional dealers; they grow tiresome to some of us. We find attraction, at times, even in a poetry of revolt against them; in a poetry which might take for its motto Omar Khayyám's [8] words: "Let us make up in the tavern for the time which we have wasted in the mosque." Or we find attractions in a poetry indifferent to them; in a poetry where the contents may be what they will, but where the form is studied and exquisite. We delude ourselves in either case; and the best cure for our delusion is to let our minds rest upon that great and inexhaustible word "life," until we learn to enter into its meaning. A poetry of revolt against moral ideas is a poetry of revolt against *life;* a poetry of indifference towards moral ideas is a poetry of indifference towards *life.*

Epictetus had a happy figure for things like the play of the senses, or literary form and finish, or argumentative ingenuity, in comparison with "the best and master thing" for us, as he called it, the concern, how to live. Some people were afraid of them, he said, or they disliked and undervalued them. Such people were wrong; they were unthankful or cowardly. But the things might also be overprized, and treated as final when they are not. They bear to life the relation which inns bear to home.

As if a man, journeying home, and finding a nice inn on the road, and liking it, were to stay forever at the inn! Man, thou hast forgotten thine object; thy journey was not *to* this, but *through* this. "But this inn is taking." And how many other inns, too, are taking, and how many fields and meadows! but as places of passage merely. You have an object, which is this: to get home, to do your duty to your family, friends, and fellow countrymen, to attain inward freedom, serenity, happiness, contentment. Style takes your fancy, arguing takes your fancy, and you forget your home and want to make your abode with them and to stay with them, on the plea that they are taking. Who denies that they are taking? but as places of passage, as inns. And when I say this, you suppose me to be attacking the care for style, the care for argument. I am not; I attack the resting in them, the not looking to the end which is beyond them.

Now, when we come across a poet like Théophile Gautier, we have a poet who has taken up his abode at an inn, and never got farther. There may be inducements to this or that one of us, at this or that moment, to find delight in him, to cleave to him; but after all, we do not change the truth about him — we only stay ourselves in his inn along with him. And when we come across a poet like Wordsworth, who sings

Of truth, of grandeur, beauty, love and hope.
And melancholy fear subdued by faith,
Of blessed consolations in distress,
Of moral strength and intellectual power,
Of joy in widest commonalty spread — [9]

then we have a poet intent on "the best and master thing," and who prosecutes his journey home. We say, for brevity's sake, that he deals with *life,* because he deals with that in which life really consists. This is what Voltaire means to praise in the English poets — this dealing with what is really life. But always it is the mark of the greatest poets that they deal with it; and to say that the English poets are remarkable for dealing with it, is only another way of saying what is true, that in poetry the English genius has especially shown its power.

Wordsworth deals with it, and his greatness lies in his dealing with it so powerfully. I have named a number of celebrated poets above all of whom he, in my opinion, deserves to be placed. He is to be placed above poets like Voltaire, Dryden, Pope, Lessing, Schiller, because these famous personages, with a thousand gifts and merits, never, or scarcely ever, attain the distinctive accent and utterance of the high and genuine poets —

*Quique pii vates et Phoebo digna locuti,*[10]

at all. Burns, Keats, Heine, not to speak of others in our list, have this accent; who can doubt it? And at the same time they have treasures of humor, felicity, passion, for which in Wordsworth we shall look in vain. Where, then, is Wordsworth's superiority? It is here; he deals with more of *life* than they do; he deals with *life,* as a whole, more powerfully.

8. **Omar Khayyám:** Persian poet (?–1123), author of the *Rubáiyát.*

9. *The Recluse,* ll. 767–71. 10. "Those pious prophets who utter things that are worthy of Phoebus" (Virgil, *Aeneid,* VI.662). Phoebus Apollo was the god of prophecy and also of poetry.

No Wordsworthian will doubt this. Nay, the fervent Wordsworthian will add, as Mr. Leslie Stephen does, that Wordsworth's poetry is precious because his philosophy is sound; that his "ethical system is as distinctive and capable of exposition as Bishop Butler's"; that his poetry is informed by ideas which "fall spontaneously into a scientific system of thought."[11] But we must be on our guard against the Wordsworthians, if we want to secure for Wordsworth his due rank as a poet. The Wordsworthians are apt to praise him for the wrong things, and to lay far too much stress upon what they call his philosophy. His poetry is the reality, his philosophy — so far, at least, as it may put on the form and habit of "a scientific system of thought," and the more that it puts them on — is illusion. Perhaps we shall one day learn to make this proposition general, and to say: Poetry is the reality, philosophy the illusion. But in Wordsworth's case, at any rate, we cannot do him justice until we dismiss his formal philosophy.

*The Excursion* abounds with philosophy, and therefore *The Excursion* is to the Wordsworthian what it never can be to the disinterested lover of poetry — a satisfactory work. "Duty exists," says Wordsworth, in *The Excursion;* and then he proceeds thus —

> . . . Immutably survive,
> For our support, the measures and the forms,
> Which an abstract Intelligence supplies,
> Whose kingdom is, where time and space are not.[12]

And the Wordsworthian is delighted, and thinks that here is a sweet union of philosophy and poetry. But the disinterested lover of poetry will feel that the lines carry us really not a step farther than the proposition which they would interpret; that they are a tissue of elevated but abstract verbiage, alien to the very nature of poetry.

Or let us come direct to the center of Wordsworth's philosophy, as "an ethical system, as distinctive and capable of systematical exposition as Bishop Butler's" —

> . . . One adequate support
> For the calamities of mortal life
> Exists, one only — an assured belief
> That the procession of our fate, howe'er
> Sad or disturbed, is ordered by a Being
> Of infinite benevolence and power;
> Whose everlasting purposes embrace
> All accidents, converting them to good.[13]

That is doctrine such as we hear in church too, religious and philosophic doctrine; and the attached Wordsworthian loves passages of such doctrine, and brings them forward in proof of his poet's excellence. But however true the doctrine may be, it has, as here presented, none of the characters of *poetic* truth, the kind of truth which we require from a poet, and in which Wordsworth is really strong.

Even the "intimations" of the famous "Ode," those cornerstones of the supposed philosophic system of Wordsworth — the idea of the high instincts and affections coming out in childhood, testifying of a divine home recently left, and fading away as our life proceeds — this idea, of undeniable beauty as a play of fancy, has itself not the character of poetic truth of the best kind; it has no real solidity. The instinct of delight in Nature and her beauty had no doubt extraordinary strength in Wordsworth himself as a child. But to say that universally this instinct is mighty in childhood, and tends to die away afterwards, is to say what is extremely doubtful. In many people, perhaps with the majority of educated persons, the love of Nature is nearly imperceptible at ten years old, but strong and operative at thirty. In general we may say of these high instincts of early childhood, the base of the alleged systematic philosophy of Wordsworth, what Thucydides says of the early achievements of the Greek race: "It is impossible to speak with certainty of what is so remote; but from all that we can really investigate, I should say that they were no very great things."

Finally, the "scientific system of thought" in Wordsworth gives us at last such poetry as this, which the devout Wordsworthian accepts —

> O for the coming of that glorious time
> When, prizing knowledge as her noblest wealth
> And best protection, this Imperial Realm,
> While she exacts allegiance, shall admit
> An obligation, on her part, to *teach*
> Them who are born to serve her and obey;
> Binding herself by statute to secure,
> For all the children whom her soil maintains,
> The rudiments of letters, and inform
> The mind with moral and religious truth.[14]

11. **"ethical . . . thought"**: The remarks appear in the essay "Wordsworth's Ethics" in Vol. III of Leslie Stephen's *Hours in a Library*. Stephen (1832–1904) was a well-known critic and man of letters, editor of *The Dictionary of National Biography* and *The English Men of Letters* Series. The Bishop Butler to whom he refers is the famous theologian (1692–1752), author of the *Analogy of Religion*. See "Written in Butler's Sermons" footnote, above. 12. *The Excursion*, IV.73–76.

13. *The Excursion*, IV.10–17. 14. *The Excursion*, IX.293–302.

Wordsworth calls Voltaire dull, and surely the production of these un-Voltairian lines must have been imposed on him as a judgment! One can hear them being quoted at a Social Science Congress; one can call up the whole scene. A great room in one of our dismal provincial towns; dusty air and jaded afternoon daylight; benches full of men with bald heads and women in spectacles; an orator lifting up his face from a manuscript written within and without to declaim these lines of Wordsworth; and in the soul of any poor child of nature who may have wandered in thither, an unutterable sense of lamentation, and mourning, and woe!

"But turn we," as Wordsworth says,[15] "from these bold, bad men," the haunters of Social Science Congresses. And let us be on our guard, too, against the exhibitors and extollers of a "scientific system of thought" in Wordsworth's poetry. The poetry will never be seen aright while they thus exhibit it. The cause of its greatness is simple, and may be told quite simply. Wordsworth's poetry is great because of the extraordinary power with which Wordsworth feels the joy offered to us in nature, the joy offered to us in the simple primary affections and duties; and because of the extraordinary power with which, in case after case, he shows us this joy, and renders it so as to make us share it.

The source of joy from which he thus draws is the truest and most unfailing source of joy accessible to man. It is also accessible universally. Wordsworth brings us word, therefore, according to his own strong and characteristic line, he brings us word

> Of joy in widest commonalty spread.

Here is an immense advantage for a poet. Wordsworth tells of what all seek, and tells of it at its truest and best source, and yet a source where all may go and draw for it.

Nevertheless, we are not to suppose that everything is precious which Wordsworth, standing even at this perennial and beautiful source, may give us. Wordsworthians are apt to talk as if it must be. They will speak with the same reverence of "The Sailor's Mother," for example, as of "Lucy Gray." They do their master harm by such lack of discrimination. "Lucy Gray" is a beautiful success; "The Sailor's Mother" is a failure. To give aright what he wishes to give, to interpret and render successfully, is not always within Wordsworth's own command. It is within no poet's command; here is the part of the Muse, the inspiration, the God, the "not ourselves." In Wordsworth's case, the accident, for so it may almost be called, of inspiration, is of peculiar importance. No poet, perhaps, is so evidently filled with a new and sacred energy when the inspiration is upon him; no poet, when it fails him, is so left "weak as is a breaking wave." I remember hearing him say that "Goethe's poetry was not inevitable enough." The remark is striking and true; no line in Goethe, as Goethe said himself, but its maker knew well how it came there. Wordsworth is right, Goethe's poetry is not inevitable, not inevitable enough. But Wordsworth's poetry, when he is at his best, is inevitable, as inevitable as Nature herself. It might seem that Nature not only gave him the matter for his poem, but wrote his poem for him. He has no style. He was too conversant with Milton not to catch at times his master's manner, and he has fine Miltonic lines; but he has no assured poetic style of his own, like Milton. When he seeks to have a style he falls into ponderosity and pomposity. In *The Excursion* we have his style, as an artistic product of his own creation; and although Jeffrey[16] completely failed to recognize Wordsworth's real greatness, he was yet not wrong in saying of *The Excursion,* as a work of poetic style: "This will never do." And yet magical as is that power, which Wordsworth has not, of assured and possessed poetic style, he has something which is an equivalent for it.

Everyone who has any sense for these things feels the subtle turn, the heightening, which is given to a poet's verse by his genius for style. We can feel it in the

> After life's fitful fever, he sleeps well[17]

of Shakespeare; in the

> . . . though fall'n on evil days,
> On evil days though fall'n, and evil tongues[18]

of Milton. It is the incomparable charm of Milton's power of poetic style which gives such worth to *Paradise Regained,* and makes a great poem of a work in which Milton's imagination does not soar high. Wordsworth has in constant possession, and at command, no style of this kind; but he had too poetic a nature, and had read the great poets too

15. In his poem "The Lady Fleming."

16. **Jeffrey:** Francis Jeffrey (1773–1850), Scottish judge and well known as a literary critic. "This will never do" is the opening sentence of his review of Wordsworth's *Excursion* in the *Edinburgh Review,* November, 1814. 17. *Macbeth,* III.ii.23. 18. *Paradise Lost,* VII.25–26. See p. 487 in Vol. I.

well, not to catch, as I have already remarked, something of it occasionally. We find it not only in his Miltonic lines; we find it in such a phrase as this, where the manner is his own, not Milton's —

> . . . the fierce confederate storm
> Of sorrow, barricadoed evermore
> Within the walls of cities —[19]

although even here, perhaps, the power of style, which is undeniable, is more properly that of eloquent prose than the subtle heightening and change wrought by genuine poetic style. It is style, again, and the elevation given by style, which chiefly makes the effectiveness of " Laodamía." Still the right sort of verse to choose from Wordsworth, if we are to seize his true and most characteristic form of expression, is a line like this from " Michael " —

> And never lifted up a single stone.

There is nothing subtle in it, no heightening, no study of poetic style, strictly so called, at all; yet it is expression of the highest and most truly expressive kind.

Wordsworth owed much to Burns, and a style of perfect plainness, relying for effect solely on the weight and force of that which with entire fidelity it utters, Burns could show him.

> The poor inhabitant below
> Was quick to learn and wise to know,
> And keenly felt the friendly glow
> And softer flame;
> But thoughtless follies laid him low
> And stain'd his name.[20]

Everyone will be conscious of a likeness here to Wordsworth; and if Wordsworth did great things with this nobly plain manner, we must remember, what indeed he himself would always have been forward to acknowledge, that Burns used it before him.

Still, Wordsworth's use of it has something unique and unmatchable. Nature herself seems, I say, to take the pen out of his hand, and to write for him with her own bare, sheer, penetrating power. This arises from two causes: from the profound sincereness with which Wordsworth feels his subject, and also from the profoundly sincere and natural character of his subject itself. He can and will treat such a subject with nothing but the most plain, first-hand, almost austere naturalness. His expression may often be called bald, as, for instance, in the poem of " Resolution and Independence "; But it is bald as the bare mountaintops are bald, with a baldness which is full of grandeur.

Wherever we meet with the successful balance, in Wordsworth, of profound truth of subject with profound truth of execution, he is unique. His best poems are those which most perfectly exhibit this balance. I have a warm admiration for " Laodamía " and for the great " Ode "; but if I am to tell the very truth, I find " Laodamía " not wholly free from something artificial, and the great " Ode " not wholly free from something declamatory. If I had to pick out poems of a kind most perfectly to show Wordsworth's unique power, I should rather choose poems such as " Michael," " The Fountain," " The Highland Reaper." And poems with the peculiar and unique beauty which distinguishes these, Wordsworth produced in considerable number, besides very many other poems of which the worth, although not so rare as the worth of these, is still exceedingly high.

On the whole, then, as I said at the beginning, not only is Wordsworth eminent by reason of the goodness of his best work, but he is eminent also by reason of the great body of good work which he has left to us. With the ancients I will not compare him. In many respects the ancients are far above us, and yet there is something that we demand which they can never give. Leaving the ancients, let us come to the poets and poetry of Christendom. Dante, Shakespeare, Molière, Milton, Goethe, are altogether larger and more splendid luminaries in the poetical heaven than Wordsworth. But I know not where else, among the moderns, we are to find his superiors.

To disengage the poems which show his power, and to present them to the English-speaking public and to the world, is the object of this volume. I by no means say that it contains all which in Wordsworth's poems is interesting. Except in the case of " Margaret," a story composed separately from the rest of *The Excursion,* and which belongs to a different part of England, I have not ventured on detaching portions of poems, or on giving any piece otherwise than as Wordsworth himself gave it. But under the conditions imposed by this reserve, the volume contains, I think, everything, or nearly everything, which may best serve him with the majority of lovers of poetry, nothing which may disserve him.

19. *The Recluse,* ll. 831–33. 20. Burns, "A Bard's Epitaph."

I have spoken lightly of Wordsworthians; and if we are to get Wordsworth recognized by the public and by the world, we must recommend him not in the spirit of a clique, but in the spirit of disinterested lovers of poetry. But I am a Wordsworthian myself. I can read with pleasure and edification " Peter Bell," and the whole series of *Ecclesiastical Sonnets,* and the address to Mr. Wilkinson's spade, and even the " Thanksgiving Ode " — everything of Wordsworth, I think, except " Vaudracour and Julia." It is not for nothing that one has been brought up in the veneration of a man so truly worthy of homage; that one has seen him and heard him, lived in his neighborhood, and been familiar with his country. No Wordsworthian has a tenderer affection for this pure and sage master than I, or is less really offended by his defects. But Wordsworth is something more than the pure and sage master of a small band of devoted followers, and we ought not to rest satisfied until he is seen to be what he is. He is one of the very chief glories of English poetry; and by nothing is England so glorious as by her poetry. Let us lay aside every weight which hinders our getting him recognized as this, and let our one study be to bring to pass, as widely as possible and as truly as possible, his own word concerning his poems: "They will cooperate with the benign tendencies in human nature and society, and will, in their degree, be efficacious in making men wiser, better, and happier."[21]

# JOHN KEATS

Arnold's essay on Keats was written as the introduction to the selections from Keats's poetry in T. H. Ward's admirable anthology in four volumes, *The English Poets,* 1880. Most modern critics would estimate Keats's character, genius, and achievement at a higher rate than Arnold does. Yet it is apparent that despite a certain principled resistance to Keats, Arnold is deeply drawn to him, and no one has ever said of Keats a truer and more significant thing than Arnold's remark that on almost everything that Keats wrote "there is that stamp of high work which is akin to character, which is character passing into intellectual production."

Poetry, according to Milton's famous saying, should be " simple, sensuous, impassioned." [1] No one can question the eminency, in Keats's poetry, of the quality of sensuousness. Keats as a poet is abundantly and enchantingly sensuous; the question with some people will be, whether he is anything else? Many things may be brought forward which seem to show him as under the fascination and sole dominion of sense, and desiring nothing better. There is the exclamation in one of his letters: [2] " O for a life of sensations rather than of thoughts! " There is the thesis, in another, " that with a great Poet the sense of Beauty overcomes every other consideration, or rather obliterates all consideration." There is Haydon's story of him, how " he once covered his tongue and throat as far as he could reach with Cayenne pepper, in order to appreciate the delicious coldness of claret in all its glory — his own expression." [3] One is not much surprised when Haydon further tells us, of the hero of such a story, that once for six weeks together he was hardly ever sober. " He had no decision of character," Haydon adds; " no object upon which to direct his great powers." [4]

Character and self-control, the *virtus verusque labor* [5] so necessary for every kind of greatness, and for the great artist, too, indispensable, appear to be wanting, certainly, to this Keats of Haydon's portraiture. They are wanting also to the Keats of the *Letters to Fanny Brawne.* [6] These letters make as unpleasing an impression as Haydon's anecdotes. The editor of Haydon's journals could not well omit what Haydon said of his friend, but for the publication of the *Letters to Fanny Brawne* I can see no good reason whatever. Their publication appears to me, I confess, inexcusable; they ought never to have been published. But published they are, and we have to take notice of them. Letters written when Keats was near his end, under the throttling and unmanning grasp of mortal disease, we will not judge. But here is a letter written some months before he was taken ill. It is printed just as Keats wrote it:

You have absorb'd me. I have a sensation at the present moment as though I was dissolving — I should be exquisitely miserable without the hope

21. From Wordsworth's "Essay, Supplementary to the Preface," in *Poems*, 1815 edition. JOHN KEATS. 1. "simple . . . impassioned": Milton, *Of Education* — but Arnold misquotes, as he often does, for Milton wrote "passionate," not "impassioned."

2. Arnold's prose quotations from Keats are all from Keats's letters. For some of the most famous of these letters, many in their entirety, see above. 3. There . . . expression: Haydon's story about the pepper is now held to be apocryphal. 4. A reading of Keats's letters will show how wrong Haydon was in this belief, and how wrong Arnold was to accept it, although Arnold does go on to qualify his opinion of Keats's character. 5. *virtus . . . labor:* "manhood and true labor." See Virgil, *Aeneid*, XII.435. 6. *Letters . . . Brawne:* Keats's letters to Fanny Brawne, his fiancée, were first published in 1878 in the edition of H. B. Forman.

of soon seeing you. I should be afraid to separate myself far from you. My sweet Fanny, will your heart never change? My love, will it? I have no limit now to my love. . . . Your note came in just here. I cannot be happier away from you. 'Tis richer than an Argosy of Pearles. Do not threat me even in jest. I have been astonished that Men could die Martyrs for religion — I have shuddered at it. I shudder no more — I could be martyred for my Religion — Love is my religion — I could die for that. I could die for you. My Creed is Love and you are its only tenet. You have ravished me away by a Power I cannot resist; and yet I could resist till I saw you; and even since I have seen you I have endeavoured often "to reason against the reasons of my Love." I can do that no more — the pain would be too great. My love is selfish. I cannot breathe without you.

A man who writes love letters in this strain is probably predestined, one may observe, to misfortune in his love affairs; but that is nothing. The complete enervation of the writer is the real point for remark. We have the tone, or rather the entire want of tone, the abandonment of all reticence and all dignity, of the merely sensuous man, of the man who "is passion's slave."[7] Nay, we have them in suchwise that one is tempted to speak even as *Blackwood* or the *Quarterly* were in the old days wont to speak: one is tempted to say that Keats's love letter is the love letter of a surgeon's apprentice.[8] It has in its relaxed self-abandonment something underbred and ignoble, as of a youth ill brought up, without the training which teaches us that we must put some constraint upon our feelings and upon the expression of them. It is the sort of love letter of a surgeon's apprentice which one might hear read out in a breach-of-promise case, or in the Divorce Court. The sensuous man speaks in it, and the sensuous man of a badly bred and badly trained sort. That many who are themselves also badly bred and badly trained should enjoy it, and should even think it a beautiful and characteristic production of him whom they call their "lovely and beloved Keats," does not make it better. These are the admirers whose pawing and fondness does not good but harm to the fame of Keats; who concentrate attention upon what in him is least wholesome and most questionable; who worship him, and would have the world worship him too, as the poet of

Light feet, dark violet eyes, and parted hair,
Soft dimpled hands, white neck, and creamy
breast.[9]

This sensuous strain Keats had, and a man of his poetic powers could not, whatever his strain, but show his talent in it. But he has something more, and something better. We who believe Keats to have been by his promise, at any rate, if not fully by his performance, one of the very greatest of English poets, and who believe also that a merely sensuous man cannot either by promise or by performance be a very great poet, because poetry interprets life, and so large and noble a part of life is outside of such a man's ken — we cannot but look for signs in him of something more than sensuousness, for signs of character and virtue. And indeed the elements of high character Keats undoubtedly has, and the effort to develop them; the effort is frustrated and cut short by misfortune, and disease, and time, but for the due understanding of Keats's worth the recognition of this effort, and of the elements on which it worked, is necessary.

Lord Houghton,[10] who praises very discriminatingly the poetry of Keats, has on his character also a remark full of discrimination. He says: "The faults of Keats's disposition were precisely the contrary of those attributed to him by common opinion." And he gives a letter written after the death of Keats by his brother George, in which the writer, speaking of the fantastic *Johnny Keats* invented for common opinion by Lord Byron and by the reviewers, declares indignantly: "John was the very soul of manliness and courage, and as much like the Holy Ghost as *Johnny Keats.*" It is important to note this testimony, and to look well for whatever illustrates and confirms it.

Great weight is laid by Lord Houghton on such a direct profession of faith as the following: "That sort of probity and disinterestedness," Keats writes to his brothers, "which such men as Bailey possess, does hold and grasp the tip-top of any spiritual honors that can be paid to anything in this world." Lord Houghton says that "never have words more effectively expressed the conviction of the superiority of virtue above beauty than those." But merely to make a profession of faith of the kind here made by Keats is not difficult; what we should rather

7. **"is . . . slave":** *Hamlet,* III.ii.77. See p. 261 in Vol. I.
8. ***Blackwood* . . . apprentice:** The reviewers of *Blackwood's Magazine* and the *Quarterly Review* had taunted Keats on his lowly origin and on his former profession.

9. The opening lines of the second of three sonnets on woman, the first of which is "Woman! when I behold thee flippant, vain!" 10. **Lord Houghton:** the editor of the *Life, Letters, and Literary Remains of Keats,* 1848. A revised edition appeared in 1867.

look for is some evidence of the instinct for character, for virtue, passing into the man's life, passing into his work.

Signs of virtue, in the true and large sense of the word, the instinct for virtue passing into the life of Keats and strengthening it, I find in the admirable wisdom and temper of what he says to his friend Bailey on the occasion of a quarrel between Reynolds and Haydon:

> Things have happened lately of great perplexity; you must have heard of them; Reynolds and Haydon retorting and recriminating, and parting forever. The same thing has happened between Haydon and Hunt. It is unfortunate; men should bear with each other; there lives not the man who may not be cut up, aye, lashed to pieces, on his weakest side. The best of men have but a portion of good in them. . . . The sure way, Bailey, is first to know a man's faults, and then be passive. If, after that, he insensibly draws you towards him, then you have no power to break the link. Before I felt interested in either Reynolds or Haydon, I was well read in their faults; yet, knowing them, I have been cementing gradually with both. I have an affection for them both, for reasons almost opposite; and to both must I of necessity cling, supported always by the hope that when a little time, a few years, shall have tried me more fully in their esteem, I may be able to bring them together.

Butler[11] has well said that "endeavoring to enforce upon our own minds a practical sense of virtue, or to beget in others that practical sense of it which a man really has himself, is a virtuous *act*." And such an "endeavoring" is that of Keats in those words written to Bailey. It is more than mere words; so justly thought and so discreetly urged as it is, it rises to the height of a virtuous *act*. It is proof of character.

The same thing may be said of some words written to his friend Charles Brown, whose kindness, willingly exerted whenever Keats chose to avail himself of it, seemed to free him from any pressing necessity of earning his own living. Keats felt that he must not allow this state of things to continue. He determined to set himself to "fag on as others do" at periodical literature, rather than to endanger his independence and his self-respect; and he writes to Brown:

> I had got into a habit of mind of looking towards you as a help in all difficulties. This very habit would be the parent of idleness and difficulties. You will see it is a duty I owe to myself to break the neck of it. I do nothing for my subsistence—make no exertion. At the end of another year you shall applaud me, not for verses, but for conduct.

He had not, alas, another year of health before him when he announced that wholesome resolve; it then wanted but six months of the day of his fatal attack. But in the brief time allowed to him he did what he could to keep his word.

What character, again, what strength and clearness of judgment, in his criticism of his own productions, of the public, and of "the literary circles"! His words after the severe reviews of *Endymion* have often been quoted; they cannot be quoted too often:

> Praise or blame has but a momentary effect on the man whose love of beauty in the abstract makes him a severe critic on his own works. My own criticism has given me pain without comparison beyond what *Blackwood* or the *Quarterly* could possibly inflict; and also, when I feel I am right, no external praise can give me such a glow as my own solitary reperception and ratification of what is fine. J. S. is perfectly right in regard to the "slip-shod Endymion." That it is so is no fault of mine. No! though it may sound a little paradoxical, it is as good as I had power to make it by myself.

And again, as if he had foreseen certain of his admirers gushing over him, and was resolved to disengage his responsibility:

> I have done nothing, except for the amusement of a few people who refine upon their feelings till anything in the un-understandable way will go down with them. I have no cause to complain, because I am certain anything really fine will in these days be felt. I have no doubt that if I had written *Othello* I should have been cheered. I shall go on with patience.

Young poets almost inevitably overrate what they call "the might of poesy," and its power over the world which now is. Keats is not a dupe on this matter any more than he is a dupe about the merit of his own performances:

> I have no trust whatever in poetry. I don't wonder at it; the marvel is to me how people read so much of it.

His attitude towards the public is that of a strong man, not of a weakling avid of praise, and made to "be snuffed out by an article":[12]

**11. Butler:** See "Wordsworth," n. 11, above.

**12. "be . . . article":** in *Don Juan*, XI.60, Byron refers to "John Keats who was kill'd off by one critique, / Just as he

I shall ever consider the public as debtors to me for verses, not myself to them for admiration, which I can do without.

And again, in a passage where one may perhaps find fault with the capital letters, but surely with nothing else:

I have not the slightest feel of humility towards the public or to anything in existence but the Eternal Being, the Principle of Beauty, and the Memory of great Men. . . . I would be subdued before my friends, and thank them for subduing me; but among multitudes of men I have no feel of stooping; I hate the idea of humility to them. I never wrote one single line of poetry with the least shadow of thought about their opinion. Forgive me for vexing you, but it eases me to tell you: I could not live without the love of my friends; I would jump down Etna for any great public good — but I hate a mawkish popularity. I cannot be subdued before them. My glory would be to daunt and dazzle the thousand jabberers about pictures and books.

Against these artistic and literary "jabberers," amongst whom Byron fancied Keats, probably, to be always living, flattering them and flattered by them, he has yet another outburst:

Just so much as I am humbled by the genius above my grasp, am I exalted and look with hate and contempt upon the literary world. Who could wish to be among the commonplace crowd of the little famous, who are each individually lost in a throng made up of themselves?

And he loves Fanny Brawne the more, he tells her, because he believes that she has liked him for his own sake and for nothing else. "I have met with women who I really think would like to be married to a Poem and to be given away by a Novel."

There is a tone of too much bitterness and defiance in all this, a tone which he with great propriety subdued and corrected when he wrote his beautiful preface to *Endymion*. But the thing to be seized is, that Keats had flint and iron in him, that he had character; that he was, as his brother George says, "as much like the Holy Ghost as *Johnny Keats*" — as that imagined sensuous weakling, the delight of the literary circles of Hampstead.

It is a pity that Byron, who so misconceived Keats, should never have known how shrewdly Keats, on the other, had characterized *him* as "a fine thing" in the sphere of "the worldly theatrical, and pantomimical." But indeed nothing is more remarkable in Keats than his clear-sightedness, his lucidity; and lucidity is in itself akin to character and to high and severe work. In spite, therefore, of his overpowering feeling for beauty, in spite of his sensuousness, in spite of his facility, in spite of his gift of expression, Keats could say resolutely:

I know nothing, I have read nothing; and I mean to follow Solomon's directions: "Get learning, get understanding." There is but one way for me. The road lies through application, study, and thought. I will pursue it.

And of Milton, instead of resting in Milton's incomparable phrases, Keats could say, although indeed all the while looking "upon fine phrases," as he himself tells us, "like a lover" —

Milton had an exquisite passion for what is properly, in the sense of ease and pleasure, poetical luxury; and with that, it appears to me, he would fain have been content, if he could, so doing, preserve his self-respect and feeling of duty performed; but there was working in him, as it were, that same sort of thing which operates in the great world to the end of a prophecy's being accomplished. Therefore he devoted himself rather to the ardours than the pleasures of song, solacing himself at intervals with cups of old wine.

In his own poetry, too, Keats felt that place must be found for "the ardours rather than the pleasures of song," although he was aware that he was not yet ripe for it —

"But my flag is not unfurl'd
On the Admirals staff, and to philosophise
I dare not yet." [13]

Even in his pursuit of "the pleasures of song," however, there is that stamp of high work which is akin to character, which is character passing into intellectual production. *"The best sort of poetry* — that," he truly says, "is all I care for, all I live for." It is curious to observe how this severe addiction of his to the best sort of poetry affects him with a

really promised something great," and goes on to say "Poor fellow! His was an untoward fate, / 'Tis strange the mind, that fiery particle, / Should let itself be snuff'd out by an article." It was a common but erroneous belief that Keats's death was brought about by the savage reviews of his *Endymion* in *Blackwood's Magazine* and the *Quarterly Review.*

13. Lines 72–74 of Keats's "Epistle to John Hamilton Reynolds." Keats wrote "and so philosophize."

certain coldness, as if the addiction had been to mathematics, towards those prime objects of a sensuous and passionate poet's regard, love and women. He speaks of "the opinion I have formed of the generality of women, who appear to me as children to whom I would rather give a sugar-plum than my time." He confesses "a tendency to class women in my books with roses and sweet-meats — they never see themselves dominant"; and he can understand how the unpopularity of his poems may be in part due to "the offence which the ladies" not unnaturally "take at him" from this cause. Even to Fanny Brawne he can write "a flint-worded letter," when his "mind is heaped to the full" with poetry:

I know the generality of women would hate me for this; that I should have so unsoftened, so hard a mind as to forget them; forget the brightest realities for the dull imaginations of my own brain. . . . My heart seems now made of iron — I could not write a proper answer to an invitation to Idalia.

The truth is that "the yearning passion for the Beautiful," which was with Keats, as he himself truly says, the master passion, is not a passion of the sensuous or sentimental man, is not a passion of the sensuous or sentimental poet. It is an intellectual and spiritual passion. It is "connected and made one," as Keats declares that in his case it was, "with the ambition of the intellect." It is, as he again says, "the mighty *abstract idea* of Beauty in all things." And in his last days Keats wrote:

If I should die, I have left no immortal work behind me — nothing to make my friends proud of my memory; *but I have loved the principle of beauty in all things,* and if I had had time I would have made myself remembered.

He *has* made himself remembered, and remembered as no merely sensuous poet could be; and he has done it by having "loved the principle of beauty in all things."

For to see things in their beauty is to see things in their truth, and Keats knew it. "What the Imagination seizes as Beauty must be Truth," he says in prose; and in immortal verse he has said the same thing —

"Beauty is truth, truth beauty" — that is all
Ye know on earth, and all ye need to know.[14]

14. Concluding lines of "Ode on a Grecian Urn." See above.

No, it is not all; but it is true, deeply true, and we have deep need to know it. And with beauty goes not only truth; joy goes with her also; and this too Keats saw and said, as in the famous first line of his *Endymion* it stands written —

A thing of beauty is a joy forever.

It is no small thing to have so loved the principle of beauty as to perceive the necessary relation of beauty with truth, and of both with joy. Keats was a great spirit, and counts for far more than many even of his admirers suppose, because this just and high perception made itself clear to him. Therefore a dignity and a glory shed gleams over his life, and happiness, too, was not a stranger to it. "Nothing startles me beyond the moment," he says. "The setting sun will always set me to rights — or if a sparrow come before my window I take part in its existence and pick about the gravel." But he had terrible bafflers — consuming disease and early death. "I think," he writes to Reynolds, "if I had a free and healthy and lasting organization of heart, and lungs as strong as an ox's, so as to be able to bear unhurt the shock of extreme thought and sensation without weariness, I could pass my life very nearly alone, though it should last eighty years. But I feel my body too weak to support me to the height; I am obliged continually to check myself, and be nothing." He had against him even more than this; he had against him the blind power which we call Fortune. "O that something fortunate," he cries in the closing months of his life, "had ever happened to me or my brothers! — then I might hope, — but despair is forced upon me as a habit." So baffled and so sorely tried — while laden, at the same time, with a mighty formative thought requiring health, and many days, and favouring circumstances, for its adequate manifestation — what wonder if the achievement of Keats be partial and incomplete?

Nevertheless, let and hindered as he was, and with a short term and imperfect experience — "young," as he says of himself, "and writing at random, straining after particles of light in the midst of a great darkness, without knowing the bearing of any one assertion, of any one opinion" — notwithstanding all this, by virtue of his feeling for beauty and of his perception of the vital connection of beauty with truth, Keats accomplished so much in poetry, that in one of the two great modes by which poetry interprets, in the faculty of naturalistic interpretation, in what we call natural magic, he ranks with Shakespeare. "The tongue of Kean," he says in an admirable criticism of that great actor and of his enchanting elocution, "the tongue of Kean must seem to have robbed the Hybla bees and left them honeyless. There is an indescribable *gusto* in his voice; in *Richard,* 'Be stirring with the lark to-morrow, gentle Norfolk!' comes from him as through the morning atmosphere towards which he yearns." This magic, this "indescribable *gusto* in the voice," Keats himself, too, exhibits in his poetic expression. No one else in English poetry, save Shakespeare, has in expression quite the fascinating felicity of Keats, his perfection of loveliness. "I think," he said humbly, "I shall be among the English poets after my death." He is; he is with Shakespeare.

For the second great half of poetic interpretation, for that faculty of moral interpretation which is in Shakespeare, and is informed by him with the same power of beauty as his naturalistic interpretation, Keats was not ripe. For the architectonics of poetry, the faculty which presides at the evolution of works like the *Agememnon* or *Lear,* he was not ripe. His *Endymion,* as he himself well saw, is a failure, and his *Hyperion,* fine things as it contains, is not a success. But in shorter things, where the matured power of moral interpretation, and the high architectonics which go with complete poetic development, are not required, he is perfect. The poems which follow prove it — prove it far better by themselves than anything which can be said about them will prove it. Therefore I have chiefly spoken here of the man, and of the elements in him which explain the production of such work. Shakespearian work it is; not imitative, indeed, of Shakespeare, but Shakespearian, because its expression has that rounded perfection and felicity of loveliness of which Shakespeare is the great master. To show such work is to praise it. Let us now end by delighting ourselves with a fragment of it, too broken to find a place among the pieces which follow, but far too beautiful to be lost. It is a fragment of an ode for May Day.[15] O might I, he cries to May, O might I

. . . thy smiles
Seek as they once were sought, in Grecian isles,
By bards who died content on pleasant sward,
  Leaving great verse unto a little clan!
O, give me their old vigour, and unheard
  Save of the quiet primrose, and the span
    Of heaven, and few years,
Rounded by thee, my song should die away,
    Content as theirs,
Rich in the simple worship of a day!

15. Arnold refers to the "Fragment of an Ode to Maia." Maia was the eldest and loveliest of the Pleiades and the mother of Hermes by Zeus. Although the month of May is named in her honor, there is no justification for Arnold to suppose that the ode was intended by Keats to be "for May Day"; the poet seems to be interested only in the charming goddess, not in the month. See above.

REUBEN A. BROWER, Editor

# George Bernard Shaw

## 1856–1950

When Shaw was once asked about his reputation, he answered, "Which reputation? I have at least fifteen different reputations." The impudence and the exaggeration of the reply are characteristic of Shaw and express very well how hard it is to describe him, for the question immediately arises as to which Shaw we are talking about. Louis Dubedat, a character in one of Shaw's plays, *The Doctor's Dilemma,* finds it equally difficult to fasten a label on his creator. Having announced himself as "a disciple of Bernard Shaw," he is asked to explain what he means:

SIR PATRICK. Bernard Shaw? I never heard of him. He's a Methodist preacher, I suppose.

LOUIS [*scandalized*]. No, no. He's the most advanced man now living: he isnt anything.

The reply is both wise and revealing; Shaw, like many writers and artists, *isn't* any *one* thing, but an expresser of many things, of many points of view, including quite contradictory ones. The only single term that might do for him is "a talker." He will be remembered, like Dr. Johnson and Coleridge, as one of the great talkers, both in his actual conversation and in his writings. Shaw stands for the free play of talk, and at his best for the free play of ideas. To the present generation, increasingly distrustful of both freedoms — and in need of being reminded of their value — Shaw may appear less sympathetic than he did to his contemporaries. It must be granted that Shaw abuses his auditors, that being an Irishman he blends blarney with sense, that he becomes intoxicated with the sound of his own voice. But who would be always for talking sense?

Though no one label is satisfactory, the "fifteen different reputations" suggest some that are partially appropriate. Thus we may describe Shaw as a socialist and propagandist for the socialist cause; a journalist-critic of music, fine arts, and drama; a novelist, a dramatist, and a director of plays; an astute manager of his own financial interests; an enormously successful lecturer, a reformer concerned with social problems (such as housing, women's rights, prison reform, and prostitution); a propounder of scientific theories and a critic of science, a philosopher, a preacher of a peculiar evolutionary religion and of socialist Christianity; an antivivisectionist, a vegetarian, and an advocate of spelling reform (the cause for which he left the bulk of his estate). The list — far from complete — suggests in its universality and freakishness the quality of Shaw's mind, and it also reflects the "advanced" views held by the first generation of Englishmen to regard themselves as "twentieth-century." Shaw was in fact an inventor of the twentieth-century temper.

Although we shall get glimpses of G.B.S. in various roles, we can consider here only the dramatist, in particular the writer of comedy and the comic poet. (We can justifiably use the term "poet" of Shaw both in the Aristotelian sense of a "maker," one who represents human life, and in the more restricted sense of a writer who uses many resources of language, including rhythm.) The basis of Shaw's comedy, as we might expect, is talk, but essentially *dramatic* talk, speech that exactly defines and projects character. The talk is not simply the conversation of the man George Bernard Shaw, transferred to the stage and headed by different names — a common criticism of Shaw's work, though certainly not applicable to his better plays. Like Shakespeare or any dramatist of the first rank, he possessed a fine talent for writing dialogue of character, a talent that puzzled late nineteenth-century actors who had grown accustomed to half-written plays and who took it for granted that they must "build up" a part by introducing their own variations of speech and manner. (Oddly enough, they thought that Shakespeare too needed a good deal of "filling out" of the same sort.) Beerbohm Tree found to his surprise that "Shaw, with his platform technique, could build up speeches by tricks that were beyond the compass of his [Tree's] voice." As an example of Shaw's art, hear how deftly the characters are defined in the opening dialogue of *Man and Superman:* [1]

RAMSDEN. . . . Well, well, Octavius, it's the common lot. We must all face it some day. Sit down. . . .

OCTAVIUS. Yes: we must face it, Mr Ramsden. But I owed him a great deal. He did everything for me that my father could have done if he had lived.

RAMSDEN. He had no son of his own, you see.

OCTAVIUS. But he had daughters; and yet he was as good to my sister as to me. And his death was so sudden! I always intended to thank him — to let him know that I had not taken all his care of me as a matter of course, as any boy takes his father's care. But I waited for an opportunity; and now he is dead — dropped without a moment's warning. He will never know what I felt. . . .

RAMSDEN. How do we know that, Octavius? He may know it: we cannot tell. Come! dont grieve. . . . Thats right. Now let me tell you something to console you. The last time I saw him — it was in this very room — he said to me: "Tavy is a generous lad and the soul of honor; and when I see how little consideration other men get from their sons, I realize how much better than a son he's been to me." There! Doesnt that do you good?

OCTAVIUS. Mr. Ramsden: he used to say to me that he had met only one man in the world who was the soul of honor, and that was Roebuck Ramsden.

Note how the sententious sermonizing tone at once fixes Ramsden as a man of the generation that regarded death as a solemn "occasion": ". . . it's the common lot. We must all face it . . . we cannot tell." The "we's" betray the voice of the public speaker, a tone that comes out clearly in Ramsden's final speech. Note also the rhetorical question ("How do we know that, Octavius?") and the studied parenthesis of the accomplished orator ("The last time I saw him — it was in this very room —"). This is no way to address a friend's son, though it might do very well in parliament. Ramsden's accent recalls one of his liberal heroes, a Gladstone or a Cobden:

Excuse me, Octavius; but there are limits to social toleration. You know that I am not a bigoted or prejudiced man. You know that I am plain Roebuck Ramsden when other men who have done less have got handles to their names, because I have stood for equality and liberty of conscience while they were truckling to the Church and to the aristocracy. Whitefield and I lost chance after chance through our advanced opinions. But I draw the line at Anarchism and Free Love and that sort of thing. If I am to be Annie's guardian, she will have to learn that she has a duty to me. I wont have it: I will not have it. She must forbid John Tanner the house; and so must you.

Here speaks the brave tolerance of the 50's and 60's, rudely shaken by the "advanced opinions" of 1900.

In musical contrast, we have Octavius talking like "any boy," with his polite "Mr Ramsden's," his naïve exclamations, and his flat repetition of obvious compliments. But he and Ramsden agree in praising the "wonderfully dutiful" Ann Whitefield. With delicious irony, which the audience readily senses, Ramsden gives us a pre-hearing of her guilefully innocent speech:

. . . I dont believe she has ever once given her own wish as a reason for doing anything or not doing it. It's always "Father wishes me to," or "Mother wouldnt like it." It's really almost a fault in her.

Their agreement is rudely broken by the "Anarchist" Tanner:

TANNER. Ramsden: do you know what that is?

RAMSDEN [*loftily*]. No, sir.

TANNER. It's a copy of Whitefield's will. Ann got it this morning.

RAMSDEN. When you say Ann, you mean, I presume, Miss Whitefield.

[1] Read Act I and preferably the rest of the play, except the dream scene of Act III.

TANNER. I mean our Ann, your Ann, Tavy's Ann, and now, Heaven help me, my Ann!

OCTAVIUS [*rising, very pale*]. What do you mean?

TANNER. Mean! [*He holds up the will.*] Do you know who is appointed Ann's guardian by this will?

RAMSDEN. [*cooly*]. I believe I am.

TANNER. You! You and I, man. I! I!! I!!! Both of us! . .

RAMSDEN. You! Impossible.

TANNER. It's only too hideously true. . . . Ramsden: get me out of it somehow. You dont know Ann as well as I do. She'll commit every crime a respectable woman can; and she'll justify every one of them by saying that it was the wish of her guardians. She'll put everything on us; and we shall have no more control over her than a couple of mice over a cat.

OCTAVIUS. Jack: I wish you wouldnt talk like that about Ann.

TANNER. This chap's in love with her: thats another complication. Well, she'll either jilt him and say I didnt approve of him, or marry him and say you ordered her to. I tell you, this is the most staggering blow that has ever fallen on a man of my age and temperament.

The outrageous curtness of Tanner's addresses to Ramsden and the ragtime swing of " our Ann, your Ann, Tavy's Ann " characterize the man who breaks all rules, who is " possibly a little mad." But he too is an orator, of the soapbox, not the rostrum, type. He is a great " teller-off " (" I tell you . . ."), who has mastered the lesson Shaw had learned from the social reformer, Robert Owen: "Never argue: repeat your assertion." Listen to his dithyrambic iterations: " She'll commit . . . she'll justify . . . She'll put . . . ," which are so typical of his talk throughout the play. The smart balance of phrasing and the coarse comparison of a woman to an animal are equally typical.

From the beginning to the end of *Man and Superman,* Shaw keeps distinct the speaking voices of Tanner and of the other characters: by deft choice of idiom and arrangement of words and sentences, he makes us hear a definite personality through the tone and rhythm imposed on the dialogue. If we read the whole play and consider especially the longer speeches, we shall see that they have a very clear rhythmical structure, that, for example, there is a good deal of symmetry in phrase and sentence pattern. (Note above the longer speeches of Ramsden and Tanner.) There is also much symmetry of sound in the exchanges of repartee. Our first and last impression of *Man and Superman* and of the best Shaw plays is one of hearing sharply contrasted tones and rhythms that build up individual voices and characters.

Now we can see what Shaw does with this expertly contrived vocal interplay, what the full comic excitement of his drama is like. The situation in the scene we are reading is farcical: a man supposedly in his right mind has left a will appointing as guardians two men who could never be joined together, but who debate the possibility with high seriousness. The fun starts with this mockery and with the contrast between the character of the debaters *heard* in their voices.

As in most comedy, we are amused by observing some incongruity in man's behavior as a social animal — here, for example, by the ironic difference between Ramsden's view of himself as an " advanced " thinker and the view that emerges from the comparison with Tanner. But what is distinctly Shavian is not this comedy of character; the excitement and amusement peculiar to Shaw are of another kind. Our attention is not focused on personalities as such, not on unique individuals, but on what they represent. The interplay of voices carries and projects an interplay of attitudes and ideas. We hear in Ramsden the noble sonority of Liberalism blended with Victorian reverence for Womanly Woman and for Respectability; in Octavius, the gentle accents of the lover-artist of the late Romantic type; in Tanner, the snap and crackle of the new intolerance that questions older political and ethical values, that exults in the harshly biological view of the relations between men and women. Shavian comedy is above all a comedy of ideas; it amuses us by exploiting the incongruities between views professed or unconsciously enacted by the characters — views of the individual and society, of art and science, of history, religion, and even the universe. We say " comedy of ideas " because we are so acutely conscious of the intellectual positions which the speakers symbolize, and which we recognize as philosophically or historically important. We are rarely tempted to regard these personages as real people, whom we might meet off the stage. We do not say, " That is what happens when Tanner meets Ramsden," but " That is what happens when revolutionary socialism meets nineteenth-century liberalism." The fun comes from watching a "sparring match" between ideas. We are talking, remember, of where our attention *mainly* rests, of a difference in emphasis in the comic art of Shaw as compared with that of Shakespeare or of Dickens. But the fun in Shaw is still dramatic: the ideas are present to our ears and eyes in the personalities created by the words, particularly in those wonderfully distinct voices and rhythms, in the gestures that the words require of the actors, and in the precise stage directions. Here is a characteristic climax:

OCTAVIUS [*rising and coming from his refuge by the wall*]. Mr Ramsden: I think you are prejudiced against Jack. He is a man of honor, and incapable of abusing —

TANNER. Dont, Tavy: youll make me ill. I am not a man of honor: I am a man struck down by a dead hand. Tavy: you must marry her after all and take her off my hands. And I had set my heart on saving you from her!

OCTAVIUS. Oh, Jack, you talk of saving me from my highest happiness.

TANNER. Yes, a lifetime of happiness. If it were only the first half hour's happiness, Tavy, I would buy it for you with my last penny. But a lifetime of happiness! No man alive could bear it: it would be hell on earth.

RAMSDEN [*violently*]. Stuff, sir. Talk sense; or else go and waste someone else's time: I have something better to do than listen to your fooleries. [*He positively kicks his way to his table and resumes his seat.*]

Two more features of Shaw's comedy come out in this dialogue: the inversion of accepted values and the isolation of the revolutionary hero. The inversion is familiar enough in comic drama; Falstaff's view of "honor" is a classic example. But the Shavian hero in his splendid isolation is more self-conscious and more devastatingly impudent in turning values upside down. He proudly proclaims his independence from everything and everybody, and unlike Falstaff has no "gang" to whom he appeals for sympathy. The only approval he seeks is of conscience and Right Reason. He is very Protestant, quite Miltonic, not unlike the archrebel of *Paradise Lost*. But there is a comic possibility in the role of the rebel, especially of the man who "knows it all," as Tanner does. Such bright ratiocination is potentially comic, the very patness of the rhetorical formulas suggesting the thought that they can't be sound. Thus Shaw's hero becomes a victim of his own wisdom, and like the heroes of classical comedy — Falstaff is again an apt example — he falls and is laughed off the stage.

As Shaw often acknowledges, he makes use of the most ancient tricks of comic drama: misunderstandings, farcical tear-jerking, absurd coincidences, discoveries of long-lost relatives, fantastic accidents that change the course of the action, eavesdroppers who pop up unexpectedly, and so on. When he is most Shavian, when the chorus of opposing voices and ideas is going full blast, he also turns on the repertory of old-fashioned stage devices. (For a fine example in *Man and Superman,* consider the scene near the end of the play, which begins with Ann Whitefield disillusioning Octavius and continues with her mother slyly insinuating that Tanner should marry Ann.) In such scenes, the audience, like Mrs. Whitefield and other naïve characters, gets an impression that what started as a reasonable world is now a mad one. But madness is essential in comedy, in Shaw no less than in Aristophanes and the Marx Brothers' films.

Madness in Shavian drama is expressed most characteristically in one of those exhilarating aria-like speeches in which the hero "tells the world," or in a throbbing duet in which two characters denounce each other or wildly proclaim a new life (as at the climax of *Major Barbara*). Granville Barker, the director and playwright, once said to the actors rehearsing a Shaw play, "Do remember, ladies and gentlemen, that this is Italian opera." There are in fact features of Shaw's plays that remind us of musical comedy and opera, as we have already suggested in observing the "interplay of voices" and the rhythmic form of the dialogue. Perhaps we might describe the peculiar blend of Shavian comedy as "*operatic* comedy of ideas." (Any such label is misleading, but, as Shaw said, "It is always necessary to overstate a case startlingly to make people sit up and listen to it.") Barker's remark is apt and points to a more or less conscious intention on Shaw's part. Certainly he was very sensitive to the way in which composers, Mozart in particular, used different voices to portray differences of character and social status. Writing as a music critic in 1893, he said:

If you look at the score of *Don Giovanni,* you will find three different male voices written for on the bass clef, and so treated as to leave no doubt that Mozart as he wrote the music, had a particular sort of voice for each part constantly in his head, and that one (Masetto's) was a rough peasant's bass, another (Leporello's) a ready, fluent, copious *basso cantante;* and the third a light fine baritone, the voice of a gentleman. I have heard public meetings addressed successively by an agricultural laborer's delegate, a representative of the skilled artisans, and a university man; and they have taught me what all the treatises on singing in the world could not about the Mozartian differentiation between Masetto, Leporello, and Don Giovanni.

This perceptive comment on Mozart gives us a hint as to how Shaw combined in a single art his love of "public meetings," of discussion of ideas, with his fondness for music drama. The form of comedy which resulted distinguishes Shaw's art from that of his contemporaries and that of earlier writers of comedy. But the reference to Mozart and his characters — types thoroughly familiar in eighteenth-century drama — may remind us that part of Shaw's originality lay in renewing traditions out of date in 1890. Though his characters seem so modern, beneath the names and new slogans we recognize older comic types: the pert servant who rules his masters, the pompous hero who is a fool, the officious mother bent on marrying off her daughters, the garrulous female who gets everything wrong, and so on. Shaw was familiar with these and similar characters in dramatists of the eighteenth century, such as Goldsmith and Sheridan, or Fielding (whom he greatly admired). These writers had inherited the tradition of the "comedy of manners" established in England by dramatists of the Restoration. (A "comedy of manners" reflects and ridicules the accepted modes of behavior, i.e., "the manners," of a particular society.) The characters of eighteenth-century comedy, like Shaw's, seem only two-dimensional if compared with the many-sided characters of Shakespeare, and they often seem to live to talk, to make a profession of wit.

In the popular sentimental drama of the 80's and the 90's the drawing room of the comedy of manners had been replaced by the Victorian parlor. But the audience had now been schooled to assume that the parlor and its inhabitants were accurate copies of their counterparts in the real world, whereas the eighteenth-century audience was more willing to regard the drawing room as an imaginary region where actors played out the game of wit. Many of Shaw's plays observe the conventions of popular parlor drama; on the surface they look like "trumpery plays of London life" (his phrase for *Man and Superman*). It was chiefly Ibsen (1828–1906), the Norwegian dramatist, who introduced a serious purpose into the writing of parlor dramas by focusing them on crises in the moral and social life of modern men and women. Although he accepted the realistic convention and though he was much influenced by Parisian dramatists with their insistence on neat construction, he made his scene a place where the most serious and most revolutionary views of personal and social morality could be presented. He showed Shaw and his contemporaries that the theater might express and help to shape the intellectual life of the audience. A drama might become a "discussion of ideas," as Shaw sometimes quite inadequately described his own plays.

But Shaw was a joker and a musician. He could "never resist a joke," and had been pleasantly corrupted by a taste for opera, the most absurd and least realistic of dramatic forms. Via opera he leaped easily back to eighteenth-century drama, with its simplified type-characters who exercise the art of witty conversation. But Shaw's more immediate inspiration was drawn from Mozart. (It should be noted, too, that the traditions of comedy and comic opera were very closely connected in the eighteenth century.) In Shaw, as in music drama, we have the constant sense that the stage is a stage and the actors quite free to step forward and sound off at length on any emotion or idea suggested by the situation. In opera, too, we expect the most preposterous and unlikely action: heroes who burst in at the window or come over the sea in ships, captures by brigand bands who live in the remote mountains, secrets of parentage suddenly revealed, and the like. (Shaw works these conventions for all they are worth, and then turns around and makes fun of them.) Finally there is in Shaw as in opera the extreme emphasis on a role as "a voice," rather than a person. Note, as evidence, Shaw's very exact directions as to the kind of voice required for each part. He maintains this operatic quality by his wonderful skill in molding the tones and rhythms of his speakers, in building up a strong sense of rhythm in whole speeches and in whole passages of the dialogue. That a man who was so obsessed with notions about society, with programs for improvement, who spent so much time in committees and meetings, should have created a dramatic style that was musical and not merely didactic, is one of the surprises of literary history.

## SOME LIVES OF G.B.S.

Shaw came to the theater and to his peculiar form of drama by a roundabout way. Before enjoying his first major success, with the 1905 performance of *Man and Superman,* he had already lived through a number of careers as a private person and a public figure. For a writer of comedy his beginning was not very auspicious — apart from the fact that he was born in Ireland (in Dublin, July 26, 1856). As he put it, he was "a downstart," the son of a respectable family that had come down in the world though still cherishing a sense of social importance. "I am a typical Irishman," Shaw once remarked. "My ancestors came from Yorkshire." In other words, he belonged to the English and Protestant governing class that had been much affected by Irish life while remaining oddly aloof from it. As Chesterton observed, Shaw owed to Ireland his asceticism and fear of physical passion, his hardness and clarity of mind, and his love of argument and speechmaking. His sense of being a "Complete Outsider" may be traced to his Protestant ancestry, or more particularly to his father, a failure in business and so terrible a drunkard that the family were cut off from decent society. The disgraceful father had an outrageous sense of humor that he indulged by mocking everything human and divine, to the delight of his equally skeptical son.

If Shaw's talent for comedy was "a Shavian inheritance," his musical gift came from his remarkable mother. A woman with a beautiful singing voice, she escaped from the horrors of life with her family by following a career as an opera singer and teacher. From hearing her performances Shaw acquired his passion for Mozart and his familiarity with the operas of the nineteenth-century repertoire. He early heard her sing one of the great roles in *Don Giovanni:*

> In my small-boyhood I by good luck had an opportunity of learning the Don thoroughly, and if it were only for the sense of the value of fine workmanship which I gained from it, I should still esteem that lesson the most important part of my education. Indeed, it educated me artistically in all sorts of ways. . . .

His formal schooling was often interrupted and included a brief period at a Wesleyan (Methodist) school and a briefer stay at a Roman Catholic one. He hated school and "learned nothing," except a distrust of efforts to force intellectual growth, a conviction that affected his own "teaching" as a pamphleteer and dramatist. His real education was in "whistling and singing," in reading "English literature from Bunyan to Byron and Dickens," and in roaming over the countryside near Dalkey, where his parents took him in summers.

At fifteen school ended, and Shaw's education as a critic of capitalistic society began with five years' dull service as a clerk and cashier in the office of a Dublin land agent. Although a highly satisfactory employee, he threw up his job and went to live with his mother in London, where he set about writing novels at the rate of exactly five pages per day. Between 1876 and 1883 he wrote five novels, none of which were accepted for publication in book form, though four came out serially. The first, appropriately entitled *Immaturity,* pictures a young man lost in London life but very sensitive to class distinctions and amusingly critical of cultural absurdities such as the current fad for the "aesthetic"[1] in art and dress. The last, *An Unsocial Socialist,* probably the first Marxist novel written in English, shows that the most important event in Shaw's intellectual history had taken place — his conversion to socialism.

Although he was "a born Communist and Iconoclast (or Quaker) without knowing it," he had not understood the reason for his dissatisfaction with society and his alienation from it, until he acquired "a clear comprehension of life in the light of an intelligible theory: in short, a religion. . . ." (He later evolved a religion of another sort.) Like Yeats,[2] Shaw's head was

[1] See p. 782. [2] See nn. 22 and 23, p. 808, below.

"full of Darwin and Tyndall," but he rejected the controversies they had fostered as "mere middle-class business" when "the importance of the economic basis dawned" on him. It "dawned" one night in 1882, when he heard a lecture by an American, Henry George, author of *Progress and Poverty* and proponent of the single-tax theory. He next read Marx and for a time was an active member of a Marxist society led by the high-minded and eloquent revolutionary, Henry M. Hyndman, the model for Tanner in *Man and Superman*. But Shaw soon broke with Hyndman and with orthodox Marxist economics and joined (1884) the new Fabian Society. Like the Roman general Fabius, who by his delaying tactics saved Rome from Hannibal, the Fabians aimed to reach their goal slowly and in the long run. They worked to bring in a socialist state by gradual changes, by infiltrating other parties and the existing government. They educated the British public in the theories of the welfare state, and they were largely responsible for the growth of the Labor party. The Society educated Shaw in practical politics and gave him the opportunity to become an expert public speaker and debater. The shy outsider now deliberately adopted the role of G.B.S., "Cool as a Cucumber," the marvelously witty and persuasive orator. "The cart and the trumpet for me," was now his cry, as speaker and writer.

He reached his most congenial platform, the theater, via the back door of criticism. For most of six years, 1888–94, Shaw delighted and horrified London newspaper readers with some of the best music criticism that has ever been written for the layman. With no fear of great names in the musical world, he reported ruthlessly and wittily on what he heard. If the prima donna was off pitch, or the conductor and singers were a half-measure apart, or if the piece had not been properly rehearsed, Shaw said so. "The true critic," he said, ". . . is the man who becomes your personal enemy on the sole provocation of a bad performance, and will only be appeased by good performances." When "appeased," Shaw would praise a great singer like Patti or a village musical society with equal enthusiasm. He campaigned for Mozart, at that time neglected and underestimated, and he led the fight to get Wagner's music heard and appreciated in England. He also wrote an enthusiastic book, *The Perfect Wagnerite,* in which he proved that Wagner was indeed the Perfect Revolutionist.

In his theatrical criticism Shaw carried on a similarly merciless campaign against star performers and fashionable playwrights. Shaw's hero in the theater was Ibsen, whom he defended against the violent attacks made by reviewers during the 80's and the 90's. *The Quintessence of Ibsenism,* in which Shaw summed up his case, is of importance here because it expresses most clearly Shaw's surprising view of "morality," a view that must be understood in reading *Man and Superman* and many other Shaw plays. By "morals" (or "ideals") Shaw means conventional, current standards. Because these standards are universal and inherited from the past, they often do not fit particular situations and present-day societies. Therefore good men — like some of Ibsen's characters — often choose to act "immorally," contrary to accepted morality. "Ibsen's attack on morality is a symptom of the revival of religion," that is, of a sense of individual moral responsibility. Shaw's own moral seriousness is that of the Biblical prophets and Bunyan, of men who summon their generation to act by a new and higher standard.

His first play, *Widowers' Houses* (1892), is just what one might expect from a man who had been exhorting Englishmen from the street corner and the newsstand to remake their society and to lead the good life. But it is not in a strict sense either a socialist or an Ibsenite drama. In fact, Shaw never wrote a play that had a socialist hero (in the admiring sense of the term) or that clearly and simply backed the setting-up of a collectivist state. In *Man and Superman,* for example, it is hard to say whether anarchists, socialists, or capitalists come out better. *Widowers' Houses,* if not a socialist tract, does remind the audience that it is nasty and wrong to live on the profits of slum housing. In the simplicity of this moral and in the exaggerated characterization, the play is nearer to Dickens than Ibsen. With *Arms and the Man* (1894), the true Shaw, the man with a purpose who is also a master of comedy, appears. The play expresses with musical gaiety the "view of romance as the great heresy to be swept off from art and life." The military hero of the play admits he is afraid in battle, while the girl who falls in love with him sheds her illusions about war and love. Shaw never struck a happier balance between seriousness of purpose and fun than in *Arms and the Man*. Here, at the outset of his career, the comedian and the philosopher are one.

Before tracing the shifting balance between these two selves in Shaw's principal comedies, we may look briefly at his later career outside the theater. In 1896, while working with the Fabians, Shaw met Charlotte Payne-Townsend, a woman of means and advanced views. Though much attracted, Shaw, like Tanner, did not rush into marriage. He did not marry Miss Townsend until two years later, after his future wife had nursed him through a long illness.

During the next twenty years, when he was not writing or rehearsing his plays, he was preparing them for the press, writing lengthy prefaces to them on topics such as married life and children (*Getting Married*), the superstitions of modern science (*The Doctor's Dilemma*), and the "true" nature of Christianity (*Androcles and the Lion*). One of the best, the Preface to *The Shewing-Up of Blanco Posnet,* was occasioned by the Censor's suppression of the play, which Shaw properly described as "a religious tract." Shaw's plea for decency in the theater and for responsible judgment rather than irresponsible censorship is the *Areopagitica* of the modern theater and should be read by all persons concerned with the present tendency to curb freedom of expression. In 1914 he infuriated and puzzled many by his pamphlet, *Common Sense about the War,* in which he oddly combined socialist analysis of the war — as a conflict between powers having similar militarist and capitalist aims — with the resolve to back England solidly in the actual fighting. In 1928 he published his most thorough exposition of socialist doctrine, *The Intelligent Woman's Guide to Socialism and Capitalism.*

In the 20's and 30's Shaw and his wife did a good deal of traveling, and finally in 1933 he came to the United States, where he delivered an address at the Metropolitan Opera House in New York, which was entitled (in England, only) "The Political Madhouse in America and Nearer Home." He continued to write plays, political pieces, and autobiographical sketches up to his death in 1950, at the age of ninety-four. Although he did not quite equal Methuselah, he did prove that the will to live was stronger in him than in most men.

## COMEDY AND IDEAS

Shaw has himself written the best defense and the best criticism of his plays in his comments on "art teaching," where he calls "attention to the fact that fine art is the only teacher except torture. . . . You cannot listen to a lesson or a sermon unless the teacher or the preacher is an artist. You cannot read the Bible if you have no sense of literary art. . . . To read a dull book; to listen to a tedious play or prosy sermon or lecture; to stare at uninteresting pictures or ugly buildings: nothing is more dreadful than this." Like Pope, he made war on dullness and ugliness; and, ironically enough, also like Pope, he could be monumentally dull when earnestness or controversy got the best of art. In his happiest mood, Shaw makes a play out of the play of ideas. Although he sometimes talks as if "ideas" and "art" were separable, this kind of talk will not do for a dramatist. He will succeed — and we shall listen — only when he has created a voice and an idiom and gestures that bring his ideas home to us, not as propositions but as dramatic presences. Failure to do so indicates more than a technical failure; it is a sign that the idea was itself limited, that it was less than human, that the writer could not live it out in any full sense.

But Shaw the comic poet — the Shaw we are concerned with here — had a peculiar and difficult problem. For the man, the Fabian socialist and reformer-orator, the iconoclastic critic of science, art, and religion, believed in his ideas, and was out to win converts to them. His avowed purpose, to judge from the prefaces to the plays, was to destroy inadequate views — say of marriage or government — and to put forward more rational theories and programs in their place. But there was also Shaw the born actor, the man of wit and lover of music, who had found his calling in the theater and who understood that "teaching" without "art" means boredom. As a comic poet his object was to combine both roles, to be an artist-philosopher in the drama. At his best, Shaw was able to satisfy his twofold aim and produce an integrated form of dramatic art, to make comedy out of his ideas.

As we consider some of his more important plays, from early to late in his career, we shall see that he did not always succeed in reaching his goal, that "ideas" sometimes got the better of "comedy." In most of the plays discussed, his success is notable, though some examples of difficulties and partial failures will appear.

When we speak of Shaw's "ideas" in the *plays* (as distinct from his critical works), we are using the term in a popular sense to cover all the varieties of opinion, theory, and belief that Shaw expresses. "Philosophy" when applied to an idea or group of ideas in the plays is an equally loose term, with one possible exception when used of the doctrine of the Life Force. In general, no coherent system of thought expressible in propositions arranged in strict logical order can be deduced from Shaw's plays. Happily for his audiences, Shaw had too keen a sense of the comic limitations of all points of view, including his *own*.

Knowing Shaw's lifelong mockery of the romantic conception of love and marriage, we are hardly surprised that in *Arms and the Man* he made drama and beautiful fun out of anti-romance. (The operatic quality of the play was recognized and overadvertised in a musical comedy version, *The Chocolate Soldier,* produced in 1908.) It is a surer sign of comic power when a dramatist of ideas takes as his subject a man representing some of his own favorite allegiances and presents him with such detachment and clarity as to make him amusing. In his next play, *Candida* (1894), Shaw depicts a type very much after his own heart, a socialist cleric, Morell, and exposes him to the ridicule of a terribly innocent young poet. The reduction of the hero is effected by typically Shavian means, *"the poet's boyish crudity of assertion telling sharply against Morell's oratory."* As the comedy ends, the poet departs with "a secret in his heart" unknown to Morell and his wife. The treatment of the poet — in contrast to Shaw's very sure handling of the cleric — is an example of how an inadequate idea is reflected in inadequate art. Shaw, as he repeatedly reveals in his plays and criticism, had a fairly crude notion of the inner life of an artist, and he shows it in *Candida* by filling his poet's mouth with second-rate Shelley. If he were content with ridicule, all might be well, but he isn't, and the result is sentimental. The play is most successful when it is most Shavian, when Shaw is exposing the limitations of Morell's moral and intellectual position. *Candida* has been much admired — in the present writer's view overadmired — for its un-Shavian qualities, the human and lifelike characterization of Candida and her husband.

No confusion and no embarrassing solemnity mar *The Devil's Disciple* (first performance in Albany, New York, 1897). It is a perfect play, the best possible introduction to the exhilarating dry light of the Shavian world. No work shows better how Shaw, like Shakespeare, takes threadbare stage conventions and makes something new out of them. On one level the play is pure melodrama, even to a last-minute rescue of the hero just as the clock is striking the hour for his hanging. It is also history, the action taking place in America at the time of Burgoyne's defeat. But what melodrama and what history! Shaw brilliantly misuses both to express values that are entirely his own, and yet he makes his points by dramatic means, using little direct statement. So the hero, a roistering rebel in a decadent Puritan community, saves the parson from hanging by giving himself up to the British. Although the parson's wife has fallen in love with the hero, he acts nobly not for love or for country, but because he "could not do" otherwise. That is "the law of his nature." Thus a parody of romantic drama comes around to a fundamentally romantic action, an action chosen by blind instinct, not by reasoning or by following some traditional moral or religious code. The hero is Shavian in still another way, one that anticipates later plays, notably *Man and Superman.* Although "the Devil's disciple," he is potentially a martyr and a saint, an illustration of "Diablonian ethics." In a society of perverted Christianity, in which hatred and joylessness have taken the place of love, he is against professed Christians and for the Devil. But his acts, which are generous and selfless, are recognizably Christian. Here in its simple and essential form is the Christianity which later plays and prefaces will elaborate, Shaw's belief in right action for its own sake, which he based on no clear theology but on the traditional Protestant appeal to the "inner light." *The Devil's Disciple* says all this in passing, through the hero's mocking speeches and daredevil gestures. The attack on an inadequate and outmoded form of belief and the advocacy of a new and better one are not separable from the melodramatic antics and half-heroic speechmaking. Shaw was never more successful in uniting an ideological attack with the fun and games of pseudo melodrama. Within a few years he would write plays that offer a richer variety of speakers and ideas (for example, *John Bull's Other Island*); but he rarely ever attained a happier blend of "art" with "teaching."

The play also shows that Shaw could exercise historical imagination and still be amusing. "Born," as he says, "in the seventeenth-century atmosphere of mid-nineteenth-century Ireland," he could appreciate the dourness and courage of the Puritan mind. Although *Caesar and Cleopatra* (1898) is fitted out with more archaeological apparatus, it does not take us so far into the past and is much less fun. If it is "better than Shakespeare" (a question Shaw raises), "better" means "better *for* us." Caesar is the vehicle for the message that revenge is futile, that the great man rises above its appeal.

But Shaw teaches us a similar lesson more delightfully in *Captain Brassbound's Conversion,* a play written merely to give a good part to an enchanting actress, Ellen Terry.[1] With her seemingly artless chitchat, the leading lady makes the bitter hero feel that the avenger's role is absurd. She also saves him from punishment for his high-handed actions by talk, talk that miraculously gets around some very ticklish legal and moral corners. Although the scene is laid in Morocco, the heroine establishes around her the comfortable and enlightened atmosphere of an English household, where life is a continuous parlor game of bright conversation.

In *Man and Superman* (1901–03), this type of conversational game is worked up into the more complex dramatic form we have already described, mainly by skillful introduction of more voices and more points of view. But as Shaw indicates in his subtitle, *A Comedy and a Philosophy,* he attached to the play views that he regarded as very important, the related doctrines of the Life Force and the Superman, which are expounded in the dream scene of Act III. This Force, a half-personified power at once reminiscent of a deity and a machine, is about as obviously comprehensible and as difficult to define as "Nature" in Pope's *Essay on Man.* It is a force, the very essence of life, working through man by an evolutionary process "to achieve higher and higher organization and completer self-consciousness." Also referred to as "the inner will of the world," it is very nearly a synonym for "Life: the force that ever strives to attain greater power of contemplating itself." In time the Force will produce a new kind of man, a Superman, "the philosophic man" who enjoys a supreme awareness of himself. One obvious manifestation of this power is sex, especially the impulse to beget children. Though the Force is "stupid" and though it seems to go on working regardless of what individuals do, Shaw insists that the philosophic man can discover it and manage it somewhat as we manage natural forces. Indeed, we can gradually breed the Superman by eugenic marriages.

These doctrines — which look dreadfully naked when exposed to flat, nondramatic treatment — have many sources, both in Shaw's experience as a reformer and in his reading of older and contemporary philosophers. His belief that society could be perfected only by the evolution of "the philosophic man . . . who seeks in contemplation to discover the inner will of the world," probably had its origin in the Fabian conviction that experts rather than the People must govern. The stress on the need for breeding Supermen reflects Shaw's loss of belief in the inevitable improvement of the whole population in a modern democratic society.

The notion of the Force as an inner will, a blind power working through man, Shaw adopted in part from the German philosopher, Schopenhauer (1788–1860), who found true reality in an impelling will that worked through each individual. Schopenhauer saw this power as the source of strife among men and reached the pessimistic conclusion that life was painful and to be lived only by limiting one's desires. But Shaw's cheerful belief in the independence of *his* personal will and his certainty that life is good made him regard the Force as making for higher intelligence and for justice in society. He found support for his hopes in Nietzsche,[2] who rejected the asceticism of Schopenhauer and who produced the dream of the Superman, a born leader of mankind, an aristocrat who scorned the masses. He was "beyond good and evil," that is, he was independent of the common

[1] See n. 8, p. 807, below.

[2] Friedrick W. Nietzsche (1844–1900), German philosopher. His greatest work, *Thus Spake Zarathustra* (1891), proclaimed the gospel of the Superman.

codes and particularly opposed to the gentleness and "weakness" of Christian morality. For Shaw the process by which we shall reach the Superman is biological and evolutionary, but he was influenced by thinkers who rejected the Darwinian concept of natural selection. Shaw found this theory objectionable because it seemed to make evolution of new species automatic and mechanical and to allow no place for mind or for the exercise of will. (It is exceedingly hard to tell where Shaw draws the line between the blind unconscious will and the individual conscious exercise of choice.) Shaw's evolutionary ideas are also partially indebted to the "creative evolution" theory of the French philosopher, Henri Bergson (1859–1941). The philosophic difficulties raised by the Life Force doctrine are obvious; for example, how is the seeming determinism of the theory consistent with Shaw's healthy assertion of freedom of the will? The essential faith that Shaw expresses through the doctrine is Arnoldian and religious, a belief in "the Eternal Power, not ourselves that makes for righteousness." (Shaw does not explicitly equate his Power with God, but he comes near to doing so.) The theoretical scaffolding—the talk of "force" and "inner will" and "evolution"—adds little proof and diminishes respect for a conviction otherwise noble and human.

The subtitle of *Man and Superman* is correct: *A Comedy* and *a Philosophy,* since the philosophy referred to, the theory of the Life Force, rarely gets into the comedy. Other ideas and attitudes do get into the drama, as we have seen from our study of the opening scene, whereas Don Juan's expositions of the Life Force lend support to the Philistine criticism of Shaw as being a preacher rather than a dramatist. But if we read the whole of Juan's part along with the responses of the Devil, we see that the preaching tone is usually undercut and that the ideas meet in dubious battle. What happened to comedy and to drama when Shaw had his eye only on philosophy can be seen in the waste stretches of *Back to Methuselah* (1921), where he attempts to provide a Genesis and a Revelation for his faith. Except when his scene moves into fantastic satire on actual English and Irish society, the prophet cries monotonously in a wilderness of words.

The true Shavian love of life comes out in *Man and Superman* in the energy and address of Shaw's debates and in the bounce of the more purely comic passages and scenes where personalities and the positions they symbolize are being brightly played off against one another. It is these qualities that made the public demand 176 performances of *Man and Superman* between 1904 and 1907. Shaw had now reached his dramatic maturity, and in the "operatic comedy of ideas" he had created a new form.

In 1904 he brought out a more perfect play of this same type, which established him as a financial success—*John Bull's Other Island.* Surprisingly enough—since the subject of the play was Ireland—it received the honor of a command performance attended by King Edward VII. More remarkable still, Shaw made out of this most topical subject a masterpiece, one of his purest and most sustained comedies. He was certainly never more resourceful in inventing situations and in orchestrating voices and roles. Take, for instance, the scene in which five different kinds of Irishmen and two kinds of Englishmen range over the sorrows and hopes of Ireland. Their mazy debate reaches a climax of high comedy in which a solemn Gladstonian Englishman, Broadbent, is chosen as the local candidate for parliament, though he is happily unaware of the reasons *why* he has been so honored.

But Broadbent is not a fool, and his English energy and know-how are seen to be necessary if Ireland is to solve her problems. There is in fact a breadth of vision in *John Bull's Other Island* rare in Shaw. For the most part he is content with the exclusive vision of comedy: he sees with relentless eye only the incongruous and illogical, and his stage is a well-lighted place, with few shadows suggesting uglier and more terrible responses to the human scene. But the unfrocked priest, Keegan, has a sense of evil that anticipates the disturbed old men of Shaw's later plays. Consider how he cross-examines Broadbent, who cheerfully "sees no evils in the world—except, of course, natural evils—that cannot be remedied by freedom, self-government, and English institutions":

> KEEGAN. You feel at home in the world, then?
> BROADBENT. Of course. Dont you?
> KEEGAN [*from the very depths of his nature*]. No.

There is more religious feeling here, more sense of mystery, than in Shaw's next play,

*Major Barbara,* with its militantly salvationist heroine. Like *The Doctor's Dilemma* (written a year later, 1906), it is a "problem" play and focused on a question involving personal conduct and a social need: "How can we save men's souls unless we have the economic power to save their bodies?" But while both of these plays have very amusing scenes, they mark no change in Shaw's comic technique. Something new and also prophetic of his later development appears with *Getting Married* (1908) and *Misalliance* (1910). Up until now Shaw had not broken completely with the conventions of popular parlor drama: his plays appeared to have some sort of "plot"; they moved toward an expected destination, a marriage, a rescue, or an exposure. They were often "operatic" in the sense of having the most preposterous and unexpected kinds of action. But in these two plays we have a whole drama made up only of operatic conversation, the play of voices and ideas almost unbroken by anything that "happens." (In *Misalliance* an airplane does fall from the sky to introduce an important character.) It was once fashionable to regard these pieces as unplayable, but the 1953 New York City Center production of *Misalliance* showed the absurdity of this view. It also proved what Shaw always insisted on, that his drama requires above all the most expert speaking style. If the performers forget the nonsense about acting like real people and come forward to "sing out" their parts with sure rhythm and timing and with tone that is dramatically appropriate, if not quite natural, the result is a unique experience of musical and ever-varying intellectual gymnastics. *Misalliance* may not be a play, but it is a successful piece of theatrical art.

Before Shaw's comedy moved further in the direction set by *Misalliance,* he wrote one more play in his earlier manner, the surest classic in his repertory, *Pygmalion* (1912). It is significant that his least didactic play is centered on the motif of the speaking voice. In *Pygmalion* a Cockney flower girl is transformed into a lady by a phonetics professor who teaches her to speak with an upper-class accent. The interplay of accents naturally evokes oppositions of personalities and manners and ultimately of ways of life, for Shaw makes speech the index of manners and of social and moral values. But changing a person's accent and manner is a revolutionary business. "Making life is making trouble," as Professor Higgins tells his pupil, Eliza. The "trouble" rebounds comically on Higgins (a knowing fellow like Tanner), when he finds that the girl is not a "block of wood," but a woman of feeling. With true Shavian independence, he rejects the possibility of falling in love with his creation, and she with equally fine disdain frees herself from her master and from all subservience to class. The closing dialogue of the play, in which Eliza and Higgins tell each other off and attain their pure if precarious freedom from sentiment and class, is perhaps the finest that Shaw ever wrote. Anyone who has watched a good actress play this scene — or who has the imagination to see and hear Eliza as she dances about the stage delivering the twists and turns of her attack with perfect balance between new cultivation and old coarseness — will know what is meant by the poetic art of Shaw. Borrowing Johnson's query to the critics of Pope, we may ask, "If this be not poetry, where is poetry to be found?"

With *Pygmalion* Shaw reached the end of his development as a writer who preserved at least the outward forms of parlor comedy. Eleven years later, in *Saint Joan,* he brought to its finish another type of Shavian drama, the heroic-historical, the kind of play first attempted years before in his tour de force on Napoleon, *The Man of Destiny* (1895), and of which *Caesar and Cleopatra* is a more perfect example. (*The Devil's Disciple* might be regarded as a parody of this type of drama.) But *Saint Joan* (1923) can hardly be treated in a discussion of comedy, though the play is one of highly ironic contrasts. Nor is it a tragedy, since it is not focused on the protagonist's situation but on a social and philosophic question: "How can a saint be fitted into a society?" An interesting comparison might be made between *Saint Joan* and Eliot's *Murder in the Cathedral,*[1] another dramatization of martyrdom and its relation to the modern world.

Shaw's early comedy and much of the early Shaw expired with World War I. During the three years following *Pygmalion* (1913–16), he was writing his obscure and yet often moving play, *Heartbreak House: A Fantasia in the Russian Manner on English Themes.* The freedom

[1] See p. 824.

of fancy and style and the musical analogy suggested by the subtitle indicate both change and continuity in Shaw's new mode. We at once feel a difference in the dialogue, for while Shaw has never etched roles more tellingly, bright neatness of speech is less common. Epigram is created, but the form of statement is less perfectly balanced: "People don't have their virtues and vices in sets: they have them anyhow: all mixed." (Mrs. Hushabye) The character who hears this does not cap it with one better, but says almost to herself, "I have a horrible fear that my heart is broken, but that heartbreak is not like what I thought it must be." The answer lacks the old Shavian symmetry of rhythmic pattern; the "music" is nearer to Stravinsky [1] than Mozart. The Shavian hero still stands alone, but now, standing in the isolation of madness, he eagerly tries to invent ways of exterminating the human race. This "Wild Old Wicked Man" [2] reminds us of the Lear-like figures of Yeats's later poems, and his world is a Waste Land [3] of twentieth-century despair. Although the play has many — perhaps too many — symbolic meanings, it expresses no distinct propositions of the older Shavian type. It is a "comedy," only in the sense in which we speak of the "bitter comedies" of Shakespeare.

Shaw did not follow this pattern with any consistency. He kicks up his heels again in the comic scenes of *Back to Methuselah* (1921) and much more entertainingly in *The Apple Cart* (1929). There is a slightly *non sequitur,* fantastic quality in these last plays that can be traced to *Heartbreak House,* but the bitter intensity is gone, and the control of dialogue is less sure. There are ideas enough — often familiar ones — and more than enough talk, but the balance, the "athletic joy," of *John Bull's Other Island* or *Pygmalion* belongs to another man and almost another century.

For the twentieth century that Shaw and the Fabians ushered in had run into another historical tide that would have seemed to the youthful Shaw not at all "advanced." Great wars and revolutions, the resurgence of primitive forms of violence and religious belief, and many other causes shattered the confidence of many in our ability to better ourselves and society by will and reason. In the period after World War I, literature reflects more often hopelessness and unreason or the longing for new faith. Yeats, as we shall see, while shocked by the "growing murderousness of the world," accepted and even welcomed the reaction against rationalism. In an interesting comparison of Yeats's prophetic book, *A Vision* [4] (1925) with Shaw's *Guide to Socialism and Capitalism* (1928), Edmund Wilson [5] says: "Here we can see unmistakably the differences between the kind of literature which was fashionable before the War and the kind which has been fashionable since." But though Shaw welcomed the advances achieved by consciously directed effort in managing the life of the human body and of the body politic, he was no cheerful eighteenth-century worshiper of Reason. He was on the contrary a sharp critic of simple trust in the miracles of science — either physical or political — and he put his faith in a determination that is deeply instinctive. *Heartbreak House* shows that he also knew what it was to have faith shaken.

But we must not turn Shaw into his opposite. His importance to his century and his more enduring value, we may prophesy, lie in his affirming the right to question, in his belief in the power of intelligence. Like Swift, though without Swift's terrible insight, his attack is a measure of his love of reason, but the scent of the Yahoo [6] is in his nostrils, too. There are unpleasant possibilities in Shaw's thought, as in Swift's: hatred of romance may conceal hatred of sex and marriage, planned societies may be planned tyrannies, the life of mere mind seems no life at all, and religion purified may seem to some no religion. Though few of Shaw's opinions are vicious, many are no longer fashionable or useful. We are just near enough to him to be annoyed by such differences, although we are able to overlook them in Ben Jonson or Shakespeare. As Shaw says in the Epistle to *Man and Superman,* his works will "have to stand," not by their "forms of thought," but "by quite amor-

1 Igor Stravinsky (1882– ), Russian composer, now an American citizen. Best known for his ballet scores, such as *Petrouchka* (1911) and *The Fire Bird* (1910). The dissonances of his music for *Le Sacre du Printemps* (*The Rite of Spring*) (1913) aroused violent demonstrations in Paris.

2 A poem by W. B. Yeats, pp. 803–04, below.

3 *The Waste Land,* a poem by T. S. Eliot, pp. 830–38, below.

4 See p. 788, below.

5 Edmund Wilson (b.1895), American critic and man of letters. Note also his essay on Shaw in the reading suggestions, below.

6 Swift, *Gulliver's Travels,* Part IV, pp. 705–37 in Vol. I.

phous qualities of temper and energy." But that is not quite the last word, because a writer's "temper and energy" reach us only through *formed* expression. The communication we call art is not "amorphous": "All the assertions get disproved sooner or later; and so we find the world full of a magnificent débris of artistic fossils, with the matter-of-fact credibility gone clean out of them, but the form still splendid." Steadily in a few plays, and by flashes in many, the "form" of Shavian comedy still shines out energetic and radiant.

## Reading Suggestions

WORKS BY SHAW

All the plays written before 1932 are included in the Ayot St. Lawrence Edition (1930–32).

*Autobiographical*

Preface to *Immaturity* (first edition, 1930).

Preface to *London Music in 1888–1889 as Heard by Corno di Bassetto* (1937).

Two very important accounts of Shaw's childhood and youth. Reprinted in *Bernard Shaw, Selected Prose,* edited by Diarmuid Russell (1952).

*Plays*

*Selected Plays of Bernard Shaw,* 3 vols. (1948). A reprint of twenty plays.

Penguin Books, Inc. (U.S.A.) has published: *Caesar and Cleopatra, Pygmalion, Saint Joan, Major Barbara, Androcles and the Lion, Arms and the Man, Candida, Man and Superman.*

Penguin Books, Ltd. (Great Britain) has published in addition to the above titles: *The Man of Destiny, You Never Can Tell* (both in *Plays Pleasant*); *The Devil's Disciple, Captain Brassbound's Conversion* (both in *Plays for Puritans*); *Plays Unpleasant* (which includes *Widowers' Houses, The Philanderer, Mrs Warren's Profession*); *Back to Methuselah.*

*Four Plays: Candida, Caesar and Cleopatra, Pygmalion, Heartbreak House,* with introduction by Louis Kronenberger (1953).

*Other Works*

*The Intelligent Woman's Guide to Socialism and Capitalism* (1928).

*Major Critical Essays* (1930). Contains "The Quintessence of Ibsenism," "The Perfect Wagnerite," "The Sanity of Art."

*Our Theatres in the Nineties* (1931). Shaw's weekly criticisms for *The Saturday Review,* 1895–98.

*The Prefaces of Bernard Shaw* (1934).

WORKS ABOUT SHAW

*Biographical*

Archibald Henderson, *Bernard Shaw, Playboy and Prophet* (1932). A complete and carefully documented biography (up to 1932), written by a fervent admirer.

Hesketh Pearson, *G.B.S., A Full Length Portrait* and *A Postscript* (1952). The two books, now published in one volume, survey the whole of Shaw's life. Pearson has written a series of collected impressions rather than a conventional biography, but he is less simply admiring than Henderson and presents a more balanced picture. Many amusing anecdotes and remarks are reported from conversations with Shaw.

*Critical*

Gilbert K. Chesterton, *George Bernard Shaw* (1910; 1935). Probably the nearest to a first-rate critical book on Shaw. An incisive portrait of the man and his mind, with fairly hasty literary criticism of the plays. Full of obvious prejudices and bright remarks.

Edmund Wilson, "Bernard Shaw at Eighty," in *The Triple Thinkers* (1938). A survey of Shaw's career, with some emphasis on his political thought, and an appreciation of his art. A good introductory essay.

Eric Bentley, *Bernard Shaw* (1947). A defense and a revaluation of Shaw's work as thinker and dramatist. For a reader familiar with the plays, useful as a help in arriving at a critical estimate. Good selected bibliography.

A. C. Ward, *Bernard Shaw* (1951). A handbook containing a life and brief comments on most of the plays and other works.

Louis Kronenberger, editor, *George Bernard Shaw; A Critical Survey* (1953).

FILMS

*Pygmalion* (1938), with Wendy Hiller and Leslie Howard.

*Major Barbara* (1941), with Wendy Hiller, Rex Harrison, and Sybil Thorndike.

Both films were produced by Gabriel Pascal, in consultation with Shaw.

RECORDINGS

*Don Juan in Hell,* Columbia, with the Drama Quartette: Charles Laughton, Sir Cedric Hardwicke, Charles Boyer, and Agnes Moorehead. Recording of the popular dramatic reading of the dream scene from *Man and Superman,* Act III.

Mozart, *Don Giovanni,* Victor, with Fritz Busch conducting the Glyndebourne Festival Orchestra. Nearly perfect singing by the famous Glyndebourne Opera of England.

# MAN AND SUPERMAN

## A Comedy and a Philosophy

*Man and Superman* might be described as "The Quintessence of Bernard Shaw." Certainly few of his works are more Shavian or more inclusive in the number of "Shaws" represented. First and foremost comes the master of operatic comedy, the creator of the peculiar form of vocal interplay, which, as we have seen, Shaw had learned from composers, singers, and street-corner orators. We see also in *Man and Superman* the writer of a popular comedy of manners, a play of "modern London life." But the story includes a "problem" that recalls Shaw's earlier interest in Ibsen, whom he now honors rather oddly by burlesquing New Women heroines. And in the Don Juan scenes, we see Shaw characteristically remaking the literature of the past to suit his own twentieth-century purposes.

But *Man and Superman* is also a comedy of ideas, of Shavian ideological bell ringing, and the thinker and the propagandist turn up in a wide variety of poses. There are expressions of an immense number of beliefs or theories about man in his social, political, and economic relations, about man as artist and philosopher, about man in relation to the universe. Many of these ideas are not Shaw's in a strict biographical sense. We can learn, for example, something from *Man and Superman* about the Womanly Woman, anarchism, and capitalism — ideals or ideas that were hardly dear to G.B.S. the man. Every position and every concept — with the possible exception of the Life Force — is exposed to the buffeting of rival positions and concepts. The fun of seeing ideas knocked about in this fashion is essentially Shavian.

In the admirable preface to the play, the "Epistle Dedicatory," we see Shaw in many of his other roles as man of letters. Here is the irreverent and admiring correspondent, the advertiser and defender of his own works, the critic of music and the theater, the theorist on art and literature. The preface is equally characteristic in another respect: it does not fit — it in part misrepresents — the work that is being introduced. In addressing his Epistle to the dramatic critic, A. B. Walkley, Shaw explains that he is writing a Don Juan play at Walkley's suggestion. Walkley may have been surprised by Shaw's also attributing to him the theme of the play: "You propound a certain social substance, sexual attraction to wit, for dramatic distillation; and I distil it for you." Readers of *Man and Superman* may feel equally surprised if they try to fit this statement to the orator-hero, Tanner, or to the heroine, Ann Whitefield, who is certainly resolved to get her man, but who makes fun of his wit and shows few signs of being sensuously responsive.

The interest of *Man and Superman* lies elsewhere, in the "comic excitement" that we have described in the Introduction. What we enjoy most is the interplay of voices and roles expressive of conflicting attitudes and ideas, for example, the noble speech of the Victorian protector of womanhood versus the insulting yaps of the iconoclast who asks for protection from women. As we move through the play we witness a series of scenes in which a male with "advanced" views gets his comeuppance from a female who looks reactionary but isn't. Even the socialist brigand, Mendoza, is reduced to maudlin versifying by thoughts of his beloved Louisa. Although many of the views ridiculed were revolutionary in the late Victorian era and though some are still regarded as subversive, the basic assumption on which the comedy depends — that the female pursues the male — is as old as the Garden of Eden and can be illustrated from many works of comedy and satire. The pursuing female has been depicted by writers as far apart in time and temperament as Shakespeare and Jane Austen. *Man and Superman,* like most of Shaw's comedies, has a place in the central tradition of comic literature.

The best way to get into the fun of *Man and Superman* — or of any Shaw play, as we have already suggested — is to read it aloud, to see how precisely Shaw has shaped idiom and rhythm so that we hear distinct persons expressing distinct attitudes. A good preparation for enjoying the play is to listen to a recording of Mozart's *Don Giovanni,* the greatest of all Don Juan dramas, the work that had the most direct influence on *Man and Superman.* Some familiarity with the opera is helpful in order to know what the legend and characters were like before Shaw took them over. It is also useful to have some measure for judging Shaw's account of his purposes as he describes them in his preface. A more important reason for listening to *Don Giovanni* is to get into the right frame of mind for approaching the play, to be ready for something like comic opera, rather than the kind of discussion drama suggested by the Superman myth. The opera, an acknowledged masterpiece, also offers an appropriate standard for evaluating *Man and Superman* as a work of art.

The story of *Don Giovanni,* as retold by Edward J. Dent, goes as follows:

In Mozart's opera Don Giovanni begins his adventures with Donna Anna; she refuses his advances, and her father, the Commendatore, who defends her honor, is killed by Don Giovanni in a duel. At a village wedding Don Giovanni attempts to seduce Zerlina, bride of the peasant Masetto, and the first act ends with a ball given to peasants by Don Giovanni during which he makes a more violent attempt on her virtue. In the first part of the second act he plays a cruel trick on Donna Elvira, a woman whom he has seduced long ago and deserted; she pursues him to Seville, and he disguises his servant Leporello in his own hat and cloak in order that he may pretend to make love to her and thus get her out of the way while Don Giovanni pursues other adventures. Lastly Don Giovanni, taking refuge in a cemetery, discovers the statue of the Commendatore and mockingly invites it to supper; the statue nods its head, accepts and finally appears at Don Giovanni's house, where it reproves the host for his vices. Devils rise from below and carry Don Giovanni off to punishment in the infernal regions, after which the other characters enter with the police to arrest Don Giovanni for the murder of the Commendatore. Leporello gives them a comic account of his master's end, and, as it is obviously too late for the police to take effective action, the survivors go their several ways.

Nothing except hearing Mozart's music can show what he made out of this commonplace plot. To anyone familiar with the opera Shaw's words will seem wonderfully apt:

> After Molière comes the artist-enchanter, the master beloved by masters, Mozart, revealing the hero's spirit in magical harmonies, elfin tones, and elate darting rhythms as of summer lightning made audible. Here you have freedom in love and in morality mocking exquisitely at slavery to them, and interesting you, attracting you, tempting you, inexplicably forcing you to range the hero with his enemy the statue on a transcendent plane, leaving the prudish daughter and her priggish lover on a crockery shelf below to live piously ever after.

But Shaw does justice to no more than one or two aspects of the opera. There is a range of emotional experience in *Don Giovanni* that can only be matched in Shakespearean tragedy, for example in *Antony and Cleopatra,* where we have a comparable blend of nobility and sensuousness and mocking gaiety. The "vicissitudes of passion," as Dr. Johnson might say, are astonishing in this Mozartean music drama — from melodramatic horror to lascivious wit, from innocent pathos to bedroom farce, from wine, women, and song to the grandeur of Christian damnation. Shaw never approached this varied and splendid art, except in a few pages of *Heartbreak House*. *Man and Superman* is a transcription of Mozart into simpler harmonies and a lower key.

Shaw discusses his borrowings from Mozart in the Epistle (pp. 700–01; 707–08), though, as often in his prefaces, he is talking in part of what he intended rather than what he performed. In the play proper (as distinct from the dialogue in Hell), the translation of the characters into modern types is quite complete. Only one, Octavius, the tender-hearted artist-lover, is "taken over unaltered from Mozart." In the opera, Ottavio, a friend of Don Giovanni, is the faithful suitor of Donna Anna and her constant supporter in her attempts to avenge her father's death. As one critic has said, he is a "sweet man," and like Octavius he is led by the nose from the first scene to the last. Violet, who is a combination of Zerlina and Elvira, instead of crying for vengeance, proudly proclaims that she is going to have a child. The other transformations of Mozart's characters, of Don Giovanni into the "political pamphleteer," Tanner, of Donna Anna into Ann, the modern Everywoman, and of Leporello into the New Man, Straker, are described quite accurately by Shaw. The Commendatore is barely recognizable in Roebuck Ramsden, the defender of Victorian propriety.

But in the Hell sequence the characters come much nearer to the aristocratic level of their Mozartean originals. The alteration in status is expressed through subtle alterations in dramatic tone. Note in the opening exchanges of the dialogue the politeness of Don Juan's way of addressing Donna Ana (Shaw's spelling; for this dialogue see p. 746), the use of correct titles, the sympathetic gestures, the leisurely balance of the rhythms. The insolence of Tanner is seen peering through the mask, but softened and refined. Donna Ana, like Ann Whitefield, speaks with directness, but it is the superior directness of a woman used to addressing her inferiors, not the brash candor of a woman among men. The "distinguished intonation" of the Statue is polite, almost regal, in contrast to the parliamentarian pomposity of Ramsden in the play:

> ANA. Father! Vanity! personal vanity! from you!
>
> THE STATUE. Ah, you outlived that weakness, my daughter: you must be nearly 80 by this time. I was cut off (by an accident) in my 64th year, and am considerably your junior in consequence. Besides, my child, in this place, what our libertine friend here would call the farce of parental wisdom is dropped. Regard me, I beg, as a fellow creature, not as a father.

The Devil is "perceptibly less well bred than the two other men," and the difference is heard immediately in the cheap form of his compliments, the chummy vulgarity of his address:

THE DEVIL [*heartily*]. Have I the pleasure of again receiving a visit from the illustrious Commander of Calatrava? [*Coldly*] Don Juan, your servant. [*Politely*] And a strange lady? My respects, Señora.

We remember unpleasantly that Mendoza, his counterpart in the play, is a waiter. The Devil is full of the inverted snobbery of manner of the English servant class. His "heart-warming" eloquence is adorned with the synthetic climaxes of the evangelist and the moral "uplift" orator:

THE DEVIL [*shaking his head*]. You flatter me, Señora; but you are mistaken. It is true that the world cannot get on without me; but it never gives me credit for that: in its heart it mistrusts and hates me. Its sympathies are all with misery, with poverty, with starvation of the body and of the heart. I call on it to sympathize with joy, with love, with happiness, with beauty—

In the earlier part of the dialogue Shaw maintains much of the same kind of comic excitement that he created in the best parts of the play proper. Ana and the Statue, Juan and the Devil, are lively dramatic "presences"; each seems really to respond to the satirical insults directed at him by the others; and if the characters express opinions of general intellectual interest, the opinions seem to belong to the person who utters them. Necessarily, there are fewer of the other sorts of complication which enriched the comedy of the play scenes, fewer farcical or melodramatic deceptions and surprises, fewer hits at contemporary manners. But while the dialogue is in these respects less like comic opera than the play, as it progresses it becomes more purely operatic in style, especially when the Devil and Don Juan launch into those tremendous speeches that are a cross between opera arias and satirical orations. The climaxes come in bravura bursts of oratory such as that of the Devil on music and horse racing (see pp. 750–51), or of Don Juan (see pp. 761–62) on the Devil's friends ("They are not clean: they are only shaved and starched. They are not dignified: they are only fashionably dressed. . . .") "Your flow of words is simply amazing," the Statue comments somewhat naïvely to Juan.

But it may be that Shaw's originality was his undoing. His power of making speeches, even very long ones, is admirable and dramatically justifiable so long as we hear a voice that we can distinguish as belonging to Don Juan or the Devil or the Statue. But when we hear a mechanical repetition of the same sentence patterns and when the verbal form of the paradox recurs so often that we can no longer register any meaning, then we begin to ask whether there is any dramatic illusion, whether all characters are one, and whether there is any genuine interplay of ideas. We may feel, when attention is focused on the single attitude or idea—say of Man as the self-destroyer (pp. 752–53)—that we are left with a platitude and that the sense of complexity which depended on the posing of various possibilities has disappeared. We may raise this question in another way by comparing this "Shavio-Socratic dialogue" (Shaw's term) with one of the dialogues of Plato—for example, the opening book of the *Republic,* or the *Euthyphro* (on holiness). How does Plato manage to illuminate a nobler concept of justice or of holiness without addressing the reader, without preaching, without sacrificing the dramatic character of Socrates? Is Shaw capable of that ultimate irony, that high sense of humor with which Plato regards even his most beautiful ideas? But Plato was a great poet, though he wrote in prose and though he condemned poets much as Shaw condemns pure artists. The reader of *Man and Superman* must decide for himself when and why the spirit of comic poetry vanishes from Shavian drama.

---

# EPISTLE DEDICATORY

To ARTHUR BINGHAM WALKLEY[1]

My dear Walkley

You once asked me why I did not write a Don Juan play. The levity with which you assumed this frightful responsibility has probably by this time enabled you to forget it; but the day of reckoning has arrived: here is your play! I say your play, because *qui facit per alium facit per se.*[2] Its profits, like its labor, belong to me: its morals, its manners, its philosophy, its influence on the young, are for you to

MAN AND SUPERMAN. **Epistle Dedicatory: 1. Walkley:** at this time (1903), dramatic critic of the *Times*, London. Fifteen years earlier, as Shaw says, Walkley was a colleague of his on the *Star*, a halfpenny newspaper, which the Fabian Society had more or less taken over and made a vehicle for their views. On Shaw's music criticism, see Intro., p. 687. The *Times* (first published in 1785; under the present name since 1788) has long been the leading paper in Great Britain. Though independent of party, it has had an enormous political influence and has generally been regarded as authoritative. The somewhat portentous style of the paper and the *Times* custom of publishing articles without signatures are referred to below. **2. *qui . . . se:*** "What a man does through another, he does through himself." (A man is legally responsible for his agent.)

justify. You were of mature age when you made the suggestion; and you knew your man. It is hardly fifteen years since, as twin pioneers of the New Journalism of that time, we two, cradled in the same new sheets, began an epoch in the criticism of the theatre and the opera house by making it the pretext for a propaganda of our own views of life. So you cannot plead ignorance of the character of the force you set in motion. You meant me to épater le bourgeois; and if he protests, I hereby refer him to you as the accountable party.

I warn you that if you attempt to repudiate your responsibility, I shall suspect you of finding the play too decorous for your taste. The fifteen years have made me older and graver. In you I can detect no such becoming change. Your levities and audacities are like the loves and comforts prayed for by Desdemona: they increase, even as your days do grow. No mere pioneering journal dares meddle with them now: the stately Times itself is alone sufficiently above suspicion to act as your chaperone; and even the Times must sometimes thank its stars that new plays are not produced every day, since after each such event its gravity is compromised, its platitude turned to epigram, its portentousness to wit, its propriety to elegance, and even its decorum into naughtiness by criticisms which the traditions of the paper do not allow you to sign at the end, but which you take care to sign with the most extravagant flourishes between the lines. I am not sure that this is not a portent of Revolution. In eighteenth century France the end was at hand when men bought the Encyclopedia [3] and found Diderot there. When I buy the Times and find you there, my prophetic ear catches a rattle of twentieth century tumbrils.

However, that is not my present anxiety. The question is, will you not be disappointed with a Don Juan play in which not one of that hero's *mille e tre* [4] adventures is brought upon the stage? To propitiate you, let me explain myself. You will retort that I never do anything else: it is your favorite jibe at me that what I call drama is nothing but explanation. But you must not expect me to adopt your inexplicable, fantastic, petulant, fastidious ways: you must take me as I am, a reasonable, patient, consistent, apologetic, laborious person, with the temperament of a schoolmaster and the pursuits of a vestryman. No doubt that literary knack of mine which happens to amuse the British public distracts attention from my character; but the character is there none the less, solid as bricks. I have a conscience; and conscience is always anxiously explanatory. You, on the contrary, feel that a man who discusses his conscience is much like a woman who discusses her modesty. The only moral force you condescend to parade is the force of your wit: the only demand you make in public is the demand of your artistic temperament for symmetry, elegance, style, grace, refinement, and the cleanliness which comes next to godliness if not before it. But my conscience is the genuine pulpit article: it annoys me to see people comfortable when they ought to be uncomfortable; and I insist on making them think in order to bring them to conviction of sin. If you dont like my preaching you must lump it. I really cannot help it.

In the preface to my Plays for Puritans I explained the predicament of our contemporary English drama, forced to deal almost exclusively with cases of sexual attraction, and yet forbidden to exhibit the incidents of that attraction or even to discuss its nature. Your suggestion that I should write a Don Juan play was virtually a challenge to me to treat this subject myself dramatically. The challenge was difficult enough to be worth accepting, because, when you come to think of it, though we have plenty of dramas with heroes and heroines who are in love and must accordingly marry or perish at the end of the play, or about people whose relations with one another have been complicated by the marriage laws, not to mention the looser sort of plays which trade on the tradition that illicit love affairs are at once vicious and delightful, we have no modern English plays in which the natural attraction of the sexes for one another is made the mainspring of the action. That is why we insist on beauty in our performers, differing herein from the countries our friend William Archer [5] holds up as examples of seriousness to our childish theatres. There the Juliets and Isoldes, the Romeos and Tristans, might be our mothers and fathers. Not so the English actress. The heroine she impersonates is not allowed to discuss the elemental relations of men and women: all her romantic twaddle about novelet-made love, all her purely legal dilemmas as to whether she

3. **Encyclopedia:** published 1751–65, edited by Diderot and d'Alembert; it exerted a revolutionary influence on the culture of Europe. 4. *mille e tre:* one thousand and three, the number of Don Juan's loves in Spain, according to the aria, "Madamina," sung by the Don's servant Leporello, in Mozart's *Don Giovanni*, I.ii.no. 4. (See Intro., p. 696.) All references are based on the edition of Boosey & Hawkes, Ltd., London.

5. **Archer:** William Archer (1856–1924), critic, translator of Ibsen, a champion of Continental drama.

was married or "betrayed," quite miss our hearts and worry our minds. To console ourselves we must just look at her. We do so; and her beauty feeds our starving emotions. Sometimes we grumble ungallantly at the lady because she does not act as well as she looks. But in a drama which, with all its preoccupation with sex, is really void of sexual interest, good looks are more desired than histrionic skill.

Let me press this point on you, since you are too clever to raise the fool's cry of paradox whenever I take hold of a stick by the right instead of the wrong end. Why are our occasional attempts to deal with the sex problem on the stage so repulsive and dreary that even those who are most determined that sex questions shall be held open and their discussion kept free, cannot pretend to relish these joyless attempts at social sanitation? Is it not because at bottom they are utterly sexless? What is the usual formula for such plays? [6] A woman has, on some past occasion, been brought into conflict with the law which regulates the relations of the sexes. A man, by falling in love with her, or marrying her, is brought into conflict with the social convention which discountenances the woman. Now the conflicts of individuals with law and convention can be dramatized like all other human conflicts; but they are purely judicial; and the fact that we are much more curious about the suppressed relations between the man and the woman than about the relations between both and our courts of law and private juries of matrons, produces that sensation of evasion, of dissatisfaction, of fundamental irrelevance, of shallowness, of useless disagreeableness, of total failure to edify and partial failure to interest, which is as familiar to you in the theatres as it was to me when I, too, frequented those uncomfortable buildings, and found our popular playwrights in the mind to (as they thought) emulate Ibsen.

I take it that when you asked me for a Don Juan play you did not want that sort of thing. Nobody does: the successes such plays sometimes obtain are due to the incidental conventional melodrama with which the experienced popular author instinctively saves himself from failure. But what did you want? Owing to your unfortunate habit — you now, I hope, feel its inconvenience — of not explaining yourself, I have had to discover this for myself. First, then, I have had to ask myself, what is a Don Juan? Vulgarly, a libertine. But your dislike of vulgarity is pushed to the length of a defect (universality of character is impossible without a share of vulgarity); and even if you could acquire the taste, you would find yourself overfed from ordinary sources without troubling me. So I took it that you demanded a Don Juan in the philosophic sense.

Philosophically, Don Juan is a man who, though gifted enough to be exceptionally capable of distinguishing between good and evil, follows his own instincts without regard to the common, statute, or canon law; and therefore, whilst gaining the ardent sympathy of our rebellious instincts (which are flattered by the brilliancies with which Don Juan associates them) finds himself in mortal conflict with existing institutions, and defends himself by fraud and force as unscrupulously as a farmer defends his crops by the same means against vermin. The prototypic Don Juan, invented early in the XVI century by a Spanish monk, was presented, according to the ideas of that time, as the enemy of God, the approach of whose vengeance is felt throughout the drama, growing in menace from minute to minute. No anxiety is caused on Don Juan's account by any minor antagonist: he easily eludes the police, temporal and spiritual; and when an indignant father seeks private redress with the sword, Don Juan kills him without an effort. Not until the slain father returns from heaven as the agent of God, in the form of his own statue, does he prevail against his slayer and cast him into hell. The moral is a monkish one: repent and reform now; for tomorrow it may be too late. This is really the only point on which Don Juan is sceptical; for he is a devout believer in an ultimate hell, and risks damnation only because, as he is young, it seems so far off that repentance can be postponed until he has amused himself to his heart's content.

But the lesson intended by an author is hardly ever the lesson the world chooses to learn from his book. What attracts and impresses us in El Burlador de Sevilla [7] is not the immediate urgency of repentance, but the heroism of daring to be the enemy of God. From Prometheus to my own Devil's Disciple, such enemies have always been popular. Don Juan became such a pet that the world could not bear his damnation. It reconciled him sentimentally to God in a second version, and clamored for his canonization for a whole century, thus treating him as English journalism has treated that comic foe of the

**6. plays:** A classic example of the type described by Shaw is *The Second Mrs. Tanqueray* (1893), by Sir Arthur Wing Pinero.

**7. El . . . Sevilla:** *The Seducer of Seville,* first dramatization of the Don Juan story, attributed to Tirso de Molina, pseudonym of Gabriel Téllez (1571–1648).

gods, Punch.[8] Molière's Don Juan [9] casts back to the original in point of impenitence; but in piety he falls off greatly. True, he also proposes to repent; but in what terms! "Oui, ma foi! il faut s'amender. Encore vingt ou trente ans de cette vie-ci, et puis nous songerons à nous." [10] After Molière comes the artist-enchanter, the master beloved by masters, Mozart, revealing the hero's spirit in magical harmonies, elfin tones, and elate darting rhythms as of summer lightning made audible. Here you have freedom in love and in morality mocking exquisitely at slavery to them, and interesting you, attracting you, tempting you, inexplicably forcing you to range the hero with his enemy the statue on a transcendent plane, leaving the prudish daughter and her priggish lover on a crockery shelf below to live piously ever after.

After these completed works Byron's fragment [11] does not count for much philosophically. Our vagabond libertines are no more interesting from that point of view than the sailor who has a wife in every port; and Byron's hero is, after all, only a vagabond libertine. And he is dumb: he does not discuss himself with a Sganarelle-Leporello [12] or with the fathers or brothers of his mistresses: he does not even, like Casanova,[13] tell his own story. In fact he is not a true Don Juan at all; for he is no more an enemy of God than any romantic and adventurous young sower of wild oats. Had you and I been in his place at his age, who knows whether we might not have done as he did, unless indeed your fastidiousness had saved you from the empress Catherine.[14] Byron was as little of a philosopher as Peter the Great: both were instances of that rare and useful, but unedifying variation, an energetic genius born without the prejudices or superstitions of his contemporaries. The resultant unscrupulous freedom of thought made Byron a bolder poet than Wordsworth just as it made Peter a bolder king than George III; but as it was, after all, only a negative qualification, it did not prevent Peter from being an appalling blackguard and an arrant poltroon, nor did it enable Byron to become a religious force like Shelley. Let us, then, leave Byron's Don Juan out of account. Mozart's is the last of the true Don Juans; for by the time he was of age, his cousin Faust had, in the hands of Goethe, taken his place and carried both his warfare and his reconciliation with the gods far beyond mere lovemaking into politics, high art, schemes for reclaiming new continents from the ocean, and recognition of an eternal womanly principle in the universe. Goethe's Faust and Mozart's Don Juan were the last words of the XVIII century on the subject; and by the time the polite critics of the XIX century, ignoring William Blake [15] as superficially as the XVIII had ignored Hogarth [16] or the XVII Bunyan, had got past the Dickens-Macaulay Dumas-Guizot stage and the Stendhal-Meredith-Turgenieff stage,[17] and were confronted with philosophic fiction by such pens as Ibsen's and Tolstoy's, Don Juan had changed his sex and become Doña Juana, breaking out of the Doll's House [18] and asserting herself as an individual instead of a mere item in a moral pageant.

Now it is all very well for you at the beginning of the XX century to ask me for a Don Juan play; but you will see from the foregoing survey that Don Juan is a full century out of date for you and for me; and if there are millions of less literate people who are still in the eighteenth century, have they not Molière and Mozart, upon whose art no human hand can improve? You would laugh at me if at this time of day I dealt in duels and ghosts and "womanly" women. As to mere libertinism, you would be the first to remind me that the Festin de Pierre of Molière is not a play for amorists, and that

**8. thus . . . Punch:** The hero of the traditional English puppet play, Punch is a rough fellow who beats and kills the heroine, Judy. In the original story, he killed Death and outsmarted the Devil. *Punch* is also the name of the English weekly devoted to humorous sketches and good-natured social and political satire. "English journalism" has thus further reduced the heroic role of the "comic foe of the gods." **9. Juan:** Molière's play, *Don Juan ou le Festin de Pierre* (1665). **10. "Oui . . . nous":** "Yes, upon my word, we must reform. Twenty or thirty years more of this life, and then we shall think of it" (*Don Juan,* IV.vii). **11. fragment:** Byron's *Don Juan* (1819–24), an uncompleted epic satire. **12. Sganarelle-Leporello:** Sganarelle is the name of Don Juan's servant in Molière's play. See also nn. 4, 9, above. **13. Casanova:** Venetian adventurer and writer (1725–98), a man of learning and taste, famed for his love affairs, author of *Memoirs* in which he "tells his own story." **14. Catherine:** Catherine the Great (1729–96), empress of Russia, an enlightened despot who had an immense number of lovers. Byron's Don Juan visits her court, and "Her majesty look'd down, the youth look'd up — / And so they fell in love" (*Don Juan,* IX.lxvii).

**15. ignoring . . . Blake:** Apparently Shaw means that the critics paid no attention to Blake's revolutionary views, in particular his criticism of traditional moral and religious concepts. In Blake's peculiar mythology, Urizen, the deviser of moral codes, is opposed by Orc, the archrebel (a sort of Shavian Don Juan). It is Urizen, not Satan, who is expelled from Heaven. **16. Hogarth:** William Hogarth (1697–1764), English painter, famous for several series of engravings satirizing eighteenth-century society, such as *The Rake's Progress, The Harlot's Progress,* and *Marriage à la Mode.* **17. Dickens . . . stage:** The "stages" referred to by this Shavian galaxy of nineteenth-century novelists and historians are apparently two phases of nineteenth-century realism in history and fiction, the first being more romantic; the second, more critical. **18. Doll's House:** Nora, the heroine of Ibsen's *A Doll's House* (1879), leaves her husband after "she sees that their whole family life has been a fiction: their home a mere doll's house in which they have been playing at ideal husband and father, wife and mother" (Shaw, *The Quintessence of Ibsenism*).

one bar of the voluptuous sentimentality of Gounod or Bizet would appear as a licentious stain on the score of Don Giovanni. Even the more abstract parts of the Don Juan play are dilapidated past use: for instance, Don Juan's supernatural antagonist hurled those who refuse to repent into lakes of burning brimstone, there to be tormented by devils with horns and tails. Of that antagonist, and of that conception of repentance, how much is left that could be used in a play by me dedicated to you? On the other hand, those forces of middle class public opinion which hardly existed for a Spanish nobleman in the days of the first Don Juan, are now triumphant everywhere. Civilized society is one huge bourgeoisie: no nobleman dares now shock his greengrocer. The women, " marchesane, principesse, cameriere, cittadine " [19] and all, are become equally dangerous: the sex is aggressive, powerful: when women are wronged they do not group themselves pathetically to sing " Protegga il giusto cielo ": [20] they grasp formidable legal and social weapons, and retaliate. Political parties are wrecked and public careers undone by a single indiscretion. A man had better have all the statues in London to supper with him, ugly as they are, than be brought to the bar of the Nonconformist Conscience by Donna Elvira.[21] Excommunication has become almost as serious a business as it was in the tenth century.

As a result, Man is no longer, like Don Juan, victor in the duel of sex. Whether he has ever really been may be doubted: at all events the enormous superiority of Woman's natural position in this matter is telling with greater and greater force. As to pulling the Nonconformist Conscience by the beard as Don Juan plucked the beard [22] of the Commandant's statue in the convent of San Francisco, that is out of the question nowadays: prudence and good manners alike forbid it to a hero with any mind. Besides, it is Don Juan's own beard that is in danger of plucking. Far from relapsing into hypocrisy, as Sganarelle feared, he has unexpectedly discovered a moral in his immorality. The growing recognition of his new point of view is heaping responsibility on him. His former jests he has had to take as seriously as I have had to take some of the jests of Mr W. S. Gilbert. His scepticism, once his least tolerated quality, has now triumphed so completely that he can no longer assert himself by witty negations, and must, to save himself from cipherdom, find an affirmative position. His thousand and three affairs of gallantry, after becoming, at most, two immature intrigues leading to sordid and prolonged complications and humiliations, have been discarded altogether as unworthy of his philosophic dignity and compromising to his newly acknowledged position as the founder of a school. Instead of pretending to read Ovid [23] he does actually read Schopenhauer and Nietzsche,[24] studies Westermarck,[25] and is concerned for the future of the race instead of for the freedom of his own instincts. Thus his profligacy and his daredevil airs have gone the way of his sword and mandoline into the rag shop of anachronisms and superstitions. In fact, he is now more Hamlet than Don Juan; for though the lines put into the actor's mouth to indicate to the pit that Hamlet is a philosopher are for the most part mere harmonious platitude which, with a little debasement of the word-music, would be properer to Pecksniff,[26] yet if you separate the real hero, inarticulate and unintelligible to himself except in flashes of inspiration, from the performer who has to talk at any cost through five acts; and if you also do what you must always do in Shakespear's tragedies: that is, dissect out the absurd sensational incidents and physical violences of the borrowed story from the genuine Shakespearian tissue, you will get a true Promethean foe of the gods, whose instinctive attitude towards women much resembles that to which Don Juan is now driven. From this point of view Hamlet was a developed Don Juan whom Shakespear palmed off as a reputable man just as he palmed poor Macbeth off as a murderer. Today the palming off is no longer necessary (at least on your plane and mine) because Don Juanism is no longer misunderstood as mere Casanovism. Don Juan himself is almost ascetic in his desire to avoid that misunderstanding; and so my attempt to bring him up to date by launching him as a modern Englishman into a modern English environment has

19. **"marchesane . . . cittadine":** "marchionesses, princesses, servant girls, city girls"; quoted from Leporello's catalogue of Don Juan's loves in Mozart's *Don Giovanni*. See n. 4, above. 20. **"Protegga . . . cielo":** "May righteous Heaven defend . . .," a phrase sung by Donna Anna in *Don Giovanni*, I.iv.no. 14. She is asking Heaven to punish Don Juan for killing her father, the Commandant (referred to in the next paragraph). 21. **Elvira:** a pious woman seduced by Don Juan, for Shaw a symbol of the puritanical morality of the Nonconformists (members of sects outside the Church of England). 22. **beard:** The beard of the statue is irreverently "plucked" by Don Juan in the cemetery of the convent of San Francisco (*Don Giovanni*, II.iii).

23. **Ovid:** referring especially to the Latin poet Ovid's *Ars Amatoria* (*The Art of Love*). 24. **Schopenhauer . . . Nietzsche:** See Intro., p. 690. 25. **Westermarck:** Edward A. Westermarck (1862–1939), authority on the history of morals and marriage customs. 26. **Pecksniff:** a hypocritical architect in Dickens' *Martin Chuzzlewit*, who was much given to "soothing reflections" on "mankind in general."

produced a figure superficially quite unlike the hero of Mozart.

And yet I have not the heart to disappoint you wholly of another glimpse of the Mozartian *dissoluto punito*[27] and his antagonist the statue. I feel sure you would like to know more of that statue — to draw him out when he is off duty, so to speak. To gratify you, I have resorted to the trick of the strolling theatrical manager who advertizes the pantomime of Sinbad the Sailor with a stock of second-hand picture posters designed for Ali Baba. He simply thrusts a few oil jars into the valley of diamonds, and so fulfils the promise held out by the hoardings to the public eye. I have adapted this easy device to our occasion by thrusting into my perfectly modern three-act play a totally extraneous act in which my hero, enchanted by the air of the Sierra, has a dream in which his Mozartian ancestor appears and philosophizes at great length in a Shavio-Socratic dialogue with the lady, the statue, and the devil.

But this pleasantry is not the essence of the play. Over this essence I have no control. You propound a certain social substance, sexual attraction to wit, for dramatic distillation; and I distil it for you. I do not adulterate the product with aphrodisiacs nor dilute it with romance and water; for I am merely executing your commission, not producing a popular play for the market. You must therefore (unless, like most wise men, you read the play first and the preface afterwards) prepare yourself to face a trumpery story of modern London life, a life in which, as you know, the ordinary man's main business is to get means to keep up the position and habits of a gentleman, and the ordinary woman's business is to get married. In 9,999 cases out of 10,000, you can count on their doing nothing, whether noble or base, that conflicts with these ends; and that assurance is what you rely on as their religion, their morality, their principles, their patriotism, their reputation, their honor and so forth.

On the whole, this is a sensible and satisfactory foundation for society. Money means nourishment and marriage means children; and that men should put nourishment first and women children first is, broadly speaking, the law of Nature and not the dictate of personal ambition. The secret of the prosaic man's success, such as it is, is the simplicity with which he pursues these ends: the secret of the artistic man's failure, such as that is, is the versatility with which he strays in all directions after secondary ideals. The artist is either a poet or a scallawag: as poet, he cannot see, as the prosaic man does, that chivalry is at bottom only romantic suicide: as scallawag, he cannot see that it does not pay to spunge and beg and lie and brag and neglect his person. Therefore do not misunderstand my plain statement of the fundamental constitution of London society as an Irishman's reproach to your nation. From the day I first set foot on this foreign soil I knew the value of the prosaic qualities of which Irishmen teach Englishmen to be ashamed as well as I knew the vanity of the poetic qualities of which Englishmen teach Irishmen to be proud. For the Irishman instinctively disparages the quality which makes the Englishman dangerous to him; and the Englishman instinctively flatters the fault that makes the Irishman harmless and amusing to him. What is wrong with the prosaic Englishman is what is wrong with the prosaic men of all countries: stupidity. The vitality which places nourishment and children first, heaven and hell a somewhat remote second, and the health of society as an organic whole nowhere, may muddle successfully through the comparatively tribal stages of gregariousness; but in nineteenth century nations and twentieth century commonwealths the resolve of every man to be rich at all costs, and of every woman to be married at all costs, must, without a highly scientific social organization, produce a ruinous development of poverty, celibacy, prostitution, infant mortality, adult degeneracy, and everything that wise men most dread. In short, there is no future for men, however brimming with crude vitality, who are neither intelligent nor politically educated enough to be Socialists. So do not misunderstand me in the other direction either: if I appreciate the vital qualities of the Englishman as I appreciate the vital qualities of the bee, I do not guarantee the Englishman against being, like the bee (or the Canaanite[28]) smoked out and unloaded of his honey by beings inferior to himself in simple acquisitiveness, combativeness, and fecundity, but superior to him in imagination and cunning.

The Don Juan play, however, is to deal with sexual attraction, and not with nutrition, and to deal with it in a society in which the serious business of sex is left by men to women, as the serious business of nutrition is left by women to men. That

27. *dissoluto punito:* "the libertine who is punished," a reference to Don Juan as portrayed in Mozart's opera.

28. **Canaanite:** inhabitant of Canaan, the Promised Land, "flowing with milk and honey," which the Israelites conquered. The Canaanites were at the time superior in culture to the Israelites.

the men, to protect themselves against a too aggressive prosecution of the women's business, have set up a feeble romantic convention that the initiative in sex business must always come from the man, is true; but the pretence is so shallow that even in the theatre, that last sanctuary of unreality, it imposes only on the inexperienced. In Shakespear's plays the woman always takes the initiative. In his problem plays and his popular plays alike the love interest is the interest of seeing the woman hunt the man down. She may do it by charming him, like Rosalind,[29] or by stratagem, like Mariana;[30] but in every case the relation between the woman and the man is the same: she is the pursuer and contriver, he the pursued and disposed of. When she is baffled, like Ophelia,[31] she goes mad and commits suicide; and the man goes straight from her funeral to a fencing match. No doubt Nature, with very young creatures, may save the woman the trouble of scheming: Prospero knows that he has only to throw Ferdinand and Miranda [32] together and they will mate like a pair of doves; and there is no need for Perdita to capture Florizel [33] as the lady doctor [34] in All's Well That Ends Well (an early Ibsenite heroine) captures Bertram. But the mature cases all illustrate the Shakespearian law. The one apparent exception, Petruchio,[35] is not a real one: he is most carefully characterized as a purely commercial matrimonial adventurer. Once he is assured that Katharine has money, he undertakes to marry her before he has seen her. In real life we find not only Petruchios, but Mantalinis [36] and Dobbins [37] who pursue women with appeals to their pity or jealousy or vanity, or cling to them in a romantically infatuated way. Such effeminates do not count in the world scheme: even Bunsby dropping like a fascinated bird into the jaws of Mrs MacStinger [38] is by comparison a true tragic object of pity and terror. I find in my own plays that Woman, projecting herself dramatically by my hands (a process over which I assure you I have no more real control than I have over my wife), behaves just as Woman did in the plays of Shakespear.

And so your Don Juan has come to birth as a stage projection of the tragi-comic love chase of the man by the woman; and my Don Juan is the quarry instead of the huntsman. Yet he is a true Don Juan, with a sense of reality that disables convention, defying to the last the fate which finally overtakes him. The woman's need of him to enable her to carry on Nature's most urgent work, does not prevail against him until his resistance gathers her energy to a climax at which she dares to throw away her customary exploitations of the conventional affectionate and dutiful poses, and claim him by natural right for a purpose that far transcends their mortal personal purposes.

Among the friends to whom I have read this play in manuscript are some of our own sex who are shocked at the "unscrupulousness," meaning the utter disregard of masculine fastidiousness, with which the woman pursues her purpose. It does not occur to them that if women were as fastidious as men, morally or physically, there would be an end of the race. Is there anything meaner than to throw necessary work upon other people and then disparage it as unworthy and indelicate. We laugh at the haughty American nation because it makes the Negro clean its boots and then proves the moral and physical inferiority of the Negro by the fact that he is a shoeblack; but we ourselves throw the whole drudgery of creation on one sex, and then imply that no female of any womanliness or delicacy would initiate any effort in that direction. There are no limits to male hypocrisy in this matter. No doubt there are moments when man's sexual immunities are made acutely humiliating to him. When the terrible moment of birth arrives, its supreme importance and its superhuman effort and peril, in which the father has no part, dwarf him into the meanest insignificance: he slinks out of the way of the humblest petticoat, happy if he be poor enough to be pushed out of the house to outface his ignominy by drunken rejoicings. But when the crisis is over he takes his revenge, swaggering as the breadwinner, and speaking of Woman's "sphere" with condescension, even with chivalry, as if the kitchen and the nursery were less important than the office in the city. When his swagger is exhausted he drivels into erotic poetry or sentimental uxoriousness; and the Tennysonian King Arthur posing at Guinevere becomes Don Quixote grovelling before Dulcinea.[39] You must admit that here Nature beats Comedy

29. **Rosalind:** in *As You Like It.* 30. **Mariana:** in *Measure for Measure.* 31. **Ophelia:** in *Hamlet.* 32. **Ferdinand . . . Miranda:** in *The Tempest.* 33. **Perdita . . . Florizel:** in *The Winter's Tale.* 34. **doctor:** Helena. 35. **Petruchio:** in *The Taming of the Shrew.* 36. **Mantalinis:** Mantalini, in Dickens' *Nicholas Nickleby*, a fop who lives on his wife's earnings. 37. **Dobbins:** Captain Dobbin, faithful lover of Amelia Sedley, in Thackeray's *Vanity Fair.* 38. **Bunsby . . . Mrs MacStinger:** in Dickens' *Dombey and Son.*

39. **Don Quixote . . . Dulcinea:** In Cervantes' novel, *Don Quixote de la Mancha*, the hero imagines himself to be a knight-errant and chooses as his ladylove a peasant girl, to whom he gives the highfalutin name, Dulcinea del Toboso.

out of the field: the wildest hominist or feminist farce is insipid after the most commonplace " slice of life." The pretence that women do not take the initiative is part of the farce. Why, the whole world is strewn with snares, traps, gins, and pitfalls for the capture of men by women. Give women the vote, and in five years there will be a crushing tax on bachelors. Men, on the other hand, attach penalties to marriage, depriving women of property, of the franchise, of the free use of their limbs, of that ancient symbol of immortality, the right to make oneself at home in the house of God by taking off the hat, of everything that he can force Woman to dispense with without compelling himself to dispense with her. All in vain. Woman must marry because the race must perish without her travail: if the risk of death and the certainty of pain, danger, and unutterable discomforts cannot deter her, slavery and swaddled ankles will not. And yet we assume that the force that carries women through all these perils and hardships, stops abashed before the primnesses of our behavior for young ladies. It is assumed that the woman must wait, motionless, until she is wooed. Nay, she often does wait motionless. That is how the spider waits for the fly. But the spider spins her web. And if the fly, like my hero, shews a strength that promises to extricate him, how swiftly does she abandon her pretence of passiveness, and openly fling coil after coil about him until he is secured for ever!

If the really impressive books and other art-works of the world were produced by ordinary men, they would express more fear of women's pursuit than love of their illusory beauty. But ordinary men cannot produce really impressive art-works. Those who can are men of genius: that is, men selected by Nature to carry on the work of building up an intellectual consciousness of her own instinctive purpose. Accordingly, we observe in the man of genius all the unscrupulousness and all the " self-sacrifice " (the two things are the same) of Woman. He will risk the stake and the cross; starve, when necessary, in a garret all his life; study women and live on their work and care as Darwin studied worms and lived upon sheep; work his nerves into rags without payment, a sublime altruist in his disregard of himself, an atrocious egotist in his disregard of others. Here Woman meets a purpose as impersonal, as irresistible as her own; and the clash is sometimes tragic. When it is complicated by the genius being a woman, then the game is one for a king of critics: your George Sand [40] becomes a mother to gain experience for the novelist and to develop her, and gobbles up men of genius, Chopins, Mussets and the like, as mere hors d'oeuvres.

I state the extreme case, of course; but what is true of the great man who incarnates the philosophic consciousness of Life and the woman who incarnates its fecundity, is true in some degree of all geniuses and all women. Hence it is that the world's books get written, its pictures painted, its statues modelled, its symphonies composed, by people who are free from the otherwise universal dominion of the tyranny of sex. Which leads us to the conclusion, astonishing to the vulgar, that art, instead of being before all things the expression of the normal sexual situation, is really the only department in which sex is a superseded and secondary power, with its consciousness so confused and its purpose so perverted, that its ideas are mere fantasy to common men. Whether the artist becomes poet or philosopher, moralist or founder of a religion, his sexual doctrine is nothing but a barren special pleading for pleasure, excitement, and knowledge when he is young, and for contemplative tranquillity when he is old and satiated. Romance and Asceticism, Amorism and Puritanism are equally unreal in the great Philistine world. The world shewn us in books, whether the books be confessed epics or professed gospels, or in codes, or in political orations, or in philosophic systems, is not the main world at all: it is only the self-consciousness of certain abnormal people who have the specific artistic talent and temperament. A serious matter this for you and me, because the man whose consciousness does not correspond to that of the majority is a madman; and the old habit of worshipping madmen is giving way to the new habit of locking them up. And since what we call education and culture is for the most part nothing but the substitution of reading for experience, of literature for life, of the obsolete fictitious for the contemporary real, education, as you no doubt observed at Oxford, destroys, by supplantation, every mind that is not strong enough to see through the imposture and to use the great Masters of Arts as what they really are and no more: that is, patentees of highly questionable methods of thinking, and manufacturers of highly questionable, and for the majority but half valid representations of life. The schoolboy who uses his Homer to throw

40. **Sand**: French novelist, mistress of "men of genius," including the composer Chopin and the poet Alfred de Musset.

at his fellow's head makes perhaps the safest and most rational use of him; and I observe with reassurance that you occasionally do the same, in your prime, with your Aristotle.

Fortunately for us, whose minds have been so overwhelmingly sophisticated by literature, what produces all these treatises and poems and scriptures of one sort or another is the struggle of Life to become divinely conscious of itself instead of blindly stumbling hither and thither in the line of least resistance. Hence there is a driving towards truth in all books on matters where the writer, though exceptionally gifted, is normally constituted, and has no private axe to grind. Copernicus had no motive for misleading his fellowmen as to the place of the sun in the solar system: he looked for it as honestly as a shepherd seeks his path in a mist. But Copernicus would not have written love stories scientifically. When it comes to sex relations, the man of genius does not share the common man's danger of capture, nor the woman of genius the common woman's overwhelming specialization. And that is why our scriptures and other art works, when they deal with love, turn from honest attempts at science in physics to romantic nonsense, erotic ecstasy, or the stern asceticism of satiety (" the road of excess leads to the palace of wisdom " said William Blake; for " you never know what is enough unless you know what is more than enough ").

There is a political aspect of this sex question which is too big for my comedy, and too momentous to be passed over without culpable frivolity. It is impossible to demonstrate that the initiative in sex transactions remains with Woman, and has been confirmed to her, so far, more and more by the suppression of rapine and discouragement of importunity, without being driven to very serious reflections on the fact that this initiative is politically the most important of all the initiatives, because our political experiment of democracy, the last refuge of cheap misgovernment, will ruin us if our citizens are ill bred.

When we two were born, this country was still dominated by a selected class bred by political marriages. The commercial class had not then completed the first twenty-five years of its new share of political power; and it was itself selected by money qualification, and bred, if not by political marriage, at least by a pretty rigorous class marriage. Aristocracy and plutocracy still furnish the figureheads of politics; but they are now dependent on the votes of the promiscuously bred masses. And this, if you please, at the very moment when the political problem, having suddenly ceased to mean a very limited and occasional interference, mostly by way of jobbing public appointments, in the mismanagement of a tight but parochial little island, with occasional meaningless prosecution of dynastic wars, has become the industrial reorganization of Britain, the construction of a practically international Commonwealth, and the partition of the whole of Africa and perhaps the whole of Asia by the civilized Powers. Can you believe that the people whose conceptions of society and conduct, whose power of attention and scope of interest, are measured by the British theatre as you know it today, can either handle this colossal task themselves, or understand and support the sort of mind and character that is (at least comparatively) capable of handling it? For remember: what our voters are in the pit and gallery they are also in the polling booth. We are all now under what Burke called " the hoofs of the swinish multitude." Burke's language gave great offence because the implied exceptions to its universal application made it a class insult; and it certainly was not for the pot to call the kettle black. The aristocracy he defended, in spite of the political marriages by which it tried to secure breeding for itself, had its mind undertrained by silly schoolmasters and governesses, its character corrupted by gratuitous luxury, its self-respect adulterated to complete spuriousness by flattery and flunkeyism. It is no better today and never will be any better: our very peasants have something morally hardier in them that culminates occasionally in a Bunyan, a Burns, or a Carlyle. But observe, this aristocracy, which was overpowered from 1832 to 1885 by the middle class, has come back to power by the votes of " the swinish multitude." Tom Paine[41] has triumphed over Edmund Burke; and the swine are now courted electors. How many of their own class have these electors sent to parliament? Hardly a dozen out of 670, and these only under the persuasion of conspicuous personal qualifications and popular eloquence. The multitude thus pronounces judgment on its own units: it admits itself unfit to govern, and will vote only for a man morphologically and generically transfigured by palatial residence and equipage, by transcendent tailoring, by the glamor of aristocratic

41. **Paine:** Thomas Paine (1737–1809), revolutionary writer, whose *Rights of Man* was published in reply to Edmund Burke's *Reflections on the Revolution in France.*

kinship. Well, we two know these transfigured persons, these college passmen,[42] these well groomed monocular Algys and Bobbies,[43] these cricketers to whom age brings golf instead of wisdom, these plutocratic products of "the nail and sarspan business as he got his money by." Do you know whether to laugh or cry at the notion that they, poor devils! will drive a team of continents as they drive a four-in-hand; turn a jostling anarchy of casual trade and speculation into an ordered productivity; and federate our colonies into a world-Power of the first magnitude? Give these people the most perfect political constitution and the soundest political program that benevolent omniscience can devise for them, and they will interpret it into mere fashionable folly or canting charity as infallibly as a savage converts the philosophical theology of a Scotch missionary into crude African idolatry.

I do not know whether you have any illusions left on the subject of education, progress, and so forth. I have none. Any pamphleteer can shew the way to better things; but when there is no will there is no way. My nurse was fond of remarking that you cannot make a silk purse out of a sow's ear; and the more I see of the efforts of our churches and universities and literary sages to raise the mass above its own level, the more convinced I am that my nurse was right. Progress can do nothing but make the most of us all as we are, and that most would clearly not be enough even if those who are already raised out of the lowest abysses would allow the others a chance. The bubble of Heredity has been pricked: the certainty that acquirements are negligible as elements in practical heredity has demolished the hopes of the educationists as well as the terrors of the degeneracy mongers; and we know now that there is no hereditary "governing class" any more than a hereditary hooliganism. We must either breed political capacity or be ruined by Democracy, which was forced on us by the failure of the older alternatives. Yet if Despotism failed only for want of a capable benevolent despot, what chance has Democracy, which requires a whole population of capable voters: that is, of political critics who, if they cannot govern in person for lack of spare energy or specific talent for administration, can at least recognize and appreciate capacity and benevolence in others, and so govern through capably benevolent representatives? Where are such voters to be found today? Nowhere. Plutocratic inbreeding has produced a weakness of character that is too timid to face the full stringency of a thoroughly competitive struggle for existence and too lazy and petty to organize the commonwealth co-operatively. Being cowards, we defeat natural selection under cover of philanthropy: being sluggards, we neglect artificial selection under cover of delicacy and morality.

Yet we must get an electorate of capable critics or collapse as Rome and Egypt collapsed. At this moment the Roman decadent phase of *panem et circenses*[44] is being inaugurated under our eyes. Our newspapers and melodramas are blustering about our imperial destiny; but our eyes and hearts turn eagerly to the American millionaire. As his hand goes down to his pocket, our fingers go up to the brims of our hats by instinct. Our ideal prosperity is not the prosperity of the industrial north, but the prosperity of the Isle of Wight, of Folkestone and Ramsgate,[45] of Nice and Monte Carlo. That is the only prosperity you see on the stage, where the workers are all footmen, parlourmaids, comic lodging-letters, and fashionable professional men, whilst the heroes and heroines are miraculously provided with unlimited dividends, and eat gratuitously, like the knights in Don Quixote's books of chivalry. The city papers prate of the competition of Bombay with Manchester and the like. The real competition is the competition of Regent Street with the Rue de Rivoli,[46] of Brighton and the south coast with the Riviera, for the spending money of the American Trusts. What is all this growing love of pageantry, this effusive loyalty, this officious rising and uncovering at a wave from a flag or a blast from a brass band? Imperialism? Not a bit of it. Obsequiousness, servility, cupidity roused by the prevailing smell of money. When Mr Carnegie rattled his millions in his pockets all England became one rapacious cringe. Only, when Rhodes (who had probably been reading my Socialism for Millionaires) left word that no idler was to inherit his estate, the bent backs straightened mistrustfully for a moment. Could it be that the Diamond King was no gentleman after all? However, it was easy to ignore a rich man's solecism. The ungentleman-

42. **college passmen:** refers to English university students who take an "ordinary" or "pass" degree instead of the more difficult honors degree. Compare the American undergraduate, who is satisfied with a "gentleman's C." 43. **monocular . . . Bobbies:** monocle-wearing young men of good society, Algernons and Roberts.

44. ***panem et circenses:*** "bread dole and circus shows," according to the satirist Juvenal, the only things that the Roman populace cared for. 45. **Isle . . . Ramsgate:** English seaside resorts. 46. **Regent . . . Rivoli:** Regent Street, London, and the Rue de Rivoli, Paris, both fashionable shopping streets.

ly clause was not mentioned again; and the backs soon bowed themselves back into their natural shape.

But I hear you asking me in alarm whether I have actually put all this tub thumping into a Don Juan comedy. I have not. I have only made my Don Juan a political pamphleteer, and given you his pamphlet in full by way of appendix.[47] You will find it at the end of the book. I am sorry to say that it is a common practice with romancers to announce their hero as a man of extraordinary genius, and then leave his works entirely to the reader's imagination; so that at the end of the book you whisper to yourself ruefully that but for the author's solemn preliminary assurance you should hardly have given the gentleman credit for ordinary good sense. You cannot accuse me of this pitiable barrenness, this feeble evasion. I not only tell you that my hero wrote a revolutionists' handbook: I give you the handbook at full length for your edification if you care to read it. And in that handbook you will find the politics of the sex question as I conceive Don Juan's descendant to understand them. Not that I disclaim the fullest responsibility for his opinions and for those of all my characters, pleasant and unpleasant. They are all right from their several points of view; and their points of view are, for the dramatic moment, mine also. This may puzzle the people who believe that there is such a thing as an absolutely right point of view, usually their own. It may seem to them that nobody who doubts this can be in a state of grace. However that may be, it is certainly true that nobody who agrees with them can possibly be a dramatist, or indeed anything else that turns upon a knowledge of mankind. Hence it has been pointed out that Shakespear had no conscience. Neither have I, in that sense.

You may, however, remind me that this digression of mine into politics was preceded by a very convincing demonstration that the artist never catches the point of view of the common man on the question of sex, because he is not in the same predicament. I first prove that anything I write on the relation of the sexes is sure to be misleading; and then I proceed to write a Don Juan play. Well, if you insist on asking me why I behave in this absurd way, I can only reply that you asked me to, and that in any case my treatment of the subject may be valid for the artist, amusing to the amateur, and at least intelligible and therefore possibly suggestive to the Philistine. Every man who records his illusions is providing data for the genuinely scientific psychology which the world still waits for. I plank down my view of the existing relations of men to women in the most highly civilized society for what it is worth. It is a view like any other view and no more, neither true nor false, but, I hope, a way of looking at the subject which throws into the familiar order of cause and effect a sufficient body of fact and experience to be interesting to you, if not to the playgoing public of London. I have certainly shewn little consideration for that public in this enterprise; but I know that it has the friendliest disposition towards you and me as far as it has any consciousness of our existence, and quite understands that what I write for you must pass at a considerable height over its simple romantic head. It will take my books as read and my genius for granted, trusting me to put forth work of such quality as shall bear out its verdict. So we may disport ourselves on our own plane to the top of our bent; and if any gentleman points out that neither this epistle dedicatory nor the dream of Don Juan in the third act of the ensuing comedy is suitable for immediate production at a popular theatre we need not contradict him. Napoleon provided Talma with a pit of kings, with what effect on Talma's[48] acting is not recorded. As for me, what I have always wanted is a pit of philosophers; and this is a play for such a pit.

I should make formal acknowledgment to the authors whom I have pillaged in the following pages if I could recollect them all. The theft of the brigand-poetaster from Sir Arthur Conan Doyle is deliberate; and the metamorphosis of Leporello into Enry Straker, motor engineer and New Man, is an intentional dramatic sketch of the contemporary embryo of Mr H. G. Wells's anticipation of the efficient engineering class[49] which will, he hopes, finally sweep the jabberers out of the way of civilization. Mr Barrie has also, whilst I am correcting my proofs, delighted London with a servant[50]

47. **appendix:** *The Revolutionist's Handbook and Pocket Companion,* by John Tanner, M.I.R.C. (Member of the Idle Rich Class), not reprinted in this anthology.

48. **Talma:** François Joseph Talma (1763–1826), French actor. In an English theater the "pit" refers to what is called the "orchestra" in the United States. "Pit" also is used as here to refer to the people who sit in that part of the theater. Napoleon bestowed kingships on his German allies and on his brothers.

49. **Wells's . . . class:** In *Anticipations of the Reaction of Mechanical and Scientific Progress upon Human Life and Thought* (1901), Wells (1866–1946) writes of "this new, great and expanding body of mechanics and engineers." Wells was an early socialist friend of Shaw's and for a time a fellow member of the Fabian Society.

50. **servant:** in *The Admirable Crichton* (1902).

who knows more than his masters. The conception of Mendoza Limited I trace back to a certain West Indian colonial secretary, who, at a period when he and I and Mr Sidney Webb [51] were sowing our political wild oats as a sort of Fabian Three Musketeers, without any prevision of the surprising respectability of the crop that followed, recommended Webb, the encyclopedic and inexhaustible, to form himself into a company for the benefit of the shareholders. Octavius I take over unaltered from Mozart; and I hereby authorize any actor who impersonates him, to sing "Dalla sua pace" [52] (if he can) at any convenient moment during the representation. Ann was suggested to me by the fifteenth century Dutch morality called Everyman, which Mr William Poel has lately resuscitated so triumphantly. I trust he will work that vein further, and recognize that Elizabethan Renascence fustian is no more bearable after medieval poesy than Scribe [53] after Ibsen. As I sat watching Everyman at the Charterhouse, I said to myself Why not Everywoman? Ann was the result: every woman is not Ann; but Ann is Everywoman.

That the author of Everyman was no mere artist, but an artist-philosopher, and that the artist-philosophers are the only sort of artists I take quite seriously, will be no news to you. Even Plato and Boswell, as the dramatists who invented Socrates and Dr Johnson, impress me more deeply than the romantic playwrights. Ever since, as a boy, I first breathed the air of the transcendental regions at a performance of Mozart's Zauberflöte,[54] I have been proof against the garish splendors and alcoholic excitements of the ordinary stage combinations of Tappertitian [55] romance with the police intelligence. Bunyan, Blake, Hogarth, and Turner (these four apart and above all the English classics), Goethe, Shelley, Schopenhauer, Wagner, Ibsen, Morris, Tolstoy, and Nietzsche [56] are among the writers whose peculiar sense of the world I recognize as more or less akin to my own. Mark the word peculiar. I read Dickens and Shakespear without shame or stint; but their pregnant observations and demonstrations of life are not co-ordinated into any philosophy or religion: on the contrary, Dickens's sentimental assumptions are violently contradicted by his observations; and Shakespear's pessimism is only his wounded humanity. Both have the specific genius of the fictionist and the common sympathies of human feeling and thought in pre-eminent degree. They are often saner and shrewder than the philosophers just as Sancho-Panza was often saner and shrewder than Don Quixote. They clear away vast masses of oppressive gravity by their sense of the ridiculous, which is at bottom a combination of sound moral judgment with lighthearted good humor. But they are concerned with the diversities of the world instead of with its unities: they are so irreligious that they exploit popular religion for professional purposes without delicacy or scruple (for example, Sydney Carton [57] and the ghost in Hamlet!): they are anarchical, and cannot balance their exposures of Angelo [58] and Dogberry,[59] Sir Leicester Dedlock [60] and Mr Tite Barnacle,[61] with any portrait of a prophet or a worthy leader: they have no constructive ideas: they regard those who have them as dangerous fanatics: in all their fictions there is no leading thought or inspiration for which any man could conceivably risk the spoiling of his hat in a shower, much less his life. Both are alike forced to borrow motives for the more strenuous actions of their personages from the common stockpot of melodramatic plots; so that Hamlet has to be stimulated by the prejudices of a policeman and Macbeth by the cupidities of a bushranger. Dickens, without the excuse of having to manufacture motives for Hamlets and Macbeths, superfluously punts his crew down the stream of his monthly parts by mechanical devices which I leave you to describe, my own memory being quite baffled by the simplest question as to Monks in Oliver Twist, or the long lost parentage of Smike,[62] or the relations between the Dorrit and Clennam families so inopportunely discovered by Monsieur Rigaud Blandois.[63] The truth is, the world was to

**51. Webb:** Sidney Webb (1859–1947), an English civil servant, a man of "encyclopedic" knowledge, particularly in economics and government. He and his wife, Beatrice Potter Webb, carried on a remarkable partnership in research and practical politics. Shaw brought Webb into the Fabian Society soon after he joined it in 1884. **52. "Dalla . . . pace":** "On her peace [mine depends]," aria sung by Don Ottavio (Octavius) in Mozart's *Don Giovanni*, I.iii.no. 11. It is a set piece, which Mozart inserted especially for the tenor part, and can be sung at almost "any convenient moment." **53. Scribe:** Augustin Eugène Scribe (1791–1861), writer of commonplace, highly successful comedies of middle-class life. He was one of the creators of the "well-made play." See Intro., p. 685. **54. Zauberflöte:** *The Magic Flute.* **55. Tappertitian:** adjective from Tapertit, an aspiring apprentice in Dickens' historical novel, *Barnaby Rudge.* **56. Bunyan . . . Nietzsche:** These writers, philosophers, painters, and musicians are cited by Shaw as examples of the "artist-philosopher" type he is here defining. **57. Carton:** in Dickens' *A Tale of Two Cities.* **58. Angelo:** in Shakespeare's *Measure for Measure.* **59. Dogberry:** in *Much Ado About Nothing.* **60. Dedlock:** in Dickens' *Bleak House.* **61. Barnacle:** in Dickens' *Little Dorrit.* **62. Smike:** in *Nicholas Nickleby.* Most of Dickens' novels were published in serial form in monthly installments, and they were written in "installments," too. **63. Dorrit . . . Blandois:** all characters in *Little Dorrit.*

Shakespear a great " stage of fools " on which he was utterly bewildered. He could see no sort of sense in living at all; and Dickens saved himself from the despair of the dream in The Chimes [64] by taking the world for granted and busying himself with its details. Neither of them could do anything with a serious positive character: they could place a human figure before you with perfect verisimilitude; but when the moment came for making it live and move, they found, unless it made them laugh, that they had a puppet on their hands, and had to invent some artificial external stimulus to make it work. This is what is the matter with Hamlet all through: he has no will except in his bursts of temper. Foolish Bardolaters make a virtue of this after their fashion: they declare that the play is the tragedy of irresolution; but all Shakespear's projections of the deepest humanity he knew have the same defect: their characters and manners are lifelike; but their actions are forced on them from without, and the external force is grotesquely inappropriate except when it is quite conventional, as in the case of Henry V. Falstaff is more vivid than any of these serious reflective characters, because he is self-acting: his motives are his own appetites and instincts and humors. Richard III, too, is delightful as the whimsical comedian who stops a funeral to make love to the corpse's son's widow; but when, in the next act, he is replaced by a stage villain who smothers babies and offs with people's heads, we are revolted at the imposture and repudiate the changeling. Faulconbridge,[65] Coriolanus, Leontes [66] are admirable descriptions of instinctive temperaments: indeed the play of Coriolanus is the greatest of Shakespear's comedies; but description is not philosophy; and comedy neither compromises the author nor reveals him. He must be judged by those characters into which he puts what he knows of himself, his Hamlets and Macbeths and Lears and Prosperos. If these characters are agonizing in a void about factitious melodramatic murders and revenges and the like, whilst the comic characters walk with their feet on solid ground, vivid and amusing, you know that the author has much to shew and nothing to teach. The comparison between Falstaff and Prospero is like the comparison between Micawber and David Copperfield. At the end of the book you know Micawber, whereas you only know what has happened to David, and are not interested enough in him to wonder what his politics or religion might be if anything so stupendous as a religious or political idea, or a general idea of any sort, were to occur to him. He is tolerable as a child; but he never becomes a man, and might be left out of his own biography altogether but for his usefulness as a stage confidant, a Horatio [67] or " Charles his friend ": what they call on the stage a feeder.

Now you cannot say this of the work of the artist-philosophers. You cannot say it, for instance, of The Pilgrim's Progress. Put your Shakespearian hero and coward, Henry V and Pistol [68] or Parolles,[69] beside Mr Valiant and Mr Fearing,[70] and you have a sudden revelation of the abyss that lies between the fashionable author who could see nothing in the world but personal aims and the tragedy of their disappointment or the comedy of their incongruity, and the field preacher who achieved virtue and courage by identifying himself with the purpose of the world as he understood it. The contrast is enormous: Bunyan's coward stirs your blood more than Shakespear's hero, who actually leaves you cold and secretly hostile. You suddenly see that Shakespear, with all his flashes and divinations, never understood virtue and courage, never conceived how any man who was not a fool could, like Bunyan's hero, look back from the brink of the river of death over the strife and labor of his pilgrimage, and say " yet do I not repent me "; or, with the panache of a millionaire, bequeath " my sword to him that shall succeed me in my pilgrimage, and my courage and skill to him that can get it." This is the true joy in life, the being used for a purpose recognized by yourself as a mighty one; the being thoroughly worn out before you are thrown on the scrap heap; the being a force of Nature instead of a feverish selfish little clod of ailments and grievances complaining that the world will not devote itself to making you happy. And also the only real tragedy in life is the being used by personally minded men for purposes which you recognize to be base. All the rest is at worst mere misfortune or mortality: this alone is misery, slavery, hell on earth; and the revolt against it is the only force that offers a man's work to the poor

64. **The Chimes:** Christmas book by Dickens, in which Toby Veck has a dream of terrible misfortunes falling on his daughter. 65. **Faulconbridge:** in *King John.* 66. **Leontes:** in *The Winter's Tale.*

67. **Horatio:** Hamlet's friend. 68. **Pistol:** a swaggering coward in *II Henry IV.* 69. **Parolles:** in *All's Well That Ends Well.* 70. **Mr Valiant . . . Mr Fearing:** characters in *The Pilgrim's Progress.*

artist, whom our personally minded rich people would so willingly employ as pander, buffoon, beauty monger, sentimentalizer and the like.

It may seem a long step from Bunyan to Nietzsche; but the difference between their conclusions is merely formal. Bunyan's perception that righteousness is filthy rags, his scorn for Mr Legality in the village of Morality, his defiance of the Church as the supplanter of religion, his insistence on courage as the virtue of virtues, his estimate of the career of the conventionally respectable and sensible Worldly Wiseman as no better at bottom than the life and death of Mr Badman: all this, expressed by Bunyan in the terms of a tinker's theology, is what Nietzsche has expressed in terms of post-Darwin, post-Schopenhauer philosophy; Wagner [71] in terms of polytheistic mythology; and Ibsen in terms of mid-XIX century Parisian dramaturgy. Nothing is new in these matters except their novelties: for instance, it is a novelty to call Justification by Faith "Wille," and Justification by Works "Vorstellung." The sole use of the novelty is that you and I buy and read Schopenhauer's treatise on Will and Representation when we should not dream of buying a set of sermons on Faith versus Works. At bottom the controversy is the same, and the dramatic results are the same. Bunyan makes no attempt to present his pilgrims as more sensible or better conducted than Mr Worldly Wiseman. Mr W. W.'s worst enemies, Mr Embezzler, Mr Never-go-to-Church-on-Sunday, Mr Bad Form, Mr Murderer, Mr Burglar, Mr Co-respondent, Mr Blackmailer, Mr Cad, Mr Drunkard, Mr Labor Agitator [72] and so forth, can read the Pilgrim's Progress without finding a word said against them; whereas the respectable people who snub them and put them in prison, such as Mr W. W. himself and his young friend Civility; Formalist and Hypocrisy; Wildhead, Inconsiderate, and Pragmatick (who were clearly young university men of good family and high feeding); that brisk lad Ignorance, Talkative, By-ends of Fairspeech and his mother-in-law Lady Feigning, and other reputable gentlemen and citizens, catch it very severely. Even Little Faith, though he gets to heaven at last, is given to understand that it served him right to be mobbed by the brothers Faint Heart, Mistrust, and Guilt, all three recognized members of respectable society and veritable pillars of the law. The whole allegory is a consistent attack on morality and respectability, without a word that one can remember against vice and crime. Exactly what is complained of in Nietzsche and Ibsen, is it not? And also exactly what would be complained of in all the literature which is great enough and old enough to have attained canonical rank, officially or unofficially, were it not that books are admitted to the canon by a compact which confesses their greatness in consideration of abrogating their meaning; so that the reverend rector can agree with the prophet Micah [73] as to his inspired style without being committed to any complicity in Micah's furiously Radical opinions. Why, even I, as I force myself, pen in hand, into recognition and civility, find all the force of my onslaught destroyed by a simple policy of nonresistance. In vain do I redouble the violence of the language in which I proclaim my heterodoxies. I rail at the theistic credulity of Voltaire,[74] the amoristic superstition of Shelley,[75] the revival of tribal soothsaying and idolatrous rites which Huxley [76] called Science and mistook for an advance on the Pentateuch, no less than at the welter of ecclesiastical and professional humbug which saves the face of the stupid system of violence and robbery which we call Law and Industry. Even atheists reproach me with infidelity and anarchists with nihilism because I cannot endure their moral tirades. And yet, instead of exclaiming "Send this inconceivable Satanist to the stake," the respectable newspapers pith me by announcing "another book by this brilliant and thoughtful writer." And the ordinary citizen, knowing that an author who is well spoken of by a respectable newspaper must be all right, reads me, as he reads Micah, with undisturbed edification from his own point of view. It is narrated that in the eighteenseventies an old lady, a very devout Methodist, moved from Colchester to a house in the neighborhood of the City Road, in London, where, mistaking the Hall of Science for a chapel, she sat at the feet of Charles

71. **Wagner**: in his opera cycle, *The Nibelung's Ring.* See Shaw's *The Perfect Wagnerite* for an account of the ideas dramatized by Wagner. 72. **Mr Embezzler . . . Mr . . . Agitator**: This group of allegorical characters, *not* to be found in *Pilgrim's Progress*, are invented by Shaw as examples of "vicious and criminal" persons in modern society. Shaw is here displaying his usual attitude toward conventional "morality" and "idealism." (See Intro., p. 687.) He asserts that Bunyan did not attack "vice and crime," but hypocritical pretensions to virtue, which passed for "morality" in his society as they do in ours. 73. **Micah**: Old Testament prophet who condemned the Israelites for their social injustice and hypocritical worship. 74. **Voltaire**: Though a skeptic in philosophy and highly critical of orthodox Christianity, Voltaire was a deist and advocated a belief in a supreme being. 75. **amoristic . . . Shelley**: referring to Shelley's belief in the power of love to transform man's moral nature. 76. **Huxley**: English biologist. See n. 22, p. 808. For Shaw's views on science worship, see Intro., p. 688.

Bradlaugh[77] for many years, entranced by his eloquence, without questioning his orthodoxy or moulting a feather of her faith. I fear I shall be defrauded of my just martyrdom in the same way.

However, I am digressing, as a man with a grievance always does. And after all, the main thing in determining the artistic quality of a book is not the opinions it propagates, but the fact that the writer has opinions. The old lady from Colchester was right to sun her simple soul in the energetic radiance of Bradlaugh's genuine beliefs and disbeliefs rather than in the chill of such mere painting of light and heat as elocution and convention can achieve. My contempt for *belles lettres,* and for amateurs who become the heroes of the fanciers of literary virtuosity, is not founded on any illusion of mine as to the permanence of those forms of thought (call them opinions) by which I strive to communicate my bent to my fellows. To younger men they are already outmoded; for though they have no more lost their logic than an eighteenth century pastel has lost its drawing or its color, yet, like the pastel, they grow indefinably shabby, will grow shabbier until they cease to count at all, when my books will either perish, or, if the world is still poor enough to want them, will have to stand, with Bunyan's, by quite amorphous qualities of temper and energy. With this conviction I cannot be a bellettrist. No doubt I must recognize, as even the Ancient Mariner did, that I must tell my story entertainingly if I am to hold the wedding guest spellbound in spite of the siren sounds of the loud bassoon. But "for art's sake" alone I would not face the toil of writing a single sentence. I know that there are men who, having nothing to say and nothing to write, are nevertheless so in love with oratory and with literature that they delight in repeating as much as they can understand of what others have said or written aforetime. I know that the leisurely tricks which their want of conviction leaves them free to play with the diluted and misapprehended message supply them with a pleasant parlor game which they call style. I can pity their dotage and even sympathize with their fancy. But a true original style is never achieved for its own sake: a man may pay from a shilling to a guinea, according to his means, to see, hear, or read another man's act of genius; but he will not pay with his whole life and soul to become a mere virtuoso in literature, exhibiting an accomplishment which will not even make money for him, like fiddle playing. Effectiveness of assertion is the Alpha and Omega of style. He who has nothing to assert has no style and can have none: he who has something to assert will go as far in power of style as its momentousness and his conviction will carry him. Disprove his assertion after it is made, yet its style remains. Darwin has no more destroyed the style of Job nor of Handel than Martin Luther destroyed the style of Giotto.[78] All the assertions get disproved sooner or later; and so we find the world full of a magnificent débris of artistic fossils, with the matter-of-fact credibility gone clean out of them, but the form still splendid. And that is why the old masters play the deuce with our mere susceptibles. Your Royal Academician thinks he can get the style of Giotto without Giotto's beliefs, and correct his perspective into the bargain. Your man of letters thinks he can get Bunyan's or Shakespear's style without Bunyan's conviction or Shakespear's apprehension, especially if he takes care not to split his infinitives. And so with your Doctors of Music, who, with their collections of discords duly prepared and resolved or retarded or anticipated in the manner of the great composers, think they can learn the art of Palestrina[79] from Cherubini's[80] treatise. All this academic art is far worse than the trade in sham antique furniture; for the man who sells me an oaken chest which he swears was made in the XIII century, though as a matter of fact he made it himself only yesterday, at least does not pretend that there are any modern ideas in it; whereas your academic copier of fossils offers them to you as the latest outpouring of the human spirit, and, worst of all, kidnaps young people as pupils and persuades them that his limitations are rules, his observances dexterities, his timidities good taste, and his emptinesses purities. And when he declares that art should not be didactic, all the people who have nothing to teach and all the people who dont want to learn agree with him emphatically.

I pride myself on not being one of these sus-

**77. Bradlaugh:** Bradlaugh (1833–91) was a social reformer and an advocate of free thought.

**78. Giotto:** Florentine painter (*c.* 1266–*c.* 1337), who broke away from the rigid Byzantine style of his predecessors and introduced a sense of more natural movement in his representation of the human figure. The reverence and the certainty of his faith are evident in all his work, particularly in the frescoes of the churches at Assisi and Padua. Luther, a leader in the Reformation, might be thought of as having "destroyed" medieval Christianity. **79. Palestrina:** Palestrina (*c.* 1525–94), great composer of church music. **80. Cherubini:** Cherubini (1760–1842), who wrote a treatise on Palestrina, composed church music in a similar polyphonic style.

ceptibles. If you study the electric light with which I supply you in that Bumbledonian [81] public capacity of mine over which you make merry from time to time, you will find that your house contains a great quantity of highly susceptible copper wire which gorges itself with electricity and gives you no light whatever. But here and there occurs a scrap of intensely insusceptible, intensely resistant material; and that stubborn scrap grapples with the current and will not let it through until it has made itself useful to you as those two vital qualities of literature, light and heat. Now if I am to be no mere copper wire amateur but a luminous author, I must also be a most intensely refractory person, liable to go out and to go wrong at inconvenient moments, and with incendiary possibilities. These are the faults of my qualities; and I assure you that I sometimes dislike myself so much that when some irritable reviewer chances at that moment to pitch into me with zest, I feel unspeakably relieved and obliged. But I never dream of reforming, knowing that I must take myself as I am and get what work I can out of myself. All this you will understand; for there is community of material between us: we are both critics of life as well as of art; and you have perhaps said to yourself when I have passed your windows "There, but for the grace of God, go I." An awful and chastening reflection, which shall be the closing cadence of this immoderately long letter from yours faithfully,

G. Bernard Shaw.

Woking, 1903.

**81. Bumbledonian:** from Bumble, an officious and domineering beadle (inferior parish officer) in charge of the workshop in Dickens' *Oliver Twist.*

*P.S.*—Amid unprecedented critical cerebration over this book of ours—alas! that your own voice should be dedicated to silence!—I find myself warned to prepare a new edition. I take the opportunity to correct a slip or two. You may have noticed (nobody else has, by the way) that I fitted you with a quotation from Othello, and then unconsciously referred it to A Winter's Tale. I correct this with regret; for half its appropriateness goes with Florizel and Perdita: still, one must not trifle with Shakespear; so I have given Desdemona [82] back her property.

On the whole, the book has done very well. The strong critics are impressed; the weak intimidated; the connoisseurs tickled by my literary bravura (put in to please you): the humorists alone, oddly enough, sermonize me, scared out of their profession into the quaintest tumults of conscience. Not all my reviewers have understood me: like Englishmen in France, confidently uttering their own island diphthongs as good French vowels, many of them offer, as samples of the Shavian philosophy, the likest article from their own stock. Others are the victims of association of ideas: they call me Pessimist because my remarks wound their self-complacency, and Renegade because I would have my mob all Caesars instead of Toms, Dicks, and Harrys. Worst of all, I have been accused of preaching a Final Ethical Superman: no other, in fact, than our old friend the Just Man Made Perfect! This misunderstanding is so galling that I lay down my pen without another word lest I should be tempted to make the postscript longer even than the letter.

**82. Desdemona:** See *Othello,* II.i.193–95. The corrected quotation appears in the second paragraph of the Epistle, above.

# Man and Superman

## Act I

*Roebuck Ramsden is in his study, opening the morning's letters. The study, handsomely and solidly furnished, proclaims the man of means. Not a speck of dust is visible: it is clear that there are at least two housemaids and a parlormaid downstairs, and a housekeeper upstairs who does not let them spare elbow-grease. Even the top of Roebuck's head is polished: on a sunshiny day he could heliograph his orders to distant camps by merely nodding. In no other respect, however, does he suggest the military man. It is in active civil life that men get his broad air of importance, his dignified expectation of deference, his determinate mouth disarmed and refined since the hour of his success by the withdrawal of opposition and the concession of comfort and precedence and power. He is more than a highly respectable man: he is marked out as a president of highly respectable men, a chairman among directors, an alderman among councillors, a mayor among aldermen. Four tufts of iron-grey hair, which will soon be as white as isinglass, and are in other respects not at all unlike it, grow in two symmetrical pairs above his ears and at the angles of his spreading jaws. He wears a black frock coat, a white waistcoat (it is bright spring weather), and trousers, neither black nor perceptibly blue, of one of those indefinitely mixed hues which the modern clothier has produced to harmonize with the religions of respectable men. He has not been out of doors yet today; so he still wears his slippers, his boots being ready for him on the hearthrug. Surmising that he has no valet, and seeing that he has no secretary with a shorthand notebook and a typewriter, one meditates on how little our great burgess domesticity has been disturbed by new fashions and methods, or by the enterprise of the railway and hotel companies which sell you a Saturday to Monday of life at Folkestone as a real gentleman for two guineas, first class fares both ways included.*

*How old is Roebuck? The question is important on the threshold of a drama of ideas; for under such circumstances everything depends on whether his adolescence belonged to the sixties or to the eighties. He was born, as a matter of fact, in 1839, and was a Unitarian and Free Trader from his boyhood, and an Evolutionist from the publication of the Origin of Species.*[1] *Consequently he has always classed himself as an advanced thinker and fearlessly outspoken reformer.*

*Sitting at his writing table, he has on his right the windows giving on Portland Place. Through these, as through a proscenium, the curious spectator may contemplate his profile as well as the blinds will permit. On his left is the inner wall, with a stately bookcase, and the door not quite in the middle, but somewhat further from him. Against the wall opposite him are two busts on pillars: one, to his left, of John Bright,*[2] *the other, to his right, of Mr Herbert Spencer.*[3] *Between them hang an engraved portrait of Richard Cobden;*[4] *enlarged photographs of Martineau,*[5] *Huxley, and George Eliot; autotypes of allegories by Mr G. F. Watts*[6] *(for Roebuck believes in the fine arts with all the earnestness of a man who does not understand them), and an impression of Dupont's engraving of Delaroche's*[7] *Beaux Arts hemicycle, representing the great men of all ages. On the wall behind him, above the mantel-shelf, is a family portrait of impenetrable obscurity.*

*A chair stands near the writing table for the convenience of business visitors. Two other chairs are against the wall between the busts.*

*A parlormaid enters with a visitor's card. Roebuck takes it, and nods, pleased. Evidently a welcome caller.*

RAMSDEN. Shew him in.

*The parlormaid goes out and returns with the visitor.*

THE MAID. Mr Robinson.

*Mr Robinson is really an uncommonly nice look-*

Act I: 1. ***Origin of Species:*** by Charles Darwin, published in 1859. 2. ***Bright:*** John Bright (1811–89), statesman of the nineteenth-century English "liberal" type, a free-trader, an advocate of laissez-faire economics, and an active fighter for the repeal of the Corn Laws. Bright and the other figures named here are representative of "advanced" views and tastes of the intellectual leaders in Ramsden's youth. 3. ***Spencer:*** Herbert Spencer (1820–1903), a philosopher who based much of his thinking on the doctrine of evolution. 4. ***Cobden:*** Richard Cobden (1804–65) worked with Bright in the Anti-Corn Law League. 5. ***Martineau:*** Harriet Martineau (1802–76), controversial writer on political science, a propagandist for Unitarianism, the abolition of slavery, and positivism. 6. ***Watts:*** George F. Watts (1817–1904), English painter of noble but solemn allegories, such as *Love and Life, Love and Death, Love Triumphant.* See Yeats, "The Mask," n. 31, p. 809, below. 7. ***Delaroche:*** Hippolyte Delaroche (1797–1856), French historical painter. The work referred to is in the hemicycle of the lecture theater of the École des beaux arts, Paris.

*ing young fellow. He must, one thinks, be the jeune premier;* [8] *for it is not in reason to suppose that a second such attractive male figure should appear in one story. The slim, shapely frame, the elegant suit of new mourning, the small head and regular features, the pretty little moustache, the frank clear eyes, the wholesome bloom on the youthful complexion, the well brushed glossy hair, not curly, but of fine texture and good dark color, the arch of good nature in the eyebrows, the erect forehead and neatly pointed chin, all announce the man who will love and suffer later on. And that he will not do so without sympathy is guaranteed by an engaging sincerity and eager modest serviceableness which stamp him as a man af amiable nature. The moment he appears, Ramsden's face expands into fatherly liking and welcome, an expression which drops into one of decorous grief as the young man approaches him with sorrow in his face as well as in his black clothes. Ramsden seems to know the nature of the bereavement. As the visitor advances silently to the writing table, the old man rises and shakes his hand across it without a word: a long, affectionate shake which tells the story of a recent sorrow common to both.*

RAMSDEN [*concluding the handshake and cheering up*]. Well, well, Octavius, it's the common lot. We must all face it some day. Sit down.

*Octavius takes the visitor's chair. Ramsden replaces himself in his own.*

OCTAVIUS. Yes: we must face it, Mr Ramsden. But I owed him a great deal. He did everything for me that my father could have done if he had lived.

RAMSDEN. He had no son of his own, you see.

OCTAVIUS. But he had daughters; and yet he was as good to my sister as to me. And his death was so sudden! I always intended to thank him — to let him know that I had not taken all his care of me as a matter of course, as any boy takes his father's care. But I waited for an opportunity; and now he is dead — dropped without a moment's warning. He will never know what I felt. [*He takes out his handkerchief and cries unaffectedly.*]

RAMSDEN. How do we know that, Octavius? He may know it: we cannot tell. Come! dont grieve. [*Octavius masters himself and puts up his handkerchief.*] Thats right. Now let me tell you something to console you. The last time I saw him — it was in this very room — he said to me: "Tavy is a generous lad and the soul of honor; and when I see how little consideration other men get from their sons, I realize how much better than a son he's been to me." There! Doesnt that do you good?

OCTAVIUS. Mr Ramsden: he used to say to me that he had met only one man in the world who was the soul of honor, and that was Roebuck Ramsden.

RAMSDEN. Oh, that was his partiality: we were very old friends, you know. But there was something else he used to say about you. I wonder whether I ought to tell you or not!

OCTAVIUS. You know best.

RAMSDEN. It was something about his daughter.

OCTAVIUS [*eagerly*]. About Ann! Oh, do tell me that, Mr Ramsden.

RAMSDEN. Well, he said he was glad, after all, you were not his son, because he thought that someday Annie and you — [*Octavius blushes vividly.*] Well, perhaps I shouldnt have told you. But he was in earnest.

OCTAVIUS. Oh, if only I thought I had a chance! You know, Mr Ramsden, I dont care about money or about what people call position; and I cant bring myself to take an interest in the business of struggling for them. Well, Ann has a most exquisite nature; but she is so accustomed to be in the thick of that sort of thing that she thinks a man's character incomplete if he is not ambitious. She knows that if she married me she would have to reason herself out of being ashamed of me for not being a big success of some kind.

RAMSDEN [*getting up and planting himself with his back to the fireplace*]. Nonsense, my boy, nonsense! Youre too modest. What does she know about the real value of men at her age? [*More seriously*] Besides, she's a wonderfully dutiful girl. Her father's wish would be sacred to her. Do you know that since she grew up to years of discretion, I dont believe she has ever once given her own wish as a reason for doing anything or not doing it. It's always "Father wishes me to," or "Mother wouldnt like it." It's really almost a fault in her. I have often told her she must learn to think for herself.

OCTAVIUS [*shaking his head*]. I couldnt ask her to marry me because her father wished it, Mr Ramsden.

RAMSDEN. Well, perhaps not. No: of course not. I see that. No; you certainly couldnt. But when you win her on your own merits, it will be a great happiness to her to fulfil her father's desire as well as her own. Eh? Come! youll ask her, wont you?

OCTAVIUS [*with sad gaiety*]. At all events I promise you I shall never ask anyone else.

RAMSDEN. Oh, you shant need to. She'll accept you, my boy — although [*Here he suddenly becomes very serious indeed*] you have one great drawback.

OCTAVIUS. [*anxiously*]. What drawback is that, Mr Ramsden? I should rather say which of my many drawbacks?

8. *jeune premier:* technical term of the French theater for the young male lead, who often has the part of a lover.

RAMSDEN. I'll tell you, Octavius. [*He takes from the table a book bound in red cloth.*] I have in my hand a copy of the most infamous, the most scandalous, the most mischievous, the most blackguardly book that ever escaped burning at the hands of the common hangman. I have not read it: I would not soil my mind with such filth; but I have read what the papers say of it. The title is quite enough for me. [*He reads it.*] The Revolutionist's Handbook and Pocket Companion. By John Tanner, M.I.R.C., Member of the Idle Rich Class.

OCTAVIUS [*smiling*]. But Jack —

RAMSDEN [*testily*]. For goodness' sake, dont call him Jack under my roof. [*He throws the book violently down on the table. Then, somewhat relieved, he comes past the table to Octavius, and addresses him at close quarters with impressive gravity.*] Now, Octavius, I know that my dead friend was right when he said you were a generous lad. I know that this man was your schoolfellow, and that you feel bound to stand by him because there was a boyish friendship between you. But I ask you to consider the altered circumstances. You were treated as a son in my friend's house. You lived there; and your friends could not be turned from the door. This man Tanner was in and out there on your account almost from his childhood. He addresses Annie by her Christian name as freely as you do. Well, while her father was alive, that was her father's business, not mine. This man Tanner was only a boy to him: his opinions were something to be laughed at, like a man's hat on a child's head. But now Tanner is a grown man and Annie a grown woman. And her father is gone. We dont as yet know the exact terms of his will; but he often talked it over with me; and I have no more doubt than I have that youre sitting there that the will appoints me Annie's trustee and guardian. [*Forcibly*] Now I tell you, once for all, I cant and I wont have Annie placed in such a position that she must, out of regard for you, suffer the intimacy of this fellow Tanner. It's not fair: it's not right: it's not kind. What are you going to do about it?

OCTAVIUS. But Ann herself has told Jack that whatever his opinions are, he will always be welcome because he knew her dear father.

RAMSDEN [*out of patience*]. That girl's mad about her duty to her parents. [*He starts off like a goaded ox in the direction of John Bright, in whose expression there is no sympathy for him. As he speaks he fumes down to Herbert Spencer, who receives him still more coldly.*] Excuse me, Octavius; but there are limits to social toleration. You know that I am not a bigoted or prejudiced man. You know that I am plain Roebuck Ramsden when other men who have done less have got handles to their names, because I have stood for equality and liberty of conscience while they were truckling to the Church and to the aristocracy. Whitefield and I lost chance after chance through our advanced opinions. But I draw the line at Anarchism and Free Love and that sort of thing. If I am to be Annie's guardian, she will have to learn that she has a duty to me. I wont have it: I will not have it. She must forbid John Tanner the house; and so must you.

*The parlormaid returns.*

OCTAVIUS. But —

RAMSDEN [*calling his attention to the servant*]. Ssh! Well?

THE MAID. Mr Tanner wishes to see you, sir.

RAMSDEN. Mr Tanner!

OCTAVIUS. Jack!

RAMSDEN. How dare Mr Tanner call on me! Say I cannot see him.

OCTAVIUS [*hurt*]. I am sorry you are turning my friend from your door like that.

THE MAID [*calmly*]. He's not at the door, sir. He's upstairs in the drawing room with Miss Ramsden. He came with Mrs Whitefield and Miss Ann and Miss Robinson, sir.

*Ramsden's feelings are beyond words.*

OCTAVIUS [*grinning*]. Thats very like Jack, Mr Ramsden. You must see him, even if it's only to turn him out.

RAMSDEN [*hammering out his words with suppressed fury*]. Go upstairs and ask Mr Tanner to be good enough to step down here. [*The parlormaid goes out, and Ramsden returns to the fireplace, as to a fortified position.*] I must say that of all the confounded pieces of impertinence — well, if these are Anarchist manners, I hope you like them. And Annie with him! Annie! A — [*He chokes.*]

OCTAVIUS. Yes: thats what surprises me. He's so desperately afraid of Ann. There must be something the matter.

*Mr John Tanner suddenly opens the door and enters. He is too young to be described simply as a big man with a beard. But it is already plain that middle life will find him in that category. He has still some of the slimness of youth; but youthfulness is not the effect he aims at: his frock coat would befit a prime minister; and a certain high chested carriage of the shoulders, a loftly pose of the head, and the Olympian majesty with which a mane, or rather a huge wisp, of hazel colored hair is thrown back from an imposing brow, suggest Jupiter rather than Apollo. He is prodigiously fluent of speech, restless, excitable (mark the snorting nostril and the restless blue eye, just the thirty-secondth of an inch too wide open), possibly a little mad. He is carefully dressed, not from the vanity that cannot resist finery, but from a sense of the importance of everything he does which leads him to make as much of paying a call as other men do of getting married or laying a foundation stone. A sensitive, susceptible, exaggerative, earnest man: a megalomaniac, who would be lost without a sense of humor.*

*Just at present the sense of humor is in abeyance. To say that he is excited is nothing: all his moods are phases of excitement. He is now in the panic-stricken phase; and he walks straight up to Ramsden as if with the fixed intention of shooting him on his own hearthrug. But what he pulls from his breast pocket is not a pistol, but a foolscap document which he thrusts under the indignant nose of Ramsden as he exclaims*

TANNER. Ramsden: do you know what that is?

RAMSDEN [*loftily*]. No, sir.

TANNER. It's a copy of Whitefield's will. Ann got it this morning.

RAMSDEN. When you say Ann, you mean, I presume, Miss Whitefield.

TANNER. I mean our Ann, your Ann, Tavy's Ann, and now, Heaven help me, my Ann!

OCTAVIUS [*rising, very pale*]. What do you mean?

TANNER. Mean! [*He holds up the will.*] Do you know who is appointed Ann's guardian by this will?

RAMSDEN [*cooly*]. I believe I am.

TANNER. You! You and I, man. I! I!! I!!! Both of us! [*He flings the will down on the writing table.*]

RAMSDEN. You! Impossible.

TANNER. It's only too hideously true. [*He throws himself into Octavius's chair.*] Ramsden: get me out of it somehow. You dont know Ann as well as I do. She'll commit every crime a respectable woman can; and she'll justify every one of them by saying that it was the wish of her guardians. She'll put everything on us; and we shall have no more control over her than a couple of mice over a cat.

OCTAVIUS. Jack: I wish you wouldnt talk like that about Ann.

TANNER. This chap's in love with her: thats another complication. Well, she'll either jilt him and say I didnt approve of him, or marry him and say you ordered her to. I tell you, this is the most staggering blow that has ever fallen on a man of my age and temperament.

RAMSDEN. Let me see that will, sir. [*He goes to the writing table and picks it up.*] I cannot believe that my old friend Whitefield would have shewn such a want of confidence in me as to associate me with — [*His countenance falls as he reads.*]

TANNER. It's all my own doing: thats the horrible irony of it. He told me one day that you were to be Ann's guardian; and like a fool I began arguing with him about the folly of leaving a young woman under the control of an old man with obsolete ideas.

RAMSDEN [*stupended*]. My ideas obsolete!!!!!!!

TANNER. Totally. I had just finished an essay called Down with Government by the Greyhaired; and I was full of arguments and illustrations. I said the proper thing was to combine the experience of an old hand with the vitality of a young one. Hang me if he didnt take me at my word and alter his will — it's dated only a fortnight after that conversation — appointing me as joint guardian with you!

RAMSDEN [*pale and determined*]. I shall refuse to act.

TANNER. Whats the good of that? Ive been refusing all the way from Richmond; but Ann keeps on saying that of course she's only an orphan; and that she cant expect the people who were glad to come to the house in her father's time to trouble much about her now. Thats the latest game. An orphan! It's like hearing an ironclad talk about being at the mercy of the winds and waves.

OCTAVIUS. This is not fair, Jack. She is an orphan. And you ought to stand by her.

TANNER. Stand by her! What danger is she in? She has the law on her side; she has popular sentiment on her side; she has plenty of money and no conscience. All she wants with me is to load up all her moral responsibilities on me, and do as she likes at the expense of my character. I cant control her; and she can compromise me as much as she likes. I might as well be her husband.

RAMSDEN. You can refuse to accept the guardianship. *I* shall certainly refuse to hold it jointly with you.

TANNER. Yes; and what will she say to that? what does she say to it? Just that her father's wishes are sacred to her, and that she shall always look up to me as her guardian whether I care to face the responsibility or not. Refuse! You might as well refuse to accept the embraces of a boa constrictor when once it gets round your neck.

OCTAVIUS. This sort of talk is not kind to me, Jack.

TANNER [*rising and going to Octavius to console him, but still lamenting*]. If he wanted a young guardian, why didnt he appoint Tavy?

RAMSDEN. Ah! why indeed?

OCTAVIUS. I will tell you. He sounded me about it; but I refused the trust because I loved her. I had no right to let myself be forced on her as a guardian by her father. He spoke to her about it; and she said I was right. You know I love her, Mr Ramsden; and Jack knows it too. If Jack loved a woman, I would not compare her to a boa constrictor in his presence, however much I might dislike her. [*He sits down between the busts and turns his face to the wall.*]

RAMSDEN. I do not believe that Whitefield was in his right senses when he made that will. You have admitted that he made it under your influence.

TANNER. You ought to be pretty will obliged to me for my influence. He leaves you two thousand five hundred for your trouble. He leaves Tavy a dowry for his sister and five thousand for himself.

OCTAVIUS [*his tears flowing afresh*]. Oh, I cant take it. He was too good to us.

TANNER. You wont get it, my boy, if Ramsden upsets the will.

RAMSDEN. Ha! I see. You have got me in a cleft stick.

TANNER. He leaves me nothing but the charge of Ann's morals, on the ground that I have already more money than is good for me. That shews that he had his wits about him, doesnt it?

RAMSDEN [*grimly*]. I admit that.

OCTAVIUS [*rising and coming from his refuge by the wall*]. Mr Ramsden: I think you are prejudiced against Jack. He is a man of honor, and incapable of abusing—

TANNER. Dont, Tavy: youll make me ill. I am not a man of honor: I am a man struck down by a dead hand. Tavy: you must marry her after all and take her off my hands. And I had set my heart on saving you from her!

OCTAVIUS. Oh, Jack, you talk of saving me from my highest happiness.

TANNER. Yes, a lifetime of happiness. If it were only the first half hour's happiness, Tavy, I would buy it for you with my last penny. But a lifetime of happiness! No man alive could bear it: it would be hell on earth.

RAMSDEN [*violently*]. Stuff, sir. Talk sense; or else go and waste someone else's time: I have something better to do than listen to your fooleries. [*He positively kicks his way to his table and resumes his seat.*]

TANNER. You hear him, Tavy! Not an idea in his head later than eighteensixty. We cant leave Ann with no other guardian to turn to.

RAMSDEN. I am proud of your contempt for my character and opinions, sir. Your own are set forth in that book, I believe.

TANNER [*eagerly going to the table*]. What! Youve got my book! What do you think of it?

RAMSDEN. Do you suppose I would read such a book, sir?

TANNER. Then why did you buy it?

RAMSDEN. I did not buy it, sir. It has been sent me by some foolish lady who seems to admire your views. I was about to dispose of it when Octavius interrupted me. I shall do so now, with your permission. [*He throws the book into the waste-paper basket with such vehemence that Tanner recoils under the impression that it is being thrown at his head.*]

TANNER. You have no more manners than I have myself. However, that saves ceremony between us. [*He sits down again.*] What do you intend to do about this will?

OCTAVIUS. May I make a suggestion?

RAMSDEN. Certainly, Octavius.

OCTAVIUS. Arnt we forgetting that Ann herself may have some wishes in this matter?

RAMSDEN. I quite intend that Annie's wishes shall be consulted in every reasonable way. But she is only a woman, and a young and inexperienced woman at that.

TANNER. Ramsden: I begin to pity you.

RAMSDEN [*hotly*]. I dont want to know how you feel towards me, Mr Tanner.

TANNER. Ann will do just exactly what she likes. And whats more, she'll force us to advise her to do it; and she'll put the blame on us if it turns out badly. So, as Tavy is longing to see her—

OCTAVIUS [*shyly*]. I am not, Jack.

TANNER. You lie, Tavy: you are. So lets have her down from the drawing room and ask her what she intends us to do. Off with you, Tavy, and fetch her. [*Tavy turns to go.*] And dont be long; for the strained relations between myself and Ramsden will make the interval rather painful. [*Ramsden compresses his lips, but says nothing.*]

OCTAVIUS. Never mind him, Mr Ramsden. He's not serious. [*He goes out.*]

RAMSDEN [*very deliberately*]. Mr Tanner: you are the most impudent person I have ever met.

TANNER [*seriously*]. I know it, Ramsden. Yet even I cannot wholly conquer shame. We live in an atmosphere of shame. We are ashamed of everything that is real about us; ashamed of ourselves, of our relatives, of our incomes, of our accents, of our opinions, of our experience, just as we are ashamed of our naked skins. Good Lord, my dear Ramsden, we are ashamed to walk, ashamed to ride in an omnibus, ashamed to hire a hansom instead of keeping a carriage, ashamed of keeping one horse instead of two and a groom-gardener instead of a coachman and footman. The more things a man is ashamed of, the more respectable he is. Why, youre ashamed to buy my book, ashamed to read it: the only thing youre not ashamed of is to judge me for it without having read it; and even that only means that youre ashamed to have heterodox opinions. Look at the effect I produce because my fairy godmother withheld from me this gift of shame. I have every possible virtue that a man can have except—

RAMSDEN. I am glad you think so well of yourself.

TANNER. All you mean by that is that you think I ought to be ashamed of talking about my virtues. You dont mean that I havnt got them; you know perfectly well that I am as sober and honest a citizen as yourself, as truthful personally, and much more truthful politically and morally.

RAMSDEN [*touched on his most sensitive point*]. I deny that. I will not allow you or any man to treat me as if I were a mere member of the British public. I detest its prejudices; I scorn its narrowness; I demand the right to think for myself. You pose as an advanced man. Let me tell you that I was an advanced man before you were born.

TANNER. I knew it was a long time ago.

RAMSDEN. I am as advanced as ever I was. I defy you to prove that I have ever hauled down the flag. I am more advanced than ever I was. I grow more advanced every day.

TANNER. More advanced in years, Polonius.

RAMSDEN. Polonius! So you are Hamlet, I suppose.

TANNER. No: I am only the most impudent person youve ever met. Thats your notion of a thoroughly bad character. When you want to give me a piece of your mind, you ask yourself, as a just and upright man, what is the worst you can fairly say of me. Thief, liar, forger, adulterer, perjurer, glutton, drunkard? Not one of these names fit me. You have to fall back on my deficiency in shame. Well, I admit it. I even congratulate myself; for if I were ashamed of my real self, I should cut as stupid a figure as any of the rest of you. Cultivate a little impudence, Ramsden; and you will become quite a remarkable man.

RAMSDEN. I have no —

TANNER. You have no desire for that sort of notoriety. Bless you, I knew that answer would come as well as I know that a box of matches will come out of an automatic machine when I put a penny in the slot: you would be ashamed to say anything else.

*The crushing retort for which Ramsden has been visibly collecting his forces is lost for ever; for at this point Octavius returns with Miss Ann Whitefield and her mother; and Ramsden springs up and hurries to the door to receive them. Whether Ann is good-looking or not depends upon your taste; also and perhaps chiefly on your age and sex. To Octavius she is an enchantingly beautiful woman, in whose presence the world becomes transfigured, and the puny limits of individual consciousness are suddenly made infinite by a mystic memory of the whole life of the race to its beginnings in the east, or even back to the paradise from which it fell. She is to him the reality of romance, the inner good sense of nonsense, the unveiling of his eyes, the freeing of his soul, the abolition of time, place, and circumstance, the etherealization of his blood into rapturous rivers of the very water of life itself, the revelation of all the mysteries and the sanctification of all the dogmas. To her mother she is, to put it as moderately as possible, nothing whatever of the kind. Not that Octavius's admiration is in any way ridiculous or discreditable. Ann is a well formed creature, as far as that goes; and she is perfectly ladylike, graceful, and comely, with ensnaring eyes and hair. Besides, instead of making herself an eyesore, like her mother, she has devised a mourning costume of black and violet silk which does honor to her late father and reveals the family tradition of brave unconventionality by which Ramsden sets such store.*

*But all this is beside the point as an explanation of Ann's charm. Turn up her nose, give a cast to her eye, replace her black and violet confection by the apron and feathers of a flower girl, strike all the aitches out of her speech, and Ann would still make men dream. Vitality is as common as humanity; but, like humanity, it sometimes rises to genius; and Ann is one of the vital geniuses. Not at all, if you please, an oversexed person: that is a vital defect, not a true excess. She is a perfectly respectable, perfectly self-controlled woman, and looks it; though her pose is fashionably frank and impulsive. She inspires confidence as a person who will do nothing she does not mean to do; also some fear, perhaps, as a woman who will probably do everything she means to do without taking more account of other people than may be necessary and what she calls right. In short, what the weaker of her own sex sometimes call a cat.*

*Nothing can be more decorous than her entry and her reception by Ramsden, whom she kisses. The late Mr Whitefield would be gratified almost to impatience by the long faces of the men (except Tanner, who is fidgety), the silent handgrasps, the sympathetic placing of chairs, the sniffing of the widow, and the liquid eye of the daughter, whose heart, apparently will not let her control her tongue to speech. Ramsden and Octavius take the two chairs from the wall, and place them for the two ladies; but Ann comes to Tanner and takes his chair, which he offers with a brusque gesture, subsequently relieving his irritation by sitting down on the corner of the writing table with studied indecorum. Octavius gives Mrs Whitefield a chair next Ann, and himself takes the vacant one which Ramsden has placed under the nose of the effigy of Mr Herbert Spencer.*

*Mrs Whitefield, by the way, is a little woman, whose faded flaxen hair looks like straw on an egg. She has an expression of muddled shrewdness, a squeak of protest in her voice, and an odd air of continually elbowing away some larger person who is crushing her into a corner. One guesses her as one of those women who are conscious of being treated as silly and negligible, and who, without having strength enough to assert themselves effectually, at any rate never submit to their fate. There is a touch of chivalry in Octavius's scrupulous attention to her, even whilst his whole soul is absorbed by Ann.*

*Ramsden goes solemnly back to his magisterial seat at the writing table, ignoring Tanner, and opens the proceedings.*

RAMSDEN. I am sorry, Annie, to force business on you, at a sad time like the present. But your poor dear father's will has raised a very serious question. You have read it, I believe?

*Ann assents with a nod and a catch of her breath, too much affected to speak.*

I must say I am surprised to find Mr Tanner named as joint guardian and trustee with myself of you and Rhoda. [*A pause. They all look portentous; but they have nothing to say. Ramsden, a little ruffled by the lack of any response, continues.*] I dont know that I can consent to act under such conditions. Mr Tanner has, I understand, some objection also; but I do not profess to understand its nature: he will no doubt speak for himself. But we are agreed that we can decide nothing until we know your views. I am afraid I shall have to ask you to choose between my sole guardianship and that of Mr Tanner; for I fear it is impossible for us to undertake a joint arrangement.

ANN [*in a low musical voice*]. Mamma—

MRS WHITEFIELD [*hastily*]. Now, Ann, I do beg you not to put it on me. I have no opinion on the subject; and if I had, it would probably not be attended to. I am quite content with whatever you three think best.

*Tanner turns his head and looks fixedly at Ramsden, who angrily refuses to receive this mute communication.*

ANN [*resuming in the same gentle voice, ignoring her mother's bad taste*]. Mamma knows that she is not strong enough to bear the whole responsibility for me and Rhoda without some help and advice. Rhoda must have a guardian; and though I am older, I do not think any young unmarried woman should be left quite to her own guidance. I hope you agree with me, Granny?

TANNER [*starting*]. Granny! Do you intend to call your guardians Granny?

ANN. Dont be foolish, Jack. Mr Ramsden has always been Grandpapa Roebuck to me: I am Granny's Annie; and he is Annie's Granny. I christened him so when I first learned to speak.

RAMSDEN [*sarcastically*]. I hope you are satisfied Mr Tanner. Go on, Annie: I quite agree with you.

ANN. Well, if I am to have a guardian, can I set aside anybody whom my dear father appointed for me?

RAMSDEN [*biting his lip*]. You approve of your father's choice, then?

ANN. It is not for me to approve or disapprove. I accept it. My father loved me and knew best what was good for me.

RAMSDEN. Of course I understand your feeling, Annie. It is what I should have expected of you; and it does you credit. But it does not settle the question so completely as you think. Let me put a case to you. Suppose you were to discover that I had been guilty of some disgraceful action—that I was not the man your poor dear father took me for! Would you still consider it right that I should be Rhoda's guardian?

ANN. I cant imagine you doing anything disgraceful, Granny.

TANNER [*to Ramsden*]. You havnt done anything of the sort, have you?

RAMSDEN [*indignantly*]. No, sir.

MRS WHITEFIELD [*placidly*]. Well, then, why suppose it?

ANN. You see, Granny, Mamma would not like me to suppose it.

RAMSDEN [*much perplexed*]. You are both so full of natural and affectionate feeling in these family matters that it is very hard to put the situation fairly before you.

TANNER. Besides, my friend, you are not putting the situation fairly before them.

RAMSDEN [*sulkily*]. Put it yourself, then.

TANNER. I will. Ann: Ramsden thinks I am not fit to be your guardian; and I quite agree with him. He considers that if your father had read my book, he wouldnt have appointed me. That book is the disgraceful action he has been talking about. He thinks it's your duty for Rhoda's sake to ask him to act alone and to make me withdraw. Say the word; and I will.

ANN. But I havnt read your book, Jack.

TANNER [*diving at the waste-paper basket and fishing the book out for her*]. Then read it at once and decide.

RAMSDEN [*vehemently*]. If I am to be your guardian, I positively forbid you to read that book, Annie. [*He smites the table with his first and rises.*]

ANN. Of course not if you dont wish it. [*She puts the book on the table.*]

TANNER. If one guardian is to forbid you to read the other guardian's book, how are we to settle it? Suppose I order you to read it! What about your duty to me?

ANN [*gently*]. I am sure you would never purposely force me into a painful dilemma, Jack.

RAMSDEN [*irritably*]. Yes, yes, Annie: this is all very well, and, as I said, quite natural and becoming. But you must make a choice one way or the other. We are as much in a dilemma as you.

ANN. I feel that I am too young, too inexperienced, to decide. My father's wishes are sacred to me.

MRS WHITEFIELD. If you two men wont carry them out I must say it is rather hard that you should put the responsibility on Ann. It seems to me that people are always putting things on other people in this world.

RAMSDEN. I am sorry you take it in that way.

ANN [*touchingly*]. Do you refuse to accept me as your ward, Granny?

RAMSDEN. No: I never said that. I greatly object to act with Mr Tanner: thats all.

MRS WHITEFIELD. Why? What's the matter with poor Jack?

TANNER. My views are too advanced for him.

RAMSDEN [*indignantly*]. They are not. I deny it.

ANN. Of course not. What nonsense! Nobody is more advanced than Granny. I am sure it is Jack himself who has made all the difficulty. Come, Jack! be kind to me in my sorrow. You dont refuse to accept me as your ward, do you?

TANNER [*gloomily*]. No. I let myself in for it; so I suppose I must face it. [*He turns away to the bookcase, and stands there, moodily studying the titles of the volumes.*]

ANN [*rising and expanding with subdued but gushing delight*]. Then we are all agreed; and my dear father's will is to be carried out. You dont know what a joy that is to me and to my mother! [*She goes to Ramsden and presses both his hands, saying*] And I shall have my dear Granny to help and advise me. [*She casts a glance at Tanner over her shoulder.*] And Jack the Giant Killer. [*She goes past her mother to Octavius.*] And Jack's inseparable friend Ricky-ticky-tavy.[9] [*He blushes and looks inexpressibly foolish.*]

MRS WHITEFIELD [*rising and shaking her widow's weeds straight*]. Now that you are Ann's guardian, Mr Ramsden, I wish you would speak to her about her habit of giving people nicknames. They cant be expected to like it. [*She moves towards the door.*]

ANN. How can you say such a thing, Mamma! [*Glowing with affectionate remorse*] Oh, I wonder can you be right! Have I been inconsiderate? [*She turns to Octavius, who is sitting astride his chair with his elbows on the back of it. Putting her hand on his forehead she turns his face up suddenly.*] Do you want to be treated like a grown-up man? Must I call you Mr Robinson in future?

OCTAVIUS [*earnestly*]. Oh please call me Ricky-ticky-tavy. "Mr Robinson" would hurt me cruelly. [*She laughs and pats his cheek with her finger, then comes back to Ramsden.*] You know I'm beginning to think that Granny is rather a piece of impertinence. But I never dreamt of its hurting you.

RAMSDEN [*breezily, as he pats her affectionately on the back*]. My dear Annie, nonsense. I insist on Granny. I wont answer to any other name than Annie's Granny.

ANN [*gratefully*]. You all spoil me, except Jack.

TANNER [*over his shoulder, from the bookcase*]. I think you ought to call me Mr Tanner.

9. **Ricky-ticky-tavy:** "Rikki-tikki-tavi" is a pet mongoose in Kipling's story of the same name in *The Jungle Book.*

ANN [*gently*]. No you dont, Jack. That's like the things you say on purpose to shock people: those who know you pay no attention to them. But, if you like, I'll call you after your famous ancestor Don Juan.

RAMSDEN. Don Juan!

ANN [*innocently*]. Oh, is there any harm in it? I didnt know. Then I certainly wont call you that. May I call you Jack until I can think of something else?

TANNER. Oh, for Heaven's sake dont try to invent anything worse. I capitulate. I consent to Jack. I embrace Jack. Here endeth my first and last attempt to assert my authority.

ANN. You see, Mamma, they all really like to have pet names.

MRS WHITEFIELD. Well, I think you might at least drop them until we are out of mourning.

ANN [*reproachfully, stricken to the soul*]. Oh, how could you remind me, mother? [*She hastily leaves the room to conceal her emotion.*]

MRS WHITEFIELD. Of course. My fault as usual! [*She follows Ann.*]

TANNER [*coming from the bookcase*]. Ramsden: we're beaten — smashed — nonentitized, like her mother.

RAMSDEN. Stuff, sir. [*He follows Mrs Whitefield out of the room.*]

TANNER [*left alone with Octavius, stares whimsically at him*]. Tavy: do you want to count for something in the world?

OCTAVIUS. I want to count for something as a poet: I want to write a great play.

TANNER. With Ann as the heroine?

OCTAVIUS. Yes: I confess it.

TANNER. Take care, Tavy. The play with Ann as the heroine is all right; but if youre not very careful, by Heaven she'll marry you.

OCTAVIUS [*sighing*]. No such luck, Jack!

TANNER. Why, man, your head is in the lioness's mouth: you are half swallowed already — in three bites — Bite One, Ricky; Bite Two, Ticky; Bite Three, Tavy; and down you go.

OCTAVIUS. She is the same to everybody, Jack: you know her ways.

TANNER. Yes: she breaks everybody's back with the stroke of her paw; but the question is, which of us will she eat? My own opinion is that she means to eat you.

OCTAVIUS [*rising, pettishly*]. It's horrible to talk like that about her when she is upstairs crying for her father. But I do so want her to eat me that I can bear your brutalities because they give me hope.

TANNER. Tavy: thats the devilish side of a woman's fascination: she makes you will your own destruction.

OCTAVIUS. But it's not destruction: it's fulfilment.

TANNER. Yes, of her purpose; and that purpose is neither her happiness nor yours, but Nature's. Vitality in a woman is a blind fury of creation. She sacrifices herself to it: do you think she will hesitate to sacrifice you?

OCTAVIUS. Why, it is just because she is self-sacrificing that she will not sacrifice those she loves.

TANNER. That is the profoundest of mistakes, Tavy. It is the self-sacrificing women that sacrifice others most recklessly. Because they are unselfish, they are kind in little things. Because they have a purpose which is not their own purpose, but that of the whole universe, a man is nothing to them but an instrument of that purpose.

OCTAVIUS. Dont be ungenerous, Jack. They take the tenderest care of us.

TANNER. Yes, as a soldier takes care of his rifle or a musician of his violin. But do they allow us any purpose or freedom of our own? Will they lend us to one another? Can the strongest man escape from them when once he is appropriated? They tremble when we are in danger, and weep when we die; but the tears are not for us, but for a father wasted, a son's breeding thrown away. They accuse us of treating them as a mere means to our pleasure; but how can so feeble and transient a folly as a man's selfish pleasure enslave a woman as the whole purpose of Nature embodied in a woman can enslave a man?

OCTAVIUS. What matter, if the slavery makes us happy?

TANNER. No matter at all if you have no purpose of your own, and are, like most men, a mere breadwinner. But you, Tavy, are an artist: that is, you have a purpose as absorbing and as unscrupulous as a woman's purpose.

OCTAVIUS. Not unscrupulous.

TANNER. Quite unscrupulous. The true artist will let his wife starve, his children go barefoot, his mother drudge for his living at seventy, sooner than work at anything but his art. To women he is half vivisector, half vampire. He gets into intimate relations with them to study them, to strip the mask of convention from them, to surprise their inmost secrets, knowing that they have the power to rouse his deepest creative energies, to rescue him from his cold reason, to make him see visions and dream dreams, to inspire him, as he calls it. He persuades women that they may do this for their own purpose whilst he really means them to do it for his. He steals the mother's milk and blackens it to make printer's ink to scoff at her and glorify ideal women with. He pretends to spare her the pangs of childbearing so that he may have for himself the tenderness and fostering that belong of right to her children. Since marriage began, the great artist has been known as a bad husband. But he is worse: he is a child-robber, a blood-sucker, a hypocrite, and a cheat. Perish the race and wither a thousand women if only the sacrifice of them enable him to act Hamlet better, to paint a finer picture, to write a deeper poem, a greater play, a profounder philosophy! For mark you, Tavy, the artist's work is to shew us ourselves as we really are. Our minds are nothing but this knowledge of ourselves; and he who adds a jot to such knowledge creates new mind as surely as any woman creates new men. In the rage of that creation he is as ruthless as the woman, as dangerous to her as she to him, and as horribly fascinating. Of all human struggles there is none so treacherous and remorseless as the struggle between the artist man and the mother woman. Which shall use up the other? that is the issue between them. And it is all the deadlier because, in your romanticist cant, they love one another.

OCTAVIUS. Even if it were so — and I dont admit it for a moment — it is out of the deadliest struggles that we get the noblest characters.

TANNER. Remember that the next time you meet a grizzly bear or a Bengal tiger, Tavy.

OCTAVIUS. I meant where there is love, Jack.

TANNER. Oh, the tiger will love you. There is no love sincerer than the love of food. I think Ann loves you that way: she patted your cheek as if it were a nicely underdone chop.

OCTAVIUS. You know, Jack, I should have to run away from you if I did not make it a fixed rule not to mind anything you say. You come out with perfectly revolting things sometimes.

*Ramsden returns, followed by Ann. They come in quickly, with their former leisurely air of decorous grief changed to one of genuine concern, and, on Ramsden's part, of worry. He comes between the two men, intending to address Octavius, but pulls himself up abruptly as he sees Tanner.*

RAMSDEN. I hardly expected to find you still here, Mr Tanner.

TANNER. Am I in the way? Good morning, fellow guardian. [*He goes towards the door.*]

ANN. Stop, Jack. Granny: he must know, sooner or later.

RAMSDEN. Octavius: I have a very serious piece of news for you. It is of the most private and delicate nature — of the most painful nature too, I am sorry to say. Do you wish Mr Tanner to be present whilst I explain?

OCTAVIUS. [*turning pale*]. I have no secrets from Jack.

RAMSDEN. Before you decide that finally, let me say that the news concerns your sister, and that it is t e r r i b l e news.

OCTAVIUS. Violet! What has happened? Is she — dead?

RAMSDEN. I am not sure that it is not even worse than that.

OCTAVIUS. Is she badly hurt? Has there been an accident?

RAMSDEN. No: nothing of that sort.

TANNER. Ann: will you have the common humanity to tell us what the matter is?

ANN [*half whispering*]. I cant. Violet has done something dreadful. We shall have to get her away somewhere. [*She flutters to the writing table and sits in Ramsden's chair, leaving the three men to fight it out between them.*]

OCTAVIUS [*enlightened*]. Is t h a t what you meant, Mr Ramsden?

RAMSDEN. Yes. [*Octavius sinks upon a chair, crushed.*] I am afraid there is no doubt that Violet did not really go to Eastbourne three weeks ago when we thought she was with the Parry Whitefields. And she called on a strange doctor yesterday with a wedding ring on her finger. Mrs Parry Whitefield met her there by chance; and so the whole thing came out.

OCTAVIUS [*rising with fists clenched*]. Who is the scoundrel?

ANN. She wont tell us.

OCTAVIUS [*collapsing into the chair again*]. What a frightful thing!

TANNER [*with angry sarcasm*]. Dreadful, Appalling. Worse than death, as Ramsden says. [*He comes to Octavius.*] What would you not give, Tavy, to turn it into a railway accident, with all her bones broken, or something equally respectable and deserving of sympathy?

OCTAVIUS. Dont be brutal, Jack.

TANNER. Brutal! Good Heavens, man, what are you crying for? Here is a woman whom we all supposed to be making bad water color sketches, practising Grieg and Brahms, gadding about to concerts and parties, wasting her life and her money. We suddenly learn that she has turned from these sillinesses to the fulfilment of her highest purpose and greatest function — to increase, multiply, and replenish the earth. And instead of admiring her courage and rejoicing in her instinct; instead of crowning the completed womanhood and raising the triumphal strain of "Unto us a child is born: unto us a son is given,"[10] here you are — you who have been as merry as grigs in your mourning for the dead — all pulling long faces and looking as ashamed and disgraced as if the girl had committed the vilest of crimes.

RAMSDEN [*roaring with rage*]. I will not have these abominations uttered in my house. [*He smites the writing-table with his fist.*]

10. "Unto . . . given": Isa. 9:6 (traditionally interpreted as referring to the birth of Christ).

TANNER. Look here: if you insult me again I'll take you at your word and leave your house. Ann: where is Violet now?

ANN. Why? Are you going to her?

TANNER. Of course I am going to her. She wants help; she wants money; she wants respect and congratulation; she wants every chance for her child. She does not seem likely to get it from you: she shall from me. Where is she?

ANN. Dont be so headstrong, Jack. She's upstairs.

TANNER. What! Under Ramsden's sacred roof! Go and do your miserable duty, Ramsden. Hunt her out into the street. Cleanse your threshold from her contamination. Vindicate the purity of your English home. I'll go for a cab.

ANN [*alarmed*]. Oh, Granny, you mustnt do that.

OCTAVIUS [*broken-heartedly, rising*]. I'll take her away, Mr Ramsden. She had no right to come to your house.

RAMSDEN [*indignantly*]. But I am only too anxious to help her. [*Turning on Tanner*] How dare you, sir, impute such monstrous intentions to me? I protest against it. I am ready to put down my last penny to save her from being driven to run to you for protection.

TANNER [*subsiding*]. It's all right, then. He's not going to act up to his principles. It's agreed that we all stand by Violet.

OCTAVIUS. But who is the man? He can make reparation by marrying her; and he shall, or he shall answer for it to me.

RAMSDEN. He shall, Octavius. There you speak like a man.

TANNER. Then you dont think him a scoundrel, after all?

OCTAVIUS. Not a scoundrel! He is a heartless scoundrel.

RAMSDEN. A damned scoundrel. I beg your pardon, Annie; but I can say no less.

TANNER. So we are to marry your sister to a damned scoundrel by way of reforming her character! On my soul, I think you are all mad.

ANN. Dont be absurd, Jack. Of course you are quite right, Tavy; but we dont know who he is: Violet wont tell us.

TANNER. What on earth does it matter who he is? He's done his part; and Violet must do the rest.

RAMSDEN [*beside himself*]. Stuff! lunacy! There is a rascal in our midst, a libertine, a villain worse than a murderer; and we are not to learn who he is! In our ignorance we are to shake him by the hand; to introduce him into our homes; to trust our daughters with him; to — to —

ANN [*coaxingly*]. There, Granny, dont talk so loud. It's most shocking: we must all admit that; but if Violet wont tell us, what can we do? Nothing. Simply nothing.

RAMSDEN. Hmph! I'm not so sure of that. If any man has paid Violet any special attention, we can easily find that out. If there is any man of notoriously loose principles among us —

TANNER. Ahem!

RAMSDEN [*raising his voice*]. Yes, sir, I repeat, if there is any man of notoriously loose principles among us —

TANNER. Or any man notoriously lacking in self-control.

RAMSDEN [*aghast*]. Do you dare to suggest that *I* am capable of such an act?

TANNER. My dear Ramsden, this is an act of which every man is capable. That is what comes of getting at cross purposes with Nature. The suspicion you have just flung at me clings to us all. It's a sort of mud that sticks to the judge's ermine or the cardinal's robe as fast as to the rags of the tramp. Come, Tavy! dont look so bewildered: it might have been me: it might have been Ramsden; just as it might have been anybody. If it had, what could we do but lie and protest — as Ramsden is going to protest.

RAMSDEN [*choking*]. I — I — I —

TANNER. Guilt itself could not stammer more confusedly. And yet you know perfectly well he's innocent, Tavy.

RAMSDEN [*exhausted*]. I am glad you admit that, sir. I admit, myself, that there is an element of truth in what you say, grossly as you may distort it to gratify your malicious humor. I hope, Octavius, no suspicion of me is possible in your mind.

OCTAVIUS. Of you! No, not for a moment.

TANNER [*drily*]. I think he suspects me just a little.

OCTAVIUS. Jack: you couldnt — you wouldnt —

TANNER. Why not?

OCTAVIUS [*appalled*]. Why not!

TANNER. Oh, well, I'll tell you why not. First, you would feel bound to quarrel with me. Second, Violet doesnt like me. Third, if I had the honor of being the father of Violet's child, I should boast of it instead of denying it. So be easy: our friendship is not in danger.

OCTAVIUS. I should have put away the suspicion with horror if only you would think and feel naturally about it. I beg your pardon.

TANNER. My pardon! nonsense! And now lets sit down and have a family council. [*He sits down. The rest follow his example, more or less under protest.*] Violet is going to do the State a service; consequently she must be packed abroad like a criminal until it's over. What's happening upstairs?

ANN. Violet is in the housekeeper's room — by herself, of course.

TANNER. Why not in the drawing room?

ANN. Don't be absurd, Jack. Miss Ramsden is in the drawing room with my mother, considering what to do.

TANNER. Oh! the housekeeper's room is the penitentiary, I suppose; and the prisoner is waiting to be brought before her judges. The old cats!

ANN. Oh, Jack!

RAMSDEN. You are at present a guest beneath the roof of one of the old cats, sir. My sister is the mistress of this house.

TANNER. She would put me in the housekeeper's room, too, if she dared, Ramsden. However, I withdraw cats. Cats would have more sense. Ann: as your guardian, I order you to go to Violet at once and be particularly kind to her.

ANN. I have seen her, Jack. And I am sorry to say I am afraid she is going to be rather obstinate about going abroad. I think Tavy ought to speak to her about it.

OCTAVIUS. How can I speak to her about such a thing? [*He breaks down.*]

ANN. Don't break down, Ricky. Try to bear it for all our sakes.

RAMSDEN. Life is not all plays and poems, Octavius. Come! face it like a man.

TANNER [*chafing again*]. Poor dear brother! Poor dear friends of the family! Poor dear Tabbies and Grimalkins! Poor dear everybody except the woman who is going to risk her life to create another life! Tavy: dont you be a selfish ass. Away with you and talk to Violet; and bring her down here if she cares to come. [*Octavius rises.*] Tell her we'll stand by her.

RAMSDEN [*rising*]. No, sir —

TANNER [*rising also and interrupting him*]. Oh, we understand: it's against your conscience; but still youll do it.

OCTAVIUS. I assure you all, on my word, I never meant to be selfish. It's so hard to know what to do when one wishes earnestly to do right.

TANNER. My dear Tavy, your pious English habit of regarding the world as a moral gymnasium built expressly to strengthen your character in, occasionally leads you to think about your own confounded principles when you should be thinking about other people's necessities. The need of the present hour is a happy mother and a healthy baby. Bend your energies on that; and you will see your way clearly enough.

*Octavius, much perplexed, goes out.*

RAMSDEN [*facing Tanner impressively*]. And Morality, sir? What is to become of that?

TANNER. Meaning a weeping Magdalen and an innocent child branded with her shame. Not in our circle, thank you. Morality can go to its father the devil.

RAMSDEN. I thought so, sir. Morality sent to the devil to please our libertines, male and female.

That is to be the future of England, is it?

TANNER. Oh, England will survive your disapproval. Meanwhile, I understand that you agree with me as to the practical course we are to take?

RAMSDEN. Not in your spirit, sir. Not for your reasons.

TANNER. You can explain that if anybody calls you to account, here or hereafter. [*He turns away, and plants himself in front of Mr Herbert Spencer, at whom he stares gloomily.*]

ANN [*rising and coming to Ramsden*]. Granny: hadnt you better go up to the drawing room and tell them what we intend to do?

RAMSDEN [*looking pointedly at Tanner*]. I hardly like to leave you alone with this gentleman. Will you not come with me?

ANN. Miss Ramsden would not like to speak about it before me, Granny. I ought not to be present.

RAMSDEN. You are right: I should have thought of that. You are a good girl, Annie.

*He pats her on the shoulder. She looks up at him with beaming eyes; and he goes out, much moved. Having disposed of him, she looks at Tanner. His back being turned to her, she gives a moment's attention to her personal appearance, then softly goes to him and speaks almost into his ear.*

ANN. Jack [*He turns with a start*]: are you glad that you are my guardian? You don't mind being made responsible for me, I hope.

TANNER. The latest addition to your collection of scapegoats, eh?

ANN. Oh, that stupid old joke of yours about me! Do please drop it. Why do you say things that you know must pain me? I do my best to please you, Jack: I suppose I may tell you so now that you are my guardian. You will make me so unhappy if you refuse to be friends with me.

TANNER [*studying her as gloomily as he studied the bust*]. You need not go begging for my regard. How unreal our moral judgments are! You seem to me to have absolutely no conscience — only hypocrisy; and you cant see the difference — yet there is a sort of fascination about you. I always attend to you, somehow. I should miss you if I lost you.

ANN [*tranquilly slipping her arm into his and walking about with him*]. But isnt that only natural, Jack? We have known each other since we were children. Do you remember —

TANNER [*abruptly breaking loose*]. Stop! I remember e v e r y t h i n g.

ANN. Oh, I daresay we were often very silly; but —

TANNER. I wont have it, Ann. I am no more that schoolboy now than I am the dotard of ninety I shall grow into if I live long enough. It is over: let me forget it.

ANN. Wasnt it a happy time? [*She attempts to take his arm again.*]

TANNER. Sit down and behave yourself. [*He makes her sit down in the chair next the writing table.*] No doubt it was a happy time for you. You were a good girl and never compromised yourself. And yet the wickedest child that ever was slapped could hardly have had a better time. I can understand the success with which you bullied the other girls: your virtue imposed on them. But tell me this: did you ever know a good boy?

ANN. Of course. All boys are foolish sometimes; but Tavy was always a really good boy.

TANNER [*struck by this*]. Yes: youre right. For some reason you never tempted Tavy.

ANN. Tempted! Jack!

TANNER. Yes, my dear Lady Mephistopheles, tempted. You were insatiably curious as to what a boy might be capable of, and diabolically clever at getting through his guard and surprising his inmost secrets.

ANN. What nonsense! All because you used to tell me long stories of the wicked things you had done — silly boy's tricks! And you call such things inmost secrets! Boys' secrets are just like men's; and you know what they are!

TANNER [*obstinately*]. No I don't. What are they, pray?

ANN. Why, the things they tell everybody, of course.

TANNER. Now I swear I told you things I told no one else. You lured me into a compact by which we were to have no secrets from one another. We were to tell one another everything. I didnt notice that you never told me anything.

ANN. You didnt want to talk about me, Jack. You wanted to talk about yourself.

TANNER. Ah, true, horribly true. But what a devil of a child you must have been to know that weakness and to play on it for the satisfaction of your own curiosity! I wanted to brag to you, to make myself interesting. And I found myself doing all sorts of mischievous things simply to have something to tell you about. I fought with boys I didnt hate; I lied about things I might just as well have told the truth about; I stole things I didnt want; I kissed little girls I didnt care for. It was all bravado: passionless and therefore unreal.

ANN. I never told of you, Jack.

TANNER. No; but if you had wanted to stop me you would have told of me. You wanted me to go on.

ANN [*flashing out*]. Oh, thats not true: it's not true, Jack. I never wanted you to do those dull, disappointing, brutal, stupid, vulgar things. I always hoped that it would be something really heroic at last. [*Recovering herself*] Excuse me, Jack; but the things you did were never a bit like the things I wanted you to do. They often gave me great uneasiness; but I could not tell of you and get you into trouble. And you were only a boy. I knew you would grow out of them. Perhaps I was wrong.

TANNER [*sardonically*]. Do not give way to remorse, Ann. At least nineteen twentieths of the exploits I confessed to you were pure lies. I soon noticed that you didnt like the true stories.

ANN. Of course I knew that some of the things couldnt have happened. But —

TANNER. You are going to remind me that some of the most disgraceful ones did.

ANN [*fondly, to his great terror*]. I dont want to remind you of anything. But I knew the people they happened to, and heard about them.

TANNER. Yes; but even the true stories were touched up for telling. A sensitive boy's humiliations may be very good fun for ordinary thick-skinned grown-ups; but to the boy himself they are so acute, so ignominious, that he cannot confess them — cannot but deny them passionately. However, perhaps it was as well for me that I romanced a bit; for, on the one occasion when I told you the truth, you threatened to tell of me.

ANN. Oh, never. Never once.

TANNER. Yes, you did. Do you remember a dark-eyed girl named Rachel Rosetree? [*Ann's brows contract for an instant involuntarily.*] I got up a love affair with her; and we met one night in the garden and walked about very uncomfortably with our arms round one another, and kissed at parting, and were most conscientiously romantic. If that love affair had gone on, it would have bored me to death; but it didnt go on; for the next thing that happened was that Rachel cut me because she found out that I had told you. How did she find it out? From you. You went to her and held the guilty secret over her head, leading her a life of abject terror and humiliation by threatening to tell on her.

ANN. And a very good thing for her, too. It was my duty to stop her misconduct; and she is thankful to me for it now.

TANNER. Is she?

ANN. She ought to be, at all events.

TANNER. It was not your duty to stop my misconduct, I suppose.

ANN. I did stop it by stopping her.

TANNER. Are you sure of that? You stopped my telling you about my adventures; but how do you know that you stopped the adventures?

ANN. Do you mean to say that you went on in the same way with other girls?

TANNER. No. I had enough of that sort of romantic tomfoolery with Rachel.

ANN [*unconvinced*]. Then why did you break off our confidences and become quite strange to me?

TANNER [*enigmatically*]. It happened just then that I got something that I wanted to keep all to myself instead of sharing it with you.

ANN. I am sure I shouldnt have asked for any of it if you had grudged it.

TANNER. It wasnt a box of sweets, Ann. It was something youd never have let me call my own.

ANN [*incredulously*]. What?

TANNER. My soul.

ANN. Oh, do be sensible, Jack. You know youre talking nonsense.

TANNER. The most solemn earnest, Ann. You didnt notice at that time that you were getting a soul too. But you were. It was not for nothing that you suddenly found you had a moral duty to chastise and reform Rachel. Up to that time you had traded pretty extensively in being a good child; but you had never set up a sense of duty to others. Well, I set one up too. Up to that time I had played the boy buccaneer with no more conscience than a fox in a poultry farm. But now I began to have scruples, to feel obligations, to find that veracity and honor were no longer goody-goody expressions in the mouths of grown-up people, but compelling principles in myself.

ANN [*quietly*]. Yes, I suppose youre right. You were beginning to be a man, and I to be a woman.

TANNER. Are you sure it was not that we were beginning to be something more? What does the beginning of manhood and womanhood mean in most people's mouths? You know: it means the beginning of love. But love began long before that for me. Love played its part in the earliest dreams and follies and romances I can remember — may I say the earliest follies and romances we can remember? — though we did not understand it at the time. No: the change that came to me was the birth in me of moral passion;[11] and I declare that according to my experience moral passion is the only real passion.

ANN. All passions ought to be moral, Jack.

TANNER. Ought! Do you think that anything is strong enough to impose oughts on a passion except a stronger passion still?

ANN. Our moral sense controls passion, Jack. Dont be stupid.

TANNER. Our moral sense! And is that not a passion? Is the devil to have all the passions as well as all the good tunes? If it were not a passion — if it were not the mightiest of the passions, all the other passions would sweep it away like a leaf before a hurricane. It is the birth of that passion that turns a child into a man.

11. **moral passion:** Cf. ". . . that dawning of moral passion in me which I have described in the first act of *Man and Superman*." Preface to *Immaturity*, p. xx.

ANN. There are other passions, Jack. Very strong ones.

TANNER. All the other passions were in me before; but they were idle and aimless — mere childish greedinesses and cruelties, curiosities and fancies, habits and superstitions, grotesque and ridiculous to the mature intelligence. When they suddenly began to shine like newly lit flames it was by no light of their own, but by the radiance of the dawning moral passion. That passion dignified them, gave them conscience and meaning, found them a mob of appetites and organized them into an army of purposes and principles. My soul was born of that passion.

ANN. I noticed that you got more sense. You were a dreadfully destructive boy before that.

TANNER. Destructive! Stuff! I was only mischievous.

ANN. Oh, Jack, you were very destructive. You ruined all the young fir trees by chopping off their leaders with a wooden sword. You broke all the cucumber frames with your catapult. You set fire to the common: the police arrested Tavy for it because he ran away when he couldnt stop you. You —

TANNER. Pooh! pooh! pooh! these were battles, bombardments, stratagems to save our scalps from the red Indians. You have no imagination, Ann. I am ten times more destructive now than I was then. The moral passion has taken my destructiveness in hand and directed it to moral ends. I have become a reformer, and, like all reformers, an iconoclast. I no longer break cucumber frames and burn gorse bushes: I shatter creeds and demolish idols.

ANN [*bored*]. I am afraid I am too feminine to see any sense in destruction. Destruction can only destroy.

TANNER. Yes. That is why it is so useful. Construction cumbers the ground with institutions made by busybodies. Destruction clears it and gives us breathing space and liberty.

ANN. It's no use, Jack. No woman will agree with you there.

TANNER. Thats because you confuse construction and destruction with creation and murder. Theyre quite different: I adore creation and abhor murder. Yes: I adore it in tree and flower, in bird and beast, even in you. [*A flush of interest and delight suddenly chases the growing perplexity and boredom from her face.*] It was the creative instinct that led you to attach me to you by bonds that have left their mark on me to this day. Yes, Ann: the old childish compact between us was an unconscious love compact —

ANN. Jack!

TANNER. Oh, dont be alarmed —

ANN. I am not alarmed.

TANNER [*whimsically*]. Then you ought to be: where are your principles?

ANN. Jack: are you serious or are you not?

TANNER. Do you mean about the moral passion?

ANN. No, no: the other one. [*Confused*] Oh! you are so silly: one never knows how to take you.

TANNER. You must take me quite seriously. I am your guardian; and it is my duty to improve your mind.

ANN. The love compact is over, then, is it? I suppose you grew tired of me?

TANNER. No; but the moral passion made our childish relations impossible. A jealous sense of my new individuality arose in me —

ANN. You hated to be treated as a boy any longer. Poor Jack!

TANNER. Yes, because to be treated as a boy was to be taken on the old footing. I had become a new person; and those who knew the old person laughed at me. The only man who behaved sensibly was my tailor: he took my measure anew every time he saw me, whilst all the rest went on with their old measurements and expected them to fit me.

ANN. You became frightfully self-conscious.

TANNER. When you go to heaven, Ann, you will be frightfully conscious of your wings for the first year or so. When you meet your relatives there, and they persist in treating you as if you were still a mortal, you will not be able to bear them. You will try to get into a circle which has never known you except as an angel.

ANN. So it was only your vanity that made you run away from us after all?

TANNER. Yes, only my vanity, as you call it.

ANN. You need not have kept away from me on that account.

TANNER. From you above all others. You fought harder than anybody against my emancipation.

ANN [*earnestly*]. Oh, how wrong you are! I would have done anything for you.

TANNER. Anything except let me get loose from you. Even then you had acquired by instinct that damnable woman's trick of heaping obligations on a man, of placing yourself so entirely and helplessly at his mercy that at last he dare not take a step without running to you for leave. I know a poor wretch whose one desire in life is to run away from his wife. She prevents him by threatening to throw herself in front of the engine of the train he leaves her in. That is what all women do. If we try to go where you do not want us to go there is no law to prevent us; but when we take the first step your breasts are under our foot as it descends: your bodies are under our wheels as we start. No woman shall ever enslave me in that way.

ANN. But, Jack, you cannot get through life without considering other people a little.

TANNER. Ay; but what other people? It is this consideration of other people — or rather this cowardly fear of them which we call consideration — that makes us the sentimental slaves we are. To consider you, as you call it, is to substitute your will for my own. How if it be a baser will than mine? Are women taught better than men or worse? Are mobs of voters taught better than statesmen or worse? Worse, of course, in both cases. And then what sort of world are you going to get, with its public men considering its voting mobs, and its private men considering their wives? What does Church and State mean nowadays? The Woman and the Ratepayer.

ANN [*placidly*]. I am so glad you understand politics, Jack: it will be most useful to you if you go into parliament. [*He collapses like a pricked bladder.*] But I am sorry you thought my influence a bad one.

TANNER. I dont say it was a bad one. But bad or good, I didnt choose to be cut to your measure. And I wont be cut to it.

ANN. Nobody wants you to, Jack. I assure you — really on my word — I dont mind your queer opinions one little bit. You know we have all been brought up to have advanced opinions. Why do you persist in thinking me so narrow minded?

TANNER. Thats the danger of it. I know you dont mind, because youve found out that it doesnt matter. The boa constrictor doesnt mind the opinions of a stag one little bit when once she has got her coils round it.

ANN [*rising in sudden enlightenment*]. O-o-o-o-oh! now I understand why you warned Tavy that I am a boa constrictor. Granny told me. [*She laughs and throws her boa round his neck.*] Doesnt it feel nice and soft, Jack?

TANNER [*in the toils*]. You scandalous woman, will you throw away even your hypocrisy?

ANN. I am never hypocritical with you, Jack. Are you angry? [*She withdraws the boa and throws it on a chair.*] Perhaps I shouldnt have done that.

TANNER [*contemptuously*]. Pooh, prudery! Why should you not, if it amuses you?

ANN [*shyly*]. Well, because — because I suppose what you really meant by the boa constrictor was this. [*She puts her arms round his neck.*]

TANNER [*staring at her*]. Magnificent audacity! [*She laughs and pats his cheeks.*] Now just to think that if I mentioned this episode not a soul would believe me except the people who would cut me for telling, whilst if you accused me of it nobody would believe my denial!

ANN [*taking her arms away with perfect dignity*]. You are incorrigible, Jack. But you should not jest about our affection for one another. Nobody could possibly misunderstand it. You do not misunderstand it, I hope.

TANNER. My blood interprets for me, Ann. Poor Ricky Ticky Tavy!

ANN [*looking quickly at him as if this were a new light*]. Surely you are not so absurd as to be jealous of Tavy.

TANNER. Jealous! Why should I be? But I dont wonder at your grip of him. I feel the coils tightening round my very self, though you are only playing with me.

ANN. Do you think I have designs on Tavy?

TANNER. I know you have.

ANN [*earnestly*]. Take care, Jack. You may make Tavy very unhappy if you mislead him about me.

TANNER. Never fear: he will not escape you.

ANN. I wonder are you really a clever man!

TANNER. Why this sudden misgiving on the subject?

ANN. You seem to understand all the things I dont understand; but you are a perfect baby in the things I do understand.

TANNER. I understand how Tavy feels for you, Ann: you may depend on that, at all events.

ANN. And you think you understand how I feel for Tavy, dont you?

TANNER. I know only too well what is going to happen to poor Tavy.

ANN. I should laugh at you, Jack, if it were not for poor papa's death. Mind! Tavy will be very unhappy.

TANNER. Yes; but he wont know it, poor devil. He is a thousand times too good for you. Thats why he is going to make the mistake of his life about you.

ANN. I think men make more mistakes by being too clever than by being too good. [*She sits down, with a trace of contempt for the whole male sex in the elegant carriage of her shoulders.*]

TANNER. Oh, I know you dont care very much about Tavy. But there is always one who kisses and one who only allows the kiss. Tavy will kiss; and you will only turn the cheek. And you will throw him over if anybody better turns up.

ANN [*offended*]. You have no right to say such things, Jack. They are not true, and not delicate. If you and Tavy choose to be stupid about me, that is not my fault.

TANNER [*remorsefully*]. Forgive my brutalities, Ann. They are levelled at this wicked world, not at you. [*She looks up at him, pleased and forgiving. He becomes cautious at once.*] All the same, I wish Ramsden would come back. I never feel safe with you: there is a devilish charm — or no: not a charm, a subtle interest [*she laughs*] — Just so: you know it; and you triumph in it. Openly and shamelessly triumph in it!

ANN. What a shocking flirt you are, Jack!

TANNER. A flirt!! I!!!

ANN. Yes, a flirt. You are always abusing and offending people; but you never really mean to let go your hold of them.

TANNER. I will ring the bell. This conversation has already gone further than I intended.

*Ramsden and Octavius come back with Miss Ramsden, a hardheaded old maiden lady in a plain brown silk gown, with enough rings, chains, and brooches to shew that her plainness of dress is a matter of principle, not of poverty. She comes into the room very determinedly: the two men, perplexed and downcast, following her. Ann rises and goes eagerly to meet her. Tanner retreats to the wall between the busts and pretends to study the pictures. Ramsden goes to his table as usual; and Octavius clings to the neighborhood of Tanner.*

MISS RAMSDEN [*almost pushing Ann aside as she comes to Mrs Whitefield's chair and plants herself there resolutely*]. I wash my hands of the whole affair.

OCTAVIUS [*very wretched*]. I know you wish me to take Violet away, Miss Ramsden. I will. [*He turns irresolutely to the door.*]

RAMSDEN. No, no —

MISS RAMSDEN. What is the use of saying no, Roebuck? Octavius knows that I would not turn any truly contrite and repentant woman from your doors. But when a woman is not only wicked, but intends to go on being wicked, she and I part company.

ANN. Oh, Miss Ramsden, what do you mean? What has Violet said?

RAMSDEN. Violet is certainly very obstinate. She wont leave London. I dont understand her.

MISS RAMSDEN. I do. It's as plain as the nose on your face, Roebuck, that she wont go because she doesnt want to be separated from this man, whoever he is.

ANN. Oh, surely, surely! Octavius: did you speak to her?

OCTAVIUS. She wont tell us anything. She wont make any arrangement until she has consulted somebody. It cant be anybody else than the scoundrel who has betrayed her.

TANNER [*to Octavius*]. Well, let her consult him. He will be glad enough to have her sent abroad. Where is the difficulty?

MISS RAMSDEN [*taking the answer out of Octavius's mouth*]. The difficulty, Mr Jack, is that when I offered to help her I didnt offer to become her accomplice in her wickedness. She either pledges her word never to see that man again, or else she finds some new friends; and the sooner the better.

*The parlormaid appears at the door. Ann hastily resumes her seat, and looks as unconcerned as possible. Octavius instinctively imitates her.*

THE MAID. The cab is at the door, ma'am.

MISS RAMSDEN. What cab?

THE MAID. For Miss Robinson.

MISS RAMSDEN. Oh! [*Recovering herself*] All right. [*The maid withdraws.*] She has sent for a cab.

TANNER. *I* wanted to send for that cab half an hour ago.

MISS RAMSDEN. I am glad she understands the position she has placed herself in.

RAMSDEN. I dont like her going away in this fashion, Susan. We had better not do anything harsh.

OCTAVIUS. No: thank you again and again; but Miss Ramsden is quite right. Violet cannot expect to stay.

ANN. Hadnt you better go with her, Tavy?

OCTAVIUS. She wont have me.

MISS RAMSDEN. Of course she wont. She's going straight to that man.

TANNER. As a natural result of her virtuous reception here.

RAMSDEN [*much troubled*]. There, Susan! You hear! and theres some truth in it. I wish you could reconcile it with your principles to be a little patient with this poor girl. She's very young; and theres a time for everything.

MISS RAMSDEN. Oh, she will get all the sympathy she wants from the men. I'm surprised at you, Roebuck.

TANNER. So am I, Ramsden, most favorably.

*Violet appears at the door. She is as impenitent and self-possessed a young lady as one could desire to see among the best behaved of her sex. Her small head and tiny resolute mouth and chin; her haughty crispness of speech and trimness of carriage; the ruthless elegance of her equipment, which includes a very smart hat with a dead bird in it, mark a personality which is as formidable as it is exquisitely pretty. She is not a siren, like Ann: admiration comes to her without any compulsion or even interest on her part; besides, there is some fun in Ann, but in this woman none, perhaps no mercy either: if anything restrains her, it is intelligence and pride, not compassion. Her voice might be the voice of a schoolmistress addressing a class of girls who had disgraced themselves, as she proceeds with complete composure and some disgust to say what she has come to say.*

VIOLET. I have only looked in to tell Miss Ramsden that she will find her birthday present to me, the filagree bracelet, in the housekeeper's room.

TANNER. Do come in, Violet; and talk to us sensibly.

VIOLET. Thank you: I have had quite enough of the family conversation this morning. So has your mother, Ann: she has gone home crying. But at all events, I have found out what some of my pretended friends are worth. Goodbye.

TANNER. No, no: one moment. I have something to say which I beg you to hear. [*She looks at him without the slightest curiosity, but waits, apparently as much to finish getting her glove on as to hear what he has to say.*] I am altogether on your side in this matter. I congratulate you, with the sincerest respect, on having the courage to do what you have done. You are entirely in the right; and the family is entirely in the wrong.

*Sensation. Ann and Miss Ramsden rise and turn towards the two. Violet, more surprised than any of the others, forgets her glove, and comes forward into the middle of the room, both puzzled and displeased. Octavius alone does not move nor raise his head: he is overwhelmed with shame.*

ANN [*pleading to Tanner to be sensible*]. Jack!

MISS RAMSDEN [*outraged*]. Well, I must say!

VIOLET [*sharply to Tanner*]. Who told you?

TANNER. Why, Ramsden and Tavy of course. Why should they not?

VIOLET. But they dont know.

TANNER. Dont know what?

VIOLET. They dont know that I am in the right, I mean.

TANNER. Oh, they know it in their hearts, though they think themselves bound to blame you by their silly superstitions about morality and propriety and so forth. But I know, and the whole world really knows, though it dare not say so, that you were right to follow your instinct; that vitality and bravery are the greatest qualities a woman can have, and motherhood her solemn initiation into womanhood; and that the fact of your not being legally married matters not one scrap either to your own worth or to our real regard for you.

VIOLET [*flushing with indignation*]. Oh! You think me a wicked woman, like the rest. You think I have not only been vile, but that I share your abominable opinions. Miss Ramsden: I have borne your hard words because I knew you would be sorry for them when you found out the truth. But I wont bear such a horrible insult as to be complimented by Jack on being one of the wretches of whom he approves. I have kept my marriage a secret for my husband's sake. But now I claim my right as a married woman not to be insulted.

OCTAVIUS [*raising his head with inexpressible relief*]. You are married!

VIOLET. Yes; and I think you might have guessed it. What business had you all to take it for granted that I had no right to wear my wedding ring? Not one of you even asked me: I cannot forget that.

TANNER [*in ruins*]. I am utterly crushed. I meant well. I apologize — abjectly apologize.

VIOLET. I hope you will be more careful in future about the things you say. Of course one does not take them seriously; but they are very disagreeable, and rather in bad taste, I think.

TANNER [*bowing to the storm*]. I have no defence: I shall know better in future than to take any woman's part. We have all disgraced ourselves in your eyes, I am afraid, except Ann. She befriended you. For Ann's sake, forgive us.

VIOLET. Yes! Ann has been kind; but then Ann knew.

TANNER [*with a desperate gesture*]. Oh!!! Unfathomable deceit! Double crossed!

MISS RAMSDEN [*stiffly*]. And who, pray, is the gentleman who does not acknowledge his wife?

VIOLET [*promptly*]. That is my business, Miss Ramsden, and not yours. I have my reasons for keeping my marriage a secret for the present.

RAMSDEN. All I can say is that we are extremely sorry, Violet. I am shocked to think of how we have treated you.

OCTAVIUS [*awkwardly*]. I beg your pardon, Violet. I can say no more.

MISS RAMSDEN [*still loth to surrender*]. Of course what you say puts a very different complexion on the matter. All the same, I owe it to myself —

VIOLET [*cutting her short*]. You owe me an apology, Miss Ramsden: thats what you owe both to yourself and to me. If you were a married woman you would not like sitting in the housekeeper's room and being treated like a naughty child by young girls and old ladies without any serious duties and responsibilities.

TANNER. Dont hit us when we're down, Violet. We seem to have made fools of ourselves; but really it was you who made fools of us.

VIOLET. It was no business of yours, Jack, in any case.

TANNER. No business of mine! Why, Ramsden as good as accused me of being the unknown gentleman.

*Ramsden makes a frantic demonstration; but Violet's cool keen anger extinguishes it.*

VIOLET. You! Oh, how infamous! how abominable! how disgracefully you have all been talking about me! If my husband knew it he would never let me speak to any of you again. [*To Ramsden*] I think you might have spared me that, at least.

RAMSDEN. But I assure you I never — at least it is a monstrous perversion of something I said that —

MISS RAMSDEN. You neednt apologize, Roebuck. She brought it all on herself. It is for her to apologize for having deceived us.

VIOLET. I can make allowances for you, Miss Ramsden: you cannot understand how I feel on this subject, though I should have expected rather better taste from people of greater experience. However, I quite feel that you have placed yourselves in a very painful position; and the most truly considerate thing for me to do is to go at once. Good morning.

*She goes, leaving them staring.*

MISS RAMSDEN. Well, I must say!

RAMSDEN [*plaintively*]. I dont think she is quite fair to us.

TANNER. You must cower before the wedding ring like the rest of us, Ramsden. The cup of our ignominy is full.

# Act II

*On the carriage drive in the park of a country house near Richmond* [1] *an open touring car has broken down. It stands in front of a clump of trees round which the drive sweeps to the house, which is partly visible through them: indeed Tanner, standing in the drive with his back to us, could get an unobstructed view of the west corner of the house on his left were he not far too much interested in a pair of supine legs in dungaree overalls which protrude from beneath the machine. He is watching them intently with bent back and hands supported on his knees. His leathern overcoat and peaked cap proclaim him one of the dismounted passengers.*

THE LEGS. Aha! I got him.

TANNER. All right now?

THE LEGS. Aw rawt nah.

*Tanner stoops and takes the legs by the ankles, drawing their owner forth like a wheelbarrow, walking on his hands, with a hammer in his mouth. He is a young man in a neat suit of blue serge, clean shaven, dark eyed, square fingered, with short well brushed black hair and rather irregular sceptically turned eyebrows. When he is manipulating the car his movements are swift and sudden, yet attentive and deliberate. With Tanner and Tanner's friends his manner is not in the least deferential, but cool and reticent, keeping them quite effectually at a distance whilst giving them no excuse for complaining of him. Nevertheless he has a vigilant eye on them always, and that, too, rather cynically, like a man who knows the world well from its seamy side. He speaks slowly and with a touch of sarcasm; and as he does not at all affect the gentleman in his speech, it may be inferred that his smart appearance is a mark of respect to himself and his own class, not to that which employs him.*

**Act II:** 1. ***Richmond:*** near London, on the Thames, once famous for its royal palace, still one of the more attractive suburbs in the London area.

*He now gets into the car to stow away his tools and divest himself of his overalls. Tanner takes off his leathern overcoat and pitches it into the car with a sigh of relief, glad to be rid of it. The chauffeur, noting this, tosses his head contemptuously, and surveys his employer sardonically.*

THE CHAUFFEUR. Had enough of it, eh?

TANNER. I may as well walk to the house and stretch my legs and calm my nerves a little. [*Looking at his watch*] I suppose you know that we have come from Hyde Park Corner to Richmond in twenty-one minutes.

THE CHAUFFEUR. I'd ha done it under fifteen if I'd had a clear road all the way.

TANNER. Why do you do it? Is it for love of sport or for the fun of terrifying your unfortunate employer?

THE CHAUFFEUR. What are you afraid of?

TANNER. The police, and breaking my neck.

THE CHAUFFEUR. Well, if you like easy going, you can take a bus, you know. It's cheaper. You pay me to save your time and give you the value of what you paid for the car. [*He sits down calmly.*]

TANNER. I am the slave of that car and of you too. I dream of the accursed thing at night.

THE CHAUFFEUR. Youll get over that all right. If youre going up to the house, may I ask how long youre goin to stay? Because if you mean to put in the whole morning in there, talkin to the ladies, I'll put the car in the garage and make myself agreeable with a view to lunching here. If not, I'll keep the car on the go about here til you come.

TANNER. Better wait here. We shant be long. Theres a young American gentleman, a Mr Malone, who is driving Mr Robinson down in his new American steam car.

THE CHAUFFEUR [*springing up and coming hastily out of the car to Tanner*]. American steam car! Wot! racin us dahn from London!

TANNER. Perhaps theyre here already.

THE CHAUFFEUR. If I'd known it! [*With deep reproach*] Why didn't you tell me, Mr Tanner?

TANNER. Because Ive been told that this car is capable of 84 miles an hour; and I already know what you are capable of when there is a rival car on the road. No, Henry: there are things it is not good for you to know; and this was one of them. However, cheer up: we are going to have a day after your own heart. The American is to take Mr Robinson and his sister and Miss Whitefield. We are to take Miss Rhoda.

THE CHAUFFEUR [*consoled, and musing on another matter*]. Thats Miss Whitefield's sister, isnt it?

TANNER. Yes.

THE CHAUFFEUR. And Miss Whitefield herself is goin in the other car? Not with you?

TANNER. Why the devil should she come with me? Mr Robinson will be in the other car. [*The Chauffeur looks at Tanner with cool incredulity, and turns to the car, whistling a popular air softly to himself. Tanner, a little annoyed, is about to pursue the subject when he hears the footsteps of Octavius on the gravel. Octavius is coming from the house, dressed for motoring, but without his overcoat.*] Weve lost the race, thank Heaven: heres Mr Robinson. Well, Tavy, is the steam car a success?

OCTAVIUS. I think so. We came from Hyde Park Corner here in seventeen minutes. [*The Chauffeur, furious, kicks the car with a groan of vexation.*] How long were you?

TANNER. Oh, about three quarters of an hour or so.

THE CHAUFFEUR [*remonstrating*]. Now, now, Mr Tanner, come now! We could ha done it easy under fifteen.

TANNER. By the way, let me introduce you. Mr Octavius Robinson: Mr Enry Straker.

STRAKER. Pleased to meet you, sir. Mr Tanner is gittin at you with is Enry Straker, you know. You call it Henery. But I dont mind, bless you!

TANNER. You think it's simply bad taste in me to chaff him, Tavy. But youre wrong. This man takes more trouble to drop his aitches than ever his father did to pick them up. It's a mark of caste to him. I have never met anybody more swollen with the pride of class than Enry is.

STRAKER. Easy, easy! A little moderation, Mr Tanner.

TANNER. A little moderation, Tavy, you observe. You would tell me to draw it mild. But this chap has been educated. Whats more, he knows that we havnt. What was that Board School [2] of yours, Straker?

STRAKER. Sherbrooke Road.

TANNER. Sherbrooke Road! Would any of us say Rugby! Harrow! Eton! [3] in that tone of intellectual snobbery? Sherbrooke Road is a place where boys learn something: Eton is a boy farm where we are sent because we are nuisances at home, and because in after life, whenever a Duke is mentioned, we can claim him as an old school-fellow.

STRAKER. You dont know nothing about it, Mr Tanner. It's not the Board School that does it: it's the Polytechnic.[4]

TANNER. His university, Octavius. Not Oxford, Cambridge, Durham, Dublin, or Glasgow. Not even those Noncomformist holes in Wales. No, Tavy. Regent Street! Chelsea! the Borough! [5]—I dont know half their confounded names: these are his universities, not mere shops for selling class limitations like ours. You despise Oxford, Enry, dont you?

STRAKER. No, I dont. Very nice sort of place, Oxford, I should think, for people that like that sort of place. They teach you to be a gentleman there. In the Polytechnic they teach you to be an engineer or such like. See?

TANNER. Sarcasm, Tavy, sarcasm! Oh, if you could only see into Enry's soul, the depth of his contempt for a gentleman, the arrogance of his pride in being an engineer, would appal you. He positively likes the car to break down because it brings out my gentlemanly helplessness and his workmanlike skill and resource.

STRAKER. Never you mind him, Mr Robinson. He likes to talk. We know him, dont we?

OCTAVIUS [*earnestly*]. But theres a great truth at the bottom of what he says. I believe most intensely in the dignity of labor.

STRAKER [*unimpressed*]. Thats because you never done any, Mr Robinson. My business is to do away with labor. Youll get more out of me and a machine than you will out of twenty laborers, and not so much to drink either.

TANNER. For Heaven's sake, Tavy, dont start him on political economy. He knows all about it; and we dont. Youre only a poetic Socialist, Tavy: he's a scientific one.

STRAKER [*unperturbed*]. Yes. Well, this conversation is very improvin; but Ive got to look after the car; and you two want to talk about your ladies. *I* know. [*He pretends to busy himself about the car, but presently saunters off to indulge in a cigaret.*]

TANNER. Thats a very momentous social phenomenon.

OCTAVIUS. What is?

TANNER. Straker is. Here have we literary and cultured persons been for years setting up a cry of the New Woman whenever some unusually old fashioned female came along and never noticing the advent of the New Man. Straker's the New Man.

OCTAVIUS. I see nothing new about him, except your way of chaffing him. But I dont want to talk about him just now. I want to speak to you about Ann.

TANNER. Straker knew even that. He learnt it at the Polytechnic, probably. Well, what about Ann? Have you proposed to her?

OCTAVIUS [*self-reproachfully*]. I was brute enough to do so last night.

TANNER. Brute enough! What do you mean?

**2. Board School**: a school under the management of a school board, corresponding to an American public school. **3.** Rugby, Harrow, and Eton are English "public schools," that is, private secondary schools comparable to American preparatory schools. By tradition, they are concerned with the education of "gentlemen." **4. Polytechnic**: technical school, London.

**5. Regent Street**: London. **Chelsea**: a borough (or quarter) of London. **the Borough**: refers especially to Southwark.

OCTAVIUS [*dithyrambically*]. Jack: we men are all coarse: we never understand how exquisite a woman's sensibilities are. How could I have done such a thing!

TANNER. Done what, you maudlin idiot?

OCTAVIUS. Yes, I a m an idiot. Jack: if you had heard her voice! If you had seen her tears! I have lain awake all night thinking of them. If she had reproached me, I could have borne it better.

TANNER. Tears! thats dangerous. What did she say?

OCTAVIUS. She asked me how she could think of anything now but her dear father. She stifled a sob — [*He breaks down.*]

TANNER [*patting him on the back*]. Bear it like a man, Tavy, even if you feel it like an ass. It's the old game: she's not tired of playing with you yet.

OCTAVIUS [*impatiently*]. Oh, dont be a fool, Jack. Do you suppose this eternal shallow cynicism of yours has any real bearing on a nature like hers?

TANNER. Hm! Did she say anything else?

OCTAVIUS. Yes; and that is why I expose myself and her to your ridicule by telling you what passed.

TANNER [*remorsefully*]. No, dear Tavy, not ridicule, on my honor! However, no matter. Go on.

OCTAVIUS. Her sense of duty is so devout, so perfect, so —

TANNER. Yes: I know. Go on.

OCTAVIUS. You see, under this new arrangement, you and Ramsden are her guardians; and she considers that all her duty to her father is now transferred to you. She said she thought I ought to have spoken to you both in the first instance. Of course she is right; but somehow it seems rather absurd that I am to come to you and formally ask to be received as a suitor for your ward's hand.

TANNER. I am glad that love has not totally extinguished your sense of humor, Tavy.

OCTAVIUS. That answer wont satisfy her.

TANNER. My official answer is, obviously, Bless you, my children: may you be happy!

OCTAVIUS. I wish you would stop playing the fool about this. If it is not serious to you, it is to me, and to her.

TANNER. You know very well that she is as free to choose as you are.

OCTAVIUS. She does not think so.

TANNER. Oh, doesnt she! just! However, say what you want me to do?

OCTAVIUS. I want you to tell her sincerely and earnestly what you think about me. I want you to tell her that you can trust her to me — that is, if you feel you can.

TANNER. I have no doubt that I can trust her to you. What worries me is the idea of trusting you to her. Have you read Maeterlinck's[6] book about the bee?

OCTAVIUS [*keeping his temper with difficulty*]. I am not discussing literature at present.

TANNER. Be just a little patient with me. *I* am not discussing literature: the book about the bee is natural history. It's an awful lesson to mankind. You think that you are Ann's suitor; that you are the pursuer and she the pursued; that it is your part to woo, to persuade, to prevail, to overcome. Fool: it is you who are the pursued, the marked down quarry, the destined prey. You need not sit looking longingly at the bait through the wires of the trap: the door is open, and will remain so until it shuts behind you for ever.

OCTAVIUS. I wish I could believe that, vilely as you put it.

TANNER. Why, man, what other work has she in life but to get a husband? It is a woman's business to get married as soon as possible, and a man's to keep unmarried as long as he can. You have your poems and your tragedies to work at: Ann has nothing.

OCTAVIUS. I cannot write without inspiration. And nobody can give me that except Ann.

TANNER. Well, hadnt you better get it from her at a safe distance? Petrarch didnt see half as much of Laura,[7] nor Dante of Beatrice, as you see of Ann now; and yet they wrote first-rate poetry — at least so I'm told. They never exposed their idolatry to the test of domestic familiarity; and it lasted them to their graves. Marry Ann; and at the end of a week youll find no more inspiration in her than in a plate of muffins.

OCTAVIUS. You think I shall tire of her!

TANNER. Not at all: you dont get tired of muffins. But you dont find inspiration in them; and you wont in her when she ceases to be a poet's dream and becomes a solid eleven stone wife. Youll be forced to dream about somebody else; and then there will be a row.

OCTAVIUS. This sort of talk is no use, Jack. You dont understand. You have never been in love.

TANNER. I! I have never been out of it. Why, I am in love even with Ann. But I am neither the slave of love nor its dupe. Go to the bee, thou poet: consider her ways and be wise. By Heaven, Tavy, if women could do without our work, and we ate their children's bread instead of making it, they would kill us as the spider kills her mate or as the bees kill the drone. And they would be right if we were good for nothing but love.

OCTAVIUS. Ah, if we were only good enough for

**6. Maeterlinck:** Maurice Maeterlinck (1862–1949), Belgian poet and dramatist, also author of a biological study, *The Life of the Bee.* **7. Laura:** beloved of the Italian poet Petrarch (1304–74).

Love! There is nothing like Love: there is nothing else but Love: without it the world would be a dream of sordid horror.

TANNER. And this—this is the man who asks me to give him the hand of my ward! Tavy: I believe we were changed in our cradles, and that you are the real descendant of Don Juan.

OCTAVIUS. I beg you not to say anything like that to Ann.

TANNER. Dont be afraid. She has marked you for her own; and nothing will stop her now. You are doomed. [*Straker comes back with a newspaper.*] Here comes the New Man, demoralizing himself with a halfpenny paper as usual.

STRAKER. Now would you believe it, Mr Robinson, when we're out motoring we take in two papers: the Times for him, the Leader or the Echo for me. And do you think I ever see my paper? Not much. He grabs the Leader and leaves me to stodge myself with his Times.

OCTAVIUS. Are there no winners in the Times?

TANNER. Enry dont old with bettin, Tavy. Motor records are his weakness. Whats the latest?

STRAKER. Paris to Biskra at forty mile an hour average, not countin the Mediterranean.

TANNER. How many killed?

STRAKER. Two silly sheep. What does it matter? Sheep dont cost such a lot: they were glad to ave the price without the trouble o sellin em to the butcher. All the same, d'y'see, therell be a clamor agin it presently; and then the French Government'll stop it; an our chance'll be gone, see? Thats what makes me fairly mad: Mr Tanner wont do a good run while he can.

TANNER. Tavy: do you remember my uncle James?

OCTAVIUS. Yes. Why?

TANNER. Uncle James had a first rate cook: he couldnt digest anything except what she cooked. Well, the poor man was shy and hated society. But his cook was proud of her skill, and wanted to serve up dinners to princes and ambassadors. To prevent her from leaving him, that poor old man had to give a big dinner twice a month, and suffer agonies of awkwardness. Now here am I; and here is this chap Enry Straker, the New Man. I loathe travelling; but I rather like Enry. He cares for nothing but tearing along in a leather coat and goggles, with two inches of dust all over him, at sixty miles an hour and the risk of his life and mine. Except, of course, when he is lying on his back in the mud under the machine trying to find out where it has given way. Well, if I dont give him a thousand mile run at least once a fortnight I shall lose him. He will give me the sack and go to some American millionaire; and I shall have to put up with a nice respectful groom-gardener-amateur, who will touch his hat and know his place. I am Enry's slave, just as Uncle James was his cook's slave.

STRAKER [*exasperated*]. Garn! I wish I had a car that would go as fast as you can talk, Mr Tanner. What I say is that you lose money by a motor car unless you keep it workin. Might as well ave a pram and a nussmaid to wheel you in it as that car and me if you dont git the last inch out of us both.

TANNER [*soothingly*]. All right, Henry, all right. We'll go out for half an hour presently.

STRAKER [*in disgust*]. Arf an ahr! [*He returns to his machine; seats himself in it; and turns up a fresh page of his paper in search of more news.*]

OCTAVIUS. Oh, that reminds me. I have a note for you from Rhoda. [*He gives Tanner a note.*]

TANNER. [*opening it*]. I rather think Rhoda is heading for a row with Ann. As a rule there is only one person an English girl hates more than she hates her eldest sister; and thats her mother. But Rhoda positively prefers her mother to Ann. She—[*indignantly*] Oh, I say!

OCTAVIUS. Whats the matter?

TANNER. Rhoda was to have come with me for a ride in the motor car. She says Ann has forbidden her to go out with me.

*Straker suddenly begins whistling his favorite air with remarkable deliberation. Surprised by this burst of larklike melody, and jarred by a sardonic note in its cheerfulness, they turn and look inquiringly at him. But he is busy with his paper; and nothing comes of their movement.*

OCTAVIUS [*recovering himself*]. Does she give any reason?

TANNER. Reason! An insult is not a reason. Ann forbids her to be alone with me on any occasion. Says I am not a fit person for a young girl to be with. What do you think of your paragon now?

OCTAVIUS. You must remember that she has a very heavy responsibility now that her father is dead. Mrs Whitefield is too weak to control Rhoda.

TANNER [*staring at him*]. In short, you agree with Ann.

OCTAVIUS. No; but I think I understand her. You must admit that your views are hardly suited for the formation of a young girl's mind and character.

TANNER. I admit nothing of the sort. I admit that the formation of a young lady's mind and character usually consists in telling her lies; but I object to the particular lie that I am in the habit of abusing the confidence of girls.

OCTAVIUS. Ann doesnt say that, Jack.

TANNER. What else does she mean?

STRAKER [*catching sight of Ann coming from the house*]. Miss Whitefield, gentlemen. [*He dismounts and strolls away down the avenue with the air of a man who knows he is no longer wanted.*]

ANN [*coming between Octavius and Tanner*].

Good morning, Jack. I have come to tell you that poor Rhoda has got one of her headaches and cannot go out with you today in the car. It is a cruel disappointment to her, poor child!

TANNER. What do you say now, Tavy?

OCTAVIUS. Surely you cannot misunderstand, Jack. Ann is shewing you the kindest consideration, even at the cost of deceiving you.

ANN. What do you mean?

TANNER. Would you like to cure Rhoda's headache, Ann?

ANN. Of course.

TANNER. Then tell her what you said just now; and add that you arrived about two minutes after I had received her letter and read it.

ANN. Rhoda has written to you!

TANNER. With full particulars.

OCTAVIUS. Never mind him, Ann. You were right—quite right. Ann was only doing her duty, Jack; and you know it. Doing it in the kindest way, too.

ANN [*going to Octavius*]. How kind you are, Tavy! How helpful! How well you understand!

*Octavius beams.*

TANNER. Ay: tighten the coils. You love her, Tavy, dont you?

OCTAVIUS. She knows I do.

ANN. Hush. For shame, Tavy!

TANNER. Oh, I give you leave. I am your guardian; and I commit you to Tavy's care for the next hour. I am off for a turn in the car.

ANN. No, Jack. I must speak to you about Rhoda. Ricky: will you go back to the house and entertain your American friend. He's rather on Mamma's hands so early in the morning. She wants to finish her housekeeping.

OCTAVIUS. I fly, dearest Ann. [*He kisses her hand.*]

ANN [*tenderly*]. Ricky Ticky Tavy!

*He looks at her with an eloquent blush, and runs off.*

TANNER [*bluntly*]. Now look here, Ann. This time youve landed yourself; and if Tavy were not in love with you past all salvation he'd have found out what an incorrigible liar you are.

ANN. You misunderstand, Jack. I didnt dare tell Tavy the truth.

TANNER. No: your daring is generally in the opposite direction. What the devil do you mean by telling Rhoda that I am too vicious to associate with her? How can I ever have any human or decent relations with her again, now that you have poisoned her mind in that abominable way?

ANN. I know you are incapable of behaving badly—

TANNER. Then why did you lie to her?

ANN. I had to.

TANNER. Had to!

ANN. Mother made me.

TANNER [*his eye flashing*]. Ha! I might have known it. The mother! Always the mother!

ANN. It was that dreadful book of yours. You know how timid mother is. All timid women are conventional: we m u s t be conventional, Jack, or we are so cruelly, so vilely misunderstood. Even you, who are a man, cannot say what you think without being misunderstood and vilified—yes: I admit it: I have had to vilify you. Do you want to have poor Rhoda misunderstood and vilified in the same way? Would it be right for mother to let her expose herself to such treatment before she is old enough to judge for herself?

TANNER. In short, the way to avoid misunderstanding is for everybody to lie and slander and insinuate and pretend as hard as they can. That is what obeying your mother comes to.

ANN. I love my mother, Jack.

TANNER [*working himself up into a sociological rage*]. Is that any reason why you are not to call your soul your own? Oh, I protest against this vile abjection of youth to age! Look at fashionable society as you know it. What does it pretend to be? An exquisite dance of nymphs. What is it? A horrible procession of wretched girls, each in the claws of a cynical, cunning, avaricious, disillusioned, ignorantly experienced, foul-minded old woman whom she calls mother, and whose duty it is to corrupt her mind and sell her to the highest bidder. Why do these unhappy slaves marry anybody, however old and vile, sooner than not marry at all? Because marriage is their only means of escape from these decrepit fiends who hide their selfish ambitions, their jealous hatreds of the young rivals who have supplanted them, under the mask of maternal duty and family affection. Such things are abominable: the voice of nature proclaims for the daughter a father's care and for the son a mother's. The law for father and son and mother and daughter is not the law of love: it is the law of revolution, of emancipation, of final supersession of the old and worn-out by the young and capable. I tell you, the first duty of manhood and womanhood is a Declaration of Independence: the man who pleads his father's authority is no man: the woman who pleads her mother's authority is unfit to bear citizens to a free people.

ANN [*watching him with quiet curiosity*]. I suppose you will go in seriously for politics some day, Jack.

TANNER [*heavily let down*]. Eh? What? Wh—? [*Collecting his scattered wits*] What has that got to do with what I have been saying?

ANN. You talk so well.

TANNER. Talk! Talk! It means nothing to you but talk. Well, go back to your mother, and help her to poison Rhoda's imagination as she has poisoned yours. It is the tame elephants who enjoy capturing the wild ones.

ANN. I am getting on. Yesterday I was a boa constrictor: today I am an elephant.

TANNER. Yes. So pack your trunk and begone: I have no more to say to you.

ANN. You are so utterly unreasonable and impracticable. What c a n I do?

TANNER. Do! Break your chains. Go your way according to your own conscience and not according to your mother's. Get your mind clean and vigorous; and learn to enjoy a fast ride in a motor car instead of seeing nothing in it but an excuse for a detestable intrigue. Come with me to Marseilles and across to Algiers and to Biskra, at sixty miles an hour. Come right down to the Cape if you like. That will be a Declaration of Independence with a vengeance. You can write a book about it afterwards. That will finish your mother and make a woman of you.

ANN [*thoughtfully*]. I dont think there would be any harm in that, Jack. You are my guardian: you stand in my father's place, by his own wish. Nobody could say a word against our travelling together. It would be delightful: thank you a thousand times, Jack. I'll come.

TANNER [*aghast*]. Youll come!!!

ANN. Of course.

TANNER. But — [*He stops, utterly appalled; then resumes feebly*] No: look here, Ann: if theres no harm in it theres no point in doing it.

ANN. How absurd you are! You dont want to compromise me, do you?

TANNER. Yes: thats the whole sense of my proposal.

ANN. You are talking the greatest nonsense; and you know it. You would never do anything to hurt me.

TANNER. Well, if you dont want to be compromised, dont come.

ANN [*with simple earnestness*]. Yes, I will come, Jack, since you wish it. You are my guardian; and I think we ought to see more of one another and come to know one another better. [*Gratefully*] It's very thoughtful and very kind of you, Jack, to offer me this lovely holiday, especially after what I said about Rhoda. You really are good — much better than you think. When do we start?

TANNER. But —

*The conversation is interrupted by the arrival of Mrs Whitefield from the house. She is accompanied by the American gentleman, and followed by Ramsden and Octavius.*

*Hector Malone is an Eastern American; but he is not at all ashamed of his nationality. This makes English people of fashion think well of him, as of a young fellow who is manly enough to confess to an obvious disadvantage without any attempt to conceal or extenuate it. They feel that he ought not to be made to suffer for what is clearly not his fault, and make a point of being specially kind to him. His chivalrous manners to women, and his elevated moral sentiments, being both gratuitous and unusual, strike them as perhaps a little unfortunate; and though they find his vein of easy humor rather amusing when it has ceased to puzzle them (as it does at first), they have had to make him understand that he really must not tell anecdotes unless they are strictly personal and scandalous, and also that oratory is an accomplishment which belongs to a cruder stage of civilization than that in which his migration has landed him. On these points Hector is not quite convinced: he still thinks that the British are apt to make merits of their stupidities, and to represent their various incapacities as points of good breeding. English life seems to him to suffer from a lack of edifying rhetoric (which he calls moral tone); English behavior to shew a want of respect for womanhood; English pronunciation to fail very vulgarly in tackling such words as world, girl, bird, etc.; English society to be plain spoken to an extent which stretches occasionally to intolerable coarseness; and English intercourse to need enlivening by games and stories and other pastimes; so he does not feel called upon to acquire these defects after taking great pains to cultivate himself in a first rate manner before venturing across the Atlantic. To this culture he finds English people either totally indifferent, as they very commonly are to all culture, or else politely evasive, the truth being that Hector's culture is nothing but a state of saturation with our literary exports of thirty years ago, reimported by him to be unpacked at a moment's notice and hurled at the head of English literature, science, and art, at every conversational opportunity. The dismay set up by these sallies encourages him in his belief that he is helping to educate England. When he finds people chattering harmlessly about Anatole France*[8] *and Nietzsche, he devastates them with Matthew Arnold, the Autocrat of the Breakfast Table,*[9] *and even Macaulay;*[10] *and as he is devoutly religious at bottom, he first leads the unwary, by humorous irreverence, to leave popular theology out of account in discussing moral questions with him, and then scatters them in confusion by demanding whether the carrying out of his ideals of conduct was not the manifest object of God Almighty in creating honest men and pure*

8. ***Anatole France:*** French novelist (1844–1924). Because of the skeptical and erotic aspects of his novels, France, like Nietzsche, would certainly have shocked and surprised Hector. 9. ***Autocrat . . . Table:*** collection of sketches (1858), by Oliver Wendell Holmes (1809–94). 10. ***Macaulay:*** Thomas Babington Macaulay (1800–59), author of a *History of England* enormously popular in its day.

*women. The engaging freshness of his personality and the dumbfoundering staleness of his culture make it extremely difficult to decide whether he is worth knowing; for whilst his company is undeniably pleasant and enlivening, there is intellectually nothing new to be got out of him, especially as he despises politics, and is careful not to talk commercial shop, in which department he is probably much in advance of his English capitalist friends. He gets on best with romantic Christians of the amoristic sect: hence the friendship which has sprung up between him and Octavius.*

*In appearance Hector is a neatly built young man of twenty-four, with a short, smartly trimmed black beard, clear, well shaped eyes, and an ingratiating vivacity of expression. He is, from the fashionable point of view, faultlessly dressed. As he comes along the drive from the house with Mrs Whitefield he is sedulously making himself agreeable and entertaining, and thereby placing on her slender wit a burden it is unable to bear. An Englishman would let her alone, accepting boredom and indifference as their common lot; and the poor lady wants to be either let alone or let prattle about the things that interest her.*

*Ramsden strolls over to inspect the motor car. Octavius joins Hector.*

ANN [*pouncing on her mother joyously*]. Oh, mamma, what do you think! Jack is going to take me to Nice in his motor car. Isnt it lovely? I am the happiest person in London.

TANNER [*desperately*]. Mrs Whitefield objects. I am sure she objects. Doesnt she, Ramsden?

RAMSDEN. I should think it very likely indeed.

ANN. You dont object, do you, mother?

MRS WHITFIELD. *I* object! Why should I? I think it will do you good, Ann. [*Trotting over to Tanner*] I meant to ask you to take Rhoda out for a run occasionally: she is too much in the house; but it will do when you come back.

TANNER. Abyss beneath abyss of perfidy!

ANN [*hastily, to distract attention from this outburst*]. Oh, I forgot: you have not met Mr Malone. Mr Tanner, my guardian: Mr Hector Malone.

HECTOR. Pleased to meet you, Mr. Tanner. I should like to suggest an extension of the travelling party to Nice, if I may.

ANN. Oh, we're all coming. Thats understood, isnt it?

HECTOR. I also am the mawdest possessor of a motor car. If Miss Rawbnsn will allow me the privilege of taking her, my car is at her service.

OCTAVIUS. Violet!

*General constraint.*

ANN [*subduedly*]. Come, mother: we must leave them to talk over the arrangements. I must see to my travelling kit.

*Mrs Whitefield looks bewildered; but Ann draws her discreetly away; and they disappear round the corner towards the house.*

HECTOR. I think I may go so far as to say that I can depend on Miss Rawbnsn's consent.

*Continued embarrassment.*

OCTAVIUS. I'm afraid we must leave Violet behind. There are circumstances which make it impossible for her to come on such an expedition.

HECTOR [*amused and not at all convinced*]. Too American, eh? Must the young lady have a chaperone?

OCTAVIUS. It's not that, Malone — at least not altogether.

HECTOR. Indeed! May I ask what other objection applies?

TANNER [*impatiently*]. Oh, tell him, tell him. We shall never be able to keep the secret unless everybody knows what it is. Mr Malone: if you go to Nice with Violet, you go with another man's wife. She is married.

HECTOR [*thunderstruck*]. You dont tell me so!

TANNER. We do. In confidence.

RAMSDEN [*with an air of importance, lest Malone should suspect a misalliance*]. Her marriage has not yet been made known: she desires that it shall not be mentioned for the present.

HECTOR. I shall respect the lady's wishes. Would it be indiscreet to ask who her husband is, in case I should have an opportunity of cawnsulting him about this trip?

TANNER. We dont know who he is.

HECTOR [*retiring into his shell in a very marked manner*]. In that case, I have no more to say.

*They become more embarrassed than ever.*

OCTAVIUS. You must think this very strange.

HECTOR. A little singular. Pardn mee for saying so.

RAMSDEN [*half apologetic, half huffy*]. The young lady was married secretly; and her husband has forbidden her, it seems, to declare his name. It is only right to tell you, since you are interested in Miss — er — in Violet.

OCTAVIUS [*sympathetically*]. I hope this is not a disappointment to you.

HECTOR [*softened, coming out of his shell again*]. Well: it is a blow. I can hardly understand how a man can leave his wife in such a position. Surely it's not custoMary. It's not manly. It's not considerate.

OCTAVIUS. We feel that, as you may imagine, pretty deeply.

RAMSDEN [*testily*]. It is some young fool who has not enough experience to know what mystifications of this kind lead to.

HECTOR [*with strong symptoms of moral repugnance*]. I hope so. A man need be very young and pretty foolish too to be excused for such conduct. You take a very lenient view, Mr Ramsden. Too lenient to my mind. Surely marriage should ennoble a man.

TANNER [*sardonically*]. Ha!

HECTOR. Am I to gather from that cachinnation that you dont agree with me, Mr Tanner?

TANNER [*drily*]. Get married and try. You may find it delightful for a while: you certainly wont find it ennobling. The greatest common measure of a man and a woman is not necessarily greater than the man's single measure.

HECTOR. Well, we think in America that a woman's morl number is higher than a man's, and that the purer nature of a woman lifts a man right out of himself, and makes him better than he was.

OCTAVIUS [*with conviction*]. So it does.

TANNER. No wonder American women prefer to live in Europe! It's more comfortable than standing all their lives on an altar to be worshipped. Anyhow, Violet's husband has not been ennobled. So whats to be done?

HECTOR [*shaking his head*]. I cant dismiss that man's cawnduct as lightly as you do, Mr Tanner. However, I'll say no more. Whoever he is, he's Miss Rawbnsn's husband; and I should be glad for her sake to think better of him.

OCTAVIUS [*touched; for he divines a secret sorrow*]. I'm very sorry, Malone. Very sorry.

HECTOR [*gratefully*]. Youre a good fellow, Rawbnsn. Thank you.

TANNER. Talk about something else. Violet's coming from the house.

HECTOR. I should esteem it a very great favor, gentlemen, if you would take the opportunity to let me have a few words with the lady alone. I shall have to cry off this trip; and it's rather a dullicate —

RAMSDEN [*glad to escape*]. Say no more. Come, Tanner. Come, Tavy. [*He strolls away into the park with Octavius and Tanner, past the motor car.*]

*Violet comes down the avenue to Hector.*

VIOLET. Are they looking?

HECTOR. No.

*She kisses him.*

VIOLET. Have you been telling lies for my sake?

HECTOR. Lying! Lying hardly describes it. I overdo it. I get carried away in an ecstasy of mendacity. Violet: I wish youd let me own up.

VIOLET [*instantly becoming serious and resolute*]. No, no, Hector: you promised me not to.

HECTOR. I'll keep my prawmis until you release me from it. But I feel mean, lying to those men, and denying my wife. Just dastardly.

VIOLET. I wish your father were not so unreasonable.

HECTOR. He's not unreasonable. He's right from his point of view. He has a prejudice against the English middle class.

VIOLET. It's too ridiculous. You know how I dislike saying such things to you, Hector; but if I were to — oh, well, no matter.

HECTOR. I know. If you were to marry the son of an English manufacturer of awffice furniture, your friends would consider it a misalliance. And here's my silly old dad, who is the biggest awffice furniture man in the world, would shew me the door for marrying the most perfect lady in England merely because she has no handle to her name. Of course it's just absurd. But I tell you, Violet, I dont like deceiving him. I feel as if I was stealing his money. Why wont you let me own up?

VIOLET. We cant afford it. You can be as romantic as you please about love, Hector; but you mustnt be romantic about money.

HECTOR [*divided between his uxoriousness and his habitual elevation of moral sentiment*]. That's very English. [*Appealing to her impulsively*] Violet: dad's bound to find us out someday.

VIOLET. Oh yes, later on of course. But dont lets go over this every time we meet, dear. You promised —

HECTOR. All right, all right, I —

VIOLET [*not to be silenced*]. It is I and not you who suffer by this concealment; and as to facing a struggle and poverty and all that sort of thing I simply will not do it. It's too silly.

HECTOR. You shall not. I'll sort of borrow the money from my dad until I get on my own feet; and then I can own up and pay up at the same time.

VIOLET [*alarmed and indignant*]. Do you mean to work? Do you want to spoil our marriage?

HECTOR. Well, I dont mean to let marriage spoil my character. Your friend Mr Tanner has got the laugh on me a bit already about that; and —

VIOLET. The beast! I hate Jack Tanner.

HECTOR [*magnanimously*]. Oh, hee's all right: he only needs the love of a good woman to ennoble him. Besides, he's proposed a motoring trip to Nice; and I'm going to take you.

VIOLET. How jolly!

HECTOR. Yes; but how are we going to manage? You see, theyve warned me off going with you, so to speak. Theyve told me in cawnfidnce that youre married. Thats just the most overwhelming cawnfidnce Ive ever been honored with.

*Tanner returns with Straker, who goes to his car.*

TANNER. Your car is a great success, Mr Malone. Your engineer is showing it off to Mr Ramsden.

HECTOR [*eagerly — forgetting himself*]. Lets come, Vi.

VIOLET [*coldly, warning him with her eyes*]. I beg

your pardon, Mr Malone: I did not quite catch—

HECTOR [*recollecting himself*]. I ask to be allowed the pleasure of shewing you my little American steam car, Miss Rawbnsn.

VIOLET. I shall be very pleased. [*They go off together down the avenue.*]

TANNER. About this trip, Straker.

STRAKER [*preoccupied with the car*]. Yes?

TANNER. Miss Whitefield is supposed to be coming with me.

STRAKER. So I gather.

TANNER. Mr Robinson is to be one of the party.

STRAKER. Yes.

TANNER. Well, if you can manage so as to be a good deal occupied with me, and leave Mr Robinson a good deal occupied with Miss Whitefield, he will be deeply grateful to you.

STRAKER [*looking round at him*]. Evidently.

TANNER. "Evidently"! Your grandfather would have simply winked.

STRAKER. My grandfather would have touched his at.

TANNER. And I should have given your good nice respectful grandfather a sovereign.

STRAKER. Five shillins, more likely. [*He leaves the car and approaches Tanner.*] What about the lady's views?

TANNER. She is just as willing to be left to Mr Robinson as Mr Robinson is to be left to her. [*Straker looks at his principal with cool scepticism; then turns to the car whistling his favorite air.*] Stop that aggravating noise. What do you mean by it? [*Straker calmly resumes the melody and finishes it. Tanner politely hears it out before he again addresses Straker, this time with elaborate seriousness.*] Enry: I have even been a warm advocate of the spread of music among the masses; but I object to your obliging the company whenever Miss Whitefield's name is mentioned. You did it this morning, too.

STRAKER [*obstinately*]. It's not a bit o use. Mr Robinson may as well give it up first as last.

TANNER. Why?

STRAKER. Garn! You know why. Course it's not my business; but you neednt start kiddin me about it.

TANNER. I am not kidding. I dont know why.

STRAKER [*cheerfully sulky*]. Oh, very well. All right. It aint my business.

TANNER [*impressively*]. I trust, Enry, that, as between employer and engineer, I shall always know how to keep my proper distance, and not intrude my private affairs on you. Even our business arrangements are subject to the approval of your Trade Union. But dont abuse your advantages. Let me remind you that Voltaire said that what was too silly to be said could be sung.

STRAKER. It wasnt Voltaire: it was Bow Mar Shay.

TANNER. I stand corrected: Beaumarchais[11] of course. Now y o u seem to think that what is too delicate to be said can be whistled. Unfortunately your whistling, though melodious, is unintelligible. Come! theres nobody listening: neither my genteel relatives nor the secretary of your confounded Union. As man to man, Enry, why do you think that my friend has no chance with Miss Whitefield?

STRAKER. Cause she's arter summun else.

TANNER. Bosh! who else?

STRAKER. You.

TANNER. Me!!!

STRAKER. Mean to tell me you didnt know? Oh, come, Mr Tanner!

TANNER [*in fierce earnest*]. Are you playing the fool, or do you mean it?

STRAKER [*with a flash of temper*]. I'm not playin no fool. [*More coolly*] Why, it's as plain as the nose on your face. If you aint spotted that, you dont know much about these sort of things. [*Serene again*] Ex-cuse me, you know, Mr Tanner; but you asked me as man to man; and I told you as man to man.

TANNER [*wildly appealing to the heavens*]. Then I—*I* am the bee, the spider, the marked down victim, the destined prey.

STRAKER. I dunno about the bee and the spider. But the marked down victim, thats what you are and no mistake; and a jolly good job for you, too, I should say.

TANNER [*momentously*]. Henry Straker: the golden moment of your life has arrived.

STRAKER. What d'y'mean?

TANNER. That record to Biskra.

STRAKER [*eagerly*]. Yes?

TANNER. Break it.

STRAKER [*rising to the height of his destiny*]. D'y'mean it?

TANNER. I do.

STRAKER. When?

TANNER. Now. Is that machine ready to start?

STRAKER [*quailing.*] But you cant—

TANNER [*cutting him short by getting into the car*]. Off we go. First to the bank for money; then to my rooms for my kit; then to your rooms for your kit; then break the record from London to Dover or Folkestone; then across the channel and away like mad to Marseilles, Gibraltar, Genoa, any port from which we can sail to a Mahometan country where men are protected from women.

STRAKER. Garn! youre kiddin.

11. **Beaumarchais:** Pierre Beaumarchais (1732–99), French dramatist, author of *The Marriage of Figaro*. The servant Figaro is an early example of the cheeky type represented by Leporello-Straker. See headnote, p. 696, above.

TANNER [*resolutely*]. Stay behind then. If you wont come I'll do it alone. [*He starts the motor.*]

STRAKER [*running after him*]. Here! Mister! arf a mo! steady on! [*He scrambles in as the car plunges forward.*]

# Act III

*Evening in the Sierra Nevada. Rolling slopes of brown with olive trees instead of apple trees in the cultivated patches, and occasional prickly pears instead of gorse and bracken in the wilds. Higher up, tall stone peaks and precipices, all handsome and distinguished. No wild nature here: rather a most aristocratic mountain landscape made by a fastidious artist-creator. No vulgar profusion of vegetation: even a touch of aridity in the frequent patches of stones: Spanish magnificence and Spanish economy everywhere.*

*Not very far north of a spot at which the high road over one of the passes crosses a tunnel on the railway from Malaga to Granada, is one of the mountain amphitheatres of the Sierra. Looking at it from the wide end of the horse-shoe, one sees, a little to the right, in the face of the cliff, a romantic cave which is really an abandoned quarry, and towards the left a little hill, commanding a view of the road, which skirts the amphitheatre on the left, maintaining its higher level on embankments and an occasional stone arch. On the hill, watching the road, is a man who is either a Spaniard or a Scotchman. Probably a Spaniard, since he wears the dress of a Spanish goatherd and seems at home in the Sierra Nevada, but very like a Scotchman for all that. In the hollow, on the slope leading to the quarry-cave, are about a dozen men who, as they recline at their ease round a heap of smouldering white ashes of dead leaf and brushwood, have an air of being conscious of themselves as picturesque scoundrels honoring the Sierra by using it as an effective pictorial background. As a matter of artistic fact they are not picturesque; and the mountains tolerate them as lions tolerate lice. An English policeman or Poor Law Guardian*[1] *would recognize them as a selected band of tramps and ablebodied paupers.*

*This description of them is not wholly contemptuous. Whoever has intelligently observed the tramp, or visited the ablebodied ward of a workhouse, will admit that our social failures are not all drunkards and weaklings. Some of them are men who do not fit the class they were born into. Precisely the same qualities that make the educated gentleman an artist may make an uneducated manual laborer an ablebodied pauper. There are men who fall helplessly into the workhouse because they are good for nothing; but there are also men who are there because they are strong-minded enough to disregard the social convention (obviously not a disinterested one on the part of the ratepayer) which bids a man live by heavy and badly paid drudgery when he has the alternative of walking into the workhouse, announcing himself as a destitute person, and legally compelling the Guardians to feed, clothe, and house him better than he could feed, clothe, and house himself without great exertion. When a man who is born a poet refuses a stool in a stockbroker's office, and starves in a garret, spunging on a poor landlady or on his friends and relatives sooner than work against his grain; or when a lady, because she is a lady, will face any extremity of parasitic dependence rather than take a situation as cook or parlormaid, we make large allowances for them. To such allowances the ablebodied pauper, and his nomadic variant the tramp, are equally entitled.*

*Further, the imaginative man, if his life is to be tolerable to him, must have leisure to tell himself stories, and a position which lends itself to imaginative decoration. The ranks of unskilled labor offer no such positions. We misuse our laborers horribly, and when a man refuses to be misused, we have no right to say that he is refusing honest work. Let us be frank in this matter before we go on with our play; so that we may enjoy it without hypocrisy. If we were reasoning, far-sighted people, four fifths of us would go straight to the Guardians for relief, and knock the whole social system to pieces with most beneficial reconstructive results. The reason we do not do this is because we work like bees or ants, by instinct or habit, not reasoning about the matter at all. Therefore when a man comes along who can and does reason, and who, applying the Kantian test*[2] *to his conduct, can truly say to us, If everybody did as I do, the world would be compelled to reform itself industrially, and abolish slavery and squalor, which exist only because everybody does as you do, let us honor that man and seriously consider the advisability of following his example. Such a man is the ablebodied, ableminded pauper. Were he a gentleman doing his best to get a pension or a sinecure instead of sweeping a crossing, nobody would blame him for deciding that so long as the alternative lies be-*

**Act III: 1. *Poor . . . Guardian:*** one of a board elected to administer the poor laws in a parish.

**2. *Kantian test:*** expressed by the philosopher, Immanuel Kant (1724–1804) in the "categorical imperative," one form of which runs, "So act as if the maxim from which you act were to become through your will a universal law of nature."

*tween living mainly at the expense of the community and allowing the community to live mainly at his, it would be folly to accept what is to him personally the greater of the two evils.*

*We may therefore contemplate the tramps of the Sierra without prejudice, admitting cheerfully that our objects — briefly, to be gentlemen of fortune — are much the same as theirs, and the difference in our position and methods merely accidental. One or two of them, perhaps, it would be wiser to kill without malice in a friendly and frank manner; for there are bipeds, just as there are quadrupeds, who are too dangerous to be left unchained and unmuzzled; and these cannot fairly expect to have other men's lives wasted in the work of watching them. But as society has not the courage to kill them, and, when it catches them, simply wreaks on them some superstitious expiatory rites of torture and degradation, and then lets them loose with heightened qualifications for mischief, it is just as well that they are at large in the Sierra, and in the hands of a chief who looks as if he might possibly, on provocation, order them to be shot.*

*This chief, seated in the centre of the group on a squared block of stone from the quarry, is a tall strong man, with a striking cockatoo nose, glossy black hair, pointed beard, upturned moustache, and a Mephistophelean affectation which is fairly imposing, perhaps because the scenery admits of a larger swagger than Piccadilly, perhaps because of a certain sentimentality in the man which gives him that touch of grace which alone can excuse deliberate picturesqueness. His eyes and mouth are by no means rascally; he has a fine voice and a ready wit; and whether he is really the strongest man in the party or not, he looks it. He is certainly the best fed, the best dressed, and the best trained. The fact that he speaks English is not unexpected, in spite of the Spanish landscape; for with the exception of one man who might be guessed as a bullfighter ruined by drink, and one unmistakable Frenchman, they are all cockney or American; therefore, in a land of cloaks and sombreros, they mostly wear seedy overcoats, woollen mufflers, hard hemispherical hats, and dirty brown gloves. Only a very few dress after their leader, whose broad sombrero with a cock's feather in the band, and voluminous cloak descending to his high boots, are as un-English as possible. None of them are armed; and the ungloved ones keep their hands in their pockets because it is their national belief that it must be dangerously cold in the open air with the night coming on. (It is as warm an evening as any reasonable man could desire.)*

*Except the bullfighting inebriate there is only one person in the company who looks more than, say, thirty-three. He is a small man with reddish whiskers, weak eyes, and the anxious look of a small tradesman in difficulties. He wears the only tall hat visible: it shines in the sunset with the sticky glow of some six penny patent hat reviver, often applied and constantly tending to produce a worse state of the original surface than the ruin it was applied to remedy. He has a collar and cuffs of celluloid; and his brown Chesterfield overcoat, with velvet collar, is still presentable. He is preeminently the respectable man of the party, and is certainly over forty, possibly over fifty. He is the corner man on the leader's right, opposite three men in scarlet ties on his left. One of these three is the Frenchman. Of the remaining two, who are both English, one is argumentative, solemn, and obstinate; the other rowdy and mischievous.*

*The chief, with a magnificent fling of the end of his cloak across his left shoulder, rises to address them. The applause which greets him shews that he is a favorite orator.*

THE CHIEF. Friends and fellow brigands. I have a proposal to make to this meeting. We have now spent three evenings in discussing the question Have Anarchists [3] or Social-Democrats [4] the most personal courage? We have gone into the principles of Anarchism and Social-Democracy at great length. The cause of Anarchy has been ably represented by our one Anarchist, who doesnt know what Anarchism means [*laughter*] —

THE ANARCHIST [*rising*]. A point of order, Mendoza —

MENDOZA [*forcibly*]. No, by thunder: your last point of order took half an hour. Besides, Anarchists dont believe in order.

THE ANARCHIST [*mild, polite but persistent: he is, in fact, the respectable looking elderly man in the celluloid collar and cuffs*]. That is a vulgar error. I can prove —

MENDOZA. Order, order.

THE OTHERS [*shouting*]. Order, order. Sit down. Chair! Shut up.

*The Anarchist is suppressed.*

MENDOZA. On the other hand we have three Social-Democrats among us. They are not on speaking terms; and they have put before us three distinct and incompatible views of Social-Democracy.

THE THREE MEN IN SCARLET TIES. 1. Mr Chairman, I protest. A personal explanation. 2. It's a lie. I

3. **Anarchists:** believers in the abolition of the state; they were at this time an active political group, particularly in the Latin countries. Their bombings and assassinations of prominent officials aroused widespread fear of anarchism in Europe and America during the early 1900's, a fear that recurred even much later, for example, at the time of the Sacco and Vanzetti case in 1927. 4. **Social-Democrats:** members of one of the socialist parties organized under the "Second International." The anarchists had contributed to the break-up of the "First International," which was founded by **Karl Marx.**

never said so. Be fair, Mendoza. 3. Je demande la parole. C'est absolument faux. C'est faux! faux!! faux!!![5] Assas-s-s-s-sin!!!!!!

MENDOZA. Order, order.

THE OTHERS. Order, order, order! Chair!

*The Social-Democrats are suppressed.*

MENDOZA. Now, we tolerate all opinions here. But after all, comrades, the vast majority of us are neither Anarchists nor Socialists, but gentlemen and Christians.

THE MAJORITY [*shouting assent*]. Hear, hear! So we are. Right.

THE ROWDY SOCIAL-DEMOCRAT [*smarting under suppression*]. You aint no Christian. Youre a Sheeny, you are.

MENDOZA [*with crushing magnanimity*]. My friend: *I* am an exception to all rules. It is true that I have the honor to be a Jew; and when the Zionists need a leader to reassemble our race on its historic soil of Palestine, Mendoza will not be the last to volunteer [*sympathetic applause*—Hear, Hear, *&c.*]. But I am not a slave to any superstition. I have swallowed all the formulas, even that of Socialism; though, in a sense, once a Socialist, always a Socialist.

THE SOCIAL-DEMOCRATS. Hear, hear!

MENDOZA. But I am well aware that the ordinary man—even the ordinary brigand, who can scarcely be called an ordinary man [Hear, hear!]—is not a philosopher. Common sense is good enough for him; and in our business affairs common sense is good enough for me. Well, what is our business here in the Sierra Nevada, chosen by the Moors as the fairest spot in Spain? Is it to discuss abstruse questions of political economy? No: it is to hold up motor cars and secure a more equitable distribution of wealth.

THE SULKY SOCIAL-DEMOCRAT. All made by labor, mind you.

MENDOZA [*urbanely*]. Undoubtedly. All made by labor, and on its way to be squandered by wealthy vagabonds in the dens of vice that disfigure the sunny shores of the Mediterranean. We intercept that wealth. We restore it to circulation among the class that produced it and that chiefly needs it: the working class. We do this at the risk of our lives and liberties, by the exercise of the virtues of courage, endurance, foresight, and abstinence—especially abstinence. I myself have eaten nothing but prickly pears and broiled rabbit for three days.

THE SULKY SOCIAL-DEMOCRAT [*stubbornly*]. No more aint we.

MENDOZA [*indignantly*]. Have I taken more than my share?

5. **Je . . . faux:** "I demand the right to speak. It's absolutely untrue. It's untrue! untrue!! untrue!!!"

THE SULKY SOCIAL-DEMOCRAT [*unmoved*]. Why should you?

THE ANARCHIST. Why should he not? To each according to his needs: from each according to his means.[6]

THE FRENCHMAN [*shaking his fist at the Anarchist*]. Fumiste![7]

MENDOZA [*diplomatically*]. I agree with both of you.

THE GENUINELY ENGLISH BRIGANDS. Hear, hear! Bravo Mendoza!

MENDOZA. What I say is, let us treat one another as gentlemen, and strive to excel in personal courage only when we take the field.

THE ROWDY SOCIAL-DEMOCRAT [*derisively*]. Shikespear.

*A whistle comes from the goatherd on the hill. He springs up and points excitedly forward along the road to the north.*

THE GOATHERD. Automobile! Automobile! [*He rushes down the hill and joins the rest, who all scramble to their feet.*]

MENDOZA [*in ringing tones*]. To arms! Who has the gun?

THE SULKY SOCIAL-DEMOCRAT [*handing a rifle to Mendoza*]. Here.

MENDOZA. Have the nails been strewn in the road?

THE ROWDY SOCIAL-DEMOCRAT. Two ahnces of em.

MENDOZA. Good! [*To the Frenchman*] With me, Duval. If the nails fail, puncture their tires with a bullet. [*He gives the rifle to Duval, who follows him up the hill. Mendoza produces an opera glass. The others hurry across to the road and disappear to the north.*]

MENDOZA [*on the hill, using his glass*]. Two only, a capitalist and his chauffeur. They look English.

DUVAL. Angliche! Aoh yess. Cochons! [*Handling the rifle*] Faut tirer, n'est-ce pas?[8]

MENDOZA. No: the nails have gone home. Their tire is down: they stop.

DUVAL [*shouting to the others*]. Fondez sur eux, nom de Dieu![9]

MENDOZA [*rebuking his excitement*]. Du calme, Duval: keep your hair on. They take it quietly. Let us descend and receive them.

*Mendoza descends, passing behind the fire and coming forward, whilst Tanner and Straker, in their motoring goggles, leather coats, and caps, are led in from the road by the brigands.*

TANNER. Is this the gentleman you describe as your boss? Does he speak English?

THE ROWDY SOCIAL-DEMOCRAT. Course e daz. Y'

6. **To . . . means:** formula first set forth by the early French socialist, Louis Blanc. 7. **Fumiste!:** "Humbug!" 8. **Cochons . . . pas?:** "Pigs! We'll have to shoot, won't we?" 9. **Fondez . . . Dieu!:** "Rush on them, in God's name!"

downt suppowz we Hinglishmen luts ahrselves be bossed by a bloomin Spenniard, do you?

MENDOZA [*with dignity*]. Allow me to introduce myself: Mendoza, President of the League of the Sierra! [*Posing loftily*] I am a brigand: I live by robbing the rich.

TANNER [*promptly*]. I am a gentleman: I live by robbing the poor. Shake hands.

THE ENGLISH SOCIAL-DEMOCRATS. Hear, hear!

*General laughter and good humor. Tanner and Mendoza shake hands. The Brigands drop into their former places.*

STRAKER. Ere! where do I come in?

TANNER [*introducing*]. My friend and chauffeur.

THE SULKY SOCIAL-DEMOCRAT [*suspiciously*]. Well, which is he? friend or show-foor? It makes all the difference, you know.

MENDOZA [*explaining*]. We should expect ransom for a friend. A professional chauffeur is free of the mountains. He even takes a trifling percentage of his principal's ransom if he will honor us by accepting it.

STRAKER. I see. Just to encourage me to come this way again. Well, I'll think about it.

DUVAL [*impulsively rushing across to Straker*]. Mon frère! [*He embraces him rapturously and kisses him on both cheeks.*]

STRAKER [*disgusted*]. Ere, git aht: dont be silly. Who are you, pray?

DUVAL. Duval: Social-Democrat.

STRAKER. Oh, youre a Social-Democrat, are you?

THE ANARCHIST. He means that he has sold out to the parliamentary humbugs and the bourgeoisie. Compromise! that is his faith.

DUVAL [*furiously*]. I understand what he say. He say Bourgeois. He say Compromise. Jamais de la vie! Misérable menteur —[10]

STRAKER. See here, Captain Mendoza, ah mach o this sort o thing do you put up with here? Are we avin a pleasure trip in the mountains, or are we at a Socialist meetin?

THE MAJORITY. Hear, hear! Shut up. Chuck it. Sit down, &c. &c. [*The Social-Democrats and the Anarchist are hustled into the background. Straker, after superintending this proceeding with satisfaction, places himself on Mendoza's left, Tanner being on his right.*]

MENDOZA. Can we offer you anything? Broiled rabbit and prickly pears —

TANNER. Thank you: we have dined.

MENDOZA [*to his followers*]. Gentlemen: business is over for the day. Go as you please until morning.

*The Brigands disperse into groups lazily. Some go into the cave. Others sit down or lie down to sleep in the open. A few produce a pack of cards and move off towards the road; for it is now starlight; and they know that motor cars have lamps which can be turned to account for lighting a card party.*

STRAKER [*calling after them*]. Dont none of you go fooling with that car, d'ye hear?

MENDOZA. No fear, Monsieur le Chauffeur. The first one we captured cured us of that.

STRAKER [*interested*]. What did it do?

MENDOZA. It carried three brave comrades of ours, who did not know how to stop it, into Granada, and capsized them opposite the police station. Since then we never touch one without sending for the chauffeur. Shall we chat at our ease?

TANNER. By all means.

*Tanner, Mendoza, and Straker sit down on the turf by the fire. Mendoza delicately waives his presidential dignity, of which the right to sit on the squared stone block is the appanage, by sitting on the ground like his guests, and using the stone only as a support for his back.*

MENDOZA. It is the custom in Spain always to put off business until tomorrow. In fact, you have arrived out of office hours. However, if you would prefer to settle the question of ransom at once, I am at your service.

TANNER. Tomorrow will do for me. I am rich enough to pay anything in reason.

MENDOZA [*respectfully, much struck by this admission*]. You are a remarkable man, sir. Our guests usually describe themselves as miserably poor.

TANNER. Pooh! Miserably poor people dont own motor cars.

MENDOZA. Precisely what we say to them.

TANNER. Treat us well: we shall not prove ungrateful.

STRAKER. No prickly pears and broiled rabbits, you know. Dont tell me you cant do us a bit better than that if you like.

MENDOZA. Wine, kids, milk, cheese, and bread can be procured for ready money.

STRAKER [*graciously*]. Now youre talkin.

TANNER. Are you all Socialists here, may I ask?

MENDOZA [*repudiating this humiliating misconception*]. Oh no, no, no: nothing of the kind, I assure you. We naturally have modern views as to the injustice of the existing distribution of wealth: otherwise we should lose our self-respect. But nothing that you could take exception to, except two or three faddists.

TANNER. I had no intention of suggesting anything discreditable. In fact, I am a bit of a Socialist myself.

STRAKER [*drily*]. Most rich men are, I notice.

MENDOZA. Quite so. It has reached us, I admit. It is in the air of the century.

10. **Jamais . . . menteur:** "Never, as long as I live! Miserable liar."

STRAKER. Socialism must be lookin up a bit if your chaps are taking to it.

MENDOZA. That is true, sir. A movement which is confined to philosophers and honest men can never exercise any real political influence: there are too few of them. Until a movement shews itself capable of spreading among brigands, it can never hope for a political majority.

TANNER. But are your brigands any less honest than ordinary citizens?

MENDOZA. Sir: I will be frank with you. Brigandage is abnormal. Abnormal professions attract two classes: those who are not good enough for ordinary bourgeois life and those who are too good for it. We are dregs and scum, sir: the dregs very filthy, the scum very superior.

STRAKER. Take care! some o the dregs'll hear you.

MENDOZA. It does not matter: each brigand thinks himself scum, and likes to hear the others called dregs.

TANNER. Come! you are a wit. [*Mendoza inclines his head, flattered.*] May one ask you a blunt question?

MENDOZA. As blunt as you please.

TANNER. How does it pay a man of your talent to shepherd such a flock as this on broiled rabbit and prickly pears? I have seen men less gifted, and I'll swear less honest, supping at the Savoy on foie gras and champagne.

MENDOZA. Pooh! they have all had their turn at the broiled rabbit, just as I shall have my turn at the Savoy. Indeed, I have had a turn there already — as waiter.

TANNER. A waiter! You astonish me!

MENDOZA [*reflectively*]. Yes: I, Mendoza of the Sierra, was a waiter. Hence, perhaps, my cosmopolitanism. [*With sudden intensity*] Shall I tell you the story of my life?

STRAKER [*apprehensively*]. If it aint too long, old chap —

TANNER [*interrupting him*]. Tsh-sh: you are a Philistine, Henry: you have no romance in you. [*To Mendoza*] You interest me extremely, President. Never mind Henry: he can go to sleep.

MENDOZA. The woman I loved —

STRAKER. Oh, this is a love story, is it? Right you are. Go on: I was only afraid you were going to talk about yourself.

MENDOZA. Myself! I have thrown myself away for her sake: that is why I am here. No matter: I count the world well lost for her. She had, I pledge you my word, the most magnificent head of hair I ever saw. She had humor; she had intellect; she could cook to perfection; and her highly strung temperament made her uncertain, incalculable, variable, capricious, cruel, in a word, enchanting.

STRAKER. A six shillin novel sort o woman, all but the cookin. Er name was Lady Gladys Plantagenet, wasnt it?

MENDOZA. No, sir: she was not an earl's daughter. Photography, reproduced by the half-tone process, has made me familiar with the appearance of the daughters of the English peerage; and I can honestly say that I would have sold the lot, faces, dowries, clothes, titles, and all, for a smile from this woman. Yet she was a woman of the people, a worker: otherwise — let me reciprocate your bluntness — I should have scorned her.

TANNER. Very properly. And did she respond to your love?

MENDOZA. Should I be here if she did? She objected to marry a Jew.

TANNER. On religious grounds?

MENDOZA. No: she was a freethinker. She said that every Jew considers in his heart that English people are dirty in their habits.

TANNER [*surprised*]. Dirty!

MENDOZA. It shewed her extraordinary knowledge of the world; for it is undoubtedly true. Our elaborate sanitary code makes us unduly contemptuous of the Gentile.

TANNER. Did you ever hear that, Henry?

STRAKER. Ive heard my sister say so. She was cook in a Jewish family once.

MENDOZA. I could not deny it; neither could I eradicate the impression it made on her mind. I could have got round any other objection; but no woman can stand a suspicion of indelicacy as to her person. My entreaties were in vain: she always retorted that she wasnt good enough for me, and recommended me to marry an accursed barmaid named Rebecca Lazarus, whom I loathed. I talked of suicide: she offered me a packet of beetle poison to do it with. I hinted at murder: she went into hysterics; and as I am a living man I went to America so that she might sleep without dreaming that I was stealing upstairs to cut her throat. In America I went out west and fell in with a man who was wanted by the police for holding up trains. It was he who had the idea of holding up motor cars in the South of Europe: a welcome idea to a desperate and disappointed man. He gave me some valuable introductions to capitalists of the right sort. I formed a syndicate; and the present enterprise is the result. I became leader, as the Jew always becomes leader, by his brains and imagination. But with all my pride of race I would give everything I possess to be an Englishman. I am like a boy: I cut her name on the trees and her initials on the sod. When I am alone I lie down and tear my wretched hair and cry Louisa —

STRAKER [*startled*]. Louisa!

MENDOZA. It is her name — Louisa — Louisa Straker —

TANNER. Straker!

STRAKER [*scrambling up on his knees most indignantly*]. Look here: Louisa Straker is my sister, see? Wot do you mean by gassing about her like this? Wotshe got to do with you?

MENDOZA. A dramatic coincidence! You are Enry, her favorite brother!

STRAKER. Oo are you callin Enry? What call have you to take a liberty with my name or with hers? For two pins I'd punch your fat edd, so I would.

MENDOZA [*with grandiose calm*]. If I let you do it, will you promise to brag of it afterwards to her? She will be reminded of her Mendoza: that is all I desire.

TANNER. This is genuine devotion. Henry. You should respect it.

STRAKER [*fiercely*]. Funk, more likely.

MENDOZA [*springing to his feet*]. Funk! Young man: I come of a famous family of fighters; and as your sister well knows, you would have as much chance against me as a perambulator against your motor car.

STRAKER [*secretly daunted, but rising from his knees with an air of reckless pugnacity*]. I aint afraid of you. With your Louisa! Louisa! Miss Straker is good enough for you, I should think.

MENDOZA. I wish you could persuade her to think so.

STRAKER [*exasperated*]. Here —

TANNER [*rising quickly and interposing*]. Oh come, Henry: even if you could fight the President you cant fight the whole League of the Sierra. Sit down again and be friendly. A cat may look at a king; and even a President of brigands may look at your sister. All this family pride is really very old fashioned.

STRAKER [*subdued, but grumbling*]. Let him look at her. But wot does he mean by makin out that she ever looked at im? [*Reluctantly resuming his couch on the turf*] Ear him talk, one ud think she was keepin company with him. [*He turns his back on them and composes himself to sleep.*]

MENDOZA [*to Tanner, becoming more confidential as he finds himself virtually alone with a sympathetic listener in the still starlight of the mountains; for all the rest are asleep by this time*]. It was just so with her, sir. Her intellect reached forward into the twentieth century: her social prejudices and family affections reached back into the dark ages. Ah, sir, how the words of Shakespear seem to fit every crisis in our emotions!

I loved Louisa: 40,000 brothers
Could not with all their quantity of love
Make up my sum.[11]

And so on. I forget the rest. Call it madness if you will — infatuation. I am an able man, a strong man: in ten years I should have owned a first-class hotel. I met her; and — you see! — I am a brigand, an outcast. Even Shakespear cannot do justice to what I feel for Louisa. Let me read you some lines that I have written about her myself. However slight their literary merit may be, they express what I feel better than any casual words can. [*He produces a packet of hotel bills scrawled with manuscript, and kneels at the fire to decipher them, poking it with a stick to make it glow.*]

TANNER [*slapping him rudely on the shoulder*]. Put them in the fire, President.

MENDOZA [*startled*]. Eh?

TANNER. You are sacrificing your career to a monomania.

MENDOZA. I know it.

TANNER. No you dont. No man would commit such a crime against himself if he really knew what he was doing. How can you look round at these august hills, look up at this divine sky, taste this finely tempered air, and then talk like a literary hack on a second floor in Bloomsbury? [12]

MENDOZA [*shaking his head*]. The Sierra is no better than Bloomsbury when once the novelty has worn off. Besides, these mountains make you dream of women — of women with magnificent hair.

TANNER. Of Louisa, in short. They will not make me dream of women, my friend: I am heartwhole.

MENDOZA. Do not boast until morning, sir. This is a strange country for dreams.

TANNER. Well, we shall see. Goodnight. [*He lies down and composes himself to sleep.*]

*Mendoza, with a sigh, follows his example; and for a few moments there is peace in the Sierra. Then Mendoza sits up suddenly and says pleadingly to Tanner —*

MENDOZA. Just allow me to read a few lines before you go to sleep. I should really like your opinion of them.

TANNER [*drowsily*]. Go on. I am listening.

MENDOZA. I saw thee first in Whitsun week
Louisa, Louisa —

TANNER [*rousing himself*]. My dear President, Louisa is a very pretty name; but it really doesnt rhyme well to Whitsun week.

MENDOZA. Of course not. Louisa is not the rhyme, but the refrain.

TANNER [*subsiding*]. Ah, the refrain. I beg your pardon. Go on.

MENDOZA. Perhaps you do not care for that one: I think you will like this better. [*He recites, in rich soft tones, and in slow time*]

Louisa, I love thee.
I love thee, Louisa.

11. **I . . . sum:** *Hamlet*, V.i.292–94. The first line reads: "I loved Ophelia. Forty thousand brothers."

12. **Bloomsbury:** The "Greenwich Village" of London, a quarter where many writers, artists, and students live.

Louisa, Louisa, Louisa, I love thee.
One name and one phrase make my music,
Louisa.
Louisa, Louisa, Louisa, I love thee.

Mendoza thy lover,
Thy lover, Mendoza,
Mendoza adoringly lives for Louisa.
Theres nothing but that in the world for
Mendoza.
Louisa, Louisa, Mendoza adores thee.

[*Affected*] There is no merit in producing beautiful lines upon such a name. Louisa is an exquisite name, is it not?

TANNER [*all but asleep, responds with a faint groan*].

MENDOZA. O wert thou, Louisa,
The wife of Mendoza,
Mendoza's Louisa, Louisa Mendoza,
How blest were the life of
Louisa's Mendoza!
How painless his longing of love
for Louisa!

That is real poetry — from the heart — from the heart of hearts. Dont you think it will move her?

*No answer.*

[*Resignedly*] Asleep, as usual. Doggrel to all the world: heavenly music to me! Idiot that I am to wear my heart on my sleeve! [*He composes himself to sleep, murmuring*] Louisa, I love thee; I love thee, Louisa; Louisa, Louisa, Louisa, I —

*Straker snores; rolls over on his side; and relapses into sleep. Stillness settles on the Sierra; and the darkness deepens. The fire has again buried itself in white ash and ceased to glow. The peaks shew unfathomably dark against the starry firmament; but now the stars dim and vanish; and the sky seems to steal away out of the universe. Instead of the Sierra there is nothing: omnipresent nothing. No sky, no peaks, no light, no sound, no time nor space, utter void. Then somewhere the beginning of a pallor, and with it a faint throbbing buzz as of a ghostly violoncello palpitating on the same note endlessly. A couple of ghostly violins presently take advantage of this bass* [13]

*and therewith the pallor reveals a man in the void, an incorporeal but visible man, seated, absurdly enough, on nothing. For a moment he raises his head as the music passes him by. Then, with a heavy sigh, he droops in utter dejection; and the violins, discouraged, retrace their melody in despair and at last give it up, extinguished by wailings from uncanny wind instruments, thus:* — [14]

*It is all very odd. One recognizes the Mozartian strain; and on this hint, and by the aid of certain sparkles of violet light in the pallor, the man's costume explains itself as that of a Spanish nobleman of the XV–XVI century. Don Juan, of course; but where? why? how? Besides, in the brief lifting of his face, now hidden by his hat brim, there was a curious suggestion of Tanner. A more critical, fastidious, handsome face, paler and colder, without Tanner's impetuous credulity and enthusiasm, and without a touch of his modern plutocratic vulgarity, but still a resemblance, even an identity. The name too: Don Juan Tenorio,*[15] *John Tanner. Where on earth — or elsewhere — have we got to from the XX century and the Sierra?*

*Another pallor in the void, this time not violet, but a disagreeable smoky yellow. With it, the whisper of a ghostly clarionet turning this tune into infinite sadness:* [16]

*The yellowish pallor moves: there is an old crone wandering in the void, bent and toothless; draped, as well as one can guess, in the coarse brown frock of some religious order. She wanders and wanders in her slow hopeless way, much as a wasp flies in*

13. ***bass:*** The musical quotation that follows is from Mozart's *Don Giovanni*, the Overture, bars 31–38. (As noted above, all references are based on the edition of Boosey & Hawkes, Ltd., London.) 14. ***thus:*** The musical quotation follows the preceding one, beginning with bar 39. Both passages are played with great rapidity. 15. ***Don . . . Tenorio:*** the full name of Don Juan in the legend. For this and other parallels between the play and the legend and Mozart's opera, see Shaw's Epistle Dedicatory, pp. 699–702 and 708 and the headnote. 16. ***sadness:*** The following theme, which introduces Dona Ana de Ulloa (Ann), is from the beginning of Donna Anna's aria, "Non mi dir" ("Say no more"), *Don Giovanni*, II.iii.no.25.

*its rapid busy way, until she blunders against the thing she seeks: companionship. With a sob of relief the poor old creature clutches at the presence of the man and addresses him in her dry unlovely voice, which can still express pride and resolution as well as suffering.*

THE OLD WOMAN. Excuse me; but I am so lonely; and this place is so awful.

DON JUAN. A new comer?

THE OLD WOMAN. Yes: I suppose I died this morning. I confessed; I had extreme unction; I was in bed with my family about me and my eyes fixed on the cross. Then it grew dark; and when the light came back it was this light by which I walk seeing nothing. I have wandered for hours in horrible loneliness.

DON JUAN [*sighing*]. Ah! you have not yet lost the sense of time. One soon does, in eternity.

THE OLD WOMAN. Where are we?

DON JUAN. In hell.

THE OLD WOMAN [*proudly*]. Hell! I in hell! How dare you?

DON JUAN [*unimpressed*]. Why not, Señora?

THE OLD WOMAN. You do not know to whom you are speaking. I am a lady, and a faithful daughter of the Church.

DON JUAN. I do not doubt it.

THE OLD WOMAN. But how then can I be in hell? Purgatory, perhaps: I have not been perfect: who has? But hell! oh, you are lying.

DON JUAN. Hell, Señora, I assure you; hell at its best: that is, its most solitary — though perhaps you would prefer company.

THE OLD WOMAN. But I have sincerely repented; I have confessed —

DON JUAN. How much?

THE OLD WOMAN. More sins than I really committed. I loved confession.

DON JUAN. Ah, that is perhaps as bad as confessing too little. At all events, Señora, whether by oversight or intention, you are certainly damned, like myself; and there is nothing for it now but to make the best of it.

THE OLD WOMAN [*indignantly*]. Oh! and I might have been so much wickeder! All my good deeds wasted! It is unjust.

DON JUAN. No: you were fully and clearly warned. For your bad deeds, vicarious atonement, mercy without justice. For your good deeds, justice without mercy. We have many good people here.

THE OLD WOMAN. Were you a good man?

DON JUAN. I was a murderer.

THE OLD WOMAN. A murderer! Oh, how dare they send me to herd with murderers! I was not as bad as that: I was a good woman. There is some mistake: where can I have it set right?

DON JUAN. I do not know whether mistakes can be corrected here. Probably they will not admit a mistake even if they have made one.

THE OLD WOMAN. But whom can I ask?

DON JUAN. I should ask the Devil, Señora: he understands the ways of this place, which is more than I ever could.

THE OLD WOMAN. The Devil! *I* speak to the Devil!

DON JUAN. In hell, Señora, the Devil is the leader of the best society.

THE OLD WOMAN. I tell you, wretch, I know I am not in hell.

DON JUAN. How do you know?

THE OLD WOMAN. Because I feel no pain.

DON JUAN. Oh, then there is no mistake: you are intentionally damned.

THE OLD WOMAN. Why do you say that?

DON JUAN. Because hell, Señora, is a place for the wicked. The wicked are quite comfortable in it: it was made for them. You tell me you feel no pain. I conclude you are one of those for whom Hell exists.

THE OLD WOMAN. Do *you* feel no pain?

DON JUAN. I am not one of the wicked, Señora; therefore it bores me, bores me beyond description, beyond belief.

THE OLD WOMAN. Not one of the wicked! You said you were a murderer.

DON JUAN. Only a duel. I ran my sword through an old man who was trying to run his through me.

THE OLD WOMAN. If you were a gentleman, that was not a murder.

DON JUAN. The old man called it murder, because he was, he said, defending his daughter's honor. By this he meant that because I foolishly fell in love with her and told her so, she screamed; and he tried to assassinate me after calling me insulting names.

THE OLD WOMAN. You were like all men. Libertines and murderers all, all, all!

DON JUAN. And yet we meet here, dear lady.

THE OLD WOMAN. Listen to me. My father was slain by just such a wretch as you, in just such a duel, for just such a cause. I screamed: it was my duty. My father drew on my assailant: his honor demanded it. He fell: that was the reward of honor. I am here: in hell, you tell me: that is the reward of duty. Is there justice in heaven?

DON JUAN. No; but there is justice in hell: heaven is far above such idle human personalities. You will be welcome in hell, Señora. Hell is the home of honor, duty, justice, and the rest of the seven deadly virtues. All the wickedness on earth is done in their name: where else but in hell should they have their reward? Have I not told you that the truly damned are those who are happy in hell?

THE OLD WOMAN. And are you happy here?

DON JUAN [*springing to his feet*]. No; and that is the enigma on which I ponder in darkness. Why am I here? I, who repudiated all duty, trampled honor underfoot, and laughed at justice!

THE OLD WOMAN. Oh, what do I care why you are here? Why am *I* here? I, who sacrificed all my inclinations to womanly virtue and propriety!

DON JUAN. Patience, lady: you will be perfectly happy and at home here. As saith the poet, "Hell is a city much like Seville."

THE OLD WOMAN. Happy! here! where I am nothing! where I am nobody!

DON JUAN. Not at all: you are a lady; and wherever ladies are is hell. Do not be surprised or terrified: you will find everything here that a lady can desire, including devils who will serve you from sheer love of servitude, and magnify your importance for the sake of dignifying their service — the best of servants.

THE OLD WOMAN. My servants will be devils!

DON JUAN. Have you ever had servants who were not devils?

THE OLD WOMAN. Never: they were devils, perfect devils, all of them. But that is only a manner of speaking. I thought you meant that my servants here would be real devils.

DON JUAN. No more real devils than you will be a real lady. Nothing is real here. That is the horror of damnation.

THE OLD WOMAN. Oh, this is all madness. This is worse than fire and the worm.

DON JUAN. For you, perhaps, there are consolations. For instance: how old were you when you changed from time to eternity?

THE OLD WOMAN. Do not ask me how old I w a s — as if I were a thing of the past. I a m 77.

DON JUAN. A ripe age, Señora. But in hell old age is not tolerated. It is too real. Here we worship Love and Beauty. Our souls being entirely damned, we cultivate our hearts. As a lady of 77, you would not have a single acquaintance in hell.

THE OLD WOMAN. How can I help my age, man?

DON JUAN. You forget that you have left your age behind you in the realm of time. You are no more 77 than you are 7 or 17 or 27.

THE OLD WOMAN. Nonsense!

DON JUAN. Consider, Señora: was not this true even when you lived on earth? When you were 70, were you really older underneath your wrinkles and your grey hairs than when you were 30?

THE OLD WOMAN. No, younger: at 30 I was a fool. But of what use is it to feel younger and look older?

DON JUAN. You see, Señora, the look was only an illusion. Your wrinkles lied, just as the plump smooth skin of many a stupid girl of 17, with heavy spirits and decrepit ideas, lies about h e r age? Well, here we have no bodies: we see each other as bodies only because we learnt to think about one another under that aspect when we were alive; and we still think in that way, knowing no other. But we can appear to one another at what age we choose. You have but to will any of your old looks back, and back they will come.

THE OLD WOMAN. It cannot be true.

DON JUAN. Try.

THE OLD WOMAN. Seventeen!

DON JUAN. Stop. Before you decide, I had better tell you that these things are a matter of fashion. Occasionally we have a rage for 17; but it does not last long. Just at present the fashionable age is 40 — or say 37; but there are signs of a change. If you were at all good-looking at 27, I should suggest your trying that, and setting a new fashion.

THE OLD WOMAN. I do not believe a word you are saying. However, 27 be it. [*Whisk! the old woman becomes a young one, magnificently attired, and so handsome that in the radiance into which her dull yellow halo has suddenly lightened one might almost mistake her for Ann Whitefield.*]

DON JUAN. Doña Ana de Ulloa!

ANA. What? You know me!

DON JUAN. And you forget me!

ANA. I cannot see your face. [*He raises his hat.*] Don Juan Tenorio! Monster! You who slew my father! even here you pursue me.

DON JUAN. I protest I do not pursue you. Allow me to withdraw [*going*].

ANA [*seizing his arm*]. You shall not leave me alone in this dreadful place.

DON JUAN. Provided my staying be not interpreted as pursuit.

ANA [*releasing him*]. You may well wonder how I can endure your presence. My dear, dear father!

DON JUAN. Would you like to see him?

ANA. My father h e r e!!!

DON JUAN. No: he is in heaven.

ANA. I knew it. My noble father! He is looking down on us now. What must he feel to see his daughter in this place, and in conversation with his murderer!

DON JUAN. By the way, if we should meet him —

ANA. How can we meet him? He is in heaven.

DON JUAN. He condescends to look in upon us here from time to time. Heaven bores him. So let me warn you that if you meet him he will be mortally offended if you speak of me as his murderer! He maintains that he was a much better swordsman than I, and that if his foot had not slipped he would have killed me. No doubt he is right: I was not a good fencer. I never dispute the point; so we are excellent friends.

ANA. It is no dishonor to a soldier to be proud of his skill in arms.

DON JUAN. You would rather not meet him, probably.

ANA. How dare you say that?

DON JUAN. Oh, that is the usual feeling here. You may remember that on earth — though of course we never confessed it — the death of anyone we knew, even those we liked best, was always mingled with a certain satisfaction at being finally done with them.

ANA. Monster! Never, never.

DON JUAN [*placidly*]. I see you recognize the feeling. Yes: a funeral was always a festivity in black, especially the funeral of a relative. At all events, family ties are rarely kept up here. Your father is quite accustomed to this: he will not expect any devotion from you.

ANA. Wretch: I wore mourning for him all my life.

DON JUAN. Yes: it became you. But a life of mourning is one thing: an eternity of it quite another. Besides, here you are as dead as he. Can anything be more ridiculous than one dead person mourning for another? Do not look shocked, my dear Ana; and do not be alarmed: there is plenty of humbug in hell (indeed there is hardly anything else); but the humbug of death and age and change is dropped because here we are all dead and all eternal. You will pick up our ways soon.

ANA. And will all the men call me their dear Ana?

DON JUAN. No. That was a slip of the tongue. I beg your pardon.

ANA [*almost tenderly*]. Juan: did you really love me when you behaved so disgracefully to me?

DON JUAN [*impatiently*]. Oh, I beg you not to begin talking about love. Here they talk of nothing else but love: its beauty, its holiness, its spirituality, its devil knows what! — excuse me; but it does so bore me. They dont know what theyre talking about: I do. They think they have achieved the perfection of love because they have no bodies. Sheer imaginative debauchery! Faugh!

ANA. Has even death failed to refine your soul, Juan? Has the terrible judgment of which my father's statue was the minister taught you no reverence?

DON JUAN. How is that very flattering statue, by the way? Does it still come to supper with naughty people and cast them into this bottomless pit?

ANA. It has been a great expense to me. The boys in the monastery school would not let it alone: the mischievous ones broke it; and the studious ones wrote their names on it. Three new noses in two years, and fingers without end. I had to leave it to its fate at last; and now I fear it is shockingly mutilated. My poor father!

DON JUAN. Hush! Listen! [*Two great chords rolling on syncopated waves of sound break forth: D minor and its dominant: a sound of dreadful joy to all musicians.*] Ha! Mozart's statue music.[17] It is your father. You had better disappear until I prepare him. [*She vanishes.*]

*From the void comes a living statue of white marble, designed to represent a majestic old man. But he waives his majesty with infinite grace; walks with a feather-like step; and makes every wrinkle in his war worn visage brim over with holiday joyousness. To his sculptor he owes a perfectly trained figure, which he carries erect and trim; and the ends of his moustache curl up, elastic as watchsprings, giving him an air which, but for its Spanish dignity, would be called jaunty. He is on the pleasantest terms with Don Juan. His voice, save for a much more distinguished intonation, is so like the voice of Roebuck Ramsden that it calls attention to the fact that they are not unlike one another in spite of their very different fashions of shaving.*

DON JUAN. Ah, here you are, my friend. Why dont you learn to sing the splendid music Mozart has written for you?

THE STATUE. Unluckily he has written it for a bass voice. Mine is a counter tenor.[18] Well: have you repented yet?

DON JUAN. I have too much consideration for you to repent, Don Gonzalo. If I did, you would have no excuse for coming from Heaven to argue with me.

THE STATUE. True. Remain obdurate, my boy. I wish I had killed you, as I should have done but for an accident. Then I should have come here; and you would have had a statue and a reputation for piety to live up to. Any news?

DON JUAN. Yes: your daughter is dead.

THE STATUE [*puzzled*]. My daughter? [*Recollecting*] Oh! the one you were taken with. Let me see: what was her name?

DON JUAN. Ana.

THE STATUE. To be sure: Ana. A goodlooking girl, if I recollect aright. Have you warned Whatshisname? her husband.

DON JUAN. My friend Ottavio? No: I have not seen him since Ana arrived.

*Ana comes indignantly to light.*

ANA. What does this mean? Ottavio here and y o u r friend! And you, father, have forgotten my name. You are indeed turned to stone.

**17. statue music:** The music, very aptly described by Shaw, accompanies the Statue of the dead Commendatore as it appears to Don Juan in the cemetery (*Don Giovanni*, II.iii.no.23). The trombones are prominent and most impressive. See the Statue's speech, "Ha ha! . . . trombones," p. 752. **18. counter tenor:** a part pitched higher than the tenor and sung by a high male voice. The voice ironically suggests the "distinguished intonation" of Ramsden as the Statue.

THE STATUE. My dear: I am so much more admired in marble than I ever was in my own person that I have retained the shape the sculptor gave me. He was one of the first men of his day: you must acknowledge that.

ANA. Father! Vanity! personal vanity! from you!

THE STATUE. Ah, you outlived that weakness, my daughter: you must be nearly 80 by this time. I was cut off (by an accident) in my 64th year, and am considerably your junior in consequence. Besides, my child, in this place, what our libertine friend here would call the farce of parental wisdom is dropped. Regard me, I beg, as a fellow creature, not as a father.

ANA. You speak as this villain speaks.

THE STATUE. Juan is a sound thinker, Ana. A bad fencer, but a sound thinker.

ANA [*horror creeping upon her*]. I begin to understand. These are devils, mocking me. I had better pray.

THE STATUE [*consoling her*]. No, no, no, my child: do not pray. If you do, you will throw away the main advantage of this place. Written over the gate here are the words "Leave every hope behind, ye who enter."[19] Only think what a relief that is! For what is hope? A form of moral responsibility. Here there is no hope, and consequently no duty, no work, nothing to be gained by praying, nothing to be lost by doing what you like. Hell, in short, is a place where you have nothing to do but amuse yourself. [*Don Juan sighs deeply.*] You sigh, friend Juan; but if you dwelt in heaven, as I do, you would realize your advantages.

DON JUAN. You are in good spirits today, Commander. You are positively brilliant. What is the matter?

THE STATUE. I have come to a momentous decision, my boy. But first, where is our friend the Devil? I must consult him in the matter. And Ana would like to make his acquaintance, no doubt.

ANA. You are preparing some torment for me.

DON JUAN. All that is superstition, Ana. Reassure yourself. Remember: the devil is not so black as he is painted.

THE STATUE. Let us give him a call.

*At the wave of the statue's hand the great chords roll out again; but this time Mozart's music gets grotesquely adulterated with Gounod's.*[20] *A scarlet halo begins to glow; and into it the Devil rises, very Mephistophelean, and not at all unlike Mendoza, though not so interesting. He looks older; is getting prematurely bald; and, in spite of an effusion of goodnature and friendliness, is peevish and sensitive when his advances are not reciprocated. He does not inspire much confidence in his powers of hard work or endurance, and is, on the whole, a disagreeably self-indulgent looking person; but he is clever and plausible, though perceptibly less well bred than the two other men, and enormously less vital than the woman.*

THE DEVIL [*heartily*]. Have I the pleasure of again receiving a visit from the illustrious Commander of Calatrava? [*Coldly*] Don Juan, your servant. [*Politely*] And a strange lady? My respects, Señora.

ANA. Are you —

THE DEVIL [*bowing*]. Lucifer, at your service.

ANA. I shall go mad.

THE DEVIL [*gallantly*]. Ah, Señora, do not be anxious. You come to us from earth, full of the prejudices and terrors of that priest-ridden place. You have heard me ill spoken of; and yet, believe me, I have hosts of friends there.

ANA. Yes: you reign in their hearts.

THE DEVIL [*shaking his head*]. You flatter me, Señora; but you are mistaken. It is true that the world cannot get on without me; but it never gives me credit for that: in its heart it mistrusts and hates me. Its sympathies are all with misery, with poverty, with starvation of the body and of the heart. I call on it to sympathize with joy, with love, with happiness, with beauty —

DON JUAN [*nauseated*]. Excuse me: I am going. You know I cannot stand this.

THE DEVIL [*angrily*]. Yes: I know that you are no friend of mine.

THE STATUE. What harm is he doing you, Juan? It seems to me that he was talking excellent sense when you interrupted him.

THE DEVIL [*warmly patting the statue's hand*]. Thank you, my friend: thank you. You have always understood me: he has always disparaged and avoided me.

DON JUAN. I have treated you with perfect courtesy.

THE DEVIL. Courtesy! What is courtesy? I care nothing for mere courtesy. Give me warmth of heart, true sincerity, the bond of sympathy with love and joy —

DON JUAN. You are making me ill.

THE DEVIL. There! [*Appealing to the statue*] You hear, sir! Oh, by what irony of fate was this cold selfish egotist sent to my kingdom, and you taken to the icy mansions of the sky!

THE STATUE. I cant complain. I was a hypocrite; and it served me right to be sent to heaven.

THE DEVIL. Why, sir, do you not join us, and leave a sphere for which your temperament is too sympathetic, your heart too warm, your capacity for enjoyment too generous?

THE STATUE. I have this day resolved to do so. In

**19. "Leave . . . enter"**: from the inscription over the Gate of Hell, Dante, *Inferno*, III.9. **20. *Gounod:*** from Gounod's *Faust*, in which Mephistopheles is a character.

future, excellent Son of the Morning, I am yours. I have left Heaven for ever.

THE DEVIL [*again touching the marble hand*]. Ah, what an honor! what a triumph for our cause! Thank you, thank you. And now, my friend — I may call you so at last — could you not persuade him to take the place you have left vacant above?

THE STATUE [*shaking his head*]. I cannot conscientiously recommend anybody with whom I am on friendly terms to deliberately make himself dull and uncomfortable.

THE DEVIL. Of course not; but are you sure he would be uncomfortable? Of course you know best: you brought him here originally; and we had the greatest hopes of him. His sentiments were in the best taste of our best people. You remember how he sang? [*He begins to sing in a nasal operatic baritone, tremendous from an eternity of misuse in the French manner*]

Vivan le femmine!
Viva il buon vino!

THE STATUE [*taking up the tune an octave higher in his counter tenor*].

Sostegno e gloria
D'umanità.[21]

THE DEVIL. Precisely. Well, he never sings for us now.

DON JUAN. Do you complain of that? Hell is full of musical amateurs: music is the brandy of the damned. May not one lost soul be permitted to abstain?

THE DEVIL. You dare blaspheme against the sublimest of the arts!

DON JUAN [*with cold disgust*]. You talk like a hysterical woman fawning on a fiddler.

THE DEVIL. I am not angry. I merely pity you. You have no soul; and you are unconscious of all that you lose. Now you, Señor Commander, are a born musician. How well you sing! Mozart would be delighted if he were still here; but he moped and went to heaven. Curious how these clever men, whom you would have supposed born to be popular here, have turned out social failures, like Don Juan!

DON JUAN. I am really very sorry to be a social failure.

THE DEVIL. Not that we dont admire your intellect, you know. We do. But I look at the matter from your own point of view. You dont get on with us. The place doesnt suit you. The truth is, you have — I wont say no heart; for we know that beneath all your affected cynicism you have a warm one —

DON JUAN [*shrinking*]. Dont, please dont.

THE DEVIL [*nettled*]. Well, youve no capacity for enjoyment. Will that satisfy you?

DON JUAN. It is a somewhat less insufferable form of cant than the other. But if youll allow me, I'll take refuge, as usual, in solitude.

THE DEVIL. Why not take refuge in Heaven? Thats the proper place for you. [*To Ana*] Come Señora! could you not persuade him for his own good to try change of air?

ANA. But can he go to Heaven if he wants to?

THE DEVIL. Whats to prevent him?

ANA. Can anybody — can *I* go to Heaven if I want to?

THE DEVIL [*rather contemptuously*]. Certainly, if your taste lies that way.

ANA. But why doesnt everybody go to Heaven, then?

THE STATUE [*chuckling*]. *I* can tell you that, my dear. It's because heaven is the most angelically dull place in all creation: thats why.

THE DEVIL. His excellency the Commander puts it with military bluntness; but the strain of living in Heaven is intolerable. There is a notion that I was turned out of it; but as a matter of fact nothing could have induced me to stay there. I simply left it and organized this place.

THE STATUE. I dont wonder at it. Nobody could stand an eternity of heaven.

THE DEVIL. Oh, it suits some people. Let us be just, Commander: it is a question of temperament. I dont admire the heavenly temperament: I dont understand it: I dont know that I particularly want to understand it; but it takes all sorts to make a universe. There is no accounting for tastes: there are people who like it. I think Don Juan would like it.

DON JUAN. But — pardon my frankness — could you really go back there if you desired to; or are the grapes sour?

THE DEVIL. Back there! I often go back there. Have you never read the book of Job?[22] Have you any canonical authority for assuming that there is any barrier between our circle and the other one?

ANA. But surely there is a great gulf fixed.

THE DEVIL. Dear lady: a parable must not be taken literally. The gulf is the difference between the angelic and the diabolic temperament. What more impassable gulf could you have? Think of what you have seen on earth. There is no physical gulf between the philosopher's class room and the bull ring; but the bull fighters do not come to the class room for all that. Have you ever been in the country where I have the largest following? England. There they have great racecourses, and also concert

**21. Vivan . . . D'umanita**: "Here's to the women all! / Here's to good wine! / They nourish and honor all mankind." This toast is sung by Don Juan as an impious and mocking reply to Donna Elvira, who has come to beg him to repent before it is too late (*Don Giovanni*, II.v.no.26, soon after Elvira's entrance).

**22. Job**: In Job 1:6, Satan comes also among "the sons of God" when they present themselves "before the Lord."

rooms where they play the classical compositions of his Excellency's friend Mozart. Those who go to the racecourses can stay away from them and go to the classical concerts instead if they like: there is no law against it; for Englishmen never will be slaves: they are free to do whatever the Government and public opinion allow them to do. And the classical concert is admitted to be a higher, more cultivated, poetic, intellectual, ennobling place than the racecourse. But do the lovers of racing desert their sport and flock to the concert room? Not they. They would suffer there all the weariness the Commander has suffered in heaven. There is the great gulf of the parable between the two places. A mere physical gulf they could bridge; or at least I could bridge it for them (the earth is full of Devil's Bridges); but the gulf of dislike is impassable and eternal. And that is the only gulf that separates my friends here from those who are invidiously called the blest.

ANA. I shall go to heaven at once.

THE STATUE. My child: one word of warning first. Let me complete my friend Lucifer's similitude of the classical concert. At every one of those concerts in England you will find rows of weary people who are there, not because they really like classical music, but because they think they ought to like it. Well, there is the same thing in heaven. A number of people sit there in glory, not because they are happy, but because they think they owe it to their position to be in heaven. They are almost all English.

THE DEVIL. Yes: the Southerners give it up and join me just as you have done. But the English really do not seem to know when they are thoroughly miserable. An Englishman thinks he is moral when he is only uncomfortable.

THE STATUE. In short, my daughter, if you go to Heaven without being naturally qualified for it, you will not enjoy yourself there.

ANA. And who dares say that I am not naturally qualified for it? The most distinguished princes of the Church have never questioned it. I owe it to myself to leave this place at once.

THE DEVIL [*offended*]. As you please, Señora. I should have expected better taste from you.

ANA. Father: I shall expect you to come with me. You cannot stay here. What will people say?

THE STATUE. People! Why, the best people are here — princes of the Church and all. So few go to Heaven, and so many come here, that the blest, once called a heavenly host, are a continually dwindling minority. The saints, the fathers, the elect of long ago are the cranks, the faddists, the outsiders of today.

THE DEVIL. It is true. From the beginning of my career I knew that I should win in the long run by sheer weight of public opinion, in spite of the long campaign of misrepresentation and calumny against me. At bottom the universe is a constitutional one; and with such a majority as mine I cannot be kept permanently out of office.

DON JUAN. I think, Ana, you had better stay here.

ANA [*jealously*]. You do not want me to go with you.

DON JUAN. Surely you do not want to enter Heaven in the company of a reprobate like me.

ANA. All souls are equally precious. You repent, do you not?

DON JUAN. My dear Ana, you are silly. Do you suppose heaven is like earth, where people persuade themselves that what is done can be undone by repentance; that what is spoken can be unspoken by withdrawing it; that what is true can be annihilated by a general agreement to give it the lie? No: heaven is the home of the masters of reality: that is why I am going thither.

ANA. Thank you: I am going to heaven for happiness. I have had quite enough of reality on earth.

DON JUAN. Then you must stay here; for hell is the home of the unreal and of the seekers for happiness. It is the only refuge from heaven, which is, as I tell you, the home of the masters of reality, and from earth, which is the home of the slaves of reality. The earth is a nursery in which men and women play at being heroes and heroines, saints and sinners; but they are dragged down from their fool's paradise by their bodies: hunger and cold and thirst, age and decay and disease, death above all, make them slaves of reality: thrice a day meals must be eaten and digested: thrice a century a new generation must be engendered: ages of faith, of romance, and of science are all driven at last to have but one prayer "Make me a healthy animal." But here you escape this tyranny of the flesh; for here you are not an animal at all: you are a ghost, an appearance, an illusion, a convention, deathless, ageless: in a word, bodiless. There are no social questions here, no political questions, no religious questions, best of all, perhaps, no sanitary questions. Here you call your appearance beauty, your emotions love, your sentiments heroism, your aspirations virtue, just as you did on earth; but here there are no hard facts to contradict you, no ironic contrast of your needs with your pretensions, no human comedy, nothing but a perpetual romance, a universal melodrama. As our German friend put it in his poem, "the poetically nonsensical here is good sense; and the Eternal Feminine draws us ever upward and on"[23] — without getting us a step farther. And yet you want to leave this paradise!

23. "the . . . on": a free translation of the last four lines of Goethe's *Faust*.

ANA. But if Hell be so beautiful as this, how glorious must heaven be!

*The Devil, the Statue, and Don Juan all begin to speak at once in violent protest; then stop abashed.*

DON JUAN. I beg your pardon.

THE DEVIL. Not at all. I interrupted you.

THE STATUE. You were going to say something.

DON JUAN. After you, gentlemen.

THE DEVIL [*to Don Juan*]. You have been so eloquent on the advantages of my dominions that I leave you to do equal justice to the drawbacks of the alternative establishment.

DON JUAN. In Heaven, as I picture it, dear lady, you live and work instead of playing and pretending. You face things as they are; you escape nothing but glamor; and your steadfastness and your peril are your glory. If the play still goes on here and on earth, and all the world is a stage, Heaven is at least behind the scenes. But Heaven cannot be described by metaphor. Thither I shall go presently, because there I hope to escape at last from lies and from the tedious, vulgar pursuit of happiness, to spend my eons in contemplation —

THE STATUE. Ugh!

DON JUAN. Señor Commander: I do not blame your disgust: a picture gallery is a dull place for a blind man. But even as you enjoy the contemplation of such romantic mirages as beauty and pleasure; so would I enjoy the contemplation of that which interests me above all things: namely, Life: the force that ever strives to attain greater power of contemplating itself. What made this brain of mine, do you think? Not the need to move my limbs; for a rat with half my brains moves as well as I. Not merely the need to do, but the need to know what I do, lest in my blind efforts to live I should be slaying myself.

THE STATUE. You would have slain yourself in your blind efforts to fence but for my foot slipping, my friend.

DON JUAN. Audacious ribald: your laughter will finish in hideous boredom before morning.

THE STATUE. Ha ha! Do you remember how I frightened you when I said something like that to you from my pedestal in Seville? It sounds rather flat without my trombones.

DON JUAN. They tell me it generally sounds flat with them, Commander.

ANA. Oh, do not interrupt with these frivolities, father. Is there nothing in Heaven but contemplation, Juan?

DON JUAN. In the Heaven I seek, no other joy. But there is the work of helping Life in its struggle upward. Think of how it wastes and scatters itself, how it raises up obstacles to itself and destroys itself in its ignorance and blindness. It needs a brain, this irresistible force, lest in its ignorance it should resist itself. What a piece of work is man! [24] says the poet. Yes; but what a blunderer! Here is the highest miracle of organization yet attained by life, the most intensely alive thing that exists, the most conscious of all the organisms; and yet, how wretched are his brains! Stupidity made sordid and cruel by the realities learnt from toil and poverty: Imagination resolved to starve sooner than face these realities, piling up illusions to hide them, and calling itself cleverness, genius! And each accusing the other of its own defect: Stupidity accusing Imagination of folly, and Imagination accusing Stupidity of ignorance: whereas, alas! Stupidity has all the knowledge, and Imagination all the intelligence.

THE DEVIL. And a pretty kettle of fish they make of it between them. Did I not say, when I was arranging that affair of Faust's, that all Man's reason has done for him is to make him beastlier than any beast. One splendid body is worth the brains of a hundred dyspeptic, flatulent philosophers.

DON JUAN. You forget that brainless magnificence of body has been tried. Things immeasurably greater than man in every respect but brain have existed and perished. The megatherium, the icthyosaurus have paced the earth with seven-league steps and hidden the day with cloud vast wings. Where are they now? Fossils in museums, and so few and imperfect at that, that a knuckle bone or a tooth of one of them is prized beyond the lives of a thousand soldiers. These things lived and wanted to live; but for lack of brains they did not know how to carry out their purpose, and so destroyed themselves.

THE DEVIL. And is Man any the less destroying himself for all this boasted brain of his? Have you walked up and down upon the earth lately? I have; and I have examined Man's wonderful inventions. And I tell you that in the arts of life man invents nothing; but in the arts of death he outdoes Nature herself, and produces by chemistry and machinery all the slaughter of plague, pestilence, and famine. The peasant I tempt today eats and drinks what was eaten and drunk by the peasants of ten thousand years ago; and the house he lives in has not altered as much in a thousand centuries as the fashion of a lady's bonnet in a score of weeks. But when he goes out to slay, he carries a marvel of mechanism that lets loose at the touch of his finger all the hidden molecular energies, and leaves the javelin, the arrow, the blowpipe of his fathers far behind. In the arts of peace Man is a bungler. I have seen his cotton factories and the like, with machinery that a greedy dog could have invented if it had wanted money instead of food.

24. **man**: "What a piece of work is a man!" *Hamlet*, II.ii.315.

I know his clumsy typewriters and bungling locomotives and tedious bicycles: they are toys compared to the Maxim gun, the submarine torpedo boat. There is nothing in Man's industrial machinery but his greed and sloth: his heart is in his weapons. This marvellous force of Life of which you boast is a force of Death: Man measures his strength by his destructiveness. What is his religion? An excuse for hating me. What is his law? An excuse for hanging you. What is his morality? Gentility! an excuse for consuming without producing. What is his art? An excuse for gloating over pictures of slaughter. What are his politics? Either the worship of a despot because a despot can kill, or parliamentary cockfighting. I spent an evening lately in a certain celebrated legislature, and heard the pot lecturing the kettle for its blackness, and ministers answering questions. When I left I chalked up on the door the old nursery saying "Ask no questions and you will be told no lies." I bought a sixpenny family magazine, and found it full of pictures of young men shooting and stabbing one another. I saw a man die: he was a London bricklayer's laborer with seven children. He left seventeen pounds club money; and his wife spent it all on his funeral and went into the workhouse with the children next day. She would not have spent sevenpence on her children's schooling: the law had to force her to let them be taught gratuitously; but on death she spent all she had. Their imagination glows, their energies rise up at the idea of death, these people: they love it; and the more horrible it is the more they enjoy it. Hell is a place far above their comprehension: they derive their notion of it from two of the greatest fools that ever lived, an Italian and an Englishman. The Italian [25] described it as a place of mud, frost, filth, fire, and venomous serpents: all torture. This ass, when he was not lying about me, was maundering about some woman whom he saw once in the street. The Englishman [26] described me as being expelled from Heaven by cannons and gunpowder; and to this day every Briton believes that the whole of his silly story is in the Bible. What else he says I do not know; for it is all in a long poem which neither I nor anyone else ever succeeded in wading through. It is the same in everything. The highest form of literature is the tragedy, a play in which everybody is murdered at the end. In the old chronicles you read of earthquakes and pestilences, and are told that these shewed the power and majesty of God and the littleness of Man. Nowadays the chronicles describe battles. In a battle two bodies of men shoot at one another with bullets and explosive shells until one body runs away, when the others chase the fugitives on horseback and cut them to pieces as they fly. And this, the chronicle concludes, shews the greatness and majesty of empires, and the littleness of the vanquished. Over such battles the people run about the streets yelling with delight, and egg their Governments on to spend hundreds of millions of money in the slaughter, whilst the strongest Ministers dare not spend an extra penny in the pound against the poverty and pestilence through which they themselves daily walk. I could give you a thousand instances; but they all come to the same thing: the power that governs the earth is not the power of Life but of Death; and the inner need that has nerved Life to the effort of organizing itself into the human being is not the need for higher life but for a more efficient engine of destruction. The plague, the famine, the earthquake, the tempest were too spasmodic in their action; the tiger and crocodile were too easily satiated and not cruel enough: something more constantly, more ruthlessly, more ingeniously destructive was needed; and that something was Man, the inventor of the rack, the stake, the gallows, the electric chair; of sword and gun and poison gas: above all, of justice, duty, patriotism, and all the other isms by which even those who are clever enough to be humanely disposed are persuaded to become the most destructive of all the destroyers.

DON JUAN. Pshaw! all this is old. Your weak side, my diabolic friend, is that you have always been a gull: you take Man at his own valuation. Nothing would flatter him more than your opinion of him. He loves to think of himself as bold and bad. He is neither one nor the other: he is only a coward. Call him tyrant, murderer, pirate, bully; and he will adore you, and swagger about with the consciousness of having the blood of the old sea kings in his veins. Call him liar and thief; and he will only take an action against you for libel. But call him coward; and he will go mad with rage: he will face death to outface that stinging truth. Man gives every reason for his conduct save one, every excuse for his crimes save one, every plea for his safety save one; and that one is his cowardice. Yet all his civilization is founded on his cowardice, on his abject tameness, which he calls his respectability. There are limits to what a mule or an ass will stand; but Man will suffer himself to be degraded until his vileness becomes so loathsome to his oppressors that they themselves are forced to reform it.

THE DEVIL. Precisely. And these are the creatures in whom you discover what you call a Life Force!

DON JUAN. Yes; for now comes the most surprising part of the whole business.

THE STATUE. Whats that?

25. **Italian:** Dante, in the *Inferno*. 26. **Englishman:** Milton, in *Paradise Lost*, VI.469–669.

DON JUAN. Why, that you can make any of these cowards brave by simply putting an idea into his head.

THE STATUE. Stuff! As an old soldier I admit the cowardice: it's as universal as sea sickness, and matters just as little. But that about putting an idea into a man's head is stuff and nonsense. In a battle all you need to make you fight is a little hot blood and the knowledge that it's more dangerous to lose than to win.

DON JUAN. That is perhaps why battles are so useless. But men never really overcome fear until they imagine they are fighting to further a universal purpose — fighting for an idea, as they call it. Why was the Crusader braver than the pirate? Because he fought, not for himself, but for the Cross. What force was it that met him with a valor as reckless as his own? The force of men who fought, not for themselves, but for Islam. They took Spain from us, though we were fighting for our very hearths and homes; but when we, too, fought for that mighty idea, a Catholic Church, we swept them back to Africa.

THE DEVIL [*ironically*]. What! you a Catholic, Señor Don Juan! A devotee! My congratulations.

THE STATUE [*seriously*]. Come, come! as a soldier, I can listen to nothing against the Church.

DON JUAN. Have no fear, Commander: this idea of a Catholic Church will survive Islam, will survive the Cross, will survive even that vulgar pageant of incompetent schoolboyish gladiators which you call the Army.

THE STATUE. Juan: you will force me to call you to account for this.

DON JUAN. Useless: I cannot fence. Every idea for which Man will die will be a Catholic idea. When the Spaniard learns at last that he is no better than the Saracen, and his prophet no better than Mahomet, he will arise, more Catholic than ever, and die on a barricade across the filthy slum he starves in, for universal liberty and equality.

THE STATUE. Bosh!

DON JUAN. What you call bosh is the only thing men dare die for. Later on, Liberty will not be Catholic enough: men will die for human perfection, to which they will sacrifice all their liberty gladly.

THE DEVIL. Ay: they will never be at a loss for an excuse for killing one another.

DON JUAN. What of that? It is not death that matters, but the fear of death. It is not killing and dying that degrades us, but base living, and accepting the wages and profits of degradation. Better ten dead men than one live slave or his master. Men shall yet rise up, father against son and brother against brother, and kill one another for the great Catholic idea of abolishing slavery.

THE DEVIL. Yes, when the Liberty and Equality of which you prate shall have made free white Christians cheaper in the labor market than black heathen slaves sold by auction at the block.

DON JUAN. Never fear! the white laborer shall have his turn too. But I am not now defending the illusory forms the great ideas take. I am giving you examples of the fact that this creature Man, who in his own selfish affairs is a coward to the backbone, will fight for an idea like a hero. He may be abject as a citizen; but he is dangerous as a fanatic. He can only be enslaved whilst he is spiritually weak enough to listen to reason. I tell you, gentlemen, if you can shew a man a piece of what he now calls God's work to do, and what he will later on call by many new names, you can make him entirely reckless of the consequences to himself personally.

ANA. Yes: he shirks all his responsibilities, and leaves his wife to grapple with them.

THE STATUE. Well said, daughter. Do not let him talk you out of your common sense.

THE DEVIL. Alas! Señor Commander, now that we have got on to the subject of Woman, he will talk more than ever. However, I confess it is for me the one supremely interesting subject.

DON JUAN. To a woman, Señora, man's duties and responsibilities begin and end with the task of getting bread for her children. To her, Man is only a means to the end of getting children and rearing them.

ANA. Is that your idea of a woman's mind? I call it cynical and disgusting animalism.

DON JUAN. Pardon me, Ana: I said nothing about a woman's whole mind. I spoke of her view of Man as a separate sex. It is no more cynical than her view of herself as above all things a Mother. Sexually, Woman is Nature's contrivance for perpetuating its highest achievement. Sexually, Man is Woman's contrivance for fulfilling Nature's behest in the most economical way. She knows by instinct that far back in the evolutional process she invented him, differentiated him, created him in order to produce something better than the single-sexed process can produce. Whilst he fulfils the purpose for which she made him, he is welcome to his dreams, his follies, his ideals, his heroisms, provided that the keystone of them all is the worship of woman, of motherhood, of the family, of the hearth. But how rash and dangerous it was to invent a separate creature whose sole function was her own impregnation! For mark what has happened. First, Man has multiplied on her hands until there are as many men as women; so that she has been unable to employ for her purposes more than a fraction of the immense energy she has left at his disposal by saving him the exhausting labor of gestation. This superfluous energy has gone to his brain and to his muscle. He has become too strong to be controlled by her bodily, and too imaginative and mentally vigorous to be content with mere self-reproduction. He has created civilization without consulting her, taking her domestic labor for granted as the foundation of it.

ANA. That is true, at all events.

THE DEVIL. Yes; and this civilization! what is it, after all?

DON JUAN. After all, an excellent peg to hang your cynical commonplaces on; but before all, it is an attempt on Man's part to make himself something more than the mere instrument of Woman's purpose. So far, the result of Life's continual effort not only to maintain itself, but to achieve higher and higher organization and completer self-consciousness, is only, at best, a doubtful campaign between its forces and those of Death and Degeneration. The battles in this campaign are mere blunders, mostly won, like actual military battles, in spite of the commanders.

THE STATUE. That is a dig at me. No matter: go on, go on.

DON JUAN. It is a dig at a much higher power than you, Commander. Still, you must have noticed in your profession that even a stupid general can win battles when the enemy's general is a little stupider.

THE STATUE [*very seriously*]. Most true, Juan, most true. Some donkeys have amazing luck.

DON JUAN. Well, the Life Force is stupid; but it is not so stupid as the forces of Death and Degeneration. Besides, these are in its pay all the time. And so Life wins, after a fashion. What mere copiousness of fecundity can supply and mere greed preserve, we possess. The survival of whatever form of civilization can produce the best rifle and the best fed riflemen is assured.

THE DEVIL. Exactly! the survival, not of the most effective means of Life but of the most effective means of Death. You always come back to my point, in spite of your wrigglings and evasions and sophistries, not to mention the intolerable length of your speeches.

DON JUAN. Oh, come! who began making long speeches? However, if I overtax your intellect, you can leave us and seek the society of love and beauty and the rest of your favorite boredoms.

THE DEVIL [*much offended*]. This is not fair, Don Juan, and not civil. I am also on the intellectual plane. Nobody can appreciate it more than I do. I am arguing fairly with you, and, I think, successfully refuting you. Let us go on for another hour if you like.

DON JUAN. Good: let us.

THE STATUE. Not that I see any prospect of your coming to any point in particular, Juan. Still, since in this place, instead of merely killing time we have to kill eternity, go ahead by all means.

DON JUAN [*somewhat impatiently*]. My point, you marbleheaded old masterpiece, is only a step ahead of you. Are we agreed that Life is a force which has made innumerable experiments in organizing itself; that the mammoth and the man, the mouse and the megatherium, the flies and the fleas and the Fathers of the Church, are all more or less successful attempts to build up that raw force into higher and higher individuals, the ideal individual being omnipotent, omniscient, infallible, and withal completely, unilludedly self-conscious: in short, a god?

THE DEVIL. I agree, for the sake of argument.

THE STATUE. I agree, for the sake of avoiding argument.

ANA. I most emphatically disagree as regards the Fathers of the Church; and I must beg you not to drag them into the argument.

DON JUAN. I did so purely for the sake of alliteration, Ana; and I shall make no further allusion to them. And now, since we are, with that exception, agreed so far, will you not agree with me further that Life has not measured the success of its attempts at godhead by the beauty or bodily perfection of the result, since in both these respects the birds, as our friend Aristophanes [27] long ago pointed out, are so extraordinarily superior, with their power of flight and their lovely plumage, and, may I add, the touching poetry of their loves and nestings, that it is inconceivable that Life, having once produced them, should, if love and beauty were her object, start off on another line and labor at the clumsy elephant and the hideous ape, whose grandchildren we are?

ANA. Aristophanes was a heathen; and you, Juan, I am afraid, are very little better.

THE DEVIL. You conclude, then, that Life was driving at clumsiness and ugliness?

DON JUAN. No, perverse devil that you are, a thousand times no. Life was driving at brains — at its darling object: an organ by which it can attain not only self-consciousness but self-understanding.

THE STATUE. This is metaphysics, Juan. Why the devil should — [*To The Devil*] I beg your pardon.

THE DEVIL. Pray dont mention it. I have always regarded the use of my name to secure additional emphasis as a high compliment to me. It is quite at your service, Commander.

THE STATUE. Thank you: thats very good of you. Even in heaven, I never quite got out of my old military habits of speech. What I was going to ask Juan was why Life should bother itself about get-

**27. Aristophanes:** ancient Greek dramatist, in his comedy, ***The Birds.***

ting a brain. Why should it want to understand itself? Why not be content to enjoy itself?

DON JUAN. Without a brain, Commander, you would enjoy yourself without knowing it, and so lose all the fun.

THE STATUE. True, most true. But I am quite content with brain enough to know that I'm enjoying myself. I dont want to understand why. In fact, I'd rather not. My experience is that one's pleasures dont bear thinking about.

DON JUAN. That is why intellect is so unpopular. But to Life, the force behind the Man, intellect is a necessity, because without it he blunders into death. Just as Life, after ages of struggle, evolved that wonderful bodily organ the eye, so that the living organism could see where it was going and what was coming to help or threaten it, and thus avoid a thousand dangers that formerly slew it, so it is evolving today a mind's eye that shall see, not the physical world, but the purpose of Life, and thereby enable the individual to work for that purpose instead of thwarting and baffling it by setting up shortsighted personal aims as at present. Even as it is, only one sort of man has ever been happy, has ever been universally respected among all the conflicts of interests and illusions.

THE STATUE. You mean the military man.

DON JUAN. Commander: I do n o t mean the military man. When the military man approaches, the world locks up its spoons and packs off its womankind. No: I sing, not arms and the hero,[28] but the philosophic man: he who seeks in contemplation to discover the inner will of the world, in invention to discover the means of fulfilling that will, and in action to do that will by the so-discovered means. Of all other sorts of men I declare myself tired. They are tedious failures. When I was on earth, professors of all sorts prowled round me feeling for an unhealthy spot in me on which they could fasten. The doctors of medicine bade me consider what I must do to save my body, and offered me quack cures for imaginary diseases. I replied that I was not a hypochondriac; so they called me Ignoramus and went their way. The doctors of divinity bade me consider what I must do to save my soul; but I was not a spiritual hypochondriac any more than a bodily one, and would not trouble myself about that either; so they called me Atheist and went their way. After them came the politician, who said there was only one purpose in nature, and that was to get him into parliament. I told him I did not care whether he got into parliament or not; so he called me Mugwump and went his way. Then came the romantic man, the Artist, with his love songs and his paintings and his poems; and with him I had great delight for many years, and some profit; for I cultivated my senses for his sake; and his songs taught me to hear better, his paintings to see better, and his poems to feel more deeply. But he led me at last into the worship of Woman.

ANA. Juan!

DON JUAN. Yes: I came to believe that in her voice was all the music of the song, in her face all the beauty of the painting, and in her soul all the emotion of the poem.

ANA. And you were disappointed, I suppose. Well, was it her fault that you attributed all these perfections to her?

DON JUAN. Yes, partly. For with a wonderful instinctive cunning, she kept silent and allowed me to glorify her: to mistake my own visions, thoughts, and feelings for hers. Now my friend the romantic man was often too poor or too timid to approach those women who were beautiful or refined enough to seem to realize his ideal; and so he went to his grave believing in his dream. But I was more favored by nature and circumstance. I was of noble birth and rich; and when my person did not please, my conversation flattered, though I generally found myself fortunate in both.

THE STATUE. Coxcomb!

DON JUAN. Yes; but even my coxcombry pleased. Well, I found that when I had touched a woman's imagination, she would allow me to persuade myself that she loved me; but when my suit was granted she never said "I am happy: my love is satisfied": she always said, first, "At last, the barriers are down," and second, "When will you come again?"

ANA. That is exactly what men say.

DON JUAN. I protest I never said it. But all women say it. Well, these two speeches always alarmed me; for the first meant that the lady's impulse had been solely to throw down my fortifications and gain my citadel; and the second openly announced that henceforth she regarded me as her property, and counted my time as already wholly at her disposal.

THE DEVIL. That is where your want of heart came in.

THE STATUE [*shaking his head*]. You shouldnt repeat what a woman says, Juan.

ANA [*severely*]. It should be sacred to you.

THE STATUE. Still, they certainly do say it. I never minded the barriers; but there was always a slight shock about the other, unless one was very hard hit indeed.

DON JUAN. Then the lady, who had been happy and idle enough before, became anxious, preoccu-

**28. I . . . hero:** except for "not" a translation of the first line of the *Aeneid*. Cf. *Arms and the Man.*

pied with me, always intriguing, conspiring, pursuing, watching, waiting, bent wholly on making sure of her prey: I being the prey, you understand. Now this was not what I had bargained for. It may have been very proper and very natural; but it was not music, painting, poetry, and joy incarnated in a beautiful woman. I ran away from it. I ran away from it very often: in fact I became famous for running away from it.

ANA. Infamous, you mean.

DON JUAN. I did not run away from you. Do you blame me for running away from the others?

ANA. Nonsense, man. You are talking to a woman of 77 now. If you had had the chance, you would have run away from me too — if I had let you. You would not have found it so easy with me as with some of the others. If men will not be faithful to their home and their duties, they must be made to be. I daresay you all want to marry lovely incarnations of music and painting and poetry. Well, you cant have them, because they dont exist. If flesh and blood is not good enough for you you must go without: thats all. Women have to put up with flesh-and-blood husbands — and little enough of that too, sometimes; and you will have to put up with flesh-and-blood wives. [*The Devil looks dubious. The Statue makes a wry face.*] I see you dont like that, any of you; but it's true, for all that; so if you dont like it you can lump it.

DON JUAN. My dear lady, you have put my whole case against romance into a few sentences. That is just why I turned my back on the romantic man with the artist nature, as he called his infatuation. I thanked him for teaching me to use my eyes and ears; but I told him that his beauty worshipping and happiness hunting and woman idealizing was not worth a dump as a philosophy of life; so he called me Philistine and went his way.

ANA. It seems that Woman taught you something, too, with all her defects.

DON JUAN. She did more: she interpreted all the other teaching for me. Ah, my friends, when the barriers were down for the first time, what an astounding illumination! I had been prepared for infatuation, for intoxication, for all the illusions of love's young dream; and lo! never was my perception clearer, nor my criticism more ruthless. The most jealous rival of my mistress never saw every blemish in her more keenly than I. I was not duped: I took her without chloroform.

ANA. But you did take her.

DON JUAN. That was the revelation. Up to that moment I had never lost the sense of being my own master; never consciously taken a single step until my reason had examined and approved it. I had come to believe that I was a purely rational creature: a thinker! I said, with the foolish philosopher, "I think; therefore I am."[29] It was Woman who taught me to say "I am; therefore I think." And also "I would think more; therefore I must be more."

THE STATUE. This is extremely abstract and metaphysical, Juan. If you would stick to the concrete, and put your discoveries in the form of entertaining anecdotes about your adventures with women, your conversation would be easier to follow.

DON JUAN. Bah! what need I add? Do you not understand that when I stood face to face with Woman, every fibre in my clear critical brain warned me to spare her and save myself. My morals said No. My conscience said No. My chivalry and pity for her said No. My prudent regard for myself said No. My ear, practised on a thousand songs and symphonies; my eye, exercised on a thousand paintings; tore her voice, her features, her color to shreds. I caught all those tell-tale resemblances to her father and mother by which I knew what she would be like in thirty years' time. I noted the gleam of gold from a dead tooth in the laughing mouth: I made curious observations of the strange odors of the chemistry of the nerves. The visions of my romantic reveries, in which I had trod the plains of heaven with a deathless, ageless creature of coral and ivory, deserted me in that supreme hour. I remembered them and desperately strove to recover their illusion; but they now seemed the emptiest of inventions: my judgment was not to be corrupted: my brain still said No on every issue. And whilst I was in the act of framing my excuse to the lady, Life seized me and threw me into her arms as a sailor throws a scrap of fish into the mouth of a seabird.

THE STATUE. You might as well have gone without thinking such a lot about it, Juan. You are like all the clever men: you have more brains than is good for you.

THE DEVIL. And were you not the happier for the experience, Señor Don Juan?

DON JUAN. The happier, no: the wiser, yes. That moment introduced me for the first time to myself, and, through myself, to the world. I saw then how useless it is to attempt to impose conditions on the irresistible force of Life; to preach prudence, careful selection, virtue, honor, chastity —

ANA. Don Juan: a word against chastity is an insult to me.

DON JUAN. I say nothing against your chastity, Señora, since it took the form of a husband and twelve children. What more could you have done had you been the most abandoned of women?

29. "I . . . am": translation of Descartes's "*Cogito, ergo sum.*"

ANA. I could have had twelve husbands and no children: thats what I could have done, Juan. And let me tell you that that would have made all the difference to the earth which I replenished.

THE STATUE. Bravo Ana! Juan: you are floored, quelled, annihilated.

DON JUAN. No; for though that difference is the true essential difference — Doña Ana has, I admit, gone straight to the real point — yet it is not a difference of love or chastity, or even constancy; for twelve children by twelve different husbands would have replenished the earth perhaps more effectively. Suppose my friend Ottavio had died when you were thirty, you would never have remained a widow: you were too beautiful. Suppose the successor of Ottavio had died when you were forty, you would still have been irresistible; and a woman who marries twice marries three times if she becomes free to do so. Twelve lawful children borne by one highly respectable lady to three different fathers is not impossible nor condemned by public opinion. That such a lady may be more law abiding than the poor girl whom we used to spurn into the gutter for bearing one unlawful infant is no doubt true; but dare you say she is less self-indulgent?

ANA. She is more virtuous: that is enough for me.

DON JUAN. In that case, what is virtue but the Trade Unionism of the married? Let us face the facts, dear Ana. The Life Force respects marriage only because marriage is a contrivance of its own to secure the greatest number of children and the closest care of them. For honor, chastity, and all the rest of your moral figments it cares not a rap. Marriage is the most licentious of human institutions —

ANA. Juan!

THE STATUE [*protesting*]. Really! —

DON JUAN [*determined*]. I say the most licentious of human institutions: that is the secret of its popularity. And a woman seeking a husband is the most unscrupulous of all the beasts of prey. The confusion of marriage with morality has done more to destroy the conscience of the human race than any other single error. Come, Ana! do not look shocked: you know better than any of us that marriage is a mantrap baited with simulated accomplishments and delusive idealizations. When your sainted mother, by dint of scoldings and punishments, forced you to learn how to play half a dozen pieces on the spinet — which she hated as much as you did — had she any other purpose than to delude your suitors into the belief that your husband would have in his home an angel who would fill it with melody, or at least play him to sleep after dinner? You married my friend Ottavio: well, did you ever open the spinet from the hour when the Church united him to you?

ANA. You are a fool, Juan. A young married woman has something else to do than sit at the spinet without any support for her back; so she gets out of the habit of playing.

DON JUAN. Not if she loves music. No: believe me, she only throws away the bait when the bird is in the net.

ANA [*bitterly*]. And men, I suppose, never throw off the mask when t h e i r bird is in the net. The husband never becomes negligent, selfish, brutal — oh, never!

DON JUAN. What do these recriminations prove, Ana? Only that the hero is as gross an imposture as the heroine.

ANA. It is all nonsense: most marriages are perfectly comfortable.

DON JUAN. "Perfectly" is a strong expression, Ana. What you mean is that sensible people make the best of one another. Send me to the galleys and chain me to the felon whose number happens to be next before mine; and I must accept the inevitable and make the best of the companionship. Many such companionships, they tell me, are touchingly affectionate; and most are at least tolerably friendly. But that does not make a chain a desirable ornament nor the galleys an abode of bliss. Those who talk most about the blessings of marriage and the constancy of its vows are the very people who declare that if the chain were broken and the prisoners left free to choose, the whole social fabric would fly asunder. You cannot have the argument both ways. If the prisoner is happy, why lock him in? If he is not, why pretend that he is?

ANA. At all events, let me take an old woman's privilege again, and tell you flatly that marriage peoples the world and debauchery does not.

DON JUAN. How if a time come when this shall cease to be true? Do you not know that where there is a will there is a way? that whatever Man really wishes to do he will finally discover a means of doing? Well, you have done your best, you virtuous ladies, and others of your way of thinking, to bend Man's mind wholly towards honorable love as the highest good, and to understand by honorable love, romance and beauty and happiness in the possession of beautiful, refined, delicate, affectionate women. You have taught women to value their own youth, health, shapeliness, and refinement above all things. Well, what place have squalling babies and household cares in this exquisite paradise of the senses and emotions? Is it not the inevitable end of it all that the human will shall say to the human brain: Invent me a means by which I can have love, beauty, romance, emotion, passion, without their wretched penalties, their expenses, their worries, their trials, their illnesses and agonies and risks of death, their retinue of servants and nurses and doctors and schoolmasters.

THE DEVIL. All this, Señor Don Juan, is realized here in my realm.

DON JUAN. Yes, at the cost of death. Man will not take it at that price: he demands the romantic delights of your hell whilst he is still on earth. Well, the means will be found: the brain will not fail when the will is in earnest. The day is coming when great nations will find their numbers dwindling from census to census; when the six roomed villa will rise in price above the family mansion; when the viciously reckless poor and the stupidly pious rich will delay the extinction of the race only by degrading it; whilst the boldly prudent, the thriftily selfish and ambitious, the imaginative and poetic, the lovers of money and solid comfort, the worshippers of success, of art, and of love, will all oppose to the Force of Life the device of sterility.

THE STATUE. That is all very eloquent, my young friend; but if you had lived to Ana's age, or even to mine, you would have learned that the people who get rid of the fear of poverty and children and all the other family troubles, and devote themselves to having a good time of it, only leave their minds free for the fear of old age and ugliness and impotence and death. The childless laborer is more tormented by his wife's idleness and her constant demands for amusement and distraction than he could be by twenty children; and his wife is more wretched than he. I have had my share of vanity; for as a young man I was admired by women; and as a statue I am praised by art critics. But I confess that had I found nothing to do in the world but wallow in these delights I should have cut my throat. When I married Ana's mother — or perhaps, to be strictly correct, I should rather say when I at last gave in and allowed Ana's mother to marry me — I knew that I was planting thorns in my pillow, and that marriage for me, a swaggering young officer thitherto unvanquished, meant defeat and capture.

ANA [*scandalized*]. Father!

THE STATUE. I am sorry to shock you, my love; but since Juan has stripped every rag of decency from the discussion I may as well tell the frozen truth.

ANA. Hmf! I suppose I was one of the thorns.

THE STATUE. By no means: you were often a rose. You see, your mother had most of the trouble you gave.

DON JUAN. Then may I ask, Commander, why you have left Heaven to come here and wallow, as you express it, in sentimental beatitudes which you confess would once have driven you to cut your throat?

THE STATUE [*struck by this*]. Egad, thats true.

THE DEVIL [*alarmed*]. What! You are going back from your word! [*To Don Juan*] And all your philosophizing has been nothing but a mask for proselytizing! [*To the Statue*] Have you forgotten already the hideous dulness from which I am offering you a refuge here? [*To Don Juan*] And does your demonstration of the approaching sterilization and extinction of mankind lead to anything better than making the most of those pleasures of art and love which you yourself admit refined you, elevated you, developed you?

DON JUAN. I never demonstrated the extinction of mankind. Life cannot will its own extinction either in its blind amorphous state or in any of the forms into which it has organized itself. I had not finished when His Excellency interrupted me.

THE STATUE. I begin to doubt whether you ever will finish, my friend. You are extremely fond of hearing yourself talk.

DON JUAN. True; but since you have endured so much, you may as well endure to the end. Long before this sterilization which I described becomes more than a clearly foreseen possibility, the reaction will begin. The great central purpose of breeding the race: ay, breeding it to heights now deemed superhuman: that purpose which is now hidden in a mephitic cloud of love and romance and prudery and fastidiousness, will break through into clear sunlight as a purpose no longer to be confused with the gratification of personal fancies, the impossible realization of boys' and girls' dreams of bliss, or the need of older people for companionship or money. The plain-spoken marriage services of the vernacular Churches will no longer be abbreviated and half suppressed as indelicate. The sober decency, earnestness, and authority of their declaration of the real purpose of marriage will be honored and accepted, whilst their romantic vowings and pledgings and until-death-do-us-partings and the like will be expunged as unbearable frivolities. Do my sex the justice to admit, Señora, that we have always recognized that the sex relation is not a personal or friendly relation at all.

ANA. Not a personal or friendly relation! What relation is more personal? more sacred? more holy?

DON JUAN. Sacred and holy, if you like, Ana, but not personally friendly. Your relation to God is sacred and holy: dare you call it personally friendly? In the sex relation the universal creative energy, of which the parties are both the helpless agents, over-rides and sweeps away all personal considerations, and dispenses with all personal relations. The pair may be utter strangers to one another, speaking different languages, differing in race and color, in age and disposition, with no bond between them but a possibility of that fecundity for the sake of which the Life Force throws them into one another's arms at the exchange of a glance. Do we not recognize this by allowing marriages to be made by parents without consulting the woman? Have you not often expressed your disgust at the immorality of the English nation, in which women and men of noble birth become acquainted and court each other like peasants? And how much does even the peasant know of his bride or she of him before he engages himself? Why, you would not make a man your lawyer or your family doctor on so slight an acquaintance as you would fall in love with and marry him!

ANA. Yes, Juan: we know the libertine's philosophy. Always ignore the consequences to the woman.

DON JUAN. The consequences, yes: they justify her fierce grip of the man. But surely you do not call that attachment a sentimental one. As well call the policeman's attachment to his prisoner a love relation.

ANA. You see you have to confess that marriage is necessary, though, according to you, love is the slightest of all human relations.

DON JUAN. How do you know that it is not the greatest of all human relations? far too great to be a personal matter. Could your father have served his country if he had refused to kill any enemy of Spain unless he personally hated him? Can a woman serve her country if she refuses to marry any man she does not personally love? You know it is not so: the woman of noble birth marries as the man of noble birth fights, on political and family grounds, not on personal ones.

THE STATUE [*impressed*]. A very clever point that, Juan: I must think it over. You are really full of ideas. How did you come to think of this one?

DON JUAN. I learnt it by experience. When I was on earth, and made those proposals to ladies which, though universally condemned, have made me so interesting a hero of legend, I was not infrequently met in some such way as this. The lady would say that she would countenance my advances, provided they were honorable. On inquiring what that proviso meant, I found that it meant that I proposed to get possession of her property if she had any, or to undertake her support for life if she had not; that I desired her continual companionship, counsel, and conversation to the end of my days, and would take a most solemn oath to be always enraptured by them: above all, that I would turn my back on all other women for ever for her sake. I did not object to these conditions because they were exorbitant and inhuman: it was their extraordinary irrelevance that prostrated me. I invariably replied with perfect frankness that I had never dreamt of any of these things; that unless the lady's character and intellect were equal or superior to my own, her conversation must degrade and her counsel mislead me; that her constant companionship might, for all I knew, become intolerably tedious to me; that I could not answer for my feelings for a week in advance, much less to the end of my life; that to cut me off from all natural and unconstrained intercourse with half my fellowcreatures would narrow and warp me if I submitted to it, and, if not, would bring me under the curse of clandestinity; that, finally, my proposals to her were wholly unconnected with any of these matters, and were the outcome of a perfectly simple impulse of my manhood towards her womanhood.

ANA. You mean that it was an immoral impulse.

DON JUAN. Nature, my dear lady, is what you call immoral. I blush for it; but I cannot help it. Nature is a pandar, Time a wrecker, and Death a murderer. I have always preferred to stand up to those facts and build institutions on their recognition. You prefer to propitiate the three devils by proclaiming their chastity, their thrift, and their loving kindness; and to base your institutions on these flatteries. Is it any wonder that the institutions do not work smoothly?

THE STATUE. What used the ladies to say, Juan?

DON JUAN. Oh, come! Confidence for confidence. First tell me what you used to say to the ladies.

THE STATUE. I! Oh, I swore that I would be faithful to the death; that I should die if they refused me; that no woman could ever be to me what she was —

ANA. She! Who?

THE STATUE. Whoever it happened to be at the time, my dear. I had certain things I always said. One of them was that even when I was eighty, one white hair of the woman I loved would make me tremble more than the thickest gold tress from the most beautiful young head. Another was that I could not bear the thought of anyone else being the mother of my children.

DON JUAN [*revolted*]. You old rascal!

THE STATUE [*stoutly*]. Not a bit; for I really believed it with all my soul at the moment, I had a heart: not like you. And it was this sincerity that made me successful.

DON JUAN. Sincerity! To be fool enough to believe a ramping, stamping, thumping lie: that is what you call sincerity! To be so greedy for a woman that you deceive yourself in your eagerness to deceive her: sincerity, you call it!

THE STATUE. Oh, damn your sophistries! I was a man in love, not a lawyer. And the women loved me for it, bless them!

DON JUAN. They made you think so. What will you say when I tell you that though I played the lawyer so callously, they made me think so too? I also had my moments of infatuation in which I gushed nonsense and believed it. Sometimes the desire to give pleasure by saying beautiful things so rose in me on the flood of emotion that I said them recklessly. At other times I argued against myself with a devilish coldness that drew tears. But I found it just as hard to escape when I was cruel as when I was kind. When the lady's instinct was set on me, there was nothing for it but life-long servitude or flight.

ANA. You dare boast, before me and my father, that every woman found you irresistible.

DON JUAN. Am I boasting? It seems to me that I cut the most pitiable of figures. Besides, I said "when the lady's instinct was set on me." It was not always so; and then, heavens! what transports of virtuous indignation! what overwhelming defiance to the dastardly seducer! what scenes of Imogen[30] and Iachimo!

ANA. I made no scenes. I simply called my father.

DON JUAN. And he came, sword in hand, to vindicate outraged honor and morality by murdering me.

THE STATUE. Murdering! What do you mean? Did I kill you or did you kill me?

DON JUAN. Which of us was the better fencer?

THE STATUE. I was.

DON JUAN. Of course you were. And yet you, the hero of those scandalous adventures you have just been relating to us, you had the effrontery to pose as the avenger of outraged morality and condemn me to death! You would have slain me but for an accident.

THE STATUE. I was expected to, Juan. That is how things were arranged on earth. I was not a social reformer; and I always did what it was customary for a gentleman to do.

DON JUAN. That may account for your attacking me, but not for the revolting hypocrisy of your subsequent proceedings as a statue.

THE STATUE. That all came of my going to Heaven.

THE DEVIL. I still fail to see, Señor Don Juan, that these episodes in your earthly career and in that of the Señor Commander in any way discredit my view of life. Here, I repeat, you have all that you sought without anything that you shrank from.

DON JUAN. On the contrary, here I have everything that disappointed me without anything that I have not already tried and found wanting. I tell you that as long as I can conceive something better than myself I cannot be easy unless I am striving to bring it into existence or clearing the way for it. That is the law of my life. That is the working within me of Life's incessant aspiration to higher organization, wider, deeper, intenser self-consciousness, and clearer self-understanding. It was the supremacy of this purpose that reduced love for me to the mere pleasure of a moment, art for me to the mere schooling of my faculties, religion for me to a mere excuse for laziness, since it had set up a God who looked at the world and saw that it was good, against the instinct in me that looked through my eyes at the world and saw that it could be improved. I tell you that in the pursuit of my own pleasure, my own health, my own fortune, I have never known happiness. It was not love for Woman that delivered me into her hands: it was fatigue, exhaustion. When I was a child, and bruised my head against a stone, I ran to the nearest woman and cried away my pain against her apron. When I grew up, and bruised my soul against the brutalities and stupidities with which I had to strive, I did again just what I had done as a child. I have enjoyed, too, my rests, my recuperations, my breathing times, my very prostrations after strife; but rather would I be dragged through all the circles of the foolish Italian's Inferno than through the pleasures of Europe. That is what has made this place of eternal pleasures so deadly to me. It is the absence of this instinct in you that makes you that strange monster called a Devil. It is the success with which you have diverted the attention of men from their real purpose, which in one degree or another is the same as mine, to yours, that has earned you the name of The Tempter. It is the fact that they are doing your will, or rather drifting with your want of will, instead of doing their own, that makes them the uncomfortable, false, restless, artificial, petulant, wretched creatures they are.

THE DEVIL [*mortified*]. Señor Don Juan: you are uncivil to my friends.

DON JUAN. Pooh! why should I be civil to them or to you? In this Palace of Lies a truth or two will not hurt you. Your friends are all the dullest dogs I know. They are not beautiful: they are only decorated. They are not clean: they are only shaved and starched. They are not dignified: they are only fashionably dressed. They are not educated: they are only college passmen. They are not religious: they are only pewrenters. They are not moral: they are only conventional. They are not virtuous: they are only cowardly. They are not even vicious: they are only "frail." They are not artistic: they are only lascivious. They are not prosperous: they are only rich. They are not loyal, they are only servile; not dutiful, only sheepish; not public spirited, only patriotic; not courageous, only quarrelsome; not determined, only obstinate; not masterful, only domineering; not self-controlled, only obtuse; not self-respecting, only vain; not kind, only sentimental; not social, only gregarious; not considerate, only polite; not intelligent, only opin-

**30. Imogen:** In Shakespeare's *Cymbeline,* the princess Imogen repulses Iachimo, who tries to win her love after slandering her absent husband.

ionated; not progressive, only factious; not imaginative, only superstitious; not just, only vindictive; not generous, only propitiatory; not disciplined, only cowed; and not truthful at all: liars every one of them, to the very backbone of their souls.

THE STATUE. Your flow of words is simply amazing, Juan. How I wish I could have talked like that to my soldiers.

THE DEVIL. It is mere talk, though. It has all been said before; but what change has it ever made? What notice has the world ever taken of it?

DON JUAN. Yes, it is mere talk. But why is it mere talk? Because, my friend, beauty, purity, respectability, religion, morality, art, patriotism, bravery, and the rest are nothing but words which I or anyone else can turn inside out like a glove. Were they realities, you would have to plead guilty to my indictment; but fortunately for your self-respect, my diabolical friend, they are not realities. As you say, they are mere words, useful for duping barbarians into adopting civilization, or the civilized poor into submitting to be robbed and enslaved. That is the family secret of the governing caste; and if we who are of that caste aimed at more Life for the world instead of at more power and luxury for our miserable selves, that secret would make us great. Now, since I, being a nobleman, am in the secret too, think how tedious to me must be your unending cant about all these moralistic figments, and how squalidly disastrous your sacrifice of your lives to them! If you even believed in your moral game enough to play it fairly, it would be interesting to watch; but you dont: you cheat at every trick; and if your opponent outcheats you, you upset the table and try to murder him.

THE DEVIL. On earth there may be some truth in this, because the people are uneducated and cannot appreciate my religion of love and beauty; but here—

DON JUAN. Oh yes: I know. Here there is nothing but love and beauty. Ugh! it is like sitting for all eternity at the first act of a fashionable play, before the complications begin. Never in my worst moments of superstitious terror on earth did I dream that Hell was so horrible. I live, like a hairdresser, in the continual contemplation of beauty, toying with silken tresses. I breathe an atmosphere of sweetness, like a confectioner's shopboy. Commander: a r e there any beautiful women in Heaven?

THE STATUE. None. Absolutely none. All dowdies. Not two pennorth of jewellery among a dozen of them. They might be men of fifty.

DON JUAN. I am impatient to get there. Is the word beauty ever mentioned; and are there any artistic people?

THE STATUE. I give you my word they wont admire a fine statue even when it walks past them.

DON JUAN. I go.

THE DEVIL. Don Juan: shall I be frank with you?

DON JUAN. Were you not so before?

THE DEVIL. As far as I went, yes. But I will now go further, and confess to you that men get tired of everything, of heaven no less than of hell; and that all history is nothing but a record of the oscillations of the world between these two extremes. An epoch is but a swing of the pendulum; and each generation thinks the world is progressing because it is always moving. But when you are as old as I am; when you have a thousand times wearied of heaven, like myself and the Commander, and a thousand times wearied of hell, as you are wearied now, you will no longer imagine that every swing from heaven to hell is an emancipation, every swing from hell to heaven an evolution. Where you now see reform, progress, fulfilment of upward tendency, continual ascent by Man on the stepping stones of his dead selves to higher things, you will see nothing but an infinite comedy of illusion. You will discover the profound truth of the saying of my friend Koheleth,[31] that there is nothing new under the sun.[32] Vanitas vanitatum—[33]

DON JUAN [*out of all patience*]. By Heaven, this is worse than your cant about love and beauty. Clever dolt that you are, is a man no better than a worm, or a dog than a wolf, because he gets tired of everything? Shall he give up eating because he destroys his appetite in the act of gratifying it? Is a field idle when it is fallow? Can the Commander expend his hellish energy here without accumulating heavenly energy for his next term of blessedness? Granted that the great Life Force has hit on the device of the clockmaker's pendulum, and uses the earth for its bob; that the history of each oscillation, which seems so novel to us the actors, is but the history of the last oscillation repeated; nay more, that in the unthinkable infinitude of time the sun throws off the earth and catches it again a thousand times as a circus rider throws up a ball, and that our agelong epochs are but the moments between the toss and the catch, has the colossal mechanism no purpose?

THE DEVIL. None, my friend. You think, because you have a purpose, Nature must have one. You might as well expect it to have fingers and toes because you have them.

DON JUAN. But I should not have them if they served no purpose. And I, my friend, am as much

**31. Koheleth:** Hebrew for "Preacher," i.e., Ecclesiastes, the name given to Solomon as the author of the book of Ecclesiastes.
**32. nothing . . . sun:** Eccles. 1:9. **33. Vanitas vanitatum:** "Vanity of vanities," Eccles. 1:2.

a part of Nature as my own finger is a part of me. If my finger is the organ by which I grasp the sword and the mandoline, my brain is the organ by which Nature strives to understand itself. My dog's brain serves only my dog's purposes; but my own brain labors at a knowledge which does nothing for me personally but make my body bitter to me and my decay and death a calamity. Were I not possessed with a purpose beyond my own I had better be a ploughman than a philosopher; for the ploughman lives as long as the philosopher, eats more, sleeps better, and rejoices in the wife of his bosom with less misgiving. This is because the philosopher is in the grip of the Life Force. This Life Force says to him "I have done a thousand wonderful things unconsciously by merely willing to live and following the line of least resistance: now I want to know myself and my destination, and choose my path; so I have made a special brain — a philosopher's brain — to grasp this knowledge for me as the husbandman's hand grasps the plough for me. And this" says the Life Force to the philosopher "must thou strive to do for me until thou diest, when I will make another brain and another philosopher to carry on the work."

THE DEVIL. What is the use of knowing?

DON JUAN. Why, to be able to choose the line of greatest advantage instead of yielding in the direction of the least resistance. Does a ship sail to its destination no better than a log drifts nowhither? The philosopher is Nature's pilot. And there you have our difference: to be in hell is to drift: to be in heaven is to steer.

THE DEVIL. On the rocks, most likely.

DON JUAN. Pooh! which ship goes oftenest on the rocks or to the bottom? the drifting ship or the ship with a pilot on board?

THE DEVIL. Well, well, go your way, Señor Don Juan. I prefer to be my own master and not the tool of any blundering universal force. I know that beauty is good to look at; that music is good to hear; that love is good to feel; and that they are all good to think about and talk about. I know that to be well exercised in these sensations, emotions, and studies is to be a refined and cultivated being. Whatever they may say of me in churches on earth, I know that it is universally admitted in good society that the Prince of Darkness is a gentleman; and that is enough for me. As to your Life Force, which you think irresistible, it is the most resistible thing in the world for a person of any character. But if you are naturally vulgar and credulous, as all reformers are, it will thrust you first into religion, where you will sprinkle water on babies to save their souls from me; then it will drive you from religion into science, where you will snatch the babies from the water sprinkling and inoculate them with disease to save them from catching it accidentally; then you will take to politics, where you will become the catspaw of corrupt functionaries and the henchman of ambitious humbugs; and the end will be despair and decrepitude, broken nerve and shattered hopes, vain regrets for that worst and silliest of wastes and sacrifices, the waste and sacrifice of the power of enjoyment: in a word, the punishment of the fool who pursues the better before he has secured the good.

DON JUAN. But at least I shall not be bored. The service of the Life Force has that advantage, at all events. So fare you well, Señor Satan.

THE DEVIL [*amiably*]. Fare you well, Don Juan. I shall often think of our interesting chats about things in general. I wish you every happiness: Heaven, as I said before, suits some people. But if you should change your mind, do not forget that the gates are always open here to the repentant prodigal. If you feel at any time that warmth of heart, sincere unforced affection, innocent enjoyment, and warm, breathing, palpitating reality —

DON JUAN. Why not say flesh and blood at once, though we have left those two greasy commonplaces behind us?

THE DEVIL [*angrily*]. You throw my friendly farewell back in my teeth, then, Don Juan?

DON JUAN. By no means. But though there is much to be learnt from a cynical devil, I really cannot stand a sentimental one. Señor Commander: you know the way to the frontier of hell and heaven. Be good enough to direct me.

THE STATUE. Oh, the frontier is only the difference between two ways of looking at things. Any road will take you across it if you really want to get there.

DON JUAN. Good. [*Saluting Doña Ana*] Señora: your servant.

ANA. But I am going with you.

DON JUAN. I can find my own way to heaven, Ana; not yours [*He vanishes*].

ANA. How annoying!

THE STATUE [*calling after him*]. Bon voyage, Juan! [*He wafts a final blast of his great rolling chords after him as a parting salute. A faint echo of the first ghostly melody comes back in acknowledgment.*] Ah! there he goes. [*Puffing a long breath out through his lips*] Whew! How he does talk! Theyll never stand it in heaven.

THE DEVIL [*gloomily*]. His going is a political defeat. I cannot keep these Life Worshippers: they all go. This is the greatest loss I have had since that Dutch painter went: a fellow who would paint a hag of 70 with as much enjoyment as a Venus of 20.

THE STATUE. I remember: he came to heaven. Rembrandt.

THE DEVIL. Ay, Rembrandt. There is something unnatural about these fellows. Do not listen to their gospel, Señor Commander: it is dangerous. Beware of the pursuit of the Superhuman: it leads to an indiscriminate contempt for the Human. To a man, horses and dogs and cats are mere species, outside the moral world. Well, to the Superman, men and women are a mere species too, also outside the moral world. This Don Juan was kind to women and courteous to men as your daughter here was kind to her pet cats and dogs; but such kindness is a denial of the exclusively human character of the soul.

THE STATUE. And who the deuce is the Superman?

THE DEVIL. Oh, the latest fashion among the Life Force fanatics. Did you not meet in Heaven, among the new arrivals, that German Polish madman? what was his name? Nietzsche?

THE STATUE. Never heard of him.

THE DEVIL. Well, he came here first, before he recovered his wits. I had some hopes of him; but he was a confirmed Life Force worshipper. It was he who raked up the Superman, who is as old as Prometheus; and the 20th century will run after this newest of the old crazes when it gets tired of the world, the flesh, and your humble servant.

THE STATUE. Superman is a good cry; and a good cry is half the battle. I should like to see this Nietzsche.

THE DEVIL. Unfortunately he met Wagner here, and had a quarrel with him.

THE STATUE. Quite right, too. Mozart for me!

THE DEVIL. Oh, it was not about music. Wagner once drifted into Life Force worship, and invented a Superman called Siegfried. But he came to his senses afterwards. So when they met here, Nietzsche denounced him as a renegade; and Wagner wrote a pamphlet to prove that Nietzsche was a Jew; and it ended in Nietzsche's going to heaven in a huff. And a good riddance too. And now, my friend, let us hasten to my palace and celebrate your arrival with a grand musical service.

THE STATUE. With pleasure: youre most kind.

THE DEVIL. This way, Commander. We go down the old trap. [*He places himself on the grave trap.*]

THE STATUE. Good. [*Reflectively*] All the same, the Superman is a fine conception. There is something statuesque about it. [*He places himself on the grave trap beside The Devil. It begins to descend slowly. Red glow from the abyss.*] Ah, this reminds me of old times.

THE DEVIL. And me also.

ANA. Stop! [*The trap stops.*]

THE DEVIL. You, Señora, cannot come this way. You will have an apotheosis. But you will be at the palace before us.

ANA. That is not what I stopped you for. Tell me: where can I find the Superman?

THE DEVIL. He is not yet created, Señora.

THE STATUE. And never will be, probably. Let us proceed: the red fire will make me sneeze. [*They descend.*]

ANA. Not yet created! Then my work is not yet done. [*Crossing herself devoutly*] I believe in the Life to Come. [*Crying to the universe*] A father! a father for the Superman!

*She vanishes into the void; and again there is nothing: all existence seems suspended infinitely. Then, vaguely, there is a live human voice crying somewhere. One sees, with a shock, a mountain peak shewing faintly against a lighter background. The sky has returned from afar; and we suddenly remember where we were. The cry becomes distinct and urgent: it says* Automobile, Automobile. *The complete reality comes back with a rush: in a moment it is full morning in the Sierra; and the brigands are scrambling to their feet and making for the road as the goatherd runs down from the hill, warning them of the approach of another motor. Tanner and Mendoza rise amazedly and stare at one another with scattered wits. Straker sits up to yawn for a moment before he gets on his feet, making it a point of honor not to shew any undue interest in the excitement of the bandits. Mendoza gives a quick look to see that his followers are attending to the alarm; then exchanges a private word with Tannner.*

MENDOZA. Did you dream?

TANNER. Damnably. Did you?

MENDOZA. Yes. I forget what. You were in it.

TANNER. So were you. Amazing!

MENDOZA. I warned you. [*A shot is heard from the road.*] Dolts! they will play with that gun. [*The brigands come running back scared.*] Who fired that shot? [*To Duval*] Was it you?

DUVAL [*breathless*]. I have not shoot. Dey shoot first.

ANARCHIST. I told you to begin by abolishing the State. Now we are all lost.

THE ROWDY SOCIAL-DEMOCRAT [*stampeding across the amphitheatre*]. Run, everybody.

MENDOZA [*collaring him; throwing him on his back; and drawing a knife*]. I stab the man who stirs. [*He blocks the way. The stampede is checked.*] What has happened?

THE SULKY SOCIAL-DEMOCRAT. A motor—

THE ANARCHIST. Three men—

DUVAL. Deux femmes—

MENDOZA. Three men and two women! Why have you not brought them here? Are you afraid of them?

THE ROWDY ONE [*getting up*]. Thyve a hescort. Ow, de-ooh luts ook it, Mendowza.

THE SULKY ONE. Two armored cars full o soldiers at the ed o the valley.

ANARCHIST. The shot was fired in the air. It was a signal.

*Straker whistles his favorite air, which falls on the ears of the brigands like a funeral march.*

TANNER. It is not an escort, but an expedition to capture you. We were advised to wait for it; but I was in a hurry.

THE ROWDY ONE [*in an agony of apprehension*]. And Ow my good Lord, ere we are, w y t i n for em! Luts tike to the mahntns.

MENDOZA. Idiot, what do you know about the mountains? Are you a Spaniard? You would be given up by the first shepherd you met. Besides, we are already within range of their rifles.

THE ROWDY ONE. Bat —

MENDOZA. Silence. Leave this to me. [*To Tanner*] Comrade: you will not betray us.

STRAKER. Oo are you callin comrade?

MENDOZA. Last night the advantage was with me. The robber of the poor was at the mercy of the robber of the rich. You offered your hand: I took it.

TANNER. I bring no charge against you, comrade. We have spent a pleasant evening with you: that is all.

STRAKER. I gev my and to nobody, see?

MENDOZA [*turning on him impressively*]. Young man: if I am tried, I shall plead guilty, and explain what drove me from England, home, and duty. Do you wish to have the respectable name of Straker dragged through the mud of a Spanish criminal court? The police will search me. They will find Louisa's portrait. It will be published in the illustrated papers. You blench. It will be your doing, remember.

STRAKER [*with baffled rage*]. I dont care about the court. It's avin our name mixed up with yours that I object to, you blackmailin swine, you.

MENDOZA. Language unworthy of Louisa's brother! But no matter: you are muzzled: that is enough for us. [*He turns to face his own men, who back uneasily across the amphitheatre towards the cave to take refuge behind him, as a fresh party, muffled for motoring, comes from the road in riotous spirits. Ann, who makes straight for Tanner, comes first; then Violet, helped over the rough ground by Hector holding her right hand and Ramsden her left. Mendoza goes to his presidential block and seats himself calmly with his rank and file grouped behind him, and his Staff, consisting of Duval and the Anarchist on his right and the two Social-Democrats on his left, supporting him in flank.*]

ANN. It's Jack!

TANNER. Caught!

HECTOR. Why, certainly it is. I said it was you, Tanner. Weve just been stopped by a puncture: the road is full of nails.

VIOLET. What are you doing here with all these men?

ANN. Why did you leave us without a word of warning?

HECTOR. I wawnt that bunch of roses, Miss Whitefield. [*To Tanner*] When we found you were gone, Miss Whitefield bet me a bunch of roses my car would not overtake yours before you reached Monte Carlo.

TANNER. But this is not the road to Monte Carlo.

HECTOR. No matter. Miss Whitefield tracked you at every stopping place: she is a regular Sherlock Holmes.

TANNER. The Life Force! I am lost.

OCTAVIUS [*bounding gaily down from the road into the amphitheatre, and coming between Tanner and Straker*]. I am so glad you are safe, old chap. We were afraid you had been captured by brigands.

RAMSDEN [*who has been staring at Mendoza*]. I seem to remember the face of your friend here. [*Mendoza rises politely and advances with a smile between Ann and Ramsden.*]

HECTOR. Why, so do I.

OCTAVIUS. I know you perfectly well, sir; but I cant think where I have met you.

MENDOZA [*to Violet*]. Do you remember me, madam?

VIOLET. Oh, quite well; but I am so stupid about names.

MENDOZA. It was at the Savoy Hotel. [*To Hector*] You, sir, used to come with this lady [*Violet*] to lunch. [*To Octavius*] You, sir, often brought this lady [*Ann*] and her mother to dinner on your way to the Lyceum Theatre. [*To Ramsden*] You, sir, used to come to supper, with [*Dropping his voice to a confidential but perfectly audible whisper*] several different ladies.

RAMSDEN [*angrily*]. Well, what is that to you, pray?

OCTAVIUS. Why, Violet, I thought you hardly knew one another before this trip, you and Malone!

VIOLET [*vexed*]. I suppose this person was the manager.

MENDOZA. The waiter, madam. I have a grateful recollection of you all. I gathered from the bountiful way in which you treated me that you all enjoyed your visits very much.

VIOLET. What impertinence! [*She turns her back on him, and goes up the hill with Hector.*]

RAMSDEN. That will do, my friend. You do not expect these ladies to treat you as an acquaintance, I suppose, because you have waited on them at table.

MENDOZA. Pardon me: it was you who claimed my acquaintance. The ladies followed your example. However, this display of the unfortunate manners of your class closes the incident. For the future, you will address me with the respect due to a stranger and fellow traveller. [*He turns haughtily away and resumes his presidential seat.*]

TANNER. There! I have found one man on my journey capable of reasonable conversation; and you all instinctively insult him. Even the New Man is as bad as any of you. Enry: you have behaved just like a miserable gentleman.

STRAKER. Gentleman! Not me.

RAMSDEN. Really, Tanner, this tone—

ANN. Dont mind him, Granny: you ought to know him by this time. [*She takes his arm and coaxes him away to the hill to join Violet and Hector. Octavius follows her, dog-like.*]

VIOLET [*calling from the hill*]. Here are the soldiers. They are getting out of their motors.

DUVAL [*panicstricken*]. Oh, nom de Dieu!

THE ANARCHIST. Fools: the State is about to crush you because you spared it at the prompting of the political hangers-on of the bourgeoisie.

THE SULKY SOCIAL-DEMOCRAT [*argumentative to the last*]. On the contrary, only by capturing the State machine—

THE ANARCHIST. It is going to capture you.

THE ROWDY SOCIAL-DEMOCRAT [*his anguish culminating*]. Ow, chack it. Wot are we ere for? Wot are we wytin for?

MENDOZA [*between his teeth*]. Go on. Talk politics, you idiots: nothing sounds more respectable. Keep it up, I tell you.

*The soldiers line the road, commanding the amphitheatre with their rifles. The brigands, struggling with overwhelming impulse to hide behind one another, look as unconcerned as they can. Mendoza rises superbly, with undaunted front. The officer in command steps down from the road into the amphitheatre; looks hard at the brigands; and then inquiringly at Tanner.*

THE OFFICER. Who are these men, Señor Ingles?

TANNER. My escort.

*Mendoza, with a Mephistophelean smile, bows profoundly. An irrepressible grin runs from face to face among the brigands. They touch their hats, except the Anarchist, who defies the State with folded arms.*

# Act IV

*The garden of a villa in Granada. Whoever wishes to know what it is like must go to Granada to see. One may prosaically specify a group of hills dotted with villas, the Alhambra*[1] *on the top of one of the hills, and a considerable town in the valley, approached by dusty white roads in which the children, no matter what they are doing or thinking about, automatically whine for halfpence and reach out little clutching brown palms for them; but there is nothing in this description except the Alhambra, the begging, and the color of the roads, that does not fit Surrey*[2] *as well as Spain. The difference is that the Surrey hills are comparatively small and ugly, and should properly be called the Surrey Protuberances; but these Spanish hills are of mountain stock: the amenity which conceals their size does not compromise their dignity.*

*This particular garden is on a hill opposite the Alhambra; and the villa is as expensive and pretentious as a villa must be if it is to be let furnished by the week to opulent American and English visitors. If we stand on the lawn at the foot of the garden and look uphill, our horizon is the stone balustrade of a flagged platform on the edge of infinite space at the top of the hill. Between us and this platform is a flower garden with a circular basin and fountain in the centre, surrounded by geometrical flower beds, gravel paths, and clipped yew trees in the genteelest order. The garden is higher than our lawn; so we reach it by a few steps in the middle of its embankment. The platform is higher again than the garden, from which we mount a couple more steps to look over the balustrade at a fine view of the town up the valley and of the hills that stretch away beyond it to where, in the remotest distance, they become mountains. On our left is the villa, accessible by steps from the left hand corner of the garden. Returning from the platform through the garden and down again to the lawn (a movement which leaves the villa behind us on our right) we find evidence of literary interests on the part of the tenants in the fact that there is no tennis net nor set of croquet hoops, but, on our left, a little iron garden table with books on it, mostly yellow-backed, and a chair beside it. A chair on the right has also a couple of open books upon it. There are no newspapers, a circumstance which, with the absence of games, might lead an intelligent spectator to the most far reaching conclusions as to the sort of people who live in the villa. Such speculations are checked, however, on*

Act IV: 1. ***Alhambra:*** group of buildings, once the citadel of the Moors. Most famous example of Moorish architecture. 2. ***Surrey:*** English county near London.

*this delightfully fine afternoon, by the appearance at a little gate in a paling on our left, of Henry Straker in his professional costume. He opens the gate for an elderly gentleman, and follows him on to the lawn.*

*This elderly gentleman defies the Spanish sun in a black frock coat, tall silk hat, trousers in which narrow stripes of dark grey and lilac blend into a highly respectable color, and a black necktie tied into a bow over spotless linen. Probably therefore a man whose social position needs constant and scrupulous affirmation without regard to climate: one who would dress thus for the middle of the Sahara or the top of Mont Blanc. And since he has not the stamp of the class which accepts as its life-mission the advertizing and maintenance of first rate tailoring and millinery, he looks vulgar in his finery, though in a working dress of any kind he would look dignified enough. He is a bullet cheeked man with a red complexion, stubbly hair, smallish eyes, a hard mouth that folds down at the corners, and a dogged chin. The looseness of skin that comes with age has attacked his throat and the laps of his cheeks; but he is still hard as an apple above the mouth; so that the upper half of his face looks younger than the lower. He has the self-confidence of one who has made money, and something of the truculence of one who has made it in a brutalizing struggle, his civility having under it a perceptible menace that he has other methods in reserve if necessary. Withal, a man to be rather pitied when he is not to be feared; for there is something pathetic about him at times, as if the huge commercial machine which has worked him into his frock coat had allowed him very little of his own way and left his affections hungry and baffled. At the first word that falls from him it is clear that he is an Irishman whose native intonation has clung to him through many changes of place and rank. One can only guess that the original material of his speech was perhaps the surly Kerry brogue; but the degradation of speech that occurs in London, Glasgow, Dublin, and big cities generally has been at work on it so long that nobody but an arrant cockney would dream of calling it a brogue now; for its music is almost gone, though its surliness is still perceptible. Straker, being a very obvious cockney, inspires him with implacable contempt, as a stupid Englishman who cannot even speak his own language properly. Straker, on the other hand, regards the old gentleman's accent as a joke thoughtfully provided by Providence expressly for the amusement of the British race, and treats him normally with the indulgence due to an inferior and unlucky species, but occasionally with indignant alarm when the old gentleman shews signs of intending his Irish nonsense to be taken seriously.*

STRAKER. I'll go tell the young lady. She said youd prefer to stay here. [*He turns to go up through the garden to the villa.*]

THE IRISHMAN [*who has been looking round him with lively curiosity*]. The young lady? Thats Miss Violet, eh?

STRAKER [*stopping on the steps with sudden suspicion*]. Well, you know, dont you?

THE IRISHMAN. Do I?

STRAKER [*his temper rising*]. Well, do you or dont you?

THE IRISHMAN. What business is that of yours?

*Straker, now highly indignant, comes back from the steps and confronts the visitor.*

STRAKER. I'll tell you what business it is of mine. Miss Robinson—

THE IRISHMAN [*interrupting*]. Oh, her name is Robinson, is it? Thank you.

STRAKER. Why, you dont know even her name?

THE IRISHMAN. Yes I do, now that youve told me.

STRAKER [*after a moment of stupefaction at the old man's readiness in repartee*]. Look here: what do you mean by gittin into my car and lettin me bring you here if youre not the person I took that note to?

THE IRISHMAN. Who else did you take it to, pray?

STRAKER. I took it to Mr Ector Malone, at Miss Robinson's request, see? Miss Robinson is not my principal: I took it to oblige her. I know Mr Malone; and he aint you, not by a long chalk. At the hotel they told me that your name is Ector Malone—

MALONE. *H*ector Malone.

STRAKER [*with calm superiority*]. Hector in your own country: thats what comes o livin in provincial places like Ireland and America. Over here youre Ector: if you avnt noticed it before you soon will.

*The growing strain of the conversation is here relieved by Violet, who has sallied from the villa and through the garden to the steps, which she now descends, coming very opportunely between Malone and Straker.*

VIOLET [*to Straker*]. Did you take my message?

STRAKER. Yes, miss. I took it to the hotel and sent it up, expecting to see young Mr Malone. Then out walks this gent, and says it's all right and he'll come with me. So as the hotel people said he was Mr Ector Malone, I fetched him. And now he goes back on what he said. But if he isnt the gentleman you meant, say the word: it's easy enough to fetch him back again.

MALONE. I should esteem it a great favor if I might have a short conversation with you, madam. I am Hector's father, as this bright Britisher would have guessed in the course of another hour or so.

STRAKER [*coolly defiant*]. No, not in another year or so. When weve ad you as long to polish up as weve ad im perhaps youll begin to look a little bit up to is mark. At present you fall a long way short. Youve got too many aitches, for one thing. [*To Violet, amiably*] All right, Miss: you want to talk to him: I shant intrude. [*He nods affably to Malone and goes out through the little gate in the paling.*]

VIOLET [*very civilly*]. I am so sorry, Mr Malone, if that man has been rude to you. But what can we do? He is our chauffeur.

MALONE. Your hwat?

VIOLET. The driver of our automobile. He can drive a motor car at seventy miles an hour, and mend it when it breaks down. We are dependent on our motor cars; and our motor cars are dependent on him; so of course we are dependent on him.

MALONE. Ive noticed, madam, that every thousand dollars an Englishman gets seems to add one to the number of people he's dependent on. However, you neednt apologize for your man: I made him talk on purpose. By doing so I learnt that youre stayin here in Grannida with a party of English, including my son Hector.

VIOLET [*conversationally*]. Yes. We intended to go to Nice; but we had to follow a rather eccentric member of our party who started first and came here. Wont you sit down? [*She clears the nearest chair of the two books on it.*]

MALONE [*impressed by this attention*]. Thank you. [*He sits down, examining her curiously as she goes to the iron table to put down the books. When she turns to him again, he says*] Miss Robinson, I believe?

VIOLET [*sitting down*]. Yes.

MALONE [*taking a letter from his pocket*]. Your note to Hector runs as follows [*Violet is unable to repress a start. He pauses quietly to take out and put on his spectacles, which have gold rims*]: "Dearest: they have all gone to the Alhambra for the afternoon. I have shammed headache and have the garden all to myself. Jump into Jack's motor: Straker will rattle you here in a jiffy. Quick, quick, quick. Your loving Violet." [*He looks at her; but by this time she has recovered herself, and meets his spectacles with perfect composure. He continues slowly*] Now I dont know on hwat terms young people associate in English society; but in America that note would be considered to imply a very considerable degree of affectionate intimacy between the parties.

VIOLET. Yes: I know your son very well, Mr Malone. Have you any objection?

MALONE [*somewhat taken aback*]. No, no objection exactly. Provided it is understood that my son is altogether dependent on me, and that I have to be consulted in any important step he may propose to take.

VIOLET. I am sure you would not be unreasonable with him, Mr Malone.

MALONE. I hope not, Miss Robinson; but at your age you might think many things unreasonable that dont seem so to me.

VIOLET [*with a little shrug*]. Oh, well, I suppose theres no use our playing at cross purposes, Mr Malone. Hector wants to marry me.

MALONE. I inferred from your note that he might. Well, Miss Robinson, he is his own master; but if he marries you he shall not have a rap from me. [*He takes off his spectacles and pockets them with the note.*]

VIOLET [*with some severity*]. That is not very complimentary to me, Mr Malone.

MALONE. I say nothing against you, Miss Robinson: I daresay you are an amiable and excellent young lady. But I have other views for Hector.

VIOLET. Hector may not have other views for himself, Mr Malone.

MALONE. Possibly not. Then he does without me: thats all. I daresay you are prepared for that. When a young lady writes to a young man to come to her quick, quick, quick, money seems nothing and love seems everything.

VIOLET [*sharply*]. I beg your pardon, Mr Malone: I do not think anything so foolish. Hector must have money.

MALONE [*staggered*]. Oh, very well, very well. No doubt he can work for it.

VIOLET. What is the use of having money if you have to work for it? [*She rises impatiently.*] It's all nonsense, Mr Malone: you m u s t enable your son to keep up his position. It is his right.

MALONE [*grimly*]. I should not advise you to marry him on the strength of that right, Miss Robinson.

*Violet, who has almost lost her temper, controls herself with an effort; unclenches her fingers; and resumes her seat with studied tranquillity and reasonableness.*

VIOLET. What objection have you to me, pray? My social position is as good as Hector's, to say the least. He admits it.

MALONE [*shrewdly*]. You tell him so from time to time, eh? Hector's social position in England, Miss Robinson, is just what I choose to buy for him. I have made him a fair offer. Let him pick out the most historic house, castle, or abbey that England contains. The very day he tells me he wants it for a wife worthy of its traditions, I buy it for him, and give him the means of keeping it up.

VIOLET. What do you mean by a wife worthy of its traditions? Cannot any well bred woman keep such a house for him?

MALONE. No: she must be born to it.

VIOLET. Hector was not born to it, was he?

MALONE. His granmother was a barefooted Irish girl that nursed me by a turf fire. Let him marry another such, and I will not stint her marriage portion. Let him raise himself socially with my money or raise somebody else: so long as there is a social profit somewhere, I'll regard my expenditure as justified. But there must be a profit for someone. A marriage with you would leave things just where they are.

VIOLET. Many of my relations would object very much to my marrying the grandson of a common woman, Mr Malone. That may be prejudice; but so is your desire to have him marry a title prejudice.

MALONE [*rising, and approaching her with a scrutiny in which there is a good deal of reluctant respect*]. You seem a pretty straightforward downright sort of a young woman.

VIOLET. I do not see why I should be made miserably poor because I cannot make profits for you. Why do you want to make Hector unhappy?

MALONE. He will get over it all right enough. Men thrive better on disappointments in love than on disappointments in money. I daresay you think that sordid; but I know what I'm talking about. Me father died of starvation in Ireland in the black 47. Maybe youve heard of it.

VIOLET. The Famine?

MALONE [*with smouldering passion*]. No, the starvation. When a country is full o food, and exporting it, there can be no famine. Me father was starved dead; and I was starved out to America in me mother's arms. English rule drove me and mine out of Ireland. Well, you can keep Ireland. Me and me like are coming back to buy England; and we'll buy the best of it. I want no middle class properties and no middle class women for Hector. Thats straightforward, isnt it, like yourself?

VIOLET [*icily pitying his sentimentality*]. Really, Mr Malone, I am astonished to hear a man of your age and good sense talking in that romantic way. Do you suppose English noblemen will sell their places to you for the asking?

MALONE. I have the refusal of two of the oldest family mansions in England. One historic owner cant afford to keep all the rooms dusted: the other cant afford the death duties. What do you say now?

VIOLET. Of course it is very scandalous; but surely you know that the Government will sooner or later put a stop to all these Socialistic attacks on property.

MALONE [*grinning*]. D'y'think theyll be able to get that done before I buy the house — or rather the abbey? Theyre both abbeys.

VIOLET [*putting that aside rather impatiently*]. Oh, well, let us talk sense, Mr Malone. You must feel that we havnt been talking sense so far.

MALONE. I cant say I do. I mean all I say.

VIOLET. Then you dont know Hector as I do. He is romantic and faddy — he gets it from you, I fancy — and he wants a certain sort of wife to take care of him. Not a faddy sort of person, you know.

MALONE. Somebody like you, perhaps?

VIOLET [*quietly*]. Well, yes. But you cannot very well ask me to undertake this with absolutely no means of keeping up his position.

MALONE [*alarmed*]. Stop a bit, stop a bit. Where are we getting to? I'm not aware that I'm asking you to undertake anything.

VIOLET. Of course, Mr Malone, you can make it very difficult for me to speak to you if you choose to misunderstand me.

MALONE [*half bewildered*]. I dont wish to take any unfair advantage; but we seem to have got off the straight track somehow.

*Straker, with the air of a man who has been making haste, opens the little gate, and admits Hector, who, snorting with indignation, comes upon the lawn, and is making for his father when Violet, greatly dismayed, springs up and intercepts him. Straker does not wait; at least he does not remain visibly within earshot.*

VIOLET. Oh, how unlucky! Now please, Hector, say nothing. Go away until I have finished speaking to your father.

HECTOR [*inexorably*]. No, Violet: I mean to have this thing out, right away. [*He puts her aside; passes her by; and faces his father, whose cheeks darken as his Irish blood begins to simmer.*] Dad: youve not played this hand straight.

MALONE. Hwat d'y mean?

HECTOR. Youve opened a letter addressed to me. Youve impersonated me and stolen a march on this lady. Thats disawnerable.

MALONE [*threateningly*]. Now you take care what youre saying, Hector. Take care, I tell you.

HECTOR. I have taken care. I am taking care. I'm taking care of my honor and my position in English society.

MALONE [*hotly*]. Your position has been got by my money: do you know that?

HECTOR. Well, youve just spoiled it all by opening that letter. A letter from an English lady, not addressed to you — a cawnfidential letter! a dullicate letter! a private letter! opened by my father! Thats a sort of thing a man cant struggle against in England. The sooner we go back together the better. [*He appeals mutely to the heavens to witness the shame and anguish of two outcasts.*]

VIOLET [*snubbing him with an instinctive dislike for scene making*]. Dont be unreasonable, Hector.

It was quite natural for Mr Malone to open my letter: his name was on the envelope.

MALONE. There! Youve no common sense, Hector. I thank you, Miss Robinson.

HECTOR. I thank you, too. It's very kind of you. My father knows no better.

MALONE [*furiously clenching his fists*]. Hector—

HECTOR [*with undaunted moral force*]. Oh, it's no use hectoring me. A private letter's a private letter, dad: you cant get over that.

MALONE [*raising his voice*]. I wont be talked back to by you, d'y'hear?

VIOLET. Ssh! please, p l e a s e. Here they all come.

*Father and son, checked, glare mutely at one another as Tanner comes in through the little gate with Ramsden, followed by Octavius and Ann.*

VIOLET. Back already!

TANNER. The Alhambra is not open this afternoon.

VIOLET. What a sell!

*Tanner passes on, and presently finds himself between Hector and a strange elder, both apparently on the verge of personal combat. He looks from one to the other for an explanation. They sulkily avoid his eye, and nurse their wrath in silence.*

RAMSDEN. Is it wise for you to be out in the sunshine with such a headache, Violet?

TANNER. Have you recovered too, Malone?

VIOLET. Oh, I forgot. We have not all met before. Mr Malone: wont you introduce your father?

HECTOR [*with Roman firmness*]. No, I will not. He is no father of mine.

MALONE [*very angry*]. You disown your dad before your English friends, do you?

VIOLET. Oh, please dont make a scene.

*Ann and Octavius, lingering near the gate, exchange an astonished glance, and discreetly withdraw up the steps to the garden, where they can enjoy the disturbance without intruding. On their way to the steps Ann sends a little grimace of mute sympathy to Violet, who is standing with her back to the little table, looking on in helpless annoyance as her husband soars to higher and higher moral eminences without the least regard to the old man's millions.*

HECTOR. I'm very sorry, Miss Rawbnsn; but I'm contending for a principle. I am a son, and, I hope, a dutiful one; but before everything I'm a Mahn!!! And when dad treats my private letters as his own, and takes it on himself to say that I shant marry you if I am happy and fortunate enough to gain your consent, then I just snap my fingers and go my own way.

TANNER. Marry Violet!

RAMSDEN. Are you in your senses?

TANNER. Do you forget what we told you?

HECTOR [*recklessly*]. I dont care what you told me.

RAMSDEN [*scandalized*]. Tut tut, sir! Monstrous! [*He flings away towards the gate, his elbows quivering with indignation.*]

TANNER. Another madman! These men in love should be locked up. [*He gives Hector up as hopeless, and turns away towards the garden; but Malone, taking offence in a new direction, follows him and compels him, by the aggressiveness of his tone, to stop.*]

MALONE. I dont understand this. Is Hector not good enough for this lady, pray?

TANNER. My dear sir, the lady is married already. Hector knows it; and yet he persists in his infatuation. Take him home and lock him up.

MALONE [*bitterly*]. So this is the highborn social tone Ive spoilt be me ignorant, uncultivated behavior! Makin love to a married woman! [*He comes angrily between Hector and Violet, and almost bawls into Hector's left ear.*] Youve picked up that habit of the British aristocracy, have you?

HECTOR. Thats all right. Dont you trouble yourself about that. I'll answer for the morality of what I'm doing.

TANNER [*coming forward to Hector's right hand with flashing eyes*]. Well said, Malone! You also see that mere marriage laws are not morality! I agree with you; but unfortunately Violet does not.

MALONE. I take leave to doubt that, sir. [*Turning on Violet*] Let me tell you, Mrs Robinson, or whatever your right name is, you had no right to send that letter to my son when you were the wife of another man.

HECTOR [*outraged*]. This is the last straw. Dad: you have insulted my wife.

MALONE. Y o u r wife!

TANNER. Y o u the missing husband! Another moral impostor! [*He smites his brow, and collapses into Malone's chair.*]

MALONE. Youve married without my consent!

RAMSDEN. You have deliberately humbugged us, sir!

HECTOR. Here: I have had just about enough of being badgered. Violet and I are married: thats the long and the short of it. Now what have you got to say—any of you?

MALONE. I know what Ive got to say. She's married a beggar.

HECTOR. No: she's married a Worker. [*His American pronunciation imparts an overwhelming intensity to this simple and unpopular word.*] I start to earn my own living this very afternoon.

MALONE [*sneering angrily*]. Yes: youre very plucky now, because you got your remittance from me yesterday or this morning, I reckon. Wait! it's spent. You wont be so full of cheek then.

HECTOR [*producing a letter from his pocket*

*book*]. Here it is [*Thrusting it on his father*]. Now you just take your remittance and yourself out of my life. I'm done with remittances; and I'm done with you. I dont sell the privilege of insulting my wife for a thousand dollars.

MALONE [*deeply wounded and full of concern*]. Hector: you dont know what poverty is.

HECTOR [*fervidly*]. Well, I wawnt to know what it is. I wawnt'be a Mahn. Violet: you come along with me, to your own home: I'll see you through.

OCTAVIUS [*jumping down from the garden to the lawn and running to Hector's left hand*]. I hope youll shake hands with me before you go, Hector. I admire and respect you more than I can say. [*He is affected almost to tears as they shake hands.*]

VIOLET [*also almost in tears, but of vexation*]. Oh, dont be an idiot, Tavy. Hector's about as fit to become a workman as you are.

TANNER [*rising from his chair on the other side of Hector*]. Never fear: theres no question of his becoming a navvy, Mrs Malone. [*To Hector*] Theres really no difficulty about capital to start with. Treat me as a friend: draw on me.

OCTAVIUS [*impulsively*]. Or on me.

MALONE [*with fierce jealousy*]. Who wants your durty money? Who should he draw on but his own father? [*Tanner and Octavius recoil, Octavius rather hurt, Tanner consoled by the solution of the money difficulty. Violet looks up hopefully.*] Hector: dont be rash, my boy. I'm sorry for what I said: I never meant to insult Violet: I take it all back. She's just the wife you want: there!

HECTOR [*patting him on the shoulder*]. Well, thats all right, dad. Say no more: we're friends again. Only, I take no money from anybody.

MALONE [*pleading abjectly*]. Dont be hard on me, Hector. I'd rather you quarrelled and took the money than made friends and starved. You dont know what the world is: I do.

HECTOR. No, no, NO. Thats fixed: thats not going to change. [*He passes his father inexorably by, and goes to Violet.*] Come, Mrs Malone: youve got to move to the hotel with me, and take your proper place before the world.

VIOLET. But I must go in, dear, and tell Davis to pack. Wont you go on and make them give you a room overlooking the garden for me? I'll join you in half an hour.

HECTOR. Very well. Youll dine with us, Dad, wont you?

MALONE [*eager to conciliate him*]. Yes, yes.

HECTOR. See you all later. [*He waves his hand to Ann, who has now been joined by Tanner, Octavius, and Ramsden in the garden, and goes out through the little gate, leaving his father and Violet together on the lawn.*]

MALONE. Youll try to bring him to his senses, Violet: I know you will.

VIOLET. I had no idea he could be so headstrong. If he goes on like that, what can I do?

MALONE. Dont be discurridged: domestic pressure may be slow; but it's sure. Youll wear him down. Promise me you will.

VIOLET. I will do my best. Of course I think it's the greatest nonsense deliberately making us poor like that.

MALONE. Of course it is.

VIOLET [*after a moment's reflection*]. You had better give me the remittance. He will want it for his hotel bill. I'll see whether I can induce him to accept it. Not now, of course, but presently.

MALONE [*eagerly*]. Yes, yes, yes: thats just the thing [*He hands her the thousand dollar bill, and adds cunningly*] Y'understand that this is only a bachelor allowance.

VIOLET [*cooly*]. Oh, quite. [*She takes it.*] Thank you. By the way, Mr Malone, those two houses you mentioned — the abbeys.

MALONE. Yes?

VIOLET. Dont take one of them until Ive seen it. One never knows what may be wrong with these places.

MALONE. I wont. I'll do nothing without consulting you, never fear.

VIOLET [*politely, but without a ray of gratitude*]. Thanks: that will be much the best way. [*She goes calmly back to the villa, escorted obsequiously by Malone to the upper end of the garden.*]

TANNER [*drawing Ramsden's attention to Malone's cringing attitude as he takes leave of Violet*]. And that poor devil is a billionaire! one of the master spirits of the age! Led in a string like a pug dog by the first girl who takes the trouble to despise him! I wonder will it ever come to that with me. [*He comes down to the lawn.*]

RAMSDEN [*following him*]. The sooner the better for you.

MALONE [*slapping his hands as he returns through the garden*]. That'll be a grand woman for Hector. I wouldnt exchange her for ten duchesses. [*He descends to the lawn and comes between Tanner and Ramsden.*]

RAMSDEN [*very civil to the billionaire*]. It's an unexpected pleasure to find you in this corner of the world, Mr Malone. Have you come to buy up the Alhambra?

MALONE. Well, I dont say I mightnt. I think I could do better with it than the Spanish government. But thats not what I came about. To tell you the truth, about a month ago I overheard a deal between two men over a bundle of shares. They differed about the price: they were young and greedy, and didnt know that if the shares were worth what was bid for them they must be worth what was asked, the margin being too small to be of any account, you see. To amuse meself, I cut in and bought the shares. Well, to this day I havnt found out what the business is. The office is in this town; and the name is Mendoza, Limited. Now whether Mendoza's a mine, or a steamboat line, or a bank, or a patent article —

TANNER. He's a man. I know him: his principles are thoroughly commercial. Let us take you round the town in our motor, Mr Malone, and call on him on the way.

MALONE. If youll be so kind, yes. And may I ask who —

TANNER. Mr Roebuck Ramsden, a very old friend of your daughter-in-law.

MALONE. Happy to meet you, Mr Ramsden.

RAMSDEN. Thank you. Mr Tanner is also one of our circle.

MALONE. Glad to know you also, Mr Tanner.

TANNER. Thanks. [*Malone and Ramsden go out very amicably through the little gate. Tanner calls to Octavius, who is wandering in the garden with Ann*] Tavy! [*Tavy comes to the steps, Tanner whispers loudly to him*] Violet's father-in-law is a financier of brigands. [*Tanner hurries away to overtake Malone and Ramsden. Ann strolls to the steps with an idle impulse to torment Octavius.*]

ANN. Wont you go with them, Tavy?

OCTAVIUS [*tears suddenly flushing his eyes*]. You cut me to the heart, Ann, by wanting me to go. [*He comes down on the lawn to hide his face from her. She follows him caressingly.*]

ANN. Poor Ricky Ticky Tavy! Poor heart!

OCTAVIUS. It belongs to you, Ann. Forgive me: I must speak of it. I love you. You know I love you.

ANN. Whats the good, Tavy? You know that my mother is determined that I shall marry Jack.

OCTAVIUS [*amazed*]. Jack!

ANN. It seems absurd, doesnt it?

OCTAVIUS [*with growing resentment*]. Do you mean to say that Jack has been playing with me all this time? That he has been urging me not to marry you because he intends to marry you himself?

ANN [*alarmed*]. No, no: you mustnt lead him to believe that I said that. I dont for a moment think that Jack knows his own mind. But it's clear from my father's will that he wished me to marry Jack. And my mother is set on it.

OCTAVIUS. But you are not bound to sacrifice yourself always to the wishes of your parents.

ANN. My father loved me. My mother loves me. Surely their wishes are a better guide than my own selfishness.

OCTAVIUS. Oh, I know how unselfish you are, Ann. But believe me — though I know I am speaking in my own interest — there is another side to this question. Is it fair to Jack to marry him if you do not love him? Is it fair to destroy my happiness as well as your own if you can bring yourself to love me?

ANN [*looking at him with a faint impulse of pity*]. Tavy, my dear, you are a nice creature — a good boy.

OCTAVIUS [*humiliated*]. Is that all?

ANN [*mischievously in spite of her pity*]. Thats a great deal, I assure you. You would always worship the ground I trod on, wouldnt you?

OCTAVIUS. I do. It sounds ridiculous; but it's no exaggeration. I do; and I always shall.

ANN. Always is a long word, Tavy. You see, I shall have to live up always to your idea of my divinity; and I dont think I could do that if we were married. But if I marry Jack, youll never be disillusioned — at least not until I grow too old.

OCTAVIUS. I too shall grow old, Ann. And when I am eighty, one white hair of the woman I love will make me tremble more than the thickest gold tress from the most beautiful young head.

ANN [*quite touched*]. Oh, thats poetry, Tavy, real poetry. It gives me that strange sudden sense of an echo from a former existence which always seems to me such a striking proof that we have immortal souls.

OCTAVIUS. Do you believe that it is true?

ANN. Tavy: if it is to come true, you must lose me as well as love me.

OCTAVIUS. Oh! [*He hastily sits down at the little table and covers his face with his hands.*]

ANN [*with conviction*]. Tavy: I wouldnt for worlds destroy your illusions. I can neither take you nor let you go. I can see exactly what will suit you. You must be a sentimental old bachelor for my sake.

OCTAVIUS [*desperately*]. Ann: I'll kill myself.

ANN. Oh no, you wont: that wouldnt be kind. You wont have a bad time. You will be very nice to women; and you will go a good deal to the opera. A broken heart is a very pleasant complaint for a man in London if he has a comfortable income.

OCTAVIUS [*considerably cooled, but believing that he is only recovering his self-control*]. I know you mean to be kind, Ann. Jack has persuaded you that cynicism is a good tonic for me. [*He rises with quiet dignity.*]

ANN [*studying him slyly*]. You see, I'm disillusionizing you already. Thats what I dread.

OCTAVIUS. You do not dread disillusionizing Jack.

ANN [*her face lighting up with mischievous ecstasy — whispering*]. I cant: he has no illusions about me. I shall surprise Jack the other way. Getting over an unfavorable impression is ever so much easier than living up to an ideal. Oh, I shall enrapture Jack sometimes!

OCTAVIUS [*resuming the calm phase of despair, and beginning to enjoy his broken heart and delicate attitude without knowing it*]. I dont doubt that. You will enrapture him always. And he — the fool! — thinks you would make him wretched.

ANN. Yes: thats the difficulty, so far.

OCTAVIUS [*heroically*]. Shall *I* tell him that you love him?

ANN [*quickly*]. Oh no: he'd run away again.

OCTAVIUS [*shocked*]. Ann: would you marry an unwilling man?

ANN. What a queer creature you are, Tavy! Theres no such thing as a willing man when you really go for him. [*She laughs naughtily.*] I'm shocking you, I suppose. But you know you are really getting a sort of satisfaction already in being out of danger yourself.

OCTAVIUS [*startled*]. Satisfaction! [*Reproachfully*] You say that to me!

ANN. Well, if it were really agony, would you ask for more of it?

OCTAVIUS. H a v e I asked for more of it?

ANN. You have offered to tell Jack that I love him. Thats self-sacrifice, I suppose; but there must be some satisfaction in it. Perhaps it's because youre a poet. You are like the bird that presses its breast against the sharp thorn to make itself sing.

OCTAVIUS. It's quite simple. I love you; and I want you to be happy. You dont love me; so I cant make you happy myself; but I can help another man to do it.

ANN. Yes: it seems quite simple. But I doubt if we ever know why we do things. The only really simple thing is to go straight for what you want and grab it. I suppose I dont love you, Tavy; but sometimes I feel as if I should like to make a man of you somehow. You are very foolish about women.

OCTAVIUS [*almost coldly*]. I am content to be what I am in that respect.

ANN. Then you must keep away from them, and only dream about them. I wouldnt marry you for worlds, Tavy.

OCTAVIUS. I have no hope, Ann: I accept my ill luck. But I dont think you quite know how much it hurts.

ANN. You are so softhearted! It's queer that you should be so different from Violet. Violet's as hard as nails.

OCTAVIUS. Oh no. I am sure Violet is thoroughly womanly at heart.

ANN [*with some impatience*]. Why do you say that? Is it unwomanly to be thoughtful and businesslike and sensible? Do you want Violet to be an idiot — or something worse, like me?

OCTAVIUS. Something worse — like y o u! What do you mean, Ann?

ANN. Oh well, I dont mean that, of course. But I have a great respect for Violet. She gets her own way always.

OCTAVIUS [*sighing*]. So do you.

ANN. Yes; but somehow she gets it without coaxing — without having to make people sentimental about her.

OCTAVIUS [*with brotherly callousness*]. Nobody could get very sentimental about Violet, I think, pretty as she is.

ANN. Oh yes they could, if she made them.

OCTAVIUS. But surely no really nice woman would deliberately practise on men's instincts in that way.

ANN [*throwing up her hands*]. Oh, Tavy, Tavy, Ricky Ticky Tavy, heaven help the woman who marries you!

OCTAVIUS [*his passion reviving at the name*]. Oh why, why, why do you say that? Dont torment me. I dont understand.

ANN. Suppose she were to tell fibs, and lay snares for men?

OCTAVIUS. Do you think *I* could marry such a woman — I, who have known and loved you?

ANN. Hm! Well, at all events, she wouldnt let you if she were wise. So thats settled. And now I cant talk any more. Say you forgive me, and that the subject is closed.

OCTAVIUS. I have nothing to forgive; and the subject is closed. And if the wound is open, at least you shall never see it bleed.

ANN. Poetic to the last, Tavy. Goodbye, dear. [*She pats his cheek; has an impulse to kiss him and then another impulse of distaste which prevents her; finally runs away through the garden and into the villa.*]

*Octavius again takes refuge at the table, bowing his head on his arms and sobbing softly. Mrs Whitefield, who has been pottering round the Granada shops, and has a net full of little parcels in her hand, comes in through the gate and sees him.*

MRS WHITEFIELD [*running to him and lifting his head*]. Whats the matter, Tavy? Are you ill?

OCTAVIUS. No, nothing, nothing.

MRS WHITEFIELD [*still holding his head, anxiously*]. But youre crying. Is it about Violet's marriage?

OCTAVIUS. No, no. Who told you about Violet?

MRS WHITEFIELD [*restoring the head to its owner*]. I met Roebuck and that awful old Irishman. Are you sure youre not ill? Whats the matter?

OCTAVIUS [*affectionately*]. It's nothing. Only a man's broken heart. Doesnt that sound ridiculous?

MRS WHITEFIELD. But what is it all about? Has Ann been doing anything to you?

OCTAVIUS. It's not Ann's fault. And dont think for a moment that I blame y o u.

MRS WHITEFIELD [*startled*]. For what?

OCTAVIUS [*pressing her hand consolingly*]. For nothing. I said I didnt blame you.

MRS WHITEFIELD. But I havnt done anything. Whats the matter?

OCTAVIUS [*smiling sadly*]. Cant you guess? I daresay you are right to prefer Jack to me as a husband for Ann; but I love Ann; and it hurts rather. [*He rises and moves away from her towards the middle of the lawn.*]

MRS WHITEFIELD [*following him hastily*]. Does Ann say that I want her to marry Jack?

OCTAVIUS. Yes: she has told me.

MRS WHITEFIELD [*thoughtfully*]. Then I'm very sorry for you, Tavy. It's only her way of saying s h e wants to marry Jack. Little she cares what *I* say or what *I* want!

OCTAVIUS. But she would not say it unless she believed it. Surely you dont suspect Ann of—of d e c e i t!!

MRS WHITEFIELD. Well, never mind, Tavy. I dont know which is best for a young man: to know too little, like you, or too much, like Jack.

*Tanner returns.*

TANNER. Well, Ive disposed of old Malone. Ive introduced him to Mendoza, Limited; and left the two brigands together to talk it out. Hullo, Tavy! anything wrong?

OCTAVIUS. I must go wash my face, I see. [*To Mrs Whitefield*] Tell him what you wish. [*To Tanner*] You may take it from me, Jack, that Ann approves of it.

TANNER [*puzzled by his manner*]. Approves of what?

OCTAVIUS. Of what Mrs Whitefield wishes. [*He goes his way with sad dignity to the villa.*]

TANNER [*to Mrs Whitefield*]. This is very mysterious. What is it you wish? It shall be done, whatever it is.

MRS WHITEFIELD [*with snivelling gratitude*]. Thank you, Jack. [*She sits down. Tanner brings the other chair from the table and sits close to her with his elbows on his knees, giving her his whole attention.*] I dont know why it is that other people's children are so nice to me, and that my own have so little consideration for me. It's no wonder I dont seem able to care for Ann and Rhoda as I do for you and Tavy and Violet. It's a very queer world. It used to be so straightforward and simple; and now nobody seems to think and feel as they ought. Nothing has been right since that speech that Professor Tyndall [3] made at Belfast.

TANNER. Yes: life is more complicated than we used to think. But what am I to do for you?

MRS WHITEFIELD. Thats just what I want to tell you. Of course youll marry Ann whether I like it or not—

TANNER [*starting*]. It seems to me that I shall presently be married to Ann whether I like it myself or not.

MRS WHITEFIELD [*peacefully*]. Oh, very likely you will: you know what she is when she has set her mind on anything. But dont put it on me: thats all I ask. Tavy has just let out that she's been saying that I am making her marry you; and the poor boy is breaking his heart about it; for he is in love with her himself, though what he sees in her so wonderful, goodness knows: *I* dont. It's no use telling Tavy that Ann puts things into people's heads by telling them that I want them when the thought of them never crossed my mind. It only sets Tavy against me. But you know better than that. So if you marry her, dont put the blame on me.

TANNER [*emphatically*]. I havnt the slightest intention of marrying her.

MRS WHITEFIELD [*slyly*]. She'd suit you better than Tavy. She'd meet her match in you, Jack. I'd like to see her meet her match.

TANNER. No man is a match for a woman, except with a poker and a pair of hobnailed boots. Not always even then. Anyhow, *I* cant take the poker to her. I should be a mere slave.

MRS WHITEFIELD. No: she's afraid of you. At all events, you would tell her the truth about herself. She wouldnt be able to slip out of it as she does with me.

TANNER. Everybody would call me a brute if I told Ann the truth about herself in terms of her own moral code. To begin with, Ann says things that are not strictly true.

MRS WHITEFIELD. I'm glad somebody sees she is not an angel.

TANNER. In short—to put it as a husband would put it when exasperated to the point of speaking out—she is a liar. And since she has plunged Tavy head over ears in love with her without any intention of marrying him, she is a coquette, according to the standard definition of a coquette as a woman who rouses passions she has no intention of gratifying. And as she has now reduced you to the point of being willing to sacrifice me at the altar for the mere satisfaction of getting me to call her a liar to her face, I may conclude that she is a bully as well. She cant bully men as she bullies women; so she habitually and unscrupulously uses her personal fascination to make men give her whatever she wants. That makes her almost something for which I know no polite name.

3. **Tyndall:** John Tyndall (1820–93), British physicist, an advocate of materialism, a doctrine that he upheld in an address before the British Association at Belfast, in 1874.

MRS WHITEFIELD [*in mild expostulation*]. Well, you cant expect perfection, Jack.

TANNER. I dont. But what annoys me is that Ann does. I know perfectly well that all this about her being a liar and a bully and a coquette and so forth is a trumped-up moral indictment which might be brought against anybody. We all lie; we all bully as much as we dare; we all bid for admiration without the least intention of earning it; we all get as much rent as we can out of our powers of fascination. If Ann would admit this I shouldnt quarrel with her. But she wont. If she has children she'll take advantage of their telling lies to amuse herself by whacking them. If another woman makes eyes at me, she'll refuse to know a coquette. She will do just what she likes herself whilst insisting on everybody else doing what the conventional code prescribes. In short, I can stand everything except her confounded hypocrisy. Thats what beats me.

MRS WHITEFIELD [*carried away by the relief of hearing her own opinion so eloquently expressed*]. Oh, she is a hypocrite. She is: she is. Isnt she?

TANNER. Then why do you want to marry me to her?

MRS WHITEFIELD [*querulously*]. There now! put it on me, of course. I never thought of it until Tavy told me she said I did. But, you know, I'm very fond of Tavy: he's a sort of son to me; and I don't want him to be trampled on and made wretched.

TANNER. Whereas I dont matter, I suppose.

MRS WHITEFIELD. Oh, you are different, somehow: you are able to take care of yourself. Youd serve her out. And anyhow, she must marry somebody.

TANNER. Aha! there speaks the life instinct. You detest her; but you feel that you must get her married.

MRS WHITEFIELD [*rising, shocked*]. Do you mean that I detest my own daughter! Surely you dont believe me to be so wicked and unnatural as that, merely because I see her faults.

TANNER [*cynically*]. You love her, then?

MRS WHITEFIELD. Why, of course I do. What queer things you say, Jack! We cant help loving our own blood relations.

TANNER. Well, perhaps it saves unpleasantness to say so. But for my part, I suspect that the tables of consanguinity have a natural basis in a natural repugnance [*he rises*].

MRS WHITEFIELD. You shouldnt say things like that, Jack. I hope you wont tell Ann that I have been speaking to you. I only wanted to set myself right with you and Tavy. I couldnt sit mumchance and have everything put on me.

TANNER [*politely*]. Quite so.

MRS WHITEFIELD [*dissatisfied*]. And now Ive only made matters worse. Tavy's angry with me because I don't worship Ann. And when it's been put into my head that Ann ought to marry you, what can I say except that it would serve her right?

TANNER. Thank you.

MRS WHITEFIELD. Now dont be silly and twist what I say into something I dont mean. I ought to have fair play—

*Ann comes from the villa, followed presently by Violet, who is dressed for driving.*

ANN [*coming to her mother's right hand with threatening suavity*]. Well, mamma darling, you seem to be having a delightful chat with Jack. We can hear you all over the place.

MRS WHITEFIELD [*appalled*]. Have you overheard—

TANNER. Never fear: Ann is only—well, we were discussing that habit of hers just now. She hasnt heard a word.

MRS WHITEFIELD [*stoutly*]. I dont care whether she has or not: I have a right to say what I please.

VIOLET [*arriving on the lawn and coming between Mrs Whitefield and Tanner*]. Ive come to say goodbye. I'm off for my honeymoon.

MRS WHITEFIELD [*crying*]. Oh, dont say that, Violet. And no wedding, no breakfast, no clothes, nor anything.

VIOLET [*petting her*]. It wont be for long.

MRS WHITEFIELD. Dont let him take you to America. Promise me that you wont.

VIOLET [*very decidedly*]. I should think not, indeed. Dont cry, dear: I'm only going to the hotel.

MRS WHITEFIELD. But going in that dress, with your luggage, makes one realize—[*She chokes, and then breaks out again*] How I wish you were my daughter, Violet!

VIOLET [*soothing her*]. There, there: so I am. Ann will be jealous.

MRS WHITEFIELD. Ann doesnt care a bit for me.

ANN. Fie, mother! Come, now: you mustnt cry any more: you know Violet doesnt like it. [*Mrs Whitefield dries her eyes, and subsides.*]

VIOLET. Goodbye, Jack.

TANNER. Goodbye, Violet.

VIOLET. The sooner you get married too, the better. You will be much less misunderstood.

TANNER [*restively*]. I quite expect to get married in the course of the afternoon. You all seem to have set your minds on it.

VIOLET. You might do worse. [*To Mrs Whitefield: putting her arm round her*] Let me take you to the hotel with me: the drive will do you good. Come in and get a wrap. [*She takes her towards the villa.*]

MRS WHITEFIELD [*as they go up through the garden*]. I dont know what I shall do when you are gone, with no one but Ann in the house; and she always occupied with the men! It's not to be expected that your husband will care to be bothered with an old woman like me. Oh, you neednt tell me: politeness is all very well; but I know what people think — [*She talks herself and Violet out of sight and hearing.*]

*Ann, alone with Tanner, watches him and waits. He makes an irresolute movement towards the gate; but some magnetism in her draws him to her, a broken man.*

ANN. Violet is quite right. You ought to get married.

TANNER [*explosively*]. Ann: I will not marry you. Do you hear? I wont, wont, wont, wont, WONT marry you.

ANN [*placidly*]. Well, nobody axd you, sir she said, sir she said, sir she said. So thats settled.

TANNER. Yes, nobody has asked me; but everybody treats the thing as settled. It's in the air. When we meet, the others go away on absurd pretexts to leave us alone together. Ramsden no longer scowls at me: his eye beams, as if he were already giving you away to me in church. Tavy refers me to your mother and gives me his blessing. Straker openly treats you as his future employer: it was he who first told me of it.

ANN. Was that why you ran away?

TANNER. Yes, only to be stopped by a lovesick brigand and run down like a truant schoolboy.

ANN. Well, if you dont want to be married, you neednt be. [*She turns away from him and sits down, much at her ease.*]

TANNER [*following her*]. Does any man want to be hanged? Yet men let themselves be hanged without a struggle for life, though they could at least give the chaplain a black eye. We do the world's will, not our own. I have a frightful feeling that I shall let myself be married because it is the world's will that you should have a husband.

ANN. I daresay I shall, someday.

TANNER. But why me? me of all men! Marriage is to me apostasy, profanation of the sanctuary of my soul, violation of my manhood, sale of my birthright, shameful surrender, ignominious capitulation, acceptance of defeat. I shall decay like a thing that has served its purpose and is done with; I shall change from a man with a future to a man with a past; I shall see in the greasy eyes of all the other husbands their relief at the arrival of a new prisoner to share their ignominy. The young men will scorn me as one who has sold out: to the women I, who have always been an enigma and a possibility, shall be merely somebody else's property — and damaged goods at that: a secondhand man at best.

ANN. Well, your wife can put on a cap and make herself ugly to keep you in countenance, like my grandmother.

TANNER. So that she may make her triumph more insolent by publicly throwing away the bait the moment the trap snaps on the victim!

ANN. After all, though, what difference would it make? Beauty is all very well at first sight; but who ever looks at it when it has been in the house three days? I thought our pictures very lovely when papa bought them; but I havent looked at them for years. You never bother about my looks: you are too well used to me. I might be the umbrella stand.

TANNER. You lie, you vampire: you lie.

ANN. Flatterer. Why are you trying to fascinate me, Jack, if you dont want to marry me?

TANNER. The Life Force. I am in the grip of the Life Force.

ANN. I dont understand in the least: it sounds like the Life Guards.

TANNER. Why don't you marry Tavy? He is willing. Can you not be satisfied unless your prey struggles?

ANN [*turning to him as if to let him into a secret*]. Tavy will never marry. Havent you noticed that that sort of man never marries?

TANNER. What! a man who idolizes women! who sees nothing in nature but romantic scenery for love duets! Tavy, the chivalrous, the faithful, the tenderhearted and true! Tavy never marry! Why, he was born to be swept up by the first pair of blue eyes he meets in the street.

ANN. Yes, I know. All the same, Jack, men like that always live in comfortable bachelor lodgings with broken hearts, and are adored by their landladies, and never get married. Men like you always get married.

TANNER [*smiting his brow*]. How frightfully, horribly true! It has been staring me in the face all my life; and I never saw it before.

ANN. Oh, it's the same with women. The poetic temperament's a very nice temperament, very amiable, very harmless and poetic, I daresay; but it's an old maid's temperament.

TANNER. Barren. The Life Force passes it by.

ANN. If thats what you mean by the Life Force, yes.

TANNER. You dont care for Tavy?

ANN [*looking round carefully to make sure that Tavy is not within earshot*]. No.

TANNER. And you do care for me?

ANN [*rising quietly and shaking her finger at him*]. Now, Jack! Behave yourself.

TANNER. Infamous, abandoned woman! Devil!

ANN. Boa-constrictor! Elephant!

TANNER. Hypocrite!

ANN [*softly*]. I must be, for my future husband's sake.

TANNER. For mine! [*Correcting himself savagely*] I mean for his.

ANN [*ignoring the correction*]. Yes, for yours. You had better marry what you call a hypocrite, Jack. Women who are not hypocrites go about in rational dress and are insulted and get into all sorts of hot water. And then their husbands get dragged in too, and live in continual dread of fresh complications. Wouldnt you prefer a wife you could depend on?

TANNER. No: a thousand times no: hot water is the revolutionist's element. You clean men as you clean milkpails, by scalding them.

ANN. Cold water has its uses too. It's healthy.

TANNER [*despairingly*]. Oh, you are witty: at the supreme moment the Life Force endows you with every quality. Well, I too can be a hypocrite. Your father's will appointed me your guardian, not your suitor. I shall be faithful to my trust.

ANN [*in low siren tones*]. He asked me who I would have as my guardian before he made that will. I chose you!

TANNER. The will is yours then! The trap was laid from the beginning.

ANN [*concentrating all her magic*]. From the beginning — from our childhood — for both of us — by the Life Force.

TANNER. I will not marry you. I will not marry you.

ANN. Oh, you will, you will.

TANNER. I tell you, no, no, no.

ANN. I tell you, yes, yes, yes.

TANNER. No.

ANN [*coaxing — imploring — almost exhausted*]. Yes. Before it is too late for repentance. Yes.

TANNER [*struck by the echo from the past*]. When did all this happen to me before? Are we two dreaming?

ANN [*suddenly losing her courage, with an anguish that she does not conceal*]. No. We are awake; and you have said no: that is all.

TANNER [*brutally*]. Well?

ANN. Well, I made a mistake: you do not love me.

TANNER [*seizing her in his arms*]. It is false: I love you. The Life Force enchants me: I have the whole world in my arms when I clasp you. But I am fighting for my freedom, for my honor, for my self, one and indivisible.

ANN. Your happiness will be worth them all.

TANNER. You would sell freedom and honor and self for happiness?

ANN. It will not be all happiness for me. Perhaps death.

TANNER [*groaning*]. Oh, that clutch holds and hurts. What have you grasped in me? Is there a father's heart as well as a mother's?

ANN. Take care, Jack: if anyone comes while we are like this, you will have to marry me.

TANNER. If we two stood now on the edge of a precipice, I would hold you tight and jump.

ANN [*panting, failing more and more under the strain*]. Jack; let me go. I have dared so frightfully — it is lasting longer than I thought. Let me go: I cant bear it.

TANNER. Nor I. Let it kill us.

ANN. Yes: I dont care. I am at the end of my forces. I dont care. I think I am going to faint.

*At this moment Violet and Octavius come from the villa with Mrs Whitefield, who is wrapped up for driving. Simultaneously Malone and Ramsden, followed by Mendoza and Straker, come in through the little gate in the paling. Tanner shamefacedly releases Ann, who raises her hand giddily to her forehead.*

MALONE. Take care. Something's the matter with the lady.

RAMSDEN. What does this mean?

VIOLET [*running between Ann and Tanner*]. Are you ill?

ANN [*reeling, with a supreme effort*]. I have promised to marry Jack. [*She swoons. Violet kneels by her and chafes her hand. Tanner runs round to her other hand, and tries to lift her head. Octavius goes to Violet's assistance, but does not know what to do. Mrs Whitefield hurries back into the villa. Octavius, Malone, and Ramsden run to Ann and crowd round her, stooping to assist. Straker coolly comes to Ann's feet, and Mendoza to her head, both upright and self-possessed.*]

STRAKER. Now then, ladies and gentlemen: she dont want a crowd round her: she wants air — all the air she can git. If you please, gents — [*Malone and Ramsden allow him to drive them gently past Ann and up the lawn towards the garden, where Octavius, who has already become conscious of his uselessness, joins them. Straker, following them up, pauses for a moment to instruct Tanner.*] Dont lift er ed, Mr Tanner: let it go flat so's the blood can run back into it.

MENDOZA. He is right, Mr Tanner. Trust to the air of the Sierra. [*He withdraws delicately to the garden steps.*]

TANNER [*rising*]. I yield to your superior knowledge of physiology, Henry. [*He withdraws to the corner of the lawn; and Octavius immediately hurries down to him.*]

TAVY [*aside to Tanner, grasping his hand*]. Jack: be very happy.

TANNER [*aside to Tavy*]. I never asked her. It is a trap for me. [*He goes up the lawn towards the garden. Octavius remains petrified.*]

MENDOZA [*intercepting Mrs Whitefield, who comes from the villa with a glass of brandy*]. What is this, madam? [*He takes it from her.*]

MRS WHITEFIELD. A little brandy.

MENDOZA. The worst thing you could give her. Allow me. [*He swallows it.*] Trust to the air of the Sierra, madam.

*For a moment the men all forget Ann and stare at Mendoza.*

ANN [*in Violet's ear, clutching her round the neck*]. Violet: did Jack say anything when I fainted?

VIOLET. No.

ANN. Ah! [*With a sigh of intense relief she relapses.*]

MRS WHITEFIELD. Oh, she's fainted again.

*They are about to rush back to her; but Mendoza stops them with a warning gesture.*

ANN [*supine*]. No. I havnt. I'm quite happy.

TANNER [*suddenly walking determinedly to her, and snatching her hand from Violet to feel her pulse*]. Why, her pulse is positively bounding. Come! get up. What nonsense! Up with you. [*He hauls her up summarily.*]

ANN. Yes: I feel strong enough now. But you very nearly killed me, Jack, for all that.

MALONE. A rough wooer, eh? Theyre the best sort, Miss Whitefield. I congratulate Mr Tanner; and I hope to meet you and him as frequent guests at the abbey.

ANN. Thank you. [*She goes past Malone to Octavius.*] Ricky Ticky Tavy: congratulate me. [*Aside to him*] I want to make you cry for the last time.

TAVY [*steadfastly*]. No more tears. I am happy in your happiness. And I believe in you in spite of everything.

RAMSDEN [*coming between Malone and Tanner*]. You are a happy man, Jack Tanner. I envy you.

MENDOZA [*advancing between Violet and Tanner*]. Sir: there are two tragedies in life. One is to lose your heart's desire. The other is to gain it. Mine and yours, sir.

TANNER. Mr Mendoza: I have no heart's desires. Ramsden: it is very easy for you to call me a happy man: you are only a spectator. I am one of the principals; and I know better. Ann: stop tempting Tavy, and come back to me.

ANN [*complying*]. You are absurd, Jack. [*She takes his proffered arm.*]

TANNER [*continuing*]. I solemnly say that I am not a happy man. Ann looks happy; but she is only triumphant, successful, victorious. That is not happiness, but the price for which the strong sell their happiness. What we have both done this afternoon is to renounce happiness, renounce freedom, renounce tranquillity, above all, renounce the romantic possibilities of an unknown future, for the cares of a household and a family. I beg that no man may seize the occasion to get half drunk and utter imbecile speeches and coarse pleasantries at my expense. We propose to furnish our own house according to our own taste; and I hereby give notice that the seven or eight travelling clocks, the four or five dressing cases, the carvers and fish slices, the copies of Patmore's Angel In The House in extra morocco, and the other articles you are preparing to heap upon us, will be instantly sold, and the proceeds devoted to circulating free copies of the Revolutionist's Handbook. The wedding will take place three days after our return to England, by special licence, at the office of the district superintendent registrar, in the presence of my solicitor and his clerk, who, like his clients, will be in ordinary walking dress—

VIOLET [*with intense conviction*]. You a r e a brute, Jack.

ANN [*looking at him with fond pride and caressing his arm*]. Never mind her, dear. Go on talking.

TANNER. Talking!

*Universal laughter.*

**REUBEN A. BROWER,** *Editor*

# *William Butler Yeats*

**1865–1939**

We value the poetry of Yeats, like other good poetry, because it fixes moments of experience in memorable image and distinctly heard rhythm, and so seems to make them timeless:

An aged man is but a paltry thing,
A tattered coat upon a stick, unless
Soul clap its hands and sing, and louder sing
For every tatter in its mortal dress. . . .
("Sailing to Byzantium")

But we also feel in Yeats, for example in these lines from "Sailing to Byzantium," a distinctly "modern" quality; his art has an additional value for us because it belongs so definitely to our own time. Yeats's achievement matters especially to present-day readers because he wrote his way out of the nineteenth century, and because he helped the first generation of the twentieth to see and feel what their world was like. But his work was so entangled in the political and literary life of Ireland that the historical and biographical view is liable to swamp our reading of his poems. He was overly aware of the connection between his life and his art and almost too conscious of what he was doing; and, although we can see some kinds of meaning and value in Yeats only by setting his work in its biographical context, we had better begin by looking at the poetry itself. (An energetic and properly skeptical student will read no further until he has first read carefully five or six poems.)[1]

[1] "The Lake Isle of Innisfree," "To a Friend Whose Work Has Come to Nothing," "No Second Troy," "The Magi," "Sailing to Byzantium," "The Second Coming."

What does Yeats sound like, to a reader coming from Arnold or Browning? To give a characteristically Irish answer, he sounds more like Tennyson, the poet he most "venerated" as a young man:

I will arise and go now, and go to Innisfree, . . .
And I shall have some peace there, for peace comes
dropping slow,
Dropping from the veils of morning to where the
cricket sings;
There midnight's all a glimmer, and noon a purple
glow,
And evening full of the linnet's wings.
("The Lake Isle of Innisfree")

We hear echoes of the earlier Tennyson who sings of the Lotos-Eaters coming "unto a land / In which it seemed always afternoon":

A land of streams! some, like a downward smoke,
Slow-dropping veils of thinnest lawn, did go . . .

The longing to reach an other-world "isle" is definitely reminiscent of Shelley, another of Yeats's early admirations; and the lonely lake that appears here and in many of Yeats's poems recalls Keats's "La Belle Dame sans Merci," as in this rather bald imitation:

I wander by the edge
Of this desolate lake
Where wind cries in the sedge. . . .
("He Hears the Cry of the Sedge")

But here is a voice that we have never found in Keats:

Now all the truth is out,
Be secret and take defeat

From any brazen throat,
For how can you compete,
Being honour bred, with one
Who, were it proved he lies,
Were neither shamed in his own
Nor in his neighbours' eyes? . . .
(" To a Friend Whose Work
Has Come to Nothing ")

Where have we heard such rudeness of attack (to a friend!) and such bitter sympathy, in short lines heavily stressed and harshly rhymed? In Swift, in his addresses to friends and enemies. The spareness in use of images and the surprising power of any single one that is admitted are also Swiftian:

And strongly shoot a radiant Dart,
To shine through Life's declining Part.[1]

The title of Yeats's poem recalls the Augustan fondness for " occasional " poetry and social verse. The austere aristocratic tone is equally characteristic of Yeats, and it is very like him to find his poetic role in an eighteenth-century writer. (He in fact came to regard Swift and Burke as ideal writers and thinkers.)

But though Yeats plays many parts in his verse — that is a sign of his scope — there are poems which could have been written by no one else:

THE MAGI

Now as at all times I can see in the mind's eye,
In their stiff, painted clothes, the pale unsatisfied ones
Appear and disappear in the blue depth of the sky
With all their ancient faces like rain-beaten stones,
And all their helms of silver hovering side by side,
And all their eyes still fixed, hoping to find once more,
Being by Calvary's turbulence unsatisfied,
The uncontrollable mystery on the bestial floor.

Two features of this poem strike us at once: the completeness with which attention focuses on the Magi, and the wavering exaltation that gradually comes into the speaker's voice. What has happened to the familiar figures of the Three Kings, and what do they mean here? How does the speaker of this brief dramatic monologue address his audience?

[1] Swift, " Stella's Birth-Day, March 13, 1726/7," ll. 33–34. The lines quoted contain one of two striking images in a poem of eighty-eight lines, which is otherwise written in a plain conversational style.

We hear at first the voice of a man talking quietly to himself, but we soon feel that the " I " of this poem is a far from ordinary person. He *sees* the Magi " in the *mind's* eye," the " inward eye " of Wordsworth — his seeing is vision. Though he speaks with extraordinary collectedness, in one long, well-ordered sentence, his voice soars far away as the lines fall into gently balanced units:

Appear and disappear . . .
With all their ancient faces . . .
And all their helms . . .
And all their eyes . . .

The strongly accented lines are further lifted out of speech by their length: six stresses with heavy pauses seem very long to ears accustomed to blank verse.

But this foreignness of sound, the sense of lines going on and on, is very nice for a poem that takes us from here and now to a " sky-scape " of the mind where the Wise Men's quest is never-ending. In part the picture is expected and traditional — the aged seer-kings in rich garments and armor seen against the sky as they go toward Bethlehem. But there is an odd and recurrent emphasis in the way in which they are described. Their clothes are " stiff " and " painted," as if artificial and not fitted to their bodies; their faces, stony, " their eyes still fixed " in an immovable gaze. These hardly human and unsubstantial (" pale," " hovering ") seekers are perpetually obsessed with the search for a " mystery." What they seek is in Christ, divinity revealed, the " mystery " that is " uncontrollable," in the sense of inconceivable, beyond man's grasp.

So far the poem seems simple enough, the Magi being taken as symbols of the unending search for the divine. But " uncontrollable " has another side, and in fact, most of the poem has " another side." " Bestial " recalls the stable of the Nativity, but with " uncontrollable " and " turbulence " it may also suggest that the divine birth was too human, linked with the primitive and subhuman. The Magi were " unsatisfied " with the Incarnation, with God made flesh; their dream was not fulfilled by a career that ended in the " turbulence " and bloodshed of Calvary. So " once more " they are " hoping to find " the Absolute uncontaminated by the human. In writing of " The Magi " and its companion piece, " The Dolls," Yeats spoke of ". . .

how all thought among us is frozen into 'something other than human life.'"

We have had a vision, but a strange one, for we have been led to feel an unexpected irony in the quest of the Magi, an irony inherent in all seeking after dehumanized, abstract truth. Other disturbing implications enter — for example, that religious revelation is inseparable from primitive violence. But note that the "I" of the poem stands apart from the Magi; he accepts, perhaps welcomes, the connection of divine being with human suffering and violence. If we now reread the poem with an ear for his voice and rhythm, we can feel their perfect appropriateness. The prose control of meditative speech rightly checks the tendency to visionary song; it goes well, too, with the critical attitude toward the Magi, and fits the far from simple reverence of this rehandling of Christian myth.

The visions of Keats or Wordsworth were certainly not like this. But "The Magi" is a poem of 1913, not 1813, and the awareness it expresses is very much of its time. Here is a poet who has rebelled against the rationality and abstraction of nineteenth-century social and scientific thought, who has been attracted by the rediscovery of primitive elements in religion, perhaps by the new comparative study of myth. The lack of simple seriousness, the blend of irony and wonder, is another sign of a twentieth-century sensibility. It is also a sign of a revolution in Yeats's poetic personality and style. Fifteen or sixteen years before, he had written very differently of the Magi in a poem to the Rose (his symbol for Passion, Intellectual Beauty, and a number of things):

> Thy great leaves enfold
> The ancient beards, the helms of ruby and gold
> Of the crowned Magi; and the kings whose eyes
> Saw the Pierced Hands and Rood of elder rise
> In Druid vapour. . . .
>
> ("The Secret Rose")

Whatever these rich and solemn lines may mean, they belong to a literary realm miles removed from Yeats's later poetry. To trace the journey by which the poet of "The Secret Rose" became the poet of "The Magi," we shall have to relate his growth to personal history and to history in the broad sense.

Yeats's development, from the late 1880's to his death in 1939, falls into four fairly distinct phases, each of which is characterized by a more or less dominant mode of poetry: (I) Solitary Pre-Raphaelite Song (1889–1904); (II) Poetry Out of the Theater (1904–16); (III) Lyric Debate and Visionary Song (1916–29); and (IV) Poetry of Madness (1929–39). Before tracing the growth of the poet it will be useful to have in mind a brief outline of his life. (See also the selections from *The Autobiography,* below.)

## PERSONAL HISTORY

The first twenty years of Yeats's life, until he became a professional writer, might be called his "Sligo" period. He was born, June 13, 1865, in Dublin; but he was never a Dubliner at heart; his home by inheritance and imaginative sympathy was in Sligo, a county of western Ireland with barren mountains overlooking the sea and exquisite Lough Gill, the lake of "Innisfree." Both his father's and mother's family had long lived in various parts of the county; and his ancestors on both sides were, like Shaw's, Protestant Irish, in the main descendants from English immigrants to Ireland. His father, John Butler Yeats, the son and grandson of clergymen, had rejected the family faith and calling to become a painter. During Yeats's boyhood his parents moved back and forth from London to Dublin, setting up their household where J. B. Y. wanted to study or paint, or where he could afford to pay the rent. During the summers and sometimes for periods of a year or more, William and the other children went to stay with their mother at her parents' home in Sligo. Here "Willie," as his father called him, first discovered the Celtic dreamland of his early poems and stories; here he saw strange lights on the nearby mountains, heard ghostly rappings and strange buzzings, and filled his head with tales about Irish heroes and fairy folk.

Yeats's career as a man of letters began in a serious way with the family's return to London in 1887, where he published his first volume of verse, *The Wanderings of Oisin and Other Poems,* in 1889, and three years later, his second, *The Countess Kathleen and Various Legends and Lyrics* (which included "The Lake Isle of Innisfree"). As these books show, Yeats had now come under the influence of late followers of the Pre-Raphaelite Brotherhood, a movement in art and literature initiated in 1848 by the poet and painter, Dante Gabriel Rossetti.[1] Rebelling

[1] On Rossetti and the Pre-Raphaelites, see "A Pre-Raphaelite's Son" in *The Autobiography,* below.

against the Royal Academy with its worship of Raphael, the founding Brothers had called themselves "*Pre*-Raphaelites." Their ideal was vaguely medieval; at least their subjects in poetry and painting were religious or allegorically "spiritual." One allegiance seems common to the men, from Rossetti to William Morris,[1] who were affected by the movement — a belief in "the life of imagination," in an ideal dream world, which they sought in protest against the materialism of nineteenth-century England.

This notion of art as a voyage out of the crass material present was also driven into Yeats's thinking by all sorts of influences that he encountered in the 80's and 90's. In 1891, he had joined a number of other poets in forming the Rhymers Club. He later said that for him and his friends in the Club "perhaps the most powerful influence" after Rossetti was Walter Pater, the high priest of the aesthetic movement. Whatever Pater may have intended, he came to represent the aim of reducing life to moments of exquisite sensations, of cultivating "aesthetic states" utterly unlike other kinds of experience. His attitude seemed to be sanctioned also by the French Symbolists,[2] to whom Yeats and the Rhymers had been introduced by Arthur Symons, author of *The Symbolist Movement in Literature*. As they sat in the "candelight," says Yeats, ". . . it never seemed very difficult to murmur Villiers de L'Isle-Adam's words, 'As for living — our servants will do that for us.'" To these literary influences were added a number of bizarre but deadly serious interests in magic and theosophy, in societies devoted to occult knowledge such as "The Order of the Golden Dawn," and in the founding of a new religion for Ireland.

But while Yeats was living in this literary and religious wonderland he was also very much alive in another world, in the political and cultural activities of the Irish National movement. Yeats proved himself an efficient organizer of societies aimed to arouse interest in old and new Irish literature (1891–92); he worked hard as a propagandist for the Nationalists, and actually joined a revolutionary group, the Irish Republican Brotherhood (1896). His two lives had been oddly linked by his falling in love (1889) with Maud Gonne, a beautiful woman and an agitator against English rule of Ireland. While Yeats was trying to interest his beloved in secret cults, she drew him into noisy and even dangerous political demonstrations, such as those against Queen Victoria's Jubilee in 1897.

In 1896 he met Lady Augusta Gregory, a member of an old Anglo-Irish landholding family and an enthusiastic collector of local traditions and folklore. In part through her influence and in part because of Maud Gonne's repeated refusals to marry him, Yeats's political activities diminished, and his interests became more closely identified with the revival of Irish literature and art, the so-called "Irish Renaissance." Toward the end of the century he joined Lady Gregory in the founding of an Irish National Theatre, the society that organized the famous Abbey Players. For the next ten years Yeats put most of his time and energy into writing and producing plays, or into explaining and defending the policies of the Theatre. He wrote and published very little lyric poetry between *The Wind among the Reeds* (1899) and *The Green Helmet and Other Poems,* a volume which came out in 1910 and marks a turning point in Yeats's career.

About this time Yeats became an intimate associate of Ezra Pound, a young American poet who introduced him to the "modern" style in verse. He continued to write plays, but for an ideal rather than an actual theater, and from this time on he concentrated more fully on the business of being a poet; nearly all his best poetry was written during the last thirty years of his life. The rest of Yeats's personal history can be quickly outlined. In 1917 he married Miss Georgie Hyde-Lees and soon after began to rebuild as a country home Thoor Ballylee, part of an ancient castle near Lady Gregory's place, Coole Park. (The castle is the original of the "Tower" symbol in Yeats's later poems.) In 1922 he was appointed to the Senate of the newly founded Irish Free State, and in 1923 he won the Nobel Prize for literature. But though Yeats's life in later years was more firmly focused on his art, after his marriage he entered on his most elaborate experiment in occult knowledge and religion, the studies and myste-

[1] See "Morris: His Antithetical Dream" in *The Autobiography,* below.

[2] On Mallarmé, the leading poet in this movement, see note 81 in *The Autobiography,* below. Villiers de L'Isle-Adam (1838–89) was a French writer whose drama, *Axel,* was "a sacred book" to Yeats. The hero is the perfect type of the Symbolist dreamer-philosopher who withdraws from society to live the life of imagination.

rious communications with spirits that led to his book of revelation, *A Vision* (first published in 1925).

The year 1929 marks the beginning of the last period of the poet's life. Because he had suffered a congestion of the lungs in the fall of 1927, he began the practice of spending his winters on the French or Italian Riviera. During the winter of 1928–29 he stayed at Rapallo, Italy, and early in 1929 he started writing an entirely new kind of lyric poem, the first of a series, "Words for Music Perhaps." The following summer was his last at Thoor Ballylee. In the remaining years Yeats continued to read and write as vigorously as ever, working on a new edition of *A Vision* (1937) and writing poems up to within a day or two of his death, on January 28, 1939, at Cap Martin, France. The variety of his life — which we have barely glimpsed — is matched by the variety of his several "careers" as a poet. As we shall see, Yeats showed a unique power of renewing and transforming his art during each of the phases that followed his first successes in poetry.

## I. SOLITARY PRE-RAPHAELITE SONG (1889–1904)

These early successes, exquisite lyrics such as "Innisfree" and "Who Goes with Fergus?" now seem rather minor, as they did to Yeats himself a few years after he had written them. The poet who interests us today and who stands among the first of our century is the one who rejected or reshaped many elements in his youthful poetic self. A composite portrait of the poet drawn from the early volumes (1889–99) would include some curious traits: he is a chanter of fairy songs that take us

> Up the airy mountain
> Down the rushy glen, . . .[1]

but he is also a melancholy singer who longs for an "isle in the water" and a weary lover who seeks consolation from "love's bitter mystery" in Celtic hero stories; finally, he is a worshiper of symbolic images such as the "Far-off, most secret, and inviolate Rose."

It is interesting to note that much of his early poetic character can be traced either to his mother or his father. To his mother's family, the Middletons, Yeats owed his taste for mystery and for Celtic other-worlds. To his father his debt as a poet was enormous both early and late in his career. Throughout his life Yeats can be seen reacting against or fulfilling his father's ideals in art and poetry, and J. B. Y. in old age might have said that Willie had come round wonderfully to the standards he had imparted in their early reading of Shelley and Shakespeare. But as often happens, the young man was first influenced by elements in his inheritance that interested his father least. For the father too had something to do with the far-awayness, the mysterious loves and symbols of his son's early verse, features that remind us less of Old Ireland than of the Pre-Raphaelites. J. B. Y. had in fact begun his career as a Pre-Raphaelite and had introduced his son to the pictures and verse of Rossetti, but while the father rejected his masters in favor of the more realistic French painters, his son had continued to love the saints and mournful beauties of the older school.

But the wanness and weariness, the insistent loneliness of Yeats's early love poetry, is Pre-Raphaelitism as transmitted through the tired but elegant and erudite conversation of the Rhymers. It is hard to say how much the cloudy symbolism of these poems — particularly the "Rose" lyrics — owes to the Rhymers' passion for the French Symbolists. Certainly the theories of *symbolisme* gave support to Yeats's own belief that a poet's images disclose a reality beyond that known to the senses. But the belief can be traced equally well to many of his early literary and religious enthusiasms — to his love of Shelley and Blake, to his interest in magic, or to the secret wisdom of the Golden Dawn.

As Yeats's poetry grew more hazily symbolic, especially in the 1899 volume, *The Wind among the Reeds,* the typical speaker of his poems resembles more and more the conventional lover of nineteenth-century Romantic poetry. "Dream" and "dream-dimmed" are words often on his lips, and if he now talks less naïvely of longing for fairyland, he is always addressing a beloved who is hardly of this world or picturing their love as a state of passionate trance. The tone he adopts is terribly solemn; the high religious unction of "I will arise and go now" becomes the rule, and too much of the time this

[1] William Allingham (1824–89), "The Fairies." Allingham was a popular Irish poet who had a considerable influence on Yeats's early work.

lover sounds like the worshiper of "The Secret Rose." Although Yeats probably intended to create a distinct "personal utterance" in these love poems, the over-all impression is one of monotony and inhuman somnolence.

Yeats felt dissatisfied with much of his youthful poetry almost as soon as he had published it; and as early as 1892 he began to eliminate the more obviously "poetical" idioms and devices from his verse. But an important change in a poet's style must come from something more than disgust with a literary fashion. It was a deeper dissatisfaction that led to the revolution in Yeats's poetry in the years following his "exile" in the Irish Theatre. The first play produced by the new society — in 1899 — was *The Countess Kathleen,* a play that Yeats had first written in 1891 and that mirrored very sharply the division in his activities during the last decade of the century. In this "ill-constructed" drama, with "dialogue turning aside at the lure of word or metaphor" (Yeats's comment), the Nationalist Yeats honored Maud Gonne as a Friend of the People, while the mystic poet subtly criticized her for wasting her life in politics. *The Countess Kathleen* points to the continuing conflict in Yeats's life and art between the dreamer and the man of action, but "out of this quarrel with himself, his poetry was born." Yeats ultimately created a new role for himself and found a new style by recognizing and expressing the conflict; but he had first to suffer a rather severe discipline both of his talent and his character.

## II. POETRY OUT OF THE THEATER (1904–16)

Yeats's progress from lonely song to lyric debate is connected with his discovery that he had been fighting a number of lost causes: Maud Gonne married another man, the Irish theatrical audience did not take kindly to being educated, a new religion was not born, and Yeats's enthusiasm for revolution waned when he saw "the little streets hurled upon the great." More important for the change in his style was his progress as a dramatist in making "characters talk to one another." We first surely detect speech breaking into song in a poem that probably reflects his difficulties in love, "The Folly of Being Comforted." With "No Second Troy," Yeats clearly has found a new voice as compared with that of the old "dream-dimmed" lover: "Why should I blame her that she filled my days / With misery . . . ?" He also begins to use a type of metaphor characteristic of his work from 1914 on. A modern feminist and city appear in the poem as another Helen in "no second Troy"; that is, a familiar symbol from myth or history refers to a present-day situation while also expressing more intimate concerns, here of a lover disappointed by his beloved and his society.

The poet who had once thought that his aim of "personal utterance" was at odds with his father's insistence on "drama" had at length found a way of being both personal and dramatic. J. B. Y., he recalled, ". . . did not care even for a fine lyric passage unless he felt some actual man behind its elaboration of beauty, and he was always looking for the lineaments of some desirable, familiar life. . . . All must be an idealization of speech, and at some moment of passionate action or somnambulistic reverie." The latter sentence describes very aptly the two modes of expression dominant in Yeats's later poetry. In *Responsibilities* (1914), the contained violence of "To a Friend" stands beside "The Magi," a poem that looks ahead to the union of both modes in lyrics focused on some great traditional symbol.

But before Yeats reached those successes he had first to make a conscious critical effort, which for him as for Keats meant also a personal and moral effort. In the period between 1912 and 1916 he set about quite deliberately to remake himself as a man and a poet, and in such a situation it is very like Yeats to seize on any source of power from the sublime to the ridiculous. He schools his inner life by the image of his "anti-self," the heroic man he would be, he rewrites his poems under the direction of Ezra Pound, a man twenty years younger than himself, and he consults a medium to talk with his attendant spirit. However comic the means, the end — the achievement of the poet — is admirable. It is not often that a poet or any man of fifty can learn from the young (an event very nearly as remarkable as communicating with another world). At the time when Yeats felt he was "drying up" and when he still had moments of longing for the fantasies of his youth,[1] he found

[1] See "Lines Written in Dejection," below.

a role in which he could positively embrace and balance both " dreams " and " responsibilities."

"The Fisherman" (1914) clearly announces Yeats's newly realized sense of himself and his audience. He will write no longer for actual Ireland, but for a man of heroic temper who will welcome poetry " cold / And passionate as the dawn." Here we see Yeats's myth-making power at its best: as the poem moves along, the " fisherman " very gradually takes on symbolic meaning; Yeats does not *make* his symbol, it makes itself. Although this man is " but a dream," he evokes a real past, the sterner Ireland of Swift and Burke. If Yeats is no longer a partisan, he is still responsive to national life. But now—and this is the important fact—he has discovered his relation to politics *as a poet.* In " Easter 1916 " he honors a group of rebels, but in his own way, candidly acknowledging that they may have been wrong, that their hearts may have been " enchanted to a stone " by fanaticism, but also recognizing that in their action and death they have become beautiful. Yeats's balancing of loyalties in the poem is wonderfully matched by his interweaving of the old dreamlike rhythms with a new hardness of speech.

## III. LYRIC DEBATE AND VISIONARY SONG (1916–29)

But Yeats attained a much subtler poise among his various selves in poetry written during the next few years, notably in the poems of *The Tower* (1928). He had at last seen how to reconcile action and reverie, speech and song, public and personal symbolism. Yeats did not " solve " anything in these poems; he succeeded rather in making poetry out of his irresolution: that is his peculiar inimitable feat. In " Sailing to Byzantium," " reverie " (in a special sense) seems the prime value, while in " Among School Children " there is an energetic balance between achievement and aiming at the unattainable. Though the two poems are so different, they disclose a similar progression, the mode of lyric debate that finally links the styles we have been tracing. So both begin with an old man talking in a matter-of-fact way (" That is no country for old men " and " I walk through the long schoolroom questioning "); each of the old men is keenly responsive to the sights and sounds of the real world, and each is ironically aware of the figure he cuts in an actual society; but they are at the same time excited by images of the soul's " magnificence " and of " heavenly glory." As they reflect, the debate between opposing desires and values becomes sharper, reaching a climax in a songlike prayer (" O sages," " O Presences "). In the strongly rhythmed lines of the close, images appear (the bird, the chestnut-tree) that symbolize a reconciliation between feelings aroused in the debate. Yeats has found his " form "—in the full athletic sense—just as Keats did in his odes. (The comparison is illuminating, because the kind of poetry first glimpsed in *Endymion* [1] culminates in " Sailing to Byzantium " and because Keats can strike a note of assurance beyond the reach of Yeats and most poets of the past fifty years.)

But the attitudes Yeats dramatizes are not wholly opposed, at least not in the poems. The singer of Byzantium hears too well the " sensual music " he neglects. The old man of " Among School Children " knows that heavenly " Presences " like children " break hearts," and he happily asserts the value of what Yeats's father called " Personality," the harmonious expression of the whole man. Other poems in *The Tower* express a poise between Yeats's private and public loyalties, often in the form of an argument between the man who withdrew to his " tower " and the man who might have fought beside his countrymen. But in poems like " Sailing to Byzantium " Yeats succeeds more fully in connecting his opposing worlds because he takes as symbols figures or cities that have long had the kind of meaning he attaches to them. It makes all the difference that he now chooses to sail to Byzantium rather than to Innisfree. He " leans out," as his father would say, to larger, more public kinds of significance and is able to say a great deal more to readers aware of their place in history.

The way in which Yeats's symbols extend his range can be seen most clearly in " Two Songs from a Play." Both are visions in pure song; in both speech rhythm almost disappears, though it still may be felt in the decorum and succinctness of the sentences:

The Roman Empire stood appalled:
It dropped the reins of peace and war

[1] See pp. 327–30, above.

When that fierce virgin and her Star
Out of the fabulous darkness called.

But what has happened to debate? Yeats is again balancing different views of Christianity and of Greco-Roman civilization, but he no longer presents his choices through distinct voices and rhythms. Debate has been compressed into symbols or allusions with double, sometimes opposite, kinds of significance. So the "virgin" is at once Athena and Mary. The peace of Augustus which marked Christ's birth is both a moment of high civilization and the moment of a fatal relaxation of control, a dropping of "the reins of peace and war." Double meanings grow out of the very center of the poem. Its key metaphor is one of alternation, of a cyclical movement pervading history and all human activity.

But Yeats's historic symbols are not only backward-looking. Like those of T. S. Eliot and James Joyce they express a surprising sense of the present *in* the past, and they make us think of our moment in history, of modern crises, while talking about the turning point between pagan and Christian, or Babylonian and Greek, civilizations. "The Second Coming" is a nightmare vision of this "simultaneous" type:

And what rough beast, its hour come round at last,
Slouches towards Bethlehem to be born?

Bethlehem is now Berlin or Moscow or Rome, any city where a new cult of violence may be revealed. By playing on "slouches" Yeats says that a revelation is at hand but that revelations are mixed blessings. Earlier in the poem, by one of his cyclical images ("gyring"), he makes us feel both that the modern world is moving toward a crisis and that it is falling apart. Yeats has finally managed to turn "dream" into prophetic "history."

The form that Yeats achieved in the 20's, through which he balanced speech and song, the personal symbol and the historic, action and contemplation, remained with him during the rest of his career. Similar or identical symbols — Byzantium and Troy, gyres and towers, caves and tremendous statues — recur quite often and express the now familiar conflicts. But by the 30's there is some change in tone and intensity, perhaps a reflection of "the smiling public man" who had become a Senator in the Free State, a Nobel prize winner, and something of a national sage. Yeats now honors his early political and literary associates in verse that has the fine detachment and public decorum of Pope or Dr. Johnson. His "tower" is no longer the retreat of "Il Penseroso,"[1] but the Anglo-Irish tradition, another country of the mind but one linked with actuality. "Vacillation," the poem that perhaps best sums up Yeats's career, is remarkable for the ripe good humor with which the poet puts behind him the old temptation to "find relief" in a life and art detached from ordinary humanity.

## IV. POETRY OF MADNESS (1929–39)

Tranquillity is hardly the keynote of the poems written during Yeats's fourth and last period. He appears in them as an old man, but as no sage, and even when descanting on the serenity that comes with his years, he surprises us: "Bodily decrepitude is wisdom."[2] The ugly facts are unblinkingly accepted; this old man, "mad as the mist and snow," has little in common with the prematurely aged singer of the 90's who found consolation in other-world fantasies. Conventional religious and sexual experiences are seen through completely, and yet the rhythm of the later songs is oddly cheerful, the singer is terribly and happily hard-boiled. This return to ballad-like rhythms recalls Yeats's early imitations of Irish popular verse only to bring out a difference: the consoling "yet's," the tear in the beer of music-hall song, have vanished.

But there is a close relation between the singer of *Last Poems* (1936–39) and the poet-philosopher of *The Tower* period. One of the best of the late lyrics, "An Acre of Grass," is a kind of noble parody of poems written ten years earlier. The progression is still the familiar one, from quiet speech to prayer, from images of here and now to symbols of a life eagerly desired, but instead of asking for a life "out of nature" or for harmonious development, this poet rudely calls for "an old man's frenzy." His ideal Presences are not Plato and Homer, but Lear and Michelangelo, mad old men who also found victory in "seeing through." A similarly exultant

[1] See ll. 85–96 of "Il Penseroso," p. 420 in Vol. I.
[2] See "After Long Silence," below.

note can be heard in "A Wild Old Wicked Man." There is the sexual heartiness of

> "Because I am mad about women
> I am mad about the hills,"

combined with bitter knowledge:

> "All men live in suffering,
> I know as few can know, . . ."

The first attitude apart from the second might be embarrassing, or at least of limited interest. Old age asserting youthful vigor is not a pleasant sight. But "a coarse old man" aware of his coarseness, who teaches his love that life is suffering, engages deeper and more complex feelings. Nevertheless, Yeats had his difficulties in managing the old men of his later poems, and, like his commentators, he often tries too hard to force the note of vitality and profundity in songs of "lust and rage." We find the richness that we miss in these songs in the symbolic meditative poems of the familiar historical and personal sort: "The Gyres," "The Statues," "The Circus Animals' Desertion," "A Bronze Head." Yeats still moves in his mysterious way around the memory of a woman or a statue or a city, and as he talks and sings he unfolds and weighs antithetical views of character or history. Resolution becomes no easier; the poems almost fall apart as Yeats opens up his mind to every pull and counterpull.

## HISTORY ON A LARGER SCALE: A POET WHO WOULD BE A PHILOSOPHER

Some critics argue that the unity of these and similar poems depends on the curious system that Yeats had evolved as a "philosopher." But we can usually grasp the meaning of Yeats's historic and cosmic symbols from the poems themselves, provided we have some familiarity with the interests in religion and history that he shared with his contemporaries. The poems are not necessarily more coherent because he had elsewhere worked out a diagram of man and the universe. But Yeats's theories — if that is the name for them — are worth looking at, since they supply some of the context in which he wrote and since they illustrate the difficulties of being a poet in the twentieth century.

Characteristics dominant in Yeats's poetry are also dominant in his thought: conflict and irresolution, combined with an intense desire to achieve reconciliation. Two themes keep recurring, the doctrines of the "anti-self" and of "Unity of Being." The dream of unity had started from his father's belief in "Personality," and Yeats's ultimate solution was to return to another attitude imparted by J. B. Y. But as usual his path was rebellious; he rejected the intellectual tradition to which his father, "a follower of John Stuart Mill," introduced him, just as he had clung to Pre-Raphaelite standards long after his father had abandoned them. Cut off from Catholic dogma by Protestant rationalism and scientific criticism, he had tried to create a cult from poetry and folklore and magic. But as the dream of finding a faith he could share with others faded, Yeats gradually evolved a private religion, and he finally produced his own Bible, *A Vision*. The search that came to this fantastic end grew out of a sensitivity to the disorder of the modern world and from a sane awareness that as a poet he needed some sort of "groundwork" on which to write. On these two counts, Yeats's thought is interesting even when absurd.

Characteristically, his beliefs were embodied in symbols. Unity of Being he saw represented by William Morris or by certain men of the Renaissance or by the characters of Chaucer, idealized figures in whom he found happy blends of art with effortlessness, intellect with physical vigor and grace, humanity with sensitivity to the supernatural. Individuals who attain Unity of Being arise most often in a society possessing a similar balance of values, in which all classes share inherited social traditions and religious beliefs. Unity of Being implies Unity of Culture. The enemy of Unity is "abstraction," the overdevelopment of one aspect of personality, or — in society — excessive specialization. The notion of the anti-self, expressed symbolically as "the Mask," is closely related to Unity, since men (and societies) achieve unity by modeling their lives after a self that is the opposite of their natural selves. Obscure as this doctrine is, it had practical importance as a private superstition by which Yeats's character was decisively shaped. He was always adopting some pose that he regarded as his opposite: he was the timid man who was trying to act boldly, the gregarious man who would be a lone thinker, the mystic longing to be a man of action. But he found it hard to decide which in fact *was* his natural self; mask and self kept interchanging.

These guiding ideas were becoming increasingly important to Yeats just when he was remaking himself as a poet between 1912 and 1916. In the years following his marriage in 1917 he translated his doctrines into a preposterous "system" that embraced history, the individual, and the universe, the full revelation being summed up in *A Vision*. The surprising experiences by which Yeats reached his goal include appearances of his personal "daemon" and communications with "voices" through his wife.

The key to the system lies in the anti-self, the tension of opposites, which is now symbolized by the "phases of the moon"[1] and the "gyre" or cycle. Types of personality are placed on a scale running from the dark of the moon (the purely objective type) to the full moon (the purely subjective type), with varying mixtures assigned to each of the twenty-eight phases. The figure is also used to classify stages in a cycle of history. For example, shortly after "the full moon" of our era (the last thousand years), in the mid-Renaissance, that happy moment occurred when unity of culture and being were attained, as seen in "the men of Shakespeare, of Titian, of Strozzi, and of Van Dyck." We are now in the twenty-third night, or later; our culture is going toward the dark of the moon that precedes a movement in the opposite direction. But the most vivid metaphor for this process in the individual and in history is the gyre, a cone-like spiral, a whirling movement that widens out as it goes. Like the phases of the moon, it represents movement from subjectivity (the point) to objectivity (the base), or vice versa. In history, progress in one direction is immediately followed by its opposite. So in the Greco-Roman cycle ending with Christ's birth, men and their culture became more and more "objective" until the single personality scarcely mattered. The coming of Christ initiated a movement of increasing emphasis on the self that reached its climax in the Renaissance.

What emerges from a look into this systematic fantasia? Certainly not a satisfactory religious belief or an adequate theory of historical change. What Yeats had done was to find in a symbolic account of history the dramatic and emotional satisfactions of religion. Here he resembles Henry Adams,[2] the American historian in whose thinking he found support for his own theories. Starting from a nightmarish vision of multiplicity in the modern world and a nostalgic admiration for the unity of the Middle Ages, Adams evolved a theory of history based on the law of acceleration in physics. Both Adams' and Yeats's views are built on physical analogies, both are ways of relating the individual modern mind to the past, and both satisfy the longing to make order out of lives disturbed by the loss of traditional beliefs. As a recent writer has observed, cyclical theories are typical of contemporary thought, just as belief in orderly progress along a line was common two generations back. In the growth of his sense of history as in his growth as a poet, Yeats made his way out of the nineteenth into the twentieth century.

While Yeats's theories are representative enough, their value is another matter. Adams' theory, which sounds equally surprising, is potentially useful because it takes into account modern science and industry, areas that Yeats happily ignored. But the exclusion is wonderfully representative, too: "I have always considered myself," Yeats writes, "a voice of what I believe to be a greater renaesance [*sic*] — the revolt of the soul against the intellect — now beginning in the world." In view of what has been happening in the last twenty years, his words now sound prophetic. If his theories were translated into practice, we might see a society notable for anti-intellectualism and the revival of folk cults, and ruled by supermen. We are not surprised to learn that Yeats at one time spoke well of Mussolini and that he gave some support to a group of Irish fascists.

But when we are reading his poetry, the absurdities and practical consequences of his system matter very little. In what sense Yeats "believed" in the statements of *A Vision* can never be determined; it seems unlikely that he regarded them as true in the sense in which the term is used of a scientific hypothesis. In the poems — with the few exceptions in which he is

[1] See "Wilson and Shaw: 'Phases of the Moon,'" in *The Autobiography*, below.

[2] See *The Education of Henry Adams* (1906) and *The Degradation of the Democratic Dogma* (1919). The second contains three essays on the philosophy of history, one of which, "The Rule of Phase Applied to History," Yeats had read. Among other historians to whom he was indebted are H. G. Wells, Arnold Toynbee, and Oswald Spengler.

versifying his theories — we are free to take his cosmic symbols much as we take the celestial geography of *Paradise Lost.* But undoubtedly Yeats's interest in his system encouraged his weakness for deliberate symbol-making in verse, and under the spell of *A Vision,* he too often wrote poems in which he tells us he has found a symbol, but the symbol does not work imaginatively. So in " Blood and the Moon " he declares " this tower is my symbol," and the reader dutifully reminds himself that a tower equals a gyre, equals a phase of history, equals eighteenth-century Ireland. But we feel nothing " tower-like " in the imagery and concepts of the poem, we feel no connection *through* the analogy. By contrast, we can clearly link various phases of the poem through images of growth and sterility. As always, the proof of the poem is not in the symbol; the proof of the symbol is in the poem. When Yeats's metaphors drawn from dreaming about history are renewed in the imagery of a poem with the effect of focusing its meanings and extending its range, they justify themselves. (For a fine example, see the metaphor of cyclical movement in " Two Songs from a Play.")

We need not conclude that in poetry any metaphor for man and his destiny, any sense of history will do. But that Yeats had a way of expressing a large historical vision makes him certainly a more satisfying writer. He is one of the poets who expresses for us our fullest and finest awareness of our time. But insofar as his vision remains private or mechanically " built into " his poems, his poetry must be ranked with verse of a cult, for initiates only. Certainly the range of his response to man and to history seems limited if we compare him with Chaucer or Milton or Shakespeare. He was too ill-educated to play such roles, and he lived at the wrong " phase of the moon." He was one of " the last Romantics," born in a country half-feudal, and, by family inheritance, like Henry Adams, a " child of the eighteenth century required to play the game of the twentieth." For a writer so born, to accept the new age and to produce works of art was hard indeed.

Yeats did not succeed in putting the modern world together, but he did put some poems together. They were, as Robert Frost says, his " stays against confusion." He attained the successes of his maturity, not by system-making, but by artistic tact, by evolving his way of dramatizing various beliefs and attitudes, by letting his dreamlike symbols materialize to express and connect conflicts he could never resolve outside his poetry. In the achieved unity of his poems — as distinct from his theories — he had come back to his father's views of how a poet " believes " and works. The belief " of the poet," his father wrote to him, " comes when the man within has found some method or manner of thinking or arrangement of fact (such as is only possible in dreams) by which to express and embody an absolute freedom. . . ." And in describing Blake, he gives an apt account of his son's best work: " Yet mysticism was never the substance of his poetry, only its machinery. . . . The substance of his poetry is himself, revolting and desiring." The substance of Yeats's poetry matters to us because he expresses with dramatic truth and musical delight dreams and renunciations to which we attach value in our own private and public worlds. To have experienced the voyage into a city of the mind's creating, where we are both alone and in the company of the great minds of the past, or to have felt both the waste and the heroic quality of political action based on abstract principles, to have entertained at once the tranquillity and the madness of age — these are among the better things that poetry can do for us.

The poems of Yeats are reprinted from *The Collected Poems of W. B. Yeats,* The Macmillan Company (New York, 1950). The dates printed below the poems at the *left* are those provided by Yeats himself as a part of the text in the *Collected Poems.* Some, if not all, of these dates are almost certainly *not* the dates of composition. Therefore, dates of composition, when they can be determined, have been printed below the poems at the *right.* These dates are based on information supplied by Yeats's biographers (Ellmann, Hone, Jeffares). Where a date has seemed no more than probable, an interrogation point follows the figure. All dating of Yeats's poems should be regarded as provisional until his letters and other unpublished material have been edited and published.

The selections from *The Autobiography of William Butler Yeats* are from the edition published by The Macmillan Company, New York, in 1938. All page references are to this edition. The *Autobiography* consists of the following sections: *Reveries over Childhood and Youth* (1914), *The Trembling of the Veil* (1922), *Dramatis Personae, 1896–1902* (1935), *Estrangement* (1926), *The Death of Synge* (1926), and *The Bounty of Sweden* (1925).

The selections from the *Essays* are from the edition published by The Macmillan Company, New York, in 1924. *Essays* consists of the following items: *Ideas of Good and Evil* (1896–1903), *The Cutting of an Agate* (1903–15), and *Per Amica Silentia Lunae* (1916–17).

## Reading Suggestions

BY YEATS AND HIS FATHER

The first two books are the most important for understanding Yeats's personality and his aims as a writer:

W. B. Yeats, *Essays* (1924).

*The Autobiography of William Butler Yeats* (1938). (See selections and notes in the present text.)

Joseph Hone, editor, *J. B. Yeats: Letters to His Son W. B. Yeats and Others, 1869–1922* (1944). The letters of J. B. Yeats are filled with fine observations on life and art, many of which had a decisive effect on his son's thinking.

BIOGRAPHIES AND LITERARY HISTORY

Edmund Wilson, *Axel's Castle* (1931). An account of Yeats (and other modern writers) in relation to the Symbolist movement.

William Gaunt, *The Pre-Raphaelite Tragedy* (1942). A history of the extraordinary persons who were leaders in the Pre-Raphaelite movement, by which Yeats was much influenced in his early career.

Joseph Hone, *W. B. Yeats, 1865–1939* (1943). A humane and often amusing biography addressed to the general reader. Hone combines an account of Yeats's poetic development with a picture of the many literary and political figures with whom he was associated.

A. Norman Jeffares, *W. B. Yeats, Man and Poet* (1949). Jeffares gives much attention to the private literary history of Yeats's work. The book is especially remarkable for the many quotations from unpublished writings of the poet.

CRITICISM

Louis MacNeice, *The Poetry of W. B. Yeats* (1941). A more casual introduction to the man and his work, with some emphasis on the ideas expressed in the poems and on the intellectual environment in which they were composed.

Richard Ellman, *Yeats, The Man and the Masks* (1948). The most complete study of the evolution of Yeats's thought and character in relation to his work as a poet and dramatist.

James Hall and Martin Steinmann, editors, *The Permanence of Yeats: Selected Criticism* (1950). This is the most convenient single book for a student who wishes to see how leading American and British critics have evaluated Yeats's poetry. Most of the essays are from books that are also worth consulting. A "select bibliography" is included.

---

## THE LAKE ISLE OF INNISFREE

This poem first appeared in the *National Observer,* December 13, 1890, and was reprinted in *The Countess Kathleen and Various Legends and Lyrics* (1892). See Introduction.

I will arise and go now, and go to Innisfree,
And a small cabin build there, of clay and wattles made:
Nine bean-rows will I have there, a hive for the honeybee,
And live alone in the bee-loud glade.

And I shall have some peace there, for peace comes dropping slow,
Dropping from the veils of the morning to where the cricket sings;
There midnight's all a glimmer, and noon a purple glow,
And evening full of the linnet's wings.

I will arise and go now, for always night and day
I hear lake water lapping with low sounds by the shore;
While I stand on the roadway, or on the pavements grey,
I hear it in the deep heart's core.

*1890?*

## WHO GOES WITH FERGUS?

Who will go drive with Fergus now,
And pierce the deep wood's woven shade,
And dance upon the level shore?

THE LAKE ISLE OF INNISFREE. **1. Innisfree:** "My father had read to me some passage out of *Walden*, and I planned to live some day in a cottage on a little island called Innisfree . . ." (*Autobiography*, p. 64).

**10. I . . . lapping:** Cf. "'I heard the water lapping on the crag, / And the long ripple washing in the reeds'" (Tennyson, *Morte d'Arthur*, ll. 116–17). WHO GOES WITH FERGUS? **1. Fergus:** legendary king of Ulster, who gave up his throne to Conchobar and later went into exile. Cf. "I feast amid my people on the hill, / And pace the woods, and drive my chariot-wheels / In the white border of the murmuring sea; / And still I feel the

Young man, lift up your russet brow,
And lift your tender eyelids, maid,
And brood on hopes and fear no more.

And no more turn aside and brood
Upon love's bitter mystery;
For Fergus rules the brazen cars,
And rules the shadows of the wood,
And the white breast of the dim sea
And all dishevelled wandering stars.

## THE FOLLY OF BEING COMFORTED

This poem was included in the volume *In the Seven Woods* (1903). The text printed here is that of *Later Poems,* by W. B. Yeats, The Macmillan Company, New York (1924).

One that is ever kind said yesterday:
" Your well-belovéd's hair has threads of grey,
And little shadows come about her eyes;
Time can but make it easier to be wise
Though now it seem impossible, and so
Patience is all that you have need of."
No,
I have not a crumb of comfort, not a grain,
Time can but make her beauty over again:
Because of that great nobleness of hers
The fire that stirs about her, when she stirs
Burns but more clearly. O she had not these ways,
When all the wild summer was in her gaze.
O heart! O heart! if she'd but turn her head,
You'd know the folly of being comforted.

## NO SECOND TROY

The opening lines refer to Maud Gonne and her revolutionary activities. See Introduction, p. 782, and "Maud Gonne" in *The Autobiography,* below. The heroic figure of the poem is not the actual woman, but a "second" Helen of Troy. The Troy symbols recur in many of Yeats's poems and often express similar parallels and contrasts between different civilizations. See "Two Songs from a Play," "Leda and the Swan," and "Among School Children," below. In this poem the contrast serves both to ennoble and to satirize Ireland and Irish politics. Compare the idiom and rhythm with those of poems immediately preceding and following. "No Second Troy" was first printed in *The Green Helmet and Other Poems* (1910).

crown upon my head" ("Fergus and the Druid," *Collected Poems,* pp. 32–33, ll. 17–20). FOLLY. **13. turn . . . head:** Consider possible interpretations of what the lover sees, and compare the similar balancing of attitudes in "No Second Troy," "Men Improve with the Years," and "After Long Silence," below.

Why should I blame her that she filled my days
With misery, or that she would of late
Have taught to ignorant men most violent ways,
Or hurled the little streets upon the great,
Had they but courage equal to desire?
What could have made her peaceful with a mind
That nobleness made simple as a fire,
With beauty like a tightened bow, a kind
That is not natural in an age like this,
Being high and solitary and most stern?
Why, what could she have done, being what she is?
Was there another Troy for her to burn?

*1908?*

## TO A FRIEND WHOSE WORK HAS COME TO NOTHING

"Lady Gregory in her *Life of Sir Hugh Lane* assumes that the poem which begins 'Now all the truth is out,' was addressed to him. It was not; it was addressed to herself. — 1922" [Yeats's note]. The Corporation of Dublin had refused to provide a building for a collection of French pictures offered to the city by Sir Hugh Lane. This poem and the two that follow were included in *Responsibilities* (1914).

Now all the truth is out,
Be secret and take defeat
From any brazen throat,
For how can you compete,
Being honour bred, with one
Who, were it proved he lies,
Were neither shamed in his own
Nor in his neighbours' eyes?
Bred to a harder thing
Than Triumph, turn away
And like a laughing string
Whereon mad fingers play
Amid a place of stone,
Be secret and exult,
Because of all things known
That is most difficult.

*1913*

## THE MAGI

For an interpretation of this poem, see Introduction, p. 780, and the headnote to "The Dolls," below.

Now as at all times I can see in the mind's eye,
In their stiff, painted clothes, the pale unsatisfied ones
Appear and disappear in the blue depth of the sky

With all their ancient faces like rain-beaten stones,
And all their helms of silver hovering side by side,
And all their eyes still fixed, hoping to find once more,
Being by Calvary's turbulence unsatisfied,
The uncontrollable mystery on the bestial floor.

*1913?*

## THE DOLLS

"The fable for this poem came into my head while I was giving some lectures in Dublin. I had noticed once again how all thought among us is frozen into 'something other than human life.' After I had made the poem, I looked up one day into the blue of the sky, and suddenly imagined, as if lost in the blue of the sky, stiff figures in procession. I remembered that they were the habitual image suggested by blue sky, and looking for a second fable called them 'The Magi,' complementary forms of those enraged dolls. — 1914" [Y]. Compare this with: "Today a grotesque twopenny doll was lying on the floor near the old woman. He [the old man] picked it up and examined it as if comparing it with her. Then he held it up: 'Is it you is after bringing that thing into the world,' he said, 'woman of the house?'" (John Synge, *The Aran Islands,* p. 42)

A doll in the doll-maker's house
Looks at the cradle and bawls:
"That is an insult to us."
But the oldest of all the dolls,
Who had seen, being kept for show,
Generations of his sort,
Out-screams the whole shelf: "Although
There's not a man can report
Evil of this place,
The man and the woman bring
Hither, to our disgrace,
A noisy and filthy thing."
Hearing him groan and stretch
The doll-maker's wife is aware
Her husband has heard the wretch,
And crouched by the arm of his chair,
She murmurs into his ear,
Head upon shoulder leant:
"My dear, my dear, O dear,
It was an accident."

*1912*

THE MAGI. **7. Calvary's turbulence:** Cf. "Galilean turbulence," in "Two Songs from a Play," l. 19n. Cf. also "The Second Coming," below.

## THE WILD SWANS AT COOLE

Notice how the metaphorical significance of the "swans" grows quite naturally out of the setting and the narrative facts of the poem. Compare the "swan" symbols in "The Tower," III, lines 19–24, and in "Leda and the Swan," below. "The Wild Swans" is a clear and harmonious piece of expression quite apart from any reference to particular places and persons. For a different type of biographical poem, see "Coole Park, 1929," below, which explains the importance of Coole to Yeats and his friends. "The Wild Swans at Coole" is the title poem of a volume published in 1917 (the Cuala Press edition), which also included the next three poems printed here.

The trees are in their autumn beauty,
The woodland paths are dry,
Under the October twilight the water
Mirrors a still sky;
Upon the brimming water among the stones
Are nine-and-fifty swans.

The nineteenth autumn has come upon me
Since I first made my count;
I saw, before I had well finished,
All suddenly mount
And scatter wheeling in great broken rings
Upon their clamourous wings.

I have looked upon those brilliant creatures,
And now my heart is sore.
All's changed since I, hearing at twilight,
The first time on this shore,
The bell-beat of their wings above my head,
Trod with a lighter tread.

Unwearied still, lover by lover,
They paddle in the cold
Companionable streams or climb the air;
Their hearts have not grown old;
Passion or conquest, wander where they will,
Attend upon them still.

But now they drift on the still water,
Mysterious, beautiful;
Among what rushes will they build,
By what lake's edge or pool
Delight men's eyes when I awake some day
To find they have flown away?

*1916*

THE WILD SWANS. **7. nineteenth autumn:** 1916, the nineteenth year since Yeats first came to stay with Lady Gregory at Coole Park. **14. my . . . sore:** There is an oblique allusion in this and the next stanza to Yeats's continuing love for Maud Gonne, who had recently again refused to marry him.

## MEN IMPROVE WITH THE YEARS

This lyric is focused on the symbolic image of the triton. Observe the many and varied connections between the image and other details of the poem, and how this interrelationship alters and enriches the meaning of the closing lines.

I am worn out with dreams;
A weather-worn, marble triton
Among the streams;
And all day long I look
Upon this lady's beauty
As though I had found in a book
A pictured beauty,
Pleased to have filled the eyes
Or the discerning ears,
Delighted to be but wise,
For men improve with the years;
And yet, and yet,
Is this my dream, or the truth?
O would that we had met
When I had my burning youth!
But I grow old among dreams,
A weather-worn, marble triton
Among the streams.

*1916*

## LINES WRITTEN IN DEJECTION

Note the way in which Yeats now combines his earlier hypnotic rhythms with the movement of plain speech. Compare this poem with "Men Improve with the Years," above, and "Sailing to Byzantium," below.

When have I last looked on
The round green eyes and the long wavering bodies
Of the dark leopards of the moon?
All the wild witches, those most noble ladies,
For all their broom-sticks and their tears,
Their angry tears, are gone.
The holy centaurs of the hills are vanished;
I have nothing but the embittered sun;
Banished heroic mother moon and vanished,
And now that I have come to fifty years
I must endure the timid sun.

*1915?*

## THE FISHERMAN

Here Yeats announces most clearly his intention of creating a new audience and a new kind of poetry. See Introduction, p. 785. The central image is a familiar one in Yeats: ". . . in boyhood when with rod and fly, / Or the humbler worm, I climbed Ben Bulben's back. . . ." ("The Tower," I, ll. 8–9, *Collected Poems,* p. 192); "And I call to the mind's eye / . . . A man climbing up to a place / The salt sea wind has swept bare" ("At the Hawk's Well," ll. 4, 7–8, *Collected Plays,* p. 208). The "man" is the hero Cuchulain. The scorn expressed in this poem and the occasional baldness of idiom and rhythm recall Swift. For further connections between "fishermen," Swift, and the Anglo-Irish tradition, see "The Tower," III, l. 2n., and notes to "Blood and the Moon," I, II, below.

Although I can see him still,
The freckled man who goes
To a grey place on a hill
In grey Connemara clothes
At dawn to cast his flies,
It's long since I began
To call up to the eyes
This wise and simple man.
All day I'd looked in the face
What I had hoped 'twould be
To write for my own race
And the reality;
The living men that I hate,
The dead man that I loved,
The craven man in his seat,

MEN IMPROVE. **11. improve:** The word takes on a different sense when it is related both to the lines that follow and to the "marble triton." The blend of opposing attitudes is characteristic. Cf. "The Folly of Being Comforted," above, and "After Long Silence," below. LINES WRITTEN IN DEJECTION. **7. centaurs:** creatures of Greek myth, half man and half horse. The most famous of the centaurs, Chiron, was a gifted musician and the teacher of Achilles, Herakles, Jason, and other heroes; hence the centaur makes an appropriate symbol for a young poet's dreams of an heroic world. But the myth had for Yeats other meanings of a more private sort: "I thought that all art should be a Centaur finding in the popular lore its back and its strong legs" ("A World of Fragments," *Autobiography*, below). Thus the poem also expresses Yeats's regret for the decline of folklore and folk poetry. **9. heroic . . . moon:** ". . . the simple unmysterious things living as in a clear moonlight are of the nature of the sun, and the vague, many-imaged things have in them the strength of the moon. Did not the Egyptian carve it on emerald that all living things have the sun for father and the moon for mother, and has it not been said that a man of genius takes the most after his mother?" ("Emotion of Multitude," *Essays*, p. 267) "Heroic" also suggests the moon as Artemis the fierce huntress; "mother," Artemis in her Asiatic form as the mother goddess. This image, like others in the poem, carries connotations of folk culture, primitive religious power, and heroic nobility. THE FISHERMAN. **4. Connemara:** a mountainous region in County Galway, for Yeats an ideal Ireland where heroic manners and the ancient art of the folk song still survived. Hence the fisherman makes an appropriate symbol for the audience Yeats would like to address. **12. the reality:** This and the following lines contain more or less specific allusions to Yeats's experiences in Irish literary circles, particularly in the theater. See Intro., p. 782. **14. The . . . man:** John Synge. Cf. "Coole Park, 1929," ll. 12–13, below, and "The Tragic Generation," *Autobiography*, below.

The insolent unreproved,
And no knave brought to book
Who has won a drunken cheer,
The witty man and his joke
Aimed at the commonest ear,
The clever man who cries
The catch-cries of the clown,
The beating down of the wise
And great Art beaten down.

Maybe a twelvemonth since
Suddenly I began,
In scorn of this audience,
Imagining a man,
And his sun-freckled face,
And grey Connemara cloth,
Climbing up to a place
Where stone is dark under froth,
And the down-turn of his wrist
When the flies drop in the stream;
A man who does not exist,
A man who is but a dream;
And cried, "Before I am old
I shall have written him one
Poem maybe as cold
And passionate as the dawn."

*1914*

## EASTER 1916

The occasion of this poem was an insurrection of extreme Irish nationalists that took place on Easter Monday, 1916. The Easter Rising, as it was called, was repressed by the English; fifteen of the leaders, including the four men named in the poem, were executed. Yeats, who had in general a dislike for revolutions, had originally not approved of the Rising, and his poem shows a far from simple attitude toward all followers of a patriotic "cause" (ll. 57–69). "Easter 1916" must not be read as a record of historical events or of Yeats's political opinions; it expresses a surprising imaginative transformation of fact. See Introduction, p. 785. First published in 1916, the poem was reprinted in *Michael Robartes and the Dancer* (1921), a volume that included "The Second Coming."

I have met them at close of day
Coming with vivid faces
From counter or desk among grey
Eighteenth-century houses.
I have passed with a nod of the head
Or polite meaningless words,
Or have lingered awhile and said
Polite meaningless words,
And thought before I had done
Of a mocking tale or a gibe
To please a companion
Around the fire at the club,
Being certain that they and I
But lived where motley is worn:
All changed, changed utterly:
A terrible beauty is born.

That woman's days were spent
In ignorant good-will,
Her nights in argument
Until her voice grew shrill.
What voice more sweet than hers
When, young and beautiful,
She rode to harriers?
This man had kept a school
And rode our wingèd horse;
This other his helper and friend
Was coming into his force;
He might have won fame in the end,
So sensitive his nature seemed,
So daring and sweet his thought.
This other man I had dreamed
A drunken, vainglorious lout.
He had done most bitter wrong
To some who are near my heart,
Yet I number him in the song;
He, too, has resigned his part
In the casual comedy;
He, too, has been changed in his turn,
Transformed utterly:
A terrible beauty is born.

Hearts with one purpose alone
Through summer and winter seem
Enchanted to a stone
To trouble the living stream.
The horse that comes from the road,
The rider, the birds that range
From cloud to tumbling cloud,
Minute by minute they change;
A shadow of cloud on the stream
Changes minute by minute;
A horse-hoof slides on the brim,
And a horse plashes within it;
The long-legged moor-hens dive,
And hens to moor-cocks call;
Minute by minute they live:
The stone's in the midst of all.

EASTER 1916. **17. That woman:** Countess Markiewicz (before her marriage, Constance Gore-Booth) took an active part in the Easter Rising and was sentenced to life imprisonment. In her youth she was famous for her beauty and ability as a rider (ll. 22–23). See "Eva Gore-Booth and Con Markiewicz," below. Cf. "A Political Prisoner," *Collected Poems*, pp. 181–82. **24. This man:** Patrick Pearse, leader in the Gaelic language movement, founder of a bilingual school, and a poet, commanded the forces of the rebels. **26. This other:** Thomas MacDonagh, a writer whose work Yeats had read and admired. **31. This . . . man:** Major John MacBride, the husband of Maud Gonne.

Too long a sacrifice
Can make a stone of the heart.
O when may it suffice?
That is Heaven's part, our part
To murmur name upon name,
As a mother names her child
When sleep at last has come
On limbs that had run wild.
What is it but nightfall?
No, no, not night but death;
Was it needless death after all?
For England may keep faith
For all that is done and said.
We know their dream; enough
To know they dreamed and are dead;
And what if excess of love
Bewildered them till they died?
I write it out in a verse —
MacDonagh and MacBride
And Connolly and Pearse
Now and in time to be,
Wherever green is worn,
Are changed, changed utterly:
A terrible beauty is born.

*September 25, 1916*

## THE SECOND COMING

The best introduction to the poem is Yeats's own comment, "A World of Fragments," in the *Autobiography,* below. This twentieth-century vision of a "second coming" recalls the familiar Christian prophecy, but as elsewhere in Yeats Christ's birth has a double significance. The Nativity marked the beginning of Christian civilization, but also brought to an end the Greco-Roman cycle (*gyre*) that had lasted for "twenty centuries." According to this view, Christ's coming entailed a revival of the bloody violence of primitive religion, a revival expressed in the poem as an awakening of a sphinx-like creature (ll. 13–16). See "Two Songs from a Play," below; "The Magi," above; "The Tragic Generation," in the *Autobiography,* below; and Introduction, p. 786.

Turning and turning in the widening gyre
The falcon cannot hear the falconer;
Things fall apart; the center cannot hold;
Mere anarchy is loosed upon the world,
The blood-dimmed tide is loosed, and everywhere
The ceremony of innocence is drowned;
The best lack all conviction, while the worst
Are full of passionate intensity.

Surely some revelation is at hand;
Surely the Second Coming is at hand.
The Second Coming! Hardly are those words out
When a vast image out of *Spiritus Mundi*
Troubles my sight: somewhere in sands of the
desert
A shape with lion body and the head of a man,
A gaze blank and pitiless as the sun,
Is moving its slow thighs, while all about it
Reel shadows of the indignant desert birds.
The darkness drops again; but now I know
That twenty centuries of stony sleep
Were vexed to nightmare by a rocking cradle,
And what rough beast, its hour come round at last,
Slouches towards Bethlehem to be born?

*1919*

## SAILING TO BYZANTIUM

"Sailing to Byzantium" is the first poem in *The Tower* (1928), the volume that marks the culminating point in the development of Yeats's later style. The next four poems also appeared in the same volume. For further interpretation, see Introduction, p. 785.

I

That is no country for old men. The young
In one another's arms, birds in the trees
— Those dying generations — at their song,
The salmon-falls, the mackerel-crowded seas
Fish, flesh, or fowl, commend all summer long
Whatever is begotten, born, and dies.
Caught in that sensual music all neglect
Monuments of unageing intellect.

**76. Connolly:** James Connolly was Pearse's partner in leading the insurrection. In the late 90's Yeats and Maud Gonne had joined him in various anti-English demonstrations. THE SECOND COMING. **1. gyre:** refers to the phase of history now moving towards completion. **4–8. anarchy . . . intensity:** with allusion to revolutionary or reactionary mass movements, such as the Russian Revolution (note the date of poem) and fascism.

**6. ceremony of innocence:** The connotations are Christian and aristocratic, "ceremony" suggesting both religious ritual and civilized behavior. **12. *Spiritus Mundi:*** or *Anima Mundi,* in the belief of Yeats and of many mystics, the Spirit or Soul of the universe, with which all individual souls are connected; it is also the Great Memory, which is the repository of all individual memories from the past. Yeats sometimes refers to the *Anima Mundi* as "the subconscious": ". . . the general mind where that mind is scarcely separable from what we have begun to call 'the subconscious' . . ." ("Anima Mundi," *Essays,* p. 507). It is accordingly the source from which the poet may draw images or symbols. SAILING TO BYZANTIUM. **1. That . . . country:** Though the imagery of the stanza (*salmon-falls, mackerel-crowded seas*) suggests Ireland, the "country" of the poem is not to be located on a map. Similarly, though "Byzantium" refers to the capital of the Eastern Roman Empire and to "the holy city" of Greek Orthodox Christianity, the city of the poem is the ideal life of the soul expressed in sts. 2–4. The historic city was an apt symbol for Yeats's purpose, since it was famous for its holiness, for the somewhat rarefied and extremely subtle character of its intellectual life, and for its exquisite art.

2

An aged man is but a paltry thing,
A tattered coat upon a stick, unless
Soul clap its hands and sing, and louder sing
For every tatter in its mortal dress,
Nor is there singing school but studying
Monuments of its own magnificence;
And therefore I have sailed the seas and come
To the holy city of Byzantium.

3

O sages standing in God's holy fire
As in the gold mosaic of a wall,
Come from the holy fire, perne in a gyre,
And be the singing-masters of my soul.
Consume my heart away; sick with desire
And fastened to a dying animal
It knows not what it is; and gather me
Into the artifice of eternity.

4

Once out of nature I shall never take
My bodily form from any natural thing,
But such a form as Grecian goldsmiths make
Of hammered gold and gold enamelling
To keep a drowsy Emperor awake;
Or set upon a golden bough to sing
To lords and ladies of Byzantium
Of what is past, or passing, or to come.

*1927* *1926*

**17–18. sages . . . wall:** an allusion to the figures in mosaic on the walls of the Church of Hagia Sophia (meaning "Holy Wisdom"), the greatest of Byzantine architectural monuments. Byzantine art tended to be geometric and abstract; the human figure was rendered in a style far from naturalistic. **19. come . . . gyre:** He begs the sage-saints to come down from the golden, fiery nimbus that surrounds them, and he sees them descend with a whirling (spool-like), spiral motion. **perne:** "When I was a child at Sligo I could see above my grandfather's trees a little column of smoke from 'the pern mill,' and was told that 'pern' was another name for the spool . . . on which the thread was wound" [Yeats's note to "Shepherd and Goatherd"]. **27. Grecian goldsmiths:** "I have read somewhere that in the Emperor's palace at Byzantium was a tree made of gold and silver, and artificial birds that sang" [Y].

## THE TOWER

"The Tower," III, is the last poem of a sequence on themes similar to those of "Sailing to Byzantium," with which it should be carefully compared. The title refers to Thoor Ballylee, part of an ancient castle that Yeats had rebuilt as a country home, where he had lived off and on since 1919; but the more important meanings of "the tower" are symbolic. In "The Tower," II, it is associated with Ireland's heroic past and with memories of local tales that Yeats had retold in the *Celtic Twilight* and similar collections; more generally, like Byzantium, it stands for the aging poet-philosopher's ideal way of life: "It seems that I must bid the Muse go pack, / Choose Plato and Plotinus for a friend / Until imagination, ear and eye, / Can be content with argument and deal / In abstract things; . . ." ("The Tower," I, ll. 11–15, *Collected Poems,* p. 192). Compare with "Blood and the Moon," below. See also "Yeats's Anti-Self," in the *Autobiography,* below.

III

It is time that I wrote my will;
I choose upstanding men
That climb the streams until
The fountain leap, and at dawn
Drop their cast at the side
Of dripping stone; I declare
They shall inherit my pride,
The pride of people that were
Bound neither to Cause nor to State,
Neither to slaves that were spat on,
Nor to the tyrants that spat,
The people of Burke and of Grattan
That gave, though free to refuse —
Pride, like that of the morn,
When the headlong light is loose,
Or that of the fabulous horn,
Or that of the sudden shower
When all streams are dry,
Or that of the hour
When the swan must fix his eye
Upon a fading gleam,
Float out upon a long
Last reach of glittering stream
And there sing his last song.
And I declare my faith:
I mock Plotinus' thought
And cry in Plato's teeth,
Death and life were not
Till man made up the whole,
Made lock, stock and barrel
Out of his bitter soul,

THE TOWER. **2. upstanding men:** Cf. "The Fisherman," above. Here the "fishermen" are regarded as inheritors of the Anglo-Irish tradition that Yeats admired increasingly in later years. See notes to "Blood and the Moon," below. **9. Cause:** referring to a religious "cause" or a political program. **12. Burke:** Edmund Burke (1729–97), British statesman, born in Dublin, who favored reconciliation with the American colonies (1775); later, a severe critic of the French Revolution. **Grattan:** Henry Grattan (1746–1820), a statesman who worked for an independent Irish parliament and for Catholic emancipation. To Yeats, he represents like Burke a moderate, aristocratic type of reformer, whose actions were "bound" neither by the Irish mob nor by the English "tyrants." **20–24. swan . . . song:** an echo of "The Dying Swan," a poem by Yeats's friend, Sturge Moore. **26–32. I . . . all:** With a characteristic reversal of feeling, Yeats rejects the philosophers whom he had earlier chosen as his instructors ("The Tower," I.12). In a note to the poem dated 1928, he confessed that he had been mistaken about Plato's and Plotinus' thought and observed that the latter had written of the soul's power to create "all living things." (Plato also expressed similar beliefs; cf. *Laws,* X.896A.)

Aye, sun and moon and star, all.
And further add to that
That, being dead, we rise,
Dream and so create
Translunar Paradise.
I have prepared my peace
With learned Italian things
And the proud stones of Greece,
Poet's imaginings
And memories of love,
Memories of the words of women,
All those things whereof
Man makes a superhuman
Mirror-resembling dream.

As at the loophole there
The daws chatter and scream,
And drop twigs layer upon layer.
When they have mounted up,
The mother bird will rest
On their hollow top,
And so warm her wild nest.

I leave both faith and pride
To young upstanding men
Climbing the mountain-side,
That under bursting dawn
They may drop a fly;
Being of that metal made
Till it was broken by
This sedentary trade.

Now shall I make my soul,
Compelling it to study
In a learned school
Till the wreck of body,
Slow decay of blood,
Testy delirium
Or dull decrepitude,
Or what worse evil come —
The death of friends, or death
Of every brilliant eye
That made a catch in the breath —
Seem but the clouds of the sky
When the horizon fades;
Or a bird's sleepy cry
Among the deepening shades.

*1926* *1925*

**36. Translunar Paradise:** Cf. "the artifice of eternity" ("Sailing to Byzantium," l. 24, above), a phrase also implying that the poet-philosopher creates his own "heaven." **45. Mirror-resembling:** producing like a mirror a reflection of the world, but a reflection in which actuality is enlarged and idealized (*a superhuman . . . dream*). **46–52: As . . . nest:** a comparison to the ways in which the speaker has "prepared his peace." **58–60. Being . . . trade:** By becoming a poet he has lost the heroic quality of "the fisherman" (ll. 2–6). **61–63. Now . . . school:** Cf. "the singing school" ("Sailing to Byzantium," l. 13, above). **67. dull decrepitude:** Cf. "Bodily decrepitude is wisdom" ("After Long Silence," l. 7, below).

## TWO SONGS FROM A PLAY

The songs were written for Yeats's play, *The Resurrection* (1927). Both songs assume a cyclical view of history, which is expressed by the symbol of the Magnus Annus (the Great Year) of the ancients, an astronomical cycle of 2000 years or more, at the end of which the heavenly bodies reach the same positions in which they stood when first set in motion. The Magnus Annus is alluded to in Virgil's fourth *Eclogue,* a poem regarded in the Middle Ages as prophesying the birth of Christ, and which Yeats probably had in mind when writing his "Songs." In *A Vision* he gives a free translation of the opening lines of the fourth *Eclogue:* "'. . . the latest age of the Cumaean song is at hand; the cycles in their vast array begin anew; Virgin Astraea comes, the reign of Saturn comes, and from the heights of Heaven a new generation of mankind descends'" (*A Vision* [1938], pp. 243–44). On the "Songs" and on Yeats's view of history, see Introduction, pp. 785 and 788.

### I

I saw a staring virgin stand
Where holy Dionysus died,
And tear the heart out of his side,
And lay the heart upon her hand
And bear that beating heart away;
And then did all the Muses sing
Of Magnus Annus at the spring,
As though God's death were but a play.

Another Troy must rise and set,
Another lineage feed the crow,
Another Argo's painted prow
Drive to a flashier bauble yet.
The Roman Empire stood appalled:
It dropped the reins of peace and war
When that fierce virgin and her Star
Out of the fabulous darkness called.

TWO SONGS. **2. Dionysus:** the god of wine, with whose cult Greek drama was closely associated. **3–5. tear . . . away:** Athena, the virgin goddess, brought the heart of the dead Dionysus to Zeus. **6–8. Muses . . . play:** Greek tragedies, depicting the death of heroes or demigods, were performed (*sung*) at spring festivals in honor of Dionysus. There is also an allusion to Easter. "Staring virgin" (l. 1) therefore may refer to both Athena and the Virgin Mary. **9. Another Troy:** Rome. Cf. Virgil, *Eclogues*, IV.34–36: "When a second Tiphys will arise, and a second Argo to carry chosen heroes; there will also be a second war, and once again a great Achilles will be sent to Troy." Cf. also "The world's great age begins anew, / The golden years return, / . . . A loftier Argo cleaves the main, / Fraught with a later prize . . ." (Shelley, Chorus from *Hellas*, ll. 1060–61, 1072–73). **13–14. Roman . . . war:** the peaceful reign of the emperor Augustus, 27 B.C.–14 A.D. **16. fabulous darkness:** Cf. "Babylonian starlight" (l. 20); see also headnote to "Leda and the Swan," below. Both phrases suggest the strange cults, such as Mithraism, that came to Rome from the East.

II

In pity for man's darkening thought
He walked that room and issued thence
In Galilean turbulence;
The Babylonian starlight brought
A fabulous, formless darkness in;
Odour of blood when Christ was slain
Made all Platonic tolerance vain
And vain all Doric discipline.

Everything that man esteems
Endures a moment or a day.
Love's pleasure drives his love away,
The painter's brush consumes his dreams;
The herald's cry, the soldier's tread
Exhaust his glory and his might:
Whatever flames upon the night
Man's own resinous heart has fed.

## LEDA AND THE SWAN

According to the Greek myth, Leda was loved by Zeus in the form of a swan and so became the mother of Helen, wife of Menelaus, and of Clytemnestra, wife of Agamemnon. When Helen was carried off to Troy by Paris, Agamemnon led an expedition of the Greeks against the Trojans in order to bring her back. After winning the war and destroying the city, he returned home and was murdered by Clytemnestra. The last two lines of Yeats's sonnet reveal most clearly what is expressed through his version of the myth, although the opposition between "knowledge" and "power" is only one of many suggested by the poem's imagery. If read in connection with "Two Songs from a Play" and "The Second Coming," "Leda and the Swan" pictures an earlier "Annunciation," a parallel to the event that ushered in the cycle of Christian civilization: ". . . when in my ignorance I try to imagine what older civilization that annunciation rejected, I can but see bird and woman blotting out some corner of the Babylonian mathematical starlight" (*A Vision,* Book V, "Dove or Swan," III, p. 268). See Introduction, p. 788.

A sudden blow: the great wings beating still
Above the staggering girl, her thighs caressed
By the dark webs, her nape caught in his bill,
He holds her helpless breast upon his breast.

How can those terrified vague fingers push
The feathered glory from her loosening thighs?
And how can body, laid in that white rush,
But feel the strange heart beating where it lies?

A shudder in the loins engenders there
The broken wall, the burning roof and tower
And Agamemnon dead.
Being so caught up,
So mastered by the brute blood of the air,
Did she put on his knowledge with his power
Before the indifferent beak could let her drop?

*1923*

**19. Galilean turbulence:** By being born and by entering the world, Christ submitted to the violence of Calvary and brought not only the light of a new belief but the darkness of superstition and intolerance. The poem expresses the view that Christianity, like other Eastern cults, helped destroy the civilized order of the Greco-Roman world. **24. Doric:** Spartan. **32. resinous:** an allusion to the pine torches brandished by the women who worshiped Dionysus in nighttime rites. **heart:** The heart, as the Dionysiac element in man, is the source of both creation and destruction. The metaphors of the fourth stanza are expressive of the paradox that all achievement is self-destructive. They thus symbolize a cyclical movement similar to that of history. For an enlightening comment on this stanza, see "The Tragic Generation," *Autobiography,* below, especially the four last sentences.

## AMONG SCHOOL CHILDREN

The poem moves through the preparatory reflections and images of the earlier stanzas to the affirmations of the closing lines: "Labour is blossoming or dancing. . . ." The ideal of "labour" in which works of "beauty" or "wisdom" are created by harmonious activity of the whole man is central in Yeats's poetry and thought. See "Unity of Being" in the *Autobiography,* below, and Introduction, p. 787. On the whole poem, see Introduction, p. 785.

I

I walk through the long schoolroom questioning;
A kind old nun in a white hood replies;
The children learn to cipher and to sing,
To study reading-books and histories,
To cut and sew, be neat in everything
In the best modern way — the children's eyes
In momentary wonder stare upon
A sixty-year-old smiling public man.

2

I dream of a Ledaean body, bent
Above a sinking fire, a tale that she
Told of a harsh reproof, or trivial event
That changed some childish day to tragedy —
Told, and it seemed that our two natures blent
Into a sphere from youthful sympathy,
Or else, to alter Plato's parable,
Into the yolk and white of the one shell.

AMONG SCHOOL CHILDREN. **9. Ledaean:** like that of Helen of Troy, daughter of Leda. Cf. "No Second Troy," and "Leda and the Swan," above. "Swan" and bird images recur in most of the following stanzas. **15. Plato's parable:** as told in the *Symposium,* 189C–193D. According to the parable, human beings were once spherical in form; though subsequently divided in half, the one half longed to rejoin the other. **16. shell:** like the "sphere," another metaphor of close relationship between two natures. The image also recalls the egg from which Helen of Troy was said to have been born.

3

And thinking of that fit of grief or rage
I look upon one child or t' other there
And wonder if she stood so at that age —
For even daughters of the swan can share
Something of every paddler's heritage —
And had that color upon cheek or hair,
And thereupon my heart is driven wild:
She stands before me as a living child.

4

Her present image floats into the mind —
Did Quattrocento finger fashion it
Hollow of cheek as though it drank the wind
And took a mess of shadows for its meat?
And I though never of Ledaean kind
Had pretty plumage once — enough of that,
Better to smile on all that smile, and show
There is a comfortable kind of old scarecrow.

5

What youthful mother, a shape upon her lap
Honey of generation had betrayed,
And that must sleep, shriek, struggle to escape
As recollection or the drug decide,
Would think her son, did she but see that shape
With sixty or more winters on its head,
A compensation for the pang of his birth,
Or the uncertainty of his setting forth?

6

Plato thought nature but a spume that plays
Upon a ghostly paradigm of things;
Solider Aristotle played the taws
Upon the bottom of a king of kings;
World-famous golden-thighed Pythagoras
Fingered upon a fiddle-stick or strings
What a star sang and careless Muses heard:
Old clothes upon old sticks to scare a bird.

7

Both nuns and mothers worship images,
But those the candles light are not as those
That animate a mother's reveries,
But keep a marble or a bronze repose.
And yet they too break hearts — O Presences
That passion, piety or affection knows,
And that all heavenly glory symbolise —
O self-born mockers of man's enterprise;

8

Labour is blossoming or dancing where
The body is not bruised to pleasure soul,
Nor beauty born out of its own despair,
Nor blear-eyed wisdom out of midnight oil.
O chestnut-tree, great-rooted blossomer,
Are you the leaf, the blossom or the bole?
O body swayed to music, O brightening glance,
How can we know the dancer from the dance?

*1926*

**26. Quattrocento:** refers to fifteenth-century artists in Italy, more particularly to Botticelli (1444?–1510), who painted his madonnas and angels with lean and hollow cheeks. **32. scarecrow:** Cf. "A tattered coat upon a stick" in "Sailing to Byzantium," l. 10, above. **33–34. What . . . betrayed:** The syntax of the lines runs: "What youthful mother, with a shape upon her lap (i.e., her child) that honey of generation had betrayed . . ." **34. honey of generation:** Yeats took the phrase from *The Cave of the Nymphs* by Porphyry (A.D. 232/3–*c.* 305). He uses it in at least two different senses. He seems to mean first the "pleasure arising from generation," which the soul experiences in coming into life. The soul of the child is said to be "betrayed" by this pleasure, because in being born, it gives up the life it has enjoyed apart from the body. As it recalls that purer life, it "struggles to escape" (ll. 35, 36). Yeats also means by "honey of generation" a "drug" that destroys the memory of "prenatal freedom." If the drug works, the struggle ceases: the child's soul "struggles to escape / As recollection *or* the drug decide." The notion of the soul's "recollection" and "prenatal freedom" is Platonic. But in the context of the whole stanza, "honey of generation" may equally well refer to sexual desire or to the mother's desire to beget children. **41–42. Plato . . . things:** Nature for Plato is mere appearance (*a spume*); reality lies beneath in the spiritual (*ghostly*) form or scheme (*the paradigm*). **43. Solider Aristotle:** In contrast to Plato, he insisted that form was immanent in matter; that is, he attributed a measure of reality to "solid" matter as well as to form. **43–44. played . . . kings:** Aristotle was tutor to Alexander the Great. "The taws" are an instrument of discipline, used in Scottish and English schools, made of a leather strap divided at the end into narrow strips (*OED*). Aristotle "spanked" his royal pupil. **45. golden-thighed Pythagoras:** The early Greek philosopher and religious teacher was regarded by his adoring disciples as a god with a "thigh of gold." The Pythagoreans combined various astronomical and musical discoveries in the doctrine of the "harmony of the spheres." Hence Yeats says that Pythagoras expressed musically "what a star sang." **48. Old clothes . . . bird:** The line refers to the achievements of all three philosophers, to their "blear-eyed wisdom" (l. 60). **49. images:** both the statues of saints and the mother's idealized images of her children. They are also "ikons" or symbols of "heavenly glory," the "Presences" addressed in l. 53, which resemble Plato's ideal forms of goodness and beauty. **56. self-born mockers:** Though the "Presences," the ideal concepts by which human achievement is measured, are created by man, they mock his efforts, since he can never realize them in fact. Cf. "Image of Unity," *Autobiography*, below. **61. chestnut-tree:** an image of creation where beauty is inseparable from the life processes that produce it. The tree in blossom symbolizes the "Unity of Being" that the whole poem celebrates. Cf. ". . . blood, imagination, intellect, running together . . ." ("Personality and the Intellectual Essences," *Essays*, below).

## IN MEMORY OF EVA GORE-BOOTH AND CON MARKIEWICZ

Eva Gore-Booth was the younger sister of Constance Markiewicz. (See "Easter 1916," l. 17n., above.) This elegy expresses a judgment of the effect of political action on personality that recurs fairly often in Yeats's later poems. It is anticipated in "Easter 1916," lines 57–58: "Too long a sacrifice / Can make a stone of the heart." As in "Sailing to Byzantium," action seems clearly inferior to contemplation. In other poems, such as "Blood and the Moon," and "Vacillation," below, Yeats very nearly reverses this evaluation. "Eva Gore-Booth and Con Markiewicz" and the next six poems were included in *The Winding Stair and Other Poems* (1933).

The light of evening, Lissadell,
Great windows open to the south,
Two girls in silk kimonos, both
Beautiful, one a gazelle.
But a raving autumn shears
Blossom from the summer's wreath;
The older is condemned to death,
Pardoned, drags out lonely years
Conspiring among the ignorant.
I know not what the younger dreams —
Some vague Utopia — and she seems,
When withered old and skeleton-gaunt,
An image of such politics.
Many a time I think to seek
One or the other out and speak
Of that old Georgian mansion, mix
Pictures of the mind, recall
That table and the talk of youth,
Two girls in silk kimonos, both
Beautiful, one a gazelle.
Dear shadows, now you know it all,
All the folly of a fight
With a common wrong or right.
The innocent and the beautiful
Have no enemy but time;
Arise and bid me strike a match
And strike another till time catch;
Should the conflagration climb,
Run till all the sages know.
We the great gazebo built,
They convicted us of guilt;
Bid me strike a match and blow.

*October, 1927*

IN MEMORY OF EVA GORE-BOOTH. **1. Lissadell:** the "old Georgian mansion" (l. 16) of the Gore-Booths, whom Yeats had visited in 1894–95. **24–27. The innocent . . . catch:** Innocence of spirit is lost in time, in the activities of this world, but it may be recovered in the state of mind known to "the sages," which is symbolized by "fire." Cf. "sages standing in God's holy fire" ("Sailing to Byzantium," l. 17, above). In "Anima Mundi," *Essays*, pp. 532–34, Yeats writes of "the Condition of Fire," the mood of pure contemplative joy in which ". . . the images from *Anima Mundi,* embodied there and drunk with that sweetness, would, like a country drunkard who has thrown a wisp into his own thatch, burn up time." He adds that he enters upon this mood ". . . the moment I cease to hate. I think the common condition of our life is hatred." **30. gazebo:** a projecting balcony with windows, built especially for commanding a wide view; cf. "great windows" (l. 2). "The great gazebo" suggests an absurd and oversized structure and so symbolizes the grandiose political programs that the speaker and the sisters had "built" in their youth.

## BLOOD AND THE MOON

In these two poems (from a sequence of four), Yeats's "tower" becomes an emblem of the lively and various Anglo-Irish culture of the eighteenth century, which he compares with the present, "a time / Half dead at the top" (I, ll. 11–12). The main significance of "blood" — crude physical energy — is clear from the opening lines of the first poem. The opposed symbol of "the moon" stands for wisdom, "the property of the dead, / A something incompatible with life" (IV, ll. 49–50). See Introduction, p. 780, for "blood"; see also "The Second Coming" and "Two Songs from a Play," above. The imediate occasion for the poem was the assassination of Kevin O'Higgins, a minister of the Irish Free State and a friend of Yeats, whom Yeats saw as an inheritor of the best Anglo-Irish traditions.

Yeats also wrote elsewhere of the four chief figures in eighteenth-century Anglo-Irish culture: "Born in such community Berkeley with his belief in perception, that abstract ideas are mere words, Swift with his love of perfect nature, of the Houyhnhnms, his disbelief in Newton's system and every sort of machine, Goldsmith and his delight in the particulars of common life that shocked his contemporaries, Burke with his conviction that all states not grown slowly like a forest tree are tyrannies, found in England an opposite that stung their own thought into expression and made it lucid" (Yeats, *Essays, 1931–1936,* p. 36).

**I**

Blessed be this place,
More blessed still this tower;
A bloody, arrogant power
Rose out of the race
Uttering, mastering it,
Rose like these walls from these
Storm-beaten cottages —
In mockery I have set
A powerful emblem up,
And sing it rhyme upon rhyme
In mockery of a time
Half dead at the top.

**II**

Alexandria's was a beacon tower, and Babylon's
An image of the moving heavens, a log-book of the
sun's journey and the moon's;

BLOOD AND THE MOON. **I: 5. Uttering, mastering:** The Anglo-Irish gained the upper hand over the native race and in time created the culture through which it became articulate. Anglo-Irish literature, for example, gave expression to the folk beliefs of the native Irish. **II:** The unity of this section arises from the "co-operation" among the allusive metaphors by which the four men are characterized. Each metaphor (except perhaps that used of Goldsmith) has links with the "blood-moon" themes. **13. Alexandria:** the famous lighthouse on Pharos, an island in the bay of Alexandria. **Babylon:** The temple towers of Babylon were said to be "like heaven," because their structure was a

And Shelley had his towers, thought's crowned powers he called them once.

I declare this tower is my symbol; I declare
This winding, gyring, spiring treadmill of a stair is my ancestral stair;
That Goldsmith and the Dean, Berkeley and Burke have travelled there.

Swift beating on his breast in sibylline frenzy blind
Because the heart in his blood-sodden breast had dragged him down into mankind,
Goldsmith deliberately sipping at the honey-pot of his mind,

And haughtier-headed Burke that proved the State a tree,
That this unconquerable labyrinth of the birds, century after century,
Cast but dead leaves to mathematical equality;

And God-appointed Berkeley that proved all things a dream,
That this pragmatical, preposterous pig of a world, its farrow that so solid seem,
Must vanish on the instant if the mind but change its theme;

*Saeva Indignatio* and the labourer's hire,
The strength that gives our blood and state magnanimity of its own desire;
Everything that is not God consumed with intellectual fire.

copy of the structure of the heavens. **15. Shelley . . . powers:** *Prometheus Unbound*, IV.103, above. **19. Swift:** See Intro., pp. 780 and 785. "Sibylline frenzy blind" refers to Swift's madness and to the lack of comprehension which he met with in England and in Ireland. **20. Because . . . mankind:** For Swift's attitude toward the Yahoos, see *Gulliver's Travels*, Book IV, in Vol. I. **21. Goldsmith . . . mind:** The metaphor hardly seems to express Goldsmith's "delight in the particulars of common life." It suggests rather a dilettante, a man whose thought was a savoring of ideas and sentiments. **22. haughtier-headed:** without Goldsmith's sympathy for the lower classes, e.g., in "The Deserted Village." **22–24. State . . . equality:** For Burke the state was a complex growth coming out of the past. He maintained his organic view against supporters of the French Revolution, who thought of the state as founded on *a priori* (*mathematical*) principles of equality. Burke's "tree-State" gives no "living" support to such theories, but does offer a home for "birds," that is, for men, not for an abstract "political man." **25–27. Berkeley . . . theme:** an eloquent expression of idealism, though not an adequate account of Berkeley's philosophy. Yeats characteristically reduces reality to dream and gives almost no place to the observing mind of God, which in Berkeley's view sustains the continuous existence of things. **28. *Saeva Indignatio:*** "savage indignation," a phrase from the Latin epitaph that Swift wrote for himself. Cf. Yeats's translation, *Collected Poems*, p. 241. **laborer's hire:** See l. 22n. **29. blood . . . state:** "The glories of our blood and state / Are shadows, not substantial things," from a song by the dramatist James Shirley (1596–1666), who lived for a time in Ireland.

## THE NINETEENTH CENTURY AND AFTER

An allusion to the English periodical of the same title. In a letter, March 2, 1929, Yeats introduced this poem with the remark, "I have come to find the world's last great poetical period is over" (A. Norman Jeffares, *W. B. Yeats, Man and Poet*, p. 254).

Though the great song return no more
There's keen delight in what we have:
The rattle of pebbles on the shore
Under the receding wave.

*1929*

## COOLE PARK, 1929

Compare this poem with "The Wild Swans at Coole," above, and with "Coole Park and Ballylee, 1931," *Collected Poems*, pp. 239–40. Also see Introduction, p. 782.

I meditate upon a swallow's flight,
Upon an aged woman and her house,
A sycamore and lime-tree lost in night
Although that western cloud is luminous,
Great works constructed there in nature's spite
For scholars and for poets after us,
Thoughts long knitted into a single thought,
A dance-like glory that those walls begot.

There Hyde before he had beaten into prose
That noble blade the Muses buckled on,
There one that ruffled in a manly pose
For all his timid heart, there that slow man,
That meditative man, John Synge, and those
Impetuous men, Shawe-Taylor and Hugh Lane,
Found pride established in humility,
A scene well set and excellent company.

THE NINETEENTH CENTURY. **1. great song:** the poetry of the Romantics. Cf. "The world's great age begins anew" (Shelley, Chorus from *Hellas*, l. 1060). Cf. "Two Songs from a Play," above. **3–4. rattle . . . wave:** Cf. ". . . you hear the grating roar / Of pebbles which the waves draw back . . ." (Matthew Arnold, "Dover Beach," ll. 9–10, above). COOLE PARK: **2. aged woman:** Lady Gregory. **9. Hyde:** Douglas Hyde, folklorist and Gaelic poet, played an important part in the revival of Irish literature. Yeats writes of him as "the great poet who died in his youth," who later "took for his model the newspaper upon his breakfast table" (*Autobiography*, p. 188). **11. one:** Yeats. See Intro., p. 787. **13. Synge:** dramatist, author of *The Playboy of the Western World*. See "The Tragic Generation," *Autobiography*, below. **14. Shawe-Taylor:** John Shawe-Taylor, a nephew of Lady Gregory, who had ". . . that instant decision of the hawk, between the movement of whose wings and the perception of whose eye no time passes capable of division" (Yeats, *Essays*, p. 426). On his initiative a conference was held that led to the Land Act of 1903, under the terms of which tenants were enabled to purchase their lands from the owners. On Lane, also a nephew of Lady Gregory, see "To a Friend Whose Work Has Come to Nothing," above.

They came like swallows and like swallows went,
And yet a woman's powerful character
Could keep a swallow to its first intent;
And half a dozen in formation there,
That seemed to whirl upon a compass-point,
Found certainty upon the dreaming air,
The intellectual sweetness of those lines
That cut through time or cross it withershins.

Here, traveller, scholar, poet, take your stand
When all those rooms and passages are gone,
When nettles wave upon a shapeless mound
And saplings root among the broken stone,
And dedicate — eyes bent upon the ground,
Back turned upon the brightness of the sun
And all the sensuality of the shade —
A moment's memory to that laurelled head.

## VACILLATION

"Vacillation," VII, VIII, are the closing sections of a poem that expresses one of Yeats's most characteristic states of mind, as he observed in reviewing his own career: "The swordsman throughout repudiates the saint, but not without vacillation. Is that perhaps the sole theme — Usheen and Patrick 'So get you gone Von Hügel though with blessings on your head'" (from a letter, June 30, 1932, quoted in Richard Ellman, *Yeats, The Man and the Masks,* p. 272). "Usheen," or Oisin, *the swordsman,* is the legendary poet-hero of Yeats's *The Wanderings of Oisin* (1889). St. Patrick once argued at length with Oisin in an unsuccessful attempt to convert him to Christianity. For another expression of the conflict between Christianity and the poet's art, see "The Tragic Generation," *Autobiography,* below.

VII

*The Soul.* Seek out reality, leave things that seem.

*The Heart.* What, be a singer born and lack a
theme?

*The Soul.* Isaiah's coal, what more can man desire?

*The Heart.* Struck dumb in the simplicity of fire!

*The Soul.* Look on that fire, salvation walks within.

*The Heart.* What theme had Homer but original
sin?

VIII

Must we part, Von Hügel, though much alike, for
we
Accept the miracles of the saints and honour sanctity?
The body of Saint Teresa lies undecayed in tomb,
Bathed in miraculous oil, sweet odours from it
come,
Healing from its lettered slab. Those self-same
hands perchance
Eternalised the body of a modern saint that once
Had scooped out Pharaoh's mummy. I — though
heart might find relief
Did I become a Christian man and choose for my
belief
What seems most welcome in the tomb — play a
predestined part.
Homer is my example and his unchristened heart.
The lion and the honeycomb, what has Scripture
said?
So get you gone, Von Hügel, though with blessings
on your head.

*1932*

## WORDS FOR MUSIC PERHAPS

### XVII. AFTER LONG SILENCE

"After Long Silence" and the following poem are from the cycle, "Words for Music Perhaps" (1929–32), which includes the "Crazy Jane" poems. See Introduction, p. 783.

**22. dreaming air:** perhaps the trancelike peace favorable to imaginative creation. **23–24. lines . . . withershins:** lines of activity in which men seem to escape from time; they move into a state outside time (*cut through it*), or they move counter to its flow and so arrest its course (*cross it withershins*). On this opposition between time and "the intellectual sweetness" of imaginative activity, see "Eva Gore-Booth and Con Markiewicz," ll. 24–27, above. **30–31. Back . . . shade:** Cf. "nature's spite" (l. 5); note the imagery of light and shade in both the first and the last stanzas. VACILLATION. **VII: 3. Isaiah's coal:** the live coal with which the seraph touched Isaiah's "unclean lips" and "purged" him from "sin" (Isa. 7:5–7).

**4. Struck . . . fire!:** Unlike Isaiah, whom the fire made more eloquent, the poet feels unable to sing of "reality." As elsewhere in Yeats, "the condition of fire" symbolizes the state of pure contemplation, untouched by the "complexities of mire or blood," in which reality is revealed to poets and sages. See "Sailing to Byzantium," above, and "Byzantium," *Collected Poems,* pp. 243–44. **VIII: 7. Von Hügel:** Roman Catholic philosopher, author of *The Mystical Element of Religion as Studied in St. Catherine of Genoa and her Friends* (1908). Here, Von Hügel has the role of "a Christian man," corresponding to "The Soul" of "Vacillation," VII. **9–13. Saint . . . mummy:** a reference to the Spanish Carmelite nun and mystic writer, 1515–82. "Why should not the old embalmers come back — as ghosts and bestow upon the saint all the care once bestowed upon Rameses: why should I doubt the tale that when St. Theresa's tomb was opened in the middle of the nineteenth century the still undecayed lady dripped with fragrant oil" (from a letter, January 3, 1932, quoted in A. Norman Jeffares, *W. B. Yeats, Man and Poet,* p. 272). **17. lion . . . honeycomb:** refers to Samson's discovery of honey "in the carcase of the lion" and to his riddle: "Out of the eater came forth meat, and out of the strong came forth sweetness" (Judg. 14:8–14).

Speech after long silence; it is right,
All other lovers being estranged or dead,
Unfriendly lamplight hid under its shade,
The curtains drawn upon unfriendly night,
That we descant and yet again descant
Upon the supreme theme of Art and Song:
Bodily decrepitude is wisdom; young
We loved each other and were ignorant.

*1929*

### XVIII. MAD AS THE MIST AND SNOW

Bolt and bar the shutter,
For the foul winds blow:
Our minds are at their best this night,
And I seem to know
That everything outside us is
*Mad as the mist and snow.*

Horace there by Homer stands,
Plato stands below,
And here is Tully's open page.
How many years ago
Were you and I unlettered lads
*Mad as the mist and snow?*

You ask what makes me sigh, old friend,
What makes me shudder so?
I shudder and I sigh to think
That even Cicero
And many-minded Homer were
*Mad as the mist and snow.*

*1929*

## AN ACRE OF GRASS

"An Acre of Grass" and the next two poems are from *Last Poems* (1936–39). See Introduction, p. 786.

Picture and book remain,
An acre of green grass
For air and exercise,
Now strength of body goes;
Midnight, an old house
Where nothing stirs but a mouse.
My temptation is quiet.
Here at life's end
Neither loose imagination,
Nor the mill of the mind
Consuming its rag and bone,
Can make the truth known.

Grant me an old man's frenzy,
Myself must I remake
Till I am Timon and Lear
Or that William Blake
Who beat upon the wall
Till Truth obeyed his call;

A mind Michael Angelo knew
That can pierce the clouds,
Or inspired by frenzy
Shake the dead in their shrouds;
Forgotten else by mankind,
An old man's eagle mind.

## THE WILD OLD WICKED MAN

"The Wild Old Wicked Man" is one of many poems from Yeats's last period that are written in a style derived from Irish folk songs and ballads. He shows here his skill in using the bald idiom and plain rhythms of popular poetry to express states of mind that are serious and far from simple. Note, for example, that the poet-speaker is both a "young man," and a "wild old man," that he is a lover who has words and knowledge "that can pierce the heart." See Introduction, p. 787.

AFTER LONG SILENCE. **7–8. Bodily . . . ignorant:** Cf. "The Folly of Being Comforted," "Men Improve with the Years," and "Sailing to Byzantium," above. MAD AS THE MIST AND SNOW. **9. Tully:** Marcus Tullius Cicero, Roman orator and philosophic writer. **17. many-minded:** or myriad-minded, an ancient epithet for Homer.

AN ACRE OF GRASS. **7. My . . . quiet:** Consider the very different meanings of this statement in relation to the preceding and the following lines. The key to the poem lies in the contrast between "quiet" and "frenzy" (l. 13). **9. loose:** i.e., of an old man; perhaps with a further reference to the uncontrolled fancies of Yeats's earlier poems. **11. rag and bone:** suggests the problems that the aging mind goes over again and again, working like a *mill.* The phrase also alludes to the refuse of past experiences, all that is left the old man when the transforming power of imagination is gone. Cf. "the foul rag-and-bone shop of the heart" ("The Circus Animals' Desertion," *Collected Poems*, pp. 335–36). **13. frenzy:** the passionate and energetic insight that is expressed and defined through the four symbolic "old men." **15. Timon:** protagonist of Shakespeare's *Timon of Athens*, who in his mad hatred exulted in perceiving the unnaturalness of "the whole race of mankind" (*Timon of Athens*, IV.i.40). Cf. Lear's vision of "unaccommodated man" (*King Lear*, III.iv.105–14). **16. Blake:** William Blake, the poet, who had mystical visions of divine "Truth." For Yeats, he was one of those near-madmen who ". . . discover symbolism to express the overflowing and bursting of the mind" (*A Vision*, p. 138). **19–22. Michael Angelo . . . shrouds:** Michelangelo's power of depicting the supernatural, especially in his Sistine Chapel fresco of *The Last Judgment* with its nightmarish scenes of the dead rising from their graves.

"Because I am mad about women
I am mad about the hills,"
Said that wild old wicked man
Who travels where God wills.
"Not to die on the straw at home,
Those hands to close these eyes,
That is all I ask, my dear,
From the old man in the skies.
*Daybreak and a candle-end.*

"Kind are all your words, my dear,
Do not the rest withhold.
Who can know the year, my dear,
When an old man's blood grows cold?
I have what no young man can have
Because he loves too much.
Words I have that can pierce the heart,
But what can he do but touch?"
*Daybreak and a candle-end.*

Then said she to that wild old man,
His stout stick under his hand,
"Love to give or to withhold
Is not at my command.
I gave it all to an older man:
That old man in the skies.
Hands that are busy with His beads
Can never close those eyes."
*Daybreak and a candle-end.*

"Go your ways, O go your ways,
I choose another mark,
Girls down on the seashore
Who understand the dark;
Bawdy talk for the fishermen;
A dance for the fisher-lads;
When dark hangs upon the water
They turn down their beds.
*Daybreak and a candle-end.*

"A young man in the dark am I,
But a wild old man in the light,
That can make a cat laugh, or
Can touch by mother wit
Things hid in their marrow-bones
From time long passed away,
Hid from all those warty lads
That by their bodies lay.
*Daybreak and a candle-end.*

"All men live in suffering,
I know as few can know,
Whether they take the upper road
Or stay content on the low,
Rower bent in his row-boat
Or weaver bent at his loom,
Horseman erect upon horseback
Or child hid in the womb.
*Daybreak and a candle-end.*

"That some stream of lightning
From the old man in the skies
Can burn out that suffering
No right-taught man denies.
But a coarse old man am I,
I choose the second-best,
I forget it all awhile
Upon a woman's breast."
*Daybreak and a candle-end.*

THE WILD OLD WICKED MAN. **9. *Daybreak . . . candle-end:*** As often in Yeats, the refrain has symbolic meaning when related to the rest of the poem. **43. warty:** in Irish popular belief, a sign of sexual potency. **47. I know:** Cf. "An old man's eagle mind" ("An Acre of Grass," l. 24, above).

## A BRONZE HEAD

"A Bronze Head" is mainly focused on the opposition suggested by "human, superhuman" (l. 2), which is echoed later in "who can tell / Which of her forms has shown her substance right?" (ll. 10, 11). The references to the statue of Maud Gonne in the Dublin Municipal Gallery and to the actual woman are of the most general sort.

Here at right of the entrance this bronze head,
Human, superhuman, a bird's round eye,
Everything else withered and mummy-dead.
What great tomb-haunter sweeps the distant sky
(Something may linger there though all else die;)
And finds there nothing to make its terror less
*Hysterica passio* of its own emptiness?

**55–62.** For the opposition between Christian and pagan attitudes, compare "Vacillation," VIII, above. A BRONZE HEAD. **1. the entrance:** of a tomb, or of a museum. **3. else:** the rest of the body. **6. there:** "the distant sky," the region beyond life known to the "tomb-haunter." **to . . . less:** "Less" may go with either "terror" or "*Hysterica passio.*" If taken with "terror" — which is the more likely reading — the phrase means "to diminish its terror"; and then "*Hysterica passio*" stands in apposition with the whole idea expressed in l. 6. **7. *Hysterica passio:*** hysteria, madness; cf. *King Lear*, II.ii.240–41. "We all have something within ourselves to batter down and get our power from this fighting. I have never 'produced' a play in verse without showing the actors that the passion of the verse comes from the fact that the speakers are holding down violence or madness — 'down Hysterica passio'" (from a letter to Dorothy Wellesley, August 5 [1936], *Letters on Poetry from W. B. Yeats to Dorothy Wellesley*, p. 94).

No dark tomb-haunter once; her form all full
As though with magnanimity of light,
Yet a most gentle woman; who can tell
Which of her forms has shown her substance right?
Or maybe substance can be composite,
Profound McTaggart thought so, and in a breath
A mouthful held the extreme of life and death.

But even at the starting-post, all sleek and new,
I saw the wildness in her and I thought
A vision of terror that it must live through
Had shattered her soul. Propinquity had brought
Imagination to that pitch where it casts out
All that is not itself: I had grown wild
And wandered murmuring everywhere, "My child, my child!"

Or else I thought her supernatural;
As though a sterner eye looked through her eye
On this foul world in its decline and fall;
On gangling stocks grown great, great stocks run dry,
Ancestral pearls all pitched into a sty,
Heroic reverie mocked by clown and knave,
And wondered what was left for massacre to save.

**10. a . . . woman:** "Her voice was ever soft, / Gentle, and low, an excellent thing in woman" (*King Lear,* V.iii.273–74). **11. substance:** essence, that which determines the essential nature of a thing. **13–14. McTaggart . . . death:** John McT. E. McTaggart (1866–1925), philosopher, an atheist and convinced believer in immortality, who argued that "substance" is divisible, i.e., "composite." Yeats seems to say that the essential nature of man includes both extremes, "life" and "death," the "human" and the "superhuman." **18–20. Propinquity . . . wild:** Through association with his beloved he had become obsessed by the view of her that his imagination had created; he could see only a reflection of the "terror" that he had himself attributed to her. **22. supernatural:** Cf. "superhuman," l. 2, and note how the meaning of the word is qualified by the lines that follow. Cf. also ". . . beauty like a tightened bow, a kind / That is not natural in an age like this" ("No Second Troy," ll. 8–9, above). **24. On . . . fall:** Cf. "Cleanse the foul body of th' infected world" (*As You Like It,* II.vii.60). Note also allusion to Edward Gibbon's *History of the Decline and Fall of the Roman Empire.* **25. gangling . . . great:** rise of lower and middle classes to power. **27. Heroic reverie:** the passionate, trancelike exaltation of a tragic hero. The phrase describes both a type of character scorned by modern society and an ideal type of drama that the Irish audience had failed to appreciate. Cf. "The Fisherman," ll. 9–26, above, and "On Those That Hated *The Playboy of the Western World,* 1907," *Collected Poems,* p. 109. **28. massacre:** the violence of "blood," which in Yeats's view is necessary for the birth of each new phase of civilization. Cf. "The Second Coming" and "Two Songs from a Play," above.

# from *THE AUTO-BIOGRAPHY*

## MIDDLETONS AND POLLEXFENS [1]

### I

Once too I was driving with my grandmother [2] a little after dark close to the channel that runs for some five miles from Sligo to the sea, and my grandmother showed me the red light of an outward-bound steamer and told me that my grandfather was on board, and that night in my sleep I screamed out and described the steamer's wreck. The next morning my grandfather arrived on a blind horse found for him by grateful passengers. He had, as I remember the story, been asleep when the captain aroused him to say they were going on the rocks. He said, "Have you tried sail on her?" and judging from some answer that the captain was demoralized took over the command and, when the ship could not be saved, got the crew and passengers into the boats. His own boat was upset and he saved himself and some others by swimming; some women had drifted ashore, buoyed up by their crinolines. "I was not so much afraid of the sea as of that terrible man with his oar," was the comment of a schoolmaster who was among the survivors. Eight men were, however, drowned and my grandfather suffered from that memory at intervals all his life, and if asked to read family prayers never read anything but the shipwreck of St. Paul.

### II

He [the stable boy] had a book of Orange [3] rhymes, and the days when we read them together in the hayloft gave me the pleasure of rhyme for the first time. Later on I can remember being told, when there was a rumor of a Fenian [4] rising, that

THE AUTOBIOGRAPHY. **1.** The first four selections are taken from *Reveries over Childhood and Youth* (1914). **2. grandmother:** Elizabeth Pollexfen. Yeats spent a good deal of time during his boyhood in county Sligo, near the town of the same name, at the home of his maternal grandparents, William and Elizabeth Pollexfen. His grandfather, with his grandmother's brother, William Middleton, ran a large and prosperous milling business at Ballisodare. The same firm owned and operated a number of ships. County Sligo had also been the home of the poet's great-grandfather, John Yeats, and of his grandfather, William Butler Yeats, both of whom were clergymen in the Established Church of Ireland (corresponding to the Church of England). **3. Orange:** the Orangemen, members of the Loyal Orange Institution, a society founded to maintain the Protestant ascendancy in Ireland. **4. Fenian:** the Fenian Brotherhood, or Irish Republican Brotherhood, a revolutionary society active in Ireland and America from the 1860's to World War I.

rifles had been served out to the Orangemen; and presently, when I had begun to dream of my future life, I thought I would like to die fighting the Fenians. I was to build a very fast and beautiful ship and to have under my command a company of young men who were always to be in training like athletes and so become as brave and handsome as the young men in the storybooks, and there was to be a big battle on the seashore near Rosses and I was to be killed. I collected little pieces of wood and piled them up in a corner of the yard, and there was an old rotten log in a distant field I often went to look at because I thought it would go a long way in the making of the ship. All my dreams were of ships; and one day a sea captain who had come to dine with my grandfather put a hand on each side of my head and lifted me up to show me Africa, and another day a sea captain pointed to the smoke from the pern[5] mill on the quays rising up beyond the trees of the lawn, as though it came from the mountain, and asked me if Ben Bulben was a burning mountain.

Once every few months I used to go to Rosses Point or Ballisodare to see another little boy, who had a piebald pony that had once been in a circus and sometimes forgot where it was and went round and round. He was George Middleton, son of my great-uncle William Middleton. Old Middleton had bought land, then believed a safe investment, at Ballisodare and at Rosses, and spent the winter at Ballisodare and the summer at Rosses. The Middleton and Pollexfen flour mills were at Ballisodare, and a great salmon weir, rapids and a waterfall, but it was more often at Rosses that I saw my cousin. We rowed in the river mouth or were taken sailing in a heavy slow schooner yacht or in a big ship's boat that had been rigged and decked. There were great cellars under the house, for it had been a smuggler's house a hundred years before, and sometimes three loud raps would come upon the drawing-room window at sundown, setting all the dogs barking: some dead smuggler giving his accustomed signal. One night I heard them very distinctly and my cousins often heard them, and later on my sister. A pilot had told me that, after dreaming three times of a treasure buried in my uncle's garden, he had climbed the wall in the middle of the night and begun to dig but grew disheartened "because there was so much earth." I told somebody what he had said and was told that it was well he did not find it for it was guarded by a spirit that looked like a flatiron. At Ballisodare there was a cleft among the rocks that I passed with terror because I believed that a murderous monster lived there that made a buzzing sound like a bee.

It was through the Middletons perhaps that I got my interest in country stories, and certainly the first faery stories that I heard were in the cottages about their houses. The Middletons took the nearest for friends and were always in and out of the cottages of pilots and of tenants. They were practical, always doing something with their hands, making boats, feeding chickens, and without ambition. . . .

## EARLY READING

My father read out poetry, for the first time, when I was eight or nine years old. Between Sligo and Rosses Point, there is a tongue of land covered with coarse grass that runs out into the sea or the mud, according to the state of the tide. It is the place where dead horses are buried. Sitting there, my father read me *The Lays of Ancient Rome*.[6] It was the first poetry that had moved me after the stable boy's *Orange Rhymes*. Later on he read me *Ivanhoe* and *The Lay of the Last Minstrel*,[7] and they are still vivid in the memory. I re-read *Ivanhoe* the other day, but it has all vanished except Gurth, the swineherd, at the outset and Friar Tuck and his venison pasty, the two scenes that laid hold of me in childhood. *The Lay of the Last Minstrel* gave me a wish to turn magician that competed for years with the dream of being killed upon the seashore. When I first went to school, he tried to keep me from reading boys' papers, because a paper, by its very nature, as he explained to me, had to be made for the average boy or man and so could not but thwart one's growth. He took away my paper, and I had not courage to say that I was but reading and delighting in a prose retelling of the *Iliad*. But after a few months, my father said he had been too anxious and became less urgent about my lessons and less violent if I had learned them badly, and he ceased to notice what I read. From that on I shared the excitement which ran through all my fellows on Wednesday afternoons when the boys' papers were published, and I read endless stories I have forgotten as I have forgotten *Grimm's Fairy Tales* that I read at Sligo, and all of Hans Andersen except the "Ugly Duckling" which my mother had read to me and to my sisters. I remember vaguely

**5. pern mill:** spool mill. See "Sailing to Byzantium," l. 19n. above.

**6.** ***The Lays of Ancient Rome*****:** by T. B. Macaulay. **7.** ***The Lay of the Last Minstrel*****:** by Sir Walter Scott.

that I liked Hans Andersen better than Grimm because he was less homely, but even he never gave me the knights and dragons and beautiful ladies that I longed for. I have remembered nothing that I read, but only those things that I heard or saw. When I was ten or twelve my father took me to see Irving play *Hamlet,* and did not understand why I preferred Irving to Ellen Terry,[8] who was, I can now see, the idol of himself and his friends. I could not think of her, as I could of Irving's Hamlet, as but myself, and I was not old enough to care for feminine charm and beauty. For many years Hamlet was an image of heroic self-possession for the poses of youth and childhood to copy, a combatant of the battle within myself.

## HIS FATHER'S INFLUENCE

My father's [9] influence upon my thoughts was at its height. We went to Dublin [10] by train every morning, breakfasting in his studio. He had taken a large room with a beautiful eighteenth-century mantelpiece in a York Street tenement house, and at breakfast he read passages from the poets, and always from the play or poem at its most passionate moment. He never read me a passage because of its speculative interests, and indeed did not care at all for poetry where there was generalization or abstraction, however impassioned. He would read out the first speeches of the *Prometheus Unbound,* but never the ecstatic lyricism of that famous fourth act; and another day the scene where Coriolanus comes to the house of Aufidius and tells the impudent servants that his home is under the canopy. I have seen *Coriolanus* played a number of times since then, and read it more than once, but that scene is more vivid than the rest, and it is my father's voice that I hear and not Irving's or Benson's.[11] He did not care even for a fine lyric passage unless he felt some actual man behind its elaboration of beauty, and he was always looking for the lineaments of some desirable, familiar life. When the spirits sang their scorn of Manfred,[12] and Manfred answered, "O sweet and melancholy voices," I was told that they could not, even in anger, put off their spiritual sweetness. He thought Keats a greater poet than Shelley, because less abstract, but did not read him, caring little, I think, for any of that most beautiful poetry which has come in modern times from the influence of painting. All must be an idealization of speech, and at some moment of passionate action or somnambulistic reverie. I remember his saying that all contemplative men were in a conspiracy to overrate their state of life, and that all writers were of them excepting the great poets. Looking backwards, it seems to me that I saw his mind in fragments, which had always hidden connections I only now begin to discover. He disliked the Victorian poetry of ideas, and Wordsworth but for certain passages or whole poems. He said one morning over his breakfast that he had discovered in the shape of the head of a Wordsworthian scholar, an old and greatly respected clergyman whose portrait he was painting, all the animal instincts of a prizefighter. He despised the formal beauty of Raphael, that calm which is not an ordered passion but an hypocrisy, and attacked Raphael's life for its love of pleasure and its self-indulgence. In literature he was always Pre-Raphaelite; [13] and carried into literature principles that, while the Academy [14] was still unbroken, had made the first attack upon academic form.

He no longer read me anything for its story, and all our discussion was of style.

## PERSONAL UTTERANCE

Some one at the Young Ireland Society [15] gave me a newspaper that I might read some article or letter. I began idly reading verses describing the shore of Ireland as seen by a returning, dying emigrant. My eyes filled with tears, and yet I know the verses were badly written — vague, abstract words such as one finds in a newspaper. I looked at the end and saw the name of some political exile who had died but a few days after his return to Ireland. They had moved me because they contained the actual thoughts of a man at a passionate moment of life, and when I met my father I was full of the discovery. We should write out our own thoughts in as nearly as possible the language we thought

**8. Terry:** Dame Ellen Terry (1848–1928), English actress, for over twenty years leading lady in Sir Henry Irving's (1838–1905) productions at the Lyceum Theatre, London. She and Irving were particularly famous for their Shakespearean roles. **9. My father:** John Butler Yeats, the painter. **10. Dublin:** The poet's family were now living at Howth, near Dublin. **11. Benson:** Sir Francis Robert ("Frank") Benson (1858–1939), actor, made his first professional appearance in Irving's *Romeo and Juliet.* He organized and for years directed his own Shakespearean company. **12. Manfred:** hero of Byron's dramatic poem, *Manfred.* See pp. 178–94, above.

**13. Pre-Raphaelite:** See Intro., pp. 781–82, and "A Pre-Raphaelite's Son," p. 808. **14. Academy:** The Royal Academy of Art, London, which maintained standards in painting. **15. Young Ireland Society:** a society to which Yeats belonged in his youth, and which was headed by John O'Leary, a famous leader in the Fenian movement. Yeats's joining the Society, which was vigorously Nationalistic, marks his departure from his father's more moderate Home Rule views. Through O'Leary, Yeats was introduced to the writings of popular Irish poets.

them in, as though in a letter to an intimate friend. We should not disguise them in any way; for our lives give them force as the lives of people in plays give force to their words. Personal utterance, which had almost ceased in English literature, could be as fine an escape from rhetoric and abstraction as drama itself. But my father would hear of nothing but drama; personal utterance was only egotism. I knew it was not, but as yet did not know how to explain the difference. I tried from that on to write out of my emotions exactly as they came to me in life, not changing them to make them more beautiful. "If I can be sincere and make my language natural, and without becoming discursive, like a novelist, and so indiscreet and prosaic," I said to myself, "I shall, if good luck or bad luck make my life interesting, be a great poet; for it will be no longer a matter of literature at all." Yet when I re-read those early poems which gave me so much trouble, I find little but romantic convention, unconscious drama. It is so many years before one can believe enough in what one feels even to know what the feeling is.

## A PRE-RAPHAELITE'S SON [16]

Yet I was in all things Pre-Raphaelite.[17] When I was fifteen or sixteen my father had told me about Rossetti [18] and Blake and given me their poetry to read; and once at Liverpool on my way to Sligo I had seen Dante's "Dream" in the gallery there, a picture painted when Rossetti had lost his dramatic power and today not very pleasing to me, and its color, its people, its romantic architecture had blotted all other pictures away. It was a perpetual bewilderment that when my father, moved perhaps by some memory of his youth, chose some theme from poetic tradition, he would soon weary and leave it unfinished. I had seen the change coming bit by bit and its defense elaborated by young men fresh from the Paris art schools. "We must paint what is in front of us," or "A man must be of his own time," they would say, and if I spoke of Blake or Rossetti they would point out his bad drawing and tell me to admire Carolus Duran [19] and Bastien-Lepage.[20] Then, too, they were very ignorant men; they read nothing, for nothing mattered but "knowing how to paint," being in reaction against a generation that seemed to have wasted its time upon so many things. I thought myself alone in hating these young men, their contempt for the past, their monoply of the future, but in a few months I was to discover others of my own age, who thought as I did, for it is not true that youth looks before it with the mechanical gaze of a well-drilled soldier. Its quarrel is not with the past, but with the present, where its elders are so obviously powerful and no cause seems lost if it seem to threaten that power. Does cultivated youth ever really love the future, where the eye can discover no persecuted Royalty [21] hidden among oak leaves, though from it certainly does come so much proletarian rhetoric?

I was unlike others of my generation in one thing only. I am very religious, and deprived by Huxley [22] and Tyndall,[23] whom I detested, of the simple-minded religion of my childhood,[24] I had made a new religion, almost an infallible church of poetic tradition, of a fardel of stories, and of personages, and of emotions, inseparable from their first expression, passed on from generation to generation by poets and painters with some help from philosophers and theologians. I wished for a world where I could discover this tradition perpetually, and not in pictures and in poems only, but in tiles round the chimney piece and in the hangings that kept out the draft. I had even created a dogma: "Because those imaginary people are created out of the deepest instinct of man, to be his measure and his norm, whatever I can imagine those mouths speaking may be the nearest I can go to truth." When I listened they seemed always to speak of one thing only: they, their loves, every incident of their lives, were steeped in the supernatural. Could even Titian's "Ariosto" [25] that I loved beyond other portraits

16. This selection and those that follow through "The Tragic Generation" are taken from *The Trembling of the Veil* (1922). **17. Pre-Raphaelite**: See n. 13, above. In 1887, the Yeats family had again come to live in London, in Bedford Park, the earliest of planned garden suburbs. "Years before we had lived there, when the crooked ostentatiously picturesque streets with great trees casting great shadows had been a new enthusiasm: the Pre-Raphaelite movement at last affecting life." **18. Rossetti:** Dante Gabriel Rossetti (1828–82), painter and poet, a founder of the Pre-Raphaelite movement. See Intro., pp. 781–82, and "The Tragic Generation," pp. 815–16.

**19. Duran:** Carolus-Duran or Charles Durand (1837–1917), French portrait painter and teacher of many famous artists. **20. Bastien-Lepage:** Jules Bastien-Lepage (1848–84), French painter of figures in the open air. **21. Royalty:** After the execution of Charles I, Prince Charles had hidden in an oak tree in order to escape from his would-be murderers. **22. Huxley:** Thomas H. Huxley (1825–95), biologist and exponent of Darwinism. **23. Tyndall:** John Tyndall (1820–93), physicist; also lecturer and writer on scientific subjects "for unscientific people." See Shaw, *Man and Superman*, IV, p. 774, n. 3. **24. religion . . . childhood:** See Intro., p. 781. **25. Titian's "Ariosto":** a painting by Titian (1477–1576) in the National Gallery, London, formerly regarded as a portrait of the Italian poet, Ariosto (1474–1533), but now described as "Portrait of a Man." For the meaning Yeats attached to this portrait, with

have its grave look, as if waiting for some perfect final event, if the painters before Titian had not learned portraiture, while painting into the corner of compositions full of saints and Madonnas, their kneeling patrons? At seventeen years old I was already an old-fashioned brass cannon full of shot, and nothing had kept me from going off but a doubt as to my capacity to shoot straight.

## MAUD GONNE

Presently [26] a hansom drove up to our door at Bedford Park with Miss Maud Gonne,[27] who brought an introduction to my father from old John O'Leary, the Fenian leader. She vexed my father by praise of war, war for its own sake, not as the creator of certain virtues but as if there were some virtue in excitement itself. I supported her against my father, which vexed him the more, though he might have understood that, apart from the fact that Carolus Duran and Bastien-Lepage were somehow involved, a man young as I could not have differed from a woman so beautiful and so young. Today, with her great height and the unchangeable lineaments of her form, she looks the sibyl I would have had played by Florence Farr,[28] but in that day she seemed a classical impersonation of the Spring, the Virgilian commendation, "She walks like a goddess," [29] made for her alone. Her complexion was luminous, like that of apple blossom through which the light falls, and I remember her standing that first day by a great heap of such blossoms in the window. In the next few years I saw her always when she passed to and fro between Dublin and Paris, surrounded, no matter how rapid her journey and how brief her stay at either end of it, by cages full of birds, canaries, finches of all kinds, dogs, a parrot, and once a full-grown hawk from Donegal. Once when I saw her to her railway carriage I noticed how the cages obstructed wraps and cushions and wondered what her fellow-travelers would say, but the carriage remained empty. It was years before I could see into the mind that lay hidden under so much beauty and so much energy.

## "THE MASK"

### 1. *Morris: His Antithetical Dream*

It was now Morris [30] himself that stirred my interest, and I took to him first because of some little tricks of speech and body that reminded me of my old grandfather in Sligo, but soon discovered his spontaneity and joy and made him my chief of men. Today I do not set his poetry very high, but for an odd altogether wonderful line, or thought; and yet, if some angel offered me the choice, I would choose to live his life, poetry and all, rather than my own or any other man's. A reproduction of his portrait by Watts [31] hangs over my mantelpiece with Henley's,[32] and those of other friends. Its grave wide-open eyes, like the eyes of some dreaming beast, remind me of the open eyes of Titian's "Ariosto," while the broad vigorous body suggests a mind that has no need of the intellect to remain sane, though it give itself to every fantasy: the dreamer of the Middle Ages. It is "the fool of fairy . . . wide and wild as a hill," the resolute European image that yet half remembers Buddha's motionless meditation, and has no trait in common with the wavering, lean image of hungry speculation, that cannot but because of certain famous Hamlets of our stage fill the mind's eye. Shakespeare himself foreshadowed a symbolic change, that is, a change in the whole temperament of the world, for though he called his Hamlet "fat" and even "scant of breath," he thrust between his fingers agile rapier and dagger.

The dream world [33] of Morris was as much the antithesis of daily life as with other men of genius, but he was never conscious of the antithesis and so knew nothing of intellectual suffering. His intellect, unexhausted by speculation or casuistry, was wholly at the service of hand and eye, and whatever he

its handsome and sensitive features and penetrating yet tranquil look, see his remarks below on Morris, and "Wilson and Shaw." **26. Presently:** January 30, 1889. **27. Maud Gonne:** a woman of revolutionary aims, who devoted herself to the cause of Ireland's independence and the destruction of the British Empire. Yeats here recalls his first meeting with her. He fell in love almost at once and for years tried without success to persuade her to marry him. She later married Major John MacBride. (See "Easter 1916," l. 31n.) Maud Gonne MacBride died in Dublin, April 27, 1953. **28. Florence Farr:** An actress and an intimate friend of Yeats and of Shaw, Miss Farr took important roles in the plays of both writers. Yeats admired her gift for poetic declamation, which Shaw mockingly described as "cantilating." Yeats believed that in her natural style of acting she had "a Sibyl's majesty," but that she perversely insisted on playing her roles in a more popular and realistic manner. **29. "goddess":** recalls such phrases of Virgil as *vera incessu patuit dea, Aeneid,* I.405: "By her walk she is revealed a true goddess."

**30. Morris:** William Morris (1834–96), a figure in the second phase of Pre-Raphaelitism, a poet, artist, and socialist, at whose house Yeats attended the debates of the Socialist League. At these gatherings, Yeats made the acquaintance of Shaw. **31. Watts:** George F. Watts (1817–1904), an eccentric painter, who knew many of the Pre-Raphaelites but remained outside the movement. See Shaw, *Man and Superman,* I, n. 6. **32. Henley:** W. E. Henley (1849–1903), poet and editor, who introduced to the literary public Kipling, Conrad, and Yeats, among others. **33. dream world:** the world of classical and medieval legends and northern sagas that Morris recreated in narrative poems such as *The Earthly Paradise* and *Sigurd the Volsung.*

pleased he did with an unheard-of ease and simplicity, and if style and vocabulary were at times monotonous, he could not have made them otherwise without ceasing to be himself. Instead of the language of Chaucer and Shakespeare, its warp fresh from field and market — if the woof were learned — his age offered him a speech, exhausted from abstraction, that only returned to its full vitality when written learnedly and slowly.

The roots of his antithetical dream were visible enough; a never-idle man of great physical strength and extremely irascible — did he not fling a badly baked plum pudding through the window upon Christmas Day? — a man more joyous than any intellectual man of our world, he called himself "the idle singer [34] of an empty day," created new forms of melancholy, and faint persons, like the knights and ladies of Burne-Jones,[35] who are never, no not once in forty volumes, put out of temper. A blunderer who had said to the only unconverted man at a Socialist picnic in Dublin, to prove that equality came easy, "I was brought up a gentleman and now as you can see associate with all sorts," and left wounds thereby that rankled after twenty years, a man of whom I have heard it said, "He is always afraid that he is doing something wrong and generally is," he wrote long stories with apparently no other object than that his persons might show to one another, through situations of poignant difficulty, the most exquisite tact.

### 2. *Yeats's Anti-self*

I have described what image — always opposite to the natural self or the natural world — Wilde,[36] Henley, Morris, copied or tried to copy, but I have not said if I found an image for myself. I know very little about myself and much less of that anti-self: probably the woman who cooks my dinner or the woman who sweeps out my study knows more than I. It is perhaps because nature made me a gregarious man, going hither and thither looking for conversation, and ready to deny from fear or favor his dearest conviction, that I love proud and lonely things. When I was a child and went daily to the sexton's daughter for writing lessons, I found one poem in her school reader that delighted me beyond all others: a fragment of some metrical translation from Aristophanes [37] wherein the birds sing scorn upon mankind. In later years my mind gave itself to gregarious Shelley's dream of a young man,[38] his hair blanched with sorrow, studying philosophy in some lonely tower, or of his old man,[39] master of all human knowledge, hidden from human sight in some shell-strewn cavern on the Mediterranean shore.

### 3. *Abstraction*

I generalized [40] a great deal and was ashamed of it. I thought it was my business in life to be an artist and a poet, and that there could be no business comparable to that. I refused to read books and even to meet people who excited me to generalization, all to no purpose. I said my prayers much as in childhood, though without the old regularity of hour and place, and I began to pray that my imagination might somehow be rescued from abstraction and became as preoccupied with life as had been the imagination of Chaucer. For ten or twelve years more I suffered continual remorse, and only became content when my abstractions had composed themselves into picture and dramatization. My very remorse helped to spoil my early poetry, giving it an element of sentimentality through my refusal to permit it any share of an intellect which I considered impure. Even in practical life I only very gradually began to use generalizations, that have since become the foundation of all I have done, or shall do, in Ireland. For all I know all men may have been so timid, for I am persuaded that our intellects at twenty contain all the truths we shall ever find, but as yet we do not know truths that belong to us from opinions caught up in casual irritation or momentary fantasy. As life goes on we discover that certain thoughts sustain us in defeat, or give us victory, whether over ourselves or others, and it is these thoughts, tested by passion, that we call convictions. Among subjective men (in all those, that is, who must spin a web out of their own bowels) the victory is an intellectual daily recreation of all that exterior fate

34. **"the idle singer"**: in his introductory stanzas to *The Earthly Paradise*. 35. **Burne-Jones**: Sir Edward Burne-Jones (1833–98), friend of Morris, one of the most famous of Pre-Raphaelite painters; also a designer in stained glass. 36. **Wilde**: Oscar Wilde (1856–1900), author and wit, one of the prime examples among Yeats's acquaintances of a man who in his life adopted a "pose" that reflected his "anti-self."

37. **Aristophanes**: Greek writer of comedy (last half of the fifth century, B.C.), author of *The Birds*, the play from which the "fragment" was translated. 38. **Shelley's . . . man**: Yeats refers to heroes of poems such as *Prince Athanase* and *Laon and Cythna* (in its revised form, *The Revolt of Islam*). These strangely old young men and the "old man," whom Yeats presently mentions, have affinities with the philosopher-poets of "The Tower" and "Blood and the Moon" (see above). 39. **old man**: Cf. the sage Ahasuerus in Shelley's *Hellas*. 40. **I generalized**: The period referred to in this and the following selection is somewhere between 1887 and 1891.

snatches away, and so that fate's antithesis; while what I have called "the Mask" is an emotional antithesis to all that comes out of their internal nature. We begin to live when we have conceived life as tragedy.

## UNITY OF BEING: UNITY OF CULTURE

### 1. *A World of Fragments*

A conviction that the world was now but a bundle of fragments possessed me without ceasing. I had tried this conviction on the Rhymers,[41] thereby plunging into greater silence an already too-silent evening. "Johnson," I was accustomed to say, "you are the only man I know whose silence has beak and claw." I had lectured on it to some London Irish society, and I was to lecture upon it later on in Dublin, but I never found but one interested man, an official of the Primrose League,[42] who was also an active member of the Fenian Brotherhood.[43] "I am an extreme conservative apart from Ireland," I have heard him explain; and I have no doubt that personal experience made him share the sight of any eye that saw the world in fragments. I had been put into a rage by the followers of Huxley, Tyndall, Carolus Duran, and Bastien-Lepage, who not only asserted the unimportance of subject whether in art or literature, but the independence of the arts from one another. Upon the other hand, I delighted in every age where poet and artist confined themselves gladly to some inherited subject matter known to the whole people, for I thought that in man and race alike there is something called "Unity of Being," using that term as Dante used it when he compared beauty in the *Convito*[44] to a perfectly proportioned human body. My father, from whom I had learned the term, preferred a comparison to a musical instrument so strung that if we touch a string all the strings murmur faintly. There is not more desire, he had said, in lust than in true love, but in true love desire awakens pity, hope, affection, admiration and, given appropriate circumstance, every emotion possible to man. When I began, however, to apply this thought to the state and to argue for a law-made balance among trades and occupations my father displayed at once the violent free trader and propagandist of liberty. I thought that the enemy of this unity was abstraction, meaning by abstraction not the distinction but the isolation of occupation, or class or faculty. . . .

I knew no medieval cathedral, and Westminster, being a part of abhorred London, did not interest me, but I thought constantly of Homer and Dante, and the tombs of Mausolus and Artemisia,[45] the great figures of King and Queen and the lesser figures of Greek and Amazon, Centaur[46] and Greek. I thought that all art should be a Centaur finding in the popular lore its back and its strong legs. I got great pleasure too from remembering that Homer was sung, and from that tale of Dante hearing a common man sing some stanza from *The Divine Comedy,* and from Don Quixote's meeting with some common man that sang Ariosto.[47] Morris had never seemed to care greatly for any poet later than Chaucer, and though I preferred Shakespeare to Chaucer I begrudged my own preference. Had not Europe shared one mind and heart, until both mind and heart began to break into fragments a little before Shakespeare's birth? Music and verse began to fall apart when Chaucer robbed verse of its speed that he might give it greater meditation, though for another generation or so minstrels were to sing his lengthy elaborated *Troilus and Criseyde;* painting parted from religion in the later Renaissance that it might study effects of tangibility undisturbed; while, that it might characterize, where it had once personified, it renounced, in our own age, all that inherited subject matter which we have named poetry. Presently I was indeed to number character itself among the abstractions, encouraged by Congreve's[48] saying that "passions are too powerful in the fair sex to let humor"—or as we say character—"have its course." Nor have we fared better under the common daylight, for pure reason has notoriously made but light of practical reason, and has been made light of in its turn from that morning when Descartes[49] discovered that he could think better in his bed than out of it; nor needed I original thought to discover, being so late of the school of Morris, that machinery had not separated from handicraft wholly for the world's good, nor to notice that the

**41. Rhymers:** The Rhymers Club, of which Yeats was a founder, included among other writers Lionel Johnson, Ernest Dowson, and Arthur Symons. See Intro., p. 782. **42. Primrose League:** an English political organization of members of the Conservative Party. **43. Fenian Brotherhood:** See n. 4, above. **44. *Convito:*** more properly, *Il Convivio, The Banquet,* a collection of odes on love and virtue with allegorical interpretations.

**45. Mausolus . . . Artemisia:** refers to the Mausoleum, the tomb of Mausolus (*c.* 376–353 B.C.), erected by his wife Artemisia. Yeats was thinking of the grand sculptures from this tomb now in the British Museum. "King" and "Queen" refer to the two rulers (in fact a Persian satrap and his wife). **46. Centaur:** See "Lines Written in Dejection," especially l. 7n., above. **47. Ariosto:** See n. 25, above. **48. Congreve:** William Congreve (1670–1729), writer of comedy. **49. Descartes:** René Descartes (1596–1650), French philosopher and scientist, author of the *Discourse on Method.*

distinction of classes had become their isolation. If the London merchants of our day competed together in writing lyrics they would not, like the Tudor merchants, dance in the open street before the house of the victor; nor do the great ladies of London finish their balls on the pavement before their doors as did the great Venetian ladies, even in the eighteenth century, conscious of an all-enfolding sympathy. Doubtless because fragments broke into even smaller fragments we saw one another in a light of bitter comedy, and in the arts, where now one technical element reigned and now another, generation hated generation, and accomplished beauty was snatched away when it had most engaged our affections. One thing I did not foresee, not having the courage of my own thought: the growing murderousness of the world.

## 2. *Image of Unity*

If abstraction had reached, or all but reached its climax, escape might be possible for many, and if it had not, individual men might still escape. If Chaucer's personages had disengaged themselves from Chaucer's crowd, forgot their common goal and shrine, and after sundry magnifications became each in turn the center of some Elizabethan play, and had after split into their elements and so given birth to romantic poetry, must I reverse the cinematograph? I thought that the general movement of literature must be such a reversal, men being there displayed in casual, temporary, contact as at the Tabard door. I had lately read Tolstoy's *Anna Karenina* and thought that where his theoretical capacity had not awakened there was such a turning back: but a nation or an individual with great emotional intensity might follow the pilgrims as it were to some unknown shrine, and give to all those separated elements and to all that abstract love and melancholy, a symbolical, a mythological coherence. Not Chaucer's rough-tongued riders, but rather an ended pilgrimage, a procession of the Gods! Arthur Symons [50] brought back from Paris stories of Verhaeren and Maeterlinck, and so brought me confirmation, as I thought, and I began to announce a poetry like that of the Sufis.[51] I could not endure, however, an international art, picking stories and symbols where it pleased. Might I not, with health and good luck to aid me, create some new *Prometheus Unbound;* [52] Patrick or Columbkil,[53] Oisin or Fion,[54] in Prometheus' stead; and, instead of Caucasus, Cro-Patric or Ben Bulben? [55] Have not all races had their first unity from a mythology, that marries them to rock and hill? We had in Ireland imaginative stories, which the uneducated classes knew and even sang, and might we not make those stories current among the educated classes, rediscovering for the work's sake what I have called "the applied arts of literature," the association of literature, that is, with music, speech, and dance; and at last, it might be, so deepen the political passion of the nation that all, artist and poet, craftsman and day laborer would accept a common design? Perhaps even these images, once created and associated with river and mountain, might move of themselves and with some powerful, even turbulent life, like those painted horses that trampled the rice-fields of Japan.

I used to tell the few friends to whom I could speak these secret thoughts that I would make the attempt in Ireland but fail, for our civilization, its elements multiplying by division like certain low forms of life, was all-powerful; but in reality I had the wildest hopes. Today I add to that first conviction, to that first desire for unity, this other conviction, long a mere opinion vaguely or intermittently apprehended: Nations, races, and individual men are unified by an image, or bundle of related images, symbolical or evocative of the state of mind, which is of all states of mind not impossible, the most difficult to that man, race, or nation; because only the greatest obstacle that can be contemplated without despair, rouses the will to full intensity.

## 3. *Shaw's* Arms and the Man

Shaw,[56] whose turn came next, had foreseen all months before, and had planned an opening that would confound his enemies. For the first few min-

**50. Symons:** See Intro., p. 782. On Verhaeren and Maeterlinck, see nn. 87, 88, below. **51. Sufis:** The Sufis were members of a Mohammedan mystic order, which included the greatest Persian poets. The lyrics of the Sufis often express symbolically the soul's union with God. Through writing a similar sort of poetry based on Irish myths, Yeats seems to have hoped to generate a unity of belief in Ireland.

**52. *Prometheus Unbound:*** Shelley's lyric drama. **53. Columbkil:** St. Columba or Columcille (*c.* 521–97), founder of monasteries in Ireland and Scotland. **54. Oisin:** legendary poet-hero of Ireland. See headnote to "Vacillation," VII, VIII, above. **Fion:** or Fionn, hero of enormous stature, father of Oisin. **55. Caucasus:** the mountain to which the hero Prometheus was chained. **Cro-Patric:** or Croagh Patrick, Ireland's holiest mountain; from here St. Patrick banished snakes and toads from Ireland. **Ben Bulben:** mountain in Sligo, visible from his grandparents' home. Mountains in the area had many associations with Irish heroes. See "Middletons and Pollexfens," above. **56. Shaw:** Yeats's account of the first performance, in 1894, of Shaw's *Arms and the Man*, at the Avenue Theatre, London, which was managed

utes *Arms and the Man* is crude melodrama and then, just when the audience are thinking how crude it is, it turns into excellent farce. At the dress rehearsal, a dramatist who had his own quarrel with the public, was taken in the noose; at the first laugh he stood up, turned his back on the stage, scowled at the audience, and even when everybody else knew what turn the play had taken, continued to scowl, and order those nearest to be silent.

On the first night the whole pit and gallery, except certain members of the Fabian Society, started to laugh at the author and then, discovering that they themselves were being laughed at, sat there not converted — their hatred was too bitter for that — but dumbfounded, while the rest of the house cheered and laughed. In the silence that greeted the author after the cry for a speech one man did indeed get his courage and boo loudly. "I assure the gentleman in the gallery," was Shaw's answer, "that he and I are of exactly the same opinion, but what can we do against a whole house who are of the contrary opinion?" And from that moment Bernard Shaw became the most formidable man in modern letters, and even the most drunken of medical students knew it. My own play,[57] which had been played with *The Comedy of Sighs,* had roused no passions, but had pleased a sufficient minority for Florence Farr to keep it upon the stage with *Arms and the Man,* and I was in the theater almost every night for some weeks. "Oh, yes, the people seem to like *Arms and the Man,*" said one of Mr. Shaw's players to me, "but we have just found out that we are all wrong. Mr. Shaw did really mean it quite seriously, for he has written a letter to say so, and we must not play for laughs any more." Another night I found the manager, triumphant and excited, the Prince of Wales and the Duke of Edinburgh [58] had been there, and the Duke of Edinburgh had spoken his dislike out loud so that the whole stalls could hear, but the Prince of Wales had been "very pleasant" and "got the Duke of Edinburgh away as soon as possible." "They asked for me," he went on, "and the Duke of Edinburgh kept on repeating, 'The man is mad,' meaning Mr. Shaw, and the Prince of Wales asked who Mr. Shaw was, and what he meant by it." I myself was almost as bewildered for though I came mainly to see how my own play went, and for the first fortnight to vex my most patient actors with new lines, I listened to *Arms and the Man* with admiration and hatred. It seemed to me inorganic, logical straightness and not the crooked road of life, yet I stood aghast before its energy as today before that of the "Stone Drill" by Mr. Epstein [59] or of some design by Mr. Wyndham Lewis.[60] He was right to claim Samuel Butler [61] for his master, for Butler was the first Englishman to make the discovery, that it is possible to write with great effect without music, without style, either good or bad, to eliminate from the mind all emotional implication and to prefer plain water to every vintage, so much metropolitan lead and solder to any tendril of the vine. Presently I had a nightmare that I was haunted by a sewing machine, that clicked and shone, but the incredible thing was that the machine smiled, smiled perpetually. Yet I delighted in Shaw the formidable man. He could hit my enemies and the enemies of all I loved, as I could never hit, as no living author that was dear to me could ever hit.

### 4. *Wilson and Shaw: "Phases of the Moon"*

Somewhere about 1450, though later in some parts of Europe by a hundred years or so, and in some earlier, men attained to personality in great numbers, "Unity of Being," and became like a "perfectly proportioned human body," and as men so fashioned held places of power, their nations had it too, prince and plowman sharing that thought and feeling. What afterwards showed for rifts and cracks were there already, but imperious impulse held all together. Then the scattering came, the seeding of the poppy, bursting of peapod, and for a time personality seemed but the stronger for it. Shakespeare's people make all things serve their passion, and that passion is for the moment the whole energy of their being — birds, beasts, men, women, landscape, society, are but symbols, and

by Florence Farr. (See n. 28 above.) Shaw's "turn came next" after Dr. John Todhunter's *The Comedy of Sighs*, which met with "boos and jeers." See pp. 687–88. **57. My . . . play:** *The Land of Heart's Desire.* **58. Wales . . . Edinburgh:** The Prince of Wales, later King Edward VII (1841–1910), was a man of the world and a patron of the arts and sciences. His tolerance of Shaw was characteristic, and in marked contrast to the proper Victorian attitude of his brother, the Duke of Edinburgh (1844–1900).

**59. Epstein:** Jacob Epstein (1880– ), American-born sculptor living in England, whose figures often show a primitive massiveness and the surprising "energy" of which Yeats speaks. **60. Wyndham Lewis:** writer and artist (1886– ), associate of Ezra Pound, a pioneer in England of Cubism, one of the earliest modern movements in abstract design. **61. Samuel Butler:** English writer (1835–1902); his novel, *The Way of All Flesh,* was highly critical of Victorian moral and religious standards. On Shaw's style, see Shaw, Intro., pp. 685–86.

metaphors, nothing is studied in itself, the mind is a dark well, no surface, depth only. The men that Titian[62] painted, the men that Jongsen painted, even the men of Van Dyck,[63] seemed at moments like great hawks at rest. In the Dublin National Gallery there hung, perhaps there still hang, upon the same wall, a portrait of some Venetian gentleman by Strozzi and Mr. Sargent's[64] painting of President Wilson. Whatever thought broods in the dark eyes of that Venetian gentleman has drawn its life from his whole body; it feeds upon it as the flame feeds upon the candle — and should that thought be changed, his pose would change, his very cloak would rustle for his whole body thinks. President Wilson lives only in the eyes, which are steady and intent; the flesh about the mouth is dead, and the hands are dead, and the clothes suggest no movement of his body, nor any movement but that of the valet, who has brushed and folded in mechanical routine. There, all was an energy flowing outward from the nature itself; here, all is the anxious study and slight deflection of external force; there man's mind and body were predominantly subjective; here all is objective, using those words not as philosophy uses them, but as we use them in conversation.

The bright part of the moon's disk, to adopt the symbolism of a certain poem,[65] is subjective mind, and the dark, objective mind, and we have eight and twenty Phases for our classification of mankind, and of the movement of its thought. At the first Phase — the night where there is no moonlight — all is objective, while when, upon the fifteenth night, the moon comes to the full, there is only subjective mind. The mid-Renaissance could but approximate to the full moon, "For there's no human life at the full or the dark," but we may attribute to the next three nights of the moon the men of Shakespeare, of Titian, of Strozzi, and of Van Dyck, and watch them grow more reasonable, more orderly, less turbulent, as the nights pass; and it is well to find before the fourth — the nineteenth moon counting from the start — a sudden change, as when a cloud becomes rain, or water freezes, for the great transitions are sudden; popular, typical men have grown more ugly and more argumentative; the face that Van Dyck called a fatal face[66] has faded before Cromwell's warty opinionated head. Henceforth no mind made like "a perfectly proportioned human body" shall sway the public, for great men must live in a portion of themselves, become professional and abstract; but seeing that the moon's third quarter is scarce passed; that abstraction has attained but not passed its climax; that a half, as I affirm it, of the twenty-second night still lingers, they may subdue and conquer, cherish even some Utopian dream, spread abstraction ever further till thought is but a film and there is no dark depth any more, surface only. But men who belong by nature to the nights near to the full are still born, a tragic minority, and how shall they do their work when too ambitious for a private station, except as Wilde of the nineteenth Phase, as my symbolism has it, did his work? He understood his weakness, true personality was impossible, for that is born in solitude, and at his moon one is not solitary; he must project himself before the eyes of others, and, having great ambition, before some great crowd of eyes; but there is no longer any great crowd that cares for his true thought. He must humor and cajole and pose, take worn-out stage situations, for he knows that he may be as romantic as he please, so long as he does not believe in his romance, and all that he may get their ears for a few strokes of contemptuous wit in which he does believe.

We Rhymers did not humor and cajole; but it was not wholly from demerit, it was in part because of different merit, that he refused our exile. Shaw, as I understand him, has no true quarrel with his time, its moon and his almost exactly coincide. He is quite content to exchange Narcissus[67] and his Pool for the signal box at a railway junction, where goods and travelers pass perpetually upon their logical glittering road. Wilde was a monarchist, though content that monarchy should turn demagogue for its own safety, and he held a theater by the means whereby he held a London dinner table. "He who can dominate a London dinner table," he had boasted, "can dominate the world." While Shaw has but carried his street-corner socialist eloquence on to the stage, and in him one discovers, in his writing and his public speech, as once — be-

62. **Titian:** See n. 25, above. 63. **Jongsen . . . Van Dyck:** probably Cornelius Johnson or Janssen van Ceulen (1593–1664?), Dutch portrait painter. **Van Dyck:** Sir Anthony Van Dyck (1599–1641), Flemish painter, best known for portraits of European nobility. He was court painter to Charles I of England (1600–49). Van Dyck's remark about King Charles (who was later beheaded) is referred to below. See n. 66. 64. **Strozzi:** Bernardo Strozzi (1581–1644), Italian painter. **Sargent:** John Singer Sargent (1856–1925), American portrait painter. 65. **a . . . poem:** "The Phases of the Moon," *Collected Poems*, pp. 160–64. The symbolism of the "phases" was further elaborated in *A Vision.* See Intro., p. 788.

66. **fatal face:** Charles I. See n. 63. 67. **Narcissus:** According to the myth, he fell in love with his own reflection; for Yeats he is an example of the "solitary," that is, the "subjective," man.

fore their outline had been softened by prosperity or the passage of the years — in his clothes and in his stiff joints, the civilization that Sargent's picture has explored. Neither his crowd nor he have yet made a discovery that brought President Wilson so near his death, that the moon draws to its fourth quarter. But what happens to the individual man whose moon has come to that fourth quarter, and what to the civilization . . . ?

I can but remember pipe music tonight, though I can half hear beyond it in the memory a weightier music, but this much at any rate is certain — the dream of my early manhood, that a modern nation can return to Unity of Culture, is false; though it may be we can achieve it for some small circle of men and women, and there leave it till the moon bring round its century.

### 5. *"The Tragic Generation"*

Two men are always at my side, Lionel Johnson [68] and John Synge [69] whom I was to meet a little later; but Johnson is to me the more vivid in memory, possibly because of the external finish, the clearly marked lineament of his body, which seemed but to express the clarity of his mind. I think Dowson's [70] best verse immortal, bound, that is, to outlive famous novels and plays and learned histories and other discursive things, but he was too vague and gentle for my affections. I understood him too well, for I had been like him but for the appetite that made me search out strong condiments. Though I cannot explain what brought others of my generation to such misfortune, I think that (falling backward upon my parable of the moon) I can explain some part of Dowson's and Johnson's dissipation —

> What portion in the world can the artist have,
> Who has awaked from the common dream,
> But dissipation and despair? [71]

When Edmund Spenser described the islands of Phaedria [72] and of Acrasia [73] he aroused the indignation of Lord Burleigh, "that rugged forehead," and Lord Burleigh was in the right if morality were our only object.

In those islands certain qualities of beauty, certain forms of sensuous loveliness were separated from all the general purposes of life, as they had not been hitherto in European literature — and would not be again, for even the historical process has its ebb and flow, till Keats wrote his *Endymion.*[74] I think that the movement of our thought has more and more so separated certain images and regions of the mind, and that these images grow in beauty as they grow in sterility. Shakespeare leaned, as it were, even as craftsman, upon the general fate of men and nations, had about him the excitement of the playhouse; and all poets, including Spenser in all but a few pages, until our age came, and when it came almost all, have had some propaganda or traditional doctrine to give companionship with their fellows. Had not Matthew Arnold [75] his faith in what he described as the best thought of his generation? Browning his psychological curiosity, Tennyson, as before him Shelley and Wordsworth, moral values that were not aesthetic values? But Coleridge of the "Ancient Mariner," and "Kubla Khan," and Rossetti in all his writing made what Arnold has called that "morbid effort," that search for "perfection of thought and feeling, and to unite this to perfection of form," sought this new, pure beauty, and suffered in their lives because of it. The typical men of the classical age (I think of Commodus,[76] with his half-animal beauty, his cruelty and his caprice), lived public lives, pursuing curiosities of appetite, and so found in Christianity, with its Thebaid and its Mariotic Sea the needed curb.[77] But what can the Christian confessor say to those who more and more must make all out of the privacy of their

**68. Johnson:** On Johnson and the Rhymers, see n. 41, above. **69. John Synge:** See "Coole Park, 1929," l. 13n., above. **70. Dowson:** Ernest C. Dowson (1867–1900), poet, member of the Rhymers, best known for his worldly and exquisite lyrics. **71. What . . . despair?:** quoted from Yeats's "Ego Dominus Tuus," ll. 49–51, *Collected Poems*, p. 159, a poem based on the theories of the Mask and the Phases of the Moon. **72. Phaedria:** the Lady of the Idle Lake, *Faerie Queene*, II.vi.9–18. See pp. 127–28 in Vol. I. **73. Acrasia:** the island of Acrasia, "Whereas the Bowre of Blisse was situate," *Faerie Queene*, II.xii.37–87. See pp. 134–38 in Vol. I.

**74. *Endymion:*** See pp. 265–68 in Vol. I, and Intro., p. 785. **75. Arnold:** in "The Function of Criticism," p. 630, above. **76. Commodus:** Roman emperor (180–92 A.D.), brutal son of Marcus Aurelius, who was fond of displaying his prowess in extraordinary gladiatorial combats, such as shooting down giraffes with a bow and arrow. Observe the implied definition of "the classical age." **77. needed curb:** Yeats is again referring to his cyclic theory of history. See Intro., p. 788, "The Second Coming," and "Two Songs from a Play," above. As each cycle of history is completed, it is followed by a new cycle whose civilization represents the antithesis of the one which has just come to an end. The "objective" (i.e., "public") man, typical of "the classical age," is followed by the "subjective" man, typical of the Christian era. Christianity thus offered a "curb" to the opposing tendency in the preceding phase of history. The exact symbolic meaning of "Thebaid and its Mariotic Sea" is obscure. The Thebaid is the region around Thebes in Egypt; the Mariotic Sea (properly the Mareotis) is a salt lake also in Egypt. Both apparently suggest the desert region and the darkness of the "rough beast," the sphinx-like creature of "The Second Coming," l. 21, above. In the present passage the region seems to symbolize the darkness and irrationality of the "subjective" phase, which was initiated by the birth of Christ. Cf. "Demon and Beast," ll. 43–50, *Collected Poems*, p. 184.

thought, calling up perpetual images of desire, for he cannot say "Cease to be artist, cease to be poet," [78] where the whole life is art and poetry, nor can he bid men leave the world, who suffer from the terrors that pass before shut-eyes. Coleridge, and Rossetti though his dull brother did once persuade him that he was an agnostic, were devout Christians, and Steinbock and Beardsley [79] were so towards their lives' end, and Dowson and Johnson always, and yet I think it but deepened despair and multiplied temptation. . . .

Why are these strange souls born everywhere today? with hearts that Christianity, as shaped by history, cannot satisfy. Our love letters wear out our love; [80] no school of painting outlasts its founders, every stroke of the brush exhausts the impulse, Pre-Raphaelitism had some twenty years; impressionism thirty perhaps. Why should we believe that religion can never bring round its antithesis? Is it true that our air is disturbed, as Mallarmé [81] said, by "the trembling of the veil of the temple," or "that our whole age is seeking to bring forth a sacred book"? Some of us thought that book near towards the end of last century, but the tide sank again.

### YEATS ON HIS OWN WRITING [82]

. . . I am but a writer of plays which are acted by players with a literary mind for a few evenings, and I have altered them so many times that I doubt the value of every passage. I am more confident of my lyrics, or of some few amongst them, but then I have got into the habit of recommending or commending myself to general company for anything rather than my gift of lyric writing, which concerns such a meager troop.

Every now and then, when something has stirred my imagination, I begin talking to myself. I speak in my own person and dramatize myself, very much as I have seen a mad old woman do upon the Dublin quays, and sometimes detect myself speaking and moving as if I were still young, or walking perhaps like an old man with fumbling steps. Occasionally, I write out what I have said in verse, and generally for no better reason than because I remember that I have written no verse for a long time. I do not think of my soliloquies as having different literary qualities. They stir my interest, by their appropriateness to the men I imagine myself to be, or by their accurate description of some emotional circumstance, more than by any aesthetic value. When I begin to write I have no object but to find for them some natural speech, rhythm and syntax, and to set it out in some pattern, so seeming old that it may seem all men's speech, and though the labor is very great, I seem to have used no faculty peculiar to myself, certainly no special gift. I print the poem and never hear about it again, until I find the book years after with a page dog-eared by some young man, or marked by some young girl with a violet, and when I have seen that I am a little ashamed, as though somebody were to attribute to me a delicacy of feeling I should but do not possess. What came so easily at first, and amidst so much drama, and was written so laboriously at the last, cannot be counted among my possessions.

78. **"poet"**: On the conflict between Christianity and poetry, see "Vacillation," above. 79. **Beardsley**: Aubrey Beardsley (1872–98), illustrator famous for black and white drawings that were often erotic but also rather terrifying in their expression of evil. He was briefly editor of the *Yellow Book*, a periodical to which Yeats and other Rhymers contributed. 80. **love**: Cf. "Two Songs from a Play," ll. 27–30, above. 81. **Mallarmé**: Stéphane Mallarmé (1842–98), one of the founders of Symbolist poetry in France. See Intro., p. 782. The phrase, "the trembling of the veil" ("*une inquiétude du voile dans le temple*") was first printed March 26, 1892, in the *National Observer*, edited by Henley, a journal in which some of Yeats's work was also published. At the death of Christ, "the veil of the temple was rent in twain" (Matt. 27:51). The phrase is used by Yeats to express his feeling that some great change was about to take place in the intellectual and religious life of Europe. 82. From *The Bounty of Sweden* (1925), a journal kept by Yeats during his trip to Sweden, when he went there to receive the Nobel Prize (1923).

## SELECTIONS FROM THE ESSAYS

### PERSONALITY AND THE INTELLECTUAL ESSENCES [83]

My work [84] in Ireland has continually set this thought before me: "How can I make my work mean something to vigorous and simple men whose attention is not given to art but to a shop, or teaching in a National School, or dispensing medicine?" I had not wanted to "elevate them" or "educate them," as these words are understood, but to make them understand my vision, and I had not wanted a large audience, certainly not what is called a national audience, but enough people for what is accidental and temporary to lose itself in the lump. In England, where there have been so many changing activities and so much systematic education, one only escapes from crudities and temporary interests

83. One of the group of essays entitled "Discoveries" (1906), in *The Cutting of an Agate*. 84. **My work**: particularly as a writer for the Irish Theatre.

among students, but here there is the right audience, could one but get its ears. I have always come to this certainty: what moves natural men in the arts is what moves them in life, and that is, intensity of personal life, intonations that show them in a book or a play, the strength, the essential moment of a man who would be exciting in the market or at the dispensary door. They must go out of the theater with the strength they live by strengthened from looking upon some passion that could, whatever its chosen way of life, strike down an enemy, fill a long stocking with money, or move a girl's heart. They have not much to do with the speculations of science, though they have a little, or with the speculations of metaphysics, though they have a little. Their legs will tire on the road if there is nothing in their hearts but vague sentiment, and though it is charming to have an affectionate feeling about flowers, that will not pull the cart out of the ditch. An exciting person, whether the hero of a play or the maker of poems, will display the greatest volume of personal energy, and this energy must seem to come out of the body as out of the mind. We must say to ourselves continually when we imagine a character: "Have I given him the roots, as it were, of all faculties necessary for life?" And only when one is certain of that may one give him the one faculty that fills the imagination with joy. I even doubt if any play had ever a great popularity that did not use, or seem to use, the bodily energies of its principal actor to the full. Villon [85] the robber could have delighted these Irishmen with plays and songs, if he and they had been born to the same traditions of word and symbol, but Shelley could not; and as men came to live in towns and to read printed books and to have many specialized activities, it has become more possible to produce Shelleys and less and less possible to produce Villons. The last Villon dwindled into Robert Burns because the highest faculties had faded, taking the sense of beauty with them, into some sort of vague heaven and left the lower to lumber where they best could. In literature, partly from the lack of that spoken word which knits us to normal man, we have lost in personality, in our delight in the whole man [86] — blood, imagination, intellect, running together — but have found a new delight, in essences, in states of mind, in pure imagination, in all that comes to us most easily in elaborate music. There are two ways before literature — upward into ever-growing subtlety, with Verhaeren,[87] with Mallarmé, with Maeterlinck,[88] until at last, it may be, a new agreement among refined and studious men gives birth to a new passion, and what seems literature becomes religion; or downward, taking the soul with us until all is simplified and solidified again. That is the choice of choices — the way of the bird until common eyes have lost us, or to the market carts; but we must see to it that the soul goes with us, for the bird's song is beautiful, and the traditions of modern imagination, growing always more musical, more lyrical, more melancholy, casting up now a Shelley, now a Swinburne, now a Wagner, are, it may be, the frenzy of those that are about to see what the magic hymn printed by the Abbé de Villars [89] has called the Crown of Living and Melodious Diamonds. If the carts have hit our fancy, we must have the soul tight within our bodies, for it has grown so fond of a beauty accumulated by subtle generations that it will for a long time be impatient with our thirst for mere force, mere personality, for the tumult of the blood. If it begin to slip away we must go after it, for Shelley's Chapel of the Morning Star [90] is better than Burns's beerhouse [91] — surely it was beer, not barleycorn — except at the day's weary end; and it is always better than that uncomfortable place where there is no beer, the machine shop of the realists.

85. **Villon:** François Villon (1431–after 1463), French poet, at one time a member of a gang of thieves, whose jargon he used in some of his ballads. 86. **the whole man:** See "Among School Children," l. 61n. above.

## RHETORICIANS, SENTIMENTALISTS, AND POETS [92]

We make out of the quarrel with others, rhetoric, but of the quarrel [93] with ourselves, poetry. Unlike the rhetoricians, who get a confident voice from remembering the crowd they have won or may win, we sing amid our uncertainty; and, smitten even in

87. **Verhaeren:** Emile Verhaeren (1855–1916), Belgian poet, who wrote in a style with affinities to that of the Symbolists. On Mallarmé, see n. 81. 88. **Maeterlinck:** Maurice Maeterlinck (1862–1949), a Belgian writer of dramas in the Symbolist manner. 89. **Abbé de Villars:** l'abbé de Villars (1635–73), author of *Comte de Gabalis,* a work critical of magic and other occult sciences. 90. **Chapel . . . Star:** According to Yeats, the Morning Star was the most important of Shelley's symbols; it is ". . . a symbol of love, or liberty, or wisdom, or beauty, or of some other expression of that Intellectual Beauty, which was to Shelley's mind the central power of the world . . ." ("Shelley's Poetry," in *Ideas of Good and Evil, Essays,* pp. 108–09). 91. **Burns's beerhouse:** referring to compositions by Burns such as "Tam o'Shanter" and "The Jolly Beggars." 92. From "Anima Hominis" (1917) in *Per Amica Silentia Lunae.* 93. **quarrel:** See Intro., p. 784.

the presence of the most high beauty by the knowledge of our solitude, our rhythm shudders. I think, too, that no fine poet, no matter how disordered his life, has ever, even in his mere life, had pleasure for his end. Johnson and Dowson, friends of my youth, were dissipated men, the one a drunkard, the other a drunkard and mad about women, and yet they had the gravity of men who had found life out and were awakening from the dream; and both, one in life and art and one in art and less in life, had a continual preoccupation with religion. Nor has any poet I have read of or heard of or met with been a sentimentalist. The other self, the anti-self [94] or the antithetical self, as one may choose to name it, comes but to those who are no longer deceived, whose passion is reality. The sentimentalists are practical men who believe in money, in position, in a marriage bell, and whose understanding of happiness is to be so busy whether at work or at play, that all is forgotten but the momentary aim. They find their pleasure in a cup that is filled from Lethe's wharf, and for the awakening, for the vision, for the revelation of reality, tradition offers us a different word — ecstasy. An old artist [95] wrote to me of his wanderings by the quays of New York, and how he found there a woman nursing a sick child, and drew her story from her. She spoke, too, of other children who had died: a long tragic story. "I wanted to paint her," he wrote, "if I denied myself any of the pain I could not believe in my own ecstasy." We must not make a false faith by hiding from our thoughts the causes of doubt, for faith is the highest achievement of the human intellect, the only gift man can make to God, and therefore it must be offered in sincerity. Neither must we create, by hiding ugliness, a false beauty as our offering to the world. He only can create the greatest imaginable beauty who has endured all imaginable pangs, for only when we have seen and foreseen what we dread shall we be rewarded by that dazzling unforeseen wing-footed wanderer.

**94. anti-self:** See "The Mask," and Intro., p. 627.

**95. old artist:** Yeats's father, J. B. Yeats. The letter, well worth looking up, is dated July 2, 1913, in *J. B. Yeats, Letters to His Son W. B. Yeats and Others*. See Reading Suggestions, p. 790, above.

ELIZABETH DREW, Editor

# T. S. Eliot

## 1888–

On June 21, 1917, *The Times Literary Supplement* of London gave a short review of a volume of poems entitled *Prufrock and Other Observations,* by T. S. Eliot. The author was an American, whose ancestors had come to Massachusetts from England in 1670. He was born in St. Louis in 1888 and had recently settled in London, where he worked as a clerk in the foreign department of Lloyds Bank in the City. The reviewer was far from enthusiastic:

> Mr Eliot's notion of poetry . . . seems to be a purely analytical treatment, verging sometimes on the catalogue, of personal relations and environments, uninspired by any glimpse beyond them and untouched by any genuine rush of feeling. As, even on this basis, he remains frequently inarticulate, his "poems" will hardly be read by many with enjoyment.

Thirty-one years later, in 1948, Eliot was awarded the Nobel prize for literature, and in the same year, in honor of his sixtieth birthday, a Symposium of tributes to him was published in London. This contained contributions from forty-seven writers from more than a dozen different countries, and hailed the poet-critic-dramatist as perhaps the most powerful literary influence in the civilized world of today. It gave several glimpses of him in his early years; first as a quiet student at Harvard, where, however, he insisted on disciplining his natural shyness by going out to parties, and resisting his natural sedentary habits by taking boxing lessons and learning "how to swarm with passion up a rope." Then, on his removal to London in 1915 (after periods in Paris, Marburg, and Oxford) we see him recognized by a small circle of intellectuals as having genius, winning a reputation as a brilliant talker, though "with a studied primness of manner and speech," marked as somewhat of a dandy in his dress, and a lover of practical jokes.

In the London of 1915 the dictator of the *avant-garde* in literary taste was Ezra Pound. Pound had come to England from the Midwest of America a few years before, full of revolutionary ideas about the reform of the language and content of poetry. Pound loved to "discover" young talent and to bring it to birth in the world of letters under his patronage. Though critics disagree violently about the value of Pound's own verse, he had a real enthusiasm for good writing, and he recognized Eliot's quality at once. He bullied Harriet Monroe into publishing "Prufrock" in her new magazine, *Poetry,* in June, 1915, and he introduced Eliot to Harriet Weaver, whose Egoist Press put out the first volume of his poems. It was he, too, when Eliot had a breakdown in health a few years later, who collected money to send him on a holiday in Switzerland, one outcome of which was the completion of *The Waste Land.* Eliot has never ceased to acknowledge his debt to Pound, though it is doubtful if his purely *literary* debt is as great as he has always declared. Eliot had developed his own literary creed, in theory and in practice, years before he met Pound. But Pound did most to get a hearing for it. It was his apostolic zeal, his dynamic enthusiasm, and his dogged determination to get the work before the public that finally launched it.

Once the early work had found publishers, Eliot needed no impresario. Slowly but steadily his reputation increased. In 1922 he founded the *Criterion,* the leading English literary review for many years, and a few years later he joined the publishing house of Faber and Gwyer (now Faber and Faber).

But the history of Eliot's mind and personality during the years since the 1920's is in his poems and essays rather than in the outward events of his life, and it is not too much to say that through them he has changed the current of taste and accomplishment of his age. If poets and critics have now ceased to value the Romantics and the Victorians as they were valued a generation ago, and have exalted in their place the Elizabethans and Metaphysicals, Dante, and the French poets of the nineteenth century, Eliot more than anyone else is responsible. He has done more than Pound himself, or than any other writer, to bring about "the revolution of the Word," which Pound declared to be his own mission. But Eliot never preached as Pound did. They shared many of the same beliefs about the reformation and renaissance of their art, but Eliot lacked entirely Pound's belligerent and self-conscious arrogance of approach. He had no desire to be a dictator; he was much too busy exploring his own problems and finding his own way. In several of his later essays, indeed, Eliot has given oblique warnings to those who *have* taken him as a dictator, who have swallowed his early dicta as if they were a complete literary credo, and have frozen into dogmas what were to him tentative and temporary positions. In "The Music of Poetry," for instance, we find him writing:

> I believe that the critical writings of poets . . . owe a great deal of their interest to the fact that at the back of the poet's mind, if not as his ostensible purpose, he is always trying to defend the kind of poetry he is writing, or to formulate the kind that he wants to write. Especially when he is young, and actively engaged in battling for the kind of poetry which he practices, he sees the poetry of the past in relation to his own: and his gratitude to those dead poets from whom he has learned, as well as his indifference to those whose aims have been alien to his own, may be exaggerated.

Elsewhere, Eliot has pointed out that, when he began to write in 1908, there were no poets in the recent past who were of any help to him as masters who could stir his own consciousness and teach him the use of his own voice. He had to go to writers of another age and to those in another language — to the English Jacobeans and to Baudelaire and the later French Symbolists. There he found models who seemed to him to be using the techniques of verse which could best communicate his own new vision.

First of all, they used the language of speech, and as Eliot says in this same essay: "while poetry attempts to convey something beyond what can be conveyed in prose rhythms, it remains, all the same, one person talking to another. . . . Every revolution in poetry is apt to be, and sometimes announces itself as, a return to common speech. That is the revolution which Wordsworth announced in his prefaces, and he was right." Eliot as a young man, like Wordsworth, wanted to refresh and renew the poetic language by replacing the worn-out tradition of "poetic diction" with the natural rhythms of the spoken word of his own day. Along with this, he was fighting against what he calls in the essay on the Metaphysical poets "the dissociation of sensibility" (see p. 850) and battling to create in its place a poetry founded on the use of what he calls in the "Hamlet" essay "the objective correlative" (see p. 846). These two phrases of his coinage, he says later, "have had a success in the world astonishing to their author," and indeed they are rather ugly and clumsy critical terms. But they contain the core of his early theories of poetry, though they are both illustrations of positions held by the young poet where "his gratitude to those dead poets from whom he has learned, as well as his indifference to those whose aims have been alien to his own," have somewhat distorted his view of the poetry of the past.

What does he mean by "the dissociation of sensibility"? His argument in "The Metaphysical Poets" is that something "happened to the mind of England" between the time of Donne and the nineteenth century, whereby "thought" and "feeling," which before were united in poetic expression, became divorced. He says: "Tennyson and Browning are poets, and they think, but they do not feel their thought as immediately as the odor of a rose." Eliot's vocabulary in this essay is a little confusing, but it is evident here that by "feeling" he means not "emotion" but "sensation." He sees the poets who have written since the seventeenth century as relying on explanation rather than on revelation in their use of language. Instead of evoking the idea directly through the sense image, he sees them as elaborating the intellectual and the sensuous as separate entities, and relating them by a process of wasteful diffusion. Eliot blames Milton and Dryden for this, and hits hard at the Victorians (though in later writings he has modified several of these judgments). But the essay on the Metaphysicals is very valuable as an illumination of his own early practice, and gives the clue to the chief difficulty of his early poetry.

This difficulty rests mainly on the absence of logical connectives between the various sense images, and the reason for this is Eliot's early dislike of "thought" in poetry if it appears in the form of what he calls variously in the essay "meditation," "reflection," or "rumination." In contradiction to these terms he praises "a direct sensuous apprehension of thought, or a recreation of thought into feeling" and "the essential quality of transmuting ideas into sensations." In fact, Eliot is urging the abolition of abstract statements in poetry, and of all analysis and interpretation. This is not really the method of the Metaphysicals, who always express a strict logical content *as well as* the pattern of images. But Eliot's method is to make the association of sensuous imagery alone imply the intellectual content of the poem, without the intrusion of logical interpretation at all. He owns himself that though the method makes for great concentration and intensity, it does so sometimes at the cost of clarity, and there are few readers who would disagree with him. He declares in this essay that modern poetry *must* be difficult because of the complexity of modern civilization, but perhaps it is more this reliance on "feeling" or "sensation" to do all the work of the intellect, than the complexity of our civilization, which is at the root of Eliot's obscurity.

Just as in the essay on Metaphysical poets he argued that the only way of expressing "thought" should be by creating it into "feeling," so in the "Hamlet" essay he argues in the same way about "emotion." It too must be created in poetry through "sensory experience."

> The only way of expressing emotion in the form of art is by finding an "objective correlative"; in other words, a set of objects, a situation, a chain of events which shall be the formula of that *particular* emotion; such that when the external facts, which must terminate in sensory experience, are given, the emotion is immediately evoked.

But this too seems an overstatement. The "Hamlet" essay ignores other elements in Shakespeare's use of language which create emotion besides "the skillful accumulations of imagined sensory impressions," and it is much more a description of Eliot's own early poetry than of Shakespeare's tragedies. We think at once of the series of vignettes embodying the plight of Prufrock; the accumulations of sensory impressions of which the Sweeney poems are constructed; of the sensations of drought created in the images of *The Waste Land* and of those of desiccated living in "The Hollow Men."

Two of the chief characteristics in Eliot's early techniques are thus the search for the rhythm of common speech and the transmuting of both thought and emotion into images of sensation. Other qualities which he admires in the Metaphysicals and which appear in his own poetry are "brief words and sudden contrasts," "telescoping of images," and the faculty (so characteristic of Donne and his followers) of unifying a great diversity of associations within the compass of a single poem. But there is another characteristic quality in his own work which he emphasizes in that of his masters. These poets, he says, "were notably erudite and were notably men who incorporated their erudition into their sensibility; their mode of feeling was directly and freshly altered by their reading and thought." Although no one has spoken more harshly of Matthew Arnold than Eliot, he would agree with Arnold that the poets of the nineteenth century "did not know enough." The young Eliot himself was erudite, and he wanted to write a personal poetry into which a sense of the poetic tradition and his debt to it could be absorbed. He possessed, like the Metaphysicals, "a mechanism of sensibility which could devour any kind of experience," and one kind of experience very valuable to him was the work of other poets. Hence his favorite device of incorporating references, allusions, and quotations from his reading into the texture of his own verse. His imagination draws almost as much of its material from the literary tradition as from his own living; indeed the two are inseparable. And this serves a double purpose in his poems. It emphasizes his belief in the immense importance of the tradition, and the fact that the past is always alive in the present, and can be changed and given new life there. But it is also a way of *contrasting* the present with the past: a quotation or allusion may combine with what the poet is showing in the present to bring an ironical reminder of a lost melody or a lost ideal.

This use of the past, too, is allied with Eliot's doctrine of the impersonality of the poet. The extreme view of this in his early essay on "Tradition and the Individual Talent" (1917) states that poetry "is not the expression of personality, but an escape from personality," that "the more perfect the artist, the more completely separate in him will be the man who suffers and the mind which creates." But later he defined the mature poet as one who "out of intense and personal experience is able to express a general truth; retaining all the particularity of his experience, to make of it a general symbol."

The faculty to do this is at the root of Eliot's enormous influence. He has never wavered from his insistence that poetry is art, not "self-expression"; "not our feelings, but the pattern we make of our feelings is the center of value." But his art has always communicated "intense and personal experience." His poetry, indeed, in spite of all its obliquities, and the disguises and ventriloquisms that he adopts to "distance" his experience, forms a spiritual autobiography, which speaks to all sensitive readers of their own emotions and conflicts. It is true that the poet appears always as a strangely lonely figure. Other persons must have been involved in the intense and personal experiences, but no subjective human relationships emerge in the poems. We find nothing, for instance, of all that Yeats reveals in his poems of love and friendship. Yet in spite of Eliot's intense reserve, behind the mask of impersonality the drama is deeply human and individual, and its conflicts are those which are common in some degree to all. This is what made the younger generation of readers and writers respond so warmly to the early poetry, though their elders dismissed it as ugly and unintelligible. Over and over again in the birthday Symposium we hear other writers and poets declare that Eliot revealed to them both themselves and their world. A Hindu writer from India declares, "he sharp-pointed us in our self-consciousness . . . he made us poetically aware of self-consciousness as a reality." Or the English poet Kathleen Raine speaks for many others:

> For my generation T. S. Eliot's early poetry, more than the work of any other poet, has enabled us to know our world imaginatively. All those who have lived in the Waste Land of London, can, I suppose, remember the particular occasion on which, reading T. S. Eliot's poems for the first time, an experience of the contemporary world that had been nameless and formless, suddenly received its apotheosis.

What was this vision of the modern world which was projected with such vividness? In Eliot's review of Joyce's *Ulysses* in 1923, he speaks of "the immense panorama of futility and anarchy which is contemporary history." Whether or not this is a just description of the modern world, it is certainly the picture of it which emerges from the poetry of Eliot. The early poems have two backgrounds. The first is that of the poet's own social environment, the world of Prufrock, which has much in common with that of the novels of Henry James. The second is the background of the ugliness and squalor of the modern metropolis, the world of Sweeney and of many scenes in *The Waste Land*. Eliot has told us that the earliest literary inspiration behind this world, with its mixture of sordid realism and fantastic nightmare, came from the poetry of Baudelaire working on Eliot's own adolescent experiences in the city of St. Louis.

The figures that move about in these worlds, whether they are Brahmin or plebeian, suffer a common impoverishment of emotional vitality. They either live by the "formulated phrases" of an empty social convention and a decadent culture, or their lives are purely sordid and sensual. Some are vaguely conscious of isolation and rootlessness and insecurity, and the poet himself shares this spiritual coloring. He is a psychologically displaced person; he feels himself imprisoned in a disintegrating, alien, and often ugly society, which fills him with a sense of frustration and disgust. But it is a symptom of his predicament that, though he senses acutely the need to discover some escape from the prison of actuality, he shrinks from the necessary action toward achieving freedom and self-fulfillment. All he can do is to escape into his poetry, where he can objectify and dramatize the situation; where he can create in his own strange fragmentary images the moods of ironic and cynical repulsion and of unromantic disillusionment which mirror his condition.

In "The Love Song of J. Alfred Prufrock," written when Eliot was only twenty-three, all the characteristics of his early vision are already in being. The hero is an aging failure, caught in an interminable self-debate between the desire to live fully and the compulsion to conform to his social milieu. Eliot dramatizes brilliantly the double conflict between character and environment and between the warring elements within a single soul. He creates the sense of the emptiness, the barrenness, and the consequent frustration of a directionless and counterfeit culture, and the need for a vital purpose and order and wholeness of living. But "Prufrock" is a dramatic tragicomedy; the poet does not speak in his own person. Nor is there any definite and unified pattern of values set over against the aridity of the hero's environment and the disorder of his own spirit, though elements suggesting vitality and order are scattered in various images drawn from nature, history, and art. But in "Sweeney among the Nightingales," which appeared in Eliot's second volume of poems, in 1920, we find the embryo of the matter and the method which he was to enlarge and elaborate and deepen in *The Waste Land*. Here "the immense panorama of futility and anarchy which is contemporary history" is juxtaposed with the timeless values of myth and religion. "Sweeney" is an illustration of how intensity and concentration are gained at the expense of clarity, but its pictures and rhythms are most powerful and compelling. The realism is of the other end of the social scale from that of "Prufrock"; it is sordid and brutal, but the characters are equally rootless, sterile, and aimless. Eliot presents them under images of animals, of non-entity, of disorder. They have no vital relationship with the natural world, or with the spiritual world, or with each other. Opposed to them, by oblique suggestion, are the orders of Greek myth and tragedy and of the Christian story — all timeless patterns within which the temporal and physical worlds are given *meaning* in terms of moral law and spiritual significance.

But again these rival forces of the secular and the spiritual are not engaged in the poet's *own* consciousness any more than they are in "Prufrock." In *The Waste Land* (1922), however, the personal element is strongly felt, though it is overlaid with disguises. Indeed, one of the great difficulties of the poem is the sense of the struggle behind it to transmute personal and private experience into the universal and impersonal. Eliot's method is to evoke the emotional barrenness and the spiritual failure of communal and personal living in the civilization of the present, and to set it against reminders of the myths and faiths of the past, and the literature inspired by those faiths. This involves a labyrinth of allusions, and it is perhaps questionable whether a poem which has needed so much reference to outside sources unknown to the average reader, and such elaborate annotation and interpretation, "succeeds" poetically. The reader must at first spend more time sleuthing than enjoying the poetry. But as Eliot says: "We all have to choose whatever subject matter allows us the most powerful and most secret release; and that is a personal affair." The poem, moreover, in spite of its difficulty has established itself as the literary symbol of the social and psychic disintegration of our age. The agonies of the shadowy protagonist arise from his horror and disgust at the life he sees around him, and from his incapacity to surrender himself to the active and self-creative elements in his being. He is torn between the desire for rebirth and the desire to drift. And in "The Hollow Men" this latter mood has triumphed. In a condition of spiritual exhaustion the poet feels himself identified with those who give up the struggle and dwindle into colorless apathy and stagnation.

"The Hollow Men" was published in 1925, and during the next few years a profound change occurred in the nature of both Eliot's poetry and prose. He describes the direction of the change in the preface he wrote in 1928 for the second edition of *The Sacred Wood,* the collection of his early essays first published in 1920. He defined the central problem of these essays as that of "the integrity of poetry" — of poetry considered primarily as poetic art and not as anything else. He does not disown anything he had written in the book, but he has passed on, he says, to another problem, " that of the relation of poetry to the spiritual and social life of its time and of other times." The early essays deal mainly with revolutionary critical attitudes towards poetry and with the revaluation of poets neglected by the Victorians. They pay homage to the Jacobean dramatists and to the poets of the seventeenth century; they attack Milton, and they dismiss the popular nineteenth-century Romantics. Whether avowed or not, Eliot's target is often Matthew Arnold and the whole concept of poetry as " criticism of life." While these essays are often brilliant in themselves, and while they had an enormous influence on contemporary literary taste, they were, as we have seen, mainly useful to Eliot himself as clarifying his own ideas about the poetry *he* wished to write. It is significant that he has written very little purely literary criticism since his own formative period. His main prose interest shifted to social and religious writing. In 1927 Eliot became a British subject, and in the same year he was confirmed in the Anglican Church. In 1929 he published his long essay on Dante, and Dante was henceforth to be the central influence in his own vision. His most substantial prose essays since then have been on the cultural problems of the relation of society to religious beliefs. These are the basis of " Thoughts after Lambeth " (1931), *The Idea of a Christian Society* (1939), and *Notes Towards the Definition of Culture* (1948). The theme of all of these writings is summed up in the conclusion of " Thoughts after Lambeth ":

> The World is trying the experiment of attempting to form a civilized but non-Christian mentality. The experiment will fail; but we must be very patient in awaiting its collapse; meanwhile redeeming the time: so that the Faith may be preserved alive through the dark ages before us. . . .

This theme, illustrated in dramatic terms, also dominates Eliot's plays. He had always been interested in the possibility of reviving poetic drama, and here too he proved himself a pioneer. He wrote an essay on " The Possibility of Poetic Drama " as early as 1920, though there he speaks of it as a " mirage." In 1933, however, we find him saying: " The ideal medium for poetry, to my mind, and the most direct means of social ' usefulness ' for poetry is the theater." Two years later *Murder in the Cathedral* was performed in Canterbury Cathedral. It was followed by *The Family Reunion* in 1939, and *The Cocktail Party* in 1949. Eliot's dramatic pattern is always the same. A single character, or a very small group, makes the choice of a way of life dedicated to ultimate values outside those of the temporal world. This way of life may lead to a martyr's death, but it is chosen " so that the Faith may be preserved alive."

All Eliot's plays are experimental and interesting, but there is a good deal of truth in his remark that " no man can invent a form, create a taste for it, and perfect it too." He says enviously: " To have, given into one's hands, a crude form, capable of indefinite refinement, and to be the person to see the possibilities — Shakespeare was very fortunate." Eliot was not so fortunate, for he had to create both new forms and new verse rhythms for the modern theater. His theme, moreover, was unfamiliar, and even unpopular, in the contemporary world. He is the first to acknowledge that he has not yet succeeded in conquering his many technical obstacles, as may be seen from his wise and witty comments on his own work in *Poetry and Drama* (1951).

Perhaps a weakness of the plays is that the central theme of repentance and regeneration, and the presentation of its process is never very convincing. We see clearly the situations that lead up to the vital choice of the way of salvation; then in *Murder in the Cathedral* we watch the resulting martyrdom, and in *The Cocktail Party* we are told of it. But the purgatorial *process* through which the characters subdue the personal will to the will of God is omitted, or is oversimplified and compressed. And this dramatic weakness is strange because it is exactly this emotional material and its conflicts that are treated with such variety and depth in Eliot's later poems.

All the poetry after " The Hollow Men " is written from within the Christian faith, but Eliot's religious poems have an atmosphere which is all their own. He has said that there is very little religious verse that reaches the highest level of poetry, and that he suspects that that is because of a " pious insincerity " in most of it. " People who write devotional verse are usually writing as they *want* to feel, rather than as they do feel." Eliot's religious poetry is never like this; indeed it is almost as much a poetry of doubt as of faith. "The Hollow Men" presents the despairing state in which the will, knowing that a choice *must* be made if any new spiritual vitality is to be kindled, is yet incapable of stirring itself to action. In the group of poems written during the next few years, the choice *has* been made, and all the later poetry creates a sense of gradual spiritual clarification, of process and progress in a new realm of being. But within that large framework there are many differing moods. This is what creates the deeply moving quality of "Ash Wednesday" (1930), and the so-called "Ariel" poems, which include the "Journey of the Magi" and "A Song for Simeon." These poems are completely different from any of the early work. The savage or satiric or despairing picture of the contemporary scene disappears altogether: the poems are all visionary dramatizations of the inner world. They alternate in moods of assurance and insecurity, of the pain of spiritual discipline and the gladness of submission, of the heaviness of doubt and conflict and the joyous sense of renewal. This sense of renewal pervades "Marina," the "Ariel" poem chosen for this volume. It is unlike any poem of its length by Eliot in that it is completely happy: it is as full of quiet ecstasy as "The Hollow Men" is full of anguished apathy. It tells of a moment of transcendence, when all that belongs to the death-haunted atmosphere of doubt and failure fades into a new radiance of hope and the sense of grace, centered in the intangible, dreamlike and only half-comprehended figure of Marina. The world of the senses still exists in the strange beauty of the seascape and the figure, but it is absorbed into a new lighting where the worlds of nature and spirit melt into one another. And this union enfolds both the individual and the universe: it is "more distant than the stars and nearer than the eye."

"Marina" is an intensely personal poem under its thin dramatic disguise, and it brings the feeling of the presence of a new spiritual center in the life of the poet. In contrast, what is emphasized in the "Coriolan" poems, of which "Triumphal March" is the first, is the complete absence of any such center in the public living of the modern world. The poem shows a social and religious structure focused entirely on a figure representing material force and secular power, while "hidden" from all the organized mechanism of the "turning world" is the "still point" which it ignores. What the still point is, is not clarified in the poem, except insofar as it is something hidden within the worlds of physical nature and of time, which is yet distinct from both.

This central symbol of "the still point in the turning world," and the concept behind it, controls the whole pattern of Eliot's latest poems, *Four Quartets.* The poems were written over the years 1935–42 and published in a single volume in 1943. They are four long poems of meditation which yet form a single unity, and it is clear from the over-all title that they have certain analogies with musical form. In content they gather up all Eliot's profoundest beliefs and insights about the life of the race and of the individual; about time, about history, about the use of the past in the present, and about the moments of illumination in which the human spirit transcends time and space and has apprehensions of a higher reality which is changeless.

Critics often speak of the "still point" as the symbol of the eternal itself, but this is inexact, and indeed contradicts Eliot's whole concept. As he says in "Burnt Norton," the first Quartet: "Only through time time is conquered." Man cannot escape time, and the still point is therefore "the point of intersection of the timeless / With time," the point of intersection between the spheres of nature and spirit, where we partake of both and can bring away "hints and guesses" of another dimension of being. The central passage of the four poems is in Part V of "The Dry Salvages," the Quartet in this selection. Here, after scornfully dismissing all the means by which man has always tried to solve the riddles of the time world, he contrasts this "curiosity" that "clings" to past and future with the "apprehension," the intuitive grasp, of the other dimension at the still point, which is, as he says in "Burnt Norton," "always present"; that is, it is always *there* and existing at the present moment.

to apprehend  
The point of intersection of the timeless  
With time, is an occupation for the saint —  
No occupation either, but something given  
And taken, in a lifetime's death in love,  
Ardour and selflessness and self-surrender.  
For most of us, there is only the unattended  
Moment, the moment in and out of time,  
The distraction fit, lost in a shaft of sunlight,

The wild thyme unseen, or the winter lightning
Or the waterfall, or music heard so deeply
That it is not heard at all, but you are the music
While the music lasts. These are only hints and guesses,
Hints followed by guesses; and the rest
Is prayer, observance, discipline, thought and action.
The hint half guessed, the gift half understood, is Incarnation.

Even the saint doesn't move in, as it were, and occupy the still point as if it were a dwelling: the apprehension is a given grace depending on the surrender of the personal will and the death of self-love and self-interest. For most of us the moment is "unattended," unexpected and not noted with attention; it comes when we are distracted, drawn away from the purely temporal. In the next lines the images carry the quality of such moments. They are flashes of ecstasy and illumination, like the shaft of sunlight and the winter lightning; they occur in memory, like the scent of the wild thyme; they are moments when the regular flow of life is interrupted and intensified, as with a waterfall in a stream. They come in our full identification with works of art. At any of these creative emotional moments, although we are still in time — for human life cannot exist anywhere except in "the turning world" — we are at the same moment in another "sphere of existence," that of spirit. Beyond such intense glimpses, the rest of the living of life must be in the *conscious* will to reach beyond the temporal, and to reconcile the pattern of daily living with the quality of the flashes of radiance by "prayer, observance, discipline, thought and action." And the ultimate symbol of the union of sense and spirit, of time and the timeless, is Incarnation. Eliot does not say *the* Incarnation, though as a Christian that is to him the central symbol of the whole concept. But all the varied moments when we reach the still point are incarnations; that is, they are revelations in a sense medium of a spiritual reality which transcends it.

In spite of the flashes of lyrical sensuous intensity, it would be difficult to find anything more different from Eliot's early poetry than this passage. The straightforward logical argument, the direct moral and psychological approach, is at the opposite extreme of expression from the tightly packed metaphors, the multiplied associations, the elliptical syntax of *The Waste Land*. This is indeed poetry which could be called "criticism of life" — the meditative and reflective poetry which Eliot had attacked so harshly in "The Metaphysical Poets." But his expanded subject matter demanded an extension of his medium. As Eliot says in his essay on Yeats: "A man who is capable of experience finds himself in a different world in every decade of his life; as he sees it with different eyes, the material of his art is continually renewed." With Eliot as with Yeats, it is not only renewed, but deepened and enriched. The theme remains the same. From *Prufrock* onwards the constant preoccupation of Eliot's poetry has been the moral and emotional bankruptcy of a world and of individuals without an active and dynamic faith, and the poetry has created the human truth of the various stages by which such a faith has been won. At every stage the width and variety in his use of language has developed. In *Four Quartets* the range is far wider than in *The Waste Land;* it reaches from the prosaic level of colloquial discussion to the richest rhetoric and the most concentrated intensity. There is a great change too in the tones of the voice we hear speaking to us. The impersonal disguises have gone. The poet is openly "one person talking to another." The form of address is quite direct, "I," "we," "you"; and the speaker places himself among the rest of the suffering human race on its journey through time, and tells of the wisdom he has himself learnt, and of the help that it may be to others.

This is Eliot's final view of the function of poetry. The poet is first and foremost artist; his medium is language. "He has the privilege of contributing to the development and maintaining the quality, the capacity of the language to express wide range and subtle gradations of feeling and emotion." He must absorb the tradition of the past and explore all possibilities of extending its scope. But this is always intertwined with, and inseparable from, the human truth which is the material he must transmute into words. Eliot says that, when the poet is concentrating on the practical problems of his craft, he is no more concerned with the social consequences than is the scientist in his laboratory. But he adds: "without the context of the use to society neither the writer nor the scientist could have the conviction which sustains him."

The task of the poet is always a dual one, that of the creation of language and of the revelation of life, and it is summed up by the "familiar compound ghost" of all the great poets, who appears in the last Quartet, "Little Gidding," and who tells his fellow poet:

> our concern was speech, and speech impelled us
> To purify the dialect of the tribe
> And urge the mind to aftersight and foresight.

Whether Eliot will be numbered among the great poets only time can prove, but there is no question that he is the living poet who has performed both these two functions with most distinction today, and that his work, in both prose and verse, is central to any understanding of both the literature and the human problems of our times.

### *Reading Suggestions*

F. O. Matthiessen, *The Achievement of T. S. Eliot* (1947). Particularly valuable for its discussion of Eliot's techniques.

Elizabeth Drew, *T. S. Eliot: The Design of his Poetry* (1949). Contains full interpretations of all the major poems.

Helen Gardner, *The Art of T. S. Eliot* (1949). This has chapters on the earlier poems and one chapter on the plays, but it is centered on a discussion of *Four Quartets.*

COLLECTIONS OF ESSAYS

B. Rajan, editor, *T. S. Eliot: A Study of His Writings by Several Hands* (1947).

Leonard Unger, editor, *T. S. Eliot: A Selected Critique* (1948). This contains essays reprinted from periodicals and extracts from books, and also a bibliography of critical articles and references to passages in books of criticism. Both this and the Rajan collection contain Cleanth Brooks's essay on *The Waste Land,* which is the most valuable help to the reading of that poem.

*T. S. Eliot: A Symposium.* Compiled by Richard March and Tambimuttu (1948). The Foreword says: "This book was conceived as a tribute to T. S. Eliot, on his sixtieth birthday, from his friends, critics and admirers in many parts of the world. . . . It has been our aim to present a picture of T. S. Eliot, the man, in the particular setting in which he has been active as poet and man of letters, against a background of poems in homage, and critical essays on his work."

---

## THE LOVE SONG OF J. ALFRED PRUFROCK

First printed in *Poetry* June, 1915 (Chicago), but written several years earlier. The title is ironic. A love song is ordinarily addressed to an individual personality, but it seems probable that the "you" of the poem is either a part of Prufrock himself, or that he is addressing other "hollow men" who are in his own condition. That condition is suggested in the epigraph, which is from Dante's *Inferno,* Canto XXVII, lines 61–66. Dante asks one of the damned souls for its name, and it replies: "If I thought my answer were to one who could return to the world, I would not reply, but as none ever did return alive from this depth, without fear of infamy I answer thee." Prufrock also is in an inferno, and he can speak of his shame only because he thinks no one who hears his confession will condemn him for his cowardice. Eliot's use of the form of dramatic monologue should be compared with that of Browning. Eliot dispenses with all logical narrative sequence, and the situation is revealed by the different qualities of the sense images, by references to various historical figures, and by literary allusions. These form a pattern of contrasts between Prufrock's incapacity to act and the self-fulfillment of those who have lived by the instinct or principle of creative activity. The most pervasive contrast is with Marvell's poem "To His Coy Mistress." This extends not only to the opposition between Marvell's direct plea for the consummation of passion and Prufrock's own neurotic self-debate, but it hints in many subtle ways also at the contrast of the ideal of active self-fulfillment in general with that of the empty forms and frustrating trivialities of Prufrock's social environment.

---

*S'io credesse che mia risposta fosse*
*A persona che mai tornasse al mondo,*
*Questa fiamma staria senza piu scosse.*
*Ma perciocche giammai di questo fondo*
*Non torno vivo alcun, s'i'odo il vero,*
*Senza tema d'infamia ti rispondo.*

Let us go then, you and I,
When the evening is spread out against the sky
Like a patient etherised upon a table;
Let us go, through certain half-deserted streets,
The muttering retreats
Of restless nights in one-night cheap hotels
And sawdust restaurants with oyster-shells:
Streets that follow like a tedious argument
Of insidious intent
To lead you to an overwhelming question . . .
Oh, do not ask, "What is it?"
Let us go and make our visit.

In the room the women come and go
Talking of Michelangelo.

The yellow fog that rubs its back upon the window-panes,
The yellow smoke that rubs its muzzle on the window-panes
Licked its tongue into the corners of the evening,
Lingered upon the pools that stand in drains,
Let fall upon its back the soot that falls from chimneys,
Slipped by the terrace, made a sudden leap,
And seeing that it was a soft October night,
Curled once about the house, and fell asleep.

And indeed there will be time
For the yellow smoke that slides along the street,
Rubbing its back upon the window-panes;
There will be time, there will be time
To prepare a face to meet the faces that you meet;
There will be time to murder and create,
And time for all the works and days of hands
That lift and drop a question on your plate;
Time for you and time for me,
And time yet for a hundred indecisions,
And for a hundred visions and revisions,
Before the taking of a toast and tea.

In the room the women come and go
Talking of Michelangelo.

And indeed there will be time
To wonder, "Do I dare?" and, "Do I dare?"
Time to turn back and descend the stair,
With a bald spot in the middle of my hair —
[They will say: "How his hair is growing thin!"]
My morning coat, my collar mounting firmly to the chin,
My necktie rich and modest, but asserted by a simple pin —
[They will say: "But how his arms and legs are thin!"]
Do I dare
Disturb the universe?
In a minute there is time
For decisions and revisions which a minute will reverse.

For I have known them all already, known them all: —
Have known the evenings, mornings, afternoons,
I have measured out my life with coffee spoons;
I know the voices dying with a dying fall
Beneath the music from a farther room.
So how should I presume?

And I have known the eyes already, known them all —
The eyes that fix you in a formulated phrase,
And when I am formulated, sprawling on a pin,
When I am pinned and wriggling on the wall,
Then how should I begin
To spit out all the butt-ends of my days and ways?
And how should I presume?

And I have known the arms already, known them all —
Arms that are braceleted and white and bare
[But in the lamplight, downed with light brown hair!]
Is it perfume from a dress
That makes me so digress?
Arms that lie along a table, or wrap about a shawl.
And should I then presume?
And how should I begin?

. . . . . . . .

Shall I say, I have gone at dusk through narrow streets
And watched the smoke that rises from the pipes
Of lonely men in shirt-sleeves, leaning out of windows? . . .

I should have been a pair of ragged claws
Scuttling across the floors of silent seas.

. . . . . . . .

And the afternoon, the evening, sleeps so peacefully!
Smoothed by long fingers,
Asleep . . . tired . . . or it malingers,
Stretched on the floor, here beside you and me.
Should I, after tea and cakes and ices,
Have the strength to force the moment to its crisis?
But though I have wept and fasted, wept and prayed,
Though I have seen my head [grown slightly bald] brought in upon a platter,
I am no prophet — and here's no great matter;
I have seen the moment of my greatness flicker,
And I have seen the eternal Footman hold my coat, and snicker,
And in short, I was afraid.

And would it have been worth it, after all,
After the cups, the marmalade, the tea,

PRUFROCK. **23. there . . . time:** Cf. Marvell's "To His Coy Mistress": "Had we but world enough and time. . . ." Marvell argues throughout the poem that there *is* no time for "indecisions." **29. works . . . days:** the title of a poem by the Greek poet Hesiod (*c.* 735 B.C.). It was addressed to his brother and urged him to work hard at farming. **46. Disturb . . . universe:** Cf. Marvell, who suggests that love can make a new universe. **52. a . . . fall:** Cf. the opening speech of Duke Orsino in Shakespeare's *Twelfth Night.*

**82. Though . . . platter:** a reference to John the Baptist, beheaded by Herod to please his wife Herodias. **85. the . . . Footman:** Death. Even his final exit will be without dignity or respect.

Among the porcelain, among some talk of you and me,
Would it have been worth while,
To have bitten off the matter with a smile,
To have squeezed the universe into a ball
To roll it toward some overwhelming question,
To say: "I am Lazarus, come from the dead,
Come back to tell you all, I shall tell you all"—
If one, settling a pillow by her head,
Should say: "That is not what I meant at all.
That is not it, at all."

And would it have been worth it, after all,
Would it have been worth while,
After the sunsets and the dooryards and the sprinkled streets,
After the novels, after the teacups, after the skirts that trail along the floor—
And this, and so much more?—
It is impossible to say just what I mean!
But as if a magic lantern threw the nerves in patterns on a screen:
Would it have been worth while
If one, settling a pillow or throwing off a shawl,
And turning toward the window, should say:
"That is not it at all,
That is not what I mean, at all."

. . . . . . . .

No! I am not Prince Hamlet, nor was meant to be;
Am an attendant lord, one that will do
To swell a progress, start a scene or two,
Advise the prince; no doubt, an easy tool,
Deferential, glad to be of use,
Politic, cautious, and meticulous;
Full of high sentence, but a bit obtuse;
At times, indeed, almost ridiculous—
Almost, at times, the Fool.

I grow old . . . I grow old . . .
I shall wear the bottoms of my trousers rolled.

Shall I part my hair behind? Do I dare to eat a peach?
I shall wear white flannel trousers, and walk upon the beach.
I have heard the mermaids singing, each to each.

I do not think that they will sing to me.

I have seen them riding seaward on the waves
Combing the white hair of the waves blown back
When the wind blows the water white and black.

We have lingered in the chambers of the sea
By sea-girls wreathed with seaweed red and brown
Till human voices wake us, and we drown.

**92. squeezed . . . ball:** Cf. Marvell: "Let us roll all our strength and all / Our sweetness up into a ball, / And tear our pleasures with rough strife / Thorough the iron gates of life"; Marvell has "the strength to force the moment to its crisis" (l. 180). For Prufrock this would break the death-in-life of his present existence and be like the return of Lazarus from the dead (John 11). **119. the Fool:** There is no Fool in *Hamlet,* but Prufrock recognizes sadly that he corresponds to all the characters in the play who are made use of by others, or are made the butt of their ridicule.

# SWEENEY AMONG THE NIGHTINGALES

The epigraph is from the *Agamemnon* of Aeschylus and is the cry of Agamemnon as he is murdered by Clytemnestra: "Alas, I am smitten deep with a mortal blow." It is unlikely that any parallel is intended between this action and the scene in the poem. It is more probable that Eliot is suggesting that the values represented in the worlds of Greek myth and tragedy have been killed in the world of Sweeney. The nightingales in the title suggest the myth of Philomela, used again in *The Waste Land.* King Tereus raped his wife's sister, Philomela, and tore out her tongue so that she should not tell. But the gods took pity on her and changed her into a nightingale, an immortal voice in the natural world, which lives on forever. See Arnold's "Philomela," p. 608, above. Sweeney and the other figures in the scene are deaf both to the song and to the significance of the story behind it.

---

ὤμοι, πέπληγμαι καιρίαν πληγὴν ἔσω.

Apeneck Sweeney spreads his knees
Letting his arms hang down to laugh,
The zebra stripes along his jaw
Swelling to maculate giraffe.

The circles of the stormy moon
Slide westward toward the River Plate,
Death and the Raven drift above
And Sweeney guards the hornèd gate.

Gloomy Orion and the Dog
Are veiled; and hushed the shrunken seas;
The person in the Spanish cape
Tries to sit on Sweeney's knees

Slips and pulls the table cloth
Overturns a coffee-cup,
Reorganised upon the floor
She yawns and draws a stocking up;

The silent man in mocha brown
Sprawls at the window-sill and gapes;

SWEENEY AMONG THE NIGHTINGALES. **6. River Plate:** the estuary between Uruguay and Argentina. **8. the . . . gate:** the gates of horn in Hades through which true dreams came to the upper world. **9. Orion . . . Dog:** the constellations.

The waiter brings in oranges
Bananas figs and hothouse grapes;

The silent vertebrate in brown
Contracts and concentrates, withdraws;
Rachel *née* Rabinovitch
Tears at the grapes with murderous paws;

She and the lady in the cape
Are suspect, thought to be in league;
Therefore the man with heavy eyes
Declines the gambit, shows fatigue,

Leaves the room and reappears
Outside the window, leaning in,
Branches of wistaria
Circumscribe a golden grin;

The host with someone indistinct
Converses at the door apart,
The nightingales are singing near
The Convent of the Sacred Heart,

And sang within the bloody wood
When Agamemnon cried aloud,
And let their liquid siftings fall
To stain the stiff dishonoured shroud.

*1918*

# THE WASTE LAND

In many ways the most influential poem of this century. Eliot dedicated it to Pound as "the better craftsman" (the words used by Guido Guinicelli about Arnaut Daniel in Canto XXVI of the *Purgatorio*). Eliot has written of his sense of debt to Pound: "It was in 1922 that I placed before him in Paris the manuscript of a sprawling chaotic poem called *The Waste Land,* which left his hands, reduced to about half its size, in the form in which it appears in print." It appeared originally in the first issue of the *Criterion,* October, 1922, and in America in the *Dial,* November, 1922.

**37. the . . . wood:** There seems to be a telescoping of suggestions here. Agamemnon, on his return from the Trojan War, was killed in a bath, not a wood. The first chapter of Frazer's *The Golden Bough* tells the story of the wood of Nemi, the scene of a bloody ritual in which the old priest of the grove was killed by a younger one, who in his turn became priest until he too was slain. Frazer regards this ritual as bound up with that of the ancient fertility cults, which linked the seasonal rhythms of winter and spring with the death and resurrection of vegetation gods, particularly the wine god, Dionysus. The origins of Greek drama have also been traced to the festival of Dionysus, and the fertility cults expanded later into the larger religious theme of death and resurrection. The bloody wood, therefore, is appropriately linked here with the nightingales' immortal song, the *Agamemnon,* and the Sacred Heart.

The epigraph, from Chapter 48 of Petronius' *Satyricon,* can be rendered in English as follows: "Indeed I saw with my own eyes the Sibyl of Cumae hanging in a cage, and when the boys cried at her, 'Sibyl, what do you want?' she would reply, 'I want to die.'"

Eliot added some notes for the first publication in book form, by Boni and Liveright, New York, December, 1922. These are here marked [E]. He prefaces the notes with some information about his source material: "Not only the title, but the plan and a good deal of the incidental symbolism of the poem were suggested by Miss Jessie L. Weston's book on the Grail legend: *From Ritual to Romance*. . . . To another work of anthropology I am indebted in general, one which has influenced our generation profoundly; I mean [J. G. Frazer's] *The Golden Bough;* I have used especially the two volumes "Adonis, Attis, Osiris." Anyone who is acquainted with these works will immediately recognize in the poem certain references to vegetation ceremonies."

The Waste Land is that of the Fisher King in the Grail legends. According to these legends, the land is under a curse of sterility and the king is impotent; the curse cannot be removed until the king is healed. The knight who can save him and the land must make his way through great dangers of body and soul to the king's castle, which stands on the bank of a river. Miss Weston found the Grail legends to be Christianized versions, via the "mystery" religions, of the ancient fertility cults. She believed the knight's "quest" to be a version of older initiation rites into religious mysteries concerned with the union of the physical with the source of spiritual being. These faiths, she thinks, were spread into western Europe by Syrian merchants and later transformed into the stories of the Grail.

The central meaning of both the fertility rituals and the later religious beliefs is that new life is preceded by death and is inseparable from it: "Except a corn of wheat fall in the ground and die, it abideth alone; but if it die, it bringeth forth much fruit," and "Whosoever will save his life shall lose it." Paradoxically, many of the death images in Eliot's poem, such as rock, dust, bones, are also used to suggest the possibility of life, just as the water image contains also the possibility of death. The central experience of "rebirth" is one of the oldest symbolic patterns of the human race, and Eliot suggests this by the number of cultures and languages, and all the spreading and proliferating associations from other writings that he plants in the poem. The most pervasive of these are the references to Shakespeare's *The Tempest,* reminding us of the theme of that play; an apparent "death by water," which leads to a "sea-change" and proves the prelude to new life.

Eliot sees the contemporary world as deaf and blind to the realities behind the old symbols and myths of its literary tradition and therefore stunted and parched in its whole emotional living. The central symbol of the fragmentariness, the moral ugliness, and the boredom of the contemporary scene is the modern City. It represents the lack of all fertility and communion between man and God, between man and man, between man and woman, and between man and his traditional cultural heritage. The central symbol of the possibility of regeneration is water. In the vegetation ceremonies it was the coming of the spring rains that restored the gods to life after their winter death. When these fertility myths developed into religions concerned with spiritual truths, their initiation ceremonies used water as the symbol of regeneration, just as the Christian religion has adopted the sacrament of baptism.

In one of his notes, Eliot tells us of the significance of Tiresias, though he does not appear until Part III of the poem: "Tiresias, although a mere spectator and not indeed a 'character,' is yet the most important personage in the poem, uniting all the rest. . . . What Tiresias *sees,* in fact, is the substance of the poem." But Tiresias is a blind seer, and since Eliot says that the one-eyed merchant, the Phoenician sailor, and Ferdinand (from *The Tempest*) "melt into" one another, and all the women are one woman, and that the two sexes meet in Tiresias, we may take it that Tiresias' vision in its largest aspect is of Man in *all* ages. Man is always a waste land unless he is redeemed from time by faith in the values that transcend time.

One of the difficulties of the poem, however, is the identity of the "I" who speaks it. In Part III he is identified with Tiresias, but elsewhere he is more particularly a representative of the consciousness of the modern world. He is someone who has set out, like a knight of the Grail, on a quest for salvation; and though in one sense he is identified with the sterility of the Waste Land and the Fisher King, in another he is aware that there is a Parsifal within himself who *can* save him if he can sustain his faith. He is committed by "the awful daring of a moment's surrender" (Part V) and cannot turn back, though he is almost overwhelmed by the forces of spiritual drought. The end is not despair, but there is no final resolution of the conflict: the healing waters of release and refreshment have not come.

The structure of the poem is in five parts, and it has been pointed out that this formal arrangement, which Eliot uses again in the *Four Quartets,* is a poetic equivalent of the movements of the classical symphony, quartet, or sonata. The hint of a musical analogy emphasizes that there is no logical or consecutive narrative line of development in Eliot's use of his mythical material. The composition is based on related themes interpreted in a series of glimpsed visions, presenting the themes in different contexts and colorings.

---

"Nam Sibyllam quidem Cumis ego ipse oculis meis vidi in ampulla pendere, et cum illi pueri dicerent: Σίβυλλα τί θέλεις; respondebat illa: ἀποθανεῖν θέλω."

For Ezra Pound
*il miglior fabbro.*

## I. THE BURIAL OF THE DEAD

April is the cruellest month, breeding
Lilacs out of the dead land, mixing
Memory and desire, stirring
Dull roots with spring rain.
Winter kept us warm, covering
Earth in forgetful snow, feeding
A little life with dried tubers.
Summer surprised us, coming over the Starnbergersee
With a shower of rain; we stopped in the colonnade,
And went on in sunlight, into the Hofgarten,
And drank coffee, and talked for an hour.
Bin gar keine Russin, stamm' aus Litauen, echt deutsch.
And when we were children, staying at the archduke's,
My cousin's, he took me out on a sled,
And I was frightened. He said, Marie,
Marie, hold on tight. And down we went.
In the mountains, there you feel free.
I read, much of the night, and go south in the winter.

What are the roots that clutch, what branches grow
Out of this stony rubbish? Son of man,
You cannot say, or guess, for you know only
A heap of broken images, where the sun beats,
And the dead tree gives no shelter, the cricket no relief,
And the dry stone no sound of water. Only
There is shadow under this red rock,
(Come in under the shadow of this red rock),
And I will show you something different from either
Your shadow at morning striding behind you
Or your shadow at evening rising to meet you;
I will show you fear in a handful of dust.

THE WASTE LAND. **I. The Burial of the Dead:** In the fertility myths the burial of the god was a prelude to his resurrection, but the atmosphere of this section is that of death without hope of rebirth. **1–4. April . . . rain:** Cf. the tone of the opening of Chaucer's Prologue: "Whan that Aprill with his shoures soote / The droghte of March hath perced to the roote" (Vol. I). See Intro., p. 823. **8–18. Summer . . . winter:** life in its superficial aspects, where the seasons are spoken of only in terms of scenery, sports, tourists, and travel. The scene is Munich and its surroundings. **12. Bin . . . deutsch:** "I am not Russian, I come from Lithuania, true German."

**20.** Cf. Ezek. 2:1 [Eliot's note]. **23. And . . . relief:** Cf. Eccles. 12:5 [E]. **25–26. There . . . rock:** In some notes contributed by John Hayward (who lives with Eliot) to a French translation of the poem, the red rock is equated with the Grail. He quotes some lines from Jessie Weston's translation of Wolfram von Eschenbach's *Parzival:*

And this stone all men call the Graal . . .
As children, the Graal doth call them,
Neath its shadow they wax and grow.

**30. fear . . . dust:** Cf. "The fear of the Lord is the beginning of wisdom" (Ps. 111:10).

*Frisch weht der Wind*
*Der Heimat zu*
*Mein Irisch Kind,*
*Wo weilest du?*
"You gave me hyacinths first a year ago;
"They called me the hyacinth girl."
—Yet when we came back, late, from the Hyacinth garden,
Your arms full, and your hair wet, I could not
Speak, and my eyes failed, I was neither
Living nor dead, and I knew nothing,
Looking into the heart of light, the silence.
*Oed' und leer das Meer.*

Madame Sosostris, famous clairvoyante,
Had a bad cold, nevertheless
Is known to be the wisest woman in Europe,
With a wicked pack of cards. Here, said she,
Is your card, the drowned Phoenician Sailor,
(Those are pearls that were his eyes. Look!)
Here is Belladonna, the Lady of the Rocks,
The lady of situations.
Here is the man with three staves, and here the Wheel,
And here is the one-eyed merchant, and this card,
Which is blank, is something he carries on his back,
Which I am forbidden to see. I do not find
The Hanged Man. Fear death by water.
I see crowds of people, walking round in a ring.
Thank you. If you see dear Mrs. Equitone,
Tell her I bring the horoscope myself:
One must be so careful these days.

Unreal City,

**31–34. *Frisch . . . du?*** "See Wagner's *Tristan und Isolde*, I.5–8" [E]. "The wind blows fresh to the homeland: my Irish child, where are you lingering?" The passage concludes (l. 42) with the words from Act III.24 of the opera: "Empty and blank the sea." Between the two quotations is another vision of frustrated love. **43. Madame Sosostris:** the debased modern counterpart of the Egyptian diviners who used the Tarot cards to predict the rising of the waters of the Nile. **46–55.** "I am not familiar with the exact constitution of the Tarot pack of cards, from which I have obviously departed to suit my own convenience. The Hanged Man, a member of the traditional pack, fits my purpose in two ways: because he is associated in my mind with the Hanged God of Frazer, and because I associate him with the hooded figure in the passage of the disciples to Emmaus in Part V" [E]. **47. drowned . . . Sailor:** symbol of the fertility god whose image was thrown annually into the sea to mark the death of summer. **48. Those . . . eyes:** *The Tempest*, I.ii.399. **49–50. Belladonna . . . situations:** The name, though meaning literally "beautiful woman," is also that of a poison which numbs the senses. The rocks suggest aridity, and she prefers "situations" to fruitful union. She is symbolic of all the other women in the poem. **52. one-eyed:** The card shows the profile only. **52–53. this . . . back:** The blank card signifies the religious mysteries the merchant used to carry to other lands. **60. Unreal City:** Cf. Baudelaire:

> *Fourmillante cité, cité pleine de rêves,*
> *Ou le spectre en plein jour raccroche le passant* [E].

"Swarming city, city full of dreams, / Where the specter in broad daylight accosts the passer-by" (*Fleurs du Mal*, No. 90).

Under the brown fog of a winter dawn,
A crowd flowed over London Bridge, so many,
I had not thought death had undone so many.
Sighs, short and infrequent, were exhaled,
And each man fixed his eyes before his feet.
Flowed up the hill and down King William Street,
To where Saint Mary Woolnoth kept the hours
With a dead sound on the final stroke of nine.
There I saw one I knew, and stopped him, crying: "Stetson!
"You who were with me in the ships at Mylae!
"That corpse you planted last year in your garden,
"Has it begun to sprout? Will it bloom this year?
"Or has the sudden frost disturbed its bed?
"Oh keep the Dog far hence, that's friend to men,
"Or with his nails he'll dig it up again!
"You! hypocrite lecteur!—mon semblable—mon frère!"

## II. A GAME OF CHESS

The Chair she sat in, like a burnished throne,
Glowed on the marble, where the glass
Held up by standards wrought with fruited vines
From which a golden Cupidon peeped out
(Another hid his eyes behind his wing)
Doubled the flames of sevenbranched candelabra

**63–64. I . . . exhaled:** Cf. *Inferno*, III. 55–57 and IV. 25–27 [E]. The souls in Canto III are those who had "lived without praise or blame" and "who never were alive." Those in Canto IV are sighing in Limbo, the hell of those who have never known the true faith. The crowd is the morning stream of workers going to their offices in the City. **67. Saint . . . Woolnoth:** an eighteenth-century church on King William Street. **68. dead sound:** "A phenomenon I have often noticed" [E]. Office hours start at nine o'clock. **69. Stetson:** probably a symbol for the average businessman. Here the figure merges with the poet himself and his readers, by the use of the quotation from Baudelaire in the last line. **70. Mylae:** the battle between the Romans and Carthaginians in the First Punic War. That war, like that of 1914–18, had an economic basis, and the suggestion is that all wars are an extension of commercial conflicts. **71–75. That . . . again:** a much annotated passage, where a fleeting reference to the buried corn god is merged with an allusion to the dirge in *The White Devil*, a play by John Webster (*c.* 1608):

> But keep the wolf far hence, that's foe to man
> For with his nails he'll dig them up again.

The suggestion seems to be that it is more likely to be the sort of deadening life represented by a suburban garden and a friendly dog that will prevent a rebirth of the spirit. **76. "You . . . frère":** That the great enemy is deadness of soul is further suggested by this quotation of the final line from the prefatory poem in Baudelaire's *Fleurs du Mal*. After describing human vices as animals, Baudelaire calls "*l'ennuie*" (boredom) the ugliest of all, and ends, "You know him, reader . . . Hypocrite reader! —my double—my brother!" **II. A Game of Chess:** Eliot refers to Act II.ii of Middleton's play, *Women Beware Women* (*c.* 1626). In this scene a game of chess is used to distract attention from a seduction. The reference to the story of Philomela (see "Sweeney among the Nightingales," l. 37n.) alludes again to this theme. But in the two scenes here, at each end of the social scale, and as in Part III, sexual relations are not even actively lustful; they are dead and meaningless. **77. The . . . throne:** Cf. *Antony and Cleopatra*, II.ii.190 [E].

Reflecting light upon the table as
The glitter of her jewels rose to meet it,
From satin cases poured in rich profusion;
In vials of ivory and coloured glass
Unstoppered, lurked her strange synthetic per-
fumes,
Unguent, powdered, or liquid — troubled, confused
And downed the sense in odours; stirred by the air
That freshened from the window, these ascended
In fattening the prolonged candle-flames,
Flung their smoke into the laquearia,
Stirring the pattern on the coffered ceiling.
Huge sea-wood fed with copper
Burned green and orange, framed by the coloured
stone,
In which sad light a carvèd dolphin swam.
Above the antique mantel was displayed
As though a window gave upon the sylvan scene
The change of Philomel, by the barbarous king
So rudely forced; yet there the nightingale
Filled all the desert with inviolable voice
And still she cried, and still the world pursues,
"Jug Jug" to dirty ears.
And other withered stumps of time
Were told upon the walls; staring forms
Leaned out, leaning, hushing the room enclosed.
Footsteps shuffled on the stair.
Under the firelight, under the brush, her hair
Spread out in fiery points
Glowed into words, then would be savagely still.

"My nerves are bad to-night. Yes, bad. Stay with
me.
"Speak to me. Why do you never speak. Speak.
"What are you thinking of? What thinking?
What?
"I never know what you are thinking. Think."

I think we are in rats' alley
Where the dead men lost their bones.

"What is that noise?"
The wind under the door.
"What is that noise now? What is the wind do-
ing?"
Nothing again nothing.
"Do
"You know nothing? Do you see nothing? Do
you remember
"Nothing?"

I remember
Those are pearls that were his eyes.
"Are you alive, or not? Is there nothing in your
head?"
But

O O O O that Shakespeherian Rag —
It's so elegant
So intelligent
"What shall I do now? What shall I do?"
"I shall rush out as I am, and walk the street
"With my hair down, so. What shall we do to-
morrow?
"What shall we ever do?"
The hot water at ten.
And if it rains, a closed car at four.
And we shall play a game of chess,
Pressing lidless eyes and waiting for a knock upon
the door.

When Lil's husband got demobbed, I said —
I didn't mince my words, I said to her myself,
HURRY UP PLEASE ITS TIME
Now Albert's coming back, make yourself a bit
smart.
He'll want to know what you done with that money
he gave you
To get yourself some teeth. He did, I was there.
You have them all out, Lil, and get a nice set,
He said, I swear, I can't bear to look at you.
And no more can't I, I said, and think of poor
Albert,
He's been in the army four years, he wants a good
time,
And if you don't give it him, there's others will, I
said.
Oh is there, she said. Something o' that, I said.
Then I'll know who to thank, she said, and give me
a straight look.
HURRY UP PLEASE ITS TIME
If you don't like it you can get on with it, I said.
Others can pick and choose if you can't.
But if Albert makes off, it won't be for lack of tell-
ing.
You ought to be ashamed, I said, to look so an-
tique.
(And her only thirty-one.)
I can't help it, she said, pulling a long face,
It's them pills I took, to bring it off, she said.

**92. *laquearia:*** the gilded spaces between crossbeams of a ceiling. Eliot takes the word from Virgil's *Aeneid,* I.726, where it appears in the description of Dido's palace. Both Cleopatra and Dido chose death rather than life without their lovers. **98. sylvan scene:** *Paradise Lost,* IV.140 [E]: the opening of the description of the Garden of Eden. **100. so . . . forced:** Cf. III.205 [E]. **103. "Jug Jug":** The inner significance of the nightingale's song is as meaningless in the modern world as this Elizabethan way of describing it. **116. rats' alley:** Cf. III.195 [E].

**128. Shakespeherian Rag:** The music and meaning of Ariel's song are equally vulgarized into an empty ragtime jingle. **135–36. The . . . four:** The life-giving water symbol appears only as "the hot water at ten," a reference to the days before modern plumbing, when cans of hot water were taken round to the bedrooms (or as the rain from which the couple will be protected in a car). **139. demobbed:** demobilized, released from army service. **141. HURRY . . . TIME:** the traditional formula in English "pubs" to announce the closing hour.

(She's had five already, and nearly died of young
George.)
The chemist said it would be all right, but I've
never been the same.
You *are* a proper fool, I said.
Well, if Albert won't leave you alone, there it is, I
said,
What you get married for if you don't want chil-
dren?
HURRY UP PLEASE ITS TIME
Well, that Sunday Albert was home, they had a
hot gammon,
And they asked me in to dinner, to get the beauty
of it hot—
HURRY UP PLEASE ITS TIME
HURRY UP PLEASE ITS TIME
Goonight Bill. Goonight Lou. Goonight May.
Goonight.
Ta ta. Goonight. Goonight.
Good night, ladies, good night, sweet ladies, good
night, good night.

### III. THE FIRE SERMON

The river's tent is broken: the last fingers of leaf
Clutch and sink into the wet bank. The wind
Crosses the brown land, unheard. The nymphs are
departed.
Sweet Thames, run softly, till I end my song.
The river bears no empty bottles, sandwich papers,
Silk handkerchiefs, cardboard boxes, cigarette ends
Or other testimony of summer nights. The nymphs
are departed.
And their friends, the loitering heirs of city di-
rectors;
Departed, have left no addresses.
By the waters of Leman I sat down and wept . . .
Sweet Thames, run softly till I end my song,
Sweet Thames, run softly, for I speak not loud or
long.
But at my back in a cold blast I hear
The rattle of the bones, and chuckle spread from
ear to ear.
A rat crept softly through the vegetation
Dragging its slimy belly on the bank
While I was fishing in the dull canal
On a winter evening round behind the gashouse
Musing upon the king my brother's wreck
And on the king my father's death before him.
White bodies naked on the low damp ground
And bones cast in a little low dry garret,
Rattled by the rat's foot only, year to year.
But at my back from time to time I hear
The sound of horns and motors, which shall
bring
Sweeney to Mrs. Porter in the spring.
O the moon shone bright on Mrs. Porter
And on her daughter
They wash their feet in soda water
*Et O ces voix d'enfants, chantant dans la coupole!*

Twit twit twit
Jug jug jug jug jug jug
So rudely forc'd.
Tereu

Unreal City
Under the brown fog of a winter noon
Mr. Eugenides, the Smyrna merchant
Unshaven, with a pocket full of currants
C.i.f. London: documents at sight,
Asked me in demotic French

**161. chemist:** druggist. **166. gammon:** a cut of bacon. **172. Good . . . night:** *Hamlet*, IV.v.72: the farewell of the mad Ophelia; a prelude to another "death by water," a self-destruction. The words are, as it were, an ironical epitaph for all these frustrated figures. **III. The Fire Sermon:** The river Thames and the city of London dominate this section, and again the theme is the degradation of sexual relations. **176. Sweet . . . song:** the refrain of Spenser's *Prothalamion*, a marriage song in which nymphs and swains on the river bank prepare gaily for a wedding. **182. By . . . wept:** Cf. Ps. 137:1: "By the rivers of Babylon, there we sat down. yea, we wept." Leman is a name for the lake of Geneva, and Eliot wrote part of the poem in Lausanne on that lake. **185. But . . . hear:** Cf. Marvell's "To His Coy Mistress":

> But at my back I always hear
> Time's wingèd chariot hurrying near.

**189–92. While . . . him:** Eliot merges the Fisher-King and Ferdinand. See *The Tempest*, I.ii.389:

> Sitting on a bank,
> Weeping again the king my father's wreck, . . .

The introduction of "the king my brother's wreck" seems to enlarge the situation to include all men, the effect is the same as that gained by the quotation from Baudelaire which ends Part I. **196–98. at . . . spring:** a fusion of Marvell's line with a passage from John Day's *The Parliament of Bees* (*c.* 1607):

> When of a sudden, listening, you shall hear,
> A noise of horns and hunting, which shall bring
> Actaeon to Diana in the spring,
> Where all shall see her naked skin. . . .

Actaeon, out hunting, saw Diana, goddess of chastity, bathing with her nymphs. For this outrage, the goddess changed him into a stag, and he was killed by his own dogs. **199–201. O . . . water:** "I do not know the origin of the ballad from which these lines are taken: it was reported to me from Sydney, Australia" [E]. **202. *Et . . . cupole!*:** At the ceremony of the foot washing which precedes the healing of Amfortas (the Fisher-King), Parsifal, in Verlaine's poem of that name, hears the voices of the children singing in the choir loft of the chapel. **203–06. Twit . . . Tereu:** Again the memory of Philomela ravished by Tereus, and its message of lust avenged by the gods, cannot assert itself. It is drowned out by the trivial syllables, just as the memory of Actaeon and Diana is drowned out by the noise of the traffic and the vulgar ballad. **209. Mr. Eugenides:** Miss Weston says of his counterparts in the ancient world: "As ardently religious as practically business-like, the Syrians introduced their native deities wherever they penetrated, founding their chapels at the same time as their counting houses" [E]. **211. C.i.f. . . . sight:** "The currants were quoted at a price 'carriage and insurance free to London,' and the Bill of Lading etc. were to be handed to the buyer upon payment of the sight draft" [E]. **212. demotic:** slangy, uneducated.

To luncheon at the Cannon Street Hotel
Followed by a weekend at the Metropole.

At the violet hour, when the eyes and back
Turn upward from the desk, when the human engine waits
Like a taxi throbbing waiting,
I Tiresias, though blind, throbbing between two lives,
Old man with wrinkled female breasts, can see
At the violet hour, the evening hour that strives
Homeward, and brings the sailor home from sea,
The typist home at teatime, clears her breakfast, lights
Her stove, and lays out food in tins.
Out of the window perilously spread
Her drying combinations touched by the sun's last rays,
On the divan are piled (at night her bed)
Stockings, slippers, camisoles, and stays.
I Tiresias, old man with wrinkled dugs
Perceived the scene, and foretold the rest —
I too awaited the expected guest.
He, the young man carbuncular, arrives,
A small house agent's clerk, with one bold stare,
One of the low on whom assurance sits
As a silk hat on a Bradford millionaire.
The time is now propitious, as he guesses,
The meal is ended, she is bored and tired,
Endeavours to engage her in caresses
Which still are unreproved, if undesired.
Flushed and decided, he assaults at once;
Exploring hands encounter no defence;
His vanity requires no response,
And makes a welcome of indifference.
(And I Tiresias have foresuffered all
Enacted on this same divan or bed;
I who have sat by Thebes below the wall
And walked among the lowest of the dead.)
Bestows one final patronising kiss,
And gropes his way, finding the stairs unlit . . .

She turns and looks a moment in the glass,
Hardly aware of her departed lover;
Her brain allows one half-formed thought to pass:
" Well now that's done: and I'm glad it's over."
When lovely woman stoops to folly and
Paces about her room again, alone,
She smoothes her hair with automatic hand,
And puts a record on the gramophone.

" This music crept by me upon the waters "
And along the Strand, up Queen Victoria Street.
O City city, I can sometimes hear
Beside a public bar in Lower Thames Street,
The pleasant whining of a mandoline
And a clatter and a chatter from within
Where fishmen lounge at noon: where the walls
Of Magnus Martyr hold
Inexplicable splendour of Ionian white and gold.

The river sweats
Oil and tar

**213. Cannon Street Hotel:** The quickest route from the Continent had at this time a terminus at Cannon Street Station in the City. The hotel was a favorite meeting place for business transactions. **214. the Metropole:** a luxury hotel at Brighton, the popular seaside resort. **218. Tiresias:** the blind seer who appears in Sophocles' *Oedipus the King*. Cf. headnote above. There he knew the cause of the curse that had made a waste land of Thebes. Ovid (*Metamorphoses*, III.322 ff.) tells the legend of Tiresias: "It chanced that Jove (as the story goes), while warmed with wine, put care aside and bandied good-humored jests with Juno in an idle hour. 'I maintain,' said he, 'that your pleasure in love is greater than that which we [the male gods] enjoy.' She held the opposite view. And so they decided to ask the judgment of the wise Tiresias. He knew both sides of love. For once, with a blow of his staff, he had outraged two huge serpents mating in the green forest; and, wonderful to relate, from man he was changed into a woman, and in that form spent seven years. In the eighth year he saw the same serpents again and said: 'Since in striking you there is such magic power as to change the nature of the giver of the blow, now will I strike you once again.' So saying, he struck the serpents, and his former state was restored, and he became as he had been born. He, therefore, being asked to arbitrate the playful dispute of the gods, took sides with Jove. Saturnia [Juno], they say, grieved more deeply than she should and than the issue warranted, and condemned the arbitrator to perpetual blindness. But the Almighty Father (for no god may undo what another god has done) in return for his loss of sight gave Tiresias the power to know the future, lightening the penalty by the honor" (translation by Frank J. Miller in the Loeb Classical Library). See Arnold's "The Strayed Reveler," l. 135n., p. 594, above. **220–21. At . . . sea:** a reference to Sappho's poem: "Hesperus (the evening star), thou bringest home all things bright morning scattered: thou bringest the sheep, the goat, the child to the mother." Eliot says: "This may not appear as exact as Sappho's lines, but I had in mind the 'longshore' or 'dory' fisherman, who returns at nightfall." **224. Out . . . spread:** Cf. Keats's "magic casements, opening on the foam / Of perilous seas . . ." ("Ode to a Nightingale," ll. 69–70). **234. Bradford:** woolen manufacturing town in Yorkshire where large profits were made from war contracts in 1914–18. **253–56. When . . . gramophone:** Cf. Goldsmith's:

When lovely woman stoops to folly
  And finds too late that men betray,
What charm can soothe her melancholy,
  What art can wash her guilt away?

The only art her guilt to cover,
  To hide her shame from every eye,
To give repentance to her lover
  And wring his bosom — is to die.

**257. "This . . . waters":** the line of Ferdinand's speech which continues from "weeping again the king my father's wreck." **258. the Strand:** so called originally because the houses of the Elizabethan nobles built along it backed onto the banks of the Thames. Now, like the nineteenth-century Queen Victoria Street, it is entirely commercial in character. **259. O . . . city:** in distinction to the Unreal City. For a moment the city becomes the unit of communal life, the Greek city. Cf. "Ionian white and gold" (l. 265). **260. Lower . . . Street:** for centuries the scene of London's central fish market. The fish is a very ancient life symbol. **264. Magnus Martyr:** one of the City churches: "The interior of St. Magnus Martyr is to my mind one of the finest among Wren's interiors" [E]. **266. "The song of the (three)

The barges drift
With the turning tide
Red sails
Wide
To leeward, swing on the heavy spar.
The barges wash
Drifting logs
Down Greenwich reach
Past the Isle of Dogs.
Weialala leia
Wallala leialala

Elizabeth and Leicester
Beating oars
The stern was formed
A gilded shell
Red and gold
The brisk swell
Rippled both shores
Southwest wind
Carried down stream
The peal of bells
White towers
Weialala leia
Wallala leialala

"Trams and dusty trees.
Highbury bore me. Richmond and Kew
Undid me. By Richmond I raised my knees
Supine on the floor of a narrow canoe."

"My feet are at Moorgate, and my heart
Under my feet. After the event
He wept. He promised 'a new start.'
I made no comment. What should I resent?"

"On Margate Sands.
I can connect
Nothing with nothing.
The broken fingernails of dirty hands.
My people humble people who expect
Nothing."
la la

To Carthage then I came

Burning burning burning burning
O Lord Thou pluckest me out
O Lord Thou pluckest

burning

## IV. DEATH BY WATER

Phlebas the Phoenician, a fortnight dead,
Forgot the cry of gulls, and the deep sea swell
And the profit and loss.
A current under sea
Picked his bones in whispers. As he rose and fell
He passed the stages of his age and youth
Entering the whirlpool.
Gentile or Jew
O you who turn the wheel and look to windward,
Consider Phlebas, who was once handsome and
tall as you.

## V. WHAT THE THUNDER SAID

After the torchlight red on sweaty faces
After the frosty silence in the gardens

Thames-daughters begins here. From ll. 292–306 inclusive they speak in turn. See *Götterdämmerung*, III.i: the Rhine-daughters" [E]. The curse on the Waste Land in the myth followed the seduction of some maidens at the court of the Fisher-King. The Rhine-daughters also had been violated and robbed of their gold, and they lament the loss of the river's beauty as the result. Eliot merges the idea of the violation of the river with that of the loss of chastity. **276. Isle of Dogs:** a district on the lower north bank of the Thames. It is not really an island, but is enclosed on three sides by a bend of the river, and occupied almost entirely by docks. The origin of the name is unknown. **279. Elizabeth . . . Leicester:** "See Froude, *Elizabeth*, Vol. I, ch. iv, letter of De Quadra to Philip of Spain: 'In the afternoon we were in a barge, watching the games on the river. (The queen) was alone with Lord Robert and myself on the poop, when they began to talk nonsense, and went so far that Lord Robert at last said, as I was on the spot there was no reason why they should not be married if the queen pleased'" [E]. **289. White towers:** those of the Tower of London. **293–94. Highbury . . . me:** Cf. *Purgatorio*, V.133. Dante meets the soul of La Pia of Siena, whose husband, wishing to marry another woman, murdered her in his castle in the Tuscan Maremma. She says: "Siena made me, Maremma unmade me." **293.** Highbury, Richmond, and Kew are suburbs of London. **296. Moorgate:** a district in the "City." **300. Margate:** a popular coast resort in Kent at the extreme end of the Thames estuary.

**307. To Carthage:** "See St. Augustine's *Confessions:* 'to Carthage then I came, where a cauldron of unholy loves sang all about mine ears'" [E]. The passage is at the opening of Book III, where Augustine blames himself for the sexual indulgence which he had substituted for the love of God. **308. Burning:** "The complete text of the Buddha's Fire Sermon (which corresponds in importance to the Sermon on the Mount) from which these words are taken will be found translated in the late Henry Clarke Warren's *Buddhism in Translation*" [E]. In the Sermon, the Buddha says that all things are on fire with lust, hatred, and infatuation. The way of the disciple is to turn from the sense world and to become "free from attachment." **309–10. O . . . . . . pluckest:** "From St. Augustine's *Confessions* again. The collocation of these two representatives of eastern and western asceticism as the culmination of this part of the poem, is not an accident" [E]. **IV. Death by Water:** Critics differ in the interpretation of this section. Some see the description as that of actual death; others as that of the surrender to the sacrificial death, or the initiation ritual, as a prelude to rebirth. The latter seems more probable. Phlebas is the symbol of the drowned fertility god who will rise again, and the condition described seems to be that "freedom from attachment" which the Fire Sermon demanded. **316. Picked . . . whispers:** Cf. Ariel's song, *The Tempest*, I.ii.398: "Of his bones are coral made"; and I.ii.379: "The wild waves whist." **V. What the Thunder Said:** "In the first part of Part V three themes are employed: the journey to Emmaus, the approach to the Chapel Perilous (see Miss Weston's book), and the present decay of eastern Europe" [E]. **322–27. After . . . mountains:** The Passion of Christ in the garden of Gethsemane, and his trial before the Crucifixion (see John 18), is fused with the vegetation myth.

After the agony in stony places
The shouting and the crying
Prison and palace and reverberation
Of thunder of spring over distant mountains
He who was living is now dead
We who were living are now dying
With a little patience

Here is no water but only rock
Rock and no water and the sandy road
The road winding above among the mountains
Which are mountains of rock without water
If there were water we should stop and drink
Amongst the rock one cannot stop or think
Sweat is dry and feet are in the sand
If there were only water amongst the rock
Dead mountain mouth of carious teeth that cannot spit
Here one can neither stand nor lie nor sit
There is not even silence in the mountains
But dry sterile thunder without rain
There is not even solitude in the mountains
But red sullen faces sneer and snarl
From doors of mudcracked houses
If there were water
And no rock
If there were rock
And also water
And water
A spring
A pool among the rock
If there were the sound of water only
Not the cicada
And dry grass singing
But sound of water over a rock
Where the hermit-thrush sings in the pine trees
Drip drop drip drop drop drop drop
But there is no water

Who is the third who walks always beside you?
When I count, there are only you and I together
But when I look ahead up the white road
There is always another one walking beside you
Gliding wrapt in a brown mantle, hooded
I do not know whether a man or a woman
— But who is that on the other side of you?

What is that sound high in the air
Murmur of maternal lamentation
Who are those hooded hordes swarming
Over endless plains, stumbling in cracked earth
Ringed by the flat horizon only
What is the city over the mountains
Cracks and reforms and bursts in the violet air
Falling towers
Jerusalem Athens Alexandria
Vienna London
Unreal

A woman drew her long black hair out tight
And fiddled whisper music on those strings
And bats with baby faces in the violet light
Whistled, and beat their wings
And crawled head downward down a blackened wall
And upside down in air were towers
Tolling reminiscent bells, that kept the hours
And voices singing out of empty cisterns and exhausted wells.

In this decayed hole among the mountains
In the faint moonlight, the grass is singing
Over the tumbled graves, about the chapel
There is the empty chapel, only the wind's home.
It has no windows, and the door swings,
Dry bones can harm no one.
Only a cock stood on the rooftree
Co co rico co co rico
In a flash of lightning. Then a damp gust
Bringing rain

Ganga was sunken, and the limp leaves
Waited for rain, while the black clouds
Gathered far distant, over Himavant.
The jungle crouched, humped in silence.
Then spoke the thunder
Da
*Datta:* what have we given?
My friend, blood shaking my heart
The awful daring of a moment's surrender

330. **patience:** used perhaps in the root meaning of "suffering." 359. **Who . . . you?:** See the account of the journey to Emmaus (Luke 24:1–32). 360–65. **When . . . you?:** "The following lines were stimulated by the account of one of the Antarctic expeditions: . . . it was related that the party of explorers, at the extremity of their strength, had the constant delusion that there was *one more member* than could actually be counted" [E]. 367. **maternal lamentation:** Cf. Luke 23:27–30. 368–76. The theme of the decay of eastern Europe.

377–84. **woman . . . wells:** In this nightmare there are references to Eccles. 12, perhaps also to the woman's hair in II.108–10, and to the towers and bells of Part III. 385–90. **In . . . one:** The trials of the knights at the Chapel Perilous are described in Chapter V of *From Ritual to Romance.* The graves are of those who have failed to survive the terrors of body and mind which the initiate must undergo. 388–89. Eliot thinks that the imagery was suggested in part by a picture of the school of the fifteenth-century Dutch painter, Hieronymus Bosch. 391. **cock . . . rooftree:** In folklore, cockcrow drives evil spirits to their lairs. 395. **Ganga:** the river Ganges. 397. **Himavant:** "Snowy Mountain"; a peak in the Himalayas. 399–400. **Then . . . Da:** This is not the "dry sterile thunder" of l. 342, but the voice of the Lord of Creation speaking to his children. It is a myth from the Hindu Upanishads, the earliest literature in the Indo-European languages. Three listeners to the voice of the thunder (represented by the syllable Da) interpret its meaning in three different Sanskrit words beginning with that syllable, which Eliot translates as Give, Sympathize, Control. See R. E. Hume, *The Thirteen Principal Upanishads* (1921), p. 150.

Which an age of prudence can never retract
By this, and this only, we have existed
Which is not to be found in our obituaries
Or in memories draped by the beneficent spider
Or under seals broken by the lean solicitor
In our empty rooms
DA
*Dayadhvam:* I have heard the key
Turn in the door once and turn once only
We think of the key, each in his prison
Thinking of the key, each confirms a prison
Only at nightfall, aethereal rumours
Revive for a moment a broken Coriolanus
DA
*Damyata:* The boat responded
Gaily, to the hand expert with sail and oar
The sea was calm, your heart would have re-
    sponded
Gaily, when invited, beating obedient
To controlling hands

                                        I sat upon the shore
Fishing, with the arid plain behind me
Shall I at least set my lands in order?
London Bridge is falling down falling down fall-
    ing down
*Poi s'ascose nel foco che gli affina*
*Quando fiam uti chelidon*—O swallow swallow
*Le Prince d'Aquitaine à la tour abolie*
These fragments I have shored against my ruins
Why then Ile fit you. Hieronymo's mad againe.
Datta. Dayadhvam. Damyata.
            Shantih shantih shantih

# THE HOLLOW MEN

The first epigraph to the poem is from Conrad's *Heart of Darkness.* In that story Mr. Kurtz, who was in charge of a French trading company, had surrendered himself to the dark powers of the African jungle. As Kurtz is dying, Marlow (who tells the story), describes how he lies "with a wide and immense stare embracing, condemning, loathing all the universe," and cries, "The horror! The horror!" Marlow goes to dinner, and the manager's boy puts his head in the doorway and says, "in a tone of scathing contempt—'Mistah Kurtz—he dead.'" But Marlow, despite all the waste and degradation of Kurtz's fate, is not contemptuous. He feels in Kurtz's cry "the appalling face of glimpsed truth. . . . It was an affirmation, a moral victory paid for by innumerable defeats. . . . But it was a victory."

The second epigraph is an allusion to Guy Fawkes Day in England, when children make straw effigies of the "Guy" and collect pennies for fireworks. In the plot to blow up the House of Commons in 1605, Guy Fawkes had the job of firing the barrels of gunpowder in the cellar. He was arrested before he could carry it out, and executed. Both Mr. Kurtz and Guy Fawkes are "lost violent souls," but they *chose* their fate, in contrast to the hollow men who cannot exercise will and choice. A remark from Eliot's essay on Baudelaire illustrates his point: "So far as we are human, what we do must be either evil or good; so far as we do evil or good, we are human; and it is better, in a paradoxical way, to do evil than to do nothing; at least we exist." See Browning's "The Statue and the Bust" for a similar attitude.

---

*Mistah Kurtz—he dead.*
*A penny for the Old Guy*

I

We are the hollow men
We are the stuffed men
Leaning together
Headpiece filled with straw. Alas!
Our dried voices, when

**407. memories . . . spider:** Cf. Webster, *The White Devil,* V.vi. 157–59:

> . . . they'll remarry
> Ere the worm pierce your winding-sheet, ere the spider
> Make a thin curtain for your epitaphs [E].

**411–12. heard . . . door:** Cf. *Inferno,* XXXIII.46 [E]. Ugolino, damned in the lowest circle of Hell for treachery to his city, hears in memory the key locking him and his children in the tower where they starved to death. Eliot connects this in his note with the reality of human isolation as expressed by the philosopher F. H. Bradley in *Appearance and Reality,* p. 346: "My external sensations are no less private to myself than are my thoughts or my feelings. In either case my experience falls within my own circle, a circle closed on the outside; and, with all its elements alike, every sphere is opaque to the others which surround it. . . . In brief, regarded as an existence which appears in a soul, the whole world for each is peculiar and private to that soul." **416. Coriolanus:** also a traitor to his city: his motive was personal egotism. **426. London . . . down:** the refrain of a familiar nursery rhyme. **427. *Poi . . . affina:* *Purgatorio,*** XXVI.148: "Then he dived back into the fire which refines them." The concluding line of the description of Arnaut Daniel, the Provençal poet, who is being purged of carnal lust, and gladly accepts his suffering. **428. *Quando . . . chelidon:*** "When shall I be like the swallow?" (from the *Pervigilium Veneris,* a late Latin poem). The poet laments that spring comes to the natural world but not to his own heart. It ends, however, with the hope that he too may love. Procne, the sister of Philomela, was changed into a swallow when Philomela became a nightingale. **429. *Le . . . abolie:*** from a sonnet by Gerard de Nerval (1808–55), *El Desdichado* (*The Disinherited*). The poet sees himself as the lost descendant of the noble medieval tradition: "I am the Prince of Aquitaine whose tower is ruined," and he prays for consolation. **431. Why . . . againe:** See Kyd's *The Spanish Tragedy* (1584), IV.i.67. The subtitle of the play is "Hieronymo's mad againe." Hieronymo, like Hamlet, feigns madness to discover the truth about a murder. Asked to provide an entertainment for the court, he replies, "Why then Ile fit you," and says he has a tragedy written in his youth, when he "plied himself to fruitless poetry." This is written in various foreign languages, and it can now be used, he thinks, to unmask the murderer. In fact it can prove fruitful, as the fragments the poet has just quoted may prove fruitful in his own quest for truth, though to others it may appear madness. **433. Shantih:** "Repeated as here, a formal ending to an Upanishad. 'The peace which passeth understanding' is our equivalent to this word" [E].

We whisper together
Are quiet and meaningless
As wind in dry grass
Or rats' feet over broken glass
In our dry cellar

Shape without form, shade without colour,
Paralysed force, gesture without motion;

Those who have crossed
With direct eyes, to death's other Kingdom
Remember us — if at all — not as lost
Violent souls, but only
As the hollow men
The stuffed men.

II

Eyes I dare not meet in dreams
In death's dream kingdom
These do not appear:
There, the eyes are
Sunlight on a broken column
There, is a tree swinging
And voices are
In the wind's singing
More distant and more solemn
Than a fading star.

Let me be no nearer
In death's dream kingdom
Let me also wear
Such deliberate disguises
Rat's coat, crowskin, crossed staves
In a field
Behaving as the wind behaves
No nearer —

Not that final meeting
In the twilight kingdom

III

This is the dead land
This is cactus land
Here the stone images
Are raised, here they receive
The supplication of a dead man's hand
Under the twinkle of a fading star.

Is it like this
In death's other kingdom
Waking alone
At the hour when we are
Trembling with tenderness
Lips that would kiss
Form prayers to broken stone.

IV

The eyes are not here
There are no eyes here
In this valley of dying stars
In this hollow valley
This broken jaw of our lost kingdoms

In this last of meeting places
We grope together
And avoid speech
Gathered on this beach of the tumid river

Sightless, unless
The eyes reappear
As the perpetual star
Multifoliate rose
Of death's twilight kingdom
The hope only
Of empty men.

V

*Here we go round the prickly pear*
*Prickly pear prickly pear*
*Here we go round the prickly pear*
*At five o'clock in the morning.*

Between the idea
And the reality
Between the motion
And the act
Falls the Shadow
*For Thine is the Kingdom*

Between the conception
And the creation
Between the emotion
And the response
Falls the Shadow
*Life is very long*

THE HOLLOW MEN. **10. our . . . cellar**: in contrast to the living Guy Fawkes in *his* cellar. **13–14 Those . . . Kingdom**: those who have crossed the river Acheron to hell. Cf. *Inferno*, III. **20. death's . . . kingdom**: This appears to be the condition of illusion and revery in which moral choice can be escaped; the condition in which Prufrock lived. **37–38. Not . . . kingdom**: Taken together with the "eyes" of the first line of this section, this seems to refer to Dante's meeting with Beatrice in *Purgatorio*, XXX. Beatrice's eyes are stern, and she upbraids Dante with his failures and weaknesses. "The twilight kingdom," therefore, may refer to the active purgation from which the protagonist shrinks.

**60. tumid river**: the river Acheron. See *Inferno*, III. Many details of the scene there are suggested in the poem. **63–64. perpetual . . . rose**: Conducted by Beatrice, whose stern eyes turn to "eyes of light," Dante sees the Divine Essence "like a star in Heaven," while Paradise forms itself into the "multifoliate rose," whose petals are the souls of the blessed. See *Paradiso*, XXVIII.30. **68. *Here . . . pear:*** The substitution of the prickly pear for the mulberry bush suggests the "cactus land" of l. 40. The going *round* indicates the lack of any *forward* movement, and perhaps the nursery-rhyme form hints at the childish world of illusion and make-believe which paralyzes the will and concludes in the "whimper" instead of the "bang" planned by the real Guy Fawkes.

Between the desire
And the spasm
Between the potency
And the existence
Between the essence
And the descent
Falls the Shadow

*For Thine is the Kingdom*

For Thine is
Life is
For Thine is the

*This is the way the world ends*
*This is the way the world ends*
*This is the way the world ends*
*Not with a bang but a whimper.*

*1925*

## MARINA

The poem appeared first as No. 29 of the "Ariel" poems. These were a series of individual poems by various authors, published over a period of years by Faber and Faber, to which Eliot contributed five. The title is the name of the heroine of Shakespeare's play *Pericles.* Marina, the daughter of Pericles, was born at sea (hence her name) and was then thought to have been murdered by those in whose charge she was left. She was miraculously restored to her father when she was a grown woman. Pericles is the speaker. In contrast to the subject of the poem, which is the discovery of life where death had been accepted, the epigraph ironically recalls an opposite experience. It is from the play *Hercules Furens* of Seneca, at the moment when Hercules, having unknowingly killed his children in a fit of madness, returns to sanity, asks where he is, and realizes his loss. (See Introduction, p. 825.)

---

*Quis hic locus, quae regio, quae mundi plaga?*

What seas what shores what grey rocks and what islands
What water lapping the bow
And scent of pine and the woodthrush singing through the fog
What images return
O my daughter.

Those who sharpen the tooth of the dog, meaning
Death
Those who glitter with the glory of the hummingbird, meaning
Death
Those who sit in the stye of contentment, meaning
Death
Those who suffer the ecstasy of the animals, meaning
Death

Are become unsubstantial, reduced by a wind,
A breath of pine, and the woodsong fog
By this grace dissolved in place

What is this face, less clear and clearer
The pulse in the arm, less strong and stronger —
Given or lent? more distant than stars and nearer than the eye

Whispers and small laughter between leaves and hurrying feet
Under sleep, where all the waters meet.

Bowsprit cracked with ice and paint cracked with heat.
I made this, I have forgotten
And remember.
The rigging weak and the canvas rotten
Between one June and another September.
Made this unknowing, half conscious, unknown, my own.
The garboard strake leaks, the seams need caulking.
This form, this face, this life
Living to live in a world of time beyond me; let me
Resign my life for this life, my speech for that unspoken,
The awakened, lips parted, the hope, the new ships.

What seas what shores what granite islands towards my timbers
And woodthrush calling through the fog
My daughter.

*1930*

## TRIUMPHAL MARCH

In the volume of *Collected Poems* this appears among "Unfinished Poems" as No. 1 under the general title "Coriolan." The second (and last) in the uncompleted series is "Difficulties of a Statesman." These poems differ from anything previously published by Eliot in that they have a direct political significance. Writing in the *Criterion* in the spring of 1929, he had declared: "We must prepare a state of mind towards something other than the facile alternatives of communist or fascist dictatorship." He saw fascistic nationalism as "a familiar conventional modern idea . . . the doctrine of success." The poem's setting is neither ancient Rome nor a modern city; it is a fusion of the

MARINA. **17–18. What . . . stronger:** Cf. *Pericles,* V.i.154: "But are you flesh and blood? Have you a working pulse?" **20. Whispers . . . feet:** This seems to be a childhood memory, associated with a sense of ecstasy. It appears again in *Burnt Norton,* I, "for the leaves were full of children, / Hidden excitedly, containing laughter." **22–28. Bowsprit . . . caulking:** At first glance this damaged and dilapidated ship seems out of keeping with the quality of the vision. But the importance seems to be in the "I made this." The presence of Marina is in some way connected with some half-understood constructive effort of the speaker, symbolized by the old ship. It has been the *means* of the revelation, and having served its purpose it can dissolve into the general sense of new life.

two, suggesting the universality of the *idea* of a central figure with which the people identify both the nation and the Godhead. This is implicitly contrasted with a pattern of values having at its center the "still point" (see Introduction, p. 825). The whole description of the Triumphal March should be contrasted with the entry of Christ into Jerusalem, riding upon an ass, with the multitudes on the way to the Temple crying: "Blessed be the King that cometh in the name of the Lord" (Mark 12, Luke 20).

Stone, bronze, stone, steel, stone, oakleaves, horses' heels
Over the paving.
And the flags. And the trumpets. And so many eagles.
How many? Count them. And such a press of people.
We hardly knew ourselves that day, or knew the City.
This is the way to the temple, and we so many crowding the way.
So many waiting, how many waiting? what did it matter, on such a day?
Are they coming? No, not yet. You can see some eagles. And hear the trumpets.
Here they come. Is he coming?
The natural wakeful life of our Ego is a perceiving.
We can wait with our stools and our sausages.
What comes first? Can you see? Tell us. It is

5,800,000 rifles and carbines,
    102,000 machine guns,
    28,000 trench mortars,
    53,000 field and heavy guns,
I cannot tell how many projectiles, mines and fuses,
    13,000 aeroplanes,
    24,000 aeroplane engines,
    50,000 ammunition waggons,
now 55,000 army waggons,
    11,000 field kitchens,
    1,150 field bakeries.

What a time that took. Will it be he now? No,
Those are the golf club Captains, these the Scouts,
And now the *société gymnastique de Poissy*
And now come the Mayor and the Liverymen. Look
There he is now, look:
There is no interrogation in his eyes
Or in the hands, quiet over the horse's neck,
And the eyes watchful, waiting, perceiving, indifferent.
O hidden under the dove's wing, hidden in the turtle's breast,
Under the palmtree at noon, under the running water
At the still point of the turning world. O hidden.

Now they go up to temple. Then the sacrifice.
Now come the virgins bearing urns, urns containing
Dust
Dust
Dust of dust, and now
Stone, bronze, stone, steel, stone, oakleaves, horses' heels
Over the paving.
That is all we could see. But how many eagles! and how many trumpets!
(And Easter Day, we didn't get to the country,
So we took young Cyril to church. And they rang a bell
And he said right out loud, *crumpets*.)
                    Don't throw away that sausage,
It'll come in handy. He's artful. Please, will you
Give us a light?
Light
Light
*Et les soldats faisaient la haie? ILS LA FAISAIENT.*

*1931*

## THE DRY SALVAGES

(See Introduction, p. 825.) The title of each of the Quartets ("Burnt Norton," "East Coker," "The Dry Salvages," and "Little Gidding") is the name of a place, associated in some way with Eliot's own experience. His family went for summer vacations to Cape Ann, and the atmosphere and scenery of that coast entered deeply into his imaginative life. It is the background of "Marina," and in Part I of "The Dry Salvages" it supplies the material for what is perhaps Eliot's finest piece of sustained descriptive imagery.

In each Quartet also, one of the elements (earth, air, fire, water) dominates the imagery of the poem and emphasizes the element in man's nature to which it is an analogy. In "The Dry Salvages" the dominating element is water. Human life appears first as the river of racial consciousness alive in man's blood, and then as the vast flux of the sea on which he is afloat. Part III, as in the other Quartets, uses metaphors of traveling to suggest man's passage through time.

It will be noticed that this is the first poem (in this selection), which is strongly and openly colored with Christian terminology and reference.

For a discussion of the parallels with musical form which Eliot uses throughout the Quartets, see *The Art of T. S. Eliot* by Helen Gardner, Chapter 2, and also Eliot's own remarks on this topic at the conclusion of "The Music of Poetry" below.

TRIUMPHAL MARCH. 44–45. **And . . . *crumpets:*** In the residential districts of London, the sellers of muffins and crumpets used to carry trays of them on their heads and ring a bell to advertise their presence. The ignorant Cyril responds thus to the ringing of the bell at Mass, at the elevation of the Host. 50. ***Et . . . FAISAIENT:*** "*Faire la haie*" is to form a military line, the "hedge" being the bayonets of the ranks of soldiers. The suggestion here is presumably that the only light is that of the gleaming steel; and the ranks of the army grow ever greater, just as the letters are enlarged on the page.

(The Dry Salvages — presumably *les trois sauvages* — is a small group of rocks, with a beacon, off the N.E. coast of Cape Ann, Massachusetts. *Salvages* is pronounced to rhyme with *assuages. Groaner:* a whistling buoy.)

## I

I do not know much about gods; but I think that the river
Is a strong brown god — sullen, untamed and intractable,
Patient to some degree, at first recognised as a frontier;
Useful, untrustworthy, as a conveyor of commerce;
Then only a problem confronting the builder of bridges.
The problem once solved, the brown god is almost forgotten
By the dwellers in cities — ever, however, implacable,
Keeping his seasons and rages, destroyer, reminder
Of what men choose to forget. Unhonoured, unpropitiated
By worshippers of the machine, but waiting, watching and waiting.
His rhythm was present in the nursery bedroom,
In the rank ailanthus of the April dooryard,
In the smell of grapes on the autumn table,
And the evening circle in the winter gaslight.

The river is within us, the sea is all about us;
The sea is the land's edge also, the granite
Into which it reaches, the beaches where it tosses
Its hints of earlier and other creation:
The starfish, the hermit crab, the whale's backbone;
The pools where it offers to our curiosity
The more delicate algae and the sea anemone.
It tosses up our losses, the torn seine,
The shattered lobsterpot, the broken oar
And the gear of foreign dead men. The sea has many voices,
Many gods and many voices.
The salt is on the briar rose,
The fog is in the fir trees.
The sea howl
And the sea yelp, are different voices
Often together heard; the whine in the rigging,
The menace and caress of wave that breaks on water,
The distant rote in the granite teeth,
And the wailing warning from the approaching headland
Are all sea voices, and the heaving groaner
Rounded homewards, and the seagull:
And under the oppression of the silent fog
The tolling bell
Measures time not our time, rung by the unhurried
Ground swell, a time
Older than the time of chronometers, older
Than time counted by anxious worried women
Lying awake, calculating the future,
Trying to unweave, unwind, unravel
And piece together the past and the future,
Between midnight and dawn, when the past is all deception,
The future futureless, before the morning watch
When time stops and time is never ending;
And the ground swell, that is and was from the beginning,
Clangs
The bell.

## II

Where is there an end of it, the soundless wailing,
The silent withering of autumn flowers
Dropping their petals and remaining motionless;
Where is there an end to the drifting wreckage,
The prayer of the bone on the beach, the unprayable
Prayer at the calamitous annunciation?

There is no end, but addition: the trailing
Consequence of further days and hours,
While emotion takes to itself the emotionless
Years of living among the breakage
Of what was believed in as the most reliable —
And therefore the fittest for renunciation.

There is the final addition, the failing
Pride or resentment at failing powers,
The unattached devotion which might pass for devotionless,
In a drifting boat with a slow leakage,
The silent listening to the undeniable
Clamour of the bell of the last annunciation.

Where is the end of them, the fishermen sailing
Into the wind's tail, where the fog cowers?
We cannot think of a time that is oceanless
Or of an ocean not littered with wastage
Or of a future that is not liable
Like the past, to have no destination.

We have to think of them as forever bailing,
Setting and hauling, while the North East lowers

DRY SALVAGES. **22. seine:** a fishing net.

**35. tolling . . . bell:** not just the reminder of death. It suggests also the Angelus, rung daily to commemorate the Annunciation to the Virgin Mary of the birth of Christ, and the bell at the consecration of the Host in the sacrament of the Eucharist; both reminders of "time not our time." **37. Ground swell:** The clue to the meaning of this is in the echo from the doxology in l. 46: "as it was from the beginning, is now and ever shall be": the ground swell is the presence of the permanence within the flux, the Trinity. **44. before . . . watch:** See Ps. 130:6: "My soul fleeth unto the Lord, before the morning watch, I say, before the morning watch."

Over shallow banks unchanging and erosionless
Or drawing their money, drying sails at dockage;
Not as making a trip that will be unpayable
For a haul that will not bear examination.

There is no end of it, the voiceless wailing,
No end to the withering of withered flowers,
To the movement of pain that is painless and motionless,
To the drift of the sea and the drifting wreckage,
The bone's prayer to Death its God. Only the hardly, barely prayable
Prayer of the one Annunciation.

It seems, as one becomes older,
That the past has another pattern, and ceases to be a mere sequence —
Or even development: the latter a partial fallacy,
Encouraged by superficial notions of evolution,
Which becomes, in the popular mind, a means of disowning the past.
The moments of happiness — not the sense of well-being,
Fruition, fulfilment, security or affection,
Or even a very good dinner, but the sudden illumination —
We had the experience but missed the meaning,
And approach to the meaning restores the experience
In a different form, beyond any meaning
We can assign to happiness. I have said before
That the past experience revived in the meaning
Is not the experience of one life only
But of many generations — not forgetting
Something that is probably quite ineffable:
The backward look behind the assurance
Of recorded history, the backward half-look
Over the shoulder, towards the primitive terror.
Now, we come to discover that the moments of agony
(Whether, or not, due to misunderstanding,
Having hoped for the wrong things or dreaded the wrong things,
Is not in question) are likewise permanent
With such permanence as time has. We appreciate this better
In the agony of others, nearly experienced,
Involving ourselves, than in our own.
For our own past is covered by the currents of action,
But the torment of others remains an experience
Unqualified, unworn by subsequent attrition.
People change, and smile: but the agony abides.
Time the destroyer is time the preserver,
Like the river with its cargo of dead Negroes, cows and chicken coops,
The bitter apple and the bite in the apple.
And the ragged rock in the restless waters,
Waves wash over it, fogs conceal it;
On a halcyon day it is merely a monument,
In navigable weather it is always a seamark
To lay a course by: but in the sombre season
Or the sudden fury, is what it always was.

III

I sometimes wonder if that is what Krishna meant —
Among other things — or one way of putting the same thing:
That the future is a faded song, a Royal Rose or a lavender spray
Of wistful regret for those who are not yet here to regret,
Pressed between yellow leaves of a book that has never been opened.
And the way up is the way down, the way forward is the way back.
You cannot face it steadily, but this thing is sure,
That time is no healer: the patient is no longer here.
When the train starts, and the passengers are settled
To fruit, periodicals and business letters
(And those who saw them off have left the platform)
Their faces relax from grief into relief,
To the sleepy rhythm of a hundred hours.
Fare forward, travellers! not escaping from the past
Into different lives, or into any future;
You are not the same people who left that station
Or who will arrive at any terminus,
While the narrowing rails slide together behind you;
And on the deck of the drumming liner
Watching the furrow that widens behind you,
You shall not think "the past is finished"
Or "the future is before us."
At nightfall, in the rigging and the aerial,
Is a voice descanting (though not to the ear,
The murmuring shell of time, and not in any language)
"Fare forward, you who think that you are voyaging;

**84. Prayer . . . Annunciation:** "Be it unto me according to thy word" (Luke 1:38). **115–17. Time . . . apple:** Time preserves in our consciousness the memory of past agonies, carried along in our racial memory as the great flood on the Mississippi carried along its load of death. The symbol of man's death is the Fall. **118. the . . . rock:** perhaps the Crucifixion; the agony which redeemed man from time. **124. Krishna:** the Hindu god and hero, worshiped as an incarnation of Vishnu, the preserver. See ll. 156–58n. **126–28. That . . . opened:** The future is part of an endless sequence that repeats itself: all the future ever brings is regret for the past. **126. Royal Rose:** a Jacobite song. **131. time . . . here:** It is not time that heals; it is the sufferer who changes. **149. you . . . voyaging:** Any real development is

You are not those who saw the harbour
Receding, or those who will disembark.
Here between the hither and the farther shore
While time is withdrawn, consider the future
And the past with an equal mind.
At the moment which is not of action or inaction
You can receive this: 'on whatever sphere of being
The mind of man may be intent
At the time of death'—that is the one action
(And the time of death is every moment)
Which shall fructify in the lives of others:
And do not think of the fruit of action.
Fare forward.
O voyagers, O seamen,
You who come to port, and you whose bodies
Will suffer the trial and judgement of the sea,
Or whatever event, this is your real destination."
So Krishna, as when he admonished Arjuna
On the field of battle.
Not fare well,
But fare forward, voyagers.

IV

Lady, whose shrine stands on the promontory,
Pray for all those who are in ships, those
Whose business has to do with fish, and
Those concerned with every lawful traffic
And those who conduct them.

Repeat a prayer also on behalf of
Women who have seen their sons or husbands
Setting forth, and not returning:
Figlia del tuo figlio,
Queen of Heaven.

Also pray for those who were in ships, and
Ended their voyage on the sand, in the sea's lips
Or in the dark throat which will not reject them
Or wherever cannot reach them the sound of the sea bell's
Perpetual angelus.

V

To communicate with Mars, converse with spirits,
To report the behaviour of the sea monster,

never in time, it is in consciousness. It is there that we can "fare forward." **156–58. 'on . . . death'**: quoted from the *Bhagavad-Gita* (the Song of the Blessed), a sacred Hindu poem. **166–67. So . . . battle**: Arjuna hesitated to fight when some kinsmen were in the opposing army. But Krishna, who was his charioteer, urged that the way of salvation is in the performing of immediate duties with complete detachment from personal interests. Such action is the equal of the other "sphere of being," which is the abstention from action, the life of contemplation. Eliot is saying, therefore, that it is the quality of disinterested thought or action in the present moment which is important. The time of death is every moment, for no moment will come again. *This* moment is our "real destination." **177. Figlia . . . figlio**: "daughter of thine own son"; the address of St. Bernard to the Virgin. *Paradiso*, XXXIII.

Describe the horoscope, haruspicate or scry,
Observe disease in signatures, evoke
Biography from the wrinkles of the palm
And tragedy from fingers; release omens
By sortilege, or tea leaves, riddle the inevitable
With playing cards, fiddle with pentagrams
Or barbituric acids, or dissect
The recurrent image into pre-conscious terrors—
To explore the womb, or tomb, or dreams; all these are usual
Pastimes and drugs, and features of the press:
And always will be, some of them especially
When there is distress of nations and perplexity
Whether on the shores of Asia, or in the Edgware Road.
Men's curiosity searches past and future
And clings to that dimension. But to apprehend
The point of intersection of the timeless
With time, is an occupation for the saint—
No occupation either, but something given
And taken, in a lifetime's death in love,
Ardour and selflessness and self-surrender.
For most of us, there is only the unattended
Moment, the moment in and out of time,
The distraction fit, lost in a shaft of sunlight,
The wild thyme unseen, or the winter lightning
Or the waterfall, or music heard so deeply
That it is not heard at all, but you are the music
While the music lasts. These are only hints and guesses,
Hints followed by guesses; and the rest
Is prayer, observance, discipline, thought and action.
The hint half guessed, the gift half understood, is Incarnation.
Here the impossible union
Of spheres of existence is actual,
Here the past and future
Are conquered, and reconciled,
Where action were otherwise movement
Of that which is only moved
And has in it no source of movement—
Driven by daemonic, chthonic
Powers. And right action is freedom
From past and future also
For most of us, this is the aim
Never here to be realised;
Who are only undefeated
Because we have gone on trying;
We, content at the last
If our temporal reversion nourish
(Not too far from the yew-tree)
The life of significant soil.

*1941*

**186. haruspicate**: to practice divination. **scry**: descry. **198. Edgware Road**: a well-known London street **223. chthonic**: relating to the earth spirits of the underworld.

# HAMLET

First entitled "Hamlet and his Problems"; a review of *The Problem of Hamlet* by J. M. Robertson. (See Introduction, pp. 820–21.)

Few critics have even admitted that *Hamlet* the play is the primary problem, and Hamlet the character only secondary. And Hamlet the character has had an especial temptation for that most dangerous type of critic: the critic with a mind which is naturally of the creative order, but which through some weakness in creative power exercises itself in criticism instead. These minds often find in Hamlet a vicarious existence for their own artistic realization. Such a mind had Goethe, who made of Hamlet a Werther; and such had Coleridge,[1] who made of Hamlet a Coleridge; and probably neither of these men in writing about Hamlet remembered that his first business was to study a work of art. The kind of criticism that Goethe and Coleridge produced, in writing of Hamlet, is the most misleading kind possible. For they both possessed unquestionable critical insight, and both make their critical aberrations the more plausible by the substitution — of their own Hamlet for Shakespeare's — which their creative gift effects. We should be thankful that Walter Pater did not fix his attention on this play.

Two writers of our own time, Mr. J. M. Robertson and Professor Stoll of the University of Minnesota, have issued small books [2] which can be praised for moving in the other direction. Mr. Stoll performs a service in recalling to our attention the labors of the critics of the seventeenth and eighteenth centuries, observing that

> they knew less about psychology than more recent Hamlet critics, but they were nearer in spirit to Shakespeare's art; and as they insisted on the importance of the effect of the whole rather than on the importance of the leading character, they were nearer, in their old-fashioned way, to the secret of dramatic art in general.

*Qua* work of art, the work of art cannot be interpreted; there is nothing to interpret; we can only criticize it according to standards, in comparison to other works of art; and for "interpretation" the chief task is the presentation of relevant historical facts which the reader is not assumed to know. Mr. Robertson points out, very pertinently, how critics have failed in their "interpretation" of *Hamlet* by ignoring what ought to be very obvious; that *Hamlet* is a stratification, that it represents the efforts of a series of men, each making what he could out of the work of his predecessors. The *Hamlet* of Shakespeare will appear to us very differently if, instead of treating the whole action of the play as due to Shakespeare's design, we perceive his *Hamlet* to be superposed upon much cruder material which persists even in the final form.

We know that there was an older play by Thomas Kyd, that extraordinary dramatic (if not poetic) genius who was in all probability the author of two plays so dissimilar as *The Spanish Tragedy* and *Arden of Feversham;* and what this play was like we can guess from three clues: from *The Spanish Tragedy* itself, from the tale of Belleforest upon which Kyd's *Hamlet* must have been based, and from a version acted in Germany in Shakespeare's lifetime which bears strong evidence of having been adapted from the earlier, not from the later, play. From these three sources it is clear that in the earlier play the motive was a revenge motive simply; that the action or delay is caused, as in *The Spanish Tragedy,* solely by the difficulty of assassinating a monarch surrounded by guards; and that the "madness" of Hamlet was feigned in order to escape suspicion, and successfully. In the final play of Shakespeare, on the other hand, there is a motive which is more important than that of revenge, and which explicitly "blunts" the latter; the delay in revenge is unexplained on grounds of necessity or expediency; and the effect of the "madness" is not to lull but to arouse the king's suspicion. The alteration is not complete enough, however, to be convincing. Furthermore, there are verbal parallels so close to *The Spanish Tragedy* as to leave no doubt that in places Shakespeare was merely *revising* the text of Kyd. And finally there are unexplained scenes — the Polonius-Laertes and the Polonius-Reynaldo scenes — for which there is little excuse; these scenes are not in the verse style of Kyd, and not beyond doubt in the style of Shakespeare. These Mr. Robertson believes to be scenes in the original play of Kyd reworked by a third hand, perhaps Chapman, before Shakespeare touched the play. And he concludes, with very strong show of reason, that the original play of Kyd was, like certain other revenge plays, in two parts of five acts each. The

HAMLET. 1. Cf. pp. 141–43, above. 2. Robertson's *The Problem of Hamlet* (1919) and Stoll's *Hamlet: An Historical and Comparative Study* (1919). Eliot's essay was a review of the former. Robertson suggests that perhaps some passages in *Hamlet* are not Shakespeare's original work.

upshot of Mr. Robertson's examination is, we believe, irrefragable: that Shakespeare's *Hamlet,* so far as it is Shakespeare's, is a play dealing with the effect of a mother's guilt upon her son, and that Shakespeare was unable to impose this motive successfully upon the " intractable " material of the old play.

Of the intractability there can be no doubt. So far from being Shakespeare's masterpiece, the play is most certainly an artistic failure. In several ways the play is puzzling, and disquieting as is none of the others. Of all the plays it is the longest and is possibly the one on which Shakespeare spent most pains; and yet he has left in it superfluous and inconsistent scenes which even hasty revision should have noticed. The versification is variable. Lines like

> Look, the morn, in russet mantle clad,
> Walks o'er the dew of yon high eastern hill.

are of the Shakespeare of *Romeo and Juliet.* The lines in Act V, Sc. ii,

> Sir, in my heart there was a kind of fighting
> That would not let me sleep . . .
> Up from my cabin,
> My sea-gown scarf'd about me, in the dark
> Grop'd I to find out them: had my desire;
> Finger'd their packet . . .

are of his quite mature style. Both workmanship and thought are in an unstable position. We are surely justified in attributing the play, with that other profoundly interesting play of " intractable " material and astonishing versification, *Measure for Measure,* to a period of crisis, after which follow the tragic successes which culminate in *Coriolanus. Coriolanus* may be not as " interesting " as *Hamlet,* but it is, with *Antony and Cleopatra,* Shakespeare's most assured artistic success. And probably more people have thought *Hamlet* a work of art because they found it interesting, than have found it interesting because it is a work of art. It is the " Mona Lisa " of literature.

The grounds of *Hamlet's* failure are not immediately obvious. Mr. Robertson is undoubtedly correct in concluding that the essential emotion of the play is the feeling of a son towards a guilty mother:

" [Hamlet's] tone is that of one who has suffered tortures on the score of his mother's degradation. . . . The guilt of a mother is an almost intolerable motive for drama, but it had to be maintained and emphasized to supply a psychological solution, or rather a hint of one."

This, however, is by no means the whole story. It is not merely the " guilt of a mother " that cannot be handled as Shakespeare handled the suspicion of Othello, the infatuation of Antony, or the pride of Coriolanus. The subject might conceivably have expanded into a tragedy like these, intelligible, self-complete, in the sunlight. *Hamlet,* like the sonnets, is full of some stuff that the writer could not drag to light, contemplate, or manipulate into art. And when we search for this feeling, we find it, as in the sonnets, very difficult to localize. You cannot point to it in the speeches; indeed, if you examine the two famous soliloquies you see the versification of Shakespeare, but a content which might be claimed by another, perhaps by the author of the *Revenge of Bussy d'Ambois,* Act V, Sc. i. [3] We find Shakespeare's Hamlet not in the action, not in any quotations that we might select, so much as in an unmistakable tone which is unmistakably not in the earlier play.

The only way of expressing emotion in the form of art is by finding an " objective correlative "; in other words, a set of objects, a situation, a chain of events which shall be the formula of that *particular* emotion; such that when the external facts, which must terminate in sensory experience, are given, the emotion is immediately evoked. If you examine any of Shakespeare's more successful tragedies, you will find this exact equivalence; you will find that the state of mind of Lady Macbeth walking in her sleep has been communicated to you by a skillful accumulation of imagined sensory impressions; the words of Macbeth on hearing of his wife's death strike us as if, given the sequence of events, these words were automatically released by the last event in the series. The artistic " inevitability " lies in this complete adequacy of the external to the emotion; and this is precisely what is deficient in *Hamlet.* Hamlet (the man) is dominated by an emotion which is inexpressible, because it is in *excess* of the facts as they appear. And the supposed identity of Hamlet with his author is genuine to this point: that Hamlet's bafflement at the absence of objective equivalent to his feelings is a prolongation of the bafflement of his creator in the face of his artistic problem. Hamlet is up against the difficulty that his disgust is occasioned by his mother, but that his mother is not an adequate equivalent for it; his disgust envelops and exceeds her. It is thus a feeling which he cannot understand; he cannot objectify it, and it therefore remains to poison life and

3. George Chapman (1559?–1634).

obstruct action. None of the possible actions can satisfy it; and nothing that Shakespeare can do with the plot can express Hamlet for him. And it must be noticed that the very nature of the *données* of the problem precludes objective equivalence. To have heightened the criminality of Gertrude would have been to provide the formula for a totally different emotion in Hamlet; it is just *because* her character is so negative and insignificant that she arouses in Hamlet the feeling which she is incapable of representing.

The "madness" of Hamlet lay to Shakespeare's hand; in the earlier play a simple ruse, and to the end, we may presume, understood as a ruse by the audience. For Shakespeare it is less than madness and more than feigned. The levity of Hamlet, his repetition of phrase, his puns, are not part of a deliberate plan of dissimulation, but a form of emotional relief. In the character Hamlet it is the buffoonery of an emotion which can find no outlet in action; in the dramatist it is the buffoonery of an emotion which he cannot express in art. The intense feeling, ecstatic or terrible, without an object or exceeding its object, is something which every person of sensibility has known; it is doubtless a subject of study for pathologists. It often occurs in adolescence: the ordinary person puts these feelings to sleep, or trims down his feelings to fit the business world; the artist keeps them alive by his ability to intensify the world to his emotions. The Hamlet of Laforgue[4] is an adolescent; the Hamlet of Shakespeare is not, he has not that explanation and excuse. We must simply admit that here Shakespeare tackled a problem which proved too much for him. Why he attempted it at all is an insoluble puzzle; under compulsion of what experience he attempted to express the inexpressibly horrible, we cannot ever know. We need a great many facts in his biography; and we should like to know whether, and when, and after or at the same time as what personal experience, he read Montaigne, II. xii, *Apologie de Raimond Sebond*. We should have, finally, to know something which is by hypothesis unknowable, for we assume it to be an experience which, in the manner indicated, exceeded the facts. We should have to understand things which Shakespeare did not understand himself.

*1919*

4. Jules Laforgue (1860–87), a French Symbolist poet who influenced Eliot strongly.

# THE METAPHYSICAL POETS

By collecting these poems[1] from the work of a generation more often named than read, and more often read than profitably studied, Professor Grierson has rendered a service of some importance. Certainly the reader will meet with many poems already preserved in other anthologies, at the same time that he discovers poems such as those of Aurelian Townshend or Lord Herbert of Cherbury here included. But the function of such an anthology as this is neither that of Professor Saintsbury's admirable edition of Caroline poets nor that of the *Oxford Book of English Verse*. Mr. Grierson's book is in itself a piece of criticism and a provocation of criticism; and we think that he was right in including so many poems of Donne, elsewhere (though not in many editions) accessible, as documents in the case of "Metaphysical poetry." The phrase has long done duty as a term of abuse or as the label of a quaint and pleasant taste. The question is to what extent the so-called Metaphysicals formed a school (in our own time we should say a "movement"), and how far this so-called school or movement is a digression from the main current.

Not only is it extremely difficult to define Metaphysical poetry, but difficult to decide what poets practice it and in which of their verses. The poetry of Donne (to whom Marvell and Bishop King are sometimes nearer than any of the other authors) is late Elizabethan, its feeling often very close to that of Chapman. The "courtly" poetry is derivative from Jonson, who borrowed liberally from the Latin; it expires in the next century with the sentiment and witticism of Prior. There is finally the devotional verse of Herbert, Vaughan, and Crashaw (echoed long after by Christina Rossetti and Francis Thompson); Crashaw, sometimes more profound and less sectarian than the others, has a quality which returns through the Elizabethan period to the early Italians. It is difficult to find any precise use of metaphor, simile, or other conceit, which is common to all the poets and at the same time important enough as an element of style to isolate these poets as a group. Donne, and often Cowley, employ a device which is sometimes considered characteristically "Metaphysical"; the elaboration (contrasted with the condensation) of a figure of speech to the farthest stage to which in-

METAPHYSICAL POETS. 1. The essay first appeared in *The Times Literary Supplement* as a review of *Metaphysical Lyrics and Poems of the Seventeenth Century: Donne to Butler*, selected and edited by Herbert J. C. Grierson.

genuity can carry it. Thus Cowley develops the commonplace comparison of the world to a chess-board through long stanzas ("To Destiny"), and Donne, with more grace, in "A Valediction," the comparison of two lovers to a pair of compasses. But elsewhere we find, instead of the mere explication of the content of a comparison, a development by rapid association of thought which requires considerable agility on the part of the reader.

On a round ball
A workman that hath copies by, can lay
An Europe, Afrique, and an Asia,
And quickly make that, which was nothing, *All,*
So doth each teare,
Which thee doth weare,
A globe, yea, world by that impression grow,
Till thy tears mixt with mine doe overflow
This world, by waters sent from thee, my heaven dissolvèd so.[2]

Here we find at least two connections which are not implicit in the first figure, but are forced upon it by the poet: from the geographer's globe to the tear, and the tear to the deluge. On the other hand, some of Donne's most successful and characteristic effects are secured by brief words and sudden contrasts:

A bracelet of bright hair about the bone,[3]

where the most powerful effect is produced by the sudden contrast of associations of "bright hair" and of "bone." This telescoping of images and multiplied associations is characteristic of the phrase of some of the dramatists of the period which Donne knew: not to mention Shakespeare, it is frequent in Middleton, Webster, and Tourneur, and is one of the sources of the vitality of their language.

Johnson, who employed the term "Metaphysical poets," apparently having Donne, Cleveland, and Cowley chiefly in mind, remarks of them that "the most heterogeneous ideas are yoked by violence together." The force of this impeachment lies in the failure of the conjunction, the fact that often the ideas are yoked but not united; and if we are to judge of styles of poetry by their abuse, enough examples may be found in Cleveland to justify Johnson's condemnation. But a degree of heterogeneity of material compelled into unity by the operation of the poet's mind is omnipresent in poetry. We need not select for illustration such a line as:

2. John Donne, "A Valediction: Of Weeping," pp. 370–71 in Vol. I. 3. "The Relique," p. 374 in Vol. I.

*Notre âme est un trois-mâts cherchant son Icarie;*[4]

we may find it in some of the best lines of Johnson himself ("The Vanity of Human Wishes"):

His fate was destined to a barren strand,
A petty fortress, and a dubious hand;
He left a name at which the world grew pale,
To point a moral, or adorn a tale.

where the effect is due to a contrast of ideas, different in degree but the same in principle, as that which Johnson mildly reprehended. And in one of the finest poems of the age (a poem which could not have been written in any other age), the "Exequy" of Bishop King, the extended comparison is used with perfect success: the idea and the simile become one, in the passage in which the Bishop illustrates his impatience to see his dead wife, under the figure of a journey:

Stay for me there; I will not faile
To meet thee in that hollow Vale.
And think not much of my delay;
I am already on the way,
And follow thee with all the speed
Desire can make, or sorrows breed.
Each minute is a short degree,
And ev'ry houre a step towards thee.
At night when I betake to rest,
Next morn I rise nearer my West
Of life, almost by eight houres sail,
Than when sleep breath'd his drowsy gale. . . .
But heark! My Pulse, like a soft Drum
Beats my approach, tells *Thee* I come;
And slow howere my marches be,
I shall at last sit down by *Thee.*

(In the last few lines there is that effect of terror which is several times attained by one of Bishop King's admirers, Edgar Poe.) Again, we may justly take these quatrains from Lord Herbert's Ode, stanzas which would, we think, be immediately pronounced to be of the Metaphysical school:

So when from hence we shall be gone,
And be no more, nor you, nor I,
As one another's mystery,
Each shall be both, yet both but one.

This said, in her up-lifted face,
Her eyes, which did that beauty crown,
Were like two starrs, that having faln down,
Look up again to find their place:

4. "Our soul is a three-master [ship] searching for her Icaria" (Charles Baudelaire [1821–67], "*Le Voyage*"). *Icarie* was the name of an imaginary Utopia created in a novel by Étienne Cabet in 1840.

While such a moveless silent peace
  Did seize on their becalmed sense,
  One would have thought some influence
Their ravished spirits did possess.

There is nothing in these lines (with the possible exception of the stars, a simile not at once grasped, but lovely and justified) which fits Johnson's general observations on the Metaphysical poets in his essay on Cowley. A good deal resides in the richness of association which is at the same time borrowed from and given to the word "becalmed"; but the meaning is clear, the language simple and elegant. It is to be observed that the language of these poets is as a rule simple and pure; in the verse of George Herbert this simplicity is carried as far as it can go — a simplicity emulated without success by numerous modern poets. The *structure* of the sentences, on the other hand, is sometimes far from simple, but this is not a vice; it is a fidelity to thought and feeling. The effect, at its best, is far less artificial than that of an ode by Gray. And as this fidelity induces variety of thought and feeling, so it induces variety of music. We doubt whether, in the eighteenth century, could be found two poems in nominally the same meter, so dissimilar as Marvell's "Coy Mistress" and Crashaw's "Saint Teresa"; the one producing an effect of great speed by the use of short syllables, and the other an ecclesiastical solemnity by the use of long ones:

  Love, thou art absolute sole lord
  Of life and death.

If so shrewd and sensitive (though so limited) a critic as Johnson failed to define Metaphysical poetry by its faults, it is worth while to inquire whether we may not have more success by adopting the opposite method: by assuming that the poets of the seventeenth century (up to the Revolution) were the direct and normal development of the precedent age; and, without prejudicing their case by the adjective "Metaphysical," consider whether their virtue was not something permanently valuable, which subsequently disappeared, but ought not to have disappeared, Johnson has hit, perhaps by accident, on one of their peculiarities, when he observes that "their attempts were always analytic"; he would not agree that, after the dissociation, they put the material together again in a new unity.

It is certain that the dramatic verse of the later Elizabethan and early Jacobean poets expresses a degree of development of sensibility which is not found in any of the prose, good as it often is. If we except Marlowe, a man of prodigious intelligence, these dramatists were directly or indirectly (it is at least a tenable theory) affected by Montaigne. Even if we except also Jonson and Chapman, these two were notably erudite, and were notably men who incorporated their erudition into their sensibility: their mode of feeling was directly and freshly altered by their reading and thought. In Chapman especially there is a direct sensuous apprehension of thought, or a recreation of thought into feeling, which is exactly what we find in Donne:

  in this one thing, all the discipline
Of manners and of manhood is contained;
A man to join himself with th' Universe
In his main sway, and make in all things fit
One with that All, and go on, round as it;
Not plucking from the whole his wretched part,
And into straits, or into nought revert,
Wishing the complete Universe might be
Subject to such a rag of it as he;
But to consider great Necessity.[5]

We compare this with some modern passage:

No, when the fight begins within himself,
A man's worth something. God stoops o'er his head,
Satan looks up between his feet — both tug —
He's left, himself, i' the middle; the soul wakes
And grows. Prolong that battle through his life![6]

It is perhaps somewhat less fair, though very tempting (as both poets are concerned with the perpetuation of love by offspring), to compare with the stanzas already quoted from Lord Herbert's Ode the following from Tennyson:

One walked between his wife and child,
With measured footfall firm and mild,
And now and then he gravely smiled.
  The prudent partner of his blood
  Leaned on him, faithful, gentle, good,
  Wearing the rose of womanhood.
And in their double love secure,
The little maiden walked demure,
Pacing with downward eyelids pure.
  These three made unity so sweet,
  My frozen heart began to beat,
  Remembering its ancient heat.[7]

The difference is not a simple difference of degree between poets. It is something which had happened to the mind of England between the time of Donne or Lord Herbert of Cherbury and the time

5. *The Revenge of Bussy d'Ambois*, IV.i.139–46. 6. Robert Browning, "Bishop Blougram's Apology." 7. Tennyson, "The Two Voices."

of Tennyson and Browning; it is the difference between the intellectual poet and the reflective poet. Tennyson and Browning are poets, and they think; but they do not feel their thought as immediately as the odor of a rose. A thought to Donne was an experience; it modified his sensibility. When a poet's mind is perfectly equipped for its work, it is constantly amalgamating disparate experience; the ordinary man's experience is chaotic, irregular, fragmentary. The latter falls in love, or reads Spinoza, and these two experiences have nothing to do with each other, or with the noise of the typewriter or the smell of cooking; in the mind of the poet these experiences are always forming new wholes.

We may express the difference by the following theory: The poets of the seventeenth century, the successors of the dramatists of the sixteenth, possessed a mechanism of sensibility which could devour any kind of experience. They are simple, artificial, difficult, or fantastic, as their predecessors were; no less nor more than Dante, Guido Cavalcanti, Guinizelli, or Cino.[8] In the seventeenth century a dissociation of sensibility set in, from which we have never recovered; and this dissociation, as is natural, was aggravated by the influence of the two most powerful poets of the century, Milton and Dryden. Each of these men performed certain poetic functions so magnificently well that the magnitude of the effect concealed the absence of others. The language went on and in some respects improved; the best verse of Collins, Gray, Johnson, and even Goldsmith satisfies some of our fastidious demands better than that of Donne or Marvell or King. But while the language became more refined, the feeling became more crude. The feeling, the sensibility, expressed in the "Country Churchyard" (to say nothing of Tennyson and Browning) is cruder than that in the "Coy Mistress."

The second effect of the influence of Milton and Dryden followed from the first, and was therefore slow in manifestation. The sentimental age began early in the eighteenth century, and continued. The poets revolted against the ratiocinative, the descriptive; they thought and felt by fits, unbalanced; they reflected. In one or two passages of Shelley's *Triumph of Life,* in the second *Hyperion,* there are traces of a struggle toward unification of sensibility. But Keats and Shelley died, and Tennyson and Browning ruminated.

8. These were all members of the thirteenth-century Tuscan school of lyric love poets.

After this brief exposition of a theory — too brief, perhaps, to carry conviction — we may ask, what would have been the fate of the "Metaphysical" had the current of poetry descended in a direct line from them, as it descended in a direct line to them? They would not, certainly, be classified as Metaphysical. The possible interests of a poet are unlimited; the more intelligent he is the better; the more intelligent he is the more likely that he will have interests: our only condition is that he turn them into poetry, and not merely meditate on them poetically. A philosophical theory which has entered into poetry is established, for its truth or falsity in one sense ceases to matter, and its truth in another sense is proved. The poets in question have, like other poets, various faults. But they were, at best, engaged in the task of trying to find the verbal equivalent for states of mind and feeling. And this means both that they are more mature, and that they wear better, than later poets of certainly not less literary ability.

It is not a permanent necessity that poets should be interested in philosophy, or in any other subject. We can only say that it appears likely that poets in our civilization, as it exists at present, must be *difficult*. Our civilization comprehends great variety and complexity, and this variety and complexity, playing upon a refined sensibility, must produce various and complex results. The poet must become more and more comprehensive, more allusive, more indirect, in order to force, to dislocate if necessary, language into his meaning. (A brilliant and extreme statement of this view, with which it is not requisite to associate oneself, is that of M. Jean Epstein, *La Poésie d'aujourd'hui.*) Hence we get something which looks very much like the conceit — we get, in fact, a method curiously similar to that of the "Metaphysical poets," similar also in its use of obscure words and of simple phrasing.

*O géraniums diaphanes, guerroyeurs sortilèges,*
*Sacrilèges monomanes!*
*Emballages, dévergondages, douches! O pressoirs*
*Des vendanges des grands soirs!*
*Layettes aux abois,*
*Thyrses au fond des bois!*
*Transfusions, représailles,*
*Relevailles, compresses et l'éternelle potion,*
*Angélus! n'en pouvoir plus*
*De débâcles nuptiales! de débâcles nuptiales!*[9]

9. Jules Laforgue, *Derniers vers X.* I am indebted for this translation to Professor Warren Ramsey (author of *Jules Laforgue and the Ironic Inheritance*). It is somewhat strange that Eliot sees a similarity between this poetry of disconnected substantives

The same poet could write also simply:

*Elle est bien loin, elle pleure,*
*Le grand vent se lamente aussi . . .*[10]

Jules Laforgue and Tristan Corbière,[11] in many of his poems, are nearer to the "school of Donne" than any modern English poet. But poets more classical than they have the same essential quality of transmuting ideas into sensations, of transforming an observation into a state of mind.

*Pour l'enfant, amoureux de cartes et d'estampes,*
*L'univers est égal à son vaste appétit.*
*Ah, que le monde est grand à la clarté des lampes!*
*Aux yeux du souvenir que le monde est petit!*[12]

In French literature the great master of the seventeenth century — Racine — and the great master of the nineteenth — Baudelaire — are in some ways more like each other than they are like any one else. The greatest two masters of diction are also the greatest two psychologists, the most curious explorers of the soul. It is interesting to speculate whether it is not a misfortune that two of the greatest masters of diction in our language, Milton and Dryden, triumph with a dazzling disregard of the soul. If we continued to produce Miltons and Drydens it might not so much matter, but as things are it is a pity that English poetry has remained so incomplete. Those who object to the "artificiality" of Milton or Dryden sometimes tell us to "look into our hearts and write." But that is not looking deep enough; Racine or Donne looked into a good deal more than the heart. One must look into the cerebral cortex, the nervous system, and the digestive tracts.

May we not conclude, then, that Donne, Crashaw, Vaughan, Herbert and Lord Herbert, Marvell, King, Cowley at his best, are in the direct current of English poetry, and that their faults should be reprimanded by this standard rather than coddled by antiquarian affection? They have been enough praised in terms which are implicit limitations because they are "Metaphysical" or "witty," "quaint" or "obscure," though at their best they have not these attributes more than other serious poets. On the other hand, we must not reject the criticism of Johnson (a dangerous person to disagree with) without having mastered it, without having assimilated the Johnsonian canons of taste. In reading the celebrated passage in his essay on Cowley we must remember that by wit he clearly means something more serious than we usually mean today; in his criticism of their versification we must remember in what a narrow discipline he was trained, but also how well trained; we must remember that Johnson tortures chiefly the chief offenders, Cowley and Cleveland. It would be a fruitful work, and one requiring a substantial book, to break up the classification of Johnson (for there has been none since) and exhibit these poets in all their difference of kind and of degree, from the massive music of Donne to the faint, pleasing tinkle of Aurelian Townshend — whose "Dialogue Between a Pilgrim and Time" is one of the few regrettable omissions from the excellent anthology of Professor Grierson.

*1921*

and the strictly controlled metaphysical "conceit":

Translucent geraniums, bellicose incantations,
Obsessed sacrileges!
Discarded wrappings, shamelessnesses, showers! O wine-presses
Of evening vintages!
O layettes at bay!
Thyrsis deep in the woods!
Transfusions, reprisals,
Churchings, compresses and the eternal medicine,
Angelus! O those intolerable
Disastrous marriages, O those ill-starred bridals!

10. "She is far away, she weeps; / the great wind grieves also" (*Derniers vers XI*, "*Sur une défunte*"). 11. Corbière: 1845–75. Another of the French Symbolist poets. 12. Baudelaire, "*Le Voyage*": "For the child, in love with maps and prints, / The universe matches his vast desires. / Ah, how big the world is, reading at night! / How small it is to the eyes of memory!"

# THE MUSIC OF POETRY

Eliot delivered the third W. P. Ker Memorial Lecture at the University of Glasgow, February 24, 1942. Printed by the Glasgow University Publications, August, 1942, and reprinted in *Partisan Review,* November–December, 1942.

I debated with myself for some time before electing, for this occasion, to talk about the subject the nature of which is vaguely indicated by my title. Circumstance and conscience conspire, in these times, to direct our attention to matters of a wider scope and perhaps of more general interest. It seems almost impertinent, even as a man of letters, to concern oneself with a purely literary subject: I find myself tempted to the opposite impertinence of talking about matters beyond my range. Even within my own field, there seem to be questions of greater urgency and relevance: the place of literature in culture, the place of culture itself in the society of the future, and all the educational problems implicit in the cultivation of letters. There are many problems of literature and the arts which lead towards political, sociological and religious speculation; and the question which is in every mind — the question of the condition of society after the war, of its limitations, necessities and possibilities, of its inevitable or of its desirable change — this insistent question might suggest, as a more suitable subject for a formal address on a distinguished foundation, some discussion of the place of literature in a changing world.

If I have resisted this temptation, it is for two reasons, the second of which supports the first. At a time when everyone is interested in the phenomena of change, and when any reflections on these phenomena, whether analytical or constructive, may command attention if only by stimulating controversy and eliciting contradictory opinion, there is a particular need to consider, now and then, problems which only seem unimportant, because they are no more important now than they always have been and always will be. The prime interest of a practitioner of verse like myself must be in the immediate future; not that we regard the future with either hope or fear, or are moved by either the aspiration or despair of excelling dead masters, but simply because our first concern is always the perennial question, what is to be done next? what direction is unexplored? what is there to be done immediately before us, which has not been done already, once and for all, as well as it can be done? When absorbed in these investigations, the poet is no more concerned with the social consequences than is the scientist in his laboratory — though without the context of the use to society, neither the writer nor the scientist could have the conviction which sustains him. This concern with the future requires a concern with the past also: for in order to know what there is to be done we need a pretty accurate knowledge of what has been done already; and this again leads to examination of those principles and conditions which hold good always, to distinguish them from those which only held good for one or another group of our predecessors.

If my subject is justifiable by its permanence, it is also the more fitting on a foundation designed to perpetuate the memory of W. P. Ker. I never met Ker: it is a cause of regret to me that I missed the one opportunity offered me, which came only a few weeks before his last journey to Switzerland. But I found myself asking the question: what would Ker prefer me to talk about, supposing that he could appraise my abilities and my limitations? Not a subject requiring a parade of learning, certainly; for he would be the first to detect, and the most qualified to denounce, such an imposture. I can think of no other great scholar who would have been more certain to perceive both the difference and the relation between his area and mine, and to condemn any trespass from one area to the other. He was a great scholar who was also a great humanist, who was always aware that the end of scholarship is understanding, and that the end of understanding poetry is enjoyment, and that this enjoyment is gusto disciplined by taste. He was remarkable, not only for the comprehensiveness and accuracy of his knowledge of medieval and modern European literature, a knowledge with a firm basis of Latin and Greek, but for his ability to enjoy the most diverse species of it, and for the intuition, fortified by a great memory, which enabled him to detect analogies or relationships which few other men, even as learned as he, would have noticed. Each compartment of his learning was at the disposal of every other: a line of modern verse could take him back to Iceland or Provence, or the rhythm of a popular Spanish ballad could evoke half a dozen modern comparisons. I recently read again the posthumous volume of lectures collected under the title of *Form and Style in Poetry* — mostly lecture notes, but Ker always wrote, and must have spoken, well. It is a book from which the poet, as much as the scholar and the general reader, can profit. I think it is worth while, before proceeding to conjectures of my own as to what we mean, or ought to mean, or can mean, when we say that a poem is musical or unmusical, to emphasize the difference between the approach of the scholar and that of the writer of verse.

The poet, when he talks or writes about poetry, has peculiar qualifications and peculiar limitations: if we allow for the latter we can better appreciate the former — a caution which I recommend to poets themselves as well as to the readers of what they say about poetry. I can never reread any of my own prose writings without acute embarrassment: I shirk the task, and consequently may not take account of all the assertions to which I have at one time or another committed myself; I may often repeat what I have said before, and I may equally well contradict myself. But I believe that the critical writings of poets, of which in the past there have been some very distinguished examples, owe a great deal of their interest to the fact that at the back of the poet's mind, if not as his ostensible purpose, he is always trying to defend the kind of poetry he is writing, or to formulate the kind that he wants to write. Especially when he is young, and actively engaged in battling for the kind of poetry which he practices, he sees the poetry of the past in relation to his own: and his gratitude to those dead poets from whom he has learned, as well as his indifference to those whose aims have been alien to his own, may be exaggerated. He is not so much a judge as an advocate. His knowledge even is likely to be partial: for his studies will have led him to concentrate on certain authors to the neglect of others. When he theorizes about poetic creation, he is likely to be generalizing one type of experience; when he ventures into aesthetics, he is likely to be less, rather than more competent than the philosopher; and he may do best merely to report, for the information of the philosopher, the data of his own introspection. What he writes about poetry, in short, must be assessed in relation to the poetry he writes. We must return to the scholar for ascertainment of facts, and to the more detached critic for impartial judgment. The critic, certainly, should be something of a scholar, and the scholar something of a critic. Ker, whose attention was devoted mainly to the literature of the past, and to problems of historical relationship, must be put in the category of scholars; but he had in a high degree the sense of value, the humane taste, the understanding of critical canons and the ability to apply them, without which the scholar's contribution can be only indirect.

There is another, more particular respect in which the scholar's and the practitioner's acquaintance with versification differs. Here, perhaps, I should be prudent to speak only of myself. I have never been able to retain the names of feet and meters, or to pay the proper respect to the accepted rules of scansion. At school, I enjoyed very much reciting Homer or Virgil — in my own fashion. Perhaps I had some instinctive suspicion that nobody really knew how Greek ought to be pronounced, or what interweaving of Greek and native rhythms the Roman ear might appreciate in Virgil; perhaps I had only an instinct of protective laziness. But certainly, when it came to applying rules of scansion to English verse, with its very different stresses and variable syllabic values, I wanted to know why one line was good and another bad; and this, scansion could not tell me. The only way to learn to manipulate any kind of English verse seemed to be by assimilation and imitation, by becoming so engrossed in the work of a particular poet that one could produce a recognizable derivative. This is not to say that I consider the analytical study of metric, of the abstract forms which sound so extraordinarily different when handled by different poets, to be an utter waste of time. It is only that a study of anatomy will not teach you how to make a hen lay eggs. I do not recommend any other way of beginning the study of Greek or Latin verse than with the aid of those rules of scansion which were established by grammarians after most of the poetry had been written: but if we could revive those languages sufficiently to be able to speak and hear them as the authors did, we could regard the rules with indifference. We have to learn a dead language by an artificial method, and we have to approach its versification by an artificial method, and our methods of teaching have to be applied to pupils most of whom have only a moderate gift for language. Even in approaching the poetry of our own language, we may find the classification of meters, of lines with different numbers of syllables and stresses in different places, useful at a preliminary stage, as a simplified map of a complicated territory: but it is only the study, not of poetry but of poems, that can train our ear. It is not from rules, or by cold-blooded imitation indeed, but by a deeper imitation that is achieved by analysis of style. When we imitated Shelley, it was not so much from a desire to write as he did, as from an invasion of the adolescent self by Shelley, which made Shelley's way, for the time, the only way in which to write.

The practice of English versification has, no doubt, been affected by awareness of the rules of prosody: it is a matter for the historical scholar to determine the influence of Latin upon those great innovators Wyatt and Surrey. The great grammarian Otto Jespersen has maintained that the structure of English grammar has been misunderstood in our attempts to make it conform to the categories of Latin — as in the supposed "subjunctive." In the history of versification, the question whether poets have misunderstood the rhythms of the language in imitating foreign models does not arise: we must accept the practices of great poets of the past, because they are practices upon which our ear has been trained and must be trained. I believe that a number of foreign influences have gone to enrich the range and variety of English verse. Some classical scholars hold the view — this is a matter beyond my competence — that the native measure of Latin poetry was accentual rather than syllabic, that it was overlaid by the influence of a very different language — Greek — and that it reverted to something approximating to its early form, in poems such as the *Pervigilium Veneris* [1] and the Christian hymns. If so, I cannot help suspecting that to the cultivated audience of the age of Virgil, part of the pleasure in the poetry arose from the presence in it of two metrical schemes in a kind of counterpoint: even though the audience may not necessarily have been able to analyze the experience. Similarly, it may be possible that the beauty of some English poetry is due to the presence of more than one metrical structure in it. Deliberate attempts to devise English meters on Latin models are usually very frigid. Among the most successful are a few exercises by Campion,[2] in his brief but too little read treatise on metrics; among the most eminent failures, in my opinion, are the experiments of Robert Bridges — I would give all his ingenious inventions for his earlier and more traditional lyrics. But when a poet has so thoroughly absorbed Latin poetry that its movement informs his verse without deliberate artifice — as with Milton and in some of Tennyson's poems — the result can be among the great triumphs of English versification.

What I think we have, in English poetry, is a kind of amalgam of systems of divers sources (though I do not like to use the word "system," for it has a suggestion of conscious invention rather than growth): an amalgam like the amalgam of races, and indeed partly due to racial origins. The rhythms of Anglo-Saxon, Celtic, Norman French, of Middle English and Scots, have all made their mark upon English poetry, together with the rhythms of Latin, and, at various periods, of French, Italian and Spanish. As with human beings in a composite race, different strains may be dominant in different individuals, even in members of the same family, so one or another element in the poetic compound may be more congenial to one or another poet or to one or another period. The kind of poetry we get is determined, from time to time, by the influence of one or another contemporary literature in a foreign language; or by circumstances which make one period of our own past more sympathetic than another; or by the prevailing emphases in education. But there is one law of nature more powerful than any of these varying currents, or influences from abroad or from the past: the law that poetry must not stray too far from the ordinary everyday language which we use and hear. Whether poetry is accentual or syllabic, rhymed or rhymeless, formal or free, it cannot afford to lose its contact with the changing language of common intercourse.

It may appear strange, that when I profess to be talking about the "music" of poetry, I put such emphasis upon conversation. But I would remind you, first, that the music of poetry is not something which exists apart from the meaning. Otherwise, we could have poetry of great musical beauty which made no sense, and I have never come across such poetry. The apparent exceptions only show a difference of degree: there are poems in which we are moved by the music and take the sense for granted, just as there are poems in which we attend to the sense and are moved by the music without noticing it. Take an apparently extreme example — the nonsense verse of Edward Lear. His nonsense is not vacuity of sense: it is a parody of sense, and that is the sense of it. "The Jumblies" is a poem of adventure, and of nostalgia for the romance of foreign voyage and exploration; "The Yongy-Bongy-Bo" and "The Dong with a Luminous Nose" are poems of unrequited passion — "blues" in fact. We enjoy the music, which is of a higher order, and we enjoy the feeling of irresponsibility towards the sense. Or take a poem of another type, the "Blue Closet" of William Morris. It is a delightful poem, though I cannot explain what it means and I doubt whether the author could have explained it. It has an effect somewhat like that of a rune or charm, but runes and charms are very practical formulae designed to produce definite results, such as getting a cow out of a bog. But its obvious intention (and I think the author succeeds) is to produce the effect of a dream. It is not necessary, in order to enjoy the poem, to know what the dream means; but human beings have an unshakable belief that dreams mean something: they used to believe — and many still believe — that dreams disclose the secrets of the future; the orthodox modern faith is that they reveal the secrets — or at least the more horrid ones — of the past. It is a commonplace to observe that the meaning of a poem may wholly escape paraphrase. It is not quite so commonplace to observe that the meaning of a poem may be something larger than its author's conscious purpose, and something remote from its origins. One of the most obscure of modern poets was the French writer Stephane Mallarmé, of whom the French

MUSIC OF POETRY. 1. **Pervigilium Veneris:** anonymous Latin love poem, probably from the 2nd century A.D. (See l. 428n., p. 838.) 2. **Campion:** Thomas Campion (1567–1620), Elizabethan poet and musician.

sometimes say that his language is so peculiar that it can be understood only by foreigners. The late Roger Fry, and his friend Charles Mauron, published an English translation with notes to unriddle the meanings: when I learn that a difficult sonnet was inspired by seeing a painting on the ceiling reflected on the polished top of a table, or by seeing the light reflected from the foam on a glass of beer, I can only say that this may be a correct embryology, but it is not the meaning. If we are moved by a poem, it has meant something, perhaps something important, to us; if we are not moved, then it is, as poetry, meaningless. We can be deeply stirred by hearing the recitation of a poem in a language of which we understand no word; but if we are then told that the poem is gibberish and has no meaning, we shall consider that we have been deluded — this was no poem, it was merely an imitation of instrumental music. If, as we are aware, only a part of the meaning can be conveyed by paraphrase, that is because the poet is occupied with frontiers of consciousness beyond which words fail, though meanings still exist. A poem may appear to mean very different things to different readers, and all of these meanings may be different from what the author thought he meant. For instance, the author may have been writing some peculiar personal experience, which he saw quite unrelated to anything outside; yet for the reader the poem may become the expression of a general situation, as well as of some private experience of his own. The reader's interpretation may differ from the author's and be equally valid — it may even be better. There may be much more in a poem than the author was aware of. The different interpretations may all be partial formulations of one thing; the ambiguities may be due to the fact that the poem means more, not less, than ordinary speech can communicate.

So, while poetry attempts to convey something beyond what can be conveyed in prose rhythms, it remains, all the same, one person talking to another; and this is just as true if you sing it, for singing is another way of talking. The immediacy of poetry to conversation is not a matter on which we can lay down exact laws. Every revolution in poetry is apt to be, and sometimes to announce itself as, a return to common speech. That is the revolution which Wordsworth announced in his prefaces, and he was right: but the same revolution had been carried out a century before by Oldham, Waller, Denham and Dryden; and the same revolution was due again something over a century later. The followers of a revolution develop the new poetic idiom in one direction or another; they polish or perfect it; meanwhile the spoken language goes on changing, and the poetic idiom goes out of date. Perhaps we do not realize how natural the speech of Dryden must have sounded to the most sensitive of his contemporaries. No poetry, of course, is ever exactly the same speech that the poet talks and hears: but it has to be in such a relation to the speech of his time that the listener or reader can say "that is how I should talk if I could talk poetry." This is the reason why the best contemporary can give us a feeling of excitement and a sense of fulfillment different from any sentiment aroused by even very much greater poetry of a past age.

The music of poetry, then, must be a music latent in the common speech of its time. And that means also that it must be latent in the common speech of the poet's *place*. It would not be to my present purpose to inveigh against the ubiquity of standardized, or "B.B.C." English. If we all came to talk alike there would no longer be any point in our not writing alike: but until that time comes — and I hope it may be long postponed — it is the poet's business to use the speech which he finds about him, that with which he is most familiar. I shall always remember the impression of W. B. Yeats reading poetry aloud. To hear him read his own works was to be made to recognize how much the Irish way of speech is needed to bring out the beauties of Irish poetry: to hear Yeats reading William Blake was an experience of a different kind, more astonishing than satisfying. Of course, we do not want the poet merely to reproduce exactly the conversational idiom of himself, his family, his friends and his particular district: but what he finds there is the material out of which he must make his poetry. He must, like the sculptor, be faithful to the material in which he works; it is out of sounds that he has heard that he must make his melody and harmony.

It would be a mistake, however, to assume that all poetry ought to be melodious, or that melody is more than one of the components of the music of words. Some poetry is meant to be sung; most poetry, in modern times, is meant to be spoken — and there are many other things to be spoken of besides the murmur of innumerable bees or the moan of doves in immemorial elms.[3] Dissonance,

3. **murmur . . . elms:** See Tennyson's *The Princess*, VII.206–07.

even cacophony, has its place: just as, in a poem of any length, there must be transitions between passages of greater and less intensity, to give rhythm of fluctuating emotion essential to the musical structure of the whole; and the passages of less intensity will be, in relation to the level on which the total poem operates, prosaic — so that, in the sense implied by that context, it may be said that no poet can write a poem of amplitude unless he is a master of the prosaic.[4]

What matters, in short, is the whole poem: and if the whole poem need not be, and often should not be, wholly melodious, it follows that a poem is not made only out of " beautiful words." I doubt whether, from the point of view of *sound* alone, any word is more or less beautiful than another — within its own language, for the question whether some languages are not more beautiful than others is quite another question. The ugly words are the words not fitted for the company in which they find themselves; there are words which are ugly because of rawness or because of antiquation; there are words which are ugly because of foreignness or ill-breeding (e.g., *television*): but I do not believe that any word well-established in its own language is either beautiful or ugly. The music of a word is, so to speak, at a point of intersection: it arises from its relation first to the words immediately preceding and following it, and indefinitely to the rest of its context; and from another relation, that of its immediate meaning in that context to all the other meanings which it has had in other contexts, to its greater or less wealth of association. Not all words, obviously, are equally rich and well-connected: it is part of the business of the poet to dispose the richer among the poorer, at the right points, and we cannot afford to load a poem too heavily with the former — for it is only at certain moments that a word can be made to insinuate the whole history of a language and a civilization. This is an " allusiveness " which is not the fashion or eccentricity of a peculiar type of poetry; but an allusiveness which is in the nature of words, and which is equally the concern of every kind of poet. My purpose here is to insist that a " musical poem " is a poem which has a musical pattern of sound and a musical pattern of the secondary meanings of the words which compose it, and that these two patterns are indissoluble and one. And if you object that it is only the pure sound, apart from the sense, to which the adjective " musical " can be rightly applied, I can only reaffirm my previous assertion that the sound of a poem is as much an abstraction from the poem as is the sense.

The history of blank verse illustrates two interesting and related points: the dependence upon speech and the striking difference, in what is prosodically the same form, between dramatic blank verse and blank verse employed for epical, philosophical, meditative and idyllic purposes. The dependence of verse upon speech is much more direct in dramatic poetry than in any other. In most kinds of poetry, the necessity for its reminding us of contemporary speech is reduced by the latitude allowed for personal idiosyncrasy: a poem by Gerard Hopkins, for instance, may sound pretty remote from the way in which you and I express ourselves — or rather, from the way in which our fathers and grandfathers expressed themselves: but Hopkins does give the impression that his poetry has the necessary fidelity to his way of thinking and talking to himself. But in dramatic verse the poet is speaking in one character after another, through the medium of a company of actors trained by a producer, and of different actors and different producers at different times: his idiom must be comprehensive of all the voices, but present at a deeper level than is necessary when the poet speaks only for himself. Some of Shakespeare's later verse is very elaborate and peculiar: but it remains the language, not of one person, but of a world of persons. It is based upon the speech of three hundred years ago, yet when we hear it well rendered we can forget the distance of time — as is brought home to us most patently in one of those plays, of which *Hamlet* is the chief, which can fittingly be produced in modern dress. By the time of Otway [5] dramatic blank verse has become artificial and at best reminiscent; and when we get to the verse plays by nineteenth-century poets, of which the greatest is probably *The Cenci,*[6] it is difficult to preserve any illusion of reality. Nearly all the greater poets of the last century tried their hands at verse plays. These plays, which few people read more than once, are treated with respect as fine poetry; and their insipidity is usually attributed to the fact that the authors, though great poets, were

4. "This is the complementary doctrine to that of the 'touchstone' line or passage of Matthew Arnold: this test of the greatness of a poet is the way he writes his less intense, but structurally vital matter" [E]. See Arnold's essay, "The Study of Poetry," pp. 653–65, above. 5. Thomas Otway (1652–85). His *Venice Preserved* (1682) is sometimes spoken of as the last "Elizabethan" tragedy. 6. By Shelley, published 1819.

amateurs in the theater. But even if the poets had had greater natural gifts for the theater, or had toiled to acquire the craft, their plays would have been just as ineffective, unless their theatrical talent and experience had shown them the necessity for a different kind of versification. It is not primarily lack of plot, or lack of action and suspense, or imperfect realization of character, or lack of anything of what is called " theater," that makes these plays so lifeless: it is primarily that their rhythm of speech is something that we cannot associate with any human being except a poetry reciter.

Even under the powerful manipulation of Dryden dramatic blank verse shows a grave deterioration. There are splendid passages in *All for Love:* yet Dryden's characters talk more naturally at times in the heroic plays which he wrote in rhymed couplets, than they do in what would seem the more natural form of blank verse — though less naturally in English than the characters of Corneille and Racine in French. The causes for the rise and decline of any form of art are always complex, and we can always trace a number of contributory causes, while there seems to remain some deeper cause incapable of formulation: I should not care to advance any one reason why prose came to supersede verse in the theater. But I feel sure that one reason why blank verse cannot be employed now in the drama is that so much nondramatic poetry, and great nondramatic poetry, has been written in it in the last three hundred years. Our minds are saturated in these nondramatic works in what is formally the same kind of verse. If we can imagine, as a flight of fancy, Milton coming before Shakespeare, Shakespeare would have had to discover quite a different medium from that which he used and perfected. Milton handled blank verse in a way which no one has ever approached or ever will approach: and in so doing did more than anyone or anything else to make it impossible for the drama: though we may also believe that dramatic blank verse had exhausted its resources, and had no future in any event. Indeed, Milton almost made blank verse impossible for any purpose for a couple of generations. It was the precursors of Wordsworth — Thomson, Young, Cowper — who made the first efforts to rescue it from the degradation to which the eighteenth-century imitators of Milton had reduced it. There is much, and varied, fine blank verse in the nineteenth century: the nearest to colloquial speech is that of Browning — but, significantly, in his monologues rather than in his plays.

To make a generalization like this is not to imply any judgment of the relative stature of poets. It merely calls attention to the profound difference between dramatic and all other kinds of verse: a difference in the music, which is a difference in the relation to the current spoken language. It leads to my next point: which is that the task of the poet will differ, not only according to his personal constitution, but according to the period in which he finds himself. At some periods, the task is to explore the musical possibilities of an established convention of the relation of the idiom of verse to that of speech; at other periods, the task is to catch up with the changes in colloquial speech, which are fundamentally changes in thought and sensibility. This cyclical movement also has a very great influence upon our critical judgment. At a time like ours, when a refreshment of poetic diction similar to that brought about by Wordsworth has been called for (whether it has been satisfactorily accomplished or not) we are inclined, in our judgments upon the past, to exaggerate the importance of the innovators at the expense of the reputation of the developers: which might account for what will seem, surely, to a later age, our undue adulation of Donne and depreciation of Milton.

I have said enough, I think, to make clear that I do not believe that the task of the poet is primarily and always to effect a revolution in language. It would not be desirable, even if it were possible, to live in a state of perpetual revolution: the craving for continual novelty of diction and metric is as unwholesome as the obstinate adherence to the idiom of our grandfathers. There are times for exploration and times for the development of the territory acquired. The poet who did most for the English language is Shakespeare: and he carried out, in one short lifetime, the task of two poets. I have attempted to indicate his dual achievement elsewhere: I can only say here, briefly, that the development of Shakespeare's verse can be roughly divided into two periods. During the first, he was slowly adapting his form to colloquial speech: so that by the time he wrote *Antony and Cleopatra* he had devised a medium in which everything that any dramatic character might have to say, whether high or low, " poetical " or " prosiac," could be said with naturalness and beauty. Having got to this point, he began to elaborate. The first period — of the poet who began with *Venus and Adonis,* but who had already, in *Love's Labor's Lost,* begun to see what he had to do — is from artificiality to simplicity, from stiffness to suppleness. The later plays move from simplicity towards elaboration. He is occupied with the other task of the poet — doing the work of two poets in one lifetime — that of experimenting to see how elaborate, how complicated, the music could be made without losing touch with colloquial speech altogether, and without his characters ceasing to be human beings. This is the poet of *Cymbeline, The Winter's Tale, Pericles,* and *The Tempest.* Of those whose exploration took them in this one direction only, Milton is the greatest master. We may think that Milton, in exploring the orchestral music of language, sometimes ceases to talk a social idiom at all; we may think that Wordsworth, in attempting to recover the social idiom, sometimes oversteps the mark and becomes pedestrian: but it is often true that only by going too far can we find out how far we can go; though one has to be a very great poet to justify such perilous adventures.

So far, I have spoken only of versification and not of poetic structure; and it is time for a reminder that the music of verse is not a line by line matter, but a question of the whole poem. Only with this in mind can we approach the vexed question of formal pattern and free verse. In the plays of Shakespeare a musical design can be discovered in particular scenes, and in his more perfect plays as wholes. It is a music of imagery as well as sound: Mr. Wilson Knight has shown in his examination of several of the plays, how much the use of recurrent imagery, and dominant imagery, throughout one play, has to do with the total effect. A play of Shakespeare is a very complex musical structure; the more easily grasped structure is that of forms such as the sonnet, the formal ode, the ballade, the villanelle, rondeau or sestina. It is sometimes assumed that modern poetry has done away with forms like these. I have seen signs of a return to them; and indeed I believe that the tendency to return to set, and even elaborate, patterns is permanent, as permanent as the need for a refrain or a chorus to a popular song. Some forms are more appropriate to some languages than to others, and all are more appropriate to some periods than to others. At one stage the stanza is a right and natural formalization of speech into pattern. But the stanza — and the more elaborate it is, the more rules to be observed in its proper execution, the more surely this happens — tends to become fixed to the idiom of the moment of its perfection. It quickly loses contact with the changing colloquial speech, being possessed by the mental outlook of a past generation; it becomes discredited when employed solely by those writers who, having no impulse to form within them, have recourse to pouring their liquid sentiment into a ready-made mold in which they vainly hope that it will set. In a perfect sonnet, what you admire is not so much the author's skill in adapting himself to the pattern as the skill and power with which he makes the pattern comply with what he has to say. Without this fitness, which is contingent upon period as well as individual genius, the rest is at best virtuosity: and where the musical element is the only element, that also vanishes. Elaborate forms return: but there have to be periods during which they are laid aside.

As for "free verse," I expressed my view twenty-five years ago by saying that no verse is free for the man who wants to do a good job. No one has better cause to know than I, that a great deal of bad prose has been written under the name of free verse: though whether its authors wrote bad prose or bad verse, or bad verse in one style or in another, seems to me a matter of indifference. But only a bad poet could welcome free verse as a liberation from form. It was a revolt against dead form, and a preparation for new form or for renewal of the old; it was an insistence upon the inner unity which is unique to every poem, against the outer unity which is typical. The poem comes before the form, in the sense that a form grows out of the attempt of somebody to say something; just as a system of prosody is only a formulation of the identities in the rhythms of a succession of poets influenced by each other.

Forms have to be broken and remade: but I believe that any language, so long as it remains the same language, imposes its laws and restrictions and permits its own license, dictates its own speech rhythms and sound patterns. And a language is always changing; its developments in vocabulary, in syntax, pronunciation and intonation — even, in the long run, its deterioration — must be accepted by the poet and made the best of. He in turn has the privilege of contributing to the development and maintaining the quality, the capacity of the language to express a wide range, and subtle gradation, of feeling and emotion; his task is both to respond to change and make it conscious, and to battle against degradation below the standards which he has learned from the past. The liberties that he may take are for the sake of order.

At what stage contemporary verse now finds itself, I must leave you to judge for yourselves. I suppose that it will be agreed that if the work of the last twenty years is worthy of being classified at all, it is as belonging to a period of search for a proper modern colloquial idiom. We have still a good way to go in the invention of a verse medium for the theater; a medium in which we shall be able to hear the speech of contemporary human beings, in which dramatic characters can express the purest poetry without highfalutin and in which they can convey the most commonplace message without absurdity. But when we reach a point at which the poetic idiom can be stabilized, then a period of musical elaboration can follow. I think that a poet may gain much from the study of music: how much technical knowledge of musical form is desirable I do not know, for I have not that technical knowledge myself. But I believe that the properties in which music concerns the poet most nearly, are the sense of rhythm and the sense of structure. I think that it might be possible for a poet to work too closely to musical analogies: the result might be an effect of artificiality; but I know that a poem, or a passage of a poem, may tend to realize itself first as a particular rhythm before it reaches expression in words, and that this rhythm may bring to birth the idea and the image; and I do not believe that this is an experience peculiar to myself. The use of recurrent themes is as natural to poetry as to music. There are possibilities for verse which bear some analogy to the development of a theme by different groups of instruments; there are possibilities of transitions in a poem comparable to the different movements of a symphony or a quartet; there are possibilities of contrapuntal arrangement of subject matter. It is in the concert room, rather than in the opera house, that the germ of a poem may be quickened. More than this I cannot say, but must leave the matter here to those who have had a musical education. But I would remind you again of the two tasks of poetry, the two directions in which language must at different times be worked: so that however far it may go in musical elaboration, we must expect a time to come when poetry will have again to be recalled to speech. The same problems arise, and always in new forms; and poetry has always before it, as F. S. Oliver said of politics, an "endless adventure."

# A Note on Versification

I have never been able to retain the names of feet and meters, or to pay the proper respect to the accepted rules of scansion. . . . This is not to say that I consider the analytical study of metric, of the abstract forms which sound so extraordinarily different when handled by different poets, to be utter waste of time. It is only that a study of anatomy will not teach you how to make a hen lay eggs . . .

— T. S. Eliot, "The Music of Poetry"

When we open a book of verse, we unconsciously prepare ourselves for a different kind of experience from what we get in a page of solid print. What is the basis of the difference? It is in the ***sound pattern*** of the language — poetry is distinguished from prose by its rhythms.

The study of versification is concerned with the ways in which the poet uses recurrent sound pattern to create formal verbal designs. In a full analysis of any poem, this is seen to be only a part of the total effect. Other topics inevitably intrude. For one thing, we can never discuss poetry without talking about its themes, its subject matter. And beyond the theme, the fact that subject and the structural form in which it realizes itself are inseparable leads to the discussion of the various forms of poetic expression: epic, drama, meditative, and lyric outlines. Then the discovery that the language of logical statement tends, in poetry, to give way to symbolic and metaphorical expression brings another large topic — perhaps the largest of all — since, as Yeats says: "It is not possible to separate an emotion or a spiritual state from the image that calls it up and gives it expression."

Since a poem is a unity, and language is the medium in which it is expressed, in practice none of these things — theme, structure, imagery — can be separated from the sound pattern through which alone we become aware of them. But a note on versification cannot go that far afield. It must limit itself to a short account of meters, rhymes, rhythms, and the word textures and values which combine to make the sound patterns. There is an infinite variety of these patterns, and different poets use the same pattern in widely different ways. They are all, however, differentiated from prose by their basis in *meter*. As we shall see later, meter is only a part of the larger subject of poetic rhythm, but since it is the part which can be stated factually, we will start with the facts.

## METER

Meter means "measure." Verse is written in lines, which are measured according to the number and arrangement of accented and unaccented syllables within them. The unit of this measurement is the *foot*. English verse has borrowed the classical names for describing the number and order and character of the syllables which form "feet." Feet may be either disyllabic (formed of two syllables), or trisyllabic (formed of three syllables). They are named as follows:

*Iamb:* an unaccented syllable followed by an accented one:

The cŭrfew tŏlls thĕ knéll ŏf párting dáy.

*Trochee:* an accented syllable followed by an unaccented one:

Téll mĕ nót ĭn móurnfŭl númbĕrs.

*Spondee:* two accented syllables together, as in the last two feet of the line,

The cumbrous elements — eárth, flóod, aír, fíre

*Dactyl:* an accented syllable followed by two unaccented ones:

Táke hĕr ŭp téndĕrly̆

*Anapest:* Two unaccented syllables followed by an accented one:

Ĭ ăm mŏnárch ŏf áll Ĭ sŭrvéy

Although it is not difficult to find illustrations of all these types of feet, by far the most popular and all-pervasive movement of English verse is the iambic. It suits the nature of the language better than any other, and probably nine-tenths of English poetry uses that foot as its basic metrical unit.

The *line* of verse is composed of one or more feet. Again, the classical names are officially used: *monometer:* one foot; *dimeter:* two feet; *trimeter:* three feet; *tetrameter:* four feet (sometimes called octosyllabics); *pentameter:* five feet;

*hexameter:* six feet (also called alexandrines); *heptameter:* seven feet; *octameter:* eight feet.

Two measurements are therefore involved in meter: the *kind* of foot and the *number* of feet. These can be combined in any possible ways. " The curfew tolls the knell of parting day " is iambic pentameter; " Tell me not in mournful numbers " is trochaic tetrameter; " Take her up tenderly " is dactylic dimeter; and " I am monarch of all I survey," anapestic trimeter.

## RHYME AND OTHER METRICAL DEVICES

Verse patterns may be either rhymed or unrhymed. Rhyme is an identity of sounds at the end of lines. This may be in the last syllable of the line (single or masculine rhyme),

> To hear the lark begin his *flight*,
> And singing startle the dull *night*,

or in the last two syllables (double or feminine rhyme),

> Then to come, in spite of *sorrow*,
> And at my window bid good-*morrow*.[1]

Dactylic verse requires a triple rhyme,

> Touch her not *scornfully*.
> Think of her *mournfully*,[2]

but in serious verse the rhyme is seldom more than double. Triple rhymes are found more often in comic or satiric verse — as in Byron's *Don Juan:*

> . . . Oh! ye lords of ladies intell*ectual*,
> Inform us truly, have they not hen*pecked you all*? [3]

or as in so many of the verses of Ogden Nash today.

The rhymes may be *internal*, within the line as well as at the end:

> Alas,
> We loved, sir — used to meet;
> How *sad* and *bad* and *mad* it was —
> But then, how it was sweet! [4]

Or the rhymes may be *half-rhymes* or *slant rhymes*, where the sounds are similar, but not identical:

> Little Tommy *Tucker*
> Sang for his *supper*.
> What did he have?
> Brown bread and *butter*.

Modern poets are fond of using *assonance*, an identity of vowel sounds only, while the consonants are different. Louis MacNeice writes:

> Not the twilight of the gods but a precise *dawn*
> Of sallow and grey bricks, and the newsboys crying *war*.

An alternative to this is *consonance*, an identity of consonants while the vowels differ. The following example is from Wilfred Owen's " Strange Meeting ":

> It seemed that out of battle I *escaped*
> Down some profound dull tunnel, long since *scooped*
> Through granites which titanic wars had *groined*.
> Yet also there encumbered sleepers *groaned*.

### RHYME SCHEMES

Lines of rhymed verse are usually grouped into patterns called rhyme schemes. These can vary from the single couplet to an elaborate arrangement such as Spenser's *Epithalamion*, which has a varying scheme of sixteen lines.

The *couplet* is any rhymed pattern of two lines, but its most popular forms are the iambic tetrameter, or octosyllabic (see the quotations from Milton's " L'Allegro " above) and the iambic pentameter. This latter form is usually called the *heroic couplet*, though that name was not used for it until late in the seventeenth century, when it was associated with the popular " heroic plays " of the time. More will be said about it later in the section on rhythm.

A three-rhymed pattern is called a *triplet* or *tercet*. The three lines may use one set of rhyming words, as in Tennyson's *The Eagle:*

> He clasps the crag with hooked hands;
> Close to the sun in lonely lands,
> Ring'd with the azure world, he stands,[5]

or the rhymes may be linked from verse to verse. This form is called *terza rima*, and the rhymes run: *aba-bcb-cdc-ded* and so on. There are not many examples of it in English poetry. The finest is Shelley's " Ode to the West Wind ":

> O wild West Wind, thou breath of Autumn's being,
> Thou, from whose unseen presence the leaves dead
> Are driven, like ghosts from an enchanter fleeing,
>
> Yellow, and black, and pale, and hectic red,
> Pestilence-stricken multitudes! O thou
> Who chariotest to their dark wintry bed
>
> The wingèd seeds, where they lie cold and low,
> Each like a corpse within its grave, until
> Thine azure sister of the Spring shall blow
>
> Her clarion o'er the dreaming earth . . .[6]

With the *quatrain* (any arrangement of four lines), we pass into patterns usually called

[1] Milton, " L'Allegro." See p. 418 in Vol. I.
[2] Thomas Hood, " The Bridge of Sighs."
[3] See p. 210, above.
[4] Browning, " Confessions." See p. 532, above.
[5] See p. 409, above.
[6] See p. 254, above.

*stanzas*, and the variations of four-, five-, six-, seven-, and eight-line stanzas are too numerous to differentiate. But there are certain "named varieties": *rhyme royal*, first used in England by Chaucer, is a seven-line stanza in iambic pentameter, with the rhymes running *ababbcc*. It is the meter of Shakespeare's *Rape of Lucrece*.

From the besieged Ardea all in post,
Borne by the trustless wings of false desire,
Lust-breathèd Tarquin leaves the Roman host,
And to Collatium bears the lightless fire,
Which, in pale embers hid, lurks to aspire,
  And girdle with embracing flames the waist
  Of Collatine's fair love, Lucrece the chaste.

*Ottava rima* was introduced from Italy in the sixteenth century. It is an eight-line stanza, also in iambic pentameter, rhyming *abababcc*. It was Byron's favorite meter.

The Angels all were singing out of tune,
  And hoarse with having little else to do,
Excepting to wind up the sun and moon,
  Or curb a runaway young star or two,
Or wild colt of a comet, which too soon
  Broke out of bounds o'er the ethereal blue,
Splitting some planet with its playful tail
As boats are sometimes by a wanton whale.[1]

*The Spenserian stanza* has nine lines, eight in iambic pentameter, and the last an alexandrine, with the rhyme scheme *ababbcbcc*.

So passeth, in the passing of a day,
  Of mortall life the leafe, the bud, the flowre;
Ne more doth florish after first decay,
  That earst was sought to deck both bed and bowre
  Of many a lady, and many a Paramowre.
Gather therefore the Rose whilest yet is prime,
  For soone comes age that will her pride deflowre;
Gather the Rose of love whilest yet is time,
Whilest loving thou mayst lovèd be with equall crime.[2]

The *sonnet* is a complete poem of fourteen lines in iambic pentameter. There are many versions of the form, but the two general types are the Petrachan and the Shakespearean. The *Petrarchan*, introduced from Italy in the sixteenth century, is divided into an octave, the first eight lines, usually playing on two rhymes, and a sestet, the last six lines, using either two or three rhymes. Wordsworth's sonnet on Westminster Bridge is a Petrarchan model.

Earth has not anything to show more fair;
Dull would he be of soul who could pass by
A sight so touching in its majesty:
This city now doth, like a garment, wear
The beauty of the morning; silent, bare,
Ships, towers, domes, theaters, and temples lie
Open unto the fields, and to the sky;
All bright and glittering in the smokeless air.

Never did sun more beautifully steep
In his first splendor, valley, rock, or hill;
Ne'er saw I, never felt, a calm so deep!
The river glideth at his own sweet will;
Dear God! the very houses seem asleep;
And all that mighty heart is lying still![3]

The *Shakespearean* sonnet form divides into three quatrains, each with its own two rhymes, and a final couplet with another rhyme.

When in disgrace with fortune and men's eyes,
I all alone beweep my outcast state,
And trouble deaf heaven with my bootless cries,
And look upon myself, and curse my fate,

Wishing me like to one more rich in hope,
Featured like him, like him with friends possessed,
Desiring this man's art and that man's scope,
With what I most enjoy contented least;

Yet in these thoughts myself almost despising —
Haply I think on thee: and then my state,
Like to the lark at break of day arising
From sullen earth, sings hymns at heaven's gate;

For thy sweet love remembered such wealth brings
That then I scorn to change my state with kings.[4]

### UNRHYMED VERSE

Any stanzaic form may be written without rhymes, but the most popular unrhymed pattern is that of *blank verse*, the iambic pentameter not broken into formal units. Along with the couplet, this will be discussed more fully later in the section on rhythm.

*Free verse* dispenses with any regular metrical pattern, either of rhyme or accent. But as T. S. Eliot states in "*The Music of Poetry*," the term itself is a misnomer: "no verse is free for the man who wants to do a good job." And as he points out in an earlier essay, there is never any escape from meter in poetry; there is only mastery of it.

We may therefore formulate as follows: the ghost of some simple meter should lurk behind the arras in even the "freest" verse; to advance menacingly as we doze, and withdraw as we rouse. Or, freedom is only true freedom when it appears against a background of an artificial limitation.[5]

In these lines from *The Waste Land*, for instance, in spite of all the extra syllables, the uneven accents, and the differences in line length, the ghost of an iambic tetrameter lurks behind the arras.

[1] "The Vision of Judgment." See p. 195, above.
[2] *The Faerie Queene*, II.xii.75. See p. 137 in Vol. I.

[3] See p. 93, above.
[4] Shakespeare, Sonnet XXIX.
[5] *The New Statesman*, March 3, 1917

My friénd, blóod sháking my heárt
The áwful dáring of a móment's surrénder
Which an áge of prúdence can néver retráct
By thís, and thís ónly, we have exísted
Which is nót to be fóund in our obítuaries
Or in mémories dráped by the benéficent spíder
Or under séals bróken by the léan solícitor
In our émpty róoms. . . .[1]

### OTHER VERBAL DEVICES

In all kinds of verse certain common devices are used to give variety to the metrical design. It will have been noted in the above examples of stanzaic and sonnet forms that in some lines the sense is enclosed in the single line, which is then called *end-stopped*. If the sense flows over into two, or several lines, they are then called *run-on*. A couplet where the sense is complete is a *closed couplet* (as in the lines from Pope below). If a sentence, or clause, ends in the middle of a line, the break which then occurs is called a *caesura*, and makes a pause in the reading of the line. In the Wordsworth sonnet quoted above, the first line is end-stopped; the second is run-on; and in the fifth there is a caesura. There is another caesura in the thirteenth, where the words "Dear God!" stand apart from the rest of the line and make a break in the sound pattern.

Other common sound effects are those of *alliteration*, the repetition of consonants; and *onomatopoeia*, the imitation of natural sounds in words. A succession of harsh, slow-moving syllables is called *cacophony;* and of light, harmonious ones, *euphony*. The following passage from Pope's *Essay on Criticism* gives illustrations of all these devices.

True ease in writing comes from art, not chance,
As those move easiest who have learned to dance.
'Tis not enough no harshness gives offense,
The sound must seem an echo to the sense:
Soft is the strain when Zephyr gently blows,
And the smooth stream in smoother numbers flows;
But when loud surges lash the sounding shore,
The hoarse, rough verse should like the torrent roar:
When Ajax strives some rock's vast weight to throw,
The line too labors, and the words move slow;
Not so, when swift Camilla scours the plain,
Flies o'er th' unbending corn, and skims along the main.[2]

[1] See pp. 837–38, above.
[2] See p. 766 in Vol. I.

There is alliteration throughout the passage (which should be read aloud), and in the fifth and sixth lines, where the repetition of the "s" sound creates the softness and smoothness of wind and stream, it is combined with onomatopoeia. The lines on the torrent and on Ajax illustrate cacophony, and those on Camilla, euphony. In all, carefully and skillfully, Pope makes the sound of the words echo the actions described.

### RHYTHM

When we have enumerated the kinds of feet and the number of feet in different lines, have named various rhyme schemes and listed verbal devices used by poets, we are not much nearer the realities of versification. We have given the mechanical framework, a set of rules and conventions which put verse apart from prose. But to attempt to reduce poetry to rules, to make the laws of versification into an authoritarian dictatorship to keep poets in order, would be quite useless. The rules do insist on the basic fact of *recurrent pattern*. They emphasize that it is the setting up of an expectation of certain returning sound effects that catches the ear and pleases it. The measurements of these sound effects is meter, but the *regular* metrical pattern is never more than a foundation, a norm from which to depart and return. It is part of a larger movement: the *rhythm*. Rhythm means *flow*, and flow is determined by considerations beyond those of the regular metrical schemes. The schemes create a formal outline, which sets a limit to the degree of variety the poet can practice, but his art is to exercise freedom within this self-imposed framework of necessity. Meter, therefore, is only one element in rhythm, and rhythm is both larger and deeper in significance than meter. Rhythms move in feeling more than in feet, and their effect may depend on irregularity as much as on regularity.

There is one unalterable rule in the study of versification: in the reading of poetry it is not the *regular* number and kind of syllables and feet which control the rhythm but the placing of the *particular* and *varied* accents or stresses or beats (these three words are interchangeable). The real direction and ordering of the rhythm comes from the poet's personal *voice*, which is heard speaking through the lines. Because the human ear is as individual in its range as any of the other senses, and the intonations it hears vary, different individuals may hear this voice differently. There are no precise rules of rhythm as there are of meter, and so no absolute laws of scansion (the placing of the stresses in reading). The poet's voice itself may have numberless different tones, but whatever tone it takes, it asserts that the regular metrical scheme it has chosen must obey the sense of what is being said, and be subordinated to the rhythmical movement required to express the thought and the feeling. To do this, the poet will vary the formal accentual pattern with reversals of the expected stress, with omissions or additions of syllables or feet, with surprises and even shocks. These are all deliberate and calculated: "It is not inspiration that exhausts one," says Yeats, "it is Art." Eliot too declares that "probably the larger part of the labor of the author is critical labor; the labor of sifting, combining, constructing, expunging, correcting, testing."

### RHYTHMICAL VARIATIONS

Many variations of rhythmical stress can be heard by reading carefully any of the stanzas or the two sonnets quoted in the section on rhyme schemes. Although the basic sound pattern in each illustration is iambic pentameter, none keep to that regular beat, and it would be very dull if they did. But perhaps the differences can be heard more clearly if we listen to several "voices" using the same verse form, and note the various rhythmical possibilities that emerge.

Take blank verse. This is what it sounded like in *Gorboduc* (1561), the earliest play written in that meter:

The royal king and eke his sons are slain;
No ruler rests within the regal seat;
The heir, to whom the scepter 'longs, unknown; . . .
Lo, Britain's realm is left an open prey,
A present spoil for conquest to ensue.

It is clumsily regular. Its iambs, all end-stopped, plod along in regimented uniformity, and the result is a lifeless monotony.

Marlowe changed all that, and brought a new ease and flexibility to blank verse by varying the accents, by breaking the line with the caesura, by indicating dramatic pauses, and by allowing the sense to flow into a freer sentence structure.

Was this the face that launched a thousand ships,
And burnt the topless towers of Ilium? —
Sweet Helen, make me immortal with a kiss, —
Her lips suck forth my soul; see, where it flies!
Come, Helen, come, give me my soul again.
Here will I dwell, for heaven is in these lips,
And all is dross that is not Helena.[1]

Shakespeare's intonations are still nearer the speaking voice.

That it should come to this!
But two months dead! Nay, not so much, not two.
So excellent a King, that was, to this,
Hyperion to a satyr. So loving to my mother
That he might not beteem the winds of heaven
Visit her face too roughly. Heaven and earth!
Must I remember? Why, she would hang on him
As if increase of appetite had grown
By what it fed on. And yet within a month ——
Let me not think on 't —[2]

This is really dramatic blank verse: no single line is entirely regular, and the almost strangling fury and disgust come out in the broken, uneven rhythms and gasps of angry pain and nausea.

Milton's blank verse is not dramatic, but epic. It depends for its magnificence on sustained rhythmic nobility and sonorous sweep. But again, his finest effects are gained by playing the thought and feeling structure of his larger rhythms against the expected regular beat. Take his description of the fall of Satan:

Him the Almighty Power
Hurled headlong flaming from the ethereal sky
With hideous ruin and combustion down
To bottomless perdition, there to dwell
In adamantine chains and penal fire,
Who durst defy the Omnipotent to arms.[3]

Here one line only, the fifth, keeps the regular metrical pattern. It supplies the conventional order against which the freedom and irregularity of the other lines are counterpointed. Their magnificent energy, indeed, is not only in the splendor of their diction, but in the movement which, in the sweep of a single sentence, creates the sense of Lucifer falling through space. The rush of the opening with its powerful beats carries through without pause to "perdition,"

[1] *Doctor Faustus*, XIII.91–97.
[2] *Hamlet*, I.ii.137–46. See p. 242 in Vol. I.
[3] *Paradise Lost*, I.44–49. See p. 455 in Vol. I.

and after this toppling descent, "there to dwell / In adamantine chains and penal fire," checks the rush into the feeling of the permanence of Satan's doom.

In *Samson Agonistes* Milton allows himself not only variations within the pentameter line, but variations of line length itself to give specific effects.

> O dark, dark, dark, amid the blaze of noon,
> Irrecoverably dark, total eclipse
> Without all hope of day![1]

Although the first line has ten syllables, it has six stresses; the second has eleven syllables, but only four beats; and the third, with only three beats, stands as a complete line. The sound goes underground, as it were, and the pause which completes the line is filled with the echo of "dark" and Samson's silent hopelessness.

If we turn to Browning from Milton, it is difficult to realize that they are both using the same meter:

> I am poor brother Lippo, by your leave!
> You [illegible]ed not clap your torches in my face.
> Zooks, what's to blame? you think you see a monk!
> What, 'tis past midnight, and you go the rounds,
> And here you catch me at an alley's end
> Where sportive ladies leave their doors ajar?
> The Carmine's my cloister; hunt it up,
> Do —[2]

Again we hear speech rhythms in individual tones. The parentheses, the quick shifts and breaks in thought, the questions, the ejaculations, carry all the immediacy and spontaneity of the natural voice. But the rhythms are facile rather than subtle.

An equal variety of rhythmic flow and tone can be heard in the heroic couplet. Marlowe loads it with descriptive richness, but the end-stopped lines tend towards monotony.

> Upon her head she wore a myrtle wreath,
> From whence her veil reached to the ground beneath.
> Her veil was artificial flowers and leaves,
> Whose workmanship both man and beast deceives.
> Many would praise the sweet smell as she passed,
> When 'twas the odor which her breath forth cast;
> And there for honey bees have sought in vain,
> And, beat from thence, have lighted there again.[3]

[illegible]onne was only nine years younger than Mar-[illegible] but his heroic couplets certainly sound [illegible]ifferent.

> On a huge hill
> Cragged, and steep, Truth stands, and he that will
> Reach her, about must, and about must go;
> And what the hill's suddenness resists, win so;
> Yet strive so, that before age, death's twilight,
> Thy soul rest, for none can work in that night.[4]

Though this is in rhymed couplets, it has more of the quality of Elizabethan blank verse than of the nondramatic poetry of the period. The pressure of the thinking mind bends the rhyme out of regularity. In some lines it is emphasized with heavy stress; in others ignored. The reader must slow up to get the force of the ideas, must identify himself, in an almost physical way, with the breath pauses, with the image of reaching and striving and resisting "the hill's suddenness" by patient struggle. In the third and fourth lines the slow, plodding effort lengthens the lines by stresses on the last two single words, and in the last line the Biblical echo, "for the night cometh when no man can work," brings home the deliberate *laboriousness* which Donne is creating in the place of that easy musical rhythm.

The rhythm of Donne's couplets moves slowly with its burden of personal emotional meaning, while that of Pope's has the brisk tone of the man of the world conversing with his friends. Instead of speaking in a sustained sentence of several lines, he makes each couplet a unit in itself, with its rhythm based on the symmetry and neat opposition of its two halves. The closed couplet is an artificial convention, but within its framework of formal decorum Pope packs it with pithy terseness.

> First slave to words, then vassal to a name,
> Then dupe to party; child and man the same;
> Bounded by Nature, narrowed still by art,
> A trifling head, and a contracted heart.[5]

In spite of its clipped trimness, this is full of subtle sound variations and acute, witty precision. But Pope can inject real intensity of feeling into couplets. In the Sporus portrait, he introduces a dramatic element which enlarges the rhythmical scope. One side of the conversation is in the negative tone of light contempt taken by Dr. Arbuthnot, while Pope himself sweeps that away in the positive, though controlled, vibrations of direct hatred.

[illegible] 504 in Vol. I.
[illegible]ippo Lippi," ll. 1–8. See p. 496, above.
[illegible] *Leander*, I.17–22.

4 Satire III, ll. 79–84. See p. 376 in Vol. I.
5 *Dunciad*, IV.501–05. See p. 840 in Vol. I.

Let Sporus tremble — "What? that thing of silk,
Sporus, that mere white curd of ass's milk?
Satire or sense, alas! can Sporus feel?
Who breaks a butterfly upon a wheel?"
Yet let me flap this bug with gilded wings,
This painted child of dirt, that stinks and stings;
Whose buzz the witty and the fair annoys,
Yet wit ne'er tastes, and beauty ne'er enjoys: . . .[1]

Browning used the couplet, as he used blank verse, to carry the tones of the ordinary speaking voice. The sense is never enclosed within the two lines; the rhymes are unaccented, and the meaning flows across them and ignores them.

Who'd stoop to blame
This sort of trifling? Even had you skill
In speech — (which I have not) — to make your will
Quite clear to such an one, and say, "Just this
Or that in you disgusts me; here you miss,
Or there exceed the mark" — [2]

## SOUND AND SENSE

From these illustrations it is clear that though the interrelation of sound and sense is the foundation of rhythm, that interrelation is much more complex than Pope's lines on the subject, quoted earlier, suggest. It is not just a matter of actions being translated into imitative sounds, but of feeling and thought coming through the flow and quality of the language and the management of the sound pattern. There cannot be much feeling and thought if the metrical convention is too rigid or if the tone and pitch remain too long at one level. A poem may become monotonous, even if it is a monotony of pleasant sounds. For instance, the opening stanza of Meredith's "Love in the Valley" is very delightful.

Under yonder beech-tree single on the green-sward,
Couched with her arms behind her golden head,
Knees and tresses folded to slip and ripple idly,
Lies my young love sleeping in the shade.
Had I the heart to slide an arm beneath her,
Press her parting lips as her waist I gather slow,
Waking in amazement she could not but embrace me:
Then would she hold me and never let me go?

But when this is followed by twenty-five stanzas of the same rippling melody, the ear cloys, and the senses become blurred and comatose; the sound pattern is *too* sweet, *too* fluid, *too* flexible.

But versification may fail, of course, from a different kind of monotony, a prosiness where neither a regular beat nor a vital speech rhythm asserts itself, and the verse becomes torpid. Milton, great verbal artist though he is, can at times be rhythmically toneless. Some of the choruses in *Samson Agonistes*, for instance, are extraordinarily flat, all liveliness of movement stifled out of the verse.

Many are the sayings of the wise
In ancient and in modern books enrolled,
Extolling patience as the truest fortitude;
And to the bearing well of all calamities,
All chances incident to man's frail life,
Consolatories writ
With studied argument, and much persuasion sought, . . .[3]

Many rhythms are bad, however, not from monotony, but because of the choice of an unsuitable meter and diction for their subject matter — a clumsy adaptation of matter to medium. Cowper, for instance, ruined his "Verses Supposed to Be Written by Alexander Selkirk," by choosing to write them in the tripping anapest.

I am monarch of all I survey,
My right there is none to dispute;
From the center all round to the sea,
I am lord of the fowl and the brute.
Oh, Solitude! where are thy charms
That sages have seen in thy face?
Better dwell in the midst of alarms,
Than reign in this horrible place.

The sound pattern is better suited to comic opera than to expressing the horrors of shipwrecked isolation.

Wordsworth makes the same fatal choice of the anapest for "The Reverie of Poor Susan," for the sense of nostalgic longing in Susan's memories fails to communicate itself in that singsong meter.

Green pastures she views in the midst of the dale,
Down which she so often has tripped with her pail;
And a single small cottage, a nest like a dove's,
The one only dwelling on earth that she loves.[4]

Or again, when Sir Ronald Ross had finally proved how the female mosquito transfers the infection of malaria, he put his sense of thrilling triumph into a poem, one stanza of which runs:

I know this little thing
A myriad men will save,
O Death, where is thy sting,
Thy victory, O grave!

No one would deny the truth of the thou[g] the sincerity of the feeling, but they [...]

[1] "Epistle to Dr. Arbuthnot," ll. 305–12. See p. 822 in Vol. I.
[2] "My Last Duchess," ll. 34–39. See p. 481, above.
[3] See p. 510 in Vol. I.
[4] See p. 30, above.

created in the words. To feel how a sense of triumph can be translated into rhythm, listen to Spenser in the *Epithalamion*.

Open the temple gates unto my love,
Open them wide that she may enter in,
And all the postes adorne as doth behove,
And all the pillours deck with girlands trim . . .
And let the roring Organs loudly play
The praises of the Lord in lively notes,
The whiles with hollow throates
The Choristers the joyous Antheme sing,
That al the woods may answere and their eccho ring.[1]

But this is a simple joyous burst: to hear the mind working with concentrated force, keeping a complex stanza pattern and packing the lines with brain stuff as well as with emotional intensity, take the first stanza of Donne's "The Anniversary."

Áll kíngs, and áll their fávorites,
Áll glóry of hónors, beáuties, wíts,
The sún itsélf, which mákes tímes, as they páss,
Is élder by a yéar, nów, than it wás
When thóu and Í first óne anóther sáw:
All óther thíngs to their destrúction dráw,
Ónly our lóve hath nó decáy;
Thís nó tomórrow háth, nor yésterday,
Rúnning it néver rúns from ús awáy,
But trúly kéeps his fírst, lást, éverlásting dáy.[2]

The sixth line is a regular iambic, but until that is reached, the accents are wrenched to enforce a slowing up in the reading, so that all the weight of the temporal, and the passing, and the material, shall contrast with the light, sweeping movement of the triumph over time in the last half of the verse. After the summing up of the theme of mortality, "All other things to their destruction draw," the firm beats of "Only our love hath no decay," announce that triumph, and then the syllables move easily, with their four chiming rhymes, to end in the long, lingering, seven-beat exultation of eternal constancy.

The rhythmic creation of the totally opposing mood of empty despair is well illustrated in the opening lines of Eliot's "The Hollow Men."

We are the hollow men
We are the stuffed men
Leaning together
Headpiece filled with straw. Alas!
Our dried voices, when
We whisper together
Are quiet and meaningless
As wind in dry grass
Or rats' feet over broken glass
In our dry cellar

Shape without form, shade without colour,
Paralysed force, gesture without motion; . . .[3]

The theme of the paragraph is the sense of banishment from human vitality, vitality either for good or for evil. That condition of meaningless neutrality is evoked in the unrhymed couplet at the end. It has no directed movement towards anything else, its language is as static and negative as its feeling, and the lifelessness of the hollow men is expressed in the very faint heartbeat of the rhythm in the introductory lines, with their halting uneven stresses. The "dried voices" are entirely without resonance or vigor; the words they whisper "lean together" with no interlocking harmony; and they are likened to the meaningless inhuman sounds of the wind in dry grass or "rats' feet over broken glass." The halting, harsh cacophony of vowels and consonants in that image carries something of the shattered fragments which is all "our dry cellar" contains.

As an example of a skillful *change* of mood within a single stanza take the first verse of Yeats's "Sailing to Byzantium."

That is no country for old men. The young
In one another's arms, birds in the trees
— Those dying generations — at their song,
The salmon-falls, the mackerel-crowded seas,
Fish, flesh, or fowl, commend all summer long
Whatever is begotten, born, and dies.
Caught in that sensual music all neglect
Monuments of unageing intellect.[4]

The poem is going to contrast the life of the body with that of the soul; the state of natural animal fertility with the inanimate creations of man's hands and minds; instinctive mortal joys with the immortal triumphs of art; transience with permanence. The contrasts are already pointed to in this stanza by the difference in the rhythm between the first six lines of the *ottava rima* and the last two.

The "country" is no place on the map; it is simply the world of nature and its delights. The abrupt opening sentence seems to dismiss it, but its beauty and sweetness come crowding in.

[1] See pp. 106–07 in Vol. I.
[2] See p. 368 in Vol. I.
[3] See p. 838, above.
[4] See p. 795, above.

The flow of the first phases, evoking the lovely summer world, is checked by the parenthesis, "those dying generations," the reminder of transience, but the "sensual music" asserts itself with the flowing, regular stress of "the salmon-falls, the mackerel-crowded seas," followed by the triple alliteration of "fish, flesh, or fowl." In the next line the ear expects "begotten, born" will lead to a parallel device, but instead, what might be called an alliterative disappointment comes. The finality of "and dies" reminds the reader again of the inevitable end of the natural cycle in which mortal music is "caught"; and the rhythm of that music is brought up short at the end of the seventh line in the hardening of the consonants in "neglect," followed by the three powerful heavily accented words which oppose the fleeting loveliness of bodies to the permanence of the immortal creations of mind and spirit.

## WORD TEXTURE AND VALUE

From the analyses of these passages, it is very apparent that the matter of word texture and value cannot be separated from that of the sound pattern. Not only the changing rhythmic design from line to line, but the quality of the words themselves, their echoes from the past, their associations, their disposal and manipulation in a poem, all play their parts in the total effect of a poem.

Every age has a particular flavor in its use of poetic vocabulary. The history of poetic language is like that of the soil. However rich, poetic language is subject to erosion, and its fertility is constantly threatened by elements which destroy its vitality and impoverish its content. Time washes away its surface freshness and use exhausts its vigor until it becomes arid and sterile. The history of poetry is, in one sense, a cyclical history of the birth, maturing and decay of various traditions of poetic diction. Each is born in revolution, runs its course of development and elaboration, and degenerates into formalism and mechanical imitation.

It is usual to give the name "poetic diction" to a peculiarly artificial use of words which became popular in the eighteenth century, when a breeze was always a zephyr; a girl a nymph; fishes, birds, and sheep, the finny prey, the feathered choir, and the fleecy care; and rats, the whiskered vermin race. We cannot by any stretch of imagination, think of Donne calling a girl a nymph, or Wordsworth or Shelley calling birds the feathered choir, or of Eliot speaking of rats as the whiskered vermin race. But it was not the eighteenth century only which evolved a poetic diction; certain marked characteristics belong to each tradition. Before the enormous development of language which the Elizabethan and Jacobean dramatists illustrate, the early Elizabethan lyrists sang in a very simple vocabulary.

> Love in my bosom like a bee
> Doth suck his sweet;
> Now with his wings he plays with me,
> Now with his feet.
> Within mine eyes he makes his nest,
> His bed amidst my tender breast;
> And yet he robs me of my rest.
> Ah, wanton, will ye? [1]

But that convention was much too easy for the complexity of thought and dramatic intensity which Donne and his followers demanded that the lyric should carry, so that in their era words became close-packed and concentrated in their condensation of emotional and intellectual meaning. At the opposite extreme from Donne, Milton changed the Elizabethan vocabulary into the Latinized eloquence of formal grandeur. But to the poets of the eighteenth century the language of both Donne or Milton was equally unsuitable. They needed a social literary medium which would communicate readily to an audience which prided itself on standards of clarity, elegance, and decorum in the use of language. That fashion in turn seemed false and artificial to Wordsworth, who demanded a return to the language of ordinary men. The later Romantics developed more particularly the sensuous suggestions of words, and loaded their poetry with them. That convention in turn weakened in the 1890's, and petered out into the ultra-sensuous.

> I have forgot much, Cynara! Gone with the wind,
> Flung roses, roses, riotously with the throng,
> Dancing to put thy pale lost lilies out of mind.[2]

The modern generation has entirely discarded such florid gestures, and if they wish to express something of the same situation they do it in a deliberately "unpoetic" vocabulary.

> I have stuttered on my feet
> Clinched to the streamlined and butter smooth trulls
> of the elite.[3]

[1] Thomas Lodge.
[2] Ernest Dowson.
[3] Louis MacNeice.

Apart from a "poetic diction" belonging in a general way to the language of every age, the problem of poetic diction in its simplest sense — the words — is at the foundation of every poem. Nature and training endow each poet with certain tendencies in his use of words. He will be thrifty like Housman or Hardy, or spendthrift like Marlowe or Swinburne; calm like Herbert or boisterous like Browning; graceful like Herrick or energetic like Hopkins. And in addition to his inherent bent, the whole conscious force of his artistry is towards the most exact equivalent he can attain between the words he uses and the effects he wishes to communicate. Hart Crane speaks for every poet: "Oh, it is hard! One must be drenched in words, literally soaked in them, to have the right ones form themselves into the proper patterns at the right moment."

Against the poet are ranged all the forces of custom and carelessness in the use of words. His readers have eyes blurred by the film of familiarity and ears muffled by common usage. Through his verbal pattern he must sharpen and intensify every significant sound, shade of meaning and association. He arranges his words so that they influence one another, like color values in painting, and work directly or obliquely on the emotions and senses in ways that *seem* inevitable.

White in the moon the long road lies
  The moon stands blank above;
White in the moon the long road lies
  That leads me from my love.

If Housman had written "that leads me *to* my love," the statement might have been factually true, but it would be poetically false. The feeling of the poem has already been created by the association of "white," "long," "blank" with the road and the moon; the forlornness and weariness and emptiness and chill are already there. The whole effect of a poem, indeed, can be ruined by a wrong word or rhyme. It is useless for Burns to prepare us for a beautiful lament with the opening,

Ae fond kiss and then we sever!
Ae fareweel, and then for ever!

if he starts the next stanza,

I'll ne'er blame my partial fancy,
Naething could resist my Nancy.

The mood is irrevocably shattered.

Poetry may work through the senses only, and appeal to eye, ear, touch, taste, and smell, as in this stanza of Ben Jonson:

Have you seen but a bright flower grow
  Before rude hands have touched it?
Have you marked but the fall of the snow
  Before the soil hath smutched it?
Have you felt the wool of the beaver,
  Or swan's down ever?
Or have smelt o' the bud of the brier,
  Or the nard in the fire?
Or have tasted the bag of the bee?
O so white, O so soft, O so sweet is she!

Or the words may generate so much activity in themselves that the reader feels almost muscularly involved in the response. As we have seen from an earlier example, Donne's verse in particular has this forceful energy.

Batter my heart, three-personed God; for, you
As yet but knock, breathe, shine, and seek to mend;
That I may rise and stand, o'erthrow me, and bend
Your force, to break, blow, burn, and make me new.[1]

Words can turn a moral platitude about the need for spiritual vitality in the face of bodily decay, into a vivid, concrete picture, as in the second stanza of "Sailing to Byzantium."

An aged man is but a paltry thing,
A tattered coat upon a stick, unless
Soul clap its hands and sing, . . .[2]

Put in their full context, leading on from the first stanza, the words take on more than their surface meaning, for the picture of the scarecrow, the "thing," in its stiff and lifeless rigidity, contrasts with the flowing grace of "the young in one another's arms"; and the soul clapping its hands and singing is parallel to the birds at *their* song, "commending" the life of "whatever is begotten, born, and dies."

Eliot weaves a very complex and subtle pattern through association and verbal allusion. The home-coming of the typist in Part III of *The Waste Land* is a good illustration.

At the violet hour, the evening hour that strives
Homeward, and brings the sailor home from sea,
The typist home at teatime, clears her breakfast, lights
Her stove, and lays out food in tins.
Out of the window perilously spread
Her drying combinations touched by the sun's last
  rays, . . .[3]

The central lines describe the sordid and unappetizing quality of the typist's "home" and slovenly manner of living in the most prosaic

[1] See p. 387 in Vol. I.
[2] See p. 796, above.
[3] See p. 855, above.

and direct words; but the picture they give is ironized and accentuated by framing it within other lines where allusive words recall memories of romantic scenes of evening, home-coming, and open windows. The "violet hour" suggests Sappho's lines to the evening star; "the sailor home from sea" echoes R. L. Stevenson's "Requiem"; while the conjunction of the window with the word "perilously" provokes a wry comparison with Keats's

> . . . magic casements, opening on the foam
> Of perilous seas, in faery lands forlorn.[1]

This juxtaposition of words calling up very different associations gives great compression of meaning by ironical contrast. Yeats gets a powerful effect of this sort in the final lines of "The Second Coming."

> And what rough beast, its hour come round at last,
> Slouches towards Bethlehem to be born?[2]

All the suggestions of Bethlehem to the Christian world — the simple shepherds, the stately Magi, the birth of the Prince of Peace — are brought into opposition with the words *rough beast* and *slouches*. The poem has established that Yeats sees a new historical cycle beginning in blood and violence, and the conclusion points to the birth of Christ as a similar era, doomed from the start to its present ending.

Even without all the weight and subtlety of suggestion which modern poets introduce, the mingling of different *qualities* of language has always made for effective musical pattern and added emotional richness. Shakespeare is the great master of the blending of the simple and the elaborate. The dying Hamlet addresses Horatio:

> If thou didst ever hold me in thy heart,
> Absent thee from felicity a while,
> And in this harsh world draw thy breath in pain
> To tell my story.[3]

Or Macbeth, returning from the murder of Duncan, cries:

> Will all great Neptune's ocean wash this blood
> Clean from my hand? No; this my hand will rather
> The multitudinous seas incarnadine
> Making the green one red.

In both these passages, the particular verbal texture of the short simple words interwoven with the dignity and resonance of latinizations is peculiarly satisfying to the ear. The same thing happens in Wordsworth's "A Slumber Did My Spirit Seal":

> No motion has she now, no force;
> She neither hears nor sees;
> Rolled round in earth's diurnal course,
> With rocks, and stones, and trees.[4]

Both the agonizing thought of the inaction of the dead, and the majesty of the eternal measured movement of the earth's rotation, come through the contrast of the three short, almost monosyllabic, lines with the force of the lengthened third line of five beats and the one formal word in the whole poem — *diurnal*.

The precise use of *epithets* by poets is in sharp contrast to their usual careless usage in speech. Dorothy Wordsworth enters in her journal: "William tired himself seeking an epithet for the cuckoo," and Keats writes to Fanny Brawne, "I want a brighter word than bright, a fairer word than fair." Keat's own description of "the tiger-moth's deep-damasked wings,"[5] concentrates in *damasked* the suggestions of the shimmer of silk, the sheen of damascened metal, and the texture of a damask rose. Arnold's final line in "To Marguerite,"[6] "The unplumbed, salt, estranging sea," is haunting in its creation of the mystery, the bitterness, the loneliness of the human situation in the flux of life and time. Tennyson reveals a similar mood entirely in descriptive epithets.

> And ghastly thro' the drizzling rain
> On the bald street breaks the blank day.[7]

Another device is to blend the abstract and the concrete so that they set off one another: "proud pied April,"[8] "the lazy, leaden-stepping hours,"[9] "the same bright, patient stars."[10]

Another way to remind poetry readers of the patient search for words of the right music and meaning, the right interrelation and precision, is to study the revisions poets have made in their work. Milton's "airy tongues that syllable men's names,"[11] was first the rather vague "airy tongues that lure night wanderers"; Poe's famous lines

> the glory that was Greece
> And the grandeur that was Rome

[1] See p. 344, above.
[2] See p. 795, above.
[3] See p. 286 in Vol. I.

[4] See p. 82, above.
[5] *The Eve of St. Agnes*. See p. 338, above.
[6] See p. 601, above.
[7] *In Memoriam*, VII. See p. 411, above.
[8] Shakespeare, Sonnet XCVIII.
[9] Milton, " On Time."
[10] Keats, *Hyperion*. See p. 336, above.
[11] Milton, *Comus*.

went through the stage of

> the beauty of fair Greece
> And the grandeur of old Rome.

The precise veracity of Keats's

> Not so much life as on a summer's day
> Robs not one light seed from the feathered grass [1]

might have remained

> Not so much life as on a summer's day
> Robs not at all the dandelion's fleece.

The great poet uses every value that he can wring from his medium; music, meaning, memory; simplicity and ornament; visual image and abstract idea; dramatic force, lyric intensity, sensuous suggestion. All these are distilled from the mass of language into the potent spirit of poetry. Or we can use Donne's image of molding metal on a forge, and say that the poet takes words to batter them, to break, blow, burn, and make them new; or that he has the power both to remint the old coinage of traditional expression and to issue new currency. But the best image of a poem is an organic one of growth. It arises and takes its own specific form out of the formless flux of life and language.

> Out of the sea of sound the life of music,
> Out of the slimy mud of words, out of the sleet and hail of verbal imprecisions,
> Approximate thoughts and feelings, words that have taken the place of thoughts and feelings,
> There spring the perfect order of speech, and the beauty of incantation.[2]

E. D.

[1] Keats, *Hyperion*. See p. 340, above.

[2] T. S. Eliot. *The Rock*, Chorus IX.

# Author-Title Index

This is a combined index for both volumes of *Major British Writers.* The appropriate volume number is indicated by a roman numeral after each entry. Author's names are in boldface type, and the page numbers of the introductions to their writings are in italics.

# Index of First Lines by Volume

## VOLUME I

## VOLUME II